LONGMAN ANNOTATED ENGLISH POETS

SPENSER
THE FAERIE QVEENE
Edited by A. C. Hamilton

Praise for previous editions:

"All in all, it is a major work of scholarship, combining a meticulously prepared text with splendid annotation. It will last, and will help inspire new generations of readers."

Tom MacFaul, *Notes & Queries*

"A volume of prime importance to Spenserians, who will find it a mine of information and insights assembled by one of the most knowledgeable of modern readers of the poem."

Spenser Newsletter

"Hamilton's introductory material is both succinct and incisive, while his notes, attentive both to language and interpretation, are immensely valuable."

Studies in English Literature

"It is a valuable volume in a valuable series."

Essays in Criticism

LONGMAN ANNOTATED ENGLISH POETS

General Editors: John Barnard and Paul Hammond
Founding Editor: F. W. Bateson

Titles available in paperback:

BLAKE: THE COMPLETE POEMS
(Third Edition)
Edited by W. H. Stevenson

DRYDEN: SELECTED POEMS
Edited by Paul Hammond and David Hopkins

THE POEMS OF ANDREW MARVELL
(Revised Edition)
Edited by Nigel Smith

MILTON: PARADISE LOST
(Second Edition)
Edited by Alastair Fowler

MILTON: COMPLETE SHORTER POEMS
(Second Edition)
Edited by John Carey

SPENSER: THE FAERIE QVEENE
(Revised Second Edition)
Edited by A. C. Hamilton

TENNYSON: A SELECTED EDITION
(Revised Edition)
Edited by Christopher Ricks

EDMUND SPENSER

THE FAERIE QVEENE

EDITED BY

A. C. HAMILTON

REVISED SECOND EDITION

TEXT EDITED BY

HIROSHI YAMASHITA
TOSHIYUKI SUZUKI

Routledge
Taylor & Francis Group

LONDON AND NEW YORK

First published 2001 by Pearson Education Limited
Revised edition published in 2007

Published 2013 by Routledge
2 Park Square, Milton Park, Abingdon, Oxon OX14 4RN
711 Third Avenue, New York, NY 10017, USA

Routledge is an imprint of the Taylor & Francis Group, an informa business

ISBN 13: 978-1-4058-3281-6 (pbk)

British Library Cataloguing in Publication Data
A CIP catalogue record for this book can be obtained from the British Library

Library of Congress Cataloging-in-Publication Data
Spenser, Edmund, 1552?–1599.
    [Faerie queene]
    The Faerie Qveene / Edmund Spenser ; edited by A.C. Hamilton ; text edited by Hiroshi Yamashita, Toshiyuki Suzuki. — Rev. ed.
      p. cm. — (Longman annotated English poets)
    Includes bibliographical references.
    ISBN-13: 978-1-4058-3281-6 (pbk.)
    ISBN-10: 1-4058-3281-9 (pbk.)
    1. Knights and knighthood—Poetry. 2. Virtues—Poetry. I. Hamilton, A. C. (Albert Charles), 1921– II. Yamashita, Hiroshi, 1944– III. Suzuki, Toshiyuki, 1944– IV. Title. V. Series.

PR2358.A3H28 2006
821'.3—dc22
                                             2006040879

Set in Galliard by Graphicraft Ltd., Hong Kong

To
Elizabeth the Second
By the Grace of God of the United Kingdom
Canada and Her other Realms and Territories
Queen
Head of the Commonwealth
Defender of the Faith

CONTENTS

Note by the General Editors   ix

Preface   xi

Acknowledgements   xiii

Chronological Table of Spenser's Life and Works   xiv

Abbreviations   xx

General Introduction   1

Textual Introduction by Hiroshi Yamashita and Toshiyuki Suzuki   21

Facsimiles of 1590 title page and 1590 dedication   26

Facsimiles of 1596 title page and 1596 dedication   27

BOOK I   The Legend of the Knight of the Red Crosse, or of Holinesse   29

BOOK II   The Legend of Sir Guyon, or of Temperaunce   157

BOOK III   The Legend of Britomartis, or of Chastity   287

Facsimile of 'The Second Part of The Faerie Queene'   408

BOOK IV   The Legend of Cambel and Telamond, or of Friendship   409

BOOK V   The Legend of Artegall, or of Iustice   507

BOOK VI   The Legend of S. Calidore, or of Courtesie   601

BOOK VII   Two Cantos of Mutabilitie   691

Letter to Raleigh   713

Commendatory Verses and Dedicatory Sonnets   719

Textual Notes by Hiroshi Yamashita and Toshiyuki Suzuki   736

Bibliography   754

The Characters of The Faerie Queene by Shohachi Fukuda   775

NOTE BY THE GENERAL EDITORS

Longman Annotated English Poets was launched in 1965 with the publication of Kenneth Allott's edition of *The Poems of Matthew Arnold*. F.W. Bateson wrote that the 'new series is the first designed to provide university students and teachers, and the general reader with complete and fully annotated editions of the major English poets'. That remains the aim of the series, and Bateson's original vision of its policy remains essentially the same. Its 'concern is primarily with the *meaning* of the extant texts in their various contexts'. The two other main principles of the series were that the text should be modernized and the poems printed 'as far as possible in the order in which they were composed'.

These broad principles still govern the series. Its primary purpose is to provide an annotated text giving the reader any necessary contextual information. However, flexibility in the detailed application has proved necessary in the light of experience and the needs of a particular case (and each poet is by definition, a particular case).

First, proper glossing of a poet's vocabulary has proved essential and not something which can be taken for granted. Second, modernization has presented difficulties, which have been resolved pragmatically, trying to reach a balance between sensitivity to the text in question and attention to the needs of a modern reader. Thus, to modernize Browning's text has a double redundancy: Victorian conventions are very close to modern conventions, and Browning had firm ideas on punctuation. Equally, to impose modern pointing on the ambiguities of Marvell would create a misleading clarity. Third, in the very early days of the series Bateson hoped that editors would be able in many cases to annotate a *textus receptus*. That has not always been possible, and where no accepted text exists or where the text is controversial, editors have been obliged to go back to the originals and create their own text. The series has taken, and will continue to take, the opportunity not only of providing thorough annotations not available elsewhere, but also of making important scholarly textual contributions where necessary. A case in point is the edition of *The Poems of Tennyson* by Christopher Ricks, the Second Edition of which (1987) takes into account a full collation of the Trinity College Manuscripts, not previously available for an edition of this kind. Yet the series' primary purpose remains annotation.

The requirements of a particular author take precedence over principle. It would make little sense to print Herbert's *Temple* in the order of composition even if it could be established. Where Ricks rightly decided that Tennyson's reader needs to be given the circumstances of composition, the attitude to Tennyson and his circle, allusions, and important variants, a necessary consequence was the exclusion of twentieth-century critical responses. Milton, however, is a very different case. John Carey and Alastair Fowler, looking to the needs of their readers, undertook synopses of the main lines of the critical debate over Milton's poetry. Finally, chronological ordering by date of composition will almost always have a greater or lesser degree of speculation or arbitrariness. The evidence is usually partial, and is confused further by the fact that poets do not always write one poem at a time and frequently revise at a later period than that of composition.

John Barnard
Paul Hammond

PREFACE

Whatever of value may be found in my annotations and commentary on *The Faerie Queene* is a testimony to twentieth-century Spenser criticism, a full and rich banquet from which, as the many references indicate, I have attempted to pick up as many crumbs as limited space and time afford. I am much indebted to the advice of old friends, even where I have failed to follow it, chiefly A. Kent Hieatt, Donald Cheney, Carol V. Kaske, Judith H. Anderson, Alastair Fowler, and Shohachi Fukuda. I am indebted also to many new friends among the critics cited in the Bibliography with whom I have corresponded extensively by email. To list a few of them in alphabetical order: Catherine Bates for clarifying my commentary on the dance of the Graces; Richard J. Berleth for explaining Spenser's chronographs; Kenneth Borris for sending me his doctoral dissertation on Book VI and for responding to my commentary on several cantos of Book VI; Jean R. Brink for advice on the Chronology; Douglas Brooks-Davies for his learned commentary on Books I and II; Donald Bruce for information on Spenser's life in London; Colin Burrow for clarifying Spenser's use of Ovid; Terence Clifford-Amos for information on the poem's English setting; John E. Curran for information on Spenser's use of the chronicles; Walter R. Davis for general help with the commentary; A. Leigh DeNeef for reviewing my commentary on the *Letter to Raleigh*; Michael F.N. Dixon for sharing his knowledge of Spenser's use of rhetoric; John Downie, with Norman Zacour, for solving my computer problems expeditiously; Wayne Erickson for information on the geography of *The Faerie Queene*; Andrew Hadfield for making me realize the importance of Spenser's life in Ireland; William M. Hamlin for advice on Spenser and the New World; Mark A. Heberle for commenting on the Introduction; Ronald Arthur Horton for his exposition of the virtues; Anthea Hume for commenting on the Introduction; Sean Kane for explaining Spenser's use of the homilies; Ross Kilpatrick for patiently and thoroughly vetting my Greek; Jeffrey Knapp for advice on Spenser and the New World; Masaru Kosako for advice on Spenser's use of rhyme; Theresa M. Krier for general advice on my comment-

ary; Kenneth J. Larsen for information on Spenser's use of the *Book of Common Prayer*; F.J. Levy for advice on the *Commendatory Verses*; George M. Logan for aiding my research when he was Head of the Queen's English Department; Ruth Samson Luborsky for help with the *1590* woodcut; Willy Maley for help with the Chronology, and all matters Scottish; Richard Mallette for commenting on the Introduction; Lawrence Manley for help on the topography of London; John Manning for his careful review of the annotations to the first Longman edition; Steven W. May for help with the *Commendatory Verses*; David Lee Miller for commenting on the *Dedicatory Sonnets*; Jerry Leath Mills for advice on Spenser's use of the chronicles; John Mulryan for sending me his translation of Conti's *Mythologiae*; James Nohrnberg for writing his indispensable *The Analogy of 'The Faerie Queene'*; William A. Oram for general advice; Charlotte Otten for explaining Spenser's use of herbs; Lawrence F. Rhu for determining Spenser's use of Tasso's *Allegoria*; J. Michael Richardson for help on Spenser's astronomical and astrological references; Maren-Sofie Røstvig for her insight into the unifying patterns of *The Faerie Queene*; Paul R. Rovang for explaining Spenser's use of Malory; Mats Rydén for advice on the Renaissance lore of plants and flowers; Naseeb Shaheen for information on Spenser's use of the Bible; David R. Shore for his comments on the 1977 annotations; Lauren Silberman for her reading of Books III and IV; Dorothy Stephens for advice on Spenser's treatment of women; Gordon Teskey for advice on the *Letter to Raleigh* and much else; Kathryn Walls for advice on the ecclesiastical history in Book I; John Watkins for his study of Spenser and Virgil; Harold L. Weatherby for clarification of Spenser's religious background; Robin Headlam Wells for information on Spenser's references to music; and Alan Young for advice on all chivalric matters. In addition, there are those to whom I am much indebted who, alas, have died: Don Cameron Allen who first encouraged me to write; F.W. Bateson whose support made the first Longman edition possible; Northrop Frye who first awakened my interest in Spenser; John E. Hankins who instructed me in Spenser's use of sources; Hugh Maclean for his sustaining friendship over many decades; and Helena Shire for lively discussions of Spenser's poetry.

As the many references to *The Spenser Encyclopedia* indicate, I am much indebted to its contributors. Reference to their scholarship has allowed me to condense the annotations very considerably. For Spenser's shorter poems, I cite the Yale edition edited by William A. Oram *et al.*; and for their valuable annotations, I have also consulted the editions by Douglas Brooks-Davies and Richard A. McCabe.

Since Spenser dedicated the first edition of *The Faerie Queene* to Queen Elizabeth, he would have rejoiced, as I do, that over four centuries later a Queen with the same name would graciously allow an annotated edition of his poem to be dedicated to her.

A.C. Hamilton
Cappon Professor Emeritus
Kingston, Canada
hamiltna@post.queensu.ca

ACKNOWLEDGEMENTS

The first edition in 1977 was published with the help of a grant from the Humanities Research Council of Canada, using funds provided by the Canada Council. The second edition in 2001 was published with the help of The Great Britain Sasakawa Foundation and The Daiwa Anglo-Japanese Foundation. This third edition has been corrected with the help of generous readers world-wide.

CHRONOLOGICAL TABLE
OF SPENSER'S LIFE AND WORKS

1552?

Born in London, 'my most kyndly Nurse, | That to me gave this Lifes first native sourse' (*Proth* 128–29). (Possibly 1553 or 1554, as conjectured from *Am* 60.) On the tradition that he was born in East Smithfield near the Tower of London, see Bruce 1995a:284. His family may have come from Lancashire, and his father may have been a cloth weaver who belonged to the Merchant Taylors' Company. (The lack of evidence is noted by Brink 1997a.) In several of his poems, he claimed kinship with 'An house of auncient fame' (*Proth*), the Spencers of Wormleighton in Warwickshire and of Althorp in Northamptonshire, who, in turn, claimed descent from the ancient house of Despencer, earls of Gloucester and Winchester. On the family's great wealth from sheep, see Finch 1956:38–65. S. may have known the possible connection with William Langland, whose father was *tenens domini le Spenser in comitatu Oxon* (fifteenth-century note in a *Piers Plowman* ms., Trinity College, Dublin).

1561

Enters Merchant Taylors' School, a newly founded boys' school in central London, as a 'poor scholar' who would not be charged full fees. On his education for the next eight years, see 'Merchant Taylors' School' in the *SEnc*, and Bruce 1994:74–78. Its first headmaster was the classical scholar and educationalist Richard Mulcaster, who was a strong defender of the English language: 'I honor the *Latin*, but I worship the *English*' (cited in 1994:xlviii). Among S.'s fellow or near-fellow students were Lancelot Andrewes, Thomas Kyd, and Thomas Lodge.

1569

Feb. Gets a gown and a shilling to attend the funeral of Robert Nowell, a wealthy Londoner and chief beneficiary of the school.

Publishes anonymously six 'Epigrams' illustrated by woodcuts (tr. from Petrarch's *Rime* 323 using Clément Marot's French version), eleven 'Sonets'

(tr. from Joachim du Bellay's *Songe* appended to *Antiquitez de Rome*), and four 'Sonets' (tr. from Noot's poems in French on visions from Revelation) for the English edition of *A theatre wherein be represented as wel the miseries and calamities that follow the voluptuous Worldlings, As also the great ioyes and plesures which the faithfull do enioy*. This militantly anti-Catholic work compiled by Jan van der Noot, a Dutch Calvinist refugee living in London, was published a year earlier in Dutch and French. See 'Noot, Jan van der' and '*A Theatre for Worldlings*' in the *SEnc*. The first two sets of poems, revised, were included at the end of *Complaints* (1591) as *The Visions of Bellay* and *The Visions of Petrarch*.

20 May Matriculates at Pembroke Hall (now Pembroke College), Cambridge, as a sizar (a poor, though not necessarily penniless, scholar required to work as a servant for his tuition). Receives a grant of ten shillings from the Nowell bequest. A formative friendship begins with Gabriel Harvey, Fellow of Pembroke from 1570.

18 Oct. Bill signed to 'Edmonde Spencer' (possibly the poet) as bearer from Tours of letters to the Queen from Sir Henry Norris, English ambassador to France.

1570–74

Receives various amounts from the Nowell bequest: e.g. *7 Nov. 1570* six shillings; *24 Apr. 1571* two shillings sixpence. On *10 Oct. 1574*, he receives four payments from Pembroke Hall. Awarded B.A. in 1573, eleventh in a list of 120 candidates.

1576

Awarded M.A., 66th in a list of 70 candidates. Since he was not required to remain in Cambridge after 1574, he may have gone down to London where the Master of Pembroke Hall, John Young, resided (Judson 1945:37; Brink 1996:55), or visited the 'Northparts', presumably the family home in Lancashire, but returned south, according to E.K. in his gloss to *SC June*, 'for his more preferment'. About this time he may have become 'enamored of a countrie lasse called Rosalinde' (E.K. gloss to *Jan.* Arg); see 'Rosalind' in the *SEnc*.

1577

1 July It is possible, though unlikely, that he was in Ireland bearing letters from Leicester to the Lord Deputy, Henry Sidney, for in the *View* 62, Irenius (who speaks for the New English in Ireland, of which S. became one) says that he witnessed the execution of 'a notable traitor', Murrogh O'Brien, at Limerick in July. Yet that claim may be only anti-Catholic polemic, as Hadfield 1999 argues.

1578

20 Dec. Harvey records that S. presented him with four jestbooks (*Till Eulenspiegel*, *Jests of Scoggin*, *Merie tales by Skelton*, and *Lazarillo de Tormes*), to be read by 1 Jan. or forfeit his four-volume Lucian; noted Stern 1979:228. In a copy of Jerome Turler's *Traueiler*, Harvey writes: 'ex dono Edmundi Spenserii, Episcopi Roffensis Secretarii' (Stern 1979:237), revealing that S. was in Bromley, Kent, as secretary to Young, who became Bishop of Rochester in April.

1579

10 Apr. Date of the Prefatory Epistle to *The Shepheardes Calender* by E.K., whose identity is not revealed. (He may be Edward Kirke who was also a sizar at Pembroke Hall at that time: see 'E.K.' in the *SEnc*, and McCarthy 2000.) Nor is S.'s identity revealed: in the Envoy, he signs himself *Immeritô* (the unworthy). The work is dedicated to Philip Sidney.
10 July Addressed by Harvey (1884:65) as 'my yunge Italianate Seignior and French Monsieur'.
5 Oct. Writes to Harvey from 'Leycester House' that he has an appointment in the household of the Earl, and intends to devote his time 'to his Honours seruice'. He also writes that he expects to be sent to France as Leicester's confidential emissary. On 23 Oct., Harvey replies that this will not happen.
15–16 Oct. Writes to Harvey from Westminster to say that he is in 'some vse of familiarity' with Sidney and Edward Dyer, who 'haue proclaimed in their ἀρείῳ πάγῳ, a generall surceasing and silence of balde Rymers' (see 'Areopagus' in the *SEnc*), that he intends to dedicate a work (presumably the *SC*) to Leicester but fears it may be 'too base for his excellent Lordship', and refers to his 'late beeing with hir Maiestie'.

27 Oct. An 'Edmounde Spenser' (probably the poet) marries Machabyas [= Maccabaeus] Chylde, aged twenty, at St Margaret's, Westminster. For his association with Westminster, see Bruce 1997. Marriage ended any chance for a college fellowship. The date of his wife's death is not known. There were two children: Sylvanus (probably named after Mulcaster's son) and Katherine (the name of Mulcaster's wife and daughter).
5 Dec. The *Shepheardes Calender* entered in the Stationers' Register. By this year S. may have written part of *Prosopopoia: Mother Hubberds Tale*. He had started to write *The Faerie Queene*, for in a letter in Apr. 1580 Harvey mentions having read one parcel of it. E.K. refers to some 'lost' works: *Dreames*, for which he has 'discoursed . . . at large in my Commentarye' (a work praised by Harvey for 'that singular extra-ordinarie veine and inuention' found in the best Greek and Italian writers), *Legendes*, *Court of Cupide* (perhaps revised in *FQ* III xi–xii, VI vii), a translation of Moschus's *Idyllion of Wandring Love* (possibly from Politian's Latin version), *Pageaunts*, *The English Poete* (a critical treatise that would be a companion to the second part of Sidney's *Defence of Poetry*), and *Sonnets*. See 'works, lost' in the *SEnc*.

1580

19 June Publication of correspondence between S. and Harvey in a two-part volume: 1. *Three proper, and wittie, Familiar letters: lately passed betwene two Vniuersitie men: touching the Earthquake in April last, and our English refourmed Versifying*; 2. *Two other, very commendable Letters, of the same mens writing: both touching the foresaid Artificiall Versifying, and certain other Particulars*. The second part contains earlier letters. S.'s two letters are dated from Leicester House, 5 October 1579 (including a letter of 15–16 October), and from Westminster, 'Quarto Nonas Aprilis 1580' (2 Apr., perhaps in error for 10 Apr.). See 'letters, Spenser's and Harvey's' in the *SEnc*, and Quitslund 1996. These are S.'s only surviving personal letters, and, fittingly, Harvey refers to S.'s *altera Rosalindula . . . mea bellissima Collina Clouta* (a changed little Rosalind, my most charming Lady Colin Clout), and S., in his Latin poem 'Ad Ornatissimum virum', names himself 'Edmundus' (Spenser 1912:638). The letters mention the *FQ* for the first time and refer to a number of his 'lost' works: *My Slomber* (which he intended to dedicate to Edward Dyer), *Dreames* (see under 1579), *Dying Pellicane* (most likely an allegory of the death of Christ), both being described by him as 'fully finished', *Epithalamion Thamesis* ('whyche Booke I dare vndertake wil be very profitable for the knowledge, and rare for the Inuention, and manner of handling'; possibly revised in *FQ* IV xi), *Nine Comoedies* (named after the nine Muses, and praised by Harvey for 'the finenesse of plausible Elocution' and 'the rarenesse of Poetical Inuention'), and the Latin *Stemmata Dudleiana* in praise of the Leicester family. The correspondence includes S.'s *Iambicum Trimetrum* and two short fragments in which he applies quantitative classical metres to English versification.

12 Aug. Appointed one of the secretaries of Arthur Lord Grey de Wilton, the newly appointed Lord Deputy of Ireland. His senior was Timothy Reynolds. It is likely that they arrived with him in Ireland, along with Geoffrey Fenton, who was appointed as the principal secretary of state. Salary £10 half-yearly. Served as Grey's amanuensis, and paymaster for his messengers (i.e. informants). He may have travelled with him, or remained in Dublin to receive information from him to send to the English court. See Rambuss 1993:25–28 and Rambuss 1996 on his career as a secretary. On whether his appointment was a preferment or exile, see McCabe 1993a, Carey and Carroll 1996, and Brink 1996; for an account of S.'s Irish experience, see Bruce 1995b, and Hadfield 1997:13–50; and for his exile as a formative influence on *FQ* I, see Breen 1996.

9 Nov. May have accompanied Grey, who entered the fort at Smerwick in Munster after Raleigh had directed what in *View* 107 is called 'that sharp execution of the Spaniards' – they were chiefly Italian filibusters with their Irish supporters – some 500–600 in all. For a contemporary account, see Maley 1997:65.

1581

The Shepheardes Calender, second edition.

Mar. Appointed registrar or clerk of faculties in the Irish Court of Chancery, for seven years. Since he continued to serve Grey, a deputy may have carried out his duties, which were to record 'faculties' (dispensations and licences) issued by the Archbishop of Dublin.

6 Dec. Leases the Abbey and Manor of Enniscorthy, in Co. Wexford, but evidently it was forfeited almost immediately. About this time he leases New Ross, a

dissolved Augustinian friary, also in Co. Wexford, which he held until 1584.

1582

24 Aug. Leases the dissolved house of friars, called New Abbey, Kilcullen in Co. Kildare, about 25 miles from Dublin at £3 annual rent. Now a landowner, he is addressed as 'Gent.' At this time he had leased a house in Dublin.

31 Aug. After repeated appeals, Grey is recalled to England – see *View* 106 – thus ending S.'s appointment with him, having served on the national level for slightly over two years. Hereafter his public role became largely regional.

1583

Appointed a commissioner of musters for Co. Kildare, and again the next year. With others, his duty was to compile a list of able-bodied men and judge their ability to fight.

6 Nov. At this time, or early in 1584, became deputy to Lodowick Bryskett, clerk of the council of Munster, at a salary of £7 10s. (His successor, Nicholas Curteys, refers to it as 'that poor and troublesome place'; cited Judson 1945:160). During the next few years it is likely that he attended council meetings at Limerick and Cork as secretary of its president, John Norris. Bryskett claims to record a conversation with him and others in *A Discourse of Civill Life* (1606 but written much earlier for Lord Grey). See 'Bryskett, Lodowick' in the *SEnc*, and Maley 1997:69–72. For the S. circle, esp. in Ireland, see Maley 1994:85–108.

1584

21 June May have travelled with Sir John Perrot, Grey's successor.

1585

26 Apr. It is likely that, with Norris, he attended the Irish Parliament, which met until 14 May, and again in the next year with Norris's brother Thomas.

1586

The Shepheardes Calender, third edition.

18 July S.'s sonnet to Harvey, signed 'Your deuoted frend, during life', dated from Dublin, and published in Harvey's *Foure Letters and certaine Sonnets* (1592).

8 Dec. Named as prebendary of Effin, attached to Limerick Cathedral. Probably a sinecure, a nonresident living that S. mocks in *Mother Hubberd* 419–22.

1589

22 May Occupies the ruined castle of Kilcolman, Co. Cork, with an estate of 3,028 acres, from the forfeited lands of the Earl of Desmond. The grant to hold this property 'for ever, in fee farm, by the name of "Hap Hazard" by fealty, in common socage [i.e. rent]' was issued on 26 Oct. 1590, about £20 annual rent. Now an undertaker, S. claims to have settled 'six households of English people upon his land'; cited Maley 1994:51. His ownership was contested by the Anglo-Irish Lord Roche. Visited by his neighbour, Raleigh, as he records in *Colin Clout.*

Oct. Having succeeded Bryskett as clerk of the council of Munster, leaves a substitute deputy to journey with Raleigh to England; see Carpenter 1923:33. Given an audience by the Queen, who was pleased to have him read the *FQ* to her, 'And it desir'd at timely houres to heare'.

1 Dec. Entered in the Stationers' Register by William Ponsonby, 'a booke intytuled *the fayrye Queene dysposed into xii. bookes, &c*'.

1590

Publication of *The Faerie Queene* Books I–III, to which was appended the *Letter to Raleigh* (dated '23 Jan. 1589' (OS) = 1590 (NS), *Commendatory Verses*, and *Dedicatory Sonnets.*

May In the Dedication to *The Ruines of Time*, pub. 1591, refers to 'my late cumming into England'. (In the preface to *Complaints*, Ponsonby refers to S.'s 'departure over Sea'.) He may have returned to Ireland to handle litigation with Lord Roche.

29 Dec. Complaints entered in the Stationers' Register.

1591

Publication of nine poems, some written much earlier, under the title: *Complaints. Containing sundrie small Poemes of the Worlds Vanitie,* 'being all complaints and meditations of the worlds vanitie, verie graue and profitable': *The Ruines of Time; The Teares of the Muses; Virgils Gnat* (a version of the pseudo-Virgilian *Culex,* said to be 'Long since dedicated To . . . the Earle of Leicester'); *Prosopopoia, or Mother Hubberds Tale; Ruines of Rome: by Bellay* (tr. of *Les Antiquitez de Rome*); *Muiopotmos, or The Fate of the Butterflie* (dated 1590); *Visions of the Worlds Vanitie; The Visions of Bellay* (rev. from the first eleven 'Sonets' in Noot's *Theatre;* see 1569 above); and *The Visions of Petrarch; formerly translated* (rev. from the Epigrams in Noot's *Theatre*). For a general account,

see '*Complaints*' in the *SEnc;* for their relation to the literary tradition, see Brown 1999.

Mother Hubberd was 'called in' (i.e. unsold copies were confiscated; see Peterson 1998:7) apparently because of its satire against Burghley. Harvey noted: 'Mother-Hubbard in heat of choller, forgetting the pure sanguine of her sweete Faery Queene, wilfully ouer-shott her malcontented selfe'; cited *Sp All* 24. On its textual history, which indicates that the publication was not authorized by S., see Brink 1991. The printer, Ponsonby, wanted to publish other poems by S.: '*Ecclesiastes,* and *Canticum canticorum* translated, *A senights slumber* [cf. *My Slomber,* under 1580], *The hell of louers, his Purgatorie* . . . Besides some other Pamphlets looselie scattered abroad: as *The dying Pellican* [see under 1580], *The howers of the Lord, The sacrifice of a sinner, The seuen Psalmes* [i.e. the penitential psalms]'. None has survived.

The Shepheardes Calender, fourth edition.

25 Feb. Granted a life pension of £50 per annum by the Queen. (Only Thomas Churchyard was so honoured two years later, but his amount, about £30, did not qualify him for the rank of gentleman.) May have returned to Ireland by this time to resume his office as deputy clerk (or clerk?), though about this time he acquired an assistant to perform his duties.

27 Dec. Dedication of *Colin Clouts Come Home Againe* to Raleigh refers to 'my late being in England' and is signed 'From my house of Kilcolman, the 27. of December. 1591'. (Yet see date of *Daphnaïda* below.) On Ireland not as exile but as home, see Lupton 1990 and Highley 1997:35.

1592

Publication of *Daphnaïda. An Elegie vpon the death of the noble and vertuous Douglas Howard.* Entered in the Stationers' Register, 29 Dec. 1590; dated from London 1 Jan. 1591. Since she died in Aug. 1590, it is less likely that the date is 1592 NS, though he claims to be in Ireland three days earlier, as noted above. See de Selincourt in Spenser 1912:xxxi. Publication of the pseudo-Platonic *Axiochus,* tr. from the Greek by way of the 1568 Latin tr. by Rayanus Welsdalius, said to be 'by *Edw. Spenser*'. See Weatherby 1986.

1594

11 June, St Barnabas' Day Married Elizabeth Boyle, by many years his junior, kinswoman of Sir Richard Boyle, later first Earl of Cork. Their one child is named Peregrine ('Lat. Strange or outlandish', according to W. Camden 1984:93, who includes it in a list of usual Christian names).

Serves as Queen's Justice for Co. Cork.

1595

Publication as one volume, *Amoretti and Epithalamion. Written not long since*, entered in the Stationers' Register 19 Nov. 1594. A record of a courtship and marriage. In *Am* 80, S. writes that he has completed the six books of the *FQ*. Dedicated by Ponsonby to Sir Robert Needham, who brought the ms. to England.

Publication of *Colin Clouts Come Home Againe*: 'this simple pastorall . . . agreeing with the truth in circumstance and matter' records Raleigh's visit, their voyage to England, and their stay at court in 1589. The volume includes *Astrophel. A Pastorall Elegie vpon the death of the most Noble and valorous Knight, Sir Philip Sidney*, and (most likely by S. though attributed to the Countess of Pembroke) *The Doleful Lay of Clorinda*, and five more elegies on Sidney's death by Bryskett, Raleigh, and others.

Commendatory sonnet prefixed to William Jones's English tr. from the Italian: *Nennio, or a Treatise of Nobility: Wherein is discoursed what true Nobilitie is, with such qualities as are required in a perfect Gentleman*.

1596

Publication of the second edition of *The Faerie Queene* Books I–III together with the first edition of Books IV–VI. The only evidence that S. was in England to enter the poem in the Stationers' Register on 20 Jan. and supervise its printing, which must have taken place some time before 12 Nov., is that *Fowre Hymnes* is dedicated from the court at 'Greenwich this first of September, 1596'. He may have been prevented from leaving Ireland except briefly by the June 1595 rebellion of the Earl of Tyrone.

Publication of *Fowre Hymnes* (*Of Love, Of Beautie, Of Heavenly Love, Of Heavenly Beautie*), the first two written, as he explains in the dedication, 'in the greener times of my youth', and the second two 'to amend, and by way of retractation to reforme them'. See Oates 1984. The volume includes the second edition of *Daphnaïda*.

Publication of *Prothalamion*, spousal verse celebrating the betrothal of two daughters of the Earl of Worcester. S. coined the title for a pre-wedding celebration.

Commendatory sonnet prefixed to Jaques de Lavardin, *The Historie of George Castriot, surnamed*

Scanderbeg, King of Albanie, tr. from the French by Z.I. (Zachary Jones).

12 Nov. Complaint by King James of Scotland that his mother was slandered as Duessa in *FQ* V ix. See V ix 38–50*n*. Sale of the poem was banned in Scotland, noted Maley 1994:67.

1597

The Shepheardes Calender, fifth edition.

Purchases the castle and lands of Renny in south Cork for his son, Peregrine. Also about this time purchases Buttevant Abbey near Kilcolman.

1598

25 Feb. A report that an Irishman, Walter Quin, was 'answering Spencers book whereat the K [King James] was offended'; noted Carpenter 1923:42.

14 Apr. Entry in the Stationers' Register: '*A viewe of the present state of Ireland. Discoursed by waye of a Dialogue betwene Eudoxus and Irenius*, vppon Condician that hee [Matthew Lownes, the printer] gett further aucthoritie before yt be prynted'. Probably written in 1596 for it was circulating in ms. at this time, but since further authority seems not to have been given, it did not appear until much later; see 1633.

30 Sept. Appointed Sheriff-designate of Cork, recommended by the Privy Council to the lords justices as 'a gentleman dwelling in the county of Cork, who is so well known unto your lordships for his good and commendable parts (being a man endowed with good knowledge in learning and not unskilful or without experience in the service of the wars)'; cited Judson 1945:200.

Oct. Kilcolman Castle sacked and burned by Irish rebels during the Tyrone Rebellion. With his wife takes refuge in Cork.

9 Dec. Leaves for London and delivers despatches from Sir Thomas Norris, President of Munster, to the Privy Council meeting at Whitehall on Christmas Eve. On behalf of the Munster planters, S. may have delivered three state papers in which he may have had a hand, *A briefe note of Ireland, To the Queene*, and *Certaine pointes to be considered of in the recouery of the Realme of Ireland*. On their attribution, see 'A Brief Note of Ireland', in the *SEnc*, and Brink 1997b.

1599

Commendatory sonnet prefixed to Cardinal Gasper Contareno, *The Commonwealth and Government of Venice*, tr. from the Italian by Lewes Lewkenor.

13 Jan. Died at Westminster. Jonson told Drummond 'That the Irish having Robd Spensers goods & burnt his house & a litle child new born [the poet's?], he and his wyfe escaped [to Cork and then to England?], & after, he died for lake of bread jn King Street' (1925–52:1.137). That he died for lack of bread, though supported by Camden, does not accord with the £8 he was said to have been paid on 30 Dec. 1598 and a pension of £25 due at Christmas. See Heffner 1933. Jonson first recorded that the funeral expenses were paid by the Earl of Essex through the intercession of Lodowick Lloyd, but Underwood 1996 cites a ms. poem by John Lane which attributes the cost to Lloyd himself. Buried in Westminster Abbey, as Camden records, 'neere *Chawcer*, at the charges of the Earle of *Essex*, all Poets carrying his body to Church, and casting their dolefull Verses, and Pens too into his graue' (*Sp All* 178–79). Elizabeth's order that a memorial be erected was not carried out until 1620.

1609

First folio edition of *The Faerie Queene* Books I–VI, together with first edition of *Two Cantos of Mutabilitie*.

1611

The Faerie Queen: The Shepheardes Calender: Together with the other Works of England's Arch-Poët, Edm. Spenser: Collected into one Volume. The first folio of S.'s collected works, excluding *Mother Hubberds Tale* in order not to offend Burghley's son, Robert Cecil, Lord Treasurer. (After Cecil's death in 1612, it was included in the 1612–13 printing; see F.R. Johnson 1933:41.)

1617

Second folio edition of the collected works.

1620

A funeral memorial, commissioned by Lady Anne Clifford and constructed by Nicholas Stone, James I's chief mason, was erected in Westminster Abbey at a cost of £40 with the inscription 'Heare lyes (expecting the second comminge of our Saviour Christ Jesus) the body of Edmond Spencer, the Prince of Poets in his tyme; whose divine spirit needs noe othir witnesse then the works which he left behinde him' (Judson 1945:207). Restored in marble 1778 and still in place.

1633

Publication of *A vewe of the present state of Irelande*, ed. Sir James Ware in *Ancient Irish Chronicles*. Possibly suppressed until this year. On the matter of S.'s authorship, see Brink 1997b:95–100 and Hadfield 1998a. In the Preface, Ware refers to 'the later part' of the *FQ* lost by a servant.

1679

Publication of *The Works of that Famous English Poet, Mr. Edmond Spenser*. The title suggests that used for Chaucer: *The Workes* (1532, 1561).

The chief facts about S.'s life are compiled by Carpenter 1923:11–22, Atkinson 1937:1–6, and comprehensively, with a full account of S.'s letters on Grey's behalf, by Maley 1994. The standard biography remains Judson 1945. See also 'Spenser, Edmund' in the *SEnc*, and Waller 1994. For a brief account, see Tonkin 1989:1–16, essays in Anderson, Cheney and Richardson 1996, and Oram 1997:1–24. On the autobiographical fiction in S.'s poetry after 1590, see D. Cheney 1984; on his effort to seek an active life of service to the common weal, see Levy 1996; on the scripting of his life as a poet, see Pask 1996:83–112. In a 1946 review of Judson's *Life*, Conyers Read noted the paucity of our knowledge: 'Outside of what Edmund Spenser himself wrote all that is positively known about his life could probably be written in a few short paragraphs. The rest is inference, surmise, and conjecture' (*AHR* 51:539). D. Cheney 1996:172 concludes that evidence for S.'s life is questionable: 'not merely doubtful but calling its own authority into question and demanding that we question it'.

ABBREVIATIONS

Spenser's poems

Am	*Amoretti*
As	*Astrophel*
Bellay	*Visions of Bellay*
Colin Clout	*Colin Clouts Come Home Againe*
Comm Sonn	*Commendatory Sonnets*
CV	*Commendatory Verses to the FQ*
Daph	*Daphnaïda*
DS	*Dedicatory Sonnets to the FQ*
Epith	*Epithalamion*
FQ	*The Faerie Queene*
Gnat	*Virgils Gnat*
HB	*An hymne in honour of beautie*
HL	*An hymne in honour of love*
HHB	*An hymne of heavenly beauty*
HHL	*An hymne of heavenly love*
LR	*A letter of the authors . . . to . . . Sir Walter Raleigh*
Mother Hubberd	*Prosopopoia: Mother Hubberds Tale*
Muiopotmos	*Muiopotmos, or The Fate of the Butterflie*
Petrarch	*The Visions of Petrarch*
Proth	*Prothalamion*
Rome	*Ruines of Rome*
SC	*The Shepheardes Calender*
Teares	*Teares of the Muses*
Theatre	*A Theatre for Worldlings*
Three Letters	*Three Proper Letters* (in Spenser 1912:609–32)
Time	*Ruines of Time*
Two Letters	*Two Commendable Letters* (in Spenser 1912:633–43)
Vanitie	*Visions of the Worlds Vanitie*
View	*A View of the Present State of Ireland*, ed. W.L. Renwick, London, 1934; rev. Oxford, 1970

Common abbreviations

1590	The first edition of Books I–III of the *FQ* together with *LR*, *CV*, and *DS*
1596	The second edition of Books I–III and first edition of Books IV–VI together with *CV 1–3*
1609	The first folio edition of Books I–VI together with the *Two Cantos of Mutabilitie*
BCP	*The Book of Common Prayer 1559: The Elizabethan Prayer Book*, ed. John E. Booty, Charlottesville, VA, 1976
EA	*Essential Articles for the Study of Edmund Spenser*, ed. A.C. Hamilton, Hamden, CT, 1972

Enc. Brit.	*Encyclopædia Britannica*, 11th edn, Cambridge
F.E.	'Faults escaped in the Print' in *1590*
NT	New Testament
OED	*The Oxford English Dictionary*
OT	Old Testament
SEnc	*The Spenser Encyclopedia*, ed. A.C. Hamilton, Donald Cheney, W.F. Blissett, David A. Richardson, and William Barker, Toronto, 1990; rev. 1992
Smith Charles G.	*Spenser's Proverb Lore: With Special Reference to His Use of the* Sententiae *of Leonard Culman and Publilius Syrus*, Cambridge, MA, 1970
Sp All	*Spenser Allusions in the Sixteenth and Seventeenth Centuries*, ed. William Wells. *SP* Texts and Studies 68–69, 1971–72
STC	*Short-title Catalogue . . . 1475–1640*, ed. A.W. Pollard and G.R. Redgrave in 1926, rev. and enl. W.A. Jackson, F.S. Ferguson, and Katharine F. Pantzer, London, 1976
Tilley	Morris Palmer Tilley, *A Dictionary of the Proverbs in England in the Sixteenth and Seventeenth Centuries*, Ann Arbor, MI, 1950
Var	*The Works of Edmund Spenser, a Variorum Edition*, ed. Edwin Greenlaw, *et al.*, 11 vols, Baltimore, MD, 1932–57

Editions

BIRCH, THOMAS 1751 *The Faerie Queene*, 3 vols, London

BROOKS-DAVIES, DOUGLAS 1977 *Spenser's 'Faerie Queene': A critical commentary on Books I and II*, Manchester

BROOKS-DAVIES, DOUGLAS 1987 *The Faerie Queene, Books I–III*, London

BROOKS-DAVIES, DOUGLAS 1995 *Selected Shorter Poems*, Longman Annotated Texts, London

CHURCH, RALPH 1758 *The Faerie Queene*, 4 vols, London

COLLIER, J. PAYNE 1862 *Works*, 5 vols, London

DODGE, R.E. NEIL 1908 *Complete Poetical Works*, Boston, MA

GOUGH, ALFRED B. 1918 *The Faerie Queene, Book V*, Oxford; rev. 1921

HUGHES, JOHN 1715 *Works*, 6 vols, London; rev. 1750

KELLOGG, ROBERT, and OLIVER STEELE 1965 *Books I and II of 'The Faerie Queene' and 'The Mutability Cantos'*, New York

KERMODE, FRANK 1965 *Selections*, London

KITCHIN, G.W. 1905 *The Faery Queene, Books I and II*, 2 vols, London [First pub. 1867]

MACLEAN, HUGH, and ANNE LAKE PRESCOTT 1993, *Edmund Spenser's Poetry*, New York

ORAM, WILLIAM A., *et al.* 1989 *The Shorter Poems*, New Haven

PERCIVAL, H.M. 1964 *The Faerie Queene, Book I*, London; first pub. 1893

RENWICK, W.L. 1923 *Selections, With Essays by Hazlitt, Coleridge, & Leigh Hunt*, Oxford

ROCHE, THOMAS P., JR with C. PATRICK O'DONNELL, JR 1978 *The Faerie Queene*, Harmondsworth

SMITH, J.C. 1909 *The Faerie Queene*, 2 vols, Oxford

SMITH, J.C. and E. DE SÉLINCOURT 1912 *Poetical Works*, Oxford

TODD, H.J. 1805 *Works*, 8 vols, London

UPTON, JOHN 1758 *Spenser's 'Faerie Queene': A New Edition with a Glossary, and Notes explanatory and critical*, 2 vols, London; ed., John Radcliffe, New York, 1987

VAR 1932–57 *The Works of Edmund Spenser, A Variorum Edition* by Edwin Greenlaw *et al.*, 11 vols, Baltimore, MD

WINSTANLEY, LILIAN 1914–15 *The Faerie Queene, Books I and II*, Cambridge

ZITNER, S.P. 1968 *The Mutabilitie Cantos*, London

GENERAL INTRODUCTION

Spenser's *Faerie Queene* is a canonical poem in the sense that for over four centuries it has remained central to the literary experience of readers, however select a group, for it continues to address directly and profoundly, as only poetry may, their most deeply held private and public values, concerns, and anxieties. It is very much of its own age, being in Milton's phrase 'doctrinal to a nation', for it addressed its first readers from the centre of their culture. There is no part of that culture, from religion to ethics and from philosophy to politics, to which it is not relevant, either directly or allusively. Yet the poem is not time-bound for it has transcended its own age to live in later ages. It has become an English classic in the sense that it is inexhaustible in its relevance to our life, as Homer's *Iliad* and *Odyssey* were to Chapman, who found in them 'all learning, government and wisedome being deduc't as from a bottomlesse fountaine', or as Petrarch's *Triumphs* were to Lord Morley: 'who that doth understande them, shall se in them comprehended al morall vertue, all Phylosophye, all storyall matters, and briefely manye devyne sentences [and] theologicall secretes declared'. To term it a classic may imply that it is to be honoured but remain unread. However, as Radcliffe's 1996 study of its reception testifies, for more than four centuries it has proven to be encyclopedic in its appeal, its comprehensiveness, and its inclusiveness – what he calls its 'monumentality'. See 'Imitations and Adaptations, Renaissance (1579–1660)' and 'Imitations and Adaptations, 1660–1800' in the *SEnc*, Wurtsbaugh 1936, Kramnick 1998:137–89, and Frushell 1999. Of course, the Spenser who is our contemporary need not have been recognizable to his first readers as their contemporary, for we recreate his poem within our culture, in our image rather than theirs, and never more thoroughly than in the second half of the twentieth century. It may be continually recreated because it is a classic in the terms argued by Kermode 1975:43: it speaks to us directly in our time by requiring us to speak to it in its own time.

As with any literary work, the words of *The Faerie Queene* first turn inward to establish the poem's own identity, however much it employs the ordinary language of its day, common literary conventions, and stock generic patterns, and takes its matter from its age. As many studies have indicated, the poem is elaborately constructed, both drawing readers intensely into its episodes, cantos, and books and requiring them to stand back to see them as parts of a whole, a single literary universe. Whether consciously or not, readers are sustained by some vision or idea of the work's wholeness. As a consequence, the first and essential context for understanding any stanza of the poem is the rest of the poem. To read it otherwise is to read it out of context. As readers have always known, the poem is uniquely 'literary' in creating its own reality in faery land rather than reflecting ordinary reality, being much closer to myth than to realism. This point was made by Lewis 1936:358 in explaining Spenser's 'true likeness to life': 'The things we read about in [*The Faerie Queene*] are not like life, but the experience of reading it is like living'. The same point is made by Spenser in the course of explaining to his chief reader, Queen Elizabeth as Gloriana, the Queen of Faery land: 'In this faire mirrhour maist behold thy face, | And thine owne realmes in lond of Faery'.

While the words that construct the world of *The Faerie Queene* turn inward to define their own meanings within the poem, of necessity they point outward to the 'real' world of the late sixteenth century. Jonson's complaint that Spenser 'writ no Language' is valid but only limitedly so. This can be illustrated by the first example that confronts the reader. From the opening line: 'A gentle Knight was pricking on the plaine', the reader anticipates the simple, direct pleasure of an exciting chivalric story of adventures, especially on being told that the knight is on a quest to slay a dragon. This is not the kind of thing that happens in life but it does happen in literature, and one may speculate that such tales have always been popular ever since human beings hunted the woolly mammoth. Yet in the course of reading, each of these terms – 'gentle', 'Knight', 'pricking', 'plaine' – acquires special and distinct meanings in the poem. For the moment, though, even without knowing anything about the appropriate attire of chivalric knights, one expects this knight to be clad 'in mightie armes and siluer shielde', and would be only momentarily puzzled on learning that he is wearing second-hand armour. The simple pleasure of reading a story, as it were for its own sake, is interrupted and complicated only when we are told that he bears 'a bloodie Crosse' on his breast as 'The deare remembrance of his dying Lord'. The 'bloodie Crosse' names him the Red Cross Knight, and, for its first readers, involves his story in the complexities of Renaissance religion, one minor example being the controversy over the use of commemorative icons, such as the proclamation by the Lord Deputy in Ireland in 1579 that every horseman wear a red cross on his breast and another on his back. (See R. Smith 1955:673.) Another such complexity is the knight's identity: after he slays the dragon, the poem's earliest annotator, John Dixon, names him 'Christe'. As meanings and associations multiply, the poem is exposed to what Spenser most feared and needed to control, 'the daunger of enuy, and suspition of present time' (*LR12*). For its early reception, see Cummings 1971.

Criticism

In the twentieth century, academic criticism of *The Faerie Queene* oscillated between a response to its words as they relate to each other and as they relate to the age. (For an account of critical approaches to the poem up to the 1960s, see Hamilton 1968.) The first half-century placed the poem in various historical contexts to show how its metaphorical language, if translated into discursive statements that treat its fiction as fact, refers to contemporary events, moral doctrine, religious beliefs, and philosophical ideas. In addition, its classical sources were thoroughly investigated, as were its native sources, particularly Chaucer. Surprisingly, its relation to Langland's *Piers Plowman* has been largely ignored, except by Hamilton 1961b, Anderson 1976, and Crowley 1992, even though – to adapt what Milton told Dryden about his relation to Spenser – Langland was, together with Chaucer, 'his Original'.

The dominance of historical scholarship brought a brief counter-movement in the third quarter of the century: the poem itself was foregrounded in a close analysis of its poetic use of words in metaphor, myth, and generic conventions. In the final quarter, a more dominant counter-movement effected a return to a renewed historical criticism, one that related the poem more broadly to its own culture and especially to ours. While its excesses have been challenged, for example by Stewart 1997:52–89, as the pendulum continues to swing, soon one may expect a consolidated interest in the poem as both a cultural and a literary artefact shaped by the intervening centuries, and shaping our perception of them.

These critical movements considered only incidentally Spenser's declared intention in writing his poem, even though he announces it on the title-page: '*THE FAERIE QUEENE. Disposed into twelue books, Fashioning XII. Morall vertues*', and at the end of the *1590* edition declares in the *Letter to Raleigh* that 'the generall end . . . of all the booke is to fashion a gentleman or noble person in vertuous and gentle discipline' (7–8). He adds that his means of doing so is 'to pourtraict in Arthure, before he was king, the image of a braue knight, perfected in the twelue priuate morall vertues, as Aristotle hath deuised' (18–19). This led earlier historical scholars to examine almost exhaustively how the virtues were defined in the classical and Christian centuries, for they assumed that Spenser inherited a tradition of the virtues that flowed from its source in Aristotle's *Nicomachean Ethics* through a pipe-line (with extensive feeder-lines along the way) directly into his poem. See 'Aristotle and his commentators' in the *SEnc*.

Earlier historical interest in Spenser's virtues culminated in Rosemond Tuve's 1966 study of medieval allegorical imagery in which she argues that the subject of each book of *The Faerie Queene* is not biography or psychological analysis or the exploration of archetypes but a virtue: 'the sought virtue is the unifying factor in *every* Book' (369). In saying this, she is countering an interest in biography by Jones 1930:129, in psychology by M. Evans 1967:143–56, and in archetypes by N. Frye 1957:200–05 and Hamilton 1961a. Also, she is drawing attention to the double title of each book, as Book I contains 'The Legend of the Knight | *of the Red Crosse*, | OR | *Of Holinesse*'. For her, the virtues treated in Spenser's poem were 'inherited' (33) from earlier books, which served as 'channels by which patristic and scholastic doctrine or classification flowed into vernacular writing' (43), as a consequence of which its virtues 'speak in the present of the timeless, and locally of the universal' (32). To illustrate her argument: in the decade in which she wrote, the most notorious crux in Spenser's poem was Guyon's destruction of Acrasia's Bower of Bliss in II xii 83, which had been treated by Grierson 1929:54 as a clash between the beauty-loving Renaissance and the moral Reformation. In the light of the medieval religious tradition examined by Tuve, Guyon destroys the Bower because he 'looks at the kind of complete seduction which means the final death of the soul' (31).

If the New Critics of the 1930s to the early 1950s had been interested in Spenser (few were), they would not have considered his intention in writing *The Faerie Queene* because that topic had been dismissed as a fallacy. For Wimsatt and Beardsley 1954:5 (first proclaimed in 1946), 'The poem is not the critic's own and not the author's (it is detached from the author at birth and goes about the world beyond his power to intend about it or control it)'. So much for any poet's intention, conscious or unconscious, realized or not. Not that it would have mattered much, for the arbiter of taste at that time, T.S. Eliot, had asked rhetorically: 'who, except scholars, and except the eccentric few who are born with a sympathy for such work, or others who have deliberately studied themselves into the right appreciation, can now read through the whole of *The Faerie Queene* with delight?' (1932:443). In *Two Letters*, Spenser acknowledges that the gods had given him the gift to delight but never to be useful (*Dii mihi, dulce diu dederant: verùm vtile numquam*), though he wishes they had; and, in the *Letter to Raleigh*, he recognizes that the general end of his poem could be achieved only through fiction, which 'the most part of men delight to read, rather for variety of matter, then for profite of the ensample' (10). As a consequence, he addresses his readers not by teaching them didactically but rather through delight. It follows that if his poem does not delight, it remains a closed book.

Several critics who first flourished in the 1950s and 1960s responded initially to Spenser's words and imagery rather than to his ideas, thought, or historical context. One is Donald Cheney, who, in *Spenser's Image of Nature* (1966), read *The Faerie Queene* 'under the intensive scrutiny which has been applied in recent decades to metaphysical lyrics', seeking out 'ironic, discordant impulses', 'rapidly shifting allusions', and the poet's 'constant insistence upon the ambiguity of his images' (7, 17, 20). Another is Paul Alpers, whose *The Poetry of 'The Faerie Queene'* (1967) demonstrated that individual stanzas of the poem may be subjected to very intense scrutiny. A third, the most influential of all, is Harry Berger, Jr, who later observed that 'when the first waves of the

"new criticism" washed across the decks of academe, he [Spenser] was quickly swept overboard because of his inability to write like Donne, Eliot, and Allen Tate' (1968:2). His extended interpretation of Book II, *The Allegorical Temper* (1957), followed by essays on the other books, traces the changing psychological or psychic development of the poem's major characters by 'reading the poem as a poem' (9) rather than as a historical document. My own book, *The Structure of Allegory in 'The Faerie Queene'* (1961a), which I regard now as the work of a historical critic partly rehabilitated by myth and archetypal criticism, examines the poem's structure through its patterns of imagery, an interest shared with Alastair Fowler, *Spenser and the Numbers of Time* (1964), and by Kathleen Williams, *Spenser's 'Faerie Queene': The World of Glass* (1966).

In any history of modern Spenser criticism – for a general account, see Hadfield 1996b – Berger may serve as a key transitional figure. In a retrospective glance at his essays on Spenser written from 1958 to 1987, he acknowledges that 'I still consider myself a New Critic, even an old-fashioned one' who has been 'reconstructed' by New Historicism (1989:208). In Berger 1988:453–56, he offers a personal account of his change, admitting that as a New Critic he had been interested 'in exploring complex representations of ethico-psychological patterns' apart from 'the institutional structures and discourses that give them historical specificity'. Even so, he had allowed that earlier historical study, which had been concerned with 'historical specificity', was 'solid and important'. For the New Historicist Louis Adrian Montrose, however, earlier historical scholarship 'merely impoverished the text' (Berger 1988:8), and he is almost as harsh towards Berger himself, complaining that his writings 'have tended to avoid direct confrontations of sociopolitical issues', though he blames 'the absence of a historically specific sociopolitical dimension' on the time they were written – a time when 'the sociopolitical study of Spenser was epitomized by the pursuit of topical identifications or the cataloguing of commonplaces' (7). In contrast, the New Historicism, of which he is the most eloquent theorist, sees a work embedded – i.e. intrinsically, inextricably fixed – not in history generally, and certainly not in 'cosmic politics' that Thomas Greene 1963:406 claims to be the concern of all epics, but in a historically specific *sociopolitical* context. (For further comments on their clash, see Hamilton 1999:103–06.)

Instead of examining how Spenser fashions the virtues in his poem, the New Historical critics consider how the poem was fashioned by his culture and also how its readers today are fashioned by their culture; see Hamilton 1995:374–75. A seminal essay is Stephen Greenblatt's 'To Fashion a Gentleman: Spenser and the Destruction of the Bower of Bliss', in *Renaissance Self-Fashioning* (1980). To illustrate that Spenser is one of the first English writers with 'a field theory of culture', he argues that Guyon's destruction of the Bower invites us 'to experience the ontogeny of our culture's violent resistance to a sensuous release for which it nevertheless yearns with a new intensity' (175). As a cultural critic, he relates Guyon's act to 'the European response to the native cultures of the New World, the English colonial struggle in Ireland, and the Reformation attack on images' (179), but not to the one that Book II offers: the knight of temperance is avenging the bloody-handed babe whose parents had been Acrasia's victims. (See Hieatt 1992:28, and II xii 83*n*.)

Greenblatt's argument has been extended by Louis Adrian Montrose. For example, in answer to his argument that the Queen was able 'at once to fashion her identity and to manipulate the identities of her followers' (1980:19), he claims that 'such fashioning and such manipulation were reciprocal': 'the refashioning of an Elizabethan subject as a laureate poet is dialectically related to the refashioning of the queen as the author's subject' (1986:318, 323). Helgerson 1983:55–100 had explained how Spenser fashions himself as England's poet-laureate within the literary tradition; Montrose explains such authorial self-fashioning in culturally-specific, psychological terms by qualifying Greenblatt's explanation of Guyon's destruction of Acrasia's Bower: 'Guyon's violent repression of his own sexual arousal' shows that what is being fashioned is Spenser himself as a male subject to a female ruler (329). Again, however, the poem is bypassed: unsupported speculation about Guyon's 'sexual arousal' in relation to the poet still replaces an interest in the virtue of which he is the patron, and of that virtue in relation to the other virtues.

Current interest in Spenser's culture has made readers aware of themselves as gendered subjects alert to the possible androcentric bias, patriarchy, and misogyny of *The Faerie Queene*, as Cavanagh 1994a has argued. It has alerted them also to 'the undercurrent of misogyny and gynophobia in much Spenser criticism' (Berger 1998:181). Yet it has also allowed them to appreciate Virginia Woolf's perceptiveness in calling Spenser a feminist; see III ii 1–3*n*. For example, Quilligan 1983:38–40 suggests that the reader who is being fashioned by the poem may be female, its first reader being Elizabeth; and Wofford 1988:6–7 claims that the female reader especially is privileged in Book III. (Their claim is contested by D.L. Miller 1988:217–18, and Gregerson 1995:124.) On the role of gender in earlier Spenser criticism, see Cohee 2000; on the effect of female authority on Spenser's use of the romance genre, especially in Books III and IV, see Eggert 2000a:22–37; and on the relation between romance's rapture and rape, see Eggert 2000b.

As one who treats the relation between the sexes in singing 'of Knights and Ladies gentle deeds', Spenser's central subject is love from which 'spring all noble deedes and neuer dying fame' (III iii 1.9). The presence of a woman on the throne may have been anathema to some on the religious right of his day but for all poets it was an enormous blessing, so I have argued:

> As the Virgin Queen, Elizabeth was courted by her courtiers, requiring their love while refusing to satisfy their desire. In her 'body natural' she was their Petrarchan mistress: faithful, unconsummated love for her legitimized their desire, releasing the creative power of lyric poets by permitting them to explore the state of loving without provoking the charge that they were encouraging lust. For the heroic poet, such as Spenser, her 'body politic', which was sacred and immortal, made her the subject of a poem worthy of England as God's elect nation governed by a godly prince. Enshrined as the Virgin Queen, Mother, and the second Mary – unconfined, then, by patriarchy – she became the Muse who inspired her poets. They found in her an ideal object on which to practice their art of praise ... thereby gaining the authority which they had lacked. Love became the central subject of Elizabethan poets, illustrating Socrates' claim in the *Symposium* (196e) that Eros is so divine a poet that he can kindle creative power in others. It is not an accident of history, then, that the miracle of Elizabeth's emergence by the late 1570s as a successful queen inspired the English literary Renaissance. (1995:385–86)

Awareness of how thoroughly *The Faerie Queene* is embedded in Elizabethan culture provides an opportunity to examine first its nature, and then how thoroughly it both contains and subverts that culture.

The moral virtues

Spenser's intention to fashion the twelve moral virtues is most directly informed and sustained by Sidney's claim in his *Defence of Poetry* 81–82: 'it is that feigning notable images of virtues, vices, or what else, with that delightful teaching, which must be the right describing note to know a poet by'. His method of doing so was expressed by Jonson: 'Wee doe not require in [the poet] meere *Elocution*; or an excellent faculty in verse; but the exact knowledge of all vertues, and their Contraries; with ability to render the one lov'd, the other hated, by his proper embattaling them' (1925–52:8.595). In this critical context, Tuve's argument may be renewed to set the stage for the reception of *The Faerie Queene* in this millennium by focusing on the virtues that Spenser inherited as they were fashioned by Elizabethan culture, and as he fashioned them in the poem.

The first step is to extend Tuve's insight that 'the sought virtue is the unifying factor in *every* Book', with its corollary in the claim by Fujii 1974:159 that a knight's adventures do not reveal 'personal growth but show different aspects of the virtue he represents'. The virtue of holiness, for example, may be examined initially in relation to Reformation doctrine, as it is by Gless 1994, but it cannot be understood apart from the book itself. The only adequate answer to the question 'What is holiness?' is to point to Book I in the relation of all its parts, and then in its relation to the other books. Tuve's claim that 'Spenser got Holiness out of Aristotle' (1966:82) should be rejected, not because he got it rather out of the biblical culture of his age, however it got there, but because he fashioned it in Book I. When he claims in the concluding canto of Book II, 'Now ginnes this goodly frame of Temperaunce | Fayrely to rise', he is preparing the reader to see that virtue finally shaped by Guyon's destruction of Acrasia's Bower in order to prevent her victims from ever being able to return to that false Eden, however unhappy all were in no longer being her beasts. Greenblatt claims that this act shows that 'Spenser understands, at the deepest level of his being, the appeal of . . . self-abandonment, erotic aestheticism, [and] the melting of the will' (1980:173), but what Spenser understands at any level of his being is simply unknown and unknowable. What is known, and what deserves critical attention, is that Guyon's act shows the full power and final limitations of the virtue of temperance.

The second step is to relate each virtue to the other virtues by following up the claim by Northrop Frye 1963:75 that the private virtues of the first three books and the public virtues of the second 'seem to run in a sort of Hegelian progression', and the claim by Nohrnberg 1976:86 that 'each of Spenser's books forms a completed rhetorical period; subsequent installments reveal the membership of a prior book in a more inclusive pattern'. The relation of temperance to holiness is inescapable, being established at the beginning of Book II: the initial encounter of Guyon and the Red Cross Knight carefully discriminates between them, and therefore between the virtues of which they are the patrons. (On the relation of the two books and their virtues, see Hamilton 1961a:90–96, A. Fowler 1964:80–85, Hume 1984:59–71, 'nature and grace' in the *SEnc*.) The relation of chastity to temperance is indicated at the beginning of Book III: after Britomart unhorses Guyon, and his 'wrathfull will' is mollified by the Palmer and Arthur, they are reconciled 'Through goodly temperaunce, and affection chaste'; and when Arthur joins their 'golden chaine of concord', 'goodly all agreed' (i 12). At the beginning of the next episode, which initially defines her virtue, Britomart aids the Red Cross Knight against the enemies of chastity, and at the end is aided by him against these same enemies, 'ioyning foot to foot, and syde to syde' (i 66.8). The relation of chastity to temperance becomes even more clear at the end of the book: instead of binding an enchantress, freeing her lover, and destroying her bower, Britomart overpowers Busirane, frees Amoret, and witnesses the self-destruction of his house. (For further on the relation between Books II and III, see Mallette 1997:86–112.) As Roche 1964 demonstrates, chastity in Book III is related to friendship in Book IV through the structuring of the two books into one. The relation of justice to temperance is examined by Nohrnberg 1976:285–425 under the rubric 'Books of the Governors'. Since Britomart's quest for Artegall extends through Book III to Book V, these three books are usually read as an integrated vision. The relation of justice to courtesy is indicated initially by the opening encounter of Calidore and Artegall, the first friendly encounter of the patrons of the virtues in the poem, and then by parallel episodes that show how Book V is countered and supplemented by Book VI. For an analysis of the parallels, see D. Cheney 1966:176–96.

Much has been done to relate the virtues, but much more needs to be done before we may begin to grasp the 'goodly golden chayne, wherewith yfere | The vertues linked are in louely wize' (I ix 1.1–2). For example, in displaying the special powers of a virtue, each book displays also its radical limitations without the other virtues, and, above all, without divine grace. No book is complete in itself, for each (after the first) critiques those that preceded it, so that understanding what has been read constantly expands and consolidates until by the end all the virtues are seen in their unifying relationships.

A general survey of all the books of *The Faerie Queene* is offered in a number of introductions to the poem: Spens 1934, Nelson 1963, R. Freeman 1970, Heale 1987, Tonkin 1989, Meyer 1991, Waller 1994, and Oram 1997. Tonkin and Oram especially offer close and perceptive readings of each book. In addition, there are studies of individual books. Book I: Rose 1975; II: Berger 1957; III and IV: Roche 1964, Silberman 1995; IV: Goldberg 1981; III, IV, and V: Broaddus 1995; V: Dunseath 1968, Aptekar 1969, Fletcher 1971; VI: A. Williams 1967, Tonkin 1972. See also the entry on each book in *The Spenser Encyclopedia*. In addition, there are general studies of the virtues: for example, Horton 1978 finds the poem's unity in the binary pairing of the books (see also his entry, 'virtues', in the *SEnc*), and M.F.N. Dixon 1996:13 argues that Spenser offers 'a grammar of virtues', i.e. 'an iterative series of interdependent virtues'. There are also many studies of the techniques used by Spenser to structure the virtues: for example, the 'resonances sounding at large throughout the poem' examined by Lewis 1967, the structural triads by A. Fowler 1973, the poem's analogical coherence by Nohrnberg 1976, its self-reflexiveness by MacCaffrey 1976, the 'echoing' by Hollander 1981, the demonic parody of the virtues by N. Frye 1963 and Fletcher 1971, the poem's ambivalence by Fletcher 1964, the structural patterns in Books I and II by Røstvig 1994, the symmetrical ring structure in Book III by Greenfield 1989, the poem's broken symmetries by Kane 1990, the use of image-patterns in which images are repeated *in bono et in malo* by Kaske 1999, the sequence of emblems which make the poem 'the most emblematic long poem in our literature' (A. Fowler 1999:23), and the narrative's self-reflectiveness by Goldberg 1981. The poem interprets and reinterprets itself endlessly, as Tonkin 1989:43 suggests in commenting on Spenser's cumulative technique: 'All the virtues

spring from the first and greatest of them, Holiness, and are summed up in Book VI, with its climactic vision of the Graces'. Clearly the poem was meant to be read as a verse in the Bible was read in Spenser's day: any stanza is the centre from which to reconstruct the whole.

A study of the virtues makes it increasingly clear that before ever Spenser began to write he had seen at least the outline of each virtue and had mapped out their relationships. (On the formal idea of each virtue, which his narrative unfolds and realizes, see Heninger 1991:147.) Early in his career, he dedicated his talents to fashion the scheme of virtues in a poem he could never expect to complete, no more than could Chaucer in projecting the *Canterbury Tales* – on its unfinished state, see Rajan 1985:44–84, and Hamilton 1990 – and he never faltered or changed. What he says about the Red Cross Knight may be applied to him: 'The noble hart, that harbours vertuous thought [i.e. knowledge of the virtues], | And is with childe of glorious great intent, | Can neuer rest, vntill it forth haue brought | Th'eternall brood of glorie excellent' (I v 1.1–4). As he testifies in the final canto of the *1596* poem: as a ship may be delayed by storms on its way to a certain shore, 'Right so it fares with me in this long way, | Whose course is often stayd, yet neuer is astray' (VI xii 1.8–9). While we may speculate that Spenser wrote for patronage, a pension, or a position at court, we know from the opening stanza of *The Faerie Queene* that 'the sacred Muse' commanded him 'To blazon broade emongst her learned throng'. Clearly he had no choice but to devote his life to writing that poem.

The third step in relating the virtues is to recognize that they are fashioned in the poem through the actions of the major characters in order to fashion readers in 'vertuous and gentle discipline'. In the *Letter to Raleigh*, Spenser distinguishes between his 'general intention and meaning', which is to fashion the virtues, and his poem's 'generall end', which is to 'fashion a gentleman or noble person in vertuous and gentle discipline' (8). Accordingly, our understanding of the nature of holiness, for example, is gained only by reading the story of the Red Cross Knight, and not by bringing to it anything more than a general awareness that the virtue relates our life in this world to God. His quest traces the process of sanctification as his will cooperates with divine grace; and, through him, we learn how to frame our lives in holy living. The virtues do not exist apart from the story, nor the story apart from our active participation in it, for, in Sidney's words, the virtues are 'so in their own natural seats laid to the view, that we seem not to hear of them, but clearly to see through them' (*Defence of Poetry* 86). In other words, we do not see beyond, or outside, the virtues to something else but rather through them as lenses. Only by so seeing through them may we share Spenser's vision of human life from his moral perspective. It follows that finally nothing outside the poem is needed to understand it, except (for us) the shared primary culture of its first audience. (I adapt the term 'primary culture' from the account by N. Frye 1990b:22–23 of 'primary mythology' or 'primary concerns' in contrast to 'secondary concerns', such as ideology.)

To gain 'an exact knowledge of the virtues' needed to write *The Faerie Queene*, Spenser calls upon the muses to reveal to him 'the sacred noursery | Of vertue' (VI proem 3.1–2). Since he goes on to claim that the nursery was first planted on earth by the Gods 'being deriu'd at furst | From heauenly seedes of bounty soueraine', for him the virtues exist transcendentally. As this nursery provides what Sidney calls 'that *idea* or fore-conceit' by which the poet's skill is to be judged rather than by the poem itself, his effort as a poet is to plant its garden of virtue in the minds of his readers so that they may share his state of being 'rauisht with rare thoughts delight'. Since 'vertues seat is deepe within the mynd', however, he does not so much plant the virtues in them as nurture what is already there.

To spell out this point using the familiar Platonic doctrine of anamnesis: while Spenser needed an exact knowledge of the virtues in order to write his poem, his readers need only to be reminded of what they already know (even today) but have largely forgotten (especially today). What he finds deep within the minds of his readers may be identified with the primary culture upon which his poem draws. It led him to use allegory, which, as Tuve cited by Roche 1964:30 explains, 'is a method of reading in which we are made to think about things we already know'; and to use proverbs extensively, as Cincotta 1983 explains, as a means to give authority to his poem. Being primary, this culture is basic: simply expressed, it is what we all know as human beings regardless of gender, race, religion, and class. It is what we just know and have always known to be fair, right, and just, both in our awareness of who we are and also our relation to society and to some higher reality outside ourselves, both what it is and what it ought to be. While that primary culture would be regarded

by all readers of Spenser's day as given by God, and by many readers today as humanly constructed, its reconstruction in the poem is where we meet.

In his *Discourse on Civil Life* (1606), Lodowick Bryskett writes that Spenser is known to be very well read in philosophy, both moral and natural, and that he intends to appeal to him to learn what moral philosophy is, 'what be the parts thereof, whereby vertues are to be distinguished from vices' (21). Spenser rightly terms his poem 'this present treatise' (in the current sense of the term) for his task is 'True vertue to aduance' (V iii 3.8–9). One chief problem is to separate virtue from vice, for what used to be called virtue 'Is now cald vice; and that which vice was hight, | Is now hight vertue, and so vs'd of all' (V proem 4.2–3). Raleigh makes the same point in the *History of the World* 1614:2.6.7: 'some vertues and some vices are so nicely distinguished, and so resembling each other, as they are often confounded, and the one taken for the other'; and he praises *The Faerie Queene* because Spenser has 'formed right true vertues face herein' (*CV* 2.3). The problem is noted in the opening cantos of the poem: in the argument to canto i, the Red Cross Knight is called 'The Patrone of true Holinesse', but he is so named only after Archimago assumes his disguise. Then readers are told – in fact, they are admonished – that '*Saint George* himselfe ye would haue deemed him to be' (ii 11.9), as even Una does.

Today Spenser's purpose may seem ideologically innocuous but in his day those who called virtue vice, and vice virtue, may well have regarded the poem as subversive. But who were they? Most likely, the pillars of society, such as Burghley (see IV proem 1.1–2*n*), theologians, such as John King who, in 1597, complained that 'instead of the writings of Moses and the prophets . . . now we have Arcadia, and the Faëry Queene' (cited Garrett 1996:139), and those religiously-minded for whom holiness meant professing correct doctrine; temperance meant life in a moral strait-jacket; chastity meant the rejection of sexual love; friendship meant patriarchal family ties; justice meant the justification of present authority; and courtesy meant the conduct of Elizabeth's courtiers – in sum, those for whom virtue meant remaining subject to external law rather living in the freedom of the gospel.

Although generally Spenser overtly endorses the claims of noble blood, his poem values individual worth over social rank by ranking middle-class nurture higher than nobility's inherited virtue. He is concerned more with moral rather than social promotion, the latter being Elizabeth's sole prerogative. In fashioning courtesy, for example, he is seeking to fashion her courtiers; see 'courtesy as a social code' in the *SEnc*. More subversively, his poem challenges doctrinal claims of God's grace at a time when, as Gless 1994:37 notes, 'the Protestant refusal to concede that men might achieve meritorious works expresses a conviction that true virtue lies beyond the reach of human capacity'. (He cites Bullinger, for whom one chief aim of the Reformation was to propagate the doctrine that belief in human merit is the most insidiously corrupting error promoted by Roman Catholicism; for counter-claims, see Mallette 1997:173–74.) Spenser wraps himself and his poem in the Queen's robes because he needed her protection to speak through her.

Holiness: Book I

As a Protestant poet writing on the virtues during the Reformation, Spenser had no choice but to begin with holiness, for that virtue distinguishes our unfallen state created in the image of God, as the Geneva gloss to Gen. 1.27 explains: 'man was created after God in righteousnes and true holines, meaning by these two wordes all perfection, as wisdome, trueth, innocencie, power, etc'. Since holiness reestablishes the right relationship of the fallen body to God upon which all the other virtues depend, the Red Cross Knight turns praise for killing the dragon from himself to God; see II i 33.1–5*n*. To display this virtue, Spenser chose the very popular (and therefore, by the learned, generally discredited) legend of St George, whose name was associated by Lydgate with holiness (see I x 61.8–9*n*) and his legend by de Malynes in 1601 with salvation by Christ (see I i 1–6*n*). A contemporary, Robert Salter, who claimed to be 'so trew a friend' of Spenser, saw 'this very *Mysterie*' deciphered in Book I, namely, that one who was first cast down finally was 'fully possessed of that Kingdome [of Christ], against which there is none to stand vp' (*Wonderfull Prophecies* 1626; cited *Sp All* 175–76).

As one would expect of Elizabethan biblical culture, the nature of holiness was a subject of intensive sectarian debate. As a consequence, Spenser needed to guide his patron of that virtue through a theological minefield, and he does so chiefly in two ways. First, he avoids religious controversy as much as possible. In the opening episode, the Red Cross Knight

is able to defeat Errour after Una tells him to 'Add faith vnto your force'. But faith in what? and whose faith? We are never told, but the effect of her cry, as Kane 1989:34 notes, affirms the general promise of the homilies that 'true faith doth give life to the works'. When the knight is freed from Orgoglio's dungeon by Arthur, we may infer that he is redeemed by God's grace, but the poem shows Arthur descending into the dungeon to rend its iron door and laboriously lift him up. When Fidelia teaches him 'Of God, of grace, of iustice, of free will', we are not told what she says. The most theologically controversial word in Book I – inescapable because predestination was reformed theology's central doctrine (see 'Predestination' in the *SEnc*) – occurs when Una tells him not to despair of salvation because he is 'chosen'. We may infer that he is among God's elect predestined to salvation, but the poem tells us only that at the court of the Faerie Queene he was chosen by her to free her parents. On every matter of faith, doctrine, and belief invited by an allegorical reading of his poem, Spenser responds: 'Thou saist it', for he only tells his story.

On the relation of Book I to the fervent Protestantism of the 1590s, see Sinfield 1983:44–48, and Hume 1984:72–106; to Reformation literary genres and modes, see King 1990a:183–226; to the multiplying perspectives on Elizabethan theological doctrines to which a contemporary reader interested in theology is asked to respond, see Gless 1994; to Elizabethan discourses of preaching, see Mallette 1997:17–49. On the book as structured by two interlocking triads, the theological virtues (faith, hope, charity) and the infernal triad (world, flesh, devil), see Cullen 1974:3–96 and Weber 1993:176–212. On the place of the Bible in Spenser's culture, see Kaske 1999:9–17; on his references to the Bible, see Shaheen 1976; and on his accommodation of his poem to Elizabethan biblical culture, see Hamilton 1992.

In addition to avoiding religious controversy as much as possible, Spenser took the structure and the framing imagery of Book I from the Revelation of St John, which allowed him to fashion holiness by telling the legend of the Red Cross Knight as a romance. In this way, he gave his poem the authority of the whole Bible without being bound by it as a pre-text. Quite deliberately, then, the knight is described in terms of holiness only once; see I x 45.6–9*n*. Instead of being directly instructed in the nature of holiness, readers see that virtue realized in what he does and in what happens to him. The virtue is shown as a way of living, which (not surprisingly) is generally compatible with the teaching of the Reformed church, and therefore with doctrines found in the Book of Common Prayer and the homilies, rather than as a system of beliefs. See J.N. Wall 1988:88–127.

Traditional interpretations of Book I have been either moral, varying between extremes of psychological and spiritual readings, or historical, varying between particular and general readings. Both were sanctioned by the interpretations given the major classical poets and sixteenth-century romance writers. For example, in 1632 Henry Reynolds praised *The Faerie Queene* as 'an exact body of the Ethicke doctrine' while wishing that Spenser had been 'a little freer of his fiction, and not so close riuetted to his Morall' (*Sp All* 186). In 1642 Henry More praised it as 'a Poem richly fraught within divine Morality as Phansy', and in 1660 offers a historical reading of Una's reception by the satyrs in I vi 11–19, saying that it 'does lively set out the condition of Christianity since the time that the Church of a Garden became a *Wilderness*' (*Sp All* 210, 249). Both kinds of readings continue today though the latter often tends to be restricted to the sociopolitical. An influential view in the earlier twentieth century, expressed by Kermode 1971:12–32, was that the historical allegory of Book I treats the history of the true church from its beginnings to the Last Judgement in its conflict with the Church of Rome. According to this reading, the Red Cross Knight's subjection to Orgoglio in canto vii refers to the popish captivity of England from Gregory VII to Wyclif (about 300 years: the three months of viii 38; but see *n*); and the six years that the Red Cross Knight must serve the Faerie Queene before he may return to Eden refers to the six years of Mary Tudor's reign when England was subject to the Church of Rome (see I xii 18.6–8*n*). While interest in the ecclesiastical history of Book I continues, e.g. in Richey 1998:16–35, usually it is directed more specifically to its immediate context in the Reformation (King 1990a; and Mallette 1997 who explores how the poem appropriates and parodies overlapping Reformation texts); or Reformation doctrines of holiness (Gless 1994); or patristic theology (Weatherby 1994); or Reformation iconoclasm (Gregerson 1995).

The moral allegory of Book I, as set down by Ruskin in *The Stones of Venice* (1853), remains generally accepted, though with reservations. For example, he identifies Orgoglio as 'Orgueil, or Carnal Pride; not the pride of life, spiritual and subtle, but the common and vulgar pride in the power of this world' (cited *Var* 1.423). Readers today, who rightly query any labelling of Spenser's characters, may query just how the knight's pride, if he is proud, is personified by Orgoglio. Does he fall through pride? Most certainly he falls: one who was on horseback lies upon the ground, first to rest in the shade and then to lie with Duessa; and although he staggers to his feet, he soon falls senseless upon the ground, and finally is placed deep underground in the giant's dungeon. The giant himself is not 'identified' until after the knight's fall, and then he is named Orgoglio, not Pride. Although he is said to be proud, pride is only one detail in a very complex description. In his size, descent, features, weapon, gait, and mode of fighting, he is seen as a particular giant rather than as a particular kind of pride. To name him such is to select a few words – and not particularly interesting ones – such as 'arrogant' and 'presumption' out of some twenty-six lines or about two hundred words, and to collapse them into pride because pride is one of the seven deadly sins. To say that the knight falls through pride ignores the complex interactions of all the words in the episode. While he is guilty of sloth and lust before he falls, he is not proud; in fact, he has just escaped from the house of Pride. Quite deliberately, Spenser seeks to prevent any such moral identification by attributing the knight's weakness before Orgoglio to his act of ignorantly drinking the enfeebling waters issuing from a nymph who, like him, rested in the midst of her quest.

Although holiness is a distinctively Christian virtue, Book I does not treat 'pilgrim's progress from this world to that which is to come', as does Bunyan, but rather the Red Cross Knight's quest in this world on a pilgrimage from error to salvation; see Prescott 1989. His slaying the dragon only qualifies him to enter the antepenultimate battle as the defender of the Faerie Queene against the pagan king (I xii 18), and only after that has been accomplished may he start his climb to the New Jerusalem. As a consequence, the whole poem is deeply rooted in the human condition: it treats our life in this world, under the aegis of divine grace, more comprehensively than any other poem in English.

Temperance: Book II

Since the virtues are founded on holiness and framed by temperance, the first two books are central to the whole poem and their relationship is crucial to understanding its allegory. In an influential essay, first published in 1949, Woodhouse argues that Book I moves with reference to the order of grace and Book II to the order of nature: 'whereas what touches the Redcross Knight bears primarily upon revealed religion, or belongs to the order of grace, whatever touches Guyon bears upon natural ethics, or belongs to the order of nature' (204). While Book I draws primarily on the Bible and Book II on classical texts, they are not isolated within the two orders. In the second canto, for example, the opening tableau of Medina and her sisters relates to the Aristotelian concept of temperance as the mean between the extremes of excess and defect (see II i 58, ii 13.7–9*n*), the confused battle between Guyon and the suitors that follows relates to the Platonic concept of temperance as the struggle between the rational part of the soul (Guyon) and the irrational (the latter being divided into the irascible Huddibras and the concupiscent Sansloy), and their final reconciliation at a feast relates to the Christian humanist concept of the virtue implicit in Milton's remark: 'Wherefore did he [God] creat passions within us, pleasures round about us, but that these rightly temper'd are the very ingredients of vertu?' (1953–82:2.527); see Kaske 1975:125. More broadly, there is a shift, marked by the intercession of the angel sent by God to aid Guyon, from an Aristotelian concept of virtue to a Christian concept, as Berger 1957:41–64 persuasively argues. Temperance is one of the four cardinal virtues, which, allied to the three theological virtues, is central to all the virtues as their sum. On its association with magnanimity or magnificence, which Spenser in the *Letter to Raleigh* calls 'the perfection of all the rest [of the virtues]' (39), see II vii 2.4–5*n*.

While Book I treats our spiritual life through our relationship to God in the vertical perspective of heaven and hell, Book II analyses our natural life through our relationship to our own nature in the horizontal perspective of the world in which we live. By exercising temperance through the rule of reason, human nature may so control its own irascible and concupiscent passions that it may control the two major forces of external nature that assault the temperate body, as represented by the two forces that assault the castle of Alma: 'two then all more huge and violent, | Beautie, and money they against that Bulwarke lent' (II xi 9.8–9). One is represented by Mammon, the other by Acrasia; accordingly, they

tempt Guyon at the climactic mid and final points of his quest. The two related moments when reason is overcome by amazement or wonder become turning-points in the narrative. The first is when Guyon is unable to cleanse Amavia's bloody-handed babe in the waters of the fountain: 'The which him into great amaz'ment droue, | And into diuerse doubt his wauering wonder cloue' (ii 3.8–9). He continues in this state until the Palmer offers 'goodly reason' by telling him a tale about its pure waters. The second is when Arthur's sword fails to kill Maleger: 'His wonder far exceeded reasons reach, | That he began to doubt his dazeled sight, | And oft of error did him selfe appeach' (xi 40.1–3). He continues in this state until he recalls the tale of Hercules slaying Antaeus, whereupon he is able to slay Maleger by casting him into 'a standing lake'. The prominence given wonder, here and elsewhere, suggests that Book II, and the whole poem, may be a critique of reason, as N. Davis 1999:75–120 argues.

Chastity: Book III

'It falls me here to write of Chastity, | The fayrest vertue, far aboue the rest', so Spenser announces startlingly in the opening lines of Book III to declare that virtue's highest place in maintaining the autonomy of the human (traditionally female) body, that is, preserving its integrity inviolate. (As the virtue is informed by charity, see Morgan 1993.) Even in the simplest sense of virtue as power or strength, the book of chastity is the climax to the first three books. The patron of holiness shows us that 'If any strength we haue, it is to ill, | But all the good is Gods, both power and eke will' (I x 1.8–9); and the patron of temperance, though addressed as 'Fayre sonne of *Mars*' (II i 8.7 and see *n*), exercises the virtue chiefly by not acting; but the patron of chastity, invincible while she wields her lance, alone remains unconquered. The virtue of holiness exists apart from the Red Cross Knight; the virtue of temperance, also external to Guyon, measures his actions and governs them, not always successfully, chiefly through the Palmer; the virtue of chastity is identified with Britomart, an inner virtue at one with her, so that, unlike the others in relation to their virtues, she is never less than chaste in all her actions. Most surprisingly, then, her quest is to yield her virginity to a stranger whose face she has seen in a looking-glass.

In the adolescent state, to which temperance especially applies, the feminine appears chiefly as the virgin Belphœbe and the whore Acrasia, states that involve either the rejection of sexual love or its abuse. Although Guyon is the servant of the 'heauenly Mayd' (II i 28.7), he never sees the one and only spies on the other before binding her and ravaging her bower. From the opening episode of Book III, it becomes evident that Guyon's binding of Acrasia has initiated an action that requires the rest of the poem to resolve, namely, how to release women from male tyranny, and therefore release men from their desire to tyrannize women. Chastity is fulfilled when its patron, Britomart, frees Amoret from Busirane's tyranny; friendship is fulfilled when Florimell's chaste love for Marinell leads to her being freed from Proteus's tyranny; and Artegall is able to fulfil the virtue of justice when his lover, Britomart, frees him from Radigund's tyranny to which he has submitted.

By destroying Acrasia's sterile bower of perpetual summer, Guyon frees Verdant, whose name invokes spring with its cycle of regeneration. The temperate body, seen in the Castle of Alma, 'had not yet felt *Cupides* wanton rage' (II ix 18.2), but with the cycle of the seasons, love enters the world: 'all liuing wights, soone as they see | The spring breake forth out of his lusty bowres, | They all doe learne to play the Paramours' (IV x 45). Once the temperate body has felt '*Cupides* wanton rage' in Book III, knights lie wounded or helpless and their ladies are either in flight or imprisoned – all except Britomart, who, though as sorely wounded by love as any, is armed with chastity, which controls her desire as she follows 'the guydaunce of her blinded guest' (III iv 6.8), that is, her love for Artegall.

Book III presents an anatomy of love, its motto being 'Wonder it is to see, in diuerse mindes, | How diuersly loue doth his pageaunts play, | And shewes his powre in variable kindes' (v 1). While there is only one Cupid, his pageants vary, then, according to diverse human states. If only because the poem is dedicated to the Virgin Queen, virginity is accorded 'the highest stayre | Of th'honorable stage of womanhead' (v 54.7–8), being represented in Book III by Belphœbe. She was 'vpbrought in perfect Maydenhed' by Diana, while her twin (yet later born) sister, Amoret, was 'vpbrought in goodly womanhed' (vi 28.4, 7) by Venus. Accordingly, Amoret occupies the central stair of chaste love, for she loves Scudamour faithfully and is rescued by Britomart, the virgin who loves Artegall faithfully. Since both are chaste, their goal is marriage in which they may lose their virginity while preserving their

chastity. A lower stair is occupied by those who love chastely but want sexual satisfaction now, for example Timias at v 48. The lowest stair is occupied by those who pervert love, either through jealousy in loving a woman as an object (as Malbecco at ix 5) or in using force to satisfy their desire (as Busirane at xi 11). Book III is aptly named 'the book of sex' by M. Evans 1970:152, for Spenser's anatomy of love extends outward to the natural order and the cosmos, and to the political order in which the 'Most famous fruites of matrimoniall bowre' (iii 3.7) are the progeny of English kings.

To fashion the virtues of the first two books, Spenser uses the motif of the single quest: a knight is guided to his goal, one by Una and the other by the Palmer, and on his way engages in chivalric action usually in the open field. To fashion chastity, he uses the romance device of *entrelacement*, the interweaving of separate love stories into a pattern of relationships. (As the stories of the four squires in Books III and IV form an interlaced narrative, see Dasenbrock 1991:52–69.) The variety of love's pageants requires multiple quests, and the action shifts to the forest, the seashore, and the sea (see 'Places, allegorical' and 'Sea' in the *SEnc*). Thus Britomart, guided by 'blind loue' (IV v 29.5), wanders not knowing where to find her lover. As she is a virgin, her love for Artegall is treated in the Belphœbe–Timias story; as she seeks to fulfil her love in marriage, her relationship to Artegall is treated in the Scudamour–Amoret story; and as her marriage has the apocalyptic import prophesied by Merlin at III iii 22–23, its significance in relation to nature is treated in the Marinell–Florimell story. Like Florimell, Britomart loves a knight faithfully; but, like Marinell (see iv 26.6), Artegall scorns love (see IV vi 28.9), neither knowing that he is loved. Yet Florimell knows whom she loves while Britomart does not, having seen only his image. In contrast to both, Amoret loves faithfully, and is loved faithfully in return; and in contrast to all, Belphœbe does not know that she is loved by Timias and does not love him. (To complete this scheme: at III vii 54, Columbell knows that she is loved by the Squire of Dames but withholds love for him.) The pattern formed by these stories fashions the virtue of chastity of which Britomart is the patron.

Since interlaced narratives take the place of the linear quest, Spenser structures Book III by balancing the opening and concluding cantos against the middle canto. Canto vi is the book's centre as it treats the source and centre of all life and loving in 'great creating Nature', *natura naturans*, in the Garden of Adonis. Perhaps because the image is largely inexpressible by the usual scholarly vocabulary, its philosophical sources and analogues in mythology have been extensively studied, confirming Kenelm Digby's judgement (*c.* 1643) that Spenser 'hath a way of expression peculiar to him selfe; he bringeth downe the highest and deepest misteries that are contained in human learning, to an easy and gentle forme of deliuery' (*Sp All* 213). Two symmetrically placed cantos enforce its place at the centre: the balancing accounts of Britain's historical destiny in Merlin's prophecy to Britomart concerning her famous progeny in canto iii, and in the account of her ancestry in canto ix.

The opening canto provides an initial statement of the nature of chastity by distinguishing its state from its opposite: both Malecasta and Britomart are infected by love through an evil casting (male-casta) of their eyes on a passing stranger (see i 41.7–9*n*), but the one is evilly chaste (see 57.4*n*), that is, not chaste at all, for she lusts after every passing stranger, while the other loves one alone. The house of Malecasta where love is promiscuous is balanced in the concluding cantos by the house of Busirane where love is bound. Amoret had been nurtured by Venus in the Garden of Adonis where she had been 'lessoned | In all the lore of loue, and goodly womanhead'. Accordingly, once she enters the world 'To be th'ensample of true loue alone, | And Lodestarre of all chaste affection' (vi 51.8–9, 52.4–5) and loves Scudamour, she refuses to yield her body to Busirane. When she is freed by Britomart, she yields herself freely to her lover – in the *1590* text – in an ecstasy of physical delight.

Friendship: Book IV

Following Erskine 1915:832, who endorses the usual view that 'Books III and IV are really one', and Lewis 1936:338, who treats Books III and IV as 'a single book on the subject of love', Roche 1964 argues that the two books form one legend in four movements of six cantos each that show the emergence of concord out of discord, moving from the inception of love in Britomart's vision of Artegall to the marriage of Florimell and Marinell. (On the parallelism of the two books, see Nohrnberg 1976:599–604, 626–47.) Yet Book IV deserves to be examined on its own terms if only because it was published six years after Book III as a separate book that fashions

the virtue of friendship, and because it introduces the second half of the poem that treats the public rather than the private virtues.

Since the virtues are based on temperance, their product is friendship, for virtue 'doth beget | True loue and faithfull friendship' (IV vi 46.8–9); and since friendship is social in being the offspring of Concord (x 34.2), it is fashioned on commonplaces, as C.G. Smith 1935:27–53 shows. Being social, it may not be described through the adventures of a single knight, or even of several knights. Spenser chooses to fashion it by the elaborate relationship of various stories, beginning with the homoerotic bonding of Britomart and Amoret that replaces the usual male contest for the woman as prize. As 'the band of vertuous mind' (ix 1.8), the virtue is paradigmatically represented in the first three cantos, which are set apart from the rest. The friendship which the 'fickle' Blandamour and 'false *Paridell*' (i 32.5, 8) are reported to have sworn (see ii 13.3) is only 'faynd' (18.9) because 'vertue is the band, that bindeth harts most sure' (29.9). Their fitting mates are 'false *Duessa*' and '*Ate*, mother of debate' (i 18.1, 19.1). In contrast, true friendship is illustrated in the bond between Triamond and Cambell, both of whom are virtuous, and is sealed by their cross marriages – Triamond to Cambell's sister, Canacee, and Cambell to Triamond's sister, Cambina – because 'true, and perfite love . . . maketh the *Flower of Friendship* betweene man and wyfe freshly to spring' (Tilney 1992:110). True friendship is also illustrated in Triamond's filial bond with his brothers, Priamond and Diamond, who live 'As if but one soule in them all did dwell' (ii 43.3). The concord achieved by true friendship is contrasted in the next two cantos by the discord among the knights in Satyrane's tournament who fight to gain the False Florimell as the victor's prize, and among their ladies in the related beauty contest to gain her girdle. In cantos vii to ix, another marriage tetrad is added in the story of the true friends Amyas and Placidas, and the marriage of the one to Æmylia and the other to Pœana, Corflambo's daughter, to form through Arthur's aid 'paires of friends' (ix 17.2). On these groupings of four, see Hieatt 1975a:75–94.

Much of what follows resolves in various ways the four chief stories of Book III: the discord between Britomart and Artegall ends with their betrothal (vi); after a separation, Belphœbe and Timias are reconciled (vii–viii); the story of Amoret's separation from Scudamour ends, apparently – see ix 39*n* – in their union, and his account of its beginning when he gained her in the Temple of Venus; and, after the marriage of the Thames and the Medway (xi), Florimell is restored to Marinell (xii). On the narrative patterning of these stories, see Tonkin 1989:136–50, and 'friendship' in the *SEnc*; on their failure to achieve definitive endings because of their incoherencies, inconsistencies, and subversions of narrative logic, see Goldberg 1981; and as they reveal the limitations of friendship because that virtue needs to be fulfilled by justice, see Heberle 1990.

Florimell's culminating role in the book is indicated by the poet's lament when Sclaunder disparages Arthur's rescue of Amoret:

> Then beautie, which was made to represent
>   The great Creatours owne resemblance bright,
>   Vnto abuse of lawlesse lust was lent,
>   And made the baite of bestiall delight:
>   Then faire grew foule, and foule grew faire in sight,
>   And that which wont to vanquish God and man,
>   Was made the vassall of the victors might;
>   Then did her glorious flowre wex dead and wan,
> Despisd and troden downe of all that ouerran. (viii 32)

This stanza traces Florimell's flight from the lustful Foster at the beginning of Book III: when the flower of her beauty is 'dead and wan', her place is taken by the snowy Florimell, and the renewal of spring and the fruitfulness of autumn found in the Garden of Adonis (III vi 42) yield to winter. See IV viii 32*n*. With the renewed harmony of nature marked by the marriage of the Thames and the Medway, which is attended by the major rivers of the world, Florimell returns to the land as '*Venus* of the fomy sea' (IV xii 2) to restore the dying Marinell. In the sunshine of her presence, he revives 'As withered weed . . . that did before decline | And gins to spread his leafe before the faire sunshine' (34.6–9). With this image of Marinell as a revived Adonis, or, more exactly, a renewed Verdant, the concord represented by the virtue of friendship extends from the human down to the natural world and up to the heavens (see x 35).

Justice: Book V

For critics who place the poem in its contemporary culture, Book V has proven to be the most interesting, as it may have been for Spenser to write. To render the virtue of justice loved and injustice hated 'by his proper embattaling them' may well have been his greatest challenge, for of all the virtues justice is the most problematic. Perhaps for this reason, he deliberately distances himself from the Queen's 'great iustice praysed ouer all' by referring to her instrument as 'thy *Artegall*' (V proem 11.8–9), as though not his. While 'Nought is on earth more sacred or diuine, | That Gods and men doe equally adore, | Then this same vertue' (V vii 1), the Red Cross Knight did not adore God's justice: it caused him to despair. Justice may comprehend all the virtues, as Aristotle declares, but all the other virtues promote and fulfil human nature, not oppress it. Justice alone, as Sidney notes in the *Defence* 84, seeks to make men good through fear of punishment rather than love of virtue, 'or, to say righter, doth not endeavour to make men good, but that their evil hurt not others; having no care, so he be a good citizen, how bad a man he be'. Spenser knew justice at first hand from serving the Lord Deputy in Ireland and being the clerk of faculties in the Irish Court of Chancery, and was sufficiently qualified in the knowledge of law to be nominated Sheriff-designate of Cork. He knew, for example, that 'laws ought to be fashioned unto the manners and condition of the people to whom they are meant, and not to be imposed upon them according to the simple rule of right' (*View* 11; see Hadfield 1997:63–65). Further, he was fashioning justice at a time when the relation of justice to equity and mercy was being determined and distributed among common-law courts and the courts of the crown. (On the plethora of courts with their conflicting jurisdictions, see O'Day 1995:149–60; on justice as an imperial virtue in conflict with common law, see 'justice and equity' in the *SEnc*.)

While *The Faerie Queene*, like the Protestant Bible, is to be read as though it were self-validating, self-authorizing, and self-referential with nothing prior to the text or beyond it, the exception would seem to be the concluding cantos of Book V, which allude to the defeat of the Spanish Armada, England's intervention in the Netherlands, the Spanish Inquisition, the Burbon affair in France, and (notoriously) 'the troubles' in Ireland, which (as Irenius complains in *View* 94) 'every day we perceive . . . growing more upon us'. Yet the first point to be made about these allusions is that they seem painfully obvious, hardly needing to be interpreted: the Souldan's armed chariot alludes to the Spanish Armada; Belge alludes to the Low Countries as a whole (which then included Belgium), her seventeen sons being the seventeen provinces (see V x 6–xi.35*n*); Burbon alludes to Henri, King of Navarre (see V xi 44–65*n*); and Irena alludes to the Anglos in the English Pale who appealed to the Queen on being besieged by the wild Irish (see V i 4.1*n*). In reading this 'darke conceit', no one could have failed to recognize these allusions. The second point is that Spenser's fiction, when compared to historical fact, is far too economical with the truth: for example, England's intervention in the Netherlands under Leicester is, as A.B. Gough 1921:289 concludes, 'entirely misrepresented'. It would seem that historical events are treated from a perspective that is 'far from univocally celebratory or optimistic', as Gregory 2000:366 argues, or in what Sidney calls their 'universal consideration', i.e. what is imminent in them, namely, their apocalyptic import, as Borris 1991:11–61 argues. The third point, which is properly disturbing to many readers in our most slaughterous age, especially since the matter is still part of our imaginative experience as Healy 1992:104–09 testifies, is that Talus's slaughter of Irena's subjects is rendered too brutally real in allegorizing, and apparently justifying, Grey's atrocities in subduing Irish rebels (see V xii 26–27*n*). Here Spenser is a product of his age, as was the Speaker of the House of Commons in 1580 in reporting the massacre of Spanish soldiers at Smerwick: 'The *Italians* pulled out by the ears at *Smirwick* in *Ireland*, and cut to pieces by the notable Service of a noble Captain and Valiant Souldiers' (D'Ewes 1682:286). As this historical matter relates to Book V, it displays the slaughter that necessarily attends the triumph of justice, illustrating the truth of the common adage, *summum ius, summa iniuria*, even as Guyon's destruction of the Bower shows the triumph of temperance. This is justice; or, at best, what justice has become, and what its executive power displayed in that rottweiler, Talus, has become, in our worse than 'stonie' age as the world moves towards its 'last ruinous decay' (proem 2.2, 6.9). In doing so, Book V confirms the claim by Thrasymachus in Plato's *Republic*: justice is the name given by those in power to keep their power. It is the one virtue in the poem that cannot be exercised by itself but within the book must be over-ruled by equity, circumvented by mercy, and, in the succeeding book, countered by courtesy.

Courtesy: Book VI

Few readers leave Book V for the triumphant opening of Book VI, to rejoice with the poet on 'The waies, through which my weary steps I guyde, | In this delightfull land of Faery', without relief and an awareness of a higher awakening, for there is a strong sense, especially in the concluding cantos, of leaving an iron world to enter a golden one. But do these ways lead to an end that triumphantly concludes the *1596* poem, or to an impasse of the poet's imaginative powers? For some readers, Book VI relates to the earlier books as Shakespeare's final romances relate to his earlier plays, a crowning and fulfilment, 'a summing up and conclusion for the entire poem and for Spenser's poetic career' (N. Frye 1963:70; cf. Tonkin 1972:11). For others, Spenser's exclamation of wonder on cataloguing the names of the waters that attend the marriage of the Thames and the Medway, 'O what an endlesse worke haue I in hand, | To count the seas abundant progeny' (IV xii 1.1–2), indicates that the poem, like such sixteenth-century romances as *Amadis of Gaul*, could now go on for ever, at least until it used up all possible virtues and the poet's life. As Nohrnberg 1976:656 aptly notes, 'we find ourselves experiencing not the romance of faith or chastity, but the romance of romance itself'. For still others, there is a decline: 'the darkening of Spenser's spirit' is a motif in many studies of the book, agreeing with Lewis 1936:353 that 'the poem begins with its loftiest and most solemn book and thence, after a gradual descent, sinks away into its loosest and most idyllic'; and with Neuse 1968:331 that 'the dominant sense of Book VI is one of disillusionment, of the disparity between the poet's ideals and the reality he envisions'; or that the return to pastoral signals the failure of chivalry in Book V to achieve reform (see DeNeef 1982b). Certainly canto x provides the strong sense of an ending. As I have suggested, 'it is as difficult not to see the poet intruding himself into the poem, as it is not to see Shakespeare in the role of Prospero with the breaking of the pipe, the dissolving of the vision, and our awareness (but surely the poet's too) that his work is being rounded out' (1961a:202).

Defined as 'doing gentle deedes with franke delight' (vii 1.2), courtesy is an encompassing virtue in a poem that sets out to 'sing of Knights and Ladies gentle deeds' (I proem 1.5). As such, its flowering would fully 'fashion a gentleman or noble person in vertuous and gentle discipline' (*Letter to Raleigh* 8). Lewis 1936:351–52 refers to it as 'the poetry of conduct, an "unbought grace of life" which makes its possessor immediately loveable to all who meet him, and which is the bloom (as Aristotle would say) – the supervenient perfection – on the virtues of charity and humility'. Certainly its patron, Calidore, is the one hero in the poem, not excepting even Arthur, whom one would like to have as a friend, a member of the family, or a guest, or whom one would call a gentleman. (The praise given him at i 3.1–5 would not apply to any other knight.) According to Colin, those who possess the virtue may be recognized by the gifts given them by the Graces: 'comely carriage, entertainment kynde, | Sweete semblaunt, friendly offices that bynde' (x 23.4–5) – or rather, according to the proem, given them by Elizabeth from whom all virtues well 'Into the rest, which round about you ring, | Faire Lords and Ladies, which about you dwell, | And doe adorne your Court, where courtesies excell' (7.7–9).

It follows, as Spenser acknowledges in the opening line of canto i, 'Of Court it seemes, men Courtesie doe call'. In its wide range of meanings, the simplest is courtly etiquette and good manners. In this sense, it is more a social than a moral virtue, and therefore open to being feigned, as evident in the 'faire dissembling curtesie' seen by Colin at Elizabeth's court (*Colin Clout* 700), which is 'nought but forgerie' (VI proem 5.3). While it is the virtue most closely associated with the Elizabethan court and Elizabethan culture generally, Spenser's treatment of it goes far beyond his own culture. As Chang 1955:202–20 shows, it has an illuminating counterpart in the Confucian concept of ritual. Spenser fashions a virtue that may best be called civility, which is the basis of civilization; see VI proem 4.5*n*. Yet civility in its political expression could legitimize violence in Ireland, as P. Stevens 1995 notes, and it is not surprising to see the patron of courtesy slaughtering the (Irish) brigands at VI xi 46. Accordingly, its link with Machiavelli's *virtù* has been rightly noted by Neuse 1968 and Danner 1998. On its general application to the uncertain human condition, see Northrop 2000. Ideally, though, it is the culminating moral virtue of *The Faerie Queene*, and, as such, has the religious sense expressed by Peter in addressing those whose faith, according to the Geneva gloss, is confirmed 'by holines of life': 'be ye all of one minde: one suffre with another: loue as brethren: be pitiful: be courteous' (1 Peter 3.8); see, for example, Morgan 1981, and Tratner 1990:147–57. Without courtesy's 'civility' there would be no civilization; without its 'friendly offices that bynde' (x 23.5), there would be no Christian community. By including courtesy among the virtues, Spenser fulfils Milton's claim in *Reason of Church Government* that poetry has the power 'beside the office of a pulpit, to

imbreed and cherish in a great people the seeds of vertu, and publick civility' (1953–82:1.816).

The sources of the virtue may be found in Renaissance moral manuals, such as Elyot's *Gouernour* (1531) with its first book treating 'the best fourme of education or bringing up of noble children' and the planned second volume aiming to cover 'all the reminant . . . apt to the perfection of a iuste publike weale' (1.2); or in Seneca's *De Beneficiis* (tr. Arthur Golding in 1578), as Archer 1987 argues; or in such courtesy books as Castiglione's *Courtier* (1528, tr. 1561) in which 'The Count with golden vertue deckes' the court, as Sackville wrote in its praise; and especially Guazzo's *Civile Conversation* (1574, tr. 1581/1586; see VI i 1.6*n*), for sections of it were included in Bryskett's *Discourse of Civill Life*, which claims to report his conversation with Spenser on moral philosophy. The full title of this last work, *A discourse, containing the ethicke part of morall philosophie: fit to instruct a gentleman in the course of a vertuous life*, could serve as a subtitle of Spenser's poem, especially since Bryskett tells Lord Grey that his end is 'to discourse upon the morall vertues, yet not omitting the intellectuall, to the end to frame a gentleman fit for civill conversation, and to set him in the direct way that leadeth him to his civill felicitie' (6). See 'courtesy books' in the *SEnc*.

As the final book of the *1596* edition, appropriately Book VI raises larger questions about the whole poem. One such question is the relation of Spenser's art to nature, and, for a generation of critics, the seminal essay has been 'A Secret Discipline' by Harry Berger, Jr, in which he concludes that 'the secret discipline of imagination is a double burden, discordant and harmonious: first, its delight in the power and freedom of art; second, the controlled surrender whereby it acknowledges the limits of artifice' (1988:242; first pub. 1961). As chastity is to Britomart, courtesy is to Calidore: the virtue is natural to him. He is courteous 'by kind' (ii 2.2): 'gentlenesse of spright | And manners mylde were planted naturall' (i 2.3–4). It is natural also to Tristram because of his noble birth (ii 24) and proper nurturing, as shown by his defence of the lady abused by her discourteous knight. Its powers are shown in the three opening cantos: Calidore may reform both Crudor when he is threatened with death, and his lady, Briana, who is 'wondrously now chaung'd, from that she was afore' (i 46.9) when she sees the change in him (41–43). Also, he may restore Aldus to his father (iii 4–6) and reconcile Priscilla to her father (18–19). Courtesy's strength and weakness first appear when Calidore's courteous behaviour to Calepine after inadvertently interrupting his love-making with Serena results in her being wounded by the Blatant Beast.

The next five cantos explore the various states of art (i.e. nurture) in relation to nature (i.e. either noble or base blood). Courtesy is shown to be natural to the Salvage Man, as evident in his courteous behaviour to Calepine and Serena after he pities them in their distress (iv 1–16), for though he lacks nurture, he is of 'gentle bloud' (v 1.2). In contrast, the savage bear's 'son' may become a knight or philosopher (iv 35.4–36.9) through nurture alone. In contrast to both, Turpine, a 'most discourteous crauen' (iv 2.6), being of 'base kind' (vii 1.9), may not be reformed even by Arthur. And in contrast to him, Mirabella, though of 'kindred base', is 'deckt with wondrous giftes of natures grace' (vii 28). The lowest level of nature is seen in the Salvage Nation: its attempt to divide and eat Serena is the demonic parody of courtly behaviour. For an analysis of these states, see Oram 1997: 252–54, and Tonkin 1989:176–81.

The four concluding cantos describe Calidore's adventures after he abandons his quest and enters the pastoral world. His vision of Pastorella culminates in his vision of the Graces, and his courtship of her culminates in their union (x 38); and only after he rescues her from the brigants, and restores her to her noble parents, does he seek to capture the Blatant Beast. This pastoral interlude surprises any reader, not because Calidore abandons his quest – the Red Cross Knight and Guyon do the same – but because he is rewarded for doing so. At the outset we are told that he would suffer 'daunger, not to be redrest, | If he for slouth forslackt so famous quest' (ix 3.4–5); he does just that, and is rewarded by seeing the Graces and gaining Pastorella. Yet the interlude is rightly justified by Lewis 1936:350 because it helps us understand courtesy: 'the shepherd's country and Mount Acidale in the midst of it are the core of the book, and the key to Spenser's whole conception of Courtesy'. In retrospect, it becomes evident that Calidore's vision is more than the allegorical core of Book VI: it is the allegorical core of the whole poem, its climactic vision, and the centre about which the whole poem turns.

Of all the books, Book VI is the closest to romance, especially popular romance, in its gathering of stock motifs such as the Salvage Man, the canni-balism of the Salvage Nation, the bear's baby, the noble child raised as a shepherdess – see 'romance' in the *SEnc* – and its stories with their aura of indefinite, mysterious meanings that seem to invite incompatible interpretations even while they resist them. One example is the story of Serena about to be divided and eaten by the Salvage Nation: it may be seen as a romance motif that draws on Spenser's knowledge of human sacrifice practised by the Irish Celts (McNeir 1968:130–35, 143), and on his experience of the Munster famine (*View* 104; see Gray 1930:423–24); or it may be interpreted as mocking the Petrarchan rhetorical dismemberment of women (Krier 1990:114–15); or parodying the Roman Catholic concept of the Real Presence in the eucharist (Nohrnberg 1976:712–13); or satirizing Protestant extremists who threaten to dismember the Church of England (Borris 1990). Another example is Calidore's rescue of Pastorella from the brigants' underground cave: the story is closer to myth than to allegory, for her descent into the cave evokes Proserpina's descent into the underworld, and her rescue a resurrection from death to life. It has been interpreted (for example, by M. Evans 1970:224) as an allegory of Christ harrowing hell, but preserved as a myth or fiction, its potential meanings remain inexhaustible. See Hamilton 1959:352–54.

Two Cantos of Mutabilitie

These two cantos, vi and vii, together with two stanzas of canto viii, first appeared in the 1609 folio edition following Books I–VI under the title: 'TWO CANTOS OF *MUTABILITIE*: Which, both for Forme and Matter, appeare | to be parcell of some following Booke of the | FAERIE QVEENE, | VNDER THE LEGEND | OF | *Constancie*. | Neuer before imprinted'. The volume ends with the date and 'At London. Printed by H.L. for Matthew Lownes'. The date of composition is not known, though it may well have been after 1590 when Spenser occupied Kilcolman Castle and came to know its countryside well (see vi 40–41n); or after Dec. 1591, the date of the dedication of *Colin Clout* (see 40.3–6n); or, most likely, after the lunar eclipse on 14 April 1595 (see 14.1–5n); or after the Tyrone rebellion in 1598 (see 55.8n). Nor is it known who provided the title, the division and numbering of the cantos (vi, vii, viii, 'vnperfite'), and the running title, 'The Seuenth Booke'. The tentative 'appeare' in the heading suggests a lack of manuscript authority, though the earlier books support the title, 'The Legend of *Constancie*'. Although that virtue is named only once before, to describe Guyon and his Palmer as they prepare to enter the Bower of Bliss (II xii 38.9), it is implicit in each virtue. Its importance is indicated in Elyot's *Gouernour* 3.19: 'that man which in childehode is brought up in sondry vertues, if eyther by nature, or els by custome, he be nat induced to be all way constant and stable, so that he meue nat for any affection, griefe, or displeasure, all his vertues will shortely decaye'. It seems inevitable also that this legend, appropriately foreshortened, should be the seventh and final book, for that number heralds the poet's day of rest to round out his six days of labour. On seven as the number of constancy and mutability, see A. Fowler 1964:58. Such traditional number symbolism would seem to determine the numbering of the cantos: vi for the days of creation evident in Mutabilitie's reign; vii for Nature's orderly control over that reign; and viii for regeneration and resurrection; see I viii Arg. 1–2*n*, Bieman 1988:233–38, and headnote to VII viii.

The fragmentary nature of the cantos, and their differences in form from the previous books, preclude any understanding of their place in a poem that fashions the virtues. One may only speculate that they provide a recapitulation or coda to certain themes in the previous books, such as mutability; or 'a detached retrospective commentary on the poem as a whole' (Blissett 1964:26); or the allegorical 'core' of a book on constancy (Lewis 1936:353). Or that they constitute 'one of the great philosophical poems of the language' (Kermode 1965:225) that may be read as an eschatology (Zitner 1968:11), or as a theodicy (Oram 1997:290–300), or as an Ovidian brief epic (Holahan 1976, C. Burrow 1988:117–19) that treats the dialectical relationship of Nature and Mutabilitie (Nohrnberg 1976:741–44), or the nature of time itself (Waller 1994:181–85).

Annotations

In discussing the problems of annotating *The Faerie Queene* in Hamilton 1975, and in trying to contribute to the philosophy of the footnote in Hamilton 1981, I came to appreciate why 'gloss' and 'gloze' are connected etymologically, why it is perhaps impossible to gloss without glozing, and why, then, the annotator is open to the charge of forcing readers to see through a gloss darkly. While Spenser was taught by Richard Mulcaster that 'when all is

done the glosse will wring the text' (1994:269), his *Shepheardes Calender* was thoroughly glossed by E.K., and his *Dreames*, as he told Harvey with some pride, had 'growen by means of the Glosse, (running continually in maner of a Paraphrase) full as great as my *Calender*' (Spenser 1912:612). In glossing *The Faerie Queene*, I have taken E.K. as my guide, sharing his apprehension that without glosses 'many excellent and proper devises both in wordes and matter would passe in the speedy course of reading, either as unknown, or as not marked' (*Epistle*). (For the historical practice that informs his glossing, see Tribble 1993:12–17, 72–87, and Snare 1995.) I limit my annotations chiefly to words that need to be explicated for readers today, selecting their meanings from the entirely indispensable *OED*, though I believe that, finally, most may be clarified by their immediate context and by their use elsewhere in the poem. For several reasons, I have avoided interpretation as much as possible. First, limitations of space do not give me any choice. Second, I agree with Hanna 1991:180 that the annotator who resorts to interpretation will 'impose his being, in a double attack, on the reader and on the text'. Third, I agree also with Krier 1994:72 that an annotator's interpretation is 'premature and deracinated, especially for pedagogical purposes'. Fourth, I believe that any interpretation of the poem – including my own – is Procrustean: a matter of finding several points common to the poem and some other discourse, and then aligning them, using whatever force is needed to spin one's own tale. All 'readings' of the poem without exception are misreadings, at best partial readings, if only because they are translations. At the same time I recognize that I am interpreting the poem in drawing the reader's attention to the meanings of its words, and adding such commentary as I think represents a consensus on how the poem may be understood today. Yet I ask only that readers appreciate Spenser's art in using words. Although his words may not always be memorable in themselves, as Heninger 1987:309–10 claims, they create images that, in Sidney's terms, 'strike, pierce [and] possess the sight of the soul' (*Defence* 85). On Spenser's art of using words, see Hamilton 1973, and the articles listed under 'language, general' in the index to the *SEnc*. Since my credo as an annotator remains unchanged since 1977, I condense what I said then.

Through his art of language Spenser seeks to purify words by restoring them to their true, original meanings. When Adam fell, he lost that natural language in which words contain and reveal the realities they name. Though corrupt, they remain divinely given and the poet's burden is to purify the language of his own tribe. Words have been 'wrested from their true calling', and the poet attempts to wrest them back in order to recreate that natural language in which the word and its reality again merge. Like Adam, he gives names to his creatures which express their natures. His word-play is a sustained and serious effort to plant true words as seeds in the reader's imagination. In Jonson's phrase, he 'makes their minds like the thing he writes' (1925–52:8.588). He shares Bacon's faith that the true end of knowledge is 'a restitution and reinvesting (in great part) of man to the sovereignty and power (for whensoever he shall be able to call the creatures by their true names he shall again command them) which he had in his first state of creation' (*Valerius Terminus*). Although his poem remains largely unfinished, he has restored at least those words that are capable of fashioning his reader in virtuous and gentle discipline. What is chiefly needed to understand the allegory of *The Faerie Queene* fully is to understand all the words. That hypothesis is the basis of my annotation.

My larger goal is to help readers understand why Spenser was honoured in his day as 'England's Arch-Poët', why he became Milton's 'Original' and the 'poet's poet' for the Romantics (see 'poet's poet' in the *SEnc*), and why today Harold Bloom 1986: 2 may claim that he 'possessed [mythopoeic power] . . . in greater measure than any poet in English except for Blake', and why Greenblatt 1990b:229 may judge him to be 'among the most exuberant, generous, and creative literary imaginations in our language'.

As I write in a year that marks a half century of my engagement with the poem, I have come to realize the profound truth of Wallace Stevens's claim that 'Anyone who has read a long poem day after day as, for example, *The Faerie Queene*, knows how the poem comes to possess the reader and how it naturalizes him in its own imagination and liberates him there' (1951:50). It has been so for me though, I also recognize, not for many critics today whose engagement with the poem I respect. With Montrose 1996:121–22, I am aware that 'the cultural politics that are currently ascendant within the academic discipline of literary studies call forth condemnations of Spenser for his racist / misogynist / elitist / imperialist biases'. I am aware also that where I see

unity, harmony, and wholeness, they see contradictions, fissures, discord, repressions, aporias, etc. Inasmuch as their response is a product of their time, so is mine for I remain caught up in a vision of the poem I had during my graduate years at the University of Cambridge when I began seriously to read it. What I had anticipated to be an obscure allegory that could be understood only by an extended study of its background became more clear the more I read it until I had the sense of standing at the centre of a whirling universe of words each in its proper order and related to all the others, its meanings constantly unfolding from within until the poem is seen to contain all literature, and all knowledge needed to guide one's personal and social life. In the intervening years, especially as a result of increasing awareness of Spenser's and his poem's involvement in Ireland, as indicated by the bibliographies compiled by Maley in 1991 and 1996a, and such later studies as McLeod 1999:32–62, but best shown in Hadfield 1997, I have come to realize also the profound truth of Walter Benjamin's observation that 'there is no document of civilization that is not at the same time a document of barbarism'. The greatness of *The Faerie Queene* consists in being both: while it ostensibly focuses on Elizabeth's court, it is impossible even to imagine it being written there, or at any place other than Ireland, being indeed 'wilde fruit, which saluage soyl hath bred' (*DS* 7.2).

If Spenser is to continue as a classic, criticism must continue to recreate the poem by holding it up as a mirror that first of all reflects our own anxieties and concerns. It may not be possible, or even desirable, to seek a perspective on the poem 'uncontaminated by late twentieth century interests and beliefs', as Stewart 1997:87 urges, and I would only ask with him that we need to be aware of 'historical voices other than our own, including Spenser's'. As far as possible criticism should serve also as a transparent glass through which to see what Spenser intended and what he accomplished in '*Fashioning* XII Morall vertues'. Of course, we cannot assume that understanding his intention as it is fulfilled in the poem necessarily provides a sufficient reading, but it may provide a focus for understanding it. Contemporary psychological interpretation of the poem's characters reads the poem out of focus, and the commendable effort to see the poem embedded in its immediate sociopolitical context, chiefly Spenser's relation to the Queen, fails to allow that he wrote it 'to liue with the eternitie of her fame'.

History of the text

The lack of any rough draft, autograph copy, fair or foul manuscripts of *The Faerie Queene* would seem to indicate that Spenser intended to establish his reputation as a professional poet through the publication of a printed text even though earlier he had circulated some parcels of it among friends. In a letter to Harvey in April 1580, he writes: 'I wil in hande forthwith with my *Faery Queene*, whyche I praye you hartily send me with al expedition: and your frendly Letters, and long expected Iudgement wythal'. From the phrase 'long expected', one may infer that he started writing it not much later than 1579 when *The Shepheardes Calender* was published. In returning the manuscript 'at the laste', Harvey commented: 'If so be the *Faerye Queene* be fairer in your eie than the *Nine Muses* [cf. *Nine Comœdies*, one of Spenser's lost works], and *Hobgoblin* runne away with the Garland from *Apollo*: Marke what I saye, and yet I wil not say that I thought, but there an End for this once, and fare you well, till God or some good Aungell putte you in a better minde' (Spenser 1912:612, 628). Unless he is referring to himself as one who would gain the poetic laurels, as Shore 1987 surmises, he may be responding both to Spenser's use of Chaucer's comic tale of Sir Thopas on which to model Arthur's quest for the Faerie Queene (see I ix 8–15*n*) and to his use of fairy tale lore (see Lamb 2000:82–83). Some part of the poem was circulating in London by 1588 for a stanza is cited in that year by Abraham Fraunce: see II iv 35*n*; and since he cites its correct book and canto, one may infer that the poem was organized in its final form at least to this point. About this time, Marlowe, in *2 Tamburlaine* 4.3.119–24, cites from the description of Arthur's helmet; see I vii 32.5–9*n*. From *DS 7*, one may conclude that some part of the first three books was written after 1580 when Spenser settled in Ireland. Bryskett's *Discourse*, published in 1606, may have been tailored to be consonant with the published poem, but if it is the record of a conversation which took place about 1583 – see Chronology 1583 *6 Nov.* – we may accept as valid Spenser's remark that he is writing a work 'in *heroical verse*, under the title of a *Faerie Queene*, to represent all the moral vertues', that he has 'already well entred into' it, and that he intends to finish it 'according to my mind' (22). Bryskett responds that his friends 'had shewed an extreme longing after his worke of the *Faerie Queene*, whereof some parcels had bin by some of them seene' (23).

For the *1596* edition, one evidence of the date of composition is the Burbon episode in Book V: its historical basis is the conversion of the Protestant Henri de Burbon to the Church of Rome in 1593 in order to gain Paris; see V xi 44–65*n*. In *Amoretti* 33, published in 1595, Spenser confesses to Bryskett that he was wrong not to complete *The Faerie Queene*, and asks: 'doe ye not thinck th'accomplishment of it | sufficient worke for one mans simple head'. In sonnet 80, he refers to its six books as 'halfe fordonne'; after rest, 'Out of my prison I will breake anew: | and stoutly will that second work assoyle, | with strong endevour and attention dew', referring to the twelve books promised on the title-page. On his plan for an additional twelve books on the political virtues, see the *Letter to Raleigh* 20–21.

These few facts provide a very uncertain foundation upon which to erect hypothetical earlier versions of the poem, though seriatim composition need not be assumed for a poem written over eighteen years. One may surmise from their titles that some of Spenser's thirty lost (projected?) works – see 'works, lost' in the *SEnc* – may have been absorbed into the one great poem that would be his life-work. That a poem composed over a long period could absorb earlier works (if it did) yet remain unified (as it is) argues for some overall plan that would allow piece-meal construction.

Whatever the process of composition, the first three books appeared first in 1590, and again with the second three books in 1596. Why these years? As good a guess as any is that the publication of the *1590* poem was meant to coincide with the publication of its prose companion, Sidney's *Arcadia*; and that the publication of the *1596* poem – it was entered in the Stationers' Register on 20 Jan. – was planned to coincide with Elizabeth's Grand Climacteric, which began on 7 Sept. 1595 (on the term, see II x 5–68.2*n*). The 63rd year in which she entered the final stage of life is answered by a poem which promises 'the eternitie of her fame'. On the revised ending of Book III, see III xii 43–45 (*1596*)*n*. On possible reasons why *1596* omitted the *Letter to Raleigh*, all but three of the *Commendatory Verses*, and all the *Dedicatory Sonnets*, see their headnotes.

The 1609 folio edition added the *Cantos of Mutabilitie* (see note above) to the reprinting of the six books; and the entire poem was reprinted in the first folio of the collected works in 1611, 1617, and 1679. It was edited in 1715 by John Hughes in

modernized spelling and brief glosses, in 1751 by
Thomas Birch, in 1758 by Ralph Church with brief
annotations, and in the same year by John Upton
'with a glossary, and notes explanatory and critical'
of over 350 pages. In 1805 Henry John Todd pro-
duced the first variorum edition. In 1897–1900 Kate
M. Warren edited the poem with brief notes. On the
earlier editions, see Wurtsbaugh 1936 and 'biblio-
graphy, critical' in the *SEnc*.

Beginning in the nineteenth century, separate
books were published for school-children, most with
the poem carefully expurgated and notes heavily
philological. The most valuable are editions of Books
I and II in 1867 and 1872 by G.W. Kitchin; Book I
by H.M. Percival in 1893 and by Lilian Winstanley
in 1914–15; Book V by Alfred B. Gough in
1918/21; and Books I and II in 1966 and 1965 by
P.C. Bayley. For a list of early editions, see Carpenter
1923:115–18; for an analysis of their contribution to
English studies, see Radcliffe 1996:104–14. The
Oxford edition of *The Faerie Queene* by J.C. Smith in
1909, which collated the first two quartos and the
first folio, was used in the edition of Spenser's poet-
ical works by Smith and E. de Selincourt, 1912, with
a glossary compiled by Henry Alexander. In the
Johns Hopkins Variorum edition of Spenser's col-
lected works, *The Faerie Queene* was edited by Edwin
Greenlaw, Charles Grosvenor Osgood, Frederick
Morgan Padelford, and Ray Heffner (1932–38). It
sought to establish an accurate text, and cited extens-
ively from earlier historical commentary, but by
deliberate policy omitted all annotation except for a
few critical cruxes. Since then Books I and II and the
Cantos of Mutabilitie have been edited with substan-
tial annotation by Robert Kellogg and Oliver Steele
in 1965; Books I and II with excellent critical com-
mentary by Douglas Brooks-Davies in 1977; selec-
tions with annotations by Frank Kermode in 1965,
by A.C. Hamilton in 1966, and by Hugh Maclean in
1968, 1982, and (with Anne Lake Prescott) 1993;
the whole poem in the Longman Annotated Poets
series by A.C. Hamilton in 1977, and with minimal
annotation by Thomas P. Roche, Jr, assisted by
C. Patrick O'Donnell, Jr, in 1978.

My frequent references to *The Spenser Encyclope-
dia*, published now over a decade ago, indicate the
continuing excellence of the entries by its distin-
guished contributors.

TEXTUAL INTRODUCTION

by Hiroshi Yamashita and Toshiyuki Suzuki

No autograph of *The Faerie Queene* survives and its text has been transmitted to us through the printed editions. Books I–III were first published in 1590 in a quarto volume, together with some supplementary matter including the 'Letter to Raleigh' (*LR*). In 1596, two quarto volumes were published, consisting of the second edition of Books I–III and the first edition of Books IV–VI. In 1609, the first folio edition of the poem included the first edition of the *Two Cantos of Mutabilitie*, which are assumed to be part of Book VII. Later editions seem to be derivative reprints without any independent authority. For bibliographical details, see F.R. Johnson 1933, the *Pforzheimer Catalogue*, Yamashita *et al.* 1990, and Yamashita *et al.* 1993.

Since J.C. Smith's Oxford edition of the poem in 1909, modern editions have been based on the two quarto volumes of 1596 for Books I–VI and on the 1609 folio for Book VII. The choice of the copy-text of Books IV–VII is indisputable because the 1596 quarto and the 1609 folio are the only substantive editions. The anomaly is that the copy-text for Books I–III has been the second edition of 1596 rather than the first edition of 1590, which certainly deserves more attention than has hitherto been given. Editors from Smith onward have thought lightly of the merits of the first edition, claiming that 'the text of 1596 shows sufficient alteration for the better to justify the opinion that Spenser was responsible for an incidental revision' (*Var* 1.516). Yet the first edition was very probably set from Spenser's own manuscript, while the second edition is for the most part a mere page-for-page reprint of the first edition.

Clearly, the 1590 text has preserved more of the generally accepted Spenserian characteristics, particularly his spellings, which have been established through studies of extant documents written by his hand. (See R.M. Smith 1958.) The correction of the 1590 errors by the 1596 edition was not thorough-going. The second edition failed to correct nearly half of the errors listed in 'Faults escaped in the Print' (*F.E.*), the errata printed on the last page (Pp8v) of the first issue of the first edition. An analysis of the 1596 corrections agreeing with *F.E.* suggests that it was not consulted in the reprinting of Books I–III. (For an analysis of *F.E.*, see T. Suzuki 1997.) The second edition ignored about 48 corrections out of the 110 listed in the errata. It would be reasonable to suppose, as did both J.C. Smith and F.M. Padelford, the textual editor of the Variorum edition, that neither Spenser nor the printer attempted to make a systematic correction using *F.E.*

Although no fewer than 83 misprints in 1590 were corrected independently of *F.E.*, 183 new misprints were introduced in 1596 (Yamashita *et al.* 1993: xii, 269–72). In addition, confusions of personages, apparently unintentional discords in rhyme and even incomplete lines (II iii 26.9 and II viii 55.9) survived the second edition. In view of the quantity and quality of its errors, we doubt that the poet himself supervised the printing of the second edition of the first three books. As F.B. Evans 1965:62 suggests, 'Spenser may well have sent ahead the necessary copy [for the revised second edition] and entrusted his publisher with the reprinting'. Probably he could neither proofread the second edition nor supervise its printing because he may have been in Ireland at that time. This might explain why *F.E.* was not consulted in the printing of the second edition. A collation of *1590* and *1596* suggests that the authorial alterations made in the latter were limited to a small number and not as extensive as it has appeared to modern editors. Major revisions, which indeed seem to be authorial, are the addition of a stanza (I xi 3) and the replacement of the last five stanzas at the end of Book III of *1590* by three newly composed ones. There are some substantive changes which may have been revised by the poet himself, but others could well have been caused by a compositor's or proof-reader's tamperings. (For an analysis of the variants between the two editions, see Yamashita *et al.* 1993.)

It seems that the influence of the second edition on contemporary readers could have been less than the first, for the number of copies was probably fewer than that for the first edition of 1590 or the Second Part (Books IV–VI) of 1596, as F.R. Johnson 1933: 19 points out in his *Bibliography*: 'probably only one-half or one-third as many copies were printed of the second edition of the First Part as were printed of the first edition of the First Part'. This edition seems to have been no more than a supplement to make good the shortage of the 1590 quarto copies, although the text includes some additions and revisions. The book appears to have been very hastily and perfunctorily made, for it reprinted, apparently just to fill up the final leaf of the volume (Oo8r–Oo8v), only three commendatory poems, omitting *LR* found in the 1590 edition. This omission has been variously interpreted (see *LR, n.*), but it was possibly made for economical reasons: the printer wanted to save the cost and time of printing the new gathering Pp, which would have been necessary if he had intended to reprint the letter. On the other hand, the publication of the first edition of Books I–III, which included *LR* plus seven commendatory poems to Spenser and seventeen dedicatory sonnets by Spenser (ten in the first issue of the quarto), was indeed monumental in many ways.

The present edition, therefore, bases its text for Books I–III on *1590*, for Books IV–VI on *1596*, and for Book VII on *1609*. What follows is a description of each edition together with related textual matters and editorial procedures we have adopted for this edition. For the entries of the copies for the early editions in the Stationers' Register, see the *Chronological Table*.

Books I–III

For the title page of *1590*, see *Facsimile*. Owing to the varying states of the dedicatory sonnets at the end, extant copies differ in the collation of the last few leaves. The one most commonly found in libraries and markets today collates as 4° in eights: A–Z⁸, Aa–Pp⁸, Qq⁴; 308 leaves. The text runs to approximately 18,500 type-lines. On the basis of the skeleton pattern and the records of John Wolfe's printing house, Johnson concluded that probably at least two presses were used for the printing of this quarto. However, his analysis of the pagination errors in gathering F led him to the erroneous conclusion that 'one compositor or pair of compositors set both the outer formes and a different pair set both the inner formes' (17). As he says, four different skeleton-formes can be identified, which pre-

cludes the supposition of printing with one press; and if we hypothesize two presses, it follows that there must have been more than one compositor.

Inquiring into the number of compositors and their stints, we have examined spelling variations, typographical characteristics such as the spacing of words and the punctuation marks (Yamashita 1981), recurring impression of identifiable types, ornamental boxes surrounding canto arguments, and so on. Among these, the first two afforded particularly useful information to identify the compositors. The space test, examining use or non-use of space before colons, semicolons and question marks, has suggested division of work between 1r–3r (the first five pages) and 3v–8v (the remaining eleven pages) in many gatherings. The spelling test has not only corroborated the results of the space test but also strongly suggested that a third compositor was probably involved in the setting of pages 6r– or 6v–8v.

The compositor who set most of the first five pages in gatherings C–Oo (designated as Wolfe's Compositor X) can be distinguished from the second (Compositor Y) and/or the third compositor (Compositor Z) by his frequent use of the following spelling forms: *else, forrest, foorth, little, whyles* and *whylome* as against *els, forest, forth, litle, whiles* and *whilome*. Among these, *litle, whiles* and *whilome* are Spenser's well-established preferences. Compositor X is more clearly identified by his persistent rejection of such Spenserian final voiceless stops as *-att, -ett, -itt* and *-ott* in favour of *-at, -et, -it* and *-ot* and of such initial or medial long vowels and diphthongs as *aid, maid, pain, spoil, grownd, rownd* and *sownd* in favour of *ayd, mayd, payn, spoyl, ground, round* and *sound*. Compositor Y, who was mainly responsible for 3v–5v in each gathering, is distinguished from Compositor Z by his use of medial *i* as in *daies, eie(s), guide* and *noise* as against Compositor Z's *dayes, eye(s), guyde* and *noyse*. Compositor Z set all of 6v–8v in gatherings C–Oo except for Y6v, which was probably set by Compositor X as the evidence from spacing suggests.

As for the 6r pages, evidence available at present is not sufficient to assign them with confidence to any of the three compositors, though it might be said that all were involved in setting these 'extra' pages. To turn to the four gatherings A, B, Pp and Qq, both the space and spelling tests suggest that the first eight pages of gathering A including the title page (A1r), Dedication (A1v) and the last page (A8v) were set by Compositor X alone, while the remaining seven pages were done by Compositor Z alone.

Gathering B was possibly divided into three sections; 2r–3r and 8v were undertaken by Compositor X, 3v–5v by Compositor Y, and 6v–8r by Compositor Z. The first two pages could not be identified. As for the last two gatherings Pp and Qq, suffice it to say that *LR* (Pp1r–Pp3r) may have been set by Compositor X. (For a fuller description of the three compositors, see Yamashita *et al.* 1990: ix–x.)

For the title page of the second edition in 1596, see *Facsimile*. The collation of this edition is 4° in eights: A–Z⁸, Aa–Oo⁸; 296 leaves. F.B. Evans 1965 identified two pairs of skeletons and a pair of compositors, designated as Richard Field's Compositors A_1 and B_1, who alternated in setting by gatherings.

In determining the text for Books I–III we have collated twelve extant copies of the 1590 quarto and have chosen the copy in possession of Yamashita as the base text because it was not only the easiest of access but also it proved to contain more corrected formes than any other copy. (For the collated copies and the states of variants, see the *Textual Notes*.) Except for the British Library copy (C12h17), all copies we have collated have blank spaces instead of the Welsh words on X7v (II x 24.8–9), which have been filled by consulting the British Library copy.

Of the two major variants between the first and the second editions, we have inserted the stanza (I xi 3) added in 1596 into our text, possibly because it was an omission by the 1590 compositor, but we have kept the last five stanzas of 1590 at the end of Book III and laid out the three stanzas newly composed for the 1596 edition after the 1590 ending. As for the two eight-line stanzas (I x 20 and III vi 45) in 1590 and 1596, we have adopted the lines added in 1609. Other revisions possibly made by Spenser for the second edition are not always adopted but are recorded in the Textual Notes.

We have adopted the corrections of *F.E.* appended to *1590*, for it is probable that Spenser was concerned in the preparation of this errata, which includes not only corrections of compositorial errors but also authorial revisions. A considerable number of revisions involve stylistic changes and adjustment of syllables to the metre. However, *F.E.* appears to have been made hurriedly and haphazardly, for, as noted above, it overlooked 83 obvious misprints and no fewer than 48 possible misprints and doubtful readings. It is notable that the number of the *F.E.* corrections in Book III, where 33 misprints and 22 doubtful readings remain uncorrected, is far fewer than those in Books I and II.

In addition, the list has its own faults; erroneous citation of pages, improper quotation and misprint of words sometimes make it difficult for the reader to locate the errors in the text. Simple citations of the definite article 'the' or the demonstrative pronoun 'that' as well as citations of spellings and capitalizations that differ between the text in the quarto and *F.E.* puzzle the reader when they occur more than once on the same page of the text.

It is probable that Spenser himself marked the corrections on the printed sheets, and a proof-reader of the printing-house compiled the corrections out of the marked sheets, noting only page numbers, errors and corrections as they were marked on the sheets.

Books IV–VI

For the title page of 'The Second Part' of *The Faerie Queene* in 1596, see *Facsimile*.

The edition collates as 4° in eights: A–Z⁸, Aa–Ii⁸, Kk⁴; 260 leaves. F.B. Evans 1965: 58, 65–67 clarified two pairs of skeletons different from those used in setting the first part and also a different pair of compositors, whom he names Field's Compositors A_2 and B_2. From the results of his spelling test, he infers that Compositor A_1, who shared the work on the first part with Compositor B_1, and Compositor A_2 are possibly one and the same compositor, whereas Compositor B_2 is different from Compositor B_1. His bibliographical evidence shows that this quarto edition was probably printed from Spenser's own manuscript and that he saw the printing through the press. We have chosen it as copy-text for Books IV–VI and collated sixteen copies including the one in possession of Yamashita. We use the Yamashita copy as the base text, adopting into it the corrected state of readings where we find press variants.

In determining the text for Books IV–VI, we have followed the editorial procedures adopted in Books I–III and tried to reproduce the copy-text as closely as possible.

Two Cantos of Mutabilitie, Book VII

The collation of the first folio edition in 1609 in which the Two Cantos of Mutabilitie appear for the first time is 2°: A–Y⁶, Aa–Hh⁶, Ii4; 184 leaves. The stanzas are numbered throughout each canto for the first time. Like the 1596 edition, it prints only three commendatory verses at the end of Book III. For the head title of the two cantos, see *Facsimile*.

Except for these cantos, which run Hh4r–Ii3r, this edition was set from the two-volume edition of 1596, but both spelling and punctuation were considerably modernized. Some substantive variants between the 1596 and 1609 texts may have been due to Spenser's marginal interpolations in the printer's copy. We have chosen the Yamashita copy as the base text and collated seven copies but have found few press variants.

Editorial procedures

The stanzas are numbered throughout each canto and the numbers for the last five stanzas of III xii are marked with an asterisk to distinguish them from those of the current editions based on the 1596 edition. All substantive and accidental emendations made to the copy-texts and substantive variants of some significance in the early texts (the editions of 1590, 1596, 1609 and occasionally 1611) are recorded in the *Textual Notes*.

The original spelling of the copy-texts has been basically preserved, but in a few cases where the old interchangeable spelling is likely to produce unnecessary confusion (e.g. *of/off*, *to/too*, *there/their*), spelling has been changed according to modern usage. Though some proper nouns are variously spelled in the copy-texts, they are not standardized except for a few cases where misprints are suspected. Contractions such as 'qd' and '&' are expanded. The tilde is also expanded and thus the form *thĕ*, for instance, is spelled out as *them* or *then*. As for the initial u and medial v, we have generally kept them. Ornamental capitals and display initials are reproduced. The long *s* is silently replaced by the short *s*. So are 'VV' by 'W' and '!' by 'l'. The initial letter of the first word in conversations, normally capitalized to demarcate the beginning of a quotation, is sometimes in minuscule in the 1590 and 1596 texts. We have capitalized such minuscules in the present text. The spacing of words in the quartos is so variable that we have often found it difficult to discern between a one-word form and a two-word form (e.g. *himselfe/him selfe*, *howeuer/how euer*, *tomorrow/to morrow*). In such cases we had to use our own judgement. Compound characters such as ligatures, diereses and accents are retained where they are used in the copy-texts.

In editing punctuation, we basically adhered to the pointing of our copy-texts and accepted their inconsistencies, unless they are obvious errors. In other words, we strictly refrained from standardizing or normalizing punctuation as we did in editing other 'accidentals', for we believe that any attempt to sweep out inconsistencies in these 'accidentals' in an old-spelling edition is historically inappropriate and editorially interpolating. Observing this principle inevitably requires accepting what J.C. Smith 1909 deemed puzzling to the modern reader and rejected in his edition, such as absence of the comma after vocatives and occurrence of the comma between modifying phrases and nouns they modify.

Padelford 1938 analyses the punctuation of the *FQ*. Since most of the 1590 punctuation has been transmitted intact to the 1596 edition, his description of the punctuation of the latter is for the most part applicable to the earlier edition, but some noticeable traits typical of the 1590 edition are as follows. (1) The most lightly punctuated of all the early editions, it economizes punctuation and often places no marks for setting off additive, adversative, concessive and relative clauses, and for setting off vocatives. (2) On the other hand, the edition frequently employs the comma for breath between subject and verb, verb and object, and noun and prepositional phrase, particularly at the end of the line, whereas later editions tend to omit these commas. (3) The comma is used for demarcating almost every kind of clause and for marking quotations. In the latter case, the 1596 edition often adopts the semicolon. (4) The parentheses breaking quotations are less often used. (5) The exclamation mark is not used in exclamatory sentences and rhetorical questions but the interrogation mark is used instead. (6) The semicolon as well as the colon is used at the end of complete sentences. The 1590 compositors seem to have considered this mark of intermediate value closer to the colon than to the comma, though the distinction between the colon and the semicolon is not clear and they were used to some extent interchangeably.

In an attempt to formulate principles of editing punctuation, we have re-examined the 1596 changes of punctuation, restricting the definition of obvious errors to the following cases: (1) omission of the period, colon, semicolon, or interrogation mark at the end of complete sentences; (2) use of the comma at the end of complete sentences; (3) use of the period or the colon where sentences are yet to be completed; and (4) use of the period or other marks at the end of interrogative sentences. Though these cases are concerned only with logical or syntactical aspects of punctuation, they are what the compositors of both editions would have commonly recognized as erroneous. The results showed that out of the total of 741 punctuation variants between the two editions, 174 obvious errors in the 1590 edition were corrected and 38 fresh errors were introduced in 1596.

To see the characteristics of the changes made in 1596, we have further analysed the variants excluding the obvious errors and classified them into three categories established purely from a syntactical viewpoint. In other words, contribution to the interest of logical value is our criterion for judging whether a change is for the better or for the worse. Accordingly, if a change clarifies the structure or meaning of a sentence to any extent, we regard it as improving the original punctuation, and conversely, if a change obscures the structure or meaning, we regard it as deteriorating. A change that has no conceivable significance in clarifying meaning is treated as indifferent. Thus, omission or addition of commas placed for breath is taken to be indifferent, regardless of the consequent effect on the metrical pattern.

While 137 changes turned out to be improvement, 350 proved indifferent and 42 deteriorating. A further analysis showed that 87 out of the total of 350 indifferent changes involved semicolons replacing commas followed by quotations, coordinate clauses, relative clauses and other subordinate clauses. On the other hand, there are 12 instances of substitution of semicolons with commas without influencing syntactic clarity. It should be also noted that while 103 commas were removed at the expense of pauses for breath, particularly at line endings, 55 additions of the comma were made both within the line and at the end of the line. Thus the indifferent changes reveal the compositors' contradictory behaviour. The figures also show that a considerable number of changes served to clarify the syntax. (See T. Suzuki 1999.) In view of this and the frequent omission of the comma placed for breath, we can say that the 1596 changes in punctuation on the whole reveal a shift from rhythmical to grammatical pointing.

We have confined our emendations of punctuation to obvious errors, adopting neither metrical value nor thought units as criteria for judging whether an emendation is necessary or not, for fear that subjective judgement contingent to these kinds of emendations would be misleading, even if they are meant to improve the reading. In emending errors, we consulted corrections made in the early texts up to 1609 and adopted them if we found them proper, on the ground that early compositors or editors were closer to and more familiar with the contemporary punctuation system. Otherwise, we emended them according to the normal practice of the copy-texts.

THE FAERIE
QVEENE.

Diſpoſed into twelue books,
Faſhioning
XII. Morall vertues.

LONDON
Printed for William Ponſonbie.
1 5 9 0.

TO THE MOST MIGH-
TIE AND MAGNIFI-
CENT EMPRESSE ELI-
ZABETH, BY THE
GRACE OF GOD QVEENE
OF ENGLAND, FRANCE
AND IRELAND DE-
FENDER OF THE FAITH
&c.

Her moſt humble

Seruant:

Ed. Spenſer.

Title Page

The Faerie Qveene: see I i 3.2–3*n*. **Disposed . . . vertues**: in the *LR*, S. explains that 'the purpose of these first twelue bookes' is to portray in Arthur 'the image of a braue knight, perfected in the twelue priuate morall vertues' (19); and that their 'generall end . . . is to fashion a gentleman or noble person in vertuous and gentle discipline' (7–8).

Device 1590: the crowned fleur-de-lis, a device of the printer, John Wolfe (McKerrow 1913:No.242), who entered the poem in the Stationers' Register on 1 December 1589. On Wolfe's career as a printer, see Huffman 1988, and Loewenstein 1988. **Ponsonbie**: S.'s (and Sidney's) 'official' publisher; see 'Ponsonby, William' in the *SEnc*.
Device 1596: *Anchora spei*: 'Anchor of (heavenly) hope' held by a hand from the clouds, the device of Richard Field (McKerrow:No.222), represented by Speranza's anchor on which she teaches the Red Cross Knight 'to take assured hold' (I x 22.2).

1590/1596 Dedications

The *1596* expansion, with the change from 8 end-stopped lines to 25 urn-shaped lines, indicates S.'s increased aggrandizement of the Queen – 'most High' is a common biblical term for God, esp. in the Psalms (e.g. Ps. 7.17) – and of himself as her subject: 'her upraising, doest thy selfe upraise' (*Colin Clout* 355). See Montrose 1996:87. He addresses her directly as 'that most sacred Empresse' in *Am* 33.2; and as 'soueraine Queene' in II x 4.1; see IV Proem 4.2*n*. He calls her by name in *Am* 74.13, but not in the *FQ* even though her presence dominates the poem. In 1541 Henry VIII assumed the title of King of Ireland; in 1585 Elizabeth allowed the recently discovered land north of Florida to be named Virginia in her honour; see II proem 2.9*n*.

THE FAERIE QVEENE.

Disposed into twelue bookes,

Fashioning

XII. Morall vertues.

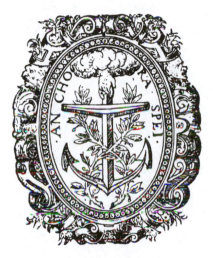

LONDON

Printed for VVilliam Ponsonbie.

1596.

TO
THE MOST HIGH,
MIGHTIE
And
MAGNIFICENT
EMPRESSE RENOVV-
MED FOR PIETIE, VER-
TVE, AND ALL GRATIOVS
GOVERNMENT ELIZABETH BY
THE GRACE OF GOD QVEENE
OF ENGLAND FRAVNCE AND
IRELAND AND OF VIRGI-
NIA, DEFENDOVR OF THE
FAITH, &c . HER MOST
HVMBLE SERVAVNT
EDMVND SPENSER
DOTH IN ALL HV-
MILITIE DEDI-
CATE, PRE-
SENT
AND CONSECRATE THESE
HIS LABOVRS TO LIVE
VVITH THE ETERNI-
TIE OF HER
FAME.

The first Booke of
the Faerie Queene.

Contayning

The Legend of the Knight
of the Red Croſſe,
O R
Of Holineſſe.

1

LO I the man, whose Muse whylome did maske,
As time her taught, in lowly Shephards weeds,
Am now enforst a farre vnfitter taske,
For trumpets sterne to chaunge mine Oaten reeds:
And sing of Knights and Ladies gentle deeds,
Whose praises hauing slept in silence long,
Me, all too meane, the sacred Muse areeds
To blazon broade emongst her learned throng:
Fierce warres and faithfull loues shall moralize my song.

Book I Title

Legend: 'The word LEGEND, so called of the Latine Gerund, *Legendum*, and signifying, by the Figure *Hexoche*, things specially worthy to be read, was anciently used in an Ecclesiast-icall sense, and restrained therein to things written in Prose, touching the Lives of Saints. Master EDMUND SPENSER was the very first among us, who transferred the use of the word, LEGEND, from Prose to Verse: nor that unfortunately; the Argument of his Bookes being of a kind of sacred Nature, as comprehending in them things as well Divine as Humane. And surely, that excellent Master, knowing the weight and use of Words, did competently answere the *Decorum* of a LEGEND, in the qualitie of his Matter, and meant to give it a kind of Consecration in the Title' (Drayton 1931–41:2.382).   **or**: the alternative title distinguishes the story from the virtue being fashioned through its patron; cf. *LR* 42: 'the knight of the Redcrosse, in whome I expresse Holynes'.

Proem*

*A term not used by S. but by editors to refer to the prefatory stanzas to each book, a device for which he lacked any precedent in classical or Italian epic. For a study of the proems, see DeNeef 1982a:91–141, 'The Faerie Queene, proems' in the *SEnc*, and Brill 1994.

Stanzas 1–4

A prologue to the whole poem rather than only to Bk I. The poet is like the 'clownish person' described in the *LR* 61–62

who assumes a quest on behalf of the Faerie Queene. Like him, he needs grace to succeed.

Stanza 1

Lines 1–4 imitate verses prefixed to the opening lines of Renaissance editions of Virgil's *Aeneid*, alluding to the *rota Virgilii* and reputed to be by him: *Ille ego, qui quondam gra-cili modulatus avena | carmen, et egressus silvis vicina coegi | ut quamvis avido parerent arva colono, | gratum opus agricolis; at nunc horrentia Martis.* (I am he who once tuned my song on a slender reed, then, leaving the woodland, constrained the neighbouring fields to serve the husbandmen, however grasping – a work welcome to farmers: but now of Mars' bristling.) In effect, he claims the title of 'the English Virgil' as he abandons pastoral for the epic. Cf. *Gnat* 9–12. Line 5 varies the opening – *Arma virumque cano* – by way of Ariosto's imitation in *Orl. Fur.*: *Le donne, i cavalieri, l'arme, gli amori, | Le cortesie, l'au-daci imprese io canto.* As Cain 1978:39–40 observes, S. begins to imitate Ariosto's matter but overgoes his form by having his ninth line cap Ariosto's eight. See 'stanza, Spenserian' in the *SEnc*.   **1–2 whylome**: some time before, the eleven years since *SC* was published.   **did maske**: went in disguise, revelling as in a masque – cf. 'maske in mirth' (*Teares* 180); also *SC Nov.* 19 – in contrast to his present high seriousness.   **As time her taught**: referring to the subject-matter of the *SC* with its 'twelve Æglogues proportionable to the twelve monethes' (title-page), or to its pastoral form befitting his poetic appren-ticeship.   **3 enforst**: compelled by the muse, as the knight is 'compeld' (i 5.9) by Una.   **4 trumpets sterne**: i.e. the trumpets

2

Helpe then, O holy virgin chiefe of nyne,
  Thy weaker Nouice to performe thy will,
  Lay forth out of thine euerlasting scryne
  The antique rolles, which there lye hidden still,
  Of Faerie knights and fayrest *Tanaquill*,
  Whom that most noble Briton Prince so long
  Sought through the world, and suffered so much ill,
  That I must rue his vndserued wrong:
O helpe thou my weake wit, and sharpen my dull tong.

3

And thou most dreaded impe of highest *Ioue*,
  Faire *Venus* sonne, that with thy cruell dart
  At that good knight so cunningly didst roue,
  That glorious fire it kindled in his hart,

Lay now thy deadly Heben bowe apart,
  And with thy mother mylde come to mine ayde:
  Come both, and with you bring triumphant *Mart*,
  In loues and gentle iollities arraid,
After his murdrous spoyles and bloudie rage allayd.

4

And with them eke, O Goddesse heauenly bright,
  Mirrour of grace and Maiestie diuine,
  Great Ladie of the greatest Isle, whose light
  Like *Phœbus* lampe throughout the world doth shine,
  Shed thy faire beames into my feeble eyne,
  And raise my thoughtes too humble and too vile,
  To thinke of that true glorious type of thine,
  The argument of mine afflicted stile:
The which to heare, vouchsafe, O dearest dread a while.

---

of the heroic poem will now proclaim the stern deeds of war. **Oaten reeds**: the pastoral pipe; cf. *SC Oct.* 7–8. **5 gentle**: noble, as they are the deeds of noble knights and their ladies. **6** Implying the traditional exordium, 'I bring things never said before' (Curtius 1953:85–86); hence the triumphant **Me**. In revealing what has been hidden, he assumes the role of the poet-prophet. **7 too meane**: of low degree. The topos of affected modesty, traced by Curtius 83–85, is used six times in the proem. **sacred**: S.'s usual epithet for the muse. **areeds**: counsels; both 'commands' as **enforst** suggests, and 'instructs' (from 'read' *OED* 12); cf. VII vii 1–2. **8 blazon broade**: make known abroad; proclaim, from 'blaze': to proclaim with a trumpet. There is a startling transformation of the lowly pastoral poet into one who throws off his disguise to thrust his work among the muses. **9 faithfull**: the word counters Ariosto's scepticism regarding love, as Watkins 1995:61 notes. **moralize**: the stories of fierce wars and faithful loves provide subject matter to illustrate general moral truths rather than provide a text for a moral. Cf. 'morall laie' (*Colin Clout* 86).

Stanza 2

1 O holy virgin: perhaps Clio, the muse of history, **chiefe** in being the 'eldest' (*Teares* 53) of the nine muses, called the 'greater Muse' at VII vii 1.1. The name links her with the 'Goddesse', Elizabeth (4.1), who is the source of the poet's inspiration. See III iii 4 and IV xi 10. More likely, Calliope, 'the firste glorye of the Heroicall verse' (E.K. on *SC Apr.* 100), as Roche 1989:181 argues. In *Teares* 459, Calliope calls herself the muse 'That lowly thoughts lift up to heavens hight'. The two are linked at VII vi 37.9. S. may invoke either (and hence does not name the goddess) or he may conflate them as the proper muse of a heroic poem of praise, which is also an 'antique history' (II proem 1.2); see I xi 5.6–9*n*, and 'Muses' in the *SEnc*. **2 weaker**: too weak, as he is 'too meane' (1.7) for the muses' task and his thoughts 'too humble and too vile' (4.6). **3–4 scryne**: 'a coffer or other lyke place wherin iewels or secreate thynges are kepte' (T. Cooper 1565); also a shrine, as Memory's 'immortall scrine' (II ix 56.6); and analogous to the Bible as *ta biblia*, scrolls kept in a chest. On S.'s uses of the term, see Anderson 1996:127–32. **euerlasting** because it preserves deeds of everlasting fame. **hidden still**: now as formerly hidden; hidden always. **5 Tanaquill**: in Roman history, Caia Tanaquil, the wife of the first Tarquin, famed as 'a very noble woman and a sad . . . her image set up . . . as a token and a sign of chastity and labour' (Vives 1912:45). At II x 76.8–9 she is named 'Glorian', referring to Queen Elizabeth.

6–7 that . . . Briton Prince: Arthur, who is not named within the poem until he reveals himself and is named by Una at ix 6.5. S. follows Virgil who introduces his hero simply as the man (*ille*). **suffered**: i.e. for whom he suffered, extending the parallel to Virgil's hero (*multum ille et terris iactatus et alto*) to clarify the nature of the hero and his mission. **9 wit**: mind or intellectual powers, which must be strengthened so that he may 'thinke' (4.7).

Stanza 3

1 impe: offspring. **3 cunningly**: skilfully, craftily. **roue**: shoot. **4 glorious fire**: suggesting his love for Gloriana and also his desire for glory, who appears as 'Praysdesire' at II ix 36–39. **5–7** Cupid without his bow is the divine Cupid, son of the celestial Venus and a principle of order and harmony in the universe. On his opposition to the armed Cupid, see Lewis 1967:18–44. Mars and Venus represent respectively war and love, the two related subjects of the poem (1.9); their union produces the goddess Harmony. On this ancient 'mystery' in Renaissance thought and painting, see Wind 1967:85–96. **deadly**: because love's wounds last until death; see ix 9. **Heben**: made of ebony whose blackness suggests sinister properties. The bow carried by the god of love's friend in *Le Roman de la Rose* 914 is made of the bitter-fruited tree, *plus noirs que meure*. Heben is also 'some substance having a poisonous juice' (*OED*); cf. '*Heben* sad' (II vii 52.2).

Stanza 4

1–4 Cf. Wisd. 7.26: 'For she is the brightnes of the euerlasting light, the vndefiled mirroure of the maiestie of God'. **Goddesse**: a common term for princes, 'Who gods (as God's viceregents) ar' (Sidney 1963:Ps. 82.1). **Mirrour**: the earthly reflection of heavenly **grace and Maiestie diuine**; also 'pattern', 'paragon', as **Goddesse** suggests. **7** i.e. in his poem he will not flatter Elizabeth – an action condemned at II vii 47.3 – but **thinke** of the glory of which she is the antitype, her **type** being '*Gloriane* great Queene of glory bright' (vii 46.6), as he declares in the *LR*. See i 3.2–3*n*. **8 argument**: matter or subject; cf. 'O Queene, the matter of my song' (III iv 3.8). In *Am* 33.3, he refers to his poem as 'her Queene of faëry'. **afflicted stile**: humble pen; also a more general reference, from Lat. *afflictus*, thrown down: hence his need to be raised; or referring to the poem itself (cf. *SC Jan.* 10). **9** The plea to the Queen to **heare** is renewed at II proem 5.8; cf. IV proem 5.1. **dread**: as the **Goddesse** whom he beholds with fear and reverence; cf. Isa. 8.13: 'let him be your dread'. See vi 2.3, IV viii 17.1.

Canto I.

The Patrone of true Holinesse,
Foule Errour doth defeate:
Hypocrisie him to entrappe,
Doth to his home entreate.

1

A Gentle Knight was pricking on the plaine,
 Ycladd in mightie armes and siluer shielde,
 Wherein old dints of deepe woundes did remaine,
 The cruell markes of many' a bloody fielde;
 Yet armes till that time did he neuer wield:
 His angry steede did chide his foming bitt,
 As much disdayning to the curbe to yield:
 Full iolly knight he seemd, and faire did sitt,
As one for knightly giusts and fierce encounters fitt.

2

And on his brest a bloodie Crosse he bore,
 The deare remembrance of his dying Lord,
 For whose sweete sake that glorious badge he wore,
 And dead as liuing euer him ador'd:
 Vpon his shield the like was also scor'd,
 For soueraine hope, which in his helpe he had:
 Right faithfull true he was in deede and word,
 But of his cheere did seeme too solemne sad;
Yet nothing did he dread, but euer was ydrad.

Book I Canto i

Canto: Ital. 'song' used, e.g. by Ariosto; here first used in English for the twelve divisions of a book, the usual epic division from Homer (24) by way of Virgil (12). Drayton 1931–41:2.5 comments: 'The Italians use *Canto's*; and so our first late great Reformer, Master Spenser'.

Argument*
*A term used by editors to refer to the epigraph to each canto. In ballad metre or the common measure of the hymn-book, it serves as a mnemonic device in its synopsis of the canto. Like the *Argomento* in Ariosto, and 'The Argument' to each book in the Geneva Bible, it stands apart from the work itself. **Patrone**: protector and defender (from Lat. *patronus*); hence Guyon is addressed as one 'that for that vertue [temperance] fights' (II xii 1.6). Bryskett 1970:22 records that S. told him that he had undertaken a work 'to represent all the moral vertues, assigning to every vertue, a Knight to be the patron and defender of the same', and in whose actions we see the operation of the virtue 'whereof he is the protector'; see *LR* 41. Only the Red Cross Knight is so called. Morgan 1986a:830–31 suggests 'pattern' or 'model', citing the account of Blanche in Chaucer, *Book of the Duchess* 910–11, as Nature's 'chef patron of beaute | And chef ensample of al hir werk'. **true** claims the virtue for the Red Cross Knight in opposition to the seeming holiness of Archimago, as again at ii 12.2. See Hume 1984:73–74. **Hypocrisie**: i.e. Archimago. A rare occasion in the poem in which the Argument provides information not found in the text. The word is never used in the poem itself.

Stanzas 1–6
On the legend of St George with the maiden and her lamb, see 'George, St' in the *SEnc*; on his cult in England, see Bengston 1997. In his note to Drayton's reference to St George as England's patron, Selden records the story of the knight's delivery of the king's daughter from the dragon and adds: 'Your more neat judgements, finding no such matter in true antiquity, rather make it symbolicall then truely proper. So that some account him an allegory of our Saviour Christ; and our admired *Spencer* hath made him an embleme of Religion' (1931–41:4.85). Lydgate 1911:145 offers two interpretations of the name: 'the first of hoolynesse, | And the secound of knighthood and renoun'. Cf. de Malynes, *Saint George for England* 1601: 'vnder the person of the noble champion Saint George our Sauiour Christ was prefigured, deliuering the Virgin (which did signifie the sinfull soules of Christians) from the dragon or diuels power' (*Sp All* 84). On the knight's armour, see 'armor of God' in the *SEnc*.

Stanza 1
1 Gentle: noble, referring to his present appearance and true nature; see VI v 1–2*n*. His rusticity before he dons Una's armour is noted in the *LR* 56. **pricking**: spurring; the word's association with sexual desire is noted by Anderson 1985:166–68. **2 mightie armes**: 'that is the armour of a Christian man specified by Saint Paul' (*LR* 64, referring to Eph. 6.11–17); cf. ii 11.3 and 'his godly armes' (xi 7.9). **siluer shielde**: the 'shield of faith' (Eph. 6.16). The silver shield with its cross of blood was known as St George's arms, as ii 11.9 indicates. Hardyng 1812:84 records that they were given to Arviragus when Joseph converted him to Christianity 'long afore sainct George was gotten or borne'. **3 dints**: dents, a S. neologism that combines the blow ('dint' *OED* 1), and its effect. The knight's unproven role corresponds to David's when he 'girded . . . his sworde vpon his rayment and began to go: for he neuer proued it' (1 Sam. 17.39). Unlike David who doffs his armour to prove his God, Una's knight wears her armour to prove himself worthy of it. **8 iolly**: a simple yet complex term with a wide range of meanings: gallant, brave, handsome, of proud bearing, amorous. **seemd**: the ambiguous use of this word warns the reader to be aware of the disparity throughout the poem between what is and what seems to be.

Stanza 2
1 And: But (*1596*) stresses the paradoxes in the knight's appearance; see Gless 1994:51–52. **a bloodie Crosse**: the anonymous knight is identified as the traditional Christian knight by his symbol, Christ's blood and cross, which is also the red cross of St George. See the woodcut at the end

3

Vpon a great aduenture he was bond,
  That greatest *Gloriana* to him gaue,
  That greatest Glorious Queene of *Faery* lond,
  To winne him worshippe, and her grace to haue,
  Which of all earthly thinges he most did craue;
  And euer as he rode his hart did earne,
  To proue his puissance in battell braue
Vpon his foe, and his new force to learne;
Vpon his foe, a Dragon horrible and stearne.

4

A louely Ladie rode him faire beside,
  Vpon a lowly Asse more white then snow,
  Yet she much whiter, but the same did hide
  Vnder a vele, that wimpled was full low,

And ouer all a blacke stole shee did throw,
As one that inly mournd: so was she sad,
And heauie sate vpon her palfrey slow:
  Seemed in heart some hidden care she had,
And by her in a line a milkewhite lambe she lad.

5

So pure and innocent, as that same lambe,
  She was in life and euery vertuous lore,
  And by descent from Royall lynage came
  Of ancient Kinges and Queenes, that had of yore
  Their scepters stretcht from East to Westerne shore,
  And all the world in their subiection held,
  Till that infernall feend with foule vprore
Forwasted all their land, and them expeld:
Whom to auenge, she had this Knight from far compeld.

---

of Bk I. By this badge, he symbolically bears the cross; cf. *HHL* 258–59 and II i 18.8–9. **2 deare**: implying also 'dire'. **his dying Lord**: cf. 2 Cor. 4.10: 'Euerie where we beare about in our bodie the dying of the Lord Iesus, that the life of Iesus might also be made manifest in our bodies'. **4 dead as liuing euer**: cf. Rev. 1.18 on John's vision of the resurrected Christ who tells him '[I] am aliue, but I was dead: and beholde, I am aliue for euermore'. The pointing may be either 'dead, as liuing euer', or 'dead, as liuing, euer'. Nelson 1963:147 notes that the paradox, 'Christ dead is Christ living', is the principal subject of Bk I. **5 scor'd**: painted or incised. **6 For soueraine hope**: i.e. to show the supreme hope. **hope** and **helpe** are linked alliteratively to indicate their causal connection. The knight's enemy Sansfoy curses 'that Crosse . . . | That keepes thy body from the bitter fitt' (ii 18.1–2). **7 Right faithfull true**: cf. Rev. 19.11: 'And I sawe heauen open, and beholde a white horse, and he that sate vpon him, was called, Faithful and true', which the Geneva Bible glosses: 'He meaneth Christ'. **Right**: upright, righteous (cf. Ps. 51.10); or it may function as an adverb. 'The faithfull knight' is his common tag, as in Arg. to cantos iv, v, and x. **8 too solemne sad**: too grave or serious; cf. Guyon who is 'Still solemne sad' (II vi 37.5) when he avoids pleasure in order to pursue his quest; and Arthur, 'somwhat sad, and solemne eke in sight' (II ix 36.8) in his desire for glory; and Una who is 'sad' (4.6) in mourning. **too** prepares for his encounter with Sansjoy. **9 ydrad**: dreaded.

Stanza 3
1 bond: obs. form of 'bound' (going); also bound by vow (cf. 54.3). **2–3** 'In that Faery Queene I meane glory in my generall intention, but in my particular I conceiue the most excellent and glorious person of our soueraine the Queene' (*LR* 32–34). On **Gloriana**, see II x 76.8–9, VI x 28.1–3, and 'Gloriana' in the *SEnc*. **Glorious** refers to Christ's cross (2.3) before being applied to the Queen. On her role in the poem, see Fruen 1987, 1994. **4 worshippe**: honour, renown. **5 earthly**: as distinct from his hope in Christ (2.6). **6 earne**: yearn, as 7 confirms. It also carries the usual sense, 'seek to deserve by merit'. **8 his new force**: either the force of the armour newly given him, or his unproven power in wielding that armour. The phrasing is scriptural: e.g. Col. 3.10.

Stanza 4
Until she is named at 45.9, Una is associated by the lowly **Asse** with Christ's humility (Matt. 21.5–6, from Zech. 9.9); by

more white then snow with truth (in Ripa 1603:501, Verità is *vestita di color bianco*) and with faith (cf. x 13.1); and by her **vele** with the truth that remains veiled to the fallen. White and black are the colours of perpetual virginity and hence the Queen's personal colours (Strong 1977:71, 74). While the **lambe** associates her with innocence and with the sacrificial lamb of John 1.29, the king's daughter leading the lamb bound by her girdle is a traditional item in the legend of St George; see 'Una's Lamb' in the *SEnc*. Una riding an ass is a familiar Renaissance emblem, *asinus portans mysteria*, which symbolizes the true church; see Steadman 1979:131–37. As an allegorical enigma, see Nohrnberg 1976:151, 207–08, 268. On Una as Holy Church in relation to Elizabeth, see Perry 1997. **1 louely**: also 'loving' and 'worthy of love'. **him faire beside**: as she is fair and rides becomingly by his side. **beside**: indicating one meaning of her name, Lat. *una* (together), because her 'wondrous faith' is 'firmest fixt' (ix 17.4–5) in her knight; see 45.9*n*. Her place is taken by Duessa who rides 'together' with him at ii 28.1. **3 the same**: i.e. the whiteness of her garment. **4 wimpled**: lying in folds. Her 'widow-like sad wimple' is not thrown away until xii 22.3. **6 inly**: inwardly, in her heart; 'entirely' (E.K. on *SC May* 38). **9 in a line**: on a lead. Buxton, in the *SEnc* 724, concludes that this detail is purely pictorial, one of the very few where S. recalls an image he had seen. A woodcut in Barclay 1955 shows a lamb on a string; see the *SEnc* 706.

Stanza 5
1 innocent: in the religious sense, 'sinless', as the virgins who follow the lamb (Rev. 14.4); also 'undeserving of punishment' from which she seems to suffer. **2 vertuous lore**: i.e. in her knowledge of, and obedience to, moral doctrine. **3 Royall lynage**: see vii 43.3–9*n*. **5 from East to Westerne shore** asserts Una's claim to be the holy Catholic Church; see ii 22.7–9*n*. The Church of England claimed that its authority derived from the Apostolic Church before it was divided with the West ruled by Rome. Cf. Drayton's prayer that Elizabeth's empire might 'stretch her Armes from East to the West' (1931–41:2.530). **6** In man's unfallen state, God 'gaue | All in his hand' (x 42.7–8) and commanded him to 'fil the earth, and subdue it' (Gen. 1.28). **7 feend**: Satan; called **infernall** because he comes from hell. **vprore**: revolt, insurrection; cf. the account of his rebellion at vii 44. **8 Forwasted**: utterly laid waste. **9 compeld**: called; with the stronger implication, 'forced to come'.

6

Behind her farre away a Dwarfe did lag,
   That lasie seemd in being euer last,
   Or wearied with bearing of her bag
   Of needments at his backe. Thus as they past,
   The day with cloudes was suddeine ouercast,
   And angry *Ioue* an hideous storme of raine
   Did poure into his Lemans lap so fast,
   That euerie wight to shrowd it did constrain,
And this faire couple eke to shroud themselues were fain.

7

Enforst to seeke some couert nigh at hand,
   A shadie groue not farr away they spide,
   That promist ayde the tempest to withstand:
   Whose loftie trees yclad with sommers pride,
   Did spred so broad, that heauens light did hide,
   Not perceable with power of any starr:
   And all within were pathes and alleies wide,
   With footing worne, and leading inward farr:
Faire harbour that them seemes, so in they entred ar.

8

And foorth they passe, with pleasure forward led,
   Ioying to heare the birdes sweete harmony,
   Which therein shrouded from the tempest dred,
   Seemd in their song to scorne the cruell sky.
   Much can they praise the trees so straight and hy,
   The sayling Pine, the Cedar proud and tall,
   The vine-propp Elme, the Poplar neuer dry,
   The builder Oake, sole king of forrests all,
The Aspine good for staues, the Cypresse funerall.

9

The Laurell, meed of mightie Conquerours
   And Poets sage, the Firre that weepeth still,
   The Willow worne of forlorne Paramours,
   The Eugh obedient to the benders will,
   The Birch for shaftes, the Sallow for the mill,
   The Mirrhe sweete bleeding in the bitter wound,
   The warlike Beech, the Ash for nothing ill,
   The fruitfull Oliue, and the Platane round,
The caruer Holme, the Maple seeldom inward sound.

Stanza 6

1–4 Dwarfe: see 'dwarfs' in the *SEnc*. S. coins **needments** to suggest that the dwarf bears what Una 'needs', though without explaining what it is. **6–7** The storm suggests the myth of the sky impregnating the earth, which marks the beginning of creation, as in Virgil, *Georg.* 2.325–26 (see Rudat 1983), and here of S.'s creation of faery land. As it initiates the action of Bk I, **hideous** anticipates Errour's 'hideous taile' (16.2) to which the storm leads. **Lemans**: beloved's. **9 fain**: obliged; glad.

Stanza 7

1 couert: a dense thicket of woods that marks a place of peril and deceit, as again at the entrance to Mammon's house (II vii 20.6) and to Acrasia's inner bower (xii 76.6). **4 pride**: magnificent adornment; the most flourishing state, referring to the leaves; linked with 5, it suggests swelling pride. See 21.2*n* and Anderson 1976:24–25. **6 power of any starr**: referring to astral influence, emanation which may be benign or malign as **any** suggests. **8 footing**: footprints. The repetition of **-ing . . . -ing in** shows how the paths lead inward. **9 harbour**: covert or place of retreat; an earlier form of 'arbour': a bower or shady retreat. As in 8, there is similar mimetic syntax, **in . . . en**, to note an enclosed state. **Faire**: the epithet is more than formulaic, as Webster 1976:86–88 shows.

Stanza 8

1–4 The elaborate alliteration sets up its own **sweete harmony** to convey the sense of an enclosed garden. **5–9.9** On the 'groue' (7.2) as a literary topos, see Curtius 1953:194–95. The list of trees displays S.'s craftsmanship as the poet of faery land. Being a traditional epic catalogue, it announces his poetical kinship with Chaucer (*Parl. Fowls* 176–82), Virgil (*Aen.* 6.179–82, *Georg.* 2.440–53), and Ovid in his story of Orpheus, the archetype of the poet's power to move trees and gather a forest around him as he plays upon his lyre (*Met.* 10.90–105). For his use of Chaucer, see Esolen 1990:306–11. The characterizing of trees by their usefulness or stock associations indicates that the Wandering Wood, like Dante's *selva oscura*, is an emblem of human life, as Upton 1758 first noted. On their order, see Røstvig in the *SEnc* 514–15, and Røstvig

1994:271. J. Dixon 1964 glosses stanzas 7–9: 'worldly delighte'. **5 can**: do, did; or 'may'. Hence: 'well may they praise'. **6 sayling Pine**: because ships or their masts were made of pine, as Virgil, *navigiis pinos* (*Georg.* 443); or itself sailing or soaring in its height; or because Chaucer 179 writes of the 'saylynge fyr'. **Cedar proud and tall**: the biblical 'cedres of Lebanon, that are hie and exalted' (Isa. 2.13); a symbol of pride, as also Ezek. 31.3–10. **7 vine-propp Elme**: because it supports the vine, as the 'piler elm' in Chaucer 177. The marriage of the masculine elm and feminine vine was a popular Renaissance emblem. **the Poplar neuer dry**: because 'poplers grow by water sides' (Turner, *Herbal* 2.98; cited *OED*), or were associated with springs (Homer, *Ody.* 6.291); or because the Heliades, weeping for their brother Phaethon's death, were transformed into poplars and their tears into its oozing amber (Ovid, *Met.* 2.340–66). **8 builder Oake**: Chaucer's 'byldere ok' (176), i.e. used in building. **9 Cypresse funerall**: Chaucer's 'cipresse, deth to playne' (179), and 'used of the old Paynims in the furnishing of their funerall Pompe. and properly the signe of all sorow and heauinesse' (E.K. on *SC Nov.* 145).

Stanza 9

2 weepeth still: exudes resin continually. **3 of forlorne Paramours**: by forsaken lovers. **4 Eugh**: Chaucer's 'shetere ew' (180), traditionally used for bows. **5 Sallow**: 'a kind of woodde like Wyllow, fit to wreath and bynde' (E.K. on *SC Dec.* 81). Placed here in contrast to the stiff birch. It is associated with stagnant water (cf. IV v 33.4–5), which would be found at a mill-pond, and may have been used to make the mill-wheel. **6 Mirrhe**: noted as an incense for its sweet smell (cf. Prov. 7.17, Song Sol. 3.6); as a herb for its bitter taste (Mark 15.23 where it is associated with Christ crucified as earlier, Matthew 2.11, with his birth); and, as the Arabian myrtle, for its medicinal gum, which preserves the body. On the birth of Adonis from the myrrh, see Ovid, *Met.* 10.503–13. **7 warlike Beech**: in Homer, *Iliad* 5.839, the axle of the war chariot is made of 'the Beechen tree' (tr. Chapman). **Ash**: 'hath so great vertue, that Serpents come not in shadowe thereof' (Bartholomaeus 1582:17.62). Its virtues and general usefulness

10

Led with delight, they thus beguile the way,
   Vntill the blustring storme is ouerblowne;
   When weening to returne, whence they did stray,
   They cannot finde that path, which first was showne,
   But wander too and fro in waies vnknowne,
   Furthest from end then, when they neerest weene,
   That makes them doubt, their wits be not their owne:
   So many pathes, so many turnings seene,
That which of them to take, in diuerse doubt they been.

11

At last resoluing forward still to fare,
   Till that some end they finde or in or out,
   That path they take, that beaten seemd most bare,
   And like to lead the labyrinth about;
   Which when by tract they hunted had throughout,
   At length it brought them to a hollowe caue,
   Amid the thickest woods. The Champion stout
   Eftsoones dismounted from his courser braue,
And to the Dwarfe a while his needlesse spere he gaue.

12

Be well aware, quoth then that Ladie milde,
   Least suddaine mischiefe ye too rash prouoke:
   The danger hid, the place vnknowne and wilde,
   Breedes dreadfull doubts: Oft fire is without smoke,
   And perill without show: therefore your stroke
   Sir knight with-hold, till further tryall made.
   Ah Ladie (sayd he) shame were to reuoke,
   The forward footing for an hidden shade:
Vertue giues her selfe light, through darkenesse for to wade.

13

Yea but (quoth she) the perill of this place
   I better wot then you, though nowe too late,
   To wish you backe returne with foule disgrace,
   Yet wisedome warnes, whilest foot is in the gate,
   To stay the steppe, ere forced to retrate.
   This is the wandring wood, this *Errours den*,
   A monster vile, whom God and man does hate:
   Therefore I read beware. Fly fly (quoth then
The fearefull Dwarfe:) this is no place for liuing men.

---

are noted by Pliny, *Nat. Hist.* 16.24. **for nothing ill**: in contrast to the beech. **8 Platane round**: Lat. *platanus*, f. *platea*, broad. It may have been suggested by the **Oliue**, to balance a Christian reference (the Mount of Olives, Matt. 24.3) with a pagan one (Socrates and his friends sat by a plane tree, *Phaedrus* 230b). **9 caruer Holme**: either the holly or the holm-oak, both suitable for carving; cf. Chaucer's 'holm to whippes lashe' (178). Of the maple **seeldom inward sound**, Lyly 1902:1.242 asks 'Is not . . . dunge [taken] out of the Maple tree by the Scorpion?' According to Sinon, the Trojan horse was made of maple (*Aen.* 2.112). Fair without but unsound within, it stands as a fitting climax to the delightful wood with the monster at its centre.

Stanza 10

1 Led with delight: completing the description of the Wandering Wood which was ominously introduced by the phrase, 'with pleasure forward led' (8.1). They no longer lead but are passively led, failing to see the wood for the trees; for the implied proverb, see Tilley W733. **3 weening**: intending. **4 was showne**: the passive tense shows how the Wood beguiles them. **6 neerest weene**: think to be nearest to it. **9 doubt**: also 'fear', as the repetition of the word suggests. **diuerse**: distracting; a usage peculiar to S., from the sense of 'divers': 'turned different ways'. What is mentally diuerse proves morally distracting and dividing.

Stanza 11

1 still: in the same direction, a persistence that leads them into the centre of the labyrinth, as later (28.5) it leads them out. **3** The same path leads to the house of Pride at iv 2.9. **4 about**: i.e. through it, for once in a labyrinth the way out is the way in. Drayton 1931–41:2.138–39 describes the labyrinth as 'an Allegorie of Mans life . . . for what liker to a Labyrinth, then the Maze of Life?' See 'labyrinths' in the *SEnc*, Diehl 1986, and Blissett 1989. **5 tract**: track; tracing. A hunting term used here with **hunted** because the maze leads to the Minotaur at its centre. That Theseus slays the Minotaur, even

as the Red Cross Knight slays Errour, to escape the labyrinth suggests that their careers are parallel; see Fike 1997. **6 caue**: for this setting, see 'caves' in the *SEnc*, and Blissett. **7 stout**: brave, undaunted. **8 Eftsoones**: forthwith. **braue**: excellent, splendid. **9 needlesse**: because the spear is used only on horseback (cf. II ii 3), except in dire need, as at II viii 34.

Stanza 12

1 aware: watchful, on your guard. J. Dixon 1964 cites Eph. 5.15: 'Take hede therefore that ye walke circumspectly, not as fooles, but as wise'. **milde**: gentle, gracious. The epithet has strong religious connotations, being commonly applied to Christ and the Virgin Mary. Cf. its use at ix 46.6. **2 mischiefe**: misfortune, calamity. **rash**: here both adv. and adj. **4–5** Una's proverbial expressions first establish her as Wisdom: cf. 'Yet wisedome warnes' (13.4), and her moral aphorisms at 32.6–7, 33.3. Her role is that of Wisdom in Ecclus. 4.17: 'first she wil walke with him by crooked waies, and bring him vnto feare'. Una inverts the common proverb: 'there is no fire without smoke' (Smith 263) in order to adapt it to the knight's state. **7–8** For the sentiment, see III xi 24.5–9. **reuoke**: draw back. **9** The proverb (Smith 820) is undone at 14.3–5, for **Vertue**, which has the primary sense of 'manly force' (24.6), proves insufficient until faith is added (19.3). The Geneva gloss to Isa. 40.30 warns those who 'trust in their owne vertue'. **wade**: proceed, though the usual sense makes **shade** a substance that impedes motion, as the biblical plague of darkness, 'euen darcknes that may be felt' (Exod. 10.21).

Stanza 13

2 wot: know. **4–5 gate**: way, applied here to the entrance of the cave. **retrate**: the obs. vb 'retrait'. **6 wandring wood**: the labyrinthine wood within which one may wander or err physically, morally, and spiritually. **Errours**: from Lat. *errare*, to wander. Hankins 1971:68 links the term to Servius's gloss on *Aen.* 6.295: *errorem syluarum*, the error of the woods, leads either to vices or to virtues. On the structural function of the pun on 'error', see Quilligan 1979:35–36. **8–9** As later the

14

But full of fire and greedy hardiment,
   The youthfull knight could not for ought be staide,
   But forth vnto the darksom hole he went,
   And looked in: his glistring armor made
   A litle glooming light, much like a shade,
   By which he saw the vgly monster plaine,
   Halfe like a serpent horribly displaide,
   But th'other halfe did womans shape retaine,
Most lothsom, filthie, foule, and full of vile disdaine.

15

And as she lay vpon the durtie ground,
   Her huge long taile her den all ouerspred,
   Yet was in knots and many boughtes vpwound,
   Pointed with mortall sting. Of her there bred,
   A thousand yong ones, which she dayly fed,
   Sucking vpon her poisnous dugs, eachone
   Of sundrie shapes, yet all ill fauored:
   Soone as that vncouth light vpon them shone,
Into her mouth they crept, and suddain all were gone.

16

Their dam vpstart, out of her den effraide,
   And rushed forth, hurling her hideous taile
   About her cursed head, whose folds displaid
   Were stretcht now forth at length without entraile.
   She lookt about, and seeing one in mayle
   Armed to point, sought backe to turne againe;
   For light she hated as the deadly bale,
   Ay wont in desert darknes to remaine,
Where plain none might her see, nor she see any plaine.

17

Which when the valiant Elfe perceiu'd, he lept
   As Lyon fierce vpon the flying pray,
   And with his trenchand blade her boldly kept
   From turning backe, and forced her to stay:
   Therewith enrag'd, she loudly gan to bray,
   And turning fierce, her speckled taile aduaunst,
   Threatning her angrie sting, him to dismay:
   Who nought aghast, his mightie hand enhaunst:
The stroke down from her head vnto her shoulder glaunst.

'wary Dwarfe' (v 45.7) counsels the knight to flee the house of Pride. **read**: counsel, or warn. As Una is Truth, **wisedome warnes**.

Stanza 14

1 hardiment: boldness. This word describes Arthur when he begins his career at ix 12.6. **2 ought**: anything whatever. **4 glistring**: shining with its own light, as the sun is described at v 2.5. The Red Cross Knight claims that 'Vertue giues her selfe light' (12.9) but it is 'the armour of light' (Rom. 13.12) that allows him to see Errour. Nohrnberg 1976:142 refers to Ecclus. 21:23: 'A foole wil pepe in at the dore into the house: but he that is wel nurtured, wil stand without'. **5 glooming**: gleaming; glowing (from 'gloom'); but cf. 'glooming': 'that appears dark' (*OED* 2); hence it is **much like a shade**. **7–9** As a type of Satan, Errour may traditionally appear as a serpent with a woman's face, as Satan in Langland, *Piers Plowman* 18.335: 'ylyke a lusarde with a lady visage'. To Shakespeare's King Lear in his madness, 'Down from the waist they [women] are Centaurs, | Though women all above' (4.6.124–25). See Trapp 1968:261–62; and 'Error' in the *SEnc*. The classical source is Echidna: see VI vi 10–12*n*; the biblical source is the locusts in Rev. 9.7–10 who have the hair of women and the tails of scorpions; and the best-known literary source is Dante's Geryon, *Inf*. 17.10–12. On the conjunction as a symbol of treachery or fraud, see Panofsky 1962:89–91. In her double aspect, Errour is the prototype of Duessa (see ii 40–41) and the house of Pride (see iv 5). **disdaine**: loathsomeness; both her disdain for him and arousing his disdain for her (as 19.6).

Stanza 15

2–4 As the dragon in Rev. 12 is said by Bullinger, *Apocalypse* (1561), to be 'wonderful subtle, and can turn himself into folds infinite, that he may deceive, and keep the deceived in error'; cited Gless 1994:67. **boughtes**: coils. **mortall sting**: the locusts in Rev. 9.10 with 'stings in their tailes' are said in the

gloss 'to infect and kil with their venemous doctrine'. **7** Each is distinct and separate from the others though all, being **ill fauored**, resemble their dam. **8–9** On the popular belief that an adder, when disturbed, swallows its young, see Pheifer 1984:131–32.

Stanza 16

1 vpstart: started up. **effraide**: alarmed. **2–4 hurling**: hurtling and whirling. Cf. the violent motion of Lucifera at iv 16.3 and of Orgoglio at viii 17.9. **hideous**: both 'huge' and 'abominable', meanings that are paired throughout the poem; cf. the dragon's tail at xi 23.1. **displaid**: extended, and therefore shown to view, as 14.7. **entraile**: coiling. **6 Armed to point**: fully armed. **7 deadly bale**: deadly injury (or by double enallage, baleful death), i.e. death. Cf. John 3.20: 'For euerie man that euil doeth, hateth the light, nether commeth to light, lest his dedes shulde be reproued'. **8 Ay wont**: ever accustomed.

Stanza 17

1 Elfe: literally a fairy but applied generally to a knight in faery land as distinct from a Briton knight. On the distinction, see Hume 1984:145–61; also 'Britain, Britons' and 'fairies' in the *SEnc*. When applied to evil characters or used by them, it suggests a 'malignant being' (*OED* 1b). While the Red Cross Knight is supposed 'a Faeries sonne', he is a changeling descended 'Of *Saxon* kinges . . . in *Britans* land' (see x 64–65). **2 As Lyon fierce**: a carefully chosen opening simile, which is later expanded in Una's adventures. When her knight abandons her and she is left without 'my Lyon, and my noble Lord' (iii 7.6), she is sustained by the lion, which she makes mild (iii Arg.), but its fierceness brings its defeat by Sansloy, etc. **3 trenchand**: sharp. **6 speckled**: the snake's colours, signifying blots of sin as do the dragon's 'bespotted' tail and 'speckled brest' (xi 11.5, 15.2). **7 dismay**: defeat, literally 'make powerless'. **8 enhaunst**: raised up.

18

Much daunted with that dint, her sence was dazd,
    Yet kindling rage her selfe she gathered round,
    And all attonce her beastly bodie raizd
    With doubled forces high aboue the ground:
    Tho wrapping vp her wrethed sterne arownd,
    Lept fierce vpon his shield, and her huge traine
    All suddenly about his body wound,
    That hand or foot to stirr he stroue in vaine:
God helpe the man so wrapt in *Errours* endlesse traine.

19

His Lady sad to see his sore constraint,
    Cride out, Now now Sir knight, shew what ye bee,
    Add faith vnto your force, and be not faint:
    Strangle her, els she sure will strangle thee.
    That when he heard, in great perplexitie,
    His gall did grate for griefe and high disdaine,
    And knitting all his force got one hand free,
    Wherewith he grypt her gorge with so great paine,
That soone to loose her wicked bands did her constraine.

20

Therewith she spewd out of her filthie maw
    A floud of poyson horrible and blacke,
    Full of great lumps of flesh and gobbets raw,
    Which stunck so vildly, that it forst him slacke,
    His grasping hold, and from her turne him backe:
    Her vomit full of bookes and papers was,
    With loathly frogs and toades, which eyes did lacke,
    And creeping sought way in the weedy gras:
Her filthie parbreake all the place defiled has.

21

As when old father *Nilus* gins to swell
    With timely pride aboue the *Aegyptian* vale,
    His fattie waues doe fertile slime outwell,
    And ouerflow each plaine and lowly dale:
    But when his later spring gins to auale,
    Huge heapes of mudd he leaues, wherin there breed
    Ten thousand kindes of creatures partly male
    And partly femall of his fruitful seed;
Such vgly monstrous shapes elswher may no man reed.

Stanza 18

1 daunted: subdued; stupefied. **dint**: blow. **dazd**: bewildered. Throughout the episode, S. wittily shows Errour herself overcome by error and doubt. **2 gathered round**: coiled. **5 Tho**: then. She wraps her coiled tail around herself, ready to wrap it around the knight. **6 traine**: tail, suggesting all that follows Errour. **9** The poet's prayer implies that only God may help the knight so caught. **traine**: treachery, deceit. Duplication of the rhyme word links the literal and allegorical significances of the monster's tail, and both with the labyrinth of the Wandering Wood. Cf. the 'endlesse error' (iii 23.9) to which Corceca wishes to condemn Una. Soon the knight will be defeated by Archimago's 'subtile traines' (vii 26.2). Moseley 1989:35 observes how the alexandrine comments on the symbolic application of the strikingly visual image in the first eight lines.

Stanza 19

1 constraint: fettered state; distress. **2–4** Una's cry breaks the encoiling rhythm: the eight words of line 2 require eight heavy stresses rising in intensity with the concluding **shew what ye bee**, followed by the surprising and rare dactyl, **Strangle her**. Her injunction comes at the moment when Errour has seized the knight's shield of faith and threatens to strangle him. His **force** is his 'virtue' (*OED* 1) or fortitude (*OED* 6) to which he now joins faith: 'ioyne moreouer vertue with your faith' (2 Pet. 1.5). This moment is repeated in the knight's battle with Sansjoy at v 12, and against the dragon at xi 40. **faith** suggests an opposition to knowledge, with which the serpent is traditionally associated. **be not faint**: be not wanting in courage or strength, as Christ urged his disciples 'not to waxe fainte' (Luke 18.5). Diehl 1986:288 cites a contemporary emblem that identifies the pleasures of the world as a labyrinth from which the human figure at the centre may escape only by an act of faith. **5 perplexitie**: literally, his entangled state (*OED* 3); morally, his distress and bewilderment (*OED* 1b) in the biblical sense: the day of destruction is marked by perplexity (Isa. 21.5). Later he refers to this moment as a time when Una was 'wont to comfort me affrayd' (52.9). **6 gall**: the source of (jealous) anger;

cf. ii 6.4. **grate**: fret. **griefe**: anger. **high disdaine** renders the Ital. *alto sdegno*, in contrast to his later 'fiery fierce disdaine' (ii 8.4). **8 paine**: labour; also as his effort leads to her pain.

Stanza 20

3 gobbets raw: chunks of undigested food. Gregerson 1995:96 notes the reference to the Catholic doctrine of transubstantiation. **6–8** Cf. Rev. 16.13: 'And I sawe thre vncleane spirits like frogges come out of the mouth of the dragon, and out of the mouth of the beast, and out of the mouth of the false prophet', to which the gloss adds: 'That is, a strong number of this great deuil the Popes ambassadours which are euer crying and croking like frogs and come out of Antichrists mouth, because they shulde speake nothing but lies'. Hume 1984:78 cites Bale, *Image of Both Churches* (1545) on the dragon's flood as an image of 'hypocrisy, errors and lies' by Satan's forces. Similarly, Milton refers to 'the new-vomited Paganisme of sensuall Idolatry' of the insufficiently reformed English Church (1953–82:1.520). **bookes and papers** may refer specifically to such published lies and Archimago's 'magick bookes' (36.8), or more generally to the learning massively promulgated by the new print technology, as Rhu 1994:101 claims. **9 parbreake**: vomit, spewing; its etymological sense, 'breaking out or forth', shows the monster's violence – cf. 'vpstart' (16.1) – which the knight must overcome. Errour is made repulsive to each sense.

Stanza 21

The poem's first epic simile is suggested by the association of the Nile with the captivity of the Israelites in Egypt and hence with the fallen world, the flesh, and bondage to sin. When Aaron stretched his hand upon the Nile 'frogges came vp, and couered the land of Egypt' (Exod. 8.6). It was a commonplace of natural history that the river breeds strange monsters, e.g. Donne, 'Satyre' 4.18–19. **1 old father**: as the Nile was known as the world's oldest river; accordingly, it leads the rivers of the world at IV xi 20.3. **2 timely pride**: seasonable flooding; 'pride' is suggested by **swell**, as though 'puffed up with pride', and refers to its most flourishing state, as the trees at 7.4.

22

The same so sore annoyed has the knight,
  That welnigh choked with the deadly stinke,
  His forces faile, ne can no lenger fight.
  Whose corage when the feend perceiud to shrinke,
  She poured forth out of her hellish sinke
  Her fruitfull cursed spawne of serpents small,
  Deformed monsters, fowle, and blacke as inke,
  Which swarming all about his legs did crall,
And him encombred sore, but could not hurt at all.

23

As gentle Shepheard in sweete euentide,
  When ruddy *Phebus* gins to welke in west,
  High on an hill, his flocke to vewen wide,
  Markes which doe byte their hasty supper best,
  A cloud of cumbrous gnattes doe him molest,
  All striuing to infixe their feeble stinges,
  That from their noyance he no where can rest,
  But with his clownish hands their tender wings,
He brusheth oft, and oft doth mar their murmurings.

24

Thus ill bestedd, and fearefull more of shame,
  Then of the certeine perill he stood in,
  Halfe furious vnto his foe he came,
  Resolud in minde all suddenly to win,

Or soone to lose, before he once would lin;
  And stroke at her with more then manly force,
  That from her body full of filthie sin
  He raft her hatefull heade without remorse;
A streame of cole black blood forth gushed from her corse.

25

Her scattred brood, soone as their Parent deare
  They saw so rudely falling to the ground,
  Groning full deadly, all with troublous feare,
  Gathred themselues about her body round,
  Weening their wonted entrance to haue found
  At her wide mouth: but being there withstood
  They flocked all about her bleeding wound,
  And sucked vp their dying mothers bloud,
Making her death their life, and eke her hurt their good.

26

That detestable sight him much amazde,
  To see th'vnkindly Impes of heauen accurst,
  Deuoure their dam; on whom while so he gazd,
  Hauing all satisfide their bloudy thurst,
  Their bellies swolne he saw with fulnesse burst,
  And bowels gushing forth: well worthy end
  Of such as drunke her life, the which them nurst;
  Now needeth him no lenger labour spend,
His foes haue slaine themselues, with whom he should contend.

---

3 fattie: fecund, fertilizing. **outwell**: pour forth. **5 later spring**: last spring-tide; or **later** may be an adverb. **auale**: abate. **6–9** This account of spontaneous generation, abiogenesis, which popular etymology linked with Lat. *nil*, closely follows Ovid, *Met.* 1.416–37; cf. III vi 8.7–9, IV xi 20.3, and VII vii 18. T. Cooper 1565 writes: 'Nilus was famous for the vertue of the water thereof, whiche ouerflowynge the countrey of Aegypte, made the grounde woonderfull fertyle many yeres after, so that without labourynge, the earth brought foorth abundaunce of sundry graynes and plantes. . . . Also beastes of sundry kyndes'. **partly**: in part; some. **seed**: semen. **reed**: see. A sense found only in S. For him, to read is to see; cf. III ix 2.3, V xii 39.9. On his more than 130 uses of this word in its multiple meanings, see DeNeef 1982a:142–56, and Ferry 1988:9–48.

Stanza 22
1 annoyed: affected injuriously. **4 feend**: applied elsewhere in Bk I to the dragon, e.g. xi 2.3. **5–6 sinke**: her womb, or organs of excretion, as a cesspool. Apparently the flood of black poison (20.2) of the monster's vomit suggested the flooding of the Nile; in turn, its 'fertile slime' (21.3) suggested the **fruitfull . . . spawne of serpents** spontaneously generated by Errour, which she now defecates upon the knight. **7 blacke as inke**: linked with the 'bookes and papers' in Errour's black vomit.

Stanza 23
The simile heralds the knight's victory. For its development in the poem, see Hamilton 1961a:218–19. On the significance of the pastoral setting suggested by such details as the gnats' **tender wings**, see Knapp 1992:113–17. The gnat, or fly, is a common emblem in the poem of what is merely troublesome, as at II ix 16, 51; V xi 58; VI i 24, xi 48. Here

the feeble stings of Errour's brood contrast with her 'mortall sting' (15.4). The simile may have been provoked by S.'s environment in southern Ireland – see II ix 16.7n – but it is also literary, e.g. Ariosto, *Orl. Fur.* 14.109 and Homer, *Iliad* 2.469–71. On the further significance of the fly, see 38.2n. Stephens 1998:61 suggests that the gnats' **murmurings** make Errour's 'bookes and papers' audible. **2 welke**: wane. **5 cumbrous**: harassing. **8 clownish**: rough; belonging to a rustic, specifically to the 'clownishe younge man' described in the *LR* 53.

Stanza 24
1 ill bestedd: in bad plight. **3 Halfe furious**: a careful qualification, for only later does he yield totally to furious ire (ii 5.8) and become subject to irrational passion (cf. ii 15, v 14). The connection of his state with Errour's is noted by Gless 1994:66–67. **5 lin**: cease, leave off. **6 manly**: human. That his force is **more then manly** alludes to the faith which he adds to his force. Force, by itself, fails him at 22.3; 'Manly' force fails him before Orgoglio (vii 6) and before Despair (ix 48). **8 raft**: struck off. **remorse**: pity.

Stanza 25
2 rudely: violently. **4** As Errour's tail surrounds her body at 18.5. **7–9** The popular legend of the pelican whose heart's blood revives her dying brood (e.g. G. Whitney 1586:87) was applied to Christ who is our pelican (e.g. Dante, *Parad.* 25.113). Here it is an emblem of ingratitude, as in Lear's reference to his 'pelican daughters' (*King Lear* 3.4.74), and brings death rather than life, in parody of the Eucharist: 'Whosoeuer . . . drinketh my blood hathe eternal life' (John 6.54). *Am* 2 alludes to the legend that the viper in giving birth to itself by eating through its mother's womb kills her. On the legend, see Pheifer 1984.

27

His Lady seeing all, that chaunst, from farre
Approcht in hast to greet his victorie,
And saide, Faire knight, borne vnder happie starre,
Who see your vanquisht foes before you lye:
Well worthie be you of that Armory,
Wherein ye haue great glory wonne this day,
And proou'd your strength on a strong enimie,
Your first aduenture: many such I pray,
And henceforth euer wish, that like succeed it may.

28

Then mounted he vpon his Steede againe,
And with the Lady backward sought to wend;
That path he kept, which beaten was most plaine,
Ne euer would to any byway bend,
But still did follow one vnto the end,
The which at last out of the wood them brought.
So forward on his way (with God to frend)
He passed forth, and new aduenture sought,
Long way he traueiled, before he heard of ought.

29

At length they chaunst to meet vpon the way
An aged Sire, in long blacke weedes yclad,
His feete all bare, his beard all hoarie gray,
And by his belt his booke he hanging had;
Sober he seemde, and very sagely sad,
And to the ground his eyes were lowly bent,
Simple in shew, and voide of malice bad,
And all the way he prayed as he went,
And often knockt his brest, as one that did repent.

30

He faire the knight saluted, louting low,
Who faire him quited, as that courteous was:
And after asked him, if he did know
Of straunge aduentures, which abroad did pas.
Ah my deare Sonne (quoth he) how should, alas,
Silly old man, that liues in hidden cell,
Bidding his beades all day for his trespas,
Tydings of warre and worldly trouble tell?
With holy father sits not with such thinges to mell.

Stanza 26

1 **amazde**: stunned, stupefied.   2 **vnkindly Impes**: unnatural offspring; 'vnkindly' includes the current sense as an ironic understatement.   **5–6** The offspring of Errour are revealed finally to be a type of Judas who, with his reward for betraying Christ, purchased a field 'and when he had thrown downe him selfe head long he brast a sondre in the middes, and all his bowels gushed out' (Acts 1.18).

Stanza 27

2 **greet**: offer congratulations on.   3 **happie**: auspicious, propitious, referring to astral influence. Cf. her greeting when he emerges from Orgoglio's dungeon: 'what euill starre | On you hath frownd, and pourd his influence bad' (viii 42.6–7).   **4–8** The repetition of **you** and **your** stresses the knight's worthiness to wear the armour of Christ (**Armory**: armour) and assume his role as the Knight of the Red Cross (armory as armorial bearings, *OED* 2). At the beginning he sought 'To proue his puissance' (3.7); now he has **proou'd** his strength by an adventure that foreshadows his final defeat of the dragon.

Stanza 28

This stanza divides the canto into two balancing episodes of twenty-seven stanzas each, as Rose 1975:14 notes. Its central fifth line marks his taking charge after being led by pleasure (8.1) and delight (10.1) – in effect, to begin his quest. As 'an emblematic centre-piece', see Røstvig 1994:275.   **1–4** As Ecclus. 4.18: Wisdom will 'returne the streight way vnto him'. **beaten** by those entering rather than leaving; cf. the way to the house of Pride: 'All bare through peoples feet, which thether traueiled. | . . . But few returned' (iv 2.9–3.3). 28.3 repeats 11.3 to round out the episode, changing 'bare' to **plaine** now that the forces of darkness in Errour have been defeated, as Gless 1994:73 suggests, though only symbolically and only for the moment.   **4–5** To escape from the wilderness the Israelites are exhorted to 'turne not aside to the right hand nor to the left, but walke in all the wayes which the Lord your God hath commanded you' (Deut. 5.32–33). The moral applica-

tion of this injunction, given at Deut. 17.20, also applies to the knight. The accumulation of monosyllables in 5, together with the steady rhythm, imitates his persistence. The use of **one** rather than 'it' would seem deliberate.   **7 to frend**: as a friend.

Stanza 29

2 **An aged Sire**: identified as 'Hypocrisie' in Arg.3, named 'Archimago' at 43.6, and exposed for what he is at xii 35–36. Wybarne 1609 names him 'Antichrist' (*Sp All* 120). In denouncing monasticism in *The Three Laws* (1538), Bale refers to 'Hypocresy lyke a graye fryre'; noted King 1990a:51.   **4 his booke**: ostensibly the Bible, but see 36.8.   **5 sagely sad**: wise and serious, a counterpart to the sad appearance of the knight (2.8) and Una (4.6).   **7–9** The posture of the penitent publican who 'wolde not lift vp so muche as his eyes to heauen, but smote his brest' (Luke 18.13).   **in shew**: in appearance; always in S. with the implication that the reality is different. **malice**: wickedness; **bad** alludes to its root (Lat. *malus*).

Stanza 30

1 **louting**: bowing humbly.   2 **quited**: returned the salutation. 4 **straunge**: out of the country (*OED* 1b), being abroad; unusual; out of the way (*OED* 8). At the end the knight tells Una's father of his 'perils straunge and hard' (xii 31.8). He seeks the **aduentures** that Una wished for him at 27.8–9. **5–9 my deare Sonne**: more than religious formality. Only after the knight overcomes the perils into which the **holy father** now betrays him may Una's father address him as 'Deare Sonne' (xii 17.2). M.F.N. Dixon, *SEnc* 192, notes the abuse of copia in Archimago's tortuous forty-word paraphrase of 'no'.   6 **Silly**: feeble, simple, lowly, so he wishes to appear. **cell**: the obs. sense, 'a compartment of the brain', the *cellula phantastica*, is relevant to the infection of the knight's fancy by this arch image-maker.   **7 Bidding his beades**: counting his prayers on his rosary.   **all day** in contrast to the heavenly Cælia who bids her beades 'All night' (x 3.8) because during the day she is busy doing good deeds.   **9 sits not**: is not fitting. **mell**: mingle, concern himself.

31

But if of daunger which hereby doth dwell,
　And homebredd euil ye desire to heare,
　Of a straunge man I can you tidings tell,
　That wasteth all this countrie farre and neare.
　Of such (saide he) I chiefly doe inquere,
　And shall thee well rewarde to shew the place,
　In which that wicked wight his dayes doth weare:
　For to all knighthood it is foule disgrace,
That such a cursed creature liues so long a space.

32

Far hence (quoth he) in wastfull wildernesse
　His dwelling is, by which no liuing wight
　May euer passe, but thorough great distresse.
　Now (saide the Ladie) draweth toward night,
　And well I wote, that of your later fight
　Ye all forwearied be: for what so strong,
　But wanting rest will also want of might?
　The Sunne that measures heauen all day long,
At night doth baite his steedes the *Ocean* waues emong.

33

Then with the Sunne take Sir, your timely rest,
　And with new day new worke at once begin:
　Vntroubled night they say giues counsell best.
　Right well Sir knight ye haue aduised bin,
　Quoth then that aged man; the way to win
　Is wisely to aduise: now day is spent;
　Therefore with me ye may take vp your In
　For this same night. The knight was well content:
So with that godly father to his home they went.

34

A litle lowly Hermitage it was,
　Downe in a dale, hard by a forests side,
　Far from resort of people, that did pas
　In traueill to and froe: a litle wyde
　There was an holy chappell edifyde,
　Wherein the Hermite dewly wont to say
　His holy thinges each morne and euentyde:
　Thereby a christall streame did gently play,
Which from a sacred fountaine welled forth alway.

pastoral romance

35

Arriued there the litle house they fill,
　Ne looke for entertainement, where none was:
　Rest is their feast, and all thinges at their will;
　The noblest mind the best contentment has.
　With faire discourse the euening so they pas:
　For that olde man of pleasing wordes had store,
　And well could file his tongue as smooth as glas,
　He told of Saintes and Popes, and euermore
He strowd an *Aue-Mary* after and before.

36

The drouping Night thus creepeth on them fast,
　And the sad humor loading their eye liddes,
　As messenger of *Morpheus* on them cast
　Sweet slombring deaw, the which to sleep them biddes:
　Vnto their lodgings then his guestes he riddes:
　Where when all drownd in deadly sleepe he findes,
　He to his studie goes, and there amiddes
　His magick bookes and artes of sundrie kindes,
He seekes out mighty charmes, to trouble sleepy minds.

Stanza 31
1–4 Archimago replies with characteristic equivocation: to the knight's request for 'straunge aduentures, which abroad did pas' (30.4), he tells of **euil** that is **homebredd** being **hereby**, yet performed by a **straunge man** (i.e. one from outside) 'Far hence' (32.1). In effect, he describes the dragon, the intruder who has ravaged Eden, but does so in terms that reduce the Red Cross Knight to a mere chivalric knight.   7 **weare**: spend.

Stanza 32
1 **wastfull**: desolate.   4–33.3 Una's words to her knight are both ironic and prophetic: night does not bring rest but only his flight from her. They express the dilemma that **might** needs rest but virtue needs ceaseless vigilance.   **later**: recent.   **forwearied**: utterly wearied.   **baite**: give food and drink to; rests, refreshes. Her nine lines counter Archimago's nine at 30.5–31.4.

Stanza 33
3 Proverbial: Smith 574.   6 **wisely to aduise**: heedfully take thought; a sarcastic riposte to Una's advice.   7 **In**: abode, as the earlier 'harbour' of the Wandering Wood where 'in they entred ar' (7.9).

Stanza 34
1–5 Archimago's hermitage **Downe in a dale** is the demonic counterpart to Contemplation's hermitage on a hill (x 46); it is **hard by a forests side** because the knight flees into its wilderness; and it is **Far from resort of people** because from here he takes 'bywaies . . . | Where neuer foote of liuing wight

did tread' (vii 50.3–4).   **edifyde**: built; with the religious sense, 'strengthened in holiness' (*OED* 3), implied ironically.   7 **thinges**: prayers, monastic offices.   9 **sacred fountaine**: the counterpart to the well of life at xi 30.

Stanza 35
2 **entertainement**: food, a feast.   3 In being content, they have all that they wish in rest itself.   5 **discourse**: conversation, which Archimago turns into a popish service by his prayers to the Virgin.   7 **file**: smooth, polish; cf. his 'fayre fyled tonge' (II i 3.6). The derogatory implications are clear from the contrast with Zele 'That well could charme his tongue' (V ix 39.3). Cf. Ps. 140 3: 'Thei haue sharpened their tongues like a serpent'.   8 His stories would be found in *The Golden Legend*, as Nohrnberg 1976:158 suggests.   9 This Protestant scorn is nicely rendered in Shakespeare, *2 Henry VI* 1.3.55–56: 'all his mind is bent to holiness, | To number Aue-Maries on his beads'.

Stanza 36
2–4 **sad humor**: heavy moisture, the **deaw** of sleep. Imitating Virgil, *Aen.* 5.854–60: Somnus, the God of Sleep, shakes over Palinurus's temples a branch dripping with the dew of Lethe, the river of forgetfulness, before plunging him to his death. S. invokes his son, Morpheus, the fashioner of dreams through which the knight will fall to his 'death'.   **slombring**: occasioning sleep.   5 **riddes**: dispatches.   6 **deadly**: like his twin, death.   8 **magick bookes**: alluding to his name, Archimago, the arch-magician.   9 **sleepy**: sleeping.

37

Then choosing out few words most horrible,
  (Let none them read) thereof did verses frame,
  With which and other spelles like terrible,
  He bad awake blacke *Plutoes* griesly Dame,
  And cursed heuen, and spake reprochful shame
  Of highest God, the Lord of life and light,
  A bold bad man, that dar'd to call by name
  Great *Gorgon*, prince of darknes and dead night,
At which *Cocytus* quakes and *Styx* is put to flight.

38

And forth he cald out of deepe darknes dredd
  Legions of Sprights, the which like litle flyes
  Fluttring about his euerdamned hedd,
  A waite whereto their seruice he applyes,
  To aide his friendes, or fray his enimies:
  Of those he chose out two, the falsest twoo,
  And fittest for to forge true-seeming lyes;
  The one of them he gaue a message too,
The other by him selfe staide other worke to doo.

39

He making speedy way through spersed ayre,
  And through the world of waters wide and deepe,
  To *Morpheus* house doth hastily repaire.
  Amid the bowels of the earth full steepe,

And low, where dawning day doth neuer peepe,
  His dwelling is; there *Tethys* his wet bed
  Doth euer wash, and *Cynthia* still doth steepe
  In siluer deaw his euer-drouping hed,
Whiles sad Night ouer him her mantle black doth spred.

40

Whose double gates he findeth locked fast,
  The one faire fram'd of burnisht Yuory,
  The other all with siluer ouercast;
  And wakeful dogges before them farre doe lye,
  Watching to banish Care their enimy,
  Who oft is wont to trouble gentle Sleepe.
  By them the Sprite doth passe in quietly,
  And vnto *Morpheus* comes, whom drowned deepe
In drowsie fit he findes: of nothing he takes keepe.

41

And more, to lulle him in his slumber soft,
  A trickling streame from high rock tumbling downe
  And euer drizling raine vpon the loft,
  Mixt with a murmuring winde, much like the sowne
  Of swarming Bees, did cast him in a swowne:
  No other noyse, nor peoples troublous cryes,
  As still are wont t'annoy the walled towne,
  Might there be heard: but carelesse Quiet lyes,
Wrapt in eternall silence farre from enimyes.

Stanza 37

4 Plutoes griesly Dame: Proserpina, the consort of Pluto and the goddess of the underworld, who is linked with Hecate (see 43.3) by Conti 1616:3.16. She is called **griesly** because her appearance arouses horror, as at ii 2.7. **6 Lord of life**: in Acts 3.15 that title refers to Christ whom 'God hathe raised from the dead', an act parodied here, as indicated by Demogorgon's epithet **dead night**. The entire phrase may be owing to Langland who refers to Christ as 'The lorde of lyf & of lighte' (18.58) at the moment of his death. **7 call**: summon by rites; or in the sense (*OED* 23b), 'call vpon the Name of the Lord', as Gen. 4.26. **8 Gorgon**: 'an inchanter, whiche was supposed to be of suche excellencie, that he had authoritie ouer all spirites that made men afearde' (T. Cooper 1565). As Demogorgon, see v 22.5*n*. In Marlowe's *Faustus* 1.3, he is one of the infernal trinity invoked with Lucifer and Beelzebub. S. here introduces this name for Demogorgon into English, as Fowler 1989a:45 notes. **9 At which**: alluding to the fear aroused by uttering a god's name, esp. the 'dreaded name | Of Demogorgon' (Milton, *Par. Lost* 2.964–65); cf. 43.2. **Cocytus**: the river of lamentation in Hades. **quakes**: because even wailing ceases. **Styx**: river goddess of the lower world whose waters are associated with death.

Stanza 38

2 Legions: the Geneva gloss to Matt. 26.53 interprets 'twelue legions' as an infinite number; in Mark 5.9, the man possessed by devils is named Legion 'for we are manie'. **flyes**: reputed to be the form assumed by demons; see Chambers 1966. The simile suggests that Archimago is Beelzebub (interpreted as 'the master of flies' in the Geneva Bible) and 'chief of the deuils' (Luke 11.15). **3 euerdamned**: eternally damned. **5 fray**: attack, terrify.

Stanza 39

1 spersed: dispersed, 'empty' (ii 32.6). **2 world of waters**: the primal world from which land first rose. **3–41.9** S. imitates the *domus et penetralia Somni* in Ovid, *Met.* 11.592–632. **6 Tethys**: 'wyfe of Neptune, called goddesse of the sea' (T. Cooper 1565); here the sea itself. **7 Cynthia**: goddess of the moon; here the moon itself. **still doth steepe**: continually bathes. **9 sad**: dark; causing sorrow.

Stanza 40

1–3 Virgil, *Aen.* 6.893–96, describes the two gates of sleep: from the one of horn truth emerges and from the other of ivory false dreams. S.'s gate of **siluer** suggests the ivory gate, *candenti perfecta nitens elephanto*, which is associated with sleep; cf. 'siluer slomber' (VI vii 19.8), 'siluer sleepe' (VI ix 22.8). Like Aeneas, Archimago's spirit does not enter the underworld through a gate; also like him, he returns through 'the Yuorie dore' (44.6). **8–9** Morpheus is seen like the knight 'drownd in deadly sleepe' (36.6), as D. Cheney 1966:29 notes. **keepe**: heed.

Stanza 41

1–5 Echoing Chaucer's description of the cave of Morpheus, e.g. water 'Came rennynge fro the clyves adoun, | That made a dedly slepynge soun' (*Book of the Duchess* 161–62). The same opiate effect of running water is noted in the Bower of Bliss, II v 30.1–4. **swowne**: an earlier spelling of 'swoon' used throughout the poem. **vpon the loft**: in the upper region of the air (*OED* 1), or the roof (*OED* 5c) of Morpheus's house; cf. V vi 27.9. **6–7** The assonance of **noyse** and **annoy** is 'a carefully calculated discord designed to express the mingling of mental impressions that precedes the coming of sleep' (N. Frye 1976b:126). **8 carelesse**: free from care.

42

The Messenger approching to him spake,
    But his waste wordes retournd to him in vaine:
    So sound he slept, that nought mought him awake.
    Then rudely he him thrust, and pusht with paine,
    Whereat he gan to stretch: but he againe
    Shooke him so hard, that forced him to speake.
    As one then in a dreame, whose dryer braine
    Is tost with troubled sights and fancies weake,
He mumbled soft, but would not all his silence breake.

43

The Sprite then gan more boldly him to wake,
    And threatned vnto him the dreaded name
    Of *Hecate*: whereat he gan to quake,
    And lifting vp his lompish head, with blame
    Halfe angrie asked him, for what he came.
    Hether (quoth he) me *Archimago* sent,
    He that the stubborne Sprites can wisely tame,
    He bids thee to him send for his intent
A fit false dreame, that can delude the sleepers sent.

44

The God obayde, and calling forth straight way
    A diuerse dreame out of his prison darke,
    Deliuered it to him, and downe did lay
    His heauie head, deuoide of careful carke,

Whose sences all were straight benumbd and starke.
    He backe returning by the Yuorie dore,
    Remounted vp as light as chearefull Larke,
    And on his litle winges the dreame he bore,
In hast vnto his Lord, where he him left afore.

45

Who all this while with charmes and hidden artes,
    Had made a Lady of that other Spright,
    And fram'd of liquid ayre her tender partes
    So liuely and so like in all mens sight,
    That weaker sence it could haue rauisht quight:
    The maker selfe for all his wondrous witt,
    Was nigh beguiled with so goodly sight:
    Her all in white he clad, and ouer it
Cast a black stole, most like to seeme for *Vna* fit.

46

Now when that ydle dreame was to him brought,
    Vnto that Elfin knight he bad him fly,
    Where he slept soundly void of euil thought,
    And with false shewes abuse his fantasy,
    In sort as he him schooled priuily:
    And that new creature borne without her dew,
    Full of the makers guyle with vsage sly
    He taught to imitate that Lady trew,
Whose semblance she did carrie vnder feigned hew.

Stanza 42

2 waste: idle, being wasted. **4 rudely**: roughly. **paine**: effort. **7 dryer**: too dry, in lacking 'Sweet slombring deaw' (36.4). As one of the four states of the mind that leads to troubled dreams, see 'dreams' in the *SEnc*. **8 fancies**: fantasies, apparitions. **9 all**: altogether.

Stanza 43

3 Hecate: an infernal deity, the female counterpart to Demogorgon. 'A name of Diana, Juno, or Proserpina' (T. Cooper 1565), or of all three (Conti 1616:3.15). As the patroness of witches and witchcraft, she is associated with magic, dreams, and apparitions; see 'Hecate' in the *SEnc*. **4 lompish**: 'heauie' (44.4). **6 Archimago**: from Lat. *archi* + *magus*, the first or chief magician, or the 'great Enchaunter' (ii Arg.) as he is frequently named; also, the architect or source of false images, and of 'guilefull semblants, which he makes vs see' (II xii 48.6). Named 'Hypocrisie' at i Arg.3. See 'Archimago' in the *SEnc*. **7 stubborne**: untamable. **wisely**: i.e. by his magic arts; or skilfully. **9 fit false dreame**: as Morpheus is 'the feyner of mannes shape' (Ovid, *Met.* 11.634, tr. Golding). **delude**: deceive, in the current sense; specifically, 'impose on with false impressions' (*OED* 1). **sent**: senses.

Stanza 44

2 diuerse: diverting or distracting; cf. the knight's 'diuerse doubt' (10.9) in the Wandering Wood. Its literal sense, 'turning different ways', is suggested when he and Una are 'diuided into double parts' (ii 9.2). **4 careful carke**: sorrowful anxiety, collapsing the paired 'care and cark' (see *OED* 'cark' 3). **5 starke**: paralysed, unfeeling. **7** The **Larke** is cited as the

harbinger of dawn – see xi 51.9*n* – when dreams were thought to take place; see 47.3–7*n*.

Stanza 45

1 hidden: occult. **2 that other Spright**: the 'other' at 38.9, possibly epicene but now a succubus. In Tasso, *Ger. Lib.* 7.99, Satan forges an aerial body like the pagan Clorinda. **3 liquid**: bright. Being incorporeal, spirits must assume a body of air to appear before men; cf. ii 3.3. **ayre** is woman's element (though also man's at ii 3.3–4), from the folk etymology, *mollis aer* (gentle air) for *mulier* (woman), cited in Shakespeare, *Cymbeline* 5.5.446–48. **4** So lifelike and so resembling life itself, i.e. so like Una. **9 Vna**: one (Lat. *una*). She is named only now when her double appears; cf. ii 12.2*n*. Usually S. withholds naming a character until the image is complete, here following Gen 3.20: Eve is not named until after the Fall. On Una as a common Irish name and a cult name for Elizabeth, see 'Una' in the *SEnc*. On the Queen's motto *semper eadem*, see 'Elizabeth, images of' in the *SEnc*.

Stanza 46

1 ydle: empty or unsubstantial (being made of air or being a dream); or vain and frivolous (describing the nature of the dream). **4 abuse**: deceive. **fantasy**: fancy or imagination, which has the power to deceive reason, as the role of Phantastes is to deliver 'all that fained is' (II ix 51.9). On Archimago's deception, see 'magic, amatory' in the *SEnc*. **5 In sort as**: in the way that. **6 borne . . . dew**: being 'miscreated' (ii 3.1) and not 'from mothers womb deriv'd by dew descent' (*Am* 74.6). **7 vsage sly**: the cunning behaviour by which she imitates Una. **9 hew**: shape, appearance.

47

Thus well instructed, to their worke they haste,
    And comming where the knight in slomber lay,
    The one vpon his hardie head him plaste,
    And made him dreame of loues and lustfull play,
    That nigh his manly hart did melt away,
    Bathed in wanton blis and wicked ioy:
    Then seemed him his Lady by him lay,
    And to him playnd, how that false winged boy,
Her chaste hart had subdewd, to learne Dame pleasures toy.

48

And she her selfe of beautie soueraigne Queene,
    Fayre *Venus* seemde vnto his bed to bring
    Her, whom he waking euermore did weene,
    To bee the chastest flowre, that aye did spring
    On earthly braunch, the daughter of a king,
    Now a loose Leman to vile seruice bound:
    And eke the *Graces* seemed all to sing,
    Hymen iō Hymen, dauncing all around,
Whylst freshest *Flora* her with Yuie girlond crownd.

49

In this great passion of vnwonted lust,
    Or wonted feare of doing ought amis,
    He starteth vp, as seeming to mistrust,
    Some secret ill, or hidden foe of his:

Lo there before his face his Ladie is,
    Vnder blacke stole hyding her bayted hooke,
    And as halfe blushing offred him to kis,
    With gentle blandishment and louely looke,
Most like that virgin true, which for her knight him took.

50

All cleane dismayd to see so vncouth sight,
    And halfe enraged at her shamelesse guise,
    He thought haue slaine her in his fierce despight,
    But hastie heat tempring with sufferance wise,
    He stayde his hand, and gan himselfe aduise
    To proue his sense, and tempt her faigned truth.
    Wringing her hands in wemens pitteous wise,
    Tho can she weepe, to stirre vp gentle ruth,
Both for her noble blood, and for her tender youth.

51

And sayd, Ah Sir, my liege Lord and my loue,
    Shall I accuse the hidden cruell fate,
    And mightie causes wrought in heauen aboue,
    Or the blind God, that doth me thus amate,
    For hoped loue to winne me certaine hate?
    Yet thus perforce he bids me do, or die.
    Die is my dew: yet rew my wretched state
    You, whom my hard auenging destinie
Hath made iudge of my life or death indifferently.

Stanza 47

3–7 Although the knight is 'void of euil thought' (46.3), he is afflicted first by an *insomnium* in which he experiences vexations similar to those that disturbed him during the day, and then by a *phantasma* which occurs between sleep and waking, and in which a succubus appears as the false Una. See Macrobius 1952:1.3.2–8. Cf. Arthur's dream at ix 13.7–8. **8 playnd**: complained, lamented. **9 Dame pleasure**: Venus. **toy**: lustful play.

Stanza 48

Presenting 47.7 as a pageant, with the action resumed in the next stanza. **1–3 of beautie soueraigne Queene**: the phrase applies to 'Una' but also to Venus, here in her role as procuress; see Manning in the *SEnc* 708. The confusing reversal of time-sequence appropriate to a dream is noted by Roberts 1992:35. **5 On earthly braunch**: cf. 'borne of heauenly brood' (iii 8.7). **6 seruice**: as the 'servant' of Love (*OED* 2c), inverting the role that is properly his; cf. 54.3. Being **loose**, she becomes **bound**. **7 the Graces**: the handmaids of Venus; cf. VI x 9.5, 21.4. **8 Hymen iō Hymen**: the Roman hymeneal chant praising the god of marriage. **9 Flora**: traditionally the flower-goddess, as at II ii 6.5; but also 'a notable harlotte, whiche with the abuse of hir bodie hauinge gotten exceeding great riches, at hir death lefte the people of Rome hir heire' (T. Cooper 1565; cf. E.K. on *SC March* 16). **Yuie**: sacred to Bacchus and signifying wantonness; see E.K. on *SC March* 111. For the parody involved, cf. her crowning with 'oliue girlond' at vi 13.9 and with 'girlond greene' at xii 8.6. On the image, see 'garlands' in the *SEnc*; and on the topos of crowning in the poem, see Røstvig 1994:297–98.

Stanza 49

1 passion: *OED* credits S. with the earliest use here of the sense, 'a fit marked by abandonment to overpowering emotion'. **2 Or**: rather than 'and' because either is sufficient to arouse the innocent knight. **3 mistrust**: suspect. **4 ill**: both an internal bodily disorder and an external evil (as a **foe**). **5** As the knight dreams Una to be, so she **is**, or so it seems to him, now in a dream and soon in a vision. Unable to distinguish between what is and what only seems to be, his nightmare continues until viii 47–49 when he sees Duessa as she is. **6 bayted hooke**: as Lechery's 'fleshly hookes' at iv 25.9. **8 blandishment**: flattering speech. **louely**: loving. **9 virgin true**: Una's state is declared now that it is doubted; cf. 46.8.

Stanza 50

1 vncouth: strange; unseemly; repellent. **2 halfe enraged**: almost frantic; cf. his state 'Halfe furious' (24.3) against Errour. **3 despight**: indignation. **5–6** In seeking to **tempt**, i.e. test, 'Una' for her fidelity, he is the one being tempted. At the beginning he seeks to 'proue his puissance' (3.7) by killing the dragon; now he seeks to prove his senses. This act proves his downfall, for when he forgoes faith and accepts the evidence of his senses, he proves himself false. In place of Truth in Una, he gains **faigned truth** in Duessa. **8 Tho can**: then did.

Stanza 51

1 my liege Lord: as the superior to whom she is in 'vile seruice bound' (48.6). That address separates his role into that of knight and lover, subverting the former and appealing only to the latter. It posits a feudal relationship in contrast to Una's freely offered service to her defenders at viii 27.5. **4 the blind**

52

Your owne deare sake forst me at first to leaue
    My Fathers kingdom, There she stopt with teares;
    Her swollen hart her speech seemd to bereaue,
    And then againe begonne, My weaker yeares
    Captiu'd to fortune and frayle worldly feares
    Fly to your fayth for succour and sure ayde:
    Let me not die in languor and long teares.
    Why Dame (quoth he) what hath ye thus dismayd?
What frayes ye, that were wont to comfort me affrayd?

53

Loue of your selfe, she saide, and deare constraint
    Lets me not sleepe, but waste the wearie night
    In secret anguish and vnpittied plaint,
    Whiles you in carelesse sleepe are drowned quight.
    Her doubtfull words made that redoubted knight
    Suspect her truth: yet since no'vntruth he knew,
    Her fawning loue with foule disdainefull spight
    He would not shend, but said, Deare dame I rew,
That for my sake vnknowne such griefe vnto you grew.

54

Assure your selfe, it fell not all to ground;
    For all so deare as life is to my hart,
    I deeme your loue, and hold me to you bound;
    Ne let vaine feares procure your needlesse smart,
    Where cause is none, but to your rest depart.
    Not all content, yet seemd she to appease
    Her mournefull plaintes, beguiled of her art,
    And fed with words, that could not chose but please,
So slyding softly forth, she turnd as to her ease.

55

Long after lay he musing at her mood,
    Much grieu'd to thinke that gentle Dame so light,
    For whose defence he was to shed his blood.
    At last dull wearines of former fight
    Hauing yrockt a sleepe his irkesome spright,
    That troublous dreame gan freshly tosse his braine,
    With bowres, and beds, and ladies deare delight:
    But when he saw his labour all was vaine,
With that misformed spright he backe returnd againe.

God: Cupid, 'that false winged boy' (47.8). **amate**: dismay; but wilily suggesting 'mate'. **5 For**: instead of. **6 perforce**: forcibly; also implying necessity. **do, or die**: the bawdy sense, copulate and have orgasm, is particularly apt to her role as his mistress. **6–8** The jangling echoes declare her falsehood. As N. Frye 1957:261 notes, 'the grammar, rhythm, and assonance could hardly be worse'. **Die is my dew**: i.e. I deserve to die. **rew**: feel sorry for, as he does at 53.8 and therefore at ii 26.8. **8 destinie**: of the three alternatives in 2–4, she accepts **fate**. The same pagan powers of fate, necessity, and destiny are invoked by Despair to defeat the knight at ix 42.

Stanza 52

1–2 In effect, she inverts his role as dragon-killer, identifying him with the dragon. **5–7** The doubling of phrases comments upon her duplicity as Duessa while the **fayth** which she seeks in him suggests her assumed name, Fidessa. Now the term means 'chivalric constancy' rather than 'religious devotion', as C. Burrow 1993:122 notes. **languor**: woeful plight, sorrow; cf. Una's 'captiue languor' at vii 49.2. **9 frayes**: frightens.

Stanza 53

1 deare: dire, but also the usual sense because of her love. **constraint**: distress; cf. the knight in the coils of Errour at 19.1. **5 doubtfull**: as her words arouse doubts in him. **redoubted**: dreaded. He does not deserve this title until xii 29.7 for slaying the dragon. Through her words, he is again assailed by doubt; cf. 10.7, 12.4. **6 truth**: fidelity, as Tuve 1966:121 argues. From testing 'her faigned truth' (50.6), he is led now to **Suspect her truth**. **7 disdainefull spight**: indignant contempt. **8 shend**: reproach; suggesting 'destroy', as he was tempted to slay her at 50.3. **9 vnknowne**: unknown to her, but suggesting that he is unknown and unproven, and hence unworthy to be her lover.

Stanza 54

3 to you bound: correcting her address to him as her 'liege Lord' (51.1). **4 procure**: cause. **6 appease**: cease, as though satisfied. **7 beguiled of her art**: being disappointed in her intent; or deprived of her cunning. **9** The line's serpentine movement declares her serpentine nature. **turnd**: returned.

Stanza 55

1 musing indicates the mental wandering which will lead him to forsake Una; see ii 5.1n. The pattern for his fall is suggested by Satan's temptation of Christ, as described by Luke 4.3–13. Christ overcomes the three sins to which the knight, as the first Adam, becomes subject: distrust (by Duessa), ambition (by Lucifera), and presumption (by Orgoglio). **2 light**: a concealed pun. Only later does he recognize Una as 'fayrest virgin, full of heauenly light' (ix 17.3). **5 irkesome**: tired; also troublesome. The knight's **spright** cannot be distinguished from Archimago's (now male) 'misformed' spright. **8–9 he**: i.e. the dream. **misformed**: being 'miscreated' (ii 3.1), or created for evil.

Cant. II.

The guilefull great Enchaunter parts
The Redcrosse Knight from Truth:
Into whose stead faire falshood steps,
And workes him woefull ruth.

1

BY this the Northerne wagoner had set
His seuenfold teme behind the stedfast starre,
That was in Ocean waues yet neuer wet,
But firme is fixt, and sendeth light from farre
To al, that in the wide deepe wandring arre:
And chearefull Chaunticlere with his note shrill
Had warned once, that *Phœbus* fiery carre,
In hast was climbing vp the Easterne hill,
Full enuious that night so long his roome did fill.

2

When those accursed messengers of hell,
That feigning dreame, and that faire-forged Spright
Came to their wicked maister, and gan tel
Their bootelesse paines, and ill succeeding night:
Who all in rage to see his skilfull might
Deluded so, gan threaten hellish paine
And sad *Proserpines* wrath, them to affright.
But when he saw his threatning was but vaine,
He cast about, and searcht his baleful bokes againe.

3

Eftsoones he tooke that miscreated faire,
And that false other Spright, on whom he spred
A seeming body of the subtile aire,
Like a young Squire, in loues and lusty hed
His wanton daies that euer loosely led,
Without regard of armes and dreaded fight:
Those twoo he tooke, and in a secrete bed,
Couered with darkenes and misdeeming night,
Them both together laid, to ioy in vaine delight.

4

Forthwith he runnes with feigned faithfull hast
Vnto his guest, who after troublous sights
And dreames gan now to take more sound repast,
Whom suddenly he wakes with fearful frights,
As one aghast with feends or damned sprights,
And to him cals, Rise rise vnhappy Swaine,
That here wex old in sleepe, whiles wicked wights
Haue knit themselues in *Venus* shamefull chaine;
Come see, where your false Lady doth her honor staine.

Book I Canto ii

Argument
1 great Enchaunter: see i 43.6*n*. **2 Truth**: explicitly identi-
fying Una, as again at iii Arg. That 'truth is one' (V ii 48.6; xi
56.8) is proverbial; see Smith 791. **4 ruth**: mischief, ruin.

Stanza 1
1–4 the Northerne wagoner: or the Wain, the constellation
Boötes (Gk βοώτης, ploughman = ox-man) viewed as the
driver of the **seuenfold teme** of Charles' Wain, the seven
bright stars in Ursa Major. **the stedfast starre**: the Pole Star,
stedfast as the centre of the revolving stars, **behind** because in
pictorial star-maps, Boötes is seen behind his wagon. Eade, in
the *SEnc* 152, concludes that the date is on or about July 11.
yet neuer wet because above the 41st parallel it never sets. The
brightest star of Boötes and the second brightest star in the
English sky is Arcturus ('the North starre' in the Geneva gloss
to Job 38.22) or Arturus. It may be associated with Arthur (see
Anglo 1969:79–80, 92–94) and be regarded as his stellification
(on the process, see A. Fowler 1996:65–67). **7 once**: i.e.
once for all, though dawn comes only at 7.1–4. **Phœbus
fiery carre**: the chariot of the sun. Its progress is noted at
6.6–9 and 29.3–6.

Stanza 2
2 feigning: dissembling; also as it causes the knight to ima-
gine erroneously (*OED* v 4b). **faire-forged**: being falsely

fashioned and counterfeit in her goodly appearance; hence
'miscreated faire' (3.1). **6 Deluded**: frustrated in its purpose.
At i 43.9, he asked for a dream that would 'delude' the knight.
7 sad: because she was carried down to the underworld to
become 'blacke *Plutoes* griesly Dame' (i 37.4); cf. iv 11.2. Also
'causing sorrow'.

Stanza 3
2 that false other Spright: the one who brought the dream
from the house of Morpheus. **3 A seeming body**: as an
incubus; see i 45.3*n*. **subtile**: rarefied. **8 misdeeming**:
deceiving, or as it causes the knight to misdeem Una or think
evil of her; cf. iv 2.2. **9 vaine**: either describing their sinful
delight, or 'useless' as their bodies are of air. Being spirits, their
only satisfaction in fornicating is to entice others into it; see
Hasker 1947:334.

Stanza 4
2–3 sights | And dreames: the two stages of the earlier tempta-
tion – the dream of love (i 47.4) and the sight of 'Una' (49.5)
– now merge in the 'vision' (iii 3.6) of copulation. On later
homologies to Archimago's dream and vision, see Quint 2000.
repast: repose. **6 Swaine**: youth or rustic, in contrast to the
'Squire' (3.4), reminding the knight of his social inferiority,
and therefore, as 3.4–6 indicates, of everything that he is not.
7 wex old in sleepe: developing the false Una's suggestion,
'you in carelesse sleepe are drowned quight', while she is over-
come by love (i 53.4). **8** The description extends the knight's

5

All in amaze he suddenly vp start
   With sword in hand, and with the old man went;
   Who soone him brought into a secret part,
   Where that false couple were full closely ment
   In wanton lust and leud embracement:
   Which when he saw, he burnt with gealous fire,
   The eie of reason was with rage yblent,
   And would haue slaine them in his furious ire,
But hardly was restreined of that aged sire.

6

Retourning to his bed in torment great,
   And bitter anguish of his guilty sight,
   He could not rest, but did his stout heart eat,
   And wast his inward gall with deepe despight,
   Yrkesome of life, and too long lingring night.
   At last faire *Hesperus* in highest skie
   Had spent his lampe, and brought forth dawning light,
   Then vp he rose, and clad him hastily;
The dwarfe him brought his steed: so both away do fly.

7

Now when the rosy fingred Morning faire,
   Weary of aged *Tithones* saffron bed,
   Had spred her purple robe through deawy aire,
   And the high hils *Titan* discouered,

The royall virgin shooke off drousy hed,
   And rising forth out of her baser bowre,
   Lookt for her knight, who far away was fled,
   And for her dwarfe, that wont to wait each howre;
Then gan she wail and weepe, to see that woeful stowre.

8

And after him she rode with so much speede,
   As her slowe beast could make; but all in vaine:
   For him so far had borne his light-foot steede,
   Pricked with wrath and fiery fierce disdaine,
   That him to follow was but fruitlesse paine;
   Yet she her weary limbes would neuer rest,
   But euery hil and dale, each wood and plaine
   Did search, sore grieued in her gentle brest,
He so vngently left her, whome she loued best.

9

But subtill *Archimago* when his guests
   He saw diuided into double parts,
   And *Vna* wandring in woods and forrests,
   Th'end of his drift, he praisd his diuelish arts,
   That had such might ouer true meaning harts:
   Yet rests not so, but other meanes doth make,
   How he may worke vnto her further smarts:
   For her he hated as the hissing snake,
And in her many troubles did most pleasure take.

---

horror at being bound by Errour's coils and his earlier dream of Una 'to vile seruice bound' (i 48.6). **Venus shameful chaine**: as Acrasia's victims are 'In chaines of lust and lewde desyres ybownd' (II i 54.3).

Stanza 5

1 amaze: bewilderment; punning on 'maze'. First lost in a labyrinth and then caught in Errour's 'endlesse traine' (i 18.9), he continues to wander, now in a mental maze; see i 55.1*n*. **vp start**: the response of Errour; cf. i 16.1 and esp. 49.3. **4 ment**: joined together, knit in sexual intercourse. **6 gealous fire**: cf. his 'gealous feare' at 12.3. **7 yblent**: blinded. **9 hardly**: with difficulty.

Stanza 6

2 his guilty sight: the guilty sight that he has seen, though his own sight is also guilty; cf. 'troublous sights' (4.2). **3** The action of jealousy: see IV vi 7.5, etc.; cf. *HL* 267–68: 'that monster Gelosie, | Which eates the hart'. Proverbial: Smith 203. **4 gall**: see i 19.6. **despight**: no longer the simple indignation of i 50.3 but settled malice. The emotion is always base. **5 Yrkesome of life**: tired of life, in contrast to his earlier confident love for Una: 'so deare as life is to my hart, | I deeme your loue' (i 54.2–3). He has begun his journey to Despaire. **6 Hesperus**: here the morning star, associated with Venus, and named with obvious irony. **in highest skie**: see III iv 51.6–9*n*.

Stanza 7

1–3 Morning is Aurora, goddess of the dawn, whose lover, Tithonus, was granted immortality but not eternal youth. To associate the virgin Aurora and Una, the classical and Christian

day-stars, S. provides a pastiche of classical sources: **rosy fingred** is a stock Homeric epithet, **saffron bed** is Virgil's *croceum cubile* (*Aen*. 3.585), purple robe is Ovid's *purpureae Aurorae* (*Met*. 3.184). Cf. xi 51.1–4. **Weary** wittily varies the set description: Aurora is not satisfied with her aged lover. **4 discouered**: revealed. **5 The royall virgin**: as Una is described at iii 5.4, viii 26.1. **6 baser**: too lowly for her. **8 wait**: attend. **9 stowre**: time of distress or turmoil.

Stanza 8

4 Referring to the knight but also to his horse, an animal commonly associated with the passions in the poem, and therefore always male. The horse controls him in contrast to its curbed pace at i 1.6–7. **disdaine**: angry indignation, which was the knight's response to Errour at i 19.6; cf. i 50.3. **9** As Una represents metaphorically the true church, the line invokes John's rebuke: 'thou hast left thy first loue' (Rev. 2.4); noted Kermode 1971:15–16.

Stanza 9

1 subtill: crafty, cunning, a strongly pejorative sense that characterizes Archimago; cf. iii 24.6, vii 26.2. **2 double**: two; also 'divided'. The knight is divided from himself, so that his mirror image appears in the false St George, and divided in himself so that aspects of him appear in Sansfoy and Sansjoy. Una's mirror image is seen in Duessa who, as Fidessa, assumes her place. On their shared iconicity as the true and false churches, see McEachern 1996:41–50. **3** The broken scansion reflects her wandering state, as N. Frye 1957:259–60 notes. At II i 19.8, she is named 'the *Errant damozell*'. **4 drift**: scheme, plot. **8** Proverbial, as *SC Jan*. 65. He hates her as he hates a snake and/or as a snake hates.

10

He then deuisde himselfe how to disguise;
   For by his mighty science he could take
   As many formes and shapes in seeming wise,
   As euer *Proteus* to himselfe could make:
   Sometime a fowle, sometime a fish in lake,
   Now like a foxe, now like a dragon fell,
   That of himselfe he ofte for feare would quake,
   And oft would flie away. O who can tell
The hidden powre of herbes, and might of Magick spel?

11

But now seemde best, the person to put on
   Of that good knight, his late beguiled guest:
   In mighty armes he was yclad anon:
   And siluer shield, vpon his coward brest
   A bloody crosse, and on his crauen crest
   A bounch of heares discoloured diuersly:
   Full iolly knight he seemde, and wel addrest,
   And when he sate vppon his courser free,
Saint George himselfe ye would haue deemed him to be.

12

But he the knight, whose semblaunt he did beare,
   The true *Saint George* was wandred far away,
   Still flying from his thoughts and gealous feare;
   Will was his guide, and griefe led him astray.

At last him chaunst to meete vpon the way
   A faithlesse Sarazin all armde to point,
   In whose great shield was writ with letters gay
   Sans foy: full large of limbe and euery ioint
He was, and cared not for God or man a point.

13

Hee had a faire companion of his way,
   A goodly Lady clad in scarlot red,
   Purfled with gold and pearle of rich assay,
   And like a *Persian* mitre on her hed
   Shee wore, with crowns and owches garnished,
   The which her lauish louers to her gaue;
   Her wanton palfrey all was ouerspred
   With tinsell trappings, wouen like a waue,
Whose bridle rung with golden bels and bosses braue.

14

With faire disport and courting dalliaunce
   She intertainde her louer all the way:
   But when she saw the knight his speare aduaunce,
   Shee soone left off her mirth and wanton play,
   And bad her knight addresse him to the fray:
   His foe was nigh at hand. He prickte with pride
   And hope to winne his Ladies hearte that day,
   Forth spurred fast: adowne his coursers side
The red bloud trickling staind the way, as he did ride.

Stanza 10
2 mighty science: as in the biblical phrase 'mighty works', the knowledge needed to perform miracles (gloss to Mark 6.2). **3–6** Proverbial: *Proteo mutabilior*, as T. Cooper 1565 notes. Proteus could change himself particularly into the four elements, as Conti 1616:8.8 notes, citing Homer (*Ody.* 4.415–18), and as S. catalogues here to indicate his power over the earth. The dragon suggests the fourth element of fire. **3 seeming**: ways of seeming or appearing. **7–8** While the humour is obvious, the lines comment on the knight who flees from himself. **9 powre of herbes**: in glossing *SC Dec.* 88, E.K. notes their use in 'enchauntments and sorceries'.

Stanza 11
1–2 I.e. to assume the knight's appearance, appearance and reality now being divided in him. As the phrases borrowed from i 1 show, Archimago appropriates his appearance and also the title he will gain after his earthly adventures when 'thou *Saint George* shalt called bee' (x 61.8). On the significance of his impersonation, see Anderson 1998:94. **that good knight** is his stock epithet throughout, as 29.1, 44.3, etc. **6 discoloured**: variously coloured. Arthur wears this plume at vii 32.1–2. **7 addrest**: attired. **8 free**: high-spirited, willing. At this same-numbered stanza and line in canto i, the Red Cross Knight dismounts from his courser. **9** As Una deems him to be at iii 26.6–9. See x 65.6–9*n.*

Stanza 12
1 semblaunt: appearance. **2 The true Saint George**: named only when his double appears; see i 45.9*n.* **wandred**: with a strong moral sense. He falls into error as he seeks to flee from himself. **4 Will**: the emphasis gained by using a trochee in the usual iambic line stresses the stronger theological sense: the infected will becomes subject to the passions once 'The eie of reason was with rage yblent' (5.7). G. Whitney 1586:6 moral-

izes the emblem of *temeritas*: 'bridle will, and reason make thy guide'. **griefe**: anger, mental distress, with the modern sense, 'regret for what has been lost'. **6 Sarazin**: Saracen specifically, or pagan generally, applied also to Sansjoy (v 4.1) and Sansloy (vi 8.6); see 'Paynims' in the *SEnc*. On the identification with militant Islam, see Heberle 1989. **to point**: completely. **8 Sans foy**: Fr. *sans foi*, i.e. **faithlesse**. **9 not . . . a point**: not at all; like the unrighteous judge in Christ's parable of loss of faith, Luke 18.2.

Stanza 13
2 goodly: often, as here, used ironically to suggest what is good only in appearance, only 'seeming glorious show' (21.5). **scarlot**: a rich cloth associated with royalty, as she is 'royall richly dight' (xii 32.4). Duessa is the great whore of Babylon, 'araied in purple and skarlat, and guilded with golde, and precious stones, and pearles' (Rev.17.4). As the gloss explains, 'this woman is the Antichrist, that is, the Pope with the whole bodie of his filthie creatures . . . whose beautie onely standeth in outwarde pompe and impudencie and craft like a strumpet', one 'whose crueltie and blood sheding is declared by skarlat'. She is Langland's Meed, daughter of Fals and wife of Falsehood, 'Purfiled with pelure the finest vpon erthe | . . . Hire robe was ful riche, of red scarlet engreyned | With ribanes of red golde and of riche stones' (*Piers Plowman* 2.9, 15–16). **3 Purfled**: embroidered. **of rich assay**: proven of rich value. **4 like a Persian mitre**: resembling a Persian head-dress, and hence suggesting 'pompous pride' (iv 7.6). **mitre**: the papal tiara or 'triple crowne' (vii 16.4, and see *n*). **5 owches**: jewels, as Lady Meed is 'Ycrounede with a corone' (2.10). Cf. the wanton and haughty daughters of Zion (Isa. 3.16). **6 lauish**: also licentious (*OED* 1b). **7–9 wanton**: unruly, frisky, in contrast to Una's 'slowe beast' (8.2); also lascivious, as the horse symbolizes her passion. **tinsell**: glittering. **wouen like a waue**: probably watered-silk that would ripple as she rode.

15

The knight of the *Redcrosse* when him he spide,
  Spurring so hote with rage dispiteous,
  Gan fairely couch his speare, and towards ride:
  Soone meete they both, both fell and furious,
  That daunted with theyr forces hideous,
  Their steeds doe stagger, and amazed stand,
  And eke themselues too rudely rigorous,
  Astonied with the stroke of their owne hand,
Doe backe rebutte, and ech to other yealdeth land.

16

As when two rams stird with ambitious pride,
  Fight for the rule of the rich fleeced flocke,
  Their horned fronts so fierce on either side,
  Doe meete, that with the terror of the shocke
  Astonied both, stand sencelesse as a blocke,
  Forgetfull of the hanging victory:
  So stood these twaine, vnmoued as a rocke,
  Both staring fierce, and holding idely,
The broken reliques of their former cruelty.

17

The *Sarazin* sore daunted with the buffe
  Snatcheth his sword, and fiercely to him flies;
  Who well it wards, and quyteth cuff with cuff:
  Each others equall puissaunce enuies,

And through their iron sides with cruell spies
Does seeke to perce: repining courage yields
No foote to foe. The flashing fier flies
As from a forge out of their burning shields,
And streams of purple bloud new dies the verdant fields.

18

Curse on that Crosse (quoth then the *Sarazin*)
  That keepes thy body from the bitter fitt;
  Dead long ygoe I wote thou haddest bin,
  Had not that charme from thee forwarned itt:
  But yet I warne thee now assured sitt,
  And hide thy head. Therewith vpon his crest
  With rigor so outrageous he smitt,
  That a large share it hewd out of the rest,
And glauncing downe his shield, from blame him fairely blest.

19

Who thereat wondrous wroth, the sleeping spark
  Of natiue vertue gan eftsoones reuiue,
  And at his haughty helmet making mark,
  So hugely stroke, that it the steele did riue,
  And cleft his head. He tumbling downe aliue,
  With bloudy mouth his mother earth did kis,
  Greeting his graue: his grudging ghost did striue
  With the fraile flesh; at last it flitted is,
Whether the soules doe fly of men, that liue amis.

Such trappings are denounced by Chaucer's Parson: 'the synne of aornement or of apparaille is in thynges that apertenen to ridynge, as in . . . bridles covered with precious clothyng . . . For which God seith by Zakarie the prophete, "I wol confounde the rideres of swiche horses" ' (*Parson's Tale* 431–34). **bosses braue**: handsome studs on each side of the bit.

Stanza 14

1 disport: wanton play, diversion that carries one from the right way. **4 soone**: without delay. **6 prickte with pride**: i.e. urged on by lust, as 16.1–4 registers. **7** Their courtship is interrupted before their troth is plighted, allowing the Red Cross Knight to take Sansfoy's place.

Stanza 15

1 Redcrosse: this first naming of the knight may have been suggested by the 'red bloud' of the previous line. Yet, as with Una, he is named when his double appears: 'Pricked with wrath' (8.4), as Sansfoy is **Spurring . . . with rage**, he meets himself. **2 dispiteous**: cruel, merciless. **3 fairely couch his speare**: expertly place his spear in its rest and lower it for attack. **5 daunted**: dazed. **7 rigorous**: violent; also 'rigid', as they hold their spears. **8 Astonied**: stunned, as though turned to stone. **9 rebutte**: recoil. The term suggests a literal butting of rams as described in the next stanza.

Stanza 16

1–9 The simile reduces the knight to the same brute level as his antagonist, in contrast to the earlier simile, 'As Lyon fierce' (i 17.2). **6 hanging**: i.e. in the balance. **9 reliques**: fragments of the spears, and hence held **idely**, i.e. in vain; or memorials of earlier cruelty.

Stanza 17

4 enuies: seeks to rival, 'each seeks to rival the other's equal force'; also in the modern sense, as **repining** suggests. Cf. iv

14.9. **5 spies**: eyes, as each watches cruelly where to thrust his sword; also the darting of their swords.

Stanza 18

2 bitter fitt: pangs of death. **4 charme**: an amulet worn to avert evil; cf. 'charmed shield' (iv 50.5). Sansfoy confuses the sign with the power it signifies; noted Maclean and Prescott 1993. The ritual of chivalric combat included an oath to abjure charms. **forwarned**: prohibited; prevented. The slightly awkward syntax allows a play on **warne** in the next line. **5 assured**: securely; advice given, of course, in mockery. The cross protects the knight's body but not his head now that his 'eie of reason was with rage yblent' (5.7); hence the 'helmet of saluation' (Eph. 6.17) may be sheared by the knight of faithlessness but his life is preserved. **7 rigor**: violence. **8 share**: a piece cut or sheared away. **9 blame**: injury, hurt; with the modern sense, 'imputation of a fault'. In a judicial combat, injury was proof of fault. **fairely**: entirely. **blest**: protected, suggesting that God's grace protects him, as his shield of faith preserves him from harm. When he adds faith to force, the combination defeats Sansfoy, as it had defeated Errour (cf. i 19). Cf. the similar phrasing and sense at IV vi 13.4.

Stanza 19

2 natiue vertue: natural courage or power (Lat. *virtus*); cf. the 'more then manly force' by which he kills Errour (i 24.6). **3 haughty**: also lofty, in the literal sense. The knight's blow upon the head is the counterpart to Sansfoy's blow. On the theological significance of the battle, see Gless 1994:81–82. **4 hugely**: mightily. **6 his mother earth**: see vii 9.1n. **7 grudging**: complaining, repining. S. imitates the closing line of the *Aeneid*: *vitaque cum gemitu fugit indignata sub umbras*. The end of Virgil's poem marks the beginning of significant action in S.'s. By killing Sansfoy, the knight gains Duessa in place of Una, and arouses the wrath of Sansjoy and Sansloy; see v 10.1–6n.

20

The Lady when she saw her champion fall,
  Like the old ruines of a broken towre,
  Staid not to waile his woefull funerall,
  But from him fled away with all her powre;
  Who after her as hastily gan scowre,
  Bidding the dwarfe with him to bring away
  The *Sarazins* shield, signe of the conqueroure,
  Her soone he ouertooke, and bad to stay,
For present cause was none of dread her to dismay.

21

Shee turning backe with ruefull countenaunce,
  Cride, Mercy mercy Sir vouchsafe to show
  On silly Dame, subiect to hard mischaunce,
  And to your mighty wil. Her humblesse low
  In so ritch weedes and seeming glorious show,
  Did much emmoue his stout heroicke heart,
  And said, Deare dame, your suddein ouerthrow
  Much rueth me; but now put feare apart,
And tel, both who ye be, and who that tooke your part.

22

Melting in teares, then gan shee thus lament;
  The wreched woman, whom vnhappy howre
  Hath now made thrall to your commandement,
  Before that angry heauens list to lowre,

And fortune false betraide me to thy powre,
  Was, (O what now auaileth that I was?)
  Borne the sole daughter of an Emperour,
  He that the wide West vnder his rule has,
And high hath set his throne, where *Tiberis* doth pas.

23

He in the first flowre of my freshest age,
  Betrothed me vnto the onely haire
  Of a most mighty king, most rich and sage;
  Was neuer Prince so faithfull and so faire,
  Was neuer Prince so meeke and debonaire;
  But ere my hoped day of spousall shone,
  My dearest Lord fell from high honors staire,
  Into the hands of hys accursed fone,
And cruelly was slaine, that shall I euer mone.

24

His blessed body spoild of liuely breath,
  Was afterward, I know not how, conuaid
  And fro me hid: of whose most innocent death
  When tidings came to mee vnhappy maid,
  O how great sorrow my sad soule assaid,
  Then forth I went his woefull corse to find,
  And many yeares throughout the world I straid,
  A virgin widow, whose deepe wounded mind
With loue, long time did languish as the striken hind.

Stanza 20

2 An image developed and expanded at viii 23 to describe Orgoglio's fall. 3 **funerall**: death. 5 Flight from Una now becomes a flight after Duessa. 7 The chivalric convention that allowed the victor to claim the arms of the defeated enemy is given special significance: in his Pyrrhic victory, the knight gains, and must later defend, a shield bearing the inscription '*Sans foy*' (12.8).

Stanza 21

1 **ruefull**: seeking to excite pity. 3–4 **silly**: helpless, and therefore subject to his **mighty wil**, as she implies suggestively; cf. 22.3. **humblesse**: humility. 5 **show**: appearance, in contrast to Archimago who appears 'Simple in shew' (i 29.7). 6 **emmoue**: move inwardly or strongly. 8 **Much rueth me**: greatly affects with pity (*OED* 4). A similar appeal from the false dream led him to rue the false Una's grief (i 53.8). Now pity will betray him further. Later he will rue this meeting with Duessa in the sense that he will regret it (*OED* 7), and suffer repentance and remorse (*OED* 9).

Stanza 22

3 **commandement**: authority. 5 Reality still enacts his dream at i 51.8–9. 7–9 **sole daughter**: the rival of Una who is her father's 'onely daughter deare, | His onely daughter, and his onely hayre' (xii 21.2–3). In this context, **Emperour** suggests the head of the Holy Roman Empire and the papal usurpation of imperial power in opposition to the 'magnificent Empresse', Elizabeth, to whom S. dedicates his poem. Una is called 'the daughter of a king' at i 48.5, iii 2.5, and vii 43.3; cf. the distinction in the phrase 'Renowmed kings, and sacred Emperours' (III iii 23.1), and the contest at II x 51 between

the Roman Emperor and the British King. In *Comm Sonn* 4.3, S. refers to Rome as 'Second *Babell* tyrant of the West'. **wide West**: in contrast to the kingdom ruled by Una's parents: their 'scepters stretcht from East to Westerne shore' (i 5.5), thus distinguishing the universal (and now English) Church from the Church of Rome. See Hankins 1971:211–12, and 'Church of Rome' in the *SEnc*. **has**: because the dragon now rules Una's parents' kingdom; see vii 43.3–9n. The gloss by J. Dixon 1964 reads: 'Antichriste taketh one hir the nam of Truth, fained to be the daughter of a persian kynge: but truth is only ment. to our Souerainge Eliz. Christe and his gospell'. **high**: suggesting pride. **Tiberis**: the Tiber, associated with Rome; cf. xii 26.3–4.

Stanza 23

4–5 Alluding to Christ – 'him hathe God lift vp with his right hand, to be a Prince' (Acts 5.31) – who refers to himself as 'the bridegrome [who] shalbe taken from them [his followers]' (Matt. 9.15). **debonaire**: gentle, gracious.

Stanza 24

Since S. associates the Church of Rome with the cult of Christ's dead body in the Mass, Duessa echoes Mary Magdalene's lament: 'They haue taken away the Lord out of the sepulchre, and we knowe not where they haue laid him' (John 20.2). Matthew records the saying 'noised among the Iewes vnto this day' that soldiers were bribed to say 'his disciples came by night and stole him away while we slept' (28.13, 15). As the disciples were exhorted, 'Why seke ye him that liueth, among the dead?' (Luke 24.5), S. associates his Protestant hero with the resurrection; hence 'And dead as liuing euer him ador'd' (i 2.4). In *HHL* 148, 259, Christ's 'blessed bodie' instructs each

25

At last it chaunced this proud *Sarazin*,
   To meete me wandring, who perforce me led
   With him away, but yet could neuer win
   The Fort, that Ladies hold in soueraigne dread.
   There lies he now with foule dishonor dead,
   Who whiles he liude, was called proud *Sans foy*,
   The eldest of three brethren, all three bred
   Of one bad sire, whose youngest is *Sans ioy*,
And twixt them both was born the bloudy bold *Sans loy*.

26

In this sad plight, friendlesse, vnfortunate,
   Now miserable I *Fidessa* dwell,
   Crauing of you in pitty of my state,
   To doe none ill, if please ye not doe well.
   He in great passion al this while did dwell,
   More busying his quicke eies, her face to view,
   Then his dull eares, to heare what shee did tell,
   And said, Faire Lady hart of flint would rew
The vndeserued woes and sorrowes, which ye shew.

27

Henceforth in safe assuraunce may ye rest,
   Hauing both found a new friend you to aid,
   And lost an old foe, that did you molest:
   Better new friend then an old foe is said.

   With chaunge of chear the seeming simple maid
   Let fal her eien, as shamefast to the earth,
   And yeelding soft, in that she nought gain-said,
   So forth they rode, he feining seemely merth,
And shee coy lookes: so dainty they say maketh derth.

28

Long time they thus together traueiled,
   Til weary of their way, they came at last,
   Where grew two goodly trees, that faire did spred
   Their armes abroad, with gray mosse ouercast,
   And their greene leaues trembling with euery blast,
   Made a calme shadowe far in compasse round:
   The fearefull Shepheard often there aghast
   Vnder them neuer sat, ne wont there sound
His mery oaten pipe, but shund th'vnlucky ground.

29

But this good knight soone as he them can spie,
   For the coole shade him thither hastly got:
   For golden *Phoebus* now ymounted hie,
   From fiery wheeles of his faire chariot
   Hurled his beame so scorching cruell hot,
   That liuing creature mote it not abide;
   And his new Lady it endured not.
   There they alight, in hope themselues to hide
From the fierce heat, and rest their weary limbs a tide.

---

individual 'in thy brest his blessed image beare'. **1 spoild of liuely breath**: robbed of the breath of life. **2 conuaid**: carried away secretly. **3 innocent**: being undeserved. **4 vnhappy**: in this context 'unfortunate'; cf. 'causing trouble', 'evil' (*OED* 5). **5 assaid**: assailed, afflicted (*OED* 14), but cited under *OED* 12: tried with afflictions. **9 as the striken hind**: as the widow Dido wanders throughout the city, raging through love even as a deer struck by an arrow (Virgil, *Aen.* 3.68–69).

Stanza 25
2 perforce: by violence. **6–9** The names and states of the three brothers may be inferred from Gal. 5.22–23: 'But the frute of the Spirit is loue, ioye . . . faith . . . temperancie: against suche there is no Law'. In their hierarchy, faithlessness comes first; its fruit is joylessness; and their product is lawlessness. In their chronological sequence in the poem, first comes Sansfoy (12), then Sansloy (iii 33), and finally Sansjoy (iv 38). See 'Sansfoy, Sansjoy, Sansloy' in the *SEnc*. On their ancestry, see v 22–23. As pagan names, see Bull 1997a. **bold** is the epithet of all three: e.g. iv 44.1, vii 26.4; as is 'proud': e.g. i 25.6, iii 35.1, and v 2.9.

Stanza 26
2 Fidessa: Faithful; Lat. *fides* + *esse*, i.e. being faith, though only seeming to be so. She perverts faith, which is 'the grounde of things, which are hoped for, and the euidence of things which are not sene' (Heb. 11.1). **5 passion**: see i 49.1*n*. Since S. rarely duplicates a rhyme word with the same sense,

dwell may signify 'to continue in a state' (*OED* 4). **6 her face to view**: in contrast to the veiled Una.

Stanza 27
1 With these words he plights himself to her. **assuraunce** carries the secondary meaning of marriage engagement (*OED* 2); later she charges that he was 'affyaunced' (xii 27.2) to her. **4** Evidently this proverb is the knight's own, its triteness befitting a rustic ready to offer himself as a **friend**, i.e. 'lover' (*OED* 4), in Sansfoy's place. **6 as shamefast**: as if modest. **8 feining**: fashioning; dissembling (as 2.2). **seemely**: suitable, with a play on 'seeming'. **9** Fastidiousness makes one precious (**derth**: costliness) to another, implying here that her coyness makes her seem more worthy to be wooed; cf. Smith 145.

Stanza 28
4–6 The **trembling leaues** (suggesting fearfulness) and the **calme shadowe** are conventional features of the *locus amoenus* – see 'bowers' in the *SEnc* – here made ominous by **gray mosse** and **shadowe far**. Cf. IV vii 38.6–9 and the setting of Bk III: 'a forest wyde, | Whose . . . sad trembling sound | Full griesly seemd' (i 14.5–7). **far in compasse round**: as the hellish tree in the garden of Proserpina 'shadowed all the ground' (II vii 56.2). **7–9** As the yew tree, 'The shadowe thereof is grievous, and slayeth such as sleepe therunder' (Bartholomaeus 1582:17.161).

Stanza 29
The sun's fiercest heat at noon is associated with temptation, fall, and judgement. See vii 4.3*n*. **9 tide**: while.

30

Faire seemely pleasaunce each to other makes,
  With goodly purposes there as they sit:
  And in his falsed fancy he her takes
  To be the fairest wight, that liued yit;
  Which to expresse, he bends his gentle wit,
  And thinking of those braunches greene to frame
  A girlond for her dainty forehead fit,
  He pluckt a bough; out of whose rifte there came
Smal drops of gory bloud, that trickled down the same.

31

Therewith a piteous yelling voice was heard,
  Crying, O spare with guilty hands to teare
  My tender sides in this rough rynd embard,
  But fly, ah fly far hence away, for feare
  Least to you hap, that happened to me heare,
  And to this wretched Lady, my deare loue,
  O too deare loue, loue bought with death too deare.
  Astond he stood, and vp his heare did houe,
And with that suddein horror could no member moue.

32

At last whenas the dreadfull passion
  Was ouerpast, and manhood well awake,
  Yet musing at the straunge occasion,
  And doubting much his sence, he thus bespake;
  What voice of damned Ghost from *Limbo* lake,
  Or guilefull spright wandring in empty aire,
  Both which fraile men doe oftentimes mistake,
  Sends to my doubtfull eares these speaches rare,
And ruefull plaints, me bidding guiltlesse blood to spare?

33

Then groning deep, Nor damned Ghost, (quoth he,)
  Nor guileful sprite to thee these words doth speake,
  But once a man *Fradubio*, now a tree,
  Wretched man, wretched tree; whose nature weake
  A cruell witch her cursed will to wreake,
  Hath thus transformd, and plast in open plaines,
  Where *Boreas* doth blow full bitter bleake,
  And scorching Sunne does dry my secret vaines:
For though a tree I seme, yet cold and heat me paines.

Stanzas 30–34

On the motif of the bleeding and speaking bush in earlier literature, see Scott 1987, the key texts for S. being Virgil's story of Polydorus (*Aen.* 3.22–48), and Ariosto's story of Astolfo (*Orl. Fur.* 6.26–53). On its significance in S. as a marvel, see Biow 1996:167–68; and as it challenges his use of marvels, see Bellamy 1985.

Stanza 30

1 pleasaunce: pleasing behaviour, courtesy; usually suggesting 'false' or 'feigned', as **seemely** here indicates. This moment is repeated at vii 4. **2 goodly purposes**: courteous conversation. **3 falsed**: deceived, proved false. **fancy**: referring to the deceiving power of the imagination; see i 46.4*n* and III xii 7.1*n*. **5 bends**: applies, directs; more powerfully, 'perverts from the right use' (*OED* 15). 7 In parody of Una who is crowned with 'a girlond greene' (xii 8.6) at her betrothal to the Red Cross Knight after he slays the dragon. If he were to crown Duessa, he would become her subject and victim. On the topos of crowning with a garland, see 'garlands' in the *SEnc*; for its use in Bk I, see Røstvig 1994:297–98. **8 rifte**: split, crack. **9 gory**: clotted.

Stanza 31

3 embard: enclosed. **4** Again the knight is urged to flee; cf. i 13.8–9. **for feare**: 'for feare to be induced by romish doctrin to leaue the true god, and so taste of his heauie Judgment' (J. Dixon 1964); cf. the dwarf's warning at i 13.8–9. **7 too deare . . . too deare**: very precious . . . too costly. In the 'Morall' to Ariosto, *Orl. Fur.* 6.26–53, where Astolfo reveals that he has been transformed into a tree by the enchantress Alcina, Harington 1591:79 notes 'how men given over to sensualitie leese in the end the verie forme of man (which is reason) and so become beastes or stockes'. In *Inf.* 13,

Dante's suicides suffer the same transformation. **8 Astond**: stunned. He suffered the same physical shock at 15.8 and 16.5. **houe**: rise; transfixed, with hair on end, he assumes the posture of the tree but is unable to speak, as Aeneas on hearing Polydorus.

Stanza 32

1 dreadfull passion: passion of dread; cf. i 49.1, ii 26.5. **3 musing**: marvelling. **5 damned Ghost**: a set term for a spirit condemned to hell. **Limbo lake**: a term used in Phaer's 1584 tr. *Aen.* 3.386, as Lotspeich 1932 notes, for the pit (Lat. *lacus*) of hell, the place of punishment for lost souls. As the traditional region of hell for the unbaptized, Limbo is a fitting place for Fradubio who must be baptized before he may be freed (43.4). **7 mistake**: ?mislead (not in *OED*); or 'err as to the nature of' (*OED* 9). Cf. the four alternatives posed at II xi 39. **8 doubtful**: full of fear; also in the current sense, as the knight's state corresponds to Fradubio's. **rare**: strange, as the voice of a ghost; thin-sounding (Lat. *rarus*), as the voice of an airy spirit. **9 guiltlesse blood**: the knight fails to hear correctly Fradubio's plea even as he fails entirely to heed his warning.

Stanza 33

3 Fradubio: 'in doubt' (37.3); Ital. *fra* (among, amongst) + *dubbio* (doubt, suspect). Or Brother Doubt (from *frate*), suggesting a kinship with the knight and Una who were 'in diuerse doubt' (i 10.9) in the Wandering Wood. See i 53.5*n* and 'Fradubio' in the *SEnc*. He is reduced to vegetable life because loss of faith through frailty is dehumanizing. **7 Boreas**: 'The Northerne wynd, that bringeth the most stormie weather' (E.K. on *SC Feb.* 226). **9** Though Fradubio claims not to be among the damned, he endures their punishment. On cold and heat as hell's torments, see, e.g. Job 24.19 (Vulg.), Dante, *Inf.*

34

Say on *Fradubio* then, or man, or tree,
　Quoth then the knight, by whose mischieuous arts
　Art thou misshaped thus, as now I see?
　He oft finds med'cine, who his griefe imparts;
　But double griefs afflict concealing harts,
　As raging flames who striueth to suppresse.
　The author then (said he) of all my smarts,
　Is one *Duessa* a false sorceresse,
That many errant knights hath broght to wretchednesse.

35

In prime of youthly yeares, when corage hott
　The fire of loue and ioy of cheualree
　First kindled in my brest, it was my lott
　To loue this gentle Lady, whome ye see,
　Now not a Lady, but a seeming tree;
　With whome as once I rode accompanyde,
　Me chaunced of a knight encountred bee,
　That had a like faire Lady by his syde,
Lyke a faire Lady, but did fowle *Duessa* hyde.

36

Whose forged beauty he did take in hand,
　All other Dames to haue exceeded farre;
　I in defence of mine did likewise stand,
　Mine, that did then shine as the Morning starre:

37

So doubly lou'd of ladies vnlike faire,
　Th'one seeming such, the other such indeede,
　One day in doubt I cast for to compare,
　Whether in beauties glorie did exceede;
　A Rosy girlond was the victors meede:
　Both seemde to win, and both seemde won to bee,
　So hard the discord was to be agreede.
　Fralissa was as faire, as faire mote bee,
And euer false *Duessa* seemde as faire as shee.

38

The wicked witch now seeing all this while
　The doubtfull ballaunce equally to sway,
　What not might right, she cast to win by guile,
　And by her hellish science raisd streight way
　A foggy mist, that ouercast the day,
　And a dull blast, that breathing on her face,
　Dimmed her former beauties shining ray,
　And with foule vgly forme did her disgrace:
Then was she fayre alone, when none was faire in place.

3.87, and Shakespeare, *Measure for Measure* 3.1.121–22. Cf. the sufferings of the mariner at iii 31.4–6.

Stanza 34
2 mischieuous: harmful. **3 as now I see**: no longer 'doubting much his sence' (32.4). **4** Proverbial: Smith 761; cf. vii 40.6–9, II i 46.9. **5** Hearts that conceal grief double it. **8 Duessa**: Double Being (Ital. *due* + Lat. *esse*), referring to the mask of beauty she wears, for she is not what she seems to be; see v 26.6. From the suffix, 'ess' (from 'essa'): Mistress Duplicity. **false** is her defining word throughout Bk I, always in opposition, direct or implied, to truth and singleness in Una in whom appearance and reality are one; see xii 8.9. In her attractive disguise, Duessa is 'faire falshood' (Arg.3). **false sorceresse** is the name given her by Una at the end, xii 33.6, alluding to the witchcraft of the Whore of Babylon in Rev. 18. See 'Duessa' in the *SEnc*.

Stanza 35
1 corage: nature; spirit; heart (Lat. *cor*; hence the etymological spelling). **8–9 like**: i.e. similarly, though 9 suggests 'what was like a fair lady'. Punning on this word is central to the episode. Because of the word-play, the initial stress on **Lyke** brings heavy stress on **but**. The paralleling of the experiences of the knight and Fradubio is noted, e.g. by Kennedy 1973:364.

Stanza 36
1 forged beauty: as the 'faire-forged Spright' (2.2), falsely fashioned to imitate beauty. **take in hand**: as a knight he is ready to take spear in hand to uphold his claim. **4 the**

Morning starre: on the larger significance of this image within Bk I, see xii 21.5–9*n*. **7 dye**: hazard. **8 prise martiall**: spoil or booty won by conflict, suggesting also 'price', alluding to the cost of his victory.

Stanza 37
1 vnlike: incomparably; diversely. **2** The clash here between **seeming such** and **such indeede** is that between Duessa and Una, which is resolved only at the end when the unveiled Una 'Did seeme such, as she was, a goodly maiden Queene' (xii 8.9). **4 Whether**: which of the two. **6 won to bee**: i.e. to be overcome; with a pun, 'to be one'. The careful balancing of the line echoes the balance of indecision in Fradubio's mind, as Percival 1964 notes. **8–9** Similarly, the knight takes Duessa to be one with Una, 'the fairest wight, that liued yit' (30.4). **Fralissa**: frail nature (Ital. *frale, fralezza*); in effect, 'Woman, thy name is Frailty'. Since she is reduced to her plight because she is doubted by her lover, the description extends to 'fraile men' (32.7), for 'all flesh doth frayltie breed' (II i 52.6).

Stanza 38
5 As in the Wandering Wood, 'heauens light' (i 7.5) is hidden before enchantments begin. **mist** signifies mental confusion; for its infection, see iv 36.7*n*. Fog raised by witches was associated with contagion. **6 dull**: dulling, in an active sense. **blast**: the blighting breath of a malignant power (*OED* 6). **8 did her disgrace**: marred her outward appearance. **9 alone**: having no equal. **in place**: a rhyming tag that here suggests 'in place of her'.

39

Then cride she out, Fye, fye, deformed wight,
　　Whose borrowed beautie now appeareth plaine
　　To haue before bewitched all mens sight;
　　O leaue her soone, or let her soone be slaine.
　　Her loathly visage viewing with disdaine,
　　Eftsoones I thought her such, as she me told,
　　And would haue kild her; but with faigned paine,
　　The false witch did my wrathfull hand with-hold:
So left her, where she now is turnd to treen mould.

40

Thens forth I tooke *Duessa* for my Dame,
　　And in the witch vnweeting ioyd long time,
　　Ne euer wist, but that she was the same,
　　Till on a day (that day is euerie Prime,
　　When Witches wont do penance for their crime)
　　I chaunst to see her in her proper hew,
　　Bathing her selfe in origane and thyme:
　　A filthy foule old woman I did vew,
That euer to haue toucht her, I did deadly rew.

41

Her neather partes misshapen, monstruous,
　　Were hidd in water, that I could not see,
　　But they did seeme more foule and hideous,
　　Then womans shape man would beleeue to bee.

Thens forth from her most beastly companie
　　I gan refraine, in minde to slipp away,
　　Soone as appeard safe opportunitie:
　　For danger great, if not assurd decay
I saw before mine eyes, if I were knowne to stray.

42

The diuelish hag by chaunges of my cheare
　　Perceiu'd my thought, and drownd in sleepie night,
　　With wicked herbes and oyntments did besmeare
　　My body all, through charmes and magicke might,
　　That all my senses were bereaued quight:
　　Then brought she me into this desert waste,
　　And by my wretched louers side me pight,
　　Where now enclosd in wooden wals full faste,
Banisht from liuing wights, our wearie daies we waste.

43

But how long time, said then the Elfin knight,
　　Are you in this misformed hous to dwell?
　　We may not chaunge (quoth he) this euill plight,
　　Till we be bathed in a liuing well;
　　That is the terme prescribed by the spell.
　　O how, sayd he, mote I that well out find,
　　That may restore you to your wonted well?
　　Time and suffised fates to former kynd
Shall vs restore, none else from hence may vs vnbynd.

Stanza 39

1 deformed: marred in appearance (*OED* 1) and therefore hateful; also marred in shape, anticipating her transformation into a tree. **6 as she me told**: in his state of doubt he thinks as he is told. **7–8** Cf. Archimago's similar restraint of the knight at 5.8–9. **9 treen mould**: the mould or form of a tree; cf. human nature as 'earthly mould' (V proem 2.4) or 'Gods owne mould' (I x 42.6). Her 'foule vgly forme' (38.8) is her arborization, a motif used by Ovid in the *Metamorphoses*. The tree with its roots suggests Duessa's own form with 'Her neather partes misshapen' (41.1). On the fallen Adamic tree, see Nohrnberg 1976:158–66.

Stanza 40

2 vnweeting: unaware. **3 the same**: as she appeared to be. **4–5** As penance, witches were forced to appear as beasts. In Ariosto, *Orl. Fur.* 43.98, the fairy Manto reveals that she is changed into an adder every seventh day. **Prime**: spring; or the first appearance of the new moon when witches gather under the aegis of their goddess, Hecate; or their Sabbath. **6 proper hew**: own shape or form. **7 origane and thyme**: to heal the scabs exposed at viii 47.8–9, as recommended in Gerarde, *Herball*; noted Todd 1805. **thyme** is the first herb recommended in Fracastoro, *Syphilis* 2.174–75, as a cure for syphilis. **9 toucht**: in a sexual sense. His remorse is greater than he realizes: it is **deadly** as she brings his death.

Stanza 41

1–4 Cf. Duessa's full exposure to the knight at viii 46. The usually erotic image of a woman waist-deep in water (cf. II xii 66) here becomes repulsive. Errour (i 14) and the house of Pride (iv 5) are similarly biformed. What had seemed fair but was not, now seems more ugly than a doubting mind can

believe. Since Fradubio still does not see, he becomes Duessa's victim. M.J. Gough 1999:50 notes that his equivocation – he claims to have seen her 'in her proper hew' (40.6) but her nether parts he **could not see** – suggests self-blindness. **5 companie**: sexual contact with her. **8 decay**: death.

Stanza 42

3–5 A parody of the ointment that preserves life at xi 48.6–9. **7 pight**: planted. **8–9** On the arborization of Adam and Eve when they hid themselves '*in medio ligni paradisi*' (Gen. 3.8, from the Vulg. interpreted as 'inside a tree'), see Nelson 1963:162–64. The duplicated rhyme, **waste**, intensifies the sense, 'spend unprofitably': they consume or destroy their lives, as later the knight 'he his better dayes hath wasted all' (viii 28.8).

Stanza 43

2 hous: a term for the body in Eccles. 12:3–5. **3 may not**: also 'cannot'. **4 liuing well**: spring of constantly flowing water (*OED* 2d), here referring to the biblical well of life, as John 4.14: 'whosoeuer drinketh of the water that I shal giue him, shal neuer be more athirst: but the water that I shal giue him, shalbe in him a well of water, springing vp into euerlasting life'. More particularly, it refers to 'the well of the water of life' proceeding out of the throne of God in Rev. 21.6, which is glossed as 'the liuelie waters of this euerlasting life'. The knight is bathed in 'that liuing well' (xi 31.6) when he battles the dragon. The sense of 'living well', rather than badly, is implicit. **6 out find**: find out, discover. **7 wonted**: accustomed, with a pun on 'wanted'. **well**: with a pun on 'well-being'. The pun is repeated at xi 2.4. **8 suffised**: satisfied, as 'fates all satisfide' (III iii 44.7); cf. 'fates expired' (v 40.3). **kynd**: human nature. **9 restore**: repeated from 7 to suggest the two senses: reinstate; free from the effects of sin.

44

The false *Duessa*, now *Fidessa* hight,
  Heard how in vaine *Fradubio* did lament,
  And knew well all was true. But the good knight
  Full of sad feare and ghastly dreriment,
  When all this speech the liuing tree had spent,
  The bleeding bough did thrust into the ground,
  That from the blood he might be innocent,
  And with fresh clay did close the wooden wound:
Then turning to his Lady, dead with feare her fownd.

45

Her seeming dead he fownd with feigned feare,
  As all vnweeting of that well she knew,
  And paynd himselfe with busie care to reare
  Her out of carelesse swowne. Her eylids blew
  And dimmed sight with pale and deadly hew
  At last she vp gan lift: with trembling cheare
  Her vp he tooke, too simple and too trew,
  And oft her kist. At length all passed feare,
He set her on her steede, and forward forth did beare.

Stanza 44

1 Duessa is pointedly named when the knight's alliance with her is about to be sealed with a kiss. **4 ghastly**: terror inspired by the sight of a ghost. **dreriment**: 'dreery and heavy cheere' (*SC Nov.* 36 gloss); coined by S. **6–7** On the literary and biblical antecedents of the knight's actions, see Kennedy 1973:366–67. **blood**: the guilt of shedding blood. Una relates to Arthur how she found the unproved knight 'Whose manly hands imbrewd in guilty blood | Had neuer bene' (vii 47.3–4). Unwittingly, his hands now are guilty (cf. 31.2) of shedding Fradubio's blood.

Stanza 45

4–6 Cf. Ecclus. 26.9: 'The whordome of a woman may be knowen in the pride of her eyes, and eyeliddes'. Cf. Prov. 6.25.

carelesse: having no care in pretending to be unconscious; uncared for; swooning from being unattended. **blew**: from the veins or from her blue eyes. A suggestive analogue is Sycorax, the 'blue-ey'd hag' in Shakespeare, *Tempest* 1.2.269, who imprisons Ariel in a tree, as Duessa does Fradubio. On the ambiguity of the description, as it suggests sexual attractiveness but of a witch, see Marcus 1996:5–17. **deadly hew**: death-like appearance. **6–7 trembling cheare**: the phrase relates the knight to the wavering Fradubio 'trembling with euery blast' (28.5), and with some emphasis because it returns to the 'a' rhyme. **too simple and too trew** describes his own gullibility; applied to Duessa, the phrase is powerfully ironic: Una's singleness (an obs. sense of **simple**) and truth are carried to excess in Duessa.

Cant. III.

Forsaken Truth long seekes her loue,
And makes the Lyon mylde,
Marres blind Deuotions mart, and fals
In hand of leachour vylde.

1

Nought is there vnder heau'ns wide hollownesse,
  That moues more deare compassion of mind,
  Then beautie brought t'vnworthie wretchednesse
  Through enuies snares or fortunes freakes vnkind:
  I, whether lately through her brightnes blynd,
  Or through alleageance and fast fealty,
  Which I do owe vnto all womankynd,
  Feele my hart perst with so great agony,
When such I see, that all for pitty I could dy.

2

And now it is empassioned so deepe,
  For fairest *Vnaes* sake, of whom I sing,
  That my frayle eies these lines with teares do steepe,
  To thinke, how she through guyleful handeling,
  Though true as touch, though daughter of a king,
  Though faire as euer liuing wight was fayre,
  Though nor in word nor deede ill meriting,
  Is from her knight diuorced in despayre
And her dew loues deryu'd to that vile witches shayre.

3

Yet she most faithfull Ladie all this while
  Forsaken, wofull, solitarie mayd
  Far from all peoples preace, as in exile,
  In wildernesse and wastfull deserts strayd,

To seeke her knight; who subtily betrayd
  Through that late vision, which th'Enchaunter wrought,
  Had her abandond. She of nought affrayd,
  Through woods and wastnes wide him daily sought;
Yet wished tydinges none of him vnto her brought.

4

One day nigh wearie of the yrkesome way,
  From her vnhastie beast she did alight,
  And on the grasse her dainty limbs did lay
  In secrete shadow, far from all mens sight:
  From her fayre head her fillet she vndight,
  And layd her stole aside. Her angels face
  As the great eye of heauen shyned bright,
  And made a sunshine in the shady place;
Did neuer mortall eye behold such heauenly grace.

5

It fortuned out of the thickest wood
  A ramping Lyon rushed suddeinly,
  Hunting full greedy after saluage blood;
  Soone as the royall virgin he did spy,
  With gaping mouth at her ran greedily,
  To haue attonce deuourd her tender corse:
  But to the pray when as he drew more ny,
  His bloody rage aswaged with remorse,
And with the sight amazd, forgat his furious forse.

Book I Canto iii

Argument

3 Marres blind Deuotions mart: i.e. ruins her trade, referring to Kirkrapine's trafficking in church spoils. The blind Corceca's piety and religious zeal are named 'blind Deuotion' only here, a term J. Dixon 1964 applies to Archimago in glossing i 29.

Stanza 1

3 vnworthie: undeserved. **5 lately**: either a personal reference or a historical one to the persecution of the reformed church under Mary Tudor. **her**: beauty's.

Stanza 2

The heightened style imitates the lament for the Church in Ps. 137. **1 empassioned**: deeply moved. **5 true as touch**: absolutely true (a proverbial phrase); cf. Ecclus. 6.21: Wisdom is 'as a fine touchstone' to test man. The phrase works almost as a pun: though 'true as touch', she is subject to **guyleful handeling**. **8 diuorced**: separated, in the specific sense that their implied contract to be married has been dissolved. **9 dew loues**: the love due her. **deryu'd**: diverted; also the legal sense, 'transferred'.

Stanza 3

3 preace: press, throng; cf. Chaucer, *Truth* 1: 'Flee fro the prees, and dwelle with sothfastnesse'. **4** Una is linked with the woman who fled into the wilderness (Rev. 12.6). The Geneva gloss reads: 'The Church was remoued from among the Iewes to the Gentiles, which were as a baren wildernes, and so it is persecuted to and fro'. **wastfull**: desolate; hence **wastnes**: an uninhabited place. **7 of nought affrayd**: 'There is no feare in loue, but perfect loue casteth out feare' (1 John 4.18). **9 none**: no one.

Stanza 4

3–4 In contrast to the earlier moment when 'she her weary limbes would neuer rest' (ii 8.6), and like her knight who, with Duessa, 'weary of their way' rest in a 'shadowe' (28.2, 6). **secrete**: secluded, concealed, or concealing. **5 fillet**: the head-piece with its veil. **7 the great eye of heauen**: the sun, *mundi oculus*. Una is being compared implicitly to the woman in the wilderness 'clothed with the sunne' (Rev. 12.1); cf. xii 23.1–2. Her brightness would be enhanced by her golden hair (x 28.6).

6

In stead thereof he kist her wearie feet,
  And lickt her lilly hands with fawning tong,
  As he her wronged innocence did weet.
  O how can beautie maister the most strong,
  And simple truth subdue auenging wrong?
  Whose yielded pryde and proud submission,
  Still dreading death, when she had marked long,
  Her hart gan melt in great compassion,
And drizling teares did shed for pure affection.

7

The Lyon Lord of euerie beast in field,
  Quoth she, his princely puissance doth abate,
  And mightie proud to humble weake does yield,
  Forgetfull of the hungry rage, which late
  Him prickt, in pittie of my sad estate:
  But he my Lyon, and my noble Lord,
  How does he find in cruell hart to hate
  Her that him lou'd, and euer most adord,
As the God of my life? why hath he me abhord?

8

Redounding teares did choke th'end of her plaint,
  Which softly ecchoed from the neighbour wood;
  And sad to see her sorrowfull constraint
  The kingly beast vpon her gazing stood;

With pittie calmd, downe fell his angry mood.
  At last in close hart shutting vp her payne,
  Arose the virgin borne of heauenly brood,
  And to her snowy Palfrey got agayne,
To seeke her strayed Champion, if she might attayne.

9

The Lyon would not leaue her desolate,
  But with her went along, as a strong gard
  Of her chast person, and a faythfull mate
  Of her sad troubles and misfortunes hard:
  Still when she slept, he kept both watch and ward,
  And when she wakt, he wayted diligent,
  With humble seruice to her will prepard:
  From her fayre eyes he tooke commandement,
And euer by her lookes conceiued her intent.

10

Long she thus traueiled through deserts wyde,
  By which she thought her wandring knight shold pas,
  Yet neuer shew of liuing wight espyde;
  Till that at length she found the troden gras,
  In which the tract of peoples footing was,
  Vnder the steepe foot of a mountaine hore;
  The same she followes, till at last she has
  A damzell spyde slow footing her before,
That on her shoulders sad a pot of water bore.

Stanza 5
1 thickest wood: as with Errour's den at i 11.7. **2 ramping**: the lion's heraldic posture, standing on its hind legs with forepaws raised in the air, is assumed here and again at its death (41.5). As a symbol of royal power, see Aptekar 1969:61–69. **3 saluage blood**: blood of wild animals. **4–6** David laments that his enemies 'gape vpon me with their mouthes, as a ramping and roaring lion' (Ps. 22.13). **corse**: body. **7–9** Common lore maintains that 'the lion will not touch the true prince' (Shakespeare, *1 Henry IV* 2.4.271–72); that it protects virgins; and, as the most compassionate of beasts, aids the faithful wearied in God's service, as when Mary Magdalen wandered in the wilderness, 'ne was lyoun ne leopart . . . | That ne fel to her feet and fauned with the tailles' (Langland, *Piers Plowman* 15.293–95). The moment invokes 2 Tim. 4.17: 'the Lord assisted me . . . and I was deliuered out of the mouth of the lion'. There may be a specific allusion to Phil. 2.7: in the incarnation, the angry God of the OT 'toke on him the forme of a seruant'; sugg. Walls 1985:17–18. **8 remorse**: pity, as 7.5; or regret for his wrong in threatening her.

Stanza 6
2 lilly hands: as always in the poem, a token of innocence. **4** G. Whitney 1586:182 records the emblem, *Pulchritudo vincit*. **can**: know how to. **6** A witty and playful use of oxymoron.

Stanza 7
1–5 The lore used here is proverbial (Smith 469), and is used again in *Am* 20.5–8: 'the Lyon that is Lord of power . . . disdeigneth to devoure | the silly lambe that to his might doth yield'. **estate**: state. **9** The language is appropriately biblical, as Ps. 42.8: 'in the night shal I sing of him, euen a praier vnto the God of my life', and Ps. 89.38: 'Thou hast reiected and abhorred, thou hast bene angrie with thine Anointed'.

abhord: implying that she has been rejected as a whore, for her knight has doubted her loyalty; cf. 27.3. At 25.3, she is accused of being a harlot.

Stanza 8
1 Redounding: overflowing; its further sense, 'to resound', from its confusion with 'rebound', suggests the image of 2. **2** The echo marks nature's sympathy for her plight. **3 constraint**: distress. **5** The repetition from 5.8 and 7.4–5 sets up these stanzas as a tableau. **7 brood**: lineage. **9 attayne**: overtake him.

Stanza 9
The lion represents England's royal power as 'Defendour of the Faith', which is Elizabeth's title in the dedication, and hence God's 'mightie power' (gloss to 2 Kings 17.25). **1 desolate**: Una's state is so described at vi 9.2, vii 50.1, and x 60.4. **5** On the lion as the symbol of watchfulness because it sleeps with its eyes open, see Rowland 1973:118; cf. 15.4. As guardian of the church, see G. Whitney 1586:120. **Still**: always.

Stanza 10
1 traueiled: with the pun, as always, on 'travail'. **2 wandring knight**: no longer the knight-errant upon a quest but a knight wandering in error, being so described at ii 12.2 and 21.4 below. **4–5** As a worn path leads to the Wandering Wood at i 7.8 and a beaten path to Errour's den at i 11.3. **tract**: trace. **6 hore**: grey with age, or barren. The mountain suggests Mount Sinai where Moses received the law under which Abessa and Corceca live. **8–9** Upton 1758 compares the woman of Samaria in John 4.7–30 who came to draw water from Jacob's well where Christ rested. When she mocks him in saying that 'our fathers worshiped in this mountaine', he prophesies the

11

To whom approching she to her gan call,
    To weet, if dwelling place were nigh at hand;
    But the rude wench her answerd nought at all,
    She could not heare, nor speake, nor vnderstand;
    Till seeing by her side the Lyon stand,
    With suddeine feare her pitcher downe she threw,
    And fled away: for neuer in that land
Face of fayre Lady she before did vew,
And that dredd Lyons looke her cast in deadly hew.

12

Full fast she fled, ne euer lookt behynd,
    As if her life vpon the wager lay,
    And home she came, whereas her mother blynd
    Sate in eternall night: nought could she say,
    But suddeine catching hold did her dismay
    With quaking hands, and other signes of feare:
    Who full of ghastly fright and cold affray,
Gan shut the dore. By this arriued there
Dame *Vna*, weary Dame, and entrance did requere.

13

Which when none yielded, her vnruly Page
    With his rude clawes the wicket open rent,
    And let her in; where of his cruell rage
    Nigh dead with feare, and faint astonishment,
    Shee found them both in darkesome corner pent;
    Where that old woman day and night did pray
    Vpon her beads deuoutly penitent;
Nine hundred *Pater nosters* euery day,
And thrise nine hundred *Aues* she was wont to say.

14

And to augment her painefull penaunce more,
    Thrise euery weeke in ashes shee did sitt,
    And next her wrinkled skin rough sackecloth wore,
    And thrise three times did fast from any bitt:
    But now for feare her beads she did forgett.
    Whose needelesse dread for to remoue away,
    Faire *Vna* framed words and count'naunce fitt:
Which hardly doen, at length she gan them pray,
That in their cotage small that night she rest her may.

15

The day is spent, and commeth drowsie night,
    When euery creature shrowded is in sleepe;
    Sad *Vna* downe her laies in weary plight,
    And at her feete the Lyon watch doth keepe:
    In stead of rest, she does lament, and weepe
    For the late losse of her deare loued knight,
    And sighes, and grones, and euermore does steepe
Her tender brest in bitter teares all night,
All night she thinks too long, and often lookes for light.

16

Now when *Aldeboran* was mounted hye
    Aboue the shinie *Cassiopeias* chaire,
    And all in deadly sleepe did drowned lye,
    One knocked at the dore, and in would fare;
    He knocked fast, and often curst, and sware,
    That ready entraunce was not at his call:
    For on his backe a heauy load he bare
Of nightly stelths and pillage seuerall,
Which he had got abroad by purchas criminall.

---

time when she will not worship there. Walls 1985:4–8 associates her with Hagar, the Egyptian bondmaid who was driven into the wilderness with a bottle of water on her shoulder (Gen. 21.14), an event allegorized by Paul as the Jewish faith rejected by Christians under the New Covenant (Gal. 4:21–31). See Bergvall 1997:24–25.   **sad**: heavy with weight; firm.

Stanza 11
3 rude: 'impolite', as the line suggests; 'ignorant', as the next line reveals.   **6–7** In contrast to the woman of Samaria who left her waterpot at the well to go into the city to bring men to Christ.   **8 Face**: appearance; presumably Una's face remains veiled.

Stanza 12
2 As if her life were at stake.   **7 affray**: terror.   **8 Gan**: did.   **9 requere**: entreat.

Stanza 13
1 Page: so called because he takes the place of her dwarf who is called her knight's page at iv 39.2.   **2 rude**: violent, rough. **wicket**: a small door.   **4 faint astonishment**: loss of 'wits' through fainting.   **6 day and night**: much like Archimago at i 30.7, and in contrast to the true devotion of Cælia who is said at x 3.8–9 to spend her day in acts of charity. The internal rhyme mocks her blind devotion.   **8–9** That Roman Catholics offer more prayers to the Virgin than to God remains a common Protestant complaint. It is made against the Irish in

View 84. On the monastic parody in this episode, see King 1990a:54–56.

Stanza 14
1–4 As in Dan. 9.3, where penance is expressed by 'fasting and sackcloth and ashes'; a parody of the knight's penance at x 26.1–7 and the fasting of Contemplation at x 52.7.   **2 Thrise**: indicating superstition, as at III ii 50.   **4** She went without three meals a day for the three days of the week on which she did penance. She is more righteous than the boasting Pharisee of Luke 18.12. For a reference to traditional Catholic practice, see Weatherby 1999:423.   **8 hardly**: with difficulty.

Stanza 15
6 her deare loued knight: Una's overwhelming love for the Red Cross Knight as her 'deare' becomes a constant refrain. Later he is simply named as such, e.g. vii 48.7, viii Arg., culminating in xi 1.7.

Stanza 16
1–3 This stellar configuration places the sun near the middle of Virgo in late August, according to Eade in the *SEnc* 153; see also Eade 1984a:173–75. Meyer 1984:121 prefers a date in September. Richard Berleth has suggested to me a date between mid-October and early November because only after midnight is **Aldeboran** high above **Cassiopeias chaire** in the northern latitudes. **Cassiopeia** is named for her blackness, as in Milton, *Il Penseroso* 17–21; or because a new star appeared

17

He was to weete a stout and sturdy thiefe,
    Wont to robbe Churches of their ornaments,
    And poore mens boxes of their due reliefe,
    Which giuen was to them for good intents;
    The holy Saints of their rich vestiments
    He did disrobe, when all men carelesse slept,
    And spoild the Priests of their habiliments,
    Whiles none the holy things in safety kept;
Then he by conning sleights in at the window crept.

18

And all that he by right or wrong could find,
    Vnto this house he brought, and did bestow
    Vpon the daughter of this woman blind,
    Abessa daughter of *Corceca* slow,
    With whom he whoredome vsd, that few did know,
    And fed her fatt with feast of offerings,
    And plenty, which in all the land did grow;
    Ne spared he to giue her gold and rings:
And now he to her brought part of his stolen things.

19

Thus long the dore with rage and threats he bett,
    Yet of those fearfull women none durst rize,
    The Lyon frayed them, him in to lett:
    He would no lenger stay him to aduize,
    But open breakes the dore in furious wize,
    And entring is; when that disdainfull beast
    Encountring fierce, him suddein doth surprize,
    And seizing cruell clawes on trembling brest,
Vnder his Lordly foot him proudly hath supprest.

20

Him booteth not resist, nor succour call,
    His bleeding hart is in the vengers hand,
    Who streight him rent in thousand peeces small,
    And quite dismembred hath: the thirsty land
    Dronke vp his life; his corse left on the strand.
    His fearefull freends weare out the wofull night,
    Ne dare to weepe, nor seeme to vnderstand
    The heauie hap, which on them is alight,
Affraid, least to themselues the like mishappen might.

---

in this constellation in Nov. 1572 (see F.R. Johnson 1937:154–55, 195*n*81), which would have an apocalyptic significance appropriate to the time of the poem. **Aldeboran** is named because the lunar mansion that contains this star causes the 'destruction and hindrances of buildings . . . and begetteth discord' (Agrippa, *Occult Philosophy*, cited Brooks-Davies 1977:39). **5 fast**: vigorously. **8 stelths**: thefts. **seuerall**: diverse, from different sources. **9 purchas criminall**: robbery.

Stanza 17

1 stout: fierce, arrogant. **sturdy**: ruthless, violent. **2 robbe Churches**: alluding to his name, Kirkrapine, which is not revealed until after his death at 22.3. **3 poore mens boxes**: alms-boxes. **5** Lewis 1954:45 assumes that S. would have found robed images of saints an abomination. Moroney 1998:117–18 finds a complaint against Protestant iconoclasts. **7 spoild**: robbed. His crime is sacrilege in the literal sense, 'stealing sacred objects'. **habiliments**: attire, but also **holy things** generally. On that term, see Weatherby 1999:427–40. The 'heauy load' (16.7) that he bears on his back suggests Una's 'needments' which the dwarf was 'wearied with bearing . . . at his backe' (i 6.3–4). **9 at the window**: referring to Christ's parable of those who come to steal, kill, and destroy: 'He that entreth not in by the dore into the shepefolde, but climeth vp another way, he is a thefe and a robber' (John 10.1). Cf. Joel's prophecy of the time of iudgement when 'they shal clime vp vpon the houses, and enter in at the windowes like the thief' (Joel 2.9).

Stanza 18

1 The point lies in his confusion of right with wrong; see iv 27.9*n*. **4 Corceca**: blindness of heart (from Lat. *cor*, heart + *caecum*, blind), for 'their foolish heart was ful of darkenes' (Rom. 1.21). Cf. Ephes. 4.18: 'hauing their cogitation darkened, and being strangers from the life of God through the ignorance that is in them, because of the hardnes of their heart'. The Geneva gloss explains that 'the hardenes of heart is the founteine of ignorance'. Here the offspring of 'blind Deuotion' (Arg.) is the deaf mute **Abessa** who, as 'abbess', represents the abbeys and monasteries, products of blind and ignorant superstition that robs the true Church; or, more generally, as *ab-essa*, those practices by Catholics then, but also Protestants now, that divert offerings from parishioners to their own purposes, such as the general abuse of benefices or absenteeism of nonresident clergy. See 'Abessa, Corceca, Kirkrapine' in the *SEnc*. **5–7** Cf. the sons of Eli who 'laye with the women that assembled at the doore of the Tabernacle' and made themselves 'fat of the first frutes of all the offrings of Israel' (1 Sam. 2.22, 29). Here **whoredome** has the biblical sense of idolatry and vnfaithfulness to God. The poet's scorn is registered in the excessive alliteration of 6. **offerings**: oblations owing to God.

Stanza 19

3 frayed: frightened. **4–6** Kirkrapine's violence parallels the lion's at 13.1–3. **disdainfull**: indignant, angry. **9 his Lordly foot**: the capital letter here and at 42.8 may be in deference to the lion as royal power. **supprest**: pressed down physically.

Stanza 20

5 strand: ground. **7–8 nor . . . hap**: in their ignorance they do not know what grievous events are happening to them. Alluding to 2 Kings 17.25: those who later became Samaritans – one of whom was the woman of Samaria (see 10.8–9*n*) – 'at the beginning of their dwelling there, thei feared not the Lord: therefore the Lord sent lyons among them, which slewe them'; noted Nohrnberg 1976:213. The gloss explains that because they did not serve God, 'he sheweth his mightie power among them by this strange punishment'. **9 mishappen**: happen amiss.

21

Now when broad day the world discouered has,
  Vp *Vna* rose, vp rose the lyon eke,
  And on their former iourney forward pas,
  In waies vnknowne, her wandring knight to seeke,
  With paines far passing that long wandring *Greeke*,
  That for his loue refused deitye;
  Such were the labours of this Lady meeke,
Still seeking him, that from her still did flye,
Then furthest from her hope, when most she weened nye.

22

Soone as she parted thence, the fearfull twayne,
  That blind old woman and her daughter dear
  Came forth, and finding *Kirkrapine* there slayne,
  For anguish great they gan to rend their heare,
  And beat their brests, and naked flesh to teare.
  And when they both had wept and wayld their fill,
  Then forth they ran like two amazed deare,
  Halfe mad through malice, and reuenging will,
To follow her, that was the causer of their ill.

23

Whome ouertaking, they gan loudly bray,
  With hollow houling, and lamenting cry,
  Shamefully at her rayling all the way,
  And her accusing of dishonesty,
  That was the flowre of faith and chastity;
  And still amidst her rayling, she did pray,
  That plagues, and mischiefes, and long misery
  Might fall on her, and follow all the way,
And that in endlesse error she might euer stray.

24

But when she saw her prayers nought preuaile,
  Shee backe retourned with some labour lost;
  And in the way, as shee did weepe and waile,
  A knight her mett in mighty armes embost,
  Yet knight was not for all his bragging bost,
  But subtill *Archimag*, that *Vna* sought
  By traynes into new troubles to haue toste:
  Of that old woman tidings he besought,
If that of such a Lady shee could tellen ought.

25

Therewith she gan her passion to renew,
  And cry, and curse, and raile, and rend her heare,
  Saying, that harlott she too lately knew,
  That causd her shed so many a bitter teare,
  And so forth told the story of her feare:
  Much seemed he to mone her haplesse chaunce,
  And after for that Lady did inquere;
  Which being taught, he forward gan aduaunce
His fair enchaunted steed, and eke his charmed launce.

26

Ere long he came, where *Vna* traueild slow,
  And that wilde Champion wayting her besyde:
  Whome seeing such, for dread hee durst not show
  Him selfe too nigh at hand, but turned wyde
  Vnto an hil; from whence when she him spyde,
  By his like seeming shield her knight by name
  Shee weend it was, and towards him gan ride:
  Approching nigh she wist, it was the same,
And with faire fearefull humblesse towards him shee came.

Stanza 21
4–6 that long wandring Greeke is Ulysses who refused the
love of the goddess Calypso for his love of Penelope (Homer,
Ody. 5.203–04). More heroic than Ulysses, Una who is herself
'of heauenly brood' (8.7), seeks a lover who has rejected her.
8 Still: always.

Stanza 22
3 Kirkrapine: literally 'church robber'. The primary reference
is to the greed of Rome through which the English Church
was pillaged, and which led to the dissolution of the monas-
teries in the 1530s. It extends to the reformed church, as
suggested by Marprelate's attack on the bishops: 'keep the
people in ignoraunce no longer: good fathers now | maintain
the dumbe ministerie no longer. Be the destruction of the
Church no longer | good sweete babes nowe: leave youre non-
residencie | . . . and suffer the trueth to have free passage'
(1588–89:34). As Kirkrapine's actions relate to John Foxe's
attack on the Church of Rome, see Walls 1984. See also 23.4*n*
and VI xii 23–25*n*. **7 amazed**: terror-stricken. **8 reuenging
will**: desire for revenge.

Stanza 23
2 hollow: cf. 'hollo', a loud shout; possibly suggesting 'false'.
4 dishonesty: unchastity; cf. 25.3. The truth of their charge is
that she had stayed in the house to which Kirkrapine brought
his stolen things, as the English Church had profited from the

dissolution of the monasteries. **6 her**: Corceca, since Abessa
can only howl. **pray**: in cursing she abuses prayer. **7 mis-
chiefes**: misfortunes. **9 error**: wandering.

Stanza 24
1 preuaile: avail, be of help. Being superstitious, she believes
curses are effective. **4 embost**: encased; adorned or decorated
sumptuously. **5 bost**: ostentation, pomp. **6–7** Cf. ii 9.6–7.
subtill: crafty. **traynes**: guile.

Stanza 25
3 too lately: i.e. only too lately. **5 her feare**: her spouse,
Kirkrapine. **9** Replicating the Red Cross Knight's 'straunge
Courser' (*LR* 67) and 'enchaunted armes' (iv 50.6).

Stanza 26
2 that wilde Champion: the lion that has taken the place of
Una's 'strayed Champion' (8.9), the Red Cross Knight.
wayting: keeping watch, attending as a guardian servant; cf.
9.6, 15.4. **6** Una recognizes her own armour (see *LR*
63–64), particularly the shield of faith, which represents her
role in relation to her knight. **by name**: own, particular; 'her
true knight' (40.4). **7–8 weend**: supposed; balanced against
wist (knew). **9 humblesse**: humility, in contrast to Duessa's
'humblesse low' (ii 21.4). Una submits herself to 'her' knight;
Duessa seeks his submission.

27

And weeping said, Ah my long lacked Lord,
    Where haue ye bene thus long out of my sight?
    Much feared I to haue bene quite abhord,
    Or ought haue done, that ye displeasen might,
    That should as death vnto my deare heart light:
    For since mine eie your ioyous sight did mis,
    My chearefull day is turnd to chearelesse night,
    And eke my night of death the shadow is;
But welcome now my light, and shining lampe of blis.

28

He thereto meeting said, My dearest Dame,
    Far be it from your thought, and fro my wil,
    To thinke that knighthood I so much should shame,
    As you to leaue, that haue me loued stil,
    And chose in Faery court of meere goodwil,
    Where noblest knights were to be found on earth:
    The earth shall sooner leaue her kindly skil
    To bring foth fruit, and make eternall derth,
Then I leaue you, my liefe, yborn of heuenly berth.

29

And sooth to say, why I lefte you so long,
    Was for to seeke aduenture in straunge place,
    Where *Archimago* said a felon strong
    To many knights did daily worke disgrace;
    But knight he now shall neuer more deface:
    Good cause of mine excuse, that mote ye please
    Well to accept, and euer more embrace
    My faithfull seruice, that by land and seas
Haue vowd you to defend. Now then your plaint appease.

30

His louely words her seemd due recompence
    Of all her passed paines: one louing howre
    For many yeares of sorrow can dispence:
    A dram of sweete is worth a pound of sowre:
    Shee has forgott, how many, a woeful stowre
    For him she late endurd; she speakes no more
    Of past: true is, that true loue hath no powre
    To looken backe; his eies be fixt before.
Before her stands her knight, for whom she toyld so sore.

31

Much like, as when the beaten marinere,
    That long hath wandred in the *Ocean* wide,
    Ofte soust in swelling *Tethys* saltish teare,
    And long time hauing tand his tawney hide,
    With blustring breath of Heauen, that none can bide,
    And scorching flames of fierce *Orions* hound,
    Soone as the port from far he has espide,
    His chearfull whistle merily doth sound,
And *Nereus* crownes with cups; his mates him pledg around.

32

Such ioy made *Vna*, when her knight she found;
    And eke th'enchaunter ioyous seemde no lesse,
    Then the glad marchant, that does vew from ground
    His ship far come from watrie wildernesse,
    He hurles out vowes, and *Neptune* oft doth blesse:
    So forth they past, and all the way they spent
    Discoursing of her dreadful late distresse,
    In which he askt her, what the Lyon ment:
Who told her all that fell in iourney, as she went.

Stanza 27
Una's speech effectively counters and corrects the offers of love made by the false dream and Duessa. **3 abhord**: as 7.9. **5 deare**: loving; also heavy, sore.

Stanza 28
1 thereto meeting: responding accordingly; with similarly kind words. **5 meere**: entire, without any merit on his part, referring to her knight's unproven state; or, as an adv., that she chose him merely out of **goodwil**: see vii 47.1–5. **7–9** A vow that is a threat, as his continuing harassment of her shows. **kindly skil**: innate, natural art. **derth**: famine. **liefe**: beloved.

Stanza 29
3 felon: villain. **5 deface**: discredit, defame. **6–7** 'This adventure is good reason to excuse my absence, which I hope you will accept graciously'. Archimago seeks to trap her into receiving as her knight one who undertakes endless adventures but never the one quest to free her captive parents. **9 appease**: cease, by being pacified.

Stanza 30
1 louely: loving. **3 dispence**: make amends; or compensate for, in its literal sense (Lat. *dispendere*, to weigh out), as the next line indicates. **4** Proverbial: Smith 743; cf. VI xi 1.8. Tung 1985:191–92 discusses S.'s use of such emblematic lore. **5 stowre**: time of distress or turmoil; terminating the time that began at ii 7.9. **8–9 her knight**: now Archimago is her knight and defender; cf. 32.1.

Stanza 31
1 beaten: i.e. weather-beaten. **3 Tethys saltish teare**: ocean spray which drenches the mariner; see i 39.6*n*. **6 fierce Orions hound**: Sirius, the Dog Star, 'the hot *Syrian* Dog' (*Mother Hubberd* 5) whose heliacal rising marks the hottest days of the year. T. Cooper 1565 notes it as the star 'unto the whiche whan the sunne commeth, the feruentnesse of heate is doubled, whereby the bodies of men become sicke with heate'. More directly, it is called **scorching** from its Gk root, σείριος; Virgil calls it *Canis aestifer* (*Georg.* 2.353). The rising of Orion marks the season of storms in Virgil, *Aen.* 1.535; cf. IV xi 13.9. **7 from far**: suggesting that the mariner is over-confident, even as Una is. Although he has endured the elements of water, air, and fire, he now approaches land with its perils. **9 Nereus**: 'th'eldest, and the best' of the children of Tethys (IV xi 18.5). **crownes with cups**: honours as a king through offering a libation to him by crowning a cup with a garland and filling it to the brim with wine. Perhaps recalling Anchises's libation on seeing Italy, *Aen.* 3.525–26.

Stanza 32
3–5 Answering the simile, now from Archimago's perspective and pointing to his over-confidence: the **ground** from which he views with joy, he shortly lies upon (35.8) close to death. On his appropriate invocation of Neptune as a seducer of women, see Thaon 1985:634. Una's quest is treated as a voyage throughout the poem – cf. esp. xii 1 – but not until the end is she seen 'As wetherbeaten ship arryu'd on happie shore' (II i 2.9). See vi 1*n*. **vowes**: prayers. **9 her . . . fell**: all that befell her.

33

They had not ridden far, when they might see
　One pricking towards them with hastie heat,
　Full strongly armd, and on a courser free,
　That through his fiersnesse fomed all with sweat,
　And the sharpe yron did for anger eat,
　When his hot ryder spurd his chauffed side;
　His looke was sterne, and seemed still to threat
　Cruell reuenge, which he in hart did hyde,
And on his shield *Sans loy* in bloody lines was dyde.

34

When nigh he drew vnto this gentle payre
　And saw the Red-crosse, which the knight did beare,
　He burnt in fire, and gan eftsoones prepare
　Himselfe to batteill with his couched speare.
　Loth was that other, and did faint through feare,
　To taste th'vntryed dint of deadly steele;
　But yet his Lady did so well him cheare,
　That hope of new good hap he gan to feele;
So bent his speare, and spurd his horse with yron heele.

35

But that proud Paynim forward came so ferce,
　And full of wrath, that with his sharphead speare
　Through vainly crossed shield he quite did perce,
　And had his staggering steed not shronke for feare,

Through shield and body eke he should him beare:
　Yet so great was the puissance of his push,
　That from his sadle quite he did him beare:
　He tombling rudely downe to ground did rush,
And from his gored wound a well of bloud did gush.

36

Dismounting lightly from his loftie steed,
　He to him lept, in minde to reaue his life,
　And proudly said, Lo there the worthie meed
　Of him, that slew *Sansfoy* with bloody knife;
　Henceforth his ghost freed from repining strife,
　In peace may passen ouer *Lethe* lake,
　When mourning altars purgd with enimies life,
　The black infernall *Furies* doen aslake:
Life from *Sansfoy* thou tookst, *Sansloy* shall from thee take.

37

Therewith in haste his helmet gan vnlace,
　Till *Vna* cride, O hold that heauie hand,
　Deare Sir, what euer that thou be in place:
　Enough is, that thy foe doth vanquisht stand
　Now at thy mercy: Mercy not withstand:
　For he is one the truest knight aliue,
　Though conquered now he lye on lowly land,
　And whilest him fortune fauourd, fayre did thriue
In bloudy field: therefore of life him not depriue.

Stanza 33

3–5 This description carefully modulates the poem's opening tableau in which the Red Cross Knight's 'angry steede did chide his foming bitt' (i 1.6) but was restrained by his 'curbe'. **free**: eager to charge, suggesting Sansloy's passionate nature; cf. ii 11.8. **sharpe yron**: the bit is roughened to infuriate the horse. **6 chauffed**: chafed, being ripped by the spur; but also the effect of spurring: angry. Cf. Sansfoy's horse at ii 14.8–9. **7 sterne**: threatening; as Wrath at iv 33.6. **9 Sans loy**: Lawlessness. See ii 25.6–9*n*, and 'law, natural and divine' in the *SEnc*.

Stanza 34

4 **couched**: lowered ready for charging. **5 faint**: lose heart. **6 taste**: try by touch; cf. 39.3. **dint**: blow. 7–9 Faith, whether true or false (as v 12), is always nurturing. **bent**: aimed. **spurd**: spurnd *1596* has the same meaning; see *OED* v.[2]

Stanza 35

1 **Paynim**: pagan, heathen; as 'Sarazin' (ii 12.6). **3 vainly crossed**: bearing the cross in vain. Cf. Sansfoy's curse on 'that Crosse . . . | That keepes thy body from the bitter fitt' (ii 18.1–2), and Duessa's complaint that the Red Cross Knight 'beares a charmed shield, | And eke enchaunted armes, that none can perce' (iv 50.5–6). In this canto S. refers only to the Enchanter's 'enchanted steed' and 'charmed launce' (25.9), neither of which avails him now, though the steed saves him from death. **5 beare**: thrust (*OED* 35), a sense different from that of 7, which allows the rhyme. Røstvig 1994:279 notes that the repetition of the 'b' rhyme of the previous stanza mirrors the sudden reversal of Archimago's fortune. **8 rudely**: violently.

Stanza 36

4 **knife**: a short sword used in battle by Pyrochles at II v 9.4. Although used by Marinell at III iv 24.9, usually an unknightly weapon associated chiefly with suicide as at ix 29.9, II i 39.6, etc. **5 strife**: pain, distress; cf. 'his grudging ghost' (ii 19.7). **6 Lethe lake**: 'a lake in hell, which the Poetes call the lake of forgetfulnes. For Lethe signifieth forgetfulnes. Wherein the soules being dipped, did forget the cares of their former lyfe' (E.K. on *SC March* 23). Usually the soul passes into Hades over the marshy river Styx (cf. Virgil, *Aen.* 6.323) unless delayed by lack of a burial. At v 10.5–6 this same soul is still 'wayling by blacke *Stygian* lake', delayed through desire for revenge, which may not be forgotten until purged by his slayer's blood; cf. iv 48.7–9. Such souls figure prominently in the poem because they were no longer imprisoned in the Catholic purgatory. On the continuing imaginative hold of purgatory, see Mazzola 1998:37–39, 54–61. **7 mourning altars**: altars of mourning. **purgd**: purified, ceremonially cleansed by having his enemy's body burned, usually alive, to propiate his ghost, as *Aen.* 10.518–20. **8 Furies**: 'the Authours of all evill and mischiefe' (gloss to *SC Nov.* 164). **aslake**: appease; a unique usage, apparently suggested by '*Lethe* lake', as though the Furies quenched their rage by its waters.

Stanza 37

3 **in place**: here; more probably, 'in rank' as 'some man of place' (IV viii 14.4). **5 withstand**: withhold; oppose, as Una is associated with mercy. **6 one the truest**: the one truest. 7–9 The argument is deliberately specious – since he killed many, don't kill him – to contrast mercy with justice which claims that 'blood must blood repay' (ix 43.6). **on lowly land**: low on the ground.

38

Her piteous wordes might not abate his rage,
　But rudely rending vp his helmet, would
Haue slayne him streight: but when he sees his age,
　And hoarie head of *Archimago* old,
　His hasty hand he doth amased hold,
　And halfe ashamed, wondred at the sight:
　For that old man well knew he, though vntold,
　In charmes and magick to haue wondrous might,
Ne euer wont in field, ne in round lists to fight.

39

And said, Why Archimago, luckelesse syre,
　What doe I see? what hard mishap is this,
That hath thee hether brought to taste mine yre?
　Or thine the fault, or mine the error is,
　In stead of foe to wound my friend amis?
　He answered nought, but in a traunce still lay,
　And on those guilefull dazed eyes of his
　The cloude of death did sit. Which doen away,
He left him lying so, ne would no lenger stay.

40

But to the virgin comes, who all this while
　Amased stands, her selfe so mockt to see
By him, who has the guerdon of his guile,
　For so misfeigning her true knight to bee:
　Yet is she now in more perplexitie,
　Left in the hand of that same Paynim bold,
　From whom her booteth not at all to flie;
　Who by her cleanly garment catching hold,
Her from her Palfrey pluckt, her visage to behold.

41

But her fiers seruant full of kingly aw
　And high disdaine, whenas his soueraine Dame
So rudely handled by her foe he saw,
　With gaping iawes full greedy at him came,

And ramping on his shield, did weene the same
Haue reft away with his sharp rending clawes:
But he was stout, and lust did now inflame
His corage more, that from his griping pawes
He hath his shield redeemd, and forth his swerd he drawes.

42

O then too weake and feeble was the forse
　Of saluage beast, his puissance to withstand:
For he was strong, and of so mightie corse,
　As euer wielded speare in warlike hand,
　And feates of armes did wisely vnderstand.
　Eftsoones he perced through his chaufed chest
　With thrilling point of deadly yron brand,
　And launcht his Lordly hart: with death opprest
He ror'd aloud, whiles life forsooke his stubborne brest.

43

Who now is left to keepe the forlorne maid
　From raging spoile of lawlesse victors will?
Her faithfull gard remou'd, her hope dismaid,
　Her selfe a yielded pray to saue or spill.
　He now Lord of the field, his pride to fill,
　With foule reproches, and disdaineful spight
　Her vildly entertaines, and will or nill,
　Beares her away vpon his courser light:
Her prayers nought preuaile, his rage is more of might.

44

And all the way, with great lamenting paine,
　And piteous plaintes she filleth his dull eares,
That stony hart could riuen haue in twaine,
　And all the way she wetts with flowing teares:
　But he enrag'd with rancor, nothing heares.
　Her seruile beast yet would not leaue her so,
　But followes her far off, ne ought he feares,
　To be partaker of her wandring woe,
More mild in beastly kind, then that her beastly foe.

Stanza 38

7 that: *F.E.*, probably referring to this line. **though vntold**: i.e. he knew him by sight without needing to be told; or, he knew also that he was a magician, etc. Either sense implies the instinctive kinship among evil characters. **9 round lists**: the enclosed ground in which tournaments were held, in contrast to the **field** where knights tilted by chance.

Stanza 39

7–8 cloude of death: rendering what his **dazed eyes** see. **Which doen away**: i.e. when the danger of death had passed.

Stanza 40

5 perplexitie: trouble, distress. **8 cleanly**: clean, pure; signifying 'morally and spiritually clean' (*OED* 1).

Stanza 41

1 kingly aw: the power of kings to inspire awe. **2 high disdaine**: indignation; see i 19.6*n*. **5 ramping**: the lion's heraldic posture (see 5.2*n*), appropriate to his seizing the

shield, the emblem of power. **weene**: intend. **9 redeemd**: recovered by force.

Stanza 42

3 For he was strong: a measure of Sansloy's strength, for 'what is stronger then a lyon' (Judg. 14.18). **6 chaufed**: chafed, angered. **7 thrilling**: piercing. **brand**: sword; used to express the nature of one who 'burnt in fire' (34.3). **8 launcht**: pierced. **opprest**: overwhelmed. **9 stubborne**: fierce, untamable.

Stanza 43

2 I.e. 'from becoming the spoil or booty of the lawless victor's raging will', naming him **lawlesse . . . will**, describing his characteristic act, which is **raging**, and showing the effect of his action: Una is his **spoile**. **4 spill**: destroy. **7 entertaines**: treats. **8 light**: quickly. **9** The repetition of the phrase from 24.1 is designed to round out the episode.

Stanza 44

1 lamenting paine: also 'painfully lamenting'; cf. **wandring woe**. **2 dull**: deaf. **9 in beastly kind**: as a beast by nature; or, being kind though a beast.

Cant. IIII.

To sinfull hous of Pryde, Duessa
guydes the faithfull knight,
Where brothers death to wreak Sansioy
doth chaleng him to fight.

1

Y Oung knight, what euer that dost armes professe,
  And through long labours huntest after fame,
  Beware of fraud, beware of ficklenesse,
  In choice, and chaunge of thy deare loued Dame,
  Least thou of her belieue too lightly blame,
  And rash misweening doe thy hart remoue:
  For vnto knight there is no greater shame,
  Then lightnesse and inconstancie in loue;
That doth this *Redcrosse* knights ensample plainly proue.

2

Who after that he had faire *Vna* lorne,
  Through light misdeeming of her loialtie,
  And false *Duessa* in her sted had borne,
  Called *Fidess'*, and so supposd to be;
  Long with her traueild, till at last they see
  A goodly building, brauely garnished,
  The house of mightie Prince it seemd to be:
  And towards it a broad high way that led,
All bare through peoples feet, which thether traueiled.

3

Great troupes of people traueild thetherward
  Both day and night, of each degree and place,
  But few returned, hauing scaped hard,
  With balefull beggery, or foule disgrace,
  Which euer after in most wretched case,
  Like loathsome lazars, by the hedges lay.
  Thether *Duessa* badd him bend his pace:
  For she is wearie of the toilsom way,
And also nigh consumed is the lingring day.

4

A stately Pallace built of squared bricke,
  Which cunningly was without morter laid,
  Whose wals were high, but nothing strong, nor thick
  And golden foile all ouer them displaid,
  That purest skye with brightnesse they dismaid:
  High lifted vp were many loftie towres,
  And goodly galleries far ouer laid,
  Full of faire windowes, and delightful bowres;
And on the top a Diall told the timely howres.

Book I Canto iv

Argument

1 sinfull hous: literally so, being full of sins. **2 the faithfull knight**: as v Arg. and x Arg.; cf. 'Right faithfull true' (i 2.7). He earns the title by defeating Sansfoy, though his acceptance of Duessa in place of Una raises the question: 'faithful to whom?' **3 wreak**: avenge.

Stanza 1

2 long labours: S.'s multiple uses of this term suggests his use of Virgil's *Georgics* as a model; see Sessions 1980:216, Ettin 1982:60–61, and Low 1985:38–43. **3 fraud**: faithlessness. **5 blame**: evil charges, accusations, as against Una at ii 4.6–9. **6 rash misweening**: rashly mistrusting; rash mistrust.

Stanza 2

1 lorne: left, leaving her 'forlorne' (iii 43.1). **2 misdeeming**: misjudging; thinking evil of. Cf. the 'misdeeming night' (ii 3.8) when he first mistrusts her, and her complaint to Arthur at vii 49.4–5. **3 borne**: taken as a companion (*OED* 1e). **5** The substance of this line is repeated from ii 28.1 where it introduces a new episode; cf. i 28.9. **6** The description fits Duessa, 'A goodly Lady' who wears a crown 'garnished' with jewels (ii 13.2, 5). The mocking use of 'goodly' at 4.7, 5.1, 13.5, etc. becomes overtly sarcastic by 37.1, and is later countered by the repeated use of 'godly' in the house of Holinesse. Similarly with **faire**: used repeatedly about Una but ironically at 4.8, 5.3, 7.9, etc. M.F.N. Dixon 1996:29 notes how such

epithets function dyslogistically in Bk I. **brauely**: splendidly; cf. 8.3. **8 a broad high way**: 'for it is the wide gate, and broad waye that leadeth to destruction: and manie there be which go in thereat' (Matt. 7.13); cf. the paths that lead to Errour's den (i 11.3) and to Corceca's hovel (iii 10.4–5).

Stanza 3

2 place: rank. **4 balefull**: painful; wretched; sorrowful. **beggery**: stressing poverty as a consequence of sin, rather than sin itself; cf. 'wasted welthes decay' (v 51.4). **6 lazars**: lepers; or, from Lazarus, those afflicted with any loathsome disease. **7 bend his pace**: direct his steps; but also 'turn from the straight way'; cf. i 28.4.

Stanza 4

1–2 squared bricke: as the Tower of Babel (Gen. 11.3), which was built because men 'were moued with pride and ambition, thinking to preferre their own glorie to Gods honour' (Geneva gloss). **squared**: being hewn, and hence worldly, in contrast to Jehovah's altar which is not built 'of hewen stones: for if thou lift vp thy tole vpon them, thou hast polluted them' (Exod. 20.25). **without morter**: as the wall 'dawbed with vntempered morter', which the Lord vows to 'bring . . . downe to the grounde, so that the fundacion thereof shal fall' (Ezek. 13.14). Since 'stones well squar'd . . . will rise strong a great way without mortar' (Jonson 1925–52:8.623), the lines may assert the palace's strength until it overreaches itself. **4 golden foile**: as Solomon's temple is 'ouerlaied . . . with golde' (1 Kings 6.22).

5

It was a goodly heape for to behould,
   And spake the praises of the workmans witt;
   But full great pittie, that so faire a mould
   Did on so weake foundation euer sitt:
   For on a sandie hill, that still did flitt,
   And fall away, it mounted was full hie,
   That euery breath of heauen shaked itt:
   And all the hinder partes, that few could spie,
Were ruinous and old, but painted cunningly.

6

Arriued there they passed in forth right;
   For still to all the gates stood open wide,
   Yet charge of them was to a Porter hight
   Cald *Maluenù*, who entrance none denide:
   Thence to the hall, which was on euery side
   With rich array and costly arras dight:
   Infinite sortes of people did abide
   There waiting long, to win the wished sight
Of her, that was the Lady of that Pallace bright.

7

By them they passe, all gazing on them round,
   And to the Presence mount; whose glorious vew
   Their frayle amazed senses did confound:
   In liuing Princes court none euer knew
   Such endlesse richesse, and so sumpteous shew;
   Ne *Persia* selfe, the nourse of pompous pride
   Like euer saw. And there a noble crew
   Of Lords and Ladies stood on euery side,
Which with their presence fayre, the place much beautifide.

8

High aboue all a cloth of State was spred,
   And a rich throne, as bright as sunny day,
   On which there sate most braue embellished
   With royall robes and gorgeous array,
   A mayden Queene, that shone as *Titans* ray,
   In glistring gold, and perelesse pretious stone;
   Yet her bright blazing beautie did assay
   To dim the brightnesse of her glorious throne,
As enuying her selfe, that too exceeding shone.

S.'s model may be the wall surrounding the city of the enchantress Alcina (Ariosto, *Orl. Fur.* 6.59), which seems to be of gold. This architectural feature suggests deception, as at IV ii 29.4–5 and v 15.1–6, particularly hypocrisy, as the robes of lead worn by the hypocrites in Dante, *Inf.* 23.58–63, are gilded with gold, as though 'ypocrita' were derived from ὑπέρ and χρυσός; see Singleton 1968:371. **5** Cf. the dazzling brightness of Lucifera (8.5–9), which also seeks to outrival Nature by deceiving art. **purest skye**: either the empyrean, the region of purest light, or the sky at its brightest. The line suggests the overweening ambition of those who built Babel: 'let vs buylde vs a citie and a tower, whose toppe may reach vnto the heauen' (Gen. 11.4). **6–9 loftie towres**: cf. II ix 21.6 and *Comm Sonn 4*. A parody of the 'lofty towres' of the New Jerusalem at x 56.8. S. refers disparagingly to the 'loftie towres' of Burghley House in *Mother Hubberd* 1172–74. **far ouer**: high above. **faire windowes**: a popular feature of Elizabethan stately homes, which became lantern-houses through the use of bay windows: e.g. Kenilworth was described by Laneham as 'glittering by glasse'; see Girouard 1983:19. **timely howres**: measured hours of the day. The **Diall** may be a sundial unless **told** = 'tolled'. It suggests time's destructive power in the house where the victims 'waiting long' (6.8) 'Consumed . . . thriftlesse howres' (v 51.8); see A. Fowler 1964:74*n*3. It may allude to the prominent three-storeyed clock tower in the courtyard of Burghley House, Northants; see Summerson 1963:Plate 19b.

Stanza 5

1 goodly: as Duessa is a 'goodly Lady' (ii 13.2). **heape**: presumably 'pile', a small castle (*OED* sb.²), as II xi 7.2. The term may have been suggested by the house's heap of galleries (4.6–7), its heaps of people (16.7), and its heap of carcasses (v 49.1–2); or because Jerusalem was reduced to 'heapes of stones' (Ps. 79.1). **2 witt**: mechanical skill. **3 mould**: frame, structure. The reference is clearly to human substance and form. See V proem 2.4, and 'body' in the *SEnc*. **5 sandie hill**: 'whosoeuer heareth these my wordes, and doeth them not, shalbe lickened vnto a foolish man, which hathe buylded his house vpon the sand: And the raine fell, and the floods

came, and the windes blewe, and beat vpon that house, and it fell, and the fall thereof was great' (Matt. 7.26–27). In *Time* 505–08, 'a statelie Towre . . . placed on a plot of sandie ground' suddenly falls; cf. *Bellay* 183–96. **still did flitt**: continually shifted or gave way. **8–9** As the 'human' form of the house of Pride, Duessa is revealed in similar terms at viii 48; cf. Errour at i 14. The **hinder partes** are described at the end of the episode, v 53, thereby fulfilling the function of tragedy, which 'teacheth . . . upon how weak foundations gilden roofs are builded' (Sidney, *Defence of Poetry* 96).

Stanza 6

1–4 As in Dante, *Inf* 14.87, where the threshold of hell is denied to none. **hight**: committed, entrusted. **Maluenù**: the opposite of Fr. *bienvenu* (welcome), implying 'ill-coming'. **6 dight**: arrayed, adorned. **7 sortes**: companies; or 'of each degree and place' (3.2). **8 waiting**: suggesting both loss of time and that all who attend are servants.

Stanza 7

The pictorial qualities of this stanza, and 8–13, are analysed by Bender 1972:124–34. **1 round**: on all sides. **2 the Presence**: the presence chamber, where the sovereign receives visitors: see May 1991:12–13; or referring to Lucifera herself; cf. 13.1. **mount**: i.e. 'proceed', but S. is preparing for the moment, here parodied, when Contemplation leads the knight 'to the highest Mount' (x 53.1). **6 nourse**: both nurse and nourisher. **7 crew**: company, in a derogatory sense.

Stanza 8

Cf. the true royalty of Mercilla at V ix 29. In Bk I, Una alone is the 'royall virgin', as ii 7.5, etc. **1 cloth of State**: canopy. **5 mayden Queene**: the 'virgine, daughter Babel' on her throne (Isa. 47.1). This title belongs also to Una who appears finally 'such, as she was, a goodly maiden Queene' (xii 8.9), to Mercilla (V viii 17.2), implicitly to '*Gloriane* great Queene of glory bright' (vii 46.6), and to Elizabeth whom S. praises in *SC Apr.* 57 as 'like a mayden Queene' who outshines the sun. Lucifera's relation to Elizabeth is examined by O'Connell 1977:52–54, Wells 1983:32–33, Suttie 1998:64–65, and

9

Exceeding shone, like *Phœbus* fayrest childe,
　That did presume his fathers fyrie wayne,
　And flaming mouthes of steedes vnwonted wilde
Through highest heauen with weaker hand to rayne;
Proud of such glory and aduancement vayne,
While flashing beames do daze his feeble eyen,
He leaues the welkin way most beaten playne,
And rapt with whirling wheeles, inflames the skyen,
With fire not made to burne, but fayrely for to shyne.

10

So proud she shyned in her princely state,
　Looking to heauen; for earth she did disdayne,
　And sitting high; for lowly she did hate:
Lo vnder neath her scornefull feete, was layne
A dreadfull Dragon with an hideous trayne,
And in her hand she held a mirrhour bright,
Wherein her face she often vewed fayne,
And in her selfe-lou'd semblance tooke delight;
For she was wondrous faire, as any liuing wight.

11

Of griesly *Pluto* she the daughter was,
　And sad *Proserpina* the Queene of hell;
　Yet did she thinke her pearelesse worth to pas
That parentage, with pride so did she swell,

And thundring *Ioue*, that high in heauen doth dwell,
And wield the world, she claymed for her syre,
Or if that any else did *Ioue* excell:
For to the highest she did still aspyre,
Or if ought higher were then that, did it desyre.

12

And proud *Lucifera* men did her call,
　That made her selfe a Queene, and crownd to be,
　Yet rightfull kingdome she had none at all,
Ne heritage of natiue soueraintie,
But did vsurpe with wrong and tyrannie
Vpon the scepter, which she now did hold:
Ne ruld her Realme with lawes, but pollicie,
And strong aduizement of six wisards old,   *witchy*
That with their counsels bad her kingdome did vphold.

13

Soone as the Elfin knight in presence came,
　And false *Duessa* seeming Lady fayre,
　A gentle Husher, *Vanitie* by name
Made rowme, and passage for them did prepaire:
So goodly brought them to the lowest stayre
Of her high throne, where they on humble knee
Making obeysaunce, did the cause declare,
Why they were come, her roiall state to see,
To proue the wide report of her great Maiestee.

Greenfield 1998:41–42, 81. **that**: i.e. her throne. **Titans**: the sun's; but also suggesting the proud, rebellious offspring of the earth, a symbol of pride; cf. II vii 41.6–8. **7 bright blazing beautie** prepares for the comparison to Phaethon in the next stanza. The throne's brightness shines, like Titan; Lucifera's brightness burns, like Phaethon. **9** The throne envied her, so the proud Queen believes, because she shines excessively.

Stanza 9
The story of Phaethon told by Ovid, *Met.* 2. According to Conti 1616:6.1, it shows how arrogance leads to great calamities. **1 Exceeding shone**: wittily naming Phaethon (Gk Φαέθων, shining) without naming him. **2 presume**: usurp. On his association with the rebellious Lucifer, see 'Phaethon' in the *SEnc*. **wayne**: wagon; cf. III viii 51.5. **3 flaming mouthes** renders Ovid's *quos [ignes] ore et naribus efflant* (*Met.* 2.85). **4 weaker**: too weak; weaker than Titan's. **7 welkin way**: the sun's path through the sky, Ovid's *tritum spatium* (*Met.* 2.167–68). **8 rapt**: carried away, morally by his pride and now physically. **9** The careful pointing of this line distinguishes heavenly light which shines from infernal fire which burns.

Stanza 10
1–2 Cf. Prov. 21.4: 'A hautie loke, and a proude heart, which is the light of the wicked, is sinne'. In contrast to Speranza whose eyes are fixed 'euer vp to heuen' (x 14.8) in hope of salvation. Cf. the lady in *Am* 13.1–3 who in her proud bearing lifts her face to the sky but looks down to the earth. **state**: high rank; throne. **3 lowly**: lowliness. **5 hideous trayne**: monstrously large and long tail; cf. the dragon's 'huge long tayle' (xi 11.1). Later Lucifera's lengthy procession of sins assumes the shape of the dragon's tail, as at 26.9, etc., forming

another labyrinth in which the knight wanders. Lucifera with the dragon under her feet suggests Duessa riding the dragon at vii 18. More precisely, she is a parody of royal power shown in Mercilla with the lion chained under her feet at V ix 33. Cf. Una accompanied by the lion, and Isis with her foot 'set vppon the Crocodile' (V vii 7.1). **6 mirrhour**: the common symbol of vanity, the chief quality of pride. See 'mirrors' in the *SEnc*. 7 **fayne**: gladly.

Stanza 11
1 **griesly**: arousing horror. The knight is betrayed when Archimago invokes 'blacke *Plutoes* griesly Dame' at i 37.4, and threatens her wrath at ii 2.7; now he meets her offspring. **3 pas**: surpass. **5–6 thundring Ioue**: Jupiter Tonans who in this form overthrew Phaethon. **wield**: rule.

Stanza 12
1 **Lucifera**: adapted from Lucifer, Satan's name in heaven, as in Isa. 14.12–14: 'How art thou fallen from heauen, O Lucifer, sonne of the morning', and applied to the proud king of Babylon: 'thou saidest in thine heart, I wil ascend into heauen, and exalt my throne aboue beside the starres of God . . . I wil ascend aboue the height of the cloudes, and I wil be like the moste high'; cf. 11.8–9. Its etymology, 'light-bringing', reveals the role to which she aspires. See 'Lucifera' in the *SEnc*. **2** Indicating that she was not appointed by God. **4 natiue**: rightful, by virtue of birth. **7 pollicie**: political cunning, expediency. **8 wisards**: wise men; used contemptuously: see 18.2.

Stanza 13
1 **in presence**: in the special sense, 'attending on royalty'. **3 Husher**: usher. **5 goodly**: graciously. **6 high throne**: as Elizabeth sat on a raised chair of state in her presence chamber.

14

With loftie eyes, halfe loth to looke so lowe,
  She thancked them in her disdainefull wise,
  Ne other grace vouchsafed them to showe
Of Princesse worthy, scarse them bad arise.
  Her Lordes and Ladies all this while deuise
  Themselues to setten forth to straungers sight:
  Some frounce their curled heare in courtly guise,
  Some prancke their ruffes, and others trimly dight
Their gay attyre: each others greater pride does spight.

15

Goodly they all that knight doe entertayne,
  Right glad with him to haue increast their crew;
  But to *Duess'* each one himselfe did payne
All kindnesse and faire courtesie to shew;
  For in that court whylome her well they knew:
  Yet the stout Faery mongst the middest crowd
  Thought all their glorie vaine in knightly vew,
  And that great Princesse too exceeding prowd,
That to strange knight no better countenance allowd.

16

Suddein vpriseth from her stately place
  The roiall Dame, and for her coche doth call;
  All hurtlen forth, and she with princely pace,
As faire *Aurora* in her purple pall,
  Out of the East the dawning day doth call:
  So forth she comes: her brightnes brode doth blaze;
  The heapes of people thronging in the hall,
  Doe ride each other, vpon her to gaze:
Her glorious glitterand light doth all mens eies amaze.

17

So forth she comes, and to her coche does clyme,
  Adorned all with gold, and girlonds gay,
  That seemd as fresh as *Flora* in her prime,
And stroue to match, in roiall rich array,
  Great *Iunoes* golden chayre, the which they say
  The Gods stand gazing on, when she does ride
  To *Ioues* high hous through heauens bras-paued way
  Drawne of fayre Pecocks, that excell in pride,
And full of *Argus* eyes their tayles dispredden wide.

7–9 **obeysaunce**: submission. **declare**: make clear. **proue**: the knight first sought to 'proue his puissance' (i 3.7) by slaying the dragon and was betrayed into seeking to 'proue his sense' (50.6); now he seeks to confirm Lucifera's fame.

Stanza 14
1 Prov. 30.13 condemns those 'whose eyes are haughtie, and their eye liddes are lifted vp'. **5 deuise**: make ready. **6 setten forth**: exhibit (*OED* 144j). **7 frounce**: gather in braids. **8 prancke**: fold, in order to display ostentatiously. **dight**: arrange. **9 gay**: usually pejorative when applied to clothes, as x 39.2. Each despises the greater pride of the others.

Stanza 15
A significant analogue to this moment is found in Cartigny 1951:32–52; and see 152–53. **4 kindnesse**: suggesting also 'natural kinship' for Duessa is of their kind. **5 whylome**: earlier. **6 stout**: firm, as he resists their vanity; also from his present mood of injured merit, 'proud' (*OED* 1). Cf. 37.7–9. **Faery**: see i 17.1n. He is so named to indicate that he is not of their kind. **middest**: the very middle; cf. 'the thickest woods' (i 11.7) where he encounters Errour. At the centre of Vanity Fair, he is able to resist vanity though not entirely. **9 strange**: foreign, not of their kind. **countenance**: manner towards him. In her bright presence, her vanity is reflected in his pique, which, from a theological perspective – see Gless 1994:93 – is a spiritual indictment of him.

Stanza 16
Lucifera's progress would seem to comment obliquely on the progresses by which Elizabeth displayed and asserted her authority; see the *SEnc* 525. **3 hurtlen**: rush jostlingly or impetuously, as sugg. by hurlen *1609*. As does **Suddein**, it indicates the violence of pride; cf. 40.1 and i 16.2–4n. **pace**: movement. **4** Here she appears as Lucifera, 'light-bearing', the morning star which heralds the sun. **purple pall**: crimson robe; see ii 7.1–3n. **8** This image of the courtiers riding each other as the sins ride their beasts is expanded at II vii 47 to show how the ambitious oppress each other in their desire to rise. Its consequences are revealed when they are seen

'together in one heape . . . throwne, | Like carkases of beastes in butchers stall' (v 49.1–2). **9 glitterand**: 'Glittering, a Participle used sometime in Chaucer, but altogether in J. Goore [Gower]' (E.K. on *SC July* 177). It suggests 'light-giving', as Arthur's armour at vii 29.4, the only other use of the word in the poem. **amaze**: dazzle, bewilder.

Stanza 17
1 **So forth she comes**: repeated from 16.6 to inflate her in her pride in order to collapse all her pretensions in the next stanza. **2–3 gold** for Juno's chariot; **girlonds** for **Flora**, the goddess of flowers (see i 48.9n). **5 chayre**: chariot. **7** From Ovid's description of the Milky Way by which the gods travel to Jove's royal dwelling, *Met.* 1.168–71. **8–9** From Ovid's description of Juno's chariot drawn by **Pecocks**, sacred to her, *Met.* 2.533–35, and a common emblem of pride. **in pride**: in the heraldic posture with tail expanded, suggesting love of ostentatious display; noted Chew 1962:96. **Argus eyes**: 'whose eyes it is sayd that Iuno for his [Argus's] eternall memory placed in her byrd the Peacocks tayle' (E.K. on *SC Oct.* 32). **dispredden**: widely spread out.

Stanzas 18–35
Each counsellor is shown in grotesque dress appropriate to his sin, holding an object which symbolizes his inner state, suffering from a deadly disease which is either a consequence of his sin or a fitting punishment for it, riding a beast that represents the passion associated with his sin, and paired in a significant manner with a second sin. Each is described in three stanzas. They ride in three pairs, one on each side of the wagon-beam: Idlenesse, Auarice, and Enuie on one side, and Gluttony, Lecherie, and Wrath on the other. Their order corresponds to the 'froward' and 'forward' passions – see II ii 38.5–8n – as Donald Stump has suggested to me. All are masculine except Lucifera who completes the traditional seven deadly sins. She opens the procession because pride is 'the original of sinne' (Ecclus. 10:14); see 'pride' in the *SEnc*. Together they form the beast with seven heads described in Rev. 17.3. Each detail may be traced to conventional iconography though, as Crossett and Stump 1984:215 conclude, S.'s procession of the

18

But this was drawne of six vnequall beasts,
　　On which her six sage Counsellours did ryde,
　　Taught to obey their bestiall beheasts,
　　With like conditions to their kindes applyde:
　　Of which the first, that all the rest did guyde,
　　Was sluggish *Idlenesse* the nourse of sin;
　　Vpon a slouthfull Asse he chose to ryde,
　　Arayd in habit blacke, and amis thin,
Like to an holy Monck, the seruice to begin.

19

And in his hand his Portesse still he bare,
　　That much was worne, but therein little redd,
　　For of deuotion he had little care,
　　Still drownd in sleepe, and most of his daies dedd;
　　Scarse could he once vphold his heauie hedd,
　　To looken, whether it were night or day:
　　May seeme the wayne was very euill ledd,
　　When such an one had guiding of the way,
That knew not, whether right he went, or else astray.

20

From worldly cares himselfe he did esloyne,
　　And greatly shunned manly exercise,
　　From euerie worke he chalenged essoyne,
　　For contemplation sake: yet otherwise,
　　His life he led in lawlesse riotise;
　　By which he grew to grieuous malady;
　　For in his lustlesse limbs through euill guise
　　A shaking feuer raignd continually:
Such one was *Idlenesse*, first of this company.

21

And by his side rode loathsome *Gluttony*,
　　Deformed creature, on a filthie swyne,
　　His belly was vpblowne with luxury;
　　And eke with fatnesse swollen were his eyne,
　　And like a Crane his necke was long and fyne,
　　With which he swallowd vp excessiue feast,
　　For want whereof poore people oft did pyne,
　　And all the way, most like a brutish beast,
He spued vp his gorge, that all did him deteast.

22

In greene vine leaues he was right fitly clad;
　　For other clothes he could not weare for heat,
　　And on his head an yuie girland had,
　　From vnder which fast trickled downe the sweat:
　　Still as he rode, he somewhat still did eat,
　　And in his hand did beare a bouzing can,
　　Of which he supt so oft, that on his seat
　　His dronken corse he scarse vpholden can,
In shape and life more like a monster, then a man.

23

Vnfit he was for any wordly thing,
　　And eke vnhable once to stirre or go,
　　Not meet to be of counsell to a king,
　　Whose mind in meat and drinke was drowned so,
　　That from his frend he seeldome knew his fo:
　　Full of diseases was his carcas blew,
　　And a dry dropsie through his flesh did flow,
　　Which by misdiet daily greater grew:
Such one was *Gluttony*, the second of that crew.

---

sins is uniquely his own. See 'sins, seven deadly' with illustrations in the *SEnc*.

Stanza 18
1 vnequall: different, because of the different sins which they represent. **4** I.e. the bestial commands were appropriate to each beast's nature, indicating that rider and beast are in harmony. **6 the nourse of sin**: idleness is traditionally 'the ministre and the norice unto vices' (Chaucer, *Second Nun's Prologue* 1), as an 'ydle dreame' (i 46.1) first tempted the knight to forsake Una. It is associated with vagrancy, an urgent social problem in the late sixteenth century. **8–9** The simile associates Idlenesse, and therefore Lucifera's pride, with the Church of Rome. **amis**: priestly vestment or monk's hood.

Stanza 19
1 Portesse: a breviary carried by priests; noted as outward popish display. **4 Still**: always, continually. A key word in the account of the sins that fixes their active and enduring state. **7–9** Sloth represents the human state before the coming of the law.

Stanza 20
1–3 esloyne: withdraw, remove himself from the jurisdiction of the law. **chalenged essoyne**: claimed exemption. The two legal terms show that he seeks to live in lawlessness. **5 riotise**: riotous conduct. A typical S. coinage which preserves the

action of the verb in the state itself. **7 lustlesse**: listless; implying that lustfulness has led to this state. **guise**: behaviour.

Stanza 21
1 Gluttony: Nashe declared that he would 'decypher at large' the excess of gluttony 'but that a new Laureat hath sau'd me the labor' (1904–10:1.199). On gluttony as traditionally the first sin, see W.I. Miller 1997. **3 luxury**: vicious indulgence. **4** 'Their eyes swell with fatnesse' (Ps. 73.7, *BCP* Psalter). **5 Crane**: a common emblem of gluttony (from Lat. *glutir*, to swallow) because its long neck extends the pleasure of swallowing (Aristotle, *Ethics* 3.10). **fyne**: scrawny. **9** I.e. he vomits up what he had swallowed. He suffers from bulimia nervosa.

Stanza 22
Gluttony resembles the drunken satyr Silenus, foster-father of Bacchus (Ovid, *Met.* 4.26–27, 11.90–99). **1 right fitly**: because ivy is sacred to Bacchus. **5 somewhat**: something.

Stanza 23
1 Vnfit: like his companion Idlenesse, Gluttony is unfit to serve the world. **wordly**: worldly *1596*, of which it is an obs. form (*OED*). **2 once**: ever. **go**: walk. **6 blew**: black or livid, the colour of diseased flesh. **7 dry dropsie**: either 'dire dropsie' (sugg. Upton 1758 from *dirus hydrops* in Horace, *Odes* 2.2.13) or 'dry' because the disease causes thirst.

24

And next to him rode lustfull *Lechery*,
 Vpon a bearded Gote, whose rugged heare,
 And whally eies (the signe of gelosy,)
 Was like the person selfe, whom he did beare:
 Who rough, and blacke, and filthy did appeare,
 Vnseemely man to please faire Ladies eye,
 Yet he of Ladies oft was loued deare,
 When fairer faces were bid standen by:
O who does know the bent of womens fantasy?

25

In a greene gowne he clothed was full faire,
 Which vnderneath did hide his filthinesse,
 And in his hand a burning hart he bare,
 Full of vaine follies, and new fanglenesse;
 For he was false, and fraught with ficklenesse,
 And learned had to loue with secret lookes,
 And well could daunce, and sing with ruefulnesse,
 And fortunes tell, and read in louing bookes,
And thousand other waies, to bait his fleshly hookes.

26

Inconstant man, that loued all he saw,
 And lusted after all, that he did loue,
 Ne would his looser life be tide to law,
 But ioyd weake wemens hearts to tempt, and proue
 If from their loyall loues he might them moue;
 Which lewdnes fild him with reprochfull pain
 Of that foule euill, which all men reproue,
 That rotts the marrow, and consumes the braine:
Such one was *Lechery*, the third of all this traine.

27

And greedy *Auarice* by him did ride,
 Vppon a Camell loaden all with gold;
 Two iron coffers hong on either side,
 With precious metall full, as they might hold,
 And in his lap an heap of coine he told;
 For of his wicked pelf his God he made,
 And vnto hell him selfe for money sold;
 Accursed vsury was all his trade,
And right and wrong ylike in equall ballaunce waide.

28

His life was nigh vnto deaths dore yplaste,
 And thred-bare cote, and cobled shoes hee ware,
 Ne scarse good morsell all his life did taste,
 But both from backe and belly still did spare,
 To fill his bags, and richesse to compare;
 Yet childe ne kinsman liuing had he none
 To leaue them to; but thorough daily care
 To get, and nightly feare to lose his owne,
He led a wretched life vnto him selfe vnknowne.

29

Most wretched wight, whom nothing might suffise,
 Whose greedy lust did lacke in greatest store,
 Whose need had end, but no end couetise,
 Whose welth was want, whose plenty made him pore,
 Who had enough, yett wished euer more,
 A vile disease, and eke in foote and hand
 A grieuous gout tormented him full sore,
 That well he could not touch, nor goe, nor stand:
Such one was *Auarice*, the fourth of this faire band.

Stanza 24
1 next to him: immediately following him, because 'after Glotonye thanne comth Lecherie, for thise two synnes been so ny cosyns that ofte tyme they wol nat departe' (Chaucer, *Parson's Tale* 836). **2** The goat is proverbially lustfull; see Rowland 1973:85. **rugged**: shaggy. **heare**: cf. Lust 'All ouergrowne with haire' (IV vii 5.4). **3 whally**: glaring, to indicate jealousy; or wall-eyed, showing white as the eye rolls in jealousy.

Stanza 25
1 greene: 'the color of lovers' (Shakespeare, *Love's Labor's Lost* 1.2.86); but also of fickleness (Chaucer, *Against Women Unconstant* 7). **8 louing bookes**: books of erotic love. One would be Ovid, *Ars amatoria*, which informs the poem's treatment of lust; see Stapleton 1998.

Stanza 26
4 tempt: make trial of. **proue**: test. **6–8 reprochfull**: deserving of reproach, besides being full of reproach for his pain. **that foule euill**: either leprosy, which was widely held to be transmitted venereally and to be a special punishment inflicted by God (cf. III v 14.8–9); or syphilis, which rots the marrow, leaving the bones hollow (as in Shakespeare, *Measure for Measure* 1.2.56).

Stanza 27
1 greedy: as the name implies (Lat. *avarus*). **by him**: Auarice and Lecherie are paired as are Mammon and Acrasia, the two

extremes of intemperance in Bk II. **2 Camell**: associated with avarice through Christ's story of the rich man seeking eternal life, Matt. 19.16–24. Treasures 'vpon the bounches of the camels' (Isa. 30.6) became an emblem of avarice; see G. Whitney 1586:18. **5 told**: counted; cf. Mammon at II vii 4.7. **6 wicked pelf**: filthy lucre. **8 Accursed**: because condemned by Scripture except to strangers, e.g. Deut. 23.19–20. **9** The error of trying to weigh right with wrong is exposed by Artegall, 'For by no meanes the false will with the truth be wayd' (V ii 45.9).

Stanza 28
The association of avarice with old age was proverbial (Tilley: M568). **5 compare**: acquire. **9 vnknowne**: i.e. he did not know how wretched he was; or he lacks self-knowledge; or living to himself he remained unknown to others.

Stanza 29
1–2 Proverbial: 'Who desires most lacks most' (Smith 175). **lacke**: want. **3 couetise**: covetousness. **4** I.e. he possesses only his covetousness as he personifies the state itself. **plenty . . . pore**: the cry of Narcissus in Ovid, *Met*. 3.466. The emblem of *SC Sept.*, which E.K. applies to Diggon Davie's plight: 'through great plentye was fallen into great penurie'. **5** Cf. the Second Beadman in the house of Holinesse: 'He had enough, what need him care for more?' (x 38.8). **6–9 disease**: his mental state is expressed as a physical disease. The pain of gout prevents him from enjoying his wealth, and its physical effect is a fitting punishment for his grasping nature.

30

And next to him malicious *Enuy* rode,
  Vpon a rauenous wolfe, and still did chaw
  Betweene his cankred teeth a venemous tode,
  That all the poison ran about his chaw;
  But inwardly he chawed his owne maw
  At neibors welth, that made him euer sad;
  For death it was, when any good he saw,
  And wept, that cause of weeping none he had,
But when he heard of harme, he wexed wondrous glad.

31

All in a kirtle of discolourd say
  He clothed was, ypaynted full of eies;
  And in his bosome secretly there lay
  An hatefull Snake, the which his taile vptyes
  In many folds, and mortall sting implyes.
  Still as he rode, he gnasht his teeth, to see
  Those heapes of gold with griple Couetyse,
  And grudged at the great felicitee
Of proud *Lucifera*, and his owne companee.

32

He hated all good workes and vertuous deeds,
  And him no lesse, that any like did vse,
  And who with gratious bread the hungry feeds,
  His almes for want of faith he doth accuse;

So euery good to bad he doth abuse:
  And eke the verse of famous Poets witt
  He does backebite, and spightfull poison spues
  From leprous mouth on all, that euer writt:
Such one vile *Enuy* was, that fifte in row did sitt.

33

And him beside rides fierce reuenging *Wrath*,
  Vpon a Lion, loth for to be led;
  And in his hand a burning brond he hath,
  The which he brandisheth about his hed;
  His eies did hurle forth sparcles fiery red,
  And stared sterne on all, that him beheld,
  As ashes pale of hew and seeming ded;
  And on his dagger still his hand he held,
Trembling through hasty rage, when choler in him sweld.

34

His ruffin raiment all was staind with blood,
  Which he had spilt, and all to rags yrent,
  Through vnaduized rashnes woxen wood;
  For of his hands he had no gouernement,
  Ne car'd for blood in his auengement:
  But when the furious fitt was ouerpast,
  His cruell facts he often would repent;
  Yet wilfull man he neuer would forecast,
How many mischieues should ensue his heedlesse hast.

Stanzas 30–35
Wrath and envy are the climactic sins through which the inhabitants of the house of Pride fall into its dungeon at v 46.7; see 39.4–6*n*. Enuie is paired with Detraction at V xii 28–32. See 'envy' in the *SEnc*.

Stanza 30
Chaucer's parson cites the two characteristics of envy described by Augustine: 'sorwe of oother mennes wele, and joye of othere mennes harm' (*Parson's Tale* 484), as S. shows Enuie provoked **At neibors welth** and **malicious**; cf. V xii 29–31. **1 next to him**: immediately following him. **2 wolfe**: usually associated with avarice but here with envy because of its reputed paralysing glance or because it was reputed to be envious (Chew 1962:109). **still**: continually. **3 cankred**: infected; possibly, 'rusted' (i.e. bloody). **venemous** was a common epithet for the toad, which was regarded as poisonous. Usually Enuie chews a snake as at V xii 30.5–9, or his own heart (G. Whitney 1586:4), though seen 'gnawing on the flesh | Of Snakes and Todes' in Ovid, *Met.* 2.768–69 (tr. Golding). Cf. 'Enuies poisnous bit' (*DS* 3.4). **4 chaw**: jaw. **5** Proverbial: Smith 215. **maw**: guts. **6 welth**: well-being, welfare; or specifically the gold of his companion, Auarice, as at 31.6–9.

Stanza 31
1 kirtle: either robes of state or a woman's gown (cf. *SC Aug*. 67), both appropriate to the state of envy. **discolourd say**: a many-coloured cloth of fine texture, showing the false colours in which Enuie sees everything, as the envious appear in *livido color* in Dante, *Purg.* 13.9. M. Craig 1967:457 finds a pun on the vicious things Enuie says. **2 full of eies**: the literal sense

of envy (Lat. *invidia*, f. *invidere*, to look maliciously upon). **4–5 Snake**: the traditional attribute of envy. **mortall**: death-dealing, as Errour's 'mortall sting' (i 15.4). **implyes**: enfolds; suggesting that what envy implies wounds deepest. **7 with griple Couetyse**: i.e. owned by grasping Auarice, implying also that he looks with covetousness. **8 grudged**: was envious; complained.

Stanza 32
2 vse: perform. **3 with gratious bread**: with bread graciously. The phrase identifies the deed and the doer, for a gracious deed manifests inner grace. **4** By claiming that good works indicate lack of faith, Enuie denies the doctrine that 'of workes a man is justified, and not of faith onely' (Jas. 2.24). **5 abuse**: misrepresent; colour falsely. **6–8** Cf. the action of the Blatant Beast at VI xii 41.

Stanza 33
1 him beside: Enuie's evil eyes lead to Wrath's fiery glances. **2–3** On the association of the lion with wrath, see Chew 1962:111. Its well-known pride makes it an unwilling mount. **burning brond**: blazing torch. **5** The stream of animal spirits emitted by Wrath's eyes infects those he looks upon with wrath. **9 choler**: the humour that causes anger.

Stanza 34
1 ruffin: befitting a ruffian or the Devil ('ruffin'); possibly red in colour (Lat. *rufus*). **3 woxen wood**: grown mad. **5 car'd for**: i.e. cared about spilling. **7 facts**: crimes, evil deeds. Wrath is the only sin associated with repentance, as Chew 1962:112–13 notes. **9 mischieues**: evil consequences, calamities.

35

Full many mischiefes follow cruell *Wrath*;
   Abhorred bloodshed, and tumultuous strife,
   Vnmanly murder, and vnthrifty scath,
   Bitter despight, with rancours rusty knife,
   And fretting griefe the enemy of life;
   All these, and many euils moe haunt ire,
   The swelling Splene, and Frenzy raging rife,
   The shaking Palsey, and Saint *Fraunces* fire:
Such one was *Wrath*, the last of this vngodly tire.

36

And after all vpon the wagon beame
   Rode *Sathan*, with a smarting whip in hand,
   With which he forward lasht the laesy teme,
   So oft as *Slowth* still in the mire did stand.
   Huge routs of people did about them band,
   Showting for ioy, and still before their way
   A foggy mist had couered all the land;
   And vnderneath their feet, all scattered lay
Dead sculls and bones of men, whose life had gone astray.

37

So forth they marchen in this goodly sort,
   To take the solace of the open aire,
   And in fresh flowring fields themselues to sport;
   Emongst the rest rode that false Lady faire,
   The foule *Duessa*, next vnto the chaire
   Of proud *Lucifer'*, as one of the traine:
   But that good knight would not so nigh repaire,
   Him selfe estraunging from their ioyaunce vaine,
Whose fellowship seemd far vnfitt for warlike swaine.

38

So hauing solaced themselues a space,
   With pleasaunce of the breathing fields yfed,
   They backe retourned to the princely Place;
   Whereas an errant knight in armes ycled,
   And heathnish shield, wherein with letters red
   Was writt *Sans ioy*, they new arriued find:
   Enflam'd with fury and fiers hardy hed,
   He seemd in hart to harbour thoughts vnkind,
And nourish bloody vengeaunce in his bitter mind.

39

Who when the shamed shield of slaine *Sans foy*
   He spide with that same Fary champions page,
   Bewraying him, that did of late destroy
   His eldest brother, burning all with rage
   He to him lept, and that same enuious gage
   Of victors glory from him snacht away:
   But th'Elfin knight, which ought that warlike wage,
   Disdaind to loose the meed he wonne in fray,
And him rencountring fierce, reskewd the noble pray.

40

Therewith they gan to hurtlen greedily,
   Redoubted battaile ready to darrayne,
   And clash their shields, and shake their swerds on hy,
   That with their sturre they troubled all the traine;
   Till that great Queene vpon eternall paine
   Of high displeasure, that ensewen might,
   Commaunded them their fury to refraine,
   And if that either to that shield had right,
In equall lists they should the morrow next it fight.

[handwritten marginal note: right to England?]

Stanza 35
3 Vnmanly: as it destroys the man, both the victim and the doer. **vnthrifty scath**: wasteful or destructive harm. **vnthrifty** may have the stronger sense, 'harmful', 'wicked'; **scath** is glossed as 'losse', 'hinderaunce' for *SC Dec.* 100. **4 despight**: malice. **rusty**: red with blood. Usually the word suggests 'filthy' or 'defiled' from use, not disuse, as at v 32.2 and ix 36.8. **5 griefe**: mental distress (*OED* 7) in a more comprehensive sense. **fretting**: gnawing, pricking. **7 swelling Splene**: outburst of hot temper, scorn and ridicule, the spleen being the seat of anger and morose feeling (Robin 1911:67). **8 Saint Fraunces fire**: presumably St Anthony's fire, erysipelas, 'a brennyng sore engendred of choler' (T. Cooper 1565). **9 tire**: 'rank', 'procession' (not in *OED*).

Stanza 36
2 Sathan: his sole appearance in the poem, perhaps in deliberate contrast to his major role in Tasso, *Ger. Lib.*, as Roche 1995:19-20 suggests. He appears here because the seven-headed beast of Rev. 17.3 was 'interpreted as Satan with his seven sins or vices or heads' (Tuve 1966:102). **4 Slowth**: the obs. spelling is used to suggest slowness. **still**: continually; not moving. **7 foggy mist**: signifying the moral confusion that leads to sin and results from it; cf. the mist that falls upon the sorcerer as punishment for his sin in Acts 13.11, and the fog that envelops Guyon on his voyage to the Bower of Bliss at II xii 34.

Stanza 37
1 sort: company. **2 solace**: pleasure. **7 that good knight**: his epic epithet (see ii 11.1-2*n*), which he deserves in this company.

8 ioyaunce: festivity; coined by S. to emphasize the (false) state of joy, and to prepare for the knight's battle with Sansjoy.

Stanza 38
2 pleasaunce: see vii 4.2*n*. **breathing**: exhaling fragrance; or (preferably) fields where they breathe to escape the stench of sin. **3 the princely Place**: S. reserves its final naming for the concluding phrase of canto v. **6 Sansjoy** appears here in response to the knight's rejection of 'ioyaunce vaine' (37.8). On the state represented by the name, see ii 25.6-9*n*. **7 hardy hed**: hardihood, over-boldness.

Stanza 39
1 shamed: in being reversed (41.9). **3 Bewraying**: revealing. **4-6** Sansjoy displays the two climactic sins of the house of Pride; see 39.4-6*n*. **enuious gage**: envied pledge of victory; the 'signe of the conqueroure' (ii 20.7) which he envied or begrudged him. **7 ought**: owned. **warlike wage**: pledge of skill in war, or spoil of war. **9 rencountring**: engaging in fight, suggesting a skirmish or accidental combat; hence Lucifera's judgement at 40.9. **pray**: booty. Instead of seeking to free Una's parents, the knight seeks to possess the shield of faithlessness, which he regards as his **noble pray**.

Stanza 40
1 hurtlen: clash violently; cf. 16.3. **2 darrayne**: engage in order to vindicate a claim (a legal term). **3** Such details suggest a pagan encounter to which the Red Cross Knight is reduced. **9 equall**: impartial, just. Unlike the chance outcome of a casual encounter, a battle in the lists was an ordeal whose outcome was considered to be a just verdict.

41

Ah dearest Dame, quoth then the Paynim bold,
    Pardon the error of enraged wight,
    Whome great griefe made forgett the raines to hold
    Of reasons rule, to see this recreaunt knight,
    No knight, but treachour full of false despight
    And shamefull treason, who through guile hath slayn
    The prowest knight, that euer field did fight,
    Euen stout *Sans foy* (O who can then refrayn?)
Whose shield he beares renuerst, the more to heap disdayn.

42

And to augment the glorie of his guile,
    His dearest loue the faire *Fidessa* loe
    Is there possessed of the traytour vile,
    Who reapes the haruest sowen by his foe,
    Sowen in bloodie field, and bought with woe:
    That brothers hand shall dearely well requight
    So be, O Queene, you equall fauour showe.
    Him litle answerd th'angry Elfin knight;
He neuer meant with words, but swords to plead his right.

43

But threw his gauntlet as a sacred pledg,
    His cause in combat the next day to try:
    So been they parted both, with harts on edg,
    To be aueng'd each on his enimy.
    That night they pas in ioy and iollity,
    Feasting and courting both in bowre and hall;
    For Steward was excessiue *Gluttony*,
    That of his plenty poured forth to all;
Which doen, the Chamberlain *Slowth* did to rest them call.

44

Now whenas darkesome night had all displayd
    Her coleblacke curtein ouer brightest skye,
    The warlike youthes on dayntie couches layd,
    Did chace away sweet sleepe from sluggish eye,
    To muse on meanes of hoped victory.
    But whenas *Morpheus* had with leaden mace,
    Arrested all that courtly company,
    Vprose *Duessa* from her resting place,
And to the Paynims lodging comes with silent pace.

45

Whom broad awake she findes, in troublous fitt,
    Forecasting, how his foe he might annoy,
    And him amoues with speaches seeming fitt:
    Ah deare *Sansioy*, next dearest to *Sansfoy*,
    Cause of my new griefe, cause of my new ioy,
    Ioyous, to see his ymage in mine eye,
    And greeud, to thinke how foe did him destroy,
    That was the flowre of grace and cheualrye;
Lo his *Fidessa* to thy secret faith I flye.

46

With gentle wordes he can her fayrely greet,
    And bad say on the secrete of her hart,
    Then sighing soft, I learne that litle sweet
    Oft tempred is (quoth she) with muchell smart:
    For since my brest was launcht with louely dart
    Of deare *Sansfoy*, I neuer ioyed howre,
    But in eternall woes my weaker hart
    Haue wasted, louing him with all my powre,
And for his sake haue felt full many an heauie stowre.

Stanza 41

3–4 A traditional emblem of the passions overpowering reason, as at III vii 2.7–9. **recreaunt**: cowardly, a term of the greatest opprobrium; cf. the charge 'Miscreant' against Sansjoy at v 13.1, and Sansloy at vi 41.1. More precisely: 'one who has yielded up his faith'. **5 treachour**: traitor, an obs. form that suggests 'treacherous'. **9 renuerst**: turned upside down, as Braggadocchio is shamed at V iii 37.

Stanza 42

3 **possessed**: i.e. sexually. **4** Proverbial: Smith 710; see also John 4.37. **5** Cf. the dwarf's account of Fidessa 'Bought with the blood of vanquisht Paynim bold' (vii 26.4). **6 That**: i.e. that act. **7 equall**: impartial, as 40.9. **8 angry**: he is brought to the level of his wrathful opponent.

Stanza 43

5–6 Not simply a duplication of terms: they **ioy** in **Feasting** in the hall, and have **iollity** (pleasure, esp. sexual pleasure, *OED* 3) in **courting** in the **bowre**. Presumably **they** refers to the courtiers but may well include the two knights. **9 Chamberlain**: the attendant at court in charge of the bedchambers, as the spelling indicates.

Stanza 44

1–2 **night**: personified to prepare for Duessa's descent to Night at v 19–20. **6–7 leaden mace**: as in Shakespeare, *Julius*

Caesar: 'O murd'rous slumber! | Layest thou thy leaden mace upon my boy?' (4.3.267–68). The term is suggested by the metal staff of office with which a sergeant or beadle tapped the person to be arrested. **Arrested** makes a simple but effective pun: until Bk VI, sleep is usually associated with death or imprisonment.

Stanza 45

2 **annoy**: injure. **3 amoues**: arouses, or seeks to move inwardly. **seeming**: suitably. **9** 'I place myself secretly in your allegiance' (playing on her name). The significance of her pledge appears at v 11.9: she perverts both knights by making herself, rather than the shield, the issue of their battle. Cf. the similar moment at i 52.6.

Stanza 46

1 **can**: did. **fayrely**: courteously. **2 secrete of her hart**: not to be known of one upon whose forehead is written 'Mysterie' (Rev. 17.5). Only God 'knoweth the secrets of the heart' (Ps. 44.21); we hear a deceiving tale. **3–4** A variation of Thomalin's emblem to *SC March*; see IV x 1.1–5*n*. **muchell**: muckle, much. **5–9** Cf. the story she tells the Red Cross Knight to move him at ii.25. **launcht**: pierced. **louely**: amorous, referring to Cupid's dart of love. **weaker**: too weak to resist love's woes. **stowre**: grievous time of turmoil.

47

At last when perils all I weened past,
　And hop'd to reape the crop of all my care,
　Into new woes vnweeting I was cast,
　By this false faytor, who vnworthie ware
　His worthie shield, whom he with guilefull snare
　Entrapped slew, and brought to shamefull graue.
　Me silly maid away with him he bare,
　And euer since hath kept in darksom caue,
For that I would not yeeld, that to *Sansfoy* I gaue.

48

But since faire Sunne hath sperst that lowring clowd,
　And to my loathed life now shewes some light,
　Vnder your beames I will me safely shroud,
　From dreaded storme of his disdainfull spight:
　To you th'inheritance belonges by right
　Of brothers prayse, to you eke longes his loue.
　Let not his loue, let not his restlesse spright,
　Be vnreueng'd, that calles to you aboue
From wandring *Stygian* shores, where it doth endlesse moue.

49

Thereto said he, Faire Dame be nought dismaid
　For sorrowes past; their griefe is with them gone:
　Ne yet of present perill be affraid:
　For needlesse feare did neuer vantage none,

And helplesse hap it booteth not to mone.
　Dead is *Sansfoy*, his vitall paines are past,
　Though greeued ghost for vengeance deep do grone:
　He liues, that shall him pay his dewties last,
And guiltie Elfin blood shall sacrifice in hast.

50

O But I feare the fickle freakes (quoth shee)
　Of fortune false, and oddes of armes in field.
　Why dame (quoth he) what oddes can euer bee,
　Where both doe fight alike, to win or yield?
　Yea but (quoth she) he beares a charmed shield,
　And eke enchaunted armes, that none can perce,
　Ne none can wound the man, that does them wield.
　Charmd or enchaunted (answerd he then ferce)
I no whitt reck, ne you the like need to reherce.

51

But faire *Fidessa*, sithens fortunes guile,
　Or enimies powre hath now captiued you,
　Returne from whence ye came, and rest a while
　Till morrow next, that I the Elfe subdew,
　And with *Sansfoyes* dead dowry you endew.
　Ay me, that is a double death (she said)
　With proud foes sight my sorrow to renew:
　Where euer yet I be, my secrete aide
Shall follow you. So passing forth she him obaid.

Stanza 47

1 Two **perils** have been told: about the knight slain by Fradubio, and about Fradubio himself (ii 35–36). **2** Echoing Sansjoy's claim at 42.4. **4 faytor**: impostor, because he wears Sansfoy's shield. Often with the epithet 'false', as xii 35.5, etc. **7 silly**: helpless, as she claimed at ii 21.3. **9 For that**: because. The great whore primly corrects Sansjoy's indelicate inference at 42.3–4.

Stanza 48

1–4 The bungled metaphor reveals her duplicity. **sperst**: dispersed. **shrowd**: take shelter; also 'conceal', for she conceals herself in 'borrowed light' (viii 49.5). **6 longes**: belongs. **7–9 wandring Stygian shores**: wandering on the banks of the Styx; see iii 36.6 and *n*. **Stygian** suggests blackness in contrast to the brother's light. **endlesse**: ceaselessly; forever.

Stanza 49

1–5 The tissue of proverbs befits his moral state. **vantage none**: benefit anyone. **helplesse**: admitting no help. **6 vitall paines**: troubles in life in contrast to those in death (not in *OED*). **8 dewties**: debts; the final obligations owed to Sansfoy: his slayer's death will 'redeeme [him] from his long wandring woe' (v 11.2).

Stanza 50

1–2 Excessive alliteration declares Duessa's duplicity. **oddes of armes**: advantage through difference of armour, not of battle as he understands. **4 alike**: as they fight 'In equall lists' (40.9) under Lucifera's 'equall fauour' (42.7).

Stanza 51

4 Elfe: suggesting a 'malignant being' (*OED* 1b). **5 dead**: qualifying Sansfoy, though it applies as well to faithlessness. **endew**: endow. Presumably the **dowry** is Sansfoy's shield.

Cant. V.

*The faithfull knight in equall field
subdewes his faithlesse foe,
Whom false Duessa saues, and for
his cure to hell does goe.*

1

THe noble hart, that harbours vertuous thought,
    And is with childe of glorious great intent,
    Can neuer rest, vntill it forth haue brought
    Th'eternall brood of glorie excellent:
    Such restlesse passion did all night torment
    The flaming corage of that Faery knight,
    Deuizing, how that doughtie turnament
    With greatest honour he atchieuen might;
Still did he wake, and still did watch for dawning light.

2

At last the golden Orientall gate
    Of greatest heauen gan to open fayre,
    And *Phoebus* fresh, as brydegrome to his mate,
    Came dauncing forth, shaking his deawie hayre:
    And hurld his glistring beams through gloomy ayre.
    Which when the wakeful Elfe perceiud, streight way
    He started vp, and did him selfe prepayre,
    In sunbright armes, and battailous array:
For with that Pagan proud he combatt will that day.

3

And forth he comes into the commune hall,
    Where earely waite him many a gazing eye,
    To weet what end to straunger knights may fall.
    There many Minstrales maken melody,
    To driue away the dull melancholy,
    And many Bardes, that to the trembling chord
    Can tune their timely voices cunningly,
    And many Chroniclers, that can record
Old loues, and warres for Ladies doen by many a Lord.

4

Soone after comes the cruell Sarazin,
    In wouen maile all armed warily,
    And sternly lookes at him, who not a pin
    Does care for looke of liuing creatures eye.
    They bring them wines of *Greece* and *Araby*,
    And daintie spices fetcht from furthest *Ynd*,
    To kindle heat of corage priuily:
    And in the wine a solemne oth they bynd
T'obserue the sacred lawes of armes, that are assynd.

Book I Canto v

Argument
1 The faithfull knight: see iv Arg.2*n*.

Stanza 1
1–4 An endorsement of the humanist faith that the highest end of self-knowledge is 'well-doing and not of well-knowing only' (Sidney, *Defence of Poetry* 83) even though here the knight's 'well-doing' is to possess the shield of faithlessness. **vertuous**: valorous, full of manly courage. **glorious**: eager for glory. **excellent**: supreme, rather than 'extremely good'. **6 corage**: mind; nature; heart. The etymological spelling, Lat. *cor*, heart, is used throughout the poem. **7–8** In contrast to Sansjoy 'Forecasting, how his foe he might annoy' (iv 45.2). See also 7.3, 6. **turnament**: usually applied to mounted knights fighting with lances; see III i 44.7*n*, and 'tournaments' in the *SEnc*. What follows here is a parody of a tilt or joust for the knights engage in a personal duel on foot using swords, seeking to kill each other rather than to score hits. **atchieuen**: finish, i.e. win.

Stanza 2
1–5 The solar imagery, which dominates Bk I as A. Fowler 1964: 63–79 argues, provides the setting for the battle between one of the 'sonnes of Day' and one of 'great *Nightes*

children' (25.7, 23.8), and prepares for the dramatic coming of Night at stanza 20. **3–5** Cf. Ps. 19.4–5: 'In them [the heauens] hathe he set a tabernacle for the sunne. Which commeth forthe as a bridegrome out of his chambre, and reioyceth like a mightie man to runne his race'. **dauncing** is a common Renaissance term for the movement of the constellations. **8** 'They that loue him shal be as the sunne when he riseth in his might' (Judg. 5.31). **sunbright**: appropriately, first recorded in S.; cf. 9.5. **battailous**: warlike.

Stanza 3
4–8 Minstrales compose the music, **Bardes** sing it, and **Chroniclers** set down the words (perhaps in rhyme as at III xii 5.5). **5** Cf. 17.6–8. This line is repeated in the account of the knight's marriage to Una at xii 38.8. **7 Can**: knew how to. **timely**: keeping time with the music.

Stanza 4
1 cruell: also fierce, savage. **Sarazin**: Saracen; as Sansfoy at ii 12.6. **2 warily**: carefully, i.e. completely; possibly 'warly': in a warlike manner. Like his brother, he is 'all armde to point' (ii 12.6), in contrast to the 'enchaunted armes' (iv 50.6) carried by the Red Cross Knight. **3–4** Also imitating his brother at ii 12.9. **5–9** The laws of arms in medieval judicial combat involved an oath, often sworn over wine, not to use charms; see ii 18.4*n*. This oath is soon violated. **daintie**: precious.

5

At last forth comes that far renowmed Queene,
    With royall pomp and princely maiestie;
    She is ybrought vnto a paled greene,
    And placed vnder stately canapee,
    The warlike feates of both those knights to see.
    On th'other side in all mens open vew
    Duessa placed is, and on a tree
    Sansfoy his shield is hangd with bloody hew:
Both those the lawrell girlonds to the victor dew.

6

A shrilling trompett sownded from on hye,
    And vnto battaill bad them selues addresse:
    Their shining shieldes about their wrestes they tye,
    And burning blades about their heades doe blesse,
    The instruments of wrath and heauinesse:
    With greedy force each other doth assayle,
    And strike so fiercely, that they doe impresse
    Deepe dinted furrowes in the battred mayle:
The yron walles to ward their blowes are weak and fraile.

7

The Sarazin was stout, and wondrous strong,
    And heaped blowes like yron hammers great:
    For after blood and vengeance he did long.
    The knight was fiers, and full of youthly heat,
    And doubled strokes, like dreaded thunders threat:
    For all for praise and honour he did fight.
    Both stricken stryke, and beaten both doe beat,
    That from their shields forth flyeth firie light,
And helmets hewen deepe shew marks of eithers might.

8

So th'one for wrong, the other striues for right:
    As when a Gryfon seized of his pray,
    A Dragon fiers encountreth in his flight,
    Through widest ayre making his ydle way,
    That would his rightfull rauine rend away:
    With hideous horror both together smight,
    And souce so sore, that they the heauens affray:
    The wise Southsayer seeing so sad sight,
Th'amazed vulgar telles of warres and mortall fight.

9

So th'one for wrong, the other striues for right,
    And each to deadly shame would driue his foe:
    The cruell steele so greedily doth bight
    In tender flesh, that streames of blood down flow,
    With which the armes, that earst so bright did show,
    Into a pure vermillion now are dyde:
    Great ruth in all the gazers harts did grow,
    Seeing the gored woundes to gape so wyde,
That victory they dare not wish to either side.

10

At last the Paynim chaunst to cast his eye,
    His suddein eye, flaming with wrathfull fyre,
    Vpon his brothers shield, which hong thereby:
    Therewith redoubled was his raging yre,
    And said, Ah wretched sonne of wofull syre,
    Doest thou sit wayling by blacke *Stygian* lake,
    Whylest here thy shield is hangd for victors hyre,
    And sluggish german doest thy forces slake,
To after-send his foe, that him may ouertake?

Stanza 5

1–2 At last: repeating 2.1 to indicate her parody of the sun's light. **far renowmed**: cf. 'the wide report of her great Maiestee' (iv 13.9). **3 paled greene**: the fenced grassy lists. **6 On th'other side**: i.e. across from Lucifera who is stationed midfield where the combatants on horse meet. Oddly, for a tournament in a tiltyard, they are on foot. **7 on a tree**: the tree of chivalry which displayed the coats of arms of knights in a tournament; see Young 1987:46 and illust. 12.

Stanza 6

4 blesse: brandish, making in the air the sign of the cross under which they fight; cf. viii 22.3. **5 heauinesse**: anger, indignation; also sadness, grief (*OED* 1.e), which is appropriate to their state of joylessness.

Stanza 7

The first three lines are carefully paralleled by the second three; then the action of each set is doubled in the seventh with the giving and receiving of blows. The difference between the two knights, which is developed from iv 45.2–3 and v 1.7–8, becomes increasingly blurred. **4 fiers**: high-spirited, brave, eager (*OED* 2, 5), or fiery (as the spelling suggests, cf. 1.6); cf. the 'Dragon fiers' at 8.3.

Stanza 8

The primary allusion is to a meteorological phenomenon known as a firedrake or flying dragon, a portent of troublous times; see Heninger 1960:95. **2 Gryfon**: a lion with eagle's wings (Dan. 7.4). In Dante, *Purg.* 29.108, it represents Christ in his twofold nature, and here suggests 'that clownish person' wearing 'the armour of a Christian man' (*LR* 64). Yet griffins 'designe | Swiftnesse, and strength' (Jonson 1925–52:7.305), and its valour and magnanimity make it 'applyable vnto Princes . . . and all heroick Commanders' (Browne 1981:1.201). As an emblem of covetousness from its guarding gold (see W.M. Carroll 1954:67, 105), it represents the knight who fights for a pagan's shield. **4 ydle**: presumably the griffin is making his way idly when suddenly attacked by the dragon, even as the Red Cross Knight was solacing himself when Sansfoy suddenly seized Sansfoy's shield at iv 38–39. **5 That**: i.e. the dragon. **rauine**: spoil. **7 souce**: strike, swoop down with heavy blows; a term from falconry. **8 sad**: lamentable, ominous.

Stanza 9

2 deadly shame: also shameful death. **5 earst**: not long ago.

Stanza 10

1–6 As in the closing scene of Virgil, *Aen.*: angered at the sight of Turnus sporting the sword-belt of his dearest friend, Pallas, Aeneas slays him to atone for guilty blood. See ii 19.7*n*. Here, however, the Red Cross Knight is linked to the victim. **blacke Stygian lake**: see iii 36.6*n*. **8 german**: addressing himself as Sansfoy's brother. **slake**: diminish the fury of.

11

Goe caytiue Elfe, him quickly ouertake,
   And soone redeeme from his long wandring woe,
   Goe guiltie ghost, to him my message make,
   That I his shield haue quit from dying foe.
   Therewith vpon his crest he stroke him so,
   That twise he reeled, readie twise to fall;
   End of the doubtfull battaile deemed tho
   The lookers on, and lowd to him gan call
The false *Duessa*, Thine the shield, and I, and all.

12

Soone as the Faerie heard his Ladie speake,
   Out of his swowning dreame he gan awake,
   And quickning faith, that earst was woxen weake,
   The creeping deadly cold away did shake:
   Tho mou'd with wrath, and shame, and Ladies sake,
   Of all attonce he cast auengd to be,
   And with so'exceeding furie at him strake,
   That forced him to stoupe vpon his knee;
Had he not stouped so, he should haue clouen bee.

13

And to him said, Goe now proud Miscreant,
   Thy selfe thy message do to german deare,
   Alone he wandring thee too long doth want:
   Goe say, his foe thy shield with his doth beare.
   Therewith his heauie hand he high gan reare,
   Him to haue slaine; when lo a darkesome clowd
   Vpon him fell: he no where doth appeare,
   But vanisht is. The Elfe him calls alowd,
But answer none receiues: the darknes him does shrowd.

women's favor

14

In haste *Duessa* from her place arose,
   And to him running sayd, O prowest knight,
   That euer Ladie to her loue did chose,
   Let now abate the terrour of your might,
   And quench the flame of furious despight,
   And bloodie vengeance; lo th'infernall powres
   Couering your foe with cloud of deadly night,
   Haue borne him hence to *Plutoes* balefull bowres.
The conquest yours, I yours, the shield, and glory yours.

15

Not all so satisfide, with greedy eye
   He sought all round about, his thristy blade
   To bathe in blood of faithlesse enimy;
   Who all that while lay hid in secret shade:
   He standes amazed, how he thence should fade.
   At last the trumpets Triumph sound on hie,
   And running Heralds humble homage made,
   Greeting him goodly with new victorie,
And to him brought the shield, the cause of enmitie.

16

Wherewith he goeth to that soueraine Queene,
   And falling her before on lowly knee,
   To her makes present of his seruice seene:
   Which she accepts, with thankes, and goodly gree,
   Greatly aduauncing his gay cheualree.
   So marcheth home, and by her takes the knight,
   Whom all the people followe with great glee,
   Shouting, and clapping all their hands on hight,
That all the ayre it fils, and flyes to heauen bright.

Stanza 11

1 caytiue: servile, captive. **2** Cf. iv 48.9. **redeeme**: ransom, as an expiatory sacrifice. **3 ghost**: applied to the living knight in anticipation of his death. **make**: i.e. deliver; or provide physically by his body; cf. 'do' (13.2). **4 quit**: recovered. **5–9** Cf. Sansfoy's stroke at ii 18.6–9. Again the knight is saved by faith. **doubtfull**: also dread. **him**: the Red Cross Knight assumes that he, not Sansjoy, is addressed.

Stanza 12

3–4 Arousing his faith, he shook off, etc. He responds to her cry as he did to Una's 'Add faith vnto your force' (i 19.3), though now, since faith is aroused by Fidessa/Duessa, he is unable to kill his enemy. **5 sake**: regard. **6 cast**: resolved.

Stanza 13

1 Miscreant: misbeliever; cf. 'faithlesse' (Arg.2, 15.3) and 'Hethen' (19.4). A fitting term of abuse, which applies to the knight himself as he now gains Duessa, Sansfoy's shield, and submits to Lucifera; see 11.3. **2 do**: deliver. **6 a darkesome clowd**: a carefully chosen term that varies the epic convention in which the gods – here 'th'infernall powres' (14.6) – protect their favourites from impending death: 'a cloud of gold' in Homer, *Iliad* 3.399 (tr. Chapman), a hollow cloud in Virgil, *Aen*. 5.809, and an 'ouglie shade' in Tasso, *Ger. Lib*. 7.45 (tr. Fairfax). It anticipates the coming of Night. For the cloud of death, cf. 41.8 and iii 39.8. The moment marks a change:

earlier the knight's 'sunbright armes' (2.8) pierced the darkness of Errour's cave (i 14.4–6). See xi 4.8*n*.

Stanza 14

5–6 Duessa identifies the knight with his enemy who sought 'blood and vengeance' (7.3). **9** She expands her call at 11.9. **glory**: the 'glorie' (iv 15.7) of the house of Pride rather than that won by slaying Errour at i 27.6.

Stanza 15

1–3 The knight's frustrated action imitates Aeneas's search for Turnus through the thick gloom (*Aen*. 12.466–67). His degradation becomes clear when Una tells Arthur how she found in him one 'Whose manly hands imbrewd in guilty blood | Had neuer beene' (vii 47.3–4). **4** Cf. the 'foggy mist' (iv 36.7) that covers the land before the pageant of the sins. **5 fade**: vanish. **6 Triumph**: the official blast to salute the victor.

Stanza 16

1–2 The traditional gesture that closes an Elizabethan tournament. **Wherewith**: with which (i.e. the shield). **2–6** His act of falling expresses his fallen state: now he becomes Lucifera's knight, riding by her and following the sins to the house of Pride, which is now his **home**. **gay** is a bitterly appropriate epithet to mark his chivalry. **seene**: shown, and so proven. **goodly gree**: courteous goodwill. **aduauncing**: extolling.

17

Home is he brought, and layd in sumptuous bed:
    Where many skilfull leaches him abide,
    To salue his hurts, that yet still freshly bled.
    In wine and oyle they wash his woundes wide,
    And softly gan embalme on euerie side.
    And all the while, most heauenly melody
    About the bed sweet musicke did diuide,
    Him to beguile of griefe and agony:
And all the while *Duessa* wept full bitterly.

18

As when a wearie traueiler that strayes
    By muddy shore of broad seuen-mouthed *Nile*,
    Vnweeting of the perillous wandring wayes,
    Doth meete a cruell craftie Crocodile,
    Which in false griefe hyding his harmefull guile,
    Doth weepe full sore, and sheddeth tender teares:
    The foolish man, that pitties all this while
    His mournefull plight, is swallowd vp vnwares,
Forgetfull of his owne, that mindes anothers cares.

19

So wept *Duessa* vntill euentyde,
    That shyning lampes in *Ioues* high house were light:
    Then forth she rose, ne lenger would abide,
    But comes vnto the place, where th'Hethen knight
    In slombring swownd nigh voyd of vitall spright,
    Lay couer'd with inchaunted cloud all day:
    Whom when she found, as she him left in plight,
    To wayle his wofull case she would not stay,
But to the Easterne coast of heauen makes speedy way.

20

Where griesly *Night*, with visage deadly sad,
    That *Phœbus* chearefull face durst neuer vew,
    And in a foule blacke pitchy mantle clad,
    She findes forth comming from her darksome mew,
    Where she all day did hide her hated hew.
    Before the dore her yron charet stood,
    Already harnessed for iourney new;
    And coleblacke steedes yborne of hellish brood,
That on their rusty bits did champ, as they were wood.

21

Who when she saw *Duessa* sunny bright,
    Adornd with gold and iewels shining cleare,
    She greatly grew amazed at the sight,
    And th'vnacquainted light began to feare:
    For neuer did such brightnes there appeare,
    And would haue backe retyred to her caue,
    Vntill the witches speach she gan to heare,
    Saying, Yet O thou dreaded Dame, I craue
Abyde, till I haue told the message, which I haue.

22

She stayd, and foorth *Duessa* gan proceede,
    O thou most auncient Grandmother of all,
    More old then *Ioue*, whom thou at first didst breede,
    Or that great house of Gods cælestiall,
    Which wast begot in *Dæmogorgons* hall,
    And sawst the secrets of the world vnmade,
    Why suffredst thou thy Nephewes deare to fall
    With Elfin sword, most shamefully betrade?
Lo where the stout *Sansioy* doth sleepe in deadly shade.

Stanza 17

1 Home: emphatically placed here, and repeated from the preceding stanza, to expose the consequences of his victory. **2 abide**: await, i.e. attend. **3 salue**: anoint. **4** The medication is biblical; see Luke 10.34. **5 gan embalme**: did anoint. The suggestion that he is being preserved in death, which is the fate of Lucifera's other victims, is uncomfortably close. **7 diuide**: in the musical sense. The melody is divided into passages of short, quick notes by separate voices singing in polyphony. In Castle Joyeous, such music is linked with sensual '*Lydian* harmony' (III i 40.1–2). In contrast, the 'heauenly noise' heard at the knight's marriage to Una (xii 39) is the resolving harmony of the music of the spheres. **8 griefe**: pain.

Stanza 18

The crocodile of medieval bestiaries, which was said to weep while (or after) it devours its victims, was a symbol of hypocrisy. It became topical from reports of the New World; see the *SEnc* 501. In comparing its craft and guile to Duessa's, the simile associates her with Egypt, and her knight as a wanderer in that fallen land. **2 seuen-mouthed Nile**: as in Virgil, *Aen.* 6.800. **8 vnwares**: suddenly; being unwary. **9 of his owne**: i.e. of his own care or preservation.

Stanza 19

1 euentyde: the time is fixed precisely at the moment of balance between the opposing forces of light and darkness. **6 inchaunted**: 'charmed' (29.4). **7 in plight**: i.e. in the same state in which she had left him; or in the same perilous state.

Stanza 20

The description of Night may be drawn from Conti 1616:3.12, as Lotspeich 1932 suggests; or from the authorities he cites, esp. Virgil. See III iv 55–60*n*, and 'Night' in the *SEnc*. The description of her steeds may be indebted to Golding's translation of Ovid; see Taylor 1987b:197. **1 griesly**: because her appearance arouses horror, as does Proserpina's at i 37.4. **deadly sad**: either sad, dismal as death, or extremely dismal. **2** Either she does not dare to look upon Phœbus, or he upon her. **4 mew**: den; dark prison. **5 hew**: both shape and colour. **9 rusty**: being stained with blood. **wood**: rabid.

Stanza 21

2 cleare: brightly. **3 amazed**: terrified. **4–6 vnacquainted**: unfamiliar, as Errour's brood shuns 'vncouth light' (i 15.8) and she retreats into her cave at i 16.5–9. **9 Abyde**: stop. As Fidessa, Duessa stops Night even as faith may 'commaund the hasty Sunne to stay' (x 20.2).

Stanza 22

2–6 The genealogy of Night is also taken from Conti 1616. **auncient**: the appropriately 'ancient' spelling of the word. **Which**: i.e. Night. **Dæmogorgon**: i.e. chaos; see i 37.8*n* and IV ii 47.7. Lotspeich 1932 observes that S.'s spelling follows Boccaccio's etymology of the name: δαίμων + γεωργός, demon of the earth. **secrets**: because properly known only by revelation. **vnmade**: i.e. before the world was formed out of chaos; see 'chaos' in the *SEnc*. **7 Nephewes**: grandsons.

23

And him before, I saw with bitter eyes
　　The bold *Sansfoy* shrinck vnderneath his speare;
　　And now the pray of fowles in field he lyes,
　　Nor wayld of friends, nor layd on groning beare,
　　That whylome was to me too dearely deare.
　　O what of Gods then boots it to be borne,
　　If old *Aveugles* sonnes so euill heare?
　　Or who shall not great *Nightes* children scorne,
When two of three her Nephews are so fowle forlorne?

24

Vp then, vp dreary Dame, of darknes Queene,
　　Go gather vp the reliques of thy race,
　　Or else goe them auenge, and let be seene,
　　That dreaded *Night* in brightest day hath place,
　　And can the children of fayre light deface.
　　Her feeling speaches some compassion mou'd
　　In hart, and chaunge in that great mothers face:
　　Yet pitty in her hart was neuer prou'd
Till then: for euermore she hated, neuer lou'd.

25

And said, Deare daughter rightly may I rew
　　The fall of famous children borne of mee,
　　And good successes, which their foes ensew:
　　But who can turne the streame of destinee,
　　Or breake the chayne of strong necessitee,
　　Which fast is tyde to *Ioues* eternall seat.
　　The sonnes of Day he fauoureth, I see,
　　And by my ruines thinkes to make them great:
To make one great by others losse, is bad excheat.

26

Yet shall they not escape so freely all;
　　For some shall pay the price of others guilt:
　　And he the man that made *Sansfoy* to fall,
　　Shall with his owne blood price, that he hath spilt.
　　But what art thou, that telst of Nephews kilt?
　　I that do seeme not I, *Duessa* ame,
　　Quoth she, how euer now in garments gilt,
　　And gorgeous gold arayd I to thee came;
Duessa I, the daughter of Deceipt and Shame.

27

Then bowing downe her aged backe, she kist
　　The wicked witch, saying, In that fayre face
　　The false resemblaunce of Deceipt, I wist
　　Did closely lurke; yet so true-seeming grace
　　It carried, that I scarse in darksome place
　　Could it discerne, though I the mother bee
　　Of falshood, and roote of *Duessæs* race.
　　O welcome child, whom I haue longd to see,
And now haue seene vnwares. Lo now I goe with thee.

28

Then to her yron wagon she betakes,
　　And with her beares the fowle welfauourd witch:
　　Through mirkesome aire her ready way she makes.
　　Her twyfold Teme, of which two blacke as pitch,
　　And two were browne, yet each to each vnlich,
　　Did softly swim away, ne euer stamp,
　　Vnlesse she chaunst their stubborne mouthes to twitch;
　　Then foming tarre, their bridles they would champ,
And trampling the fine element, would fiercely ramp.

Stanza 23

3–4 'And thy carkeis shal be meat vnto all foules of the ayre' (Deut. 28.26). As the Geneva gloss explains, 'thou shalt be curst . . . in thy death, for buryal is a testimonie of the resurrection'. Cf. II i 59.8–9.　**4 groning**: because attended by mourners.　**7 Aveugle**: Fr. 'blind, sightlesse' (Cotgrave 1611); also an English word: 'to blind, hoodwink'. She may be Night herself or the son / husband of Night; cf. '*Aueugles* sonne' (44.6).　**so euill heare**: such evil is reported. Duessa appeals to Night's concern for the reputation of her house. **9 so fowle forlorne**: later Arthur learns how the Red Cross Knight is 'so fowle forlore' (viii 39.4) and saves him, as Night here aids his foe.

Stanza 24

1 dreary: melancholy, dreadful.　**4 place**: high rank.　**5 children of fayre light**: cf. 'sonnes of Day' (25.7). Later Arthur prophesies that 'The children of day' [Dayes dearest children 1596] be the blessed seed, | Which darknesse shall subdue, and heauen win' (III iv 59.5–6). Cf. John 12.36: 'While ye haue light, beleue in the light, that ye may be the children of the light'; also Eph. 5.8 and 1 Thess. 5.5.　**deface**: destroy, defame, outface, outshine by contrast.　**8 prou'd**: experienced.

Stanza 25

5 chayne: the golden chain by which Jove controls all creation: see ix 1.1–2n; not here the linking of everything in universal concord under God's providence but a binding chain of necessity. On this distinction, see 'providence' in the *SEnc*, and

McCabe 1989a *passim*, esp. 159–60.　**9 excheat**: spoil, gain; or simply exchange.

Stanza 26

1 freely: without punishment.　**2 some**: includes one who cannot be named in the lower world, i.e. Christ; but also Arthur: see viii 40.4–6.　**4 price**: pay for. In his debate with Despaire, the knight invokes justice as simple revenge: 'With thine owne blood to price his blood' (ix 37.9), only to be overcome by Despaire's argument that 'blood must blood repay' (43.6).　**5** Night's ultimate question is the ultimate matrilinear question, as Roche 1995:23 notes.　**6** Duessa's state parodies that of Una who 'Did seeme such, as she was' (xii 8.9), and of God who declares 'I am that I am' (Exod. 3.14). When Duessa is stripped, she is seen 'Such as she was' (viii 46.6).　**7 how euer**: although.　**gilt**: gilded. The rhyme with **guilt** conveys its secondary meaning.　**9 Shame**: the first of the four degrees of death, the guiltiness that is the first effect of Adam and Eve's sinning in Gen. 3.7, 10.

Stanza 27

3 false: even the image of Deceit is not true.　**4 closely**: secretly.　**6–7** Conti 1616:3.12 lists Fraud among the descendants of Night.　**falshood**: a nice pun – Duessa wears a false hood.

Stanza 28

2 fowle welfauourd: a variant of the usual 'false-fair' oxymoron.　**3 mirkesome**: coined by S. to suggest dense, heavy,

29

So well they sped, that they be come at length
   Vnto the place, whereas the Paynim lay,
   Deuoid of outward sence, and natiue strength,
   Couerd with charmed cloud from vew of day,
   And sight of men, since his late luckelesse fray.
   His cruell wounds with cruddy bloud congeald,
   They binden vp so wisely, as they may,
   And handle softly, till they can be heald:
So lay him in her charett, close in night conceald.

30

And all the while she stood vpon the ground,
   The wakefull dogs did neuer cease to bay,
   As giuing warning of th'vnwonted sound,
   With which her yron wheeles did them affray,
   And her darke griesly looke them much dismay;
   The messenger of death, the ghastly owle
   With drery shriekes did also her bewray;
   And hungry wolues continually did howle,
At her abhorred face, so filthy and so fowle.

31

Thence turning backe in silence softe they stole,
   And brought the heauy corse with easy pace
   To yawning gulfe of deepe *Auernus* hole.
   By that same hole an entraunce darke and bace

With smoake and sulphur hiding all the place,
   Descends to hell: there creature neuer past,
   That backe retourned without heauenly grace;
   But dreadfull *Furies*, which their chaines haue brast,
And damned sprights sent forth to make ill men aghast.

32

By that same way the direfull dames doe driue
   Their mournefull charett, fild with rusty blood,
   And downe to *Plutoes* house are come biliue:
   Which passing through, on euery side them stood
   The trembling ghosts with sad amazed mood,
   Chattring their iron teeth, and staring wide
   With stony eies; and all the hellish brood
   Of feends infernall flockt on euery side,
To gaze on erthly wight, that with the Night durst ride.

33

They pas the bitter waues of *Acheron*,
   Where many soules sit wailing woefully,
   And come to fiery flood of *Phlegeton*,
   Whereas the damned ghosts in torments fry,
   And with sharp shrilling shriekes doe bootlesse cry,
   Cursing high *Ioue*, the which them thither sent.
   The house of endlesse paine is built thereby,
   In which ten thousand sorts of punishment
The cursed creatures doe eternally torment.

---

polluted, so that air becomes an element in which the horses swim. **ready**: lying directly before her; or the adv. 'readily'. **4 twyfold**: indicating her duplicity. **5 browne**: dark. **vnlich**: unlike. Night's steeds resemble Luna's which, according to Conti 1616:3.17, are drawn by horses *discoloribus albo et nigro*. **9** The **element** is air, which is **fine** in relation to the other elements. **ramp**: rear on their hind legs.

Stanza 29

6 cruddy: clotted. **7 wisely**: skilfully; carefully. **9 in night**: S.'s allegorical technique allows him to shift from personifying night to referring to it.

Stanza 30

2–5 As in Virgil, *Aen*. 6.257–58, where dogs howl at the coming of Hecate. **6–7 owle**: the traditional bird of ill omen that inhabits desolation and wilderness, as in Isa. 34.11–15 and *Teares* 283–84; an omen of death in Chaucer, *Parl. Fowls* 343, and II vii 23.3–5. **ghastly**: causing terror; cf. ix 33.6–8. **bewray**: reveal.

Stanza 31

3 Auernus: a dark lake by a deep cave with a hole that leads down to hell (*Aen*. 6.237–38). **4 By**: by means of. **bace**: low in height. **6–7** In *Aen*. 6.126–31, the Sibyl tells Aeneas that those who have returned from hell either have been loved by Jove or have been raised by their own merit. In contrast, **heauenly grace** alludes to Christ's descent into hell to free the imprisoned souls by his merit not their own. **8 Furies**: the hellish spirits of discord; see iii 36.8. **chaines**: this detail may be original, as Lotspeich 1932 claims, but it is suggested by

Aen. 6.555–58. See also ix 24.5. **brast**: burst. **9 ill**: wicked. **aghast**: terrified (by death).

Stanza 32

The inflated diction and the exaggerated details indicate a parody of the classical descent to hell, esp. in Virgil, *Aen*. 6. See Hamilton 1961a:70–71, and Gless 1994:101–02. As a motif in the poem, see Maresca 1979:13–73. **1 direfull dames**: suggested by the 'dreadfull *Furies*' of 31.8 (Lat. *Dirae*). **2** Night's chariot, at 28.1 and 29.9, is now also Duessa's. **fild**: defiled; also filled. **rusty**: blood-blackened; defiled. See iv 35.4*n*. **3 biliue**: quickly; or a pun on being alive, as 9 may suggest. **7 stony**: fixed.

Stanza 33

1–6 Two of the four rivers of Hades are named while line 5 describes the behaviour of those on the banks of Cocytus, the river of lamentation (cf. II vii 56.8–9), and the Styx was alluded to obliquely at 10.6. The epithet given each river suggests the Greek name. **Acheron**: from ἄχος pain, the woeful river of death, **bitter** in being full of grief. According to Badius, *Virgilii Opera* 255ʳ (cited Nelson 1963:155), the name is derived from the Gk ἀ + χαρά: *absque laetitia*, i.e. sans joy; or *sine gaudio* in Servius's note to *Aen*. 6.107. **Phlegeton**: φλέγω burn, the river of fire, as in *Aen*. 6.551 (cf. II vi 50.9), which is also the 'lake of fyre, burning with brimstone' (Rev. 19.20) into which the damned are cast. **bootlesse**: as the ghosts are helpless, or their crying is without avail. **7** Cf. the infernal castle in *Aen*. 6.548–72 where the dead are tortured; and the house of grief and pain in Tasso, *Ger. Lib*. 9.59.

34

Before the threshold dreadfull *Cerberus*
    His three deformed heads did lay along,
    Curled with thousand adders venemous,
    And lilled forth his bloody flaming tong:
    At them he gan to reare his bristles strong,
    And felly gnarre, vntill Dayes enemy
    Did him appease; then downe his taile he hong
    And suffered them to passen quietly:
For she in hell and heauen had power equally.

35

There was *Ixion* turned on a wheele,
    For daring tempt the Queene of heauen to sin;
    And *Sisyphus* an huge round stone did reele
    Against an hill, ne might from labour lin;
    There thristy *Tantalus* hong by the chin;
    And *Tityus* fed a vultur on his maw;
    Typhoeus ioynts were stretched on a gin,
    Theseus condemned to endlesse slouth by law
And fifty sisters water in leke vessels draw.

36

They all beholding worldly wights in place,
    Leaue off their worke, vnmindfull of their smart,
    To gaze on them; who forth by them doe pace,
    Till they be come vnto the furthest part:

Where was a Caue ywrought by wondrous art,
    Deepe, darke, vneasy, dolefull, comfortlesse,
    In which sad *Aesculapius* far apart
    Emprisond was in chaines remedilesse,
For that *Hippolytus* rent corse he did redresse.

37

Hippolytus a iolly huntsman was,
    That wont in charett chace the foming bore;
    He all his Peeres in beauty did surpas,
    But Ladies loue as losse of time forbore:
    His wanton stepdame loued him the more,
    But when she saw her offred sweets refusd
    Her loue she turnd to hate, and him before
    His father fierce of treason false accusd,
And with her gealous termes his open eares abusd.

38

Who all in rage his Sea-god syre besought,
    Some cursed vengeaunce on his sonne to cast:
    From surging gulf two Monsters streight were brought,
    With dread whereof his chacing steedes aghast,
    Both charett swifte and huntsman ouercast.
    His goodly corps on ragged cliffs yrent,
    Was quite dismembred, and his members chast
    Scattered on euery mountaine, as he went,
That of *Hippolytus* was lefte no moniment.

Stanza 34

1 Cerberus: the three-headed dog that guards the entrance to hell in *Aen.* 6.417–23; cf. *Gnat* 345–52, 440. **2 along**: at full length. **4 lilled forth**: lolled out. **6 felly gnarre**: fiercely snarl, 'r' being 'the *Dogs* Letter', according to Jonson 1925–52:8.491. **7 appease**: either by a cake laced with a drug, as in *Aen.* 6.420; or by a clod of earth, as in Dante, *Inf.* 6.26–27. **9** Echoing Virgil, *Aen.* 6.247: *caeloque Erboque potentem* describes Hecate's power.

Stanza 35

The punishments of these traditional sufferers in hell are drawn indirectly from Seneca, Virgil, and Ovid, and ultimately from Homer (*Ody.* 11.576–635), though Renaissance mythological handbooks and dictionaries made them common knowledge. S. follows Conti's (1616) order, as Lotspeich 1932 notes. For **Ixion** to **Typhoeus** he follows his list of those who seek what cannot be obtained from the gods (6.16–22); he adds **Theseus** from his list of illustrious men (7.9), and the fifty sisters from 9.17. Three are guilty of sexual assault against goddesses, three of scorning or rebelling against the gods, and the fifty sisters of slaying their husbands. **2 the Queene of heauen**: Juno. See 'Juno' in the *SEnc*. **3 reele**: cause to roll. **4 lin**: cease. **5 hong by the chin**: as though suspended up to the chin in water; see II vii 58.1. **6 maw**: liver. **7 gin**: rack. The punishment may have been devised by S. For **Typhoeus** (or Typhon), see III vii 47.6–9 and VI vi 10–12*n*. **8 Theseus**: condemned to sit forever in the chair of forgetfulness; see II vii 63.6–9*n*. See 'Theseus' in the *SEnc*, and i 11.5*n*. **9 fifty sisters**: the Danaides (or Belides) who murdered their husbands on their wedding night; see *Gnat* 393–96.

Stanza 36

1–3 In Ovid, *Met.* 10.40–44, the damned pause in their toil to wonder at Orpheus's music. **in place**: present. **worldly**: mortal. **6 vneasy**: entirely without ease or comfort, emphasized by its central place in a line which is itself **ywrought by wondrous art**, applying more to S. than to Æsculapius. **comfortlesse**: helpless; desolate. **Aesculapius** is not one to whom Christ's promise – 'I wil not leaue you comfortles' (John 14.18) – is given; cf. vi 6.1. **7–9** As he is the false Christ who heals the body but not the soul, see Hamilton 1961a:70–71, Nohrnberg 1976:172–73, and Røstvig 1994:302–04. His epithet, **sad**, allies him with the Red Cross Knight, Sansjoy, and Night, as Gless 1994:103 notes. **remedilesse**: beyond all remedy; without hope of release. Cf. vii 51.8. **redresse**: restore, deliver from death.

Stanzas 37–40

The story of Hippolytus who was slain by the treachery of his stepmother Phaedra but restored to life by Æsculapius, the god of healing, was well-known; see 'Aesculapius' in the *SEnc*. It is told again at V viii 43. That Phaedra killed herself with a knife is added by S., as Lotspeich 1932 notes.

Stanza 37

1 iolly: gallant; brave. **9 gealous termes**: words arousing jealousy.

Stanza 38

1 Theseus's **Sea-god syre** is Neptune. **3 two Monsters**: from the sea monsters in Virgil, *Aen.* 7.780, but here they suggest two tsunamis: the first overturns the chariot and the

39

His cruell stepdame seeing what was donne,
  Her wicked daies with wretched knife did end,
  In death auowing th'innocence of her sonne.
  Which hearing his rash Syre, began to rend
  His heare, and hasty tong, that did offend:
  Tho gathering vp the relicks of his smart
  By *Dianes* meanes, who was *Hippolyts* frend,
Them brought to *Aesculape*, that by his art
Did heale them all againe, and ioyned euery part.

40

Such wondrous science in mans witt to rain
  When *Ioue* auizd, that could the dead reuiue,
  And fates expired could renew againe,
  Of endlesse life he might him not depriue,
  But vnto hell did thrust him downe aliue,
  With flashing thunderbolt ywounded sore:
  Where long remaining, he did alwaies striue
Him selfe with salues to health for to restore,
And slake the heauenly fire, that raged euermore.

41

There auncient Night arriuing, did alight
  From her nigh weary wayne, and in her armes
  To *AEsculapius* brought the wounded knight:
  Whome hauing softly disaraid of armes,
  Tho gan to him discouer all his harmes,
  Beseeching him with prayer, and with praise,
  If either salues, or oyles, or herbes, or charmes
A fordonne wight from dore of death mote raise,
He would at her request prolong her nephews daies.

42

Ah Dame (quoth he) thou temptest me in vaine,
  To dare the thing, which daily yet I rew,
  And the old cause of my continued paine
  With like attempt to like end to renew.
  Is not enough, that thrust from heauen dew
  Here endlesse penaunce for one fault I pay,
  But that redoubled crime with vengeaunce new
Thou biddest me to eeke? Can Night defray
The wrath of thundring *Ioue*, that rules both night and day?

43

Not so (quoth she) but sith that heauens king
  From hope of heauen hath thee excluded quight,
  Why fearest thou, that canst not hope for thing,
  And fearest not, that more thee hurten might,
  Now in the powre of euerlasting Night?
  Goe to then, O thou far renowmed sonne
  Of great *Apollo*, shew thy famous might
In medicine, that els hath to thee wonne
Great pains, and greater praise, both neuer to be donne.

44

Her words preuaild: And then the learned leach
  His cunning hand gan to his wounds to lay,
  And all things els, the which his art did teach:
  Which hauing seene, from thence arose away
  The mother of dredd darkenesse, and let stay
  Aueugles sonne there in the leaches cure,
  And backe retourning tooke her wonted way,
To ronne her timely race, whilst *Phoebus* pure
In westerne waues his weary wagon did recure.

---

second mangles the huntsman. **7 chast**: an implied pun. Following the chase, rather than love, proves his chastity, but his **members chast** are destroyed by his **chacing steedes**. **9 moniment**: trace, identifying mark.

Stanza 39

6 Then gathering up the fragments of the body which cause his grief.

Stanza 40

1 science: skill. **2 auizd**: observed. **3 fates expired**: the completed term of life determined by the Fates; cf. 'suffised fates' (ii 43.8). **7–9** The biblical injunction, 'Physician, heal thyself', is implicit here: Æsculapius may heal Hippolytus's wounds but not his own.

Stanza 41

2 nigh weary wayne: the horses of Night's chariot are exhausted either because night is far spent (for the pun on 'wane', cf. III viii 51.5) or because of their unusual journey down to earth (cf. 30.3) and then to hell. **5 discouer**: literally, 'lay bare'. **8 fordonne**: utterly overcome.

Stanza 42

5 dew: deserved as an immortal, or for his art. **6** His state is the human condition before the coming of Christ. **penaunce**: punishment. **7–8 eeke**: augment. **redoubled** may be pro-

leptic: 'you bid me to add to my crime by redoubling it'; but it is simpler to refer **eeke** to **vengeaunce**. **defray**: settle, appease.

Stanza 43

3 **thing**: i.e. anything. She argues for despair. **4 that**: referring to herself, or her power. **5 euerlasting**: asserting her own immortality over that of the gods. **6–9** Apollo 'first inuented the use of phisike, and therby deserued the name of a God' (T. Cooper 1565); cf. Ovid, *Met.* 1.521–22, and III iv 41.3. At IV xii 25.4 he is named 'King of Leaches'. **els**: already, formerly. **donne**: ended; surpassed.

Stanza 44

4–6 The further fortunes of Sansjoy need not be told: none return from hell 'without heauenly grace' (31.7). **cure**: charge, care; combined with the current sense (as Arg.4). **8–9 timely race**: in the astronomical sense, the measured course through the heavens which is fulfilled in time, and in contrast to her journey to hell. A reference to **Phoebus pure** fittingly concludes the episode which began with Duessa's journey to Night 'That *Phœbus* chearefull face durst neuer vew' (20.2). The natural cycle of the sun's renewal contrasts with Sansjoy's infernal descent to be renewed, and the state of Aesculapius who remains 'remedilesse' (36.8). **pure**: purified and purifying light limits the reign of foul darkness. **recure**: restore to health, refresh.

45

The false *Duessa* leauing noyous Night,
    Returnd to stately pallace of Dame *Pryde*;
    Where when she came, she found the Faery knight
    Departed thence, albee his woundes wyde
    Not throughly heald, vnready were to ryde.
    Good cause he had to hasten thence away;
    For on a day his wary Dwarfe had spyde,
    Where in a dungeon deepe huge nombers lay
Of caytiue wretched thralls, that wayled night and day.

46

A ruefull sight, as could be seene with eie;
    Of whom he learned had in secret wise
    The hidden cause of their captiuitie,
    How mortgaging their liues to *Couetise*,
    Through wastfull Pride, and wanton Riotise,
    They were by law of that proud Tyrannesse
    Prouokt with *Wrath*, and *Enuyes* false surmise,
    Condemned to that Dongeon mercilesse,
Where they should liue in wo, and dye in wretchednesse.

47

There was that great proud king of *Babylon,*
    That would compell all nations to adore,
    And him as onely God to call vpon,
    Till through celestiall doome thrown out of dore,
    Into an Oxe he was transformd of yore:
    There also was king *Crœsus*, that enhaunst
    His hart too high through his great richesse store;
    And proud *Antiochus*, the which aduaunst
His cursed hand gainst God, and on his altares daunst.

48

And them long time before, great *Nimrod* was,
    That first the world with sword and fire warrayd;
    And after him old *Ninus* far did pas
    In princely pomp, of all the world obayd;
    There also was that mightie Monarch layd
    Low vnder all, yet aboue all in pride,
    That name of natiue syre did fowle vpbrayd,
    And would as *Ammons* sonne be magnifide,
Till scornd of God and man a shamefull death he dide.

Stanza 45

1 noyous: obnoxious, causing harm; as xi 50.9. **4 albee**: although. **7 wary**: the term defines the dwarf's allegorical function; cf. his response to Errour's den at i 13.8–9. In observing that Bateman's *Travayled Pylgrime* (1569) is the only other published Protestant allegory that describes the journey of a knight from error to salvation, Prescott 1989:184 notes that he leaves the 'palace of disordered livers' when Memory, who looks like Reason, holds up a mirror that shows his sins. **9 caytiue**: captive, and therefore wretched.

Stanza 46

4 mortgaging: in its etymological sense, 'offering a death-pledge'. **Couetise**: covetousness or avarice described at iv 27–29. **5 wastfull**: causing desolation. **wanton**: undisciplined. **Riotise**: riotous conduct, the life of Idlenesse at iv 20.5. **6–7** 'For the Law causeth wrath' (Rom. 4.15). Here envy carries the larger sense: malignant feeling, ill-will (*OED* 1), as Wisd. Sol. 2.24 records that 'thorow enuy of the deuil came death into the worlde'. **surmise**: charge, imputation; possibly suspicion. Enuie and Wrath ride together, the final pair of councillors in Lucifera's procession of sins. If **wanton** includes Gluttony and Lecherie, all the deadly sins are included in this stanza. **Tyrannesse**: the female tyrant (Lucifera), a term first attrib. to S. by the *OED* and first used here. **8 mercilesse**: without hope of mercy. **9** 'For when we were in the flesh, the motions of sinnes, which were by the Law, had force in our membres, to bring forthe frute vnto death' (Rom. 7.5).

Stanzas 47–50

A catalogue of the fall of 'mightie men' (50.1), as in Boccaccio, *De casibus virorum illustrium* and Chaucer, *Monk's Tale*. The historical counterpart to the mythological figures catalogued in 35, and the classical counterpart to the 'wofull falles' (51.3) of corresponding English figures in *A Mirror for Magistrates*. Of

the 'huge nombers' (45.8), S. names three proud kings (47), three world conquerors (48), ten Roman emperors (49), and three queens (50).

Stanza 47

1–5 king of Babylon: Nebuchadnezzar; see Dan. 3–6. The golden image that he had set up to be worshipped is taken to be his own image. For such idolatry, he has first place. As does Gower 1980:1.2993–96, S. assumes that since he 'did eat grasse as the oxen' (Dan. 4.30), he was transformed into an ox. **4 doome**: judgement. **6–7 Crœsus**: the last king of Lydia, proverbial for his wealth. S. assumes that he was proud because of his wealth. **enhaunst**: lifted up in pride. **8–9 Antiochus**: S. assumes that when he desecrated the altar, as recorded in 1 Macc. 1.23, he danced upon it, perhaps suggested by 2 Macc. 6.4–5.

Stanza 48

1–2 Nimrod: the name means 'cruel oppressor and tyrant' (Geneva gloss); **great** as the first giant: 'Nimrod who began to be mighty in the earth' (Gen. 10.8), a verse taken to refer to the origin of giants. The founder of Babylon (T. Cooper 1565) who 'moued with pride and ambition' (Geneva gloss to Gen. 11.4) built the tower of Babel. **warrayd**: ravaged. **3–4 Ninus**: 'the fyrst that made warre. He conquered vnto Indie' (Cooper). Famous as the founder of the great but wicked city (see Jonah 1.1) but notorious for 'old Ninny's tomb'. Cf. II ix 21.5–6, 56.8. **5–9 that mightie Monarch** is Alexander the Great, fittingly left unamed, and **layd | Low vnder all** as fitting punishment for his **shamefull death**. Through pride, he found fault with (**vpbrayd**) his natural father and claimed to be the son of Jupiter Ammon. In proclaiming himself a god, 'he fell into suche crueltie and pryde . . . that he became odious to his owne people . . . at the laste whan he was in his most glory at the citie of Babylon . . . [he] was poisoned by drinkyng out of a cup' (Cooper).

49

All these together in one heape were throwne,
  Like carkases of beastes in butchers stall.
  And in another corner wide were strowne
  The Antique ruins of the *Romanes* fall: *ruins of empire*
  Great *Romulus* the Grandsyre of them all,
  Proud *Tarquin*, and too lordly *Lentulus*,
  Stout *Scipio*, and stubborne *Hanniball*,
  Ambitious *Sylla*, and sterne *Marius*,
High *Cæsar*, great *Pompey*, and fiers *Antonius*.

50

Amongst these mightie men were wemen mixt,
  Proud wemen vaine, forgetfull of their yoke:
  The bold *Semiramis*, whose sides transfixt
  With sonnes own blade, her fowle reproches spoke;
  Fayre *Sthenobœa*, that her selfe did choke
  With wilfull chord, for wanting of her will;
  High minded *Cleopatra*, that with stroke
  Of Aspes sting her selfe did stoutly kill:
And thousands moe the like, that did that dongeon fill.

51

Besides the endlesse routes of wretched thralles,
  Which thether were assembled day by day,
  From all the world after their wofull falles,
  Through wicked pride, and wasted welthes decay.

But most of all, which in that Dongeon lay
  Fell from high Princes courtes, or Ladies bowres,
  Where they in ydle pomp, or wanton play,
  Consumed had their goods, and thriftlesse howres,
And lastly thrown themselues into these heauy stowres.

52

Whose case whenas the carefull Dwarfe had tould,
  And made ensample of their mournfull sight
  Vnto his maister, he no lenger would
  There dwell in perill of like painefull plight,
  But early rose, and ere that dawning light
  Discouered had the world to heauen wyde,
  He by a priuy Posterne tooke his flight,
  That of no enuious eyes he mote be spyde:
For doubtlesse death ensewed, if any him descryde.

53

Scarse could he footing find in that fowle way,
  For many corses, like a great Lay-stall
  Of murdred men which therein strowed lay,
  Without remorse, or decent funerall:
  Which al through that great Princesse pride did fall
  And came to shamefull end. And them besyde
  Forth ryding vnderneath the castell wall,
  A Donghill of dead carcases he spyde,
The dreadfull spectacle of that sad house of *Pryde*.

Stanza 49

1–2 in one heape: a fitting death for the builders of towers and cities. It is fitting, too, that Nimrod who in life hunted men like beasts in death lies like a beast. **3–9** These Roman emperors, seen lying apart (**wide**), would be well known to any Elizabethan schoolboy. Most of the material is in T. Cooper 1565 and Plutarch. Except for Lentulus, they are grouped in roughly chronological order from the founding of Rome to the end of the republic, and each is given a fitting epithet. **Great Romulus** was the first king of Rome, and therefore the **Grandsyre**; the last was **Proud Tarquin**, 'for his proud and sterne behauiour surnamed *superbus*' (Cooper). **too lordly Lentulus**: Cornelius, who attempted to set Rome on fire. **Stout Scipio** is Scipio Africanus, known for his martial prowess in vanquishing Hannibal and the people of Africa; his courage is noted by Cooper. **Hanniball** gains the epithet **stubborne** for his constant war against the Romans: he took poison rather than become their prisoner. **Ambitious Sylla** because he was 'desirous of glorie' (Cooper) and became dictator of Rome. He was engaged in civil war with **Marius** who is called **sterne** for his courage. 'Of this man [Cæsar] and Pompei it was saide, that they weare of so haute courages, that the one could not abyde an equall, the other a superiour' (Cooper). **great Pompey**: Pompey the Great. By his war with Caesar, 'al the world almost was vexed and troubled' (Cooper). **fiers Antonius**: 'fierce' in love and war.

Stanza 50

3–4 bold Semiramis: after her husband Ninus died, fearing that the people 'would be loth to be gouerned by a woman', she disguised herself as her son and became famous for her bravery. 'At the last falling from noblenesse to sensuall luste,

she desired the companie of hir owne sonne, and of him was slayne' (T. Cooper 1565); cf. II x 56.2. The lustful in the second circle of Dante, *Inf.* 5, are led by Semiramis, followed by Dido and Cleopatra. **5–6 Fayre Sthenobœa** lusted after her brother-in-law, Bellerophon, but was refused by him. **With wilfull chord**: i.e. with cord wilfully, suggesting her despair, which may account for her death by hanging rather than by poison; see ix 22.7*n*.

Stanza 51

1–2 Cf. iv 3.1–2. **4 welthes**: in the more general sense of the term, 'well-being', though its usual sense is suggested by 8. **decay**: downfall. **9 stowres**: afflictions.

Stanza 52

1 carefull: 'wary' (45.7). **2 ensample**: warning. **3** The line breaks at the end to fit the sense. **7 priuy Posterne**: secret back door, as the 'backgate' of the castle of Alma (II ix 32.7–9), and the cleft of the rock by which Dante is excreted from Satan's body (*Inf.* 34.85). **8 enuious**: malicious.

Stanza 53

2 Lay-stall: a burial place, literally a place where the dead are laid; cf. 'butchers stall' (49.2). **4 decent**: fitting. Lacking burial, Lucifera's victims lack the promise of resurrection; see 23.3–4*n*. **8–9 spectacle** refers to the completed vision of the house of Pride from the towering turrets above to the dungeon below and the garbage-heap round about. **that sad house of Pryde**: finally named, after two cantos of description in which its name was either not mentioned, or referred to by the indefinite article (iv 2.6 and 4.1) or no article at all (v 45.2).

Cant. VI.

From lawlesse lust by wondrous grace
fayre Vna is releast:
Whom saluage nation does adore,
and learnes her wise beheast.

1

A S when a ship, that flyes fayre vnder sayle,
  An hidden rocke escaped hath vnwares,
  That lay in waite her wrack for to bewaile,
  The Marriner yet halfe amazed stares
  At perill past, and yet in doubt ne dares
  To ioy at his foolhappie ouersight:
  So doubly is distrest twixt ioy and cares
  The dreadlesse corage of this Elfin knight,
Hauing escapt so sad ensamples in his sight.

2

Yet sad he was, that his too hastie speed
  The fayre *Duess'* had forst him leaue behind;
  And yet more sad, that *Vna* his deare dreed
  Her truth had staynd with treason so vnkind;
  Yet cryme in her could neuer creature find,
  But for his loue, and for her own selfe sake,
  She wandred had from one to other *Ynd,* *indies*
  Him for to seeke, ne euer would forsake,
Till her vnwares the fiers *Sansloy* did ouertake.

3

Who after *Archimagoes* fowle defeat,
  Led her away into a forest wilde,
  And turning wrathfull fyre to lustfull heat,
  With beastly sin thought her to haue defilde,
  And made the vassall of his pleasures vilde.
  Yet first he cast by treatie, and by traynes,
  Her to persuade, that stubborne fort to yilde:
  For greater conquest of hard loue he gaynes,
That workes it to his will, then he that it constraines.

4

With fawning wordes he courted her a while,
  And looking louely, and oft sighing sore,
  Her constant hart did tempt with diuerse guile:
  But wordes, and lookes, and sighes she did abhore,
  As rock of Diamond stedfast euermore.
  Yet for to feed his fyrie lustfull eye,
  He snatcht the vele, that hong her face before;
  Then gan her beautie shyne, as brightest skye,
And burnt his beastly hart t'efforce her chastitye.

Book I Canto vi

Argument

3 saluage nation: see 11.3*n.* **4 wise beheast**: in contrast to the 'bestiall beheasts' (iv 18.3) of Lucifera's councillors.

Stanza 1

The simile extends iii 31–32 and again marks a point at which perils seem past but in fact lie ahead. **3** The context suggests simply, 'to cause the ship's wreck'. Yet **bewaile** may be an error for 'assayle' (cf. 5.3), i.e. assault (cf. II ii 24.1–3); or derive from 'wale', i.e. 'choose': the rock chooses the ship to wreck it; or it may suggest the consequences of the wreck: the rock causes the ship's wreck to be bewailed; or, since Duessa is linked to the rock, her crocodile tears may be implied (cf. v 18): the rock only appears to be sorry for the wreck it causes (see Tilley C831); or a wave-washed rock may be said to be weeping, as Cymoent wails so piteously 'That the hard rocks could scarse from tears refraine' (III iv 35.7). **5 doubt**: fear. **6 foolhappie**: plain lucky or fortunate. **8 dreadlesse corage**: apparently he deserves this epithet even when he flees from danger. **9 ensamples**: warnings; cf. v 52.2.

Stanza 2

3 dreed: object of reverence and awe; cf. the address to Gloriana at proem 4.9. **4 vnkind**: contrary to her nature. **5 cryme**: wrong-doing, sin. **7 one to other Ynd**: East to the West Indies, proverbial for 'throughout the world'. **8** The echo **seeke / forsake** recalls God's frequent vow to his people that 'he wil not forsake thee' (Deut. 4.31).

Stanza 3

2 a forest wilde: the poem's allegorical landscape for violent, primitive, and archetypal experience, in contrast to the plain on which knights may fight on horseback to uphold their virtues. See 'woods' in the *SEnc*. **5 vassall**: in this context, suggesting a play on 'vessel'. **6 treatie**: entreaty. **traynes**: guile.

Stanza 4

1 fawning wordes: see 12.9*n.* **2 louely**: lovingly. **3 diuerse**: of different kinds; also as it seeks to lead her astray; cf. i 44.2*n.* **5 rock of Diamond**: see vii 33.5–9*n.* It is associated with truth, as Maplet 1930:18 records: 'Iorach calleth it an other eie: such certaintie and truth giveth it in things done in his presence'. As Una is associated with truth and faith, it refers to the rock upon which Christ promises to build his church at Matt.16:18. **7–9** As Solomon's bride complains that 'the watchemen of the walles toke away my vaile from me' (Song Sol. 5.7). The Geneva gloss explains that the bride is the Church, the watchmen 'false teachers'. Sansloy's action parallels that of Kirkrapine who disrobed the saints, iii 17.5–6. See iv 9.9 for the distinction, used here, between heavenly light that shines and infernal fire that burns. **efforce**: overcome by force.

5

So when he saw his flatt'ring artes to fayle,
  And subtile engines bett from batteree,
  With greedy force he gan the fort assayle,
  Whereof he weend possessed soone to bee,
  And win rich spoile of ransackt chastitee.
  Ah heauens, that doe this hideous act behold,
  And heauenly virgin thus outraged see,
  How can ye vengeance iust so long withhold,
And hurle not flashing flames vpon that Paynim bold?

6

The pitteous mayden carefull comfortlesse,
  Does throw out thrilling shriekes, and shrieking cryes,
  The last vaine helpe of wemens great distresse,
  And with loud plaintes importuneth the skyes,
  That molten starres doe drop like weeping eyes;
  And Phœbus flying so most shamefull sight,
  His blushing face in foggy cloud implyes,
  And hydes for shame. What witt of mortall wight
Can now deuise to quitt a thrall from such a plight?

7

Eternall prouidence exceeding thought,
  Where none appeares can make her selfe a way:
  A wondrous way it for this Lady wrought,
  From Lyons clawes to pluck the gryped pray.

Her shrill outcryes and shrieks so loud did bray,
  That all the woodes and forestes did resownd;
  A troupe of Faunes and Satyres far a way
  Within the wood were dauncing in a rownd,
Whiles old Syluanus slept in shady arber sownd.

8

Who when they heard that pitteous strained voice,
  In haste forsooke their rurall meriment,
  And ran towards the far rebownded noyce,
  To weet, what wight so loudly did lament.
  Vnto the place they come incontinent:
  Whom when the raging Sarazin espyde,
  A rude, mishapen, monstrous rablement,
  Whose like he neuer saw, he durst not byde,
But got his ready steed, and fast away gan ryde.

9

The wyld woodgods arriued in the place,
  There find the virgin doolfull desolate,
  With ruffled rayments, and fayre blubbred face,
  As her outrageous foe had left her late,
  And trembling yet through feare of former hate;
  All stand amazed at so vncouth sight,
  And gin to pittie her vnhappie state,
  All stand astonied at her beautie bright,
In their rude eyes vnworthy of so wofull plight.

Stanza 5
2 subtile engines: cleverly contrived machines of warfare – the courtly wiles – used to assault 'that stubborne fort' (3.7). **bett from batteree**: beaten from their battering. **3** One such historical moment is prophesied by Merlin: a Norwegian King shall overrun Britain 'And holy Church with faithlesse handes deface' (III iii 34.2). **7 outraged**: violated.

Stanza 6
1 carefull: full of grief. **comfortlesse**: helpless, desolate. The word signals the intervention of 'wondrous grace' (Arg.1) according to God's promise: 'I wil not leaue you comfortles' (John 14.18); see v 36.6n. **2 thrilling**: piercing. **5–8** Signs of the Last Judgement: 'immediatly after the tribulations of those dayes, shal the sunne be darkened . . . and the starres shal fall from heauen' (Matt. 24.29); also signs of nature's sympathy for her 'goddess'. **molten**: both liquefied by heat and dissolved into tears. **implyes**: conceals. **8–9** S. wittily alludes to his own **witt**: what other poet would devise fawns and satyrs as instruments of God's grace to rescue the Church in its moment of greatest peril? **9 quitt**: set free.

Stanza 7
1–2 A major doctrine of the poem, repeated at III v 27.1, and based on Eph 3.19: 'the loue of Christ . . . passeth knowledge'. See 'providence' in the SEnc. **7 Faunes and Satyres**: Lat. and Gk woodland deities. E.K. glosses 'the holy Faunes' (SC July 77): 'of Poetes feigned to be Gods of the Woode'. Although they mingle here, they are distinguished by name and nature: Conti 1616:10 explains that 'Faunes' are tutelary deities who protect those in their territory, for 'nothing can happen, even in field or forest, without the knowledge of God';

noted Lemmi 1929:275. **Satyres** are half men and half goats traditionally characterized by their uninhibited sexual passion and virility, and therefore symbolize concupiscence (see 'satyrs' in the SEnc). They are associated with the desolation of Palestine when 'the Satyrs shal dance there' (Isa. 13.21), and their presence here has been variously identified: historically, as ignorant Christians (Steadman 1979:133), the Jews (Jordan 1977), savage people responding to religion (Hume 1984:88–89), the Gaelic population of Ireland (Jardine 1993:69); morally, as 'nature without nurture' (Nohrnberg 1976:221), or uncorrupted human nature (Gless 1994:106–08). **8 rownd**: either the circle into which they draw Una (13.6) or the name of their dance. See 'dance' in the SEnc. **9 old Syluanus**: their sylvan god shares their twofold nature being the son of Faunus, the Roman Pan, and the father of satyrs; the epithet is from Virgil 2.494, and always accompanies his name. Being old, he is senile, as silva-vanus.

Stanza 8
3 rebownded: re-echoed. **5 incontinent**: headlong, intemperate in their haste.

Stanza 9
2 desolate: her state when she is befriended by the Lion at iii 9.1; cf. vii 50.1, x 60.4. **3 blubbred**: wet with tears (with no suggestion of the ludicrous). **4 outrageous**: violent; as one who 'outraged' her at 5.7. **5 hate**: both one who hated her, and one whom she hated. **6 vncouth**: strange; marvellous, as 8 suggests; but cf. i 50.1. **8 astonied**: stunned; as Job declares that the righteous will be 'astonied' when they see his suffering state (17.8).

10

She more amazd, in double dread doth dwell;
   And euery tender part for feare does shake:
   As when a greedy Wolfe through honger fell
   A seely Lamb far from the flock does take,
   Of whom he meanes his bloody feast to make,
   A Lyon spyes fast running towards him,
   The innocent pray in hast he does forsake,
   Which quitt from death yet quakes in euery lim
With chaunge of feare, to see the Lyon looke so grim.

11

Such fearefull fitt assaid her trembling hart,
   Ne word to speake, ne ioynt to moue she had:
   The saluage nation feele her secret smart,
   And read her sorrow in her count'nance sad;
   Their frowning forheades with rough hornes yclad,
   And rustick horror all a syde doe lay,
   And gently grenning, shew a semblance glad
   To comfort her, and feare to put away,
Their backward bent knees teach her humbly to obay.

12

The doubtfull Damzell dare not yet committ,
   Her single person to their barbarous truth,
   But still twixt feare and hope amazd does sitt,
   Late learnd what harme to hasty trust ensu'th:
   They in compassion of her tender youth,
   And wonder of her beautie souerayne,
   Are wonne with pitty and vnwonted ruth,
   And all prostrate vpon the lowly playne,
Doe kisse her feete, and fawne on her with count'nance fayne.

13

Their harts she ghesseth by their humble guise,
   And yieldes her to extremitie of time;
   So from the ground she fearelesse doth arise,
   And walketh forth without suspect of crime:
   They all as glad, as birdes of ioyous Pryme,
   Thence lead her forth, about her dauncing round,
   Shouting, and singing all a shepheards ryme,
   And with greene braunches strowing all the ground,
Do worship her, as Queene, with oliue girlond cround.

14

And all the way their merry pipes they sound,
   That all the woods with doubled Eccho ring,
   And with their horned feet doe weare the ground,
   Leaping like wanton kids in pleasant Spring.
   So towards old *Syluanus* they her bring;
   Who with the noyse awaked, commeth out,
   To weet the cause, his weake steps gouerning,
   And aged limbs on Cypresse stadle stout,
And with an yuie twyne his waste is girt about.

15

Far off he wonders, what them makes so glad,
   Or *Bacchus* merry fruit they did inuent,
   Or *Cybeles* franticke rites haue made them mad;
   They drawing nigh, vnto their God present
   That flowre of fayth and beautie excellent:
   The God himselfe vewing that mirrhour rare,
   Stood long amazd, and burnt in his intent;
   His owne fayre *Dryope* now he thinkes not faire,
And *Pholoe* fowle, when her to this he doth compaire.

Stanza 10

1 amazd: terrified. Cf. her plight at iii 40. **3–7** The wolf and the lion are traditional symbols of brute power; cf. Jer. 5.6: 'Wherefore a lion out of the forest shal slay them, and a wolfe of the wildernes shal destroye them'. The wolf is the traditional symbol of predatory power against the Church. **seely**: innocent, helpless. **9 chaunge of feare**: i.e. from fear of the wolf to fear of the lion. The protective role of the lion, which Sansloy abused (cf. 7.4), is now assumed by the fawns. **grim**: fierce, savage.

Stanza 11

1 assaid: assailed; tested. **3 saluage nation**: from Ital. *selvaggio*, 'sauage, wild . . . of the field' (Florio 1598), as VI viii 35.2, etc. Cf. the 'saluage nation' of 'hideous Giaunts, and halfe beastly men' at II x 7; also VI iv 6.6 and viii 35.2. In the present context, it suggests 'heathen' (as in Deut. 4.27): their 'barbarous truth' (12.2) confronts truth itself in the person of Una. Ireland is so described in *View* 1, which suggests that their worship of Una mirrors the submission of the people of the 'saluage Island' (V xi 39.3) to Irena (Hadfield 1996a:31), or specifically to Catholicism (Coughlan 1989b:51), or to the Anglican church (Highley 1997:127–28). **6 horror**: roughness, referring to the ruggedness of their looks with their bristling hair and horns. **7–9 grenning** provokes her **feare** because of its association with lust, as at III viii 24.6 and IV vii 24.9, etc. **backward bent**: because they have the legs of a

goat. Their kneeling teaches her to humbly obey their desire that she put away fear.

Stanza 12

2 single: as 'single Truth' (*Colin Clout* 727) but playing on various senses of the word: 'solitary' in contrast to their numbers as a nation, and hence 'weak'; 'plain', or 'free from duplicity' in contrast to their uncivilized state; and 'unmarried', as holy church relates to this ignorant nation ready to worship her, or her ass, as their own. **truth**: allegiance, expressed in their act of kneeling. **barbarous** may refer to their lack of language. **9 kisse her feete**: as does the lion at iii 6.1. **fawne**: punning on their nature as fauns and on their fawning worship, as the lion that licked her hands 'with fawning tong' (iii 6.2) reveals his nature, and as Sansloy's 'fawning wordes' (4.1) express his inner lawlessness. **fayne**: glad.

Stanza 13

1 guise: behaviour. **2 to . . . time**: i.e. as time demands. **4 without suspect of crime**: without any apprehension of guilt or without suspicion or fear of being reproached for wrongdoing; as the Red Cross Knight in the house of Holinesse learns to frame his life in righteousness 'without rebuke or blame' (x 45.9). **9 oliue girlond**: the traditional emblem of peace (as II ii 31.7, IV iii 42.5), here signifying the peace between her truth and their 'barbarous truth' (12.2). Cf. the 'girlond greene' with which she is crowned at xii 8.6.

16

The woodborne people fall before her flat,
    And worship her as Goddesse of the wood;
    And old *Syluanus* selfe bethinkes not, what
    To thinke of wight so fayre, but gazing stood,
    In doubt to deeme her borne of earthly brood;
    Sometimes Dame *Venus* selfe he seemes to see,
    But *Venus* neuer had so sober mood;
    Sometimes *Diana* he her takes to be,
But misseth bow, and shaftes, and buskins to her knee.

[handwritten margin note: idolatory/ virtue?]

17

By vew of her he ginneth to reuiue
    His ancient loue, and dearest *Cyparisse*,
    And calles to mind his pourtraiture aliue,
    How fayre he was, and yet not fayre to this,
    And how he slew with glauncing dart amisse
    A gentle Hynd, the which the louely boy
    Did loue as life, aboue all worldly blisse;
    For griefe whereof the lad n'ould after ioy,
But pynd away in anguish and selfewild annoy.

18

The wooddy Nymphes, faire *Hamadryades*
    Her to behold do thether runne apace,
    And all the troupe of light-foot *Naiades*,
    Flocke all about to see her louely face:

But when they vewed haue her heauenly grace,
    They enuy her in their malitious mind,
    And fly away for feare of fowle disgrace:
    But all the *Satyres* scorne their woody kind,
And henceforth nothing faire, but her on earth they find.

19

Glad of such lucke, the luckelesse lucky mayd,
    Did her content to please their feeble eyes,
    And long time with that saluage people stayd,
    To gather breath in many miseryes.
    During which time her gentle wit she plyes,
    To teach them truth, which worship't her in vaine,
    And made her th'Image of Idolatryes;
    But when their bootlesse zeale she did restrayne
From her own worship, they her Asse would worship fayn.

20

It fortuned a noble warlike knight
    By iust occasion to that forrest came,
    To seeke his kindred, and the lignage right,
    From whence he tooke his weldeserued name:
    He had in armes abroad wonne muchell fame,
    And fild far landes with glorie of his might,
    Plaine, faithfull, true, and enimy of shame,
    And euer lou'd to fight for Ladies right,
But in vaine glorious frayes he litle did delight.

Stanza 14

4 wanton: lively, playful. **7–8 gouerning**: i.e. guiding his steps and supporting his limbs, referring figuratively to his love of Cyparissus which sustains him in his feeble age. **stadle**: a tree trunk used as a staff; or a standing tree (*OED* 2), which infers that Sylvanus's life is rooted in his lost love. That it is **Cypresse** (from Virgil, *Georg*.1.20) is explained at 17. **yuie**: sacred to Bacchus and symbol of his festivities; here it refers to his love.

Stanza 15

2 Bacchus merry fruit: grapes; hence wine. **inuent**: find. **3 Cybeles franticke rites**: the mad rites of the Corybantes to honour the Phrygian 'mother of the Gods' (see IV xi 28.1–6*n*). His second guess is close to the truth. **5 excellent**: supreme. **6 mirrhour**: paragon, as a mirror that reflects heavenly faith and beauty. **7** Since Una remains unveiled, her shining beauty burns Sylvanus as it 'burnt . . . [Sansloy's] beastly hart' (4.9). **intent**: also gaze, intense observation. **8–9** Since **Dryope** was the consort of Faunus and **Pholoe** was a nymph beloved of Pan, both may be associated with Sylvanus in his double nature.

Stanza 16

3 bethinkes not: cannot decide, does not know. **6–9** A Renaissance commonplace that derives from Virgil, *Aen*. 1.314–28: Aeneas meets his mother Venus disguised as the virgin huntress Diana but takes her to be a goddess. On the significance of the Venus–Virgo allusion, see DiMatteo 1992:54–56.

Stanza 17

The story of Cyparissus derives ultimately from Ovid, *Met*. 10.106–42. See 'Cyparissus' in the *SEnc*. **3 pourtraiture aliue**: figure or likeness when alive. **8 n'ould**: would not.

9 pynd away: a pun on his metamorphosis into a cypress; see i 8.9*n*. **selfewild annoy**: self-imposed suffering or harm in contrast to the accidental slaying of the deer.

Stanza 18

1 Hamadryades: wood-nymphs, spirits of the trees in which they live. **3 Naiades**: freshwater-nymphs; **light-foot** as shown in their dancing. **5 heauenly grace**: cf. iii 4.9. **8 woody kind**: woodborn race.

Stanza 19

1 The word-play gains point through its context: such **lucke** is 'wondrous grace' (Arg.1) that comes to aid the earthly expression of 'heauenly grace' (18.5). **luckelesse** is a key term in the Red Cross Knight's adventures; cf. vii 26.8, viii 2.4, ix 45.4, xii 16.4. **2 feeble**: because they may gaze upon her unveiled beauty without being dazzled; or because they fail to see beyond her beauty as their 'Goddesse of the wood' (16.2). **6–9 in vaine**: profanely, in the biblical sense (Exod. 20.7), for they worship her as an idol, as the Israelites turned from God to worship a golden calf (Exod. 32.4). Jardine 1993:69 sees an allusion to the degeneration of Christianity into paganism in Ireland; see also Hadfield 1997:133–34. Purdon 1988 notes the traditional symbolism of the ass as an emblem of the flesh. **Image of Idolatryes**: the idol of their worship. See 'idols, idolatry' in the *SEnc*. **fayn**: gladly; or 'desired to worship'. By worshipping Una and then the ass, they turn from 'the glorie of the incorruptible God to the similitude of the image of . . . foure foted beastes' (Rom. 1.23); noted Gless 1994:108, and Bergvall 1997:27.

Stanza 20

2 iust occasion: in contrast to Sansloy who enters the forest at 3.2 to rape Una. **7** As Una's defender, he shares the Red Cross Knight's epithets: **faithfull, true** (i 2.7).

21

A Satyres sonne yborne in forrest wyld,
　By straunge aduenture as it did betyde,
　And there begotten of a Lady myld,
　Fayre *Thyamis* the daughter of *Labryde*,
　That was in sacred bandes of wedlocke tyde
　To *Therion*, a loose vnruly swayne;
　Who had more ioy to raunge the forrest wyde,
　And chase the saluage beast with busie payne,
Then serue his Ladies loue, and waste in pleasures vayne.

22

The forlorne mayd did with loues longing burne,
　And could not lacke her louers company,
　But to the wood she goes, to serue her turne,
　And seeke her spouse, that from her still does fly,
　And followes other game and venery:
　A Satyre chaunst her wandring for to finde,
　And kindling coles of lust in brutish eye,
　The loyall linkes of wedlocke did vnbinde,
And made her person thrall vnto his beastly kind.

23

So long in secret cabin there he held
　Her captiue to his sensuall desyre,
　Till that with timely fruit her belly sweld,
　And bore a boy vnto that saluage syre:
　Then home he suffred her for to retyre,
　For ransome leauing him the late-borne childe;
　Whom till to ryper yeares he gan aspyre,
　He noursled vp in life and manners wilde,
Emongst wild beastes and woods, from lawes of men exilde.

24

For all he taught the tender ymp was but
　To banish cowardize and bastard feare;
　His trembling hand he would him force to put
　Vpon the Lyon and the rugged Beare,
　And from the she Beares teats her whelps to teare;
　And eke wyld roring Buls he would him make
　To tame, and ryde their backes not made to beare;
　And the Robuckes in flight to ouertake,
That euerie beast for feare of him did fly and quake.

25

Thereby so fearelesse, and so fell he grew,
　That his owne syre and maister of his guise
　Did often tremble at his horrid vew,
　And oft for dread of hurt would him aduise,
　The angry beastes not rashly to despise,
　Nor too much to prouoke: for he would learne
　The Lyon stoup to him in lowly wise,
　(A lesson hard) and make the Libbard sterne
Leaue roaring, when in rage he for reuenge did earne.

26

And for to make his powre approued more,
　Wyld beastes in yron yokes he would compell;
　The spotted Panther, and the tusked Bore,
　The Pardale swift, and the Tigre cruell;
　The Antelope, and Wolfe both fierce and fell;
　And them constraine in equall teme to draw.
　Such ioy he had, their stubborne harts to quell,
　And sturdie courage tame with dreadfull aw,
That his beheast they feared, as a tyrans law.

Stanza 21

2 aduenture: chance. **4–6** Their Greek names reveal their natures, as Percival 1964 notes: **Thyamis**: θυμός, passion; **Labryde**: λάβρος, turbulent, greedy; **Therion**: θηρίον, wild beast. **7–9** A prototype of the apparently reluctant Adonis at III i 35 and the even more reluctant Adonis in Shakespeare, *Venus and Adonis*.

Stanza 22

1–4 That Una is also a 'forlorne maid' (iii 43.1) seeking her knight 'that from her still did flye' (21.8) is noted by Levin 1991:12. **lacke**: do without. **serue her turne**: answer her need, i.e. satisfy her desire. **5 game**: for its sexual significance, see III xi 38.8, V vii 16.5. **venery**: wild animals, with the common play on love-making.

Stanza 23

1 cabin: cave (*OED* 4); cf. Despaire's cabin at ix 32.4, which is a cave (33.2). **3 timely**: occurring in the course of time; or 'ripening' (cf. *OED* 1). **5 retyre**: return. **7 aspyre**: grow up. **8 noursled**: reared; combining 'nurse', and 'nousle' (raise).

Stanza 24

1 ymp: child. **2 bastard**: base-born, and therefore contemptible but natural to him as a bastard; cf. Sansloy's charge at 42.1. **4 the Lyon and the . . . Beare** are the two animals

killed by David to prove himself worthy to fight Goliath (1 Sam. 17.34–37). Artegall also practises on wild beasts; see V i 7.7–9 and *n*. **8 Robuckes**: noted for their speed, as at II x 7.5.

Stanza 25

2 maister: leader, tutor. **guise**: behaviour. **3 horrid vew**: his rough appearance as half-beast, seen in his 'rugged armes' (27.9) and the 'rustick horror' (11.6) of his race. **5 despise**: treat with contempt. **6 learne**: teach. **9 he**: either Satyrane or the leopard. **earne**: yearn.

Stanza 26

1 approued: proved; demonstrated. **2 compell**: drive together. **3–5** The six animals broadly denote Satyrane's lineage, each being identified by its traditional epithet from natural history lore. **spotted Panther** because it attracts its prey by its spotted hide: cf. *Am* 53.1–4; the **Bore** by its tusks, as IV vii 5.6; the **Tigre** is always cruel, as II v 8.9, etc.; the **Pardale** or female leopard known for its swiftness; **Antelope** is the Lat. *antalops*, a savage creature capable of cutting down trees with its horns. **6 in equall teme**: level, side by side in three teams. Compare the six 'vnequall beasts' (iv 18.1) in three teams that draw Lucifera's coach. **9 as a tyrans law**: cf. Lucifera's victims who suffer as beasts 'by law of that proud Tyrannesse' (v 46.6).

27

His louing mother came vpon a day
   Vnto the woodes, to see her little sonne;
   And chaunst vnwares to meet him in the way,
   After his sportes, and cruell pastime donne,
   When after him a Lyonesse did runne,
   That roaring all with rage, did lowd requere
   Her children deare, whom he away had wonne:
   The Lyon whelpes she saw how he did beare,
And lull in rugged armes, withouten childish feare.

28

The fearefull Dame all quaked at the sight,
   And turning backe, gan fast to fly away,
   Vntill with loue reuokt from vaine affright,
   She hardly yet perswaded was to stay,
   And then to him these womanish words gan say;
   Ah *Satyrane*, my dearling, and my ioy,
   For loue of me leaue off this dreadfull play;
   To dally thus with death, is no fit toy,
Go find some other play-fellowes, mine own sweet boy.

29

In these and like delightes of bloody game
   He trayned was, till ryper yeares he raught,
   And there abode, whylst any beast of name
   Walkt in that forrest, whom he had not taught,
   To feare his force: and then his courage haught
   Desyrd of forreine foemen to be knowne,
   And far abroad for straunge aduentures sought:
   In which his might was neuer ouerthrowne,
But through al Faery lond his famous worth was blown.

30

Yet euermore it was his maner faire,
   After long labours and aduentures spent,
   Vnto those natiue woods for to repaire,
   To see his syre and ofspring auncient.
   And now he thether came for like intent;
   Where he vnwares the fairest *Vna* found,
   Straunge Lady, in so straunge habiliment,
   Teaching the Satyres, which her sat around
Trew sacred lore, which from her sweet lips did redound.

31

He wondred at her wisedome heuenly rare,
   Whose like in womens witt he neuer knew;
   And when her curteous deeds he did compare,
   Gan her admire, and her sad sorrowes rew,
   Blaming of Fortune, which such troubles threw,
   And ioyd to make proofe of her cruelty
   On gentle Dame, so hurtlesse, and so trew:
   Thenceforth he kept her goodly company,
And learnd her discipline of faith and verity.

32

But she all vowd vnto the *Redcrosse* knight,
   His wandring perill closely did lament,
   Ne in this new acquaintaunce could delight,
   But her deare heart with anguish did torment,
   And all her witt in secret counsels spent,
   How to escape. At last in priuy wise
   To *Satyrane* she shewed her intent;
   Who glad to gain such fauour, gan deuise,
How with that pensiue Maid he best might thence arise.

Stanzas 27–28
This humorous interlude – stanza 29 follows directly after 26 – is borrowed from the account in Statius, *Achilleid* 1.158–70, of Thetis's fears when she sees Achilles harass wild beasts.

Stanza 27
5–9 A biblical simile of a beast's extreme anger, as Hos. 13.8 and 2 Sam. 17.8. **requere**: demand. **rugged**: rough with hair.

Stanza 28
3 **reuokt**: called back; restrained. 6 **Satyrane**: i.e. like a satyr, being 'A Satyres sonne' (21.1); see 'Satyrane' in the *SEnc*. When he becomes a knight, his shield bears 'a Satyres hedd' (III vii 30.6). **dearling**: darling.

Stanza 29
2 **raught**: reached. 3 **of name**: noted, known. The twelve beasts in stanzas 24–26 – counting the bear and she-bear as two – include most of the traditional forest animals known for their fierceness. 5 **haught**: haughty; or high-minded, lofty.

Stanza 30
3 **repaire**: return. 4 **ofspring**: origin, 'lignage' (20.3). 7 **Straunge**: as not belonging to the race of satyrs. **habili-**

ment: array, referring here to the satyrs who surround her. 9 **redound**: proceed, issue (*OED* 9c); the etymological sense, from Lat. *redundare*, to flow, is implied since Una is the fount of wisdom.

Stanza 31
2 His cynicism towards women, which becomes fully manifest at III vii 57.5–9 and ix 6–7.9, reflects his one-fourth beastly origin. 3 **compare**: i.e. compared to those of other women; or when he compared her deeds to her words, or her deeds to her present plight. 4 **admire**: with its etymology, 'to wonder at'. 7 **hurtlesse**: harmless, innocent. 9 **discipline**: teaching, with the added suggestion of the ecclesiastical polity of the reformed church.

Stanza 32
1 **vowd**: in the sense that she has chosen him as 'her knight' (i 49.9), a frequently repeated term, e.g. ii 7.7 and iii 2.8. 2 **closely**: secretly. 4 **deare**: loving. 9 **arise**: depart. The simpler sense, 'stand up', is present: she is plucked from her palfrey by Sansloy (iii 40.9); but with the satyrs 'from the ground she fearelesse doth arise' (13.3). Later the satyrs 'her sat around' (30.8), and now she is ready to 'arise' with Satyrane.

33

So on a day when Satyres all were gone,
    To doe their seruice to *Syluanus* old,
    The gentle virgin left behinde alone
    He led away with corage stout and bold.
    Too late it was, to Satyres to be told,
    Or euer hope recouer her againe:
    In vaine he seekes that hauing cannot hold.
    So fast he carried her with carefull paine,
That they the woods are past, and come now to the plaine.

34

The better part now of the lingring day,
    They traueild had, whenas they far espide
    A weary wight forwandring by the way,
    And towards him they gan in hast to ride,
    To weete of newes, that did abroad betide,
    Or tidings of her knight of the *Redcrosse*.
    But he them spying, gan to turne aside,
    For feare as seemd, or for some feigned losse;
More greedy they of newes, fast towards him do crosse.

35

A silly man, in simple weeds forworne,
    And soild with dust of the long dried way;
    His sandales were with toilsome trauell torne,
    And face all tand with scorching sunny ray,
    As he had traueild many a sommers day,
    Through boyling sands of *Arabie* and *Ynde*;
    And in his hand a *Iacobs* staffe, to stay
    His weary limbs vpon: and eke behind,
His scrip did hang, in which his needments he did bind.

36

The knight approching nigh, of him inquerd
    Tidings of warre, and of aduentures new;
    But warres, nor new aduentures none he herd.
    Then *Vna* gan to aske, if ought he knew,

Or heard abroad of that her champion trew,
    That in his armour bare a croslet red.
    Ay me, Deare dame (quoth he) well may I rew
    To tell the sad sight, which mine eies haue red:
These eies did see that knight both liuing, and eke ded.

37

That cruell word her tender hart so thrild,
    That suddein cold did ronne through euery vaine,
    And stony horrour all her sences fild
    With dying fitt, that downe she fell for paine.
    The knight her lightly reared vp againe,
    And comforted with curteous kind reliefe:
    Then wonne from death, she bad him tellen plaine
    The further processe of her hidden griefe;
The lesser pangs can beare, who hath endur'd the chief.

38

Then gan the Pilgrim thus, I chaunst this day,
    This fatall day, that shall I euer rew,
    To see two knights in trauell on my way
    (A sory sight) arraung'd in batteill new,
    Both breathing vengeaunce, both of wrathfull hew:
    My fearefull flesh did tremble at their strife,
    To see their blades so greedily imbrew,
    That dronke with blood, yet thristed after life:
What more? the *Redcrosse* knight was slain with Paynim knife.

39

Ah dearest Lord (quoth she) how might that bee,
    And he the stoutest knight, that euer wonne?
    Ah dearest dame (quoth hee) how might I see
    The thing, that might not be, and yet was donne?
    Where is (said *Satyrane*) that Paynims sonne,
    That him of life, and vs of ioy hath refte?
    Not far away (quoth he) he hence doth wonne
    Foreby a fountaine, where I late him lefte
Washing his bloody wounds, that through the steele were cleft.

Stanza 33
9 **plaine**: in the poem's moralized landscape, the setting for chivalric encounters, as i 1.1. See 3.2*n*.

Stanza 34
3 **forwandring**: wandering far and wide; or, as an intensive, 'utterly astray'. 8 I.e. he pretends to search for something lost. He makes a similar cowardly gesture at iii 26.3–5.

Stanza 35
1 **silly**: simple, without guile. The same pose as i 30.6 where he appears as a hermit. Here he appears as the pilgrim, one who comes from abroad though he is not named for what he seems to be until 38.1, and for what he is, 'that false *Pilgrim*', until 48.1. Presumably he has been wandering in search of Una. 7 **Iacobs staffe**: a venerable pilgrim's staff, associated with St James. **stay**: support. 9 **scrip**: small bag.

Stanza 36
5 **champion**: in the specific sense, one who defends another; cf. iii 8.9. 6 **croslet**: small cross; a heraldic term. 8 **red**: seen.

Stanza 37
Cf. her similar response to news of her knight's death at vii 20–21, 24–25, 39.4–6. 1–4 **thrild**: pierced. **dying fitt**: death-like swoon. 5 **lightly**: quickly. 7–9 I.e. she asks him to tell the rest of the 'tale' (**processe**: *OED* 4), which, though still unknown to her, will cause further grief.

Stanza 38
1 **this day**: a detail designed to make his story 'plaine' (37.7). 4–9 **sory**: grievous, painful. **new**: anew, after jousting with spears. Very cunningly, Archimago tells as though true what nearly happened to him in his disguise as the Red Cross Knight: he was nearly killed by Sansloy 'with bloody knife' (iii 36.4). **imbrew**: soak or stain themselves in blood.

Stanza 39
1–4 **Ah dearest Lord**: presumably addressed to God; possibly addressed to the Red Cross Knight: cf. her address to him at viii 28.7, 42.6. Presumptuously, Archimago applies it to himself by his parallel, **Ah dearest dame**. His involved playing on **might** in 3–4 seeks to change her appeal in 1 to what should

40

Therewith the knight thence marched forth in hast,
　　Whiles *Vna* with huge heauinesse opprest,
　　Could not for sorrow follow him so fast;
　　And soone he came, as he the place had ghest,
　　Whereas that *Pagan* proud him selfe did rest,
　　In secret shadow by a fountaine side:
　　Euen he it was, that earst would haue supprest
　　Faire Vna: whom when *Satyrane* espide,
With foule reprochfull words he boldly him defide.

41

And said, Arise thou cursed Miscreaunt,
　　That hast with knightlesse guile and trecherous train
　　Faire knighthood fowly shamed, and doest vaunt
　　That good knight of the *Redcrosse* to haue slain:
　　Arise, and with like treason now maintain
　　Thy guilty wrong, or els thee guilty yield.
　　The Sarazin this hearing, rose amain,
　　And catching vp in hast his three square shield,
And shining helmet, soone him buckled to the field.

42

And drawing nigh him said, Ah misborn Elfe,
　　In euill houre thy foes thee hither sent,
　　Anothers wrongs to wreak vpon thy selfe:
　　Yet ill thou blamest me, for hauing blent
　　My name with guile and traiterous intent;
　　That *Redcrosse* knight, perdie, I neuer slew,
　　But had he beene, where earst his armes were lent,
　　Th'enchaunter vaine his errour should not rew:
But thou his errour shalt, I hope now prouen trew.

43

Therewith they gan, both furious and fell,
　　To thunder blowes, and fiersly to assaile
　　Each other, bent his enimy to quell,
　　That with their force they perst both plate and maile,
　　And made wide furrowes in their fleshes fraile,
　　That it would pitty any liuing eie.
　　Large floods of blood adowne their sides did raile;
　　But floods of blood could not them satisfie:
Both hongred after death: both chose to win, or die.

44

So long they fight, and fell reuenge pursue,
　　That fainting each, them selues to breathen lett,
　　And ofte refreshed, battell oft renue:
　　As when two Bores with rancling malice mett,
　　Their gory sides fresh bleeding fiercely frett,
　　Til breathlesse both them selues aside retire,
　　Where foming wrath, their cruell tuskes they whett,
　　And trample th'earth, the whiles they may respire;
Then backe to fight againe, new breathed and entire.

45

So fiersly, when these knights had breathed once,
　　They gan to fight retourne, increasing more
　　Their puissant force, and cruell rage attonce,
　　With heaped strokes more hugely, then before,
　　That with their drery wounds and bloody gore
　　They both deformed, scarsely could bee known.
　　By this sad *Vna* fraught with anguish sore,
　　Led with their noise, which through the aire was thrown,
Arriu'd, wher they in erth their fruitles blood had sown.

be, thereby to accept his story as fact. **euer wonne**: ever lived. J. Dixon 1964 glosses 3–4: 'The eternall diuinitie of Jesus Christe is here plainly declared with his manhod and victorie ouer death'. **7 wonne**: stay. **8 Foreby**: close by. As the Red Cross Knight is soon found 'foreby a fountaine syde' (vii 2.7).

Stanzas 40–48
S. draws on an episode in Ariosto, *Orl. Fur.* 2.3–12, in which Rinaldo and Sacripant fight over Angelica, who flees from both.

Stanza 40
2 heauinesse: sadness, grief; here taken literally. **7 supprest**: violated; literally, 'pressed down by force'.

Stanza 41
1 And said: the run-on speech registers his haste. **Miscreaunt**: as he is a pagan; see v 13.1*n*. **2 knightlesse**: unknightly. **train**: trickery. **5 treason**: treachery. A similar charge is made against the Red Cross Knight at iv 41.4–7. **maintain**: defend. **7 amain**: at once. **8 three square**: with three equal sides, either straight or slightly curved; the traditional shape of the chivalric shield in the Middle Ages, as seen in monumental brasses. See III i 4.4*n*.

Stanza 42
1 misborn Elfe: base-born creature, being born out of wedlock; but see 47.1*n*. A counter-charge to Satyrane's 'Miscreant' (41.1). **4 blent**: mingled; hence, tainted, defiled. **8–9 vaine**: foolish. **his errour**: either Archimago's error in wearing the Red Cross Knight's armour in fighting Sansloy, or the Red Cross Knight's error in slaying Sansfoy. **rew**: cf. 36.7, 38.2. **hope**: think, expect. **prouen trew**: i.e. through judicial combat.

Stanza 43
3 Each was determined to kill his opponent. **6 pitty**: move to pity. **7 Large**: copious. **raile**: flow.

Stanza 44
4–9 The extended simile shows how the two knights both reduced to bestiality are difficult to distinguish, in their actions becoming one by the climactic line, 45.6. **gory**: gored, and therefore bloody. **frett**: gnaw, tear. **entire**: refreshed.

Stanza 45
5 drery: bloody. **6 deformed**: disfigured, but used here almost literally.

46

Whom all so soone as that proud Sarazin
  Espide, he gan reuiue the memory
  Of his leud lusts, and late attempted sin,
  And lefte the doubtfull battell hastily,
  To catch her, newly offred to his eie:
  But *Satyrane* with strokes him turning, staid,
  And sternely bad him other businesse plie,
Then hunt the steps of pure vnspotted Maid:
Wherewith he al enrag'd, these bitter speaches said.

47

O foolish faeries sonne, what fury mad
  Hath thee incenst, to hast thy dolefull fate?
  Were it not better, I that Lady had,
  Then that thou hadst repented it too late?

Most sencelesse man he, that himselfe doth hate,
  To loue another. Lo then for thine ayd
  Here take thy louers token on thy pate.
  So they to fight; the whiles the royall Mayd
Fledd farre away, of that proud Paynim sore afrayd.

48

But that false *Pilgrim*, which that leasing told,
  Being in deed old *Archimage*, did stay
  In secret shadow, all this to behold,
  And much reioyced in their bloody fray:
  But when he saw the Damsell passe away
  He left his stond, and her pursewd apace,
  In hope to bring her to her last decay.
  But for to tell her lamentable cace,
And eke this battels end, will need another place.

Stanza 46
4 doubtfull: dreaded; undecided.

Stanza 47
1 faeries sonne: oddly used of a satyr's son, perhaps because he is Una's champion. Elsewhere in Bk I, the term is applied only to the Red Cross Knight, as ix 47.9, etc. **6–7** I.e. as a reward for aiding Una, and in place of the lover's token worn on the helmet, take this blow on the head. **8 So they to**

fight: two *1596*, i.e. the two return to fighting. The *1590* reading is supported by 44.1 and 45.2.

Stanza 48
1 leasing: falsehood. **6 stond**: stand, place of ambush. **7 last decay**: death. **8 lamentable**: accented on the first and third syllables, as always in the poem. **9** Since **another place** is not given, one infers that the battle never ends.

Cant. VII.

The Redcrosse knight is captiue made
By Gyaunt proud opprest,
Prince Arthure meets with Vna great-
ly with those newes distrest.

1

WHat man so wise, what earthly witt so ware,
  As to discry the crafty cunning traine,
By which deceipt doth maske in visour faire,
And cast her coulours di_e_d deepe in graine,
To seeme like truth, whose shape she well can faine,
And fitting gestures to her purpose frame,
  The guiltlesse man with guile to entertaine?
  Great maistresse of her art was that false Dame,
The false *Duessa*, cloked with *Fidessaes* name.

2

Who when returning from the drery *Night*,
  She fownd not in that perilous hous of *Pryde*,
Where she had left, the noble *Redcross* knight,
Her hoped pray; she would no lenger byde,

But forth she went, to seeke him far and wide.
Ere long she fownd, whereas he wearie sate,
To rest him selfe, foreby a fountaine syde,
Disarmed all of yron-coted Plate,
And by his side his steed the grassy forage ate.

3

Hee feedes vpon the cooling shade, and bayes
  His sweatie forehead in the breathing wynd,
Which through the trembling leaues full gently playes
Wherein the chearefull birds of sundry kynd
Doe chaunt sweet musick, to delight his mynd:
  The witch approching gan him fayrely greet,
  And with reproch of carelesnes vnkynd,
Vpbrayd, for leauing her in place vnmeet,
With fowle words tempring faire, soure gall with hony sweet.

Book I Canto vii

Argument
2 proud: the only explicit linking of Orgoglio with pride.
opprest: taken by surprise; harassed; overwhelmed.

Stanza 1
1–3 ware: vigilant; prudent.   **traine**: guile, a term that links her to Errour (i 18.6, 9), Lucifera's dragon (iv 10.5), and the procession of sins (26.9, etc.). It refers also to the robe in which **deceipt doth maske**, and by which Duessa, 'the daughter of Deceipt', deceives even 'the mother . . . | Of falshood' (v 27.6–7). **4 cast her coulours**: dispose her colours, a term in painting. Also 'lose colour', for Duessa 'clad in scarlot red' (ii 13.2) appears in Una's **visour faire**. Wearing a false hood, she becomes Falsehood, being so named in ii Arg. etc. **died deepe in graine**: fast dyed; also 'dyed scarlet', referring to her robe. **8 maistresse**: an earlier spelling of 'mistress' fittingly used only for Duessa.

Stanza 2
1 drery Night: as v 24.1. **7** The posture of Sansfoy at vi 39.8, 40.6. On the general significance of the setting, see 'fountains' in the *SEnc*. **8** The knight's rejection of 'the whole armour of God' (Eph. 6.11), now dismissed as **yron-coted Plate** too heavy to bear, reveals his spiritual state. In Ariosto, *Orl. Fur.* 6.24, Ruggiero removes his shield, helmet and gauntlets; in Tasso, *Ger. Lib.* 14.59, Rinaldo removes his helmet. By disarming **all**, S.'s knight loses his wholeness and

holiness. See 'armor of God' in the *SEnc*. **9** This detail, repeated at 19.2, suggests the usual link between the horse and its rider's passions: as it feeds on **grassy forage**, the knight 'feedes vpon the cooling shade' (3.1).

Stanza 3
1–5 cooling shade, **breathing wynd**, **trembling leaues**, and **chearefull birds** are features of the *locus amoenus*, e.g. in Ariosto, *Orl. Fur.* 6.21, 24, where it is the setting for Ruggiero's enslavement to the witch Alcina. Trembling leaves and cool shade at ii 28–29 provide the setting for Fradubio's story of his enslavement to Duessa; repeated here, they herald the knight's seduction by the same witch. Feeding upon the shade of the trees and later drinking from the fountain parody the 'feeding' on the tree of life and drinking from the well of life through which he finally triumphs over the dragon. **1 bayes**: bathes from 'embay'; cf. 'embayd' (ix 13.5). **3** Cf. Jer. 2.20: 'like an harlot thou runnest about . . . vnder all grene trees'. **4–5** Cf. 'the birdes sweete harmony' (i 8.2) which leads him astray in the Wandering Wood. In Bks I and II esp., the charm of birds conspires to occasion a fall into sin; cf. II v 31, vi 13, xii 71. Turning from the eye to the ear indicates the knight's yielding to the inner passions. The association of the song of birds with sensuality is noted by Wells 1994:31. **6 fayrely**: courteously; with fair words. Duessa's reproach contrasts with Una's 'faire fearefull humblesse' (iii 26.9) to her supposed knight; cf. viii 42.6–9.   **7 carelesnes**: indifference to her plight. Ironically, her words apply to him, for he lies 'carelesse of his health' (7.3).

4

Vnkindnesse past, they gan of solace treat,
   And bathe in pleasaunce of the ioyous shade,
   Which shielded them against the boyling heat,
   And with greene boughes decking a gloomy glade,
   About the fountaine like a girlond made;
   Whose bubbling waue did euer freshly well,
   Ne euer would through feruent sommer fade:
   The sacred Nymph, which therein wont to dwell,
Was out of *Dianes* fauor, as it then befell.

5

The cause was this: one day when *Phœbe* fayre
   With all her band was following the chace,
   This Nymph, quite tyr'd with heat of scorching ayre
   Satt downe to rest in middest of the race:
   The goddesse wroth gan fowly her disgrace,
   And badd the waters, which from her did flow,
   Be such as she her selfe was then in place.
   Thenceforth her waters wexed dull and slow,
And all that drinke thereof, do faint and feeble grow.

6

Hereof this gentle knight vnweeting was,
   And lying downe vpon the sandie graile,
   Dronke of the streame, as cleare as christall glas;
   Eftsoones his manly forces gan to fayle,
   And mightie strong was turnd to feeble frayle:
   His chaunged powres at first them selues not felt,
   Till crudled cold his corage gan assayle,
   And chearefull blood in fayntnes chill did melt,
Which like a feuer fit through all his body swelt.

7

Yet goodly court he made still to his Dame,
   Pourd out in loosnesse on the grassy grownd,
   Both carelesse of his health, and of his fame:
   Till at the last he heard a dreadfull sownd,
   Which through the wood loud bellowing, did rebownd,
   That all the earth for terror seemd to shake,
   And trees did tremble. Th'Elfe therewith astownd,
   Vpstarted lightly from his looser make,
And his vnready weapons gan in hand to take.

Stanza 4

1 solace: pleasure, with the usual sense, alleviation of sorrow. **2 pleasaunce**: pleasantness. An ominous term associated with Duessa at I ii 30.1, with the house of Pride at iv 38.2, and now the scene of the knight's fall. In Bk II, it is associated with Phædria at II vi 6.9, and the Bower of Bliss at xii 50.3. **ioyous shade**: in S.'s idiom, a powerful oxymoron. **3 boyling heat** suggests noon. Without God's truth as his shield, the knight lies helpless before 'the plague that destroyeth at noone daye' (Ps. 91.6). On noon as the locus of the *demonium meridianum*, see A. Fowler 1964:72, and P.A. Parker 1979:62. **5 girlond**: see ii 30.7n. **7 fade**: shrink, dry up. **8 sacred**: her title as the nymph of the fountain; cf. i 34.9. The alternate sense of *sacer*, listed by T. Cooper 1565 as 'cursed', applies to the present state of her waters. **Nymph** denotes a follower of Diana, the *nympha nympharum*.

Stanza 5

1 Phœbe: Diana as goddess of the moon. The feminine of Phœbus whose heat causes the knight to drink. **4 in middest of the race**: see stanzas 12–13n. The weary nymph is an Ovidian counterpart to the weary knight who also rests in the middle of his race. For the biblical resonance, see Heb. 12.1: 'let vs runne with pacience the race that is set before vs'; and on its relevance to the life of holiness, see Gless 1994:117–18. **5 disgrace**: disfigure; bring into disgrace; literally, deprive of the graces infused into the water. Cf. the Palmer's account of the 'secret vertues' (II ii 5.6–9) in fountains. The nymph prefigures the knight's state at 11.6. This enfeebling fountain is an emblem of idleness, perhaps taken directly from Ovid's story of Hermaphroditus and Salmacis, *Met.* 4.285–386, 15.319–21: he gives up toil and she gives up Diana's chase. Ovid's vain nymph is esp. lazy and self-indulgent in Golding's tr., nicely laying herself 'On soft sweete hearbes or soft greene leaues' (4.380). S.'s use of the myth assumes its standard interpretation, e.g. by Golding, Epistle: 'that idlenesse | Is cheefest nurce and cherisher of all volupteousnesse, | And that voluptuous lyfe breedes sin: which linking all tooghter | Make men too bee effeminate, unweeldy, weake and lither' (113–16). **7 in place**: there. **9 faint**: wanting in courage; wanting in

strength; in both senses opposed to the working of faith at i 19.3.

Stanza 6

1 vnweeting: cf. 49.3, xi 29.2. **2–3 lying downe**: a further stage of his fall. First he sits in the shade to rest and then to lie with Duessa; now he is totally prostrate. **graile**: gravel, suggesting a pun on 'grail' (Hamilton 1961a:74) to note an infernal communion by which the knight is metamorphosed into the fallen state. Tuve 1966:124n disagrees. Cf. Prov. 25.26: 'a righteous man falling downe before the wicked is like . . . a corrupt spring'. **cleare as christall glas**: in parody of the water of life which is 'clear as crystal' (Rev. 22.1). Waters 1970:64–67 interprets this action as spiritual fornication associated with the dulling effects of the Roman mass. Shroeder 1962:144–46 sees an overt sexual significance: the knight's drinking signifies the act of copulation that causes loss of bodily heat. Silberman 1995:55 cites the mythographic tradition 'which holds that the fountain of Salmacis is aphrodisiac and promotes impotence through sexual overindulgence'. On Duessa as Eve's succuba-like rival, Lilith, see Nohrnberg 1976:228–39. **4 manly**: human; see i 24.6n. **5** Playing on the supporting sense: strong might . . . frail feebleness. **feeble frayle** defines man's fallen nature; see ix 53.1n. **7 crudled**: congealing. **corage**: vital powers. **8 chearefull**: lively, living. **did melt**: was reduced to the polluted water which he drank by losing its heat, the element of fire. There may be a precise medical sense: congealed blood has separated from the watery serum, as the 'watery token' of 'corrupted blood' reveals Lucrece's polluted state in Shakespeare, *Lucrece* 1748. The knight suffers both chill and fever, contrasting states that anticipate the suffering of the damned; see ii 33.9n. **9 swelt**: raged.

Stanza 7

1 his Dame: the possessive confirms his commitment to her. She is his mistress, as ii 40.1, xii 20.5; cf. 'his Ladie' (v 12.1). **2 Pourd out**: Lat. *effusus*, spread out, or stretched out, indicating his dissipation: sexually expended and exhausted, he is like the water he drank. Una refers to him as 'dissolute' (51.3),

8

But ere he could his armour on him dight,
  Or gett his shield, his monstrous enimy
  With sturdie steps came stalking in his sight,
  An hideous Geaunt horrible and hye,
  That with his tallnesse seemd to threat the skye,
  The ground eke groned vnder him for dreed;
  His liuing like saw neuer liuing eye,
  Ne durst behold: his stature did exceed
The hight of three the tallest sonnes of mortall seed.

9

The greatest Earth his vncouth mother was,
  And blustring *AEolus* his boasted syre,
  Who with his breath, which through the world doth pas,
  Her hollow womb did secretly inspyre,
  And fild her hidden caues with stormie yre,
  That she conceiu'd; and trebling the dew time,
  In which the wombes of wemen doe expyre,
  Brought forth this monstrous masse of earthly slyme,
Puft vp with emptie wynd, and fild with sinfull cryme.

10

So growen great through arrogant delight
  Of th'high descent, whereof he was yborne,
  And through presumption of his matchlesse might,
  All other powres and knighthood he did scorne.
  Such now he marcheth to this man forlorne,
  And left to losse: his stalking steps are stayde
  Vpon a snaggy Oke, which he had torne
  Out of his mothers bowelles, and it made
His mortall mace, wherewith his foemen he dismayde.

---

which includes the sense 'dissolved' (*OED* 1). Water is traditionally associated with the lustful passions, e.g. the biblical cry of death: 'I am like water powred out' (Ps. 22.14). The knight's symbolic descent through the four elements is noted by Hamilton 1961a:76. **loosnesse**: licentiousness. **3 Both**: both are careless, he is careless both, etc. **carelesse**: the state of *acedia*, the non-caring state. **health** and **fame** refer to the private and public virtues, the former signifying spiritual and moral well-being, welfare, safety. **4 at the last**: finally; evoking in this context death and the Day of Judgement. **5 loud bellowing**: as Typhon, another offspring of the Earth (cf. III vii 47), approaches his victims with 'the noise of a bull bellowing aloud' (Hesiod, *Theog.* 832). The link may have been suggested by the name: Typhon or Typhœus signifies 'A great whirle winde' (T. Cooper 1565). **7 tremble**: extending the image of 'the trembling leaues' (3.3), now with apocalyptic overtones. **astownd**: confounded. **8 lightly**: quickly, for he lacks his armour. **looser make**: too loose mate.

Stanza 8
3 sturdie: furious, violent; also 'vigorous', in contrast to the knight's feebleness. **stalking**: lumbering with great strides, suggesting the hunter after his prey. The alliteration marks his steps; cf. 10.6. **4 hideous**: huge, immense; also 'abominable'. **Geant**: the etymological spelling points to his origin as son of Gaea (or Ge), the Earth. See II i 10.6*n*. He is one of the Titans, giants traditionally associated with pride and rebellion against God; see III vii 47.3–5, VI vii 41.6–8.

Stanza 9
Orgoglio's conception is like that of an earthquake, to which his blow is compared at viii 8.9. Harvey attributed the earthquake in England in 1580 to 'great aboundance of wynde . . . emprysoned in the Caues, and Dungeons of the Earth' (Spenser 1912:616). See 'winds' in the *SEnc*. As an omen of the Last Judgement, see Rev. 6.12, 8.5, etc.; as an embodiment of the Red Cross Knight's fallen state, see Hamilton 1961a:75. **1 greatest Earth**: 'great mother', *omniparens*, is the traditional epithet of the earth, as at II i 10.6. She is also the mother of Sansfoy (ii 19.6), Maleger (II xi 45.2), Argante (III vii 47.8), Grantorto (V xii 23.7), and Mutabilitie (VII vi 26.4–6). In Bk I, the earth is associated with earthly man (as

in 1 Cor. 15.47) and therefore with 'the Popes kingdome [which] is of the earth and leadeth to perdition' (Geneva gloss to Rev. 13.11). **vncouth**: vile; strange, marvellous. **2 AEolus**: here the wind. The earth was generally held to be hollow (cf. II vii 8.9), winds being caused by exhalations from its bowels. S. mocks the giant for such boasting, as Jonson mocks Vulcan: 'Sonne of the Wind! for so thy mother gone | With lust conceiv'd thee; Father thou hadst none' (1925–52:8.208). J. Watkins 1995:100 notes the allegorical tradition that associated AEolus with the destruction of the spirit. **4 inspyre**: breathe into; breathe life into (as Gen. 2.7), a parody of divine inspiration. **5 yre**: a pun on air. **7 expyre**: give birth after full term; also 'breathing out'. **8 earthly slyme**: applied to the human body in general as a mixture of earth and water; cf. Prometheus's creation of man out of earth and water (Ovid, *Met.* 1.80–83). In Gen. 2.7, *de limo terrae* (Vulg.) suggests Lat. *limus*, slime. Cf. 'fleshly slime' (II x 50.2, III vi 3.5). The third element, air, puffs him up, and alludes to the Greek root of Orgoglio, ὀργάω, 'to be swollen with lust', here with wind in parody of man's creation by the breath of life; cf. viii 24.8–9*n*. He is man 'rashly puft vp with his fleshlie minde' (Col. 2.18). The fourth element, fire (associated with the soul), is necessarily missing. On the giants, formed of primeval slime, interpreted as our bodies, see Seznec 1953:91. **9 fild**: i.e. filled, as seen when he implodes at viii 24.7–9; also 'filed': defiled, corrupted.

Stanza 10
5 forlorne: left alone; morally lost; doomed to destruction. Cf. 'so fowle forlore' (viii 39.4), and see 19.4*n*. **6 losse**: perdition; destruction; death. He is 'that which was lost', one whom 'the Sonne of man is come to seke, and to saue' (Luke 19.10). **stayde**: supported, suggesting that Orgoglio is maintained by power not by right. **7 snaggy**: knotty. The oak is cited for its strength; cf. viii 18.6. For its association with Druidism and paganism, see Selden's note on δρῦς, oak, in Drayton 1931–41:4.192. Virgil's Polyphemus supports his steps by a lopped pine (*Aen.* 3.659); cf. Homer, *Ody.* 9.319–20. For the club as an attribute of the Wild Man, see 'Salvage Man' in the *SEnc*. Lust carries 'a tall young oake' with 'knottie snags' at IV vii 7.4–5. **9 dismayde**: for the play on the word, see 11.6*n*.

11

That when the knight he spyde, he gan aduaunce
    With huge force and insupportable mayne,
    And towardes him with dreadfull fury praunce;
    Who haplesse, and eke hopelesse, all in vaine
    Did to him pace, sad battaile to darrayne,
    Disarmd, disgraste, and inwardly dismayde,
    And eke so faint in euery ioynt and vayne,
    Through that fraile fountain, which him feeble made,
That scarsely could he weeld his bootlesse single blade.

12

The Geaunt strooke so maynly mercilesse,
    That could haue ouerthrowne a stony towre,
    And were not heuenly grace, that him did blesse,
    He had beene pouldred all, as thin as flowre:
    But he was wary of that deadly stowre,
    And lightly lept from vnderneath the blow:
    Yet so exceeding was the villeins powre
    That with the winde it did him ouerthrow,
And all his sences stoond, that still he lay full low.

13

As when that diuelish yron Engin wrought
    In deepest Hell, and framd by *Furies* skill,
    With windy Nitre and quick Sulphur fraught,
    And ramd with bollet rownd, ordaind to kill,

Conceiueth fyre, the heauens it doth fill
    With thundring noyse, and all the ayre doth choke,
    That none can breath, nor see, nor heare at will,
    Through smouldry cloud of duskish stincking smok,
That th'onely breath him daunts, who hath escapt the stroke.

14

So daunted when the Geaunt saw the knight,
    His heauie hand he heaued vp on hye,
    And him to dust thought to haue battred quight,
    Vntill *Duessa* loud to him gan crye;
    O great *Orgoglio*, greatest vnder skye,
    O hold thy mortall hand for Ladies sake,
    Hold for my sake, and doe him not to dye,
    But vanquisht thine eternall bondslaue make,
And me thy worthy meed vnto thy Leman take.

15

He hearkned, and did stay from further harmes,
    To gayne so goodly guerdon, as she spake:
    So willingly she came into his armes,
    Who her as willingly to grace did take,
    And was possessed of his newfound make.
    Then vp he tooke the slombred sencelesse corse,
    And ere he could out of his swowne awake,
    Him to his castle brought with hastie forse,
And in a Dongeon deep him threw without remorse.

Stanza 11

1 That: i.e. his mace. Emphasis falls awkwardly but strongly upon this word to emphasize the blow which is the subject of stanzas 11–14. **aduaunce**: lift up. **2 insupportable**: irresistible. The accent on the second syllable together with the three heavy accents before the caesura emphasize that no human power may resist this giant. **mayne**: strength, force. It suggests the power of the sea. **3 praunce**: strut, in contrast to the knight's slow pace. **5 darrayne**: engage; fight. **6 disgraste**: put to shame, as the nymph (see 5.5*n*); more strongly, out of God's grace, for the knight is **hopelesse**. **dismayde**: with a pun on 'un-made'; cf. Una's catalogue of his state: 'dis-auenturous' (48.7) and 'disarmed, dissolute, dismaid' (51.3). Alluding to this moment, Despaire adds 'defild' (ix 46.9). The negations place the knight in the power of Dis. **8 fraile**: i.e. causing frailness; cf. 6.5. **9 bootlesse**: useless. **single**: because he has the sword alone and lacks defence. Only his shield and armour are such that 'none can wound the man, that does them wield' (iv 50.7).

Stanzas 12–13

These two stanzas mark the arithmetical centre (excluding the proem) of the *1590* Bk I: the fall of the hero who, like the nymph, is 'in middest of the race' (5.4). (*1596* has an extra stanza: xi 3.) For similar midpoints, see II vii 53–55*n*, III vi 43*n*. Each is found in a *locus amoenus*. See Baybak *et al.* 1969:231; also Hieatt 1973:19–25. On the extended centre of Bk I, see Røstvig 1994:292–97.

Stanza 12

1 maynly: mightily. **mercilesse**: both adv. and adj. (with such merciless might), in contrast to heavenly grace. **2 That**: i.e. the stroke. The comparison is developed at viii 23 to describe Orgoglio's own fall. **3 heuenly grace**: cf. viii 1.3.

See II viii 1*n*. The term prepares for Arthur's entrance as its agent. **blesse**: preserve. **4 pouldred**: obs. form of 'powdered', i.e. pulverized; cf. 14.3. **5 stowre**: assault. **7 villeins**: used precisely here as he is low-born, being born of the earth and in bondage to the flesh. **8 winde**: as he is the son of Æolus. A parody of the breath of the Holy Ghost: by this wind the knight is created as was Orgoglio and reduced to a 'slombred sencelesse corse' (15.6). **9 stoond**: stunned.

Stanza 13

Except for occasional similes, e.g. IV ii 16, V x 34, S. tends to ignore contemporary warfare; see A. Fowler 1989b:151. **1–2 yron Engin**: the cannon; **diuelish** because invented by the devil in hell (Ariosto, *Orl. Fur.* 9.91). On the **Furies**, see iii 36.8*n*. **3 windy**: producing wind. **Nitre**: potassium nitrate, the principal ingredient of gunpowder. **quick**: fiery. **4 ordaind**: devised; also the military sense, 'drawn up in order of battle'. **5 Conceiueth**: catches; breeds within. **8 smouldry**: smothering. **9** The smoke or smell alone overcomes him.

Stanza 14

2 This strongly alliterative line mimes the act of raising the weapon. **5 Orgoglio**: Ital. 'pride, disdaine, haughtines' (Florio 1598); cf. Eng. 'orgueil', 'orgulus'. The name contains the root of the knight's name, 'Georgos': see x 66.5–6*n*. Only after defeating the knight is he named; see viii 8.4–6*n*. **9 meed**: Duessa plays the role of Lady Meed; see ii 13.2*n*. As the Red Cross Knight won her as his 'guerdon' (iii 40.3) for defeating Sansfoy, Orgoglio wins her as his 'guerdon' (15.2) for defeating the Red Cross Knight.

Stanza 15

1 stay: refrain. **4 to grace**: into his favour. **5** In possessing her, he is possessed by her. **6 slombred**: unconscious.

16
From that day forth *Duessa* was his deare,
   And highly honourd in his haughtie eye,
   He gaue her gold and purple pall to weare,
   And triple crowne set on her head full hye,
   And her endowd with royall maiestye:
   Then for to make her dreaded more of men,
   And peoples hartes with awfull terror tye,
A monstrous beast ybredd in filthy fen
He chose, which he had kept long time in darksom den.

17
Such one it was, as that renowmed Snake
   Which great *Alcides* in *Stremona* slew,
   Long fostred in the filth of *Lerna* lake,
   Whose many heades out budding euer new,
   Did breed him endlesse labor to subdew:
   But this same Monster much more vgly was;
   For seuen great heads out of his body grew,
An yron brest, and back of scaly bras,
And all embrewd in blood, his eyes did shine as glas.

18
His tayle was stretched out in wondrous length,
   That to the hous of heuenly gods it raught,
   And with extorted powre, and borrow'd strength,
   The euerburning lamps from thence it braught,
   And prowdly threw to ground, as things of naught;
   And vnderneath his filthy feet did tread,
   The sacred thinges, and holy heastes foretaught.
Vpon this dreadfull Beast with seuenfold head
He sett the false *Duessa*, for more aw and dread.

19
The wofull Dwarfe, which saw his maisters fall,
   Whiles he had keeping of his grasing steed,
   And valiant knight become a caytiue thrall,
   When all was past, tooke vp his forlorne weed,
   His mightie Armour, missing most at need;
   His siluer shield, now idle maisterlesse;
   His poynant speare, that many made to bleed,
The ruefull moniments of heauinesse,
And with them all departes, to tell his great distresse.

Stanzas 16–17
Based on Rev. 17.3–5: 'I sawe a woman sit vpon a skarlat coloured beast, full of names of blasphemie, which had seuen heads, and ten hornes. And the woman was araied in purple and skarlat, and guilded with golde, and precious stones, and pearles'. Then she is named 'great Babylon, the mother of whoredomes', as later she is named by S. 'That scarlot whore' (viii 29.2). See ii 13.2*n*, viii 14.1–5*n*. The Geneva gloss notes that 'the beast signifieth the ancient Rome; the woman that sitteth thereon, the new Rome which is the Papistrie, whose crueltie and blood sheding is declared by skarlat'. In Alciati 1985:emblem 6, she is an emblem of false religion. See the woodcut in Noot's *Theatre* accompanying S.'s *sonn* 12.

Stanza 16
3 **purple pall**: the crimson robe of royalty. 4 **triple crowne**: the Pope's three-tiered crown; cf. viii 25.3. It was taken to symbolize temporal power over the world, as Ovid's *triplex mundus* (land, sea, and sky) or east, south, and west (the north belongs to Satan), or the three continents (Europe, Africa, and Asia). King 1990a:96 concludes that S. draws on Reformation visual propaganda. On the opposition of the royal crown and papal tiara, see King 1989:116–81. Duessa's crowning, which lasts until her defeat at viii 25, sixty stanzas later, may allude to the six-year reign of the Catholic Mary Tudor. 5 Cf. Rev. 18.7: 'for she saith in her heart, I sit being a quene, and am no widowe, and shal se no mourning'. Duessa first appeared as a 'virgin widow' (ii 24.8) mourning her lover's death. 7 **tye**: enthral.

Stanza 17
1–2 S. finds authority for the dragon in classical mythology rather than in the Bible. **that renowmed Snake**: the Lernean hydra slain by Hercules (**Alcides**) as the second of his labours. According to Ovid, *Met.* 9.68–74, the hydra has 100 heads. At VI xii 32.4 it has 1000. Its connection with **Stremona**, or Strymon (a river in Thrace), remains unknown. 3 **filth**: because 'in this lake the people . . . dyd throwe all the ordure

and sweepynges of theyr streetes and houses' (T. Cooper 1565). In *The Golden Legend*, the dragon slain by St George lived in 'a stagne or a ponde lyke a see' (app. Barclay 1955); in Barclay 501, it was bred in 'a foule infernall lake'. 5 **breed**: as their breeding bred his labour. 7 **seuen great heads**: 'And I sawe a beast rise out of the sea, hauing seuen heads' (Rev. 13.1; cf. *Theatre, sonn* 8.13). The Geneva gloss reads: 'meaning Rome, because it was first gouerned by seuen Kings or Emperours after Nero, and also is compassed about with seuen mountaines'. Geneva glosses the dragon of Rev. 12.3 as ' the deuil, and al his power'. 8 **back of scaly bras**: cf. the dragon's 'bras-scaly back' (xi 11.2). 9 **embrewd**: stained; defiled. The shining eyes suggest the etymology of dragon (from Gk δράκων); cf. the dragon's 'blazing eyes, like two bright shining shieldes' (xi 14.1); also the Leviathan whose eyes 'are like the eye lids of the morning' (Job 41.9).

Stanza 18
Cf. Daniel's vision of the goat whose horn 'grewe vp vnto the hoste of heauen, and it cast downe some of the hoste, and of the starres to the grounde, and trode vpon them . . . and the place of his Sanctuarie was cast downe' (Dan. 8.10–11; cf. 7.23); cf. also Rev. 12.3–4. 2 **raught**: reached. 3 **extorted powre**: power wrongfully obtained, implying that papal tyranny usurps civil power, as Upton 1758 notes. **borrow'd**: assumed, counterfeit; cf. Duessa's 'borrowed light' (viii 49.5) and 'borrowd beauty' (II i 22.7). Possibly also 'loaned' by God to fulfil his purposes. 7 **heastes**: commands. **foretaught**: previously taught; i.e. he treads underfoot holy doctrines that earlier had been reverenced. 'Untaught' and 'mistaught' are possible readings. 9 Repeating 16.6–7.

Stanza 19
4 **forlorne**: forsaken by the knight; cf. 'forlorne reliques' (48.1). **weed**: armour. 5 **most at need**: when most needed. 7 **poynant**: piercing. 8 **moniments of heauinesse**: tokens, or reminders of grief, as 'reliques sad' (24.9); cf. 'heauie record' (48.8).

20

He had not trauaild long, when on the way
   He wofull Lady, wofull *Vna* met,
   Fast flying from that Paynims greedy pray,
   Whilest *Satyrane* him from pursuit did let:
   Who when her eyes she on the Dwarf had set,
   And saw the signes, that deadly tydinges spake,
   She fell to ground for sorrowfull regret,
   And liuely breath her sad brest did forsake,
Yet might her pitteous hart be seene to pant and quake.

21

The messenger of so vnhappie newes,
   Would faine haue dyde: dead was his hart within,
   Yet outwardly some little comfort shewes:
   At last recouering hart, he does begin
   To rubb her temples, and to chaufe her chin,
   And euerie tender part does tosse and turne:
   So hardly he the flitted life does win,
   Vnto her natiue prison to retourne:
Then gins her grieued ghost thus to lament and mourne.

22

Ye dreary instruments of dolefull sight,
   That doe this deadly spectacle behold,
   Why do ye lenger feed on loathed light,
   Or liking find to gaze on earthly mould,
   Sith cruell fates the carefull threds vnfould,
   The which my life and loue together tyde?
   Now let the stony dart of sencelesse cold
   Perce to my hart, and pas through euerie side,
And let eternall night so sad sight fro me hyde.

23

O lightsome day, the lampe of highest *Ioue*,
   First made by him, mens wandring wayes to guyde,
   When darknesse he in deepest dongeon droue,
   Henceforth thy hated face for euer hyde,
   And shut vp heauens windowes shyning wyde:
   For earthly sight can nought but sorow breed,
   And late repentance, which shall long abyde.
   Mine eyes no more on vanitie shall feed,
But seeled vp with death, shall haue their deadly meed.

24

Then downe againe she fell vnto the ground;
   But he her quickly reared vp againe:
   Thrise did she sinke adowne in deadly swownd,
   And thrise he her reviu'd with busie paine:
   At last when life recouer'd had the raine,
   And ouer-wrestled his strong enimy,
   With foltring tong, and trembling euerie vaine,
   Tell on (quoth she) the wofull Tragedy,
The which these reliques sad present vnto mine eye.

25

Tempestuous fortune hath spent all her spight,
   And thrilling sorrow throwne his vtmost dart;
   Thy sad tong cannot tell more heauy plight,
   Then that I feele, and harbour in mine hart:
   Who hath endur'd the whole, can beare ech part.
   If death it be, it is not the first wound,
   That launched hath my brest with bleeding smart.
   Begin, and end the bitter balefull stound;
If lesse, then that I feare, more fauour I haue found.

Stanza 20
3 **greedy pray**: i.e. his preying greedily on her. 4 **let**: hinder. 7 **regret**: sorrow caused by an external event. 8 **liuely breath**: the breath of life.

Stanza 21
5–6 **chin**: rhyme may force this synecdoche for 'face'. *OED* cites an earlier use in which the word seems to signify 'cheek'. **tender part**: at i 45.3, the term seems to apply to the body generally, as vi 10.2 and 'tender corse' at iii 5.6. Decorum forbids specificity. **tosse**: shake. 7 **So hardly**: with such difficulty. **win**: persuade. 8 **natiue prison**: her natural body which encloses her spirit (**ghost**) from birth; cf. Ps. 142.7.

Stanzas 22–23
The pathos of Una's lament lies in her association with light. Bajazeth's lament in Marlowe, *1 Tamburlaine* 5.2.196–241, is a pastiche of these stanzas. On the differences, see P. Cheney 1997:271.

Stanza 22
1 Addressing her 'eyes' (20.5). 2 **deadly**: as sign of his death and cause of hers. 4 **liking**: pleasure. **earthly mould**: mortal things. 5 The three Fates who spin and cut the thread of life; see IV ii 48 and *n*. **carefull**: sorrowful. 7 **dart**: referring

to 'deathes eternall dart' (III x 59.9); hence **sencelesse cold** refers to the numbing cold of death. 9 Una's lament takes literally love's extravagant claim that without her knight who is her 'light, and shining lampe of blis', her 'chearefull day is turnd to chearelesse night' (iii 27.7, 9).

Stanza 23
1–3 Alluding to Gen. 1.3–4. **deepest dongeon**: cf. the 'Dongeon deep' (15.9) into which Orgoglio has cast her knight. 6 Una's cry echoes throughout the poem; cf. Arthur's lesson 'That blisse may not abide in state of mortall men' (viii 44.9). 7 **late**: i.e. too late. The term expresses the state of despair. 9 **seeled vp**: closed, as the stitched eyelids of a hawk. **deadly meed**: reward of death.

Stanza 24
3–4 In any life-and-death struggle, three is the inevitable number.

Stanza 25
5 Cf. vi 37.9. 7 **launched**: pierced. Una alludes to her earlier knights, the 'Full many' (45.1) who have died in their quest to slay the dragon. 8 **stound**: time; here, time of trial or sorrow. 9 **more**: i.e. more than I expect.

26

Then gan the Dwarfe the whole discourse declare,
  The subtile traines of *Archimago* old;
  The wanton loues of false *Fidessa* fayre,
  Bought with the blood of vanquisht Paynim bold:
  The wretched payre transformd to treen mould;
  The house of *Pryde*, and perilles round about;
  The combat, which he with *Sansioy* did hould;
  The lucklesse conflict with the Gyaunt stout,
Wherein captiu'd, of life or death he stood in doubt.

27

She heard with patience all vnto the end,
  And stroue to maister sorrowfull assay,
  Which greater grew, the more she did contend,
  And almost rent her tender hart in tway;
  And loue fresh coles vnto her fire did lay:
  For greater loue, the greater is the losse.
  Was neuer Lady loued dearer day,
  Then she did loue the knight of the *Redcrosse*;
For whose deare sake so many troubles her did tosse.

28

At last when feruent sorrow slaked was,
  She vp arose, resoluing him to find,
  Aliue or dead: and forward forth doth pas,
  All as the Dwarfe the way to her assynd:

And euermore in constant carefull mind
  She fedd her wound with fresh renewed bale;
  Long tost with stormes, and bet with bitter wind,
  High ouer hills, and lowe adowne the dale,
She wandred many a wood, and measurd many a vale.

29

At last she chaunced by good hap to meet
  A goodly knight, faire marching by the way
  Together with his Squyre, arayed meet:
  His glitterand armour shined far away,
  Like glauncing light of *Phœbus* brightest ray;
  From top to toe no place appeared bare,
  That deadly dint of steele endanger may:
  Athwart his brest a bauldrick braue he ware,
That shind, like twinkling stars, with stones most pretious rare.

30

And in the midst thereof one pretious stone
  Of wondrous worth, and eke of wondrous mights,
  Shapt like a Ladies head, exceeding shone,
  Like *Hesperus* emongst the lesser lights,
  And stroue for to amaze the weaker sights;
  Thereby his mortall blade full comely hong
  In yuory sheath, ycaru'd with curious slights;
  Whose hilts were burnisht gold, and handle strong
Of mother perle, and buckled with a golden tong.

Stanza 26
The semicolons divide the knight's 'wofull Tragedy' (24.8) into five acts. I: line 2 (canto i and the opening of canto ii); II: lines 3–5 (the rest of canto ii, gaining Duessa with its consequences shown in Fradubio); III: line 6 (canto iv); IV: line 7 (canto v); V: lines 8–9 (canto vii). **1 discourse**: sequence of events. **2 subtile traines**: crafty wiles; cf. iii 24.7. **5 treen mould**: the form and substance of a tree; see ii 39.9*n*. **8 stout**: also 'proud', 'haughty'.

Stanza 27
2 assay: affliction; trial. **7 loued dearer day**: loved life more dearly in an exact sense, for he is her 'light, and shining lampe of blis' (iii 27.9).

Stanza 28
Duessa as the 'virgin widow' (ii 24.8) who seeks in sorrow the body of her dead lover is the type of which Una in her present quest is the antitype. **1 slaked**: abated, relieved; but more literally, 'quenched', for her **feruent** (burning) sorrow is caused by 'her fire' (27.5) of love. **4 assynd**: pointed out; cf. 52.9. The line marks the reversal of the opening tableau when he was 'euer last' (i 6.2). **5 carefull**: sorrowful. **7 bet**: buffeted. **9 measurd**: traversed (*OED* 11). The line measures the tedium of her travel as she resumes the quest which began at ii 8.

Stanzas 29–36
An extended blazon commensurate with Arthur's virtue of magnificence, which includes the perfection of all the virtues (see *LR* 19, 39). He is not named, except in the Arguments, until ix 6.5.

Stanza 29
2 faire: as an adj., 'pleasing to the eye'; as an adv., 'becomingly', 'gently'. **4–5 glitterand**: sparkling with light; cf.

his light-giving shield, 34.5. The present participle is used to suggest 'light-giving' in contrast to 'glittering' or light-reflecting. Lucifera's 'glitterand light' (iv 16.9, and see *n*) is associated with the usurping Phaethon (iv 9) in contrast to the Phœbus image used here. **glauncing**: flashing, dazzling. **7 dint**: stroke. **8–9 bauldrick**: the ornamented belt worn from the right shoulder across the breast to support the sword. Its central stone (30.1) covers the heart. As a belt of **twinkling stars**, which lies **Athwart his brest**, it suggests the obliquity of the zodiac, 'heauens bright-shining baudricke' (V i 11.7). On the baldric, or *cingulum militare*, as the chief emblem of knighthood, see Leslie 1983:169–74. On Arthur as a sun-god, see A. Fowler 1964:214–15, and Brooks-Davies 1977:74–75.

Stanza 30
1 in the midst: the phrase notes the sovereignty of the centre (see A. Fowler 1970:27–33) with Arthur's shield bearing one precious stone shaped like a lady's head, thus constituting a second midpoint in Bk I; see 12–13*n*. **2 mights**: powers, virtues, referring to the magical powers possessed by certain precious stones; see 'stones, precious' in the *SEnc*. Here its power is gained from its shape: an effigy of the Faerie Queene, as does Guyon's shield at II i 28.7–8. Geoffrey of Monmouth 1891:9.4 records that the device on Arthur's shield was a picture of the Virgin Mary. **4 Hesperus**: Venus, to indicate the place and power of love in Arthur's quest. For the association of Venus with Astræa-Virgo-Elizabeth, see Yates 1977:59–69. **5 amaze**: dazzle, bewilder. **weaker sights**: eyes too weak to endure its brightness. **7 curious slights**: elaborately wrought designs, perhaps suggesting some magical inscription but avoiding any power such as that given the scabbard by Merlin in Malory 1.25. **9 tong**: pin.

31

His haughtie Helmet, horrid all with gold,
    Both glorious brightnesse, and great terrour bredd,
    For all the crest a Dragon did enfold
    With greedie pawes, and ouer all did spredd
    His golden winges: his dreadfull hideous hedd
    Close couched on the beuer, seemd to throw
    From flaming mouth bright sparckles fiery redd,
    That suddeine horrour to faint hartes did show;
And scaly tayle was stretcht adowne his back full low.

32

Vpon the top of all his loftie crest,
    A bounch of heares discolourd diuersly,
    With sprincled pearle, and gold full richly drest,
    Did shake, and seemd to daunce for iollity,
    Like to an Almond tree ymounted hye
    On top of greene *Selinis* all alone,
    With blossoms braue bedecked daintily;
    Whose tender locks do tremble euery one
At euerie little breath, that vnder heauen is blowne.

33

His warlike shield all closely couer'd was,
    Ne might of mortall eye be euer seene;
    Not made of steele, nor of enduring bras,
    Such earthly mettals soone consumed beene:
    But all of Diamond perfect pure and cleene
    It framed was, one massy entire mould,
    Hewen out of Adamant rocke with engines keene,
    That point of speare it neuer percen could,
Ne dint of direfull sword diuide the substance would.

34

The same to wight he neuer wont disclose,
    But when as monsters huge he would dismay,
    Or daunt vnequall armies of his foes,
    Or when the flying heauens he would affray:
    For so exceeding shone his glistring ray,
    That *Phœbus* golden face it did attaint,
    As when a cloud his beames doth ouer-lay
    And siluer *Cynthia* wexed pale and faynt,
As when her face is staynd with magicke arts constraint.

Stanza 31

1 haughtie: lofty (in the literal sense); cf. ii 19.3. **horrid**: rough, bristling. **3–9** Geoffrey of Monmouth 1891:8.14–9.4 relates that a star 'darting forth a ray, at the end of which was a globe of fire in form of a dragon', foretold to Uther that he should have 'a most potent son'. When he carried a dragon made of gold to the wars, he became known as Uther Pendragon, i.e. Uther with the dragon's head; see II x 68.1–2*n*. Consequently his son, Arthur, 'placed a golden helmet upon his head, on which was engraven the figure of a dragon'. The chief classical models are Turnus's helmet in Virgil, *Aen.* 7.785–86, and the Soldan's helmet in Tasso, *Ger. Lib.* 9.25; on their differences, see Leslie 1983:53–54. Kaske 1999:37 notes that the caesura-less alexandrine mimes the trailing length of the tail. **greedie**: displaying its intense desire, as does Arthur at viii 6.9, 29.3. **couched**: *couchant*, lying; a heraldic term usually applied to an animal with head and tail erect, as III ii 25.1; see the *SEnc* 354. **beuer**: the visor.

Stanza 32

1 crest: top of the helmet; more specifically, the attached upright plume, a badge worn 'in tokne he was a kniht' (Gower 1980:5.6044). As the symbol of knighthood, it deserves its own stanza. See the woodcut of St George (at the end of Bk I). **2 discolourd diuersly**: of many colours. Repeated from ii 11.6, which describes the crest worn by Archimago disguised as the Red Cross Knight. **5–9** Aaron's rod that blossomed and bore ripe almonds was the sign that he had been chosen by God, Num. 17.5–8. The **Almond tree** is connected with the miraculous in the popular legend of Phyllis, who, having died through grief at her lover's long absence, was changed into an almond tree; upon being embraced by him, it sprouted fresh leaves and flowers. According to folk etymology, the name yields *al monde*, Lord of the World; noted Bailey 1912:2.277. The almond is also a symbol of age: that 'the almonde tre shal florish' (Eccles. 12.5) signifies white hair that crowns old age (Geneva gloss). Marlowe quotes these lines to describe Tamburlaine's triumphant appearance in *2 Tamburlaine* 4.3.119–24; see 'Marlowe' in the *SEnc*, and P. Cheney

1997:132. **6 Selinis**: from Virgil's *palmosa Selinus* (*Aen.* 3.705), the town of the victor's palm. **8 locks**: leaves (E.K. on *SC Nov.* 125); also 'hairs'.

Stanzas 33–35

Atlante's enchanted shield in Ariosto, *Orl. Fur.* 2.55–56, 8.11, 22.84–86, which is similarly veiled because its light blinds all who see it, is interpreted by Harington 1591:39 as 'the great pompes of the world' that blind vain people. For a comparison with Arthur's shield, see Alpers 1967:166–79, and Wiggins 1991; on the heraldry, see Berman 1983:2.

Stanza 33

1 The blank shield is the mark of an unproven knight, appropriate for Arthur who is still a prince; noted Leslie 1983:14–15. **2 be euer seene**: because its brightness is greater than the sun's (34.5–6). **5–9** On the **Diamond** as an emblem of fortitude in Valeriano, see de Tervarent 1958:147. The shield is hewen **out of Adamant rocke**, and hence is called 'th'Adamantine shield' at V xi 10.7, because adamant is a substance of supreme hardness, as indicated by its etymology, Gk ἀδάμας, unconquerable, which it shares with its derivative 'diamond'; see vi 4.5*n*. It suggests 'the shield of faith, wherewith ye may quench all the fyrie dartes of the wicked' (Eph. 6.16). In Tasso, *Ger. Lib.* 7.82, the diamond shield that defends God's faithful is taken by an angel to aid the Christian champion. It is said to be among the weapons used by Michael to slay the dragon. In his 'Allegorie of the Poem', Tasso identifies the shield as 'the special safegard of the Lord God'; see Hankins 1971:32. The magical properties of the diamond are listed by T. Cooper 1565 under 'Adamas'. The three descriptive terms in line 5 are not distinct in meaning: **perfect** functions either as an adj. or adv; **cleene**: clear, without any device or symbol engraved upon it, and therefore **pure**. **6** I.e. it was shaped wholly of one piece. **7 engines**: instruments.

Stanza 34

1 to wight: to any creature. **2 dismay**: defeat; literally, render powerless. **3 daunt**: vanquish; daze. **vnequall**: dispropor-

35

No magicke arts hereof had any might,
   Nor bloody wordes of bold Enchaunters call,
   But all that was not such, as seemd in sight,
   Before that shield did fade, and suddeine fall:
   And when him list the raskall routes appall,
   Men into stones therewith he could transmew,
   And stones to dust, and dust to nought at all;
   And when him list the prouder lookes subdew
He would them gazing blind, or turne to other hew.

36

Ne let it seeme that credence this exceedes,
   For he that made the same, was knowne right well
   To haue done much more admirable deedes.
   It *Merlin* was, which whylome did excell
   All liuing wightes in might of magicke spell:
   Both shield, and sword, and armour all he wrought
   For this young Prince, when first to armes he fell,
   But when he dyde, the Faery Queene it brought
To Faerie lond, where yet it may be seene, if sought.

37

A gentle youth, his dearely loued Squire
   His speare of heben wood behind him bare,
   Whose harmeful head, thrise heated in the fire,
   Had riuen many a brest with pikehead square;
   A goodly person, and could menage faire,
   His stubborne steed with curbed canon bitt,
   Who vnder him did amble as the aire,
   And chauft, that any on his backe should sitt;
The yron rowels into frothy fome he bitt.

38

Whenas this knight nigh to the Lady drew,
   With louely court he gan her entertaine;
   But when he heard her aunswers loth, he knew
   Some secret sorrow did her heart distraine:
   Which to allay and calme her storming paine,
   Faire feeling words he wisely gan display,
   And for her humor fitting purpose faine,
   To tempt the cause it selfe for to bewray;
Wherewith enmoud, these bleeding words she gan to say.

tionate, being otherwise more than a match for him. Heb. 11.34 records that faith has 'turned to flight the armies of the aliantes [aliens]'. **4 the flying heauens**: a claim commonly made of epic heroes, e.g. Turnus in Virgil, *Aen.* 11.351, but the line implies that the constellations revolve through fear of the power of Arthur's shield. Cf. Fidelia's power over the heavens at x 20.2–3. **5 glistring**: see i 14.4*n*; used of the sun's rays at v 2.5, ix 18.2. **6 attaint**: sully, obscure by surpassing in brilliance. **8–9** The power of witchcraft to eclipse the moon is noted at VII vi 16.5–6; see Ovid, *Met.* 7.207–08.

Stanza 35
1 hereof: concerning this, i.e. the shield. **2 bloody**: as they seek to shed blood. **5 raskall routes**: base rabble, vulgar mob. **6–7** While Atlante's shield, which has Medusa's head at its centre, petrifies observers, and Orgoglio's club batters his enemies to dust (14.3), Arthur's shield reduces them to nothing, in effect, reversing creation *ex nihilo*, as shown at viii 24.6–9. On its magical power, see Gross 1985:135–39. **8 prouder**: most proud. **9 hew**: shape.

Stanza 36
3 admirable: amazing, marvellous. **4–7** On Merlin as the maker of Arthur's arms, see II viii 20. His reputation as 'the great magicien' (ix 5.1) was established by Geoffrey of Monmouth and medieval romance writers. See 'Merlin' in the *SEnc*. On his role as a 'Prophet' (III iii 21.4), see Dobin 1990:19–60. **8–9** Before ever Arthur acts in the poem, he is distanced from us by his death; see Anderson 1988:199. **it**: that is, the **armes**, which would include the shield, sword, and armour though apparently not the spear noted at 37.2–4. Hieatt 1990:338 claims that the reference is to the shield, which has been described in the three previous stanzas; Roche 1990a:345 counters that the reference is to the armour. **if sought**: as Caesar's sword, which S. claims at II x 49.5 is 'yet to be seene this day' (without saying where).

Stanza 37
1 gentle: the usual epithet for Timias, often serving instead of his name, as II xi 29.8, IV viii 1.2, etc. **2 His speare**: i.e. Arthur's spear, carried by Timias here and at II viii 17.6. Such a spear is not used until wielded by Britomart who becomes the 'Knight of the Hebene speare' (IV v 8.2, etc.). For her connection with Arthur, see III i 8.6*n*. **heben wood**: ebony, noted for its extreme hardness. Its association with Cupid's bow (see proem 3.5) links Arthur with love. **5 menage**: manège, direct a horse through its paces; denoting his temperance. **6–9 curbed**: fastened at the ends with a chain. **canon bitt**: a smooth round bit. **amble**: trample *1596*. **as the aire**: nimbly, as Trevisan's steed 'did tread the wynd' (ix 21.8). **rowels**: knobs for the bit. **frothy fome**: hence his name, Spumador; see II xi 19.6–9*n*.

Stanza 38
2 louely: loving, kind. **court** signifies courteous attention or regard; cf. his 'gentle court' of Guyon at II ix 2.5, and the Red Cross Knight's 'goodly court' (7.1) of Duessa. **4 distraine**: afflict; tear asunder (cf. 27.4). **5–8** His 'well guided speach' (42.1) to save Una from despair is as powerful as Despaire's in canto ix to lead the Red Cross Knight into despair. **display**: pour forth, utter. **purpose**: speech. **bewray**: reveal. **9 enmoud**: moved inwardly or strongly. **bleeding words**: words that express 'her wound' (28.6).

Stanzas 39–41
For comment on the 'marvelous stichomythic exchange of proverb and *sententia*' in these stanzas, see the *SEnc* 564. Cincotta 1983:26–28 notes ten variations of seven proverbial forms. The proverb, 'counsel is a sovereign remedy' (Smith 123), which Arthur invokes at 40.8, is the most important for Elizabethan poets in establishing their authority to preserve their culture's wisdom and values persuasively and therefore memorably. Cf. II i 44.2–3, III iii 5.4–5, etc.

39

What worlds delight, or ioy of liuing speach
  Can hart, so plungd in sea of sorrowes deep,
  And heaped with so huge misfortunes, reach?
  The carefull cold beginneth for to creep,
  And in my heart his yron arrow steep,
  Soone as I thinke vpon my bitter bale:
  Such helplesse harmes yts better hidden keep,
  Then rip vp griefe, where it may not auaile,
My last left comfort is, my woes to weepe and waile.

40

Ah Lady deare, quoth then the gentle knight,
  Well may I ween, your grief is wondrous great;
  For wondrous great griefe groneth in my spright,
  Whiles thus I heare you of your sorrowes treat.
  But woefull Lady, let me you intrete,
  For to vnfold the anguish of your hart:
  Mishaps are maistred by aduice discrete,
  And counsell mitigates the greatest smart;
Found neuer help, who neuer would his hurts impart.

41

O but (quoth she) great griefe will not be tould,
  And can more easily be thought, then said.
  Right so (quoth he) but he, that neuer would,
  Could neuer: will to might giues greatest aid.

dialogue!

But griefe (quoth she) does greater grow displaid,
  If then it find not helpe, and breeds despaire.
  Despaire breeds not (quoth he) where faith is staid.
  No faith so fast (quoth she) but flesh does paire.
Flesh may empaire (quoth he) but reason can repaire.

42

His goodly reason, and well guided speach
  So deepe did settle in her gracious thought,
  That her perswaded to disclose the breach,
  Which loue and fortune in her heart had wrought,
  And said; Faire Sir, I hope good hap hath brought
  You to inquere the secrets of my griefe,
  Or that your wisedome will direct my thought,
  Or that your prowesse can me yield reliefe:
Then heare the story sad, which I shall tell you briefe.

43

The forlorne Maiden, whom your eies haue seene
  The laughing stocke of fortunes mockeries,
  Am th'onely daughter of a King and Queene,
  Whose parents deare whiles equal destinies,
  Did ronne about, and their felicities
  The fauourable heauens did not enuy,
  Did spred their rule through all the territories,
  Which *Phison* and *Euphrates* floweth by,
And *Gehons* golden waues doe wash continually.

Stanza 39

1–3 The abrupt beginning shows just how much she is 'enmoud' (38.9). We are not told what Arthur has said to which she replies unless **worlds delight** refers to his 'louely court' and **ioy of liuing speach** to his 'Faire feeling words' (38.6). **4–5 carefull cold**: 'for care is sayd to coole the blood' (E.K. on *SC Dec*. 133); see III x 59.6*n*. Cf. Una's state at vi 37.1–2 and vii 22.7–8, which culminates in her present despair. **7–8 helplesse**: admitting no help, preparing for Arthur's rejoinder at 40.7.

Stanza 40

8 Cf. Prov. 11.14: 'Where no counsel is, the people fall'.

Stanza 41

1 This same claim rounds out her complaint at 51.9. **2** The first stage of rescuing her from despair: at 39.4–6 her grief was too great to 'thinke vpon', now she allows the possibility that her state is not 'helplesse' (39.7). **7 staid**: constant, sustained. **8 paire**: impair; or, from 'appair': weaken. **9 reason**: after his sympathetic counsel, Arthur asserts first the powers of will and faith, and now of reason.

Stanza 42

1 **goodly reason**: attributed to the Palmer at II ii 5.2. That divine grace, for which Arthur is the instrument, operates through human reason rather than in defiance of it, makes a precise point in the extended controversy on their relationship; see 'nature and grace' in the *SEnc*. **2 gracious**: probably with overtones of 'receiving grace' (cf. *OED* 6: 'endowed with

divine grace'), which rescues her from despair. **thought**: in the earlier, more general sense, 'mind', which permits the repetition of the rhyme word in 7. **5–6** Her hope is sound; see 29.1. **secrets**: the plural suggests the biblical sense in Ps. 44.21: 'Shal not God search this out? for he knoweth the secrets of the heart'. **7 Or**: either.

Stanza 43

1 **forlorne**: as iii 43.1. **3 th'onely daughter**: in opposition to Duessa who claims to be 'the sole daughter of an Emperour' (ii 22.7–9 and see *n*); cf. xii 21.2–3. Nohrnberg 1976:128 cites Song Sol. 6.8: 'my dooue is alone [i.e. one], and my vndefiled, she is the onelie daughter of her mother', which was generally interpreted to refer to the one catholic church. Although not named, presumably her parents are Adam and Eve, the **King and Queene** of Eden; see xii 26.1. **4–5** I.e. while the impartial fates ran their course. A reference to the fixed stars which, before the Fall, revolved justly in their orbits. For the cosmic disorder after the Fall, see V proem 4–9. **6 fauourable**: well disposed in their astral influence. **7–9 territories**: at i 5.3–6 these are said to include 'all the world', which is identified as Eden by naming three of its four rivers, from Gen. 2.11–14. The fourth, the Tigris, joins the Euphrates, as the map in the Geneva Bible shows; the gloss explains how the names of the four rivers interchange. Commentators took Gen. 2.5 to mean that the whole earth was watered from Paradise; yet **floweth by** suggests that the rivers did not take their source in Eden but only flowed through it. **9** The Phison, not the Gehon, is associated with gold at Gen. 2.11–2, as Upton 1758 notes; but S. prefers alliteration to fact.

44

Till that their cruell cursed enemy,
   An huge great Dragon horrible in sight,
   Bred in the loathly lakes of *Tartary*,
   With murdrous rauine, and deuouring might
   Their kingdome spoild, and countrey wasted quight:
   Themselues, for feare into his iawes to fall,
   He forst to castle strong to take their flight,
   Where fast embard in mighty brasen wall,
He has them now fowr years besiegd to make them thrall.

45

Full many knights aduenturous and stout
   Haue enterprizd that Monster to subdew;
   From euery coast that heauen walks about,
   Haue thither come the noble Martial crew,
   That famous harde atchieuements still pursew,
   Yet neuer any could that girlond win,
   But all still shronke, and still he greater grew:
   All they for want of faith, or guilt of sin,
The pitteous pray of his fiers cruelty haue bin.

46

At last yled with far reported praise,
   Which flying fame throughout the world had spred,
   Of doughty knights, whom Fary land did raise,
   That noble order hight of maidenhed,
   Forthwith to court of *Gloriane* I sped,
   Of *Gloriane* great Queene of glory bright,
   Whose kingdomes seat *Cleopolis* is red,
   There to obtaine some such redoubted knight,
That Parents deare from tyrants powre deliuer might.

47

Yt was my chaunce (my chaunce was faire and good)
   There for to find a fresh vnproued knight,
   Whose manly hands imbrewd in guilty blood
   Had neuer beene, ne euer by his might
   Had throwne to ground the vnregarded right:
   Yet of his prowesse proofe he since hath made
   (I witnes am) in many a cruell fight;
   The groning ghosts of many one dismaide
Haue felt the bitter dint of his auenging blade.

48

And ye the forlorne reliques of his powre,
   His biting sword, and his deuouring speare,
   Which haue endured many a dreadfull stowre,
   Can speake his prowesse, that did earst you beare,
   And well could rule: now he hath left you heare,
   To be the record of his ruefull losse,
   And of my dolefull disauenturous deare:
   O heauie record of the good *Redcrosse*,
Where haue yee left your lord, that could so well you tosse?

Stanza 44

This stanza expands the substance of i 5.7–8. **3** Cf. 'the squalid lakes of *Tartarie*' (*Gnat* 543), Tartarus being the region in the underworld reserved for the damned; see II xii 6.4–6. At xi 40.3, the dragon is said to be 'hell-bred'. **4 rauine**: violence, force; or as 'ravin': preying, voracity. **8 embard**: imprisoned. **brasen**: see xi 3n. **9 fowr years**: when the dragon or Satan was cast down to the earth, he droue the woman into the wilderness where she was nourished 'for a time, and times, and halfe a time, from the presence of the serpent' (Rev. 12.14). In verse 6, the time is given as 1,260 days, or about three and a half years. Upton 1758 notes that S. elegantly uses a round number. Or the figure may represent 4,000 years: in 'A Perfite Supputation of the Yeres and Times from Adam vnto Christ', the Geneva Bible demonstrates that from creation to the birth of Christ was 3,974 years, 6 months and 10 days. Metre, if not elegance, requires this figure to be rounded, as it is in 'Adam lay y-bounden'.

Stanza 45

1–3 Cf. xi 17.9. **enterprizd**: undertaken. **coast**: part of the world. **walks**: moves. The astronomy is, of course, Ptolemaic. **7** The dragon grows greater because the knights wither or shrivel in sin and death, as seen in the Red Cross Knight with 'al his flesh shronk vp like withered flowres' (viii 41.9). Cf. the description of the dragon 'swolne with blood of late' (viii 12.4). **8 want of faith . . . guilt of sin**: the two key phrases in the moral allegory of Bk I.

Stanza 46

4–7 The order . . . of maidenhed is the type or pattern of the Elizabethan Order of the Garter; see Strong 1977:164–85. Its sovereign was the Virgin Queen, its collar and ribbon displayed St George killing the dragon, and its star was the Red Cross; see *Enc. Brit.* 15.856, Plate I. Guyon belongs to the Order (II ii 42.3–4) as does Artegall (II ix 6.9), and its knights triumph in the first day of Satyrane's tournament; see IV iv 17–25n. Bennett 1942:39–46 discusses the relation of the two orders; see also Leslie 1983:138–46. On their relation to the Knights Templars, which S. may have sought to rehabilitate, see Wilkin 1994. **Queene of glory**: see i 3.2–3n. **Cleopolis**: signifying the city of Fame or Glory; see x 58.2–4n. **red**: named.

Stanza 47

2 vnproued: untried in battle; see i 3.7–8. **3 imbrewd . . . blood**: stained, and hence defiled, by blood shed guiltily. **8 dismaide**: defeated. **9 bitter**: biting, cutting (as 48.2). **dint**: stroke.

Stanza 48

A poignant address to the armour that she brought to the court of Gloriana; see *LR* 63–64. Hence Bk I's unique reference to the Red Cross Knight as **Redcrosse**. **1 forlorne**: forsaken by the knight, as 19.4. **3 stowre**: conflict. **6–8 record** (6): evidence; proof; witness. **record** (8): memorial; cf. 'ruefull moniments' (19.8). **disauenturous**: unfortunate. At the beginning the knight was 'aduenturous' (45.1); cf. ix 11.8, 45.4. **deare**: beloved; cf. viii Arg. **9 tosse**: brandish, wield.

49

Well hoped I, and faire beginnings had,
  That he my captiue languor should redeeme,
  Till all vnweeting, an Enchaunter bad
  His sence abusd, and made him to misdeeme
  My loyalty, not such as it did seeme
  That rather death desire, then such despight.
  Be iudge ye heauens, that all things right esteeme,
  How I him lou'd, and loue with all my might,
So thought I eke of him, and think I thought aright.

50

Thenceforth me desolate he quite forsooke,
  To wander, where wilde fortune would me lead,
  And other bywaies he himselfe betooke,
  Where neuer foote of liuing wight did tread,
  That brought not backe the balefull body dead;
  In which him chaunced false *Duessa* meete,
  Mine onely foe, mine onely deadly dread,
  Who with her witchcraft and misseeming sweete,
Inueigled him to follow her desires vnmeete.

51

At last by subtile sleights she him betraid
  Vnto his foe, a Gyaunt huge and tall,
  Who him disarmed, dissolute, dismaid,
  Vnwares surprised, and with mighty mall
  The monster mercilesse him made to fall,
  Whose fall did neuer foe before behold;
  And now in darkesome dungeon, wretched thrall,
  Remedilesse, for aie he doth him hold;
This is my cause of griefe, more great, then may be told.

52

Ere she had ended all, she gan to faint:
  But he her comforted, and faire bespake,
  Certes, Madame, ye haue great cause of plaint,
  That stoutest heart, I weene, could cause to quake.
  But be of cheare, and comfort to you take:
  For till I haue acquitt your captiue knight,
  Assure your selfe, I will you not forsake.
  His chearefull words reuiu'd her chearelesse spright,
So forth they went, the Dwarfe them guiding euer right.

Stanza 49

2 captiue languor: languishment in captivity; or their languorous (distressing) captivity. If 'captiue' is given its weaker sense from 'caitiff', she refers simply to their wretched plight (see *OED* 3). Cf. the false Una's complaint at i 52.7. **3 vnweeting**: unknown to the knight; cf. 6.1. **4 misdeeme**: misjudge, think evil of; see iv 2.2*n*. **6 despight**: outrage against her **loyalty**. **7 esteeme**: judge. Fittingly, Una appeals to the heavens and leaves all judgement to God.

Stanza 50

3–5 He took a by-path from which no one returns alive. According to Prov. 2.13–19, those who have left 'the waies of righteousnes to walke in the waies of darkenes' must be delivered by Wisdom 'from the strange woman, euen from the stranger, which flattereth with her wordes. . . . Surely her house tendeth to death, and her paths vnto the dead. All thei that go vnto her returne not againe'. **he himselfe betooke**: alternatively, he betook himself, leading himself into sin. See Jer. 2.6 on Egypt as 'a land that no man passed through, and where no man dwelt'. Una refers to spiritual death in this life: 'dead in trespasses and sinnes, wherein, in time past ye walked, according to the course of this worlde' (Eph. 2.1–2); cf. man's state in hell at v 31.6–33.9 **onely**: chief, greatest; cf. the use of the term at 43.3. The second use in the line has the adverbial sense, 'specially', 'pre-eminently'. Una first names Duessa

here and indicates her duplicity by the repeated phrase. **8 misseeming**: false appearance, unless **sweete** is a substantive. On such double syntax, see Kosako 1993:134. **9 Inueigled**: beguiled, more specifically, 'blinded in judgement', from Fr. *aveugle*, alluding to Duessa's relation to Night and Aveugle, v 23.7; cf. xii 32.5.

Stanza 51

3 dissolute: enfeebled, relaxed, careless, debauched; and even literally 'dissolved' (*OED* I); see 7.2*n*. Weatherby 1994:9–10 notes that this word is a literal translation of St John Chrysostom's adjective for those who discard Christian armour. **dismaid**: see 11.6*n*. This catalogue of the knight's deprivations began with her reference to him as her 'disauenturous deare' (48.7). **4 mall**: 'mace' (10.9). **5** Alliteration and internal echoes make this line esp. powerful. **8 Remedilesse, for aie**: forever without hope of rescue, which is the state of Æsculapius at v 36.8, except that Una brings Arthur 'to redeeme her deare' (viii Arg.).

Stanza 52

6 acquitt: delivered; inferring the legal sense: he will pay the ransom or debt needed to release the knight. Cf. the use of the word in viii 1.4, and the Ferryman's prayer: 'God doe vs well acquitt' (II xii 3.3).

Cant. VIII.

Faire virgin to redeeme her deare
Brings Arthure to the fight:
Who slayes the Gyaunt, wounds the beast,
And strips Duessa quight.

1

AY me, how many perils doe enfold
The righteous man, to make him daily fall?
Were not that heauenly grace doth him vphold,
And stedfast truth acquite him out of all:
Her loue is firme, her care continuall,
So oft as he thorough his own foolish pride,
Or weaknes is to sinfull bands made thrall:
Els should this *Redcrosse* knight in bands haue dyde,
For whose deliuerance she this Prince doth thether guyd.

2

They sadly traueild thus, vntill they came
Nigh to a castle builded strong and hye:
Then cryde the Dwarfe, lo yonder is the same,
In which my Lord my liege doth lucklesse ly,
Thrall to that Gyaunts hatefull tyranny:
Therefore, deare Sir, your mightie powres assay.
The noble knight alighted by and by
From loftie steed, and badd the Ladie stay,
To see what end of fight should him befall that day.

3

So with his Squire, th'admirer of his might,
He marched forth towardes that castle wall;
Whose gates he fownd fast shutt, ne liuing wight
To warde the same, nor answere commers call.
Then tooke that Squire an horne of bugle small,
Which hong adowne his side in twisted gold,
And tasselles gay. Wyde wonders ouer all
Of that same hornes great vertues weren told,
Which had approued bene in vses manifold.

4

Was neuer wight, that heard that shrilling sownd,
But trembling feare did feel in euery vaine;
Three miles it might be easy heard arownd,
And Ecchoes three aunswerd it selfe againe:
No false enchauntment, nor deceiptfull traine
Might once abide the terror of that blast,
But presently was void and wholly vaine:
No gate so strong, no locke so firme and fast,
But with that percing noise flew open quite, or brast.

Book I Canto viii

Argument
1–2 redeeme: rescue, save; also deliver from sin. Una chose the Red Cross Knight in the hope 'That he my captiue languor should redeeme' (vii 49.2); now she must bring Arthur to redeem him. Arthur intervenes in the eighth canto of each book (except Bk III), since eight is the number of regeneration. See A. Fowler 1964:53. The number of times he intervenes is determined by the number of the book; see II xi 16.1–3*n*, III v 27*n*, IV viii 18*n*, V viii Arg.*n*, VI viii Arg.*n*. On the stanza-total, 50, as the number associated with the advent of the Holy Spirit and with liberation, see Fowler 54*n*4.

Stanza 1
This testimony to the power and working of truth in our life answers the power and working of deceit as seeming truth at vii 1. A similar testimony to the power and working of God's grace is given at the corresponding point of Bk II. **3** Arthur as **heauenly grace** must literally **vphold** the Red Cross Knight at 40.4–8. Cf. Una's role at x 2.8–9. **4 acquite**: cf. vii 52.6. Una, here identified as truth, may be said to 'acquite' her knight when she absolves him from all blame at 42.6–9, 43.3–6, and 49.3–5. Cf. John 8.32: 'the trueth shal make you fre'. **6–7 pride, | Or weaknes**: these terms link respectively with the 'guilt of sin' or 'want of faith' (vii 45.8) through which Una's earlier champions were defeated by the dragon. **sinfull bands**: bondage to sin. **9** Una assumes the dwarf's role at vii 52.9.

Stanza 2
3–6 The climax to the dwarf's role in Bk I. At first he bears Una's needments (i 6.1–4), and then the knight's armour (vii 19.4–9); and later he guides Una and then Arthur (vii 28.4 and 52.9) to rescue the imprisoned knight. His gesture marks the mid-point of an action that is completed when Una points to the castle where her parents are imprisoned (xi 3). **6 assay**: put to trial; prove. **7 by and by**: immediately. **8** A knight's steed is usually called **loftie** to indicate chivalric pride in controlling passion; it is named a horse if passion is not controlled, as iii 34.9, II v 3.5, etc.

Stanza 3
4 warde: guard. **5 horne of bugle small**: hunting-horn made of the horn of a wild ox (bugle). **7 ouer all**: everywhere. **8 vertues**: powers. **9 approued**: proved.

Stanza 4
The enchanted horn in Italian romance, e.g. the horn given the English duke Astolfo in Ariosto, *Orl. Fur.* 15.14–15, and that given Huon by Gloriande in *Huon of Burdeux* (as McCabe 1989a:98 notes), here becomes the horn of salvation, the word of God whose 'sounde went out through all the earth' (Rom. 10.18). In Josh. 6.3–20, the walls of Jericho are brought down by the sound of a ram's horns, thus attributing the victory to God, as the Geneva gloss explains. Cf. also the seven apocalyptic trumpets of Rev. 8–9 that proclaim the final resurrection. **5 traine**: deception. **7 presently**: immediately. **void**: ineffective, useless. **9 brast**: burst open; shattered.

5

The same before the Geaunts gate he blew,
　That all the castle quaked from the grownd,
　And euery dore of freewill open flew:
　The Gyaunt selfe dismaied with that sownd,
　Where he with his *Duessa* dalliaunce fownd,
　In hast came rushing forth from inner bowre,
　With staring countenance sterne, as one astownd,
　And staggering steps, to weet, what suddein stowre,
Had wrought that horror strange, and dar'd his dreaded powre.

6

And after him the proud *Duessa* came,
　High mounted on her many headed beast,
　And euery head with fyrie tongue did flame,
　And euery head was crowned on his creast,
　And bloody mouthed with late cruell feast.
　That when the knight beheld, his mightie shild
　Vpon his manly arme he soone addrest,
　And at him fiersly flew, with corage fild,
And eger greedinesse through euery member thrild.

7

Therewith the Gyant buckled him to fight,
　Inflamd with scornefull wrath and high disdaine,
　And lifting vp his dreadfull club on hight,
　All armd with ragged snubbes and knottie graine,

Him thought at first encounter to haue slaine.
　But wise and wary was that noble Pere,
　And lightly leaping from so monstrous maine,
　Did fayre auoide the violence him nere;
It booted nought, to thinke, such thunderbolts to beare.

8

Ne shame he thought to shonne so hideous might:
　The ydle stroke, enforcing furious way,
　Missing the marke of his misaymed sight
　Did fall to ground, and with his heauy sway
　So deepely dinted in the driuen clay,
　That three yardes deepe a furrow vp did throw:
　The sad earth wounded with so sore assay,
　Did grone full grieuous vnderneath the blow,
And trembling with strange feare, did like an erthquake show.

9

As when almightie *Ioue* in wrathfull mood,
　To wreake the guilt of mortall sins is bent,
　Hurles forth his thundring dart with deadly food,
　Enrold in flames, and smouldring dreriment,
　Through riuen cloudes and molten firmament;
　The fiers threeforked engin making way,
　Both loftie towres and highest trees hath rent,
　And all that might his angry passage stay,
And shooting in the earth, castes vp a mount of clay.

Stanza 5

2–3 The horn has the same effect on Alma's castle at II ix 11.3–5. **euery dore**: i.e. of Orgoglio's castle but not the 'yron doore' of his dungeon in which the Red Cross Knight is seen imprisoned at 37.4–5. 4–7 Orgoglio is surprised in the same act as was the knight. **dismaied**: cf. vii 11.6, 51.3. **staring**: glaring in fury. **astownd**: cf. vii 7.7. 8 **stowre**: uproar.

Stanza 6

2–5 See vii 16–17*n*. The **fyrie tongue** (cf. 12.6) belongs to the fire-breathing dragon of folklore, the **crowned . . . creast** to the beast in Rev. 12.3, with **bloody mouthed** transferred from its rider to 'the woman drunken with the blood of Saintes, and with the blood of the Martyrs of Iesus' (Rev. 17.6). **late**: as 12.4 and xi 13.4, suggests some topical reference, possibly to the St Bartholomew's Day massacre in France in 1572, or to the executions by Alva's Council of Blood in the Netherlands in 1567, or to the persecution of Protestants during the reign of Mary I. See Hume 1984:94–95, King 1990a:91. 6–9 Arthur's readiness contrasts at each point with the Red Cross Knight's lack of readiness when confronted by Orgoglio. **addrest**: made ready. **eger greedinesse**: intense eagerness for battle; also 'biting', 'sharp', referring to the piercing effect of the emotion. Hence **thrild**, 'penetrated', is close to the current sense, 'caught up in emotion'. The phrase indicates his state of Praysdesire at II ix 39; cf. his 'greedie great desyre' at 29.3.

Stanza 7

2 **disdaine**: indignation, anger; see i 19.6*n*. 4 **snubbes**: root snags; cf. 'snaggy Oke' (vii 10.7). 6 **Pere**: champion, or rival

(*OED* 3). 7–8 The Red Cross Knight was 'wary' (vii 12.5) but his defence ended with his **lightly leaping** away from Orgoglio's blow (cf. vii 12.6), for he could not avoid the **violence him nere**. **maine**: force; see vii 11.2 and *n*. **fayre**: quite, clean. On the differences between the two battles, see Gless 1994:134–36. 9 **thunderbolts** were thought to contain stones (*OED* 3).

Stanza 8

1 **hideous**: immense. 4–6 Alluding to Orgoglio's name: 'orge', from 'tilling' which is also the etymology of George, according to *The Golden Legend* (see x 66.5–6*n*), 'so george is to saye as tilyenge the erthe | that is his flesshe' (112). **sway**: the impetus of the blow. 7 **sad**: heavy; or melancholy, the humour with which the earth is associated (see 'elements' in the *SEnc*); or sad because she is hit by her son. **assay**: attack.

Stanza 9

Orgoglio's blow was compared to cannon-fire at vii 13 in his fight with the Red Cross Knight. That it is now compared to a thunderbolt and an earthquake (8.9) indicates that the fight with Arthur is more elemental. 2 **wreake**: punish. **mortall sins**: the sins of mortals; the sins that cause (and deserve) death. 3 **food**: feud, i.e. hatred, hostility. 4 **smouldring dreriment**: smothering gloom or darkness, in contrast to the flames; cf. 'smouldry cloud' (vii 13.8). For **dreriment**, see ii 44.4*n*. 6 **threeforked**: Ovid's *ignes trisulci* (*Met.* 2.848–49). **engin**: machine used in warfare; here a battering-ram.

10

His boystrous club, so buried in the grownd,
 He could not rearen vp againe so light,
 But that the knight him at aduantage fownd,
 And whiles he stroue his combred clubbe to quight,
 Out of the earth, with blade all burning bright
 He smott off his left arme, which like a block
 Did fall to ground, depriu'd of natiue might;
 Large streames of blood out of the truncked stock
Forth gushed, like fresh water streame from riuen rocke.

11

Dismayed with so desperate deadly wound,
 And eke impatient of vnwonted payne,
 He lowdly brayd with beastly yelling sownd,
 That all the fieldes rebellowed againe,
 As great a noyse, as when in Cymbrian plaine
 An heard of Bulles, whom kindly rage doth sting,
 Doe for the milky mothers want complaine,
 And fill the fieldes with troublous bellowing,
The neighbor woods arownd with hollow murmur ring.

12

That when his deare *Duessa* heard, and saw
 The euill stownd, that daungerd her estate,
 Vnto his aide she hastily did draw
 Her dreadfull beast, who swolne with blood of late
 Came ramping forth with proud presumpteous gate,
 And threatned all his heades like flaming brandes.
 But him the Squire made quickly to retrate,
 Encountring fiers with single sword in hand,
And twixt him and his Lord did like a bulwarke stand.

13

The proud *Duessa* full of wrathfull spight,
 And fiers disdaine, to be affronted so,
 Enforst her purple beast with all her might
 That stop out of the way to ouerthroe,
 Scorning the let of so vnequall foe:
 But nathemore would that corageous swayne
 To her yeeld passage, gainst his Lord to goe,
 But with outrageous strokes did him restraine,
And with his body bard the way atwixt them twaine.

14

Then tooke the angrie witch her golden cup,
 Which still she bore, replete with magick artes;
 Death and despeyre did many thereof sup,
 And secret poyson through their inner partes,
 Th'eternall bale of heauie wounded harts;
 Which after charmes and some enchauntments said,
 She lightly sprinkled on his weaker partes;
 Therewith his sturdie corage soone was quayd,
And all his sences were with suddein dread dismayd.

15

So downe he fell before the cruell beast,
 Who on his neck his bloody clawes did seize,
 That life nigh crusht out of his panting brest:
 No powre he had to stirre, nor will to rize.
 That when the carefull knight gan well auise,
 He lightly left the foe, with whom he fought,
 And to the beast gan turne his enterprise;
 For wondrous anguish in his hart it wrought,
To see his loued Squyre into such thraldom brought.

Stanza 10

1 boystrous: massive; perhaps chosen because it is associated with wind (*OED* 8). **2 light**: quickly. **3 at aduantage**: in a favourable position. **4 combred**: encumbered, because held fast in the ground. His mother Earth aids his downfall. **8–9** As Moses 'lift vp his hand, and with his rod he smote the rocke twise, and the water came out abundantly' (Num. 20.11). This allusion, first noted by Percival 1964, is confirmed by **fresh**. As interpreted typologically by Paul, 'they dranke of the spiritual Rocke . . . and the Rocke was Christ' (1 Cor. 10.4); noted Nohrnberg 1976:274. **truncked stock**: i.e. his truncated body.

Stanza 11

2 impatient: unable to bear the suffering, as 17.4. **3–4** Cf. the 'bellowing' that precedes his appearance at vii 7.4–5. **5–8 Cymbrian plaine**: apparently named here for the land (Denmark and Norway) occupied by the Cimbri, a savage Teutonic tribe. **kindly rage**: natural lust. **want**: absence. **9 murmur**: complaint.

Stanza 12

2 stownd: time of peril. **estate**: state. **4 of late**: see 6.2–5*n*. **5 ramping**: bounding. **8 with single sword**: i.e. with sword alone, as the Red Cross Knight confronted Orgoglio with 'single blade' (vii 11.9).

Stanza 13

1–2 Cf. Orgoglio's state at 7.2. **affronted**: faced in defiance. **3 Enforst**: both 'compelled' and 'added (her) force to'. The double syntax is noted by Alpers 1967:86. **5 let**: obstruction. **6 nathemore**: not at all.

Stanza 14

1–5 Cf. the great whore upon her scarlet-coloured beast, who 'had a cup of golde in her hand, ful of abominations, and filthines of her fornication . . . all nations haue dronken of the wine of the wrath of her fornication' (Rev. 17.4–18.3); cf. Jer. 51.7. On the contrast to Fidelia's 'cup of gold', see x 13.2–5*n*. **still**: always. **3 Death** and **despeyre** are distinguished as physical and spiritual death. **5 wounded**: i.e. by sin. **6** On the identification of Duessa with the Church of Rome, and the association of her with Circe, particularly in her use of magic in Ovid, *Met.* 14.55–58, see Roberts 1978:433–34, and the *SEnc* 166, 229. **7 weaker**: too weak. **8–9** Cf. the effect on the Red Cross Knight of drinking from the poisoned fountain at vii 6. His fall is now re-enacted. **quayd**: subdued, daunted.

Stanza 15

2 seize: fasten. **4 nor will**: because his will is infected. **5 carefull**: full of care (for his squire). **auise**: observe. **9 his loued Squyre**: as vii 37.1.

16

And high aduauncing his blood-thirstie blade,
    Stroke one of those deformed heades so sore,
    That of his puissaunce proud ensample made;
    His monstrous scalpe downe to his teeth it tore,
    And that misformed shape misshaped more:
    A sea of blood gusht from the gaping wownd,
    That her gay garments staynd with filthy gore,
    And ouerflowed all the field arownd;
That ouer shoes in blood he waded on the grownd.

17

Thereat he rored for exceeding paine,
    That to haue heard, great horror would haue bred,
    And scourging th'emptie ayre with his long trayne,
    Through great impatience of his grieued hed
    His gorgeous ryder from her loftie sted
    Would haue cast downe, and trodd in durty myre,
    Had not the Gyaunt soone her succoured;
    Who all enrag'd with smart and frantick yre,
Came hurtling in full fiers, and forst the knight retyre.

18

The force, which wont in two to be disperst,
    In one alone left hand he now vnites,
    Which is through rage more strong then both were erst;
    With which his hideous club aloft he dites,
    And at his foe with furious rigor smites,
    That strongest Oake might seeme to ouerthrow:
    The stroke vpon his shield so heauie lites,
    That to the ground it doubleth him full low:
What mortall wight could euer beare so monstrous blow?

19

And in his fall his shield, that couered was,
    Did loose his vele by chaunce, and open flew:
    The light whereof, that heuens light did pas,
    Such blazing brightnesse through the ayer threw,
    That eye mote not the same endure to vew.
    Which when the Gyaunt spyde with staring eye,
    He downe let fall his arme, and soft withdrew
    His weapon huge, that heaued was on hye,
For to haue slain the man, that on the ground did lye.

20

And eke the fruitfull-headed beast, amazd
    At flashing beames of that sunshiny shield,
    Became stark blind, and all his sences dazd
    That downe he tumbled on the durtie field,
    And seemd himselfe as conquered to yield.
    Whom when his maistresse proud perceiu'd to fall,
    Whiles yet his feeble feet for faintnesse reeld,
    Vnto the Gyaunt lowdly she gan call,
O helpe *Orgoglio*, helpe, or els we perish all.

21

At her so pitteous cry was much amoou'd,
    Her champion stout, and for to ayde his frend,
    Againe his wonted angry weapon proou'd:
    But all in vaine: for he has redd his end
    In that bright shield, and all their forces spend
    Them selues in vaine: for since that glauncing sight,
    He hath no poure to hurt, nor to defend;
    As where th'Almighties lightning brond does light,
It dimmes the dazed eyen, and daunts the sences quight.

Stanza 16
1 aduauncing: lifting up. **2–6** Cf. Rev. 13.3: 'And I sawe one of his heads as it were wounded to death'. Yet this stroke is only a warning (**ensample**) of what will happen to the dragon's **puissance proud**, for the verse adds that the head heals. The stroke is only a token, then, of God's promise that the seed of man 'shal breake thine [the Serpent's] head' (Gen. 3.15). S. records this moment in his earliest verse, the first of four visions from Revelation in *Theatre*, *sonn* 12. Its editor, Noot, interpreted the wound as 'places where gods word is preached . . . a manifest token of his fall to come' (26v). **scalpe**: skull. **misformed**: suggesting also 'formed for evil'; cf. 'misformed spright' (i 55.9).

Stanza 17
3 trayne: tail. **4 impatience**: inability to endure suffering; cf. 11.2. **grieued**: afflicted with pain; injured. **5 sted**: place. **9 hurtling**: see iv 16.3*n*.

Stanza 18
2 left: i.e. remaining. **4 hideous**: huge. **dites**: lifts; makes ready to strike by lifting. **5 rigor**: violence. **7 lites**: strikes. **8–9** Since the Red Cross Knight 'lay full low' at vii 12.9 totally defeated, the question suggests that Arthur wields power more than **mortall wight**.

Stanza 19
1–5 On the shield, see vii 33–35*n*. **vele**: this term for 'covering' links the shield with the brightness of Una's face when her veil is removed (vi 4.7–9, xii 21.5–9). Cf. the veil of the temple, which was rent at the crucifixion (Matt. 27.51) to signify 'an end of all the ceremonies of the Lawe' (Geneva gloss), and Paul's account of 'the brightnes of his [Christ's] comming' (2 Thess. 2.8). **pas**: surpass, indicating supernatural power. In contrast, Lucifera's throne shines only 'as bright as sunny day' (iv 8.2). **through . . . threw**: the internal echo registers the light's bursting violence. **7 soft**: after the bellowing, the stalking steps, and the violence, this word superbly modulates the action to a close. **8–9** His posture at the moment of the Red Cross Knight's defeat at vii 14.2–3.

Stanza 20
1 fruitfull-headed: because the beast is like the Lernean hydra with its 'many heades out budding euer new' (vii 17.4). **5** By falling prostrate, the wounded dragon only **seemd** to be slain, for it is not slain until canto xi. **9** Orgoglio is first named by Duessa in her cry of triumph at vii 14.5, and now for the second time in her cry of defeat.

Stanza 21
2 frend: paramour. **3 proou'd**: tried, i.e. tried to strike (cf. 22.2). **4 redd**: i.e. seen as in a mirror, referring to God's word; see Gless 1994:138. **6 glauncing**: flashing, dazzling; cf. vii 29.5. **8–9 Almighties**: in contrast to the 'almightie *Ioue*' (9.1) to whose thunderbolt the giant's blow is compared. **light**: descend; shine. **dazed**: dazzled.

22

Whom when the Prince, to batteill new addrest,
    And threatning high his dreadfull stroke did see,
    His sparkling blade about his head he blest,
    And smote off quite his right leg by the knee,
    That downe he tombled; as an aged tree,
    High growing on the top of rocky clift,
    Whose hartstrings with keene steele nigh hewen be,
    The mightie trunck halfe rent, with ragged rift
Doth roll adowne the rocks, and fall with fearefull drift.

23

Or as a Castle reared high and round,
    By subtile engins and malitious slight
    Is vndermined from the lowest ground,
    And her foundation forst, and feebled quight,
    At last downe falles, and with her heaped hight
    Her hastie ruine does more heauie make,
    And yields it selfe vnto the victours might;
    Such was this Gyaunts fall, that seemd to shake
The stedfast globe of earth, as it for feare did quake.

24

The knight then lightly leaping to the pray,
    With mortall steele him smot againe so sore,
    That headlesse his vnweldy bodie lay,
    All wallowd in his owne fowle bloody gore,
    Which flowed from his wounds in wondrous store.
    But soone as breath out of his brest did pas,
    That huge great body, which the Gyaunt bore,
    Was vanisht quite, and of that monstrous mas
Was nothing left, but like an emptie blader was.

25

Whose grieuous fall, when false *Duessa* spyde,
    Her golden cup she cast vnto the ground,
    And crowned mitre rudely threw asyde;
    Such percing griefe her stubborne hart did wound,
    That she could not endure that dolefull stound,
    But leauing all behind her, fled away:
    The light-foot Squyre her quickly turnd around,
    And by hard meanes enforcing her to stay,
So brought vnto his Lord, as his deserued pray.

26

The roiall Virgin, which beheld from farre,
    In pensiue plight, and sad perplexitie,
    The whole atchieuement of this doubtfull warre,
    Came running fast to greet his victorie,
    With sober gladnesse, and myld modestie,
    And with sweet ioyous cheare him thus bespake;
    Fayre braunch of noblesse, flowre of chevalrie,
    That with your worth the world amazed make,
How shall I quite the paynes, ye suffer for my sake?

27

And you fresh budd of vertue springing fast,
    Whom these sad eyes saw nigh vnto deaths dore,
    What hath poore Virgin for such perill past,
    Wherewith you to reward? Accept therefore
    My simple selfe, and seruice euermore;
    And he that high does sit, and all things see
    With equall eye, their merites to restore,
    Behold what ye this day haue done for mee,
And what I cannot quite, requite with vsuree.

Stanza 22

The battle is renewed from stanza 18 to show that Arthur triumphs through the power of grace. Then Orgoglio's blow would overthrow the 'strongest Oake'; now he is **an aged tree** cut down by Arthur. **3 blest**: brandished; making the sign of the cross in the air. **5–9** S. imitates the well-known simile in Virgil, *Aen.* 2.626–31, in which the fall of Troy is compared to the fall of an ancient ash. **rift**: splitting. **drift**: impetus.

Stanza 23

2 subtile engins: cleverly devised machines of warfare. Not open battery, as vi 5.2, but covert tunnelling. **malitious slight**: clever strategy. **4 forst**: broken down. **6 ruine**: the action of falling (Lat. *ruina*). **8–9** A climactic assertion of the earth's terror before her son; see vii 7.6, 8.6, viii 8.7–9.

Stanza 24

8–9 Orgoglio is dismissed with an etymological play upon his name; see vii 9.8*n*. **monstrous mas** and **blader** return to the opening terms that define his state: 'this monstrous masse of earthly slyme, | Puft up with emptie wynd' (vii 9.8–9). Chaucer's Saint Cecile dismisses her persecutor's power because 'every mortal mannes power nys | But lyk a bladdre ful of wynd' (*Second Nun's Tale* 438–39), as Kellogg and Steele 1965 note. Cf. *Colin Clout* 717–18.

Stanza 25

1 fall . . . false: the internal echo suggests her own fall. **3** She reverses the moment at vii 16.4 when Orgoglio placed the papal 'triple crowne' on her head. **rudely**: violently. Tudor iconography showing how royal power, represented here by Arthur, defeated the papacy is examined by King 1990a:97.

Stanza 26

1–4 Una first stands aside while her champion battles the enemy and then comes forward to congratulate (**greet**) him at i 27.1–2, and for the third time in his battle against the dragon at xi 5.5, 55.3–7. **pensiue**: anxious. **perplexitie**: anguish. **doubtfull**: also 'dreaded'. **5 myld**: gracious. **9 quite**: repay. **for my sake**: cf. ix 2.8, xi 1.8.

Stanza 27

1 Una addresses the squire who is the bud to Arthur's 'flowre' (26.7). **vertue**: also 'manliness' (from Lat. *vir*, man), valour. **3–5 poore Virgin**: a poignant use of the word, recognizing that the whore Duessa knew how to offer **seruice** to her benefactors. **6–7** This claim persuades the Red Cross Knight to despair at ix 47.1–2. **equall**: impartial, just. **restore**: make amends for, compensate. **8 Behold**: the optative, 'may He behold'. She speaks with the authority of the church. **9 vsuree**: interest.

28

But sith the heauens, and your faire handeling
  Haue made you master of the field this day,
  Your fortune maister eke with gouerning,
  And well begonne end all so well, I pray,
  Ne let that wicked woman scape away;
  For she it is, that did my Lord bethrall,
  My dearest Lord, and deepe in dongeon lay,
  Where he his better dayes hath wasted all.
O heare, how piteous he to you for ayd does call.

29

Forthwith he gaue in charge vnto his Squyre,
  That scarlot whore to keepen carefully;
  Whyles he himselfe with greedie great desyre
  Into the Castle entred forcibly,
  Where liuing creature none he did espye;
  Then gan he lowdly through the house to call:
  But no man car'd to answere to his crye.
  There raignd a solemne silence ouer all,
Nor voice was heard, nor wight was seene in bowre or hall.

30

At last with creeping crooked pace forth came
  An old old man, with beard as white as snow,
  That on a staffe his feeble steps did frame,
  And guyde his wearie gate both too and fro;

For his eye sight him fayled long ygo,
  And on his arme a bounch of keyes he bore,
  The which vnused rust did ouergrow:
  Those were the keyes of euery inner dore,
But he could not them vse, but kept them still in store.

31

But very vncouth sight was to behold,
  How he did fashion his vntoward pace,
  For as he forward mooud his footing old,
  So backward still was turnd his wrincled face,
  Vnlike to men, who euer as they trace,
  Both feet and face one way are wont to lead.
  This was the auncient keeper of that place,
  And foster father of the Gyaunt dead;
His name *Ignaro* did his nature right aread.

32

His reuerend heares and holy grauitee
  The knight much honord, as beseemed well,
  And gently askt, where all the people bee,
  Which in that stately building wont to dwell.
  Who answerd him full soft, he could not tell.
  Againe he askt, where that same knight was layd,
  Whom great *Orgoglio* with his puissaunce fell
  Had made his caytiue thrall; againe he sayde,
He could not tell: ne euer other answere made.

Stanza 28

1–3 The distinction is important: the heavens joined with Arthur's own skill have made him the victor; now he alone must master his fortune. **4 all so**: just as. **5** At 45.9, Una urges 'let her fly', but only after Duessa has been revealed for what she is. **6–7** Cf. xii 33.7–9. **8 his better dayes**: the better part of his life; possibly, days 'that might have been better spent' (sugg. Percival 1964). **wasted**: consumed, destroyed; see ii 42.8–9*n*. **9** As the true church, she hears him call; Arthur hears nothing (29.8). She hears him call to Arthur for aid; Arthur hears him call for death (38.3–9).

Stanza 29

2 That scarlot whore: the traditional name for 'the great whore'; see vii 16–17*n*. **3 greedie great desyre**: cf. his 'eger greedinesse' at 6.9. **6 house**: the place of the dead, as Job 30.23. **8 a solemne silence**: evoking the emptiness of Virgil's underworld (*Aen.* 6.269); cf. also III xi 53.5–7. Such awe-inspiring silence is the precise antithetical point to the 'solemne feast' (xii 40 2) that celebrates the knight's marriage to Una.

Stanza 30

1 The movement of this line mimics the sense. **3 frame**: support, direct. **5** Cf. Corceca's blindness at iii 18.4 and see *n*. **6–9 keyes**: the general reference is to 'the keyes of the king-dome of heauen' (Matt. 16.19) now claimed by the reformed church whose ministers 'open the gates of heauen with the word of God' (Geneva gloss). See Gless 1994:138–39. The specific reference is to 'the keye of the bottomles pit' given the fallen angel, Rev. 9.1. As the Geneva gloss explains, 'This autoritie chiefly is committed to the Pope in signe whereof he beareth the keyes in his armes'. Cf. x 50.7. See King 1990a:99.

vnused rust: rusty because unused. Brooks-Davies 1977:82 cites Luke's condemnation of those who 'haue taken away the keye of knowledge' (11.52), to which the Geneva gloss adds: 'they hid and toke away the pure doctrine and true vnder-standing of the Scriptures'. **euery**: every one, that is, except the iron door (37.3–5) for which he has no key. **in store**: laid up for future use.

Stanza 31

1 vncouth: strange; repellent; indecorous. **2 vntoward**: i.e. awkward, because he looks back while he comes towards Arthur, as though going 'un-towards'. **5–6** While readers need not be told that usually they look where they are going, S. needs to clarify the nature of Ignaro according to Isa. 44.25 where God declares that he will 'turne the wise men backward, and make their knowledge foolishnes'. **trace**: walk. **8 foster father**: i.e. nourishing father. Although born of earth and wind, Orgoglio is nourished by ignorance, which S. calls the 'Image of hellish horrour' and 'the enemie of grace' (*Teares* 259, 497). **9 Ignaro**: Ignorance (Ital. *ignorante*). He reveals his nature by repeating 'he could not tell' in response to Arthur's queries. Eph. 4.18 warns against those who have 'their cogitation darkened . . . through the ignorance that is in them'. Specifically, he represents ignorance of the true faith, and is therefore associated with the spiritual ignorance of the Church of Rome. See 'Ignaro' in the *SEnc*. More generally, he represents the ignorance which Conti 1616:3.12 describes as the night of the mind, and the parents and nurse of all the plagues that afflict human kind. **aread**: declare.

Stanza 32

3 gently: courteously. **8 caytiue**: captive; also 'wretched'. Cf. the 'caytiue wretched thralls' (v 45.9) in the house of Pride.

33

Then asked he, which way he in might pas:
    He could not tell, againe he answered.
    Thereat the courteous knight displeased was,
    And said, Old syre, it seemes thou hast not red
    How ill it sits with that same siluer hed,
    In vaine to mocke, or mockt in vaine to bee:
    But if thou be, as thou art pourtrahed
    With natures pen, in ages graue degree,
Aread in grauer wise, what I demaund of thee.

34

His answere likewise was, he could not tell.
    Whose sencelesse speach, and doted ignorance
    When as the noble Prince had marked well,
    He ghest his nature by his countenance,
    And calmd his wrath with goodly temperance.
    Then to him stepping, from his arme did reach
    Those keyes, and made himselfe free enterance.
    Each dore he opened without any breach;
There was no barre to stop, nor foe him to empeach.

35

There all within full rich arayd he found,
    With royall arras and resplendent gold,
    And did with store of euery thing abound,
    That greatest Princes presence might behold.
    But all the floore (too filthy to be told)
    With blood of guiltlesse babes, and innocents trew,
    Which there were slaine, as sheepe out of the fold,
    Defiled was, that dreadfull was to vew,
And sacred ashes ouer it was strowed new.

36

And there beside of marble stone was built
    An Altare, caru'd with cunning ymagery,
    On which trew Christians blood was often spilt,
    And holy Martyres often doen to dye,
    With cruell malice and strong tyranny:
    Whose blessed sprites from vnderneath the stone
    To God for vengeance cryde continually,
    And with great griefe were often heard to grone,
That hardest heart would bleede, to heare their piteous mone.

37

Through euery rowme he sought, and euerie bowr,
    But no where could he find that wofull thrall:
    At last he came vnto an yron doore,
    That fast was lockt, but key found not at all
    Emongst that bounch, to open it withall;
    But in the same a little grate was pight,
    Through which he sent his voyce, and lowd did call
    With all his powre, to weet, if liuing wight
Were housed therewithin, whom he enlargen might.

38

Therewith an hollow, dreary, murmuring voyce
    These pitteous plaintes and dolours did resound;
    O who is that, which brings me happy choyce
    Of death, that here lye dying euery stound,
    Yet liue perforce in balefull darkenesse bound?
    For now three Moones haue changed thrice their hew,
    And haue beene thrice hid vnderneath the ground,
    Since I the heauens chearefull face did vew:
O welcome thou, that doest of death bring tydings trew.

Stanza 33

3 the courteous knight: his title at ix 7.8, and its first use in the poem. **4 red**: perceived, learned. **5 sits**: agrees. **7 pourtrahed**: an etymological spelling from Lat. *protrahere*, to draw forth. **8 ages graue degree**: the stage of life at which 'grauitee' (32.1) is befitting. On similar grounds, Duessa's ugliness is judged 'as in hate of honorable eld' (47.2). **9 Aread**: declare. **demaund**: inquire.

Stanza 34

2 doted: stupid. **4 countenance**: behaviour. **5 temperance**: Bk II's virtue of temperance is first associated with Arthur. **8–9 breach**: forcing. **empeach**: hinder.

Stanza 35

1–4 The castle is equipped with all that the greatest prince would find worthy to behold, or with what would befit a prince's court. Cf. the presence chamber in the house of Pride decked 'With rich array and costly arras' (iv 6.6). **6 innocents trew**: applied to all Christian martyrs but particularly to those slain by Herod after the birth of Christ, Matt. 2.16. **9 sacred**: hallowed, being the ashes of 'holy Martyres' (36.4). **new** alludes to recent martyrs; see 6.2–5*n*.

Stanza 36

'I sawe vnder the altar the soules of them, that were killed for the worde of God, and for the testimonie which they mainteined. And they cryed with a lowde voyce, saying, How long, Lord, holie and true! doest not thou iudge and auenge our blood on them that dwell on the earth?' (Rev. 6.9–10). **2 ymagery**: images. **3 often**: twice repeated in this stanza, the word notes 'the continual persecution of the Church' (Geneva gloss to Rev. 6.9) recorded in Foxe's 'Book of Martyrs', as King 1990a:91 suggests.

Stanza 37

1 bowr: an inner private room. **3 yron doore**: cf. Ps. 107.16, 'For he hathe broken the gates of brasse, and brast the barres of yron asunder'. **6 grate**: the ear through which God's word, esp. for Protestants, comes to free man. **pight**: placed. **9 enlargen**: set at large.

Stanza 38

1 murmuring: repining. **2 dolours**: lamentations. **3–9** The knight's outburst contrasts with his silence throughout his adventures. He spoke to Fradubio at ii 43.1–2, 6–7, to Sansjoy at v 13.1–4, and his cry for aid is reported at 28.9; but does not speak again until ix 17. **choyce | Of death**: the chance or right to choose death. He speaks ironically: 'What choice do I have: death or a living death?'; or in despair: 'Now I may choose death'. He echoes Paul's cry: 'O wretched man that I am, who shal deliuer me from the bodie of this death?' (Rom. 7.24), for he lives in those final days when 'men seke death, and shal not finde it, and shal desire to dye, and death shal flee from them' (Rev. 9.6). Despaire reminds him of this time when he 'for death so oft did call' (ix 45.6). At x 27.9, he is

39

Which when that Champion heard, with percing point
  Of pitty deare his hart was thrilled sore,
  And trembling horrour ran through euery ioynt,
  For ruth of gentle knight so fowle forlore:
  Which shaking off, he rent that yron dore,
  With furious force, and indignation fell;
  Where entred in, his foot could find no flore,
  But all a deepe descent, as darke as hell,
That breathed euer forth a filthie banefull smell.

40

But nether darkenesse fowle, nor filthy bands,
  Nor noyous smell his purpose could withhold,
  (Entire affection hateth nicer hands)
  But that with constant zele, and corage bold,
  After long paines and labors manifold,
  He found the meanes that Prisoner vp to reare;
  Whose feeble thighes, vnhable to vphold
  His pined corse, him scarse to light could beare,
A ruefull spectacle of death and ghastly drere.

41

His sad dull eies deepe sunck in hollow pits,
  Could not endure th'vnwonted sunne to view;
  His bare thin cheekes for want of better bits,
  And empty sides deceiued of their dew,

Could make a stony hart his hap to rew;
  His rawbone armes, whose mighty brawned bowrs
  Were wont to riue steele plates, and helmets hew,
  Were clene consum'd, and all his vitall powres
Decayd, and al his flesh shronk vp like withered flowres.

42

Whome when his Lady saw, to him she ran
  With hasty ioy: to see him made her glad,
  And sad to view his visage pale and wan,
  Who earst in flowres of freshest youth was clad.
  Tho when her well of teares she wasted had,
  She said, Ah dearest Lord, what euill starre
  On you hath frownd, and pourd his influence bad,
  That of your selfe ye thus berobbed arre,
And this misseeming hew your manly looks doth marre?

43

But welcome now my Lord, in wele or woe,
  Whose presence I haue lackt too long a day;
  And fie on Fortune mine auowed foe,
  Whose wrathful wreakes them selues doe now alay.
  And for these wronges shall treble penaunce pay
  Of treble good: good growes of euils priefe.
  The chearelesse man, whom sorow did dismay,
  Had no delight to treaten of his griefe;
His long endured famine needed more reliefe.

---

rightly named 'The man that would not liue': he seeks death in the Despaire episode (ix 51), in the house of Penaunce (x 21–22), on the hill of Contemplation (x 63.1–5), and in his battle against the dragon (xi 28.4). His state is that of despair (cf. ix 54.8–9), or the living death that is hell: 'he in hell doth lie, | That liues a loathed life, and wishing cannot die' (IV vii 11.8–9), for he is among those 'that dwell in darkenes and in the shadowe of death, being bounde in miserie and yron, because they rebelled against the wordes of the Lord' (Ps. 107.10–11). Yet the Psalmist continues: 'Then they cryed vnto the Lord in their trouble, and he deliuered them from their distres. He broght them out of darkenes, and out of the shadowe of death, and brake their bands asunder' (13–14). For an analysis of his state, see Nohrnberg 1976:260–82. **stound**: moment. **balefull**: full of evil; full of suffering. **6–7** Possibly three months but most likely nine (suggested by **three** and **thrice**), the period of gestation (cf. II i 53) which leads to fulfilment (cf. IV vi 43.9), or rebirth (see ix 15.9*n*). The three-month period is clearly expressed at II ii 44.1–2. The time may allude to the nearly 300 years from Gregory VII to Wyclif during which England was subjected to popish captivity (sugg. Kermode 1971:48), or to the reign of Mary Tudor (sugg. O'Connell 1977:54–55).

Stanza 39

2 deare: heart-felt; grievous; dire. **3 trembling horrour**: the adj. stresses the noun's Lat. root, *horreo*, to tremble. **4 fowle forlore**: grievously lost, doomed to destruction, as he is 'this man forlorne' (vii 10.5). **5** Horror paralyses Arthur (cf. ii 31.9) but by shaking it off, he may shake off the door. Woodhouse 1949:203 interprets the act as the violence of grace. **7–9** Arthur's descent re-enacts Christ's harrowing of hell with

its bottomless pit (Rev. 9.2, etc.), thick smoke, and traditional stench. See 'hell' in the *SEnc*. S. refers to this moment at x 40.8–9 and *Am* 68.1–4; his chief literary source is Langland, *Piers Plowman* 18. For an image of Christ's triumph in hell on a 1592 title-page, see Prescott 1994. **9 banefull**: poisonous.

Stanza 40

The fortieth stanza is chosen for the knight's redemption because that number marks the limit of wandering: e.g. the forty years that the children of Israel wandered in the wilderness (Josh. 5.6), and the forty days that Christ was tempted in the wilderness (Mark 1.13). See II vii 26.5*n*. **1 bands**: bonds. **2 noyous**: noxious. **3 Entire affection**: a stock phrase always used approvingly for love that is total, e.g. Britomart to Artegall at III ii 44.4, and Artegall to Arthur at V viii 12.9. **nicer**: too fastidious. **4–6 long paines and labors manifold**: these are not spelled out, but when Christ descended into hell he 'preached vnto the spirits that were in prison' (1 Pet. 3.19). In *Piers Plowman* 18.319, Christ demands that the gates of hell be opened, 'And with that breth helle brake with Beliales barres'. Cf. Ps. 74.12, 107.14. In the same numbered stanza in canto x, S. refers to Christ's harrowing of hell; see x 40.8–9 and *n*. **8–9 pined corse**: wasted body; cf. ix 35.8. **to light**: also as he is brought to Una who is 'full of heauenly light' (ix 17.3). **drere**: sadness, wretchedness.

Stanza 41

3 better bits: proper food; more precisely, larger bites of food to fill out his cheeks. **4 deceiued of their dew**: cheated out of what is owing to human nature. **6 brawned bowrs**: brawny muscles. **8 vitall powres**: for the Elizabethan doctrine of the bodily spirits relevant to this term, see the *SEnc* 565–67.

44

Faire Lady, then said that victorious knight,
　The things, that grieuous were to doe, or beare,
　Them to renew, I wote, breeds no delight;
　Best musicke breeds delight in loathing eare:
　But th'only good, that growes of passed feare,
　Is to be wise, and ware of like agein.
　This daies ensample hath this lesson deare
　Deepe written in my heart with yron pen,
That blisse may not abide in state of mortall men.

45

Henceforth Sir knight, take to you wonted strength,
　And maister these mishaps with patient might;
　Loe wher your foe lies stretcht in monstrous length,
　And loe that wicked woman in your sight,
　The roote of all your care, and wretched plight,
　Now in your powre, to let her liue, or die.
　To doe her die (quoth *Vna*) were despight,
　And shame t'auenge so weake an enimy;
But spoile her of her scarlot robe, and let her fly.

46

So as she bad, that witch they disaraid,
　And robd of roiall robes, and purple pall,
　And ornaments that richly were displaid;
　Ne spared they to strip her naked all.
　Then when they had despoyld her tire and call,
　Such as she was, their eies might her behold,
　That her misshaped parts did them appall,
　A loathly, wrinckled hag, ill fauoured, old,
Whose secret filth good manners biddeth not be told.

47

Her crafty head was altogether bald,
　And as in hate of honorable eld,
　Was ouergrowne with scurfe and filthy scald;
　Her teeth out of her rotten gummes were feld,
　And her sowre breath abhominably smeld;
　Her dried dugs, lyke bladders lacking wind,
　Hong downe, and filthy matter from them weld;
　Her wrizled skin as rough, as maple rind,
So scabby was, that would haue loathd all womankind.

Stanza 42

3 wan: expressing his state of wanhope or despair; see ix 22.4–5*n*.　**7 influence**: referring to astral influence or power, the fluid flowing from the stars which determines one's destiny.　**9 misseeming hew**: unseemly appearance.

Stanza 43

1 In welcoming him as her lord whether in his former well-being or in his present woeful state, she renews the marriage vow, 'in sickness, and in health'.　**3** Una blamed an 'euill starre' (42.6) for his plight rather than him; to excuse him further, she blames fortune for her plight rather than Duessa who is her **auowed foe** (cf. vii 50.7), as Arthur claims at 45.4–5.　**4 wreakes**: acts of vengeance; also acts that vent her wrath.　**5 penaunce**: satisfaction.　**6** By her proverbial counsel, she seeks to rescue him from despair. **of euils priefe**: through experiencing evil and thereby being tested.　**8 griefe**: mental pain, distress.

Stanza 44

3 renew: go over again.　**4 delight**: 'dislike' (sugg. Jortin 1734); 'no delight' (sugg. Church 1758). If the text is kept, possible paraphrases are: 'music best breeds delight, not a recital of grievous matters'; or 'only the best music, not a recital etc., may breed delight'.　**5 only**: chief.　**6 ware**: wary; beware.　**7 deare**: grievous, dire; cf. 39.2.　**8 yron pen**: a biblical phrase, as Job 19.24, Jer. 17.1.　**9** A common motif in the poem, as vii 23.6, III i 10.7, etc. Cf. the refrain 'Nothing is sure, that growes on earthly grownd' (I ix 11.5) with its variants at II ix 21.9, xi 30.3–4, etc.

Stanza 45

2 The line prepares for the role of Patience at x 24. Cf. his advice to Una at vii 40.7.　**5 care**: trouble, grief.　**7–9** Una's sentiment is in accord with Christ's mission to destroy 'the workes of the deuil' rather than the devil (1 John 3.8). **despight**: vindictiveness.　**spoile**: despoil.

Stanzas 46–48

S's chief literary analogue is Ariosto, *Orl. Fur.* 7.72–74: the ugliness of the seemingly beautiful witch Alcina; his source is Scripture: Rev. 17.16 prophesies that the great whore shall be made 'desolate [i.e. laid waste] and naked'. Cf. Isa. 3.17, 24: 'Therefore shal the Lord make the heads of the daughters of Zion balde, and the Lord shal discouer their secret partes. In that day shal the Lord take away . . . the calles, and the round tyres . . . And in stead of swete sauour, there shalbe stinke, and in stead of a girdle, a rent, and in stead of dressing of the heere, baldnes . . . and burning in stead of beautie'. Duessa is first seen 'in her proper hew' at ii 40.6–41.4. Krier 1990:134 notes the parody of the usual blazon of the female anatomy; Cavanagh 1994a:29 finds a gynophobic attitude to women; Silberman 1995:57 notes S.'s delight in human grossness: female, as here, and male in the description of Lust at IV vii 5–7.

Stanza 46

1 they: said to be Prince Arthur alone at II i 22.6–7.　**5 tire and call**: head-dress; or attire and head-dress.

Stanza 47

2 I.e. such as would cause hatred for those whose old age would otherwise claim honour (sugg. Upton 1758); or, in contempt of honourable age.　**3 scurfe**: scabs. **scald**: scall, a scabby disease of the scalp.　**4** The one detail taken from Ariosto; S. adds the **rotten gummes**. **feld**: fallen.　**5 abhominably**: the spelling preserves the etymological sense, Lat. *ab homine*, from man, and hence like a beast.　**6–9** Paster 1993:206 notes that metonymy transforms Duessa's breasts 'into the lower parts, an oozing, excretory bladder-womb', in contrast to the 'good' breasts of Charissa (x.30) who is an image of conspicuous maternal display. **wrizled**: wrinkled. **maple**: 'seeldom inward sound' (i 9.9). **scabby**: indicates God's curse (Deut. 28.27); a symptom of syphilis in Fracastoro, *Syphilis* 1.400–04. **haue loathd**: i.e. would have caused **all womankind** to have loathed her.

48

Her neather parts, the shame of all her kind,
    My chaster Muse for shame doth blush to write;
    But at her rompe she growing had behind
    A foxes taile, with dong all fowly dight;
    And eke her feete most monstrous were in sight;
    For one of them was like an Eagles claw,
    With griping talaunts armd to greedy fight,
    The other like a beares vneuen paw:
More vgly shape yet neuer liuing creature saw.

49

Which when the knights beheld, amazd they were,
    And wondred at so fowle deformed wight.
    Such then (said *Vna*) as she seemeth here,
    Such is the face of falshood, such the sight

Of fowle *Duessa*, when her borrowed light
    Is laid away, and counterfesaunce knowne.
    Thus when they had the witch disrobed quight,
    And all her filthy feature open showne,
They let her goe at will, and wander waies vnknowne.

50

Shee flying fast from heauens hated face,
    And from the world that her discouered wide,
    Fled to the wastfull wildernesse apace,
    From liuing eies her open shame to hide,
    And lurkt in rocks and caues long vnespide.
    But that faire crew of knights, and *Vna* faire
    Did in that castle afterwards abide,
    To rest them selues, and weary powres repaire,
Where store they fownd of al, that dainty was and rare.

Stanza 48

1 Her neather parts: the privy members or 'parts of shame' (*OED* 7). **of all her kind**: as Silberman 1995:58 observes, **her** is ambiguous: the phrase may refer to all evil witches, to all womankind, or to all humankind. Cavanagh 1994a:37 suggests 'women of many kinds'. **2 chaster**: too chaste. (Yet not too chaste not to continue.) **3–9** The animal imagery is conventional: the crafty fox, the predatory eagle, the cruel bear. Duessa is a blazon of craftiness from her 'crafty head' (47.1) to tail, her tail being emphasized as she is a whore. Rowland 1973:78 notes that the fox's outstretched tail symbolizes fraud. **talaunts**: talons. **vneuen**: rugged, rough. In Rev. 13.2, the beast from the sea has 'fete like a beares' because such feet are unclean, according to Lev. 11.26–27.

Stanza 49

3–4 Cf. v 26.6. **5 borrowed light**: cf. 'of proud ornaments | And borrowd beauty spoyld' (II i 22.6–7). **6 counterfesaunce**: deceit, dissimulation; coined by S. from Fr. *contrefaisance*, as though literally 'false face', for her **falshood** is exposed. **8 feature**: shape, body.

Stanza 50

2 discouered: exposed to view. **3 wastfull**: desolate. The line echoes Rev. 12.6 on 'the woman fled into wildernes', which had been Una's state before it was Duessa's; see iii 3.4. **6 crew**: company; used for the first time not pejoratively. **9 dainty**: precious.

Cant. IX.

His loues and lignage Arthure tells:
the knights knitt friendly bands:
Sir Trevisan flies from Despeyre,
Whom Redcros knight withstands.

1

O Goodly golden chayne, wherewith yfere
　The vertues linked are in louely wize:
　And noble mindes of yore allyed were,
　In braue poursuitt of cheualrous emprize,
　That none did others safety despize,
　Nor aid enuy to him, in need that stands,
　But friendly each did others praise deuize,
　How to aduaunce with fauourable hands,
As this good Prince redeemd the *Redcrosse* knight from bands.

2

Who when their powres empayrd through labor long,
　With dew repast they had recured well,
　And that weake captiue wight now wexed strong,
　Them list no lenger there at leasure dwell,
　But forward fare, as their aduentures fell,
　But ere they parted, *Vna* faire besought
　That straunger knight his name and nation tell;
　Least so great good, as he for her had wrought,
Should die vnknown, and buried be in thankles thought.

3

Faire virgin (said the Prince) yee me require
　A thing without the compas of my witt:
　For both the lignage and the certein Sire,
　From which I sprong, from mee are hidden yitt.
　For all so soone as life did me admitt
　Into this world, and shewed heuens light,
　From mothers pap I taken was vnfitt:
　And streight deliuered to a Fary knight,
To be vpbrought in gentle thewes and martiall might.

4

Vnto old *Timon* he me brought byliue,
　Old *Timon*, who in youthly yeares hath beene
　In warlike feates th'expertest man aliue,
　And is the wisest now on earth I weene;
　His dwelling is low in a valley greene,
　Vnder the foot of *Rauran* mossy hore,
　From whence the riuer *Dee* as siluer cleene
　His tombling billowes rolls with gentle rore:
There all my daies he traind mee vp in vertuous lore.

Book I Canto ix

Argument

2 bands: corr. from *hands* in *F.E.* The uncorrected reading is supported by 1.8 and 'right hands together ioynd' (18.9); **friendly bands** contrast with the 'bands' (1.9) which had bound the knight (cf. viii 1.7, 40.1).

Stanza 1

1–2 golden chayne: derives ultimately from the golden chain by which Homer's Zeus threatens to draw up the entire uniuerse into Olympus (*Iliad* 8.18–27), and which was interpreted as a symbol of universal concord; cf. the 'golden chaine of concord' (III i 12.8), and the works of Concord at IV x 35. See v 25.5*n*, II vii 46.2*n*. S.'s chain which links in loving manner (**in louely wize**) suggests Chaucer's 'faire cheyne of love' (*Knight's Tale* 2988) which links the elements. It symbolizes the linking of the virtues in Arthur whose virtue of magnificence 'is the perfection of all the rest, and conteineth in it them all' (*LR* 39). See D.L. Miller 1988:159–60. **yfere**: together. **4 emprize**: adventure, from Ariosto's *l'audaci imprese* (*Orl. Fur.* 1.2), for chivalric enterprise that brings renown and glory. **5 despize**: disregard, set at nought. **6 enuy**: refuse to give. **9 redeemd**: as viii Arg.

Stanza 2

1–3 Yet see 20.4–9*n*, x 18.1–2*n*. **repast**: refreshment and repose. **recured**: restored to health. **8–9** Arthur's rescue of the Red Cross Knight is interpreted as a service to Una rather than to him; cf. viii 26.9.

Stanza 3

1 require: ask. **2 without**: beyond. **3–4** Arthur's lineage is given at II x 68 – his **certein Sire** is Uther Pendragon, the son of Constantine II – but is not made explicit perhaps because of the controversy over his grandfather; see II x 62*n*. In Malory 1.6, Arthur believes Sir Ector to be his father. In the *LR* 30, S. reveals that he 'was borne of the Lady Igrayne'; see III iii 27*n*. On his effort to gain his identity, see Bellamy 1989:801; on the isolation that he shares with Braggadocchio, see Mazzola 1996. **7–9 vnfitt**: because not weaned. In Malory 1.3–5, 'Sir Ectors wyf nourysshed hym with her owne pappe'. Bellamy 797 notes that Arthur is the first protagonist in epic to be given a neonatal infancy. He is a changeling, as are the Red Cross Knight (I x 65.6–9) and Artegall (III iii 26.4–7). Unlike the Red Cross Knight, who is 'sprong out from English race' (I x 60.1), he is a Briton, as are Artegall, Britomart, and Tristram. See 'Britain, Britons' in the *SEnc*. **gentle thewes**: 'vertuous lore' (4.9), i.e. manners and qualities befitting one of noble birth. His education corresponds on the secular level to that given by the heavenly virtues, x 4.3–4.

Stanza 4

1 Timon: from the Gk τιμή honour. **he**: presumably not the 'Sire' (3.3) who is Uther Pendragon; possibly Malory's Sir Ector; but most likely Merlin, who is named in the next stanza. Arthur's 'long education by Timon, to whom he was by Merlin deliuered to be brought vp, so soone as he was borne' is noted in the *LR* 29–30. The confusion may be Arthur's, or S.'s in inventing Timon's role. **byliue**: forthwith. **5–8** Selden cites this 'Fiction of the Muses best pupil' and observes

5

Thether the great magicien *Merlin* came,
　As was his vse, ofttimes to visitt mee:
　For he had charge my discipline to frame,
　And Tutors nouriture to ouersee.
　Him oft and oft I askt in priuity,
　Of what loines and what lignage I did spring.
　Whose aunswere bad me still assured bee,
　That I was sonne and heire vnto a king,
As time in her iust term the truth to light should bring.

6

Well worthy impe, said then the Lady gent,
　And Pupill fitt for such a Tutors hand.
　But what aduenture, or what high intent
　Hath brought you hether into Fary land,
　Aread Prince *Arthure*, crowne of Martiall band?
　Full hard it is (quoth he) to read aright
　The course of heauenly cause, or vnderstand
　The secret meaning of th'eternall might,
That rules mens waies, and rules the thoughts of liuing wight.

7

For whether he through fatal deepe foresight
　Me hither sent, for cause to me vnghest,
　Or that fresh bleeding wound, which day and night
　Whilome doth rancle in my riuen brest,
　With forced fury following his behest,
　Me hether brought by wayes yet neuer found,
　You to haue helpt I hold my selfe yet blest.
　Ah courteous knight (quoth she) what secret wound
Could euer find, to grieue the gentlest hart on ground?

8

Deare Dame (quoth he) you sleeping sparkes awake,
　Which troubled once, into huge flames will grow,
　Ne euer will their feruent fury slake,
　Till liuing moysture into smoke do flow,
　And wasted life doe lye in ashes low.
　Yet sithens silence lesseneth not my fire,
　But told it flames, and hidden it does glow,
　I will reuele, what ye so much desire:
Ah Loue, lay down thy bow, the whiles I may respyre.

---

that 'this *Rauran-Vaur* hill is there by in *Merioneth*' (in Drayton 1931–41:4.210), which Bruce 1985:466 notes was 'one of the last strongholds of the Welsh in their war against the Saxons'. Arthur's association with North Wales, which was sovereign over South Wales, links him to the ancestral seat of the Tudors. **mossy hore**: hoary with moss. **Dee**: the ancient boundary between Wales and England. This reference links the two countries and the river's divine waters (see IV xi 39.3–4*n*) with Arthur. **siluer cleene**: bright (and pure) as silver. **9 vertuous lore**: knowledge of the virtues, which includes their practice; cf. Una's purity 'in life and euery vertuous lore' (i 5.2).

Stanza 5

3 discipline: instruction, education. **4 nouriture**: upbringing, nurture. S. echoes Caxton's rubric to chap. iii of 'The Tale of King Arthur': 'Of the byrthe of kyng Arthur and of his nouryture'. At II viii 20.3, Arthur is called Merlin's 'noursling'. The **Tutor** is 'old *Timon*' (4.1); cf. *LR* 29. **9 iust term**: due course, time being the womb which in full term gives birth to events; cf. 14.4. On the motif 'Truth unveiled by Time', see Panofsky 1962:83–91. Smith 769 records the proverb 'Time brings the truth to light'.

Stanza 6

1 impe: child, scion (*OED* 3), naming him the offspring of a noble house. **gent**: high-born; also 'gracious' in her response; cf. 16.5. **3 aduenture**: chance. **5 Aread**: declare. Arthur does not give his name despite Una's request (2.7); appropriately, she first names him in the poem. As truth, she brings the 'truth to light' (5.9). **6–9** Cf. Rom. 11.33: 'how vnsearcheable are his iudgements, and his wayes past finding out'. **cause**: used in a theological sense, e.g. as God is the first and final cause. **secret**: beyond ordinary apprehension.

Stanza 7

1 he: God. **fatal**: ordained by fate; prophetic. **4 Whilome**: 'incessantly', in this context, rather than 'at one time'.

5 forced fury: force and fury; compelled fury; furious compulsion. **his behest**: the command of the wound, or love, or God. In submitting to the power of love, Arthur obeys God's rule. **6 by wayes**: echoing the 'bywaies' taken by the Red Cross Knight 'Where neuer foote of liuing wight did tread' (vii 50.4). **8 courteous**: see viii 33.3*n*. **9 find**: contrive; find the means to. **on ground**: on the earth; cf. 16.9.

Stanzas 8–15

Celtic folkore provides numerous analogues to the fairy mistress theme; see *Var* 1.267–68. S.'s immediate source is Chaucer's Sir Thopas, that gay knight who so 'wery was | For prikyng on the softe gras' that he 'leyde him in that plas' where he 'dremed al this nyght' that 'An elf-qeene shal my lemman be' and vows 'Alle othere wommen I forsake, | And to an elf-qeene I me take | By dale and eek by downe' (*Tale of Sir Thopas* 778–96). On S.'s use of Chaucer's tale, see Anderson 1985:169–72, Esolen 1990:299–302, Higgins 1990:24–27, and esp. C.A. Berry 1994:153–66. The classical analogue is the sleeping Endymion visited by Diana, to which S. alludes in *SC July* 63–64. The biblical analogue is Adam's 'heauie slepe' (Gen. 2.21) out of which he awoke to find Eve. On Arthur's dream, see D.L. Miller 1988:130–42, 'dreams' in the *SEnc*, and Bellamy 1992:212–21.

Stanza 8

3–5 liuing moysture: radical or essential moisture, the humours that compose the body. Love's fury will endure until its heat consumes the vital juices of his body: 'as the heat consumes the water, so doth Love dry up his radical moisture' (Burton, *Anat.* 3.2.3.1); or until the elements melt with the heat of the final fire (2 Pet. 3.12). On the physiological need to control love-sickness, see the *SEnc* 461. The sentiment is expressed in the Song Sol. 8.6: 'loue is strong as death'. **wasted**: spent unprofitably and therefore consumed. **9 respyre**: take breath.

9

It was in freshest flowre of youthly yeares,
 When corage first does creepe in manly chest,
 Then first that cole of kindly heat appeares
 To kindle loue in euery liuing brest;
 But me had warnd old *Timons* wise behest,
 Those creeping flames by reason to subdew,
 Before their rage grew to so great vnrest,
As miserable louers vse to rew,
Which still wex old in woe, whiles wo stil wexeth new.

10

That ydle name of loue, and louers life,
 As losse of time, and vertues enimy
 I euer scornd, and ioyd to stirre vp strife,
 In middest of their mournfull Tragedy,
 Ay wont to laugh, when them I heard to cry,
 And blow the fire, which them to ashes brent:
 Their God himselfe, grieud at my libertie,
 Shott many a dart at me with fiers intent,
But I them warded all with wary gouernment.

11

But all in vaine: no fort can be so strong,
 Ne fleshly brest can armed be so sownd,
 But will at last be wonne with battrie long,
 Or vnawares at disauantage fownd:
 Nothing is sure, that growes on earthly grownd:
 And who most trustes in arme of fleshly might,
 And boastes, in beauties chaine not to be bownd,
 Doth soonest fall in disauentrous fight,
And yeeldes his caytiue neck to victours most despight.

12

Ensample make of him your haplesse ioy,
 And of my selfe now mated, as ye see;
 Whose prouder vaunt that proud auenging boy
 Did soone pluck downe, and curbd my libertee.
 For on a day prickt forth with iollitee
 Of looser life, and heat of hardiment,
 Raunging the forest wide on courser free,
 The fields, the floods, the heauens with one consent
Did seeme to laugh on me, and fauour mine intent.

13

For wearied with my sportes, I did alight
 From loftie steed, and downe to sleepe me layd;
 The verdant gras my couch did goodly dight,
 And pillow was my helmett fayre displayd:
 Whiles euery sence the humour sweet embayd,
 And slombring soft my hart did steale away
 Me seemed, by my side a royall Mayd
 Her daintie limbes full softly down did lay:
So fayre a creature yet saw neuer sunny day.

14

Most goodly glee and louely blandishment
 She to me made, and badd me loue her deare;
 For dearely sure her loue was to me bent,
 As when iust time expired should appeare.
 But whether dreames delude, or true it were,
 Was neuer hart so rauisht with delight,
 Ne liuing man like wordes did euer heare,
 As she to me deliuered all that night;
And at her parting said, She Queene of Faries hight.

Stanza 9
1–4 Fradubio's state at ii 35.1–3. **kindly heat**: natural feeling.
5 **Timons**: *Cleons 1590* (corr. *F.E.*) signifies glory (Gk κλέος).
9 By this excessive playing with the letter 'w', even beginning and ending the line with the same letter, Arthur mocks a state that soon mocks him.

Stanza 10
7 **Their God**: Cupid. 9 **gouernment**: conduct; governing his passions.

Stanza 11
1–3 Proverbial: Smith 281; cf. III x 10.1–2. **battrie**: battering. 5 Smith 91; see viii 44.9n. 6 As Jer. 17.5: 'Cursed be the man that . . . maketh flesh his arme'. 8 **disauentrous**: unfortunate; see vii 48.6–8n. 9 **most despight**: greatest outrage. Once conquered, he must yield to the most contemptuous treatment.

Stanza 12
1–2 This paralleling comments on the Red Cross Knight's fall: he became bound 'in beauties chaine' (11.7) by yielding to Duessa, and trusted 'in arme of fleshly might' (11.6) by abandoning Una and his armour. **mated**: confounded; matched; also, as a term from chess: he has been mated by a queen; cf. *SC Dec.* 53: 'Love they him called, that gave me checkmate'. 3 **prouder**: over-proud. 5 **prickt forth**: decked out; also

'spurred on' like his horse. The parallel with the Red Cross Knight at i.1.1 and vii 2.6–7 is noted by Roche 1984:74–75. 6 **looser**: too loose, being free from all bonds; too wanton. **hardiment**: boldness. 7 **forest wide**: on the significance of this forest setting, see vi 3.2n. **free**: willing and ready to go; suggesting his youthful nature. 8–9 With this harmony of natural powers which encourages the lover, cf. Venus whom Scudamour saw 'laugh at me, and fauour my pretence' (IV x 56.4) to seize Amoret. **floods**: waters. **intent**: frame of mind; will.

Stanza 13
1 **For wearied**: utterly wearied. 3 **dight**: adorn. 5–6 Sleep is described as a yielding of the senses to love. **humour**: dew of sleep. **embayd**: bathed, suffused. 9 Either she is fairer than any other woman in this world; or, since he is dreaming, she does not exist in this world.

Stanza 14
The double obscurity of the *concubitus* is noted by Lewis 1966:158–59. Either the experience was a dream or it took place (as the 'pressed gras' (15.2) would suggest). The *LR* 30 refers to Arthur's 'dream or vision'. The echoes set up with Archimago's 'fit false dreame' (i 43.9) are noted by P.A. Parker 1979:84–85. 1 **glee**: entertainment; joy, describing its effect upon him. **louely blandishment**: loving flattery. 4 I.e. in due course of time, or 'As time in her iust term' (5.9) will

15

When I awoke, and found her place deuoyd,
    And nought but pressed gras where she had lyen,
I sorrowed all so much, as earst I ioyd,
    And washed all her place with watry eyen.
    From that day forth I lou'd that face diuyne;
    From that day forth I cast in carefull mynd,
    To seeke her out with labor, and long tyne,
    And neuer vowd to rest, till her I fynd,
Nyne monethes I seek in vain yet ni'll that vow vnbynd.

16

Thus as he spake, his visage wexed pale,
    And chaunge of hew great passion did bewray;
    Yett still he stroue to cloke his inward bale,
    And hide the smoke, that did his fire display,
    Till gentle *Vna* thus to him gan say;
    O happy Queene of Faries, that hast fownd
    Mongst many, one that with his prowesse may
    Defend thine honour, and thy foes confownd:
True Loues are often sown, but seldom grow on grownd.

17

Thine, O then, said the gentle *Redcrosse* knight,
    Next to that Ladies loue, shalbe the place,
    O fayrest virgin, full of heauenly light,
    Whose wondrous faith, exceeding earthly race,

Was firmest fixt in myne extremest case.
    And you, my Lord, the Patrone of my life,
    Of that great Queene may well gaine worthie grace:
    For onely worthie you through prowes priefe
Yf liuing man mote worthie be, to be her liefe.

18

So diuersly discoursing of their loues,
    The golden Sunne his glistring head gan shew,
    And sad remembraunce now the Prince amoues,
    With fresh desire his voyage to pursew:
    Als *Vna* earnd her traueill to renew.
    Then those two knights, fast frendship for to bynd,
    And loue establish each to other trew,
    Gaue goodly gifts, the signes of gratefull mynd,
And eke as pledges firme, right hands together ioynd.

19

Prince *Arthur* gaue a boxe of Diamond sure,
    Embowd with gold and gorgeous ornament,
    Wherein were closd few drops of liquor pure,
    Of wondrous worth, and vertue excellent,
    That any wownd could heale incontinent:
    Which to requite, the *Redcrosse* knight him gaue
    A booke, wherein his Saueours testament
    Was writt with golden letters rich and braue;
A worke of wondrous grace, and hable soules to saue.

---

reveal. Being projected into the future, the love of the Faerie Queene is distinguished from that offered the dreaming Red Cross Knight by the false Una: e.g. the 'gentle blandishment and louely looke' (i 49.8) that seeks immediate satisfaction. Fruen 1994:54–56 compares Wisd. Sol. 8.2: 'I haue loued her, and soght her from my youth: I desired to marye her, suche loue had I vnto her beautie'. **7** As 13.9, implying that in his visionary state, he heard what no living man has ever heard, perhaps echoing 1 Cor. 2.9: 'nether eare hathe heard' the things that God has prepared for them that love him.

Stanza 15
1 deuoyd: empty. **2** The 'reality' of the vision is confirmed here, in contrast to the dreamer's 'Me seemed' (13.7). **6 cast**: resolved. **7 tyne**: trouble, suffering (S.'s variant of 'teen'). **8 neuer vowd to rest**: vowed never to rest. **9 Nyne monethes**: the time of fulfilment or gestation, as III ii 11.6; see viii 38.6–7 n. One stage of his search for the Faerie Queene is fulfilled when he serves her by aiding Una. At II ix 7.5–6 the elapsed time is seven years (*1590*) or one year (*1596*); at II ix 38.9 it is three years (*1590*) or twelve months (*1596*).

Stanza 16
3 bale: fire; sorrow, grief. **9 on grownd**: on earth, as 7.9, and suggesting 'earthly'; referring also to Arthur's vision while lying on the grass.

Stanza 17
1–3 Ambiguity of precedence is required by the allegory, as Upton 1758 suggests: the knight declares that he will place his love for Una before – or more likely – next after his love for the Faerie Queene. Levin 1991:16 infers that he declares

'that his love for Una shall henceforth match Arthur's love for the Faerie Queene'. **4 faith**: loyalty. He had left her 'Through light misdeeming of her loialtie' (iv 2.2); cf. vii 49.4–5. **5 case**: fortune, plight. **6 Patrone**: protector, defender; cf. Guyon's similar tribute to Arthur at the corresponding moment in his adventure, II viii 55.4. **7 worthie**: excellent; fitting, deserved. **8** I.e. you alone deserve her grace by proof of your valour. **9 liefe**: beloved, used of a superior.

Stanza 18
5 earnd: yearned. **6** The virtue of Bk IV is here first named. **9** Cf. II i 34.2.

Stanza 19
These 'giftes of healing' (1 Cor. 12:9) are complementary: the first heals bodily wounds, the second saves souls. Their difference is that between the water from the well of life and the balm from the tree of life; see xi 46–48 n. DuRocher 1984:186–87 links Arthur's gift to his magnificence. **1 Diamond**: either the stone or the rock adamant. Both signify unconquerable faith; see vii 33.5–9 n. **sure**: sound, true (referring to **Diamond**); secure (referring to the **boxe**). Weatherby 1994:20 compares the 'boxe of verie costelie ointement' (Matt. 26.7) with which the woman anointed Christ, and identifies the **liquor pure** with unction that heals both sin and sickness. **2 Embowd**: arched, i.e. surrounded or encircled. **3–5 liquor pure**: cf. the blood of Christ which 'clenseth vs from all sinne' (1 John 1.7). **excellent**: pre-eminent, supreme. **incontinent**: straightway. The word also modifies **wownd**, referring to the sin of concupiscence which the liquor heals. Hence Arthur uses a 'few drops' to cure Amoret's wounds at IV viii 20. **7–9** Since the book is the NT, the

20

Thus beene they parted, *Arthur* on his way
  To seeke his loue, and th'other for to fight
  With *Vnaes* foe, that all her realme did pray.
  But she now weighing the decayed plight,
  And shrunken synewes of her chosen knight,
  Would not a while her forward course pursew,
  Ne bring him forth in face of dreadfull fight,
  Till he recouered had his former hew:
For him to be yet weake and wearie well she knew.

21

So as they traueild, lo they gan espy
  An armed knight towards them gallop fast,
  That seemed from some feared foe to fly,
  Or other griesly thing, that him aghast.
  Still as he fledd, his eye was backward cast,
  As if his feare still followed him behynd;
  Als flew his steed, as he his bandes had brast,
  And with his winged heeles did tread the wynd,
As he had beene a fole of *Pegasus* his kynd.

22

Nigh as he drew, they might perceiue his head
  To bee vnarmd, and curld vncombed heares
  Vpstaring stiffe, dismaid with vncouth dread;
  Nor drop of blood in all his face appeares

Nor life in limbe: and to increase his feares,
  In fowle reproch of knighthoodes fayre degree,
  About his neck an hempen rope he weares,
  That with his glistring armes does ill agree;
But he of rope or armes has now no memoree.

23

The *Redcrosse* knight toward him crossed fast,
  To weet, what mister wight was so dismayd:
  There him he findes all sencelesse and aghast,
  That of him selfe he seemd to be afrayd,
  Whom hardly he from flying forward stayd,
  Till he these wordes to him deliuer might;
  Sir knight, aread who hath ye thus arayd,
  And eke from whom make ye this hasty flight:
For neuer knight I saw in such misseeming plight.

24

He answerd nought at all, but adding new
  Feare to his first amazment, staring wyde
  With stony eyes, and hartlesse hollow hew,
  Astonisht stood, as one that had aspyde
  Infernall furies, with their chaines vntyde.
  Him yett againe, and yett againe bespake
  The gentle knight, who nought to him replyde,
  But trembling euery ioynt did inly quake,
And foltring tongue at last these words seemd forth to shake.

---

relation between the two gifts may be suggested by Matt. 26.28: 'For this is my blood of the Newe testament, that is shed for manie, for the remission of sinnes'. Kellogg and Steele 1965 suggest that the two gifts answer the blood and book of the old Covenant, Exod. 24.6–8. At x 13.8–9, Fidelia holds this book 'signd and seald with blood'. The separation of the OT from the NT becomes central in the Red Cross Knight's encounter with Despaire; see 37–51n. **his Saueours**: this Saueours *1590* (corr. F.E). An interesting error if it is the poet's. **braue**: splendid.

Stanza 20

3 **pray**: plunder. **4–9** Cf. 2.1–2. The substance of these lines is repeated at x 2.1–6 to set the Despaire episode apart as a prefatory interlude to the knight's experience in the house of Holinesse. **her chosen knight**: as explained in the *LR* 63–66, Una chose him when her armour fitted him. The phrase prepares for the resolution of the episode at 53.5; but the question, 'chosen for what?' leads him into Despaire's mental maze. The dilemma that one should be saved from death only to become subject to despair is expressed at III v 42.7–9.

Stanza 21

1 **gan**: did. **4 griesly** and **aghast** suggest fear aroused by infernal spirits. **6 his feare**: what he feared; or Fear itself, described at III xii 12; or suggesting that Despaire is his 'fere' or companion. **9 kynd**: breed. **Pegasus** suggests swift flight. Possibly Pegasus's flight to the heavens suggests the knight's flight to 'Gods deare loue' (25.1) through which alone he may be saved from despair.

Stanza 22

Trevisan appears as did the Red Cross Knight before his fall: 'Disarmd, disgraste, and inwardly dismayde' (vii 11.6); and also immediately after it: 'pale and wan' (viii 42.3). **1–2** His head is **vnarmd** because despair is an error of reason; hence his loss of memory. In the state of despair, he lacks the helmet which is 'the hope of saluation' (1 Thess. 5.8). That S. has this text in mind is suggested by the verse that follows: 'For God hathe not appointed vs vnto wrath, but to obteine saluation'. **3 Vpstaring**: standing on end, suggesting that his hairs stare like eyes. **vncouth**: strange, repellent; also 'unknown'. **4–5** Pallidness expresses the state of wan-hope or despair. **7 hempen**: indicating that he wears the hangman's halter; cf. 54.4–5. Chew 1947:113 notes that the suicide of Judas Iscariot made the rope or halter the chief image of despair.

Stanza 23

2 **what mister wight**: a common formula for 'what kind of person are you?'; see E.K. on *SC July* 201. **7 aread**: declare. **9 misseeming**: cf. his own 'misseeming hew' (viii 42.9) upon emerging from Orgoglio's dungeon.

Stanza 24

2–4 **amazment**: overwhelming fear; mental stupefaction, with its literal force: he has been led into a mental maze by Despaire; see 49.1. His eyes indicate his state of despair; see 35.6–7. **stony**: fixed; cf. v 32.7. **hartlesse**: lacking heart or courage; hence 'Nor drop of blood in all his face appeares' (22.4); cf. 29.7. For the importance of the heart in this episode, see 48.2n. **5** On the **furies**, see iii 36.8n.

25

For Gods deare loue, Sir knight, doe me not stay;
    For loe he comes, he comes fast after mee.
    Eft looking back would faine haue runne away;
    But he him forst to stay, and tellen free
    The secrete cause of his perplexitie,
    Yet nathemore by his bold hartie speach,
    Could his blood frosen hart emboldened bee,
    But through his boldnes rather feare did reach,
Yett forst, at last he made through silence suddein breach.

26

And am I now in safetie sure (quoth he)
    From him, that would haue forced me to dye?
    And is the point of death now turnd fro mee,
    That I may tell this haplesse history?
    Feare nought:(quoth he) no daunger now is nye.
    Then shall I you recount a ruefull cace,
    (Said he) the which with this vnlucky eye
    I late beheld, and had not greater grace
Me reft from it, had bene partaker of the place.

27

I lately chaunst (Would I had neuer chaunst)
    With a fayre knight to keepen companee,
    Sir *Terwin* hight, that well himselfe aduaunst
    In all affayres, and was both bold and free,
    But not so happy as mote happy bee:
    He lou'd, as was his lot, a Lady gent,
    That him againe lou'd in the least degree:
    For she was proud, and of too high intent,
And ioyd to see her louer languish and lament.

28

From whom retourning sad and comfortlesse,
    As on the way together we did fare,
    We met that villen (God from him me blesse)
    That cursed wight, from whom I scapt whyleare,
    A man of hell, that calls himselfe *Despayre*:
    Who first vs greets, and after fayre areedes
    Of tydinges straunge, and of aduentures rare:
    So creeping close, as Snake in hidden weedes,
Inquireth of our states, and of our knightly deedes.

29

Which when he knew, and felt our feeble harts
    Embost with bale, and bitter byting griefe,
    Which loue had launched with his deadly darts,
    With wounding words and termes of foule repriefe,
    He pluckt from vs all hope of dew reliefe,
    That earst vs held in loue of lingring life;
    Then hopelesse hartlesse, gan the cunning thiefe
    Perswade vs dye, to stint all further strife:
To me he lent this rope, to him a rusty knife.

30

With which sad instrument of hasty death,
    That wofull louer, loathing lenger light,
    A wyde way made to let forth liuing breath.
    But I more fearefull, or more lucky wight,
    Dismayd with that deformed dismall sight,
    Fledd fast away, halfe dead with dying feare:
    Ne yet assur'd of life by you, Sir knight,
    Whose like infirmity like chaunce may beare:
But God you neuer let his charmed speaches heare.

Stanza 25

1 For Gods deare loue: a curious exclamation from one who has almost yielded to despair. Even uttered unwittingly, however, it may save him: at 26.8 he recognizes God's grace, and at 28.3 he invokes God's blessing. **doe me not stay**: this inverted construction with the four heavy and rising stresses indicates the knight's terror. It balances the opening exclamation: he flees from Despaire to God's love. **3 Eft**: again. **5 perplexitie**: trouble, distress; also mental bewilderment. **6 nathemore**: not at all. **hartie**: encouraging; courageous; also literally 'full of heart' as he seeks to revive the knight's **blood frosen hart**. **8 reach**: succeed in arousing; in Trevisan, apparently, although the loose reference in 7–8 transfers **feare** to the Red Cross Knight.

Stanza 26

4 haplesse: a key word in the Red Cross Knight's history; see vii 11.4, ix 12.1. **6 cace**: event. **8–9** The confusing response betrays Trevisan's trepidation, as Percival 1964 notes. **greater grace**: greater than his companion enjoyed. By **grace** he seems to refer to his fear or luck; cf. 30.4. **partaker of the place**: i.e. 'I would have shared my companion's fate in that place'.

Stanza 27

3 Terwin: possibly from 'terwyn', to weary, fatigue; or coined from 'ter' + 'won': i.e. thrice – and therefore totally –

conquered; see Hebert 1974. Alice Fox 1975:39 suggests an anagram for 'Winter'. Roche 1984:77–78 suggests 'thrice-winner', and, as he is 'a thrice-loser', relates his despair to the poet-lover's in Elizabethan sonnet sequences. For further on the name, see 32.5*n*. **7 againe**: in return. **8 intent**: mind, will; suggesting 'aim', 'ambition'.

Stanza 28

1 comfortlesse: implying the stronger sense, helpless, desolate. **3 blesse**: protect by his blessing. **4 whyleare**: a while before, 'late' (31.3). **6 areedes**: tells. **8 in hidden weedes**: hidden in weeds; in weeds that hide.

Stanza 29

1 our: its third use in two lines shows that Trevisan, for reasons not given, is infected by his companion's despair. **2 Embost with bale**: exhausted by sorrow; suggested by the pun on **harts**, as Collier 1862 observes: an exhausted hart is embossed when it foams with fatigue. **3 launched**: pierced. **4 repriefe**: insult, scorn. **5** Alluding to the etymology of despair, 'depriving of hope'. **9** In Skelton, *Magnificence* 2309, Despair offers the hero the same weapons for suicide.

Stanza 30

5 deformed: hateful; or referring to his disfigured friend. **dismall**: causing terror. **6 dying feare**: fear of dying, which here preserves him from death. **9 God you neuer let**: i.e.

31

How may a man (said he) with idle speach
  Be wonne, to spoyle the Castle of his health?
  I wote (quoth he) whom tryall late did teach,
  That like would not for all this worldes wealth:
  His subtile tong, like dropping honny, mealt'th
  Into the heart, and searcheth euery vaine,
  That ere one be aware, by secret stealth
  His powre is reft, and weaknes doth remaine.
O neuer Sir desire to try his guilefull traine.

32

Certes (sayd he) hence shall I neuer rest,
  Till I that treachours art haue heard and tryde;
  And you Sir knight, whose name mote I request,
  Of grace do me vnto his cabin guyde.
  I that hight *Treuisan* (quoth he) will ryde
  Against my liking backe, to doe you grace:
  But nor for gold nor glee will I abyde
  By you, when ye arriue in that same place;
For leuer had I die, then see his deadly face.

33

Ere long they come, where that same wicked wight
  His dwelling has, low in an hollow caue,
  Far vnderneath a craggy clift ypight,
  Darke, dolefull, dreary, like a greedy graue,

That still for carrion carcases doth craue:
  On top whereof ay dwelt the ghastly Owle,
  Shrieking his balefull note, which euer draue
  Far from that haunt all other chearefull fowle;
And all about it wandring ghostes did wayle and howle.

34

And all about old stockes and stubs of trees,
  Whereon nor fruite, nor leafe was euer seene,
  Did hang vpon the ragged rocky knees;
  On which had many wretches hanged beene,
  Whose carcases were scattred on the greene,
  And throwne about the cliffs. Arriued there,
  That bare-head knight for dread and dolefull teene,
  Would faine haue fled, ne durst approchen neare,
But th'other forst him staye, and comforted in feare.

35

That darkesome caue they enter, where they find
  That cursed man, low sitting on the ground,
  Musing full sadly in his sullein mind;
  His griesie lockes, long growen, and vnbound,
  Disordred hong about his shoulders round,
  And hid his face; through which his hollow eyne
  Lookt deadly dull, and stared as astound;
  His raw-bone cheekes through penurie and pine,
Were shronke into his iawes, as he did neuer dyne.

---

may God never let you. **charmed speaches**: speeches that charm; cf. 48.8.

Stanza 31
1 idle: foolish, in the biblical sense: 'euerie idle worde that men shal speake' (Matt. 12.36). **2 spoyle**: despoil. **the Castle of his health**: 'our earthlie house of this tabernacle' (2 Cor. 5.1). **health**: well-being. **4** That like trial would not undergo again. Or **like** may refer to taking one's own life. **5** Cf. Prov. 5.3: 'the lippes of a strange woman drop as an honie combe'. **mealt'th**: melts. **9 try**: make trial of. **traine**: wiles.

Stanza 32
1–2 His vow is ironic, for Despaire offers him 'eternall rest' (40.1) and urges him 'to thy rest betake' (44.2). **treachours**: traitor's, an obs. form that suggests 'treacherous'. **4, 6 grace**: the limited sense, 'favour', clears the way for the religious significance at 53.6 after the knight has **tryde** Despaire's art and shown his need for grace. **4 cabin**: cave. **5 Treuisan**: from Gk τρέω flee, sugg. Belson 1964:361, which is supported by 21.6; or 'dread', which is supported by 22.3. Since 'u' corresponds to 'w', it may be an anagram: 'as Terwin'. Ruthven's suggestion, in the *SEnc* 256, that the name derives from L. *ter* thrice + *visi* I have seen, because he encounters Despaire three times, is supported by the many references to sight, e.g. 32.9. In noticing that these are the only two names in Bk I not obviously labels, O'Connor 1990 argues that they are the names of two European cities: Terwin, an English version of Thérouanne, a Protestant stronghold razed by the Catholic forces of Charles V in 1553; and Trevisan, derived from Treves, a Roman Catholic stronghold from which the Reformers were expelled during the early 1560s. See also Meyer 1975. **7 glee**: bright colour, beauty; possibly the glitter of gold. Church 1758 suggests 'fee' as at x 43.6 but alliteration supports the text. Moreover, the phrase refers to the two major temptations of Bk II: money (Mammon) and beauty (Acrasia). **9 leuer**: rather.

Stanza 33
3 ypight: pitched. **4–5** Cf. Aesculapius's cave at v 36.5–6. In contrast, Despaire's cave is actively malignant. **6–8 the ghastly Owle**: see v 30.6–7n on the owl as the messenger of death.

Stanza 34
1 stockes: stumps (unique to S. in this sense). **3 knees**: cliffs, crags (unique to S. in this sense). **5 greene**: common land (*OED* 12b), usually grassy (as 36.4), here a graveyard where the dead lie unburied. **7 teene**: grief.

Stanza 35
1 Trevisan has no further place in the story. **3 sullein**: gloomy; morose; cf. 'solein' (*OED* 5). Despaire displays the outward symptoms of melancholy described by Burton, *Anat. Mel.* 1.3.1.1, and therefore of Saturn (see II ix 52.8–9n). **4 griesie**: grey, grizzled; horrible, hideous; filthy. **8–9** Cf. the appearance of the Red Cross Knight upon emerging from Orgoglio's dungeon at viii 41. **penurie and pine**: lack of food and the suffering that follows.

36

His garment nought but many ragged clouts,
　With thornes together pind and patched was,
　The which his naked sides he wrapt abouts;
　And him beside there lay vpon the gras
　A dreary corse, whose life away did pas,
　All wallowd in his own yet luke-warme blood,
　That from his wound yet welled fresh alas;
　In which a rusty knife fast fixed stood,
And made an open passage for the gushing flood.

37

Which piteous spectacle, approuing trew
　The wofull tale, that *Trevisan* had told,
　When as the gentle *Redcrosse* knight did vew,
　With firie zeale he burnt in courage bold,
　Him to auenge, before his blood were cold,
　And to the villein sayd, Thou damned wight,
　The authour of this fact, we here behold,
　What iustice can but iudge against thee right,
With thine owne blood to price his blood, here shed in sight.

38

What franticke fit (quoth he) hath thus distraught
　Thee, foolish man, so rash a doome to giue?
　What iustice euer other iudgement taught,
　But he should dye, who merites not to liue?

None els to death this man despayring driue,
　But his owne guiltie mind deseruing death.
　Is then vniust to each his dew to giue?
　Or let him dye, that loatheth liuing breath?
Or let him die at ease, that liueth here vneath?

39

Who trauailes by the wearie wandring way,
　To come vnto his wished home in haste,
　And meetes a flood, that doth his passage stay,
　Is not great grace to helpe him ouer past,
　Or free his feet, that in the myre sticke fast?
　Most enuious man, that grieues at neighbours good,
　And fond, that ioyest in the woe thou hast,
　Why wilt not let him passe, that long hath stood
Vpon the bancke, yet wilt thy selfe not pas the flood?

40

He there does now enioy eternall rest
　And happy ease, which thou doest want and craue,
　And further from it daily wanderest:
　What if some little payne the passage haue,
　That makes frayle flesh to feare the bitter waue?
　Is not short payne well borne, that bringes long ease,
　And layes the soule to sleepe in quiet graue?
　Sleepe after toyle, port after stormie seas,
Ease after warre, death after life does greatly please.

Stanza 36

1–3 His clothes display his abandoned state; cf. the 'olde rotten ragges, and olde worne cloutes' worn by Jeremiah on being taken from the dungeon at Jer. 38.11. The garment pinned with thorns is worn by the abandoned Achaemenides in Virgil, *Aen.* 3.594, a detail selected by Ovid, *Met.* 14.166, to mark his state. The **thornes** signify Despaire's cursed state without hope of redemption, according to God's curse (Gen. 3.18). **clouts**: rags. **abouts**: obs. form of 'about'. **5 dreary**: gory, bloody. **6 wallowd**: lying prostrate; literally rolled in his blood. **8 rusty**: bloody, as 29.9.

Stanzas 37–51

The Red Cross Knight's encounter with Despaire is a major display of S.'s rhetorical powers in rendering persuasively classical and Christian commonplaces on living in despair of God's judgement, and through loss of hope of God's grace being tempted by suicide. It is his allegorical version of Hamlet's soliloquy, 'To be, or not to be'. For a brief rhetorical analysis, see Vickers 1970:157–60 and M.F.N. Dixon 1996:37–42. Sirluck 1949–50 discusses the prejudicial use of enthymeme in Despaire's argument by which God's justice is stressed while his mercy is ignored. See also Cullen 1974:59–61, Nohrnberg 1976:152–55, Goeglein 1994:5–8 and Mallette 1997:37–41. The argument is analysed by Imbrie 1987:146–50 as a parody of biblical interpretation; its rhetorical cunning is analysed by Skulsky in the *SEnc* 213. See also 'dialogue, poetic' in the *SEnc*.

Stanza 37

1 approuing: proving, finding by experience. **4** Arthur's 'constant zele, and corage bold' (viii 40.4) that led him to

rescue the Red Cross Knight now lead to the knight's defeat. **5 his**: Terwin's (cf. 36.6); yet applied also to the knight burning with **firie zeale**. **7 fact**: crime. **8–9** Cf. Gen. 9.6: 'Whoso shedeth mans blood, by man shal his blood be shed'. As does Despaire at 43.6, Night uses this same argument at v 26.3–4, and her prophecy is almost fulfilled when the knight himself invokes the justice which condemns him. Cf. Rom. 2.1: 'Therefore thou art inexcusable, O man, whosoeuer thou art that iudgest: for in that thou iudgest another, thou condemnest thy self'. **price**: pay for. **in sight**: not a mere rhyming tag, for again the knight is betrayed by his sight.

Stanza 38

1 franticke: mad with rage; guilty of extreme folly. **2 foolish man**: in response to the knight's 'damned wight', noting his want of judgement. **doome**: judgement. **5 driue**: either the earlier form of 'drove', or the present tense, 'drives', to intensify Despaire's argument. **8–9 let him die**: i.e. is it unjust to let him die? **die at ease**: i.e. die and be at ease. **vneath**: in unease.

Stanza 39

3–5 Cf. Ps. 69.1–2: 'Saue me, O God: for the waters are entred euen to my soule. I sticke fast in the depe myre, where no staie is: I am come into depe waters, and the streames runne ouer me'. **grace**: favour, in parody of God's saving grace. **7 fond**: foolish. **8–9** The ironic allusion to the crossing of the Jordan – the traditional figure for baptism – is noted by Brooks-Davies 1977:91.

Stanza 40

6 well borne: well worth bearing. **7** Unless **soule** refers to the whole person, Despaire rejects the distinction made in the

41

The knight much wondred at his suddeine wit,
  And sayd, The terme of life is limited,
  Ne may a man prolong, nor shorten it;
  The souldier may not moue from watchfull sted,
  Nor leaue his stand, vntill his Captaine bed.
  Who life did limit by almightie doome,
  (Quoth he) knowes best the termes established;
  And he, that points the Centonell his roome,
Doth license him depart at sound of morning droome.

42

Is not his deed, what euer thing is donne,
  In heauen and earth? did not he all create,
  To die againe? all ends that was begonne.
  Their times in his eternall booke of fate
  Are written sure, and haue their certein date.
  Who then can striue with strong necessitie,
  That holds the world in his still chaunging state,
  Or shunne the death ordaynd by destinie?
When houre of death is come, let none aske whence, nor why.

43

The lenger life, I wote the greater sin,
  The greater sin, the greater punishment:
  All those great battels, which thou boasts to win,
  Through strife, and blood-shed, and auengement,

Now praysd, hereafter deare thou shalt repent:
For life must life, and blood must blood repay.
Is not enough thy euill life forespent?
For he, that once hath missed the right way,
The further he doth goe, the further he doth stray.

44

Then doe no further goe, no further stray,
  But here ly downe, and to thy rest betake,
  Th'ill to preuent, that life ensewen may.
  For what hath life, that may it loued make,
  And giues not rather cause it to forsake?
  Feare, sicknesse, age, losse, labour, sorrow, strife,
  Payne, hunger, cold, that makes the hart to quake;
  And euer fickle fortune rageth rife,
All which, and thousands mo do make a loathsome life.

45

Thou wretched man, of death hast greatest need,
  If in true ballaunce thou wilt weigh thy state:
  For neuer knight, that dared warlike deed,
  More luckless dissauentures did amate:
  Witnes the dungeon deepe, wherein of late
  Thy life shutt vp, for death so oft did call;
  And though good lucke prolonged hath thy date,
  Yet death then, would the like mishaps forestall,
Into the which heareafter thou maist happen fall.

---

burial service in the *BCP*: the soul is taken by God, the body is committed to the ground. **8–9** The echoing **seas** / **Ease** rounded out with **please** characterizes the highly rhetorical nature of the commonplaces used by Despaire. Crampton 1974:124 notes how 'ease' echoes through the lines, even replacing the expected 'peace' in 9.

Stanza 41

1 wondred: with a pun on 'wandered'. By not answering Despaire's biblical verses with biblical verses, he becomes lost in a mental labyrinth. **suddeine wit**: quick mind. **2–5** The knight is given only these four lines in response to Despaire's three stanzas followed by six more. His argument against suicide is a classical commonplace, used, e.g. by Pyrocles in Sidney, *Old Arcadia* 294. **4 watchfull sted**: the post or station of watch assigned to him. **5 stand**: post. **bed**: bids. **8–9 roome**: assigned place or station. Life is reduced to the sentinel's weary role of keeping watch; cf. Ps. 130.6: 'My soule waiteth on the Lord more then the morning watche watcheth for the morning'. **morning droome**: with the pun on 'mourning', the knight's argument shifts from 'leaving when time expires' to 'leaving when mourning'.

Stanza 42

The knight's voice blends with Despaire's as he yields to despair. The proverbs in Despaire's speech are listed by Smith, e.g. line 2: 179; 3: 12, 53; 5: 260; 6: 570; 9: 155. On the use of cultural memory, see Anderson 1996:177–78. **4–5** Despaire invokes Ps. 31.15: 'My times are in thine hand' while ignoring the context which indicates that God's rule is a cause for joy,

as Imbrie 1987:147 notes. **certein date**: fixed duration. The argument is Night's at v 25.5.

Stanza 43

1 wote: know; with the stronger sense, 'know for certain'. The necessity of sinning is supported by 1 John 1.8: 'If we say that we haue no sinne, we deceiue our selues, and trueth is not in vs'. Again Despaire ignores the context, for John adds: 'If we acknowledge our sinnes, he is faithful and iust, to forgiue vs our sinnes, and to clense vs from all vnrighteousnes'. **4 auengement**: vengeance. The word undercuts the knight's ambition to fight for worship and grace (cf. i 3.4). **6** See 37.8–9*n*. Despaire invokes the knight's concept of retributive justice to condemn him. **7 forespent**: previously spent; entirely spent, i.e. worn out, wasted; misspent.

Stanza 44

3 . . . that follows if you happen to live; or that results from life. **7 makes**: the singular indicates that each of the ten listed ills is sufficient by itself to cause his heart to quake.

Stanza 45

1 Thou: i.e. you especially. **4 dissauentures**: mishaps. Despaire echoes Una's lament for her 'dolefull disauenturous deare' (vii 48.7); cf. xi 28.3. **amate**: daunt; also match, hinting that the knight and bad luck are inseparably linked. **6 for . . . call**: see viii 38.3–9*n*. **7** Despaire reduces 'heauenly grace' (viii 1.3) to **good lucke**, the 'good hap' of vii 29.1. **date**: term of life, the time 'given' us in life. **8 then**: i.e. when you called **of late**; also 'consequently'. **forestall**: prevent by anticipation.

46

Why then doest thou, O man of sin, desire
   To draw thy dayes forth to their last degree?
   Is not the measure of thy sinfull hire
   High heaped vp with huge iniquitee,
   Against the day of wrath, to burden thee?
   Is not enough, that to this Lady mild
   Thou falsed hast thy faith with periuree,
   And sold thy selfe to serue *Duessa* vild,
With whom in al abuse thou hast thy selfe defild?

47

Is not he iust, that all this doth behold
   From highest heuen, and beares an equall eie?
   Shall he thy sins vp in his knowledge fold,
   And guilty be of thine impietie?
   Is not his lawe, Let euery sinner die:
   Die shall all flesh? what then must needs be donne,
   Is it not better to doe willinglie,
   Then linger, till the glas be all out ronne?
Death is the end of woes: die soone, O faries sonne.

48

The knight was much enmoued with his speach,
   That as a swords poynt through his hart did perse,
   And in his conscience made a secrete breach,
   Well knowing trew all, that he did reherse,

And to his fresh remembraunce did reuerse,
   The vgly vew of his deformed crimes,
   That all his manly powres it did disperse,
   As he were charmed with inchaunted rimes,
That oftentimes he quakt, and fainted oftentimes.

49

In which amazement, when the Miscreaunt
   Perceiued him to wauer weake and fraile,
   Whiles trembling horror did his conscience daunt,
   And hellish anguish did his soule assaile,
   To driue him to despaire, and quite to quaile,
   Hee shewd him painted in a table plaine,
   The damned ghosts, that doe in torments waile,
   And thousand feends that doe them endlesse paine
With fire and brimstone, which for euer shall remaine.

50

The sight whereof so throughly him dismaid,
   That nought but death before his eies he saw,
   And euer burning wrath before him laid,
   By righteous sentence of th'Almighties law:
   Then gan the villein him to ouercraw,
   And brought vnto him swords, ropes, poison, fire,
   And all that might him to perdition draw;
   And bad him choose, what death he would desire:
For death was dew to him, that had prouokt Gods ire.

Stanza 46

1 O man of sin: a terrible final naming, applied to the Antichrist at 2 Thess. 2.3. Only the knight in despair judges himself guilty of his crimes: Una blames an evil star and fortune (viii 42–43); Arthur blames the uncertainty of worldly bliss (viii 44.9), and the weakness of the flesh (ix 11–12); and Una's parents blame fate (xii 16.5–6). Later he admits his weakness against Duessa's 'wicked arts' (xii 32.6). **3–5 sinfull hire**: echoing Rom. 6.23: 'For the wages of sinne is death'; cf. Rom. 2.3–5: 'And thinkest thou this, O thou man, that iudgest them which do suche things, and doest the same, that thou shalt escape the iudgement of God? . . . But thou . . . heapest vnto thyself wrath against the day of wrath'. **the day of wrath**: citing Rom. 2.5, the day 'when the wicked shalbe condemned' (Geneva gloss). **burden**: playing on its double sense: as God's word lays a 'charge' (*OED* 2) on the knight, he carries its weight. **6 this Lady mild**: Una's presence is indicated again at 52.1 for only in the presence of her 'wondrous faith, exceeding earthly race' (17.4) is the knight's sin fully manifest to him. **7 falsed**: violated, betrayed. **8–9** Despaire names the two faults that have overcome Una's earlier champions: 'want of faith, or guilt of sin' (vii 45.8).

Stanza 47

1–2 As God through Ezekiel asks: 'Is not my waie equall?' (18.25). If the knight were not paralysed by guilt, he could reply: 'The Lord is good to all, and his mercies are ouer all his workes' (Ps. 145.9). **equall**: impartial, just; cf. Una's statement at viii 27.6–7. **3–4** Despaire's rhetorical question suggests the solution to all these riddles: 'Christ dyed for our sinnes according to the Scriptures' (1 Cor. 15.3), answering the Old Covenant by the New; cf. 1 Pet. 3.18. **5** 'The soule that sinneth, it shal dye' (Ezek. 18.4). Despaire suppresses half of the verse: 'The wages of sinne is death; but the gifte of God

is eternal life through Iesus Christ our Lord' (Rom. 6.23). **6** 'All flesh shal perish together' (Job 34.15). **8 glas**: the hour-glass. **9** Proverbial: Smith 153. **soone**: straightway. **O faries sonne**: see x 33.2*n*.

Stanza 48

2–3 his hart did perse: the sign that he is overcome by despair. In effect, he has drunk from Duessa's cup: 'Death and despeyre did many thereof sup, | . . . Th'eternall bale of heauie wounded harts' (viii 14.3–5). The extended play on the wounded heart in this episode reaches a climax in these closing stanzas, for Despaire's words have appropriated God's word which is 'sharper then anie two edged sworde' (Heb. 4.12). See Imbrie 1987:148–49, and Dughi 1997:27–28. **conscience**: inward knowledge, consciousness, mind. Once breached by Despaire, it must be cured in the house of Holinesse; see x 23.8–9, 29.3. **4 reherse**: say; also the current sense for Despaire repeats what the knight has done and recites Scripture. **5 reuerse**: bring back. **8–9 inchaunted rimes**: cf. his 'charmed speaches' (30.9) and Archimago's verses framed with 'mighty charmes' (i 36.9). The relation of this moment to the knight's earlier failures is noted by Mikics 1994:56.

Stanza 49

1 amazement: see 24.2–4*n* and 41.1*n*. **Miscreaunt**: misbeliever, in the literal sense. **2 weake and fraile**: the terms define his fleshly state; cf. 53.1. **3 trembling horror**: the adj. stresses the noun's Lat. root, as viii 39.3. **daunt**: overcome. **4 hellish anguish**: i.e. fear of hell. **6 table**: picture. **7–9** In his despair the knight no longer regards death as 'the end of woes' (47.9). 'But the fearefull and vnbeleuing . . . shal haue their parte in the lake, which burneth with fyre and brimstone, which is the seconde death' (Rev. 21.8). **for euer**: Rev. 20.10.

51

But whenas none of them he saw him take,
    He to him raught a dagger sharpe and keene,
    And gaue it him in hand: his hand did quake,
    And tremble like a leafe of Aspin greene,
    And troubled blood through his pale face was seene
    To come, and goe with tidings from the heart,
    As it a ronning messenger had beene.
At last resolu'd to worke his finall smart,
He lifted vp his hand, that backe againe did start.

52

Which whenas *Vna* saw, through euery vaine
    The crudled cold ran to her well of life,
    As in a swowne: but soone reliu'd againe,
    Out of his hand she snatcht the cursed knife,
    And threw it to the ground, enraged rife,
    And to him said, Fie fie, faint hearted knight,
    What meanest thou by this reprochfull strife?
Is this the battaile, which thou vauntst to fight
With that fire-mouthed Dragon, horrible and bright?

53

Come, come away, fraile, feeble, fleshly wight,
    Ne let vaine words bewitch thy manly hart,
    Ne diuelish thoughts dismay thy constant spright.
    In heauenly mercies hast thou not a part?
    Why shouldst thou then despeire, that chosen art?
    Where iustice growes, there grows eke greter grace,
    The which doth quench the brond of hellish smart,
And that accurst hand-writing doth deface.
Arise, Sir knight arise, and leaue this cursed place.

54

So vp he rose, and thence amounted streight.
    Which when the carle beheld, and saw his guest
    Would safe depart, for all his subtile sleight,
    He chose an halter from among the rest,
    And with it hong him selfe, vnbid vnblest.
    But death he could not worke himselfe thereby;
    For thousand times he so him selfe had drest,
    Yet nathelesse it could not doe him die,
Till he should die his last, that is eternally.

Stanza 50

5 ouercraw: exalt over.   **7 perdition**: as the place of damnation of the beast (Rev. 17.8) and as eternal death.

Stanza 51

1–3 The knight seems incapable of choosing but accepts a dagger because his heart is already pierced (48.2). **raught**: reached, held out.   **4** Such is the doubting state of Fradubio at ii 28.5. The simile is proverbial: Smith 29.   **9** . . . i.e., that started to come down to stab him. As in Skelton, *Magnificence* 2321–27: after the hero is convinced by Despair that he has no hope of God's grace and is handed a knife by Mischief, he is about to stab himself when Good Hope snatches it from him. Cf. the similar moment at VI viii 49.2 when Calepine interrupts the sacrifice of Serena as the priest's 'right hand adowne descends'.

Stanza 52

The 'b' rhyme repeats the 'c' rhyme of stanza 29 to recall the similar moment in Trevisan's story, as Roche 1984:83–85 notes.   **2 well of life**: heart.   **3 reliu'd**: revived.   **7 reprochfull**: deserving of reproach; also strife 'in which you reproach yourself'.

Stanza 53

After being 'enraged rife' (52.5), Una speaks more persuasively than Despaire for she must move her knight's infected will. Instead of instructing him, she reminds him of what he already knows but has forgotten: that he lives under the New Covenant, not the Old. In his first battle, she urged him to 'Add faith vnto your force' (i 19.3); now to add hope; and soon she will lead him to where he may add charity. On the five major types of homily in her speech, see Mallette 1997:41–42. **1 fraile, feeble, fleshly**: cf. Rom. 8.1–13 on the sinful flesh; also Matt. 26.41 on its weakness.   **2** Una echoes Paul's warning against 'entising wordes' (Col. 2.4); cf. the knight's speech to Trevisan, 31.1–2.   **3 diuelish thoughts**: literally thoughts of devils, 49.8.   **constant**: perhaps 'constantly', or referring to the virtue of constancy, which all the heroes must uphold. **4 heauenly mercies**: the repressed term in Despaire's argument. Later despair 'Made him forget all, that *Fidelia* told' (x 22.5).   **5 that chosen art**: cf. 2 Thess. 2.13: 'God hathe from the beginning chosen you to saluacion, through sanctificacion of the Spirit, and the faith of trueth'; cf. Mark 13.20, and see x 57.1–4.   **chosen** may refer to the salvation open to all though few chosen (cf. x 10); or that he is 'her chosen knight' (20.5; cf. i 49.9); or that, as St George, he represents the nation chosen by God to defend the faith. See 'predestination' in the *SEnc*.   **6** Cf. Rom. 5.20: 'the Law entred thereupon that the offence shulde abunde: neuertheles where sinne abunded, there grace abunded muche more'.   **7** Cf. Eph. 6.16: 'Aboue all, take the shield of faith, wherewith ye may quench all the fyrie dartes of the wicked'.   **8** Cf. Col. 2.14: 'And putting out the hand writing of ordinances that was against vs, which was contrarie to vs, he euen toke it out of the way, and fastened it vpon the crosse'.

Stanza 54

2 carle: churl.   **3 for**: in spite of.   **5 vnbid vnblest**: i.e. without prayer and blessing, as given in the burial service in the *BCP*.   **7 drest**: made ready.   **9** The line invokes *BCP*: 'whosoever liueth, and believeth in him, shall not die eternally'.

Cant. X.

Her faithfull knight faire Vna brings
To house of Holinesse,
Where he is taught repentaunce, and
The way to heuenly blesse.

1

WHat man is he, that boasts of fleshly might,
  And vaine assuraunce of mortality,
Which all so soone, as it doth come to fight,
Against spirituall foes, yields by and by,
Or from the fielde most cowardly doth fly?
Ne let the man ascribe it to his skill,
That thorough grace hath gained victory.
If any strength we haue, it is to ill,
But all the good is Gods, both power and eke will.

2

By that, which lately hapned, *Vna* saw,
  That this her knight was feeble, and too faint;
And all his sinewes woxen weake and raw,
Through long enprisonment, and hard constraint,
Which he endured in his late restraint,
That yet he was vnfitt for bloody fight:
Therefore to cherish him with diets daint,
She cast to bring him, where he chearen might,
Till he recouered had his late decayed plight.

3

There was an auncient house not far away,
  Renowmd throughout the world for sacred lore,
And pure vnspotted life: so well they say
It gouernd was, and guided euermore,
Through wisedome of a matrone graue and hore;
Whose onely ioy was to relieue the needes
Of wretched soules, and helpe the helpeless pore:
All night she spent in bidding of her bedes,
And all the day in doing good and godly deedes.

4

Dame *Cælia* men did her call, as thought
  From heauen to come, or thether to arise,
The mother of three daughters, well vpbrought
In goodly thewes, and godly exercise:
The eldest two most sober, chast, and wise,
Fidelia and *Speranza* virgins were,
Though spousd, yet wanting wedlocks solemnize;
But faire *Charissa* to a louely fere
Was lincked, and by him had many pledges dere.

Book I Canto x

Argument

4 blesse: bliss; also blessing, the need of which is stressed in Trevisan's prayer, 'God from him [Despaire] me blesse' (ix 28.3).

Stanza 1

1–2 WHat man is he: implying, 'how foolish is that man', for 'Cursed be the man that trusteth in man, and maketh flesh his arme' (Jer. 17.5). In a superscription to *Am* 58, unique in the sequence, the poet charges his lady for being 'most assured to her selfe'. **4–5** This comment upon Terwin yielding to Despaire and Trevisan fleeing from him applies also to the Red Cross Knight: he yielded to Despaire instead of fighting the dragon, as Una charges at ix 52.8–9. **by and by**: immediately. **6–9** 'For by grace are ye saued through faith, and that not of your selues: it is the gifte of God, not of workes, lest any man shulde boaste himself' (Eph. 2.8–9). Line 9 combines two texts: 'there is no power but of God' (Rom. 13.1) and 'it is God which worketh in you, bothe the wil and the dede' (Phil. 2.13). In discussing the theological implications of the line, Wells 1983:45 allows the anomaly; Hume 1984:68–69 limits its application to the unregenerate; Schiavoni 1992 shows how the canto relates predestination and free will; Gless

1994:148–49 concludes that it allows the renewed human will a role in doing good works; and Kaske 1999:142–45 traces the contradiction to the Bible.

Stanza 2

1–6 See ix 20.4–9*n*. **faint**: wanting in courage; wanting in strength. Una had once enjoined him to 'Add faith . . . and be not faint' (i 19.3); now she takes him to Fidelia to be strengthened. **raw**: cf. his 'rawbone armes' (viii 41.6). **constraint**: confinement; or affliction, referring to his imprisonment in Orgoglio's dungeon, viii 38.6–9. **7–9** In contrast to Duessa who brought the knight to the house of Pride because she was 'wearie of the toilsom way' (iv 3.8). Cf. 11.4–5. **cherish**: foster; also cheer, gladden, as he is a victim of despair. **daint**: dainty, choice; cf. 18.2, 26.3. **9 recouered**: got over.

Stanza 3

1–3 Cf. the 'spiritual house', 1 Pet. 2.5, and see 'Holiness, house of' in the *SEnc*. Una, who is pure 'in life and euery vertuous lore' (i 5.2), taught the satyrs 'Trew sacred lore' at vi 30.9. Since she now guides the knight, his experience in the house of Holinesse reverses that in the house of Pride. On the relation of the two houses to the two conflicting cities of Augustine's *City of God*, see 'cities' in the *SEnc* and Bergvall

5

Arriued there, the dore they find fast lockt;
　For it was warely watched night and day,
　For feare of many foes: but when they knockt,
　The Porter opened vnto them streight way:
　He was an aged syre, all hory gray,
　With lookes full lowly cast, and gate full slow,
　Wont on a staffe his feeble steps to stay,
　Hight *Humiltá*. They passe in stouping low;
For streight and narrow was the way, which he did shew.

6

Each goodly thing is hardest to begin,
　But entred in a spatious court they see,
　Both plaine, and pleasaunt to be walked in,
　Where them does meete a francklin faire and free,
　And entertaines with comely courteous glee,
　His name was *Zele*, that him right well became,
　For in his speaches and behaueour hee
　Did labour liuely to expresse the same,
And gladly did them guide, till to the Hall they came.

7

There fayrely them receiues a gentle Squyre,
　Of myld demeanure, and rare courtesee,
　Right cleanly clad in comely sad attyre;
　In word and deede that shewd great modestee,
　And knew his good to all of each degree,
　Hight *Reuerence*. He them with speaches meet
　Does faire entreat; no courting nicetee,
　But simple trew, and eke vnfained sweet,
As might become a Squyre so great persons to greet.

8

And afterwardes them to his Dame he leades,
　That aged Dame, the Lady of the place:
　Who all this while was busy at her beades:
　Which doen, she vp arose with seemely grace,
　And toward them full matronely did pace.
　Where when that fairest *Vna* she beheld,
　Whom well she knew to spring from heuenly race,
　Her heart with ioy vnwonted inly sweld,
As feeling wondrous comfort in her weaker eld.

9

And her embracing said, O happy earth,
　Whereon thy innocent feet doe euer tread,
　Most vertuous virgin borne of heuenly berth,
　That to redeeme thy woefull parents head,
　From tyrans rage, and euer-dying dread,
　Hast wandred through the world now long a day;
　Yett ceassest not thy weary soles to lead,
　What grace hath thee now hether brought this way?
Or doen thy feeble feet vnweeting hether stray?

1993:34–35. With her, the house lies **not far away**; with Duessa, he 'Long with her traueild, till at last they see | A goodly building' (iv 2.5–6). **5 hore**: hoar, venerable; cf. 5.5. **6–7** Cf. the works of mercy, Matt. 25.35; see 36–43*n*. **onely**: chief. **8–9** She spends **All night . . . bidding of her bedes**, i.e. saying her prayers, in contrast to the blind devotion of Corceca who spends both 'day and night' (iii 13.6), and Archimago who spends 'all day' (i 30.7). Yet see 8.3–4. On the distinctions involved, see Kaske 1999:83–85.

Stanza 4

1 Cælia: or '*Cælia*' (1596) i.e. 'the heavenly one'. **3–9** Based on 1 Cor. 13.13: 'And now abideth faith, hope and loue, euen these thre [the three theological virtues], but the chiefest of these is loue'; 'chiefest', as the Geneva gloss explains: 'because it serueth bothe here and in the life to come: but faith and hope apperteine onely to this life'. Charity is the youngest according to the Protestant doctrine, 'Faith before good works', though 'faith without workes is dead' (Jas. 2:26). See 12.6–9*n*. **thewes**: manners, discipline. **godly exercise**: i.e. 'godly deedes' (3.9). **solemnize**: solemnization. Cf. the state of Una and the Red Cross Knight described at xii 19.9 and 37. **louely fere**: loving husband. **pledges**: i.e. children as tokens of their parents' love, a meaning coined by the poet of married love.

Stanza 5

4 'Knocke, and it shalbe opened vnto you' (Matt. 7.7). **7 stay**: support. **8–9** 'The gate is streicte, and the way narowe that leadeth vnto life' (Matt. 7.14). **Humiltá**: Ital. *humiltà*, a name parodied in Malvenù, the porter of the house of Pride at iv 6.4. He serves as porter because 'whosoeuer wil humble himself, shalbe exalted' (Matt. 23.12).

Stanza 6

1 Proverbial: Smith 52. **2 a spatious court**: a glancing allusion to the uncluttered Protestant church; but also, being a court, marked by **comely courteous glee**, 'rare courtesee' (7.2) and 'all the court'sies' (11.8). See Bates 1992:167. **4 francklin**: freeholder, referring to his state of Christian liberty. **free**: 'in the libertie wherewith Christ hathe made vs fre' (Gal. 5.1). **6 His name was**: a common formula in a canto where disguise is not needed; cf. 17.9, 23.9, etc.

Stanza 7

1 fayrely: courteously; an adverb used six times in the canto to mark the gracious formality of the house of Holinesse. **3 sad**: sober-coloured. **5** 'He knew how to behave with the respect suitable to each class of society and each member in it'. His virtue of civility is closely linked to courtesy; see VI proem 4.5*n*. **6 Reuerence**: his name sums up his contrast to Vanitie, the usher of the house of Pride at iv 13.3. **7 entreat**: treat. **courting nicetee**: affectation in paying court. **8 simple trew**: simple true behaviour; or simple truth.

Stanza 8

9 comfort: physical strength, invigoration. **weaker eld**: too weak age.

Stanza 9

2 euer: as the Church is *semper eadem* and *semper una*, i.e. 'one, continued from the first beginning of the world to the last end' (Hooker, *Lawes* 3.1.3). **3 borne of heuenly berth** enforces the claim at 8.7 that she springs 'from heauenly race'; cf. iii 8.7. **5 euer-dying dread**: constant fear of (eternal) death. **7 soles**: a pun on 'souls', as Una on earth is the Church Militant.

10

Straunge thing it is an errant knight to see
  Here in this place, or any other wight,
  That hether turnes his steps. So few there bee,
  That chose the narrow path, or seeke the right:
  All keepe the broad high way, and take delight
  With many rather for to goe astray,
  And be partakers of their euill plight,
  Then with a few to walke the rightest way;
O foolish men, why hast ye to your owne decay?

11

Thy selfe to see, and tyred limbes to rest,
  O matrone sage (quoth she) I hether came,
  And this good knight his way with me addrest,
  Ledd with thy prayses and broad-blazed fame,
  That vp to heuen is blowne. The auncient Dame,
  Him goodly greeted in her modest guyse,
  And enterteynd them both, as best became,
  With all the court'sies, that she could deuyse,
Ne wanted ought, to shew her bounteous or wise.

12

Thus as they gan of sondrie thinges deuise,
  Loe two most goodly virgins came in place,
  Ylinked arme in arme in louely wise,
  With countenance demure, and modest grace,
  They numbred euen steps and equall pace:
  Of which the eldest, that *Fidelia* hight,
  Like sunny beames threw from her Christall face,
  That could haue dazd the rash beholders sight,
And round about her head did shine like heuens light.

13

She was araied all in lilly white,
  And in her right hand bore a cup of gold,
  With wine and water fild vp to the hight,
  In which a Serpent did himselfe enfold,
  That horrour made to all, that did behold;
  But she no whitt did chaunge her constant mood:
  And in her other hand she fast did hold
  A booke that was both signd and seald with blood,
Wherin darke things were writt, hard to be vnderstood.

14

Her younger Sister, that *Speranza* hight,
  Was clad in blew, that her beseemed well;
  Not all so chearefull seemed she of sight,
  As was her sister; whether dread did dwell,
  Or anguish in her hart, is hard to tell:
  Vpon her arme a siluer anchor lay,
  Whereon she leaned euer, as befell:
  And euer vp to heuen, as she did pray,
Her stedfast eyes were bent, ne swarued other way.

Stanza 10
4 chose: i.e. choose. **5 the broad high way**: the 'broad waye that leadeth to destruction: and manie there be which go in thereat' (Matt. 7.13). At iv 2.8, it leads to the house of Pride. **8 a few**: the 'chosen' of ix 53.5, and repeated from 3 to stress that 'manie are called, but fewe chosen' (Matt. 20.16). **rightest**: the only right way; also the most direct way instead of going astray. Cf. 'the paths of righteousnes' (Prov. 4.11).

Stanza 11
3 addrest: directed. **4–5** In contrast to his reason for visiting Lucifera at iv 13.8–9.

Stanza 12
1 deuise: converse. **2–5 louely**: loving. This brief allegorical pageant contrasts with the monstrously yoked procession of the sins in the house of Pride. **6–9** Faith is **the eldest** because Faith comes before Hope as 'the grounde of things, which are hoped for, and the euidence of things which are not sene' (Heb. 11.1). Yet they are paired as though one, as line 5 carefully spells out. On S.'s use of the traditional iconography of the three Christian virtues, see King 1990a:61–62. **Like sunny beames**: what seemed like sunbeams; cf. Moses's face at Exod. 34.29–30, and Christ's face at Matt. 17.2. **Christall**: clear, luminous, with a pun on 'Christ'. Her aureole **dazd**, i.e. dazzled, beholders, as does Arthur's shield at vii 35.8–9.

Stanza 13
1 lilly white: 'in signe of puritie' (Geneva gloss to Rev. 7.9). **2–5** St John the Evangelist is usually represented carrying a chalice out of which issues a serpent, and an open book. The *Golden Legend* tells how he drank a cup of poison to prove his faith. At Mark 16.18, serpents are associated with poisoned drink. **cup of gold**: the cup of the holy sacrament containing **wine and water**, referring to the healing blood and baptismal water that issued from the side of the crucified Christ; see John 19.34 and 1 John 5.6. According to the Geneva gloss, water and blood 'declare that we haue our sinnes washed by him, and he hathe made ful satisfaction for the same'. **Serpent**: the emblem of Aesculapius, the symbol of healing; also of the crucified Christ, the symbol of redemption. The serpent lifted up by Moses (Num. 21.9) was interpreted typologically as Christ lifted up on the cross (John 3.14). Fidelia holds the symbol of true healing, which is parodied by the healing powers of Aesculapius at v 36–44. Both the wine and water and the Serpent 'answer' the death and despair which many drink from Duessa's golden cup (viii 14). On the distinction between the two cups, which is that between 'the cup of the Lord, and the cup of the deuils' (1 Cor. 10.21), see Kaske 1999:41–49. **6** 'Let vs kepe the profession of our hope, without wauering' (Heb. 10.23). **8 booke**: either the New Testament which is sealed with Christ's blood (cf. Mark 14.24, Rev. 5.1), or the whole Bible, as Kaske suggests in the *SEnc* 88. **9** Cf. Peter on Paul's epistles: 'among the which some things are hard to be vnderstand' (2 Pet. 3.16); applied here particularly to Revelation.

Stanza 14
2 blew: Hope's traditional colour, 'For the hopes sake, which is layd vp . . . in heauen' (Col. 1.5). **4–5 dread** and **anguish** are complementary emotions afflicting those without hope, i.e. in despair; cf. ix 22.3, 49.4. **6** Cf. Heb. 6.18–19: 'to holde fast the hope that is set before vs, which we haue, as an ancre of the soule, both sure and stedfast'. **siluer**: for purity, as Ps.

15

They seeing *Vna*, towardes her gan wend,
  Who them encounters with like courtesee;
  Many kind speeches they betweene them spend,
  And greatly ioy each other for to see:
  Then to the knight with shamefast modestie
  They turne them selues, at *Vnaes* meeke request,
  And him salute with well beseeming glee;
  Who faire them quites, as him beseemed best,
And goodly gan discourse of many a noble gest.

16

Then *Vna* thus; But she your sister deare,
  The deare *Charissa* where is she become?
  Or wants she health, or busie is elswhere?
  Ah no, said they, but forth she may not come:
  For she of late is lightned of her wombe,
  And hath encreast the world with one sonne more,
  That her to see should be but troublesome.
  Indeed (quoth she) that should her trouble sore,
But thankt be God, and her encrease so euermore.

17

Then saide the aged *Cælia*, Deare dame,
  And you good Sir, I wote that of youre toyle,
  And labors long, through which ye hether came,
  Ye both forwearied be: therefore a whyle

I read you rest, and to your bowres recoyle.
  Then called she a Groome, that forth him ledd
  Into a goodly lodge, and gan despoile
  Of puissant armes, and laid in easie bedd;
His name was meeke *Obedience* rightfully aredd.

18

Now when their wearie limbes with kindly rest,
  And bodies were refresht with dew repast,
  Fayre *Vna* gan *Fidelia* fayre request,
  To haue her knight into her schoolehous plaste,
  That of her heauenly learning he might taste,
  And heare the wisedom of her wordes diuine.
  She graunted, and that knight so much agraste,
  That she him taught celestiall discipline,
And opened his dull eyes, that light mote in them shine.

19

And that her sacred Booke, with blood ywritt,
  That none could reade, except she did them teach,
  She vnto him disclosed euery whitt,
  And heauenly documents thereout did preach,
  That weaker witt of man could neuer reach,
  Of God, of grace, of iustice, of free will,
  That wonder was to heare her goodly speach:
  For she was hable, with her wordes to kill,
And rayse againe to life the hart, that she did thrill.

12.6: 'The wordes of the Lord are pure wordes, as the siluer, tryed in a fornace of erth, fired seuen folde'. For the *ancora spei*, see *1596* title-page. **7 as befell**: as was fitting. Not a rhyming tag: stress is placed throughout the pageant of virtues on what is fitting and seemly.

Stanza 15

2 encounters: goes to meet (*OED* 6). **7** Their **well beseeming glee** repeats the 'comely courteous glee' (6.5) with which Zele welcomes the knight. **8** He returns their salutation courteously. **9 gest**: deed.

Stanza 16

The stanza's leisurely unfolding suggests that her new son is the Red Cross Knight; see 29.7–9*n*. **2 deare**: stressed as she is Love. **become**: i.e. 'gone to'; or, 'what has happened to her?' **8** Courteously suggesting that the visit would trouble Charissa rather than it would Una. **9 her encrease**: i.e. may God give her increase.

Stanza 17

4 forwearied: utterly wearied, the knight's state at i 32.6 when his resting began his descent into Orgoglio's dungeon. **5 read**: counsel. **recoyle**: retire. **9 aredd**: told; understood.

Stanza 18

1–2 Repeated from ix 2.1–2 to mark the next stage in the knight's adventure; see ix 20.4–9*n*. **kindly**: natural; owing to nature, as **dew** also suggests, and in contrast to the 'deadly sleepe' that overpowered the knight in Archimago's hermitage

(i 36.6). **repast**: refreshment on the physical level, preparing for 'spirituall repast' (48.8). **6 heare**: because 'faith is by hearing, and hearing by the worde of God' (Rom. 10.17). The line, enforced by 19.1–4, registers the Protestant emphasis on preaching. See 'homiletics' in the *SEnc*, and D.L. Miller 1988:89–92. **7 agraste**: favoured with grace. **9** As Christ sent Paul to the Gentiles 'To open their eyes, that they may turne from darkenes to light, and from the power of Satan vnto God, that they may receiue forgiuenes of sinnes, and inheritance among them, which are sanctified by faith in me' (Acts 26.18); cf. Eph. 1.17–18. **in**: both 'into' and 'in'.

Stanza 19

1–3 Cf. Rev. 5.1, 3: 'A Boke written within, and on the backeside, sealed with seuen seales. . . . and no man in heauen, nor in earth, nether vnder the earth, was able to open the Boke nether to loke thereon'. **blood**: the blood of Christ; cf. Heb. 9.20. **reade**: discover the meaning of (*OED* 1.2). Line 2 refers to the law of exegesis: *Credo ut intelligam*; **euery whitt** indicates the fullness of understanding gained through faith. In arguing that Augustine's theory of signs is central to the interpretation of Bk I, Bergvall 1993:35 notes that here the knight's understanding of the words of the Bible leads him to the Word, the transcendent signifier through which all other signs may be interpreted. **4 documents**: teachings. **6** These four intensely controversial terms are interlinked: God: justice; God's grace: human will. See Gless 1994:154–55, and 'nature and grace' in the *SEnc*. **8–9** 2 Cor. 3.6: 'for the letter killeth, but the Spirit giueth life'. **thrill**: pierce.

20

And when she list poure out her larger spright,
 She would commaund the hasty Sunne to stay,
 Or backward turne his course from heuens hight,
 Sometimes great hostes of men she could dismay,
 Dry-shod to passe, she parts the flouds in tway;
 And eke huge mountaines from their natiue seat
 She would commaund, themselues to beare away,
 And throw in raging sea with roaring threat.
Almightie God her gaue such powre, and puissaunce great.

21

The faithfull knight now grew in litle space,
 By hearing her, and by her sisters lore,
 To such perfection of all heuenly grace;
 That wretched world he gan for to abhore,
 And mortall life gan loath, as thing forlore,
 Greeud with remembrance of his wicked wayes,
 And prickt with anguish of his sinnes so sore,
 That he desirde, to end his wretched dayes:
So much the dart of sinfull guilt the soule dismayes.

22

But wise *Speranza* gaue him comfort sweet,
 And taught him how to take assured hold
 Vpon her siluer anchor, as was meet;
 Els had his sinnes so great, and manifold
 Made him forget all, that *Fidelia* told.
 In this distressed doubtfull agony,
 When him his dearest *Vna* did behold,
 Disdeining life, desiring leaue to dye,
She found her selfe assayld with great perplexity.

23

And came to *Cælia* to declare her smart,
 Who well acquainted with that commune plight,
 Which sinfull horror workes in wounded hart,
 Her wisely comforted all, that she might,
 With goodly counsell and aduisement right;
 And streightway sent with carefull diligence,
 To fetch a Leach, the which had great insight
 In that disease of grieued conscience,
And well could cure the same; His name was *Patience*.

24

Who comming to that sowle-diseased knight,
 Could hardly him intreat, to tell his grief:
 Which knowne, and all that noyd his heauie spright,
 Well searcht, eftsoones he gan apply relief
 Of salues and med'cines, which had passing prief,
 And there to added wordes of wondrous might:
 By which to ease he him recured brief,
 And much aswag'd the passion of his plight,
That he his paine endur'd, as seeming now more light.

25

But yet the cause and root of all his ill,
 Inward corruption, and infected sin,
 Not purg'd nor heald, behind remained still,
 And festring sore did ranckle yett within,
 Close creeping twixt the marow and the skin.
 Which to extirpe, he laid him priuily
 Downe in a darksome lowly place far in,
 Whereas he meant his corrosiues to apply,
And with streight diet tame his stubborne malady.

Stanza 20

Line **5**, added *1609*, refers to Moses's parting the waters of the Red Sea; see 53.2–5. If omitted, the stanza offers three lines of miracles from the OT balanced by three from the NT. Also, it makes the witty point that even the poet's verse halts before the power of faith; see A. Fowler 1964:145*n*1. For these miracles of faith, see for line 2: Josh. 10.12–13; line 3: 2 Kings 20.10–11; line 4: Judg. 7.21; lines 5–7: Matt. 21.21. **1 larger spright**: greater power, the biblical 'spirit of the Lord'. **4** Cf. Merlin's similar power at III iii 12.5. **dismay**: defeat. **8 roaring threat**: also 'threatening roar'.

Stanza 21

3 That the knight's **perfection** is indicated by a desire to take his own life, from which earlier (ix 51) in despair he had been saved by Una, marks the first stage of his regeneration. Cf. 45.6, and see Gless 1994:155. **5 forlore**: doomed to destruction; or, 'which he had abandoned'. **6–9** Now guided by grace he repents the sin itself rather than, as earlier, fearing punishment for the sin: 'For godlie sorowe causeth repentance vnto saluacion, not to be repented of: but the worldlie sorowe causeth death' (2 Cor. 7.10).

Stanza 22

1 comfort sweet: such as Una offers to save the knight from despair at ix 53.4–8. **2 assured**: alluding to 'the full assurance of hope' (Heb. 6.11) that he needs. **6 doubtfull**: fearful. **agony**: Christ's agony in the garden of Gethsemane (Luke

22.44) provides the pattern for the knight's experience. The Geneva gloss reads: 'the worde signifieth that horrour [cf. 23.3] that Christ had conceiued not onely for feare of death, but of his fathers iudgment and wrath against sinne'. **9 perplexity**: distress; also bewilderment. Greater curative power than the church may provide is needed.

Stanza 23

3 sinfull horror: horror of sin; 'sinfull guilt' (21.9). **5 aduisement**: advice. **7–9 Leach**: surgeon. **conscience**: see ix 48.2–3*n*; cf. 'sowle-diseased' (24.1). **Patience**: Christian patience, continued faith in God's mercy; cf. Rev. 14.12 which Geneva glosses as 'The faithful are exhorted to pacience'. See 'Patience' in the *SEnc*; and on his assuming the traditional role of penance, see Low 1998:16–17.

Stanza 24

2 intreat: persuade. **3 Which knowne**: confession is necessary for salvation but being private is only preliminary to godly deeds. For this reason, S.'s account is brief. **noyd**: troubled. **4 searcht**: probed, as a wound. **5 passing prief**: surpassing efficacy; cf. Jas. 1.4: 'And let pacience haue her perfite worke, that ye may be perfite and entire, lacking nothing'. **6–9** Through absolution the knight is **recured**, i.e. restored to health. **brief** suggests both 'quickly' and 'only for a moment'. **passion**: suffering.

Stanza 25

1–5 infected sin: apparently referring to original sin which, according to Article 9 of the *Thirty-nine Articles*, 'doth remain,

26

In ashes and sackcloth he did array
   His daintie corse, proud humors to abate,
   And dieted with fasting euery day,
   The swelling of his woundes to mitigate,
   And made him pray both early and eke late:
   And euer as superfluous flesh did rott
   Amendment readie still at hand did wayt,
   To pluck it out with pincers fyrie whott,
That soone in him was lefte no one corrupted iott.

27

And bitter *Penaunce* with an yron whip,
   Was wont him once to disple euery day:
   And sharpe *Remorse* his hart did prick and nip,
   That drops of blood thence like a well did play;
   And sad *Repentance* vsed to embay,
   His blamefull body in salt water sore,
   The filthy blottes of sin to wash away.
   So in short space they did to health restore
The man that would not liue, but erst lay at deathes dore.

28

In which his torment often was so great,
   That like a Lyon he would cry and rore,
   And rend his flesh, and his owne synewes eat.
   His owne deare *Vna* hearing euermore
   His ruefull shriekes and gronings, often tore
   Her guiltlesse garments, and her golden heare,
   For pitty of his payne and anguish sore;
   Yet all with patience wisely she did beare;
For well she wist, his cryme could els be neuer cleare.

29

Whom thus recouer'd by wise Patience,
   And trew *Repentaunce* they to *Vna* brought;
   Who ioyous of his cured conscience,
   Him dearely kist, and fayrely eke besought
   Himselfe to chearish, and consuming thought
   To put away out of his carefull brest.
   By this *Charissa*, late in child-bed brought,
   Was woxen strong, and left her fruitfull nest;
To her fayre *Vna* brought this vnacquainted guest.

---

yea in them that are regenerated'; cf. 'all loathly crime, | That is ingenerate in fleshly slime' (III vi 3.4–5). *HHL* 166–68 tells how Christ died to 'clense the guilt of that infected cryme | Which was enrooted in all fleshly slyme'. Cf. 57.3–7; II x 50.2–4. Or it may refer to the knight's actual sins which physically and morally contaminate him, as Weatherby 1994:168–69 argues. **ranckle**: a festering, incurable wound; see VI iv 9.9*n*. **6 extirpe**: root out, in the surgical sense (cf. 26.8) and hence in a moral sense. **7–9** The knight 'returns' to Orgoglio's dungeon and Despaire's cave to root out the sins which placed him there. **corrosiues**: metre requires 'corsives' (an obs. form; cf. IV ix 14.4) or elision of the final phrase. The term signifies both a corrosive drug and a caustic remedy. **streight diet**: strict way of living. The two stages of the knight's mortification of the flesh in the house of Penance are marked by the duplication of terms throughout this stanza.

Stanza 26

1–4 In ashes and sackcloth: not only an ascetical practice but a biblical phrase for repentance, as Matt. 11.21. Cf. Corceca's penance at iii 14.2–4: her outward acts of indulgence become the means used by the knight to renovate his body. **daintie corse**: handsome body. **humors**: the bodily fluids whose proportions, according to Renaissance physiology, determine one's temperament. **proud humors** signify the state of pride; in particular, the swelling of concupiscence. **abate**: put an end to. **6 superfluous flesh**: like 'proud flesh', a term for the swelling of a wound. **7 Amendment**: here personifying his decision to sin no more as he is now ready to 'bring forthe . . . frutes worthie amendement of life' (Matt. 3.8).

Stanza 27

1 bitter: because of his biting whip. **2 disple**: punish or subject to penance by scourging. **3 sharpe Remorse**: alluding to its derivation from Lat. *remorsus*, f. *remordere*, to sting, torture, here from the prick of conscience. **5–7** line 6: 'His bodie in salt water smarting sore' *1596*. Cf. Ps. 51.2: 'Wash me throughly

from mine iniquitie, and clense me from my sinne'. The Geneva gloss adds: 'My sinnes sticke so fast in me, that I haue nede of some singular kinde of washing'. **embay**: drench, referring to the salt tears of repentance. **salt** increases the agony but it is also cleansing; and in this context may suggest the practice of rubbing a new-born child with salt. **9 The man that would not liue**: i.e. who otherwise would not have lived and who did not wish to live; see viii 38.3–9*n*, and cf. the repetition of this moment at xi 28.4.

Stanza 28

1–3 He acts as though he were casting out 'the deuil as a roaring lyon [who] walketh about, seking whome he may deuoure' (1 Pet. 5.8). Cf. Joel 2.13: 'Rent your heart'. The Geneva gloss reads: 'Mortifie your affections and serue God with purenes of heart'. **4–9** The knight's shrieks and groanings are assimilated to Una's suffering, as Alpers 1967:37 notes. She endures with patience so that he may recover by patience. **cryme**: charge or accusation (Lat. *crimen*).

Stanza 29

4–5 Una offers him the 'kysse of loue' (1 Pet. 5.14), the holy kiss of greeting in the NT. Low 1998:17 interprets her passive role in her knight's cure to the privatization of sin in the Reformation. **fayrely**: 'courteously', as it modifies **besought**; 'properly', as it modifies **chearish**, i.e. cheer, gladden, or hold himself dear. The history of the knight's adventures focuses on this word from the moment he enters 'too solemne sad' (i 2.8), to his 'sad feare' (ii 44.4) when he hears Fradubio's story, to his meeting with Sansjoy, until, overcome by despair, grief for his sins causes him to seek his own death. Now, as Paul enjoined the Ephesians, 'his owne flesh . . . he nourisheth and cherisheth'. **7–9 By this**: i.e. by this time. Also, it points to the knight's renewed faith and suggests that he is the child to whom Charissa has given birth. After faith comes charity, for 'if I had all faith, so that I colde remoue mountaines [cf. 20.6–8] and had not loue, I were nothing' (1 Cor. 13.2). **vnacquainted**: not known to her.

30

She was a woman in her freshest age,
  Of wondrous beauty, and of bounty rare,
  With goodly grace and comely personage,
  That was on earth not easie to compare;
  Full of great loue, but *Cupids* wanton snare
  As hell she hated, chaste in worke and will;
  Her necke and brests were euer open bare,
  That ay thereof her babes might sucke their fill;
The rest was all in yellow robes arayed still.

31

A multitude of babes about her hong,
  Playing their sportes, that ioyd her to behold,
  Whom still she fed, whiles they were weak and young,
  But thrust them forth still, as they wexed old:
  And on her head she wore a tyre of gold,
  Adornd with gemmes and owches wondrous fayre,
  Whose passing price vneath was to be told;
  And by her syde there sate a gentle payre
Of turtle doues, she sitting in an yuory chayre.

32

The knight and *Vna* entring, fayre her greet,
  And bid her ioy of that her happy brood;
  Who them requites with court'sies seeming meet,
  And entertaynes with friendly chearefull mood.
  Then *Vna* her besought, to be so good,
  As in her vertuous rules to schoole her knight,
  Now after all his torment well withstood,
  In that sad house of *Penaunce*, where his spright
Had past the paines of hell, and long enduring night.

33

She was right ioyious of her iust request,
  And taking by the hand that Faeries sonne,
  Gan him instruct in euerie good behest,
  Of loue, and righteousnes, and well to donne,
  And wrath, and hatred warely to shonne,
  That drew on men Gods hatred, and his wrath,
  And many soules in dolours had fordonne:
  In which when him she well instructed hath,
From thence to heauen she teacheth him the ready path.

34

Wherein his weaker wandring steps to guyde,
  An auncient matrone she to her does call,
  Whose sober lookes her wisedome well descryde:
  Her name was *Mercy*, well knowne ouer all,
  To be both gratious, and eke liberall:
  To whom the carefull charge of him she gaue,
  To leade aright, that he should neuer fall
  In all his waies through this wide worldes waue,
That Mercy in the end his righteous soule might saue.

35

The godly Matrone by the hand him beares
  Forth from her presence, by a narrow way,
  Scattred with bushy thornes, and ragged breares,
  Which still before him she remou'd away,
  That nothing might his ready passage stay:
  And euer when his feet encombred were,
  Or gan to shrinke, or from the right to stray,
  She held him fast, and firmely did vpbeare,
As carefull Nourse her child from falling oft does reare.

Stanza 30

2 bounty: goodness, virtue. **3 personage**: personal appearance. **4 compare**: match; rival. **8–9** The image is biblical: 'As new borne babes desire the syncere milke of the worde' (1 Pet. 2.2). On the role of godly women to breast-feed their children, also metaphorically by catechizing them, see McManus 1997. **yellow**: the colour of marriage, fertility, fruitfulness, and maternity. For the iconographical details here and in stanza 31, see Brooks-Davies 1977:97–98.

Stanza 31

2 Suggesting also 'whom she rejoiced to behold'. **5 tyre**: head-dress, diadem. **6 owches**: jewels. 7 Whose surpassing worth was difficult to calculate. **8–9 turtle doues**: the emblem here of a chaste Venus, the symbol of true love (cf. III xi 2.9) and of innocence (cf. Matt. 10.16); the **yuory chayre** suggests Solomon's regal throne (1 Kings 10.18).

Stanza 32

3 requites: greets in return. **seeming meet**: for 'loue doeth not boast itself: it is not puffed vp: it disdaineth not' (1 Cor. 13.4–5). The courtesy in the house of Holinesse contrasts with the disdain in the house of Pride; see 7.1*n*. **4 entertaynes**: receives. **8 that sad house of Penaunce**: in opposition to 'that sad house of *Pryde*' (v 53.9). **9 past**: passed through; suffered.

Stanza 33

2 that Faeries sonne: repeated at 52.3 and 60.2 to prepare for the revelation of his true identity at 65. **4 well to**

donne: well-doing. **5–7** Cf. Col. 3.6, 8. **dolours**: sorrows. **fordonne**: overcome, ruined. **9 teacheth**: shows. **ready**: direct; also a path he is now ready to take.

Stanza 34

1 weaker: too weak. **3 descryde**: revealed. **4** 'The Lord is good to all, and his mercies are ouer all his workes' (Ps. 145.9). **7–9** Mercy's role in saving the knight so that he may never fall from grace refers, appropriately, to the public baptismal service: 'being steadfast in faith, joyful through hope, and rooted in charity, may so pass the waves of this troublesome world, that finally they may come to the land of everlasting life' (*BCP*).

Stanza 35

1 Mercie is called **Matrone** in the specific sense of one having knowledge of childbirth (*OED* 2). **2 a narrow way**: see 5.8–9*n*; called 'that painfull way' (46.1). It is 'The way to heauenly blesse' (Arg.), for 'through the workes was the faith made perfite' (Jas. 2.22). **3 thornes** 'procede of the corruption of sinne' (Geneva gloss to Gen. 3.18).

Stanzas 36–43

The **seuen Bead-men**, literally seven men of prayer who respond to the prayers of others through works of mercy, counter the seven deadly sins in the house of Pride. Their life of good works, praised in Matt. 5.16, is broadly based on Matt. 25.35–41, which names the six works of mercy that separate the saved from the damned. Later tradition added 'burying the dead'. All

36

Eftsoones vnto an holy Hospitall,
 That was foreby the way, she did him bring,
 In which seuen Bead-men that had vowed all
 Their life to seruice of high heauens king
 Did spend their daies in doing godly thing:
 Their gates to all were open euermore,
 That by the wearie way were traueiling,
To call in commers-by, that needy were and pore.

37

The first of them that eldest was, and best,
 Of all the house had charge and gouernement,
 As Guardian and Steward of the rest:
 His office was to giue entertainement
 And lodging, vnto all that came, and went:
 Not vnto such, as could him feast againe,
 And double quite, for that he on them spent,
But such, as want of harbour did constraine:
Those for Gods sake his dewty was to entertaine.

38

The second was as Almner of the place,
 His office was, the hungry for to feed,
 And thristy giue to drinke, a worke of grace:
 He feard not once him selfe to be in need,
 Ne car'd to hoord for those, whom he did breede:
 The grace of God he layd vp still in store,
 Which as a stocke he left vnto his seede;
 He had enough, what need him care for more?
And had he lesse, yet some he would giue to the pore.

39

The third had of their wardrobe custody,
 In which were not rich tyres, nor garments gay,
 The plumes of pride, and winges of vanity,
 But clothes meet to keepe keene cold away,
 And naked nature seemely to aray;
 With which bare wretched wights he dayly clad,
 The images of God in earthly clay;
 And if that no spare clothes to giue he had,
His owne cote he would cut, and it distribute glad.

40

The fourth appointed by his office was,
 Poore prisoners to relieue with gratious ayd,
 And captiues to redeeme with price of bras,
 From Turkes and Sarazins, which them had stayd;
 And though they faulty were, yet well he wayd,
 That God to vs forgiueth euery howre
 Much more then that, why they in bands were layd,
 And he that harrowd hell with heauie stowre,
The faulty soules from thence brought to his heauenly bowre.

41

The fift had charge sick persons to attend,
 And comfort those, in point of death which lay;
 For them most needeth comfort in the end,
 When sin, and hell, and death doe most dismay
 The feeble soule departing hence away.
 All is but lost, that liuing we bestow,
 If not well ended at our dying day.
 O man haue mind of that last bitter throw;
For as the tree does fall, so lyes it euer low.

---

seven, as they fulfil Cælia's life (see 3.6–9), are given here: (1) lodging strangers, (2) feeding the hungry and giving drink to the thirsty, (3) clothing the naked, (4) relieving prisoners and redeeming captives, (5) comforting the sick and counselling the dying, (6) burying the dead, and (7) taking care of widows and orphans. (5) and (6) are rites in the *BCP*, (7) is a special chivalric theme (see III ii 14.6) enjoined by Scripture; see 43.2–3*n*. Kaske 1979:130–35 notes how the Red Cross Knight enacts the fourth work and Guyon the next three. See 'Bead-men' in the *SEnc*.

Stanza 36

1 **Hospitall**: hostel or hospice. 2 **foreby**: close by; see 3.1–3*n*. 8 Although not named, this **one** who serves as porter suggests by his posture that he counters the hypocritical alms-giver of Matt. 6.1–4. **wayting**: watching.

Stanza 37

1 **best**: chiefest, as explained at 44.2–3. 4–6 As did Job (Job 31.32). **office**: duty. **entertainement**: provisions; provision for wants; reception. **feast** has the general sense 'entertain hospitably'. 6–8 Cf. Luke 14:13–14. **againe**: in return. **double quite**: repay double. **constraine**: afflict; or 'force to come to him'.

Stanza 38

1 **Almner**: one who distributes charitable relief among the poor, as Christ directs: 'Sel that ye haue, and giue almes' (Luke 12.33). 2–3 'For I was an hungred, and ye gaue me meat: I

thursted, and ye gaue me drinke' (Matt. 25.35). 5–6 **breede**: i.e. **his seede**. 7 **stocke**: fund, capital, referring to works of supererogation, as at 51.7–9; see Schiavoni 1992:182. 9 **lesse**: too little (a Latinism).

Stanza 39

4–5 **meet, seemely**: on this twofold need of clothes, cf. Shakespeare, *King Lear* 2.4.264–70. 7 As Gen. 1.27, 2.7. 9 Cf. Luke 3.11: 'He that hathe two coates, let him parte with him that hathe none'.

Stanza 40

3–5 **price of bras**: payment of money. **stayd**: imprisoned. **they**: the prisoners; also **captiues**. On the topicality of this work, see Chew 1937:385–86, Heberle 1989:83–84. 7 **why**: for which. 8–9 After his crucifixion Christ descended into hell which he **harrowd**, i.e. robbed or despoiled by ransoming the prisoners; cf. *Am* 68.1–4, and see xi 53.7*n*. On the appropriate number of this stanza, see viii 40*n*. **stowre**: assault, referring to 'the gates of hell broken vp' by Christ in his descent (E.K. on *SC May* 54; cf. Ps. 107.16). In this context, 'conflict with death' (*OED* 2) is a relevant sense. **faulty**: guilty.

Stanza 41

6 **bestow**: 'store up'; also give to others (38.6–7) in accord with the second work of mercy, as Kaske 1979:140 maintains. 8 **throw**: throe, the agony of death, also 'overthrow'. 9 Eccles. 11.3: 'In the place that the tre falleth, there it shalbe'.

42

The sixt had charge of them now being dead,
    In seemely sort their corses to engraue,
    And deck with dainty flowres their brydall bed,
    That to their heauenly spouse both sweet and braue
    They might appeare, when he their soules shall saue.
    The wondrous workmanship of Gods owne mould,
    Whose face he made, all beastes to feare, and gaue
All in his hand, euen dead we honour should.
Ah dearest God me graunt, I dead be not defould.

43

The seuenth now after death and buriall done,
    Had charge the tender Orphans of the dead
    And wydowes ayd, least they should be vndone:
    In face of iudgement he their right would plead,
    Ne ought the powre of mighty men did dread
    In their defence, nor would for gold or fee
    Be wonne their rightfull causes downe to tread:
And when they stood in most necessitee,
He did supply their want, and gaue them euer free.

44

There when the Elfin knight arriued was,
    The first and chiefest of the seuen, whose care
    Was guests to welcome, towardes him did pas:
    Where seeing *Mercie*, that his steps vpbare,
    And alwaies led, to her with reuerence rare
    He humbly louted in meeke lowlinesse,
    And seemely welcome for her did prepare:
For of their order she was Patronesse,
Albe *Charissa* were their chiefest founderesse.

45

There she awhile him stayes, him selfe to rest,
    That to the rest more hable he might bee:
    During which time, in euery good behest
    And godly worke of Almes and charitee
    Shee him instructed with great industree;
    Shortly therein so perfect he became,
    That from the first vnto the last degree,
His mortall life he learned had to frame
In holy righteousnesse, without rebuke or blame.

46

Thence forward by that painfull way they pas,
    Forth to an hill, that was both steepe and hy;
    On top whereof a sacred chappell was,
    And eke a litle Hermitage thereby.
    Wherein an aged holy man did lie,
    That day and night said his deuotion,
    Ne other worldly busines did apply;
    His name was heuenly *Contemplation*;
Of God and goodnes was his meditation.

47

Great grace that old man to him giuen had;
    For God he often saw from heauens hight,
    All were his earthly eien both blunt and bad,
    And through great age had lost their kindly sight,
    Yet wondrous quick and persaunt was his spright,
    As Eagles eie, that can behold the Sunne:
    That hill they scale with all their powre and might,
    That his fraile thighes nigh weary, and fordonne
Gan faile, but by her helpe the top at last he wonne.

Stanza 42

This sixth work has its basis in Tobit 12.12: 'when thou didest burye the dead, I was with thee likewise'.   **3–5** Rev. 21.2 tells of the redeemed who are prepared to meet Christ the bridegroom 'as a bride trimmed for her housband'.   **sweet and braue** is typically Spenserian.   **6** Gen. 1.27; cf. V x 28.7.   **mould**: image (as 39.7); suggesting 'moulding'.   **7–8** 'Also the feare of you, and the dread of you shalbe vpon euerie beast of the earth . . . into your hand are thei deliuered' (Gen. 9.2).   **9** A rare personal intrusion into the poem, perhaps prompted by fear of dying in Ireland where the starving 'did eat of the dead carrions' (*View* 104); cf. II i 59.8–9.   **defould**: defiled. Cf. Ps. 16.10: 'Nether wilt thou suffer thine holie one to se corruption'.

Stanza 43

2–3 As Isa. 1.17: 'Seke iudgement, relieue the oppressed: iudge the fatherles and defend the widowe'; cf. Jas. 1.27. Such is Guyon's task at II i 61.6–8, Artegall's at III ii 14.6, and Arthur's at V x 14–15.   **4** I.e. in open court.   **6 fee**: bribe.   **7 wonne**: persuaded, i.e. bribed.

Stanza 44

8–9 Patronesse: protector (Lat. *patronus*); founder (of a religious order); and defender before a court of justice, as she pleads for humanity before God (51.7–9). Her office is distinct from that of Charissa who, as **chiefest founderesse**, would have established and endowed the hospital.

Stanza 45

3–4 good behest refers to a promise to do well, **godly worke** to doing charitable acts; see 3.9, 4.4, 36.5. Cf. 33.3–4.   **6–9 so perfect**: the term distinguishes the first stage of his perfection (21.3–9). Cook 1996:92 notes that line 7 marks a new type of the knight's exemplary life in opposition to the moment when Despaire urged him not 'To draw thy dayes forth to their last degree' (ix 46.2).   **In holy righteousnesse**: for the first and only time the knight is linked directly with the virtue of holiness.   **without**: beyond.

Stanza 46

1 that painfull way: described at 35.2–3.   **3–4** In contrast to Archimago's hermitage 'Downe in a dale' with its chapel 'a litle wyde' (i 34.2, 4).   **7** He did not attend to any worldly concern.   **8–9 Contemplation**: the state of meditation beyond but not in opposition to the active life in the holy Hospital; accordingly, he lives apart on a steep, high hill that leads to the knight's vision (from Lat. *contemplare*, to see) on 'the highest Mount' (53.1). See 'Contemplation' in the *SEnc*.

Stanza 47

3 All: although.   **4 kindly**: natural.   **5–6 persaunt**: piercing. The eagle's sharp sight is proverbial (Smith 199) for it 'perseth the sonne' (Chaucer, *Parl. Fowls* 331; cf. HHB 138–40). See xi 34.3–9*n*. The eagle is the iconographical attribute of the 'contemplative' St John the Divine whose visions, recorded in Revelation, are seen by Contemplation.   **8 fordonne**: exhausted.

48

There they doe finde that godly aged Sire,
  With snowy lockes adowne his shoulders shed,
  As hoary frost with spangles doth attire
  The mossy braunches of an Oke halfe ded.
  Each bone might through his body well be red,
  And euery sinew seene through his long fast:
  For nought he car'd his carcas long vnfed;
  His mind was full of spirituall repast,
And pyn'd his flesh, to keepe his body low and chast.

49

Who when these two approching he aspide,
  At their first presence grew agrieued sore,
  That forst him lay his heuenly thoughts aside;
  And had he not that Dame respected more,
  Whom highly he did reuerence and adore,
  He would not once haue moued for the knight.
  They him saluted standing far afore;
  Who well them greeting, humbly did requight,
And asked, to what end they clomb that tedious hight.

50

What end (quoth she) should cause vs take such paine,
  But that same end, which euery liuing wight
  Should make his marke, high heauen to attaine?
  Is not from hence the way, that leadeth right
  To that most glorious house, that glistreth bright
  With burning starres, and euerliuing fire,
  Whereof the keies are to thy hand behight
  By wise *Fidelia*? shee doth thee require,
To shew it to this knight, according his desire.

51

Thrise happy man, said then the father graue,
  Whose staggering steps thy steady hand doth lead,
  And shewes the way, his sinfull soule to saue.
  Who better can the way to heauen aread,
  Then thou thy selfe, that was both borne and bred
  In heuenly throne, where thousand Angels shine?
  Thou doest the praiers of the righteous sead
  Present before the maiesty diuine,
And his auenging wrath to clemency incline.

52

Yet since thou bidst, thy pleasure shalbe donne.
  Then come thou man of earth, and see the way,
  That neuer yet was seene of Faries sonne,
  That neuer leads the traueiler astray,
  But after labors long, and sad delay,
  Brings them to ioyous rest and endlesse blis.
  But first thou must a season fast and pray,
  Till from her bands the spright assoiled is,
And haue her strength recur'd from fraile infirmitis.

53

That done, he leads him to the highest Mount;
  Such one, as that same mighty man of God,
  That blood-red billowes like a walled front
  On either side disparted with his rod,
  Till that his army dry-foot through them yod,
  Dwelt forty daies vpon; where writt in stone
  With bloody letters by the hand of God,
  The bitter doome of death and balefull mone
He did receiue, whiles flashing fire about him shone.

Stanza 48
5 red: seen. **7 car'd**: took care of. **carcas** retains the etymo-logical sense, 'dead flesh', as II viii 12.5, for his body is dead to sin. **9 pyn'd**: starved; cf. Rom. 8.13: 'if ye mortifie the dedes of the bodie by the Spirit, ye shal liue'. **low**: weak, and therefore humble.

Stanza 49
4 more: also 'greatly'. **7 far afore**: as a token of respect (cf. xii 5.6), or in order not to disturb his privacy.

Stanza 50
6 euerliuing fire: in the New Jerusalem, which 'hathe no nede of the sunne, nether of the moone to shine in it: for the glorie of God did light it' (Rev. 21.23). **7 keies**: 'the keyes of the kingdome of heauen' (Matt. 16.19) given Peter for his great faith, in contrast to the keys carried by Ignaro at viii 30.6–9. **behight**: delivered. **8 require**: request. **9 according**: consenting to, granting.

Stanza 51
1 Thrise happy: i.e. exceedingly fortunate; cf. xii 40.6. **4 aread**: make known; show (cf. 50.9). **6** See Rev. 5.11. **7 righteous sead**: the redeemed.

Stanza 52
2 thou man of earth: so called being made of the dust of the ground (Gen. 2.7); also referring to his name: see 66.5–6n. **3** Suggesting that he is not a **Faries sonne**. **7 a season**: for a

time, perhaps referring to Lent, as *Am* 22.1: 'This holy season fit to fast and pray'. **8–9** The bonds from which the knight's spirit must be delivered are those of the flesh, the old Adam: 'the first man is of the earth, earthlie' (1 Cor. 15.47). **assoiled**: released, in the etymological sense, f. Lat. *absolvere*: loosened. **recur'd**: restored to health.

Stanza 53
1 the highest Mount: the very top of the mountain, inferring that the revelation it provides is higher than that provided clas-sical poets on 'that pleasaunt Mount' (54.6). It is both the OT 'mountaine of the house of the Lord' where 'he wil teache vs his waies, and we will walke in his paths' (Isa. 2.2–3), and the NT 'great and an hie mountaine' from which John is shown the New Jerusalem at Rev. 21.10. On the connection with Mount Tabor, see Nohrnberg 1976:180–81. As a sequence of specific moments in which God has acted in history, see J.N. Wall 1988:101–02. **2–9** Mount Sinai upon which Moses spent forty days (Exod. 24.18), received the tablets of the law, and was transfigured (Exod. 34.39). Apart from the detail of the **blood-red billowes**, lines 2–5 are close to the account in Exod. 14.21–31 of Moses's parting the waters of the Red Sea. **man of God**: Deut. 33.1; here in apposition to 'man of earth' (52.2). **disparted**: parted asunder. **yod**: went; cf. 20.5. **bloody**: 'the blood of the couenant' (Exod. 24.8). **doome of death**: 'the ministration of death written with letters and ingrauen in stones' (2 Cor. 3.7). For line 9, see Deut. 4.11, 'and the mountaine burnt with fire'.

54

Or like that sacred hill, whose head full hie,
  Adornd with fruitfull Oliues all arownd,
  Is, as it were for endlesse memory
  Of that deare Lord, who oft thereon was fownd,
  For euer with a flowring girlond crownd:
  Or like that pleasaunt Mount, that is for ay
  Through famous Poets verse each where renownd,
  On which the thrise three learned Ladies play
Their heuenly notes, and make full many a louely lay.

55

From thence, far off he vnto him did shew
  A litle path, that was both steepe and long,
  Which to a goodly Citty led his vew;
  Whose wals and towres were builded high and strong
  Of perle and precious stone, that earthly tong
  Cannot describe, nor wit of man can tell;
  Too high a ditty for my simple song:
  The City of the greate king hight it well,
Wherein eternall peace and happinesse doth dwell.

56

As he thereon stood gazing, he might see
  The blessed Angels to and fro descend
  From highest heuen, in gladsome companee,
  And with great ioy into that Citty wend,

As commonly as frend does with his frend.
  Whereat he wondred much, and gan enquere,
  What stately building durst so high extend
  Her lofty towres vnto the starry sphere,
And what vnknowen nation there empeopled were.

57

Faire knight (quoth he) *Hierusalem* that is,
  The new *Hierusalem*, that God has built
  For those to dwell in, that are chosen his,
  His chosen people purg'd from sinful guilt,
  With pretious blood, which cruelly was spilt
  On cursed tree, of that vnspotted lam,
  That for the sinnes of al the world was kilt:
  Now are they Saints all in that Citty sam,
More dear vnto their God, then younglings to their dam.

58

Till now, said then the knight, I weened well,
  That great *Cleopolis*, where I haue beene,
  In which that fairest *Fary Queene* doth dwell,
  The fairest City was, that might be seene;
  And that bright towre all built of christall clene,
  Panthea, seemd the brightest thing, that was:
  But now by proofe all otherwise I weene;
  For this great Citty that does far surpas,
And this bright Angels towre quite dims that towre of glas.

Stanza 54

The three mountains (Parnassus, Sinai, and Olivet) are linked
to the three traditional dispensations – nature, law, and grace
– by Kaske 1975:147 and Bergvall 1997:30. By associating the
Mount of Olives (Matt. 24.3, esp. 26.30) with Parnassus, S.
links Christ with the muses, and through them with poetry.
The **heuenly notes** and songs of love (**louely lay**) contrast the
'balefull mone' which results from Moses's sojourn on Mount
Sinai. **3–5 memory**: probably 'memorial' rather than
'remembrance'. **girlond crownd** is not from the Bible but
is suggested by the head of the hill with olives **all arownd**.
oft: from Luke 21.37, 22.39. The 'mount of oliues' is asso-
ciated with Christ's ascension (Acts 1.9,12). **7 each where**:
everywhere.

Stanza 55

3–5 Rev. 21.10–21: 'And he shewed me the great citie, holie
Ierusalem . . . her shining was like vnto a stone most precious
. . . And had a great wall and hie . . . And the fundacions of the
wall of the citie were garnished with all maner of precious
stones . . . And the twelue gates were twelue pearles'. Cf.
Theatre, sonn 15, and see 'Jerusalem, New' in the *SEnc*. This
vision is analysed by J.N. Wall 1988:89–127 to show how the
poem teaches the reader. **7** S. invokes the topos of inexpress-
ibility for what is ineffable; see Curtius 1953:159–62. **ditty**:
subject. **8** Ps. 48.2: 'Mount Zion . . . is the ioye of the whole
earth, and the citie of the great King'.

Stanza 56

2–5 Cf. Jacob's vision of the ladder stretching from earth to
heaven 'and lo, the Angels of God went vp and downe by it'
(Gen. 28.12). Here **descend** indicates that the ladder stretches

from heaven to earth. The vision moved Jacob to accept the
Lord, as it here moves the knight. Christ's prophecy of the
time when 'ye se heauen open, and the Angels of God ascend-
ing, and descending vpon the Sonne of man' (John 1.51) is
applied to God's elect ascending to Heaven to be greeted by
the descending angels. Cf. Heb. 12.22. **5 commonly**: famil-
iarly; cf. Exod. 33.11. **7–9** On the significance of the ensuing
dialogue between the knight and Contemplation that begins
here, and leads to the 'transformative moment' in 58–61 that
culminates in 62–64, see Goeglein 1994:8–16. **lofty towres**:
cf. 58.9 and II ix 47.5–6.

Stanza 57

1–4 Hierusalem: so spelled in the Bishops' Bible (1568);
noted Shaheen 1976:188. Cf. Rev. 21.2: 'And I John sawe the
holie citie newe Ierusalem come downe from God out of
heauen'. The Geneva gloss adds: 'the holie companie of the
elect'. **4 chosen people**: as 1 Pet. 2.9: 'Ye are a chosen gen-
eracion, a royal Priesthode, an holie nacion, a peculiar people'.
Cf. Rev. 17.14 and Una's reminder to the knight that he is
chosen, ix 53.5. **purg'd . . . guilt**: cf. Heb. 1.3. **5–7** Cf. 1
Pet.1.19: 'the precious blood of Christ, as of a Lambe
vndefiled, and without spot'; 1 Pet. 2.24: 'Who his owne self
bare our sinnes in his bodie on the tre, that we being deliuered
from sinne shulde liue in righteousnes'; John 1.29: 'Beholde
the lambe of God, which taketh away the sinne of the worlde'.
cursed tree: as Gal. 3.13: 'Christ hathe redemed vs from the
curse of the Law, when he was made a curse for vs (for it is
written, Cursed is euerie one that hangeth on tre)'. **8 sam**:
'together' (E.K. on *SC May* 168); cf. Eph. 2.19: 'Ye are no
more strangers and foreners: but citizens with the Saintes, and
of the housholde of God'.

59

Most trew, then said the holy aged man;
   Yet is *Cleopolis* for earthly frame,
   The fairest peece, that eie beholden can:
   And well beseemes all knights of noble name,
   That couett in th'immortall booke of fame
   To be eternized, that same to haunt,
   And doen their seruice to that soueraigne Dame,
   That glory does to them for guerdon graunt:
For she is heuenly borne, and heauen may iustly vaunt.

60

And thou faire ymp, sprong out from English race,
   How euer now accompted Elfins sonne,
   Well worthy doest thy seruice for her grace,
   To aide a virgin desolate foredonne.
   But when thou famous victory hast wonne,
   And high emongst all knights hast hong thy shield,
   Thenceforth the suitt of earthly conquest shonne,
   And wash thy hands from guilt of bloody field:
For blood can nought but sin, and wars but sorrows yield.

61

Then seek this path, that I to thee presage,
   Which after all to heauen shall thee send;
   Then peaceably thy painefull pilgrimage
   To yonder same *Hierusalem* doe bend,

Where is for thee ordaind a blessed end:
   For thou emongst those Saints, whom thou doest see,
   Shalt be a Saint and thine owne nations frend
   And Patrone: thou Saint *George* shalt called bee,
Saint George of mery England, the signe of victoree.

62

Vnworthy wretch (quoth he) of so great grace,
   How dare I thinke such glory to attaine?
   These that haue it attaynd, were in like cace
   As wretched men, and liued in like paine.
   But deeds of armes must I at last be faine,
   And Ladies loue to leaue so dearely bought?
   What need of armes, where peace doth ay remaine,
   (Said he) and bitter battailes all are fought?
As for loose loues they'are vaine, and vanish into nought.

63

O let me not (quoth he) then turne againe
   Backe to the world, whose ioyes so fruitlesse are,
   But let me heare for aie in peace remaine,
   Or streight way on that last long voiage fare,
   That nothing may my present hope empare.
   That may not be (said he) ne maist thou yitt
   Forgoe that royal maides bequeathed care,
   Who did her cause into thy hand committ,
Till from her cursed foe thou haue her freely quitt.

Stanza 58

2–4 **Cleopolis**: city of fame (Gk κλέος + πόλις); cf. vii 46.7, II x 72.7–8. Historically, London (i.e. Troynovant), though distinguished from it at III ix 51.5; or Westminster, as Hankins 1971:201 suggests. See 'Cleopolis' in the *SEnc*. **5–9 Panthea**: from Gk πᾶν, all + θεά, sight: i.e. 'the best of sights', being built of **glas**; cf. 'all of Christall' (II x 73.4). In Rev. 21.11, John sees the New Jerusalem shining 'cleare as cristal'; cf. *Bellay* 20. Various historical models have been suggested: Westminster Abbey with its Royal Chapel, which is an English Pantheon because it contains the tombs of Elizabeth's ancestors (see II x 73.3–4n); Windsor Castle where she resided; or her Palace at Richmond, known as Shene (= bright). See 'Panthea' in the *SEnc*; and, for similar marvels, see A. Fowler 1996:94–99. **clene**: clear, pure.

Stanza 59

2 **for earthly frame**: considered as an earthly structure. 3 **peece**: structure; masterpiece. **7–9 that soueraigne Dame** is Gloriana/Elizabeth. Like Una, who is 'borne of heauenly brood' (iii 8.7), she may **vaunt** – i.e. boast – that heauen is her home. The **glory** she offers is distinct from the 'glory' (62.2) the knight is promised in the New Jerusalem. On the distinction, see Bergvall 1997:19–20.

Stanza 60

2 **accompted**: accounted. 3 **grace**: favour; cf. i 3.4. A sense distinct from 62.1 but merging with it. 6 **high**: inferring that the knight will have the most honoured position; cf. xi 2.9. 7 **suitt**: pursuit.

Stanza 61

1 **presage**: show prophetically (cf. 55.1); predict, i.e. that it will take you to heaven. **3–5** The pattern for the knight's role as a pilgrim – see 66.5–6n – is outlined in Heb. 11.13–16.

ordaind: as he is 'chosen' (ix 53.5). **6–8** Cf. II i 32.3–5. **Patrone**: guardian saint. **shalt called bee**: referring to Rev. 3.12: 'Him that ouercometh . . . I wil write vpon him my new Name'. He gains that name only **after all**, i.e. at the end of his pilgrimage. **8–9 Saint**: i.e. one of God's chosen people (*OED* 3) who has been **ordaind** to special sainthood, as Kaske 1999:119 notes; cf. II i 32.5. **signe**: mark or token (Lat. *signum*); signal or battle cry: 'Our ancient word of courage, fair Saint George' (Shakespeare, *Richard III* 5.3.349). On his legend, see i 1–6n.

Stanza 62

The knight's first question (1–2) is answered by Contemplation (3–4); his second question (5–6) has two parts: the first is parried by a double question (7–8) and the second dismissed with reproof (9). S.'s *1596* revisions show his difficulties with this stanza: 4 '(Quoth he) as wretched, and liu'd in like paine'; 8 'battailes none are to be fought'; 9 'are'. **5 faine**: content to leave. **6 Ladies loue**: referring to his love for Una and/or for the Faerie Queene; see ix 17.1–3. **9** The echo of **vaine** and **vanish** suggests that loves vanish because they are vain; or because 'in the resurrection they nether marie wiues, nor wiues are bestowed in marriage' (Matt. 22.30).

Stanza 63

6 **That**: i.e. to remain here as a hermit, or take the path to the New Jerusalem as a pilgrim. Contemplation proposes the georgic alternative taken by the author of *Piers Plowman*, 'the Pilgrim that the Ploughman playde a whyle' (*SC* envoy). 7 **bequeathed care**: the **cause** entrusted to him by Una; or her distress which he has undertaken to relieve. What faith has revealed to him, and he holds in **present hope**, must now be perfected in charity. **9** The conditions for entry into his pilgrimage are expanded at xii 18. **freely quitt**: entirely freed; or delivered to make her free; or released by the knight's free will.

64

Then shall I soone, (quoth he) so God me grace,
  Abett that virgins cause disconsolate,
  And shortly back returne vnto this place,
  To walke this way in Pilgrims poore estate.
  But now aread, old father, why of late
  Didst thou behight me borne of English blood,
  Whom all a Faeries sonne doen nominate?
  That word shall I (said he) auouchen good,
Sith to thee is vnknowne the cradle of thy brood.

65

For well I wote, thou springst from ancient race
  Of *Saxon* kinges, that haue with mightie hand
  And many bloody battailes fought in place
  High reard their royall throne in *Britans* land
  And vanquisht them, vnable to withstand:
  From thence a Faery thee vnweeting reft,
  There as thou slepst in tender swadling band,
  And her base Elfin brood there for thee left.
Such men do Chaungelings call, so chaungd by Faeries theft.

66

Thence she thee brought into this Faery lond,
  And in an heaped furrow did thee hyde,
  Where thee a Ploughman all vnweeting fond,
  As he his toylesome teme that way did guyde,

And brought thee vp in ploughmans state to byde,
  Whereof *Georgos* he thee gaue to name;
  Till prickt with courage, and thy forces pryde,
  To Fary court thou cam'st to seeke for fame,
And proue thy puissaunt armes, as seemes thee best became.

67

O holy Sire (quoth he) how shall I quight
  The many fauours I with thee haue fownd,
  That hast my name and nation redd aright,
  And taught the way that does to heauen bownd?
  This saide, adowne he looked to the grownd,
  To haue returnd, but dazed were his eyne,
  Through passing brightnes, which did quite confound
  His feeble sence, and too exceeding shyne.
So darke are earthly thinges compard to things diuine.

68

At last whenas himselfe he gan to fynd,
  To *Vna* back he cast him to retyre;
  Who him awaited still with pensiue mynd.
  Great thankes and goodly meed to that good syre,
  He thens departing gaue for his paynes hyre.
  So came to *Vna*, who him ioyd to see,
  And after litle rest, gan him desyre,
  Of her aduenture myndfull for to bee.
So leaue they take of *Cælia*, and her daughters three.

Stanza 64

2 Abett: maintain. **3 shortly**: see xii 18.6–8*n*. **5 aread**: tell. **6 behight**: name. **7 nominate**: call or name. **8 auouchen**: prove. **9 cradle of thy brood**: place from which his race derives.

Stanza 65

1–5 Being 'sprong out from English race' (60.1), the Red Cross Knight is the only character in the poem who is a Saxon, and the only one who belongs to an earlier century (the fourth) rather than with Arthur and the Britons in the sixth. In glossing this stanza, Tristram White 1614 notes: 'In S. *Georges* English birth the Poet followes the vulgar errour, of purpose, to fit his fabulous morall argument the rather' (*Sp All* 139). **in place**: there. **in Britans land**: i.e. Wales and Cornwall (also known as West Wales). See Erickson 1996:87–89. **them**: the Britons. **6–7 vnweeting**: modifying **thee** (i.e. without your knowing), or **reft** (without anyone knowing); cf. 66.3. A similar story is told of Artegall at III iii 26. Cf. Arthur's upbringing at ix 3.5–9. **6–9** On the folklore of **Chaungelings**, see 'foundlings' in the *SEnc*. **tender**: infant. Changelings could be made only before christening. **chaungd**: exchanged. When Archimago disguises himself as the knight, '*Saint George* himselfe ye would haue deemed him to be' (ii 11.9), which suggests that the knight celebrated as St George is only of **base Elfin brood**.

Stanza 66

2 White 1614 seems to allude to this line in claiming that S. 'playing vpon the Etymologie of this Name [George], doth also allude to *Tilth*' (*Sp All* 139). **3 vnweeting**: inadvertently; or, as 65.6, referring to the knight who does not remember.

5–6 According to *The Golden Legend*, 'George is sayd of geos | whiche is as moche to saye as erthe and orge | that is tilyenge | so george is to saye as tilyenge the erthe | that is his flesshe | . . . Or George may be sayd of gera: that is holy | and of gyon that is a wrasteler | that is an holy wrasteler. For he wrasteled with the dragon. or it is sayd of george that is a pylgrim | and geyr that is cut or detrenched out and us that is a counseyllour. He was a pylgryme in the syght of the worlde | and he was cut and detrenched by the crowne of martyrdome | and he was a good counseyllour in prechynge' (app. Barclay 1955:112). **6 Whereof**: wherefore. **to name**: as a name. **7 forces pryde**: natural powers in their prime. **9** . . . as best suited you.

Stanza 67

1 quight: repay. **4 bownd**: lead. **6–9** The surpassing brightness of heavenly revelation, emphasized by the inverted construction, is further enforced by the concluding moral summary. There may be a distinction between eyes dazzled by the brightness of **earthly thinges** and senses confounded by the **shyne** (the brilliance of the source of light) of **things diuine**. Cf. the dazzling of the senses of another man of earth, Orgoglio, by the brightness of Arthur's shield at viii 19.

Stanza 68

1 to fynd: to recover from his bright vision. Also noting that he has found himself: in the past, his name and nation; in the present, his commitment to Una's cause; in the future, after serving the Faerie Queene, his pilgrimage to the heavenly Jerusalem; and after his death as St George of England. **3 pensiue**: anxious. **4–5 Great thankes** would be the only **goodly meed** that Contemplation would accept as payment for his efforts. **hyre**: reward.

Cant. XI.

The knight with that old Dragon fights
two dayes incessantly:
The third him ouerthrowes, and gayns
most glorious victory.

1

High time now gan it wex for *Vna* fayre,
  To thinke of those her captiue Parents deare,
  And their forwasted kingdom to repayre:
  Whereto whenas they now approched neare,
  With hartie wordes her knight she gan to cheare,
  And in her modest maner thus bespake;
  Deare knight, as deare, as euer knight was deare,
  That all these sorrowes suffer for my sake,
High heuen behold the tedious toyle, ye for me take.

2

Now are we come vnto my natiue soyle,
  And to the place, where all our perilles dwell;
  Here hauntes that feend, and does his dayly spoyle,
  Therefore henceforth bee at your keeping well,
  And euer ready for your foeman fell.
  The sparke of noble corage now awake,
  And striue your excellent selfe to excell;
  That shall ye euermore renowmed make,
Aboue all knights on earth, that batteill vndertake.

3

And pointing forth, lo yonder is (said she)
  The brasen towre in which my parents deare
  For dread of that huge feend emprisond be
  Whom I from far, see on the walles appeare
  Whose sight my feeble soule doth greatly cheare:
  And on the top of all I do espye
  The watchman wayting tydings glad to heare,
  That ô my parents might I happily
Vnto you bring, to ease you of your misery.

4

With that they heard a roaring hideous sownd,
  That all the ayre with terror filled wyde,
  And seemd vneath to shake the stedfast ground.
  Eftsoones that dreadfull Dragon they espyde,
  Where stretcht he lay vpon the sunny side,
  Of a great hill, himselfe like a great hill.
  But all so soone, as he from far descryde
  Those glistring armes, that heuen with light did fill,
He rousd himselfe full blyth, and hastned them vntill.

Book I Canto xi

Argument

1 that old Dragon: first named with the indefinite article (i 3.9) and later called 'that fire-mouthed Dragon' (ix 52.9), but now named, as in Rev. 12.9, 'the great dragon, that olde serpent, called the deuil and Satan'. On the association with Pope Gregory XIII whose personal *impresa* was a winged dragon, see E.S. Watson 2000.

Stanza 1

1 HIgh time has the apocalyptic force of Rev. 1.3, 22.10: 'the time is at hand'.   **3 forwasted**: utterly laid waste; cf. i 5.8 and vii 44.5.   **repayre**: restore; heal.   **5 hartie**: bold, full of courage, to arouse his heart, the seat of courage; cf. ix 25.6–7.   **7 Deare**: repeated twice in her first impassioned address to the Red Cross Knight, it conveys the sense of 'thrice-dear', i.e. exceedingly dear.

Stanza 2

1 natiue soyle: applies properly only to '*Eden* landes' (II i 1.5). Its rulers, Una's parents, are never named Adam and Eve. It is 'the world of recovered human nature, as it originally was and still can be when sin is removed' (N. Frye 1963:78). As distinct from faery land, see Erickson 1996:77.   **3 feend**: the devil (*OED* 2).   **4** . . . be well on your guard. With the seriously witty pun: the **keeping well** is the well of life that alone may keep him well; cf. ii 43.7. Her words are more of a benediction than a caution.   **7 excellent**: pre-eminent, excelling, as the word-play and accent indicate.   **8 That**: referring to his coming battle.

Stanza 3

Omitted *1590* by the printer; or, less likely, added by S. in *1596*. Some description of the **brasen towre** that imprisons Una's parents is needed to establish its connection with the brazen dragon, as indicated at vii 44.8 and xii 3.6.   **2–3** The knight returns to the active life to perform the fourth work of mercy, the release of captives (x 40), as Kaske 1979:130 notes.   **6–7** 'Watche therefore: for ye know nether the day, nor the houre, when the Sonne of man wil come' (Matt. 25.13). Kaske 1969:631n23 notes that an OT prophet is often pictured as a watchman on a tower, e.g. Hab. 2.1, and that the **tydings glad**, which he awaits to announce at xii 3.4, is the gospel, as at Rom. 10.15.

Stanza 4

3 vneath: almost. As used here, it may be a contraction of 'underneath'; or indicate that the earth shakes 'uneasily', as with Orgoglio's bellowing 'all the earth for terror seemd to shake' (vii 7.6).   **6** The striking effect of the two spondees in **great hill**, each preceded by a pyrrhic foot, is noted by Percival 1964. Traditionally, Eden is a great hill, as Ezekiel's 'holy mountaine of God' (Ezek. 28.14).   **7** The dragon's vigilance is traditional.   **8** The knight has travelled far from that first moment before Errour's cave when 'his glistring armor made | A litle glooming light, much like a shade' (i 14.4–5).   **9 rousd himselfe**: 'raised himself' rather than the technical sense at 9.6, 9.   **blyth**: joyfully; perhaps with the earlier sense, 'kindly', for the dragon appears as a courteous host hurrying to greet his guest, as at 15.4.   **them vntill**: towards them.

5

Then badd the knight his Lady yede aloof,
   And to an hill her selfe withdraw asyde,
   From whence she might behold that battailles proof
   And eke be safe from daunger far descryde:
   She him obayd, and turnd a litle wyde.
   Now O thou sacred Muse, most learned Dame,
   Fayre ympe of *Phœbus*, and his aged bryde,
   The Nourse of time, and euerlasting fame,
That warlike handes ennoblest with immortall name;

6

O gently come into my feeble brest,
   Come gently, but not with that mightie rage,
   Wherewith the martiall troupes thou doest infest,
   And hartes of great Heroes doest enrage,
   That nought their kindled corage may aswage,
   Soone as thy dreadfull trompe begins to sownd;
   The God of warre with his fiers equipage
   Thou doest awake, sleepe neuer he so sownd,
And scared nations doest with horror sterne astownd.

7

Fayre Goddesse lay that furious fitt asyde,
   Till I of warres and bloody *Mars* doe sing,
   And Bryton fieldes with Sarazin blood bedyde,
   Twixt that great faery Queene and Paynim king,

That with their horror heuen and earth did ring,
   A worke of labour long, and endlesse prayse:
   But now a while lett downe that haughtie string,
   And to my tunes thy second tenor rayse,
That I this man of God his godly armes may blaze.

8

By this the dreadfull Beast drew nigh to hand,
   Halfe flying, and halfe footing in his haste,
   That with his largenesse measured much land,
   And made wide shadow vnder his huge waste;
   As mountaine doth the valley ouercaste.
   Approching nigh, he reared high afore
   His body monstrous, horrible, and vaste,
   Which to increase his wondrous greatnes more,
Was swoln with wrath, and poyson, and with bloody gore.

9

And ouer, all with brasen scales was armd,
   Like plated cote of steele, so couched neare,
   That nought mote perce, ne might his corse bee harmd
   With dint of swerd, nor push of pointed speare,
   Which as an Eagle, seeing pray appeare,
   His aery plumes doth rouze, full rudely dight,
   So shaked he, that horror was to heare,
   For as the clashing of an Armor bright,
Such noyse his rouzed scales did send vnto the knight.

Stanza 5

The stanza is divided into two parts as both the knight and poet prepare for battle, for **warlike handes** applies to both. The analogy extends to the next stanza to form a rare double stanza befitting this solemn moment. **1 yede aloof**: go aside. She sees the battle 'from farre' (32.1), as she saw his battle with Errour at i 27.1 and Arthur's battle with Orgoglio at viii 26.1. **3 proof**: issue. **6–9 sacred Muse**: possibly Clio, the muse of history, offspring of Phœbus or Apollo and Mnemosyne or Memory (cf. IV xi 10.1–2) who is the **Nourse of . . . fame** because she cherishes the memory of famous deeds; see III iii 4. Or Calliope: see proem 2.1*n* and VII vii 1.1. As Galbraith 2000:5 notes, their relationship 'registers an elaborately figured intrication of poetry and history' in the poem. Apollo is named **Phœbus** because light battles darkness.

Stanza 6

3 infest: attack, in the sense 'make fierce' or 'inspire', from Lat. *infestare*. Often confused with 'infect', according to *OED*, as may be implied here: the rage so infects the heroes that they fight. **6–8 equipage**: equipment; 'order' (E.K. on *SC Oct.* 114).

Stanza 7

1 that furious fitt: strain of music, as line 7 suggests. It parallels the hero's 'mightie rage' (6.2). **2–6** Later the knight reveals his promise to serve the Faerie Queene 'Gainst that proud Paynim king, that works her teene' (xii 18.8; see xii Arg.*n*.). In the historical allegory, that pagan king would be Philip II of Spain, and the apocalyptic battle against him would end in the defeat of Antichrist, i.e. the Church of Rome. In *DS* 6, using language that echoes his praise of Leicester in *SC Oct.* 43–48, S. promises to write a poem in which his muse 'shall

dare alofte to sty | To the last praises of this Faery Queene', presumably in the projected second twelve books, which would treat King Arthur's conquest of Rome (and hence of the Church of Rome), as treated by Hardyng, *Chronicle* (1543) and Malory, *Morte Darthur*. See Hieatt 1988 (and Roche 1990a), Hieatt 1990, Hieatt 1991, and Rovang 1996:77–83. See also II x 49.8*n*. **7 lett downe** by loosening the string to lower the pitch. **haughtie**: high; hence high-pitched. **8 second tenor**: i.e. a lower or less taut tuning. As the middle style of the georgic, see 'georgic' in the *SEnc*. In *SC Oct.* 50, Piers says that the muse being tired of war 'Hast somewhat slackt the tenor of thy string', referring to an intermediate pitch (*OED* B.1). **rayse**: produce (a sound), *OED* 13b citing S. as the first use in this sense. **9** S. adapts the Virgilian formula, *arma virumque cano*: his man is **of God** and his arms **godly**; moreover, he sings of arms rather than the man, as the contest reveals. Cf. the earlier distinction between the knight as 'man of earth' and Moses as 'man of God' (x 52.2, 53.2). **blaze**: proclaim.

Stanza 8

3 The indefinite size creates the horror, as does Milton's Satan who lay floating 'many a rood' (*Par. Lost* 1.196) and Virgil's Tityos who covers nine acres (*Aen.* 6.596). Murrin 1969:142–43 notes that the dragon's size varies. **4 waste**: waist, referring to its vast body; also to the devastation to which the land has been reduced under his shadow; cf. vii 44.5.

Stanza 9

1 I.e. 'and over his body, all', etc.; or the pointing may be: 'And, over all', i.e. 'and everywhere his body', etc. **brasen**: proverbial for hardness and indestructibility. **2–4** The dragon resembles the Leviathan in Job 41.6–8 but also the great red

10

His flaggy winges when forth he did display,
    Were like two sayles, in which the hollow wynd
    Is gathered full, and worketh speedy way:
    And eke the pennes, that did his pineons bynd,
    Were like mayne-yardes, with flying canuas lynd,
    With which whenas him list the ayre to beat,
    And there by force vnwonted passage fynd,
    The clowdes before him fledd for terror great,
And all the heuens stood still amazed with his threat.

11

His huge long tayle wownd vp in hundred foldes,
    Does ouerspred his long bras-scaly back,
    Whose wreathed boughtes when euer he vnfoldes,
    And thick entangled knots adown does slack,
    Bespotted as with shieldes of red and blacke,
    It sweepeth all the land behind him farre,
    And of three furlongs does but litle lacke;
    And at the point two stinges in fixed arre,
Both deadly sharp, that sharpest steele exceeden farr.

12

But stinges and sharpest steele did far exceed
    The sharpnesse of his cruel rending clawes;
    Dead was it sure, as sure as death in deed,
    What euer thing does touch his rauenous pawes,

Or what within his reach he euer drawes.
    But his most hideous head my tongue to tell,
    Does tremble: for his deepe deuouring iawes
    Wyde gaped, like the griesly mouth of hell,
Through which into his darke abysse all rauin fell.

13

And that more wondrous was, in either iaw
    Threeranckes of yron teeth enraunged were,
    In which yett trickling blood and gobbets raw
    Of late deuoured bodies did appeare,
    That sight thereof bredd cold congealed feare:
    Which to increase, and all atonce to kill,
    A cloud of smoothering smoke and sulphure seare
    Out of his stinking gorge forth steemed still,
That all the ayre about with smoke and stench did fill.

14

His blazing eyes, like two bright shining shieldes,
    Did burne with wrath, and sparkled liuing fyre;
    As two broad Beacons, sett in open fieldes,
    Send forth their flames far off to euery shyre,
    And warning giue, that enimies conspyre,
    With fire and sword the region to inuade;
    So flam'd his eyne with rage and rancorous yre:
    But far within, as in a hollow glade,
Those glaring lampes were sett, that made a dreadfull shade.

---

dragon of the Apocalypse (Rev. 12.3), the harlot's beast of Rev. 19, the ten-horned beast of Dan. 7, and the 'specled serpent' with its 'knottie rolles of scales' that 'bending into bunchie boughts', lifts itself 'above the wast . . . unto the Skie' (Ovid, *Met.* 3.46–49, tr. Golding; noted Taylor 1987a:199). See 'dragons' in the *SEnc*, and 13.2*n*. **so couched neare**: placed so closely. **dint**: blow. **6 rouze**: ruffle in anger. **rudely dight**: ruggedly arrayed. **8–9** Cf. Rev. 9.9. The detail is repeated at 15.7–8 in order to appal all the senses.

Stanza 10

1 flaggy: drooping. **2 hollow wynd**: as wind makes the sails hollow. **4 pennes**: the ribs of his wings. **7 vnwonted**: as the air is unaccustomed to such beating. **9** With the spondee the line stands still at its centre. **threat**: thrust or pressure from the beating wings.

Stanza 11

1 long: for 'his taile drue the third parte of the starres of heauen, and cast them to the earth' (Rev. 12.4); cf. vii 18.1–5. **3 boughtes**: coils; cf. Errour, i 15.3. **5 Bespotted** suggests defilement by spots of sin. **shieldes**: scales, as the Leviathan (Job 41.6); cf. Errour's speckled tail (i 17.6), and the dragon's 'speckled brest' (15.2). Since **red and blacke** were the dominant colours of Philip II's arms, there may be a reference to the ensigns of the Spanish Armada, esp. since the dragon's wings are said to be 'like two sayles' and its feathers 'like mayne-yards'; noted A. Fowler 1989b:156–57. See Leslie in the *SEnc* 354. Or since the imagery is biblical, there may be a reference to the apocalyptic red and black horses of Rev. 6.4–5. **8–9** Cf. the locusts of Rev. 9.10. The **two stinges** may be the 'want

of faith, or guilt of sin' (vii 45.8) through which the dragon has always triumphed over Una's champions; or 'Death and despeyre' (viii 14.3) which Duessa carries in her cup; or Sin and Death over which the transfigured Christ is seen to triumph in Holbein's title-page to Coverdale's Bible of 1535 (rpt King 1982: Fig.2); or simply the duplicity that symbolizes evil.

Stanza 12

1–2 sharpnesse is the subject of the sentence. **3 in deed**: in its effect. **8** 'Therefore gapeth hell' (Isa. 5.14, Bishops' Bible). For the common iconography of the dragon's gaping mouth as the mouth of hell, see 'dragons' in the *SEnc*. **griesly**: horrible. **9 abysse**: hell, the bowels of the earth, in its etymological sense, 'bottomless', as the 'bottomles pit' of Rev. 20.3; see viii 39.7–9*n*, and IV ii 47.6–7. **rauin**: plunder, prey.

Stanza 13

2 As the 'three rowes of teeth' of the snake killed by Cadmus (*Met.* 3.34, tr. Golding); the 'great yron teeth' of the beast in Dan. 7.7; and the 'teeth . . . fearful round about' of Leviathan (Job 41.5). **enraunged**: placed in a row. **3 gobbets raw**: chunks of undigested food, as Errour's vomit at i 20.3. **4 late**: see viii 6.2–5*n*. **7 smoke** and **sulphure** suggest hell-fire, as v. 31.5. **seare**: searing; see 26.7, 50.6. **9 fill**: also 'file': pollute.

Stanza 14

1 His blazing eyes: see vii 17.9*n*. **3–6** The simile, which links the danger and the warning against it, also describes the vigilant eyes of the castle of Alma at II ix 46.3–4, and of Disdaine at VI vii 42.2.

15

So dreadfully he towardes him did pas,
  Forelifting vp a loft his speckled brest,
  And often bounding on the brused gras,
  As for great ioyaunce of his newcome guest.
  Eftsoones he gan aduaunce his haughty crest,
  As chauffed Bore his bristles doth vpreare,
  And shoke his scales to battaile ready drest;
  That made the *Redcrosse* knight nigh quake for feare,
As bidding bold defyaunce to his foeman neare.

16

The knight gan fayrely couch his steady speare,
  And fiersely ran at him with rigorous might:
  The pointed steele arriuing rudely theare,
  His harder hyde would nether perce, nor bight,
  But glauncing by foorth passed forward right;
  Yet sore amoued with so puissaunt push,
  The wrathfull beast about him turned light,
  And him so rudely passing by, did brush
With his long tayle, that horse and man to ground did rush.

17

Both horse and man vp lightly rose againe,
  And fresh encounter towardes him addrest:
  But th'ydle stroke yet backe recoyld in vaine,
  And found no place his deadly point to rest.
  Exceeding rage enflam'd the furious beast,
  To be auenged of so great despight;
  For neuer felt his imperceable brest
  So wondrous force, from hand of liuing wight;
Yet had he prou'd the powre of many a puissant knight.

18

Then with his wauing wings displayed wyde,
  Himselfe vp high he lifted from the ground,
  And with strong flight did forcibly diuyde
  The yielding ayre, which nigh too feeble found
  Her flitting parts, and element vnsound,
  To beare so great a weight: he cutting way
  With his broad sayles, about him soared round:
  At last low stouping with vnweldy sway,
Snatcht vp both horse and man, to beare them quite away.

19

Long he them bore aboue the subiect plaine,
  So far as Ewghen bow a shaft may send,
  Till struggling strong did him at last constraine,
  To let them downe before his flightes end:
  As hagard hauke presuming to contend
  With hardy fowle, aboue his hable might,
  His wearie pounces all in vaine doth spend,
  To trusse the pray too heauy for his flight;
Which comming down to ground, does free it selfe by fight.

20

He so disseized of his gryping grosse,
  The knight his thrillant speare againe assayd
  In his bras-plated body to embosse,
  And three mens strength vnto the stroake he layd;
  Wherewith the stiffe beame quaked, as affrayd,
  And glauncing from his scaly necke, did glyde
  Close vnder his left wing, then broad displayd.
  The percing steele there wrought a wound full wyde,
That with the vncouth smart the Monster lowdly cryde.

Stanza 15

1 pas: pace. **4 ioyaunce**: joy; coined by S. to emphasize the state of joy. **guest**: not simply wry humour, for the knight is a guest at various 'houses', e.g. of Archimago, Pride, Despaire, Penance, and Una's father. **5 haughty**: lofty; also proud. **7 ready drest**: made ready. **8 That**: i.e. that shaking, the formal defiance before battle.

Stanza 16

The contest for Eden, which begins here, lasts for forty stanzas, as Nohrnberg 1976:187 notes. On the significance of that number, see I viii 40*n*. **2 rigorous**: violent; also 'stiff', referring to the **steady speare**. **3, 8 rudely**: violently. **4 harder**: too hard; also, harder than the spear; cf. 24.4–6. **7 light**: quickly. **8–9** In the initial contest, S. distinguishes between the knight's spear that idly passes **forward right** and the dragon's tail **passing by** (*en passant*). **horse**: not the usual chivalric 'steed', and most likely used here because in Rev. 6.2, 19.19, Christ rides a horse. **to ground**: see 11.1*n*.

Stanza 17

6 despight: outrage, insulting action. **9** Cf. vii 45. **prou'd**: tested.

Stanza 18

The dragon's flight relates him to 'the prince that ruleth in the aire' (Eph. 2.2). **5 flitting**: moving, unstable; or yielding, as

II viii 2.4. **vnsound**: lacking solidity. **7–8 sayles**: cf. 10.2. As a term for the wings of a hawk, it introduces **stouping**, a term for a hawk swooping down on its prey. **vnweldy**: implying also that the knight cannot wield his force against the dragon's. **sway**: force.

Stanza 19

1 subiect: as lying below. **5 hagard hauke**: an untamed, adult hawk noted for its powerful flight, in contrast to the young 'Eyas hauke' (34.6) to which the knight is compared. **6 hable**: proper; powerful (*OED* 5). **7 pounces**: anterior claws. **8 trusse**: seize and carry off.

Stanza 20

1 . . . rid of his heavy grasping. **2 thrillant**: piercing. **3 embosse**: plunge; coined by S. to indicate the knight's effort to sheathe his spear in the dragon's body. **4 three mens strength**: marking the greatest human strength, signified by the spear's third thrust (following 16.3–5 and 17.3–4). Cf. the dragon's 'hable might' (19.6). Both exert maximum natural power until the knight triumphs through supernatural power. **5 beame**: the spear's wooden shaft. Since the knight's armour fills heaven with light, 'beam of light' is implied. **7–9** Since the wing had been 'displayed wyde' (18.1) in flight, the knight triumphs over the powers of the air. It is evident from 36.8–9 that the dragon's body is not wounded.

21

He cryde, as raging seas are wont to rore,
    When wintry storme his wrathful wreck does threat,
    The rolling billowes beat the ragged shore,
    As they the earth would shoulder from her seat,
    And greedy gulfe does gape, as he would eat
    His neighbour element in his reuenge:
    Then gin the blustring brethren boldly threat,
    To moue the world from off his stedfast henge,
And boystrous battaile make, each other to auenge.

22

The steely head stuck fast still in his flesh,
    Till with his cruell clawes he snatcht the wood,
    And quite a sunder broke. Forth flowed fresh
    A gushing riuer of blacke gory blood,
    That drowned all the land, whereon he stood;
    The streame thereof would driue a water-mill.
    Trebly augmented was his furious mood
    With bitter sence of his deepe rooted ill,
That flames of fire he threw forth from his large nosethril.

23

His hideous tayle then hurled he about,
    And therewith all enwrapt the nimble thyes
    Of his froth-fomy steed, whose courage stout
    Striuing to loose the knott, that fast him tyes,
    Himselfe in streighter bandes too rash implyes,
    That to the ground he is perforce constraynd
    To throw his ryder: who can quickly ryse
    From off the earth, with durty blood distaynd,
For that reprochfull fall right fowly he disdaynd.

24

And fercely tooke his trenchand blade in hand,
    With which he stroke so furious and so fell,
    That nothing seemd the puissaunce could withstand:
    Vpon his crest the hardned yron fell,
    But his more hardned crest was armd so well,
    That deeper dint therein it would not make;
    Yet so extremely did the buffe him quell,
    That from thenceforth he shund the like to take,
But when he saw them come, he did them still forsake.

25

The knight was wroth to see his stroke beguyld,
    And smot againe with more outrageous might;
    But backe againe the sparcling steele recoyld,
    And left not any marke, where it did light;
    As if in Adamant rocke it had beene pight.
    The beast impatient of his smarting wound,
    And of so fierce and forcible despight,
    Thought with his winges to stye aboue the ground;
But his late wounded wing vnseruiceable found.

26

Then full of griefe and anguish vehement,
    He lowdly brayd, that like was neuer heard,
    And from his wide deuouring ouen sent
    A flake of fire, that flashing in his beard,
    Him all amazd, and almost made afeard:
    The scorching flame sore swinged all his face,
    And through his armour all his body seard,
    That he could not endure so cruell cace,
But thought his armes to leaue, and helmet to vnlace.

Stanza 21

The dragon is associated with the elements of water, earth, and air. The next stanza adds the fourth element, fire. **2 wreck**: ruin, adding the comic (and apocalyptic) note that the raging seas bring their own ruin. **5 greedy gulfe**: the eddies made by the waves after they break; or the yawning chasm of the oncoming wave. **6 His neighbour element**: the earth. **8 henge**: axis. **9 boystrous**: violently fierce, savage.

Stanza 22

1–4 The alliteration of 's' and 'f' in each half of 1, divided by the strong caesura, shows how fast the head stuck. The breaking of the spear in line 3 is indicated by the break in the line, appropriately after **broke**. The flowing of the blood is rendered by the alliteration **Forth flowed fresh**. **4–6** The superb extravagance registers the poet's joy as the knight's victory approaches. **8 sence**: feeling. **ill**: injury, wound; perhaps also his own evil nature.

Stanza 23

1 hideous: huge. **hurled**: 'hurtling' and 'whirling', as Errour 'hurling her hideous taile' (i 16.2). **5 streighter**: tighter. **too rash**: all too quickly; or too hasty, referring to the horse. Either way, he cooperates in his fall. **implyes**: entangles. **7 can**: did. **8 durty blood**: i.e. with dirt and blood. **distaynd**: deeply stained or defiled. **9 disdaynd**: was indignant about.

Stanza 24

Being deprived of horse and spear, the knight fights on foot with his sword; and since the dragon cannot fly, both fight on equal terms on the ground. Unlike the traditional St George who slays the dragon while on horseback, the Red Cross Knight fights on foot, as the Archangel Michael is usually seen in medieval art when he slays the dragon. **1 trenchand**: sharp; cf. i 17.3. **7 buffe**: blow. **9 still forsake**: ever shun.

Stanza 25

1 beguyld: foiled. **5** As if thrust at **Adamant rocke**. See vii 33.5–9n. **6 impatient**: unable to bear the suffering. **7 forcible despight**: powerful injury; combining the injury and its cause in the knight's contemptuous defiance of the dragon. **8 stye**: mount.

Stanza 26

1 griefe: pain. **3–7 flake**: flame. The apocalyptic imagery describing this battle suggests that the dragon's fire expresses God's punishment of the sinful, such as the vials of wrath by which the fourth angel torments them so that 'men boyled in great heat' (Rev. 16.8–9); or John's prophecy that one will come who 'wil baptize you . . . with fyre' (Matt. 3.11). **flashing in his beard**: as the Leviathan's 'breath maketh the coles burne; for a flame goeth out of his mouth' (Job 41.12). On the theological implications of this detail with its aftermath, see

27

Not that great Champion of the antique world,
　Whom famous Poetes verse so much doth vaunt,
　And hath for twelue huge labours high extold,
　So many furies and sharpe fits did haunt,
　When him the poysoned garment did enchaunt
With *Centaures* blood, and bloody verses charmd,
　As did this knight twelue thousand dolours daunt,
　Whom fyrie steele now burnt, that erst him armd,
That erst him goodly armd, now most of all him harmd.

28

Faynt, wearie, sore, emboyled, grieued, brent
　With heat, toyle, wounds, armes, smart, and inward fire
　That neuer man such mischiefes did torment;
　Death better were, death did he oft desire,
　But death will neuer come, when needes require.
Whom so dismayd when that his foe beheld,
　He cast to suffer him no more respire,
　But gan his sturdy sterne about to weld,
And him so strongly stroke, that to the ground him feld.

29

It fortuned (as fayre it then befell,)
　Behynd his backe vnweeting, where he stood,
　Of auncient time there was a springing well,
　From which fast trickled forth a siluer flood,
　Full of great vertues, and for med'cine good.
Whylome, before that cursed Dragon got
　That happy land, and all with innocent blood
　Defyld those sacred waues, it rightly hot
The well of life, ne yet his vertues had forgot.

30

For vnto life the dead it could restore,　*Christ*
　And guilt of sinfull crimes cleane wash away,
　Those that with sicknesse were infected sore,
　It could recure, and aged long decay
　Renew, as one were borne that very day.
Both *Silo* this, and *Iordan* did excell,
　And th'English *Bath*, and eke the german *Spau*,
　Ne can *Cephise*, nor *Hebrus* match this well:
Into the same the knight back ouerthrowen, fell.

Kaske 1999:134–35. **almost**: perhaps the intensive, 'indeed' (*OED* 4); cf. 15.8. **swinged**: singed, scorched; also whipped by the lash of its tail. **7–9 seard**: literally, 'burned by hot iron'. **cace**: plight; with a pun on the armour which encloses him. The witty word-play points to the paradox: putting off the armour led to his defeat by Orgoglio; now put on, it causes him to be defeated. **armes** are linked with his battle against Orgoglio; the **helmet**, which is 'the hope of saluation' (1 Thess. 5.8), with his battle against Despaire; but 'the shield of faith, wherewith ye may quench all the fyrie dartes of the wicked' (Eph. 6.16) is not employed until the second day. Røstvig 1994:300–02 contrasts the 'wooden wals' (ii 42.8) enclosing Fradubio and Fralissa through which they suffer 'cold and heat' (33.9). **thought**: intended. For further on the theological implications, see Gless 1994:163–71; on the problems raised by allegorical reading, see Krier 1994:72.

Stanza 27

1–6 that great Champion: Hercules. When he put on a garment soaked in a centaur's poisoned blood, his flesh burned and he died in great agony; and since it was given him as a love-charm, it is said to be **With . . . bloody verses charmd**. See Ovid, *Met.* 9.134–272; and on S.'s use of the Hercules myth, see Cook 1996:101–02. The comparison is apt because the knight's armour is also 'charmed' (cf. iv 50.5–6), and because Hercules's fiery death was interpreted as punishment for concupiscence, e.g. by Conti 1616:7.1. **the antique world**: referring generally to the classical world; see V proem 1*n*. **extold**: the context suggests the obs. sense, 'made too much of'. **7 twelue thousand**: alluding to Hercules's twelue renowned labours, suggesting that the Red Cross Knight accomplishes them all at once while the **dolours** (pains) are multiplied a thousandfold. **8, 9 armd . . . harmd**: the jingle, which Percival 1964 notes as 'a perfectly serious euphuistic pun', enforces the paradox noted in the previous stanza.

Stanza 28

1–2 Faynt . . . fire: faint with heat, weary with toil, etc. **emboyled**: literally 'boiled' in his armour. The echo of Isa.

40.30, 'Euen the yong men shal faint, and be wearie, and the yong men shal stumble and fall', is noted by MacGillivray 1992. For the promise of restoration in the next verse, see 34.3–9*n* below. **3 mischiefes**: misfortunes; cf. ix 45.3–4. Now he is beyond despair. **4** On his frequent desire for death, now fulfilled by the dragon's blow, see viii 38.3–9*n*. **6–9 dismayd**: he relives his earlier plight; see vii 11.6*n*. **suffer**: answering the knight's sufferings through which he desires death. **respire**: live. **weld**: wield.

Stanza 29

1 fayre: auspiciously. **2 vnweeting**: i.e. not known to him. **5 vertues**: powers. **8 hot**: was called. **9 The well of life**: glossed by J. Dixon 1964 as 'spirituall graces giuen to the Church under the kingdom of Christe'. Cf. John 4.14: 'The water that I shal giue him, shalbe in him a well of water, springing vp into euerlasting life', which Geneva glosses as 'spiritual grace'. The 'pure riuer of water of life' (Rev. 22.1) is taken to represent baptism by Jonson 1995, and to Christ's doctrine by Hume 1984:104. The association with Solomon's description of his bride as the 'well of liuing waters' (Song Sol. 4.15) is noted by Quint 1983:160. See 46–48*n*.

Stanza 30

1 'Euen when we were dead by sinnes, [God] hathe quickened vs together in Christ, by whose grace ye are saued' (Eph. 2.5). **2** 'Arise, and be baptized, and washe away thy sinnes' (Acts 22.16). The knight is purged of that 'guilt of sin' (vii 45.8) by which all Una's previous champions had been defeated. **3–5** *The Golden Legend* (see x 66.5–6*n*) records that after the dragon was bound the people were baptized and a church built 'In the whiche yet sourdeth [springs] a fountayne of lyuynge [running] water | whiche heleth the seke people that drynken therof'. Cf. John 3.5: 'Except that a man be borne of water and of the Spirit, he can not enter into the kingdome of God'. **6–8** These waters are famous either for their healing powers or their purity. The man born blind was cured by washing in the pool of Siloam 'which is by interpretation, Sent' (John 9.7); the Geneva gloss adds: 'Hereby was prefigured the

31

Now gan the golden *Phœbus* for to steepe
   His fierie face in billowes of the west,
   And his faint steedes watred in Ocean deepe,
   Whiles from their iournall labours they did rest,
   When that infernall Monster, hauing kest
   His wearie foe into that liuing well,
   Can high aduaunce his broad discoloured brest,
   Aboue his wonted pitch, with countenance fell,
And clapt his yron wings, as victor he did dwell.

32

Which when his pensiue Lady saw from farre,
   Great woe and sorrow did her soule assay,
   As weening that the sad end of the warre,
   And gan to highest God entirely pray,
   That feared chaunce from her to turne away;
   With folded hands and knees full lowly bent
   All night shee watcht, ne once adowne would lay
   Her dainty limbs in her sad dreriment,
But praying still did wake, and waking did lament.

33

The morrow next gan earely to appeare,
   That *Titan* rose to runne his daily race;
   But earely ere the morrow next gan reare
   Out of the sea faire *Titans* deawy face,
   Vp rose the gentle virgin from her place,
   And looked all about, if she might spy
   Her loued knight to moue his manly pace:
   For she had great doubt of his safety,
Since late she saw him fall before his enimy.

34

At last she saw, where he vpstarted braue
   Out of the well, wherein he drenched lay;
   As Eagle fresh out of the Ocean waue,
   Where he hath lefte his plumes all hory gray,
   And deckt himselfe with fethers youthly gay,
   Like Eyas hauke vp mounts vnto the skies,
   His newly budded pineons to assay,
   And merueiles at him selfe, stil as he flies:
So new this new-borne knight to battell new did rise.

Messias, who shulde be sent vnto them'. S. prefers the Vulg. form **Silo**. In the **Iordan**, Naaman was cured of his leprosy (2 Kings 5.14), but its waters are associated chiefly with John's baptism of Christ (Matt. 3.16). After the two spiritual waters, the two contemporary European waters are given precedence over the classical. The waters of **Bath** are described at II x 26. **Cephise**: its purifying waters were used to sprinkle Deucalion and Pyrrha before they restored the human race, Ovid, *Met.* 1.369–70. Sandys 1970:69 refers to its 'holywater'. See Yiavis 1998. **Hebrus**: its healing powers are noted by Horace, *Epi.* 1.16.13–14.

Stanza 31

1–4 faint: lacking in strength; as the knight at 28.1. **steepe** implies both cleansing and renewal. While the dragon's victory over the knight is the victory of the west over the sun, **iournall** ('daily'; cf. 33.2) reminds us that dawn will follow. Both the sun and the knight are bathed as they rest for renewed labours. Their relation is extended throughout the battle until it achieves its climactic expression in stanza 52. On the knight's role as *Sol iustitiæ*, see A. Fowler 1964:69. **5 infernall Monster**: 'infernall feend' at i 5.7. **6 liuing**: constantly flowing; alluding to its name as it gives life. **7 Can**: did. **discoloured**: variously coloured; 'speckled' (15.2); also 'stained'. **8 pitch**: height; also blackness. **9 dwell**: remain.

Stanza 32

1 pensiue: anxious, as x 68.3. **2 assay**: assail; also 'test', as an attack tests or proves endurance. **3 weening that**: i.e. believing that to be. **4 entirely**: earnestly, whole-heartedly. **5 chaunce**: mischance, mishap. **7–9** Matt. 26.41: 'watch, and pray'. **dreriment**: dismal plight.

Stanza 33

1–5 A prolepsis to relate Una to the new dawn (cf. 51), or to the morning star (cf. xii 21) which precedes the sun's rising.

The lines prepare for the knight's resurrection: the sun rears **Out of the sea**, the renewed eagle 'out of the Ocean waue' (34.3) and the knight 'Out of the well' (34.2). **race**: the sun's daily course. Lines 1–2 may mark the solstitial point that heralds the imminent victory of light over darkness; or the beginning of a cloudless day in contrast to the black clouds at the end, 44.3, 8–9. **7 moue his manly pace**: the formality of the phrase suggests the ordered movement of the sun. **manly** is the key word. The knight's manly heart melted at Archimago's dream (i 47.5), his manly force failed him before Orgoglio (vii 6.4), his manly looks were marred by imprisonment (viii 42.9), Despaire's arguments dispersed his manly powers and bewitched his manly heart (ix 48.7, 53.2), but now he becomes fully man, and more than man.

Stanza 34

1–2 The context suggests an allusion to Ps. 19.4: the sun 'commeth forthe as a bridegrome out of his chambre, and reioyceth like a mightie man to runne his race'; noted Weatherby 1994:52. **braue**: courageous; also 'splendidly dressed' like the eagle. **drenched**: submerged, which suggests Protestant baptism by immersion in running water; see 46–48*n*. **3–9** According to popular lore, the eagle, which renewed its youth every ten years by plunging into the ocean, became a type of the crucifixion and resurrection of Christ, and also of baptism; see Rowland 1978:52–53. The comparison of the dragon to the eagle at 9.5–7 now serves to place the old dragon, the old eagle, and the old Adam in opposition to the renewed eagle and the **new-borne knight**. Cf. Ps. 103.4–5: '[God] redemeth thy life from the graue, and crowneth thee with mercie and compassions . . . and thy youth is renued like the egles'. **Eyas hauke**: a young untamed hawk, 'King of fowles in maiesty and powre' (VI x 6.9). **to battell new**: here **new** also modifies knight, as the word-play suggests. Cf. public baptism (*BCP*): 'grant that the old Adam in these children may be so buried, that the new man may be raised up in them'.

35

Whom when the damned feend so fresh did spy,
　　No wonder, if he wondred at the sight,
　　And doubted, whether his late enimy
　　It were, or other new supplied knight.
　　He, now to proue his late renewed might,
　　High brandishing his bright deaw-burning blade,
　　Vpon his crested scalp so sore did smite,
　　That to the scull a yawning wound it made:
The deadly dint his dulled sences all dismaid.

36

I wote not, whether the reuenging steele
　　Were hardned with that holy water dew,
　　Wherein he fell, or sharper edge did feele,
　　Or his baptized hands now greater grew;
　　Or other secret vertue did ensew;
　　Els neuer could the force of fleshly arme,
　　Ne molten mettall in his blood embrew:
　　For till that stownd could neuer wight him harme,
By subtilty, nor slight, nor might, nor mighty charme.

37

The cruell wound enraged him so sore,
　　That loud he yelded for exceeding paine;
　　As hundred ramping Lions seemd to rore,
　　Whom rauenous hunger did thereto constraine:
　　Then gan he tosse aloft his stretched traine,
　　And therewith scourge the buxome aire so sore,
　　That to his force to yielden it was faine;
　　Ne ought his sturdy strokes might stand afore,
That high trees ouerthrew, and rocks in peeces tore.

38

The same aduauncing high aboue his head,
　　With sharpe intended sting so rude him smott,
　　That to the earth him droue, as stricken dead,
　　Ne liuing wight would haue him life behott:
　　The mortall sting his angry needle shott
　　Quite through his shield, and in his shoulder seasd,
　　Where fast it stucke, ne would thereout be gott:
　　The griefe thereof him wondrous sore diseasd,
Ne might his rancling paine with patience be appeasd.

39

But yet more mindfull of his honour deare,
　　Then of the grieuous smart, which him did wring,
　　From loathed soile he can him lightly reare,
　　And stroue to loose the far infixed sting:
　　Which when in vaine he tryde with struggeling,
　　Inflam'd with wrath, his raging blade he hefte,
　　And strooke so strongly, that the knotty string
　　Of his huge taile he quite a sonder clefte,
Fiue ioints thereof he hewd, and but the stump him lefte.

40

Hart cannot thinke, what outrage, and what cries,
　　With fowle enfouldred smoake and flashing fire,
　　The hell-bred beast threw forth vnto the skies,
　　That all was couered with darknesse dire:
　　Then fraught with rancour, and engorged yre,
　　He cast at once him to auenge for all,
　　And gathering vp himselfe out of the mire,
　　With his vneuen wings did fiercely fall,
Vpon his sunne-bright shield, and grypt it fast withall.

Stanza 35
6 deaw-burning: shining with 'that holy water dew' (36.2); cf. '*Titans* deawy face' (33.4).   **7–9** As Arthur's similar blow at viii 16 wounds Duessa's beast.

Stanza 36
1–5 S. offers four possible explanations without endorsing any. (1) The sword is tempered by **holy water dew** from the '*well of life*' (29.9; cf. xii 37.5), **dew** being associated, through the miracle of manna, with God's providential care; cf. 48.5. (2) The sword is sharpened by the dew, as 'deaw-burning blade' (35.6) suggests. Cf. 1 Heb. 41.2: 'The worde of God is . . . sharper then anie two edged sword'. (3) The knight's **baptized hands** – baptized in the literal sense of the Lat. and Gk root of βαπτίζω, to drench or bathe. (4) Some other secret power resulting from the knight's fall into the well. For comment on these explanations, see Gless 1994:165–67. In all earlier battles against Una's knights, the dragon 'still . . . greater grew' (vii 45.7), where 'greater' suggests also proud, arrogant (*OED* 4); now applied to this knight, it signifies 'stronger', or more 'full-grown' (*OED* 7).   **7 molten mettall**: the forging of weapons from melted metal contrasts the tempering (or sharpening) of the knight's sword in the well of life.   **embrew**: steep.   **8–9** See 20.7–9n.   **stownd**: moment. The four terms in line 9 relate to the four explanations in 1–5 in their order.   **slight**: deception.

Stanza 37
The knight's blow is prologue to a battle in which the dragon employs each of his three weapons in turn: tail, claws, and

mouth; noted Rose 1975:141.   **1–4** After Israel forsook 'the fountaine of liuing waters', 'the lyons roared vpon him, and yelled, and they haue made his land waste' (Jer. 2.13–15; cf. 31.58). Only lions yell in the Bible. See x 28.1–3n.   **5–8 traine**: tail.   **buxome**: unresisting.   **faine**: obliged.   **sturdy**: violent.

Stanza 38
2 intended: aimed; but also 'extended' (*OED* 2).   **rude**: violently.   **3** As earlier: 23.6–7 and 28.9.   **4** . . . would have held out hope of life.   **5–6 sting**: the term suggests the proverbial 'sting of lust' as IV ii 5.5, and '*Venus* sting' (II xii 39.3).   **6 seasd**: penetrated.   **8 griefe**: pain.   **diseasd**: tormented.   **9** In contrast to his earlier disease which could be cured by patience, x 23.8–9.   **rancling**: its use for a festering wound is particularly appropriate, for it derives from med. Lat. *dranculus*, dim. of *draco* dragon; noted *OED*. See x 25.1–5n.

Stanza 39
2 wring: vex; or afflict with pain.   **3 loathed**: because defeat brings dishonour which he loathes; cf. 23.9.   **soile** suggests 'defiling'.   **6 hefte**: heaved.   **8** This stage of the battle may be marked by the question: 'O death, where is thy sting?' (1 Cor. 15.55).   **9 Fiue**: corresponding to the five fallen heads of the beast in Rev. 17.10.

Stanza 40
1 outrage: violent clamour.   **2 enfouldred**: charged with thunderbolts; black as a thunder cloud. The word enwraps

41

Much was the man encombred with his hold,
  In feare to lose his weapon in his paw,
  Ne wist yett, how his talaunts to vnfold;
  Nor harder was from *Cerberus* greedy iaw
  To plucke a bone, then from his cruell claw
  To reaue by strength, the griped gage away:
  Thrise he assayd it from his foote to draw,
  And thrise in vaine to draw it did assay,
It booted nought to thinke, to robbe him of his pray.

42

Tho when he saw no power might preuaile,
  His trusty sword he cald to his last aid,
  Wherewith he fiersly did his foe assaile,
  And double blowes about him stoutly laid,
  That glauncing fire out of the yron plaid;
  As sparckles from the Anduile vse to fly,
  When heauy hammers on the wedg are swaid;
  Therewith at last he forst him to vnty
One of his grasping feete, him to defend thereby.

43

The other foote, fast fixed on his shield,
  Whenas no strength, nor stroks mote him constraine
  To loose, ne yet the warlike pledg to yield,
  He smott thereat with all his might and maine,

That nought so wondrous puissaunce might sustaine;
  Vpon the ioint the lucky steele did light,
  And made such way, that hewd it quite in twaine;
  The paw yett missed not his minisht might,
But hong still on the shield, as it at first was pight.

44

For griefe thereof, and diuelish despight,
  From his infernall fournace forth he threw
  Huge flames, that dimmed all the heuens light,
  Enrold in duskish smoke and brimstone blew;
  As burning *Aetna* from his boyling stew
  Doth belch out flames, and rockes in peeces broke,
  And ragged ribs of mountaines molten new,
  Enwrapt in coleblacke clowds and filthy smoke,
That al the land with stench, and heuen with horror choke.

45

The heate whereof, and harmefull pestilence
  So sore him noyd, that forst him to retire
  A litle backeward for his best defence,
  To saue his body from the scorching fire,
  Which he from hellish entrailes did expire.
  It chaunst (eternall God that chaunce did guide)
  As he recoiled backeward, in the mire
  His nigh foreweried feeble feet did slide,
And downe he fell, with dread of shame sore terrifide.

---

its epithet, **fowle**. **4 darknesse**: a mark of the Last Days, as Rev. 9.2, etc. **5 engorged**: swallowed, and hence swollen; the same sense as **fraught**. **8 vneuen wings**: because one is wounded. **9 withall**: as well. The dragon first attacks the knight with fire, almost defeating him because of his armour; next he pierces his shoulder through his shield; now he attacks the shield itself.

Stanza 41

4–5 Cerberus: the dog that guards the entrance to hell (see v 34). Its defeat by **Hercules** (see VI xii 35 and *n*), which was interpreted as a victory over hell and death (Conti 1616:3.5), is the classical analogue of the knight's victory over the dragon. **6 gage**: the pawn or 'warlike pledg' (43.3) for which they fight.

Stanza 42

5 yron: referring to the dragon's iron claws. **7 wedg**: metal ingot. **swaid**: swung. **8 vnty**: relax his hold.

Stanza 43

6–7 'For the worde of God is . . . sharper then anie two edged sworde, and entreth through, euen vnto the diuiding asonder . . . of the ioynts' (Heb. 4.12). **8 minisht**: diminished. **9 pight**: fixed.

Stanza 44

1 griefe: pain. **2–4** Cf. the end of the first day's battle, 26.3–7 and see *n*. **blew**: the colour of burning brimstone or sulphur, symbolically the colour of **diuelish** flame. Finally the dragon will be cast into the lake of fire 'burning with brimstone' (Rev. 19.20). **5–9** The dragon's infernal nature becomes evident by comparing this simile with its source in

Aen. 3.571–77. To Virgil's horrific details, S. adds the defilement in 9. **stew**: cauldron.

Stanza 45

1–5 The immediate context suggests an allusion to Ps. 91.3: 'Surely he wil deliuer thee . . . from the noisome pestilence'. **noyd**: harmed. **expire**: breathe out; here suggesting 'to breathe one's last in death'. **7** On the first day the dragon 'to the ground him feld' (28.9), and 'It fortuned' (29.1) that the ground was watered by the well of life; now **It chaunst** through God's guidance that the knight co-operates with saving grace. Through his backsliding, grace aids him, not to support him but to occasion his fall. See McCabe 1989a:154–69 on the relation between providence and fortune.

Stanzas 46–48

On the sacramental imagery that associates '*The well of life*' (29.9) with baptism, and 'The tree of life' (46.9) with holy communion (though the knight does not feed on its fruit), as derived from Rev. 22.1–2, see 'sacraments' in the *SEnc*. Stanza 48 is glossed by J. Dixon 1964 as 'a fiction of the incarnation of Christe', and by Jonson 1995 as the 'Euch[arist]'. Identification with specific theological doctrine, whether traditional or reformed, remains moot: see, e.g. Tuve 1966:110–12, Hume 1984:105, Gless 1994:164–65, Weatherby 1994:25–43, and Weatherby 1999:424–25. Yet distinctions between the two are specific: the well bestows 'life' (30.1) and the tree 'happy life . . . | And life eke euerlasting' (46.5–6; cf. 48.6); the well cures chronic disabilities, 'sicknesse' and 'aged long decay' (30.3–4), and the tree 'deadly wounds' (48.7), etc. For similar distinctions between the gifts exchanged by Arthur and the Red Cross Knight, see ix 19*n*. On the relation of the knight's fall to militantly biblical Protestantism, see Dughi 1997.

46

There grew a goodly tree him faire beside,
   Loaden with fruit and apples rosy redd,
   As they in pure vermilion had beene dide,
   Whereof great vertues ouer all were redd:
   For happy life to all, which thereon fedd,
   And life eke euerlasting did befall:
   Great God it planted in that blessed stedd
   With his Almighty hand, and did it call
The tree of life, the crime of our first fathers fall.

47

In all the world like was not to be fownd,
   Saue in that soile, where all good things did grow,
   And freely sprong out of the fruitfull grownd,
   As incorrupted Nature did them sow,
   Till that dredd Dragon all did ouerthrow.
   Another like faire tree eke grew thereby,
   Whereof who so did eat, eftsoones did know
   Both good and ill: O mournfull memory:
That tree through one mans fault hath doen vs all to dy.

48

From that first tree forth flowd, as from a well,
   A trickling streame of Balme, most soueraine
   And dainty deare, which on the ground still fell,
   And ouerflowed all the fertile plaine,
   As it had deawed bene with timely raine:
   Life and long health that gracious ointment gaue,
   And deadly wounds could heale, and reare againe
   The sencelesse corse appointed for the graue.
Into that same he fell: which did from death him saue.

49

For nigh thereto the euer damned Beast
   Durst not approch, for he was deadly made,
   And al that life preserued, did detest:
   Yet he it oft aduentur'd to inuade.
   By this the drouping day-light gan to fade,
   And yield his rowme to sad succeeding night,
   Who with her sable mantle gan to shade
   The face of earth, and wayes of liuing wight,
And high her burning torch set vp in heauen bright.

50

When gentle *Vna* saw the second fall
   Of her deare knight, who weary of long fight,
   And faint through losse of blood, moou'd not at all,
   But lay as in a dreame of deepe delight,
   Besmeard with pretious Balme, whose vertuous might
   Did heale his woundes, and scorching heat alay,
   Againe she stricken was with sore affright,
   And for his safetie gan deuoutly pray;
And watch the noyous night, and wait for ioyous day.

51

The ioyous day gan early to appeare,
   And fayre *Aurora* from the deawy bed
   Of aged *Tithone* gan her selfe to reare,
   With rosy cheekes, for shame as blushing red;
   Her golden locks for hast were loosely shed
   About her eares, when *Vna* her did marke
   Clymbe to her charet, all with flowers spred,
   From heuen high to chace the chearelesse darke;
With mery note her lowd salutes the mounting larke.

Stanza 46
Based on Gen. 2.8–9: 'The Lord God planted a garden . . .
The tree of life also in the middes of the garden'. **1 faire
beside**: close by; auspiciously. Cf. 29.1–2. **2** 'The tre of life
. . . bare twelue maner of frutes' (Rev 22.2). **apples**: see
'apples' in the *SEnc*. **4** . . . everywhere were told. **7 stedd**:
place. **9** I.e. it was a cause of reproach, or accusation (Lat.
crimen), against Adam. After eating of the tree of knowledge
of good and evil, he was banished 'lest he put forthe his hand,
and take also of the tre of life and eat and liue for euer' (Gen. 3.22).
In this sense, the tree was the cause of his expulsion from Eden.

Stanza 47
6 thereby: according to Gen. 2.9, 'the tre of life [was] also in
the middes of the garden'. **8 memory**: memorial, memento;
also a witty play on the usual sense: **mournfull memory**
records the knowledge of **good and ill**. **9** 'By one man sinne
entred into the worlde, and death by sinne, and so death went
ouer all men' (Rom. 5.12).

Stanza 48
2 soueraine: applied to a remedy of supreme healing powers.
3 dainty deare: exceedingly precious. **6–8** The leaves of the
tree of life 'serued to heale the nations' (Rev. 22.2). **health**:
spiritual and moral well-being. **gracious**: endowed with
God's grace. **ointment**: as 2 Esd. 2.12: 'They shal haue at wil
the tre of life, smelling of ointement: they shal nether labour

nor be weary'. In the apocryphal Gospel of Nicodemus, Seth is
promised oil from the tree of life that will heal the dying Adam;
noted Hankins 1971:119. **appointed**: made ready.

Stanza 49
2 deadly made: i.e. being made for death, belonging to it.
4 aduentur'd: dared, attempted.

Stanza 50
On Rev. 2.11: 'He that ouercometh shal not be hurt of the
seconde death', the Geneva gloss reads: 'the first death is the
natural death of the bodie, the seconde is the eternal death'.
From this second death of the soul, the knight is saved by the
tree that gives 'life eke euerlasting' (46.6). **4** His previous
dream was an erotic nightmare of an unchaste Una (i 47–48;
cf. 55.7), which, after waking, seemed to be true. His present
dreame of deepe delight is not described but after his present
agony he will awake to find it true and enjoy 'deare delights'
(xii 41.4) on the pattern of Arthur's dream of the Faerie
Queene at ix 14. See Nohrnberg 1976:197–98. **5–6** In con-
trast to Duessa's ointment at ii 42.3–5. **vertuous**: efficacious
in healing. **9 noyous**: irksome.

Stanza 51
1–5 On **Aurora**, see ii 7.1–3 for the dawning of a different
day, which this stanza answers. As at 33.1–5, dawn is associated
with Una, here through her 'golden heare' (x 28.6). **9** The

52

Then freshly vp arose the doughty knight,
   All healed of his hurts and woundes wide,
   And did himselfe to battaile ready dight;
   Whose early foe awaiting him beside
   To haue deuourd, so soone as day he spyde,
   When now he saw himselfe so freshly reare,
   As if late fight had nought him damnifyde,
   He woxe dismaid, and gan his fate to feare;
Nathlesse with wonted rage he him aduaunced neare.

53

And in his first encounter, gaping wyde,
   He thought attonce him to haue swallowd quight,
   And rusht vpon him with outragious pryde;
   Who him rencountring fierce, as hauke in flight,
   Perforce rebutted backe. The weapon bright
   Taking aduantage of his open iaw,
   Ran through his mouth with so importune might,
   That deepe emperst his darksom hollow maw,
And back retyrd, his life blood forth with all did draw.

54

So downe he fell, and forth his life did breath,
   That vanisht into smoke and cloudes swift;
   So downe he fell, that th'earth him vnderneath
   Did grone, as feeble so great load to lift;
   So downe he fell, as an huge rocky clift,
   Whose false foundacion waues haue washt away,
   With dreadfull poyse is from the mayneland rift,
   And rolling downe, great *Neptune* doth dismay;
So downe he fell, and like an heaped mountaine lay.

55

The knight him selfe euen trembled at his fall,
   So huge and horrible a masse it seemd;
   And his deare Lady, that beheld it all,
   Durst not approch for dread, which she misdeemd,
   But yet at last, whenas the direfull feend
   She saw not stirre, off-shaking vaine affright,
   She nigher drew, and saw that ioyous end:
   Then God she praysd, and thankt her faithfull knight,
That had atchieude so great a conquest by his might.

larke is the traditional herald of the day; see Rowland 1978:98–99.

Stanza 52

2 'The third day [of the resurrection] I shalbe perfited' (Luke 13.32). **4 awaiting**: keeping watch. **5 as day he spyde**: as the knight is one of 'The children of day' (III iv 59.5). **7 damnifyde**: injured.

Stanza 53

4 rencountring: charging in return. **as hauke in flight**: see 34.3–9*n*. **5–9** Personification of the weapon would seem to imply that it kills the dragon rather than the knight, as he explains: God 'made my hand the organ of his might' (II i 33.3); see 55.8–9*n*. The unidentified weapon could be his 'charmed launce' (iii 25.9) as at 16 and 20, and as the image here suggests; or his sword, which he uses at 24, etc., once he is on foot. His model is John's vision of one called Faithful and True, identified by the gloss as Christ, who, sitting on a horse, slays the beast with the sword out of his mouth (Rev. 19.11–21). **7 importune**: grievous, violent. On the dragon's mouth as an emblem of hell, see 12.8*n*. Symbolically, the knight enters hell and leaves triumphant, enacting Christ's harrowing of hell; see I x 40.8–9*n*. **9 back retyrd**: i.e. on being drawn back by the knight, identifying him with his weapon, as McDermott 1996 notes.

Stanza 54

So downe he fell is thrice repeated in imitation of Rev. 14.8 and 18.2: 'It is fallen, it is fallen, Babylon the great citie'. The deliberate use of *anaphora* is designed to connect the dragon's fall with air, earth, and sea. **3–4** In *Comm Sonn 4*, S. refers to Rome as 'Second *Babell* tyrant of the West' which now has fallen 'that all the earth did feare'. **8 Neptune** is dismayed because the victory heralds the end of time when there shall be no sea (Rev. 21.1). **6 false**: treacherous, having been made such by the waves. **7 poyse**: weight; force. **rift**: split.

Stanza 55

4 which she misdeemd: she misjudged, or was mistaken in fearing either for her knight's safety or that the dragon was not dead. While she hastens to congratulate him on his first victory over Errour (i 27.2), and also Arthur on his victory over Orgoglio (viii 26.4), this present victory is greater than faith itself may believe. **8–9** There is a deliberate equivocation in **his**: it refers both to God and to the knight – as Alpers 1967:336 first noted – in agreement with Phil. 2.13: 'it is God which worketh in you, both the wil and the dede'; see II i 33.2–5. Roche 1990b:12 notes that here the allegorical and tropological senses are at one. Human might and God's grace merge as the knight is revealed in the lineaments of Christ, the dragon-killer, even as Michael, the dragon-killer of Rev. 12.7, is identified by the Geneva gloss as Christ.

Cant. XII.

Fayre Vna to the Redcrosse knight
betrouthed is with ioy:
Though false Duessa it to barre
Her false sleightes doe imploy.

1

Behold I see the hauen nigh at hand,
To which I meane my wearie course to bend;
Vere the maine shete, and beare vp with the land,
The which afore is fayrly to be kend,
And seemeth safe from storms, that may offend;
There this fayre virgin wearie of her way
Must landed bee, now at her iourneyes end:
There eke my feeble barke a while may stay,
Till mery wynd and weather call her thence away.

2

Scarsely had *Phœbus* in the glooming East
Yett harnessed his fyrie-footed teeme,
Ne reard aboue the earth his flaming creast,
When the last deadly smoke aloft did steeme,
That signe of last outbreathed life did seeme,
Vnto the watchman on the castle wall;
Who thereby dead that balefull Beast did deeme,
And to his Lord and Lady lowd gan call,
To tell, how he had seene the Dragons fatall fall.

3

Vprose with hasty ioy, and feeble speed
That aged Syre, the Lord of all that land,
And looked forth, to weet, if trew indeed
Those tydinges were, as he did vnderstand,
Which whenas trew by tryall he out fond,
He badd to open wyde his brasen gate,
Which long time had beene shut, and out of hond
Proclaymed ioy and peace through all his state;
For dead now was their foe, which them forrayed late.

4

Then gan triumphant Trompets sownd on hye,
That sent to heuen the ecchoed report
Of their new ioy, and happie victory
Gainst him, that had them long opprest with tort,
And fast imprisoned in sieged fort.
Then all the people, as in solemne feast,
To him assembled with one full consort,
Reioycing at the fall of that great beast,
From whose eternall bondage now they were releast.

Book I Canto xii

Argument

J. Dixon 1964 glosses: 'a fiction of our Queene Eliz: the maintainer of the gospell of Christe, to be by god himselfe betrouthed unto Christe, though by k[ing] p[hilip] and r[oman] c[atholics] for 6 yeares it was debared'. On the six years, see 18.6–8n. **sleightes**: wiles.

Stanza 1

On this traditional figure of the poet undertaking a voyage, see 'ship imagery' in the *SEnc*. On its dominance in the poem, see Edwards 1997:19–49. The motif by which S. relates himself to his poem by comparing his **wearie course** to Una **wearie of her way** concludes Bk I, and, most notably, introduces the final canto of Bk VI. 3 To **Vere** the sail is to let it out so that it holds less wind (cf. V xii 18.8); to **beare vp** 'is to bring the ship to goe large or before the wind' (J. Smith 1970:56). S. will no longer tack but run before the wind, steering directly towards the land. **5 offend**: harm, strike. **8 barke**: a small sailing vessel. **9 mery**: favourable.

Stanza 2

1–4 This is the dawn at xi 51 that heralds the knight's defeat of the dragon. **glooming**: gleaming, glowing. **6 the**

watchman: see xi 3.6–7 and *n*. **9 fatall**: also 'ordained by fate', i.e. by prophecy.

Stanza 3

2 That aged Syre: addressed as the 'king of *Eden*' (26.1), a figure, therefore, of Adam, though never so named, who is described chiefly in terms of his age, as 'auncient' (5.1) and 'hoarie' (12.2), while his Queen appears only once as 'aged' (5.1). **5 tryall**: investigation. **out fond**: found out. **7 out of hond**: immediately. **8** As the 'eternall peace and happinesse' (x 55.9) of the New Jerusalem, the type of Adam's state; cf. Lev. 25.10 which announces the jubilee: 'proclaime libertie in the land to all the inhabitants thereof'. **9 forrayed**: plundered.

Stanza 4

4 tort: wrong, injustice. **6–9** The general happiness, the playing of musical instruments, the singing, and the dancing recall Langland's account in *Piers Plowman* 18 of the joy following Christ's harrowing hell. **solemne feast**: sacred or holy festival. **consort**: accord; also the musical sense, 'concert'. **eternall**: balancing the 'long time' of 3.7. Now they are released for ever while the devil is to be tormented 'for euermore' (Rev. 20.10).

5

Forth came that auncient Lord and aged Queene,
  Arayd in antique robes downe to the grownd,
  And sad habiliments right well beseene;
  A noble crew about them waited rownd
  Of sage and sober Peres, all grauely gownd;
  Whom far before did march a goodly band
  Of tall young men, all hable armes to sownd,
  But now they laurell braunches bore in hand;
Glad signe of victory and peace in all their land.

6

Vnto that doughtie Conquerour they came,
  And him before themselues prostrating low,
  Their Lord and Patrone loud did him proclame,
  And at his feet their lawrell boughes did throw.
  Soone after them all dauncing on a row
  The comely virgins came, with girlands dight,
  As fresh as flowres in medow greene doe grow,
  When morning deaw vpon their leaues doth light:
And in their handes sweet Timbrels all vpheld on hight.

7

And them before, the fry of children yong
  Their wanton sportes and childish mirth did play,
  And to the Maydens sownding tymbrels song
  In well attuned notes, a ioyous lay,
  And made delightfull musick all the way,
  Vntill they came, where that faire virgin stood;
  As fayre *Diana* in fresh sommers day,
  Beholdes her Nymphes, enraung'd in shady wood,
Some wrestle, some do run, some bathe in christall flood.

8

So she beheld those maydens meriment
  With chearefull vew; who when to her they came,
  Themselues to ground with gracious humblesse bent
  And her ador'd by honorable name,
  Lifting to heuen her euerlasting fame:
  Then on her head they sett a girlond greene,
  And crowned her twixt earnest and twixt game;
  Who in her self-resemblance well beseene,
Did seeme such, as she was, a goodly maiden Queene.

9

And after all the raskall many ran,
  Heaped together in rude rablement,
  To see the face of that victorious man:
  Whom all admired, as from heauen sent,
  And gazd vpon with gaping wonderment.
  But when they came, where that dead Dragon lay,
  Stretcht on the ground in monstrous large extent,
  The sight with ydle feare did them dismay,
Ne durst approch him nigh, to touch, or once assay.

10

Some feard, and fledd; some feard and well it faynd;
  One that would wiser seeme, then all the rest,
  Warnd him not touch, for yet perhaps remaynd
  Some lingring life within his hollow brest,
  Or in his wombe might lurke some hidden nest
  Of many Dragonettes, his fruitfull seede;
  Another saide, that in his eyes did rest
  Yet sparckling fyre, and badd thereof take heed;
Another said, he saw him moue his eyes indeed.

Stanza 5
3 And sober-coloured attire very attractive to be seen.
beseene may signify 'appointed'; or, as 'beseem', appropriate
to their state (cf. 8.8). **7** . . . all able to strike arms in battle,
i.e. to fight, as knights clash their shields at iv 40.3; cf. xi 9.8.
tall: also comely, handsome; good at arms.

Stanza 6
1 Conquerour: S.'s choice of this term may have been sug-
gested by Langland, who speaks of Christ as 'conquerour
called of quikke & of ded' because he gave Adam and Eve
'blisse, | That longe hadde leyne bifore as lucyferes cherles'
(19.53–55). Skeat 2.266 notes that Langland supposed that
the name 'Christ' signifies 'conquerour'. Only Arthur is also so
named, at II viii 51.2 and xi 48.1. **3–4** Cf. Christ's entry into
Jerusalem at John 12.13. See 13.4*n*. **Patrone**: protector,
defender; as the Red Cross Knight addresses Arthur, 'my Lord,
the Patrone of my life' at ix 17.6. **8 light**: settle; shine.
9 Timbrels: tambourines. Associated with giving thanks to
God for victory, as Exod. 15.20. At 1 Sam. 18.6, the women
come 'singing and dancing to mete King Saul, with timbrels,
with instruments of ioye'.

Stanza 7
2 wanton: playful. **4–5** On the linking of vocal and instrumental
music also at 13.2–3, see 38.6–39.9*n*. **8 enraung'd**: ranging.

Stanza 8
3 humblesse: humility. **4 by honorable name**: with titles of
honour. **6–9** In contrast to the earlier mock crowning with
'Yuie girlond' at i 48.9 and 'oliue girlond' at vi 13.9. **greene**
because 'the greene is for maydens meete' (*SC Aug.* 68). **her
self-resemblance**: i.e. resembling her true self. **well beseene**:
see 5.3*n*. Her state is parodied by Duessa: 'I that do seeme not
I' (v 26.6). Crowned in the pastoral game, she appears as she
is, a **maiden Queene**, as does Elisa in the *SC Apr.* 57, and the
bride in *Epith* 157–58. See 'appearance' in the *SEnc*.

Stanza 9
1 raskall many: rabble throng. **2 rablement**: confusion.
3 that victorious man: glossed 'Christe' by J. Dixon 1964.
4 admired: viewed with wonder. **8 ydle**: baseless. **9 once
assay**: i.e. even venture to touch.

Stanza 10
1 faynd: concealed. **6 Dragonettes**: young dragons.

11

One mother, whenas her foolehardy chyld
  Did come too neare, and with his talants play
  Halfe dead through feare, her litle babe reuyld,
  And to her gossibs gan in counsell say;
  How can I tell, but that his talants may
  Yet scratch my sonne, or rend his tender hand.
  So diuersly them selues in vaine they fray;
  Whiles some more bold, to measure him nigh stand,
To proue how many acres he did spred of land.

12

Thus flocked all the folke him rownd about,
  The whiles that hoarie king, with all his traine,
  Being arriued, where that champion stout
  After his foes defeasaunce did remaine,
  Him goodly greetes, and fayre does entertayne,
  With princely gifts of yuory and gold,
  And thousand thankes him yeeldes for all his paine.
  Then when his daughter deare he does behold,
Her dearely doth imbrace, and kisseth manifold.

13

And after to his Pallace he them bringes,
  With shaumes, and trompets, and with Clarions sweet;
  And all the way the ioyous people singes,
  And with their garments strowes the paued street:
  Whence mounting vp, they fynd purueyaunce meet
  Of all, that royall Princes court became,
  And all the floore was vnderneath their feet
  Bespredd with costly scarlott of great name,
On which they lowly sitt, and fitting purpose frame.

14

What needes me tell their feast and goodly guize,
  In which was nothing riotous nor vaine?
  What needes of dainty dishes to deuize,
  Of comely seruices, or courtly trayne?

My narrow leaues cannot in them contayne
  The large discourse of roiall Princes state.
  Yet was their manner then but bare and playne:
  For th'antique world excesse and pryde did hate;
Such proud luxurious pompe is swollen vp but late.

15

Then when with meates and drinkes of euery kinde
  Their feruent appetites they quenched had,
  That auncient Lord gan fit occasion finde,
  Of straunge aduentures, and of perils sad,
  Which in his trauell him befallen had,
  For to demaund of his renowmed guest:
  Who then with vtt'rance graue, and count'nance sad,
  From poynt to poynt, as is before exprest,
Discourst his voyage long, according his request.

16

Great pleasure mixt with pittifull regard,
  That godly King and Queene did passionate,
  Whyles they his pittifull aduentures heard,
  That oft they did lament his lucklesse state,
  And often blame the too importune fate,
  That heapd on him so many wrathfull wreakes:
  For neuer gentle knight, as he of late,
  So tossed was in fortunes cruell freakes;
And all the while salt teares bedeawd the hearers cheaks.

17

Then sayd that royall Pere in sober wise;
  Deare Sonne, great beene the euils, which ye bore
  From first to last in your late enterprise,
  That I note, whether praise, or pitty more:
  For neuer liuing man, I weene, so sore
  In sea of deadly daungers was distrest;
  But since now safe ye seised haue the shore,
  And well arriued are, (high God be blest)
Let vs deuize of ease and euerlasting rest.

Stanza 11

4 gossibs: earlier form of gossips *1596*, i.e. cronies. **in counsell**: privately. **7 fray**: frighten.

Stanza 12

4 defeasaunce: defeat, adapting the earlier legal sense, 'to render a claim null and void' to mark the end of the dragon's usurpation of Una kingdom. **6 yuory and gold**: traditional gifts, as 1 Kings 10.22. **9 manifold**: many times over, rather than 'in many ways', as the *OED* claims.

Stanza 13

2 shaumes: a kind of oboe; cf. Ps. 98.6: 'With shalmes and sounde of trumpets sing loude before the Lord the King'. **4** Cf. Luke 19.36: 'And as he [Christ] went, they spred their clothes in the way'. J. Dixon 1964 cites Rev. 19.4, 5. **5 purueyaunce**: provisions. **8 scarlott**: a rich cloth. **of great name**: well-known, of great value. **9 fitting purpose**: seemly conversation.

Stanza 14

1 guize: behaviour. **3 deuize**: tell. **4 seruices**: courses. **6 large discourse**: lengthy account. **8 th'antique world**: see

V proem 1*n*. **9 luxurious**: extravagant; excessive. **but late**: apparently alluding to Elizabeth's court. Elsewhere S. refers more diplomatically to the corruption of 'later ages' (II vii 16.6) or of 'later age' (III i 13.8).

Stanza 15

1–2 In accord with the epic convention of eating before telling stories. **7 sad**: grave, serious, in keeping with his tale of **perils sad**. **8 as . . . exprest**: addressed to the reader of Bk I, for the knight does not tell the whole story, **From poynt to poynt** or 'From first to last' (17.3); see 31.8–9*n*. **9 according**: granting.

Stanza 16

2 passionate: express with passion; possibly, 'fill with compassion'. **5 importune**: grievous. **6 wrathfull wreakes**: injuries or vengeful acts that express fate's wrath; cf. viii 43.3. Only Despaire claims that the knight suffers by his own fault. **7 of late**: a topical reference for S.'s first readers, as 14.9, 33.5, and viii 6.5.

Stanza 17

1 that royall Pere: both Una's *père* and head of the 'Peres' at 5.5, here marking the supremacy of British kings over the

18

Ah dearest Lord, said then that doughty knight,
  Of ease or rest I may not yet deuize;
  For by the faith, which I to armes haue plight,
  I bownden am streight after this emprize,
  As that your daughter can ye well aduize,
  Backe to retourne to that great Faery Queene,
  And her to serue six yeares in warlike wize,
  Gainst that proud Paynim king, that works her teene:
Therefore I ought craue pardon, till I there haue beene.

19

Vnhappy falls that hard necessity,
  (Quoth he) the troubler of my happy peace,
  And vowed foe of my felicity;
  Ne I against the same can iustly preace:
  But since that band ye cannot now release,
  Nor doen vndoe; (for vowes may not be vayne)
  Soone as the terme of those six yeares shall cease,
  Ye then shall hether backe retourne agayne,
The marriage to accomplish vowd betwixt you twayn.

20

Which for my part I couet to performe,
  In sort as through the world I did proclame,
  That who so kild that monster most deforme,
  And him in hardy battayle ouercame,
  Should haue mine onely daughter to his Dame,
  And of my kingdome heyre apparaunt bee:
  Therefore since now to thee perteynes the same,
  By dew desert of noble cheualree,
Both daughter and eke kingdome, lo I yield to thee.

21

Then forth he called that his daughter fayre,
  The fairest *Vn'* his onely daughter deare,
  His onely daughter, and his only hayre;
  Who forth proceeding with sad sober cheare,
  As bright as doth the morning starre appeare
  Out of the East, with flaming lockes bedight,
  To tell that dawning day is drawing neare,
  And to the world does bring long wished light;
So faire and fresh that Lady shewd her selfe in sight.

22

So faire and fresh, as freshest flowre in May;
  For she had layd her mournefull stole aside,
  And widow-like sad wimple throwne away,
  Wherewith her heauenly beautie she did hide,
  Whiles on her wearie iourney she did ride;
  And on her now a garment she did weare,
  All lilly white, withoutten spot, or pride,
  That seemd like silke and siluer wouen neare,
But neither silke nor siluer therein did appeare.

---

church, as Cain 1978:76 notes. **2 euils**: misfortunes. **4 note**: know not. **5–6** Agreeing with Despaire at ix 45.3–4 but not with his inference. **7–9 safe**: also 'saved' in the theological sense, 'delivered from sin'. **seised**: reached. **deuize**: talk. **euerlasting rest**: his state in heaven; cf. x 62.7.

Stanza 18
4 streight: immediately. At x 63.4, 64.3, he had promised to begin his 'last long voiage' to heaven 'shortly' after aiding Una. **emprize**: enterprise; see ix 1.4*n*. **6–8 sixe**: possibly referring to the six years of Mary Tudor's reign; see xi 7.2–6*n* and xii Arg.*n*. Or to the six days of the creation before the seventh day of 'euerlasting rest' (17.9); see Heb. 4.1–9. Or to the last of the traditional seven ages of the world from Adam to Christ, as in the 'Supputation [calculation] of the yeares' in the Geneva Bible. **teene**: harm, injury.

Stanza 19
4 preace: press, contend. **6 not be vayne**: i.e. not be made vain, as enjoined at Num. 30.3. The stress on the knight's vow prepares for the revelation of his 'bloody vowes' (30.1) to Duessa. **9 accomplish**: the term distinguishes wedlock that is contracted or performed (as the next line indicates; cf. 'betrouthed', Arg.2) and that which is completed, i.e. consummated; cf. III ix 42.4–7. See 40.4–5*n*. The distinction is clear in the Geneva gloss to Rev. 19.7: 'God made Christ the bridgrome of his Church at the beginning, and at the last day it shalbe fully accomplished when we shal be ioyned with our head'. The fulfilment of a life of holiness in marriage was an Elizabethan commonplace.

Stanza 20
2–5 That a dragon-slayer be rewarded by a princess **to his Dame**, i.e. as his wife, is a familiar romance motif. S. would

have found it in *Bevis of Hamtoun* (see *Var* 1.395–96), or Hawes, *The Example of Vertue* (see Kaske 1989:129–33). **In sort as**: in the way that; even as. **9** J. Dixon 1964 glosses: 'the true Church and heauen'.

Stanza 21
1–5 Earlier Una is called 'th'onely daughter of a King and Queene' (vii 43.3). **onely** gives her her name and suggests also that she is 'peerless', 'incomparable' (*OED* 5). Repeated twice with the final emphasis on **only hayre**, she is named as the one true church of the English nation, as McEachern 1996:82 notes. In Song Sol. 6.8–9, the bride, traditionally identified as the church, is praised as 'the onelie daughter of her mother' . . . [who] loketh forthe as the morning'. **sad sober cheare** expresses her womanhood; see IV x 49.5–9. **sad**: steadfast, constant. **5–9** In Rev. 2.28, Christ promises to give his followers the morning star. In *View* 84, Eudoxus laments that the papists have not been 'lightened with the morning star of truth', implying, of course, that protestants have.

Stanza 22
Cf. Rev. 19.7–8: 'the mariage of the Lambe is come, and his wife hathe made her self readie. And to her was granted, that she shulde be araied with pure fyne linen and shining'. **7 All lilly white**: as Fidelia appears; see x 13.1*n*. **withoutten**: an emphatic form, 'entirely without'. **spot, or pride**: blemish or ostentatious ornament, indicating that she is immaculate as is the church in Song Sol. 4.7: 'Thou art all faire, my loue, and there is no spot in thee', and as the Queen in *SC Apr.* 50. At III iv 59.8, Truth is called 'Most sacred virgin, without spot of sinne'. On the association with the iconography of the Virgin Mary as the Bride of Christ, and the cult of Elizabeth as the second Virgin Mary, see Wells 1983:31, and McClure and Wells 1990:43. **8 neare**: closely.

23

The blazing brightnesse of her beauties beame,
    And glorious light of her sunshyny face
    To tell, were as to striue against the streame.
    My ragged rimes are all too rude and bace,
    Her heauenly lineaments for to enchace.
    Ne wonder; for her own deare loued knight,
    All were she daily with himselfe in place,
    Did wonder much at her celestiall sight:
Oft had he seene her faire, but neuer so faire dight.

24

So fairely dight, when she in presence came,
    She to her Syre made humble reuerence,
    And bowed low, that her right well became,
    And added grace vnto her excellence:
    Who with great wisedome, and graue eloquence
    Thus gan to say. But eare he thus had sayd,
    With flying speede, and seeming great pretence,
    Came running in, much like a man dismayd,
A Messenger with letters, which his message sayd.

25

All in the open hall amazed stood,
    At suddeinnesse of that vnwary sight,
    And wondred at his breathlesse hasty mood.
    But he for nought would stay his passage right,
    Till fast before the king he did alight;
    Where falling flat, great humblesse he did make,
    And kist the ground, whereon his foot was pight;
    Then to his handes that writt he did betake,
Which he disclosing, read thus, as the paper spake.

26

To thee, most mighty king of *Eden* fayre,
    Her greeting sends in these sad lines addrest,
    The wofull daughter, and forsaken heyre
    Of that great Emperour of all the West;
    And bids thee be aduized for the best,
    Ere thou thy daughter linck in holy band
    Of wedlocke to that new vnknowen guest:
    For he already plighted his right hand
Vnto another loue, and to another land.

27

To me sad mayd, or rather widow sad,
    He was affyaunced long time before,
    And sacred pledges he both gaue, and had,
    False erraunt knight, infamous, and forswore:
    Witnesse the burning Altars, which he swore,
    And guilty heauens of his bold periury,
    Which though he hath polluted oft of yore,
    Yet I to them for iudgement iust doe fly,
And them coniure t'auenge this shamefull iniury.

28

Therefore since mine he is, or free or bond,
    Or false or trew, or liuing or else dead,
    Withhold, O souerayne Prince, your hasty hond
    From knitting league with him, I you aread;
    Ne weene my right with strength adowne to tread,
    Through weakenesse of my widowhed, or woe:
    For truth is strong, her rightfull cause to plead,
    And shall finde friends, if need requireth soe.
So bids thee well to fare, Thy neither friend, nor foe,
                                   Fidessa.

Stanza 23

1–3 At *HHB* 170, light from eternal truth is said to be 'many thousand times more bright, more cleare' than that of the sun. At last Una is seen by her knight as she really is: 'clothed with the sunne' (Rev. 12.1). Cf. the 'blazing brightnesse' of Arthur's unveiled shield at viii 19.4.   **4 ragged**: rough to the ear; cf. III ii 3.6.   **5 for to enchace**: to serve as a setting for; hence 'display' or 'adorn'.

Stanza 24

1 in presence: in the sense of attending upon royalty. **5–6** He is about to bid the banns, as 36.6–7 makes clear, when Archimago enters with an impediment why the knight and Una may not be lawfully joined together in matrimony. **7 pretence**: purpose; claim to importance.

Stanza 25

2 vnwary: unexpected. A unique usage adapted from the current sense, 'unguarded', 'incautious' referring to the spectators.   **4 right**: direct, straightforward.   **5 alight**: arrive, stop. Another unique usage, either forced by the rhyme or doggedly literal: he descends from his 'flying speede' (24.7).   **8 betake**: deliver.   **9 disclosing**: unfolding.

Stanzas 26–28

Duessa's letter, which stands apart from the other stanzas by its hypermetric signature, *Fidessa*, was interpreted by one of its earliest readers, J. Dixon, as a challenge by Mary Queen of Scots 'that the religion by hir maintained to be the truth'. Jonson told Drummond that in a paper given to Raleigh 'by the false Duessa [was understood] the Q of Scots' (1925–52:1.137).

Stanza 26

3–4 Cf. ii 22.7–9.   **8–9** Donne employs this metaphor in 'Batter my heart': 'dearely I love you, and would be loved faine, | But am betroth'd unto your enemie'. **to another land**: i.e. the fallen world, which the knight is 'in' but not 'of'.

Stanza 27

1 widow: cf. her role as a 'virgin widow' (ii 24.8).   **4 infamous**: with the earlier stress on the second syllable. **forswore**: forsworn.   **5 which**: by which (a Latinism). The altars burn with sacrifices that confirm the marriage vows.   **6** 'And witness also the heavens by which he swore and so made guilty', etc., implying that the heavens will punish his guilt. Cf. Despaire's charge: 'Thou falsed hast thy faith with periurie' (ix 46.7).   **9 coniure**: implore; also invoke by supernatural power, as she is a witch.   **iniury**: also offensive speech, specifically perjury.

Stanza 28

1 bond: bound.   **4 league**: a marriage covenant, as II iv 18.6, *Am* 65.10.   **aread**: counsel.   **7** Proverbial: Smith 792; cf. III i 29.8.   **9 well to fare**: farewell.

29

When he these bitter byting wordes had red,
 The tydings straunge did him abashed make,
 That still he sate long time astonished
 As in great muse, ne word to creature spake.
 At last his solemne silence thus he brake,
 With doubtfull eyes fast fixed on his guest;
 Redoubted knight, that for myne only sake
 Thy life and honor late aduenturest,
Let nought be hid from me, that ought to be exprest.

30

What meane these bloody vowes, and idle threats,
 Throwne out from womanish impatient mynd?
 What heuens? what altars? what enraged heates
 Here heaped vp with termes of loue vnkynd,
 My conscience cleare with guilty bands would bynd?
 High God be witnesse, that I guiltlesse ame.
 But if your selfe, Sir knight, ye faulty fynd,
 Or wrapped be in loues of former Dame,
With cryme doe not it couer, but disclose the same.

31

To whom the *Redcrosse* knight this answere sent,
 My Lord, my king, be nought hereat dismayd,
 Till well ye wote by graue intendiment,
 What woman, and wherefore doth me vpbrayd
 With breach of loue, and loialty betrayd.
 It was in my mishaps, as hitherward
 I lately traueild, that vnwares I strayd
 Out of my way, through perils straunge and hard;
That day should faile me, ere I had them all declard.

32

There did I find, or rather I was fownd
 Of this false woman, that *Fidessa* hight,
 Fidessa hight the falsest Dame on grownd,
 Most false *Duessa*, royall richly dight,
 That easy was t'inueigle weaker sight:
 Who by her wicked arts, and wiely skill,
 Too false and strong for earthly skill or might,
 Vnwares me wrought vnto her wicked will,
And to my foe betrayd, when least I feared ill.

33

Then stepped forth the goodly royall Mayd,
 And on the ground her selfe prostrating low,
 With sober countenaunce thus to him sayd;
 O pardon me, my soueraine Lord, to sheow
 The secret treasons, which of late I know
 To haue bene wrought by that false sorceresse.
 Shee onely she it is, that earst did throw
 This gentle knight into so great distresse,
That death him did awaite in daily wretchednesse.

34

And now it seemes, that she suborned hath
 This crafty messenger with letters vaine,
 To worke new woe and improuided scath,
 By breaking of the band betwixt vs twaine;
 Wherein she vsed hath the practicke paine
 Of this false footman, clokt with simplenesse,
 Whome if ye please for to discouer plaine,
 Ye shall him *Archimago* find, I ghesse,
The falsest man aliue; who tries shall find no lesse.

Stanza 29
4 muse: astonishment. **5** In Orgoglio's castle, the 'solemne silence' at viii 29.8 similarly marks a turning-point in the knight's progress. **7 Redoubted**: dread, with a pun on 'being doubted', as i 53.5. **for myne only sake**: for my sake alone.

Stanza 30
4 vnkynd: ungrateful; unnaturally wicked. **6** 'That godly King' (16.2) calls upon **High God**, not the pagan 'heauens' of 27.6. **7 faulty**: guilty. **8 former Dame**: Duessa was 'his Dame' at vii 7.1; as Una is now, 20.5. **9 cryme**: i.e. the crime of perjury.

Stanza 31
1 answere: in the legal sense, 'a reply made to a charge' (*OED* 1). **2** The possessives reject Duessa's claim that he is plighted 'to another land' (26.9). **3 intendiment**: careful consideration. **7 vnwares**: without his knowledge; or 'suddenly', referring to his hasty flight from Una; cf. 32.8. **8–9** The omission of any reference to Duessa in his 'poynt to poynt' account of his 'straunge aduentures, and of perils sad' (15.4, 8) indicates that the knight is not yet wedded to truth. Even the memory of his sin seems to have been purged in the house of Holinesse until he is now reminded of it. At 32.9, he recalls the precise moment when he lay with Duessa, vii 7. See J. Miller 1986b:279–81, and Suttie 1998:71–73.

Stanza 32
4 royall richly dight: royally and richly dressed; dressed with royal richness. **5 inueigle**: beguile; blind; cf. vii 50.9. **weaker**: too weak. **6–7** I.e. her arts were too strong for earthly might, and her skill too false for earthly skill.

Stanza 33
1 Being named the **royall Mayd**, in contrast to Duessa who is only dressed as such, proclaims her the one to whom the knight owes his allegiance. **4 pardon me**: give me leave. Her humble posture contrasts with Duessa's proud presumption in counselling the King of Eden at 26.5. **7–9** Cf. viii 28.6–7.

Stanza 34
In a suit of law, an appellant was required to abjure enchantments and rely only on the justness of the cause. Duessa's case is overturned by showing that her messenger is disguised. As she is 'the falsest Dame on grownd' (32.3), he is **The falsest man aliue**. **2 vaine**: i.e. in vain or false. **3 improuided**: unforeseen. **scath**: harm. **5 practicke paine**: crafty pains. **7 discouer**: literally, 'remove the cover from'.

35

The king was greatly moued at her speach,
    And all with suddein indignation fraight,
    Bad on that Messenger rude hands to reach.
    Eftsoones the Gard, which on his state did wait,
    Attacht that faytor false, and bound him strait:
    Who seeming sorely chauffed at his band,
    As chained beare, whom cruell dogs doe bait,
    With ydle force did faine them to withstand,
And often semblaunce made to scape out of their hand.

36

But they him layd full low in dungeon deepe,
    And bound him hand and foote with yron chaines.
    And with continual watch did warely keepe;
    Who then would thinke, that by his subtile trains
    He could escape fowle death or deadly pains?
    Thus when that Princes wrath was pacifide,
    He gan renew the late forbidden bains,
    And to the knight his daughter deare he tyde,
With sacred rites and vowes for euer to abyde.

37

His owne two hands the holy knotts did knitt,
    That none but death for euer can diuide;
    His owne two hands, for such a turne most fitt,
    The housling fire did kindle and prouide,

And holy water thereon sprinckled wide;
    At which the bushy Teade a groome did light,
    And sacred lamp in secret chamber hide,
    Where it should not be quenched day nor night,
For feare of euill fates, but burnen euer bright.

38

Then gan they sprinckle all the posts with wine,
    And made great feast to solemnize that day;
    They all perfumde with frankincense diuine,
    And precious odours fetcht from far away,
    That all the house did sweat with great aray:
    And all the while sweete Musicke did apply
    Her curious skill, the warbling notes to play,
    To driue away the dull Melancholy;
The whiles one sung a song of loue and iollity.

39

During the which there was an heauenly noise
    Heard sownd through all the Pallace pleasantly,
    Like as it had bene many an Angels voice,
    Singing before th'eternall maiesty,
    In their trinall triplicities on hye;
    Yett wist no creature, whence that heuenly sweet
    Proceeded, yet eachone felt secretly
    Himselfe thereby refte of his sences meet,
And rauished with rare impression in his sprite.

Stanza 35
5 **Attacht**: seized. **faytor**: impostor. **6–9** In his falseness, he only pretended (**did faine**) to resist, as he only **seeming**, i.e. seemingly, chafed at his bonds, and made only **semblaunce** to escape. The reference to the popular sport of bear-baiting – see II xi 33.3–6 – suggests to the contrary that he was angered and sought without avail to resist the guard. **ydle force**: force used idly.

Stanza 36
1–5 The pattern for the action is given by Rev. 20.1–3: 'I sawe an Angel come downe from heauen, hauing . . . a great chaine in his hand. And he toke the dragon that olde serpent, which is the devil and Satan, and he bounde him a thousand yeres, And cast him into the bottomles pit . . . til the thousand yeres were fulfilled'. The question in 4–5 indicates that Archimago will escape; see II i 1 and the rest of Rev. 20.3: 'for after that he must be losed for a litle season'; cf. 1 John 2.18. According to the Geneva gloss, 'the thousand yeres' refers to the time from Christ's nativity to Pope Sylvester II during which 'the pure doctrine shulde after a sorte remaine'. Roughly the same length of time separates the time of Arthur in the sixth century from Elizabeth's reign in the sixteenth century; see III iii 26–50n. **warely**: watchfully. **subtile trains**: as vii 26.2. **7–9** Writing c. 1597 and alluding to Elizabeth's accession in 1558, J. Dixon 1964 glosses: 'The Church and the Lambe Christe united by god himsellfe. a happy knotte wherby peace hath beine Continewed 39 yea[res]'. **renew**: repeat. **bains**: banns of marriage. **rites and vowes**: cancelling what Duessa claimed to be her 'right' (28.5) to him and his 'bloody vowes' (30.1).

Stanza 37
3 **turne**: act; task. **4–5** The fire and water of the Roman marriage rites are adapted for a Christian marriage: **housling fire**:

'sacramental' fire (OED 2) may allude to the Easter eucharist, as Weatherby 1994:65–68 argues, in contrast to Duessa's 'burning Altars' (27.5); and **holy water** to baptism that sanctifies wedded love. Una's father serves as priest in order to confirm that she is the true church; see I ii 22.7–9n, and McAuley 1974. **6 Teade**: the nuptial torch. **7–9** Cf. Lev. 6.13: 'The fire shal euer burne vpon the altar, and neuer go out'.

Stanza 38
1–5 Cf. *Epith* 253–54: 'sprinkle all the postes and wals with wine, | That they may sweat, and drunken be withall'. The Roman custom in which the bride anoints the doorposts of her new home becomes a festive act by the wedding guests who anoint the bridal bed to promote fertility. **all**: if not taken absolutely, as 'all being perfumed', but objectively, 'everything', **sweat** refers to the sprinkled perfumes of the marriage preparations. **diuine**: the epithet is deserved since the gift was given to the Christ child at Matt. 2.11. **6–39.9** The progression from the music of timbrels (7.3–5) attuned to human voices, to the wind instruments orchestrated with voices (13.2–3), to personified **sweete Musicke**, and finally, in response, the heavenly harmonies is noted by Hollander 1971:227–28. See II xii 71n. **7 curious**: elaborate, intricate. **8** This line describes the festivities at the house of Pride at v 3.5. **9** The song is the epithalamium.

Stanza 39
Alluding to the song at the marriage of the Lamb (Rev. 19.6–7), with Christ typified in the knight and the church in Una. It may suggest the earlier view of marriage as a sacrament at which God's grace was bestowed upon a couple. The music of the spheres in its ninefold harmony has not been audible since the Fall, and in the poem is heard only here. The

40

Great ioy was made that day of young and old,
 And solemne feast proclaymd throughout the land,
 That their exceeding merth may not be told:
 Suffice it heare by signes to vnderstand
 The vsuall ioyes at knitting of loues band.
 Thrise happy man the knight himselfe did hold,
 Possessed of his Ladies hart and hand,
 And euer, when his eie did her behold,
His heart did seeme to melt in pleasures manifold.

41

Her ioyous presence and sweet company
 In full content he there did long enioy,
 Ne wicked enuy, ne vile gealosy
 His deare delights were hable to annoy:

Yet swimming in that sea of blisfull ioy,
 He nought forgott, how he whilome had sworne,
 In case he could that monstrous beast destroy,
 Vnto his Faery Queene backe to retourne:
The which he shortly did, and *Vna* left to mourne.

42

Now strike your sailes yee iolly Mariners,
 For we be come vnto a quiet rode,
 Where we must land some of our passengers,
 And light this weary vessell of her lode.
 Here she a while may make her safe abode,
 Till she repaired haue her tackles spent,
 And wants supplide. And then againe abroad
 On the long voiage whereto she is bent:
Well may she speede and fairely finish her intent.

Faery Queen

---

apocalyptic dimensions of the moment are noted by H. Hendrix 1990:166. As a sacred marriage (in Jungian terms), which unites not only man and woman 'but also conscious and unconscious, light and dark, heaven and earth', see Lockerd 1987:121. **1 noise**: melodious sound; parodied at v 17.6–7. **5 trinall triplicities**: triple triad, the nine orders of angels divided into three threefold hierarchies. See *HHL* 64–70, and 'angels' in the *SEnc*. **6 sweet**: sweet sound.

Stanza 40

The stanza number is associated with marriage because Isaac was forty when he married Rebecca (Gen. 25.20), or because it marks the fulfilment of love: 'the sphaere of Cupid fourty yeares containes' (*Am* 60.10). **1** J. Dixon 1964 glosses: 'The daye of the Crownation of our bleesed princess Eliz'. W. Camden records that the Queen spoke of that day as her marriage 'unto an Husband, which is the Kingdome of England'; noted but challenged by King 1990b:33–36. **2 solemne feast**: sacred festival, as 4.6. **4–5 signes**: tokens; but more

specifically indications of a coming event. The betrothal celebrated now is only a token of the later consummation of the marriage. The **knitting of loues band** comes only after the knight is free from all other bonds. **9** The line recalls the parody of his present state at i 47.4–6.

Stanza 41

5 Cf. the 'sea of deadly daungers' (17.6) which had distressed him. **6–8** Recalling his vow revealed at 18.3–8; cf. II i 1.4–6.

Stanza 42

The number has apocalyptic significance for Antichrist's tyranny ends after forty-two months, according to Rev. 11.2 and gloss; noted Cain 1978:81–82. The vered sails of the opening stanza are struck now the ship is **safe** (cf. i 5). The King of Eden notes that the knight, having suffered 'In sea of deadly daungers . . . now safe ye seised haue the shore' (17.6–7). **2 rode**: roadstead, place of safe anchorage. **8 the long voiage**: preparing for Guyon's voyage at II i 34.3, etc.

The image of St George killing the dragon is the only woodcut in the *1590* and *1596* editions. As reproduced here, it appears on a page by itself, the verso side of the last page of Bk I facing the opening of Bk II. The printer, John Wolfe, had used it earlier, and used it again to illustrate news pamphlets, one treating the popular French Protestant king, Henri IV; see V xi 44–65*n*, Voss 1996:66–67, and Luborsky and Ingram 1998:1.311. On the continuing popularity of the story of George and the Dragon, see Murrin 1997:6–9.

The second Booke

of the Faerie Queene.

Contayning

The Legend of Sir Guyon.

OR

Of Temperaunce.

1

Ight well I wote most mighty Soueraine,
That all this famous antique history,
Of some th'aboundance of an ydle braine
Will iudged be, and painted forgery,
Rather then matter of iust memory,
Sith none, that breatheth liuing aire, does know,
Where is that happy land of Faery,
Which I so much doe vaunt, yet no where show,
But vouch antiquities, which no body can know.

first-person narrator

2

But let that man with better sence aduize,
That of the world least part to vs is red:
And daily how through hardy enterprize,
Many great Regions are discouered,
Which to late age were neuer mentioned.
Who euer heard of th'Indian *Peru*?
Or who in venturous vessell measured
The *Amazons* huge riuer now found trew?
Or fruitfullest *Virginia* who did euer vew?

Book II Title

Sir: the accepted title of a knight but used on the title-page only for Guyon.

Proem

Stanza 1

2 antique history: see V proem 1*n*. **4 painted forgery**: deceiving invention. On S.'s fear that his poem would be dismissed as such, see Hulse 1994:95–96. **5 iust memory**: i.e. as a true record. **6–9** At VI proem 2.9, S. claims that no one can find the strange ways in faery land 'but who was taught them by the Muse'. **land of Faery**: see Murrin 1980:131–52, J. Miller 1986a:90–101, 'fairyland' in the *SEnc*, and Erickson 1996:60–64. As Hedley 1988:18 notes, it is at once an 'an-tique image' and a 'new world'. Its connection with India and therefore with nascent British imperialism is argued by Bellamy 2000. **vaunt**: display; praise. **antiquities**: referring to the muse's 'antique rolles' that he seeks at I proem 2.4 and her 'records of antiquitie' at IV xi 10.1–5.

Stanza 2

Parallels with Humphrey Gilbert's 1576 account of New World discoveries are noted by S. Miller 1998:36–37. **1 aduize**: consider; reflect. **2 red**: told, and therefore 'made known'. **6 th'Indian Peru**: Peru was believed to be India. Martin Cortés boasts of Spanish discoveries: 'Who before this tyme ever harde .. of . . . *Peru*?' in *Arte of Navigation*, tr. Richard Eden, 1561; noted Hutson 1996:30. **7 measured**: travelled; also, 'deter-mined its length'. **8 now found trew**: in 1541 by Orellana. In 1555 Eden referred to 'the myghty ryuer cauled Flumen Amazonum, found of late'; noted Read 2000:136*n*9.

direct address

3

Yet all these were when no man did them know,
    Yet haue from wisest ages hidden beene
    And later times thinges more vnknowne shall show.
    Why then should witlesse man so much misweene
    That nothing is but that which he hath seene?
    What if within the Moones fayre shining spheare,
    What if in euery other starre vnseene
    Of other worldes he happily should heare?
He wonder would much more, yet such to some appeare.

4

Of faery lond yet if he more inquyre
    By certein signes here sett in sondrie place
    He may it fynd; ne let him then admyre
    But yield his sence to bee too blunt and bace

That no'te without an hound fine footing trace.
    And thou, O fayrest Princesse vnder sky,
    In this fayre mirrhour maist behold thy face
    And thine owne realmes in lond of Faery,
And in this antique ymage thy great auncestry.

5

The which O pardon me thus to enfold
    In couert vele and wrap in shadowes light,
    That feeble eyes your glory may behold
    Which ells could not endure those beames bright
    But would bee dazled with exceeding light.
    O pardon and vouchsafe with patient eare
    The braue aduentures of this faery knight
    The good Sir *Guyon* gratiously to heare
In whom great rule of Temp'raunce goodly doth appeare.

---

9 Virginia: this reference, and the addition 'and of Virginia' to the titles of Elizabeth in the *1596* dedication, are among the first in literature. **fruitfullest**: in an early account of Virginia, Barlowe refers to its soil as 'the most . . . fruitfull . . . of all the world'; cited J.N. Wall 1984:2*n*6.

Stanza 3
4–5 Cf. Ariosto's mockery, *Orl. Fur.* 7.1, of the foolish throng that rejects travellers' reports of strange sights together with his poem because they believe only what they see. Chaucer makes much the same complaint in the *Legend of Good Women, Prol.* 12–15. As line 6 suggests, **witlesse** may refer specifically to those on the moon who have lost their wits in *Orl. Fur.* 34. **misweene**: wrongly judge. **6–9** S.'s first question expresses a contemporary interest in the moon as habitable; see Nicolson 1936:36–43. The second is one of the earliest references to a possible plurality of worlds; see Kocher 1953:86. Extraterrestrial life is suggested by Bruno in *Del'infinito universo et mondi* (1584), which was written and published in England. On S.'s own world-making, see R. Greene 2000. **vnseene**: i.e. worlds at present unseen. **happily**: by chance.

Stanza 4
1–3 As Christ mocks those who 'except ye se signes and wonders, ye wil not beleue' (John 4.48), S. mocks those who **inquyre** – i.e. seek after – **certein signes**, a phrase that refers to the many topical allusions in the poem but also to the twelve zodiacal signs traced by Guyon's journey, as Fisher 1993b and 1993c argues. **in sondrie place**: in different places. **admyre**: i.e. wonder at what his own senses have revealed. **5** I.e., does not know how to track faint or cunning footsteps without a hound, implying that the poet's **fine footing** in his use of metre is sufficient. **6–9 this fayre mirrhour** is the poem itself, which does more than reflect but reveals by its transparency. See 'mirrors' in the *SEnc*. The shift from I

proem 4.2 in which the mirror is the Queen is noted by Rambuss 1993:71. The Queen is invited to see her **face** in Belphœbe in canto iii, her **realmes** in 'Briton moniments' (x 5–68.2), and her **great auncestry** in the 'Antiquitee of Faery lond' (x 70–76).

Stanza 5
1–2 O pardon me: give me leave, so Una addresses the King of Eden at I xii 33.4. The **vele** may be compared to the covering that Moses put upon his face because it 'shone bright' after God had talked with him, so that the children of Israel 'were afraide to come nere him' (Exod. 34.30). In 2 Cor. 3.7, Paul writes that 'the children of Israel colde not beholde the face of Moses for the glorie of his countenance'; see Nohrnberg 1976:54–55. The common Renaissance view that poetry veils truth in its fiction – e.g. Boccaccio 1976:14.7, and S. in *DS 1* and *DS 3* – is inverted here: the poet veils light in order that his readers may see. He must reveil Elizabeth so that she may be revealed as the type of which the absent Gloriana is the antitype; see Fruen 1987. That Elizabeth was known as 'sweet sister *Temperance*', as W. Camden 1630:6 records, makes the address to her esp. fitting. **couert**: covering, concealing. **light**: with a pun, for the shadows give light. **7 this faery knight**: contrasts with the emphasis on Britain in Bk 1. **8 Guyon**: the name of a romance hero, e.g. Guy of Warwick, or Guy of Burgundy who is called 'the good Gyoun' in *Sir Firumbras* 465. It may have been chosen for its etymology for it signifies 'wrestler', according to *The Golden Legend* (see I x 66.5–6*n*): 'George may be sayd . . . of gyon that is a wrasteler'. W. Camden 1984:67 derives 'Guy' from Lat. *guido* and Fr. *guide*: 'A Guide, Leader, or Director to other'. Guyon, however, is himself guided both by the Palmer and by God (i 34.4, 32.8). A. Fowler 1960a notes that Gihon, the second of the four rivers of Eden (Gen. 2.13), was interpreted as the virtue of temperance because 'it cleanses the worthless body, and quenches the fire of vile flesh'. See 'Guyon' in the *SEnc*.

Cant. I.

Guyon by Archimage abusd,
the Redcrosse knight awaytes,
Fyndes Mordant and Amauia slaine
With pleasures poisoned baytes.

1

That conning Architect of cancred guyle,
  Whom Princes late displeasure left in bands,
For falsed letters and suborned wyle,
Soone as the *Redcrosse* knight he vnderstands,
To beene departed out of *Eden* landes,
To serue againe his soueraine Elfin Queene,
His artes he moues, and out of caytiues handes
Himselfe he frees by secret meanes vnseene;
His shackles emptie lefte, him selfe escaped cleene.

2

And forth he fares full of malicious mynd,
  To worken mischiefe and auenging woe,
Where euer he that godly knight may fynd,
His onely hart sore, and his onely foe,
Sith *Vna* now he algates must forgoe,
Whom his victorious handes did earst restore
To natiue crowne and kingdom late ygoe:
Where she enioyes sure peace for euermore,
As wetherbeaten ship arryu'd on happie shore.

3

Him therefore now the obiect of his spight
  And deadly food he makes: him to offend
By forged treason, or by open fight
He seekes, of all his drifte the aymed end:

Thereto his subtile engins he does bend
His practick witt, and his fayre fyled tonge,
With thousand other sleightes: for well he kend,
His credit now in doubtfull ballaunce hong;
For hardly could bee hurt, who was already stong.

4

Still as he went, he craftie stales did lay,
  With cunning traynes him to entrap vnwares,
And priuy spyals plast in all his way,
To weete what course he takes, and how he fares;
To ketch him at a vauntage in his snares.
But now so wise and wary was the knight
By tryall of his former harmes and cares,
That he descryde, and shonned still his slight:
The fish that once was caught, new bait wil hardly byte.

5

Nath'lesse th'Enchaunter would not spare his payne,
  In hope to win occasion to his will;
Which when he long awaited had in vayne,
He chaungd his mynd from one to other ill:
For to all good he enimy was still.
Vpon the way him fortuned to meet,
Fayre marching vnderneath a shady hill,
A goodly knight, all armd in harnesse meete,
That from his head no place appeared to his feete.

Book II Canto i

Argument

1 abusd: deceived; misused. **2 awaytes**: waylays, ambushes. **3 Mordant**: *Mortdant* at 49.9 in *1590, 1596*. **Amauia** is not named until the end of their story at ii. 45.8. On the names, see 55.4–5*n*. **4 pleasures**: i.e. Acrasia's; cf. ii 45.4. She is named 'Pleasure' at xii 1.8, 48.8; cf. iii 41.8.

Stanza 1

1 That conning Architect: alluding to his name, Archimago; see I i 43.6*n*. On his escape, see Rev. 20.1–3 (cited I xii 36.1–5*n*). **cancred**: venomous; infectious. **3** Duessa suborned Archimago to break the bond between Una and the Red Cross Knight 'with letters vaine' at I xii 34.1–2. These are **falsed** as they seek to break loyalty, and Archimago's **wyle** is **suborned** as he was engaged to bear false witness. **5 Eden landes**: see I xi 2.1*n*. **7 moues**: applies. **caytiues handes**: the hands of those who held him captive, or the hands of menials; cf. 'rude hands' (I xii 35.3).

Stanza 2

4 onely: chief, special. **5 algates**: altogether. **7 late ygoe**: lately; indicating that chronologically Bk II follows Bk I. **9** On the ship imagery in the poem, see I xii 1*n*. Here it refers back to I xii 42 and forward to 32.9.

Stanza 3

2 food: i.e. feud: hatred, hostility. This early spelling suggests 'food for death'; cf. 'pleasures poisoned baytes' (Arg.4). **offend**: injure, harm. **3 forged**: made up, invented by the 'conning Architect' (1.1). **4 drifte**: plot, purpose; as I ii 9.4 where 'Th'end of his drift' is Una. **5 subtile engins**: cunning wiles; also machines of warfare, extending the metaphor of **aymed end**. **6 practick**: crafty; cf. his 'practicke paine' (I xii 34.5). **fayre fyled**: smooth, as I i 35.7. **8 credit**: credibility.

Stanza 4

1 stales: baits, decoys. **2 traynes**: stratagems; specifically, as 1 suggests, a trail of bait to lure his prey into a trap (*OED* sb.¹ II 7). **3 priuy spyals**: hidden spies. **5 at a vauntage**: i.e. at his advantage and the knight's disadvantage. **9** Proverbial: Smith 266.

Stanza 5

7 vnderneath a shady hill: as the Wandering Wood encloses the wandering Red Cross Knight before he enters upon his quest. **8 A goodly knight**: in contrast to 'that godly knight' (2.3), noting the chief difference between Guyon and the Red Cross Knight. **all armd**: armed cap-à-pie, as Arthur at I vii 29.6, pointing here to Guyon's apparent invulnerability to external attack. **harnesse meete**: fitting armour, i.e. appropriate; also close-fitting.

6

His carriage was full comely and vpright,
  His countenance demure and temperate,
  But yett so sterne and terrible in sight,
  That cheard his friendes, and did his foes amate:
  He was an Elfin borne of noble state,
  And mickle worship in his natiue land;
  Well could he tourney and in lists debate,
  And knighthood tooke of good Sir *Huons* hand,
When with king *Oberon* he came to Fary land.

7

Him als accompanyd vpon the way
  A comely Palmer, clad in black attyre,
  Of rypest yeares, and heares all hoarie gray,
  That with a staffe his feeble steps did stire,
  Least his long way his aged limbes should tire:
  And if by lookes one may the mind aread,
  He seemd to be a sage and sober syre,
  And euer with slow pace the knight did lead,
Who taught his trampling steed with equall steps to tread.

8

Such whenas *Archimago* them did view,
  He weened well to worke some vncouth wyle,
  Eftsoones vntwisting his deceiptfull clew,
  He gan to weaue a web of wicked guyle,
  And with faire countenance and flattring style,
  To them approching, thus the knight bespake:
  Fayre sonne of *Mars*, that seeke with warlike spoyle,
  And great atchieu'ments great your selfe to make,
Vouchsafe to stay your steed for humble misers sake.

9

He stayd his steed for humble misers sake,
  And badd tell on the tenor of his playnt;
  Who feigning then in euery limb to quake,
  Through inward feare, and seeming pale and faynt
  With piteous mone his percing speach gan paynt;
  Deare Lady how shall I declare thy cace,
  Whom late I left in languorous constraynt?
  Would God thy selfe now present were in place,
To tell this ruefull tale; thy sight could win thee grace.

10

Or rather would, O would it so had chaunst,
  That you, most noble Sir, had present beene,
  When that lewd rybauld with vyle lust aduaunst
  Laid first his filthie hands on virgin cleene,
  To spoyle her dainty corps so faire and sheene,
  As on the earth, great mother of vs all,
  With liuing eye more fayre was neuer seene,
  Of chastity and honour virginall:
Witnes ye heauens, whom she in vaine to help did call.

11

How may it be, sayd then the knight halfe wroth,
  That knight should knighthood euer so haue shent?
  None but that saw (quoth he) would weene for troth,
  How shamefully that Mayd he did torment.
  Her looser golden lockes he rudely rent,
  And drew her on the ground, and his sharpe sword,
  Against her snowy brest he fiercely bent,
  And threatned death with many a bloodie word;
Tounge hates to tell the rest, that eye to see abhord.

Stanza 6

2 demure: serious or grave, suggesting modesty or Shame-fastnes (ix 43.9), corresponding to the Red Cross Knight's sadness. The term describes Fidelia and Speranza (I x 12.4), its only other use in the poem. **temperate**: referring to the proper mingling of the humours as it expresses the 'great rule of Temp'raunce' (Pr. 5.9) in him. **4 amate**: daunt; cf. Artegall whose 'manly face . . . did his foes agrize' (III ii 24.4). **5–6 Elfin**: Elf or Fay, to distinguish Guyon's race from the Red Cross Knight's: see I x 65; hence **his natiue land** is faery land. On the distinction, see I i 17.1*n*. **mickle worship**: much honour. **7 debate**: fight. **8–9 Sir Huon**: the hero of the thirteenth-century romance *Huon of Burdeux* (English tr. 1534), favoured by Oberon, whom S. names king of faery land and father of Tanaquill or Gloriana at x 75, 76.

Stanza 7

2 comely: decent, decorous, as also applied to Guyon at 6.1; or, adverbially, 'suitably clad'. **Palmer**: a pilgrim (cf. 52.8); more specifically, one who has returned from the Holy Land. **black** is his identifying epithet at 34.4, etc., in contrast to Una's whiteness. **4 stire**: steer, guide. **6 aread**: know or guess. **8–9** A Platonic emblem of the temperate person who controls the passions – cf. iv 2.1–2 – through the exercise of right reason, a faculty associated with the Palmer; see Hoopes 1962:150–52, and 'Palmer' in the *SEnc*. **with slow**

pace: in contrast to the Red Cross Knight's angry steed 'much disdayning to the curbe to yield' (I i.6). **with equall steps**: once Guyon quickens his pace, he becomes intemperate; cf. 13.1–2.

Stanza 8

3–4 clew: ball of thread. Not the ball of thread that led Theseus out of the labyrinth but a web to enclose Guyon. The web is an emblem of Mammon's house at vii 28.7–9, and the insignia on Acrasia's dress at xii 77.7–9. **7–8** He appeals to Guyon as the traditional heroic (and classical) warrior, a role denied him by the virtue of which he is the patron, e.g. he binds an old woman (iv 12), kills Pyrochles's horse (v 4), and sets out on a quest to bind a naked woman. He is the only hero who does not kill anyone. **9 misers**: wretch's.

Stanza 9

5 paynt: depict vividly but also falsely. **7 languorous constraynt**: sorrowful distress; also referring to her alleged rape, as ii 8.3. The phrase offers an erotic analogue to the Red Cross Knight's adventure to redeem Una's parents from 'captiue languor' (I vii 49.2).

Stanza 10

3–5 Archimago refers to the stripping of Duessa by Arthur and the Red Cross Knight at I viii 46. **rybauld**: a licentious

12

Therewith amoued from his sober mood,
   And liues he yet (said he) that wrought this act,
   And doen the heauens afford him vitall food?
   He liues, (quoth he) and boasteth of the fact,
   Ne yet hath any knight his courage crackt.
   Where may that treachour then (sayd he) be found,
   Or by what meanes may I his footing tract?
   That shall I shew (sayd he) as sure, as hound
The stricken Deare doth chaleng by the bleeding wound.

13

He stayd not lenger talke, but with fierce yre
   And zealous haste away is quickly gone,
   To seeke that knight, where him that crafty Squyre
   Supposd to be. They do arriue anone,
   Where sate a gentle Lady all alone,
   With garments rent, and heare discheueled,
   Wringing her handes, and making piteous mone;
   Her swollen eyes were much disfigured,
And her faire face with teares was fowly blubbered.

14

The knight approching nigh, thus to her said,
   Fayre Lady, through fowle sorrow ill bedight,
   Great pitty is to see you thus dismayd,
   And marre the blossom of your beauty bright:
   For thy appease your griefe and heauy plight,
   And tell the cause of your conceiued payne:
   For if he liue, that hath you doen despight,
   He shall you doe dew recompence agayne,
Or els his wrong with greater puissance maintaine.

15

Which when she heard, as in despightfull wise,
   She wilfully her sorrow did augment,
   And offred hope of comfort did despise:
   Her golden lockes most cruelly she rent,
   And scratcht her face with ghastly dreriment,
   Ne would she speake, ne see, ne yet be seene,
   But hid her visage, and her head downe bent,
   Either for grieuous shame, or for great teene,
As if her hart with sorow had transfixed beene.

16

Till her that Squyre bespake, Madame my liefe,
   For Gods deare loue be not so wilfull bent,
   But doe vouchsafe now to receiue reliefe,
   The which good fortune doth to you present.
   For what bootes it to weepe and to wayment,
   When ill is chaunst, but doth the ill increase,
   And the weake minde with double woe torment?
   When she her Squyre heard speake, she gan appease
Her voluntarie paine, and feele some secret ease.

17

Eftsoone she said, Ah gentle trustie Squyre,
   What comfort can I wofull wretch conceaue,
   Or why should euer I henceforth desyre,
   To see faire heauens face, and life not leaue,
   Sith that false Traytour did my honour reaue?
   False traytour certes (saide the Faerie knight)
   I read the man, that euer would deceaue
   A gentle Lady, or her wrong through might:
Death were too little paine for such a fowle despight.

---

person. **aduaunst**: incited, pricked, in contrast to the temperate knight's restraint. **cleene**: pure. **sheene**: beautiful. **6 great mother**: an appropriate term for Archimago to use; see I vii 9.1*n*. In Bk II, the earth is associated with man's fall into intemperance; see vii 17.1–4.

Stanza 11
1 halfe wroth: cf 13.1–2. At 25.8, he is 'inflam'd with wrathfulnesse'. **2 shent**: disgraced. **5 looser**: loose, 'discheueled' (13.6), in contrast to Medina's braided locks at ii. 15.7–9. **7 bent**: levelled.

Stanza 12
1–3 The chivalric code is expressed in Malory 6.10: 'What, said Sir Launcelot, is he a theef and a knyght and a rauyssher of wymmen? He doth shame vnto the ordre of knyghthode and contrary vnto his othe; hit is pyte that he lyueth'. **vitall**: life-giving. **4 fact**: crime. **6 treachour**: obs. form of 'traitor', suggesting 'treacherous'. **7–9** Archimago becomes Guyon's guide in place of the Palmer. **tract**: trace. **chaleng**: bay (upon picking up the scent).

Stanza 13
1–4 Instead of leading Guyon to the Red Cross Knight, as he promised, Archimago leads him to Duessa in order to incite

him further by seeing her violated state. **Squyre**: see 21.8–9. **9 blubbered**: disfigured.

Stanza 14
On Guyon as a homilist, see Mallette 1997:52–55. **2 ill bedight**: ill-arrayed, referring to her disfiguring tears; also sexually abused. **3 pitty**: the emotion that confounds Guyon throughout his quest; see Morgan 1986b:32–33. **dismayd**: the pun on 'dis-maid' is the poet's. **5 For thy**: therefore. **7 despight**: injury, outrage.

Stanza 15
4 golden lockes: as she mocks Una in Bk I – see I x 28.6 – and now Medina at ii 15.7, Belphœbe at iii 30.1, and Alma at ix 19.6. **5 dreriment**: grief. **8 teene**: woe.

Stanza 16
1 liefe: dear; corresponding to 'Sir' as an address to a woman. **5–7** The construction is confusing because Archimago answers his question as he asks it. **wayment**: lament. **9 voluntarie**: self-inflicted.

Stanza 17
7 read: consider. **8** The description of Duessa as **gentle**, also at 13.5 and 19.3, indicates that rape of a lower-class woman would be condoned.

18

But now, fayre Lady, comfort to you make,
   And read, who hath ye wrought this shamfull plight;
   That short reuenge the man may ouertake,
   Where so he be, and soone vpon him light.
   Certes (saide she) I wote not, how he hight,
   But vnder him a gray steede he did wield,
   Whose sides with dapled circles weren dight;
   Vpright he rode, and in his siluer shield
He bore a bloodie Crosse, that quartred all the field.

19

Now by my head (saide *Guyon*) much I muse,
   How that same knight should do so fowle amis,
   Or euer gentle Damzell so abuse:
   For may I boldly say, he surely is
   A right good knight, and trew of word ywis,
   I present was, and can it witnesse well,
   When armes he swore, and streight did enterpris
   Th'aduenture of the *Errant damozell*,
In which he hath great glory wonne, as I heare tell.

20

Nathlesse he shortly shall againe be tryde,
   And fairely quit him of th'imputed blame,
   Els be ye sure he dearely shall abyde,
   Or make you good amendment for the same:
   All wrongs haue mendes, but no amendes of shame.
   Now therefore Lady, rise out of your paine,
   And see the saluing of your blotted name.
   Full loth she seemd thereto, but yet did faine,
For she was inly glad her purpose so to gaine.

21

Her purpose was not such, as she did faine,
   Ne yet her person such, as it was seene,
   But vnder simple shew and semblant plaine
   Lurkt false *Duessa* secretly vnseene,
   As a chaste Virgin, that had wronged beene:
   So had false *Archimago* her disguysd,
   To cloke her guile with sorrow and sad teene;
   And eke himselfe had craftily deuisd
To be her Squire, and do her seruice well aguisd.

22

Her late forlorne and naked he had found,
   Where she did wander in waste wildernesse,
   Lurking in rockes and caues far vnder ground,
   And with greene mosse cou'ring her nakednesse,
   To hide her shame and loathly filthinesse,
   Sith her Prince *Arthur* of proud ornaments
   And borrowd beauty spoyld. Her nathelesse
   Th'enchaunter finding fit for his intents,
Did thus reuest, and deckt with dew habiliments.

23   *what is shame?*

For all he did, was to deceiue good knights,
   And draw them from pursuit of praise and fame,
   To slug in slouth and sensuall delights,
   And end their daies with irrenowmed shame.
   And now exceeding griefe him ouercame,
   To see the *Redcrosse* thus aduaunced hye;
   Therefore this craftie engine he did frame,
   Against his praise to stirre vp enmitye
Of such, as vertues like mote vnto him allye.

Stanza 18

2 read: tell. **3 short**: speedy. **reuenge**: a key word in the first eight cantos where it occurs fourteen times but not in the next four, as MacLaughlan 1980:157 notes. **6 gray**: since the lustful Argante rides a grey horse at III vii 37.3, the colour may represent the lust with which the Red Cross Knight is charged. **wield**: manage. **8–9** The description is heraldic: the red cross divides the whole **field** or surface of the shield into quarters. **Vpright**: as Guyon at 6.1.

Stanza 19

1 by my head: a classical oath, as Virgil's *per caput hoc iuro* (*Aen.* 9.300). Apart from the proem, and excluding the argument, Guyon is first named when he abandons the Palmer. Cf. the naming of the Red Cross Knight at I ii 12.2. **muse**: wonder. **2 amis**: evil deed. **3 abuse**: violate. **5 ywis**: indeed; I know. **6–9** Only the *LR* records the moment when the Red Cross Knight, 'taking on him knighthood' (66–67), **did enterpris** – i.e. undertook – his adventure. **Errant damozell**: so named at III i 24.7. The term is used in two senses: like a knight errant she undertakes an adventure to release her parents, and also wanders in search of her knight.

Stanza 20

2 fairely quit him: fully prove himself innocent. **blame**: charge. **3 abyde**: suffer; pay the penalty. **4 amendment**: reparation. **5 mendes**: recompense. Wrong may be amended by punishing the wrong-doer though the one wronged still suffers shame. Or shame may be imputed to the wrong-doer: while wrongful acts may be amended, shameful ones may never be. **shame** is a key term to describe this 'shamefast' knight (ix 43.9), as this opening episode makes clear; cf. 27.4, 30.1, 9. **7 saluing**: vindication, clearing.

Stanza 21

3 semblant plaine: honest appearance. **5 a chaste Virgin**: the tautology indicates her duplicity. **9 aguisd**: arrayed, i.e. disguised.

Stanza 22

1–7 For Duessa's unveiling, see I viii 46–48*n* and 50.1–5. **borrowd beauty**: in Bk I where the central conflict is between powers of light and darkness, the phrase is 'borrowed light' (viii 49.5); in Bk II, 'beauty' becomes a key term when Duessa's role is assumed by Acrasia. **9 reuest**: clothe again. **dew habiliments**: fitting attire.

Stanza 23

3 delights: suggests the plural of 'delice', sensual pleasure. Another key term in Bk II; cf. v 27.2, 33.1, xii 1.8, etc. **4 irrenowmed**: adds to 'unrenowned' an intensive sense to note a negation of all praise. **6 aduaunced**: raised or extolled, as the Palmer testifies at 32.1–5. **7 engine**: plot, snare to deceive the mind. **9 as vertues like**: as those of similarly

24

So now he *Guyon* guydes an vncouth way
  Through woods and mountaines, till they came at last
  Into a pleasant dale, that lowly lay
  Betwixt two hils, whose high heads ouerplast,
  The valley did with coole shade ouercast;
  Through midst thereof a little riuer rold,
  By which there sate a knight with helme vnlaste,
  Himselfe refreshing with the liquid cold,
After his trauell long, and labours manifold.

25

Lo yonder he, cryde *Archimage* alowd,
  That wrought the shamefull fact, which I did shew,
  And now he doth himselfe in secret shrowd,
  To fly the vengeaunce for his outrage dew;
  But vaine: for ye shall dearely do him rew,
  So God ye speed, and send you good successe;
  Which we far off will here abide to vew.
  So they him left, inflam'd with wrathfulnesse,
That streight against that knight his speare he did addresse.

26

Who seeing him from far so fierce to pricke,
  His warlike armes about him gan embrace,
  And in the rest his ready speare did sticke;
  Tho when as still he saw him towards pace,

He gan rencounter him in equall race:
  They bene ymett; both ready to affrap,
  When suddeinly that warrior gan abace
  His threatned speare, as if some new mishap
Had him betide, or hidden danger did entrap.

27

And cryde, Mercie Sir knight, and mercie Lord,
  For mine offence and heedelesse hardiment,
  That had almost committed crime abhord,
  And with reprochfull shame mine honour shent,
  Whiles cursed steele against that badge I bent,
  The sacred badge of my Redeemers death,   *Christ + Engl*
  Which on your shield is set for ornament:
  But his fierce foe his steed could stay vneath,
Who prickt with courage kene, did cruell battell breath.

28

But when he heard him speake, streight way he knew
  His errour, and himselfe inclyning sayd,
  Ah deare Sir *Guyon*, well beecommeth you,
  But me behoueth rather to vpbrayd,
  Whose hastie hand so far from reason strayd,
  That almost it did haynous violence
  On that fayre ymage of that heauenly Mayd,   *Queen*
  That decks and armes your shield with faire defence:
Your court'sie takes on you anothers dew offence,

---

virtuous nature, referring to the relationships among the virtues.

Stanza 24

1 So now he Guyon guydes: the verbal echo and heavy alliterative stress indicate the ominous change from 7.8–9. **vncouth**: strange, wild. **4–7** A topographical emblem of temperance, as Brooks-Davies 1977:119 suggests: the Red Cross Knight represents the mean between two extremes, the **two hils**. **ouerplast**: overhanging.

Stanza 25

2 fact: crime. **5 But vaine**: i.e. he hides in vain. **do**: cause. **6** Not 'may God prosper you' but 'may God hasten you [i.e. into intemperate speed]'; in contrast to the Palmer's benediction, 'God guide thee' at 32.8. **8–9** I.e., so angry that. **addresse**: aim.

Stanza 26

2 embrace: put on, buckle. **3 rest**: a support for the spear when levelled for charging. **5 rencounter**: charging in return. **race**: charge. **6 affrap**: strike. **7–9 that warriour**: purposefully vague though Guyon is meant. A fitting term for this 'sonne of *Mars*' (8.7); cf. 39.1 and vii 32.6. **abace**: lower. **His threatned speare**: both threatening the knight and being threatened by his spear. **betide**: befallen.

Stanza 27

1 Guyon's prayer is twofold: first to the Red Cross Knight: 'pardon me Sir knight'; and second to God on seeing the red

cross (as described to him at 18.8–9): 'grant me mercy Lord'. The different meanings of **mercie** are indicated by the different stresses, the first being the Fr. *merci*, as v 12.7. The chivalric code does not endorse unprovoked aggression; cf. IV vi 4.1–3. As Staton 1987:156 notes, playing by the Old Boys' Rules takes precedence over a woman's rape. **2 offence**: attack; transgression; also 'occasion of doubt', here referring to his misjudging the Red Cross Knight. **hardiment**: boldness, rashness. **4** While defending a lady who claimed that a knight 'did my honour reaue' (17.5), Guyon almost loses his own. **shent**: disgraced. The charge that he made against the Red Cross Knight at 11.2, he now takes upon himself. **6 my Redeemers death**: the possessive indicates that Guyon's classical virtue of temperance has a Christian framework. In Gal. 5.22–23, temperance is 'vnder the Spirit or grace' (Geneva gloss). **8–9** Since the **steed** manifests the Red Cross Knight's passion, **Who** may refer to either. **vneath**: only with difficulty. **kene**: fierce.

Stanza 28

2 inclyning: turning his spear aside (from Guyon). **4** It is more fitting that you should upbraid me rather than yourself. **5 reason**: an important key term fittingly introduced by the knight of holiness. **7–8 that heauenly Mayd**: presumably the Faerie Queene, as on Arthur's baldric at I vii 30.1–3, though not so identified until viii 43.3. Named 'the Saint' at v 11.7; cf. ix 2.7–9. **decks**: ornaments, as does the cross on his own shield (27.7). **armes**: protects, as shown at viii 43.1–6.

29

So beene they both at one, and doen vpreare
    Their beuers bright, each other for to greet;
    Goodly comportaunce each to other beare,
    And entertaine themselues with court'sies meet;
    Then saide the *Redcrosse* knight, Now mote I weet,
    Sir *Guyon*, why with so fierce saliaunce,
    And fell intent ye did at earst me meet;
    For sith I know your goodly gouernaunce,
Great cause, I weene, you guided, or some vncouth chaunce.

30

Certes (said he) well mote I shame to tell
    The fond encheason, that me hether led.
    A false infamous faitour late befell
    Me for to meet, that seemed ill bested,
    And playnd of grieuous outrage, which he red
    A knight had wrought against a Ladie gent;
    Which to auenge, he to this place me led,
    Where you he made the marke of his intent,
And now is fled, foule shame him follow, wher he went.

31

So can he turne his earnest vnto game,
    Through goodly handling and wise temperaunce.
    By this his aged Guide in presence came,
    Who soone as on that knight his eye did glaunce,

Eftsoones of him had perfect cognizaunce,
    Sith him in Faery court he late auizd;
    And sayd, Fayre sonne, God giue you happy chaunce,
    And that deare Crosse vppon your shield deuizd,
Wherewith aboue all knights ye goodly seeme aguizd.

32

Ioy may you haue, and euerlasting fame,
    Of late most hard atchieu'ment by you donne,
    For which enrolled is your glorious name
    In heauenly Regesters aboue the Sunne,
    Where you a Saint with Saints your seat haue wonne:
    But wretched we, where ye haue left your marke,
    Must now anew begin, like race to ronne;
    God guide thee, *Guyon*, well to end thy warke,
And to the wished hauen bring thy weary barke.

33

Palmer, him answered the *Redcrosse* knight,
    His be the praise, that this atchieu'ment wrought,
    Who made my hand the organ of his might;
    More then goodwill to me attribute nought:
    For all I did, I did but as I ought.
    But you, faire Sir, whose pageant next ensewes,
    Well mote yee thee, as well can wish your thought,
    That home ye may report thrise happy newes;
For well ye worthy bene for worth and gentle thewes.

Stanza 29
1 at one: reconciled. **3 comportaunce**: behaviour; coined by S. to emphasize their mutual response. **4 entertaine**: conduct. **6 saliaunce**: assault, onslaught; coined to stress the hasty violence of Guyon's attack made without a formal challenge. See v 3.2, and Arthur's rebuke of Pyrochles for his unprovoked attack at viii 31.6–9. Cf. 'salied' (vi 38.5, xii 38.4). **8 gouernaunce**: self-control, wise behaviour; a term used only in this Bk. It indicates control of the passions by temperance, as at 54.6, iv 7.2, 36.4, and defines the role of the Palmer. Bks II and V are analysed by Nohrnberg 1976:285–351 under the rubric 'Books of the Governors'. See Bates 1989 on Bk II's images of government.

Stanza 30
2 fond encheason: foolish occasion. **3 infamous**: the earlier stress on the second syllable adds alliterative force to Guyon's indignation. **faitour**: so named at I xii 35.5. **4 ill bested**: in bad plight. **5 red**: declared. **8 intent**: Archimago's intent became his at 29.7.

Stanza 31
1 can he: does he; or knows he how to. **3 By this**: an allegorical pointer which collapses 'by this time' into 'by this means'. With temperance restored, Guyon's guide returns. **5–6 cognizaunce**: recognition and understanding; in heraldry, the device by which a person is known. The Palmer instantly knows the knight by his Red Cross and confirms Guyon's belated recognition at 27.5–7. **auizd**: observed. **7–9** Either 'may God give happy chance to that dear cross' or, with a run-on stanza, 'of that dear cross may you have joy'. **deuizd**: drawn or painted as a device. **aguizd**: arrayed, i.e. armed.

The Palmer honours the **Crosse** more than the image of 'that heauenly Mayd' (28.7).

Stanza 32
4 heauenly Regesters: the Book of Life in Rev. 3.5, etc. **Ioy** alludes to Luke 10.20. 'reioyce, because your names are written in heauen'. **5** I.e., among those predestined to salvation, he is canonized for his **atchieu'ment**, as Kaske 1999:120 argues. **6–7** Either Guyon begins where the Red Cross Knight left off, as in a relay race, or where he began. **race**: course in a tournament. Also in the biblical sense, as the race of life in 1 Cor. 9.24–27, and Heb. 12.1: 'Let us runne with pacience the race that is set before vs'. In *Am* 80.1–2, S. refers to the 'long . . . race . . . I have run | Through Faery land'. It is rendered in moral terms at 34.7. **8 God guide thee**: alluding to one etymology of Guyon's name, from 'guide'. See proem 5.8n; cf 34.4, and note the Ferryman's appeal at xii 3.3.

Stanza 33
1–5 The knight corrects the Palmer's claim that he has 'wonne' (32.5) his seat in heaven: the dragon was slain by God's **might**, not his own, in agreement with I x 1.6–9. Hence **organ** refers to his spiritual armour, specifically the sword or lance that he wielded. Meaning remains indeterminate, however, because S. is negotiating a theological controversy on whether, or if, and if how much, **goodwill** may cooperate with God's grace. See Gless 1994:179–80, and Kaske 1999:111. **6 Sir**: in opposition to 'Saint' (32.5). **pageant**: Guyon's 'race' is regarded as an allegorical procession. **next**: on the second day of the Faerie Queene's annual feast, according to the *LR* 70–74. **7 thee**: prosper. **8 report**: bring, carry back. **9 gentle thewes**: virtuous habits befitting one of noble birth; see I ix 3.7–9n.

34

So courteous conge both did giue and take,
With right hands plighted, pledges of good will.
Then *Guyon* forward gan his voyage make,
With his blacke Palmer, that him guided still.
Still he him guided ouer dale and hill,
And with his steedy staffe did point his way:
His race with reason, and with words his will,
From fowle intemperaunce he ofte did stay,
And suffred not in wrath his hasty steps to stray.

35

In this faire wize they traueild long yfere,
Through many hard assayes, which did betide,
Of which he honour still away did beare,
And spred his glory through all countryes wide.
At last as chaunst them by a forest side
To passe, for succour from the scorching ray,
They heard a ruefull voice, that dearnly cride,
With percing shriekes, and many a dolefull lay;
Which to attend, awhile their forward steps they stay.

36

But if that carelesse heuens (quoth she) despise
The doome of iust reuenge, and take delight
To see sad pageaunts of mens miseries,   *pageaunts*
As bownd by them to liue in liues despight,
Yet can they not warne death from wretched wight.
Come then, come soone, come sweetest death to me,
And take away this long lent loathed light:
Sharpe be thy wounds, but sweete the medicines be,
That long captiued soules from weary thraldome free.

37

But thou, sweete Babe, whom frowning froward fate
Hath made sad witnesse of thy fathers fall,
Sith heuen thee deignes to hold in liuing state,
Long maist thou liue, and better thriue withall,
Then to thy lucklesse parents did befall:
Liue thou, and to thy mother dead attest,
That cleare she dide from blemish criminall;
Thy litle hands embrewd in bleeding brest
Loe I for pledges leaue. So giue me leaue to rest.

38

With that a deadly shrieke she forth did throw,
That through the wood reechoed againe,
And after gaue a grone so deepe and low,
That seemd her tender heart was rent in twaine,
Or thrild with point of thorough piercing paine;
As gentle Hynd, whose sides with cruell steele
Through launched, forth her bleeding life does raine,
Whiles the sad pang approching shee does feele,
Braies out her latest breath, and vp her eies doth seele.

39

Which when that warriour heard, dismounting straict
From his tall steed, he rusht into the thick,
And soone arriued, where that sad pourtraict
Of death and dolour lay, halfe dead, halfe quick,
In whose white alabaster brest did stick
A cruell knife, that made a griesly wownd,
From which forth gusht a stream of goreblood thick,
That all her goodly garments staind arownd,
And into a deepe sanguine dide the grassy grownd.

Stanza 34

1 conge: a ceremonious farewell.   **2** Cf. the plighting of the Red Cross Knight and Arthur at I ix 18.9. At iii 11.8, the knight is said to be 'with *Guyon* knitt in one consent'.   **4 Still**: always.   **7–9** Distinguishing the two kinds of passions, which are treated later: the irascible would cause him to stray with **hasty steps** from his forward path (**race**) unless controlled by **reason**; and the concupiscible would lead him into **fowle intemperaunce** unless **words** controlled his **will**.

Stanza 35

1 yfere: together.   **2 assayes**: trials.   **5–6** The setting for Fradubio's warning tale at I ii 29 is abbreviated to alert the reader to its correspondence with Amavia's tale. **succour**: shelter.   **7 dearnly**: 'earnestly', so the context suggests; or 'grievously' as at III i 14.4.   **8 lay**: strain, tune (*OED* 2), i.e. a lament.

Stanza 36

1–2 carelesse: uncaring. **doome**: judgement, execution. **iust reuenge**: such Guyon sought for Duessa at 18.1–4, and at 61.5–8 seeks for Amavia and Mordant. On Guyon as an avenger of blood, see MacLachlan 1980:139–51, esp. 143. **3 pageaunts**: a tableau shown on the (world's) stage, a 'spectacle' (40.1). The role of theatrical pageant in Bk II is examined by Dolven 1999:181–90.   **4 bownd**: obliged. **in liues despight**: either we must live even though we scorn life, or our state scorns life in its **miseries**. In lovingly wooing death,

Amavia reverses the state revealed in her name: 'love to live' or 'live to love'. See 55.4–5*n*.   **5 warne**: forbid.

Stanza 37

1 froward: adverse, unfavourable.   **3 thee**: the heavy stress excludes her.   **6 attest**: bear witness to; a legal term, suggested by **witnesse**, to emphasize her oath.   **8–9** In the legal sense, the babe's bloody hands are sureties to be forfeited if he does not attest that his mother died free from **blemish criminall**. It is a witty paradox that bloody hands should be **pledges** of innocence. **embrewd**: plunged; stained; implying also 'infected', 'defild' (50.9). She may stab herself at this moment as does Dido upon concluding her lament in Virgil, *Aen.* 4.660, as Upton 1758 first noted.

Stanza 38

5 thrild: pierced.   **8 the sad pang**: i.e. death.   **9 Braies**: breathes out with a cry. **latest**: last. **seele**: close, as the stitched eyelids of a hawk; see I vii 23.9*n*.

Stanza 39

2 the thick: the thickest part; here the centre.   **4 dolour**: labour 1596 may have been suggested by her search for her lover, by her efforts to release him from Acrasia's power, or by her labour in child-birth. Yet alliteration demands the *1590* reading, as at vii 23.5 and viii 7.7. **quick**: alive.   **6 griesly**: arousing horror.   **7 goreblood**: clotted blood.   **9 sanguine**: blood red.

40

Pitifull spectacle of deadly smart,
    Beside a bubling fountaine low she lay,
    Which shee increased with her bleeding hart,
    And the cleane waues with purple gore did ray;
    Als in her lap a louely babe did play
    His cruell sport, in stead of sorrow dew;
    For in her streaming blood he did embay
    His litle hands, and tender ioints embrew;
Pitifull spectacle, as euer eie did vew.

41

Besides them both, vpon the soiled gras
    The dead corse of an armed knight was spred,
    Whose armour all with blood besprincled was;
    His ruddy lips did smyle, and rosy red
    Did paint his chearefull cheekes, yett being ded,
    Seemd to haue beene a goodly personage,
    Now in his freshest flowre of lusty hed,
    Fitt to inflame faire Lady with loues rage,
But that fiers fate did crop the blossome of his age.

42

Whom when the good Sir *Guyon* did behold,
    His hart gan wexe as starke, as marble stone,
    And his fresh blood did frieze with fearefull cold,
    That all his sences seemd berefte attone:
    At last his mighty ghost gan deepe to grone,
    As Lion grudging in his great disdaine,
    Mournes inwardly, and makes to him selfe mone,
    Til ruth and fraile affection did constraine,
His stout courage to stoupe, and shew his inward paine.

43

Out of her gored wound the cruell steel
    He lightly snatcht, and did the floodgate stop
    With his faire garment: then gan softly feel
    Her feeble pulse, to proue if any drop
    Of liuing blood yet in her veynes did hop;
    Which when he felt to moue, he hoped faire
    To call backe life to her forsaken shop;
    So well he did her deadly wounds repaire,
That at the last shee gan to breath out liuing aire.

44

Which he perceiuing greatly gan reioice,
    And goodly counsell, that for wounded hart
    Is meetest med'cine, tempred with sweete voice;
    Ay me, deare Lady, which the ymage art
    Of ruefull pitty, and impatient smart,
    What direfull chaunce, armd with auenging fate,
    Or cursed hand hath plaid this cruell part,
    Thus fowle to hasten your vntimely date;
Speake, O dear Lady speake: help neuer comes too late.

45

Therewith her dim eie-lids she vp gan reare,
    On which the drery death did sitt, as sad
    As lump of lead, and made darke clouds appeare;
    But when as him all in bright armour clad
    Before her standing she espied had,
    As one out of a deadly dreame affright,
    She weakely started, yet she nothing drad:
    Streight downe againe her selfe in great despight,
She groueling threw to ground, as hating life and light.

Stanza 40

1 spectacle: also in the dramatic sense; cf. 'pageaunts' (36.3). **4 ray**: defile. Since the water (**waues**: *OED* I i c) may not 'with any filth be dyde' (ii 9.8), there is a paradox, one that becomes even more inexplicable when the water is said to be complicit in Mordant's death at 55.9 and refuses to cleanse the babe's bloody hands at ii 3. For a theological explanation that derives from the account in Ezek. 16 of Jerusalem as a bloody new-born babe whom God washes, see Kaske 1976:203–09. Gregerson 1995:28 suggests that the nymph in the water becomes 'a creature with blood on her hands'. **7–9** S. draws upon Gower's story of the incestuous Canace whose child, when she stabs herself through the heart, 'lay bathende in hire blod | Out rolled fro the moder barm' (1980:3.312–13); see Sanders 1992:201. The simile of the 'gentle Hynd' (38.6–7), extended in **bleeding hart**, suggests the ritual act in which hunters wash their hands in the blood of the deer they have slain. **embay**: bathe. **embrew**: see 37.8–9*n*.

Stanza 41

1–3 soiled: stained, suggesting 'defiled'; an important motif in Bk II: e.g. the soiled arms of Phaon (iv 16.4), Atin (iv 37.7), and Pyrochles (v 4.9). See v 22.4*n*, vi 41.6–8*n*. **5 yett being ded**: having just died; or 'though dead'. **7 lusty hed**: youthful vigour; also 'lustfulness'.

Stanza 42

2–4 starke: hard. **fearefull cold**: i.e. cold caused by fear. Fear and pity are a fitting response to Amavia's 'sad Tragedie' (ii 1.3). Through sympathy caused by his own **fraile affection**, Guyon almost dies himself; cf. 48.9. Pity balances the anger he felt in his encounter with Duessa. **attone**: together; at once. **6–7** The lion reveals its compassionate nature to Una at I iii 8.3–5. **grudging**: growling. **disdaine**: indignation. **9 courage**: spirit, nature.

Stanza 43

5 hop: spring; a precise term to describe pulsating blood. **7 shop**: body; the place where the heart operates (*OED* 3c).

Stanza 44

2–3 Proverbial: Smith 123, to which the need to rhyme appends **with sweete voice**. In comforting the dying, Guyon is performing the fifth work of mercy; see I x 36–43*n*. **4–5 ymage**: emblem; pattern; embodiment. As a 'pourtraict' (39.3) or 'spectacle' (40.1), Amavia is interpreted in moral terms by the Palmer when he calls her 'the ymage of mortalitie' (57.2). **impatient smart**: unendurable pain. **8 date**: end of life. **9** Also proverbial: Smith 379.

46

The gentle knight her soone with carefull paine
    Vplifted light, and softly did vphold:
    Thrise he her reard, and thrise she sunck againe,
    Till he his armes about her sides gan fold,
    And to her said; Yet if the stony cold
    Haue not all seized on your frozen hart,
    Let one word fall that may your griefe vnfold,
    And tell the secrete of your mortall smart;
He oft finds present helpe, who does his griefe impart.

47

Then casting vp a deadly looke, full low
    Shee sight from bottome of her wounded brest,
    And after, many bitter throbs did throw
    With lips full pale and foltring tong opprest,
    These words she breathed forth from riuen chest;
    Leaue, ah leaue off, what euer wight thou bee,
    To lett a weary wretch from her dew rest,
    And trouble dying soules tranquilitee.
Take not away now got, which none would giue to me.

48

Ah far be it (said he) Deare dame fro mee,
    To hinder soule from her desired rest,
    Or hold sad life in long captiuitee:
    For all I seeke, is but to haue redrest
    The bitter pangs, that doth your heart infest.
    Tell then O Lady tell, what fatall priefe
    Hath with so huge misfortune you opprest:
    That I may cast to compas your reliefe,
Or die with you in sorrow, and partake your griefe.

49

With feeble hands then stretched forth on hye,
    As heuen accusing guilty of her death,
    And with dry drops congealed in her eye,
    In these sad wordes she spent her vtmost breath:
    Heare then, O man, the sorrowes that vneath
    My tong can tell, so far all sence they pas:
    Loe this dead corpse, that lies here vnderneath,
    The gentlest knight, that euer on greene gras
Gay steed with spurs did pricke, the good Sir *Mortdant* was.

50

Was, (ay the while, that he is not so now)
    My Lord my loue; my deare Lord, my deare loue,
    So long as heuens iust with equall brow,
    Vouchsafed to behold vs from aboue,
    One day when him high corage did emmoue,
    As wont ye knightes to seeke aduentures wilde,
    He pricked forth his puissaunt force to proue,
    Me then he left enwombed of this childe,
This luckles childe, whom thus ye see with blood defild.

51

Him fortuned (hard fortune ye may ghesse)
    To come, where vile *Acrasia* does wonne,
    Acrasia a false enchaunteresse,
    That many errant knightes hath fowle fordonne:
    Within a wandring Island, that doth ronne
    And stray in perilous gulfe, her dwelling is;
    Fayre Sir, if euer there ye trauell, shonne
    The cursed land where many wend amis,
And know it by the name; it hight the *Bowre of blis*.

Stanza 45
S. imitates Virgil's account of Dido's death in *Aen*. 4; see 37.8–9*n*. The many echoes, here and in the following stanzas, are traced by J. Watkins 1995:120–26. One chief difference is that Dido seeks the light, Amavia the dark. See 'Dido' in the *SEnc*. **2 sad**: heavy. **8–9 despight**: contempt of life. **groueling**: prostrate, face down. In **hating life**, she denies her nature, which is 'to love to live'; and in **hating . . . light**, to which she is first attracted by Guyon's bright appearance in 4–7, again she denies her nature, which is 'to live to love'. She acts out the state she calls upon at 36.6–7.

Stanza 46
3–4 As Una thrice falls down in a swoon and is thrice revived by the dwarf at I vii 24.1–4. Amavia's name indicates that she may revive only when Guyon embraces her; see 55.4–5*n*. **9** As the Red Cross Knight says to Fradubio at I ii 34.4, and Arthur to Una at I vii 40.9, in analogous episodes. For the proverb, here varied, see Smith 761.

Stanza 47
2 sight: an earlier form of 'sighed'. **7 lett**: prevent. **9 now got**: i.e. the peace of death.

Stanza 48
4 redrest: remedied, by exacting revenge; cf. 61.7. **5 infest**: assail; infect. **6 priefe**: experience, trial. **8 cast to compas**: plan to accomplish.

Stanza 49
3 She is now beyond grief. **4 vtmost**: last. **5–56.1** Amavia's lament, just short of 60 lines, has the poignancy and authority proverbially given 'last words'; see Tilley M514. **vneath**: scarcely. **7 dead corpse**: i.e. dead body; as Isa. 37.36, etc. **9 Mortdant**: see 55.4–5*n*.

Stanza 50
2 The repetition manifests Amavia's loving nature. That her love brings death relates her to Fradubio's lament: 'O too deare loue, loue bought with death too deare' (I ii 31.7). **3–4** As Matt. 5.45: 'he maketh his sunne to arise on the euil, and the good, and sendeth raine on the iuste, and vniuste'. Amavia invokes Ezekiel's complaint that 'the waie of the Lord is not equal' (18.25). **equall**: impartial, just. **6 ye knightes**: a rare complaint in the poem by a woman against men.

Stanza 51
2–4 Acrasia: on the name, see xii 69.8*n*. **wonne**: dwell. **false enchaunteresse**: her chief title, as 55.1, etc. As such, she combines the roles of the false Duessa (see I ii 34.8–9) and the enchanter Archimago. **false**: refers also to the vanity of her delights. **fordonne**: killed (cf. ii 44.9); ruined. **5–6 wandring Island**: see xii 11–12. **9 know it by the name**: i.e. the name declares its nature. On that name, see xii 42.1–4*n*.

52

Her blis is all in pleasure and delight,
 Wherewith she makes her louers dronken mad,
 And then with words and weedes of wondrous might,
 On them she workes her will to vses bad:
 My liefest Lord she thus beguiled had
 For he was flesh: (all flesh doth frayltie breed)
 Whom when I heard to beene so ill bestad
Weake wretch I wrapt my selfe in Palmers weed,
And cast to seek him forth through danger and great dreed.

53

Now had fayre *Cynthia* by euen tournes
 Full measured three quarters of her yeare,
 And thrise three tymes had fild her crooked hornes,
 Whenas my wombe her burdein would forbeare,
 And bad me call *Lucina* to me neare.
 Lucina came: a manchild forth I brought:
 The woods, the Nymphes, my bowres, my midwiues weare,
Hard helpe at need. So deare thee babe I bought,
Yet nought too dear I deemd, while so my deare I sought.

54

Him so I sought, and so at last I fownd
 Where him that witch had thralled to her will,
 In chaines of lust and lewde desyres ybownd
 And so transformed from his former skill,

That me he knew not, nether his owne ill;
 Till through wise handling and faire gouernaunce,
 I him recured to a better will,
Purged from drugs of fowle intemperaunce:
Then meanes I gan deuise for his deliuerance.

55

Which when the vile Enchaunteresse perceiu'd,
 How that my Lord from her I would repriue,
 With cup thus charmd, him parting she deceiud;
 Sad verse, giue death to him that death does giue,
 And losse of loue, to her that loues to liue,
 So soone as Bacchus with the Nymphe does lincke:
 So parted we, and on our iourney driue,
Till comming to this well, he stoupt to drincke:
The charme fulfild, dead suddeinly he downe did sincke.

56

Which when I wretch, Not one word more she sayd
 But breaking off, the end for want of breath,
 And slyding soft, as downe to sleepe her layd,
 And ended all her woe in quiet death.
 That seeing good Sir *Guyon*, could vneath
 From teares abstayne, for griefe his hart did grate,
 And from so heauie sight his head did wreath,
Accusing fortune, and too cruell fate,
Which plonged had faire Lady in so wretched state.

Stanza 52

3 Acrasia's **words** counter the Palmer's words that keep Guyon's will from intemperance at 34.7–8. Her **weedes** are herbs or 'drugs' (54.8, v 34.9), such as used by Circe in Virgil, *Aen.* 7.19, to change her victims into beasts, in contrast to Amavia who assumes **Palmers weed** to rescue Mordant. **5 liefest:** dearest. **6** Matt. 26.41: 'the flesh is weake'. **7 so ill bestad:** in such bad plight.

Stanza 53

1–4 An elaborate periphrasis for the nine lunar months of pregnancy. **burdein:** the child borne in the womb (*OED* 4). **forbeare:** give up; ill-bear any longer. **5 Lucina:** Diana in her role as goddess of childbirth; cf. 'of wemens labours thou hast charge, | And generation goodly dost enlarge' (*Epith* 383–84). The setting alludes to one etymology of her name, from Lat. *lucus*, a grove.

Stanza 54

2 that witch: Acrasia inherits this title – cf. xii 26.4 – from Duessa at I ii 33.5, etc. **4 skill:** reason, power of discernment; in a wider sense 'knowledge', particularly of what is right or fitting, by which temperance is maintained. **6 gouernaunce:** either his temperate behaviour (cf. 29.8) or, preferably, her governing. In her disguise, she plays the Palmer's role; cf. 31.2. **7 recured:** restored. **8 drugs:** as Cymochles was 'Made dronke with drugs of deare voluptuous receipt' (v 34.9).

Stanza 55

2 repriue: take back; rescue. **3** The cup replicates Duessa's cup 'replete with magick artes' (I viii 14.2), which is S.'s rendering of the cup borne by the whore of Rev. 18.3 from which

'all nations haue dronken of the wine of the wrath of her fornication'. Either the cup is charmed, as Gregerson 1995:27 claims, or it contains 'the charme and veneme (ii 4.6) which poison Mordant and Amavia. **4–5 Sad verse:** a strong or powerful incantation or charm, 'words . . . of wondrous might' (52.3); also Lat. *tristis*, ill-omened: hence a fatal charm. **that death does giue:** the etymology of Mordant, which associates him with Adam by whom 'sinne entred into the worlde, and death by sinne, and so death went ouer all men' (Rom. 5.12). As 'he was flesh' (52.6), he is given to death, his counterpart being Verdant; cf. 41.7 and xii 79.7–9. **that loues to liue:** the etymology of Amavia, *ama-via / ama-vita*, suggests that she is the counterpart to Mordant, being one who loves in order to live or who lives to love – loving and living being one in her. Their conjunction is found in Matt. 5:44–45. Nelson 1963:189 finds an allusion to Virgil's Amata, the suicide mother of Lavinia. Her name is suggested in the epigraph but is not given in the poem until ii 45.8. **6** Since **Bacchus** signifies wine and the **Nymphe** water, S. inverts one proverbial emblem of temperance, the mixing of wine and water; see the sources cited by A. Fowler 1960b, and Nohrnberg 1976:495–96. In drinking from Acrasia's charmed bacchic cup, Mordant enacts the Red Cross Knight's drinking from the enfeebling fountain. Both acts parody the mingling of wine and water in the communion chalice. Here the pure water will not be corrupted by wine even as it will not cleanse the babe's bloody hands at ii 3. See ii 7–9. **8** At ii 4.6, it is assumed that both parents drank from the cup, as **lincke** here suggests.

Stanza 56

1 The witty point is that her story of Mordant's death coincides with her own death. The effectiveness of the caesura is

57

Then turning to his Palmer said, Old syre
    Behold the ymage of mortalitie,
    And feeble nature cloth'd with fleshly tyre
    When raging passion with fierce tyranny
    Robs reason of her dew regalitie,
    And makes it seruaunt to her basest part:
    The strong it weakens with infirmitie,
    And with bold furie armes the weakest hart;
The strong through pleasure soonest falles, the weake
               (through smart.

58

But temperaunce (said he) with golden squire
    Betwixt them both can measure out a meane,
    Nether to melt in pleasures whott desyre,
    Nor frye in hartlesse griefe and dolefull tene.
    Thrise happy man, who fares them both atweene.
    But sith this wretched woman ouercome
    Of anguish, rather then of crime hath bene,
    Reserue her cause to her eternall doome,
And in the meane vouchsafe her honorable toombe.

59

Palmer, quoth he, death is an equall doome
    To good and bad, the commen In of rest;
    But after death the tryall is to come,   *heaven/hell*
    When best shall bee to them, that liued best:
    But both alike, when death hath both supprest,
    Religious reuerence doth buriall teene,
    Which who so wants, wants so much of his rest:
    For all so greet shame after death I weene,
As selfe to dyen bad, vnburied bad to beene.

60

So both agree their bodies to engraue;
    The great earthes wombe they open to the sky,
    And with sad Cypresse seemely it embraue,
    Then couering with a clod their closed eye,
    They lay therein those corses tenderly,
    And bid them sleepe in euerlasting peace.
    But ere they did their vtmost obsequy,
    Sir *Guyon* more affection to increace,
Bynempt a sacred vow, which none should ay releace.

---

noted by Fried 1981:267. **6** Until he wastes the Bower of Bliss 'with rigour pittilesse' (xii 83.2), Guyon is much given to pity that leads to 'womanish teares' (III xi 44.6), as also at 61.9 and ii 1.9. In Bk I, except for the aged King of Eden at xii 16.9, only women weep. On his compassion, see Buhler 1999:233–36. **grate**: fret. **7 wreath**: turn, twist.

Stanza 57
A rare stanza that unfolds the moral significance of an episode. The actions of Mordant and Amavia together provide **the ymage of mortalitie** – i.e. of fleshly nature – from the perspective of temperance, and offer an initial insight into that virtue. As Gless 1994:182 observes, Guyon's aphorisms take no account of Mordant's death which happens only *after* he had been 'Purged from drugs of fowle intemperaunce' (54.8). Yet drinking from Acrasia's cup indicates his backsliding. **3 tyre**: attire, vesture. **6 basest**: lowest, referring to the passions. Reason should exercise sovereign authority over her subjects, namely, the passions. This is the lesson that Timon taught Arthur at I ix 9.5–7. **7–9** Distinguishing between the two kinds of passions, the irascible and the concupiscent, later expressed in Pyrochles and Cymochles; see 34.7–9n, iv 41n.

Stanza 58
1 said he: i.e. the Palmer rather than Guyon, as MacLachlan 1984:112 suggests, though here they speak almost with one voice. **golden squire**: referring to the golden set-square, *norma temperantiae*, a common emblem of temperance as the 'golden mean'; also to the instrument used by masons to determine the precise proportion of a building, as Sadowski 2000:107–15 argues. **4 frye**: burn. 'fryze', sugg. Church 1758, would provide a fitting antithesis to **melt**, and describe the effects of excessive grief, e.g. 'his fresh blood did frieze with fearefull cold' (42.3) and Amavia's 'frozen hart' (46.6).

hartlesse griefe: i.e. grief that lacks the courage to endure. **tene**: suffering, anguish. **6–7** Mordant is **ouercome | . . . of crime** by having yielded to concupiscence even though he was restored, while Amavia though guilty of the crime of suicide is excused by Guyon at 48.1–5. **9 in the meane**: in the meantime. Implying also that the mean between judging her case (**cause**) and reserving judgement to God is to bury her.

Stanza 59
In the matter of burial, Guyon refuses to submit to the Palmer's judgement: burial customs, though here pagan, are too deeply felt to yield to reason. Claiming that both the good and the bad deserve burial, he proceeds to perform the sixth work of mercy; see I x 42. Kaske 1979:130–33 comments on the Christian and pagan elements here – esp. in lines 8–9 and in the ensuing episode – and notes a parallel in Sophocles, *Antigone*. **2 To good and bad**: presumably Amavia and Mordant respectively. **In of rest**: as burial is a temporary resting place until the **tryall** of the Last Judgement. **6 teene**: grant, afford, or 'require'; so the context implies. **7–9** Guyon's sentiment is particularly pagan (see Virgil, *Aen.* 6.329–30), as Kaske 135 notes. It prepares for the later irony when he is not given proper burial; see viii 12–17. **selfe to dyen bad**: possibly a reference to the sin of self-slaughter; yet see 37.7, 58.7. For the importance of burial, see I v 53.4n.

Stanza 60
1 engraue: place in a grave, with the next line suggesting that death is rebirth. **2 great earthes wombe**: as 'the earth [is] great mother of vs all' (10.6). **3 Cypresse**: see I i 8.9n. These rituals are classical in contrast to the Christian burial provided by the sixth bead-man at I x 42. **embraue**: adorn beautifully (a S. neologism). **6 euerlasting**: i.e. until the end of time. **8 affection**: deep feeling, piety. **9 Bynempt**: swore. This obs. form makes the occasion more solemn. **releace**: revoke.

61

The dead knights sword out of his sheath he drew,
   With which he cutt a lock of all their heare,
   Which medling with their blood and earth, he threw
   Into the graue, and gan deuoutly sweare;

Such and such euil God on *Guyon* reare,
   And worse and worse young Orphane be thy payne,
   If I or thou dew vengeance doe forbeare,
   Till guiltie blood her guerdon doe obtayne:
So shedding many teares, they closd the earth agayne.

Stanza 61

1–4 all: presumably not only the dead but also Guyon, the Palmer, and Ruddymane in a pagan burial rite that may also be a magical rite serving to identify the living with the dead, as Jordan 1989:41 suggests. **medling**: mingling. **5–9** The heightened language is biblical, as 1 Sam. 3.17: 'God do so to thee, and more also, if thou hide anie thing from me'. **dew vengeance**: cf. the 'iust reuenge' (36.2) against Acrasia which Amavia believes the heavens will not provide. Guyon assumes the chivalric role of 'Defending . . . Orphans right' (III ii 14.6), which is the seventh work of mercy; see I x 43.2. As his virtue allows, he ignores God's claim that 'vengeaunce is mine' (Rom. 12.19), though his solemnity shows that he does not 'giue place vnto wrath'. Presumably after his upbringing in the house of Medina, Ruddymane wearing his father's arms will seek revenge. **guiltie blood**: blood shed guiltily, though the blood itself is guilty; see ii 4.5.

Cant. II.

Babes bloody handes may not be clensd,
the face of golden Meane.
Her sisters two Extremities
striue her to banish cleane.

1

Thus when Sir Guyon with his faithful guyde
  Had with dew rites and dolorous lament
The end of their sad Tragedie vptyde,
The litle babe vp in his armes he hent;
Who with sweet pleasaunce and bold blandishment
Gan smyle on them, that rather ought to weepe,
As carelesse of his woe, or innocent
Of that was doen, that ruth emperced deepe
In that knightes hart, and wordes with bitter teares did steepe.

2

Ah lucklesse babe, borne vnder cruell starre,
  And in dead parents balefull ashes bred,
Full little weenest thou, what sorrowes are
Left thee for porcion of thy liuelyhed,
Poore Orphane in the wide world scattered,
As budding braunch rent from the natiue tree,
And thrown forth, till it be withered:
Such is the state of men: Thus enter we
Into this life with woe, and end with miseree.

3

Then soft him selfe inclyning on his knee
  Downe to that well, did in the water weene
(So loue does loath disdainefull nicitee.)
His guiltie handes from bloody gore to cleene;
He washt them oft and oft, yet nought they beene
For all his washing cleaner. Still he stroue,
Yet still the litle hands were bloody seene;
The which him into great amaz'ment droue,
And into diuerse doubt his wauering wonder cloue.

Book II Canto ii

Argument

2–4 face: outward appearance or form. In the architectural sense, the façade of the castle (12.6) flanked by opposing bastions which are its **Extremities**; see A. Fowler 1989b:151. **golden Meane**: *aurea mediocritas* (Horace, *Odes* 2.10.5). As **Extremities** opposed to the mean (cf. 38.4), they indicate, figuratively, the hands – cf. the 'two brethren Gyauntes' at xi 15.6 who defend the castle of Alma – in relation to the **face**. Cf. the architectural image at xii 1.1–5.

Stanza 1

4 hent: took. **7 innocent**: referring to the babe's 'innocence' (4.3) until the syntax restricts the meaning in the next line.

Stanza 2

1 cruell starre: evil astral influence; cf. I viii 42.6–7. **2** Alluding to the legend of the phoenix that, after immolating itself, emerges from its ashes with renewed youth. The suggestion of renewal is qualified by the sight of the babe's 'guiltie handes' (3.4). **balefull**: full of evil; also, from the legend, suggesting 'bale': funeral pyre. In his account of an epigram of Meleager, as Kaske 1976:197–99 notes, Conti 1616:5.12 says that the nymphs take Bacchus born from his dead parent's ashes and wash him. **4 liuelyhed**: inheritance. **5 scattered**: cast down, dropped at random. **6–7** 'He is cast forthe as a branche, and withereth' (John 15.6). **8–9** 'Man that is borne of woman hath but a short time to liue, and is ful of miserie' (Job 14.1, Bishops').

Stanzas 3–4

Guyon's vain attempt to cleanse Ruddymane's hands at the 'well' – referring to 'this well' at i 55.8 or 'bubling fountaine'

(i 40.2) – is taken by Weatherby 1994:172–79 to allude generally to the curse of mortality. Then 'bloodguiltinesse' may be taken to refer to the corruption of human nature – concupiscence in Mordant and love's rage leading to suicide in Amavia – as in David's cry in Ps. 51.2: 'Wash me throughly from mine iniquitie, and clense me from my sinne', which is glossed by Geneva: 'My sinnes sticke so fast in me, that I haue nede of some singular kinde of washing'. More specifically, Guyon's act has been related to baptism, e.g. by A. Fowler 1961a:97. In terms of this analogy, the babe has 'guiltie handes' because stained hands and the failure to wash them are traditional symbols of guilt, as Pilate at vii 61, and because failure to cleanse them indicates the limits of baptism. While 'all men be conceived and born in sin', and may be 'born anew of water' (public baptism, *BCP*), original sin remains, as Article 16 of the *Thirty-nine Articles* declares. See I x 25.1–5*n*. The hands may not be cleansed 'with water' because God has imprinted the stain, and not 'with bath' because the infection has spread throughout the parents' bodies. Then 'bloody gore' may be taken to refer to the blood's continuing corruption (cf. i 40.4; I viii 16.7, 24.4), and 'purgd' carries both the physical sense (as at i 54.8) and the religious sense (as at I x 25.1–3, 57.4). Kaske 1976:204–05 compares the babe to the bloody babe in Ezek. 16; and in Kaske 1999:165–73 interprets the well as Mosaic law, and the blood as afterbirth. See also her entry, 'Amavia, Mortdant, Ruddymane' in the *SEnc*. Guyon's attempted cleansing is read by Mazzola 1994:9–11 as a ritual interruption that delays his return to the Faery Queene.

Stanza 3

3 nicitee: fastidiousness; cf. I viii 40.3. **9 diuerse**: distracting. **cloue**: divided.

4

He wist not whether blott of fowle offence
    Might not be purgd with water nor with bath;
    Or that high God, in lieu of innocence,
    Imprinted had that token of his wrath,
    To shew how sore bloodguiltinesse he hat'th;
    Or that the charme and veneme, which they dronck,
    Their blood with secret filth infected hath,
    Being diffused through the sencelesse tronck,
That through the great contagion direfull deadly stonck.

5

Whom thus at gaze, the Palmer gan to bord
    With goodly reason, and thus fayre bespake;
    Ye bene right hard amated, gratious Lord,
    And of your ignorance great merueill make,
    Whiles cause not well conceiued ye mistake.
    But know, that secret vertues are infusd
    In euery fountaine, and in euerie lake,
    Which who hath skill them rightly to haue chusd,
To proofe of passing wonders hath full often vsd.

6

Of those some were so from their sourse indewd
    By great Dame Nature, from whose fruitfull pap
    Their welheads spring, and are with moisture deawd;
    Which feedes each liuing plant with liquid sap,

And filles with flowres fayre *Floraes* painted lap:
    But other some by guifte of later grace,
    Or by good prayers, or by other hap,
    Had vertue pourd into their waters bace,
And thenceforth were renowmd, and sought from place
                                              (to place.

7

Such is this well, wrought by occasion straunge,
    Which to her Nymph befell. Vpon a day,
    As she the woodes with bow and shaftes did raunge,
    The hartlesse Hynd and Robucke to dismay,
    Dan Faunus chaunst to meet her by the way,
    And kindling fire at her faire burning eye,
    Inflamed was to follow beauties chace,
    And chaced her, that fast from him did fly;
As Hynd from her, so she fled from her enimy.

8

At last when fayling breath began to faint,
    And saw no meanes to scape, of shame affrayd,
    She set her downe to weepe for sore constraint,
    And to *Diana* calling lowd for ayde,
    Her deare besought, to let her die a mayd.
    The goddesse heard, and suddeine where she sate,
    Welling out streames of teares, and quite dismayd
    With stony feare of that rude rustick mate,
Transformd her to a stone from stedfast virgins state.

Stanza 4

3 Or: either.   **in lieu of innocence**: see i 37.8–9*n*.   **5 blood-guiltinesse**: 'guiltie blood' (i 61.8) rather than the sin of bloodshed (as at 30.3); cf vii 19.5.   **6 charme and veneme**: Acrasia's 'words and weedes' (i 52.3).   **veneme** may suggest venereal disease. Together they suggest that Mordant's drinking is to be interpreted as sexual; see i 55.6*n*.   **7–9** The stench from bodies recently dead confirms the natural explanation, i.e. their mortality; but it implies a supernatural working, i.e. their sin.

Stanza 5

After Guyon has speculated on the nature of the stigma, the Palmer offers an etiological myth, similar to the one at I vii 5, which he moralizes to explain why the stain cannot be removed.   **1 at gaze**: standing in bewilderment.   **bord**: address.   **3 amated**: dismayed, confounded.   **6 secret vertues**: hidden powers that were held to be in all things but esp. water, as the well of life is 'Full of great vertues, and for med'cine good', and which can 'guilt of sinfull crimes cleane wash away' (I xi 29.5, 30.2). Either Guyon lacks such purifying water, or the **skill** to use it.   **infusd**: 'pour'd' (6.8).   **9 To proofe of**: to effect, and hence prove, their powers.   **passing**: surpassing.

Stanza 6

The Palmer posits two kinds of waters: virtuous liquid from Nature's breast to which moisture is added, and **waters bace** or ordinary to which virtue is added. On the distinction, see Weatherby 1996a:243–45, 253–57.   **1 indewd**: also in the literal sense, moisture added to the well.   **5 Flora**: the goddess of flowers.   **6–8** This well's **vertue** is gained from all three sources: **by guifte of later grace** from Diana; **by good prayers**

of the nymph at 8.4–5; and **by other hap**, i.e. 'by occasion straunge' (7.1).   **other some**: some others.   **later**: either at some later date or later in its course.

Stanza 7

4 hartlesse: timid, lacking heart; a repressed pun. The **Robucke** is noted for its swiftness, as in 1 Chron. 12.8; cf x 7.5.   **5 Dan**: a highly complimentary form of address used by S. chiefly of the gods, as here of **Faunus** as the wood god. From his proclivity for chasing nymphs (Horace, *Odes* 3.18.1), he is named Luxuria by the emblem writers, e.g. Ripa 1603:295; see VII vi 42.7–9. His attempted union with the nymph relates to Acrasia's charm at i 55.6.   **6** I.e., her **faire** eye causes lustful **burning** in him.   **7 chace**: 'pray' (i.e. prey), sugg. Collier 1862 from Drayton's note in the *1611* folio, preserves the 'b' rhyme but sacrifices the play on the word in the next line. The imperfect rhyme may have been intentional, as Kellogg and Steele 1965 suggest; or it may note Faunus's failed rape, as Røstvig 1994:313 suggests; or serve to emphasize the poem's major motif: **beauties chace** in Arthur and the other knights is understood as preying on women because of their beauty.

Stanza 8

3 constraint: distress; also compulsion, alluding to the rape she fears.   **5 deare**: earnestly.   **7–9 Welling**: as she becomes a well.   **dismayd**: overwhelmed with fear; with a double pun: she is 'dis-made' and 'dis-maid'. Through **stony feare** she is changed to stone as her emotional state becomes physical. On this Ovidian metamorphosis, see C. Burrow 1988:104–07. It is paralleled by Daphne's in Ovid, *Met.* 1.548–552 (cf. esp. her prayer at 486–87), and by Arethusa's in *Met.* 5.621–23.

9

Lo now she is that stone, from whose two heads,
  As from two weeping eyes, fresh streames do flow,
  Yet colde through feare, and old conceiued dreads;
  And yet the stone her semblance seemes to show,
  Shapt like a maide, that such ye may her know;
  And yet her vertues in her water byde:
  For it is chaste and pure, as purest snow,
  Ne lets her waues with any filth be dyde,
But euer like her selfe vnstayned hath beene tryde.

10

From thence it comes, that this babes bloody hand
  May not be clensd with water of this well:
  Ne certes Sir striue you it to withstand,
  But let them still be bloody, as befell,
  That they his mothers innocence may tell,
  As she bequeathd in her last testament;
  That as a sacred Symbole it may dwell
  In her sonnes flesh, to mind reuengement,
And be for all chaste Dames an endlesse moniment.

[handwritten: blood as symbol of innocence – christ?]

11

He hearkned to his reason, and the childe
  Vptaking, to the Palmer gaue to beare;
  But his sad fathers armes with blood defilde,
  An heauie load himselfe did lightly reare,

And turning to that place, in which whyleare
  He left his loftie steed with golden sell,
  And goodly gorgeous barbes, him found not theare.
  By other accident that earst befell,
He is conuaide, but how or where, here fits not tell.

12

Which when Sir *Guyon* saw, all were he wroth,
  Yet algates mote he soft himselfe appease,
  And fairely fare on foot, how euer loth;
  His double burden did him sore disease.
  So long they traueiled with litle ease,
  Till that at last they to a Castle came,
  Built on a rocke adioyning to the seas;
  It was an auncient worke of antique fame,
And wondrous strong by nature, and by skilfull frame.

13

Therein three sisters dwelt of sundry sort,
  The children of one syre by mothers three;
  Who dying whylome did diuide this fort
  To them by equall shares in equall fee:
  But stryfull mind, and diuerse qualitee
  Drew them in partes, and each made others foe:
  Still did they striue, and daily disagree;
  The eldest did against the youngest goe,
And both against the middest meant to worken woe.

Stanza 9

3–4 **Yet**: still. 9 **tryde**: proven, found to be.

Stanza 10

5–6 At i 37.6–9, the dying Amavia prays that the babe's bloody hands be seen as pledges 'That cleare she dide from blemish criminall'. 7–8 **Symbole**: sign or token (recorded in *OED* as the first use in this sense). Guyon's contract with the babe to seek revenge suggests its earlier sense, 'a confession of faith', as Mikics 1994:224 suggests. **sacred** may suggest 'accursed', as the blood is 'filth' (9.8) and the 'token of his [God's] wrath' (4.4). If **dwell** is taken in the biblical sense of 'the sinne that dwelleth in me' (Rom. 7.17), **In** may refer to indwelling sin, diffused through the babe's body as through his parents' bodies (4.7–9), rather than the obs. sense 'on'. Tribble 1996:30–32 notes the semiotic complexity of the Palmer's interpretation of the sign. The 'bloody hand . . . is O'Neale's badge', as S. notes in *View* 54, referring to the Irish rebel Hugh O'Neil, which suggested to Upton 1758 a topical reference in the episode. Hadfield and Maley 1997:59 note that the bloody hand is the traditional symbol of Ulster. 9 **moniment**: token of remembrance; warning.

Stanza 11

2 According to the *LR* 70, 'a Palmer bearing an Infant with bloody hands' to the court of the Faerie Queene was the occasion of Guyon's adventure; cf. 43. 3 **sad**: heavy, referring to the **armes**. **with blood defilde**: see i 41.3. The babe is also 'with blood defild' (i 50.9). 6 **sell**: saddle, the seat of authority. **golden**: associated with the 'golden Meane' (Arg.) of temperance. On the horse's name, Brigadore, i.e. golden bridle, see V iii 34.3n. 7 **barbes**: protective covering

for the breast and flanks. 8 **accident**: chance; event. 9 **conuaide**: stolen.

Stanza 12

2 **algates**: nevertheless. 3 From now on Guyon acts outside the chivalric tradition, for 'What is a knyght but whan he is on horsebak? I sett not by a knyght whanne he is on fote' (Malory 10.48), as shown throughout his adventures; see i 8.7–8n. 4 **disease**: trouble. 7 The castle's setting indicates the control of temperance over the temptations of land and sea. **on a rocke**: as the 'wise man, which hathe buylded his house on a rocke' (Matt. 7.24). 9 Its strength **by nature** is shown by its foundations, referring to the natural body which is subject to upheaval, as at 20.6–7; its strength **by . . . frame** refers to its 'goodly gouernaunce' (i 29.8) by temperance; cf. xii 1.

Stanza 13

1–2 In accord with traditional classical theory in which the castle is the human body ruled by the soul, the **syre** is reason or mind; the **mothers three** are the three souls: rational, sensible, and vegetable; or their three faculties: rational, irascible and concupiscible. See 'psychology, Platonic' in the *SEnc*. **sundry**: different, individually distinct. 4 **in equall fee**: in equal possession as a heritable right. The temperate state is not the victory of the mean over the two extremes but their shared governing, which the mean keeps in harmony. 6 **partes**: factions. 7–9 Again in accord with traditional classical theory, specifically, Aristotle, *Ethics* 2.8, in which virtue is the mean between warring contrary vices of excess and deficiency; and Plato, *Republic* 430–31, in which the three parts or powers of the soul – reason, 'spirit', and appetite – are kept in harmony by self-control or temperance. Cf. Thomalin's emblem to *SC July*: '*In medio virtus*'.

14

Where when the knight arriu'd, he was right well
   Receiu'd, as knight of so much worth became,
   Of second sister, who did far excell
   The other two; *Medina* was her name,
   A sober sad, and comely courteous Dame;
   Who rich arayd, and yet in modest guize,
   In goodly garments, that her well became,
   Fayre marching forth in honorable wize,
Him at the threshold mett, and well did enterprize.

15

She led him vp into a goodly bowre,
   And comely courted with meet modestie,
   Ne in her speach, ne in her hauiour,
   Was lightnesse seene, or looser vanitie,
   But gratious womanhood, and grauitie,
   Aboue the reason of her youthly yeares:
   Her golden lockes she roundly did vptye
   In breaded tramels, that no looser heares
Did out of order stray about her daintie eares.

16

Whilest she her selfe thus busily did frame,
   Seemely to entertaine her new-come guest,
   Newes hereof to her other sisters came,
   Who all this while were at their wanton rest,
   Accourting each her frend with lauish fest:
   They were two knights of perelesse puissaunce,
   And famous far abroad for warlike gest,
   Which to these Ladies loue did countenaunce,
And to his mistresse each himselfe stroue to aduaunce.

17

He that made loue vnto the eldest Dame,
   Was hight Sir *Huddibras*, an hardy man;
   Yet not so good of deedes, as great of name,
   Which he by many rash aduentures wan,
   Since errant armes to sew he first began;
   More huge in strength, then wise in workes he was,
   And reason with foole-hardize ouer ran;
   Sterne melancholy did his courage pas,
And was for terrour more, all armd in shyning bras.

18

But he that lou'd the youngest, was *Sansloy*,
   He that faire *Vna* late fowle outraged,
   The most vnruly, and the boldest boy,
   That euer warlike weapons menaged,
   And to all lawlesse lust encouraged,
   Through strong opinion of his matchlesse might:
   Ne ought he car'd, whom he endamaged
   By tortious wrong, or whom bereau'd of right.
He now this Ladies Champion chose for loue to fight.

19

These two gay knights, vowd to so diuerse loues,
   Each other does enuy with deadly hate,
   And daily warre against his foeman moues,
   In hope to win more fauour with his mate,
   And th'others pleasing seruice to abate,
   To magnifie his owne. But when they heard,
   How in that place straunge knight arriued late,
   Both knightes and ladies forth right angry far'd,
And fercely vnto battell sterne themselues prepar'd.

Stanza 14

1–5 Until his presence is noted at 43.1, the Palmer is pointedly excluded while his role is explored through **Medina** whose name declares her nature: from Lat. *medium* or *mediana*, the middle or mean, which is not simply the Aristotelian arithmetical mean between two extremes but their union. **sober sad**: severely grave; balanced (as she is the mean) by **comely courteous**; cf. Una's 'sad sober cheare' (I xii 21.4). As the middle sister, she represents, in ecclesiastical terms, what was later called the *via media* of the reformed church; her elder half-sister, Elissa, represents the Church of Rome or, in her austerity, the Puritans; and the younger Perissa represents the 'lawless' Anabaptists or, in her sensuousness, the Church of Rome. See 'Medina, Elissa, Perissa' in the *SEnc*. **6–7** Medina's apparel may reflect the reformed church's approval of canonical dress; see Magill 1970:174. **9 enterprize**: take in hand.

Stanza 15

4 looser: too loose. **6 Aboue the reason**: Lat. *ultra rationem*, beyond the proportion to be expected. **7–8 roundly**: in a circle. **breaded tramels**: braids rather than nets (cf. III ix 20.4–6), though either contrasts with her 'tresses torne' at 27.2 when the knights fight, and with Duessa's 'discheueled' hair at i 13.6. Cf. Alma's golden hair 'trimly wouen' and in tresses (ix 19.6–7).

Stanza 16

1 frame: apply. **5 Accourting**: courting, to stress their affectation in contrast to Medina who 'comely courted' (15.2)

her guest. **fest**: festivity; or literally 'a feast', which is called **lauish** again in contrast to Medina who 'attempered her feast' (39.1). **7 gest**: deeds. **8 countenaunce**: make a show of; possibly 'pretend', though Medina appeals to their love at 27.6.

Stanza 17

Sir Huddibras is **great of name** as he bears the name of a British king; see x 25.4. His name suggests 'hardi-bras' i.e. 'hard as brass' as in Job's complaint: 'is my flesh of brasse?' (6.12), but also **foole-hardize**. The **shyning bras** he wears – the only knight so armed – signifies endurance or hardness. **8 melancholy**: also irascibility, anger. **pas**: surpass.

Stanza 18

1–3 Sansloy: as the sole survivor of the three Sans brothers in the fashioning of holiness in Bk I – see I ii 25.6–9 – he has his place in the fashioning of temperance in Bk II. **boy** is used as a term of contempt (*OED* 4). That he **chose for loue to fight** indicates the lack of any inner, binding law. **4 menaged**: wielded. **8 tortious**: injurious, illegal.

Stanza 19

1 gay: excellent, fine; used ironically. **2–3** For an explanation of their enmity, see 13.7–9*n*. **enuy**: regard with hatred. **5 abate**: bring down in estimation.

20

But ere they could proceede vnto the place,
    Where he abode, themselues at discord fell,
    And cruell combat ioynd in middle space:
    With horrible assault, and fury fell,
    They heapt huge strokes, the scorned life to quell,
    That all on vprore from her settled seat,
    The house was raysd, and all that in did dwell;
    Seemd that lowde thunder with amazement great
Did rend the ratling skyes with flames of fouldring heat.

21

The noyse thereof cald forth that straunger knight,
    To weet, what dreadfull thing was there in hand;
    Where when as two braue knightes in bloody fight
    With deadly rancour he enraunged fond,
    His sunbroad shield about his wrest he bond,
    And shyning blade vnsheathd, with which he ran
    Vnto that stead, their strife to vnderstond;
    And at his first arriuall, them began
With goodly meanes to pacifie, well as he can.

22

But they him spying, both with greedy forse
    Attonce vpon him ran, and him beset
    With strokes of mortall steele without remorse,
    And on his shield like yron sledges bet:
    As when a Beare and Tygre being met
    In cruell fight on lybicke Ocean wide,
    Espye a traueiler with feet surbet,
    Whom they in equall pray hope to diuide,
They stint their strife, and him assayle on euerie side.

23

But he, not like a weary traueilere,
    Their sharp assault right boldly did rebut,
    And suffred not their blowes to byte him nere,
    But with redoubled buffes them backe did put:
    Whose grieued mindes, which choler did englut,
    Against themselues turning their wrathfull spight,
    Gan with new rage their shieldes to hew and cut;
    But still when *Guyon* came to part their fight,
With heauie load on him they freshly gan to smight.

24

As a tall ship tossed in troublous seas,
    Whom raging windes threatning to make the pray
    Of the rough rockes, doe diuersly disease,
    Meetes two contrarie billowes by the way,
    That her on either side doe sore assay,
    And boast to swallow her in greedy graue;
    Shee scorning both their spights, does make wide way,
    And with her brest breaking the fomy waue,
Does ride on both their backs, and faire her self doth saue.

25

So boldly he him beares, and rusheth forth
    Betweene them both, by conduct of his blade.
    Wondrous great prowesse and heroick worth
    He shewd that day, and rare ensample made,
    When two so mighty warriours he dismade:
    Attonce he wards and strikes, he takes and paies,
    Now forst to yield, now forcing to inuade,
    Before, behind, and round about him laies:
So double was his paines, so double be his praise.

Stanza 20

3 middle space relates their contest to the temperate mean. Extremes meet at the middle or mean where Guyon may try to pacify them, as at 21.9; cf. iv 32.4. The term is used in the same sense in Bk V of the balance of justice (e.g. x 32.1). **5 quell**: kill, as they scorned the other's life and as their rage is suicidal. **8 with amazement great**: i.e. to the great consternation of the inhabitants. **9 fouldring**: thundering, flashing; see I xi 40.2*n*.

Stanza 21

4 enraunged: standing in battle order. **5 sunbroad shield**: cf. the Red Cross Knight's 'sunne-bright shield' at I xi 40.9. Here size seems the point of the description; see i 28.7–8. **7 stead**: place. **vnderstond**: also 'come between'. The consequence of his intercession suggests the sense, 'prop up' (*OED* 1.9). **9 meanes**: with a pun on the temperate 'mean', as he acts as Medina's 'Champion' (18.9).

Stanza 22

3 remorse: also 'mitigation'. **5–9** Bears and tigers are commonly linked, as at IV vii 2.6–7, viii 4.9, V v 40.6. Both are associated with violence, esp. sexual, and are traditional enemies: 'Beres and Tygres, that maken fiers warre' decorate the mazer

in *SC Aug.* 26–28. Their traditional association with the concupiscible and irascible emotions – see Rowland 1973:33, 151 – relates them to Huddibras and Sansloy respectively. **lybicke Ocean**: the Libyan desert. Aeneas wandered 'emongst the Lybick sandes' (III ix 41.6). Topsell 1967:1.28 lists '*Lybican*' as an epithet of the bear. **surbet**: sore.

Stanza 23

5 choler: one of the four humours. Its excess causes anger; see *SEnc* 566. **englut**: fill; devour.

Stanza 24

The handling of the alliterative line in this stanza as it illustrates the working of the temperate mean is esp. noteworthy. To imitate the sense, line 8 breaks in the middle with the accent on the second syllable of **breaking** to echo **backs** at the caesura in line 9. **3 disease**: distress. **5 assay**: assail; put to the test. **6 boast**: threaten.

Stanza 25

2 conduct: skilful handling, displaying virtue in battle. **5 dismade**: defeated. **7 forcing to inuade**: i.e. exerting force in order to attack.

26

Straunge sort of fight, three valiaunt knights to see
   Three combates ioine in one, and to darraine
   A triple warre with triple enmitee,
   All for their Ladies froward loue to gaine,
   Which gotten was but hate. So loue does raine
   In stoutest minds, and maketh monstrous warre;
   He maketh warre, he maketh peace againe,
   And yett his peace is but continuall iarre:
O miserable men, that to him subiect arre.

27

Whilst thus they mingled were in furious armes,
   The faire *Medina* with her tresses torne,
   And naked brest, in pitty of their harmes,
   Emongst them ran, and falling them beforne,
   Besought them by the womb, which them had born,
   And by the loues, which were to them most deare,
   And by the knighthood, which they sure had sworn,
   Their deadly cruell discord to forbeare,
And to her iust conditions of faire peace to heare.

28

But her two other sisters standing by,
   Her lowd gainsaid, and both their champions bad
   Pursew the end of their strong enmity,
   As euer of their loues they would be glad.
   Yet she with pitthy words and counsell sad,
   Still stroue their stubborne rages to reuoke,
   That at the last suppressing fury mad,
   They gan abstaine from dint of direfull stroke,
And hearken to the sober speaches, which she spoke.

29

Ah puissaunt Lords, what cursed euill Spright,
   Or fell *Erinnys*, in your noble harts
   Her hellish brond hath kindled with despight,
   And stird you vp to worke your wilfull smarts?
   Is this the ioy of armes? be these the parts
   Of glorious knighthood, after blood to thrust,
   And not regard dew right and iust desarts?
   Vaine is the vaunt, and victory vniust,
That more to mighty hands, then rightful cause doth trust.

30

And were there rightfull cause of difference,
   Yet were not better, fayre it to accord,
   Then with bloodguiltnesse to heape offence,
   And mortal vengeaunce ioyne to crime abhord?
   O fly from wrath, fly, O my liefest Lord:
   Sad be the sights, and bitter fruites of warre,
   And thousand furies wait on wrathfull sword;
   Ne ought the praise of prowesse more doth marre,
Then fowle reuenging rage, and base contentious iarre.

31

But louely concord, and most sacred peace
   Doth nourish vertue, and fast friendship breeds;
   Weake she makes strong, and strong thing does increace,
   Till it the pitch of highest praise exceeds:
   Braue be her warres, and honorable deeds,
   By which she triumphes ouer yre and pride,
   And winnes an Oliue girlond for her meeds:
   Be therefore, O my deare Lords, pacifide,
And this misseeming discord meekely lay aside.

Stanza 26
1–5 Guyon is included because the relationships among the three knights, each fighting for his lady's love, define classical temperance. **darraine**: wage; also the legal sense, 'to vindicate a claim by wager of battle'. **triple warre**: as each knight fights the other two. **froward**: perverse, ungovernable. **9 miserable**: wretchedly unhappy.

Stanza 27
2–3 Her **tresses torne** are in contrast to her coiffured hair at 15.7–9, and her **naked brest** to her 'modest guize' at 14.6. **9 heare**: the judicial sense, 'listen to in a court of law'. Her plea establishes a new law of harmony; cf. 32.8.

Stanza 28
4 As euer: i.e. even as, with the threat: 'if ever'. **5 sad**: grave, serious. **6 stubborne**: fierce. **reuoke**: check, restrain.

Stanza 29
2–4 Erinnys: the Furies, 'the Authours of all evill and mischiefe' (gloss to *SC Nov.* 164), who are 'nothinge but the wringinges, tourmentes, and gnawinges of yll consciences that vexed naughty men' (T. Cooper 1565). Their traditional

number three is appropriate to the three knights provoked by 'fury mad' (28.7). Medina seeks to replace vengeance, with which the Furies are associated, with **dew right**, **iust desarts** and **rightfull cause**. Cf. 30.7. **6 thrust**: also 'thirst'.

Stanza 30
3 bloodguiltnesse: see 4.5n. **5** She addresses the three lords as one, or each alone; cf. 31.8. Her warning against **mortal vengeaunce** is esp. pertinent to Guyon who seeks 'dew vengeance' (i 61.7) against Acrasia.

Stanza 31
1–2 I.e., **concord** nourishes **vertue** in the individual and **peace** breeds **friendship** with others. The concord she seeks by preparing 'Their minds to pleasure' (33.9) is perverted by Phædria and Acrasia. Its role in establishing friendship is elaborated at IV x 34–35. **louely**: loving. **most sacred peace**: for 'Blessed are the peace makers: for they shalbe called the children of God' (Matt. 5.9). **3–4** Her role expands from the Aristotelian mean between two vices to a moderator of the passions and a peacemaker; suggested Nelson 1963:194, in noting that her name derives from Lat. *medens*, healer. **7 Oliue girlond**: 'Olives bene for peace' (*SC Apr.* 124). **meeds**: reward.

32

Her gracious words their rancour did appall,
    And suncke so deepe into their boyling brests,
    That downe they lett their cruell weapons fall,
    And lowly did abase their lofty crests
    To her faire presence, and discrete behests.
    Then she began a treaty to procure,
    And stablish termes betwixt both their requests,
    That as a law for euer should endure;
Which to obserue in word of knights they did assure.

33

Which to confirme, and fast to bind their league,
    After their weary sweat and bloody toile,
    She them besought, during their quiet treague,
    Into her lodging to repaire a while,
    To rest themselues, and grace to reconcile.
    They soone consent: so forth with her they fare,
    Where they are well receiud, and made to spoile
    Themselues of soiled armes, and to prepare
Their minds to pleasure, and their mouths to dainty fare.

34

And those two froward sisters, their faire loues
    Came with them eke, all were they wondrous loth,
    And fained cheare, as for the time behoues,
    But could not colour yet so well the troth,
    But that their natures bad appeard in both:
    For both did at their second sister grutch,
    And inly grieue, as doth an hidden moth
    The inner garment frett, not th'vtter touch;
One thought her cheare too litle, th'other thought too
                       (mutch.

35

Elissa (so the eldest hight) did deeme
    Such entertainment base, ne ought would eat,
    Ne ought would speake, but euermore did seeme
    As discontent for want of merth or meat;
    No solace could her Paramour intreat
    Her once to show, ne court, nor dalliaunce,
    But with bent lowring browes, as she would threat,
    She scould, and frownd with froward countenaunce,
Vnworthy of faire Ladies comely gouernaunce.

36

But young *Perissa* was of other mynd,
    Full of disport, still laughing, loosely light,
    And quite contrary to her sisters kynd;
    No measure in her mood, no rule of right,
    But poured out in pleasure and delight;
    In wine and meats she flowd aboue the banck,
    And in excesse exceeded her owne might;
    In sumptuous tire she ioyd her selfe to pranck,
But of her loue too lauish (litle haue she thanck.)

37

Fast by her side did sitt the bold *Sansloy*,
    Fitt mate for such a mincing mineon,
    Who in her loosenesse tooke exceeding ioy;
    Might not be found a francker franion,
    Of her leawd parts to make companion:
    But *Huddibras*, more like a Malecontent,
    Did see and grieue at his bold fashion;
    Hardly could he endure his hardiment,
Yett still he satt, and inly did him selfe torment.

[handwritten marginal note: 2 opposing evils]

Stanza 32

1 appall: quell. **6 procure**: endeavour to arrange. **7 both their requests**: as extended to more than two persons (*OED* B.1.b), or as she sets up three separate treaties, each between two knights. Here she acts as an officer of the court of requests. **8** The limit of her law is revealed by Rom. 7.23: 'I se another law in my membres, rebelling against the law of my minde, and leading me captiue vnto the law of sinne, which is in my membres'.

Stanza 33

3 treague: truce; evidently coined by S. by combining 'league' and 'truce', from Ital. *tregua*, 'a truce, a league, an atonement' (Florio 1598). **5 grace to reconcile**: to regain each other's favour, Lat. *gratiam reconciliare*.

Stanza 34

1 froward: perverse, ungovernable (as 26.4) because they turn away from the mean; see 38.5–8*n*. **6 grutch**: grumble. **7–8 frett**: consume; cf. Ps. 39.12: when man is rebuked for sin, 'he waxeth wo and wan, | As doth a cloth that moths haue fret' (Sternhold and Hopkins 1562). The sisters are eaten inwardly by their emotions while outwardly seeming unchanged. **9 One** is the excessive Perissa; **th'other**, the deficient Elissa. Their states correspond to the pride and weakness that leads to sin; see I viii 1.6–7.

Stanza 35

1 Elissa: from Gk ἐλάσσων, too little, i.e. taking too little delight in bodily things (Aristotle, *Ethics* 7.9); or from the Phoenician name of Virgil's outraged Dido, as Nelson 1963:181 suggests. **2 entertainment**: provisions; more broadly, 'hospitality'. **4 meat**: i.e. food; its usual sense, as 39.3. **5 solace**: pleasure. **intreat**: persuade. **6 court**: courtesy. **9 gouernaunce**: behaviour.

Stanza 36

1 Perissa: Excess, from Gk περισσός, too much, excessive; the Aristotelian counterpart to Elissa. **of other mynd**: literally so; see 13.7–9*n*. **2 disport**: merriment that carries one from the mean. **still**: ever. Her laughing anticipates Phædria's at vi 3.4. **3 kynd**: disposition. **5 poured out**: for the sexual sense, see I vii 7.2*n*. Cf. Cymochles in the Bower at v 28.5.

Stanza 37

1 bold: his defining epithet at I ii 25.9. **2 Fitt mate**: as he also personifies 'no rule of right' (36.4). **mincing mineon**: excessively dainty mistress; used ironically as the alliteration indicates. **4 francker franion**: looser paramour. **6 Malecontent**: a type of melancholic humour. See 'melancholy' in the *SEnc*. **8 his hardiment**: referring to Sansloy's boldness in love, in contrast to his own 'foole-hardize' in fighting (17.7).

38

Betwixt them both the faire *Medina* sate
  With sober grace, and goodly carriage:
  With equall measure she did moderate
  The strong extremities of their outrage,
  That forward paire she euer would asswage,
  When they would striue dew reason to exceed;
  But that same froward twaine would accorage,
  And of her plenty adde vnto their need:
So kept she them in order, and her selfe in heed.

39

Thus fairely shee attempered her feast,
  And pleasd them all with meete satiety:
  At last when lust of meat and drinke was ceast,
  She *Guyon* deare besought of curtesie,
  To tell from whence he came through ieopardy,
  And whether now on new aduenture bownd.
  Who with bold grace, and comely grauity,
  Drawing to him the eies of all arownd,
From lofty siege began these words aloud to sownd.

40

This thy demaund, O Lady, doth reuiue
  Fresh memory in me of that great Queene,
  Great and most glorious virgin Queene aliue,
  That with her soueraine powre, and scepter shene

All Faery lond does peaceably sustene.
  In widest Ocean she her throne does reare,
  That ouer all the earth it may be seene;
  As morning Sunne her beames dispredden cleare,
And in her face faire peace, and mercy doth appeare.

41

In her the richesse of all heauenly grace,
  In chiefe degree are heaped vp on hye:
  And all that els this worlds enclosure bace,
  Hath great or glorious in mortall eye,
  Adornes the person of her Maiestye;
  That men beholding so great excellence,
  And rare perfection in mortalitye,
  Doe her adore with sacred reuerence,
As th'Idole of her makers great magnificence.

FQ

42

To her I homage and my seruice owe,
  In number of the noblest knightes on ground,
  Mongst whom on me she deigned to bestowe
  Order of *Maydenhead*, the most renownd,
  That may this day in all the world be found:
  An yearely solemne feast she wontes to make
  The day that first doth lead the yeare around;
  To which all knights of worth and courage bold
Resort, to heare of straunge aduentures to be told.

virginity

Stanza 38

On **Medina** as peacemaker, see 31.3–4*n*. In seeking harmony rather than a mean – a state that is dynamic rather than static – her role as hostess is more Platonic than Aristotelian. **3 equall**: also 'just'. **4 extremities**: violent outbursts; also the 'two Extremities' of Arg.3. **outrage**: excesses, want of moderation. **5–8** The **forward paire** is Perissa–Sansloy; the **froward twaine**, Elissa–Huddibras, though see 34.1. **froward**: perverse; but also 'from-ward'. On the 'forward–froward' distinction, see Nelson 1963:182–83. **accorage**: encourage; the double stress suggests 'urge to take heart'. **9 in heed**: heeded, respected; also 'takes care of herself', for the mean exists only in relation to the extremes.

Stanza 39

1 attempered: controlled, alluding to the tempering of temperance, as Alma's banquet is 'Attempred goodly well for health and for delight' (xi 2.9). **3–4** On this epic convention, see I xii 15.1–2*n*. **lust**: desire. **8–9** This moment recalls Dido's banquet in *Aen.* 1.753–56: when Aeneas is asked by her to tell his story, all eyes turn to him as he speaks from his lofty couch. His story lasts until dawn. See J. Watkins 1995:127–28. Dido's request leads her to love him; Medina's request arouses Guyon's worship of the Faerie Queene. **siege**: seat, throne.

Stanza 40

4 shene: bright. At III iii 49, the Queen's **scepter** is called 'her white rod' by which she establishes 'sacred Peace'. **8 dispredden**: spread abroad or far. **9 peace, and mercy**: two of the four daughters or graces of God, from Ps. 85.10, who seek

forgiveness for man against the claims of Truth and Justice for satisfaction, as in Langland, *Piers Plowman* 18.416–21. At V ix 32, Mercilla, whose name suggests mercy, is attended by Eirene (Peace).

Stanza 41

1–2 The Queen in her **richesse** [i.e. wealth] **of all heauenly grace** is parodied by Lucifera's 'endlesse richesse' (I iv 7.5) and by the 'rich hils of welth' in Mammon's 'house of Richesse' (II vii 7.3, 24.9). As 'Mirrour of grace' (I proem 4.2), she is seen in Belphœbe as the 'glorious mirrhour of celestiall grace' (iii 25.6). As a symbol of God-created glory and her relation to biblical Wisdom, see Fruen 1994:77–78. On praise of her as overt celebration and implied criticism of the Queen, see Hackett 1995:142–43. **3 bace**: low, being of the earth. **7** Exempting the Queen from 'the ymage of mortalitie' described at i 57. **8–9 sacred**: suggests that they respect the injunction: 'kepe your selues from idoles' (1 John 5.21). **Idole**: image; an earthly embodiment of the divine, one made in the image of God; cf. IV vi 17.5. **magnificence**: sovereign bounty, glory, splendour, grandeur, imposing beauty. It describes Arthur's virtue in the *LR* 38, and is used once again at V v 4.2 to describe Radigund who parodies Gloriana's rule.

Stanza 42

4–5 On the **Order of Maydenhead**, see I vii 46.4–7*n*. **6–7** On the Faerie Queene's **yearely solemne feast** see the *LR* 50–51. **make**: the verb used at I xii 38.2; 'hold', sugg. Collier 1862 from Drayton's note in the *1611* folio has been adopted by some editors for the sake of the rhyme.

43

There this old Palmer shewd himselfe that day,
 And to that mighty Princesse did complaine
 Of grieuous mischiefes, which a wicked <u>Fay</u> *fayre*
 Had wrought, and many whelmd in deadly paine,
 Whereof he crau'd redresse. My Soueraine,
 Whose glory is in gracious deeds, and ioyes
 Throughout the world her mercy to maintaine,
 Eftsoones deuisd redresse for such annoyes;
Me all vnfitt for so great purpose she employes.

44

Now hath faire *Phebe* with her siluer face
 Thrise seene the shadowes of the neather world,
 Sith last I left that honorable place,
 In which her roiall presence is entrold;
 Ne euer shall I rest in house nor hold,
 Till I that false *Acrasia* haue wonne;
 Of whose fowle deedes, too hideous to bee told,
 I witnesse am, and this their wretched sonne,
Whose wofull parents she hath wickedly fordonne.

45

Tell on, fayre Sir, said she, that dolefull tale,
 From which sad ruth does seeme you to restraine,
 That we may pitty such vnhappie bale,
 And learne from pleasures poyson to abstaine:
 Ill by ensample good doth often gayne.
 Then forward he his purpose gan pursew,
 And told the story of the mortall payne,
 Which *Mordant* and *Amauia* did rew;
As with lamenting eyes him selfe did lately vew.

46

Night was far spent, and now in *Ocean* deep
 Orion, flying fast from hissing snake,
 His flaming head did hasten for to steep,
 When of his pitteous tale he end did make;
 Whilst with delight of that he wisely spake,
 Those guestes beguyled, did beguyle their eyes
 Of kindly sleepe, that did them ouertake.
 At last when they had markt the chaunged skyes,
They wist their houre was spent; then each to rest him hyes.

Stanza 43
1–4 Cf. Guyon's account to Arthur at ix 9.5–8; see 11.2*n*.
3 Fay: fairy. **4 whelmd**: destroyed; also 'drowned', 'buried'.
deadly paine: referring not to Acrasia's victims who enjoy their
captivity but to those, such as Mordant, who seek to escape but
lacking temperance suffer 'mortall payne' (45.7). **6** Alluding
to her name, Gloriana. **8 annoyes**: injuries.

Stanza 44
1–4 This elaborate paraphrase for 'three months have
passed' is appropriate to the formal taking of a vow. On the
significance of measuring time by the moon, see I viii 38.6–7*n*.
J.N. Wall 1990:333 notes that a period of three lunar cycles
earlier fits 1 Jan. as the day Guyon begins his quest. See ix
7.5–6*n*. **entrold**: either 'enrolled', i.e. celebrated (cf. i 32.3);
or 'encircled', extending the image of the Queen surrounded
by her knights. The **place**, then, would be the presence cham-
ber, as at V ix 27.2, etc. **5 hold**: place of refuge; fort.
6 wonne: subdued. **9 fordonne**: killed.

Stanza 45
4 pleasures poyson: cf. 'pleasures poisoned baytes' (i Arg.4).
6 purpose: discourse. **8 Amauia**: here first named; see i
55.4–5*n*. **rew**: 'suffer' is the required sense; i.e. suffering
which they regretted (*OED* 7) or lamented (*OED* 11).

Stanza 46
1–3 As Scorpion rises in the east, Orion the hunter sets
in the west pursued by his slayer (see VII vii 39.6–8). They
are seldom in the same sky at the same time. **Orion**: the
'starre [that] bringeth in winter' (Geneva gloss to Job 38.31).
hissing snake: the Hydra which occupies the interval between
Scorpio and Orion in the conventional representations of
the stars; noted in *SEnc* 189. On the date indicated by the
constellations, see note on the Queen's 'Annuall feaste' in
the *LR* 50–51. **8 the chaunged skyes**: i.e. the changed posi-
tion of the stars.

Cant. III.

*Vaine Braggadocchio getting Guyons
horse is made the scorne
Of knighthood trew, and is of fayre
Belphœbe fowle forlorne.*

1

SOone as the morrow fayre with purple beames
Disperst the shadowes of the misty night,
  And *Titan* playing on the eastern streames,
  Gan cleare the deawy ayre with springing light,
  Sir *Guyon* mindfull of his vow yplight,
  Vprose from drowsie couch, and him addrest
  Vnto the iourney which he had behight:
  His puissaunt armes about his noble brest,
And many-folded shield he bound about his wrest.

2

Then taking *Congé* of that virgin pure,
  The bloody-handed babe vnto her truth
  Did earnestly committ, and her coniure,
  In vertuous lore to traine his tender youth,
  And all that gentle noriture ensueth:
  And that so soone as ryper yeares he raught,
  He might for memory of that dayes ruth,
  Be called *Ruddymane*, and thereby taught,
T'auenge his Parents death on them, that had it wrought.

3

So forth he far'd, as now befell, on foot,
  Sith his good steed is lately from him gone;
  Patience perforce: helplesse what may it boot
  To frett for anger, or for griefe to mone?

His Palmer now shall foot no more alone:
  So fortune wrought, as vnder greene woodes syde
  He lately heard that dying Lady grone,
  He left his steed without, and speare besyde,
And rushed in on foot to ayd her, ere she dyde.

4

The whyles a losell wandring by the way,
  One that to bountie neuer cast his mynd,
  Ne thought of honour euer did assay
  His baser brest, but in his kestrell kynd
  A pleasing vaine of glory he did fynd,
  To which his flowing toung, and troublous spright
  Gaue him great ayd, and made him more inclynd:
  He that braue steed there finding ready dight,
Purloynd both steed and speare, and ran away full light.

5

Now gan his hart all swell in iollity,
  And of him selfe great hope and help conceiu'd
  That puffed vp with smoke of vanity,
  And with selfe-loued personage deceiu'd,
  He gan to hope, of men to be receiu'd
  For such, as he him thought, or faine would bee:
  But for in court gay portaunce he perceiu'd,
  And gallant shew to be in greatest gree,
Eftsoones to court he cast t'aduaunce his first degree.

Book II Canto iii

Argument

1 Vaine: foolish; his stock epithet: see 4.5*n*. **4 Belphœbe**: Ital. *bella*, handsome + Gk φοίβη, pure, radiant. At ii 44.1, 'faire *Phebe*' incorporates her name; see 22.1–3*n*. Apart from this rubric, she is not named in Bk II. For further on her name, see III v 27.9*n*. At III vi 28.5, Dame Phœbe (Diana) 'of her selfe her name *Belphœbe* red'. In the *LR* 36–37, S. speaks of 'fashioning her name according to your owne excellent conceipt of Cynthia, (Phœbe and Cynthia being both names of Diana)'. **fayre**: her stock epithet. **fowle forlorne**: disgracefully put to shame; deserted; see 43.7–9.

Stanza 1

1 purple beames: the stock classical description of dawn, as at I ii 7.1–3. **7 behight**: vowed. **9 many-folded**: a standard multi-layered classical shield; see v 6.3*n*.

Stanza 2

1 Congé: ceremonious farewell, as i 34.1. **virgin pure**: as Alma is 'a virgin bright' (ix 18.1 and see *n*). **2 truth**: trust; virtue. **3 coniure**: solemnly entreat; charge. Literally, 'to

swear together'. **4** As Arthur was trained in **vertuous lore**, i.e. moral doctrine; see I ix 4.9. **5 gentle noriture**: noble upbringing. **8 Ruddymane**: i.e. **bloody-handed** being 'with blood defild' (i 50.9), a traditional sign of guilt. **9** Confirming the vow Guyon made for him at i 61.5–8.

Stanza 3

2 lately: at ii 11.5–9. **3 Patience perforce**: proverbial (Smith 598). **perforce**: upon compulsion; through necessity. Guyon follows the injunction to join temperance with patience (1 Pet. 1.5). **4 anger** and **griefe** uncontrolled by temperance are illustrated in the Phaon episode; see iv 33.3–6 and vi 1.6–7*n*. On these two vices in relation to patience, see 'patience' in the *SEnc*. On the Red Cross Knight's grief cured by Patience, see I x 24.

Stanza 4

1–2 losell: scoundrel. **bountie**: valour; munificence. **cast**: applied. **4 baser**: most base. **kestrell kynd**: a small hawk of poor breed and base nature; a term of contempt for one who preys on others. **5 glory**: boasting, vainglory. **glory he**: glory vaine *1596* is preferred by J.C. Smith, in Spenser 1912, for the play on words.

6

And by the way he chaunced to espy
  One sitting ydle on a sunny banck,
  To whom auaunting in great brauery,
  As Peacocke, that his painted plumes doth pranck,
  He smote his courser in the trembling flanck,
  And to him threatned his hart-thrilling speare:
  The seely man seeing him ryde so ranck,
  And ayme at him, fell flatt to ground for feare,
And crying Mercy loud, his pitious handes gan reare.

7

Threat the Scarcrow wexed wondrous prowd,
  Through fortune of his first aduenture fayre,
  And with big thundring voice reuyld him lowd;
  Vile Caytiue, vassall of dread and despayre,
  Vnworthie of the commune breathed ayre,
  Why liuest thou, dead dog, a lenger day,
  And doest not vnto death thy selfe prepayre.
  Dy, or thy selfe my captiue yield for ay;
Great fauour I thee graunt, for aunswere thus to stay.

8

Hold, O deare Lord, hold your dead-doing hand,
  Then loud he cryde, I am your humble thrall.
  Ah wretch (quoth he) thy destinies withstand
  My wrathfull will, and doe for mercy call.

I giue thee life: therefore prostrated fall,
  And kisse my stirrup; that thy homage bee.
  The Miser threw him selfe, as an Offall,
  Streight at his foot in base humilitee,
And cleeped him his liege, to hold of him in fee.

9

So happy peace they made and faire accord:
  Eftsoones this liegeman gan to wexe more bold,
  And when he felt the folly of his Lord,
  In his owne kind he gan him selfe vnfold:
  For he was wylie witted, and growne old
  In cunning sleightes and practick knauery.
  From that day forth he cast for to vphold
  His ydle humour with fine flattery,
And blow the bellowes to his swelling vanity.

10

Trompart fitt man for *Braggadochio*,
  To serue at court in view of vaunting eye;
  Vaineglorious man, when fluttring wind does blow
  In his light winges, is lifted vp to skye:
  The scorne of knighthood and trew cheualrye,
  To thinke without desert of gentle deed,
  And noble worth to be aduaunced hye:
  Such prayse is shame; but honour vertues meed
Doth beare the fayrest flowre in honourable seed.

Stanza 5
1 iollity: presumptuous self-reliance (*OED* 4). **2–4** His moral state parodies Guyon's at vii 2.4–5. **selfe-loued personage**: love of his own image or impersonation. **7 portaunce**: bearing, demeanour. At 21.9, he is confronted by Belphœbe's 'stately portance'. **8 gree**: favour, goodwill. **9 his first degree**: the first stage in attaining knighthood or promotion, later represented by Philotime's chain of ambition in which each link is 'a step of dignity' (vii 46.9). Yet his means t'aduaunce consists only in his 'auaunting' (6.3).

Stanza 6
3 auaunting: advancing; boasting; hence, 'advancing boastfully'. **brauery**: the term gathers a range of meanings, e.g. 'bravado'; 'splendour' or 'finery' in referring to armour; mere outward show without inner worth; and 'valour' or 'courage', which is mocked by the simile in the next line. Its only two uses in the poem refer to him: here he is seen **auaunting in great brauery** and at the end his 'great vaunt of brauerie' (V iii 39.7) is exposed. See Quint 1992:414–16. **4 pranck**: proudly display. **7 seely**: mean, miserable, helpless. **ranck**: fiercely, proudly. **9 Mercy loud**: he calls for mercy loudly; or he calls 'Mercy Lord' (sugg. Upton 1758), which would echo Guyon's appeal to the Red Cross Knight at i 27.1; cf. 8.1–2. **his pitious handes**: a witty play on hands appealing for pity.

Stanza 7
1 Scarcrow: as one dressed in another's clothes, and fit only to scare crows. **4 Caytiue**: wretch; captive. **6 The dog** is regarded with contempt throughout the poem, perhaps because it is abhorred in the Bible, e.g. **dead dog** is a term of infamy in 2 Sam. 9.8. **a lenger day**: i.e. a day longer.

Stanza 8
7 Miser: wretch. **Offall**: refuse, something thrown down; from 'off fall' as the stress shows. Perhaps a play on 'oaf', an elf's child; hence 'misbegotten'. **9 in fee**: in absolute possession, i.e. to be his feudal **thrall**.

Stanza 9
4 kind: nature. **6 practick**: crafty. **9 blow the bellowes**: alluding to his name and to Braggadocchio's puffed-up state; cf. 5.3, 10.3–4.

Stanza 10
1 Trompart: the deceiver (cf. 'trompant': cheating, deceiving, and 'trump': to deceive); or the flatterer ready to 'blow the bellowes' (9.9) of Braggadocchio's vanity. See 'Trompart' in the *SEnc*. **Braggadochio**: brag, bragard, braggart + *occhio*, the Ital. suffix; 'brag' also signifies 'show', 'pomp'. Or Ital. *occhio*, eye, referring to his **vaunting eye**, as Jerome Saulnier has suggested to me. He is Aristotle's rash man who is boastful and only pretends to be courageous (*Ethics* 3.7), the *alazon* or *miles gloriosus*. His name soon entered the English language: in a copy of *Till Eulenspiegel* given him by S. – see Chronology 1578 *20 Dec.* – Harvey noted in 1588 that the host in one tale is 'A great braggadocia'. (I owe this information to William Barker and Henry Woudhuysen.) His usual title is 'the boaster' as 18.8, III x 24.1, etc. Quint 1992:414–20 relates him to the newfangled vanity of the court. See 'Braggadocchio' in the *SEnc*. **5** Repeating Arg.2–3. **8–9** I.e., honour, which is the reward of valour, flourishes best among the nobility. See iv 1.

11

So forth they pas, a well consorted payre,
  Till that at length with *Archimage* they meet:
  Who seeing one that shone in armour fayre,
  On goodly courser thondring with his feet,
  Eftsoones supposed him a person meet,
  Of his reuenge to make the instrument:
  For since the *Redcrosse* knight he erst did weet,
  To beene with *Guyon* knitt in one consent,
The ill, which earst to him, he now to *Guyon* ment.

12

And comming close to *Trompart* gan inquere
  Of him, what mightie warriour that mote bee,
  That rode in golden sell with single spere,
  But wanted sword to wreake his enmitee.
  He is a great aduenturer, (said he)
  That hath his sword through hard assay forgone,
  And now hath vowd, till he auenged bee,
  Of that despight, neuer to wearen none;
That speare is him enough to doen a thousand grone.

13

Th'enchaunter greatly ioyed in the vaunt,
  And weened well ere long his will to win,
  And both his foen with equall foyle to daunt.
  Tho to him louting lowly did begin
  To plaine of wronges, which had committed bin
  By *Guyon*, and by that false *Redcrosse* knight,
  Which two through treason and deceiptfull gin,
  Had slayne Sir *Mordant*, and his Lady bright:
That mote him honour win, to wreak so foule despight.

14

Therewith all suddeinly he seemd enragd,
  And threatned death with dreadfull countenaunce,
  As if their liues had in his hand beene gagd;
  And with stiffe force shaking his mortall launce,

To let him weet his doughtie valiaunce,
  Thus said; Old man, great sure shalbe thy meed,
  If where those knights for feare of dew vengeaunce
  Doe lurke, thou certeinly to mee areed,
That I may wreake on them their hainous hateful deed.

15

Certes, my Lord, (said he) that shall I soone,
  And giue you eke good helpe to their decay.
  But mote I wisely you aduise to doon;
  Giue no ods to your foes, but doe puruay
  Your selfe of sword before that bloody day:
  For they be two the prowest knights on grownd,
  And oft approu'd in many hard assay,
  And eke of surest steele, that may be fownd,
Doe arme your self against that day, them to confownd.

16

Dotard, (saide he) let be thy deepe aduise;
  Seemes that through many yeares thy wits thee faile,
  And that weake eld hath left thee nothing wise,
  Els neuer should thy iudgement be so frayle,
  To measure manhood by the sword or mayle.
  Is not enough fowre quarters of a man,
  Withouten sword or shield, an hoste to quayle?
  Thou litle wotest, what this right-hand can:
Speake they, which haue beheld the battailes, which it wan.

17

The man was much abashed at his boast;
  Yet well he wist, that who so would contend
  With either of those knightes on euen coast,
  Should neede of all his armes, him to defend;
  Yet feared least his boldnesse should offend,
  When *Braggadocchio* saide, Once I did sweare,
  When with one sword seuen knightes I brought to end,
  Thence forth in battaile neuer sword to beare,
But it were that, which noblest knight on earth doth weare.

Stanza 11
8 in one consent: in mutual accord; in one fellowship; see i 34.2. **9 ment**: directed.

Stanza 12
3 golden sell: as ii 11.6. **single spere**: i.e. spear alone. **6 assay**: encounter. **forgone**: forfeited. At 17.6–9 the Boaster offers a more flattering explanation.

Stanza 13
3 with equall foyle: i.e. by defeating both. Or **foyle** refers to a sword (*OED* 5). At 18.1–7 Archimago vows to bring Arthur's sword to Braggadocchio the next day, and at viii 19.1–4 he is asked by Pyrochles, who lacks a sword, that it be brought to him. Then the fight would be **equall**: sword against sword. **7 gin**: device, craft. **9 wreak**: punish.

Stanza 14
1 all suddeinly marks his intemperate rashness; cf. Guyon's response to a similar tale at i 11–12. **3 gagd**: i.e. given as pledges. **5 valiaunce**: valour. **8 areed**: tell.

Stanza 15
2 decay: death. **3 wisely**: referring to his advice; or how Braggadocchio should act. **4 puruay**: supply. **7 approu'd**: tested.

Stanza 16
6 The traditional four parts of the body, each with a limb, together constituting one complete man, suggesting here the four quarters of a shield.

Stanza 17
3 euen coast: i.e. equal ground or level playing-field; or, as 'cost': equal terms; cf. IV iii 24.8. **6 Once**: once for all. **7** This mock knight is mocked by the story of Jack who became known as the Brave Tailor when his boast that he had killed seven at one swat was taken to refer to giants not flies. See 'folklore' in the *SEnc*.

18

Perdy Sir knight, saide then th'enchaunter bliue,
    That shall I shortly purchase to your hond:
    For now the best and noblest knight aliue,
    Prince *Arthur* is, that wonnes in Faerie lond;
    He hath a sword, that flames like burning brond.
    The same by my deuice I vndertake
    Shall by to morrow by thy side be fond.
    At which bold word that boaster gan to quake,
And wondred in his minde, what mote that Monster make.

19

He stayd not for more bidding, but away
    Was suddein vanished out of his sight:
    The Northerne winde his wings did broad display
    At his commaund, and reared him vp light
    From off the earth, to take his aerie flight.
    They lookt about, but no where could espye
    Tract of his foot: then dead through great affright
    They both nigh were, and each bad other flye:
Both fled attonce, ne euer backe retourned eye.

20

Till that they come vnto a forrest greene,
    In which they shrowd themselues from causeles feare;
    Yet feare them followes still, where so they beene,
    Each trembling leafe, and whistling wind they heare,

As ghastly bug does greatly them affeare:
    Yet both doe striue their fearefulnesse to faine.
    At last they heard a horne, that shrilled cleare
    Throughout the wood, that ecchoed againe,
And made the forrest ring, as it would riue in twaine.

21

Eft through the thicke they heard one rudely rush;
    With noyse whereof he from his loftie steed
    Downe fell to ground, and crept into a bush,
    To hide his coward head from dying dreed:
    But *Trompart* stoutly stayd to taken heed,
    Of what might hap. Eftsoone there stepped foorth
    A goodly Ladie clad in hunters weed,
    That seemd to be a woman of great worth,
And by her stately portance, borne of heauenly birth.

22

Her face so faire as flesh it seemed not,
    But heuenly pourtraict of bright Angels hew,
    Cleare as the skye, withouten blame or blot,
    Through goodly mixture of complexions dew;
    And in her cheekes the vermeill red did shew
    Like roses in a bed of lillies shed,
    The which ambrosiall odours from them threw,
    And gazers sence with double pleasure fed,
Hable to heale the sicke, and to reuiue the ded.

Stanza 18

1 Perdy: assuredly; or an oath to confirm Braggadocchio's vow. **bliue**: quickly. **2 purchase**: procure. **3–4** He praises Arthur in similar terms at viii 18.3–4. **6 deuice**: devising. **9** . . . how that marvel (Lat. *monstrum*) could be accomplished.

Stanza 19

1–5 A supernatural action rare in the poem. Archimago is like Satan, 'the prince that ruleth in the aire' (Eph. 2.2) and who is associated with the north (as in Isa. 14.13).

Stanza 20

2–5 Cf. Ps. 53.5: 'They were afraied for feare, where no feare was'; Lev. 26.36: 'The sounde of a leafe shaken shal chase them'; and Song Sol. 17.14, 17: the wicked are 'troubled with monstrous visions' and bound with terror by 'an hyssing winde'. **ghastly bug**: terrifying apparition. **6 faine**: conceal.

Stanzas 21–31

The poem's longest and most ecstatic blazon, a vision of innocence and beauty designed to sustain readers against the assaults of Acrasia. In the *LR* 35–36, S. declares that Belphoebe mirrors Elizabeth as 'a most vertuous and beautifull Lady'; and in III proem 5.9 that she is a mirror of the Queen's 'rare chastitee'. His use of imagery from the Song of Solomon, which he was said to have translated, is noted below. As a blazon, see Quilligan 1987:164–65; as an icon, see Cain 1978:86–91. On the relation of the blazon to Virgil's description of Venus disguised as Diana appearing before her son, Aeneas (*Aen.* 1.314–24), see Bono 1984:71–74; on its relation also to Ariosto's description of Alcina when she first appears to Ruggiero (*Orl. Fur.* 7.9–16), see J. Watkins 1995:114–19; and on its relation to Ovidian voyeurism, see Krier 1990:71–76. See 'Belphoebe' in the *SEnc.* Hageman

1971 notes that the blazon begins at stanza 22, a number associated with temperance; see ix 22*n*.

Stanza 21

1 Eft: afterwards; or **Eftsoone**: forthwith. **thicke**: thicket. **rudely**: violently. **4 dying dreed**: fear of dying; or he is like Sidney's Dametas who thrust himself into a bush when wild beasts appear 'resolved not to see his own death' (*New Arcadia* 115). **8 worth**: rank, dignity. **9 stately portance**: majestic bearing. The next ten stanzas define this term.

Stanza 22

1–3 Wittily alluding to the etymology of Belphoebe's name without naming her; see Arg.4*n*. **Cleare**: brightly shining, Lat. *clarus*. **withouten**: used for emphasis. **blame**: fault. **blot**: as Una at I xii 22.7; and as the beloved in the Song Sol. 4.7: 'Thou art all faire, my loue, and there is no spot in thee'. **4** The temperate combination of colours in her face expresses the temperate combination of the four humours in her body in opposition to their bad mixture (Gk ἀκρασία) in Acrasia; see xii 69.8*n*. **5–9** 'Lilly white, and Cremsin redde' are 'Colours meete to clothe a mayden Queene' (*SC Feb.* 130, 132). In particular, the **vermeill red** of her cheeks expresses her sanguine nature as one unaffected by passion, and manifests her shamefastness; cf. ix 41.3–7 and Song Sol. 5.10. The internal rhyme of line 6 draws attention to their beauty so that the **double pleasure** of seeing and smelling attests to the extraordinary physical and spiritual power of her face: the mere sight of her combines the powers of the well of life and the tree of life (I xi 30, 48). She is seen, then, as Britomart is seen: 'The maker selfe resembling in her feature' (IV vi 17.5). **ambrosiall**: divinely fragrant, as Diana's locks are sprinkled 'with sweet *Ambrosia*' (III vi 18.9); from Venus's *ambrosiae comae* (*Aen.* 1.403).

23

In her faire eyes two liuing lamps did flame,
    Kindled aboue at th'heuenly makers light,
    And darted fyrie beames out of the same,
    So passing persant, and so wondrous bright,
    That quite bereau'd the rash beholders sight:
    In them the blinded god his lustfull fyre
    To kindle oft assayd, but had no might;
    For with dredd Maiestie, and awfull yre,
She broke his wanton darts, and quenched bace desyre.

24

Her yuorie forhead, full of bountie braue,
    Like a broad table did it selfe dispred,
    For Loue his loftie triumphes to engraue,
    And write the battailes of his great godhed:
    All good and honour might therein be red:
    For there their dwelling was. And when she spake,
    Sweete wordes, like dropping honny she did shed,
    And twixt the perles and rubins softly brake
A siluer sound, that heauenly musicke seemd to make.

25

Vpon her eyelids many Graces sate,
    Vnder the shadow of her euen browes,
    Working belgardes, and amorous retrate,
    And euerie one her with a grace endowes:

And euerie one with meekenesse to her bowes.
    So glorious mirrhour of celestiall grace,
    And soueraine moniment of mortall vowes,
    How shall frayle pen descriue her heauenly face,
For feare through want of skill her beauty to disgrace?

26

So faire, and thousand thousand times more faire
    She seemd, when she presented was to sight,
    And was yclad, for heat of scorching aire,
    All in a silken Camus lylly whight,
    Purfled vpon with many a folded plight,
    Which all aboue besprinckled was throughout,
    With golden aygulets, that glistred bright,
    Like twinckling starres, and all the skirt about
Was hemd with golden fringe

27

Below her ham her weed did somewhat trayne,
    And her streight legs most brauely were embayld
    In gilden buskins of costly Cordwayne,
    All bard with golden bendes, which were entayld
    With curious antickes, and full fayre aumayld:
    Before they fastned were vnder her knee
    In a rich iewell, and therein entrayld
    The ends of all the knots, that none might see,
How they within their fouldings close enwrapped bee.

Stanza 23
Belphœbe's eyes have the blinding power of the sun from whose beams she was conceived (see III vi 6–7), of Arthur's shield (I vii 35.9), and of Fidelia's face 'That could haue dazd the rash beholders sight' (I x 12.8). **4 passing persant**: exceedingly piercing. **5 rash**: lustful. Her eyes have the power of Medusa's head on Minerva's shield, which, according to Conti 1616:4.5, signifies the power of virginity over lust. It is fitting, then, that Cupid is called **the blinded god**. Cf. Acrasia's eyes whose 'fierie beames . . . thrild | Fraile harts, yet quenched not' (xii 78.7–8).

Stanza 24
1 bountie braue: excellent goodness. **2 table**: surface for painting. **4–5** Not as the 'blinded god' of 23.6 but as one whose wars record **All good and honour**. **7** Cf. Song Sol. 4.11: 'Thy lippes, my spouse, droppe as honie combes'. **8 rubins**: rubies, i.e. her lips. **9** That **siluer sound** is S.'s in *SC June* 61.

Stanza 25
1–2 Cf. *Am* 40.3–4: 'on each eyelid sweetly doe appeare | an hundred Graces as in shade to sit'. **3** I.e., fashioning loving looks and amorous countenance. **belgardes**: coined by S. from Ital. *bel* + *guardo*, but suggesting also beauty's guard against love; cf. *HB* 255–56. **retrate**: from Ital. *ritratto*, 'a picture' (Florio 1598; cf. ix 4.2), referring to her looks which arouse love but suggesting also the lover's retreat (see *OED* 'retrait'). **6–9** The praise becomes more openly owing to Elizabeth. With line 6, cf. the praise of her at I proem iv 2. At II proem 4.7, S. tells her that she 'maist behold thy face' in his poem but now after four stanzas describing it, he must resort

to the topos of inexpressibility. **descriue**: describe, in the special sense, 'represent', 'picture'.

Stanza 26
1–2 I.e., she is **more faire** than any image of her could possibly be. The same claim is made of the Faerie Queene at ix 3.7. **4 Camus**: a light loose dress. **lylly whight**: denoting her virginity; cf. Alma at ix 19.1. **5 Purfled**: embroidered. **plight**: pleat. The pleats express her modesty as does Shamefastnes's attire at ix 40.6. **7–9** One expects Diana's colour, silver (cf. III vi 18.3), but the repeated **golden** declares her kinship with her father, the sun; see III vi 6–7. **aygulets**: tags or sequins. Line 9, a rare half-line, is authorized by Virgil's half-lines. At the centre of the ten stanzas of the icon, it either confirms the topos of inexpressibility or indicates the poet's distraction when he contemplates Belphœbe's genitalia, and necessarily moves lower. See Montrose 1986:327; and on his use of *occupatio*, see Betts 1998:160–61.

Stanza 27
1 I.e., her skirt extends below her thigh, unlike Radigund's at V v 2.7; or to the back of her knee (see **ham**, *OED* 1). **trayne**: hang down. Display of the legs is associated with male, and therefore Amazonian, fashion; see V v 3.1–3. **2 embayld**: enclosed; from 'bail', a ring; or 'embay', enclose. **3 gilden**: gilded. **Cordwayne**: cordovan, a Spanish leather. **4 bendes**: bars or straps, a heraldic term. **entayld**: engraved. **5 curious antickes**: elaborate, grotesque figures. These charms suggest the magical power that protects her virginity. **aumayld**: enamelled. **6–9** The hidden ends suggest that her armour cannot be undone, being a virgin's knot, in contrast to Venus's girdle which may be loosened. **Before**: i.e. in front, to declare her virginity. **entrayld**: entwined.

28

Like two faire marble pillours they were seene,
  Which doe the temple of the Gods support,
  Whom all the people decke with girlands greene,
  And honour in their festiuall resort;
  Those same with stately grace, and princely port
  She taught to tread, when she her selfe would grace,
  But with the woody Nymphes when she did play,
  Or when the flying Libbard she did chace,
She could them nimbly moue, and after fly apace.

29

And in her hand a sharpe bore-speare she held,
  And at her backe a bow and quiuer gay,
  Stuft with steele-headed dartes, wherewith she queld
  The saluage beastes in her victorious play,
  Knit with a golden bauldricke, which forelay
  Athwart her snowy brest, and did diuide
  Her daintie paps; which like young fruit in May
  Now little gan to swell, and being tide,
Through her thin weed their places only signifide.

30

Her yellow lockes crisped, like golden wyre,
  About her shoulders weren loosely shed,
  And when the winde emongst them did inspyre,
  They waued like a penon wyde dispred
  And low behinde her backe were scattered:
  And whether art it were, or heedelesse hap,
  As through the flouring forrest rash she fled,
  In her rude heares sweet flowres themselues did lap,
And flourishing fresh leaues and blossomes did enwrap.

31

Such as *Diana* by the sandy shore
  Of swift *Eurotas*, or on *Cynthus* greene,
  Where all the Nymphes haue her vnwares forlore,
  Wandreth alone with bow and arrowes keene,
  To seeke her game: Or as that famous Queene
  Of *Amazons*, whom *Pyrrhus* did destroy,
  The day that first of *Priame* she was seene,
  Did shew her selfe in great triumphant ioy,
To succour the weake state of sad afflicted *Troy*.

32

Such when as hartlesse *Trompart* her did vew,
  He was dismayed in his coward minde,
  And doubted, whether he himselfe should shew,
  Or fly away, or bide alone behinde:
  Both feare and hope he in her face did finde,
  When she at last him spying thus bespake;
  Hayle Groome; didst not thou see a bleeding Hynde,
  Whose right haunch earst my stedfast arrow strake?
If thou didst, tell me, that I may her ouertake.

33

Wherewith reviu'd, this answere forth he threw;
  O Goddesse, (for such I thee take to bee)
  For nether doth thy face terrestriall shew,
  Nor voyce sound mortall; I auow to thee,
  Such wounded beast, as that, I did not see,
  Sith earst into this forrest wild I came.
  But mote thy goodlyhed forgiue it mee,
  To weete, which of the Gods I shall thee name,
That vnto thee dew worship I may rightly frame.

Stanza 28

1–2 Cf. Song Sol. 5.15: 'His leggs are as pillers of marble'. The simile is suggested by the Pauline doctrine of the body as the 'temple of the holie Gost' (1 Cor. 6.19); cf. VI viii 42.7–9. **5–6** She graced herself when she walked **with stately grace**, as Venus reveals herself to be a goddess by her step (Virgil, *Aen.* 1.405). **7 play**: 'sport', sugg. Church 1758 for the rhyme; cf. VI x 9.5, and see ii.7.7*n*. **8 Libbard**: leopard. The emblem of incontinence in Dante, *Inf.* 1.32, which virginity seeks to destroy, as again at IV vii 23.7.

Stanza 29

1 bore-speare: for slaying the boar, which traditionally denotes lust. **3 queld**: killed. **5 Knit**: fastened. The Amazon warrior Penthesilea wears a golden girdle fastened below her bare breast in Virgil, *Aen.* 1.492; cf. Radigund's belt at V v 3.5. It is distinct from a **bauldricke** worn over the shoulder, e.g. by Arthur at I vii 29.8 and Britomart at III iii 59.9. See Leslie 1983:172–74. **7–8** The month of May in the OS extends into our June, though that does not help much. In *Am* 76.9, the beloved's paps are 'like early fruit in May'. **young fruit**: as the *pome acerbe* of Ariosto's Alcina, *Orl. Fur.* 7.14.

Stanza 30

1 crisped: curled. **3 inspyre**: breathe, as Venus allowed her hair to be scattered by the winds in Virgil, *Aen.* 1.319. **7–9** Botticelli's *Primavera* seems the closest analogue to this startling image. For a general comparison of his paintings with S.'s descriptions, see W.B.C. Watkins 1961:236–38, and Roston 1987:179–87. **flouring**: 'flourishing' and 'flowering', which

mean the same in Belphœbe as in Flora. **rash**: quickly. **rude**: disordered, being loosely flowing.

Stanza 31

The simile is developed from Virgil, *Aen.* 1.498–99: while Aeneas gazes upon a picture of Penthesilea defending Troy, Dido approaches him 'even as on Eurotas' or along the heights of Cynthus Diana guides her dancing bands'. On Belphœbe as a threatening Amazonian figure, see Villeponteaux 1993:33–37; and on her relation to Elizabeth as a *divina virago*, see Schleiner 1978:176–78. **3 forlore**: left. **6** The story of Penthesilea's death by **Pyrrhus** follows popular legend. That she shows herself **in great triumphant ioy** is added by S. to associate her appearance with Belphœbe's.

Stanzas 32–33

Venus's encounter with Aeneas in *Aen.* 1.321–24 and his reply (327–28) are the model for Belphœbe's encounter with Trompart. Their exchange is used for the emblems to *SC Apr.*, which E.K. in his gloss relates to 'the excelency of Elisa', i.e. Elizabeth. It may allude to the courtship of the Queen by the Duc d'Alençon (Braggadocchio) through his agent Simier (Trompart) from 1579 to 1581, as Upton 1758 first suggested. See 'Alençon' in the *SEnc*.

Stanza 32

8 stedfast: steady.

Stanza 33

7 thy goodlyhed: a respectful form of address.

34

To whom she thus, but ere her words ensewd,
  Vnto the bush her eye did suddein glaunce,
  In which vaine *Braggadocchio* was mewd,
  And saw it stirre: she lefte her percing launce,
  And towards gan a deadly shafte aduaunce,
  In mind to marke the beast. At which sad stowre,
  Trompart forth stept, to stay the mortall chaunce,
  Out crying, O what euer heuenly powre,
Or earthly wight thou be, withhold this deadly howre.

35

O stay thy hand, for yonder is no game
  For thy fiers arrowes, them to exercize,
  But loe my Lord, my liege, whose warlike name,
  Is far renowmd through many bold emprize;
  And now in shade he shrowded yonder lies.
  She staid: with that he crauld out of his nest,
  Forth creeping on his caitiue hands and thies,
  And standing stoutly vp, his lofty crest
Did fiercely shake, and rowze, as comming late from rest.

36

As fearfull fowle, that long in secret caue
  For dread of soring hauke her selfe hath hid,
  Not caring how her silly life to saue,
  She her gay painted plumes disorderid,
  Seeing at last her selfe from daunger rid,
  Peepes forth, and soone renews her natiue pride;
  She gins her feathers fowle disfigured
  Prowdly to prune, and sett on euery side,
So shakes off shame, ne thinks how erst she did her hide.

37

So when her goodly visage he beheld,
  He gan himselfe to vaunt: but when he vewd
  Those deadly tooles, which in her hand she held,
  Soone into other fitts he was transmewd,

Till she to him her gracious speach renewd;
  All haile, Sir knight, and well may thee befall,
  As all the like, which honor haue pursewd
  Through deeds of armes and prowesse martiall;
All vertue merits praise, but such the most of all.

38

To whom he thus, O fairest vnder skie,
  Trew be thy words, and worthy of thy praise,
  That warlike feats doest highest glorifie.
  Therein I haue spent all my youthly daies,
  And many battailes fought, and many fraies
  Throughout the world, wher so they might be found,
  Endeuoring my dreaded name to raise
  Aboue the Moone, that fame may it resound
In her eternall tromp, with laurell girlond cround.

39

But what art thou, O Lady, which doest raunge
  In this wilde forest, where no pleasure is,
  And doest not it for ioyous court exchaunge,
  Emongst thine equall peres, where happy blis
  And all delight does raigne, much more then this?
  There thou maist loue, and dearly loued be,
  And swim in pleasure, which thou here doest mis;
  There maist thou best be seene, and best maist see:
The wood is fit for beasts, the court is fitt for thee.

40

Who so in pompe of prowd estate (quoth she)
  Does swim, and bathes him selfe in courtly blis,
  Does waste his dayes in darke obscuritee,
  And in obliuion euer buried is:
  Where ease abownds, yt's eath to doe amis;
  But who his limbs with labours, and his mynd
  Behaues with cares, cannot so easy mis.
  Abroad in armes, at home in studious kynd
Who seekes with painfull toile, shal honor soonest fynd.

Stanza 34
3 vaine: foolish; as Arg.1. **mewd**: shut up as a caged hawk. The term prepares for 'nest' (35.6) and the extended simile at 36. **4 lefte**: lifted. More likely, she put it aside to use her 'fiers arrowes' (35.2). **5 towards**: in his direction. **6 marke**: strike as a target. **stowre**: peril.

Stanza 35
2 exercize: use; or 'harass', if **them** refers to **game**. **4 emprize**: chivalric enterprise. **9 rowze**: applied to a bird, it means 'ruffle the feathers'; applied to Braggadocchio, 'waken from sleep', or, as he is Belphœbe's game, 'rise from cover'.

Stanza 36
'An excell.[ent] Simile to expresse . . . cowardnesse' (Jonson 1995). **3 silly**: helpless. **7 fowle**: as the 'Peacocke' (6.4), 'Scarcrow' (7.1), and now **fearfull fowle**, Braggadocchio deserves this pun. **8 prune**: preen.

Stanza 37
2 vaunt: bear proudly; see 6.3*n*. **3 tooles**: weapons. **4 transmewd**: changed; perhaps echoing 'mewd' (34.3) to note his present transformation.

Stanza 38
2 I.e., you are worthy of praise in praising those worthy of praise. **5 fraies**: conflicts. **8 Aboue the Moone**: vaunting his superiority over one who is fairest **vnder skie**.

Stanza 39
7 mis: lack.

Stanzas 40–42.1
With notable irony, S. has one in whom he mirrors the Queen – see 21–31*n* – attack the courtier's slothful life. Belphœbe's argument is based on the usual opposition of the active life in the world and the contemplative life withdrawn from it, as shown in the exchange between the Red Cross Knight and Contemplation at I x 60–64, but expands it, with considerable personal fervour, into a third life: the active life of the scholar-poet who enters public service to pursue two careers, as Rambuss 1993 argues. On the active life in service of the commonweal, see Levy 1996. S.'s argument answers G. Harvey's complaint that scholars in our age are 'rather active then contemplative philosophers' (1884–85:1.136). On the 'mixed life' of action informed by contemplation, see 'triplex vita' in the *SEnc*.

41

In woods, in waues, in warres she wonts to dwell,
  And wilbe found with perill and with paine;
  Ne can the man, that moulds in ydle cell,
  Vnto her happy mansion attaine:
  Before her gate high God did Sweate ordaine,
  And wakefull watches euer to abide:
  But easy is the way, and passage plaine
  To pleasures pallace; it may soone be spide,
And day and night her dores to all stand open wide.

42

In Princes court. The rest she would haue sayd,
  But that the foolish man, fild with delight
  Of her sweete words, that all his sence dismayd,
  And with her wondrous beauty rauisht quight,
  Gan burne in filthy lust, and leaping light,
  Thought in his bastard armes her to embrace.
  With that she swaruing backe, her Iauelin bright
  Against him bent, and fiercely did menace:
So turned her about, and fled away apace.

43

Which when the Pesaunt saw, amazd he stood,
  And grieued at her flight; yet durst he nott
  Pursew her steps, through wild vnknowen wood;
  Besides he feard her wrath, and threatned shott
  Whiles in the bush he lay, not yet forgott:
  Ne car'd he greatly for her presence vayne,
  But turning said to *Trompart*, What fowle blott
  Is this to knight, that Lady should agayne
Depart to woods vntoucht, and leaue so proud disdayne?

44

Perdy (said *Trompart*) lett her pas at will,
  Least by her presence daunger mote befall.
  For who can tell (and sure I feare it ill)
  But that shee is some powre celestiall?
  For whiles she spake, her great words did apall
  My feeble corage, and my heart oppresse,
  That yet I quake and tremble ouer all.
  And I (said *Braggadocchio*) thought no lesse,
When first I heard her horn sound with such ghastlinesse.

45

For from my mothers wombe this grace I haue
  Me giuen by eternall destiny,
  That earthly thing may not my corage braue
  Dismay with feare, or cause on foote to flye,
  But either hellish feends, or powres on hye:
  Which was the cause, when earst that horne I heard,
  Weening it had beene thunder in the skye,
  I hid my selfe from it, as one affeard;
But when I other knew, my selfe I boldly reard.

46

But now for feare of worse, that may betide,
  Let vs soone hence depart. They soone agree;
  So to his steed he gott, and gan to ride,
  As one vnfitt therefore, that all might see
  He had not trayned bene in cheualree.
  Which well that valiaunt courser did discerne;
  For he despisd to tread in dew degree,
  But chaufd and fom'd, with corage fiers and sterne,
And to be easd of that base burden still did erne.

Stanza 40
7 **Behaues**: regulates, governs. **cares**: study, thought. **mis: err; or,** referring to Braggadocchio's use of the term, 'lack honour'. 8 **kynd**: fashion, manner, referring to the scholar's life.

Stanza 41
4 **mansion**: dwelling-place. 5 Gen. 3.19: 'In the sweat of thy face shalt thou eat bread, til thou returne to the earth'. 7–9 Alluding to Acrasia's 'Pallace' whose gate 'euer open stood to all' (xii 83.1, 46.2); possibly also to Painter's *Palace of Pleasure* (1566–75) and Pettie's *Petite Pallace of Pettie his Pleasure* (1576), popular collections of tales that lack the moral and spiritual dimensions of S.'s poem.

Stanza 42
1 A diplomatic interruption: Belphœbe is about to associate the **Princes court** with 'pleasures pallace' (41.8). 2–4 Being **rauisht** by the sound of her **sweete words** – see 24.6–9 – and by her beauty, he seeks to ravish her. 6 **bastard**: mean, base; as he is a spurious knight, a 'Pesaunt' (43.1). 7 **swaruing backe**: retreating.

Stanza 43
1 **Pesaunt**: knave, a term of abuse with strong class overtones. 6 **vayne**: i.e. useless to him because she rejects his assault; or because he is unable, being base, 'loue to entertaine' (iv 1.6). 9 **vntoucht**: in the sexual sense, *intacta*; cf. IV vii 18.8. His presumption is broadly humorous.

Stanza 44
9 **ghastlinesse**: terror induced by a spirit.

Stanza 45
Braggadocchio is a coward on instinct. 5 **But**: i.e. unless it be. 9 **other**: otherwise.

Stanza 46
2 **soone**: without delay. Later S. recalls how Belphœbe 'made him fast out of the forest ronne' (III v 27.8). 4 **therefore**: for that. 5 **cheualree**: horsemanship. 7 **in dew degree**: 'with equall steps' (i 7.9). 9 **erne**: yearn.

Cant. IIII.

Guyon does Furor bind in chaines,
And stops Occasion:
Deliuers Phaon, and therefore
By Strife is rayld vppon.

1

IN braue poursuitt of honorable deed,
There is I know not (what) great difference
Betweene the vulgar and the noble seed,
Which vnto things of valorous pretence
Seemes to be borne by natiue influence;
As feates of armes, and loue to entertaine,
But chiefly skill to ride seemes a science
Proper to gentle blood; some others faine
To menage steeds, as did this vaunter; but in vaine.

classism

2

But he the rightfull owner of that steede,
Who well could menage and subdew his pride,
The whiles on foot was forced for to yeed,
With that blacke Palmer, his most trusty guide;
Who suffred not his wandring feete to slide.

But when strong passion or weake fleshlinesse,
Would from the right way seeke to draw him wide,
He would through temperaunce and stedfastnesse,
Teach him the weak to strengthen, and the strong
                                          (suppresse.

3

It fortuned forth faring on his way,
He saw from far, or seemed for to see
Some troublous vprore or contentious fray,
Whereto he drew in hast it to agree.
A mad man, or that feigned mad to bee,
Drew by the heare along vpon the grownd,
A handsom stripling with great crueltee,
Whom sore he bett, and gor'd with many a wownd,
That cheekes with teares, and sydes with blood did all
                                          (abownd.

Book II Canto iv

Argument
3 Phaon: *Phedon* 1596. See 36.7*n*.

Stanza 1
On the genetic superiority of **noble seed**, see the praise
of 'honourable seed' at iii 10.8–9, VI iii 1–2 (and see *n*).
4 pretence: design; what may rightly claim to be valorous.
5 natiue influence: i.e. ability inherited from one's ancestors
rather than from the disposition of the stars at one's birth.
6 entertaine: engage in. **9 menage**: manège, direct a horse
through its paces.

Stanza 2
1–2 rightfull in being 'borne of noble state' (i 6.5); cf. 6.1
below. **3** Guyon's **pride** is at issue because walking may
suggest that 'in lucklesse warre | His forlorne steed from him
the victour wan' (vi 41.3–4). Or that he is not a knight, as Atin
suggests at 39.2; see ii 12.3*n*. **yeed**: go. **5 slide**: slip; err
morally. **6–9** The extremes of **strong passion** and **weake
fleshlinesse** were revealed in Mordant and Amavia (see i 57);
now the corresponding and combined states of 'griefe and
fury' (33.4) are revealed in Phaon.

Stanza 3
2 seemed for to see: a correction to indicate the allegorical
nature of an encounter that projects the mental and moral

forces that need to be disciplined by temperance. **4 agree**:
conciliate; a more active role than at ii 21. **6** This icono-
graphical detail – in Botticelli, *The Calumny of Apelles*, a female
Calumny drags Apelles by the hair – is examined by Bull
1997b.

Stanzas 4–5
Although Occasion as a classical deity had accumulated stock
descriptions and associations upon which S. draws, his figure
remains puzzlingly original. She is conflated with fortune
(Kiefer 1979), esp. 'Misfortune' (17.4) or bad fortune (Burch-
more 1981), and her iconographical attributes include those of
Penitence (Manning and Fowler 1976). As the mother of
Furor – on their relationship, see Wofford 1992:270–72 – she
is the 'roote of all wrath and despight' (10.9); and at v 1, she
is identified with 'stubborne perturbation', the greatest enemy
of temperance. Traditionally, she embodies the proverb 'Take
time (Occasion) by the forelock' (Smith 777), according to
which her hair hangs before her face so that she may not be
recognized until she has passed; and she is bald behind so that
she cannot be grasped once she has passed. Yet that proverb is
inverted, as Burchmore 95 notes: 'Shee comes vnsought, and
shonned followes eke' (44.3). On her relation to Impotence
and Impatience, see xi 23.8–9*n*; on her role in Bk II, which
begins when Archimago seeks to 'win occasion to his will' (i
5.2) to destroy Guyon, see Nohrnberg 1976:305–26. See also
'Occasion' and 'Fortune' in the *SEnc*, Steppat 1990:103–08,
and Nohrnberg 1998:37–38, 55–57.

4

And him behynd, a wicked Hag did stalke,
   In ragged robes, and filthy disaray,
   Her other leg was lame, that she no'te walke,
   But on a staffe her feeble steps did stay;
   Her lockes, that loathly were and hoarie gray,
   Grew all afore, and loosly hong vnrold,
   But all behinde was bald, and worne away,
   That none thereof could euer taken hold,
And eke her face ill fauourd, full of wrinckles old.

5

And euer as she went, her toung did walke
   In fowle reproch, and termes of vile despight,
   Prouoking him by her outrageous talke,
   To heape more vengeance on that wretched wight;
   Somtimes she raught him stones, wherwith to smite,
   Sometimes her staffe, though it her one leg were,
   Withouten which she could not goe vpright;
   Ne any euill meanes she did forbeare,
That might him moue to wrath, and indignation reare.

6

The noble *Guyon* mou'd with great remorse,
   Approching, first the Hag did thrust away,
   And after adding more impetuous forse,
   His mighty hands did on the madman lay,
   And pluckt him backe; who all on fire streight way,
   Against him turning all his fell intent,
   With beastly brutish rage gan him assay,
   And smott, and bitt, and kickt, and scratcht, and rent,
And did he wist not what in his auengement.

7

And sure he was a man of mickle might,
   Had he had gouernaunce, it well to guyde:
   But when the frantick fitt inflamd his spright,
   His force was vaine, and strooke more often wyde,

Then at the aymed marke, which he had eyde:
   And oft himselfe he chaunst to hurt vnwares,
   Whylest reason blent through passion, nought descryde
   But as a blindfold Bull at randon fares,
And where he hits, nought knowes, and whom he hurts,
                    (nought cares.

8

His rude assault and rugged handeling
   Straunge seemed to the knight, that aye with foe
   In fayre defence and goodly menaging
   Of armes was wont to fight, yet nathemoe
   Was he abashed now not fighting so,
   But more enfierced through his currish play,
   Him sternly grypt, and hailing to and fro,
   To ouerthrow him strongly did assay,
But ouerthrew him selfe vnwares, and lower lay.

9

And being downe the villein sore did beate,
   And bruze with clownish fistes his manly face:
   And eke the Hag with many a bitter threat,
   Still cald vpon to kill him in the place.
   With whose reproch and odious menace
   The knight emboyling in his haughtie hart,
   Knitt all his forces, and gan soone vnbrace
   His grasping hold: so lightly did vpstart,
And drew his deadly weapon, to maintaine his part.

10

Which when the Palmer saw, he loudly cryde,   *wisdom*
   Not so O *Guyon*, neuer thinke that so
   That Monster can be maistred or destroyd:
   He is not, ah, he is not such a foe,
   As steele can wound, or strength can ouerthroe.
   That same is *Furor*, cursed cruel wight,
   That vnto knighthood workes much shame and woe;
   And that same Hag, his aged mother, hight
Occasion, the roote of all wrath and despight.

Stanza 4
1 stalke: walk with stiff steps, as her lameness suggests; walk stealthily after game; cf. Orgoglio's stride at I vii 8.3.   **3 other leg**: one of her legs, or possibly the left or unlucky leg; cf. Impotence at xi 23.6.   **no'te**: could not.   **4 stay**: support.

Stanza 5
1 walke: move briskly (*OED* I.3.g), in contrast to her feet.   **5 raught**: reached.   **9 reare**: arouse.

Stanza 6
1 remorse: pity, compassion.   **4 His mighty hands**: a striking phrase that distinguishes Guyon from the Red Cross Knight's 'mightie armes' (I i 1.2), which refers to his spiritual armour.   **7 assay**: attack.   **9 auengement**: vengeance, alluding to the 'vengeaunce' (29.2) that Phaon finally embodies.

Stanza 7
2 gouernaunce: self-control; see i 29.8*n*.   **5 eyde**: aimed at.   **7 blent**: blinded; cf. 'The eie of reason was with rage yblent' (I ii 5.7).   **8 at randon**: heedlessly; suggesting speed and violence.

Stanza 8
3 goodly menaging: fighting according to rule.   **4 nathemoe**: not at all.   **6 more enfierced**: made more fierce, thus sharing Furor's wrath.   **7–9** Guyon has become the 'wrestler', which is one etymological significance of his name; see proem 5.8*n*. In this *psychomachia*, he overthrows himself, as Furor who 'oft himselfe he chaunst to hurt vnwares' (7.6).

Stanza 9
2 clownish: coarse, rustic, as opposed to **manly**, in a difference of class.   **4 in the place**: on the spot, at once.   **6 emboyling**: boiling with rage. Later Guyon advises Pyrochles to 'quench thy whott emboyling wrath' (v 18.5).

Stanza 10
6 Furor: personifying **wrath and despight** or any excess emotion that leads to frenzy; hence the variety of descriptive adjectives: 'bold' (i 57.8), 'fell' (ii 20.4), 'mad' (28.7), 'raging' (iv 11.1), 'ydle' (11.7) and 'hellish' (30.2).

11

With her, who so will raging *Furor* tame,
  Must first begin, and well her amenage:
  First her restraine from her reprochfull blame,
  And euill meanes, with which she doth enrage
  Her frantick sonne, and kindles his corage,
  Then when she is withdrawne, or strong withstood,
  It's eath his ydle fury to aswage,
  And calme the tempest of his passion wood;
The bankes are ouerflowne, when stopped is the flood.

12

Therewith Sir *Guyon* left his first emprise,
  And turning to that woman, fast her hent
  By the hoare lockes, that hong before her eyes,
  And to the ground her threw: yet n'ould she stent
  Her bitter rayling and foule reuilement,
  But still prouokt her sonne to wreake her wrong;
  But nathelesse he did her still torment,
  And catching hold of her vngratious tonge,
Thereon an yron lock, did fasten firme and strong.

13

Then whenas vse of speach was from her reft,
  With her two crooked handes she signes did make,
  And beckned him, the last help she had left:
  But he that last left helpe away did take,
  And both her handes fast bound vnto a stake,
  That she note stirre. Then gan her sonne to flye
  Full fast away, and did her quite forsake;
  But *Guyon* after him in hast did hye,
And soone him ouertooke in sad perplexitye.

14

In his strong armes he stifly him embraste,
  Who him gainstriuing, nought at all preuaild:
  For all his power was vtterly defaste,
  And furious fitts at earst quite weren quaild:
  Oft he re'nforst, and oft his forces fayld,
  Yet yield he would not, nor his rancor slack.
  Then him to ground he cast, and rudely hayld,
  And both his hands fast bound behind his backe,
And both his feet in fetters to an yron rack.

15

With hundred yron chaines he did him bind,
  And hundred knots that did him sore constraine:
  Yet his great yron teeth he still did grind,
  And grimly gnash, threatning reuenge in vaine:
  His burning eyen, whom bloody strakes did staine,
  Stared full wide, and threw forth sparkes of fyre,
  And more for ranck despight, then for great paine,
  Shakt his long locks, colourd like copper-wyre,
And bitt his tawny beard to shew his raging yre.

16

Thus whenas *Guyon Furor* had captiud,
  Turning about he saw that wretched Squyre,
  Whom that mad man of life nigh late depriud,
  Lying on ground, all soild with blood and myre:
  Whom whenas he perceiued to respyre,
  He gan to comfort, and his woundes to dresse.
  Being at last recured, he gan inquyre,
  What hard mishap him brought to such distresse,
And made that caytiues thrall, the thrall of wretchednesse.

Stanza 11
The Palmer takes his lesson from 2 Cor. 11.12: 'Cut away occasion from them which desire occasion'.   **2 amenage**: control; from manège, as at 1.9, 2.2.   **5 corage**: anger.   **8 passion wood**: mad outburst of anger.   **9** Furor may be controlled only when the 'roote' (10.9) of his wrath is stopped. (For the proverb, see Smith 731.) To stop him only increases his fury, as a river overflows if blocked before blocking its source.

Stanza 12
1 emprise: undertaking.   **2–3** Guyon obeys the proverb 'to take time (Occasion) by the forelock'; see 4–5*n*.   **4 n'ould**: would not.   **8 vngratious**: rude, both wicked in itself and denying virtue in others. Appropriate to his virtue, he fits her with a scold's bridle, or 'branks'. A picture from the British Library, repr. in Fraser 1984, shows an iron framework to enclose the head with a metal bit to restrain the tongue and a key to secure it. See Isa. 37.29.

Stanza 13
3 the last help: referring to **him**, i.e. Furor, but in the next line to her **handes**. Once she is totally helpless, he is overcome.   **6 note**: could not; knew not how to.   **9 perplexitye**: distress.

Stanza 14
2 gainstriuing: striving against.   **3 defaste**: destroyed.   **4 at earst**: at once.   **quaild**: subdued.   **5 re'nforst**: renewed his force.

Stanza 15
1–2 As Furor is bound by a hundred knots in Virgil, *Aen.* 1.294–96, to mark the end of war.   **6 Stared**: opened wide in fury, revealing an inner unquenchable burning; shone. Cf. Mammon's fiends at vii 37.6, and the lustful Argante whose 'fyrie eyes with furious sparkes did stare' (III vii 39.8).   **7 ranck**: excessive.   **8–9** Red is inevitably associated with anger, as Wrath's eyes at I iv 33.5, and Pyrochles's steed at v 2.8.

Stanza 16
4 soild: see i 41.1–3*n*.

Stanzas 17–35
In analysing Shakespeare's use of the Phaon story in *Much Ado about Nothing*, Bullough 1957–75:2.533 lists thirteen adaptations up to 1590. S.'s immediate source is Ariosto's story of Ariodante and Ginevra in *Orl. Fur.* 4.42–6.61; for a comparison, see Alpers 1967:54–69, and Rhu 1993b. Used here, it extends the false tale of the 'violated' Duessa in the Bk's opening episode that led Guyon into intemperance. On the story as a critique of temperance offered by the Palmer at 34–35, see Silberman 1988a and Berger 1991:16–32. Fisher 1993a charts a general correspondence of stanzas between Phaon's story and Lucifera's similarly numbered pageant at I iv 17–35.

Stanza 17
4 Misfortune: see 4–5*n*.   **waites aduantage**: watches for the opportunity or occasion.   **5 whelming lap**: as the common

17

With hart then throbbing, and with watry eyes,
    Fayre Sir (quoth he) what man can shun the hap,
    That hidden lyes vnwares him to surpryse?
    Misfortune waites aduantage to entrap
    The man most wary in her whelming lap.
    So me weake wretch, of many weakest wretch,
    Vnweeting, and vnware of such mishap,
    She brought to mischiefe through her guilful trech,
Where this same wicked villein did me wandring ketch.

18

It was a faithlesse Squire, that was the sourse
    Of all my sorrow, and of these sad teares,
    With whom from tender dug of commune nourse,
    Attonce I was vpbrought, and eft when yeares
    More rype vs reason lent to chose our Peares,
    Our selues in league of vowed loue wee knitt:
    In which we long time without gealous feares,
    Or faultie thoughts contynewd, as was fitt;
And for my part I vow, dissembled not a whitt.

19

It was my fortune, commune to that age,
    To loue a Lady fayre of great degree,
    The which was borne of noble parentage,
    And set in highest seat of dignitee,
    Yet seemd no lesse to loue, then loued to bee:
    Long I her seru'd, and found her faithfull still,
    Ne euer thing could cause vs disagree:
    Loue that two harts makes one, makes eke one will:
Each stroue to please, and others pleasure to fulfill.

20

My friend, hight *Philemon*, I did partake,
    Of all my loue and all my priuitie;
    Who greatly ioyous seemed for my sake,
    And gratious to that Lady, as to mee,

    Ne euer wight, that mote so welcome bee,
    As he to her, withouten blott or blame,
    Ne euer thing, that she could thinke or see,
    But vnto him she would impart the same:
O wretched man, that would abuse so gentle Dame.

21

At last such grace I found, and meanes I wrought,
    That I that Lady to my spouse had wonne;
    Accord of friendes, consent of Parents sought,
    Affyaunce made, my happinesse begonne,
    There wanted nought but few rites to be donne,
    Which mariage make; that day too farre did seeme:
    Most ioyous man, on whom the shining Sunne,
    Did shew his face, my selfe I did esteeme,
And that my falser friend did no lesse ioyous deeme.

22

But ere that wished day his beame disclosd,
    He either enuying my toward good,
    Or of him selfe to treason ill disposd,
    One day vnto me came in friendly mood,
    And told for secret how he vnderstood
    That Lady whom I had to me assynd,
    Had both distaind her honorable blood,
    And eke the faith, which she to me did bynd;
And therfore wisht me stay, till I more truth should fynd.

23

The gnawing anguish and sharp gelosy,
    Which his sad speach infixed in my brest,
    Ranckled so sore, and festred inwardly,
    That my engreeued mind could find no rest,
    Till that the truth thereof I did out wrest,
    And him besought by that same sacred band
    Betwixt vs both, to counsell me the best.
    He then with solemne oath and plighted hand
Assurd, ere long the truth to let me vnderstand.

---

phrase, 'fall into the lap of', but also the bawdy sense. **6–9** The 'c' rhyme was revised in *1596* to read: 'one', 'occasion', 'light vpon'. **mischiefe**: misfortune, evil plight.

Stanza 18
4 eft: afterwards. **5 Peares**: companions. **6 league of vowed loue**: the 'sacred band' (23.6) between friends that takes precedence to married love.

Stanza 19
5 Yet marks his surprise that love should cross boundaries of class. His ancestry is praiseworthy (36.7–9) but not **noble** or 'honorable' (22.7).

Stanza 20
1 Philemon: Gk Φιλήμων, affectionate; and, as they are knit in love, 'love of self'. **partake**: inform, make partaker. **2 priuitie**: personal affairs. **9 abuse**: malign, revile, suggested by Occasion's 'foule reuilement' (12.5; cf. 5.2); but also

'violate' (24.9, 27.9). The theme of the violated body, introduced by Archimago's lying tale (cf i 19.3), is central to the virtue of temperance which centres on the unviolated and inviolable body.

Stanza 21
1 grace: favour. **4 Affyaunce**: betrothal. **5–6 make**: i.e. 'are the essential criteria of' (*OED* 24). Cf. *Epith* 216–17: 'The sacred ceremonies . . . which do endlesse matrimony make'. **9 that**: i.e. the marriage day. **falser**: most false.

Stanza 22
2 toward: coming. **6 assynd**: appointed, chosen (for marriage). **7 distaind**: defiled.

Stanza 23
2 sad: causing sorrow. **5 out wrest**: draw out. **8 plighted hand**: pledge sworn by the clasping of hands. **9 Assurd**: pledged.

24

Ere long with like againe he boorded mee,
   Saying, he now had boulted all the floure,
   And that it was a groome of base degree,
   Which of my loue was partener Paramoure:
   Who vsed in a darkesome inner bowre
   Her oft to meete: which better to approue,
   He promised to bring me at that howre,
   When I should see, that would me nearer moue,
And driue me to withdraw my blind abused loue.

25

This gracelesse man for furtherance of his guile,
   Did court the handmayd of my Lady deare,
   Who glad t'embosome his affection vile,
   Did all she might, more pleasing to appeare.
   One day to worke her to his will more neare,
   He woo'd her thus: *Pryene* (so she hight)
   What great despight doth fortune to thee beare,
   Thus lowly to abase thy beautie bright,
That it should not deface all others lesser light?

26

But if she had her least helpe to thee lent,
   T'adorne thy forme according thy desart,
   Their blazing pride thou wouldest soone haue blent,
   And staynd their prayses with thy least good part;
   Ne should faire *Claribell* with all her art,
   Though she thy Lady be, approch thee neare:
   For proofe thereof, this euening, as thou art,
   Aray thy selfe in her most gorgeous geare,
That I may more delight in thy embracement deare.

27

The Mayden proud through praise, and mad through loue
   Him hearkned to, and soone her selfe arayd,
   The whiles to me the treachour did remoue
   His craftie engin, and as he had sayd,

Me leading, in a secret corner layd,
   The sad spectatour of my Tragedie;
   Where left, he went, and his owne false part playd,
   Disguised like that groome of base degree,
Whom he had feignd th'abuser of my loue to bee.

28

Eftsoones he came vnto th'appointed place,
   And with him brought *Pryene*, rich arayd,
   In *Claribellaes* clothes. Her proper face
   I not descerned in that darkesome shade,
   But weend it was my loue, with whom he playd.
   Ah God, what horrour and tormenting griefe
   My hart, my handes, mine eyes, and all assayd?
   Me liefer were ten thousand deathes priefe,
Then wounde of gealous worme, and shame of such repriefe.

29

I home retourning, fraught with fowle despight,
   And chawing vengeaunce all the way I went,
   Soone as my loathed loue appeard in sight,
   With wrathfull hand I slew her innocent;
   That after soone I dearely did lament:
   For when the cause of that outrageous deede
   Demaunded, I made plaine and euident,
   Her faultie Handmayd, which that bale did breede,
Confest, how *Philemon* her wrought to chaunge her weede.

30

Which when I heard, with horrible affright
   And hellish fury all enragd, I sought
   Vpon my selfe that vengeable despight
   To punish: yet it better first I thought,
   To wreake my wrath on him, that first it wrought.
   To *Philemon*, false faytour *Philemon*
   I cast to pay, that I so dearely bought;
   Of deadly drugs I gaue him drinke anon,
And washt away his guilt with guilty potion.

Stanza 24

1 boorded: accosted; addressed. **2 boulted**: sifted. Proverbial: he has found the matter out. **3** Class distinctions figure here: Phaon, who is a 'Squyre' (33.8), learns that his lady 'of great degree' (19.2) is having an affair with a **groome of base degree**. **6 approue**: show to be true. **8** . . . what would affect me more deeply.

Stanza 25

3 embosome: cherish; literally, 'fix in the bosom'. **6 Pryene**: suggesting fire (Gk πῦρ) as she is 'mad through loue'(27.1); or the means by which Philemon seeks to 'pry' into her mistress's affairs; or Lat. *prae + iens* as she wishes to go before, i.e. rival, her lady (see the *SEnc* 516). **9 deface**: outshine, and therefore disfigure; alluding to the etymology of Claribell.

Stanza 26

3 blent: blinded; blemished. **4 staynd**: eclipsed; defaced. Continuing the image of 25.9. **5 Claribell**: famous or bright in beauty (Lat. *clara + bella*). **7 as thou art**: as you truly are, her lady's clothes showing that she is her equal.

Stanza 27

3 treachour: traitor, to their 'vowed loue' (18.6). **did remoue**: moved again; cf. 24.1. **4 engin**: plot.

Stanza 28

This moment repeats the Red Cross Knight's deception at I ii 4 when Archimago led him to believe that Una was copulating with a squire. **3 proper**: own. **7 assayd**: assailed. **8 priefe**: proof, experience. **9 gealous worme**: the serpent of jealousy. **repriefe**: disgrace.

Stanza 29

1 His mood reveals him to be a victim of Occasion, 'the roote of all . . . despight' (10.9). **2 chawing**: meditating, a fig. sense that is secondary to the physical sense of chewing, as jealousy in Enuie (I iv 30.2–3), Malbecco (III x 18.1), and Britomart (V vi 19.2). **5 That**: i.e. that action. **6–9** I.e., when I made it clear, on being asked, why I killed Claribell, Pryene confessed etc. **faultie**: guilty of wrong-doing.

31

Thus heaping crime on crime, and griefe on griefe,
　　To losse of loue adioyning losse of frend,
　　I meant to purge both with a third mischiefe,
　　And in my woes beginner it to end:
　　That was *Pryene*; she did first offend,
　　She last should smart: with which cruell intent,
　　When I at her my murdrous blade did bend,
　　She fled away with ghastly dreriment,
And I poursewing my fell purpose, after went.

32

Feare gaue her winges, and rage enforst my flight;
　　Through woods and plaines so long I did her chace,
　　Till this mad man, whom your victorious might
　　Hath now fast bound, me met in middle space,
　　As I her, so he me poursewd apace,
　　And shortly ouertooke: I breathing yre,
　　Sore chauffed at my stay in such a cace,
　　And with my heat kindled his cruell fyre;
Which kindled once, his mother did more rage inspyre.

33

Betwixt them both, they haue me doen to dye,
　　Through wounds, and strokes, and stubborne handeling,
　　That death were better, then such agony,
　　As griefe and fury vnto me did bring;
　　Of which in me yet stickes the mortall sting,
　　That during life will neuer be appeasd.
　　When he thus ended had his sorrowing,
　　Said *Guyon*, Squyre, sore haue ye beene diseasd;
But all your hurts may soone through temperance be easd.

34

Then gan the Palmer thus, Most wretched man,
　　That to affections does the bridle lend;
　　In their beginning they are weake and wan,
　　But soone through suff'rance growe to fearefull end;
　　Whiles they are weake betimes with them contend:
　　For when they once to perfect strength do grow,
　　Strong warres they make, and cruell battry bend
Gainst fort of Reason, it to ouerthrow:
Wrath, gelosy, griefe, loue haue laid this Squyre thus low.

didactic – temperance

reason as virtue

35

Wrath, gealosie, griefe, loue do thus expell:
　　Wrath is a fire, and gealosie a weede,
　　Griefe is a flood, and loue a monster fell;
　　The fire of sparkes, the weede of little seede,
　　The flood of drops, the Monster filth did breede:
　　But sparks, seed, drops, and filth do thus delay;
　　The sparks soone quench, the springing seed outweed,
　　The drops dry vp, and filth wipe cleane away:
So shall wrath, gealosy, griefe, loue die and decay.

36

Vnlucky Squire (said *Guyon*) sith thou hast
　　Falne into mischiefe through intemperaunce,
　　Henceforth take heede of that thou now hast past,
　　And guyde thy waies with warie gouernaunce,
　　Least worse betide thee by some later chaunce.
　　But read how art thou nam'd, and of what kin.
　　Phaon I hight (quoth he) and do aduaunce
　　Mine auncestry from famous *Coradin*,
Who first to rayse our house to honour did begin.

Stanza 30
1 affright: terror. **3 vengeable despight**: cruel outrage, as 46.2. **6 faytour**: impostor. **9** The potion becomes **guilty** by washing away Philemon's **guilt**. Berger 1991:27 finds a 'nasty little pun on absolution'. It extends to 'purge' (31.3).

Stanza 31
2 adioyning: adding. **8 ghastly dreriment**: fearful horror.

Stanza 32
1 enforst: gave fresh vigour to; compelled. **4 in middle space**: where the temperate mean may be asserted on meeting Guyon; see ii 20.3n. **7 stay**: hindrance. **9 inspyre**: blow into.

Stanza 33
1 doen to dye: i.e. he is about to take his own life, as he had planned at 30.2–4. **2 stubborne**: fierce. **4 griefe and fury**: see vi 1.6–7n. **5 mortall**: deadly, belonging to man. **8 diseasd**: tormented. **9** As Amavia failed to cure Mordant's concupiscence by 'faire gouernaunce' (i 54.6), Guyon may dress Phaon's wounds (see 16.6) but not cure them.

Stanza 34
2 affections: passions, violent emotions. **bridle**: a common emblem of temperance; cf. xii 53.5. **4 suff'rance**: toleration, indulgence. **5 betimes**: speedily. **contend**: struggle with the

affections in order to expel or purge them, as he counsels in the next stanza. **7–8** Cf. xi 1.1–4.

Stanza 35
Quoted by book and canto by Fraunce in 1588 (1950:60) to illustrate 'conceipted kindes of verses'. Specifically, it is correlative verse with the four passions and their sources forming interlocked pairs that culminate in love. The mischiefs that follow Wrath in Lucifera's pageant of sins culminate in 'griefe the enemy of life' (I iv 35.5). The four correspond to the four humours: choler, phlegm, melancholy, and blood respectively. **3** On love as a **monster**, see III xi 51.7–9. **5** Cf. the 'monstrous shapes' bred from the mud of the Nile (I i 21.6–9); cf. also the dragon (I vii 17.3). **6 do thus delay**: i.e. allay or remove the sparks by quenching them, etc.

Stanza 36
2 mischiefe: misfortune; evil plight, as 17.8. **4 gouernaunce**: self-control; wise behaviour, as i 29.8. **5** Guyon takes his lesson from John 5.14: 'Sinne no more, lest a worse thing come vnto thee'. **chaunce**: i.e. Occasion. **6 read**: tell. **7 Phaon**: 'the name of a fayre yonge man' (T. Cooper 1565) who was the boatman of Mitylene loved by Sappho. Aphrodite gave him youth and beauty; hence he is 'A handsom stripling' (3.7). *Phedon 1596* may be taken from the handsome youth whom Socrates saved from prostitution; see the *SEnc* 516. **aduaunce**: claim; boast. **8 Coradin**: Lat. *cor*, heart + Gk ἀδυναμία, lack of power; hence his son's weakness.

37

Thus as he spake, lo far away they spyde
  A varlet ronning towardes hastily,
   Whose flying feet so fast their way applyde,
  That round about a cloud of dust did fly,
  Which mingled all with sweate, did dim his eye.
  He soone approched, panting, breathlesse, whot,
  And all so soyld, that none could him descry;
  His countenaunce was bold, and bashed not
For *Guyons* lookes, but scornefull eyglaunce at him shot.

38

Behind his backe he bore a brasen shield,
  On which was drawen faire, in colours fit,
  A flaming fire in midst of bloody field,
  And round about the wreath this word was writ,
  Burnt I doe burne. Right well beseemed it,
  To be the shield of some redoubted knight;
  And in his hand two dartes exceeding flit,
  And deadly sharp he held, whose heads were dight
In poyson and in blood, of malice and despight.

39

When he in presence came, to *Guyon* first
  He boldly spake, Sir knight, if knight thou bee,
  Abandon this forestalled place at erst,
  For feare of further harme, I counsell thee,

Or bide the chaunce at thine owne ieopardee.
  The knight at his great boldnesse wondered,
  And though he scornd his ydle vanitee,
  Yet mildly him to purpose answered;
For not to grow of nought he it coniectured.

40

Varlet, this place most dew to me I deeme,
  Yielded by him, that held it forcibly.
  But whence shold come that harme, which thou dost seeme
  To threat to him, that mindes his chaunce t'abye?
  Perdy (sayd he) here comes, and is hard by
  A knight of wondrous powre, and great assay,
  That neuer yet encountred enemy,
  But did him deadly daunt, or fowle dismay;
Ne thou for better hope, if thou his presence stay.

41

How hight he then (sayd *Guyon*) and from whence?
  Pyrochles is his name, renowned farre
  For his bold feates and hardy confidence,
  Full oft approud in many a cruell warre,
  The brother of *Cymochles*, both which arre
  The sonnes of old *Acrates* and *Despight*,
  Acrates sonne of *Phlegeton* and *Iarre*;
  But Phlegeton is sonne of Herebus and Night;
But Herebus sonne of Aeternitie is hight.

Stanza 37

2 varlet: an attendant upon a knight; a squire. **5 his eye**: his countenance; or one's sight of him, as 7. **7 soyld**: see i 41.1–3*n*. **8 bashed**: daunted; literally, he did not lower his eyes.

Stanza 38

1 brasen: noting the shield's indestructibility. Fear bears such a shield in the masque of Cupid at III xii 12.8. **2–4** The terms are heraldic: the shield's device, **A flaming fire**, alludes to the name of its owner, Pyrochles (see 41*n*); **colours fit**: proper heraldic tinctures; **field**: the shield's surface; **wreath**: an ornamental band along its edge bearing its motto (**word**), **Burnt I doe burne**, which is literally fulfilled at vi 44 when the fire that burns others burns him. See 'heraldry' in the *SEnc*. **7–9** The **dartes** serve to identify him, as at 46 and v 36.1, each being double-pronged; cf. 'forckhead' (46.8). **flit**: swift. The heads were **dight**, i.e. prepared, by being dipped in poisoned or polluted blood, as the blood on Ruddymane's hands are 'with secret filth infected' (ii 4.7).

Stanza 39

3 forestalled: taken beforehand, i.e. the 'middle space' (32.4) earlier claimed by Furor and now by Pyrochles but which Guyon must claim for temperance; cf. 'this fearfull stead' (42.8). **at erst**: at once. **7 ydle**: empty, from the etymology of **vanitee** (Lat. *vanus*). **8 mildly**: demonstrating his control over Furor. **to purpose**: to the point at issue.

Stanza 40

4 . . . who intends to 'bide the chaunce' (39.5). **6 assay**: proven worth. **8 deadly daunt**: vanquish by death. **9 stay**: await.

Stanza 41

The nature of each character is revealed by name and genealogy. **Pyrochles**, as corrected *F.E.* from 'Pyrrhochles' (*1590, 1596*), derives from πῦρ, fire + ὀχλέω, to disturb, cause annoyance, i.e. the fiery temper troubling to himself and others; or πῦρ + κλέυς, fame, glory, i.e. the fiery temper that seeks fame. In this latter role he parodies '*Praysdesire*' in Arthur at ix 39.8. First described in terms of light 'Vpon the trembling waue' (v 2.5), he is linked to **Cymochles** whose name derives from κῦμα, wave, which also indicates his unstable nature in canto vi, changing from lust to wrath and then back again, illustrating the pun in Jas. 1.6: 'he that wauereth is like a waue of the sea'. Or from καῦμα, burning, glow, as Gilbert 1933:230 suggests in noting that Cymochles is often associated with 'burning, glow'. See 'Pyrochles, Cymochles' in the *SEnc*. Their relation to temperance is indicated in S.'s poem to Harvey: the safe middle road is found between the two extremes where 'here the wave would overwhelm, there the fire consume you' (tr. *Var* 10.257). In Ripa 1603:482, Temperance holds a burning iron in her right hand to be tempered by a vase of water in her left; noted Brooks-Davies 1977:138. Yet S.'s allusions are as popular as they are learned: the same figure appears in a window of Canterbury Cathedral, as Rossi 1985:45 notes. The two elements, fire and water, which are linked in the proverb 'as false as water, as rash as fire' (Tilley W86), here represent the irascible and concupiscent parts of the irrational soul warring against the rational soul, as suggested by Jas. 4.1: 'From whence are warres and contentions among you? are they not hence, euen of your lustes, that fight in your members?' Their lack of control is inherited from **Acrates**, Gk ἀκρατής, 'without control', the adjectival form of ἀκρασία, intemperance; see xii 69.8*n*. The elements themselves are derived from

42

So from immortall race he does proceede,
    That mortall hands may not withstand his might,
    Drad for his derring doe, and bloody deed;
    For all in blood and spoile is his delight.
    His am I *Atin*, his in wrong and right,
    That matter make for him to worke vpon,
    And stirre him vp to strife and cruell fight.
    Fly therefore, fly this fearfull stead anon,
Least thy foolhardize worke thy sad confusion.

43

His be that care, whom most it doth concerne,
    (Sayd he) but whether with such hasty flight
    Art thou now bownd? for well mote I discerne
    Great cause, that carries thee so swifte and light.
    My Lord (quoth he) me sent, and streight behight
    To seeke *Occasion*; where so she bee:
    For he is all disposd to bloody fight,
    And breathes out wrath and hainous crueltee;
Hard is his hap, that first fals in his ieopardee.

44

Mad man (said then the Palmer) that does seeke
    Occasion to wrath, and cause of strife;
    Shee comes vnsought, and shonned followes eke.
    Happy, who can abstaine, when Rancor rife

Kindles Reuenge, and threats his rusty knife;
    Woe neuer wants, where euery cause is caught,
    And rash *Occasion* makes vnquiet life.
    Then loe, wher bound she sits, whom thou hast sought,
Said *Guyon*, let that message to thy Lord be brought.

45

That when the varlett heard and saw, streight way
    He wexed wondrous wroth, and said, Vile knight,
    That knights and knighthood doest with shame vpbray,
    And shewst th'ensample of thy childishe might,
    With silly weake old woman that did fight.
    Great glory and gay spoile sure hast thou gott,
    And stoutly prou'd thy puissaunce here in sight;
    That shall *Pyrrhochles* well requite, I wott,
And with thy blood abolish so reprochfull blott.

46

With that one of his thrillant darts he threw,
    Headed with yre and vengeable despight;
    The quiuering steele his aymed end wel knew,
    And to his brest it selfe intended right:
    But he was wary, and ere it empight
    In the meant marke, aduaunst his shield atweene,
    On which it seizing, no way enter might,
    But backe rebownding, left the forckhead keene;
Eftsoones he fled away, and might no where be seene.

Phlegeton, the infernal river of burning fire; see I v 33.1–6*n*. On **Aeternitie** and her progeny, see Lotspeich 1932:34. **3 confidence**: fearlessness; overboldness. **4 approud**: tested. **6 Despight**: cf. Despetto at VI v 13.6–9 and see *n*. **7 Iarre**: discord, dissent. **8–9 Herebus** the lowest region of hell or the god of darkness. At III iv 55.7–8, he is addressed as the husband of Night and 'the foe | Of all the Gods'. Among their offspring are the Fates; see Starnes and Talbert 1955:356. The double alexandrine emphasizes the genealogy.

Stanza 42
3 derring doe: daring deeds; 'manhoode and chevalrie' (E.K. on *SC Oct.* 65). **5 Atin**: from Ate, the classical goddess of discord, 'mother of debate, | And all dissention' (IV i 19.1–2), or 'Strife' (Arg.4). See 'Ate' in the *SEnc*. Hieatt 1975a:185 derives the name from OF *atine*, 'incitement to battle', which suggests that the name is linked to 'tine', trouble, 'suffering', a variant of 'teen', as at I ix 15.7, and to 'tynd', inflamed; see viii 11.4–5*n*. **8 stead**: place. **9 foolhardize**: foolhardiness, as ii 17.7. **confusion**: ruin.

Stanza 43
5 behight: commanded.

Stanza 44
5 rusty: rusty with blood.

Stanza 45
2–7 As Juno mocks Aeneas for subduing Dido, *Aen.* 4.93–95. Cf. Pyrochles's reproach at v 5.3–7. **vpbray**: upbraid, bring reproach on. **silly**: helpless.

Stanza 46
This sudden ending may be a consequence of S.'s decision to limit cantos ii–iv to 46 stanzas. **1 thrillant**: piercing. **2** Cf. 38.8–9. **4 intended**: aimed; made its way. **5 empight**: implanted itself. **6–8** Cf. Eph. 6.16: 'Aboue all, take the shield of faith, wherewith ye may quench all the fyrie dartes of the wicked'. The shaft rebounds while the head remains stuck on the shield. The emblem in G. Whitney 1586:138 shows that slander's arrows cannot hurt virtue.

Cant. V.

*Pyrrhochles does with Guyon fight,
And Furors chayne vntyes,
Who him sore wounds, whiles Atin to
Cymochles for ayd flyes.*

1

Who euer doth to temperaunce apply
    His stedfast life, and all his actions frame,
Trust me, shal find no greater enimy,
Then stubborne perturbation, to the same;
To which right wel the wise doe giue that name,
For it the goodly peace of staied mindes
Does ouerthrow, and troublous warre proclame:
His owne woes author, who so bound it findes,
As did *Pirrhocles*, and it wilfully vnbindes.

2

After that varlets flight, it was not long,
    Ere on the plaine fast pricking *Guyon* spide
One in bright armes embatteiled full strong,
That as the Sunny beames doe glaunce and glide
Vpon the trembling waue, so shined bright,
And round about him threw forth sparkling fire,
That seemd him to enflame on euery side:
His steed was bloody red, and fomed yre,
When with the maistring spur he did him roughly stire.

3

Approching nigh, he neuer staid to greete,
    Ne chaffar words, prowd corage to prouoke,
But prickt so fiers, that vnderneath his feete
The smouldring dust did rownd about him smoke,
Both horse and man nigh able for to choke;
And fayrly couching his steeleheaded speare,
Him first saluted with a sturdy stroke:
It booted nought Sir *Guyon* comming neare
To thincke, such hideous puissaunce on foot to beare.

4

But lightly shunned it, and passing by,
    With his bright blade did smite at him so fell,
That the sharpe steele arriuing forcibly
On his broad shield, bitt not, but glauncing fell
On his horse necke before the quilted sell,
And from the head the body sundred quight.
So him dismounted low, he did compell
On foot with him to matchen equall fight;
The truncked beast fast bleeding, did him fowly dight.

5

Sore bruzed with the fall, he slow vprose,
    And all enraged, thus him loudly shent;
Disleall knight, whose coward corage chose
To wreake it selfe on beast all innocent,
And shund the marke, at which it should be ment,
Therby thine armes seem strong, but manhood frayl:
So hast thou oft with guile thine honor blent;
But litle may such guile thee now auayl,
If wonted force and fortune doe me not much fayl.

6

With that he drew his flaming sword, and strooke
    At him so fiercely, that the vpper marge
Of his seuenfolded shield away it tooke,
And glauncing on his helmet, made a large
And open gash therein: were not his targe,
That broke the violence of his intent,
The weary sowle from thence it would discharge,
Nathelesse so sore a buff to him it lent,
That made him reele, and to his brest his beuer bent.

Book II Canto v

Argument
2–4 *1596* reads: . . . *vnbinds| Of whom sore hurt, for his reuenge
| Attin Gymochles finds.* The *1590* reading is suggested by 19.1
and 25.8–9; the revision extends the action beyond stanza 25
to the discovery of Cymochles in the Bower of Bliss.

Stanza 1
3 **Trust me**: a unique injunction by the poet asking the reader
to accept his authority.   4 **stubborne**: fierce; implacable.
5 The **wise** include Cicero who, in *De Finibus* 3.10, names
four kinds of perturbation, which Upton 1758 distributes
as follows: sorrow in Amavia, fearfulness in Braggadocchio,
lasciviousness in Cymochles, and idle pleasure in Phædria.
6 **staied**: staid, steadfast.

Stanza 2
3 **embatteiled**: armed for battle.   4–8 This image of a raging
fire in motion is an emblem of Pyrochles's nature; see iv 41*n*.
9 **stire**: incite.

Stanza 3
2 **chaffar**: exchange. On the required challenge before an
encounter, which Pyrochles fails to offer, see i 29.6*n*. That a
knight **on foot** should be **saluted** with a blow is esp. heinous.
4 **smouldring**: suffocating. The line develops iv 37.3–5 on
Atin's approach, for Pyrochles follows in his steps.   5 . . . they
were nearly choked.   7 **sturdy**: violent.

Stanza 4
9 **truncked**: truncated.   **him**: Pyrochles, but possibly Guyon.
dight: soil, defile.

7

Exceeding wroth was *Guyon* at that blow,
    And much ashamd, that stroke of liuing arme
    Should him dismay, and make him stoup so low,
    Though otherwise it did him litle harme:
    Tho hurling high his yron braced arme,
    He smote so manly on his shoulder plate,
    That all his left side it did quite disarme;
    Yet there the steele stayd not, but inly bate
Deepe in his flesh, and opened wide a red floodgate.

8

Deadly dismayd, with horror of that dint
    Pyrrhochles was, and grieued eke entyre;
    Yet nathemore did it his fury stint,
    But added flame vnto his former fire,
    That welnigh molt his hart in raging yre;
    Ne thenceforth his approued skill, to ward,
    Or strike, or hurtle rownd in warlike gyre,
    Remembred he, ne car'd for his saufgard,
But rudely rag'd, and like a cruel tygre far'd.

9

He hewd, and lasht, and foynd, and thondred blowes,
    And euery way did seeke into his life,
    Ne plate, ne male could ward so mighty throwes,
    But yeilded passage to his cruell knife.
    But *Guyon*, in the heat of all his strife,
    Was wary wise, and closely did awayt
    Auauntage, whilest his foe did rage most rife;
    Sometimes a thwart, sometimes he strook him strayt,
And falsed oft his blowes, t'illude him with such bayt.

10

Like as a Lyon, whose imperiall powre
    A prowd rebellious Vnicorne defyes,
    T'auoide the rash assault and wrathfull stowre
    Of his fiers foe, him to a tree applyes,
    And when him ronning in full course he spyes,
    He slips aside; the whiles that furious beast
    His precious horne, sought of his enimyes
    Strikes in the stocke, ne thence can be releast,
But to the mighty victor yields a bounteous feast.

11

With such faire sleight him *Guyon* often fayld,
    Till at the last all breathlesse, weary, faint
    Him spying, with fresh onsett he assayld,
    And kindling new his corage seeming queint,
    Strooke him so hugely, that through great constraint
    He made him stoup perforce vnto his knee,
    And doe vnwilling worship to the Saint,
    That on his shield depainted he did see;
Such homage till that instant neuer learned hee.

12

Whom *Guyon* seeing stoup, poursewed fast
    The present offer of faire victory,
    And soone his dreadfull blade about he cast,
    Wherewith he smote his haughty crest so hye,
    That streight on grownd made him full low to lye;
    Then on his brest his victor foote he thrust,
    With that he cryde, Mercy, doe me not dye,
    Ne deeme thy force by fortunes doome vniust,
That hath (maugre her spight) thus low me laid in dust.

Stanza 5
2 shent: reproached; (verbally) defiled; cf. i 11.2. **3–7** As Galahad was shamed when accidentally he smote off the head of Palomydes's horse (Malory 10.42); cf. Atin's charge against Guyon's knighthood at iv 45. **ment**: aimed. **blent**: mingled; defiled.

Stanza 6
1–2 He is acting out the device on his shield: 'A flaming fire in midst of bloody field' (iv 38.3). **3 seuenfolded shield**: the standard classical shield of Ajax (Homer, *Iliad* 7.220) and Turnus (Virgil, *Aen.* 12.925) though for the knight of temperance the number suggests the protection given by the four cardinal and three theological virtues (see 'virtues' in the *SEnc*) against the seven deadly sins. Cf. Artegall's shield at III ii 25.7 and the fashioning of Arthur's sword at II viii 20.7–9. **5 targe**: shield. **9 beuer**: visor of the helmet.

Stanza 7
5 hurling: the term renders the violence of whirling and hurtling as the blow begins to descend. **7–8 left** has its customary associations with the sinister. **inly bate**: cut inward.

Stanza 8
1 Deadly dismayd: going beyond Guyon's state at 7.3. **dint**: blow. **2 entyre**: entirely; inwardly; exceedingly, as the context suggests. **7 gyre**: the action of closely wheeling around a

foe (Lat. *gyrus*) in an effort to strike. **8 saufgard**: safeguard, the guard in fencing. **9 far'd**: acted.

Stanza 9
1 foynd: lunged. **3 throwes**: thrusts; blows; attacks. **6 closely**: secretly. **8–9** As the intemperate battle at ii 25.6–9. **falsed**: feinted. **illude**: deceive.

Stanza 10
The **Vnicorne** is cited in Job 39.12–15 as a beast that may not be tamed but could be defeated by its traditional enemy, the lion. Traditional lore, as in Topsell 1967:1.557, records that a unicorn attacking a treed lion would impale its horn in the tree. Its self-destructive fury is noted in Shakespeare, *Timon of Athens* 4.3.336–37. **3 stowre**: encounter. **4 applyes**: makes his way. **7 precious**: being full of marvellous medicinal virtues.

Stanza 11
1 fayld: deceived; caused to fail. **4 queint**: quenched; referring to Pyrochles's fiery nature. **7 Saint**: 'ymage of that heauenly Mayd' (i 28.7), i.e. the Faerie Queene, who is addressed as 'that sacred Saint' at IV proem 4.2. **8 depainted**: depicted.

Stanza 12
4–5 so hye: with such extreme force, so the context suggests; or the phrase may modify the **haughty** (high) crest in order to

13

Eftsoones his cruel hand Sir *Guyon* stayd,
　　Tempring the passion with aduizement slow,
　　And maistring might on enimy dismayd:
　　For th'equall die of warre he well did know;
　　Then to him said, Liue and alleagaunce owe,
　　To him, that giues thee life and liberty,
　　And henceforth by this daies ensample trow,
　　That hasty wroth, and heedlesse hazardry
Doe breede repentaunce late, and lasting infamy.

14

So vp he let him rise, who with grim looke
　　And count'naunce sterne vpstanding, gan to grind
　　His grated teeth for great disdeigne, and shooke
　　His sandy lockes, long hanging downe behind,
　　Knotted in blood and dust, for griefe of mind,
　　That he in ods of armes was conquered;
　　Yet in himselfe some comfort he did find,
　　That him so noble knight had maystered,
Whose bounty more then might, yet both he wondered.

15

Which *Guyon* marking said, Be nought agrieu'd,
　　Sir knight, that thus ye now subdewed arre:
　　Was neuer man, who most conquestes atchieu'd
　　But sometimes had the worse, and lost by warre,
　　Yet shortly gaynd, that losse exceeded farre:
　　Losse is no shame, nor to bee lesse then foe,
　　But to bee lesser, then himselfe, doth marre
　　Both loosers lott, and victours prayse alsoe.
Vaine others ouerthrowes, who selfe doth ouerthrow.

16

Fly, O *Pyrrhochles*, fly the dreadfull warre,
　　That in thy selfe thy lesser partes doe moue,
　　Outrageous anger, and woe working iarre,
　　Direfull impatience, and hartmurdring loue;
　　Those, those thy foes, those warriours far remoue,
　　Which thee to endlesse bale captiued lead.
　　But sith in might thou didst my mercy proue,
　　Of courtesie to mee the cause aread,
That thee against me drew with so impetuous dread.

17

Dreadlesse (said he) that shall I soone declare:
　　It was complaind, that thou hadst done great tort
　　Vnto an aged woman, poore and bare,
　　And thralled her in chaines with strong effort,
　　Voide of all succour and needfull comfort:
　　That ill beseemes thee, such as I thee see,
　　To worke such shame. Therefore I thee exhort,
　　To chaunge thy will, and set *Occasion* free,
And to her captiue sonne yield his first libertee.

18

Thereat Sir *Guyon* smylde, And is that all
　　(Said he) that thee so sore displeased hath?
　　Great mercy sure, for to enlarge a thrall,
　　Whose freedom shall thee turne to greatest scath.
　　Nath'lesse now quench thy whott emboyling wrath:
　　Loe there they bee; to thee I yield them free.
　　Thereat he wondrous glad, out of the path
　　Did lightly leape, where he them bound did see,
And gan to breake the bands of their captiuitee.

---

stress Pyrochles's fall **full low** – line 5 measures his length upon the ground.　**8–9** While Pyrochles's general point that fortune, not Guyon's force, has defeated him is clear, the word-play, **deeme . . . doome** and the apparent meaning of **maugre**, which is unique, according to *OED*, confuse the syntax. The simplest reading is: 'Do not judge your force according to the unjust judgement of fortune, for it is she – a curse upon her spite! – who has defeated me'.

Stanza 13

2 aduizement: deliberation.　**3** Guyon masters his might by knowing when not to use it; cf. xii 53.5.　**dismayd**: defeated.
4 equall die: equal hazard or chance, a gaming metaphor; cf. 'ods of armes' (14.6).　**die** is used here with a scarcely repressed pun.　**8 hazardry**: risk; the same gaming metaphor: playing at hazard or dicing.　**9 late**: i.e. too late.

Stanza 14

3 grated: clenched, as a grate; or gnashing, as Furor's teeth at iv 15.3–4.　**4** As Furor's 'long locks, coloured like copper-wyre' (iv 15.8).　**9** I.e., Guyon's generosity in granting Pyrochles life is greater than his force, as (in a repeat of this battle) Arthur is said to be 'full of princely bounty' (viii 51.1) in also granting him life.　**wondered**: wondered at.

Stanza 15

3 most: also greatest.　**6–8** 'There is no shame in losing a battle against a foe, but to lose a battle against oneself mars not only oneself but, in being unworthy, also the victor'.
9 'He who overthrows himself, overthrows others in vain'.

Stanza 16

2 lesser partes: the body's inner parts that produce the passions.　**3–4** Guyon's moralizing extends Medina's exhortation to fly from 'rage, and . . . iarre' (ii 30.9) and parallels the Palmer's exhortation to Phaon to expel 'Wrath, gealosie, griefe, loue' (iv 35.1).　**iarre**: discord; named an ancestor of Pyrochles at iv 41.7.　**impatience**: inability to bear grief or suffering; personified as Maleger's hag at xi 23.9.　**hartmurdring loue**: as seen in Amavia.　**8 aread**: declare.　**9 dread**: dreadfulness. Guyon refers to Pyrochles's failure to challenge him to battle at 3.1–2.

Stanza 17

1 Dreadlesse: fearless one, picking up Guyon's closing word.
2 tort: wrong; a legal term used here for a major breach of knightly code.　**3 bare**: defenceless.　**with strong effort**: with excessive use of force.　**comfort**: aid.　**9 first**: i.e. as he was at first.

19

Soone as *Occasion* felt her selfe vntyde,
 Before her sonne could well assoyled bee,
 She to her vse returnd, and streight defyde
 Both *Guyon* and *Pyrrhochles*: th'one (said shee)
 Bycause he wonne; the other because hee
 Was wonne: So matter did she make of nought,
 To stirre vp strife, and garre them disagree:
 But soone as *Furor* was enlargd, she sought
To kindle his quencht fyre, and thousand causes wrought.

20

It was not long, ere she inflam'd him so,
 That he would algates with *Pyrrhochles* fight,
 And his redeemer chalengd for his foe,
 Because he had not well mainteind his right,
 But yielded had to that same straunger knight:
 Now gan *Pyrrhochles* wex as wood, as hee,
 And him affronted with impatient might:
 So both together fiers engrasped bee,
Whyles *Guyon* standing by, their vncouth strife does see.

21

Him all that while *Occasion* did prouoke
 Against *Pyrrhochles*, and new matter fram'd
 Vpon the old, him stirring to bee wroke
 Of his late wronges, in which she oft him blam'd
 For suffering such abuse, as knighthood sham'd,
 And him dishabled quyte. But he was wise,
 Ne would with vaine occasions be inflam'd;
 Yet others she more vrgent did deuise:
Yet nothing could him to impatience entise.

22

Their fell contention still increased more,
 And more thereby increased *Furors* might,
 That he his foe has hurt, and wounded sore,
 And him in blood and durt deformed quight.
 His mother eke, more to augment his spight,
 Now brought to him a flaming fyer brond,
 Which she in *Stygian* lake, ay burning bright
 Had kindled: that she gaue into his hond,
That armd with fire, more hardly he mote him withstond.

23

Tho gan that villein wex so fiers and strong,
 That nothing might sustaine his furious forse;
 He cast him downe to ground, and all along
 Drew him through durt and myre without remorse,
 And fowly battered his comely corse,
 That *Guyon* much disdeignd so loathly sight.
 At last he was compeld to cry perforse,
 Help, O Sir *Guyon*, helpe most noble knight,
To ridd a wretched man from handes of hellish wight.

24

The knight was greatly moued at his playnt,
 And gan him dight to succour his distresse,
 Till that the Palmer, by his graue restraynt,
 Him stayd from yielding pitifull redresse;
 And said, Deare sonne, thy causelesse ruth represse,
 Ne let thy stout hart melt in pitty vayne:
 He that his sorow sought through wilfulnesse,
 And his foe fettred would release agayne,
Deserues to taste his follies fruit, repented payne.

Stanza 18
3–4 Great mercy: great favour it is! Guyon's irony proves double-edged: freeing Pyrochles turns to **greatest scath** (harm) against himself.   **7 out of the path**: i.e. from the path of temperance.

Stanza 19
2 assoyled: set free.   **3 vse**: customary behaviour.   **6 wonne**: defeated.   **7 garre**: cause (as E.K. on *SC Apr.* 1); do *1596*.

Stanza 20
2 algates: at all costs.   **3** On this motif in Bk II, see viii 22.5–9*n*.   **6 wood**: frantic.   **7 affronted**: attacked.   **impatient**: unable to be contained.   **9 vncouth**: strange; marvellous; unseemly.

Stanza 21
3 wroke: wreaked, i.e. revenged.   **6–7 dishabled**: dishonoured. That Guyon is no longer **with vaine occasions . . . inflam'd** resolves the theme of the opening episode. He was 'inflam'd with wrathfulnesse' at i 25.8 when Archimago, 'In hope to win occasion to his will' (i 5.2), tells him a false tale; now he proves that he is no longer an errant knight and may 'his voyage to poursew' (25.3).   **9 entise**: provoke.

Stanza 22
4 Pyrochles is increasingly defiled: he enters in a cloud of dust (3.4), becomes soiled with blood (4.9), falls to the ground to rise with his hair 'Knotted in blood and dust' (14.5), and now is deformed **in blood and durt**. See vi 41.6–8*n*.
5–9 Illustrating Jas. 3.6: 'And the tongue is fyre, yea, a worlde of wickednes: so is the tongue set among our members, that it defileth the whole bodie, and setteth on fyre the course of nature, and it is set on fyre of hel'. Cf. the effect of her tongue at iv 5.1–4.   **Stygian lake**: usually the fiery river Phlegeton is named, as at IV ii 1.1, but S. associates wrath with hatred and therefore with the 'blacke *Stygian* lake' (I v 10.6): Στύξ, hateful.   **hardly**: hardily; vigorously.

Stanza 23
4 remorse: pity.   **6 disdeignd**: was indignant at.

Stanza 24
4 The occasion to anger is succeeded by an occasion to pity. Both were illustrated in the opening episode when Guyon was moved to anger by pity for the 'violated' Duessa, his opening words to her being 'Great pitty is to see you thus dismayd' (i 14.3). He had intervened when he saw Phaon suffering under Furor (iv 3.5–9), as here Pyrochles suffers, but now he is restrained by the Palmer whose motto is 'Let *Gryll* be *Gryll*' (xii 87.8).   **pitifull redresse**: aid given out of pity.   **9 repented payne**: i.e. pain which he repents.

25

Guyon obayd; So him away he drew
    From needlesse trouble of renewing fight
    Already fought, his voyage to poursew.
    But rash *Pyrrhochles* varlett, *Atin* hight,
    When late he saw his Lord in heauie plight,
    Vnder Sir *Guyons* puissaunt stroke to fall,
    Him deeming dead, as then he seemd in sight,
    Fledd fast away, to tell his funerall
Vnto his brother, whom *Cymochles* men did call.

26

He was a man of rare redoubted might,
    Famous throughout the world for warlike prayse,
    And glorious spoiles, purchast in perilous fight:
    Full many doughtie knightes he in his dayes
    Had doen to death, subdewde in equall frayes,
    Whose carkases, for terrour of his name,
    Of fowles and beastes he made the piteous prayes,
    And hong their conquerd armes for more defame
On gallow trees, in honour of his dearest Dame.

27

His dearest Dame is that Enchaunteresse,
    The vyle *Acrasia*, that with vaine delightes,
    And ydle pleasures in her *Bowre of Blisse*,
    Does charme her louers, and the feeble sprightes
    Can call out of the bodies of fraile wightes:
    Whom then she does transforme to monstrous hewes,
    And horribly misshapes with vgly sightes,
    Captiu'd eternally in yron mewes,
And darksom dens, where *Titan* his face neuer shewes.

28

There *Atin* fownd *Cymochles* soiourning,
    To serue his Lemans loue: for he by kynd,
    Was giuen all to lust and loose liuing,
    When euer his fiers handes he free mote fynd:
    And now he has pourd out his ydle mynd
    In daintie delices, and lauish ioyes,
    Hauing his warlike weapons cast behynd,
    And flowes in pleasures, and vaine pleasing toyes,
Mingled emongst loose Ladies and lasciuious boyes.

29

And ouer him, art stryuing to compayre,
    With nature, did an Arber greene dispred,
    Framed of wanton Yuie, flouring fayre,
    Through which the fragrant Eglantine did spred
    His prickling armes, entrayld with roses red,
    Which daintie odours round about them threw,
    And all within with flowres was garnished,
    That when myld *Zephyrus* emongst them blew,
Did breath out bounteous smels, and painted colors shew.

30

And fast beside, there trickled softly downe
    A gentle streame, whose murmuring waue did play
    Emongst the pumy stones, and made a sowne,
    To lull him soft a sleepe, that by it lay;
    The wearie Traueiler, wandring that way,
    Therein did often quench his thristy heat,
    And then by it his wearie limbes display,
    Whiles creeping slomber made him to forget
His former payne, and wypt away his toilsom sweat.

Stanza 25
8 funerall: death.

Stanza 26
1–5 Cf. the description of Pyrochles at iv 41.2–4. **glorious
spoiles**: conquests that bring him glory. **purchast**: got by
conquest in war. **6–7** On despoiling the dead body, see vi
28.7–9 and *n*. **8–9 defame**: disgrace. **On gallow trees**: in
mockery of the tree of chivalry; see I v 5.7*n*.

Stanza 27
Enchaunteresse and **vyle** are Acrasia's name and epithet at i
51.2–3 and 55.1. On her name, see xii 69.8*n*. She is worse than
Homer's Circe who transforms her lovers' bodies but not their
minds; see xii 85.5*n*. **6–8 monstrous hewes**: the shapes of
monsters. **sightes**: appearances. **mewes**: prisons, as Lucifera's
victims are confined to a 'Dongeon mercilesse' (I v 46.8).

Stanza 28
The same 'c' rhyme is used at xii 60 to describe the pleasures
of the Bower of Bliss. **2 by kynd**: by his nature. **6 delices**:
delights, sensual pleasures; cf. xii 85.7. **7 cast behynd**: i.e.
'hong vp' (35.7), as Verdant has done at xii 80.1–2. **8–9
flowes . . . | Mingled**: indicating his watery nature; see iv 41*n*.
Cf. the Red Cross Knight with Duessa 'Pourd out in loosnesse
on the grassy grownd' (I vii 7.2). **toyes**: amorous dallyings;

cf. xii 72.9. In a preview to the Bower of Bliss, the next six
stanzas show Cymochles enjoying a banquet of all the senses;
see 'senses, five' in the *SEnc*. **lasciuious boyes**: as xii 72.8, an
overt reference to paederasty.

Stanza 29
1–2 On the rivalry between art and nature in the Bower, see xii
59 and *n*. **compayre**: vie. **3–5 wanton**: as ivy is luxuriant
in growth, wanders and clings, and is sacred to Bacchus; cf. xii
61.2. **flouring**: flourishing. **Yuie** and **Eglantine** (sweet-
briar) also flourish on Venus's mount in the garden of Adonis
at III vi 44.5–6. For the **roses**, see xii 77.1. **prickling**: from
the etymology of Eglantine, Lat. *aculeus*, prickle. **entrayld**:
entwined. **8 Zephyrus**: the west wind, which also blows at xii
33.5 (see *n*).

Stanza 30
3 pumy stones: pumice, chosen because being porous it
softens the sound of flowing water. As a feature of the *locus
amoenus*, see Nohrnberg 1976:502–07; as a feature of Italianate
gardens in England, see the *SEnc* 324. **sowne**: the obs.
spelling avoids the harsh dental of 'sound'. **7 display**: extend.

Stanza 31
1–5 the stately tree: either the oak, which is dedicated to Jove
(as Homer, *Ody*. 19.296–97), or the poplar, which is linked to

31

And on the other syde a pleasaunt groue
  Was shott vp high, full of the stately tree,
  That dedicated is t'*Olympick Ioue*,
  And to his sonne *Alcides*, whenas hee
  In *Nemus* gayned goodly victoree;
  Therein the mery birdes of euery sorte
  Chaunted alowd their chearefull harmonee:
  And made emongst them selues a sweete consort,
That quickned the dull spright with musicall comfort.

32

There he him found all carelesly displaid,
  In secrete shadow from the sunny ray,
  On a sweet bed of lillies softly laid,
  Amidst a flock of Damzelles fresh and gay,
  That rownd about him dissolute did play
  Their wanton follies, and light meriment;
  Euery of which did loosely disaray
  Her vpper partes of meet habiliments,
And shewd them naked, deckt with many ornaments.

33

And euery of them stroue, with most delights,
  Him to aggrate, and greatest pleasures shew;
  Some framd faire lookes, glancing like euening lights,
  Others sweet wordes, dropping like honny dew;
  Some bathed kisses, and did soft embrew
  The sugred licour through his melting lips:
  One boastes her beautie, and does yield to vew
  Her dainty limbes aboue her tender hips;
Another her out boastes, and all for tryall strips.

34

He, like an Adder, lurking in the weedes,
  His wandring thought in deepe desire does steepe,
  And his frayle eye with spoyle of beauty feedes;
  Sometimes he falsely faines himselfe to sleepe,
  Whiles through their lids his wanton eies do peepe,
  To steale a snatch of amorous conceipt,
  Whereby close fire into his heart does creepe:
  So, he them deceiues, deceiud in his deceipt,
Made dronke with drugs of deare voluptuous receipt.

35

Attin arriuing there, when him he spyde,
  Thus in still waues of deepe delight to wade,
  Fiercely approching, to him lowdly cryde,
  Cymochles, oh no, but *Cymochles* shade,
  In which that manly person late did fade,
  What is become of great *Acrates* sonne?
  Or where hath he hong vp his mortall blade,
  That hath so many haughty conquests wonne?
Is all his force forlorne, and all his glory donne?

36

Then pricking him with his sharp-pointed dart,
  He saide; Vp, vp, thou womanish weake knight,
  That here in Ladies lap entombed art,
  Vnmindfull of thy praise and prowest might,
  And weetlesse eke of lately wrought despight,
  Whiles sad *Pyrrhochles* lies on sencelesse ground,
  And groneth out his vtmost grudging spright,
  Through many a stroke, and many a streaming wound,
Calling thy help in vaine, that here in ioyes art dround.

Alcides, i.e. Hercules (as Virgil, *Ecl.* 7.61). Here associated first with victories at the Olympic games and then with Hercules's victories, the first over the Nemean lion and (by inference) the last over hell, which is symbolized by the crown of poplar leaves he wore on his return, as in Alciati 1985:emblem 212. These references emphasize Cymochles's rejection of the active, heroic life, as the tree **shott vp high** contrasts with his prone state. **Olympick Ioue** points to the free state of the gods on Olympus in contrast to the knight's bound state in the Bower. Hence the grove is **on the other syde**, set apart from the slothful knight. **6–9** On the association of the song of birds with sensuality, see I vii 3.4–5*n*. **consort**: company; accord. **comfort**: the term cancels the effect of **quickned**. Instead of the awakening call that hurries Chaucer's pilgrims on their way, the birds, like the waters, lull the traveller.

Stanza 32
2 As at vi 14.1–4, led there by Acrasia in anticipation of the 'darksom dens' (27.9) in which she finally places her lovers. **3 bed of lillies**: a deliberately perverse use of this flower of chastity. **6 follies**: lewd actions. **9 ornaments**: jewellery, such as Duessa wears, in contrast to Amoret's naked breast 'Without adorne of gold or siluer bright' (III xii 20.2).

Stanza 33
1–2 most: greatest. **delights**: sensual pleasures, as 'delices' (28.6). **aggrate**: please, gratify. **shew**: cf. xii 68.9. **4** Cf. Prov. 5.3: 'For the lippes of a strange woman drop as an honie

combe'. **5 embrew**: thrust, in kissing. **7–9** Repeated with embellishments at xii 66. **tryall**: examination; and challenging him to 'try all'.

Stanza 34
2 wandring: wanton. **3 spoyle of beauty**: referring to the damsels stripping themselves but also despoiling their beauty through their wantonness. **6 snatch**: quick grab, hasty glimpse; which leads to his 'entanglement' (*OED* 2). **conceipt**: thought, image. **7 close**: secret. **8–9** As Acrasia's lovers become 'dronken mad' by her 'drugs of fowle intemperaunce' (i 52.2, 54.8). **deare**: dire, grievous; possibly 'precious'. **receipt**: recipe (*OED* 1.1), as the fatal potion Acrasia gives Mordant at i 55, but referring primarily to the sight he receives (*OED* 3.4.b).

Stanza 35
2 Alluding to the etymology of his name; see iv 41*n*. **4–9** Atin's reproof parallels admonitions to warriors who yielded to sensuality, as Mercury to Aeneas subject to Dido in Libya (Virgil, *Aen.* 4.265–76), Melissa to Ruggiero on Alcina's island (Ariosto, *Orl. Fur.* 7.57–64), and Ubaldo to Rinaldo in Armida's bower (Tasso, *Ger. Lib.* 16.32–33). **shade**: image or ghost. **fade**: vanish. **forlorne**: lost.

Stanza 36
3 lap: with the erotic implications of its use at xii 76.9. **7** . . . his last complaining (or tormented) breath.

37

Suddeinly out of his delightfull dreame
　　The man awoke, and would haue questiond more;
　　But he would not endure that wofull theame
　　For to dilate at large, but vrged sore
　　With percing wordes, and pittifull implore,
　　Him hasty to arise. As one affright
　　With hellish feends, or *Furies* mad vprore,
He then vprose, inflamd with fell despight,
And called for his armes; for he would algates fight.

38

They bene ybrought; he quickly does him dight,
　　And lightly mounted, passeth on his way,
　　Ne Ladies loues, ne sweete entreaties might
　　Appease his heat, or hastie passage stay,
　　For he has vowd, to beene auengd that day,
　　(That day it selfe him seemed all too long:)
　　On him, that did *Pyrrhochles* deare dismay:
So proudly pricketh on his courser strong,
And *Attin* ay him pricks with spurs of shame and wrong.

Stanza 37
4 dilate at large: relate at length.　**5 pittifull implore**: appeal
for pity.　**6** The caesura marks his hasty rising.　**8** The dart
(36.1) is poisoned by 'despight' (iv 38.9).

Stanza 38
2 lightly: quickly.　**7 deare dismay**: grievously vanquish.
8–9 A fresh rendering of the stock figure of the rider
ridden.

Cant. VI.

Guyon is of immodest Merth,
led into loose desyre,
Fights with Cymochles, whiles his bro-
ther burnes in furious fyre.

1

A Harder lesson, to learne Continence
In ioyous pleasure, then in grieuous paine:
For sweetnesse doth allure the weaker sence
So strongly, that vneathes it can refraine
From that, which feeble nature couets faine;
But griefe and wrath, that be her enemies,
And foes of life, she better can abstaine;
Yet vertue vauntes in both her victories,
And *Guyon* in them all shewes goodly maysteries.

2

Whom bold *Cymochles* traueiling to finde,
With cruell purpose bent to wreake on him
The wrath, which *Atin* kindled in his mind,
Came to a riuer, by whose vtmost brim
Wayting to passe, he saw whereas did swim
A long the shore, as swift as glaunce of eye,
A litle Gondelay, bedecked trim
With boughes and arbours wouen cunningly,
That like a litle forrest seemed outwardly.

3

And therein sate a Lady fresh and fayre,
Making sweete solace to her selfe alone;
Sometimes she song, as lowd as larke in ayre,
Sometimes she laught, as merry as Pope Ione,
Yet was there not with her else any one,
That to her might moue cause of meriment:
Matter of merth enough, though there were none
She could deuise, and thousand waies inuent,
To feede her foolish humour, and vaine iolliment.

4

Which when far off *Cymochles* heard, and saw,
He lowdly cald to such, as were abord,
The little barke vnto the shore to draw,
And him to ferry ouer that deepe ford:
The merry mariner vnto his word
Soone hearkned, and her painted bote streightway
Turnd to the shore, where that same warlike Lord
She in receiu'd; but *Atin* by no way
She would admit, albe the knight her much did pray.

Book II Canto vi

Argument

1 immodest: improper, lewd; also the sense of Lat. *immodestus*, intemperate, excessive; cf. 37.4, its only other use in the poem.

Stanza 1

1–2 Adapting Aristotle's comment, in *Ethics* 2.3, on Heraclitus's claim that it is harder to fight pleasure than anger. The irascible passions are treated chiefly in the first half of Bk II, the concupiscent in the second half. **Continence**: 'a vertue whiche kepeth the pleasaunt appetite of man under the yoke of reason' (Elyot 1907:3.17), as shown in Arthur 'who goodly learned had of yore | The course of loose affection to forstall' (IV ix 19.2–3). The term 'continence of life' – its only other use in the poem – is linked with 'stedfast chastity' at V vii 9.8, 9; cf. 'continent and chast' at V iii 28.8. On S.'s choice of the term 'temperance' for the virtue in Bk II, see Weatherby 1996b. **3 weaker**: too weak. **4 vneathes**: hardly. **5 faine**: willingly. **6–7 griefe and wrath**: a traditional pair as **foes of life**, esp. in Bk II, as the grief and anger which Guyon restrains at the loss of his horse at iii 3.4. See also i 57–58, iv 33.4, and viii 33.1–2. **abstaine**: 'hold back', an obs. sense that relates temperance to self-control. restraine *1596*.

Stanza 2

4 vtmost brim: extreme edge; perhaps the mouth of the river where it debouches into the Idle Lake; or the shore of the lake itself. Cf. 'that deepe ford' (4.4) and 'wide strond' (19.2). **7 Gondelay**: its suggestion of sexual licence is noted by Crossley and Edwards 1973:315–16. Phædria's humour depends on the obscene significance of her boat with its pin, and the use to which she is very willing to put it. **8–9** Cf. the description of the Bower of Bliss at v 29.1–3. **arbours**: vines or trailing shrubs. **forrest**: in this context, the spelling suggests 'for-rest'.

Stanza 3

2 sweete solace: narcissistic amusement. **3** Phædria's connection with birds is made again at 5.2 and 25.1. The common expression, **lowd as larke**, is used at *SC Nov.* 71. **4 as merry as Pope Ione**: alluding to the legendary female Pope – see Patrides 1982:152–81 – who became proverbial (Smith 529). 'that nigh her breth was gone' *1596* befits this airhead. **7–9** As Occasion 'matter [of anger] did . . . make of nought' (v 19.6; cf. 21.2). As Phædria's title, 'immodest Merth' (Arg.), would suggest, loud laughter characterizes her, and therefore her island (24.6); hence her laughter at xii 15.4. Her self-indulgent frivolity distinguishes her from Acrasia's heavy-breathing, soul-destroying sex. Cf. Perissa 'still [i.e. always] laughing' (ii 36.2). **foolish humour**: her self-regarding disposition of wanton idleness or obsessive frivolity.

Stanza 4

6 painted: i.e. with 'painted blossomes' (12.7), as she is at 7.4; cf. 2.7–9.

5
Eftsoones her shallow ship away did slide,
   More swift, then swallow sheres the liquid skye,
   Withouten oare or Pilot it to guide,
   Or winged canuas with the wind to fly,
   Onely she turnd a pin, and by and by
   It cut away vpon the yielding waue,
   Ne cared she her course for to apply:
   For it was taught the way, which she would haue,
And both from rocks and flats it selfe could wisely saue.

6
And all the way, the wanton Damsell found
   New merth, her passenger to entertaine:
   For she in pleasaunt purpose did abound,
   And greatly ioyed merry tales to faine,
   Of which a store-house did with her remaine,
   Yet seemed, nothing well they her became;
   For all her wordes she drownd with laughter vaine,
   And wanted grace in vtt'ring of the same,
That turned all her pleasaunce to a scoffing game.

7
And other whiles vaine toyes she would deuize,
   As her fantasticke wit did most delight,
   Sometimes her head she fondly would aguize
   With gaudy girlonds, or fresh flowrets dight
   About her necke, or rings of rushes plight;
   Sometimes to do him laugh, she would assay
   To laugh at shaking of the leaues light,
   Or to behold the water worke, and play
About her little frigot, therein making way.

8
Her light behauiour, and loose dalliaunce
   Gaue wondrous great contentment to the knight,
   That of his way he had no souenaunce,
   Nor care of vow'd reuenge, and cruell fight,
   But to weake wench did yield his martiall might.
   So easie was to quench his flamed minde
   With one sweete drop of sensuall delight.
   So easie is, t'appease the stormy winde
Of malice in the calme of pleasaunt womankind.

9
Diuerse discourses in their way they spent,
   Mongst which *Cymochles* of her questioned,
   Both what she was, and what that vsage ment,
   Which in her cott she daily practized.
   Vaine man (saide she) that wouldest be reckoned
   A straunger in thy home, and ignoraunt
   Of *Phædria* (for so my name is red)
   Of *Phædria*, thine owne fellow seruaunt;
For thou to serue *Acrasia* thy selfe doest vaunt.

10
In this wide Inland sea, that hight by name
   The *Idle lake*, my wandring ship I row,
   That knowes her port, and thether sayles by ayme,
   Ne care, ne feare I, how the wind do blow,
   Or whether swift I wend, or whether slow:
   Both slow and swift a like do serue my tourne,
   Ne swelling *Neptune*, ne lowd thundring *Ioue*
   Can chaunge my cheare, or make me euer mourne;
My little boat can safely passe this perilous bourne.

Stanza 5
2 The swallow's swiftness is proverbial (Smith 748) and is cited here because swiftness characterizes Phædria's boat, as 2.6, 20.3 and 38.1, etc. **liquid**: clear, bright; a Virgilian phrase (cf. *Aen.* 5.217) used here to note the mingling of water and sky. **5 pin**: like the throttle on the brass steed in Chaucer, *Squire's Tale* 127. In Homer, *Ody.* 8.557–63, the Phaeacian ships need not be steered for they know men's thoughts, as Phædria's ship moves 'obaying to her mind' (20.3). For similar magical boats, see Ariosto, *Orl. Fur.* 30.11; and Tasso, *Ger. Lib.* 14.57–65, 15.6–9. **by and by**: immediately. **6 waue**: water, as 18.7, 47.1, for there are no waves on this lake. **7 apply**: steer. **9 wisely**: skilfully.

Stanza 6
1 wanton: undisciplined, frivolous, gay, carefree, in addition to 'lasciuious'. It is her usual appellation, e.g. 40.8, viii 3.3, xii 17.1, as Acrasia whom she serves is 'That wanton Lady' (xii 76.8). **3 purpose**: speech, punning on her own lack of purpose. **4 merry tales**: possibly alluding to a jestbook, such as the *Merie tales by Skelton*, which S. loaned Harvey (see Chronology 1578 *20 Dec.*), though the tales she feigns would be more amorous. **6–9** She tells off-colour stories, like one of Aristotle's buffoons, in *Ethics* 4.8, who seek to raise a laugh rather than to say what is becoming. **the same**: i.e. her words. **pleasaunce**: pleasing behaviour.

Stanza 7
1 other whiles: at times. **toyes**: amorous sports, tricks. **2 fantasticke wit**: extravagant fantasy. **3 fondly**: foolishly. **aguize**: array. **4 gaudy**: showy. **flowrets**: 'young blossomes' (E.K. on *SC Feb.* 182). **5 plight**: pleated, woven.

Stanza 8
3 souenaunce: memory. **6–7** These lines prepare for Pyrochles's failure to quench his inner fire in the Idle Lake at 49–50.

Stanza 9
1 Diuerse: various; distracting; hence diverting him from his way. **4 cott**: a small Irish boat; 'shelter' (*OED* sb.¹ 2) is preferable. Decked 'like a litle forrest' (2.9), it is like Cymochles's **home**, the Bower of Bliss. **5 Vaine**: foolish. **7 Phædria**: glittering, cheerful (Gk φαιδρός), referring to her superficial pleasure and superfluous frivolity. See 'Phaedria' in the *SEnc*. In her lightness and variability, she is linked to the element of air, in opposition to Mammon who is linked to earth. **red**: called. **8–9** Implying that 'since you serve Acrasia, I serve you', a preferable reading to 'I am a servant of Acrasia even as you are'.

Stanza 10
1–2 Inland sea: i.e. the Mediterranean, an appropriate reference in the classical scheme of Bk II. For the association

11

Whiles thus she talked, and whiles thus she toyd,
    They were far past the passage, which he spake,
    And come vnto an Island, waste and voyd,
    That floted in the midst of that great lake,
    There her small Gondelay her port did make,
    And that gay payre issewing on the shore
    Disburdned her. Their way they forward take
    Into the land, that lay them faire before,
Whose pleasaunce she him shewd, and plentifull great store.

12

It was a chosen plott of fertile land,
    Emongst wide waues sett, like a litle nest,
    As if it had by Natures cunning hand,
    Bene choycely picked out from all the rest,
    And laid forth for ensample of the best:
    No dainty flowre or herbe, that growes on grownd,
    No arborett with painted blossomes drest,
    And smelling sweete, but there it might be fownd
To bud out faire, and throwe her sweete smels al arownd.

13

No tree, whose braunches did not brauely spring;
    No braunch, whereon a fine bird did not sitt:
    No bird, but did her shrill notes sweetely sing;
    No song but did containe a louely ditt:

Trees, braunches, birds, and songs were framed fitt,
    For to allure fraile mind to carelesse ease.
    Carelesse the man soone woxe, and his weake witt
    Was ouercome of thing, that did him please;
So pleased, did his wrathfull purpose faire appease.

14

Thus when shee had his eyes and sences fed
    With false delights, and fild with pleasures vayn,
    Into a shady dale she soft him led,
    And laid him downe vpon a grassy playn;
    And her sweete selfe without dread, or disdayn,
    She sett beside, laying his head disarmd
    In her loose lap, it softly to sustayn,
    Where soone he slumbred, fearing not be harmd,
The whils with a loue lay she thus him sweetely charmd.

15

Behold, O man, that toilesome paines doest take
    The flowrs, the fields, and all that pleasaunt growes,
    How them them selues doe thine ensample make,
    Whiles nothing enuious nature them forth throwes
    Out of her fruitfull lap; how no man knowes,
    They spring, they bud, they blossome fresh and faire,
    And decke the world with their rich pompous showes;
    Yet no man for them taketh paines or care,
Yet no man to them can his carefull paines compare.

---

with the Dead Sea, or what Wybarne 1609 calls Phædria's 'dead sea of pleasure' (*Sp All* 120), see 46.6–9*n*. See 'Idle Lake' in the *SEnc*. The spelling 'Ydle' at vii 2.2 suggests the Pythagorean letter Υ (Gk *upsilon*), its two shafts representing the diverging paths of virtue and vice open to Guyon. S. Miller 1998:41 notes that Phædria seeks to contain Guyon within the known European world. **9 perilous bourne**: referring to the 'riuer' (2.4) or 'that deepe ford' (4.4), though the term suggests 'boundary' or 'limit', particularly of life itself. Cf. 'perlous foord' (19.9) and 'perlous shard' (38.9). See 38.9*n*.

Stanza 11
3–4 As Acrasia's 'wandring Island . . . in perilous gulfe' (i 51.5–6). **waste and voyd**: both words signify 'uninhabited' in contrast to the 'fertile land' (12.1) which has **plentifull great store**, as Webster 1994:89 notes. In this feature, it suggests the New World. **9 pleasaunce**: pleasantness (as 6.9, 21.6), or with reference to a secluded garden.

Stanza 12
3–5 As the Bower of Bliss is said at xii 42.3–4 to be the best choice of Nature that art could imitate; but here only **As if** because art only mocks nature. **6–9** As an earthly paradise, it contains all plant life; cf. Gen. 2.5 and see IV x 22.1–5*n*. **arborett**: shrub; evidently coined by S.

Stanza 13
This finely crafted stanza was included in Robert Allott, *England's Parnassus* (1600) to illustrate 'the choysest Flowers of our Moderne Poets'. In 1593, Thomas Watson appropriated its first six lines in *The Tears of Fancie* 51. **4 ditt**: ditty,

as subject matter, theme. **6 carelesse**: free from care. At v 31.6–9, the song of birds provides 'musicall comfort' but now its danger is manifest; see I vii 3.4–5*n*.

Stanza 14
2 **fild**: also defiled (from 'file'); cf. vii 24.4. **7** He is seen in this posture at v 36.3. **9 loue lay**: cf. 'louely lay' (xii 74.1), i.e. a song of love; loud lay *1596* is supported by her singing 'as lowd as larke' (3.3). **charmd**: from Lat. *carmen*, song.

Stanzas 15–17
Phædria's song replicates the Siren's song to Rinaldo on Armida's enchanted island, which urges him to follow nature (Tasso, *Ger. Lib.* 14.62–64) by mocking Christ's sermon on the mount (Matt. 6.25–34), esp. vv. 28–29: 'Learne, how the lilies of the field do growe: they labour not, nether spinne: yet I say vnto you, that euen Solomon in all his glorie was not arayed like one of these'. It is echoed in the song heard in Acrasia's Bower at xii 74–75. In urging Cymochles not to care, she assigns God's role to nature, as Stambler 1977:64 notes; in rejecting 'toile' (17.9), she seeks to escape God's penalty that 'In the sweat of thy face shalt thou eat bread, til thou returne to the earth' (Gen. 3.19); and in urging idleness, the first of the sins in the house of Pride, she opposes the best use of time through temperance, as its connection with Lat. *tempus* suggests. As a parody of Reformation sermons, see Imbrie 1987:150–51 and Mallette 1997:66–67.

Stanza 15
4 **nothing enuious**: in no way grudging; a Latinism for 'all-bountifull'.

16

The lilly, Lady of the flowring field,
 The flowre deluce, her louely Paramoure,
 Bid thee to them thy fruitlesse labors yield,
 And soone leaue off this toylsome weary stoure;
 Loe loe how braue she decks her bounteous boure,
 With silkin curtens and gold couerletts,
 Therein to shrowd her sumptuous Belamoure,
 Yet nether spinnes nor cards, ne cares nor fretts,
But to her mother Nature all her care she letts.

17

Why then doest thou, O man, that of them all
 Art Lord, and eke of nature Soueraine,
 Wilfully make thy selfe a wretched thrall,
 And waste thy ioyous howres in needelesse paine,
 Seeking for daunger and aduentures vaine?
 What bootes it al to haue, and nothing vse?
 Who shall him rew, that swimming in the maine,
 Will die for thrist, and water doth refuse?
Refuse such fruitlesse toile, and present pleasures chuse.

18

By this she had him lulled fast a sleepe,
 That of no wordly thing he care did take;
 Then she with liquors strong his eies did steepe,
 That nothing should him hastily awake:
 So she him lefte, and did herselfe betake
 Vnto her boat again, with which she clefte
 The slouthfull waue of that great griesy lake;
 Soone shee that Island far behind her lefte,
And now is come to that same place, where first she wefte.

19

By this time was the worthy *Guyon* brought
 Vnto the other side of that wide strond,
 Where she was rowing, and for passage sought:
 Him needed not long call, shee soone to hond

Her ferry brought, where him she byding fond,
 With his sad guide; him selfe she tooke a boord,
 But the *Blacke Palmer* suffred still to stond,
 Ne would for price, or prayers once affoord,
To ferry that old man ouer the perlous foord.

20

Guyon was loath to leaue his guide behind,
 Yet being entred, might not backe retyre;
 For the flitt barke, obaying to her mind,
 Forth launched quickly, as she did desire,
 Ne gaue him leaue to bid that aged sire
 Adieu, but nimbly ran her wonted course
 Through the dull billowes thicke as troubled mire,
 Whom nether wind out of their seat could forse,
Nor timely tides did driue out of their sluggish sourse.

21

And by the way, as was her wonted guize,
 Her mery fitt shee freshly gan to reare,
 And did of ioy and iollity deuize,
 Her selfe to cherish, and her guest to cheare:
 The knight was courteous, and did not forbeare
 Her honest merth and pleasaunce to partake;
 But when he saw her toy, and gibe, and geare,
 And passe the bonds of modest merimake,
Her dalliaunce he despisd, and follies did forsake.

22

Yet she still followed her former style,
 And said, and did all that mote him delight,
 Till they arriued in that pleasaunt Ile,
 Where sleeping late she lefte her other knight.
 But whenas *Guyon* of that land had sight,
 He wist him selfe amisse, and angry said;
 Ah Dame, perdy ye haue not doen me right,
 Thus to mislead mee, whiles I you obaid:
Me litle needed from my right way to haue straid.

Stanza 16

1–2 The **lilly** is called the 'mistress of the field' in Shakespeare, *Henry VIII* 3.1.152. By its etymology, **flowre deluce** was taken to be the *flos deliciae*, the iris, a flower of chastity, which E.K. glosses as 'Flowre delice, that which they use to misterme, Flowre de luce, being in Latine called Flos delitiarum' (*SC Apr.* 144). The parodic mating of the 'virgin Lillie' (*Proth* 32) with the phallic-like fleur-de-lis is noted by Hieatt 1975b:102–06. **louely**: loving. **3 to them**: i.e. before them; in the face of their ease. **4 stoure**: time of turmoil, struggle. **7 Belamoure**: a Spenserian nonce-word meaning 'fair lover'; from Fr. *bel* + *amour*. A flower at *Am* 64.7. **9 letts**: leaves.

Stanza 17

1–2 Cf. Ps. 8.6–8. **6** In urging **vse**, she omits the key term 'right', opposing Guyon's concern with 'right vsaunce' (vii 7.4).

Stanza 18

2 wordly: worldly *1596*, of which it is an obs. form. **7 griesy**: horrible; also 'sluggish', for the waters are 'thicke as troubled mire' (20.7) and 'Engrost with mud' (46.7). Cf. the description at 20.7, 38.3, 46.6. griesly *1596*: arousing horror, as

its waters are said to 'fowle agrise' Pyrochles and Atin at 46.7. **9 wefte**: sailed; its association with 'wefte', as at III x 36.3, suggests 'wandering'.

Stanza 19

2 the other side: Cymochles travels from the Bower, Guyon to it. **strond**: sea, lake; or 'shore' as at 27.9, 38.2. **6 sad**: grave; in contrast to 'immodest Merth' (Arg.1) who now guides Guyon. **tooke a boord**: a flirtatious use of the bawdy sense; cf. III x 6.4 and 38.1 below. **8–9** As she treats Atin at 4.8–9. **affoord**: grant.

Stanza 20

3 flitt: swift. **9 timely**: i.e. obedient to time; see 26.9*n*.

Stanza 21

1 wonted guize: customary manner. **2 reare**: commence. **3 iollity**: pleasure, esp. sexual pleasure. **4** I.e., to make herself cherished; or to cheer herself. **7 gibe, and geare**: jest and joke (or jeer); cf. V iii 39.4. **8 bonds**: bounds. **modest**: as she is 'immodest Merth' (Arg.). **9 follies**: lewd desires or actions. **forsake**: decline, shun.

23

Faire Sir (quoth she) be not displeasd at all;
    Who fares on sea, may not commaund his way,
    Ne wind and weather at his pleasure call:
    The sea is wide, and easy for to stray;
    The wind vnstable, and doth neuer stay.
    But here a while ye may in safety rest,
    Till season serue new passage to assay;
    Better safe port, then be in seas distrest.
Therewith she laught, and did her earnest end in iest.

24

But he halfe discontent, mote nathelesse
    Himselfe appease, and issewd forth on shore:
    The ioyes whereof, and happy fruitfulnesse,
    Such as he saw, she gan him lay before,
    And all though pleasaunt, yet she made much more:
    The fields did laugh, the flowres did freshly spring,
    The trees did bud, and early blossomes bore,
    And all the quire of birds did sweetly sing,
And told that gardins pleasures in their caroling.

25

And she more sweete, then any bird on bough,
    Would oftentimes emongst them beare a part,
    And striue to passe (as she could well enough)
    Their natiue musicke by her skilful art:
    So did she all, that might his constant hart
    Withdraw from thought of warlike enterprize,
    And drowne in dissolute delights apart,
    Where noise of armes, or vew of martiall guize
Might not reuiue desire of knightly exercize.

26

But he was wise, and wary of her will,
    And euer held his hand vpon his hart:
    Yet would not seeme so rude, and thewed ill,
    As to despise so curteous seeming part,
    That gentle Lady did to him impart,
    But fairly tempring fond desire subdewd,
    And euer her desired to depart.
    She list not heare, but her disports poursewd,
And euer bad him stay, till time the tide renewd.

27

And now by this, *Cymochles* howre was spent,
    That he awoke out of his ydle dreme,
    And shaking off his drowsy dreriment,
    Gan him auize, howe ill did him beseme,
    In slouthfull sleepe his molten hart to steme,
    And quench the brond of his conceiued yre.
    Tho vp he started, stird with shame extreme,
    Ne staied for his Damsell to inquire,
But marched to the Strond, there passage to require.

28

And in the way he with Sir *Guyon* mett,
    Accompanyde with *Phædria* the faire,
    Eftsoones he gan to rage, and inly frett,
    Crying, Let be that Lady debonaire,
    Thou recreaunt knight, and soone thy selfe prepaire
    To batteile, if thou meane her loue to gayn:
    Loe, loe already, how the fowles in aire
    Doe flocke, awaiting shortly to obtayn
Thy carcas for their pray, the guerdon of thy payn.

Stanza 22
8 **whiles I you obaid**: as her boat 'obaying to her mind' does 'as she did desire' (20.3, 4).

Stanza 23
8–9 If her jest is about the frustrated sailor ready to enter any port in a storm (of passion), it was still circulating among those at sea in the early 1940s.

Stanza 24
1–2 He exercises the same restraint at ii 12.2. **4–5 gan him lay before**: bring to his sight, or describe to him, adding to nature by her art. 6 Ultimately a biblical expression: in Ps. 65.13, the pastures 'showte for ioye'.

Stanza 25
1–4 The same blending of sounds is heard in the Bower at xii 71 (and see *n*). 8 **martiall guize**: knightly armour.

Stanza 26
1–2 Against the passion of anger at v 21.6–9, he was 'wise'; now against desire's corrupt **will**, he is also **wary**. His posture declares his control over the fountain of affections in contrast to his state at i 42.2, 56.6, ii 1.8–9, iv 9.6, etc. 3–5 As he was courteous towards her at 21.5–6. **thewed ill**: ill-mannered. **part**: referring to her treatment of him, or to the feigning role she plays. 6 I.e., properly governing himself, he subdued foolish desire. 7 **to depart**: i.e. to let him depart, as 36.8. 8 **disports**: merriment, sports; suggesting its etymological sense, 'to carry away', for her diversions have led him from the 'right way' (22.9). 9 **tide**: i.e. 'the right moment' (so she would have him believe), but in fact 'never' for her world is tideless (20.9) and therefore timeless.

Stanza 27
1 **howre**: appointed time, signalled by Guyon's desire to leave. 3 **dreriment**: heaviness, replacing his earlier merriment. 5 **steme**: 'steep', or 'dissolve in steam' (so the context suggests).

Stanza 28
2 **Accompanyde with**: inferring 'cohabiting with' (*OED* 2. 4), so Cymochles's outrage suggests and Phædria's claim that the two knights fight for her love (33.4). 4 **debonaire**: of pleasing disposition. 5 **recreaunt**: cowardly, a term of the greatest opprobrium. **soone**: immediately. 7–9 **Loe, loe**: Look! look! He invokes God's curse on those who disobey his laws: 'thy carkeis shal be meat vnto all foules of the ayre' (Deut. 28.26). Since the body's wholeness is the goal of temperance, corresponding to its holiness in Bk I, its despoiling is a central theme in Bk II and provides the climax to Guyon's adventures in the first half; see viii 12–13, 16, etc.

29

And therewith all he fiersly at him flew,
    And with importune outrage him assayld;
    Who soone prepard to field, his sword forth drew,
    And him with equall valew counteruayld:
    Their mightie strokes their haberieons dismayld,
    And naked made each others manly spalles;
    The mortall steele despiteously entayld
    Deepe in their flesh, quite through the yron walles,
That a large purple stream adown their giambeux falles.

30

Cymocles, that had neuer mett before,
    So puissant foe, with enuious despight
    His prowd presumed force increased more,
    Disdeigning to bee held so long in fight;
    Sir *Guyon* grudging not so much his might,
    As those vnknightly raylinges, which he spoke,
    With wrathfull fire his corage kindled bright,
    Thereof deuising shortly to be wroke,
And doubling all his powres, redoubled euery stroke.

31

Both of them high attonce their hands enhaunst,
    And both attonce their huge blowes down did sway;
    Cymochles sword on *Guyons* shield yglaunst,
    And there of nigh one quarter sheard away;
    But *Guyons* angry blade so fiers did play
    On th'others helmett, which as *Titan* shone,
    That quite it cloue his plumed crest in tway,
    And bared all his head vnto the bone;
Wherewith astonisht, still he stood, as sencelesse stone.

32

Still as he stood, fayre *Phædria*, that beheld
    That deadly daunger, soone atweene them ran;
    And at their feet her selfe most humbly feld,
    Crying with pitteous voyce, and count'nance wan;

Ah well away, most noble Lords, how can
    Your cruell eyes endure so pitteous sight,
    To shed your liues on ground? wo worth the man,
    That first did teach the cursed steele to bight
In his owne flesh, and make way to the liuing spright.

33

If euer loue of Lady did empierce
    Your yron brestes, or pittie could find place,
    Withhold your bloody handes from battaill fierce,
    And sith for me ye fight, to me this grace
    Both yield, to stay your deadly stryfe a space.
    They stayd a while: and forth she gan proceed:
    Most wretched woman, and of wicked race,
    That am the authour of this hainous deed,
And cause of death betweene two doughtie knights do breed.

34

But if for me ye fight, or me will serue,
    Not this rude kynd of battaill, nor these armes
    Are meet, the which doe men in bale to sterue,
    And doolefull sorrow heape with deadly harmes:
    Such cruell game my scarmoges disarmes:
    Another warre, and other weapons I
    Doe loue, where loue does giue his sweet Alarmes,
    Without bloodshed, and where the enimy
Does yield vnto his foe a pleasaunt victory.

35

Debatefull strife, and cruell enmity
    The famous name of knighthood fowly shend;
    But louely peace, and gentle amity,
    And in Amours the passing howres to spend,
    The mightie martiall handes doe most commend;
    Of loue they euer greater glory bore,
    Then of their armes: *Mars* is *Cupidoes* frend,
    And is for *Venus* loues renowmed more,
Then all his wars and spoiles, the which he did of yore.

Stanza 29

1 therewith all: that being said. **2 importune outrage**: violent fury. **3 to field**: to fight. **4 valew**: valour. **counteruayld**: resisted; counter-attacked. **5 haberieons**: a sleeveless coat of mail. **dismayld**: stripped the mail off. **6 spalles**: shoulders. **7 entayld**: cut into, carved. **9 giambeux**: S.'s spelling of 'jambeux', leg-armour, perhaps from Chaucer, *Sir Thopas* 875.

Stanza 30

2 enuious despight: malicious anger. **3 presumed force**: i.e. force upon which he relies presumptuously. **5–6 grudging**: being vexed at. Force may be countered with force but against slander temperance may only exercise patience, as at v 21.

Stanza 31

1 enhaunst: raised. **2 sway**: swing. **6 which as Titan shone**: as does Pyrochles's armour at v 2.4–5. **9 astonisht**: stunned; turned to **stone**.

Stanza 32

Phædria's intercession contrasts Medina's at ii 27; see ii 31.1–2*n*, and 36.2*n* below. For a close analysis, see Hieatt 1975b:114–17. **7–9 wo worth**: may evil befall. **In his owne flesh**: i.e. in human flesh, emphasizing the internal battle. See 'psychomachia' in the *SEnc*.

Stanza 33

4 grace: favour.

Stanza 34

3 . . . which cause men to die in grief. **5** Either 'your **scarmoges** (skirmishes) prevent my **warre** (of love)', or, as she goes on to claim, 'my war stops yours'. **7 Alarmes**: assaults.

Stanza 35

1 Debatefull: contentious. **2 shend**: disgrace. **3 louely**: loving. **4 Amours**: love-making, playing on 'armours'. **7–9** Phædria echoes I proem in which S. addresses triumphant Mars 'In loues and gentle iollities arraid' (3.8).

36

Therewith she sweetly smyld. They though full bent,
    To proue extremities of bloody fight,
    Yet at her speach their rages gan relent,
    And calme the sea of their tempestuous spight,
    Such powre haue pleasing wordes: such is the might
    Of courteous clemency in gentle hart.
    Now after all was ceast, the Faery knight
    Besought that Damzell suffer him depart,
And yield him ready passage to that other part.

37

She no lesse glad, then he desirous was
    Of his departure thence; for of her ioy
    And vaine delight she saw he light did pas,
    A foe of folly and immodest toy,
    Still solemne sad, or still disdainfull coy,
    Delighting all in armes and cruell warre,
    That her sweet peace and pleasures did annoy,
    Troubled with terrour and vnquiet iarre,
That she well pleased was thence to amoue him farre.

38

Tho him she brought abord, and her swift bote
    Forthwith directed to that further strand;
    The which on the dull waues did lightly flote
    And soone arriued on the shallow sand,
    Where gladsome *Guyon* salied forth to land,
    And to that Damsell thankes gaue for reward.
    Vpon that shore he spyed *Atin* stand,
    There by his maister left, when late he far'd
In *Phædrias* flitt barck ouer that perlous shard.

39

Well could he him remember, sith of late
    He with *Pyrrhochles* sharp debatement made;
    Streight gan he him reuyle, and bitter rate,
    As Shepheards curre, that in darke eueninges shade
    Hath tracted forth some saluage beastes trade;
    Vile Miscreaunt (said he) whether dost thou flye
    The shame and death, which will thee soone inuade?
    What coward hand shall doe thee next to dye,
That art thus fowly fledd from famous enimy?

40

With that he stifly shooke his steelhead dart:
    But sober *Guyon*, hearing him so rayle,
    Though somewhat moued in his mightie hart,
    Yet with strong reason maistred passion fraile,
    And passed fayrely forth. He turning taile,
    Backe to the strond retyrd, and there still stayd,
    Awaiting passage, which him late did faile;
    The whiles *Cymochles* with that wanton mayd
The hasty heat of his auowd reuenge delayd.

41

Whylest there the varlet stood, he saw from farre
    An armed knight, that towardes him fast ran,
    He ran on foot, as if in lucklesse warre
    His forlorne steed from him the victour wan;
    He seemed breathlesse, hartlesse, faint, and wan,
    And all his armour sprinckled was with blood,
    And soyld with durtie gore, that no man can
    Discerne the hew thereof. He neuer stood,
But bent his hastie course towards the ydle flood.

Stanza 36

2 I.e., to fight to the death. **extremities**: the extreme degree, in contrast to the mean. While Medina 'did moderate | The strong extremities of their outrage' (ii 38.3–4) to include the warring states in the temperate mean, Phædria seeks to reduce them to the **calme** of her Idle Lake. **3 relent**: cool (*OED* 2c); give way (*OED* 2b). **5** The biblical proverb (Prov. 15.1) is important to any poet, but esp. to S. who uses it six times, as Smith 23 notes. **9 to that other part**: 'that further strand' (38.2), across from the side at which he arrived at 19.2. The way to the Bower of Bliss lies through and beyond the Idle Lake.

Stanza 37

3 **light did pas**: easily disregarded; made light of. **4 folly**: wantonness. **immodest**: see Arg.1*n*. **5 Still**: ever. **solemne sad**: grave, serious, applied to the Red Cross Knight at I i 2.8 (see *n*) and to Arthur at II ix 36.8. **coy**: distant, being **disdainfull**. **8 iarre**: discord.

Stanza 38

5 **gladsome**: gladly. **salied**: leaped (from Lat. *salio*) rather than 'issued forth'; cf. xii 38.4, and see i 29.6*n*. **9 shard**: its usual sense, 'cleft' or 'gap', applies to the channel of water across which Guyon must be ferried to the Bower of Bliss; cf.

'ford' (4.4, 19.9, 47.8). Other possible senses are 'dividing water' (sugg. *OED*), as 'perilous bourne' (10.9); 'dung', which refers to the water's filth: cf. 46.6–7; and 'boundary' or 'division', which refers to temperance as a voyage between boundaries or extremities.

Stanza 39

2 **debatement**: strife. **5 trade**: track, tread that he has **tracted**, i.e. pursued. **6 Miscreaunt**: wretch. **7 inuade**: attack.

Stanza 40

The stanza, fittingly by its number (see vii 26.5*n*) and at its middle line, indicates that the patron of temperance has mastered the irascible passions while Cymochles remains unchanged. **4 passion fraile**: i.e. passions that make human nature frail. **5 fayrely**: peaceably. **9 delayd**: allayed, quenched, relented (cf. 36.3); 'postponed' may be implied for his anger is allayed only for the moment.

Stanza 41

4 **forlorne**: lost. **6–8** A climax to his staining in contrast to his brilliant first appearance at v 2; see v 22.4*n*. While 'blood and filth' may be washed away at 42.8, inwardly he remains unchanged until Archimago restores him to health at 51.9. **stood**: stopped.

42

The varlett saw, when to the flood he came,
  How without stop or stay he fiersly lept,
  And deepe him selfe beducked in the same,
  That in the lake his loftie crest was stept,
  Ne of his safetie seemed care he kept,
  But with his raging armes he rudely flasht,
  The waues about, and all his armour swept,
  That all the blood and filth away was washt,
Yet still he bet the water, and the billowes dasht.

43

Atin drew nigh, to weet, what it mote bee;
  For much he wondred at that vncouth sight;
  Whom should he, but his own deare Lord, there see,
  His owne deare Lord *Pyrrhochles*, in sad plight,
  Ready to drowne him selfe for fell despight.
  Harrow now out, and well away, he cryde,
  What dismall day hath lent but this his cursed light,
  To see my Lord so deadly damnifyde?
Pyrrhochles, O *Pyrrhochles*, what is thee betyde?

44

I burne, I burne, I burne, then lowd he cryde,
  O how I burne with implacable fyre,
  Yet nought can quench mine inly flaming syde,
  Nor sea of licour cold, nor lake of myre,
  Nothing but death can doe me to respyre.
  Ah be it (said he) from *Pyrrhochles* farre
  After pursewing death once to requyre,
  Or think, that ought those puissant hands may marre:
Death is for wretches borne vnder vnhappy starre.

45

Perdye, then is it fitt for me (said he)
  That am, I weene, most wretched man aliue,
  Burning in flames, yet no flames can I see,
  And dying dayly, dayly yet reuiue:

O *Atin*, helpe to me last death to giue.
  The varlet at his plaint was grieued so sore,
  That his deepe wounded hart in two did riue,
  And his owne health remembring now no more,
Did follow that ensample, which he blam'd afore.

46

Into the lake he lept, his Lord to ayd,
  (So Loue the dread of daunger doth despise)
  And of him catching hold him strongly stayd
  From drowning. But more happy he, then wise
  Of that seas nature did him not auise.
  The waues thereof so slow and sluggish were,
  Engrost with mud, which did them fowle agrise,
  That euery weighty thing they did vpbeare,
Ne ought mote euer sinck downe to the bottom there.

47

Whiles thus they strugled in that ydle waue,
  And stroue in vaine, the one him selfe to drowne,
  The other both from drowning for to saue,
  Lo, to that shore one in an auncient gowne,
  Whose hoary locks great grauitie did crowne,
  Holding in hand a goodly arming sword,
  By fortune came, ledd with the troublous sowne:
  Where drenched deepe he fownd in that dull ford
The carefull seruaunt, stryuing with his raging Lord.

48

Him *Atin* spying, knew right well of yore,
  And lowdly cald, Help helpe, O *Archimage*,
  To saue my Lord, in wretched plight forlore;
  Helpe with thy hand, or with thy counsell sage:
  Weake handes, but counsell is most strong in age.
  Him when the old man saw, he woundred sore,
  To see *Pyrrhochles* there so rudely rage:
  Yet sithens helpe, he saw, he needed more
Then pitty, he in hast approched to the shore.

Stanza 42
6 flasht: splashed; also referring to his burning.

Stanza 43
6 Pyrochles's cry of alarm is followed by a cry of grief.   **7 dismall day**: one of the evil or cursed days, a play on *dies mali*; hence often the day of death, as vii 26.7, viii 51.5.   **8 damnifyde**: injured; suggesting also 'damned'.   **9** . . . what has happened to you?

Stanza 44
1–3 The motto on his shield, '*Burnt I doe burne*' (iv 38.5), is now confirmed: outer fire manifests his inner burning. **implacable**: that cannot be assuaged.   **5** The paradox is indicated by **respyre**: only through death may he breathe again, i.e. have new life as promised in Rom. 6. Cf. Phaon's lament at iv 33.5–6.   **7 requyre**: call upon; seek after. **9 vnhappy**: inauspicious.

Stanza 45
8 health: safety.

Stanza 46
4–5 I.e., in leaping into the sea, not knowing that it would not drown Pyrochles, Atin was more lucky than wise. **6–9** Analogues to Phædria's 'lake of myre' (44.4) are Cocytus's muddy waters that confine the damned souls in hell, in Virgil, *Aen.* 6.323–30; the asphalt lake around Armida's castle in which nothing sinks, in Tasso, *Ger. Lib.* 10.61–62; the black mire of the Stygian marsh that covers those overcome by anger, in Dante, *Inf.* 7.108–30; and the Salt or Dead Sea, 'the Sea of the wildernes' in Josh. 3.16: its 'heavie waters [are] hardly to be moved by the winds' (Sandys 1615:142).   **Engrost**: made thick.   **which . . . agrise**: which rendered them fowly horrible; or 'which terrified them', taking **fowle** as an adj.   **them**: referring to the waves, Pyrochles, and Atin.

Stanza 47
6 arming: a technical term for a sword as part of knightly arms. The sword is Arthur's, which Archimago promised to procure for Braggadocchio at iii 18; see viii 19.3–4.   **8 drenched**: submerged.   **9 carefull**: full of care.

49

And cald, *Pyrrhochles*, what is this, I see?
    What hellish fury hath at earst thee hent?
    Furious euer I thee knew to bee,
    Yet neuer in this straunge astonishment.
    These flames, these flames (he cryde) do me torment.
    What flames (quoth he) when I thee present see,
    In daunger rather to be drent, then brent?
    Harrow, the flames, which me consume (said hee)
Ne can be quencht, within my secret bowelles bee.

50

That cursed man, that cruel feend of hell,
    Furor, oh *Furor* hath me thus bedight:
    His deadly woundes within my liuers swell,
    And his whott fyre burnes in mine entralles bright,
    Kindled through his infernall brond of spight,
    Sith late with him I batteill vaine would boste,
    That now I weene *Ioues* dreaded thunder light
    Does scorch not halfe so sore, nor damned ghoste
In flaming *Phlegeton* does not so felly roste.

51

Which when as *Archimago* heard, his griefe
    He knew right well, and him attonce disarmd:
    Then searcht his secret woundes, and made a priefe
    Of euery place, that was with bruzing harmd,
    Or with the hidden fier inly warmd.
    Which doen, he balmes and herbes thereto applyde,
    And euermore with mightie spels them charmd,
    That in short space he has them qualifyde,
And him restor'd to helth, that would haue algates dyde.

Stanza 48
3 **forlore**: ruined.   5 **Weake handes**: i.e. hands are weak.

Stanza 49
2 **at earst**: now. **hent**: seized.   4 **straunge astonishment**: extreme dismay or loss of wits. **7–9 drent**: drenched, drowned. Fire that cannot be quenched by water was a popular motif. It is found, e.g. in Shakespeare, *Venus and Adonis* 94: Venus 'bathes in water, yet her fire must burn'; and in Gascoigne's entertainment for Elizabeth at Kenilworth: fireballs burning in water signify Leicester's unquenchable desire for her (1907–10:2.95, 99). It is hell-fire, 'the fyre that neuer shal be quenched' (Mark 9.43).

Stanza 50
2 **bedight**: treated; i.e. maltreated.   3 **liuers**: liuer *1609*, the traditional seat of violent passion; see Hoeniger 1992:166. Plural because of its five lobes or because the rhyme so requires.   4 Refined by fire, his body becomes translucent, like a clay pot heated in a kiln.   5 As v 22.6–9.   7 **thunder light**: lightning.   **8–9 Phlegeton**: the infernal river of fire – see I v 33.1–6*n* – from which Pyrochles derives, iv 41.7. **felly**: fiercely.

Stanza 51
3 **searcht**: probed. **priefe**: examination.   8 **qualifyde**: moderated, assuaged.   9 **algates**: otherwise.

Cant. VII.

Guyon findes Mamon in a delue,
sunning his threasure hore:
Is by him tempted, and led downe,
To see his secrete store.

1

AS Pilot well expert in perilous waue,
    That to a stedfast starre his course hath bent,
When foggy mistes, or cloudy tempests haue
The faithfull light of that faire lampe yblent,
And couer'd heauen with hideous dreriment,
Vpon his card and compas firmes his eye,
The maysters of his long experiment,
And to them does the steddy helme apply,
Bidding his winged vessell fairely forward fly.

2

So *Guyon* hauing lost his trustie guyde,
    Late left beyond that *Ydle lake*, proceedes
Yet on his way, of none accompanyde;
And euermore himselfe with comfort feedes,
Of his owne vertues, and praise-worthie deedes.
So long he yode, yet no aduenture found,
Which fame of her shrill trompet worthy reedes:
For still he traueild through wide wastfull ground,
That nought but desert wildernesse shewed all around.

3

At last he came vnto a gloomy glade,
    Couer'd with boughes and shrubs from heauens light,
Whereas he sitting found in secret shade
An vncouth, saluage, and vnciuile wight,
Of griesly hew, and fowle ill fauour'd sight;
His face with smoke was tand and eies were bleard,
His head and beard with sout were ill bedight,
His cole-blacke hands did seeme to haue ben seard
In smythes fire-spitting forge, and nayles like clawes appeard.

4

His yron cote all ouergrowne with rust,
    Was vnderneath enueloped with gold,
Whose glistring glosse darkned with filthy dust,
Well yet appeared, to haue beene of old
A worke of rich entayle, and curious mould,
Wouen with antickes and wyld ymagery:
And in his lap a masse of coyne he told,
And turned vpside downe, to feede his eye
And couetous desire with his huge threasury.

Book II Canto vii

Argument

1 Mam[m]on: see 8.1–4*n*. **delue**: i.e. 'glade' (3.1); cf. 20.6, viii 4.6. **2** His hoard is **hore** (grey) because it is not gold; he suns it that it may become gold, so Lewis 1964:106 suggests. (Phœbus is called the 'God of Gold' in Chapman, *Hero and Leander* 3.24 'since the vertue of his beams creates it'.) Yet **hore** may signify grey with age through lack of 'right vsaunce' (7.4), or with 'rust' (4.1) like his coat; hence the hoard needs to be 'turned vpside downe' (4.8) to show its beauty. His confrontation with Guyon suggests folk-tales of gnomes surprised by strangers as they sun their treasures. The substance of the line is repeated at viii 4.7.

Stanza 1

2 a stedfast starre: cf. 'the stedfast starre' at I ii 1.2, which is the Pole star, or 'the Northern starre' (x 4.7), or the 'Lodestar' (III iv 53.3). **4 yblent**: hid. **6 card**: the mariner's geographical chart, possibly the graduated compass card though either sense may apply; see Falconer 1964:89. **firmes**: firmly fixes. **7 maysters**: instruments; instructors. **experiment**: experience, referring to his art of navigation. **8 apply**: steer.

Stanza 2

4–5 Like the mariner, Guyon turns from sure, heavenly guidance to depend on his own resources. His self-assurance is shown by Pyrocles in Sidney, *Old Arcadia* 289: 'the confidence in oneself is the chief nurse of true magnanimity'. (Both heroes display the distinguishing characteristic of the magnanimous man in Aristotle, *Ethics* 4.3.) It is parodied by Braggadocchio at iii 5.2–4. **comfort**: aid, support. **feedes**: a common metaphor in the canto, e.g. 4.8, 9.3, 24.4, and 65.3 when Guyon faints partly through want of food. **6 yode**: went. **7 reedes**: considers. **8–9 traueild**: with the usual play on 'travail'. **wastfull**: desolate. Limitless expanse suggests the absence of the bounds of temperance, as xii 35.3. **desert wildernesse** suggests the wilderness in which Christ was tempted, Matt. 4.1; see 9–63*n*.

Stanza 3

2 As trees hide 'heauens light' in the Wandering Wood, I i 7.5. **4 vncouth**: strange; repellent; clumsy. **saluage**: wild, as a woodland creature and the 'saluage man' at VI iv 2.2. **vnciuile**: barbarous. **5 griesly hew**: shape that arouses horror. **6–9** Mammon appears as a blacksmith, showing his kinship with Care at IV v 34.4–9. **bleard**: inflamed, as Leah is 'bleare eied' (Geneva gloss to Gen. 29.17); here induced by smoke, or lack of sleep from caring for his wealth. Cf. the 'two blered eyghen' of Langland's Avarice (*Piers Plowman* 5.191). **ill bedight**: ill-arrayed; disfigured. **seard**: scorched. **nayles like clawes**: like Auarice's gouty hands at I iv 29.6–7.

5

And round about him lay on euery side
    Great heapes of gold, that neuer could be spent:
    Of which some were rude owre, not purifide
    Of *Mulcibers* deuouring element;
    Some others were new driuen, and distent
    Into great Ingowes, and to wedges square;
    Some in round plates withouten moniment:
    But most were stampt, and in their metal bare
The antique shapes of kings and kesars straung and rare.

6

Soone as he *Guyon* saw, in great affright
    And haste he rose, for to remoue aside
    Those pretious hils from straungers enuious sight,
    And downe them poured through an hole full wide,
    Into the hollow earth, them there to hide.
    But *Guyon* lightly to him leaping, stayd
    His hand, that trembled, as one terrifyde;
    And though him selfe were at the sight dismayd,
Yet him perforce restraynd, and to him doubtfull sayd.

7

What art thou man, (if man at all thou art)
    That here in desert hast thine habitaunce,
    And these rich hils of welth doest hide apart
    From the worldes eye, and from her right vsaunce?
    Thereat with staring eyes fixed askaunce,
    In great disdaine, he answerd, Hardy Elfe,
    That darest vew my direfull countenaunce,
    I read thee rash, and heedlesse of thy selfe,
To trouble my still seate, and heapes of pretious pelfe.

8

God of the world and worldlings I me call,
    Great *Mammon*, greatest god below the skye,
    That of my plenty poure out vnto all,
    And vnto none my graces do enuye:
    Riches, renowme, and principality,
    Honour, estate, and all this worldes good,
    For which men swinck and sweat incessantly,
    Fro me do flow into an ample flood,
And in the hollow earth haue their eternall brood.

Stanza 4

4 yet: i.e. 'even though it was darkened'; it *1596*. **5–6** The embroidered surcoat that Mammon wears over his **yron cote** indicates that he is protected by charms. The **entayle** (carving, engraving) and **curious mould** (elaborately wrought pattern or design) woven into it correspond to the heraldic arms of a knight's surcoat. **antickes**: fantastic figures. As an example of Renaissance 'grotesque' art, see Evett 1982:198–99. Cf. Belphœbe's buskins 'entayld | With curious antickes' (iii 27.4–5), and the arras in the house of Busirane wrought 'with wilde Antickes' (III xi 51.5). **ymagery**: images; hence **wyld** suggests 'fantastic' or 'grotesque'; cf. Acrasia's fountain wrought 'with curious ymageree' (xii 60.5). **7** As Auarice is seen at I iv 27.5. **told**: counted. **9 treasury**: treasure.

Stanza 5

1–2 The setting invokes Christ's warning in Matt. 6.19–24: 'Lay not vp treasures for your selues vpon the earth' for 'ye can not serue God and riches [i.e. Mammon]'. Mammon's coins are not legal currency; cf. 7.4. Chaucer's Parson defines avarice as the desire to keep things 'withoute rightful nede' (*Parson's Tale* 744). **4 deuouring element**: fire, the element whose deity is Mulciber (the purifier of metals); or Vulcan, as at 36.5. **5 driuen, and distent**: beaten out and extended; or smelted and beaten, as described at 35–36. **6 Ingowes**: S.'s variant of 'ingot' that suggests the Elizabethan word for Incas (Sp. *Ingas*) and their city of gold, El Dorado; see *SEnc* 510. **wedges**: ingots of gold. **7 moniment**: identifying mark, superscription. **9 kings and kesars**: always paired terms, the latter signifying the absolute monarch; cf. III xi 29.9, IV vii 1.4, etc. The allusion to Matt. 22.20–21 reveals to whom this wealth is owing.

Stanza 6

3 hils: as 7.3. At 5.2, only 'heapes' but by 9.2 expanded to 'mountaines'. **5 hollow earth**: as 8.9, 20.8. **9 perforce**: forcibly. **to him doubtfull**: i.e. to the fearful Mammon; but referring chiefly to Guyon who is doubtful about Mammon's identity.

Stanza 7

3 hils: heapes *1596*. **4 right vsaunce**: proper use, invoking the parable of the talents, Matt. 25.14–30. **5 Threat**: because of that. **staring**: glaring. **askaunce**: 'askewe or asquint' (E.K. on *SC March* 21); here suggesting disdain, and distrust. Cf. the glance of Malbecco at III ix 27.3, Suspect at III xii 15.2, Enuie at V xii 29.2, and Disdaine at VI vii 42.3–4. In Malecasta, at III i 41.6, it suggests wanton guile. As an infernal creature, Mammon has the full staring eyes of the dragon (I xi 14) and Despaire (I ix 35.7). **6–9** In answer to Guyon's question, Mammon implies that he is no man at all but a god whose face may not be looked upon with impunity. Accordingly, Guyon is rightly called **Hardy**, i.e. rashly bold or foolhardy in undertaking a 'hardy enterprize' (65.7). The term is applied to Huddibras at ii 17.2; cf. 27.1 below. **Elfe**: as Guyon is a faery knight. **read**: consider. **seate**: throne, rather than abode. His sitting upon the earth establishes him as the 'God of the world' (8.1).

Stanza 8

1–4 Mammon: so named in all the major Elizabethan bibles except Geneva (see Shaheen 1976:191) where he is named 'Richesse' as at 24.9, corresponding to 'riches' in Matt. 6.24 and Luke 16.13. He is named the 'Money God' at 39.1, corresponding to 'the god of this worlde' (2 Cor. 4.4) and 'the prince of this worlde' (John 12.31). In *Theatre* 91ᵛ, Mammon is included in the generation of Antichrist. Plutus, the classical god of riches, was often identified with Pluto, god of the underworld, e.g. by Milton who refers to 'the den of *Plutus*, or the cave of *Mammon*' (1953–82:1.719). See 'Mammon' in the *SEnc*. His hyperbolic claims are examined by Dillon 1998:24–27. On the need for money by those in the Renaissance who lacked land, see Shepherd 1989:51–55. On the fierce consumerism of the European Renaissance, see Jardine 1996:*passim*. **enuye**: refuse. **5–6 renowme** is linked with **Honour**; **principality** (exalted rank or dignity) with **estate**; and **Riches** with **all this worldes good**. Hence Mammon's daughter rewards her followers with 'Honour and dignitie . . . and all this worldes blis' (48.7–8). **7 swinck**: labour. **9 brood**: birth or breeding-place.

9

Wherefore if me thou deigne to serue and sew,
    At thy commaund lo all these mountaines bee;
    Or if to thy great mind, or greedy vew
    All these may not suffise, there shall to thee
    Ten times so much be nombred francke and free.
    Mammon (said he) thy godheads vaunt is vaine,
    And idle offers of thy golden fee;
    To them, that couet such eye-glutting gaine,
Proffer thy giftes, and fitter seruaunts entertaine.

10

Me ill besits, that in derdoing armes,
    And honours suit my vowed daies do spend,
    Vnto thy bounteous baytes, and pleasing charmes,
    With which weake men thou witchest, to attend:
    Regard of worldly mucke doth fowly blend,
    And low abase the high heroicke spright,
    That ioyes for crownes and kingdomes to contend;
    Faire shields, gay steedes, bright armes be my delight:
Those be the riches fit for an aduent'rous knight.

11

Vaine glorious Elfe (saide he) doest not thou weet,
    That money can thy wantes at will supply?
    Sheilds, steeds, and armes, and all things for thee meet
    It can puruay in twinckling of an eye;
    And crownes and kingdomes to thee multiply.
    Doe not I kings create, and throw the crowne
    Sometimes to him, that low in dust doth ly?
    And him that raignd, into his rowme thrust downe,
And whom I lust, do heape with glory and renowne?

12

All otherwise (saide he) I riches read,
    And deeme them roote of all disquietnesse;
    First got with guile, and then preseru'd with dread,
    And after spent with pride and lauishnesse,
    Leauing behind them griefe and heauinesse.
    Infinite mischiefes of them doe arize,
    Strife, and debate, bloodshed, and bitternesse,
    Outrageous wrong, and hellish couetize,
That noble heart as great dishonour doth despize.

Stanzas 9–63

Guyon must be tempted by Mammon because virtue must be tested by trial, as Milton declares that S. 'describing true temperance under the person of *Guion*, brings him in with his palmer through the cave of Mammon . . . that he might see and know, and yet abstain' (1953–82:2.516). The temptation is carefully structured. First, Mammon offers wealth, which Guyon rejects for the pursuit of glory. In the debate that follows, wealth is offered as the means to glory but rejected as the source of evil. Then he renews his offer, allowing Guyon to choose from the wealth that he sees. Guyon rejects it with reservations: he will not accept wealth until he knows how and where it was obtained. From this debate follow three temptations: (1) At the house of Richesse, Mammon tempts him with wealth as the 'worldes blis' (32.7), which he rejects for another bliss, the life of chivalry. He rejects also the source of wealth, 'the fountaine of the worldes good' (38.6), for he is content with what he can use. (2) Mammon tempts him with worldly advancement through marriage to Philotime. Guyon chooses not to accept. (3) When Mammon invites him to eat the golden fruit and sit on the silver stool, he simply refuses. The three temptations have been variously interpreted, e.g. as lust, pride, and curiosity by Kermode 1971:68–71 in arguing that 'Guyon undergoes . . . a *total* temptation parallel to that of Christ in the wilderness'. See 26.5*n*. (The parallel is rejected, e.g. by Hume 1984:117 and Jordan 1989:32–33, but is generally endorsed, e.g. by Weatherby 1994:147–49 and Oram 1997:102–03.) On Guyon's progress through Mammon's four 'rooms', see W.R. Davis 1981:133–35. Spanish control of the gold mines in the New World influences certain details of this episode, e.g. 'Ingowes' that were 'new driuen' (5.6); see 'New World' in the *SEnc*, and Read 2000:66–78.

Stanza 9

1 serue and sew: give suit and service. The attendance owing from **seruaunts** to the feudal lord is used here of worshippers to their god. Mammon tempts Guyon as Satan tempted Christ: 'All these wil I giue thee, if thou wilt fall downe, and worship me' (Matt. 4.9). The final temptation in Matthew is preliminary here. **3 great mind**: i.e. 'huge desire' (17.6) or ambition,

perverting Aristotle's magnanimity or great-mindedness; see viii 51.1*n*. **5 francke and free**: i.e. as a gift rather than an obligation. **6 godheads vaunt**: boast to be a god. **7 idle offers**: i.e. your offers are idle; but here suggesting idolatry. **fee**: money, bribe. **9 entertaine**: keep, retain; used of Guyon's service to the Faerie Queene at ix 6.5.

Stanza 10

Eight words in this stanza 'have made their first appearance in the sixteenth century, or at any rate their first appearance in this meaning or form' (Bolton 1967:21–22): **derdoing, heroicke**, and **contend** are new words; new meanings are **suit**: pursuit of honour (*OED* 6); **witch**: charm, entice (*OED* 3). **1–2** I.e., your offer does not suit me, for I have vowed to spend my days in arms pursuing honour by doing daring deeds. Since this response makes him appear 'Vaine glorious' (11.1) and thus akin to Braggadocchio (cf. iii 10.3), it introduces his second temptation. **3 bounteous baytes**: temptations of bounty displayed earlier in Phædria and later in Acrasia to tempt the weak into intemperance in opposition to God's 'soueraine bounty' (16.4). **5 Regard of**: respect for; attention to. **mucke**: manure; cf. 'mucky pelfe' (III ix 4.1). **blend**: blind; defile. **8** As Phædria at vi 37.6 had good reason to complain.

Stanza 11

4 Cf. Luke 4.5: 'The deuil . . . shewed him all the kingdomes of the worlde in the twinkeling of an eye'. **puruay**: provide. **6** Mammon arrogates God's role: 'By me, Kings reigne' (Prov. 8.15), as the Geneva gloss spells out: 'honors, dignitie or riches come not of mans wisdome or industrie, but by the prouidence of God'. **8 rowme**: the particular place to which he properly belongs. **9 lust**: choose.

Stanza 12

The stanza glosses 1 Tim. 6.9–10: 'For they that wil be riche, fall into temptation and snares, and into many foolish and noysome lustes, which drowne men in perdition and destruction. For the desire of money is the roote of all euil'. **1 read**: consider. **8 couetize**: covetousness.

13

Ne thine be kingdomes, ne the scepters thine;
 But realmes and rulers thou doest both confound,
 And loyall truth to treason doest incline;
 Witnesse the guiltlesse blood pourd oft on ground,
 The crowned often slaine, the slayer cround,
 The sacred Diademe in peeces rent,
 And purple robe gored with many a wound;
 Castles surprizd, great citties sackt and brent:
So mak'st thou kings, and gaynest wrongfull gouernment.

14

Long were to tell the troublous stormes, that tosse
 The priuate state, and make the life vnsweet:
 Who swelling sayles in Caspian sea doth crosse,
 And in frayle wood on *Adrian* gulf doth fleet,
 Doth not, I weene, so many euils meet.
 Then *Mammon* wexing wroth, And why then, sayd,
 Are mortall men so fond and vndiscreet,
 So euill thing to seeke vnto their ayd,
And hauing not complaine, and hauing it vpbrayd?

15

Indeede (quoth he) through fowle intemperaunce,
 Frayle men are oft captiu'd to couetise:
 But would they thinke, with how small allowaunce
 Vntroubled Nature doth her selfe suffise,
 Such superfluities they would despise,
 Which with sad cares empeach our natiue ioyes:
 At the well head the purest streames arise:
 But mucky filth his braunching armes annoyes,
And with vncomely weedes the gentle waue accloyes.

16

The antique world, in his first flowring youth,
 Fownd no defect in his Creators grace,
 But with glad thankes, and vnreproued truth,
 The guifts of soueraine bounty did embrace:
 Like Angels life was then mens happy cace;
 But later ages pride, like corn-fed steed,
 Abusd her plenty, and fat swolne encreace
 To all licentious lust, and gan exceed
The measure of her meane, and naturall first need.

17

Then gan a cursed hand the quiet wombe
 Of his great Grandmother with steele to wound,
 And the hid treasures in her sacred tombe,
 With Sacriledge to dig. Therein he fownd
 Fountaines of gold and siluer to abownd,
 Of which the matter of his huge desire
 And pompous pride eftsoones he did compownd;
 Then auarice gan through his veines inspire
His greedy flames, and kindled life-deuouring fire.

18

Sonne (said he then) lett be thy bitter scorne,
 And leaue the rudenesse of that antique age
 To them, that liu'd therin in state forlorne;
 Thou that doest liue in later times, must wage
 Thy workes for wealth, and life for gold engage.
 If then thee list my offred grace to vse,
 Take what thou please of all this surplusage;
 If thee list not, leaue haue thou to refuse:
But thing refused, doe not afterward accuse.

Stanza 13

Mammon's godhead is denied because he does not properly govern the kingdoms he claims to control. **2 confound**: overthrow. **3 incline**: bend. **9 So**: in this manner (strongly contemptuous).

Stanza 14

2 priuate state: the private life in contrast to public office described in the previous stanza. **3–5** The Caspian and the Adriatic were proverbial for their violence. **fleet**: sail. **9 vpbrayd**: i.e. speak reproachfully against riches; or be reproached for having them.

Stanza 15

A close rendering of Lady Philosophy's argument in Boethius, *De Consol. Phil.* 2 Prosa 5: 'For with ful fewe thynges and with ful litel thynges nature halt hir apayed; and yif thow wolt achoken the fulfillynge of nature with superfluytees, certes thilke thynges that thow wolt thresten or powren into nature schulle ben unjoyeful to the, or elles anoyous' (tr. Chaucer). 'achoken' suggests the metaphor in 6–9. See 'Boethius' in the *SEnc*. **6 empeach**: impair. **8 braunching armes**: the mouths of the river rather than its tributaries. **annoyes**: harms.

Stanza 16

On S.'s frequent praise of the **antique world**, or past golden age, to measure present corruption, perhaps prompted here by Lady Philosophy's argument in 2 Met. 5, see V proem 1*n*. **3 vnreproued**: i.e. without condemning or reproaching the giver; answering Mammon's charge at 14.9. **truth**: sincerity; faith, trust. **5 cace**: state. **6 corn-fed steed**: proverbial. Smith 121 aptly cites Gascoigne: 'cornfed beasts, whose bellie is their God' (1907–10:2.170). **8 licentious**: lawless. **9 measure of her meane**: i.e. the temperate mean.

Stanza 17

Mining marks the corrupt iron age, as in Ovid, *Met.* 1.135–40. As Barkan 1975:212 notes, the image in the stanza 'moves from an anthropomorphic cosmos to a cosmomorphic human body'. **2 great Grandmother**: i.e. female ancestor; cf. 'the earth, great mother of vs all' (i 10.6). **4 Sacriledge**: in the etymological sense, 'to take away sacred objects', here from Nature's **sacred tombe**. **8** Those who search the earth's veins for wealth open their own veins to infection, mixing their blood with **gold and siluer**. **inspire**: breathe.

Stanza 18

4 wage: put out to hire. **5 engage**: pledge. **7 surplusage**: superabundance. The offer now allows a measure of choice.

19

Me list not (said the Elfin knight) receaue
　　Thing offred, till I know it well be gott,
　　Ne wote I, but thou didst these goods bereaue
　　From rightfull owner by vnrighteous lott,
　　Or that bloodguiltnesse or guile them blott.
　　Perdy (quoth he) yet neuer eie did vew,
　　Ne tong did tell, ne hand these handled not,
　　But safe I haue them kept in secret mew,
From heuens sight, and powre of al which them poursew.

20

What secret place (quoth he) can safely hold
　　So huge a masse, and hide from heauens eie?
　　Or where hast thou thy wonne, that so much gold
　　Thou canst preserue from wrong and robbery?
　　Come thou (quoth he.) and see. So by and by
　　Through that thick couert he him led, and fownd
　　A darkesome way, which no man could descry,
　　That deep descended through the hollow grownd,
And was with dread and horror compassed arownd.

21

At length they came into a larger space,
　　That stretcht it selfe into an ample playne,
　　Through which a beaten broad high way did trace,
　　That streight did lead to *Plutoes* griesly rayne:

By that wayes side, there sate internall Payne,
And fast beside him sat tumultuous Strife:
The one in hand an yron whip did strayne,
The other brandished a bloody knife,
And both did gnash their teeth, and both did threten life.

22

On thother side in one consort there sate,
　　Cruell Reuenge, and rancorous Despight,
　　Disloyall Treason, and hart-burning Hate,
　　But gnawing Gealosy out of their sight
　　Sitting alone, his bitter lips did bight,
　　And trembling Feare still to and fro did fly,
　　And found no place, wher safe he shroud him might,
　　Lamenting Sorrow did in darknes lye.
And shame his vgly face did hide from liuing eye.

23

And ouer them sad horror with grim hew,
　　Did alwaies sore, beating his yron wings;
　　And after him Owles and Night-rauens flew,
　　The hatefull messengers of heauy things,
　　Of death and dolor telling sad tidings;
　　Whiles sad *Celeno*, sitting on a clifte,
　　A song of bale and bitter sorrow sings,
　　That hart of flint a sonder could haue rifte:
Which hauing ended, after him she flyeth swifte.

Stanza 19

Guyon's refusal is necessarily qualified for he must live in the world with its temptations, giving to Mammon the things that are Mammon's, according to Mark 12.17, without becoming his victim. **1 2** The argument is basically Aristotle's: the liberal man will not accept money from a tainted source (*Ethics* 4.1). **3 bereaue**: take away by violence. **4 lott**: share of plunder acquired either by slaying the rightful owner or by cheating him. **5 bloodguiltnesse**: the sin of bloodshed; see ii 4.5*n*. **6** This claim, confirmed at 31.5, 37.4–5, and 38.2, mocks Paul's report to the Corinthians that for those who love him God has prepared 'the things which eye hathe not sene' (1 Cor. 2.9). **7** The double negative remains doubly negative. **tell**: count. **8 mew**: place of concealment.

Stanza 20

3–4 wonne: dwelling place; or 'riches' (*OED* sb.³ 5), for Guyon's second question concerns the source of Mammon's wealth. See 38.3–5. **5** An ironic echo of Christ's answer to the disciples who ask 'where dwellest thou?': 'He said vnto them, Come, and se' (John 1.38–39), as Kellogg and Steele 1965 note. **by and by**: immediately. **6 he him led**: the three words get equal stress: Mammon, not the Palmer, now guides Guyon. Variations on the phrase mark further stages of temptation at 35.1, 39.9, and 51.2.

Stanzas 21–23

Similar figures are described by Boccaccio 1976:8.6, in interpreting Virgil's Dis (*Aen.* 6.541) as a house of riches; noted Lotspeich 1932. They illustrate the evils catalogued by Guyon at 12.7–8.

Stanza 21

3 broad high way: like the 'broad high way' (I iv 2.8) that leads to the house of Pride, in contrast to the 'litle dore' (24.5) that leads out. **beaten**: cf. the path to the garden of Proserpina at 51.3. **4 Plutoes griesly rayne**: hell, the horrifying realm ruled by Pluto; called '*Plutoes* balefull bowres' at I v 14.8, and 'Plutoes griesly land' at IV iii 13.3. **5 Payne**: Punishment, corresponding to Poena, the goddess of punishment; appropriately named here to personify what is, in effect, the 'house of endlesse paine' (I v 33.7). **internall** *1590* applies to punishment in hell; infernall *1596* to pain which Pyrochles suffers. **7 strayne**: grasp tightly and hold extended; cf. the fiend at 27.5–6.

Stanza 22

1 On thother side: in Virgil, *Aen.* 6.278–81, War and Strife are on the opposite side of the threshold from the horrors they cause. **consort**: company. **7 shroud**: conceal. **9 shame**: a frequent presence in the poem, threatening almost everyone except the shameless.

Stanza 23

1 ouer them: i.e. over the fiends, but also over Mammon and Guyon. So also **after him**: i.e. after Horror, but also after Guyon. **hew**: appearance. **3–5** Both are traditional birds of evil omen because they prefer darkness to light. On the **Owle** as the messenger of death, see I v 30.6–7*n*; on the **Night-rauen**, cf. *Epith* 346. The reference in *SC June* 23–24 to 'Ravens . . . [and] gastly owles' is glossed by E.K. to mean 'all misfortunes (Whereof they be tokens) flying every where'. They assault Guyon and the Palmer at xii 36.4–5. **dolor**: pain

24
All these before the gates of *Pluto* lay,
　By whom they passing, spake vnto them nought.
　But th'Elfin knight with wonder all the way
　Did feed his eyes, and fild his inner thought.
　At last him to a litle dore he brought,
　That to the gate of Hell, which gaped wide,
　Was next adioyning, ne them parted nought:
　Betwixt them both was but a litle stride,
That did the house of Richesse from hellmouth diuide.

25
Before the dore sat selfe-consuming Care,
　Day and night keeping wary watch and ward,
　For feare least Force or Fraud should vnaware
　Breake in, and spoile the treasure there in gard:
　Ne would he suffer Sleepe once thether-ward
　Approch, albe his drowsy den were next;
　For next to death is Sleepe to be compard:
　Therefore his house is vnto his annext;
Here Sleep, ther Richesse, and Helgate them both betwext.

26
So soone as *Mammon* there arriud, the dore
　To him did open, and affoorded way;
　Him followed eke Sir *Guyon* euermore,
　Ne darkenesse him, ne daunger might dismay.

Soone as he entred was, the dore streight way
　Did shutt, and from behind it forth there lept
　An vgly feend, more fowle then dismall day,
　The which with monstrous stalke behind him stept,
And euer as he went, dew watch vpon him kept.

27
Well hoped hee, ere long that hardy guest,
　If euer couetous hand, or lustfull eye,
　Or lips he layd on thing, that likte him best,
　Or euer sleepe his eiestrings did vntye,
　Should be his pray. And therefore still on hye
　He ouer him did hold his cruell clawes,
　Threatning with greedy gripe to doe him dye
　And rend in peeces with his rauenous pawes,
If euer he transgrest the fatall *Stygian* lawes.

28
That houses forme within was rude and strong,
　Lyke an huge caue, hewne out of rocky clifte,
　From whose rough vaut the ragged breaches hong,
　Embost with massy gold of glorious guifte,
　And with rich metall loaded euery rifte,
　That heauy ruine they did seeme to threatt;
　And ouer them *Arachne* high did lifte
　Her cunning web, and spred her subtile nett,
Enwrapped in fowle smoke and clouds more black then Iett.

rather than grief. **6–9 Celeno**: chief of the harpies, 'prophets of sad destiny' (xii 36.9), and associated here with defiling greed. Her presence implies that Guyon may not eat. In Virgil, *Aen.* 3.245–46, she perches on a rock and utters ill omens; and in Boccaccio 1976:10.61, she is associated with avarice, as Lotspeich 1932 notes. The pathos of her song may relate to Guyon's misplaced pity at i 14.3 and xii 28.3. **rifte**: riven.

Stanza 24
2 As in Ovid, *Met.* 4.432–33, where the way to the infernal realm leads *per muta silentia*. Guyon's silence (cf. 31.1) is associated with resisting temptation: to speak at this stage of his ordeal would be to desire – in effect, to lay his lips on what he sees (as 27.3) – and thereby become a victim of Mammon's fiend (26.7–9). His initiation is comparable to that in the Eleusinian mysteries; see 26.6–9n, 63.6–9n. **6 gaped wide**: as the gates of hell in Virgil, *Aen.* 6.127, and where Ate dwells (IV i 20.1). 7 I.e., nothing separated them. To avoid duplicating the rhyme, *1596* has 'ought'. **9 house**: so called at 29.5 and viii 3.2, as it is the infernal counterpart to the castle of Alma. Not a cave, then, but only 'Lyke an huge caue' (28.2) in being a mine, as Read 2000:72–73 notes.

Stanza 25
3 **Force or Fraud**: traditionally paired (e.g. xi 7.4, V iv 31.1, and esp. V vii 7.3–4), the *forza* and *froda* in Dante's *Inferno*, which, with concupiscence, correspond to the three beasts that confront Dante at the beginning of his quest. As a literary theme, see N. Frye 1976a:65–93. **4 spoile**: plunder. **gard**: keeping. **5–6 selfe-consuming Care**, which does not permit Guyon to sleep, is the second of his two privations; see 27.4, 65.3. **next**: i.e. 'next adioyning' (24.7). **7–8 death** and

Sleepe are usually linked in the poem, as in the phrase 'deadly sleepe' at I i 36.6, iii 16.3, etc.

Stanza 26
5 The forty stanzas that describe Guyon's three temptations in Mammon's house – from here to 66.4 – correspond to the forty days of Christ's three temptations in the wilderness, as Hieatt 1973:51 has noted. See I xi 16n. **6–9** This **feend**, a name given the dragon at 1 i 5.7 and to Errour at 22.4, is akin to the Fury who follows initiates in the Eleusinian mysteries to ensure that they do not transgress 'the fatall *Stygian* lawes' (27.9). **dismall day**: day of death; see vi 43.7n.

Stanza 27
3 **likte**: pleased. **9 Stygian lawes**: laws of the infernal kingdom, named from the river Styx over which souls pass into hell; **fatall** because they control human destiny.

Stanza 28
3 **vaut**: vault. **breaches**: projecting arches of rock rather than fissures. **4 Embost**: adorned; raised. **glorious guifte**: rich or brilliant quality. **5 rifte**: also a projecting fragment or vein of ore rather than a fissure, as xii 4.5; or possibly a gap between protruding rocks. **6 ruine**: downfall. **7–9** Arachne's web is associated with 'dust and old decay' (29.2), noting the lack of 'right vsaunce' (7.4) of Mammon's wealth; but **high did lifte** suggests that it is an emblem of ambitious envy, from Ovid's story of Arachne's challenge to Minerva, in *Met.* 6.5–145, which S. revises in *Muiopotmos* 257–352. **subtile**: artfully contrived, suggesting that Mammon's house is a trap; cf. Acrasia's covering veil at xii 77.7.

29

Both roofe, and floore, and walls were all of gold,
But ouergrowne with dust and old decay,
And hid in darkenes, that none could behold
The hew thereof: for vew of cherefull day
Did neuer in that house it selfe display,
But a faint shadow of vncertein light;
Such as a lamp, whose life does fade away:
Or as the Moone cloathed with clowdy night,
Does shew to him, that walkes in feare and sad affright.

30

In all that rowme was nothing to be seene,
But huge great yron chests and coffers strong,
All bard with double bends, that none could weene
Them to efforce by violence or wrong:
On euery side they placed were along.
But all the grownd with sculs was scattered,
And dead mens bones, which round about were flong,
Whose liues, it seemed, whilome there were shed,
And their vile carcases now left vnburied.

31

They forward passe, ne *Guyon* yet spoke word,
Till that they came vnto an yron dore,
Which to them opened of his owne accord,
And shewd of richesse such exceeding store,
As eie of man did neuer see before,
Ne euer could within one place be fownd,
Though all the wealth, which is, or was of yore,
Could gathered be through all the world arownd,
And that aboue were added to that vnder grownd.

32

The charge thereof vnto a couetous Spright
Commaunded was, who thereby did attend,
And warily awaited day and night,
From other couetous feends it to defend,

Who it to rob and ransacke did intend.
Then *Mammon* turning to that warriour, said;
Loe here the worldes blis, loe here the end,
To which al men doe ayme, rich to be made:
Such grace now to be happy, is before thee laid.

33

Certes (sayd he) I n'ill thine offred grace,
Ne to be made so happy doe intend:
Another blis before mine eyes I place,
Another happines, another end.
To them, that list, these base regardes I lend:
But I in armes, and in atchieuements braue,
Do rather choose my flitting houres to spend,
And to be Lord of those, that riches haue,
Then them to haue my selfe, and be their seruile sclaue.

34

Thereat the feend his gnashing teeth did grate,
And grieu'd, so long to lacke his greedie pray;
For well he weened, that so glorious bayte
Would tempt his guest, to take thereof assay:
Had he so doen, he had him snatcht away,
More light then Culuer in the Faulcons fist.
Eternall God thee saue from such decay.
But whenas *Mammon* saw his purpose mist,
Him to entrap vnwares another way he wist.

35

Thence forward he him ledd, and shortly brought
Vnto another rowme, whose dore forthright,
To him did open, as it had beene taught:
Therein an hundred raunges weren pight,
And hundred fournaces all burning bright;
By euery fournace many feendes did byde,
Deformed creatures, horrible in sight,
And euery feend his busie paines applyde,
To melt the golden metall, ready to be tryde.

Stanza 29
4 hew: appearance, form. **6–9** The use of chiaroscuro is memorable here as elsewhere in the canto, e.g. 37.1–7, 42.2, 45.2–3. The second simile is drawn, appropriately, from Virgil, *Aen.* 6.270–72, which describes Aeneas's descent into hell.

Stanza 30
3 bends: bands. **6–9** As Guyon claimed at 13.4, and as the land over which the deadly sins ride 'all scattered lay | Dead sculs and bones of men, whose life had gone astray' (I iv 36.8–9); see vi 28.7–9n.

Stanza 31
1 On Guyon's silence, see 24.2n. **3** Doors open on their own, as again at 35.3, to lead deeper into the dungeon, in contrast to the iron gate that opened spontaneously to allow Peter, guided by the Angel, to escape from prison in Acts 12.10.

Stanza 32
2 Commaunded: committed. **3 awaited**: kept watch.

Stanza 33
1–4 Guyon answers with the opening argument of Aristotle's *Ethics*, that happiness is the chief good desired for its own sake and the end of all we do. Mammon offers him now what others strive for, but he will not (**n'ill**) take it. He does not want to be thus **happy** (i.e. rich) because **Another blis** (presumably chivalric honour) is the end of what he does. **5 base regardes**: heed for low matters; cf. 47.4. **8–9** Cicero, *De Senectute* 16.56, is the *locus classicus* of the popular story of Marcus Curius who 'had leuer haue dominion ouer them that be riche than he him selfe to haue richesse' (Elyot 1907:3.17). **sclaue**: obs. form of 'slave'.

Stanza 34
1–4 feend: the 'vgly feend' at 26.7 rather than Mammon, though no distinction is needed here. **his greedie pray**: i.e. the prey for which he is greedy. **assay**: trial by touching, as suggested at 27.2–3; but also testing of metals to determine their quality. **6 light**: quickly. **Culuer**: a dove. **fist**: grip. **7** Cf. S.'s response to the Red Cross Knight's predicament at

36

One with great bellowes gathered filling ayre,
  And with forst wind the fewell did inflame;
  Another did the dying bronds repayre
  With yron tongs, and sprinckled ofte the same
  With liquid waues, fiers *Vulcans* rage to tame,
  Who maystring them, renewd his former heat;
  Some scumd the drosse, that from the metall came.
  Some stird the molten owre with ladles great;
And euery one did swincke, and euery one did sweat.

37

But when an earthly wight they present saw,
  Glistring in armes and battailous aray,
  From their whot work they did themselues withdraw
  To wonder at the sight: for till that day,
  They neuer creature saw, that cam that way.
  Their staring eyes sparckling with feruent fyre,
  And vgly shapes did nigh the man dismay,
  That were it not for shame, he would retyre,
Till that him thus bespake their soueraine Lord and syre.

38

Behold, thou Faeries sonne, with mortall eye,
  That liuing eye before did neuer see:
  The thing, that thou didst craue so earnestly,
  To weet, whence all the wealth late shewd by mee,
  Proceeded, lo now is reueald to thee:
  Here is the fountaine of the worldes good:
  Now therefore, if thou wilt enriched bee,
  Auise thee well, and chaunge thy wilfull mood,
Least thou perhaps hereafter wish, and be withstood.

39

Suffise it then, thou Money God (quoth hee)
  That all thine ydle offers I refuse.
  All that I need I haue; what needeth mee
  To couet more, then I haue cause to vse?
  With such vaine shewes thy worldlinges vyle abuse:
  But giue me leaue to follow mine emprise.
  Mammon was much displeasd, yet no'te he chuse,
  But beare the rigour of his bold mesprise,
And thence him forward ledd, him further to entise.

40

He brought him through a darksom narrow strayt,
  To a broad gate, all built of beaten gold:
  The gate was open, but therein did wayt
  A sturdie villein, stryding stiffe and bold,
  As if that highest God defy he would;
  In his right hand an yron club he held,
  And he himselfe was all of yron mould,
  Yet had both life and sence, and well could weld
That cursed weapon, when his cruell foes he queld.

41

Disdayne he called was, and did disdayne
  To be so cald, and who so did him call:
  Sterne was his looke, and full of stomacke vayne,
  His portaunce terrible, and stature tall,
  Far passing th'hight of men terrestriall;
  Like an huge Gyant of the *Titans* race,
  That made him scorne all creatures great and small,
  And with his pride all others powre deface:
More fitt emongst black fiendes, then men to haue his place.

I i 18.9. **decay**: death. **8 purpose**: with a pun on the sense, 'speech'. Guyon is tempted by the eye and the ear. **9 vnwares**: unexpectedly; or as an adj., 'unwary', to stress Guyon's need for vigilance.

Stanza 35
1 he him ledd marks the second stage of the temptation (see 20.6*n*). Control of the source of riches would make Guyon 'Lord of those, that riches haue' (33.8). The two stages differ as the mine and the furnace, or as the pioneer and the smith. **4 pight**: placed. **9 tryde**: purified.

Stanza 36
Details are drawn from Virgil's Cyclopean furnaces under Mount Aetna (*Aen.* 8.416–22, 449–51), and from contemporary mining activity; see Quilligan 1983:57 and Read 2000:72–73. **3 bronds**: embers. **5 fiers Vulcans rage**: i.e. fire; see 5.4. **7 scumd**: skimmed off.

Stanza 37
2 Glistring suggests that the arms outshine the furnace; cf. 42.1–2. **battailous**: warlike. **6 staring**: also shining; see iv 15.6*n*; cf. Mammon's 'staring eyes' (7.5).

Stanza 38
3–5 Mammon refers to Guyon's question at 20.3–4 but adds **earnestly** to imply that Guyon is intemperate. **6 worldes good**: as 'worldes blis' (32.7), the *summum bonum*. **8 Auise thee**: consider. **9** As he warned him at 18.9.

Stanza 39
1 Mammon's claim that his riches are 'the fountaine of the worldes good' (38.6), which he may offer his **worldlinges**, prompts Guyon to name him as the **Money God** and to separate himself from those who worship him, as his repeated use of **I** and **mee** indicates. **2 ydle**: vain; worthless. **5 abuse**: deceive. **6 emprise**: adventure. **7 no'te**: could not. **8 mesprise**: scorn.

Stanza 40
1–2 strayt: confined passageway. It leads out of the house of Richesse as the 'litle dore' (24.5) leads in. The **broad gate** suggests 'the gate of Hell, which gaped wide' (24.6). **4 sturdie**: ruthless, violent. **villein**: villain; also a serf, a bondsman to his disdain of others. **7 yron** is appropriate to Mammon's iron age; revised to golden *1596*, which is appropriate to the house supported by 'golden pillours' (43.5). (The revision required that 'And' *1590* be changed to 'But'.) Perhaps revised to agree with Disdaine's 'golden feete' at VI viii 26.6. **8** The allegorist insists that his most allegorical figure is not merely allegorical. **weld**: wield. **9** . . . when he cruelly killed his foes.

Stanza 41
1 Disdayne manifests Mammon's 'great disdaine' at 7.6, and now is summoned up by Guyon's 'bold mesprise' (39.8). Cf. his genealogy at VI vii 41.5–8. See 'Disdain' in the *SEnc*. **3 stomacke**: pride, haughtiness. **4 portaunce**: bearing. **6 Titans race**: see III vii 47.3–5*n*. **8 deface**: 'abash' (42.8).

42

Soone as those glitterand armes he did espye,
  That with their brightnesse made that darknes light,
  His harmefull club he gan to hurtle hye,
  And threaten batteill to the Faery knight;
  Who likewise gan himselfe to batteill dight,
  Till *Mammon* did his hasty hand withhold,
  And counseld him abstaine from perilous fight:
  For nothing might abash the villein bold,
Ne mortall steele emperce his miscreated mould.

43   *reason without the palmer*

So hauing him with (reason) pacifyde,
  And the fiers Carle commaunding to forbeare,
  He brought him in. The rowme was large and wyde,
  As it some Gyeld or solemne Temple weare:
  Many great golden pillours did vpbeare
  The massy roofe, and riches huge sustayne,
  And euery pillour decked was full deare
  With crownes and Diademes, and titles vaine,
Which mortall Princes wore, whiles they on earth did rayne.

44

A route of people there assembled were,
  Of euery sort and nation vnder skye,
  Which with great vprore preaced to draw nere
  To th'vpper part, where was aduaunced hye
  A stately siege of soueraine maiestye,
  And thereon satt a woman gorgeous gay,
  And richly cladd in robes of royaltye,
  That neuer earthly Prince in such aray
His glory did enhaunce and pompous pryde display.

45

Her face right wondrous faire did seeme to bee,
  That her broad beauties beam great brightnes threw
  Through the dim shade, that all men might it see:
  Yet was not that same her owne natiue hew,

Guyon is ambitious —
is ambition for virtue sin?

But wrought by art and counterfetted shew,
  Thereby more louers vnto her to call;
  Nath'lesse most heuenly faire in deed and vew
  She by creation was, till she did fall;
Thenceforth she sought for helps to cloke her crime withall.

46

There as in glistring glory she did sitt,
  She held a great gold chaine ylincked well,
  Whose vpper end to highest heuen was knitt,
  And lower part did reach to lowest Hell,
  And all that preace did rownd about her swell,
  To catchen hold of that long chaine, thereby
  To climbe aloft, and others to excell:
  That was *Ambition*, rash desire to sty,
And euery linck thereof a step of dignity.

47

Some thought to raise themselues to high degree,
  By riches and vnrighteous reward,
  Some by close shouldring, some by flatteree;
  Others through friendes, others for base regard;
  And all by wrong waies for themselues prepard.
  Those that were vp themselues, kept others low,
  Those that were low themselues, held others hard,
  Ne suffred them to ryse or greater grow,
But euery one did striue his fellow downe to throw.

48

Which whenas *Guyon* saw, he gan inquire,
  What meant that preace about that Ladies throne,
  And what she was that did so high aspyre.
  Him *Mammon* answered, That goodly one,
  Whom all that folke with such contention,
  Doe flock about, my deare my daughter is;
  Honour and dignitie from her alone,
  Deriued are, and all this worldes blis
For which ye men doe striue: few gett, but many mis.

Stanza 42
1 **glitterand**: 'Glistring' (37.2); cf. xi 17.1, and see I vii
29.4–5*n*.   3 **hurtle**: violently brandish.   6–9 Mammon plays
the Palmer's role at iv 10.2–5, esp. in using reason to pacify
Guyon (43.1; cf. i 34.7, etc.), but he does so in order to sub-
ject him to greater temptations. Nothing can **abash**, i.e. con-
found Disdayne: to disdain him only increases his power.
miscreated mould: unnaturally created body, being made of
metal.

Stanza 43
2 **Carle**: churl.   4 **Gyeld**: guildhall.   **solemne**: grand, sump-
tuous.   7 **deare**: richly.

Stanza 44
4–9 Cf. Lucifera's court at I iv 7.4–7 and her attire at 8.3–4.
siege: throne; suggested by the siege of suitors.

Stanza 45
2–3 The juxtaposition of **threw | Through** projects her
brightness against **the dim shade**.   8–9 Her brightness and

fall associate her with Satan: 'How art thou fallen from heauen,
O Lucifer, sonne of the morning' (Isa. 14.12). Her **crime** is
clearly '*Ambition*' (46.8).

Stanza 46
1 **glistring glory**: as she is a demonic Gloriana/Elizabeth; cf.
proem 5.3–5.   2 The **great gold chaine** replicates the golden
chain by which Zeus controls all creation; see I ix 1.1–2*n*. It
was interpreted by Chapman, following Conti 1616:2.4, as
'Ambition . . . or cursed auarice' (*Hymnus in Noctem* 159–60).
5 The suitors act out the etymology of 'ambition': 'to go
around'.   **preace**: throng.   **swell**: also behave proudly; here,
ambitiously.   8 **sty**: mount up.   9 **step of dignity**: also social
rank or class; see iii 5.9*n*.

Stanza 47
The evident satire on the English court is repeated in *Colin
Clout* 690–730.   4 **base regard**: the 'base regardes' that
Guyon leaves to Mammon's worldlings at 33.5, i.e. bribes or
vnrighteous reward.

49

And fayre *Philotime* she rightly hight,
  The fairest wight that wonneth vnder skye,
  But that this darksom neather world her light
  Doth dim with horror and deformity,
  Worthie of heuen and hye felicitie,
  From whence the gods haue her for enuy thrust:
  But sith thou hast found fauour in mine eye,
  Thy spouse I will her make, if that thou lust,
That she may thee aduance for works and merits iust.

50

Gramercy *Mammon* (said the gentle knight)
  For so great grace and offred high estate,
  But I, that am fraile flesh and earthly wight,
  Vnworthy match for such immortall mate   *humility*
  My selfe well wote, and mine vnequall fate,
  And were I not, yet is my trouth yplight,
  And loue auowd to other Lady late,
  That to remoue the same I haue no might:
To chaunge loue causelesse is reproch to warlike knight.

51

Mammon emmoued was with inward wrath;
  Yet forcing it to fayne, him forth thence ledd
  Through griesly shadowes by a beaten path,
  Into a gardin goodly garnished
  With hearbs and fruits, whose kinds mote not be redd.
  Not such, as earth out of her fruitfull woomb
  Throwes forth to men sweet and well savored,
  But direfull deadly black both leafe and bloom,
Fitt to adorne the dead and deck the drery toombe.

52

There mournfull *Cypresse* grew in greatest store,
  And trees of bitter *Gall*, and *Heben* sad,
  Dead sleeping *Poppy*, and black *Hellebore*,
  Cold *Coloquintida*, and *Tetra* mad,
  Mortall *Samnitis*, and *Cicuta* bad,
  With which th'vniust *Atheniens* made to dy
  Wise *Socrates*, who thereof quaffing glad
  Pourd out his life, and last Philosophy
To the fayre *Critias* his dearest Belamy.

Stanza 48
7–9 For a chivalric knight who 'through long labours huntest after fame' (I iv 1.2), fame is more tempting than the riches offered at 32.7–9.

Stanza 49
1 Philotime: Gk φίλο + τιμή, love of honour, or rather, mere worldly honour. See 'Philotime' in the *SEnc*. To her suit Guyon would seem to have vowed himself at 10.2.   5–6 As happened to Night, III iv 55.3–4.   8 lust: wish; also implying its modern sense.   9 As Mammon offers 'great grace' (50.2), his daughter offers salvation by **works** which he considers **Worthie of heuen**. The nature of such works is revealed in the various 'wrong waies' catalogued at 47.   merits: 'good works viewed as entitling reward from God' (*OED* 5); see I viii 27.7. On the Protestant emphasis on salvation through faith alone and the rejection of merit even though **iust**, see *SEnc* 506. Cf. the Faerie Queene's freely offered grace to advance her servants at ix 5.4–5.

Stanza 50
Guyon's answer shows how he 'did beguile the Guyler of his pray' (64.9): he is tempted by Mammon as a worldling, and as such, he rejects his offer to marry an **immortall mate**. Yet the 'confession' that he is **fraile flesh** is a prelude to his defeat at 65.   1 Gramercy: i.e. 'Great reward that would be!' mocking Mammon's 'so great grace' (50.2).   5 vnequall: i.e. not being an equal match for her.   7 Presumably the **Lady** is 'the mighty Queene of *Faery*' (ix 4.1), and **late** refers to his presence at her court more than three months earlier; see ii 44.1–4n.
9 causelesse: without good cause; cf. I iv 1.

Stanza 51
2 him . . . ledd: formally announcing the final temptation by skilfully varying earlier statements; see 20.6n.   5 redd: told.

Stanza 52
1–5 For these plants whose deadly powers were described by sixteenth-century herbalists, see 'plants, herbs' in the *SEnc*. **Cypresse**: the traditional funereal tree, as at I i 8.9, II i 60.3. **Gall**: an oak whose fruit is called oak-gall, **bitter** from its name. **Heben**: either the ebony-tree or Hebenon called by Gower 'that slepi Tree' (*Conf. Aman.* 4.3017), and by T. Cooper 1565 'a tree wherof the wodde is blacke as iette within, and beareth nor leaues nor fruite'. See Rydén 1984:159. **Hellebore**: its name suggests 'hell-born', and is therefore **black**. **Coloquintida**: the poisonous wild gourd of 2 Kings 4.39–40, glossed in the Geneva Bible as 'moste vehement and dangerous in purging'. **Cold**: perhaps suggested by the name. **Tetra mad**: *totrum solanum* or *atropa helladonna*, deadly nightshade, which causes madness. **Samnitis**: a unique usage, but since the Samnites were neighbours of the Sabines, Upton 1758 conjectures that it is the savine tree, *arbor Sabina*. Called **Mortall** because it procures abortion. **Cicuta**: hemlock.   6–9 If S. wrote **Critias** and knew that he became Socrates's enemy, **dearest Belamy** must be taken as ironical; or **dearest** read in the sense of 'direst', i.e. 'most grievous'. It is simpler to allow a mistake for Crito, the friend present at Socrates's death; or a simple conflation with the parallel story of Theramenes who, according to Xenophon, *Hellenica* 2.3.56, drank hemlock to the health of his beloved Critias. See IV proem 3.6–8n, and 'Socrates' in the *SEnc*. **last Philosophy**: because he is dying and because in *Phaedo* he discusses the immortality of the soul.   **Belamy**: sweet friend (Fr. *bel ami*) used in the sense of 'Belamoure' (vi 16.7).

Stanzas 53–55
Baybak *et al.* 1969:231 note that these three stanzas constitute the numerical midpoint of the *1590* edition (not counting the proems): hence the phrase 'in the midst' (53.2). The central stanza describes the fruit that Mammon offers Guyon in a final temptation. On the centres of Bks I and III, each describing a *locus amoenus*, here reversed, see I vii 12–13n, III vi 43n.

53

The *Gardin of Proserpina* this hight;
    And in the midst thereof a siluer seat,
    With a thick Arber goodly ouerdight,
    In which she often vsd from open heat
    Her selfe to shroud, and pleasures to entreat.
    Next thereunto did grow a goodly tree,
    With braunches broad dispredd and body great,
    Clothed with leaues, that none the wood mote see
And loaden all with fruit as thick as it might bee.

54

Their fruit were golden apples glistring bright,
    That goodly was their glory to behold,
    On earth like neuer grew, ne liuing wight
    Like euer saw, but they from hence were sold;
    For those, which *Hercules* with conquest bold
    Got from great *Atlas* daughters, hence began,
    And planted there, did bring forth fruit of gold
    And those, with which th'*Eubœan* young man wan
Swift *Atalanta*, when through craft he her out ran.

55

Here also sprong that goodly golden fruit,
    With which *Acontius* got his louer trew,
    Whom he had long time sought with fruitlesse suit:
    Here eke that famous golden Apple grew,
    The which emongst the Gods false *Ate* threw:
    For which th'*Idæan* Ladies disagreed,
    Till partiall *Paris* dempt it *Venus* dew,
    And had of her, fayre *Helen* for his meed,
That many noble *Greekes* and *Troians* made to bleed.

56

The warlike Elfe, much wondred at this tree,
    So fayre and great, that shadowed all the ground,
    And his broad braunches, laden with rich fee,
    Did stretch themselues without the vtmost bound
    Of this great gardin, compast with a mound,
    Which ouer-hanging, they themselues did steepe,
    In a blacke flood which flow'd about it round;
    That is the riuer of *Cocytus* deepe,
In which full many soules do endlesse wayle and weepe.

57

Which to behold, he clomb vp to the bancke,
    And looking downe, saw many damned wightes,
    In those sad waues, which direfull deadly stancke,
    Plonged continually of cruell Sprightes,
    That with their piteous cryes, and yelling shrightes,
    They made the further shore resounden wide:
    Emongst the rest of those same ruefull sightes,
    One cursed creature, he by chaunce espide,
That drenched lay full deepe, vnder the Garden side.

58

Deepe was he drenched to the vpmost chin,
    Yet gaped still as coueting to drinke,
    Of the cold liquour which he waded in,
    And stretching forth his hand, did often thinke
    To reach the fruit which grew vpon the brincke:
    But both the fruit from hand, and flood from mouth
    Did fly abacke, and made him vainely swincke:
    The whiles he steru'd with hunger, and with drouth
He daily dyde, yet neuer throughly dyen couth.

Stanza 53

The **Gardin** is modelled on the grove of **Proserpina**, 'the Queene of hell' (I iv 11.2), at the entrance to the lower world in Homer, *Ody.* 10.509–10; and its **goodly tree** laden with **fruit** on the golden fruit consecrated to her in Claudian, *De Raptu Proserpinae* 2.290–92. Her consort, Plutus, is associated with Mammon; see 8.1–4*n*. **2 siluer seat**: see 63.6–9*n*. **3 ouerdight**: overspread. **5 entreat**: occupy herself in; entice others to indulge in.

Stanza 54

1–2 The **fruit**, inevitably forbidden in this context, suggests the fruit of the tree of knowledge of good and evil in Gen. 2.17, traditionally identified as **apples** from Lat. *malum* (apple) and *malum* (evil); also, from its association with love, as in Song Sol. 2.5, and therefore with temptation. See 'apples' in the *SEnc*. **goodly**: ironical in this context, as 51.4. **4 sold**: procured; stolen. **5–9** Hercules's **conquest bold** was his eleventh labour: he slew the guardian dragon to fetch the apples from the garden of **great Atlas daughters** who were known as the Hesperides. It is balanced against the craft by which Hippomenes, from Eubœa, outran **Atalanta** by throwing down golden apples, which she paused to gather (Ovid, *Met.* 4.560–680). The two stories are linked again in *Am* 77.7–8, most likely indebted to Conti 1616:7.7 who interprets the apples as symbols of wealth that test the soul.

Stanza 55

1–3 Acontius tricked Cydippe into speaking aloud their marriage vow inscribed on an apple (Ovid, *Heroides* 20–21).

fruitlesse: an irresistible pun. **4–9 that famous golden Apple** was inscribed 'to the fairest', and thrown by Eris here identified as **Ate**, goddess of discord, among the guests at the marriage of Peleus and Thetis. When Venus, Minerva, and Juno quarrelled over its possession, Paris awarded it to Venus on Mount Ida; his reward, Helen, led to the Trojan war. See III ix 34 and *n*. On his choice, see Nohrnberg 1976:720–23, and Stewart 1991:179–88. On **Ate**, see IV i 19–30*n*; and on the importance of the marriage, see VII vii 12*n*. The story of Eve and the apple is made prominent by being omitted. **dempt**: judged.

Stanza 56

3 fee: wealth. **4 without**: beyond. **5 mound**: embankment; here a ditch. **8–9 Cocytus**: one of the four rivers of hell; see I v 33.1–6*n*, and cf. III iv 55.4–6. It is associated with the wailing of damned souls from its name, Κωκυτός, wailing.

Stanza 57

3 sad: alluding to the etymology of Cocytus but suggesting also 'dark', 'deep'. **waues**: waters. **direfull deadly stancke**: describing the waters or possibly the damned wights themselues; cf. the bodies of Amavia and Mordant which 'direfull deadly stonck' (ii 4.9), and Pyrochles and Atin in the Idle Lake 'Engrost with mud, which did them fowle agrise' (vi 46.7). **4 of**: by. **5 shrightes**: shrieks. **9 drenched**: submerged.

Stanza 58

3 liquour: liquid. **8 drouth**: thirst. **9** The state of Despaire at I ix 54.8. **couth**: could.

59

The knight him seeing labour so in vaine,
   Askt who he was, and what he ment thereby:
   Who groning deepe, thus answerd him againe;
   Most cursed of all creatures vnder skye,
   Lo *Tantalus*, I here tormented lye:
   Of whom high *Ioue* wont whylome feasted bee,
   Lo here I now for want of food doe dye:
   But if that thou be such, as I thee see,
Of grace I pray thee, giue to eat and drinke to mee.

60

Nay, nay, thou greedy *Tantalus* (quoth he)
   Abide the fortune of thy present fate,
   And vnto all that liue in high degree,
   Ensample be of mind more temperate,
   To teach them how to vse their present state.
   Then gan the cursed wretch alowd to cry,
   Accusing highest *Ioue* and gods ingrate,
   And eke blaspheming heauen bitterly,
As authour of vniustice, there to let him dye.

61

He lookt a litle further, and espyde
   Another wretch, whose carcas deepe was drent
   Within the riuer, which the same did hyde:
   But both his handes most filthy feculent,

Aboue the water were on high extent,
   And faynd to wash themselues incessantly,
   Yet nothing cleaner were for such intent,
   But rather fowler seemed to the eye,
So lost his labour vaine and ydle industry.

62

The knight him calling, asked who he was,
   Who lifting vp his head, him answerd thus:
   I *Pilate* am the falsest Iudge, alas,
   And most vniust that by vnrighteous
   And wicked doome to Iewes despiteous,
   Deliuered vp the Lord of life to dye,
   And did acquite a murdrer felonous,
   The whiles my handes I washt in purity,
The whiles my soule was soyld with fowle iniquity.

[handwritten: Apathy]

63

Infinite moe, tormented in like paine
   He there beheld, too long here to be told:
   Ne *Mammon* would there let him long remayne,
   For terrour of the tortures manifold,
   In which the damned soules he did behold,
   But roughly him bespake. Thou fearefull foole
   Why takest not of that same fruite of gold,
   Ne sittest downe on that same siluer stoole,
To rest thy weary person, in the shadow coole.

Stanza 59
3 againe: in reply. **4–5** From Homer, *Ody.* 11.582–92, Tantalus became a traditional type of avarice and greed; and from Conti 1616:6.18, of blasphemous or intemperate knowledge. He was **cursed** either because he invited the gods to a banquet of his own son's flesh to test their omniscience; or because he betrayed their secrets (T. Cooper 1565; cf. *Gnat* 386); or because he became ambitious not knowing 'how to vse [his] present state' (60.5). Cf. I v 35.5. His gardens are a symbol of *vanitas* in Erasmus, *Adagia*, as Nohrnberg 1976:493 notes. **6 Of whom**: 'Who of', sugg. Upton 1758, to agree with the usual account that Jove was the host. Yet Tantalus was the host, according to Conti, and therefore he may complain at 60.7 that Jove is ungrateful.

Stanza 60
2 Abide: suffer. **6–9** That he does not repent even though punished indicates that he is confirmed in his sin, as the stubborn sinners of Rev. 16.9 'blasphemed the Name of God'. **let him dye**: i.e. suffer eternally; or until he dies.

Stanza 61
One may only speculate why, of the infinite numbers of damned souls tormented in Cocytus, S. should name only Tantalus and Pilate, though each has his place in Bk II, the first as a figure of intemperance and the second as one whose hands, like Ruddymane's at ii 3, cannot be cleansed. A connection between them is indicated by their similar postures: both extend their hands above the water, one being submerged to the chin and the other totally; and both act in vain, as Oram 1997:103–04 notes. See 'Tantalus, Pilate' in the *SEnc*. Among many other sins, ambition has been associated also with Pilate, e.g. by Marlorat in his 1570 commentary on St Matthew, as Hume 1984:176 notes. **2 drent**: submerged, drowned. **4–9** 'Pilate . . . toke water and wasshed his hands before the

multitude, saying, I am innocent of the blood of this iust man' (Matt. 27.24). That his hands being above the water must remain **feculent**, i.e. covered with faeces, shows how futile his feigned washing is, and how defiled he remains inwardly (62.8–9). Cf. Isa. 1.15: 'And when you shal stretch out your hands, I wil hide mine eyes from you . . . for your hands are ful of blood'. **extent**: extended. **faynd**: desired; or pretended, as they are held out of the water. The motif of outstretched hands describes Philotime's suitors (46.6) and Guyon's fiend (27.5–6).

Stanza 62
A medieval legend records that after his suicide, Pilate was plunged in a gulf near Lucerne from which his body is raised every Good Friday so he may try in vain to wash his hands; see *Enc. Brit.* 21.602. **5–7** Cf. Acts 3.14–15, from which S. takes the title, **the Lord of life. despiteous**: spiteful, cruel. **felonous**: wicked. **8 in purity**: the ceremonial cleansing, as Ps. 26.6: 'I wil wash my hands in innocencie'.

Stanza 63
2 too . . . told because S. is nearing the end of the forty stanzas on Guyon's temptation by Mammon; see 26.5*n*. **6–9 foole**: 'whosoeuer shal say, Foole, shalbe worthie to be punished with hel fyre' (Matt. 5.22). **fruite of gold**: the traditional forbidden fruit; see 54.1–2*n*. The **siluer stoole** suggests the temptation to idleness or sloth; in effect, to remain in the underworld, sharing Proserpina's seat of authority. Theseus was 'condemned to endlesse slouth by law' (I v 35.8) by sitting on this same chair of forgetfulness to which his flesh grew (cf. Virgil, *Aen.* 6.617–18; see Nohrnberg 1976:342–43). Upton 1758 compares it to the forbidden seat of the goddess Ceres in the Eleusinian mysteries; see Kermode 1971:74–75. The first 'sinfull bayt' (64.2) relates to the starving Tantalus, the second to Pilate who cannot rest.

64

All which he did, to do him deadly fall,
   In frayle intemperaunce through sinfull bayt,
   To which if he inclyned had at all,
   That dreadfull feend, which did behinde him wayt,
   Would him haue rent in thousand peeces strayt:
   But he was wary wise in all his way,
   And well perceiued his deceiptfull sleight,
   Ne suffred lust his safety to betray;
So goodly did beguile the Guyler of his pray.

65

And now he has so long remained theare,
   That vitall powres gan wexe both weake and wan,
   For want of food, and sleepe, which two vpbeare,
   Like mightie pillours, this frayle life of man,
   That none without the same enduren can.
   For now three dayes of men were full outwrought,
   Since he this hardy enterprize began:
   For thy great *Mammon* fayrely he besought,
Into the world to guyde him backe, as he him brought.

66

The God, though loth, yet was constraynd t'obay,
   For lenger time, then that, no liuing wight
   Below the earth, might suffred be to stay:
   So backe againe, him brought to liuing light.
   But all so soone as his enfeebled spright,
   Gan sucke this vitall ayre into his brest,
   As ouercome with too exceeding might,
   The life did flit away out of her nest,
And all his sences were with deadly fit opprest.

Stanza 64

2 frayle: alluding to the frailty of the flesh (cf. 50.3) through which he needs food and rest. **bayt**: temptation (cf. 34.3). **3 inclyned**: both literally and metaphorically. **5** On the threat of despoiling, see vi 28.7–9*n*. **8 lust**: both desire and appetite. **9 Guyler**: beguiler. The line has proverbial force (see Smith 352). It is used most pertinently by Langland in describing Satan's defeat by Christ in *Piers Plowman* 18.159–60, as Anderson 1976:64 notes.

Stanza 65

6 outwrought: completed. **8 For thy**: therefore. **fayrely**: courteously. Otherwise Guyon would be overcome by Disdayne.

Stanza 66

2–3 'For as Ionas was thre dayes, and thre nights in the whales bellie: so shal the Sonne of man be thre dayes and thre nights in the heart of the earth' (Matt. 12.40). **5–9** The difficulty of crossing the threshold from the underworld invokes the Sibyl's warning to Aeneas: the descent is easy but to return to the upper air is difficult. See I v 31.6–7. In an unpub. paper, Broaddus explains Guyon's faint in terms of Renaissance psychology: according to Galenic respiratory theory, Guyon faints when his heart, overwhelmed by the **vitall ayre** which he suddenly sucks in, oppresses his vital spirits; cf. Jordan 1989:31. **deadly fit**: the trance of death.

Cant. VIII.

Sir Guyon layd in swowne is by
Acrates sonnes despoyld,
Whom Arthure soone hath reskewed
And Paynim brethren foyld.

1

A Nd is there care in heauen? and is there loue
In heauenly spirits to these creatures bace,
That may compassion of their euilles moue?
There is: else much more wretched were the cace
Of men then beasts. But O th'exceeding grace
Of highest God, that loues his creatures so,
And all his workes with mercy doth embrace,
That blessed Angels, he sends to and fro,
To serue to wicked man, to serue his wicked foe.

2

How oft do they, their siluer bowers leaue,
To come to succour vs, that succour want,
How oft do they with golden pineons, cleaue
The flitting skyes, like flying Pursuiuant,
Against fowle feendes to ayd vs militant?
They for vs fight, they watch and dewly ward,
And their bright Squadrons round about vs plant,
And all for loue, and nothing for reward:
O why should heuenly God to men haue such regard?

3

During the while, that *Guyon* did abide
In *Mamons* house, the Palmer, whom whyleare
That wanton Mayd of passage had denide,
By further search had passage found elsewhere,
And being on his way, approched neare,
Where *Guyon* lay in traunce, when suddeinly
He heard a voyce, that called lowd and cleare,
Come hether, come hether, O come hastily;
That all the fields resounded with the ruefull cry.

4

The Palmer lent his eare vnto the noyce,
To weet, who called so importunely:
Againe he heard a more efforced voyce,
That bad him come in haste. He by and by
His feeble feet directed to the cry;
Which to that shady delue him brought at last,
Where *Mammon* earst did sunne his threasury:
There the good *Guyon* he found slumbring fast
In senceles dreame; which sight at first him sore aghast.

Book II Canto viii

Argument

2 despoyld: stripped of his armour (*OED* II 5).

Stanza 1

This stanza marks the only moment in the poem when God intervenes directly into the narrative. Elsewhere divine intervention is attributed indirectly to the heavens, heavenly grace, or heavenly providence. The corresponding stanza in Bk I also marks the entrance of Arthur as the instrument of heavenly grace to rescue the fallen hero. **1 And**: parallels the previous line to show that man's defeat is answered by God's grace. S.'s rhetorical question invokes 1 Pet. 5.7: 'he careth for you'. **2 creatures bace**: 'low', but implying the moral sense. Mammon's 'worldlings' (vii 8.1) are claimed by God as **his workes**. **3 euilles**: misfortunes. **5 exceeding**: glorious, of surpassing excellence. **7** Ps. 145.9: 'His mercies are ouer all his workes'. **8–9** Alluding to the Gk root of angel, ἄγγελος, a messenger; cf. Heb. 1.14: 'Are they not all ministring spirits, sent forthe to minister, for their sakes which shalbe heires of saluation?' S. extends their ministry to all. Cf. I ix 53.5, *HHL* 64–68. **serue**: the biblical 'minister to'.

Stanza 2

S.'s text is Matt. 4.11: 'the deuil left him [Christ]: and beholde, the Angels came, and ministred vnto him'. **1–5** In contrast to the upward striving in Mammon's golden kingdom with its betraying silver seat, now there is the contrary motion from God to humanity as angels from **siluer bowers** fly down on **golden** wings. **succour**: supply, aid, in the military sense. On the use of this word, see 8.5, 25.7, ix 9.3. **want**: lack; desire. **flitting**: yielding, shifting. **Pursuiuant**: a royal messenger, here from God the King. **militant**: warring, referring to the angels who fight on our behalf but also to warfare on earth. **6–7** 'The Angel of the Lord pitcheth rounde about them, that feare him, and deliuereth them' (Ps. 34.7). **Squadrons**: the square military formation taken up to guard the four sides or four quarters of the human body. **9** 'Lord, what is man that thou regardest him?' (Ps. 144.3).

Stanza 3

2 whyleare: some time ago – 100 stanzas earlier. **3 That wanton Mayd**: Phædria; see vi 6.1*n*. **8** The urgency of the call is conveyed by the unusual stress: two opening amphibrachs followed by a trochee and ending with an amphimacer.

Stanza 4

2 importunely: persistently. **3 more efforced**: uttered with more effort. **4 by and by**: immediately. **6–7** Repeating vii Arg.1–2.

5

Beside his head there satt a faire young man,
    Of wondrous beauty, and of freshest yeares,
    Whose tender bud to blossome new began,
    And florish faire aboue his equall peares;
    His snowy front curled with golden heares,
    Like *Phœbus* face adornd with sunny rayes,
    Diuinely shone, and two sharpe winged sheares,
    Decked with diuerse plumes, like painted Iayes,
Were fixed at his backe, to cut his ayery wayes.

6

Like as *Cupido* on *Idæan* hill,
    When hauing laid his cruell bow away,
    And mortall arrowes, wherewith he doth fill
    The world with murdrous spoiles and bloody pray,
    With his faire mother he him dights to play,
    And with his goodly sisters, *Graces* three;
    The Goddesse pleased with his wanton play,
    Suffers her selfe through sleepe beguild to bee,
The whiles the other Ladies mind theyr mery glee.

7

Whom when the Palmer saw, abasht he was
    Through fear and wonder, that he nought could say,
    Till him the childe bespoke, Long lackt, alas,
    Hath bene thy faithfull aide in hard assay,
    Whiles deadly fitt thy pupill doth dismay;
    Behold this heauy sight, thou reuerend Sire,
    But dread of death and dolor doe away;
    For life ere long shall to her home retire,
And he that breathlesse seems, shal corage bold respire.

8

The charge, which God doth vnto me arrett,
    Of his deare safety, I to thee commend;
    Yet will I not forgoe, ne yet forgett
    The care thereof my selfe vnto the end,
    But euermore him succour, and defend
    Against his foe and mine: watch thou I pray;
    For euill is at hand him to offend.
    So hauing said, eftsoones he gan display
His painted nimble wings, and vanisht quite away.

9

The Palmer seeing his lefte empty place,
    And his slow eies beguiled of their sight,
    Woxe sore affraid, and standing still a space,
    Gaz'd after him, as fowle escapt by flight;
    At last him turning to his charge behight,
    With trembling hand his troubled pulse gan try,
    Where finding life not yet dislodged quight,
    He much reioyst, and courd it tenderly,
As chicken newly hatcht, from dreaded destiny.

10

At last he spide, where towards him did pace
    Two Paynim knights, al armd as bright as skie,
    And them beside an aged Sire did trace,
    And far before a light-foote Page did flie,
    That breathed strife and troublous enmitie;
    Those were the two sonnes of *Acrates* old,
    Who meeting earst with *Archimago* slie,
    Foreby that idle strond, of him were told,
That he, which earst them combatted, was *Guyon* bold.

Stanza 5
The guardian angel who sits by the right side of Christ's tomb is a young man (Mark 16.5). Matt. 28.3 records that 'his countenance was like lightning, and his raiment white as snowe'. **4 equall peares**: companions of the same age or rank. **7–9** Wings denote the cherubim (see Exod. 25.20), the second of the nine orders of angels: 'those bright *Cherubins*, | Which all with golden wings are overdight' (*HHB* 92–93). The brightness of angel wings is traditional, as in Chaucer, *Parl. Fowls* 356: 'the pekok, with his aungels fetheres bryghte'. Cupid appears 'With spotted winges like Peacocks trayne' in *SC March* 80. The Palmer, who is associated with reason (see i 7.8–9*n*), is brought to aid Guyon by a cherub because that order was reputed to excel in knowledge, esp. in the knowledge of God. See 'angels' in the *SEnc*. **sheares**: wings. **diuerse**: variously coloured. The jay is noted because of its beautiful feathers.

Stanza 6
1–5 Cupido: the divine Cupid, son of the celestial Venus, invoked at I proem 3.5–7 (and see *n*), the unarmed Cupid who is allowed into the castle of Alma (ix 34.6–9) and the garden of Adonis (III vi 49.3–9). On the pictorial conventions of the angel as Cupid, see 'angel, Guyon's' in the *SEnc*. **on Idæan hill**: on Mount Ida near Troy Paris awarded the apple of beauty to the goddess of love; see vii 55.4–9. **6 Graces three**: in making them sisters of Cupid and hence daughters of Venus, S. follows Boccaccio 1976:3.22, and Conti 1616:4.13. Cf. their parentage at VI x 22 and *Teares* 401–06.

Stanza 7
3 childe: youth of gentle birth; see 56.1–3*n*. **4 assay**: affliction; trial. **5 dismay**: defeat. **6 reuerend**: for the Palmer is worthy to be revered even by God's messenger. **8 retire**: return. **9 corage**: spirit, life; i.e. 'he shall regain the breath of life'. Throughout this episode, Guyon is regarded as both alive and dead (e.g. 11.7, 14.9, 15.2–3, 9, 16.4), analogous on the religious level to being 'dead in trespasses and sinnes' (Eph. 2.1). His state is interpreted as spiritual death by MacLachlan 1984:105; see also Gless 1994:188–89.

Stanza 8
1–2 'For he shal giue his Angels charge ouer thee to kepe thee in all thy waies' (Ps. 91.11). **arrett**: entrust, lay to the charge of. **3–6** The Angel prepares the Palmer for the intercession of Arthur, whose **succour**, as it expresses that offered by God through his angels at 2.2, is sought at 25.7, offered at 26.9, and then renewed at ix 9.3. **6** Cf. Mark 13.33: 'Take hede: watche, and pray'. **7 offend**: attack, harm.

Stanza 9
5 ... to the charge committed, commended (cf. 8.2), or 'assind' (11.7) to him. **8–9 courd**: covered, as the simile suggests, in a gesture of hovering over Guyon to protect him. **it**: i.e. **his charge**. A biblical simile, e.g. Matt. 23.37: 'I haue gathered thy children together, as the henne gathereth her chickens vnder her wings'. Or **it** refers to Guyon's heart beat or pulse, as Broaddus argues in an unpublished paper.

11

Which to auenge on him they dearly vowd,
  Where euer that on ground they mote him find;
  False *Archimage* prouokte their corage prowd,
  And stryful *Atin* in their stubborne mind
  Coles of contention and whot vengeaunce tind.
  Now bene they come, whereas the Palmer sate,
  Keeping that slombred corse to him assind;
  Well knew they both his person, sith of late
With him in bloody armes they rashly did debate.

12

Whom when *Pyrochles* saw, inflam'd with rage,
  That sire he fowl bespake, Thou dotard vile,
  That with thy brutenesse shendst thy comely age,
  Abandon soone, I read, the caytiue spoile
  Of that same outcast carcas, that ere while
  Made it selfe famous through false trechery,
  And crownd his coward crest with knightly stile;
  Loe where he now inglorious doth lye,
To prooue he liued il, that did thus fowly dye.

13

To whom the Palmer fearlesse answered,
  Certes, Sir knight, ye bene too much to blame,
  Thus for to blott the honor of the dead,
  And with fowle cowardize his carcas shame,
  Whose liuing handes immortalizd his name.
  Vile is the vengeaunce on the ashes cold,
  And enuy base, to barke at sleeping fame:
  Was neuer wight, that treason of him told;
Your self his prowesse prou'd and found him fiers and bold.

14

Then sayd *Cymochles*, Palmer, thou doest dote,
  Ne canst of prowesse, ne of knighthood deeme,
  Saue as thou seest or hearst. But well I wote,
  That of his puissaunce tryall made extreeme;
  Yet gold al is not, that doth golden seeme,
  Ne all good knights, that shake well speare and shield:
  The worth of all men by their end esteeme,
  And then dew praise, or dew reproch them yield;
Bad therefore I him deeme, that thus lies dead on field.

15

Good or bad, gan his brother fiers reply,
  What doe I recke, sith that he dide entire?
  Or what doth his bad death now satisfy,
  The greedy hunger of reuenging yre,
  Sith wrathfull hand wrought not her owne desire?
  Yet since no way is lefte to wreake my spight,
  I will him reaue of armes, the victors hire,
  And of that shield, more worthy of good knight;
For why should a dead dog be deckt in armour bright?

16

Fayr Sir, said then the Palmer suppliaunt,
  For knighthoods loue, doe not so fowle a deed,
  Ne blame your honor with so shamefull vaunt
  Of vile reuenge. To spoile the dead of weed
  Is sacrilege, and doth all sinnes exceed;
  But leaue these relicks of his liuing might,
  To decke his herce, and trap his tomblacke steed.
  What herce or steed (said he) should he haue dight,
But be entombed in the rauen or the kight?

Stanza 10

The four figures merge into an image of intemperance. Atin, the spirit of discord, flies ahead to seek occasion for enmity. **Archimago** is called **an aged Sire** because he parodies the Palmer who is so addressed at vi 20.5, ix 60.8, and is called 'reuerend Sire' at 7.6. He is seen to **trace**: i.e. walk; but also 'stalk' or 'pursue', referring to his designs against Guyon. Pyrochles and Cymochles are called **Paynim** (pagan) knights, a term used in Bk I to describe the enemies of the Red Cross Knight – and used only in this canto in Bk II (again at 45.3, 50.1) – to note that Guyon's enemies are God's, as the Angel has declared at 8.6. They are named **sonnes of Acrates** (cf. Arg.2) as they oppose the knight of temperance; cf. iv 41.6. They **pace** because the irascible and concupiscible emotions, which they embody, move steadily together to destroy Guyon. **8 that idle strond**: 'the shallow sand' (vi 38.4) of Phædria's Idle Lake.

Stanza 11

1 dearly: earnestly; direly. **2 on ground**: with a pun, for they find him on the ground. **4–5** Cf. Prov. 26.21: 'As the cole maketh burning coles, and wood a fyre, so the contentious man is apt to kindle strife'. **stubborne**: implacable, ruthless. **tind**: inflamed (alluding to the etymology of Atin). **7 slombred**: unconscious. **9 debate**: fight.

Stanza 12

3 brutenesse: stupidity, in seeking to protect Guyon. **shendst**: disgrace. **comely**: what is comely for. **4 soone**: without

delay. **read**: advise. **caytiue**: wretched. **5 carcas**: as 13.4, 27.8, 28.5; used in its etymological sense: Lat. *caro* + *casa*, fallen flesh. **6–7** He refers to the binding of Occasion (iv 45, v 17), and to the killing of his horse (v 4–5). **stile**: title; outward appearance.

Stanza 13

1 fearelesse: in contrast to his response to the Angel at 7.2, 9.3. **7 barke**: envy is traditionally associated with the dog; or the wolf, as I iv 30.2 and *SC* 'To His Booke'.

Stanza 14

5 Proverbial: Smith 336. **6 shake**: brandish threateningly.

Stanza 15

1 gan: did. **2 entire**: wholly, completely; or unbroken (Lat. *integer*), and hence not mortally wounded. **9 dead dog**: a biblical term of ignominy; see iii 7.6*n*.

Stanza 16

The chivalric code allowed the victor the arms of a defeated knight, as at IV iv 31.2–3, though not if the knight had been slain. In general, it was an offence to reave the dead, though Arthur allows it as a 'right' at 27.7; cf. VI ii 39.1–2. Here the Palmer defends Guyon's **relicks** as Una preserves 'the forlorne reliques' of the Red Cross Knight's armour at I vii 48.1. His claim that reaving the dead of arms exceeds all sins suggests that Pyrochles and Cymochles seek to disarm and then despoil Guyon's body (see 25.3), as Achilles first despoils

17

With that, rude hand vpon his shield he laid,
And th'other brother gan his helme vnlace,
Both fiercely bent to haue him disaraid;
Till that they spyde, where towards them did pace
An armed knight, of bold and bounteous grace,
Whose squire bore after him an heben launce,
And couerd shield. Well kend him so far space
Th'enchaunter by his armes and amenaunce,
When vnder him he saw his Lybian steed to praunce.

18

And to those brethren sayd, Rise rise byliue,
And vnto batteil doe your selues addresse;
For yonder comes the prowest knight aliue,
Prince *Arthur*, flowre of grace and nobilesse,
That hath to Paynim knights wrought gret distresse,
And thousand Sar'zins fowly donne to dye.
That word so deepe did in their harts impresse,
That both eftsoones vpstarted furiously,
And gan themselues prepare to batteill greedily.

19

But fiers *Pyrrhochles*, lacking his owne sword,
The want thereof now greatly gan to plaine,
And *Archimage* besought, him that afford,
Which he had brought for *Braggadochio* vaine.
So would I (said th'enchaunter) glad and faine
Beteeme to you this sword, you to defend,
Or ought that els your honor might maintaine,
But that this weapons powre I well haue kend,
To be contrary to the worke, which ye intend.

20

For that same knights owne sword this is of yore,
Which *Merlin* made by his almightie art,
For that his noursling, when he knighthood swore,
Therewith to doen his foes eternall smart.
The metall first he mixt with *Medæwart*,
That no enchauntment from his dint might saue;
Then it in flames of *Aetna* wrought apart,
And seuen times dipped in the bitter waue
Of hellish *Styx*, which hidden vertue to it gaue.

21

The vertue is, that nether steele, nor stone
The stroke thereof from entraunce may defend;
Ne euer may be vsed by his fone,
Ne forst his rightful owner to offend,
Ne euer will it breake, ne euer bend.
Wherefore *Morddure* it rightfully is hight.
In vaine therefore, *Pyrhochles*, should I lend
The same to thee, against his lord to fight,
For sure yt would deceiue thy labor, and thy might.

22

Foolish old man, said then the Pagan wroth,
That weenest words or charms may force withstond:
Soone shalt thou see, and then beleeue for troth,
That I can carue with this inchaunted brond
His Lords owne flesh. Therewith out of his hond
That vertuous steele he rudely snatcht away,
And *Guyons* shield about his wrest he bond;
So ready dight, fierce battaile to assay,
And match his brother proud in battailous aray.

---

the dead Hector of his arms and then desecrates his corpse in Homer, *Iliad* 22.375–404. He calls their intent 'Vnworthie vsage' (25.4); Arthur calls it 'rude' (26.1, and see 29.6–9). S. may draw on Langland: after Longinus has wounded Christ's body on the cross, Faith declares: 'Cursed caytyue! knighthod was it neuere | To mysdo a ded body by day or by nyghte' (*Piers Plowman* 18.96–97). **1 suppliaunt**: humbly. **3 blame**: bring into disrepute. **4–5 vile reuenge** is associated with Guyon's antagonists in contrast to his seeking 'dew vengeance' at i 61.7. **7–9 herce**: bier or corpse. **trap**: adorn. **tomblacke**: referring to the funereal black trappings of the horse. On this threat, see vi 28.7–9*n*. **dight**: i.e. dressed for him.

Stanza 17
4–5 Till that: answering 10.1 to claim that through Arthur, God's grace comes to save Guyon. Hence **bold and bounteous grace** refers to 'th'exceeding grace | Of highest God' (1.5–6) to his creatures. Cf. Archimago's reference to him as 'flowre of grace' (18.4), and the Palmer's hope for his 'timely grace' at 25.6. **6–7** The lance and shield, described at Arthur's entrance (I vii 37, 33–34), serve as identifying insignia. **8 amenaunce**: noble bearing. **9** Arthur's horse is first mentioned here as an emblem of temperance: a horse under control signifies the rider's control of the passions; see i 7.8–9*n*. **Lybian**: Arabian; evidently a type of excellence.

Stanza 18
1 For the *psychomachia* that follows, his address to Pyrochles and Cymochles includes the prostrate Guyon. **byliue**: at once. **6 Sar'zins**: Saracens; see I ii 12.6*n*.

Stanza 19
1–2 Pyrochles may have abandoned his sword when he abandoned his horse at vi 41. **plaine**: lament. **3–4** Cf. iii 18.1–7, vi 47.6. **vaine**: foolish, as iii 34.3. **5 faine**: willingly. **6 Beteeme**: grant. **8 kend**: found out.

Stanza 20
1–3 As told at I vii 36.2–7. **5–6** Herbs were held to possess particular powers against enchantments. **Medæwart**: medewart, the meadow-plant or meadow-sweet. In Bk I, the shield (vii 35.1–4) and horn (viii 4.5–6) are given this power. **dint**: blow. **7–9** The flames of **Aetna** are associated with Vulcan's forge where Aeneas's arms were made. Turnus's sword, made by Vulcan for his father, was dipped into the Stygian lake, *Aen.* 12.90–91, as was Furor's sword (v 22.7–8). **seuen times**: therefore proof against the seven deadly sins; see v 6.3*n*. It is also the number of completion: Namaan was dipped seven times in the Jordan, 2 Kings 5:10. **vertue**: power.

Stanza 21
3 fone: foes. **4 offend**: injure. **6 Morddure**: i.e. hard-biter (Lat. *mordere*, to bite + *durus*, hard) as Eng. 'mordant' (*OED*

23

By this that straunger knight in presence came,
    And goodly salued them; who nought againe
    Him answered, as courtesie became,
    But with sterne lookes, and stomachous disdaine,
    Gaue signes of grudge and discontentment vaine:
    Then turning to the Palmer, he gan spy
    Where at his feet, with sorrowfull demayne
    And deadly hew, an armed corse did lye,
In whose dead face he redd great magnanimity.

24

Sayd he then to the Palmer, Reuerend syre,
    What great misfortune hath betidd this knight?
    Or did his life her fatall date expyre,
    Or did he fall by treason, or by fight?
    How euer, sure I rew his pitteous plight.
    Not one, nor other, sayd the Palmer graue,
    Hath him befalne, but cloudes of deadly night
    A while his heauy eylids couer'd haue,
And all his sences drowned in deep sencelesse waue.

25

Which, those his cruell foes, that stand hereby,
    Making aduauntage, to reuenge their spight,
    Would him disarme, and treaten shamefully,
    Vnworthie vsage of redoubted knight.
    But you, faire Sir, whose honourable sight
    Doth promise hope of helpe, and timely grace,
    Mote I beseech to succour his sad plight,
    And by your powre protect his feeble cace.
First prayse of knighthood is, fowle outrage to deface.

26

Palmer, (said he) no knight so rude, I weene,
    As to doen outrage to a sleeping ghost:
    Ne was there euer noble corage seene,
    That in aduauntage would his puissaunce bost:
    Honour is least, where oddes appeareth most.
    May bee, that better reason will aswage,
    The rash reuengers heat. Words well dispost
    Haue secrete powre, t'appease inflamed rage:
If not, leaue vnto me thy knights last patronage.

27

Tho turning to those brethren, thus bespoke,
    Ye warlike payre, whose valorous great might
    It seemes, iust wronges to vengeaunce doe prouoke,
    To wreake your wrath on this dead seeming knight,
    Mote ought allay the storme of your despight,
    And settle patience in so furious heat?
    Not to debate the challenge of your right,
    But for this carkas pardon I entreat,
Whom fortune hath already laid in lowest seat.

28

To whom *Cymochles* said, For what art thou,
    That mak'st thy selfe his dayes-man, to prolong
    The vengeaunce prest? Or who shall let me now,
    On this vile body from to wreak my wrong,
    And make his carkas as the outcast dong?
    Why should not that dead carrion satisfye
    The guilt, which if he liued had thus long,
    His life for dew reuenge should deare abye?
The trespas still doth liue, albee the person dye.

---

1), though that reading of the name confirms only the first of its four virtues. On its failure to 'bite' Arthur, see 38.4, 44.8.

Stanza 22
2 words: possibly referring to the sword's name as possessing magical power. **4 inchaunted brond**: also as it overcomes all enchantments. **5–9** That Guyon's enemy is armed with Guyon's shield and Arthur's sword indicates that at first human power, passive and active respectively, resists his rescue; see 40n. **vertuous**: possessing certain virtues or powers, as said of the balm from the tree of life at I xi 50.5 and of the Palmer's staff at II xii 26.6, 86.1.

Stanza 23
2 goodly salued: courteously greeted. **4 stomachous**: resentful. **7 demayne**: demeanour; also behaviour. **9 great magnanimity**: its outward expression is 'magnificence', which the *LR* 39 calls 'the perfection of all the rest [of the virtues], and conteineth in it them all' (see *n*). In its only other use in the poem, Scudamour praises Britomart's 'huge heroicke magnanimity' (III xi 19.2) when she vows to rescue Amoret. It applies to Arthur in its literal sense, 'doing great deeds'; cf. the praise of his 'great mind' at 51.1.

Stanza 24
1 Reuerend syre: echoing the Angel at 7.6. **3 fatall date**: i.e. the term of life given by fate; cf. I ix 42.4–5.

Stanza 25
5 sight: appearance. **8 cace**: condition, referring to Guyon's body and his armour. **9 deface**: destroy; prevent (sugg. by the context).

Stanza 26
2 ghost: person; spirit. **5 most**: i.e. most in one's favour. **7–8** Proverbial: see vi 36.5n. **9 patronage**: defence; more specifically, guardianship: the 'charge' and 'care' (8.1, 4) over Guyon assumed by the Angel; cf. 55.4.

Stanza 27
3 To allay the passions by reason, Arthur allows that the brothers may be justly angry for wrongs done to them. Yet **iust wronges** implies that wrongs done to them are **iust**. **7 debate the chalenge**: contest the claim.

Stanza 28
2 dayes-man: mediator. Job's appeal for a 'dayes man' to intervene between him and God's wrath (Job 9.33, Bishops'), and assumed by Christ, becomes the model for Arthur's role on Guyon's behalf. **prolong**: delay. **3 prest**: at hand. **let**: hinder. **6 dead carrion**: rejecting Arthur's 'dead seeming' (27.4). **8 abye**: pay for.

29

Indeed, then said the Prince, the euill donne
   Dyes not, when breath the body first doth leaue,
   But from the grandsyre to the Nephewes sonne,
   And all his seede the curse doth often cleaue,
   Till vengeaunce vtterly the guilt bereaue:
   So streightly God doth iudge. But gentle knight,
   That doth against the dead his hand vpreare,
   His honour staines with rancour and despight,
And great disparagment makes to his former might.

30

Pyrrhochles gan reply the second tyme,
   And to him said, Now felon sure I read,
   How that thou art partaker of his cryme:
   Therefore by *Termagaunt* thou shalt be dead.
   With that his hand, more sad then lomp of lead,
   Vplifting high, he weened with *Morddure*,
   His owne good sword *Morddure*, to cleaue his head.
   The faithfull steele such treason no'uld endure,
But swaruing from the marke, his Lordes life did assure.

31

Yet was the force so furious and so fell,
   That horse and man it made to reele asyde;
   Nath'lesse the Prince would not forsake his sell:
   For well of yore he learned had to ryde,

But full of anger fiersly to him cryde;
   False traitour miscreaunt, thou broken hast
   The law of armes, to strike foe vndefide.
   But thou thy treasons fruit, I hope, shalt taste
Right sowre, and feele the law, the which thou hast defast.

32

With that his balefull speare, he fiercely bent
   Against the Pagans brest, and therewith thought
   His cursed life out of her lodg haue rent:
   But ere the point arriued, where it ought,
   That seuen fold shield, which he from *Guyon* brought
   He cast between to ward the bitter stownd:
   Through all those foldes the steelehead passage wrought
   And through his shoulder perst; wherwith to ground
He groueling fell, all gored in his gushing wound.

33

Which when his brother saw, fraught with great griefe
   And wrath, he to him leaped furiously,
   And fowly saide, By *Mahoune*, cursed thiefe,
   That direfull stroke thou dearely shalt aby.
   Then hurling vp his harmefull blade on hy,
   Smote him so hugely on his haughtie crest,
   That from his saddle forced him to fly:
   Els mote it needes downe to his manly brest
Haue cleft his head in twaine, and life thence dispossest.

Stanza 29

1–6 Exod. 20.5: 'I am the Lord thy God, a ielouse God, visiting the iniquitie of the fathers vpon the children, vpon the third generacion and vpon the fourth of them that hate me'. Line 6 gently reminds the pair that vengeance belongs to God; see i 61.5–9*n*. **3 Nephewes**: grandson's. **5–6** Earlier Guyon vows to seek 'dew vengeance . . . | Till guiltie blood her guerdon doe obtayne' (i 61.7–8); his enemies seek revenge (11.5, 13.6, 27.3, 28.3), which Arthur renounces at 51.1–4. **streightly**: rigorously. **7 vpreare**: 'vpheaue' would satisfy the 'b' rhyme though that word is never used in the poem while 'vpreare' is common, e.g. IV i 54.8. The failure to rhyme may mark the perversity of the act, as Røstvig 1994:313 suggests.

Stanza 30

2 felon: villain; accusing him of committing a felony by defending Guyon. **read**: discern. **3 partaker of his cryme**: as Arthur serves as Guyon's 'dayes-man' (28.2). **4 Termagaunt**: the 'thrice-great' Saracen god. His brother adds '*Mahoune*' at 33.3. This pair of gods is invoked again at VI vii 47.9 to mark their duplicity and distinguish their religion from the worship of the one true God. **5 sad**: heavy. **8 no'uld**: would not. **9 assure**: render secure.

Stanzas 31–39

The five strokes in 'the whole debate' (54.6) over Guyon's body are carefully orchestrated: (1) Pyrochles strikes at Arthur with his own sword at 31.1–3, and, though missing his head, causes him and his horse to reel; (2) in response, Arthur wounds him in the shoulder and unhorses him at 32.8–9; (3) Cymochles strikes Arthur on the head with his sword, unhors-

ing him at 33.5–7; (4) in response, Arthur wounds him in the thigh at 36.5, though severing his spear; (5) both brothers strike together: Pyrochles strikes the shield without effect, Cymochles further severs the spear that had wounded him and pierces Arthur's right side at 38–39. Five may be chosen to suggest the five senses; or it may conventional, as the 'five memorable strokes' by Pyrocles and Musidorus in fighting the rebels in Sidney, *New Arcadia* 2.25 title. The allusions to Virgil's *Aeneid* are noted by Leslie 1983:92–100.

Stanza 31

6–9 The laws of chivalry require that a challenge be given and accepted before a blow is struck. Cf. the charge of unknightly conduct made by Pyrochles against Guyon at v 5.3–7. See i 29.6*n*. **traitour**: as 46.6, a most severe charge made even worse by adding **miscreaunt**: misbeliever; cf. 'Paynim' (10.2). **defast**: defamed, discredited.

Stanza 32

5 seuen fold shield: see v 6.3*n*. **6 stownd**: attack. **9 groueling**: face down.

Stanza 33

1–2 griefe | And wrath: see vi 1.6–7*n*. **3 Mahoune**: Mohammed; see 30.4*n*. **thiefe**: a general term of reproach (*OED* 2), though it may be taken as an epithet of his god. **4 aby**: pay for, as 28.8. **5 hurling**: see v 7.5*n*. **6–7** The stroke at 31.3, delivered now by the concupiscible Cymochles, has greater effect on Arthur because of his love for Gloriana, the *psychomachia* being his as well as Guyon's. From this point all fight on foot.

34

Now was the Prince in daungerous distresse,
  Wanting his sword, when he on foot should fight:
His single speare could doe him small redresse,
  Against two foes of so exceeding might,
  The least of which was match for any knight.
And now the other, whom he earst did daunt,
  Had reard him selfe againe to cruel fight,
  Three times more furious, and more puissaunt,
Vnmindfull of his wound, of his fate ignoraunt.

35

So both attonce him charge on either syde,
  With hideous strokes, and importable powre,
That forced him his ground to trauerse wyde,
  And wisely watch to ward that deadly stowre:
  For in his shield, as thicke as stormie showre,
Their strokes did raine, yet did he neuer quaile,
  Ne backward shrinke, but as a stedfast towre,
  Whom foe with double battry doth assaile,
Them on her bulwarke beares, and bids them nought auaile.

36

So stoutly he withstood their strong assay,
  Till that at last, when he aduantage spyde,
His poynant speare he thrust with puissant sway
  At proud *Cymochles*, whiles his shield was wyde,
  That through his thigh the mortall steele did gryde:
He swaruing with the force, within his flesh
  Did breake the launce, and let the head abyde:
  Out of the wound the redblood flowed fresh,
That vnderneath his feet soone made a purple plesh.

37

Horribly then he gan to rage, and rayle,
  Cursing his Gods, and him selfe damning deepe:
Als when his brother saw the redblood rayle
  Adowne so fast and all his armour steepe,
  For very felnesse lowd he gan to weepe,
And said, Caytiue, cursse on thy cruell hond,
  That twise hath spedd; yet shall it not thee keepe
  From the third brunt of this my fatall brond:
Lo where the dreadfull Death behynd thy backe doth stond.

38

With that he strooke, and thother strooke withall,
  That nothing seemd mote beare so monstrous might:
The one vpon his couered shield did fall,
  And glauncing downe would not his owner byte:
  But th'other did vpon his troncheon smyte,
Which hewing quite a sunder, further way
  It made, and on his hacqueton did lyte,
  The which diuiding with importune sway,
It seizd in his right side, and there the dint did stay.

39

Wyde was the wound, and a large lukewarme flood,
  Red as the Rose, thence gushed grieuously,
That when the Paynym spyde the streaming blood,
  Gaue him great hart, and hope of victory.
  On thother side, in huge perplexity,
The Prince now stood, hauing his weapon broke;
  Nought could he hurt, but still at warde did ly:
  Yet with his troncheon he so rudely stroke
Cymochles twise, that twise him forst his foot reuoke.

Stanza 34
1–4 In contrast to Guyon who also fought on foot but had a sword and fought only Pyrochles at v 4. **single speare**: i.e. spear alone. **redresse**: aid. **6 daunt**: subdue. **9 ignoraunt**: ignoring, not knowing or caring.

Stanza 35
2 **importable**: unbearable. **3** . . . to shift his ground, in order to dodge without retreating. **4 stowre**: assault. **7–9** Arthur demonstrates how the castle of Alma resists the assault of the senses on its bulwarks at xi 7–14. **double battry**: i.e. two battering rams; possibly two cannon. **bids**: allows?

Stanza 36
1 **assay**: attack; also testing. **3–5 poynant**: piercing. **sway**: force. **wyde**: not close to his body, or to one side. It is fitting that the lustful Cymochles should himself cause the head of the lance to be embedded in his own thigh. **proud**: suggests lascivious; yet cf. 11.3, 22.9. **gryde**: pierce (E.K. on *SC Feb.* 4). **9 plesh**: pool.

Stanza 37
3 **rayle**: flow. The different sense allows the duplication of the rhyme. **5 felnesse**: fury. **7 spedd**: attained its purpose.

8 third brunt: presumably, the first blow was delivered with his own sword against Guyon at v 6, the second with Arthur's sword against Arthur himself.

Stanza 38
1 **withall**: as well; at the same time. **3–4 couered shield**: repeated from 17.7 to note the contrast with I viii 19 when Orgoglio's stroke loosens the veil by chance and he is defeated by its supernatural light. Again the shield saves Arthur but, since it remains couered, he must continue to fight. **5 troncheon**: the broken spear shaft. **7 hacqueton**: a jacket worn under the armour. **8–9** Cymochles fulfils Pyrochles's boast at 22.4–5. **importune sway**: grievous, violent force. **seizd**: penetrated. Arthur's **right side** is wounded because it is not protected by his shield but also because traditionally the crucified Christ is wounded on the right (heart) side, an analogy supported by the graphic imagery in the next stanza.

Stanza 39
5 **perplexity**: distress. **7 at warde**: on guard; a defensive posture. **9 reuoke**: withdraw.

40

Whom when the Palmer saw in such distresse,
  Sir *Guyons* sword he lightly to him raught,
  And said, Fayre Sonne, great god thy right hand blesse,
  To vse that sword so well, as he it ought.
  Glad was the knight, and with fresh courage fraught,
  When as againe he armed felt his hond;
  Then like a Lyon, which hath long time saught
  His robbed whelpes and at the last them fond
Emongst the shepeheard swaynes, then wexeth wood and
                                              (yond.

41

So fierce he laid about him, and dealt blowes
  On either side, that neither mayle could hold,
  Ne shield defend the thunder of his throwes:
  Now to *Pyrrhochles* many strokes he told;
  Eft to *Cymochles* twise so many fold:
  Then backe againe turning his busie hond,
  Them both atonce compeld with courage bold,
  To yield wide way to his hart-thrilling brond;
And though they both stood stiffe, yet could not both
                                              (withstond.

42

As saluage Bull, whom two fierce mastiues bayt,
  When rancour doth with rage him once engore,
  Forgets with wary warde them to awayt,
  But with his dreadfull hornes them driues afore,
  Or flings aloft or treades downe in the flore,
  Breathing out wrath, and bellowing disdaine,
  That all the forest quakes to heare him rore:
  So rag'd Prince *Arthur* twixt his foemen twaine,
That neither could his mightie puissaunce sustaine.

43

But euer at *Pyrrhochles* when he smitt,
  Who *Guyons* shield cast euer him before,
  Whereon the Faery Queenes pourtract was writt,
  His hand relented, and the stroke forbore,
  And his deare hart the picture gan adore,
  Which oft the Paynim sau'd from deadly stowre.
  But him henceforth the same can saue no more;
  For now arriued is his fatall howre,
That no'te auoyded be by earthly skill or powre.

44

For when *Cymochles* saw the fowle reproch,
  Which them appeached, prickt with guiltie shame,
  And inward griefe, he fiercely gan approch,
  Resolu'd to put away that loathly blame,
  Or dye with honour and desert of fame;
  And on the haubergh stroke the Prince so sore,
  That quite disparted all the linked frame,
  And pierced to the skin, but bit not thore,
Yet made him twise to reele, that neuer moou'd afore.

45

Whereat renfierst with wrath and sharp regret,
  He stroke so hugely with his borrowd blade,
  That it empierst the Pagans burganet,
  And cleauing the hard steele, did deepe inuade
  Into his head, and cruell passage made
  Quite through his brayne. He tombling downe on ground,
  Breathd out his ghost, which to th'infernall shade
  Fast flying, there eternall torment found,
For all the sinnes, wherewith his lewd life did abound.

Stanza 40
The 'redemptive' stanza (see I viii 40*n*) as it marks the turning-point in the battle when the Palmer blesses Arthur and in God's name hands him Guyon's sword. **2 raught**: handed. **3** Cf. his blessing the Red Cross Knight: 'Fayre sonne, God giue you happy chaunce' (i 31.7), and to Guyon at 32.8. **4 well, as he it ought**: wisely as it ought *1596*. Whatever the reading, the essential point is that he gives him Guyon's sword. **7–9** A biblical simile to express God's wrath at 2 Sam. 17.8. **wood**: mad. **yond**: fierce, savage.

Stanza 41
3 throwes: thrusts, blows. **4 told**: counted. **5** Cymochles receives twice as many strokes as Pyrochles because he wounded Arthur twice; cf. 39.8–9. (Neither of Pyrochles's strokes wounds him.) **8 hart-thrilling**: heart-piercing.

Stanza 42
Alluding to the popular sport of bull-baiting, as at VI v 19 (see *n*); a variant of bear-baiting alluded to at xi 33.3–6 where again it applies to Arthur. **2** Rancour and rage **engore** him, provoking him to engore his enemies.

Stanza 43
3 See i 28.7–8, v 11.7–8. **writt**: drawn. **5 deare**: loving. **adore** suggests the sacred nature of the royal portrait in

Elizabethan England; cf. ii 41.8, and see Strong 1963:33–41. **6 deadly stowre**: death. **9 no'te**: may not.

Stanza 44
Pyrochles's battle with Arthur is interrupted so that he may be overcome by his own irascibility provoked by his brother's death. Arthur's failure to strike Guyon's shield because it bears his love's image leads to his wounding by the concupiscible Cymochles. **2 appeached**: brought as a charge against them. Defeat would dishonour them, as it did Guyon at 14.7–9. **6 haubergh**: chain-mail that covers the neck. **8 not thore**: i.e. not through; hence only a token wound. no more *1596*. **9 twise**: as 39.9, the prelude to a third and final effort. Cymochles has retreated twice and now delivers the stroke that results in his own death.

Stanza 45
1 renfierst: re-enforced; rendered more fierce. **regret**: pain; sorrow. **3 burganet**: helmet; elsewhere in the poem only by the lustful Timias. **6 through**: completing Cymochles's blow that 'bit not thore' (44.8). **7–9** A classical motif used, e.g. in the death of Turnus at *Aen*. 12.951–52, though the soul suffering **eternall torment** provides a Christian perspective.

46

Which when his german saw, the stony feare,
    Ran to his hart, and all his sence dismayd,
    Ne thenceforth life ne corage did appeare,
    But as a man, whom hellish feendes haue frayd,
    Long trembling still he stoode: at last thus sayd,
    Traytour what hast thou doen? how euer may
    Thy cursed hand so cruelly haue swayd
    Against that knight: Harrow and well away,
After so wicked deede why liu'st thou lenger day?

47

With that all desperate as loathing light,   *(Reason'!)*
    And with reuenge desyring soone to dye,
    Assembling all his force and vtmost might,
    With his owne swerd he fierce at him did flye,
    And strooke, and foynd, and lasht outrageously,
    Withouten reason or regard. Well knew
    The Prince, with pacience and sufferaunce sly
    So hasty heat soone cooled to subdew:
Tho when this breathlesse woxe, that batteil gan renew.

48

As when a windy tempest bloweth hye,
    That nothing may withstand his stormy stowre,
    The clowdes, as thinges affrayd, before him flye;
    But all so soone as his outrageous powre
    Is layd, they fiercely then begin to showre,
    And as in scorne of his spent stormy spight,
    Now all attonce their malice forth do poure;
    So did Sir *Guyon* beare himselfe in fight,
And suffred rash *Pyrrhochles* waste his ydle might.

49

At last when as the Sarazin perceiu'd,
    How that straunge sword refusd, to serue his neede,
    But when he stroke most strong, the dint deceiu'd,
    He flong it from him, and deuoyd of dreed,

Vpon him lightly leaping without heed,
    Twixt his two mighty armes engrasped fast,
    Thinking to ouerthrowe and downe him tred:
    But him in strength and skill the Prince surpast,
And through his nimble sleight did vnder him down cast.

50

Nought booted it the Paynim then to striue;
    For as a Bittur in the Eagles clawe,
    That may not hope by flight to scape aliue,
    Still waytes for death with dread and trembling aw;
    So he now subiect to the victours law,
    Did not once moue, nor vpward cast his eye,
    For vile disdaine and rancour, which did gnaw
    His hart in twaine with sad melancholy,
As one that loathed life, and yet despysd to dye.

51

But full of princely bounty and great mind,
    The Conquerour nought cared him to slay,
    But casting wronges and all reuenge behind,
    More glory thought to giue life, then decay,
    And sayd, Paynim, this is thy dismall day;
    Yet if thou wilt renounce thy miscreaunce,
    And my trew liegeman yield thy selfe for ay,
    Life will I graunt thee for thy valiaunce,
And all thy wronges will wipe out of my souenaunce.

52

Foole (sayd the Pagan) I thy gift defye,
    But vse thy fortune, as it doth befall,
    And say, that I not ouercome doe dye,
    But in despight of life, for death doe call.
    Wroth was the Prince, and sory yet withall,
    That he so wilfully refused grace;
    Yet sith his fate so cruelly did fall,
    His shining Helmet he gan soone vnlace,
And left his headlesse body bleeding all the place.

Stanza 46
1 german: full brother. **4 frayd**: terrified. **7 swayd**: swung.
8 Harrow and well away: Atin's cry at vi 43.6. **9 lenger
day**: i.e. a day longer; or longer life.

Stanza 47
4 his owne: Arthur's. **5 foynd**: thrust. **7 sufferaunce sly**:
wise forbearance. **9 this**: Pyrochles. **that**: Arthur.

Stanza 48
2 stowre: tumult. **5 Is layd**: has subsided. **7 malice**: power
to harm. **8 Sir Guyon**: *1590, 1596*; corr. *1609*. The slip may
have occurred because Arthur fights on Guyon's behalf the
battle that Guyon had fought against the same foes: e.g. at
v 9.1, Pyrochles 'hewd, and lasht, and foynd, and thondred
blowes' as he does in the stanza above, while Guyon waited as
Arthur does here.

Stanza 49
2 straunge: belonging to another. **3 deceiu'd**: as Archimago
had warned him at 21.9. **5–9** Again there is a significant
reversal of Guyon's previous battle; cf. iv 8.6–9. **sleight**:
dexterity.

Stanza 50
2 The bittern was a symbol of baseness; noted Rowland
1978:10. **4 aw**: terror. **8 melancholy**: irascibility, anger.

Stanza 51
1 bounty: virtue, goodness. **great mind**: i.e. Aristotle's
high-mindedness (*Ethics* 4.3), seen in Guyon's 'great mag-
nanimity' at 23.9. **2 Conquerour**: see I xii 6.1*n*. **4 decay**:
death. **5 dismall day**: i.e. day of death; see vi 43.7*n*. **6 mis-
creaunce**: false faith; cf. 'miscreaunt' (31.6). **8 valiaunce**:
valour. **9 souenaunce**: memory.

Stanza 52
1–4 Foole: the biblical text cited at vii 63.6–9*n* confirms that
Pyrochles is 'worthie to be punished with hel fyre', as is his
brother at 45.7–9. Line 2 echoes Turnus's words before his death
(*Aen* 12.931–32), associating Arthur's **Wroth** with Aeneas's.
At the comparable moment, v 12.7–9, Pyrochles pleads not to
die. C. Burrow 1993:127–31 shows how S. imitates Virgil via
Tasso's imitation of Virgil in his account of Tancred killing
Argante in *Ger. Lib.* 19.26. **despight**: scorn. **8–9** The ges-
ture completes the action begun when Cymochles 'gan his
[Guyon's] helme vnlace' (17.2). **shining Helmet**: cf. vi 31.6.

53

By this Sir *Guyon* from his traunce awakt,
    Life hauing maystered her sencelesse foe;
    And looking vp, when as his shield he lakt,
    And sword saw not, he wexed wondrous woe:
    But when the Palmer, whom he long ygoe
    Had lost, he by him spyde, right glad he grew,
    And saide, Deare sir, whom wandring to and fro
    I long haue lackt, I ioy thy face to vew;
Firme is thy faith, whom daunger neuer fro me drew.

54

But read, what wicked hand hath robbed mee
    Of my good sword and shield? The Palmer glad,
    With so fresh hew vprysing him to see,
    Him answered; Fayre sonne, be no whit sad
    For want of weapons, they shall soone be had.
    So gan he to discourse the whole debate,
    Which that straunge knight for him sustained had,
    And those two Sarazins confounded late,
Whose carcases on ground were horribly prostrate.

55

Which when he heard, and saw the tokens trew,
    His hart with great affection was embayd,
    And to the Prince bowing reuerence dew,
    As to the Patrone of his life, thus sayd;
    My Lord, my liege, by whose most gratious ayd
    I liue this day, and see my foes subdewd,
    What may suffise, to be for meede repayd
    Of so great graces, as ye haue me shewd,
But to be euer bound

56

To whom the Infant thus, Fayre Sir, what need
    Good turnes be counted, as a seruile bond,
    To bind their dooers, to receiue their meed?
    Are not all knightes by oath bound, to withstond
    Oppressours powre by armes and puissant hond?
    Suffise, that I haue done my dew in place.
    So goodly purpose they together fond,
    Of kindnesse and of courteous aggrace;
The whiles false *Archimage* and *Atin* fled apace.

Stanza 53
1–2 By this: the phrase connects the slaying of Guyon's enemies to his restoration to life by Arthur. **4 woe**: woeful. **9** The Red Cross Knight pays much the same tribute to Una at I ix 17.4–5.

Stanza 54
1 read: declare. **4 Fayre sonne**: as he addresses Arthur at 40.3. **6 debate**: fight. **8 confounded**: defeated.

Stanza 55
2 embayd: suffused; literally, bathed. **4 the Patrone of his life**: i.e. protector, as Arthur at 26.9 had vowed to be. The Red Cross Knight also addresses Arthur as 'the Patrone of my life'

at I ix 17.6, and so does Alma at II xi 16.9. **5 my liege**: offering the submission just refused by Pyrochles. **9** Church 1758 suggests perceptively that Guyon's speech is unfinished because Arthur interrupts him.

Stanza 56
1–3 Arthur stresses grace as an absolute gift, which any reward would render a **seruile bond**, even as God's angels watch and protect us 'all for loue, and nothing for reward' (2.8). **Infant**: youth of noble birth (*OED* 3), from Span. *infante*, prince; it is applied to Arthur again at xi 25.7. On Arthur as 'child', see IV viii 44.8*n*. Cf. the Angel as 'the childe' (7.3). **6 dew**: duty. **in place**: here. **7 purpose**: conversation. **fond**: devised. **8 aggrace**: favour.

Cant. IX.

The house of Temperance, in which
doth sober Alma dwell,
Besiegd of many foes, whom straunger
knightes to flight compell.

1

OF all Gods workes, which doe this world adorne,
    There is no one more faire and excellent,
Then is mans body both for powre and forme,
Whiles it is kept in sober gouernment;
But none then it, more fowle and indecent,
Distempred through misrule and passions bace:
It growes a Monster, and incontinent
Doth loose his dignity and natiue grace.
Behold, who list, both one and other in this place.

2

After the Paynim brethren conquer'd were,
    The *Briton* Prince recou'ring his stolne sword,
And *Guyon* his lost shield, they both yfere
Forth passed on their way in fayre accord,
Till him the Prince with gentle court did bord;
Sir knight, mote I of you this court'sy read,
To weet why on your shield so goodly scord
Beare ye the picture of that Ladies head?
Full liuely is the semblaunt, though the substance dead.

3

Fayre Sir (sayd he) if in that picture dead
    Such life ye read, and vertue in vaine shew,
What mote ye weene, if the trew liuely-head
Of that most glorious visage ye did vew?
But yf the beauty of her mind ye knew,
That is her bounty, and imperiall powre,
Thousand times fairer then her mortal hew,
O how great wonder would your thoughts deuoure,
And infinite desire into your spirite poure.

4

Shee is the mighty Queene of *Faery*,
    Whose faire retraitt I in my shield doe beare;
Shee is the flowre of grace and chastity,
Throughout the world renowmed far and neare,
My liefe, my liege, my Soueraine, my deare,
Whose glory shineth as the morning starre,
And with her light the earth enlumines cleare;
Far reach her mercies, and her praises farre,
As well in state of peace, as puissaunce in warre.

Book II Canto ix

Argument

2 sober: a quality of moderate or temperate behaviour, shared also by the Palmer at i 7.7 and Medina at ii 14.5.

Stanza 1

In the previous canto, readers are asked, in effect, to **Behold** God's care over 'all his workes' (viii 1.7) in defending Guyon's body through the intercession of the Angel, the Palmer, and Arthur; now they are asked to behold temperance's care of the body, the most excellent **Of all God's workes**. The castle of Alma displays 'The wondrous workmanship of Gods owne mould' (I x 42.6) in showing how 'God hath tempered the bodie together' (1 Cor. 12.24). See Farmer 1993:81–82. **3 powre and forme**: the two divisions of the house of temperance, its structure (21–46) and its faculties (47–58). **4 sober gouernment**: temperate behaviour or conduct under the rule of 'sober Alma' (Arg.); cf. Guyon's 'goodly gouernaunce' (i 29.8). In the temperate body, 'the soule [Alma] doth rule the earthly masse, | And all the seruice of the bodie frame' (IV ix 2.6–7). **5 indecent**: uncomely; in the etymological sense, 'not fitting'. **6 Distempred**: disordered, and therefore disturbing the proper temper of the bodily humours. **7 incontinent**: immediately; being concupiscent. **8 loose**: also, 'do away with', 'violate'. When reason does not rule, the soul 'loseth hir dignite, and becommith ministre vnto the sences. . . . And so Man . . . is become equalle or rather infer- ior to brute beastes' (Elyot 1946:119–20). **9 one and other**: i.e. Alma's house of temperance described in this canto and Maleger described at 13–17, xi 5–47.

Stanza 2

3 yfere: together. **5 gentle court**: courteous regard; cf. 20.3. **6 read**: ?ask. On S.'s complex use of this word, see I i 21.6–9*n*. **7 scord**: painted or incised. **9 liuely**: lifelike, in contrast to the 'picture dead' (3.1). **semblaunt**: image.

Stanza 3

1 Fayre Sir: answering Arthur's address at viii 56.1. **2 vertue**: power. **3 liuely-head**: living original; literally, the living head rather than its picture. D.L. Miller 1988:145–46 notes the chiastic repetition in Guyon's response to Arthur's comment at 2.9. **6 bounty**: goodness, as 5.4, and IV proem 4.3, though not excluding 'Great guerdon' (6.7). **7 hew**: shape.

Stanza 4

2 retraitt: portrait, coined by S. to suggest that the image is twice redrawn: its beauty reflects Gloriana's beauty, which, in turn, reflects 'the beauty of her mind' (3.5), as D.L. Miller 1988:146 suggests. **5** The four terms are counterpoised with the stress on the personal rather than the political; cf. his address to Arthur at viii 55.5. **liefe**: beloved. **liege**: cf. viii 55.5. **6–7** As she is praised at I proem 4.3–4, and as Una appears at I xii 21.5–9 (and see *n*).

5

Thrise happy man, (said then the *Briton* knight)
    Whom gracious lott, and thy great valiaunce
    Haue made thee soldier of that Princesse bright,
    Which with her bounty and glad countenaunce
    Doth blesse her seruaunts, and them high aduaunce.
    How may straunge knight hope euer to aspire,
    By faithfull seruice, and meete amenaunce,
    Vnto such blisse? sufficient were that hire
For losse of thousand liues, to die at her desire.

6

Said *Guyon*, Noble Lord, what meed so great,
    Or grace of earthly Prince so soueraine,
    But by your wondrous worth and warlike feat
    Ye well may hope, and easely attaine?
    But were your will, her sold to entertaine,
    And numbred be mongst knights of *Maydenhed*,
    Great guerdon, well I wote, should you remaine,
    And in her fauor high bee reckoned,
As *Arthogall*, and *Sophy* now beene honored.

7

Certes (then said the Prince) I God auow,
    That sith I armes and knighthood first did plight,
    My whole desire hath beene, and yet is now,
    To serue that Queene with al my powre and might.
    Seuen times the Sunne with his lamp-burning light,
    Hath walkte about the world, and I no lesse,
    Sith of that Goddesse I haue sought the sight,
    Yet no where can her find: such happinesse
Heuen doth to me enuy, and fortune fauourlesse.

8

Fortune, the foe of famous cheuisaunce
    Seldome (said *Guyon*) yields to vertue aide,
    But in her way throwes mischiefe and mischaunce,
    Whereby her course is stopt, and passage staid.
    But you, faire Sir, be not herewith dismaid,
    But constant keepe the way, in which ye stand;
    Which were it not, that I am els delaid
    With hard adventure, which I haue in hand,
I labour would to guide you through al Fary land.

9

Gramercy Sir (said he) but mote I wote,
    What straunge aduenture doe ye now pursew?
    Perhaps my succour, or aduizement meete
    Mote stead you much your purpose to subdew.
    Then gan Sir *Guyon* all the story shew
    Of false *Acrasia*, and her wicked wiles,
    Which to auenge, the Palmer him forth drew
    From Faery court. So talked they, the whiles
They wasted had much way, and measurd many miles.

10

And now faire *Phoebus* gan decline in haste
    His weary wagon to the Westerne vale,
    Whenas they spide a goodly castle, plaste
    Foreby a riuer in a pleasaunt dale,
    Which choosing for that euenings hospitale,
    They thether marcht: but when they came in sight,
    And from their sweaty Coursers did auale,
    They found the gates fast barred long ere night,
And euery loup fast lockt, as fearing foes despight.

Stanza 5

2 valiaunce: valour; praised by Arthur in Pyrochles at viii 51.8.
4–5 In contrast to Philotime, whose suitors advance through
their own 'works and merits iust' (vii 49.9). **glad**: bright,
shining.   **7 meete amenaunce**: proper conduct. It marks
Arthur's bearing at viii 17.8.   **9 die**: not excluding the sexual
sense.

Stanza 6

5 I.e., if you should wish to be paid as her servant.   **6 knights
of Maydenhed**: see I vii 46.4–7 and *n*.   **7 remaine**: await.
9 Sophy, Gk σοφία, wisdom. Presumably the hero of a pro-
jected book, as **Arthogall** (or Artegall) is of Bk V. A holy Welsh
king of this name is recorded in Drayton 1931–41:4.482.

Stanza 7

5–6 Seuen times: i.e. seven years, the time that the castle of
Alma has been besieged; see 12.8–9 and *n*. Now hath *1596*
marks one full year, agreeing with 'twelue moneths' *1596*
at 38.9. Since Arthur rescues the Red Cross Knight after
searching for Gloriana for nine months (I ix 15.9), three
months have elapsed since then, according to the *1596* com-
putation, which is the time that Guyon has been searching for

Acrasia; see ii 44.1–4 and *n*. One, seven, and nine indicate
completed cycles of time.   **9 Heuen** and **enuy** (begrudge) are
monosyllabic.

Stanza 8

1–4 On **Fortune**, see iv 4.4–5*n*.   **cheuisaunce**: chivalric
enterprise or achievement; 'sometime of Chaucer used for
gaine: sometime of other for spoyle, or bootie, or enterprise,
and sometime for chiefdome' (E.K. on *SC May* 92).

Stanza 9

3 aduizement: counsel.   **4 stead**: help, i.e. stand you in good
stead.   **subdew**: attain; achieve (by effort).   **5–8** Cf. the
account given at ii 43.1–4.

Stanza 10

3–4 As distinguished from the castle of Medina 'Built on
a rocke adioyning to the seas' (ii 12.7).   **5 hospitale**: hostel.
7 Evidently Guyon has recovered not only his sword and shield
but also his horse, which he lost at ii 11.5–9. Since the horse is
commonly associated with the passions, one may infer, as the
capital of **Coursers** may suggest, that Guyon's temperate state
has been confirmed.   **auale**: dismount.   **9 loup**: loop-hole.

11

Which when they saw, they weened fowle reproch
  Was to them doen, their entraunce to forstall,
  Till that the Squire gan nigher to approch,
  And wind his horne vnder the castle wall,
  That with the noise it shooke; as it would fall.
  Eftsoones forth looked from the highest spire
  The watch, and lowd vnto the knights did call,
  To weete, what they so rudely did require.
Who gently answered, They entraunce did desire.

12

Fly fly, good knights, (said he) fly fast away
  If that your liues ye loue, as meete ye should;
  Fly fast, and saue your selues from neare decay,
  Here may ye not haue entraunce, though we would:
  We would and would againe, if that we could;
  But thousand enemies about vs raue,
  And with long siege vs in this castle hould:
  Seuen yeares this wize they vs besieged haue,
And many good knights slaine, that haue vs sought to saue.

13

Thus as he spoke, loe with outragious cry
  A thousand villeins rownd about them swarmd
  Out of the rockes and caues adioyning nye,
  Vile caitiue wretches, ragged, rude, deformd,
  All threatning death, all in straunge manner armd,
  Some with vnweldy clubs, some with long speares,
  Some rusty knifes, some staues in fier warmd.
  Sterne was their looke, like wild amazed steares,
Staring with hollow eies, and stiffe vpstanding heares.

14

Fiersly at first those knights they did assayle,
  And droue them to recoile: but when againe
  They gaue fresh charge, their forces gan to fayle,
  Vnhable their encounter to sustaine;

For with such puissaunce and impetuous maine
  Those Champions broke on them, that forst them fly,
  Like scattered Sheepe, whenas the Shepherds swaine
  A Lyon and a Tigre doth espye,
With greedy pace forth rushing from the forest nye.

15

A while they fled, but soone retournd againe
  With greater fury, then before was fownd;
  And euermore their cruell Captaine
  Sought with his raskall routs t'enclose them rownd,
  And ouerronne to tread them to the grownd.
  But soone the knights with their bright-burning blades
  Broke their rude troupes, and orders did confownd,
  Hewing and slashing at their idle shades;
For though they bodies seem, yet substaunce from them fades.

16

As when a swarme of Gnats at euentide
  Out of the fennes of Allan doe arise,
  Their murmuring small trompetts sownden wide,
  Whiles in the aire their clustring army flies,
  That as a cloud doth seeme to dim the skies;
  Ne man nor beast may rest, or take repast,
  For their sharpe wounds, and noyous iniuries,
  Till the fierce Northerne wind with blustring blast
Doth blow them quite away, and in the *Ocean* cast.

17

Thus when they had that troublous rout disperst,
  Vnto the castle gate they come againe,
  And entraunce crau'd, which was denied erst.
  Now when report of that their perlous paine,
  And combrous conflict, which they did sustaine,
  Came to the Ladies eare, which there did dwell,
  Shee forth issewed with a goodly traine
  Of Squires and Ladies equipaged well,
And entertained them right fairely, as befell.

Stanza 11
5 The power of the Squire's horn is described at I viii 4.
9 gently: courteously.

Stanza 12
3 neare decay: approaching death. **6 raue**: rage. **8–9 Seuen** may allude to the traditional seven ages of human life (see Chew 1962:163–69; J. Burrow 1986:36–54), or of the world. The same number notes the length of confinement of Amoret and Florimell; see III xi 10.8*n*. On seven as the ruling number of human life, see Macrobius 1952:1.6.62.

Stanza 13
2 villeins: peasants or serfs, such as S. encountered in Ireland, as M. West 1988:661–62 notes; or the rabble representing 'misrule and passions bace' (1.6) that attacks Ruggiero on his way to the realm of Logistilla (Ariosto, *Orl. Fur*. 6.60–67). Jonson 1995 glosses: 'By these sorte I conceive to be ment Errors and vanities which beseidge Alma that is our reason'. See 'villeins' in the *SEnc*. **7 warmd**: and therefore hardened.

Stanza 14
5 maine: force.

Stanza 15
3 Captaine: the spelling stresses Maleger's role as head of the troops that assault the head of the temperate body. Capitaine *1609* better serves the metre; cf. xi 14.6. **4 raskall routs**: base rabble. In Bk I, Arthur's shield overthrows 'the raskall routes' (vii 35.5); now he is seen **Hewing and slashing** at shades that cannot be injured. Virgil saves Aeneas from this frustration; see *Aen*. 6.290–94. **7 orders**: ranks. **8 idle**: empty.

Stanza 16
2 the fennes of Allan: the great bog close to New Abbey, which S. leased in 1582. **7 noyous**: annoying. Gnats 'do more annoy the naked rebels . . . and do more sharply wound them than all their enemies' swords or spears' (*View* 52). **9** The line predicts Arthur's defeat of Maleger in 'a standing lake' at xi 46.6.

Stanza 17
4 paine: pains, efforts. **5 combrous**: harassing; suggested by the gnats: cf. the 'cloud of cumbrous gnattes' at I i 23.5. **8 equipaged**: arrayed; or being furnished with the **goodly traine**. **9 entertained**: received. **as befell**: as was fitting.

18

Alma she called was, a virgin bright;
    That had not yet felt *Cupides* wanton rage,
    Yet was shee wooed of many a gentle knight,
    And many a Lord of noble parentage,
    That sought with her to lincke in marriage:
    For shee was faire, as faire mote euer bee,
    And in the flowre now of her freshest age;
    Yet full of grace and goodly modestee,
That euen heuen reioyced her sweete face to see.

19

In robe of lilly white she was arayd,
    That from her shoulder to her heele downe raught,
    The traine whereof loose far behind her strayd,
    Braunched with gold and perle, most richly wrought,
    And borne of two faire Damsels, which were taught
    That seruice well. Her yellow golden heare
    Was trimly wouen, and in tresses wrought,
    Ne other tire she on her head did weare,
But crowned with a garland of sweete Rosiere.

20

Goodly shee entertaind those noble knights,
    And brought them vp into her castle hall;
    Where gentle court and gracious delight
    Shee to them made, with mildnesse virginall,

    Shewing her selfe both wise and liberall:
    Then when they rested had a season dew,
    They her besought of fauour speciall,
    Of that faire Castle to affoord them vew;
Shee graunted, and them leading forth, the same did shew.

21

First she them led vp to the Castle wall,
    That was so high, as foe might not it clime,
    And all so faire, and fensible withall,
    Not built of bricke, ne yet of stone and lime,
    But of thing like to that *AEgyptian* slime,
    Whereof king *Nine* whilome built *Babell* towre,
    But O great pitty, that no lenger time
    So goodly workemanship should not endure:
Soone it must turne to earth; no earthly thing is sure.

22

The frame thereof seemd partly circulare,
    And part triangulare, O worke diuine;
    Those two the first and last proportions are,
    The one imperfect, mortall, foeminine;
    Th'other immortall, perfect, masculine;
    And twixt them both a quadrate was the base,
    Proportioned equally by seuen and nine;
    Nine was the circle sett in heauens place,
All which compacted made a goodly diapase.

Stanza 18

1 Alma: 'the soule of man' (Florio 1598), as xi 1.4. More specifically, the rational soul or mind, which 'doth rule the earthly masse, | And all the seruice of the bodie frame' (IV ix 2.6–7), making the temperate body 'the forte of reason' (xi 1.3). More precisely, she includes the three souls; on their function, see W.R. Davis 1981:121–27, and 22*n* below. Cf. Langland's castle, '*caro*', which means 'man with a soule', for the flesh contains the Lady *Anima* 'that lyf is ynempned' (*Piers Plowman* 9.48–53). The term also signifies 'a mayden' (T. Cooper 1565), from Heb. *almah*. Lat. *alma* means 'gracious'; hence Alma is 'full of grace' (18.8); also 'that [which] norisheth; fayre; beautifull' (Cooper), as 18.6–7. See 'Alma, castle of' and 'soul' in the *SEnc*. On its relation to the house of Mammon, see 33.1–4*n*, Nohrnberg 1976:343–51, and Davis 131–38. As a hermetic word-emblem, see Szőnyi 1984:364–84. The literary tradition of the metaphor of the body is examined by Barkan 1975:116–74. Helkiah Crooke structures his anatomical textbook *Microcosmographia* (1615) on the description of the castle of Alma, as Sawday 1995:167–68 notes. Since the soul is incorporeal, Alma herself is described as little as possible.

Stanza 19

As those 'araied in long white robes' before God's throne in Rev. 7.9, 13, 'in signe of puritie' (Geneva gloss), to denote their virginity, as does Una's robe 'All lilly white' (I xii 22.7) and Belphœbe's 'Camus' (II iii 26.4). **4 Braunched**: embroidered, referring to branch-like figured patterns. **5** Presumably the irascible and concupiscible faculties which, properly governed, attend the temperate soul. **6–7** Cf. Medina's braided golden locks at ii 15.7–9. **8 tire**: head-dress. **9 Rosiere**:

roses, or rose bush, sacred to Venus; significantly, in a bush and not gathered, in contrast to Acrasia who lies on a bed of roses at xii 77.1. It is linked by Hume 1984:124 to 'the rose of the field' (Song Sol. 2.1) and therefore to the sweet-smelling wild rose.

Stanza 20

4 mildnesse virginall: i.e. graciousness befitting a virgin. **5 liberall**: free in bestowing bounty (*OED* 2); cf. Mercy 'both gratious, and eke liberall' (I x 34.5).

Stanza 21

1–2 The height suggests the body's erect, unfallen state. **3 fensible**: able to be defended. **4–6 Babell towre** was built of brick and slime: Gen. 11.3. **slime** because the body was made *de limo terrae* (Gen. 2.7 Vulg.); see I vii 9.8*n*. **AEgyptian** because Babylon was a name for Cairo. On 'the antique *Babel*, Empresse of the East', see *Comm Sonn* 4. **Nine**: Ninus, the eponymous founder of Nineveh (see I v 48.3–4*n*), a parody of the nine from which the temperate body is proportioned at 22.8. S. links him with Nimrod, 'the beginning of [whose] kingdome was Babél' (Gen. 10.10); see I v 48.1–2*n*. **9** A frequent motif in the poem; see I viii 44.9*n*.

Stanza 22

Glossing of this stanza – the most extensively glossed in the poem – began with William Austin in 1636 (see C. Camden 1943) and notably by Kenelm Digby's lengthy *Observations* in 1643/44 (rpt *Var* 2.472–78), which Riddell and Stewart 1995:101–06 argue was based partly on Jonson's glosses. Its number, 22, is associated with the soul (A. Fowler 1964:286), or with moderation or temperance (J.L. Mills 1967, Hageman

23

Therein two gates were placed seemly well:
  The one before, by which all in did pas,
  Did th'other far in workmanship excell;
  For not of wood, nor of enduring bras,
  But of more worthy substance fram'd it was;
  Doubly disparted, it did locke and close,
  That when it locked, none might thorough pas,
  And when it opened, no man might it close,
Still open to their friendes, and closed to their foes.

24

Of hewen stone the porch was fayrely wrought,
  Stone more of valew, and more smooth and fine,
  Then Iett or Marble far from Ireland brought;
  Ouer the which was cast a wandring vine,

Enchaced with a wanton yuie twine.
  And ouer it a fayre Portcullis hong,
  Which to the gate directly did incline,
  With comely compasse, and compacture strong,
Nether vnseemly short, nor yet exceeding long.

25

Within the Barbican a Porter sate,
  Day and night duely keeping watch and ward,
  Nor wight, nor word mote passe out of the gate,
  But in good order, and with dew regard;
  Vtterers of secrets he from thence debard,
  Bablers of folly, and blazers of cryme.
  His larumbell might lowd and wyde be hard,
  When cause requyrd, but neuer out of time;
Early and late it rong, at euening and at prime.

1971). Sadowski 2000:122 links it to the φ ratio of the stanza-total of the canto.

By one reading, **circulare** refers to the head, the **quadrate** to the main body, and **triangulare** to the lower body with legs astride. As a primary figure (**Proportioned**) without beginning or end, the circle is **perfect**, and **immortall** as it refers to God and eternity. Being less simple and stable, the triangle is **imperfect**, and, by contrast, **mortall**. As creation imposes form upon matter, the one is **masculine** and the other **fœminine** (the spelling suggests that the feminine is 'foe to man'). Their union by the quadrate **twixt them both** indicates the castle's androgynous state. The circle and triangle also refer to spirit and matter, or soul and body, with the **quadrate** (a square area, applied to a building) being the **base** or trunk of the body. These three figures refer to the three human souls: the circle to the rational soul, the quadrate to the sensible, and the triangle to the vegetable. Further, the quadrate is associated with the four elements and the four humours that connect the body to the soul, indicating that the **frame** refers also to the body's temperament, i.e. the proper tempering of its elements, which constitutes its state of temperance. This notion is expressed by Puttenham, who refers to the constant-minded man as '*hominem quadratum*, a square man' (1936:100). Clifford-Amos 1999:258–71 finds a topographical reference to Castle Quadrate in Plymouth, which is described by William Browne in *Britannia's Pastorals* 1.5.85–110. On the circle, square, and triangle as an emblem of the universe, see Heninger 1974:159.

For **seuen** as the number of the body, see 12.8–9*n*. It is also the number of the planets, each governing a part of the body. **Nine** is the number of mind or soul because there are nine spheres in the Ptolemaic system and nine orders of angels which govern the soul. Seven and nine have architectural significance as female and male proportions in Vitruvius, *De Arch.* 4.1.7–8. Their product, the number **Proportioned equally by seuen and nine**, is 63, the 'Grand Climacteric' of bodily life; on the term, see Hamilton 1996:452*n*3. The quadrate 4 is connected with 7 and 9 because its square is their sum.

The **circle sett in heauens place** is the ninth sphere of the fixed stars which encloses the universe. The body and soul are held in harmony even as the octave 8 is the arithmetic mean between 7 and 9. Being so **compacted**, there is **a goodly diapase** or the complete harmony of the musical octave in which, as Røstvig 1994:16 notes, the last note returns to the first, but in a higher register. Bryskett 1970:203–05 records his conversation with S. on the relation between the body and soul, which J.L. Mills 1973:183–84 expresses as a diagram: the circle encloses a **quadrate** (quadrangle, the usual shape of a castle) divided into two triangles. The triangles represent the vegetative soul and part of the sensitive soul, the circle expresses the perfection of the *mens*, or spiritual faculty of the mind, and the quadrate is to be taken as the four virtues and the square of reason. The most complete account of the stanza remains A. Fowler 1964:260–89. See also Sadowski 122–27.

Stanza 23

2–3 The one before is the mouth; **th'other** is the anus, the 'backgate' at 32.7. **6 Doubly disparted**: referring to the upper and lower jaws. **7–9** Cf. Ps. 141.3: 'Set a watche, O Lord, before my mouth, and kepe the dore of my lippes'. At xi 6.6, this gate is attacked by more than half of Maleger's forces.

Stanza 24

The **porch** is the jaw or chin; the **vine**, the beard; the **yuie twine**, the moustache; and the **Portcullis** (a grating that closes the gateway of a castle), the nose, whose length observes the golden mean (not unreasonably resembling S.'s own in the Pembroke College portrait). **1 fayrely**: beautifully. **3 Iett**: black marble. Todd 1805 notes that there was a red and grey marble quarry near Kilcolman Castle. **far from Ireland** associates Alma's castle with English country houses. **5 Enchaced**: adorned. **wanton**: luxuriant in growth. **8 compasse**: proportion. **compacture**: compact structure.

Stanza 25

The **Barbican** is a castle's outer defences; here, the oral cavity. The **Porter** in charge of the **larumbell** is the tongue. **5** A witty personal reference to S.'s career as a keeper of state secrets. **6 blazers**: proclaimers. **8 out of time**: i.e. at an inappropriate time, agreeing with the role of temperance to keep time, as Nohrnberg 1976:307 notes.

26

And rownd about the porch on euery syde
   Twise sixteene warders satt, all armed bright,
   In glistring steele, and strongly fortifyde:
   Tall yeomen seemed they, and of great might,
   And were enraunged ready, still for fight.
   By them as *Alma* passed with her guestes,
   They did obeysaunce, as beseemed right,
   And then againe retourned to their restes:
The Porter eke to her did lout with humble gestes.

27

Thence she them brought into a stately Hall,
   Wherein were many tables fayre dispred,
   And ready dight with drapets festiuall,
   Against the viaundes should be ministred.
   At th'upper end there sate, yclad in red
   Downe to the ground, a comely personage,
   That in his hand a white rod menaged,
   He Steward was, hight *Diet*; rype of age,
And in demeanure sober, and in counsell sage.

28

And through the Hall there walked to and fro
   A iolly yeoman, Marshall of the same,
   Whose name was *Appetite*; he did bestow
   Both guestes and meate, when euer in they came,

And knew them how to order without blame,
   As him the Steward badd. They both attone
   Did dewty to their Lady, as became;
   Who passing by, forth ledd her guestes anone
Into the kitchin rowme, ne spard for nicenesse none.

29

It was a vaut ybuilt for great dispence,
   With many raunges reard along the wall;
   And one great chimney, whose long tonnell thence,
   The smoke forth threw. And in the midst of all
   There placed was a caudron wide and tall,
   Vpon a mightie fornace, burning whott,
   More whott, then *Aetn'*, or flaming *Mongiball*:
   For day and night it brent, ne ceased not,
So long as any thing it in the caudron gott.

30

But to delay the heat, least by mischaunce
   It might breake out, and set the whole on fyre,
   There added was by goodly ordinaunce,
   An huge great payre of bellowes, which did styre
   Continually, and cooling breath inspyre.
   About the Caudron many Cookes accoyld,
   With hookes and ladles, as need did requyre;
   The whyles the viaundes in the vessell boyld
They did about their businesse sweat, and sorely toyld.

Stanza 26

1–5 A witty play on the **porch** as a double-pillared colonnade used as a place of debate (*OED* 3). **warders**: the teeth. **Twise sixteene**: the one factual detail in this allegorical pageant, to prepare for the teeth coming forward to bow. Jonson notes that 'it was excellently said of that Philosopher [Plutarch]; that there was a Wall, or Parapet of teeth set in our mouth, to restraine the petulancy of our words' (1925–52:8.573). **Tall**: comely; bold, valiant. 7 **as beseemed right**: as was rightly fitting. 9 **lout**: obeisance. **gestes**: gestures.

Stanza 27

1–4 **a stately Hall**: the throat. **dispred**: spread out. **drapets**: cloths. **Against**: for the time when. 5–9 The **Steward** is described at length because he was the chief officer responsible for the court's well-being. Also because S. may wittily praise his own name, which derives from the office of the 'spencer' or 'steward', as W. Camden 1984:123 records, an allusion supported by the description of the kitchen 'ybuilt for great dispence' (29.1) and the reference to S. as 'this rare dispenser of your [the muses'] graces' in *CV* 5.3, as D.L. Miller 1988:176 notes. (In 1598 Richard Carey referred to S. as *Muses despencier*, cited Cummings 1971:95.) As he represents the back of the throat, the Steward is **yclad in red**, his colour dramatically set off by his **white rod**, the uvula, here the symbol of royal power; see III iii 49.6–9*n*. He is in charge of the stew or cauldron (*OED* 1), i.e. the stomach; and he is named **Diet** as he personifies the temperate course of life (*OED* 1). **menaged**: wielded. Since Milton's 'sage and serious Poet' is here on holiday, **sage** may allude to the herb, *Salvia officinalis*, much valued in Elizabethan cooking; called 'wholsome' in *Muiopotmos* 187.

Stanza 28

2 **yeoman**: an assistant to an official. 3 **bestow**: place. 4 **meate**: i.e. food in general. 5 **order**: arrange. 6 **attone**: together. 7 **their Lady**: for the soul maintains the nutritive part of the body, functioning as the vegetative soul, which has its seat in the stomach. 8 **anone**: straightway. 9 **nicenesse**: fastidiousness.

Stanza 29

In the ensuing Cook's tour from kitchen to parlor to turret, Guyon and Arthur visit the three vital organs: the stomach, which is the seat of the passions; the heart, of the affections; and the brain, of reason. These are linked with the natural, animal, and vital spirits; or with the three souls: vegetable, sensible, and rational (see 22*n*) in the body's three parts. Except for the humorous digression in 32, the sexual organs are not included because Alma 'had not yet felt *Cupides* wanton rage' (18.2). As 'the temple of the holie Gost' (1 Cor. 6.19), the human body is epicene, containing only what both sexes have in common. On the Renaissance physiology of digestion, see Robin 1911:76–106. 1 **vaut**: vault. **dispence**: expenditure, consumption. 3 **chimney**: fireplace and flue; also a psychological term for 'a vent for humour' or 'fumosities' of the body (*OED* 6b). 7 **Mongiball**: another name for Aetna.

Stanza 30

1 **delay**: allay, temper, as in du Bartas 1979:1.6.693–94: 'the Lungs, whose motions light, | Our inward heat doo temper day and night'. 3 **ordinaunce**: planning, management. 4 **styre**: stir, move to and fro. 5 **inspyre**: breathe in. 6 **accoyld**: gathered together.

31

The maister Cooke was cald *Concoction*,
  A carefull man, and full of comely guyse:
  The kitchin clerke, that hight *Digestion*,
  Did order all th'Achates in seemely wise,
  And set them forth, as well he could deuise.
  The rest had seuerall offices assynd,
  Some to remoue the scum, as it did rise;
  Others to beare the same away did mynd;
And others it to vse according to his kynd.

32

But all the liquour, which was fowle and waste,
  Not good nor seruiceable elles for ought,
  They in another great rownd vessell plaste,
  Till by a conduit pipe it thence were brought:
  And all the rest, that noyous was, and nought,
  By secret wayes, that none might it espy,
  Was close conuaid, and to the backgate brought,
  That cleped was *Port Esquiline*, whereby
It was auoided quite, and throwne out priuily.

33

Which goodly order, and great workmans skill
  Whenas those knightes beheld, with rare delight,
  And gazing wonder they their mindes did fill;
  For neuer had they seene so straunge a sight.

Thence backe againe faire *Alma* led them right,
  And soone into a goodly Parlour brought,
  That was with royall arras richly dight,
  In which was nothing pourtrahed, nor wrought,
Not wrought, nor pourtrahed, but easie to be thought.

34

And in the midst thereof vpon the floure,
  A louely beuy of faire Ladies sate,
  Courted of many a iolly Paramoure,
  The which them did in modest wise amate,
  And eachone sought his Lady to aggrate:
  And eke emongst them litle *Cupid* playd
  His wanton sportes, being retourned late
  From his fierce warres, and hauing from him layd
His cruel bow, wherewith he thousands hath dismayd.

35

Diuerse delights they fownd them selues to please;
  Some song in sweet consort, some laught for ioy,
  Some plaid with strawes, some ydly satt at ease,
  But other some could not abide to toy,
  All pleasaunce was to them griefe and annoy:
  This fround, that faund, the third for shame did blush,
  Another seemed enuious, or coy,
  Another in her teeth did gnaw a rush:
But at these straungers presence euery one did hush.

Stanza 31

Renaissance physiology divided digestion into three stages: the first in which food is turned into chylus is called **Concoction**, who is the **maister Cooke**, from Lat. *con* + *coquere*, to boil or cook together; the second, in which the chylus is turned into blood and distributed to the body, is called **Digestion**, from Lat. *digerere*, to distribute; and the third is elimination treated in the next stanza. **2 guyse**: behaviour. **4 order**: arrange, as 28.5. **Achates**: provisions; used for organs that receive nourishment from the stomach. **6 seuerall offices**: particular duties. **7–8** Robin 1911:78, 82 notes that in concoction the liver produces a fermentation that escapes as yellow bile (choler) and is strained off from the blood to be lodged in the gall bladder.

Stanza 32

1–4 S. avoids naming the attendant – the Sewer who was in charge of tasting the liquor – in order to turn to more fundamental matters. **vessell**: the bladder. **conduit pipe**: the urinary canal (for the male, including the penis). **5 noyous**: noxious. **nought**: useless; bad in condition. **7 close**: covertly. **8 Port Esquiline**: a gate in ancient Rome, its anus as it gave passage to the city dump. It may have been suggested by the office of the Esquiller, one in charge of the scullery. Schoenfeldt 1999:62 concludes that the ejection of noxious material accomplished by the stomach is necessary to S.'s portrait of the temperate body. Cf. Schoenfeldt 2000:237–38. **9 auoided**: also excreted. **priuily**: with a pun on 'privy'.

Stanza 33

1–4 Countering Mammon's repeated claim (vii 19.6–7, etc.) that he would show Guyon **so straunge a sight**. Again

'th'Elfin knight with wonder all the way | Did feed his eyes, and fild his inner thought' (vii 24.3–4). Earlier, he descends deep into hell but here, having reached the bottom, he makes his way back through the stomach up to the heart. **6–9 goodly Parlour**: the privy chamber (as the Queen's private rooms), here the heart as the seat of the affections and the sensible soul; its **royall arras** (appropriately red) notes that Alma, the soul, resides here. The absence of elaborate mythological representations, usual in Elizabethan tapestries, indicates that it contains only what is **easie to be thought**, i.e. what is easily apprehended by the senses.

Stanza 34

3 iolly: amorous; also splendid, handsome, gay, lively, etc. **4 amate**: keep company. **5 aggrate**: please, gratify. **8–9** On the unarmed Cupid not in his 'wanton rage' (18.2), see I proem 3.5–7*n*.

Stanza 35

Nine affections or moods are displayed emblematically: the four forward or concupiscible passions, earlier associated with Perissa, are shown together in groups; the five froward or irascible passions, earlier associated with Elissa, are seen alone. See ii 38.5–8*n*. Both are ordered in degrees of inwardness. Later both knights choose from the second group. **2 consort**: harmony; concert. **3 plaid with strawes**: possibly the game of jack-straws or pick-up-sticks. **5 pleasaunce**: pleasing behaviour. **6 faund**: cringed; not in servility but in refusing to be pleased. **7 enuious**: full of ill-will. **coy**: disdainful.

36

Soone as the gracious *Alma* came in place,
    They all attonce out of their seates arose,
    And to her homage made, with humble grace:
    Whom when the knights beheld, they gan dispose
    Themselues to court, and each a damzell chose:
    The Prince by chaunce did on a Lady light,
    That was right faire and fresh as morning rose,
    But somwhat sad, and solemne eke in sight,
As if some pensiue thought constraind her gentle spright.

37

In a long purple pall, whose skirt with gold,
    Was fretted all about, she was arayd;
    And in her hand a Poplar braunch did hold:
    To whom the prince in courteous maner sayd,
    Gentle Madame, why beene ye thus dismayd,
    And your faire beautie doe with sadnes spill?
    Liues any, that you hath thus ill apayd?
    Or doen you loue, or doen you lack your will?
What euer bee the cause, it sure beseemes you ill.

38

Fayre Sir, said she halfe in disdainefull wise,
    How is it, that this word in me ye blame,
    And in your selfe doe not the same aduise?
    Him ill beseemes, anothers fault to name,
    That may vnwares bee blotted with the same:
    Pensiue I yeeld I am, and sad in mind,
    Through great desire of glory and of fame;
    Ne ought I weene are ye therein behynd,
That haue three years sought one, yet no where can her find.

39

The Prince was inly moued at her speach,
    Well weeting trew, what she had rashly told,
    Yet with faire semblaunt sought to hyde the breach,
    Which chaunge of colour did perforce vnfold,
    Now seeming flaming whott, now stony cold.
    Tho turning soft aside, he did inquyre
    What wight she was, that Poplar braunch did hold:
    It answered was, her name was *Praysdesire*,
That by well doing sought to honour to aspyre.

40

The whyles, the *Faery* knight did entertayne
    Another Damsell of that gentle crew,
    That was right fayre, and modest of demayne,
    But that too oft she chaung'd her natiue hew:
    Straunge was her tyre, and all her garment blew,
    Close rownd about her tuckt with many a plight:
    Vpon her fist the bird, which shonneth vew
    And keepes in couerts close from liuing wight,
Did sitt, as yet ashamd, how rude *Pan* did her dight.

41

So long as *Guyon* with her commoned,
    Vnto the grownd she cast her modest eye,
    And euer and anone with rosy red
    The bashfull blood her snowy cheekes did dye,
    That her became, as polisht yuory,
    Which cunning Craftesman hand hath ouerlayd
    With fayre vermilion or pure Castory.
    Great wonder had the knight, to see the mayd
So straungely passioned, and to her gently said.

Stanza 36

1 gracious: full of grace; cf. 'natiue grace' (1.8). **8 sad, and solemne**: as the Red Cross Knight first appears 'too solemne sad' at I i 2.8, and Guyon 'Still [always] solemne sad' at II vi 37.5. **9 constraind**: distressed.

Stanza 37

1–3 purple and **gold** indicate her sovereignty (as I vii 16.3) among Arthur's passions. In Ripa 1603:202, *Honore* is dressed in purple; noted Brooks-Davies 1977:167. Her emblem, the **Poplar braunch**, is Hercules's tree; see v 31.1–5*n*. Appropriate to Arthur's desire for Gloriana, its bicolour leaves, black and white, were Elizabeth's personal colours; see I i 4*n*. It associates her with 'great desire of glory and of fame' (38.7); cf. *LR* 32–33: 'In that Faery Queene I meane glory in my generall intention'. **fretted**: adorned. **6 spill**: spoil. **7 ill apayd**: requited.

Stanza 38

2 this word: i.e. 'sadnes' (37.6), which she defends. **3 aduise**: perceive. **4–5** Proverbial: Smith 244. **9 three years**: twelue monethes *1596*. See 7.5–6*n*.

Stanza 39

3 semblaunt: appearance, demeanour. **8 Praysdesire**: the desire for praise or fame. A common motif in the poem, e.g. 'all for praise and honour he did fight' (I v 7.6), 'pursuit of praise and fame' (II i 23.2), 'To hunt for glory and renowmed prayse' (III i 3.3), etc. As it personifies Arthur as courtly ambition, see Mueller 1991:761–62.

Stanza 40

The two damsels are paired by Elyot 1907:1.9 to explain why shamefastnes and desire for praise are two most necessary qualities in children: 'By shamfastnes, as it were with a bridell, they rule as well theyr dedes as their appetites. And desire of prayse addeth to a sharpe spurre to their disposition towarde lernyng and vertue'. See Nohrnberg 1976:324–25. Sawday 1995:164–65 remarks on the knights' interior voyage by which their social identities are displayed within a mirror of themselves. **3 demayne**: demeanour. **5–6** Her **blew** garment may indicate her withdrawal from the world for heaven; its pleats her modesty, as Belphœbe's dress at II iii 26.5. **7–9** The bird has been variously identified as the owl, cuckoo, wryneck, nightingale, or the turtle-dove which is described by Valeriano, in *Hieroglyphica*, as the bird that 'spends its life in secret places far from the multitude, seeking out lonely mountains or coverts removed from the meeting-place of the other birds'; noted A. Fowler 1961b:235–36. **dight**: abuse sexually. If the myth is S.'s own, as it seems to be, even the bird's name is kept from **vew**. **ashamd** refers equally to the bird and the damsel.

Stanza 41

1 commoned: conversed. **2** She retains this womanly posture of modesty at IV x 50.2, as does the lady in *Am* 13.3, in accord with Paul's injunction in 1 Tim. 2.9 that women 'araye themselues . . . with shamefastnes and modestie'. **3–7** Blushing, which indicates her fear of shame, is the usual sign and proof of innocence; see D.L. Miller 1988:172–74, 'shame' in the *SEnc*, and Krier 1990:157–62. **Castory**: apparently a red dye.

42

Fayre Damzell, seemeth, by your troubled cheare,
  That either me too bold ye weene, this wise
  You to molest, or other ill to feare
  That in the secret of your hart close lyes,
  From whence it doth, as cloud from sea aryse.
  If it be I, of pardon I you pray;
  But if ought else that I mote not deuyse,
  I will, if please you it discure, assay,
To ease you of that ill, so wisely as I may.

43

She answerd nought, but more abasht for shame,
  Held downe her head, the whiles her louely face,
  The flashing blood with blushing did inflame,
  And the strong passion mard her modest grace,
  That *Guyon* meruayld at her vncouth cace;
  Till *Alma* him bespake, Why wonder yee
  Faire Sir at that, which ye so much embrace?
  She is the fountaine of your modestee;
You shamefast are, but *Shamefastnes* it selfe is shee.

44

Thereat the Elfe did blush in priuitee,
  And turnd his face away; but she the same
  Dissembled faire, and faynd to ouersee.
  Thus they awhile with court and goodly game,

Themselues did solace each one with his Dame,
  Till that great Lady thence away them sought,
  To vew her Castles other wondrous frame.
  Vp to a stately Turret she them brought,
Ascending by ten steps of Alablaster wrought.

45

That Turrets frame most admirable was,
  Like highest heauen compassed around,
  And lifted high aboue this earthly masse,
  Which it suruewd, as hils doen lower ground;
  But not on ground mote like to this be found,
  Not that, which antique *Cadmus* whylome built
  In *Thebes*, which *Alexander* did confound;
  Nor that proud towre of *Troy*, though richly guilt,
From which young *Hectors* blood by cruell *Greekes* was spilt.

46

The roofe hereof was arched ouer head,
  And deckt with flowers and herbars daintily;
  Two goodly Beacons, set in watches stead,
  Therein gaue light, and flamd continually:
  For they of liuing fire most subtilly,
  Were made, and set in siluer sockets bright,
  Couer'd with lids deuiz'd of substance sly,
  That readily they shut and open might.
O who can tell the prayses of that makers might?

Stanza 42
4 the secret of your hart: a biblical phrase, e.g. Ps. 51.6.
6–9 The piling-up of monosyllables reveals Guyon's awkward
shamefastness. **deuyse**: guess. **discure**: discover.

Stanza 43
5 vncouth: strange; unseemly. **7 embrace**: cultivate; cherish.
8 modestee: also moderation, keeping due measure.
9 shamefast: held fast by shame. Guyon's horror of shame,
appropriate to a chivalric shame-culture, is frequently noted,
e.g. i 27.4, 30.1, etc. **Shamefastnes** sits on the (honoured)
right-hand side of Womanhood in the temple of Venus at IV x
50, being associated with Lat. *verecundia* or *pudicitia* and
therefore with chastity. She is present here because 'shame and
shamefastnes are . . . ioyned with this vertue of Temperance'
(La Primaudaye 1586:256; cited Hume 1984:107). See
'Shamefastnesse' in the *SEnc*.

Stanza 44
1 in priuitee: privately. **3 ouersee**: overlook. **5 solace**: take
enjoyment. **6 sought**: entreated. **8–9 stately Turret**: the
head, the seat of the rational soul. The **ten steps of Alablaster**
(alabaster) correspond to the vertebrae, the seven cervical and
the three thoracic needed to move from the heart to the head
in a natural and easy ascent from the feminine part of the body
to the masculine (22.4–5).

Stanza 45
1 admirable: marvellous, evoking wonder. **4 suruewd**: sur-
veyed. **6–7** Cadmus built Thebes, as Ovid, *Met.* 3.1–130,
records; Alexander **did confound** (i.e. demolished) it, as
T. Cooper 1565 records. **8–9** As told in *Met.* 14.415–17.
Cooper notes that 'the Greekes cruelly threwe [Astyanax]

downe from a towre, so that his braynes cleaued to the walles'.
guilt: gilded.

Stanza 46
1 ouer head: a heady pun but unavoidable. **2 herbars**:
herbar or arbour, a garden of herbs as a covering, here the hair.
3–6 The eyes, serving here as watchmen, were thought to emit
rather than simply receive light; see IV viii 39*n*. **subtilly**:
ingeniously. **7 sly**: cleverly or finely made.

Stanzas 47–58
The three rooms with the three sages correspond to the three
ventricles or cells of the brain with its three interior senses
of the mind or higher faculties of the sensitive soul. S. names
only the first and the third sages; the second is glossed by
Jonson as 'Judg[ment]'. Prudence, one of the four cardinal
virtues, relates the three stages of human life (youth, maturity,
and old age), and therefore of time ('things to come', 'pre-
sent', and 'past') to the three faculties (foresight, judgement or
understanding, and memory), as in Cicero, *De inventione* 2.53.
See Panofsky 1955:149 on Titian's 'Allegory of Prudence'.
On their relation to Chaucer's Prudence, see Anderson
1995:35–37. On the three figures as an emblem of prudence,
see J.L. Mills 1978:85–89; as they symbolize the process of
ratio, see Reid 1981:515–20. S. indicates their relationship and
ranking by interlocking the stanzas that describe them, and by
the number of lines given each (31, 16, 36). On the kinds of
personification used, see Paxson 1994:139–49. The **present**
(49.2) may receive least attention because it is the most fleet-
ing; or because its sage in being the most rational is the most
orderly; or because it is the poet's space, i.e. 'the middest', as
S. explains in the *LR* 47. For a reading of Bk II as an allegory
of prudence, see Black 1999, and Cooney 2000.

47

Ne can I tell, ne can I stay to tell
　　This parts great workemanship, and wondrous powre,
　　That all this other worldes worke doth excell,
　　And likest is vnto that heauenly towre,
　　That God hath built for his owne blessed bowre.
　　Therein were diuers rowmes, and diuers stages,
　　But three the chiefest, and of greatest powre,
　　In which there dwelt three honorable sages,
The wisest men, I weene, that liued in their ages.

48

Not he, whom *Greece*, the Nourse of all good arts,
　　By *Phœbus* doome, the wisest thought aliue,
　　Might be compar'd to this by many parts:
　　Nor that sage *Pylian* syre, which did suruiue
　　Three ages, such as mortall men contriue,
　　By whose aduise old *Priams* cittie fell,
　　With these in praise of pollicies mote striue,
　　These three in these three rowmes did sondry dwell,
And counselled faire *Alma*, how to gouerne well.

49

The first of them could things to come foresee;
　　The next could of thinges present best aduize;
　　The third things past could keepe in memoree,
　　So that no time, nor reason could arize,
　　But that the same could one of these comprize.
　　For thy the first did in the forepart sit,
　　That nought mote hinder his quicke preiudize:
　　He had a sharpe foresight, and working wit,
That neuer idle was, ne once would rest a whit.

50

His chamber was dispainted all with in,
　　With sondry colours, in the which were writ
　　Infinite shapes of thinges dispersed thin;
　　Some such as in the world were neuer yit,
　　Ne can deuized be of mortall wit;
　　Some daily seene, and knowen by their names,
　　Such as in idle fantasies doe flit:
　　Infernall Hags, *Centaurs*, feendes, *Hippodames*,
Apes, Lyons, Aegles, Owles, fooles, louers, children, Dames.

51

And all the chamber filled was with flyes,
　　Which buzzed all about, and made such sound,
　　That they encombred all mens eares and eyes,
　　Like many swarmes of Bees assembled round,
　　After their hiues with honny do abound:
　　All those were idle thoughtes and fantasies,
　　Deuices, dreames, opinions vnsound,
　　Shewes, visions, sooth-sayes, and prophesies;
And all that fained is, as leasings, tales, and lies.

52

Emongst them all sate he, which wonned there,
　　That hight *Phantastes* by his nature trew,
　　A man of yeares yet fresh, as mote appere,
　　Of swarth complexion, and of crabbed hew,
　　That him full of melancholy did shew;
　　Bent hollow beetle browes, sharpe staring eyes,
　　That mad or foolish seemd: one by his vew
　　Mote deeme him borne with ill disposed skyes,
When oblique *Saturne* sate in the house of agonyes.

Stanza 47

2 On the distinction between **workemanship** and **powre**, see 1.3 and *n*. **4–5 that heauenly towre**: the New Jerusalem seen by the Red Cross Knight at I x 55–57, and now by Guyon and Arthur in its human form.

Stanza 48

1–2 'Apollo beynge demaunded who was the wysest man lyuynge, aunswered, Socrates' (T. Cooper 1565). **doome**: judgement. **3 parts**: times. **4–6** Nestor, whom Homer praises as the Pylian orator who had ruled over three ages or generations of men, *Iliad* 1.247–52. Largely through his counsel, Troy fell. **contriue**: wear away, spend (time). **7 in praise of pollicies**: i.e. in whatever is praiseworthy in statecraft. **8 sondry**: separately.

Stanza 49

5 **comprize**: comprehend. **6 For thy**: therefore. **7 preiudize**: prejudgement, forethought. **8 working**: active.

Stanza 50

1 **dispainted**: diversely painted. **3 thin**: widely; or insubstantially, referring to the **shapes** whose substance, like that of fire, is 'thin and slight' (VII vi 7.7). This detail is related to Renaissance grotesque by Evett 1990:312*n*26. **4** Cf. Sidney's praise of poets who invent 'forms such as never were in nature' (*Defence of Poetry*:78). **7–9** At the first reading of this extended and witty use of *asyndeton* (the omission of grammatical connections between words), all the creatures seem lumped together: four fantastical creatures (the second and fourth being mythological are in italics), four animals, and four of inferior humankind, reaching a climax in the contemptuous reference to **Dames**. At second reading, however, it becomes clear that the first eight are found in the **idle fantasies** of the last four. (The disorganized first reading is appropriate to the first chamber; the organized second reading to the second.) These fantasies anticipate the deformed creatures who later assault the castle. **Hippodames**: perhaps a humorous variant of 'hippotame', the earlier spelling of 'hippopotamus'. **Lyons** and **Aegles** are juxtaposed as they combine in the griffin.

Stanza 51

1–5 'A head full of bees' is a proverbial expression for one full of whims and idle fantasies. **flyes**: a symbol of persistence, such as the 'swarme of Gnats' (16.1) to which the attack of Maleger and his forces is compared; see I i 23*n*, and 38.2*n*. Since this chamber contains **all that fained is**, S. may be commenting on his act of composing his poem, the swarms of thoughts which he needed to organize, as he wrote like a honey bee 'Working her formall rowmes in Wexen frame' (*SC Dec*. 68). **7–9** Another twelve-unit catalogue wittily alternating **idle thoughtes**, such as **Deuices** (conceits), **opinions**, etc., and **fantasies**, such as **dreames**, **Shewes**, etc. **sooth-sayes**: predictions. **leasings**: falsehoods.

53

Whom *Alma* hauing shewed to her guestes,
    Thence brought them to the second rowme, whose wals
    Were painted faire with memorable gestes,
    Of famous Wisards, and with picturals
    Of Magistrates, of courts, of tribunals,
    Of commen wealthes, of states, of pollicy,
    Of lawes, of iudgementes, and of decretals;
    All artes, all science, all Philosophy,
And all that in the world was ay thought wittily.

54

Of those that rowme was full, and them among
    There sate a man of ripe and perfect age,
    Who did them meditate all his life long,
    That through continuall practise and vsage,
    He now was growne right wise, and wondrous sage.
    Great plesure had those straunger knightes, to see
    His goodly reason, and graue personage,
    That his disciples both desyrd to bee;
But *Alma* thence them led to th'hindmost rowme of three.

55

That chamber seemed ruinous and old,
    And therefore was remoued far behind,
    Yet were the wals, that did the same vphold,
    Right firme and strong, though somwhat they declind;

And therein sat an old oldman, halfe blind,
    And all decrepit in his feeble corse,
    Yet liuely vigour rested in his mind,
    And recompenst him with a better scorse:
Weake body well is chang'd for minds redoubled forse.

56

This man of infinite remembraunce was,
    And things foregone through many ages held,
    Which he recorded still, as they did pas,
    Ne suffred them to perish through long eld,
    As all things els, the which this world doth weld,
    But laid them vp in his immortall scrine,
    Where they for euer incorrupted dweld:
    The warres he well remembred of king *Nine*,
Of old *Assaracus*, and *Inachus* diuine.

57

The yeares of *Nestor* nothing were to his,
    Ne yet *Mathusalem* though longest liu'd;
    For he remembred both their infancis:
    Ne wonder then, if that he were depriu'd
    Of natiue strength now, that he them suruiu'd.
    His chamber all was hangd about with rolls,
    And old records from auncient times deriud,
    Some made in books, some in long parchment scrolls,
That were all worm-eaten, and full of canker holes.

Stanza 52
Phantastes: Gk φανταστής; cf. Eng. 'fantast, phantast': 'a visionary, a dreamer' (*OED* 1). Cf. also Phædria's 'fantasticke wit' (vi 7.2) and the 'phantasies | In wauering wemens witt' (III xii 26.3–4) suffered by Amoret. See III xii 7.1*n*, and 'melancholy' in the *SEnc*. **5–6** On the tradition that associates Saturn with **melancholy**, see I ix 35.1*n*. **sharpe staring eyes** signify his 'sharpe foresight' (49.8). **8–9 oblique Saturne** may refer to the planet's astrologically unfavourable position in the zodiac and its latitude, here suggesting its perverse influence upon Phantastes's life. On Saturn as the lord of melancholy, see Klibansky *et al.* 1964:127–95, and Richardson 1989:91–121. Of the horoscope's twelve houses, the twelfth is the worst; see 'astronomy, 'astrology' in the *SEnc*. In Chaucer, *Knight's Tale* 2456–69, Saturn lists his baleful effects upon mankind 'Whil I dwelle in the signe of the leoun'. **house** refers to the twelfth house of the horoscope, which was associated with adversity (A. Fowler 1964:289–91); **agonyes** refers to the belief that under Saturn strife and contentions (Gk ἀγῶνες) prevail, as Kitchin 1872 notes.

Stanza 53
3–9 A third twelve-unit catalogue if **Philosophy** is a summative term as its capital seems to indicate, divided equally between the deeds (**gestes**) of wise men and the pictures (**picturals**) of magistrates. **decretals**: decrees. **science**: knowledge. **ay thought wittily**: ever wisely thought, using 'wit' in its older sense of 'intellectual power'.

Stanza 54
2–5 This unnamed sage is like Diet, who is 'rype of age, | . . . and in counsell sage', and therefore like the poet – see 27.8–9

and *n* – who receives and digests images of sense experience, as his room full of murals indicates. **perfect age**: full age. **7 personage**: appearance.

Stanza 55
2–4 Memory is popularly associated with the back of the mind, with what is farthest away. The chamber fits its inhabitant: although both appear physically decrepit, one is strongly founded and the other mentally vigorous. The extended description of his person, in contrast to the brief descripion of the first two, is designed to make him memorable. **declind**: in sloping down to the vertebrae; in being decayed. **8 scorse**: exchange.

Stanza 56
5 weld: have to do with; rule over. **6 immortall scrine**: the storehouse from which S. derives his poem – cf. the 'heauenly Registers aboue the Sunne' (i 32.4) – rather than the 'books' and 'scrolls' mentioned in the next stanza. See I proem 2.3–4*n*. **8–9 Nine**: Ninus of Babylon, 'the fyrst that made warre' (T. Cooper 1565); see 21.4–6*n*. **Assaracus**: son of the founder of Troy, the great-grandfather of Aeneas; cf. x 9.7. **Inachus diuine**: a river god, first King of Argos. Eumnestes's memory extends to the beginnings of biblical, classical, and mythical history.

Stanza 57
2 Mathusalem lived 969 years, according to Gen. 5.27. T. Cooper 1565 records that Nestor was almost 300 years old when he went to Troy.

58

Amidst them all he in a chaire was sett,
　　Tossing and turning them withouten end;
　　But for he was vnhable them to fett,
　　A litle boy did on him still attend,
　　To reach, when euer he for ought did send;
　　And oft when thinges were lost, or laid amis,
　　That boy them sought, and vnto him did lend.
　　Therefore he *Anamnestes* cleped is,
And that old man *Eumnestes*, by their propertis.

59

The knightes there entring, did him reuerence dew
　　And wondred at his endlesse exercise,
　　Then as they gan his Library to vew,
　　And antique Regesters for to auise,

There chaunced to the Princes hand to rize,
　　An auncient booke, hight *Briton moniments*,
　　That of this lands first conquest did deuize,
　　And old diuision into Regiments,
Till it reduced was to one mans gouernements.

60

Sir *Guyon* chaunst eke on another booke,
　　That hight, *Antiquitee* of *Faery* lond.
　　In which whenas he greedily did looke,
　　Th'ofspring of Elues and Faryes there he fond,
　　As it deliuered was from hond to hond:
　　Whereat they burning both with feruent fire,
　　Their countreys auncestry to vnderstond,
　　Crau'd leaue of *Alma*, and that aged sire,
To read those bookes; who gladly graunted their desire.

Stanza 58
3 fett: fetch. **7 lend**: give. **8–9 Anamnestes**: cf. Gk
ἀναμνηστικός, able to call to mind; hence the Re-minder.
Eumnestes: Gk εὐμνηστος, well-remembering, **laid amis**
points to memory as recollection, a distinction found in
Plato, *Phaedrus* 275a. See 'memory' in the *SEnc*. Demaray
1991:157–59 notes a contemporary analogue in Leicester's
account of the 'office of Arms' in London's round Temple
church.

Stanza 59
4 auise: look at. **5 rize**: happen; come to hand. **6 Briton
moniments**: records or chronicles of Britain; see x Arg.
7 deuize: recount. **8 Regiments**: independent kingdoms.
9 one mans: i.e. King Arthur's.

Stanza 60
2 Antiquitee of Faery lond: 'rolls of Elfin Emperours' (x
Arg.3). **4 ofspring**: origin.

Cant. X.

A chronicle of Briton kings,
From Brute to Vthers rayne.
And rolls of Elfin Emperours,
Till time of Gloriane.

1

WHo now shall giue vnto me words and sound,
  Equall vnto this haughty enterprise?
Or who shall lend me wings, with which from ground
My lowly verse may loftily arise,
And lift it selfe vnto the highest skyes?
More ample spirit, then hetherto was wount,
Here needes me, whiles the famous auncestryes
Of my most dreaded Soueraigne I recount,
By which all earthly Princes she doth far surmount.

2

Ne vnder Sunne, that shines so wide and faire,
  Whence all that liues, does borrow life and light,
  Liues ought, that to her linage may compaire,
  Which though from earth it be deriued right,
Yet doth it selfe stretch forth to heuens hight,
And all the world with wonder ouerspred;
A labor huge, exceeding far my might:
How shall fraile pen, with feare disparaged,
Conceiue such soueraine glory, and great bountyhed?

3

Argument worthy of *Mæonian* quill,
  Or rather worthy of great *Phoebus* rote,
  Whereon the ruines of great *Ossa* hill,
  And triumphes of *Phlegræan Ioue* he wrote,
That all the Gods admird his lofty note.
But if some relish of that heuenly lay
His learned daughters would to me report,
To decke my song withall, I would assay,
Thy name, O soueraine Queene, to blazon far away.

Book II Canto x

Argument

1–2 To fashion his **chronicle** of Elizabeth's 'auncestryes' (1.7) – his preferred terms are '*moniments*' and '*Antiquitee*' (ix 59.6, 60.2) – S. consulted a number of sources, chiefly Geoffrey of Monmouth, *Historia Regum Britanniae* (*c.* 1135); John Hardyng, *Chronicle* (1543); John Stow, *Chronicles of England, Scotland, and Ireland* (1580); Raphael Holinshed, *Chronicles* (1577, 1587); and *A Mirror for Magistrates* (1559, later rev. and enlarged). On the chronicle tradition, see Levy 1967:167–201; the standard study of S.'s use of them remains Harper 1910, abstracted in *Var* 2.302–34. The chronicles are cited below chiefly when S.'s use of them, or departure from them, is noteworthy. See also 'chronicles' in the *SEnc*. In the first of his three-part chronicle, S. 'thrusteth [himself] into the middest' (*LR* 47) by having Arthur read the history from the arrival in Britain of the Trojan Brute, the eponymous founder of Britain, to the reign of his own father. In III iii 26–50, 'diuining of thinges to come', the prophet Merlin continues the history from Arthur to the coming of Elizabeth; and in III ix 33–51, 'recoursing to the thinges forepaste', Paridell goes back to the beginning, from the fall of Troy to the arrival of the Trojans in Britain.

  On the distinction between **kings** and **Emperours**, see I ii 22.7–9*n*; on the distinction between **Briton** and **Elfin**, see I i 17.1*n*. **rolls**: records, as a register or catalogue; distinct from a **chronicle**. The claim by Berger 1957:110 that the **chronicle** and the **rolls** present two different worlds, for in the second 'all difficulties are left out, and the good works are made much better', remains for critics the point of departure for relating the two; see esp. D.L. Miller 1988:199–209. Mazzola 1995 explores their separate ontologies. On the textual patterning of the stanzas, which shows how the chronicle becomes a story of redemption, see Røstvig 1994:347–54.

Stanza 1

S. closely paraphrases Ariosto, *Orl. Fur.* 3.1, and in his ninth line overgoes Ariosto's eight-line stanza in order to claim that his Queen overgoes Ariosto's Duke d'Este. **2 haughty**: exalted.

Stanza 2

1–2 That S. follows Ariosto 3.2.3 may explain this surprising claim: the power attributed to the **Sunne** belongs to 'the Sunne of righteousnes' (Mal. 4.2). **4 deriued right** asserts Elizabeth's claim to be England's rightful Queen. **5** Expanded at III iii 22.5–6 to introduce the second part of the history. **8–9 disparaged**: cast down, degraded. **bountyhed**: naming Elizabeth the head or fountain of goodness; cf. VI proem 7.6–7. S.'s question is answered by this canto, as O'Connell 1977:75 notes.

Stanza 3

1 Mœonian: from Homer's surname Mæonides. **quill**: plectrum, pipe, or pen. **2–5 Phoebus rote**: the lyre or harp of Apollo, the god of music and poetry. In their assault upon heaven, the giants tried to pile **Ossa** on Pelion and top it with Olympus (Virgil, *Georg.* 1.281–83). **ruines** implies the defeat of the giants; see Ovid, *Met.* 1.151–55. **Phlegræan**: because the battle took place 'in the Phlegrean plaine' (V vii 10.5) – information found in Stephanus's *Dictionarium*, as Starnes and Talbert 1955:75 note. **wrote**: i.e. composed and set to music. S. still follows Ariosto 3.3. **admird**: wondered at. **6 relish**: trace. **7 His learned daughters**: the muses; see I xi 5.6–9*n*. **report**: bring back. **9 blazon**: proclaim by trumpet; hence with a louder note than that given by Homer's pipe or Apollo's lyre.

4

Thy name O soueraine Queene, thy realme and race,
　　From this renowmed Prince deriued arre,
　　Who mightily vpheld that royall mace,
　　Which now thou bear'st, to thee descended farre
　　From mighty kings and conquerours in warre,
　　Thy fathers and great Grandfathers of old,
　　Whose noble deeds aboue the Northern starre
　　Immortall fame for euer hath enrold;
As in that old mans booke they were in order told.

5

The land, which warlike Britons now possesse,
　　And therein haue their mighty empire raysd,
　　In antique times was saluage wildernesse,
　　Vnpeopled, vnmannurd, vnproud, vnpraysd,
　　Ne was it Island then, ne was it paysd
　　Amid the *Ocean* waues, ne was it sought
　　Of merchaunts farre, for profits therein praysd,
　　But was all desolate, and of some thought
By sea to haue bene from the *Celticke* mayn-land brought.

6

Ne did it then deserue a name to haue,
　　Till that the venturous Mariner that way
　　Learning his ship from those white rocks to saue,
　　Which all along the Southerne sea-coast lay,
　　Threatning vnheedy wrecke and rash decay,
　　For safety that same his sea-marke made,
　　And namd it *Albion*. But later day
　　Finding in it fit ports for fishers trade,
Gan more the same frequent, and further to inuade.

7

But far in land a saluage nation dwelt,
　　Of hideous Giaunts, and halfe beastly men,
　　That neuer tasted grace, nor goodnes felt,
　　But like wild beastes lurking in loathsome den,
　　And flying fast as Roebucke through the fen,
　　All naked without shame, or care of cold,
　　By hunting and by spoiling liueden;
　　Of stature huge, and eke of corage bold,
That sonnes of men amazd their sternesse to behold.

8

But whence they sprong, or how they were begott,
　　Vneath is to assure, vneath to wene
　　That monstrous error, which doth some assott,
　　That *Dioclesians* fifty daughters shene
　　Into this land by chaunce haue driuen bene,
　　Where companing with feends and filthy Sprights
　　Through vaine illusion of their lust vnclene,
　　They brought forth Geaunts and such dreadfull wights,
As far exceeded men in their immeasurd mights.

Stanza 4

1–2 The careful repetition of the first half of 3.9 registers S.'s claim to be the Queen's (and England's) 'Poet historical'. **this renowmed Prince**: Arthur. Although by strict genealogy Arthur does not descend from Brutus, whose progeny 'left no moniment' (36.8), he does uphold royal power **descended farre**. Further, as the chronicle at III iii 26–50 shows, the Queen derives her race from Arthur's half-brother, Artegall. **3 royall mace**: the sceptre of sovereignty. **6 Grandfathers**: forefathers. **7 the Northern starre**: 'the stedfast starre' in being the centre of the revolving stars; see I ii 1.1–4*n*.

Stanzas 5–68.2

The chronicle of British history is divided into four dynasties by a failure to establish a male heir: 5–36 ends Brutus's progeny; 37–54 ends with the death of Lucius following the Roman invasion; 55–61 ends with the invasion of the Huns and Picts during which Maximinian 'dying left none heire them to withstand'; and 62–68.2 ends with the coming of Arthur – and therefore of Elizabeth who also lacked an heir. The 63 stanzas name 62 kings from Brute to Uther, making Arthur the 63rd, a number that marks the 'Grand Climacteric' of human life. On that number, the divisions, and their numerological ordering according to multiples of seven and nine, which are the ratios of body and mind respectively in the temperate body, see ix 22*n*. On their thematic ordering to reveal God's providence, see J.L. Mills 1976. On the Roman Britain history within this chronology, see 47–63*n*. Rossi 1985 interprets the chronicle as S.'s definition of temperance in history.

Stanza 5

1 possesse: inhabit. **2 empire**: supreme command (*OED* 1.1.2), alluding to England's sovereignty under Elizabeth.

4 Vnpeopled because its people were 'a saluage nation' (7.1). **vnmannurd**: uncultivated. **vnproud**: untried as a place to live. **5 paysd**: poised. **7 praysd**: appraised. **8–9 of some thought**: referring to the chroniclers, e.g. Holinshed 1807–08:1.427, who records that England was 'ioined without any separation of sea to the maine land'.

Stanza 6

Cf. T. Cooper 1565: 'It was named *Albion, ab albis rupibus*, of white rockes, because that vnto them, that come by sea, from the east or southe, the bankes and rockes of this Ile doe appeare whyte'. He notes also that Greek adventurers 'reioysinge at their good and fortunate arriuall, named this yle in greeke *Olbion*, which in englishe signifieth happy, in latine *Fælix*'. For other explanations, see III iii 56.2–7 and III ix 47.9. **5** I.e., threatning **wrecke** if he should be **vnheedy**, and **decay** if **rash**. **9 inuade**: enter.

Stanza 7

1–2 Cf. III ix 49.8–9. On the role of giants in the poem, see 'giants' in the *SEnc*; on the ambivalence about the political system which they expose, see Wofford 1992:334–53. On the relation of Brutus's conquests to the role of the New English in Ireland, see Ivic 1999:153–55. **hideous**: huge. **5** For the simile, see ii 7.4*n*. **9 sternesse**: fierceness; formidableness.

Stanza 8

2 'It is difficult to affirm, difficult to believe'. T. Cooper 1565 relates the fable but adds that it is one in which 'is neither similitude of trouth, reasone, nor honestie'. **3 That monstrous error**: with the added sense, the daughters' error by which monsters were conceived. **assott**: befool. **4** The chroniclers record that all but one of Dioclesian's fifty daughters killed their husbands on their wedding-night, the exception

9

They held this land, and with their filthinesse
  Polluted this same gentle soyle long time:
  That their owne mother loathd their beastlinesse,
  And gan abhorre her broods vnkindly crime,
  All were they borne of her owne natiue slime;
  Vntil that *Brutus* anciently deriu'd
  From roiall stocke of old *Assaracs* line,
  Driuen by fatall error, here arriu'd,
And them of their vniust possession depriu'd.

10

But ere he had established his throne,
  And spred his empire to the vtmost shore,
  He fought great batteils with his saluage fone;
  In which he them defeated euermore,
  And many Giaunts left on groning flore,
  That well can witnes yet vnto this day
  The westerne Hogh, besprincled with the gore
  Of mighty *Goëmot*, whome in stout fray
Corineus conquered, and cruelly did slay.

11

And eke that ample Pitt, yet far renownd,
  For the large leape, which *Debon* did compell
  Coulin to make, being eight lugs of grownd;
  Into the which retourning backe, he fell,

But those three monstrous stones doe most excell
  Which that huge sonne of hideous *Albion*,
  Whose father *Hercules* in Fraunce did quell,
  Great *Godmer* threw, in fierce contention,
At bold *Canutus*, but of him was slaine anon.

12

In meed of these great conquests by them gott,
  Corineus had that Prouince vtmost west,
  To him assigned for his worthy lott,
  Which of his name and memorable gest
  He called *Cornwaile*, yet so called best:
  And *Debons* shayre was, that is *Deuonshyre*:
  But *Canute* had his portion from the rest,
  The which he cald *Canutium*, for his hyre;
Now *Cantium*, which Kent we comenly inquyre.

13

Thus *Brute* this Realme vnto his rule subdewd,
  And raigned long in great felicity,
  Lou'd of his freends, and of his foes eschewd,
  He left three sonnes, his famous progeny,
  Borne of fayre *Inogene* of *Italy*;
  Mongst whom he parted his imperiall state,
  And *Locrine* left chiefe Lord of *Britany*.
  At last ripe age bad him surrender late
His life, and long good fortune vnto finall fate.

---

being Albine who gave birth to Albion, a detail not mentioned because S. prefers the fable of Albion's descent from Neptune; see IV xi 16.1. Since the chroniclers did not agree whether Dioclesian had thirty or thirty-three daughters, S. felt free to choose the classical version, the story of Danao's fifty daughters. **shene**: beautiful. **6 companing**: copulating. The biblical analogue is the story in Gen. 6.1–7 of the 'gyantes in the earth' whose fathers were 'sonnes of God', reputed to be fallen angels. Their wickedness provoked God to destroy them by the Flood. **7** I.e., they were deceived by their lust. **9 immeasurd**: immeasurable.

Stanza 9

At III ix 49.8–9, it is revealed that the giants were guilty of cannibalism. S. stresses their moral **filthinesse** in order to claim that their possession of their own land is **vniust**, and their extermination just, as Waswo 1987–88:556 notes. **2–4 their owne mother**: the **soyle** of Albion. Holinshed 1807–08:1.432 notes that these giants 'tooke their name of the soile where they were borne: for *Gigantes* signifieth the sons of the earth'. **vnkindly**: unnatural. **7 Assarac**: the founder of Troy and great-grandfather of Aeneas (see ix 56.9) who was Brutus's great-grandfather. **8 fatall error**: wandering ordained by fate; from *Aen.* 1.2. He was directed to England by a vision after he had accidentally killed his father; cf. III ix 48.4–5 and the phrase 'by fatall course' (49.1). A cancelled passage in *View* 197 notes that the tale of Brutus conquering and inhabiting this land is 'impossible to prove'.

Stanza 10

For a similar account, see III ix 50. **3 fone**: foes. **7–9** So described by Geoffrey 1891:1.16. The place of the battle,

Plymouth Hoe, agrees with local tradition preserved in Carew 1602:2ᵛ. It may be seen **vnto this day** because their effigies were cut into the hillside and preserved.

Stanza 11

1–4 I.e., **that ample Pitt** also bears witness to the battle against the giants: **Debon** forced **Coulin** to jump across its **eight lugs** or rods of width. **retourning backe**, i.e. falling back. Their battle is mentioned briefly at III ix 50.4–5 where again it follows the story of Goëmot or Gogmagog. Forste-Grupp 1999 argues that S. took Coulin's name and manner of death from Irish traditions. **5–9** I.e., the **three . . . stones** best bear witness to the battle against the giants. **hideous Albion**: one of the 'hideous Giaunts' (7.2), after whom his country was named (6.7), was killed in France by Hercules as described in Holinshed 1807–08:1.7, and by T. Cooper 1565; see IV xi 16. S. may have invented the story that his son, **Godmer**, threw the stones at **Canutus** and was killed by him. **quell**: kill.

Stanza 12

Geoffrey 1891:1.16 suggests that **Corineus** was the eponymous founder of Cornwall; S. invents the rest through assumed etymologies. **5 so called best**: referring to the preferred spelling, **Cornwaile**. **7 from the rest**: apart from the others. **9 inquyre**: call (so the context would suggest).

Stanza 13

3 eschewd: avoided. **5 of Italy**: traditionally of Greece. S.'s authority may be alliteration and rhyme, as Harper 1910:53 suggests. **7 Britany**: Britain.

14

Locrine was left the soueraine Lord of all;
But *Albanact* had all the Northerne part,
Which of him selfe *Albania* he did call;
And *Camber* did possesse the Westerne quart,
Which *Seuerne* now from *Logris* doth depart:
And each his portion peaceably enioyd,
Ne was there outward breach, nor grudge in hart,
That once their quiet gouernment annoyd,
But each his paynes to others profit still employd.

15

Vntill a nation straung, with visage swart,
And corage fierce, that all men did affray,
Which through the world then swarmd in euery part,
And ouerflow'd all countries far away,
Like *Noyes* great flood, with their importune sway,
This land inuaded with like violence,
And did themselues through all the North display:
Vntill that *Locrine* for his Realmes defence,
Did head against them make, and strong munificence.

16

He them encountred, a confused rout,
Foreby the Riuer, that whylome was hight
The ancient *Abus*, where with courage stout
He them defeated in victorious fight,
And chaste so fiercely after fearefull flight,
That forst their Chiefetain, for his safeties sake,
(Their Chiefetain *Humber* named was aright,)
Vnto the mighty streame him to betake,
Where he an end of batteill, and of life did make.

17

The king retourned proud of victory,
And insolent wox through vnwonted ease,
That shortly he forgot the ieopardy,
Which in his land he lately did appease,

And fell to vaine voluptuous disease:
He lou'd faire Ladie *Estrild*, leudly lou'd,
Whose wanton pleasures him too much did please,
That quite his hart from *Guendolene* remou'd,
From *Guendolene* his wife, though alwaies faithfull prou'd.

18

The noble daughter of *Corineus*
Would not endure to bee so vile disdaind,
But gathering force, and corage valorous,
Encountred him in batteill well ordaind,
In which him vanquisht she to fly constraind:
But she so fast pursewd, that him she tooke,
And threw in bands, where he till death remaind;
Als his faire Leman, flying through a brooke,
She ouerhent, nought moued with her piteous looke.

19

But both her selfe, and eke her daughter deare,
Begotten by her kingly Paramoure,
The faire *Sabrina* almost dead with feare,
She there attached, far from all succoure;
The one she slew vpon the present floure,
But the sad virgin innocent of all,
Adowne the rolling riuer she did poure,
Which of her name now *Seuerne* men do call:
Such was the end, that to disloyall loue did fall.

20

Then for her sonne, which she to *Locrin* bore,
Madan was young; vnmeet the rule to sway,
In her owne hand the crowne she kept in store,
Till ryper yeares he raught, and stronger stay:
During which time her powre she did display
Through all this realme, the glory of her sex,
And first taught men a woman to obay:
But when her sonne to mans estate did wex,
She it surrendred, ne her selfe would lenger vex.

Stanza 14

3 **Albania**: Scotland. **4 possesse**: inhabit. **quart**: region, quarter, referring to Cambria, i.e. Wales. **5 Logris**: England, as IV xi 36.6, derived from **Locrine**. **depart**: separate.

Stanza 15

1 **straung**: foreign; referring to the Huns. **5** The simile befits the nation's leader, Humber, who gave his name to that tidal river; also it aligns British and human history, as Røstvig 1994:349 notes. **importune sway**: heavy force. **7 display**: spread out. **9 munificence**: subsidies, aid; munificence *1596*, i.e. 'fortification' (coined by S. from 'munify') may be preferred.

Stanza 16

7 Humber **named was aright** because the river was named after him; cf. IV xi 38.5–7.

Stanza 17

2 **insolent**: intemperate; proud. **4 appease**: settle; pacify. **5 disease**: disturbed state; or referring to his voluptuousness as an affliction.

Stanza 18

4 **ordaind**: drawn up, set in order. **6–7** Invented by S.; so also praise of her as 'the glory of her sex' (20.6). **9 ouerhent**: overtook.

Stanza 19

4 **attached**: seized. **5–9 vpon the present floure**: in that very place. in that impatient stoure *1596*, i.e. impatient in the tumult. Eldevik 1998:210–11 suggests a reference to the swiftly-rushing Stour – cf. IV xi 32.1–4 – where Gwendolen defeated Locrinus and drowned Estrildis. The drowning of **Sabrina** provides S. with an example of an English river that 'Had vertue pourd into [its] waters bace' (ii 6.8). Cf. Bladud's act of infusing virtue into the waters at Bath at 26. **poure**: a nonce use for sending down the stream to identify **Sabrina** with her waters. A revised version of her story, attributed to Meliboeus (i.e. S.), is told by the Attendant Spirit in Milton, *Comus* 820–34.

Stanza 20

1 **for**: because. **2 sway**: wield. **4 stay**: strength. **5 display**: extend.

21

Tho *Madan* raignd, vnworthie of his race:
    For with all shame that sacred throne he fild:
    Next *Memprise*, as vnworthy of that place,
    In which being consorted with *Manild*,
    For thirst of single kingdom him he kild.
    But *Ebranck* salued both their infamies
    With noble deedes, and warreyd on *Brunchild*
    In *Henault*, where yet of his victories
Braue moniments remaine, which yet that land enuies.

22

An happy man in his first dayes he was,
    And happy father of faire progeny:
    For all so many weekes, as the yeare has,
    So many children he did multiply;
    Of which were twentie sonnes, which did apply,
    Their mindes to prayse, and cheualrous desyre:
    Those germans did subdew all *Germany*,
    Of whom it hight; but in the end their Syre
With foule repulse from Fraunce was forced to retyre.

23

Which blott his sonne succeeding in his seat,
    The second *Brute*, the second both in name,
    And eke in semblaunce of his puissaunce great,
    Right well recur'd, and did away that blame
    With recompence of euerlasting fame.
    He with his victour sword first opened,
    The bowels of wide *Fraunce*, a forlorne Dame,
    And taught her first how to be conquered;
Since which, with sondrie spoiles she hath bene ransacked.

24

Let *Scaldis* tell, and let tell *Hania*,
    And let the marsh of *Estham bruges* tell,
    What colour were their waters that same day,
    And all the moore twixt *Eluersham* and *Dell*,
    With blood of *Henalois*, which therein fell.
    How oft that day did sad *Brunchildis* see
    The greene shield dyde in dolorous vermell?
    That not *Scuith guiridh* it mote seeme to bee,
But rather *y Scuith gogh*, signe of sad crueltee.

25

His sonne king *Leill* by fathers labour long,
    Enioyd an heritage of lasting peace,
    And built *Cairleill*, and built *Cairleon* strong.
    Next *Huddibras* his realme did not encrease,
    But taught the land from wearie wars to cease.
    Whose footsteps *Bladud* following, in artes
    Exceld at *Athens* all the learned preace,
    From whence he brought them to these saluage parts
And with sweet science mollifide their stubborne harts.

26

Ensample of his wondrous faculty,
    Behold the boyling Bathes at *Cairbadon*,
    Which seeth with secret fire eternally,
    And in their entrailles, full of quick Brimston,
    Nourish the flames, which they are warmd vpon,
    That to their people wealth they forth do well,
    And health to euery forreyne nation:
    Yet he at last contending to excell
The reach of men, through flight into fond mischief fell.

Stanza 21
2 **fild**: also defiled.   5 **single**: undivided; i.e. he wanted to rule alone.   6 He made amends for (**salued**) the evil deeds of both his father **Memprise** and his father **Madan**.   7 **warreyd**: made war.   8 **Henault**: Hainaut, a province in Belgium.   9 **enuies**: regards with dislike.

Stanza 22
3–8 S. adds two children to Ebranck's reputed fifty; etymology requires Germany to be named from the **germans** or brothers.

Stanza 23
4 **recur'd**: remedied.   6–7 The facts are from Stow, as Harper 1910:68–69 notes, but the brutal expression and the granting of **euerlasting fame** for disembowelling France are the poet's. 9 **spoiles**: plunderings.

Stanza 24
The only stanza of S.'s chronicle cited in Milton's *History of Britain* with the comment: '*Henault*, and *Brunchild* [see 21.7–8], and *Greenesheild*, seeme newer names then for a Story pretended thus Antient' (1953–82:5.21).   1–4 Referring to the rivers Scheldt (**Scaldis**) and **Hania** (from the province of Hainaut) and the marshes of the town of Bruges (named **Estham bruges**, the camp of Brutus).   **Eluersham** and **Dell** are added by S.   5 **Henalois**: men of 'Henault' (21.8).

7 **vermell**: vermilion.   8–9 I.e., not 'the green shield' (Brutus's surname) as it may seem to be but 'the red shield', i.e. red with blood. On these Welsh phrases, see Bruce 1985:466, and 'Wales' in the *SEnc*. The use of Welsh, which S. adds to his sources, seems designed to allude to Elizabeth's Welsh descent.

Stanza 25
3 Since Stow records that Leill only repaired **Cairleon**, the *Var* editors suggest that the phrase means he 'made it strong'. Yet S. may have him build it because Arthur was crowned there, so Malory 1.7 claims.   5 **wearie wars**: wars of aggression, as Harper 1910:71 suggests.   7 **preace**: throng.   9 **science**: knowledge, learning.   **mollifide**: softened.

Stanza 26
1 **wondrous faculty**: referring to Bladud's magical 'artes' (25.6).   2 **Cairbadon**: the city of Bath.   4 **quick Brimston**: fiery sulphur.   6 **wealth**: well-being.   **well**: the fig. sense, 'pour out as a stream' (*OED* 7b) is appropriate here.   8–9 In attempting to fly with artificial wings, as did Icarus, he broke his neck.   **fond mischief**: foolish death.

Stanzas 27–32
S.'s chief source for the story of **king Leyr** is Geoffrey, as Harper 1910:75–84 shows. His story became, in turn, a chief source of Shakespeare's *King Lear*. See 'Lear' in the *SEnc* and Weiner 1991:261–66.

27

Next him king *Leyr* in happie peace long raynd,
　But had no issue male him to succeed,
　But three faire daughters, which were well vptraind,
　In all that seemed fitt for kingly seed:
　Mongst whom his realme he equally decreed
　To haue diuided. Tho when feeble age
　Nigh to his vtmost date he saw proceed,
　He cald his daughters; and with speeches sage
Inquyrd, which of them most did loue her parentage.

28

The eldest *Gonorill* gan to protest,
　That she much more then her owne life him lou'd:
　And *Regan* greater loue to him profest,
　Then all the world, when euer it were proou'd;
　But *Cordeill* said she lou'd him, as behoou'd:
　Whose simple answere, wanting colours fayre
　To paint it forth, him to displeasaunce moou'd,
　That in his crown he counted her no hayre,
But twixt the other twain his kingdom whole did shayre.

29

So wedded th'one to *Maglan* king of Scottes,
　And thother to the king of *Cambria*,
　And twixt them shayrd his realme by equall lottes:
　But without dowre the wise *Cordelia*,
　Was sent to *Aggannip* of *Celtica*.
　Their aged Syre, thus eased of his crowne,
　A priuate life ledd in *Albania*,
　With *Gonorill*, long had in great renowne,
That nought him grieu'd to beene from rule deposed downe.

30

But true it is that when the oyle is spent,
　The light goes out, and weeke is throwne away;
　So when he had resignd his regiment,
　His daughter gan despise his drouping day,
　And wearie wax of his continuall stay.
　Tho to his daughter *Regan* he repayrd,
　Who him at first well vsed euery way;
　But when of his departure she despayrd,
Her bountie she abated, and his cheare empayrd.

31

The wretched man gan then auise to late,
　That loue is not, where most it is profest,
　Too truely tryde in his extremest state;
　At last resolu'd likewise to proue the rest,
　He to *Cordelia* him selfe addrest,
　Who with entyre affection him receau'd,
　As for her Syre and king her seemed best;
　And after all an army strong she leau'd,
To war on those, which him had of his realme bereau'd.

32

So to his crowne she him restord againe,
　In which he dyde, made ripe for death by eld,
　And after wild, it should to her remaine:
　Who peaceably the same long time did weld:
　And all mens harts in dew obedience held:
　Till that her sisters children, woxen strong,
　Through proud ambition against her rebeld,
　And ouercommen kept in prison long,
Till weary of that wretched life, her selfe she hong.

33

Then gan the bloody brethren both to raine:
　But fierce *Cundah* gan shortly to enuy
　His brother *Morgan*, prickt with proud disdaine,
　To haue a pere in part of souerainty,
　And kindling coles of cruell enmity,
　Raisd warre, and him in batteill ouerthrew:
　Whence as he to those woody hilles did fly,
　Which hight of him *Glamorgan*, there him slew:
Then did he raigne alone, when he none equall knew.

34

His sonne *Riuall'* his dead rowme did supply,
　In whose sad time blood did from heauen rayne:
　Next great *Gurgustus*, then faire *Caecily*,
　In constant peace their kingdomes did contayne,
　After whom *Lago*, and *Kinmarke* did rayne,
　And *Gorbogud*, till far in yeares he grew:
　Then his ambitious sonnes vnto them twayne,
　Arraught the rule, and from their father drew,
Stout *Ferrex* and sterne *Porrex* him in prison threw.

Stanza 27
9 **parentage**: parents; here, parent.

Stanza 28
4 **proou'd**: put to the test.   5 **as behoou'd**: as was fitting (to a father).   7 **displeasaunce**: displeasure.

Stanza 29
2 **Cambria**: Wales.   5 **Celtica**: France.   7 **Albania**: Scotland.

Stanza 30
1–2 Proverbial: Smith 588.   **weeke**: wick; with a pun on 'weak', alluding to Lear's 'feeble age' (27.6).   3 **regiment**: office.   9 **cheare**: kindly reception.

Stanza 31
1 **auise**: reflect.   3 **tryde**: proven.   6–7 I.e., she 'lou'd him, as behoou'd' (28.5).   **entyre**: sincere; perfect.   8 **after all**: afterwards.   **leau'd**: levied.

Stanza 32
3 **after wild**: willed that afterwards.   4 **weld**: wield.   9 S.'s major departure from his sources. Hanging is his emblem for dying in despair; see I ix 22.7*n*.

Stanza 33
4 **pere**: peer, equal.

Stanza 34
1 **dead rowme**: his office after he died.   4 **contayne**: keep.   6 **Gorbogud**: Gorboduc.   8 **Arraught**: seized by force.

35

But O, the greedy thirst of royall crowne,
   That knowes no kinred, nor regardes no right,
   Stird *Porrex* vp to put his brother downe;
   Who vnto him assembling forreigne might,
   Made warre on him, and fell him selfe in fight:
   Whose death t'auenge, his mother mercilesse,
   Most mercilesse of women, *Wyden* hight,
   Her other sonne fast sleeping did oppresse,
And with most cruell hand him murdred pittilesse.

36

Here ended *Brutus* sacred progeny,
   Which had seuen hundred yeares this scepter borne,
   With high renowme, and great felicity;
   The noble braunch from th'antique stocke was torne
   Through discord, and the roiall throne forlorne:
   Thenceforth this Realme was into factions rent,
   Whilest each of *Brutus* boasted to be borne,
   That in the end was left no moniment
Of *Brutus*, nor of Britons glorie auncient.

37

Then vp arose a man of matchlesse might,
   And wondrous wit to menage high affayres,
   Who stird with pitty of the stressed plight
   Of this sad realme, cut into sondry shayres
   By such, as claymd themselues *Brutes* rightfull hayres,
   Gathered the Princes of the people loose,
   To taken counsell of their common cares;
   Who with his wisdom won, him streight did choose
Their king, and swore him fealty to win or loose.

38

Then made he head against his enimies,
   And *Ymner* slew, of *Logris* miscreate;
   Then *Ruddoc* and proud *Stater*, both allyes,
   This of *Albany* newly nominate,
   And that of *Cambry* king confirmed late,
   He ouerthrew through his owne valiaunce;
   Whose countries he redus'd to quiet state,
   And shortly brought to ciuile gouernaunce,
Now one, which earst were many, made through variaunce.

39

Then made he sacred lawes, which some men say
   Were vnto him reueald in vision,
   By which he freed the Traueilers high way,
   The Churches part, and Ploughmans portion,
   Restraining stealth, and strong extortion;
   The gratious *Numa* of great *Britany*:
   For till his dayes, the chiefe dominion
   By strength was wielded without pollicy;
Therefore he first wore crowne of gold for dignity.

40

Donwallo dyde (for what may liue for ay?)
   And left two sonnes, of pearelesse prowesse both;
   That sacked *Rome* too dearely did assay,
   The recompence of their periured oth,
   And ransackt *Greece* wel tryde, when they were wroth;
   Besides subiected *France*, and *Germany*,
   Which yet their praises speake, all be they loth,
   And inly tremble at the memory
Of *Brennus* and *Belinus*, kinges of Britany.

---

drew: withdrew. **9** S.'s invention, as Harper 1910:89 notes.
Stout: proud; fierce; rebellious. **sterne**: cruel.

Stanza 35
8 oppresse: take by surprise.

Stanza 36
In concluding the first dynasty of British history, S. departs from the chronicles in order to draw upon Eubulus's concluding lament in the *Tragedy of Gorboduc* (1565); see Harper 1910:91. **1 sacred**: because descended from the Trojan kings who claimed kinship with the gods. **2 seuen hundred yeares**: see 70–76*n*. **5 forlorne**: abandoned. **8 moniment**: record.

Stanza 37
1–2 In not naming the man but listing his achievements, S. marks a new dynasty that begins with Donwallo, the first British king (39.9) who combines courage and wisdom. His **matchlesse might** is shown in 38, his **wondrous wit** in 39. **3 stressed**: afflicted. **4 sondry shayres**: cf. 'old diuision into Regiments' (ix 59.8). **6 loose**: disunited. **8–9** This detail, not found in the chronicles, is suggested by the legend of Numa (see 39.6) who 'was chosen by the people and Senate of Rome . . . for his excellent vertues and learning' (T. Cooper 1565). Numa ruled after Romulus, the founder of Rome as

Donwallo succeeds Brutus, the eponymous founder of Britain.

Stanza 38
2 miscreate: unlawfully made king, or created unnaturally (being illegitimate). **4–5 Albany** is Scotland and **Cambry** is Wales, separate countries at 29 that now form the union of 'great *Britany*' (39.6). **8 gouernaunce**: order. **9 variaunce**: dissension.

Stanza 39
5 stealth: theft. **6 Numa** 'by his policie and ceremonies, brought the Romaines . . . in . . . a wonderfull quietnesse and honest fourme of lyuing' (T. Cooper 1565). The title is confirmed by noting that Donwallo's laws were divinely revealed, as Numa claimed his were: 'that the people myght haue in more estimation, he feigned that he deuised them [the laws] by the instruction of the goddesse or nymph *Aegeria*' (Cooper); see 42.8. **8 pollicy**: political cunning, expediency.

Stanza 40
3 I.e., Rome, which they sacked, too dearly learned of their prowess by experience. **4 periured**: falsely sworn, referring to their oath of allegiance to them. **5** I.e., Greece, which they ransacked, well proved their prowess.

41

Next them did *Gurgunt*, great *Belinus* sonne
    In rule succeede, and eke in fathers praise;
He Easterland subdewd, and Denmarke wonne,
    And of them both did foy and tribute raise,
    The which was dew in his dead fathers daies:
He also gaue to fugitiues of *Spayne*,
    Whom he at sea found wandring from their waies,
    A seate in *Ireland* safely to remayne,
Which they should hold of him, as subiect to *Britayne*.

42

After him raigned *Guitheline* his hayre,
    The iustest man and trewest in his daies,
Who had to wife Dame *Mertia* the fayre,
    A woman worthy of immortall praise,
    Which for this Realme found many goodly layes,
And wholesome Statutes to her husband brought:
    Her many deemd to haue beene of the *Fayes*,
    As was *Aegerie*, that *Numa* tought:
Those yet of her be *Mertian* lawes both nam'd and thought.

43

Her sonne *Sisillus* after her did rayne,
    And then *Kimarus*, and then *Danius*;
    Next whom *Morindus* did the crowne sustayne,
Who, had he not with wrath outrageous,
    And cruell rancour dim'd his valorous
    And mightie deedes, should matched haue the best:
As well in that same field victorious
    Against the forreine *Morands* he exprest;
Yet liues his memorie, though carcas sleepe in rest.

44

Fiue sonnes he left begotten of one wife,
    All which successiuely by turnes did rayne;
First *Gorboman* a man of vertuous life;
    Next *Archigald*, who for his proud disdayne,
    Deposed was from princedome souerayne,
And pitteous *Elidure* put in his sted;
    Who shortly it to him restord agayne,
    Till by his death he it recouered;
But *Peridure* and *Vigent* him disthronized.

45

In wretched prison long he did remaine,
    Till they outraigned had their vtmost date,
    And then therein reseized was againe,
And ruled long with honorable state,
    Till he surrendred Realme and life to fate.
    Then all the sonnes of these fiue brethren raynd
By dew successe, and all their Nephewes late,
    Euen thrise eleuen descents the crowne retaynd,
Till aged *Hely* by dew heritage it gaynd.

46

He had two sonnes, whose eldest called *Lud*
    Left of his life most famous memory,
    And endlesse moniments of his great good:
The ruin'd wals he did reædifye
    Of *Troynouant*, gainst force of enimy,
    And built that gate, which of his name is hight,
By which he lyes entombed solemnly.
    He left two sonnes, too young to rule aright,
Androgeus and *Tenantius*, pictures of his might.

Stanza 41
3 Easterland: from Holinshed 1807–08 who claims that the merchants of Norway and Denmark are called *Ostomanni* because they come from the east; noted Harper 1910:97, and see 63.2*n*. Vink 1990:102 suggests a reference to the land of the Lowland Scots and the Picts in Ireland and Northumberland. **4 foy**: fealty; or specifically the tribute paid as a sign of allegiance. **6–9** On S.'s claim that Ireland should be **subiect to Britayne** by right of conquest, see *View* 46: 'King Arthur, and before him Gurgunt, had all that island in his allegiance and subjection'; and see Maley 1997:102–04.

Stanza 42
5 found: established; 'discovered', suggested Benson 1992:270 because Mertia was a fay. **layes**: laws. The specific sense, 'religious law' (*OED* sb.³), is suggested by **goodly**. **7–9 Fayes**: fairies. **thought**: i.e. conceived by her.

Stanza 43
3 sustayne: bear. **9** S. differs from the chroniclers who record that **Morindus** was swallowed by a sea-monster.

Stanza 44
4–5 Archigald: a prototype of Artegall; see V i 3*n*. **6 pitteous**: pious, because he was surnamed Pius; full of pity,

because of his pity for his brother; exciting pity, because he was dethroned twice and was imprisoned. **9 Peridure**: see III viii 28.2*n*.

Stanza 45
3 reseized: reinstated; in the legal sense of 'seise': 'put in legal possession'. **7 By dew successe**: by rightful succession. **Nephewes**: descendants. **late**: i.e. later. **8 descents**: generations.

Stanza 46
4–5 Troynouant: New Troy or London founded by Brutus; see III ix 46. **6 that gate**: Ludgate. A topical reference to its rebuilding in 1586 is noted by Steggle 2000. **7 solemnly**: sumptuously.

Stanzas 47–63
On the late sixteenth-century interest in Roman Britain, chiefly owing to Camden's *Britannia* (1586), which effectively challenged many of Geoffrey's claims about British history, e.g. that the Trojans founded Britain, see Kendrick 1950:108–09, and esp. Curran 1996.

47

Whilst they were young, *Cassibalane* their Eme
   Was by the people chosen in their sted,
   Who on him tooke the roiall Diademe,
   And goodly well long time it gouerned,
   Till the prowde *Romanes* him disquieted,
   And warlike *Cæsar*, tempted with the name
   Of this sweet Island, neuer conquered,
   And enuying the Britons blazed fame,
(O hideous hunger of dominion) hether came.

48

Yet twise they were repulsed backe againe,
   And twise renforst, backe to their ships to fly,
   The whiles with blood they all the shore did staine,
   And the gray *Ocean* into purple dy:
   Ne had they footing found at last perdie,
   Had not *Androgeus*, false to natiue soyle,
   And enuious of Vncles soueraintie,
   Betrayd his countrey vnto forreine spoyle:
Nought els, but treason, from the first this land did foyle.

49

So by him *Cæsar* got the victory,
   Through great bloodshed, and many a sad assay,
   In which himselfe was charged heauily
   Of hardy *Nennius*, whom he yet did slay,
   But lost his sword, yet to be seene this day.
   Thenceforth this land was tributarie made
   T'ambitious *Rome*, and did their rule obay,
   Till *Arthur* all that reckoning defrayd;
Yet oft the Briton kings against them strongly swayd.

50

Next him *Tenantius* raignd, then *Kimbeline*,
   What time th'eternall Lord in fleshly slime
   Enwombed was, from wretched *Adams* line
   To purge away the guilt of sinfull crime:
   O ioyous memorie of happy time,
   That heauenly grace so plenteously displayd;
   (O too high ditty for my simple rime.)
   Soone after this the *Romanes* him warrayd;
For that their tribute he refusd to let be payd.

51

Good *Claudius*, that next was Emperour,
   An army brought, and with him batteile fought,
   In which the king was by a Treachetour
   Disguised slaine, ere any thereof thought:
   Yet ceased not the bloody fight for ought;
   For *Aruirage* his brothers place supplyde,
   Both in his armes, and crowne, and by that draught
   Did driue the *Romanes* to the weaker syde,
That they to peace agreed. So all was pacifyde.

52

Was neuer king more highly magnifide,
   Nor dredd of *Romanes*, then was *Aruirage*,
   For which the Emperour to him allide
   His daughter *Genuiss'* in marriage:
   Yet shortly he renounst the vassallage
   Of *Rome* againe, who hether hastly sent
   Vespasian, that with great spoile and rage
   Forwasted all, till *Genuissa* gent
Persuaded him to ceasse, and her lord to relent.

Stanza 47

1–4 That **Cassibalane was by the people chosen** suggests that he was not of royal line, though he was the **Eme** (uncle) of Lud's sons. **8 blazed**: published. **9 of dominion**: for power to rule.

Stanza 48

2 renforst: forced again; or reinforced. **3–4** Geoffrey 1891:4.3 notes only that the ground was drenched with blood as though it had been washed by the tide. **5 perdie**: assuredly. Geoffrey claims that the Britons repulsed the Romans through the blessing of God. **9 foyle**: overthrow, defeat; defile, pollute.

Stanza 49

2 sad assay: heavy attack. **5** Geoffrey 1891:4.4 records that Caesar's sword was buried with Nennius at the north gate of Troynovant. On S.'s treatment of this legendary British hero as fiction, see Curran 1996:287–88; on Arthur's sword on display in faery land, see I vii 36.8–9*n*. **8** Arthur would even the account either by withholding 'tribute' (50.9) or by conquering Rome in a victory that heralds Christ's birth in the next stanza. See I xi 7.2–6*n*. Like history in the Bible, S.'s history here becomes prophetic. The point is sufficiently important for

him to ignore the narrative awkwardness of having Arthur read about his future. **9 swayd**: moved hostilely.

Stanza 50

On this stanza as a climax to the system of concords set up between profane and sacred history, see Røstvig 1994:347. As the number of the jubilee, announced in Lev. 25.10: 'proclaime libertie in the land to all the inhabitants thereof', see I viii Arg.1–2*n*. **2–4** Cf. Rom. 8.3: 'God sending his owne Sonne, in the similitude of sinfull flesh, and for sinne, condemned sinne in the flesh'. **fleshly slime**: the human body; see I vii 9.8*n*; cf. III vi 3.4–5. **8 warrayd**: made war upon.

Stanza 51

1 next: after 'warlike *Cæsar*' (47.6). **3 Treachetour**: traitor. Possibly an error for 'treacherour', i.e. a treacher or traitor (cf. i 12.6), as *OED* suggests, though the word occurs again at VI viii 7.4. Possibly a blend of 'treachour' (traitor) and *ME* 'tregetour' (deceiver). See 'neologism' in the *SEnc*. **7 draught**: stratagem; representation.

Stanza 52

1 magnifide: extolled. **2 dredd**: dreaded. **8 Forwasted**: utterly wasted. **gent**: noble.

53

He dide; and him succeeded *Marius*,
   Who ioyd his dayes in great tranquillity.
   Then *Coyll*, and after him good *Lucius*,
   That first receiued Christianity,
   The sacred pledge of Christes Euangely:
   Yet true it is, that long before that day
   Hither came *Ioseph* of *Arimathy*,
Who brought with him the holy grayle, (they say)
And preacht the truth; but since it greatly did decay.

54

This good king shortly without issew dide,
   Whereof great trouble in the kingdome grew,
   That did her selfe in sondry parts diuide,
   And with her powre her owne selfe ouerthrew,
   Whilest *Romanes* daily did the weake subdew:
   Which seeing stout *Bunduca*, vp arose,
   And taking armes, the *Britons* to her drew;
   With whom she marched streight against her foes,
And them vnwares besides the *Seuerne* did enclose.

55

There she with them a cruell batteill tryde,
   Not with so good successe, as shee deseru'd;
   By reason that the Captaines on her syde,
   Corrupted by *Paulinus*, from her sweru'd:
   Yet such, as were through former flight preseru'd,
   Gathering againe, her Host she did renew,
   And with fresh corage on the victor seru'd:
   But being all defeated, saue a few,
Rather then fly, or be captiu'd, her selfe she slew.

56

O famous moniment of womens prayse,
   Matchable either to *Semiramis*,
   Whom antique history so high doth rayse,
   Or to *Hypsiphil'*, or to *Thomiris*:
   Her Host two hundred thousand numbred is;
   Who whiles good fortune fauoured her might,
   Triumphed oft against her enemis;
   And yet though ouercome in haplesse fight,
Shee triumphed on death, in enemies despight.

57

Her reliques *Fulgent* hauing gathered,
   Fought with *Seuerus*, and him ouerthrew;
   Yet in the chace was slaine of them, that fled:
   So made them victors, whome he did subdew.
   Then gan *Carausius* tirannize anew,
   And gainst the *Romanes* bent their proper powre,
   But him *Allectus* treacherously slew,
   And tooke on him the robe of Emperoure:
Nath'lesse the same enioyed but short happy howre:

58

For *Asclepiodate* him ouercame,
   And left inglorious on the vanquisht playne,
   Without or robe, or rag, to hide his shame.
   Then afterwards he in his stead did raigne;
   But shortly was by *Coyll* in batteill slaine:
   Who after long debate, since *Lucies* tyme,
   Was of the *Britons* first crownd Soueraine:
   Then gan this Realme renew her passed prime;
He of his name *Coylchester* built of stone and lime.

Stanza 53
The advent of Christianity marks a major climacteric in S.'s chronicle, being the 49th stanza from stanza 5; see J.L. Mills 1976:283. **5 sacred pledge**: i.e. baptism. **Euangely**: Gospel. **6 long before that day**: S. is claiming that Christianity in England, and therefore the English Church, came directly from Jerusalem rather than by way of Rome. **Ioseph of Arimathy**: the disciple who buried Jesus at Matt. 27.57–60. Holinshed 1807–08:1.486 records that he first taught the gospel in England; legend and medieval romance associate him with the holy grail, which he was reputed to have carried to Glastonbury Abbey (Malory 2.16), the site of Arthur's tomb (Malory 21.11).

Stanzas 54–56
S. transfers the story of **Bunduca** or Boadicea from before Marius's reign to after Lucius's death; noted Harper 1910:117–20, who observes that stanza 56, which follows the chroniclers in praising her victories, 'in part contradicts and in part repeats the narrative in the preceding stanzas'. One explanation may be that 54 marks the end of the second dynasty of British history; see 5–68.2n. Another may be S.'s desire to single her out as a prototype of Elizabeth, and (for which he has no authority) to point to the dangers of corruption by Rome even at the cost of destroying stanza 56 with its absurd fifth line. Any analogy must remain oblique, for Bunduca succeeds Lucius, England's first Christian king, as Elizabeth succeeds Henry VIII, the first defender of the faith, but Lucius died 'without issew' (54.1). S. refers to her story again at III

iii 54.7–8, and *Time* 106–12. On her early reception, see Mikalachki 1998, esp. 119–28.

Stanza 54
3–4 her: the three uses mark the emerging kingdom as feminine under Bunduca, in contrast to the use of 'it' at 5.5–6. **6 stout**: valiant. **9 besides the Seuerne**: by the side of the Severn, a detail invented by S., perhaps to associate her with another British heroine; see 19.5–9n.

Stanza 55
4 sweru'd: deserted. **6 Host**: army. **7 seru'd**: brought action.

Stanza 56
1 prayse: virtue, excellence. **2–5 Semiramis**: the famous queen who, disguised as her son, performed 'many noble enterprices and valiaunt actes' (T. Cooper 1565). For her ambition, she is imprisoned in the dungeon of the house of Pride at I v 50.3–4. **Hypsiphil'**: the queen of Lemnos who saved her father when her female subjects killed their male relatives. **Thomiris**: the savage Queen of Scythia who, aided by 200,000 Persians (Cooper), killed Cyrus. Bunduca's ambiguous reputation may explain S.'s conflicting comparisons.

Stanza 57
1 reliques: the residue of her army, the 'few' at 55.8. **6 proper**: own.

59

Which when the *Romanes* heard, they hether sent
  Constantius, a man of mickle might,
  With whome king *Coyll* made an agreement,
  And to him gaue for wife his daughter bright,
  Fayre *Helena*, the fairest liuing wight;
  Who in all godly thewes, and goodly praise,
  Did far excell, but was most famous hight
  For skil in Musicke of all in her daies,
Aswell in curious instruments as cunning laies.

60

Of whom he did great *Constantine* begett,
  Who afterward was Emperour of *Rome*;
  To which whiles absent he his mind did sett,
  Octauius here lept into his roome,
  And it vsurped by vnrighteous doome:
  But he his title iustifide by might,
  Slaying *Traherne*, and hauing ouercome
  The *Romane* legion in dreadfull fight:
So settled he his kingdome, and confirmd his right.

61

But wanting yssew male, his daughter deare,
  He gaue in wedlocke to *Maximian*,
  And him with her made of his kingdome heyre,
  Who soone by meanes thereof the Empire wan,
  Till murdred by the freends of *Gratian*,
  Then gan the Hunnes and Picts inuade this land,
  During the raigne of *Maximinian*;
  Who dying left none heire them to withstand,
But that they ouerran all parts with easy hand.

62

The weary *Britons*, whose war-hable youth
  Was by *Maximian* lately ledd away,
  With wretched miseryes, and woefull ruth,
  Were to those Pagans made an open pray,
  And daily spectacle of sad decay:
  Whome *Romane* warres, which now fowr hundred yeares,
  And more had wasted, could no whit dismay;
  Til by consent of Commons and of Peares,
They crownd the second *Constantine* with ioyous teares,

63

Who hauing oft in batteill vanquished
  Those spoylefull Picts, and swarming Easterlings,
  Long time in peace his realme established
  Yet oft annoyd with sondry bordragings.
  Of neighbour Scots, and forrein Scatterlings,
  With which the world did in those dayes abound:
  Which to outbarre, with painefull pyonings
  From sea to sea he heapt a mighty mound,
Which from *Alcluid* to *Panwelt* did that border bownd.

64

Three sonnes he dying left, all vnder age;
  By meanes whereof, their vncle *Vortigere*
  Vsurpt the crowne, during their pupillage;
  Which th'Infants tutors gathering to feare,
  Them closely into *Armorick* did beare:
  For dread of whom, and for those Picts annoyes,
  He sent to *Germany*, straunge aid to reare,
  From whence eftsoones arriued here three hoyes
Of *Saxons*, whom he for his safety imployes.

Stanza 58

5 **Coyll**: Coyll II; not the merry old soul of 53.3. 7 This claim lacks authority, as Harper 1910:126 notes.

Stanza 59

4 **bright**: beautiful. 6 **thewes**: manners, qualities. **goodly praise**: i.e. what deserves goodly praise; cf. 56.1. 7 **hight**: named. 9 **curious**: requiring skill.

Stanza 60

1–2 **great Constantine**: Constantine the Great, the first Christian Roman Emperor. He was compared to Elizabeth because his mother was English, because he was head of both church and state, and because he ruled Rome; see Yates 1977:41–45. 4 **roome**: office. 5 **doome**: law or act.

Stanza 61

6 **Picts**: the Scots, but a general term for the borderers on the northern fringe of the British Isles; see Vink 1990:105. 7 **Maximinian**: a variant of **Maximian** to avoid duplication.

Stanza 62

The utter desolation of England prepares for the beginning of the fourth dynasty and the coming of Arthur. 1 **war-hable**: fit for war. 3 **ruth**: sorrow; ruin. 5 **decay**: death. 8 For the military, as in Holinshed, S. substitutes the two Houses of Parliament, i.e. the **Commons** and **Peares**.

Stanza 63

2 **spoylefull**: plundering. **Easterlings**: identified by Vink 1990:102 as Picts in Ireland who practised Columban, i.e. non-Roman, Christianity; see 41.3*n*. 4 **bordragings**: raids; specifically border raids. 5 **Scatterlings**: vagrants; presumably the Easterlings who have been scattered by English power. They are identified as a subset of **Scots** by Vink 104. See Maley 1997:150–51. 7–9 The Picts Wall was built by the Romans but attributed by S. (alone, as Harper 1910:134 notes) to Constantine II, 'That Romaine Monarch' (IV xi 36.2), who is Arthur's grandfather. **pyonings**: excavations, the work of pioneers.

Stanza 64

3 **pupillage**: minority. 4 **gathering to feare**: gathering cause to fear, coming to fear; or **to feare**: 'tofere', together. 5 **closely**: secretly. **Armorick**: Armorica, i.e. Brittany. 7 **He**: Vortigern. **straunge**: foreign. 8–9 The Saxons now replace the Romans as the chief enemy of the Britons. Their triumph is recorded again at III iii 41. **hoyes**: small boats.

65

Two brethren were their Capitayns, which hight
   Hengist and *Horsus*, well approu'd in warre,
   And both of them men of renowmed might;
   Who making vantage of their ciuile iarre,
   And of those forreyners, which came from farre,
   Grew great, and got large portions of land,
   That in the Realme ere long they stronger arre,
   Then they which sought at first their helping hand,
And *Vortiger* haue forst the kingdome to aband.

66

But by the helpe of *Vortimere* his sonne,
   He is againe vnto his rule restord,
   And *Hengist* seeming sad, for that was donne,
   Receiued is to grace and new accord,
   Through his faire daughters face, and flattring word,
   Soone after which, three hundred Lords he slew
   Of British blood, all sitting at his bord;
   Whose dolefull moniments who list to rew,
Th'eternall marks of treason may at *Stonheng* vew.

67

By this the sonnes of *Constantine*, which fled,
   Ambrose and *Vther* did ripe yeares attayne,
   And here arriuing, strongly challenged
   The crowne, which *Vortiger* did long detayne:

Who flying from his guilt, by them was slayne,
And *Hengist* eke soone brought to shamefull death.
Thenceforth *Aurelius* peaceably did rayne,
Till that through poyson stopped was his breath;
So now entombed lies at Stoneheng by the heath.

68

After him Vther, which *Pendragon* hight,
   Succeeding There abruptly it did end,
   Without full point, or other Cesure right,
   As if the rest some wicked hand did rend,
   Or th'Author selfe could not at least attend
   To finish it: that so vntimely breach
   The Prince him selfe halfe seemed to offend,
   Yet secret pleasure did offence empeach,
And wonder of antiquity long stopt his speach.

69

At last quite rauisht with delight, to heare
   The royall Ofspring of his natiue land,
   Cryde out, Deare countrey, O how dearely deare
   Ought thy remembraunce, and perpetual band
   Be to thy foster Childe, that from thy hand
   Did commun breath and nouriture receaue?
   How brutish is it not to vnderstand,
   How much to her we owe, that all vs gaue,
That gaue vnto vs all, what euer good we haue.

Stanza 65

2 well approu'd: well-tried.   **9 aband**: abandon.

Stanza 66

9 marks: stones standing as a memorial (*OED* sb.[1] 5). According to Geoffrey 1891:8.11, the stone circle of **Stoneheng** was the Giant's Dance, mystical stones of a medicinal virtue that Merlin through his magic transported from Ireland to Salisbury Plain.

Stanza 67

3 challenged: laid claim to.   **7 Aurelius**: i.e. Ambrose. **9 the heath**: Salisbury Plain.

Stanza 68

1–2 The coming of Arthur marks another major climacteric in S.'s chronicle, being $7 \times 9 \times 9$ lines from the beginning at stanza 5; see J.L. Mills 1976:283. The chronicle breaks here because history does: time is now the present; see III iii 52.5–9 and *n*. On **Vther**, who is Arthur's father named **Pendragon**, a Welsh term for the chief leader in war (*Pen*, head + *dragon*), see I vii 31.3–9*n*. Presumably Arthur remains ignorant of his parentage (see I ix 3.3–4) though his **secret pleasure** and his delight in hearing about 'his natiue land' (69.2) would suggest otherwise. On his descent from the Roman Constantine II, his grandfather, see Curran 1996:284–87. The chronicle resumes through prophecy in the story of Arthur's half-brother, Artegall, at III iii 27, and ends in a similarly abrupt manner at 50.1.   **abruptly**: a new word in *1590*, used in the sense of the Lat. *abruptus*, broken off.   **3** 'Without full stop or proper formal break'. The caesura in the line marks the caesura in chronology, the moment when the past yields to the present.

See Fried 1981:267; also D.L. Miller 1988:205–06 who interprets S.'s use of aposiopesis in its literal sense, 'becoming silent' as a challenge to Arthur to perfect imperfect history by completing it. That he is left 'between nations', a present and a transcendent Britain, is argued by Baker 1997:169–73. **5 th'Author selfe**: a possible pun since the account ends with the coming of Arthur.   **at least**: at the last.   **6 breach**: break, interruption of the history.   **7 to offend**: i.e. to be offended. **8 empeach**: prevent.

Stanza 69

2 royall Ofspring: ancestry or descent of the kings.   **5 foster Childe**: because he was nurtured by the land as though one of her own, although from his birth he has lived in faery land; see I ix 3.5–9.   **7** An allusion to Britain's assumed Trojan ancestry through Brutus – see 9.8*n* – is inescapable.

Stanzas 70–76

The seven nine-line stanzas of the 'rolls of Elfin Emperours' (Arg.) incorporate the proportions of seven and nine in the temperate human body – see 5–68.2*n* – and their total of 63 lines registers the major climacteric in human life; see J.L. Mills 1976:285. In Holinshed 1807–08:1.49–51, Harrison notes that changes in the government and the religion of Britain occur in cycles, each a multiple of seven or nine. Accordingly, Brutus's progeny ruled for 700 years (36.1–2), seven kings are listed at 72–73, and 'seuen hundred Princes' are mentioned at 74.3. As a teleological and triumphalist history, its uninterrupted succession of the Elfin kings – in contrast to the four dynasties of the 'chronicle of Briton kings' (Arg.), which is marked by the lack of a successor – is noted by the various suffixes added to **Elfe**. The identification of the seven named in 72–73, generally

70

But *Guyon* all this while his booke did read,
　Ne yet has ended: for it was a great
　And ample volume, that doth far excead
　My leasure, so long leaues here to repeat:
　It told, how first *Prometheus* did create
　A man, of many parts from beasts deryu'd,
　And then stole fire from heuen, to animate
　His worke, for which he was by *Ioue* depryu'd
Of life him self, and hart-strings of an Aegle ryu'd.

71

That man so made, he called *Elfe*, to weet
　Quick, the first author of all Elfin kynd:
　Who wandring through the world with wearie feet,
　Did in the gardins of *Adonis* fynd
　A goodly creature, whom he deemd in mynd
　To be no earthly wight, but either Spright,
　Or Angell, th'authour of all woman kynd;
　Therefore a *Fay* he her according hight,
Of whom all *Faryes* spring, and fetch their lignage right.

72

Of these a mighty people shortly grew,
　And puissant kinges, which all the world warrayd,
　And to them selues all Nations did subdew:
　The first and eldest, which that scepter swayd,

Was *Elfin*; him all *India* obayd,
　And all that now *America* men call:
　Next him was noble *Elfinan*, who laid
　Cleopolis foundation first of all:
But *Elfiline* enclosd it with a golden wall.

73

His sonne was *Elfinell*, who ouercame
　The wicked *Gobbelines* in bloody field:
　But *Elfant* was of most renowmed fame,
　Who all of Christall did *Panthea* build:
　Then *Elfar*, who two brethren gyauntes kild,
　The one of which had two heades, th'other three:
　Then *Elfinor*, who was in magick skild;
　He built by art vpon the glassy See
A bridge of bras, whose sound heuens thunder seem'd to bee.

74

He left three sonnes, the which in order raynd,
　And all their Ofspring, in their dew descents,
　Euen seuen hundred Princes, which maintaynd
　With mightie deedes their sondry gouernments;
　That were too long their infinite contents
　Here to record, ne much materiall:
　Yet should they be most famous moniments,
　And braue ensample, both of martiall,
And ciuil rule to kinges and states imperiall.

---

alternating from conqueror to constructor, remains moot; see D.L. Miller 1988:209–14. Rathborne 1937:65–128 suggested figures from Roman history but modified her claims in correspondence in *TLS* 1948:79, 233, 275, and 373. In stanza 74, after the three unnamed kings followed by their 700 successors, the historical analogues emerge more clearly in 75–76, which trace Elizabeth's 'famous auncestryes' (1.7) in the Tudors. Elferon, or Prince Arthur, is included even though he did not become king, and the reigns of Edward VI and Mary Tudor are ignored in order to maintain Elizabeth's unbroken line of succession; see Christian 1991:74.

Stanza 70

2 The '*Antiquitee* of *Faerie* lond' (ix 60.2) **[n]e yet has ended** because it extends to the present reign of Elizabeth. **5–9** See 'Prometheus' in the *SEnc*. On his creation as the beginning of human civilization, see Roche 1964:35–37; on his origin in violence, see J. Miller 1986a:90. **depryu'd | Of life**: as he was deprived of happiness, or separated from heaven by being bound upon a rock. Jove's role seems to be invented by S. **hart-strings**: the tendons that were held to sustain the heart. Usually Prometheus's liver is devoured, though Cooper names the heart.

Stanza 71

1–2 The etymology of **Elfe**, i.e. **Quick** (i.e. a living thing), is S.'s. Since the term was applied to supernatural and infernal creatures, he finds his own kind in a **Fay**, so named because she is a 'fay' (*OED* sb.[2]) or fairy. **authour**: ancestor. **4 the gardins of Adonis**: see III vi 30–50 and *n*; here it provides an analogue to Eden, to which it is linked by etymology. **8 according**: fittingly.

Stanza 72

2 warrayd: ravaged by war. **4–6 Elfin**: identified with Osiris-Bacchus by Rathborne 1937:108–11; possibly Bacchus-Hercules who conquered the East and West (see V i 2), named **India** and **America** as the boundaries of faery land. **7–9 Next**: i.e. next in importance in the Elfin line. **Elfinan**: possibly Brutus, the founder of London. **Cleopolis**: see I vii 46.7, x 58.2. **Elfiline**: possibly Lud who restored London wall (46.4–5).

Stanza 73

1–2 His sonne: i.e. Elfinan's son; possibly Locrine, son of Brutus. The **Gobbelines**, as enemies of the Elfs (after the analogy of the Italian Guelfs and Ghibellines) would be the Huns whom Locrine overthrew at 15. See E.K. on *SC June* 25. **3–4 Elfant**: probably Lucius, the first British king (53.3–5). If so, **Panthea** would be Westminster Abbey, which was built by Lucius (Holinshed 1807–08:1.512); or Windsor Castle (but see I x 58.5–9*n*); or the towers of London: see IV xi 27.6–9. **5–6 Elfar**: possibly Constantine the Great who became 'Emperour of *Rome*' (60.2). If so, the two-headed giant would refer to his defeat of Maxentius and Licinius, and the three-headed giant his defeat of pagan religion. **7–9 Elfinor**: possibly Constantine II. The **bridge of bras** upon **the glassy See** suggests an idealized London Bridge over the Thames; its **thunder**, the roar of tidal water against its piers; see III ix 45. Since the 'glassie sea' of Rev. 15.2 is glossed in the Geneva Bible as 'this brittel and inconstant worlde', the lines suggest a consolidation of empire.

Stanza 74

1 three sonnes: associated with the three sons of Constantine II; see 64.1. **6 ne much materiall**: nor of much consequence.

75

After all these *Elficleos* did rayne,
    The wise *Elficleos* in great Maiestie,
    Who mightily that scepter did sustayne,
    And with rich spoyles and famous victorie,
    Did high aduaunce the crowne of *Faery*.
    He left two sonnes, of which faire *Elferon*
    The eldest brother did vntimely dy;
    Whose emptie place the mightie *Oberon*
Doubly supplide, in spousall, and dominion.

76

Great was his power and glorie ouer all,
    Which him before, that sacred seate did fill,
    That yet remaines his wide memoriall:
    He dying left the fairest *Tanaquill*,

Him to succeede therein, by his last will:
    Fairer and nobler liueth none this howre,
    Ne like in grace, ne like in learned skill;
    Therefore they *Glorian* call that glorious flowre,
Long mayst thou *Glorian* liue, in glory and great powre.

77

Beguyld thus with delight of nouelties,
    And naturall desire of countryes state,
    So long they redd in those antiquities,
    That how the time was fled, they quite forgate,
    Till gentle *Alma* seeing it so late,
    Perforce their studies broke, and them besought
    To thinke, how supper did them long awaite.
    So halfe vnwilling from their bookes them brought,
And fayrely feasted, as so noble knightes she ought.

Stanza 75
Elficleos is Henry VII; his two sons are **Elferon** or Prince Arthur who died young, and **Oberon** or Henry VIII who **Doubly supplide** his brother's place by assuming his rule and marrying his widow.

Stanza 76
3 memoriall: memory. **4 Tanaquill**: Elizabeth; see I proem 2.5*n*. **5 by his last will**: referring to Henry's final will in which he declared that 'the said imperyall crowne . . . *shall*

wholely remaine and come to our said daughter Elizabeth' (cited Kitchin 1872). **6 liueth none**: as at 68.2, there is a sudden shift from the past to the present.

Stanza 77
1–2 The same motive led them to read the chronicles: 'burning both with feruent fire, | Their countreys auncestry to vnderstond' (ix 60.6–7). **desire**: i.e. to know their country's history, but also their love of their country.

Cant. XI.

The enimies of Temperaunce
besiege her dwelling place:
Prince Arthure them repelles, and fowle
Maleger doth deface.

1

WHat warre so cruel, or what siege so sore,
　　As that, which strong affections doe apply
Against the forte of reason euermore,
To bring the sowle into captiuity:
Their force is fiercer through infirmity
Of the fraile flesh, relenting to their rage,
And exercise most bitter tyranny
Vpon the partes, brought into their bondage:
No wretchednesse is like to sinfull vellenage.

2

But in a body which doth freely yeeld
　　His partes to reasons rule obedient,
And letteth her that ought the scepter weeld,
All happy peace and goodly gouernment
Is setled there in sure establishment,
There *Alma* like a virgin Queene most bright,
Doth florish in all beautie excellent:
And to her guestes doth bounteous banket dight,
Attempred goodly well for health and for delight.

3

Early before the Morne with cremosin ray,
　　The windowes of bright heauen opened had,
Through which into the world the dawning day
Might looke, that maketh euery creature glad,

Vprose Sir *Guyon*, in bright armour clad,
　　And to his purposd iourney him prepar'd:
With him the Palmer eke in habit sad,
Him selfe addrest to that aduenture hard:
So to the riuers syde they both together far'd.

4

Where them awaited ready at the ford
　　The *Ferriman*, as *Alma* had behight,
With his well rigged bote: They goe abord,
And he eftsoones gan launch his barke forthright.
Ere long they rowed were quite out of sight,
And fast the land behynd them fled away.
But let them pas, whiles winde and wether right
Doe serue their turnes: here I a while must stay,
To see a cruell fight doen by the prince this day.

5

For all so soone, as *Guyon* thence was gon
　　Vpon his voyage with his trustie guyde,
That wicked band of villeins fresh begon
That castle to assaile on euery side,
And lay strong siege about it far and wyde.
So huge and infinite their numbers were,
That all the land they vnder them did hyde;
So fowle and vgly, that exceeding feare
Their visages imprest, when they approched neare.

Book II Canto xi

Argument
4 deface: destroy.

Stanza 1
1–4 The **siege** of the temperate body – see ix 12.7–8 – by the **affections**, i.e. 'passions bace', is announced at ix 1.5–8. In the sixteenth century, siege warfare had replaced chivalric combat; see M. West 1988:654–55, 661–65. Cf. Paul on 'the infirmities of [the] flesh' (Rom. 6.19), esp. 7.23: 'I se another law in my membres, rebelling against the law of my minde, and leading me captiue vnto the law of sinne, which is in my membres'. **6 relenting**: yielding. **9 sinfull vellenage**: bondage of the flesh to sin through the corrupt will (Lat. *velle*). Aided by a 'thousand villeins' (ix 13.2), Maleger is called a 'villein' at 26.6, 29.4, 35.3 to indicate his state of bondage.

Stanza 2
The male body, which is identified with the affections, ruled by the female soul, which is identified with reason, is analogous to the body politic, i.e. Elizabeth the **virgin Queene** ruling her subjects. **5 establishment**: established condition. **8 boun-**

teous banket: cf. the feast at the house of Medina at ii 39.1–2. The 'firme foundation' of temperance is 'true bountyhed' (xii 1.5). **dight**: prepare. **9 Attempred**: controlled, as ii 39.1, indicating the exercise of temperance. **health**: spiritual and moral well-being.

Stanza 3
The matter of iii 1, which marks the beginning of Guyon's journey to the Bower, is repeated here to note his renewed effort. Accordingly, he returns to the river reached at ix 10.3–4.

Stanza 4
2 Ferriman: see xii 10*n*. **behight**: commanded, indicating that he is the will, which, being directed by reason, keeps the body 'in sober gouernment' (ix 1.4).

Stanza 5
3 That wicked band: the 'thousand villeins' or serfs at ix 13.2. That they cover **all the land** indicates that they represent the world. **8–9 So fowle and vgly**: from the poet's perspective as he sees them from the castle, 4.8–9. Hence **imprest** has the psychological sense, imprinted.

6

Them in twelue troupes their Captein did dispart,
  And round about in fittest steades did place,
  Where each might best offend his proper part,
  And his contrary obiect most deface,
  As euery one seem'd meetest in that cace.
  Seuen of the same against the Castle gate,
  In strong entrenchments he did closely place,
  Which with incessaunt force and endlesse hate,
They battred day and night, and entraunce did awate.

7

The other fiue, fiue sondry wayes he sett,
  Against the fiue great Bulwarkes of that pyle,
  And vnto each a Bulwarke did arrett,
  T'assayle with open force or hidden guyle,
  In hope thereof to win victorious spoile.
  They all that charge did feruently apply,
  With greedie malice and importune toyle,
  And planted there their huge artillery,
With which they dayly made most dreadfull battery.

8

The first troupe was a monstrous rablement
  Of fowle misshapen wightes, of which some were
  Headed like Owles, with beckes vncomely bent,
  Others like Dogs, others like Gryphons dreare,

And some had wings, and some had clawes to teare,
  And euery one of them had Lynces eyes,
  And euery one did bow and arrowes beare:
  All those were lawlesse lustes, corrupt enuyes,
And couetous aspects, all cruel enimyes.

9

Those same against the bulwarke of the *Sight*
  Did lay strong siege, and battailous assault,
  Ne once did yield it respitt day nor night,
  But soone as *Titan* gan his head exault,
  And soone againe as he his light withhault,
  Their wicked engins they against it bent:
  That is each thing, by which the eyes may fault,
  But two then all more huge and violent,
Beautie, and money they against that Bulwarke lent.

10

The second Bulwarke was the *Hearing* sence,
  Gainst which the second troupe assignment makes,
  Deformed creatures, in straunge difference,
  Some hauing heads like Harts, some like to Snakes,
  Some like wilde Bores late rouzd out of the brakes,
  Slaunderous reproches, and fowle infamies,
  Leasinges, backbytinges, and vaineglorious crakes,
  Bad counsels, prayses, and false flatteries,
All those against that fort did bend their batteries.

Stanza 6
1 Of the **twelue**, seven are the deadly sins, which assault the soul, and five are the vices, which assault the body through the five senses. That Arthur is left alone as conqueror at 48.1 with the death of Maleger and his two hags indicates that the twelve troops are included in their captain. **dispart**: divide. 2 **steades**: positions. 3 **offend**: attack. 6 **Castle gate** the mouth (see ix 23) as it provides an entrance to the heart. 7 **closely**: secretly.

Stanza 7
2 **great Bulwarkes**: the five senses as fortifications or powers of defence; cf. 'fort' (10.9) and 'breaches' (14.7). **pyle**: castle. 3 **arrett**: commit in charge. 4 **force . . . guyle**: the traditional pair; see vii 25.3*n*. 6 **apply**: attend. 7 **importune**: ceaseless; grievous. 8 **huge artillery**: the 'hideous Ordinaunce' of 14.3; also bows (*OED* 2), as shown at 18.1–2.

Stanzas 8–13
On the five senses given here in their traditional order, see 'senses, five' in the *SEnc*. On the traditional association of each with an animal emblematic of its power, see Bloomfield 1952:245–49. Ripa 1603:449 links the boar with hearing, the lynx with sight, the ape with taste, the vulture with smell, and the spider with touch. A literary analogue is Alcina's animal-headed crew that attacks Ruggiero in Ariosto, *Orl. Fur.* 6.61–64, interpreted by Harington 1591:80 as 'those seauen sinnes which be called the deadly sinnes'. Three animals are associated with each of the five senses and then with three (or three groups) of moral faults generally appropriate to the sense.

Stanza 8
1 **monstrous rablement**: also 'rabble of monsters'. 2 **fowle**: hardly a pun in this context. 3–4 **Owles**: generally a bird of

ill-omen; see I v 30.6–7*n*; cf. the 'ill-faste Owle' at xii 36.4. **beckes**: beaks. **Gryphons**: a lion with eagle's wings, traditionally sharp-sighted and associated with covetousness; see I v 8.2*n*. **dreare**: dreadful. 6–7 The keen sight of the lynx was proverbial (Smith 510). 8–9 The three moral faults are **lawlesse lustes**: the 'fleshlie lustes, which fight against the soule' (1 Pet. 2.11); **enuyes**: in the etymological sense, 'to look upon (with malice)'; and **couetous aspects**: looks that express covetousness. They form part of Lucifera's pageant at I iv 18–35.

Stanza 9
5 **withhault**: withheld. 6 **engins**: machines used in warfare but also snares that deceive the mind (Lat. *ingenium*); cf. 'open force or hidden guyle' (7.4). 7 The attack from without is interpreted as an attack from within. **fault**: sin. 9 **Beautie, and money**: the two chief objects of appetite in the world which the passive mind seeks as ends in themselves, as N. Frye 1963:81 notes. Guyon's two chief foes are Acrasia and Mammon, the powers of Cupid and cupidity, which oppose the temperate body's form and function respectively. **lent**: pressed against; rent *1596* is more appropriate to 'breaches' (14.7).

Stanza 10
2 **assignment**: dessignment *1596* is a military term for design or plan of attack. 3–5 **in straunge difference**: i.e. strangely different from each other. The hart is opposed to the boar and both to the snake. Harvey, in Spenser 1912:626, refers to the 'Hartes hearing'. Actaeon wearing the stag's head is usually an emblem of man transformed by desire; here, perhaps, the victim of (sexual?) slander. **brakes**: bushes. 6–8 The first two lines list the three kinds of vices: **infamies** or slanders, **Leasinges** or lies, and **crakes** or braggings. The third gives examples of each in the same order.

11

Likewise that same third Fort, that is the *Smell*
    Of that third troupe was cruelly assayd:
    Whose hideous shapes were like to feendes of hell,
    Some like to houndes, some like to Apes, dismayd,
    Some like to Puttockes, all in plumes arayd:
    All shap't according their conditions,
    For by those vgly formes weren pourtrayd,
    Foolish delights and fond abusions,
Which doe that sence besiege with light illusions.

12

And that fourth band which cruell battry bent,
    Against the fourth Bulwarke, that is the *Taste*,
    Was as the rest a grysie rablement,
    Some mouth'd like greedy Oystriges, some faste
    Like loathly Toades, some fashioned in the waste
    Like swine; for so deformd is luxury,
    Surfeat, misdiet, and vnthriftie waste,
    Vaine feastes, and ydle superfluity:
All those this sences Fort assayle incessantly.

13

But the fift troupe most horrible of hew,
    And ferce of force, is dreadfull to report:
    For some like Snailes, some did like spyders shew,
    And some like vgly Vrchins thick and short:
    Cruelly they assayed that fift Fort,
    Armed with dartes of sensuall delight,
    With stinges of carnall lust, and strong effort
    Of feeling pleasures, with which day and night
Against that same fift bulwarke they continued fight.

14

Thus these twelue troupes with dreadfull puissaunce
    Against that Castle restlesse siege did lay,
    And euermore their hideous Ordinaunce
    Vpon the Bulwarkes cruelly did play,
    That now it gan to threaten neare decay.
    And euermore their wicked Capitayn
    Prouoked them the breaches to assay,
    Somtimes with threats, somtimes with hope of gayn,
Which by the ransack of that peece they should attayn.

15

On th'other syde, th'assieged Castles ward
    Their stedfast stonds did mightily maintaine,
    And many bold repulse, and many hard
    Atchieuement wrought with perill and with payne,
    That goodly frame from ruine to sustaine:
    And those two brethren Gyauntes did defend
    The walles so stoutly with their sturdie mayne,
    That neuer entraunce any durst pretend,
But they to direfull death their groning ghosts did send.

16

The noble Virgin, Ladie of the Place,
    Was much dismayed with that dreadful sight:
    For neuer was she in so euill cace,
    Till that the Prince seeing her wofull plight,
    Gan her recomfort from so sad affright,
    Offring his seruice, and his dearest life
    For her defence, against that Carle to fight,
    Which was their chiefe and th'authour of that strife:
She him remercied as the Patrone of her life.

Stanza 11

2 assayd: assaulted. **3–5 dismayd**: as the first troop is 'mis-shapen' (8.2) and the second 'Deformed' (10.3), the hounds and apes are **hideous** in being 'dis-made' or 'mis-made' in being half of each, with the puttocks 'mis-made' in wearing false feathers. **houndes** and **Puttockes** (kites or buzzards) have acute smell; **Apes** are usually associated with taste but also with hearing, because of their short ears, in *Mother Hubberd* 1383. **in plumes arayd**: perhaps because smell is associated with the air. **6 according their conditions**: suitable to their natures, i.e. to their allegorical functions. **8 fond abusions**: foolish deceptions.

Stanza 12

3 grysie: terrible, fearful; or, as 'grisly': horrible to see, hideous. **4–8** This troop is deformed in mouth, face, and body; cf. 10.3. **Oystriges**: ostriches; **greedy** because they were reputed to eat anything. **faste**: faced. **Toades**: appropriate here in being regarded as poisonous. **luxury**: vicious indulgence, illustrated by 7. **misdiet**: improper feeding. **Vaine feastes** describes **Surfeat** and **misdiet**. **vnthriftie waste**: because the vice is embodied in the waistless swine.

Stanza 13

The only sense not directly named, perhaps because touch is the temptation of the Bower of Bliss. **1 hew**: appearance, shape. **3–4** Harvey, in Spenser 1912:626, cites the 'spiders touching'. **Vrchins**: the hedgehog; cited for its bristling spines. **7 effort**: power. **8 feeling**: tactile, sentient.

Stanza 14

2 restlesse: never ceasing, but suggesting 'not to be resisted'. **3–4 Ordinaunce**: applied to a cannon, ballistic catapult, or battering ram. **play**: fire; batter. **5 decay**: destruction. **6 Capitayn**: see ix 15.3*n*. **7 assay**: assault. **9 peece**: fortress or castle; masterpiece.

Stanza 15

1 assieged: besieged. **ward**: garrison. **2 stonds**: posts; used here in the military sense: 'holding one's ground against an enemy' (*OED* 4). **6–9** The **two brethren Gyauntes** are the hands; noted Gilbert 1955. **mayne**: a bilingual pun on Fr. *main*, hand. Hands are 'the kepers of the house' (Eccles. 12.3), which the Geneva gloss spells out as 'the hands, which kepe the bodie'. See iv 6.4*n*. **pretend**: attempt.

Stanza 16

1–3 At this lowest point of Alma's fortunes (cf. 14.5), Arthur may assume his traditional role as the instrument of divine grace. The book's number determines that he must intervene a second time; see I viii Arg.1–2*n*. **Place**: fortress. **5 affright**: terror. **6 his dearest life**: i.e. life most precious to him, life itself. **7 Carle**: villain. **9 remercied**: thanked (for his mercy). **Patrone**: protector; see viii 55.4*n*.

17

Eftsoones himselfe in glitterand armes he dight,
    And his well proued weapons to him hent;
    So taking courteous conge he behight,
    Those gates to be vnbar'd, and forth he went.
    Fayre mote he thee, the prowest and most gent,
    That euer brandished bright steele on hye:
    Whom soone as that vnruly rablement,
    With his gay Squyre issewing did espye,
They reard a most outrageous dreadfull yelling cry.

18

And therewithall attonce at him let fly
    Their fluttring arrowes, thicke as flakes of snow,
    And round about him flocke impetuously,
    Like a great water flood, that tombling low
    From the high mountaines, threates to ouerflow
    With suddein fury all the fertile playne,
    And the sad husbandmans long hope doth throw,
    A downe the streame and all his vowes make vayne,
Nor bounds nor banks his headlong ruine may sustayne.

19

Vpon his shield their heaped hayle he bore,
    And with his sword disperst the raskall flockes,
    Which fled a sonder, and him fell before,
    As withered leaues drop from their dryed stockes,
    When the wroth Western wind does reaue their locks;
    And vnder neath him his courageous steed,
    The fierce *Spumador* trode them downe like docks,
    The fierce *Spumador* borne of heauenly seed:
Such as *Laomedon* of *Phœbus* race did breed.

20

Which suddeine horrour and confused cry,
    When as their Capteine heard, in haste he yode,
    The cause to weet, and fault to remedy,
    Vpon a Tygre swift and fierce he rode,
    That as the winde ran vnderneath his lode,
    Whiles his long legs nigh raught vnto the ground,
    Full large he was of limbe, and shoulders brode,
    But of such subtile substance and vnsound,
That like a ghost he seem'd, whose graue-clothes were
                                              (vnbound.

21

And in his hand a bended bow was seene,
    And many arrowes vnder his right side,
    All deadly daungerous, all cruell keene,
    Headed with flint, and fethers bloody dide,
    Such as the *Indians* in their quiuers hide,
    Those could he well direct and streight as line,
    And bid them strike the marke, which he had eyde,
    Ne was their salue ne was their medicine,
That mote recure their wounds: so inly they did tine.

22

As pale and wan as ashes was his looke,
    His body leane and meagre as a rake,
    And skin all withered like a dryed rooke,
    Thereto as cold and drery as a Snake,
    That seemd to tremble euermore, and quake:
    All in a canuas thin he was bedight,
    And girded with a belt of twisted brake,
    Vpon his head he wore an Helmet light,
Made of a dead mans skull, that seemd a ghastly sight.

Stanza 17

1 glitterand: sparkling with light; cf. 'Glistring in armes' (24.2), and see I vii 29.4–5*n*. **2 hent**: seized. **3 conge**: leave. **behight**: commanded. **5** I.e., 'auspiciously may he thrive', as the Red Cross Knight blesses Guyon at i 33.7. This rare intrusion by S. into his story indicates the larger import of Arthur's battle with Maleger. Cf. his personal address at 30.6–9. **gent**: valiant; courteous; noble.

Stanza 18

The similes are ostentatiously Virgilian. The first (1–3) on the arrows **thicke as flakes of snow** translates the hurling of darts *crebra nivis ritu* that opens the final battle in Virgil, *Aen.* 11.611. The second (4–9) conflates the simile used by Aeneas to describe his first impression of Troy's fall (*Aen.* 2.305–08), and that used to describe the bursting of Troy's gate (496–99). **8 vowes**: prayers for a good harvest. **9 ruine**: fall, applied both to the water and to the farm's destruction.

Stanza 19

3 before: in the causal sense, they fell by his hand. **5** After the harvest in England, 'the Westerne wynde beareth most swaye' (E.K. on *SC Sept.* 49). **6–9** See viii 17.9*n*. **Spumador**: the foamer (Lat. *spuma*); or foam-gilded or golden (Ital *spuma* + *d'oro*). The name, used only here, may have been suggested by the simile imitated in 18: *spumeus amnis* (*Aen.* 2.496). Froth or foam is commonly linked with a horse, as *Aen.* 6.881, though in S.'s poem only with Arthur's horse, as at III i 5.5.

Most other horses are described as lofty. **docks**: weeds. **Laomedon**: grandfather of Aeneas. Jupiter gave his grandfather, Tros, heavenly horses, which S. links with the horses of the sun in Ovid, *Met.* 2.154, as Lotspeich 1932 notes. Cf. the horses chosen for Aeneas at *Aen.* 7.280–83.

Stanza 20

2 yode: went. **4–5 a Tygre swift**: 'the Tiger gets his name from his speedy pace; for the Persians, Greeks and Medes used to call an arrow "tygris"' (T.H. White 1954:12); cf. 26.1–2. **8–9** Cf. ix 15.8–9. **subtile**: rarefied; in contrast to the firm substance of the castle of Alma. **vnsound**: i.e. as man's life at 30.3, and therefore linked with death.

Stanza 21

The arrow is a common emblem of sin which assaults the body, e.g. Ps. 11.2, Ephes. 6.16. **5** See John White's drawing, 'Indian with Body Paint', in the *SEnc*, 'visual arts': Fig. 1; see also Hamlin 1995:71, 73, 165*n*16. **9 tine**: hurt, give pain.

Stanza 22

1 The proverbial pallor of death, as at VI vii 17.8. **2 leane and meagre**: alluding to his name. **meagre**: emaciated; fleshless, like the skeleton Death. The comparison to a rake is also proverbial: Smith 451. **3–4** His bodily humour is cold and dry, the worst of all humours, associating him with mental illness, e.g. melancholy, as Nohrnberg 1976:297 suggests. See 'melancholy' in the *SEnc*. **rooke**: a stack of hay or a stook. With his clothes tied by bracken, he appears as a lifeless harvest

23

Maleger was his name, and after him,
　There follow'd fast at hand two wicked Hags,
　With hoary lockes all loose, and visage grim;
　Their feet vnshod, their bodies wrapt in rags,
　And both as swift on foot, as chased Stags,
　And yet the one her other legge had lame,
　Which with a staffe, all full of litle snags
　She did support, and *Impotence* her name:
But th'other was *Impatience*, arm'd with raging flame.

24

Soone as the Carle from far the Prince espyde,
　Glistring in armes and warlike ornament,
　His Beast he felly prickt on either syde,
　And his mischieuous bow full readie bent,
　With which at him a cruell shaft he sent:
　But he was warie, and it warded well
　Vpon his shield, that it no further went,
　But to the ground the idle quarrell fell:
Then he another and another did expell.

25

Which to preuent, the Prince his mortall speare
　Soone to him raught, and fierce at him did ride,
　To be auenged of that shot whyleare:
　But he was not so hardy to abide
　That bitter stownd, but turning quicke aside
　His light-foot beast, fled fast away for feare:
　Whom to poursue, the Infant after hide,
　So fast as his good Courser could him beare,
But labour lost it was, to weene approch him neare.

26

For as the winged wind his Tigre fled,
　That vew of eye could scarse him ouertake,
　Ne scarse his feet on ground were seene to tred;
　Through hils and dales he speedy way did make,
　Ne hedge ne ditch his readie passage brake,
　And in his flight the villein turn'd his face,
　(As wonts the *Tartar* by the *Caspian* lake,
　When as the *Russian* him in fight does chace)
Vnto his Tygres taile, and shot at him apace.

27

Apace he shot, and yet he fled apace,
　Still as the greedy knight nigh to him drew,
　And oftentimes he would relent his pace,
　That him his foe more fiercely should poursew:
　But when his vncouth manner he did vew,
　He gan auize to follow him no more,
　But keepe his standing, and his shaftes eschew,
　Vntill he quite had spent his perlous store,
And then assayle him fresh, ere he could shift for more.

28

But that lame Hag, still as abroad he strew
　His wicked arrowes, gathered them againe,
　And to him brought fresh batteill to renew:
　Which he espying, cast her to restraine
　From yielding succour to that cursed Swaine,
　And her attaching, thought her hands to tye;
　But soone as him dismounted on the plaine,
　That other Hag did far away espye
Binding her sister, she to him ran hastily.

figure, to be blown by Arthur who is compared to the western
wind at 19.4–5. **Thereto**: moreover. **drery**: horrid.

Stanza 23

1 Maleger: Lat. *mal*, evil + *aeger*, 'sicke, sorowfull, pensiffe, or
heauie' (T. Cooper 1565), i.e. desperately diseased; or *male* +
gerens, evil-bearing, sugg. Roche 1978. Accordingly, he has
been identified generally as sin; or specifically as original sin by
Woodhouse 1949:221; or sin manifest as lust, 'the olde man,
which is corrupt through the deceiueable lustes' (Eph. 4.22),
glossed in the Geneva Bible as 'all the natural corruption that
is in vs'; or the effects of sin in physical decay, disease, and
death, as 'the bodie of this death' (Rom. 7.24), glossed as 'this
fleshlie lump of sinne and death'; or as 'misrule and passions
bace' (ix 1.6) that make the body a monster, sugg. Rollinson
1987:107–08. See 'Maleger' in the *SEnc*. Harris 1998:28 sug-
gests that Maleger's appearance shows symptoms of syphilis.
6 other legge: either one of her legs, or her left (unlucky) leg;
cf. Occasion at iv 4.3. **8–9** The two **Hags** are paired in their
relation to temperance. **Impotence**: unruliness, intemper-
ance (Lat. *impotentia*); also 'feebleness' (Lat. *im-potens*, unable
to do), earlier manifest in Mordant (i 58.3, 52.6) and in
Cymochles (v 28.2–4). Defined by Cooper as the condition of
one 'that can not bridle his lustes and affections . . . vnhable to
rule himselfe'; see xii 69.8*n*. The two senses, unruliness and
feebleness, suggest that Maleger's strength is his weakness, and
his weakness his strength, making him 'most strong in most
infirmitee' (40.8), as the force of 'strong affections . . . is
fiercer through infirmity | Of the fraile flesh' (1.2–6).

Impatience: from Lat. *impatiens*, 'that cannot suffer or abide'
(Cooper), manifest in Amavia at i 44.4–5, and in Pyrochles at
v 16.4. Her **raging flame** is the emblem of her irascible state,
as in Pyrochles at vi 45.3.

Stanza 24

2 ornament: attire. **3 felly**: fiercely. **4 mischieuous**: cap-
able of inflicting injury. **8–9 quarrell**: a square-headed arrow
shot from a cross-bow; noted for its speed and accuracy. Also
the current sense: the shot is an occasion to wrath. **idle**:
because shot in vain. **expell**: shoot.

Stanza 25

5 stownd: encounter; moment of peril. **7 Infant**: Prince; see
viii 56.1–3*n*.

Stanza 26

5 readie: straight. **brake**: stopped. **6–9** This strategy, used
by Parthian horse-archers in flight, befits Maleger's paradoxical
state noted in 40.

Stanza 27

3 relent: slacken. **6 gan auize**: determined. **7 keepe his
standing**: as the castle of Alma maintains its 'stedfast stonds'
(15.2); cf. his standing 'as a stedfast towre' at viii 35.7.
8 perlous: perilous.

Stanza 28

4 cast: resolved. **6 attaching**: seizing.

29

And catching hold of him, as downe he lent,
    Him backeward ouerthrew, and downe him stayd
    With their rude handes and gryesly graplement,
    Till that the villein comming to their ayd,
    Vpon him fell, and lode vpon him layd;
    Full litle wanted, but he had him slaine,
    And of the battell balefull end had made,
    Had not his gentle Squire beheld his paine,
And commen to his reskew, ere his bitter bane.

30

So greatest and most glorious thing on ground
    May often need the helpe of weaker hand;
    So feeble is mans state, and life vnsound,
    That in assuraunce it may neuer stand,
    Till it dissolued be from earthly band.
    Proofe be thou Prince, the prowest man alyue,
    And noblest borne of all in *Britayne* land,
    Yet thee fierce Fortune did so nearely driue,
That had not grace thee blest, thou shouldest not suruiue.

31

The Squyre arriuing, fiercely in his armes
    Snatcht first the one, and then the other Iade,
    His chiefest letts and authors of his harmes,
    And them perforce withheld with threatned blade,
    Least that his Lord they should behinde inuade;
    The whiles the Prince prickt with reprochful shame,
    As one awakte out of long slombring shade,
    Reuiuyng thought of glory and of fame,
Vnited all his powres to purge him selfe from blame.

32

Like as a fire, the which in hollow caue
    Hath long bene vnderkept, and down supprest,
    With murmurous disdayne doth inly raue,
    And grudge, in so streight prison to be prest,
    At last breakes forth with furious infest,
    And striues to mount vnto his natiue seat;
    All that did earst it hinder and molest,
    Yt now deuoures with flames and scorching heat,
And carries into smoake with rage and horror great.

33

So mightely the *Briton* Prince him rouzd
    Out of his holde, and broke his caytiue bands,
    And as a Beare whom angry curres haue touzd,
    Hauing off-shakt them, and escapt their hands,
    Becomes more fell, and all that him withstands
    Treads down and ouerthrowes. Now had the Carle
    Alighted from his Tigre, and his hands
    Discharged of his bow and deadly quar'le,
To seize vpon his foe flatt lying on the marle.

34

Which now him turnd to disauantage deare,
    For neither can he fly, nor other harme,
    But trust vnto his strength and manhood meare,
    Sith now he is far from his monstrous swarme,
    And of his weapons did him selfe disarme.
    The knight yet wrothfull for his late disgrace,
    Fiercely aduaunst his valorous right arme,
    And him so sore smott with his yron mace,
That groueling to the ground he fell, and fild his place.

Stanza 29
3 gryesly graplement: horrible grappling. **6 wanted**: was
lacking. **9 bane**: death.

Stanza 30
1–2 Cf. the help that Timias gives Arthur at I viii 12.9. **on
ground**: on earth; punning on Arthur's present position.
4–5 Cf. gloss to 2 Cor. 5.1: 'After this bodie shalbe dissolued,
it shalbe made incorruptible and immortal'. **assuraunce**:
security. **6** Cf. S.'s praise of him at 17.5, and Archimago's at
viii 18.3. **7 in Britayne land**: i.e. Wales; see I x 65.1–5*n*.
8 so nearely driue: press so hard. **9 blest**: saved.

Stanza 31
3 letts: hindrances. **4 perforce**: forcibly. **6–9** As
Cymochles is seen at v 32.2 lying 'In secrete shadow' until
pricked with shame by Atin at 38.9. Arthur is saved by Timias
even as he saved '*Guyon* . . . slumbring fast' (viii 4.8). In
Reuiuyng thought of glory and of fame, he remembers the
'great desire of glory and of fame' (ix 38.7), which is named his
'*Praysdesire*' at 39.8.

Stanza 32
3 disdayne: indignation. **4 grudge**: grumble. **streight**:
narrow; confining. **5 infest**: hostility, assuming that the adj.
signifying 'hostile' is used as a substantive; vnrest *1596* is

preferable: cf. I ix 9.7. **6 natiue seat**: above the other
elements. Volcanic eruption was explained as the result of fire
imprisoned underground seeking its natural place just below
the sphere of the moon.

Stanza 33
2 his holde: i.e. the bonds that held him. **caytiue bands**:
captive (or vile) bonds; the 'chaines and bands' (47.4) carried
by Impatience. **3–6** On the popular sport of bear-baiting
in Elizabethan England, see Lee 1916. **touzd**: worried.
8 Discharged: rid; literally 'having discharged his arrows'.
9 marle: earth.

Stanza 34
1 deare: grievous, dire. **2 other harme**: i.e. harm the other
(Arthur); do other harm; or otherwise harm. **3 meare**: solely.
8 The yron mace is used by evil characters, such as Orgoglio
at I vii 10.9 and Argante at III vii 40.1, but here by Arthur to
show that brute force cannot defeat Maleger. **9 groueling**:
prostrate, face downward; the posture in which he gains susten-
ance from his mother earth. **fild his place**: suggesting that
Maleger fills Arthur's place at 30.1. The phrase may refer to
each man's place in the ground; or it may be the common
rhyming tag, for the writing in 36–40, as evident in the repeti-
tion and internal echoes, is weak.

35

Wel weened hee, that field was then his owne,
  And all his labor brought to happy end,
  When suddein vp the villeine ouerthrowne,
  Out of his swowne arose, fresh to contend,
  And gan him selfe to second battaill bend,
  As hurt he had not beene. Thereby there lay
  An huge great stone, which stood vpon one end,
  And had not bene remoued many a day;
Some land-marke seemd to bee, or signe of sundry way.

36

The same he snatcht, and with exceeding sway
  Threw at his foe, who was right well aware
  To shonne the engin of his meant decay;
  It booted not to thinke that throw to beare,
  But grownd he gaue, and lightly lept areare:
  Efte fierce retourning, as a faulcon fayre
  That once hath failed of her souse full neare,
  Remounts againe into the open ayre,
And vnto better fortune doth her selfe prepayre.

37

So braue retourning, with his brandisht blade,
  He to the Carle him selfe agayn addrest,
  And strooke at him so sternely, that he made
  An open passage through his riuen brest,
  That halfe the steele behind his backe did rest;
  Which drawing backe, he looked euermore
  When the hart blood should gush out of his chest,
  Or his dead corse should fall vpon the flore;
But his dead corse vpon the flore fell nathemore.

38

Ne drop of blood appeared shed to bee,
  All were the wownd so wide and wonderous,
  That through his carcas one might playnly see:
  Halfe in amaze with horror hideous,

And halfe in rage, to be deluded thus,
  Again through both the sides he strooke him quight,
  That made his spright to grone full piteous:
  Yet nathemore forth fled his groning spright,
But freshly as at first, prepard himselfe to fight.

39

Thereat he smitten was with great affright,
  And trembling terror did his hart apall,
  Ne wist he, what to thinke of that same sight,
  Ne what to say, ne what to doe at all;
  He doubted, least it were some magicall
  Illusion, that did beguile his sense,
  Or wandring ghost, that wanted funerall,
  Or aery spirite vnder false pretence,
Or hellish feend raysd vp through diuelish science.

40

His wonder far exceeded reasons reach,
  That he began to doubt his dazeled sight,
  And oft of error did him selfe appeach:
  Flesh without blood, a person without spright,
  Wounds without hurt, a body without might,
  That could doe harme, yet could not harmed bee,
  That could not die, yet seemd a mortall wight,
  That was most strong in most infirmitee;
Like did he neuer heare, like did he neuer see.

41

A while he stood in this astonishment,
  Yet would he not for all his great dismay
  Giue ouer to effect his first intent,
  And th'vtmost meanes of victory assay,
  Or th'vtmost yssew of his owne decay.
  His owne good sword *Mordure*, that neuer fayld
  At need, till now, he lightly threw away,
  And his bright shield, that nought him now auayld,
And with his naked hands him forcibly assayld.

Stanza 35
5 **bend**: apply. 6–9 The **great stone** recalls the ancient giant stone set up for a landmark that Turnus hurls at Aeneas before his death, *Aen.* 12.896–98. Or it may mark a choice of paths.

Stanza 36
1 **sway**: force. 2 **aware**: watchful. 7 **souse**: swoop. **full neare**: only by a very little.

Stanza 37
1 **with his brandisht blade**: i.e. brandishing his sword, the gesture for which he is praised at 17.6. 3 **sternely**: fiercely.

Stanza 38
2 **All**: although. 4 **in amaze**: in amazement; suggesting 'being in a maze'; cf. 44.1. 7–9 A demon suffers pain when his body is cut, but he is soon healed; see R. West 1955:146–47.

Stanza 39
5 **doubted**: feared. 7 The soul cannot enter Hades until the body is properly buried; see I iii 36.6n. **wanted**: lacked.

8 **aery**: belonging to the air, or having assumed a body of air; see I i 45.3n. **pretence**: appearance.

Stanza 40
The seven riddles are carefully posed to challenge and defeat **reasons reach**. Answers are not given though one would be death, as Weatherby 1994:180–82 suggests; or, more precisely, 'the bodie of this death', that is, 'our olde man', 'the bodie of sinne' (Rom. 6.6, 7.24) from which Paul asks to be delivered. Maleger is like Furor in not being one whom 'steele can wound, or strength can ouerthroe' (iv 10.5). His paradoxical state is summed up in such phrases as 'lifelesse shadow' (44.3) and 'dead-liuing swayne' (44.7). 3 **appeach**: accuse. 7 **mortall**: and therefore subject to death.

Stanza 41
3 **Giue ouer**: give up trying. 9 **naked hands**: cf. 'puissant hands' (46.1). Arthur becomes the wrestler in place of Guyon; see proem 5.8n, and iv 6.4n.

42

Twixt his two mighty armes him vp he snatcht,
    And crusht his carcas so against his brest,
    That the disdainfull sowle he thence dispatcht,
    And th'ydle breath all vtterly exprest:
    Tho when he felt him dead, adowne he kest
    The lumpish corse vnto the sencelesse grownd,
    Adowne he kest it with so puissant wrest,
    That backe againe it did alofte rebownd,
And gaue against his mother earth a gronefull sownd.

43

As when *Ioues* harnesse-bearing Bird from hye
    Stoupes at a flying heron with proud disdayne,
    The stone-dead quarrey falls so forciblye,
    That yt rebownds against the lowly playne,
    A second fall redoubling backe agayne.
    Then thought the Prince all peril sure was past,
    And that he victor onely did remayne;
    No sooner thought, then that the Carle as fast
Gan heap huge strokes on him, as ere he down was cast.

44

Nigh his wits end then woxe th'amazed knight,
    And thought his labor lost and trauell vayne,
    Against this lifelesse shadow so to fight:
    Yet life he saw, and felt his mighty mayne,
    That whiles he marueild still, did still him payne:
    For thy he gan some other wayes aduize,
    How to take life from that dead-liuing swayne,
    Whom still he marked freshly to arize
From th'earth, and from her womb new spirits to reprize.

45

He then remembred well, that had bene sayd,
    How th'Earth his mother was, and first him bore,
    Shee eke so often, as his life decayd,
    Did life with vsury to him restore,
    And reysd him vp much stronger then before,
    So soone as he vnto her wombe did fall;
    Therefore to grownd he would him cast no more,
    Ne him committ to graue terrestriall,
But beare him farre from hope of succour vsuall.

46

Tho vp he caught him twixt his puissant hands,
    And hauing scruzd out of his carrion corse
    The lothfull life, now loosd from sinfull bands,
    Vpon his shoulders carried him perforse
    Aboue three furlongs, taking his full course,
    Vntill he came vnto a standing lake;
    Him thereinto he threw without remorse,
    Ne stird, till hope of life did him forsake;
So end of that Carles dayes, and his owne paynes did make.

47

Which when those wicked Hags from far did spye,
    Like two mad dogs they ran about the lands,
    And th'one of them with dreadfull yelling crye,
    Throwing away her broken chaines and bands,
    And hauing quencht her burning fier brands,
    Hedlong her selfe did cast into that lake;
    But *Impotence* with her owne wilfull hands,
    One of *Malegers* cursed darts did take,
So ryu'd her trembling hart, and wicked end did make.

Stanza 42

4 exprest: squeezed out.   **5–6** I.e., he cast the heavy, sense-less corpse to the earth.   **7 wrest**: throw.   **9 his mother earth**: see I vii 9.1*n*.

Stanza 43

1–3 I.e., the eagle that bears Jove's armour (his thunderbolts) in its claws.   **Stoupes**: swoops; a term in falconry.   **quarrey**: a bird flown at and killed by a hawk.

Stanza 44

1–2 Cf. the dragon's response at I xi 35.2 and 52.8 on seeing the Red Cross Knight rise restored from the earth where he had been cast.   **3 this**: 'his' *1590*, corrected *F.E.*, indicates that the battle is a *psychomachia*.   **6 For thy**: therefore. **aduize**: consider.   **9 reprize**: take anew.

Stanzas 45–46

Arthur wrestling with Maleger is analogous to Hercules wrestling with Antaeus, which was reputed to be one of his most difficult labours. As interpreted in the Renaissance, e.g. by Fulgentius 1971:69 (noted Lotspeich 1932), Hercules's victory shows how virtue conquers fleshly lusts. Antaeus is

killed when his crushed body is held off the ground until he dies; Maleger must also be cast into the lake.

Stanza 45

4 vsury: interest.

Stanza 46

2 scruzd: screwed and squeezed; a portmanteau word devised by S.   **3 lothfull**: loathsome; reluctant to die.   **sinfull bands**: i.e. bondage to sin.   **5 Aboue three furlongs**: Arthur paces out the length of the dragon's tail and beyond, I xi 11.7.   **taking his full course**: measuring the full distance.   **6 a standing lake**: one whose waters neither ebb nor flow; hence not renewing, in contrast to the 'liuing well' of I ii 43.4, xi 31.6.

Stanza 47

2 lands: country (cf. *OED* 7).   **4 chaines and bands**: perhaps those used by Arthur to bind Impotence at 28.6, and by which he was bound at 33.2.   **6** In Mark 5.13, the Gadarene swine invaded by the devils whom Christ had cast out from a demo-niac 'ran headling from the high banke into the sea'. Geneva offers alternative readings, which S. uses: 'ran with violence headlong . . . in the lake'; noted Hankins 1971:86–87.

48

Thus now alone he conquerour remaines;
    Tho cumming to his Squyre, that kept his steed,
    Thought to haue mounted, but his feeble vaines
    Him faild thereto, and serued not his need,
    Through losse of blood, which from his wounds did bleed,
    That he began to faint, and life decay:
    But his good Squyre him helping vp with speed,
    With stedfast hand vpon his horse did stay,
And led him to the Castle by the beaten way.

49

Where many Groomes and Squyres ready were,
    To take him from his steed full tenderly,
    And eke the fayrest *Alma* mett him there
    With balme and wine and costly spicery,
    To comfort him in his infirmity;
    Eftesoones shee causd him vp to be conuayd,
    And of his armes despoyled easily,
    In sumptuous bed shee made him to be layd,
And al the while his wounds were dressing, by him stayd.

Stanza 48
1 conquerour: see I xii 6.1*n*.   **7–9** Timias ministers to Arthur as the Angel does to Guyon after his struggle against Mammon. **stay**: support.

Stanza 49
4 spicery: spices.   **5 infirmity**: Maleger's state at 40.8.

Cant. XII.

Guyon through Palmers gouernaunce,
through passing perilles great,
Doth ouerthrow the Bowre of blis,
and Acrasy defeat.

1

Now ginnes this goodly frame of Temperaunce
    Fayrely to rise, and her adorned hed
    To pricke of highest prayse forth to aduaunce,
    Formerly grounded, and fast setteled
    On firme foundation of true bountyhed;
    And this braue knight, that for that vertue fightes,
    Now comes to point of that same perilous sted,
    Where Pleasure dwelles in sensuall delights,
Mongst thousand dangers, and ten thousand Magick mights.

2

Two dayes now in that sea he sayled has,
    Ne euer land beheld, ne liuing wight,
    Ne ought saue perill, still as he did pas:
    Tho when appeared the third *Morrow* bright,
    Vpon the waues to spred her trembling light,
    An hideous roring far away they heard,
    That all their sences filled with affright,
    And streight they saw the raging surges reard
Vp to the skyes, that them of drowning made affeard.

3

Said then the Boteman, Palmer stere aright,
    And keepe an euen course; for yonder way
    We needes must pas (God doe vs well acquight,)
    That is the *Gulfe of Greedinesse*, they say,
    That deepe engorgeth all this worldes pray:
    Which hauing swallowd vp excessiuely,
    He soone in vomit vp againe doth lay,
    And belcheth forth his superfluity,
That all the seas for feare doe seeme away to fly.

4

On thother syde an hideous Rock is pight,
    Of mightie *Magnes* stone, whose craggie clift
    Depending from on high, dreadfull to sight,
    Ouer the waues his rugged armes doth lift,
    And threatneth downe to throw his ragged rift,
    On whoso cometh nigh; yet nigh it drawes
    All passengers, that none from it can shift:
    For whiles they fly that Gulfes deuouring iawes,
They on this Rock are rent, and sunck in helples wawes.

Book II Canto xii

Argument

1–2 gouernaunce: see i 29.8*n*. **through . . . through passing**: the paralleling suggests that by resisting the temptations that lead him to the Bower, Guyon is able to overthrow it; by . . . passing through *1596* leaves the two experiences separate.

Stanza 1

1 frame: structure, as at ix 22.1, 44.7, xi 15.5. Also the structuring of the body by temperance: see ii 12.9*n*; and of the virtue itself. **2 Fayrely**: handsomely. **3** To the highest point of praise . . . **4 Formerly**: first of all. **5 bountyhed**: goodness, virtue. **7 point**: the same metaphor informs **pricke**: the mark aimed at in shooting, the bull's eye. **8 Pleasure**: Acrasia, as 48.8; see i Arg.4*n*.

Stanzas 2–41

The chief precedents for Guyon's voyage are the voyage of Ulysses in Homer, *Ody.* 12; of Aeneas in Virgil, *Aen.* 2–3; and of Carlo and Ubaldo to Armida's enchanted garden in Tasso, *Ger. Lib.* 15, esp. the first two as they were moralized, e.g. by Conti 1616, and the third by Tasso. These are supplemented by narratives of sea-travel: e.g. classical sources, such as Jason's search for the Golden Fleece, the medieval legendary voyage of St Brendan, and esp. narratives of the New World explorers, such as Peter Martyr's account of the early Spanish voyagers: see L. Whitney 1921–22, and Read 2000:95–97. The forty stanzas that treat the dangers – the traditional number in a full temptation (see vii 26.5*n*) – thirty-six at sea and four on land

(38–41), divide into groups of four (except that the Quicksand and Whirlpool have two each), alternating between peril and pleasure. The first four dangers (Gulf and Rock, Wandring Islands and Phædria) lead to a second inserted four (see 18–29*n*) and culminate in four that comprise all the dangers of sea (mermaids), air (fog and fowls), and land (beasts).

Stanza 2

1 Two dayes: since temperance is linked to time (from Lat. *tempus*), one may infer that the battle with Maleger extends over two days, the first ending with Arthur's defeat at xi 29, followed by his awakening as out of sleep at 31. Guyon's victory comes, then, on the traditional **third Morrow**, as does the Red Cross Knight's defeat of the dragon.

Stanza 3

3 Cf. the Palmer's injunction at i 32.8. **acquight**: deliver; a role given in Bk I to Arthur (vii 52.6) and to Truth (viii 1.4). **4–9.9** The **Gulfe of Greedinesse** and the **hideous Rock** derive from Homer's Charybdis and Scylla (*Ody.* 12.73–110, 234–59) by way of Virgil (*Aen.* 3.420–32, 555–67). Conti 1616:8.12 interprets the passage between them as virtue's mean between two extremes of vice. On S.'s witty use of language in these stanzas, see M. Craig 1967:465. **6–8 excessiuely**: also 'greedily'. **lay**: throw; cf. Gluttony at I iv 21.8–9. **9** Cf. Ps. 114.3: 'The sea sawe it and fled'.

Stanza 4

1–2 A medieval parallel to Scylla's further transformation from a rock into a magnet or loadstone (Lat. *magnes*), which

5

Forward they passe, and strongly he them rowes,
  Vntill they nigh vnto that Gulfe arryue,
  Where streame more violent and greedy growes:
  Then he with all his puisaunce doth stryue
  To strike his oares, and mightily doth dryue
  The hollow vessell through the threatfull waue,
  Which gaping wide, to swallow them alyue,
  In th'huge abysse of his engulfing graue,
Doth rore at them in vaine, and with great terrour raue.

6

They passing by, that grisely mouth did see,
  Sucking the seas into his entralles deepe,
  That seemd more horrible then hell to bee,
  Or that darke dreadfull hole of *Tartare* steepe,
  Through which the damned ghosts doen often creep
  Backe to the world, bad liuers to torment:
  But nought that falles into this direfull deepe,
  Ne that approcheth nigh the wyde descent,
May backe retourne, but is condemned to be drent.

7

On thother side, they saw that perilous Rocke,
  Threatning it selfe on them to ruinate,
  On whose sharp cliftes the ribs of vessels broke,
  And shiuered ships, which had beene wrecked late,
  Yet stuck, with carcases exanimate
  Of such, as hauing all their substance spent
  In wanton ioyes, and lustes intemperate,
  Did afterwardes make shipwrack violent,
Both of their life, and fame for euer fowly blent.

8

For thy this hight *The Rock of* vile *Reproch*,
  A daungerous and detestable place,
  To which nor fish nor fowle did once approch,
  But yelling Meawes, with Seagulles hoars and bace,
  And Cormoyraunts, with birds of rauenous race,
  Which still sat wayting on that wastfull clift,
  For spoile of wretches, whose vnhappy cace,
  After lost credit and consumed thrift,
At last them driuen hath to this despairefull drift.

9

The Palmer seeing them in safetie past,
  Thus saide, Behold th'ensamples in our sightes,
  Of lustfull luxurie and thriftlesse wast:
  What now is left of miserable wightes,
  Which spent their looser daies in leud delightes,
  But shame and sad reproch, here to be red,
  By these rent reliques, speaking their ill plightes?
  Let all that liue, hereby be counselled,
To shunne *Rock of Reproch* and it as death to dread.

10

So forth they rowed, and that *Ferryman*
  With his stiffe oares did brush the sea so strong,
  That the hoare waters from his frigot ran,
  And the light bubles daunced all along,
  Whiles the salt brine out of the billowes sprong.
  At last far off they many Islandes spy,
  On euery side floting the floodes emong:
  Then said the knight, Lo I the land descry,
Therefore old Syre thy course doe thereunto apply.

captures ships by the iron in them, is found in *Huon of Burdeux*, cited *Var* 2.353. **hideous**: immense. **pight**: placed. **3 Depending**: hanging down. **5 rift**: projecting fragments rather than fissures; cf. vii 28.5. **7 passengers**: passers by, as again at 12.6. **8–9** T. Cooper 1565 cites the proverb: *Decidit in Scyllam cupiens vitare Charybdim*. One becomes victim of the one by fleeing the other, as the avoidance of Mammon's greedy labour for riches is the sensual sloth of Acrasia's Bower, and as Gluttony is followed by Lecherie in the pageant of the sins in the house of Pride. **in helples wawes**. waves (suggesting 'woes') in which one is sunk helplessly.

Stanza 5

7–8 Cf. Prov. 1.12: 'We wil swallowe them vp aliue like a graue euen whole, as those that go downe into the pit'. In *Gnat* 542, S. refers to 'deep *Charybdis* gulphing in and out', which emphasizes the point here and 3.6–8, and also I iv 21.6–9, which describes Gluttony's gorging and vomiting.

Stanza 6

4–6 Tartare: Tartarus, the classical hell, where sinners are punished; see I vii 44.3*n*. **9 drent**: drenched; drowned.

Stanza 7

2 ruinate: fall down and bring ruin. **3 broke**: suggesting 'made bankrupt'. **5 exanimate**: in its literal sense, deprived of their souls. **6–9** Cf. 1 Tim. 6.9: 'For they that wil be riche, fall into temptation and snares, and into many foolish and noysome lustes, which drowne men in perdition and destruction'. **blent**: despoiled.

Stanza 8

1 For thy: therefore. **2 daungerous**: includes the obs. sense, 'being in debt' (*OED* 1). **4 Meawes**: the common gull. **Seagulles**: a symbol of greed and trickery; hence the epithet **bace**. **5 Cormoyraunts**: the voracious sea-raven associated with the fallen Edom in Isa. 34.11, and a symbol of gluttony in Chaucer, *Parl. Fowls* 362. Applied to usurers and the rapacious; hence the pun on **rauenous**. **6 wayting**: watching. **wastfull**: desolate; causing devastation. A fitting punishment for the wasteful; cf. 35.3, 80.7. **7 spoile**: ruin; booty. **8 thrift**: savings; or 'what they thrived on'. **9 drift**: course; with the sense of 'driving' victims to their desperate end.

Stanza 9

3 luxurie: vicious indulgence (Lat. *luxuria*). **thriftlesse wast**: as 'vnthriftie waste' assaults the castle of Alma at xi 12.7. **4 miserable**: poverty-stricken; wretchedly unhappy. **5 looser**: too loose. **6 red**: seen; interpreted. **7 plightes**: state; offences.

Stanza 10

The classical ferryman, Charon, is interpreted by Conti 1616:3.4 as clearness of conscience, or confidence in God's mercy, that helps the dead across the troubled stream of their regrets; noted Lemmi 1929:278. Cf. the Red Cross Knight's 'cured conscience' (I x 29.3) at the parallel point in his quest. An aged though vigorous man in Virgil, *Aen.* 6.304; hence Guyon's address to him as **old Syre** and the reference to his 'puisaunce' at 5.4, etc. See 'Ferryman' in the *SEnc*. **2 stiffe**: strong, rigid; with reference to the Ferryman: steadfast. **3 hoare**: white with foam. **9 apply**: steer.

11

That may not bee, said then the *Ferryman*
　　Least wee vnweeting hap to be fordonne:
　　For those same Islands, seeming now and than,
　　Are not firme land, nor any certein wonne,
　　But stragling plots, which to and fro doe ronne
　　In the wide waters: therefore are they hight
　　The *wandring Islands*. Therefore doe them shonne;
　　For they haue ofte drawne many a wandring wight
Into most deadly daunger and distressed plight.

12

Yet well they seeme to him, that farre doth vew,
　　Both faire and fruitfull, and the grownd dispred,
　　With grassy greene of delectable hew,
　　And the tall trees with leaues appareled,
　　Are deckt with blossoms dyde in white and red,
　　That mote the passengers thereto allure;
　　But whosoeuer once hath fastened
　　His foot thereon, may neuer it recure,
But wandreth euer more vncertein and vnsure.

13

As th'Isle of *Delos* whylome men report
　　Amid th'*Aegaean* sea long time did stray,
　　Ne made for shipping any certeine port,
　　Till that *Latona* traueiling that way,
　　Flying from *Iunoes* wrath and hard assay,
　　Of her fayre twins was there deliuered,
　　Which afterwards did rule the night and day;
　　Thenceforth it firmely was established,
And for *Apolloes* temple highly herried.

14

They to him hearken, as beseemeth meete,
　　And passe on forward: so their way does ly,
　　That one of those same Islands, which doe fleet
　　In the wide sea, they needes must passen by,

Which seemd so sweet and pleasaunt to the eye,
　　That it would tempt a man to touchen there:
　　Vpon the banck they sitting did espy
　　A daintie damsell, dressing of her heare,
By whom a little skippet floting did appeare.

15

She them espying, loud to them can call,
　　Bidding them nigher draw vnto the shore;
　　For she had cause to busie them withall;
　　And therewith lowdly laught: But nathemore
　　Would they once turne, but kept on as afore:
　　Which when she saw, she left her lockes vndight,
　　And running to her boat withouten ore,
　　From the departing land it launched light,
And after them did driue with all her power and might.

16

Whom ouertaking, she in merry sort
　　Them gan to bord, and purpose diuersly,
　　Now faining dalliaunce and wanton sport,
　　Now throwing forth lewd wordes immodestly;
　　Till that the Palmer gan full bitterly
　　Her to rebuke, for being loose and light:
　　Which not abiding, but more scornfully
　　Scoffing at him, that did her iustly wite,
She turnd her bote about, and from them rowed quite.

17

That was the wanton *Phædria*, which late
　　Did ferry him ouer the *Idle lake*:
　　Whom nought regarding, they kept on their gate,
　　And all her vaine allurements did forsake,
　　When them the wary Boteman thus bespake;
　　Here now behoueth vs well to auyse,
　　And of our safety good heede to take;
　　For here before a perlous passage lyes,
Where many Mermayds haunt, making false melodies.

Stanza 11

2 fordonne: ruined, killed.　**3** . . . appearing here and there.　**4 certein wonne**: fixed dwelling-place.　**7 wandring Islands** such as Acrasia's 'wandring Island, that doth ronne | And stray in perilous gulfe' (i 51.5–6) and Phædria's floating island (vi 11), which relate to the Planctae or Drifters in *Ody.* 12.61 (called 'Rovers' in Chapman's tr.), were occasionally reported in travel literature.

Stanza 12

3 delectable: with the earlier stress on the first and third syllables.　**5 white and red**: traditionally associated with (feminine) beauty, e.g. *HB* 71.　**8 recure**: recover.

Stanza 13

The story of how **Latona** (or Leto) on the floating island of **Delos** gave birth to Diana and Apollo who as the sun and moon **rule the night and day** is told by Ovid, *Met.* 6.186–91, 332–34; Virgil, *Aen.* 3.73–77; and Conti 1616:9.6 who associates the island with Eden.　**4 traueiling**: also 'being in labour' (*OED* 3).　**5 assay**: pursuit.　**9 temple**: honor *1596*. The revision notes correctly that Delos, not the temple, is praised in honour of Apollo.　**herried**: praised.

Stanza 14

3 fleet: float.　**6 touchen**: stay in passing; but also 'lay a hand on' sexually.　**9 skippet**: a small boat; a coinage that combines 'ship' and 'skiff'.

Stanza 15

1 can: did.　**3–4** On her loud laughter, see vi 3.7–9*n*. She laughs at her bawdy pun: **cause** = her 'case'.　**7 withouten ore**: as vi 5.3.　**8 departing land**: cf. 'fast the land behynd them fled away' (xi 4.6); but also the island floated away. **light**: quickly.

Stanza 16

1 sort: manner.　**2 bord**: accost; also the nautical sense, 'come alongside to attack'; also 'jest'.　**purpose diuersly**: talk of various matters; engage in small talk.　**8 wite**: blame. **9 rowed**: since her boat moves swiftly 'withouten ore' (15.7), the Palmer may have defeated her (will) power; or the term is metaphorical.

Stanza 17

3 gate: way, journey.　**6 auyse**: take thought; cf. 69.6.

18

But by the way, there is a great Quicksand,
  And a whirlpoole of hidden ieopardy,
  Therefore, Sir Palmer, keepe an euen hand;
  For twixt them both the narrow way doth ly.
  Scarse had he saide, when hard at hand they spy
  That quicksand nigh with water couered;
  But by the checked waue they did descry
  It plaine, and by the sea discoloured:
It called was the quicksand of *Vnthriftyhed*.

19

They passing by, a goodly Ship did see,
  Laden from far with precious merchandize,
  And brauely furnished, as ship might bee,
  Which through great disauenture, or mesprize,
  Her selfe had ronne into that hazardize;
  Whose mariners and merchants with much toyle,
  Labour'd in vaine, to haue recur'd their prize,
  And the rich wares to saue from pitteous spoyle,
But neither toyle nor traueill might her backe recoyle.

20

On th'other side they see that perilous Poole,
  That called was the *Whirlpoole of decay*,
  In which full many had with haplesse doole
  Beene suncke, of whom no memorie did stay:
  Whose circled waters rapt with whirling sway,
  Like to a restlesse wheele, still ronning round,
  Did couet, as they passed by that way,
  To draw their bote within the vtmost bound
Of his wide *Labyrinth*, and then to haue them dround.

21

But th'earnest Boteman strongly forth did stretch
  His brawnie armes, and all his bodie straine,
  That th'vtmost sandy breach they shortly fetch,
  Whiles the dredd daunger does behind remaine.
  Suddeine they see from midst of all the Maine,
  The surging waters like a mountaine rise,
  And the great sea puft vp with proud disdaine,
  To swell aboue the measure of his guise,
As threatning to deuoure all, that his powre despise.

22

The waues come rolling, and the billowes rore
  Outragiously, as they enraged were,
  Or wrathfull *Neptune* did them driue before
  His whirling charet, for exceeding feare:
  For not one puffe of winde there did appeare,
  That all the three thereat woxe much afrayd,
  Vnweeting, what such horrour straunge did reare.
  Eftsoones they saw an hideous hoast arrayd,
Of huge Sea monsters, such as liuing sence dismayd.

23

Most vgly shapes, and horrible aspects,
  Such as Dame Nature selfe mote feare to see,
  Or shame, that euer should so fowle defects
  From her most cunning hand escaped bee;
  All dreadfull pourtraicts of deformitee:
  Spring-headed *Hydres*, and sea-shouldring Whales,
  Great whirlpooles, which all fishes make to flee,
  Bright Scolopendraes, arm'd with siluer scales,
Mighty *Monoceros*, with immeasured tayles.

Stanzas 18–29

These 'inserted' stanzas describe the 'perlous passage' that lies 'here before' (17.8) the 'calmy bay' (30.3) of the mermaids. The four dangers clarify the nature of the four earlier ones, e.g. 'the *Gulfe of Greedinesse*' (3.4) is seen as 'the *Whirlepoole of decay*' (20.2).

Stanza 18

3 **keepe an euen hand**: i.e. straight or direct, referring to the path; or a mean between extremes, as S. does by allotting thirteen lines to each. 7 **checked**: restrained by the sand and therefore 'checkered'. 9 **Vnthriftyhed**: thriftlessness, extravagance; cf. the 'thriftlesse wast' (9.3) which brings ships to ruin upon '*The Rock of* vile *Reproch*' (8.1). Cf. 'unthrift': dissolute conduct (*OED* 2).

Stanza 19

4 **disauenture**: mishap. **mesprize**: mistake; failure to value. 5 **hazardize**: hazardous situation. 7 **recur'd**: recovered. **prize**: used of a stranded vessel whose cargo may be claimed as booty. J.N. Wall 1984:3 notes a topical reference to ships stranded off the coast of North Carolina in the 1580s. 9 **backe recoyle**: draw back.

Stanza 20

3 **doole**: grief, suffering, guile, fraud. 5 **circled**: circling. **sway**: motion in a circle.

Stanza 21

1 **earnest**: heedfull *1596*, in line with his advice: 'of our safety good heede to take' (17.7). 3 **sandy breach**: i.e. where the waves break upon the sand; presumably the channel between the edge of the quicksand and the whirlpool. **fetch**: reach, in the nautical sense. 8 **guise**: custom, usual manner.

Stanza 22

1–4 I.e., the waves roar in great fear as though Neptune were driving them before his chariot. **Outragiously**: intemperately, from the obs. sense of 'outrage'; hence violence that goes beyond all bounds. Cf. 39.2. 6 **all the three**: only Guyon at 25.6, in accord with the allegorical nature of the encounter. 7 **horrour**: the roughness or ruffling of the water and its effect upon the beholders. **reare**: bring about.

Stanza 23

Nature's **cunning hand** is illustrated in such compilations of animal lore as Pliny, *Historia Naturalis*, Conrad Gesner, *Historia Animalium*; and Olaus Magnus, *Description of the Northern Peoples* 1555. See 'natural history' with its illustrations in the *SEnc*. 6 **Spring-headed Hydres**: related to the Lernean hydra with its 'many heades out budding euer new' (I vii 17.4). **sea-shouldring Whales**: i.e. lifting the sea before them; identified as the Leviathan by the Geneva gloss to Job 40.20 7 **whirlpooles**: the spouting whale. 8 **Scolopendraes**: S.'s own fabulous sea-fish, not to be confused with the bait-vomiting annelid centipede that fascinated the natural historians. 9 **Monoceros**: a one-horned fish, such as the narwhal. 'Monoceroses' has been suggested for the metre but Upton 1758 notes the witty point: the verse is **immeasured**, i.e. immeasurable.

24

The dreadfull Fish, that hath deseru'd the name
    Of Death, and like him lookes in dreadfull hew,
    The griesly Wasserman, that makes his game
    The flying ships with swiftnes to pursew,
    The horrible Sea-satyre, that doth shew
    His fearefull face in time of greatest storme,
    Huge *Ziffius*, whom Mariners eschew
    No lesse, then rockes, (as trauellers informe,)
And greedy *Rosmarines* with visages deforme.

25

All these, and thousand thousands many more,
    And more deformed Monsters thousand fold,
    With dreadfull noise, and hollow rombling rore,
    Came rushing in the fomy waues enrold,
    Which seem'd to fly for feare, them to behold:
    Ne wonder, if these did the knight appall;
    For all that here on earth we dreadfull hold,
    Be but as bugs to fearen babes withall,
Compared to the creatures in the seas entrall.

26

Feare nought, then saide the Palmer well auiz'd;
    For these same Monsters are not these in deed,
    But are into these fearefull shapes disguiz'd
    By that same wicked witch, to worke vs dreed,
    And draw from on this iourney to proceed.
    Tho lifting vp his vertuous staffe on hye,
    He smote the sea, which calmed was with speed,
    And all that dreadfull Armie fast gan flye
Into great *Tethys* bosome, where they hidden lye.

27

Quit from that danger, forth their course they kept,
    And as they went, they heard a ruefull cry
    Of one, that wayld and pittifully wept,
    That through the sea the resounding plaints did fly:

At last they in an Island did espy
    A seemely Maiden, sitting by the shore,
    That with great sorrow and sad agony,
    Seemed some great misfortune to deplore,
And lowd to them for succour called euermore.

28

Which *Guyon* hearing, streight his Palmer bad,
    To stere the bote towards that dolefull Mayd,
    That he might know, and ease her sorrow sad:
    Who him auizing better, to him sayd;
    Faire Sir, be not displeasd if disobayd:
    For ill it were to hearken to her cry;
    For she is inly nothing ill apayd,
    But onely womanish fine forgery,
Your stubborne hart t'affect with fraile infirmity.

29

To which when she your courage hath inclind
    Through foolish pitty, then her guilefull bayt
    She will embosome deeper in your mind,
    And for your ruine at the last away.
    The Knight was ruled, and the Boteman strayt
    Held on his course with stayed stedfastnesse,
    Ne euer shroncke, ne euer sought to bayt
    His tyred armes for toylesome wearinesse,
But with his oares did sweepe the watry wildernesse.

30

And now they nigh approched to the sted,
    Where as those Mermayds dwelt: it was a still
    And calmy bay, on th'one side sheltered
    With the brode shadow of an hoarie hill,
    On th'other side an high rocke toured still,
    That twixt them both a pleasaunt port they made,
    And did like an halfe Theatre fulfill:
    There those fiue sisters had continuall trade,
And vsd to bath themselues in that deceiptfull shade.

Stanza 24
This second group of five 'Sea monsters' (22.9) is drawn chiefly from the depths of Gesner. **Death**: the walrus or morse, from *mors* (Lat. death). **Wasserman**: *homo marinus*, a merman. **Sea-satyre**: Pan or *satyrus marinus*, a sea-monster part satyr in form. **Ziffius**: the Xiphias or sword-fish, a kind of whale. **Rosmarines**: the sea-horse; **greedy** because it climbs on rocks to feed on grass, or on dew (Lat. *ros*).

Stanza 25
1–2 On their numbers, see IV xii 1. 7–9 S. endorses the common notion that the sea contains every kind of creature found on land. **bugs**: bugbears. **entrall**: entrails, bowels.

Stanza 26
1 **well auiz'd**: very wary; also keen-sighted. 3 **disguiz'd**: transformed. 6–7 The Palmer's act suggests Moses dividing the Red Sea with his rod at Exod. 14.16, and Christ

calming the sea at Matt. 8.26. **vertuous**: possessing magical powers; cf. 40.3. 9 **Tethys**: the sea itself, as I i 39.6. At IV xi 18.1–4, she is named as the mother of all that live in the sea.

Stanza 27
4 The definite article is added to make **resounding** resound. 6 **seemely**: fair, pleasing to see; but with a play on 'seeming'.

Stanza 28
4 **him auizing better**: taking better thought than Guyon had; or better counselling Guyon. 7 **ill apayd**: distressed. 8 **fine forgery**: cunning deception.

Stanza 29
1 **courage**: heart, mind. 2 **foolish pitty**: to which Guyon had yielded at i 14.3. 3 **embosome**: infix. 6 **stayed**: staid, constant. 7 **bayt**: rest.

31

They were faire Ladies, till they fondly striu'd
  With th'*Heliconian* maides for maystery;
  Of whom they ouer-comen, were depriu'd
  Of their proud beautie, and th'one moyity
  Transformd to fish, for their bold surquedry,
  But th'vpper halfe their hew retayned still,
  And their sweet skill in wonted melody;
  Which euer after they abusd to ill,
T'allure weake traueillers, whom gotten they did kill.

32

So now to *Guyon*, as he passed by,
  Their pleasaunt tunes they sweetly thus applyde;
  O thou fayre sonne of gentle *Faery*,
  That art in mightie armes most magnifyde
  Aboue all knights, that euer batteill tryde,
  O turne thy rudder hetherward a while:
  Here may thy storme-bett vessell safely ryde;
  This is the Port of rest from troublous toyle,
The worldes sweet In, from paine and wearisome turmoyle.

33

With that the rolling sea resounding soft,
  In his big base them fitly answered,
  And on the rocke the waues breaking aloft,
  A solemne Meane vnto them measured,

The whiles sweet *Zephyrus* lowd whisteled
  His treble, a straunge kinde of harmony;
  Which *Guyons* senses softly tickeled,
  That he the boteman bad row easily,
And let him heare some part of their rare melody.

34

But him the Palmer from that vanity,
  With temperate aduice discounselled,
  That they it past, and shortly gan descry
  The land, to which their course they leueled;
  When suddeinly a grosse fog ouer spred
  With his dull vapour all that desert has,
  And heauens chearefull face enueloped,
  That all things one, and one as nothing was,
And this great Vniuerse seemd one confused mas.

35

Thereat they greatly were dismayd, ne wist
  How to direct theyr way in darkenes wide,
  But feard to wander in that wastefull mist,
  For tombling into mischiefe vnespide.
  Worse is the daunger hidden, then descride.
  Suddeinly an innumerable flight
  Of harmefull fowles about them fluttering, cride,
  And with their wicked wings them ofte did smight,
And sore annoyed, groping in that griesly night.

Stanza 30
1–2 Picking up from 17.8–9. **sted**: place. **those Mermayds**: the Sirens (from Homer, *Ody.* 12.39–54, 165–200) 'whom poets feigned to be mermaydens' (T. Cooper 1565). **fiue** rather than the usual three because they tempt the five senses; interpreted by Conti 1616:7.13 as all voluptuous desire. Their fishlike 'hew' (31.6) is interpreted by Boccaccio 1976:7.20 as female concupiscence; noted Lotspeich 1932. The same reading is found in Renaissance dictionaries, as Starnes and Talbert 1955:109–10 note. **2–9** S. borrows details from the bay of nymphs in Virgil, *Aen.* 1.157–68, which Aeneas and his followers reach during their voyage, and which leads them to the lustful Dido. **still** as the antithesis of Guyon's forward movement is stressed by the unusual syntactical break at the end of line 2 and enforced by its repetition in line 5. **bay**: suggesting a retreat from the active life, and also a place of last extremity. **like an halfe Theatre**: i.e. the hill and rock formed a semicircle rather than an amphitheatre. **fulfill**: fill full, in the etymological sense. **trade**: referring to their manner of life or resort; hence, where they always lived. **deceiptfull**: because here they practise their deceit.

Stanza 31
1–5 fondly: foolishly. **th'Heliconian maides**: the muses on Mount Helicon. Conti 1616:7.13 tells of a contest in which the sirens having dared to challenge the muses in song were defeated and punished by having their wings plucked. **moyity**: half. **surquedry**: presumption. **6 hew**: shape.

Stanza 32
2 applyde: addressed (*OED* 26); also 'adapted' (cf. *OED* 4). **3–9** Conti 1616:7.13 notes how the Sirens tempt their

victims to sloth, and through flattery lure them to their deaths. Their song is a prelude to the song at 74–75. **magnifyde**: extolled.

Stanza 33
2–4 big: sonorous. **solemne Meane**: middle part or tenor of the waves, which is proportioned between the bass (the sea) and the alto (the Sirens). Four-part harmony is gained by the treble of the west wind. The lines themselves seek **a straunge kinde of harmony** by breaking the regular iambic rhythm at **breaking**. **measured**: proportioned. **5 Zephyrus**: associated with sexual desire by Conti 1616:4.12; hence it blows through the Bower of Bliss at v 29.8–9.

Stanza 34
1–3 A deliberate contrast to Ulysses, in *Ody.* 12.178–96, who needed to be bound hand and foot, and then bound more, in order not to yield to the temptations of the voluptuous life offered by the Sirens. **temperate aduice**: advice counselling temperance. **5 fog**: cf. the 'foggy mist' that covers all the land before the procession of the deadly sins at I iv 36.7, and the smoke encountered by Ulysses after passing the Sirens (202). **6 has**: i.e. has overspread. **8–9** The repetition of **one** suggests a play on the etymological sense of **Vniuerse**, 'one-turning', 'turning into one', to mark a return to primal chaos.

Stanza 35
3 wastefull: desolate; causing desolation. Limitless expanse suggests the lack of bounds in intemperance; cf. vii 2.8. **4 For**: for fear of.

36

Euen all the nation of vnfortunate
    And fatall birds about them flocked were,
    Such as by nature men abhorre and hate,
    The ill-faste Owle, deaths dreadfull messengere,
    The hoars Night-rauen, trump of dolefull drere,
    The lether-winged Batt, dayes enimy,
    The ruefull Strich, still waiting on the bere,
    The whistler shrill, that who so heares, doth dy,
The hellish Harpyes, prophets of sad destiny.

37

All those, and all that els does horror breed,
    About them flew, and fild their sayles with feare:
    Yet stayd they not, but forward did proceed,
    Whiles th'one did row, and th'other stifly steare;
    Till that at last the weather gan to cleare,
    And the faire land it selfe did playnly sheow.
    Said then the Palmer, Lo where does appeare
    The sacred soile, where all our perills grow;
Therfore, Sir knight; your ready arms about you throw.

38

He hearkned, and his armes about him tooke,
    The whiles the nimble bote so well her sped,
    That with her crooked keele the land she strooke,
    Then forth the noble *Guyon* sallied,
    And his sage Palmer, that him gouerned;
    But th'other by his bote behind did stay.
    They marched fayrly forth, of nought ydred,
    Both firmely armd for euery hard assay,
With constancy and care, gainst daunger and dismay.

39

Ere long they heard an hideous bellowing
    Of many beasts, that roard outrageously,
    As if that hungers poynt, or *Venus* sting
    Had them enraged with fell surquedry;
    Yet nought they feard, but past on hardily,
    Vntill they came in vew of those wilde beasts:
    Who all attonce, gaping full greedily,
    And rearing fercely their vpstaring crests,
Ran towards, to deuoure those vnexpected guests.

40

But soone as they approcht with deadly threat,
    The Palmer ouer them his staffe vpheld,
    His mighty staffe, that could all charmes defeat:
    Eftesoones their stubborne corages were queld,
    And high aduaunced crests downe meekely feld,
    Instead of fraying, they them selues did feare,
    And trembled, as them passing they beheld:
    Such wondrous powre did in that staffe appeare,
All monsters to subdew to him, that did it beare.

41

Of that same wood it fram'd was cunningly,
    Of which *Caduceus* whilome was made,
    Caduceus the rod of *Mercury*,
    With which he wonts the *Stygian* realmes inuade,
    Through ghastly horror, and eternall shade;
    Th'infernall feends with it he can asswage,
    And *Orcus* tame, whome nothing can persuade,
    And rule the *Furyes*, when they most doe rage:
Such vertue in his staffe had eke this Palmer sage.

Stanza 36

1–2 As the fallen Babylon became 'a cage of euerie vncleane and hateful byrde' (Rev. 18.2); noted Wells 1994:38. **nation**: class, kind. **vnfortunate**: ill-omened, inauspicious. **4–5** Both birds guard the entrance to Mammon's house at vii 23.3–5; see *n*. **ill-faste**: evil-faced; cf. xi 8.3. **trump**: trumpet. **drere**: sadness. **7 Strich**: the lich-owl, so called because its screech portends death ('lich': corpse), and it was known to wait near the bier in a funeral procession. See Harrison 1956:64–65. **8 whistler**: known only by this description, but the name was applied to a curlew, as Harrison 65 notes. The Seven Whistlers are well known in folklore as birds of death. **9 Harpyes**: see vii 23.6–9*n*. Virgil calls them *obscenae volucres* (*Aen*. 3.262) and places them in hell (6.289).

Stanza 37

4 stifly: resolutely, steadily. **8 sacred**: also 'accursed' (*OED* 6); cf. 'cursed land' (i 51.8) and *View* 92 where the ancient name of Ireland is said to be '*Sacra Insula*, taking *sacra* for *accursed*'. **where all our perills grow**: the comparable moment to I xi 2.1–2 when the Red Cross Knight reaches the land 'where all our perilles dwell'. **soile** suggests a pun on 'defiling'.

Stanza 38

3 crooked: curved at the prow. **4 sallied**: leaped (*OED* v.[1]), or 'issued forth' (*OED* v.[2] 1). Cf. vi 38.5, and see i 29.6*n*. **5 gouerned**: guided. **8 firmely armd**: armed with the **constancy and care** of temperance. **assay**: attack, trial.

Stanza 39

1–5 The assault on Guyon's senses – chiefly hearing – by the beasts in the sea (23–25) and the birds in the air (35.6–37.2), and now by the beasts on the land, prepares for the assault upon his sight in the Bower. S. differs from his sources – in Homer, *Ody*. 10.210–19, Circe's beasts fawn upon the visitors; in Virgil, *Aen*. 7.15–20, they are heard to rage in the distance; and in Ovid, *Met*. 14.254–59, their rage suddenly collapses into fawning – in order to demonstrate the power of the Palmer's staff. **outrageously**: cf. 22.2. **Venus sting**: *Veneris stimuli* or sexual desire; cf. III viii 25.2, IV ii 5.5. **fell surquedry**: fierce arrogance; here suggesting sexual indulgence, as III x 2.5. **9 towards**: in their direction.

Stanza 40

6 fraying: frightening (others). **8–9** S.'s immediate model is Tasso, *Ger. Lib.* 15.49–52: the rod given Ubaldo to subdue Armida's wild beasts. His classical model is Homer, *Ody*. 10.287–94: Odysseus's magical charm, moly, protects him from Circe's wand and her charms.

Stanza 41

1–3 cunningly: skilfully. **Mercury**: the messenger of the gods. On his role as the *psychopompos*, or guide of souls, see Brooks-Davies 1983:33–42. His **Caduceus** is given power over the living and the dead in Virgil, *Aen*. 4.242–44; cf. the power of Cambina's 'rod of peace' at IV iii 42. On its connection with the virtue of prudence through which Guyon overcomes concupiscence, see Black 1999:76–77.

42

Thence passing forth, they shortly doe arryue,
　Whereas the Bowre of *Blisse* was situate;
　A place pickt out by choyce of best alyue,
　That natures worke by art can imitate:
　In which what euer in this worldly state
　Is sweete, and pleasing vnto liuing sense,
　Or that may dayntest fantasy aggrate,
Was poured forth with plentifull dispence,
And made there to abound with lauish affluence.

43

Goodly it was enclosed rownd about,
　Aswell their entred guestes to keep within,
　As those vnruly beasts to hold without;
　Yet was the fence thereof but weake and thin;
　Nought feard theyr force, that fortilage to win,
　But wisedomes powre, and temperaunces might,
　By which the mightiest things efforced bin:
And eke the gate was wrought of substaunce light,
Rather for pleasure, then for battery or fight.

44

Yt framed was of precious yuory,
　That seemd a worke of admirable witt;
　And therein all the famous history
　Of *Iason* and *Medæa* was ywritt;
　Her mighty charmes, her furious louing fitt,
　His goodly conquest of the golden fleece,
　His falsed fayth, and loue too lightly flitt,
The wondred *Argo*, which in venturous peece
First through the *Euxine* seas bore all the flowr of *Greece*.

45

Ye might haue seene the frothy billowes fry
　Vnder the ship, as thorough them she went,
　That seemd the waues were into yuory,
　Or yuory into the waues were sent;
　And otherwhere the snowy substaunce sprent
　With vermell, like the boyes blood therein shed,
　A piteous spectacle did represent,
And otherwhiles with gold besprinkeled;
Yt seemd thenchaunted flame, which did *Creusa* wed.

Stanza 42

1–4 of best alyue: i.e. the best artisans alive picked out the place, in contrast to Phædria's island 'by Natures cunning hand . . . picked out from all the rest' (vi 12.3–4). Or 'from the best of any that exists', which still points to art, rather than nature, as the agent that chooses. For poets, **art** is primarily the literary tradition of the *locus amoenus* which, for S., is chiefly Alcinous's garden in Homer, *Ody.* 7.112–32; Alcina's isle in Ariosto, *Orl. Fur.* 6.19–25; and esp. Armida's isle in Tasso, *Ger. Lib.* 15.53–66 with its enclosed garden at 16.1–26. Antecedents in classical literature are traced by Curtius 1953:195–200, and in Italian romance by Giamatti 1966:268–90. In addition to the literary tradition, the **art** includes contemporary Renaissance gardens: see Leslie 1992:3–22 and Beretta 1993:135–39; and the idealized descriptions of contemporary Virginia: see J.N. Wall 1984:4–12. Guyon and the Palmer, who have now arrived at Acrasia's 'wandring Island' (i 51.5), move inward, first to the plain with its pleasure-grounds at 50.1, and then to the paradise or garden at 58.1, and not until 69.4 do they 'come nigh' the Bower itself, presumably at its centre. **7 fantasy**: a term with strongly negative associations; see III xii 7.1*n*. **aggrate**: please; cf. v 33.2. **8 dispence**: liberality. Praise of nature's abundance is a reminder that nature herself is good, though here abused by art: 'For the earth is the Lords, and all that therein is' (1 Cor. 10.26).

Stanza 43

1 enclosed introduces the theme of the *hortus conclusus*, the 'garden inclosed' of the Song of Solomon 4.12; see Stewart 1966:41–45. **5–6** I.e., it was not at all feared that the physical force of the beasts without could conquer that **fortilage** (i.e. fortress); what was feared was **wisedomes powre** (associated with the Palmer) and **temperaunces might** (associated with Guyon).

Stanza 44

Cf. the gate of ivory through which Archimago's spright brings the lustful dream to delude the Red Cross Knight; see I i 40.1–3*n*. **2 admirable witt**: marvellous skill. **3–9** S.'s model is the gate leading to Armida's garden in Tasso, *Ger. Lib.* 16.2–7. In place of the stories of Hercules and Iole, and Antony and Cleopatra, he substitutes **the famous history | Of Iason and Medæa**. With choice Grecian warriors, Jason sailed in the Argo to obtain King Aeetes's golden fleece at Colchis, where he was aided by the **mighty charmes** of his daughter Medæa, who passionately loved him. After he obtained the fleece and fled with her, they escaped pursuit when, in **her furious louing fitt**, she threw pieces of her brother's body into the sea for their father to retrieve. When she was abandoned by Jason, she sent his new bride, Creüsa, an enchanted garment which burned her to death; in this sense, Creüsa 'wed' the flame (45.9). Medæa inherits her magic and sensuality from her aunt Circe, as does Acrasia; see 85.5*n*. For a close analysis of the *ecphrasis* here and in stanza 45, see DuBois 1982:75–78, and Heffernan 1993:71–72. On Acrasia's murderousness, see Hieatt 1992:30. **falsed**: violated. **flitt**: altering. **venturous peece**: adventurous ship. **First**: the **Argo** was the first ocean-going ship.

Stanza 45

On the pictorial description used here, see Hulse 1994:102–03. **1 fry**: foam. **5 otherwhere**: elsewhere. **sprent**: sprinkled. **6 vermell**: vermilion.

Stanzas 46–48

First seen sitting in the porch, Genius assumes the role of guardian of the garden of love in the *Roman de la Rose*, called 'Ydelnesse', tr. Chaucer 593. With his bowl of wine at 49.2–3, he assumes the role of the young Bacchus described in Cartari, *Le imagini de i dei*; see J.L. Klein 1985:97–98. The distinction between this figure and Agdistes, the porter of the garden of Adonis at III vi 31–33, is traced by Lewis 1936:361–63. To distinguish between the god of generation and the good individual genius, Lewis 1966:172–74 proposes that 47.2–4 be read as a parenthetical account of the former. Conti 1616:4.3, whom S. follows perhaps too closely in these stanzas, notes that 'genius' is so called either because he is born with us or because the care of generation was thought to be entrusted to

46

All this, and more might in that goodly gate
   Be red; that euer open stood to all,
   Which thether came: but in the Porch there sate
   A comely personage of stature tall,
   And semblaunce pleasing, more then naturall,
   That traueilers to him seemd to entize;
   His looser garment to the ground did fall,
   And flew about his heeles in wanton wize,
Not fitt for speedy pace, or manly exercize.

47

They in that place him *Genius* did call:
   Not that celestiall powre, to whom the care
   Of life, and generation of all
   That liues, perteines in charge particulare,
   Who wondrous things concerning our welfare,
   And straunge phantomes doth lett vs ofte forsee,
   And ofte of secret ill bids vs beware:
   That is our Selfe, whom though we doe not see,
Yet each doth in him selfe it well perceiue to bee.

48

Therefore a God him sage Antiquity
   Did wisely make, and good *Agdistes* call:
   But this same was to that quite contrary,
   The foe of life, that good enuyes to all,
   That secretly doth vs procure to fall,
   Through guilefull semblants, which he makes vs see.
   He of this Gardin had the gouernall,
   And Pleasures porter was deuizd to bee,
Holding a staffe in hand for more formalitee.

49

With diuerse flowres he daintily was deckt,
   And strowed rownd about, and by his side
   A mighty Mazer bowle of wine was sett,
   As if it had to him bene sacrifide;
   Wherewith all new-come guests he gratyfide:
   So did he eke Sir *Guyon* passing by:
   But he his ydle curtesie defide,
   And ouerthrew his bowle disdainfully;
And broke his staffe, with which he charmed semblants sly.

50

Thus being entred, they behold arownd
   A large and spacious plaine, on euery side
   Strowed with pleasauns, whose fayre grassy grownd
   Mantled with greene, and goodly beautifide
   With all the ornaments of *Floraes* pride,
   Wherewith her mother Art, as halfe in scorne
   Of niggard Nature, like a pompous bride
   Did decke her, and too lauishly adorne,
When forth from virgin bowre she comes in th'early morne.

---

him by the gods. Cf. the 'glad Genius' of the 'geniall bed' who helps produce 'fruitfull progeny' in *Epith* 398–403, as its etymology, from Lat. *gignere*, 'to give birth' suggests. The good Genius shows us *spectra et imagines* in contrast to the evil genius whose images tempt us to evil. See 'Genius' in the *SEnc*.

Stanza 46
3 the Porch, here and at 54.1, marks a liminal moment in Guyon's rite of passage; see 'thresholds' in the *SEnc*. **5 more then naturall**: in contrast to Agdistes who is associated with nature. **7–9** As Idlenesse 'greatly shunned manly exercise' (I iv 20.2). **looser**: too loose, suggesting his effeminate appearance.

Stanza 47
8 our Selfe: i.e. a person's *daemon*, the essential being, which, as S. says, each of us perceives within.

Stanza 48
2 Agdistes: Genius is so named by Conti 1616. **3–6** The same distinction is made today between one's good and evil genius/ angel/ or self. **enuyes**: begrudges. **procure**: cause. **which he makes vs see**: the key phrase, for the Bower forces us to see and thereby be overwhelmed by its spectacle. Archimago exercises such power over the Red Cross Knight at I i 47, ii 5. On the Bower as a spectacle of desire that is also a *trompe-l'œil*, see Belsey 1994:155–58. **7–8 gouernall**: management. As each place has its genius, he is the tutelary or guardian spirit of the Bower. **Pleasures porter**: because the evil Genius leads one into lust, according to Conti; or because the *Geruli* (porters) were associated with Genii and genial gods

in Renaissance dictionaries. In Chaucer, *Second Nun's Prologue* 3, Idleness is said to be the 'porter of the gate . . . of delices'. **deuizd**: appointed; contrived, referring to his artful appearance. **9 for more formalitee**: i.e. only as an emblem of his office, in contrast to the Palmer's staff used to subdue the beasts at 40.

Stanza 49
1–4 S. still follows Conti 1616, who follows Horace, in associating the worship of Agdistes with flowers and bowls of wine. **Mazer bowle**: a drinking-cup made of maple. In *SC Aug.* 26–30, its trail of 'wanton Yvie' associates it with intemperance. **Mazer**: associated with 'maze', bewilder, and with 'mazer', to knock on the head, referring to the wine's potency. At i 55, Mordant dies after drinking from Acrasia's bacchic cup. Cf. the effect of Duessa's cup at I viii 14.1–5. The **bowle** and **staffe** (or wand) are Circe's attributes and carry the same sexual significance. **sacrifide**: offered as a sacrifice, consecrated. **5 gratyfide**: welcomed; also gave pleasure to. **9 charmed semblants sly**: i.e. conjured up the 'guilefull semblants, which he makes vs see' (48.6). **sly**: as an adv., in a cunning manner; as an adj., cleverly or finely made.

Stanza 50
3 pleasauns: pleasure-grounds or small parks. **5 Floraes pride**: the goddess of flowers in her most flourishing state; see I i 48.9*n*. **6–8** Art's scorn of nature is implicit in the claim that the golden age was lost when man 'gan exceed | The measure of her [nature's] meane, and naturall first need' (vii 16.8–9), and becomes central in the description of the Bower; see 59*n*.

51

Therewith the Heauens alwayes Iouiall,
　　Lookte on them louely, still in stedfast state,
　　Ne suffred storme nor frost on them to fall,
　　Their tender buds or leaues to violate,
　　Nor scorching heat, nor cold intemperate
　　T'afflict the creatures, which therein did dwell,
　　But the milde ayre with season moderate
　　Gently attempred, and disposd so well,
That still it breathed forth sweet spirit and holesom smell.

52

More sweet and holesome, then the pleasant hill
　　Of *Rhodope*, on which the Nimphe, that bore
　　A gyaunt babe, her selfe for griefe did kill:
　　Or the Thessalian *Tempe*, where of yore
　　Fayre *Daphne Phœbus* hart with loue did gore;
　　Or *Ida*, where the Gods lou'd to repayre,
　　When euer they their heauenly bowres forlore;
　　Or sweet *Parnasse*, the haunt of Muses fayre;
Or *Eden* selfe, if ought with *Eden* mote compayre.

53

Much wondred *Guyon* at the fayre aspect
　　Of that sweet place, yet suffred no delight
　　To sincke into his sence, nor mind affect,
　　But passed forth, and lookt still forward right,
　　Brydling his will, and maystering his might:
　　Till that he came vnto another gate,
　　No gate, but like one, being goodly dight
　　With bowes and braunches, which did broad dilate
Their clasping armes, in wanton wreathings intricate.

54

So fashioned a Porch with rare deuice,
　　Archt ouer head with an embracing vine,
　　Whose bounches hanging downe, seemd to entice
　　All passers by, to taste their lushious wine,
　　And did them selues into their hands incline,
　　As freely offering to be gathered:
　　Some deepe empurpled as the *Hyacint*,
　　Some as the Rubine, laughing sweetely red,
Some like faire Emeraudes, not yet well ripened.

55

And them amongst, some were of burnisht gold,
　　So made by art, to beautify the rest,
　　Which did themselues emongst the leaues enfold,
　　As lurking from the vew of couetous guest,
　　That the weake boughes, with so rich load opprest,
　　Did bow adowne, as ouerburdened.
　　Vnder that Porch a comely dame did rest,
　　Clad in fayre weedes, but fowle disordered,
And garments loose, that seemd vnmeet for womanhed.

Stanza 51

1–2 Therewith: Thereto *1596*, i.e. added to that. **Iouiall**: joyous, serene, being under the influence of Jove. Since his rule brought seasonal change (Ovid, *Met.* 1.113–18), **always** notes that the Bower endures eternal summer without spring's renewal and autumn's fruition. Hence **still**: always; implying a static, sterile state. **louely**: lovingly. **4 violate**: damage by violence. **5–9** The topoi used here may be drawn from Tasso, *Ger. Lib.* 15.53–54, but more likely from Chaucer, *Parl. Fowls* 204–06, 210: 'Th'air of that place so attempre was | That nevere was ther grevaunce of hot ne cold; | There wex ek every holsom spice and gras; . . . But ay cler day'. As the language echoes *Axiochus*, see Weatherby 1986:96. **attempred**: modified its temperature; cf. the birds' song at 71.2. **disposd**: regulated. **spirit**: breath.

Stanza 52

The five *loci amoeni* evoke scenes of natural beauty which, except for **Parnasse** (the earlier form of Parnassus, home of the muses: see I x 54.6–9), are marred by sin and death. Two legends of **Rhodope** become one: that she was transformed into the mountain because she and her brother assumed the names of the gods (Ovid, *Met.* 6.87–89); and that, after she gave birth to a **gyaunt babe** by Neptune, she assumed the name of Juno. **Rhodope** is the **pleasant hill** where Orpheus sang (*Met.* 10.86–105) and where he was torn to pieces (*Met.* 11.39–43). The love of **Phœbus** for **Daphne** (*Met.* 1.452–567), his first love, led to her metamorphosis, a type of all that follow in Ovid. **Ida** is the mountain where the three goddesses appeared before Paris in a judgement that led to the war of Troy; see vii 55.4–9*n*. **Eden** was commonly taken to signify 'pleasure', the *paradisum voluptatis* of Gen. 2.8 (Vulg.), and place of the Fall. For its relation to other earthly paradises,

esp. the garden of Adonis, see Nohrnberg 1976:507–19. **7 forlore**: left. **9 compayre**: be compared.

Stanza 53

4 forward right: straight ahead, obeying the injunction: 'Let thine eyes behold the right, and let thine eyeliddes direct thy way before thee' (Prov. 4.25). **forward** is a key word in this canto: cf. 5.1, 14.2, 37.3, 57.9, 69.3; its climax comes in the phrase: 'kept their forward way' (76.5). **5 Brydling**: see iv 34.2*n*. **maystering his might**: continuing the emblem of temperance as the rider who controls his horse or passions. Paradoxically, Guyon exercises his might by restraining its use (cf. v 13.3) until the moment he destroys the Bower. **8 dilate**: extend. **9** The line conveys the labyrinthine twisting it describes.

Stanza 54

1 deuice: design. **7–9** The reversal of the three seasons of grapes from ripened to turning, to unripened, and then to artificial in 55, is noted by Brooks-Davies 1977:192. **Hyacint**: hyacinth or jacinth. 'Hyacine' *1611*, and a variant in *1590*, provides the 'c' rhyme, but S. may have wanted to avoid an internal echo with **Rubine**; or to surprise us with a non-rhyming word. **Rubine**: ruby. **Emeraudes**: emeralds. Perhaps climactic: Drayton 1931–41:3.319 refers to 'The Emerauld then, most deepely greene, | For beauty most excelling'. Cain 1978:92 notes that emeralds recently discovered in Peru were held 'to ripen chemically in their lode, like fruit'.

Stanza 55

1–4 Reports of the New World told of Incan gardens with plants made of gold; noted Cain 1978:92–93. **9** As Genius wears a loose garment not fit for 'manly exercize' (46.9).

56

In her left hand a Cup of gold she held,
　And with her right the riper fruit did reach,
　Whose sappy liquor, that with fulnesse sweld,
　Into her cup she scruzd, with daintie breach
　Of her fine fingers, without fowle empeach,
　That so faire winepresse made the wine more sweet:
　Thereof she vsd to giue to drinke to each,
　Whom passing by she happened to meet:
It was her guise, all Straungers goodly so to greet.

57

So she to *Guyon* offred it to tast,
　Who taking it out of her tender hond,
　The cup to ground did violently cast,
　That all in peeces it was broken fond,
　And with the liquor stained all the lond:
　Whereat *Excesse* exceedingly was wroth,
　Yet no'te the same amend, ne yet withstond,
　But suffered him to passe, all were she loth;
Who nought regarding her displeasure, forward goth.

58

There the most daintie Paradise on ground,
　It selfe doth offer to his sober eye,
　In which all pleasures plenteously abownd,
　And none does others happinesse enuye:
　The painted flowres, the trees vpshooting hye,
　The dales for shade, the hilles for breathing space,
　The trembling groues, the christall running by;
　And that, which all faire workes doth most aggrace,
The art, which all that wrought, appeared in no place.

59

One would haue thought, (so cunningly, the rude
　And scorned partes were mingled with the fine,)
　That nature had for wantonesse ensude
　Art, and that Art at nature did repine;
　So striuing each th'other to vndermine,
　Each did the others worke more beautify;
　So diff'ring both in willes, agreed in fine:
　So all agreed through sweete diuersity,
This Gardin to adorne with all variety.

60

And in the midst of all, a fountaine stood,
　Of richest substance, that on earth might bee,
　So pure and shiny, that the siluer flood
　Through euery channell running one might see;
　Most goodly it with curious ymageree
　Was ouerwrought, and shapes of naked boyes,
　Of which some seemd with liuely iollitee,
　To fly about, playing their wanton toyes,
Whylest others did them selues embay in liquid ioyes,

61

And ouer all, of purest gold was spred,
　A trayle of yuie in his natiue hew:
　For the rich metall was so coloured,
　That wight, who did not well auis'd it vew,
　Would surely deeme it to bee yuie trew:
　Low his lasciuious armes adown did creepe,
　That themselues dipping in the siluer dew,
　Their fleecy flowres they fearefully did steepe,
Which drops of Christall seemd for wantones to weep.

Stanza 56

1 left: from its association with the left, or heart, side, to indicate the temptation of sensual indulgence. **4 scruzd**: screwed and squeezed. **breach**: crushing. The erotic significance of her action is noted by Paglia 1990:187. **5 without fowle empeach**: without injury to the fruit; or without foul injury to her appearance by soiling her fingers. The context suggests 'hindrance'. **9 guise**: custom. **all**: as Genius offers wine to 'all new-come guests' (49.5); and as the bathing maidens display their beauty to 'any, which them eyd' (63.9).

Stanza 57

1–5 At 49.7–9, Guyon rejects a similar temptation 'disdainfully', but now **violently**, and finally with 'rigour pittilesse' (83.2). The religious sanction for his present action, which characterizes **Excesse** as intemperate, is given in Eph. 5.18: 'Be not drunke with wine, wherein is excesse but be fulfilled with the Spirit'. **7 no'te**: could not.

Stanza 58

The final two lines all but translate Tasso's final two lines on Armida's garden in *Ger. Lib.* 16.9, and yet remain original, as Durling 1954 demonstrates. **1–2 daintie**: choice, excellent. **on ground**: implying an earthly paradise. Line 2 shows how actively the garden tempts all passers-by, as at 54.3–6. **5 painted flowres**: referring to hybrids, which became popular in the 1590s, as Beretta 1993:136 notes. **7 christall**:

crystal streams. **8–9 aggrace**: add grace to; an intensification of Tasso's *accresce*.

Stanza 59

Developing and extending *Ger. Lib.* 16.10 on the relation between art and nature: not only does art imitate nature but nature imitates art, as in Ovid, *Met.* 3.158–59. Cf. v 29.1–2, and the harmony of art and nature on the island of the temple of Venus at IV x 21.6–9. See 'nature and art' in the *SEnc*. **3 wantonesse**: playfulness, unruliness, the literal sense of intemperance; also arrogance. **ensude**: imitated. **4 repine**: fret. **7 in fine**: in the end.

Stanza 60

The **fountaine** – in this context, inevitably phallic, esp. in being called 'vpright' (62.9) – is S.'s addition to Tasso's pool with its bathing virgins, *Ger. Lib.* 15.58–66, perhaps prompted by actual gardens, as Leslie 1992:18 notes; or by Acratia's fountain of concupiscence in Trissino, *Italia liberata da' Goti*, as A. Fowler 1964:94 suggests. **3 pure**: clear, transparent; cf. the altar in the temple of Venus at IV x 39.7–9. **4 channell**: referring also to the stream. **6–9** The 'c' rhyme (**boyes**, **toyes**, **ioyes**) is repeated from the description of the Bower at v 28, and is repeated again at stanza 72, with the order (1–2–3) reversed here, and then inverted (1–3–2); noted Downing 1982:66. In the first and third use, the boys are called 'lasciuious'; here they are sculptures but **naked**. **ouerwrought**: wrought all over; excessively wrought. **toyes**: amorous sports. **embay**: bathe.

62

Infinit streames continually did well
  Out of this fountaine, sweet and faire to see,
  The which into an ample lauer fell,
  And shortly grew to so great quantitie,
  That like a litle lake it seemd to bee;
  Whose depth exceeded not three cubits hight,
  That through the waues one might the bottom see,
  All pau'd beneath with Iaspar shining bright,
That seemd the fountaine in that sea did sayle vpright.

63

And all the margent round about was sett,
  With shady Laurell trees, thence to defend
  The sunny beames, which on the billowes bett,
  And those which therein bathed, mote offend:
  As *Guyon* hapned by the same to wend,
  Two naked Damzelles he therein espyde,
  Which therein bathing, seemed to contend,
  And wrestle wantonly, ne car'd to hyde,
Their dainty partes from vew of any, which them eyd.

64

Sometimes the one would lift the other quight
  Aboue the waters, and then downe againe
  Her plong, as ouer maystered by might,
  Where both awhile would couered remaine,

And each the other from to rise restraine;
  The whiles their snowy limbes, as through a vele,
  So through the christall waues appeared plaine:
  Then suddeinly both would themselues vnhele,
And th'amarous sweet spoiles to greedy eyes reuele.

65

As that faire Starre, the messenger of morne,
  His deawy face out of the sea doth reare:
  Or as the *Cyprian* goddesse, newly borne
  Of th'Oceans fruitfull froth, did first appeare:
  Such seemed they, and so their yellow heare
  Christalline humor dropped downe apace.
  Whom such when *Guyon* saw, he drew him neare,
  And somewhat gan relent his earnest pace;
His stubborne brest gan secret pleasaunce to embrace.

66

The wanton Maidens him espying, stood
  Gazing a while at his vnwonted guise;
  Then th'one her selfe low ducked in the flood,
  Abasht, that her a straunger did auise:
  But thother rather higher did arise,
  And her two lilly paps aloft displayd,
  And all, that might his melting hart entyse
  To her delights, she vnto him bewrayd:
The rest hidd vnderneath, him more desirous made.

Stanza 61

2 trayle of yuie: trailing ornament of ivy. As a symbol of lust, see v 29.3–5*n*. **4 well auis'd**: carefully. **8 fearefully**: apparently for the alliteration; tenderly *1596* is associated with flowers, as 51.3.

Stanza 62

In S.'s allegorical landscape, the **fountaine** is often associated with concupiscence, as at I vii 2.7. Here its **Infinit streames** parody the chaste bride of Song Sol. 4.12 who is described as 'a fountaine sealed vp'. **3–9** In parody of John's vision of the 'sea of glasse like vnto cristal' with God's throne in the midst, and of the New Jerusalem 'shining . . . like vnto .. a Iasper stone cleare as cristal' (Rev. 4.6, 21.11). **lauer**: the basin of the fountain. **three cubits**: less than five feet; about breast-high, as we soon see. **sayle**: 'project' is a relevant sense.

Stanza 63

1–4 margent: margin. The association of **Laurell** with the preservation of the fearful Daphne's virginity – see III v 40.2*n* – counters the superbly shameless exhibitionism of the two damsels. **defend**: ward off. **offend**: harm. **6–9** The **Two naked Damzelles** are borrowed from Tasso, *Ger. Lib.* 15.58–66, where they exhibit themselves before another upright pair, though here, being more lascivious, they are more effective, as Durling 1954:338 notes. In Tasso, the maidens engage in a swimming contest; in his translation of Tasso, evidently influenced by S., Fairfax shows them wrestling; but only in S. is there the homoerotic appeal of having them wrestle **wantonly** before **any, which them eyd**. Their actions invoke the innocent vision of Diana watching her nymphs as 'Some wrestle . . . some bathe in christall flood' (I xii 7.9) now made erotic by Guyon's voyeurism, as H. Hendrix 1992 argues. Frantz 1989:245 cites this scene to support his claim that no

other poet of the English Renaissance recognized more clearly the power of sight to arouse erotic impulses. Kosako 1998:152 notes that the unusual use of transitive verbs in the rhymes invites Guyon's response.

Stanza 64

6 as through a vele: the decorum of vision in this episode, which involves gazing on secret sights, is examined by Krier 1990:105–09; the aesthetics of veiling/unveiling in the Bower by Dauber 1980; and the veil in relation to image-making by Gregerson 1995:112–25. See also 'veils' in the *SEnc*. On the motif of gazing in the poem, see also DeNeef 1994. **8 vnhele**: expose to view. **9 amarous**: lovely; arousing desire; but implying the Lat. *amarus*, bitter, as Hale 1997:107 notes. **spoiles**: cf. Cymochles who 'his fraile eye with spoyle of beauty feedes' at v 34.3.

Stanza 65

1–4 A parody of the Red Cross Knight's wondrous vision of Una as the morning star at I xii 21.5–9. In contrast, Guyon must turn aside from his vision, only barely titillated. **the messenger of morne**: because its rising 'tell[s] that dawning day is drawing neare' (I xii 21.7). **His**: to be taken as neuter; noted Daniels 1990:174. **the Cyprian goddesse**: '*Venus* of the fomy sea' (IV xii 2.2), so called because she was born from the foam of the sea. She appears here as *Aphrodite anadyomene* (Venus rising from the sea) as does the morning star. **6 humor**: moisture. **8 relent**: slacken; cf. 68.4.

Stanza 66

2 guise: behaviour; with a pun on 'gaze'. **4 auise**: view. **6 lilly paps**: the phrase collapses the simile, 'Her paps lyke lyllies budded' (*Epith* 176). **8 bewrayd**: exposed.

67

With that, the other likewise vp arose,
    And her faire lockes, which formerly were bownd
    Vp in one knott, she low adowne did lose:
    Which flowing long and thick, her cloth'd arownd,
    And th'yuorie in golden mantle gownd:
    So that faire spectacle from him was reft,
    Yet that, which reft it, no lesse faire was fownd:
    So hidd in lockes and waues from lookers theft,
Nought but her louely face she for his looking left.

68

Withall she laughed, and she blusht withall,
    That blushing to her laughter gaue more grace,
    And laughter to her blushing, as did fall:
    Now when they spyde the knight to slacke his pace,
    Them to behold, and in his sparkling face
    The secrete signes of kindled lust appeare,
    Their wanton meriments they did encreace,
    And to him beckned, to approch more neare,
And shewd him many sights, that corage cold could reare.

69

On which when gazing him the Palmer saw,
    He much rebukt those wandring eyes of his,
    And counseld well, him forward thence did draw.
    Now are they come nigh to the *Bowre of blis*

Of her fond fauorites so nam'd amis:
    When thus the Palmer, Now Sir, well auise;
    For here the end of all our traueill is:
    Here wonnes *Acrasia*, whom we must surprise,
Els she will slip away, and all our drift despise.

70

Eftsoones they heard a most melodious sound,
    Of all that mote delight a daintie eare,
    Such as attonce might not on liuing ground,
    Saue in this Paradise, be heard elswhere:
    Right hard it was, for wight, which did it heare,
    To read, what manner musicke that mote bee:
    For all that pleasing is to liuing eare,
    Was there consorted in one harmonee,
Birdes, voices, instruments, windes, waters, all agree.

71

The ioyous birdes shrouded in chearefull shade,
    Their notes vnto the voice attempred sweet;
    Th'Angelicall soft trembling voyces made
    To th'instruments diuine respondence meet:
    The siluer sounding instruments did meet
    With the base murmure of the waters fall:
    The waters fall with difference discreet,
    Now soft, now loud, vnto the wind did call:
The gentle warbling wind low answered to all.

Stanza 67

This **faire spectacle** of the maiden who is nude but not naked
because part of her body is clothed by her hair and the rest by
water is esp. close to Tasso 15.61 until the final line: S. omits
the virgin's enticing shame of exposure, replacing it in the
next line with laughter, for S. the mark of lust in any sexual
context.

Stanza 68

1 Withall . . . withall: with that . . . because of that. **9 corage**: sexual desire. **reare**: arouse; or in the explicitly erotic
sense, 'cause to stand up'.

Stanza 69

1 The pacing phrases of the line mime the Palmer's sternness.
3 Cf. the similar transition at 29.5, 34.1–3. **6 Now**: the
heavy stress, esp. following its use in 4, announces that the
time has come for Guyon to act. **auise**: consider. **7 traueill**:
also travail. **8 Acrasia**: the name is adapted from the
enchantress Acratia in Trissino, *Italia liberata* 5 who imprisons
knights in her garden. According to *OED*, the obs. word
'acrasy' derives from med. Lat. *acrasia*, which confuses two
forms of Gk ἀκρασία: badly mixed (f. ἄκρατος, unmixed,
intemperate) and want of self-command (f. ἀκρατής, incontinent). Acrasia's bad mixture is suggested by the charmed
cup she gives Mordant to drink; see i 55.6*n*. Accordingly,
she combines the bad mixture of the humours and the figure
Impotence who attends Maleger. In Matt. 23.25, Christ compares hypocrites to a cup clean on the outside but within 'ful
of . . . excesse', a term that translates the Gk ἀκρασία, which
Geneva glosses as 'intemperancie'; noted Esolen 1993:281.
Wybarne 1609 identifies Acrasia as intemperance; see *Sp All*
119. For the link with Acrates – only a link because, surprisingly, Acrasia's ancestry is not disclosed – and hence with

Impatience who also attends Maleger, see iv 41*n*. Relevant is
the cognate form 'acraze', to weaken or enfeeble, i.e. to make
others powerless. See 'Acrasia' in the *SEnc*. The influential
claim by Greenblatt 1980:185 that Acrasia represents the
threat to the colonists in Ireland by the native women is countered by S. Wilson 1995:73–74, who claims that she represents
the mistress in the *Amoretti* and even the Queen. **9 drift**:
purpose; plot. **despise**: set at nought.

Stanza 70

Following the temptation of sight comes the temptation of
hearing. **3 attonce**: together, at one time. **4 this Paradise**:
a parody of 'the bowre of blisse, the paradice of pleasure' of the
poet's beloved in *Am* 76.3. **6 read**: discern. **8–9 consorted**:
harmoniously combined; cf. v 31.8. The five listed musical elements, each with its own tonal colour, suggest the pentatonic
scale, and introduce the mixed consort in the next stanza.

Stanza 71

The harmony of what N. Frye 1976b:132 calls 'a five-part
madrigal' is revealed, as he notes, by the harmony of the
stanza: the interlocking repetition and skilful variation of each
sound, and the final concord of **meet** rhymed with **meet** at the
centre. Wells 1994:28 notes the 'emphasis on the co-operative
alliance between natural and artificial forms of music'. With
this quintet, cf. the four-part harmony at 33. Hollander
1971:230, 238 argues that it is 'marked by a morally unwholesome blending of its musical categories', and concludes that it
represents 'the total undermining of modes of recognition, of
the travesties of variety, through which the Bower's ultimately
deadly attractiveness is manifested'. Rooks 1988:29 counters
that such music displays a 'very considerable delicacy' if viewed
in the context of its precursors. See also *SEnc* 483–84. **1 ioyous birdes**: cf. their singing at v 31.6–9, and their sing-along

72

There, whence that Musick seemed heard to bee,
  Was the faire Witch her selfe now solacing,
  With a new Louer, whom through sorceree
  And witchcraft, she from farre did thether bring:
  There she had him now laid a slombering,
  In secret shade, after long wanton ioyes:
  Whilst round about them pleasauntly did sing
  Many faire Ladies, and lasciuious boyes,
That euer mixt their song with light licentious toyes.

73

And all that while, right ouer him she hong,
  With her false eyes fast fixed in his sight,
  As seeking medicine, whence she was stong,
  Or greedily depasturing delight:
  And oft inclining downe with kisses light,
  For feare of waking him, his lips bedewd,
  And through his humid eyes did sucke his spright,
  Quite molten into lust and pleasure lewd;
Wherewith she sighed soft, as if his case she rewd.

74

The whiles some one did chaunt this louely lay;
  Ah see, who so fayre thing doest faine to see,
  In springing flowre the image of thy day;
  Ah see the Virgin Rose, how sweetly shee

Doth first peepe foorth with bashfull modestee,
  That fairer seemes, the lesse ye see her may;
  Lo see soone after, how more bold and free
  Her bared bosome she doth broad display;
Lo see soone after, how she fades, and falls away.

75

So passeth, in the passing of a day,
  Of mortall life the leafe, the bud, the flowre,
  Ne more doth florish after first decay,
  That earst was sought to deck both bed and bowre,
  Of many a Lady', and many a Paramowre:
  Gather therefore the Rose, whilest yet is prime,
  For soone comes age, that will her pride deflowre:
  Gather the Rose of loue, whilest yet is time,
Whilest louing thou mayst loued be with equall crime.

76

He ceast, and then gan all the quire of birdes
  Their diuerse notes t'attune vnto his lay,
  As in approuaunce of his pleasing wordes,
  The constant payre heard all, that he did say,
  Yet swarued not, but kept their forward way,
  Through many couert groues, and thickets close,
  In which they creeping did at last display
  That wanton Lady, with her louer lose,
Whose sleepie head she in her lap did soft dispose.

---

with Phædria at vi 25.1–4. **chearefull shade**: for S., an oxymoron; cf. 'ioyous shade' (I vii 4.2). **2 attempred**: attuned; cf. 76.2. **4 respondence meet**: fitting response. **5 meet**: blend. **6 base**: with a pun. **7 The waters fall**: S.'s poetic signature – see VI x 7.9*n* – inserted to stamp the art of the Bower as his own, perhaps because he so deliberately overgoes Tasso, *Ger. Lib.* 16.12. **8 difference discreet**: distinct variation.

Stanza 72

2 the faire Witch: a particularly dangerous paradox, as Roberts 1997:71 notes, for elsewhere witches are ugly, e.g. Duessa at I viii 46–48. **9 toyes**: amorous play; 'free musical compositions', sugg. Hollander 1971:235.

Stanza 73

3 medicine: cure; as though the therapy she seeks were homœopathy, which here becomes anticipatory necrophilia, as Gregerson 1995:121 observes. **4 depasturing**: consuming, from Lat. *depascere*. A more powerful term than the usual image of the man feeding on the woman, as in Tasso, *Ger. Lib.* 16.19, which this stanza imitates. (On the influence of Lucretius, *De Rerum Natura* 1.31–40 which Tasso imitates, see Esolen 1993:274–79.) For the male reader, the horror is that he becomes her pasture, as one of 'her louers, which her lustes did feed' (85.3), like Venus who 'reape[s] sweet pleasure' of Adonis at III vi 46.3. **6–7** Fixing her eyes upon him, she literally draws his spirit through his closed eyes, as though sucking the soul from his dying body, in an action described by Giamatti 1966:279 as 'vampirish'. Cf. Venus's similar posture over the sleeping Adonis: she would 'with ambrosiall kisses bathe his eyes' while her eyes search his body (III i 36.4–6). **8 pleasure**: sensual gratification. **9** Her apparent pity for his degenerate state contrasts with the poet's moral disapproval at 80.9.

Stanzas 74–75

A brilliant imitation of the parrot's song in Armida's garden, in Tasso, *Ger. Lib.* 16.14–15. It follows Tasso closely but becomes original as a poignant expression of the topos, *carpe diem*. The answer to it is given by the Faerie Queene's one speech in the poem as reported by Arthur: 'dearely sure her loue was to me bent, | As when iust time expired should appeare' (I ix 14.3–4). Cf. Phædria's song at vi 15–17 and see *n.*

Stanza 74

1 louely lay: lay of love. **2 faine**: delight. **4–8** The rose imitates the coyness and then the bare display by the two damsels at 66.

Stanza 75

6–9 prime: the flower's most flourishing state; the 'springtime' of human life. **pride**: i.e. her **prime**. **deflowre**: the resonance of this word in Bk II is noted by Gohlke 1978:136–37. **with equall crime**: the undercutting phrase places the pagan tradition in a Christian perspective, for **crime** suggests both sin and judgement on it, in contrast to Tasso's song, which concludes: '*amiamo or quando | esser si puote riamato amando*' (rendered by Fairfax as 'Louing, be lou'd; embrasing, be embrast'). As D. Cheney 1966:100–01 observes, the phrase 'conveys the sense less of "mutual enjoyment (and hence no crime at all)" than of "a reprobate guilt to be shared by all"'. It also suggests the joy in sinning, that special mark of sin recorded in Augustine, *Confessions* 2.4. Cf. Acrasia ready for 'pleasant sin' at 77.2.

Stanza 76

4 constant: steadfast, resolute; also in the etymological sense, 'standing' or 'standing together', in contrast to the posture of Acrasia's victims. **7** While only by **creeping** may they

77

Vpon a bed of Roses she was layd,
  As faint through heat, or dight to pleasant sin,
  And was arayd, or rather disarayd,
  All in a vele of silke and siluer thin,
  That hid no whit her alablaster skin,
  But rather shewd more white, if more might bee:
  More subtile web *Arachne* cannot spin,
  Nor the fine nets, which oft we wouen see
Of scorched deaw, do not in th'ayre more lightly flee.

78

Her snowy brest was bare to ready spoyle
  Of hungry eies, which n'ote therewith be fild,
  And yet through languour of her late sweet toyle,
  Few drops, more cleare then Nectar, forth distild,
  That like pure Orient perles adowne it trild,
  And her faire eyes sweet smyling in delight,
  Moystened their fierie beames, with which she thrild
  Fraile harts, yet quenched not; like starry light
Which sparckling on the silent waues, does seeme more bright.

79

The young man sleeping by her, seemd to be
  Some goodly swayne of honorable place,
  That certes it great pitty was to see
  Him his nobility so fowle deface;
  A sweet regard, and amiable grace,
  Mixed with manly sternesse did appeare
  Yet sleeping, in his well proportiond face,
  And on his tender lips the downy heare
Did now but freshly spring, and silken blossoms beare.

80

His warlike Armes, the ydle instruments
  Of sleeping praise, were hong vpon a tree,
  And his braue shield, full of old moniments,
  Was fowly ra'st, that none the signes might see,
  Ne for them, ne for honour cared hee,
  Ne ought, that did to his aduauncement tend,
  But in lewd loues, and wastfull luxuree,
  His dayes, his goods, his bodie he did spend:
O horrible enchantment, that him so did blend.

[handwritten marginal note: no agency]

bushwhack through the **couert groues**, their posture is un-heroic: Ignaro creeps at I viii 30.1, and so does Braggadocchio at II iii 35.7, Malbecco at III x 44.1, and Defetto at VI v 20.5. **display**: discover; cited by *OED* as an erroneous use of the term as if 'to unfold to one's own view'. Yet the active form, used with passive significance, conveys the assault that beauty once uncovered makes upon the eyes and leads to the further sight of her in 77–78. **9 dispose**: lay down, in the etymological sense. Verdant's posture is like Cymochles's at vi 14.7; at 79.1, in a post-coital state, he is 'sleeping by her'. In Lucretius, Mars reclines on Venus's breast, cradled in her arms in a parody of the *pietà*; in Tasso, the enchantress hangs over her lover as he lays his head in her soft lap. S. follows Tasso even verbally: 'right ouer him she hong' (73.1) translates *'sovra lui pende'*; and his line preserves Tasso's *'grembe molle'*. **lap** has the obvious bawdy implications found, e.g. in Hamlet's request that he lie in Ophelia's lap (3.2.114); cf. v 36.3, and esp. vi 14.6–7.

Stanza 77

On the perceptual contradictions of S.'s pictorialism displayed in this stanza, see 'pictorialism' in the *SEnc* and Van Dyke 1985:247–250. For the description of the veil, which is not in Tasso, S. draws on Chaucer's description of Venus in *Parl. Fowls* 265–73: except for her naked breast, her body is covered 'with a subtyl coverchef of Valence – | Ther nas no thikkere cloth of no defense'; see Anderson 1994:642. Cf. Arachne's 'subtile nett' (vii 28.7–9) suspended over Mammon's gold. On the threat posed by Arachnean art, see Macfie 1990. As the spider is a traditional emblem of touch, Acrasia is seen as a spider in her web. Or her body may be taken as her Bower; see DuBois 1980:55. **2 dight to**: made ready for. **8–9 the fine nets**: gossamer, cobwebs thought to be formed by scorched (i.e. dried-up) dew, here anticipating the 'subtile net' (81.4) used by the Palmer to capture her.

Stanza 78

2 n'ote: could not. **3–5 languour**: weariness. Her lover sleeps 'after long wanton ioyes' (72.6). The term may have

been suggested by Tasso's *langue per vezzo* (16.18) which also prompts a description of the enchantress's sweat. **sweet toyle**: an aptly chosen phrase for love's sports. **Orient**: lustrous, sparkling; applied to the brilliant pearls of the East, and given emphasis by **pure**. **trild**: trickled. **6–8 fierie beames**: the emission of spirits from the eyes, particularly the eyes of lovers. See IV viii 39.1–6, and cf. the 'fyrie beames' from Belphœbe's eyes which quench desire (iii 23.3–9). **thrild**: pierced. **quenched**: also killed. Since the Bower is described in terms of earth and air, and Acrasia is linked with fire and water, all four elements resist Guyon's temperance.

Stanza 79

2 place: rank. **4 deface**: disgrace. **5 regard**: demeanour. **7 Yet sleeping**: even as he slept. **8–9** Alluding to his name, Verdant.

Stanza 80

1–2 As arms are the means to gain praise, being left **ydle**, praise also 'sleeps'. The lines invoke classical heroes who laid their arms aside to lie in their mistress's arms, as Mars with Venus, and Hercules with Omphale; or romance heroes, as Ruggiero with Alcina (Ariosto, *Orl. Fur.* 6.24), and Rinaldo with Armida (Tasso, *Ger. Lib.* 16.30). For other examples, see V viii 1–2. At v 28.7–9, Cymochles enjoys the Bower's pleasures 'Hauing his warlike weapons cast behynd' (v 28.7–9); but Verdant's arms hung up in a tree are a trophy of Acrasia's victory and his defeat, as later Artegall's arms are 'hang'd on high' (V v 21.7) as a trophy of Radigund's victory. On this mock tree of chivalry, see I v 5.7*n*. P.A. Parker 1987:54–66 finds a context in Ps. 137 where the Israelites are said to hang their harps upon willows to signify their refusal to sing songs of mirth for their captors. (In the Sternhold-Hopkins version, 'We hang'd our harps and instruments | the willow trees upon'.) A more immediate context is Colin's decision to 'hang my pype upon this tree' (*SC Dec.* 141) to mark his refusal to sing more pastoral songs. Parker hears phallic overtones in Verdant's suspended instruments, signifying Elizabeth's domination of her courtiers.

81

The noble Elfe, and carefull Palmer drew
  So nigh them, minding nought, but lustfull game,
  That suddein forth they on them rusht, and threw
  A subtile net, which only for that same
  The skilfull Palmer formally did frame.
  So held them vnder fast, the whiles the rest
  Fled all away for feare of fowler shame.
The faire Enchauntresse, so vnwares opprest,
Tryde all her arts, and all her sleights, thence out to wrest.

82

And eke her louer stroue: but all in vaine;
  For that same net so cunningly was wound,
  That neither guile, nor force might it distraine.
  They tooke them both, and both them strongly bound
  In captiue bandes, which there they readie found:
  But her in chaines of adamant he tyde;
  For nothing else might keepe her safe and sound;
  But *Verdant* (so he hight) he soone vntyde,
And counsell sage in steed thereof to him applyde.

83

But all those pleasant bowres and Pallace braue,
  Guyon broke downe, with rigour pittilesse;
  Ne ought their goodly workmanship might saue
  Them from the tempest of his wrathfulnesse,
  But that their blisse he turn'd to balefulnesse:
  Their groues he feld, their gardins did deface,
  Their arbers spoyle, their Cabinets suppresse,
  Their banket houses burne, their buildings race,
And of the fayrest late, now made the fowlest place.

84

Then led they her away, and eke that knight
  They with them led, both sorrowfull and sad:
  The way they came, the same retourn'd they right,
  Till they arriued, where they lately had
  Charm'd those wild-beasts, that rag'd with furie mad.
  Which now awaking, fierce at them gan fly,
  As in their mistresse reskew, whom they lad;
  But them the Palmer soone did pacify.
Then *Guyon* askt, what meant those beastes, which there
                            (did ly.

---

3 moniments: identifying marks, the records of heroic deeds. **4 ra'st**: erased by scraping, as Braggadocchio's arms are 'blotted out' when he is baffled at V iii 37.7. The term is used again at 83.8 to describe Guyon's fitting revenge for this disgrace. **7 luxuree**: licentiousness. **8 spend**: with the bawdy sense, 'expend sexually'. **9 blend**: blind (shown by his sleeping); defile.

Stanza 81

3–5 The prototype of the Palmer's net is the snare fine as Arachne's web fashioned by Vulcan to capture Venus in bed with Mars (Homer, *Ody.* 8.272–84); cf. Ovid, *Met.* 4.176–81. **they**: as both act as one. **subtile**: finely woven and skilfully devised, covering her in place of the 'subtile web' to which her veil is compared at 77.7. **for that same**: for that purpose. **formally**: expressly, i.e. just for that purpose; or describing how it was framed: skilfully, in good form. **7 fowler**: referring also to the fowler's net; cf. V ix 13–14. **8 opprest**: taken by surprise. Its other relevant sense, 'violate' or 'ravish', suggests a reversal of roles.

Stanza 82

2 wound: woven. **3 distraine**: tear asunder. **6 adamant**: cited for its surpassing hardness – see I vii 33.5–9*n* – but possibly alluding to the 'Adamantine chaines' of love in *HL* 89 by which the warring elements are bound in creation; cf. *Am* 42.10. **8 Verdant**: literally one who gives spring or life (Lat. *ver + dans*); hence the counterpart to Acrasia's earlier lover, Mordant, 'one who gives death': see i 55.4–5*n*. From Ital. *verde*, green, he is associated with Acrasia's garden, which is 'Mantled with greene' (50.4). See 'Verdant' in the *SEnc*.

Stanza 83

Guyon's destructive act is sanctioned by the destruction wrought by Josiah: 'he broght out the groue . . . and burnt it . . . and stampt it to powdre, and cast the dust thereof vpon the graues of the children of the people. And he brake downe the houses of the sodomites . . . and defiled the hie places . . . and destroied the hie places of the gates. . . . He defiled also Topheth. . . . Moreouer the King defiled the hie places . . . which Salomon the King of Israel had buylt for Ashtoreth. . . . And he brake the images in pieces, and cut downe the groues' (2 Kings 23:6–14); cf. Isa. 13.9. Esolen 1993:270 notes that the site of most of this grove-burning is also the site of 'the final defeat of Satan and the Last Judgment'. In Tasso, *Ger. Lib.* 16.68–69, the enchantress Armida herself destroys her garden. On Guyon's need to destroy the Bower for its temptation to lust, see Strauss 1995:67–70. **1 braue**: splendid, showy. **2 rigour**: violence. **pittilesse** indicates that Guyon has mastered the pity to which he was formerly subject. **4 tempest**: the only other use of the term in Bk II describes 'the tempest of [Furor's] passion wood' (iv 11.8). In addition to the sense, 'inner turmoil', it suggests that the unnatural Bower is destroyed as though by a natural force, as the destroying north wind at V xi 58.7–9. S. would be aware of its etymological connection with temperance. **5 balefulnesse**: distress; full of grief. **6–9 deface**: destroy. Guyon's counter-action to Acrasia's destruction of her lover: 'his nobility so fowle deface' (79.4); as Arthur 'fowle Maleger doth deface' (xi Arg.) in response to his attempt to 'deface' the castle of Alma (xi 6.4). **spoyle**: ravage; the term describes the dragon's plundering of Eden, I vii 44.5. **Cabinets**: garden bowers, as the 'cabins' where Cupid may be concealed at III vi 23.3. **suppresse**: put down. **banket houses**: their shady moral reputation in the Elizabethan age is noted by Girouard 1983:48. **race**: raze; literally, 'root out'.

Stanza 84

2 both sorrowfull and sad: as applied to Verdant, possibly 'for inward shame' (86.4), which afflicts some of Acrasia's other johns, in addition to their regret, though the phrase is common.

85

Sayd he, These seeming beasts are men indeed,
    Whom this Enchauntresse hath transformed thus,
    Whylome her louers, which her lustes did feed,
    Now turned into figures hideous,
    According to their mindes like monstruous.
    Sad end (quoth he) of life intemperate,
    And mournefull meed of ioyes delicious:
    But Palmer, if it mote thee so aggrate,
Let them returned be vnto their former state.

86

Streight way he with his vertuous staffe them strooke,
    And streight of beastes they comely men became;
    Yet being men they did vnmanly looke,
    And stared ghastly, some for inward shame,

(margin, handwritten: reasons power)

And some for wrath, to see their captiue Dame:
    But one aboue the rest in speciall,
    That had an hog beene late, hight *Grylle* by name,
    Repyned greatly, and did him miscall,
That had from hoggish forme him brought to naturall.

87

Saide *Guyon*, See the mind of beastly man,
    That hath so soone forgot the excellence
    Of his creation, when he life began,
    That now he chooseth, with vile difference,
    To be a beast, and lacke intelligence.
    To whom the Palmer thus, The donghill kinde
    Delights in filth and fowle incontinence:
    Let *Gryll* be *Gryll*, and haue his hoggish minde;
But let vs hence depart, whilest wether serues and winde.

Stanza 85

3 which: suggesting also 'upon which'.   **5** I.e., even as their minds were similarly monstrous. In Homer, *Ody.* 10.238–41, Circe's victims retain the minds of men, but S. follows Conti 1616:6.6 who claims that each of them took the shape to which he was inclined: the libidinous into swine, the wrathful into lions or bears, etc., as seen in Maleger's bands at xi 8–13. **7 delicious**: voluptuous.   **8 aggrate**: please.

Stanza 86

1 vertuous: possessing 'wondrous powre' (40.8); cf. 26.6. **7 Grylle**: the companion of Ulysses who was transformed by Circe into a hog – hence his name γρύλλος, hog, a type of lechery – and refused to be changed back to human shape. This is the closest S. comes to identifying Acrasia with Circe, the archetype of the enchantress traditionally identified as lust; see 'Circe' in the *SEnc*. Since S. never uses that name, he may want his character to take her place. The story of Grille derives from Plutarch's *Gryllus*, and Gelli's *Circe*. In English, the name signifies 'fierce', 'cruel'. See 'Grill' in the *SEnc*. **8 miscall**: revile.   **9 naturall**: i.e. human.

Stanza 87

1–5 The reference is generic: 'See the mind of man which is beastly'. Since none of Acrasia's victims is happy in his renewed state, **2–3** would seem to allude to the briefness of man's unfallen state. In G. Whitney 1586:82, all Circe's victims prefer their animal form, choosing to serve her and 'burne in theire desire'.   **4 vile difference**: vile discrimination or preference.   **8 Let Gryll be Gryll**: let Grille be himself, i.e. a hog. Cf. Rev. 22.11: 'he which is filthie, let him be filthie stil'; and 2 Pet. 2.22: 'It is come vnto them, according to the true prouerbe . . . the sowe that was washed [is returned] to the wallowing in the myer'. S. may have been influenced by the moral, here very appropriate, as swine are to gardens, etc. **9** Cf. the voyaging metaphor that concludes Bk I.

The thirde Booke
of the Faerie Queene.

Contayning

The Legend of Britomartis.

O R

Of Chastity.

1

I T falls me here to write of Chastity,
The fayrest vertue, far aboue the rest;
For which what needes me fetch from *Faery*
Forreine ensamples, it to haue exprest?
Sith it is shrined in my Soueraines brest,
And formd so liuely in each perfect part,
That to all Ladies, which haue it profest,
Neede but behold the pourtraict of her hart,
If pourtrayd it might bee by any liuing art.

2

But liuing art may not least part expresse,
Nor life-resembling pencill it can paynt,
All were it *Zeuxis* or *Praxiteles*:
His dædale hand would faile, and greatly faynt,
And her perfections with his error taynt:
Ne Poets witt, that passeth Painter farre
In picturing the parts of beauty daynt,
So hard a workemanship aduenture darre,
For fear through want of words her excellence to marre.

Book III Proem

see Morgan 1993. **6 formd**: bodied forth. **liuely**: lifelike. **9 liuing art**: i.e. art that may counterfeit life.

Stanza 1
2 The fayrest vertue: the phrase acknowledges that virtue is associated with *virtu*, manliness, but also, as it belongs to the Queen, that it is associated with woman's beauty; see Cavanagh 1994a:75–76. Until now, virtue has been associated chiefly with male characters, e.g. I viii 27.1, II i 23.9 and xii 1.6. **the rest**: referring primarily to the virtues of holiness and temperance, which chastity unifies, as the relation of Britomart to the Red Cross Knight and Guyon in the opening episodes illustrates. Cf. Milton's ordering of faith, hope, and chastity in *Comus* 212–14 in which chastity is the love or charity extolled in 1 Cor. 13.13. On the relation of charity as a theological virtue to chastity as a supernatural though still a moral virtue,

Stanza 2
1–3 The dilemma of the poet and painter is expressed in *Am* 17. See D.L. Miller 1988:150–51. **expresse**: portray, depict; referring to painting and sculpture. **life-resembling**: life-representing. **pencill**: the artist's brush. **Zeuxis** and **Praxiteles**: the painter (see *DS 17*.1–4) and the sculptor of antiquity famed for rendering ideal female beauty. **4 dædale**: skilful, as though belonging to Daedalus whose name signifies 'cunning worker'. **6–7** In the *paragone* between the two arts – see '*ut pictura poesis*' in the *SEnc*, Hulse 1990, esp. 9–19, and Dundas 1993 *passim* – poets generally agreed that 'the Pen is more noble, then the Pencill' (Jonson 1925–52:8.610). **daynt**: choice, excellent.

3

How then shall I, Apprentice of the skill,
   That whilome in diuinest wits did rayne,
   Presume so high to stretch mine humble quill?
   Yet now my luckelesse lott doth me constrayne
   Hereto perforce. But O dredd Souerayne
   Thus far forth pardon, sith that choicest witt
   Cannot your glorious pourtraict figure playne,
   That I in colour showes may shadow itt,
And antique praises vnto present persons fitt.

4

But if in liuing colours, and right hew,
   Thy selfe thou couet to see pictured,
   Who can it doe more liuelie, or more trew,
   Then that sweete verse, with *Nectar* sprinckeled,

In which a gracious seruaunt pictured
   His *Cynthia*, his heauens fayrest light?
   That with his melting sweetnes rauished,
   And with the wonder of her beames bright,
My sences lulled are in slomber of delight.

5

But let that same delitious Poet lend
   A little leaue vnto a rusticke Muse
   To sing his mistresse prayse, and let him mend,
   If ought amis her liking may abuse:
   Ne let his fayrest *Cynthia* refuse,
   In mirrours more then one her selfe to see,
   But either *Gloriana* let her chuse,
   Or in *Belphœbe* fashioned to bee:
In th'one her rule, in th'other her rare chastitee.

Stanza 3

The topos of inadequacy, which usually applies to the poet, extends now to poetry itself in a topos of inexpressibility. See DeNeef 1982a:111–112. **4–5** Cf. 'It falls me' (1.1), indicating that the order of the virtues requires S. to treat chastity. **8 shadow**: portray; represent by an imperfect image; cf. *LR* 34–35: 'in some places els, I doe otherwise shadow her'. Also in the Platonic sense: the shadow is related to reality as the phenomenal world to the heavenly world of ideas. The Queen is foreshadowed in Gloriana as 'the Lawe [is] the shadowe of good things to come, and not the very image of the things' (Heb. 10.1). The Geneva gloss explains: 'which was as it were the first draught and purtrait of the liuelie paterne to come'. **colourd showes**: in the *LR* 9, S. says that his poem is 'coloured with an historicall fiction'. On the problems of representing Elizabeth, see Montrose 1986:324–25. On his not naming her, see Bellamy 1987:8–9. Fruen 1987:171 argues that within the typology of the poem, the partially fictionalized Elizabeth prefigures her entirely fictive counterpart in Gloriana. **9 antique**: fanciful or imaginative, as **colourd**

showes suggests, though primarily 'ancient' as the contrast to **present** suggests.

Stanza 4

3–9 The **gracious seruaunt** is Sir Walter Raleigh whose 'song was all a lamentable lay, | Of great unkindnesse, and of usage hard, | Of *Cynthia* the Ladie of the sea' (*Colin Clout* 164–66). The surviving fragment of the poem is entitled 'The 21th and last booke of the Ocean to Scinthia'. **liuely**: lifelike; cf. II ix 3.

Stanza 5

In *DS 14*, S. offers Raleigh his 'rusticke Madrigale' 'till that thou thy Poeme wilt make knowne'. In *CV 2*, Raleigh responds to S.'s claims here. Among the works to be imitated by contemporary poets, Harvey notes that Raleigh's 'Cynthia' is 'Excellent matter of emulation for Spencer' (*Sp All* 4). **1 delitious**: i.e. delightful. **7–9** See *LR* 32–37. On **Gloriana**, see I i 3.2–3*n*; on **Belphœbe**, see II iii 21–31*n*; on Britomart, unnamed in the proem, as a portrait of Elizabeth, see Walker 1998b:74–76.

Cant. I

Guyon encountreth Britomart,
Fayre Florimell is chaced:
Duessaes traines and Malecastaes
champions are defaced.

1

T He famous Briton Prince and Faery knight,
  After long wayes and perilous paines endur'd,
  Hauing their weary limbes to perfect plight
  Restord, and sory wounds right well recur'd,
  Of the faire *Alma* greatly were procur'd,
  To make there lenger soiourne and abode;
  But when thereto they might not be allur'd,
  From seeking praise, and deeds of armes abrode,
They courteous conge tooke, and forth together yode.

2

But the captiu'd *Acrasia* he sent,
  Because of traueill long, a nigher way,
  With a strong gard, all reskew to preuent,
  And her to Faery court safe to conuay,
  That her for witnes of his hard assay,
  Vnto his Faery Queene he might present:
  But he him selfe betooke another way,
  To make more triall of his hardiment,
And seeke aduentures, as he with Prince Arthure went.

3

Long so they traueiled through wastefull wayes,
  Where daungers dwelt, and perils most did wonne,
  To hunt for glory and renowmed prayse;
  Full many Countreyes they did ouerronne,
  From the vprising to the setting Sunne,
  And many hard aduentures did atchieue;
  Of all the which they honour euer wonne,
  Seeking the weake oppressed to relieue,
And to recouer right for such, as wrong did grieue.

4

At last as through an open plaine they yode,
  They spide a knight, that towards pricked fayre,
  And him beside an aged Squire there rode,
  That seemd to couch vnder his shield three-square,
  As if that age badd him that burden spare,
  And yield it those, that stouter could it wield:
  He them espying, gan him selfe prepare,
  And on his arme addresse his goodly shield
That bore a Lion passant in a golden field.

5

Which seeing good Sir *Guyon,* deare besought
  The Prince of grace, to let him ronne that turne.
  He graunted: then the Faery quickly raught
  His poynant speare, and sharply gan to spurne
  His fomy steed, whose fiery feete did burne
  The verdant gras, as he thereon did tread;
  Ne did the other backe his foote returne,
  But fiercely forward came withouten dread,
And bent his dreadful speare against the others head.

Book III Canto i

Argument

1 encountreth: implying the military sense, 'meets as an adversary'. **3 Duessaes traines**: in Bk II, Duessa is the instrument of Archimago's 'traynes' (i 4.2), i.e. stratagems, to deceive Guyon. In Bk III, her intention to deceive Britomart is announced even though she need not appear, her role being assumed by Malecasta; see 57.4–5. **4 defaced**: defeated.

Stanza 1

As Upton 1758 inferred, Guyon, having captured Acrasia, returned to the castle of Alma where Arthur was recuperating after having slain Maleger (II xi 49). Lines 2–3 apply to Guyon, 4 to Arthur. **4 sory**: painful. **recur'd**: healed. **5 procur'd**: urged. **9 conge**: farewell. **yode**: went.

Stanza 2

4–6 This motif is found, e.g. in Malory 7.18: the defeated Red Knight goes to King Arthur's court to seek forgiveness. **assay**: endeavour.

Stanza 3

1 wastefull: desolate. **3** Arthur's 'great desire of glory and of fame' (II ix 38.7), which links him to Praysdesire, is shared by Guyon; cf. II i 35.3–4.

Stanza 4

1 an open plaine: cf. 'equall plaine' (8.5). This chief setting for chivalric encounters in the first two books is largely replaced after this episode by the forest; see 14.5–9*n*, 20.5–7*n*. **2 towards**: in their direction. **4 couch**: stoop. **three-square**: with three equal sides; cf. I vi 41.8. Upton 1758 notes: 'like the shield of our English kings: for Britomart is a British princess'. It is wielded by Marinell at iv 16.3. **8 addresse**: make ready. **9 a Lion passant**: the heraldic description of a lion walking, looking towards the dexter side, with the dexter fore-paw raised, against a golden background. A lion *passant gules* (red), in a field *or* (gold) was displayed on the arms of Brutus from whom Britomart is descended; see the illustration in Leslie 1983:34. It describes her royal offspring at iii 30.

Stanza 5

1 good Sir Guyon: his title in the opening of Bk II, e.g. proem 5.8, i 42.1, etc. **2 of grace**: as a matter of favour, alluding

6

They beene ymett, and both theyr points arriu'd,
  But *Guyon* droue so furious and fell,
  That seemd both shield and plate it would haue riu'd;
  Nathelesse it bore his foe not from his sell,
  But made him stagger, as he were not well:
  But *Guyon* selfe, ere well he was aware,
  Nigh a speares length behind his crouper fell,
  Yet in his fall so well him selfe he bare,
That mischieuous mischaunce his life and limbs did spare.

7

Great shame and sorrow of that fall he tooke;
  For neuer yet, sith warlike armes he bore,
  And shiuering speare in bloody field first shooke,
  He fownd him selfe dishonored so sore.
  Ah gentlest knight, that euer armor bore,
  Let not thee grieue dismounted to haue beene,
  And brought to grownd, that neuer wast before;
  For not thy fault, but secret powre vnseene,
That speare enchaunted was, which layd thee on the greene.

8

But weenedst thou, what wight thee ouerthrew,
  Much greater griefe and shamefuller regrett
  For thy hard fortune then thou wouldst renew,
  That of a single damzell thou wert mett
On equall plaine, and there so hard besett;
  Euen the famous *Britomart* it was,
  Whom straunge aduenture did from *Britayne* fett,
  To seeke her louer (loue far sought alas,)
Whose image shee had seene in *Venus* looking glas.

9

Full of disdainefull wrath, he fierce vprose,
  For to reuenge that fowle reprochefull shame,
  And snatching his bright sword began to close
  With her on foot, and stoutly forward came;
  Dye rather would he, then endure that same.
  Which when his Palmer saw, he gan to feare
  His toward perill and vntoward blame,
  Which by that new rencounter he should reare:
For death sate on the point of that enchaunted speare.

10

And hasting towards him gan fayre perswade,
  Not to prouoke misfortune, nor to weene
  His speares default to mend with cruell blade;
  For by his mightie Science he had seene
  The secrete vertue of that weapon keene,
  That mortall puissaunce mote not withstond:
  Nothing on earth mote alwaies happy beene.
  Great hazard were it, and aduenture fond,
To loose long gotten honour with one euill hond.

---

to Arthur's role in the poem as the instrument of divine grace.
3 raught: seized. **4 poynant**: sharp. **spurne**: spur. **5 His
fomy steed**: the epithet identifies Arthur's horse, Spumador, as
at iv 48.2. Since Guyon's horse was stolen at II iii 3–4 and not
recovered until V iii 35 (though see II ix 10.7), he may have
joined Arthur on his horse, which he now borrows together
with Arthur's spear, as D. Cheney suggests in *SpN* 1978:22–23,
noting that in Ariosto, *Orl. Fur.* 1.22, Rinaldo and Ferraù ride
on one horse to pursue Angelica. At 18.4, Arthur and Guyon
pursue Florimell, possibly on one horse. At iv 45.4–6, they are
still together though in the next stanza they separate with
Arthur on his own horse, which would leave Guyon once more
on foot. It may be simpler not to seek narrative consistency, for
the allegorical point of having Guyon on foot has already been
made. **9 bent**: aimed.

Stanza 6

1 They beene ymett: repeated from the encounter between
the Red Cross Knight and Guyon at II i 26.6. As that
encounter relates holiness to temperance, this relates chastity
to temperance. See 12.7–9n. **7 The speares length** measures
chastity's power; cf. her blow at iv 16.7. **crouper**: crupper,
the horse's rump.

Stanza 7

3 shiuering speare: capable of splitting; quivering while
poised to strike. The weapon of the classical warrior: as Aeneas's
tremibunda hasta in Virgil, *Aen.* 10.522, and Turnus's quiver-
ing (*trementem*) spear at 12.94. **shooke**: wielded; brandished.
5 Ah gentlest knight: a curious epithet for one notorious for
'the tempest of his wrathfulnesse' at II xii 83.4, but S. tends to
reserve it for a knight in defeat: e.g. Arthur struck down by
love at I ix 7.9, the dead Mordant at II i 49.8, and the dying
Timias at III v 26.6. There are two exceptions: it describes

Britomart when she aids Scudamour in his moment of defeat
at III xi 19.1, and Calidore when Pastorella has been made the
spoil of thieves at VI x 40.8. **9** Britomart becomes known as
the 'Knight of the Hebene speare' (see IV v 8.2n), as the spear
expresses **secret powre vnseene**, which is her chastity. In
Ariosto, *Orl. Fur.* 23.15, the warrior maiden Bradamante
wields a spear that may unseat any knight. The conjunction
of chastity and power as it relates the Virgin Queen to her
subjects is considered by Montrose 1986:324–32, and P. Berry
1989:153–65.

Stanza 8

6 the famous Britomart: echoing 'The famous Briton Prince'
(1.1) to indicate her role as the female Arthur. Her name sug-
gests Brito-Mart (Mars), the martial Britoness. Hence she is
called 'the Britonesse' at 58.5 (a word apparently coined by
S.), 'Briton Maid' at ii 4.5, and 'martiall Mayd' at ii 9.4. One
source of her name is the pseudo-Virgilian *Ciris* 295–305:
Britomartis (cf. 67.2, iii 19.5) who is associated with Diana.
It is a fitting name, then, for the knight of chastity; see ii
30–51n and 'Britomart' in the *SEnc.* **7 aduenture**: chance.
Britayne: Wales, rather than England (which S. calls Logris);
see ii 7.9n. **fett**: fetch. **9 Venus looking glas**: see ii 18.8n.

Stanza 9

1 disdainefull: indignant. **4 on foot**: the mode in which he
asserts his virtue in Bk II. **7 toward**: approaching; playing
against **vntoward** because his unlucky shame is imminent.
blame: injury; shame (as 7.1, 9.2). **8 rencounter**: encounter
between two knights; also 're-encounter'. **reare**: bring about.

Stanza 10

1 perswade: urge. **3 default**: fault. **4 Science**: knowledge,
such as possessed by Archimago at I ii 10.2, Duessa at I ii 38.4,

11
By such good meanes he him discounselled,
    From prosecuting his reuenging rage;
    And eke the Prince like treaty handeled,
    His wrathfull will with reason to aswage,
    And laid the blame, not to his carriage,
    But to his starting steed, that swaru'd asyde,
    And to the ill purueyaunce of his page,
    That had his furnitures not firmely tyde:
So is his angry corage fayrly pacifyde.

12
Thus reconcilement was betweene them knitt,
    Through goodly temperaunce, and affection chaste,
    And either vowd with all their power and witt,
    To let not others honour be defaste,
    Of friend or foe, who euer it embaste,
    Ne armes to beare against the others syde:
    In which accord the Prince was also plaste,
    And with that golden chaine of concord tyde.
So goodly all agreed, they forth yfere did ryde.

13
O goodly vsage of those antique tymes,
    In which the sword was seruaunt vnto right;
    When not for malice and contentious crymes,
    But all for prayse, and proofe of manly might,
    The martiall brood accustomed to fight:
    Then honour was the meed of victory,
    And yet the vanquished had no despight:
    Let later age that noble vse enuy,
Vyle rancor to avoid, and cruel surquedry.

14
Long they thus traueiled in friendly wise,
    Through countreyes waste, and eke well edifyde,
    Seeking aduentures hard, to exercise
    Their puissaunce, whylome full dernly tryde:
    At length they came into a forest wyde,
    Whose hideous horror and sad trembling sownd
    Full griesly seemd: Therein they long did ryde,
    Yet tract of liuing creature none they fownd,
Saue Beares, Lyons, and Buls, which romed them arownd.

15
All suddenly out of the thickest brush,
    Vpon a milkwhite Palfrey all alone,
    A goodly Lady did foreby them rush,
    Whose face did seeme as cleare as Christall stone,
    And eke through feare as white as whales bone:
    Her garments all were wrought of beaten gold,
    And all her steed with tinsell trappings shone,
    Which fledd so fast, that nothing mote him hold,
And scarse them leasure gaue, her passing to behold.

---

and Merlin at III ii 18.7. **5 vertue**: the spear's power is its virtue. **7 happy**: fortunate. **8 aduenture fond**: foolish risk. **9 hond**: act.

Stanza 11
1 discounselled: dissuaded. **2 reuenging rage**: the mood in which Guyon trashes the Bower of Bliss in fulfilling his vow to seek 'dew vengeance' (II i 61.7) against Acrasia. He does not yet control 'fowle reuenging rage' (II ii 30.9) against which he had been warned by Medina. Arthur's damage-control is more tactful; Guyon has difficulty managing his horse, i.e. his passions. **3 treaty**: entreaty. **5 carriage**: conduct or action. **7–9 purueyaunce**: preparation. **furnitures**: harness. **corage**: spirit. **fayrly**: entirely.

Stanza 12
3 witt: skill. **5 embaste**: degraded. **7–9** Their **reconcilement** expresses the 'goodly golden chayne, wherewith yfere | The vertues linked are in louely wize' (I ix 1.1–2). The linking of Arthur, Guyon, and Britomart includes the Red Cross Knight when Britomart comes to his aid at 28–30 and he to hers at 66.7–9, and they vow 'frendly league of loue perpetuall' at iv 4.4–5.

Stanza 13
S. invokes Ariosto's comment on the reconciliation of Rinaldo and Ferraù: '*O gran bontà de' caualieri antiqui*' (*Orl. Fur.* 1.22) to indicate one way in which he intended to 'ouergo' Ariosto, as he boasted to Harvey (see Spenser 1912:628, and *LR13n*). In place of the 'concupiscent concord' (Silberman 1988b:26) between Ariosto's knights, he sets up the **goodly vsage of those antique tymes**. On his imitation of Ariosto, see Wiggins 1988, 'Ariosto' in the *SEnc*, and C. Burrow 1993:102–20. **8 enuy**: seek to rival. **9 rancor**: applies to the malice of the defeated (cf. II viii 50.7), **surquedry** to the arrogance of the victor (cf. iii 46.9).

Stanza 14
1–4 A return to the story after the introductory matter, which took place on 'an open plaine' (4.1). **edifyde**: built up. **whylome**: at times. **dernly**: grievously (sugg. by the context). **5–9** On the significance of the forest setting, see I vi 3.2n. The beasts are cited for their extreme violence: on **Beares**, see II ii 22.5–9n; on **Lyons**, see I iv 33.2–3n; on **Buls**, see Ps. 22.12–13 where they are compared to 'a ramping and roaring lion'. **griesly**: horrible. **tract**: track.

Stanza 15
2 As Una rides a 'snowy Palfrey' at I iii 8.8. **3 foreby**: close by. **4–5** The description is courtly and conventional: e.g. 'your throte as clere as crystall stone . . . & your neke as whyte as whalles bone' (Robbins 1952:130.25–27). **cleare**: brightly shining. The simile in 5 associates Florimell with the sea into which she descends. **6–7** Florimell in her garments **of beaten gold** and her palfrey **with tinsell trappings** lures knights as powerfully as does Duessa in her 'garments gilt, | And gorgeous gold arayd' at I v 26.7–8 and her palfrey 'ouerspred | With tinsell trappings' at I ii 13.7–8. The **milkwhite Palfrey** is Florimell's chief allegorical marker while she is on land, as v 5.6, vii 2.7, 30.8.

16

Still as she fledd, her eye she backward threw,
    As fearing euill, that poursewd her fast;
    And her faire yellow locks behind her flew,
    Loosely disperst with puff of euery blast:
    All as a blazing starre doth farre outcast
    His hearie beames, and flaming lockes dispredd,
    At sight whereof the people stand aghast:
    But the sage wisard telles, as he has redd,
That it importunes death and dolefull dreryhedd.

17

So as they gazed after her a whyle,
    Lo where a griesly foster forth did rush,
    Breathing out beastly lust her to defyle:
    His tyreling Iade he fiersly forth did push,
    Through thicke and thin, both ouer banck and bush
    In hope her to attaine by hooke or crooke,
    That from his gory sydes the blood did gush:
    Large were his limbes, and terrible his looke,
And in his clownish hand a sharp bore speare he shooke.

18

Which outrage when those gentle knights did see,
    Full of great enuy and fell gealosy,
    They stayd not to auise, who first should bee,
    But all spurd after fast, as they mote fly,

To reskew her from shamefull villany.
    The Prince and *Guyon* equally byliue
    Her selfe pursewd, in hope to win thereby
    Most goodly meede, the fairest Dame aliue:
But after the foule foster *Timias* did striue.

19

The whiles faire *Britomart*, whose constant mind,
    Would not so lightly follow beauties chace,
    Ne reckt of Ladies Loue, did stay behynd,
    And them awayted there a certaine space,
    To weet if they would turne backe to that place:
    But when she saw them gone, she forward went,
    As lay her iourney, through that perlous Pace,
    With stedfast corage and stout hardiment;
Ne euil thing she feard, ne euill thing she ment.

20

At last as nigh out of the wood she came,
    A stately Castle far away she spyde,
    To which her steps directly she did frame.
    That Castle was most goodly edifyde,
    And plaste for pleasure nigh that forrest syde:
    But faire before the gate a spatious playne,
    Mantled with greene, it selfe did spredden wyde,
    On which she saw six knights, that did darrayne
Fiers battaill against one, with cruel might and mayne.

Stanza 16

1–5 The description is indebted to Golding's tr. of Ovid's account of the fleeing Daphne, *Met.* 1.642–65; noted Taylor 1985:20. **a blazing starre**: a comet, *stella comata*; its etymology, 'long-haired', is noted in the next line. The effect of its appearance is noted in *SC Dec.* 55–60: Colin relates how a comet stirred up 'unkindly heate' in him, which E.K. glosses as 'a blasing starre, meant of beautie, which was the cause of his whole love'. **7–9** The rarity of comets suggests the wonder aroused by Florimell's beauty, as Heninger 1960:89 notes. **redd**: predicted; interpreted. **importunes**: portends. **dreryhedd**: disaster.

Stanza 17

1 So as suggests that the comet's raging heat arouses the fire of love in Guyon and Arthur, provoking them to join the Foster in pursuit of Florimell. **2 foster**: forester, personifying the forest's violence; hence the repetition of **griesly** from 14.7. See 'Foster' in the *SEnc*. **4 tyreling Iade**: tired horse. **7 gory**: pierced, and therefore bloody, applied to the horse and its rider. **9 clownish**: rough, belonging to a rustic. The **bore speare** is associated with lust from the story of Adonis wounded by the boar at 38.1–3.

Stanza 18

1–5 The Palmer is pointedly excluded from the emotional tumult that overcomes Arthur and Guyon, for while **enuy** carries the sense of 'hostility' and **gealosy** of 'indignation', their 'chivalric motive is not entirely free of sexual desire' (Berger 1989:224); see Cavanagh 1994a:15–16. **auise**: consider. **villany**: ill-usage. **6–8** This pursuit, called 'beauties chace' (19.2) or the 'chace of beauty excellent' (iv 45.5), is joined by 'All the braue knightes' (viii 46.7) at the court of the Faerie Queene, and is called 'this Quest' at viii 50.8. At iv 45.4–6,

they are said to pursue the Foster but, in the next stanza, they are seen pursuing Florimell. **byliue**: eagerly. **the fairest** is Florimell's stock epithet. It associates her with Una (I iii 2.2), Tanaquill (I proem 2.5), the Faerie Queene (2 proem 4.6), and Britomart (III ix 21.9). It is claimed for Malecasta at 27.4 below. (Her chief literary progenitor is Angelica, in Ariosto, *Orl. Fur.* 1, whom Harington dubs 'the faire' in his 1591 tr.) See v 8.7n. **9 Timias**: Arthur's squire, whose name signifies 'honoured', from Gk τιμήεις, named here for the first time. See 'Timias' in the *SEnc*. His pursuit of the Foster rather than Florimell is explained at iv 47.2.

Stanza 19

2 beauties chace: when Faunus sees the nymph, he 'Inflamed was to follow beauties chace, | And chaced her' (II ii 7.7–8), but by Diana's intervention, she remains 'chaste' (9.7). There is the implied pun that one who is chaste is not chased. **3 Ladies Loue**: the capital letters point to the significance of Florimell's dramatic entrance: love is aroused by the sight of beauty, and those who pursue her seek her love; cf. iv 47.2. **7 perlous Pace**: perilous passage. Cf. 'the Paas Perillous' in Malory 7.9. **8 stedfast** defines chaste love. It is applied to Florimell at v 8.5, Belphœbe at v 55.1, Amoret at vi 53.8, Psyche at vi 50.6, and Britomart at xii 2.9 and 37.5. In Bk IV it is used only once, to describe the eyes of Womanhood at x 49.7. **9 ment**: 'intended' is a possible sense. However, her constancy in her quest makes the contrast clear: Florimell fears even Arthur who 'ment | To her no euill thought, nor euill deed' (iv 50.2–3).

Stanza 20

3 frame: direct. **4 edifyde**: built. **5–7** That the castle is placed **nigh that forrest syde** suggests that the **pleasure** is sexual. The **spatious playne, | Mantled with greene** associates

21

Mainely they all attonce vpon him laid,
  And sore beset on euery side arownd,
  That nigh he breathlesse grew, yet nought dismaid,
  Ne euer to them yielded foot of grownd
  All had he lost much blood through many a wownd,
  But stoutly dealt his blowes, and euery way
  To which he turned in his wrathfull stownd,
  Made them recoile, and fly from dredd decay,
That none of all the six before, him durst assay.

22

Like dastard Curres, that hauing at a bay
  The saluage beast embost in wearie chace,
  Dare not aduenture on the stubborne pray,
  Ne byte before, but rome from place to place,
  To get a snatch, when turned is his face.
  In such distresse and doubtfull ieopardy,
  When *Britomart* him saw, she ran apace
  Vnto his reskew, and with earnest cry,
Badd those same six forbeare that single enimy.

23

But to her cry they list not lenden eare,
  Ne ought the more their mightie strokes surceasse,
  But gathering him rownd about more neare,
  Their direfull rancour rather did encreasse;
  Till that she rushing through the thickest preasse,
  Perforce disparted their compacted gyre,
  And soone compeld to hearken vnto peace:
  Tho gan she myldly of them to inquyre
The cause of their dissention and outrageous yre.

24

Whereto that single knight did answere frame;
  These six would me enforce by oddes of might,
  To chaunge my liefe, and loue another Dame,
  That death me liefer were, then such despight,
  So vnto wrong to yield my wrested right:
  For I loue one, the truest one on grownd,
  Ne list me chaunge; she th'*Errant damzell* hight,
  For whose deare sake full many a bitter stownd,
I haue endurd, and tasted many a bloody wownd.

25

Certes (said she) then beene ye sixe to blame,
  To weene your wrong by force to iustify:
  For knight to leaue his Lady were great shame,
  That faithfull is, and better were to dy.
  All losse is lesse, and lesse the infamy,
  Then losse of loue to him, that loues but one;
  Ne may loue be compeld by maistery;
  For soone as maistery comes, sweet loue anone
Taketh his nimble winges, and soone away is gone.

26

Then spake one of those six, There dwelleth here
  Within this castle wall a Lady fayre,
  Whose soueraine beautie hath no liuing pere,
  Thereto so bounteous and so debonayre,
  That neuer any mote with her compayre.
  She hath ordaind this law, which we approue,
  That euery knight, which doth this way repayre,
  In case he haue no Lady, nor no loue,
Shall doe vnto her seruice neuer to remoue.

---

it with the 'spacious plaine . . . | Mantled with greene' that surrounds the Bower of Bliss at II xii 50.2–4. **8 six knights**: their number is repeated eight times before it is explained at 45, which suggests that Malecasta's 'Champions' (63.1) correspond to Lucifera's 'six sage Counsellours' (I iv 18.2). **darrayne**: wage. **9 one**: until named the Red Cross Knight at 42.6, he remains anonymous: 'that single knight' at 24.1 and 'that other knight' at 29.3.

Stanza 21
1 Mainely: mightily; with main. **7 stownd**: storm, referring here to his wrathful mood; cf. 24.8. **8 decay**: death. **9 before**: i.e. in front of him, in contrast to 'gathering him rownd about' at 23.3. **assay**: assail.

Stanza 22
1 at a bay: at bay, the close quarters where a hunted animal turns to face its pursuers. **2 embost**: driven to extremity; exhausted. **3 stubborne**: fierce. **6 doubtfull**: dread. **7 apace**: quickly. **9 forbeare**: leave alone.

Stanza 23
2 surceasse: stop. **6 Perforce**: forcibly. **compacted gyre**: the action of wheeling around a foe, as Pyrochles 'hurtle[s] rownd in warlike gyre' in fighting Guyon at II v 8.7.

Stanza 24
2 oddes: advantage. **3–4** The Red Cross Knight has learned the lesson given him at I iv 1. His resistance here anticipates Amoret's steadfast suffering in the house of Busirane because she will not forsake Scudamour. **liefe**: beloved. **liefer**: preferable. **6–7 one** names Una; **truest one** names her Truth. She is called 'the *Errant damozell*' at II i 19.8, a role assumed by Britomart as she wanders in search of Artegall. **8 stownd**: time of peril.

Stanza 25
4 That faithfull is: a proviso that permits the Red Cross Knight to leave 'Faithlesse *Duessa*' (IV i 32.8). **7–9** S. paraphrases Chaucer, *Franklin's Tale* 764–66: 'Love wol nat been constreyned by maistrye. | Whan maistrie comth, the God of Love anon | Beteth his wynges, and farewel, he is gon!' On Chaucer's treatment of *maistrye*, see Mann 1991:86–127. Duessa mocks this central doctrine of the poem at IV i 46.8–9, Satyrane applies it at IV v 25.7–9, and Arthur endorses it at IV ix 37.6–8. See Hamilton 1961a:180–86, J. Craig 1988:15–16, C. Burrow 1996:87–90, and Hieatt 1998:156–58. On domination in relation to ethics and politics, see E. Fowler 1995:56–59. There is strong irony for the speaker is one in whom love holds the **maistery**. Hieatt 1975a:91 notes that Britomart first speaks here.

Stanza 26
For the competition to lodge in the castle, S. imitates the Castle of Tristram episode in Ariosto, *Orl. Fur.* 32.65–107: only the strongest knight and the most beautiful woman may stay there. **3 pere**: rival. **4 debonayre**: affable, generous in her favours, as **bounteous** suggests. **6 approue**: make good, uphold.

27

But if he haue a Lady or a Loue,
　Then must he her forgoe with fowle defame,
　Or els with vs by dint of sword approue,
　That she is fairer, then our fairest Dame,
　As did this knight, before ye hether came.
　Perdy (said *Britomart*) the choise is hard:
　But what reward had he, that ouercame?
　He should aduaunced bee to high regard,
(Said they) and haue our Ladies loue for his reward.

28

Therefore a read Sir, if thou haue a loue.
　Loue haue I sure, (quoth she) but Lady none;
　Yet will I not fro mine owne loue remoue,
　Ne to your Lady will I seruice done,
　But wreake your wronges wrought to this knight alone,
　And proue his cause. With that her mortall speare
　She mightily auentred towards one,
　And downe him smot, ere well aware he weare,
Then to the next she rode, and downe the next did beare.

29

Ne did she stay, till three on ground she layd,
　That none of them himselfe could reare againe;
　The fourth was by that other knight dismayd,
　All were he wearie of his former paine,
　That now there do but two of six remaine;
　Which two did yield, before she did them smight.
　Ah (sayd she then) now may ye all see plaine,
　That truth is strong, and trew loue most of might,
That for his trusty seruaunts doth so strongly fight.

30

Too well we see, (saide they) and proue too well
　Our faulty weakenes, and your matchlesse might:
　For thy, faire Sir, yours be the Damozell,
　Which by her owne law to your lot doth light,
　And we your liegemen faith vnto you plight.
　So vnderneath her feet their swords they mard,
　And after her besought, well as they might,
　To enter in, and reape the dew reward:
She graunted, and then in they all together far'd.

31

Long were it to describe the goodly frame,
　And stately port of *Castle Ioyeous*,
　(For so that Castle hight by commun name)
　Where they were entertaynd with courteous
　And comely glee of many gratious
　Faire Ladies, and of many a gentle knight,
　Who through a Chamber long and spacious,
　Eftsoones them brought vnto their Ladies sight,
That of them cleeped was the *Lady of delight*.

32

But for to tell the sumptuous aray
　Of that great chamber, should be labour lost:
　For liuing wit, I weene, cannot display
　The roiall riches and exceeding cost,
　Of euery pillour and of euery post;
　Which all of purest bullion framed were,
　And with great perles and pretious stones embost,
　That the bright glister of their beames cleare
Did sparckle forth great light, and glorious did appeare.

Stanza 27

Infidelity is the law of Castle Joyeous, as it is of courtly love; see Lewis 1936:340. Evidently the Red Cross Knight sought to prove by force of arms that Una is the fairest lady; but if he had won, he would have gained Malecasta as his love, as in I ii when he defeated Sansfoy and thereby gained Duessa as his love. Without Britomart's intercession, he would have endured an endless succession of such encounters. **3 approue**: prove, confirm; close to the legal sense at 26.6. The same legal imagery as in 'proue' (28.6, 30.1).

Stanza 28

1 a read: tell. **2** Britomart turns their law into a riddle. **5 alone**: i.e. 'single' (22.9). **7 auentred**: i.e. aimed her spear by setting it in its rest, so the context suggests; 'thrust forward' is suggested by its use at IV iii 9.1, as Ital. *aventare*: 'to darte' (Florio 1598). **8 aware**: on his guard; cf. 6.6.

Stanza 29

3 dismayd: defeated. **8** The two proverbs (Smith 793 and 481) are linked by the play on **truth** as 'troth'.

Stanza 30

2 faulty weakenes: i.e. weakness because they are at fault, as Britomart infers. **3 For thy**: therefore. **6 mard**: damaged, to indicate that they will not seek to harm her, as Artegall's

sword is broken 'for feare of further harmes' at V v 21.8; or as Braggadocchio's sword is broken to indicate his disgrace at V iii 37.9. Possibly they debased (the honour of) their swords by placing them under Britomart's feet in a vow of loyalty they do not mean to keep. Cf. the action at V iv 16.7–8.

Stanza 31

1 frame: structure. **2 port**: appearance; or style of living within the castle. As with the Bower of Bliss at II xii 69.5, its true name is withheld though presumably it would have been known to Elizabeth's courtiers. Its **commun name, Castle Ioyeous**, suggests the *Palazo Zoioso* in Boiardo, *Orl. Inn.* 1.8.1–14; or 'Joyous Gard' where Tristram and Isolde 'maade grete ioye dayly togyders' (Malory 10.52). See 'Castle Joyous' in the *SEnc*. Bulger 1987:12 suggests an analogue in Malory 13.15–16: in the Castle of Maidens, the seven champions, identified as the seven deadly sins, are defeated by the chaste Galahad. Whatever its true name, it is a house of lust corresponding to Lucifera's house of Pride at I iv 7–8; see 41.4*n*. **4–6** A rare example of double run-on lines; perhaps to emphasize excessive courtliness. Kosako 1995:219 notes that in the Cambridge Univ. Lib. database, *English Poetry*, the rhyming adj. **courteous**, which premodifies **glee** in enjambment, appears only in S., and that the combination of the rhyming adj. **gratious**, which with **Faire** modifies **Ladies** in enjambment, appears for the first time in S. **glee**: entertainment. **7–9** See

33

These stranger knights through passing, forth were led
    Into an inner rowme, whose royaltee
    And rich purueyance might vneath be red;
    Mote Princes place be seeme so deckt to bee.
    Which stately manner when as they did see,
    The image of superfluous riotize,
    Exceeding much the state of meane degree,
    They greatly wondred, whence so sumpteous guize
Might be maintaynd, and each gan diuersely deuize.

34

The wals were round about appareiled
    With costly clothes of *Arras* and of *Toure*,
    In which with cunning hand was pourtrahed
    The loue of *Venus* and her Paramoure,
    The fayre *Adonis*, turned to a flowre,
    A worke of rare deuice, and wondrous wit.
    First did it shew the bitter balefull stowre,
    Which her assayd with many a feruent fit,
When first her tender hart was with his beautie smit.

35

Then with what sleights and sweet allurements she
    Entyst the Boy, as well that art she knew,
    And wooed him her Paramoure to bee;
    Now making girlonds of each flowre that grew,
    To crowne his golden lockes with honour dew;
    Now leading him into a secret shade
    From his Beauperes, and from bright heauens vew,
    Where him to sleepe she gently would perswade,
Or bathe him in a fountaine by some couert glade.

36

And whilst he slept, she ouer him would spred
    Her mantle, colour'd like the starry skyes,
    And her soft arme lay vnderneath his hed,
    And with ambrosiall kisses bathe his eyes;
    And whilst he bath'd, with her two crafty spyes,
    She secretly would search each daintie lim,
    And throw into the well sweet Rosemaryes,
    And fragrant violets, and Paunces trim,
And euer with sweet Nectar she did sprinkle him.

---

the plan of the Queen's chambers at Hampton Court with its long gallery, rpt in S. Frye 1993:125. **the Lady of delight:** later named Malecasta; see 57.4*n*.

Stanza 32

6 bullion: solid gold or silver.

Stanza 33

2 royaltee: magnificence. **3** 'Its rich furnishings may hardly be told'. Cf. the 'rich purueaunce' of the house of Busirane at xi 53.9. The first of many comparisons between the two in order to relate the opening and closing episodes of Bk III. **6** 'The image of immoderate extravagance'. Cf. the 'wanton Riotise' of the house of Pride at I v 46.5, and esp. 'Consuming *Riotise*' in Cupid's masque at xii 25.7. **7 meane:** moderate. **8 guize:** conduct; fashion. **9 deuize:** guess.

Stanzas 34–38

The myth of Venus and Adonis was known from contemporary tapestries – see 'tapestries' and 'visual arts' in the *SEnc* – but chiefly from Ovid, *Met.* 10.519–739 (influenced by Golding's tr.), and its interpretation by Conti 1616:5.16. See vi 46–49*n*. The four panels of the tapestry are carefully balanced. (*a*) 34.7–9: three lines on Venus's strong passion. (*b*) 35–37: three stanzas on her art of love. In 35.1–3, that art is introduced by 'Then' and divided by 'Now' at 4 and 6. His sleep (8) and bathing (9) are described separately (36.1–4, 5–8) and then together (9). (*c*) 38.1–6: his wounding and death. (*d*) 7–9: three lines on his transformation. On S.'s art, see Hollander 1995:16–18. After being acted out in Malecasta's wooing of Britomart, the myth provides the pattern for the love stories that follow in Bk III: e.g. Venus succours the wounded Adonis as Cymoent succours the wounded Marinell at iv 40–43, and Belphœbe the wounded Timias at v 31–33.

Stanza 34

2 Cf. the 'goodly arras' in the house of Busirane at xi 28–46. Arras and Tournai were famous for their cloth. **3 pour-**

trahed: the earlier etymological spelling (Lat. *protrahere*) provides the extra syllable and the rhyme. **6** The line points to the mysteries concealed in the myth. **deuice:** design. **wit:** skill. **7 First:** this temporal signifier, followed in 35 by 'Then', 'Now', and 'Now', and culminating in 'Lo' at 38.1, highlights a picture, in imitation of those that preface each canto of late sixteenth-century editions of Ariosto's *Orlando Furioso* and Harington's tr. **stowre:** time of turmoil. **8 assayd:** assailed.

Stanza 35

1–2 Venus's aggressive wooing is indicated by the stress on **she | Entyst**, and Adonis's reluctance by her **sleights and sweet allurements**, which together suggest the characters in Shakespeare, *Venus and Adonis*. **Boy** notes his youthfulness. Female dominance here is countered by male dominance in the concluding Busirane episode, as C. Burrow 1988:108 notes. **4–9 girlonds, shade, bathe,** and **fountaine** provide the setting for Duessa's seduction of the Red Cross Knight at I vii 3–4, and Acrasia's triumph over Verdant at II xii 72–73. **a secret shade:** unlike Ovid's poplar, which (according to Venus) invites them to rest in its shade. Line 7 is carefully balanced to note Adonis's dangerous state. **Beauperes:** companions; literally those who equal him in beauty or hunting.

Stanza 36

2 Venus's garment hides Adonis from 'bright heauens vew' (35.7) by covering him with the night sky. Cf. 'Venus' mantle lined with stars' (*View* 50). **4** The antique custom of kissing the eyelids, though her action may be more therapeutic than erotic. **ambrosiall** points to her divinity, as does **Nectar**. **5–6** Alluding to the story of Salmacis and Hermaphroditus in Ovid, *Met.* 4.285–380, esp. 344–45. Cf. Acrasia's posture at II xii 73.1–2. **spyes:** i.e. her eyes. **7–8 Rosemaryes:** associated with remembrance. **fragrant violets:** the *viola odorata*, the white violet; associated with Venus, it has erotic connotations, perhaps of languor. **Paunces:** the pansy, hearts-ease, or love-in-idleness.

37

So did she steale his heedelesse hart away,
    And ioyd his loue in secret vnespyde.
    But for she saw him bent to cruell play,
    To hunt the saluage beast in forrest wyde,
    Dreadfull of daunger, that mote him betyde,
    She oft and oft aduiz'd him to refraine
    From chase of greater beastes, whose brutish pryde
    Mote breede him scath vnwares: but all in vaine;
For who can shun the chance, that dest'ny doth ordaine?

38

Lo, where beyond he lyeth languishing,
    Deadly engored of a great wilde Bore,
    And by his side the Goddesse groueling
    Makes for him endlesse mone, and euermore
    With her soft garment wipes away the gore,
    Which staynes his snowy skin with hatefull hew:
    But when she saw no helpe might him restore,
    Him to a dainty flowre she did transmew,
Which in that cloth was wrought, as if it liuely grew.

39

So was that chamber clad in goodly wize,
    And rownd about it many beds were dight,
    As whylome was the antique worldes guize,
    Some for vntimely ease, some for delight,
    As pleased them to vse, that vse it might:
    And all was full of Damzels, and of Squyres,
    Dauncing and reueling both day and night,
    And swimming deepe in sensuall desyres,
And *Cupid* still emongest them kindled lustfull fyres.

40

And all the while sweet Musicke did diuide
    Her looser notes with *Lydian* harmony;
    And all the while sweet birdes thereto applide
    Their daintie layes and dulcet melody,
    Ay caroling of loue and iollity,
    That wonder was to heare their trim consort.
    Which when those knights beheld, with scornefull eye,
    They sdeigned such lasciuious disport,
And loath'd the loose demeanure of that wanton sort.

41

Thence they were brought to that great Ladies vew,
    Whom they found sitting on a sumptuous bed,
    That glistred all with gold and glorious shew,
    As the proud *Persian* Queenes accustomed:
    She seemd a woman of great bountihed,
    And of rare beautie, sauing that askaunce
    Her wanton eyes, ill signes of womanhed,
    Did roll too highly, and too often glaunce,
Without regard of grace, or comely amenaunce.

42

Long worke it were, and needlesse to deuize
    Their goodly entertainement and great glee:
    She caused them be led in courteous wize
    Into a bowre, disarmed for to be,
    And cheared well with wine and spiceree:
    The *Redcrosse* Knight was soone disarmed there,
    But the braue Mayd would not disarmed bee,
    But onely vented vp her vmbriere,
And so did let her goodly visage to appere.

Stanza 37
5 Dreadfull: fearful.   **8 scath**: harm.

Stanza 38
1 beyond: i.e. in a farther tapestry.   **languishing**: growing
faint; wasting away through lust.   **2 Deadly**: fatally.
3 groueling: lying prostrate.   **8 dainty flowre**: the anemone.
transmew: transform; suggesting confinement in a mew or
prison, in contrast to Acrasia who 'transformed' her lovers into
beasts (II xii 85.2).   **9 liuely**: as a living thing.

Stanza 39
2 beds: couches, chiefly for love-making.   **dight**: arranged.
3 guize: custom.   **4 vntimely**: probably referring to the day-
time when those in bed should be up and about.   **6–9** These
lines shift from narrative action to moral comment and finally
to mythological description in order to relate the tapestries to
the courtiers.

Stanza 40
1–2 diuide: i.e. dividing a melody into passages of notes with
shorter time values. Cf. the music in the house of Pride at I v
17.7 and see *n*.   **Lydian harmony**: a mode of Greek music
condemned by Plato (*Republic* 398e), and in the sixteenth
century thought to 'turne our gallants to *Hermaphrodites*'

(Guilpin 1974:59).   **3–6** On the association of the song of
birds with sensuality, see I vii 3.4–5*n*.   **trim consort**: pleasing
harmony; a well-balanced instrumental ensemble.   **8 sdeigned**:
disdained (Ital. *sdegnare*).   **disport**: entertainment.   **9 sort**:
company.

Stanza 41
4 Persian: as Duessa at I ii 13.4, and Lucifera at I iv 7.6.
5 bountihed: generosity, liberal in bestowing her favours as
at 26.4.   **6 askaunce**: sidelong; suggesting wanton guile.
Cf. Mammon's glance at II vii 7.5 and see *n*.   **7–9** Alluding
to her name, Malecasta, i.e. casting lewd love-glances; see
50.6–7, 57.4*n*. Upton 1758 cites 2 Pet. 2.14: 'Hauing eyes ful
of adulterie, and that can not cease to sinne, beguiling vnstable
soules'.   **highly**: as Lucifera's 'loftie eyes, halfe loth to looke
so lowe' (I iv 14.1). lightly *1609* is consonant with Malecasta's
lasciviousness, and is supported by the praise of Womanhood:
'For stedfast still her eyes did fixed rest' (IV x 49.7).   **amen-
aunce**: noble bearing. Cf. the bride in *Epith* 236–37 'That suf-
fers not one looke to glaunce awry'.

Stanza 42
1 deuize: describe.   **5** I.e. with spiced wine.   **8** I.e. she only
lifted up her visor for air.

43

As when fayre *Cynthia*, in darkesome night,
    Is in a noyous cloud enueloped,
    Where she may finde the substance thin and light,
    Breakes forth her siluer beames, and her bright hed
    Discouers to the world discomfited;
    Of the poore traueiler, that went astray,
    With thousand blessings she is heried;
    Such was the beautie and the shining ray,
With which fayre *Britomart* gaue light vnto the day.

44

And eke those six, which lately with her fought,
    Now were disarmd, and did them selues present
    Vnto her vew, and company vnsought;
    For they all seemed courteous and gent,
    And all six brethren, borne of one parent,
    Which had them traynd in all ciuilitee,
    And goodly taught to tilt and turnament;
    Now were they liegmen to this Ladie free,
And her knights seruice ought, to hold of her in fee.

45

The first of them by name *Gardante* hight,
    A iolly person, and of comely vew;
    The second was *Parlante*, a bold knight,
    And next to him Iocante did ensew;

Basciante did him selfe most courteous shew;
    But fierce *Bacchante* seemd too fell and keene;
    And yett in armes *Noctante* greater grew:
    All were faire knights, and goodly well beseene,
But to faire *Britomart* they all but shadowes beene.

46

For shee was full of amiable grace,
    And manly terror mixed therewithall,
    That as the one stird vp affections bace,
    So th'other did mens rash desires apall,
    And hold them backe, that would in error fall;
    As hee, that hath espide a vermeill Rose,
    To which sharpe thornes and breres the way forstall,
    Dare not for dread his hardy hand expose,
But wishing it far off, his ydle wish doth lose.

47

Whom when the Lady saw so faire a wight,
    All ignorant of her contrary sex,
    (For shee her weend a fresh and lusty knight)
    Shee greatly gan enamoured to wex,
    And with vaine thoughts her falsed fancy vex:
    Her fickle hart conceiued hasty fyre,
    Like sparkes of fire, that fall in sclender flex,
    That shortly brent into extreme desyre,
And ransackt all her veines with passion entyre.

Stanza 43

While Artegall's face is compared to the sun at ii 24.6–7, Britomart's face, as she is the knight of chastity, is aptly compared to the moon, though see ix 20.4–9 for the description of her hair. This is the first and most muted (the cloud remains) of four occasions on which gazers are startled by seeing her; cf. ix 20–23, IV i 13–14, and vi 19–21. (The reasons for the unveilings are carefully discriminated.) The chivalric romance motif of the vision produced by the gesture of raising a visor or helmet, which is found, e.g. in Ariosto, *Orl. Fur.* 32.79–81, when Bradamante doffs her helmet, is discussed by Giamatti 1984:76–88. **2 noyous**: troublesome. **5 discomfited**: disconcerted by the loss of light. **7 heried**: praised.

Stanza 44

4 gent: noble. **6 ciuilitee**: proper behaviour, politeness. **7 tilt**: jousting usually between two mounted knights who from either end of the lists ran at each other with lances set. **turnament**: cavalry combat between groups of knights (its earlier sense) or single combat with swords, usually on foot (its sense in the later sixteenth century). **8–9 liegmen**: the term stresses the feudal nature of Castle Joyeous (cf. 30.5). **free**: the stock epithet for a lady of noble birth, which here suggests both her liberality in offering her favours and the bondage of her knights. **ought**: did owe. **to . . . fee**: i.e. being her knights, they are obliged to serve her.

Stanza 45

The names of these knights mark the six rungs of the *gradus amoris*, the ladder of lechery: gazing, conversing, courtly playing, kissing, drunken revelling, and sexual play at night. S. reinterprets the traditional five stages (seeing, speaking, toying, kissing, and copulating), and adds revelling as the special mark of Castle Joyeous. See A. Fowler 1959 and Friedman 1965–66.

As **Gardante** denotes loving glances upon beauty, he himself is handsome (**iolly**) and of pleasant appearance (**vew**). Glances lead to boldness of seductive speaking (Ital. **Parlante**); then to **Iocante**'s 'courtly play' (56.9; f. Ital. *giocare*, to dally, to jest); then to kissing (**Basciante**, Ital. *basciare*, to kiss; and see 56.8*n*) by which, in the intoxication of desire, lovers become fierce votaries of Bacchus; and finally to the culminating sexual act itself. **Bacchante** is **keene** in being bold or fierce in desire, and **Noctante** – **in armes** refers to sexual groping, for he is disarmed (44.2) – **greater grew**, alluding to erection in his increased sexual excitement. In courting Britomart, Malecasta hopes to act out these stages of seduction. **8 goodly well beseene**: of good appearance. **9 shadowes**: ironic, for she loves a shadow; see ii 44.3, 9.

Stanza 46

1–5 amiable: pleasing, as she arouses love; worthy to be loved. Her **amiable grace** complements Artegall's 'Heroicke grace' at ii 24.9. Although she arouses love in others, her chastity prevents the pursuit which leads Florimell's lovers into **error**, i.e. wandering. Cf. the power of Belphœbe's eyes at II iii 23. **6 vermeill Rose**: esp. associated with love, as in *Proth* 33–35. **7 forstall**: obstruct.

Stanza 47

The ensuing bedroom farce is indebted to Ariosto's bawdy tale of Fiordispina who lusts after Bradamante, taking her for a man, *Orl. Fur.* 25.29–70, as Alpers 1967:180–85 and Silberman 1995:30–33 demonstrate. As a variant of the bedtrick popular in drama in the late 1590s, see Desens 1994:18–35. **3 lusty**: vigorous; but also (she hopes) lustful. **5 fancy**: the power of imagination to produce deceiving images of love, as at I ii 30.3. **9 entyre**: inward, as an 'inburning fire' (53.3); or as her passion entirely possesses her.

48

Eftsoones shee grew to great impatience
  And into termes of open outrage brust,
  That plaine discouered her incontinence,
  Ne reckt shee, who her meaning did mistrust;
  For she was giuen all to fleshly lust,
  And poured forth in sensuall delight,
  That all regard of shame she had discust,
  And meet respect of honor putt to flight:
So shamelesse beauty soone becomes a loathly sight.

49

Faire Ladies, that to loue captiued arre,
  And chaste desires doe nourish in your mind,
  Let not her fault your sweete affections marre,
  Ne blott the bounty of all womankind;
  'Mongst thousands good one wanton Dame to find:
  Emongst the Roses grow some wicked weeds;
  For this was not to loue, but lust inclind;
  For loue does alwaies bring forth bounteous deeds,
And in each gentle hart desire of honor breeds.

50

Nought so of loue this looser Dame did skill,
  But as a cole to kindle fleshly flame,
  Giuing the bridle to her wanton will,
  And treading vnder foote her honest name:
  Such loue is hate, and such desire is shame.
  Still did she roue at her with crafty glaunce
  Of her false eies, that at her hart did ayme,
  And told her meaning in her countenaunce;
But *Britomart* dissembled it with ignoraunce.

51

Supper was shortly dight and downe they satt,
  Where they were serued with all sumptuous fare,
  Whiles fruitfull *Ceres*, and *Lyæus* fatt
  Pourd out their plenty, without spight or spare:

Nought wanted there, that dainty was and rare;
  And aye the cups their bancks did ouerflow,
  And aye betweene the cups, she did prepare
  Way to her loue, and secret darts did throw;
But *Britomart* would not such guilfull message know.

52

So when they slaked had the feruent heat
  Of appetite with meates of euery sort,
  The Lady did faire *Britomart* entreat,
  Her to disarme, and with delightfull sport
  To loose her warlike limbs and strong effort,
  But when shee mote not thereunto be wonne,
  (For shee her sexe vnder that straunge purport
  Did vse to hide, and plaine apparaunce shonne:)
In playner wise to tell her grieuaunce she begonne.

53

And all attonce discouered her desire
  With sighes, and sobs, and plaints, and piteous griefe,
  The outward sparkes of her inburning fire;
  Which spent in vaine, at last she told her briefe,
  That but if she did lend her short reliefe,
  And doe her comfort, she mote algates dye.
  But the chaste damzell, that had neuer priefe
  Of such malengine and fine forgerye,
Did easely beleeue her strong extremitye.

54

Full easy was for her to haue beliefe,
  Who by self-feeling of her feeble sexe,
  And by long triall of the inward griefe,
  Wherewith imperious loue her hart did vexe,
  Could iudge what paines doe louing harts perplexe.
  Who meanes no guile, be-guiled soonest shall,
  And to faire semblaunce doth light faith annexe;
  The bird, that knowes not the false fowlers call,
Into his hidden nett full easely doth fall.

Stanza 48
The stanza shows her to be evilly chaste, as her name declares, and indicates why she is called 'the *Lady of delight*' at 31.9. **2 termes**: state, condition. **outrage**: intemperance, the 'strong extremity' (53.9) of passion. **4 mistrust**: suspect. **6 poured forth**: in the sexual sense; see I vii 7.2*n*. **7 discust**: shaken off.

Stanza 49
S.'s apostrophe to **Faire Ladies**, also at vi 1.1 and xi 2.6, imitates Ariosto's address to 'Donne', *Orl. Fur.* 28.1, prefatory to his delightfully misogynist tale, but is influenced more by Sidney's similar address throughout the early books of the *Old Arcadia*. Cf. the address to 'Fayre ympes' at v 53.1, and to 'honorable Dames' at ix 1.1–2. On S.'s direct appeal to female readers, see Quilligan 1983:185–99. **4 bounty**: goodness. **8–9** Love is defined by the virtuous action to which it leads; cf. ii 7.1–5, iii 1.7–9, and v 1.8–9; cf. also IV Pr. 2.6–9. **bounteous**: full of goodness, virtuous.

Stanza 50
1 looser: too loose. **skill**: i.e. have knowledge. **6–7** Alluding to her name; cf. 41.7–9 and see 57.4*n*. **roue**: the sense,

'shoot an arrow at a mark selected at pleasure', fits the amatory situation. **crafty glaunce**: cf. Venus's 'crafty spyes' at 36.5. Malecasta acts out Venus's role as wooer at 35.1–3.

Stanza 51
1 dight: prepared. **3 Ceres** signifies food, **Lyæus** (an epithet for Bacchus) wine. Upton 1758 cites the proverb: *sine Cerere et Baccho friget Venus*; see Tilley C 211. **4 spight or spare**: grudging or frugality. **5 dainty**: precious.

Stanza 52
3–5 Malecasta's excited state is revealed by her use of *zeugma*: she asks Britomart to unloose **her warlike limbs** by disarming and to relax her **strong effort** (i.e. power) by turning to **delightfull sport**. **loose** suggests moral laxity. **7 purport**: i.e. her appearance as it expresses her intent.

Stanza 53
1 discouered: revealed, exhibited. **5 but if**: unless. **6 algates**: otherwise. **7 priefe**: experience. **8 malengine**: deceit; personified at V ix 5. **fine forgerye**: consummate deception.

55

For thy she would not in discourteise wise,
 Scorne the faire offer of good will profest;
 For great rebuke it is, loue to despise,
 Or rudely sdeigne a gentle harts request;
 But with faire countenaunce, as beseemed best,
 Her entertaynd; nath'lesse shee inly deemd
 Her loue too light, to wooe a wandring guest:
Which she misconstruing, thereby esteemd
That from like inward fire that outward smoke had steemd.

56

Therewith a while she her flit fancy fedd,
 Till she mote winne fit time for her desire,
 But yet her wound still inward freshly bledd,
 And through her bones the false instilled fire
 Did spred it selfe, and venime close inspire.
 Tho were the tables taken all away,
 And euery knight, and euery gentle Squire
Gan choose his dame with *Bascimano* gay,
With whom he ment to make his sport and courtly play.

57

Some fell to daunce, some fel to hazardry,
 Some to make loue, some to make meryment,
 As diuerse witts to diuerse things apply;
 And all the while faire *Malecasta* bent

Her crafty engins to her close intent.
 By this th'eternall lampes, wherewith high *Ioue*
 Doth light the lower world, were halfe yspent,
 And the moist daughters of huge *Atlas* stroue
Into the *Ocean* deepe to driue their weary droue.

58

High time it seemed then for euerie wight
 Them to betake vnto their kindly rest;
 Eftesoones long waxen torches weren light,
 Vnto their bowres to guyden euery guest:
 Tho when the Britonesse saw all the rest
 Auoided quite, she gan her selfe despoile,
 And safe committ to her soft fethered nest,
 Wher through long watch, and late daies weary toile,
She soundly slept, and carefull thoughts did quite assoile.

59

Now whenas all the world in silence deepe
 Yshrowded was, and euery mortall wight
 Was drowned in the depth of deadly sleepe,
 Faire *Malecasta*, whose engrieued spright
 Could find no rest in such perplexed plight,
 Lightly arose out of her wearie bed,
 And vnder the blacke vele of guilty Night,
 Her with a scarlott mantle couered,
That was with gold and Ermines faire enueloped.

Stanza 54
4 **vexe**: trouble, afflict. 5 **perplexe**: torment. 7–9 I.e. one who believes too readily in appearances will be beguiled the soonest, as she has been in falling in love with Artegall's 'semblant' (ii 38.1–5), and now in being deceived by Malecasta's grief, even as an unwary bird is easily caught by a fowler. **light**: also 'ready'. **annexe**: join.

Stanza 55
1 **For thy**: accordingly. 3–4 The contest between temperance and courtesy is seen in Guyon at II vi 26.3–5, and the contest between chastity and courtesy is seen in Belphœbe at v 55. **rebuke**: shame. 5 **faire countenaunce**: courteous behaviour.

Stanza 56
1 **flit**: changing. 4–5 Cf. Cupid's 'poysned arrow, | That wounds the life, and wastes the inmost marrow' (*HB* 62–63). **close**: secretly. 8 **Bascimano**: Basciomani *1596*, from the phrase, *bascio le mani*. They have now reached the third and fourth rungs of the ladder of lechery. 9 **sport**: amorous dalliance or intercourse.

Stanza 57
1 **hazardry**: dicing. 4 **Malecasta**: now named when her nature is fully manifest. She is evilly unchaste: Lat. *malus* (wicked, lewd) + *castus* (chaste), as shown in the lewd casting of her love on any stranger, in her lewd loving glances (see 41.7–9*n*), and in her lewd 'casts', i.e. 'artifice', 'tricks' (*OED* 24). Britomart also loves a stranger, but her sight of him in the mirror was 'Led with eternall prouidence' (iii 24.4), and she remains constant to him, thereby distinguishing her sexual

desire from lust. 5 **engins**: wiles. **close intent**: secret purpose. 6–9 This *chronographia* fixes the time and date. Since the stars are **halfe yspent**, the time is midnight; and since **the moist daughters** – the Hyades or rainy ones (so called because they 'rayse stormes and wyndes', T. Cooper 1565) – are setting at this time, the date is near the vernal equinox. See A. Fowler 1964:145–46 and Eade 1984a:180. As Cooper also notes, 'Poetes name them the daughters of *Atlas*'. **droue** refers to the Pleiades, which being before the Hyades would seem to be driven by them into the sea. The image anticipates Florimell's descent into the sea at viii 37. Britomart is again tested at midnight in the house of Busirane; see xii 2.7*n*.

Stanza 58
2 **kindly**: natural; owing to nature. 5 **the Britonesse**: Britomart's title alone in the poem, as is 'Briton Maid' at ii 4.5, first used here and then to introduce her second temptation in the house of Busirane at xii 2.8. 6 **Auoided**: retired. **despoile**: undress; and suggesting that despoiling herself leads to her wounding, in contrast to remaining in armour and not sleeping at Dolon's castle, V vi 23.4–5, 24.7–9. 9 **assoile**: dispel, set herself free. Loosening her armour loosens thoughts for her own care.

Stanza 59
6 **Lightly**: quickly; also unchastely in contrast to Britomart's action at 62.2. 7–9 Malecasta is covered by **Night** in contrast to Britomart who 'gaue light vnto the day' at 43.9. The **scarlott mantle** associates her with Duessa who wore a 'scarlot robe' (I viii 45.9) to betray the Red Cross Knight. **Ermines**: a traditional emblem of chastity – see ii 25.7–9*n*; but also associated with lust, e.g. Alciati 1985:emblem 79.

60

Then panting softe, and trembling euery ioynt,
    Her fearfull feete towards the bowre she mou'd.
    Where she for secret purpose did appoynt
    To lodge the warlike maide vnwisely loou'd,
    And to her bed approching, first she proou'd,
    Whether she slept or wakte, with her softe hand
    She softely felt, if any member moou'd,
    And lent her wary eare to vnderstand,
If any puffe of breath, or signe of sence shee fond.

61

Which whenas none she fond, with easy shifte,
    For feare least her vnwares she should abrayd,
    Th'embroderd quilt she lightly vp did lifte,
    And by her side her selfe she softly layd,
    Of euery finest fingers touch affrayd;
    Ne any noise she made, ne word she spake,
    But inly sigh'd. At last the royall Mayd
    Out of her quiet slomber did awake,
And chaungd her weary side, the better ease to take.

62

Where feeling one close couched by her side,
    She lightly lept out of her filed bedd,
    And to her weapon ran, in minde to gride
    The loathed leachour. But the Dame halfe dedd
    Through suddein feare and ghastly drerihedd,
    Did shrieke alowd, that through the hous it rong,
    And the whole family therewith adredd,
    Rashly out of their rouzed couches sprong,
And to the troubled chamber all in armes did throng.

63

And those six knights that ladies Champions,
    And eke the *Redcrosse* knight ran to the stownd,
    Halfe armd and halfe vnarmd, with them attons:
    Where when confusedly they came, they fownd
    Their lady lying on the sencelesse grownd;
    On thother side, they saw the warlike Mayd
    Al in her snow-white smocke, with locks vnbownd,
    Threatning the point of her auenging blaed,
That with so troublous terror they were all dismayd.

64

About their Ladye first they flockt arownd,
    Whom hauing laid in comfortable couch,
    Shortly they reard out of her frosen swownd;
    And afterwardes they gan with fowle reproch
    To stirre vp strife, and troublous contecke broch:
    But by ensample of the last dayes losse,
    None of them rashly durst to her approch,
    Ne in so glorious spoile themselues embosse,
Her succourd eke the Champion of the bloody Crosse.

65

But one of those six knights, *Gardante* hight,
    Drew out a deadly bow and arrow keene,
    Which forth he sent with felonous despight,
    And fell intent against the virgin sheene:
    The mortall steele stayd not, till it was seene
    To gore her side, yet was the wound not deepe,
    But lightly rased her soft silken skin,
    That drops of purple blood thereout did weepe,
Which did her lilly smock with staines of vermeil steep.

loss of virginity?

Stanza 60

5 proou'd: tested. **8 wary**: weary *1590*, *1596* is supported by Upton 1758, for she would be weary of being unsatisfied – cf. 'her wearie bed' (59.6) – and weary of listening. However, the *1609* reading better suits the context.

Stanza 61

1 shifte: change of position; movement. **2 abrayd**: arouse, startle. **7 the royall Mayd**: a title bestowed elsewhere only on Una and the Faerie Queene.

Stanza 62

2 filed: defiled. **3–4 gride**: pierce through. Not the kind of stabbing that Malecasta had anticipated. Cf. love's wound at ii 37.8–9. Britomart is as deceived as Malecasta about the other's sex. **5 ghastly drerihedd**: fearful terror. **7 family**: retinue (*OED* 1b). **8 Rashly**: hastily.

Stanza 63

2 stownd: uproar; place. **3 attons**: together. **7** Britomart's **snow-white smocke** – called 'lilly' at 65.9 – is emblematic of her purity. It is quite unlike the elaborately embroidered undergarment worn by Elizabethan women; see Ashelford 1988: figs. 4, 11.

Stanza 64

5 contecke: discord. **8 embosse**: cover, decorate. I.e. none tries to possess her as his spoil or booty. Its sense at I xi 20.3 suggests 'plunge' his weapon into her body, which refers to sexual invasion. **9** The title distinguishes him from 'that ladies Champions' (63.1).

Stanza 65

3 felonous: fierce, cruel. **4 sheene**: beautiful, shining; cf. 43.8. **5–9** This token wound manifests her inner wound (cf. ii 39.1–6) by the sight of Artegall, mentioned at 8.9; hence only **Gardante**, of Malecasta's six champions, wounds her. The gored side is a sexual wound, here relating to the womb, as ii 11.7, vi 27.9, etc., and corresponding to the male sexual wound in the thigh. Cf. the gore that stains Adonis's snowy skin at 38.5–6, and Britomart's wounding by Busirane at xii 33.4–5. On her two wounds, see M. Suzuki 1989:155–59. **rased**: cut, scratched.

66

Wherewith enrag'd, she fiercely at them flew,
  And with her flaming sword about her layd,
  That none of them foule mischiefe could eschew,
  But with her dreadfull strokes were all dismayd:
  Here, there, and euery where about her swayd
  Her wrathfull steele, that none mote it abyde;
  And eke the *Redcrosse* knight gaue her good ayd,
  Ay ioyning foot to foot, and syde to syde,
That in short space their foes they haue quite terrifyde.

67

Tho whenas all were put to shamefull flight,
  The noble *Britomartis* her arayd,
  And her bright armes about her body dight:
  For nothing would she lenger there be stayd,
  Where so loose life, and so vngentle trade
  Was vsd of knights and Ladies seeming gent:
  So earely ere the grosse Earthes gryesy shade,
  Was all disperst out of the firmament,
They tooke their steeds, and forth vpon their iourney went.

Stanza 66
3 mischiefe: harm, evil. **eschew**: escape. **5 swayd**: swung.

Stanza 67
5 vngentle trade: discourteous conduct, not befitting those of gentle birth. **7 gryesy**: grey; horrible, being grey.

Cant. II.

The Redcrosse knight to Britomart
describeth Artegall:
The wondrous myrrhour, by which she
in loue with him did fall.

1

Ere haue I cause, in men iust blame to find,
   That in their proper praise too partiall bee,
And not indifferent to woman kind,
To whom no share in armes and cheualree,
They doe impart, ne maken memoree
Of their braue gestes and prowesse martiall;
Scarse doe they spare to one or two or three,
Rowme in their writtes; yet the same writing small
Does all their deedes deface, and dims their glories all,

2

But by record of antique times I finde,
   That wemen wont in warres to beare most sway,
And to all great exploites them selues inclind:
Of which they still the girlond bore away,
Till enuious Men fearing their rules decay,
Gan coyne streight lawes to curb their liberty,
Yet sith they warlike armes haue laide away,
They haue exceld in artes and pollicy,
That now we foolish men that prayse gin eke t'enuy.

3

Of warlike puissaunce in ages spent,
   Be thou faire *Britomart*, whose prayse I wryte,
But of all wisedom bee thou precedent,
   O soueraine Queene, whose prayse I would endyte,

Endite I would as dewtie doth excyte;
But ah my rymes too rude and rugged arre,
When in so high an obiect they doe lyte,
And striuing, fit to make, I feare doe marre:
Thy selfe thy prayses tell, and make them knowen farre.

4

She traueiling with *Guyon* by the way,
   Of sondry thinges faire purpose gan to find,
T'abridg their iourney long, and lingring day;
Mongst which it fell into that Fairies mind,
To aske this Briton Maid, what vncouth wind,
Brought her into those partes, and what inquest
Made her dissemble her disguised kind:
Faire Lady she him seemd, like Lady drest,
But fairest knight aliue, when armed was her brest.

5

Thereat she sighing softly, had no powre
   To speake a while, ne ready answere make,
But with hart-thrilling throbs and bitter stowre,
As if she had a feuer fitt, did quake,
And euery daintie limbe with horrour shake,
And euer and anone the rosy red,
Flasht through her face, as it had beene a flake
Of lightning, through bright heuen fulmined;
At last the passion past she thus him answered.

Book III Canto ii

Stanzas 1–3
S.'s praise of women and defence of Elizabeth, also at iv 1–3, imitates Ariosto, *Orl. Fur.* 20.1–3, 37.1–23. See 'women, defense of' and 'heroine' in the *SEnc*, Benson 1992:281–306, Stump 1999:401–15, and Villeponteaux 1995:53–60. On women warriors in Ariosto, Tasso, and Spenser, see Robinson 1985.

Stanza 1
2 proper: own.   **3 indifferent**: just, impartial; also, men treat women differently even though they are the same **kind**, as Villeponteaux 1995:55 suggests.   **8** I.e. the deeds of a few women though recorded briefly. Or **small** suggests minimizing 'great exploites' (2.3).   **9 deface**: outshine by contrast.

Stanza 2
1–4 S. offers examples in Guendolene who 'first taught men a woman to obay' (II x 20.7) and Boadicea (54–56).   **still**: always.
6 streight: strict.   **8 pollicy**: administration of public affairs.

Stanza 3
1–3 An injunction addressed to Britomart.   **precedent**: pattern, model; president.   **4 endyte**: put into written words (*OED* 4);

cf. *Am* 4.14.   **6 rugged**: rough to the ear. Cf. the apology at *SC Nov.* 51.   **8 fit to make**: i.e. to compose fitting verses.

Stanza 4
1 Guyon: an error for '*Redcrosse*', so named at 16.8 and iii 62.3, though the full name is always used except at I vii 48.8 and II i 23.6 where it has special religious significance. Since a book's opening episode defines the protagonist's virtue in relation to the predecessor's, it may be that S. 'returned' to i 12 where Guyon is singled out; or that Britomart's story of her 'rape' is similar to that told to Guyon at II i 9–11; see 8.6–9*n*.   **Fairies mind** fits Guyon but applies more to the Red Cross Knight who is known as 'a Faeries sonne' (I x 64.7).
2 purpose: conversation.   **5–6** The proverb (Smith 852) applies to her passion-driven state; cf. iv 10.   **inquest**: quest. The form suggests an inner quest, referring to her love and her questioning.   **7 kind**: sex.   **9 armed was her brest**: in opposition to the Amazon's naked breast, as Virgil, *Aen.* 1.491–93.

Stanza 5
Cf. Malecasta's state of loving and confession of her love at i 53, which Britomart entertained because of her own 'long

6

Faire Sir, I let you weete, that from the howre
   I taken was from nourses tender pap,
   I haue beene trained vp in warlike stowre,
   To tossen speare and shield, and to affrap
   The warlike ryder to his most mishap;
   Sithence I loathed haue my life to lead,
   As Ladies wont, in pleasures wanton lap,
   To finger the fine needle and nyce thread;
Me leuer were with point of foemans speare be dead.

7   *masculine*

All my delight on deedes of armes is sett,
   To hunt out perilles and aduentures hard,
   By sea, by land, where so they may be mett,
   Onely for honour and for high regard,
   Without respect of richesse or reward.
   For such intent into these partes I came,
   Withouten compasse, or withouten card,
   Far fro my natiue soyle, that is by name
The greater *Brytayne*, here to seeke for praise and fame.

8

Fame blazed hath, that here in Faery lond
   Doe many famous knightes and Ladies wonne,
   And many straunge aduentures to bee fond,
   Of which great worth and worship may be wonne;
   Which to proue, I this voyage haue begonne.
   But mote I weet of you, right courteous knight,
   Tydings of one, that hath vnto me donne
   Late foule dishonour and reprochfull spight,
The which I seeke to wreake, and *Arthegall* he hight.

9

The word gone out, she backe againe would call,
   As her repenting so to haue missayd,
   But that he it vptaking ere the fall,
   Her shortly answered; Faire martiall Mayd
   Certes ye misauised beene, t'vpbrayd,
   A gentle knight with so vnknightly blame:
   For weet ye well of all, that euer playd
   At tilt or tourney, or like warlike game,
The noble *Arthegall* hath euer borne the name.

10

For thy great wonder were it, if such shame
   Should euer enter in his bounteous thought,
   Or euer doe, that mote deseruen blame:
   The noble corage neuer weeneth ought,
   That may vnworthy of it selfe be thought.
   Therefore, faire Damzell, be ye well aware,
   Least that too farre ye haue your sorrow sought:
   You and your countrey both I wish welfare,
And honour both; for each of other worthy are.

11

The royall Maid woxe inly wondrous glad,
   To heare her Loue so highly magnifyde,
   And ioyd that euer she affixed had,
   Her hart on knight so goodly glorifyde,
   How euer finely she it faind to hyde:
   The louing mother, that nine monethes did beare,
   In the deare closett of her painefull syde,
   Her tender babe, it seeing safe appeare,
Doth not so much reioyce, as she reioyced theare.

---

triall of . . . inward griefe' (54.3) through love. **3 stowre:** convulsion; inner emotional struggle, in contrast to her outward 'warlike stowre' (6.3) before she fell in love; cf. Venus's 'bitter balefull stowre' at i 34.7. **7 flake:** flash. **8 fulmined:** sent forth, flashed out.

Stanza 6
Britomart's false story – the truth emerges later in the canto and at iii 53 – derives in part from Tasso's account of the Amazon, Clorinda, whose 'loftie hand would of it selfe refuse | To touch the daintie needle, or nice thred' (*Ger. Lib.* 2.39, tr. Fairfax, his wording being influenced by S.). Cf. also Camilla in Virgil, *Aen.* 7.805–07. **4 tossen:** brandish. **affrap:** strike down. **5 mishap:** misfortune. **6 Sithence:** ever since. **8 nyce:** thin. **9** I had rather . . .

Stanza 7
7 As Guyon at II vii 1.6 is compared to a mariner who sails only by card and compass. Britomart is not so complete: cf. 49.2–3, iv 9.6–9. **9 greater Brytayne:** as distinct from Britain the less or Brittany; but here Wales rather than England. At i 8.7, she is said to come 'from *Britayne*', which is identified as South Wales at 18.4 below. On the geography, see Erickson 1996:89.

Stanza 8
2 wonne: dwell. **4 worth and worship** match 'honour and . . . high regard' (7.4). **6–9** At 12.6–9, the accusation of rape is more overt. Her story is as slanderous as Duessa's, which

deceives Guyon at II i, and yet true when compared to her earlier inviolate state. On **Arthegall**, see iii 26.2*n*.

Stanza 9
2 missayd: spoken abusively. **3 ere the fall:** before her voice lowered at the end of her speech, or before she had finished speaking. **4 martiall Mayd:** combining the roles of Diana (or Venus) and Mars; see i 8.6*n*. **5 misauised:** wrongly informed. **8 tilt or tourney:** see i 44.7*n*. **9 borne the name:** won the prize.

Stanza 10
1 For thy: therefore. **2 bounteous thought:** valiant, virtuous mind. **4–5** Repeating 1–2, as the repetition of **thought** indicates. The noble nature (**corage**) never even thinks (**weeneth**) any unworthy act. The Red Cross Knight is also reproving Britomart. **6–7** His advice is lost on Britomart for she has no defence against her love for Artegall; see 26.4, 38.9, iii 24.2. **aware:** vigilant. **8–9** Cf. the benediction he gives Guyon at II i 33.6–9. Again he speaks as the future patron saint of England. **welfare:** to fare well.

Stanza 11
2 magnifyde: extolled. **5 finely:** cunningly. **6–9** A paraphrase of John 16.21. **closett:** alluding to her womb, as does **syde** (*OED* I 1b); cf. vi 27.9. See Wofford 1988:8 for other relevant meanings. On maternity as a central thematic concern in Bk III, see Goldberg 1975; and in the whole poem, see J. Craig 2000. **theare:** i.e. on that occasion.

12

But to occasion him to further talke,
    To feed her humor with his pleasing style,
    Her list in stryfull termes with him to balke,
    And thus replyde, How euer, Sir, ye fyle
    Your courteous tongue, his prayses to compyle,
    It ill beseemes a knight of gentle sort,
    Such as ye haue him boasted, to beguyle
    A simple maide, and worke so hainous tort,
In shame of knighthood, as I largely can report.

13

Let bee therefore my vengeaunce to disswade,
    And read, where I that faytour false may find.
    Ah, but if reason faire might you perswade,
    To slake your wrath, and mollify your mind,
    (Said he) perhaps ye should it better find:
    For hardie thing it is, to weene by might,
    That man to hard conditions to bind,
    Or euer hope to match in equall fight,
Whose prowesse paragone saw neuer liuing wight.

14

Ne soothlich is it easie for to read,
    Where now on earth, or how he may be fownd;
    For he ne wonneth in one certeine stead,
    But restlesse walketh all the world arownd,
    Ay doing thinges, that to his fame redownd,
    Defending Ladies cause, and Orphans right,
    Where so he heares, that any doth confownd
    Them comfortlesse, through tyranny or might;
So is his soueraine honour raisde to heuens hight.

15

His feeling wordes her feeble sence much pleased,
    And softly sunck into her molten hart;
    Hart that is inly hurt, is greatly eased
    With hope of thing, that may allegge his smart;

For pleasing wordes are like to Magick art,
    That doth the charmed Snake in slomber lay:
    Such secrete ease felt gentle *Britomart,*
    Yet list the same efforce with faind gainesay;
So dischord ofte in Musick makes the sweeter lay.

16

And sayd, Sir knight, these ydle termes forbeare,
    And sith it is vneath to finde his haunt,
    Tell me some markes, by which he may appeare,
    If chaunce I him encounter parauaunt;
    For perdy one shall other slay, or daunt:
    What shape, what shield, what armes, what steed, what
    And what so else his person most may vaunt?   (stedd,
    All which the *Redcrosse* knight to point aredd,
And him in euerie part before her fashioned.

17

Yet him in euerie part before she knew,
    How euer list her now her knowledge fayne,
    Sith him whylome in *Brytayne* she did vew,
    To her reuealed in a mirrhour playne,
    Whereof did grow her first engraffed payne,
    Whose root and stalke so bitter yet did taste,
    That but the fruit more sweetnes did contayne,
    Her wretched dayes in dolour she mote waste,
And yield the pray of loue to lothsome death at last.

18

By straunge occasion she did him behold,
    And much more straungely gan to loue his sight,
    As it in bookes hath written beene of old.
    In *Deheubarth* that now South-wales is hight,
    What time king *Ryence* raign'd, and dealed right,
    The great Magitien *Merlin* had deuiz'd,
    By his deepe science, and hell-dreaded might,
    A looking glasse, right wondrously aguiz'd,
Whose vertues through the wyde worlde soone were
                                        (solemniz'd.

Stanza 12
3 **balke**: bandy words.   8 . . . such wicked harm or torment.
Her charge is all the more slanderous in being directed against
the patron of justice.

Stanza 13
2 **read**: tell.   **faytour**: deceiver.   4 **mollify**: allay the anger of.
6–7 These lines prepare for V iv 51.4 when Artegall is bound
by Radigund's **hard conditions** outlined at 49.1–5 and sub-
mits to her, overcome not **by might** but by his own free will.
9 I.e. no one has seen the match or rival of his prowess.

Stanza 14
1 **soothlich**: truly.   3–4 J. Dixon 1964 glosses: 'Justice not
tyed to one place'.   **stead**: place.   5–8 See I x 43.2–3*n.*
confownd: overthrow.   **comfortlesse**: helpless.

Stanza 15
1 **feeling**: i.e. affecting her emotionally.   4 **allegge**: allay;
bring forward as a legal ground.   5–6 Cf. Ps. 58.4–5, Jer.
8.17.   8 **efforce**: force or struggle against. For her greater

gratification, she chose to struggle against the ease she felt.
9 proverbial (Smith 185), as *SC,* Epistle: 'So ofentimes a
dischorde in Musick maketh a comely concordaunce'.

Stanza 16
2 **vneath**: difficult.   4 **parauaunt**: before, i.e. openly; or
a short form of 'paraventure': by chance.   5 **daunt**: subdue.
6 **shape**: as she recalls at iv 5.5.   **stedd**: mark or imprint, such
as the hound on the crest of Artegall's helmet at 25.1.
7 **vaunt**: proudly display.   8 **to point aredd**: exactly declared.

Stanza 17
A transitional stanza to mark a break in the story until iv 4.
2 **fayne**: conceal.   4 **playne**: i.e. plainly.   5–7 **engraffed**:
engrafted; suggesting the image of a tree growing out of her
body; see iii 18.3, 22.2–4.

Stanza 18
4 **Deheubarth**: Dehenbarth, now commonly named South
Wales; see W. Harrison in Holinshed 1807–08:1.26.   5 **king**
Ryence: a king of North Wales. The name is adapted from

19

It vertue had, to shew in perfect sight,
  What euer thing was in the world contaynd,
  Betwixt the lowest earth and heuens hight,
  So that it to the looker appertaynd;
  What euer foe had wrought, or frend had faynd,
  Therein discouered was, ne ought mote pas,
  Ne ought in secret from the same remaynd;
  For thy it round and hollow shaped was,
Like to the world it selfe, and seemd a world of glas.

20

Who wonders not, that reades so wonderous worke?
  But who does wonder, that has red the Towre,
  Wherein th'Aegyptian *Phao* long did lurke
  From all mens vew, that none might her discoure,
  Yet she might all men vew out of her bowre?
  Great *Ptolomæe* it for his lemans sake
  Ybuilded all of glasse, by Magicke powre,
  And also it impregnable did make;
Yet when his loue was false, he with a peaze it brake.

21

Such was the glassy globe that *Merlin* made,
  And gaue vnto king *Ryence* for his gard,
  That neuer foes his kingdome might inuade,
  But he it knew at home before he hard

Tydings thereof, and so them still debar'd.
  It was a famous Present for a Prince,
  And worthy worke of infinite reward,
  That treasons could bewray, and foes conuince;
Happy this Realme, had it remayned euer since.

22

One day it fortuned, fayre *Britomart*
  Into her fathers closet to repayre;
  For nothing he from her reseru'd apart,
  Being his onely daughter and his hayre:
  Where when she had espyde that mirrhour fayre,
  Her selfe awhile therein she vewd in vaine;
  Tho her auizing of the vertues rare,
  Which thereof spoken were, she gan againe
Her to bethinke of, that mote to her selfe pertaine.

23

But as it falleth, in the gentlest harts
  Imperious Loue hath highest set his throne,
  And tyrannizeth in the bitter smarts
  Of them, that to him buxome are and prone:
  So thought this Mayd (as maydens vse to done)
  Whom fortune for her husband would allot,
  Not that she lusted after any one;
  For she was pure from blame of sinfull blot,
Yet wist her life at last must lincke in that same knot.

Malory; see VI i 13*n*. **dealed**: governed. **6** As **The great Magitien** who uses his powers only for good, such as fashioning Arthur's shield (I vii 36) and sword (II viii 20), **Merlin** is the counterpart to Archimago and Busirane. See 'Merlin' and 'magic' in the *SEnc*. As a deeply suspect figure for Protestant readers, see Highley 1997:15–20. **8** His **looking glasse** is called '*Venus* looking glas' at i 8.9 and a 'charmed looking glas' at iii 24.2. At a first glance, it is a reflecting mirror, or cosmological glass, as Demaray 1991:110–13 argues; then it becomes a transparent 'glassy globe' (21.1), or a magic crystal ball in which one sees images, such as used by Elizabeth's astrologer, John Dee, and now in the British Museum: for a photograph, see Deacon 1968:230. See 'mirrors' in the *SEnc*. **aguiz'd**: equipped. **9 solemniz'd**: celebrated.

Stanza 19

As the 'brood mirour of glas' in Chaucer, *Squire's Tale* 132–41, reveals any adversity that will befall its owner: it shows men 'openly who is youre freend or foo', and any lady her lover's disloyalty. Cf. Genius who reveals 'wondrous things concerning our welfare' (II xii 47.5). **4 So that**: provided that, as it shows Britomart what 'mote to her selfe pertaine' (22.9).

Stanza 20

1–2 In Chaucer, some 'wondred on the mirour, | That born was up into the maister-tour', and one tells of various magical mirrors 'As knowen they that han hir bookes herd' (225–35). **reades . . . has red**: sees . . . has seen (a sense unique to S.). **3–7 Phao**: one of the sea-nymphs added by S. to the Nereides

at IV xi 49.5 but here named from the Gk φάος, light. Her viewing **all men** suggests Malecasta's erotic gazing at i 41.6–9. Presumably, the lover of **Ptolomæe**, the second-century Alexandrian astronomer and geographer who built her the glass tower so that she could see without being seen. **discoure**: discover. **9 peaze**: heavy blow.

Stanza 21

3–5 This feature explains why Britomart sees Artegall in the mirror: he invades her kingdom. **8** The mirror has the power to **bewray**, i.e. reveal, **treasons** within, and **conuince**, i.e. expose or convict and hence overpower, **foes** without.

Stanza 22

4 She shares the title given to Una at I xii 21.3. **5–6** In Plato, *Phaedrus* 255d, the lover is said to be a mirror in which he beholds himself; cf. the 'mirrour perilous' (*Romaunt of the Rose* 1601–04) in which Narcissus sees himself. Britomart's inward-looking gaze projects an image of beauty, an idealized self-projection, which arouses love for Artegall; hence the vision of him follows. As it brings self-division, she compares herself to Narcissus at 44.6–9. Gregerson 1993:16 sees the second as 'another version of the narcissistic first'. **7–9** The mirror's change from reflection to transparency (indicated by **againe**) is a feature of glass, which may have been a novelty to S. A Lacanian analysis of the change is given by Bellamy 1992:203–07. **auizing**: remembering.

Stanza 23

4 buxome: yielding. **7 any one**: i.e. any particular person.

24

Eftsoones there was presented to her eye
　A comely knight, all arm'd in complete wize,
　Through whose bright ventayle lifted vp on hye
　His manly face, that did his foes agrize,
　And frends to termes of gentle truce entize,
　Lookt foorth, as *Phœbus* face out of the east,
　Betwixt two shady mountaynes doth arize;
　Portly his person was, and much increast
Through his Heroicke grace, and honorable gest.

25

His crest was couered with a couchant Hownd,
　And all his armour seemd of antique mould,
　But wondrous massy and assured sownd,
　And round about yfretted all with gold,
　In which there written was with cyphres old,
　Achilles armes, which Arthogall did win.
　And on his shield enueloped seuenfold
　He bore a crowned litle Ermilin,
That deckt the azure field with her fayre pouldred skin.

26

The Damzell well did vew his Personage,
　And liked well, ne further fastned not,
　But went her way; ne her vnguilty age
　Did weene, vnwares, that her vnlucky lot

Lay hidden in the bottome of the pot;
　Of hurt vnwist most daunger doth redound:
　But the false Archer, which that arrow shot
　So slyly, that she did not feele the wound,
Did smyle full smoothly at her weetlesse wofull stound.

27

Thenceforth the fether in her lofty crest,
　Ruffed of loue, gan lowly to auaile,
　And her prowd portaunce, and her princely gest,
　With which she earst tryumphed, now did quaile:
　Sad, solemne, sowre, and full of fancies fraile
　She woxe; yet wist she nether how, nor why,
　She wist not, silly Mayd, what she did aile,
　Yet wist, she was not well at ease perdy,
Yet thought it was not loue, but some melancholy.

28

So soone as Night had with her pallid hew
　Defaste the beautie of the shyning skye,
　And reft from men the worldes desired vew,
　She with her Nourse adowne to sleepe did lye;
　But sleepe full far away from her did fly:
　In stead thereof sad sighes, and sorrowes deepe
　Kept watch and ward about her warily,
　That nought she did but wayle, and often steepe
Her dainty couch with teares, which closely she did weepe.

Stanza 24
Britomart's vision of Artegall is patterned on Arthur's vision of the Faerie Queene: 'From that day forth I lou'd that face diuyne' (I ix 15.5). It impels them on their quests.　**2** I.e. he is armed cap-à-pie, as Arthur at I vii 29.6, and Guyon at II i 5.8.　**3 ventayle**: the beaver, or movable part of a helmet that a knight lifts up to be identified, as at IV vi **25**.8–9 and V viii 12.5.　**4–5** As said of Guyon at II i 6.3–4. **agrize**: terrify. **frends**: used generally of those who become allies; cf. 19.5. **8–9 Portly**: handsome, dignified.　**gest**: bearing.

Stanza 25
The description is given in the style of an Elizabethan *impresa*-portrait, as Leslie 1985:28–29 notes.　**1 couchant**: a heraldic term for lying with the body resting on the legs and the head lifted up ready to spring. The **Hownd** may herald the victory over 'the pagan hound' (V viii 42.5) who is Philip II of Spain. **4 yfretted**: adorned; in heraldry, interlaced. **5 cyphres**: characters.　**6** As Mandricardo won the arms of Hector, in Ariosto, *Orl. Fur.* 14.31. The first of many references to declare that Artegall, being a Briton and therefore a descendant of the Trojans, is greater than their enemy, Achilles.　**7–9** This classical shield is carried by Guyon; see II v 6.3n. **Ermilin**: ermine, a heraldic term for white powdered with spots, here in the shape of an ermine, a traditional emblem of chastity. The crowned ermine is associated with British royalty, specifically with the Virgin Queen, e.g. the 'Ermine' portrait, which displays an ermine with a crown around its neck; see Strong 1963:plate 21b. In *SC Apr.* 57–58, Elissa appears 'like a may-den Queene' in 'Ermines white'.　**azure**: associated with the heavens, as in the stock phrase, 'azure sky' (IV xii 1.4), here symbolizing 'heauenly iustice' (V ii 36.1). Dunseath 1968:58 cites the shield of justice with its field blue in Legh, *Accendence*

of Armorie (1591).　**pouldred**: powdered, but unspotted, as **fayre** suggests.

Stanza 26
1 Personage: image.　**2** I.e. she gave no further thought to him, being only at that second stage of loving: 'I saw and liked, I liked but loued not' (Sidney, *Astrophil and Stella* 2.5). **3 vnguilty**: S.'s only use of the term. It suggests that she will soon reach the guilty age when 'she | in loue with him did fall' (Arg.).　**4–5 vnwares**: immediately; or as she was unwary. Merlin explains Britomart's plight more decorously at iii 24.1–5.　**6 redound**: proceed, arise.　**9 stound**: time of trial.

Stanza 27
1–4 lofty crest: the symbol of knightly prowess; cf. iv 7.3, ix 20.3, and see I vii 32.1n.　**Ruffed**: ruffled; suggesting 'made rough'.　**auaile**: fall, drop down (applied to the helmet). **portaunce**: demeanour. **quaile**: decline. In effect, she becomes crest-fallen.　**5 Sad, solemne**: the dominant mood of the male knight; see I i 2.8n.　**sowre**: applied to those in love at 17.6.　**full of fancies fraile**: as Amoret in the house of Busirane suffers all the 'phantasies | In wauering wemens witt' (xii 26.3–4).　**7 silly**: innocent.　**9 melancholy**: her state is that of love-melancholy for which she displays all the traditional symptoms analysed in Burton, *Anat.* 3.2.1.2. See 'melancholy' in the *SEnc.*

Stanza 28
1 pallid: apparently coined by S. from Lat. *pallidus*, pale. As one would expect from a poet of light and life, the term is associated with night and death, as at V xi 45.5.　**8–9** Cf. Ps. 6.6: 'I cause my bed euery night to swimme, and watter my couche with my teares'.　**closely**: secretly.

29

And if that any drop of slombring rest
    Did chaunce to still into her weary spright,
    When feeble nature felt her selfe opprest,
    Streight way with dreames, and with fantastick sight
    Of dreadfull things the same was put to flight,
    That oft out of her bed she did astart,
    As one with vew of ghastly feends affright:
    Tho gan she to renew her former smart,
And thinke of that fayre visage, written in her hart.

30

One night, when she was tost with such vnrest,
    Her aged Nourse, whose name was *Glauce* hight,
    Feeling her leape out of her loathed nest,
    Betwixt her feeble armes her quickly keight,
    And downe againe her in her warme bed dight;
    Ah my deare daughter, ah my dearest dread,
    What vncouth fit (sayd she) what euill plight
    Hath thee opprest, and with sad drearyhead
Chaunged thy liuely cheare, and liuing made thee dead?

31

For not of nought these suddein ghastly feares
    All night afflict thy naturall repose,
    And all the day, when as thine equall peares
    Their fit disports with faire delight doe chose,
    Thou in dull corners doest thy selfe inclose,
    Ne tastest Princes pleasures, ne doest spred
    Abroad thy fresh youths fayrest flowre, but lose
    Both leafe and fruite, both too vntimely shed,
As one in wilfull bale for euer buried.

32

The time, that mortall men their weary cares
    Do lay away, and all wilde beastes do rest,
    And euery riuer eke his course forbeares,
    Then doth this wicked euill thee infest,

And riue with thousand throbs thy thrilled brest;
    Like an huge *Aetn'* of deepe engulfed gryefe,
    Sorrow is heaped in thy hollow chest,
    Whence foorth it breakes in sighes and anguish ryfe,
As smoke and sulphure mingled with confused stryfe.

33

Ay me, how much I feare, least loue it bee,
    But if that loue it be, as sure I read
    By knowen signes and passions, which I see,
    Be it worthy of thy race and royall sead,
    Then I auow by this most sacred head
    Of my deare foster childe, to ease thy griefe,
    And win thy will: Therefore away doe dread;
    For death nor daunger from thy dew reliefe
Shall me debarre, tell me therefore my liefest liefe.

34

So hauing sayd, her twixt her armes twaine
    Shee streightly straynd, and colled tenderly,
    And euery trembling ioynt, and euery vaine
    Shee softly felt, and rubbed busily,
    To doe the frosen cold away to fly;
    And her faire deawy eies with kisses deare
    Shee ofte did bathe, and ofte againe did dry;
    And euer her importund, not to feare
To let the secret of her hart to her appeare.

35

The Damzell pauzd, and then thus fearfully;
    Ah Nurse, what needeth thee to eke my paine?
    Is not enough, that I alone doe dye,
    But it must doubled bee with death of twaine?
    For nought for me, but death there doth remaine.
    O daughter deare (said she) despeire no whit,
    For neuer sore, but might a salue obtaine:
    That blinded God, which hath ye blindly smit,
Another arrow hath your louers hart to hit.

Stanza 29

2 **still**: distil; also as the dew of sleep makes her still.   **4 fantastick**: i.e. produced by her fancy.   **6 astart**: start up.

Stanzas 30–51

An imitation, at times very close, of the pseudo-Virgilian *Ciris* 220–377, which tells how the aged Carme counsels the love-stricken Scylla. In place of that lust-crazed woman willing to destroy her own city, S. substitutes Carme's virgin daughter, Britomartis, whose flight into the sea to escape Minos's lust associates her with chastity.

Stanza 30

2 **Glauce**: the mother of Diana in Cicero, *De natura deorum* 3.58. Since Britomart is associated with Minerva (see ix 22), her nurse may be associated with the traditional companion of that goddess, the owl (Gk γλαύξ, γλαυκός); see Aptekar 1969:189, A. Fowler 1964:126*n*4. Or the name may derive

from γλαυκή, grey, referring to her age, for her common epithet is 'aged' or 'old'. See 'Glauce' in the *SEnc*.   **5 dight**: placed.   **8 drearyhead**: sorrow.

Stanza 32

4 **infest**: assail; infect; swarm about.   **5 thrilled**: pierced; affected with emotion.

Stanza 33

2 **read**: discern.   **9 liefest liefe**: dearest love.

Stanza 34

2 **streightly straynd**: tightly clasped.   **colled**: embraced. 6–7 As Venus bathes Adonis's eyes with kisses at i 36.4.

Stanza 35

2 **eke**: increase.   7 The proverb (Smith 672) does not apply to Britomart's love, as Glauce learns at iii 5.1–5.

36

But mine is not (quoth she) like other wownd;
  For which no reason can finde remedy.
  Was neuer such, but mote the like be fownd,
  (Said she) and though no reason may apply
  Salue to your sore, yet loue can higher stye,
  Then reasons reach, and oft hath wonders donne.
  But neither God of loue, nor God of skye
  Can doe (said she) that, which cannot be donne.
Things ofte impossible (quoth she) seeme ere begonne.

37

These idle wordes (said she) doe nought aswage
  My stubborne smart, but more annoiaunce breed.
  For no no vsuall fire, no vsuall rage
  Yt is, O Nourse, which on my life doth feed,
  And sucks the blood, which from my hart doth bleed.
  But since thy faithfull zele lets me not hyde
  My crime, (if crime it be) I will it reed.
  Nor Prince, nor pere it is, whose loue hath gryde
My feeble brest of late, and launched this wound wyde.

38

Nor man it is, nor other liuing wight;
  For then some hope I might vnto me draw,
  But th'only shade and semblant of a knight,
  Whose shape or person yet I neuer saw,
  Hath me subiected to loues cruell law:
  The same one day, as me misfortune led,
  I in my fathers wondrous mirrhour saw,
  And pleased with that seeming goodly-hed,
Vnwares the hidden hooke with baite I swallowed.

[handwritten annotation: neo-platonic ideal]

39

Sithens it hath infixed faster hold
  Within my bleeding bowells, and so sore
  Now ranckleth in this same fraile fleshly mould,
  That all mine entrailes flow with poisnous gore,

[handwritten annotation: love makes one sick?]

And th'vlcer groweth daily more and more;
  Ne can my ronning sore finde remedee,
  Other then my hard fortune to deplore,
  And languish as the leafe faln from the tree,
Till death make one end of my daies and miseree.

40

Daughter (said she) what need ye be dismayd,
  Or why make ye such Monster of your minde?
  Of much more vncouth thing I was affrayd;
  Of filthy lust, contrary vnto kinde:
  But this affection nothing straunge I finde;
  For who with reason can you aye reproue,
  To loue the semblaunt pleasing most your minde,
  And yield your heart, whence ye cannot remoue?
No guilt in you, but in the tyranny of loue.

41

Not so th'*Arabian Myrrhe* did sett her mynd,
  Nor so did *Biblis* spend her pining hart,
  But lou'd their natiue flesh against al kynd,
  And to their purpose vsed wicked art:
  Yet playd *Pasiphaë* a more monstrous part,
  That lou'd a Bul, and learnd a beast to bee;
  Such shamefull lusts who loaths not, which depart
  From course of nature and of modestee?
Swete loue such lewdnes bands from his faire companee.

42

But thine my Deare (welfare thy heart my deare)
  Though straunge beginning had, yet fixed is
  On one, that worthy may perhaps appeare;
  And certes seemes bestowed not amis:
  Ioy thereof haue thou and eternall blis.
  With that vpleaning on her elbow weake,
  Her alablaster brest she soft did kis,
  Which all that while shee felt to pant and quake,
As it an Earth-quake were, at last she thus bespake.

Stanza 36
An accomplished handling of stichomythia with the lines carefully distributed: 2 + 4, 2 + 1. **2 For which**: i.e. mine is such for which. **5 stye**: ascend. **7 God of skye**: 'sky-ruling Ioue' at VI x 22.1.

Stanza 37
3 Upton 1758 conj. 'For know', but **no no** conveys the intensity of Britomart's passion. **7 reed**: tell. **8 pere**: member of the nobility. **gryde**: pierced. **9 launched**: cut.

Stanza 38
3 But only the illusion and image of a knight. **8 goodly-hed**: goodly appearance.

Stanza 39
1 Sithens: since that time. **2–5** In contrast to Bk II which treats the body largely from the waist up (see II ix 29*n*), Bk III includes the body's lower half, here specifically the bowels as the seat of love and compassion. Britomart's moment of falling in love is associated with the onset of menstruation – see

Hamilton 1961a:142, Wofford 1988:9, Silberman 1995:20 – leading Glauce to diagnose her complaint as a young woman's green-sickness. **2 bleeding bowells**: cf. 'troubled bowels' (iv 8.9). **3 ranckleth** describes the incurable wound of love in Arthur at I ix 7.4, and in Marinell at IV xii 22.7. **fleshly mould**: the body.

Stanza 40
2 The **Monster** is seen in the 'monstrous formes' (xi 51.7) of love in the house of Busirane, and finally in Isis's crocodile at V vii 6.8–9, 15–16.

Stanza 41
1–6 Abetted by her nurse, **th'Arabian Myrrhe** tricked her father into committing incest with her (Ovid, *Met.* 10.431–80). See 'Myrrha' in the *SEnc*. On her story in relation to Britomart, see Nohrnberg 1976:442–50, and Rapaport 1986:162–68. The reference, from *Ciris* 238–40, leads to a second traditional example of an unnatural love, **Biblis**, who lusted after her brother (*Met.* 9.454–634), and to an example of bestial love, **Pasiphaë**, who enjoyed a bull by positioning

43

Beldame, your words doe worke me litle ease;
  For though my loue be not so lewdly bent,
  As those ye blame, yet may it nought appease
  My raging smart, ne ought my flame relent,
  But rather doth my helpelesse griefe augment.
  For they, how euer shamefull and vnkinde,
  Yet did possesse their horrible intent:
  Short end of sorowes they therby did finde;
So was their fortune good, though wicked were their minde.

44

But wicked fortune mine, though minde be good,
  Can haue no end, nor hope of my desire,
  But feed on shadowes, whiles I die for food,
  And like a shadow wexe, whiles with entire
  Affection, I doe languish and expire.
  I fonder, then *Cephisus* foolish chyld,
  Who hauing vewed in a fountaine shere
  His face, was with the loue thereof beguyld;
I fonder loue a shade, the body far exyld.

45

Nought like (quoth shee) for that same wretched boy
  Was of him selfe the ydle Paramoure;
  Both loue and louer, without hope of ioy,
  For which he faded to a watry flowre.
  But better fortune thine, and better howre,
  Which lou'st the shadow of a warlike knight;
  No shadow, but a body hath in powre:
  That body, wheresoeuer that it light,
May learned be by cyphres, or by Magicke might.

46

But if thou may with reason yet represse
  The growing euill, ere it strength haue gott,
  And thee abandond wholy doe possesse,
  Against it strongly striue, and yield thee nott,
  Til thou in open fielde adowne be smott.
  But if the passion mayster thy fraile might,
  So that needs loue or death must bee thy lott,
  Then I auow to thee, by wrong or right
To compas thy desire, and find that loued knight.

47

Her chearefull words much cheard the feeble spright
  Of the sicke virgin, that her downe she layd
  In her warme bed to sleepe, if that she might;
  And the old-woman carefully displayd
  The clothes about her round with busy ayd,
  So that at last a litle creeping sleepe
  Surprisd her sence: Shee therewith well apayd,
  The dronken lamp down in the oyl did steepe,
And sett her by to watch, and sett her by to weepe.

48

Earely the morrow next, before that day
  His ioyous face did to the world reuele,
  They both vprose, and tooke their ready way
  Vnto the Church, their praiers to appele,
  With great deuotion, and with litle zele:
  For the faire Damzell from the holy herse
  Her loue-sicke hart to other thoughts did steale;
  And that old Dame said many an idle verse,
Out of her daughters hart fond fancies to reuerse.

---

herself within a model of a cow (*Met.* 9.735–40). **9 bands**: bans; banishes (sugg. by the context).

Stanza 42
1 Cf. the Red Cross Knight's benediction, 10.8. **7** As Paglia 1990:181 observes, 'these intimacies are maternal and then some'. **8–9** Continuing the image at 32.6–9. The derangement of the earth's body in an earthquake was related to the derangement of the human body by violent emotion; see Heninger 1960:130–31.

Stanza 43
1 Beldame: good mother (a respectful form of address). **4 relent**: abate, cool. **6 vnkinde**: contrary to nature, 'against al kynd' (41.3). **7 possesse**: gain.

Stanza 44
1 minde: echoing **mine** and answering 40.2; cf. 41.1. **4 entire**: sincere; complete; blameless. The emphasis on that word, by separating it from its subject, is designed to contrast her with Myrrha and her ilk. **6–9 Cephisus foolish chyld**: Narcissus. See Ovid, *Met.* 3.407–36, and 'Narcissus' in the *SEnc*. **fonder**: more foolish (Ovid's *credule*); more loving. He loved the shadow thinking it substance (417) while she loves only a shadow not knowing whom it reflects. **shere**: clear.

Stanza 45
2 ydle: vain; unable to act (in contrast to Britomart who may act). **4 watry flowre**: the narcissus 'that likes the watry shore' (vi 45.5). **6 shadow**: reflected image; playing on 'shadowes' (44.3). **7 in powre**: i.e. casting and therefore controlling it. **9 cyphres**: 'characters', specifically, the 'cyphres old' (25.5) on Artegall's armour. The **Magicke might** proves to be Merlin's at iii 11.8.

Stanza 46
1–5 The Nurse returns to her exchange with Britomart at 36 on the inability of reason, i.e. temperance, to control love. **possesse**: suggesting demonic possession by the god of love; cf. 36.4–6. Line 5 is expanded in the battle between Britomart and Artegall at IV vi, specifically 12–13, 19.

Stanza 47
7 apayd: satisfied. **8 dronken lamp**: because it drinks oil; translating *bibulum . . . lumen* (*Ciris* 344).

Stanza 48
3 ready: direct. **4 appele**: offer. **6 herse**: ceremony. **8 verse**: incantation or charm, as Busirane's 'sad verse' at xii 36.4. **9 reuerse**: turn away, in the etymological sense.

49

Retourned home, the royall Infant fell
    Into her former fitt; for why no powre,
    Nor guidaunce of her selfe in her did dwell.
    But th'aged Nourse her calling to her bowre,
    Had gathered Rew, and Sauine, and the flowre
    Of *Camphora*, and Calamint, and Dill,
    All which she in a earthen Pot did poure,
    And to the brim with Colt wood did it fill,
And many drops of milk and blood through it did spill.

50

Then taking thrise three heares from off her head,
    Them trebly breaded in a threefold lace,
    And round about the Pots mouth, bound the thread,
    And after hauing whispered a space
    Certein sad words, with hollow voice and bace,
    Shee to the virgin sayd, thrise sayd she itt;
    Come daughter come, come; spit vpon my face,
    Spitt thrise vpon me, thrise vpon me spitt;
Th'vneuen nomber for this busines is most fitt.

51

That sayd, her rownd about she from her turnd,
    She turned her contrary to the Sunne,
    Thrise she her turnd contrary, and returnd,
    All contrary; for she the right did shunne,
    And euer what she did, was streight vndonne.
    So thought she to vndoe her daughters loue:
    But loue, that is in gentle brest begonne,
    No ydle charmes so lightly may remoue,
That well can witnesse, who by tryall it does proue.

52

Ne ought it mote the noble Mayd auayle,
    Ne slake the fury of her cruell flame,
    But that shee still did waste, and still did wayle,
    That through long languour, and hart-burning brame
    She shortly like a pyned ghost became,
    Which long hath waited by the Stygian strond.
    That when old *Glauce* saw, for feare least blame
    Of her miscarriage should in her be fond,
She wist not how t'amend, nor how it to withstond.

[handwritten marginal note: sickness as virtue rather than sin]

Stanza 49

1 Infant: Princess; used elsewhere only for Arthur; see II viii
56.1–3*n*. **2 for why**: because. **3** She is guided by Cupid;
see iv 9.6–8*n*. **5–9** For Carme's narcissus, cassia, and savoury
herbs, in *Ciris* 369–70, Glauce substitutes English equivalents.
Maplet 1930 notes that **Rew** is 'the Medicinable Herbe' (104);
Sauine is used 'to remedie and help all griefs in the inward
partes and bowels' (105); **Calamint** or Mint 'stoppeth and
stencheth all kinde of swellings' (91); and **Dill** is 'a hinderance
to issue' (75). In discussing the cure of love melancholy,
Burton, *Anat. Mel.* 3.2.5.1, records that **Camphora** is most
inimical to lust. **Colt wood**: *hippomanes*, one of the herbs
used by the priestess, in Virgil, *Aen.* 4.515–16, to exorcize
Dido's love for Aeneas; see 'magic, amatory' in the *SEnc*. The
milk and blood, also used by Medea in Ovid, *Met.* 7.245–47,
are added to propitiate Hecate. On Glauce's white magic, see
P. Cheney 1988:15–16.

Stanza 50

5 sad: serious, solemn. **7 spit vpon my face**: S.'s imitation of
Carme's injunction to Scylla, *ter in gremium mecum despue*
(*Ciris* 372), seems a schoolboy's joke, esp. when followed by
her comic withershins.

Stanza 51

7–9 It was generally allowed that magic has no power over
love. Cf. Amoret's resistance to Busirane's charms at xi 16.6–
17.4. In *SC Aug.* 104, Willye laments that 'love is a curelesse
sorrowe'.

Stanza 52

4 languour: affliction. **brame**: desire. **5–6 long hath waited**:
because it is unable to cross the Styx until its body has been
buried or its death avenged; see I iii 36.6*n*. **8 miscarriage**:
failure in managing.

Cant. III.

Merlin bewrayes to Britomart,
The state of Arthegall.
And shews the famous Progeny
Which from them springen shall.

1

M Ost sacred fyre, that burnest mightily
  In liuing brests, ykindled first aboue,
Emongst th'eternall spheres and lamping sky,
And thence pourd into men, which men call Loue;
Not that same, which doth base affections moue
In brutish mindes, and filthy lust inflame,
But that sweete fit, that doth true beautie loue,
And choseth vertue for his dearest Dame,
Whence spring all noble deedes and neuer dying fame:

2

Well did Antiquity a God thee deeme,
  That ouer mortall mindes hast so great might,
To order them, as best to thee doth seeme,
And all their actions to direct aright;
The fatall purpose of diuine foresight,
Thou doest effect in destined descents,
Through deepe impression of thy secret might,
And stirredst vp th'Heroes high intents,
Which the late world admyres for wondrous moniments.

3

But thy dredd dartes in none doe triumph more,
  Ne brauer proofe in any, of thy powre
Shew'dst thou, then in this royall Maid of yore,
Making her seeke an vnknowne Paramoure,
From the worlds end, through many a bitter stowre:
From whose two loynes thou afterwardes did rayse
Most famous fruites of matrimoniall bowre,
Which through the earth haue spredd their liuing prayse,
That fame in tromp of gold eternally displayes.

4

Begin then, O my dearest sacred Dame,
  Daughter of *Phœbus* and of *Memorye*,
That doest ennoble with immortall name
The warlike Worthies, from antiquitye,
In thy great volume of Eternitye:
Begin, O *Clio*, and recount from hence
My glorious Soueraines goodly auncestrye,
Till that by dew degrees and long protense,
Thou haue it lastly brought vnto her Excellence.

Book III Canto iii

Argument
1 bewrayes: reveals.

Stanza 1
The subject of this stanza is prompted in the reference at ii 51.7 to 'loue, that is in gentle brest begonne'. It uses the familiar neoplatonic distinctions between heavenly love, human love, and bestial love, with the twin doctrines that love is the desire for beauty and that virtue is expressed in beauty. Yet love does not lead, neoplatonically, to heaven but to virtuous action on earth; see Ellrodt 1960:34. It is one and the same power but appears differently in the 'baser wit' and 'braue sprite' (v 1.4, 8). The distinction implicit in 7–8 between the love of true beauty and the love of virtue leads to the separate stories of Florimell and the False Florimell; see i 49.8–9n. On the conjunction of beauty–love–virtue, see 'beauty' in the *SEnc*. **3 lamping**: shining; coined by S. from Ital. *lampante*. **4 men**: used generically, for only women in the poem love without lust, as Una at I vii 49.8, the Faerie Queene at ix 14.3, and Britomart at III ii 51.7–9. **5 affections**: passions.

Stanza 2
1 As Phaedrus, in Plato, *Symposium* 178a, claims that love is a great god. **5 fatall**: ordained by fate. Cf. 'th'eternall

might' that guides Arthur 'through fatal deepe foresight' (I ix 6.8, 7.1). **6 destined descents**: lines of descent fixed by fate. **9** The 'antique world' is often praised by S.; see V proem 1*n*.

Stanza 3
2 brauer: more glorious. **4 Paramoure**: lover. **5 stowre**: struggle; time of turmoil. **7 matrimoniall bowre**: in deliberate contrast to the Bower of Bliss.

Stanza 4
Cf. the invocation at I xi 5.6–9 (and see *n*). **4 Worthies**: the Nine Worthies, though S. boasts at ix 50.9 that the three British 'all the antique Worthies merits far did passe'. **6 O Clio**: for the first time S. names his muse, as Roche 1989:166 notes. On her role as the muse of history, see Roche 177–88. Her **great volume of Eternitye** is the 'euerlasting scryne' of I proem 2.3; cf. Eumnestes's 'immortall scrine' at II ix 56.6. **8 dew degrees**: as 'destined descents' (2.6) to stress the Queen's legitimate succession. **protense**: extension in time (from Lat. *protendere*, to stretch forth); or a shortened form of 'protension'. pretence *1596* is an unfortunate (and most dangerous) slip. **9 lastly**: at the end, ultimately.

5

Full many wayes within her troubled mind,
　　Old *Glauce* cast, to cure this Ladies griefe:
　　Full many waies she sought, but none could find,
　　Nor herbes, nor charmes, nor counsel that is chiefe,
　　And choisest med'cine for sick harts reliefe:
　　For thy great care she tooke, and greater feare,
　　Least that it should her turne to fowle repriefe,
　　And sore reproch, when so her father deare
Should of his dearest daughters hard misfortune heare.

6

At last she her auisde, that he, which made
　　That mirrhour, wherein the sicke Damosell
　　So straungely vewed her straunge louers shade,
　　To weet, the learned *Merlin*, well could tell,
　　Vnder what coast of heauen the man did dwell,
　　And by what means his loue might best be wrought:
　　For though beyond the *Africk Ismael*,
　　Or th'Indian *Peru* he were, she thought
Him forth through infinite endeuour to haue sought.

7

Forthwith them selues disguising both in straunge
　　And base atyre, that none might them bewray,
　　To *Maridunum*, that is now by chaunge
　　Of name *Cayr-Merdin* cald, they tooke their way:
　　There the wise *Merlin* whylome wont (they say)
　　To make his wonne, low vnderneath the ground,
　　In a deepe delue, farre from the vew of day,
　　That of no liuing wight he mote be found,
When so he counseld with his sprights encompast round.

8

And if thou euer happen that same way
　　To traueill, go to see that dreadfull place:
　　It is an hideous hollow caue (they say)
　　Vnder a Rock that lyes a litle space

From the swift *Barry*, tombling downe apace,
　　Emongst the woody hilles of *Dyneuowre*:
　　But dare thou not, I charge, in any cace,
　　To enter into that same balefull Bowre,
For feare the cruell Feendes should thee vnwares deuowre.

9

But standing high aloft, low lay thine eare,
　　And there such ghastly noyse of yron chaines,
　　And brasen Caudrons thou shalt rombling heare,
　　Which thousand sprights with long enduring paines
　　Doe tosse, that it will stonn thy feeble braines,
　　And oftentimes great grones, and grieuous stownds,
　　When too huge toile and labour them constraines:
　　And oftentimes loud strokes, and ringing sowndes
From vnder that deepe Rock most horribly rebowndes.

10

The cause some say is this: A litle whyle
　　Before that *Merlin* dyde, he did intend,
　　A brasen wall in compas to compyle
　　About *Cairmardin*, and did it commend
　　Vnto these Sprights, to bring to perfect end.
　　During which worke the Lady of the Lake,
　　Whom long he lou'd, for him in hast did send,
　　Who thereby forst his workemen to forsake,
Them bownd till his retourne, their labour not to slake.

11

In the meane time through that false Ladies traine,
　　He was surprisd, and buried vnder beare,
　　Ne euer to his worke returnd againe:
　　Nath'lesse those feends may not their work forbeare,
　　So greatly his commandement they feare,
　　But there doe toyle and traueile day and night,
　　Vntill that brasen wall they vp doe reare:
　　For *Merlin* had in Magick more insight,
Then euer him before or after liuing wight.

Stanza 5

2 cast: considered. **4–5** These three means are used by the witch at vii 21.2. On **counsel** as **choisest med'cine**, see I vii 40.8, II i 44.2–3. **6–9** The repetition of ii 52.7–8 indicates that a digression follows. **For thy**: therefore. **care**: concern; grief. **repriefe**: reproof.

Stanza 6

1 her auisde: recalled. **5 coast**: region. **7–8 the Africk Ismael**: northern Africa, so called because the Saracens were held to be descendants of Ishmael. Named as the southern boundary of faery land. Its western boundary is **th'Indian Peru**; see II proem 2.6n. At II x 72.5–6, they are named India and America. On the boundaries of empire, see V x 3.6–7.

Stanza 7

2 bewray: discover; betray. **3–6 Cayr-Merdin**: Carmarthen in Wales; i.e. Merlin's Fort. **they say**: i.e. the chroniclers; see 26–50n. **7 deepe delue**: corresponding to Merlin's *grotta* in Ariosto, *Orl. Fur.* 3.10, which Bradamante visits to hear his

prophecy (16–19) of her royal progeny, such as Britomart now hears from him. **9 counseld**: took counsel.

Stanzas 8–11

A whimsical interlude; hence the tag 'they say' (8.3) repeated from 7.5; cf. 'some say' (10.1), 'men say' (13.1). Merlin's story is found in Malory 4.1. Bono 1984:77 notes that S.'s wry humour in describing the cave into which Britomart and Glauce descend contrasts with the horror of the classical descent into hell, such as Aeneas's in Virgil, *Aen.* 6.

Stanza 8

4–6 a litle space: more than 50 miles, according to Osgood (*Var* 3.224–25), who also notes that Dynevor Castle lies some 14 miles upstream on the river that runs through Carmarthen, and that the Towy, not the Barry, should have been named.

Stanza 9

6 stownds: roars; suggesting roars provoked by pain. **7 constraines**: afflicts.

12

For he by wordes could call out of the sky
  Both Sunne and Moone, and make them him obay:
  The Land to sea, and sea to maineland dry,
  And darksom night he eke could turne to day:
  Huge hostes of men he could alone dismay,
  And hostes of men of meanest thinges could frame,
  When so him list his enimies to fray:
  That to this day for terror of his fame,
The feends do quake, when any him to them does name.

13

And sooth, men say that he was not the sonne
  Of mortall Syre, or other liuing wight,
  But wondrously begotten, and begonne
  By false illusion of a guilefull Spright,
  On a faire Lady Nonne, that whilome hight
  Matilda, daughter to *Pubidius*,
  Who was the Lord of *Mathraual* by right,
  And coosen vnto king *Ambrosius*:
Whence he indued was with skill so merueilous.

14

They here ariuing, staid a while without,
  Ne durst aduenture rashly in to wend,
  But of their first intent gan make new dout
  For dread of daunger, which it might portend:
  Vntill the hardy Mayd (with loue to frend)
  First entering, the dreadfull Mage there fownd
  Deepe busied bout worke of wondrous end,
  And writing straunge characters in the grownd,
With which the stubborne feendes he to his seruice bownd.

15

He nought was moued at their entraunce bold:
  For of their comming well he wist afore,
  Yet list them bid their businesse to vnfold,
  As if ought in this world in secrete store
  Were from him hidden, or vnknowne of yore.
  Then *Glauce* thus, Let not it thee offend,
  That we thus rashly through thy darksom dore,
  Vnwares haue prest: for either fatall end,
Or other mightie cause vs two did hether send.

16

He bad tell on; And then she thus began.
  Now haue three Moones with borrowd brothers light,
  Thrise shined faire, and thrise seemd dim and wan,
  Sith a sore euill, which this virgin bright
  Tormenteth, and doth plonge in dolefull plight,
  First rooting tooke; but what thing it mote bee,
  Or whence it sprong, I can not read aright:
  But this I read, that but if remedee,
Thou her afford, full shortly I her dead shall see.

17

Therewith th'Enchaunter softly gan to smyle
  At her smooth speeches, weeting inly well,
  That she to him dissembled womanish guyle,
  And to her said, Beldame, by that ye tell,
  More neede of leach-crafte hath your Damozell,
  Then of my skill: who helpe may haue elswhere,
  In vaine seekes wonders out of Magick spell.
  Th'old woman wox half blanck, those words to heare;
And yet was loth to let her purpose plaine appeare.

Stanza 10
3 in compas: in a circle. **compyle**: build. **4 commend**: commit to their charge. **9 slake**: slacken.

Stanza 11
1–2 The Lady's **traine**, i.e. treachery, is described by Malory 4.1 as 'her subtyle wyrchynge' when she had Merlin go **vnder beare**, i.e. 'vnder a grete stone'.

Stanza 12
A secular analogue to the power God gave Fidelia at I x 20. Similarly, Arthur's shield defeats armies of men, terrifies the heavens, and changes men into stones, dust, and nothing at all (I vii 34–35). In Virgil, *Ecl.* 8.69, songs are said to have the power to draw the moon from the sky. On the diabolism of Merlin's art, see Fike 1999:91–93. **5 dismay**: defeat. **7 fray**: terrify; attack.

Stanza 13
Geoffrey of Monmouth 1891:6.18 records that an incubus in the shape of a young man lay with Merlin's mother who lived among nuns. S. invents her name **Matilda** – on which see VI iv 29.3*n* – and also her father's name. **3 begotten, and begonne** suggest two stages of conception and birth; or procreation and conception; cf. 'begot, and bred' (vi 6.1). **7–8 Mathraual**: one of the three divisions of Wales. **coosen**:

kinsman. **Ambrosius**: the brother of Uther, named at II x 67.2.

Stanza 14
5 to frend: as a friend. Cf. the Red Cross Knight who goes forward 'with God to frend' at I i 28.7. **6 Mage**: magician. **8 characters**: letters with the magical power to bind his fiends, as she surprises Busirane 'Figuring straunge characters of his art' (xii 31.2) to bind Amoret. Cf. Christ's act on confronting the accusers of the adulterous woman: he 'stouped downe, and with his finger wrote on the grounde' (John 8.6). **9 stubborne**: untamable, fierce; cf. Archimago's power to tame sprites at I i 43.7.

Stanza 15
8 fatall end: 'fatall purpose' (2.5); cf. 19.7, 21.6.

Stanza 16
2–3 On this period of gestation, see I viii 38.6–7*n*. **7 read**: guess. **8 read**: predict. **but if**: unless.

Stanza 17
1 th'Enchaunter: Merlin shares this title with Archimago, e.g. I ii Arg.; but in contrast also to 'the vile Enchaunter' Busirane (xii 31.1), he applies his magic to good ends. **5 leach-crafte**: medical healing.

18

And to him said, Yf any leaches skill,
    Or other learned meanes could haue redrest
    This my deare daughters deepe engraffed ill,
    Certes I should be loth thee to molest:
    But this sad euill, which doth her infest,
    Doth course of naturall cause farre exceed,
    And housed is within her hollow brest,
    That either seemes some cursed witches deed,
Or euill spright, that in her doth such torment breed.

19

The wisard could no lenger beare her bord,
    But brusting forth in laughter, to her sayd;
    Glauce, what needes this colourable word,
    To cloke the cause, that hath it selfe bewrayd?
    Ne ye fayre *Britomartis*, thus arayd,
    More hidden are, then Sunne in cloudy vele;
    Whom thy good fortune, hauing fate obayd,
    Hath hether brought, for succour to appele:
The which the powres to thee are pleased to reuele.

20

The doubtfull Mayd, seeing her selfe descryde,
    Was all abasht, and her pure yuory
    Into a cleare Carnation suddeine dyde;
    As fayre *Aurora* rysing hastily,
    Doth by her blushing tell, that she did lye
    All night in old *Tithonus* frosen bed,
    Whereof she seemes ashamed inwardly.
    But her olde Nourse was nought dishartened,
But vauntage made of that, which *Merlin* had ared.

21

And sayd, Sith then thou knowest all our griefe,
    (For what doest not thou knowe?) of grace I pray,
    Pitty our playnt, and yield vs meet reliefe.
    With that the Prophet still awhile did stay,

And then his spirite thus gan foorth display;
    Most noble Virgin, that by fatall lore
    Hast learn'd to loue, let no whit thee dismay
    The hard beginne, that meetes thee in the dore,
And with sharpe fits thy tender hart oppresseth sore.

22

For so must all things excellent begin,
    And eke enrooted deepe must be that Tree,
    Whose big embodied braunches shall not lin,
    Till they to heuens hight forth stretched bee.
    For from thy wombe a famous Progenee
    Shall spring, out of the auncient Troian blood,
    Which shall reuiue the sleeping memoree
    Of those same antique Peres, the heuens brood,
Which *Greeke* and *Asian* riuers stayned with their blood.

23

Renowmed kings, and sacred Emperours,
    Thy fruitfull Ofspring, shall from thee descend;
    Braue Captaines, and most mighty warriours,
    That shall their conquests through all lands extend,
    And their decayed kingdomes shall amend:
    The feeble Britons, broken with long warre,
    They shall vpreare, and mightily defend
    Against their forren foe, that commes from farre,
Till vniuersall peace compound all ciuill iarre.

24

It was not, *Britomart*, thy wandring eye,
    Glauncing vnwares in charmed looking glas,
    But the streight course of heuenly destiny,
    Led with eternall prouidence, that has
    Guyded thy glaunce, to bring his will to pas:
    Ne is thy fate, ne is thy fortune ill,
    To loue the prowest knight, that euer was.
    Therefore submit thy wayes vnto his will,
And doe by all dew meanes thy destiny fulfill.

Stanza 18

2 redrest: healed. **3 engraffed ill**: cf. 'engraffed payne' (ii 17.5). Glauce's evasions distinguish Alma's external foes, who could be controlled by temperance aided by grace in Arthur because she 'had not yet felt *Cupides* wanton rage' (II ix 18.2), from Britomart's far greater **euill**, her love for Artegall, which has become **deepe engraffed** in her. **5 infest**: assail; infect. Cf. ii 32.4.

Stanza 19

1 bord: idle tale; deception. **3 colourable**: deceiving.

Stanza 20

1 doubtfull: apprehensive. **descryde**: revealed. **3–7** At I ii 7 and xi 51, the coming of Aurora associates Una with the coming of light but here Britomart's blushing reveals her hidden desires and fears; see Krier 1990:166–69. **Carnation** is cited as a symbol of love; see Rydén 1978. Also, as a var. of 'coronation', a symbol of royalty; hence it is associated with Elizabeth in *SC Apr.* 138. **9 vauntage**: opportunity. **ared**: divined.

Stanza 21

2 of grace: as a favour. **4 still**: a solemn state, in contrast to the Sibyl's frenzy in Virgil, *Aen.* 6.78–80. **5 display**: pour forth. **6 fatall lore**: the teaching of fate; cf. 2.5, 19.7. **7–9** I.e. 'do not let the hard beginning in any way dismay you', referring (prophetically) to the flames at the entrance to the house of Busirane which leave her 'dismayd' (xi 22.1).

Stanza 22

1–4 enrooted extends the image of Britomart's grief since love 'First rooting tooke' (16.6). **embodied**: a tree composed of human bodies, as the Tree of Jesse which terminated – ironically for S.'s use here – in the Virgin and Child rather than 'a royall Virgin' (49.6) without progeny. Cf. iv 3.6–9. **lin**: cease. Line 4 is repeated from II x 2.5 where the first part of the story is told. **5–6** As in the Arg. but adding **out of . . . blood** to make the polemical stand that in Wales is found 'the true remnant of the ancient Britons' (Sidney, *Defence of Poetry* 76) who are descendants of the Trojans through Brute. **8 heuens brood**: referring to the divine origin of the Trojans; cf. 'sacred progeny' (II x 36.1). **9 their**: i.e. the Greek and Asian enemies.

25

But read (saide *Glauce*) thou Magitian
    What meanes shall she out seeke, or what waies take?
    How shall she know, how shall she finde the man?
    Or what needes her to toyle, sith fates can make
    Way for themselues, their purpose to pertake?
    Then *Merlin* thus, Indeede the fates are firme,
    And may not shrinck, though all the world do shake:
    Yet ought mens good endeuours them confirme,
And guyde the heauenly causes to their constant terme.

26

The man whom heauens haue ordaynd to bee
    The spouse of *Britomart*, is *Arthegall*:
    He wonneth in the land of *Fayeree*,
    Yet is no *Fary* borne, ne sib at all
    To Elfes, but sprong of seed terrestriall,
    And whylome by false *Faries* stolne away,
    Whyles yet in infant cradle he did crall;
    Ne other to himselfe is knowne this day,
But that he by an Elfe was gotten of a Fay.

27

But sooth he is the sonne of *Gorlois*,
    And brother vnto *Cador* Cornish king,
    And for his warlike feates renowmed is,
    From where the day out of the sea doth spring,
    Vntill the closure of the Euening.
    From thence, him firmely bound with faithfull band,
    To this his natiue soyle thou backe shalt bring,
    Strongly to ayde his countrey, to withstand
The powre of forreine Paynims, which invade thy land.

28

Great ayd thereto his mighty puissaunce,
    And dreaded name shall giue in that sad day:
    Where also proofe of thy prow valiaunce
    Thou then shalt make, t'increase thy louers pray.
    Long time ye both in armes shall beare great sway,
    Till thy wombes burden thee from them do call,
    And his last fate him from thee take away,
    Too rathe cut off by practise criminall,
Of secrete foes, that him shall make in mischiefe fall.

Stanza 23
A summary of Merlin's prophecy up to the 'sacred Peace' of Elizabeth's reign at 49.1–5. On the dangers of S.'s use of political prophecy, see van Es 2000:8–11, 28–31. **1** On the distinction, see I ii 22.7–9*n*. **5 amend**: restore. **9 compound**: settle.

Stanza 24
3 streight: strict; straight, in contrast to **wandring**. Cf. Luke 3.4: 'Prepare ye the way of the Lord: make his paths straight'. **5 Guyded thy glaunce**: on the significance of the image, see DuRocher 1993:335–39. **6** Answering Britomart's complaints against **fortune** at ii 38.6, 39.7, and 44.1. **7** Arthur is so praised at II viii 18.3 and xi 30.6. **8–9** S. stresses the cooperation of predestination and free will rather than their traditional opposition; see I v 25.5*n*. Accordingly, **his will** (5) is God's and **his will** (8) is Artegall's. By submitting to Artegall's will, Britomart brings God's will to its 'constant terme' (25.9), i.e. to its fixed goal or end. Cf. Ps. 37.5: 'Commit thy waye vnto the Lord . . . and he shal bring it to passe'.

Stanza 25
Of Glauce's five questions, the last invokes a popular classical tag, *Fata viam invenient*, which Merlin answers by declaring that the work of fate and human will are subject to the will of providence. See McCabe 1989a:186–87. On the three **fates**, see IV ii 48 and *n*. **1 read**: declare. **5 pertake**: fulfil (sugg. by the context).

Stanzas 26–50
For Merlin's chronicle, S. continues to draw on Geoffrey 1891, Holinshed 1807–08, and Hardyng 1812; see II x Arg.1–2*n*. His use of them, which is analysed by Harper 1910:142–68 (abstracted in *Var* 3.228–34), is cited only when noteworthy. S.'s chief literary antecedents are the vision that Anchises reveals to Aeneas of his descendants up to the rule of Augustus who brought peace to the world (*Aen.* 6.756–853), and the vision that Melissa, inspired by Merlin, reveals to Bradamante of her descendants, the house of Este (*Orl. Fur.* 3.23–59). The vision revealed to Britomart begins with the historical Artegall in the sixth century – and therefore with his half-brother, Arthur – and concludes with Merlin's rapturous sight of the coming of Elizabeth roughly a thousand years later. The first cycle of sixteen stanzas (26–41), divided by Berger 1988:121–24 into two cycles of eight stanzas, ends with the triumph of the Saxons over the Britons. After a stanza of Merlin's lament, a second cycle of eight stanzas (43–50) covers the 800 years until the restoration of the rule of the Britons in the house of Tudor (see 44.5–6). On Elizabeth's Arthurian descent, see Millican 1932:37–105.

Stanza 26
2 Arthegall: on the 'historical' Arthgallo in Geoffrey, see V i 3*n*. Arthgal of Cargueit or Warguit (Warwick) is included in his list of consuls who attend Arthur (9.12), and is cited by Hardyng 1812:137 as a knight of the Round Table. **4 sib**: kin. **6–7** At I x 65, a similar story is told of the Red Cross Knight who was brought from '*Britans* land'. **8–9** As Arthur is ignorant of his lineage at I ix 3.

Stanza 27
The chronicle at II x 5–68 ends with the succession of Uther Pendragon. Geoffrey 1891:8.19 tells how he lusted after Igerna – called 'the Lady Igrayne' in the *LR* 30 – wife of Gorlois, Duke of Cornwall: transformed by Merlin into the likeness of her husband, he lay with her and begot Arthur. See also Malory 1.2. The classical analogue is Jove's similar deception of Alcmena that led to the birth of Hercules. Since Artegall is the legitimate son of Gorlois, he is half-brother to Arthur. Accordingly, he is 'Art-egall' or 'equal to Arthur', taking Arthur's place in the chronicle, as Harper 1910:144 notes. **6 From thence**: from faery land. **9 forreine Paynims**: the Saxons, Britons' 'forren foe' (23.8); see 52.5–9.

Stanza 28
Cf. the prophecy by the priest of Isis at V vii 23. **3 prow valiaunce**: brave valour. **4 pray**: prey, spoils. **8–9** Who killed Artegall, or how, is not revealed, but his death may parallel Arthur's through Mordred's treachery in Malory 21. **Too rathe**: too soon or prematurely. **practise**: treachery. **9 mischiefe**: evil plight.

29

With thee yet shall he leaue for memory
  Of his late puissaunce, his ymage dead,
  That liuing him in all actiuity
  To thee shall represent. He from the head
  Of his coosen *Constantius* without dread
Shall take the crowne, that was his fathers right,
  And therewith crowne himselfe in th'others stead:
  Then shall he issew forth with dreadfull might,
Against his Saxon foes in bloody field to fight.

30

Like as a Lyon, that in drowsie caue
  Hath long time slept, himselfe so shall he shake,
  And comming forth, shall spred his banner braue
  Ouer the troubled South, that it shall make
  The warlike *Mertians* for feare to quake:
Thrise shall he fight with them, and twise shall win,
  But the third time shall fayre accordaunce make:
  And if he then with victorie can lin,
He shall his dayes with peace bring to his earthly In.

31

His sonne, hight *Vortipore*, shall him succeede
  In kingdome, but not in felicity;
  Yet shall he long time warre with happy speed,
  And with great honour many batteills try:
  But at the last to th'importunity
Of froward fortune shall be forst to yield.
  But his sonne *Malgo* shall full mightily
  Auenge his fathers losse, with speare and shield,
And his proud foes discomfit in victorious field.

32

Behold the man, and tell me *Britomart*,
  If ay more goodly creature thou didst see;
  How like a Gyaunt in each manly part
  Beares he himselfe with portly maiestee,
  That one of th'old *Heroes* seemes to bee:
He the six Islands, comprouinciall
  In auncient times vnto great Britainee,
  Shall to the same reduce, and to him call
Their sondry kings to doe their homage seuerall.

33

All which his sonne *Careticus* awhile
  Shall well defend, and *Saxons* powre suppresse,
  Vntill a straunger king from vnknowne soyle
  Arriuing, him with multitude oppresse;
  Great *Gormond*, hauing with huge mightinesse
Ireland subdewd, and therein fixt his throne,
  Like a swift Otter, fell through emptinesse,
  Shall ouerswim the sea with many one
Of his Norueyses, to assist the Britons fone.

34

He in his furie all shall ouerronne,
  And holy Church with faithlesse handes deface,
  That thy sad people vtterly fordonne,
  Shall to the vtmost mountaines fly apace:
  Was neuer so great waste in any place,
Nor so fowle outrage doen by liuing men:
  For all thy Cities they shall sacke and race,
  And the greene grasse, that groweth, they shall bren,
That euen the wilde beast shall dy in starued den.

Stanza 29
Since Arthur died without issue, S. deuises a plausible yet
deliberately vague line of descent from him to his nephew,
Constantius, son of his half-brother Cador; then to another
nephew, Conan, son of his other half-brother Artegall; and
then to Conan's son, Vortipore. Artegall's son is not named
but Geoffrey 1891:11.4–5 records that Conanus (or Conan)
killed his cousin, Constantine, who had succeeded Arthur as
king. See Hume 1984:152–53.

```
       Gorlois = Igrayne       = Uther Pendragon
                 |                  |
      ┌──────────┼──────────┐       |
   Artegall    Cador      Arthur
      |           |
   Conan      Constantius (or Constantine)
      |
   Vortipore
```

2 his ymage dead: the image of him (Artegall) when he is
dead. The same elliptical expression is found at v 54.9, *Am*
33.4. **3 in all actiuity**: i.e. as he really was, as shown in his
actions.

Stanza 30
1–2 Holinshed 1807–08:1.583 cites Gildas's comparison of
Conan to a lion's whelp. The simile is biblical: Jacob prophe-
sies the victory of Judah who comes 'as a lions whelpe' (Gen.
49.9); cf. V vii 23.7–9. **3 shall spred his banner**: an action
that provokes terror, as in Song Sol. 6.3: 'terrible as an armie

with banners'. **4–9** S. invents Conan's wars against the
Mertians who are warlike because of their name. Hence the
folklore motif of three attempts, and the odd use of **if** in a
prophecy. **lin**: leave off.

Stanza 31
3 **speed**: success. 4 **try**: undergo, experience. 5 **importunity**:
cruelty; grievous demands. 7 S. invents this relationship,
perhaps to legitimize the northern European Union. 9 **dis-
comfit**: entirely defeat.

Stanza 32
1–5 **Behold the man**: a resonant biblical phrase from John
19.5. Geoffrey 1891:11.7 says that Malgo was the most hand-
some of men and of great strength. **th'old Heroes**: a highly
approbatory term, as IV xi 13.2 and *DS* 8.4. 6 **comprouin-
ciall**: belonging to the same province. 8 **reduce**: make sub-
ject. 9 **seuerall**: particular; or (as adv.) separately.

Stanza 33
1–2 S. improves upon history by claiming genealogical succes-
sion and by making **Careticus** at first triumphant. 3–9 The
simile is S.'s, playing upon **Gormond**: gourmand, glutton.
oppresse: overwhelm. **Norueyses**: Norwegians. **fone**: earlier
pl. of 'foe'.

Stanza 34
2 **deface**: ruin, lay waste. 7 **race**: raze. 9 **in starued den**:
i.e. starved in its den.

35

Whiles thus thy Britons doe in languour pine,
   Proud *Etheldred* shall from the North arise,
   Seruing th'ambitious will of *Augustine*,
   And passing *Dee* with hardy enterprise,
   Shall backe repulse the valiaunt *Brockwell* twise,
   And *Bangor* with massacred Martyrs fill;
   But the third time shall rew his foolhardise:
   For *Cadwan* pittying his peoples ill,
Shall stoutly him defeat, and thousand *Saxons* kill.

36

But after him, *Cadwallin* mightily
   On his sonne *Edwin* all those wrongs shall wreake;
   Ne shall auaile the wicked sorcery
   Of false *Pellite*, his purposes to breake,
   But him shall slay, and on a gallowes bleak
   Shall giue th'enchaunter his vnhappy hire:
   Then shall the Britons, late dismayd and weake,
   From their long vassallage gin to respire,
And on their Paynim foes auenge theirranckled ire.

37

Ne shall he yet his wrath so mitigate,
   Till both the sonnes of *Edwin* he haue slayne,
   Offricke and *Osricke*, twinnes vnfortunate,
   Both slaine in battaile vpon Layburne playne,
   Together with the king of *Louthiane*,
   Hight *Adin*, and the king of *Orkeny*,
   Both ioynt partakers of their fatall payne:
   But *Penda*, fearefull of like desteny,
Shall yield him selfe his liegeman, and sweare fealty.

38

Him shall he make his fatall Instrument,
   T'afflict the other *Saxons* vnsubdewd;
   He marching forth with fury insolent
   Against the good king *Oswald*, who indewd

With heauenly powre, and by Angels reskewd,
   Al holding crosses in their hands on hye,
   Shall him defeate withouten blood imbrewd:
   Of which, that field for endlesse memory,
Shall *Heuenfield* be cald to all posterity.

39

Whereat *Cadwallin* wroth, shall forth issew,
   And an huge hoste into Northumber lead,
   With which he godly *Oswald* shall subdew,
   And crowne with martiredome his sacred head.
   Whose brother *Oswin*, daunted with like dread,
   With price of siluer shall his kingdome buy,
   And *Penda* seeking him adowne to tread,
   Shall tread adowne, and doe him fowly dye,
But shall with guifts his Lord *Cadwallin* pacify.

40

Then shall *Cadwallin* die, and then the raine
   Of *Britons* eke with him attonce shall dye;
   Ne shall the good *Cadwallader* with paine,
   Or powre, be hable it to remedy,
   When the full time prefixt by destiny,
   Shalbe expird of *Britons* regiment.
   For heuen it selfe shall their successe enuy,
   And them with plagues and murrins pestilent
Consume, till all their warlike puissaunce be spent.

41

Yet after all these sorrowes, and huge hills
   Of dying people, during eight yeares space,
   Cadwallader not yielding to his ills,
   From *Armoricke*, where long in wretched cace
   He liu'd, retourning to his natiue place,
   Shalbe by vision staide from his intent:
   For th'heauens haue decreed, to displace
   The *Britons*, for their sinnes dew punishment,
And to the *Saxons* ouer-giue their gouernment.

Stanza 35

1 **languour**: woeful plight; or 'long vassallage' (36.8).
3 **Augustine**: the first Archbishop of Canterbury. Even in the seventh century, the papal emissary was the enemy of the Britons and therefore of 'holy Church' (34.2). 6 **massacred**: stressed by S. on the second syllable. 7 **foolhardise**: foolhardiness.

Stanza 36

2 **his sonne**: i.e. Ethelred's son. 5–6 S. substitutes hanging for Geoffrey's stabbing. **hire**: reward. 7 **dismayd**: defeated; discouraged. 8 **respire**: recover courage.

Stanza 37

7 **fatall payne**: i.e. the pain of death; or endeavours that resulted in death.

Stanza 38

3 **insolent**: proud, arrogant. 4–5 History records only that the 'godly *Oswald*' (39.3) set up a cross on the battlefield; for S., he heralds a more famous 'godly knight' (II i 2.3), also a

Saxon, who was **indewd** [i.e. invested] | **With heauenly powre**. 7 **imbrewd**: i.e. being spilled, or staining their hands.

Stanza 39

5 **like dread**: dread of suffering the like. 6 **buy**: ransom. 7–8 I.e. Oswin, whom Penda sought to tread down, will tread him down and kill him.

Stanza 40

2 To hasten **the full time**, S. ignores the twelve years that Cadwallader ruled peacefully. 6 **regiment**: rule. 7 **enuy**: begrudge. 8 **murrins**: pestilences.

Stanza 41

4 **Armoricke**: Armorica, i.e. Brittany. Cf. II x 64.5. 5–9 Geoffrey 1891:12.17 records that an angel told Cadwallader that 'God was not willing that the Britons should reign any longer in the island, before the time came of which Merlin prophetically foretold Arthur'. **retourning**: i.e. intending to return. **ouer-giue**: give over.

42

Then woe, and woe, and euerlasting woe,
  Be to the Briton babe, that shalbe borne,
  To liue in thraldome of his fathers foe;
  Late king, now captiue, late lord, now forlorne,
  The worlds reproch, the cruell victors scorne,
  Banisht from princely bowre to wasteful wood:
  O who shal helpe me to lament, and mourne
The royall seed, the antique *Troian* blood,
Whose empire lenger here, then euer any stood.

43

The Damzell was full deepe empassioned,
  Both for his griefe, and for her peoples sake,
  Whose future woes so plaine he fashioned,
  And sighing sore, at length him thus bespake;
  Ah but will heuens fury neuer slake,
  Nor vengeaunce huge relent it selfe at last?
  Will not long misery late mercy make,
But shall their name for euer be defaste,
And quite from off the earth their memory be raste?

44

Nay but the terme (sayd he) is limited,
  That in this thraldome *Britons* shall abide,
  And the iust reuolution measured,
  That they as Straungers shalbe notifide.
  For twise fowre hundreth yeares shalbe supplide,
  Ere they vnto their former rule restor'd shalbee,
  And their importune fates all satisfide:
Yet during this their most obscuritee,
Their beames shall ofte breake forth, that men then faire
                        (may see.

45

For *Rhodoricke*, whose surname shalbe Great,
  Shall of him selfe a braue ensample shew,
  That Saxon kings his frendship shall intreat;
  And *Howell Dha* shall goodly well indew

The saluage minds with skill of iust and trew;
  Then *Griffyth Conan* also shall vp reare
  His dreaded head, and the old sparkes renew
Of natiue corage, that his foes shall feare,
Least back againe the kingdom he from them should
                        (beare.

46

Ne shall the Saxons selues all peaceably
  Enioy the crowne, which they from Britons wonne
  First ill, and after ruled wickedly:
  For ere two hundred yeares be full outronne,
  There shall a Rauen far from rising Sunne,
  With his wide wings vpon them fiercely fly,
  And bid his faithlesse chickens oueronne
The fruitfull plaines, and with fell cruelty,
In their auenge, tread downe the victors surquedry.

47

Yet shall a third both these, and thine subdew;
  There shall a Lion from the sea-bord wood
  Of *Neustria* come roring, with a crew
  Of hungry whelpes, his battailous bold brood,
  Whose clawes were newly dipt in cruddy blood,
  That from the Daniske Tyrants head shall rend
  Th'vsurped crowne, as if that he were wood,
And the spoile of the countrey conquered
Emongst his young ones shall diuide with bountyhed.

48

Tho when the terme is full accomplishid,
  There shall a sparke of fire, which hath long-while
  Bene in his ashes raked vp, and hid,
  Bee freshly kindled in the fruitfull Ile
  Of *Mona*, where it lurked in exile;
  Which shall breake forth into bright burning flame,
  And reach into the house, that beares the stile
Of roiall maiesty and soueraine name;
So shall the Briton blood their crowne agayn reclame.

Stanza 42
1 The language of Rev. 8.13: 'Wo, wo, wo, to the inhabitants of the earth'. **6 wasteful**: desolate. **9** About 1800 years from the arrival of Brutus, *c.* 1100 BC, and the death of Cadwaller in AD 689, according to Geoffrey.

Stanza 43
2 In Geoffrey 1891:7.3, Merlin bursts into tears when his prophetical spirit reveals the disasters that will befall the Britons. **9 raste**: erased.

Stanza 44
3 **the iust reuolution**: the full cycle; cf. 48.1. **4 Straungers**: in the biblical sense as used, e.g. by Jeremiah in prophesying to the Jews that 'ye may liue a long time in the land where ye be strangers' (35.7). **notifide**: denoted, known. **5** The interval between Cadwallader's death and Henry VII's succession in 1485 is about 800 years, double the time that God's seed 'shulde be a soiourner in a strange land [Egypt]' (Acts 7.6). **supplide**: completed. **7 importune**: grievous; cruel.

Stanza 45
The reigns of the three Welsh kings cover almost three hundred years of the interregnum of the rule of the Britons, and their resistance to the Saxons heralds the coming of Arthur from North Wales (I ix 4) and Britomart from South Wales (III ii 18.4). As ancestors of the founder of the Tudors, they have their place as ancestors of Elizabeth. In the absence of any English or Latin source, Bruce 1985:466 suggests that S. drew upon a Welsh ms.; see 48.2–5*n*. **5 skill**: knowledge.

Stanza 46
5–9 The **Rauen** of the arms of Denmark; **his faithlesse chickens**, the heathen brood of Danes. **auenge**: vengeance. **surquedry**: arrogance.

Stanza 47
2–4 The **Lion . . . | Of Neustria** is William the Conqueror who led the Norman Conquest of England in 1066. The image is taken from Merlin's speech in Geoffrey 1891:7.3. **sea-bord**: bordering on the sea. **5 cruddy**: clotted. **7 wood**: insane. **9 bountyhed**: liberality.

49

Thenceforth eternall vnion shall be made
  Betweene the nations different afore,
  And sacred Peace shall louingly persuade
  The warlike minds, to learne her goodly lore,
  And ciuile armes to exercise no more:
  Then shall a royall Virgin raine, which shall
  Stretch her white rod ouer the *Belgicke* shore,
  And the great Castle smite so sore with all,
That it shall make him shake, and shortly learne to fall.

50

But yet the end is not. There *Merlin* stayd,
  As ouercomen of the spirites powre,
  Or other ghastly spectacle dismayd,
  That secretly he saw, yet note discoure:
  Which suddein fitt, and halfe extatick stoure
  When the two fearefull wemen saw, they grew
  Greatly confused in behaueoure;
  At last the fury past, to former hew
Hee turnd againe, and chearfull looks did shew.

51

Then, when them selues they well instructed had
  Of all, that needed them to be inquird,
  They both conceiuing hope of comfort glad,
  With lighter hearts vnto their home retird;

Where they in secret counsell close conspird,
  How to effect so hard an enterprize,
  And to possesse the purpose they desird:
  Now this, now that twixt them they did deuize,
And diuerse plots did frame, to maske in strange disguise.

52

At last the Nourse in her foolhardy wit
  Conceiud a bold deuise, and thus bespake;
  Daughter, I deeme that counsel aye most fit,
  That of the time doth dew aduauntage take;
  Ye see that good king *Vther* now doth make
  Strong warre vpon the Paynim brethren, hight
  Octa and *Oza*, whome hee lately brake
  Beside *Cayr Verolame*, in victorious fight,
That now all *Britany* doth burne in armes bright.

53

That therefore nought our passage may empeach,
  Let vs in feigned armes our selues disguize,
  And our weake hands (need makes good schollers) teach
  The dreadfull speare and shield to exercize:
  Ne certes daughter that same warlike wize
  I weene, would you misseeme; for ye beene tall,
  And large of limbe, t'atchieue an hard emprize,
  Ne ought ye want, but skil, which practize small
Wil bring, and shortly make you a mayd Martiall.

Stanza 48
The restoration of the rule of the Britons, which Merlin prophesied at 44, was fulfilled with the victory at Bosworth Field of Henry of Richmond, the future Henry VII who was born in the Isle of Anglesey (**Mona**). J.L. Mills 1976:283–84 counts 81 chronicle stanzas – 63 (II x 5–68) + 18 (III iii 29–47, omitting stanza 43) – leading to the advent of the Tudors, that number being the third climacteric or critical age in British history. See II x 5–68.2*n*. **2–5** The image may be indebted to the Carmarthen poet Lewis Glyn Cothi; see Millican 1932:144 and Bruce 1985:466. **his ashes**: referring to the **sparke of fire** and therefore to the Britons. **7 stile**: title.

Stanza 49
1 eternall vnion: the term suggests *imperium sine fine*, referring primarily to the Act of Union of England and Wales in 1536. **2 different**: differing. **5 ciuile armes**: civil dissension between England and Wales, and within England, as in the War of the Roses; cf. 'ciuill iarre' (23.9). **6–9** The **royall Virgin** is Elizabeth who was celebrated for preserving **sacred Peace** in England during her reign. Her **white rod** or sceptre, as at II ii 40.4–5, suggests Mercury's caduceus – called a 'white rod' by T. Cooper 1565 – used to make peace; see IV iii 42.1–7*n*. It is also the traditional symbol of royal power that she wielded over the **Belgicke shore** in defending the Netherlands, shown when Mercilla sends Arthur to aid Belge at V x 6–xi 35. It is held by her Lord Deputy in Ireland; see the frontispiece to John Derricke, *The Image of Ireland* (1581). See V vii 7.4–5*n*. On Elizabeth as the Mercurian monarch, see Brooks-Davies 1983:1–14. **the great Castle** alludes to Philip II, whose arms, as he was King of Castile, show a castle. In *DS* 8.7, S. refers to the Spanish Armada as 'those huge castles of Castilian king'.

Stanza 50
1 Merlin cites Christ's words to his disciples telling them of the things that must come to pass before the end of the world: 'but the end is not yet' (Matt. 24.6). **5 halfe extatick stoure**: Merlin's earlier ecstatic trance after the quiet beginning (see 21.4–5) and the grief of his lament at 42 suggest a vision that he **note discoure**, i.e. he could not reveal, either because S. does not know what will happen; or because Merlin was overcome by his vision of the future British Empire; or because he saw **other ghastly spectacle**, such as the chaos that would follow if the Queen died without a successor (sugg. Dobin 1990:6, J. Watkins 1995:154–55, and J. Watkins 2000:158–62). Whatever it is, there is no return to the golden age, as in Ariosto, *Orl. Fur.* 3.18.

Stanza 51
2 I.e. of all they needed to ask. **7 possesse**: achieve. **9** Britomart is seen in 'straunge | And base atyre' at 7.1–2; cf. IV i 14.8, V vii 21.1.

Stanza 52
5–9 These events, freely adapted from Geoffrey 1891: 8.18–24, surround his account of the birth of Arthur at 19–20: **lately** to the time when Octa and Oza were taken prisoners by Uther at Mount Damen (18); **now** to the present time when, having gained their freedom, they are being attacked by him at **Cayr Verolame** or St Albans (22–23). In *Time* 113–116, Verulam recalls the defeat of the Saxon general who had occupied her city. S. conflates the two battles in order to connect them to the end of the chronicle at II x 67–68. **brake**: defeated.

Stanza 53
1 empeach: hinder. **2 feigned**: i.e. serving to disguise. **3** The *1596* revision – (whom need new strength shall

54

And sooth, it ought your corage much inflame,
To heare so often, in that royall hous,
From whence to none inferior ye came:
Bards tell of many wemen valorous,
Which haue full many feats aduenturous,
Performd, in paragone of proudest men:
The bold *Bunduca*, whose victorious
Exployts made *Rome* to quake, stout *Guendolen*,
Renowmed *Martia*, and redoubted *Emmilen*.

55

And that, which more then all the rest may sway,
Late dayes ensample, which these eyes beheld,
In the last field before *Meneuia*
Which *Vther* with those forrein Pagans held,
I saw a *Saxon* Virgin, the which feld
Great *Vlfin* thrise vpon the bloodly playne,
And had not *Carados* her hand withheld
From rash reuenge, she had him surely slayne,
Yet *Carados* himselfe from her escapt with payne.

56

Ah read, (quoth *Britomart*) how is she hight?
Fayre *Angela* (quoth she) men do her call,
No whit lesse fayre, then terrible in fight:
She hath the leading of a Martiall
And mightie people, dreaded more then all
The other *Saxons*, which doe for her sake
And loue, themselues of her name *Angles* call.
Therefore faire Infant her ensample make
Vnto thy selfe, and equall corage to thee take.

57

Her harty wordes so deepe into the mynd
Of the yong Damzell sunke, that great desire
Of warlike armes in her forthwith they tynd,
And generous stout courage did inspyre,

That she resolu'd, vnweeting to her Syre,
Aduent'rous knighthood on her selfe to don,
And counseld with her Nourse, her Maides attyre
To turne into a massy habergeon,
And bad her all things put in readinesse anon.

58

Th'old woman nought, that needed, did omit;
But all thinges did conueniently puruay:
It fortuned (so time their turne did fitt)
A band of Britons ryding on forray
Few dayes before, had gotten a great pray
Of Saxon goods, emongst the which was seene
A goodly Armour, and full rich aray,
Which long'd to *Angela*, the Saxon Queene,
All fretted round with gold, and goodly wel beseene.

59

The same, with all the other ornaments,
King *Ryence* caused to be hanged hy
In his chiefe Church, for endlesse moniments
Of his successe and gladfull victory:
Of which her selfe auising readily,
In th'euening late old *Glauce* thether led
Faire *Britomart*, and that same Armory
Downe taking, her therein appareled,
Well as she might, and with braue bauldrick garnished.

60

Beside those armes there stood a mightie speare,
Which *Bladud* made by Magick art of yore,
And vsd the same in batteill aye to beare;
Sith which it had beene here preseru'd in store,
For his great vertues proued long afore:
For neuer wight so fast in sell could sit,
But him perforce vnto the ground it bore:
Both speare she tooke, and shield, which hong by it;
Both speare and shield of great powre, for her purpose fit.

---

teach) – improves the sense but destroys the syntax, as *Var* 3.423 notes. **4 exercize**: use. **6 misseeme**: misbecome. **7 emprize**: enterprise. **8–9** The contradiction with ii 6 where Britomart tells the Red Cross Knight that after being weaned she was trained in martial skill is noted by Candido 1977 as evidence of revision. **a mayd Martiall**: at this point Britomart forsakes one etymology of her name for a more comprehensive one; see i 8.6*n*.

Stanza 54
6 paragone: emulation. **7–9** The first three have their place in the Briton chronicle at II x 54–56, 18–20, and 42 respectively. **Emmilen** may be the Queen of Cornwall and mother of Tristram at VI ii 29.

Stanza 55
3 last field: when fighting the Saxons at **Meneuia**, Uther learns of the death of Aurelius – see II x 67–68 – from whom he inherits the throne. **5–9** The chronicles provide barely more than the name, Angela, for the story about the **Saxon**

Virgin, as Harper 1910:168 notes. The help given Uther by **Great Vlfin** (Ulfius) to bed Igerna in the disguise of her recently slain husband is sufficient reason for Britomart to wear the armour of **a Saxon Virgin**. **payne**: difficulty.

Stanza 56
1 read: tell. **6–7** For other etymologies of England, see ix 47.9.

Stanza 57
1 harty: bold (cf. 52.2); also as they give her heart or courage. **3 tynd**: kindled. **4 generous**: high-born (cf. 54.1–3); high-spirited. **8 habergeon**: a sleeveless coat of mail.

Stanza 58
2 conueniently: fittingly. **puruay**: furnish. **5 pray**: plunder. **9** Artegall's armour is similarly adorned at ii 25.4. The only other character so attired is Praysdesire at II ix 37.2. **goodly wel beseene**: of good appearance.

61

Thus when she had the virgin all arayd,
  Another harnesse, which did hang thereby,
  About her selfe she dight, that the yong Mayd
  She might in equall armes accompany,
  And as her Squyre attend her carefully:
  Tho to their ready Steedes they clombe full light,
  And through back waies, that none might them espy,
  Couered with secret cloud of silent night,
Themselues they forth conuaid, and passed forward right.

62

Ne rested they, till that to Faery lond
  They came, as *Merlin* them directed late:
  Where meeting with this *Redcrosse* knight, she fond
  Of diuerse thinges discourses to dilate,
  But most of *Arthegall*, and his estate.
  At last their wayes so fell, that they mote part:
  Then each to other well affectionate,
  Frendship professed with vnfained hart,
The *Redcrosse* knight diuerst, but forth rode *Britomart*.

Stanza 59
5 auising readily: seeing ready at hand. **7 Armory**: armour. **9 braue bauldrick**: a chief emblem of knighthood elsewhere worn only by Arthur at I vii 29.8, and Belphœbe at II iii 29.5.

Stanza 60
1 a mightie speare: see i 7.9*n*. **2 Bladud**: a Briton king whose magical powers are told at II x 25–26. The powers of the Saxons and the Britons are thus united in Britomart's armour. **7 perforce**: forcibly.

Stanza 61
2 harnesse: suit of armour. **6 clombe**: see iv 61.6*n*. **9 conuaid**: stole away. **forward right**: while the phrase is applied to Guyon at II xii 53.4, it is characteristic of Britomart; see iv 18.1–3*n*.

Stanza 62
1–2 As Merlin is said to have sent Arthur to faery land at I ix 7.1–2. **5 estate**: state, fortune. **7–8** Stressing the bond between chastity and holiness, as again at iv 4.4–5. See i 12.7–9*n*. **9 diuerst**: turned aside; cf. iv 4.6–9. **forth**: 'forward right' (61.9), to signal the renewed beginning of her quest; cf. iv 5.1.

Cant. IIII.

Bold Marinell of Britomart,
Is throwne on the Rich strond:
Faire Florimell of Arthure is
Long followed, but not fond.

1

WHere is the Antique glory now become,
    That whylome wont in wemen to appeare?
Where be the braue atchieuements doen by some?
Where be the batteilles, where the shield and speare,
And all the conquests, which them high did reare,
That matter made for famous Poets verse,
And boastfull men so oft abasht to heare?
Beene they all dead, and laide in dolefull herse?
Or doen they onely sleepe, and shall againe reuerse?

2

If they be dead, then woe is me therefore:
    But if they sleepe, O let them soone awake:
    For all too long I burne with enuy sore,
    To heare the warlike feates, which *Homere* spake
    Of bold *Penthesilee*, which made a lake
    Of *Greekish* blood so ofte in *Troian* plaine;
    But when I reade, how stout *Debora* strake
    Proud *Sisera*, and how *Camill'* hath slaine
The huge *Orsilochus*, I swell with great disdaine.

3

Yet these, and all that els had puissaunce,
    Cannot with noble *Britomart* compare,
    Aswell for glorie of great valiaunce,
    As for pure chastitie and vertue rare,
    That all her goodly deedes do well declare.
    Well worthie stock, from which the branches sprong,
    That in late yeares so faire a blossome bare,
    As thee, O Queene, the matter of my song,
Whose lignage from this Lady I deriue along.

4

Who when through speaches with the *Redcrosse* knight,
    She learned had th'estate of *Arthegall*,
    And in each point her selfe informd aright,
    A frendly league of loue perpetuall
    She with him bound, and *Congé* tooke withall.
    Then he forth on his iourney did proceede,
    To seeke aduentures, which mote him befall,
    And win him worship through his warlike deed,
Which alwaies of his paines he made the chiefest meed.

5

But *Britomart* kept on her former course,
    Ne euer dofte her armes, but all the way
    Grew pensiue through that amarous discourse,
    By which the *Redcrosse* knight did earst display
    Her louers shape, and cheualrous aray;
    A thousand thoughts she fashiond in her mind,
    And in her feigning fancie did pourtray
    Him such, as fittest she for loue could find,
Wise, warlike, personable, courteous, and kind.

6

With such selfe-pleasing thoughts her wound she fedd,
    And thought so to beguile her grieuous smart;
    But so her smart was much more grieuous bredd,
    And the deepe wound more deep engord her hart,
    That nought but death her dolour mote depart.
    So forth she rode without repose or rest,
    Searching all lands and each remotest part,
    Following the guydaunce of her blinded guest,
Till that to the seacoast at length she her addrest.

Book III Canto iv

Stanza 1
S. continues his defence of women, esp. of Elizabeth; see ii 1–3
(and *n*). The stanza is structured on the elegiac *ubi sunt* topos,
as the repeated **where** indicates. **1 become**: gone. **9**
reuerse: return.

Stanza 2
4–9 Not Homer but Virgil, in *Aen.* 1.490–93, describes
Penthesilee (and see II iii 31.5–9), and at 11.690–98 tells how
Camill' slew **Orsilochus**. For **Debora**, see Judg. 4: through
her the Lord delivered **Sisera** into the hands of Jáel who drove
a tent-pin into his temple. As a cult-name of Elizabeth, see
E.C. Wilson 1939:61–95. **9 disdaine**: i.e. either pride for

women, or contempt for men; or indignation that he does not
have such matter for his song.

Stanza 3
4 The first reference to Britomart's chastity, made explicit now
that her love for Artegall is known. **pure** is strongly assertive,
perhaps because chastity may be queried in one who seeks to
lose her virginity to an unknown paramour. **5** As virtue is
always manifest by virtuous action. **6–9** For the image, see iii
22. **along**: continuously; directly.

Stanza 4
4–9 Giving final honour (**worship**) to the Red Cross Knight,
which is said at I i 3.4 to be the chief reward of his endeavours,
and marking the beginning of Britomart's quest.

7

There she alighted from her light-foot beast,
  And sitting downe vpon the rocky shore,
  Badd her old Squyre vnlace her lofty creast;
  Tho hauing vewd a while the surges hore,
  That gainst the craggy clifts did loudly rore,
  And in their raging surquedry disdaynd,
  That the fast earth affronted them so sore,
  And their deuouring couetize restraynd,
Thereat she sighed deepe, and after thus complaynd.

8

Huge sea of sorrow, and tempestuous griefe,
  Wherein my feeble barke is tossed long,
  Far from the hoped hauen of reliefe,
  Why doe thy cruel billowes beat so strong,
  And thy moyst mountaines each on others throng,
  Threatning to swallow vp my fearefull lyfe?
  O doe thy cruell wrath and spightfull wrong
  At length allay, and stint thy stormy stryfe,
Which in thy troubled bowels raignes, and rageth ryfe.

9

For els my feeble vessell crazd, and crackt
  Through thy strong buffets and outrageous blowes,
  Cannot endure, but needes it must be wrackt
  On the rough rocks, or on the sandy shallowes,
  The whiles that loue it steres, and fortune rowes;
  Loue my lewd Pilott hath a restless minde
  And fortune Boteswaine no assuraunce knowes,
  But saile withouten starres, gainst tyde and winde:
How can they other doe, sith both are bold and blinde?

10

Thou God of windes, that raignest in the seas,
  That raignest also in the Continent,
  At last blow vp some gentle gale of ease,
  The which may bring my ship, ere it be rent,
  Vnto the gladsome port of her intent:
  Then when I shall my selfe in safety see,
  A table for eternall moniment
  Of thy great grace, and my great ieopardee,
Great *Neptune*, I avow to hallow vnto thee.

Stanza 5
2 Recalling i 58.6 when she doffed her arms in Castle Joyeous.
3 amorous: the spelling, from Lat. *amarus*, bitter, refers to
the 'bitter stowre' (ii 5.3) she suffers for her love.
7–9 Britomart's catalogue proceeds from the private virtue in
Wise to the public virtue in **warlike**, to **personable** in his
handsome appearance and courteous bearing, and finally to
kind, i.e. well-born, and (above all) loving.

Stanza 6
2 beguile: divert attention from. **4** The metaphor is acted
out in Amoret's heart 'transfixed with a deadly dart' at xii 21.3.
5 Arthur claims as much at I ix 8.3–5 but Britomart's love
expresses the marriage vow 'to love . . . till death us depart'.
dolour: physical pain; grief. **depart**: remove. **8 her blinded
guest**: Cupid; cf. 'making blind loue her guide' (IV v 29.5).
9 her addrest: made her way.

Stanza 7
4 surges hore: white waves. **5–8 surquedry**: arrogance.
disdaynd: angered. **fast**: firmly fixed. **affronted**: confronted;
suggesting the etymological sense, 'to strike in the face'. **cou-
etize**: covetousness.

Stanzas 8–10
Britomart's three-stanza complaint is the first of three that
structure the canto, the other two being Cymoent's four
stanzas at 36–39 and Arthur's six stanzas at 55–60. (As elegiac
moments that mark their dedication to their quests, see Martin
1987:100–01.) It is properly termed an allegory by Gil
1621:99 because, in addressing the sea, Britomart translates
her emotional disorder into nature's disorder, their corres-
pondence being enforced by the change of **thy** (8.9) to these
1596. Walker 1998b:89–90 notes how Britomart internal-
izes nature's disorder. On the relation to its subtext, Petrarch,
Rime sparse 189, see Wofford 1987:40–47. Cf. her complaint
at ii 39, and Florimell's complaint against the sea at IV xii 9.

The topos derives from Ps. 69.15: 'Let not the waterflood
drowne me, nether let the depe swallowe me vp'. For its use in
sermons relevant to Britomart's complaints, see Christian
2000:133–46, and cf. *Am* 34, and 53.1–4 below. The motif
of the storm-tossed ship describes temperance at II ii 24, but
here the billows express Britomart's sorrow and the raging
winds her sighs.

Stanza 8
8 stint: stop. **9 troubled bowels**: both the sea's and her own
'bleeding bowells' (ii 39.2).

Stanza 9
1 crazd: battered. **4** The wrecked metre enforces the mean-
ing. **6–8** The metaphor clarifies the earlier statement that
Britomart is 'Following the guydaunce of her blinded guest'
(6.8) for 'no powre, | Nor guidaunce of her selfe in her did
dwell' (ii 49.2–3). It contrasts her state with Guyon's when
guided by the Ferryman who holds his course 'with stayed
stedfastnesse' at II xii 29.6. At iii 14.5, she proceeds 'with loue
to frend' but, as Merlin reveals, her love is guided by pro-
vidence. **lewd**: ignorant, unskilful; wicked; unchaste. **assur-
aunce**: steadiness. **withouten starres**: cf. ii 7.7, and Arthur at
53.3–4.

Stanza 10
1–2 Continent: land, with the obvious pun; cf. 30.5 and v
25.7. Britomart prays to Aeolus, who, according to Conti
1616:8.10, represents reason because he controls the winds,
i.e. the passions; see Weld 1951:550. Yet her love is stronger
than reason may control; see ii 46. The sea and the land are the
realms of Marinell and Florimell respectively. **7–9 table**:
votive tablet to the god, or picture of her suffering.
Neptune, to whom Britomart pleads for release from her
'Huge sea of sorrow' (8.1), releases Florimell from her impris-
onment under the sea at IV xii 32. **hallow**: consecrate.

11

Then sighing softly sore, and inly deepe,
    She shut vp all her plaint in priuy griefe;
    For her great courage would not let her weepe,
    Till that old *Glauce* gan with sharpe repriefe,
    Her to restraine, and giue her good reliefe,
    Through hope of those, which *Merlin* had her told
    Should of her name and nation be chiefe,
And fetch their being from the sacred mould
Of her immortall womb, to be in heauen enrold.

12

Thus as she her recomforted, she spyde,
    Where far away one all in armour bright,
    With hasty gallop towards her did ryde;
    Her dolour soone she ceast, and on her dight
    Her Helmet, to her Courser mounting light:
    Her former sorrow into suddein wrath,
    Both coosen passions of distroubled spright,
    Conuerting, forth she beates the dusty path;
Loue and despight attonce her courage kindled hath.

13

As when a foggy mist hath ouercast
    The face of heuen, and the cleare ayre engroste,
    The world in darkenes dwels, till that at last
    The watry Southwinde from the seabord coste
    Vpblowing, doth disperse the vapour lo'ste,
    And poures it selfe forth in a stormy showre;
    So the fayre *Britomart* hauing disclo'ste
    Her clowdy care into a wrathfull stowre,
The mist of griefe dissolu'd, did into vengeance powre.

14

Eftsoones her goodly shield addressing fayre,
    That mortall speare she in her hand did take,
    And vnto battaill did her selfe prepayre.
    The knight approching, sternely her bespake;

Sir knight, that doest thy voyage rashly make
    By this forbidden way in my despight,
    Ne doest by others death ensample take,
    I read thee soone retyre, whiles thou hast might,
Least afterwards it be too late to take thy flight.

15

Ythrild with deepe disdaine of his proud threat,
    She shortly thus; Fly they, that need to fly;
    Wordes fearen babes. I meane not thee entreat
    To passe; but maugre thee will passe or dy.
    Ne lenger stayd for th'other to reply,
    But with sharpe speares the rest made dearly knowne.
    Strongly the straunge knight ran, and sturdily
    Strooke her full on the brest, that made her downe
Decline her head, and touch her crouper with her crown.

16

But she againe him in the shield did smite
    With so fierce furie and great puissaunce,
    That through his threesquare scuchin percing quite,
    And through his mayled hauberque, by mischaunce
    The wicked steele through his left side did glaunce;
    Him so transfixed she before her bore
    Beyond his croupe, the length of all her launce,
    Till sadly soucing on the sandy shore,
He tombled on an heape, and wallowd in his gore.

17

Like as the sacred Oxe, that carelesse stands,
    With gilden hornes, and flowry girlonds crownd,
    Proud of his dying honor and deare bandes,
    Whiles th'altars fume with frankincense arownd,
    All suddeinly with mortall stroke astownd,
    Doth groueling fall, and with his streaming gore
    Distaines the pillours, and the holy grownd,
    And the faire flowres, that decked him afore;
So fell proud *Marinell* vpon the pretious shore.

Stanza 11
4 repriefe: reproof. **8–9** Her **wombe** is the **mould** of her progeny in being their form or container (*OED* sb.³ 10), but also in providing their pattern (sb.³ 1).

Stanza 12
4 dolour: lamentation. **7–9** The four emotions correspond to Phaon's at II iv 34 that have 'laide [him] . . . low' except that, instead of jealousy, Britomart feels **despight** or indignation in being attacked, and then counter-attacks. **distroubled**: greatly troubled.

Stanza 13
1–6 engroste: thickened. **lo'ste**: loosed, i.e. dissolved by dispersal or precipitation. The simile is used of Arthur at II viii 48. **7 disclo'ste**: set free; converted. **8 care**: grief. **stowre**: fury, storm. **9 powre**: the gathering strength of the line forces the pun.

Stanza 14
1 addressing fayre: arranging properly. **6 in my despight**: in contemptuous defiance of me. The custom in medieval romance of denying a knight passage until he proved his

manhood by combat is noted by Upton 1758. **7 ensample**: warning. **8 read**: advise. **soone**: straightway.

Stanza 15
1 Ythrild: pierced. **3 fearen**: frighten. **7 sturdily**: violently. **8** The blow on the breast is as appropriate to Bk III as the wound in the head to Bk II (e.g. v 4.6, viii 45.5) in order to distinguish the wound of love from an attack on reason. Cf. her 'thrilled brest' at ii 32.5 and her 'feeble brest' wounded by love at 37.9. **9 crouper**: crupper, the horse's rump; cf. her blow at i 6.7.

Stanza 16
1 againe: in return. **3 threesquare scuchin**: triangular shield; see i 4.4*n*. **4 mayled hauberque**: long coat of chain mail. **mischaunce**: evil fate. **5** The wound in the **left** or heart side here indicates a love-wound; cf. v 20.7. Not the thigh because Marinell is not wounded by lust. **glaunce**: stronger than 'grazing', though the blow's full effect is muted. **7 Beyond** the crupper indicates that her blow is stronger than his (15.9). **the length of all her launce**: he is measured by chastity, as was Guyon at i 6.7. **8 sadly soucing**: heavily falling. **9 on**: in.

18

The martiall Mayd stayd not him to lament,
  But forward rode, and kept her ready way
  Along the strond, which as she ouer-went,
  She saw bestrowed all with rich aray
  Of pearles and pretious stones of great assay,
  And all the grauell mixt with golden owre;
  Whereat she wondred much, but would not stay
For gold, or perles, or pretious stones an howre,
But them despised all; for all was in her powre.

19

Whiles thus he lay in deadly stonishment,
  Tydings hereof came to his mothers eare;
  His mother was the blacke-browd *Cymoent*,
  The daughter of great *Nereus*, which did beare
  This warlike sonne vnto an earthly peare,
  The famous *Dumarin*; who on a day
  Finding the Nymph a sleepe in secret wheare,
  As he by chaunce did wander that same way,
Was taken with her loue, and by her closely lay.

20

There he this knight of her begot, whom borne
  She of his father *Marinell* did name,
  And in a rocky caue as wight forlorne,
  Long time she fostred vp, till he became
  A mighty man at armes, and mickle fame
  Did get through great aduentures by him donne:
  For neuer man he suffred by that same
  Rich strond to trauell, whereas he did wonne,
But that he must do battail with the Sea-nymphes sonne.

21

An hundred knights of honorable name
  He had subdew'd, and them his vassals made,
  That through all Farie lond his noble fame
  Now blazed was, and feare did all inuade,
  That none durst passen through that perilous glade.
  And to aduaunce his name and glory more,
  Her Sea-god syre she dearely did perswade,
  T'endow her sonne with threasure and rich store,
Boue all the sonnes, that were of earthly wombes ybore.

22

The God did graunt his daughters deare demaund,
  To doen his Nephew in all riches flow;
  Eftsoones his heaped waues he did commaund,
  Out of their hollow bosome forth to throw
  All the huge threasure, which the sea below
  Had in his greedy gulfe deuoured deepe,
  And him enriched through the ouerthrow
  And wreckes of many wretches, which did weepe,
And often wayle their wealth, which he from them did keepe.

23

Shortly vpon that shore there heaped was,
  Exceeding riches and all pretious things,
  The spoyle of all the world, that it did pas
  The wealth of th'East, and pompe of *Persian* kings;
  Gold, amber, yuorie, perles, owches, rings,
  And all that els was pretious and deare,
  The sea vnto him voluntary brings,
  That shortly he a great Lord did appeare,
As was in all the lond of Faery, or else wheare.

Stanza 17
The killing of a castrated bull is a fitting simile for the consequences of Marinell's mother-dominated state, as also is his 'sacrifice' by a martial maid. On its significance, see Davies 1986:62–64. **1 sacred**: appointed for sacrifice. **carelesse**: free from care or unattended, to indicate a willing sacrifice. **3 dying honor**: i.e. honour gained by dying. **deare**: precious; grievous. **5 astownd**: stunned. **7 Distaines**: deeply stains.

Stanza 18
1–3 ready: direct; cf. 5.1, 44.9, iii 61.9, 62.9. Like Guyon, she keeps the straight path; unlike him, she is not tempted by wealth. See 21.5n. In Ripa 1603:66, Chastity is said to stand on coins to signify her defeat of avarice; and in Horace, *Odes* 2.2, wisdom gives true power to those who may pass by great heaps of treasure without looking longingly. **5 assay**: value. **8 an howre**: i.e. a moment.

Stanza 19
1 deadly stonishment: death-like numbness. **3 Cymoent**: as also at 33.2, but Cymodoce at IV xi 53.7 and xii 3.6. In Homer, she is a daughter of the sea god Nereus who comforts Achilles (*Iliad* 18.39); cf. Virgil, *Aen.* 5.826. Her name suggests 'flowing', or 'a wave' (κῦμα), or 'wave-tamer', as shown at 31.8–9; see IV xi 53.7n. On the parallel story of Thetis, mother of Achilles, see 'Cymoent, Cymodoce' in the *SEnc*. **4 great Nereus**: Homer's Old Man of the Sea called *grandaeuus* in Virgil, *Geog.* 4.392. See IV xi 18.5–19.9. **5 peare**: mate. **6 Dumarin**: i.e. of the sea. **7 wheare**: place. **9 closely**: secretly.

Stanza 20
2 Marinell: his name links the sea (from his father Dumarin) and the land (from Florimell's love for him), as does his **Rich strond** which, as tideland, is both sea and land; see 'rich strond' in the *SEnc*. The name also suggests 'Mars' and 'martial prowess'; and Fr. *mari*, husband + nill, i.e. unwilling to marry, as Nohrnberg 1976:587 suggests. See 'Marinell' in the *SEnc*. **3 rocky caue**: see viii 37n, IV xii 7.3n.

Stanza 21
1 hundred: a generalized large number, as at IV iv 31.6, etc. **4 inuade**: take possession of. **5 perilous glade**: this inappropriate term for a sea coast is used to associate it with the 'gloomy glade' (II vii 3.1) where Mammon tempts Guyon. In not pursuing beauty in Florimell and in ignoring the wealth of the rich strond, Britomart triumphs over Guyon's two major temptations; see II xi 9.9n. **7 dearely**: earnestly. **perswade**: urge.

Stanza 22
1 deare: earnest; expensive. **2 Nephew**: grandson. **4 hollow bosome**: the troughs between the waves. **8–9** The excessive alliteration mocks their grief over lost wealth.

Stanza 23
5 amber: an alloy of gold and silver, as in Ezek. 1.4. **owches**: jewels. **7 voluntary**: i.e. spontaneously. The term identifies the sea with its god.

24

Thereto he was a doughty dreaded knight,
    Tryde often to the scath of many Deare,
    That none in equall armes him matchen might,
    The which his mother seeing, gan to feare
    Least his too haughtie hardines might reare
    Some hard mishap, in hazard of his life:
    For thy she oft him counseld to forbeare
    The bloody batteill, and to stirre vp strife,
But after all his warre, to rest his wearie knife.

25

And for his more assuraunce, she inquir'd
    One day of *Proteus* by his mighty spell,
    (For *Proteus* was with prophecy inspir'd)
    Her deare sonnes destiny to her to tell,
    And the sad end of her sweet *Marinell.*
    Who through foresight of his eternall skill,
    Bad her from womankind to keepe him well:
    For of a woman he should haue much ill,
A virgin straunge and stout him should dismay, or kill.

26

For thy she gaue him warning euery day,
    The loue of women not to entertaine;
    A lesson too too hard for liuing clay,
    From loue in course of nature to refraine:
    Yet he his mothers lore did well retaine,
    And euer from fayre Ladies loue did fly;
    Yet many Ladies fayre did oft complaine,
    That they for loue of him would algates dy:
Dy, who so list for him, he was loues enimy.

27

But ah, who can deceiue his destiny,
    Or weene by warning to auoyd his fate?
    That when he sleepes in most security,
    And safest seemes, him soonest doth amate,
    And findeth dew effect or soone or late.
    So feeble is the powre of fleshly arme.
    His mother bad him wemens loue to hate,
    For she of womans force did feare no harme;
So weening to haue arm'd him, she did quite disarme.

28

This was that woman, this that deadly wownd,
    That *Proteus* prophecide should him dismay,
    The which his mother vainely did expownd,
    To be hart-wownding loue, which should assay
    To bring her sonne vnto his last decay.
    So ticle be the termes of mortall state,
    And full of subtile sophismes, which doe play
    With double sences, and with false debate,
T'approue the vnknowen purpose of eternall fate.

29

Too trew the famous *Marinell* it fownd,
    Who through late triall, on that wealthy Strond
    Inglorious now lies in sencelesse swownd,
    Through heauy stroke of *Britomartis* hond.
    Which when his mother deare did vnderstond,
    And heauy tidings heard, whereas she playd
    Amongst her watry sisters by a pond,
    Gathering sweete daffadillyes, to haue made
Gay girlonds, from the Sun their forheads fayr to shade,

30

Eftesoones both flowres and girlonds far away
    Shee flong, and her faire deawy locks yrent,
    To sorrow huge she turnd her former play,
    And gamesome merth to grieuous dreriment:
    Shee threw her selfe downe on the Continent,
    Ne word did speake, but lay as in a swowne,
    Whiles al her sisters did for her lament,
    With yelling outcries, and with shrieking sowne;
And euery one did teare her girlond from her crowne.

31

Soone as shee vp out of her deadly fitt
    Arose, shee bad her charett to be brought,
    And all her sisters, that with her did sitt,
    Bad eke attonce their charetts to be sought;
    Tho full of bitter griefe and pensife thought,
    She to her wagon clombe; clombe all the rest,
    And forth together went, with sorow fraught.
    The waues obedient to theyr beheast,
Them yielded ready passage, and their rage surceast.

Stanza 24

1 Thereto: in addition to that.   **2** Grievously proven so to the harm of many.   **5 hardines**: boldness.   **7 For thy**: therefore.

Stanza 25

1 assuraunce: security.   **2–9** On Proteus as a prophet, see viii 30.1–4*n*. His ambiguous prophecy applies also to Florimell. **eternall skill**: art of knowing eternal matters.   **straunge**: foreign; cf. v 9.8.   **dismay**: overthrow.

Stanza 26

5 lore: teaching.   **6** In defiance of Britomart's edict, 'great rebuke it is, loue to despise' (i 55.3), Marinell scorns love; see v 9.5–7, and esp. IV xi 5.3–4. Male chastity is Britomart's chief threat in seeking to conquer the similarly love-despising Artegall; see IV vi 28.7–9.   **8 algates**: by all means; otherwise.

Stanza 27

1–5 deceiue: frustrate, cheat.   **security**: culpable carelessness. **amate**: cast down.   **effect**: fulfilment.

Stanza 28

3 vainely: foolishly, for she was wrong.   **5 last decay**: death. **6 ticle**: uncertain.   **8 debate**: wrangling, fallacious arguments. **9 approue**: make good.

Stanza 29

7 her watry sisters: the Nereides, the daughters of Nereus; see IV xi 48–52. All fifty gather at the beginning and end of Marinell's story; hence the otherwise surprising emphasis on 'all' at 30.7, 31.3, 6, etc.   **8 sweete daffadillyes**: presumably named for the flower into which Narcissus was transformed; see vi 45.5. The connection is suggested because Marinell is like Narcissus, not in loving himself but in rejecting love for another.

32

Great *Neptune* stoode amazed at their sight,
  Whiles on his broad rownd backe they softly slid
  And eke him selfe mournd at their mournfull plight,
  Yet wist not what their wailing ment, yet did
  For great compassion of their sorow, bid
  His mighty waters to them buxome bee:
  Eftesoones the roaring billowes still abid,
  And all the griesly Monsters of the See
Stood gaping at their gate, and wondred them to see.

33

A teme of Dolphins raunged in aray,
  Drew the smooth charett of sad *Cymoent*;
  They were all taught by *Triton*, to obay
  To the long raynes, at her commaundement:
  As swifte as swallowes, on the waues they went,
  That their brode flaggy finnes no fome did reare,
  Ne bubling rowndell they behinde them sent;
  The rest of other fishes drawen weare,
Which with their finny oars the swelling sea did sheare.

34

Soone as they bene arriu'd vpon the brim
  Of the *Rich strond*, their charets they forlore,
  And let their temed fishes softly swim
  Along the margent of the fomy shore,
  Least they their finnes should bruze, and surbate sore
  Their tender feete vpon the stony grownd:
  And comming to the place, where all in gore
  And cruddy blood enwallowed they fownd
The lucklesse *Marinell*, lying in deadly swownd;

35

His mother swowned thrise, and the third time
  Could scarce recouered bee out of her paine;
  Had she not beene deuoide of mortall slime,
  Shee should not then haue bene relyu'd againe;

But soone as life recouered had the raine,
  Shee made so piteous mone and deare wayment,
  That the hard rocks could scarse from tears refraine,
  And all her sister Nymphes with one consent
Supplide her sobbing breaches with sad complement.

36

Deare image of my selfe, (she sayd) that is,
  The wretched sonne of wretched mother borne,
  Is this thine high aduauncement, O is this
  Th'immortall name, with which thee yet vnborne
  Thy Gransire *Nereus* promist to adorne?
  Now lyest thou of life and honor refte;
  Now lyest thou a lumpe of earth forlorne,
  Ne of thy late life memory is lefte,
Ne can thy irreuocable desteny bee wefte?

37

Fond *Proteus*, father of false prophecis,
  And they more fond, that credit to thee giue,
  Not this the worke of womans hand ywis,
  That so deepe wound through these deare members driue.
  I feared loue: but they that loue doe liue,
  But they that dye, doe nether loue nor hate.
  Nath'lesse to thee thy folly I forgiue,
  And to my selfe, and to accursed fate
The guilt I doe ascribe: deare wisedom bought too late.

38

O what auailes it of immortall seed
  To beene ybredd and neuer borne to dye?
  Farre better I it deeme to die with speed,
  Then waste in woe and waylfull miserye.
  Who dyes the vtmost dolor doth abye,
  But who that liues, is lefte to waile his losse:
  So life is losse, and death felicity.
  Sad life worse then glad death: and greater crosse
To see frends graue, then dead the graue self to engrosse.

what is going on?

Stanza 30
4 **dreriment**: sorrow.   5 **Continent**: shore, claimed by the continent Marinell. See 10.1–2n.

Stanza 31
5 **pensife**: sorrowful.

Stanza 32
A mythological explanation of the two previous lines.   6 **buxome**: yielding.   7 **still abid**: remained (or became) still.   9 **their gate**: the manner in which they proceed.

Stanza 33
1–4 Triton was reputed to train dolphins.   5 The simile is apt because swallows also skim the water.   7 **bubling rowndell**: circles or swirls of foam.

Stanza 34
2 **forlore**: left.   5 **surbate**: batter.   8 **cruddy**: clotted.

Stanza 35
4 **relyu'd**: restored to life.   6 **deare wayment**: grievous lamentation.   7 Allegorizing a realistic detail.   8 **consent**: accord, in full harmony.   9 Their cries supplement hers by filling up the intervals between her sobs.

Stanza 36
7 **lumpe of earth**: in contrast to 'liuing clay' (26.3).   9 **irreuocable**: fittingly, the word cannot be scanned.   **wefte**: avoided.

Stanza 37
1 **Fond**: foolish; ignorant.   3 **ywis**: certainly; or 'I know', in contrast to Proteus's ignorance.   4 **members**: limbs.

Stanza 38
2 In contrast to mortal seed which is **borne to dye**.   5 **abye**: endure.   8–9 It is a greater burden to see a friend's grave than to fill one's own.

39

But if the heauens did his dayes enuie,
   And my short blis maligne, yet mote they well
   Thus much afford me, ere that he did die
   That the dim eies of my deare *Marinell*
   I mote haue closed, and him bed farewell,
   Sith other offices for mother meet
   They would not graunt.
   Yett maulgre them farewell, my sweetest sweet;
Farewell my sweetest sonne, till we againe may meet.

40

Thus when they all had sorowed their fill,
   They softly gan to search his griesly wownd:
   And that they might him handle more at will,
   They him disarmd, and spredding on the grownd
   Their watchet mantles frindgd with siluer rownd,
   They softly wipt away the gelly blood
   From th'orifice; which hauing well vpbownd,
   They pourd in soueraine balme, and Nectar good,
Good both for erthly med'cine, and for heuenly food.

41

Tho when the lilly handed *Liagore*,
   (This *Liagore* whilome had learned skill
   In leaches craft, by great *Appolloes* lore,
   Sith her whilome vpon high *Pindus* hill,
   He loued, and at last her wombe did fill
   With heuenly seed, whereof wise *Pæon* sprong)
   Did feele his pulse, shee knew there staied still
   Some litle life his feeble sprites emong;
Which to his mother told, despeyre she from her flong.

42

Tho vp him taking in their tender hands,
   They easely vnto her charett beare:
   Her teme at her commaundement quiet stands,
   Whiles they the corse into her wagon reare,
   And strowe with flowres the lamentable beare:
   Then all the rest into their coches clim,
   And through the brackish waues their passage shear;
   Vpon great *Neptunes* necke they softly swim,
And to her watry chamber swiftly carry him.

43

Deepe in the bottome of the sea, her bowre
   Is built of hollow billowes heaped hye,
   Like to thicke clouds, that threat a stormy showre,
   And vauted all within, like to the Skye,
   In which the Gods doe dwell eternally:
   There they him laide in easy couch well dight;
   And sent in haste for *Tryphon*, to apply
   Salues to his wounds, and medicines of might:
For *Tryphon* of sea gods the soueraine leach is hight.

44

The whiles the *Nymphes* sitt all about him rownd,
   Lamenting his mishap and heauy plight;
   And ofte his mother vewing his wide wownd,
   Cursed the hand, that did so deadly smight
   Her dearest sonne, her dearest harts delight.
   But none of all those curses ouertooke
   The warlike Maide, th'ensample of that might,
   But fairely well shee thryud, and well did brooke
Her noble deeds, ne her right course for ought forsooke.

Stanza 39

1 enuie: regard with dislike. On heaven's envy, see IV viii 16.5–6 and VI iv 31.1.   **2 maligne**: begrudge, or regard with envy.   **4–5** Euryalus's mother claims this office to the dead in Virgil, *Aen.* 9.486–87.   **7** An incomplete line, perhaps to show the mother's grief, as Collier 1862 suggests, as she stops cursing the heavens to bid her son farewell.   **8 maulgre**: in spite of.   **9** . . . sith we no more shall meet *1596* increases the pathos.

Stanza 40

2 search: probe.   **5 watchet**: light blue, the colour of water, as IV xi 27.2.   **8–9** As Venus washes Aeneas's wound in Virgil, *Aen.* 12.418–19, and Thetis preserves Patroclus's body in Homer, *Iliad* 19.38–39. Nymphs are skilled in the art of healing, as at v 32.3–4.

Stanza 41

S. adapts Ovid's story, in *Heroides* 5.145–50, of Apollo who taught Oenone the arts of healing. He seems to have invented the story of Pæon's birth.   **1 Liagore**: one of the Nereides at IV xi 51.4.   **lilly handed**: a mark of a maiden's purity, as Una's 'lilly hands' at I iii 6.2, Belphœbe's at III v 33.3, Amoret's at IV x 53.9, and esp. Florimell's at IV xii 33.3.

3 lore: teaching.   **6 Pæon**: 'an excellent phisition' (T. Cooper 1565) who serves the gods in Homer, *Iliad* 5.401–02.

Stanza 42

2 easely: gently.   **5 lamentable**: causing the nymphs to lament.   **6 clim**: an early spelling of 'climb'.

Stanza 43

1–5 When the nymph Cyrene brings her mortal son to her bower beneath the water, in Virgil, *Georg.* 4.359–73, the arching waves stand as mountains to allow them to enter. There he is cured of his grief, as Marinell has been cured of his wound when he appears at IV xii 3.8.   **vauted**: vaulted. **7–9 Tryphon**: a brother of Aesculapius, according to Boccaccio 1976:7.36; noted Lotspeich 1932. S. infers that he, too, was 'the seagods surgeon' (IV xi 6.6), for which he is praised by Selden: 'justifiable . . . as wel as to make *Tryphon* their Surgeon, which our excellent *Spenser* hath done' (Drayton 1931–41:4.233).

Stanza 44

7 ensample of that might: example of 'womans force' (27.8) that overcame Marinell.   **8 fairely**: fully.   **brooke**: bear up, ply.   **9 her right course**: as 5.1, fitly repeated here as her role is assumed by surrogates until ix 12.

Spong

45

Yet did false *Archimage* her still pursew,
  To bring to passe his mischieuous intent,
  Now that he had her singled from the crew
  Of courteous knights, the Prince, and Fary gent,
  Whom late in chace of beauty excellent
  Shee lefte, pursewing that same foster strong;
  Of whose fowle outrage they impatient,
  And full of firy zele, him followed long,
To reskew her from shame, and to reuenge her wrong.

46

(playns,
Through thick and thin, through mountains and through
  Those two gret champions did attonce pursew
  The fearefull damzell, with incessant payns:
  Who from them fled, as light-foot hare from vew
  Of hunter swifte, and sent of howndes trew.
  At last they came vnto a double way,
  Where, doubtfull which to take, her to reskew,
  Themselues they did dispart, each to assay,
Whether more happy were, to win so goodly pray.

47

But *Timias*, the Princes gentle Squyre,
  That Ladies loue vnto his Lord forlent,
  And with proud enuy, and indignant yre,
  After that wicked foster fiercely went.
  So beene they three three sondry wayes ybent.
  But fayrest fortune to the Prince befell,
  Whose chaunce it was, that soone he did repent,
  To take that way, in which that Damozell
Was fledd afore, affraid of him, as feend of hell.

48

At last of her far off he gained vew:
  Then gan he freshly pricke his fomy steed,
  And euer as he nigher to her drew,
  So euermore he did increase his speed,
  And of each turning still kept wary heed:
  Alowd to her he oftentimes did call,
  To doe away vaine doubt, and needlesse dreed:
  Full myld to her he spake, and oft let fall
Many meeke wordes, to stay and comfort her withall.

49

But nothing might relent her hasty flight;
  So deepe the deadly feare of that foule swaine
  Was earst impressed in her gentle spright:
  Like as a fearefull Doue, which through the raine,
  Of the wide ayre her way does cut amaine,
  Hauing farre off espyde a Tassell gent,
  Which after her his nimble winges doth straine,
  Doubleth her hast for feare to bee for-hent,
And with her pineons cleaues the liquid firmament.

50

With no lesse hast, and eke with no lesse dreed,
  That fearefull Ladie fledd from him, that ment
  To her no euill thought, nor euill deed;
  Yet former feare of being fowly shent,
  Carried her forward with her first intent;
  And though oft looking backward, well she vewde,
  Her selfe freed from that foster insolent,
  And that it was a knight, which now her sewde,
Yet she no lesse the knight feard, then that villein rude.

Stanza 45
1–6 **Archimage**: in pursuing Britomart, he appears for the last time, making only a nominal appearance in the Bk, as does Duessa (see i Arg.3*n*), though both maintain an absent presence. His role is assumed by Busirane in cantos xi and xii. 4 **gent**: noble, valiant. 5 **chace of beauty excellent**: cf. i 19.2. 6 At i 18. 6–8, and 46.2–3 below, Arthur and Guyon pursue Florimell as their 'goodly pray' (46.9) while Timias alone pursues the Foster. Cf. v 13.3–6. 8 **zele**: ardour in pursuit, i.e. ardent love of Florimell.

Stanza 46
2 **attonce**: together. 3 **The fearefull damzell**: her identifying epithet, as at vi 54.2, vii 24.1; cf. 'fearefull Ladie' (50.2). 4 **hare**: prized for the chase because of its swiftness, and known for its fearfulness: cf. 'hartlesse hare' (*SC Dec.* 29); named here as the traditional amorous hunt of Venus. 5 **trew**: sure, applied to scent; trusty or reliable, applied to the hounds. 8 **dispart**: separate. 9 I.e. which of the two would be more fortunate.

Stanza 47
2 **forlent**: gave up entirely; i.e. he leaves the love of Florimell to Arthur. 3 **enuy**: desire, longing; here, ostensibly, to perform a chivalric deed. 5 **three sondry wayes**: at the 'double way' (46.6), Guyon takes the wrong one, next (very appropriately) seeing his horse at V iii 29, while Arthur sees Florimell at 48.1 and Timias the Foster at v 13. **ybent**: bent, directed. 6 **fayrest fortune** falls to Arthur because he follows the fairest, the Faerie Queene. 9 **him**: not now the Foster, from whom Arthur may claim, at v 6.4, to have rescued her, but Arthur himself, whom the quite rightly fearful Florimell sees 'freshly pricke' towards her at 48.2.

Stanza 48
2 **his fomy steed**: see i 5.5*n*. 7 **vaine doubt**: 'idle feare' (vi 54.9). Cf. her 'vaine feare' (vii 1.6 and see *n*).

Stanza 49
1 **relent**: slacken. 4–9 The dove's flight from the eagle or falcon is a traditional motif to contrast the present to the antique age when 'the Doue sate by the Faulcons side' (IV viii 31.2). The motif is apt for Florimell because she is 'Carried away with wings of speedy feare' (v 6.6); see vii 26.9*n*. **raine**: region. **amaine**: with all her might; at full speed. **Tassell gent**: the tercel-gentle, a male falcon. **for-hent**: overtaken and seized. **liquid**: clear, bright.

Stanza 50
4 **shent**: defiled. 7 **insolent**: lustful. 8 **sewde**: pursued.

51

His vncouth shield and straunge armes her dismayd,
    Whose like in Faery lond were seldom seene,
    That fast she from him fledd, no lesse afrayd,
    Then of wilde beastes if she had chased beene:
    Yet he her followd still with corage keene,
    So long that now the golden *Hesperus*
    Was mounted high in top of heauen sheene,
    And warnd his other brethren ioyeous,
To light their blessed lamps in *Ioues* eternall hous.

52

All suddeinly dim wox the dampish ayre,
    And griesly shadowes couered heauen bright,
    That now with thousand starres was decked fayre;
    Which when the Prince beheld, a lothfull sight,
    And that perforce, for want of lenger light,
    He mote surceasse his suit, and lose the hope
    Of his long labour, he gan fowly wyte
    His wicked fortune, that had turnd aslope,
And cursed night, that reft from him so goodly scope.

53

Tho when her wayes he could no more descry,
    But to and fro at disauenture strayd;
    Like as a ship, whose Lodestar suddeinly
    Couered with cloudes, her Pilott hath dismayd;
    His wearisome pursuit perforce he stayd,
    And from his loftie steed dismounting low,
    Did let him forage. Downe himselfe he layd
    Vpon the grassy ground, to sleepe a throw;
The cold earth was his couch, the hard steele his pillow.

54

But gentle Sleepe enuyde him any rest;
    In stead thereof sad sorow, and disdaine
    Of his hard hap did vexe his noble brest,
    And thousand fancies bett his ydle brayne
    With their light wings, the sights of semblants vaine:
    Oft did he wish, that Lady faire mote bee
    His faery Queene, for whom he did complaine:
    Or that his Faery Queene were such, as shee:
And euer hasty Night he blamed bitterlie.

55

Night thou foule Mother of annoyaunce sad,
    Sister of heauie death, and nourse of woe,
    Which wast begot in heauen, but for thy bad
    And brutish shape thrust downe to hell below,
    Where by the grim floud of *Cocytus* slow
    Thy dwelling is, in *Herebus* black hous,
    (Black *Herebus* thy husband is the foe
    Of all the Gods) where thou vngratious,
Halfe of thy dayes doest lead in horrour hideous.

56

What had th'eternall Maker need of thee,
    The world in his continuall course to keepe,
    That doest all thinges deface, ne lettest see
    The beautie of his worke? Indeed in sleepe
    The slouthfull body, that doth loue to steep
    His lustlesse limbes, and drowne his baser mind,
    Doth praise thee oft, and oft from *Stygian* deepe
    Calles thee, his goddesse in his errour blind,
And great Dame Natures handmaide, chearing euery kind.

Stanza 51

1 vncouth: strange, being covered with a veil. **5 corage keene**: the erotic implications of the phrase explain her fear. **6–9 Hesperus**: the evening star, Venus's 'lampe of love' (*Epith* 288). Its place in mid-heaven marks the ascendancy of love over Arthur; see I vii 30.4*n*. The reference is called 'a fine astronomical howler' by Kouwenhoven 1983:216 because, being near the sun, Venus cannot be **mounted high** as night approaches, unless line 7 means only 'in the sky', as at I ii 6.6–7. Or, as J.M. Richardson has suggested to me, the planet has reached its highest visible position at sunset. On his apparent misplacing of Hesperus in *Epith* 286–87, see Hieatt 1960:24–25. It is highly unlikely that S. has made a howler because he boasts through Colin in *SC Dec.* 83–84 that he knows the signs of heaven 'where *Venus* sittes and when'.

Stanza 52

6 suit: both pursuit and courtship. **7 wyte**: blame. **9 scope**: sight; target.

Stanza 53

2 at disauenture: aimlessly, implying misfortune. **3–4** As Britomart at 9.6–8. **6–9** The connection with Chaucer, *Tale of Sir Thopas* – see I ix 8–15*n* – is suggested esp. by **forage**; noted Anderson 1994:646–47. **a throw**: a while.

Stanza 54

1 enuyde: refused. **2 disdaine**: vexation, indignation. **4–5** As Phantastes's chamber is filled with flies (II ix 51); here echoing 5.6. **semblants**: appearances. **6–8** Of his dream-vision of Gloriana, Arthur says 'So fayre a creature yet saw neuer sunny day' (I ix 13.9). While Gloriana is fair, Florimell is fairness itself. Cf. IV ii 23.2–4. There may be a Platonic significance in Arthur's desire to find in an earthly image satisfaction for the spiritual *eros* that leads him to seek divine glory, as Lewis 1967:132–35 suggests; or a critique of it, as P. Cheney 1989:318 suggests. On Arthur's quest as a search for ultimate (Platonic) truth, see Mueller 1991. **complaine**: lament.

Stanzas 55–60

Arthur's complaint belongs to the moral tradition of the medieval complaint. As an aubade, it inverts the usual complaint on the brevity of night, as in Chaucer, *Troilus and Criseyde* 3.1429–42, 1450–56. **Night** appears at I v 20; her genealogy is given at I v 22.2–6 and II iv 41.8–9. As a poet who celebrates 'The children of day' (59.5), S.'s epithets for her are consistently negative except when he anticipates his wedding night in *Epith* 315–333.

Stanza 55

3–7 On **Cocytus**, see II vii 56.6–9. On **Herebus**, see II iv 41.8–9, and *n*. **8 vngratious**: wicked, devoid of spiritual grace.

57

But well I wote, that to an heauy hart
    Thou art the roote and nourse of bitter cares,
    Breeder of new, renewer of old smarts:
    In stead of rest thou lendest rayling teares,
    In stead of sleepe thou sendest troublous feares,
    And dreadfull visions, in the which aliue
    The dreary image of sad death appeares:
    So from the wearie spirit thou doest driue
Desired rest, and men of happinesse depriue.

58

Vnder thy mantle black there hidden lye,
    Light-shonning thefte, and traiterous intent,
    Abhorred bloodshed, and vile felony,
    Shamefull deceipt, and daunger imminent;
    Fowle horror, and eke hellish dreriment:
    All these I wote in thy protection bee,
    And light doe shonne, for feare of being shent:
    For light ylike is loth'd of them and thee,
And all that lewdnesse loue, doe hate the light to see.

59

For day discouers all dishonest wayes,
    And sheweth each thing, as it is in deed:
    The prayses of high God he faire displayes,
    And his large bountie rightly doth areed.

The children of day be the blessed seed,
    Which darknesse shall subdue, and heauen win:
    Truth is his daughter; he her first did breed,
    Most sacred virgin, without spot of sinne.
Our life is day, but death with darknesse doth begin.

60

O when will day then turne to me againe,
    And bring with him his long expected light?
    O *Titan*, hast to reare thy ioyous waine:
    Speed thee to spred abroad thy beames bright,
    And chace away this too long lingring night,
    Chace her away, from whence she came, to hell.
    She, she it is, that hath me done despight:
    There let her with the damned spirits dwell,
And yield her rowme to day, that can it gouerne well.

61

Thus did the Prince that wearie night outweare,
    In restlesse anguish and vnquiet paine:
    And early, ere the morrow did vpreare
    His deawy head out of the *Ocean* maine,
    He vp arose, as halfe in great disdaine,
    And clombe vnto his steed. So forth he went,
    With heauy looke and lumpish pace, that plaine
    In him bewraid great grudge and maltalent:
His steed eke seemd t'apply his steps to his intent.

Stanza 56
6 lustlesse: listless. **baser**: too base. 7–9 To remain sleeping, the slothful call upon Night as their goddess, etc. There may be a topical allusion to what became known as 'the school of night' (Shakespeare, *Love's Labor's Lost* 4.3.251); see Bradbrook 1936.

Stanza 57
4 **rayling**: gushing; also the tears of those who rail. 7 **dreary**: horrid.

Stanza 58
2 **Light-shonning thefte**: cf. 'the patronesse of loue-stealth fayre' (x 16.6). 3 **felony**: treachery. 4 **daunger**: mischief, harm or the power to harm. 7–9 'For euerie man that euil doeth, hateth the light, nether commeth to light, lest his dedes shulde be reproued' (John 3.20). **shent**: put to shame. **lewdnesse**: wickedness.

Stanza 59
1–2 Cf. 1 Cor. 3.13. 4 **areed**: make known. 5 **The children of day**: Dayes dearest children *1596*. Apparently revised to improve the metre but at the expense of the biblical source: 'Ye are all the children of light, and the children of the day: we are not of the night nether of darkenes. Therefore let vs not slepe as do other' (1 Thess. 5.5–6). See I v 24.5*n*. 7 A poetic variant of the proverb, 'Time brings the truth to light'; see I ix 5.9*n*.

Stanza 60
3 **waine**: chariot.

Stanza 61
5 **disdaine**: vexation, indignation; cf. 54.2. 6 **clombe**: indicating – surely humorously – the labour of mounting; cf. IV v 46.1. 8–9 That plainly in him revealed great resentment and ill-temper. **apply**: adapt. **intent**: frame of mind.

Cant. V.

Prince Arthur heares of Florimell:
three fosters Timias wound,
Belphebe findes him almost dead,
and reareth out of sownd.

1

WOnder it is to see, in diuerse mindes,
　　How diuersly loue doth his pageaunts play,
And shewes his powre in variable kindes:
The baser wit, whose ydle thoughts alway
Are wont to cleaue vnto the lowly clay,
It stirreth vp to sensuall desire,
And in lewd slouth to wast his carelesse day:
But in braue sprite it kindles goodly fire,
That to all high desert and honour doth aspire.

2

Ne suffereth it vncomely idlenesse,
　　In his free thought to build her sluggish nest:
Ne suffereth it thought of vngentlenesse,
Euer to creepe into his noble brest,
But to the highest and the worthiest
Lifteth it vp, that els would lowly fall:
It lettes not fall, it lettes it not to rest:
It lettes not scarse this Prince to breath at all,
But to his first poursuit him forward still doth call.

3

Who long time wandred through the forest wyde,
　　To finde some issue thence, till that at last
He met a Dwarfe, that seemed terrifyde
With some late perill, which he hardly past,
Or other accident, which him aghast;
Of whom he asked, whence he lately came,
And whether now he traueiled so fast:
For sore he swat, and ronning through that same
Thicke forest, was bescracht, and both his feet nigh lame.

4

Panting for breath, and almost out of hart,
　　The Dwarfe him answerd, Sir, ill mote I stay
To tell the same. I lately did depart
From Faery court, where I haue many a day
Serued a gentle Lady of great sway,
And high accompt through out all Elfin land,
Who lately left the same, and tooke this way:
Her now I seeke, and if ye vnderstand
Which way she fared hath, good Sir tell out of hand.

5

What mister wight (saide he) and how arayd?
　　Royally clad (quoth he) in cloth of gold,
As meetest may beseeme a noble mayd;
Her faire lockes in rich circlet be enrold,
A fayrer wight did neuer Sunne behold,
And on a Palfrey rydes more white then snow,
Yet she her selfe is whiter manifold:
The surest signe, whereby ye may her know,
Is, that she is the fairest wight aliue, I trow.

6

Now certes swaine (saide he) such one I weene,
　　Fast flying through this forest from her fo,
A foule ill fauoured foster, I haue seene;
Her selfe, well as I might, I reskewd tho,
But could not stay; so fast she did foregoe,
Carried away with wings of speedy feare.
Ah dearest God (quoth he) that is great woe,
And wondrous ruth to all, that shall it heare.
But can ye read Sir, how I may her finde, or where?

Book III Canto v

Argument
2 fosters: foresters; see i 17.2*n*.　**4 sownd**: swoon.

Stanza 1
2 I.e. acts his parts, as later displayed in the house of Busirane in the tapestries (xi 28–46) and in Cupid's masque (xii 7–25). **3 variable kindes**: diverse natures.　**4–9** The **baser wit** is openly displayed in the witch's son at vii 12–17, the Fisher at viii 22–27, and Paridell, esp. at ix 28–31 and x 35, but equivocally in Timias towards Belphœbe at 48 and Amoret at IV vii 35. The **braue sprite** includes Arthur and Britomart. The opening stanza of canto iii contrasts love from above and lust from below but here the receiving natures differ. For the doctrine that love leads to virtuous action, see i 49.8–9*n*.

Stanza 2
3 vngentlenesse: discourtesy, boorishness; cf. Paridell's 'vngentlenesse' at x 6.9.　**9** Arthur's **first poursuit**, declared at I ix 15.5–9, is for the Faerie Queene who, as Elizabeth, is both **the highest and the worthiest**. By 12.1, he has turned back to pursue Florimell, which implies that, for him, they are the same.

Stanza 3
4 hardly: with difficulty.　**5 accident**: event (*OED* 1a), but close to the current sense.　**aghast**: terrified.

Stanza 4
6 accompt: account, estimation.

Stanza 5
1 mister wight: kind of person.　**4 rich circlet**: the circle into which her locks are coiled. At vii 11.3, she dresses her hair

7

Perdy me leuer were to weeten that,
  (Saide he) then ransome of the richest knight,
  Or all the good that euer yet I gat:
  But froward fortune, and too forward Night
  Such happinesse did, maulgre, to me spight,
  And fro me reft both life and light attone.
  But Dwarfe aread, what is that Lady bright,
  That through this forrest wandreth thus alone;
For of her errour straunge I haue great ruth and mone.

8

That Ladie is (quoth he) where so she bee,
  The bountiest virgin, and most debonaire,
  That euer liuing eye I weene did see;
  Liues none this day, that may with her compare
  In stedfast chastitie and vertue rare,
  The goodly ornaments of beautie bright;
  And is ycleped *Florimell* the fayre,
  Faire *Florimell* belou'd of many a knight,
Yet she loues none but one, that *Marinell* is hight.

9

A Sea-nymphes sonne, that *Marinell* is hight,
  Of my deare Dame is loued dearely well;
  In other none, but him, she sets delight,
  All her delight is set on *Marinell*;
  But he sets nought at all by *Florimell*:
  For Ladies loue his mother long ygoe
  Did him, they say, forwarne through sacred spell.
  But fame now flies, that of a forreine foe
He is yslaine, which is the ground of all our woe.

10

Fiue daies there be, since he (they say) was slaine,
  And fowre, since *Florimell* the Court forwent,
  And vowed neuer to returne againe,
  Till him aliue or dead she did inuent.

Therefore, faire Sir, for loue of knighthood gent,
  And honour of trew Ladies, if ye may
  By your good counsell, or bold hardiment,
  Or succour her, or me direct the way,
Do one, or other good, I you most humbly pray.

11

So may ye gaine to you full great renowme,
  Of all good Ladies through the world so wide,
  And haply in her hart finde highest rowme,
  Of whom ye seeke to be most magnifide:
  At least eternall meede shall you abide.
  To whom the Prince; Dwarfe, comfort to thee take,
  For till thou tidings learne, what her betide,
  I here auow thee neuer to forsake.
Ill weares he armes, that nill them vse for Ladies sake.

12

So with the Dwarfe he backe retourn'd againe,
  To seeke his Lady, where he mote her finde;
  But by the way he greatly gan complaine
  The want of his good Squire late left behinde,
  For whom he wondrous pensiue grew in minde,
  For doubt of daunger, which mote him betide;
  For him he loued aboue all mankinde,
  Hauing him trew and faithfull euer tride,
And bold, as euer Squyre that waited by knights side.

13

Who all this while full hardly was assayd
  Of deadly daunger, which to him betidd;
  For whiles his Lord pursewd that noble Mayd,
  After that foster fowle he fiercely ridd,
  To bene auenged of the shame, he did
  To that faire Damzell: Him he chaced long
  Through the thicke woods, wherein he would haue hid
  His shamefull head from his auengement strong,
And oft him threatned death for his outrageous wrong.

'With golden wreath and gorgeous ornament'. The description associates her with the sun. **8–9** See i 18.6–8*n*.

Stanza 6
5 foregoe: go on before. **8 ruth**: occasion for sorrow. **9 read**: tell.

Stanza 7
1 Truly I would rather know that. **4 froward**: perverse; with a play on **forward**: fortune leaves the knight, night comes on him too quickly. **5 maulgre**: a general imprecation = 'A curse upon . . . !' (*OED* B 1); see II v 12.8–9*n*. **6 attone**: together. **7 aread**: declare. **9 errour**: wandering.

Stanza 8
1–6 The praise of Florimell distinguishes her from Malecasta who is 'so bounteous and so debonayre' (i 26.4) but for whom love's liberality is licentiousness. It relates her to Britomart who is known 'for pure chastitie and vertue rare' (iv 3.4), and to Belphœbe who is trained 'In all chaste vertue, and true bounti-hed' (vi 3.8). **7 Florimell**: the name, which links her with Flora, the goddess of flowers, suggests Lat. *flos*, flower + *mel*, honey. Her role links her with Proserpina, who is also associated with flowers. See 'Florimell' in the *SEnc*.

Stanza 9
6 For: against. **8 fame**: rumour.

Stanza 10
1–4 This precise fixing of the time contradicts the chronology of Florimell's actions: she was seen fleeing *before* Marinell was wounded; cf. viii 46.5–6. **the Court**: i.e. of the Faerie Queene by whom Arthur seeks 'to be most magnifide' (11.4). **forwent**: left. **inuent**: discover.

Stanza 11
3 rowme: place. **5** If not renown in this world, reward in heaven awaits you. **8** At I vii 52.7, Arthur makes a similar promise to rescue the Red Cross Knight, and at II viii 26.9 to save Guyon. **9 nill**: will not, is unwilling.

Stanza 12
4 late left behinde: at i 18.6–9. **6 doubt**: fear. **8 tride**: proven.

Stanza 13
1 assayd: assailed. **3–6** See iv 45.6*n*.

14

Nathlesse the villein sped himselfe so well,
    Whether through swiftnesse of his speedie beast,
    Or knowledge of those woods, where he did dwell,
    That shortly he from daunger was releast,
    And out of sight escaped at the least;
    Yet not escaped from the dew reward
    Of his bad deedes, which daily he increast,
    Ne ceased not, till him oppressed hard
The heauie plague, that for such leachours is prepard.

15

For soone as he was vanisht out of sight,
    His coward courage gan emboldned bee,
    And cast t'auenge him of that fowle despight,
    Which he had borne of his bold enimee.
    Tho to his brethren came: for they were three
    Vngratious children of one gracelesse syre,
    And vnto them complaynd, how that he
    Had vsed beene of that foolehardie Squyre;
So them with bitter words he stird to bloodie yre.

16

Forthwith themselues with their sad instruments
    Of spoyle and murder they gan arme byliue,
    And with him foorth into the forrest went,
    To wreake the wrath, which he did earst reuiue
    In their sterne brests, on him which late did driue
    Their brother to reproch and shamefull flight:
    For they had vow'd, that neuer he aliue
    Out of that forest should escape their might;
Vile rancour their rude harts had fild with such despight.

17

Within that wood there was a couert glade,
    Foreby a narrow foord, to them well knowne,
    Through which it was vneath for wight to wade,
    And now by fortune it was ouerflowne:
    By that same way they knew that Squyre vnknowne
    Mote algates passe; for thy themselues they set
    There in await, with thicke woods ouer growne,
    And all the while their malice they did whet
With cruell threats, his passage through the ford to let.

18

It fortuned, as they deuized had,
    The gentle Squyre came ryding that same way,
    Vnweeting of their wile and treason bad,
    And through the ford to passen did assay;
    But that fierce foster, which late fled away,
    Stoutly foorth stepping on the further shore,
    Him boldly bad his passage there to stay,
    Till he had made amends, and full restore
For all the damage, which he had him doen afore.

19

With that at him a quiu'ring dart he threw,
    With so fell force and villeinous despite,
    That through his habericon the forkehead flew,
    And through the linked mayles empierced quite,
    But had no powre in his soft flesh to bite:
    That stroke the hardy Squire did sore displease,
    But more that him he could not come to smite;
    For by no meanes the high banke he could sease,
But labour'd long in that deepe ford with vaine disease.

Stanza 14
5 at the least: at last. **9 heauie plague**: mortal blow or wound (*OED* 1), the punishment given him at 23.4–7; or syphilis, 'that foule euill' at I iv 26.7.

Stanza 15
3 cast: determined. **5–6** The three brothers represent 'the luste of the flesh, the luste of the eyes, and the pride of life' (1 John 2.16), which suggests their kinship with the six brothers in Castle Joyeous at i 45. Presumably the Foster who pursues Florimell is lust of the flesh, and is therefore armed with a boarspear (i 17.9), but also a dart by which he is able to pierce Timias's armour at 19.3–4 though not wound him. The second brother being lust of the eyes is armed with love's arrow by which Timias may be wounded with lust, as happens when he sees Belphœbe at 42; see 28*n*. The third, 'pride of life', poses no danger to the 'gentle Squyre' (18.2), and therefore is the first killed. S. would expect his readers to enjoy discriminating among the three in their choice of weapons, their effect on Timias, the nature and order of their deaths, and their relation to the squire's qualities of being 'trew', 'faithfull' and 'bold' (12.8–9). **Vngratious**: wicked, devoid of spiritual grace.

Stanza 16
1 sad: causing sorrow; heavy. **2 byliue**: immediately. **5 sterne**: cruel.

Stanza 17
2 Foreby a narrow foord: in *View* 98, Irenius notes that the Irish rebels would lie in wait to ambush the English at a 'perilous ford' where the English 'must needs pass', and here S. seems to allude to a notorious event in 1581 when Raleigh was ambushed by rebels at such a ford. He killed them, and later their instigators, the Earl of Desmond and his two brothers, were executed. S. profited from the rebellion: Kilcolman Castle with its land was part of Desmond's confiscated estate, which he was granted; see Chronology 1589 *22 May*. For the topical allusion, see Bednarz 1984:52–58. **3 vneath**: difficult. **5 vnknowne**: i.e. unknown to him. **6 algates**: in any case. **for thy**: therefore. **7 await**: ambush. **9 let**: prevent.

Stanza 18
1 deuized: schemed. **8 restore**: restitution.

Stanza 19
1 dart: a light spear or javelin. **3 habericon** = habergeon; see iii 57.8*n*. **forkehead**: the barbed head. **6 displease**: deeply annoy or grieve. **8 sease**: reach. **9 disease**: distress.

Stanza 20
2 . . . as he wished. **5 vnlucky**: causing harm. **7** Timias's wound in the **left thigh** suggests the wound of lust. Although he is only threatened by lust's traditional weapon, the

20

And still the foster with his long bore-speare
  Him kept from landing at his wished will;
  Anone one sent out of the thicket neare
  A cruell shaft, headed with deadly ill,
  And fethered with an vnlucky quill;
  The wicked steele stayd not, till it did light
  In his left thigh, and deepely did it thrill:
Exceeding griefe that wound in him empight,
But more that with his foes he could not come to fight.

21

At last through wrath and vengeaunce making way,
  He on the bancke arryud with mickle payne,
  Where the third brother him did sore assay,
  And drove at him with all his might and mayne
  A forest bill, which both his hands did strayne;
  But warily he did auoide the blow,
  And with his speare requited him agayne,
  That both his sides were thrilled with the throw,
And a large streame of bloud out of the wound did flow.

22

He tombling downe, with gnashing teeth did bite
  The bitter earth, and bad to lett him in
  Into the balefull house of endlesse night,
  Where wicked ghosts doe waile their former sin.
  Tho gan the battaile freshly to begin;
  For nathemore for that spectacle bad,
  Did th'other two their cruell vengeaunce blin,
  But both attonce on both sides him bestad,
And load vpon him layd, his life for to haue had.

23

Tho when that villayn he auiz'd, which late
  Affrighted had the fairest *Florimell*,
  Full of fiers fury, and indignant hate,
  To him he turned, and with rigor fell
  Smote him so rudely on the Pannikell,
  That to the chin he clefte his head in twaine:
  Downe on the ground his carkas groueling fell;
  His sinfull sowle with desperate disdaine,
Out of her fleshly ferme fled to the place of paine.

24

That seeing now the only last of three,
  Who with that wicked shafte him wounded had,
  Trembling with horror, as that did foresee
  The fearefull end of his auengement sad,
  Through which he follow should his brethren bad,
  His bootelesse bow in feeble hand vpcaught,
  And therewith shott an arrow at the lad;
  Which fayntly fluttring, scarce his helmet raught,
And glauncing fel to ground, but him annoyed naught.

25

With that he would haue fled into the wood;
  But *Timias* him lightly ouerhent,
  Right as he entring was into the flood,
  And strooke at him with force so violent,
  That headlesse him into the foord he sent:
  The carcas with the streame was carried downe,
  But th'head fell backeward on the Continent.
  So mischief fel vpon the meaners crowne;
They three be dead with shame, the Squire liues with renowne.

26

He liues, but takes small ioy of his renowne;
  For of that cruell wound he bled so sore,
  That from his steed he fell in deadly swowne;
  Yet still the blood forth gusht in so great store,
  That he lay wallowd all in his owne gore.
  Now God thee keepe, thou gentlest squire aliue,
  Els shall thy louing Lord thee see no more,
  But both of comfort him thou shalt depriue,
And eke thy selfe of honor, which thou didst atchiue.

27

Prouidence heuenly passeth liuing thought,
  And doth for wretched mens reliefe make way;
  For loe great grace or fortune thether brought
  Comfort to him, that comfortlesse now lay.
  In those same woods, ye well remember may,
  How that a noble hunteresse did wonne,
  Shee, that base *Braggadochio* did affray,
  And made him fast out of the forest ronne;
Belphœbe was her name, as faire as *Phœbus* sunne.

bore-speare, he has never been cured of the poison 'sprinkled on his weaker partes' by Duessa at I viii 14.7. **thrill**: pierce. **8 griefe**: pain. **empight**: implanted.

Stanza 21
3 **assay**: assail. 5 **forest bill**: long-bladed axe or sickle. **strayne**: grasp tightly. 7 **his speare**: presumably Arthur's 'heben' spear, which he carries at I vii 37.2. **8 throw**: thrust.

Stanza 22
1–2 See V ii 18.6*n*. 7 **blin**: stop. 8 **bestad**: beset.

Stanza 23
1 **auiz'd**: observed. 4 **rigor**: violence. 5–6 Presumably Timias slices the Foster's **Pannikell** (skull, brain-pan) with a sword. 9 **ferme**: enclosure (sugg. by the context); cf. 'seat' (31.4), 'shop' (II i 43.7).

Stanza 25
2 **lightly ouerhent**: swiftly or easily overtook. 7 S. inverts Ovid's account, in *Met.* 11.50–51, of the death of Orpheus: his limbs were scattered on the land while his head was carried down the Hebrus. 8 **meaners crowne**: the heads of those who meant mischief.

Stanza 26
5 As Marinell is seen at iv 16.9, 34.7–9. 8–9 Since his name signifies honour (see i 18.9*n*), to be deprived of honour would result in loss of name and identity. At this moment of crisis, he may be preserved by God's 'great grace' (27.3) through Belphœbe.

Stanza 27
In agreement with the number of the book (see I viii Arg.1–2*n*) – though uniquely not in Bk III through Arthur – grace

28

She on a day, as shee pursewd the chace
  Of some wilde beast, which with her arrowes keene
  She wounded had, the same along did trace
  By tract of blood, which she had freshly seene,
  To haue besprinckled all the grassy greene,
  By the great persue, which she there perceau'd,
  Well hoped shee the beast engor'd had beene,
  And made more haste, the life to haue bereav'd:
But ah, her expectation greatly was deceau'd.

29

Shortly she came, whereas that woefull Squire
  With blood deformed, lay in deadly swownd:
  In whose faire eyes, like lamps of quenched fire,
  The Christall humor stood congealed rownd;
  His locks, like faded leaues fallen to grownd,
  Knotted with blood, in bounches rudely ran,
  And his sweete lips, on which before that stownd
  The bud of youth to blossome faire began,
Spoild of their rosy red, were woxen pale and wan.

30

Saw neuer liuing eie more heauy sight,
  That could haue made a rocke of stone to rew,
  Or riue in twaine: which when that Lady bright
  Besides all hope with melting eies did vew,

All suddeinly abasht shee chaunged hew,
  And with sterne horror backward gan to start:
  But when shee better him beheld, shee grew
  Full of soft passion and vnwonted smart:
The point of pitty perced through her tender hart.

31

Meekely shee bowed downe, to weete if life
  Yett in his frosen members did remaine,
  And feeling by his pulses beating rife,
  That the weake sowle her seat did yett retaine,
  She cast to comfort him with busy paine:
  His double folded necke she reard vpright,
  And rubd his temples, and each trembling vaine;
  His mayled habericon she did vndight,
And from his head his heauy burganet did light.

32

Into the woods thenceforth in haste shee went,
  To seeke for hearbes, that mote him remedy;
  For shee of herbes had great intendiment,
  Taught of the Nymphe, which from her infancy
  Her nourced had in trew Nobility:
  There, whether yt diuine *Tobacco* were,
  Or *Panachæa*, or *Polygony*,
  Shee fownd, and brought it to her patient deare
Who al this while lay bleeding out his hart-blood neare.

---

intercedes three times: Belphœbe succours Timias, Proteus saves Florimell at viii 29–31, and Britomart intervenes at xi 14, 16 to free Amoret. **1** See I vi 7.1–2*n*. **4 Comfort**: aid, succour; hence **comfortlesse** indicates his helplessness. **5–8** Referring to Braggadocchio's encounter with Belphœbe at II iii 21–46 in order to contrast Timias's response to her. **ye.** a direct address to the reader that becomes increasingly common in Bk III, as vi 1.2, 53.9, etc. **9 Phœbus sunne**: i.e. Phœbus Apollo who, being Belphœbe's father, provides one etymology of her name; see vi 6–7. For further on her name, see II iii Arg.4*n*. Cf. the description of Florimell at 5.4–5.

Stanza 28
The **tract** (track) of blood **freshly seene** associates Timias with the beast wounded by Belphœbe's arrow, as at II iii 34 when Braggadocchio was taken by her to be the hind she had wounded. The connection is stressed at 37.1–6: she comes to kill the beast, and, through love of her caused by the 'vnwary dart' (42.5) from her eyes, Timias is 'destroyed quight' (41.9). **6 persue**: the track of blood left by a wounded beast. **9 But ah**: a rare moment in the poem where S. poses as spectator of what he writes; cf. 43.8–9.

Stanza 29
2 deformed: disfigured. **4 humor**: fluid, referring to his eyes glazing over in his state near death. **7 stownd**: hard time; cf. 38.5.

Stanza 30
3 bright: a traditional epithet for a lady, applied even to Hellenore at x 21.8, but esp. appropriate to Belphœbe; see 27.9*n*. **4–9 Besides all hope**: beyond or contrary to hope,

i.e. having no hope that he was alive. She responds with the two contradictory emotions aroused by tragedy, terror and pity; but on pitying him, she retreats in horror because 'pity melts the mind to love'; for the proverb, see Smith 611. While she rejects love, Marinell 'learne[s] to loue, by learning louers paines to rew' at IV xii 13.9. S.'s literary model is Ariosto, *Orl. Fur.* 19.20: Angelica's unwonted pity (*insolita pietade*) for the wounded Medoro causes her to love him; see C. Burrow 1993:110–15. **abasht**: checked with shame. **sterne**: merciless; threatening. **passion**: affection aroused through pity.

Stanza 31
3 rife: frequently; strongly. **4 her seat**: see 23.9*n*. **5 cast**: sought. By her **paine**, i.e. trouble, she seeks to cure his, but she succeeds only in causing him fresh pain, hence her 'vnfruitfull paine' (42.1); cf. 50.1. **9** I.e. she lightens his head by removing his heavy helmet.

Stanza 32
This stanza is heavily marked in a copy of S.'s poem owned by Raleigh's son; noted Oakeshott 1971:10. On Timias's relation to Belphœbe, here and at IV vii–viii, as it may allude to Raleigh's relation to the Queen, see IV vii 36.8–9*n*. **3 intendiment**: understanding. **4–5** By this (unnamed) nymph, she is 'vpbrought in perfect Maydenhed' (vi 28.4). Cf. vi 3.7–8. **trew Nobility** is praised by S. in his commendatory sonnet prefixed to *Nenno, or a Treatise of Nobility* (1595). **6–7** On the medicinal properties of herbs, see 'plants, herbs' in the *SEnc*. S. is guilty of being the first English poet to praise **Tobacco**; **diuine** refers to its Lat. name, *sacra herba* or *sancta herba*, for it was believed to cure serious wounds. On its contemporary importance, see Knapp 1992:134–74. **Panachæa**, or All-Heal, was given by Venus to cure Aeneas in Virgil, *Aen.*

33

The soueraine weede betwixt two marbles plaine
  Shee pownded small, and did in peeces bruze,
  And then atweene her lilly handes twaine,
  Into his wound the iuice thereof did scruze,
  And round about, as she could well it vze,
  The flesh therewith shee suppled and did steepe,
  T'abate all spasme, and soke the swelling bruze,
  And after hauing searcht the intuse deepe,
She with her scarf did bind the wound from cold to keepe.

34

By this he had sweet life recur'd agayne,
  And groning inly deepe, at last his eies,
  His watry eies, drizling like deawy rayne,
  He vp gan lifte toward the azure skies,
  From whence descend all hopelesse remedies:
  Therewith he sigh'd, and turning him aside,
  The goodly Maide ful of diuinities,
  And gifts of heauenly grace he by him spide,
Her bow and gilden quiuer lying him beside.

35

Mercy deare Lord (said he) what grace is this,
  That thou hast shewed to me sinfull wight,
  To send thine Angell from her bowre of blis,
  To comfort me in my distressed plight?
  Angell, or Goddesse doe I call thee right?
  What seruice may I doe vnto thee meete,
  That hast from darkenes me returnd to light,
  And with thy heuenly salues and med'cines sweete,
Hast drest my sinfull wounds? I kisse thy blessed feete.

36

Thereat she blushing said, Ah gentle Squire,
  Nor Goddesse I, nor Angell, but the Mayd,
  And daughter of a woody Nymphe, desire
  No seruice, but thy safety and ayd,
  Which if thou gaine, I shalbe well apayd.
  Wee mortall wights, whose liues and fortunes bee
  To commun accidents stil open layd,
  Are bownd with commun bond of frailtee,
To succor wretched wights, whom we captiued see.

37

By this her Damzells, which the former chace
  Had vndertaken after her, arryu'd,
  As did *Belphœbe*, in the bloody place,
  And thereby deemd the beast had bene depriu'd
  Of life, whom late their ladies arrow ryu'd:
  For thy the bloody tract they followd fast,
  And euery one to ronne the swiftest stryu'd;
  But two of them the rest far ouerpast,
And where their Lady was, arriued at the last.

38

Where when they saw that goodly boy, with blood
  Defowled, and their Lady dresse his wownd,
  They wondred much, and shortly vnderstood,
  How him in deadly case theyr Lady fownd,
  And reskewed out of the heauy stownd.
  Eftsoones his warlike courser, which was strayd
  Farre in the woodes, whiles that he lay in swownd,
  She made those Damzels search, which being stayd,
They did him set theron, and forth with them conuayd.

12. 419, and may have been given by Angelica to cure Medoro in Ariosto, *Orl. Fur.* 19.22, for it was used to treat deep wounds. **Polygony** was applied to fresh wounds. S. does not name the 'soueraine weede' (33.1) gathered by Belphœbe – the three she mentions being only possible ones – but it could have been moly, which was given Odysseus in Homer, *Odyssey* 10.302–04, to cure concupiscence (Golding tr. Ovid, *Met.*, Epistle 278–79), and would have been appropriate to cure Timias's arrow wound in the left thigh; see 20.7*n*.

Stanza 33

1–4 **soueraine**: supremely efficacious. **plaine**: flat or smooth. **bruze**: crush. **scruze**: squeeze. **lilly handes**: not just the usual token of a maiden's purity – see iv 41.1*n* – but a 'realistic' detail: she cups her hands like a lily to hold the powder. 6 **suppled**: softened, massaged. 8 **searcht**: probed. **intuse**: bruise.

Stanza 34

1 **recur'd**: recovered. **3 His watry eies**: tears denote restored life; cf. 29.3–4. 5 **hopelesse**: unhoped for; for the hopeless. 6–9 He looks to heaven for God's grace but finds it by **turning him aside** and seeing the maiden **ful of diuinities** (i.e. divine qualities) and **heauenly grace**. Cf. the praise of Britomart at ix 24.4, and esp. of the Queen as 'Mirrour of grace and Maiestie diuine' (I proem 4.2). **gilden**: golden; see II iii 26.7–9*n*.

Stanza 35

5–6 Echoing Aeneas's address to Venus masquerading as Diana in Virgil, *Aen.* 1.327–28, and recalling Trompart's address to Belphœbe at II iii 33.2–4. The erotic suggestion of **seruice**, overt in the Squire of Dames at vii 54.6, is implied here. 7 The language is appropriately biblical: 'that hathe called you out of darkenes into his marueilous light' (1 Pet. 2.9). 9 **sinfull**: because they signify the wound of concupiscence, or as he is a **sinfull wight**; cf. 'foule sore' (41.8).

Stanza 36

1 **blushing**: on Belphœbe's abashedness, see Krier 1990:164–76. 2 The definite article stresses her virginity. 3 **woody**: woodland; referring to the nymph who raised her (see 32.4–5), not to her mother who 'A Faerie was, yborne of high degree' (vi 4.3). 5 **apayd**: requited. 6–9 Belphœbe's admission that she is mortal and subject to **frailtee** as are other mortals (such as Timias) incites his desire.

Stanza 37

5 **ryu'd**: pierced. **8 two of them**: a curious detail. Possibly the three nymphs counter the three fosters.

Stanza 38

1 **that goodly boy**: at IV vii 23.6, he is introduced as 'that louely boy'. The term, usually reserved for Cupid, links him to Adonis, as at i 35.2.

39

Into that forest farre they thence him led,
    Where was their dwelling, in a pleasant glade,
    With mountaines rownd about enuironed,
    And mightie woodes, which did the valley shade,
    And like a stately Theatre it made,
    Spreading it selfe into a spatious plaine.
    And in the midst a little riuer plaide
    Emongst the pumy stones, which seemd to plaine
With gentle murmure, that his cours they did restraine.

40

Beside the same a dainty place there lay,
    Planted with mirtle trees and laurells greene,
    In which the birds song many a louely lay
    Of gods high praise, and of their sweet loues teene,
    As it an earthly Paradize had beene:
    In whose enclosed shadow there was pight
    A faire Pauilion, scarcely to be seene,
    The which was al within most richly dight,
That greatest Princes liuing it mote well delight.

41

Thether they brought that wounded Squyre, and layd
    In easie couch his feeble limbes to rest;
    He rested him a while, and then the Mayd
    His readie wound with better salues new drest;
    Daily she dressed him, and did the best
    His grieuous hurt to guarish, that she might,
    That shortly she his dolour hath redrest,
    And his foule sore reduced to faire plight:
It she reduced, but himselfe destroyed quight.

42

O foolish physick, and vnfruitfull paine,
    That heales vp one and makes another wound:
    She his hurt thigh to him recurd againe,
    But hurt his hart, the which before was sound,
    Through an vnwary dart, which did rebownd
    From her faire eyes and gratious countenaunce.
    What bootes it him from death to be vnbownd,
    To be captiued in endlesse duraunce
Of sorrow and despeyre without aleggeaunce?

43

Still as his wound did gather, and grow hole,
    So still his hart woxe sore, and health decayd:
    Madnesse to saue a part, and lose the whole.
    Still whenas he beheld the heauenly Mayd,
    Whiles dayly playsters to his wownd she layd,
    So still his Malady the more increast,
    The whiles her matchlesse beautie him dismayd.
    Ah God, what other could he doe at least,
But loue so fayre a Lady, that his life release?

44

Long while he stroue in his corageous brest,
    With reason dew the passion to subdew,
    And loue for to dislodge out of his nest:
    Still when her excellencies he did vew,
    Her soueraine bountie, and celestiall hew,
    The same to loue he strongly was constraynd:
    But when his meane estate he did reuew,
    He from such hardy boldnesse was restraynd,
And of his lucklesse lott and cruell loue thus playnd.

Stanza 39

5–6 In *Ruines* 519–25, 'a pleasant Paradize' is compared to a garden 'which *Merlin* by his Magicke slights | Made for the gentle squire, to entertaine | His fayre *Belphœbe*'. The description invokes such *loci amoeni* as the dwelling of the mermaids at II xii 30.2–7 and the site of the Bower of Bliss at II xii 50.2–5 with its counterpart in the setting of Castle Joyeous at i 20.5–7. Its primary literary source is Ovid's description of Gargaphie, the haunt of Diana, within which is her grotto (*Met.* 3.157–64), for here Actaeon, seeing her naked, is overwhelmed by passion. **8–9 pumy stones**: pumice-stones. **plaine**: complain. A curious variation of the same detail in the Bower of Bliss: at II v 30.1–4, the sound of water falling over pumice lulls the traveller asleep.

Stanza 40

1 dainty: delightful, excellent. **2 mirtle** and **laurell** are cited for their fragrance in Virgil, *Ecl.* 2.54–55, but here for their emblematic significance in marking Belphœbe's state. The former is sacred to Venus (*Ecl.* 7.62) because it shielded her when she was surprised bathing (Ovid, *Fasti* 4.139–44); see Panofsky 1962:161. The latter is associated with the protection of virginity because Daphne (δάφνη = laurel) was transformed into a laurel to preserve her from being raped by Apollo (see Ovid, *Met.* 1.548–52). Only the mirtle is found on Venus's mount at vi 43.3. **3–4 louely lay**: song of love. They sing in praise either of God or Cupid. **teene**: grief.

Stanza 41

4 readie: properly dressed. **6 guarish**: heal. **7 dolour**: pain. **redrest**: relieved. **8 reduced**: restored.

Stanza 42

In Ariosto – see 30.4–9*n* – Angelica cures Medoro but is wounded by love for him. **1 paine**: labour. **4–6** In contrast to the ineffectual dart hurled by the foster who represents the lust of the eye (19.1–5), the dart that is said to proceed (**rebownd**) from Belphœbe's **faire eyes** wounds his heart. Or 'beauty darts beams into his eyes and heart, his heart sends back the dart as desire' (Berger 1989:230). **vnwary**: unexpected. **7–9** An erotic analogue to the Red Cross Knight who was released from Orgoglio's dungeon only to become a victim of despair. **duraunce**: constraint, imprisonment. **aleggeaunce**: relief; in the legal sense, 'allegation', for Timias is unable to plead his love. Cf. ii 15.4.

Stanza 43

1–2 A curious expression, for a wound is said to **gather** when it becomes infected; and **hole** suggests an open wound. S.'s point is that 'love is a curelesse sorrow' (*SC Aug.* 104), which herbs cannot heal (Ovid, *Met.* 1.523). Any attempt to cure Timias only wounds him further. **9 release**: i.e. delivered from death, 'saued' (45.3).

45

Vnthankfull wretch (said he) is this the meed,
    With which her souerain mercy thou doest quight?
    Thy life she saued by her gratious deed,
    But thou doest weene with villeinous despight,
    To blott her honour, and her heauenly light.
    Dye rather, dye, then so disloyally
    Deeme of her high desert, or seeme so light:
    Fayre death it is to shonne more shame, to dy:
Dye rather, dy, then euer loue disloyally.

46

But if to loue disloyalty it bee,
    Shall I then hate her, that from deathes dore
    Me brought? ah farre be such reproch fro mee.
    What can I lesse doe, then her loue therefore,
    Sith I her dew reward cannot restore?
    Dye rather, dye, and dying doe her serue,
    Dying her serue, and liuing her adore;
    Thy life she gaue, thy life she doth deserue:
Dye rather, dye, then euer from her seruice swerue.

47

But foolish boy, what bootes thy seruice bace
    To her, to whom the heuens doe serue and sew?
    Thou a meane Squyre, of meeke and lowly place,
    She heuenly borne, and of celestiall hew.
    How then? of all loue taketh equall vew:
    And doth not highest God vouchsafe to take
    The loue and seruice of the basest crew?
    If she will not, dye meekly for her sake;
Dye rather, dye, then euer so faire loue forsake.

48

Thus warreid he long time against his will,
    Till that through weaknesse he was forst at last,
    To yield himselfe vnto the mightie ill:
    Which as a victour proud, gan ransack fast
    His inward partes, and all his entrayles wast,
    That neither blood in face, nor life in hart
    It left, but both did quite drye vp, and blast;
    As percing leuin, which the inner part
Of euery thing consumes, and calcineth by art.

49

Which seeing fayre *Belphœbe*, gan to feare,
    Least that his wound were inly well not heald,
    Or that the wicked steele empoysned were:
    Litle shee weend, that loue he close conceald;
    Yet still he wasted, as the snow congeald,
    When the bright sunne his beams theron doth beat;
    Yet neuer he his hart to her reueald,
    But rather chose to dye for sorow great,
Then with dishonorable termes her to entreat.

50

She gracious Lady, yet no paines did spare,
    To doe him ease, or doe him remedy:
    Many Restoratiues of vertues rare,
    And costly Cordialles she did apply,
    To mitigate his stubborne malady:
    But that sweet Cordiall, which can restore
    A loue-sick hart, she did to him enuy;
    To him, and to all th'vnworthy world forlore
She did enuy that soueraine salue, in secret store.

Stanza 44

2 dew: fitting, proper; with a play on **subdew**: 'it is fitting that reason subdue passion'. **5 bountie**: goodness; liberality; see 8.1–6*n*. **hew**: appearance.

Stanzas 45–47

Timias's formal complaint is the counterpart of Britomart's lament at iv 8–10. Each stanza moves from query to command, and the three interlinked stanzas move from a resolve not to love Belphœbe to a resolve to love and serve her but not show his love. It expresses the dilemma of Elizabeth's courtiers: she encouraged their love but denied them sexual satisfaction. As it expresses the Petrarchan bind, see Dasenbrock 1991:54–55; as an imitation of Raleigh's poetry to Elizabeth, see Bednarz 1996:287–90.

Stanza 45

2 quight: requite. **8** It is a fair death to die in order to shun more shame.

Stanza 46

6–9 The bawdy double meaning through the repetition of **dye** and **serue** is noted by Oram 1990:352 in querying Elizabeth's treatment of Raleigh as Timias. Finke 1994:222 interprets Timias's love as a metaphor for an economic relationship.

Stanza 47

2 sew: do homage.

Stanza 48

1 warreid: made war. **will**: also lust. **7 blast**: wither. **8–9 percing leuin**: piercing lightning, so described because its intense heat was thought to cause death by disintegrating the body's internal parts; see Heninger 1960:79. **calcineth**: reduces to powder. **by art**: analogous to alchemical art which reduced metals from their oxides by heat. See 'alchemy' in the *SEnc*.

Stanza 49

5–6 In Ariosto, *Orl. Fur.* 19.29, Angelica, not her lover, wastes away as snow melted by the sun. That she then allows him to gather her 'rose' becomes the point of S.'s imitation, as the next stanza makes clear.

Stanza 50

4 Cordialles: the repetition of the word points to its etymological meaning: medicine that invigorates the heart (Lat. *cor*). **7 enuy**: refuse. The consequences of her refusal are told when their story is resumed at IV vii 23. **8 forlore**: wretched, forsaken (by her).

Stanzas 51–55

Praise of Belphœbe's virginity – though S. never uses the word – praises the Virgin Queen, as S. explains in the *LR* 35–36: the Queen as 'a most vertuous and beautifull Lady . . . I doe expresse in Belphœbe'. Virginity as the rose to be preserved answers the song in Acrasia's Bower of Bliss at II xii 74–75. For God's garden of virtue, see VI proem 3.

51

That daintie Rose, the daughter of her Morne,
    More deare then life she tendered, whose flowre
    The girlond of her honour did adorne:
    Ne suffred she the Middayes scorching powre,
    Ne the sharp Northerne wind thereon to showre,
    But lapped vp her silken leaues most chayre,
    When so the froward skye began to lowre;
    But soone as calmed was the christall ayre,
She did it fayre dispred, and let to florish fayre.

52

Eternall God in his almightie powre,
    To make ensample of his heauenly grace,
    In Paradize whylome did plant this flowre;
    Whence he it fetcht out of her natiue place,
    And did in stocke of earthly flesh enrace,
    That mortall men her glory should admyre:
    In gentle Ladies breste, and bounteous race
    Of woman kind it fayrest flowre doth spyre,
And beareth fruit of honour and all chast desyre.

53

Fayre ympes of beautie, whose bright shining beames
    Adorne the world with like to heauenly light,
    And to your willes both royalties and Reames
    Subdew, through conquest of your wondrous might,

With this fayre flowre your goodly girlonds dight,
    Of chastity and vertue virginall,
    That shall embellish more your beautie bright,
    And crowne your heades with heauenly coronall,
Such as the Angels weare before Gods tribunall.

54

To youre faire selues a faire ensample frame,
    Of this faire virgin, this *Belphebe* fayre,
    To whom in perfect loue, and spotlesse fame
    Of chastitie, none liuing may compayre:
    Ne poysnous Enuy iustly can empayre
    The prayse of her fresh flowring Maydenhead;
    For thy she standeth on the highest stayre
    Of th'honorable stage of womanhead,
That Ladies all may follow her ensample dead.

55

In so great prayse of stedfast chastity,
    Nathlesse she was so courteous and kynde,
    Tempred with grace, and goodly modesty,
    That seemed those two vertues stroue to fynd
    The higher place in her Heroick mynd:
    So striuing each did other more augment,
    And both encrease the prayse of woman kynde,
    And both encrease her beautie excellent;
So all did make in her a perfect complement.

Stanza 51

The **Rose** suggests her virginity but is not equated with it, being untranslatable, as D. Cheney 1966:102 notes, though fittingly applied to the Tudor rose. **the daughter of her Morne**: this metaphorical description is linked to the description of Truth, that 'Most sacred virgin' (iv 59.8) who is the daughter of Day. **2 tendered**: cherished. **4–5** Alluding to her own conception when her mother displayed her naked body to the sun's generative powers at vi 7. In his gloss to *SC Apr.* 122, E.K. interprets Zephyrus's love for Chloris as the generative power of the wind. The north wind 'cannot blast | The tender and the delicately-grac't | Flesh of the virgin . . . kept within | Close by her mother' (Hesiod, *Geor* 2.232–35, tr. Chapman). **showre**, as it rhymes with **powre** and followed by **lapped**, may allude to Jove's 'golden showre' (xi 31.1) that impregnates Danaë. Cf. the description of Venus's mount, the *mons Veneris*, as a place where 'nether *Phœbus* beams could through them [the flowers] throng, | Nor *Aeolus* sharp blast could worke them any wrong' (vi 44.8–9). **6 chayre**: charily, carefully. **7 froward**: adverse. **8–9** Cf. Glauce's complaint to the love-sick Britomart that she does not 'spred | Abroad thy fresh youths fayrest flowre' (ii 31.6–7).

Stanza 52

5 enrace: implant. **6 admyre**: wonder at. **8 spyre**: shoot forth.

Stanza 53

1 Fayre ympes: offspring; here, literally, shoots or slips. Cf. the address to 'Faire Ladies' at i 49 (and see *n*). **3 Reames**: obs.

var. of Realmes *1596*. **6–7 chastity** belongs to those who marry, **vertue virginall** to those who remain single. **embellish**: as outward beauty manifests inner virtue. **8–9** Cf. 1 Pet. 1.4, 5.4.

Stanza 54

The praise of Florimell at 8.4–5 and viii 43 is extended here to compliment Elizabeth. At xi 2.6–9, 'faire Ladies' are exhorted to imitate Britomart. **7 stayre**: position; step, degree. **9 dead**: i.e. when she is dead; cf. 'his ymage dead' at iii 29.2. Or 'her dead, or lifeless, example', as Anderson 1982a:56 suggests in noting that **none liuing** may indicate that Belphœbe is only a mythic ideal. The contradiction that qualifies praise of virginity has been noted to me by David Shore: if **Ladies all** followed the example of Belphœbe, there would be no more virgins, as the Wife of Bath warns: 'if ther were no seed ysowe,| Virginitee, than wherof sholde it growe?'

Stanza 55

1–5 prayse: excellence, praiseworthiness. **Nathlesse**: the potential paradox from the erotic meanings of **courteous** and **kynde** is noted by O'Connell 1977:113–14. **kynde** claims that her virgin state while natural is **Tempred** (i.e. mingled in proper balance) with her second virtue, courtesy. On the relation of the two virtues, see IV x 50–51*n* and VI x 27.5–6. **8** As 53.7. **excellent**: supreme. **9 complement**: completeness, fulfilment.

Cant. VI.

The birth of fayre Belphoebe and
Of Amorett is told.
The Gardins of Adonis fraught
With pleasures manifold.

1

WEll may I weene, faire Ladies, all this while
   Ye wonder, how this noble Damozell
So great perfections did in her compile,
Sith that in saluage forests she did dwell,
So farre from court and royall Citadell,
The great schoolmaistresse of all courtesy:
Seemeth that such wilde woodes should far expell
All ciuile vsage and gentility,
And gentle sprite deforme with rude rusticity.

2

But to this faire *Belphœbe* in her berth
   The heuens so fauorable were and free,
   Looking with myld aspect vpon the earth,
   In th'*Horoscope* of her natiuitee,

That all the gifts of grace and chastitee
On her they poured forth of plenteous horne;
Ioue laught on *Venus* from his souerayne see,
And *Phœbus* with faire beames did her adorne,
And all the *Graces* rockt her cradle being borne.

3

Her berth was of the wombe of Morning dew,
   And her conception of the ioyous Prime,
   And all her whole creation did her shew
   Pure and vnspotted from all loathly crime,
That is ingenerate in fleshly slime.
So was this virgin borne, so was she bred,
So was she trayned vp from time to time,
In all chaste vertue, and true bounti-hed
Till to her dew perfection she was ripened.

Book III Canto vi

Argument

3 Gardins: the plural is used again at II x 71.4, and *Colin Clout* 804.

Stanza 1

1 faire Ladies: see i 49*n* and 54.1. S. knows that such an audience is more interested in others of their sex rather than in the love-agonies of a lowly squire. **3 compile**: gather together, or compose, to form 'a perfect complement' (v 55.9). **4 saluage**: wilde.

Stanzas 2–3

From these nativity stanzas, Berleth 1973 constructs Belphœbe's horoscope – it would also be Amoret's, who is her twin – to account for her 'great perfections' (1.3) and her 'identification' with Elizabeth. The etiological tale that follows shows how these perfections are natural to the sisters, though one is nurtured by Diana's nymph (28.3–4) and the other by Psyche (28.7, 51.3–5).

Stanza 2

2 free: generous. **3 myld aspect**: referring to the favourable relationship of the planets at the moment of her birth. **6 plenteous horne**: the cornucopia, Amalthea's horn of plenty; here the constellation Capricorn. **7–8** In neoplatonic mythology, **Ioue, Venus**, and **Phœbus** were held to correspond to the three Graces; noted A. Fowler 1964:83*n*2. For

their analogical relationship to Belphœbe/Florimell/Amoret, see Nohrnberg 1976:461–70. **from** indicates that Venus and Jove are in their most felicitous aspect; see DeLacy 1934:537. **laught on**: cf. IV x 56.4. Berleth 1973:488–89 notes that this astrological aspect indicates perfect harmony and friendship among the planets, and that **souerayne see** (throne) 'confirms that Jove is dominant to Venus'. Line 8 is read by Berger 1994:99 as a polite periphrasis for a solar rape.

Stanza 3

1–2 Cf. Ps. 110.3 (*BCP*): 'Thy birthes dew is the dew that doth from wombe of morning fall'. Roche 1964:105–06 notes that this verse was taken to refer to the begetting of Christ, and concludes that the miraculous birth here is analogous to the Incarnation. See 27.1–3*n*. **Prime**: spring; 'a Sommers ... day' (6.4). **3–5 vnspotted**: as Elisa (i.e. the Queen) is 'without spotte' (*SC Apr.* 50). **ingenerate**: inborn, innate; alluding to original sin, which was held to be transmitted by sexual intercourse. **fleshly slime**: see I vii 9.8*n*. Belphœbe's immaculate conception answers Catholic polemic that Elizabeth was the child of an incestuous, carnal union; see Hackett 1995:141–42. **6 bred** separates her conception from nourishment in the womb and from birth. **7 from time to time**: at all times. **8 bounti-hed**: goodness; as Alma's castle is established 'On firme foundation of true bountyhed' (II xii 1.5). **9 dew perfection**: the pun stresses her perfection from her original innocence at birth, in implied contrast to the perfection which a woman was held to gain through marriage.

4

Her mother was the faire *Chrysogonee*,
    The daughter of *Amphisa*, who by race
    A Faerie was, yborne of high degree,
    She bore *Belphœbe*, she bore in like cace
    Fayre *Amoretta* in the second place:
    These two were twinnes, and twixt them two did share
    The heritage of all celestiall grace.
    That all the rest it seemd they robbed bare
Of bounty, and of beautie, and all vertues rare.

5

It were a goodly storie, to declare,
    By what straunge accident faire *Chrysogone*
    Conceiu'd these infants, and how them she bore,
    In this wilde forrest wandring all alone,
    After she had nine moneths fulfild and gone:
    For not as other wemens commune brood,
    They were enwombed in the sacred throne
    Of her chaste bodie, nor with commune food,
As other wemens babes, they sucked vitall blood.

6

But wondrously they were begot, and bred
    Through influence of th'heuens fruitfull ray,
    As it in antique bookes is mentioned.
    It was vpon a Sommers shinie day,
    When *Titan* faire his beames did display,
    In a fresh fountaine, far from all mens vew,
    She bath'd her brest, the boyling heat t'allay;
    She bath'd with roses red, and violets blew,
And all the sweetest flowres, that in the forrest grew.

7

Till faint through yrkesome wearines, adowne
    Vpon the grassy ground her selfe she layd
    To sleepe, the whiles a gentle slombring swowne
    Vpon her fell all naked bare displayd;
    The sunbeames bright vpon her body playd,
    Being through former bathing mollifide,
    And pierst into her wombe, where they embayd
    With so sweet sence and secret power vnspide,
That in her pregnant flesh they shortly fructifide.

8

Miraculous may seeme to him, that reades
    So straunge ensample of conception,
    But reason teacheth that the fruitfull seades
    Of all things liuing, through impression
    Of the sunbeames in moyst complexion,
    Doe life conceiue and quickned are by kynd:
    So after *Nilus* inundation,
    Infinite shapes of creatures men doe fynd,
Informed in the mud, on which the Sunne hath shynd.

9

Great father he of generation
    Is rightly cald, th'authour of life and light;
    And his faire sister for creation
    Ministreth matter fit, which tempred right
    With heate and humour, breedes the liuing wight.
    So sprong these twinnes in womb of *Chrysogone*,
    Yet wist she nought thereof, but sore affright,
    Wondred to see her belly so vpblone,
Which still increast, till she her terme had full outgone.

Stanza 4

1 Chrysogonee: Gk χρυσο-γόνη golden-born (Draper 1932:100), alluding to the myth of Danaë who conceived when Jove came down upon her in a golden shower; or 'gold-producing', from Lat. *chrysogonum*: 'that bryngeth foorth golde' (T. Cooper 1565). See 'Chrysogone' in the *SEnc*. On gold produced by the sun, see II vii Arg.2*n*. **2 Amphisa**: ἄμ + φυσις, of double nature (Draper 1932:99), either as she is both mortal and immortal, or as her daughter gives birth to the antithetical but complementary states of Belphœbe and Amoret. Lewis 1966:158 suggests 'Both Equal' or 'Equally Both', as her descendants are the two archetypes, the Terrible Huntress and the Yielding Bride. However, as also at 51.2, Belphœbe is called the first-born, which suggests either that she is superior, or that virginity precedes chaste love. At v 54.7–8, her virginity places her 'on the highest stayre | Of th'honorable stage of womanhead'. On their ontological hierarchy as paradigmatic figures, see MacCaffrey 1976:271–81.

Stanza 5

2 accident: event.

Stanza 6

2 influence: the infusion of ethereal fluid, emanation from the heavens as they 'poured forth' (2.6) their gifts; see Silberman 1995:43–44. **3** A set phrase designed to provide impersonal authority to S.'s story, esp. where it may be challenged; and, as at ii 18.3, to announce that he is presenting his own 'goodly storie' (5.1). As an original fiction, see C. Burrow 1988:109–10. **8–9 roses** and **violets** are singled out for their traditional associations, respectively with love and virginity, Venus and Diana, and Amoret and Belphœbe.

Stanza 7

3 swowne: deep sleep. **5 playd**: suggesting the erotic sense; cf. Danaë's conception at xi 31.1–4. On Chrysogone's innocent display of her body, which resembles Belphœbe's at v 51.8–9, see Krier 1990:137–39. **6 mollifide**: made tender, as seed softened by moisture is germinated by the sun. **7–8 embayd**: steeped. **sence**: sensation. The terms are drawn from Arthur's dream of the Faerie Queene 'Whiles euery sence the humour sweet embayd' (I ix 13.5).

Stanza 8

On S.'s use of the abiogenetic origin of life in Ovid, *Met.* 1.416–37, see C. Burrow 1993:116–19. Here the birth is a variant of the marriage of the sky and the earth, which marks the beginning of creation; see I i 6.6–7*n*. **3–4 fruitfull seades | Of all things**: Ovid's *fecunda semina rerum*. **5 moyst complexion**: i.e. when the body's humour is predominantly moist; cf. 'moysture mixt with equall heate all living things createth' (*Met.* 1.516, tr. Golding). **6 by kynd**: naturally; according to their species. **7–9** See I i 21.6–9 and *n*. **Infinite shapes**: Ovid's *innumeras species*. **Informed**: formed within; impregnated, as *Epith* 386.

10

Whereof conceiuing shame and foule disgrace,
  Albe her guiltlesse conscience her cleard,
  She fled into the wildernesse a space,
  Till that vnweeldy burden she had reard,
  And shund dishonor, which as death she feard:
  Where wearie of long traueill, downe to rest
  Her selfe she set, and comfortably cheard;
  There a sad cloud of sleepe her ouerkest,
And seized euery sence with sorrow sore opprest.

11

It fortuned, faire *Venus* hauing lost
  Her little sonne, the winged god of loue,
  Who for some light displeasure, which him crost,
  Was from her fled, as flit as ayery Doue,
  And left her blisfull bowre of ioy aboue,
  (So from her often he had fled away,
  When she for ought him sharpely did reproue,
  And wandred in the world in straunge aray,
Disguiz'd in thousand shapes, that none might him bewray.)

12

Him for to seeke, she left her heauenly hous,
  The house of goodly formes and faire aspects,
  Whence all the world deriues the glorious
  Features of beautie, and all shapes select,
  With which high God his workmanship hath deckt;
  And searched euerie way, through which his wings
  Had borne him, or his tract she mote detect:
  She promist kisses sweet, and sweeter things,
Vnto the man, that of him tydings to her brings.

13

First she him sought in Court, where most he vs'd
  Whylome to haunt, but there she found him not;
  But many there she found, which sore accus'd
  His falshood, and with fowle infamous blot
  His cruell deedes and wicked wyles did spot:
  Ladies and Lordes she euery where mote heare
  Complayning, how with his empoysned shot
  Their wofull harts he wounded had whyleare,
And so had left them languishing twixt hope and feare.

14

She then the Cities sought from gate to gate,
  And euerie one did aske, did he him see;
  And euerie one her answerd, that too late
  He had him seene, and felt the crueltee
  Of his sharpe dartes and whot artilleree;
  And euery one threw forth reproches rife
  Of his mischieuous deedes, and sayd, That hee
  Was the disturber of all ciuill life,
The enimy of peace, and authour of all strife.

15

Then in the countrey she abroad him sought,
  And in the rurall cottages inquir'd,
  Where also many plaintes to her were brought,
  How he their heedelesse harts with loue had fir'd,
  And his false venim through their veines inspir'd;
  And eke the gentle Shepheard swaynes, which sat
  Keeping their fleecy flockes, as they were hyr'd,
  She sweetly heard complaine, both how and what
Her sonne had to them doen; yet she did smile thereat.

Stanza 9
1–5 The moon provides matter because it controls mortal bodies, esp. woman's body and her womb. **2 rightly cald**: by Conti 1616:5.17, who identifies Adonis with the sun because he nourishes all things and is the author of germination. **4 Ministreth**: provides.

Stanza 10
1 conceiuing: with the pun. **4 burden**: the child borne in the womb (*OED* 4). **reard**: brought into existence. **6 traueill**: also 'travail', referring to the labour of child-birth. **7 comfortably**: consolingly.

Stanzas 11–26
Venus's search for the runaway Cupid is the subject of Moschus's idyll, 'The Fugitive Love', which E.K. notes in his gloss to *SC March* 79 was translated into Latin by Politianus and 'very wel translated also into English Rymes' by S. It was expanded by Tasso in an epilogue to *Aminta* (1581), and now from both. Stanzas 13–15 carefully discriminate among the effects of love: Petrarchan love in the court, civic disorder in the cities, and pastoral complaint in the country. On the taxonomy of genre elaborated here, see Hollander 1988:105–06.

Stanza 11
4 Doue: cited as Venus's bird. **8–9** Cf. Jove's wandering through love at xi 30.3–4. **bewray**: reveal.

Stanza 12
1–5 Venus's **heauenly hous** is her planetary house or orb, as at 2.7; hence **aspects** has the astrological sense, as at 2.3. **select**: choice. **7 tract**: track. **8–9** In Moschus, a less liberal Venus offers only one kiss for tidings of Cupid, and better guerdon only for his capture and return.

Stanza 13
5 spot: vilify. **8 whyleare**: a while before.

Stanza 14
5 artilleree: shot. **8 ciuill life**: also in the sense, 'ciuile vsage' (1.8).

Stanza 15
5 inspir'd: breathed. **9** Venus smiles with pleasure at the shepherds' sweet verse; or with disdain that they should complain of love (cf. *Colin Clout* 795–98); or with pride in her son's waggish exploits. See L. Hendrix 1993:128; for *Venus ridens*, see IV x 56.4n.

16

But when in none of all these she him got,
   She gan auize, where els he mote him hyde:
   At last she her bethought, that she had not
   Yet sought the saluage woods and forests wyde,
   In which full many louely Nymphes abyde,
   Mongst whom might be, that he did closely lye,
   Or that the loue of some of them him tyde:
   For thy she thether cast her course t'apply,
To search the secret haunts of *Dianes* company.

17

Shortly vnto the wastefull woods she came,
   Whereas she found the Goddesse with her crew,
   After late chace of their embrewed game,
   Sitting beside a fountaine in a rew,
   Some of them washing with the liquid dew
   From off their dainty limbs the dusty sweat,
   And soyle which did deforme their liuely hew,
   Others lay shaded from the scorching heat;
The rest vpon her person gaue attendance great.

18

She hauing hong vpon a bough on high
   Her bow and painted quiuer, had vnlaste
   Her siluer buskins from her nimble thigh,
   And her lanck loynes vngirt, and brests vnbraste,
   After her heat the breathing cold to taste;
   Her golden lockes, that late in tresses bright
   Embreaded were for hindring of her haste,
   Now loose about her shoulders hong vndight,
And were with sweet *Ambrosia* all besprinckled light.

19

Soone as she *Venus* saw behinde her backe,
   She was asham'd to be so loose surpriz'd
   And woxe halfe wroth against her damzels slacke,
   That had not her thereof before auiz'd,

But suffred her so carelesly disguiz'd
   Be ouertaken. Soone her garments loose
   Vpgath'ring, in her bosome she compriz'd,
   Well as she might, and to the Goddesse rose,
Whiles all her Nymphes did like a girlond her enclose.

20

Goodly she gan faire *Cytherea* greet,
   And shortly asked her, what cause her brought
   Into that wildernesse for her vnmeet,
   From her sweete bowres, and beds with pleasures fraught:
   That suddein chaung she straung aduenture thought.
   To whom halfe weeping, she thus answered,
   That she her dearest sonne *Cupido* sought,
   Who in his frowardnes from her was fled;
That she repented sore, to haue him angered.

21

Thereat *Diana* gan to smile, in scorne
   Of her vaine playnt, and to her scoffing sayd;
   Great pitty sure, that ye be so forlorne
   Of your gay sonne, that giues ye so good ayd
   To your disports: ill mote ye bene apayd.
   But she was more engrieued, and replide;
   Faire sister, ill beseemes it to vpbrayd
   A dolefull heart with so disdainfull pride;
The like that mine, may be your paine another tide.

22

As you in woods and wanton wildernesse
   Your glory sett, to chace the saluage beasts,
   So my delight is all in ioyfulnesse,
   In beds, in bowres, in banckets, and in feasts:
   And ill becomes you with your lofty creasts,
   To scorne the ioy, that *Ioue* is glad to seeke;
   We both are bownd to follow heauens beheasts,
   And tend our charges with obeisaunce meeke:
Spare, gentle sister, with reproch my paine to eeke.

Stanza 16
2 auize: consider. **6 closely**: secretly. **8 For thy**: therefore.

Stanzas 17–19
Although Diana is neither naked nor bathing, S. is drawing on Ovid's story, in *Met*. 3.180–82, of the naked goddess surprised while bathing by Actaeon, a story he draws on again at VII vi 42–53. See Quilligan 1987:165–66, and Krier 1990:118–21.

Stanza 17
1 wastefull: desolate. **3 embrewed**: blood-stained.

Stanza 18
3 siluer: Diana's colour as goddess of the moon. **4 lanck loynes**: slender waist. **7 Embreaded**: braided. **for hindring**: lest they should hinder. **9 Ambrosia** anoints the gods to signify their immortality, as in Virgil's reference to Venus's ambrosial hair at *Aen*. 1.403, and *Mother Hubberd* 1267–68. Cf. the 'ambrosiall odours' (II iii 22.7) from Belphœbe's cheeks.

Stanza 19
As Diana's garments are **loose** about her, so her nymphs are **slacke**, i.e. 'remiss' but also 'loose'; and when she has gathered

(**compriz'd**) her clothes about her, her nymphs enclose her. Here we see the rose of maidenhead whose leaves, spread out at a time of safety, are gathered up at a time of danger (v 51). **5 disguiz'd**: undressed.

Stanza 20
1–5 The implied answer is her search for Adonis, as in Ovid, *Met*. 10.529–36. **Goodly**: courteously, with a sarcastic edge as **shortly** (quickly or curtly) suggests. **Cytherea**: so named because she arose from the sea off this island (see 29.4), and therefore does not belong in the woods. **sweete bowres**: the garden of Adonis rather than Venus's 'blisfull bowre of ioy aboue' (11.5). **aduenture**: chance. **8 frowardnes**: being ungovernable.

Stanza 21
3 forlorne: bereft. **5 disports**: sports; suggesting 'missports'. Diana's concluding words are either sarcastic: 'you must be really suffering', or condemning: 'may you be ill-rewarded'. **9 tide**: time.

Stanza 22
1 wanton: luxuriant; wild. **3** As she is 'The ioy of Gods and men' (IV x 44.2). **4 banckets**: carousals. **feasts** suggests

23

And tell me, if that ye my sonne haue heard,
    To lurke emongst your Nimphes in secret wize;
    Or keepe their cabins: much I am affeard,
    Least he like one of them him selfe disguize,
    And turne his arrowes to their exercize:
    So may he long him selfe full easie hide:
    For he is faire and fresh in face and guize,
    As any Nimphe (let not it be enuide.)
So saying euery Nimph full narrowly shee eide.

24

But *Phœbe* therewith sore was angered,
    And sharply saide, Goe Dame, goe seeke your boy,
    Where you him lately lefte, in *Mars* his bed;
    He comes not here, we scorne his foolish ioy,
    Ne lend we leisure to his idle toy:
    But if I catch him in this company,
    By *Stygian* lake I vow, whose sad annoy
    The Gods doe dread, he dearly shall abye:
Ile clip his wanton wings, that he no more shall flye.

25

Whom whenas *Venus* saw so sore displeasd,
    Shee inly sory was, and gan relent,
    What shee had said: so her she soone appeasd,
    With sugred words and gentle blandishment,
    From which a fountaine from her sweete lips went,
    And welled goodly forth, that in short space
    She was well pleasd, and forth her damzells sent
    Through all the woods, to search from place to place,
If any tract of him or tidings they mote trace.

26

To search the God of loue her Nimphes she sent,
    Throughout the wandring forest euery where:
    And after them her selfe eke with her went
    To seeke the fugitiue, both farre and nere.
    So long they sought, till they arriued were
    In that same shady couert, whereas lay
    Faire *Crysogone* in slombry traunce whilere:
    Who in her sleepe (a wondrous thing to say)
Vnwares had borne two babes, as faire as springing day.

27

Vnwares she them conceiud, vnwares she bore:
    She bore withouten paine, that she conceiu'd
    Withouten pleasure: ne her need implore
    Lucinaes aide: which when they both perceiu'd,
    They were through wonder nigh of sence bereu'd,
    And gazing each on other, nought bespake:
    At last they both agreed, her seeming grieu'd
    Out of her heauie swowne not to awake,
But from her louing side the tender babes to take.

28

Vp they them tooke, eachone a babe vptooke,
    And with them carried, to be fostered;
    Dame *Phœbe* to a Nymphe her babe betooke,
    To be vpbrought in perfect Maydenhed,
    And of her selfe her name *Belphœbe* red:
    But *Venus* hers thence far away conuayd,
    To be vpbrought in goodly womanhed,
    And in her litle loues stead, which was strayd,
Her *Amoretta* cald, to comfort her dismayd.

[margin annotation: Demi-god]

---

the banquet of the senses, such as Cymochles enjoys at II v
29–34.   **5 lofty creasts** suggests pride in her virgin state; cf.
ii 27.1.   **6** Jove's Venerean pursuits in beds and bowers are
displayed at xi 30–35.   **9 eeke**: increase.

Stanza 23
3 cabins: cf. the 'Cabinets' in the Bower of Bliss that Guyon
destroys at II xii 83.7.   **5 exercize**: customary practice;
suggesting that he may cause Diana's nymphs to fall in love.
8 . . . do not begrudge him such praise.

Stanza 24
1 Phœbe: Diana.   **3** Referring to Venus's affair with Mars; see
xi 36.4–5.   **5 toy**: game.   **7–9 By Stygian lake**: an oath
sworn by this name is kept even by the gods for fear of grievous
punishment (Virgil, *Aen.* 6.323–24); cf. 46.7.   **abye**: suffer,
pay the penalty. As Belphœbe at II iii 23.9 breaks 'his wanton
darts'.

Stanza 25
2 relent: soften in temper, qualify.   **3–7** One of Venus's tra-
ditional roles is to preserve concord.

Stanza 26
1 search: try to find.   **7 whilere**: a while before.   **8 a won-
drous thing to say**: a classical tag, *mirabile dictu.*   **9 spring-
ing**: dawning.

Stanza 27
1–3 The Christian analogue is the Virgin Mary's conception
and the birth of Christ: see 3.1–2*n*. The tradition, noted by
Hankins 1971:137, that she did not suffer Eve's curse – 'In
sorowe shalt thou bring forthe children' (Gen. 3.16) – suggests
that Chrysogone gives birth as Eve would have done before
her fall. On the concept of the virgin birth, see Warner
1976:34–49.   **4 Lucina**: Diana in her role as goddess of
childbirth; see II i 53.5*n*.   **9** Since **side** may signify the womb
(*OED* 1.1.b), there is the suggestion that they participate in
the birth.

Stanza 28
The twinned and complementary states of militant virginity in
Belphœbe and marital chastity in Amoret, as they share the
inheritance of their virgin mother, are carefully discriminated
throughout the central books: e.g. with 3–4, cf. v 32.4–5,
54.1–4, and 3.7–8 above; with 6–7, cf. 51–52. Cf. the paired
terms, 'chastity and vertue virginall' at v 53.6.   **3 betooke**:
gave in charge.   **5** For further on the etymology, see II iii Arg.
4*n*.   **red**: named.   **8–9** Since she takes the place of Cupid
(Lat. *amor*), she is named Amoretta, a little love (Ital.
amoretto), and serves as 'th'ensample of true loue alone'
(52.4). Accordingly, the search for Cupid at 26.5–6 leads
directly to her, and introduces the garden of Adonis where
Cupid is seen unarmed at 49.8–9.

29

Shee brought her to her ioyous Paradize,
  Wher most she wonnes, when she on earth does dwell.
  So faire a place, as Nature can deuize:
  Whether in *Paphos*, or *Cytheron* hill,
  Or it in *Gnidus* bee, I wote not well;
  But well I wote by triall, that this same
  All other pleasant places doth excell,
  And called is by her lost louers name,
The *Gardin* of *Adonis*, far renowmd by fame.

30

In that same Gardin all the goodly flowres,
  Wherewith dame Nature doth her beautify,
  And decks the girlonds of her Paramoures,
  Are fetcht: there is the first seminary
  Of all things, that are borne to liue and dye,
  According to their kynds. Long worke it were,
  Here to account the endlesse progeny
  Of all the weeds, that bud and blossome there;
But so much as doth need, must needs be counted here.

31

It sited was in fruitfull soyle of old,
  And girt in with two walls on either side;
  The one of yron, the other of bright gold,
  That none might thorough breake, nor ouer-stride:
  And double gates it had, which opened wide,
  By which both in and out men moten pas;
  Th'one faire and fresh, the other old and dride:
  Old *Genius* the porter of them was,
Old *Genius*, the which a double nature has.

32

He letteth in, he letteth out to wend,
  All that to come into the world desire;
  A thousand thousand naked babes attend
  About him day and night, which doe require,
  That he with fleshly weeds would them attire:
  Such as him list, such as eternall fate
  Ordained hath, he clothes with sinfull mire,
  And sendeth forth to liue in mortall state,
Till they agayn returne backe by the hinder gate.

Stanza 29

3 deuize: fashion.   **4–5 Paphos** and **Cytheron hill** are haunts of Venus, taken from Boccaccio 1976:3.22, as Lotspeich 1932 notes; or from Chaucer, *Knight's Tale* 1936–37: 'al the mount of Citheroun, | Ther Venus hath hir principal dwellynge'. **Gnidus** (or Cnidus): 'a city of Caria, where Venus was woorshipped' (T. Cooper 1565).   **6–7 by triall**: for a poet, personal experience of sex would be joined to literary experience.

Stanzas 30–50

The book 'That hight, *Antiquitee* of *Faery* lond' (II ix 60.2), which Guyon reads in the castle of Alma, records that 'th'author of all woman kynd' from whom 'all *Faryes* spring' was found by Elfe, in 'the gardins of *Adonis*' (II x 71). As Venus nursed Cupid in this garden where 'he his own perfection wrought' (*Colin Clout* 803–06), so here Amoret is 'vpbrought in goodly womanhed' (28.7). In Conti 1616:5.16, certain orchards are said to be called *hortos Adonios* because Adonis took pleasure in them, but originally it was the name of a forcing-bed of quick-growing herbs (Plato, *Phaedrus* 276b) and thus became proverbial of ephemerality. By the etymological conjunction of Adonis and Eden, it became a 'ioyous Paradize' (29.1), a place that preserves the species despite death. S. claims not to know where the garden may be found, except that it is 'far away' (28.6), but he does know 'by triall' that it excels all other pleasant places (29.6), as do readers who view it as a poetic image, though not one that can be visualized, as Roche 1964:119 observes. Its complexity has led to efforts to see it as a number of gardens, e.g. D. Cheney 1966:119–40; or from differing perspectives, e.g. Broaddus 1995:72–79. On its argument, see Horton 1991. On attempts to explain S.'s occasionally philosophical language through various conceptual systems, see 'Adonis, gardens of' in the *SEnc*.

Stanza 30

4–5 The suggestion in Gen. 2.5 that the garden of Eden contained every plant and herb before it grew implies that creation was instantaneous and included an everlasting store of pre-formed beings, or seminal reasons, that would come into existence in orderly succession; see Ellrodt 1960:76–79.   **seminary**: seed-plot, i.e. the womb.   **6 According to their kynds**: the language of Gen. 1.24–25.   **7 account**: relate.   **8 weeds**: plants.   **9 counted**: recounted.

Stanza 31

1 sited: placed.   **fruitfull soyle**: cf. the 'fruitfull grownd' of Eden at I xi 47.2–4.   **2–7** Either there is one double wall, an outer wall of iron which may not be broken and a concentric inner wall of gold which may not be surmounted; or, as on **either side** would suggest, there are two end walls, one golden with a fair and fresh gate and the other iron with an old and dried gate. Cf. the two gates of the castle of Alma at II ix 23.1–3. On the doubling, see D.L. Miller 1988:265. Gates are a natural image of birth, as 'the dores of my mothers wombe' (Job 3.10), but also of death (Ps. 9.13). Double gates of life and death appear in Plato's myth of Er (*Republic* 614c-e).   **men**: presumably a generic use, as in Gen. 1.27.   **8–9 Old Genius**: presumably the 'celestiall powre', Agdistes; see II xii 46–48n.   **double nature** refers to his double office or service in birth and death; or as in his office he resembles the double-headed Janus; see Nohrnberg 1976:529–30.

Stanza 32

1–3 Expanding 31.6: Genius lets human beings at their death into the garden but also at their birth into the world. If the term **naked babes** is not taken as a metaphor, it may refer to souls in their pre-existent state, either vegetative (Ellrodt 1960:82) or rational (Lewis 1966:154); or to the homuncule in semen. Only some babes desire to be born, that is, to change from the vegetative to the human state, and of these only those are born – 'born' in the human sense of being 'borne to die' – as Genius wishes and fate ordains.   **4 require**: ask, request.   **5 fleshly weeds**: the flesh, in contrast to 'weedes, that bud and blossome' (30.8), or the **sinfull mire**, 'like to that *AEgyptian* slime' (II ix 21.5) of the castle of Alma; cf. Job 10.11: 'Thou hast clothed me with skinne and flesh'.

33

After that they againe retourned beene,
  They in that Gardin planted bee agayne;
  And grow afresh, as they had neuer seene
  Fleshly corruption, nor mortall payne.
  Some thousand yeares so doen they there remayne,
  And then of him are clad with other hew,
  Or sent into the chaungefull world agayne,
  Till thether they retourne, where first they grew:
So like a wheele arownd they ronne from old to new.

34

Ne needs there Gardiner to sett, or sow,
  To plant or prune: for of their owne accord
  All things, as they created were, doe grow,
  And yet remember well the mighty word,
  Which first was spoken by th'Almighty lord,
  That bad them to increase and multiply:
  Ne doe they need with water of the ford,
  Or of the clouds to moysten their roots dry;
For in themselues eternall moisture they imply.

35

Infinite shapes of creatures there are bred,
  And vncouth formes, which none yet euer knew,
  And euery sort is in a sondry bed
  Sett by it selfe, and ranckt in comely rew:
  Some fitt for reasonable sowles t'indew,
  Some made for beasts, some made for birds to weare,
  And all the fruitfull spawne of fishes hew
  In endlesse rancks along enraunged were,
That seemd the *Ocean* could not containe them there.

36

Daily they grow, and daily forth are sent
  Into the world, it to replenish more,
  Yet is the stocke not lessened, nor spent,
  But still remaines in euerlasting store,
  As it at first created was of yore.
  For in the wide wombe of the world there lyes,
  In hatefull darknes and in deepe horrore,
  An huge eternal *Chaos*, which supplyes
The substaunces of natures fruitfull progenyes.

37

All things from thence doe their first being fetch,
  And borrow matter, whereof they are made,
  Which whenas forme and feature it does ketch,
  Becomes a body, and doth then inuade
  The state of life, out of the griesly shade.
  That substaunce is eterne, and bideth so,
  Ne when the life decayes, and forme does fade,
  Doth it consume, and into nothing goe,
But chaunged is, and often altred to and froe.

Stanza 33
5 As in Virgil, *Aen.* 6.743–51, souls dwell in Elysium for a thousand years in order to be purified before being **clad with other hew**, i.e. returned to new bodies. Cf. *HB* 201–03 on the soul's pre-existence. **6 hew:** form. **7 Or:** a puzzling term; one expects 'and'. There may be the suggestion, as in Virgil, that some souls exempt from rebirth remain in Elysium; see 32.1–3*n*. **9** The image of the wheel is found in Plato, *Timaeus* 79, as Upton 1758 notes, though, for S., change is a means of regeneration rather than decay.

Stanza 34
1–3 In contrast to the garden of Eden, which needed Adam and Eve to subdue it (Gen. 1.28). **4–6** Gen. 1.22. **7–9** As in Eden when the earth and heavens were created: 'the Lord God had not caused it to raine vpon the earth. . . . But a myst went vp from the earth, and watred all the earth' (Gen. 2.5–6). **eternall moisture** suggests the 'radical moisture' inherent in all plants and animals, its presence being a necessary condition of their vitality (*OED*). The absence of water makes the garden unique among earthly paradises, as Neuse 1990:82 notes. **ford:** stream. **imply:** contain.

Stanza 35
1 Infinite shapes of creatures: as are bred in the Nile mud at 8.8, and found in Phantastes's chamber at II ix 50.2–4. **2** Agreeing with Augustine's concept of the pre-existent seminal seeds which include creatures not yet born; noted Ellrodt 1960:79. **vncouth:** strange. **3–7** 'All flesh is not the same flesh, but there is one flesh of men, and another flesh of beastes, and another of fishes, and another of birdes' (1 Cor. 15.39). **sondry:** separate, different. In Renaissance botanical gardens, beds were arranged in rows, each species to itself; noted Leslie 1992:28. **reasonable sowles:** i.e. human beings. **indew:** assume, put on (as a garment). **hew:** shape.

Stanza 36
3–9 stocke: the matter (cf. **substaunces**) which, drawn from **Chaos**, supplies material existence to the forms in the garden; or the pure forms themselves before becoming matter; or both, as Hankins 1971.259–63 argues. Accordingly, the earth is called 'great *Chaos* child' at VII vi 26.6. Cf. *Rome* 307–08: 'The seedes, of which all things at first were bred, | Shall in great *Chaos* wombe againe be hid'. Ovid's primeval chaos (*Met.* 1.5–20) was reconciled with the account of matter **first created** in Genesis (e.g. by Golding, Epistle 346–71) except for its being **eternal** (e.g. by Sandys 1970:49). See 'chaos' in the *SEnc*.

Stanza 37
3 forme and feature: the physical shape and 'outward fashion' (38.2) as distinct from the 'goodly formes and faire aspects' kept in Venus's 'heauenly hous' (12.1–2). **ketch:** take; assume; seize. **4 inuade:** enter, but implying the stronger sense, 'make a hostile incursion into'. **6 substaunce:** used here and at 38.1, 3 for matter. The etymological sense suggests that which lies under being, the pre-existing matter before the imposition of form. **8** I.e. **That substaunce** is not consumed.

38

The substaunce is not chaungd, nor altered,
　　But th'only forme and outward fashion;
　　For euery substaunce is conditioned
　　To chaunge her hew, and sondry formes to don
　　Meet for her temper and complexion:
　　For formes are variable and decay,
　　By course of kinde, and by occasion;
　　And that faire flowre of beautie fades away,
As doth the lilly fresh before the sunny ray.

39

Great enimy to it, and to all the rest,
　　That in the *Gardin of Adonis* springs,
　　Is wicked *Tyme*, who with his scyth addrest,
　　Does mow the flowring herbes and goodly things,
　　And all their glory to the ground downe flings,
　　Where they do wither, and are fowly mard:
　　He flyes about, and with his flaggy winges
　　Beates downe both leaues and buds without regard,
Ne euer pitty may relent his malice hard.

40

Yet pitty often did the gods relent,
　　To see so faire thinges mard, and spoiled quight:
　　And their great mother *Venus* did lament
　　The losse of her deare brood, her deare delight:
　　Her hart was pierst with pitty at the sight,
　　When walking through the Gardin, them she spyde,
　　Yet no'te she find redresse for such despight:
　　For all that liues, is subiect to that law:
All things decay in time, and to their end doe draw.

41

But were it not, that *Time* their troubler is,
　　All that in this delightfull Gardin growes,
　　Should happy bee, and haue immortall blis:
　　For here all plenty, and all pleasure flowes,
　　And sweete loue gentle fitts emongst them throwes,
　　Without fell rancor, or fond gealosy;
　　Franckly each Paramor his leman knowes,
　　Each bird his mate, ne any does enuy
Their goodly meriment, and gay felicity.

42

There is continuall Spring, and haruest there
　　Continuall, both meeting at one tyme:
　　For both the boughes doe laughing blossoms beare,
　　And with fresh colours decke the wanton Pryme,
　　And eke attonce the heauenly trees they clyme,
　　Which seeme to labour vnder their fruites lode:
　　The whiles the ioyous birdes make their pastyme
　　Emongst the shady leaues, their sweet abode,
And their trew loues without suspition tell abrode.

43

Right in the middest of that Paradise,
　　There stood a stately Mount, on whose round top
　　A gloomy groue of mirtle trees did rise,
　　Whose shady boughes sharp steele did neuer lop,
　　Nor wicked beastes their tender buds did crop,
　　But like a girlond compassed the hight,
　　And from their fruitfull sydes sweet gum did drop,
　　That all the ground with pretious deaw bedight,
Threw forth most dainty odours, and most sweet delight.

Stanza 38

2 But only its form and appearance or **hew**, as illustrated in
8–9. **3 conditioned**: has the capacity or nature; possibly
'required', 'bound'. **5** I.e. fitting her temperament and nature,
referring to the combination of humours in the body. The
repeated **her** regards matter as female; see 47.8–9*n*. **7 kinde**:
nature. **occasion**: necessity.

Stanza 39

In its ephemerality (see 30–50*n*), the garden of Adonis is sub-
ject to time, a figure traditionally armed with a scythe, as at VII
viii 1.9. Even in the garden, all things find in him their **Great
enimy** because birth is the beginning of death, as Lewis
1966:154 notes, though the cycle from life to death makes
death 'the grene path way to lyfe' (E.K.'s gloss to *SC Dec.*
Emblem). **3 addrest**: armed. **7 flaggy**: drooping. **9 relent**:
cause to relent.

Stanza 40

Only at the end of the Mutabilitie Cantos is there hope that
All things decay in time in order that they may be fulfilled,
and only then does Nature interpret **end** as the completion
to which all things move (VII vii 58.7). **3 great mother
Venus**: *Venus genetrix*, cf. IV x 5.4. **6 spyde**: saw, sugg.
Church 1758 for the rhyme. **7 no'te**: could not; knew not
how to.

Stanza 41

5 fitts: surges of passion. **6 fond**: foolish. **7** Lovers enjoy
the same freedom in the garden that surrounds the temple of
Venus at IV x 25.7–28.2. **Franckly**: freely; openly. **leman**:
mistress. **knowes**: in the sexual sense.

Stanza 42

1–6 continuall Spring and autumn (**haruest**) at the same
time are traditional features of the *locus amoenus*, both in the
classical tradition, from Homer's garden of Alcinous (*Ody.*
7.112–19), and in the biblical, from God's command in Gen.
1.12 that the earth produce at the same time the bud of the
herb and the fruit of the tree. Cf., e.g. Ovid's golden age (*Met.*
1.107–10), Ariosto's earthly paradise (*Orl. Fur.* 34.49),
Tasso's garden of Armida (*Ger. Lib.* 16.10), and S.'s Mount
Acidale (VI x 6.5). **Pryme**: spring. **5 heauenly**: heauy *1596*
seems the correct reading, and supports the image of boughs
heavy with fruit climbing the trees.

Stanza 43

Baybak *et al.* 1969:228 note that this stanza with its opening
phrase **Right in the middest** occupies the exact midpoint of
the *1590* Bk III, being the 340th of 679 stanzas (excluding the
proem and the arguments to the cantos). See I vii 12–13*n*, II
vii 53–55*n*, and D. Cheney 1986:268. Being the centre of the
garden, here Venus conceals Adonis whose anatomical centre,
his penis, is its generative source, and here is displayed Venus's

44

And in the thickest couert of that shade,
  There was a pleasant Arber, not by art,
  But of the trees owne inclination made,
  Which knitting their rancke braunches part to part,
  With wanton yuie twyne entrayld athwart,
  And Eglantine, and Caprifole emong,
  Fashiond aboue within their inmost part,
That nether *Phoebus* beams could through them throng,
Nor *Aeolus* sharp blast could worke them any wrong.

45

And all about grew euery sort of flowre,
  To which sad louers were transformde of yore;
  Fresh *Hyacinthus*, *Phœbus* paramoure,
  And dearest loue,
  Foolish *Narcisse*, that likes the watry shore,
  Sad *Amaranthus*, made a flowre but late,
  Sad *Amaranthus*, in whose purple gore
Me seemes I see *Amintas* wretched fate,
To whom sweet Poets verse hath giuen endlesse date.

46

There wont fayre *Venus* often to enioy
  Her deare *Adonis* ioyous company,
  And reape sweet pleasure of the wanton boy:
  There yet, some say, in secret he does ly,
  Lapped in flowres and pretious spycery,
  By her hid from the world, and from the skill
  Of *Stygian* Gods, which doe her loue enuy;
  But she her selfe, when euer that she will,
Possesseth him, and of his sweetnesse takes her fill.

---

anatomical centre, the *mons Veneris*. Being the centre of the book, it is balanced by the perversion of sexual love in Castle Joyeous at the beginning and in the house of Busirane at the end. **1 middest** is carefully placed as the middle word of its line. **3** On the **mirtle tree** as sacred to Venus, see v 40.2*n*. A. Fowler 1964:137 cites Valeriano, *Hieroglyphica*: 'It should not be disguised that the myrtle signifies the female pudendum'.

Stanza 44

2 not by art: this natural garden, like Nature's pavilion at VII vii 8.3–9, counters the artificial Bower of Bliss, as Lewis 1936:324–33 argues. Cf. 29.3, 30.1–4. **3–4 inclination**: i.e. their leaning position; also their natural disposition. **rancke**: dense. Cf. the branches in the Bower at II xii 53.8–9. **5–6 yuie** and **Eglantine** are found in the Bower of Bliss; see II v 29.3–5*n*. **wanton**: luxuriant in growth. **entrayld**: entwined. **Caprifole**: the honeysuckle or woodbine. **8–9** See v 51.4–5*n*. **throng**: press. **Aeolus**: the wind.

Stanza 45

1 euery sort: i.e. every kind or species, which endures even though the individual flowers cited here die without reproducing themselves. **3–4** When his quoit, blown off its course by the wind's jealousy, killed his lover, **Hyacinthus**, **Phœbus** caused the hyacinth to spring from his blood (Ovid, *Met*. 10.162–219). See 'Hyacinthus' in the *SEnc*. The death illustrates the dangers of the sun and wind named at 44.8–9. **dearest loue**: as Ovid's *ante omnes* (167). There may be a witty point in the truncated line 4 added in *1609*: the poet's verse is cut short even as lovers' lives have been cut short both **of yore** and **but late**. **5 Narcisse** died through love of his own reflection in the water; see ii 44.6–9*n*. The flower to which he gives his name grows near water. **Foolish**: as Britomart calls him at ii 44.6. **6–9 Amaranthus**: a symbol of **endlesse date**, being associated with the 'incorruptible [Gk ἀμαράντινος, unfading] crowne of glorie' (1 Pet. 5.4). **Amintas**: alluding, most likely, to Sidney, whose death **but late** (in 1586) had been marked with elegies by most poets of the time, including S.; see Quitslund 1997:27–28. In *As* 152, Sidney is shown as Adonis 'With crudled blood and filthie gore deformed'. Or to Thomas Watson's Latin *Amyntas* (1585); see 'Watson,

Thomas' in the *SEnc* and D. Cheney 1984:14. Or its English paraphrase by Abraham Fraunce (1587) in which Amintas, having died through grief for Phillis, was transformed into the Amaranthus, and became a cult figure in the three parts of *The Countess of Pembrokes Yuychurch* (1591–92); see Lamb 1990:33–40. **purple gore**: the entire plant is purple; hence the reference to 'Red *Amaranthus*' (*Gnat* 677). Its common name is 'Love-lies-a-bleeding'.

Stanzas 46–49

The reference to lovers transformed into flowers leads directly to the myth of Adonis who, though not 'turned to a flowre' (i 34.5) as in Ovid, *Met*. 10.735–39, lies 'Lapped in flowres' (46.5) as though dead. At 29.8, he is named Venus's 'lost louer'; and at 47.1–2, he is said to live where 'he may not | For euer dye'. According to one traditional interpretation, he is the sun, the boar winter, and the grieving Venus the earth during his absence. See, e.g. Sandys 1970:493 and Conti 1616:5.16. Since Adonis does not remain buried 'In balefull night' (47.3) and the boar is imprisoned, the garden enjoys 'continuall Spring' (42.1). The repeated 'some say' (46.4), 'they say' (47.1), 'they call' (47.8), 'they say' (48.8), after the confident 'Me seemes I see' (45.8), distinguishes the myth from S.'s contribution to it, and invokes an impersonal authority, as Neuse 1990:87 claims.

Stanza 46

2 company: as a sexual partner (*OED* 2). **3 reape**: cf. Acrasia 'greedily depasturing delight' upon Verdant at II xii 73.4. **5** His state suggests (sexual) death, as in Donne's 'First Anniversary' 110: 'Wee kill our selves to propagate our kinde'. His passivity is Verdant's seen from a perspective 'that insists on the cosmic legitimacy of the female Eros's triumph over the male Thanatos' (Quilligan 1983:196). Since Venus is spoken of in the active voice, Davies 1986:89 concludes that in their act of coition they 'make up an androgyne within the feminine gender'. **spycery**: spices. On the association of Adonis with myrrh, see I i 9.6*n*. **6 skill**: knowledge. **7 Stygian Gods**: the infernal gods; from Styx, a river of hell. **9 sweetnesse**: refers to the etymology of Adonis, ἡδονή. **takes her fill**: in the erotic sense of being impregnated.

47

And sooth it seemes they say: for he may not
    For euer dye, and euer buried bee
    In balefull night, where all thinges are forgot;
    All be he subiect to mortalitie,
    Yet is eterne in mutabilitie,
    And by succession made perpetuall,
    Transformed oft, and chaunged diuerslie:
    For him the Father of all formes they call;
Therfore needs mote he liue, that liuing giues to all.

48

There now he liueth in eternall blis,
    Ioying his goddesse, and of her enioyd:
    Ne feareth he henceforth that foe of his,
    Which with his cruell tuske him deadly cloyd:
    For that wilde Bore, the which him once annoyd,
    She firmely hath emprisoned for ay,
    That her sweet loue his malice mote auoyd,
    In a strong rocky Caue, which is they say,
Hewen vnderneath that Mount, that none him losen may.

49

There now he liues in euerlasting ioy,
    With many of the Gods in company,
    Which thether haunt, and with the winged boy
    Sporting him selfe in safe felicity:
    Who when he hath with spoiles and cruelty
    Ransackt the world, and in the wofull harts
    Of many wretches set his triumphes hye,
    Thether resortes, and laying his sad dartes
Asyde, with faire Adonis plays his wanton partes.

50

And his trew loue faire Psyche with him playes,
    Fayre Psyche to him lately reconcyld,
    After long troubles and vnmeet vpbrayes,
    With which his mother Venus her reuyld,
    And eke himselfe her cruelly exyld:
    But now in stedfast loue and happy state
    She with him liues, and hath him borne a chyld,
    Pleasure, that doth both gods and men aggrate,
Pleasure, the daughter of Cupid and Psyche late.

51

Hether great Venus brought this infant fayre,
    The yonger daughter of Chrysogonee,
    And vnto Psyche with great trust and care
    Committed her, yfostered to bee,
    And trained vp in trew feminitee:
    Who no lesse carefully her tendered,
    Then her owne daughter Pleasure, to whom shee
    Made her companion, and her lessoned
In all the lore of loue, and goodly womanhead.

52

In which when she to perfect ripenes grew,
    Of grace and beautie noble Paragone,
    She brought her forth into the worldes vew,
    To be th'ensample of true loue alone,
    And Lodestarre of all chaste affection,
    To all fayre Ladies, that doe liue on grownd.
    To Faery court she came, where many one
    Admyrd her goodly haueour, and fownd
His feeble hart wide launched with loues cruel wownd.

Stanza 47

1 And it seems true what they say   **5–6** The distinction is found, e.g. in Boethius, De Consol. Phil. 5 Prosa 6: 'lat us seyen thanne sothly that God is "eterne," and that the world is "perpetuel"' (tr. Chaucer). **8–9** S. identifies Adonis with matter and Venus with form, here and at 12.1–5 – in contrast to 9.1–4 – 'in defiance of all tradition', as Lewis 1966:155 notes. Benson 1992:254–56 concludes that S. is profeminist. **the Father of all formes** alludes to Adonis as 'the first seminary | Of all things' (30.4–5), as Nohrnberg 1976:519–62 argues.

Stanza 48

2 Ioying: enjoying, as 49.1 stresses, to balance the 'sweet pleasure' (46.3) she reaps. **4 cloyd**: gored; 'in his codds', as Golding spells out in describing Adonis's wound (Ovid, Met. 10.839); or 'surfeited' through excessive gratification of desire. See i 34–38n. **5–9 that wilde Bore** within the mons Veneris is interpreted by Silberman 1995:48 as the vagina dentata, 'an icon of fearsome venereal power'. **annoyd**: injured.

Stanza 49

8–9 On the unarmed Cupid, see I proem 3.5–7n.

Stanza 50

The tale of Cupid and Psyche is told in Apuleius tr. 1566:93–125. After Psyche was persuaded by her wicked sisters that her nightly lover, Cupid, whom she had agreed not to see, was a serpent, she saw him asleep, was abandoned, and not reunited with him in heaven until she endured severe trials imposed by Venus. When she became immortal and married him, she bore his child, Voluptas or Pleasure. See 'Pleasure' in the SEnc, and Lockerd 1987:73–78. For Renaissance interpretations of the tale as an allegory of the sufferings of the human soul, see Allen 1960:26–31, and 'Apuleius' in the SEnc; on S.'s use of it, see Hamilton 1961a:138–48. **lately** and **late** prepare for its rendering in the story of Amoret. **1 playes**: suggests sexual pleasures, such as the continuous sexual activity between Venus and Adonis which sustains creation. **3 vpbrayes**: upbraidings. **8 aggrate**: please.

Stanza 51

2 yonger daughter: as 4.5. **5 feminitee**: femininity, womanliness. **6 tendered**: cared for. **8–9** This claim is shown at IV x 49–52 in the vision of Amoret in the lap of Womanhood surrounded by the feminine virtues. Cf. 28.6–7. **lore**: doctrine. **womanhead**: cf. Belphœbe at v 54.6–8.

Stanza 52

2 As she is seen 'Shyning with beauties light, and heauenly vertues grace' at IV x 52.9. **4–5** As Belphœbe is held up as a 'faire ensample' of 'perfect love, and spotlesse fame | Of chastitie' at v 54.1–4. **Lodestarre**: the guiding star as a centre of attraction. **7–9** These lines prepare for the concluding cantos of the Book where she herself suffers such pain; see xi 10.7n. **haueour**: behaviour. **launched**: pierced.

53

But she to none of them her loue did cast,
  Saue to the noble knight Sir *Scudamore*,
  To whom her louing hart she linked fast
  In faithfull loue, t'abide for euermore,
  And for his dearest sake endured sore,
  Sore trouble of an hainous enimy,
  Who her would forced haue to haue forlore
  Her former loue, and stedfast loialty,
As ye may elswhere reade that ruefull history.

54

But well I weene, ye first desire to learne,
  What end vnto that fearefull Damozell,
  Which fledd so fast from that same foster stearne,
  Whom with his brethren *Timias* slew, befell:
  That was to weet, the goodly *Florimell*,
  Who wandring for to seeke her louer deare,
  Her louer deare, her dearest *Marinell*,
  Into misfortune fell, as ye did heare,
And from Prince *Arthure* fled with wings of idle feare.

Stanza 53
7 **haue forlore**: forsake.

Stanza 54
3 **stearne**: cruel.   9 See iv 49.

Cant. VII.

The witches sonne loues Florimell:
She flyes, he faines to dy.
Satyrane saues the Squyre of Dames
From Gyaunts tyranny.

1

Ike as an Hynd forth singled from the heard,
L̷ That hath escaped from a rauenous beast,
   Yet flyes away of her owne feete afeard,
   And euery leafe, that shaketh with the least
   Murmure of winde, her terror hath encreast;
   So fledd fayre *Florimell* from her vaine feare,
   Long after she from perill was releast:
   Each shade she saw, and each noyse she did heare,
Did seeme to be the same, which she escapt whileare.

2

All that same euening she in flying spent,
   And all that night her course continewed:
   Ne did she let dull sleepe once to relent,
   Nor wearinesse to slack her hast, but fled
   Euer alike, as if her former dred
   Were hard behind, her ready to arrest:
   And her white Palfrey hauing conquered
   The maistring raines out of her weary wrest,
Perforce her carried, where euer he thought best.

3

So long as breath, and hable puissaunce
   Did natiue corage vnto him supply,
   His pace he freshly forward did aduaunce,
   And carried her beyond all ieopardy,

But nought that wanteth rest, can long aby.
   He hauing through incessant traueill spent
   His force, at last perforce adowne did ly,
   Ne foot could further moue: The Lady gent
Thereat was suddein strook with great astonishment.

4

And forst t'alight, on foot mote algates fare,
   A traueiler vnwonted to such way:
   Need teacheth her this lesson hard and rare,
   That fortune all in equall launce doth sway,
   And mortall miseries doth make her play.
   So long she traueild, till at length she came
   To an hilles side, which did to her bewray
   A litle valley, subiect to the same,
All couerd with thick woodes, that quite it ouercame.

5

Through the tops of the high trees she did descry
   A litle smoke, whose vapour thin and light,
   Reeking aloft, vprolled to the sky:
   Which, chearefull signe did send vnto her sight,
   That in the same did wonne some liuing wight.
   Eftsoones her steps she thereunto applyd,
   And came at last in weary wretched plight
   Vnto the place, to which her hope did guyde,
To finde some refuge there, and rest her wearie syde.

Book III Canto vii

Argument

2 faines: desires.

Stanza 1

1–5 A variation of the simile that describes her flight at iv 49.4–9 in order to continue her story. The **rauenous beast** becomes the witch's 'hideous beast' (22.2) from which she flees. **6 vaine feare**: in Ariosto, *Orl. Fur.* 1.33–34, Angelica fleeing her pursuers, and fearful of the movement of leaves, is compared to a frightened deer. The echo of Horace, *Ode* 1.23, in which the ardent lover assures Chloe that he is not a tiger from whom she must flee as a fawn, is noted by Curran 1998.

Stanza 2

1–2 The night endured by the sleepless Arthur at iv 52–60. **3 relent**: slacken, as iv 49.1. **6 arrest**: seize. **7–9** The traditional emblem of passion overpowering reason marks the beginning of her metamorphosis.

Stanza 3

1 hable puissaunce: able or sufficient strength. **5** Proverbial: Smith 652. **aby**: abide. **8 gent**: noble; beautiful. **9 aston-**

ishment: dismay; also (anticipating her later plight) numbness, deadness; cf. viii 35.6.

Stanza 4

1 algates: necessarily; at all events. **3** Proverbial: Smith 571. **rare**: unusual in its severity. **4–5 launce**: balance; apparently coined by S. from Lat. *lanx*. **sway**: rule. The lesson taught Florimell is that fortune weighs all equally, even a 'Lady gent', in making sport of human miseries. At viii 20.3, fortune teaches her to play the mariner. Her story is summed up in the *LR* 81 as 'the misery of Florimell'; cf. viii 1.9, and esp. IV xii 12.9. **7 bewray**: reveal. **8 subiect to**: lying below. **9 ouercame**: overspread.

Stanza 5

1 the tops: th'tops *1609*, as the metre requires. **3 Reeking**: rising. **6 applyd**: directed.

Stanza 6

4–9 'The most complete witch in the regular English tradition' (Briggs 1962:75). See 'witches' in the *SEnc*. She is accompanied by the usual loutish son and a beast who is her familiar. **envide**: bore a grudge against.

6

There in a gloomy hollow glen she found
  A little cottage, built of stickes and reedes
  In homely wize, and wald with sods around,
  In which a witch did dwell, in loathly weedes,
  And wilfull want, all carelesse of her needes,
  So choosing solitarie to abide,
  Far from all neighbours, that her diuelish deedes
  And hellish arts from people she might hide,
And hurt far off vnknowne, whom euer she envide.

7

The Damzell there arriuing entred in;
  Where sitting on the flore the Hag she found,
  Busie (as seem'd) about some wicked gin:
  Who soone as she beheld that suddein stound,
  Lightly vpstarted from the dustie ground,
  And with fell looke and hollow deadly gaze
  Stared on her awhile, as one astound,
  Ne had one word to speake, for great amaze,
But shewd by outward signes, that dread her sence did daze.

8

At last turning her feare to foolish wrath,
  She askt, what deuill had her thether brought,
  And who she was, and what vnwonted path
  Had guided her, vnwelcomed, vnsought.
  To which the Damzell full of doubtfull thought,
  Her mildly answer'd; Beldame be not wroth
  With silly Virgin by aduenture brought
  Vnto your dwelling, ignorant and loth,
That craue but rowme to rest, while tempest ouerblo'th.

9

With that adowne out of her christall eyne
  Few trickling teares she softly forth let fall,
  That like two orient perles, did purely shyne
  Vpon her snowy cheeke; and therewithall

She sighed soft, that none so bestiall,
  Nor saluage hart, but ruth of her sad plight
  Would make to melt, or pitteously appall;
  And that vile Hag, all were her whole delight
In mischiefe, was much moued at so pitteous sight.

10

And gan recomfort her in her rude wyse,
  With womanish compassion of her plaint,
  Wiping the teares from her suffused eyes,
  And bidding her sit downe, to rest her faint
  And wearie limbs a while. She nothing quaint
  Nor s'deignfull of so homely fashion,
  Sith brought she was now to so hard constraint,
  Sate downe vpon the dusty ground anon,
As glad of that small rest, as Bird of tempest gon.

11

Tho gan she gather vp her garments rent,
  And her loose lockes to dight in order dew,
  With golden wreath and gorgeous ornament;
  Whom such whenas the wicked Hag did vew,
  She was astonisht at her heauenly hew,
  And doubted her to deeme an earthly wight,
  But or some Goddesse, or of *Dianes* crew,
  And thought her to adore with humble spright;
T'adore thing so diuine as beauty, were but right.

12

This wicked woman had a wicked sonne,
  The comfort of her age and weary dayes,
  A laesy loord, for nothing good to donne,
  But stretched forth in ydlenesse always,
  Ne euer cast his mind to couet prayse,
  Or ply him selfe to any honest trade,
  But all the day before the sunny rayes
  He vs'd to slug, or sleepe in slothfull shade:
Such laesinesse both lewd and poore attonce him made.

Stanza 7
2 the Hag: her common title as a black witch. **3 gin**: device, stratagem. **4–7 stound**: appearance, which leaves her **astound**, i.e. stunned.

Stanza 8
5 doubtfull: fearful. **6–9** The first cited speech by one who is usually silent – cf. her similar address to the Fisher whom she calls 'father' and 'good man' at viii 23.7, 24.1 – until her eloquent soliloquy at IV xii 6–11. **Beldame**: good mother. **silly**: helpless. **by aduenture**: by chance. **while**: until.

Stanza 9
3 two: 'to', conj. Hughes 1715. **4 snowy cheeke**: anticipating her *alter ego*, the snowy Florimell. Cf. Shamefastnes's 'snowy cheekes' at II ix 41.4. **7 pitteously appall**: quell with pity.

Stanza 10
3 suffused: i.e. with tears, rendering Virgil's description of Venus *lacrimis oculos suffusa* (*Aen.* 1.228). **5 quaint**: fastidious. **6 s'deignfull**: disdainful. **7 constraint**: distress; com-

pulsion. **8 dusty ground**: repeated from 7.5, and again at 13.3, to mark another stage of her descent.

Stanza 11
1–3 Her garments, 'all . . . wrought of beaten gold' (i 15.6), which had been **rent** in her flight, may now be gathered, though soon some of 'her rich spoyles' are either destroyed by the hyena, or left behind (viii 2.8, 9.1–2) for the False Florimell to wear (12.2), and the rest are despoiled (26.9). In her flight, her hair was 'Loosely disperst' (i 16.4); now it is gathered up as it was at first (v 5.4). **dight**: arrange. **4–9** Florimell appears to the witch as Venus disguised as Diana appears to Aeneas in Virgil, *Aen.* 1.328–29. DiMatteo 1992:61–62 notes the changes in the witch's response: from dread to wrath to pity and now to astonishment and adoration, which is intensified at 14.5–9. Cf. Artegall's response to the sight of Britomart at IV vi 22.1–5.

Stanza 12
3 A lazy lout good for nothing. **6 ply**: apply. **8** As Acrasia's knights 'slug in slouth and sensuall delights' at II i 23.3. **9 lewd**: ignorant; implying also the sexual sense, as 20.1.

13

He comming home at vndertime, there found
  The fayrest creature, that he euer saw,
  Sitting beside his mother on the ground;
  The sight whereof did greatly him adaw,
  And his base thought with terrour and with aw
  So inly smot, that as one, which hath gaz'd
  On the bright Sunne vnwares, doth soone withdraw
  His feeble eyne, with too much brightnes daz'd,
So stared he on her, and stood long while amaz'd.

14

Softly at last he gan his mother aske,
  What mister wight that was, and whence deriu'd,
  That in so straunge disguizement there did maske,
  And by what accident she there arriu'd:
  But she, as one nigh of her wits depriu'd,
  With nought but ghastly lookes him answered,
  Like to a ghost, that lately is reuiu'd
  From *Stygian* shores, where late it wandered;
So both at her, and each at other wondered.

15

But the fayre Virgin was so meeke and myld,
  That she to them vouchsafed to embace
  Her goodly port, and to their senses vyld,
  Her gentle speach applyde, that in short space
  She grew familiare in that desert place.
  During which time, the Chorle through her so kind
  And courteise vse conceiu'd affection bace,
  And cast to loue her in his brutish mind;
No loue, but brutish lust, that was so beastly tind.

16

Closely the wicked flame his bowels brent,
  And shortly grew into outrageous fire;
  Yet had he not the hart, nor hardiment,
  As vnto her to vtter his desire;

His caytiue thought durst not so high aspire,
  But with soft sighes, and louely semblaunces,
  He ween'd that his affection entire
  She should aread; many resemblaunces
To her he made, and many kinde remembraunces.

17

Oft from the forrest wildings he did bring,
  Whose sides empurpled were with smyling red,
  And oft young birds, which he had taught to sing
  His maistresse praises, sweetly caroled,
  Girlonds of flowres sometimes for her faire hed
  He fine would dight; sometimes the squirrell wild
  He brought to her in bands, as conquered
  To be her thrall, his fellow seruant vild;
All which, she of him tooke with countenance meeke and mild.

18

But past awhile, when she fit season saw
  To leaue that desert mansion, she cast
  In secret wize her selfe thence to withdraw,
  For feare of mischiefe, which she did forecast
  Might by the witch or by her sonne compast:
  Her wearie Palfrey closely, as she might,
  Now well recouered after long repast,
  In his proud furnitures she freshly dight,
His late miswandred wayes now to remeasure right.

19

And earely ere the dawning day appeard,
  She forth issewed, and on her iourney went;
  She went in perill, of each noyse affeard,
  And of each shade, that did it selfe present;
  For still she feared to be ouerhent,
  Of that vile hag, or her vnciuile sonne:
  Who when too late awaking, well they kent,
  That their fayre guest was gone, they both begonne
To make exceeding mone, as they had beene vndonne.

Stanza 13

1 **vndertime**: the term applies to various times of the day but since Florimell rode all night, morning would be appropriate, specifically the testing time, noon. One who loves to lie 'before the sunny rayes' (12.7) now gazes on one who, like **the bright Sunne**, dazzles his eyes. 4 **adaw**: daunt; confound.

Stanza 14

2 **mister wight**: kind of creature. 3 The language suggests the masque of Cupid in the house of Busirane. 7–9 A witty adaptation of a common classical motif, e.g. at I iv 48.7–9, to contrast the state of the witch and her son with that of Florimell in her 'heauenly hew' (11.5). While a ghost **lately** revived from the Styx where it wandered **late** might well be astonished at the sight of Florimell, there may be a larger reference to the 'recent' freeing of souls imprisoned in purgatory; see I iii **36.6n**.

Stanza 15

2 **embace**: make base, humble; marking another stage in her descent. 3 **vyld**: vile. 5 **familiare**: i.e. on a family footing. 6–7 Cf. Belphœbe 'so courteous and kynde' at v 55.2. **vse**: habit, behaviour. 8 **cast**: determined. 9 **tind**: inflamed.

Stanza 16

1 **Closely**: secretly. 3–5 A low-life version of Timias's dilemma in loving Belphœbe at v 44–47. **caytiue**: vile. 6 **louely semblaunces**: shows of love. 7 **entire**: inward; sincere. 8 **aread**: guess. **resemblaunces**: demonstrations of affection, unlike Timias's restraint.

Stanza 17

1–2 **wildings**: wild fruit. **empurpled**: the erotic implications of the colour are evident from its use at II xii 54.7 and IV vii 6.6. 6 **dight**: prepare. **squirrell**: cf. the 'wanton squirrels' that Coridon gives Pastorella to woo her at VI ix 40.3.

Stanza 18

1 After some time had passed. 2 **mansion**: lodging. 5 **compast**: i.e. be compassed or contrived. 6 **closely**: secretly. 7 **repast**: repose. 8 **furnitures**: harness, with **proud** recalling its 'tinsell trappings' (i 15.7). 9 **miswandred**: in which he had gone astray. **remeasure**: retrace.

Stanza 19

3–4 Cf. her state at 1.4–9. Her fear of all things soon appears as Proteus who assumes 'euery shape' at viii 40.2. 5 **still**:

20

But that lewd louer did the most lament
    For her depart, that euer man did heare;
    He knockt his brest with desperate intent,
    And scratcht his face, and with his teeth did teare
    His rugged flesh, and rent his ragged heare:
    That his sad mother seeing his sore plight,
    Was greatly woe begon, and gan to feare,
    Least his fraile senses were emperisht quight,
And loue to frenzy turnd, sith loue is franticke hight.

21   *reason vs passion*

All wayes shee sought, him to restore to plight,
    With herbs, with charms, with counsel, and with teares,
    But tears, nor charms, nor herbs, nor counsell might
    Asswage the fury, which his entrails teares:
    So strong is passion, that no reason heares.
    Tho when all other helpes she saw to faile,
    She turnd her selfe backe to her wicked leares
    And by her diuelish arts thought to preuaile,
To bring her backe againe, or worke her finall bale.

22   *love vs reason*

Eftesoones out of her hidden caue she cald
    An hideous beast, of horrible aspect,
    That could the stoutest corage haue appald;
    Monstrous, mishapt, and all his backe was spect
    With thousand spots of colours queint elect,
    Thereto so swifte, that it all beasts did pas:
    Like neuer yet did liuing eie detect;
    But likest it to an *Hyena* was,
That feeds on wemens flesh, as others feede on gras.

23

It forth she cald, and gaue it streight in charge,
    Through thicke and thin her to poursew apace,
    Ne once to stay to rest, or breath at large,
    Till her he had attaind, and brought in place,

Or quite deuourd her beauties scornefull grace.
    The Monster swifte as word, that from her went,
    Went forth in haste, and did her footing trace
    So sure and swiftly, through his perfect sent,
And passing speede, that shortly he her ouerhent.

24

Whom when the fearefull Damzell nigh espide,
    No need to bid her fast away to flie;
    That vgly shape so sore her terrifide,
    That it she shund no lesse, then dread to die,
    And her flitt Palfrey did so well apply
    His nimble feet to her conceiued feare,
    That whilest his breath did strength to him supply,
    From perill free he her away did beare:
But when his force gan faile, his pace gan wex areare.

25

Which whenas she perceiu'd, she was dismayd
    At that same last extremity ful sore,
    And of her safety greatly grew afrayd;
    And now she gan approch to the sea shore,
    As it befell, that she could flie no more,
    But yield her selfe to spoile of greedinesse.
    Lightly she leaped, as a wight forlore,
    From her dull horse, in desperate distresse,
And to her feet betooke her doubtfull sickernesse.

26

Not halfe so fast the wicked *Myrrha* fled
    From dread of her reuenging fathers hond:
    Nor halfe so fast to saue her maydenhed,
    Fled fearfull *Daphne* on th'*AEgaean* strond,
    As *Florimell* fled from that Monster yond,
    To reach the sea, ere she of him were raught:
    For in the sea to drowne her selfe she fond,
    Rather then of the tyrant to be caught:
Thereto fear gaue her wings, and need her corage taught.

always. **ouerhent**: overtaken. **6 vnciuile**: barbarous, uncouth. **7 kent**: kenned, knew.

Stanza 20
2 depart: departure. **8 emperisht**: enfeebled. **9** Cf. 'that mad fit, which fooles call love' (*HHL* 9).

Stanza 21
1–2 As Glauce used herbs and charms at ii 48–50 to cure Britomart's love after counsel failed, but at iii 5.3–4 found them of no use. **plight**: health. **7 leares**: lore; magic. **9 her finall bale**: her death.

Stanza 22
5 queint elect: strangely or cleverly chosen either for disguise or to arouse fear. The **spots** signify spots of sin or its 'corrupted flesh' (32.6), specifically concupiscence, which Florimell fears most. **6 Thereto**: in addition. **pas**: surpass. **8–9 Hyena**: traditionally linked with witches, it is cited in the Geneva gloss to Ecclus. 13.19 as a wild beast that lures men out of their houses to devour them, which is how Florimell rightly regards all men except Marinell. See Rowland

1973:112–13. The association of cannibalism with lust is seen in Lust who 'fed on fleshly gore' at IV vii 5.8, and in the lecherous savage nation ready to eat Serena at VI viii 35–44.

Stanza 23
1 streight: strictly; immediately. **4 in place**: here, in her presence. **7 footing**: footprints. **9 passing**: surpassing all, including Florimell.

Stanza 24
5 flitt: swift. **apply**: accommodate, adapt. **9** . . . i.e. he began to slow down.

Stanza 25
1 dismayd: the implicit pun expresses her fears. **7 forlore**: doomed to destruction; lost. **9** She sought safety (**sickernesse**), which was doubtful, by fleeing on foot.

Stanza 26
1–4 Myrrha and **Daphne** are cited as extremes of guilt and innocence, the one associated with incestuous lust (see ii 41.1–6n) and the other with fearing loss of her virginity.

27

It fortuned (high God did so ordaine)
　　As shee arriued on the roring shore,
　　In minde to leape into the mighty maine,
　　A little bote lay houing her before,
　　In which there slept a fisher old and pore,
　　The whiles his nets were drying on the sand:
　　Into the same shee lept, and with the ore
　　Did thrust the shallop from the floting strand:
So safety fownd at sea, which she fownd not at land.

28

The Monster ready on the pray to sease,
　　Was of his forward hope deceiued quight,
　　Ne durst assay to wade the perlous seas,
　　But greedily long gaping at the sight,
　　At last in vaine was forst to turne his flight,
　　And tell the idle tidings to his Dame:
　　Yet to auenge his diuelishe despight,
　　He sett vpon her Palfrey tired lame,
And slew him cruelly, ere any reskew came.

29

And after hauing him embowelled,
　　To fill his hellish gorge, it chaunst a knight
　　To passe that way, as forth he traueiled;
　　Yt was a goodly Swaine, and of great might,
　　As euer man that bloody field did fight;
　　But in vain sheows, that wont yong knights bewitch,
　　And courtly seruices tooke no delight,
　　But rather ioyd to bee, then seemen sich:
For both to be and seeme to him was labor lich.

30

It was to weete the good Sir *Satyrane*,
　　That raungd abrode to seeke aduentures wilde,
　　As was his wont in forest, and in plaine;
　　He was all armd in rugged steele vnfilde,
　　As in the smoky forge it was compilde,
　　And in his Scutchin bore a Satyres hedd:
　　He comming present, where the Monster vilde
　　Vpon that milke-white Palfreyes carcas fedd,
Vnto his reskew ran, and greedily him spedd.

31

There well perceiud he, that it was the horse,
　　Whereon faire *Florimell* was wont to ride,
　　That of that feend was rent without remorse:
　　Much feared he, least ought did ill betide
　　To that faire Maide, the flowre of wemens pride;
　　For her he dearely loued, and in all
　　His famous conquests highly magnifide:
　　Besides her golden girdle, which did fall
From her in flight, he fownd, that did him sore apall.

32

Full of sad feare, and doubtfull agony,
　　Fiercely he flew vpon that wicked feend,
　　And with huge strokes, and cruell battery
　　Him forst to leaue his pray, for to attend
　　Him selfe from deadly daunger to defend:
　　Full many wounds in his corrupted flesh
　　He did engraue, and muchell blood did spend,
　　Yet might not doe him die, but aie more fresh
And fierce he still appeard, the more he did him thresh.

Myrrha's flight from her father parallels Florimell's rejection of the Fisher whom she calls 'father' (viii 23.7), incest being implicit in any old man's lust for a young girl. Daphne is saved by the waters of her father, Peneus (Ovid, *Met.* 1.543–52), as Florimell in her attempt to drown herself is saved by the sea. The same comparisons describe Amoret's flight from Lust at IV vii 22.8–9. **5 yond**: fierce, savage. **7 fond**: would try; 'In minde to' (27.3). **9** The first proverb (Smith 247) is associated with her at v 6.6 and vi 54.9. Images of flight and flying surround her; and that **fear gaue her wings** is expressed in comparing her to 'a fearefull Doue' at iv 49.4, a 'Bird of tempest gon' (vii 10.9), and a partridge at viii 33.3. The second proverb refers back to 4.3.

Stanza 27

1 A common romance formula to allow fortune to take charge, e.g. I xi 45.6, as she does again at viii 20.6–9. **4 houing**: hovering, floating. **7–9** S. uses the story, from Diodorus, *Biblio. Hist.* 5.76.3–4, of Britomartis who fled from Minos to find safety by leaping into the sea from which she was saved by fishermen with their nets; see ii 30–51*n*. On Florimell's movement from earth to water, see Christian 2000:146–55. **floting strand**: the shore off which the boat was floating. Florimell's story is continued at viii 20.

Stanza 28

2 forward: chief; well advanced in being almost gratified.

Stanza 29

1 The bowels are the seat of the passions; repeated at viii 49.4. **8–9** It was as difficult for him to pretend to be a good knight as to be one.

Stanza 30

1 to weete: namely. **Satyrane** gains the epithet **good** from his defence of Una at I vi. He may defeat the beast because he is 'Plaine, faithfull, true, and enimy of shame' (I vi 20.7), as the details of his armour in 4–5 confirm. **4 vnfilde**: unpolished. **5 compilde**: fashioned. **6 Scutchin**: shield. At I vi 21.1, the **Satyres hedd** announces his name and nation as a satyr's son. **8 milke-white Palfreyes** rounds out the initial description at i 15.2.

Stanza 31

5 The phrase provides one etymology of Florimell's name; see v 8.7*n*, and IV v 5.7. **7 magnifide**: glorified by fighting on her behalf. **8–9** Florimell's loss of the **golden girdle**, or 'golden ribband' (36.1), may be read as a token of her loss of maidenhead, as is Persephone's loss of her girdle when she is raped by Pluto (Ovid, *Met.* 5.468–70). It is interpreted by Roche 1964 as the loss of 'the outward sign of her chastity'. Cf. the 'riband' worn by the bride in *Epith* 44, and its loosening, e.g. in Homer, *Ody.* 11.245. Worn by Venus 'to bind lasciuous desire', it was left by her 'On *Acidalian* mount' when she visited Mars, and was brought from there by Florimell; see IV v 3–5 and *n*. Benson 1986:93 interprets its loss as the loss of social support.

33

He wist not, how him to despoile of life,
  Ne how to win the wished victory,
  Sith him he saw still stronger grow through strife,
  And him selfe weaker through infirmity;
  Greatly he grew enrag'd, and furiously
  Hurling his sword away, he lightly lept
  Vpon the beast, that with great cruelty
  Rored, and raged to be vnderkept:
Yet he perforce him held, and strokes vpon him hept.

34

As he that striues to stop a suddein flood,
  And in strong bancks his violence enclose,
  Forceth it swell aboue his wonted mood,
  And largely ouerflow the fruitfull plaine,
  That all the countrey seemes to be a Maine,
  And the rich furrowes flote, all quite fordonne:
  The wofull husbandman doth lowd complaine,
  To see his whole yeares labor lost so soone,
For which to God he made so many an idle boone.

35

So him he held, and did through might amate:
  So long he held him, and him bett so long,
  That at the last his fiercenes gan abate,
  And meekely stoup vnto the victor strong:
  Who to auenge the implacable wrong,
  Which he supposed donne to *Florimell*,
  Sought by all meanes his dolor to prolong,
  Sith dint of steele his carcas could not quell:
His maker with her charmes had framed him so well.

36

The golden ribband, which that virgin wore
  About her sclender waste, he tooke in hand,
  And with it bownd the beast, that lowd did rore
  For great despight of that vnwonted band,
  Yet dared not his victor to withstand,
  But trembled like a lambe, fled from the pray,
  And all the way him followd on the strand,
  As he had long bene learned to obay;
Yet neuer learned he such seruice, till that day.

37

Thus as he led the Beast along the way,
  He spide far off a mighty Giauntesse,
  Fast flying on a Courser dapled gray,
  From a bold knight, that with great hardinesse
  Her hard pursewd, and sought for to suppresse;
  She bore before her lap a dolefull Squire,
  Lying athwart her horse in great distresse,
  Fast bounden hand and foote with cords of wire,
Whom she did meane to make the thrall of her desire.

38

Which whenas *Satyrane* beheld, in haste
  He lefte his captiue Beast at liberty,
  And crost the nearest way, by which he cast
  Her to encounter, ere she passed by:
  But she the way shund nathemore for thy,
  But forward gallopt fast, which when he spyde,
  His mighty speare he couched warily,
  And at her ran: she hauing him descryde,
Her selfe to fight addrest, and threw her lode aside.

Stanza 32

6–9 The hyena is like Maleger who is 'most strong in most infirmitee' (II xi 40.8); cf. esp. 35.8 and II xi 37–38. Its **corrupted flesh** suggests the 'Fleshly corruption' of those who put on 'fleshly weeds' (vi 33.4, 32.5) when they leave the garden of Adonis. **engraue**: cut deeply.

Stanza 33

5–9 In throwing away his sword to grapple with his foe, Satyrane imitates Arthur in his battle with Maleger. **cruelty**: excessive suffering; also in the usual sense, as viii 21.2.

Stanza 34

The simile comments on Satyrane's efforts to subdue the hyena at 32.8–9: the restraint of violence causes greater violence. The same simile is applied to Furor at II iv 11.9. Its use here may have been suggested by the flight of Florimell: as her name suggests, she is the **fruitfull plaine** overwhelmed by the sea, as may happen in tideland where the present action takes place. 2 **enclose**: 'containe', in the obs. sense: 'confine' (cf. V xii 1.4), seems to be the word that S. intended; otherwise the 'b' rhyme is left (appropriately) unenclosed, as Fried 1981:276 notes. 5–6 **Maine**: sea. **flote**: are flooded. **fordonne**: laid waste. 9 **boone**: prayer.

Stanza 35

1 **amate**: subdue. 2 **bett**: beat with his fists. 5 **implacable**: not to be assuaged, irremediable; cf. II vi 44.2. 7 **dolor**: pain. 8 **quell**: kill.

Stanza 36

1–3 In *The Golden Legend*, the defeated dragon bound by St George with his lady's girdle meekly follows her. That detail may suggest the simile, **like a lambe**, for the lady leads a lamb on a line, as does Una at I i 4.9. 6 **pray**: one who preys. 9 **till that day** suggests some topical significance, perhaps connected with the Order of the Garter, of which St George was the patron. On the Order, see I vii 46.4–7*n*.

Stanza 37

8 **cords of wire**: unless dictated by the rhyme, the detail indicates the usual plight of the lover 'wrapt in fetters of a golden tresse' (V viii 1.7). Elsewhere used only for a woman's hair (e.g. viii 7.6), the yellow locks of the False Florimell are made of 'golden wyre'. This point having been made, the cords become 'yron bands' at 46.6.

Stanza 38

3 **cast**: determined, planned. 5 She did not change her way because of that.

39

Like as a Goshauke, that in foote doth beare
      A trembling Culuer, hauing spide on hight
      An Eagle, that with plumy wings doth sheare
      The subtile ayre, stouping with all his might,
      The quarrey throwes to ground with fell despight,
      And to the batteill doth her selfe prepare:
      So ran the Geauntesse vnto the fight;
      Her fyrie eyes with furious sparkes did stare,
And with blasphemous bannes high God in peeces tare.

40

She caught in hand an huge great yron mace,
      Wherewith she many had of life depriu'd;
      But ere the stroke could seize his aymed place,
      His speare amids her sun-brode shield arriu'd,
      Yet nathemore the steele a sonder riu'd,
      All were the beame in bignes like a mast,
      Ne her out of the stedfast sadle driu'd,
      But glauncing on the tempred metall, brast
In thousand shiuers, and so forth beside her past.

41

Her Steed did stagger with that puissant strooke;
      But she no more was moued with that might,
      Then it had lighted on an aged Oke;
      Or on the marble Pillour, that is pight
      Vpon the top of Mount *Olympus* hight,
      For the braue youthly Champions to assay,
      With burning charet wheeles it nigh to smite:
      But who that smites it, mars his ioyous play,
And is the spectacle of ruinous decay.

42

Yet therewith sore enrag'd, with sterne regard
      Her dreadfull weapon she to him addrest,
      Which on his helmet martelled so hard,
      That made him low incline his lofty crest,

And bowd his battred visour to his brest:
      Wherewith hee was so stund, that he n'ote ryde
      But reeled to and fro from east to west:
      Which when his cruell enimy espyde,
She lightly vnto him adioyned syde to syde;

43

And on his collar laying puissaunt hand,
      Out of his wauering seat him pluckt perforse,
      Perforse him pluckt, vnable to withstand,
      Or helpe himselfe, and laying thwart her horse,
      In loathly wise like to a carrion corse,
      She bore him fast away. Which when the knight,
      That her pursewed, saw with great remorse,
      He nere was touched in his noble spright,
And gan encrease his speed, as she encreast her flight.

44

Whom when as nigh approching she espyde,
      She threw away her burden angrily;
      For she list not the batteill to abide,
      But made her selfe more light, away to fly:
      Yet her the hardy knight pursewd so nye
      That almost in the backe he oft her strake:
      But still when him at hand she did espy,
      She turnd, and semblaunce of faire fight did make;
But when he stayd, to flight againe she did her take.

45

By this the good Sir *Satyrane* gan wake
      Out of his dreame, that did him long entraunce,
      And seeing none in place, he gan to make
      Exceeding mone, and curst that cruell chaunce,
      Which reft from him so faire a cheuisaunce:
      At length he spyde, whereas that wofull Squyre,
      Whom he had reskewed from captiuaunce
      Of his strong foe, lay tombled in the myre,
Vnable to arise, or foot or hand to styre.

Stanza 39
The **Goshauke** serves here as a symbol of female aggressiveness and the **Eagle** of male strength, as at V iv 42. **2 Culuer**: dove. **4–5 subtile**: rarefied. **stouping**: descending swiftly on its prey (**quarrey**). **8** Her eyes seek to infect the beholder, as do Corflambo's eyes at IV viii 39. **stare**: shine. **9 bannes**: curses, specifically naming God's body, as the rioters in Chaucer, *Pardoner's Tale* 474, 'Oure blissed Lordes body . . . totere'.

Stanza 40
1 The weapon of choice for sexual predators. Orgoglio's 'mortall mace' (I vii 10.9), Lust's club (IV vii 25), and Corflambo's 'massie yron mace' (IV viii 43.6) bear similar phallic import. **3 seize**: reach, penetrate. **4 her sun-brode shield**: referring to its size; see II ii 21.5*n*. **6** In Tasso, *Ger. Lib.* 6.40, Tancredi and Argante carry masts instead of spears. In 1 Sam. 17.7, Goliath's spear is 'like a weauers beame'.

Stanza 41
4–9 It was commonly assumed that the Olympic games were held on **Mount Olympus**, e.g. Sidney, *Defence of Poetry* 97; cf. *Rome* 20. The game played here is the classical equivalent to the grand slalom in which the course-marker to be rounded is

a **marble Pillour**. **nigh to smite**: i.e. to come as close as possible without hitting it. **decay**: destruction.

Stanza 42
1 sterne regard: terrible and threatening aspect. **2 addrest**: aimed. **3 martelled**: hammered. **6 n'ote**: could not. **9 adioyned**: joined herself to him by approaching alongside, suggesting sexual intimacy, as the concluding semicolon may also suggest. *Double entendre* is used throughout this episode.

Stanza 43
1–6 Perforse: forcibly. The inversion in **3** is for comic effect. At **4**, he takes the place of Argante's previous victim, and as **a carrion corse** may be compared to the 'dead' Adonis tended by Venus. **7 remorse**: compassion.

Stanza 44
The repeated **he** and **him**, as 43.8–9, prepares for the surprise when 'his' identity is revealed at 52. **9 when he stayd**: to allow his foe to run a tilt. The same comic action takes place at viii 18.

Stanza 45
5 cheuisaunce: chivalric enterprise; see II ix 8.1–4*n*. **7 captiuaunce**: captivity. **9 styre**: stir.

46

To whom approching, well he mote perceiue
   In that fowle plight a comely personage,
   And louely face, made fit for to deceiue
   Fraile Ladies hart with loues consuming rage,
   Now in the blossome of his freshest age:
   He reard him vp, and loosd his yron bands,
   And after gan inquire his parentage,
   And how he fell into the Gyaunts hands,
And who that was, which chaced her along the lands.

47

Then trembling yet through feare, the Squire bespake,
   That Geauntesse *Argante* is behight,
   A daughter of the *Titans* which did make
   Warre against heuen, and heaped hils on hight,
   To scale the skyes, and put *Ioue* from his right:
   Her syre *Typhoeus* was, who mad through merth,
   And dronke with blood of men, slaine by his might,
   Through incest, her of his owne mother Earth
Whylome begot, being but halfe twin of that berth.

48

For at that berth another Babe she bore,
   To weet the mightie *Ollyphant*, that wrought
   Great wreake to many errant knights of yore,
   Till him Chylde *Thopas* to confusion brought.
   These twinnes, men say, (a thing far passing thought)
   Whiles in their mothers wombe enclosd they were,
   Ere they into the lightsom world were brought,
   In fleshly lust were mingled both yfere,
And in that monstrous wise did to the world appere.

49

So liu'd they euer after in like sin,
   Gainst natures law, and good behaueoure:
   But greatest shame was to that maiden twin,
   Who not content so fowly to deuoure
   Her natiue flesh, and staine her brothers bowre,
   Did wallow in all other fleshly myre,
   And suffred beastes her body to deflowre:
   So whot she burned in that lustfull fyre,
Yet all that might not slake her sensuall desyre.

50

But ouer all the countrie she did raunge,
   To seeke young men, to quench her flaming thrust,
   And feed her fancy with delightfull chaunge:
   Whom so she fittest findes to serue her lust,
   Through her maine strength, in which she most doth trust,
   She with her bringes into a secret Ile,
   Where in eternall bondage dye he must,
   Or be the vassall of her pleasures vile,
And in all shamefull sort him selfe with her defile.

51

Me seely wretch she so at vauntage caught,
   After she long in waite for me did lye,
   And meant vnto her prison to haue brought,
   Her lothsom pleasure there to satisfye;
   That thousand deathes me leuer were to dye,
   Then breake the vow, that to faire *Columbell*
   I plighted haue, and yet keepe stedfastly:
   As for my name, it mistreth not to tell;
Call me the *Squyre of Dames* that me beseemeth well.

Stanza 46
7–9 The Squire of Dames answers Satyrane's first question by revealing only the name he assumes; see 51.9*n*. **along the lands**: throughout the country; cf. II xi 47.2.

Stanza 47
2 **Argante** inherits her incestuous nature from **Typhoeus** (on whom see VI vi 10–12*n*). S. may have taken the name directly from Tasso's Argante (see 40.6*n*) who is as fierce an enemy of Christians as she is of chastity. In Layamon's *Brut*, Argante is the Faerie Queen of Avalon, as Belson 1964:35 notes; see also Anderson 1988:195–96. As the lustful Morgana of romance, and therefore a demonic Faerie Queene, see 'Argante, Ollyphant' in the *SEnc*. The spelling **Geauntesse** indicates her earth-born nature, from Gea, the earth. 3–5 The *locus classicus* of the wars of the giants/**Titans** against Jove is Ovid, *Met.* 1.151–53 and Hesiod, *Theog.* 617–735, though S. would have consulted Renaissance dictionaries; see Starnes and Talbert 1955:74–75. See 'Titans' in the *SEnc*. References to these wars figure prominently throughout the poem. On the place it gives to titanism as a challenge to authority, see Teskey 1996:180–87. 8 **incest**: in fact and in etymology 'incest' is the extreme degree of unchastity (Lat. *incestus*).

Stanza 48
2 **Ollyphant**: from Chaucer, *Tale of Sir Thopas* 807–09: 'a greet geaunt, | His name was sire Olifaunt, | A perilous man of dede'. As the Renaissance spelling of 'elephant', the name suggests this creature's size; and as the name of Roland's ivory horn, it suggests his phallic dimension. The story of these twins

– a demonic version of the birth of Belphœbe and Amoret at vi 2–4 – is told again at xi 3.4–4.4. 3 **wreake**: harm. 4 **Till him Chylde Thopas**: And many hath to foule *1596*. Revision was needed because Chaucer's tale breaks off before Child Thopas slays Ollyphant. **confusion**: ruin. 5 **men say**: perhaps only S., though Plutarch records that Isis and Osiris copulated in the womb. 8 **yfere**: together.

Stanza 49
4 **deuoure**: make a prey of, in the sexual sense.

Stanza 50
2 **thrust**: thirst, though 'thrust' applies to a nymphomaniac's desire. 7–9 Argante's captives have a choice, as does Florimell in Proteus's bower at viii 42, and Amoret in Busirane's house at xi 17: either yield (under duress) or endure **eternall bondage**. Neither death nor rape is threatened. From 51.4, it is clear that Argante expects him to yield.

Stanza 51
1 **seely**: miserable, pitiable. 5 **me leuer were**: I would rather. 6 **Columbell**: Fr. *colombelle*, 'yong dove' (Cotgrave 1611), which is Venus's bird; or Lat. *columba*, dove + *bella*, pretty; or 'bell' may be eulogistic: among ladies she bears the bell. 8 **it mistreth not**: it is not needful. 9 **Squyre of Dames**: his name is attributed by *OED* to S., who derived it from 'the Squire of the body', an officer who attended the queen's person (*OED* 3a). See 'Squire of Dames' in the *SEnc*, and on his literary history, see Kennedy 2000.

52

But that bold knight, whom ye pursuing saw
   That Geauntesse, is not such, as she seemd,
   But a faire virgin, that in martiall law,
   And deedes of armes aboue all Dames is deemd,
   And aboue many knightes is eke esteemd,
   For her great worth; She *Palladine* is hight:
   She you from death, you me from dread redeemd.
   Ne any may that Monster match in fight,
But she, or such as she, that is so chaste a wight.

53

Her well beseemes that Quest (quoth *Satyrane*)
   But read, thou *Squyre of Dames*, what vow is this,
   Which thou vpon thy selfe hast lately ta'ne.
   That shall I you recount (quoth he) ywis,
   So be ye pleasd to pardon all amis.
   That gentle Lady, whom I loue and serue,
   After long suit and wearie seruicis,
   Did aske me, how I could her loue deserue,
And how she might be sure, that I would neuer swerue.

54

I glad by any meanes her grace to gaine,
   Badd her commaund my life to saue, or spill.
   Eftsoones she badd me, with incessaunt paine
   To wander through the world abroad at will,
   And euery where, where with my power or skill
   I might doe seruice vnto gentle Dames,
   That I the same should faithfully fulfill,
   And at the twelue monethes end should bring their names
And pledges; as the spoiles of my victorious games.

55

So well I to faire Ladies seruice did,
   And found such fauour in their louing hartes,
   That ere the yeare his course had compassid,
   Three hundred pledges for my good desartes,

And thrise three hundred thanks for my good partes
   I with me brought, and did to her present:
   Which when she saw, more bent to eke my smartes,
   Then to reward my trusty true intent,
She gan for me deuise a grieuous punishment.

56

To weet, that I my traueill should resume,
   And with like labour walke the world arownd,
   Ne euer to her presence should presume,
   Till I so many other Dames had fownd,
   The which, for all the suit I could propownd,
   Would me refuse their pledges to afford,
   But did abide for euer chaste and sownd.
   Ah gentle Squyre (quoth he) tell at one word,
How many fowndst thou such to put in thy record?

57

In deed Sir knight (said he) one word may tell
   All, that I euer fownd so wisely stayd;
   For onely three they were disposd so well,
   And yet three yeares I now abrode haue strayd,
   To fynd them out. Mote I (then laughing sayd
   The knight) inquire of thee, what were those three,
   The which thy proffred curtesie denayd?
   Or ill they seemed sure auizd to bee,
Or brutishly brought vp, that neu'r did fashions see.

58

The first which then refused me (said hee)
   Certes was but a common Courtisane,
   Yet flat refusd to haue a doe with mee,
   Because I could not giue her many a Iane.
   (Thereat full hartely laughed *Satyrane*)
   The second was an holy Nunne to chose,
   Which would not let me be her Chappellane,
   Because she knew, she sayd, I would disclose
Her counsell, if she should her trust in me repose.

Stanza 52
6 **Palladine**: from 'paladin', a knightly hero. The name is linked with Pallas Athena and hence with Minerva, the classical goddess of chastity, with whom Britomart is compared at ix 22.1 (*1596*). Hence her role as the chaste warrior feared by Argante is duplicated in Britomart feared by Ollyphant at xi 6.

Stanza 53
2 **read**: declare. 4–5 In *Orl. Fur.* 28.1, Ariosto apologizes for the host's scurrilous tale of female infidelity. In his translation, Harington comments: 'The hosts tale . . . is a bad one: M. *Spencers* tale . . . is to the like effect, sharpe and well conceyted' (*Sp All* 22). S. delays his apology until viii 44.2–3. On his imitation of Ariosto, see Rhu 1993c:32–35. **ywis**: assuredly.

Stanza 54
1 **grace**: favour. 2 **spill**: destroy. 6 **doe seruice**: i.e. become their lover. Columbell's demands on him are captious but ideal for a roué: he must prove that he deserves her love by sexually serving other courtly ladies, in effect, proving himself faithful by being unfaithful. On the similar demand at Castle Joyeous, see i 27*n*.

Stanza 55
5 **partes**: suggesting privy parts.

Stanza 56
1 **traueill**: the usual play on 'travail' is most appropriate for his Herculean labour, as line 2 suggests.

Stanza 57
2 **stayd**: resolute. 3 **three**: Ariosto's lovers do not find even one. 5 **laughing**, as again at 58.5 and the smile at ix 6.6, betray his satyr descent. Cf. Faunus's lustful laughter at VII vi 46.5. 7 **denayd**: refused. 8 **auizd**: counselled.

Stanza 58
2 **Courtisane**: suggesting one who responds to 'proffred curtesie' (57.7). 3 **haue a doe**: in the bawdy sense. 4 **Iane**: a small silver coin, a possible echo of 'many a jane' in Chaucer, *Tale of Sir Thopas* 735. 6 **to chose**: by choice (*OED* 12); or 'if you please', as Dodge 1908 suggests. 7–9 With the Protestant innuendo on a nun's relation to her confessor. **repose**: place.

59

The third a Damzell was of low degree,
  Whom I in countrey cottage fownd by chaunce;
  Full litle weened I, that chastitee
  Had lodging in so meane a maintenaunce,
  Yet was she fayre, and in her countenaunce
  Dwelt simple truth in seemely fashion.
  Long thus I woo'd her with dew obseruaunce,
  In hope vnto my pleasure to haue won,
But was as far at last, as when I first begon.

60

Safe her, I neuer any woman found,
  That chastity did for it selfe embrace,
  But were for other causes firme and sound,
  Either for want of handsome time and place,
  Or else for feare of shame and fowle disgrace.
  Thus am I hopelesse euer to attaine
  My Ladies loue, in such a desperate case,
  But all my dayes am like to waste in vaine,
Seeking to match the chaste with th'vnchaste Ladies traine.

61

Perdy, (sayd *Satyrane*) thou *Squyre of Dames*,
  Great labour fondly hast thou hent in hand,
  To get small thankes, and therewith many blames,
  That may emongst *Alcides* labours stand.
  Thence backe returning to the former land,
  Where late he left the Beast, he ouercame,
  He found him not; for he had broke his band,
  And was returnd againe vnto his Dame,
To tell what tydings of fayre *Florimell* became.

Stanza 59
4 maintenaunce: state or means of subsistence.

Stanza 60
1 Safe: save.   **4 handsome**: suitable.

Stanza 61
2 fondly: foolishly.   **hent**: taken.   **4** As a warm-up to his first labour, according to Pausanias, *Hellados Periegesis* 9.27.6, Hercules bedded all fifty virgin daughters of Thestius in a single night.   **7 broke his band**: either broke the girdle, as 'broken' (viii 2.7:*1596*) indicates, or broke free of it.

Cant. VIII.

The Witch creates a snowy Lady,
like to Florimell,
Who wrongd by Carle by Proteus sau'd,
is sought by Paridell.

1

S O oft as I this history record,
  My hart doth melt with meere compassion,
  To thinke, how causelesse of her owne accord
  This gentle Damzell, whom I write vpon,
  Should plonged be in such affliction,
  Without all hope of comfort or reliefe,
  That sure I weene, the hardest hart of stone,
  Would hardly finde to aggrauate her griefe;
For misery craues rather mercy, then repriefe.

2

But that accursed Hag, her hostesse late,
  Had so enranckled her malitious hart,
  That she desyrd th'abridgement of her fate,
  Or long enlargement of her painefull smart.
  Now when the Beast, which by her wicked art
  Late foorth she sent, she backe retourning spyde,
  Tyde with her golden girdle, it a part
  Of her rich spoyles, whom he had earst destroyd,
She weend, and wondrous gladnes to her hart applyde.

3

And with it ronning hast'ly to her sonne,
  Thought with that sight him much to haue reliu'd;
  Who thereby deeming sure the thing as donne,
  His former griefe with furie fresh reuiu'd,

Much more then earst, and would haue algates riu'd
  The hart out of his brest: for sith her dedd
  He surely dempt, himselfe he thought depriu'd
  Quite of all hope, wherewith he long had fedd
His foolish malady, and long time had misledd.

4

With thought whereof, exceeding mad he grew,
  And in his rage his mother would haue slaine,
  Had she not fled into a secret mew,
  Where she was wont her Sprightes to entertaine
  The maisters of her art: there was she faine
  To call them all in order to her ayde,
  And them coniure vpon eternall paine,
  To counsell her so carefully dismayd,
How she might heale her sonne, whose senses were decayd.

5

By their deuice, and her owne wicked wit,
  She there deuiz'd a wondrous worke to frame,
  Whose like on earth was neuer framed yit,
  That euen Nature selfe enuide the same,
  And grudg'd to see the counterfet should shame
  The thing it selfe: In hand she boldly tooke
  To make another like the former Dame,
  Another *Florimell*, in shape and looke
So liuely and so like, that many it mistooke.

Book III Canto viii

Argument
3 Carle: a churl.

Stanza 1
2 meere: entire.   **3** . . . not through her own assent (and hence not deserving reproof); or, through no blame of her own act (*Var*). Florimell is unable to avoid either loving or arousing love in others.   **5 affliction**: in the etymological sense, 'thrown down'. Finally she is thrown down to the bottom of the sea.   **7 hardest hart of stone**: preparing for the stone walls that imprison her under the sea until Marinell's 'stony heart' (IV xii 13.1) softens with love for her.   **8 finde**: find the means to; be hard-hearted enough; also 'invent', referring to the poet's ingenuity in devising ways to increase her misery. **aggrauate**: in the literal sense, add weight to, increase. **9 repriefe**: reproof.

Stanza 2
2 enranckled: embittered.   **3 fate**: the length of life allotted by the fates.   **7 golden**: as at vii 36.1, viii 49.8, IV ii 27.2,

etc.; broken *1596*, apparently to agree with the claim that the beast 'had broke his band' (vii 61.7).

Stanza 3
2 reliu'd: revived.   **4–5** Intensifying his state at vii 20.3–5. **algates**: altogether.   **7 dempt**: deemed.

Stanza 4
3 mew: hiding-place, 'her hidden caue' (vii 22.1).   **5 maisters**: means or instruments.   **faine**: accustomed.   **7 coniure**: charge, adjure.   **8 carefully**: with care or grief.

Stanza 5
1 deuice: probably a printer's error prompted by **deuiz'd**, and correctly changed to aduise *1596*, for she asks her sprights only for their counsel.   **5–9** Citing Euripides, *Helena*, A.B. Gough 1921:197 compares the false Helen, the phantom made of clouds and sunbeams that Paris carried to Troy instead of Helen who remained with King Proteus. This myth of Helen is the model for S.'s story of Florimell and her eidolon, as Roche 1964:152–67 argues.   **So liuely and so like**: so lifelike and so resembling life itself , i.e. so like Florimell. The same is said of the succubus fashioned by Archimago at I i 45.4.

6

The substance, whereof she the body made,
    Was purest snow in massy mould congeald,
    Which she had gathered in a shady glade
    Of the *Riphœan* hils, to her reueald
    By errant Sprights, but from all men conceald:
    The same she tempred with fine Mercury,
    And virgin wex, that neuer yet was seald,
    And mingled them with perfect vermily,
That like a liuely sanguine it seemd to the eye.

7

In stead of eyes two burning lampes she set
    In siluer sockets, shyning like the skyes,
    And a quicke mouing Spirit did arret
    To stirre and roll them, like to womens eyes;
    In stead of yellow lockes she did deuyse,
    With golden wyre to weaue her curled head;
    Yet golden wyre was not so yellow thryse
    As *Florimells* fayre heare: and in the stead
Of life, she put a Spright to rule the carcas dead.

8

A wicked Spright yfraught with fawning guyle,
    And fayre resemblance aboue all the rest,
    Which with the Prince of Darkenes fell somewhyle,
    From heauens blis and euerlasting rest,
    Him needed not instruct, which way were best
    Him selfe to fashion likest *Florimell*,
    Ne how to speake, ne how to vse his gest;
    For he in counterfesaunce did excell,
And all the wyles of wemens wits knew passing well.

9

Him shaped thus, she deckt in garments gay,
    Which *Florimell* had left behind her late,
    That who so then her saw, would surely say,
    It was her selfe, whom it did imitate,
    Or fayrer then her selfe, if ought algate
    Might fayrer be. And then she forth her brought
    Vnto her sonne, that lay in feeble state;
    Who seeing her gan streight vpstart, and thought
She was the Lady selfe, who he so long had sought.

10

Tho fast her clipping twixt his armes twayne,
    Extremely ioyed in so happy sight,
    And soone forgot his former sickely payne;
    But she, the more to seeme such as she hight,
    Coyly rebutted his embracement light;
    Yet still with gentle countenaunce retain'd,
    Enough to hold a foole in vaine delight:
    Him long she so with shadowes entertain'd,
As her Creatresse had in charge to her ordain'd.

11

Till on a day, as he disposed was
    To walke the woodes with that his Idole faire,
    Her to disport, and idle time to pas,
    In th'open freshnes of the gentle aire,
    A knight that way there chaunced to repaire;
    Yet knight he was not, but a boastfull swaine,
    That deedes of armes had euer in despaire,
    Proud *Braggadocchio*, that in vaunting vaine
His glory did repose, and credit did maintaine.

Stanza 6

1–4 **purest snow**: hence her name, 'The snowy *Florimell*' at IV ii 4.7, etc. Cf. Florimell's frigidity at 34.7. **massy**: solid. **the Riphœan hils**: 'mountaines in Scythia, where as is continuall wynter, and snow with huge wyndes' (T. Cooper 1565). 6–9 **Mercury**: traditionally one of the body's three basic substances. **fine** suggests the philosophical mercury or *prima materia*. On the process used to create the False Florimell, see 'alchemy' in the *SEnc*. In Sidney's blazon of Philoclea, in the *Old Arcadia* 240, her navel is described as 'a dainty seal of virgin-wax | Where nothing but impression lacks'; and at Theobalds in 1593–94, a hermit presented the Queen with 'a candle of virgin's wax, meete for a Virgin Queene' (Nichols 1823:3.245). **vermily**: vermilion. **sanguine**: a blood-red colour. As one of the body's four complexions, its predominance produces an amorous disposition.

Stanza 7

In noting the pseudo-blazon in 1–2 and 5–6, Ferry 1988:166–67 compares the blazon of Belphœbe at II iii 23.1–2 and 30.1. 3 **quicke**: living. **arret**: place in charge. 7 **thryse**: i.e. by many times.

Stanza 8

1–4 Referring to the fall of the red dragon and his angels recorded in Rev. 12.3–4, 7–9, which Geneva glosses as the devil, 'prince of this worlde'. **the Prince of Darkenes**: a mocking allusion to Satan's name, 'Lucifer, sonne of the morning' (Isa. 14.12), before he fell from heaven. The False Florimell's trans-sexual state with a masculine spirit inhabiting a female body parodies the hermaphroditic Venus. Roberts 1997:74 aptly compares the expertise at female impersonation by the Elizabethan boy actor. **somewhyle**: at one time. 5 **instruct**: i.e. to be instructed. 7 **gest**: bearing. 8 **counterfesaunce**: counterfeiting. 9 **passing**: exceedingly.

Stanza 9

3–4 As the observer is warned at I ii 11.9 about the sight of the false Red Cross Knight. 5 **algate**: by any means.

Stanza 10

5 **rebutted**: repelled. **light**: nimbly; or as an adj. 'wanton'.

Stanza 11

2 **Idole**: as she is the (false) god, image, or magic counterfeit whom he worships; used again at IV v 15.7. Wisd. Sol. 15.5 warns against the image whose sight leads the ignorant to covet 'the forme that hathe no life, of a dead image'. The counterfeit woman now attracts the counterfeit knight. 3 **disport**: entertain. 7 He despaired ever to perform deeds of arms. 9 **repose**: put, establish.

364364364364364

12

He seeing with that Chorle so faire a wight,
 Decked with many a costly ornament,
 Much merueiled thereat, as well he might,
 And thought that match a fowle disparagement:
 His bloody speare eftesoones he boldly bent
 Against the silly clowne, who dead through feare,
 Fell streight to ground in great astonishment;
 Villein (sayd he) this Lady is my deare,
Dy, if thou it gainesay: I will away her beare.

13

The fearefull Chorle durst not gainesay, nor dooe,
 But trembling stood, and yielded him the pray;
 Who finding litle leasure her to wooe,
 On *Tromparts* steed her mounted without stay,
 And without reskew led her quite away.
 Proud man himselfe then *Braggadochio* deem'd,
 And next to none, after that happy day,
 Being possessed of that spoyle, which seem'd
The fairest wight on ground, and most of men esteem'd.

14

But when hee saw him selfe free from poursute,
 He gan make gentle purpose to his Dame,
 With termes of loue and lewdnesse dissolute;
 For he could well his glozing speaches frame
 To such vaine vses, that him best became:
 But she thereto would lend but light regard,
 As seeming sory, that she euer came
 Into his powre, that vsed her so hard,
To reaue her honor, which she more then life prefard.

15

Thus as they two of kindnes treated long,
 There them by chaunce encountred on the way
 An armed knight, vpon a courser strong,
 Whose trampling feete vpon the hollow lay
 Seemed to thunder, and did nigh affray
 That Capons corage: yet he looked grim,
 And faynd to cheare his lady in dismay,
 Who seemd for feare to quake in euery lim,
And her to saue from outrage, meekely prayed him.

16

Fiercely that straunger forward came, and nigh
 Approching, with bold words and bitter threat,
 Bad that same boaster, as he mote, on high
 To leaue to him that lady for excheat,
 Or bide him batteill without further treat.
 That challenge did too peremptory seeme,
 And fild his senses with abashment great;
 Yet seeing nigh him ieopardy extreme,
He it dissembled well, and light seemd to esteeme.

17

Saying, Thou foolish knight, that weenst with words
 To steale away, that I with blowes haue wonne,
 And broght throgh points of many perilous swords:
 But if thee list to see thy Courser ronne,
 Or proue thy selfe, this sad encounter shonne,
 And seeke els without hazard of thy hedd.
 At those prowd words that other knight begonne
 To wex exceeding wroth, and him aredd
To turne his steede about, or sure he should be dedd.

18

Sith then (said *Braggadochio*) needes thou wilt
 Thy daies abridge, through proofe of puissaunce,
 Turne we our steeds, that both in equall tilt
 May meete againe, and each take happy chaunce.
 This said, they both a furlongs mountenaunce
 Retird their steeds, to ronne in euen race:
 But *Braggadochio* with his bloody launce
 Once hauing turnd, no more returnd his face,
But lefte his loue to losse, and fled him selfe apace.

19

The knight him seeing flie, had no regard
 Him to poursew, but to the lady rode,
 And hauing her from *Trompart* lightly reard,
 Vpon his Courser sett the louely lode,
 And with her fled away without abode.
 Well weened he, that fairest *Florimell*
 It was, with whom in company he yode,
 And so her selfe did alwaies to him tell;
So made him thinke him selfe in heuen, that was in hell.

Stanza 12
4 disparagement: the dishonour of marriage to one of inferior rank. **5 bloody speare**: as his sword is named '*Sanglamort*' (x 32.5); cf. 18.7. **bent**: aimed. **8 Villein**: serf.

Stanza 13
4 stay: delay; hindrance. **7 next to none**: i.e. second to none. **8–9** False Florimell assumes both Florimell's title, 'the fairest Dame aliue' (i 18.8), though she only **seem'd** such, and her reputation to be such, as at IV v 14.

Stanza 14
2 gentle purpose: polite conversation. **9 reaue**: take away by force.

Stanza 15
1 kindnes: affection. **4 lay**: ground. **6 Capon**: a term of reproach; 'eunuch' (*OED* 2) suits Braggadocchio's failed effort to be her lover.

Stanza 16
2–3 with bold words: alluding to his name, Ferraugh, which may have been taken from 'Ferragh', an Irish battle-cry noted in *View* 54; hence he shouts **on high**, i.e. as loudly as he could. He shares Braggadocchio's 'big thundring voice' (II iii 7.3). But see IV ii 4.5–9*n*. **4 excheat**: forfeit. **5 bide him batteill**: challenge him to fight, endure battle with him. **treat**: parley.

Stanza 17
4–6 I.e. if you wish ever again . . . **els**: elsewhere. **8 aredd**: advised.

Stanza 18
3 tilt: see i 44.7*n*. **4 happy chaunce**: the chance of fortune. **5 mountenaunce**: measure. **8 returnd**: turned back.

20

But *Florimell* her selfe was far away,
  Driuen to great distresse by fortune straunge,
  And taught the carefull Mariner to play,
  Sith late mischaunce had her compeld to chaunge
  The land for sea, at randon there to raunge:
  Yett there that cruell Queene auengeresse,
  Not satisfyde so far her to estraunge
  From courtly blis and wonted happinesse,
Did heape on her new waues of weary wretchednesse.

21

For being fled into the fishers bote,
  For refuge from the Monsters cruelty,
  Long so she on the mighty maine did flote,
  And with the tide droue forward carelesly,
  For th'ayre was milde, and cleared was the skie,
  And all his windes *Dan Aeolus* did keepe,
  From stirring vp their stormy enmity,
  As pittying to see her waile and weepe;
But all the while the fisher did securely sleepe.

22

At last when droncke with drowsinesse, he woke,
  And saw his drouer driue along the streame,
  He was dismayd, and thrise his brest he stroke,
  For marueill of that accident extreame;
  But when he saw, that blazing beauties beame,
  Which with rare light his bote did beautifye,
  He marueild more, and thought he yet did dreame
  Not well awakte, or that some extasye
Assotted had his sence, or dazed was his eye.

23

But when her well auizing, hee perceiu'd
  To be no vision, nor fantasticke sight,
  Great comfort of her presence he conceiu'd,
  And felt in his old corage new delight
  To gin awake, and stir his frosen spright:
  Tho rudely askte her, how she thether came.
  Ah (sayd she) father I note read aright,
  What hard misfortune brought me to this same;
Yet am I glad that here I now in safety ame.

24

But thou good man, sith far in sea we bee,
  And the great waters gin apace to swell,
  That now no more we can the mayn-land see,
  Haue care, I pray, to guide the cock-bote well,
  Least worse on sea then vs on land befell.
  Thereat th'old man did nought but fondly grin,
  And saide, his boat the way could wisely tell:
  But his deceiptfull eyes did neuer lin,
To looke on her faire face, and marke her snowy skin.

25

The sight whereof in his congealed flesh,
  Infixt such secrete sting of greedy lust,
  That the drie withered stocke it gan refresh,
  And kindled heat, that soone in flame forth brust:
  The driest wood is soonest burnt to dust.
  Rudely to her he lept, and his rough hand
  Where ill became him, rashly would haue thrust,
  But she with angry scorne him did withstond,
And shamefully reprou'd for his rudenes fond.

Stanza 19

1 regard: interest. **3 lightly**: easily; indicating the transfer of her affections. The true Florimell prefers death to the charge that 'she lightly did remoue' (42.5). **5 abode**: delay. **7 yode**: went. **9** She has a similar effect on his successor at IV ii 9.8–9.

Stanza 20

3 I.e. fortune, **that cruell Queene auengeresse**, taught her to play the role of a mariner when she launches the Fisher's boat at vii 27.7–9. **carefull**: full of care. **9 waues**: referring to her woes, but anticipating her descent under water; cf. IV xi 3.

Stanza 21

6 Dan: a respectful form of address; see II ii 7.5*n*. **Aeolus**: god of the winds. **9 securely**: free from care, as Florimell rides **carelesly**; suggesting that both are over-confident (*OED* A I 1).

Stanza 22

2 drouer: a fishing boat. **streame**: the tide. **4 accident**: event. **5–6** Cf. 'The blazing brightnesse of her beauties beame' (I xii 23.1) when Una is unveiled; cf. also i 16.5. **8 extasye**: madness which produces a 'fantasticke sight' (23.2). **9 Assotted**: infatuated.

Stanzas 23–33

Florimell nearly raped by the old Fisher and rescued by Proteus through heavenly grace is modelled on Una nearly raped by Sansloy and rescued by satyrs through eternal providence at I vi.3–7, as Bruhn 1995:280–81 notes in detail. It is modelled also on Angelica nearly raped by the impotent hermit and rescued by pirates, in Ariosto, *Orl. Fur.* 8.31, 47–64. On the action of grace, see Benson 1986, and 'Fisher' in the *SEnc*.

Stanza 23

1 auizing: observing. **2 fantasticke sight**: imaginary sight or phantasm. **3–5 comfort**: physical strengthening or invigoration. **corage**: spirit; also in the bawdy sense, 'sexual vigour', as the naked maidens at II xii 68.9 'corage cold could reare'. **7 note read**: cannot tell.

Stanza 24

4 cock-bote: a small ship's boat too dangerous for use at sea (Falconer 1964:98), which the Fisher takes in its bawdy sense, for he also **gin[s] apace to swell**. **6 fondly**: foolishly; lovingly. **grin**: associated with lust, as Lust's 'grenning laughter' at IV vii 24.9. **7 wisely**: cunningly. **8 lin**: cease.

Stanza 25

S. seeks to overgo Ariosto's bawdy play on the hermit's vain effort to have his fallen steed hold its head high. **9 fond**: doting.

26

But he, that neuer good nor maners knew,
   Her sharpe rebuke full litle did esteeme;
   Hard is to teach an old horse amble trew.
   The inward smoke, that did before but steeme,
   Broke into open fire and rage extreme,
   And now he strength gan adde vnto his will,
   Forcyng to doe, that did him fowle misseeme:
   Beastly he threwe her downe, ne car'd to spill
Her garments gay with scales of fish, that all did fill.

27

The silly virgin stroue him to withstand,   *why silly?*
   All that she might, and him in vaine reuild:
   Shee strugled strongly both with foote and hand,
   To saue her honor from that villaine vilde,
   And cride to heuen, from humane helpe exild.
   O ye braue knights, that boast this Ladies loue,
   Where be ye now, when she is nigh defild
   Of filthy wretch? well may she you reproue
Of falsehood or of slouth, when most it may behoue.

28

But if that thou, Sir *Satyran*, didst weete,
   Or thou, Sir *Peridure*, her sory state,
   How soone would yee assemble many a fleete,
   To fetch from sea, that ye at land lost late;
   Towres, citties, kingdomes ye would ruinate,
   In your auengement and dispiteous rage,
   Ne ought your burning fury mote abate;
   But if Sir *Calidore* could it presage,
No liuing creature could his cruelty asswage.

29

But sith that none of all her knights is nye,
   See how the heauens of voluntary grace,
   And soueraine fauor towards chastity,
   Doe succor send to her distressed cace:
   So much high God doth innocence embrace.
   It fortuned, whilest thus she stifly stroue,
   And the wide sea importuned long space
   With shrilling shriekes, *Proteus* abrode did roue,
Along the fomy waues driuing his finny droue.

30

Proteus is Shepheard of the seas of yore,
   And hath the charge of *Neptunes* mighty heard,
   An aged sire with head all frory hore,
   And sprinckled frost vpon his deawy beard:
   Who when those pittifull outcries he heard,
   Through all the seas so ruefully resownd,
   His charett swifte in hast he thether steard,
   Which with a teeme of scaly *Phocas* bownd
Was drawne vpon the waues, that fomed him arownd.

31

And comming to that Fishers wandring bote,
   That went at will, withouten card or sayle,
   He therein saw that yrkesome sight, which smote
   Deepe indignation and compassion frayle
   Into his hart attonce: streight did he hayle
   The greedy villein from his hoped pray,
   Of which he now did very litle fayle,
   And with his staffe, that driues his heard astray,
Him bett so sore, that life and sence did much dismay.

Stanza 26
3 The proverb (Smith 755) is suggested by the hermit's steed.
5 rage: sexual passion.   **7** Using force to do what foully mis-
became him.   **8 Beastly**: acting like a beast; or treating her as
though she were a beast.   **ne . . . spill**: nor cared if he defiled.
9 As though she were being transformed into a mermaid, her
'garments gay' (9.1) have now become **gay with scales of fish**.
fill: also defile; cf. 32.2.

Stanza 27
1 silly: helpless.   **9** . . . when it is most fitting to aid her.

Stanza 28
2 Sir Peridure: cited in the chronicle of British kings at II
x 44.9. He is one of Arthur's knights in Geoffrey of
Monmouth 1891:9.12, and singled out because his name
signifies 'one who endures'.   **5 Towres**: 'Townes', conj.
Church 1758, fits the sequence; cf. VI ix 3.7. Also it allows
the line to be scanned.   **ruinate**: lay waste.   **6 dispiteous**:
merciless.   **8–9 Sir Calidore**: the knight of courtesy in
Bk VI, perhaps singled out because one etymology of his name
is Lat. *calidus*, fierce, which describes his **cruelty**.   **presage**:
have a presentiment of.

Stanza 29
2 voluntary: to stress that God's grace is freely offered and not
because of Florimell's appeal at 27.5.   **5 embrace**: accept;
protect.

Stanza 30
1–4 A parenthetical footnote.   **Proteus** is 'the god of the sea,
whom Homere nameth to be the heardman of the fyshes called
Phocae' (T. Cooper 1565). See 'Proteus' in the *SEnc*. On
his relation to the passions and to the cycle of the seasons,
see Giamatti 1984:115–20; as prime matter, see Nohrnberg
1976:583–86.   **frory hore**: frosty with foam. *1590, 1596* have
'frowy', which in *SC July* 111 means 'musty'. The revision,
now generally adopted, is supported by 35.2, and relates
Florimell to her snowy counterpart; see 34.7–9.   **8 Phocas**:
seals, as *Colin Clout* 248–51.   **scaly**: perhaps because his
chariot is often drawn by fishes, as Virgil, *Georg.* 4.388–89.

Stanza 31
1–2 As the wanton Phædria's 'wandring ship' (II vi 10.2) moves
without pilot or wind.   **will**: associated with the Fisher's
now unrestrained lust; cf. 24.7.   **card**: chart or compass card.
3 yrkesome: loathsome.   **4 frayle**: tender.   **8 astray**: on their
way.   **9 dismay**: overwhelm.

32

The whiles the pitteous Lady vp did ryse,
  Ruffled and fowly raid with filthy soyle,
  And blubbred face with teares of her faire eyes:
  Her heart nigh broken was with weary toyle,
  To saue her selfe from that outrageous spoyle,
  But when she looked vp, to weet, what wight
  Had her from so infamous fact assoyld,
For shame, but more for feare of his grim sight,
Downe in her lap she hid her face, and lowdly shright.

33

Herselfe not saued yet from daunger dredd
  She thought, but chaung'd from one to other feare;
  Like as a fearefull partridge, that is fledd
  From the sharpe hauke, which her attached neare,
  And fals to ground, to seeke for succor theare,
  Whereas the hungry Spaniells she does spye,
  With greedy iawes her ready for to teare;
  In such distresse and sad perplexity
Was *Florimell*, when *Proteus* she did see her by.

34

But he endeuored with speaches milde
  Her to recomfort, and accourage bold,
  Bidding her feare no more her foeman vilde,
  Nor doubt himselfe; and who he was her told.
  Yet all that could not from affright her hold,
  Ne to recomfort her at all preuayld;
  For her faint hart was with the frosen cold
  Benumbd so inly, that her wits nigh fayld,
And all her sences with abashment quite were quayld.

35

Her vp betwixt his rugged hands he reard,
  And with his frory lips full softly kist,
  Whiles the cold ysickles from his rough beard,
  Dropped adowne vpon her yuory brest:
  Yet he him selfe so busily addrest,
  That her out of astonishment he wrought,
  And out of that same fishers filthy nest
  Remouing her, into his charet brought,
And there with many gentle termes her faire besought.

36

But that old leachour, which with bold assault
  That beautie durst presume to violate,
  He cast to punish for his hainous fault;
  Then tooke he him yet trembling sith of late,
  And tyde behind his charet, to aggrate
  The virgin, whom he had abusde so sore:
  So drag'd him through the waues in scornfull state,
  And after cast him vp, vpon the shore;
But *Florimell* with him vnto his bowre he bore.

37

His bowre is in the bottom of the maine,
  Vnder a mightie rocke, gainst which doe raue
  The roring billowes in their proud disdaine,
  That with the angry working of the waue,
  Therein is eaten out an hollow caue,
  That seemes rough Masons hand with engines keene
  Had long while laboured it to engraue:
  There was his wonne, ne liuing wight was seene,
Saue one old *Nymph*, hight *Panope* to keepe it cleane.

38

Thether he brought the sory *Florimell*,
  And entertained her the best he might
  And *Panope* her entertaind eke well,
  As an immortall mote a mortall wight,
  To winne her liking vnto his delight:
  With flattering wordes he sweetly wooed her,
  And offered faire guiftes, t'allure her sight,
  But she both offers and the offerer
Despysde, and all the fawning of the flatterer.

Stanza 32
1–3 **raid**: defiled; arrayed. **soyle**: stain or filth, alluding to the fish scales that cover her, in contrast to the virgin's immaculate state. **blubbred**: disfigured from weeping. Cf. Una's 'ruffled rayments, and fayre blubbred face' (I vi 9.3) when she is nearly raped by Sansloy. 5 **spoyle**: rape; or becoming his spoil. 7 **fact**: evil deed. **assoyld**: set free. 9 **shright**: shrieked.

Stanza 33
3–7 A falconer captured birds by having 'a conspiracye (as it were) betwixt the dogges and Hawkes' (Turbervile, *Booke of Faulconrie* 1575; cited Harrison 1956:70). The simile illustrates the dangers of Florimell's flight from one element to another. 4 **sharpe**: eager for prey. **attached neare**: nearly seized.

Stanza 34
2 **accourage bold**: boldly take heart. The neologism is used here for its etymology, Lat. *cor*, heart, because 'Her heart nigh broken was' (32.4). 4 **doubt**: also 'fear'. 9 **quayld**: overpowered.

Stanza 35
2 **frory**: frozen; cf. 30.3. His kisses seal her fate and her replacement by the Snowy Florimell. 5–8 Her change from 34.9 allows her removal, as the repetition of **out of** indicates. **addrest**: applied. **astonishment**: dismay; numbness.

Stanza 36
3 **cast**: resolved. 5 **aggrate**: please.

Stanza 37
In Virgil, *Georg.* 4.418–22, Proteus shelters himself on the seashore behind a huge rock in a cave hollowed out of the mountain side; cf. Cymoent's bower 'Deepe in the bottome of the sea' (iv 43.1). This submarine cave suggests that Florimell is, like Proserpina, imprisoned in Pluto's 'balefull house' (xi 1.2). 7 **engraue**: cut. 9 **Panope**: a Nereid at IV xi 49.8. S. seems to have invented her role as an elderly housekeeper, perhaps from Gk παν + Lat. *ops*, 'all-worker'.

39

Dayly he tempted her with this or that,
    And neuer suffred her to be at rest:
    But euermore she him refused flat,
    And all his fained kindnes did detest.
    So firmely she had sealed vp her brest.
    Sometimes he boasted, that a God he hight:
    But she a mortall creature loued best:
    Then he would make him selfe a mortall wight;
But then she said she lou'd none, but a Faery knight.

40

Then like a Faerie knight him selfe he drest;
    For euery shape on him he could endew:
    Then like a king he was to her exprest,
    And offred kingdoms vnto her in vew,
    To be his Leman and his Lady trew:
    But when all this he nothing saw preuaile,
    With harder meanes he cast her to subdew,
    And with sharpe threates her often did assayle,
So thinking for to make her stubborne corage quayle.

41

To dreadfull shapes he did him selfe transforme,
    Now like a Gyaunt, now like to a feend,
    Then like a Centaure, then like to a storme,
    Raging within the waues: thereby he weend
    Her will to win vnto his wished eend.
    But when with feare, nor fauour, nor with all
    He els could doe, he saw him selfe esteemd,
    Downe in a Dongeon deepe he let her fall,
And threatned there to make her his eternall thrall.

42

Eternall thraldome was to her more liefe,
    Then losse of chastitie, or chaunge of loue:
    Dye had she rather in tormenting griefe,
    Then any should of falseness her reproue,
    Or loosenes, that she lightly did remoue.
    Most vertuous virgin, glory be thy meed,
    And crowne of heauenly prayse with Saintes aboue,
    Where most sweet hymmes of this thy famous deed
Are still emongst them song, that far my rymes exceed.

43

Fit song of Angels caroled to bee,
    But yet what so my feeble Muse can frame,
    Shalbe t'aduance thy goodly chastitee,
    And to enroll thy memorable name,
    In th'heart of euery honourable Dame,
    That they thy vertuous deedes may imitate,
    And be partakers of thy endlesse fame.
    Yt yrkes me, leaue thee in this wofull state,
To tell of *Satyrane*, where I him left of late.

44

Who hauing ended with that *Squyre of Dames*
    A long discourse of his aduentures vayne,
    The which himselfe, then Ladies more defames,
    And finding not th'*Hyena* to be slayne,
    With that same *Squyre*, retourned back agayne
    To his first way. And as they forward went,
    They spyde a knight fayre pricking on the playne,
    As if he were on some aduenture bent,
And in his port appeared manly hardiment.

45

Sir *Satyrane* him towardes did addresse,
    To weet, what wight he was, and what his quest:
    And comming nigh, eftsoones he gan to gesse
    Both by the burning hart, which on his brest
    He bare, and by the colours in his crest,
    That *Paridell* it was. Tho to him yode,
    And him saluting, as beseemed best,
    Gan first inquire of tydinges farre abrode;
And afterwardes, on what aduenture now he rode.

Stanza 39

4 kindnes: affection. Proteus as the lover-rapist may derive from Ariosto, *Orl. Fur.* 8.52. **5** Her **sealed . . . brest** marks her imprisoned state, in contrast to the wide wound of Amoret's breast at xii 20.5. **7** Guyon offers this same excuse to reject Philotime at II vii 50.3–5.

Stanza 40

On his shape-changing, see I ii 10.3–6*n*. **2 endew**: assume, put on. **3 exprest**: revealed. **6 preuaile**: avail.

Stanza 41

3 Centaure: a traditional symbol of lust (being half horse). **8** Called 'lowest hell' at IV xii 6.7. **9 eternall thrall**: see vii 50.7–9*n*.

Stanza 42

1 more liefe: preferable. **5** The vow never to **remoue** – i.e. change or leave – one's love, is a central motif in the poem, e.g. i 26.9, ii 40.8, and esp. xii 31.9. Its importance is indicated by S.'s direct address to Florimell at 43. Her concern for her reputation relates to her future as a heavenly saint; see Benson 1986:90–91. **9** That S. invokes the topos of inexpressibility – see proem 3*n* – indicates Florimell's relation to Elizabeth; see II iii 25.6–9*n*.

Stanza 43

1 of: by. **3 aduance**: extol. **4–7** Cf. the praise of Belphœbe at v 54.7–9. **8** Yet he ignores her state until IV xi 1.

Stanza 44

4 to be slayne: i.e. to slay it, which he found, at vii 32.7–9, he was unable to do. **6 To his first way**: referring to his quest 'to seeke aduentures wilde' (vii 30.2) before he encountered the hyena; cf. 'my forward way' at 50.4. **7 fayre pricking** indicates Paridell's (amorous) impulsiveness, seen again at his next entrance when he comes 'pricking fast' (x 35.2).

Stanza 45

1 addresse: direct his course. **4–6** The insignia of the **burning hart** associates Paridell with lechery: see I iv 25.3; hence the first object of his adventures is 'faire ladies loue' (ix 37.7). His name marks his descent from the Trojan Paris (see ix 36–37), and may suggest 'Paris-idell' (A. Fowler 1959: 585*n*3); or, 'Par-idle', now that Troy has become an 'idle name' (ix 33.1). See 'Paridell' in the *SEnc*. **yode**: went.

46

Who thereto answering said, The tydinges bad,
　Which now in Faery court all men doe tell,
　Which turned hath great mirth, to mourning sad,
　Is the late ruine of proud *Marinell*,
　And suddein parture of faire *Florimell*,
　To find him forth: and after her are gone
　All the braue knightes, that doen in armes excell,
　To sauegard her, ywandred all alone;
Emongst the rest my lott (vnworthy') is to be one.

47

Ah gentle knight (said then Sir *Satyrane*)
　Thy labour all is lost, I greatly dread,
　That hast a thanklesse seruice on thee ta'ne,
　And offrest sacrifice vnto the dead:
　For dead, I surely doubt, thou maist aread
　Henceforth for euer *Florimell* to bee,
　That all the noble knights of *Maydenhead*,
　Which her ador'd, may sore repent with mee,
And all faire *Ladies* may for euer sory bee.

48

Which wordes when *Paridell* had heard, his hew
　Gan greatly chaung and seemd dismaid to bee,
　Then said, Fayre Sir, how may I weene it trew,
　That ye doe tell in such vncerteintee?
　Or speake ye of report, or did ye see
　Iust cause of dread, that makes ye doubt so sore?
　For perdie elles how mote it euer bee,
　That euer hand should dare for to engore
Her noble blood? the heuens such crueltie abhore.

49

These eyes did see, that they will euer rew
　To haue seene, (quoth he) when as a monstrous beast
　The Palfrey, whereon she did trauell, slew,
　And of his bowels made his bloody feast:

Which speaking token sheweth at the least
　Her certeine losse, if not her sure decay:
　Besides, that more suspicion encreast,
　I found her golden girdle cast astray,
Distaynd with durt and blood, as relique of the pray.

50

Ay me, (said *Paridell*) the signes be sadd,
　And but God turne the same to good sooth say,
　That Ladies safetie is sore to be dradd:
　Yet will I not forsake my forward way,
　Till triall doe more certeine truth bewray.
　Faire Sir (quoth he) well may it you succeed,
　Ne long shall *Satyrane* behind you stay,
　But to the rest, which in this Quest proceed
My labour adde, and be partaker of their speed.

51

Ye noble knights (said then the *Squyre of Dames*)
　Well may yee speede in so praiseworthy payne:
　But sith the Sunne now ginnes to slake his beames,
　In deawy vapours of the westerne mayne,
　And lose the teme out of his weary wayne,
　Mote not mislike you also to abate
　Your zealous hast, till morrow next againe
　Both light of heuen, and strength of men relate:
Which if ye please, to yonder castle turne your gate.

52

That counsell pleased well; so all yfere
　Forth marched to a Castle them before,
　Where soone arryuing, they restrained were
　Of ready entraunce, which ought euermore
　To errant knights be commune: wondrous sore
　Thereat displeasd they were, till that young Squyre
　Gan them informe the cause, why that same dore
　Was shut to all, which lodging did desyre:
The which to let you weet, will further time requyre.

Stanza 46
4 proud Marinell: recalling the superb phrase that describes
his **ruine** or fall: 'So fell proud *Marinell*' (iv 17.9).   **5–6** See
v 10.1–4*n*.   **parture**: departure.

Stanza 47
5 surely: 'sorely', conj. Upton 1758, from Paridell's response
at 48.6; cf. 'Right sore I feare' (ix 1.3). Yet the emendation
would jar with **sore** and **sory**.   **doubt**: fear.   **aread**: deem.
8 repent: mourn (*OED* 2c, citing only this instance); or the
usual sense, 'be contrite', as 27.8–9 suggests.

Stanza 48
5 report: rumour.   **8 engore**: stain itself in; shed.

Stanza 49
5 speaking token: significant sign.   **6 decay**: death.   **9 Dis-
taynd**: deeply stained, defiled.

Stanza 50
2 but: unless.   **sooth say**: omen.   **5 bewray**: reveal.
9 speed: success; also the usual sense, as 51.7 suggests.

Stanza 51
2 speede: succeed.   **payne**: effort.   **5 lose**: loosen.   **wayne**:
wagon; but also a pun on 'wane', decrease; cf. I v 41.2.
6 May it not displease you.   **8 relate**: restore.

Stanza 52
4–6 The law of open hospitality, which required that food,
drink, and lodging be given esp. to strangers, was an important
social virtue in the sixteenth century, as Heal 1990 shows.
9 A romance formula used extensively in the later books; see
IV ii 54.8–9*n*.

Cant. IX.

Malbecco will no straunge knights host,
For peeuish gealosy:
Paridell giusts with Britomart:
both shew their auncestry.

1

REdoubted knights, and honorable Dames,
  To whom I leuell all my labours end,
  Right sore I feare, least with vnworthie blames
This odious argument my rymes should shend,
  Or ought your goodly patience offend,
  Whiles of a wanton Lady I doe write,
  Which with her loose incontinence doth blend
The shyning glory of your soueraine light,
And knighthood fowle defaced by a faithlesse knight.

2

But neuer let th'ensample of the bad
  Offend the good: for good by paragone
  Of euill, may more notably be rad,
  As white seemes fayrer, macht with blacke attone;
  Ne all are shamed by the fault of one:
  For lo in heuen, whereas all goodnes is,
  Emongst the Angels, a whole legione
Of wicked Sprightes did fall from happy blis;
What wonder then, if one of women all did mis?

3

Then listen Lordings, if ye list to weet
  The cause, why *Satyrane* and *Paridell*
  Mote not be entertaynd, as seemed meet,
  Into that Castle (as that Squyre does tell.)

Therein a cancred crabbed Carle does dwell,
  That has no skill of Court nor courtesie,
  Ne cares, what men say of him ill or well;
  For all his dayes he drownes in priuitie,
Yet has full large to liue, and spend at libertie.

4

But all his mind is set on mucky pelfe,
  To hoord vp heapes of euill gotten masse,
  For which he others wrongs and wreckes himselfe;
  Yet is he lincked to a louely lasse,
  Whose beauty doth her bounty far surpasse,
  The which to him both far vnequall yeares,
  And also far vnlike conditions has;
  For she does ioy to play emongst her peares,
And to be free from hard restraynt and gealous feares.

5

But he is old, and withered like hay,
  Vnfit faire Ladies seruice to supply;
  The priuie guilt whereof makes him alway
  Suspect her truth, and keepe continuall spy
  Vpon her with his other blincked eye;
  Ne suffreth he resort of liuing wight
  Approch to her, ne keepe her company,
  But in close bowre her mewes from all mens sight,
Depriu'd of kindly ioy and naturall delight.

Book III Canto ix

Argument
2 **peeuish**: perverse, obstinate.

Stanzas 1–3.4
Cf. the apology to women prefacing the story of Malecasta at i 49. Here both **knights** and **Dames** are first addressed, but then only **Lordings**, which would suggest that women are expected to skip the story. The slander of 'honorable Dames' at vii 57–60 by the Squire of Dames makes it fitting that he should take over at 3.5.

Stanza 1
4 **argument**: subject. **shend**: disgrace. 7 **blend**: dim; conceal.

Stanza 2
2 **paragone**: comparison. 3 **rad**: discerned. 4 **attone**: together. 7 **legione**: vast host (*OED* 3); an infinite number in the Geneva gloss to Matt. 26.53. 9 **mis**: err.

Stanza 3
3 **entertaynd**: received as guests. 5 **cancred**: ill-tempered. **Carle**: churl; also with the sense, 'miser'; repeated at 12.9,

17.8. 6 **skill**: knowledge. 8 **priuitie**: seclusion. The importance of this word with its cognates in this canto is noted by Dubrow 1990:319. Malbecco hoards himself, his castle, his wealth, and esp. his wife, whom, in a total perversion of love, he treats as an object to be jealously and exclusively possessed. 9 **large**: largesse, which brings freedom; cf. 'bounty' (4.5).

Stanza 4
1 **mucky pelfe**: filthy lucre. 2 **masse**: treasure. 5 **bounty**: virtue. The proper balance of the two qualities is found in Cambina, who 'with her beautie bountie did compare [vie]' (IV iii 39.8). 7 **conditions**: manners. 8–9 Anticipating the joyous ending of her story when she finds her **peares** in the satyrs, free from jealousy. **play**: sport amorously, as at x 48.4.

Stanza 5
1 **withered like hay**: as the Fisher's 'drie withered stocke' at viii 25.3. 2 **seruice**: such as the Squire of Dames knows best; see vii 55.1. 3 **priuie**: secret; punning on privy parts. 5 **his other blincked eye**: i.e. his one, or left, eye which is either affected with a blink or dim with age. Since he has a 'blinde eie' (27.6), he is said to be 'halfen eye' (x 5.2, 3; cf. 58.6–7). For the folklore motif, 'The Husband's One Good Eye Covered', see 'folklore' in the *SEnc*. His blindness relates to his jealousy:

6

Malbecco he, and *Hellenore* she hight,
　Vnfitly yokt together in one teeme,
　That is the cause, why neuer any knight
　Is suffred here to enter, but he seeme
　Such, as no doubt of him he neede misdeeme.
　Thereat Sir *Satyrane* gan smyle, and say;
　Extremely mad the man I surely deeme,
That weenes with watch and hard restraynt to stay
A womans will, which is disposd to go astray.

7

In vaine he feares that, which he cannot shonne:
　For who wotes not, that womans subtiltyes
　Can guylen *Argus*, when she list misdonne?
　It is not yron bandes, nor hundred eyes,
　Nor brasen walls, nor many wakefull spyes,
　That can withhold her wilfull wandring feet,
　But fast goodwill with gentle courtesyes,
And timely seruice to her pleasures meet
May her perhaps containe, that else would algates fleet.

8

Then is he not more mad (sayd *Paridell*)
　That hath himselfe vnto such seruice sold,
　In dolefull thraldome all his dayes to dwell?
　For sure a foole I doe him firmely hold,
　That loues his fetters, though they were of gold.
　But why doe wee deuise of others ill,
　Whyles thus we suffer this same dotard old,
To keepe vs out, in scorne of his owne will,
And rather do not ransack all, and him selfe kill?

9

Nay let vs first (sayd *Satyrane*) entreat
　The man by gentle meanes, to let vs in,
　And afterwardes affray with cruell threat,
　Ere that we to efforce it doe begin:

Then if all fayle, we will by force it win,
　And eke reward the wretch for his mesprise,
　As may be worthy of his haynous sin.
　That counsell pleasd: then *Paridell* did rise,
And to the Castle gate approcht in quiet wise.

10

Whereat soft knocking, entrance he desyrd.
　The good man selfe, which then the Porter playd,
　Him answered, that all were now retyrd
　Vnto their rest, and all the keyes conuayd
　Vnto their maister, who in bed was layd,
　That none him durst awake out of his dreme;
　And therefore them of patience gently prayd.
Then *Paridell* began to chaunge his theme,
And threatned him with force and punishment extreme.

11

But all in vaine; for nought mote him relent,
　And now so long before the wicket fast
　They wayted, that the night was forward spent,
　And the faire welkin fowly ouercast,
　Gan blowen vp a bitter stormy blast,
　With showre and hayle so horrible and dred,
　That this faire many were compeld at last,
To fly for succour to a little shed,
The which beside the gate for swyne was ordered.

12

It fortuned, soone after they were gone,
　Another knight, whom tempest thether brought,
　Came to that Castle, and with earnest mone,
　Like as the rest, late entrance deare besought;
　But like so as the rest he prayd for nought,
　For flatly he of entrance was refusd.
　Sorely thereat he was displeasd, and thought
How to auenge himselfe so sore abusd,
And euermore the Carle of courtesie accusd.

---

cf. the aged Januarie's sudden blindness which heralds his jealousy of fresh May in Chaucer, *Merchant's Tale* 2069–76; but also to being a miser: cf. 'misers blinde' (x 15.9), and Mammon's 'bleard' eyes (II vii 3.6). **8 mewes**: imprisons, implying that she is a caged falcon. The term prepares for her release; see x 35.7–9 and *n*. **9 kindly**: natural. Since he is impotent, she is deprived of sex.

Stanza 6
1 Malbecco: from Lat. *malus*, wicked + Ital. *becco*, he-goat or cuckold (Florio 1598); so named because he earns the cuckold's 'faire hornes' at x 47.4. See 'Malbecco' in the *SEnc*. **Hellenore**: a debased 'second *Helene*' of Troy (x 13.1), 'Helen-o'er', or 'Helen-whore' (sugg. A. Fowler 1959:585*n*3), and a fitting companion to a debased Paris. See 'Hellenore' in the *SEnc*. **5 misdeeme**: suspect.

Stanza 7
Apparently spoken by the Squire of Dames, endorsing Satyrane's misogyny while allowing the possible effectiveness of courteous behaviour in keeping women chaste. **1** Proverbial (Smith 250). **3 guylen**: beguile. **Argus**: 'of the Poets

devised to be full of eyes' (E.K. on *SC July* 154). Cited to note the helplessness of the one-eyed Malbecco. **8–9 timely seruice** includes regular sexual satisfaction. **containe**: keep under control; keep chaste. **algates**: otherwise.

Stanza 8
4–5 Proverbial (Smith 258); used in *Am* 37.13–14. **6 deuise**: talk. **8** . . . in his scornful will; or scornfully and wilfully.

Stanza 9
4 efforce: gain by force. **6 mesprise**: contempt.

Stanza 10
2 good man: the title of the head of a household.

Stanza 11
2 wicket fast: locked gate. **3 forward spent**: i.e. far spent. **7 many**: company. **8 succour**: refuge. **9 ordered**: prepared.

Stanza 12
3 mone: complaint, i.e. plea. **4 deare**: earnestly. **9 of courtesie accusd**: i.e. accused him in the name of courtesy.

13

But to auoyde th'intollerable stowre,
    He was compeld to seeke some refuge neare,
    And to that shed, to shrowd him from the showre,
    He came, which full of guests he found whyleare,
    So as he was not let to enter there:
    Whereat he gan to wex exceeding wroth,
    And swore, that he would lodge with them yfere,
    Or them dislodg, all were they liefe or loth;
And so defyde them each, and so defyde them both.

14

Both were full loth to leaue that needfull tent,
    And both full loth in darkenesse to debate;
    Yet both full liefe him lodging to haue lent,
    And both full liefe his boasting to abate;
    But chiefely *Paridell* his hart did grate,
    To heare him threaten so despightfully,
    As if he did a dogge in kenell rate,
    That durst not barke; and rather had he dy,
Then when he was defyde, in coward corner ly.

15

Tho hastily remounting to his steed,
    He forth issew'd; like as a boystrous winde,
    Which in th'earthes hollow caues hath long ben hid,
    And shut vp fast within her prisons blind,
    Makes the huge element against her kinde
    To moue, and tremble as it were aghast,
    Vntill that it an issew forth may finde;
    Then forth it breakes, and with his furious blast
Confounds both land and seas, and skyes doth ouercast.

16

Their steel-hed speares they strongly coucht, and met
    Together with impetuous rage and forse,
    That with the terrour of their fierce affret,
    They rudely droue to ground both man and horse,

That each awhile lay like a sencelesse corse.
    But *Paridell* sore brused with the blow,
    Could not arise, the counterchaunge to scorse,
    Till that young Squyre him reared from below;
Then drew he his bright sword, and gan about him throw.

17

But *Satyrane* forth stepping, did them stay
    And with faire treaty pacifide their yre;
    Then when they were accorded from the fray,
    Against that Castles Lord they gan conspire,
    To heape on him dew vengeaunce for his hire.
    They beene agreed, and to the gates they goe
    To burne the same with vnquenchable fire,
    And that vncurteous Carle their commune foe
To doe fowle death to die, or wrap in grieuous woe.

18

Malbecco seeing them resolud in deed
    To flame the gates, and hearing them to call
    For fire in earnest, ran with fearfull speed,
    And to them calling from the castle wall,
    Besought them humbly, him to beare with all,
    As ignorant of seruants bad abuse,
    And slacke attendaunce vnto straungers call.
    The knights were willing all things to excuse,
Though nought beleu'd, and entraunce late did not refuse.

19

They beene ybrought into a comely bowre,
    And serud of all things that mote needfull bee;
    Yet secretly their hoste did on them lowre,
    And welcomde more for feare, then charitee;
    But they dissembled, what they did not see,
    And welcomed themselues. Each gan vndight
    Their garments wett, and weary armour free,
    To dry them selues by *Vulcanes* flaming light,
And eke their lately bruzed parts to bring in plight.

Stanza 13
The nearly dozen uses of **he**, **him**, **himselfe** in the dozen lines from 12.5 to 13.7, and four uses in the next stanza, prepare for the surprise of 'his' identity.   **1 stowre**: storm.   **4 whyleare**: i.e. the pigsty had been filled a while before.   **8 liefe or loth**: willing or not.   **9 both**: Paridell and the Squire of Dames, as 14.1.

Stanza 14
2 debate: fight.   **3–4 full liefe** is repeated to balance the repeated **full loth** in 1–2. From 13.5, however, the sense requires that both were **loth** to grant 'him' lodging.   **5 grate**: fret.   **6 despightfully**: contemptuously.

Stanza 15
2–9 On wind as the cause of earthquakes, see I vii 9*n*. The simile links Britomart's victory over Paridell with her victory over the storm which drives her to seek refuge, and prepares for her resistance to the whirlwind in the house of Busirane at xii 3. Cf. the inner storm that she overcomes before she meets Marinell at iv 8–10, 13. On the relation to the storm in Virgil,

Aen. 1.50–63, which brings Aeneas to Carthage and to Dido, see M. Suzuki 1989:160–61.   **5 kinde**: nature.

Stanza 16
3 affret: onslaught; apparently coined by S., from 'fret', or from Ital. *affretare*: 'to hasten', to describe a hasty, violent encounter.   **4 rudely**: violently.   **5** Britomart's 'enchaunted' spear at i 7.9 unhorses Guyon, and being 'That mortall speare' (iv 14.2) almost mortally wounds Marinell. Here it lacks that power, and for this reason may be called a **steel-hed**, as is Paridell's.   **7** . . . the requital to exchange; i.e. to trade return blows.   **8 from below**: either from the ground, or (preferably, because of the symbolism) from below his horse.   **9 throw**: brandish.

Stanza 17
2 treaty: entreat.   **5 hire**: reward.

Stanza 19
5 They pretended not to notice Malbecco's want of hospitality.   **8 Vulcanes flaming light**: metonymy for fire, its god being named here as he is Venus's cuckolded husband; see IV v 4–5.   **9 in plight**: into good condition, i.e. to heal.

20

And eke that straunger knight emongst the rest,
　　Was for like need enforst to disaray:
　　Tho whenas vailed was her lofty crest,
　　Her golden locks, that were in tramells gay
　　Vpbounden, did them selues adowne display,
　　And raught vnto her heeles; like sunny beames,
　　That in a cloud their light did long time stay,
　　Their vapour vaded, shewe their golden gleames,
And through the persant aire shoote forth their azure streames.

21

Shee also dofte her heauy haberieon,
　　Which the faire feature of her limbs did hyde,
　　And her well plighted frock, which she did won
　　To tucke about her short, when she did ryde,
　　Shee low let fall, that flowd from her lanck syde
　　Downe to her foot, with carelesse modestee.
　　Then of them all she plainly was espyde,
　　To be a woman wight, vnwist to bee,
The fairest woman wight, that euer eie did see.

22

Like as *Bellona*, being late returnd
　　From slaughter of the Giaunts conquered;
　　Where proud *Encelade*, whose wide nosethrils burnd
　　With breathed flames, like to a furnace redd,

Transfixed with her speare, downe tombled dedd
　　From top of *Hemus*, by him heaped hye;
　　Hath loosd her helmet from her lofty hedd,
　　And her *Gorgonian* shield gins to vntye
From her lefte arme, to rest in glorious victorye.

23

Which whenas they beheld, they smitten were
　　With great amazement of so wondrous sight,
　　And each on other, and they all on her
　　Stood gazing, as if suddein great affright
　　Had them surprizd. At last auizing right,
　　Her goodly personage and glorious hew,
　　Which they so much mistooke, they tooke delight
　　In their first error, and yett still anew
With wonder of her beauty fed their hongry vew.

24

Yet note their hongry vew be satisfide,
　　But seeing still the more desir'd to see,
　　And euer firmely fixed did abide
　　In contemplation of diuinitee:
　　But most they meruaild at her cheualree,
　　And noble prowesse, which they had approu'd,
　　That much they faynd to know, who she mote bee;
　　Yet none of all them her thereof amou'd,
Yet euery one her likte, and euery one her lou'd.

Stanza 20
On Britomart's revelation of her beauty, see i 43*n*. Her reason for unveiling is practical: she needs to dry her hair, in contrast to IV i 13 where she lets it hang down to declare her sex. Long hair in a woman is praised at 1 Cor. 11.15 because, as the Geneva gloss explains, God gave it to women 'to the end she shulde trusse it vp aboue her head, whereby she declareth that she must couer her head'. Coiffure distinguishes the moral state of S.'s heroines: e.g. Medina's golden locks are tied up in 'breaded tramels' (II ii 15.8), Belphœbe's curled yellow locks 'About her shoulders weren loosely shed' (iii 30.2), Alma's golden hair is 'trimly wouen, and in tresses wrought' (ix 19.6–7), and Florimell's 'faire yellow lockes' are 'Loosely disperst' in her flight (III i 16.4) but later 'dight in order dew' (vii 11.2). See 'hair' in the *SEnc*. **3 vailed**: taken off. **4 tramells**: braids. **6–9 raught vnto her heeles**: this detail is repeated at IV i 13.3. For the simile, cf. Bradamante's unveiling in Ariosto, *Orl. Fur.* 32.79–81, and esp. the sight of Armida's hair in Tasso, *Ger. Lib.* 4.29. **vaded**: vanished, dispersed. Unless **persant** and **azure** changed places in the printing, as Collier 1862 suggests, **persant aire** means 'piercing through the air', and **azure streames** suggests 'lines of firie light', as at IV i 13.6–9.

Stanza 21
1–2 Reversing her disguise at iii 57.7–8. **feature**: shape. **3 plighted**: pleated. On this detail, see II iii 26.5*n*. **did won**: was accustomed. **5 lanck**: slender. **6 carelesse modestee**: artless or carefree in contrast to the expected epithets of modesty, such as 'shamefast' (I x 15.5), 'goodly' (II ix 18.8), or 'bashfull' (xii 74.5). Strategically oxymoronic, according to Boehrer 1992:81, but it defines Britomart's state as a 'martiall Mayd' (iv 18.1). **8 vnwist to bee**: without it

having been known. **9** As Florimell is 'the fairest Dame aliue' (i 18.8).

Stanza 22
1 Bellona: identified by E.K., in glossing *SC Oct.* 114, as 'the goddesse of battaile, that is Pallas [Minerva]'. The same comparison is made at IV i 14.6–7 when Britomart again unveils herself. The change to *Minerua 1596* may have been suggested by the serpent-headed gorgon, Medusa, depicted on Minerva's shield, which turned male gazers to stone, as the sight of Britomart's hair amazes the knights; or because that shield was associated with chastity, as in Petrarch, *Triumph of Chastity* 181–82. (In Conti 1616:4.5, it is said to symbolize power over lustful eyes.) Cf. *Epith* 185–90. On Bellona as a name for Elizabeth, see E.C. Wilson 1939:88. **3–6 Enceladus**: S. follows Conti 6.21 in having Minerva rather than Jove battle Enceladus. He has no authority for placing the battle on Mount Haemus where Jove killed Typhoeus. He may have done so because Haemus was changed into a mountain for daring to assume the name of the gods (Ovid, *Met.* 6.87–89); or because he associates the mountain with the marriage of Peleus and Thetis, which led to the fall of Troy; see VII vii 12*n*. The simile prepares for Britomart's victory over Busirane's flames with her sword and shield at xi 25.

Stanza 23
5 auizing: observing. **6 hew**: also shape.

Stanza 24
1 note: could not. **4** Cf. Belphœbe seen by Timias as 'ful of diuinities' at v 34.7. **6 approu'd**: tested by experience. **7 faynd**: desired. **8–9** She was not moved to know any of them even though they all liked and loved her. The lines distance her from a discreditable group.

25

And *Paridell* though partly discontent
   With his late fall, and fowle indignity,
   Yet was soone wonne his malice to relent,
   Through gratious regard of her faire eye,
   And knightly worth, which he too late did try,
   Yet tried did adore. Supper was dight;
   Then they *Malbecco* prayd of courtesy,
   That of his lady they might haue the sight,
And company at meat, to doe them more delight.

26

But he to shifte their curious request,
   Gan causen, why she could not come in place;
   Her crased helth, her late recourse to rest,
   And humid euening ill for sicke folkes cace,
   But none of those excuses could take place;
   Ne would they eate, till she in presence came.
   Shee came in presence with right comely grace,
   And fairely them saluted, as became,
And shewd her selfe in all a gentle courteous Dame.

27

They sate to meat, and *Satyrane* his chaunce,
   Was her before, and *Paridell* beside;
   But he him selfe sate looking still askaunce,
   Gainst *Britomart*, and euer closely eide
   Sir *Satyrane*, that glaunces might not glide:
   But his blinde eie, that sided *Paridell*,
   All his demeasnure from his sight did hide:
   On her faire face so did he feede his fill,
And sent close messages of loue to her at will.

28

And euer and anone, when none was ware,
   With speaking lookes, that close embassage bore,
   He rou'd at her, and told his secret care:
   For all that art he learned had of yore.

Ne was she ignoraunt of that leud lore,
   But in his eye his meaning wisely redd,
   And with the like him aunswerd euermore:
   Shee sent at him one fyrie dart, whose hedd
Empoisned was with priuy lust, and gealous dredd.

29

He from that deadly throw made no defence,
   But to the wound his weake heart opened wyde;
   The wicked engine through false influence,
   Past through his eies, and secretly did glyde
   Into his heart, which it did sorely gryde.
   But nothing new to him was that same paine,
   Ne paine at all; for he so ofte had tryde
   The powre thereof, and lou'd so oft in vaine,
That thing of course he counted, loue to entertaine.

30

Thenceforth to her he sought to intimate
   His inward griefe, by meanes to him well knowne,
   Now *Bacchus* fruit out of the siluer plate
   He on the table dasht, as ouerthrowne,
   Or of the fruitfull liquor ouerflowne,
   And by the dauncing bubbles did diuine,
   Or therein write to lett his loue be showne;
   Which well she redd out of the learned line,
A sacrament prophane in mistery of wine.

31

And when so of his hand the pledge she raught,
   The guilty cup she fained to mistake,
   And in her lap did shed her idle draught,
   Shewing desire her inward flame to slake:
   By such close signes they secret way did make
   Vnto their wils, and one eie watch escape;
   Two eies him needeth, for to watch and wake,
   Who louers will deceiue. Thus was the ape,
By their faire handling, put into *Malbeccoes* cape.

Stanza 25

2 indignity: because defeated by a woman; cf. i 8.1–5.
3 relent: soften; qualify. **6 dight**: set out.

Stanza 26

1 shifte: evade. **their curious request**: i.e. asked out of
curiosity. **2 Gan causen**: gave causes or reasons. **3 crased**:
broken. **late recourse**: recently betaking herself. **5 take
place**: find acceptance. **8 fairely**: courteously. **saluted**:
kissed, as a salutation. **as became**: as was fitting.

Stanza 27

1–5 In this careful seating arrangement, Malbecco is at one
end of the table with Britomart at the other. Satyrane **Was her
before**, i.e. across from Hellenore who sits on Malbecco's left
(and blind) side with Paridell beside her. **he him selfe**: i.e.
Malbecco, who watches Satyrane on his right side with his one
good eye and looks **askaunce** – the glance of Suspect at xii
15.2 – at Britomart across the table because in his jealous
desire to possess his wife he fears a woman as much as he does
a man. Presumably, the Squire of Dames sits on Satyrane's

right side, across from Paridell. **7 demeasnure**: demeanour,
behaviour. **8 so**: by that means. **9 close**: secret.

Stanza 28

1 ware: watchful. **2** The line repeats two lines above; hence
close embassage = secret messages. **3 rou'd**: shot glances; cf.
i 50.6. **care**: also passion (Lat. *cura*). **5 leud lore**: doctrine
of love; specifically courtly love, as he is 'The learned louer'
(x 6.1). **9** Her glance arouses **priuy lust** in Paridell and (pre-
sumably) **gealous dredd** in Malbecco.

Stanza 29

1 throw: thrust. **3 false influence**: deceiving influx or
infusion. **5 gryde**: pierce gratingly. **9 of course**: to be
expected, as a matter of course.

Stanzas 30

This game, a variant of 'wine-throw' (κότταβος), is played
here because Hellenore's namesake, Helen, in Ovid, *Heroides*
17.75–90, recalls that she played it with Paris: he wrote her
name in spilt wine followed by *amo*. It is dismissed as sluttish

32

Now when of meats and drinks they had their fill,
  Purpose was moued by that gentle Dame,
  Vnto those knights aduenturous, to tell
  Of deeds of armes, which vnto them became,
  And euery one his kindred, and his name.
  Then *Paridell*, in whom a kindly pride
  Of gratious speach, and skill his words to frame
  Abounded, being yglad of so fitte tide
Him to commend to her, thus spake, of al well eide.

33

Troy, that art now nought, but an idle name,
  And in thine ashes buried low dost lie,
  Though whilome far much greater then thy fame,
  Before that angry Gods, and cruell skie
  Vpon thee heapt a direfull destinie,
  What boots it boast thy glorious descent,
  And fetch from heuen thy great genealogie,
  Sith all thy worthie prayses being blent,
Their ofspring hath embaste, and later glory shent.

34

Most famous Worthy of the world, by whome
  That warre was kindled, which did *Troy* inflame,
  And stately towres of *Ilion* whilome
  Brought vnto balefull ruine, was by name

Sir *Paris* far renowmd through noble fame,
  Who through great prowesse and bold hardinesse,
  From *Lacedaemon* fetcht the fayrest Dame,
  That euer *Greece* did boast, or knight possesse,
Whom *Venus* to him gaue for meed of worthinesse.

35

Fayre *Helene*, flowre of beautie excellent,
  And girlond of the mighty Conquerours,
  That madest many Ladies deare lament
  The heauie losse of their braue Paramours,
  Which they far off beheld from *Troian* toures,
  And saw the fieldes of faire *Scamander* strowne
  With carcases of noble warrioures,
  Whose fruitlesse liues were vnder furrow sowne,
And *Xanthus* sandy bankes with blood all ouerflowne.

36

From him my linage I deriue aright,
  Who long before the ten yeares siege of *Troy*,
  Whiles yet on *Ida* he a shepeheard hight,
  On faire *Oenone* got a louely boy,
  Whom for remembrance of her passed ioy,
  She of his Father *Parius* did name;
  Who, after *Greekes* did *Priams* realme destroy,
  Gathred the *Troian* reliques sau'd from flame,
And with them sayling thence, to th'Isle of *Paros* came.

---

in Castiglione, *Courtier* 252, and, for Harington 1591:12, it marks a 'slovenly sutor'. Since wine is the visible sign of the **mistery** of the Eucharist, which celebrates Christ's love for mankind, its use here is **prophane**, as Tuve 1947:221 notes, and travesties Fidelia's cup filled with wine and water at I x 13.2–3. **3 plate**: cup.

Stanza 31

1 Such indecorum is noted by Vives 1912:47: 'And worse becometh a good woman to taste a cup of drink in a feast or a banket, reached vnto her by another man'. **2 mistake**: take wrongly, and hence cause to spill. **7 wake**: guard. **8–9** 'To put an ape in a man's hood is to dupe him' (*OED* 4).

Stanza 32

2 A proposal was made . . . **4 became**: befell. **6 kindly**: native. **8 tide**: opportunity.

Stanzas 33–51

The two competing versions of the story of Troy, Paridell's formal 'complaint' (40.1) about its fall and Britomart's vision of its renewal as Troynovant, complete the three-part history of Britain; see II x Arg.1–2*n*. After his genealogy (33–37), her three stanzas (38–40) on the renewal of the Trojan stock introduce his three (41–43) on the second Troy, which are answered by her three (44–46) on the third Troy. On the differences between them, see 'Troy' in the *SEnc*. On London as Troynovant and its significance in the poem, see 'London' in the *SEnc*, and Manley 1995:173–211.

Stanza 33

7 from heuen: its founder, Dardanos, was a son of Jove. **8 blent**: obscured; blemished. **9 embaste**: made base. **shent**: disgraced; confounded.

Stanza 34

Paris is not, of course, one of the Nine Worthies; his **worthinesse** lay in choosing Venus's bribe over those offered by the other goddesses, as recorded at II vii 55.4–9. His rape of Helen is the archetypal story of adultery, which Paridell aspires to imitate. How he **fetcht** Helen is told again at IV xi 19.3–7; in *SC July* 145–48, Morrell tells how Paris left his flock 'to fetch a lasse'. On S.'s use of the judgement of Paris tradition, see Stewart 1991.

Stanza 35

1 excellent: supreme. **3 deare**: dearly. **6–9 Scamander**: the name given by mortals to the river of Troy but called **Xanthus** by the gods (Homer, *Iliad* 20.74). Paridell, but not S. (see IV xi 20.6–7), seems to regard the former as a plain.

Stanza 36

1 aright: directly; but also commenting ironically on his bastardy. **6 Parius**: changed from Corythus (Ovid, *Met.* 7.361) in order to introduce variations on Paris, as with Elfe at II x 72–75. On the echoing of the names, see Mikics 1994:108–09. **9 Paros**: corresponding to Buthrotum visited by Aeneas in his flight from Troy (*Aen.* 3.293).

37   *descent*

That was by him cald *Paros*, which before
   Hight *Nausa*, there he many yeares did raine,
   And built *Nausicle* by the *Pontick* shore,
   The which he dying lefte next in remaine
   To *Paridas* his sonne.
   From whom I *Paridell* by kin descend;
   But for faire ladies loue, and glories gaine,
   My natiue soile haue lefte, my dayes to spend
In seewing deeds of armes, my liues and labors end.

38

Whenas the noble *Britomart* heard tell
   Of *Troian* warres, and *Priams* citie sackt,
   The ruefull story of Sir *Paridell*,
   She was empassiond at that piteous act,
   With zelous enuy of *Greekes* cruell fact,
   Against that nation, from whose race of old
   She heard, that she was lineally extract:
   For noble *Britons* sprong from *Troians* bold,
And *Troynouant* was built of old *Troyes* ashes cold.

39

Then sighing soft awhile, at last she thus:
   O lamentable fall of famous towne,
   Which raignd so many yeares victorious,
   And of all *Asie* bore the soueraine crowne,
   In one sad night consumd, and throwen downe:
   What stony hart, that heares thy haplesse fate,
   Is not empierst with deepe compassiowne,
   And makes ensample of mans wretched state,
That floures so fresh at morne, and fades at euening late?

40

Behold, Sir, how your pitifull complaint
   Hath fownd another partner of your payne:
   For nothing may impresse so deare constraint,
   As countries cause, and commune foes disdayne.

But if it should not grieue you, backe agayne
   To turne your course, I would to heare desyre,
   What to *Aeneas* fell; sith that men sayne
   He was not in the cities wofull fyre
Consum'd, but did him selfe to safety retyre.

41

Anchyses sonne begott of *Venus* fayre,
   Said he, out of the flames for safegard fled,
   And with a remnant did to sea repayre,
   Where he through fatall errour long was led
   Full many yeares, and weetlesse wandered
   From shore to shore, emongst the Lybick sandes,
   Ere rest he fownd. Much there he suffered,
   And many perilles past in forreine landes,
To saue his people sad from victours vengefull handes.

42

At last in *Latium* he did arryue,
   Where he with cruell warre was entertaind
   Of th'inland folke, which sought him backe to driue,
   Till he with old *Latinus* was constraind,
   To contract wedlock: (so the fates ordaind.)
   Wedlocke contract in blood, and eke in blood
   Accomplished, that many deare complaind:
   The riuall slaine, the victour through the flood
Escaped hardly, hardly praisd his wedlock good.

43

Yet after all, he victour did suruiue,
   And with *Latinus* did the kingdom part.
   But after, when both nations gan to striue,
   Into their names the title to conuart,
   His sonne *Iulus* did from thence depart,
   With all the warlike youth of *Troians* bloud,
   And in long *Alba* plast his throne apart,
   Where faire it florished, and long time stoud,
Till *Romulus* renewing it, to *Rome* remoud.

Stanza 37
2 **Nausa**: there is no authority for the name but Gk ναῦς, ship, fits the Trojan story, as Roche 1964:63 suggests. 3 The shift from Troy to an island in the Aegean sea and then to the shore of the Black Sea indicates that he travels in the opposite direction to Aeneas. 4 **next in remaine**: as the next remaining representative. 5 The short line may suggest a break in Paridell's ancestry to correct his claim at 36.1; sugg. Fried 1981:271. 9 **seewing**: pursuing.

Stanza 38
4 **empassiond**: deeply moved, as she was at iii 43.1. 5 **enuy**: hostile feeling. **fact**: evil deed. 7 **extract**: descended. 9 **Troynouant**: New Troy or London; see II x 46.4–5. The line suggests the phoenix rising from its ashes.

Stanza 39
9 Cf. Ps. 90.6: 'In the morning it [man's life] florisheth and groweth, in the euening it is cut downe and withereth'.

Stanza 40
3 **so deare constraint**: such grievous distress.

Stanzas 41–43
Paridell offers some of the best-known trots from the *Aeneid*, e.g. **a remnant**: *reliquias* (1.30), **through fatall errour**: *fato profugus* (2), **Much there he suffered**: *multum ille . . . multa quoque et bello passus* (3, 5). He addresses Hellenore chiefly, as Aeneas addresses Dido in *Aen.* 2–3, also at a banquet and arousing lust, while decorously omitting the Dido episode. See J. Watkins 1995:163–67.

Stanza 41
2 **safegard**: safety. 5 **weetlesse**: in ignorance. 6 **Lybick**: Libyan.

Stanza 42
2 **entertaind**: received. 7 **deare**: grievously. 8–9 The **riuall** is Turnus; **flood** refers to their final battle. To appeal to Hellenore, Paridell claims that Aeneas regretted **wedlock**. **hardly**: with difficulty.

Stanza 43
Based on the prophecy in *Aen.* 1.267–77. 2 **part**: divide into parts. 4 **conuart**: convert. Each tried to gain the title of sovereignty by having the country named after him. 7–8 **long Alba**: Alba Longa, in Latium. **long time** is three hundred years.

44

There there (said *Britomart*) a fresh appeard
  The glory of the later world to spring,
  And *Troy* againe out of her dust was reard,
  To sitt in second seat of soueraine king,
  Of all the world vnder her gouerning.
  But a third kingdom yet is to arise,
  Out of the *Troians* scattered ofspring,
  That in all glory and great enterprise,
Both first and second *Troy* shall dare to equalise.

Britain!!

45

It *Troynouant* is hight, that with the waues
  Of wealthy *Thamis* washed is along,
  Vpon whose stubborne neck whereat he raues
  With roring rage, and sore him selfe does throng,
  That all men feare to tempt his billowes strong,
  She fastned hath her foot, which standes so hy,
  That it a wonder of the world is song
  In forreine landes, and all which passen by,
Beholding it from farre, doe thinke it threates the skye.

46

The *Troian Brute* did first that citie fownd,
  And Hygate made the meare thereof by west,
  And *Ouert* gate by North: that is the bownd
  Toward the land; two riuers bownd the rest.
  So huge a scope at first him seemed best,
  To be the compasse of his kingdomes seat:
  So huge a mind could not in lesser rest,
  Ne in small meares containe his glory great,
That *Albion* had conquered first by warlike feat.

47

Ah fairest Lady knight, (said *Paridell*)
  Pardon I pray my heedlesse ouersight,
  Who had forgot, that whylome I heard tell
  From aged *Mnemon*; for my wits beene light.
  Indeed he said (if I remember right,)
  That of the antique *Troian* stocke, there grew
  Another plant, that raught to wondrous hight,
  And far abroad his mightie braunches threw,
Into the vtmost Angle of the world he knew.

48

For that same *Brute*, whom much he did aduaunce
  In all his speach, was *Syluius* his sonne,
  Whom hauing slain, through luckles arrowes glaunce
  He fled for feare of that he had misdonne,
  Or els for shame, so fowle reproch to shonne,
  And with him ledd to sea an youthly trayne,
  Where wearie wandring they long time did wonne,
  And many fortunes prou'd in th'*Ocean* mayne,
And great aduentures found, that now were long to sayne.

49

At last by fatall course they driuen were
  Into an Island spatious and brode,
  The furthest North, that did to them appeare:
  Which after rest they seeking farre abrode,
  Found it the fittest soyle for their abode,
  Fruitfull of all thinges fitt for liuing foode,
  But wholy waste, and void of peoples trode,
  Saue an huge nation of the Geaunts broode,
That fed on liuing flesh, and dronck mens vitall blood.

Stanza 44

1 There there: a rhetorical device (*epizeuxis*) to register vehemence, here to a prophetic vision, specifically Brutus's of *Troia Nova* in Geoffrey of Monmouth 1891:1.11, 17. **4–6** Troy became the ruler of the world for a second time when Aeneas founded Rome; and for a third time when his grandson, Brutus, founded 'Troynouant' (38.9); cf. iii 22–23. **third kingdom** would seem to refer to Joachim of Fiore's third, apocalyptic age. On the Joachimist tradition in Reformation England, see King 1982:197–203. **9 equalise**: equal.

Stanza 45

3–5 whereat . . . strong is parenthetical within a larger parenthesis, **that with . . . foot**, which results in the awkward syntax of a foot standing high. (London Bridge appeared immense when the six-storied Nonesuch House was built on it in 1577, as Donald Bruce has told me.) The channel of water under the bridge, which its piers had reduced to less than a third, produced such dangerous currents when the tide was running that Frobisher refers to 'the waterfall of London Bridge' (Hakluyt 1903–05:7.334). At II x 73.9, it is called 'A bridge of bras, whose sound heuens thunder seem'd to bee'. Troynovant's foot on Thamis's neck is an emblem of royal power; or, more generally, 'a symbol of human triumph over time' (Manley 1995:178). **throng**: press. **tempt**: try; venture upon.

Stanza 46

2–4 Of the two gates, which provide the city's **bownd** (boundary), **Ouert gate** has not been identified. **Hygate**

refers to the village of that name, as in Drayton 1931–41:4.319 who writes that it was 'Appointed for a gate of *London* to have been, | When first the mighty *Brute*, that City did begin'. (I owe this reference to Lawrence Manley.) One would expect, instead, a reference to Ludgate, which S. names at II x 46.6. Of the **two riuers**, only the Thames has been identified. Stow 1956:12 names the Thames and the 'river of the Wells' (possibly the earlier name of the Fleet river). Manley suggests the Lee (or Lea), from the map in *Poly-Olbion* for Song 16; cf. the river of that name in IV xi 29.7 and *Proth* 38. **8 containe**: confine. **9 Albion**: Britain, rather than the giant of that name. **first**: i.e. was the first to conquer. Cf. II x 9–11.

Stanza 47

4 Mnemon: Gk. μνήμων, mindful. **7 raught**: reached. **9 the vtmost Angle**: corner, outlying place. W. Harrison in Holinshed 1807–08:1.9 notes – but rejects – the derivation of England 'ab Angulo, as from a corner of the world'.

Stanzas 48–51

Part of this **famous history**, based chiefly on Geoffrey 1891:1.3–17, is told at II x 9.6–11.4. See Harper 1910:168–71.

Stanza 48

1 aduaunce: extol. **7 wonne**: remain. **8 prou'd**: suffered.

Stanza 49

1 fatall: destined; cf. 41.4. **7 waste**: uninhabited. **trode**: tread.

50

Whom he through wearie wars and labours long,
  Subdewd with losse of many *Britons* bold:
  In which the great *Goemagot* of strong
  Corineus, and *Coulin* of *Debon* old
  Were ouerthrowne, and laide on th'earth full cold,
  Which quaked vnder their so hideous masse,
  A famous history to bee enrold
  In euerlasting moniments of brasse,
That all the antique Worthies merits far did passe.

51

His worke great *Troynouant*, his worke is eke
  Faire *Lincolne*, both renowmed far away,
  That who from East to West will endlong seeke,
  Cannot two fairer Cities find this day,
  Except *Cleopolis*: so heard I say
  Old *Mnemon*. Therefore Sir, I greet you well
  Your countrey kin, and you entyrely pray
  Of pardon for the strife, which late befell
Betwixt vs both vnknowne. So ended *Paridell*.

52

But all the while, that he these speeches spent,
  Vpon his lips hong faire Dame *Hellenore*,
  With vigilant regard, and dew attent,
  Fashioning worldes of fancies euermore
  In her fraile witt, that now her quite forlore:
  The whiles vnwares away her wondring eye,
  And greedy eares her weake hart from her bore:
  Which he perceiuing, euer priuily
In speaking, many false belgardes at her let fly.

53

So long these knightes discoursed diuersly,
  Of straunge affaires, and noble hardiment,
  Which they had past with mickle ieopardy,
  That now the humid night was farforth spent,
  And heuenly lampes were halfendeale ybrent:
  Which th'old man seeing wel, who too long thought
  Euery discourse and euery argument,
  Which by the houres he measured, besought
Them go to rest. So all vnto their bowres were brought.

Stanza 50
6 hideous: huge. **9 the antique Worthies**: the Nine
Worthies; see iii 4.4*n*.

Stanza 51
1–2 Geoffrey 1891:1.17 claims that Brutus founded **Troynouant**,
as at 46.1. Since there is no authority for the claim that he also
founded Lincoln, there may be a topical reference to Paridell's
'identity' associating him with that city. **3 endlong**: from
end to end. **5 Cleopolis**: see I x 58.2–4*n*. **7 countrey kin**:
countryman, kinsman. **entyrely**: earnestly.

Stanza 52
Hellenore responds to Paridell as Dido does to Aeneas at *Aen*.
4.1–5. Her **worldes of fancies** parody Amoret's suffering
in the house of Busirane at xii 26.3–5. **3 attent**: attention.
5 forlore: forsook. **9 belgardes**: loving looks; see II iii
25.3*n*.

Stanza 53
2 hardiment: bold exploits. **4 humid night**: as the dewy
night is speeding from the sky when Aeneas ends his story
(*Aen*. 2.8). **farforth**: far. **5 halfendeale**: half.

Cant. X.

Paridell rapeth Hellenore:
Malbecco her poursewes:
Fynds emongst Satyres, whence with him
To turne she doth refuse.

1

THe morow next, so soone as *Phœbus* Lamp
  Bewrayed had the world with early light,
  And fresh *Aurora* had the shady damp
  Out of the goodly heuen amoued quight,
  Faire *Britomart* and that same Faery knight
  Vprose, forth on their iourney for to wend:
  But *Paridell* complaynd, that his late fight
  With *Britomart*, so sore did him offend,
That ryde he could not, till his hurts he did amend.

2

So foorth they far'd, but he behind them stayd,
  Maulgre his host, who grudged grieuously,
  To house a guest, that would be needes obayd,
  And of his owne him left not liberty:
  Might wanting measure moueth surquedry.
  Two things he feared, but the third was death;
  That fiers youngmans vnruly maystery;
  His money, which he lou'd as liuing breath;
And his faire wife, whom honest long he kept vneath.

3

But patience perforce he must abie,
  What fortune and his fate on him will lay,
  Fond is the feare, that findes no remedie;
  Yet warily he watcheth euery way,

By which he feareth euill happen may:
  So th'euill thinkes by watching to preuent;
  Ne doth he suffer her, nor night, nor day,
  Out of his sight her selfe once to absent.
So doth he punish her and eke himselfe torment.

4

But *Paridell* kept better watch, then hee,
  A fit occasion for his turne to finde,
  False loue, why do men say, thou canst not see,
  And in their foolish fancy feigne thee blinde,
  That with thy charmes the sharpest sight doest binde,
  And to thy will abuse? Thou walkest free,
  And seest euery secret of the minde;
  Thou seest all, yet none at all sees thee;
All that is by the working of thy Deitee.

5

So perfect in that art was *Paridell*,
  That he *Malbeccoes* halfen eye did wyle,
  His halfen eye he wiled wondrous well,
  And *Hellenors* both eyes did eke beguyle,
  Both eyes and hart attonce, during the whyle
  That he there soiourned his woundes to heale,
  That *Cupid* selfe it seeing, close did smyle,
  To weet how he her loue away did steale,
And bad, that none their ioyous treason should reueale.

Book III Canto x

Argument
1 rapeth: carries off; cf. 13.8–9. **4 turne**: return.

Stanza 1
2 Bewrayed: revealed by the sun's rays. **3 damp**: fog.
5 that same Faery knight: i.e. Satyrane, named a 'faeries
sonne' at I vi 47.1. **8 offend**: hurt.

Stanza 2
2 Maulgre: in spite of. **grudged**: complained. **5** Power not
controlled leads to presumption, here specifically sexual indul-
gence (**surquedry**, *OED* 2). **6–9** The lines prepare for the
final irony. He feared two things – Paridell's sexual prowess
(**maystery**) and the loss of his money – but the loss of his wife
would be his death. By the end he has suffered all three and yet

'can . . . neuer dye' (60.1). **honest**: chaste. **vneath**: with
difficulty.

Stanza 3
1 patience perforce: the same proverbial advice (Smith 598)
offered Guyon at II iii 3.3 for the loss of his horse and spear.
abie: endure. **3** Proverbial (Smith 250). **Fond**: foolish.
4–6 Denying the proverb (Smith 826) that 'Good watch pre-
vents misfortune'.

Stanza 4
3–4 As S. himself does, e.g. I i 51.4, II iii 23.6.

Stanza 5
2 halfen eye: his one 'blincked eye' (ix 5.5); half his eyesight.
wyle: beguile. **7 close**: secretly.

6

The learned louer lost no time nor tyde,
    That least auantage mote to him afford,
    Yet bore so faire a sayle, that none espyde
    His secret drift, till he her layd abord.
    When so in open place, and commune bord,
    He fortun'd her to meet, with commune speach
    He courted her, yet bayted euery word,
That his vngentle hoste n'ote him appeach
Of vile vngentlenesse, or hospitages breach.

7

But when apart (if euer her apart)
    He found, then his false engins fast he plyde,
    And all the sleights vnbosomd in his hart;
    He sigh'd, he sobd, he swownd, he perdy dyde,
    And cast himselfe on ground her fast besyde:
    Tho when againe he him bethought to liue,
    He wept, and wayld, and false laments belyde,
    Saying, but if she Mercie would him giue
That he mote algates dye, yet did his death forgiue.

8

And otherwhyles with amorous delights,
    And pleasing toyes he would her entertaine,
    Now singing sweetly, to surprize her sprights,
    Now making layes of loue and louers paine,
    Bransles, Ballads, virelayes, and verses vaine;
    Oft purposes, oft riddles he deuysd,
    And thousands like, which flowed in his braine,
    With which he fed her fancy, and entysd
To take with his new loue, and leaue her old despysd.

9

And euery where he might, and euerie while
    He did her seruice dewtifull, and sewd
    At hand with humble pride, and pleasing guile,
    So closely yet, that none but she it vewd,
    Who well perceiued all, and all indewd.
    Thus finely did he his false nets dispred,
    With which he many weake harts had subdewd,
    Of yore, and many had ylike misled:
What wonder then, if she were likewise carried?

10

No fort so fensible, no wals so strong,
    But that continuall battery will riue,
    Or daily siege through dispuruayaunce long,
    And lacke of reskewes will to parley driue;
    And Peece, that vnto parley eare will giue,
    Will shortly yield it selfe, and will be made
    The vassall of the victors will byliue:
    That stratageme had oftentimes assayd
This crafty Paramoure, and now it plaine displayd.

11

For through his traines he her intrapped hath,
    That she her loue and hart hath wholy sold
    To him, without regard of gaine, or scath,
    Or care of credite, or of husband old,
    Whom she hath vow'd to dub a fayre Cucquold.
    Nought wants but time and place, which shortly shee
    Deuized hath, and to her louer told.
    It pleased well. So well they both agree;
So readie rype to ill, ill wemens counsels bee.

12

Darke was the Euening, fit for louers stealth,
    When chaunst *Malbecco* busie be elsewhere,
    She to his closet went, where all his wealth
    Lay hid: thereof she countlesse summes did reare,
    The which she meant away with her to beare;
    The rest she fyr'd for sport, or for despight;
    As *Hellene*, when she saw aloft appeare
    The *Troiane* flames, and reach to heuens hight
Did clap her hands, and ioyed at that dolefull sight.

Stanza 6
4 drift: purpose; also drifting, suggested by the image of sailing. **layd abord**: the nautical sense, 'run alongside to board', has a bawdy innuendo. **7 bayted**: bated (moderated), or baited. I.e. he spoke courteously, or with *double entendre*. **8–9** I.e. could not accuse him of discourtesy or breach of his host's hospitality.

Stanza 7
2 engins: wiles. **3 sleights**: cunning tricks. **4 perdy dyde**: assuredly would die. **7 belyde**: counterfeited. **8 but if**: unless. **9 algates**: altogether; otherwise. Yet he would pardon her for causing his death.

Stanza 8
1 otherwhyles: at other times. **2 toyes**: amorous sports. **3–6** Paridell plays the role of Lechery who 'well could . . . sing . . . and read in louing bookes' (I iv 25.7–8) in order to **surprize**, i.e. overcome or ambush, Hellenore. He sings **Bransles**: a song for dance music, or the French brawl, associated with love; **Ballads**: a dance tune; **virelayes**: 'a light kind of song' (E.K. on *SC Nov.* 21); and he reads **purposes**: a game con-

sisting of questions and answers, associated with love, as are **riddles**.

Stanza 9
2 sewd: did homage. **5 indewd**: took in, 'inwardly digested'. **6 finely**: cunningly.

Stanza 10
1–2 Proverbial (Smith 281). **fensible**: well-fortified, able to be defended. **3 dispuruayaunce**: lack of provisions. **5 Peece**: fort; with a pun on 'peace'. **7 byliue**: quickly. **8 assayd**: tried, proven.

Stanza 11
1 traines: guile; literally, snares to trap an animal or bird (cf. 9.6). **3 scath**: harm. **4 credite**: reputation.

Stanza 12
4 reare: collect. **7–9** In Virgil, *Aen.* 6.517–19, Deiphobus tells of Helen's bacchic dance to celebrate Troy's fall. As Vance 1986:349 argues, the actions of 'This second *Helene*' (13.1) in re-enacting the events in Troy are as much a 'translation' of the legend as that given by Paridell.

13

This second *Helene*, fayre Dame *Hellenore*,
  The whiles her husband ran with sory haste,
  To quench the flames, which she had tyn'd before,
  Laught at his foolish labour spent in waste;
  And ran into her louers armes right fast;
  Where streight embraced, she to him did cry,
  And call alowd for helpe, ere helpe were past,
  For lo that Guest did beare her forcibly,
And meant to rauish her, that rather had to dy.

14

The wretched man hearing her call for ayd,
  And ready seeing him with her to fly,
  In his disquiet mind was much dismayd:
  But when againe he backeward cast his eye,
  And saw the wicked fire so furiously
  Consume his hart, and scorch his Idoles face,
  He was therewith distressed diuersely,
  Ne wist he how to turne, nor to what place;
Was neuer wretched man in such a wofull cace.

15

Ay when to him she cryde, to her he turnd,
  And left the fire; loue money ouercame:
  But when he marked, how his money burnd,
  He left his wife; money did loue disclame:
  Both was he loth to loose his loued Dame,
  And loth to leaue his liefest pelfe behinde,
  Yet sith he n'ote saue both, he sau'd that same,
  Which was the dearest to his dounghill minde,
The God of his desire, the ioy of misers blinde.

16

Thus whilest all things in troublous vprore were,
  And all men busie to suppresse the flame,
  The louing couple neede no reskew feare,
  But leasure had, and liberty to frame

Their purpost flight, free from all mens reclame;
  And Night, the patronesse of loue-stealth fayre,
  Gaue them safe conduct, till to end they came:
  So beene they gone yfere, a wanton payre
Of louers loosely knit, where list them to repayre.

17

Soone as the cruell flames yslaked were,
  Malbecco seeing, how his losse did lye,
  Out of the flames, which he had quencht whylere
  Into huge waues of griefe and gealosye
  Full deepe emplonged was, and drowned nye,
  Twixt inward doole and felonous despight;
  He rau'd, he wept, he stampt, he lowd did cry,
  And all the passions, that in man may light,
Did him attonce oppresse, and vex his caytiue spright.

18

Long thus he chawd the cud of inward griefe,
  And did consume his gall with anguish sore,
  Still when he mused on his late mischiefe,
  So still the smart thereof increased more,
  And seemd more grieuous, then it was before:
  At last when sorrow he saw booted nought,
  Ne griefe might not his loue to him restore,
  He gan deuise, how her he reskew mought,
Ten thousand wayes he cast in his confused thought.

19

At last resoluing, like a Pilgrim pore,
  To search her forth, where so she might be fond,
  And bearing with him treasure in close store,
  The rest he leaues in ground: So takes in hond
  To seeke her endlong, both by sea and lond.
  Long he her sought, he sought her far and nere,
  And euery where that he mote vnderstond,
  Of knights and ladies any meetings were,
And of eachone he mett, he tidings did inquere.

Stanza 13
3 **tyn'd**: kindled.   4 **in waste**: in vain.

Stanza 14
6 **Consume his hart**: for his heart lies in his money, which is his **Idol**. His heart becomes the subject of an elaborate play, e.g. 21.9, 26.6, 45.4, and 48.6, until it is literally consumed at 59.6.

Stanza 15
Malbecco stands between the love of beauty and the love of money, Cupid and cupidity, the two most violent forces that assault the bulwark of sight in the castle of Alma; see II xi 9.9 and *n*.   1 **Ay**: ever.   4 **disclame**: in the legal sense, renounce the claims of (*OED* 3).   5 **loose**: lose; allow to become loose. Cf. 16.9, 36.1.   6–9 **liefest pelfe**: most beloved wealth, which is more dear to him than **his loued Dame**. As a consequence, love is replaced by its negation, jealousy, as in Song Sol. 8.6:

'loue is strong as death: ielousie is cruel as the graue'.   **n'ote**: might not; knew not how to.

Stanza 16
4 **frame**: set out upon.   5 **reclame**: i.e. to call back, a term used of hawks (*OED* 1); see 35.7–9*n*.   6 A more formal statement of 12.1.   8 **yfere**: together. The internal rhyme registers S.'s scorn.   9 **loosely**: suggesting also 'immorally'.

Stanza 17
6 **doole**: grief.   **felonous**: fierce, cruel.

Stanza 18
2 **gall**: the source of bitter, jealous anger; cf. 59.7.   3 **mischiefe**: misfortune.   9 **cast**: pondered.

Stanza 19
5 **endlong**: from end to end of the country.

20

But all in vaine, his woman was too wise,
　Euer to come into his clouch againe,
　And hee too simple euer to surprise
　The iolly *Paridell*, for all his paine.
　One day, as hee forpassed by the plaine
　With weary pace, he far away espide
　A couple, seeming well to be his twaine,
　Which houed close vnder a forest side,
As if they lay in wait, or els them selues did hide.

21

Well weened hee, that those the same mote bee,
　And as he better did their shape auize,
　Him seemed more their maner did agree;
　For th'one was armed all in warlike wize,
　Whom, to be *Paridell* he did deuize;
　And th'other al yclad in garments light,
　Discolourd like to womanish disguise,
　He did resemble to his lady bright,
And euer his faint hart much earned at the sight.

22

And euer faine he towards them would goe,
　But yet durst not for dread approchen nie,
　But stood aloofe, vnweeting what to doe,
　Till that prickt forth with loues extremity,
　That is the father of fowle gealosy,
　He closely nearer crept, the truth to weet:
　But, as he nigher drew, he easily
　Might scerne, that it was not his sweetest sweet,
Ne yet her Belamour, the partner of his sheet.

23

But it was scornefull *Braggadochio*,
　That with his seruant *Trompart* houerd there,
　Sith late he fled from his too earnest foe:
　Whom such whenas *Malbecco* spyed clere,
　He turned backe, and would haue fled arere;
　Till *Trompart* ronning hastely, him did stay,
　And bad before his soueraine Lord appere:
　That was him loth, yet durst he not gainesay,
And comming him before, low louted on the lay.

24

The Boaster at him sternely bent his browe,
　As if he could haue kild him with his looke,
　That to the ground him meekely made to bowe,
　And awfull terror deepe into him strooke,
　That euery member of his body quooke.
　Said he, Thou man of nought, what doest thou here,
　Vnfitly furnisht with thy bag and booke,
　Where I expected one with shield and spere,
To proue some deeds of armes vpon an equall pere.

25

The wretched man at his imperious speach,
　Was all abasht, and low prostrating, said;
　Good Sir, let not my rudenes be no breach
　Vnto your patience, ne be ill ypaid;
　For I vnwares this way by fortune straid,
　A silly Pilgrim driuen to distresse,
　That seeke a Lady, There he suddein staid,
　And did the rest with grieuous sighes suppresse,
While teares stood in his eies, few drops of bitternesse.

26

What Lady, man? (said *Trompart*) take good hart,
　And tell thy griefe, if any hidden lye;
　Was neuer better time to shew thy smart,
　Then now, that noble succor is thee by,
　That is the whole worlds commune remedy.
　That chearful word his weak heart much did cheare,
　And with vaine hope his spirits faint supply,
　That bold he sayd, O most redoubted Pere,
Vouchsafe with mild regard a wretches cace to heare.

27

Then sighing sore, It is not long (saide hee)
　Sith I enioyd the gentlest Dame aliue;
　Of whom a knight, no knight at all perdee,
　But shame of all, that doe for honor striue,
　By treacherous deceipt did me depriue;
　Through open outrage he her bore away,
　And with fowle force vnto his will did driue,
　Which al good knights, that armes do bear this day,
Are bownd for to reuenge, and punish if they may.

Stanza 20

2 clouch: i.e., clutch; also 'claw' (*OED* 2), anticipating his transformation at 57.8. **4 iolly**: amorous; lively, as are the lustful satyrs at 44.3. **5 forpassed by**: passed over. **8 houed**: waited; cf. 'houerd' (23.2). The term suggests a falcon waiting to seize its prey.

Stanza 21

2 auize: observe. **5 deuize**: guess. **6–8** On the implied transvestism, see 'sex' in the *SEnc*. **Discolourd**: variously coloured. **disguise**: fashion. **resemble**: liken. **9 earned**: yearned; grieved.

Stanza 22

1 faine: desirous. **5 fowle gealosy**: heralding his transformation; see xi 1.5*n*. **8 scerne**: discern. **9 Belamour**: fair lover, as II vi 16.7.

Stanza 23

3 Referring to his flight from Ferraugh at viii 18.8–9. **9 . . . lowly bowed to the ground.** The first of his three deep bows in three stanzas to make his abasement complete.

Stanza 24

7 booke: if not carried for the rhyme, it belongs to his attire as a pilgrim.

Stanza 25

3 Two negatives strengthen the negation. **4 ill ypaid**: displeased. **6 silly**: humble. **9** As their source is his gall at 18.2.

Stanza 27

2 gentlest: extending her description at ix 26.9 to prepare for her bestiality.

28

And you most noble Lord, that can and dare
　Redresse the wrong of miserable wight,
　Cannot employ your most victorious speare
　In better quarell, then defence of right,
　And for a Lady gainst a faithlesse knight,
　So shall your glory bee aduaunced much,
　And all faire Ladies magnify your might,
　And eke my selfe, albee I simple such,
Your worthy paine shall wel reward with guerdon rich.

29

With that out of his bouget forth he drew
　Great store of treasure, therewith him to tempt;
　But he on it lookt scornefully askew,
　As much disdeigning to be so misdempt,
　Or a war-monger to be basely nempt;
　And sayd, Thy offers base I greatly loth,
　And eke thy words vncourteous and vnkempt;
　I tread in dust thee and thy money both,
That, were it not for shame, So turned from him wroth.

30

But *Trompart*, that his maistres humor knew,
　In lofty looks to hide an humble minde,
　Was inly tickled with that golden vew,
　And in his eare him rownded close behinde:
　Yet stoupt he not, but lay still in the winde,
　Waiting aduauntage on the pray to sease;
　Till *Trompart* lowly to the grownd inclinde,
　Besought him his great corage to appease,
And pardon simple man, that rash did him displease.

31

Big looking like a doughty Doucepere,
　At last he thus, Thou clod of vilest clay,
　I pardon yield, and that with rudenes beare;
　But weete henceforth, that all that golden pray,

And all that els the vaine world vaunten may,
　I loath as doung, ne deeme my dew reward:
　Fame is my meed, and glory vertuous pray.
　But minds of mortal men are muchell mard,
And mou'd amisse with massy mucks vnmeet regard.

32

And more, I graunt to thy great misery
　Gratious respect, thy wife shall backe be sent,
　And that vile knight, who euer that he bee,
　Which hath thy lady reft, and knighthood shent,
　By *Sanglamort* my sword, whose deadly dent
　The blood hath of so many thousands shedd,
　I sweare, ere long shall dearly it repent;
　Ne he twixt heuen and earth shall hide his hedd,
But soone he shalbe fownd, and shortly doen be dedd.

33

The foolish man thereat woxe wondrous blith,
　As if the word so spoken, were halfe donne,
　And humbly thanked him a thousand sith,
　That had from death to life him newly wonne.
　Tho forth the Boaster marching, braue begonne
　His stolen steed to thunder furiously,
　As if he heauen and hell would oueronne,
　And all the world confound with cruelty,
That much *Malbecco* ioyed in his iollity.

34

Thus long they three together traueiled,
　Through many a wood, and many an vncouth way,
　To seeke his wife, that was far wandered:
　But those two sought nought, but the present pray,
　To weete the treasure, which he did bewray,
　On which their eies and harts were wholly sett,
　With purpose, how they might it best betray;
　For sith the howre, that first he did them lett
The same behold, therwith their keene desires were whett.

Stanza 28
6 **aduaunced**: praised. 7 **magnify**: extol. 8 . . . although I am so humble.

Stanza 29
1 **bouget**: 'bag' (24.7). 3 **askew**: sidelong, expressing contempt. 4 **misdempt**: misjudged; thought evil of. 5 **war-monger**: mercenary soldier. **nempt**: called. 7 **vnkempt**: rude. 9 An implied threat to slay him, if it were not shameful for a knight to slay a peasant.

Stanza 30
2 **humble**: base, low. 4 **rownded**: whispered. 5 **stoupt**: swooped, a term from falconry. Braggadocchio hovered above his prey; see 20.8*n*. 8 **corage**: anger.

Stanza 31
1 . . . like an illustrious knight, one of the twelve peers (*les douze pairs*) of France. 4 **pray**: booty. 7–9 The sentiment is worthy of Guyon at II vii 10, and of Britomart at ii 7.1–5,

but the excessive alliteration mocks his vain boasting. **vertu-ous**: correctly changed to 'vertues' *1596*. **pray**: since a duplic-ated rhyme should not have the same meaning, pay *1609* is probably correct. **muchell mard**: much corrupted.

Stanza 32
2 **Gratious**: implying the benevolent response of a ruler to his inferior. **respect**: regard, consideration. 4 **shent**: disgraced. 5 **Sanglamort**: Bloody Death. His vow not to use a sword since it was forfeited is recorded at II iii 12.6–8. **dent**: stroke.

Stanza 33
3 **sith**: times. 6 **stolen steed**: referring to his theft at II iii 4. 8 **confound**: overthrow. 9 **iollity**: gallant appearance (cf. 'braue' at 35.4); gallantry; presumption.

Stanza 34
5 **bewray**: reveal. 7 **betray**: i.e. deliver (Lat. *tradere*) it out of his possession.

35

It fortuned as they together far'd,
  They spide, where *Paridell* came pricking fast
  Vpon the plaine, the which him selfe prepar'd
  To giust with that braue straunger knight a cast,
  As on aduenture by the way he past:
  Alone he rode without his Paragone;
  For hauing filcht her bells, her vp he cast
  To the wide world, and let her fly alone,
He nould be clogd. So had he serued many one.

36

The gentle Lady, loose at randon lefte,
  The greene-wood long did walke, and wander wide
  At wilde aduenture, like a forlorne wefte,
  Till on a day the *Satyres* her espide
  Straying alone withouten groome or guide;
  Her vp they tooke, and with them home her ledd,
  With them as housewife euer to abide,
  To milk their gotes, and make them cheese and bredd,
And euery one as commune good her handeled.

37

That shortly she *Malbecco* has forgott,
  And eke Sir *Paridell*, all were he deare;
  Who from her went to seeke another lott,
  And now by fortune was arriued here,
  Where those two guilers with *Malbecco* were:
  Soone as the oldman saw Sir *Paridell*,
  He fainted, and was almost dead with feare,
  Ne word he had to speake, his griefe to tell,
But to him louted low, and greeted goodly well.

38

And after asked him for *Hellenore*,
  I take no keepe of her (sayd *Paridell*)
  She wonneth in the forrest there betore.
  So forth he rode, as his aduenture fell;

39

Perdy nay (said *Malbecco*) shall ye not:
  But let him passe as lightly, as he came:
  For litle good of him is to be got,
  And mickle perill to bee put to shame.
  But let vs goe to seeke my dearest Dame,
  Whom he hath left in yonder forest wyld:
  For of her safety in great doubt I ame,
  Least saluage beastes her person haue despoyld:
Then all the world is lost, and we in vaine haue toyld.

40

They all agree, and forward them addrest:
  Ah but (said crafty *Trompart*) weete ye well,
  That yonder in that wastefull wildernesse
  Huge monsters haunt, and many dangers dwell;
  Dragons, and Minotaures, and feendes of hell,
  And many wilde woodmen, which robbe and rend
  All traueilers; therefore aduise ye well,
  Before ye enterprise that way to wend:
One may his iourney bring too soone to euill end.

41

Malbecco stopt in great astonishment,
  And with pale eyes fast fixed on the rest,
  Their counsell crau'd, in daunger imminent.
  Said *Trompart*, You that are the most opprest
  With burdein of great treasure, I thinke best
  Here for to stay in safetie behynd;
  My Lord and I will search the wide forest.
  That counsell pleased not *Malbeccoes* mynd;
For he was much afraid, him selfe alone to fynd.

The whiles the Boaster from his loftie sell
  Faynd to alight, something amisse to mend;
  But the fresh Swayne would not his leasure dwell,
  But went his way; whom when he passed kend,
He vp remounted light, and after faind to wend.

Stanza 35
4 braue: referring to his outward show; cf. 33.5. **cast**: throw, bout. **6 Paragone**: companion; consort. **7–9 filcht her bells**: a hawking metaphor. Bells and jesses confine the hawk (cf. VI iv 19.7–9) as the marriage bond restrained Hellenore until she was 'free from all mens reclame' (16.5). **filcht** indicates that Paridell took what he wanted from her and let her go, as a falconer takes the bells from a hawk to let it go. The sense, 'to steal things of small value' (*OED* 1), is entirely fitting for her bells were not worth much. S. rings further changes upon the term at 48.9. **cast**: as a hawk is let loose to fly. See 'falconry' in the *SEnc*. **9 nould**: would not.

Stanza 36
1 at randon: at liberty, free from restraint; a hawking term for prey that fails to rise for the hawk. **3 At wilde aduenture**: at hazard in the wilderness. **wefte**: waif; in the legal sense; see IV ii 4.5–9*n*. **9 good**: property.

Stanza 37
3 lott: prize. **5 guilers**: deceivers.

Stanza 38
2 keepe: care to preserve; another falconry term. **5 Boaster**: his common title; see II iii 10.1*n*. **7 fresh Swayne**: lusty lover, in contrast to 'oldman' (37.6). **dwell**: abide. **8 But went his way**: repeated from 4 to indicate that Paridell expected to joust with Braggadocchio.

Stanza 39
2 lightly: quickly; also commenting on Paridell's fickleness. **8–9** Florimell's knights fear the same for her at viii 47–49 but Malbecco's fears are comically confirmed when the **saluage beastes** are the satyrs whose despoiling Hellenore enjoys.

Stanza 40
1 . . . and made their way. **6 woodmen**: savages. **7 aduise**: consider. **8 enterprise**: attempt.

42

Then is it best (said he) that ye doe leaue
  Your treasure here in some security,
  Either fast closed in some hollow greaue,
  Or buried in the ground from ieopardy,
  Till we returne againe in safety:
  As for vs two, least doubt of vs ye haue,
  Hence farre away we will blyndfolded ly,
Ne priuy bee vnto your treasures graue.
It pleased: so he did. Then they march forward braue.

43

Now when amid the thickest woodes they were,
  They heard a noyse of many bagpipes shrill,
  And shrieking Hububs them approching nere,
  Which all the forest did with horrour fill:
  That dreadfull sound the bosters hart did thrill,
  With such amazment, that in hast he fledd,
  Ne euer looked back for good or ill,
  And after him eke fearefull *Trompart* spedd;
The old man could not fly, but fell to ground half dedd.

44

Yet afterwardes close creeping, as he might,
  He in a bush did hyde his fearefull hedd,
  The iolly *Satyres* full of fresh delight,
  Came dauncing forth, and with them nimbly ledd
  Faire *Helenore*, with girlonds all bespredd,
  Whom their May-lady they had newly made:
  She proude of that new honour, which they redd,
  And of their louely fellowship full glade,
Daunst liuely, and her face did with a Lawrell shade.

45

The silly man that in the thickett lay
  Saw all this goodly sport, and grieued sore,
  Yet durst he not against it doe or say,
  But did his hart with bitter thoughts engore,

To see th'vnkindnes of his *Hellenore*.
  All day they daunced with great lusty hedd,
  And with their horned feet the greene gras wore,
  The whiles their Gotes vpon the brouzes fedd,
Till drouping *Phœbus* gan to hyde his golden hedd.

46

Tho vp they gan their mery pypes to trusse,
  And all their goodly heardes did gather rownd,
  But euery *Satyre* first did giue a busse
  To *Hellenore*: so busses did abound.
  Now gan the humid vapour shed the grownd
  With perly deaw, and th'Earthes gloomy shade
  Did dim the brightnesse of the welkin rownd,
  That euery bird and beast awarned made,
To shrowd themselues, whiles sleepe their sences did inuade.

47

Which when *Malbecco* saw, out of his bush
  Vpon his hands and feete he crept full light,
  And like a Gote emongst the Gotes did rush,
  That through the helpe of his faire hornes on hight,
  And misty dampe of misconceyuing night,
  And eke through likenesse of his gotish beard,
  He did the better counterfeite aright:
  So home he marcht emongst the horned heard,
That none of all the *Satyres* him espyde or heard.

48

At night, when all they went to sleepe, he vewd,
  Whereas his louely wife emongst them lay,
  Embraced of a *Satyre* rough and rude,
  Who all the night did minde his ioyous play:
  Nine times he heard him come aloft ere day,
  That all his hart with gealosy did swell;
  But yet that nights ensample did bewray,
  That not for nought his wife them loued so well,
When one so oft a night did ring his matins bell.

Stanza 41
1 astonishment: dismay, dread. **2 pale eyes**: an absence of colour associated with fear at xii 12.6.

Stanza 42
3 greaue: grove or glade.

Stanza 43
2 bagpipes: a traditional emblem of lust, from their shape. **5 thrill**: pierce. **6 amazment**: overwhelming fear.

Stanza 44
3 iolly: also amorous. **7 redd**: declared (in making her their May-lady). **8 louely**: loving. **9 Lawrell** declares that they have crowned her their queen.

Stanza 45
5 vnkindnes: unnatural conduct. **6 lusty hedd**: lustiness; lustfulness. **7** As they danced around Una at I vi 14.3. **8 brouzes**: young shoots.

Stanza 46
3 busse: kiss, employing the distinction used by Herrick in *Hesperides*: 'We busse our Wantons, but our Wives we kisse'.

Stanza 47
3 The proverbially lustful goat is associated with the lustful Satyrs, the impotent Malbecco being only **like** one. **4** Malbecco now earns his name, the horns signifying the cuckold; see ix 6.1*n*. For Hazlitt 1910:42, this line is the only jest in the poem. **5 misconceyuing**: causing misconception.

Stanza 48
2 louely: loving. **3–5** According to Pliny, the satyr gets his name – here he earns it – from his *membrum virile*. The satyr imitates Ovid who took Corinna nine times in one short night (*Amores* 3.7.25–26). **8–9** In the comic resolution to this fabliau 'of a wanton Lady' (ix 1.6), Hellenore is no longer 'Depriu'd of kindly ioy and naturall delight' (ix 5.9). Free at last though at some cost: like Argante, she 'suffred beastes her body to deflowre' (vii 49.7).

49

So closely as he could, he to them crept,
    When wearie of their sport to sleepe they fell,
    And to his wife, that now full soundly slept,
    He whispered in her eare, and did her tell,
    That it was he, which by her side did dwell,
    And therefore prayd her wake, to heare him plaine.
    As one out of a dreame not waked well,
    She turnd her, and returned backe againe:
Yet her for to awake he did the more constraine.

50

At last with irkesom trouble she abrayd;
    And then perceiuing, that it was indeed
    Her old *Malbecco*, which did her vpbrayd,
    With loosenesse of her loue, and loathly deed,
    She was astonisht with exceeding dreed,
    And would haue wakt the *Satyre* by her syde;
    But he her prayd, for mercy, or for meed,
    To saue his life, ne let him be descryde,
But hearken to his lore, and all his counsell hyde.

51

Tho gan he her perswade, to leaue that lewd
    And loathsom life, of God and man abhord,
    And home returne, where all should be renewd
    With perfect peace, and bandes of fresh accord,
    And she receiud againe to bed and bord,
    As if no trespas euer had beene donne:
    But she it all refused at one word,
    And by no meanes would to his will be wonne,
But chose emongst the iolly *Satyres* still to wonne.

52

He wooed her, till day spring he espyde;
    But all in vaine: and then turnd to the heard,
    Who butted him with hornes on euery syde,
    And trode downe in the durt, where his hore beard
    Was fowly dight, and he of death afeard.
    Early before the heauens fairest light
    Out of the ruddy East was fully reard,
    The heardes out of their foldes were loosed quight,
And he emongst the rest crept forth in sory plight.

53

So soone as he the Prison dore did pas,
    He ran as fast, as both his feet could beare,
    And neuer looked, who behind him was,
    Ne scarsely who before: like as a Beare
    That creeping close, amongst the hiues to reare
    An hony combe, the wakefull dogs espy,
    And him assayling, sore his carkas teare,
    That hardly he with life away does fly,
Ne stayes, till safe him selfe he see from ieopardy.

54

Ne stayd he, till he came vnto the place,
    Where late his treasure he entombed had,
    Where when he found it not (for *Trompart* bace
    Had it purloyned for his maister bad:)
    With extreme fury he became quite mad,
    And ran away, ran with him selfe away:
    That who so straungely had him seene bestadd,
    With vpstart haire, and staring eyes dismay,
From Limbo lake him late escaped sure would say.

55

High ouer hilles and ouer dales he fledd,
    As if the wind him on his winges had borne,
    Ne banck nor bush could stay him, when he spedd
    His nimble feet, as treading still on thorne:
    Griefe, and despight, and gealosy, and scorne
    Did all the way him follow hard behynd,
    And he himselfe himselfe loath'd so forlorne,
    So shamefully forlorne of womankynd;
That as a Snake, still lurked in his wounded mynd.

56

Still fled he forward, looking backward still,
    Ne stayd his flight, nor fearefull agony,
    Till that he came vnto a rocky hill,
    Ouer the sea, suspended dreadfully,
    That liuing creature it would terrify,
    To looke adowne, or vpward to the hight:
    From thence he threw him selfe dispiteously,
    All desperate of his fore-damned spright,
That seemd no help for him was left in liuing sight.

Stanza 49
6 plaine: complain.   **9 constraine**: exert himself.

Stanza 50
1 abrayd: awoke.

Stanza 51
1 perswade: urge.   **5 to bed and bord**: as wife and mistress
of the household.   **7 at one word**: at once.   **9 still**: always,
as she is the female counterpart of Grille at II xii 86–87.

Stanza 52
2 turnd: returned.   **4 hore**: grey with age.   **5 dight**: soiled.

Stanza 53
5 reare: take away.

Stanza 54
6 The line points to his disintegration; cf. 55.7.   **7** That who
had seen him so strangely disposed.   **8 dismay**: dismayed; or
staring in dismay.   **9** I.e. as a lost soul; see I ii 32.5 and *n*.

Stanza 55
Jealousy is commonly associated with the **thorne**, e.g. Sidney,
Astrophil and Stella 78.11: the jealous husband's 'nimble feet
. . . stirre still, [as] though on thornes'. Cf. Doubt in Cupid's
pageant at xii 10.6, and the jealous Scudamour at IV v 31.3.
Jealousy is also associated with a **Snake**, e.g. in Ariosto, *Orl.
Fur*. 42.47: Rinaldo's jealousy is objectified as a monster
encoiled by a serpent and with a swarm of serpents for hair.
5–6 These personifications suggest the fragmenting of
Malbecco's person.   **9 That**: i.e. the thought that Hellenore
preferred the satyrs to him.

57

But through long anguish, and selfe-murdring thought
   He was so wasted and forpined quight,
   That all his substance was consum'd to nought,
   And nothing left, but like an aery Spright,
   That on the rockes he fell so flit and light,
   That he thereby receiu'd no hurt at all,
   But chaunced on a craggy cliff to light;
   Whence he with crooked clawes so long did crall,
That at the last he found a caue with entrance small.

58

Into the same he creepes, and thenceforth there
   Resolu'd to build his balefull mansion,
   In drery darkenes, and continuall feare
   Of that rocks fall, which euer and anon
   Threates with huge ruine him to fall vpon,
   That he dare neuer sleepe, but that one eye
   Still ope he keepes for that occasion;
   Ne euer rests he in tranquillity,
The roring billowes beat his bowre so boystrously.

59

Ne euer is he wont on ought to feed,
   But todes and frogs, his pasture poysonous,
   Which in his cold complexion doe breed
   A filthy blood, or humour rancorous,
   Matter of doubt and dread suspitious,
   That doth with curelesse care consume the hart,
   Corrupts the stomacke with gall vitious,
   Croscuts the liuer with internall smart,
And doth transfixe the soule with deathes eternall dart.

60

Yet can he neuer dye, but dying liues,
   And doth himselfe with sorrow new sustaine,
   That death and life attonce vnto him giues.
   And painefull pleasure turnes to pleasing paine.
   There dwels he euer, miserable swaine,
   Hatefull both to him selfe, and euery wight;
   Where he through priuy griefe, and horrour vaine,
   Is woxen so deform'd that he has quight
Forgot he was a man, and *Gelosy* is hight.

Stanza 56

1 **looking backward still**: in contrast to 53.3, to signal his continuing metamorphosis. 7 **dispiteously**: mercilessly. Expecting no mercy, he shows no mercy to himself. 8 I.e. in his despair he does not care that his **spright** (or soul) would be utterly damned by suicide.

Stanza 57

2 **forpined**: wasted away. 5 **flit**: unsubstantial. 8 When Daedalion threw himself from a cliff, he was transformed into an eagle with curved claws (Ovid, *Met.* 11.342); noted Nelson 1963:324–25. C. Burrow 1988:113–14 adds another Ovidian parallel, the metamorphosis of Aesacus into a bird (*Met.* 11.783–86) when he threw himself from a cliff into the sea through grief of his lost love.

Stanza 58

3–5 As Despaire's cave is placed 'vnderneath a craggy clift' (I ix 33.3), and the house of Care lies 'Vnder a steepe hilles side' (IV v 33.1). **that rocks fall** or **ruine** may mean the overhanging cliff that threatens to fall, or the roof of the cave. 6 **that one eye**: i.e. his one eye.

Stanza 59

Malbecco's diet is analysed by Alpers 1967:222–24. **todes and frogs** are found in Errour's vomit at I i 20.7; their association with sexual jealousy is examined by Adler 1981:260. 2 **pasture**: food. 3 **complexion**: temperament. 4 **filthy blood**: excess or corrupt humour in the blood which causes illness. **humour rancorous**: associated with despite at II vii 22.2, etc. 5 **Matter**: also blood, or excrement from it. 6 **curelesse care** puns on the etymology of 'cure' (from Lat. *cura*). The rest of the line refers to the well-known etymology of care: *cura quod cor edat*. 7 **vitious**: noxious. 8 Jealous love is centred in the liver, which is the centre of the lower affections; cf. II vi 50.3.

Stanza 60

Malbecco shares Despaire's immortality at I ix 54.8–9, and Adonis's at III vi 47. On his metamorphosis into an abstract entity, see Skulsky 1981:131–34, and L.G. Freeman 2000:319–26. 7 **priuy griefe**: the secret suffering of jealousy which began with his 'priuie guilt' at ix 5.3. 9 As Grille 'forgot the excellence | Of his creation' (II xii 87.2–3). Metamorphosis is self-inflicted, as the play on 'him selfe' at 54.6 and 55.7 indicates. Cf. 'selfe-murdring thought' (57.1).

Cant. XI.

*Britomart chaceth Ollyphant,
findes Scudamour distrest:
Assayes the house of Busyrane,
where loues spoyles are exprest.*

1

O Hatefull hellish Snake, what furie furst
    Brought thee from balefull house of *Proserpine*,
    Where in her bosome she thee long had nurst,
    And fostred vp with bitter milke of tine,
    Fowle Gealosy, that turnest loue diuine
    To ioylesse dread, and mak'st the louing hart
    With hatefull thoughts to languish and to pine,
    And feed it selfe with selfe-consuming smart?
Of all the passions in the mind thou vilest art.

2

O let him far be banished away,
    And in his stead let Loue for euer dwell,
    Sweete Loue, that doth his golden wings embay
    In blessed Nectar, and pure Pleasures well,
    Vntroubled of vile feare, or bitter fell.
    And ye faire Ladies, that your kingdomes make
    In th'harts of men, them gouerne wisely well,
    And of faire *Britomart* ensample take,
That was as trew in loue, as Turtle to her make.

3

Who with Sir *Satyrane*, as earst ye red,
    Forth ryding from *Malbeccoes* hostlesse hous,
    Far off aspyde a young man, the which fled
    From an huge Geaunt, that with hideous

And hatefull outrage long him chaced thus;
    It was that *Ollyphant*, the brother deare
    Of that *Argante* vile and vitious,
    From whom the *Squyre of Dames* was reft whylere;
This all as bad as she, and worse, if worse ought were.

4

For as the sister did in feminine
    And filthy lust exceede all woman kinde,
    So he surpassed his sex masculine,
    In beastly vse all, that I euer finde:
    Whom when as *Britomart* beheld behinde
    The fearefull boy so greedily poursew,
    She was emmoued in her noble minde,
    T'employ her puissaunce to his reskew,
And pricked fiercely forward, where she did him vew.

5

Ne was Sir *Satyrane* her far behinde,
    But with like fiercenesse did ensew the chace:
    Whom when the Gyaunt saw, he soone resinde
    His former suit, and from them fled apace;
    They after both, and boldly bad him bace,
    And each did striue the other to outgoe;
    But he them both outran a wondrous space,
    For he was long, and swift as any Roe,
And now made better speed, t'escape his feared foe.

Book III Canto xi

Argument

3 Assayes: assails. **4 loues spoyles**: referring generally to Cupid's booty gained by preying upon mankind, as at 45.7, but specifically here to Amoret, his 'proud spoile' at xii 22.7, Lust's spoil at IV vii 25.5, and Scudamour's spoil at IV x 3.3. **exprest**: portrayed, set forth.

Stanza 1

1–4 Proserpine: 'the Queene of hell' (I iv 11.2), one of the Furies whose hair is entwined with snakes, e.g. Virgil, *Aen.* 7.346; cf. *Am* 86.2–3. **tine**: affliction. **5 Fowle Gealosy**: seen in Malbecco's transformation into 'an aery Spright' (x 57.4) with crooked claws.

Stanza 2

3 embay: steep. **4 blessed Nectar**: the drink of the gods, its sweetness contrasts with the 'bitter milke' (1.4) of jealousy. **5 fell**: rancour, a product of the gall (Lat. *fel*), which is the source of jealous anger; see x 18.2. **6–9** Cf. the exhortation to 'Fayre ympes of beautie' to take Belphœbe as 'a faire

ensample' at v 53–54. On the address to **faire Ladies**, see i 49n. **Turtle**: the turtle-dove. **make**: mate.

Stanza 3

1 as earst ye red: at x 1. **2 hostlesse**: inhospitable. **6–8** Referring to vii 37–51; see vii **47.2n**, **48.2n**. **reft**: taken away.

Stanza 4

4 all, that I euer: unless S. refers to what he has read, he records personal testimony, provoked by the figure of masculine lust. That may explain the rhythmic lapse that required revision: that I did euer *1596*.

Stanza 5

2 ensew: pursue. **4 suit**: pursuit. **5 bad him bace**: challenged him. Alluding to the popular children's game, prisoner's base, also played at V viii 5.4–5, 33.7–8, and VI x 8.4. See 'games, Renaissance' in the *SEnc*. It is cited here because the pursuer becomes the pursued, and because it is an exciting game of love if the teams are divided into girls and boys, as in the version 'Rover, Red Rover'. **8 swift as any Roe**: noted for its speed; see II ii 7.4n.

6

It was not *Satyrane*, whom he did feare,
   But *Britomart* the flowre of chastity;
   For he the powre of chaste hands might not beare,
   But alwayes did their dread encounter fly:
   And now so fast his feet he did apply,
   That he has gotten to a forrest neare,
   Where he is shrowded in security.
The wood they enter, and search euerie where,
They searched diuersely, so both diuided were.

7

Fayre *Britomart* so long him followed,
   That she at last came to a fountaine sheare,
   By which there lay a knight all wallowed
   Vpon the grassy ground, and by him neare
   His haberieon, his helmet, and his speare;
   A little off his shield was rudely throwne,
   On which the winged boy in colours cleare
   Depeincted was, full easie to be knowne,
And he thereby, where euer it in field was showne.

8

His face vpon the grownd did groueling ly,
   As if he had beene slombring in the shade,
   That the braue Mayd would not for courtesy,
   Out of his quiet slomber him abrade,
   Nor seeme too suddeinly him to inuade:
   Still as she stood, she heard with grieuous throb
   Him grone, as if his hart were peeces made,
   And with most painefull pangs to sigh and sob,
That pitty did the Virgins hart of patience rob.

9

At last forth breaking into bitter plaintes
   He sayd, O souerayne Lord that sit'st on hye,
   And raignst in blis emongst thy blessed Saintes,
   How suffrest thou such shamefull cruelty,
   So long vnwreaked of thine enimy?
   Or hast thou, Lord, of good mens cause no heed?
   Or doth thy iustice sleepe, and silent ly?
   What booteth then the good and righteous deed,
If goodnesse find no grace, nor righteousnes no meed?

10

If good find grace, and righteousnes reward,
   Why then is *Amoret* in caytiue band,
   Sith that more bounteous creature neuer far'd
   On foot, vpon the face of liuing land?
   Or if that heuenly iustice may withstand
   The wrongfull outrage of vnrighteous men,
   Why then is *Busirane* with wicked hand
   Suffred, these seuen monethes day in secret den
My Lady and my loue so cruelly to pen?

Stanza 6
9 diuersely: in different directions.

Stanzas 7–25
In Tasso, *Rinaldo* 5, the hero finds the despairing lover prostrate on the ground; and, after hearing him lament that his lady has been imprisoned, both enter a cave of love, the entrance to which is barred by enchanted fire. The parallels are noted in *Var* 3.288–89. To this story, S. adds details from Ariosto, *Orl. Fur.* 2.34–43: the chaste heroine finds by a fountain a lover in despair because his lady has been imprisoned in an enchanted castle, and then frees her. Lovers who need to be purged before they may pass through an enchanted fire that guards the gate of a forbidden castle is a popular romance motif, as the City of Flame in Tasso, *Ger. Lib.* 13.33–36, and the wall of fire through which Dante must pass to be purged of the sin of lust in *Purg.* 27. It is a common motif in *Amadis de Gaule*, as O'Connor 1970:172–73 notes; and in *Prolusion* 6, Milton writes of King Arthur's knights overcoming the enchantments of a fire- and flame-girdled castle. The episode corresponds in length and placing to the masque of Cupid which Britomart sees at xii 7–25.

Stanza 7
1–2 so long and **at last** associate Ollyphant with Scudamour. The **fountaine** is associated with love and the lover throughout the poem, e.g. II xii 60–68. **sheare**: clear, pure. **3 wallowed**: lying prostrate; the posture of the wounded Adonis at i 38.1, and of the dead lover at I ix 36.6. **6–9** The details identify the knight as Scudamour: Fr. *écu* (or *éscu*), shield + *d'amour*, of love; or, as Scudamore: Ital. *scudo* + *amore*. They are displayed again at IV i 39.1–3 and x 55.1–4. See 'Scudamour' and 'Scudamore family', in the *SEnc*. (Both spellings are used in this canto but afterwards only the first.)

Depeincted: depicted; suggesting 'painted'. **field**: referring to tilt or tournament but with the heraldic sense: Cupid's man is known wherever the surface of the shield displays the winged boy.

Stanza 8
4 abrade: arouse. **5 inuade**: intrude upon.

Stanza 9
2–7 In challenging God's providence, Scudamour ignores S.'s frequent claim that it exceeds human thought, e.g. I vi 7.1 and III v 27.1. See McCabe 1989a:166–67. **vnwreaked**: unavenged. **9 righteousnes**: just deeds.

Stanza 10
2 Amoret: on the name, see vi 28.8–9n and 'Amoret' in the *SEnc*. **3 bounteous**: virtuous. **7 Busirane**: the name, used only here in Bk III, is that of Busiris, a king of Egypt famous for his cruelty (as Warton 1762 first noted), and identified as the Pharaoh of Exodus (e.g. by Sandys 1970:428); and hence a symbol of tyranny (e.g. in Fraunce 1967:4.33, Cupid is called a tyrant whose cruelty surpasses 'Busiris beastlie behauiour'). As a rejected suitor of the daughters of Atlas, he sent pirates to carry them off, as Conti 1616:7.7 records; noted Nohrnberg 1976:477, 643. As the owner of man-eating horses (e.g. Chaucer, *Monk's T.* 2103–04), he was an apt symbol for flesh-devouring lust. In Ovid, *Ars Amat.* 1.657–52, the story of Busiris who slew one who sought the deaths of others illustrates the moral that a woman should feel the wound that first she inflicted; hence Amoret who once wounded her lovers (vi 52.7–9), now suffers under one of them; noted K. Williams 1966:109–10. On the medieval Busire pictured as a wizard who watches murder, see Tuve 1970:133–34. On the link with Osyris, see V vii 2–4n. See also 48.6–9n below. The name has

11

My Lady and my loue is cruelly pend
  In dolefull darkenes from the vew of day,
  Whilest deadly torments doe her chast brest rend,
  And the sharpe steele doth riue her hart in tway,
  All for she *Scudamore* will not denay.
  Yet thou vile man, vile *Scudamore* art sound,
  Ne canst her ayde, ne canst her foe dismay;
  Vnworthy wretch to tread vpon the ground,
For whom so faire a Lady feeles so sore a wound.

12

There an huge heape of singulfes did oppresse
  His strugling soule, and swelling throbs empeach
  His foltring toung with pangs of drerinesse,
  Choking the remnant of his plaintife speach,
  As if his dayes were come to their last reach.
  Which when she heard, and saw the ghastly fit,
  Threatning into his life to make a breach,
  Both with great ruth and terrour she was smit,
Fearing least from her cage the wearie soule would flit.

13

Tho stouping downe she him amoued light;
  Who therewith somewhat starting, vp gan looke,
  And seeing him behind a stranger knight,
  Whereas no liuing creature he mistooke,
  With great indignaunce he that sight forsooke,
  And downe againe himselfe disdainefully
  Abiecting, th'earth with his faire forhead strooke:
  Which the bold Virgin seeing, gan apply
Fit medcine to his griefe, and spake thus courtesly.

14

Ah gentle knight, whose deepe conceiued griefe
  Well seemes t'exceede the powre of patience,
  Yet if that heuenly grace some good reliefe
  You send, submit you to high prouidence,
  And euer in your noble hart prepense,
  That all the sorrow in the world is lesse,
  Then vertues might, and values confidence.
  For who nill bide the burden of distresse,
Must not here thinke to liue: for life is wretchednesse.

15

Therefore, faire Sir, doe comfort to you take,
  And freely read, what wicked felon so
  Hath outrag'd you, and thrald your gentle make.
  Perhaps this hand may helpe to ease your woe,
  And wreake your sorrow on your cruell foe,
  At least it faire endeuour will apply.
  Those feeling words so neare the quicke did goe,
  That vp his head he reared easily,
And leaning on his elbowe, these few words lett fly.

16

What boots it plaine, that cannot be redrest,
  And sow vaine sorrow in a fruitlesse eare,
  Sith powre of hand, nor skill of learned brest,
  Ne worldly price cannot redeeme my deare,
  Out of her thraldome and continuall feare?
  For he the tyrant, which her hath in ward
  By strong enchauntments and blacke Magicke leare,
  Hath in a dungeon deepe her close embard,
And many dreadfull feends hath pointed to her gard.

---

been interpreted as 'Busy-reign', referring to the male imagination seeking to dominate woman's will by art (Berger 1988:173); or involving earlier senses of abuse as 'an imposture, ill-usage, delusion' (Roche 1964:82). See 'Busirane' in the *SEnc*. **8 seuen monethes day**: i.e. seven months (as IV i 4.1), which is given as the length of Florimell's imprisonment at IV xi 4.6. Cf. the seven-year siege of the castle of Alma at II ix 12.8. As a length of time that leads to generation, see Macrobius 1952:1.6.46. **9** The question invokes the answer: 'Loue suffreth long' (1 Cor. 13.4). **to pen**: to imprison but also 'to write with a pen', as Quilligan 1983:198 suggests in noting that Busirane exercises phallic power by 'Figuring straunge characters of his art' with Amoret's blood at xii 31.2. For the implicit pun on 'pen/penis', see also Wofford 1992:308–10, and S. Frye 1993:128–131, 1994:65–68.

Stanza 11

3–5 Amoret's physical state expresses her psychological state. **for**: because. **denay**: in two senses, according to Silberman 1995:63–64: she will not deny her commitment to Scudamour, and not deny him anything. In both senses, her lover and tormentor merge; see xii 31.7n. An obvious third sense is given at 17.3: she denies Busirane her love. **6 vile**: Busirane's epithet at xii 31.1, etc. **7 dismay**: defeat.

Stanza 12

1 singulfes: sobs, apparently coined by S. for its onomatopoetic sob-sound, as Osgood suggests in *Var* 3.426. **2 empeach**: hinder; also 'accuse of treason' (as he is guilty of

her suffering). **3 drerinesse**: anguish. **4 plaintife**: sad; also as he is a plaintiff in his suit. **8** As Belphœbe feels pity and horror when she comes upon the wounded Timias at v 30.5–9: **ruth** or pity leads to love, and **terrour** follows here because Britomart encounters Cupid's man, to whose lord she is victim. In contrast to her shocked response to Malecasta's lust at i 62, she is now prepared to aid love.

Stanza 13

1 amoued: aroused; touched. **3–5** Since he takes her to be a goddess rather than a living creature, he turns away, for in his state of despair he has rejected heavenly aid. Cf. Timias's response to Belphœbe at v 35. **mistooke**: supposed wrongly to be. **indignaunce**: indignation (apparently coined by S.); cf. IV i 30.5. **7 Abiecting**: throwing, suggesting self-abasement; cf. his response to greater grief at 27.6.

Stanza 14

2 Referring also to her own loss of patience at 8.9. **3–4** Repeating Merlin's advice to her at iii 24. **5 prepense**: consider beforehand. **7 values**: valour's. **8 nill**: will not.

Stanza 15

2 read: tell. **3 make**: companion; beloved. **8 easily**: readily.

Stanza 16

1 plaine: to complain. For the proverb that rounds out his complaint, see Smith 14. **3–5** In Bk I, the dragon cannot be wounded 'By subtilty, nor slight, nor might, nor mighty

17

There he tormenteth her most terribly,
   And day and night afflicts with mortall paine,
   Because to yield him loue she doth deny,
   Once to me yold, not to be yolde againe:
   But yet by torture he would her constraine
   Loue to conceiue in her disdainfull brest;
   Till so she doe, she must in doole remaine,
   Ne may by liuing meanes be thence relest:
What boots it then to plaine, that cannot be redrest?

18

With this sad hersall of his heauy stresse,
   The warlike Damzell was empassiond sore,
   And sayd, Sir knight, your cause is nothing lesse,
   Then is your sorrow, certes if not more;
   For nothing so much pitty doth implore,
   As gentle Ladyes helplesse misery.
   But yet, if please ye listen to my lore,
   I will with proofe of last extremity,
Deliuer her fro thence, or with her for you dy.

19

Ah gentlest knight aliue, (sayd *Scudamore*)
   What huge heroicke magnanimity
   Dwells in thy bounteous brest? what couldst thou more,
   If shee were thine, and thou as now am I?

O spare thy happy daies, and them apply
   To better boot, but let me die, that ought;
   More is more losse: one is enough to dy.
   Life is not lost, (said she) for which is bought
Endlesse renowm, that more then death is to be sought.

20

Thus shee at length persuaded him to rise,
   And with her wend, to see what new successe
   Mote him befall vpon new enterprise;
   His armes, which he had vowed to disprofesse,
   She gathered vp, and did about him dresse,
   And his forwandred steed vnto him gott:
   So forth they both yfere make their progresse,
   And march not past the mountenaunce of a shott,
Till they arriu'd, whereas their purpose they did plott.

21

There they dismounting, drew their weapons bold
   And stoutly came vnto the Castle gate;
   Whereas no gate they found, them to withhold,
   Nor ward to wait at morne and euening late,
   But in the Porch, that did them sore amate,
   A flaming fire, ymixt with smouldry smoke,
   And stinking Sulphure, that with griesly hate
   And dreadfull horror did all entraunce choke,
Enforced them their forward footing to reuoke.

---

charme' (I xi 36.9), and the Red Cross Knight triumphs through **powre of hand** empowered by grace. In Bk II, Guyon triumphs over Acrasia by **skill of learned brest**, specifically the power of reason represented by the Palmer. To triumph over Busirane, Britomart must substitute herself as his victim by first passing through the fire that cannot be quenched 'by any witt or might' (23.7). She offers what is for her beyond **worldly price**, namely herself, as ransom or sacrifice, a phrase that in this context invokes 1 Cor. 6.20: 'For ye are boght for a price'. Hence she tells Scudamour that she is ready 'with her for you dy' (18.9). Line 5 suggests that Amoret's **thraldome** is her **continuall feare**, though **For** links her fear to Busirane's **strong enchauntments**, as P. Cheney 1988:21 notes. **6 in ward**: under guard as a prisoner. **7 leare**: lore; art. Cf. the witch's 'wicked leares' at vii 21.7. Amoret's resistance (cf. xii 31.8–9) recapitulates Britomart's: 'loue, that is in gentle brest begonne, | No ydle charmes so lightly may remoue' (ii 51.7–8). Cf. vii 21.1–5. **9 pointed**: appointed.

Stanza 17

1–3 'Busirane had in hand a most faire Lady called Amoretta, whom he kept in most grieuous torment, because she would not yield him the pleasure of her body' (*LR* 74–76). Cf. vi 53, xii 31.6. **4 yolde**: yielded. Repeated to stress her betrothal, as told at IV i 3. **5 torture**: repeated at xii 21.8, and used elsewhere only for the suffering of the damned at II vii 63.4, and of Protestant martyrs during the Inquisition at V xi 19.8. **7 doole**: physical pain; grief or mental distress. **8 liuing meanes**: any living person; anything short of death.

Stanza 18

1 hersall: rehearsal. **stresse**: affliction. **2** As the 'Virgin', she pities him (cf. 8.9); as 'the bold Virgin' (13.8), she seeks the cause of his suffering; as the **warlike Damzell**, she offers herself in battle. **3–4** Your cause is as worthy as your sorrow is great, even more so. **7 lore**: in opposition to Busirane's 'Magicke leare' (16.7). **8** . . . i.e. at the extreme peril of my life, to the utmost point of suffering.

Stanza 19

1 gentlest: noblest; most generous. **2 magnanimity**: lofty courage; literally, doing great deeds. See II viii 23.9*n*. The virtue that appears in Guyon's face dwells in Britomart's breast. **6 boot**: advantage.

Stanza 20

2 successe: fortune. **4 disprofesse**: renounce. **5–6** She anticipates her maternal aid to Artegall at V vii 41. **dresse**: array. **forwandred**: wandered away. **7 progresse**: journey. **8** . . . i.e. a distance not greater than a bow-shot, a unit of measure appropriate for a 'tilt' against Cupid's house, and within a distance that ensures an effective attack.

Stanza 21

4 Nor guard to keep watch . . . **5 amate**: daunt. **6–8** The smoke and burning sulphur suggest hell-fire, as at I v 31.5. **smouldry**: smothering. **hate** implies active malignancy. **choke**: also as it chokes all who enter. **9 reuoke**: draw back.

22

Greatly threat was *Britomart* dismayd,
　Ne in that stownd wist, how her selfe to beare;
　For dāger vaine it were, to haue assayd
　That cruell element, which all things feare,
　Ne none can suffer to approchen neare:
　And turning backe to *Scudamour*, thus sayd;
　What monstrous enmity prouoke we heare,
　Foolhardy, as the Earthes children, which made
Batteill against the Gods? so we a God inuade.

23

Daunger without discretion to attempt,
　Inglorious and beastlike is: therefore Sir knight,
　Aread what course of you is safest dempt,
　And how we with our foe may come to fight.
　This is (quoth he) the dolorous despight,
　Which earst to you I playnd: for neither may
　This fire be quencht by any witt or might,
　Ne yet by any meanes remou'd away;
So mighty be th'enchauntments, which the same do stay.

24

What is there ells, but cease these fruitlesse paines,
　And leaue me to my former languishing?
　Faire *Amorett* must dwell in wicked chaines,
　And *Scudamore* here die with sorrowing.
　Perdy not so; (saide shee) for shameful thing
　Yt were t'abandon noble cheuisaunce,
　For shewe of perill, without venturing:
　Rather let try extremities of chaunce,
Then enterprised praise for dread to disauaunce.

25

Therewith resolu'd to proue her vtmost might,
　Her ample shield she threw before her face,
　And her swords point directing forward right,
　Assayld the flame, the which eftesoones gaue place,
　And did it selfe diuide with equall space,
　That through she passed, as a thonder bolt
　Perceth the yielding ayre, and doth displace
　The soring clouds into sad showres ymolt;
So to her yold the flames, and did their force reuolt.

26

Whome whenas *Scudamour* saw past the fire,
　Safe and vntoucht, he likewise gan assay,
　With greedy will, and enuious desire, *not chast*
　And bad the stubborne flames to yield him way:
　But cruell *Mulciber* would not obay
　His threatfull pride, but did the more augment
　His mighty rage, and with imperious sway
　Him forst (maulgre) his fercenes to relent,
And backe retire, all scorcht and pitifully brent.

27

With huge impatience he inly swelt,
　More for great sorrow, that he could not pas,
　Then for the burning torment, which he felt,
　That with fell woodnes he effierced was,
　And wilfully him throwing on the gras,
　Did beat and bounse his head and brest ful sore;
　The whiles the Championesse now decked has
　The vtmost rowme, and past the formest dore,
The vtmost rowme, abounding with all precious store.

Stanza 22
1 dismayd: the implicit pun becomes overt at xii 37.3. The mood is temporary for soon she follows Merlin's advice: 'let no whit thee dismay | The hard beginne, that meetes thee in the dore' (iii 21.7–8).　**2 stownd**: time of sudden peril.　**7 prouoke**: challenge, defy; also the usual sense, for Scudamour's approach arouses the flames.　**8–9** On the war of the Titans against the Gods, see vii 47.3–5n. The **God** is either Mulciber, the God of fire (26.5), or Cupid who arouses the flames of love. The Titans were defeated by Jove's thunderbolt, to which Britomart's spear is compared at 25.6.

Stanza 23
3 Aread: declare.　**dempt**: deemed.　**9 stay**: support.

Stanza 24
6 cheuisaunce: chivalric enterprise to gain booty; see II ix 8.1–4n.　**9** 'Than retreat through dread from praiseworthy action already begun'. She summarizes her claim at 5–7, and confirms her vow at 18.8–9.

Stanza 25
Her earlier despair that nothing could 'my flame relent' (ii 43.4) describes Scudamour's present state, but now she controls the flame that love aroused in her at ii 37, 52. Sexual symbolism requires that the fire be at the porch rather than

surrounding the house. On the significance of crossing the threshold, see Gross 1985:157–60, and 'thresholds' in the *SEnc*.　**3** Since Britomart is on foot, her extended sword substitutes for her 'enchaunted speare' (i 9.9). There are Christian overtones of the shield of faith that quenches 'all the fyrie dartes of the wicked' (Eph. 6.16).　**5** . . . i.e. equally on both sides.　**8 sad showres**: heavy downpour.　**ymolt**: melted.　**9 reuolt**: turn back.

Stanza 26
3 He fails because Amoret's love of him has caused her to be wounded, as he acknowledges at 11.9; and also because his **will** and **desire** have caused the flames, as Evans 1970:160 notes; cf. Spens 1934:105.　**enuious desire**: also desire to emulate Britomart.　**8 maulgre**: in spite of himself, or of his fierceness.

Stanzas 27–xii 29
After passing through the fire, Britomart progresses through three rooms. The first displays tapestries depicting the loves of the gods and contains a statue of Cupid. Behind the statue (see 50.1–4n) is a door over which is written, '*Bee bold*', and, on its other side, the same motto repeated many times. Through it, she enters a room overlaid with gold, decorated with monstrous forms of love, and adorned with the spoils of captains and conquerors. On – rather than above – an iron door leading to

28

For round about, the walls yclothed were
  With goodly arras of great maiesty,
  Wouen with gold and silke so close and nere,
  That the rich metall lurked priuily,
  As faining to be hidd from enuious eye;
  Yet here, and there, and euery where vnwares
  It shewd it selfe, and shone vnwillingly;
  Like to a discoulourd Snake, whose hidden snares
Through the greene gras his long bright burnisht back
                         (declares.

29

And in those Tapets weren fashioned
  Many faire pourtraicts, and many a faire feate,
  And all of loue, and al of lusty-hed,
  As seemed by their semblaunt did entreat;
  And eke all *Cupids* warres they did repeate,
  And cruell battailes, which he whilome fought
  Gainst all the Gods, to make his empire great;
  Besides the huge massacres, which he wrought
On mighty kings and kesars, into thraldome brought.

30

Therein was writt, how often thondring *Ioue*
  Had felt the point of his hart percing dart,
  And leauing heauens kingdome, here did roue
  In straunge disguize, to slake his scalding smart;
  Now like a Ram, faire *Helle* to peruart,
  Now like a Bull, *Europa* to withdraw:
  Ah, how the fearefull Ladies tender hart
  Did liuely seeme to tremble, when she saw
The huge seas vnder her t'obay her seruaunts law.

31

Soone after that into a golden showre
  Him selfe he chaung'd, faire *Danaë* to vew,
  And through the roofe of her strong brasen towre
  Did raine into her lap an hony dew,
  The whiles her foolish garde, that litle knew
  Of such deceipt, kept th'yron dore fast bard,
  And watcht, that none should enter nor issew;
  Vaine was the watch, and bootlesse all the ward,
Whenas the God to golden hew him selfe transfard.

the third, inmost room is written, '*Be not too bold*' (54.8), and from it issues Cupid's masque. She enters this room at midnight of the second night, i.e. at the beginning of the third day, and there sees Amoret being tortured by Busirane.

Stanza 27

1 inly swelt: inwardly burned, corresponding to being outwardly burned; the two merging in **burning torment**. **4 fell woodnes**: fierce fury. **effierced**: maddened, made more fierce. **6 bounse**: thump. **7 the Championesse**: Britomart's title, reserved for her alone. **decked**: entered *1596*. The *1590* reading was defended by Collier 1862 because Britomart adorned the room, but the revision is clearly correct. **8 vtmost**: outermost. **formest**: foremost.

Stanzas 28–46

The tapestries, which show 'How diuersly loue doth his pageaunts play' (v 1.2; cf. 35.5 below), are drawn from Ovid, *Met.*, chiefly 6.103–28, which describes those woven by Arachne in her contest with Minerva; from mythological handbooks and dictionaries (see Starnes and Talbert 1955); and from contemporary tapestries (see 'visual arts' in the *SEnc*). For the technique of describing a painting in words, see DuBois 1982:81–86, and 'ecphrasis' and 'pictorialism' in the *SEnc*. A. Fowler 1964:150–53 traces a numerological pattern similar to that in the masque of Cupid (see xii 7–25*n*) in the total of thirty-three gods and lovers.

Stanza 28

1–2 The similar description of the tapestries seen by Britomart in Castle Joyeous at i 34.1–2 links the two episodes. **of great maiesty**: implying that it would befit a sovereign. **3 nere**: tightly-woven. **4–7** The description carefully distinguishes the arras from Medua's dress at IV xi 45.8–9, and from the false art of the Bower of Bliss at II xii 58.9. **faining**: desiring and feigning not to be seen; 'its bad faith is deconstructed in

its very manifestation', as Hollander 1995:17 notes. Cf. Barkan 1986:236–37. **vnwares**: unexpectedly. **8 discolourd**: variously coloured. **9** The line's movement measures the snake's length.

Stanza 29

1 Tapets: tapestries. **2 pourtraicts**: pictures, designs. **4 entreat**: treat; entice others to indulge in, as at II vii 53.5. **5–7** In his war against the gods, Cupid acts as another Titan; cf. 22.8–9. **repeate**: celebrate; recount.

Stanza 30

1 writt: drawn, i.e. woven. **5** This story of the first of Jove's twelve metamorphoses seems to have been invented by S. Ovid, *Fasti* 3.851–76, records that Helle was saved from being sacrificed when a golden ram carried her away, though not to safety because she fell into what became known as the Hellespont. See V proem 5.6–7. It may have been suggested to him by Boccaccio 1976:4.68, as Lotspeich 1932 notes, who associates the constellation Aries (the Ram) with Jove as a lover. **peruart**: turn away, both literally and morally. **6–9** The **Bull** is the zodiacal sign of Taurus, which follows the Ram; see VII vii 32–33. Hence the paralleling of lines 5 and 6. **liuely**: lifelike. **seruaunts**: lover's. Instead of fearing rape, she fears her own power.

Stanza 31

Ovid notes only that Jupiter *aureus ut Danaen . . . luserit*. S. may have taken the details from Conti 1616:7.18, as Lotspeich 1932 claims; or from Stephanus, *Dictionarium*, as Starnes and Talbert 1955:85 claim. **1 Soone after**: i.e. in another part of the tapestry. **4 hony dew**: 'an ideally sweet or luscious substance; often like dew, represented as falling' (*OED* 2). **9 hew**: shape. **transfard**: i.e. transformed; or transferred into another body; cf. 'transmoue' (43.5).

32

Then was he turnd into a snowy Swan,
　To win faire *Leda* to his louely trade:
　O wondrous skill, and sweet wit of the man,
　That her in daffadillies sleeping made,
　From scorching heat her daintie limbes to shade:
　Whiles the proud Bird ruffing his fethers wyde,
　And brushing his faire brest, did her inuade;
　Shee slept, yet twixt her eielids closely spyde,
How towards her he rusht, and smiled at his pryde.

33

Then shewd it, how the *Thebane Semelee*
　Deceiud of gealous *Iuno*, did require
　To see him in his souerayne maiestee,
　Armd with his thunderbolts and lightning fire,
　Whens dearely she with death bought her desire.
　But faire *Alcmena* better match did make,
　Ioying his loue in likenes more entire;
　Three nights in one, they say, that for her sake
He then did put, her pleasures lenger to partake.

34

Twise was he seene in soaring Eagles shape,
　And with wide winges to beat the buxome ayre,
　Once, when he with *Asterie* did scape,
　Againe, when as the *Troiane* boy so fayre
　He snatch from *Ida* hill, and with him bare:
　Wondrous delight it was, there to behould,
　How the rude Shepheards after him did stare,
　Trembling through feare, least down he fallen should
And often to him calling, to take surer hould.

35

In *Satyres* shape *Antiopa* he snatch:
　And like a fire, when he *Ægin'* assayd.
　A shepeheard, when *Mnemosyne* he catcht:
　And like a Serpent to the *Thracian* mayd.

Whyles thus on earth great *Ioue* these pageaunts playd,
　The winged boy did thrust into his throne,
　And scoffing, thus vnto his mother sayd,
　Lo now the heuens obey to me alone,
And take me for their *Ioue*, whiles *Ioue* to earth is gone.

36

And thou, faire *Phœbus*, in thy colours bright
　Wast there enwouen, and the sad distresse,
　In which that boy thee plonged, for despight,
　That thou bewray'dst his mothers wantonnesse,
　When she with *Mars* was meynt in ioyfulnesse:
　For thy he thrild thee with a leaden dart,
　To loue faire *Daphne*, which thee loued lesse:
　Lesse she thee lou'd, then was thy iust desart,
Yet was thy loue her death, and her death was thy smart.

37

So louedst thou the lusty *Hyacinct*,
　So louedst thou the faire *Coronis* deare:
　Yet both are of thy haplesse hand extinct,
　Yet both in flowres doe liue; and loue thee beare,
　The one a Paunce, the other a sweet breare:
　For griefe whereof, ye mote haue liuely seene
　The God himselfe rending his golden heare,
　And breaking quite his garlond euer greene,
With other signes of sorrow and impatient teene.

38

Both for those two, and for his owne deare sonne,
　The sonne of *Climene* he did repent,
　Who bold to guide the charet of the Sunne,
　Himselfe in thousand peeces fondly rent,
　And all the world with flashing fire brent:
　So like, that all the walles did seeme to flame.
　Yet cruell *Cupid*, not herewith content,
　Forst him eftsoones to follow other game,
And loue a Shephards daughter for his dearest Dame.

Stanza 32
2 louely trade: amorous dealings.　**3 wit**: ingenuity. The **sweet wit** is S.'s as he expands Ovid's six words (109) into six lines.　**6–7 ruffing**: ruffling; bristling.　**brushing**: preening itself in (sexual) pride.　**inuade**: in the Lat. sense, 'enter'.　**9** The smile conveys her **pryde** at his, with the specific sense, 'sexual desire' (*OED* 11).

Stanza 33
2 require: request.　**6–9 better match**: because she enjoyed three nights of love rather than being instantly consumed as was Semele; or because Hercules was conceived rather than Bacchus.　**entire**: perfect, containing all that is desirable because he appeared to her in the likeness of her husband. Conti 1616:6.1 grants him the extra night.

Stanza 34
2 buxome: yielding, unresisting.　**4–9** Virgil, *Aen.* 5.252–57, places Jove's rape of Ganymede on Mount Ida and tells of his guardians pleading for him with outstretched hands.

Stanza 35
1–4 Following Ovid's order but omitting Alcmena and Danaë whose rapes have already been recorded.　**the Thracian mayd** is Proserpina.

Stanza 36
4–9 According to *Met.* 4.171–97, **Phœbus** (or Apollo) was punished for revealing Venus's adultery to Vulcan by being made to dote upon Leucothoë. In her place, S. substitutes his first love, Daphne (*Met.* 1.452–76); and for Cupid's golden dart, the leaden dart which causes unhappy love: see 48.4. As a result, he causes the death of the first four of the eight whom he loves.　**meynt**: joined in sexual intercourse.　**For thy**: therefore.　**thrild**: pierced.　**lesse**: too little, as shown by her flight.

Stanza 37
1 lusty: beautiful. On **Hyacinct**, see vi 45.3–4*n*.　**2** In *Met.* 2.600, the laurel garland only falls from his head when he learns of her unchastity.　**5 Paunce**: the pansy, or love-in-

39

He loued *Isse* for his dearest Dame,
    And for her sake her cattell fedd a while,
    And for her sake a cowheard vile became,
    The seruant of *Admetus* cowheard vile,
    Whiles that from heauen he suffered exile.
    Long were to tell his other louely fitt,
    Now like a Lyon, hunting after spoile,
    Now like a Stag, now like a faulcon flit:
All which in that faire arras was most liuely writ.

40

Next vnto him was *Neptune* pictured,
    In his diuine resemblance wondrous lyke:
    His face was rugged, and his hoarie hed
    Dropped with brackish deaw; his threeforkt Pyke
    He stearnly shooke, and therewith fierce did stryke
    The raging billowes, that on euery syde
    They trembling stood, and made a long broad dyke,
    That his swift charet might haue passage wyde,
Which foure great *Hippodames* did draw in temewise tyde.

41

His seahorses did seeme to snort amayne,
    And from their nosethrilles blow the brynie streame,
    That made the sparckling waues to smoke agayne,
    And flame with gold, but the white fomy creame,
    Did shine with siluer, and shoot forth his beame.
    The God himselfe did pensiue seeme and sad,
    And hong adowne his head, as he did dreame:
    For priuy loue his brest empierced had,
Ne ought but deare *Bisaltis* ay could make him glad.

42

He loued eke *Iphimedia* deare,
    And *Aeolus* faire daughter *Arne* hight,
    For whom he turnd him selfe into a Steare,
    And fedd on fodder, to beguile her sight.
    Also to win *Deucalions* daughter bright,
    He turnd him selfe into a Dolphin fayre;
    And like a winged horse he tooke his flight,
    To snaky-locke *Medusa* to repayre,
On whom he got faire *Pegasus*, that flitteth in the ayre.

43

Next *Saturne* was, (but who would euer weene,
    That sullein *Saturne* euer weend to loue?
    Yet loue is sullein, and *Saturnlike* seene,
    As he did for *Erigone* it proue.)
    That to a *Centaure* did him selfe transmoue.
    So prou'd it eke that gratious God of wine,
    When for to compasse *Philliras* hard loue,
    He turnd himselfe into a fruitfull vine,
And into her faire bosome made his grapes decline.

44

Long were to tell the amorous assayes,
    And gentle pangues, with which he maked meeke
    The mightie *Mars*, to learne his wanton playes:
    How oft for *Venus*, and how often eek
    For many other Nymphes he sore did shreek,
    With womanish teares, and with vnwarlike smarts,
    Priuily moystening his horrid cheeke.
    There was he painted full of burning dartes,
And many wide woundes launched through his inner partes.

---

idleness, which is purple, like the hyacinth into which he was transformed. **sweet breare**, or eglantine; not in Ovid but an appropriate choice because of its association with Elizabeth; see Strong 1977:68–71. **6 liuely**: lifelike.

Stanza 38

2 sonne of Climene: Phaethon; see I iv 9 and *n*. **4 fondly rent**: i.e. was torn because, foolishly, he wished to guide the sun's chariot. **6 like**: lifelike.

Stanza 39

1–5 Two stories about Phœbus are combined: his disguise as a shepherd to trick **Isse**, and 'being exiled out of heauen by Jupiter, [he] came for reliefe [to Admetus] and kept his cattel' (T. Cooper 1565). **Admetus** is a shepherd in Conti 1616:4.10 but deserves to be called **cowheard vile** because he allowed his wife to descend into hell in his place. **6 louely fitt**: amorous passion. **7–8** Ovid mentions Phœbus's transformations only into a hawk and a lion. Jortin 1734 supports the emendation of Hag *1590*, *1596* to **Stag** by citing Conti 4.10.

Stanza 40

The description of **Neptune** as God of the Seas with his trident and chariot is traditional – cf. Virgil, *Aen*. 1.145–56, 5.817–24 – except for naming the sea horses who draw his

chariot **Hippodames**: see II ix 50.7–9*n*.   **9 in temewise**: as a team.

Stanza 41

1 amayne: with all their might.   **6–9** Based on three words in *Met*. 6.117.

Stanza 42

S. expands Ovid, perhaps by consulting Regius's commentary, as Lotspeich 1932 suggests. **7–9 snaky-locke**: Medusa's punishment for defiling Minerva's temple when she was ravished there by Neptune, *Met*. 4.798–803.

Stanza 43

The stories of **Erigone** and **Phillira** (Philyra) are juxtaposed in Ovid, but their names have been reversed, perhaps by the printer, as Upton 1758 suggests. **1 weene**: suppose. **2 sullein**: a characterizing epithet; see II ix 52.8–9*n*. **weend**: was minded. **5 Centaure**: a type of lust. **transmoue**: transform, literally move into another; cf. 31.9. **6 gratious**: attractive. **8–9** In Ovid, Bacchus only offers grapes to Erigone. A similar temptation is found at the porch of the Bower of Bliss (II xii 54).

Stanza 44

1 assayes: assaults.   **7 horrid**: rough, bristling.

45

Ne did he spare (so cruell was the Elfe)
    His owne deare mother, (ah why should he so?)
    Ne did he spare sometime to pricke himselfe,
    That he might taste the sweet consuming woe,
    Which he had wrought to many others moe.
    But to declare the mournfull Tragedyes,
    And spoiles, wherewith he all the ground did strow,
    More eath to number, with how many eyes
High heuen beholdes sad louers nightly theeueryes.

46

Kings Queenes, Lords Ladies, Knights and Damsels gent
    Were heap'd together with the vulgar sort,
    And mingled with the raskall rablement,
    Without respect of person or of port,
    To shew Dan *Cupids* powre and great effort:
    And round about a border was entrayld,
    Of broken bowes and arrowes shiuered short,
    And a long bloody riuer through them rayld,
So liuely and so like, that liuing sence it fayld.

47

And at the vpper end of that faire rowme,
    There was an Altar built of pretious stone,
    Of passing valew, and of great renowme,
    On which there stood an Image all alone,
    Of massy gold, which with his owne light shone;
    And winges it had with sondry colours dight,
    More sondry colours, then the proud *Pauone*
    Beares in his boasted fan, or *Iris* bright,
When her discolourd bow she spreds through heuen bright.

48

Blyndfold he was, and in his cruell fist
    A mortall bow and arrowes keene did hold,
    With which he shot at randon, when him list,
    Some headed with sad lead, some with pure gold;
    (Ah man beware, how thou those dartes behold)
    A wounded Dragon vnder him did ly,
    Whose hideous tayle his lefte foot did enfold,
    And with a shaft was shot through either eye,
That no man forth might draw, ne no man remedye.

49

And vnderneath his feet was written thus,
    Vnto the Victor of the Gods this bee:
    And all the people in that ample hous
    Did to that image bowe their humble knee,
    And oft committed fowle Idolatree,
    That wondrous sight faire *Britomart* amazd,
    Ne seeing could her wonder satisfie,
    But euermore and more vpon it gazd,
The whiles the passing brightnes her fraile sences dazd.

50

Tho as she backward cast her busie eye,
    To search each secrete of that goodly sted,
    Ouer the dore thus written she did spye
    Bee bold: she oft and oft it ouer-red,
    Yet could not find what sence it figured:
    But what so were therein, or writ or ment,
    She was no whit thereby discouraged,
    From prosecuting of her first intent,
But forward with bold steps into the next roome went.

Stanza 45
7 **ground**: background of the mythological scenes; the fabric itself   **8–9** A close rendering of Ariosto, *Orl. Fur.* 14.99.7–8, and a reminder that God 'counteth the number of the starres' (Ps. 147.4).   **eath**: easy.

Stanza 46
1 **gent**: noble, gentle.   **2 sort**: company.   **4 port**: social position.   **5 effort**: strength.   **6–9** The usual decorative border of a Renaissance tapestry is here doubly **entrayld** (i.e. entwined or woven), first, with Diana's **arrowes**, which are broken to signify Cupid's power over chastity (as in Chaucer, *Parl. Fowls* 281–84, where broken bows hang on the wall of the temple of Venus 'in dispit of Dyane the chaste'); second, with a **bloody riuer** that is associated with the death of Adonis (as in Lucian, *The Goddesse of Surrye* 8). **rayld**: flowed. **like**: lifelike. **fayld**: deceived; caused to fail.

Stanza 47
3 **passing**: surpassing.   **5 massy**: solid.   **6 dight**: adorned. **7–9** Both comparisons suggest that Cupid's wings are spread wide, as they are on Scudamour's shield at IV i 39.3. In *SC March* 80, Cupid appears 'With spotted winges like Peacocks trayne'. **Pauone**: Ital. peacock. **discolourd**: many-coloured.

Stanza 48
On the blindfolded (e.g. xii 22.6) or blind (e.g. iv 9.9) Cupid, see Panofsky 1962:95–128, Wind 1967:53–80, and 'Cupid' in

the *SEnc*. On the theodicy of Cupid in the Busirane episode, see Hyde 1986:173–75.   **4** These arrows are interpreted by E.K. on *SC March* 79 as 'both pleasure for the gracious and loved, and sorow for the lover that is disdayned or forsaken'. **sad**: heavy; causing sorrow.   **6–9** As the guardian of chastity who protects the golden fruit of the Hesperian tree, the **Dragon** serves the virgin goddess Minerva: see Alciati 1985: emblem 22: *Custodiendas virgines* (Virgins must be guarded); see also 'dragon, Cupid's', and the illus. in the *SEnc*. Now serving Cupid and blinded by his arrows, it no longer guards chastity. Its tail placed over Cupid's left foot marks their collusion. Its incurable wound suggests that Amoret's wound through love of '*Cupids* man' (IV x 54.7) will never be healed.

Stanza 49
6–9 A comparable moment is Psyche's first vision of Cupid: 'shee greatly feared, and amazed in mind, with a pale countenance all trembling fel on her knees' (Apuleius tr. 1566:108). **passing**: surpassing.

Stanza 50
1–4 backward: i.e. behind the statue rather than back to the door through which she entered the room; 'that same dore' (54.2) indicates that this door, which is inscribed **Bee bold** on the side facing the first room, leads into the next room where its other side repeats that inscription many times. **sted**: place. **9** At the outset of her quest, the love that guides Britomart is called 'bold and blinde' (iv 9.9), and now is seen as the blindfolded Cupid who claims to be '*the Victor of the Gods*' (49.2).

51

Much fayrer, then the former, was that roome,
  And richlier by many partes arayd:
  For not with arras made in painefull loome,
  But with pure gold it all was ouerlayd,
  Wrought with wilde Antickes, which their follies playd,
  In the rich metall, as they liuing were:
  A thousand monstrous formes therein were made,
  Such as false loue doth oft vpon him weare,
For loue in thousand monstrous formes doth oft appeare.

52

And all about, the glistring walles were hong
  With warlike spoiles, and with victorious prayes,
  Of mightie Conquerours and Captaines strong,
  Which were whilome captiued in their dayes,
  To cruell loue, and wrought their owne decayes:
  Their swerds and speres were broke, and hauberques rent
  And their proud girlonds of tryumphant bayes,
  Troden in dust with fury insolent,
To shew the victors might and mercilesse intent.

53

The warlike Mayd beholding earnestly
  The goodly ordinaunce of this rich Place,
  Did greatly wonder, ne could satisfy
  Her greedy eyes with gazing a long space,

But more she meruaild that no footings trace,
  Nor wight appear'd, but wastefull emptinesse,
  And solemne silence ouer all that place:
  Straunge thing it seem'd, that none was to possesse
So rich purueyaunce, ne them keepe with carefulnesse.

54

And as she lookt about, she did behold,
  How ouer that same dore was likewise writ,
  Be bolde, be bolde, and euery where *Be bold,*
  That much she muz'd, yet could not construe it
  By any ridling skill, or commune wit.
  At last she spyde at that rowmes vpper end,
  Another yron dore, on which was writ,
  Be not too bold; whereto though she did bend
Her earnest minde, yet wist not what it might intend.

55

Thus she there wayted vntill euentyde,
  Yet liuing creature none she saw appeare:
  And now sad shadowes gan the world to hyde
  From mortall vew, and wrap in darkenes dreare;
  Yet nould she d'off her weary armes, for feare
  Of secret daunger, ne let sleepe oppresse
  Her heauy eyes with natures burdein deare,
  But drew her selfe aside in sickernesse,
And her welpointed wepons did about her dresse.

At the beginning of the episode, she is called 'the bold Virgin' (13.8); now she obeys the motto on the door as she enters the second room **with bold steps**. For Scudamour's corresponding boldness, which requires her present boldness, see IV x 4.6n, 54.2n.

Stanza 51
2 . . . i.e. by many times. 3 . . . made painstakingly on a loom. **4–6** These figures seem to be embossed or in bas-relief, in contrast to the 'deepe impression' (iii 2.7) made by true love. Cf. the 'figures hideous' into which Acrasia's victims are turned at II xii 85.4. **Antickes**: grotesque figures, the product of fancy. The pun on the antique source of the representation is noted by Barkan 1986:234. **playd**: acted out. **as they liuing were**: in contrast to the tapestry figures that are only 'liuely', i.e. lifelike, as 30.8, 37.6, etc. **7–9 A thousand monstrous formes**: referring to Love's 'straunge aray, | Disguiz'd in thousand shapes' (vi 11.8–9) when he wanders in the world.

Stanza 52
2 **prayes**: booty. **5 decayes**: downfall; implying suicide, as in the house of Pride (I v 51.9).

Stanza 53
2 **ordinaunce**: warlike equipment. **5–7** Apparently those who live in the house of Busirane crowd into the first room (49.3–5), leaving this room **wastefull**, i.e. uninhabited. **solemne silence**: as in the house of Orgoglio (I viii 29.8). **9 purueyaunce**: array, furnishings.

Stanza 54
The mottoes derive from the 'old tale' of Bluebeard to which Shakespeare refers in *Much Ado* 1.1.216, as earlier editors have noted. See 'folklore' in the *SEnc*. According to one English nursery tale version, when Lady Mary visited the eerily empty castle of her betrothed, the mysterious Mr Fox, she saw written over the portal of the hall and elsewhere, 'Be bold, be bold but not too bold', until she came to a door on which the inscription added: 'lest that your heart's blood should run cold'. Upon opening this door, she found the room filled with the skeletons and tubs of blood of his former brides. For a comparison of Lady Mary's situation and Britomart's, see Watson 1999:287–88 and Lamb 2000:97–99. The sexual significance of the **yron dore** gives **bold** the sense of 'immodest'. Again Britomart obeys Merlin's injunction at iii 21.7–9. That she will ignore the injunction, **Be not too bold**, is shown by her resolve to 'try extremities of chaunce' (24.8). Analogous is Venus's advice to Adonis to 'Bee bold' in hunting small game but to 'forbeare too bold too bee' in hunting the boar (Ovid, *Met.* 10.628–30, tr. Golding). **5 commune wit**: common sense. See IV x 2.4n. **7** The distinction between **on which** as distinct from **ouer** (cf. 50.3) may be owing to the folktale or the demands of the decasyllabic line. **9 intend**: mean.

Stanza 55
5–9 In contrast to her action at Castle Joyeous, III i 58.6–9. **nould**: would not. **sickernesse**: security. **welpointed**: ready at hand; sharp, as 25.3. **dresse**: make ready.

Cant. XII.

The maske of Cupid, and th'enchanted
Chamber are displayd,
Whence Britomart redeemes faire
Amoret, through charmes decayd.

1

THo when as chearelesse Night ycouered had
  Fayre heauen with an vniuersall clowd,
  That euery wight dismayd with darkenes sad,
  In silence and in sleepe themselues did shrowd,
  She heard a shrilling Trompet sound alowd,
  Signe of nigh battaill, or got victory;
  Nought therewith daunted was her courage prowd,
  But rather stird to cruell enmity,
Expecting euer, when some foe she might descry.

2

With that, an hideous storme of winde arose,
  With dreadfull thunder and lightning atwixt,
  And an earthquake, as if it streight would lose
  The worlds foundations from his centre fixt;
  A direfull stench of smoke and sulphure mixt
  Ensewd, whose noyaunce fild the fearefull sted,
  From the fourth howre of night vntill the sixt;
  Yet the bold *Britonesse* was nought ydred,
Though much emmou'd, but stedfast still perseuered.

3

All suddeinly a stormy whirlwind blew
  Throughout the house, that clapped euery dore,
  With which that yron wicket open flew,
  As it with mighty leuers had bene tore:
  And forth yssewd, as on the readie flore
  Of some Theatre, a graue personage,
  That in his hand a braunch of laurell bore,
  With comely haueour and count'nance sage,
Yclad in costly garments, fit for tragicke Stage.

4

Proceeding to the midst, he stil did stand,
  As if in minde he somewhat had to say,
  And to the vulgare beckning with his hand,
  In signe of silence, as to heare a play,
  By liuely actions he gan bewray
  Some argument of matter passioned;
  Which doen, he backe retyred soft away,
  And passing by, his name discouered,
Ease, on his robe in golden letters cyphered.

Book III Canto xii

Argument

1 The maske of Cupid: here a form of a masque (called 'that mask of loue' at IV i 3.6) in which emblematic figures remain mute (see 7–25n) and the presenter is dressed 'fit for tragicke Stage' of 'some Theatre' (3.5–9). It combines the medieval processional form of the court of Love, with his followers and victims, and the Renaissance triumph in which Cupid displays his spoils. See E.B. Fowler 1921:108–31. As a form of a Petrarchan triumph, it is announced by a trumpet at 1.5. On its similarities to the masque of Cupid in *Amadis de Gaule*, see O'Connor 1970:173–81. See 'masque' in the *SEnc*. **4 decayd**: physically wasted away.

Stanza 1

8 cruell: fierce. **9 Expecting euer**: always waiting and remaining on guard.

Stanza 2

1–6 Heralding the appearance of the god of love, as the appearance of God in 1 Kings 19.11–12 is heralded by strong wind, earthquake, and fire, and in Exod. 19.16–18 by thunder, lightning, thick cloud, and 'the sound of the trumpet exceding loude'. (There may be a topical allusion to the earthquake in England on 6 April 1580, which is treated by Harvey in the *Three Letters*, as a *cause célèbre*; see Snare 1970.) As always, smoke and sulphur suggest hell-fire; cf. xi 21.6–7. **atwixt**: i.e. accompanying the wind. **centre fixt**: fixed centre. **noyaunce**: annoyance. **fild**: also defiled. **sted**: place. **7** Night was divided into four watches, each of three hours, beginning at 6 p.m. See, e.g. the Geneva gloss to Matt. 14.25, and the four divisions at Mark 13.35. Following the two-hour storm, the masque begins at midnight; cf. 29.6. In Castle Joyeous, Britomart was also tested at midnight; see i 57.6–9. **8 bold**: as the inscription (xi 54.3) demands; cf. 29.8, and see xi 50.9n. **9 perseuered**: remained.

Stanza 3

2 clapped: slammed. **3 that yron wicket**: the 'yron dore' at xi 54.7. **5 readie**: i.e. awaiting the performance, applied to the stage and to the assumed audience. **8 haueour**: bearing.

Stanza 4

2 somewhat: something. **3 vulgare**: the groundlings, here represented by Britomart though she remains concealed (27.4–5). **5–9** In his role as presenter, Ease functions as does Idleness in the pageant of the sins in the house of Pride (I iv 18–20). Since he introduces the masque by leading it, his name is **cyphered** (written) on the back of his robe. As in a dumb show, he mimes its **argument** through gestures. **passioned**: expressing passion.

5

The noble Mayd, still standing all this vewd,
  And merueild at his straunge intendiment;
  With that a ioyous fellowship issewd
  Of Minstrales, making goodly meriment,
  With wanton Bardes, and Rymers impudent,
  All which together song full chearefully
  A lay of loues delight, with sweet concent:
  After whom marcht a iolly company,
In manner of a maske, enranged orderly.

6

The whiles a most delitious harmony,
  In full straunge notes was sweetly heard to sound,
  That the rare sweetnesse of the melody
  The feeble sences wholy did confound,
  And the frayle soule in deepe delight nigh drownd:
  And when it ceast, shrill trompets lowd did bray,
  That their report did far away rebound,
  And when they ceast, it gan againe to play,
The whiles the maskers marched forth in trim aray.

7

The first was Fansy, like a louely Boy,
  Of rare aspect, and beautie without peare,
  Matchable ether to that ympe of *Troy*,
  Whom *Ioue* did loue, and chose his cup to beare,

Or that same daintie lad, which was so deare
To great *Alcides*, that when as he dyde,
He wailed womanlike with many a teare,
And euery wood, and euery valley wyde
He fild with *Hylas* name; the Nymphes eke *Hylas* cryde.

8

His garment nether was of silke nor say,
  But paynted plumes, in goodly order dight,
  Like as the sunburnt *Indians* do aray
  Their tawney bodies, in their proudest plight:
  As those same plumes, so seemd he vaine and light,
  That by his gate might easily appeare;
  For still he far'd as dauncing in delight,
  And in his hand a windy fan did beare,
That in the ydle ayre he mou'd still here and theare.

9

And him beside marcht amorous *Desyre*,
  Who seemd of ryper yeares, then th'other Swayne,
  Yet was that other swayne this elders syre,
  And gaue him being, commune to them twayne:
  His garment was disguysed very vayne,
  And his embrodered Bonet sat awry;
  Twixt both his hands few sparks he close did strayne,
  Which still he blew, and kindled busily,
That soone they life conceiu'd, and forth in flames did fly.

Stanza 5

2 intendiment: purpose, intent. **3 fellowship**: company. **5 impudent**: shameless. **7 concent**: harmony; but also, as consent *1596* suggests, yielding to love. **9 enranged**: arranged.

Stanza 6

1–5 The same enervating music is heard in Castle Joyeous at i 40.1–6. **7 rebound**: re-echo.

Stanzas 7–25

As in the pageant of the sins in the house of Pride, the masquers move 'enranged orderly' (5.9) in couples and in two lines. All couples march except Fansy who dances. Arranged in six pairs, they provide an anatomy of sexual corruption, as Broaddus 1995:91–93 argues. Each carries an appropriate emblem and, except for the final pair, each is symbolically arrayed. On their order and significance, see Roche 1964:78–80 and A. Fowler 1964:148–50. Except for the two leading male couples (Fansy and Desyre, Doubt and Daunger), they are male and female, wittily varied as either well or evilly matched. They act out Amoret's suffering, corresponding to Scudamour's suffering; see xi 7–25*n*.

Cupid is at the centre both of his own party and of the masquers, as he should be in a triumph of love, forming a party of thirteen described in thirteen stanzas (4, 7–18), as Fowler notes. See xi 28–46*n*. Amoret, in a group of three, is thirteenth, described in three stanzas (19–21), followed by Cupid (22–23), and (in an anti-masque) three figures who are described (24) and thirteen who are catalogued (25). On the

numerical significance of this 13/3/Cupid/3/13 grouping, see A. Fowler 1970:47–58. Britomart is 'maske[d] in strange disguise' (iii 51.9) but remains apart as a hidden spectator. On the relation of the masque to *Amoretti*, see W.C. Johnson 1992. See also 'masque of Cupid' in the *SEnc*.

Stanza 7

1 Fansy: the power of the imagination to deceive with false images, here of love, as 'falsed fancy' (I ii 30.3) leads the Red Cross Knight to prefer Duessa to Una; or love of a capricious and wanton nature, as in Malecasta's 'flit fancy' (i 56.1). When Britomart first sees Artegall, she is left 'full of fancies fraile' (ii 27.5; cf. 48.8–9, iv 5.7–9). See 'imagination' in the *SEnc*. **3 that ympe of Troy**: Ganymede; see xi 34.4–9. **5–9 that same daintie lad**: Hylas. When he was drowned, Hercules 'lefte the Argonautes, and went ouer all Mysia seekyng and criyng for [him]' (T. Cooper 1565).

Stanza 8

1 say: a cloth of fine texture worn by Enuie at I iv 31.1. **3–4** On S.'s knowledge of **the sunburnt Indians** of the Americas, see II xi 21.5*n*. **plight**: attire. **7 far'd**: conducted himself. **8–9** The **fan** gives Fansy his attribute by means of a pun. **windy**: causing wind; suggesting vain. **ydle**: empty; idly.

Stanza 9

1–3 Desyre seems older than Fansy but is his son, for fancy gives birth to desire. **5** . . . was very fantastically (or foolishly) designed. **7–9** Such kindling of fire/desire is seen in Malecasta at i 47.5–9. **strayne**: clasp.

10

Next after him went *Doubt*, who was yclad
In a discolour'd cote, of straunge disguyse,
That at his backe a brode Capuccio had,
And sleeues dependaunt *Albanese*-wyse:
He lookt askew with his mistrustfull eyes,
And nycely trode, as thornes lay in his way
Or that the flore to shrinke he did auyse
And on a broken reed he still did stay,
His feeble steps, which shrunck, when hard thereon he lay.

11

With him went *Daunger*, cloth'd in ragged weed,
Made of Beares skin, that him more dreadfull made,
Yet his owne face was dreadfull, ne did need
Straunge horrour, to deforme his griesly shade;
A net in th'one hand, and a rusty blade
In th'other was, this Mischiefe, that mishap;
With th'one his foes he threatned to inuade,
With th'other he his friends ment to enwrap:
For whom he could not kill, he practizd to entrap.

12

Next him was *Feare*, all arm'd from top to toe,
Yet thought himselfe not safe enough thereby,
But feard each shadow mouing to or froe,
And his owne armes when glittering he did spy,
Or clashing heard, he fast away did fly,
As ashes pale of hew, and winged heeld;
And euermore on daunger fixt his eye,
Gainst whom he alwayes bent a brasen shield,
Which his right hand vnarmed fearefully did wield.

13

With him went *Hope* in rancke, a handsome Mayd,
Of chearefull looke and louely to behold;
In silken samite she was light arayd,
And her fayre lockes were wouen vp in gold;
She alway smyld, and in her hand did hold
An holy water Sprinckle, dipt in deowe,
With which she sprinckled fauours manifold,
On whom she list, and did great liking sheowe,
Great liking vnto many, but true loue to feowe.

14

And after them *Dissemblaunce*, and *Suspect*
Marcht in one rancke, yet an vnequall paire:
For she was gentle, and of milde aspect,
Courteous to all, and seeming debonaire,
Goodly adorned, and exceeding faire:
Yet was that all but paynted, and pourloynd,
And her bright browes were deckt with borrowed haire:
Her deeds were forged, and her words false coynd,
And alwaies in her hand two clewes of silke she twynd.

15

But he was fowle, ill fauoured, and grim,
Vnder his eiebrowes looking still askaunce;
And euer as *Dissemblaunce* laught on him,
He lowrd on her with daungerous eyeglaunce;
Shewing his nature in his countenaunce;
His rolling eies did neuer rest in place,
But walkte each where, for feare of hid mischaunce,
Holding a lattis still before his face,
Through which he stil did peep, as forward he did pace.

Stanza 10

1 Next after him: i.e. after Desyre, though after Fansy if the line parallels 9.1. **Doubt** and his companion '*Daunger*' (11.1) oppose Scudamour in his effort to win Amoret at IV x 12, 17. **2 discolour'd**: many-coloured. **disguyse**: fashion. **3 Capuccio**: Ital. 'a hood or cowle' (Florio 1598); a well-known emblem of fraud, as Chew 1962:341 notes. **4** . . . hanging down in Albanian (i.e. Scottish) fashion, as a manche or university gown. There may be a topical reference to the long-sleeved dress worn by (disloyal) Celts, as de Marly 1985 suggests. In *View* 61, Irish women are said to wear 'the deep smock sleeve hanging to the ground'. **6 nycely**: cautiously. **7 shrinke**: give way. **auyse**: perceive. **8–9** 'Lo, thou trustest now in this broken staffe of rede . . . on which if a man leane, it wil go into his hand' (2 Kings 18.21). **stay**: support. **shrunck**: collapsed.

Stanza 11

In this anatomy, **Daunger** refers chiefly to the male lover's power to hurt through force and fraud – as a traditional pair, see II vii 25.3*n* – represented respectively by a **rusty blade** (i.e. red with blood) and a **net**. The blade threatens **Mischiefe** (i.e. evil-doing) to his foes; the net, an instrument of Guile at V ix 11.6, threatens **mishap** to his friends. Daunger refers also to the lady's resistance to her lover, as at IV x 16.5–19.9 where he helps guard the gate leading to Amoret in the temple of

Venus. See 'Daunger' in the *SEnc*. **2** On the significance of the bear, see II ii 22.5–9*n*. **4 Straunge**: added from outside. **shade**: image or appearance. **7 inuade**: attack. **9 practizd**: plotted.

Stanza 12

1 Next him: i.e. after Daunger. **8** Cf. the brazen shield carried by Atin at II iv 38.1. **bent**: turned. **9** Being too fearful to attack, he holds his shield on his sword arm to defend himself.

Stanza 13

By her name, **Hope** is associated with Speranza at I x 14, but her role and appearance associate her with Dame Gladnesse in the *Romaunt of the Rose* 867–76, a beautiful blonde crowned with a golden garland and dressed in silk interwoven with gold. **1 in rancke**: by his side. **3 samite**: a rich fabric. **6–9 Sprinckle**: an aspergillum, a brush to sprinkle holy water. **deowe**: traditionally associated with God's providence. S. is mocking popish practice; cf. I xii 37.5.

Stanza 14

1–4 Suspect: Suspicion. **For she**: i.e. **Dissemblaunce**, or dissimulation. **debonaire**: gracious. **7 borrowed haire**: since hair is praiseworthy in a woman (see ix 20*n*), a wig, also

16

Next him went *Griefe*, and *Fury* matcht yfere;
  Griefe all in sable sorrowfully clad,
  Downe hanging his dull head, with heauy chere,
  Yet inly being more, then seeming sad:
  A paire of Pincers in his hand he had,
  With which he pinched people to the hart,
  That from thenceforth a wretched life they ladd,
In wilfull languor and consuming smart,
Dying each day with inward wounds of dolours dart.

17

But *Fury* was full ill appareiled,
  In rags, that naked nigh she did appeare,
  With ghastly looks and dreadfull drerihed;
  For from her backe her garments she did teare,
  And from her head ofte rent her snarled heare:
  In her right hand a firebrand shee did tosse
  About her head, still roming here and there;
  As a dismayed Deare in chace embost,
Forgetfull of his safety, hath his right way lost.

18

After them went *Displeasure* and *Pleasaunce*,
  He looking lompish and full sullein sad,
  And hanging downe his heauy countenaunce;
  She chearfull fresh and full of ioyaunce glad,
  As if no sorrow she ne felt ne dread;
  That euill matched paire they seemd to bee:
  An angry Waspe th'one in a viall had,
  Th'other in hers an hony-lady Bee;
Thus marched these six couples forth in faire degree.

19

After all these there marcht a most faire Dame,
  Led of two grysie villeins, th'one *Despight*,
  The other cleped *Cruelty* by name:
  She dolefull Lady, like a dreary Spright,
  Cald by strong charmes out of eternall night,
  Had Deathes owne ymage figurd in her face,
  Full of sad signes, fearfull to liuing sight,
  Yet in that horror shewd a seemely grace,
And with her feeble feete did moue a comely pace.

20

Her brest all naked, as nett yuory,
  Without adorne of gold or siluer bright,
  Wherewith the Craftesman wonts it beautify,
  Of her dew honour was despoyled quight,
  And a wide wound therein (O ruefull sight)
  Entrenched deep with knyfe accursed keene,
  Yet freshly bleeding forth her fainting spright,
  (The worke of cruell hand) was to be seene,
That dyde in sanguine red her skin all snowy cleene.

21

At that wide orifice her trembling hart
  Was drawne forth, and in siluer basin layd,
  Quite through transfixed with a deadly dart,
  And in her blood yet steeming fresh embayd:
  And those two villeins, which her steps vpstayd,
  When her weake feete could scarcely her sustaine,
  And fading vitall powres gan to fade,
  Her forward still with torture did constraine,
And euermore encreased her consuming paine.

---

worn by Duessa at I viii 47.1, is deceptive and therefore loath-some. **9 clewes**: balls of thread, such as the 'deceiptfull clew' used by Archimago 'to weaue a web of wicked guyle' at II i 8.3–4.

Stanza 15
2 askaunce: with distrust; see II vii 7.5*n*. **3 laught on**: i.e. in encouragement. **4 daungerous**: severe, threatening harm. **7 walkte each where**: moved everywhere. **8–9** Alluding to Ital. *gelosia*, 'iealousie, . . . a letteise window' (Florio 1589; cf. Eng. 'jalousie'), through which a jealous person may see without being seen, as Upton 1758 notes.

Stanza 16
1 Next him: i.e. following Dissemblaunce. **yfere**: together. **5–9** As Scudamour is pinched by Care at IV v 44. **languor**: woeful plight; possibly illness.

Stanza 17
Cf. Wrath at I iv 33–34, and Furor at II iv 7. **3 drerihed**: utter wretchedness. **6 shee did tosse** (i.e. brandish); 'she tost', conj. Church 1758, for the rhyme and rhythm. Cf. Furor's fire-brand at II v 22.6–9. **8 embost**: driven to extremity, or into the woods.

Stanza 18
2 lompish: dejected, low-spirited. **sullein**: gloomy, morose. See I ix 35.3*n*. **8 hony-lady Bee**: either a honey-bee or honey-laden bee. **9 faire degree**: fair order; called 'the euill ordered' at 23.4.

Stanza 19
The lady's **Despight** and **Cruelty** is the courtly lover's complaint against her, e.g. *Am* 25, 31, 45, etc., but here she becomes the victim. See Roche 1964:74. **2 grysie**: horrible, grim. **9 comely**: pleasing.

Stanza 20
1 nett: clear, pure. **2 adorne**: adornment. **4 dew honour**: either adornment befitting her honour, or referring to her wounded breast. **6 Entrenched**: coined by S., according to *OED*, to describe a wound made by cutting. As expressed by Scudamour, 'deadly torments doe her chast brest rend' (xi 11.3). **accursed**: i.e. through enchantments.

Stanza 21
As Lechery bears 'a burning hart' in his hand at I iv 25.3, for he 'ioyd weake wemens hearts to tempt, and proue | If from their loyall loues he might them moue' (26.4–5). **4 embayd**: steeped.

22

Next after her, the winged God him selfe
   Came riding on a Lion rauenous,
   Taught to obay the menage of that Elfe,
   That man and beast with powre imperious
   Subdeweth to his kingdome tyrannous:
   His blindfold eies he bad a while vnbinde,
   That his proud spoile of that same dolorous
   Faire Dame he might behold in perfect kinde,
Which seene, he much reioyced in his cruell minde.

23

Of which ful prowd, him selfe vp rearing hye,
   He looked round about with sterne disdayne;
   And did suruay his goodly company:
   And marshalling the euill ordered trayne,
   With that the darts which his right hand did straine,
   Full dreadfully he shooke that all did quake,
   And clapt on hye his coulourd winges twaine,
   That all his many it affraide did make:
Tho blinding him againe, his way he forth did take.

24

Behinde him was *Reproch, Repentaunce, Shame*;
   Reproch the first, *Shame* next, *Repent* behinde:
   Repentaunce feeble, sorowfull, and lame:
   Reproch despightful, carelesse, and vnkinde;
   Shame most ill fauourd, bestiall, and blinde:
   Shame lowrd, *Repentaunce* sigh'd, *Reproch* did scould;
   Reproch sharpe stings, *Repentaunce* whips entwinde,
   Shame burning brond-yrons in her hand did hold:
All three to each vnlike, yet all made in one mould.

25

And after them a rude confused rout
   Of persons flockt, whose names is hard to read:
   Emongst them was sterne *Strife*, and *Anger* stout,
   Vnquiet *Care*, and fond *Vnthriftyhead*,
   Lewd *Losse of Time*, and *Sorrow* seeming dead,
   Inconstant *Chaunge*, and false *Disloyalty*,
   Consuming *Riotise*, and guilty *Dread*
   Of heauenly vengeaunce, faint *Infirmity*,
Vile *Pouerty*, and lastly *Death* with infamy.

26

There were full many moe like maladies,
   Whose names and natures I note readen well;
   So many moe, as there be phantasies
   In wauering wemens witt, that none can tell,
   Or paines in loue, or punishments in hell;
   All which disguized marcht in masking wise,
   About the chamber by the Damozell,
   And then returned, hauing marched thrise,
Into the inner rowme, from whence they first did rise.

27

So soone as they were in, the dore streight way
   Fast locked, driuen with that stormy blast,
   Which first it opened; nothing did remayne.
   Then the braue Maid, which al this while was plast,
   In secret shade, and saw both first and last,
   Issewed forth, and went vnto the dore,
   To enter in, but fownd it locked fast:
   It vaine she thought with rigorous vprore
For to efforce, when charmes had closed it afore.

Stanza 22

1 **the winged God**: Cupid, who need not be named for he was portrayed in the tapestry and his image set up in the first room (xi 45–48). **2 riding on a Lion**: as does Wrath at I iv 33.1–2, to mark Love's rage but also his power, as Alciati 1985:emblem 106 shows Cupid driving a chariot drawn by two lions with the motto, *Potentissimus affectus amor*. Cf. G. Whitney 1586:63. In *SC Dec.* 57–58, S. refers to 'the raging fyre' of love in summer, 'For loue then in the Lyons house did dwell'. **3 menage**: manège, horsemanship. **Elfe**: as xi 45.1. **7 his proud spoile**: as xi Arg.4. **8 in perfect kinde**: in perfect manner, i.e. clearly; or, (for him) in perfect condition being mortally wounded by him.

Stanza 23

2 **sterne**: cruel, threatening. **5 With that**: whereupon. **straine**: clasp. **6 shooke**: brandished. **8 many**: company.

Stanza 24

S.'s artistry in bringing together three figures and then distributing them is noted by Upton 1758. The order (1, 2, 3) in the first line is varied in the rest of the stanza (1, 3, 2; 2, 1, 3; 3, 2, 1; 1, 2, 3) to relate them through their differences. After the initial naming (1) and significant ordering (2), three descriptive terms are given each figure in three lines (3–5); then a characteristic action of each in one line (6), an emblem for each in two lines (7–8), with **Shame** stressed by giving it one whole line, and a concluding line which confirms that

the three though different are one. On the central figure, see 'Shame' in the *SEnc*. **4 carelesse**: not caring whom he attacks. **8 brond-yrons**: a nonce-word used by S. for a sword at VI viii 10.4. Since Busirane marks characters in Amoret's flesh, it may carry the sense of 'branding-iron' to mark her 'dread of shame' at IV i 8.6.

Stanza 25

In this group of thirteen, **Chaunge** is at the centre, as the Mutabilitie Cantos would lead one to expect. **2 read**: distinguish; guess; interpret (from their appearance). **3 stout**: fierce. **4 fond Vnthriftyhead**: foolish thriftlessness. In the procession of the sins 'vnthrifty scath' follows Wrath at I iv 35.1–3. **5 Lewd**: wicked. **7 Riotise**: riotousness.

Stanza 26

2 **note**: know not how to. **4 witt**: mind. **wauering** seems to apply to women in general rather than those who waver. **tell**: count; describe. **6 in masking wise**: in the manner of a masque; cf. 5.9. **7 by the**: with that *1596*. *1590* indicates more clearly that Amoret is a surrogate for Britomart who is often referred to as a 'Damzell', e.g. 32.8, i 8.4. **9 rise**: issue.

Stanza 27

3 **nothing did remayne**: and bore all away *1596*, revised for the rhyme. **6 Issewed forth**: used at 3.5 and 5.3 to describe the formal beginning of the masque. **8 rigorous vprore**: violent force; applies also to wind or storm.

28

Where force might not auaile, there sleights and art
　　She cast to vse, both fitt for hard emprize;
　　For thy from that same rowme not to depart
　　Till morrow next, shee did her selfe auize,
　　When that same Maske againe should forth arize.
　　The morrowe next appeard with ioyous cheare,
　　Calling men to their daily exercize,
Then she, as morrow fresh, her selfe did reare
Out of her secret stand, that day for to outweare.

29

All that day she outwore in wandering,
　　And gazing on that Chambers ornament,
　　Till that againe the second euening
　　Her couered with her sable vestiment,
　　Wherewith the worlds faire beautie she hath blent:
　　Then when the second watch was almost past,
　　That brasen dore flew open, and in went
Bold *Britomart*, as she had late forecast,
Nether of ydle showes, nor of false charmes aghast.

30

So soone as she was entred, rownd about
　　Shee cast her eies, to see what was become
　　Of all those persons, which she saw without:
　　But lo, they streight were vanisht all and some,
　　Ne liuing wight she saw in all that roome,
　　Saue that same woefull Lady, both whose hands
　　Were bounden fast, that did her ill become,
And her small waste girt rownd with yron bands,
Vnto a brasen pillour, by the which she stands.

31

And her before the vile Enchaunter sate,
　　Figuring straunge characters of his art,
　　With liuing blood he those characters wrate,
　　Dreadfully dropping from her dying hart,
　　Seeming transfixed with a cruell dart,
　　And all perforce to make her him to loue.
　　Ah who can loue the worker of her smart?
A thousand charmes he formerly did proue;
Yet thousand charmes could not her stedfast hart remoue.

32

Soone as that virgin knight he saw in place,
　　His wicked bookes in hast he ouerthrew,
　　Not caring his long labours to deface,
　　And fiercely running to that Lady trew,
　　A murdrous knife out of his pocket drew,
　　The which he thought, for villeinous despight,
　　In her tormented bodie to embrew:
But the stout Damzell to him leaping light,
His cursed hand withheld, and maistered his might.

33

From her, to whom his fury first he ment,
　　The wicked weapon rashly he did wrest,
　　And turning to the next his fell intent,
　　Vnwares it strooke into her snowie chest,
　　That litle drops empurpled her faire brest.
　　Exceeding wroth therewith the virgin grew,
　　Albe the wound were nothing deepe imprest,
And fiercely forth her mortall blade she drew,
To giue him the reward for such vile outrage dew.

Stanza 28

1–2 Britomart must resort to **sleights and art** (i.e. stratagems and wile) because neither 'powre of hand, nor skill of learned brest' (xi 16.3) can redeem Amoret. **cast**: determined. **emprize**: undertaking; see I ix 1.4*n*. **3 For thy**: accordingly. **4 auize**: counsel. **9 stand**: place; post as a sentinel, in contrast to her 'wandering' in the next line.

Stanza 30

4 all and some: every one of them. **8–9** Amoret's **yron bands** may be compared to the 'golden girdle' that falls from Florimell's waist at vii 31.8–9, to '*Venus* shameful chaine' (I ii 4.8) that binds lovers, to 'loues soft bands' at *Am* 1.3 with its implied reference to the marriage ring, and to 'this lovely band' of marriage in *Epith* 396. The **pillour** may represent the erect phallus: as a bride wedded but not bedded (as told at IV i 3), Amoret is bound by what she fears to what she fears. Cf. the 'lamenting cryes' and 'dolefull teares' of the bedded bride in *Epith* 334. As such, when she is freed, it 'detumesces' at 37.9, as Maclean and Prescott 1993 put it. Or it may represent male mastery from which Britomart releases her.

Stanza 31

On this scene as 'a formal spectacle of eroticized masochism', see Paglia 1990:186; and as it reveals the metaphysical implications of gender characteristic of allegory, see Teskey 1996:19. **1 vile Enchaunter**: so Busirane is called in the *LR* 74. **2 As** 'th'Enchaunter' Merlin is seen 'writing straunge characters in the grownd' at iii 17.1, 14.8. The **characters** are linked with those in the tapestry in the first room, and the bas-relief and the masquers in the second room. **5 Seeming**: a key word in contrast to 'Quite through transfixed' at 21.3; cf. xi 11.4. **6 perforce**: by force. **7** The **worker of her smart** is as much Scudamour as Busirane. Cf. *HL* 31–32: 'And ye faire Nimphs, which oftentimes haue loued | The cruell worker of your kindly smarts'. At VI x 31.6–7, love compels Calidore 'to returne againe | To his wounds worker'. **8 charmes**: verses with magical powers. **thousand**: corresponding to the 'thousand monstrous formes' of false love at xi 51.7. **proue**: try.

Stanza 32

1 in place: present. **3** He does not care if he destroys **his long labours**, referring to the charms in his books (cf. 43.9) and to Amoret whose love he has laboured to win. **7 embrew**: plunge.

Stanza 33

1 ment: directed. **2 rashly**: suddenly; in a slashing manner. **wrest**: twist. **4–7** Corresponding to her wound 'not deepe' by Gardante at i 65.6. In effect, she suffers Amoret's wound by Busirane's knife (see 20.5–9); hence the reference to her **snowie** breast, as Amoret's breast is 'nett yuory' (20.1). **imprest**: imprinted. Busirane seeks to mark in her flesh characters that charm Amoret. **Vnwares**: her state when she first sees Artegall at ii 26.4; cf. 38.9, iii 24.2.

(handwritten margin note: Can't kill the source of pain)

So mightily she smote him, that to ground
 He fell halfe dead; next stroke him should haue slaine,
 Had not the Lady, which by him stood bound,
 Dernly vnto her called to abstaine,
 From doing him to dy. For else her paine
 Should be remedilesse, sith none but hee,
 Which wrought it, could the same recure againe.
 Therewith she stayd her hand, loth stayd to bee;
For life she him enuyde, and long'd reuenge to see.

35

And to him said, Thou wicked man, whose meed
 For so huge mischiefe, and vile villany
 Is death, or if that ought doe death exceed,
 Be sure, that nought may saue thee from to dy,
 But if that thou this Dame doe presently
 Restore vnto her health, and former state;
 This doe and liue, els dye vndoubtedly.
 He glad of life, that lookt for death but late,
Did yield him selfe right willing to prolong his date.

36

And rising vp, gan streight to ouerlooke
 Those cursed leaues, his charmes back to reuerse;
 Full dreadfull thinges out of that balefull booke
 He red, and measur'd many a sad verse,
 That horrour gan the virgins hart to perse,
 And her faire locks vp stared stiffe on end,
 Hearing him those same bloody lynes reherse;
 And all the while he red, she did extend
Her sword high ouer him, if ought he did offend.

37

Anon she gan perceiue the house to quake,
 And all the dores to rattle round about;
 Yet all that did not her dismaied make,
 Nor slack her threatfull hand for daungers dout,
 But still with stedfast eye and courage stout,
 Abode to weet, what end would come of all.
 At last that mightie chaine, which round about
 Her tender waste was wound, adowne gan fall,
And that great brasen pillour broke in peeces small.

38

The cruell steele, which thrild her dying hart,
 Fell softly forth, as of his owne accord,
 And the wyde wound, which lately did dispart
 Her bleeding brest, and riuen bowels gor'd,
 Was closed vp, as it had not beene sor'd,
 And euery part to safety full sownd,
 As she were neuer hurt, was soone restor'd:
 Tho when she felt her selfe to be vnbownd,
And perfect hole, prostrate she fell vnto the grownd.

39

Before faire *Britomart*, she fell prostrate,
 Saying, Ah noble knight, what worthy meede
 Can wretched Lady, quitt from wofull state,
 Yield you in lieu of this your gracious deed?
 Your vertue selfe her owne reward shall breed,
 Euen immortall prayse, and glory wyde
 Which I your vassall, by your prowesse freed,
 Shall through the world make to be notifyde,
And goodly well aduaunce that goodly well was tryde.

Stanza 34
4 Dernly: earnestly or dismally (sugg. *OED*) as the dying Amavia 'dearnly cride' at II i 35.7; but most likely 'secretly' (from *OED* 'dern' A1) so that Busirane would not hear. If he did hear, Britomart's threat at 35.4–7 would be empty. **7 recure**: heal. **8** Britomart's restraint contrasts with Guyon's wrathful destruction of the Bower of Bliss at II xii 83, as do their actions: he binds Acrasia, she frees Amoret; see 42.3–4n. **9 enuyde**: begrudged.

Stanza 35
1–6 'Since you deserve death, or worse if there is anything worse, you may be sure that you are going to die unless you restore Amoret to her former well-being'. **9 date**: term of life.

Stanza 36
1 ouerlooke: look over. **2** In Ovid, *Met.* 14.300–01, Circe strikes her beasts with her reversed rod and retracts her charms to restore them to manhood. On Busirane as a male Circe and Britomart who defeats him as a female Ulysses, see Roberts 1997:73. **reuerse** suggests that Amoret is being led out of a maze. **4 measur'd**: read through; implying also 'according to its correct metre'. **sad verse**: a strong or powerful incantation or charm, as at II i 55.4. **5–7** Britomart suffers Amoret's torture by having her heart pierced with horror through hearing Busirane's charms. **vp stared**: stood up. A formidable sight

for her hair extends to her ankles; see ix. 20.6. **reherse**: say over again what he said previously to charm Amoret. S. Frye 1994:62 notes how the feminine pronouns serve to conflate Britomart and Amoret into a single unstable feminine figure.

Stanza 37
4 Nor relax her threatening hand through fear of danger. **6 Abode**: waited. **8 Her**: a deliberately ambiguous reference.

Stanza 38
1 thrild: pierced. **3 dispart**: divide. **4 riuen bowels gor'd**: as Britomart's 'bleeding bowells' are said to be pierced at ii 39.2. Bellamy 1997:408 suggests that there is a 'metonymic displacement for the hymen that must be penetrated'. **7 soone**: immediately. **8–9 Tho**: then; also 'though', to read: 'though whole, she falls'. Goldberg 1981:78–79, supported by Quilligan 1983:199, suggests a pun on 'hole', referring to her vaginal readiness as a new bride. S. Frye 1994:67 infers that 'her violated hymen is restored'. Hieatt 1998:163n9 rejects the possibility of such a pun, and suspects that no early modern English text uses **hole** to mean 'vagina'.

Stanza 39
4 in lieu of: as reward for. **5 Your vertue selfe**: your virtue itself (or your virtuous self), invoking the proverb: 'Virtue is its own reward' (Smith 818). **9 aduaunce**: extol. **that**: that which, referring to Britomart's virtue.

40

But *Britomart* vprearing her from grownd,
  Said, Gentle Dame, reward enough I weene
  For many labours more, then I haue found,
  This, that in safetie now I haue you seene,
  And meane of your deliuerance haue beene:
  Henceforth faire Lady comfort to you take,
  And put away remembraunce of late teene;
  In sted thereof know, that your louing Make,
Hath no lesse griefe endured for your gentle sake.

41

She much was cheard to heare him mentiond,
  Whom of all liuing wightes she loued best.
  Then laid the noble Championesse strong hond
  Vpon th'enchaunter, which had her distrest
  So sore, and with foule outrages opprest:
  With that great chaine, wherewith not long ygoe
  He bound that pitteous Lady prisoner, now relest,
  Himselfe she bound, more worthy to be so,
And captiue with her led to wretchednesse and wo.

42

Returning back, those goodly rowmes, which erst
  She saw so rich and royally arayd,
  Now vanisht vtterly, and cleane subuerst
  She found, and all their glory quite decayd,
  That sight of such a chaunge her much dismayd.
  Thenceforth descending to that perlous Porch,
  Those dreadfull flames she also found delayd,
  And quenched quite, like a consumed torch,
That erst all entrers wont so cruelly to scorch.

43*

At last she came vnto the place, where late
  She left Sir *Scudamour* in great distresse,
  Twixt dolour and despight halfe desperate,
  Of his loues succour, of his owne redresse,
  And of the hardie *Britomarts* successe:
  There on the cold earth him now thrown she found,
  In wilfull anguish, and dead heauinesse,
  And to him cald; whose voices knowen sound
Soone as he heard, himself he reared light from ground.

44*

There did he see, that most on earth him ioyd,
  His dearest loue, the comfort of his dayes,
  Whose too long absence him had sore annoyd,
  And wearied his life with dull delayes:
  Straight he vpstarted from the loathed layes,
  And to her ran with hasty egernesse,
  Like as a Deare, that greedily embayes
  In the coole soile, after long thirstinesse,
Which he in chace endured hath, now nigh breathlesse.

45*

Lightly he clipt her twixt his armes twaine,
  And streightly did embrace her body bright,
  Her body, late the prison of sad paine,
  Now the sweet lodge of loue and deare delight:
  But she faire Lady ouercommen quight
  Of huge affection, did in pleasure melt,
  And in sweete rauishment pourd out her spright:
  No word they spake, nor earthly thing they felt,
But like two senceles stocks in long embracement dwelt.

Stanza 40

5 meane: instrument; intercessor, for she has received the wound intended for Amoret. **6** She offers the same advice to Scudamour at xi 15.1. **7 teene**: injury, affliction. **8 Make**: mate. **9** Referring to Scudamour's 'deepe conceiued griefe' (xi 14.1) for her, which was more than he could endure.

Stanza 41

1 A rare rhythmically faulty line occasioned by the need to rhyme with **hond** and thereby fulfil Britomart's vow that Busirane's hand would be opposed by hers (xi 10.7, 15.4). Cf. 32.9, 34.8 and 37.4. **7** Unless the six feet measure the chain, **pitteous**, **Lady**, or **prisoner** should be omitted, though, as the line stands, it stresses Amoret's earlier plight.

Stanza 42

2 She: He *1590*, also at 4, and 'him' in 5 (corrected *F.E.*) may indicate that S. is anticipating Amoret's error about Britomart's sex in the opening episode of Bk IV. **3–4** The sudden vanishing of an enchanted palace is a romance motif – e.g. in Ariosto, *Orl. Fur.* 4.38 – used here to contrast Guyon's deliberate razing of the 'goodly workmanship' of the Bower of Bliss at II xii 83.3. **subuerst**: razed. **decayd**: destroyed; as before Amoret was 'through charmes decayd' (Arg.4). **7 delayd**: quenched.

Stanza 43*

3–5 Echoing Malbecco's state 'Twixt inward doole and felonous despight' (x 17.6) to note Scudamour's jealousy; cf.

his 'great despight' at IV i 52.1 when again he has cause to envy Britomart's **successe**. **redresse**: aid. **6** His posture at xi 7.3–4 and 13.6–7 when first found by Britomart; as it is Amoret's at 38.9 above. **7 heauinesse**: torpor; grief.

Stanza 44*

5 layes: ground. **7–9** Proverbial for the point of last extremity, and also of relief after a chase. **soile**: a pool of water, suggesting Salmacis in the next stanza. The same simile describes their 'first' union at IV x 55.8 where again, in a reversal of the usual roles, he is the deer and she is his refuge.

Stanza 45*

2 streightly: tightly. **5–7** Similar language is used in Castiglione, *Courtier* 315, to describe the kiss by which the souls of lovers 'poure them selves by turne the one into the others bodie, and bee so mingled together, that each of them hath two soules'. **melt** suggests orgasm, as does **pourd out** – cf. the Red Cross Knight with Duessa 'Pourd out in loosnesse' at I vii 7.2 – but goes as far beyond it as **rauishment** does rape. **9** In Ovid, *Met.* 4.373–79, the physical melding of Hermaphroditus and Salmacis when he dives into the pool of which she is its nymph is described as 'Two twigges both growing into one and still togither holde' (tr. Golding); but S. alludes primarily to marriage in which man 'shal cleaue to his wife, and they shalbe one flesh' (Gen. 2.24), as Lewis 1967:38 notes. See 'Hermaphrodite' in the *SEnc*, R. Axton 1990, and Silberman 1995:67–70.

46*

Had ye them seene, ye would haue surely thought,
  That they had beene that faire *Hermaphrodite*,
  Which that rich *Romane* of white marble wrought,
  And in his costly Bath causd to bee site:
  So seemd those two, as growne together quite,
  That *Britomart* halfe enuying their blesse,
  Was much empassiond in her gentle sprite,
  And to her selfe oft wisht like happinesse,
In vaine she wisht, that fate n'ould let her yet possesse.

47*

Thus doe those louers with sweet counteruayle,
  Each other of loues bitter fruit despoile.
  But now my teme begins to faint and fayle,
  All woxen weary of their iournall toyle:
  Therefore I will their sweatie yokes assoyle
  At this same furrowes end, till a new day:
  And ye faire Swayns, after your long turmoyle,
  Now cease your worke, and at your pleasure play;
Now cease your worke; to morrow is an holy day.

FINIS.

Stanza 46*
1–4 No such statue has been identified, as D. Cheney 1972:194 notes, and that may be S.'s witty point in his address to the reader. Cf. his comment on the whereabouts of Arthur's armour at I vii 36.9. **Bath** recalls Salmacis's fountain that made men effeminate but may allude to the alchemical bath that fused a hermaphrodite; see Cheney 195.   **9 n'ould**: would not.

Stanza 47*
1 counteruayle: reciprocation.   **3–6** This common georgic topos of conclusion – it is used, e.g. in Chaucer, *Knight's Tale*

A 886–87 – is appropriate for one in an agricultural society, esp. for a poet whose feet always follow a straight line. It is used later, e.g. IV v 46.8–9, and V iii 40.6–9; cf. VI ix 1. **woxen**: possibly a witty allusion to the team of 'oxen' pulling his plough. **iournall**: daily, in opposition to **holy day**. **assoyle**: set free.   **7 ye faire Swayns**: Scudamour and Amoret. This surprising address links the lovers to S.'s **teme** and therefore to his muses. At VI ix 1, and presumably here, some 'iolly swayne', rather than the poet, is the ploughboy who drives his team.

[The ending of Book III in the *1596* edition]

43

More easie issew now, then entrance late
    She found: for now that fained dreadfull flame,
    Which chokt the porch of that enchaunted gate,
    And passage bard to all, that thither came,
    Was vanisht quite, as it were not the same,
    And gaue her leaue at pleasure forth to passe.
    Th'Enchaunter selfe, which all that fraud did frame,
    To haue efforst the loue of that faire lasse,
Seeing his worke now wasted deepe engrieued was.

44

But when the victoresse arriued there,
    Where late she left the pensife *Scudamore*,
    With her owne trusty Squire, both full of feare,
    Neither of them she found where she them lore:
    Thereat her noble hart was stonisht sore;
    But most faire *Amoret*, whose gentle spright
    Now gan to feede on hope, which she before
    Conceiued had, to see her owne deare knight,
Being thereof beguyld was fild with new affright.

45

But he sad man, when he had long in drede
    Awayted there for *Britomarts* returne,
    Yet saw her not nor signe of her good speed,
    His expectation to despaire did turne,
    Misdeeming sure that her those flames did burne;
    And therefore gan aduize with her old Squire,
    Who her deare nourslings losse no lesse did mourne,
    Thence to depart for further aide t'enquire:
Where let them wend at will, whilest here I doe respire.

Stanzas 43–45 (*1596*)
These stanzas displaced 43–47 (*1590*), which presumably were written to provide an interim ending to the *1590* poem. 43.1–6, in repeating the substance of 42.6–9, would suggest that S. is picking up his subject again. At 44.3, either he has forgotten, or he assumes that readers have, that Glauce, who has not appeared since the end of canto iii, was not left with Scudamour.

Stanza 43
2 **fained**: being imaginary; only imagined to be dreadful. 8 **efforst**: compelled.

Stanza 44
2 **pensife**: apprehensive; sad.   4 **lore**: left.

Stanza 45
3 **speed**: success.   5 **Misdeeming**: mistakenly supposing. 6 **aduize**: consult.

THE SECOND

PART OF THE

FAERIE QVEENE.

Containing

THE FOVRTH,
FIFTH, AND
SIXTH BOOKES.

By Ed. Spenser.

Imprinted at London for VVilliam
Ponsonby. 1 5 96.

THE FOVRTH
BOOKE OF THE
FAERIE QVEENE.

Containing

The Legend of CAMBEL and TELAMOND,

OR

OF FRIENDSHIP.

1

He rugged forhead that with graue foresight
Welds kingdomes causes, and affaires of state,
My looser rimes (I wote) doth sharply wite,
For praising loue, as I haue done of late,
And magnifying louers deare debate;
By which fraile youth is oft to follie led,
Through false allurement of that pleasing baite,
That better were in vertues discipled,
Then with vaine poemes weeds to haue their fancies fed.

2

Such ones ill iudge of loue, that cannot loue,
Ne in their frosen hearts feele kindly flame:
For thy they ought not thing vnknowne reproue,
Ne naturall affection faultlesse blame,
For fault of few that haue abusd the same.
For it of honor and all vertue is
The roote, and brings forth glorious flowres of fame,
That crowne true louers with immortall blis,
The meed of them that loue, and do not liue amisse.

Book IV Title

Telamond: elsewhere Triamond, but the name is supported by Roche 1964:16–17 because its etymology, 'perfect world' (Gk τέλειος + Lat. *mundus*), is consonant with the Bk's metaphysics of friendship. Leslie 1983:177, supported by Kouwenhoven 1983:75, suggests τελαμών, band or baldric, referring to Florimell's cestus and the chivalric *cingulum militare*. More likely would be a fusion of the two words to suggest 'perfect band' as a substitute name for Tria*mond* who shares the souls of Priamond and Diamond.

Proem

Stanza 1

1–2 Apparently alluding to William Cecil, Lord Burghley, Elizabeth's Lord Treasurer, as again at the end of Bk VI which refers to 'a mighty Peres displeasure'. See *DS 2* and *n*. Anyone in his official capacity may well have been offended by the erotic ending of Bk III, enough for S. to cancel it. **rugged**: furrowed, frowning. **forhead**: associated with foresight at II ix 49.1. **Welds**: wields; governs. **3 looser**: too loose. **wite**: blame. **4 of late**: in *HHL* 8–11, S. confesses that he had written 'Many lewd layes . . . | In praise of that mad fit, which fooles call love, | . . . That in light wits did loose affection move'. **5 magnifying**: extolling; treating at length. **deare debate**: grievous or loving strife. **6 follie**: lewdness. **8–9** Cf. *LR* 21–23: 'To some I know this Methode will seeme displeasaunt, which had rather haue good discipline deliuered plainly in way of precepts, or sermoned at large, as they vse, then thus clowdily enwrapped in Allegoricall deuises'. **discipled**: taught; made subject to discipline. **weeds**: the garment of poetry; or noxious growth.

3

Which who so list looke backe to former ages,
    And call to count the things that then were donne,
    Shall find, that all the workes of those wise sages,
    And braue exploits which great Heroes wonne,
    In loue were either ended or begunne:
    Witnesse the father of Philosophie,
    Which to his *Critias*, shaded oft from sunne,
    Of loue full manie lessons did apply,
The which these Stoicke censours cannot well deny.

4

To such therefore I do not sing at all,
    But to that sacred Saint my soueraigne Queene,
    In whose chast breast all bountie naturall,
    And treasures of true loue enlocked beene,

Boue all her sexe that euer yet was seene;
    To her I sing of loue, that loueth best,
    And best is lou'd of all aliue I weene:
    To her this song most fitly is addrest,
The Queene of loue, and Prince of peace from heauen blest.

5

Which that she may the better deigne to heare,
    Do thou dred infant, *Venus* dearling doue,
    From her high spirit chase imperious feare,
    And vse of awfull Maiestie remoue:
    In sted thereof with drops of melting loue,
    Deawd with ambrosiall kisses, by thee gotten
    From thy sweete smyling mother from aboue,
    Sprinckle her heart, and haughtie courage soften,
That she may hearke to loue, and reade this lesson often.

Stanza 2

1–2 The charge that Burghley **cannot loue** would have surprised Mildred Cecil, who bore him three children during the 43 years of their marriage. His inscription on her tomb in Westminster Abbey records his deep grief at her death. **kindly flame**: i.e. **naturall affection**. **3 For thy**: therefore. **6–9** S. defends love at III i 49.8–9, iii 1–2, and v 1.8–9, and now defends his poem by adding to the *1590* dedication the claim that it will 'liue with the eternitie of her [Elizabeth's] fame'.

Stanza 3

4–5 The association of **Heroes** with love (Gk ἥρως, hero; ἔρως, love) was common, e.g. T. Cooper 1565 defines 'Heros' as 'he that for the loue of vertue susteineth great labours'. Its tri-syllabic form suggests the malady of *hereos* or heroical love; see Rose 1968:11–12. **6–8** Socrates discoursed on love to Phaedrus, not to **Critias**, in the shade of a plane tree (Plato, *Phaedrus* 230b). See II vii 52.6–9*n*. Unless S. errs, it is not clear why he should name the latter except that Critias appears in several dialogues, and the etymology of his name, κριτικός, judge, implies that he is a judge of love, as M.F.N. Dixon 1996:55 suggests. **father of Philosophie**: *parens philosophiae* is his traditional title. **9 Stoicke**: used loosely for those who repress emotion, here of love.

Stanza 4

2 In the previous proems, S. addresses the Queen directly as his muse (Bk I), or subject (Bk II), or Queen (Bk III), but now as a reader. See Quilligan 1983:202. On S.'s new role as tutor to the Queen, see Rambuss 1993:103–07. **3 bountie**: goodness. **9** The title, **The Queene of loue**, which is Venus's chief title at *Am* 39.1 and *Proth* 96, declares Elizabeth to be his poem's sponsor. **Prince of peace**, which is the future Messiah's title at Isa. 9.6, declares her to be the sponsor of the virtue of friendship.

Stanza 5

1 deigne to heare: perhaps alluding to the moment, recounted in *Colin Clout* 358–67, when he read some part of the poem to the Queen who was delighted and judged it to be of 'wondrous worth'. **2 dearling**: darling. **doue**: this unusual naming of Cupid as Venus's bird anticipates the dove's role in leading Belphœbe's 'mightie hart' (viii 17.6) to accept Timias's service. **3 imperious feare**: majesty which arouses fear in others, but implying that the Virgin Queen herself fears love. **5 melting loue**: as Amoret 'in pleasure melt' at III xii 45.6. **7 smyling mother**: Venus, 'Mother of laughter' at x 47.8; cf. x 44.4. **9 this lesson**: Cupid's lesson, which is not to fear love.

Cant. I.

Fayre Britomart saues Amoret,
Duessa discord breedes
Twixt Scudamour and Blandamour:
Their fight and warlike deedes.

1

OF louers sad calamities of old,
　　Full many piteous stories doe remaine,
　　But none more piteous euer was ytold,
　　Then that of *Amorets* hart-binding chaine,
　　And this of *Florimels* vnworthie paine:
　　The deare compassion of whose bitter fit
　　My softened heart so sorely doth constraine,
　　That I with teares full oft doe pittie it,
And oftentimes doe wish it neuer had bene writ.

2

For from the time that *Scudamour* her bought
　　In perilous fight, she neuer ioyed day,
　　A perilous fight when he with force her brought
　　From twentie Knights, that did him all assay:
　　Yet fairely well he did them all dismay:
　　And with great glorie both the shield of loue,
　　And eke the Ladie selfe he brought away,
　　Whom hauing wedded as did him behoue,
A new vnknowen mischiefe did from him remoue.

3

For that same vile Enchauntour *Busyran*,
　　The very selfe same day that she was wedded,
　　Amidst the bridale feast, whilest euery man
　　Surcharg'd with wine, were heedlesse and ill hedded,
All bent to mirth before the bride was bedded,
　　Brought in that mask of loue which late was showen:
　　And there the Ladie ill of friends bestedded,
　　By way of sport, as oft in maskes is knowen,
Conueyed quite away to liuing wight vnknowen.

4

Seuen moneths he so her kept in bitter smart,
　　Because his sinfull lust she would not serue,
　　Vntill such time as noble *Britomart*
　　Released her, that else was like to sterue,
　　Through cruell knife that her deare heart did kerue.
　　And now she is with her vpon the way,
　　Marching in louely wise, that could deserue
　　No spot of blame, though spite did oft assay
To blot her with dishonor of so faire a pray.

5

Yet should it be a pleasant tale, to tell
　　The diuerse vsage and demeanure daint,
　　That each to other made, as oft befell.
　　For *Amoret* right fearefull was and faint,
　　Lest she with blame her honor should attaint,
　　That euerie word did tremble as she spake,
　　And euerie looke was coy, and wondrous quaint,
　　And euerie limbe that touched her did quake:
Yet could she not but curteous countenance to her make.

Book IV Canto i

Stanza 1

5 vnworthie: undeserued. **6 bitter fit**: pangs of extreme grief. **7 My softened heart**: alluding to proem 5.8. K. Williams 1969:139 compares S.'s grief for Florimell at III viii 1.2 and infers that he 'experiences his poem as the simplest of readers might do'. **constraine**: afflict.

Stanza 2

Scudamour's fight is told at x 7–10; his seizure of Amoret at x 53–57. **1 bought**: set free by paying a price; cf. 'redeemed' (8.4). **4 assay**: assail. **5 fairely**: fully. **dismay**: defeat.

Stanza 3

The failure of friendship, which allows Amoret to be abducted, links her story with the virtue of Bk IV, as Alpers 1967:110 notes. Her oxymoronic state as 'a virgine wife' (6.9), i.e. wedded but not bedded and therefore about to change her allegiance from Diana to Venus, is clarified by Jonson, *Hymenæi*, where humours and affections, imaged as men, upset the marriage ceremonies. As he explains, 'These, therefore, were *tropically* brought in, before *Marriage*, as disturbers of that *mysticall bodie*, and the *rites*, which were *soule* vnto it' (1925–52:7.213). **1 vile Enchauntour**: his title at III xii 31.1. **2** Feminine rhyme, rare in the first three books, now becomes frequent. On its use, see Quilligan 1990:315–20. **7 bestedded**: attended.

Stanza 4

1 Seuen moneths: see III xi 10.8*n*. **2** See III xi 17.1–3*n*. **4 sterue**: die. **5 kerue**: cut; pierce. **7 louely**: affectionate. **9 her**: i.e. Britomart. Being taken for a male knight, she may be slandered for travelling with Amoret.

Stanza 5

2 diuerse vsage: different, or diverting, conduct. **5 attaint**: taint; convict. **7 quaint**: prim. **9 countenance**: demeanour.

6

For well she wist, as true it was indeed,
    That her liues Lord and patrone of her health
    Right well deserued as his duefull meed,
    Her loue, her seruice, and her vtmost wealth.
    All is his iustly, that all freely dealth:
    Nathlesse her honor dearer then her life,
    She sought to saue, as thing reseru'd from stealth;
    Die had she leuer with Enchanters knife,
Then to be false in loue, profest a virgine wife.

7

Thereto her feare was made so much the greater
    Through fine abusion of that Briton mayd:
    Who for to hide her fained sex the better,
    And maske her wounded mind, both did and sayd
    Full many things so doubtfull to be wayd,
    That well she wist not what by them to gesse,
    For other whiles to her she purpos made
    Of loue, and otherwhiles of lustfulnesse,
That much she feard his mind would grow to some excesse.

8

His will she feard; for him she surely thought
    To be a man, such as indeed he seemed,
    And much the more, by that he lately wrought,
    When her from deadly thraldome he redeemed,
    For which no seruice she too much esteemed,
    Yet dread of shame, and doubt of fowle dishonor
    Made her not yeeld so much, as due she deemed.
    Yet *Britomart* attended duly on her,
As well became a knight, and did to her all honor.

9

It so befell one euening, that they came
    Vnto a Castell, lodged there to bee,
    Where many a knight, and many a louely Dame
    Was then assembled, deeds of armes to see:

Amongst all which was none more faire then shee,
    That many of them mou'd to eye her sore.
    The custome of that place was such, that hee
    Which had no loue nor lemman there in store,
Should either winne him one, or lye without the dore.

10

Amongst the rest there was a iolly knight,
    Who being asked for his loue, auow'd
    That fairest *Amoret* was his by right,
    And offred that to iustifie alowd.
    The warlike virgine seeing his so prowd
    And boastfull chalenge, wexed inlie wroth,
    But for the present did her anger shrowd;
    And sayd, her loue to lose she was full loth,
But either he should neither of them haue, or both.

11

So foorth they went, and both together giusted;
    But that same younker soone was ouerthrowne,
    And made repent, that he had rashly lusted
    For thing vnlawfull, that was not his owne:
    Yet since he seemed valiant, though vnknowne,
    She that no lesse was courteous then stout,
    Cast how to salue, that both the custome showne
    Were kept, and yet that Knight not locked out,
That seem'd full hard t'accord two things so far in dout.

12

The Seneschall was cal'd to deeme the right,
    Whom she requir'd, that first fayre *Amoret*
    Might be to her allow'd, as to a Knight,
    That did her win and free from chalenge set:
    Which straight to her was yeelded without let.
    Then since that strange Knights loue from him was quitted,
    She claim'd that to her selfe, as Ladies det,
    He as a Knight might iustly be admitted;
So none should be out shut, sith all of loues were fitted.

Stanza 6
2 Britomart relates to Amoret as Arthur to the Red Cross Knight at I ix 17.6 and to Guyon at II viii 55.4. **patrone of her health**: both defender of her well-being and one who heals her wounded body; cf. III xii 35.6. **3 duefull**: due; emphasizing what is fully due, as she is Britomart's 'conquests part' (33.4). **5 dealth**: for 'dealeth', i.e. bestows. **7 stealth**: plundering.

Stanza 7
1 **Thereto**: moreover. **2 fine abusion**: cunning deception. **7–8 other whiles**: at one time, etc. **purpos**: conversation.

Stanza 8
1 **will**: sexual desire, lust. **5 seruice**: implying sexual service. **6 doubt**: fear. **8–9** The feminine rhyme mocks the love-game comedy.

Stanza 9
2 **a Castell**: it need not be named because it is a variant of Castle Joyeous with its similar custom; see III i 26–27. **6 sore**: presumably 'sorely' out of envy rather than her 'sore . . . wound' (III xi 11.9) which has been healed. **7–9** Woman

as the prize or booty of chivalric prowess is a central theme in the poem, but esp. Bk IV.

Stanza 10
1 **iolly**: handsome; gallant; amorous, as he 'rashly lusted' (11.3). **3 by right**: see 12.4n. **4 alowd**: loudly; publicly. **8–9** Britomart must quibble, for if he gains her love (Amoret), he would also gain her.

Stanza 11
2 **younker**: 'young Knight' (15.1). **6** On the conjunction of courtesy and chivalry, see VI i 2.7–9n. **stout**: brave. **7–9** I.e. she pondered how to reconcile (**accord**) a matter so difficult (**so far in dout**), i.e. to uphold the custom of the castle and yet include the knight. **salue** suggests healing. **showne**: decreed.

Stanza 12
1 **Seneschall**: the household official who administers justice. **deeme**: judge. **2 Of whom she asked . . . 4 free from chalenge set**: freed from any claim, referring to ownership gained through knightly combat. Britomart won Amoret in

13

With that her glistring helmet she vnlaced;
  Which doft, her golden lockes, that were vp bound
  Still in a knot, vnto her heeles downe traced,
  And like a silken veile in compasse round
  About her backe and all her bodie wound:
  Like as the shining skie in summers night,
  What time the dayes with scorching heat abound,
  Is creasted all with lines of firie light,
That it prodigious seemes in common peoples sight.

14

Such when those Knights and Ladies all about
  Beheld her, all were with amazement smit,
  And euery one gan grow in secret dout
  Of this and that, according to each wit:
  Some thought that some enchantment faygned it;
  Some, that *Bellona* in that warlike wise
  To them appear'd, with shield and armour fit;
  Some, that it was a maske of strange disguise:
So diuersely each one did sundrie doubts deuise.

15

But that young Knight, which through her gentle deed
  Was to that goodly fellowship restor'd,
  Ten thousand thankes did yeeld her for her meed,
  And doubly ouercommen, her ador'd:
  So did they all their former strife accord;
  And eke fayre *Amoret* now freed from feare,
  More franke affection did to her afford,
  And to her bed, which she was wont forbeare,
Now freely drew, and found right safe assurance theare.

16

Where all that night they of their loues did treat,
  And hard aduentures twixt themselues alone,
  That each the other gan with passion great,
  And griefull pittie priuately bemone.
  The morow next so soone as *Titan* shone,
  They both vprose, and to their waies them dight:
  Long wandred they, yet neuer met with none,
  That to their willes could them direct aright,
Or to them tydings tell, that mote their harts delight.

17

Lo thus they rode, till at the last they spide
  Two armed Knights, that toward them did pace,
  And ech of them had ryding by his side
  A Ladie, seeming in so farre a space,
  But Ladies none they were, albee in face
  And outward shew faire semblance they did beare;
  For vnder maske of beautie and good grace,
  Vile treason and fowle falshood hidden were,
That mote to none but to the warie wise appeare.

18

The one of them the false *Duessa* hight,
  That now had chang'd her former wonted hew:
  For she could d'on so manie shapes in sight,
  As euer could Cameleon colours new;
  So could she forge all colours, saue the trew.
  The other no whit better was then shee,
  But that such as she was, she plaine did shew;
  Yet otherwise much worse, if worse might bee,
And dayly more offensiue vnto each degree.

---

combat, as had Scudamour; see 39.6. **5 let**: hindrance. **7–9** Britomart claims him as he would have claimed Amoret if she had lost. Now in a *ménage à trois*, he enjoys them both as friends, as she allows at 10.9.

Stanza 13
The third of Britomart's four unveilings in the poem; see III i 43*n*, and cf. esp. III ix 20.3–9. This is the only time she voluntarily lets her hair down to declare her womanhood. **4 in compasse**: encompassing. **6–9** Summer lightning seen, as William Fulke writes in *A Goodly Gallery* (1571), 'on sommer nights and eveninges, after a whote daie . . . terrible to beholde, not hurtful to any thing'; cited Heninger 1960:75. **prodigious**: ominous, as Florimell's hair stretched out like a comet causes beholders to fear at III i 16.5–9.

Stanza 14
5–9 Of the three explanations, the third is comically wrong for Britomart resolved to 'maske in strange disguise' (III iii 51.9) by putting *on* armour. **Bellona**: the goddess of war to whom Britomart is compared at III ix 22.1.

Stanza 15
4 doubly: by her prowess and courtesy as a knight and by her beauty as a woman. Cf. the twofold response of men to her at III i 46.1–5. **6** For a second time 'Britomart saues Amoret' (Arg.), marking a change from her rejection of Malecasta as a bedfellow. **8 forbeare**: avoid, shun.

Stanza 16
The homoerotic relationship between Britomart and Amoret is noted by Paglia 1990:182. Stephens 1998:38 judges it 'the one happy bed scene in the whole poem', though at III x 48 both Hellenore and her satyr have good reason to be happier. **6 dight**: went.

Stanza 17
1 Lo thus: 'Long thus', sugg. Church 1758 who compares 16.7. **4** I.e. appearing at that distance to be a lady.

Stanza 18
4–5 Proverbial (Smith 92). **7** Change affects even this claim: Ate is said to wear a 'maske of beautie' at 17.6–7 (cf. 31.5–8) but at 48.1 Scudamour addresses her, though perhaps only pejoratively, as 'Vile hag'. **9 vnto each degree**: to people of all classes.

Stanzas 19–30
A twelve-stanza digression on the nature of **Ate**, the chief enemy of friendship: her house (20–24), her garden (25–26), and a description of four of her senses (27–29). It reaches its climax in her opposition to Concord. Her ancestors include Homer's goddess of discord (*Iliad* 19.91–94, 126–31), Virgil's Allecto (*Aen.* 7.324–29), and Ariosto's Discordia (*Orl. Fur.* 14.83–84). See 'Ate' in the *SEnc*. She is the female counterpart to Atin; see II iv 42.5*n*.

19

Her name was *Ate*, mother of debate,
    And all dissention, which doth dayly grow
    Amongst fraile men, that many a publike state
    And many a priuate oft doth ouerthrow.
    Her false *Duessa* who full well did know,
    To be most fit to trouble noble knights,
    Which hunt for honor, raised from below,
    Out of the dwellings of the damned sprights,
Where she in darknes wastes her cursed daies and nights.

20

Hard by the gates of hell her dwelling is,
    There whereas all the plagues and harmes abound,
    Which punish wicked men, that walke amisse:
    It is a darksome delue farre vnder ground,
    With thornes and barren brakes enuirond round,
    That none the same may easily out win;
    Yet many waies to enter may be found,
    But none to issue forth when one is in:
For discord harder is to end then to begin.

21

And all within the riuen walls were hung
    With ragged monuments of times forepast,
    All which the sad effects of discord sung:
    There were rent robes, and broken scepters plast,
    Altars defyl'd, and holy things defast,
    Disshiuered speares, and shields ytorne in twaine,
    Great cities ransackt, and strong castles rast,
    Nations captiued, and huge armies slaine:
Of all which ruines there some relicks did remaine.

22

There was the signe of antique Babylon,
    Of fatall Thebes, of Rome that raigned long,
    Of sacred Salem, and sad Ilion,
    For memorie of which on high there hong

The golden Apple, cause of all their wrong,
    For which the three faire Goddesses did striue:
    There also was the name of *Nimrod* strong,
    Of *Alexander*, and his Princes fiue,
Which shar'd to them the spoiles that he had got aliue.

23

And there the relicks of the drunken fray,
    The which amongst the *Lapithees* befell,
    And of the bloodie feast, which sent away
    So many *Centaures* drunken soules to hell,
    That vnder great *Alcides* furie fell:
    And of the dreadfull discord, which did driue
    The noble *Argonauts* to outrage fell,
    That each of life sought others to depriue,
All mindlesse of the Golden fleece, which made them striue.

24

And eke of priuate persons many moe,
    That were too long a worke to count them all;
    Some of sworne friends, that did their faith forgoe;
    Some of borne brethren, prov'd vnnaturall;
    Some of deare louers, foes perpetuall:
    Witnesse their broken bandes there to be seene,
    Their girlonds rent, their bowres despoyled all;
    The moniments whereof there byding beene,
As plaine as at the first, when they were fresh and greene.

25

Such was her house within; but all without,
    The barren ground was full of wicked weedes,
    Which she her selfe had sowen all about,
    Now growen great, at first of little seedes,
    The seedes of euill wordes, and factious deedes;
    Which when to ripenesse due they growen arre,
    Bring foorth an infinite increase, that breedes
    Tumultuous trouble and contentious iarre,
The which most often end in bloudshed and in warre.

Stanza 19
1 debate: strife. **7–9** In Homer, Ate is thrown from heaven down to earth but S. insists on her hellish origins; cf. 26.7–9, ii 1.1–3. At V ix 47.3 she is 'that old hag of hellish hew'.

Stanza 20
4 delue: pit or cave. **5 thornes and barren brakes**: as 'thornes and briars' show earth to be cursed (Heb. 6.8). Hence **brakes**, linked with briers at VI v 17.3, is either bracken growing on barren ground (cf. 25.2) or barren of fruit. **6–9** The apparent contradiction led Church 1758 to suggest 'few' for line 8. Yet the proverbial line 9 indicates that the paths are one-way: all lead in, none leads out; but see Olmsted 1994:125. **out win**: get out of.

Stanza 21
3 effects: also signs, outward manifestations. **sung**: proclaimed, but suggesting the musical sense. **6 Disshiuered**: shattered. **7 rast**: razed.

Stanza 22
1–3 Babylon and **Salem** (Jerusalem, and therefore **sacred**) are the archetypal, antithetical biblical cities. Their classical counterparts are **Thebes** (**fatall** because of the curse upon it through Oedipus) and **Ilion** (Troy), which are linked at II ix 45.6–9. In *Comm Sonn* 4, 'antique *Babel*, Empresse of the East' is linked with 'Second *Babell* tyrant of the West', i.e. **Rome**. **signe**: emblem, token, monument, as 21.2, 24.8. **4–6** See II vii 55.4–9 and *n*. **7 Nimrod**: see I v 48.1–2*n*. **8–9** Cf. 1 Macc. 1.7. **fiue**: only four are listed in the Geneva gloss to the vision in Dan. 8.8–9 but a fifth, Antiochus, is inferred from the prophecy that 'out of one of them came forthe a litle horne'. **to them**: i.e. among themselves.

Stanza 23
1–5 As do T. Cooper 1565 and others, S. conflates the battle between the Lapithae and the Centaurs at the marriage of Pirithous (Ovid, *Met.* 12.210–535) and Hercules's fight with the Centaurs (536–41). See VI x 13*n*. On S.'s treatment of the battles, see Cook 1996:105–06. **6–9** See ii 1.7–9. **which . . . striue**: i.e. for which they had striven.

Stanza 24
6–7 Correlative verse: **bandes** refers to **friends**; **girlonds** to **brethren**; and **bowres** to **louers**. The three kinds of relationship are listed at ix 1.5–7. **8 byding beene**: remain.

26

And those same cursed seedes doe also serue
  To her for bread, and yeeld her liuing food:
  For life it is to her, when others sterue
  Through mischieuous debate, and deadly feood,
  That she may sucke their life, and drinke their blood,
  With which she from her childhood had bene fed.
  For she at first was borne of hellish brood,
  And by infernall furies nourished,
That by her monstrous shape might easily be red.

27

Her face most fowle and filthy was to see,
  With squinted eyes contrarie wayes intended,
  And loathly mouth, vnmeete a mouth to bee,
  That nought but gall and venim comprehended,
  And wicked wordes that God and man offended:
  Her lying tongue was in two parts diuided,
  And both the parts did speake, and both contended;
  And as her tongue, so was her hart discided,
That neuer thoght one thing, but doubly stil was guided.

28

Als as she double spake, so heard she double,
  With matchlesse eares deformed and distort,
  Fild with false rumors and seditious trouble,
  Bred in assemblies of the vulgar sort,
  That still are led with euery light report.
  And as her eares so eke her feet were odde,
  And much vnlike, th'one long, the other short,
  And both misplast; that when th'one forward yode,
The other backe retired, and contrarie trode.

29

Likewise vnequall were her handes twaine,
  That one did reach, the other pusht away,
  That one did make, the other mard againe,
  And sought to bring all things vnto decay;

Whereby great riches gathered manie a day,
  She in short space did often bring to nought,
  And their possessours often did dismay.
  For all her studie was and all her thought,
How she might ouerthrow the things that Concord wrought.

30

So much her malice did her might surpas,
  That euen th'Almightie selfe she did maligne,
  Because to man so mercifull he was,
  And vnto all his creatures so benigne,
  Sith she her selfe was of his grace indigne:
  For all this worlds faire workmanship she tride,
  Vnto his last confusion to bring,
  And that great golden chaine quite to diuide,
With which it blessed Concord hath together tide.

31

Such was that hag, which with *Duessa* roade,
  And seruing her in her malitious vse,
  To hurt good knights, was as it were her baude,
  To sell her borrowed beautie to abuse.
  For though like withered tree, that wanteth iuyce,
  She old and crooked were, yet now of late,
  As fresh and fragrant as the floure deluce
  She was become, by chaunge of her estate,
And made full goodly ioyance to her new found mate.

32

Her mate he was a iollie youthfull knight,
  That bore great sway in armes and chiualrie,
  And was indeed a man of mickle might:
  His name was *Blandamour*, that did descrie
  His fickle mind full of inconstancie.
  And now himselfe he fitted had right well,
  With two companions of like qualitie,
  Faithlesse *Duessa*, and false *Paridell*,
That whether were more false, full hard it is to tell.

Stanza 25
The garden of Ate is designed as an infernal garden of Adonis. 5–9 Another example of correlative verse: **wordes** breed **trouble** which ends in **bloudshed**, **deedes** breed **iarre** which ends in **warre**.

Stanza 26
1–6 In parody of 'the liuing bread' (John 6.51) and blood of the Eucharist upon which men may feed and live for ever. **liuing food**: food that nourishes life. **mischieuous debate**: injurious conflict. **feood** (feud): hatred, hostility. **9 red**: seen.

Stanza 27
2 intended: directed. **4 comprehended**: contained. **6–8** Ate's double tongue invokes the warning in Ecclus. 28.13–21 against the double-tongued; her double heart invokes the lament in Ps. 12.2 against those who 'speake with a double heart'. **discided**: cut asunder.

Stanza 28
2 matchlesse: unmatched. **3 Fild**: also defiled. **5 still**: always. **6–9** The witty play in 7 on the metrical foot, trochee, is noted by Fried 1981:274. **odde**: unequal. **yode**: went.

Stanza 29
2, 3 **That**: what.

Stanza 30
2 maligne: regard with hatred. **3–4** Cf. II viii 1.5–7. **5 indigne**: unworthy. **7 confusion**: overthrow. **8–9 that great golden chaine**: see I v 25.5*n*. As in Chaucer, *Knight's Tale* 2987–93, it serves as a symbol of cosmic concord.

Stanza 31
1 that hag: a title inherited from the witch at III vii 9.8. **4 her borrowed beautie**: may be Duessa's, as at II i 22.7; or inherited from her. **to abuse**: to be defiled. **7 floure deluce**: the fleur-de-lis; see II vi 16.1–2*n*. **9 ioyance**: sexual pleasure, as at VI xi 7.4.

Stanza 32
1–5 Blandamour: flattering lover (from Lat. *blandus* + *amor*), one whose 'false allurements' have gained him the love of a thousand women (ii 10.3–5). As one who prefers to gain love by flattery rather than by conquest (see 39.6 and iv 4.1–5), he represents 'fayned blandishment', which is noted as absent in the temple of Venus at x 26.7, and may be taken as the male version of Blandina; see VI iii 42.6*n*. His name notes his

33

Now when this gallant with his goodly crew,
    From farre espide the famous *Britomart*,
    Like knight aduenturous in outward vew,
    With his faire paragon, his conquests part,
    Approching nigh, eftsoones his wanton hart
    Was tickled with delight, and iesting sayd;
    Lo there Sir *Paridel*, for your desart,
    Good lucke presents you with yond louely mayd,
For pitie that ye want a fellow for your ayd.

34

By that the louely paire drew nigh to hond:
    Whom when as *Paridel* more plaine beheld,
    Albee in heart he like affection fond,
    Yet mindfull how he late by one was feld,
    That did those armes and that same scutchion weld,
    He had small lust to buy his loue so deare,
    But answerd, Sir him wise I neuer held,
    That hauing once escaped perill neare,
Would afterwards afresh the sleeping euill reare.

35

This knight too late his manhood and his might,
    I did assay, that me right dearely cost,
    Ne list I for reuenge prouoke new fight,
    Ne for light Ladies loue, that soone is lost.
    The hot-spurre youth so scorning to be crost,
    Take then to you this Dame of mine (quoth hee)
    And I without your perill or your cost,
    Will chalenge yond same other for my fee:
So forth he fiercely prickt, that one him scarce could see.

36

The warlike Britonesse her soone addrest,
    And with such vncouth welcome did receaue
    Her fayned Paramour, her forced guest,
    That being forst his saddle soone to leaue,

Him selfe he did of his new loue deceaue:
    And made him selfe thensample of his follie.
    Which done, she passed forth not taking leaue,
    And left him now as sad, as whilome iollie,
Well warned to beware with whom he dar'd to dallie.

37

Which when his other companie beheld,
    They to his succour ran with readie ayd:
    And finding him vnable once to weld,
    They reared him on horsebacke, and vpstayd,
    Till on his way they had him forth conuayd:
    And all the way with wondrous griefe of mynd,
    And shame, he shewd him selfe to be dismayd,
    More for the loue which he had left behynd,
Then that which he had to Sir *Paridel* resynd.

38

Nathlesse he forth did march well as he might,
    And made good semblance to his companie,
    Dissembling his disease and euill plight;
    Till that ere long they chaunced to espie
    Two other knights, that towards them did ply
    With speedie course, as bent to charge them new.
    Whom when as *Blandamour* approching nie,
    Perceiu'd to be such as they seemd in vew,
He was full wo, and gan his former griefe renew.

39

For th'one of them he perfectly describe,
    To be Sir *Scudamour*, by that he bore
    The God of loue, with wings displayed wide,
    Whom mortally he hated euermore,
    Both for his worth, that all men did adore,
    And eke because his loue he wonne by right:
    Which when he thought, it grieued him full sore,
    That through the bruses of his former fight,
He now vnable was to wreake his old despight.

---

fickleness shown at ii 5.1–3 and ix 21.5–6. Draper 1932:100 suggests Lat. *blandus*, enticing. It may have been taken from Chaucer's Pleyndamour (Blayndamour in Thynne's 1532 edn) in the *Tale of Sir Thopas* 900. See 'Blandamour' in the *SEnc*. **descrie**: disclose; describe. **9 whether**: which of the two couples.

Stanza 33
4 paragon: companion. **conquests part**: booty, reward of conquest. **9 ayd**: sexual, rather than military.

Stanza 34
1 louely: affectionate. **4** Referring to his encounter with Britomart at III ix 14–16. **5 scutchion**: shield.

Stanza 35
1 Since Paridell was present when Britomart revealed herself 'To be a woman wight' (III ix 21.8), he may regard her as male because he regards **manhood** and **might** as masculine. **5–9 hot-spurre**: because he **fiercely prickt**. In offering Ate to Paridell, Blandamour begins to earn the title 'faithlesse' at V ix 41.3. **chalenge**: claim. **fee**: prize; rightful possession.

Stanza 36
1 addrest: made ready. **2 vncouth**: unpleasing; rude. **3–5** The pronouns in 3 may refer to Britomart or to Amoret, as Anderson 1971:191 notes, while Stephens 1998:38 concludes that **his new loue** refers to Amoret. Yet in seeking Amoret as **his new loue**, he seeks Britomart's love, for any encounter with her is a courtship, as here **dallie** (i.e. flirt) suggests. **deceaue**: cheat out of.

Stanza 37
1 other companie: companions. **3 once to weld**: even to move.

Stanza 38
2 And assumed a fair demeanour . . . **3 disease**: distress. **5 ply**: move.

Stanza 39
1–3 For Scudamour's shield, see III xi 7.6–9*n*. **descride**: perceived. **6** Scudamour claims Amoret **by right** of conquest, as he relates in canto x; cf. ix 38.8. His right to her is denied by Blandamour and Duessa at 51.2, 7.

40

For thy he thus to *Paridel* bespake,
  Faire Sir, of friendship let me now you pray,
  That as I late aduentured for your sake,
  The hurts whereof me now from battell stay,
  Ye will me now with like good turne repay,
  And iustifie my cause on yonder knight.
  Ah Sir (said *Paridel*) do not dismay
  Your selfe for this, my selfe will for you fight,
As ye haue done for me: the left hand rubs the right.

41

With that he put his spurres vnto his steed,
  With speare in rest, and toward him did fare,
  Like shaft out of a bow preuenting speed.
  But *Scudamour* was shortly well aware
  Of his approch, and gan him selfe prepare
  Him to receiue with entertainment meete.
  So furiously they met, that either bare
  The other downe vnder their horses feete,
That what of them became, themselues did scarsly weete.

42

As when two billowes in the Irish sowndes,
  Forcibly driuen with contrarie tydes
  Do meete together, each abacke rebowndes
  With roaring rage; and dashing on all sides,
  That filleth all the sea with fome, diuydes
  The doubtfull current into diuers wayes:
  So fell those two in spight of both their prydes,
  But *Scudamour* himselfe did soone vprayse,
And mounting light his foe for lying long vpbrayes.

43

Who rolled on an heape lay still in swound,
  All carelesse of his taunt and bitter rayle,
  Till that the rest him seeing lie on ground,
  Ran hastily, to weete what did him ayle.
  Where finding that the breath gan him to fayle,
  With busie care they stroue him to awake,
  And doft his helmet, and vndid his mayle:
  So much they did, that at the last they brake
His slomber, yet so mazed, that he nothing spake.

44

Which when as *Blandamour* beheld, he sayd,
  False faitour *Scudamour*, that hast by slight
  And foule aduantage this good Knight dismayd,
  A Knight much better then thy selfe behight,
  Well falles it thee that I am not in plight
  This day, to wreake the dammage by thee donne:
  Such is thy wont, that still when any Knight
  Is weakned, then thou doest him ouerronne:
So hast thou to thy selfe false honour often wonne.

45

He little answer'd, but in manly heart
  His mightie indignation did forbeare,
  Which was not yet so secret, but some part
  Thereof did in his frouning face appeare:
  Like as a gloomie cloud, the which doth beare
  An hideous storme, is by the Northerne blast
  Quite ouerblowne, yet doth not passe so cleare,
  But that it all the skie doth ouercast
With darknes dred, and threatens all the world to wast.

46

Ah gentle knight, then false *Duessa* sayd,
  Why do ye striue for Ladies loue so sore,
  Whose chiefe desire is loue and friendly aid
  Mongst gentle Knights to nourish euermore?
  Ne be ye wroth Sir *Scudamour* therefore,
  That she your loue list loue another knight,
  Ne do your selfe dislike a whit the more;
  For Loue is free, and led with selfe delight,
Ne will enforced be with maisterdome or might.

47

So false *Duessa*, but vile *Ate* thus;
  Both foolish knights, I can but laugh at both,
  That striue and storme with stirre outrageous,
  For her that each of you alike doth loth,
  And loues another, with whom now she goth
  In louely wise, and sleepes, and sports, and playes;
  Whilest both you here with many a cursed oth,
  Sweare she is yours, and stirre vp bloudie frayes,
To win a willow bough, whilest other weares the bayes.

Stanza 40
The aphorism, 'To beg a thing at a friend's hand, is to buy it', indicates the absence of true friendship between Blandamour and Paridell, as L.J. Mills 1937:432 notes. **1 For thy**: therefore. **9** Proverbial: Smith 355.

Stanza 41
3 preuenting speed: passing speed itself in being swifter.

Stanza 42
1 sowndes: with the pun, as **roaring** suggests, appropriate to the narrow waters of a strait. **9 vpbrayes**: upbraids.

Stanza 43
1 on: in. **2 rayle**: railing.

Stanza 44
2 faitour: villain; impostor. **slight**: trickery. **4 behight**: esteemed. **5 plight**: good condition.

Stanza 45
2 forbeare: control.

Stanza 46
1 Ah gentle knight: addressing Blandamour. **8–9** Duessa mocks Britomart's claim, 'Ne may loue be compeld by maistery' (III i 25.7–9 and see *n*), by declaring love to be self-regarding. **maisterdome**: masterful behaviour.

Stanza 47
6 louely: amorous. **9 willow bough**: 'worne of forlorne Paramours' (I i 9.3). **bayes**: the laurel, 'meed of mightie Conquerours' (I i 9.1).

48

Vile hag (sayd *Scudamour*) why dost thou lye?
  And falsly seekst a vertuous wight to shame?
  Fond knight (sayd she) the thing that with this eye
  I saw, why should I doubt to tell the same?
  Then tell (quoth *Blandamour*) and feare no blame,
  Tell what thou saw'st, maulgre who so it heares.
  I saw (quoth she) a stranger knight, whose name
  I wote not well, but in his shield he beares
(That well I wote) the heads of many broken speares.

49

I saw him haue your *Amoret* at will,
  I saw him kisse, I saw him her embrace,
  I saw him sleepe with her all night his fill,
  All manie nights, and manie by in place,
  That present were to testifie the case.
  Which when as *Scudamour* did heare, his heart
  Was thrild with inward griefe, as when in chace
  The Parthian strikes a stag with shiuering dart,
The beast astonisht stands in middest of his smart.

50

So stood Sir *Scudamour*, when this he heard,
  Ne word he had to speake for great dismay,
  But lookt on *Glauce* grim, who woxe afeard
  Of outrage for the words, which she heard say,
  Albee vntrue she wist them by assay.
  But *Blandamour*, whenas he did espie
  His chaunge of cheere, that anguish did bewray,
  He woxe full blithe, as he had got thereby,
And gan thereat to triumph without victorie.

51

Lo recreant (sayd he) the fruitlesse end
  Of thy vaine boast, and spoile of loue misgotten,
  Whereby the name of knight-hood thou dost shend,
  And all true louers with dishonor blotten,

All things not rooted well, will soone be rotten.
  Fy fy false knight (then false *Duessa* cryde)
  Vnworthy life that loue with guile hast gotten,
  Be thou, where euer thou do go or ryde,
Loathed of ladies all, and of all knights defyde.

52

But *Scudamour* for passing great despight
  Staid not to answer, scarcely did refraine,
  But that in all those knights and ladies sight,
  He for reuenge had guiltlesse *Glauce* slaine:
  But being past, he thus began amaine;
  False traitour squire, false squire, of falsest knight,
  Why doth mine hand from thine auenge abstaine,
  Whose Lord hath done my loue this foule despight?
Why do I not it wreake, on thee now in my might?

53

Discourteous, disloyall *Britomart*,
  Vntrue to God, and vnto man vniust,
  What vengeance due can equall thy desart,
  That hast with shamefull spot of sinfull lust
  Defil'd the pledge committed to thy trust?
  Let vgly shame and endlesse infamy
  Colour thy name with foule reproaches rust.
  Yet thou false Squire his fault shalt deare aby,
And with thy punishment his penance shalt supply.

54

The aged Dame him seeing so enraged,
  Was dead with feare, nathlesse as neede required,
  His flaming furie sought to haue assuaged
  With sober words, that sufferance desired,
  Till time the tryall of her truth expyred:
  And euermore sought *Britomart* to cleare.
  But he the more with furious rage was fyred,
  And thrise his hand to kill her did vpreare,
And thrise he drew it backe: so did at last forbeare.

Stanza 48
3 **Fond**: foolish.   4 **doubt**: fear.   6 **maulgre**: notwithstanding.
9 The sign of many conquests of knights, thereby gaining their
ladies; cf. III xi 52.6.

Stanza 49
4 **in place**: there.   7–9 Perhaps suggested by Virgil, *Aen.*
12.856–59: the Parthian arrow armed with an incurable
poison is here the wound of slander; and by Prov. 25.18: 'A
man that beareth false witnes against his neighbour is like a
sharpe arrowe'. The **stag** suggests cuckold's horns.   **shiuering**:
quivering; or capable of splitting.

Stanza 50
5 **assay**: trial, i.e. knowledge.   8 **got**: profited; i.e. gained the
victory.

Stanza 51
1–4 **recreant**: coward, a term of the greatest opprobrium.
misgotten: having been gained by **guile**. Scudamour boasts of
gaining Amoret as his **spoile** at x 3.3, 58.3.   **shend**: disgrace.
5 Proverbial: Smith 666.

Stanza 52
1 **passing**: exceeding.   5 **But being past**: i.e. in getting over
the anger that would have led him to kill Glauce; or, having left
the others (though they are together at ii 3).   **amaine**: vehe-
mently.   7 **thine auenge**: i.e. revenge upon you.

Stanza 53
The stanza is structured on twin charges against Britomart: as
a (male) knight who has defiled his pledge, he is discourteous
and untrue to God; as a person who is guilty of lust, he is
disloyal and unjust to man, etc.   1 **disloyall**: unfaithful; as he
dreams at v 43.8, reversing his praise of Britomart as 'gentlest
knight aliue' at III xi 19.1.   6–7 He transfers to Britomart the
charges made against him at 51.3–9.   8 **aby**: pay the penalty
for.

Stanza 54
4 **sufferance**: forbearance.   5 I.e. until the passing of time
brought proof of Britomart's loyalty by revealing the truth, as
happens at vi 28.1–5. Instead of being told here that Britomart
is a woman, Scudamour must see her as one.

Cant. II.

Blandamour winnes false Florimell,
Paridell for her striues,
They are accorded: Agape
doth lengthen her sonnes liues.

1

Firebrand of hell first tynd in Phlegeton,
  By thousand furies, and from thence out throwen
  Into this world, to worke confusion,
  And set it all on fire by force vnknowen,
  Is wicked discord, whose small sparkes once blowen
  None but a God or godlike man can slake;
  Such as was *Orpheus*, that when strife was growen
  Amongst those famous ympes of Greece, did take
His siluer Harpe in hand, and shortly friends them make.

2

Or such as that celestiall Psalmist was,
  That when the wicked feend his Lord tormented,
  With heauenly notes, that did all other pas,
  The outrage of his furious fit relented.
  Such Musicke is wise words with time concented,
  To moderate stiffe minds, disposd to striue:
  Such as that prudent Romane well inuented,
  What time his people into partes did riue,
Them reconcyld againe, and to their homes did driue.

3

Such vs'd wise *Glauce* to that wrathfull knight,
  To calme the tempest of his troubled thought:
  Yet *Blandamour* with termes of foule despight,
  And *Paridell* her scornd, and set at nought,

As old and crooked and not good for ought.
  Both they vnwise, and warelesse of the euill,
  That by themselues vnto themselues is wrought,
  Through that false witch, and that foule aged dreuill,
The one a feend, the other an incarnate deuill.

4

With whom as they thus rode accompanide,
  They were encountred of a lustie Knight,
  That had a goodly Ladie by his side,
  To whom he made great dalliance and delight.
  It was to weete the bold Sir *Ferraugh* hight,
  He that from *Braggadocchio* whilome reft
  The snowy *Florimell*, whose beautie bright
  Made him seeme happie for so glorious theft;
Yet was it in due triall but a wandring weft.

5

Which when as *Blandamour*, whose fancie light
  Was alwaies flitting as the wauering wind,
  After each beautie, that appeard in sight,
  Beheld, eftsoones it prickt his wanton mind
  With sting of lust, that reasons eye did blind,
  That to Sir *Paridell* these words he sent;
  Sir knight why ride ye dumpish thus behind,
  Since so good fortune doth to you present
So fayre a spoyle, to make you ioyous meriment?

Book IV Canto ii

Argument
3 accorded: reconciled.

Stanza 1
1–3 Furor's firebrand was kindled (**tynd**) in the Stygian lake at II v 22.6–8. **Phlegeton**: the infernal river of fire; see I v 33.1–6*n*. **confusion**: ruin, destruction. **7–9** The **famous ympes** (youths) of Greece are the Argonauts. Their **discord**, which is told at i 23.6–9, is given its musical sense because it was quelled by Orpheus's lyre, **siluer** referring to the beauty of its sound. For the story, see Apollonius, *Argonautica* 1.492–516.

Stanza 2
1–4 'When the euil spirit of God came vpon Saul, Dauid toke an harpe and plaied with his hand, and Saul was refreshed, and was eased: for the euil spirit departed from him' (1 Sam. 16.23). **relented**: abated. **5–6 with time concented**: harmonized; fitting for the time. **stiffe**: obstinate. **7–9** When the Romans quarrelled among themselves, Menenius Agrippa reconciled them with his fable of the belly. Sidney, *Defence of*

Poetry 93, cites this 'so often remembered' tale to prove the effects of poetical invention.

Stanza 3
1–2 Glauce's pacifying role associates her with Orpheus, as Stephens 1998:66–72 notes. **6 warelesse**: unaware; unwary. **8 dreuill**: a dirty person.

Stanza 4
2 lustie: young; vigorous. **5–9 Ferraugh**: or '*Ferrau*' (iv 8.2), the name of a pagan knight who pursues Angelica in Ariosto, *Orl. Fur.* 1.14–21. It suggests 'ferray', an obs. form of 'foray'. See III viii 16.2–3*n*. **whilome**: at III viii 19. His **so glorious theft** anticipates Scudamour's theft of Amoret. **in due triall**: when duly tried. **wandring weft**: in its legal sense, property left ownerless (as III x 36.3). It suggests something not worth claiming. The true waif is Florimell, who is so named at xii 31.3.

Stanza 5
7–9 At i 33.7–9, Blandamour challenged Paridell to fight Britomart, which he refused because he had been defeated by her at III ix 14–16; and in fighting her himself, he was

6

But *Paridell* that had too late a tryall
    Of the bad issue of his counsell vaine,
    List not to hearke, but made this faire denyall;
    Last turne was mine, well proued to my paine,
    This now be yours, God send you better gaine.
    Whose scoffed words he taking halfe in scorne,
    Fiercely forth prickt his steed as in disdaine,
    Against that Knight, ere he him well could torne;
By meanes whereof he hath him lightly ouerborne.

7

Who with the sudden stroke astonisht sore,
    Vpon the ground a while in slomber lay;
    The whiles his loue away the other bore,
    And shewing her, did *Paridell* vpbray;
    Lo sluggish Knight the victors happie pray:
    So fortune friends the bold: whom *Paridell*
    Seeing so faire indeede, as he did say,
    His hart with secret enuie gan to swell,
And inly grudge at him, that he had sped so well.

8

Nathlesse proud man himselfe the other deemed,
    Hauing so peerelesse paragon ygot:
    For sure the fayrest *Florimell* him seemed,
    To him was fallen for his happie lot,
    Whose like aliue on earth he weened not:
    Therefore he her did court, did serue, did wooe,
    With humblest suit that he imagine mot,
    And all things did deuise, and all things dooe,
That might her loue prepare, and liking win theretoo.

9

She in regard thereof him recompenst
    With golden words, and goodly countenance,
    And such fond fauours sparingly dispenst:
    Sometimes him blessing with a light eye-glance,
    And coy lookes tempring with loose dalliance;
    Sometimes estranging him in sterner wise,
    That hauing cast him in a foolish trance,
    He seemed brought to bed in Paradise,
And prou'd himselfe most foole, in what he seem'd most wise.

10

So great a mistresse of her art she was,
    And perfectly practiz'd in womans craft,
    That though therein himselfe he thought to pas,
    And by his false allurements wylie draft,
    Had thousand women of their loue beraft,
    Yet now he was surpriz'd: for that false spright,
    Which that same witch had in this forme engraft,
    Was so expert in euery subtile slight,
That it could ouerreach the wisest earthly wight.

11

Yet he to her did dayly seruice more,
    And dayly more deceiued was thereby;
    Yet *Paridell* him enuied therefore,
    As seeming plast in sole felicity:
    So blind is lust, false colours to descry.
    But *Ate* soone discouering his desire,
    And finding now fit opportunity
    To stirre vp strife, twixt loue and spight and ire,
Did priuily put coles vnto his secret fire.

12

By sundry meanes thereto she prickt him forth,
    Now with remembrance of those spightfull speaches,
    Now with opinion of his owne more worth,
    Now with recounting of like former breaches
    Made in their friendship, as that Hag him teaches:
    And euer when his passion is allayd,
    She it reuiues and new occasion reaches:
    That on a time as they together way'd,
He made him open chalenge, and thus boldly sayd.

13

Too boastfull *Blandamour*, too long I beare
    The open wrongs, thou doest me day by day;
    Well know'st thou, when we friendship first did sweare,
    The couenant was, that euery spoyle or pray
    Should equally be shard betwixt vs tway:
    Where is my part then of this Ladie bright,
    Whom to thy selfe thou takest quite away?
    Render therefore therein to me my right,
Or answere for thy wrong, as shall fall out in fight.

---

defeated. At i 40.1–6 he challenged him to fight Scudamour, which he accepted, and was defeated. Now he challenges him to fight Ferraugh, which he refuses, but in fighting him himself, he wins.

Stanza 6
6 **scoffed**: spoken in scoff.   **8–9** Blandamour attacks without any formal challenge.   **lightly**: easily.

Stanza 7
2 in slomber: unconscious.   **4 vpbray**: upbraid.

Stanza 8
2 paragon: companion.   **7 mot**: might, could.

Stanza 9
8 As she did with Ferraugh: 'So made him thinke him selfe in heuen, that was in hell' (III viii 19.9).

Stanza 10
3 pas: excel.   **4 draft**: power of attraction.   **6–9** As told at III viii 7–8.   **surpriz'd**: overcome.   **slight**: cunning trick.

Stanza 12
3 opinion: favourable estimate.   **7 reaches**: gives.   **8 way'd**: journeyed; made their way.

Stanza 13
3–5 Proverbial: Smith 307.

14

Exceeding wroth thereat was *Blandamour*,
    And gan this bitter answere to him make;
    Too foolish *Paridell*, that fayrest floure
    Wouldst gather faine, and yet no paines wouldst take:
    But not so easie will I her forsake;
    This hand her wonne, this hand shall her defend.
    With that they gan their shiuering speares to shake,
    And deadly points at eithers breast to bend,
Forgetfull each to haue bene euer others frend.

15

Their firie Steedes with so vntamed forse
    Did beare them both to fell auenges end,
    That both their speares with pitilesse remorse,
    Through shield and mayle, and haberieon did wend,
    And in their flesh a griesly passage rend,
    That with the furie of their owne affret,
    Each other horse and man to ground did send;
    Where lying still a while, both did forget
The perilous present stownd, in which their liues were
                        (set.

16

As when two warlike Brigandines at sea,
    With murdrous weapons arm'd to cruell fight,
    Doe meete together on the watry lea,
    They stemme ech other with so fell despight,
    That with the shocke of their owne heedlesse might,
    Their wooden ribs are shaken nigh a sonder;
    They which from shore behold the dreadfull sight
    Of flashing fire, and heare the ordenance thonder,
Do greatly stand amaz'd at such vnwonted wonder.

17

At length they both vpstarted in amaze;
    As men awaked rashly out of dreme,
    And round about themselues a while did gaze,
    Till seeing her, that *Florimell* did seme,

In doubt to whom she victorie should deeme,
    Therewith their dulled sprights they edgd anew,
    And drawing both their swords with rage extreme,
    Like two mad mastiffes each on other flew,
And shields did share, and mailes did rash, and helmes did
                        (hew.

18

So furiously each other did assayle,
    As if their soules they would attonce haue rent
    Out of their brests, that streames of bloud did rayle
    Adowne, as if their springs of life were spent;
    That all the ground with purple bloud was sprent,
    And all their armours staynd with bloudie gore,
    Yet scarcely once to breath would they relent,
    So mortall was their malice and so sore,
Become of fayned friendship which they vow'd afore.

19

And that which is for Ladies most besitting,
    To stint all strife, and foster friendly peace,
    Was from those Dames so farre and so vnfitting,
    As that in stead of praying them surcease,
    They did much more their cruelty encrease;
    Bidding them fight for honour of their loue,
    And rather die then Ladies cause release.
    With which vaine termes so much they did them moue,
That both resolu'd the last extremities to proue.

20

There they I weene would fight vntill this day,
    Had not a Squire, euen he the Squire of Dames,
    By great aduenture trauelled that way;
    Who seeing both bent to so bloudy games,
    And both of old well knowing by their names,
    Drew nigh, to weete the cause of their debate:
    And first laide on those Ladies thousand blames,
    That did not seeke t'appease their deadly hate,
But gazed on their harmes, not pittying their estate.

Stanza 14
4 **faine**: gladly. 7 **shiuering**: quivering; capable of splitting. 8 **bend**: aim.

Stanza 15
2 . . . to cruel revenge. 3 **remorse**: cutting force. 4 **wend**: go. 6 **affret**: onslaught; see III ix 16.3*n*. 9 **stownd**: moment of peril.

Stanza 16
1 **warlike Brigandines**: brigantines equipped for war. 3 **lea**: meadow, as a calm ocean appears to a land-lubber. A sense coined by S. 4 **stemme**: ram.

Stanza 17
1 **amaze**: bewilderment. 2 **rashly**: suddenly. 6–7 I.e. with their dulled spirits newly sharpened by sight of her, they fight with swords. 9 **share**: cut. **rash**: slash.

Stanza 18
3 **rayle**: flow. 5 **sprent**: besprinkled. 7 **relent**: slacken. 8–9 Their malice against each other is deadly because their friendship is only feigned. For the proverb, see Smith 303.

Stanza 19
1 **besitting**: befitting. 3 **vnfitting**: i.e. to their natures. 4 **surcease**: stop. 9 Both resolved to fight to the death.

Stanza 20
1 Not the poet's whimsy but recognition that discord caused by feigned friendship may be interrupted but never ends. 3 **aduenture**: chance. 6 **debate**: also strife. 9 **estate**: state.

21

And then those Knights he humbly did beseech,
　　To stay their hands, till he a while had spoken:
　　Who lookt a little vp at that his speech,
　　Yet would not let their battell so be broken,
　　Both greedie fiers on other to be wroken.
　　Yet he to them so earnestly did call,
　　And them coniur'd by some well knowen token,
　　That they at last their wrothfull hands let fall,
Content to heare him speake, and glad to rest withall.

22

First he desir'd their cause of strife to see:
　　They said, it was for loue of *Florimell*.
　　Ah gentle knights (quoth he) how may that bee,
　　And she so farre astray, as none can tell.
　　Fond Squire, full angry then sayd *Paridell*,
　　Seest not the Ladie there before thy face?
　　He looked backe, and her aduizing well,
　　Weend as he said, by that her outward grace,
That fayrest *Florimell* was present there in place.

23

Glad man was he to see that ioyous sight,
　　For none aliue but ioy'd in *Florimell*,
　　And lowly to her lowting thus behight;
　　Fayrest of faire, that fairenesse doest excell,
　　This happie day I haue to greete you well,
　　In which you safe I see, whom thousand late
　　Misdoubted lost through mischiefe that befell;
　　Long may you liue in health and happie state.
She litle answer'd him, but lightly did aggrate.

24

Then turning to those Knights, he gan a new;
　　And you Sir *Blandamour* and *Paridell*,
　　That for this Ladie present in your vew,
　　Haue rays'd this cruell warre and outrage fell,

Certes me seemes bene not aduised well,
　　But rather ought in friendship for her sake
　　To ioyne your force, their forces to repell,
　　That seeke perforce her from you both to take,
And of your gotten spoyle their owne triumph to make.

25

Thereat Sir *Blandamour* with countenance sterne,
　　All full of wrath, thus fiercely him bespake;
　　A read thou Squire, that I the man may learne,
　　That dare fro me thinke *Florimell* to take.
　　Not one (quoth he) but many doe partake
　　Herein, as thus. It lately so befell,
　　That *Satyran* a girdle did vptake,
　　Well knowne to appertaine to *Florimell*,
Which for her sake he wore, as him beseemed well.

26

But when as she her selfe was lost and gone,
　　Full many knights, that loued her like deare,
　　Thereat did greatly grudge, that he alone
　　That lost faire Ladies ornament should weare,
　　And gan therefore close spight to him to beare:
　　Which he to shun, and stop vile enuies sting,
　　Hath lately caus'd to be proclaim'd each where
　　A solemne feast, with publike turneying,
To which all knights with them their Ladies are to bring.

27

And of them all she that is fayrest found,
　　Shall haue that golden girdle for reward,
　　And of those Knights who is most stout on ground,
　　Shall to that fairest Ladie be prefard.
　　Since therefore she her selfe is now your ward,
　　To you that ornament of hers pertaines,
　　Against all those, that chalenge it to gard,
　　And saue her honour with your ventrous paines;
That shall you win more glory, then ye here find gaines.

Stanza 21
5 wroken: wreaked, avenged.　**7** Since the unidentified **token** anticipates the power of Cambina's 'rod of peace' (iii 42.1) to end strife, **coniur'd** suggests that he stopped their fighting by magical means.

Stanza 22
5 Fond: foolish.　**6–7** Either **before thy face** is added to **there** to provide the 'c' rhyme, or the ladies are standing back while their knights fight. Or since he has been pursuing Florimell, he must look back to see her mirrored in the False Florimell.　**aduizing**: looking upon.

Stanza 23
3 lowting: bowing, in an act of homage.　**behight**: addressed.
7 Misdoubted: feared.　**9** She thanked him in slighting fashion.

Stanza 25
1 sterne: threatening.　**3 A read**: tell.　**learne**: teach (a lesson).
6–9 Florimell's girdle, which she lost in fleeing the witch's

beast, was found by Satyrane at III vii 31.8–9 (as he reported to Paridell at viii 49.8–9), and he used it at vii 36.1–3 to bind the beast. At viii 2.5–8, the beast returned it, broken, to the witch who showed it to her son. Satyrane must wear its *eidolon*, then, as the False Florimell is Florimell's *eidolon*; see III viii 5.5–9*n*.

Stanza 26
5 close: secret.

Stanza 27
1–4 be prefard: i.e. in addition to gaining Florimell's girdle as her prize for winning the beauty contest, the **fairest Ladie** will be offered to the winner of the tournament as his 'Paramore' (v 8.9).　**6–8** I.e. it concerns you to guard Florimell's girdle against all who lay claim to it. On its association with Florimell's honour, see v 3–5*n*.

Stanza 28
9 saue they alone: evidently they agree that she 'equally be shard' (13.5).

28

When they the reason of his words had hard,
  They gan abate the rancour of their rage,
  And with their honours and their loues regard,
  The furious flames of malice to asswage.
  Tho each to other did his faith engage,
  Like faithfull friends thenceforth to ioyne in one
  With all their force, and battell strong to wage
Gainst all those knights, as their professed fone,
That chaleng'd ought in *Florimell*, saue they alone.

29

So well accorded forth they rode together
  In friendly sort, that lasted but a while;
  And of all old dislikes they made faire weather,
  Yet all was forg'd and spred with golden foyle,
  That vnder it hidde hate and hollow guyle.
  Ne certes can that friendship long endure,
  How euer gay and goodly be the style,
  That doth ill cause or euill end enure:
For vertue is the band, that bindeth harts most sure.

30

Thus as they marched all in close disguise,
  Of fayned loue, they chaunst to ouertake
  Two knights, that lincked rode in louely wise,
  As if they secret counsels did partake;
  And each not farre behinde him had his make,
  To weete, two Ladies of most goodly hew,
  That twixt themselues did gentle purpose make,
  Vnmindfull both of that discordfull crew,
The which with speedie pace did after them pursew.

31

Who as they now approched nigh at hand,
  Deeming them doughtie as they did appeare,
  They sent that Squire afore, to vnderstand,
  What mote they be: who viewing them more neare
  Returned readie newes, that those same weare
  Two of the prowest Knights in Faery lond;
  And those two Ladies their two louers deare,
  Couragious *Cambell*, and stout *Triamond*,
With *Canacee* and *Cambine* linckt in louely bond.

32

Whylome as antique stories tellen vs,
  Those two were foes the fellonest on ground,
  And battell made the dreddest daungerous,
  That euer shrilling trumpet did resound;
  Though now their acts be no where to be found,
  As that renowmed Poet them compyled,
  With warlike numbers and Heroicke sound,
  Dan *Chaucer*, well of English vndefyled,
On Fames eternall beadroll worthie to be fyled.

33

But wicked Time that all good thoughts doth waste,
  And workes of noblest wits to nought out weare,
  That famous moniment hath quite defaste,
  And robd the world of threasure endlesse deare,
  The which mote haue enriched all vs heare.
  O cursed Eld the cankerworme of writs,
  How may these rimes, so rude as doth appeare,
  Hope to endure, sith workes of heauenly wits
Are quite deuourd, and brought to nought by little bits?

Stanza 29

1 accorded: reconciled; as Arg.3.   **3 made faire weather**: made a show of friendliness.   **4 golden foyle**: suggests deception, as at v 15.1–6.   **7 style**: outward demeanour; mere appearance. **8 enure**: put into practice.   **9** Proverbial: Smith 311.

Stanza 30

In contrast to the **discordfull crew**, which enters at i 17.2 with each knight having his lady by his side (cf. iv 2.6–9, 14.9), the true friends ride together with their ladies not far behind. On their matching, see iii 52*n*.   **3 louely**: loving.   **7 gentle purpose**: polite gossip.

Stanza 31

8–9 The name **Cambell** is derived from Camballo in Chaucer's *Squire's Tale* – hence the occasional spelling 'Cambello' – and is adapted to link with Lat. *bellum* to mark his warlike nature.   **Canacee** is the name of Camballo's sister. For **Triamond**, see 41.7–9*n*.   **Cambine** – elsewhere Cambina – is derived from Ital. *cambiare*, 'to exchange, to change' (Florio 1598) because she changes hatred to love; or from 'combine' because she joins the others in love (sugg. Belson 1964:118). See 'Cambell, Canacee, Cambina' in the *SEnc*.

Stanza 32

S.'s continuation of Chaucer's *Squire's Tale*, by which he declares himself to be Chaucer's heir, begins by imitating the opening line of the first Canterbury tale told by the Squire's father: 'Whilom, as olde stories tellen us'. On his use of the *Knight's Tale*, see Hieatt 1975a:75–78, and 'Chaucer' in the *SEnc*. On his completion of the *Squire's Tale*, see P. Cheney 1985. The verbal echoes, which show how S. found his Chaucerian heritage an inspiration but also a burden, are noted by Berry 1998:111–12. Stubblefield 1998 notes that S. imitates Chaucer in delaying the tale until the third part or canto.   **2 fellonest**: fiercest.   **8–9 Dan**: Master. A highly complimentary form of address used by S. of the classical gods, Chaucer being the only exception. The anomaly of using the title with a surname is noted by Higgins 1990:19.   **well . . . vndefyled**: cf. 'That old *Dan Geffrey* (in whose gentle spright | The pure well head of Poesie did dwell)' (VII vii 9.3–4). See Anderson 1989:30–31.   **beadroll**: catalogue.   **fyled**: placed for preservation.

Stanza 33

Thynne's 1561 edition of Chaucer's works, which most likely S. read (Hieatt 1975a:19–28), records that 'There can be founde no more of this foresaid tale'.   **6–9** S. compliments Chaucer by imitating his complaint: 'This olde storie, in Latyn which I fynde, | . . . That elde, which that al can frete and bite, | As hit hath freten mony a noble storie, | Hath nygh devoured out of oure memorie' (*Anelida and Arcite* 10–14).

34
Then pardon, O most sacred happie spirit,
    That I thy labours lost may thus reuiue,
    And steale from thee the meede of thy due merit,
    That none durst euer whilest thou wast aliue,
    And being dead in vaine yet many striue:
    Ne dare I like, but through infusion sweete
    Of thine owne spirit, which doth in me suruiue,
    I follow here the footing of thy feete,
That with thy meaning so I may the rather meete.

35
Cambelloes sister was fayre *Canacee,*
    That was the learnedst Ladie in her dayes,
    Well seene in euerie science that mote bee,
    And euery secret worke of natures wayes,
    In wittie riddles, and in wise soothsayes,
    In power of herbes, and tunes of beasts and burds;
    And, that augmented all her other prayse,
    She modest was in all her deedes and words,
And wondrous chast of life, yet lou'd of Knights and Lords.

36
Full many Lords, and many Knights her loued,
    Yet she to none of them her liking lent,
    Ne euer was with fond affection moued,
    But rul'd her thoughts with goodly gouernement,
    For dread of blame and honours blemishment;
    And eke vnto her lookes a law she made,
    That none of them once out of order went,
    But like to warie Centonels well stayd,
Still watcht on euery side, of secret foes affrayd.

37
So much the more as she refusd to loue,
    So much the more she loued was and sought,
    That oftentimes vnquiet strife did moue
    Amongst her louers, and great quarrels wrought,
    That oft for her in bloudie armes they fought.
    Which whenas *Cambell,* that was stout and wise,
    Perceiu'd would breede great mischiefe, he bethought
    How to preuent the perill that mote rise,
And turne both him and her to honour in this wise.

38
One day, when all that troupe of warlike wooers
    Assembled were, to weet whose she should bee,
    All mightie men and dreadfull derring dooers,
    (The harder it to make them well agree)
    Amongst them all this end he did decree;
    That of them all, which loue to her did make,
    They by consent should chose the stoutest three,
    That with himselfe should combat for her sake,
And of them all the victour should his sister take.

39
Bold was the chalenge, as himselfe was bold,
    And courage full of haughtie hardiment,
    Approued oft in perils manifold,
    Which he atchieu'd to his great ornament:
    But yet his sisters skill vnto him lent
    Most confidence and hope of happie speed,
    Conceiued by a ring, which she him sent,
    That mongst the manie vertues, which we reed,
Had power to staunch al wounds, that mortally did bleed.

Stanza 34
1 happie: blessed.   **6–9** S.'s success in continuing Chaucer's tale is noted by Speght in *Works of Chaucer* (1598): in 'his like naturall disposition that Chaucer had, hee sheweth that none that liued with him, nor none that came after him, durst presume to reuiue Chaucers lost labours in that vnperfite tale of the Squire, but only himselfe' (*Sp All* 62).   **Ne . . . like**: nor would I dare to strive.   **infusion**: pouring in. Cf. the working of 'traduction' at iii 13.6, and *SC June* 93–94 where S. pleads that 'some little drops would flowe' on him from the spring in Chaucer's head. In *Defence of Poetry* 1579, Thomas Lodge records that Ennius 'dreamed that he received the soule of Homer into him'.   **I follow here**: in contrast to *SC Epilogue* where he follows Chaucer's 'high steppes' only 'farre off'. **feete**: also metrical divisions, specifically the iambic pentameter line. Line 9 may be read: 'So that I may agree with your meaning'.

Stanza 35
S. begins where Chaucer's tale ends: 'And after wol I speke of Cambalo, | That faught in lystes with the bretheren two | For Canacee er that he myghte hire wynne', but avoids any suspicion of incest by having Cambell marry Cambina, and by

having Canacee refer to him as 'her dearest frend' (iii 35.5). For the story of Canacee 'That loved hir owene brother synfully' (Introduction to the *Man of Law's Tale* 79), see Ovid, *Heroides* 11; on S.'s use of Gower's version in *Conf. Aman.* 3.143–360, see Sanders 1992.   **3–6** By her ring, Chaucer's Canacee (149–55) understood the songs of birds and knew the healing powers of herbs. S. invents the rest. **seene**: skilled. **7 that**: that which.   **9 yet** points to the tension between the two states: she remains chaste even though she is loved; and even though she remains chaste, she is loved.

Stanza 36
4 gouernement: on its association with temperance, see II i 29.8*n*, ix 1.4*n*.

Stanza 38
3 derring dooers: i.e. in doing daring deeds.

Stanza 39
2 courage: heart, spirit. **hardiment**: boldness. **8–9** As Chaucer records, a 'vertu of the ryng' is that it could tell which herbs would heal one 'Al be his woundes never so depe and wyde' (146, 155).

40

Well was that rings great vertue knowen to all,
　　That dread thereof, and his redoubted might
　　Did all that youthly rout so much appall,
　　That none of them durst vndertake the fight;
　　More wise they weend to make of loue delight,
　　Then life to hazard for faire Ladies looke,
　　And yet vncertaine by such outward sight,
　　Though for her sake they all that perill tooke,
Whether she would them loue, or in her liking brooke.

41

Amongst those knights there were three brethren bold,
　　Three bolder brethren neuer were yborne,
　　Borne of one mother in one happie mold,
　　Borne at one burden in one happie morne,
　　Thrise happie mother, and thrise happie morne,
　　That bore three such, three such not to be fond;
　　Her name was *Agape* whose children werne
　　All three as one, the first hight *Priamond*,
The second *Dyamond*, the youngest *Triamond*.

42

Stout *Priamond*, but not so strong to strike,
　　Strong *Diamond*, but not so stout a knight,
　　But *Triamond* was stout and strong alike:
　　On horsebacke vsed *Triamond* to fight,
　　And *Priamond* on foote had more delight,
　　But horse and foote knew *Diamond* to wield:
　　With curtaxe vsed *Diamond* to smite,
　　And *Triamond* to handle speare and shield,
But speare and curtaxe both vsd *Priamond* in field.

43

These three did loue each other dearely well,
　　And with so firme affection were allyde,
　　As if but one soule in them all did dwell,
　　Which did her powre into three parts diuyde;
　　Like three faire branches budding farre and wide,
　　That from one roote deriu'd their vitall sap:
　　And like that roote that doth her life diuide,
　　Their mother was, and had full blessed hap,
These three so noble babes to bring forth at one clap.

44

Their mother was a Fay, and had the skill
　　Of secret things, and all the powres of nature,
　　Which she by art could vse vnto her will,
　　And to her seruice bind each liuing creature,
　　Through secret vnderstanding of their feature.
　　Thereto she was right faire, when so her face
　　She list discouer, and of goodly stature;
　　But she as Fayes are wont, in priuie place
Did spend her dayes, and lov'd in forests wyld to space.

45

There on a day a noble youthly knight
　　Seeking aduentures in the saluage wood,
　　Did by great fortune get of her the sight;
　　As she sate carelesse by a cristall flood,
　　Combing her golden lockes, as seemd her good:
　　And vnawares vpon her laying hold,
　　That stroue in vaine him long to haue withstood,
　　Oppressed her, and there (as it is told)
Got these three louely babes, that prov'd three champions
　　　　　　　　　　　　　　　　　　　　　　　　(bold.

Stanza 40

7 by such outward sight: by what they could see.　**9 brooke**: hold.

Stanza 41

4 burden: applied to childbirth.　**7–9 Agape**: Gk ἀγάπη, charity or love, the 'bonde of perfectnes' (Col. 3.14); specifically that expressed in brotherly love. The names of the brothers signify generally first, second, and third world, as Lat. *prima* + *mundus* for **Priamond**, etc. More specifically, **Priamond**, who is, presumably, the first-born of the triplets, has only one life; **Dyamond** has two lives when Priamond's soul joins his, but loses both at the same time. **Triamond** enjoys three lives at iii 22 when Diamond's double soul joins his, but only briefly. See iii 3–49*n*. The three brothers serve as an emblem of concord, as does the three-bodied Geryon; see V x 9–11*n*. On the relation of their names to the three worlds of Renaissance cosmology (variously named but traditionally the physical world in which we live, the higher nature from which we fell, and the heavenly world), to an individual's 'one soule' in 'three parts' (43.3, 4: vegetative, sensitive, and rational), and to the three kinds of love named at ix 1.5–7, see Nohrnberg 1976:612–19, 769 (also in the *SEnc* 278–29), Burchmore 1985, and 'Triamond' in the *SEnc*.

Stanza 42

Correlative verse, with the pattern 1–2–3, 3–1–2, 2–3–1, which circles back on itself to form three pairs: 3,3; 2,2; 1,1. **7 curtaxe**: curtal-axe, a shortened battle-axe.

Stanza 43

3–6 That friends have 'one soul in bodies twain' is proverbial (Smith 306), but one in three suggests the unity of the Trinity. In choosing his story, S. may have known Sidney's celebration of his friendship with Dyer and Greville as 'A happy blessed Trinitie . . . one Minde in Bodies three' (1962:260–61).　**9 at one clap**: at once.

Stanza 44

1–5 Agape's magical powers are shared by Canacee (see 35.2–6) and inherited by her daughter (see iii 40.1–5). **Fay**: fairy. **skill**: understanding. **feature**: form, or nature. **6 Thereto**: also; but see iii 40.1–5*n*. **7 discouer**: uncover. **9 space**: roam.

Stanza 45

2 saluage: wild.　**8 Oppressed**: raped.

46

Which she with her long fostred in that wood,
  Till that to ripenesse of mans state they grew:
  Then shewing forth signes of their fathers blood,
  They loued armes, and knighthood did ensew,
  Seeking aduentures, where they anie knew.
  Which when their mother saw, she gan to dout
  Their safetie, least by searching daungers new,
  And rash prouoking perils all about,
Their days mote be abridged through their corage stout.

47

Therefore desirous th'end of all their dayes
  To know, and them t'enlarge with long extent,
  By wondrous skill, and many hidden wayes,
  To the three fatall sisters house she went.
  Farre vnder ground from tract of liuing went,
  Downe in the bottome of the deepe *Abysse*,
  Where *Demogorgon* in dull darknesse pent,
  Farre from the view of Gods and heauens blis,
The hideous *Chaos* keepes, their dreadfull dwelling is.

48

There she them found, all sitting round about
  The direfull distaffe standing in the mid,
  And with vnwearied fingers drawing out
  The lines of life, from liuing knowledge hid.
  Sad *Clotho* held the rocke, the whiles the thrid
  By griesly *Lachesis* was spun with paine,
  That cruell *Atropos* eftsoones vndid,
  With cursed knife cutting the twist in twaine:
Most wretched men, whose dayes depend on thrids so vaine.

49

She them saluting, there by them sate still,
  Beholding how the thrids of life they span:
  And when at last she had beheld her fill,
  Trembling in heart, and looking pale and wan,

Her cause of comming she to tell began.
  To whom fierce *Atropos*, Bold Fay, that durst
  Come see the secret of the life of man,
  Well worthie thou to be of *Ioue* accurst,
And eke thy childrens thrids to be a sunder burst.

50

Whereat she sore affrayd, yet her besought
  To graunt her boone, and rigour to abate,
  That she might see her childrens thrids forth brought,
  And know the measure of their vtmost date,
  To them ordained by eternall fate.
  Which *Clotho* graunting, shewed her the same:
  That when she saw, it did her much amate,
  To see their thrids so thin, as spiders frame,
And eke so short, that seemd their ends out shortly came.

51

She then began them humbly to intreate,
  To draw them longer out, and better twine,
  That so their liues might be prolonged late.
  But *Lachesis* thereat gan to repine,
  And sayd, Fond dame that deem'st of things diuine
  As of humane, that they may altred bee,
  And chaung'd at pleasure for those impes of thine.
  Not so; for what the Fates do once decree,
Not all the gods can chaunge, nor *Ioue* him self can free.

52

Then since (quoth she) the terme of each mans life
  For nought may lessened nor enlarged bee,
  Graunt this, that when ye shred with fatall knife
  His line, which is the eldest of the three,
  Which is of them the shortest, as I see,
  Eftsoones his life may passe into the next;
  And when the next shall likewise ended bee,
  That both their liues may likewise be annext
Vnto the third, that his may so be trebly wext.

Stanza 46
4 ensew: follow.   **6 dout**: fear.

Stanza 47
5 . . . from the track of any living creature's path.
6–7 Abysse: the bowels of the earth; see I xi 12.9*n*. **Demogorgon**: an infernal deity; see I i 37.8*n*. Either Demogorgon pent in darkness keeps Chaos or Chaos keeps Demogorgon pent in darkness, as A. Fowler 1989b:46 notes.

Stanza 48
The three Fates or Parcae, named **Clotho, Lachesis**, and **Atropos**, who govern respectively an individual's birth, life, and death, are called 'Ladies of destenie' by T. Cooper 1565 , who writes that 'The first of them is deuised to beare the distaffe, the seconde to spynne out the threade of mans lyfe so longe as it doth continue, the third breaketh of the thread, and endeth the mans life'. See E.K. on 'the fatall sisters' (*SC Nov.*

148) and 'Fates' in the *SEnc*.   **5 Sad**: steadfast; grave.   **rocke**: distaff.   **9 vaine**: useless, being frail.

Stanza 50
2 boone: request.   **4 date**: 'the terme of each mans life' (52.1).   **7 amate**: dismay.

Stanza 51
7 impes: children.   **8–9** Cf. Merlin on the fates at III iii 25.6–9.   **free**: get rid of.

Stanza 52
In Virgil, *Aen.* 8.564–67, Feronia gives her son, Erulus, three lives with threefold armour in order that he would need to be killed three times, while Triamond is given a threefold life, allowing him to lead 'a long . . . life' (iii 52.5).   **3 shred**: cut in two.

53

They graunted it; and then that carefull Fay
  Departed thence with full contented mynd;
  And comming home, in warlike fresh aray
  Them found all three according to their kynd:
  But vnto them what destinie was assynd,
  Or how their liues were eekt, she did not tell;
  But euermore, when she fit time could fynd,
  She warned them to tend their safeties well,
And loue each other deare, what euer them befell.

54

So did they surely during all their dayes,
  And neuer discord did amongst them fall;
  Which much augmented all their other praise.
  And now t'increase affection naturall,
  In loue of *Canacee* they ioyned all:
  Vpon which ground this same great battell grew,
  Great matter growing of beginning small;
  The which for length I will not here pursew,
But rather will reserue it for a Canto new.

Stanza 53
1 carefull: full of care.   **3–4** Each is arrayed according to his ability: Diamond with a curtaxe, etc., as described at 42.7–9. **6 eekt**: lengthened.

Stanza 54
4–5 Their brotherly love distinguishes them from the usual clash between friendship and love, as in Chaucer, *Knight's Tale*. **8–9** The poet intrudes himself again at the conclusion to cantos iv–vii and ix–xii to say that he will continue his story.

Cant. III.

*The battell twixt three brethren with
Cambell for Canacee:
Cambina with true friendships bond
doth their long strife agree.*

1

O Why doe wretched men so much desire,
    To draw their dayes vnto the vtmost date,
And doe not rather wish them soone expire,
Knowing the miserie of their estate,
And thousand perills which them still awate,
Tossing them like a boate amid the mayne,
That euery houre they knocke at deathes gate?
And he that happie seemes and least in payne,
Yet is as nigh his end, as he that most doth playne.

2

Therefore this Fay I hold but fond and vaine,
    The which in seeking for her children three
Long life, thereby did more prolong their paine.
Yet whilest they liued none did euer see
More happie creatures, then they seem'd to bee,
Nor more ennobled for their courtesie,
That made them dearely lou'd of each degree;
Ne more renowmed for their cheualrie,
That made them dreaded much of all men farre and nie.

3

These three that hardie chalenge tooke in hand,
    For *Canacee* with *Cambell* for to fight:
The day was set, that all might vnderstand,
And pledges pawnd the same to keepe a right,

That day, the dreddest day that liuing wight
Did euer see vpon this world to shine,
So soone as heauens window shewed light,
These warlike Champions all in armour shine,
Assembled were in field, the chalenge to define.

4

The field with listes was all about enclos'd,
    To barre the prease of people farre away;
And at th'one side sixe iudges were dispos'd,
To view and deeme the deedes of armes that day;
And on the other side in fresh aray,
Fayre *Canacee* vpon a stately stage
Was set, to see the fortune of that fray,
And to be seene, as his most worthie wage,
That could her purchase with his liues aduentur'd gage.

5

Then entred *Cambell* first into the list,
    With stately steps, and fearelesse countenance,
As if the conquest his he surely wist.
Soone after did the brethren three aduance,
In braue aray and goodly amenance,
With scutchins gilt and banners broad displayd·
And marching thrise in warlike ordinance,
Thrise lowted lowly to the noble Mayd,
The whiles shril trompets and loud clarions sweetly playd.

Book IV Canto iii

Argument
4 agree: conciliate.

Stanza 1
1–7 S.'s question is Despaire's at I ix 46.1–2, 47.7–8. **vtmost date**: term of life, as ii 50.4. **expire**: brought to an end. **9 playne**: lament.

Stanza 2
1 **fond**: foolish. **vaine**: thoughtless. **6–9** On the conjunction of courtesy and chivalry, see VI i 2.7–9*n*. **of each degree**: by all social classes.

Stanzas 3–49
In the three battles, the souls of two brothers are transferred in succession to the third, as Agape had asked of the Fates at ii 52. More particularly, when Priamond is slain, his soul enters Diamond (13); when Diamond is beheaded, both his soul and Priamond's enter Triamond (22). Triamond loses one soul from a throat-wound (30) and a second (apparently) from a wound in the arm-pit (33). Although he falls dead, he starts up

'breathing now another spright' (35.8), which is his own. The battles are carefully varied in the weapons used (spear, axe, sword), in the nature and number of the wounds, and in stanza length (8, 8, 16), as are the inset stanza-length similes at 16, 19, 27 and the shorter similes (1 to 4 lines) at 15.8, 23.7–9, etc.

Stanza 3
8 shine: shining; or 'sheen': bright. **9 define**: decide.

Stanza 4
1 **listes**: barriers; cf. 'raile' 46.2. **3–4** Since usually four judges, though at times two or three, attended an Elizabethan tournament – see Strong 1977:206–12 – **sixe** may be chosen to match the six parties to the contest. **deeme**: judge. **8 wage**: reward. **9** . . . by offering his life as a pledge.

Stanza 5
5 amenance: bearing; more particularly, noble bearing. **6 scutchins**: shields. **7 ordinance**: array. **8** The customary act of obeisance to the sovereign at a tournament. **9 sweetly**: referring to the **clarions** – as I xii 13.2 – **trompets** being for S. almost always **shril**.

6

Which doen the doughty chalenger came forth,
All arm'd to point his chalenge to abet:
Gainst whom Sir *Priamond* with equall worth,
And equall armes himselfe did forward set.
A trompet blew; they both together met,
With dreadfull force, and furious intent,
Carelesse of perill in their fiers affret,
As if that life to losse they had forelent,
And cared not to spare, that should be shortly spent.

7

Right practicke was Sir *Priamond* in fight,
And throughly skild in vse of shield and speare;
Ne lesse approued was *Cambelloes* might,
Ne lesse his skill in weapons did appeare,
That hard it was to weene which harder were.
Full many mightie strokes on either side
Were sent, that seemed death in them to beare,
But they were both so watchfull and well eyde,
That they auoyded were, and vainely by did slyde.

8

Yet one of many was so strongly bent
By *Priamond*, that with vnluckie glaunce
Through *Cambels* shoulder it vnwarely went,
That forced him his shield to disadauance:
Much was he grieued with that gracelesse chaunce,
Yet from the wound no drop of bloud there fell,
But wondrous paine, that did the more enhaunce
His haughtie courage to aduengement fell:
Smart daunts not mighty harts, but makes them more to swell.

9

With that his poynant speare he fierce auentred,
With doubled force close vnderneath his shield,
That through the mayles into his thigh it entred,
And there arresting, readie way did yield,

For bloud to gush forth on the grassie field;
That he for paine himselfe not right vpreare,
But too and fro in great amazement reel'd,
Like an old Oke whose pith and sap is seare,
At puffe of euery storme doth stagger here and theare.

10

Whom so dismayd when *Cambell* had espide,
Againe he droue at him with double might,
That nought mote stay the steele, till in his side
The mortall point most cruelly empight:
Where fast infixed, whilest he sought by slight
It forth to wrest, the staffe a sunder brake,
And left the head behind: with which despight
He all enrag'd, his shiuering speare did shake,
And charging him a fresh thus felly him bespake.

11

Lo faitour there thy meede vnto thee take,
The meede of thy mischalenge and abet:
Not for thine owne, but for thy sisters sake,
Haue I thus long thy life vnto thee let:
But to forbeare doth not forgiue the det.
The wicked weapon heard his wrathfull vow,
And passing forth with furious affret,
Pierst through his beuer quite into his brow,
That with the force it backward forced him to bow.

12

Therewith a sunder in the midst it brast,
And in his hand nought but the troncheon left,
The other halfe behind yet sticking fast,
Out of his headpeece *Cambell* fiercely reft,
And with such furie backe at him it heft,
That making way vnto his dearest life,
His weasand pipe it through his gorget cleft:
Thence streames of purple bloud issuing rife,
Let forth his wearie ghost and made an end of strife.

Stanza 6
2 to point: completely. **abet**: maintain. **7 affret**: onslaught. **8 forelent**: given up beforehand.

Stanza 7
1 practicke: skilled. **2** Noting his powers of defence and attack. In this first stage of the battle, apparently fought on foot using the sword, which Priamond at ii 42.5 is said to prefer, the wounded Cambell must resort to the spear as though fighting on horseback. **5 harder**: capable of greater exertion; or 'hardier'.

Stanza 8
1 bent: aimed. **3 vnwarely**: unexpectedly; as he was unwary. **4 disadauance**: lower. **5 gracelesse**: cruel.

Stanza 9
1 poynant: piercing. **auentred**: thrust forward (sugg. by the context), as though he were aiming a spear by setting it in its rest, as at vi 11.3. **4 arresting**: stopping. **6 not**: n'ote *1609*:

a variant of 'ne wote', i.e. 'knew not (how to)'. **7 amazement**: loss of self-possession; overwhelming fear. **9 stagger**: sway.

Stanza 10
4 empight: implanted itself. **5 he**: i.e. Priamond. **slight**: skilful handling. **8 shiuering**: capable of splitting; or shivered.

Stanza 11
1 faitour: villain. **2** 'The reward for your maintaining a wrongful challenge'. It is not clear why Cambell's challenge, which is called 'Bold' at ii 39.1, is wrong. **4 let**: granted possession; allowed. **5** Proverbial: Smith 279. **to forbeare**: to abstain from enforcing an over-due payment. **forgiue**: give up the claim to.

Stanza 12
2–3 troncheon: the remaining part of Priamond's spear. Its **other halfe** kills him. **5 heft**: heaved, hurled. **7 weasand pipe**: windpipe or throat. **gorget**: throat armour.

13

His wearie ghost assoyld from fleshly band,
　Did not as others wont, directly fly
　Vnto her rest in Plutoes griesly land,
　Ne into ayre did vanish presently,
　Ne chaunged was into a starre in sky:
　But through traduction was eftsoones deriued,
　Like as his mother prayd the Destinie,
Into his other brethren, that suruiued,
In whom he liu'd a new, of former life depriued.

14

Whom when on ground his brother next beheld,
　Though sad and sorie for so heauy sight,
　Yet leaue vnto his sorrow did not yeeld,
　But rather stird to vengeance and despight,
　Through secret feeling of his generous spright,
　Rusht fiercely forth, the battell to renew,
　As in reuersion of his brothers right;
　And chalenging the Virgin as his dew.
His foe was soone addrest: the trompets freshly blew.

15

With that they both together fiercely met,
　As if that each ment other to deuoure;
　And with their axes both so sorely bet,
　That neither plate nor mayle, whereas their powre
　They felt, could once sustaine the hideous stowre,
　But riued were like rotten wood a sunder,
　Whilest through their rifts the ruddie bloud did showre
　And fire did flash, like lightning after thunder,
That fild the lookers on attonce with ruth and wonder.

16

As when two Tygers prickt with hungers rage,
　Haue by good fortune found some beasts fresh spoyle,
　On which they weene their famine to asswage,
　And gaine a feastfull guerdon of their toyle,

Both falling out doe stirre vp strifefull broyle,
　And cruell battell twixt themselues doe make,
　Whiles neither lets the other touch the soyle,
　But either sdeignes with other to partake:
So cruelly these Knights stroue for that Ladies sake.

17

Full many strokes, that mortally were ment,
　The whiles were enterchaunged twixt them two;
　Yet they were all with so good wariment
　Or warded, or auoyded and let goe,
　That still the life stood fearelesse of her foe:
　Till *Diamond* disdeigning long delay
　Of doubtfull fortune wauering to and fro,
　Resolu'd to end it one or other way;
And heau'd his murdrous axe at him with mighty sway.

18

The dreadfull stroke in case it had arriued,
　Where it was ment, (so deadly it was ment)
　The soule had sure out of his bodie riued,
　And stinted all the strife incontinent.
　But *Cambels* fate that fortune did preuent:
　For seeing it at hand, he swaru'd asyde,
　And so gaue way vnto his fell intent:
　Who missing of the marke which he had eyde,
Was with the force nigh feld whilst his right foot did slyde.

19

As when a Vulture greedie of his pray,
　Through hunger long, that hart to him doth lend,
　Strikes at an Heron with all his bodies sway,
　That from his force seemes nought may it defend;
　The warie fowle that spies him toward bend
　His dreadfull souse, auoydes it shunning light,
　And maketh him his wing in vaine to spend;
　That with the weight of his owne weeldlesse might,
He falleth nigh to ground, and scarse recouereth flight.

Stanza 13

1 assoyld: set free. **2–6** The soul on being separated from the body may descend to hell, rise in the air, ascend to the heavens – its 'natiue home' (30.9) – or remain on earth by entering another body. Each state differs: unchanged in hell, evaporated into air, stellified in the heavens, or united with another soul in a body. The first three are illustrated, respectively, by the death of Turnus in Virgil, *Aen.* 12.952, of Dido in *Aen.* 4.705, and of Caesar in Ovid, *Met.* 15.845–46. The fourth involves Pythagorean metempsychosis; see 'Pythagoras' in the *SEnc.* **presently**: at once. **traduction**: transmission or transmigration of the soul; cf. 'infusion' (ii 34.6). **deriued**: conveyed; transferred. **8 his other brethren**: either 'the next' (ii 52.6) or referring to its double flight.

Stanza 14

1 his brother next: his second brother, Diamond. **5 his**: his brother's or his own, for the two are joined. **generous**: high-spirited; vigorous; courageous, as he is noted for being 'Stout' at ii 42.1; or in the usual sense: it freely offers itself to him. **7 in reuersion of**: in the legal sense, 'the right of succession to an office after the death of the holder'. **9 addrest**: prepared.

Stanza 15

3 their axes: Diamond's weapon of choice at ii 42.7. **4 whereas**: where. **5 stowre**: conflict. **8** Thunder precedes lightning for it was believed to be caused by clouds clashing together. **9 ruth and wonder**: the emotions aroused by tragedy; cf. III xi 12.8.

Stanza 16

The tiger, S.'s usual emblem for savage cruelty, is doubled to describe a battle marked by its savage cruelty, as 10.4, 39.4, 50.4. **7 soyle**: the ground on which the **spoyle** lies.

Stanza 17

3 wariment: wariness. **5 her foe**: Death. **9 sway**: impetus, force.

Stanza 18

1 in case: if. **4 incontinent**: immediately; also as an adj., 'intemperate'. **5 preuent**: anticipate.

Stanza 19

5 bend: aim. **6 souse**: swoop. **light**: quickly; nimbly. **8 weeldlesse**: unwieldy.

20

Which faire aduenture when *Cambello* spide,
　Full lightly, ere himselfe he could recouer,
　From daungers dread to ward his naked side,
　He can let driue at him with all his power,
　And with his axe him smote in euill hower,
　That from his shoulders quite his head he reft:
　The headlesse tronke, as heedlesse of that stower,
　Stood still a while, and his fast footing kept,
Till feeling life to fayle, it fell, and deadly slept.

21

They which that piteous spectacle beheld,
　Were much amaz'd the headlesse tronke to see
　Stand vp so long, and weapon vaine to weld,
　Vnweeting of the Fates diuine decree,
　For lifes succession in those brethren three.
　For notwithstanding that one soule was reft,
　Yet, had the bodie not dismembred bee,
　It would haue liued, and reuiued eft;
But finding no fit seat, the lifelesse corse it left.

22

It left; but that same soule, which therein dwelt,
　Streight entring into *Triamond*, him fild
　With double life, and griefe, which when he felt,
　As one whose inner parts had bene ythrild
　With point of steele, that close his hartbloud spilld,
　He lightly lept out of his place of rest,
　And rushing forth into the emptie field,
　Against *Cambello* fiercely him addrest;
Who him affronting soone to fight was readie prest.

23

Well mote ye wonder how that noble Knight,
　After he had so often wounded beene,
　Could stand on foot, now to renew the fight.
　But had ye then him forth aduauncing seene,
　Some newborne wight ye would him surely weene:
　So fresh he seemed and so fierce in sight;
　Like as a Snake, whom wearie winters teene,
　Hath worne to nought, now feeling sommers might,
Casts off his ragged skin and freshly doth him dight.

24

All was through vertue of the ring he wore,
　The which not onely did not from him let
　One drop of bloud to fall, but did restore
　His weakned powers, and dulled spirits whet,
　Through working of the stone therein yset.
　Else how could one of equall might with most,
　Against so many no lesse mightie met,
　Once thinke to match three such on equall cost,
Three such as able were to match a puissant host.

25

Yet nought thereof was *Triamond* adredde,
　Ne desperate of glorious victorie,
　But sharpely him assayld, and sore bestedde,
　With heapes of strokes, which he at him let flie,
　As thicke as hayle forth poured from the skie:
　He stroke, he soust, he foynd, he hewd, he lasht,
　And did his yron brond so fast applie,
　That from the same the fierie sparkles flasht,
As fast as water-sprinkles gainst a rocke are dasht.

26

Much was *Cambello* daunted with his blowes:
　So thicke they fell, and forcibly were sent,
　That he was forst from daunger of the throwes
　Backe to retire, and somewhat to relent,
　Till th'heat of his fierce furie he had spent:
　Which when for want of breath gan to abate,
　He then afresh with new encouragement
　Did him assayle, and mightily amate,
As fast as forward erst, now backward to retrate.

27

Like as the tide that comes fro th'Ocean mayne,
　Flowes vp the Shenan with contrarie forse,
　And ouerruling him in his owne rayne,
　Driues backe the current of his kindly course,
　And makes it seeme to haue some other sourse:
　But when the floud is spent, then backe againe
　His borrowed waters forst to redisbourse,
　He sends the sea his owne with double gaine,
And tribute eke withall, as to his Soueraine.

Stanza 20
1 aduenture: chance, i.e. opportunity; cf. 'aduantage' (30.1). **3 his naked side**: i.e. his right side, the left being protected by his shield, which is now exposed when 'his right foot did slyde' (18.9). **4 can**: began. **7 stower**: blow. **9 deadly**: i.e. in death.

Stanza 21
3 weld: wield. **8** The references are confusing, also at 22.1–3, because the three souls are one. **eft**: again.

Stanza 22
1–3 It: i.e. Priamond's soul, **that same soule** being Diamond's own soul. **double life**: referring to Priamond's and Diamond's soul(s). **5 close**: secretly; completely. **9 affronting**: confronting. **prest**: prepared.

Stanza 23
7 teene: affliction.

Stanza 24
6 I.e. of no more than average strength. **8 on equall cost**: either 'on even terms' (cf. II iii 17.3) or 'equal coast', i.e. on a level playing field.

Stanza 25
1 adredde: terrified. **2 desperate**: despairing. **3 bestedde**: beset. **6 soust**: dealt heavy blows. **foynd**: lunged. **7 yron brond**: sword.

Stanza 26
3 throwes: thrusts, blows. **4 relent**: yield. **8 amate**: dismay.

Stanza 27
2 the Shenan: Ireland's largest tidal river, said to be 'spreading like a sea' at xi 41.3. **3 rayne**: realm. **4 kindly**: natural. **6–9** That the estuary of a tidal river gives water to the sea, which is returned when the tide floods, and then given back double when the tide ebbs, is used by S. to define his relation

28
Thus did the battell varie to and fro,
　With diuerse fortune doubtfull to be deemed:
　Now this the better had, now had his fo;
　Then he halfe vanquisht, then the other seemed,
　Yet victors both them selues alwayes esteemed.
　And all the while the disentrayled blood
　Adowne their sides like litle riuers stremed,
　That with the wasting of his vitall flood,
Sir *Triamond* at last full faint and feeble stood.

29
But *Cambell* still more strong and greater grew,
　Ne felt his blood to wast, ne powres emperisht,
　Through that rings vertue, that with vigour new,
　Still when as he enfeebled was, him cherisht,
　And all his wounds, and all his bruses guarisht,
　Like as a withered tree through husbands toyle
　Is often seene full freshly to haue florisht,
　And fruitfull apples to haue borne awhile,
As fresh as when it first was planted in the soyle.

30
Through which aduantage, in his strength he rose,
　And smote the other with so wondrous might,
　That through the seame, which did his hauberk close,
　Into his throate and life it pierced quight,
　That downe he fell as dead in all mens sight:
　Yet dead he was not, yet he sure did die,
　As all men do, that lose the liuing spright:
　So did one soule out of his bodie flie
Vnto her natiue home from mortall miserie.

31
But nathelesse whilst all the lookers on
　Him dead behight, as he to all appeard,
　All vnawares he started vp anon,
　As one that had out of a dreame bene reard,
　And fresh assayld his foe, who halfe affeard
　Of th'vncouth sight, as he some ghost had seene,
　Stood still amaz'd, holding his idle sweard;
　Till hauing often by him stricken beene,
He forced was to strike, and saue him selfe from teene.

32
Yet from thenceforth more warily he fought,
　As one in feare the Stygian gods t'offend,
　Ne followd on so fast, but rather sought
　Him selfe to saue, and daunger to defend,
　Then life and labour both in vaine to spend.
　Which *Triamond* perceiuing, weened sure
　He gan to faint, toward the battels end,
　And that he should not long on foote endure,
A signe which did to him the victorie assure.

33
Whereof full blith, eftsoones his mightie hand
　He heav'd on high, in mind with that same blow
　To make an end of all that did withstand:
　Which *Cambell* seeing come, was nothing slow
　Him selfe to saue from that so deadly throw;
　And at that instant reaching forth his sweard
　Close vnderneath his shield, that scarce did show,
　Stroke him, as he his hand to strike vpreard,
In th'arm-pit full, that through both sides the wound
　　　　　　　　　　　　　　　　　　　　(appeard.

34
Yet still that direfull stroke kept on his way,
　And falling heauie on *Cambelloes* crest,
　Strooke him so hugely, that in swowne he lay,
　And in his head an hideous wound imprest:
　And sure had it not happily found rest
　Vpon the brim of his brode plated shield,
　It would haue cleft his braine downe to his brest.
　So both at once fell dead vpon the field,
And each to other seemd the victorie to yield.

35
Which when as all the lookers on beheld,
　They weened sure the warre was at an end,
　And Iudges rose, and Marshals of the field
　Broke vp the listes, their armes away to rend;
　And *Canacee* gan wayle her dearest frend.
　All suddenly they both vpstarted light,
　The one out of the swownd, which him did blend,
　The other breathing now another spright,
And fiercely each assayling, gan afresh to fight.

---

to the court at VI proem 7.4–5 (and see *n*). **redisbourse**: pay
back again.

Stanza 28
6 **disentrayled**: drawn from the entrails; also 'interlacing'
streams. 8 **vitall**: a technical term for the bodily spirit that
preserves one's 'spright' or life.

Stanza 29
2 **emperisht**: enfeebled. 5 **guarisht**: healed. 6 **husbands**:
farmer's. 8 **apples**: applied to any fruit (*OED* 2).

Stanza 30
3 **hauberk**: chain-mail that covers the neck. The stroke that
killed Priamond at 12.6–9 in effect kills him again. 5 **sight**:
judgement.

Stanza 31
2 **behight**: esteemed. 6 **vncouth**: marvellous. 9 **teene**:
injury.

Stanza 32
2 As Venus fears 'the skill | Of *Stygian* Gods' (III vi 46.6–7)
who control man's destiny; cf. II vii 27.9. 4 **defend**: keep off.

Stanza 33
5 **throw**: blow. 6–9 Cambell raises his shield to anticipate
Triamond's downward blow on his head, at the same time
reaching, i.e. thrusting, his sword, which could hardly be seen
(being just under the shield) into Triamond's armpit.

Stanza 34
4 **imprest**: imprinted; pressed in; cf. III xii 33.7.

36

Long while they then continued in that wize,
   As if but then the battell had begonne:
   Strokes, wounds, wards, weapons, all they did despise,
   Ne either car'd to ward, or perill shonne,
   Desirous both to haue the battell donne;
   Ne either cared life to saue or spill,
   Ne which of them did winne, ne which were wonne.
   So wearie both of fighting had their fill,
That life it selfe seemd loathsome, and long safetie ill.

37

Whilst thus the case in doubtfull ballance hong,
   Vnsure to whether side it would incline,
   And all mens eyes and hearts, which there among
   Stood gazing, filled were with rufull tine,
   And secret feare, to see their fatall fine,
   All suddenly they heard a troublous noyes,
   That seemd some perilous tumult to desine,
   Confusd with womens cries, and shouts of boyes,
Such as the troubled Theaters oftimes annoyes.

38

Thereat the Champions both stood still a space,
   To weeten what that sudden clamour ment;
   Lo where they spyde with speedie whirling pace,
   One in a charet of straunge furniment,
   Towards them driuing like a storme out sent.
   The charet decked was in wondrous wize,
   With gold and many a gorgeous ornament,
   After the Persian Monarks antique guize,
Such as the maker selfe could best by art deuize.

39

And drawne it was (that wonder is to tell)
   Of two grim lyons, taken from the wood,
   In which their powre all others did excell;
   Now made forget their former cruell mood,
   T'obey their riders hest, as seemed good.
   And therein sate a Ladie passing faire
   And bright, that seemed borne of Angels brood,
   And with her beautie bountie did compare,
Whether of them in her should haue the greater share.

40

Thereto she learned was in Magicke leare,
   And all the artes, that subtill wits discouer,
   Hauing therein bene trained many a yeare,
   And well instructed by the Fay her mother,
   That in the same she farre exceld all other.
   Who vnderstanding by her mightie art,
   Of th'euill plight, in which her dearest brother
   Now stood, came forth in hast to take his part,
And pacifie the strife, which causd so deadly smart.

41

And as she passed through th'vnruly preace
   Of people, thronging thicke her to behold,
   Her angrie teame breaking their bonds of peace,
   Great heapes of them, like sheepe in narrow fold,
   For hast did ouer-runne, in dust enrould,
   That thorough rude confusion of the rout,
   Some fearing shriekt, some being harmed hould,
   Some laught for sport, some did for wonder shout,
And some that would seeme wise, their wonder turnd to dout.

Stanza 35
3–4 According to Thomas of Woodstock's rules, the **Marshals** at a Tudor judicial combat received the **listes**, and the Constable the **armes**. See McNeir 1966:103, 108. **7 blend**: blind; confound. **8 another spright**: i.e. his own.

Stanza 36
3 For **wards**, Church 1758 conj. 'swords' to avoid the tautology in line 4, but that would introduce one in line 3, as Collier 1862 notes. As the text stands, **wards** counters **Strokes**: the knights neither attack nor defend themselves as they should. **6 spill**: destroy.

Stanza 37
2 **whether**: which. **4 rufull tine**: pitiful sorrow. **5 fatall fine**: destined death; or fatal end. **7 desine**: indicate. **8–9** As a record of contemporary London theatre, see Gurr 1987:207–09. Dolven 1999:196 sees anti-theatricalism at stake in the clash between popular spectacle and masque elements. **Confusd**: mingled together.

Stanza 38
4 **furniment**: fittings. **8 Persian Monarks**: traditionally associated with wealth, as at I iv 7.5–6.

Stanza 39
1–5 In traditional iconography, a chariot drawn by lions is an emblem of brute power under control, as Cupid's chariot is shown by Alciati (see III xii 22.2*n*), and Cybele's chariot by Cartari, *Le imagini de i dei* (see A. Fowler 1964: Plate 16a). Cf. the lion tamed by the sight of Una at I iii 5, and the lion chained under Mercilla's feet at V ix 33. On the relation of Cambina – not identified until 51.6 – to Cybele, see Roche 1964:23–27, and Hawkins 1981:59–61. **that wonder is to tell**: a classical tag, *mirabile dictu*. **hest**: command. **8 bountie**: goodness. **compare**: vie.

Stanza 40
1–5 On Agape's magical power, see ii 44.1–5. **Thereto**: also; but, as at ii 44.6, suggesting that Cambina has magical power because of her beauty and goodness. **leare**: lore.

Stanza 41
4–5 I.e. in her haste, the team tramples on great heaps of the people, enfolding them in dust. The violence suggests 'Cybeles franticke rites' (I vi 15.3); see Esolen 1994:32–35. Clearly the harmony that she achieves excludes the rabble, whom S. almost always disparages, e.g. V ii 33. **7 hould**: howled. **9 dout**: fear.

42

In her right hand a rod of peace shee bore,
  About the which two Serpents weren wound,
  Entrayled mutually in louely lore,
  And by the tailes together firmely bound,
  And both were with one oliue garland crownd,
  Like to the rod which *Maias* sonne doth wield,
  Wherewith the hellish fiends he doth confound.
  And in her other hand a cup she hild,
The which was with Nepenthe to the brim vpfild.

43

Nepenthe is a drinck of souerayne grace,
  Deuized by the Gods, for to asswage
  Harts grief, and bitter gall away to chace,
  Which stirs vp anguish and contentious rage:
  In stead thereof sweet peace and quiet age
  It doth establish in the troubled mynd.
  Few men, but such as sober are and sage,
  Are by the Gods to drinck thereof assynd;
But such as drinck, eternall happinesse do fynd.

44

Such famous men, such worthies of the earth,
  As *Ioue* will haue aduaunced to the skie,
  And there made gods, though borne of mortall berth,
  For their high merits and great dignitie,
  Are wont, before they may to heauen flie,
  To drincke hereof, whereby all cares forepast
  Are washt away quite from their memorie.
  So did those olde Heroes hereof taste,
Before that they in blisse amongst the Gods were plaste.

45

Much more of price and of more gratious powre
  Is this, then that same water of Ardenne,
  The which *Rinaldo* drunck in happie howre,
  Described by that famous Tuscane penne:

For that had might to change the hearts of men
  Fro loue to hate, a change of euill choise:
  But this doth hatred make in loue to brenne,
  And heauy heart with comfort doth reioyce.
Who would not to this vertue rather yeeld his voice?

46

At last arriuing by the listes side,
  Shee with her rod did softly smite the raile,
  Which straight flew ope, and gaue her way to ride.
  Eftsoones out of her Coch she gan auaile,
  And pacing fairely forth, did bid all haile,
  First to her brother, whom she loued deare,
  That so to see him made her heart to quaile:
  And next to *Cambell*, whose sad ruefull cheare
Made her to change her hew, and hidden loue t'appeare.

47

They lightly her requit (for small delight
  They had as then her long to entertaine,)
  And eft them turned both againe to fight,
  Which when she saw, downe on the bloudy plaine
  Her selfe she threw, and teares gan shed amaine;
  Amongst her teares immixing prayers meeke,
  And with her prayers reasons to restraine,
  From bloudy strife, and blessed peace to seeke,
By all that vnto them was deare, did them beseeke.

48

But when as all might nought with them preuaile,
  Shee smote them lightly with her powrefull wand.
  Then suddenly as if their hearts did faile,
  Their wrathfull blades downe fell out of their hand,
  And they like men astonisht still did stand.
  Thus whilest their minds were doubtfully distraught,
  And mighty spirites bound with mightier band,
  Her golden cup to them for drinke she raught,
Whereof full glad for thirst, ech drunk an harty draught.

Stanza 42

1–7 Mercury's snaky-entwined caduceus is called **a rod of peace** because it is 'vsed goyng to intreate of peace' (T. Cooper 1565). It is that 'With which the damned ghosts he governeth, | And furies rules, and Tartare tempereth' (*Mother Hubberd* 1293–94). Cf. its use at VII vi 18.1–3. In Conti 1616:5.5, it signifies concord, as Lotspeich 1932 notes. The Palmer's wand is said to be made of the same wood when he pacifies Acrasia's beasts at II xii 41. As Elizabeth's 'white rod', see III iii 49.6–9*n*. **Entrayled**: entwined. **mutually** heralds the 'mutuall couplement' of the four at 52.3. **in louely lore**: in amorous fashion (sugg. by the context); or in loving instruction, i.e. instructing others to love, as Cambina offers 'reasons' (47.7) for the knights to become friends.

Stanza 43

This explanatory gloss imitates Virgil's gloss on Mercury's use of the caduceus in *Aen*. 4.242–44. **1 Nepenthe**: a variation of 'nepenthes', the first recorded use in the *OED*. More than 'dispelling grief', as its etymology indicates, it brings **eternall happinesse**. **5 quiet age**: quietude.

Stanza 44

4 dignitie: desert, merit.

Stanza 45

1 price: worth. **gratious powre**: power to bestow grace and favour. **2–6** Referring to the fountain of hate from which Ranaldo first drank in Boiardo, *Orl. Inn*. 1.3.34–36; or the stream of love from which he drank in 2.15.59–61; or to the fountains of love and hate from which Rinaldo drank in Ariosto, *Orl. Fur*. 1.78–79, 42.63. See 'Boiardo' in the *SEnc*. **7 brenne**: burn.

Stanza 46

4 auaile: descend. **5** Her salutation expresses her health-giving role.

Stanza 47

1 requit: saluted in return. **5 amaine**: vehemently. **6 immixing**: mingling. **9 beseeke**: beseech.

49

Of which so soone as they once tasted had,
   Wonder it is that sudden change to see:
   Instead of strokes, each other kissed glad,
   And louely haulst from feare of treason free,
   And plighted hands for euer friends to be.
   When all men saw this sudden change of things,
   So mortall foes so friendly to agree,
   For passing ioy, which so great maruaile brings,
They all gan shout aloud, that all the heauen rings.

50

All which, when gentle *Canacee* beheld,
   In hast she from her lofty chaire descended,
   To weet what sudden tidings was befeld:
   Where when she saw that cruell war so ended,
   And deadly foes so faithfully affrended,
   In louely wise she gan that Lady greet,
   Which had so great dismay so well amended,
   And entertaining her with curt'sies meet,
Profest to her true friendship and affection sweet.

51

Thus when they all accorded goodly were,
   The trumpets sounded, and they all arose,
   Thence to depart with glee and gladsome chere.
   Those warlike champions both together chose,
   Homeward to march, themselues there to repose,
   And wise *Cambina* taking by her side
   Faire *Canacee*, as fresh as morning rose,
   Vnto her Coch remounting, home did ride,
Admir'd of all the people, and much glorifide.

52

Where making ioyous feast theire daies they spent
   In perfect loue, deuoide of hatefull strife,
   Allide with bands of mutuall couplement;
   For *Triamond* had *Canacee* to wife,
   With whom he ledd a long and happie life;
   And *Cambel* tooke *Cambina* to his fere,
   The which as life were each to other liefe.
   So all alike did loue, and loued were,
That since their days such louers were not found elswere.

Stanza 48
6 distraught: distracted; 'drawn apart' so their spirits may be bound in friendship.

Stanza 49
4 louely haulst: lovingly embraced.

Stanza 50
5 affrended: made friends, suggesting compulsion. **6 greet**: congratulate upon her victory. **7 so great dismay** combines the event with its effect upon the beholders.

Stanza 51
1 accorded: reconciled.

Stanza 52
Their complex interlocking relationship is seen at ii 30. Each is linked to the other three by the three kinds of love listed at ix 1: affection among kindred, heterosexual love, and friendship.

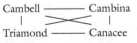

Cambell ——— Cambina
Triamond ——— Canacee

Cambell and **Triamond** change from hate to love for each other; **Canacee**, who loves her brother as 'her dearest frend' (35.5) and had rejected her suitors' love at ii 37.1, now loves Triamond; and **Cambina**, who comes to aid 'her dearest brother' (40.7), now loves Cambell. See 'tetrads' in the *SEnc*.
3 couplement: union of pairs. **6 to his fere**: as his wife. **7 liefe**: dear. **9 elswere**: earlier spelling of *elswhere 1609*.

Cant. IIII.

Satyrane makes a Turneyment
For loue of Florimell:
Britomart winnes the prize from all,
And Artegall doth quell.

1

IT often fals, (as here it earst befell)
    That mortall foes doe turne to faithfull frends,
    And friends profest are chaungd to foemen fell:
    The cause of both, of both their minds depends,
    And th'end of both likewise of both their ends.
    For enmitie, that of no ill proceeds,
    But of occasion, with th'occasion ends;
    And friendship, which a faint affection breeds
Without regard of good, dyes like ill grounded seeds.

2

That well (me seemes) appeares, by that of late
    Twixt *Cambell* and Sir *Triamond* befell,
    As els by this, that now a new debate
    Stird vp twixt *Scudamour* and *Paridell*,
    The which by course befals me here to tell:
    Who hauing those two other Knights espide
    Marching afore, as ye remember well,
    Sent forth their Squire to haue them both descride,
And eke those masked Ladies riding them beside.

3

Who backe returning, told as he had seene,
    That they were doughtie knights of dreaded name;
    And those two Ladies, their two loues vnseene;
    And therefore wisht them without blot or blame,

To let them passe at will, for dread of shame.
    But *Blandamour* full of vainglorious spright,
    And rather stird by his discordfull Dame,
    Vpon them gladly would haue prov'd his might,
But that he yet was sore of his late lucklesse fight.

4

Yet nigh approching, he them fowle bespake,
    Disgracing them, him selfe thereby to grace,
    As was his wont, so weening way to make
    To Ladies loue, where so he came in place,
    And with lewd termes their louers to deface.
    Whose sharpe prouokement them incenst so sore,
    That both were bent t'auenge his vsage base,
    And gan their shields addresse them selues afore:
For euill deedes may better then bad words be bore.

5

But faire *Cambina* with perswasions myld,
    Did mitigate the fiercenesse of their mode,
    That for the present they were reconcyld,
    And gan to treate of deeds of armes abrode,
    And strange aduentures, all the way they rode:
    Amongst the which they told, as then befell,
    Of that great turney, which was blazed brode,
    For that rich girdle of faire *Florimell*,
The prize of her, which did in beautie most excell.

Book IV Canto iv

Stanza 1
3 profest: i.e. merely pretended.

Stanza 2
3 As els: defended by J.C. Smith 1909 against As als *1609* because the proposition illustrated is twofold, concerning enmity and friendship: 'Reading "As als" we have two illustrations of this twofold proposition. Reading "As els" we have an independent illustration of each of its parts.' The point remains moot.   **That well** may refer to 'enmitie, that of no ill proceeds' (as between Cambell and Triamond), and 'As als' to 'friendship, which a faint affection breeds' (as between Blandamour and Paridell).   **4 Scudamour**: an error for Blandamour whom Scudamour left quarrelling with Paridell at i 52.5 (and see *n*). Goldberg 1981:45–46 discusses the implications of the error. Scudamour has no place viewing the beauty contest at which Amoret is displayed at v 13.1–6. However, there is no **new debate** between Blandamour and Paridell until v 24.
6–9 Referring to ii 30–31.   **their Squire**: i.e. the Squire of

Dames.   **masked**: to prepare for their unmasking at v.10.   **beside**: close by, 'not farre behinde' (ii 30.5).

Stanza 3
3 vnseene: unknown because 'masked' (2.9).   **7–9 discordfull Dame**: Ate, as i 32.   **late lucklesse fight**: his fight with Paridell at ii 14–20 rather than with Britomart at i 36.

Stanza 4
1–5 Referring to the flattering speech by which he is known; see i 32.1–5*n*.   **Disgracing**: reviling, literally seeking to mar their grace.   **deface**: defame.   **6 prouokement**: provocation.
9 Agreeing with the proverb, 'Words cut deeper than swords' (Smith 879).   **bore**: borne.

Stanza 5
2 mode: mood, referring to their anger.   **7–9 that great turney**: the contest to determine who is the strongest knight followed by the contest to decide who is the fairest lady. See 16.2, ii 27.1–4*n*. The two merge as 'that Turneyment for beauties prise' (vii 3.2). By romance convention, a knight

6

To which folke-mote they all with one consent,
  Sith each of them his Ladie had him by,
  Whose beautie each of them thought excellent,
  Agreed to trauell, and their fortunes try.
  So as they passed forth, they did espy
  One in bright armes, with ready speare in rest,
  That toward them his course seem'd to apply,
  Gainst whom Sir *Paridell* himselfe addrest,
Him weening, ere he nigh approcht to haue represt.

7

Which th'other seeing, gan his course relent,
  And vaunted speare eftsoones to disaduaunce,
  As if he naught but peace and pleasure ment,
  Now falne into their fellowship by chance,
  Whereat they shewed curteous countenaunce.
  So as he rode with them accompanide,
  His rouing eie did on the Lady glaunce,
  Which *Blandamour* had riding by his side:
Whom sure he weend, that he somwhere tofore had eide.

8

It was to weete that snowy *Florimell*,
  Which *Ferrau* late from *Braggadochio* wonne,
  Whom he now seeing, her remembred well,
  How hauing reft her from the witches sonne,
  He soone her lost: wherefore he now begunne
  To challenge her anew, as his owne prize,
  Whom formerly he had in battell wonne,
  And proffer made by force her to reprize,
Which scornefull offer, *Blandamour* gan soone despize.

9

And said, Sir Knight, sith ye this Lady clame,
  Whom he that hath, were loth to lose so light,
  (For so to lose a Lady, were great shame)
  Yee shall her winne, as I haue done in fight:
  And lo shee shall be placed here in sight
  Together with this Hag beside her set,
  That who so winnes her, may her haue by right:
  But he shall haue the Hag that is ybet,
And with her alwaies ride, till he another get.

10

That offer pleased all the company,
  So *Florimell* with *Ate* forth was brought,
  At which they all gan laugh full merrily:
  But *Braggadochio* said, he neuer thought
  For such an Hag, that seemed worse then nought,
  His person to emperill so in fight,
  But if to match that Lady they had sought
  Another like, that were like faire and bright,
His life he then would spend to iustifie his right.

11

At which his vaine excuse they all gan smile,
  As scorning his vnmanly cowardize:
  And *Florimell* him fowly gan reuile,
  That for her sake refus'd to enterprize
  The battell, offred in so knightly wize.
  And *Ate* eke prouokt him priuily,
  With loue of her, and shame of such mesprize.
  But naught he car'd for friend or enemy,
For in base mind nor friendship dwels nor enmity.

---

would challenge all others that his lady is the most beautiful, his victory proving that she is so; see V iii 4.7–9, 15.8–9. Ideally, the noblest knight would triumph and be chosen by the most virtuous (and therefore the most beautiful) lady as her defender, as VI vii 29.9: 'noblest she, that serued is of noblest knight'. Their conjunction, which is noted at v 1, would represent, then, concord in love and war. Here, in a parody of that convention, the one judged to be the fairest lady is awarded a prize that is a test of virtue, which she cannot wear; and when she is awarded to the fourth runner-up, Satyrane, at v 26.8–9, she chooses Braggadocchio, the parody of knighthood. The outcome is discord in both contests because masculine strength does not serve right, and feminine beauty does not manifest virtue. The consequent female diminishment, noted by Cavanagh 1994a:88–89, extends to the knights. See 'tournaments' in the *SEnc*; and on the tournament as a triumph, see Hamilton 1996:462–69. **blazed brode**: proclaimed widely. **prize**: used in this canto and throughout the book for both reward or sign of superiority and booty or plunder gained by force.

Stanza 6
1 folke-mote: 'a place for people to meet or talk of anything that concerned any difference between parties' (*View* 77), here

'the place of turneyment' (13.6) and 'The controuerse of beauties soueraine grace' (v 2.3). **3 excellent**: supreme.

Stanza 7
1 relent: slacken. **2 vaunted**: thrust forward boastfully. That word alone is sufficient to identify the 'vaunter' (II iv 1.9), Braggadocchio. **disaduaunce**: lower. **9 tofore**: before.

Stanza 8
6 challenge: claim. **8 proffer**: offer; attempt. **reprize**: take back again as his **prize** or booty. **9 soone**: immediately. **despize**: treat with contempt.

Stanza 9
8 ybet: beaten.

Stanza 10
7–9 Since Florimell is reputed to have no equal, Braggadocchio's offer is safe for him to make.

Stanza 11
4 enterprize: undertake. **7 mesprize**: scorn.

12

But *Cambell* thus did shut vp all in iest,
    Braue Knights and Ladies, certes ye doe wrong
    To stirre vp strife, when most vs needeth rest,
    That we may vs reserue both fresh and strong,
    Against the Turneiment which is not long.
    When who so list to fight, may fight his fill,
    Till then your challenges ye may prolong;
    And then it shall be tried, if ye will,
Whether shall haue the Hag, or hold the Lady still.

13

They all agreed, so turning all to game,
    And pleasaunt bord, they past forth on their way,
    And all that while, where so they rode or came,
    That masked Mock-knight was their sport and play.
    Till that at length vpon th'appointed day,
    Vnto the place of turneyment they came;
    Where they before them found in fresh aray
    Manie a braue knight, and manie a daintie dame
Assembled, for to get the honour of that game.

14

There this faire crewe arriuing, did diuide
    Them selues asunder: *Blandamour* with those
    Of his, on th'one; the rest on th'other side.
    But boastfull *Braggadocchio* rather chose,

For glorie vaine their fellowship to lose,
That men on him the more might gaze alone.
The rest them selues in troupes did else dispose,
Like as it seemed best to euery one;
The knights in couples marcht, with ladies linckt attone.

15

Then first of all forth came Sir *Satyrane*,
    Bearing that precious relicke in an arke
    Of gold, that bad eyes might it not prophane:
    Which drawing softly forth out of the darke,
    He open shewd, that all men it mote marke.
    A gorgeous girdle, curiously embost
    With pearle and precious stone, worth many a marke;
    Yet did the workmanship farre passe the cost:
It was the same, which lately *Florimel* had lost.

16

That same aloft he hong in open vew,
    To be the prize of beautie and of might;
    The which eftsoones discouered, to it drew
    The eyes of all, allur'd with close delight,
    And hearts quite robbed with so glorious sight,
    That all men threw out vowes and wishes vaine.
    Thrise happie Ladie, and thrise happie knight,
    Them seemd that could so goodly riches gaine,
So worthie of the perill, worthy of the paine.

Stanza 12

5–6 Against: in preparation for.   **list**: a pun on this word may be Cambell's **iest**.   **7 prolong**: postpone.   **9 Whether**: which one.

Stanza 13

2 bord: jesting.   **4 masked**: as he is a **Mock-knight**.

Stanza 14

1–3 The initial disposition of forces that precedes a tournament's formal procession before the spectators in line 9: Blandamour with 'his goodly crew' (i 33.1; cf. ii 30.8) on one side, the true friends on the other. In the tournament itself, both sides oppose Satyrane who comes from 'the other band' (17.3) of the Knights of Maidenhead. When Artegall enters 'on the other side' (39.1), he defeats them all until he is defeated by Britomart who comes 'out of the thickest rout' (43.7), apparently from neither side.   **6 alone**: i.e. being alone he will be more gazed on.   **9 attone**: together.

Stanza 15

2–8 On Florimell's girdle, see v 3–5*n*; on the significance of its loss, see III vii 31.8–9*n*. At ii 25.9, Satyrane is said to wear it; now he bears it in a chest as an idol to be worshipped. What had been the 'relique of the [hyena's] pray' at III viii 49.9, is now **that precious relicke** enshrined in an **arke | Of gold** now to be seen by **all men**. As such, it blasphemes the ark of the Covenant 'ouerlaide rounde about with gold' (Heb. 9.4), which was held to represent the presence of God, and was not to be seen except by the high priest. As Florimell's *alter ego* is called an 'Idole' at III viii 11.2, her girdle becomes a fetish to be worshipped. For Silberman 1995:101, it 'represents female genitalia and signals the presence of the hymen as it substitutes

for the absent woman'. The girdle is **curiously embost**, i.e. elaborately ornamented, according to the etymology of Lat. *cestus*, embroidered.   **pearle and precious stone**: a set phrase for what is most valuable, as at I x 55.5 and IV x 31.8, but here **pearle** carries its traditional association with purity.   **9 lately**: at III vii 31.8–9. See ii 25.6–9*n*.

Stanza 16

4 close: secret, inner.   **5 robbed**: ravished.

Stanzas 17–48

The three-day tournament is elaborately patterned. A. Fowler 1964:175–80 concludes that it is 'a poetic imitation of a *balletic* tournament, of a kind which actually took place in the sixteenth century', though it would have been a very debased one. Leslie 1983:148–58 links it to the tournament that established the Order of the Garter which, according to a contemporary account, celebrated 'Virtue, Friendship and Concord'. See 17–25*n*, 26–36*n*, 37–48*n*.

Stanzas 17–25

On the first day of the tournament, the opening encounter between Satyrane and Bruncheual ends in a draw. On behalf of Satyrane and the Knights of Maidenhead, Ferramont defeats three knights (Blandamour, Paridell, and Braggadocchio who declines to fight) only to be defeated by the fourth, Triamond. Then Triamond, in turn, defeats three knights (Deuon, Douglas, and Palimord) only to be defeated by the fourth, Satyrane. Masculine aggressiveness on this day is expressed by the 'huge great speare' (17.2; cf. 24.1). While there may be a witty point in having the phallic spear defend maidenhead, the weapon is linked with chastity in Bks III and IV; see III i 7.9*n*.

17

Then tooke the bold Sir *Satyrane* in hand
    An huge great speare, such as he wont to wield,
    And vauncing forth from all the other band
    Of knights, addrest his maiden-headed shield,
    Shewing him selfe all ready for the field.
    Gainst whom there singled from the other side
    A Painim knight, that well in armes was skild,
    And had in many a battell oft bene tride,
Hight *Bruncheual* the bold, who fiersly forth did ride.

18

So furiously they both together met,
    That neither could the others force sustaine;
    As two fierce Buls, that striue the rule to get
    Of all the heard, meete with so hideous maine,
    That both rebutted, tumble on the plaine:
    So these two champions to the ground were feld,
    Where in a maze they both did long remaine,
    And in their hands their idle troncheons held,
Which neither able were to wag, or once to weld.

19

Which when the noble *Ferramont* espide,
    He pricked forth in ayd of *Satyran*;
    And him against Sir *Blandamour* did ride
    With all the strength and stifnesse that he can.
    But the more strong and stiffely that he ran,
    So much more sorely to the ground he fell,
    That on an heape were tumbled horse and man.
    Vnto whose rescue forth rode *Paridell*;
But him likewise with that same speare he eke did quell.

20

Which *Braggadocchio* seeing, had no will
    To hasten greatly to his parties ayd,
    Albee his turne were next; but stood there still,
    As one that seemed doubtfull or dismayd.
    But *Triamond* halfe wroth to see him staid,
    Sternly stept forth, and raught away his speare,
    With which so sore he *Ferramont* assaid,
    That horse and man to ground he quite did beare,
That neither could in hast themselues againe vpreare.

21

Which to auenge, Sir *Deuon* him did dight,
    But with no better fortune then the rest:
    For him likewise he quickly downe did smight,
    And after him Sir *Douglas* him addrest,
    And after him Sir *Palimord* forth prest,
    But none of them against his strokes could stand,
    But all the more, the more his praise increst.
    For either they were left vppon the land,
Or went away sore wounded of his haplesse hand.

22

And now by this, Sir *Satyrane* abraid,
    Out of the swowne, in which too long he lay;
    And looking round about, like one dismaid,
    When as he saw the mercilesse affray,
    Which doughty *Triamond* had wrought that day,
    Vnto the noble Knights of Maidenhead,
    His mighty heart did almost rend in tway,
    For very gall, that rather wholly dead
Himselfe he wisht haue beene, then in so bad a stead.

Stanza 17
2 At III vii 38–40, Satyrane wields his spear, in 'bignesse like a mast', against Argante, but with little effect. **3 vauncing:** advancing. **4 addrest:** i.e. put on his arm. **maiden-headed shield:** as Guyon's shield bears the 'ymage of that heauenly Mayd' (II i 28.7) who is the Faerie Queene. It is carried now by Satyrane as the champion of the Knights of Maidenhead, the Order for which he speaks at III viii 47.7–9. (At III vii 30.6, his shield bears 'a Satyres hedd' in token of his race.) **7 Painim:** pagan, as he opposes the religion of love. **9 Bruncheual:** dark knight (Fr. *brun* + *chevalier*). Hankins 1971:146 interprets the name as 'dark horse' to identify him with the concupiscible faculty that corresponds to the (presumably) dark horse in Plato, *Phaedrus* 246. He is called **bold**, as is Satyrane in 1, to indicate that their encounter will end in a draw.

Stanza 18
3–5 The first of the animal images to define male sexuality. The knights are compared to boars (29.8–9), a lion (32.5, 41.5), and wolves (35.6–8). Animal imagery extends to their names: see 17.9*n*, 40.3*n*, 40.7–9*n*. See also Dunseath 1968:33–36. **maine:** force. **rebutted:** driven back; literally butted back. **8 troncheons:** the broken spear shafts. **9 wag:** brandish.

Stanza 19
1 **Ferramont:** from Lat. *ferramenta*, implements of iron, or Iron Mount. **4 stifnesse:** force, referring to the firmness with which he holds his spear though in the present context it carries erotic overtones.

Stanza 20
5 **staid:** standing still. 6 It is not clear why Triamond snatched (**raught**) the spear that Braggadocchio had stolen from Guyon at II iii 4.9, unless to have Guyon's arms defend the Knights of Maidenhead, an order to which he belongs; see II ix 6. At V iii 10.9, Artegall changes shields with Braggadocchio to preserve his disguise. **7 assaid:** assailed.

Stanza 21
The names may be topical; or they may refer to the three parts of Gloriana's kingdom: **Deuon** for England (cf. Debon who gave his name to Devonshire at II x 12.6); **Douglas** for Albania, i.e. Scotland; and **Palimord** for Wales. **1 dight:** make ready. **7 But all the more:** i.e. the more there were. **9 haplesse:** dealing mishap.

Stanza 22
1 **abraid:** awoke. **4 affray:** attack; or the panic that follows. **9 stead:** position.

23

Eftsoones he gan to gather vp around
   His weapons, which lay scattered all abrode,
   And as it fell, his steed he ready found.
   On whom remounting, fiercely forth he rode,
   Like sparke of fire that from the anduile glode,
   There where he saw the valiant *Triamond*
   Chasing, and laying on them heauy lode,
   That none his force were able to withstond,
So dreadfull were his strokes, so deadly was his hond.

24

With that at him his beamlike speare he aimed,
   And thereto all his power and might applide:
   The wicked steele for mischiefe first ordained,
   And hauing now misfortune got for guide,
   Staid not, till it arriued in his side,
   And therein made a very griesly wound,
   That streames of bloud his armour all bedide.
   Much was he daunted with that direfull stound,
That scarse he him vpheld from falling in a sound.

25

Yet as he might, himselfe he soft withdrew
   Out of the field, that none perceiu'd it plaine,
   Then gan the part of Chalengers anew
   To range the field, and victorlike to raine,
   That none against them battell durst maintaine.
   By that the gloomy euening on them fell,
   That forced them from fighting to refraine,
   And trumpets sound to cease did them compell,
So *Satyrane* that day was iudg'd to beare the bell.

26

The morrow next the Turney gan anew,
   And with the first the hardy *Satyrane*
   Appear'd in place, with all his noble crew,
   On th'other side, full many a warlike swaine,

Assembled were, that glorious prize to gaine.
   But mongst them all, was not Sir *Triamond*,
   Vnable he new battell to darraine,
   Through grieuaunce of his late receiued wound,
That doubly did him grieue, when so himselfe he found.

27

Which *Cambell* seeing, though he could not salue,
   Ne done vndoe, yet for to salue his name,
   And purchase honour in his friends behalue,
   This goodly counterfesaunce he did frame.
   The shield and armes well knowne to be the same,
   Which *Triamond* had worne, vnwares to wight,
   And to his friend vnwist, for doubt of blame,
   If he misdid, he on himselfe did dight,
That none could him discerne, and so went forth to fight.

28

There *Satyrane* Lord of the field he found,
   Triumphing in great ioy and iolity;
   Gainst whom none able was to stand on ground;
   That much he gan his glorie to enuy,
   And cast t'auenge his friends indignity.
   A mightie speare eftsoones at him he bent;
   Who seeing him come on so furiously,
   Met him mid-way with equall hardiment,
That forcibly to ground they both together went.

29

They vp againe them selues can lightly reare,
   And to their tryed swords them selues betake;
   With which they wrought such wondrous maruels there,
   That all the rest it did amazed make,
   Ne any dar'd their perill to partake;
   Now cuffling close, now chacing to and fro,
   Now hurtling round aduantage for to take:
   As two wild Boares together grapling go,
Chaufing and foming choler each against his fo.

Stanza 23
4–5 Echoing Chaucer, *Tale of Sir Thopas* 903–05: 'His goode steede al he bistrood, | And forth upon his wey he glood | As sparcle out of the bronde'. **glode**: glided.

Stanza 24
8 **stound**: attack; stunning blow. **9 sound**: swoon.

Stanza 25
3 **part**: faction.

Stanzas 26–36
Day 2 reverses Day 1: on behalf of (male) friendship, Cambell and Triamond defeat the Knights of Maidenhead. Cambell, wearing Triamond's armour, defeats Satyrane; and when he is captured by Satyrane's rescuers, he is saved by Triamond wearing his armour. First they fight with spears, then with swords.

Stanza 26
7 **darraine**: engage in. **8 grieuaunce**: pain.

Stanza 27
1 **salue**: remedy what had been done (*OED* v.¹ 3). **2 salue**: preserve (*OED* v.² 4). **3 behalue**: behalf. **4 counterfesaunce**: deception; literally putting on a false front. **7–8** The explanation is not clear. He does not tell anyone that he wears Triamond's armour for fear (**doubt**) of blame if he **misdid**. Yet if that should happen, Triamond would be blamed. S. may be preparing for 33.6 when Triamond wears Cambell's arms: in an exemplum of erotic friendship, they fight in one another's arms.

Stanza 28
5 **cast**: resolved. 6 Presumably this **mightie speare** is Guyon's. **bent**: aimed.

Stanza 29
1 **can**: did. **6 cuffling**: scuffling or fighting at close quarters. 7–9 The same simile is used of Satyrane in fighting Sansloy at I vi 44.4–9. **hurtling**: dashing or skirmishing.

30

So as they courst, and turneyd here and theare,
  It chaunst Sir *Satyrane* his steed at last,
  Whether through foundring or through sodein feare
  To stumble, that his rider nigh he cast;
  Which vauntage *Cambell* did pursue so fast,
  That ere him selfe he had recouered well,
  So sore he sowst him on the compast creast,
That forced him to leaue his loftie sell,
And rudely tumbling downe vnder his horse feete fell.

31

Lightly *Cambello* leapt downe from his steed,
  For to haue rent his shield and armes away,
  That whylome wont to be the victors meed;
  When all vnwares he felt an hideous sway
  Of many swords, that lode on him did lay.
  An hundred knights had him enclosed round,
  To rescue *Satyrane* out of his pray;
  All which at once huge strokes on him did pound,
In hope to take him prisoner, where he stood on ground.

32

He with their multitude was nought dismayd,
  But with stout courage turnd vpon them all,
  And with his brondiron round about him layd;
  Of which he dealt large almes, as did befall:
  Like as a Lion that by chaunce doth fall
  Into the hunters toile, doth rage and rore,
  In royall heart disdaining to be thrall.
  But all in vaine: for what might one do more?
They haue him taken captiue, though it grieue him sore.

33

Whereof when newes to *Triamond* was brought,
  There as he lay, his wound he soone forgot,
  And starting vp, streight for his armour sought:
  In vaine he sought; for there he found it not;

Cambello it away before had got:
  Cambelloes armes therefore he on him threw,
  And lightly issewd forth to take his lot.
  There he in troupe found all that warlike crew,
Leading his friend away, full sorie to his vew.

34

Into the thickest of that knightly preasse
  He thrust, and smote downe all that was betweene,
  Caried with feruent zeale, ne did he ceasse,
  Till that he came, where he had *Cambell* seene,
  Like captiue thral two other Knights atweene,
  There he amongst them cruell hauocke makes;
  That they which lead him, soone enforced beene
  To let him loose, to saue their proper stakes,
Who being freed, from one a weapon fiercely takes.

35

With that he driues at them with dreadfull might,
  Both in remembrance of his friends late harme,
  And in reuengement of his owne despight,
  So both together giue a new allarme,
  As if but now the battell wexed warme.
  As when two greedy Wolues doe breake by force
  Into an heard, farre from the husband farme,
  They spoile and rauine without all remorse,
So did these two through all the field their foes enforce.

36

Fiercely they followd on their bolde emprize,
  Till trumpets sound did warne them all to rest;
  Then all with one consent did yeeld the prize
  To *Triamond* and *Cambell* as the best.
  But *Triamond* to *Cambell* it relest.
  And *Cambell* it to *Triamond* transferd;
  Each labouring t'aduance the others gest,
  And make his praise before his owne preferd:
So that the doome was to another day differd.

Stanza 30

1 **courst**: ran their courses. 3 **foundring**: falling through lameness. 7 So sorely he struck him on his round helmet.

Stanza 31

2–3 On reaving the dead, see II viii 16*n*. 4 **sway**: force, referring to downward blows. 6 **hundred**: a generalized large number, as at v 11.8 and V iii 11.5. 7 . . . i.e. from being Cambell's prey.

Stanza 32

3 **brondiron**: sword. 4 I.e. with which he freely gave out blows. The metaphor suggests that the knights surround him as though petitioning him for money. 6 **toile**: net or trap.

Stanza 33

8 **in troupe**: either as a troop or in great number.

Stanza 34

8 I.e. they freed him to save their own lives that were at hazard.

Stanza 35

4 **allarme**: assault. 7 **husband farme**: farmer's house; possibly the tilled (husbanded) land. 8 **all**: any. 9 **enforce**: drive by force.

Stanza 36

1 **emprize**: enterprise. 7 **gest**: exploit. 9 **doome**: judgement. **differd**: deferred.

Stanzas 37–48

On the third and final day, Satyrane and the Knights of Maidenhead triumph until they encounter Artegall, the example of 'sole manhood' (43.2), who defeats them in three encounters (against Sangliere, Brianor, and a group of seven knights) only to be defeated in the fourth by Britomart. She triumphs over four knights (Artegall, Cambell, Triamond, and Blandamour), plus 'Full many others' (46.1), i.e. over manhood, friendship, false friendship, and any other male force.

37

The last day came, when all those knightes againe
  Assembled were their deedes of armes to shew.
  Full many deedes that day were shewed plaine:
  But *Satyrane* boue all the other crew,
  His wondrous worth declared in all mens view.
  For from the first he to the last endured,
  And though some while Fortune from him withdrew,
  Yet euermore his honour he recured,
And with vnwearied powre his party still assured.

38

Ne was there Knight that euer thought of armes,
  But that his vtmost prowesse there made knowen,
  That by their many wounds, and carelesse harmes,
  By shiuered speares, and swords all vnder strowen,
  By scattered shields was easie to be showen.
  There might ye see loose steeds at randon ronne,
  Whose luckelesse riders late were ouerthrowen;
  And squiers make hast to helpe their Lords fordonne,
But still the Knights of Maidenhead the better wonne.

39

Till that there entred on the other side,
  A straunger knight, from whence no man could reed,
  In quyent disguise, full hard to be describe.
  For all his armour was like saluage weed,
  With woody mosse bedight, and all his steed
  With oaken leaues attrapt, that seemed fit
  For saluage wight, and thereto well agreed
  His word, which on his ragged shield was writ,
Saluagesse sans finesse, shewing secret wit.

40

He at his first incomming, charg'd his spere
  At him, that first appeared in his sight:
  That was to weet, the stout Sir *Sangliere*,
  Who well was knowen to be a valiant Knight,
  Approued oft in many a perlous fight.
  Him at the first encounter downe he smote,
  And ouerbore beyond his crouper quight,
  And after him another Knight, that hote
Sir *Brianor*, so sore, that none him life behote.

41

Then ere his hand he reard, he ouerthrew
  Seuen Knights one after other as they came:
  And when his speare was brust, his sword he drew,
  The instrument of wrath, and with the same
  Far'd like a lyon in his bloodie game,
  Hewing, and slashing shields, and helmets bright,
  And beating downe, what euer nigh him came,
  That euery one gan shun his dreadfull sight,
No lesse then death it selfe, in daungerous affright.

42

Much wondred all men, what, or whence he came,
  That did amongst the troupes so tyrannize;
  And each of other gan inquire his name,
  But when they could not learne it by no wize,
  Most answerable to his wyld disguize
  It seemed, him to terme the saluage knight.
  But certes his right name was otherwize,
  Though knowne to few, that *Arthegall* he hight,
The doughtiest knight that liv'd that day, and most of
                                                    (might.

Stanza 37
7 **some while**: at times.   8 **recured**: recovered.   9 **still assured**: always rendered secure.

Stanza 38
3 **carelesse harmes**: untended injuries.   8 **fordonne**: overcome, i.e. overthrown.

Stanza 39
2 **reed**: guess.   3–7 **quyent disguise**: strange disguise (cf. 42.5, v 29.9), as Britomart appears 'in strange disguise' at III iii 51.9; cf. 'queint disguise' at V vii 21.1.   **describe**: described; 'made out'; interpreted. A savage man was a traditional figure in Elizabethan tournaments, e.g. the wild man 'full of withered leaves' at the Iberian jousts in Sidney, *New Arcadia* 256. The **woody mosse** (representing hair) and the **oaken leaues** express Artegall's savage state, long hair and the oak being associated with lust; see vii 7.1–4n.   **attrapt**: furnished as trappings.   8–9 **word**: motto.   **ragged**: being emblazoned with the oak leaves found on the horse's trappings, as Franke 1980–81:322 suggests. I owe this reference to Berman 1983:5.   **Saluagesse sans finesse**: wildness or savagery with-

out refinement or art. It was customary for the **wit** (i.e. meaning) of mottos to be **secret**.

Stanza 40
1 **charg'd**: aimed.   3 **Sangliere**: Fr. wild boar; fittingly the Salvage Knight's first foe, and his first foe in Bk V.   7–9 **ouerbore**: the play on words – Artegall overbore the boar – triggers the jingle, **Sir Brianor, so sore**.   **crouper**: crupper, the back of the saddle. Artegall's opening blow is like Britomart's opening blow at III i 6.7. He gets the same from her at 44.4–5.   **hote**: was called.   **Brianor**: Bear (Bruin). An Irish name, according to Henley 1928:127; an appropriate antagonist, then, for the defender of Irena in Bk V. Possibly alluding to Murrogh O'Brien; see Chronology 1577 *1 July*.   **behote**: promised.

Stanza 41
1 I.e. before he raised his sword, he levelled his spear against seven knights in succession, as Braggadocchio claimed to do; see II iii 17.7n.   3 **brust**: burst, shivered.   5 **Far'd**: raged.

Stanza 42
8 **Arthegall**: on the name, see III iii 27*n*, V i 3*n*.   9 As he is praised by Merlin at III iii 24.7.

43

Thus was Sir *Satyrane* with all his band
　By his sole manhood and atchieuement stout
　Dismayd, that none of them in field durst stand,
　But beaten were, and chased all about.
　So he continued all that day throughout,
　Till euening, that the Sunne gan downward bend.
　Then rushed forth out of the thickest rout
　A stranger knight, that did his glorie shend:
So nought may be esteemed happie till the end.

44

He at his entrance charg'd his powrefull speare
　At *Artegall*, in middest of his pryde,
　And therewith smote him on his Vmbriere
　So sore, that tombling backe, he downe did slyde
　Ouer his horses taile aboue a stryde;
　Whence litle lust he had to rise againe.
　Which *Cambell* seeing, much the same enuyde,
　And ran at him with all his might and maine;
But shortly was likewise seene lying on the plaine.

45

Whereat full inly wroth was *Triamond*,
　And cast t'auenge the shame doen to his freend:
　But by his friend himselfe eke soone he fond,
　In no lesse neede of helpe, then him he weend.
　All which when *Blandamour* from end to end
　Beheld, he woxe therewith displeased sore,
　And thought in mind it shortly to amend:
　His speare he feutred, and at him it bore;
But with no better fortune, then the rest afore.

46

Full many others at him likewise ran:
　But all of them likewise dismounted were,
　Ne certes wonder; for no powre of man
　Could bide the force of that enchaunted speare,
　The which this famous *Britomart* did beare;
　With which she wondrous deeds of arms atchieued,
　And ouerthrew, what euer came her neare,
　That all those stranger knights full sore agrieued,
And that late weaker band of chalengers relieued.

47

Like as in sommers day when raging heat
　Doth burne the earth, and boyled riuers drie,
　That all brute beasts forst to refraine fro meat,
　Doe hunt for shade, where shrowded they may lie,
　And missing it, faine from themselues to flie;
　All trauellers tormented are with paine:
　A watry cloud doth ouercast the skie,
　And poureth forth a sudden shoure of raine,
That all the wretched world recomforteth againe.

48

So did the warlike *Britomart* restore
　The prize, to knights of Maydenhead that day,
　Which else was like to haue bene lost, and bore
　The prayse of prowesse from them all away.
　Then shrilling trompets loudly gan to bray,
　And bad them leaue their labours and long toyle,
　To ioyous feast and other gentle play,
　Where beauties prize shold win that pretious spoyle:
Where I with sound of trompe will also rest a whyle.

Stanza 43
2 **manhood**: manliness, or the 'powre of man' at 46.3, which is about to be defeated by a female knight whose disguise displays 'manhood and . . . might' (i 35.1). **sole**: unrivalled; standing alone. 3 **Dismayd**: overthrown. 5–6 The male power of the sun, now beginning to set, is about to be replaced by the female power of the moon. On the comparisons, see III i 43*n*. 8 **A stranger knight**: being 'Attyr'd in forraine armes and straunge aray' (vi 9.3). **shend**: destroy; put to shame.

Stanza 44
1–6 **He**: the prominently placed pronoun, enforced by the repeated **his** and **him**, prepares for the revelation of 'his' identity, as at III ix 13–14. **pryde**: most flourishing state, which denies his excuse at vi 6.8. **Vmbriere**: the visor of his helmet. Her blow anticipates her defeat of him by the sight of her beauty at vi 19–22. The measurement of his fall varies from Guyon's at III i 6.7 (and see *n*) by associating him with his

horse. **lust**: desire; playing on **pryde** as sexual prowess. 7 **enuyde**: was indignant at.

Stanza 45
4 **weend**: i.e. thought in need of help. 8 **feutred**: put in its rest.

Stanza 46
4 **that enchaunted speare**: see III i 7.9*n*.

Stanza 47
This simile associates Artegall with the sun, as at 43.5–6. The beasts flee the sun's power, as the knights flee Artegall at 41.8–9. Britomart is compared to 'a stormy showre' at III iv 13.6 when she defeats Marinell.

Stanza 48
8 **beauties prize**: i.e. the most beautiful lady.

Cant. V.

*The Ladies for the girdle striue
of famous Florimell:
Scudamour comming to Cares house,
doth sleepe from him expell.*

1

I T hath bene through all ages euer seene,
    That with the praise of armes and cheualrie,
    The prize of beautie still hath ioyned beene;
    And that for reasons speciall priuitie:
    For either doth on other much relie.
    For he me seemes most fit the faire to serue,
    That can her best defend from villenie;
    And she most fit his seruice doth deserue,
That fairest is and from her faith will neuer swerue.

2

So fitly now here commeth next in place,
    After the proofe of prowesse ended well,
    The controuerse of beauties soueraine grace;
    In which to her that doth the most excell,
    Shall fall the girdle of faire *Florimell*:
    That many wish to win for glorie vaine,
    And not for vertuous vse, which some doe tell
    That glorious belt did in it selfe containe,
Which Ladies ought to loue, and seeke for to obtaine.

3

That girdle gaue the vertue of chast loue,
    And wiuehood true, to all that did it beare;
    But whosoeuer contrarie doth proue,
    Might not the same about her middle weare,

But it would loose, or else a sunder teare.
    Whilome it was (as Faeries wont report)
    Dame *Venus* girdle, by her steemed deare,
    What time she vsd to liue in wiuely sort;
But layd aside, when so she vsd her looser sport.

4

Her husband *Vulcan* whylome for her sake,
    When first he loued her with heart entire,
    This pretious ornament they say did make,
    And wrought in *Lemno* with vnquenched fire:
    And afterwards did for her loues first hire,
    Giue it to her, for euer to remaine,
    Therewith to bind lasciuious desire,
    And loose affections streightly to restraine;
Which vertue it for euer after did retaine.

5

The same one day, when she her selfe disposd
    To visite her beloued Paramoure,
    The God of warre, she from her middle loosd,
    And left behind her in her secret bowre,
    On *Acidalian* mount, where many an howre
    She with the pleasant *Graces* wont to play
    There *Florimell* in her first ages flowre
    Was fostered by those *Graces*, (as they say)
And brought with her from thence that goodly belt away.

Book IV Canto v

Stanza 1

1–4 On the conjunction of chivalry and beauty, see iv 5.7–9*n*. Reason esp. knows that one depends on the other, and that the fairest must remain faithful.

Stanza 2

3 controuerse: controversy.

Stanzas 3–5

The embroidered girdle or *cestus* is worn by Venus in Homer, *Iliad* 14.214–21, to note her power over love; it is worn by Armida in Tasso, *Ger. Lib.* 16.24–25, to note her Circean wiles. In Boccaccio 1976:3.22 whom S. follows, it becomes a chastity belt worn to restrain promiscuous desire, and is discarded by Venus when she **vsd her looser sport**. Its appearance in seventeenth-century bawdy works is noted in Thompson 1979:30–31. S. may have invented the story that it was fashioned by Vulcan in order to relate this classical type of the jealous husband to Scudamour who is about to suffer

under the Vulcan-like Care. T. Cooper 1565 defines the cestus as 'a mariage gyrdle full of studdes, wherwith the husbande gyrded his wyfe at hir fyrst weddynge'. As interpreted by S., though he is careful to attribute the story to others ('Faeries' at 3.6, and the anonymous 'they' at 4.3 and 5.8), it was presented to Venus **for her loues first hire**, i.e. when her marriage was consummated, apparently to bind the passions loosened in marriage. See III vii 31.8–9*n*, IV ii 27.6–8*n*.

Stanza 3

1–5 The power that the girdle 'did in it selfe containe' (2.8) is repeated at V iii 28.6–9. **7 steemed**: esteemed. **9 vsd**: engaged in. **sport**: amorous dalliance.

Stanza 4

8 streightly: strictly.

Stanza 5

1–3 Their love is notorious, as I proem 3.7–9, II vi 35.7–9, etc. **4–6** On the **Acidalian mount**, see VI x 6–9*n*.

6

That goodly belt was *Cestus* hight by name,
    And as her life by her esteemed deare.
    No wonder then, if that to winne the same
    So many Ladies sought, as shall appeare;
    For pearelesse she was thought, that did it beare.
    And now by this their feast all being ended,
    The iudges which thereto selected were,
    Into the Martian field adowne descended,
To deeme this doutfull case, for which they all contended.

7

But first was question made, which of those Knights
    That lately turneyd, had the wager wonne:
    There was it iudged by those worthie wights,
    That *Satyrane* the first day best had donne:
    For he last ended, hauing first begonne.
    The second was to *Triamond* behight,
    For that he sau'd the victour from fordonne:
    For *Cambell* victour was in all mens sight,
Till by mishap he in his foemens hand did light.

8

The third dayes prize vnto that straunger Knight,
    Whom all men term'd Knight of the Hebene speare,
    To *Britomart* was giuen by good right;
    For that with puissant stroke she downe did beare
    The *Saluage* Knight, that victour was whileare,
    And all the rest, which had the best afore,
    And to the last vnconquer'd did appeare;
    For last is deemed best. To her therefore
The fayrest Ladie was adiudgd for Paramore.

9

But thereat greatly grudged *Arthegall*,
    And much repynd, that both of victors meede,
    And eke of honour she did him forestall.
    Yet mote he not withstand, what was decreede;
    But inly thought of that despightfull deede
    Fit time t'awaite auenged for to bee.
    This being ended thus, and all agreed,
    Then next ensew'd the Paragon to see
Of beauties praise, and yeeld the fayrest her due fee.

10

Then first *Cambello* brought vnto their view
    His faire *Cambina*, couered with a veale;
    Which being once withdrawne, most perfect hew
    And passing beautie did eftsoones reueale,
    That able was weake harts away to steale.
    Next did Sir *Triamond* vnto their sight
    The face of his deare *Canacee* vnheale;
    Whose beauties beame eftsoones did shine so bright,
That daz'd the eyes of all, as with exceeding light.

11

And after her did *Paridell* produce
    His false *Duessa*, that she might be seene,
    Who with her forged beautie did seduce
    The hearts of some, that fairest her did weene;
    As diuerse wits affected diuers beene.
    Then did Sir *Ferramont* vnto them shew
    His *Lucida*, that was full faire and sheene,
    And after these an hundred Ladies moe
Appear'd in place, the which each other did outgoe.

12

All which who so dare thinke for to enchace,
    Him needeth sure a golden pen I weene,
    To tell the feature of each goodly face.
    For since the day that they created beene,
    So many heauenly faces were not seene
    Assembled in one place: ne he that thought
    For *Chian* folke to pourtraict beauties Queene,
    By view of all the fairest to him brought,
So many faire did see, as here he might haue sought.

13

At last the most redoubted *Britonesse*,
    Her louely *Amoret* did open shew;
    Whose face discouered, plainely did expresse
    The heauenly pourtraict of bright Angels hew.
    Well weened all, which her that time did vew,
    That she should surely beare the bell away,
    Till *Blandamour*, who thought he had the trew
    And very *Florimell*, did her display:
The sight of whom once seene did all the rest dismay.

Stanza 7
6 behight: granted; adjudged. **7 fordonne**: i.e. being overcome.

Stanza 8
2 Britomart's title, first given here and repeated at 20.5 and vi 6.4, associates her with Hebe, the goddess of youth and fertility, with Cupid who bears a 'deadly Heben bowe' (I proem 3.5), and with Arthur (see I vii 37.2*n*). See III i 7.9*n*. It is also appropriate because Hebe is celebrated as the wife of Hercules, as in *Ruines* 384–85, with whom Britomart's spouse, Artegall, is associated; see, e.g. V i 2.8–9*n*. **6** . . . which had been the best.

Stanza 9
1 grudged: complained. **3 forestall**: deprive. **8 Paragon**: pattern, model.

Stanza 10
4 passing: surpassing. **7 vnheale**: expose to view.

Stanza 11
3 forged beautie: counterfeit, being made by art; cf. 15.9. **5** As different minds are affected differently. **7 Lucida**: signifying **faire and sheene** (bright).

Stanza 12
1 enchace: portray; describe. **6–8** S. attributes to Apelles, who was famous for his painting of Venus rising from the sea (noted *HHB* 211–14), the method used by Zeuxis of Chios, who found a model for Helen of Troy by selecting the best feature from each of five maidens; see 'Apelles' in the *SEnc*.

Stanza 13
4 A topos used, e.g. to describe Una at I iii 4.6–8, Belphœbe at II iii 22.2, and the poet's beloved at *Am* 17.1.

14

For all afore that seemed fayre and bright,
　　Now base and contemptible did appeare,
　　Compar'd to her, that shone as Phebes light,
　　Amongst the lesser starres in euening cleare.
　　All that her saw with wonder rauisht weare,
　　And weend no mortall creature she should bee,
　　But some celestiall shape, that flesh did beare:
　　Yet all were glad there *Florimell* to see;
Yet thought that *Florimell* was not so faire as shee.

15

As guilefull Goldsmith that by secret skill,
　　With golden foyle doth finely ouer spred
　　Some baser metall, which commend he will
　　Vnto the vulgar for good gold insted,
　　He much more goodly glosse thereon doth shed,
　　To hide his falshood, then if it were trew:
　　So hard, this Idole was to be ared,
　　That *Florimell* her selfe in all mens vew
She seem'd to passe: so forged things do fairest shew.

16

Then was that golden belt by doome of all
　　Graunted to her, as to the fayrest Dame.
　　Which being brought, about her middle small
　　They thought to gird, as best it her became;
　　But by no meanes they could it thereto frame.
　　For euer as they fastned it, it loos'd
　　And fell away, as feeling secret blame.
　　Full oft about her wast she it enclos'd;
And it as oft was from about her wast disclos'd.

17

That all men wondred at the vncouth sight,
　　And each one thought, as to their fancies came.
　　But she her selfe did thinke it doen for spight,
　　And touched was with secret wrath and shame
　　Therewith, as thing deuiz'd her to defame.
　　Then many other Ladies likewise tride,
　　About their tender loynes to knit the same;
　　But it would not on none of them abide,
But when they thought it fast, eftsoones it was vntide.

18

Which when that scornefull *Squire of Dames* did vew,
　　He lowdly gan to laugh, and thus to iest;
　　Alas for pittie that so faire a crew,
　　As like can not be seene from East to West,
　　Cannot find one this girdle to inuest.
　　Fie on the man, that did it first inuent,
　　To shame vs all with this, *Vngirt vnblest*.
　　Let neuer Ladie to his loue assent,
That hath this day so many so vnmanly shent.

19

Thereat all Knights gan laugh, and Ladies lowre:
　　Till that at last the gentle *Amoret*
　　Likewise assayd, to proue that girdles powre;
　　And hauing it about her middle set,
　　Did find it fit, withouten breach or let.
　　Whereat the rest gan greatly to enuie:
　　But *Florimell* exceedingly did fret,
　　And snatching from her hand halfe angrily
The belt againe, about her bodie gan it tie.

20

Yet nathemore would it her bodie fit;
　　Yet nathelesse to her, as her dew right,
　　It yeelded was by them, that iudged it:
　　And she her selfe adiudged to the Knight,
　　That bore the Hebene speare, as wonne in fight.
　　But *Britomart* would not thereto assent,
　　Ne her owne *Amoret* forgoe so light
　　For that strange Dame, whose beauties wonderment
She lesse esteem'd, then th'others vertuous gouernment.

21

Whom when the rest did see her to refuse,
　　They were full glad, in hope themselues to get her:
　　Yet at her choice they all did greatly muse.
　　But after that the Iudges did arret her
　　Vnto the second best, that lou'd her better;
　　That was the *Saluage* Knight: but he was gone
　　In great displeasure, that he could not get her.
　　Then was she iudged *Triamond* his one;
But *Triamond* lou'd *Canacee*, and other none.

Stanza 15
1–6 An apt simile, for Florimell's clothes are 'wrought of
beaten gold' (III i 15.6) and her hair bound 'With golden
wreath' (III vii 11.3). **7 Idole**: image; see III viii 11.2*n*.
ared: made known; i.e. as a counterfeit.

Stanza 16
7 blame: fault or blameworthiness. **9 disclos'd**: unfastened.

Stanza 17
6–9 When this chastity test is repeated at V iii 28, not surpris-
ingly the ladies still prove not to be 'continent and chast'.

Stanza 18
1–2 As Satyrane laughs heartily at III vii 57.5 and 58.5 on
hearing of the unchaste ladies wooed by the Squire of Dames.
5 inuest: put on. **7 Vngirt vnblest**: proverbial (Smith 805).
9 shent: disgraced.

Stanza 19
5 . . . i.e. without any impediment to her keeping it on. Yet
breach may allude to the girdle having been 'broken'; see III
viii 2.7 (*1596*). **6 enuie**: grudge.

Stanza 20
1 **nathemore**: never the more. **9 gouernment**: behaviour;
proven by the girdle fitting her.

Stanza 21
3 **muse**: wonder. **4 arret her**: commit her to the charge.
7 S. may be breaking his rule against repeating a rhyme with
the same meaning, unless at 2 **get her** means to be awarded her
and at 7 to win her by his own effort. More likely, however, he
is mocking the contest, as the playful feminine rhyme shows.
8 his one: his own; his only.

22

Tho vnto *Satyran* she was adiudged,
 Who was right glad to gaine so goodly meed:
 But *Blandamour* thereat full greatly grudged,
 And litle prays'd his labours euill speed,
 That for to winne the saddle, lost the steed.
 Ne lesse thereat did *Paridell* complaine,
 And thought t'appeale from that, which was decreed,
 To single combat with Sir *Satyrane*.
Thereto him *Ate* stird, new discord to maintaine.

23

And eke with these, full many other Knights
 She through her wicked working did incense,
 Her to demaund, and chalenge as their rights,
 Deserued for their perils recompense.
 Amongst the rest with boastfull vaine pretense
 Stept *Braggadochio* forth, and as his thrall
 Her claym'd, by him in battell wonne long sens:
 Whereto her selfe he did to witnesse call;
Who being askt, accordingly confessed all.

24

Thereat exceeding wroth was *Satyran*;
 And wroth with *Satyran* was *Blandamour*;
 And wroth with *Blandamour* was *Eriuan*;
 And at them both Sir *Paridell* did loure.
 So all together stird vp strifull stoure,
 And readie were new battell to darraine.
 Each one profest to be her paramoure,
 And vow'd with speare and shield it to maintaine;
Ne Iudges powre, ne reasons rule mote them restraine.

25

Which troublous stirre when *Satyrane* auiz'd,
 He gan to cast how to appease the same,
 And to accord them all, this meanes deuiz'd:
 First in the midst to set that fayrest Dame,
 To whom each one his chalenge should disclame,
 And he himselfe his right would eke releasse:
 Then looke to whom she voluntarie came,
 He should without disturbance her possesse:
Sweete is the loue that comes alone with willingnesse.

26

They all agreed, and then that snowy Mayd
 Was in the middest plast among them all;
 All on her gazing wisht, and vowd, and prayd,
 And to the Queene of beautie close did call,
 That she vnto their portion might befall.
 Then when she long had lookt vpon each one,
 As though she wished to haue pleasd them all,
 At last to *Braggadochio* selfe alone
She came of her accord, in spight of all his fone.

27

Which when they all beheld they chaft and rag'd,
 And woxe nigh mad for very harts despight,
 That from reuenge their willes they scarse asswag'd:
 Some thought from him her to haue reft by might;
 Some proffer made with him for her to fight.
 But he nought car'd for all that they could say:
 For he their words as wind esteemed light.
 Yet not fit place he thought it there to stay,
But secretly from thence that night her bore away.

28

They which remaynd, so soone as they perceiu'd,
 That she was gone, departed thence with speed,
 And follow'd them, in mind her to haue reau'd
 From wight vnworthie of so noble meed.
 In which poursuit how each one did succeede,
 Shall else be told in order, as it fell.
 But now of *Britomart* it here doth neede,
 The hard aduentures and strange haps to tell;
Since with the rest she went not after *Florimell*.

29

For soone as she them saw to discord set,
 Her list no longer in that place abide;
 But taking with her louely *Amoret*,
 Vpon her first aduenture forth did ride,
 To seeke her lou'd, making blind loue her guide.
 Vnluckie Mayd to seeke her enemie,
 Vnluckie Mayd to seeke him farre and wide,
 Whom, when he was vnto her selfe most nie,
She through his late disguizement could him not descrie.

Stanza 22
4 euill speed: ill success. **5** Proverbial (Smith 401). Blandamour won False Florimell from Ferraugh at ii 7 only to lose her at the tournament.

Stanza 23
3 chalenge: claim. **5 pretense**: false claim.

Stanza 24
3 Eriuan: vain strife (Gk ἔρις, strife + Lat. *vanus*, vain), as A. Fowler 1964:178 suggests. **5 stoure**: tumult. **6 darraine**: wage.

Stanza 25
1 auiz'd: perceived. **9 alone**: i.e. **voluntarie**, 'of her accord' (26.9).

Stanza 26
4 close: secretly.

Stanza 28
5–6 else: at another time; elsewhere. This promise is kept (in part) at ix 20–21: Paridell and Blandamour appear **in order** through their relation to various states of loving. **7–30.6** This brief insert invokes the opening of Bk III where Britomart continues on her quest for Artegall while the other knights pursue Florimell, and the opening of Bk IV where she continues that quest accompanied by Amoret on their quest for Scudamour.

Stanza 29
5 As she is seen 'Following the guydaunce of her blinded guest' at III iv 6.8.

30

So much the more her griefe, the more her toyle:
 Yet neither toyle nor griefe she once did spare,
 In seeking him, that should her paine assoyle;
 Whereto great comfort in her sad misfare
 Was *Amoret*, companion of her care:
 Who likewise sought her louer long miswent,
 The gentle *Scudamour*, whose hart whileare
 That stryfull hag with gealous discontent
Had fild, that he to fell reueng was fully bent.

31

Bent to reuenge on blamelesse *Britomart*
 The crime, which cursed *Ate* kindled earst,
 The which like thornes did pricke his gealous hart,
 And through his soule like poysned arrow perst,
 That by no reason it might be reuerst,
 For ought that *Glauce* could or doe or say.
 For aye the more that she the same reherst,
 The more it gauld, and grieu'd him night and day,
That nought but dire reuenge his anger mote defray.

32

So as they trauelled, the drouping night
 Couered with cloudie storme and bitter showre,
 That dreadfull seem'd to euery liuing wight,
 Vpon them fell, before her timely howre;
 That forced them to seeke some couert bowre,
 Where they might hide their heads in quiet rest,
 And shrowd their persons from that stormie stowre.
 Not farre away, not meete for any guest
They spide a little cottage, like some poore mans nest.

33

Vnder a steepe hilles side it placed was,
 There where the mouldred earth had cav'd the banke;
 And fast beside a little brooke did pas
 Of muddie water, that like puddle stanke,

By which few crooked sallowes grew in ranke:
 Whereto approaching nigh, they heard the sound
 Of many yron hammers beating ranke,
 And answering their wearie turnes around,
That seemed some blacksmith dwelt in that desert ground.

34

There entring in, they found the goodman selfe,
 Full busily vnto his worke ybent;
 Who was to weet a wretched wearish elfe,
 With hollow eyes and rawbone cheekes forspent,
 As if he had in prison long bene pent:
 Full blacke and griesly did his face appeare,
 Besmeard with smoke that nigh his eye-sight blent;
 With rugged beard, and hoarie shagged heare,
The which he neuer wont to combe, or comely sheare.

35

Rude was his garment, and to rags all rent,
 Ne better had he, ne for better cared:
 With blistred hands emongst the cinders brent,
 And fingers filthie, with long nayles vnpared,
 Right fit to rend the food, on which he fared.
 His name was *Care*; a blacksmith by his trade,
 That neither day nor night, from working spared,
 But to small purpose yron wedges made;
Those be vnquiet thoughts, that carefull minds inuade.

36

In which his worke he had six seruants prest,
 About the Andvile standing euermore,
 With huge great hammers, that did neuer rest
 From heaping stroakes, which thereon soused sore:
 All sixe strong groomes, but one then other more;
 For by degrees they all were disagreed;
 So likewise did the hammers which they bore,
 Like belles in greatnesse orderly succeed,
That he which was the last, the first did farre exceede.

Stanza 30

3 **assoyle**: dispel. 4 **misfare**: misfortune; literally, going astray. 6 **miswent**: gone astray. **7–31.9** Reviewing Scudamour's jealousy aroused by Ate and vented on Glauce at i 50–54.

Stanza 31

2 **crime**: accusation. 5 **reuerst**: removed. 7 **reherst**: related.

Stanza 32

7 **stowre**: time of turmoil.

Stanza 33

1–2 Cf. the jealous Malbecco's cave under a cliff at III x 58. On the elaborate iconography of 'Cares house' (Arg.) in the following stanzas, see 'Care' in the *SEnc*. **4–5** The lover's willow, crooked and growing in stagnant water, becomes an apt emblem of the jealous lover's state. **puddle**: polluted water. **ranke**: a pun is forced by the rhyme with **stanke**. 7 **ranke**: violently; in order. 8 **wearie turnes**: referring to the ceaseless echoes.

Stanza 34

1 **the goodman selfe**: referring to the master blacksmith (cf. 44.1), an ironic use (*OED* 3b). 3 **wearish**: wizened; suggesting weary (like the sound of his hammers at 33.8); worn away, as he causes others to become. **elfe**: a malignant being. 4 Care looks like Despaire at I ix 35.6–9; or, more exactly, like one despairing in love, as Terwin at I ix 29. **forspent**: wasted away, as Care is 'selfe-consuming' (II vii 25.1).

Stanza 36

1–5 six seruants: in accord with Pythagoras's discovery that tones produced by six different weights of a blacksmith's hammer could yield musical harmony, as Nelson 1963:250 notes. An image traditionally associated with concord becomes an exemplum of discord, as Steadman 1979:157 shows. **prest**: at hand. **hammers**: suggested by Ital. *martello*, 'a hammer . . . Also iealousie or suspition in loue: panting or throbbing of the hart' (Florio 1598). **soused**: fell heavily. 6 I.e. they were unlike, each differing from the next by a fixed quantity; hence the play on **degrees . . . disagreed**.

37

He like a monstrous Gyant seem'd in sight,
　　Farre passing *Bronteus*, or *Pyracmon* great,
　　The which in *Lipari* doe day and night
　　Frame thunderbolts for *Ioues* auengefull threate.
　　So dreadfully he did the anduile beat,
　　That seem'd to dust he shortly would it driue:
　　So huge his hammer and so fierce his heat,
　　That seem'd a rocke of Diamond it could riue,
And rend a sunder quite, if he thereto list striue.

38

Sir *Scudamour* there entring, much admired
　　The manner of their worke and wearie paine;
　　And hauing long beheld, at last enquired
　　The cause and end thereof: but all in vaine;
　　For they for nought would from their worke refraine,
　　Ne let his speeches come vnto their eare.
　　And eke the breathfull bellowes blew amaine,
　　Like to the Northren winde, that none could heare:
Those *Pensifenesse* did moue; and *Sighes* the bellows weare.

39

Which when that warriour saw, he said no more,
　　But in his armour layd him downe to rest:
　　To rest he layd him downe vpon the flore,
　　(Whylome for ventrous Knights the bedding best)
　　And thought his wearie limbs to haue redrest.
　　And that old aged Dame, his faithfull Squire,
　　Her feeble ioynts layd eke a downe to rest;
　　That needed much her weake age to desire,
After so long a trauell, which them both did tire.

40

There lay Sir *Scudamour* long while expecting,
　　When gentle sleepe his heauie eyes would close;
　　Oft chaunging sides, and oft new place electing,
　　Where better seem'd he mote himselfe repose;

And oft in wrath he thence againe vprose;
　　And oft in wrath he layd him downe againe.
　　But wheresoeuer he did himselfe dispose,
　　He by no meanes could wished ease obtaine:
So euery place seem'd painefull, and ech changing vaine.

41

And euermore, when he to sleepe did thinke,
　　The hammers sound his senses did molest;
　　And euermore, when he began to winke,
　　The bellowes noyse disturb'd his quiet rest,
　　Ne suffred sleepe to settle in his brest.
　　And all the night the dogs did barke and howle
　　About the house, at sent of stranger guest:
　　And now the crowing Cocke, and now the Owle
Lowde shriking him afflicted to the very sowle.

42

And if by fortune any litle nap
　　Vpon his heauie eye-lids chaunst to fall,
　　Eftsoones one of those villeins him did rap
　　Vpon his headpeece with his yron mall;
　　That he was soone awaked therewithall,
　　And lightly started vp as one affrayd;
　　Or as if one him suddenly did call.
　　So oftentimes he out of sleepe abrayd,
And then lay musing long, on that him ill apayd.

43

So long he muzed, and so long he lay,
　　That at the last his wearie sprite opprest
　　With fleshly weaknesse, which no creature may
　　Long time resist, gaue place to kindly rest,
　　That all his senses did full soone arrest:
　　Yet in his soundest sleepe, his dayly feare
　　His ydle braine gan busily molest,
　　And made him dreame those two disloyall were:
The things that day most minds, at night doe most appeare.

Stanza 37
1 He: i.e. Care. **2–4** Two Cyclops in Vulcan's cave in Lipara (Virgil, *Aen*. 8.424–28), selected for their associations: **Bronteus**, 'interpreted thunder' (T. Cooper 1565), **Pyracmon**, Gk πῦρ, fire + ἄκμων, anvil.

Stanza 38
1 admired: wondered at. **9 Pensifenesse**: also 'full of thought', i.e. apprehensiveness; cf. 'thoughts vnkind' at vi 1.3.

Stanza 39
2 Not doffing armour registers apprehension and care, as at V vi 23.5. **5 redrest**: restored, i.e. refreshed. **8 That**: i.e. rest. **9 trauell**: travel; travail.

Stanza 40
Scudamour is a victim of Ate's double tongue against which Ecclesiasticus warns: 'Whoso hearkeneth vnto it, shal neuer find rest' (28.16). **1 expecting**: waiting.

Stanza 41
3 winke: close his eyes. Care is the enemy of Morpheus at I i 40.5.

Stanza 42
8 abrayd: awoke with a start. **9** . . . on what ill-pleased him.

Stanza 43
4 kindly: natural, owing to nature. **5 arrest**: seize. **6–9 dayly feare**: the fears of the day. Traditional dream psychology held that 'A Dreame is nothing els but the Eccho of our conceipts in the day' (Nashe 1904–10:1.356). The echo of the Red Cross Knight's state at I i 55 is noted by Anderson 1976:27.

44

With that, the wicked carle the maister Smith
    A paire of redwhot yron tongs did take
    Out of the burning cinders, and therewith
    Vnder his side him nipt, that forst to wake,
    He felt his hart for very paine to quake,
    And started vp auenged for to be
    On him, the which his quiet slomber brake:
    Yet looking round about him none could see;
Yet did the smart remaine, though he himselfe did flee.

45

In such disquiet and hartfretting payne,
    He all that night, that too long night did passe.
    And now the day out of the Ocean mayne
    Began to peepe aboue this earthly masse,
    With pearly dew sprinkling the morning grasse:
    Then vp he rose like heauie lumpe of lead,
    That in his face, as in a looking glasse,
    The signes of anguish one mote plainely read,
And ghesse the man to be dismayd with gealous dread.

46

Vnto his lofty steede he clombe anone,
    And forth vpon his former voiage fared,
    And with him eke that aged Squire attone;
    Who whatsoeuer perill was prepared,
    Both equall paines and equall perill shared:
    The end whereof and daungerous euent
    Shall for another canticle be spared.
    But here my wearie teeme nigh ouer spent
Shall breath it selfe awhile, after so long a went.

Stanza 44

4–5 Scudamour relives the moment when 'his heart | Was thrild with inward griefe' (i 49.6–7), rendered here emblematically as Grief's 'paire of Pincers' that nip the heart (III xii 16.5–6).

Stanza 45

1 hartfretting payne: on the etymology of care as that which corrodes the heart, see III x 59.6*n*.

Stanza 46

1 clombe: indicating the labour of mounting. The loss of Florimell has the same effect on Arthur at III iv 61.6. **3 attone**: together. **6 euent**: outcome. **7 canticle**: canto, adapted by S. from its current sense, a little song. **8–9** On this georgic topos of conclusion, see III xii 47.3–6*n*. The poet shares his subject's weariness. **went**: journey.

Cant. VI.

Both Scudamour and Arthegall
Doe fight with Britomart,
He sees her face; doth fall in loue,
and soone from her depart.

1

WHat equall torment to the griefe of mind,
    And pyning anguish hid in gentle hart,
    That inly feeds it selfe with thoughts vnkind,
    And nourisheth her owne consuming smart?
    What medicine can any Leaches art
    Yeeld such a sore, that doth her grieuance hide,
    And will to none her maladie impart?
    Such was the wound that *Scudamour* did gride;
For which *Dan Phebus* selfe cannot a salue prouide.

2

Who hauing left that restlesse house of *Care*,
    The next day, as he on his way did ride,
    Full of melancholie and sad misfare,
    Through misconceipt; all vnawares espide
    An armed Knight vnder a forrest side,
    Sitting in shade beside his grazing steede;
    Who soone as them approaching he descride,
    Gan towards them to pricke with eger speede,
That seem'd he was full bent to some mischieuous deede.

3

Which *Scudamour* perceiuing, forth issewed
    To haue rencountred him in equall race;
    But soone as th'other nigh approaching, vewed
    The armes he bore, his speare he gan abase,

And voide his course: at which so suddain case
    He wondred much. But th'other thus can say;
    Ah gentle *Scudamour*, vnto your grace
    I me submit, and you of pardon pray,
That almost had against you trespassed this day.

4

Whereto thus *Scudamour*, Small harme it were
    For any knight, vpon a ventrous knight
    Without displeasance for to proue his spere.
    But reade you Sir, sith ye my name haue hight,
    What is your owne, that I mote you requite.
    Certes (sayd he) ye mote as now excuse
    Me from discouering you my name aright:
    For time yet serues that I the same refuse,
But call ye me the *Saluage Knight*, as others vse.

5

Then this, Sir *Saluage Knight* (quoth he) areede;
    Or doe you here within this forrest wonne,
    That seemeth well to answere to your weede?
    Or haue ye it for some occasion donne?
    That rather seemes, sith knowen armes ye shonne.
    This other day (sayd he) a stranger knight
    Shame and dishonour hath vnto me donne;
    On whom I waite to wreake that foule despight,
When euer he this way shall passe by day or night.

Book IV Canto vi

Stanza 1
3 vnkind: unnatural, because self-destroying. **5 Leaches**: physician's. **8 gride**: pierce gratingly. **9 Dan Phebus**: '*Apollo* King of Leaches' (xii 25.4).

Stanza 2
3 sad misfare: grief caused by misfortune or by going astray. Britomart also suffers 'sad misfare' at v 30.4 but is comforted by Amoret. **4 misconceipt**: misconception, for he believes Britomart to be a man. **6 Sitting, shade**, and **grazing steede** invoke the Red Cross Knight's posture at I vii 2–3 before he is defeated by Orgoglio in order to prepare for Artegall's defeat by Britomart at 22.2–3.

Stanza 3
2 rencountred: counter-engaged in battle. **race**: a technical term for a chivalric encounter. **4 abase**: lower. **5 voide**: turn aside. **6 can**: did. **7–9** His refusal to fight one whose

shield bears 'The God of loue' (i 39.3) marks the first stage of his submission to love; cf. his apology at 22.6–7.

Stanza 4
1–3 Chivalric code sanctioned unprovoked aggression provided both parties agreed. **displeasance**: cause of grievance. **proue**: test. **4 reade**: tell. **5 requite**: salute in return. **7 discouering**: revealing.

Stanza 5
1 areede: declare. **2–5** Do you live in the forest, as your 'saluage weed' (iv 39.4) would suggest? Or have you come here for some particular reason? It would seem the latter since you shun known arms. (That he carries arms indicates that he comes from the court, but that the shield is 'ragged' and its motto obscure (iv 39.8–9) indicates that he has assumed disguise.) **8–9** Nursing a grudge and plotting revenge show Artegall's virtue of justice at its most primitive level. Cf. v 9.5–6. His ambush of Britomart contrasts with her search for him.

6

Shame be his meede (quoth he) that meaneth shame.
  But what is he, by whom ye shamed were?
  A stranger knight, sayd he, vnknowne by name,
  But knowne by fame, and by an Hebene speare,
  With which he all that met him, downe did beare.
  He in an open Turney lately held,
  Fro me the honour of that game did reare;
  And hauing me all wearie earst, downe feld,
The fayrest Ladie reft, and euer since withheld.

7

When *Scudamour* heard mention of that speare,
  He wist right well, that it was *Britomart*,
  The which from him his fairest loue did beare.
  Tho gan he swell in euery inner part,
  For fell despight, and gnaw his gealous hart,
  That thus he sharply sayd; Now by my head,
  Yet is not this the first vnknightly part,
  Which that same knight, whom by his launce I read,
Hath doen to noble knights, that many makes him dread.

8

For lately he my loue hath fro me reft,
  And eke defiled with foule villanie
  The sacred pledge, which in his faith was left,
  In shame of knighthood and fidelitie;
  The which ere long full deare he shall abie.
  And if to that auenge by you decreed
  This hand may helpe, or succour ought supplie,
  It shall not fayle, when so ye shall it need.
So both to wreake their wrathes on *Britomart* agreed.

9

Whiles thus they communed, lo farre away
  A Knight soft ryding towards them they spyde,
  Attyr'd in forraine armes and straunge aray:
  Whom when they nigh approcht, they plaine descryde

To be the same, for whom they did abyde.
  Sayd then Sir *Scudamour*, Sir *Saluage* knight
  Let me this craue, sith first I was defyde,
  That first I may that wrong to him requite:
And if I hap to fayle, you shall recure my right.

10

Which being yeelded, he his threatfull speare
  Gan fewter, and against her fiercely ran.
  Who soone as she him saw approching neare
  With so fell rage, her selfe she lightly gan
  To dight, to welcome him, well as she can:
  But entertaind him in so rude a wise,
  That to the ground she smote both horse and man;
  Whence neither greatly hasted to arise,
But on their common harmes together did deuise.

11

But *Artegall* beholding his mischaunce,
  New matter added to his former fire;
  And eft auentring his steeleheaded launce,
  Against her rode, full of despiteous ire,
  That nought but spoyle and vengeance did require.
  But to himselfe his felonous intent
  Returning, disappointed his desire,
  Whiles vnawares his saddle he forwent,
And found himselfe on ground in great amazement.

12

Lightly he started vp out of that stound,
  And snatching forth his direfull deadly blade,
  Did leape to her, as doth an eger hound
  Thrust to an Hynd within some couert glade,
  Whom without perill he cannot inuade,
  With such fell greedines he her assayled,
  That though she mounted were, yet he her made
  To giue him ground, (so much his force preuayled)
And shun his mightie strokes, gainst which no armes auayled.

Stanza 6
1 Scudamour cites the motto of the Knights of the Garter: *Honi soit qui mal y pense*, which here judges Artegall. **meaneth**: intends.   7 **reare**: take away.

Stanza 7
3 **his fairest loue**: distinguishes Amoret from 'The fayrest Ladie' (6.9), Florimell.   5 **gnaw . . . hart**: cf. 'hartfretting payne' (v 45.1) and 'gnawing Gealosy' (II vii 22.4).   6 **by my head**: a classical oath, as at II i 19.1.   8 **read**: make out; know.   9 . . . that makes many dread him.

Stanza 8
2–3 His charge against Britomart at i 53.4–5.   5 **abie**: make amends for.   6 **auenge**: vengeance. **decreed**: determined, with the legal sense, 'decided judicially'.

Stanza 9
1 **communed**: consulted.   2 **soft**: at a slow pace, in contrast to Artegall's 'eger speede' (2.8) and Scudamour's 'equall race' (3.2).   4 **when they**: referring to Artegall and Scudamour, for Britomart is alone, contrary to what one expects from v 29.   9 **recure**: recover.

Stanza 10
2 **fewter**: put into its rest.   4 **lightly**: quickly.   5 **dight**: make ready. . . . i.e. as well as she can, or as she knows well.   6 **entertaind**: received.   9 **deuise**: confer. A male knight on horseback with spear in rest bearing down upon a female knight, or thrusting at her with his sword as at 12, suggests sexual harassment, the comic, even bawdy, implications of which are potential in all Britomart's chivalric encounters.

Stanza 11
3 **eft**: again; in return. **auentring**: aiming by setting in its rest; or thrusting forward. See III i 28.7*n*. **steeleheaded launce**: so named as it opposes Britomart's 'Hebene speare' (6.4).   5 **require**: seek.   6 **felonous**: fierce, cruel.   8 **forwent**: left.

Stanza 12
1 **stound**: state of amazement.   3–5 An appropriate simile for one identified at III ii 25.1 by 'a couchant Hownd' on his helmet's crest. **eger**: fierce, savage. **Thrust to**: lunge towards.   6 **assayled**: wooed (*OED* 10) points to an allegory of courtship.

13

So as they coursed here and there, it chaunst
    That in her wheeling round, behind her crest
    So sorely he her strooke, that thence it glaunst
    Adowne her backe, the which it fairely blest
    From foule mischance; ne did it euer rest,
    Till on her horses hinder parts it fell;
    Where byting deepe, so deadly it imprest,
    That quite it chynd his backe behind the sell,
And to alight on foote her algates did compell.

14

Like as the lightning brond from riuen skie,
    Throwne out by angry *Ioue* in his vengeance,
    With dreadfull force falles on some steeple hie;
    Which battring, downe it on the church doth glance,
    And teares it all with terrible mischance.
    Yet she no whit dismayd, her steed forsooke,
    And casting from her that enchaunted lance,
    Vnto her sword and shield her soone betooke;
And therewithall at him right furiously she strooke.

15

So furiously she strooke in her first heat,
    Whiles with long fight on foot he breathlesse was,
    That she him forced backward to retreat,
    And yeeld vnto her weapon way to pas:
    Whose raging rigour neither steele nor bras
    Could stay, but to the tender flesh it went,
    And pour'd the purple bloud forth on the gras;
    That all his mayle yriv'd, and plates yrent,
Shew'd all his bodie bare vnto the cruell dent.

16

At length when as he saw her hastie heat
    Abate, and panting breath begin to fayle,
    He through long sufferance growing now more great,
    Rose in his strength, and gan her fresh assayle,

Heaping huge strokes, as thicke as showre of hayle,
    And lashing dreadfully at euery part,
    As if he thought her soule to disentrayle.
    Ah cruell hand, and thrise more cruell hart,
That workst such wrecke on her, to whom thou dearest art.

17

What yron courage euer could endure,
    To worke such outrage on so faire a creature?
    And in his madnesse thinke with hands impure
    To spoyle so goodly workmanship of nature,
    The maker selfe resembling in her feature?
    Certes some hellish furie, or some feend
    This mischiefe framd, for their first loues defeature,
    To bath their hands in bloud of dearest freend,
Thereby to make their loues beginning, their liues end.

18

Thus long they trac'd, and trauerst to and fro,
    Sometimes pursewing, and sometimes pursewed,
    Still as aduantage they espyde thereto:
    But toward th'end Sir *Arthegall* renewed
    His strength still more, but she still more decrewed.
    At last his lucklesse hand he heau'd on hie,
    Hauing his forces all in one accrewed,
    And therewith stroke at her so hideouslie,
That seemed nought but death mote be her destinie.

19

The wicked stroke vpon her helmet chaunst,
    And with the force, which in it selfe it bore,
    Her ventayle shard away, and thence forth glaunst
    A downe in vaine, ne harm'd her any more.
    With that her angels face, vnseene afore,
    Like to the ruddie morne appeard in sight,
    Deawed with siluer drops, through sweating sore,
    But somewhat redder, then beseem'd aright,
Through toylesome heate and labour of her weary fight.

Stanza 13

3 it: the stroke of the sword. **4 fairely blest**: i.e. entirely protected from serious injury; cf. I ii 18.9. His second stroke at 19.1–4 similarly glances down her front, indicating that her chaste body is inviolate. **6–9** Since the horse – more usually called a steed – serves throughout the poem as the symbol of passion, the wounding of its hind quarters is sexually significant. **chynd his backe**: split or broke the back (chine). **algates**: altogether.

Stanza 14

6–9 Britomart is about to heed Glauce's advice: 'yield thee nott [to love], | Til thou in open fielde adowne be smott' (III ii 46.4–5). Being on foot and without the power of chastity represented by her 'enchaunted speare' (III i 9.9), she must rely on her shield and sword alone, as she did when she entered the house of Busirane at III xi 25.2–3.

Stanza 15

5 rigour: hardness; violence. **8 mayle**: the pun on 'male' becomes explicit with the claim that **all his bodie** is laid bare. **9 dent**: blow.

Stanza 16

7 disentrayle: draw forth from the inward parts. **9 wrecke**: vengeance (cf. 11.5), and 'wrack' (as 21.2), i.e. injury or outrage, thus combining 'wreak' (revenge) and its consequences in 'wreck' (ruin).

Stanza 17

The rare duplication of the 'a' and 'b' rhymes, the latter (most appropriately) feminine, seems designed to highlight this crucial moment in the love between Britomart and Artegall. **4–5** As she is praised at 24.5–6. **7 defeature**: undoing, in contrast to God's **workmanship**. **8 freend**: lover.

Stanza 18

1 I.e. pursued, and then turned aside on being pursued, as line 2 explains. **5–7 decrewed**: decreased; the opposite of **accrewed**: gathered up.

Stanza 19

As in Tasso, *Ger. Lib.* 3.21–22: Tancred unhelms the Amazon Clorinda only to be overcome by her beauty and yield to her. On the revelation of Britomart's beauty, see III i 43*n*.

20

And round about the same, her yellow heare
  Hauing through stirring loosd their wonted band,
  Like to a golden border did appeare,
  Framed in goldsmithes forge with cunning hand:
  Yet goldsmithes cunning could not vnderstand
  To frame such subtile wire, so shinie cleare.
  For it did glister like the golden sand,
  The which *Pactolus* with his waters shere,
Throwes forth vpon the riuage round about him nere.

21

And as his hand he vp againe did reare,
  Thinking to worke on her his vtmost wracke,
  His powrelesse arme benumbd with secret feare
  From his reuengefull purpose shronke abacke,
  And cruell sword out of his fingers slacke
  Fell downe to ground, as if the steele had sence,
  And felt some ruth, or sence his hand did lacke,
  Or both of them did thinke, obedience
To doe to so diuine a beauties excellence.

22

And he himselfe long gazing thereupon,
  At last fell humbly downe vpon his knee,
  And of his wonder made religion,
  Weening some heauenly goddesse he did see,
  Or else vnweeting, what it else might bee;
  And pardon her besought his errour frayle,
  That had done outrage in so high degree:
  Whilest trembling horrour did his sense assayle,
And made ech member quake, and manly hart to quayle.

23

Nathelesse she full of wrath for that late stroke,
  All that long while vpheld her wrathfull hand,
  With fell intent, on him to bene ywroke,
  And looking sterne, still ouer him did stand,

Threatning to strike, vnlesse he would withstand:
  And bad him rise, or surely he should die.
  But die or liue for nought he would vpstand
  But her of pardon prayd more earnestlie,
Or wreake on him her will for so great iniurie.

24

Which when as *Scudamour*, who now abrayd,
  Beheld, whereas he stood not farre aside,
  He was therewith right wondrously dismayd,
  And drawing nigh, when as he plaine descride
  That peerelesse paterne of Dame natures pride,
  And heauenly image of perfection,
  He blest himselfe, as one sore terrifide,
  And turning his feare to faint deuotion,
Did worship her as some celestiall vision.

25

But *Glauce*, seeing all that chaunced there,
  Well weeting how their errour to assoyle,
  Full glad of so good end, to them drew nere,
  And her salewd with seemely belaccoyle,
  Ioyous to see her safe after long toyle.
  Then her besought, as she to her was deare,
  To graunt vnto those warriours truce a whyle;
  Which yeelded, they their beuers vp did reare,
And shew'd themselues to her, such as indeed they were.

26

When *Britomart* with sharpe auizefull eye
  Beheld the louely face of *Artegall*,
  Tempred with sternesse and stout maiestie,
  She gan eftsoones it to her mind to call,
  To be the same which in her fathers hall
  Long since in that enchaunted glasse she saw.
  Therewith her wrathfull courage gan appall,
  And haughtie spirits meekely to adaw,
That her enhaunced hand she downe can soft withdraw.

Fittingly, her lover unveils her.   **3 ventayle**: the movable front
of her helmet. She first saw him when his was lifted up at III ii
24.3–4.   **shard**: cut.

Stanza 20
5 vnderstand: know how.   **6 subtile**: fine.   **7–9 Pactolus**:
'a ryuer in Lydia, hauyng golden grauel' (T. Cooper 1565).
shere: clear.   **riuage**: banks.

Stanza 21
2 his vtmost wracke: the greatest destruction he could inflict;
see 16.9*n*.   **3–6** Britomart's beauty exerts the same force as
Cambina's magic at iii 48.2–5.   **7 sence**: capacity to feel.

Stanza 22
3 I.e. his wonder was turned to religious adoration, as when
Timias saw Belphœbe at III v 35, and the witch saw Florimell
at III vii 4–9. On this romance motif, see III i 43*n*, and
Hamlin 1994.   **8 trembling**: stressing the Lat. sense of **horrour**, shuddering.

Stanza 23
3 ywroke: avenged.   **4 sterne**: threatening.

Stanza 24
1 abrayd: awoke, i.e. revived after his fall.   **8** His conversion
compares to Artegall's at 22.3 for he shares his 'secret feare'
(21.3) or awe.   **faint**: because he is **dismayd** and **terrifide**.

Stanza 25
2 assoyle: purge; absolve from sin.   **4** And saluted her with an
appropriately kind greeting. As Britomart's go-between,
Glauce fulfils her vow 'To compas thy desire, and find that
loued knight' (III ii 46.9).

Stanza 26
1 auizefull: attentive.   **2 louely**: also loving.   **4–6** Recalling
III ii 24–25.   **7–8** As she responded at III ii 27.1–4 to her
first sight of him.   **appall**: fail, wax faint.   **adaw**: become
subdued.   **9 enhaunced**: uplifted.

27

Yet she it forst to haue againe vpheld,
  As fayning choler, which was turn'd to cold:
  But euer when his visage she beheld,
  Her hand fell downe, and would no longer hold
  The wrathfull weapon gainst his countnance bold:
  But when in vaine to fight she oft assayd,
  She arm'd her tongue, and thought at him to scold;
  Nathlesse her tongue not to her will obayd,
But brought forth speeches myld, when she would haue
                                            (missayd.

28

But *Scudamour* now woxen inly glad,
  That all his gealous feare he false had found,
  And how that Hag his loue abused had
  With breach of faith and loyaltie vnsound,
  The which long time his grieued hart did wound,
  He thus bespake; Certes Sir *Artegall*,
  I ioy to see you lout so low on ground,
  And now become to liue a Ladies thrall,
That whylome in your minde wont to despise them all.

29

Soone as she heard the name of *Artegall*,
  Her hart did leape, and all her hart-strings tremble,
  For sudden ioy, and secret feare withall,
  And all her vitall powres with motion nimble,
  To succour it, themselues gan there assemble,
  That by the swift recourse of flushing blood
  Right plaine appeard, though she it would dissemble,
  And fayned still her former angry mood,
Thinking to hide the depth by troubling of the flood.

30

When *Glauce* thus gan wisely all vpknit;
  Ye gentle Knights, whom fortune here hath brought,
  To be spectators of this vncouth fit,
  Which secret fate hath in this Ladie wrought,

Against the course of kind, ne meruaile nought,
  Ne thenceforth feare the thing that hethertoo
  Hath troubled both your mindes with idle thought,
  Fearing least she your loues away should woo,
Feared in vaine, sith meanes ye see there wants theretoo.

31

And you Sir *Artegall*, the saluage knight,
  Henceforth may not disdaine, that womans hand
  Hath conquered you anew in second fight:
  For whylome they haue conquerd sea and land,
  And heauen it selfe, that nought may them withstand.
  Ne henceforth be rebellious vnto loue,
  That is the crowne of knighthood, and the band
  Of noble minds deriued from aboue,
Which being knit with vertue, neuer will remoue.

32

And you faire Ladie knight, my dearest Dame,
  Relent the rigour of your wrathfull will,
  Whose fire were better turn'd to other flame;
  And wiping out remembrance of all ill,
  Graunt him your grace, but so that he fulfill
  The penance, which ye shall to him empart:
  For louers heauen must passe by sorrowes hell.
  Thereat full inly blushed *Britomart*;
But *Artegall* close smyling ioy'd in secret hart.

33

Yet durst he not make loue so suddenly,
  Ne thinke th'affection of her hart to draw
  From one to other so quite contrary:
  Besides her modest countenance he saw
  So goodly graue, and full of princely aw,
  That it his ranging fancie did refraine,
  And looser thoughts to lawfull bounds withdraw;
  Whereby the passion grew more fierce and faine,
Like to a stubborne steede whom strong hand would
                                            (restraine.

Stanza 27

2 choler: associated with heat. **4–5** Her arm and hand rebel as did Artegall's at 21. **bold**: applied to the lover rather than to the warrior. **9** As when she slandered Artegall but repented 'so to haue missayd' (III ii 9.2), i.e. to have spoken abusively.

Stanza 28

4 Recalling 8.1–4. **6 He**: Her *1596*; 'Him', sugg. Upton 1758, as 34.5. Artegall may be named because his identity was revealed at 25.9.

Stanza 29

3 Britomart's **secret feare** mirrors Artegall's at 21.3, as noted by Walker 1998b:99–100, who suggests that both fear losing power. **6–9** Her blushing recalls Shamefastnes's at II ix 43.1–3. **recourse**: flow. **flushing**: rushing.

Stanza 30

3 vncouth fit: strange, painful experience. **5 kind**: nature. **7–9** Artegall is included because he has suffered jealousy; see v 21.5–7, vi 6.9. **meanes**: such bawdy bluntness is expected of a nurse. That she ignores a possible homoerotic relationship is noted by Sedinger 2000:104.

Stanza 31

4–5 A compliment to Elizabeth, as Upton 1758 first noted. **8 deriued from aboue**: cf. III iii 1.1–4.

Stanza 32

5 grace: favour. **6 empart**: impose. **7 by**: through. **9 close**: secretly.

Stanza 33

8–9 faine: eager. **stubborne**: untamable, fierce.

34

But *Scudamour* whose hart twixt doubtfull feare
  And feeble hope hung all this while suspence,
  Desiring of his *Amoret* to heare
  Some gladfull newes and sure intelligence,
  Her thus bespake; But Sir without offence
  Mote I request you tydings of my loue,
  My *Amoret*, sith you her freed fro thence,
  Where she captiued long, great woes did proue;
That where ye left, I may her seeke, as doth behoue.

35

To whom thus *Britomart*, Certes Sir knight,
  What is of her become, or whether reft,
  I can not vnto you aread a right.
  For from that time I from enchaunters theft
  Her freed, in which ye her all hopelesse left,
  I her preseru'd from perill and from feare,
  And euermore from villenie her kept:
  Ne euer was there wight to me more deare
Then she, ne vnto whom I more true loue did beare.

36

Till on a day as through a desert wyld
  We trauelled, both wearie of the way
  We did alight, and sate in shadow myld;
  Where fearelesse I to sleepe me downe did lay.
  But when as I did out of sleepe abray,
  I found her not, where I her left whyleare,
  But thought she wandred was, or gone astray.
  I cal'd her loud, I sought her farre and neare;
But no where could her find, nor tydings of her heare.

37

When *Scudamour* those heauie tydings heard,
  His hart was thrild with point of deadly feare;
  Ne in his face or bloud or life appeard,
  But senselesse stood, like to a mazed steare,

That yet of mortall stroke the stound doth beare.
  Till *Glauce* thus; Faire Sir, be nought dismayd
  With needelesse dread, till certaintie ye heare:
  For yet she may be safe though somewhat strayd;
Its best to hope the best, though of the worst affrayd.

38

Nathlesse he hardly of her chearefull speech
  Did comfort take, or in his troubled sight
  Shew'd change of better cheare: so sore a breach
  That sudden newes had made into his spright;
  Till *Britomart* him fairely thus behight;
  Great cause of sorrow certes Sir ye haue:
  But comfort take: for by this heauens light
  I vow, you dead or liuing not to leaue,
Till I her find, and wreake on him that her did reaue.

39

Therewith he rested, and well pleased was.
  So peace being confirm'd amongst them all,
  They tooke their steeds, and forward thence did pas
  Vnto some resting place, which mote befall,
  All being guided by Sir *Artegall*.
  Where goodly solace was vnto them made,
  And dayly feasting both in bowre and hall,
  Vntill that they their wounds well healed had,
And wearie limmes recur'd after late vsage bad.

40

In all which time, Sir *Artegall* made way
  Vnto the loue of noble *Britomart*,
  And with meeke seruice and much suit did lay
  Continuall siege vnto her gentle hart,
  Which being whylome launcht with louely dart,
  More eath was new impression to receiue,
  How euer she her paynd with womanish art
  To hide her wound, that none might it perceiue:
Vaine is the art that seekes it selfe for to deceiue.

Stanza 34
2 suspence: i.e. in suspense; literally suspended. **5 Sir**: a title applied to women (*OED* 9) but owing to Britomart as a knight. **8 proue**: suffer, endure.

Stanza 35
2 whether: whither. **5 all hopelesse**: refers to Scudamour's state at III xi 16.1–5, and xii 45.4 (*1596*). **7 villenie**: ill-usage; dishonour. **8–9** Since Amoret is **true loue**, Britomart plays upon her name in order to declare her love for Artegall at the moment that love is no longer guarded by her.

Stanza 36
1–4 This moment is described again at vii 3.5–9. Britomart was **fearelesse** in contrast to her 'secret feare' (29.3) on seeing Artegall. **5 abray**: awake. **8–9** Britomart's search for Amoret is described again at ix 38.1–5.

Stanza 37
4–5 The mortally wounded **steare** indicates Scudamour's impotence. At i 49.7–9, he is compared to a struck stag.

stound: shock. **6–9** After her extended advice to Artegall and Scudamour at 30, to Artegall alone at 31, and to Britomart at 32, Glauce leaves the poem with a concluding example of her proverbial wisdom (Smith 399).

Stanza 38
2 sight: appearance. **5–9 behight**: vowed, though 'addressed' better fits the context. She extends the vow she made at III xi 18.7–9. Now that she has accepted Artegall's love, she is ready to accompany Cupid's man.

Stanza 39
3 Britomart's steed has recovered from having its back broken at 13. **5** Artegall replaces Cupid who guided Britomart at III iv 6.8 and IV v 29.5. **6 solace**: pleasure, entertainment. **9 recur'd**: restored.

Stanza 40
5 . . . pierced with the dart of love (referring to her wound on first seeing his image at III ii 26.7–9). **6 eath**: easy. **7 How euer**: how ever much. **paynd**: took pains.

41

So well he woo'd her, and so well he wrought her,
  With faire entreatie and sweet blandishment,
  That at the length vnto a bay he brought her,
  So as she to his speeches was content
  To lend an eare, and softly to relent.
  At last through many vowes which forth he pour'd,
  And many othes, she yeelded her consent
  To be his loue, and take him for her Lord,
Till they with mariage meet might finish that accord.

42

Tho when they had long time there taken rest,
  Sir *Artegall*, who all this while was bound
  Vpon an hard aduenture yet in quest,
  Fit time for him thence to depart it found,
  To follow that, which he did long propound;
  And vnto her his congee came to take.
  But her therewith full sore displeasd he found,
  And loth to leaue her late betrothed make,
Her dearest loue full loth so shortly to forsake.

43

Yet he with strong perswasions her asswaged,
  And wonne her will to suffer him depart;
  For which his faith with her he fast engaged,
  And thousand vowes from bottome of his hart,
  That all so soone as he by wit or art
  Could that atchieue, whereto he did aspire,
  He vnto her would speedily reuert:
  No longer space thereto he did desire,
But till the horned moone three courses did expire.

44

With which she for the present was appeased,
  And yeelded leaue, how euer malcontent
  She inly were, and in her mind displeased.
  So early in the morrow next he went

Forth on his way, to which he was ybent.
  Ne wight him to attend, or way to guide,
  As whylome was the custome ancient
  Mongst Knights, when on aduentures they did ride,
Saue that she algates him a while accompanide.

45

And by the way she sundry purpose found
  Of this or that, the time for to delay,
  And of the perils whereto he was bound,
  The feare whereof seem'd much her to affray:
  But all she did was but to weare out day.
  Full oftentimes she leaue of him did take;
  And eft againe deuiz'd some what to say,
  Which she forgot, whereby excuse to make:
So loth she was his companie for to forsake.

46

At last when all her speeches she had spent,
  And new occasion fayld her more to find,
  She left him to his fortunes gouernment,
  And backe returned with right heauie mind,
  To *Scudamour*, who she had left behind,
  With whom she went to seeke faire *Amoret*,
  Her second care, though in another kind;
  For vertues onely sake, which doth beget
True loue and faithfull friendship, she by her did set.

47

Backe to that desert forrest they retyred,
  Where sorie *Britomart* had lost her late;
  There they her sought, and euery where inquired,
  Where they might tydings get of her estate;
  Yet found they none. But by what haplesse fate,
  Or hard misfortune she was thence conuayd,
  And stolne away from her beloued mate,
  Were long to tell; therefore I here will stay
Vntill another tyde, that I it finish may.

Stanza 41

1 wrought: prevailed upon; persuaded. **3 vnto a bay**: to the last extremity when a hunted animal is forced to face its pursuer. The phrase continues the image of his 'siege vnto her gentle hart' (40.4), punning on 'hart'. **8** A key line in the battle for 'maistery' (see III i 25.7–9*n*): in becoming her 'thrall' (28.8), he becomes **her Lord**. Cf. V vi 18.8, vii 40.1, etc.

Stanza 42

3 in quest: i.e. uncompleted. **5 propound**: purpose or intend. **6 congee**: farewell; suggesting 'leave to depart': cf. 44.2. **8 make**: mate.

Stanza 43

7 reuert: return. **9 three** suggests fulfilment, as the three lunar months between betrothal and marriage are marked by

the three concluding sonnets to *Amoretti* on the lover's absence; see J.N. Brown 1973:6. **horned moone** may allude to Isis, whom Britomart sees wearing a 'Moon-like Mitre' at V vii 13.6, and into whom she sees herself transformed.

Stanza 44

6–8 As V i 30.8–9 and iv 3.8–9.

Stanza 45

1 sundry purpose: various subjects of conversation.

Stanza 46

7–9 She cares for Amoret not out of personal love, as she does Artegall, but primarily for the sake of (her) virtue.

Stanza 47

4 estate: state. **9 tyde**: suitable opportunity.

Cant. VII.

Amoret rapt by greedie lust
Belphebe saues from dread,
The Squire her loues, and being blam'd
his dayes in dole doth lead.

1

G Reat God of loue, that with thy cruell dart
Doest conquer greatest conquerors on ground,
And setst thy kingdome in the captiue harts
Of Kings and Keasars, to thy seruice bound,
What glorie, or what guerdon hast thou found
In feeble Ladies tyranning so sore;
And adding anguish to the bitter wound,
With which their liues thou lanchedst long afore,
By heaping stormes of trouble on them daily more?

2

So whylome didst thou to faire *Florimell*;
And so and so to noble *Britomart*:
So doest thou now to her, of whom I tell,
The louely *Amoret*, whose gentle hart
Thou martyrest with sorow and with smart,
In saluage forrests, and in deserts wide,
With Beares and Tygers taking heauie part,
Withouten comfort, and withouten guide,
That pittie is to heare the perils, which she tride.

3

So soone as she with that braue Britonesse
Had left that Turneyment for beauties prise,
They trauel'd long, that now for wearinesse,
Both of the way, and warlike exercise,

Both through a forest ryding did deuise
T'alight, and rest their wearie limbs awhile.
There heauie sleepe the eye-lids did surprise
Of *Britomart* after long tedious toyle,
That did her passed paines in quiet rest assoyle.

4

The whiles faire *Amoret*, of nought affeard,
Walkt through the wood, for pleasure, or for need;
When suddenly behind her backe she heard
One rushing forth out of the thickest weed,
That ere she backe could turne to taken heed,
Had vnawares her snatched vp from ground.
Feebly she shriekt, but so feebly indeed,
That *Britomart* heard not the shrilling sound,
There where through weary trauel she lay sleeping sound.

5

It was to weet a wilde and saluage man,
Yet was no man, but onely like in shape,
And eke in stature higher by a span,
All ouergrowne with haire, that could awhape
An hardy hart, and his wide mouth did gape
With huge great teeth, like to a tusked Bore:
For he liu'd all on rauin and on rape
Of men and beasts; and fed on fleshly gore,
The signe whereof yet stain'd his bloudy lips afore.

Book IV Canto vii

Argument

1 rapt: carried off. **2 The Squire**: Timias; see 23.6*n*. **her**: the antecedent is either Belphœbe or Amoret, as Bednarz 1984:62 notes. **4 dole**: grief, sorrow.

Stanza 1

6 tyranning: playing the tyrant, as Cupid is seen at III xii 22.1–5, and is commonly described, e.g. III ii 23.1–4. **8 lanchedst**: wounded.

Stanza 2

1–4 faire, **noble**, and **louely** are the defining epithets of the three. **so and so**: in like manner; thus and thus again. **7 Beares** and **Tygers** symbolize violence; see II ii 22.5–9*n*. **taking heauie part**: i.e. contributing to her fear. **8 comfort**: aid, succour. **9 tride**: underwent.

Stanza 3

5–9 Repeating vi 36.1–4. **assoyle**: dispel.

Stanza 4

1 of nought affeard: as Britomart at vi 36.4. At 8.9, she is 'nought fearing', being unconscious; and soon she lapses into the fear that marks her state, as 21.1. **2 need**: a euphemism, being a 'little bathroom joke' as Silberman 1995:118 suggests; or indicating that Amoret exposes herself to rape from inner compulsion; or a means to blame the victim, as Cavanagh 1994a:5 suggests; or because of the requirements of the allegory: she is enacting the role of Proserpina who was suddenly seized by Dis, as told by Ovid, *Met.* 5.391–98. **4 weed**: undergrowth. **7 Feebly**: in contrast to Una's 'thrilling shriekes, and shrieking cryes' at I vi 6.2, and marking the helplessness of 'feeble Ladies' (i.6) tyrannized by Cupid.

Stanza 5

1 saluage man: on his type, see VI iv 2.2*n*. He personifies lust, as Arg.1 suggests though not so named, as C. Burrow 1996:46 notes. See 'Lust' in the *SEnc*. On the characteristics he shares with American natives, see Hamlin 1995:74. **4** Cf. the 'rugged heare' of Lechery's goat at I iv 24.2. **awhape**: terrify; utterly confound. **6 Bore**: the usual figure of lust. **7 rauin**: plunder.

6

His neather lip was not like man nor beast,
    But like a wide deepe poke, downe hanging low,
    In which he wont the relickes of his feast,
    And cruell spoyle, which he had spard, to stow:
    And ouer it his huge great nose did grow,
    Full dreadfully empurpled all with bloud;
    And downe both sides two wide long eares did glow,
    And raught downe to his waste, when vp he stood,
More great then th'eares of Elephants by *Indus* flood.

7

His wast was with a wreath of yuie greene
    Engirt about, ne other garment wore:
    For all his haire was like a garment seene;
    And in his hand a tall young oake he bore,
    Whose knottie snags were sharpned all afore,
    And beath'd in fire for steele to be in sted.
    But whence he was, or of what wombe ybore,
    Of beasts, or of the earth, I haue not red:
But certes was with milke of Wolues and Tygres fed.

8

This vgly creature in his armes her snatcht,
    And through the forrest bore her quite away,
    With briers and bushes all to rent and scratcht;
    Ne care he had, ne pittie of the pray,
    Which many a knight had sought so many a day.
    He stayed not, but in his armes her bearing
    Ran, till he came to th'end of all his way,
    Vnto his caue farre from all peoples hearing,
And there he threw her in, nought feeling, ne nought fearing.

9

For she deare Ladie all the way was dead,
    Whilest he in armes her bore; but when she felt
    Her selfe downe soust, she waked out of dread
    Streight into griefe, that her deare hart nigh swelt,

And eft gan into tender teares to melt.
    Then when she lookt about, and nothing found
    But darknesse and dread horrour, where she dwelt,
    She almost fell againe into a swound,
Ne wist whether aboue she were, or vnder ground.

10

With that she heard some one close by her side
    Sighing and sobbing sore, as if the paine
    Her tender hart in peeces would diuide:
    Which she long listning, softly askt againe
    What mister wight it was that so did plaine?
    To whom thus aunswer'd was: Ah wretched wight
    That seekes to know anothers griefe in vaine,
    Vnweeting of thine owne like haplesse plight:
Selfe to forget to mind another, is ouersight.

11

Aye me (said she) where am I, or with whom?
    Emong the liuing, or emong the dead?
    What shall of me vnhappy maid become?
    Shall death be th'end, or ought else worse, aread.
    Vnhappy mayd (then answerd she) whose dread
    Vntride, is lesse then when thou shalt it try:
    Death is to him, that wretched life doth lead,
    Both grace and gaine; but he in hell doth lie,
That liues a loathed life, and wishing cannot die.

12

This dismall day hath thee a caytiue made,
    And vassall to the vilest wretch aliue,
    Whose cursed vsage and vngodly trade
    The heauens abhorre, and into darkenesse driue.
    For on the spoile of women he doth liue,
    Whose bodies chast, when euer in his powre
    He may them catch, vnable to gainestriue,
    He with his shamefull lust doth first deflowre,
And afterwards themselues doth cruelly deuoure.

---

8 His bestiality is found in Argante at III vii 49.7, and his cannibalism in the Salvage Nation at VI viii 35–49.

Stanza 6
An anatomizing of the male genitalia. **2 poke**: bag, here the scrotum, but possibly with distinctively female associations, making Lust bisexual, as Oram 1984:42 suggests. **4 spard**: saved. **7 glow**: like the nose (penis) engorged with blood, the ears burn with passion (*OED* 6). **9 by Indus flood**: apparently alluding to their favourite habitation because they copulate in water. The Indian species was reputed to be the greatest, and strongest (Topsell 1967:1.150). A medieval tr. of the French *Yvain* describes Lust as having 'eres als ane olyfant'; noted Freeman 1970:238.

Stanza 7
1–4 Wearing ivy and having long hair (in a man) denotes lust, e.g. Sylvanus's waist is girt with ivy at I vi 14.9, and Timias overcome by lust is covered with hair at IV vii 40. On the oak, see I vii 10.7*n*; **young** marks Lust's virility. **6** And heated in fire to be hardened and serve in place of steel.

Stanza 8
3 all to: entirely.

Stanza 9
3 soust: thrown. **4 swelt**: swooned. **8 swound**: swoon.

Stanza 10
4 againe: in response. **5 What mister**: what kind of. **plaine**: lament. **7 in vaine**: foolishly. **9** The opening trochee and the iambic **another** stress the reversal at 20.1 to note one quality of friendship.

Stanza 11
4 aread: tell. **6 try**: undergo, experience. **7–9** The answer to Amoret's two double questions – 'Am I among the living or among the dead in hell? Shall I suffer death or worse?' – is that she is living in a hell worse than death.

Stanza 12
1 dismall day: an unlucky day, *dies mali*. **caytiue**: captive, as she was held 'in caytiue band' by Busirane at III xi 10.2. **3 trade**: practice. **7 gainestriue**: oppose.

13

Now twenty daies, by which the sonnes of men
  Diuide their works, haue past through heuen sheene,
  Since I was brought into this dolefull den;
  During which space these sory eies haue seen
  Seauen women by him slaine, and eaten clene.
  And now no more for him but I alone,
  And this old woman here remaining beene;
  Till thou cam'st hither to augment our mone,
And of vs three to morrow he will sure eate one.

14

Ah dreadfull tidings which thou doest declare,
  (Quoth she) of all that euer hath bene knowen:
  Full many great calamities and rare
  This feeble brest endured hath, but none
  Equall to this, where euer I haue gone.
  But what are you, whom like vnlucky lot
  Hath linckt with me in the same chaine attone?
  To tell (quoth she) that which ye see, needs not;
A wofull wretched maid, of God and man forgot.

15

But what I was, it irkes me to reherse;
  Daughter vnto a Lord of high degree;
  That ioyd in happy peace, till fates peruerse
  With guilefull loue did secretly agree,
  To ouerthrow my state and dignitie.
  It was my lot to loue a gentle swaine,
  Yet was he but a Squire of low degree;
  Yet was he meet, vnlesse mine eye did faine,
By any Ladies side for Leman to haue laine.

16

But for his meannesse and disparagement,
  My Sire, who me too dearely well did loue,
  Vnto my choise by no meanes would assent,
  But often did my folly fowle reproue.

Yet nothing could my fixed mind remoue,
  But whether willed or nilled friend or foe,
  I me resolu'd the vtmost end to proue,
  And rather then my loue abandon so,
Both sire, and friends, and all for euer to forgo.

17

Thenceforth I sought by secret meanes to worke
  Time to my will, and from his wrathfull sight
  To hide th'intent, which in my heart did lurke,
  Till I thereto had all things ready dight.
  So on a day vnweeting vnto wight,
  I with that Squire agreede away to flit,
  And in a priuy place, betwixt vs hight,
  Within a groue appointed him to meete;
To which I boldly came vpon my feeble feete.

18

But ah vnhappy houre me thither brought:
  For in that place where I him thought to find,
  There was I found, contrary to my thought,
  Of this accursed Carle of hellish kind,
  The shame of men, and plague of womankind,
  Who trussing me, as Eagle doth his pray,
  Me hether brought with him, as swift as wind,
  Where yet vntouched till this present day,
I rest his wretched thrall, the sad *AEmylia*.

19

Ah sad *AEmylia* (then sayd *Amoret,*)
  Thy ruefull plight I pitty as mine owne.
  But read to me, by what deuise or wit,
  Hast thou in all this time, from him vnknowne
  Thine honor sau'd, though into thraldome throwne.
  Through helpe (quoth she) of this old woman here
  I haue so done, as she to me hath showne.
  For euer when he burnt in lustfull fire,
She in my stead supplide his bestiall desire.

Stanza 13
1 twenty is the number of knights who stand between Scudamour and Amoret; see x 7.6*n*. **5 Seauen** suggests the completion of a cycle, as the number of months that Amoret was tortured by Busirane as reported at III xi 10.8. **8 mone**: state of grief.

Stanza 15
On the story of her love of Amyas, **a Squire of low degree** (the title of an English version of a medieval French romance published *ca.* 1555–60), who is first named together with his look-alike friend, Placidas, at viii 59.2–4, see 'Aemylia' in the *SEnc*. **1 irkes**: troubles; grieves. **reherse**: relate. **5 dignitie**: honour, or **high degree**. **8 faine**: mistake.

Stanza 16
At viii 50–51, her story is told by Placidas. **1 meannesse**: humble rank. **disparagement**: the disgrace of marriage to an

inferior. **4 fowle**: grievously; as an adj., referring to her father's (or the poet's) judgement. **5 fixed**: stubborn rather than constant. **6 willed or nilled**: agreeing or not.

Stanza 17
2 will: purpose; carnal desire; wilfulness. **4 dight**: prepared. **7 hight**: named.

Stanza 18
6 trussing: a term from falconry to describe the action of a hawk seizing its prey in the air. **8 vntouched**: not sexually violated; 'from him vnknowne' (19.4). **9 sad AEmylia**: a vaguely romantic name and epithet, esp. when given four syllables as here; cf. 34.1, viii 63.1.

Stanza 19
3 read: relate. **9 supplide**: satisfied.

20

Thus of their euils as they did discourse,
   And each did other much bewaile and mone;
   Loe where the villaine selfe, their sorrowes sourse,
   Came to the caue, and rolling thence the stone,
   Which wont to stop the mouth thereof, that none
   Might issue forth, came rudely rushing in,
   And spredding ouer all the flore alone,
   Gan dight him selfe vnto his wonted sinne;
Which ended, then his bloudy banket should beginne.

21

Which when as fearefull *Amoret* perceiued,
   She staid not the vtmost end thereof to try,
   But like a ghastly Gelt, whose wits are reaued,
   Ran forth in hast with hideous outcry,
   For horrour of his shamefull villany.
   But after her full lightly he vprose,
   And her pursu'd as fast as she did flie:
   Full fast she flies, and farre afore him goes,
Ne feeles the thorns and thickets pricke her tender toes.

22

Nor hedge, nor ditch, nor hill, nor dale she staies,
   But ouerleapes them all, like Robucke light,
   And through the thickest makes her nighest waies;
   And euermore when with regardfull sight
   She looking backe, espies that griesly wight
   Approching nigh, she gins to mend her pace,
   And makes her feare a spur to hast her flight:
   More swift then *Myrrh'* or *Daphne* in her race,
Or any of the Thracian Nimphes in saluage chase.

23

Long so she fled, and so he follow'd long;
   Ne liuing aide for her on earth appeares,
   But if the heauens helpe to redresse her wrong,
   Moued with pity of her plenteous teares.
It fortuned *Belphebe* with her peares
   The woody Nimphs, and with that louely boy,
   Was hunting then the Libbards and the Beares,
   In these wild woods, as was her wonted ioy,
To banish sloth, that oft doth noble mindes annoy.

24

It so befell, as oft it fals in chace,
   That each of them from other sundred were,
   And that same gentle Squire arriu'd in place,
   Where this same cursed caytiue did appeare,
   Pursuing that faire Lady full of feare,
   And now he her quite ouertaken had;
   And now he her away with him did beare
   Vnder his arme, as seeming wondrous glad,
That by his grenning laughter mote farre off be rad.

25

Which drery sight the gentle Squire espying,
   Doth hast to crosse him by the nearest way,
   Led with that wofull Ladies piteous crying,
   And him assailes with all the might he may,
   Yet will not he the louely spoile downe lay,
   But with his craggy club in his right hand,
   Defends him selfe, and saues his gotten pray.
   Yet had it bene right hard him to withstand,
But that he was full light and nimble on the land.

26

Thereto the villaine vsed craft in fight;
   For euer when the Squire his iauelin shooke,
   He held the Lady forth before him right,
   And with her body, as a buckler, broke
   The puissance of his intended stroke.
   And if it chaunst, (as needs it must in fight)
   Whilest he on him was greedy to be wroke,
   That any little blow on her did light,
Then would he laugh aloud, and gather great delight.

Stanza 20

7–9 While Lust's **wonted sinne** is to rape, kill, and eat virgins (12.8–9), or satisfy his desire on the accommodating old woman, his act here suggests masturbation, which illustrates lust's self-centredness in its entire negation of friendship.

Stanza 21

2 **the vtmost end**: with the obvious bawdy reference to Lust's nose. The comedy continues throughout the stanza. 3 **ghastly Gelt**: fearful lunatic. Attr. to S. by *OED*, f. Irish *geilt*.

Stanza 22

1 **she staies**: she stays for; or stops her. 2 On the **Robucke**, see II ii 7.4*n*. 8–9 Florimell's flight is also compared to Myrrha's and Daphne's at III vii 26.1–4. Both allusions apply to Æmylia who flees her father's wrath as does the first, and her lover's lust as does the second. **the Thracian Nimphes**: presumably the Thracian Amazons in Virgil, *Aen.* 11.659–60.

Stanza 23

3–4 Amoret's need for heavenly grace signals Belphœbe's intervention, as she enters to aid Timias at III v 27. **But if**:

unless. 5 **peares**: companions. 6 **that louely boy** is the loving Timias who throughout Bk IV is called the 'gentle Squire', a name first given him by Belphœbe at III v 36.1. 7 **Libbards**: leopards; cf. II iii 28.8.

Stanza 24

3–4 The parallel **that** and **this** relates Timias to Lust, as Goldberg 1981:56 notes. 9 **grenning laughter** is a mark of lust or savagery, as at III viii 24.6; see L. Hendrix 1993:129–31. **rad**: perceived.

Stanza 25

1 **drery**: grievous. 5 **the louely spoile**: as she is Cupid's 'proud spoile' at III xii 22.7 and Scudamour's 'beauties spoile' at IV x 3.3. 9 **But that**: because. **on the land**: on the ground, i.e. on his feet.

Stanza 26

The reflexive quality of the fighting blurs the distinction between the antagonists, as Oram 1984:41 notes. 2 **shooke**: brandished in order to strike. 4 **buckler**: used to catch the blow of an adversary. 7 **wroke**: avenged.

27

Which subtill sleight did him encumber much,
    And made him oft, when he would strike, forbeare;
    For hardly could he come the carle to touch,
    But that he her must hurt, or hazard neare:
    Yet he his hand so carefully did beare,
    That at the last he did himselfe attaine,
    And therein left the pike head of his speare.
A streame of coleblacke bloud thence gusht amaine,
That all her silken garments did with bloud bestaine.

28

With that he threw her rudely on the flore,
    And laying both his hands vpon his glaue,
    With dreadfull strokes let driue at him so sore,
    That forst him flie abacke, himselfe to saue:
    Yet he therewith so felly still did raue,
    That scarse the Squire his hand could once vpreare,
    But for aduantage ground vnto him gaue,
    Tracing and trauersing, now here, now there;
For bootlesse thing it was to think such blowes to beare.

29

Whilest thus in battell they embusied were,
    Belphebe raunging in that forrest wide,
    The hideous noise of their huge strokes did heare,
    And drew thereto, making her eare her guide.
    Whom when that theefe approching nigh espide,
    With bow in hand, and arrowes ready bent,
    He by his former combate would not bide,
    But fled away with ghastly dreriment,
Well knowing her to be his deaths sole instrument.

30

Whom seeing flie, she speedily poursewed
    With winged feete, as nimble as the winde,
    And euer in her bow she ready shewed,
    The arrow, to his deadly marke desynde.
    As when *Latonaes* daughter cruell kynde,
    In vengement of her mothers great disgrace,
    With fell despight her cruell arrowes tynde
    Gainst wofull *Niobes* vnhappy race,
That all the gods did mone her miserable case.

31

So well she sped her and so far she ventred,
    That ere vnto his hellish den he raught,
    Euen as he ready was there to haue entred,
    She sent an arrow forth with mighty draught,
    That in the very dore him ouercaught,
    And in his nape arriuing, through it thrild
    His greedy throte, therewith in two distraught,
    That all his vitall spirites thereby spild,
And all his hairy brest with gory bloud was fild.

32

Whom when on ground she groueling saw to rowle,
    She ran in hast his life to haue bereft:
    But ere she could him reach, the sinfull sowle
    Hauing his carrion corse quite sencelesse left,
    Was fled to hell, surcharg'd with spoile and theft.
    Yet ouer him she there long gazing stood,
    And oft admir'd his monstrous shape, and oft
    His mighty limbs, whilest all with filthy bloud
The place there ouerflowne, seemd like a sodaine flood.

Stanza 27

1 sleight: cunning trick. **4 hazard**: endanger. **5–9** In the implied allegory of sexual intercourse, **he** in 4–6 refers to Timias who wounds Amoret when she is overcome by lust. (The ambiguity of the pronouns is noted by D. Cheney 1984:22.) His blow is described later as a wound; see 35.5–9n. The same euphemism for **hand** describes the Fisher's attack on Florimell at III viii 25.6–9. **did himselfe attaine**: in contrast to the Squire of Dames who was 'hopelesse euer to attaine | My Ladies loue' (III vii 60.6–7). S.'s model may be the lover's assault upon the lady's shrine with his staff in the *Roman de la Rose* 21633–72. For a topical allusion, see 36.8–9n. **coleblacke bloud**: a startling image, for it describes Errour's blood at I i 24.9 – cf. the black blood of the dragon at I xi 22.4 and of Geryoneo at V xi 14.6 – esp. since her blood had been described as 'sanguine red' (III xii 20). As a sign of pollution by lust, M.J. Craig 1996:333–34 compares the black blood of Shakespeare's Lucrece stained by Tarquin (1743); cf. Hamilton 1967:173, 178.

Stanza 28

2 glaue: halbert; here his club (25.6). **5 felly**: fiercely. **8 Tracing and trauersing**: pursuing and then turning aside, as vi 18.1.

Stanza 29

6 bent: aimed.

Stanza 30

2 She equals Lust's speed at 18.7. **4 desynde**: destined; or aimed. **5–9** In his gloss to *SC Apr.* 86–87, E.K. tells Ovid's story, *Met.* 6.206–312, of how Latona, offended by Niobe's boasting of her seven sons and seven daughters compared to Latona's two, ordered her son, Phoebus, to slay all the sons, and her daughter, Diana, to slay all the daughters with their arrows. **cruell kynde**: of cruel nature; or cruel to Niobe but kind to her mother. **tynde**: pointed, from the tines of the arrows; or 'kindled' by her anger.

Stanza 31

1 ventred: ventured. **4 draught**: drawing of the bow. **7 distraught**: sundered, i.e. split. **9 fild**: defiled.

Stanza 32

5 surcharg'd: weighed down. **7 admir'd**: wondered at. **and oft**: 'and eft', conj. Upton 1758, for the sake of the rhyme.

33

Thenceforth she past into his dreadfull den,
   Where nought but darkesome drerinesse she found,
   Ne creature saw, but hearkned now and then
   Some litle whispering, and soft groning sound.
   With that she askt, what ghosts there vnder ground
   Lay hid in horrour of eternall night?
   And bad them, if so be they were not bound,
   To come and shew themselues before the light,
Now freed from feare and danger of that dismall wight.

34

Then forth the sad *AEmylia* issewed,
   Yet trembling euery ioynt through former feare;
   And after her the Hag, there with her mewed,
   A foule and lothsome creature did appeare;
   A leman fit for such a louer deare.
   That mou'd *Belphebe* her no lesse to hate,
   Then for to rue the others heauy cheare;
   Of whom she gan enquire of her estate.
Who all to her at large, as hapned, did relate.

35

Thence she them brought toward the place, where late
   She left the gentle Squire with *Amoret*:
   There she him found by that new louely mate,
   Who lay the whiles in swoune, full sadly set,
   From her faire eyes wiping the deawy wet,
   Which softly stild, and kissing them atweene,
   And handling soft the hurts, which she did get.
   For of that Carle she sorely bruz'd had beene,
Als of his owne rash hand one wound was to be seene.

36

Which when she saw, with sodaine glauncing eye,
   Her noble heart with sight thereof was fild
   With deepe disdaine, and great indignity,
   That in her wrath she thought them both haue thrild,
   With that selfe arrow, which the Carle had kild:
   Yet held her wrathfull hand from vengeance sore,
   But drawing nigh, ere he her well beheld;
   Is this the faith, she said, and said no more,
But turnd her face, and fled away for euermore.

37

He seeing her depart, arose vp light,
   Right sore agrieued at her sharpe reproofe,
   And follow'd fast: but when he came in sight,
   He durst not nigh approch, but kept aloofe,
   For dread of her displeasures vtmost proofe.
   And euermore, when he did grace entreat,
   And framed speaches fit for his behoofe,
   Her mortall arrowes, she at him did threat,
And forst him backe with fowle dishonor to retreat.

38

At last when long he follow'd had in vaine,
   Yet found no ease of griefe, nor hope of grace,
   Vnto those woods he turned backe againe,
   Full of sad anguish, and in heauy case:
   And finding there fit solitary place
   For wofull wight, chose out a gloomy glade,
   Where hardly eye mote see bright heauens face,
   For mossy trees, which couered all with shade
And sad melancholy: there he his cabin made.

Stanza 33

1 **Thenceforth**: from that place onward.   9 **dismall**: terrible; causing terror.

Stanza 34

3 **the Hag**: 'this old woman', at 13.7 and 19.6, now shares Ate's appellation at i 31.1.   **mewed**: caged, a hawking term that extends Æmylia's reference to Lust 'trussing me, as Eagle doth his pray' (18.6).

Stanza 35

3 **mate**: lover, paramour.   **louely**: loving, Amoret's defining epithet (e.g. v 13.2), which is used here because she is seen with Belphœbe's 'louely boy' (23.6) as his **new** lover in her place.   5–9 As condensed by the Arg: 'The Squire her loues'. On the wound, which is interpreted as 'the effect of defloration' by Oram 1990:357, see 27.5–9, viii 19.8–9.   **stild**: trickled down.   **atweene**: i.e. between wiping her eyes and handling her hurts.

Stanza 36

1 **sodaine**: quick.   3 **indignity**: indignation, anger provoked by a shameful act.   5 **With that selfe arrow**: because both the squire and her twin sister are guilty of lust.   8–9 Belphœbe's reproof of Timias's inconstancy in serving a 'new louely mate'

(35.3) in place of her, which leads to his effort to regain her favour, has been taken as a topical reference to Elizabeth's banishment of Sir Walter Raleigh in 1592 for secretly marrying the pregnant Elizabeth Throckmorton, one of the Queen's maids of honour. This *cause célèbre*, which may be alluded to in *Colin Clout* 164–71, is discussed by Oakeshott 1960:93–98. (In Oakeshott 1971, he cites annotations of these stanzas in Lady Raleigh's copy of the poem, probably by her; but see Beal 1980:2.369.) See VI iii 23.2*n* and v 16.9*n*. For other possible references to Raleigh, see III v 17.2*n* and 32*n*. See also Bednarz 1984:61–65, Krier 1990:200–04, Oram 1990:355–58, and 'Raleigh, Walter' in the *SEnc*. For a countering argument that insists on the primacy of the moral allegory to a possible topical allegory, see Lethbridge 1992, and M.J. Craig 1996:328 who claims that S. universalizes Raleigh's behaviour as an essential ingredient of virtue.

Stanza 37

1 **light**: quickly; or as he is unchaste.   6 **grace**: favour. 7 **behoofe**: advantage.   9 Since Timias's name signifies honour – see III i 18.9*n* – **dishonor** makes him 'like a pined ghost' (41.4; cf. viii 12.7).

Stanza 38

9 **cabin**: rude dwelling; also cell of an anchorite.

39

His wonted warlike weapons all he broke,
    And threw away, with vow to vse no more,
    Ne thenceforth euer strike in battell stroke,
    Ne euer word to speake to woman more;
    But in that wildernesse, of men forlore,
    And of the wicked world forgotten quight,
    His hard mishap in dolor to deplore,
    And wast his wretched daies in wofull plight;
So on him selfe to wreake his follies owne despight.

40

And eke his garment, to be thereto meet,
    He wilfully did cut and shape anew;
    And his faire lockes, that wont with ointment sweet
    To be embaulm'd, and sweat out dainty dew,
    He let to grow and griesly to concrew,
    Vncomb'd, vncurl'd, and carelesly vnshed;
    That in short time his face they ouergrew,
    And ouer all his shoulders did dispred,
That who he whilome was, vneath was to be red.

41

There he continued in this carefull plight,
    Wretchedly wearing out his youthly yeares,
    Through wilfull penury consumed quight,
    That like a pined ghost he soone appeares.
    For other food then that wilde forrest beares,
    Ne other drinke there did he euer tast,
    Then running water, tempred with his teares,
    The more his weakened body so to wast:
That out of all mens knowledge he was worne at last.

42

For on a day, by fortune as it fell,
    His owne deare Lord Prince *Arthure* came that way,
    Seeking aduentures, where he mote heare tell;
    And as he through the wandring wood did stray,

Hauing espide this Cabin far away,
    He to it drew, to weet who there did wonne;
    Weening therein some holy Hermit lay,
    That did resort of sinfull people shonne;
Or else some woodman shrowded there from scorching sunne.

43

Arriuing there, he found this wretched man,
    Spending his daies in dolour and despaire,
    And through long fasting woxen pale and wan,
    All ouergrowen with rude and rugged haire;
    That albeit his owne deare Squire he were,
    Yet he him knew not, ne auiz'd at all,
    But like strange wight, whom he had seene no where,
    Saluting him, gan into speach to fall,
And pitty much his plight, that liu'd like outcast thrall.

44

But to his speach he aunswered no whit,
    But stood still mute, as if he had beene dum,
    Ne signe of sence did shew, ne common wit,
    As one with griefe and anguishe ouercum,
    And vnto euery thing did aunswere mum:
    And euer when the Prince vnto him spake,
    He louted lowly, as did him becum,
    And humble homage did vnto him make,
Midst sorrow shewing ioyous semblance for his sake.

45

At which his vncouth guise and vsage quaint
    The Prince did wonder much, yet could not ghesse
    The cause of that his sorrowfull constraint;
    Yet weend by secret signes of manlinesse,
    Which close appeard in that rude brutishnesse,
    That he whilome some gentle swaine had beene,
    Traind vp in feats of armes and knightlinesse;
    Which he obseru'd, by that he him had seene
To weld his naked sword, and try the edges keene.

Stanza 39

1 wonted: customary. **5 forlore**: abandoned. **9 follies**: lewdness, wantonness.

Stanza 40

Timias assumes the traditional guise of the love-melancholic. **4 embaulm'd**: anointed. **5 concrew**: mat together. **6** He appears as Lust at 7.3; or as an anchorite upon whom heaven bestows a protecting coat of hair; or, with 'heary glib' (viii 12.6), like the Irish: see V ix 10.6–9*n*. **vnshed**: unparted; cf. 43.4. **9** . . . with difficulty was to be known.

Stanza 41

1 carefull: sorrowful. **3 penury**: lack of food, 'long fasting' (43.3). **4** As Britomart becomes in her love-longing at III ii 52.5–6. **7** There is a possible historical allusion: in lamenting his estrangement from the Queen, in 'Like to a Hermite poore', Raleigh laments that 'My drink nought else but teares

falne from mine eies'; noted Oakeshott 1960:169–70. See viii 4.4–5*n*.

Stanza 42

On Arthur's appearance, see viii 18*n*.

Stanza 43

6 auiz'd: recognized.

Stanza 44

Except for the outburst to Belphœbe at viii 16–17, he remains silent through shame for the rest of the poem, as at VI v 24 (where his 'gracious speaches' go unreported), and viii 5, 27. **5 mum**: not a word. **9 semblance**: demeanour.

Stanza 45

1 vsage quaint: odd behaviour. **3 constraint**: distress. **8–9** The despairing Timias who at 39.1–3 vowed never to use his broken weapons is now considering suicide.

46

And eke by that he saw on euery tree,
　How he the name of one engrauen had,
　Which likly was his liefest loue to be,
　For whom he now so sorely was bestad;
　Which was by him *BELPHEBE* rightly rad.
　Yet who was that *Belphebe*, he ne wist;
　Yet saw he often how he wexed glad,
　When he it heard, and how the ground he kist,
Wherein it written was, and how himselfe he blist:

47

Tho when he long had marked his demeanor,
　And saw that all he said and did, was vaine,
　Ne ought mote make him change his wonted tenor,
　Ne ought mote ease or mitigate his paine,
　He left him there in languor to remaine,
　Till time for him should remedy prouide,
　And him restore to former grace againe.
　Which for it is too long here to abide,
I will deferre the end vntill another tide.

Stanza 46
In his *Booke of the Ocean to Scinthia* 327, Raleigh laments that Elizabeth 'a Queen shee was to mee, no more Belphebe'. It may be pertinent, then, that the spelling 'Belphebe' is used for the rest of the poem. **3 liefest**: dearest. **4 bestad**: beset. **6** Cf. viii 22.1–6. **9 blist**: either blessed, by crossing himself at that holy name, or 'blasted', i.e. cursed.

Stanza 47
5 languor: sorrow. **6** Timias's fortunes are again linked with time at viii 1.6 and 18.1, supporting the claim by D. Cheney 1986:277 that 'time' is one meaning of his name. Even Arthur, the vehicle of grace in Bks I and II, cannot save or even recognize him.

Cant. VIII.

The gentle Squire recouers grace,
Sclaunder her guests doth staine:
Corflambo chaseth Placidas,
And is by Arthure slaine.

1

WEll said the wiseman, now prou'd true by this,
　Which to this gentle Squire did happen late,
That the displeasure of the mighty is
Then death it selfe more dread and desperate.
For naught the same may calme ne mitigate,
Till time the tempest doe thereof delay
With sufferaunce soft, which rigour can abate,
And haue the sterne remembrance wypt away
Of bitter thoughts, which deepe therein infixed lay.

2

Like as it fell to this vnhappy boy,
　Whose tender heart the faire *Belphebe* had,
With one sterne looke so daunted, that no ioy
In all his life, which afterwards he lad,
He euer tasted, but with penaunce sad
And pensiue sorrow pind and wore away,
Ne euer laught, ne once shew'd countenance glad;
But alwaies wept and wailed night and day,
As blasted bloosme through heat doth languish and decay;

3

Till on a day, as in his wonted wise
　His doole he made, there chaunst a turtle Doue
To come, where he his dolors did deuise,
That likewise late had lost her dearest loue,
Which losse her made like passion also proue.
Who seeing his sad plight, her tender heart
With deare compassion deeply did emmoue,
That she gan mone his vndeserued smart,
And with her dolefull accent beare with him a part.

4

Shee sitting by him as on ground he lay,
　Her mournefull notes full piteously did frame,
And thereof made a lamentable lay,
So sensibly compyld, that in the same
Him seemed oft he heard his owne right name.
With that he forth would poure so plenteous teares,
And beat his breast vnworthy of such blame,
And knocke his head, and rend his rugged heares,
That could haue perst the hearts of Tigres and of Beares.

5

Thus long this gentle bird to him did vse,
　Withouten dread of perill to repaire
Vnto his wonne, and with her mournefull muse
Him to recomfort in his greatest care,
That much did ease his mourning and misfare:
And euery day for guerdon of her song,
He part of his small feast to her would share;
That at the last of all his woe and wrong
Companion she became, and so continued long.

6

Vpon a day as she him sate beside,
　By chance he certaine miniments forth drew,
Which yet with him as relickes did abide
Of all the bounty, which *Belphebe* threw
On him, whilst goodly grace she did him shew:
Amongst the rest a iewell rich he found,
That was a Ruby of right perfect hew,
Shap'd like a heart, yet bleeding of the wound,
And with a litle golden chaine about it bound.

Book IV Canto viii

Stanza 1

1–4 The familiar tag 'Indignatio principis mors est' is more appropriate to Elizabeth than to Belphœbe, as O'Connell 1977:116 notes. The **wiseman** is Solomon: 'The wrath of a King is as messengers of death' (Prov.16.14).　**6 delay**: allay.　**7 sufferaunce**: patient endurance.

Stanza 2

1 this vnhappy boy: see vii 23.6*n*.　**9 bloosme**: blossom.

Stanza 3

2 doole: dole, lamentation.　**turtle Doue**: sacred to Venus as a symbol of faithful and enduring love; see proem 5.2*n*.　**3 . . .** where he recounted his griefs.　**5 passion**: suffering.　**proue**: experience.　**9 accent**: sound. I.e. she sings in tune with his complaint.

Stanza 4

3 lamentable: mournful.　**4–5 sensibly compyld**: feelingly composed. There may be a witty allusion here, and esp. at 13.3–4, to the nickname 'Water' given Raleigh by the Queen, a name that echoes 'Walter' and refers to him as the ocean which she, as Cynthia, controls in *The Ocean to Scinthia*. That name pronounced with a burr may sound to a demented mind like a dove's cooing. Appropriately, he responds with water.　**8 rugged**: ragged.　**9 Tigres and of Beares**: see II ii 22.5–9*n*.

Stanza 5

4 care: sorrow.　**5 misfare**: misfortune.

7

The same he tooke, and with a riband new,
    In which his Ladies colours were, did bind
    About the turtles necke, that with the vew
    Did greatly solace his engrieued mind.
    All vnawares the bird, when she did find
    Her selfe so deckt, her nimble wings displaid,
    And flew away, as lightly as the wind:
    Which sodaine accident him much dismaid,
And looking after long, did marke which way she straid.

8

But when as long he looked had in vaine,
    Yet saw her forward still to make her flight,
    His weary eie returnd to him againe,
    Full of discomfort and disquiet plight,
    That both his iuell he had lost so light,
    And eke his deare companion of his care.
    But that sweet bird departing, flew forth right
    Through the wide region of the wastfull aire,
Vntill she came where wonned his *Belphebe* faire.

9

There found she her (as then it did betide)
    Sitting in couert shade of arbors sweet,
    After late weary toile, which she had tride
    In saluage chase, to rest as seem'd her meet.
    There she alighting, fell before her feet,
    And gan to her her mournfull plaint to make,
    As was her wont, thinking to let her weet
    The great tormenting griefe, that for her sake
Her gentle Squire through her displeasure did pertake.

10

She her beholding with attentiue eye,
    At length did marke about her purple brest
    That precious iuell, which she formerly
    Had knowne right well with colourd ribbands drest:
    Therewith she rose in hast, and her addrest
    With ready hand it to haue reft away.
    But the swift bird obayd not her behest,
    But swaru'd aside, and there againe did stay;
She follow'd her, and thought againe it to assay.

11

And euer when she nigh approcht, the Doue
    Would flit a litle forward, and then stay,
    Till she drew neare, and then againe remoue;
    So tempting her still to pursue the pray,
    And still from her escaping soft away:
    Till that at length into that forrest wide,
    She drew her far, and led with slow delay.
    In th'end she her vnto that place did guide,
Whereas that wofull man in languor did abide.

12

Eftsoones she flew vnto his fearelesse hand,
    And there a piteous ditty new deuiz'd,
    As if she would haue made him vnderstand,
    His sorrowes cause to be of her despis'd.
    Whom when she saw in wretched weedes disguiz'd,
    With heary glib deform'd, and meiger face,
    Like ghost late risen from his graue agryz'd,
    She knew him not, but pittied much his case,
And wisht it were in her to doe him any grace.

Stanza 6

2 miniments: articles; in the specific legal sense: evidences or proofs of Belphœbe's bounty and his former right to it. **6–9 The Ruby** was believed to control amorous desires of the wearer; see 'stones, precious' in the *SEnc*. It was returned to Belphœbe by the dove because its red colour removes anger. The choice of jewel may be literary: in Chaucer, *Troilus and Criseyde* 3.1371, Criseyde gives Troilus a brooch 'In which a ruby set was lik an herte'. More likely, there is a topical allusion: Arthur Throckmorton hoped to soften the Queen's displeasure over his sister's marriage to Raleigh by presenting her with a heart-shaped ruby with the inscription *Elizabetha potest*, as Brink 1972 shows; and as S. does in writing this episode: see O'Connell 1977:122.

Stanza 7

2 colours: her insignia or device. **8 accident**: event.

Stanza 8

4 discomfort: distress. **5 light**: easily; carelessly.

Stanza 9

3 tride: undergone. **9 pertake**: partake; endure.

Stanza 10

9 assay: touch; try.

Stanza 11

The dove is the means through which Timias regains Belphœbe's favour because it is a symbol of reconciliation through its role in the story of Noah (Gen. 8.8–12), and in the baptism of Jesus (Matt. 3.16). Its use is esp. appropriate because he seeks 'grace' (vii 37.6) from one whom he regards as a 'Goddesse' (III v 35.5). The relevant classical analogue is Virgil, *Aen.* 6.190–204: Venus's doves guide Aeneas to the golden bough that will save him. More relevant is Cupid's role in proem 5.2, 4: as '*Venus* dearling doue', he may 'vse of awfull Maiestie remoue'. On the dove as Belphœbe's *alter ego* and surrogate, see Goldberg 1981:54–55; on its symbolic significance as a strategy of S.'s self-presentation, see P. Cheney 1993:111–48.

Stanza 12

1 fearelesse: referring to the dove. **3 him**: 'her', sugg. Church 1758 correctly. **6 glib**: see vii 40.6*n*. It serves here as the large-brimmed hat that hides the love-melancholic, e.g. the well-known portrait of Donne 'taken in shadows', as a victim of 'Lover's Melancholy', with a Lat. inscription that reads: 'Lighten our darkness, Mistress'. Cf. his plea at 17.5. **7 agryz'd**: horrified; and of horrible appearance.

13

He her beholding, at her feet downe fell,
    And kist the ground on which her sole did tread,
    And washt the same with water, which did well
    From his moist eies, and like two streames procead,
    Yet spake no word, whereby she might aread
    What mister wight he was, or what he ment,
    But as one daunted with her presence dread,
    Onely few ruefull lookes vnto her sent,
As messengers of his true meaning and intent.

14

Yet nathemore his meaning she ared,
    But wondred much at his so selcouth case,
    And by his persons secret seemlyhed
    Well weend, that he had beene some man of place,
    Before misfortune did his hew deface:
    That being mou'd with ruth she thus bespake.
    Ah wofull man, what heauens hard disgrace,
    Or wrath of cruell wight on thee ywrake?
Or selfe disliked life doth thee thus wretched make?

15

If heauen, then none may it redresse or blame,
    Sith to his powre we all are subiect borne:
    If wrathfull wight, then fowle rebuke and shame
    Be theirs, that haue so cruell thee forlorne;
    But if through inward griefe or wilfull scorne
    Of life it be, then better doe aduise.
    For he whose daies in wilfull woe are worne,
    The grace of his Creator doth despise,
That will not vse his gifts for thanklesse nigardise.

16

When so he heard her say, eftsoones he brake
    His sodaine silence, which he long had pent,
    And sighing inly deepe, her thus bespake;
    Then haue they all themselues against me bent:
    For heauen, first author of my languishment,
    Enuying my too great felicity,
    Did closely with a cruell one consent,
    To cloud my daies in dolefull misery,
And make me loath this life, still longing for to die.

17

Ne any but your selfe, ô dearest dred,
    Hath done this wrong, to wreake on worthlesse wight
    Your high displesure, through misdeeming bred:
    That when your pleasure is to deeme aright,
    Ye may redresse, and me restore to light.
    Which sory words her mightie hart did mate
    With mild regard, to see his ruefull plight,
    That her inburning wrath she gan abate,
And him receiu'd againe to former fauours state.

18

In which he long time afterwards did lead
    An happie life with grace and good accord,
    Fearlesse of fortunes chaunge or enuies dread,
    And eke all mindlesse of his owne deare Lord
    The noble Prince, who neuer heard one word
    Of tydings, what did vnto him betide,
    Or what good fortune did to him afford,
    But through the endlesse world did wander wide,
Him seeking euermore, yet no where him descride.

Stanza 13
5 aread: guess. **6 mister**: kind of.

Stanza 14
1 ared: guessed. **2 selcouth**: seldom known; strange.
3–5 Arthur guesses the same at vii 45.4–9. **secret seemlyhed**: disguised seemliness or pleasing appearance. **of place**: of rank. **hew**: form. **8 ywrake**: wreaked.

Stanza 15
Belphœbe's farewell speech on the three possible causes of human misfortune stated in the three previous lines is carefully crafted as the use of *anaphora* indicates. The first two get two lines each and the third five, an emphasis appropriate to her opening defence of the active life in pursuit of honour at II iii 40–41, and appropriate also in being addressed to Timias (or any courtier) guilty of despising God's grace by 'wilfully' (vii 40.2; cf. 41.3) withdrawing from a life of virtuous action. **3 rebuke**: disgrace. **4 forlorne**: brought to ruin. **9 nigardise**: niggardliness.

Stanza 16
1–2 I.e. suddenly he broke his silence. **4 they**: alluding to the three causes of his misfortune, blaming the first two but (in typically male fashion) not himself, before going on (in typically male fashion) to blame the object of his love. **5 languishment**: suffering. **7 closely**: secretly.

Stanza 17
1 ô dearest dred: the address to Elizabeth in I proem 4.9. **3 misdeeming**: a veiled critique of the Queen for her response to the Raleigh–Throckmorton marriage; see vii 36.8–9*n*. It puts her with those who 'ill iudge of loue' (proem 2.1), as Kaplan 1997:44 notes. **5 restore to light**: also literally, for he lives in darkness (vii 38.6–9). **6 mate**: join; overcome.

Stanza 18
Arthur appears in canto viii as usual, except in Bk III, the number of times being determined by the number of the book; see I viii Arg.1–2*n*. Here he rescues Æmylia and Amoret, and saves them from Sclaunder; he slays Corflambo and unites the two friends with Æmylia and Pœana; he resolves the discord at the tournament by pacifying the six knights; and presumably he restores Amoret to Scudamour (between ix 39 and 40, as Upton 1758 first conjectured). **4–9** They remain separated until they are seen together at VI v 11.

19

Till on a day as through that wood he rode,
    He chaunst to come where those two Ladies late,
    Æmylia and *Amoret* abode,
    Both in full sad and sorrowfull estate;
    The one right feeble through the euill rate
    Of food, which in her duresse she had found:
    The other almost dead and desperate
Through her late hurts, and through that haplesse wound,
With which the Squire in her defence her sore astound.

20

Whom when the Prince beheld, he gan to rew
    The euill case in which those Ladies lay;
    But most was moued at the piteous vew
    Of *Amoret*, so neare vnto decay,
    That her great daunger did him much dismay.
    Eftsoones that pretious liquour forth he drew,
    Which he in store about him kept alway,
Her wounds, that vnto strength restor'd her soone anew.

21

Tho when they both recouered were right well,
    He gan of them inquire, what euill guide
    Them thether brought, and how their harmes befell.
    To whom they told all, that did them betide,
    And how from thraldome vile they were vntide
    Of that same wicked Carle, by Virgins hond;
    Whose bloudie corse they shew'd him there beside,
And eke his caue, in which they both were bond:
At which he wondred much, when all those signes he fond.

22

And euermore he greatly did desire
    To know, what Virgin did them thence vnbind;
    And oft of them did earnestly inquire,
    Where was her won, and how he mote her find.

But when as nought according to his mind
He could outlearne, he them from ground did reare:
    No seruice lothsome to a gentle kind;
    And on his warlike beast them both did beare,
Himselfe by them on foot, to succour them from feare.

23

So when that forrest they had passed well,
    A litle cotage farre away they spide,
    To which they drew, ere night vpon them fell;
    And entring in, found none therein abide,
    But one old woman sitting there beside,
    Vpon the ground in ragged rude attyre,
    With filthy lockes about her scattered wide,
    Gnawing her nayles for felnesse and for yre,
And there out sucking venime to her parts entyre.

24

A foule and loathly creature sure in sight,
    And in conditions to be loath'd no lesse:
    For she was stuft with rancour and despight
    Vp to the throat, that oft with bitternesse
    It forth would breake, and gush in great excesse,
    Pouring out streames of poyson and of gall
    Gainst all, that truth or vertue doe professe,
    Whom she with leasings lewdly did miscall,
And wickedly backbite: Her name men *Sclaunder* call.

25

Her nature is all goodnesse to abuse,
    And causelesse crimes continually to frame,
    With which she guiltlesse persons may accuse,
    And steale away the crowne of their good name;
    Ne euer Knight so bold, ne euer Dame
    So chast and loyall liu'd, but she would striue
    With forged cause them falsely to defame;
    Ne euer thing so well was doen aliue,
But she with blame would blot, and of due praise depriue.

Stanza 19
5 **euill rate**: poor, unsatisfactory allowance. 6 **duresse**: imprisonment. 9 **astound**: i.e. stunned with his stroke.

Stanza 20
4 **decay**: death. 6–9 Arthur gave the Red Cross Knight 'few drops of liquor pure . . . | That any wownd could heale incontinent' (I ix 19; see *n*).

Stanza 21
4 A version of the story told to Amoret at vii 13–18 and to Belphœbe at 34.9.

Stanza 22
1–4 Arthur's ignorance of Belphœbe, as at vii 46.6, with the desire now to know her, associates her with the Faerie Queene (see II iii 21–31*n*) whom he seeks in Bk I (see ix 15.5–9) and Bk II (see ix 7.5–8). He seeks Florimell in Bk III (see esp.

v 11.7–9), and Timias in Bk IV (see 18.8–9 above). Only after aiding Amoret is he 'Resolued to pursue his former quest' (ix 17.5). **won**: dwelling-place. 6 **outlearne**: find out. 7 Cf. I viii 40.3. **kind**: nature. 8 **warlike**: equipped for war.

Stanza 23
8 **felnesse**: malignity. 9 **parts entyre**: 'inward parts' (26.4).

Stanza 24
2 **in conditions**: with characteristics. 8 Whom she with lies wickedly reviled. 9 **Sclaunder**: the earlier spelling of slander suggests 'scandal'. See 'Sclaunder, slander' and Figure 1 in the *SEnc*.

Stanza 25
2 **causelesse**: not having any basis in fact, being a **forged cause**. 8 **aliue**: i.e. by any living person.

26

Her words were not, as common words are ment,
    T'expresse the meaning of the inward mind,
    But noysome breath, and poysnous spirit sent
    From inward parts, with cancred malice lind,
    And breathed forth with blast of bitter wind;
    Which passing through the eares, would pierce the hart,
    And wound the soule it selfe with griefe vnkind:
    For like the stings of Aspes, that kill with smart,
Her spightfull words did pricke, and wound the inner part.

27

Such was that Hag, vnmeet to host such guests,
    Whom greatest Princes court would welcome fayne,
    But neede, that answers not to all requests,
    Bad them not looke for better entertayne;
    And eke that age despysed nicenesse vaine,
    Enur'd to hardnesse and to homely fare,
    Which them to warlike discipline did trayne,
    And manly limbs endur'd with litle care
Against all hard mishaps and fortunelesse misfare.

28

Then all that euening welcommed with cold,
    And chearelesse hunger, they together spent;
    Yet found no fault, but that the Hag did scold
    And rayle at them with grudgefull discontent,
    For lodging there without her owne consent:
    Yet they endured all with patience milde,
    And vnto rest themselues all onely lent,
    Regardlesse of that queane so base and vilde,
To be vniustly blamd, and bitterly reuilde.

29

Here well I weene, when as these rimes be red
    With misregard, that some rash witted wight,
    Whose looser thought will lightly be misled,
    These gentle Ladies will misdeeme too light,
    For thus conuersing with this noble Knight;
    Sith now of dayes such temperance is rare
    And hard to finde, that heat of youthfull spright
    For ought will from his greedie pleasure spare,
More hard for hungry steed t'abstaine from pleasant lare.

30

But antique age yet in the infancie
    Of time, did liue then like an innocent,
    In simple truth and blamelesse chastitie,
    Ne then of guile had made experiment,
    But voide of vile and treacherous intent,
    Held vertue for it selfe in soueraine awe:
    Then loyall loue had royall regiment,
    And each vnto his lust did make a lawe,
From all forbidden things his liking to withdraw.

31

The Lyon there did with the Lambe consort,
    And eke the Doue sate by the Faulcons side,
    Ne each of other feared fraud or tort,
    But did in safe securitie abide,
    Withouten perill of the stronger pride:
    But when the world woxe old, it woxe warre old
    (Whereof it hight) and hauing shortly tride
    The traines of wit, in wickednesse woxe bold,
And dared of all sinnes the secrets to vnfold.

Stanza 26
3 noysome: ill-smelling; suggesting also its noxious effects.
8–9 The comparison links her to Detraction at V xii 36.3–4,
and to slander at VI vi 1.1–4.

Stanza 27
2 fayne: gladly. **4 entertayne**: reception. **5 that age**: the
antique age praised in 30–31. **nicenesse**: luxury. **8 manly**,
after the repeated **them**, must be gender-neutral. **endur'd**:
sustained; hardened. **9** . . . and unfortunate mischance.

Stanza 28
7 I.e. denied hospitality, they took themselves to rest.
8 queane: Hag.

Stanza 29
2 misregard: lack of care; misconstruction. **3 looser**: too
loose. **5 conuersing**: associating; but the **rash witted** reader,
assuming the role of Sclaunder, infers 'cohabiting with' (cf.
OED 2b). **7–9** It is hard to find a youth who will abstain
from pleasure because it is harder for him to abstain than for a
hungry steed, etc. **lare**: pasture.

Stanza 30
On S.'s praise of the **antique age**, see V proem 1*n*. **7 regi-
ment**: self-control. **8–9** S. is engaging in a Renaissance
debate on the legitimacy of pleasure, specifically the claim in
Tasso, *Aminta* 1.2, that in the golden age *S'ei piace, ei lice* (if
it pleases, it is lawful), which had been countered by Guarini in
Il Pastor Fido 4 Chorus: *Piaccia, se lice* (it pleases only if it is
lawful). Both were published in England in 1591.

Stanza 31
1–5 Cf. Isa. 11.6: 'The wolfe also shal dwell with the lambe,
and the leoparde shal lye with the kid, and the calfe, and the
lyon, and the fat beast together'. The dove's flight from the
falcon is noted at III iv 49.4–9. **there**: then, conj. Upton
1758, is preferable, as 30.2, 32.1, 5, 8. **tort**: wrong, injustice.
stronger pride: pride or tyranny of the stronger. **6–7** The
world's degeneration is explained by its supposed etymology,
warre old, as suggested by OE 'worold'. (*SC Sept.* 108, 'They
sayne the world is much war then it wont' is glossed 'worse' by
E.K. Or 'wax old', as Ps. 102:25–26: 'the fundation of the
earth, and the heauens . . . shal waxe olde as doeth a garment'.
That the world gets worse as it gets older is the lesson of 2 Esd.
9. **8 traines**: wiles.

32

Then beautie, which was made to represent
　　The great Creatours owne resemblance bright,
　　Vnto abuse of lawlesse lust was lent,
　　And made the baite of bestiall delight:
　　Then faire grew foule, and foule grew faire in sight,
　　And that which wont to vanquish God and man,
　　Was made the vassall of the victors might;
　　Then did her glorious flowre wex dead and wan,
Despisd and troden downe of all that ouerran.

33

And now it is so vtterly decayd,
　　That any bud thereof doth scarse remaine,
　　But if few plants preseru'd through heauenly ayd,
　　In Princes Court doe hap to sprout againe,
　　Dew'd with her drops of bountie Soueraine,
　　Which from that goodly glorious flowre proceed,
　　Sprung of the auncient stocke of Princes straine,
　　Now th'onely remnant of that royall breed,
Whose noble kind at first was sure of heauenly seed.

34

Tho soone as day discouered heauens face
　　To sinfull men with darknes ouerdight,
　　This gentle crew gan from their eye-lids chace
　　The drowzie humour of the dampish night,
　　And did themselues vnto their iourney dight.
　　So forth they yode, and forward softly paced,
　　That them to view had bene an vncouth sight;
　　How all the way the Prince on footpace traced,
The Ladies both on horse, together fast embraced.

35

Soone as they thence departed were afore,
　　That shamefull Hag, the slaunder of her sexe,
　　Them follow'd fast, and them reuiled sore,
　　Him calling theefe, them whores; that much did vexe

His noble hart; thereto she did annexe
False crimes and facts, such as they neuer ment,
That those two Ladies much asham'd did wexe:
　　The more did she pursue her lewd intent,
And rayl'd and rag'd, till she had all her poyson spent.

36

At last when they were passed out of sight,
　　Yet she did not her spightfull speach forbeare,
　　But after them did barke, and still backbite,
　　Though there were none her hatefull words to heare:
　　Like as a curre doth felly bite and teare
　　The stone, which passed straunger at him threw;
　　So she them seeing past the reach of eare,
　　Against the stones and trees did rayle anew,
Till she had duld the sting, which in her tongs end grew.

37

They passing forth kept on their readie way,
　　With easie steps so soft as foot could stryde,
　　Both for great feeblesse, which did oft assay
　　Faire *Amoret*, that scarcely she could ryde,
　　And eke through heauie armes, which sore annoyd
　　The Prince on foot, not wonted so to fare;
　　Whose steadie hand was faine his steede to guyde,
　　And all the way from trotting hard to spare,
So was his toyle the more, the more that was his care.

38

At length they spide, where towards them with speed
　　A Squire came gallopping, as he would flie,
　　Bearing a litle Dwarfe before his steed,
　　That all the way full loud for aide did crie,
　　That seem'd his shrikes would rend the brasen skie:
　　Whom after did a mightie man pursew,
　　Ryding vpon a Dromedare on hie,
　　Of stature huge, and horrible of hew,
That would haue maz'd a man his dreadfull face to vew.

Stanza 32
A brief allegory of the story of Florimell: beauty was abused by lust when she was pursued by the Foster and the hyena, and made the bait of bestial delight by the witch's son and the Fisher; it grew foul, and foul grew fair, when her role was taken by the False Florimell and she became the vassal of Proteus. On her association with flowers, see III v 8.7*n*. **1 represent**: make visible or manifest.

Stanza 33
3 But if: unless. **4–9** This elaborate praise of Elizabeth's beauty expands the claim at II x 76.8 that she is 'that glorious flowre' and therefore called Gloriana. See 'beauty' in the *SEnc*. Lines 7–8 assert her sole legitimacy to the throne, while **th'onely** implicitly laments her lack of offspring. **straine**: lineage.

Stanza 34
2 ouerdight: covered over. **6 yode**: went. **7 vncouth**: strange. **8** . . . went at a walking pace.

Stanza 35
2 slaunder of her sexe: wittily turning her condition against herself. **4** The basis of her slander is that Arthur did not gain Amoret and Æmylia rightfully through conquest. **5 annexe**: join, add. **6 facts**: evil deeds. **8 lewd**: evil.

Stanza 36
3 backbite: metaphorically at 24.9 but here she literally bites behind their backs. **5–6** An emblematic use of the proverb 'A dog bites the stone, not the man who throws it' (Smith 190) to show Slander's frenzy, as Tung 1985:191 notes.

Stanza 37
3–4 feeblesse: feebleness. Her wound was cured at 20.9 but not its infection caused by slander from which she now suffers. **assay**: afflict. **7 faine**: wont; obliged. **8 spare**: refrain; restrain.

Stanza 38
7 The dromedary is noted for its speed from its etymology, δρομάς, running. A symbol of sin in Jeremiah's denunciation of the children of Israel for playing the harlot: 'Thou art like a swift dromedarie, that runneth by his wayes' (2.23).

39

For from his fearefull eyes two fierie beames,
   More sharpe then points of needles did proceede,
   Shooting forth farre away two flaming streames,
   Full of sad powre, that poysonous bale did breede
   To all, that on him lookt without good heed,
   And secretly his enemies did slay:
   Like as the Basiliske of serpents seede,
   From powrefull eyes close venim doth conuay
Into the lookers hart, and killeth farre away.

40

He all the way did rage at that same Squire,
   And after him full many threatnings threw,
   With curses vaine in his auengefull ire:
   But none of them (so fast away he flew)
   Him ouertooke, before he came in vew.
   Where when he saw the Prince in armour bright,
   He cald to him aloud, his case to rew,
   And rescue him through succour of his might,
From that his cruell foe, that him pursewd in sight.

41

Eftsoones the Prince tooke downe those Ladies twaine
   From loftie steede, and mounting in their stead
   Came to that Squire, yet trembling euery vaine:
   Of whom he gan enquire his cause of dread;
   Who as he gan the same to him aread,
   Loe hard behind his backe his foe was prest,
   With dreadfull weapon aymed at his head,
   That vnto death had doen him vnredrest,
Had not the noble Prince his readie stroke represt.

42

Who thrusting boldly twixt him and the blow,
   The burden of the deadly brunt did beare
   Vpon his shield, which lightly he did throw
   Ouer his head, before the harme came neare.

Nathlesse it fell with so despiteous dreare
And heauie sway, that hard vnto his crowne
The shield it droue, and did the couering reare,
Therewith both Squire and dwarfe did tomble downe
Vnto the earth, and lay long while in senselesse swowne.

43

Whereat the Prince full wrath, his strong right hand
   In full auengement heaued vp on hie,
   And stroke the Pagan with his steely brand
   So sore, that to his saddle bow thereby
   He bowed low, and so a while did lie:
   And sure had not his massie yron mace
   Betwixt him and his hurt bene happily,
   It would haue cleft him to the girding place,
Yet as it was, it did astonish him long space.

44

But when he to himselfe returnd againe,
   All full of rage he gan to curse and sweare,
   And vow by *Mahoune* that he should be slaine.
   With that his murdrous mace he vp did reare,
   That seemed nought the souse thereof could beare,
   And therewith smote at him with all his might.
   But ere that it to him approched neare,
   The royall child with readie quicke foresight,
Did shun the proofe thereof and it auoyded light.

45

But ere his hand he could recure againe,
   To ward his bodie from the balefull stound,
   He smote at him with all his might and maine,
   So furiously, that ere he wist, he found
   His head before him tombling on the ground.
   The whiles his babling tongue did yet blaspheme
   And curse his God, that did him so confound;
   The whiles his life ran foorth in bloudie streame,
His soule descended downe into the Stygian reame.

Stanza 39
The power of Corflambo (see 49.1) and of the basilisk derives from the popular view that rays are emitted from the eye to the object seen, as the 'fierie beames' of Acrasia's eyes 'thrild | Fraile harts' (II xii 78.7–8). On extramissive sight, see Krier 1990:30, 52–53. It was common lore that the basilisk or cockatrice 'kill[s] with looks' (*Am* 49.10); see Robin 1932:84–95. **4 sad**: heavy, causing sorrow. **8 close**: secret.

Stanza 40
4–5 The squire is fleeing at supersonic speed. **7 rew**: succour. **9 in sight** defines the nature of his antagonist.

Stanza 41
5 aread: tell. **6 prest**: at hand. **8 vnredrest**: i.e. without hope of remedy. **9 represt**: forced back.

Stanza 42
2 brunt: stroke. **5 dreare**: direfulness; dire. **6–9** It is not clear what happens. When Arthur first enters the poem, 'His warlike shield all closely couer'd was' (I vii 33.1); and when he falls under Orgoglio's blow, 'his shield, that couered was, | Did

loose his vele by chaunce, and open flew' (viii 19.1–2), blinding Orgoglio by its light. See V viii 37.6–9*n*. Yet here Corflambo, who is himself a source of fiery light, is not blinded, nor are Placidas and the dwarf who are under the shield, and would seem to fall because it is bashed down on their heads. **couering** may apply to Arthur's shield, which covers them until knocked away and uncovered by Corflambo's blow, causing them to be blinded. Or to Placidas's helmet, which is either knocked off or its visor raised, causing him (and the dwarf?) to be struck by the laser beams from Corflambo's eyes.

Stanza 43
6 mace: see III vii 40.1*n*. **8 girding place**: the waist. **9 astonish**: stun.

Stanza 44
3 Mahoune: Mohammed, god of the Saracens or pagans generally; see II viii 30.4*n*. **5 souse**: downward blow. **8 child**: applied to a youth of noble birth or to a knight in the prime of manhood but by S. chiefly to Arthur, e.g. V viii 32.1, xi 8.8. Cf. 'Infant' at II viii 56.1. **9 proofe**: issue.

46

Which when that Squire beheld, he woxe full glad
  To see his foe breath out his spright in vaine:
  But that same dwarfe right sorie seem'd and sad,
  And howld aloud to see his Lord there slaine,
  And rent his haire and scratcht his face for paine.
  Then gan the Prince at leasure to inquire
  Of all the accident, there hapned plaine,
  And what he was, whose eyes did flame with fire;
All which was thus to him declared by that Squire.

47

This mightie man (quoth he) whom you haue slaine,
  Of an huge Geauntesse whylome was bred;
  And by his strength rule to himselfe did gaine
  Of many Nations into thraldome led,
  And mightie kingdomes of his force adred;
  Whom yet he conquer'd not by bloudie fight,
  Ne hostes of men with banners brode dispred,
  But by the powre of his infectious sight,
With which he killed all, that came within his might.

48

Ne was he euer vanquished afore,
  But euer vanquisht all, with whom he fought;
  Ne was there man so strong, but he downe bore,
  Ne woman yet so faire, but he her brought
  Vnto his bay, and captiued her thought.
  For most of strength and beautie his desire
  Was spoyle to make, and wast them vnto nought,
  By casting secret flakes of lustfull fire
From his false eyes, into their harts and parts entire.

49

Therefore *Corflambo* was he cald aright,
  Though namelesse there his bodie now doth lie,
  Yet hath he left one daughter that is hight
  The faire *Pœana*; who seemes outwardly
  So faire, as euer yet saw liuing eie:
  And were her vertue like her beautie bright,
  She were as faire as any vnder skie.
  But ah she giuen is to vaine delight,
And eke too loose of life, and eke of loue too light.

50

So as it fell there was a gentle Squire,
  That lou'd a Ladie of high parentage,
  But for his meane degree might not aspire
  To match so high, her friends with counsell sage,
  Dissuaded her from such a disparage.
  But she, whose hart to loue was wholly lent,
  Out of his hands could not redeeme her gage,
  But firmely following her first intent,
Resolu'd with him to wend, gainst all her friends consent.

51

So twixt themselues they pointed time and place,
  To which when he according did repaire,
  An hard mishap and disauentrous case
  Him chaunst; in stead of his *AEmylia* faire
  This Gyants sonne, that lies there on the laire
  An headlesse heape, him vnawares there caught,
  And all dismayd through mercilesse despaire,
  Him wretched thrall vnto his dongeon brought,
Where he remaines, of all vnsuccour'd and vnsought.

Stanza 45

1 recure: recover.   **2 stound**: attack.   **9 the Stygian reame**: the realm of Hades or hell.

Stanza 46

7 accident: event.

Stanza 47

1 This mightie man: as first described at 38.6 to note his power.   **2 Geauntesse**: not named but she may well be the lustful Argante whose 'fyrie eyes with furious sparkes did stare', and who also wields an iron mace at III vii 39.8, 40.1.   **7 with banners brode dispred**: to provoke terror; see III iii 30.3*n*.   **9 killed**: as 39.6; or held captive, as ix 8, until they died.

Stanza 48

5 Vnto his bay: to close quarters before him, used of a hunter's quarry surrounded by the hounds.   **6 strength and beautie**: i.e. over men and women. Corflambo is the final victor in the contests 'of beautie and of might' (iv 16.2) in cantos iv and v.   **9 parts entire**: i.e. throughout the body.

Stanza 49

1 Corflambo: Lat. *cor*, heart + Fr. *flambeau*, flaming torch. As **Therefore** indicates, the significance of his name is revealed in the two previous lines; cf. 39.7–9.   **2** Perhaps referring to the anonymity of death, which Virgil applies even to Priam when he lies headless at *Aen.* 2.558; but without his eyes, Corflambo is indeed **namelesse**.   **4–7 Pœana**: from Lat. *poena*, 'paine; punishment' (T. Cooper 1565), alluding to her grief from rejected love at ix 6.3–4. At ix 9.6 and 13.2, her name appears as 'Pæana' (*1596*), f. paean, i.e. a shout of joy, as her grief turns to joy at 13–16. She only **seemes** to be **faire**; if she were virtuous, she would be. See 'Corflambo, Poeana' in the *SEnc*.

Stanzas 50–51

At vii 15–18, Æmylia tells what happened to her when she kept her tryst with the Squire of low degree; now his story is told by his friend. She tells how her father opposed the marriage; he tells how her friends opposed it.

Stanza 50

5 disparage: unequal match: cf. 'disparagement' (vii 16.1).

Stanza 51

1 pointed: appointed.   **2 according**: accordingly; or, as they had agreed.   **3 disauentrous case**: unfortunate event.   **5 This Gyants sonne**: Corflambo, so called as the sonne 'Of an huge Geauntesse' (47.2). **laire**: ground.   **7 mercilesse**: an intensive that defines **despaire**. Being in despair, he is without hope of mercy, as 64.5; cf. Æmylia's state at vii 11.7–9.

52

This Gyants daughter came vpon a day
　Vnto the prison in her ioyous glee,
　To view the thrals, which there in bondage lay:
　Amongst the rest she chaunced there to see
　This louely swaine the Squire of low degree;
　To whom she did her liking lightly cast,
　And wooed him her paramour to bee:
　From day to day she woo'd and prayd him fast,
And for his loue him promist libertie at last.

53

He though affide vnto a former loue,
　To whom his faith he firmely ment to hold,
　Yet seeing not how thence he mote remoue,
　But by that meanes, which fortune did vnfold,
　Her graunted loue, but with affection cold
　To win her grace his libertie to get.
　Yet she him still detaines in captiue hold,
　Fearing least if she should him freely set,
He would her shortly leaue, and former loue forget.

54

Yet so much fauour she to him hath hight,
　Aboue the rest, that he sometimes may space
　And walke about her gardens of delight,
　Hauing a keeper still with him in place,
　Which keeper is this Dwarfe, her dearling base,
　To whom the keyes of euery prison dore
　By her committed be, of speciall grace,
　And at his will may whom he list restore,
And whom he list reserue, to be afflicted more.

55

Whereof when tydings came vnto mine eare,
　Full inly sorie for the feruent zeale,
　Which I to him as to my soule did beare;
　I thether went where I did long conceale
　My selfe, till that the Dwarfe did me reueale,
　And told his Dame, her Squire of low degree
　Did secretly out of her prison steale;
　For me he did mistake that Squire to bee;
For neuer two so like did liuing creature see.

56

Then was I taken and before her brought,
　Who through the likenesse of my outward hew,
　Being likewise beguiled in her thought,
　Gan blame me much for being so vntrew,
　To seeke by flight her fellowship t'eschew,
　That lou'd me deare, as dearest thing aliue.
　Thence she commaunded me to prison new;
　Whereof I glad did not gainesay nor striue,
But suffred that same Dwarfe me to her dongeon driue.

57

There did I finde mine onely faithfull frend
　In heauy plight and sad perplexitie;
　Whereof I sorie, yet my selfe did bend,
　Him to recomfort with my companie.
　But him the more agreeu'd I found thereby:
　For all his ioy, he said, in that distresse
　Was mine and his *Æmylias* libertie.
　Æmylia well he lou'd, as I mote ghesse;
Yet greater loue to me then her he did professe.

58

But I with better reason him auiz'd,
　And shew'd him how through error and mis-thought
　Of our like persons eath to be disguiz'd,
　Or his exchange, or freedome might be wrought.
　Whereto full loth was he, ne would for ought
　Consent, that I who stood all fearelesse free,
　Should wilfully be into thraldome brought,
　Till fortune did perforce it so decree.
Yet ouerrul'd at last, he did to me agree.

59

The morrow next about the wonted howre,
　The Dwarfe cald at the doore of *Amyas*,
　To come forthwith vnto his Ladies bowre.
　In steed of whom forth came I *Placidas*,
　And vndiscerned, forth with him did pas.
　There with great ioyance and with gladsome glee,
　Of faire *Pœana* I receiued was,
　And oft imbrast, as if that I were hee,
And with kind words accoyd, vowing great loue to mee.

Stanza 52

1 This Gyants daughter: paralleling 51.5 but referring to Pœana. **8 fast**: earnestly.

Stanza 53

1 affide: betrothed. **8 freely set**: set free. **9 former loue**: parallels the phrase in 1 in order to relate Æmylia and Pœana. When Æmylia and the squire elope, each is imprisoned by the other's lust. See ix Arg.1–2*n*.

Stanza 54

1 hight: granted. **2 space**: roam. **3 her gardens of delight**: the phrase conveys erotic overtones of the woman's body as the garden where her lover may roam. **5 dearling**: favourite. **8–9 restore**: i.e. to liberty; in contrast to **reserue**: keep in his possession.

Stanza 55

2 zeale: ardent love, as ix 1.7. **3** As Jonathan loved David 'as his owne soule' (1 Sam. 18.1), a phrase made memorable by its repetition at 18.3, 20.17. **8 did mistake**: supposed in error. **9** Since true friendship involves 'one soul in bodies twain', ideally friends are identical twins.

Stanza 56

2 hew: shape.

Stanza 57

1 onely: one, above all others. **2 perplexitie**: distress; also 'bewilderment' for he must choose between Æmylia and Pœana, and between them and his friend. **8–9** Within the conventions of friendship, he makes the correct choice.

60

Which I, that was not bent to former loue,
　As was my friend, that had her long refusd,
　Did well accept, as well it did behoue,
　And to the present neede it wisely vsd.
　My former hardnesse first I faire excusd;
　And after promist large amends to make.
　With such smooth termes her error I abusd,
　To my friends good, more then for mine owne sake,
For whose sole libertie I loue and life did stake.

61

Thenceforth I found more fauour at her hand,
　That to her Dwarfe, which had me in his charge,
　She bad to lighten my too heauie band,
　And graunt more scope to me to walke at large.
　So on a day as by the flowrie marge
　Of a fresh streame I with that Elfe did play,
　Finding no meanes how I might vs enlarge,
　But if that Dwarfe I could with me conuay,
I lightly snatcht him vp, and with me bore away.

62

Threat he shriekt aloud, that with his cry
　The Tyrant selfe came forth with yelling bray,
　And me pursew'd; but nathemore would I
　Forgoe the purchase of my gotten pray,

But haue perforce him hether brought away.
Thus as they talked, loe where nigh at hand
Those Ladies two yet doubtfull through dismay
In presence came, desirous t'vnderstand
Tydings of all, which there had hapned on the land.

63

Where soone as sad *Æmylia* did espie
　Her captiue louers friend, young *Placidas*;
　All mindlesse of her wonted modestie,
　She to him ran, and him with streight embras
　Enfolding said, And liues yet *Amyas*?
　He liues (quoth he) and his *Æmylia* loues.
　Then lesse (said she) by all the woe I pas,
　With which my weaker patience fortune proues.
But what mishap thus long him fro my selfe remoues?

64

Then gan he all this storie to renew,
　And tell the course of his captiuitie;
　That her deare hart full deepely made to rew,
　And sigh full sore, to heare the miserie,
　In which so long he mercilesse did lie.
　Then after many teares and sorrowes spent,
　She deare besought the Prince of remedie:
　Who thereto did with readie will consent,
And well perform'd, as shall appeare by his euent.

Stanza 58
2 **mis-thought**: mistaken opinion.　3 **eath**: easy.　9 **agree**: accede to my proposal.

Stanza 59
2–4 **Amyas**: Lat. *amo* + Fr. *ami*, as he combines love and friendship.　**Placidas**: Lat. *placidus*, peaceful, friendly; 'gentill, meeke' (T. Cooper 1565). Together they may reflect Concord's twins, 'Peace, and Friendship' (x 34.2), as Nohrnberg 1976:624 suggests.　9 **accoyd**: appeased, soothed, for having been placed in the dungeon.

Stanza 60
9 **sole libertie**: liberty alone.

Stanza 61
5 **marge**: margin, edge.　8 **But if**: unless.

Stanza 62
4 That the dwarf is prized as **purchase**, i.e. booty gained in the chase (*OED* 8), indicates why he wasn't jettisoned, as Argante jettisoned Satyrane in order to flee more quickly from Palladine at III vii 44. He is the means to escape the prison, and presumably evidence that he fled in scorn of Pœana's favours (ix 3.7–9).　7 **doubtfull**: fearful.

Stanza 63
4 **streight**: close.　7 Since he lives, I mind less the woes I suffer.　8 **weaker**: too weak.

Stanza 64
1 **renew**: repeat.　5 **mercilesse**: without hope of mercy, as 51.7, pointing to the need for Arthur's grace.　9 **by his euent**: by what happened to him.

Cant. IX.

The Squire of low degree releast
Pœana takes to wife:
Britomart fightes with many Knights,
Prince Arthur stints their strife.

1

Hard is the doubt, and difficult to deeme,
  When all three kinds of loue together meet,
  And doe dispart the hart with powre extreme,
  Whether shall weigh the balance downe; to weet
  The deare affection vnto kindred sweet,
  Or raging fire of loue to woman kind,
  Or zeale of friends combynd with vertues meet.
But of them all the band of vertuous mind
Me seemes the gentle hart should most assured bind.

2

For naturall affection soone doth cesse,
  And quenched is with *Cupids* greater flame:
  But faithfull friendship doth them both suppresse,
  And them with maystring discipline doth tame,
  Through thoughts aspyring to eternall fame.
  For as the soule doth rule the earthly masse,
  And all the seruice of the bodie frame,
So loue of soule doth loue of bodie passe,
No lesse then perfect gold surmounts the meanest brasse.

3

All which who list by tryall to assay,
  Shall in this storie find approued plaine;
  In which these Squires true friendship more did sway,
  Then either care of parents could refraine,

Or loue of fairest Ladie could constraine.
  For though *Pœana* were as faire as morne,
  Yet did this trustie Squire with proud disdaine
  For his friends sake her offred fauours scorne,
And she her selfe her syre, of whom she was yborne.

4

Now after that Prince *Arthur* graunted had,
  To yeeld strong succour to that gentle swayne,
  Who now long time had lyen in prison sad,
  He gan aduise how best he mote darrayne
  That enterprize, for greatest glories gayne.
  That headlesse tyrants tronke he reard from ground,
  And hauing ympt the head to it agayne,
  Vpon his vsuall beast it firmely bound,
And made it so to ride, as it aliue was found.

5

Then did he take that chaced Squire, and layd
  Before the ryder, as he captiue were,
  And made his Dwarfe, though with vnwilling ayd,
  To guide the beast, that did his maister beare,
  Till to his castle they approched neare.
  Whom when the watch, that kept continuall ward
  Saw comming home; all voide of doubtfull feare,
  He running downe, the gate to him vnbard;
Whom straight the Prince ensuing, in together far'd.

Book IV Canto ix

Argument
1–2 Pœana: Æmylia, sugg. Church 1758, though the only
marriage mentioned is that between Placidas and Pœana at
15.3–9. A double marriage, which would constitute a tetrad
corresponding to the double marriage of Cambell–Cambina
and Triamond–Canacee, is suggested at 15.1 and 17.2. The
'error' may be intentionally witty: unlike Æmylia, Pœana can-
not distinguish between the look-alike friends who, like Titus
and Gesippus (see x 27.5n), would hold their loves in com-
mon.   **4 stints**: stops.

Stanza 1
1 deeme: judge; decide.   **3 dispart**: divide.   **4 Whether**:
which.   **5–9 zeale of friends** is a mean between **deare affec-
tion** between kindred and the **raging fire of loue** between
the sexes; cf. iv 34.3, viii 55.2, and x 26.8. It follows that the
heart divided by the first two kinds of love may be bound by
the **vertuous mind** of friendship, for 'vertue is the band, that
bindeth harts most sure' (ii.29.9). See iii 52n. At vi 31.7–9,

love 'being knit with vertue' is said to be 'the band | Of noble
minds'.

Stanza 2
9 surmounts: excels.

Stanza 3
2 approued: proved; commended.   **4 refraine**: restrain.
6–9 If this trustie Squire is Amyas, he refuses Pœana's love
For his friends sake, namely Placidas, or possibly Æmylia. If
the Squire is Placidas (as at 15.3), which is more likely, he flees
from Pœana, thus scorning her love, in order to find the means
to free his friend, Amyas. She scorns her sire by freeing her
lover from his prison.

Stanza 4
4 aduise: consider.   **darrayne**: arrange.   **7 ympt**: fixed.

Stanza 5
9 ensuing: following.

6

There he did find in her delitious boure
    The faire *Pœana* playing on a Rote,
    Complayning of her cruell Paramoure,
    And singing all her sorrow to the note,
    As she had learned readily by rote.
    That with the sweetnesse of her rare delight,
    The Prince halfe rapt, began on her to dote:
    Till better him bethinking of the right,
He her vnwares attacht, and captiue held by might.

7

Whence being forth produc'd, when she perceiued
    Her owne deare sire, she cald to him for aide.
    But when of him no aunswere she receiued,
    But saw him sencelesse by the Squire vpstaide,
    She weened well, that then she was betraide:
    Then gan she loudly cry, and weepe, and waile,
    And that same Squire of treason to vpbraide.
    But all in vaine, her plaints might not preuaile,
Ne none there was to reskue her, ne none to baile.

8

Then tooke he that same Dwarfe, and him compeld
    To open vnto him the prison dore,
    And forth to bring those thrals, which there he held.
    Thence forth were brought to him aboue a score
    Of Knights and Squires to him vnknowne afore:
    All which he did from bitter bondage free,
    And vnto former liberty restore.
    Amongst the rest, that Squire of low degree
Came forth full weake and wan, not like him selfe to bee.

9

Whom soone as faire *AEmylia* beheld,
    And *Placidas*, they both vnto him ran,
    And him embracing fast betwixt them held,
    Striuing to comfort him all that they can,
    And kissing oft his visage pale and wan.
    That faire *Pœana* them beholding both,
    Gan both enuy, and bitterly to ban;
    Through iealous passion weeping inly wroth,
To see the sight perforce, that both her eyes were loth.

10

But when a while they had together beene,
    And diuersly conferred of their case,
    She, though full oft she both of them had seene
    A sunder, yet not euer in one place,
    Began to doubt, when she them saw embrace,
    Which was the captiue Squire she lou'd so deare,
    Deceiued through great likenesse of their face,
    For they so like in person did appeare,
That she vneath discerned, whether whether weare.

11

And eke the Prince, when as he them auized,
    Their like resemblaunce much admired there,
    And mazd how nature had so well disguized
    Her worke, and counterfet her selfe so nere,
    As if that by one patterne seene somewhere,
    She had them made a paragone to be,
    Or whether it through skill, or errour were.
    Thus gazing long, at them much wondred he,
So did the other knights and Squires, which him did see.

12

Then gan they ransacke that same Castle strong,
    In which he found great store of hoorded threasure,
    The which that tyrant gathered had by wrong
    And tortious powre, without respect or measure.
    Vpon all which the Briton Prince made seasure,
    And afterwards continu'd there a while,
    To rest him selfe, and solace in soft pleasure
    Those weaker Ladies after weary toile;
To whom he did diuide part of his purchast spoile.

13

And for more ioy, that captiue Lady faire
    The faire *Pœana* he enlarged free;
    And by the rest did set in sumptuous chaire,
    To feast and frollicke; nathemore would she
    Shew gladsome countenaunce nor pleasaunt glee:
    But grieued was for losse both of her sire,
    And eke of Lordship, with both land and fee:
    But most she touched was with griefe entire,
For losse of her new loue, the hope of her desire.

Stanza 6

1 **her delitious boure**: 'her gardens of delight' at viii 54.3. 2 **Rote**: lyre, lute, or harp. **6–7** As her father infected anyone who saw him, she enchants anyone who hears her. 9 **attacht**: seized.

Stanza 7

8 **preuaile**: avail; be of use. 9 **ne none to baile**: in contrast to Amyas who has a friend willing to serve as bail for him at viii 58.

Stanza 9

6 **Pœana**: unless a compositor's error, the *1596* spelling, 'Pæana', also at 6.2, 13.2, indicates her changed state; see viii 49.4–7*n*. **ban**: curse.

Stanza 10

9 She hardly knew which was which.

Stanza 11

1 **auized**: observed. 2 **admired**: wondered at. 3 **mazd**: marvelled. **disguized**: decked out (*OED* 1). 6 **paragone**: match. 9 **him**: 'them' conj. Hughes 1715, but the text may stand: being clones, the two are essentially one.

Stanza 12

4 **tortious**: wrongful, i.e. wrongfully used. **without respect**: without discrimination, as 'all' at viii 48.2 indicates. 8 **weaker**: too weak. 9 **purchast**: procured; obtained by conquest.

Stanza 13

7 **fee**: possessions; wealth. 8 **entire**: sincere; total; inward. 9 **new loue**: presumably Placidas who has replaced Amyas.

14

But her the Prince through his well wonted grace,
  To better termes of myldnesse did entreat,
  From that fowle rudenesse, which did her deface;
  And that same bitter corsiue, which did eat
  Her tender heart, and made refraine from meat,
  He with good thewes and speaches well applyde,
  Did mollifie, and calme her raging heat.
For though she were most faire, and goodly dyde,
Yet she it all did mar with cruelty and pride.

15

And for to shut vp all in friendly loue,
  Sith loue was first the ground of all her griefe,
  That trusty Squire he wisely well did moue
  Not to despise that dame, which lou'd him liefe,
  Till he had made of her some better priefe,
  But to accept her to his wedded wife.
  Thereto he offred for to make him chiefe
  Of all her land and lordship during life:
He yeelded, and her tooke; so stinted all their strife.

16

From that day forth in peace and ioyous blis,
  They liu'd together long without debate,
  Ne priuate iarre, ne spite of enemis
  Could shake the safe assuraunce of their state.
  And she whom Nature did so faire create,
  That she mote match the fairest of her daies,
  Yet with lewd loues and lust intemperate
  Had it defaste; thenceforth reformd her waies,
That all men much admyrde her change, and spake her praise.

17

Thus when the Prince had perfectly compylde
  These paires of friends in peace and setled rest,
  Him selfe, whose minde did trauell as with chylde,
  Of his old loue, conceau'd in secret brest,

Resolued to pursue his former quest;
  And taking leaue of all, with him did beare
  Faire *Amoret*, whom Fortune by bequest
  Had left in his protection whileare,
Exchanged out of one into an other feare.

18

Feare of her safety did her not constraine,
  For well she wist now in a mighty hond,
  Her person late in perill, did remaine,
  Who able was all daungers to withstond.
  But now in feare of shame she more did stond,
  Seeing her selfe all soly succourlesse,
  Left in the victors powre, like vassall bond;
  Whose will her weakenesse could no way represse,
In case his burning lust should breake into excesse.

19

But cause of feare sure had she none at all
  Of him, who goodly learned had of yore
  The course of loose affection to forstall,
  And lawlesse lust to rule with reasons lore;
  That all the while he by his side her bore,
  She was as safe as in a Sanctuary;
  Thus many miles they two together wore,
  To seeke their loues dispersed diuersly,
Yet neither shewed to other their hearts priuity.

20

At length they came, whereas a troupe of Knights
  They saw together skirmishing, as seemed:
  Sixe they were all, all full of fell despight,
  But foure of them the battell best beseemed,
  That which of them was best, mote not be deemed.
  Those foure were they, from whom false *Florimell*
  By *Braggadochio* lately was redeemed.
  To weet, sterne *Druon*, and lewd *Claribell*,
Loue-lauish *Blandamour*, and lustfull *Paridell*.

Stanza 14
4 corsiue: corrosive, a word linked to the heart (Lat. *cor*) and to the heart-devouring emotion of jealousy; see I ii 6.3*n*. **6 thewes**: behaviour. **8 dyde**: coloured; hence of fine complexion.

Stanza 15
4 liefe: dearly. **5 priefe**: proof. **9** Arthur **stinted . . . strife** in love by persuading Placidas to marry Pœana through bribing him with her wealth, which he has expropriated. His subsequent and comparable act, as Arg. 3–4 indicates, is to stint strife in a chivalric mêlée.

Stanza 16
2 debate: strife. **7–9** As said of her at viii 49.8–9. She was bound because, like Acrasia, she emasculated lovers imprisoned in 'her gardens of delight' (viii 54.3). Now reformed, she may be 'enlarged free' (13.2) as Placidas's 'wedded wife' (15.6).

Stanza 17
1 compylde: composed. **3 trauell**: travail; labour in birth, anticipating **conceau'd** in the next line.

Stanza 18
5 feare of shame: continuing her 'dread of shame' when attended by Britomart at i 8.6.

Stanza 19
3 forstall: obstruct; subdue. **5–6 safe as in a Sanctuary**: a striking simile with proverbial force that signals her return to her original state in the temple of Venus. That she is **by his side** indicates that they ride together in contrast to the earlier stage when she rode and he walked. That his care of her has extended for a complete canto – it began at viii 19 – heralds its end. **9 priuity**: private thought.

Stanzas 20–31
An interlude to illustrate the conflicting states of loving as defined by the epithets at 20.8–9: 'sterne *Druon*' is constant in rejecting love while 'lewd *Claribell*' is constant in loving excessively; 'Loue-lauish *Blandamour*' loves excessively but inconstantly, while 'lustfull *Paridell*' rejects love for inconstant lust. First Paridell and Blandamour fight Druon and Claribell, setting inconstancy against constancy; then the two who reject love fight those who accept it; and finally the two who reject

21

Druons delight was all in single life,
    And vnto Ladies loue would lend no leasure:
    The more was *Claribell* enraged rife
    With feruent flames, and loued out of measure:
    So eke lou'd *Blandamour*, but yet at pleasure
    Would change his liking, and new Lemans proue:
    But *Paridell* of loue did make no threasure,
    But lusted after all, that him did moue.
So diuersly these foure disposed were to loue.

22

But those two other which beside them stoode,
    Were *Britomart*, and gentle *Scudamour*,
    Who all the while beheld their wrathfull moode,
    And wondred at their impacable stoure,
    Whose like they neuer saw till that same houre:
    So dreadfull strokes each did at other driue,
    And laid on load with all their might and powre,
    As if that euery dint the ghost would riue
Out of their wretched corses, and their liues depriue.

23

As when *Dan AEolus* in great displeasure,
    For losse of his deare loue by *Neptune* hent,
    Sends forth the winds out of his hidden threasure,
    Vpon the sea to wreake his fell intent;
    They breaking forth with rude vnruliment,
    From all foure parts of heauen doe rage full sore,
    And tosse the deepes, and teare the firmament,
    And all the world confound with wide vprore,
As if in stead thereof they *Chaos* would restore.

24

Cause of their discord, and so fell debate,
    Was for the loue of that same snowy maid,
    Whome they had lost in Turneyment of late,
    And seeking long, to weet which way she straid,
    Met here together, where through lewd vpbraide
    Of *Ate* and *Duessa* they fell out,
    And each one taking part in others aide,
    This cruell conflict raised thereabout,
Whose dangerous successe depended yet in dout.

25

For sometimes *Paridell* and *Blandamour*
    The better had, and bet the others backe,
    Eftsoones the others did the field recoure,
    And on their foes did worke full cruell wracke:
    Yet neither would their fiendlike fury slacke,
    But euermore their malice did augment;
    Till that vneath they forced were for lacke
    Of breath, their raging rigour to relent,
And rest themselues for to recouer spirits spent.

26

There gan they change their sides, and new parts take;
    For *Paridell* did take to *Druons* side,
    For old despight, which now forth newly brake
    Gainst *Blandamour*, whom alwaies he enuide:
    And *Blandamour* to *Claribell* relide.
    So all afresh gan former fight renew.
    As when two Barkes, this caried with the tide,
    That with the wind, contrary courses sew,
If wind and tide doe change, their courses change anew.

---

virtuous love either by loving excessively or inconstantly fight the chaste Britomart who loves only Artegall, and the two who reject love itself fight the knight of love, Scudamour. On their alignments as tetrads, see A. Fowler 1964:31–32.

Stanza 20
4 Four of them seemed best fit for battle. **8–9 Druon:** i.e. cruel, from Lat. *durus*, hard; or Gk δρῦς, oak, which links him to the savage Artegall (iv 39.6) and Lust (vii 7.4). **Claribell:** Lat. *clarus + bellum*, famous in war; or suggesting that he is a lady's man for he bears a woman's name (as at II iv 26.5 and VI xii 4.1); or famous in beauty, referring to the 'famous prize of beauty' (28.9) for which he fights. Evidently they are among the 'full many other Knights' at v 23.1 who are offended when Braggadocchio claims the False Florimell as his own. **Loue-lauish:** flattering love, as his name suggests; see i 32.1–5n.

Stanza 21
1–2 Druon's state replicates that of Marinell, who is 'loues enimy' (III iv 26.9), and of Artegall at vi 28.6–9. **3–4 The more:** greatly; or Claribell's womanizing is a function of Druon's male chastity: as much as the one rejects love, the other accepts it. **6 proue:** try.

Stanza 22
4 impacable stoure: implacable tumult. Only Arthur may placate them. **8 dint:** blow.

Stanza 23
The four raging winds, which represent the chaos of human passions in Britomart's lament at III iv 8–10, now represent four kinds of love. Paridell is compared to a boisterous wind at III ix 15. Neptune's love for Æolus's daughter, Arne, is told at III xi 42.2–4. **2 hent:** taken away. **3 threasure:** store; cf. Ps. 135.7: 'He draweth forthe the winde out of his treasures'. **5 vnruliment:** unruliness.

Stanza 24
5 vpbraide: reproach. **9 successe:** outcome. **depended:** hung.

Stanza 25
3 recoure: recover. **7 vneath:** only with difficulty. **8 rigour:** violence.

Stanza 26
5 relide: rallied. **8 sew:** follow.

27
Thenceforth they much more furiously gan fare,
   As if but then the battell had begonne,
   Ne helmets bright, ne hawberks strong did spare,
   That through the clifts the vermeil bloud out sponne,
   And all adowne their riuen sides did ronne.
   Such mortall malice, wonder was to see
   In friends profest, and so great outrage donne:
   But sooth is said, and tride in each degree,
Faint friends when they fall out, most cruell fomen bee.

28
Thus they long while continued in fight,
   Till *Scudamour*, and that same Briton maide,
   By fortune in that place did chance to light:
   Whom soone as they with wrathfull eie bewraide,
   They gan remember of the fowle vpbraide,
   The which that Britonesse had to them donne,
   In that late Turney for the snowy maide;
   Where she had them both shamefully fordonne,
And eke the famous prize of beauty from them wonne.

29
Eftsoones all burning with a fresh desire
   Of fell reuenge, in their malicious mood
   They from them selues gan turne their furious ire,
   And cruell blades yet steeming with whot bloud,
   Against those two let driue, as they were wood:
   Who wondring much at that so sodaine fit,
   Yet nought dismayd, them stoutly well withstood;
   Ne yeelded foote, ne once abacke did flit,
But being doubly smitten likewise doubly smit.

30
The warlike Dame was on her part assaid,
   Of *Claribell* and *Blandamour* attone;
   And *Paridell* and *Druon* fiercely laid
   At *Scudamour*, both his professed fone.
   Foure charged two, and two surcharged one;
   Yet did those two them selues so brauely beare,
   That the other litle gained by the lone,
   But with their owne repayed duely weare,
And vsury withall: such gaine was gotten deare.

31
Full oftentimes did *Britomart* assay
   To speake to them, and some emparlance moue;
   But they for nought their cruell hands would stay,
   Ne lend an eare to ought, that might behoue,
   As when an eager mastiffe once doth proue
   The tast of bloud of some engored beast,
   No words may rate, nor rigour him remoue
   From greedy hold of that his blouddy feast:
So litle did they hearken to her sweet beheast.

32
Whom when the Briton Prince a farre beheld
   With ods of so vnequall match opprest,
   His mighty heart with indignation sweld,
   And inward grudge fild his heroicke brest:
   Eftsoones him selfe he to their aide addrest,
   And thrusting fierce into the thickest preace,
   Diuided them, how euer loth to rest,
   And would them faine from battell to surcesse,
With gentle words perswading them to friendly peace.

33
But they so farre from peace or patience were,
   That all at once at him gan fiercely flie,
   And lay on load, as they him downe would beare;
   Like to a storme, which houers vnder skie
   Long here and there, and round about doth stie,
   At length breakes downe in raine, and haile, and sleet,
   First from one coast, till nought thereof be drie;
   And then another, till that likewise fleet;
And so from side to side till all the world it weet.

34
But now their forces greatly were decayd,
   The Prince yet being fresh vntoucht afore;
   Who them with speaches milde gan first disswade
   From such foule outrage, and them long forbore:
   Till seeing them through suffrance hartned more,
   Him selfe he bent their furies to abate,
   And layd at them so sharpely and so sore,
   That shortly them compelled to retrate,
And being brought in daunger, to relent too late.

Stanza 27
4 clifts: clefts or chinks in chain mail. **sponne**: spurted.
8–9 Proverbial: Smith 303.

Stanza 28
4 bewraide: discovered. **8 fordonne**: overcome.

Stanza 29
5 wood: mad.

Stanza 30
1–4 assaid: attacked. **attone**: together, at the same time. **laid**: struck. **5–9** The elaborate word-play is noted by Orange 1958. **charged**: attacked / made a pecuniary charge; **surcharged**: made an overwhelming attack / overcharged; **beare**: endure the attack / the financial burden; **gained by the lone**: gained by their blows / by lending money; **repayed**: with blows / money; **duely**: fittingly / legally due; **vsury**: more blows than were received / interest; **gaine**: additional blows received / financial gain; **deare**: physically / financially costly.

Stanza 31
1 assay: endeavour (*OED* 17b). The sense, 'test by tasting' (*OED* 5), prompts the simile in 5–8. **2 emparlance**: parleying. **5 eager**: fierce, savage. **proue**: find out. **7 rate**: reprove.

Stanza 32
4 grudge: resentment. **8** And desired them to desist from battle.

Stanza 33
1–3 they excludes Britomart and Scudamour for they seek Arthur's pardon for the others at 35.3–4. **5 stie**: rise. **7 coast**: place, quarter. **8 fleet**: floats, i.e. covered with water. **9 weet**: wets.

35

But now his courage being throughly fired,
  He ment to make them know their follies prise,
  Had not those two him instantly desired
  T'asswage his wrath, and pardon their mesprise.
  At whose request he gan him selfe aduise
  To stay his hand, and of a truce to treat
  In milder tearmes, as list them to deuise:
  Mongst which the cause of their so cruell heat
He did them aske, who all that passed gan repeat,

36

And told at large how that same errant Knight,
  To weet faire *Britomart*, them late had foyled
  In open turney, and by wrongfull fight
  Both of their publicke praise had them despoyled,
  And also of their priuate loues beguyled,
  Of two full hard to read the harder theft.
  But she that wrongfull challenge soone assoyled,
  And shew'd that she had not that Lady reft,
(As they supposd) but her had to her liking left.

37

To whom the Prince thus goodly well replied;
  Certes sir Knight, ye seemen much to blame,
  To rip vp wrong, that battell once hath tried;
  Wherein the honor both of Armes ye shame,
  And eke the loue of Ladies foule defame;
  To whom the world this franchise euer yeelded,
  That of their loues choise they might freedom clame,
  And in that right should by all knights be shielded:
Gainst which me seemes this war ye wrongfully haue wielded.

38

And yet (quoth she) a greater wrong remaines:
  For I thereby my former loue haue lost,
  Whom seeking euer since with endlesse paines,
  Hath me much sorrow and much trauell cost;

Aye me to see that gentle maide so tost.
  But *Scudamour* then sighing deepe, thus saide,
  Certes her losse ought me to sorrow most,
  Whose right she is, where euer she be straide,
Through many perils wonne, and many fortunes waide.

39

For from the first that I her loue profest,
  Vnto this houre, this present lucklesse howre,
  I neuer ioyed happinesse nor rest,
  But thus turmoild from one to other stowre,
  I wast my life, and doe my daies deuowre
  In wretched anguishe and incessant woe,
  Passing the measure of my feeble powre,
  That liuing thus, a wretch I and louing so,
I neither can my loue, ne yet my life forgo.

40

Then good sir *Claribell* him thus bespake,
  Now were it not sir *Scudamour* to you,
  Dislikefull paine, so sad a taske to take,
  Mote we entreat you, sith this gentle crew
  Is now so well accorded all anew;
  That as we ride together on our way,
  Ye will recount to vs in order dew
  All that aduenture, which ye did assay
For that faire Ladies loue: past perils well apay.

41

So gan the rest him likewise to require,
  But *Britomart* did him importune hard,
  To take on him that paine: whose great desire
  He glad to satisfie, him selfe prepar'd
  To tell through what misfortune he had far'd,
  In that atchieuement, as to him befell.
  And all those daungers vnto them declar'd,
  Which sith they cannot in this Canto well
Comprised be, I will them in another tell.

Stanza 34
5 Until seeing that by forbearing to fight they recover their strength. **9 relent**: give way; slacken.

Stanza 35
3 instantly: urgently. **4 mesprise**: scorn (of him).

Stanza 36
6 read: guess. **7–9** Britomart may acquit herself of their second charge because she refused to accept the False Florimell at v 20.6–9.

Stanza 37
2 Knight: 'Knights' conj. Upton 1758, so that blame may be distributed. Also, it deflects any direct disagreement between Arthur and Britomart. **6–9** See III i 25.7–9*n*.

Stanza 38
2 thereby: in addition to that, i.e. to the wrong described at 37.3. **former loue** associates Amoret with Britomart's love, with **former** functioning as an adverb. **9 waide**: weighed or valued; cf. x 1.3. Or 'made way', as ii 12.8.

Stanza 39
To illustrate his claim that 'all knights' (37.8) agree that a lady should be free to choose her love, Arthur could present Amoret and allow her to choose. Yet that claim is about to be denied by Scudamour in his story of how he seized Amoret against her will (cf. esp. x 57.5), his 'right' taking priority over her 'right' (37.8). Possibly Arthur did present her, for there may be a hiatus in the narrative; see x 3.3*n*. After she chose Scudamour, S. could insert a version of the five stanzas that conclude Bk III in *1590*. Or he may have planned to reserve that moment of closure until all Gloriana's knights return to her court at the end of the projected Bk XII. **4 turmoild**: driven, tossed; as Amoret at 38.5. **stowre**: disturbance.

Stanza 40
1 good sir Claribell: apparently 'lewd *Claribell*' (20.8) is reformed by Arthur's presence, even as the others are **so well accorded**. **9** . . . perils when past please in their telling.

Stanza 41
1 require: request.

Cant. X.

Scudamour doth his conquest tell,
Of vertuous Amoret:
Great Venus Temple is describ'd,
And louers life forth set.

1

True he it said, what euer man it sayd,
    That loue with gall and hony doth abound,
But if the one be with the other wayd,
For euery dram of hony therein found,
A pound of gall doth ouer it redound.
That I too true by triall haue approued:
For since the day that first with deadly wound
My heart was launcht, and learned to haue loued,
I neuer ioyed howre, but still with care was moued.

2

And yet such grace is giuen them from aboue,
    That all the cares and euill which they meet,
    May nought at all their setled mindes remoue,
    But seeme gainst common sence to them most sweet;
    As bosting in their martyrdome vnmeet.
    So all that euer yet I haue endured,
    I count as naught, and tread downe vnder feet,
    Since of my loue at length I rest assured,
That to disloyalty she will not be allured.

3

Long were to tell the trauell and long toile,
    Through which this shield of loue I late haue wonne,
    And purchased this peerelesse beauties spoile,
    That harder may be ended, then begonne.

But since ye so desire, your will be donne.
    Then hearke ye gentle knights and Ladies free,
    My hard mishaps, that ye may learne to shonne;
    For though sweet loue to conquer glorious bee,
Yet is the paine thereof much greater then the fee.

4

What time the fame of this renowmed prise
    Flew first abroad, and all mens eares possest,
    I hauing armes then taken, gan auise
    To winne me honour by some noble gest,
    And purchase me some place amongst the best.
    I boldly thought (so young mens thoughts are bold)
    That this same braue emprize for me did rest,
    And that both shield and she whom I behold,
Might be my lucky lot; sith all by lot we hold.

5

So on that hard aduenture forth I went,
    And to the place of perill shortly came.
    That was a temple faire and auncient,
    Which of great mother *Venus* bare the name,
    And farre renowmed through exceeding fame;
    Much more then that, which was in *Paphos* built,
    Or that in *Cyprus*, both long since this same,
    Though all the pillours of the one were guilt,
And all the others pauement were with yuory spilt.

Book IV Canto x

Stanza 1
1–5 Thomalin's proverbial emblem – see Smith 389 – in *SC March* claims only that love has more gall than honey, but here the odds are 96 to 1 (troy weight); cf. VI xi 1.8–9. **redound**: preponderate. **6 approued**: shown to be true. **7–9** Repeating ix 39.1–4. Amoret suffers the same: 'from the time that *Scudamour* her bought | In perilous fight, she neuer ioyed day' (i 2.1–2). **launcht**: pierced. **still**: always.

Stanza 2
1–3 As Amoret proves in the house of Busirane: 'thousand charmes could not her stedfast hart remoue' (III xii 31.9). **them**: i.e. lovers. **4 common sence**: 'commune wit' (III xi 54.5).

Stanza 3
1 trauell: travail. **3 this peerelesse beauties spoile**: referring to Amoret who would seem to be present, as suggested by the parallel phrase, **this shield of loue**, which clearly is; cf. 4.1, and esp. 4.8 and 8.3. She is the **spoile** – suggesting 'rape' (cf. 55.9,

58.3) – that he acquired by pillaging the temple of Venus. **4 That**: i.e. the **trauell and long toile**. **6 free**: of gentle birth; also, not captive as Amoret has been. **9 His judgement** is opposed to the poet's in *Am* 63.13–14. **fee**: reward.

Stanza 4
4 gest: deed. **6 boldly** and **bold** link Scudamour's actions to Amoret's imprisonment in Busirane's house whose inner doors are inscribed, 'Bee bold', '*Be not too bold*' (III xi 50.4, 54.3, 8); cf. 54.2*n*. See Hamilton 1961a:166–67, Hieatt 1962, 1999. **7 emprize**: chivalric enterprise; see I ix 1.4*n*. **9 lot** shifts in meaning from prize (*OED* 5) to what is given by destiny (*OED* 2d), as Shepherd 1989:57 notes.

Stanza 5
2 the place of perill: a description used of the dragon's lair at I xi 2.2, and the island at II xii 37.8 which contains Acrasia's Bower. **4 great mother Venus**: as she is called at III vi 40.3, the *Venus genetrix* of the garden of Adonis. **6–9** Two well-known temples dedicated to Venus. Two rival temples are added at 30. **spilt**: covered or overlaid in mosaic.

6

And it was seated in an Island strong,
    Abounding all with delices most rare,
    And wall'd by nature gainst inuaders wrong,
    That none mote haue accesse, nor inward fare,
    But by one way, that passage did prepare.
    It was a bridge ybuilt in goodly wize,
    With curious Corbes and pendants grauen faire,
    And arched all with porches, did arize
On stately pillours, fram'd after the Doricke guize.

7

And for defence thereof, on th'other end
    There reared was a castle faire and strong,
    That warded all which in or out did wend,
    And flancked both the bridges sides along,
    Gainst all that would it faine to force or wrong.
    And therein wonned twenty valiant Knights;
    All twenty tride in warres experience long;
    Whose office was, against all manner wights
By all meanes to maintaine, that castels ancient rights.

8

Before that Castle was an open plaine,
    And in the midst thereof a piller placed;
    On which this shield, of many sought in vaine,
    The shield of Loue, whose guerdon me hath graced,
    Was hangd on high with golden ribbands laced;
    And in the marble stone was written this,
    With golden letters goodly well enchaced,
    Blessed the man that well can vse his blis:
Whose euer be the shield, faire Amoret be his.

9

Which when I red, my heart did inly earne,
    And pant with hope of that aduentures hap:
    Ne stayed further newes thereof to learne,
    But with my speare vpon the shield did rap,
    That all the castle ringed with the clap.
    Streight forth issewd a Knight all arm'd to proofe,
    And brauely mounted to his most mishap:
    Who staying nought to question from aloofe,
Ran fierce at me, that fire glaunst from his horses hoofe.

10

Whom boldly I encountred (as I could)
    And by good fortune shortly him vnseated.
    Eftsoones out sprung two more of equall mould;
    But I them both with equall hap defeated:
    So all the twenty I likewise entreated,
    And left them groning there vpon the plaine.
    Then preacing to the pillour I repeated
    The read thereof for guerdon of my paine,
And taking downe the shield, with me did it retaine.

11

So forth without impediment I past,
    Till to the Bridges vtter gate I came:
    The which I found sure lockt and chained fast.
    I knockt, but no man aunswred me by name;
    I cald, but no man answerd to my clame.
    Yet I perseuer'd still to knocke and call,
    Till at the last I spide within the same,
    Where one stood peeping through a creuis small,
To whom I cald aloud, halfe angry therewithall.

Stanza 6

2 delices: delights; delicacies. **3 wall'd by nature**: as the sea was commonly said to be England's wall built by nature. **4 fare**: passage. **5 prepare**: provide. **7 curious Corbes**: skilfully wrought corbels or projecting supports. **pendants**: supporting shafts on which the corbels rest, or which rest on the corbels. **9 the Doricke guize** suggests manlike appearance, according to Vitruvius, *De Arch.* 4.1.6, being based on the proportions of a man's body. See 'architecture' and 'bridges' in the *SEnc*.

Stanza 7

1–5 In contrast to the fence enclosing the Bower of Bliss, which is 'but weake and thin' (II xii 43.2–4). **th'other end**: i.e. across from the island. **warded**: protected. **flancked**: in the military sense, fortified to protect the sides. **faine**: desire. **6 twenty**: as i 2.4. The number may allude to the 'full twenty yeares' that Ulysses took to return to Penelope (V vii 39.6) and hence represent the obstacles between Scudamour and his love. Cf. Æmylia's twenty days in Lust's cave at vii 13.1.

Stanza 8

8–9 A general axiom with particular reference to the repeated vow in the marriage ceremony, 'to have and to hold'. **vse** is the key term, as Hieatt 1962:509 argues. Scudamour's failure to use his bliss properly adds gall to love's honey (1.2), as it does to Orpheus; see 58.4–5*n*. According to Silberman

1995:79, he fails to understand the challenge of the optative mood in the inscription: **faire Amoret be his**.

Stanza 9

1 earne: yearn. **2 hap**: good fortune, success; cf. 'lot' (4.9) and 'fortune' (10.2, esp. 17.5). **6–7** I.e. he was fully armed and well mounted against the greatest misfortune.

Stanza 10

1 as I could: as I knew how to do; or as boldly as I could. **3 of equall mould**: of similar stature. **5 entreated**: dealt with. **7–8** 'I recited aloud the inscription concerning the reward for my labour.' In his overboldness, Scudamour interprets only the second line, limiting **paine** to his effort to gain the shield. In contrast, Britomart ponders the mystery in the mottos at III xi 50.4–6 and 54.4–5, and Calidore knows how to 'wisely vse, and well apply' (VI i 3.6) what he gains. Cf. Una's advice to Arthur: 'Your fortune maister eke with gouerning' (I viii 28.3).

Stanza 11

1 impediment: alluding to the needed assurance in the service of matrimony that there is no impediment why a couple may not be married. **2 vtter**: outer. **5 clame**: call. Also, he announces his claim to Amoret, ignoring Arthur's injunction that women 'might freedom clame' (ix 37.7) in their choice of love.

12

That was to weet the Porter of the place,
   Vnto whose trust the charge thereof was lent:
   His name was *Doubt*, that had a double face,
   Th'one forward looking, th'other backeward bent,
   Therein resembling *Ianus* auncient,
   Which hath in charge the ingate of the yeare:
   And euermore his eyes about him went,
   As if some proued perill he did feare,
Or did misdoubt some ill, whose cause did not appeare.

13

On th'one side he, on th'other sate *Delay*,
   Behinde the gate, that none her might espy;
   Whose manner was all passengers to stay,
   And entertaine with her occasions sly,
   Through which some lost great hope vnheedily,
   Which neuer they recouer might againe;
   And others quite excluded forth, did ly
   Long languishing there in vnpittied paine,
And seeking often entraunce, afterwards in vaine.

14

Me when as he had priuily espide,
   Bearing the shield which I had conquerd late,
   He kend it streight, and to me opened wide.
   So in I past, and streight he closd the gate.
   But being in, *Delay* in close awaite
   Caught hold on me, and thought my steps to stay,
   Feigning full many a fond excuse to prate,
   And time to steale, the threasure of mans day,
Whose smallest minute lost, no riches render may.

15

But by no meanes my way I would forslow,
   For ought that euer she could doe or say,
   But from my lofty steede dismounting low,
   Past forth on foote, beholding all the way

The goodly workes, and stones of rich assay,
   Cast into sundry shapes by wondrous skill,
   That like on earth no where I recken may:
   And vnderneath, the riuer rolling still
With murmure soft, that seem'd to serue the workmans will.

16

Thence forth I passed to the second gate,
   The *Gate of good desert*, whose goodly pride
   And costly frame, were long here to relate.
   The same to all stoode alwaies open wide:
   But in the Porch did euermore abide
   An hideous Giant, dreadfull to behold,
   That stopt the entraunce with his spacious stride,
   And with the terrour of his countenance bold
Full many did affray, that else faine enter would.

17

His name was *Daunger* dreaded ouer all,
   Who day and night did watch and duely ward,
   From fearefull cowards, entrance to forstall,
   And faint-heart-fooles, whom shew of perill hard
   Could terrifie from Fortunes faire adward:
   For oftentimes faint hearts at first espiall
   Of his grim face, were from approaching scard;
   Vnworthy they of grace, whom one deniall
Excludes from fairest hope, withouten further triall.

18

Yet many doughty warriours, often tride
   In greater perils to be stout and bold,
   Durst not the sternnesse of his looke abide,
   But soone as they his countenance did behold,
   Began to faint, and feele their corage cold.
   Againe some other, that in hard assaies
   Were cowards knowne, and litle count did hold,
   Either through gifts, or guile, or such like waies,
Crept in by stouping low, or stealing of the kaies.

Stanza 12
3 Doubt's **double face** derives from his etymology: Lat. *dubius*, moving two ways. **5–6** Cf. *SC* Arg.: 'Januarie . . . so called tanquam Janua anni the gate and entraunce of the yere, or of the name of the god Janus'. **Doubt** appears in the masque of Cupid at III xii 10. **9 misdoubt**: suspect; playing on his name.

Stanza 13
Delay and 'Daunger' (17) correspond to the obstacles between the courtly lover and his lady, such as Shame and Daunger in the *Romaunt of the Rose* 3130–256. See 'Romance of the Rose' in the *SEnc*. **3 manner**: custom. **passengers**: passers-by. **4 occasions**: pretexts. **5 vnheedily**: heedlessly. **7 forth**: from going forward, being shut out.

Stanza 14
1 priuily: stealthily. **3 kend**: recognized. **5 close awaite**: secret ambush. **9 minute**: the smallest unit of time in the sixteenth century. **render**: restore.

Stanza 15
1 forslow: delay. **5 of rich assay**: proven of rich quality. **8–9** The river obeys the builder of the bridge as though tamed by art.

Stanza 16
1 Thence forth: from that place onwards, rather than 'afterwards'. **2** As the Red Cross Knight by 'dew desert' gains Una in marriage at I xii 20.8. **6 hideous**: huge. **7 spacious stride**: the straddle of his legs.

Stanza 17
1 Daunger: refusal to grant love, as **deniall** indicates. In the *Romaunt of the Rose* 3130–66, he is a large, hideous churl who guards the path to the rose with his club, causing the lover to flee. In the masque of Cupid at III xii 11, he is also paired with Doubt. **ouer all**: everywhere; especially. **3 forstall**: bar. **5 adward**: award.

Stanza 18
1 tride: proven. **6 assaies**: endeavours. **7** . . . and held in low esteem.

19

But I though meanest man of many moe,
　　Yet much disdaining vnto him to lout,
　　Or creepe betweene his legs, so in to goe,
　　Resolu'd him to assault with manhood stout,
　　And either beat him in, or driue him out.
　　Eftsoones aduauncing that enchaunted shield,
　　With all my might I gan to lay about:
　　Which when he saw, the glaiue which he did wield
He gan forthwith t'auale, and way vnto me yield.

20

So as I entred, I did backeward looke,
　　For feare of harme, that might lie hidden there;
　　And loe his hindparts, whereof heed I tooke,
　　Much more deformed fearefull vgly were,
　　Then all his former parts did earst appere.
　　For hatred, murther, treason, and despight,
　　With many moe lay in ambushment there,
　　Awayting to entrap the warelesse wight,
Which did not them preuent with vigilant foresight.

21

Thus hauing past all perill, I was come
　　Within the compasse of that Islands space;
　　The which did seeme vnto my simple doome,
　　The onely pleasant and delightfull place,
　　That euer troden was of footings trace.
　　For all that nature by her mother wit
　　Could frame in earth, and forme of substance base,
　　Was there, and all that nature did omit,
Art playing second natures part, supplyed it.

22

No tree, that is of count, in greenewood growes,
　　From lowest Iuniper to Ceder tall,
　　No flowre in field, that daintie odour throwes,
　　And deckes his branch with blossomes ouer all,
　　But there was planted, or grew naturall:
　　Nor sense of man so coy and curious nice,
　　But there mote find to please it selfe withall;
　　Nor hart could wish for any queint deuice,
But there it present was, and did fraile sense entice.

23

In such luxurious plentie of all pleasure,
　　It seem'd a second paradise to ghesse,
　　So lauishly enricht with natures threasure,
　　That if the happie soules, which doe possesse
　　Th'Elysian fields, and liue in lasting blesse,
　　Should happen this with liuing eye to see,
　　They soone would loath their lesser happinesse,
　　And wish to life return'd againe to bee,
That in this ioyous place they mote haue ioyance free.

24

Fresh shadowes, fit to shroud from sunny ray;
　　Faire lawnds, to take the sunne in season dew;
　　Sweet springs, in which a thousand Nymphs did play;
　　Soft rombling brookes, that gentle slomber drew;
　　High reared mounts, the lands about to vew;
　　Low looking dales, disloignd from common gaze;
　　Delightfull bowres, to solace louers trew;
　　False Labyrinthes, fond runners eyes to daze;
All which by nature made did nature selfe amaze.

Stanza 19
2 lout: bow. **8 glaiue**: bill or halberd. **9 auale**: lower.

Stanza 20
3–9 That 'true loue hath no powre | To looken backe; his eies be fixt before' (I iii 30.7–8) does not apply after Doubt with one face 'backeward bent' (12.4) has appeared. Cf. Fradubio's inferred sight of Duessa's 'neather partes' at I ii 41.1–4. **warelesse**: unwary. **preuent**: anticipate.

Stanza 21
1 all perill: i.e. of the two gates. Now he must pass the peril of the island; cf. 36.9. **3 doome**: judgement. **4 onely**: one alone, 'none other' (28.3). **6–9** In contrast to their rivalry in the Bower of Bliss at II xii 59; here nature and art work together. **mother wit**: natural powers. On art playing **second natures part**, see Sidney, *Defence of Poetry*:78 on the poet who grows 'another nature'.

Stanza 22
1–5 The island is implicitly compared to the garden of Eden, which contained 'euerie tre pleasant to the sight, and good for meat' (Gen. 2.9), and within the poem to Mount Acidale, which contains 'all trees of honour' (VI x 6.4), and to the garden of Adonis which has 'euery sort of flowre' (III vi 45.1). In contrast, the Bower of Bliss has only 'trees vpshooting hye' (II xii 58.5). Cf. the flowers on Phædria's island at II vi 12.6–9. **count**: note. **growes**: groves or growths. **6–7** . . . however reserved and overly fastidious. The garden satisfies man's senses instead of merely arousing them as does the Bower. **8 queint**: skilfully designed, and thus beautiful.

Stanza 23
1 luxurious: extravagant. **pleasure**: with its emphatic placing, the word invokes Eden, which was interpreted as 'pleasure'. **2 to ghesse**: one might suppose it to be. **4–9 Elysian fields**: 'devised of Poetes to be a place of pleasure like Paradise, where the happye soules doe rest in peace and eternal happynesse' (E.K. on *SC Nov.* 179). **happie**: blessed. **ioyance**: delight.

Stanza 24
1 Fresh: cool, refreshing. **2 lawnds**: launds, open spaces between woods. **6 disloignd**: remote. **7 solace**: delight; please. **8 Labyrinthes**: a maze formed by paths bordered by high hedges, used in contemporary landscape gardening. **False**: deceiving. Eden is described as an 'end-less Maze' in du Bartas 1979:2.1.1.552; more pertinent, in the *SC*, Epistle, E.K. refers to 'the common Labyrinth of Love'. **fond**: foolish; loving.

25

And all without were walkes and alleyes dight,
    With diuers trees, enrang'd in euen rankes;
    And here and there were pleasant arbors pight,
    And shadie seates, and sundry flowring bankes,
    To sit and rest the walkers wearie shankes,
    And therein thousand payres of louers walkt,
    Praysing their god, and yeelding him great thankes,
Ne euer ought but of their true loues talkt,
Ne euer for rebuke or blame of any balkt.

26

All these together by themselues did sport
    Their spotlesse pleasures, and sweet loues content.
    But farre away from these, another sort
    Of louers lincked in true harts consent;
    Which loued not as these, for like intent,
    But on chast vertue grounded their desire,
    Farre from all fraud, or fayned blandishment;
    Which in their spirits kindling zealous fire,
Braue thoughts and noble deedes did euermore aspire.

27

Such were great *Hercules*, and *Hylas* deare;
    Trew *Ionathan*, and *Dauid* trustie tryde;
    Stout *Theseus*, and *Pirithous* his feare;
    Pylades and *Orestes* by his syde;
    Myld *Titus* and *Gesippus* without pryde;
    Damon and *Pythias* whom death could not seuer;
    All these and all that euer had bene tyde,
    In bands of friendship there did liue for euer,
Whose liues although decay'd, yet loues decayed neuer.

28

Which when as I, that neuer tasted blis,
    Nor happie howre, beheld with gazefull eye,
    I thought there was none other heauen then this;
    And gan their endlesse happinesse enuye,
    That being free from feare and gealosye,
    Might frankely there their loues desire possesse;
    Whilest I through paines and perlous ieopardie,
    Was forst to seeke my lifes deare patronesse:
Much dearer be the things, which come through hard
                                            (distresse.

29

Yet all those sights, and all that else I saw,
    Might not my steps withhold, but that forthright
    Vnto that purposd place I did me draw,
    Where as my loue was lodged day and night:
    The temple of great *Venus*, that is hight
    The Queene of beautie, and of loue the mother,
    There worshipped of euery liuing wight;
    Whose goodly workmanship farre past all other
That euer were on earth, all were they set together.

30

Not that same famous Temple of *Diane*,
    Whose hight all *Ephesus* did ouersee,
    And which all *Asia* sought with vowes prophane,
    One of the worlds seuen wonders sayd to bee,
    Might match with this by many a degree:
    Nor that, which that wise King of *Iurie* framed,
    With endlesse cost, to be th'Almighties see;
    Nor all that else through all the world is named
To all the heathen Gods, might like to this be clamed

Stanza 25
1 dight: adorned.   **4 sundry**: 'sunny', conj. Upton 1758, as 'the opposition and sense requires'; cf. 24.1–2.   **7 their god**: Cupid, anticipating the praise of Venus at 44–47.   **9** As the lovers in paradise, in *HL* 288, play their sports 'without rebuke or blame'.   **balkt**: stopped talking. Hence their pleasures remain 'spotlesse' (26.2), and they enjoy their love 'free from feare and gealosye' (28.5).

Stanza 26
1 by themselues: apart from the others.   **3** That the friends are **farre away** is evident in the interpolation of stanzas 26–27 into Scudamour's sight of the lovers.   **sort**: company; kind.   **4 consent**: harmony.   **8–9 Which**: i.e. **their desire**. On love as the source of virtuous action, see IV proem 2.6–9, and III i 49.8–9*n*.   **aspire**: inspire.

Stanza 27
The catalogue is traditional except for the biblical pair, so also is the description except for the epithets applied to Titus and Gesippus, on which see Hamilton 1967:119–20. Four of the five pairs are found in Lyly 1902:1.198, with the final three stressed because they were willing to die for each other.   **1 Hylas**: Hyllus *1596* is Hercules's son. He is correctly named at III xii 7.5–9.   **2** See 1 Sam. 18.1.   **trustie**: faithfully.   **3 Theseus** aided **Pirithous** in his battle against the Centaurs and later descended into hell to help him carry off Proserpina.   **feare**: companion.   **4 Pylades** was willing to be sacrificed in place of **Orestes**.   **5 Gesippus** offered his betrothed to his look-alike friend, **Titus**, upon learning that he loved her. Later under penalty of death, he was saved by Titus who offered to die in his stead.   **Myld**: kind, gracious.   **6** When the one was condemned to death, the other was willing to take his place and be executed if he did not return. He did return and both were pardoned.

Stanza 28
2 gazefull: coined by S. to stress the intensity of Scudamour's gaze.   **4–6** As in the garden of Adonis where 'Without fell rancor, or fond gealosy; | Franckly each Paramor his leman knowes' (III vi 41.6–7). In the garden, however, '*Time* their troubler is' while here lovers enjoy **endlesse happinesse**. Outside the island, **feare** overwhelms Amoret, and **gealosye** Scudamour.   **8** Amoret as patron of Scudamour's life suggests Arthur's relationship with the Red Cross Knight at I ix 17.6 and with Guyon at II viii 55.4.   **9 dearer**: more precious.

Stanza 29
6 Venus is named the **Queene of beautie** at 44.1, v 26.4, I i 48.1, etc.

Stanza 30
1–7 The 'temple of the great goddesse Diana', whose magnificence 'all Asia and the worlde worshippeth' (Acts 19.27) is the secular counterpart to the temple of Jerusalem built by Solomon, King of the Jews, as the house of the Lord

31

I much admyring that so goodly frame,
  Vnto the porch approcht, which open stood;
  But therein sate an amiable Dame,
  That seem'd to be of very sober mood,
  And in her semblant shewed great womanhood:
  Strange was her tyre; for on her head a crowne
  She wore much like vnto a Danisk hood,
  Poudred with pearle and stone, and all her gowne
Enwouen was with gold, that raught full low a downe.

32

On either side of her, two young men stood,
  Both strongly arm'd, as fearing one another;
  Yet were they brethren both of halfe the blood,
  Begotten by two fathers of one mother,
  Though of contrarie natures each to other:
  The one of them hight *Loue*, the other *Hate*,
  Hate was the elder, *Loue* the younger brother;
  Yet was the younger stronger in his state
Then th'elder, and him maystred still in all debate.

33

Nathlesse that Dame so well them tempred both,
  That she them forced hand to ioyne in hand,
  Albe that *Hatred* was thereto full loth,
  And turn'd his face away, as he did stand,
  Vnwilling to behold that louely band.
  Yet she was of such grace and vertuous might,
  That her commaundment he could not withstand,
  But bit his lip for felonous despight,
And gnasht his yron tuskes at that displeasing sight.

34

Concord she cleeped was in common reed,
  Mother of blessed *Peace*, and *Friendship* trew;
  They both her twins, both borne of heauenly seed,
  And she her selfe likewise diuinely grew;
  The which right well her workes diuine did shew:
  For strength, and wealth, and happinesse she lends,
  And strife, and warre, and anger does subdew:
  Of litle much, of foes she maketh frends,
And to afflicted minds sweet rest and quiet sends.

35

By her the heauen is in his course contained,
  And all the world in state vnmoued stands,
  As their Almightie maker first ordained,
  And bound them with inuiolable bands;
  Else would the waters ouerflow the lands,
  And fire deuoure the ayre, and hell them quight,
  But that she holds them with her blessed hands.
  She is the nourse of pleasure and delight,
And vnto *Venus* grace the gate doth open right.

36

By her I entring halfe dismayed was,
  But she in gentle wise me entertayned,
  And twixt her selfe and *Loue* did let me pas;
  But *Hatred* would my entrance haue restrayned,
  And with his club me threatned to haue brayned,
  Had not the Ladie with her powrefull speach
  Him from his wicked will vneath refrayned;
  And th'other eke his malice did empeach,
Till I was throughly past the perill of his reach.

(1 Kings 6). O'Brien 1999:148 notes that Paul urges that the former 'shulde be destroyed' because of the idolatry practised there. **see**: dwelling-place. **9 clamed**: called; proclaimed.

Stanza 31
3 amiable: friendly (Fr. *amiable*); also, as *aimable*, worthy to be loved, 'loueable' (Cotgrave 1611). **5–9** Concord's **semblant** or demeanour compares to Womanhood's at 49.5–8. That her **Strange . . . tyre** (head-dress) is **like vnto a Danisk hood** may allude to the hood worn by the Danish princess Anna who married James VI in 1589/90. Their marriage was part of Elizabeth's effort to set up a league of nations to oppose Spain, and, accordingly, may be associated with Concord, as Dollerup 1985 suggests.

Stanza 32
4–5 The relation of Love and Hate to Concord is explained by Wind 1967:211 as the 'infolding' of opposites into one, which is then 'unfolded' into Peace and Friendship at 34.2. On the consequent *discordia concors* that holds unlikely opposites in unity, see Roche 1964:17, 23. **7–9** On the power of Love to reduce chaos to cosmos, see *HL* 57–91. **still**: always.

Stanza 33
1 tempred: governed. **5 louely band**: loving bond. Their hands join where Concord sits. **7 commaundment**: authority. **8 felonous**: fierce; cruel.

Stanza 34
1–2 Concord, the Lat. *Concordia*, a popular personification and emblem (see G. Whitney 1586:76) is extolled by Medina: 'louely concord, and most sacred peace | Doth nourish vertue, and fast friendship breeds' (II ii 31.1–2). She corresponds to Dame Peace who sits at the door of the temple of Venus in Chaucer, *Parl. Fowls* 239–40; see Hume 1984:128–29. **reed**: speech. **6 wealth**: well-being.

Stanza 35
On the traditional cosmogony which informs Concord's power to reconcile the warring elements through love, see 'cosmogony' and 'elements' in the *SEnc*. **2 vnmoued**: steadfast. **6** . . . i.e. and hell requite (or retaliate) against the waters and fire by reducing them to original chaos. If **deuoure** is understood to follow **hell**, the line reads: and hell devour them (land, air and water) entirely (sugg. *Var*). If **hell** is an obs. form of 'hele' (to conceal; cf. 'vnhele' at II xii 64.8, IV v 10.7), it reads: and water and fire would entirely cover land and air. **9 Venus grace**: those to whom Venus offers her gift of love.

Stanza 36
2 entertayned: received. **6–8** Concord restrained with difficulty Hate's power to act, Love prevented his malice.

37

Into the inmost Temple thus I came,
    Which fuming all with frankensence I found,
    And odours rising from the altars flame.
    Vpon an hundred marble pillors round
    The roofe vp high was reared from the ground,
    All deckt with crownes, and chaynes, and girlands gay,
    And thousand pretious gifts worth many a pound,
    The which sad louers for their vowes did pay;
And all the ground was strow'd with flowres, as fresh as May.

38

An hundred Altars round about were set,
    All flaming with their sacrifices fire,
    That with the steme thereof the Temple swet,
    Which rould in clouds to heauen did aspire,
    And in them bore true louers vowes entire:
    And eke an hundred brasen caudrons bright,
    To bath in ioy and amorous desire,
    Euery of which was to a damzell hight;
For all the Priests were damzels, in soft linnen dight.

39

Right in the midst the Goddesse selfe did stand
    Vpon an altar of some costly masse,
    Whose substance was vneath to vnderstand:
    For neither pretious stone, nor durefull brasse,

Nor shining gold, nor mouldring clay it was;
    But much more rare and pretious to esteeme,
    Pure in aspect, and like to christall glasse,
    Yet glasse was not, if one did rightly deeme,
But being faire and brickle, likest glasse did seeme.

40

But it in shape and beautie did excell
    All other Idoles, which the heathen adore,
    Farre passing that, which by surpassing skill
    Phidias did make in *Paphos* Isle of yore,
    With which that wretched Greeke, that life forlore
    Did fall in loue: yet this much fairer shined,
    But couered with a slender veile afore;
    And both her feete and legs together twyned
Were with a snake, whose head and tail were fast combyned.

41

The cause why she was couered with a vele,
    Was hard to know, for that her Priests the same
    From peoples knowledge labour'd to concele.
    But sooth it was not sure for womanish shame,
    Nor any blemish, which the worke mote blame;
    But for, they say, she hath both kinds in one,
    Both male and female, both vnder one name:
    She syre and mother is her selfe alone,
Begets and eke conceiues, ne needeth other none.

Stanza 37

1–4 The **inmost Temple** may be compared to the temple of Venus Physizoa in Francesco Colonna, *Hypnerotomachia Poliphili*, as MacColl 1989:31 suggests. For an illustration, see Hieatt 1992:11; see also Leslie 1991:87–88. The **hundred** pillars recall the vision of the building with 100 pillars in *Theatre*, *sonn* 2. **round** indicates that the temple is circular. Within it, the hundred altars (and presumably the hundred cauldrons) form a circle with the altar of Venus 'Right in the midst' (39.1), i.e. at the centre. **8 sad**: also steadfast, constant; cf. III xi 45.9.

Stanza 38

1–4 As the hundred altars in the temple of Venus in Virgil, *Aen.* 1.416–17, steam with Sabaean incense. **5 entire**: unbroken; earnest. **6 caudrons**: cauldrons, baths. Cf. the ten cauldrons and the hundred basins in the temple of Solomon (2 Chron. 4.6–8). **8 Euery**: each. **hight**: assigned.

Stanza 39

1 Right in the midst: as Venus's mount is displayed in the garden of Adonis at III vi 43.1. O'Brien 1999:149 notes that she occupies the place of the ark of the covenant in Solomon's temple. **3–9 Whose substance**: referring to the altar or possibly the statue. **vneath to vnderstand**: difficult to be known. If **vnderstand** conveys its etymological sense, the line would read: it was difficult to know how the **substance** (i.e. what 'stands under' the statue) could prop it up. It is not glass, as Merlin's 'glassy globe' at III ii 21.1, but only **likest glasse** in being **brickle** (i.e. brittle), as the fragile altar 'built of brickle

clay' in *Time* 499. It may be crystal. As a symbol of the hymen, e.g. in the *Hypnerotomachia*, see Nohrnberg 1976:475*n*95. **durefull**: durable, enduring. **to esteeme**: to be valued. **Pure**: clear, transparent. S. associates rich substance with transparency in his description of Acrasia's fountain at II xii 60.2–4.

Stanza 40

2 Idoles: images, statues; suggesting objects of idolatry. **3–6 Phidias**: 'an excellent woorkeman in makying great ymages of golde or Iuorie' (T. Cooper 1565). A similar story is told by Pliny, *Nat. Hist.* 36.21, of a statue of the naked Venus on Cnidus by Praxiteles. **8–9** On Venus with her feet and legs bound as an ancient symbol of marital concord, see Manning in the *SEnc* 248, 709. The tail-devouring serpent (*ouroboros*) is an emblem of the perpetual cycle of generation, here of matrimonial fidelity; or of the union of the male and female genitals, as suggested by the caduceus and by Scudamour and Amoret embracing as 'that faire *Hermaphrodite*' at III xii 46.2. See A. Fowler 1964:164. **slender**: 'thin', to allow the statue to shine; 'long', to cover the main (sexual) part of her body, as Venus in Chaucer, *Parl. Fowls* 269–73, is thinly covered from her breast down. See Anderson 1994:653–54.

Stanza 41

4 not sure: to be sure not. **6–9 kinds**: sexes, as she is 'Great God of men and women' (47.7). As *Venus hermaphroditos* 'doth soly couples seeme, | Both male and female through commixture joynd' (*Colin Clout* 801–02). See Paglia 1979, and 'androgyne' in the *SEnc*; also III xii 46*n*. Cf. androgynous Nature at VII vii 5.5–9.

42

And all about her necke and shoulders flew
  A flocke of litle loues, and sports, and ioyes,
  With nimble wings of gold and purple hew;
  Whose shapes seem'd not like to terrestriall boyes,
  But like to Angels playing heauenly toyes;
  The whilest their eldest brother was away,
  Cupid their eldest brother; he enioyes
  The wide kingdome of loue with Lordly sway,
And to his law compels all creatures to obay.

43

And all about her altar scattered lay
  Great sorts of louers piteously complayning,
  Some of their losse, some of their loues delay,
  Some of their pride, some paragons disdayning,
  Some fearing fraud, some fraudulently fayning,
  As euery one had cause of good or ill.
  Amongst the rest some one through loues constrayning,
  Tormented sore, could not containe it still,
But thus brake forth, that all the temple it did fill.

44

Great *Venus*, Queene of beautie and of grace,
  The ioy of Gods and men, that vnder skie
  Doest fayrest shine, and most adorne thy place,
  That with thy smyling looke doest pacifie
  The raging seas, and makst the stormes to flie;
  Thee goddesse, thee the winds, the clouds doe feare,
  And when thou spredst thy mantle forth on hie,
  The waters play and pleasant lands appeare,
And heauens laugh, and al the world shews ioyous cheare.

45

Then doth the dædale earth throw forth to thee
  Out of her fruitfull lap aboundant flowres,
  And then all liuing wights, soone as they see
  The spring breake forth out of his lusty bowres,

They all doe learne to play the Paramours;
  First doe the merry birds, thy prety pages
  Priuily pricked with thy lustfull powres,
  Chirpe loud to thee out of their leauy cages,
And thee their mother call to coole their kindly rages.

46

Then doe the saluage beasts begin to play
  Their pleasant friskes, and loath their wonted food;
  The Lyons rore, the Tygres loudly bray,
  The raging Buls rebellow through the wood,
  And breaking forth, dare tempt the deepest flood,
  To come where thou doest draw them with desire:
  So all things else, that nourish vitall blood,
  Soone as with fury thou doest them inspire,
In generation seeke to quench their inward fire.

47

So all the world by thee at first was made,
  And dayly yet thou doest the same repayre:
  Ne ought on earth that merry is and glad,
  Ne ought on earth that louely is and fayre,
  But thou the same for pleasure didst prepayre.
  Thou art the root of all that ioyous is,
  Great God of men and women, queene of th'ayre,
  Mother of laughter, and welspring of blisse,
O graunt that of my loue at last I may not misse.

48

So did he say: but I with murmure soft,
  That none might heare the sorrow of my hart,
  Yet inly groning deepe and sighing oft,
  Besought her to graunt ease vnto my smart,
  And to my wound her gratious help impart,
  Whilest thus I spake, behold with happy eye
  I spyde, where at the Idoles feet apart
  A beuie of fayre damzels close did lye,
Wayting when as the Antheme should be sung on hye.

Stanza 42
1–5 **litle loues**: suggests Amoretta; see III vi 28.8–9. **sports**: amorous play; here personified as *amorini* who attend Venus. **gold and purple**: the colours of sovereignty at I vii 16.3. At *SC March* 33, Cupid's wings are 'purple and blewe'. **toyes**: sports, games.

Stanza 43
2 **sorts**: companies. 4 Referring to the pride and disdain of their mistresses.

Stanzas 44–47
A paraphrase of the hymn to Venus in Lucretius, *De Rerum Natura*. For an analysis, see Esolen 1994:39–44. On the association of Venus with Wisdom who was present at the creation (Prov. 8.27), who is 'the mother of beautiful loue', and who 'possessed the waues of the sea' (Ecclus. 24.20, 9), see Wells 1983:101.

Stanza 44
2 **vnder skie**: i.e. beneath the highest heaven of the universe. 4 Cf. 'thy sweete smyling mother from aboue' (proem 5.7).

Stanza 45
1 **dædale**: fruitful, fertile. 4 **breake forth**: such bursting energy is expressed by the complaining lover at 43.9, and the animals at 46.5. **lusty**: joyful; lustful; vigorous. 5 **play**: sport amorously. 7 **Priuily pricked**: secretly urged or driven; as Chaucer's singing birds 'so priketh hem nature'. 9 **kindly rages**: natural desire or lust.

Stanza 46
5 **tempt**: risk the perils of.

Stanza 47
1–2 For Venus as the world's creator and preserver, both *genetrix* (or *paradigma*) and *alma*, S. draws on Conti 1616:4.13, as Lotspeich 1932 notes. 7–8 The middle two epithets are also from Conti.

Stanza 48
1 **murmure**: complaint. 2 In contrast to the hymn to Venus that fills the temple at 43.9. 7–8 **apart**: i.e. to one side, though still close to her; or **close** may suggest close together; or hidden, being under her protection.

49

The first of them did seeme of ryper yeares,
  And grauer countenance then all the rest;
  Yet all the rest were eke her equall peares,
  Yet vnto her obayed all the best.
  Her name was *Womanhood*, that she exprest
  By her sad semblant and demeanure wyse:
  For stedfast still her eyes did fixed rest,
  Ne rov'd at randon after gazers guyse,
Whose luring baytes oftimes doe heedlesse harts entyse.

50

And next to her sate goodly *Shamefastnesse*,
  Ne euer durst her eyes from ground vpreare,
  Ne euer once did looke vp from her desse,
  As if some blame of euill she did feare,
  That in her cheekes made roses oft appeare:
  And her against sweet *Cherefulnesse* was placed,
  Whose eyes like twinkling stars in euening cleare,
  Were deckt with smyles, that all sad humors chaced,
And darted forth delights, the which her goodly graced.

51

And next to her sate sober *Modestie*,
  Holding her hand vpon her gentle hart;
  And her against sate comely *Curtesie*,
  That vnto euery person knew her part;

And her before was seated ouerthwart
  Soft *Silence*, and submisse *Obedience*,
  Both linckt together neuer to dispart,
  Both gifts of God not gotten but from thence,
Both girlonds of his Saints against their foes offence.

52

Thus sate they all a round in seemely rate:
  And in the midst of them a goodly mayd,
  Euen in the lap of *Womanhood* there sate,
  The which was all in lilly white arayd,
  With siluer streames amongst the linnen stray'd;
  Like to the Morne, when first her shyning face
  Hath to the gloomy world it selfe bewray'd,
  That same was fayrest *Amoret* in place,
Shyning with beauties light, and heauenly vertues grace.

53

Whom soone as I beheld, my hart gan throb,
  And wade in doubt, what best were to be donne:
  For sacrilege me seem'd the Church to rob,
  And folly seem'd to leaue the thing vndonne,
  Which with so strong attempt I had begonne.
  Tho shaking off all doubt and shamefast feare,
  Which Ladies loue I heard had neuer wonne
  Mongst men of worth, I to her stepped neare,
And by the lilly hand her labour'd vp to reare.

Stanza 49

3–4 I.e. since she was *prima inter pares*, they obeyed her over the others. **6** By her grave countenance . . . **7–8** In contrast to Malecasta's 'wanton eyes, ill signes of womanhed' (III i 41.7), and the False Florimell's 'light eye-glance' (IV ii 9.4). **guyse**: fashion.

Stanzas 50–51

The seating arrangement is carefully spelled out. In 50: **And next to her** places Shamefastnesse beside Womanhood; **her against**: directly opposite Shamefastnesse is Cherefulnesse, the countering and complimentary state. In 51: **And next to her**: next to Shamefastnesse is Modestie who shares her sobriety; on their association, see II ix 41.2*n*. **And her against**: directly opposite Modestie is her balancing virtue, Curtesie. The vertical halves of the circle divide the private and public virtues.

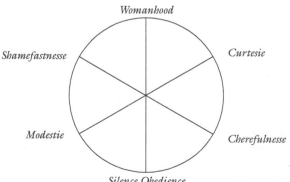

The linked Silence and Obedience, who are apart from the tetrad of natural virtues in being **gifts of God**, are seated before Curtesie but **ouerthwart**: i.e. across from her but to the side. The climax of the six virtues that comprise Womanhood is Obedience in accord with the marriage vow.

Silence is associated with Modestie, and Obedience with Cherefulnesse, for silence is the mark of modesty, and being cheerful in obeying shows true obedience. The lines allotted each virtue are carefully distributed, and the virtues are related by a defining gesture and adjective. *Epith* 191–93 offers a different set of traditional female virtues. See 'Womanhood' in the *SEnc* for a different diagram and explanation of the seating arrangement.

Stanza 50

1–5 On **Shamefastnesse**, see II ix 40–43. For Tilney 1992:132, 'if so be that there were but one onely vertue in a woman, it might well be shamefastnesse'. **desse**: dais.

Stanza 51

4 knew her part: knew how to behave with the respect owing each person, which is the virtue of civility; see VI proem 4.5*n*. **6 submisse**: submissive. **7 dispart**: separate.

Stanza 52

1 All sat in a circle in a fitting manner. **2 in the midst** suggests another seating arrangement with the six virtues infolded in 'vertuous Amoret' (Arg.), as though composing her garland. **3** As she was 'vpbrought in goodly womanhed' (III vi 28.7; cf. 51.5–9). **4–5 lilly white**: denoting her virginity, as also 53.9. **linnen** associates her with Venus's 'Priests' at 38.9. **6–9** The

54

Threat that formost matrone me did blame,
    And sharpe rebuke, for being ouer bold;
    Saying it was to Knight vnseemely shame,
    Vpon a recluse Virgin to lay hold,
    That vnto *Venus* seruices was sold.
    To whom I thus, Nay but it fitteth best,
    For *Cupids* man with *Venus* mayd to hold,
    For ill your goddesse seruices are drest
By virgins, and her sacrifices let to rest.

55

With that my shield I forth to her did show,
    Which all that while I closely had conceld;
    On which when *Cupid* with his killing bow
    And cruell shafts emblazond she beheld,
    At sight thereof she was with terror queld,
    And said no more: but I which all that while
    The pledge of faith, her hand engaged held,
    Like warie Hynd within the weedie soyle,
For no intreatie would forgoe so glorious spoyle.

56

And euermore vpon the Goddesse face
    Mine eye was fixt, for feare of her offence,
    Whom when I saw with amiable grace
    To laugh at me, and fauour my pretence,

I was emboldned with more confidence,
    And nought for nicenesse nor for enuy sparing,
    In presence of them all forth led her thence,
    All looking on, and like astonisht staring,
Yet to lay hand on her, not one of all them daring.

57

She often prayd, and often me besought,
    Sometime with tender teares to let her goe,
    Sometime with witching smyles: but yet for nought,
    That euer she to me could say or doe,
    Could she her wished freedome fro me wooe;
    But forth I led her through the Temple gate,
    By which I hardly past with much adoe:
    But that same Ladie which me friended late
In entrance, did me also friend in my retrate.

58

No lesse did daunger threaten me with dread,
    When as he saw me, maugre all his powre,
    That glorious spoyle of beautie with me lead,
    Then *Cerberus*, when *Orpheus* did recoure
    His Leman from the Stygian Princes boure.
    But euermore my shield did me defend,
    Against the storme of euery dreadfull stoure:
    Thus safely with my loue I thence did wend.
So ended he his tale, where I this Canto end.

---

simile is suggested by her conception by the sun's beams at III vi 6–7. She shines as does the statue at 40.6. **bewray'd**: revealed, with a pun on 'ray'. **in place**: no mere rhyming tag, as the disastrous sequel shows.

Stanza 53

3 sacrilege: the purloining of sacred objects, Amoret being 'a recluse Virgin' (54.4). **6–8 shamefast**: bashful; perhaps 'shameful'. He acts out the proverb: 'Faint heart never won fair lady' (Smith 233). **men of worth**: in contrast to his earlier status as 'meanest man of many moe' (19.1). **9** As Orpheus seeks to rescue Eurydice; see 58.4–5n. On the parallel to the story of Paris's sacrilege in abducting Helen from the temple of Venus, e.g. Gower, *Conf. Aman.* 5.7523–7590, see Nohrnberg 1976:641–42.

Stanza 54

1 Threat: because of that. **2** That Scudamour is **ouer bold** in seizing Amoret relates to the motto over the door to the inmost room of the house of Busirane, '*Be not too bold*' (see 4.6n), which Britomart must ignore in order to free her. **5 sold**: given; dedicated. **8–9 drest**: ordered, performed. **let to rest**: allowed to cease.

Stanza 55

6–7 Referring to the marriage ceremony before the exchange of vows in which the man takes the woman by the right hand. At *Epith* 238–39, the act is called 'the pledge of all our band'. **8–9 soyle**: the marsh in which the hunted deer seeks refuge. Either Amoret is the **spoyle** that Scudamour has ambushed, or he himself is the ambushed deer as at III xii 44.7–8; see Anderson 1994:656–57. On the relationship of the hunter and hunted, see Prescott 1986:33–37.

Stanza 56

2 offence: displeasure. **3 amiable**: see 31.3n. **4 To laugh at me**: as though the statue were animate. Cf. her 'smyling looke' (44.4), and Nature's encouragement of Arthur at I ix 12.8–9. **at me**: i.e. on me, favouring me. Or she laughs in scorn at Scudamour's folly, as the gods laugh at Mirabella at VI vii 32.4; sugg. L. Hendrix 1993:130–31. **pretence**: claim; asserting a right. **6** Neither for modesty in Amoret nor for envy in the others. **8 like**: equally; all alike.

Stanza 57

5 freedome: see III i 25.7–9n. Scudamour's dominion over Amoret against her desire for freedom conflicts with the equality in sexual relations seen in the loves of Cambina and Canacee, as E. Fowler 1995:56–57 argues. **7–9** By which I would have passed only with much difficulty had not that same Lady, etc.

Stanza 58

3 That glorious spoyle of beautie: paralleling 'this peerelesse beauties spoile' at 3.3. to round out his story. **4–5** When Orpheus descended into hell to recover Eurydice from Pluto's bower, he was opposed by its guardian, Cerberus. S. may refer to the less common version of the myth in which Orpheus recovered Eurydice, as he seems to do in *SC Oct.* 28–30, though the subsequent history of Scudamour's courtship parallels the more common version: Orpheus lost Eurydice, as Scudamour loses Amoret, because he was overcome by desire. On the irony of the reference, see Cain 1978:166–67, and Quilligan 1983:204–05. The myth relates also to Amoret who was seized and wounded on her wedding-night as Eurydice was mortally wounded in her heel on her wedding-night, by which 'is meant lustfull love' (E.K. on *SC March* 97). **recoure**: recover. **7 stoure**: assault.

Cant. XI.

Marinells former wound is heald,
he comes to Proteus hall,
Where Thames doth the Medway wedd,
and feasts the Sea-gods all.

1

BVt ah for pittie that I haue thus long
  Left a fayre Ladie languishing in payne:
    Now well away, that I haue doen such wrong,
    To let faire *Florimell* in bands remayne,
    In bands of loue, and in sad thraldomes chayne;
    From which vnlesse some heauenly powre her free
    By miracle, not yet appearing playne,
    She lenger yet is like captiu'd to bee:
That euen to thinke thereof, it inly pitties mee.

2

Here neede you to remember, how erewhile
  Vnlouely *Proteus*, missing to his mind
    That Virgins loue to win by wit or wile,
    Her threw into a dongeon deepe and blind,
    And there in chaynes her cruelly did bind,
    In hope thereby her to his bent to draw:
    For when as neither gifts nor graces kind
    Her constant mind could moue at all he saw,
He thought her to compell by crueltie and awe.

3

Deepe in the bottome of an huge great rocke
  The dongeon was, in which her bound he left,
    That neither yron barres, nor brasen locke
    Did neede to gard from force, or secret theft
    Of all her louers, which would her haue reft.
    For wall'd it was with waues, which rag'd and ror'd
    As they the cliffe in peeces would haue cleft;
    Besides ten thousand monsters foule abhor'd
Did waite about it, gaping griesly all begor'd.

4

And in the midst thereof did horror dwell,
  And darkenesse dredd, that neuer viewed day,
    Like to the balefull house of lowest hell,
    In which old *Styx* her aged bones alway,
    Old *Styx* the Grandame of the Gods, doth lay.
    There did this lucklesse mayd seuen months abide,
    Ne euer euening saw, ne mornings ray,
    Ne euer from the day the night descride,
But thought it all one night, that did no houres diuide.

5

And all this was for loue of *Marinell*,
  Who her despysd (ah who would her despyse?)
    And wemens loue did from his hart expell,
    And all those ioyes that weake mankind entyse.
    Nathlesse his pride full dearely he did pryse;
    For of a womans hand it was ywroke,
    That of the wound he yet in languor lyes,
    Ne can be cured of that cruell stroke
Which *Britomart* him gaue, when he did her prouoke.

6

Yet farre and neare the Nymph his mother sought,
  And many salues did to his sore applie,
    And many herbes did vse. But when as nought
    She saw could ease his rankling maladie,
    At last to *Tryphon* she for helpe did hie,
    (This *Tryphon* is the seagods surgeon hight)
    Whom she besought to find some remedie:
    And for his paines a whistle him behight
That of a fishes shell was wrought with rare delight.

Book IV Canto xi

Stanza 1
S. continues from his last words to Florimell about her imprisonment fourteen cantos earlier: 'Yt yrkes me, leaue thee in this wofull state' (III viii 43.8). He is not sufficiently irked, though, not to let her languish for another canto. **5 bands of loue**: referring to the bonds of her love for Marinell which leads her to choose 'Eternall thraldome' (III viii 42.1) rather than yield to Proteus. **8 like**: likely.

Stanza 2
2 Vnlouely: ugly, and (therefore) unloved; cf. 'his grim sight' (III viii 32.8). **missing**: failing. **4 blind**: dark. **6 bent**: purpose. **9 awe**: behaviour that inspires fear.

Stanza 3
9 begor'd: stained with gore.

Stanza 4
4–5 Styx: river goddess of the lower world; cf. I i 37.9. **6 seuen months**: also the period of time that Amoret is imprisoned in the house of Busirane. As the passage of time that leads to renewal, see III xi 10.8*n*. **8 descride**: distinguished.

Stanza 5
2–4 As III v 9.5–7. **5 pryse**: pay for. **6 ywroke**: inflicted. **7 languor**: illness; woeful plight. **9** Referring to his defiance of her at III iv 14.4–9.

Stanza 6
4 rankling: used by S. for a festering, incurable wound; see I x 25.1–5*n*. **maladie**: used by S. chiefly for love-sickness. **5–7** Recalling III iv 43.7–9. **8 behight**: promised.

7

So well that Leach did hearke to her request,
   And did so well employ his carefull paine,
   That in short space his hurts he had redrest,
   And him restor'd to healthfull state againe:
   In which he long time after did remaine
   There with the Nymph his mother, like her thrall;
   Who sore against his will did him retaine,
   For feare of perill, which to him mote fall,
Through his too ventrous prowesse proued ouer all.

8

It fortun'd then, a solemne feast was there
   To all the Sea-gods and their fruitfull seede,
   In honour of the spousalls, which then were
   Betwixt the *Medway* and the *Thames* agreed.
   Long had the *Thames* (as we in records reed)
   Before that day her wooed to his bed;
   But the proud Nymph would for no worldly meed,
   Nor no entreatie to his loue be led;
Till now at last relenting, she to him was wed.

9

So both agreed, that this their bridale feast
   Should for the Gods in *Proteus* house be made;
   To which they all repayr'd, both most and least,
   Aswell which in the mightie Ocean trade,
   As that in riuers swim, or brookes doe wade.
   All which not if an hundred tongues to tell,
   And hundred mouthes, and voice of brasse I had,
   And endlesse memorie, that mote excell,
In order as they came, could I recount them well.

10

Helpe therefore, O thou sacred imp of *Ioue*,
   The noursling of Dame *Memorie* his deare,
   To whom those rolles, layd vp in heauen aboue,
   And records of antiquitie appeare,
   To which no wit of man may comen neare;
   Helpe me to tell the names of all those floods,
   And all those Nymphes, which then assembled were
   To that great banquet of the watry Gods,
And all their sundry kinds, and all their hid abodes.

Stanza 7
6 like her thrall: even as Florimell is Proteus's 'eternall thrall' at III viii 41.9. **9 ouer all**: everywhere.

Stanzas 8–53
The marriage of the Thames and the Medway rivers was the subject of S.'s unpublished *Epithalamion Thamesis* which, as he told Harvey in 1580, was a work 'very profitable for the knowledge, and rare for the Inuention, and manner of handling' (Spenser 1912:612). In giving all the English rivers 'their righte names' through placing them in geographical order, as he also told him, Holinshed's *Chronicles* 'hath muche furthered and aduantaged me'. Paxson 1994:55–57 notes that the catalogue combines a procession of rivers and a list of Rivers, being both anthropomorphisms and prosopopoetic characters. S.'s generic model is the river-marriage poem, e.g. Leland, *Cygnea Cantio* (1545), and esp. Camden, *De Connubio Tamae et Isis*, fragments of which appear in *Britannia* (1586); see Herendeen 1986:242–50, and 'Camden' and 'rivers' in the *SEnc*. In *SC July* 81–84, S. refers to 'The salt Medway, that trickling stremis | adowne the dales of Kent: | Till with his elder brother Themis | his brackish waves be meynt'. The two rivers join at Rochester where S. served as the Bishop of Rochester's secretary. That he should change the sex of the Medway, and celebrate its union with the Thames in the Thames estuary where their waters mingle with the ocean, was explained by Upton 1758 as a compliment to the Sidney family: the Medway flows by Sidney's home at Penshurst. A. Fowler 1964:174 notes that it was the centre of naval operations in the 1590s, being so praised by Drayton 1931–41:4.366.

Stanza 8
6 bed: the delightful pun follows naturally from the marriage of the two rivers.

Stanza 9
2–3 The rivers meet **in Proteus house** – necessarily he is absent – because their waters flow into the sea. **most and**
least: the highest and lowest in rank. **4 trade**: go. **6–8** A Homeric motif, as in *Iliad* 2.484–93, adapted from Virgil, *Aen.* 6.623–26: e.g. voice of iron (*ferrea vox*) becomes **voice of brasse**. S. adds **endlesse memorie** to introduce the muses as daughters of Memory.

Stanza 10
1–2 Invoking Clio, the muse of history, who is the offspring of Jove and Mnemosyne, though see I proem 2.1*n* and I xi 5.6–9*n*. **4–5** Cf. II proem 1.9.

Stanzas 11–53
The wedding pageant describes the sea-gods and their seed 'In order as they came' (9.9; cf. xii 3.4–5), as the numerological analysis by A. Fowler 1964:182–91 shows. Its 'count | Of Gods, of Nymphs, of riuers' (xii 2.6–7) marks its main divisions.
I. Neptune and his seed (11–16). Neptune and Amphitrite preceded by Triton (11–12), and far after them, their offspring: the 17 sea-gods (13–14) who rule the waves, and the 9 founders of nations (15–16) who possess the world.
II. Ocean and his seed (18–52). Ocean and Tethys followed by their eldest son, Nereus (18–19), and
  i. rivers: (1) 18 world rivers (20–21)
    (2) English and Irish rivers (24–47)
      (a) led by Arion (23) and preceded by the Bridegroom's parents with their two grooms (24–26) the Bridegroom (27–28) with his 6 pages (29) followed by 34 neighbour floods (30–39) and 18 Irish rivers (40–44)
      (b) the Bride (45–46) with her 2 handmaids, preceded by 2 pages (45–47)
  ii. sea nymphs: the 50 daughters of Nereus and Doris (48–52).
Fowler 191 concludes that the high degree of formal organization is such that 'there would literally be no room for a single additional stanza or an extra river'.

11

First came great *Neptune* with his threeforkt mace,
    That rules the Seas, and makes them rise or fall;
    His dewy lockes did drop with brine apace,
    Vnder his Diademe imperiall:
    And by his side his Queene with coronall,
    Faire *Amphitrite*, most diuinely faire,
    Whose yuorie shoulders weren couered all,
    As with a robe, with her owne siluer haire,
And deckt with pearles, which th'Indian seas for her prepaire.

12

These marched farre afore the other crew;
    And all the way before them as they went,
    Triton his trompet shrill before them blew,
    For goodly triumph and great iollyment,
    That made the rockes to roare, as they were rent.
    And after them the royall issue came,
    Which of them sprung by lineall descent:
    First the Sea-gods, which to themselues doe clame
The powre to rule the billowes, and the waues to tame.

13

Phorcys, the father of that fatall brood,
    By whom those old Heroes wonne such fame;
    And *Glaucus*, that wise southsayes vnderstood;
    And tragicke *Inoes* sonne, the which became

A God of seas through his mad mothers blame,
    Now hight *Palemon*, and is saylers frend;
    Great *Brontes*, and *Astraeus*, that did shame
    Himselfe with incest of his kin vnkend;
And huge *Orion*, that doth tempests still portend.

14

The rich *Cteatus*, and *Eurytus* long;
    Neleus and *Pelias* louely brethren both;
    Mightie *Chrysaor*, and *Caïcus* strong;
    Eurypulus, that calmes the waters wroth;
    And faire *Euphœmus*, that vpon them goth
    As on the ground, without dismay or dread:
    Fierce *Eryx*, and *Alebius* that know'th
    The waters depth, and doth their bottome tread;
And sad *Asopus*, comely with his hoarie head.

15

There also some most famous founders were
    Of puissant Nations, which the world possest;
    Yet sonnes of *Neptune*, now assembled here:
    Ancient *Ogyges*, euen th'auncientest,
    And *Inachus* renowmd aboue the rest;
    Phœnix, and *Aon*, and *Pelasgus* old,
    Great *Belus*, *Phœax*, and *Agenor* best;
    And mightie *Albion*, father of the bold
And warlike people, which the *Britaine* Islands hold.

Stanza 11

1–2 his threeforkt mace: his trident by which he raises and calmes storms, though not usually the tides. **5–9 Amphitrite**: 'daughter to Nereus, and wyfe to Neptunus, God of the sea, And some tyme it is taken for the sea' (T. Cooper 1565). She shares her name with a nereid at 49.2. **coronall**: coronet.

Stanza 12

3 Triton: herald of the sea-gods and son of Neptune, whose horn causes the waters in flood to retreat to their natural state in Ovid, *Met*. 1.331–47. He is heard 'blowing loud his wreathed horne' in *Colin Clout* 245. **8–9** They assume this power from Neptune (11.2).

Stanzas 13–14

To the catalogue of the sea-gods in Conti 1616:2.8, S. adds Glaucus, and selects his names in order to tell 'Onely what needeth' (17.7).

Stanza 13

1–2 Phorcys: one of his **fatall brood** opposed by the **old Heroes** is Medusa slain by Perseus, to which S. alludes in *Time* 647–49. Another is the dragon, slain by Hercules, that guarded the garden of the Hesperides, to which S. alludes at II vii 54.5–6. **3 Glaucus** was known for his prophetic powers. **4–6** In *Met*. 4.512–42, Ovid tells the story of how the maddened Ino threw herself and her son Melicerta from a cliff into the sea; **mad mother** renders *conita mater* (519). **blame**: fault. **Now hight Palemon**: the climax of the story when the son is saved and became a new god, *Palaemona dixit*. **saylers frend**: from Conti 1616:8.4. **7–8 Great Brontes**: *maxime Brontes* (Conti 9.8), one of the Cyclops. **Astraeus** committed

incest with his sister, as Conti 2.8 records. **9 huge Orion**: referring to the large, conspicuous constellation, called 'great' at VII vii 39.8.

Stanza 14

1 Cteatus is **rich** from Gk κτέανα, possessions, wealth. **Eurytus** is **long** from εὐρύς, long. **2 louely**: not in Conti 1616. **3 Chrysaor** is **Mightie** as the father of Geryon; or because it is an epithet of Apollo: see V i 9.5–9*n*. **Caïcus** may be strong because a Trojan of that name defended Troy; see Virgil, *Aen*. 9.35–38. **4–8** S. invents the power given **Eurypulus** but follows Conti closely in the power given **Euphœmus**. The biblical echoes are noted by MacColl 1989:39. David says that God 'turneth the storme to calme, so that the waues thereof are stil' (Ps. 107.29), and Job says that God 'walketh vpon the height of the sea' (Job 9.8) and 'couereth the bottome of the sea' (36.30). **Fierce Eryx**: possibly *acer Eryx* in Virgil, *Aen*. 5.402, but more likely his ancestor, named by T. Cooper 1565 as the son of Neptune and Venus. **Alebius**: only named by Conti. His powers counter those of Euphœmus. **9 Asopus** is **sad** because his daughter Aegina was raped by Jove; see III xi 35.2.

Stanzas 15–16

While S. draws the catalogue of the famous founders of nations from Conti 1616:2.8, he orders them from the most ancient to the most recent, adds Inachus, the story of Albion whom Conti only names, and most of the characterizing descriptions.

Stanza 15

4 Ogyges: founder of Thebes (T. Cooper 1565), reputed the oldest city in the world. **5** In Alma's castle, Eumnestes's

16

For *Albion* the sonne of *Neptune* was,
  Who for the proofe of his great puissance,
  Out of his *Albion* did on dry-foot pas
  Into old *Gall*, that now is cleeped *France*,
  To fight with *Hercules*, that did aduance
  To vanquish all the world with matchlesse might,
  And there his mortall part by great mischance
  Was slaine: but that which is th'immortall spright
Liues still: and to this feast with *Neptunes* seed was dight.

17

But what doe I their names seeke to reherse,
  Which all the world haue with their issue fild?
  How can they all in this so narrow verse
  Contayned be, and in small compasse hild?
  Let them record them, that are better skild,
  And know the moniments of passed times:
  Onely what needeth, shall be here fulfild,
  T'expresse some part of that great equipage,
Which from great *Neptune* do deriue their parentage.

18

Next came the aged *Ocean*, and his Dame,
  Old *Tethys*, th'oldest two of all the rest,
  For all the rest of those two parents came,
  Which afterward both sea and land possest:

Of all which *Nereus* th'eldest, and the best,
  Did first proceed, then which none more vpright,
  Ne more sincere in word and deed profest;
  Most voide of guile, most free from fowle despight,
Doing him selfe, and teaching others to doe right.

19

Thereto he was expert in prophecies,
  And could the ledden of the Gods vnfold,
  Through which, when *Paris* brought his famous prise
  The faire Tindarid lasse, he him fortold,
  That her all *Greece* with many a champion bold
  Should fetch againe, and finally destroy
  Proud *Priams* towne. So wise is *Nereus* old,
  And so well skild; nathlesse he takes great ioy
Oft-times amongst the wanton Nymphs to sport and toy.

20

And after him the famous riuers came,
  Which doe the earth enrich and beautifie:
  The fertile Nile, which creatures new doth frame;
  Long Rhodanus, whose sourse springs from the skie;
  Faire Ister, flowing from the mountaines hie;
  Diuine Scamander, purpled yet with blood
  Of Greekes and Troians, which therein did die;
  Pactolus glistring with his golden flood,
And Tygris fierce, whose streames of none may be withstood.

---

memory goes back to '*Inachus* diuine' (II ix 56.9) who was the founder of Argos. Called *celeberrimum* by Conti 1616:8.22. **6–7 Phœnix**: the founder of Phoenicia; named third as he is third in line from Neptune, and the son of Agenor who rounds out this two-line grouping. **Aon**: founder of Aonia. **Pelasgus** is **old** because the Pelasgi, named after him, are 'people whiche came out of Greece' (Cooper), i.e. they were its earliest inhabitants. **Belus** is **Great** because he was 'an auncient kynge of Assyria, to whom the fyrst ymage or ydole to be honoured, was made' (Cooper); or because he was reputed to be the founder of Babylon. **Phœax**: founder of Phaeacia. **Agenor** is **best** either as founder of Carthage (*Aen.* 1.338) or as the father of Cadmus who built Thebes (Cooper).

Stanza 16

Albion: named 'the sonne of Neptune' in Holinshed 1807–08:1.6. On his defeat by Hercules, see II x 11.5–9*n*. **3 on dry-foot**: see II x 5.5–9. **4 Gall**: Lat. form of Gaul. **5 aduance**: go forward; propose; boast. **9 was dight**: i.e. made its way.

Stanza 17

This stanza of authorial comment is added to divide Neptune's seed from Ocean's, the break being marked by pointers: 'First came' (11.1) and 'Next came' (18.1). **1 reherse**: recount in order. **6 times**: 'age', conj. Church 1758 for the rhyme, but S.'s word suggests a pun on 'Thames', whose monument he is building in this canto. **8 equipage**: following. **9 deriue**: the playful etymological pun, 'cause to flow away' (*OED* 1.2), is noted by Silberman 1995:131.

Stanza 18

1–4 Ocean and **Tethys** are the source of all waters, for 'from the Ocean all riuers spring' (VI proem 7.4). **4** refers back to the gods who govern the sea (12.8–9) and the founders of nations who possess the world (15.2), and then forward to the rivers that possess the land in being possessed by it, a syntactical ambiguity noted by Berger 1988:206.

Stanza 19

1–2 Nereus is the counterpart to 'Fond *Proteus*, father of false prophecis' (III iv 37.1). **ledden**: speech. **3–7 Tindarid lasse**: Helen of Troy, so named as the daughter of Tyndareus, e.g. by Virgil, *Aen.* 2.601. Troy is 'named' by the pun on **destroy**. On the story of Paris, see II vii 55.4–9*n*. **fortold**: warned beforehand. **Nereus old**: *grandaevus Nereus* (Virgil, *Georg.* 4.392).

Stanza 20

3 On the Nile's fertility, see I i 21.6–9*n*. **4–5 Rhodanus**: the Rhone; its source lies in the high Alps, as does the **Ister** or Danube. **6–7 Scamander**, the scene of battles in the Trojan war, is called **Diuine** because the gods named it Xanthus; see III ix 35.6–9*n*. **8 Pactolus**: see vi 20.7–9. **9 Tygris fierce**: the epithet derives from the name. 'From him [the tiger] the River Tigris is named, because it is the most rapid of all rivers' (T.H. White 1954:12). Two other rivers of Eden are named in the next line. Together with the **Nile**, they encompass Eden and therefore the whole world. See I vii 43.7–9, and *Rome* 424.

21
Great Ganges, and immortall Euphrates,
  Deepe Indus, and Mæander intricate,
  Slow Peneus, and tempestuous Phasides,
  Swift Rhene, and Alpheus still immaculate:
  Ooraxes, feared for great *Cyrus* fate;
  Tybris, renowmed for the Romaines fame,
  Rich Oranochy, though but knowen late;
  And that huge Riuer, which doth beare his name
Of warlike Amazons, which doe possesse the same.

22
Ioy on those warlike women, which so long
  Can from all men so rich a kingdome hold;
  And shame on you, ô men, which boast your strong
  And valiant hearts, in thoughts lesse hard and bold,
  Yet quaile in conquest of that land of gold.
  But this to you, ô Britons, most pertaines,
  To whom the right hereof it selfe hath sold;
  The which for sparing litle cost or paines,
Loose so immortall glory, and so endlesse gaines.

23
Then was there heard a most celestiall sound,
  Of dainty musicke, which did next ensew
  Before the spouse: that was *Arion* crownd;
  Who playing on his harpe, vnto him drew

The eares and hearts of all that goodly crew,
That euen yet the Dolphin, which him bore
Through the Ægæan seas from Pirates vew,
Stood still by him astonisht at his lore,
And all the raging seas for ioy forgot to rore.

24
So went he playing on the watery plaine.
  Soone after whom the louely Bridegroome came,
  The noble Thamis, with all his goodly traine,
  But him before there went, as best became,
  His auncient parents, namely th'auncient Thame.
  But much more aged was his wife then he,
  The Ouze, whom men doe Isis rightly name;
  Full weake and crooked creature seemed shee,
And almost blind through eld, that scarce her way could see.

25
Therefore on either side she was sustained
  Of two smal grooms, which by their names were hight
  The *Churne*, and *Charwell*, two small streames, which pained
  Them selues her footing to direct aright,
  Which fayled oft through faint and feeble plight:
  But *Thame* was stronger, and of better stay;
  Yet seem'd full aged by his outward sight,
  With head all hoary, and his beard all gray,
Deawed with siluer drops, that trickled downe alway.

Stanza 21
1 Ganges: 'a great ryuer . . . called in holy scripture *Phison*, one of the fowre ryuers whiche come out of Paradise' (T. Cooper 1565). The **Euphrates** or Perath appears as a major river in the Geneva map for Gen. 2.10–14. **2 Indus**: 'A noble ryuer, that . . . incloseth Indie on the west' (Cooper). **Mæander**: the epithet provides the etymology of the name; 'hereof all crooked and subtylle tournyng wayes, meanes and diuises be called *Mæandri*' (Cooper). A. Fowler 1989a:41 notes how the epithet weaves with the name. **3 Peneus**: 'a ryuer in Greece' (Cooper), **Slow** because old, as at *Proth* 78; called *Peneus senex* by Ovid, *Met.* 2.243. **Phasides**: its swift waters are mentioned in *Met.* 7.6. **4 Rhene**: the Rhine; perhaps **Swift** because 'renish' means 'fierce', 'wild'. **Alpheus** is called **immaculate** because the river flows under the sea from Arcadia to Sicily without mingling with salt water (Virgil, *Aen.* 3.694–96). **still**: always. **5** Cyrus's decision to cross the **Ooraxes** resulted in his death, as Herodotus, *History* 1.201–14 records. **6 Tybris**: on the association of the Tiber with Rome, see, e.g. I ii 22.7–9. **7–9 Oranochy**: the Orinoco, **Rich** because Raleigh hoped it would lead him to El Dorado, as he reported in *Discovery of Guiana* (1596). **that huge Riuer**: the Amazon, so described at II proem 2.8. **his name**: the gender is cited as an example of women triumphing over men, as Knapp 1992:178 notes.

Stanza 22
5–9 that land of gold is Guiana with the empire of the Amazons on its southern border, the **right** to it allegedly given by its inhabitants to England. Raleigh 1965:165 complains that Guiana 'hath yet her maidenhead' and urges Elizabeth to possess it. S.'s exhortation was topical, e.g. Chapman, *De*

Guiana (1596). See S. Miller 1998:170–72. On Raleigh and the Amazons, see Montrose 1993:201–05.

Stanza 23
3–9 The story of Arion is told by Ovid in *Fasti* 2.79–118; cf. *Am* 38.1–4. **lore**: song; learning or skill.

Stanzas 24–47
The twenty-four stanzas that catalogue the English and Irish rivers as parties of the bridegroom are examined by Osgood 1920 (extracted in *Var* 4.250–73), to which the annotations below on S.'s sources are indebted.

Stanza 24
3–7 Holinshed 1807–08:1.79 notes that the river is called the Isis or Ouse at its source but later joins the Thame to receive the composite name, Thamesis or Thames. W. Camden 1637:384 refers to the confluence of the Tame and the Isis as 'joynd in Wedlocke'. They precede Thames being his parents and as their waters join upstream (near Dorchester) to his. Saxton's 1579 map of England shows the crooked course of the Isis. **7–9** Isis is **eld** because she bears the name of an Egyptian divinity invented by 'the antique world' (V vii 2.1).

Stanza 25
3 Holinshed 1807–08:1.79 records that the Ouze 'runneth directlie toward the east . . . and meeteth with the Cirne or Churne. . . . it passeth at length by Oxford . . . where it meeteth with the Charwell'. He also records that the Chirne joins the Isis 'on the left side' (which would be west) and that the Charwell joins it from the east at Oxford (79, 82, 84). **6 stay**: strength.

26

And eke he somewhat seem'd to stoupe afore
    With bowed backe, by reason of the lode,
    And auncient heauy burden, which he bore
    Of that faire City, wherein make abode
    So many learned impes, that shoote abrode,
    And with their braunches spred all Britany,
    No lesse then do her elder sisters broode.
Ioy to you both, ye double noursery,
Of Arts, but Oxford thine doth *Thame* most glorify.

27

But he their sonne full fresh and iolly was,
    All decked in a robe of watchet hew,
    On which the waues, glittering like Christall glas,
    So cunningly enwouen were, that few
    Could weenen, whether they were false or trew.
    And on his head like to a Coronet
    He wore, that seemed strange to common vew,
    In which were many towres and castels set,
That it encompast round as with a golden fret.

28

Like as the mother of the Gods, they say,
    In her great iron charet wonts to ride,
    When to *Ioues* pallace she doth take her way;
    Old *Cybele*, arayd with pompous pride,

Wearing a Diademe embattild wide
    With hundred turrets, like a Turribant.
    With such an one was Thamis beautifide;
    That was to weet the famous Troynouant,
In which her kingdomes throne is chiefly resiant.

29

And round about him many a pretty Page
    Attended duely, ready to obay;
    All little Riuers, which owe vassallage
    To him, as to their Lord, and tribute pay:
    The chaulky Kenet, and the Thetis gray,
    The morish Cole, and the soft sliding Breane,
    The wanton Lee, that oft doth loose his way,
    And the still Darent, in whose waters cleane
Ten thousand fishes play, and decke his pleasant streame.

30

Then came his neighbour flouds, which nigh him dwell,
    And water all the English soile throughout;
    They all on him this day attended well;
    And with meet seruice waited him about;
    Ne none disdained low to him to lout:
    No not the stately Seuerne grudg'd at all,
    Ne storming Humber, though he looked stout;
    But both him honor'd as their principall,
And let their swelling waters low before him fall.

Stanza 26

1–4 Referring to the bend in the Isis (rather than the Thame) at Oxford, which appears on the map as though the river were borne down by the weight of the city. **7 her elder sister:** Cambridge, founded earlier than Oxford, so the Cantabrigian S. prefers to believe while allowing that Oxford scholars **spred all Britany** (i.e. Britain), including, presumably, Cambridge. Hence **impes,** which refers to scholars in *Teares* 75, refers also to shoots that are engrafted (*OED* v.1).

Stanza 27

1 **full fresh** would seem to describe the river in spring flood. 2 **watchet:** light blue. **6–9 like to a Coronet:** Saxton's map shows London on the Thames as a crowded cluster of towers arranged like a coronet. **fret:** an ornamental border of intersecting lines; here the streets. A. Fowler 1970:67*n*4 observes that the bridegroom is honoured by appearing in the canto's central stanza.

Stanza 28

1–6 **Cybele:** 'named of Paynims the mother of the goddes' (T. Cooper 1565). For her role in the poem, see P.A. Parker 1987:59–60 and 'Cybele' in the *SEnc.* She appears with towered crown because she first taught men to fortify cities. (A crown marks the chief cities on Elizabethan maps.) In Virgil, *Aen.* 6.784–87, the simile heralds famed Rome (*incluta Roma*); used here, it suggests that **famous Troynouant** or London replaces Rome; cf. *Rome* 71–74. **pompous:** stately, ceremonious. **embattild:** having its sides shaped like battlements. **hundred turrets:** as the hundred gods held by Cybele, *Aen.* 6.786. **Turribant:** turban; literally, a band of turrets. **9 her:** referring to Cybele whose throne now resides chiefly in London.

Stanza 29

1–2 As Cybele in Virgil is shown clasping her offspring. 5–9 These six rivers **tribute pay** to the Thames because they are its tributaries, here named in order as they join the Thames. The **Kenet** is **chaulky** because its source is near Marlborough (from 'marl', chalk) and it is joined by the Chalkburne (Holinshed 1807–08:1.85). The **Thetis** may be called **gray** to make him a fitting companion to the Kenet. The **Cole** is **morish,** i.e. moorish or marshy, in contrast to the **Breane.** The **Lee** is called **wanton** from his devious route, as **loose** suggests. It appears in *Proth* 38. **Darent:** derived from Lat. *dare,* to give; hence its fruitfulness.

Stanzas 30–39

The **34 neighbour flouds** catalogued here plus the 6 tributaries of the Thames as 'their principall' (30.8) make up 40 English rivers. The generative and harmonic properties of this *tetractys* are noted by A. Fowler 1964:189. Herendeen 1986:248 notes that S. mentions the Seuerne and the Humber first because they are the Thames's two greatest rivals, and begins his catalogue in the west as does Camden, 'spirals east and north, and then south along the west coast to the Dee and Conway'.

Stanza 30

6 The **Seuerne** is **stately** because 'severane' is an obs. form of 'sovereign'. It forms the boundary between England and Wales; see II x 14.5. That it **grudg'd** [not] **at all** signifies the peaceful unification of the two countries in the Tudor line, as Erickson 1996:90 notes. 7 **storming Humber:** from Gk ὄμβρος, storm, as shown at 37.8–9. **stout:** arrogant; fierce.

31

There was the speedy Tamar, which deuides
    The Cornish and the Deuonish confines;
    Through both whose borders swiftly downe it glides,
    And meeting Plim, to Plimmouth thence declines:
    And Dart, nigh chockt with sands of tinny mines.
    But Auon marched in more stately path,
    Proud of his Adamants, with which he shines
    And glisters wide, as als' of wondrous Bath,
And Bristow faire, which on his waues he builded hath.

32

And there came Stoure with terrible aspect,
    Bearing his six deformed heads on hye,
    That doth his course through Blandford plains direct,
    And washeth Winborne meades in season drye.
    Next him went Wylibourne with passage slye,
    That of his wylinesse his name doth take,
    And of him selfe doth name the shire thereby:
    And Mole, that like a nousling Mole doth make
His way still vnder ground, till Thamis he ouertake.

33

Then came the Rother, decked all with woods
    Like a wood God, and flowing fast to Rhy:
    And Sture, that parteth with his pleasant floods
    The Easterne Saxons from the Southerne ny,
    And Clare, and Harwitch both doth beautify:
    Him follow'd Yar, soft washing Norwitch wall,
    And with him brought a present ioyfully
    Of his owne fish vnto their festiuall,
Whose like none else could shew, the which they Ruffins call.

34

Next these the plenteous Ouse came far from land,
    By many a city, and by many a towne,
    And many riuers taking vnder hand
    Into his waters, as he passeth downe,
    The Cle, the Were, the Grant, the Sture, the Rowne.
    Thence doth by Huntingdon and Cambridge flit,
    My mother Cambridge, whom as with a Crowne
    He doth adorne, and is adorn'd of it
With many a gentle Muse, and many a learned wit.

35

And after him the fatall Welland went,
    That if old sawes proue true (which God forbid)
    Shall drowne all Holland with his excrement,
    And shall see Stamford, though now homely hid,
    Then shine in learning, more then euer did
    Cambridge or Oxford, Englands goodly beames.
    And next to him the Nene downe softly slid;
    And bounteous Trent, that in him selfe enseames
Both thirty sorts of fish, and thirty sundry streames.

36

Next these came Tyne, along whose stony bancke
    That Romaine Monarch built a brasen wall,
    Which mote the feebled Britons strongly flancke
    Against the Picts, that swarmed ouer all,
    Which yet thereof Gualseuer they doe call:
    And Twede the limit betwixt Logris land
    And Albany: And Eden though but small,
    Yet often stainde with bloud of many a band
Of Scots and English both, that tyned on his strand.

Stanza 31
1–4 The **Tamar**, which forms the boundary between Devonshire and Cornwall, 'taketh his course with a swift running streame southward' (W. Camden 1637:196). S. errs in saying that it meets the **Plim**, as Osgood 1920:75 notes. 5 Sand from tin mines 'choketh the depth' of the **Dart** (Holinshed 1807–08:1.103). 6–9 The **Auon** is 'growne to be verie famous' (Holinshed 1.115), as marked by its **stately path** in contrast to the swift and the sluggish courses of the other two. **Adamants**: Bristol-diamonds, rock crystal or quartz.

Stanza 32
1–4 Holinshed 1807–08:1.98 notes that the **Stoure** 'riseth of six heads' but not the other facts given here. It has a **terrible aspect** because its name signifies 'tumult'. 8–9 The **Mole** 'maketh himselfe a way under the ground in manner of mouldwarpe . . . whereof it may seeme it tooke name, seeing that creature living within the ground, is called also in English a *Mole*' (W. Camden 1637:296).

Stanza 33
1–2 The region where the Rother takes its rise 'by reason of the woods was hardly passable' (W. Camden 1637:306). 3–5 'The Sture or Stoure parteth Essex from Suffolke' (Holinshed 1807–08:1.177). 6–9 On Saxton's map, the **Yar** seems to touch Norwich. It brings fish to the wedding because the name signifies a fishgarth, an enclosure in a river to catch fish (*OED*). Also it teems with ruff, as Camden 476 observes.

Stanza 34
1 **Ouse**: the Great Ouse in the East Midlands. 5 These five tributaries are named generally in order as the Ouse flows to the sea. **Grant**: the Granta or Cam. **Rowne**: 'Downe', conj. Osgood 1920:81, or the Little Ouse. 6 Referring to the river system, for the towns are not on the same river. 7 **My mother Cambridge**: a fitting description for S.'s *alma mater*. Its official crest is a woman with flowing breasts.

Stanza 35
1–3 Drayton 1931–41:4.477 records the prophecy 'from Ages past' that the **Welland** should drown that part of Norfolk called Holland, as its name, which signifies 'pouring forth on the land', suggests. See Tilley W266. **excrement** is suggested by a pun on **Holland**, hole-land. 4–6 In Drayton 4.154, Selden records 'that suppos'd prophesie of *Merlin*' that the University of Stamford would rival Oxford, 'which you shall have *Englished* in that solemnized marriage of *Thames* and *Medway*, by a most admired Muse of our nation'. 7 The **Nene** (or Avon) **softly slid** because 'it diuideth it selfe into sundrie armes, and those into seuerall branches and draines, among the fennes and medowes, not possible almost to be numbred' (Holinshed 1807–08:1.172). 8–9 **thirty**: as **Trent** signifies thirty (Fr. *trente*). **enseames**: contains.

Stanza 36
1–5 **That Romaine Monarch** is Constantine II who, according to S., built the Picts Wall; see II x 63.7–9. **brasen**: as

37

Then came those six sad brethren, like forlorne,
  That whilome were (as antique fathers tell)
  Six valiant Knights, of one faire Nymphe yborne,
  Which did in noble deedes of armes excell,
  And wonned there, where now Yorke people dwell;
  Still Vre, swift Werfe, and Oze the most of might,
  High Swale, vnquiet Nide, and troublous Skell;
  All whom a Scythian king, that Humber hight,
Slew cruelly, and in the riuer drowned quight.

38

But past not long, ere *Brutus* warlicke sonne
  Locrinus them aueng'd, and the same date,
  Which the proud Humber vnto them had donne,
  By equall dome repayd on his owne pate:
  For in the selfe same riuer, where he late
  Had drenched them, he drowned him againe;
  And nam'd the riuer of his wretched fate;
  Whose bad condition yet it doth retaine,
Oft tossed with his stormes, which therein still remaine.

39

These after, came the stony shallow Lone,
  That to old Loncaster his name doth lend;
  And following Dee, which Britons long ygone
  Did call diuine, that doth by Chester tend;

And Conway which out of his streame doth send
  Plenty of pearles to decke his dames withall,
  And Lindus that his pikes doth most commend,
  Of which the auncient Lincolne men doe call,
All these together marched toward *Proteus* hall.

40

Ne thence the Irishe Riuers absent were,
  Sith no lesse famous then the rest they bee,
  And ioyne in neighbourhood of kingdome nere,
  Why should they not likewise in loue agree,
  And ioy likewise this solemne day to see?
  They saw it all, and present were in place;
  Though I them all according their degree,
  Cannot recount, nor tell their hidden race,
Nor read the saluage cuntries, thorough which they pace.

41

There was the Liffy rolling downe the lea,
  The sandy Slane, the stony Aubrian,
  The spacious Shenan spreading like a sea,
  The pleasant Boyne, the fishy fruitfull Ban,
  Swift Awniduff, which of the English man
  Is cal'de Blacke water, and the Liffar deep,
  Sad Trowis, that once his people ouerran,
  Strong *Allo* tombling from Slewlogher steep,
And *Mulla* mine, whose waues I whilom taught to weep.

---

strong as brass. **flancke**: defend on the flank. **Gualseuer**: i.e. the wall of Severus. **6–7** The boundary between England and Scotland; cf. II x 14.5. **7–9** The drowning of border-raiders in the **Eden** is recorded by W. Camden 1637:776. **tyned**: perished, as the river's name indicates.

Stanza 37

2 The unique reference to **antique fathers** indicates that the tale, which S. devises to explain why the six tributaries of the Ouse are literally **drowned** when they flow into the Humber, is his own. **6–7** While not in geographical order, as Osgood 1920:87 notes, there is a climactic order of adjectives in each line, mixing geographical and etymological detail. W. Camden 1637:701, 696 records that the **Vre** flows gently; the **Werfe** is **swift** from its etymology: 'the word *Guer* . . . in British signifieth *Swift* and *Violent*'; and the **Oze** is **most of might** because the others join it. The **Swale** is **High** because its name is an obs. form of 'swell'; the **Nide** is **vnquiet** because the name is an obs. form of 'need', i.e. disturbance; and the **Skell** is **troublous** because 'skellum' means rascal. **8 Scythian**: evidently so-called in being a barbarian, one of the nation that had inhabited northern Europe, including England and Ireland; see *View* 37–38, and Shuger 1997:495–501.

Stanza 38

This history is recorded at II x 15–16. **2 date**: thing given or done (from Lat. *datum*); or limit to the term of life. **4** Cf. Ps. 7.16: 'His crueltie shal fall vpon his owne pate'. **dome**: punishment or death. **6 drenched**: drowned. **8–9** See 30.7*n*. **condition**: nature.

Stanza 39

1–2 Loncaster: as though from 'loan' (or lone) + Lat. *castra*, camp. **3–4** W. Camden 1637:602 records that the **Dee** (from Lat. *diva*) was held to possess power of divination. **tend**: make its way. **7–8 Lindus** was an old name of Witham, which was famous throughout England for its pike, according to Holinshed 1807–08:1.169.

Stanzas 40–44

From S.'s descriptions of the Irish rivers, Joyce 1911:72–114 concludes that his chief authority is personal experience. The parallel between the 18 Irish rivers and the 18 world rivers in 20–21 is indicated by 'famous' (20.1, 40.2). See the map in Judson 1933:59.

Stanza 40

7 according: fitting. **8 race**: also rush of water. **9 saluage**: S.'s frequent epithet for Ireland; see V xi 39.3*n*. **cuntreis**: i.e. counties or regions, as 42.9.

Stanza 41

The rivers are named in their order, as Joyce 1911:85–86 notes. For the **stony Aubrian**, which he could not identify, R. Smith 1944 suggests the Aherlow. **7 Sad Trowis**: from Irish *truaghas*, sadness (Joyce 79). The legend of its flooding is recorded by earlier Irish writers. **9 Mulla mine**: celebrated in *Colin Clout*; see VII vi 40.3–6*n*.

42

And there the three renowmed brethren were,
   Which that great Gyant *Blomius* begot,
   Of the faire Nimph *Rheusa* wandring there.
   One day, as she to shunne the season whot,
   Vnder Slewbloome in shady groue was got,
   This Gyant found her, and by force deflowr'd,
   Whereof conceiuing, she in time forth brought
   These three faire sons, which being thence forth powrd
In three great riuers ran, and many countreis scowrd.

43

The first, the gentle Shure that making way
   By sweet Clonmell, adornes rich Waterford;
   The next, the stubborne Newre, whose waters gray
   By faire Kilkenny and Rosseponte boord,
   The third, the goodly Barow, which doth hoord
   Great heapes of Salmons in his deepe bosome:
   All which long sundred, doe at last accord
   To ioyne in one, ere to the sea they come,
So flowing all from one, all one at last become.

44

There also was the wide embayed Mayre,
   The pleasaunt Bandon crownd with many a wood,
   The spreading Lee, that like an Island fayre
   Encloseth Corke with his deuided flood;
   And balefull Oure, late staind with English blood:
   With many more, whose names no tongue can tell.
   All which that day in order seemly good
   Did on the Thamis attend, and waited well
To doe their duefull seruice, as to them befell.

45

Then came the Bride, the louely *Medua* came,
   Clad in a vesture of vnknowen geare,
   And vncouth fashion, yet her well became;
   That seem'd like siluer, sprinckled here and theare
   With glittering spangs, that did like starres appeare,
   And wau'd vpon, like water Chamelot,
   To hide the metall, which yet euery where
   Bewrayd it selfe, to let men plainely wot,
It was no mortall worke, that seem'd and yet was not.

46

Her goodly lockes adowne her backe did flow
   Vnto her waste, with flowres bescattered,
   The which ambrosiall odours forth did throw
   To all about, and all her shoulders spred
   As a new spring; and likewise on her hed
   A Chapelet of sundry flowers she wore,
   From vnder which the deawy humour shed,
   Did tricle downe her haire, like to the hore
Congealed litle drops, which doe the morne adore.

47

On her two pretty handmaides did attend,
   One cald the *Theise*, the other cald the *Crane*;
   Which on her waited, things amisse to mend,
   And both behind vpheld her spredding traine;
   Vnder the which, her feet appeared plaine,
   Her siluer feet, faire washt against this day:
   And her before there paced Pages twaine,
   Both clad in colours like, and like array,
The *Doune* and eke the *Frith*, both which prepard her way.

Stanza 42

This etiological tale is S.'s. As Joyce 1911:86 notes, only the Barrow has its source in the Slieve Bloom Mountains, personified as **Blomius**. W. Camden 1637 calls them the Three Sisters. **Rheusa** is named from Gk ῥέω, to flow, as Joyce notes.

Stanza 43

1 the gentle Shure: called 'the faire *Shure*' at VII vi 54.9. **2** The **Clonmell** is **sweet** because of its name, Lat. *mel*, honey. **3 stubborne**: fierce, untamable. **4 boord**: border on. **5–6 Barow**: the name suggests barrow, a mountain or hill, and hence its **Great heapes** of salmon.

Stanza 44

1 embayed: formed into bays. **5 Oure**: the Avonbeg in Glenmalure called **balefull** because Lord Grey's forces were severely defeated there by Irish rebels in 1580.

Stanza 45

1 Medua: 'The Midwaie water is called in Latine Medeuia (as some write) bicause the course therof is midwaie in a manner betweene London and . . . Canturburie' (Holinshed 1807–08:1.90). **2 geare**: material. **5 spangs**: spangles. **6** I.e. with an undulating design shimmering in the light like camlet, a fabric with a moiré or wavy finish. **7–9** In contrast to the arras in the house of Busirane at III xi 28.4–7. **Bewrayd**: revealed.

Stanza 46

1–2 At II iii 30.5–9, Belphœbe's hair is seen enwrapped with flowers, and at 22.7 her cheeks throw forth 'ambrosiall odours'. **7–8 humour**: moisture. **like to the hore**: i.e. like hoar-frost. **adore**: adorn.

Stanza 47

1–4 The two rivers that join the Medway – see Holinshed 1807–08:1.90–91 – are (for S.) appropriately named: **Theise**: from Gk θεῖσα, dedicated; and **Crane**, an emblem of diligence in Ripa 1603:502–03. **6** Wittily adapts the ceremonial feet-washing at marriage.

Stanzas 48–52

As daughters of Nereus, the **Nereides** form a separate group that returns the cycle of waters to 18.5–19.9. The major classical sources for their names are Homer, *Iliad* 18.39–49, Virgil, *Aen.* 5.825–26, and esp. Hesiod, *Theog.* 240–64 in Mombritius's Lat. tr. in which epithets were added (rpt *Var* 4.274–75). See 'Nereids' in the *SEnc*. S. differs from his sources by adding **Phao** and **Poris** (in place of two he omitted) in order to make a full complement of 50, and goes beyond them in devising a significant epithet for all except seven, as Lotspeich 1932 notes. Starnes and Talbert 1955:106–07 show similar etymologizing in contemporary dictionaries. Some epithets translate Mombritius; some unfold the Greek root of the name; and some depend on literary associations. Only a few

48

And after these the Sea Nymphs marched all,
   All goodly damzels, deckt with long greene haire,
   Whom of their sire *Nereides* men call,
   All which the Oceans daughter to him bare
   The gray eyde *Doris*: all which fifty are;
   All which she there on her attending had.
   Swift *Proto*, milde *Eucrate*, *Thetis* faire,
   Soft *Spio*, sweete *Eudore*, *Sao* sad,
Light *Doto*, wanton *Glauce*, and *Galene* glad.

49

White hand *Eunica*, proud *Dynamene*,
   Ioyous *Thalia*, goodly *Amphitrite*,
   Louely *Pasithee*, kinde *Eulimene*,
   Light foote *Cymothoe*, and sweete *Melite*,
   Fairest *Pherusa*, *Phao* lilly white,
   Wondred *Agaue*, *Poris*, and *Nesæa*,
   With *Erato* that doth in loue delite,
   And *Panopæ*, and wise *Protomedæa*,
And snowy neckd *Doris*, and milkewhite *Galathæa*.

50

Speedy *Hippothoe*, and chaste *Actea*,
   Large *Lisianassa*, and *Pronæa* sage,
   Euagore, and light *Pontoporea*,
   And she, that with her least word can asswage
   The surging seas, when they do sorest rage,
   Cymodoce, and stout *Autonoe*,
   And *Neso*, and *Eione* well in age,
   And seeming still to smile, *Glauconome*,
And she that hight of many heastes *Polynome*.

51

Fresh *Alimeda*, deckt with girlond greene;
   Hyponeo, with salt bedewed wrests:
   Laomedia, like the christall sheene;
   Liagore, much praisd for wise behests;
   And *Psamathe*, for her brode snowy brests;
   Cymo, *Eupompe*, and *Themiste* iust;
   And she that vertue loues and vice detests
   Euarna, and *Menippe* true in trust,
And *Nemertea* learned well to rule her lust.

52

All these the daughters of old *Nereus* were,
   Which haue the sea in charge to them assinde,
   To rule his tides, and surges to vprere,
   To bring forth stormes, or fast them to vpbinde,
   And sailers saue from wreckes of wrathfull winde.
   And yet besides three thousand more there were
   Of th'Oceans seede, but *Ioues* and *Phœbus* kinde;
   The which in floods and fountaines doe appere,
And all mankinde do nourish with their waters clere.

53

The which, more eath it were for mortall wight,
   To tell the sands, or count the starres on hye,
   Or ought more hard, then thinke to reckon right.
   But well I wote, that these which I descry,
   Were present at this great solemnity:
   And there amongst the rest, the mother was
   Of luckelesse *Marinell Cymodoce*,
   Which, for my Muse her selfe now tyred has,
Vnto an other Canto I will ouerpas.

examples are noted below. For a more full account, see Braden 1975:31–34, and the thirteen etymologies listed by Lotspeich.

Stanza 48
7 **Proto** heads the list as her name suggests Gk πρῶτος, first; she is **Swift** from προ-ωθέω, rush on. **Eucrate** is **milde** because εὔκρατος signifies good temperament.

Stanza 49
2 **Thalia** is **Ioyous** from her namesake, the muse of comedy; cf. '*Thalia* merry' (VI x 22.8). 3 **Pasithee** is **Louely** because she shares the name of the fourth Grace, as E.K. notes in glossing *SC Apr.* 109. 4 **Cymothoe** is **Light foote** because her name signifies 'wave-swift'. 5–6 **Phao** is **lilly white** from Gk φάω, root of φαίνω, to shine. **Poris**: from πορίζω, travel, as Braden 1975:34 suggests; or πόρις, a young maiden. 9 **milkewhite** translates **Galathæa**, as in Theocritus, *Idyll* 11.

Stanza 50
9 As she has many names (**heastes**).

Stanza 51
9 **lust**: desire.

Stanza 52
3 **surges**: waves. 6–8 The three thousand more nymphs found **in floods and fountaines** are Ocean's offspring though akin to sun and sky, as R. Smith 1944 suggests.

Stanza 53
1–2 **eath**: easy. To **tell**, i.e. count, the sands, see Ps. 139.18; to **count the starres**, see Ps. 147.4. The difficulty of both tasks is proverbial; Smith 720. Drayton 1931–41:4.366 notes that the rivers 'first, by *Spenser* numbred were'. 4 **descry**: describe. 7 **Cymodoce**: earlier called Cymoent; see III iv 19.3*n*. The change of name prepares for her change of role in relation to her son, as suggested by her name, which signifies 'wave-tamer' because 'with her least word [she] can asswage | The surging seas, when they do sorest rage' (50. 4–5). She is the means through which Florimell is freed from 'waues, which rag'd and ror'd' (3.6) about her.

Cant. XII.

Marin for loue of Florimell,
In languor wastes his life:
The Nymph his mother getteth her,
And giues to him for wife.

1

O What an endlesse worke haue I in hand,
  To count the seas abundant progeny,
Whose fruitfull seede farre passeth those in land,
And also those which wonne in th'azure sky?
For much more eath to tell the starres on hy,
Albe they endlesse seeme in estimation,
Then to recount the Seas posterity:
So fertile be the flouds in generation,
So huge their numbers, and so numberlesse their nation.

2

Therefore the antique wisards well inuented,
  That *Venus* of the fomy sea was bred;
  For that the seas by her are most augmented.
Witnesse th'exceeding fry, which there are fed,
And wondrous sholes, which may of none be red.
Then blame me not, if I haue err'd in count
Of Gods, of Nymphs, of riuers yet vnred:
For though their numbers do much more surmount,
Yet all those same were there, which erst I did recount.

3

All those were there, and many other more,
  Whose names and nations were too long to tell,
  That *Proteus* house they fild euen to the dore;
  Yet were they all in order, as befell,

According their degrees disposed well.
Amongst the rest, was faire *Cymodoce,*
The mother of vnlucky *Marinell,*
Who thither with her came, to learne and see
The manner of the Gods when they at banquet be.

4

But for he was halfe mortall, being bred
  Of mortall sire, though of immortall wombe,
He might not with immortall food be fed,
Ne with th'eternall Gods to bancket come;
But walkt abrode, and round about did rome,
To view the building of that vncouth place,
That seem'd vnlike vnto his earthly home:
Where, as he to and fro by chaunce did trace,
There vnto him betid a disauentrous case.

5

Vnder the hanging of an hideous clieffe,
  He heard the lamentable voice of one,
  That piteously complaind her carefull grieffe,
Which neuer she before disclosd to none,
But to her selfe her sorrow did bemone.
So feelingly her case she did complaine,
That ruth it moued in the rocky stone,
And made it seeme to feele her grieuous paine,
And oft to grone with billowes beating from the maine.

Book IV Canto xii

Argument
2 languor: woeful plight.

Stanza 1
Repeating the claim of xi 53.1–3 to indicate the poet's recuperation from being tired. **2 abundant**: echoing 'in abundance' in the story of creation in Gen. 1. 10, 11, as MacColl 1989:44–45 notes. **3** This claim is based on the commonplace notion that being the source of life the sea contains replicas of all creatures found on land. **6 seeme**: not 'is' because the universe was held to be finite.

Stanza 2
1 antique wisards: ancient wisemen. **2–3 Venus of the fomy sea**: referring to her conception when Saturn's genitals were thrown into the ocean, as told by Hesiod, *Theogony* 176–201; cf. II xii 65.3–4 and Ovid, *Met.* 4.537–38. **5 sholes**: schools. **red**: counted. **7 vnred**: unseen; uncounted. **8 surmount**: exceed.

Stanza 3
2 nations: classes; kinds. **5** Well arranged in order by rank.

Stanza 4
1–2 As told at III iv 19.3–9. **8 trace**: go. **9 disauentrous case**: unfortunate event, but suggesting also not accidental in not being 'adventurous' (*OED* 1), as Silberman 1995:139 suggests.

Stanza 5
1 Emblematic of Florimell's despair, as at I ix 33.3. **2 lamentable**: lamenting. **3 carefull**: full of care.

Stanzas 6–11
Other notable complaints are allowed full, uninterrupted stanzas, e.g. Britomart's at III iv 8–10, Cymoent's at 36–39, and Arthur's at 55–60, but Florimell's is broken at the middle and truncated at the end to increase the pathos of her state. Her complaint is a rare instance of one that is effective, as Frantz 1986:118 observes in arguing that hearing, and not only the sight of beauty, may arouse love.

6

Though vaine I see my sorrowes to vnfold,
   And count my cares, when none is nigh to heare,
   Yet hoping griefe may lessen being told,
   I will them tell though vnto no man neare:
   For heauen that vnto all lends equall eare,
   Is farre from hearing of my heauy plight;
   And lowest hell, to which I lie most neare,
   Cares not what euils hap to wretched wight;
And greedy seas doe in the spoile of life delight.

7

Yet loe the seas I see by often beating,
   Doe pearce the rockes, and hardest marble weares;
   But his hard rocky hart for no entreating
   Will yeeld, but when my piteous plaints he heares,
   Is hardned more with my aboundant teares.
   Yet though he neuer list to me relent,
   But let me waste in woe my wretched yeares,
   Yet will I neuer of my loue repent,
But ioy that for his sake I suffer prisonment.

8

And when my weary ghost with griefe outworne,
   By timely death shall winne her wished rest,
   Let then this plaint vnto his eares be borne,
   That blame it is to him, that armes profest,
   To let her die, whom he might haue redrest.
   There did she pause, inforced to giue place,
   Vnto the passion, that her heart opprest,
   And after she had wept and wail'd a space,
She gan afresh thus to renew her wretched case.

9

Ye Gods of seas, if any Gods at all
   Haue care of right, or ruth of wretches wrong,
   By one or other way me woefull thrall,
   Deliuer hence out of this dungeon strong,

In which I daily dying am too long.
   And if ye deeme me death for louing one,
   That loues not me, then doe it not prolong,
   But let me die and end my daies attone,
And let him liue vnlou'd, or loue him selfe alone.

10

But if that life ye vnto me decree,
   Then let mee liue, as louers ought to do,
   And of my lifes deare loue beloued be:
   And if he shall through pride your doome vndo,
   Do you by duresse him compell thereto,
   And in this prison put him here with me:
   One prison fittest is to hold vs two:
   So had I rather to be thrall, then free;
Such thraldome or such freedome let it surely be.

11

But ô vaine iudgement, and conditions vaine,
   The which the prisoner points vnto the free,
   The whiles I him condemne, and deeme his paine,
   He where he list goes loose, and laughes at me.
   So euer loose, so euer happy be.
   But where so loose or happy that thou art,
   Know *Marinell* that all this is for thee.
   With that she wept and wail'd, as if her hart
Would quite haue burst through great abundance of her smart.

12

All which complaint when *Marinell* had heard,
   And vnderstood the cause of all her care
   To come of him, for vsing her so hard,
   His stubborne heart, that neuer felt misfare
   Was toucht with soft remorse and pitty rare;
   That euen for griefe of minde he oft did grone,
   And inly wish, that in his powre it weare
   Her to redresse: but since he meanes found none
He could no more but her great misery bemone.

Stanza 6

2 **count**: recount; number. 3 Proverbial: Smith 761.
5 **equall**: impartial; or, to all equally. 9 **spoile**: plundering.

Stanza 7

3 **his hard rocky hart**: cf. 'his stony heart' (13.1). The expression relates Marinell to the 'rocky stone' (5.7) that imprisons Florimell. As it pities her at 5.7–9, so will he. 5 **aboundant**: punning on the etymology, 'flowing in waves'; cf. 11.9. Like the seas, her tears will wear down his marble heart.

Stanza 8

1 **ghost**: spirit. 2 **timely**: early; hence untimely. 5 **redrest**: delivered from death. 9 **renew**: go over again. She begins anew first with a prayer and then with a direct address to Marinell.

Stanza 9

8 **attone**: i.e. at once, or once for all, rather than **daily dying**. 9 **vnlou'd**: not loving another.

Stanza 10

4 As 'proud *Marinell*' (III iv 17.9) is said at xi 5.3–5 to reject woman's love through pride.

Stanza 11

2 **points**: appoints; ordains. 3 **deeme his paine**: decree his punishment.

Stanza 12

2 **care**: grief. 4 **misfare**: mishap. Only his body was wounded by Britomart; cf. 19.6. 9 **her great misery**: summing up what the *LR* 80 calls 'the misery of Florimell'.

13

Thus whilst his stony heart with tender ruth
    Was toucht, and mighty courage mollifide,
    Dame *Venus* sonne that tameth stubborne youth
    With iron bit, and maketh him abide,
    Till like a victor on his backe he ride,
    Into his mouth his maystring bridle threw,
    That made him stoupe, till he did him bestride:
    Then gan he make him tread his steps anew,
And learne to loue, by learning louers paines to rew.

14

Now gan he in his grieued minde deuise,
    How from that dungeon he might her enlarge;
    Some while he thought, by faire and humble wise
    To *Proteus* selfe to sue for her discharge:
    But then he fear'd his mothers former charge
    Gainst womens loue, long giuen him in vaine.
    Then gan he thinke, perforce with sword and targe
    Her forth to fetch, and *Proteus* to constraine:
But soone he gan such folly to forthinke againe.

15

Then did he cast to steale her thence away,
    And with him beare, where none of her might know.
    But all in vaine: for why he found no way
    To enter in, or issue forth below:
    For all about that rocke the sea did flow.
    And though vnto his will she giuen were,
    Yet without ship or bote her thence to row,
    He wist not how her thence away to bere;
And daunger well he wist long to continue there.

16

At last when as no meanes he could inuent,
    Backe to him selfe, he gan returne the blame,
    That was the author of her punishment;
    And with vile curses, and reprochfull shame
    To damne him selfe by euery euill name;
    And deeme vnworthy or of loue or life,
    That had despisde so chast and faire a dame,
    Which him had sought through trouble and long strife;
Yet had refusde a God that her had sought to wife.

17

In this sad plight he walked here and there,
    And romed round about the rocke in vaine,
    As he had lost him selfe, he wist not where;
    Oft listening if he mote her heare againe;
    And still bemoning her vnworthy paine.
    Like as an Hynde whose calfe is falne vnwares
    Into some pit, where she him heares complaine,
    An hundred times about the pit side fares,
Right sorrowfully mourning her bereaued cares.

18

And now by this the feast was throughly ended,
    And euery one gan homeward to resort.
    Which seeing, *Marinell* was sore offended,
    That his departure thence should be so short,
    And leaue his loue in that sea-walled fort.
    Yet durst he not his mother disobay,
    But her attending in full seemly sort,
    Did march amongst the many all the way:
And all the way did inly mourne, like one astray.

19

Being returned to his mothers bowre,
    In solitary silence far from wight,
    He gan record the lamentable stowre,
    In which his wretched loue lay day and night,
    For his deare sake, that ill deseru'd that plight:
    The thought whereof empierst his hart so deepe,
    That of no worldly thing he tooke delight;
    Ne dayly food did take, ne nightly sleepe,
But pyn'd, and mourn'd, and languisht, and alone did weepe.

20

That in short space his wonted chearefull hew
    Gan fade, and liuely spirits deaded quight:
    His cheeke bones raw, and eie-pits hollow grew,
    And brawney armes had lost their knowen might,
    That nothing like himselfe he seem'd in sight.
    Ere long so weake of limbe, and sicke of loue
    He woxe, that lenger he note stand vpright,
    But to his bed was brought, and layd aboue,
Like ruefull ghost, vnable once to stirre or moue.

Stanza 13

The Petrarchan topos of Cupid riding the lover (e.g. *Rime* 161.9–11) and used, e.g. in Sidney, *Astrophil and Stella* 49, is wittily varied: Cupid gains control through the lover's pity. See III v 30.4–9*n*. **2 courage**: spirit, heart.   **mollifide**: softened; made less obdurate.

Stanza 14

5–6 Cf. III iv 26.1–2.   **7 perforce**: forcibly.   **9 forthinke**: renounce.

Stanza 15

1 cast: resolve.   **3 for why**: because.

Stanza 16

1 inuent: discover.

Stanza 17

5 vnworthy: undeserved; cf i 1.5.   **9 her bereaued cares**: i.e. the object of her cares (the calf) of which she has been deprived.

Stanza 18

4 short: near at hand.   **8 many**: company.

Stanza 19

1 his mothers bowre is 'Deepe in the bottome of the sea' (III iv 43.1), as Proteus's bower where Florimell is imprisoned is 'in the bottom of the maine' (viii 37.1). In effect, Marinell undergoes her suffering.   **3** He began to go over in his mind her lamentable distress.

21

Which when his mother saw, she in her mind
  Was troubled sore, ne wist well what to weene,
  Ne could by search nor any meanes out find
  The secret cause and nature of his teene,
  Whereby she might apply some medicine;
  But weeping day and night, did him attend,
  And mourn'd to see her losse before her eyne,
  Which grieu'd her more, that she it could not mend:
To see an helpelesse euill, double griefe doth lend.

22

Nought could she read the roote of his disease,
  Ne weene what mister maladie it is,
  Whereby to seeke some meanes it to appease.
  Most did she thinke, but most she thought amis,
  That that same former fatall wound of his
  Whyleare by *Tryphon* was not throughly healed,
  But closely rankled vnder th'orifis:
  Least did she thinke, that which he most concealed,
That loue it was, which in his hart lay vnreuealed.

23

Therefore to *Tryphon* she againe doth hast,
  And him doth chyde as false and fraudulent,
  That fayld the trust, which she in him had plast,
  To cure her sonne, as he his faith had lent:
  Who now was falne into new languishment
  Of his old hurt, which was not throughly cured.
  So backe he came vnto her patient,
  Where searching euery part, her well assured,
That it was no old sore, which his new paine procured.

24

But that it was some other maladie,
  Or griefe vnknowne, which he could not discerne:
  So left he her withouten remedie.
  Then gan her heart to faint, and quake, and earne,

And inly troubled was, the truth to learne.
  Vnto himselfe she came, and him besought,
  Now with faire speches, now with threatnings sterne,
  If ought lay hidden in his grieued thought,
It to reueale: who still her answered, there was nought.

25

Nathlesse she rested not so satisfide,
  But leauing watry gods, as booting nought,
  Vnto the shinie heauen in haste she hide,
  And thence *Apollo* King of Leaches brought.
  Apollo came; who soone as he had sought
  Through his disease, did by and by out find,
  That he did languish of some inward thought,
  The which afflicted his engrieued mind;
Which loue he red to be, that leads each liuing kind.

26

Which when he had vnto his mother told,
  She gan thereat to fret, and greatly grieue.
  And comming to her sonne, gan first to scold,
  And chyde at him, that made her misbelieue:
  But afterwards she gan him soft to shrieue,
  And wooe with faire intreatie, to disclose,
  Which of the Nymphes his heart so sore did mieue.
  For sure she weend it was some one of those,
Which he had lately seene, that for his loue he chose.

27

Now lesse she feared that same fatall read,
  That warned him of womens loue beware:
  Which being ment of mortall creatures sead,
  For loue of Nymphes she thought she need not care,
  But promist him, what euer wight she weare,
  That she her loue, to him would shortly gaine:
  So he her told: but soone as she did heare
  That *Florimell* it was, which wrought his paine,
She gan a fresh to chafe, and grieue in euery vaine.

Stanza 20
1–5 His appearance marks his despair as it does the Red Cross Knight's on emerging from Orgoglio's dungeon at I viii 41 with 'rawbone armes' and 'his vitall powres | Decayd'. 7 **note**: could not.

Stanza 21
4 **teene**: grief.   9 **helpelesse**: beyond help.

Stanza 22
1 **read**: discover.   2 **what mister**: what kind of.   3 **appease**: relieve.

Stanza 23
5 **languishment**: illness.   9 **procured**: caused.

Stanza 24
4 **earne**: grieve.

Stanza 25
4 On **Apollo** as the god of medicine, see I v 43.6–9*n*. He taught the nymph who attended the wounded Marinell at III iv 41; but even he cannot cure love's wound, as told at vi 1.9. 9 **red**: interpreted.

Stanza 26
5 **shrieue**: question; also, persuade him to confess.   7 **mieue**: obs. form of 'move'.

Stanza 27
1–2 **fatall read**: prophetic or foreboding counsel, referring to Proteus's prophecy that 'A virgin straunge and stout him should dismay, or kill' (III iv 25.9), which she continues to misinterpret.   5 Cymodoce uses **wight** in its restricted sense, 'an unearthly being' (*OED* 1b), but Marinell takes advantage of its extended sense, **mortall creature** (*OED* 2).

28

Yet since she saw the streight extremitie,
    In which his life vnluckily was layd,
    It was no time to scan the prophecie,
    Whether old *Proteus* true or false had sayd,
    That his decay should happen by a mayd.
    It's late in death of daunger to aduize,
    Or loue forbid him, that is life denayd:
    But rather gan in troubled mind deuize,
How she that Ladies libertie might enterprize.

29

To *Proteus* selfe to sew she thought it vaine,
    Who was the root and worker of her woe:
    Nor vnto any meaner to complaine,
    But vnto great king *Neptune* selfe did goe,
    And on her knee before him falling lowe,
    Made humble suit vnto his Maiestie,
    To graunt to her, her sonnes life, which his foe
    A cruell Tyrant had presumpteouslie
By wicked doome condemn'd, a wretched death to die.

30

To whom God *Neptune* softly smyling, thus;
    Daughter me seemes of double wrong ye plaine,
    Gainst one that hath both wronged you, and vs:
    For death t'adward I ween'd did appertaine
    To none, but to the seas sole Soueraine.
    Read therefore who it is, which this hath wrought,
    And for what cause; the truth discouer plaine.
    For neuer wight so euill did or thought,
But would some rightfull cause pretend, though rightly
                                                        (nought.

31

To whom she answerd, Then it is by name
    Proteus, that hath ordayn'd my sonne to die;
    For that a waift, the which by fortune came
    Vpon your seas, he claym'd as propertie:
    And yet nor his, nor his in equitie,
    But yours the waift by high prerogatiue.
    Therefore I humbly craue your Maiestie,
    It to repleuie, and my sonne repriue:
So shall you by one gift saue all vs three aliue.

32

He graunted it: and streight his warrant made,
    Vnder the Sea-gods seale autenticall,
    Commaunding *Proteus* straight t'enlarge the mayd,
    Which wandring on his seas imperiall,
    He lately tooke, and sithence kept as thrall.
    Which she receiuing with meete thankefulnesse,
    Departed straight to *Proteus* therewithall:
    Who reading it with inward loathfulnesse,
Was grieued to restore the pledge, he did possesse.

33

Yet durst he not the warrant to withstand,
    But vnto her deliuered *Florimell*.
    Whom she receiuing by the lilly hand,
    Admyr'd her beautie much, as she mote well:
    For she all liuing creatures did excell;
    And was right ioyous, that she gotten had
    So faire a wife for her sonne *Marinell*.
    So home with her she streight the virgin lad,
And shewed her to him, then being sore bestad.

34

Who soone as he beheld that angels face,
    Adorn'd with all diuine perfection,
    His cheared heart eftsoones away gan chace
    Sad death, reuiued with her sweet inspection,
    And feeble spirit inly felt refection;
    As withered weed through cruell winters tine,
    That feeles the warmth of sunny beames reflection,
    Liftes vp his head, that did before decline
And gins to spread his leafe before the faire sunshine.

35

Right so himselfe did *Marinell* vpreare,
    When he in place his dearest loue did spy;
    And though his limbs could not his bodie beare,
    Ne former strength returne so suddenly,
    Yet chearefull signes he shewed outwardly.
    Ne lesse was she in secret hart affected,
    But that she masked it with modestie,
    For feare she should of lightnesse be detected:
Which to another place I leaue to be perfected.

Stanza 28
1 **streight**: severe.   5 **decay**: downfall. The prophecy applied to Britomart applies now to Florimell.   6 **aduize**: take thought.   9 **enterprize**: attempt to gain.

Stanza 30
2 **plaine**: complain.   6 **Read**: tell.

Stanza 31
3–6 **waift**: waif, in the obs. sense 'wafted', carried over water; but chiefly in the legal sense, property left ownerless, as Hellenore at III x 36.3. If left at sea, it reverts to the crown, here Neptune, to be granted at his pleasure; see Knight 1970:269.   8 **repleuie**: recover, or command to be restored, by bailing from prison. The term plays against **repriue** (reprieve): 'rescue from death' (*OED* 4).

Stanza 32
2 **autenticall**: authentic: having legal force.   4 **his seas imperiall**: referring to his sovereign power over the sea; cf. xi 11.4, V iv 19.6.   8 **loathfulnesse**: reluctance.

Stanza 33
3 By just this gesture Scudamour seizes Amoret at x 53.9.

Stanza 34
1–2 His sight of her corresponds to the vision of Amoret's 'bright Angels hew' at v 13.4 and Britomart's 'angels face' at vi 19.5 when they are unveiled.   4 **her . . . inspection**: both his sight of her and her sight of him, as she is **the faire sunshine**.   5 **refection**: refreshment; restoration.   6 **tine**: affliction.

Stanza 35
8 **detected**: accused.

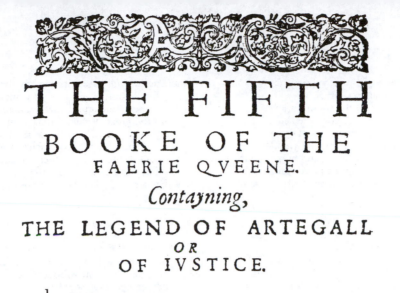

THE FIFTH
BOOKE OF THE
FAERIE QVEENE.

Contayning,

THE LEGEND OF ARTEGALL
OR
OF IVSTICE.

1

 O oft as I with state of present time,
The image of the antique world compare,
When as mans age was in his freshest prime,
And the first blossome of faire vertue bare,
Such oddes I finde twixt those, and these which are,
As that, through long continuance of his course,
Me seemes the world is runne quite out of square,
From the first point of his appointed sourse,
And being once amisse growes daily wourse and wourse.

2

For from the golden age, that first was named,
It's now at earst become a stonie one;
And men themselues, the which at first were framed
Of earthly mould, and form'd of flesh and bone,
Are now transformed into hardest stone:
Such as behind their backs (so backward bred)
Were throwne by *Pyrrha* and *Deucalione*:
And if then those may any worse be red,
They into that ere long will be degendered.

Book V Proem

Stanza 1

S. was chided by Harvey because 'You suppose the first age was the goulde age. . . . You suppose it a foolish madd worlde, wherein all thinges ar overrulid by fansye' (1884:86). The motif that 'the world hathe lost his youth, and the times beginne to waxe olde' (2 Esd. 14.9) is found in all the books – see esp. I xii 14.8–9, II vii 16–17, III i 13, and IV viii 31.6–7 (and *n*) – and is treated fully in Bk V because its virtue, justice, confronts the fallen world directly, and because it was generally believed that the world's increasing degeneration heralds the Last Judgement. See 'antique world' and 'eschatology' in the *SEnc* and Anderson 1987. **5 oddes**: difference. **7 out of square**: into disorder, referring to the set square as the emblem of justice. Cf. *SC Feb.* 11–14.

Stanza 2

2–7 at earst: at length. **stonie**: adding a final age to Ovid's account in *Met*. 1.89–127 of the descent from the first golden age to the silver, bronze, and iron ages, as suggested by the story of Pyrrha and Deucalion in *Met*. 1.395–415. Golding renders its concluding lines: 'Of these are we the crooked ympes, and stonie race in deede, | Bewraying by our toyling life, from whence we doe proceede'. **earthly mould**: i.e. a body of earth. **8–9 red**: supposed. **degendered**: degenerated; downward bred; suggesting 'made sterile'.

3

Let none then blame me, if in discipline
    Of vertue and of ciuill vses lore,
  I doe not forme them to the common line
  Of present dayes, which are corrupted sore,
  But to the antique vse, which was of yore,
    When good was onely for it selfe desyred,
    And all men sought their owne, and none no more;
  When Iustice was not for most meed outhyred,
But simple Truth did rayne, and was of all admyred.

4

For that which all men then did vertue call,
    Is now cald vice; and that which vice was hight,
    Is now hight vertue, and so vs'd of all:
  Right now is wrong, and wrong that was is right,
  As all things else in time are chaunged quight.
    Ne wonder; for the heauens reuolution
    Is wandred farre from, where it first was pight,
  And so doe make contrarie constitution
Of all this lower world, toward his dissolution.

5

For who so list into the heauens looke,
    And search the courses of the rowling spheares,
    Shall find that from the point, where they first tooke
  Their setting forth, in these few thousand yeares
  They all are wandred much; that plaine appeares.
    For that same golden fleecy Ram, which bore
    Phrixus and *Helle* from their stepdames feares,
  Hath now forgot, where he was plast of yore,
And shouldred hath the Bull, which fayre *Europa* bore.

6

And eke the Bull hath with his bow-bent horne
    So hardly butted those two twinnes of *Ioue*,
    That they haue crusht the Crab, and quite him borne
  Into the great *Nemæan* lions groue.
  So now all range, and doe at randon roue
    Out of their proper places farre away,
    And all this world with them amisse doe moue,
  And all his creatures from their course astray,
Till they arriue at their last ruinous decay.

7

Ne is that same great glorious lampe of light,
    That doth enlumine all these lesser fyres,
    In better case, ne keepes his course more right,
  But is miscaried with the other Spheres.
  For since the terme of fourteene hundred yeres,
    That learned *Ptolomæe* his hight did take,
    He is declyned from that marke of theirs,
  Nigh thirtie minutes to the Southerne lake;
That makes me feare in time he will vs quite forsake.

8

And if to those Ægyptian wisards old,
    Which in Star-read were wont haue best insight,
    Faith may be giuen, it is by them told,
  That since the time they first tooke the Sunnes hight,
  Foure times his place he shifted hath in sight,
    And twice hath risen, where he now doth West,
    And wested twice, where he ought rise aright.
  But most is *Mars* amisse of all the rest,
And next to him old *Saturne*, that was wont be best.

Stanza 3
1–2 discipline: instruction. **ciuill vses lore**: the art of polit-
ical wisdom. The term announces the further shift from the
private to the public virtues that began in Bk IV; on the dis-
tinction, see *LR* 18–21. **3 line**: standard of practice. **8**
When justice was not bought by one with the largest bribe.

Stanza 4
1–5 S.'s most powerful statement on why he needed to
fashion the virtues, and why his poem counters traditional
morality. In commenting on the chiasms in 1–4, Hollander
1988:126 notes the syntactical ambiguity of 5. **6–9** S. posits
a causal relationship between moral and political degeneration
and the physical disorder of the universe. The wandering of the
heauens reuolution may refer either to the effect of the pre-
cession of the equinoxes, i.e. the apparent shifting of the con-
stellations of the zodiac though their astrological 'signs' remain
the same, or to trepidation; see *SEnc* 73. On the apocalyptic
significance of the change as it derives from the sibylline
oracles that prophesied the return of Astraea, see Bull 1998.

Stanza 5
2 the rowling spheares: the transparent hollow concentric
spheres in which the heavenly bodies were assumed to be fixed.
4 these few thousand: fewer than six thousand according to
the calendar in the Geneva Bible. **6–9** The constellation
Aries, which in the time of Ptolemy occupied the compartment
of the zodiac to which it gave its name, had moved by the six-
teenth century one place east to Taurus. Its place, marking the

vernal equinox ostensibly at the time of creation, was almost
occupied by Pisces. At III xi 30.5–6 the tapestries in the house
of Busirane show how Jove bore Helle as a ram and Europa as
a bull.

Stanza 6
1–4 In 5.6–9 and here, S. refers to the first five signs of the
zodiacal constellations through their common names: Aries the
Ram, Taurus the Bull, Gemini the twins (Castor and Pollux),
Cancer the Crab, and Leo the Lion. The sixth is Virgo or
Astræa, the classical goddess of justice, who appears at i 11.5 in
her 'euerlasting place'. **hardly**: violently; perhaps closely.

Stanza 7
1–4 these lesser fyres are the stars and planets whose source
of light was held to be the sun, which S. fears has **miscaried**,
i.e. gone astray. **5–9** By the late sixteenth century, the obliqu-
ity of the ecliptic had declined $21^{1}/_{2}$ minutes from the time of
its measurement by Ptolemy, as A.B. Gough 1921 notes. The
figure was much debated, and S.'s **thirtie minutes**, or half a
degree, is a modest decline over 1400 years. **theirs**: referring
to the ancient astronomers. **the Southerne lake**: the south-
ern hemisphere of water.

Stanza 8
1–7 According to **those Ægyptian wisards**, 'these strange
alterations were marked in the Sunne at four sundry times.
Two sundry times it was seene to rise from that place where it

9

For during *Saturnes* ancient raigne it's sayd,
　　That all the world with goodnesse did abound:
　　All loued vertue, no man was affrayd
　　Of force, ne fraud in wight was to be found:
　　No warre was knowne, no dreadfull trompets sound,
　　Peace vniuersall rayn'd mongst men and beasts,
　　And all things freely grew out of the ground:
　　Iustice sate high ador'd with solemne feasts,
And to all people did diuide her dred beheasts.

10

Most sacred vertue she of all the rest,
　　Resembling God in his imperiall might;
　　Whose soueraine powre is herein most exprest,
　　That both to good and bad he dealeth right,

And all his workes with Iustice hath bedight.
　　That powre he also doth to Princes lend,
　　And makes them like himselfe in glorious sight,
　　To sit in his owne seate, his cause to end,
And rule his people right, as he doth recommend.

11

Dread Soucrayne Goddesse, that doest highest sit
　　In seate of iudgement, in th'Almighties place,
　　And with magnificke might and wondrous wit
　　Doest to thy people righteous doome aread,
　　That furthest Nations filles with awfull dread,
　　Pardon the boldnesse of thy basest thrall,
　　That dare discourse of so diuine a read,
　　As thy great iustice praysed ouer all:
The instrument whereof loe here thy *Artegall*.

is now wont to fall, and in like manner to set in those regions from whence it now ariseth, which also came to passe two several times' (*The Faymous Hystory of Herodotus*, tr. 1584; cited *Var* 5.159). **Star-read**: star-lore, astronomy. **8–9** That planetary orbits are elliptical rather than circular was not established until Kepler, *De Motibus Stellae Martis* (1609). On the apparent eccentricity of Mars and Saturn, see VII vii 52. The problem of Mars was notorious; see, e.g. Shakespeare, *1 Henry VI* 1.2.1–2.

Stanza 9

1 Ovid, *Met.* 1.89–112, describes the age of Saturn as the time when all men kept faith and did what was right. There was no fear of punishment and no alarm of trumpets, for men lived secure from war, and the earth freely gave all things needful. **9 diuide**: dispense, distribute. Unlike Ovid's golden age in which all did what was right without law, S.'s age exists *sub lege*, which he shows in Astræa's 'stedfast doome' (i 12.3) executed by Talus.

Stanza 10

4 Cf. Matt. 5.45: 'he maketh his sunne to arise on the euil, and the good, and sendeth raine on the iuste, and uniuste'. **5 bedight**: adorned; also ordered (sugg. by the context) because what is fitly ordered may be said to adorn. **6–9** S. is making a case for justice as a natural law derived from God and upheld by the Queen in opposition to common law derived from custom. On the distinction, see Kermode 1971:50–54, Altman in the *SEnc* 415, and R. White 1996:60. Cf. Prov. 8.15: 'By me [God's Wisdom], Kings reigne, and princes decree iustice'; also 2 Chron. 9.8: 'to set thee on his throne as King, in the stead of the Lord thy God'. In dedicating his poem to Elizabeth, S. uses the formulaic phrase, 'by the grace of God Queene'. **end**: fulfil. **recommend**: give in charge.

Stanza 11

1 Cf. the address to Elizabeth at I proem 4.1. On Elizabeth as Astræa, see i 5.4*n*. **3 magnificke**: renowned. **4 aread**: declare. **7 read**: subject; matter (sugg. by the context).

Cant. I.

*Artegall trayn'd in Iustice lore
Irenaes quest pursewed,
He doeth auenge on Sanglier
his Ladies bloud embrewed.*

1

Though vertue then were held in highest price,
   In those old times, of which I doe intreat,
Yet then likewise the wicked seede of vice
Began to spring which shortly grew full great,
And with their boughes the gentle plants did beat.
But euermore some of the vertuous race
Rose vp, inspired with heroicke heat,
   That cropt the branches of the sient base,
And with strong hand their fruitfull rancknes did deface.

2

Such first was *Bacchus*, that with furious might
   All th'East before vntam'd did ouerronne,
   And wrong repressed, and establisht right,
   Which lawlesse men had formerly fordonne.
   There Iustice first her princely rule begonne.
   Next *Hercules* his like ensample shewed,
   Who all the West with equall conquest wonne,
   And monstrous tyrants with his club subdewed;
The club of Iustice dread, with kingly powre endewed.

3

And such was he, of whom I haue to tell,
   The Champion of true Iustice *Artegall*.
   Whom (as ye lately mote remember well)
   An hard aduenture, which did then befall,
   Into redoubted perill forth did call;
   That was to succour a distressed Dame,
   Whom a strong tyrant did vniustly thrall,
   And from the heritage, which she did clame,
Did with strong hand withhold: *Grantorto* was his name.

4

Wherefore the Lady, which *Eirena* hight,
   Did to the Faery Queene her way addresse,
   To whom complayning her afflicted plight,
   She her besought of gratious redresse.
   That soueraine Queene, that mightie Emperesse,
   Whose glorie is to aide all suppliants pore,
   And of weake Princes to be Patronesse,
   Chose *Artegall* to right her to restore;
For that to her he seem'd best skild in righteous lore.

Book V Canto i

Argument

1 Iustice lore: the doctrine or 'rules of iustice' (5.9).
4 embrewed: shed.

Stanza 1

1 price: esteem, regard. **2 intreat**: treat. **6–9** The
metaphor, together with **deface** (i.e. lay waste), recalls Guyon's
destruction of the Bower of Bliss; cf. II xii 83.6. **fruitfull
rancknes** suggests the luxuriant growth of whatever is proud
and therefore rebellious. **the vertuous race** would include
the Elizabethan nobility, such as those addressed in the *DS*.
On nobility as a topic of Bk V, see Stillman 1981. **sient base**:
base shoots.

Stanza 2

Bacchus and his son **Hercules** are commonly linked – e.g.
by S. in *Teares* 461, and by the mythographers, e.g. Conti
1616:5.13 – for having established justice, the one in the east
and the other in the west. **4 fordonne**: destroyed. **8–9 The
club of Iustice**: an instrument of oppression when wielded by
Orgoglio, Disdaine, Lust, and Hatred but of justice when
wielded by Hercules against oppressors.

Stanza 3

At II ix 6.9, Artegall is praised by Guyon as a knight highly
honoured among the Knights of Maidenhead. In Merlin's

chronicle, he is revealed to be the son of Gorlois, and therefore
Arthur's half-brother; see III iii 27*n*. The preferred spelling of
his name, 'Arthegall' in Bk III and the first part of Bk IV (so
spelled in Hardyng 1812:137), suggests that he is 'Arth-egall',
i.e. 'equal or peer to Arthur'; see x 15.2. The second half of his
name suggests Fr. *égal*, 'fair', 'just', as he is 'best skild in righ-
teous lore' (4.9; cf. 7.1–3) and 'iudge of equity' (iii 36.7). In
Geoffrey of Monmouth, his namesake Arthgallo was an unjust
king until, having been deposed and restored, he began 'exer-
cising strict justice towards all men' (1891:3.17). A millennium,
from the sixth to the sixteenth century (a time of fulfilment
according to Rev. 20.1–4), separates him from his reincarna-
tion as Gloriana's knight; see Hankins 1971:150. **1** On
Hercules and his twelve labours as the model for Artegall and
his adventures, see Aptekar 1969:153–71, and 'Artegall' and
'Hercules' in the *SEnc*. As that model contributes to S.'s ana-
lysis of justice, see Cook 1996:107–14. **4 An hard aduen-
ture**: referring to IV vi 42.3. **9 Grantorto**: Ital. *gran torto*,
great wrong. He is commonly named a **tyrant**, a key term in
Bk V, to signify his opposition to God's power delegated to the
monarch. In contemporary political terms, he represents, *inter
alia*, Spanish aggression supported by the Pope in Ireland. See
'Grantorto' in the *SEnc*. A contemporary identified him as the
rebel leader, the Earl of Desmond; see *N&Q* 202:513.

Stanza 4

1 Eirena ('Irena' *1609*) referring to Éire (genitive Éireann),
the Gaelic name of Ireland; see 'Ireland, the cultural context',

5

For *Artegall* in iustice was vpbrought
  Euen from the cradle of his infancie,
  And all the depth of rightfull doome was taught
  By faire *Astræa*, with great industrie,
  Whilest here on earth she liued mortallie.
  For till the world from his perfection fell
  Into all filth and foule iniquitie,
  Astræa here mongst earthly men did dwell,
And in the rules of iustice them instructed well.

6

Whiles through the world she walked in this sort,
  Vpon a day she found this gentle childe,
  Amongst his peres playing his childish sport:
  Whom seeing fit, and with no crime defilde,
  She did allure with gifts and speaches milde,
  To wend with her. So thence him farre she brought
  Into a caue from companie exilde,
  In which she noursled him, till yeares he raught,
And all the discipline of iustice there him taught.

7

There she him taught to weigh both right and wrong
  In equall ballance with due recompence,
  And equitie to measure out along,
  According to the line of conscience,

origin of authority?

When so it needs with rigour to dispence.
  Of all the which, for want there of mankind,
  She caused him to make experience
  Vpon wyld beasts, which she in woods did find,
With wrongfull powre oppressing others of their kind.

8

Thus she him trayned, and thus she him taught,
  In all the skill of deeming wrong and right,
  Vntill the ripenesse of mans yeares he raught;
  That euen wilde beasts did feare his awfull sight,
  And men admyr'd his ouerruling might;
  Ne any liu'd on ground, that durst withstand
  His dreadfull heast, much lesse him match in fight,
  Or bide the horror of his wreakfull hand,
When so he list in wrath lift vp his steely brand.

9

Which steely brand, to make him dreaded more,
  She gaue vnto him, gotten by her slight
  And earnest search, where it was kept in store
  In *Ioues* eternall house, vnwist of wight,
  Since he himselfe it vs'd in that great fight
  Against the *Titans*, that whylome rebelled
  Gainst highest heauen; *Chrysaor* it was hight;
  Chrysaor that all other swords excelled,
Well prou'd in that same day, when *Ioue* those Gyants quelled.

---

in the *SEnc*. Since Gk εἰρήνη signifies 'peace', she represents a peaceful Ireland paying homage to the English Queen, as 'myld *Eirene*' attends Mercilla at ix 32.6. More specifically, she represents a delegation from the English Pale (known earlier as 'the land of peace', as Shire 1978:63 notes) who, besieged by the wild Irish, appealed directly to Elizabeth for aid; see Brady 1989a:32–33. That 'the worke of iustice shalbe peace, euen the worke of iustice and quietnes, and assurance for euer' (Isa. 32.17) indicates that Artegall is the instrument of the 'royall Virgin', Elizabeth, who will establish 'sacred Peace' (III iii 49. 6, 3) as a prelude to the restoration of the golden age when 'Peace vniuersall rayn'd mongst men and beasts' (proem 9.6). On the political violence involved in his quest, see McCabe 1989b:120–23, and Cavanagh 1994b. **4 redresse**: aid. **9 in righteous lore**: as the instrument of Elizabeth's 'righteous doome' (proem 11.4), Artegall acquires his dominant epithet, as at ii 39.2 and vii 22.4, even claiming it himself at iv 16.3.

Stanza 5

4 Astræa: 'the daughter of . . . Jupiter and Themis. It is taken for iustice, as the woorde doth signifie. She detesting the naughtie and uniust liuinge of men, flewe to heauen' (T. Cooper 1565). As the constellation Virgo, she was identified as the righteous Virgin next to Libra with her scales of justice (11.4–9). The chief classical source of her story in 5–9, which is repeated at 11.1–4, VII vii 37.6–9, and *Mother Hubberd* 1–4, is Ovid, *Met.* 1.149–50. In the *Theatre*, Noot tells Elizabeth that 'the Virgin *Astrea* is descended from heauen to builde hir a seate in this your moste happie countrey of *England*' (A vi). Elizabeth was commonly celebrated as Astræa but only obliquely by S.; see 'Elizabeth, Images of', and 'Astraea' in the *SEnc*. **5 mortallie**: as a mortal.

Stanza 6

1 sort: manner. **2 gentle**: nobly born. **3 peres**: companion. **5–6** Appropriately, the career of the knight of justice is initiated by bribery and in exile from humanity. See 9.2n. **8 noursled**: trained. **yeares**: mature age; cf. 8.3.

Stanza 7

1–5 Two aspects of justice are described here: justice absolute and equity (though mercy may be a part, as Phillips 1970:105–06 argues). Weighing justice and along with it measuring equity should be a single activity in imitation of God who 'with righteousnes shal . . . iudge the world, and the people with equitie' (Ps. 98.9). Traditionally, the latter is the conscience of the law; on their relation, see 'justice and equity' in the *SEnc*. **dispence**: either 'administer' by applying the letter of the law with **rigour**, or 'dispense with' rigour by easing punishment. **7–9** His classical counterpart is Chiron, who instructed Achilles in the precepts of divine justice after first practising on beasts (Statius, *Achilleid* 2.96–167). His biblical counterpart is Nimrod, who was 'a mighty hunter before the Lord' (Gen. 10.9) before he tyrannized humanity.

Stanza 8

2 deeming: distinguishing. **5 admyr'd**: marvelled at. **7 heast**: command. **8 bide**: endure. **wreakfull**: avenging. **9 steely brand**: sword.

Stanza 9

2 slight: craft. That justice should be administered by a purloined sword need not have, but most likely does have, ironical overtones. **5–9** On the battles of the Titans and/or the giants against the Olympians, see III vii 47.3–5n. **Chrysaor**:

10

For of most perfect metall it was made,
   Tempred with Adamant amongst the same,
   And garnisht all with gold vpon the blade
   In goodly wise, whereof it tooke his name,
   And was of no lesse vertue, then of fame.
   For there no substance was so firme and hard,
   But it would pierce or cleaue, where so it came;
   Ne any armour could his dint out ward,
But wheresoeuer it did light, it throughly shard.

11

Now when the world with sinne gan to abound,
   Astraea loathing lenger here to space
   Mongst wicked men, in whom no truth she found,
   Return'd to heauen, whence she deriu'd her race;
   Where she hath now an euerlasting place,
   Mongst those twelue signes, which nightly we doe see
   The heauens bright-shining baudricke to enchace;
   And is the *Virgin*, sixt in her degree,
And next her selfe her righteous ballance hanging bee.

12

But when she parted hence, she left her groome
   An yron man, which did on her attend
   Alwayes, to execute her stedfast doome,
   And willed him with *Artegall* to wend,

And doe what euer thing he did intend.
   His name was *Talus*, made of yron mould,
   Immoueable, resistlesse, without end.
   Who in his hand an yron flale did hould,
With which he thresht out falshood, and did truth vnfould.

13

He now went with him in this new inquest,
   Him for to aide, if aide he chaunst to neede,
   Against that cruell Tyrant, which opprest
   The faire *Irena* with his foule misdeede,
   And kept the crowne in which she should succeed.
   And now together on their way they bin,
   When as they saw a Squire in squallid weed,
   Lamenting sore his sorowfull sad tyne,
With many bitter teares shed from his blubbred eyne.

14

To whom as they approched, they espide
   A sorie sight, as euer seene with eye;
   An headlesse Ladie lying him beside,
   In her owne blood all wallow'd wofully,
   That her gay clothes did in discolour die.
   Much was he moued at that ruefull sight;
   And flam'd with zeale of vengeance inwardly,
   He askt, who had that Dame so fouly dight;
Or whether his owne hand, or whether other wight?

Gk χρυσός + ἄορ, golden sword. (The other notably named sword in the poem is Arthur's Morddure; see II viii 21.6.) Appropriately, an epithet of Apollo (Jove), e.g. Homer, *Iliad* 5.509; less appropriately but revealingly, of the father of Geryon, the enemy of Justice; see IV xi 14 3n. Its classical counterpart is the thunderbolt wielded by Jove against the Titans; its biblical counterpart is the sword of gold that Jeremias gave Judas, telling him: 'Take this holie sworde, a gifte from God, wherewith thou shalt wounde the aduersaries' (2 Macc. 15.16). **Ioues eternall house** suggests God's armoury, as in Jer. 50.25: 'The Lord hathe opened his treasure, and hathe broght forthe the weapons of his wrath'.

Stanza 10

1–5 gold is named as the most perfect of the metals; **Adamant** for its surpassing hardness; see I vii 33.5–9*n*. **his name**: referring both to the sword and to Jove, as A. Fowler 1964:201 notes. **vertue**: power, efficacy. **8 dint**: blow. **9 shard**: cut.

Stanza 11

2 space: walk. **6–9 those twelue signes**: the twelve zodiacal signs. The zodiac or the Milky Way, which runs diagonally across the heavens and in which most of the constellations are placed, suggests the richly ornamented sword-belt worn diagonally across a knight's shoulder; cf. Arthur's belt at I vii 29.8–9. **enchace**: adorn. **sixt in her degree**: as Virgo, the sign of August, the sixth month after March, which begins the year. **her righteous ballance**: the constellation Libra, the sign of September; see 5.4*n*, VII vii 38.7–9.

Stanza 12

1–6 Talus is fashioned from Talos in the pseudo-Platonic *Minos* 320C: he upheld the laws inscribed in brazen tablets, and therefore was named 'brazen'; or from the man of bronze

in Apollonius, *Argonautica* 4.1638–48. He is an **yron man** because he belongs to the iron age. His connection with the giant made of gold, silver, bronze, iron, and clay in Nebuchadnezzar's dream in Dan. 2.32–33 is noted by Fletcher 1971:141. When Astraea fled with the coming of the iron age, according to Conti 1616:2.2 (as noted by Lotspeich 1932), she left in her place a 'testamentum' of laws, which suggests that Talus may be regarded as the law itself in place of original righteousness. See *Var* 5.276–80, and *View* 33: 'the laws ought to be like to stony tables, plain, steadfast, and unmoveable'. Hence his name suggests Gk τλάω, to endure steadfastly. Or, as 'talion', retaliation or simple retributive justice, from Lat. *talio*: 'an equall or like payne in recompence of an hurte' (T. Cooper 1565). Since Artegall is said to go on his way 'Ne wight him to attend' (IV vi 44.6, but cf. V iv 3.8–9 and viii 3.8–9), his robocop may be regarded as the impersonal power that enforces justice. **7 without end**: immortal. Unlike Talos who was vulnerable in the ankle. **8–9 yron flale**: a Renaissance military weapon adapted from the wooden flail or 'thresher' (vi 29.7), though see iv 44.2. Since Astraea is associated with the harvest, as at VII vii 37, her **groome** is associated with the threshing of the harvester-God of the OT, as Aptekar 1969:49–51 suggests. See also Nohrnberg 1976:418–19.

Stanza 13

1 inquest: quest; suggesting a judicial inquiry. **7 squallid**: foul through neglect, suggesting extreme personal degradation, as the lady's gay clothes are discoloured with blood at 14.5; cf. iv 34.6, xii 12.2. **8 tyne**: trouble.

Stanza 14

3 On the **headlesse Ladie** as a hieroglyph of justice, see Manning 1985:66–70. **7** Artegall's characteristic response; see IV vi 5.8–9*n*. **8 dight**: abused.

15

Ah woe is me, and well away (quoth hee)
   Bursting forth teares, like springs out of a banke,
   That euer I this dismall day did see:
   Full farre was I from thinking such a pranke;
   Yet litle losse it were, and mickle thanke,
   If I should graunt that I haue doen the same,
   That I mote drinke the cup, whereof she dranke:
   But that I should die guiltie of the blame,
The which another did, who now is fled with shame.

16

Who was it then (sayd *Artegall*) that wrought?
   And why? doe it declare vnto me trew.
   A knight (said he) if knight he may be thought,
   That did his hand in Ladies bloud embrew,
   And for no cause, but as I shall you shew.
   This day as I in solace sate hereby
   With a fayre loue, whose losse I now do rew,
   There came this knight, hauing in companie
This lucklesse Ladie, which now here doth headlesse lie.

17

He, whether mine seem'd fayrer in his eye,
   Or that he wexed weary of his owne,
   Would change with me; but I did it denye;
   So did the Ladies both, as may be knowne,
   But he, whose spirit was with pride vpblowne,
   Would not so rest contented with his right,
   But hauing from his courser her downe throwne,
   Fro me reft mine away by lawlesse might,
And on his steed her set, to beare her out of sight.

18

Which when his Ladie saw, she follow'd fast,
   And on him catching hold, gan loud to crie
   Not so to leaue her, nor away to cast,
   But rather of his hand besought to die.
   With that his sword he drew all wrathfully,
   And at one stroke cropt off her head with scorne,
   In that same place, whereas it now doth lie.
   So he my loue away with him hath borne,
And left me here, both his and mine owne loue to morne.

19

Aread (sayd he) which way then did he make?
   And by what markes may he be knowne againe?
   To hope (quoth he) him soone to ouertake,
   That hence so long departed, is but vaine:
   But yet he pricked ouer yonder plaine,
   And as I marked, bore vpon his shield,
   By which it's easie him to know againe,
   A broken sword within a bloodie field;
Expressing well his nature, which the same did wield.

20

No sooner sayd, but streight he after sent
   His yron page, who him pursew'd so light,
   As that it seem'd aboue the ground he went:
   For he was swift as swallow in her flight,
   And strong as Lyon in his Lordly might.
   It was not long, before he ouertooke
   Sir *Sanglier*; (so cleeped was that Knight)
   Whom at the first he ghessed by his looke,
And by the other markes, which of his shield he tooke.

21

He bad him stay, and backe with him retire;
   Who full of scorne to be commaunded so,
   The Lady to alight did eft require,
   Whilest he reformed that vnciuill fo:
   And streight at him with all his force did go.
   Who mou'd no more therewith, then when a rocke
   Is lightly stricken with some stones throw;
   But to him leaping, lent him such a knocke,
That on the ground he layd him like a sencelesse blocke.

22

But ere he could him selfe recure againe,
   Him in his iron paw he seized had;
   That when he wak't out of his warelesse paine,
   He found him selfe vnwist, so ill bestad,
   That lim he could not wag. Thence he him lad,
   Bound like a beast appointed to the stall:
   The sight whereof the Lady sore adrad,
   And fain'd to fly for feare of being thrall;
But he her quickly stayd, and forst to wend withall.

Stanza 15
3 dismall day: unlucky or evil day. **4 pranke**: malicious deed. **5 mickle thanke**: much favour or occasion for thanks. 7 A stock saying but biblical, e.g. Matt. 20.22–23, as Shaheen 1976:140 notes.

Stanza 16
4 embrew: imbrue, stain; cf. Arg.4.

Stanza 19
1 Aread: declare. **8–9 A broken sword** is a sign of a knight's disgrace, as at iii 37.9 and v 21.8. Manning 1985:68 relates it to an emblem in Valeriano, *Hieroglyphica*: justice dragging a captive woman who holds a broken sword signifies excessive judicial severity. **bloodie field** refers both to the surface of the shield and to the field of battle. It indicates his name, Sanglier, from Fr. *sang*, blood.

Stanza 20
2 light: quickly. He inherits his speed from the classical Talos. **7 Sanglier**: Artegall's first opponent in Satyrane's tournament at IV iv 40.3. He provides a transition from the 'wyld beasts' (7.8) upon which Artegall has exercised justice. See 'Sanglier' in the *SEnc*. Artegall's victory over him parallels Hercules's first labour, subduing the Erymanthean boar, as Dunseath 1968:73–76 notes.

Stanza 21
3 eft: in turn. **4 reformed**: punished. **vnciuill**: barbarous, uncouth.

Stanza 22
1 recure: recover. **3 warelesse paine**: his painful plight of which, being unconscious, he was unaware; or against which he could not guard himself. **4 vnwist**: not knowing how. **8 fain'd**: sought. **9 wend**: turn around.

23

When to the place they came, where *Artegall*
  By that same carefull Squire did then abide,
  He gently gan him to demaund of all,
  That did betwixt him and that Squire betide.
  Who with sterne countenance and indignant pride
  Did aunswere, that of all he guiltlesse stood,
  And his accuser thereupon defide:
  For neither he did shed that Ladies bloud,
Nor tooke away his loue, but his owne proper good.

24

Well did the Squire perceiue him selfe too weake,
  To aunswere his defiaunce in the field,
  And rather chose his challenge off to breake,
  Then to approue his right with speare and shield.
  And rather guilty chose him selfe to yield.
  But *Artegall* by signes perceiuing plaine,
  That he it was not, which that Lady kild,
  But that strange Knight, the fairer loue to gaine,
Did cast about by sleight the truth thereout to straine.

25

And sayd, Now sure this doubtfull causes right
  Can hardly but by Sacrament be tride,
  Or else by ordele, or by blooddy fight;
  That ill perhaps mote fall to either side.
  But if ye please, that I your cause decide,
  Perhaps I may all further quarrell end,
  So ye will sweare my iudgement to abide.
  Thereto they both did franckly condiscend,
And to his doome with listfull eares did both attend.

26

Sith then (sayd he) ye both the dead deny,
  And both the liuing Lady claime your right,
  Let both the dead and liuing equally
  Deuided be betwixt you here in sight,
  And each of either take his share aright.
  But looke who does dissent from this my read,
  He for a twelue moneths day shall in despight
  Beare for his penaunce that same Ladies head;
To witnesse to the world, that she by him is dead.

27

Well pleased with that doome was *Sangliere*,
  And offred streight the Lady to be slaine.
  But that same Squire, to whom she was more dere,
  When as he saw she should be cut in twaine,
  Did yield, she rather should with him remaine
  Aliue, then to him selfe be shared dead;
  And rather then his loue should suffer paine,
  He chose with shame to beare that Ladies head.
True loue despiseth shame, when life is cald in dread.

28

Whom when so willing *Artegall* perceaued;
  Not so thou Squire, (he sayd) but thine I deeme
  The liuing Lady, which from thee he reaued:
  For worthy thou of her doest rightly seeme.
  And you, Sir Knight, that loue so light esteeme,
  As that ye would for little leaue the same,
  Take here your owne, that doth you best beseeme,
  And with it beare the burden of defame;
Your owne dead Ladies head, to tell abrode your shame.

Stanza 23

2 carefull: sorrowful. **3 gently**: courteously. **demaund**: ask. **7 defide**: challenged to judicial combat. **9 proper good**: private property.

Stanza 24

3 challenge: claim. To refuse to fight is to admit guilt; see iii 32.1–4. **4 approue**: show to be true (by his victory). **5 yield**: acknowledge, admit. **9** The end, to discover the truth, justifies the means, as Astræa used 'slight' at 9.2 to acquire Chrysaor.

Stanza 25

1–4 Artegall names the customary, non-judicial means to discover truth in a dispute. **Sacrament**: an oath by which an accused sought to be cleared of any offence, as used by Duessa at I xii 30.6; **ordele**: a trial usually by fire, as the flaming porch of Busirane's house through which Britomart must pass at III xi 25; **blooddy fight**: a tilt, to which Guyon challenges Braggadocchio at iii 31.6. On judicial combat, which assumed that might is right, see McNeir 1966, esp. 108–09. **8 franckly condiscend**: freely and openly consent. **9 listfull**: attentive.

Stanza 26

Artegall's 'doome' (27.1) replicates Solomon's judgement at 1 Kings 3.16–27 by which he proved that his wisdom was given him by God. It is the first judgement of both, as Dunseath 1968:81–82 notes. **3–5** Artegall may be equivocating: to divide both ladies equally could mean that the living lady would be awarded to the victor and the dead one to the vanquished, but both Sanglier and the squire assume he means that each would be awarded half of each lady. **6–9** Artegall uses 'sleight' to achieve justice: by dissenting from his counsel, the squire proves that he is innocent of murdering the knight's lady and worthy of having his own. By not dissenting, Sanglier proves that he is guilty of murdering his lady and must carry her head. By this means Artegall upholds justice by his **read** and distributes equity by his 'doome' (29.1). **day**: space of time. **in despight**: i.e. to his own scorn.

Stanza 27

9 . . . is put in danger.

Stanza 28

2–5 thou and **Sir** mark the difference in rank between a squire and a knight. **8 defame**: disgrace.

29

But *Sangliere* disdained much his doome,
  And sternly gan repine at his beheast;
  Ne would for ought obay, as did become,
  To beare that Ladies head before his breast.
  Vntill that *Talus* had his pride represt,
  And forced him, maulgre, it vp to reare.
  Who when he saw it bootelesse to resist,
  He tooke it vp, and thence with him did beare,
As rated Spaniell takes his burden vp for feare.

30

Much did that Squire Sir *Artegall* adore,
  For his great iustice, held in high regard;
  And as his Squire him offred euermore
  To serue, for want of other meete reward,
  And wend with him on his aduenture hard.
  But he thereto would by no meanes consent;
  But leauing him forth on his iourney far'd:
  Ne wight with him but onely *Talus* went.
They two enough t'encounter an whole Regiment.

Stanza 29
6 maulgre: in spite of himself. **8–9** Punishment for cutting off a lady's head is found in Malory: Gawain must carry it 'hanged aboute hys neck' (3.8), and Pedyvere must carry it and her body on his back (6.17). The simile suggests the common punishment of a dog by making it carry any animal or bird it has killed.

Stanza 30
1 adore: praise. **8** As IV vi 44.6–8 and V iv 3.8–9.

Cant. II.

Artegall heares of Florimell,
Does with the Pagan fight:
Him slaies, drownes Lady Munera,
Does race her castle quight.

1

NOught is more honorable to a knight,
   Ne better doth beseeme braue cheualry,
Then to defend the feeble in their right,
And wrong redresse in such as wend awry.
Whilome those great Heroes got thereby
Their greatest glory, for their rightfull deedes,
And place deserued with the Gods on hy.
Herein the noblesse of this knight exceedes,
Who now to perils great for iustice sake proceedes.

2

To which as he now was vppon the way,
   He chaunst to meet a Dwarfe in hasty course;
   Whom he requir'd his forward hast to stay,
   Till he of tidings mote with him discourse.
   Loth was the Dwarfe, yet did he stay perforse,
   And gan of sundry newes his store to tell,
   As to his memory they had recourse:
   But chiefly of the fairest *Florimell*,
How she was found againe, and spousde to *Marinell*.

3

For this was *Dony*, *Florimels* owne Dwarfe,
   Whom hauing lost (as ye haue heard whyleare)
   And finding in the way the scattred scarfe,
   The fortune of her life long time did feare.

But of her health when *Artegall* did heare,
And safe returne, he was full inly glad,
And askt him where, and when her bridale cheare
Should be solemniz'd: for if time he had,
He would be there, and honor to her spousall ad.

4

Within three daies (quoth hee) as I do here,
   It will be at the Castle of the strond;
   What time if naught me let, I will be there
   To doe her seruice, so as I am bond.
   But in my way a little here beyond
   A cursed cruell Sarazin doth wonne,
   That keepes a Bridges passage by strong hond,
   And many errant Knights hath there fordonne;
That makes all men for feare that passage for to shonne.

5

What mister wight (quoth he) and how far hence
   Is he, that doth to trauellers such harmes?
   He is (said he) a man of great defence;
   Expert in battell and in deedes of armes;
   And more emboldned by the wicked charmes,
   With which his daughter doth him still support;
   Hauing great Lordships got and goodly farmes,
   Through strong oppression of his powre extort;
By which he stil them holds, and keepes with strong effort.

Book V Canto ii

Argument

The canto's two episodes treat distributive justice, though the second – the Giant with the Scales (29–54) – is not mentioned here. That subject determines the careful distribution of the stanzas: 9 on preparation (2–10), 9 on the Pagan (11–19), and 9 on Munera (20–28). Guizor being a base groom is given only nine lines (6.6–9, 11.5–9).   **4 race**: raze.

Stanza 1

5–9 those great Heroes: at i 2–3, Bacchus, Hercules, and Artegall are cited.   **noblesse**: nobility. The term is used of Arthur at I viii 26.7 and II viii 18.4.

Stanza 2

3 requir'd: requested.   **7** I.e. as he recalled.   **9 spousde**: betrothed.

Stanza 3

1 Dony: from 'donzel', Ital. *donzello*, a page, squire. Possibly a diminutive of Adonio (in Ariosto, *Orl. Fur.* 43.71), or of

Adonis.   **2 Whom hauing lost**: referring to Florimell whom he had lost, as he told Arthur at III v 3–12.   **3 the scattred scarfe**: the broken girdle dropped when Florimell fled from the hyena at III vii 31.8–9, and found not by Dony but by Satyrane. Cf. iii 27.4–7.   **5 health**: safety.   **7 cheare**: reception.

Stanza 4

2 the strond: the '*Rich strond*' (III iv 20.8) guarded by Marinell.   **3 let**: prevent.   **6 Sarazin**: Saracen or 'Pagan' (12.1).   **8 fordonne**: ruined.

Stanza 5

1 mister wight: kind of person.   **3 defence**: ability to defend himself.   **5–9** As she supports him by magic, he supports her by spoils (9.1–2). On the contemporary evils of 'livery and maintenance', which they embody, see 'Munera, Pollente' in the *SEnc*.   **Lordships**: estates belonging to lords.   **farmes**: land for cultivation; also the collecting of rents.   **extort**: wrongly obtained.

6

And dayly he his wrongs encreaseth more,
 For neuer wight he lets to passe that way,
 Ouer his Bridge, albee he rich or poore,
 But he him makes his passage-penny pay:
 Else he doth hold him backe or beat away.
 Thereto he hath a groome of euill guize,
 Whose scalp is bare, that bondage doth bewray,
 Which pols and pils the poore in piteous wize;
But he him selfe vppon the rich doth tyrannize.

7

His name is hight *Pollente*, rightly so
 For that he is so puissant and strong,
 That with his powre he all doth ouergo,
 And makes them subiect to his mighty wrong;
 And some by sleight he eke doth vnderfong.
 For on a Bridge he custometh to fight,
 Which is but narrow, but exceeding long;
 And in the same are many trap fals pight,
Through which the rider downe doth fall through ouersight.

8

And vnderneath the same a riuer flowes,
 That is both swift and dangerous deepe withall;
 Into the which whom so he ouerthrowes,
 All destitute of helpe doth headlong fall,
 But he him selfe, through practise vsuall,
 Leapes forth into the floud, and there assaies
 His foe confused through his sodaine fall,
 That horse and man he equally dismaies,
And either both them drownes, or trayterously slaies.

9

Then doth he take the spoile of them at will,
 And to his daughter brings, that dwels thereby:
 Who all that comes doth take, and therewith fill
 The coffers of her wicked threasury;
 Which she with wrongs hath heaped vp so hy,
 That many Princes she in wealth exceedes,
 And purchast all the countrey lying ny
 With the reuenue of her plenteous meedes,
Her name is *Munera*, agreeing with her deedes.

10

Thereto she is full faire, and rich attired,
 With golden hands and siluer feete beside,
 That many Lords haue her to wife desired:
 But she them all despiseth for great pride.
 Now by my life (sayd he) and God to guide,
 None other way will I this day betake,
 But by that Bridge, whereas he doth abide:
 Therefore me thither lead. No more he spake,
But thitherward forthright his ready way did make.

11

Vnto the place he came within a while,
 Where on the Bridge he ready armed saw
 The Sarazin, awayting for some spoile.
 Who as they to the passage gan to draw,
 A villaine to them came with scull all raw,
 That passage money did of them require,
 According to the custome of their law.
 To whom he aunswerd wroth, Loe there thy hire;
And with that word him strooke, that streight he did expire.

Stanza 6
3 his Bridge: the possessive indicates that private property conflicts with public right-of-way. In Malory 6.10, Lancelot is challenged by a churl because he rides over a bridge without a permit; and in Ariosto, *Orl. Fur.* 29.33, the Saracen Rodomonte confronts travellers on his narrow bridge. The abuse of toll bridges in England in the sixteenth century is noted by M.L. Neff in *Var* 5.170–71. The reference extends to the abuse of any monopoly at any time, as the poll-money required of the disciples at Matt. 17.24, the poll-tax levied in England since 1531, and, as Milton complained, the 'narrow bridge of licencing where the challenger should passe' (1953–82:2.562). **albee**: whether. **6–8 guize**: behaviour; alluding to his name, Guizor, which is given at vi 33.6. **bewray**: reveal. As he shaves his head (*OED* poll I i) and skin (pill, v.[1] 9) to declare his state of bondage, he **pols and pils** (i.e. robs) **the poore**, alluding to the name of his master, Pollente, who, in a fitting distribution of extortion, preys on the rich.

Stanza 7
1 Pollente: Lat. *pollentia*, 'might, puissance, power' (T. Cooper 1565). **5 vnderfong**: entrap, alluding to the traps in the bridge. **8 trap fals**: trapdoors that fall, as at 12.6. **9 ouersight**: i.e. seeing over or across but not under.

Stanza 8
5 practise vsuall: habitual practice or treachery, as noted at 13.5–7. **6 assaies**: assails. **8 dismaies**: defeats by sudden onslaught.

Stanza 9
8 meedes: corrupt gain. **9 Munera**: Lat. rewards or gifts, here offered as bribes. She is the offspring of Lady Meed in Langland, *Piers Plowman* 2.8–17: e.g. her 'golden hands' (10.2) suggest Meed's fingers 'fretted with golde wyre'; her 'goodly hew' (25.8), Meed's rich attire; and she is seized 'by the sclender wast' (27.1) as Meed is taken 'bi the Middel' (3.10). See Nohrnberg 1976:392. At 23.3, she confirms her name in seeking to corrupt Talus with 'goodly meede'.

Stanza 11
5 A villaine: i.e. a villein, one in bondage, as noted at 6.7. **7 custome**: referring also to the toll, as again at 28.8. **8 hire**: payment, alluding to the 'passage-penny pay' (6.4) that he asks of others.

12

Which when the Pagan saw, he wexed wroth,
  And streight him selfe vnto the fight addrest,
  Ne was Sir *Artegall* behinde: so both
  Together ran with ready speares in rest.
  Right in the midst, whereas they brest to brest
  Should meete, a trap was letten downe to fall
  Into the floud: streight leapt the Carle vnblest,
  Well weening that his foe was falne withall:
But he was well aware, and leapt before his fall.

13

There being both together in the floud,
  They each at other tyrannously flew;
  Ne ought the water cooled their whot bloud,
  But rather in them kindled choler new.
  But there the Paynim, who that vse well knew
  To fight in water, great aduantage had,
  That oftentimes him nigh he ouerthrew:
  And eke the courser, whereuppon he rad,
Could swim like to a fish, whiles he his backe bestrad.

14

Which oddes when as Sir *Artegall* espide,
  He saw no way, but close with him in hast;
  And to him driuing strongly downe the tide,
  Vppon his iron coller griped fast,
  That with the straint his wesand nigh he brast.
  There they together stroue and struggled long,
  Either the other from his steede to cast;
  Ne euer *Artegall* his griple strong
For any thing wold slacke, but still vppon him hong.

15

As when a Dolphin and a Sele are met,
  In the wide champian of the Ocean plaine:
  With cruell chaufe their courages they whet,
  The maysterdome of each by force to gaine,

And dreadfull battaile twixt them do darraine:
  They snuf, they snort, they bounce, they rage, they rore,
  That all the sea disturbed with their traine,
  Doth frie with fome aboue the surges hore.
Such was betwixt these two the troublesome vprore.

16

So *Artegall* at length him forst forsake
  His horses backe, for dread of being drownd,
  And to his handy swimming him betake.
  Eftsoones him selfe he from his hold vnbownd,
  And then no ods at all in him he fownd:
  For *Artegall* in swimming skilfull was,
  And durst the depth of any water sownd.
  So ought each Knight, that vse of perill has,
In swimming be expert through waters force to pas.

17

Then very doubtfull was the warres euent,
  Vncertaine whether had the better side.
  For both were skild in that experiment,
  And both in armes well traind and throughly tride.
  But *Artegall* was better breath'd beside,
  And towards th'end, grew greater in his might,
  That his faint foe no longer could abide
  His puissance, ne beare him selfe vpright,
But from the water to the land betooke his flight.

18

But *Artegall* pursewd him still so neare,
  With bright Chrysaor in his cruell hand,
  That as his head he gan a litle reare
  Aboue the brincke, to tread vpon the land,
  He smote it off, that tumbling on the strand
  It bit the earth for very fell despight,
  And gnashed with his teeth, as if he band
  High God, whose goodnesse he despaired quight,
Or curst the hand, which did that vengeance on him dight.

Stanza 12

7 vnblest: unblessed, because he is a **Pagan**, and hence accursed. Cf. 18.8. **8 withall**: as well, i.e. with the trap. **9 aware**: wary.

Stanza 14

5 straint: strain, pressure. **wesand**: windpipe. **8 griple**: grasp.

Stanza 15

1–2 Dolphin: signifying guile, particularly that used to overcome a guileful opponent, as Aptekar 1969:127 notes, citing Ripa who represents *Stratagemma Militare* by an armed man whose helmet is crested with a dolphin's head. **Sele**: 'stinking Seales' (*Colin Clout* 249) suggests why that animal is compared to Pollente. **champian**: open stretches. **5 darraine**: wage. **6 bounce**: thump, as 21.6. **7 traine**: the track made by their bodies. **8 frie**: boil.

Stanza 16

3 handy: with his hands; or in which he was handy. **4–5** I.e. even after being released from Artegall's hold, Pollente had

no advantage over him. **6–9** For Renaissance lore on the often-scorned art of swimming and the claims by some military writers that knights should learn to swim in full armour, see M. West 1973. **vse**: frequent experience.

Stanza 17

1 euent: outcome. **2 whether**: which. **3 experiment**: experience, i.e. of swimming.

Stanza 18

1–5 While Talus's flail enforces justice throughout Bk V, Artegall's Chrysaor is used only three times: here, likely at the tournament (see iii 22.1), and against Grantorto at xii 23. **cruell**: severe, strict, rigorous. A surprising epithet; cf. iii 22.1, v 13.1, etc., and esp. Isa. 13.9. **6** More than a classical detail, as it is in Virgil, *Aen.* 11.418: the curse upon the serpent is that it shall eat dust (Gen. 3.14). It is repeated at the fall of Geryoneo at xi 14.7, and of Grantorto at xii 23.7. **7 band**: cursed. **9 that vengeance**: Artegall's vengeance is also God's, as Aptekar 1969:33–34 notes. **dight**: execute.

19

His corps was carried downe along the Lee,
  Whose waters with his filthy bloud it stayned:
  But his blasphemous head, that all might see,
  He pitcht vpon a pole on high ordayned;
  Where many years it afterwards remayned,
  To be a mirrour to all mighty men,
  That none of them the feeble ouerren,
But alwaies doe their powre within iust compasse pen.

20

That done, vnto the Castle he did wend,
  In which the Paynims daughter did abide,
  Guarded of many which did her defend:
  Of whom he entrance sought, but was denide,
  And with reprochfull blasphemy defide,
  Beaten with stones downe from the battilment,
  That he was forced to withdraw aside;
  And bad his seruant *Talus* to inuent
Which way he enter might, without endangerment.

21

Eftsoones his Page drew to the Castle gate,
  And with his iron flale at it let flie,
  That all the warders it did sore amate,
  The which erewhile spake so reprochfully,
  And made them stoupe, that looked earst so hie.
  Yet still he bet, and bounst vppon the dore,
  And thundred strokes thereon so hideouslie,
  That all the peece he shaked from the flore,
And filled all the house with feare and great vprore.

22

With noise whereof the Lady forth appeared
  Vppon the Castle wall, and when she saw
  The daungerous state, in which she stood, she feared
  The sad effect of her neare ouerthrow;
  And gan entreat that iron man below,
  To cease his outrage, and him faire besought,
  Sith neither force of stones which they did throw,
  Nor powr of charms, which she against him wrought,
Might otherwise preuaile, or make him cease for ought.

23

But when as yet she saw him to proceede,
  Vnmou'd with praiers, or with piteous thought,
  She ment him to corrupt with goodly meede;
  And causde great sackes with endlesse riches fraught,
  Vnto the battilment to be vpbrought,
  And powred forth ouer the Castle wall,
  That she might win some time, though dearly bought
  Whilest he to gathering of the gold did fall.
But he was nothing mou'd, nor tempted therewithall.

24

But still continu'd his assault the more,
  And layd on load with his huge yron flaile,
  That at the length he has yrent the dore,
  And made way for his maister to assaile.
  Who being entred, nought did then auaile
  For wight, against his powre them selues to reare:
  Each one did flie; their hearts began to faile,
  And hid them selues in corners here and there;
And eke their dame halfe dead did hide her self for feare.

25

Long they her sought, yet no where could they finde her,
  That sure they ween'd she was escapt away:
  But *Talus*, that could like a limehound winde her,
  And all things secrete wisely could bewray,
  At length found out, whereas she hidden lay
  Vnder an heape of gold. Thence he her drew
  By the faire lockes, and fowly did array,
  Withouten pitty of her goodly hew,
That *Artegall* him selfe her seemelesse plight did rew.

26

Yet for no pitty would he change the course
  Of Iustice, which in *Talus* hand did lye;
  Who rudely hayld her forth without remorse,
  Still holding vp her suppliant hands on hye,
  And kneeling at his feete submissiuely.
  But he her suppliant hands, those hands of gold,
  And eke her feete, those feete of siluer trye,
  Which sought vnrighteousnesse, and iustice sold,
Chopt off, and nayld on high, that all might them behold.

Stanza 19

1–2 **Lee**: river, as 'watry lea' (IV ii 16.3), referring to water as open ground; or to the English Lee, a tributary of the Thames (see IV xi 29.7); or possibly to the Irish Lee (see IV xi 44.3–4). The river which was the means of his injustice becomes the means of his just punishment, and is punished itself. Cf. 27.4–5, 9. 4–9 A common form of disgrace, e.g. the head of Desmond – see III v 17.2*n* – was publicly displayed at Dublin Castle in 1582 as a warning to rebels; see *Var* 5.173. **vpon a pole**: the punishment fits his crime and his name. **mirrour**: reminder; warning. **right**: the pun suggests why power is symbolized by the right hand.

Stanza 20

5 **blasphemy**: slander, specifically against God's minister.
8 **inuent**: find out.

Stanza 21

3 **amate**: dismay. 4 **reprochfully**: abusively. 8 **peece**: fortress.

Stanza 22

4 **effect**: accomplishment.

Stanza 25

3 Like a bloodhound, Talus could get the wind of her. 7 **array**: afflict. 8 **hew**: appearance; also colour, here of gold and silver. 9 **seemelesse**: unseemly.

Stanza 26

6–9 Correlative verse: he chopped off her feet which **sought vnrighteousnesse** and her hands which **iustice sold**. In being unable to receive bribes, the handless Munera becomes a traditional icon of justice; see Nohrnberg 1976:392, and Manning 1985:71. **of siluer trye**: of refined silver (to indic-ate her rich bribes).

27

Her selfe then tooke he by the sclender wast,
    In vaine loud crying, and into the flood
    Ouer the Castle wall adowne her cast,
    And there her drowned in the durty mud:
    But the streame washt away her guilty blood.
    Thereafter all that mucky pelfe he tooke,
    The spoile of peoples euill gotten good,
    The which her sire had scrap't by hooke and crooke,
And burning all to ashes, powr'd it downe the brooke.

28

And lastly all that Castle quite he raced,
    Euen from the sole of his foundation,
    And all the hewen stones thereof defaced,
    That there mote be no hope of reparation,
    Nor memory thereof to any nation.
    All which when *Talus* throughly had perfourmed,
    Sir *Artegall* vndid the euill fashion,
    And wicked customes of that Bridge refourmed.
Which done, vnto his former iourney he retourned.

29

In which they measur'd mickle weary way,
    Till that at length nigh to the sea they drew;
    By which as they did trauell on a day,
    They saw before them, far as they could vew,

Full many people gathered in a crew;
    Whose great assembly they did much admire.
    For neuer there the like resort they knew.
    So towards them they coasted, to enquire
What thing so many nations met, did there desire.

30

There they beheld a mighty Gyant stand
    Vpon a rocke, and holding forth on hie
    An huge great paire of ballance in his hand,
    With which he boasted in his surquedrie,
    That all the world he would weigh equallie,
    If ought he had the same to counterpoys.
    For want whereof he weighed vanity,
    And fild his ballaunce full of idle toys:
Yet was admired much of fooles, women, and boys.

31

He sayd that he would all the earth vptake,
    And all the sea, deuided each from either:
    So would he of the fire one ballaunce make,
    And one of th'ayre, without or wind, or wether:
    Then would he ballaunce heauen and hell together,
    And all that did within them all containe;
    Of all whose weight, he would not misse a fether.
    And looke what surplus did of each remaine,
He would to his owne part restore the same againe.

Stanza 27

2–4 The punishment fits her attempted bribery of Talus at 23.4–6. **6 mucky pelfe**: 'filthy lucre', used here for pilfered property. **9** As Moses burned the golden calf and cast its dust into the river, Deut. 9.21.

Stanza 28

1 raced: razed, as Arg.4. Cf. Job 15.34: 'Fyre shal deuoure the houses of bribes', which the Geneva gloss identifies as those 'which were buylt or mainteined by powling, and briberie'; noted Dunseath 1968:94. **3 defaced**: destroyed. **4 reparation**: repair.

Stanzas 29–54

The second half of the canto balances the first by turning from the excesses of early capitalist society, represented by Pollente's private monopoly, to the dangers of early communism, represented by the Giant; see Meyer 1991:98. The emblem of justice in the handless Munera is replaced by the Giant holding the scales of justice. His egalitarianism arouses 'the vulgar' (33.1) to revolt, which was much feared in the sixteenth century; see 'radicalism in Spenser' in the *SEnc*. A version of these stanzas was printed in *The Faerie Leveller* (1648) to attack the Levellers, a sect 'discryed long agoe in Queene *Elizabeths* days, and then graphically described by the Prince of English Poets' (*Sp All* 223). See King 1985, and Greenfield 1998:124–29. As an attack on the Anabaptists, see Padelford in *Var* 5.336–41.

The Giant's debate with Artegall, which pits polarized opposites concerning hierarchy, as Kane 1989:14–15 notes, is carefully weighted in the latter's favour: his two stanzas (31–32) are answered by Artegall's three (34–36); his two stanzas of rebuttal (37–38) by Artegall's five (39–43); and after an exchange of arguments in 44–45, Artegall continues to speak

in 46–48 while he remains silent. Yet his argument has proven surprisingly persuasive, and, for many, Talus's resort to force remains disturbing. E.g. in his last poem, and his only political one, Keats added a stanza 55 in his copy of Spenser: reconstituted by Typographus and educated by the sage, the Giant meets Artegall and Talus, 'The one he struck stone blind, the other's eyes wox dim'. Hadfield 1998b:179 suggests that S. also may have been on the Giant's side.

Stanza 29

1 measur'd: travelled. **6 great assembly**: a pejorative term that suggests a mob, as in *View* 77 and IV i 28.4. See Patterson 1993:99–101. **admire**: wonder at. **8 coasted**: approached; 'travelled along the coast' fits the context, for their destination is 'the Castle of the [rich] strond' (4.2), an appropriate setting for the ensuing debate.

Stanza 30

1 a mighty Gyant: not named but usually identified as the Giant with the scales by his **paire of ballance**, which usurps Astræa's 'righteous ballance' (i 11.9) and God's balance (see 35*n*). Or as the Egalitarian Giant from his argument; see 29–54*n*. He corresponds to the apocalyptic figure with 'balances in his hand' riding a black horse in Rev. 6.5, as Dunseath 1968:98 notes; or to the giants of Gen. 6.4 who are glossed as tyrants in the Geneva Bible, and as 'seditious and rebellious subiects in a common wealth' by Fraunce 1975:23–24. See 'Giant with the scales' in the *SEnc*. **4 surquedrie**: arrogance, presumption. **5–6** He echoes Archimedes's boast: 'Give me a place to stand and I will move the earth'. **7–9** Cf. Ps. 62.9: 'Yet the children of men are vanitie, the chief men are lies: to lay them vpon a balance thei are altogether lighter then vanitie'. Weighing **vanity** alludes to its etymology, Lat. *vanus*, empty.

32

For why, he sayd they all vnequall were,
    And had encroched vppon others share,
    Like as the sea (which plaine he shewed there)
    Had worne the earth, so did the fire the aire,
    So all the rest did others parts empaire.
    And so were realmes and nations run awry.
    All which he vndertooke for to repaire,
    In sort as they were formed aunciently;
And all things would reduce vnto equality.

33

Therefore the vulgar did about him flocke,
    And cluster thicke vnto his leasings vaine,
    Like foolish flies about an hony crocke,
    In hope by him great benefite to gaine,
    And vncontrolled freedome to obtaine.
    All which when *Artegall* did see, and heare,
    How he mis-led the simple peoples traine,
    In sdeignfull wize he drew vnto him neare,
And thus vnto him spake, without regard or feare.

34

Thou that presum'st to weigh the world anew,
    And all things to an equall to restore,
    In stead of right me seemes great wrong dost shew,
    And far aboue thy forces pitch to sore.

For ere thou limit what is lesse or more
    In euery thing, thou oughtest first to know,
    What was the poyse of euery part of yore:
    And looke then how much it doth ouerflow,
Or faile thereof, so much is more then iust to trow.

35

For at the first they all created were
    In goodly measure, by their Makers might,
    And weighed out in ballaunces so nere,
    That not a dram was missing of their right.
    The earth was in the middle centre pight,
    In which it doth immoueable abide,
    Hemd in with waters like a wall in sight;
    And they with aire, that not a drop can slide:
Al which the heauens containe, and in their courses guide.

Spenser?

36

Such heauenly iustice doth among them raine,
    That euery one doe know their certaine bound,
    In which they doe these many yeares remaine,
    And mongst them al no change hath yet beene found.
    But if thou now shouldst weigh them new in pound,
    We are not sure they would so long remaine:
    All change is perillous, and all chaunce vnsound.
    Therefore leaue off to weigh them all againe,
Till we may be assur'd they shall their course retaine.

Stanza 31

The Giant may claim that he seeks only to restore the world as it was when first created, but by reweighing the four elements he threatens to return it to its earlier state 'without forme and voyde' (Gen. 1.2). Hence line 2 refers to the third day of creation when God divided the earth from the sea. The danger of what he proposes is expressed by Jeremiah: 'Thus saith the Lord, If the heauens can be measured, or the fundacions of the earth be searched out beneth, then wil I cast of all the sede of Israel' (Jer. 31.37; noted Dunseath 1968:102). **4 wether**: tempest. I.e. he claims to be able to weigh air without regard to its motion.

Stanza 32

1 For why: because. **3–4** Mutabilitie argues the same at VII vii 25.4–9; cf. *HL* 78–83 on the original chaos. **8 In sort as**: in the manner. **9 reduce**: bring back, restore. **equality**: a term associated with the Anabaptists who were denounced in 1589 by Bishop Cooper because they sought 'a general equality, most dangerous to the society of men'; cited in the *SEnc* 579. On the connection with gavilkind or tanistry, whereby the Irish transformed private property into communal property of the clan, see C. Carroll 1990:180.

Stanza 33

1–5 The lines reflect the fear of the Elizabethan ruling class that any popular uprising, however minor and for whatever cause, threatened the rigidly hierarchical society. **leasings**: lies.

Stanza 34

1–4 an equall: a state of equality. The Giant's argument depends on the sense of Lat. *aequus*, fair, equitable. Since arithmetical equality need not be just, Astræa's scales 'equall gaue to each as Iustice duly scann'd' (VII vii 38.9), where 'equall' allows proportional distribution. See Fletcher 1971:244. **pitch**: the height to which a falcon soars before swooping upon its prey. **5–9** I.e. only by knowing the original weight (**poyse**) of each thing may one know what is more or less than just or right.

Stanza 35

To the Giant's claim that at the beginning all things were created equal, Artegall answers that God created each thing in its proper place by measuring and weighing. For the cosmic balance by which God created the universe, see 2 Esd. 4.36, Isa. 40.12, and esp. Job 28.23–25, 38.4–6. **1 at the first**: referring to the creation. **5–9** For the sake of his argument, Artegall invokes Ptolemy's geocentric theory in which the earth being the centre of the universe is surrounded by successive concentric spheres of water, air, and fire.

Stanza 36

4 For the sake of his argument, Artegall ignores the physical effects of the Fall described in Proem 4; or he may invoke the concept of entropy: in the closed system of creation, the nature and quantity of the elements have not changed, as he goes on to claim at 39.4–9. **5 new in pound**: anew in the balance. **7** As *View* 94: 'all innovation is perilous'. A truism of conservatism that extends back to Plato, *Laws* 797d–e, and is confirmed by the mob at 51.9.

37

Thou foolishe Elfe (said then the Gyant wroth)
  Seest not, how badly all things present bee,
  And each estate quite out of order goth?
  The sea it selfe doest thou not plainely see
  Encroch vppon the land there vnder thee;
  And th'earth it selfe how daily its increast,
  By all that dying to it turned be?
  Were it not good that wrong were then surceast,
And from the most, that some were giuen to the least?

38

Therefore I will throw downe these mountaines hie,
  And make them leuell with the lowly plaine:
  These towring rocks, which reach vnto the skie,
  I will thrust downe into the deepest maine,
  And as they were, them equalize againe.
  Tyrants that make men subiect to their law,
  I will suppresse, that they no more may raine;
  And Lordings curbe, that commons ouer-aw;
And all the wealth of rich men to the poore will draw.

39

Of things vnseene how canst thou deeme aright,
  Then answered the righteous *Artegall*,
  Sith thou misdeem'st so much of things in sight?
  What though the sea with waues continuall
  Doe eate the earth, it is no more at all:
  Ne is the earth the lesse, or loseth ought,
  For whatsoeuer from one place doth fall,
  Is with the tide vnto an other brought:
For there is nothing lost, that may be found, if sought.

40

Likewise the earth is not augmented more,
  By all that dying into it doe fade.
  For of the earth they formed were of yore,
  How euer gay their blossome or their blade

Doe flourish now, they into dust shall vade.
  What wrong then is it, if that when they die,
  They turne to that, whereof they first were made?
  All in the powre of their great Maker lie:
All creatures must obey the voice of the most hie.

41

They liue, they die, like as he doth ordaine,
  Ne euer any asketh reason why.
  The hils doe not the lowly dales disdaine;
  The dales doe not the lofty hils enuy.
  He maketh Kings to sit in souerainty;
  He maketh subiects to their powre obay;
  He pulleth downe, he setteth vp on hy;
  He giues to this, from that he takes away.
For all we haue is his: what he list doe, he may.

42

What euer thing is done, by him is donne,
  Ne any may his mighty will withstand;
  Ne any may his soueraine power shonne,
  Ne loose that he hath bound with stedfast band.
  In vaine therefore doest thou now take in hand,
  To call to count, or weigh his workes anew,
  Whose counsels depth thou canst not vnderstand,
  Sith of things subiect to thy daily vew
Thou doest not know the causes, nor their courses dew.

43

For take thy ballaunce, if thou be so wise,
  And weigh the winde, that vnder heauen doth blow;
  Or weigh the light, that in the East doth rise;
  Or weigh the thought, that from mans mind doth flow.
  But if the weight of these thou canst not show,
  Weigh but one word which from thy lips doth fall.
  For how canst thou those greater secrets know,
  That doest not know the least thing of them all?
Ill can he rule the great, that cannot reach the small.

Stanza 37
3 estate: state. **4** His atrocious pun rightly determines his punishment at 49.9. **8 surceast**: entirely stopped. **9 most**: greatest.

Stanza 38
1–5 The Giant assumes an apocalyptic role: 'Euerie valley shalbe filled, and euerie mountaine, and hil shalbe broght lowe' (Luke 3.5, citing Isa. 40.4). **leuell**: another highly charged term in a hierarchical society, alluding to the Levellers. **8–9 Lordings**: petty lords. The Giant's argument has expanded from 'some' (37.9) to **all**.

Stanza 40
4–5 The imagery is scriptural, as Jas. 1.10: 'As the flower of the grasse shal he vanish away'. **vade**: vanish.

Stanza 41
1–2 Cf. Dan. 4.32: 'According to his wil he worketh . . . and none can stay his hand, nor say vnto him, What doest thou?'. **5–6** Cf. Prov. 8.15: 'By me, Kings reigne' and Rom. 13.1–2: 'Let euerie soule be subiect vnto the higher powers: for there

is no power but of God . . . Whosoeuer therefore resisteth the power, resisteth the ordinance of God'. **maketh** shifts in meaning from 'appoints' to 'compels'. **7–8** Cf. Sam. 2.7: 'The Lord maketh poore and maketh riche: bringeth lowe, and exalteth'; also Job 1.21: 'The Lord hathe giuen, and the Lord hathe taken it'. **9** As Job finally admits to God: 'I knowe that thou canst do all things' (42.2). **may**: can; but with the threat that he will.

Stanza 42
Artegall's argument implies that God's absolute dominion is delegated to secular authority, as E. Fowler 1995:62 notes. Cf. P. Stevens 1995:160. **2** Cf. 2 Chron. 20 6: 'In thine hand is power and might, and none is able to withstand thee'. **5–9** As Uriel rebukes Esdras: 'Thine owne things . . . canst thou not knowe: how shulde thy vessel then be able to comprehend the wayes of the Hiest?' (2 Esd. 4.10–11). On S.'s use of this apocalyptic book, see Hazard 2000. **count**: account.

Stanza 43
1–2 Cf. 2 Esd. 4.5: 'Weigh me the weight of the fyre, or measure me the blast of the winde'. Cf. Job 28.25. **7 secrets**: the

44

Therewith the Gyant much abashed sayd;
    That he of little things made reckoning light,
    Yet the least word that euer could be layd
    Within his ballaunce, he could way aright.
    Which is (sayd he) more heauy then in weight,
    The right or wrong, the false or else the trew?
    He answered, that he would try it streight,   ??
    So he the words into his ballaunce threw,
But streight the winged words out of his ballaunce flew.

collapse of metaphor

45

Wroth wext he then, and sayd, that words were light,
    Ne would within his ballaunce well abide.
    But he could iustly weigh the wrong or right.
    Well then, sayd *Artegall*, let it be tride.
    First in one ballance set the true aside.
    He did so first; and then the false he layd
    In th'other scale; but still it downe did slide,
    And by no meane could in the weight be stayd.
For by no meanes the false will with the truth be wayd.

46

Now take the right likewise, sayd *Artegale*,
    And counterpeise the same with so much wrong.
    So first the right he put into one scale;
    And then the Gyant stroue with puissance strong
    To fill the other scale with so much wrong.
    But all the wrongs that he therein could lay,
    Might not it peise; yet did he labour long,
    And swat, and chauf'd, and proued euery way:
Yet all the wrongs could not a litle right downe way.

47

Which when he saw, he greatly grew in rage,
    And almost would his balances haue broken:
    But *Artegall* him fairely gan asswage,
    And said; Be not vpon thy balance wroken:
    For they doe nought but right or wrong betoken;
    But in the mind the doome of right must bee;
    And so likewise of words, the which be spoken,
    The eare must be the ballance, to decree
And iudge, whether with truth or falshood they agree.

48

But set the truth and set the right aside,
    For they with wrong or falshood will not fare;
    And put two wrongs together to be tride,
    Or else two falses, of each equall share;
    And then together doe them both compare.
    For truth is one, and right is euer one.
    So did he, and then plaine it did appeare,
    Whether of them the greater were attone.
But right sate in the middest of the beame alone.

49

But he the right from thence did thrust away,
    For it was not the right, which he did seeke;
    But rather stroue extremities to way,
    Th'one to diminish, th'other for to eeke.
    For of the meane he greatly did misleeke.
    Whom when so lewdly minded *Talus* found,
    Approching nigh vnto him cheeke by cheeke,
    He shouldered him from off the higher ground,
And down the rock him throwing, in the sea him dround.

---

hidden workings of God, known only through revelation. In contrast to the Giant, Arthur confesses that he does not 'vnderstand | The secret meaning of th'eternall might' (I ix 6.7–8).

Stanzas 44–47
Artegall asks his questions with the authority of one who has 'the skill of deeming wrong and right' because Astraea taught him 'to weigh both right and wrong | In equall ballance' (i 8.2, 7.1–2) . Hence he knows that the true and the false cannot be weighed together, nor can right and wrong, but only separately, the difference between them being known only by the mind. It follows that hearing alone – though only after hearing the word of God, as his biblical citations indicate – may judge if words are true or false. The Giant exposes his ignorance when he seeks to weigh right against wrong, even as Auarice reveals his moral state when he 'right and wrong ylike in equall ballance waide' (I iv 27.9). On the material substantiality of language at issue here, see Anderson 1996:180–85.

Stanza 44
9 This consequence is esp. persuasive to a poet who uses 'sweet numbers and melodious measures | . . . the winged words to tie' (*Teares* 547–48).

Stanza 45
1 **light**: implying also 'of no consequence', as 44.2. **7–8 it**: i.e. **the true**, for **the false**, like Belshazzar being 'wayed in the balance', is 'founde to light' (Dan. 5.27). **weight**: scales.

Stanza 46
7 **peise**: counterbalance. 8 **proued**: tried.

Stanza 47
3 **fairely**: courteously. 4 **wroken**: avenged. 5 **betoken**: signify; cf. *Am* 62.4. On its use, see Anderson 1996:182–83. 8–9 Implying a judicial hearing, as at iii 32.1 and ix 36.5, at which the opposing arguments of Artegall and the Giant would be heard.

Stanza 48
4 **falses**: falsehoods. 6 Proverbial: Smith 791; cf. 'truth is one in all' (xi 56.8). 8 'Which of them is the greater when brought together'. A.B. Gough 1921 finds an allusion to the Aristotelian theory of virtue as a mean between two contrary vices.

Stanza 49
4 **eeke**: increase. 6 **lewdly**: ignorantly, evilly. 7–9 Talus's gesture recalls Aries who 'shouldred hath the Bull' in proem 5.9. In effect, he tips the scales against the giant, making him lose his balance. One who wished to thrust the towering rocks into the sea at 38.3–9 is himself thrown from his rock into the sea. The 'allegorical separation of rhetoric and violence', noted by Greenblatt 1990a:123, is that between the judge and the executioner. After persuasion fails, force must be used, as much as needed.

50

Like as a ship, whom cruell tempest driues
   Vpon a rocke with horrible dismay,
   Her shattered ribs in thousand peeces riues,
   And spoyling all her geares and goodly ray,
   Does make her selfe misfortunes piteous pray.
   So downe the cliffe the wretched Gyant tumbled;
   His battred ballances in peeces lay,
   His timbered bones all broken rudely rumbled,
So was the high aspyring with huge ruine humbled.

51

That when the people, which had there about
   Long wayted, saw his sudden desolation,
   They gan to gather in tumultuous rout,
   And mutining, to stirre vp ciuill faction,
   For certaine losse of so great expectation.
   For well they hoped to haue got great good,
   And wondrous riches by his innouation.
   Therefore resoluing to reuenge his blood,
They rose in armes, and all in battell order stood.

52

Which lawlesse multitude him comming too
   In warlike wise, when *Artegall* did vew,
   He much was troubled, ne wist what to doo.
   For loth he was his noble hands t'embrew
In the base blood of such a rascall crew;
   And otherwise, if that he should retire,
   He fear'd least they with shame would him pursew.
   Therefore he *Talus* to them sent, t'inquire
The cause of their array, and truce for to desire.

53

But soone as they him nigh approching spide,
   They gan with all their weapons him assay,
   And rudely stroke at him on euery side:
   Yet nought they could him hurt, ne ought dismay.
   But when at them he with his flaile gan lay,
   He like a swarme of flyes them ouerthrew;
   Ne any of them durst come in his way,
   But here and there before his presence flew,
And hid themselues in holes and bushes from his vew.

54

As when a Faulcon hath with nimble flight
   Flowne at a flush of Ducks, foreby the brooke,
   The trembling foule dismayd with dreadfull sight
   Of death, the which them almost ouertooke,
   Doe hide themselues from her astonying looke,
   Amongst the flags and couert round about.
   When *Talus* saw they all the field forsooke
   And none appear'd of all that raskall rout,
To *Artegall* he turn'd, and went with him throughout.

Stanza 50
The Giant's death recalls the death of Antiochus: 'All the membres of his bodie were bruised with the great fall. And thus he that a litle afore thoght he might . . . weigh the hie mountaines in ye balance, was now cast on the ground . . . declaring vnto all the manifest power of God' (2 Macc. 9.7–8). **2 dismay**: referring to the effect upon her crew. **4 geares**: rigging. **ray**: array. **8 timbered**: massive, being structured like a ship or his own balances. **9** Confirming Christ's condemnation of the ambitious: 'Whosoeuer wil exalt himself, shalbe broght low' (Matt. 23.12), though the simile allows that the Giant is **misfortunes piteous pray**. **ruine**: downfall.

Stanza 51
7 innouation: another highly charged term that suggests 'revolution' or 'insurrection'; see Patterson 1993:107. **9 in**

battell order stood: indicating that 'the simple peoples traine' (33.7) has turned into an armed insurrection.

Stanza 52
4–5 A knight was forbidden by chivalric code to fight with his social inferiors. **embrew**: stain. **rascall**: knavish; villainous; belonging to the rabble.

Stanza 53
1–2 soone: forthwith. Their rejection of a truce justifies Talus's use of force without even reading the riot act. **assay**: assail.

Stanza 54
2 flush: flight of birds suddenly started up. **5 astonying**: paralysing. **6 flags**: reeds. **9 turn'd**: returned.

Cant. III.

The spousals of faire Florimell,
where turney many knights:
There Braggadochio is vncas'd
in all the Ladies sights.

1
After long stormes and tempests ouerblowne,
The sunne at length his ioyous face doth cleare:
So when as fortune all her spight hath showne,
Some blisfull houres at last must needes appeare;
Else should afflicted wights oftimes despeire.
So comes it now to *Florimell* by tourne,
After long sorrowes suffered whyleare,
In which captiu'd she many moneths did mourne,
To tast of ioy, and to wont pleasures to retourne.

2
Who being freed from *Proteus* cruell band
By *Marinell*, was vnto him affide,
And by him brought againe to Faerie land;
Where he her spous'd, and made his ioyous bride.
The time and place was blazed farre and wide;
And solemne feasts and giusts ordain'd therefore.
To which there did resort from euery side
Of Lords and Ladies infinite great store;
Ne any Knight was absent, that braue courage bore.

3
To tell the glorie of the feast that day,
The goodly seruice, the deuicefull sights,
The bridegromes state, the brides most rich aray,
The pride of Ladies, and the worth of knights,

The royall banquets, and the rare delights
Were worke fit for an Herauld, not for me:
But for so much as to my lot here lights,
That with this present treatise doth agree,
True vertue to aduance, shall here recounted bee.

4
When all men had with full satietie
Of meates and drinkes their appetites suffiz'd,
To deedes of armes and proofe of cheualrie
They gan themselues addresse, full rich aguiz'd,
As each one had his furnitures deuiz'd.
And first of all issu'd Sir *Marinell*,
And with him six knights more, which enterpriz'd
To chalenge all in right of *Florimell*,
And to maintaine, that she all others did excell.

5
The first of them was hight Sir *Orimont*,
A noble Knight, and tride in hard assayes:
The second had to name Sir *Bellisont*,
But second vnto none in prowesse prayse;
The third was *Brunell*, famous in his dayes;
The fourth *Ecastor*, of exceeding might;
The fift *Armeddan*, skild in louely layes;
The sixt was *Lansack*, a redoubted Knight:
All six well seene in armes, and prou'd in many a fight.

Book V Canto iii

Argument
3 vncas'd: exposed literally when stripped of his armour at 37.8; and figuratively when his 'counterfeits were thus vncased' at 39.1, one being his lady.

Stanza 1
6 by tourne: alluding to fortune's wheel. **9 wont**: wonted, accustomed.

Stanza 2
1–2 Recalling the warrant by which Cymodoce freed Florimell from Proteus's power, and got 'So faire a wife for her sonne *Marinell*' (IV xii 33.7). **affide**: betrothed. **3** Florimell was taken from faery land when Proteus took her to his bower at III viii 36.9. **6 solemne**: ceremonial.

Stanza 3
2 deuicefull sights: referring to the ingenious spectacles, masques, and triumphs associated with Elizabethan tournaments. **6** The distinction is made by Jonson: 'I a *Poet* here,

no *Herald* am' (1925–52:8.29). **8–9 treatise**: story (*OED* 1b) but also 'a book containing a methodical exposition of the principles of a subject' (*OED* 1a), here of the virtue of justice, which S. records. The poem has the power given religion in *Colin Clout* 323, namely, 'Advancing vertue'.

Stanza 4
4 aguiz'd: arrayed. **5 furnitures**: equipment or suit of armour. **7 enterpriz'd**: undertook.

Stanza 5
The names may veil compliments to living knights, as S. promises in *DS 3*, esp. the first: **Orimont**, the Earl of Ormond; see *DS 7n*. **Bellisont**: 'wager of war', from Lat. *bellare*; sugg. Draper 1932:100. **Brunell**: Ital. *brunello*, 'little brown man'; sugg. A.B. Gough 1921. **Ecastor**: from Castor, 'breaker of horses' (Homer, *Ody*. 11.300). As an oath used by women (T. Cooper 1565), the name fits one skilled in **louely layes**, i.e. in lays of love. **Armeddan**: from Span. *armada*, army; or the 'armed one'. **Lansack**: 'a land-sacker'. **2** . . . proven in hard assaults. **9 seene**: skilled.

6

And them against came all that list to giust,
From euery coast and countrie vnder sunne:
None was debard, but all had leaue that lust.
The trompets sound; then all together ronne.
Full many deedes of armes that day were donne,
And many knights vnhorst, and many wounded,
As fortune fell; yet litle lost or wonne:
But all that day the greatest prayse redounded
To *Marinell*, whose name the Heralds loud resounded.

7

The second day, so soone as morrow light
Appear'd in heauen, into the field they came,
And there all day continew'd cruell fight,
With diuers fortune fit for such a game,
In which all stroue with perill to winne fame.
Yet whether side was victor, note be ghest:
But at the last the trompets did proclame
That *Marinell* that day deserued best.
So they disparted were, and all men went to rest.

8

The third day came, that should due tryall lend
Of all the rest, and then this warlike crew
Together met, of all to make an end.
There *Marinell* great deeds of armes did shew;
And through the thickest like a Lyon flew,
Rashing off helmes, and ryuing plates a sonder,
That euery one his daunger did eschew.
So terribly his dreadfull strokes did thonder,
That all men stood amaz'd, and at his might did wonder.

9

But what on earth can alwayes happie stand?
The greater prowesse greater perils find.
So farre he past amongst his enemies band,
That they haue him enclosed so behind,
As by no meanes he can himselfe outwind.
And now perforce they haue him prisoner taken;
And now they doe with captiue bands him bind;
And now they lead him thence, of all forsaken,
Vnlesse some succour had in time him ouertaken.

10

It fortun'd whylest they were thus ill beset,
Sir *Artegall* into the Tilt-yard came,
With *Braggadochio*, whom he lately met
Vpon the way, with that his snowy Dame.
Where when he vnderstood by common fame,
What euill hap to *Marinell* betid,
He much was mou'd at so vnworthie shame,
And streight that boaster prayd, with whom he rid,
To change his shield with him, to be the better hid.

11

So forth he went, and soone them ouer hent,
Where they were leading *Marinell* away,
Whom he assayld with dreadlesse hardiment,
And forst the burden of their prize to stay.
They were an hundred knights of that array;
Of which th'one halfe vpon himselfe did set,
Th'other stayd behind to gard the pray.
But he ere long the former fiftie bet;
And from th'other fiftie soone the prisoner fet.

12

So backe he brought Sir *Marinell* againe;
Whom hauing quickly arm'd againe anew,
They both together ioyned might and maine,
To set afresh on all the other crew.
Whom with sore hauocke soone they ouerthrew,
And chaced quite out of the field, that none
Against them durst his head to perill shew.
So were they left Lords of the field alone:
So *Marinell* by him was rescu'd from his fone.

13

Which when he had perform'd, then backe againe
To *Braggadochio* did his shield restore:
Who all this while behind him did remaine,
Keeping there close with him in pretious store
That his false Ladie, as ye heard afore.
Then did the trompets sound, and Iudges rose,
And all these knights, which that day armour bore,
Came to the open hall, to listen whose
The honour of the prize should be adiudg'd by those.

Stanza 6
2 coast: region. 3 lust: chose. 4 all together ronne: as in a medieval mêlée rather than an Elizabethan formal joust or tilt. On the distinction, see Young 1987:32–33.

Stanza 7
1 morrow: morning. 6 whether: which. note: could not. 9 disparted: parted asunder.

Stanza 8
6 Rashing: shearing. 7 daunger: power to inflict injury; the reach of his weapons.

Stanza 9
5 outwind: extricate; suggesting a labyrinth.

Stanza 10
5 fame: report. 9 In a comparable moment at IV iv 20, Triamond seizes the spear that Braggadocchio had stolen from Guyon.

Stanza 11
1 ouer hent: overtook. 3 hardiment: courage. 5 an hundred is the number of knights defeated by Marinell to defend his rich strond at III iv 21.1, and of the Knights of Maidenhead at Satyrane's tournament at IV iv 31.6; cf. viii 50.6. As the marriage tournament restages and revises Satyrane's tournament, see Celovsky 1994–95. array: a military force. 9 fet: fetched.

14

And thether also came in open sight
　　Fayre *Florimell*, into the common hall,
　　To greet his guerdon vnto euery knight,
　　And best to him, to whom the best should fall.
　　Then for that stranger knight they loud did call,
　　To whom that day they should the girlond yield.
　　Who came not forth: but for Sir *Artegall*
　　Came *Braggadochio*, and did shew his shield,
Which bore the Sunne brode blazed in a golden field.

15

The sight whereof did all with gladnesse fill:
　　So vnto him they did addeeme the prise
　　Of all that Tryumph. Then the trompets shrill
　　Don *Braggadochios* name resounded thrise:
　　So courage lent a cloke to cowardise.
　　And then to him came fayrest *Florimell*,
　　And goodly gan to greet his braue emprise,
　　And thousand thankes him yeeld, that had so well
Approu'd that day, that she all others did excell.

16

To whom the boaster, that all knights did blot,
　　With proud disdaine did scornefull answere make;
　　That what he did that day, he did it not
　　For her, but for his owne deare Ladies sake,
　　Whom on his perill he did vndertake,
　　Both her and eke all others to excell:
　　And further did vncomely speaches crake.
　　Much did his words the gentle Ladie quell,
And turn'd aside for shame to heare, what he did tell.

17

Then forth he brought his snowy *Florimele*,
　　Whom *Trompart* had in keeping there beside,
　　Couered from peoples gazement with a vele.
　　Whom when discouered they had throughly eide,
　　With great amazement they were stupefide;
　　And said, that surely *Florimell* it was,
　　Or if it were not *Florimell* so tride,
　　That *Florimell* her selfe she then did pas.
So feeble skill of perfect things the vulgar has.

18

Which when as *Marinell* beheld likewise,
　　He was therewith exceedingly dismayd;
　　Ne wist he what to thinke, or to deuise,
　　But like as one, whom feends had made affrayd,
　　He long astonisht stood, ne ought he sayd,
　　Ne ought he did, but with fast fixed eies
　　He gazed still vpon that snowy mayd;
　　Whom euer as he did the more auize,
The more to be true *Florimell* he did surmize.

19

As when two sunnes appeare in the azure skye,
　　Mounted in *Phœbus* charet fierie bright,
　　Both darting forth faire beames to each mans eye,
　　And both adorn'd with lampes of flaming light,
　　All that behold so strange prodigious sight,
　　Not knowing natures worke, nor what to weene,
　　Are rapt with wonder, and with rare affright.
　　So stood Sir *Marinell*, when he had seene
The semblant of this false by his faire beauties Queene.

Stanza 13
4–5 I.e. he conceals the False Florimell from view – see 17.3 – as though she were some precious thing. **as ye heard afore**: Braggadocchio seized the False Florimell from the witch's son at III viii 12, lost her to Ferraugh at 19, but was awarded her and freely chosen by her at IV v 26.

Stanza 14
3 To congratulate each knight upon his reward.
8–9 Braggadocchio's boasting is recorded on his shield: only royalty may display the sun on their arms, as in Arthur's 'sun-like shield' at viii 41.2; cf. I vii 34. Upton 1758 notes the heraldic impossibility of the device: metal cannot be laid upon metal, as a gold sun upon a gold field would require. It is a false sun, then, which has reached its zenith, as has his companion, the False Florimell, who is seen as such at 19. There may well be an allusion to the Duc d'Alençon: at Antwerp in 1581–82, he distributed gold coins with 'a devise of the Sunne' (Nichols 1823:2.365–66). **blazed**: blazoned, described heraldically.

Stanza 15
2 **addeeme**: award. 3 **that Tryumph**: on Satyrane's tournament as a triumph, the discordful consequences of which Artegall now corrects, see IV iv 5.7–9*n*. 5 I.e. his reputation of being the best knight disguises his cowardice. 7 **emprise**: enterprise. 9 **Approu'd**: shown to be true, according to the chivalric convention expressed at 4.7–9.

Stanza 16
7 **crake**: utter boastfully. 8 **quell**: cause to quail, disconcert. 9 Nature complained at III viii 5.4–6 that the False Florimell would shame Florimell; cf. 23.3–5.

Stanza 17
7 **so tride**: i.e. when examined. 9 **skill**: power of discrimination.

Stanza 18
8 **auize**: regard.

Stanza 19
1–7 The simile is 'very just', as Upton 1758 observes: the false Florimell is the mock sun, or parhelion, Florimell is the true sun to which she is often compared, e.g. IV xii 34.6–9. The effect is registered by Sidney 1962:81: 'When two Sunnes do appeare | Some say it doth betoken wonders neare'. **prodigious**: ominous. 9 **semblant**: appearance, suggesting false appearance or resemblance.

20

All which when *Artegall*, who all this while
   Stood in the preasse close couered, well aduewed,
   And saw that boasters pride and gracelesse guile,
   He could no longer beare, but forth issewed,
   And vnto all himselfe there open shewed,
   And to the boaster said; Thou losell base,
   That hast with borrowed plumes thy selfe endewed,
   And others worth with leasings doest deface,
When they are all restor'd, thou shalt rest in disgrace.

21

That shield, which thou doest beare, was it indeed,
   Which this dayes honour sau'd to *Marinell*;
   But not that arme, nor thou the man I reed,
   Which didst that seruice vnto *Florimell*.
   For proofe shew forth thy sword, and let it tell,
   What strokes, what dreadfull stoure it stird this day:
   Or shew the wounds, which vnto thee befell;
   Or shew the sweat, with which thou diddest sway
So sharpe a battell, that so many did dismay.

22

But this the sword, which wrought those cruell stounds,
   And this the arme, the which that shield did beare,
   And these the signes, (so shewed forth his wounds)
   By which that glorie gotten doth appeare.
   As for this Ladie, which he sheweth here,
   Is not (I wager) *Florimell* at all;
   But some fayre Franion, fit for such a fere,
   That by misfortune in his hand did fall.
For proofe whereof, he bad them *Florimell* forth call.

23

So forth the noble Ladie was ybrought,
   Adorn'd with honor and all comely grace:
   Whereto her bashfull shamefastnesse ywrought
   A great increase in her faire blushing face;

As roses did with lillies interlace.
   For of those words, the which that boaster threw,
   She inly yet conceiued great disgrace.
   Whom when as all the people such did vew,
They shouted loud, and signes of gladnesse all did shew.

24

Then did he set her by that snowy one,
   Like the true saint beside the image set,
   Of both their beauties to make paragone,
   And triall, whether should the honor get.
   Streight way so soone as both together met,
   Th'enchaunted Damzell vanisht into nought:
   Her snowy substance melted as with heat,
   Ne of that goodly hew remayned ought,
But th'emptie girdle, which about her wast was wrought.

25

As when the daughter of *Thaumantes* faire,
   Hath in a watry cloud displayed wide
   Her goodly bow, which paints the liquid ayre;
   That all men wonder at her colours pride;
   All suddenly, ere one can looke aside,
   The glorious picture vanisheth away,
   Ne any token doth thereof abide:
   So did this Ladies goodly forme decay,
And into nothing goe, ere one could it bewray.

26

Which when as all that present were, beheld,
   They stricken were with great astonishment,
   And their faint harts with senselesse horrour queld,
   To see the thing, that seem'd so excellent,
   So stolen from their fancies wonderment;
   That what of it became, none vnderstood.
   And *Braggadochio* selfe with dreriment
   So daunted was in his despeyring mood,
That like a lifelesse corse immoueable he stood.

Stanza 20

2 aduewed: the obs. form notes his formal examination, and a penetrating sight/insight, which the others lack. **3 gracelesse**: wicked. **5** He reveals himself publicly for the first time in order that the False Florimell and Braggadocchio may be revealed publicly for the first time. **6 losell**: scoundrel. The word first defined him, at II iii 4.1, and has been reserved for this climactic moment and 35.5. **7 borrowed plumes**: from Aesop's fable of the jackdaw that clothed itself with peacock feathers. When Braggadocchio first appeared, at II iii 6.4, he was compared to a peacock.

Stanza 21

3 reed: declare. **6 stoure**: turmoil of battle. **9 dismay**: defeat.

Stanza 22

1 Presumably the sword is Chrysaor; see i 9. **stounds**: times of trial; fierce attacks. **6 wager**: a formal oath to challenge anyone who denies his claim. **7** The excessive alliteration conveys Artegall's contempt. **Franion**: loose woman. **fere**: companion.

Stanza 23

4–5 The simile is used of Belphœbe's cheeks at II iii 22.5–6.

Stanza 24

The False or Snowy Florimell was mistaken for Florimell by the witch's son at III viii 9.8–9, and by the knights at Satyrane's tournament at IV v 14–15. Since she is an 'Idole', being so called at III viii 11.2 and IV v 15.7, they are guilty of idolatry. Now Florimell is placed by the False Florimell (according to the etymology of parhelion, Gk παρά, beside + ἥλιος, sun), the two being weighed in the scales of justice, confirming that 'by no meanes the false will with the truth be wayd' (ii 45.9), and showing that those guilty of idolatry 'coueteth the forme that hathe no life, of a dead image' (Wisd. Sol. 15.5). **3 paragone**: comparison. **4 whether**: which. **9** At IV v 16, the girdle was awarded her though she could not wear it. She wears it here when her false claim to virginity and true beauty are to be uncased by justice.

Stanza 25

1–4 Referring to Iris, called Thaumantias by T. Cooper 1565, from Gk θαῦμα, a wonder, and here invoked for the rainbow's

27

But *Artegall* that golden belt vptooke,
  The which of all her spoyle was onely left;
  Which was not hers, as many it mistooke,
  But *Florimells* owne girdle, from her reft,
  While she was flying, like a weary weft,
  From that foule monster, which did her compell
  To perils great; which he vnbuckling eft,
  Presented to the fayrest *Florimell*;
Who round about her tender wast it fitted well.

28

Full many Ladies often had assayd,
  About their middles that faire belt to knit;
  And many a one suppos'd to be a mayd:
  Yet it to none of all their loynes would fit,
  Till *Florimell* about her fastned it.
  Such power it had, that to no womans wast
  By any skill or labour it would sit,
  Vnlesse that she were continent and chast,
But it would lose or breake, that many had disgrast.

29

Whilest thus they busied were bout *Florimell*,
  And boastfull *Braggadochio* to defame,
  Sir *Guyon* as by fortune then befell,
  Forth from the thickest preasse of people came,
  His owne good steed, which he had stolne, to clame;
  And th'one hand seizing on his golden bit,
  With th'other drew his sword: for with the same
  He ment the thiefe there deadly to haue smit:
And had he not bene held, he nought had fayld of it.

30

Thereof great hurly burly moued was
  Throughout the hall, for that same warlike horse.
  For *Braggadochio* would not let him pas;
  And *Guyon* would him algates haue perforse,

Or it approue vpon his carrion corse.
  Which troublous stirre when *Artegall* perceiued,
  He nigh them drew to stay th'auengers forse,
  And gan inquire, how was that steed bereaued,
Whether by might extort, or else by slight deceaued.

31

Who all that piteous storie, which befell
  About that wofull couple, which were slaine,
  And their young bloodie babe to him gan tell;
  With whom whiles he did in the wood remaine,
  His horse purloyned was by subtill traine:
  For which he chalenged the thiefe to fight.
  But he for nought could him thereto constraine.
  For as the death he hated such despight,
And rather had to lose, then trie in armes his right.

32

Which *Artegall* well hearing, though no more
  By law of armes there neede ones right to trie,
  As was the wont of warlike knights of yore,
  Then that his foe should him the field denie,
  Yet further right by tokens to descrie,
  He askt, what priuie tokens he did beare.
  If that (said *Guyon*) may you satisfie,
  Within his mouth a blacke spot doth appeare,
Shapt like a horses shoe, who list to seeke it there.

33

Whereof to make due tryall, one did take
  The horse in hand, within his mouth to looke:
  But with his heeles so sorely he him strake,
  That all his ribs he quite in peeces broke,
  That neuer word from that day forth he spoke.
  Another that would seeme to haue more wit,
  Him by the bright embrodered hedstall tooke:
  But by the shoulder him so sore he bit,
That he him maymed quite, and all his shoulder split.

---

opposition to the sun, as indicated in the motto '*Adverso sole*'. Virgil's Thaumantias (*Aen.* 5,5) was interpreted as Eris, the goddess of Discord; see Manning 1985:75. **liquid ayre**: clear, bright air; see I i 45.3*n*. **9 bewray**: reveal, point to.

Stanza 26
3 senselesse: as it takes away their senses. **5** As the Red Cross Knight's 'falsed fancy' at I ii 30.3 led him to prefer Duessa to Una.

Stanza 27
4–5 from her reft: as told at III vii 22–31. It was used by Satyrane to bind the hyena, and brought back to the witch who used it to dress the False Florimell; see III viii 2, 9. **weft**: waif; cf. IV xii 31.3. **7 eft**: afterwards. The traditional undoing (and clasping) of the virgin's girdle, or bridal knot, by the bridegroom on the marriage night is performed symbolically by the knight of justice.

Stanza 28
Recalling IV v 16–19 where only Amoret could wear it. **6–9** On the power of the girdle, see IV v 3–5*n*. Those who are not con-

tinent cannot be contained; not being **chast**, the girdle that 'gaue the vertue of chast loue' (IV v 3.1) cannot gird them.

Stanza 29
3–4 Guyon emerges from anonymity as Artegall did at 20.1–2.

Stanza 30
4 algates: nevertheless. **5 approue**: prove. **8 bereaued**: carried off. **9** I.e. whether it was wrongly obtained by force or by trickery.

Stanza 31
1–5 The story is told at II i 35–55, the theft at II ii 11 and iii 4 (**in the wood** recalls 'vnder greene woodes syde' at 3.6). **traine**: guile. **8 despight**: defiance.

Stanza 32
1–4 well hearing: i.e. hearing judicially. On Artegall's rejection of judicial combat, see i 25.1–4 and *n*.

Stanza 33
7 hedstall: halter.

34

Ne he his mouth would open vnto wight,
  Vntill that *Guyon* selfe vnto him spake,
  And called *Brigadore* (so was he hight)
  Whose voice so soone as he did vndertake,
  Eftsoones he stood as still as any stake,
  And suffred all his secret marke to see:
  And when as he him nam'd, for ioy he brake
  His bands, and follow'd him with gladfull glee,
And friskt, and flong aloft, and louted low on knee.

35

Thereby Sir *Artegall* did plaine areed,
  That vnto him the horse belong'd, and sayd;
  Lo there Sir *Guyon*, take to you the steed,
  As he with golden saddle is arayd;
  And let that losell, plainely now displayd,
  Hence fare on foot, till he an horse haue gayned.
  But the proud boaster gan his doome vpbrayd,
  And him reuil'd, and rated, and disdayned,
That iudgement so vniust against him had ordayned.

36

Much was the knight incent with his lewd word,
  To haue reuenged that his villeny;
  And thrise did lay his hand vpon his sword,
  To haue him slaine, or dearely doen aby.
  But *Guyon* did his choler pacify,
  Saying, Sir knight, it would dishonour bee
  To you, that are our iudge of equity,
  To wreake your wrath on such a carle as hee:
It's punishment enough, that all his shame doe see.

37

So did he mitigate Sir *Artegall*,
  But *Talus* by the backe the boaster hent,
  And drawing him out of the open hall,
  Vpon him did inflict this punishment.
  First he his beard did shaue, and fowly shent:
  Then from him reft his shield, and it renuerst,
  And blotted out his armes with falshood blent,
  And himselfe baffuld, and his armes vnherst,
And broke his sword in twaine, and all his armour sperst.

38

The whiles his guilefull groome was fled away:
  But vaine it was to thinke from him to flie.
  Who ouertaking him did disaray,
  And all his face deform'd with infamie,
  And out of court him scourged openly.
  So ought all faytours, that true knighthood shame,
  And armes dishonour with base villanie,
  From all braue knights be banisht with defame:
For oft their lewdnes blotteth good deserts with blame.

39

Now when these counterfeits were thus vncased
  Out of the foreside of their forgerie,
  And in the sight of all men cleane disgraced,
  All gan to iest and gibe full merilie
  At the remembrance of their knauerie.
  Ladies can laugh at Ladies, Knights at Knights,
  To thinke with how great vaunt of brauerie
  He them abused, through his subtill slights,
And what a glorious shew he made in all their sights.

40

There leaue we them in pleasure and repast,
  Spending their ioyous dayes and gladfull nights,
  And taking vsurie of time forepast,
  With all deare delices and rare delights,
  Fit for such Ladies and such louely knights:
  And turne we here to this faire furrowes end
  Our wearie yokes, to gather fresher sprights,
  That when as time to *Artegall* shall tend,
We on his first aduenture may him forward send.

Stanza 34
3 **Brigadore**: from Brigliadoro, the name of Orlando's horse in Ariosto, *Orl. Fur.* viii 24, etc. As 'bridle of gold' (*briglia + d'oro*), it indicates the rule of temperance, the golden mean, over the wilful passions symbolized by the horse; cf. its 'golden bit' (29.6) and 'golden saddle' (35.4; cf. II ii 11.6). 4 **vndertake**: hear.

Stanza 35
1 **areed**: decide.

Stanza 36
1 **lewd**: evil, wicked. 4 **aby**: i.e. suffer for it. 7 **iudge of equity**: reminding him that he is 'Art-egall'; see i 3*n*.

Stanza 37
2 **hent**: seized. 5–9 On the elaborate ritual described here, see 'baffling and degradation' in the *SEnc*. **his beard did shaue**: as David's servants were shamed at 2 Sam. 10.4–5. **shent**: disfigured, soiled; or perhaps cut in the middle, as were

their clothes. **renuerst**: turned upside down 'to heap disdayn' (I iv 41.9). **blent**: stained. **baffuld**: digraced; cf. VI vii 27.2–3. **vnherst**: removed piece by piece. **sperst**: scattered.

Stanza 38
4 **face**: external appearance. 5 **him**: i.e. Braggadocchio. 6 **faytours**: impostors. 8 **defame**: dishonour. 9 **lewdnes**: evil behaviour.

Stanza 39
2 **foreside**: outward appearance; façade. 6 **can**: began to, did. **at**: with. 9 **glorious**: also boastful, vainglorious; cf. II iii 4.5.

Stanza 40
1 **repast**: repose. 3 **vsurie**: interest, gain; hence, taking reward for their former labours. 4 **delices**: pleasures. 5 **louely**: loving. 6–7 On this georgic topos of conclusion, see III xii 47.3–6*n*. **sprights**: vigour of mind.

Cant. IIII.

Artegall dealeth right betwixt
two brethren that doe striue,
Saues Terpine from the gallow tree,
and doth from death repriue.

1

WHo so vpon him selfe will take the skill
True Iustice vnto people to diuide,
Had neede haue mightie hands, for to fulfill
That, which he doth with righteous doome decide,
And for to maister wrong and puissant pride.
For vaine it is to deeme of things aright,
And makes wrong doers iustice to deride,
Vnlesse it be perform'd with dreadlesse might.
For powre is the right hand of Iustice truely hight.

2

Therefore whylome to knights of great emprise
The charge of Iustice giuen was in trust,
That they might execute her iudgements wise,
And with their might beat downe licentious lust,
Which proudly did impugne her sentence iust.
Whereof no brauer president this day
Remaines on earth, preseru'd from yron rust
Of rude obliuion, and long times decay,
Then this of *Artegall*, which here we haue to say.

3

Who hauing lately left that louely payre,
Enlincked fast in wedlockes loyall bond,
Bold *Marinell* with *Florimell* the fayre,
With whom great feast and goodly glee he fond,

Departed from the Castle of the strond,
To follow his aduentures first intent,
Which long agoe he taken had in hond:
Ne wight with him for his assistance went,
But that great yron groome, his gard and gouernment.

4

With whom as he did passe by the sea shore,
He chaunst to come, whereas two comely Squires,
Both brethren, whom one wombe together bore,
But stirred vp with different desires,
Together stroue, and kindled wrathfull fires:
And them beside two seemely damzels stood,
By all meanes seeking to asswage their ires,
Now with faire words; but words did little good,
Now with sharpe threats; but threats the more increast
                                                  (their mood.

5

And there before them stood a Coffer strong,
Fast bound on euery side with iron bands,
But seeming to haue suffred mickle wrong,
Either by being wreckt vppon the sands,
Or being carried farre from forraine lands.
Seem'd that for it these Squires at ods did fall,
And bent against them selues their cruell hands.
But euermore, those Damzels did forestall
Their furious encounter, and their fiercenesse pall.

Book V Canto iv

Argument
4 repriue: reprieve.

Stanza 1
A retrospective comment particularly on Talus's punishment of the Giant at ii 49.8–9 but more generally on the physical force needed to impose justice, making it unique among the virtues. **1–2 skill**: the art of discrimination by which the ruler may **diuide**, i.e. dispense, justice.

Stanza 2
1 whylome: in time past. **emprise**: martial prowess. **4 licentious**: lawless. **5 impugne**: oppose. **6 brauer**: more glorious. **president**: precedent; pattern; model.

Stanza 3
1 louely: loving. **3** Their names and epithets are coupled as they were at the beginning, III iv Arg. **6** The line repeats iii 40.9 and is repeated at 20.9 in order to bracket the story of the two brothers as a digression in Artegall's quest. **9 gouernment**: i.e. means of governing, his executive power; cf. viii 3.9. Used of temperance (see II i 29.8*n*), it extends that private virtue to its public exercise.

Stanza 4
The sea shore upon which Neptune cast wealth for Marinell at III iv 22–23, and where the Giant urged that wealth be redistributed at V ii 29.2, now provides an appropriate setting for the judicial problem of alluvion (the formation of new land by the action of water), and of salvage (the recovery of goods lost at sea). Steadman 1996:75–77 notes how this problem is combined with two common types of domestic litigation, disputes over inherited lands and suits over dowries. **3 together**: i.e. both. They are not twins as their equal inheritance would suggest. **6 seemely**: fair. **9 mood**: anger.

Stanza 5
4 wreckt: cast ashore, having been 'Sea-beaten' (11.6). **7 them selues**: also each other, for each injures himself in the quarrel. **8 forestall**: seek to hinder. **9 pall**: abate.

6

But firmely fixt they were, with dint of sword,
  And battailes doubtfull proofe their rights to try,
  Ne other end their fury would afford,
  But what to them Fortune would iustify.
  So stood they both in readinesse thereby
  To ioyne the combate with cruell intent;
  When *Artegall* arriuing happily,
  Did stay a while their greedy bickerment,
Till he had questioned the cause of their dissent.

7

To whom the elder did this aunswere frame;
  Then weete ye Sir, that we two brethren be,
  To whom our sire, *Milesio* by name,
  Did equally bequeath his lands in fee,
  Two Ilands, which ye there before you see
  Not farre in sea; of which the one appeares
  But like a little Mount of small degree;
  Yet was as great and wide ere many yeares,
As that same other Isle, that greater bredth now beares.

[margin annotation: 2 islands]
[margin annotation: Irish legend]

8

But tract of time, that all things doth decay,
  And this deuouring Sea, that naught doth spare,
  The most part of my land hath washt away,
  And throwne it vp vnto my brothers share:
  So his encreased, but mine did empaire.
  Before which time I lou'd, as was my lot,
  That further mayd, hight *Philtera* the faire,
  With whom a goodly doure I should haue got,
And should haue ioyned bene to her in wedlocks knot.

9

Then did my younger brother *Amidas*
  Loue that same other Damzell, *Lucy* bright,
  To whom but little dowre allotted was;
  Her vertue was the dowre, that did delight.

What better dowre can to a dame be hight?
  But now when *Philtra* saw my lands decay,
  And former liuelod fayle, she left me quight,
  And to my brother did ellope streight way:
Who taking her from me, his owne loue left astray.

10

She seeing then her selfe forsaken so,
  Through dolorous despaire, which she conceyued,
  Into the Sea her selfe did headlong throw,
  Thinking to haue her griefe by death bereaued.
  But see how much her purpose was deceaued,
  Whilest thus amidst the billowes beating of her
  Twixt life and death, long to and fro she weaued,
  She chaunst vnwares to light vppon this coffer,
Which to her in that daunger hope of life did offer.

11

The wretched mayd that earst desir'd to die,
  When as the paine of death she tasted had,
  And but halfe seene his vgly visnomie,
  Gan to repent, that she had beene so mad,
  For any death to chaunge life though most bad:
  And catching hold of this Sea-beaten chest,
  The lucky Pylot of her passage sad,
  After long tossing in the seas distrest,
Her weary barke at last vppon mine Isle did rest.

12

Where I by chaunce then wandring on the shore,
  Did her espy, and through my good endeuour
  From dreadfull mouth of death, which threatned sore
  Her to haue swallow'd vp, did helpe to saue her.
  She then in recompence of that great fauour,
  Which I on her bestowed, bestowed on me
  The portion of that good, which Fortune gaue her,
  Together with her selfe in dowry free;
Both goodly portions, but of both the better she.

Stanza 6
1 dint of sword: force of arms.   **2 doubtfull**: because ordeal by combat allows fortune rather than justice to determine right; see i 25.1–4*n*. Fortune has given them their new possessions; justice must decide their right to them.   **5 thereby**: by that means.

Stanzas 7–8
The story may have its source in early Irish legend and legal tradition. After the two sons of Mil or Milesius inherited his island, they quarrelled when one wife desired a valley belonging to the other; see A.B. Gough 1921. It is related to the legend of Milesius, the King of Spain, who conquered Ireland, as recounted in *View* 42 but dismissed as a fable. On S.'s use of various Gaelic sources, see R. Smith 1942, and C. Carroll 1996:286–89.

Stanza 7
4 in fee: in fee-simple, as an absolute and rightful possession for ever.   **8** . . . not long ago.

Stanza 8
1 tract of time: the passage or course of time (*tractus temporum*).   **5 empaire**: 'decay' (9.6); become less.   **7 Philtera**: Gk φιλ, love + Lat. *terra*, land, as 9.6–7 reveals. Bracidas mistakes her for φίλτέρᾱ, dearer; sugg. Draper 1932:103.

Stanza 9
1 Amidas: Lat. *am*- + Gk ἴδια, fond of possessions (sugg. Osgood, *Var* 5.195); or an allusion to King Midas (sugg. Belson 1964:21).   **2 Lucy bright**: the epithet interprets the name.   **5 hight**: committed, assigned.   **6–7** Hence his name, Bracidas; see 18.2*n*. **decay**: decrease. **liuelod**: livelihood; property; inheritance.

Stanza 10
7 weaued: wandered, tossed by the waves.   **8 light**: a punning reference to her name.

Stanza 11
3 visnomie: physiognomy, face.

13

Yet in this coffer, which she with her brought,
  Great threasure sithence we did finde contained;
  Which as our owne we tooke, and so it thought.
  But this same other Damzell since hath fained,
  That to her selfe that threasure appertained;
  And that she did transport the same by sea,
  To bring it to her husband new ordained,
  But suffred cruell shipwracke by the way.
But whether it be so or no, I can not say.

14

But whether it indeede be so or no,
  This doe I say, that what so good or ill
  Or God or Fortune vnto me did throw,
  Not wronging any other by my will,
  I hold mine owne, and so will hold it still.
  And though my land he first did winne away,
  And then my loue (though now it little skill,)
  Yet my good lucke he shall not likewise pray;
But I will it defend, whilst euer that I may.

15

So hauing sayd, the younger did ensew;
  Full true it is, what so about our land
  My brother here declared hath to you:
  But not for it this ods twixt vs doth stand,
  But for this threasure throwne vppon his strand;
  Which well I proue, as shall appeare by triall,
  To be this maides, with whom I fastned hand,
  Known by good markes, and perfect good espiall,
Therefore it ought be rendred her without deniall.

16

When they thus ended had, the Knight began;
  Certes your strife were easie to accord,
  Would ye remit it to some righteous man.
  Vnto your selfe, said they, we giue our word,

To bide what iudgement ye shall vs afford.
  Then for assuraunce to my doome to stand,
  Vnder my foote let each lay downe his sword,
  And then you shall my sentence vnderstand.
So each of them layd downe his sword out of his hand.

17

anti-colonial?

Then *Artegall* thus to the younger sayd;
  Now tell me *Amidas*, if that ye may,
  Your brothers land the which the sea hath layd
  Vnto your part, and pluckt from his away,
  By what good right doe you withhold this day?
  What other right (quoth he) should you esteeme,
  But that the sea it to my share did lay?
  Your right is good (sayd he) and so I deeme,
That what the sea vnto you sent, your own should seeme.

18

Then turning to the elder thus he sayd;
  Now *Bracidas* let this likewise be showne.
  Your brothers threasure, which from him is strayd,
  Being the dowry of his wife well knowne,
  By what right doe you claime to be your owne?
  What other right (quoth he) should you esteeme,
  But that the sea hath it vnto me throwne?
  Your right is good (sayd he) and so I deeme,
That what the sea vnto you sent, your own should seeme.

19

For equall right in equall things doth stand,
  For what the mighty Sea hath once possest,
  And plucked quite from all possessors hand,
  Whether by rage of waues, that neuer rest,
  Or else by wracke, that wretches hath distrest,
  He may dispose by his imperiall might,
  As thing at randon left, to whom he list.
  So *Amidas*, the land was yours first hight,
And so the threasure yours is *Bracidas* by right.

Stanza 12
3–4 The 'deuouring Sea' (8.2) that had seized his land now threatens his new bride. He may claim her as flotsam, i.e. wreckage floating on the sea. **7 that good**: Philtera's 'goodly doure' (8.8) in contrast to her own 'little dowre' (9.3).

Stanza 13
7 **ordained**: chosen.

Stanza 14
7 **little skill**: i.e. matters little. **8 pray**: prey upon, take as booty.

Stanza 15
1 **ensew**: follow. **4 ods**: strife. **7 fastned hand**: handfasted, i.e. have betrothed myself. **8 espiall**: close observation.

Stanza 16
8 A ponderous pun, yet **vnderstand** implies 'cause his judge-ment (**doome**) to stand'.

Stanzas 17–18
The stanzas are as similar as different evidence permits, even sharing the same 'a' and 'c' rhymes, in order to declare Artegall's equity. Only after he hears the two brothers does he measure their rights, illustrating his claim at ii 47.7–9.

Stanza 18
2 **Bracidas**: few possessions, from Gk βραχύς + ἴδια; or possessions thrown up (by the sea), from βράσσω + ἴδια (sugg. Padelford in *Var* 5.195). Evidently a proverbial figure for boldness, as the common phrase 'as bold as brass'.

Stanza 19
According to the Elizabethan law of alluvion, Amidas has the right to land thrown up by the sea. According to the law of wreck (*wrecum maris*), by which Florimell belongs to Neptune at IV xii 31.3–6, treasure washed ashore belongs to the Queen, to be distributed at her pleasure, here by her agent, Artegall. On the relation of justice and equity involved here, see 'Bracidas, Amidas' in the *SEnc*. On Artegall's application of corrective justice, see Altman in the *SEnc* 414. His judgement is anticip-ated by his response to the Giant with the Scales at ii 39.4–9.

20

When he his sentence thus pronounced had,
    Both *Amidas* and *Philtra* were displeased:
    But *Bracidas* and *Lucy* were right glad,
    And on the threasure by that iudgement seased.
    So was their discord by this doome appeased,
    And each one had his right. Then *Artegall*
    When as their sharpe contention he had ceased,
    Departed on his way, as did befall,
To follow his old quest, the which him forth did call.

21

So as he trauelled vppon the way,
    He chaunst to come, where happily he spide
    A rout of many people farre away;
    To whom his course he hastily applide,
    To weete the cause of their assemblaunce wide.
    To whom when he approched neare in sight,
    (An vncouth sight) he plainely then descride
    To be a troupe of women warlike dight,
With weapons in their hands, as ready for to fight.

22

And in the midst of them he saw a Knight,
    With both his hands behinde him pinnoed hard,
    And round about his necke an halter tight,
    As ready for the gallow tree prepard:
    His face was couered, and his head was bar'd,
    That who he was, vneath was to descry;
    And with full heauy heart with them he far'd,
    Grieu'd to the soule, and groning inwardly,
That he of womens hands so base a death should dy.

23

But they like tyrants, mercilesse the more,
    Reioyced at his miserable case,
    And him reuiled, and reproched sore
    With bitter taunts, and termes of vile disgrace.

Now when as *Artegall* arriu'd in place,
    Did aske, what cause brought that man to decay,
    They round about him gan to swarme apace,
    Meaning on him their cruell hands to lay,
And to haue wrought vnwares some villanous assay.

24

But he was soone aware of their ill minde,
    And drawing backe deceiued their intent;
    Yet though him selfe did shame on womankinde
    His mighty hand to shend, he *Talus* sent
    To wrecke on them their follies hardyment:
    Who with few sowces of his yron flale,
    Dispersed all their troupe incontinent,
    And sent them home to tell a piteous tale,
Of their vaine prowesse, turned to their proper bale.

25

But that same wretched man, ordaynd to die,
    They left behind them, glad to be so quit:
    Him *Talus* tooke out of perplexitie,
    And horrour of fowle death for Knight vnfit,
    Who more then losse of life ydreaded it;
    And him restoring vnto liuing light,
    So brought vnto his Lord, where he did sit,
    Beholding all that womanish weake fight;
Whom soone as he beheld, he knew, and thus behight.

26

Sir *Turpine*, haplesse man, what make you here?
    Or haue you lost your selfe, and your discretion,
    That euer in this wretched case ye were?
    Or haue ye yeelded you to proude oppression
    Of womens powre, that boast of mens subiection?
    Or else what other deadly dismall day
    Is falne on you, by heauens hard direction,
    That ye were runne so fondly far astray,
As for to lead your selfe vnto your owne decay?

Stanza 20
3 right glad: because each is judged right.   **4 seased**: seized, took legal possession.

Stanza 21
2 happily: by chance.   **4 applide**: directed.   **5 assemblaunce**: assembly. On its pejorative associations, see ii 29.6*n*.

Stanza 22
2 pinnoed: pinned and pinioned.   **6 vneath**: difficult.   **9** As Abimelech feared that men would say of him, a woman slew him (Judg. 9.54); called a 'fowle death' at 25.4.

Stanza 23
6 decay: ruin.   **9 assay**: assault.

Stanza 24
3–4 I.e. he would be ashamed to disgrace himself by attacking women, though by 41 he is swimming in his slaughter of them. **5 wrecke**: wreak; suggesting also the effect of his action, the ruin to which he would reduce them.   **hardyment**: boldness.

6 sowces: blows.   **7 incontinent**: at once; with a pun on 'intemperate'.   **9 proper bale**: own harm.

Stanza 25
3 perplexitie: physical and mental distress.   **6 liuing light**: i.e. 'the light of the liuing' (Ps. 56.13).   **9 behight**: addressed.

Stanza 26
1 Turpine *1596*, so spelled only here, may have been suggested by its etymology, Lat. *turpis*, shameful. (Turpine appears in Bk VI; see Characters.) Elsewhere 'Terpine' or 'Terpin', signifying 'thrice-wretched' in being thrice-defeated by Radigund (32.6, 39–41, and v 18); or referring to Artegall's three possible explanations for his shameful fate, as D. Cheney 1966:203 suggests. (The second is not true of him, as he declares at 32.8–9, but becomes true of Artegall; see v 17.1–2.) **6 dismall day**: unlucky day.   **8–9 fondly**: foolishly; also amorously, as his defeat by the Amazons implies and the charge that he leads himself to his death.

27

Much was the man confounded in his mind,
　　Partly with shame, and partly with dismay,
　　That all astonisht he him selfe did find,
　　And little had for his excuse to say,
　　But onely thus; Most haplesse well ye may
　　Me iustly terme, that to this shame am brought,
　　And made the scorne of Knighthod this same day.
　　But who can scape, what his owne fate hath wrought?
The worke of heauens will surpasseth humaine thought.

28

Right true: but faulty men vse oftentimes
　　To attribute their folly vnto fate,
　　And lay on heauen the guilt of their owne crimes.
　　But tell, Sir *Terpin*, ne let you amate
　　Your misery, how fell ye in this state.
　　Then sith ye needs (quoth he) will know my shame,
　　And all the ill, which chaunst to me of late,
　　I shortly will to you rehearse the same,
In hope ye will not turne misfortune to my blame.

29

Being desirous (as all Knights are woont)
　　Through hard aduentures deedes of armes to try,
　　And after fame and honour for to hunt,
　　I heard report that farre abrode did fly,
　　That a proud Amazon did late defy
　　All the braue Knights, that hold of Maidenhead,
　　And vnto them wrought all the villany,
　　That she could forge in her malicious head,
Which some hath put to shame, and many done be dead.

30

The cause, they say, of this her cruell hate,
　　Is for the sake of *Bellodant* the bold,
　　To whom she bore most feruent loue of late,
　　And wooed him by all the waies she could:
　　But when she saw at last, that he ne would
　　For ought or nought be wonne vnto her will,
　　She turn'd her loue to hatred manifold,
　　And for his sake vow'd to doe all the ill
Which she could doe to Knights, which now she doth fulfill.

31

For all those Knights, the which by force or guile
　　She doth subdue, she fowly doth entreate.
　　First she doth them of warlike armes despoile,
　　And cloth in womens weedes: And then with threat
　　Doth them compell to worke, to earne their meat,
　　To spin, to card, to sew, to wash, to wring;
　　Ne doth she giue them other thing to eat,
　　But bread and water, or like feeble thing,
Them to disable from reuenge aduenturing.

32

But if through stout disdaine of manly mind,
　　Any her proud obseruaunce will withstand,
　　Vppon that gibbet, which is there behind,
　　She causeth them be hang'd vp out of hand;
　　In which condition I right now did stand.
　　For being ouercome by her in fight,
　　And put to that base seruice of her band,
　　I rather chose to die in liues despight,
Then lead that shamefull life, vnworthy of a Knight.

Stanza 27
9 Referring to heavenly providence, as at I vi 7.1, III v 27.1, etc.

Stanza 28
1–3 Artegall's words turn against himself when he lays the guilt of his own crime on the heavens at xi 41.6–9. For the proverb, see Smith 4; and cf. *View* 1: 'it is the manner of men that when they are fallen into any absurdity . . . they are ready always to impute the blame thereof unto the heavens'. **faulty**: guilty. **4–5** I.e. do not let your misery overwhelm you. **8 rehearse**: relate.

Stanza 29
5–6 The Amazon in sixteenth-century literature is examined by Wright 1940, and in relation to Elizabeth by Schleiner 1978. A contemporary account is given by Painter 1813:2.159–65; and a modern perspective in defence of Radigund by Woods 1991. S. praises 'those warlike women' at IV xi 22.1–4. **hold of**: maintain allegiance to. On the Order of **Maidenhead**, see I vii 46.4–7n. **9** . . . and many put to death.

Stanza 30
1–2 The cruelty of Amazons, noted at 23.8 and v 47.1, is traditional. As in Ariosto, *Orl. Fur.* 20.22–27, it derives from sexual frustration. **Bellodant**: 'given to war' (Lat. *bellum* + *dare*) rather than to love; or 'giving war' (*bellum* + *dant*), as happens when he rejects her.

Stanza 31
1 **force or guile**: on this traditional pair, see II vii 25.3n and V vii 7.1–4n. **2 entreate**: treat. **3–9** Radigund's treatment of her prisoners combines traditional stories of the slavery of men by Amazons (as in *Orl. Fur.* 19.57–58) and Omphale's treatment of Hercules (see v 24n). **feeble**: mean, scanty; enfeebling.

Stanza 32
1 **manly** describes Artegall at III ii 24.4, IV vi 22.9, and V vii 40.3, 7. It is used here because his response to women is about to be further tested. **2 obseruaunce**: rule. **7 band**: bond. **8–9 in liues despight**: in scorn of life. To prefer death to dishonour has proverbial force (Smith 157); see, e.g. III vi 10.5, V xi 55.9.

33

How hight that Amazon (sayd *Artegall*)?
  And where, and how far hence does she abide?
  Her name (quoth he) they *Radigund* doe call,
  A Princesse of great powre, and greater pride,
  And Queene of Amazons, in armes well tride,
  And sundry battels, which she hath atchieued
  With great successe, that her hath glorifide,
  And made her famous, more then is belieued;
Ne would I it haue ween'd, had I not late it prieued.

34

Now sure (said he) and by the faith that I
  To Maydenhead and noble knighthood owe,
  I will not rest, till I her might doe trie,
  And venge the shame, that she to Knights doth show.
  Therefore Sir *Terpin* from you lightly throw
  This squalid weede, the patterne of dispaire,
  And wend with me, that ye may see and know,
  How Fortune will your ruin'd name repaire,
And knights of Maidenhead, whose praise she would empaire.

35

With that, like one that hopelesse was repryu'd
  From deaths dore, at which he lately lay,
  Those yron fetters, wherewith he was gyu'd,
  The badges of reproch, he threw away,
  And nimbly did him dight to guide the way
  Vnto the dwelling of that Amazone.
  Which was from thence not past a mile or tway:
  A goodly citty and a mighty one,
The which of her owne name she called *Radegone*.

36

Where they arriuing, by the watchmen were
  Descried streight, who all the citty warned,
  How that three warlike persons did appeare,
  Of which the one him seem'd a Knight all armed,

And th'other two well likely to haue harmed.
  Eftsoones the people all to harnesse ran,
  And like a sort of Bees in clusters swarmed:
  Ere long their Queene her selfe, halfe like a man
Came forth into the rout, and them t'array began.

37

And now the Knights being arriued neare,
  Did beat vppon the gates to enter in,
  And at the Porter, skorning them so few,
  Threw many threats, if they the towne did win,
  To teare his flesh in peeces for his sin.
  Which when as *Radigund* there comming heard,
  Her heart for rage did grate, and teeth did grin:
  She bad that streight the gates should be vnbard,
And to them way to make, with weapons well prepard.

38

Soone as the gates were open to them set,
  They pressed forward, entraunce to haue made.
  But in the middle way they were ymet
  With a sharpe showre of arrowes, which them staid,
  And better bad aduise, ere they assaid
  Vnknowen perill of bold womens pride.
  Then all that rout vppon them rudely laid,
  And heaped strokes so fast on euery side,
And arrowes haild so thicke, that they could not abide.

39

But *Radigund* her selfe, when she espide
  Sir *Terpin*, from her direfull doome acquit,
  So cruell doale amongst her maides diuide,
  T'auenge that shame, they did on him commit,
  All sodainely enflam'd with furious fit,
  Like a fell Lionesse at him she flew,
  And on his head-peece him so fiercely smit,
  That to the ground him quite she ouerthrew,
Dismayd so with the stroke, that he no colours knew.

Stanza 33

3 Radigund: the name may allude to the sixth-century French nun Radegund, who refused to consummate a forced marriage. (It would be known to S. from Jesus College, Cambridge, the college of 'the glorious Virgin Saint Radigund'; in *Mother Hubberd* 497, she is called 'Saintlike'.) Or to the valorous Persian queen Rhodogune, in Philostratus, *Imagines* 2.5, who prays to conquer men. Or to Rhodogune who killed her nurse for even suggesting that she remarry (T. Cooper 1565). See 'Radigund' in the *SEnc*. Among possible etymologies are: Gk ῥᾳδία, reckless + γυνή, woman (sugg. Draper 1932:103); or Lat. *radere* + Gk γυνή, offended wife (sugg. Nohrnberg 1976:379*n*182); or 'Favourable Councell' (noted W. Camden 1984:86), for her counsel at 49.1–5 defeats knights. On her relation to Britomart, see vii 30*n*; to Elizabeth, see, e.g. Villeponteaux 1998; to the Irish, see C. Carroll 1990:182–84.   **9 prieued**: proved.

Stanza 34

1–2 A radical change from IV iv 39–43 when he defeats the Knights of Maidenhead by his 'sole manhood'.   **4 venge the shame**: the shame with which Radigund is associated is a central motif in Bk V; see Gregerson 1993:35*n*41.   **6 This squalid weede**: the halter (22.3) and the 'yron fetters' (35.3).

Stanza 35

1 repryu'd: reprieved.   **3 gyu'd**: fettered.   **5 dight**: make ready.   **7–9 A goodly citty**: on its relation to *la cité des dames*, see 'Christine de Pisan' in the *SEnc*.

Stanza 36

6 harnesse: arms.   **7 sort**: i.e. swarm.   **8 halfe like a man**: as she is an Amazon; or 'arm'd like a man' *1609*.

Stanza 37

7 grate: fret. . . . and her teeth bared in anger (*OED* 1a).

Stanza 38

6 pride is associated with all the enemies of justice, as Sanglier at i 17.5, Munera at ii 10.4, the 'surquedrie' of the Giant at ii 30.4, 'proud *Radigund*' at v 26.2, and Grantorto at xii 24.3. It is the last word said of her at vii 33.9 and 41.6.

Stanza 39

2 doome: sentence of punishment. She usurps Artegall's role; cf. 'her iudg'ment' (40.5).   **acquit**: released.   **3** . . . dealing out such cruel blows on her maids.   **doale** combines the dealing of blows and the grief that follows.

40

Soone as she saw him on the ground to grouell,
  She lightly to him leapt, and in his necke
  Her proud foote setting, at his head did leuell,
  Weening at once her wrath on him to wreake,
  And his contempt, that did her iudg'ment breake.
  As when a Beare hath seiz'd her cruell clawes
  Vppon the carkasse of some beast too weake,
  Proudly stands ouer, and a while doth pause,
To heare the piteous beast pleading her plaintiffe cause.

41

Whom when as *Artegall* in that distresse
  By chaunce beheld, he left the bloudy slaughter,
  In which he swam, and ranne to his redresse.
  There her assayling fiercely fresh, he raught her
  Such an huge stroke, that it of sence distraught her:
  And had she not it warded warily,
  It had depriu'd her mother of a daughter.
  Nathlesse for all the powre she did apply,
It made her stagger oft, and stare with ghastly eye.

42

Like to an Eagle in his kingly pride,
  Soring through his wide Empire of the aire,
  To weather his brode sailes, by chaunce hath spide
  A Goshauke, which hath seized for her share
  Vppon some fowle, that should her feast prepare;
  With dreadfull force he flies at her byliue,
  That with his souce, which none enduren dare,
  Her from the quarrey he away doth driue,
And from her griping pounce the greedy prey doth riue.

43

But soone as she her sence recouer'd had,
  She fiercely towards him her selfe gan dight,
  Through vengeful wrath and sdeignfull pride half mad:
  For neuer had she suffred such despight.

But ere she could ioyne hand with him to fight,
  Her warlike maides about her flockt so fast,
  That they disparted them, maugre their might,
  And with their troupes did far a sunder cast:
But mongst the rest the fight did vntill euening last.

44

And euery while that mighty yron man,
  With his strange weapon, neuer wont in warre,
  Them sorely vext, and courst, and ouerran,
  And broke their bowes, and did their shooting marre,
  That none of all the many once did darre
  Him to assault, nor once approach him nie,
  But like a sort of sheepe dispersed farre
  For dread of their deuouring enemie,
Through all the fields and vallies did before him flie.

45

But when as daies faire shinie-beame, yclowded
  With fearefull shadowes of deformed night,
  Warn'd man and beast in quiet rest be shrowded,
  Bold *Radigund* with sound of trumpe on hight,
  Causd all her people to surcease from fight,
  And gathering them vnto her citties gate,
  Made them all enter in before her sight,
  And all the wounded, and the weake in state,
To be conuayed in, ere she would once retrate.

46

When thus the field was voided all away,
  And all things quieted, the Elfin Knight
  Weary of toile and trauell of that day,
  Causd his pauilion to be richly pight
  Before the city gate, in open sight;
  Where he him selfe did rest in safety,
  Together with sir *Terpin* all that night:
  But *Talus* vsde in times of ieopardy
To keepe a nightly watch, for dread of treachery.

Stanza 40
2–3 A traditional gesture of victory, as Josh. 10.24. 4–5 . . .
to vent her wrath on him and avenge his contempt for her.
9 **plaintiffe**: being the plaintiff in her suit, and being plaintive.

Stanza 41
2–6 The witty use of feminine rhyme, enforced by the internal
rhyme of **mother** . . . **daughter** in a context inimical to patri-
archy, is noted by Quilligan 1987:168 and 1990:315. It is
signalled by the image of Artegall swimming in **bloudy
slaughter**. 3 **redresse**: aid, extending the legal imagery of the
previous stanza. 5 **distraught**: distracted; deprived.

Stanza 42
The same simile, adapted to its present context, is used at III
vii 39 to describe Satyrane's encounter with Argante, the **Eagle**
being a symbol of male strength and the **Goshauke** of female
aggressiveness. A version of it is inverted at v.15 when Artegall
yields to Radigund. 3–9 The simile prompts the falconry
terms, e.g. **weather**: air; **byliue**: with speed; **souce**: the down-
ward swoop of a bird of prey; **quarrey**: the bird flown at by a
bird of prey; **pounce**: the talons of a bird of prey; **greedy prey**:
i.e. the prey greedily seized.

Stanza 43
2 **gan dight**: made way. 7 **disparted**: separated.

Stanza 44
1 **euery while**: always, all the while. 2 That the Amazons
were not accustomed to a military weapon that 'amongst them
thondred' (v 19.2) suggests that Talus uses musketry or can-
nons; see Daly 1960:49 and i 12.8–9n. 3 **courst**: thrashed.
ouerran: trampled down. 5 **many**: both 'meanie' (i.e. many)
and 'meinie' (mob). **darre**: dare. 7–9 The simile is used
again of Talus at vi 30.4–6 and includes Artegall at xii 38.5–6.
sort: flock.

Stanza 45
Artegall's prowess endures until the coming of night, accord-
ing to the pattern established in his battle against Britomart;
see IV iv 43.5–6n. 4 **on hight**: on high; hence loud.
5 **surcease**: entirely cease.

Stanza 46
1 **voided**: cleared. 2 **the Elfin Knight**: so called because he
'wonneth in the land of *Fayeree*', though he is 'no *Fary* borne'
but a Briton, as Merlin explains at III iii 26. On the distinction,
see I i 17.1n. 3 **trauell**: travail.

47

But *Radigund* full of heart-gnawing griefe,
  For the rebuke, which she sustain'd that day,
  Could take no rest, ne would receiue reliefe,
  But tossed in her troublous minde, what way
  She mote reuenge that blot, which on her lay.
  There she resolu'd her selfe in single fight
  To try her Fortune, and his force assay,
  Rather then see her people spoiled quight,
As she had seene that day a disauenterous sight.

48

She called forth to her a trusty mayd,
  Whom she thought fittest for that businesse,
  Her name was *Clarin*, and thus to her sayd;
  Goe damzell quickly, doe thy selfe addresse,
  To doe the message, which I shall expresse.
  Goe thou vnto that stranger Faery Knight,
  Who yeester day droue vs to such distresse,
  Tell, that to morrow I with him wil fight,
And try in equall field, whether hath greater might.

49

But these conditions doe to him propound,
  That if I vanquishe him, he shall obay
  My law, and euer to my lore be bound,
  And so will I, if me he vanquish may;

What euer he shall like to doe or say:
  Goe streight, and take with thee, to witnesse it,
  Sixe of thy fellowes of the best array,
  And beare with you both wine and iuncates fit,
And bid him eate, henceforth he oft shall hungry sit.

50

The Damzell streight obayd, and putting all
  In readinesse, forth to the Towne-gate went,
  Where sounding loud a Trumpet from the wall,
  Vnto those warlike Knights she warning sent.
  Then *Talus* forth issuing from the tent,
  Vnto the wall his way did fearelesse take,
  To weeten what that trumpets sounding ment:
  Where that same Damzell lowdly him bespake,
And shew'd, that with his Lord she would emparlaunce make.

51

So he them streight conducted to his Lord,
  Who, as he could, them goodly well did greete,
  Till they had told their message word by word:
  Which he accepting well, as he could weete,
  Them fairely entertaynd with curt'sies meete,
  And gaue them gifts and things of deare delight.
  So backe againe they homeward turnd their feete.
  But *Artegall* him selfe to rest did dight,
That he mote fresher be against the next daies fight.

Stanza 47
1 griefe: anger; bitterness.   **2 rebuke**: disgrace; a severe blow (*OED* 1.3b), referring to Artegall's 'huge stroke' at 41.5, which disgraced her.   **9 disauenterous**: unfortunate, disastrous.

Stanza 48
3 Clarin: short for Clarinda (v 29.3), named after Clorinda, an Amazon in Tasso, *Ger. Lib.* 1.47. From Lat. *clarus*, loud: see 50.8; or *claro*, to make known (T. Cooper 1565), from her role as Radigund's messenger; or 'clarion' from the trumpet she sounds at 50.3. See 'Clarinda' in the *SEnc.*   **5 doe**: deliver.   **9 whether**: which.

Stanza 49
2–5 Radigund proposes a 'heads-I-win, tails-you-lose' contest, for either way her law is upheld and she becomes his mistress. **My law**: called 'that Amazons proud law' at v 22.3, and in

accepting it together with her **lore**, Artegall abandons Astræa's 'righteous lore' (i 4.9). It is an improper law, as Craun 1994:157–58 notes. She is one of the tyrants who make men 'subiect to their law' (ii 38.6) rather than to God's law. **7–9 Sixe**: the number suggests the ladder of lechery (see III i 45*n*), as the wine and the **iuncates** (delicacies, sweet dishes), which she **bid him eate**, suggest the fruit of the forbidden tree that Eve gave Adam to eat.

Stanza 50
9 emparlaunce: parleying.

Stanza 51
2 as he could: as he knew well how to do; or, as well as he knew how.   **4** Artegall accepts single combat, which he had rejected at i 25.3–4.   **as he could weete**: as he knew how. His affability bodes ill.   **5 fairely**: courteously.

Cant. V.

Artegall fights with Radigund
And is subdewd by guile:
He is by her emprisoned,
But wrought by Clarins wile.

1

SO soone as day forth dawning from the East,
Nights humid curtaine from the heauens withdrew,
And earely calling forth both man and beast,
Comaunded them their daily workes renew,
These noble warriors, mindefull to pursew
The last daies purpose of their vowed fight,
Them selues thereto preparde in order dew;
The Knight, as best was seeming for a Knight,
And th'Amazon, as best it likt her selfe to dight.

2

All in a Camis light of purple silke
Wouen vppon with siluer, subtly wrought,
And quilted vppon sattin white as milke,
Trayled with ribbands diuersly distraught
Like as the workeman had their courses taught;
Which was short tucked for light motion
Vp to her ham, but when she list, it raught
Downe to her lowest heele, and thereupon
She wore for her defence a mayled habergeon.

3

And on her legs she painted buskins wore,
Basted with bends of gold on euery side,
And mailes betweene, and laced close afore:
Vppon her thigh her Cemitare was tide,
With an embrodered belt of mickell pride;
And on her shoulder hung her shield, bedeckt
Vppon the bosse with stones, that shined wide,
As the faire Moone in her most full aspect,
That to the Moone it mote be like in each respect.

4

So forth she came out of the citty gate,
With stately port and proud magnificence,
Guarded with many damzels, that did waite
Vppon her person for her sure defence,
Playing on shaumes and trumpets, that from hence
Their sound did reach vnto the heauens hight.
So forth into the field she marched thence,
Where was a rich Pauilion ready pight,
Her to receiue, till time they should begin the fight.

5

Then forth came *Artegall* out of his tent,
All arm'd to point, and first the Lists did enter:
Soone after eke came she, with fell intent,
And countenaunce fierce, as hauing fully bent her,
That battels vtmost triall to aduenter.
The Lists were closed fast, to barre the rout
From rudely pressing to the middle center;
Which in great heapes them circled all about,
Wayting, how Fortune would resolue that daungerous dout.

Book V Canto v

Argument
2 guile: at iv 31.1, Radigund is said to subdue knights 'by force or guile'.   **4 wrought**: practised on, worked over.

Stanza 1
6 Referring to the conditions of the fight which Artegall accepted at iv 49.1–5.

Stanza 2
Radigund's dress conforms to the pictorial tradition of the Amazon described by Tuve 1970:120–27. It resembles Belphœbe's at II iii 26–27 in order to distinguish them. Radigund's **Camis** is **purple** (Lat. *purpurea*, crimson) to indicate her aspirations to sovereignty (cf. I vii 16.3), and to associate her with Dido who wears a *purpuream vestem* (Virgil, *Aen.* 4.139) to meet Aeneas; and it is tucked **Vp to her ham**. Belphœbe's is lily-white to indicate her virginity, and extends modestly 'Below her ham'.   **4** Decorated with a trailing ornament of ribbons drawn in different directions.

Stanza 3
2 Sewn with bands . . . **3 mailes**: lace-holes.   **4 Cemitare**: the scimitar, a weapon curved like the moon and associated with pagans. In Ripa 1603:231, it is the weapon of injustice. **5** Radigund's **belt** corresponds to the cestus worn by Hippolyta, Queen of the Amazons, which was taken from her by Hercules in an act interpreted as the triumph of virtue over lust; see Aptekar 1969:176–77.   **8–9** Radigund's shield with the decorative stones at its raised centre associates her with the full moon – cf. 12.8–9 – in contrast to Artegall who is likened to the setting sun at IV iv 43.6–7. Described frontally, it relates to the crescent-shaped shield carried by the Amazons in Virgil, *Aen.* 1.490.

Stanza 4
2 Cf. Belphœbe's 'princely port' (II iii 28.5).   **magnificence**: display of splendour.   **5 shaumes and trumpets** are ready to herald her victory; cf. I xii 13.2.

Stanza 5
2 to point: completely.   **4 countenaunce**: bearing.   **bent her**: determined.   **5 aduenter**: venture herself.

6

The Trumpets sounded, and the field began;
  With bitter strokes it both began, and ended.
  She at the first encounter on him ran
  With furious rage, as if she had intended
  Out of his breast the very heart haue rended:
  But he that had like tempests often tride,
  From that first flaw him selfe right well defended.
  The more she rag'd, the more he did abide;
She hewd, she foynd, she lasht, she laid on euery side.

7

Yet still her blowes he bore, and her forbore,
  Weening at last to win aduantage new;
  Yet still her crueltie increased more,
  And though powre faild, her courage did accrew,
  Which fayling he gan fiercely her pursew.
  Like as a Smith that to his cunning feat
  The stubborne mettall seeketh to subdew,
  Soone as he feeles it mollifide with heat,
With his great yron sledge doth strongly on it beat.

8

So did Sir *Artegall* vpon her lay,
  As if she had an yron anduile beene,
  That flakes of fire, bright as the sunny ray,
  Out of her steely armes were flashing seene,
  That all on fire ye would her surely weene.
  But with her shield so well her selfe she warded,
  From the dread daunger of his weapon keene,
  That all that while her life she safely garded:
But he that helpe from her against her will discarded.

9

For with his trenchant blade at the next blow
  Halfe of her shield he shared quite away,
  That halfe her side it selfe did naked show,
  And thenceforth vnto daunger opened way.

Much was she moued with the mightie sway
  Of that sad stroke, that halfe enrag'd she grew,
  And like a greedie Beare vnto her pray,
  With her sharpe Cemitare at him she flew,
That glauncing downe his thigh, the purple bloud forth drew.

10

Thereat she gan to triumph with great boast,
  And to vpbrayd that chaunce, which him misfell,
  As if the prize she gotten had almost,
  With spightfull speaches, fitting with her well;
  That his great hart gan inwardly to swell
  With indignation, at her vaunting vaine,
  And at her strooke with puissance fearefull fell;
  Yet with her shield she warded it againe,
That shattered all to peeces round about the plaine.

11

Hauing her thus disarmed of her shield,
  Vpon her helmet he againe her strooke,
  That downe she fell vpon the grassie field,
  In sencelesse swoune, as if her life forsooke,
  And pangs of death her spirit ouertooke.
  Whom when he saw before his foote prostrated,
  He to her lept with deadly dreadfull looke,
  And her sunshynie helmet soone vnlaced,
Thinking at once both head and helmet to haue raced.

12

But when as he discouered had her face,
  He saw his senses straunge astonishment,
  A miracle of natures goodly grace,
  In her faire visage voide of ornament,
  But bath'd in bloud and sweat together ment;
  Which in the rudenesse of that euill plight,
  Bewrayd the signes of feature excellent:
  Like as the Moone in foggie winters night,
Doth seeme to be her selfe, though darkned be her light.

Stanza 6

1 **field**: battle.   7 **flaw**: sudden squall of wind.   9 **foynd**: lunged.

Stanza 7

1 **forbore**: spared.   4 **accrew**: gather; i.e. remain.   5 **Which**: i.e. her **powre**.   6–9 The erotic implications of the encounter are exploited in *Am* 32.   **feat**: art.

Stanza 8

9 **discarded**: forced away.

Stanza 9

1 **trenchant**: cutting.   2 At 3.8–9, her shield is compared to the full moon; its power is now waning; by 10.9, it is eclipsed. **shared**: cut.   3 **naked**: also unarmed.   5 **sway**: force.   6 **sad**: heavy.   9 A sexual wound, as at III v 20.7.

Stanza 10

8 **it**: the stroke.

Stanza 11

7 **deadly**: preparing for the **looke** that soon proves deadly to

him.   8 Her (masculine) armour is now associated with the sun, her person at 12.8–9 with the moon.   9 **raced**: cut off.

Stanza 12

Similarities with differences indicate that S. expects this moment to be read against IV vi where Artegall unhelms Britomart only to be defeated by the sight of her beauty. E.g. line 2: that what he saw strangely astonished his senses repeats his astonishment when he first saw Britomart's face (21). Line 3: Britomart is addressed in similar terms as 'That peerelesse paterne of Dame natures pride' but also as the 'heauenly image of perfection' (24.5–6). Line 5: as the silver and red of Britomart's face are **ment**, i.e. mingled, at 19.6–9. Lines 8–9: in contrast to the darkened moon, Britomart's face appears 'Like to the ruddie morne' (19.6). More broadly, Radigund is compared to the moon while Britomart is compared to the full moon in its brightness at III i 43, and her hair, which is given a full stanza (20) but notably absent in the description of Radigund, to the sun's beams at III ix 20.6–9; cf. IV i 13.6–9. On the differences, see Cincotta 1983:48–51, Woods 1985:153.   4 That she is **voide of ornament** (here probably cosmetics) is a mark of praise; see II v 32.9*n*.

13

At sight thereof his cruell minded hart
  Empierced was with pittifull regard,
  That his sharpe sword he threw from him apart,
  Cursing his hand that had that visage mard:
  No hand so cruell, nor no hart so hard,
  But ruth of beautie will it mollifie.
  By this vpstarting from her swoune, she star'd
  A while about her with confused eye;
Like one that from his dreame is waked suddenlye.

14

Soone as the knight she there by her did spy,
  Standing with emptie hands all weaponlesse,
  With fresh assault vpon him she did fly,
  And gan renew her former cruelnesse:
  And though he still retyr'd, yet nathelesse
  With huge redoubled strokes she on him layd;
  And more increast her outrage mercilesse,
  The more that he with meeke intreatie prayd,
Her wrathfull hand from greedy vengeance to haue stayd.

15

Like as a Puttocke hauing spyde in sight
  A gentle Faulcon sitting on an hill,
  Whose other wing, now made vnmeete for flight,
  Was lately broken by some fortune ill;
  The foolish Kyte, led with licentious will,
  Doth beat vpon the gentle bird in vaine,
  With many idle stoups her troubling still:
  Euen so did *Radigund* with bootlesse paine
Annoy this noble Knight, and sorely him constraine.

16

Nought could he do, but shun the dred despight
  Of her fierce wrath, and backward still retyre,
  And with his single shield, well as he might,
  Beare off the burden of her raging yre;

And euermore he gently did desyre,
  To stay her stroks, and he himselfe would yield:
  Yet nould she hearke, ne let him once respyre,
  Till he to her deliuered had his shield,
And to her mercie him submitted in plaine field.

17

So was he ouercome, not ouercome,
  But to her yeelded of his owne accord;
  Yet was he iustly damned by the doome
  Of his owne mouth, that spake so warelesse word,
  To be her thrall, and seruice her afford.
  For though that he first victorie obtayned,
  Yet after by abandoning his sword,
  He wilfull lost, that he before attayned.
No fayrer conquest, then that with goodwill is gayned.

18

Tho with her sword on him she flatling strooke,
  In signe of true subiection to her powre,
  And as her vassall him to thraldome tooke.
  But *Terpine* borne to'a more vnhappy howre,
  As he, on whom the lucklesse starres did lowre,
  She causd to be attacht, and forthwith led
  Vnto the crooke t'abide the balefull stowre,
  From which he lately had through reskew fled:
Where he full shamefully was hanged by the hed.

19

But when they thought on *Talus* hands to lay,
  He with his yron flaile amongst them thondred,
  That they were fayne to let him scape away,
  Glad from his companie to be so sondred;
  Whose presence all their troups so much encombred
  That th'heapes of those, which he did wound and slay,
  Besides the rest dismayd, might not be nombred:
  Yet all that while he would not once assay,
To reskew his owne Lord, but thought it iust t'obay.

Stanza 13

3 Extending the comparison at 12: on seeing Britomart's beauty, Artegall's 'cruell sword out of his fingers slacke | Fell downe to ground' (IV vi 21.5–6); now through pity, he wilfully throws it away.

Stanza 15

1–2 Artegall is no longer the royal eagle driving the scavenger goshawk from its prey, as at iv 42, but a **gentle Faulcon**, a *female* peregrine falcon beaten by a buzzard. The stages by which he is feminized are noted by E.D. Harvey 1992:35–38. 3 **Whose other**: i.e. one of whose. 7–9 **stoups**: the swoops of a bird of prey upon its quarry; **idle** because they are **in vaine**: Artegall does not respond. Her effort is **bootlesse**, i.e. to no purpose, because he has already yielded. **constraine**: distress.

Stanza 16

3 **single shield**: i.e. shield alone. 7 Yet she would not listen . . . 9 **in plaine field**: i.e. openly, publicly.

Stanza 17

1–2 Instead of being defeated by her, he chooses to be

defeated, as he did after defeating Britomart at IV vi 21–22 and became her 'thrall' (28.8). One difference is his prior agreement to be Radigund's thrall if defeated. Another is that Britomart seeks his love, Radigund his servitude. 3 **damned**: condemned, with obvious religious overtones. 4 **warelesse**: imprudent. 5 **seruice her afford**: including sexual performance, such as that promised by the Squire of Dames at III vii 54.6. 8 **He wilfull lost**, i.e. voluntarily, of his own **goodwill**; cf. 20.2, 32.2–3, vi 1.3, 16.4–5. The obvious, pressing analogy is Adam's submission to Eve.

Stanza 18

1–2 She dubs him her vassal, as A.B. Gough 1921 notes, in order to treat him as does Argante when she makes men 'the vassall of her pleasures vile' at III vii 50.8. **flatling**: with the flat side. 5 **lucklesse**: referring to malign astral influence. 6 **attacht**: seized; legally arrested. She assumes Artegall's role as the knight of justice. 7 **the crooke**: 'that gibbet' (iv 32.3). **balefull stowre**: pain of death.

Stanza 19

3 **fayne**: glad. 7 **dismayd**: routed. 9 **iust**: according to Artegall's vow at iv 49.2–3 to obey her if defeated.

20

Then tooke the Amazon this noble knight,
    Left to her will by his owne wilfull blame,
    And caused him to be disarmed quight,
    Of all the ornaments of knightly name,
    With which whylome he gotten had great fame:
    In stead whereof she made him to be dight
    In womans weedes, that is to manhood shame,
    And put before his lap a napron white,
In stead of Curiets and bases fit for fight.

21

So being clad, she brought him from the field,
    In which he had bene trayned many a day,
    Into a long large chamber, which was sield
    With moniments of many knights decay,
    By her subdewed in victorious fray:
    Amongst the which she causd his warlike armes
    Be hang'd on high, that mote his shame bewray;
    And broke his sword, for feare of further harmes,
With which he wont to stirre vp battailous alarmes.

22

There entred in, he round about him saw
    Many braue knights, whose names right well he knew,
    There bound t'obay that Amazons proud law,
    Spinning and carding all in comely rew,
    That his bigge hart loth'd so vncomely vew.
    But they were forst through penurie and pyne,
    To doe those workes, to them appointed dew:
    For nought was giuen them to sup or dyne,
But what their hands could earne by twisting linnen twyne.

23

Amongst them all she placed him most low,
    And in his hand a distaffe to him gaue,
    That he thereon should spin both flax and tow;
    A sordid office for a mind so braue.

So hard it is to be a womans slaue.
    Yet he it tooke in his owne selfes despight,
    And thereto did himselfe right well behaue,
    Her to obay, sith he his faith had plight,
Her vassall to become, if she him wonne in fight.

24

Who had him seene, imagine mote thereby,
    That whylome hath of *Hercules* bene told,
    How for *Iolas* sake he did apply
    His mightie hands, the distaffe vile to hold,
    For his huge club, which had subdew'd of old
    So many monsters, which the world annoyed;
    His Lyons skin chaungd to a pall of gold,
    In which forgetting warres, he onely ioyed
In combats of sweet loue, and with his mistresse toyed.

25

Such is the crueltie of womenkynd,
    When they haue shaken off the shamefast band,
    With which wise Nature did them strongly bynd,
    T'obay the heasts of mans well ruling hand,
    That then all rule and reason they withstand,
    To purchase a licentious libertie.
    But vertuous women wisely vnderstand,
    That they were borne to base humilitie,
Vnlesse the heauens them lift to lawfull soueraintie.

26

Thus there long while continu'd *Artegall*,
    Seruing proud *Radigund* with true subiection;
    How euer it his noble heart did gall,
    T'obay a womans tyrannous direction,
    That might haue had of life or death election:
    But hauing chosen, now he might not chaunge.
    During which time, the warlike Amazon,
    Whose wandring fancie after lust did raunge,
Gan cast a secret liking to this captiue straunge.

Stanza 20

2 wilfull blame doubly stresses his fault: he suffers blame through his own blameful will when he 'wilfull lost' (17.8), disarmed by her beauty. **8 before his lap**: suggesting impotence. Wearing a **napron** (apron) marks his fallen state, as Adam and Eve after disobeying God 'made them apurns' (Gen. 3.7, tr. Coverdale). **9 Curiets**: cuirasses or body armour. **bases**: the skirt of mail worn by knights on horseback.

Stanza 21

3–4 sield: ceiled or lined, as are the walls of the house of Busirane at III xi 52. **decay**: overthrow. **6–8** As Verdant's 'warlike Armes . . . were hong vpon a tree' by Acrasia at II xii 80.1–2, and Braggadocchio's sword was broken to disgrace him at iii 37.9. **bewray**: reveal. **9 battailous**: warlike.

Stanza 22

5 bigge: stout. **6 penurie and pyne**: a stock phrase, e.g. *SC Sept.* 65 and I ix 35.8. Literally, lack of food and the consequent suffering.

Stanza 23

4 sordid: menial; debasing; foul. **6** In contrast to Terpine who 'rather chose to die in liues despight' (iv 32.8) than suffer such shame; cf. 26.5. **7 behaue**: conduct, manage.

Stanza 24

S. may have confused Iole and Omphale, as did his contemporaries, e.g. T. Cooper 1565, who writes of Iole: 'whome Hercules loued so much, that he serued hir in a womans apparaile, and spanne on a distaffe', and of Omphale: 'whom Hercules dyd serue, and she caused him to spinne on a rocke [distaff]'; see Aptekar 1969:177–79. Or he may have conflated them; see Skretkowicz 1980. C. Carroll 1990:182 notes a similar degendering of the Old English in Ireland, as noted in *View* 69–70. **7** For the first of his labours, Hercules killed the Nemean lion and wore its skin as a sign of victory; see viii 2.4–5. **pall**: robe.

Stanza 25

The subject of the stanza determines its careful placing: the twenty-fifth stanza in the fifth canto of Bk V, five being the number of justice; see A. Fowler 1964:34. While its matter is

27

Which long concealing in her couert brest,
    She chaw'd the cud of louers carefull plight;
    Yet could it not so thoroughly digest,
    Being fast fixed in her wounded spright,
    But it tormented her both day and night:
    Yet would she not thereto yeeld free accord,
    To serue the lowly vassall of her might,
    And of her seruant make her souerayne Lord:
So great her pride, that she such basenesse much abhord.

28

So much the greater still her anguish grew,
    Through stubborne handling of her loue-sicke hart;
    And still the more she stroue it to subdew,
    The more she still augmented her owne smart,
    And wyder made the wound of th'hidden dart.
    At last when long she struggled had in vaine,
    She gan to stoupe, and her proud mind conuert
    To meeke obeysance of loues mightie raine,
And him entreat for grace, that had procur'd her paine.

29

Vnto her selfe in secret she did call
    Her nearest handmayd, whom she most did trust,
    And to her said; *Clarinda* whom of all
    I trust a liue, sith I thee fostred first;
    Now is the time, that I vntimely must
    Thereof make tryall, in my greatest need:
    It is so hapned, that the heauens vniust,
    Spighting my happie freedome, haue agreed,
To thrall my looser life, or my last bale to breed.

30

With that she turn'd her head, as halfe abashed,
    To hide the blush which in her visage rose,
    And through her eyes like sudden lightning flashed,
    Decking her cheeke with a vermilion rose:

But soone she did her countenance compose,
    And to her turning, thus began againe;
    This griefes deepe wound I would to thee disclose,
    Thereto compelled through hart-murdring paine,
But dread of shame my doubtfull lips doth still restraine.

31

Ah my deare dread (said then the faithfull Mayd)
    Can dread of ought your dreadlesse hart withhold,
    That many hath with dread of death dismayd,
    And dare euen deathes most dreadfull face behold?
    Say on my souerayne Ladie, and be bold;
    Doth not your handmayds life at your foot lie?
    Therewith much comforted, she gan vnfold
    The cause of her conceiued maladie,
As one that would confesse, yet faine would it denie.

32

Clarin (sayd she) thou seest yond Fayry Knight,
    Whom not my valour, but his owne braue mind
    Subiected hath to my vnequall might;
    What right is it, that he should thraldome find,
    For lending life to me a wretch vnkind;
    That for such good him recompence with ill?
    Therefore I cast, how I may him vnbind,
    And by his freedome get his free goodwill;
Yet so, as bound to me he may continue still.

33

Bound vnto me, but not with such hard bands
    Of strong compulsion, and streight violence,
    As now in miserable state he stands;
    But with sweet loue and sure beneuolence,
    Voide of malitious mind, or foule offence.
    To which if thou canst win him any way,
    Without discouerie of my thoughts pretence,
    Both goodly meede of him it purchase may,
And eke with gratefull seruice me right well apay.

thoroughly traditional, e.g. the inference that a woman is subject to a man's spiritual authority and that Elizabeth is the divinely-ordained exception, Wynne-Davies 1996:92 juxtaposes III ii 2 to claim that S. is taking part in the *querelle des femmes*. On the background, see Phillips 1941–42. **2 shamefast band**: bond of modesty, i.e. bonds that restrain from shame. As woman's chief virtue, see IV x 50.1–5*n*. **4 heasts**: behests. **7–9 base**: low, humble. Not necessarily implying mean though the word so disturbed the author of *Hic Mulier* 1620 that he substituted 'milde'; see *Sp All* 157. **lawfull** affirms Elizabeth's claim to the crown.

Stanza 26
3 How euer: however much. **9 straunge**: foreign.

Stanza 28
2 stubborne: fierce, harsh. **7 stoupe**: in contrast to her 'stoups' to attack him at 15.7. Now she is being preyed on. **9 procur'd**: caused.

Stanza 29
6 Thereof: i.e. of my trust in you. **8 Spighting**: regarding with ill-will. **9 looser**: too loose. **last bale**: death.

Stanza 30
9 doubtfull: fearful.

Stanza 31
1–4 Clarinda's repeated puns on **dread** are noted by Upton 1758.

Stanza 32
5 vnkind: unnatural. **7 cast**: consider.

Stanza 33
2 streight: severe. **4 beneuolence**: affection. **7 pretence**: intent, as 35.1. **9 seruice**: see 17.5*n*. **apay**: requite.

34

Which that thou mayst the better bring to pas,
    Loe here this ring, which shall thy warrant bee,
    And token true to old *Eumenias*,
    From time to time, when thou it best shalt see,
    That in and out thou mayst haue passage free.
    Goe now, *Clarinda*, well thy wits aduise,
    And all thy forces gather vnto thee;
    Armies of louely lookes, and speeches wise,
With which thou canst euen *Ioue* himselfe to loue entise.

35

The trustie Mayd, conceiuing her intent,
    Did with sure promise of her good indeuour,
    Giue her great comfort, and some harts content.
    So from her parting, she thenceforth did labour
    By all the meanes she might, to curry fauour
    With th'Elfin Knight, her Ladies best beloued;
    With daily shew of courteous kind behauiour,
    Euen at the markewhite of his hart she roued,
And with wide glauncing words, one day she thus him proued.

36

Vnhappie Knight, vpon whose hopelesse state
    Fortune enuying good, hath felly frowned,
    And cruell heauens haue heapt an heauy fate;
    I rew that thus thy better dayes are drowned
    In sad despaire, and all thy senses swowned
    In stupid sorow, sith thy iuster merit
    Might else haue with felicitie bene crowned:
    Looke vp at last, and wake thy dulled spirit,
To thinke how this long death thou mightest disinherit.

37

Much did he maruell at her vncouth speach,
    Whose hidden drift he could not well perceiue;
    And gan to doubt, least she him sought t'appeach
    Of treason, or some guilefull traine did weaue,
    Through which she might his wretched life bereaue.
    Both which to barre, he with this answere met her;
    Faire Damzell, that with ruth (as I perceaue)
    Of my mishaps, art mou'd to wish me better,
For such your kind regard, I can but rest your detter.

38

Yet weet ye well, that to a courage great
    It is no lesse beseeming well, to beare
    The storme of fortunes frowne, or heauens threat,
    Then in the sunshine of her countenance cleare
    Timely to ioy, and carrie comely cheare.
    For though this cloud haue now me ouercast,
    Yet doe I not of better times despeyre;
    And, though vnlike, they should for euer last,
Yet in my truthes assurance I rest fixed fast.

39

But what so stonie mind (she then replyde)
    But if in his owne powre occasion lay,
    Would to his hope a windowe open wyde,
    And to his fortunes helpe make readie way?
    Vnworthy sure (quoth he) of better day,
    That will not take the offer of good hope,
    And eke pursew, if he attaine it may.
    Which speaches she applying to the scope
Of her intent, this further purpose to him shope.

40

Then why doest not, thou ill aduized man,
    Make meanes to win thy libertie forlorne,
    And try if thou by faire entreatie, can
    Moue *Radigund*? who though she still haue worne
    Her dayes in warre, yet (weet thou) was not borne
    Of Beares and Tygres, nor so saluage mynded,
    As that, albe all loue of men she scorne,
    She yet forgets, that she of men was kynded:
And sooth oft seene, that proudest harts base loue hath blynded.

41

Certes *Clarinda*, not of cancred will,
    (Sayd he) nor obstinate disdainefull mind,
    I haue forbore this duetie to fulfill:
    For well I may this weene, by that I fynd,
    That she a Queene, and come of Princely kynd,
    Both worthie is for to be sewd vnto,
    Chiefely by him, whose life her law doth bynd,
    And eke of powre her owne doome to vndo,
And als' of princely grace to be inclyn'd thereto.

Stanza 34
3 **Eumenias**: Gk εὐμενία, good will, which Radigund seeks in Artegall at 32.8.   8 **louely**: loving.

Stanza 35
1 **conceiuing**: apprehending; also suggesting that she shares Radigund's desire for Artegall; cf. 43.8.   8–9 **markewhite**: white bull's eye of a target.   **roued**: shot.   **wide glauncing**: indirect, as a roving arrow is aimed high to drop down to a target rather than directly at it.   **proued**: tested.

Stanza 36
4–5 She echoes Una's lament at I viii 28.8 that the Red Cross Knight 'his better dayes hath wasted all' in Orgoglio's dungeon. Like him, Artegall endures a **long death** from which he must be redeemed by grace.   6 **stupid**: that which stuns.   **iuster**: most just.

Stanza 37
1 **vncouth**: strange.   3 **doubt**: fear.   **appeach**: accuse.   4 **traine**: treachery.

Stanza 38
8 And though it is unlikely that **fortunes frowne, or heauens threat** should last for ever, etc.

Stanza 39
9 **purpose**: proposal.   **shope**: shaped, addressed.

Stanza 40
2 **forlorne**: lost.   6–8 Although she scorns the love of men, she is not so savage-minded as to forget, etc.   **kynded**: begotten.   9 **base**: low, humble; also debasing.

42

But want of meanes hath bene mine onely let,
From seeking fauour, where it doth abound;
Which if I might by your good office get,
I to your selfe should rest for euer bound,
And readie to deserue, what grace I found.
She feeling him thus bite vpon the bayt,
Yet doubting least his hold was but vnsound,
And not well fastened, would not strike him strayt,
But drew him on with hope, fit leasure to awayt.

43

But foolish Mayd, whyles heedlesse of the hooke,
She thus oft times was beating off and on,
Through slipperie footing, fell into the brooke,
And there was caught to her confusion.
For seeking thus to salue the Amazon,
She wounded was with her deceipts owne dart,
And gan thenceforth to cast affection,
Conceiued close in her beguiled hart,
To *Artegall*, through pittie of his causelesse smart.

44

Yet durst she not disclose her fancies wound,
Ne to himselfe, for doubt of being sdayned,
Ne yet to any other wight on ground,
For feare her mistresse shold haue knowledge gayned,
But to her selfe it secretly retayned,
Within the closet of her couert brest:
The more thereby her tender hart was payned.
Yet to awayt fit time she weened best,
And fairely did dissemble her sad thoughts vnrest.

45

One day her Ladie, calling her apart,
Gan to demaund of her some tydings good,
Touching her loues successe, her lingring smart.
Therewith she gan at first to change her mood,
As one adaw'd, and halfe confused stood;
But quickly she it ouerpast, so soone
As she her face had wypt, to fresh her blood:
Tho gan she tell her all, that she had donne,
And all the wayes she sought, his loue for to haue wonne.

46

But sayd, that he was obstinate and sterne,
Scorning her offers and conditions vaine;
Ne would be taught with any termes, to lerne
So fond a lesson, as to loue againe.
Die rather would he in penurious paine,
And his abridged dayes in dolour wast,
Then his foes loue or liking entertaine:
His resolution was both first and last,
His bodie was her thrall, his hart was freely plast.

47

Which when the cruell Amazon perceiued,
She gan to storme, and rage, and rend her gall,
For very fell despight, which she conceiued,
To be so scorned of a base borne thrall,
Whose life did lie in her least eye-lids fall;
Of which she vow'd with many a cursed threat,
That she therefore would him ere long forstall.
Nathlesse when calmed was her furious heat,
She chang'd that threatfull mood, and mildly gan entreat.

48

What now is left *Clarinda*? what remaines,
That we may compasse this our enterprize?
Great shame to lose so long employed paines,
And greater shame t'abide so great misprize,
With which he dares our offers thus despize.
Yet that his guilt the greater may appeare,
And more my gratious mercie by this wize,
I will a while with his first folly beare,
Till thou haue tride againe, and tempted him more neare.

49

Say, and do all, that may thereto preuaile;
Leaue nought vnpromist, that may him perswade,
Life, freedome, grace, and gifts of great auaile,
With which the Gods themselues are mylder made;
Thereto adde art, euen womens witty trade,
The art of mightie words, that men can charme;
With which in case thou canst him not inuade,
Let him feele hardnesse of thy heauie arme:
Who will not stoupe with good, shall be made stoupe with harme.

Stanza 42
Artegall equivocates as does Amyas when wooed by Pœana: although he loves Æmylia, 'Her graunted loue, but with affection cold | To win her grace his libertie to get' (IV viii 53.5–6). **1 let**: hindrance. **8 strike**: i.e. jerk the line to fix the hook.

Stanza 43
2 beating off and on: an angling term for strikes to test the hold on the bait. **5 salue**: heal.

Stanza 44
1 fancies wound: i.e. love's wound, as Radigund's fancy at 26.8. **2 doubt**: fear. **sdayned**: disdained.

Stanza 45
5 adaw'd: daunted. **7** The deceptive secrecy marked by this unprecedented 'realistic' detail is noted by Krier 1990:219.

It is seen in Radigund at 27.1, and in Clarinda at 43.8, esp. 44.6.

Stanza 46
4 fond: foolish; amorous. **againe**: in return. **5 penurious paine**: the pain of starvation.

Stanza 47
2 gall: the seat of anger. **7 forstall**: deprive.

Stanza 48
4 misprize: scorn.

Stanza 49
1 As she wooed Bellodant 'by all the waies she could' (iv.30.4). **3–4** Cf. the proverb, 'gifts move the gods' (Smith 321). **auaile**: benefit. **5 witty**: cunning, clever.

50

Some of his diet doe from him withdraw;
 For I him find to be too proudly fed.
 Giue him more labour, and with streighter law,
 That he with worke may be forwearied.
 Let him lodge hard, and lie in strawen bed,
 That may pull downe the courage of his pride;
 And lay vpon him, for his greater dread,
 Cold yron chaines, with which let him be tide;
And let, what euer he desires, be him denide.

51

When thou hast all this doen, then bring me newes
 Of his demeane: thenceforth not like a louer,
 But like a rebell stout I will him vse.
 For I resolue this siege not to giue ouer,
 Till I the conquest of my will recouer.
 So she departed, full of griefe and sdaine,
 Which inly did to great impatience moue her.
 But the false mayden shortly turn'd againe
Vnto the prison, where her hart did thrall remaine.

52

There all her subtill nets she did vnfold,
 And all the engins of her wit display;
 In which she meant him warelesse to enfold,
 And of his innocence to make her pray.
 So cunningly she wrought her crafts assay,
 That both her Ladie, and her selfe withall,
 And eke the knight attonce she did betray:
 But most the knight, whom she with guilefull call
Did cast for to allure, into her trap to fall.

53

As a bad Nurse, which fayning to receiue
 In her owne mouth the food, ment for her chyld,
 Withholdes it to her selfe, and doeth deceiue
 The infant, so for want of nourture spoyld:
 Euen so *Clarinda* her owne Dame beguyld,
 And turn'd the trust, which was in her affyde,
 To feeding of her priuate fire, which boyld
 Her inward brest, and in her entrayles fryde,
The more that she it sought to couer and to hyde.

54

For comming to this knight, she purpose fayned,
 How earnest suit she earst for him had made
 Vnto her Queene, his freedome to haue gayned;
 But by no meanes could her thereto perswade:
 But that in stead thereof, she sternely bade
 His miserie to be augmented more,
 And many yron bands on him to lade.
 All which nathlesse she for his loue forbore:
So praying him t'accept her seruice euermore.

55

And more then that, she promist that she would,
 In case she might finde fauour in his eye,
 Deuize how to enlarge him out of hould.
 The Fayrie glad to gaine his libertie,
 Can yeeld great thankes for such her curtesie,
 And with faire words, fit for the time and place,
 To feede the humour of her maladie,
 Promist, if she would free him from that case,
He wold by all good means he might, deserue such grace.

56

So daily he faire semblant did her shew,
 Yet neuer meant he in his noble mind,
 To his owne absent loue to be vntrew:
 Ne euer did deceiptfull *Clarin* find
 In her false hart, his bondage to vnbind;
 But rather how she mote him faster tye.
 Therefore vnto her mistresse most vnkind
 She daily told, her loue he did defye,
And him she told, her Dame his freedome did denye.

57

Yet thus much friendship she to him did show,
 That his scarse diet somewhat was amended,
 And his worke lessened, that his loue mote grow:
 Yet to her Dame him still she discommended,
 That she with him mote be the more offended.
 Thus he long while in thraldome there remayned,
 Of both beloued well, but litle frended;
 Vntill his owne true loue his freedome gayned,
Which in an other Canto will be best contayned.

Stanza 50
3 streighter: more strict. **4 forwearied**: utterly wearied.

Stanza 51
2 demeane: behaviour. **3 a rebell**: a political category that justifies any force to quell. **6 sdaine**: disdain.

Stanza 52
1 subtill: finely woven; skilfully devised; crafty. **2 engins**: snares. **3 warelesse**: unwary. **5 assay**: endeavour; best effort. **8–9** As a fowler nets birds by making imitative calls. **cast**: scheme.

Stanza 53
6 affyde: confided.

Stanza 54
1 purpose: discourse; a story. **7 lade**: load.

Stanza 55
3 hould: confinement. **5 Can**: did.

Stanza 56
1 faire semblant: favourable countenance. **8 defye**: reject.

Cant. VI.

Talus brings newes to Britomart,
of Artegals mishap,
She goes to seeke him, Dolon meetes,
who seekes her to entrap.

1

SOme men, I wote, will deeme in *Artegall*
Great weaknesse, and report of him much ill,
For yeelding so himselfe a wretched thrall,
To th'insolent commaund of womens will;
That all his former praise doth fowly spill.
But he the man, that say or doe so dare,
Be well aduiz'd, that he stand stedfast still:
For neuer yet was wight so well aware,
But he at first or last was trapt in womens snare.

2

Yet in the streightnesse of that captiue state,
This gentle knight himselfe so well behaued,
That notwithstanding all the subtill bait,
With which those Amazons his loue still craued,
To his owne loue his loialtie he saued:
Whose character in th'Adamantine mould
Of his true hart so firmely was engraued,
That no new loues impression euer could
Bereaue it thence: such blot his honour blemish should.

3

Yet his owne loue, the noble *Britomart*,
Scarse so conceiued in her iealous thought,
What time sad tydings of his balefull smart
In womans bondage, *Talus* to her brought;

Brought in vntimely houre, ere it was sought.
For after that the vtmost date, assynde
For his returne, she waited had for nought,
She gan to cast in her misdoubtfull mynde
A thousand feares, that loue-sicke fancies faine to fynde.

4

Sometime she feared, least some hard mishap
Had him misfalne in his aduenturous quest;
Sometime least his false foe did him entrap
In traytrous traine, or had vnwares opprest:
But most she did her troubled mynd molest,
And secretly afflict with iealous feare,
Least some new loue had him from her possest;
Yet loth she was, since she no ill did heare,
To thinke of him so ill: yet could she not forbeare.

5

One while she blam'd her selfe; another whyle
She him condemn'd, as trustlesse and vntrew:
And then, her griefe with errour to beguyle,
She fayn'd to count the time againe anew,
As if before she had not counted trew.
For houres but dayes; for weekes, that passed were,
She told but moneths, to make them seeme more few:
Yet when she reckned them, still drawing neare,
Each hour did seeme a moneth, and euery moneth a yeare.

Book V Canto vi

Stanza 1

4 insolent: proud, overbearing. **5 spill**: destroy. **6–9** The lines invoke 1 Cor. 10. 12: 'let him that thinketh he standeth, take hede lest he fall' in order to indicate that Artegall's weakness is the human condition. Cf. viii 1–2. **aware**: vigilant.

Stanza 2

1 streightnesse: strictness, hardship. **2** Repeating v 23.7 because his behaviour in the interim has become moot. **6 character**: figure; **impression**. **Adamantine**: suggesting also 'loving', from the popular etymology, Lat. *ad-amantem*. **9 Bereaue**: remove.

Stanzas 3–18

S. models this episode on Ariosto, *Or. Fur.* 32.10–49: Bradamante watches from a window and counts the time until Ruggiero's return. Later upon learning that he is to be married to Marfisa, she throws herself on her bed in full armour,

stuffing the sheets into her mouth so not to scream, and accuses him of being unfaithful to her. After failing to kill herself because she is in armour, she resolves to kill him, or perhaps be killed by him after she kills Marfisa. See 39*n* and vii 34.6*n*.

Stanza 3

6 the vtmost date: the three lunar months, on which they agreed at IV vi 43.8–9. **8 cast**: contrive. **misdoubtfull**: suspicious. **9 faine**: wont.

Stanza 4

2 aduenturous: perilous. **4 traine**: trap (a pleonasm enforcing **entrap**). **opprest**: taken by surprise. **7 possest**: taken.

Stanza 5

4 fayn'd: sought; desired; also, in so doing, feigned. **6–7** To make time seem shorter, she counted it in days rather than hours, and in months rather than weeks. **8 neare**: i.e. to an end.

6

But when as yet she saw him not returne,
　　She thought to send some one to seeke him out;
　　But none she found so fit to serue that turne,
　　As her owne selfe, to ease her selfe of dout.
　　Now she deuiz'd amongst the warlike rout
　　Of errant Knights, to seeke her errant Knight;
　　And then againe resolu'd to hunt him out
　　Amongst loose Ladies, lapped in delight:
And then both Knights enuide, and Ladies eke did spight.

7

One day, when as she long had sought for ease
　　In euery place, and euery place thought best,
　　Yet found no place, that could her liking please,
　　She to a window came, that opened West,
　　Towards which coast her loue his way addrest.
　　There looking forth, shee in her heart did find
　　Many vaine fancies, working her vnrest;
　　And sent her winged thoughts, more swift then wind,
To beare vnto her loue the message of her mind.

8

There as she looked long, at last she spide
　　One comming towards her with hasty speede:
　　Well weend she then, ere him she plaine descride,
　　That it was one sent from her loue indeede.
　　Who when he nigh approcht, shee mote arede
　　That it was *Talus*, *Artegall* his groome;
　　Whereat her heart was fild with hope and drede;
　　Ne would she stay, till he in place could come,
But ran to meete him forth, to know his tidings somme.

9

Euen in the dore him meeting, she begun;
　　And where is he thy Lord, and how far hence?
　　Declare at once; and hath he lost or wun?
　　The yron man, albe he wanted sence
　　And sorrowes feeling, yet with conscience
　　Of his ill newes, did inly chill and quake,
　　And stood still mute, as one in great suspence,
　　As if that by his silence he would make
Her rather reade his meaning, then him selfe it spake.

10

Till she againe thus sayd; *Talus* be bold,
　　And tell what euer it be, good or bad,
　　That from thy tongue thy hearts intent doth hold.
　　To whom he thus at length. The tidings sad,
　　That I would hide, will needs, I see, be rad.
　　My Lord, your loue, by hard mishap doth lie
　　In wretched bondage, wofully bestad.
　　Ay me (quoth she) what wicked destinie?
And is he vanquisht by his tyrant enemy?

11

Not by that Tyrant, his intended foe;
　　But by a Tyrannesse (he then replide,)
　　That him captiued hath in haplesse woe.
　　Cease thou bad newes-man, badly doest thou hide
　　Thy maisters shame, in harlots bondage tide.
　　The rest my selfe too readily can spell.
　　With that in rage she turn'd from him aside,
　　Forcing in vaine the rest to her to tell,
And to her chamber went like solitary cell.

12

There she began to make her monefull plaint
　　Against her Knight, for being so vntrew;
　　And him to touch with falshoods fowle attaint,
　　That all his other honour ouerthrew.
　　Oft did she blame her selfe, and often rew,
　　For yeelding to a straungers loue so light,
　　Whose life and manners straunge she neuer knew;
　　And euermore she did him sharpely twight
For breach of faith to her, which he had firmely plight.

13

And then she in her wrathfull will did cast,
　　How to reuenge that blot of honour blent;
　　To fight with him, and goodly die her last:
　　And then againe she did her selfe torment,
　　Inflicting on her selfe his punishment.
　　A while she walkt, and chauft; a while she threw
　　Her selfe vppon her bed, and did lament;
　　Yet did she not lament with loude alew,
As women wont, but with deepe sighes, and singulfs few.

Stanza 6
6 her errant Knight: implying that he is morally erring.
8 lapped: implying that he is 'enjoying their laps' in the sexual sense. **9 enuide**: regarded with dislike. **did spight**: regarded with spite.

Stanza 7
4 West: the direction of the setting sun; in the political allegory, the direction of Ireland; cf. 22.4. **5 coast**: direction.

Stanza 8
5 arede: perceive.

Stanza 9
5 conscience: knowledge, consciousness.

Stanza 10
2–3 I.e. tell what you know in your heart (**intent** = meaning) but your tongue won't say. A circumlocution needed to persuade Talus to speak directly for the first and only time, as C. Burrow 1996:93 has noted. **5 rad**: discovered. **7 bestad**: placed.

Stanza 11
1 that Tyrant: Grantorto. **2 Tyrannesse**: the title given Lucifera at I v 46.6. **8 Forcing**: striving.

Stanza 12
6 light: lightly. **8 twight**: twit, reproach.

Stanza 13
2–3 How to revenge his honour (and hers) stained by his falsehood. **8 alew**: halloo. **9 singulfs**: sobs; see III xi 12.1*n*.

14

Like as a wayward childe, whose sounder sleepe
    Is broken with some fearefull dreames affright,
    With froward will doth set him selfe to weepe;
    Ne can be stild for all his nurses might,
    But kicks, and squals, and shriekes for fell despight:
    Now scratching her, and her loose locks misusing;
    Now seeking darkenesse, and now seeking light;
    Then crauing sucke, and then the sucke refusing.
Such was this Ladies fit, in her loues fond accusing.

15

But when she had with such vnquiet fits
    Her selfe there close afflicted long in vaine,
    Yet found no easement in her troubled wits,
    She vnto *Talus* forth return'd againe,
    By change of place seeking to ease her paine;
    And gan enquire of him, with mylder mood,
    The certaine cause of *Artegals* detaine;
    And what he did, and in what state he stood,
And whether he did woo, or whether he were woo'd.

16

Ah wellaway (sayd then the yron man,)
    That he is not the while in state to woo;
    But lies in wretched thraldome, weake and wan,
    Not by strong hand compelled thereunto,
    But his owne doome, that none can now vndoo.
    Sayd I not then (quoth shee) erwhile aright,
    That this is things compacte betwixt you two,
    Me to deceiue of faith vnto me plight,
Since that he was not forst, nor ouercome in fight?

17

With that he gan at large to her dilate
    The whole discourse of his captiuance sad,
    In sort as ye haue heard the same of late.
    All which when she with hard enduraunce had
    Heard to the end, she was right sore bestad,
    With sodaine stounds of wrath and griefe attone:
    Ne would abide, till she had aunswere made,
    But streight her selfe did dight, and armor don;
And mounting to her steede, bad *Talus* guide her on.

18

So forth she rode vppon her ready way,
    To seeke her Knight, as *Talus* her did guide:
    Sadly she rode, and neuer word did say,
    Nor good nor bad, ne euer lookt aside,
    But still right downe, and in her thought did hide
    The felnesse of her heart, right fully bent
    To fierce auengement of that womans pride,
    Which had her Lord in her base prison pent,
And so great honour with so fowle reproch had blent.

19

So as she thus melancholicke did ride,
    Chawing the cud of griefe and inward paine,
    She chaunst to meete toward th'euen-tide
    A Knight, that softly paced on the plaine,
    As if him selfe to solace he were faine.
    Well shot in yeares he seem'd, and rather bent
    To peace, then needlesse trouble to constraine.
    As well by view of that his vestiment,
As by his modest semblant, that no euill ment.

20

He comming neare, gan gently her salute
    With curteous words, in the most comely wize;
    Who though desirous rather to rest mute,
    Then termes to entertaine of common guize,
    Yet rather then she kindnesse would despize,
    She would her selfe displease, so him requite.
    Then gan the other further to deuize
    Of things abrode, as next to hand did light,
And many things demaund, to which she answer'd light.

21

For little lust had she to talke of ought,
    Or ought to heare, that mote delightfull bee;
    Her minde was whole possessed of one thought,
    That gaue none other place. Which when as hee
    By outward signes, (as well he might) did see,
    He list no lenger to vse lothfull speach,
    But her besought to take it well in gree,
    Sith shady dampe had dimd the heauens reach,
To lodge with him that night, vnles good cause empeach.

Stanza 14
Britomart re-experiences the nightmare from which she suffered on first seeing Artegall in Merlin's mirror at III ii 29. See J. Miller 1997:195–96.

Stanza 15
7 detaine: detention.

Stanza 16
7 compacte: compacted.

Stanza 17
1 dilate: relate. **2 discourse**: account. **captiuance**: captivity. **6 stounds**: pangs. **wrath and griefe**: see II vi 1.6–7*n*. **attone**: at the same time.

Stanza 18
9 blent: stained; cf. 13.2.

Stanza 19
2 As does Radigund at v 27.2. On the bovine introspection they share only with the jealous Malbecco at III x 18.1–2, see Cavanagh 1994a:164–65. **6 shot**: advanced. **8 vestiment**: garb. **9 semblant**: outward appearance.

Stanza 20
1 gently: courteously. **4** I.e. than engage in 'small talk'. **6 requite**: i.e. she greeted him in return. **7 deuize**: converse. **9 light**: lightly; little.

Stanza 21
1 lust: desire. **7 well in gree**: in good part, with good will. **8 dampe**: fog. **reach**: height. **9 empeach**: prevented.

22

The Championesse, now seeing night at dore,
  Was glad to yeeld vnto his good request:
  And with him went without gaine-saying more.
  Not farre away, but little wide by West,
  His dwelling was, to which he him addrest;
  Where soone arriuing they receiued were
  In seemely wise, as them beseemed best:
For he their host them goodly well did cheare,
And talk't of pleasant things, the night away to weare.

23

Thus passing th'euening well, till time of rest,
  Then *Britomart* vnto a bowre was brought;
  Where groomes awayted her to haue vndrest.
  But she ne would vndressed be for ought,
  Ne doffe her armes, though he her much besought.
  For she had vow'd, she sayd, not to forgo
  Those warlike weedes, till she reuenge had wrought
  Of a late wrong vppon a mortall foe;
Which she would sure performe, betide her wele or wo.

24

Which when their Host perceiu'd, right discontent
  In minde he grew, for feare least by that art
  He should his purpose misse, which close he ment:
  Yet taking leaue of her, he did depart.
  There all that night remained *Britomart*,
  Restlesse, recomfortlesse, with heart deepe grieued,
  Not suffering the least twinckling sleepe to start
  Into her eye, which th'heart mote haue relieued,
But if the least appear'd, her eyes she streight reprieued.

25

Ye guilty eyes (sayd she) the which with guyle
  My heart at first betrayd, will ye betray
  My life now to, for which a little whyle
  Ye will not watch? false watches, wellaway,

I wote when ye did watch both night and day
  Vnto your losse: and now needes will ye sleepe?
  Now ye haue made my heart to wake alway,
  Now will ye sleepe? ah wake, and rather weepe,
To thinke of your nights want, that should yee waking keepe.

26

Thus did she watch, and weare the weary night
  In waylfull plaints, that none was to appease;
  Now walking soft, now sitting still vpright,
  As sundry chaunge her seemed best to ease.
  Ne lesse did *Talus* suffer sleepe to seaze
  His eye-lids sad, but watcht continually,
  Lying without her dore in great disease;
  Like to a Spaniell wayting carefully
Least any should betray his Lady treacherously.

27

What time the natiue Belman of the night,
  The bird, that warned *Peter* of his fall,
  First rings his siluer Bell t'each sleepy wight,
  That should their mindes vp to deuotion call,
  She heard a wondrous noise below the hall.
  All sodainely the bed, where she should lie,
  By a false trap was let adowne to fall
  Into a lower roome, and by and by
The loft was raysd againe, that no man could it spie.

28

With sight whereof she was dismayd right sore,
  Perceiuing well the treason, which was ment:
  Yet stirred not at all for doubt of more,
  But kept her place with courage confident,
  Wayting what would ensue of that euent.
  It was not long, before she heard the sound
  Of armed men, comming with close intent
  Towards her chamber; at which dreadfull stound
She quickly caught her sword, and shield about her bound.

Stanza 22

4 little wide by West: i.e. a little away from the west, which is the direction she travels in renewing her journey to find Artegall; cf. 7.4. **5 addrest**: made his way.

Stanza 23

4–5 As she conducts herself in the house of Busirane at III xi 55.5–9.

Stanza 24

2 art: device, means. **3 close**: secretly. **6 recomfortlesse**: without comfort; not to be comforted. **9 streight reprieued**: severely reproved.

Stanza 25

Britomart's thrice-repeated question is patterned after Christ's three visits to his sleeping disciples with the injunction, 'What? colde ye not watche with me one houre? Watch, and pray' (Matt. 26.40–41), and leads to the allusion to Peter's fall at 27.2. **1–2** Recalling her first sight of Artegall in Merlin's mirror at III ii 18.1–2, 24–26. **3 for which**: because. **9 your nights want**: i.e. the need I have of you tonight. Church's

emendation (1758), 'Knights want', emphasizes the implicit play on the phrase.

Stanza 26

2 I.e. no complaint could pacify her. **5** I.e. Talus watched no less than she did, for he did not suffer sleep, etc. **6 sad**: heavy. **7 disease**: disquiet.

Stanza 27

1–5 natiue Belman: Nature's night-watchman, the cock, referring specifically to Peter's **fall** in denying Christ three times before the cock crew (Matt. 26.34, 75). Unlike Peter, Britomart remains faithful to her 'Lord' (18.8). **6–9** Dolon's bed-trick may allude to one of the many attempts devised by Philip II to assassinate Elizabeth; or to the rumour that Leonard des Trappes planned to blow her up in bed, as Graziani 1964a:387–89 claims. See 33.6*n*. It is associated with the earlier moment when love led Britomart to 'leape out of her loathed nest' (III ii 30.3), and at Castle Joyeous where she 'lightly lept out of her filed bedd' (III i 62.2). **false . . . fall**: a deliberate echo that invokes the trap in the bridge at ii 7.8 where Artegall encountered Pollente. Before crossing at ii 12, he killed Pollente's

29

With that there came vnto her chamber dore
   Two Knights, all arm'd ready for to fight,
   And after them full many other more,
   A raskall rout, with weapons rudely dight.
   Whom soone as *Talus* spide by glims of night,
   He started vp, there where on ground he lay,
   And in his hand his thresher ready keight.
   They seeing that, let driue at him streight way,
And round about him preace in riotous aray.

30

But soone as he began to lay about
   With his rude yron flaile, they gan to flie,
   Both armed Knights, and eke vnarmed rout:
   Yet *Talus* after them apace did plie,
   Where euer in the darke he could them spie;
   That here and there like scattred sheepe they lay.
   Then backe returning, where his Dame did lie,
   He to her told the story of that fray,
And all that treason there intended did bewray.

31

Wherewith though wondrous wroth, and inly burning,
   To be auenged for so fowle a deede,
   Yet being forst to abide the daies returning,
   She there remain'd, but with right wary heede,
   Least any more such practise should proceede.
   Now mote ye know (that which to *Britomart*
   Vnknowen was) whence all this did proceede,
   And for what cause so great mischieuous smart
Was ment to her, that neuer euill ment in hart.

32

The goodman of this house was *Dolon* hight,
   A man of subtill wit and wicked minde,
   That whilome in his youth had bene a Knight,
   And armes had borne, but little good could finde,

And much lesse honour by that warlike kinde
   Of life: for he was nothing valorous,
   But with slie shiftes and wiles did vnderminde
   All noble Knights, which were aduenturous,
And many brought to shame by treason treacherous.

33

He had three sonnes, all three like fathers sonnes,
   Like treacherous, like full of fraud and guile,
   Of all that on this earthly compasse wonnes:
   The eldest of the which was slaine erewhile
   By *Artegall*, through his owne guilty wile;
   His name was *Guizor*, whose vntimely fate
   For to auenge, full many treasons vile
   His father *Dolon* had deuiz'd of late
With these his wicked sons, and shewd his cankred hate.

34

For sure he weend, that this his present guest
   Was *Artegall*, by many tokens plaine;
   But chiefly by that yron page he ghest,
   Which still was wont with *Artegall* remaine;
   And therefore ment him surely to haue slaine.
   But by Gods grace, and her good heedinesse,
   She was preserued from their traytrous traine.
   Thus she all night wore out in watchfulnesse,
Ne suffred slothfull sleepe her eyelids to oppresse.

35

The morrow next, so soone as dawning houre
   Discouered had the light to liuing eye,
   She forth yssew'd out of her loathed bowre,
   With full intent t'auenge that villany,
   On that vilde man, and all his family.
   And comming down to seeke them, where they wond,
   Nor sire, nor sonnes, nor any could she spie:
   Each rowme she sought, but them all empty fond:
They all were fled for feare, but whether, nether kond.

---

groom, Guizor, one of Dolon's sons; hence the form of Dolon's revenge against Britomart whom he assumes to be Artegall, as explained at 34.1–4. **loft**: floor of the room.

Stanza 28
2 treason: so called being treachery against a guest. **3 doubt**: fear. **8 stound**: time of trial.

Stanza 29
4 raskall rout: base rabble. **dight**: furnished. **5 glims**: glimpse. **7 keight**: caught.

Stanza 30
4 plie: wield his weapon vigorously; pursue. **9 bewray**: reveal.

Stanza 31
5 practise: 'treason' (28.2).

Stanza 32
1 goodman: master; an ironic use (*OED* 3b), as at IV v 34.1.
Dolon: chosen as the name of the Trojan spy in Homer, *Iliad*

10.314–459; or because of its associations: Gk δόλος, treachery; Lat. *dolus*, guile; and Eng. dole: guile, fraud. **7 vnderminde**: undermine.

Stanza 33
1–3 All three are like their father in being the most treacherous of all who live on earth. **6 Guizor**: though apparently a knight, he is the 'groome of euill guize' who served Pollente and was killed by Artegall at ii 6.6, 11.9. His name suggests the disguise of treachery, and may allude to the French Dukes of Guise, the family of Mary, Queen of Scots, portrayed as Duessa at ix 38; see A.B. Gough 1921.

Stanza 34
6 Since the phrase, **by Gods grace**, lacks any support in the poem, it indicates a topical allusion, specifically to Elizabeth saved from treachery. Cf. viii 23.5. **heedinesse**: heedfulness.

Stanza 35
9 . . . but where they fled neither she nor Talus knew.

36

She saw it vaine to make there lenger stay,
　　But tooke her steede, and thereon mounting light,
　　Gan her addresse vnto her former way.
　　She had not rid the mountenance of a flight,
　　But that she saw there present in her sight,
　　Those two false brethren, on that perillous Bridge,
　　On which *Pollente* with *Artegall* did fight.
　　Streight was the passage like a ploughed ridge,
That if two met, the one mote needes fall ouer the lidge.

37

There they did thinke them selues on her to wreake:
　　Who as she nigh vnto them drew, the one
　　These vile reproches gan vnto her speake;
　　Thou recreant false traytor, that with lone
　　Of armes hast knighthood stolne, yet Knight art none,
　　No more shall now the darkenesse of the night
　　Defend thee from the vengeance of thy fone,
　　But with thy bloud thou shalt appease the spright
Of *Guizor*, by thee slaine, and murdred by thy slight.

38

Strange were the words in *Britomartis* eare;
　　Yet stayd she not for them, but forward fared,
　　Till to the perillous Bridge she came, and there
　　Talus desir'd, that he might haue prepared

The way to her, and those two losels scared.
　　But she thereat was wroth, that for despight
　　The glauncing sparkles through her beuer glared,
　　And from her eies did flash out fiery light,
Like coles, that through a siluer Censer sparkle bright.

39

She stayd not to aduise which way to take;
　　But putting spurres vnto her fiery beast,
　　Thorough the midst of them she way did make.
　　The one of them, which most her wrath increast,
　　Vppon her speare she bore before her breast,
　　Till to the Bridges further end she past,
　　Where falling downe, his challenge he releast:
　　The other ouer side the Bridge she cast
Into the riuer, where he drunke his deadly last.

40

As when the flashing Leuin haps to light
　　Vppon two stubborne oakes, which stand so neare,
　　That way betwixt them none appeares in sight;
　　The Engin fiercely flying forth, doth teare
　　Th'one from the earth, and through the aire doth beare;
　　The other it with force doth ouerthrow,
　　Vppon one side, and from his rootes doth reare.
　　So did the Championesse those two there strow,
And to their sire their carcasses left to bestow.

Stanza 36
2 light: nimbly.　**4 the mountenance of a flight**: the distance an arrow flies; the same distance takes her to the house of Busirane at III xi 20.8.　**8 Streight**: also narrow, as at ii 7.7, but without its many traps.　**9 lidge**: ledge.

Stanza 37
4–5 Referring to '*Achilles armes, which Arthogall did win*' (III ii 25.6).　**9 slight**: sleight, wile.

Stanza 38
5 scared: drive off.

Stanza 39
S. is still drawing on Ariosto, *Orl. Fur.* 35.47–48: in her journey to find Ruggiero, Bradamante encounters Rodomonte on a narrow bridge and defeats him.　**7 releast**: withdrew.

Stanza 40
1 Leuin: lightning.　**2 stubborne**: also hard.　**4 Engin**: comparing lightning to a battering-ram.　**9 bestow**: dispose of.

Cant. VII.

Britomart comes to Isis Church,
Where shee strange visions sees:
She fights with Radigund, her slaies,
And Artegall thence frees.

1

Ought is on earth more sacred or diuine,
    That Gods and men doe equally adore,
    Then this same vertue, that doth right define:
    For th'heuens themselues, whence mortal men implore
    Right in their wrongs, are rul'd by righteous lore
    Of highest Ioue, who doth true iustice deale
    To his inferiour Gods, and euermore
    Therewith containes his heauenly Common-weale:
The skill whereof to Princes hearts he doth reueale.

2

Well therefore did the antique world inuent,
    That Iustice was a God of soueraine grace,
    And altars vnto him, and temples lent,
    And heauenly honours in the highest place;
    Calling him great *Osyris*, of the race
    Of th'old Ægyptian Kings, that whylome were;
    With fayned colours shading a true case:
    For that *Osyris*, whilest he liued here,
The iustest man aliue, and truest did appeare.

3

His wife was *Isis*, whom they likewise made
    A Goddesse of great powre and souerainty,
    And in her person cunningly did shade
    That part of Iustice, which is Equity,
    Whereof I haue to treat here presently.
    Vnto whose temple when as *Britomart*
    Arriued, shee with great humility
    Did enter in, ne would that night depart;
But *Talus* mote not be admitted to her part.

4

There she receiued was in goodly wize
    Of many Priests, which duely did attend
    Vppon the rites and daily sacrifize,
    All clad in linnen robes with siluer hemd;
    And on their heads with long locks comely kemd,
    They wore rich Mitres shaped like the Moone,
    To shew that *Isis* doth the Moone portend;
    Like as *Osyris* signifies the Sunne.
For that they both like race in equall iustice runne.

Book V Canto vii

Stanza 1
The same claims are made in proem 10 except that within the poem's fiction 'God' may be named **highest Ioue** and **his inferiour Gods** to whom he delegates power on earth, **Princes**. **8 Therewith**: i.e. with justice. **containes**: keeps under control. **heauenly Common-weale**: the adj. distinguishes the state as a body of people ruled according to God's justice, such as Britomart establishes at 42.4, from the mob incited by the Giant with the Scales at ii 30. **9 skill**: art, understanding, as iv 1.1–2.

Stanzas 2–4
The matter of these stanzas is derived chiefly from Plutarch, *De Iside*, Diodorus, *Biblio. Hist.* 1.11–22, and Apuleius, *The Golden Asse* (see Macey 1999). The Egyptian king, Osiris, and his wife, Isis, paragons of justice and equity respectively, persuaded their subjects to practise their virtues, for which they were rewarded after their death by being identified as the sun and moon. Cf. the deification of 'olde Heroes' at IV iii 44; and see 'Isis, Osiris' and 'gods and goddesses' in the *SEnc*.

Stanza 2
1 inuent: feign. **2 soueraine**: supreme; befitting a sovereign. **3 lent**: gave. **7 shading**: obscuring but also shadowing forth.

Stanza 3
3 shade: shadow forth, as 2.7; symbolize; signify, as 4.8. **4 Equity**: see i 7.1–5*n*. **5 presently**: now. The word serves to mark the unique absence in the poem of a formal approach to a major house, castle, or church. Britomart's departure in the middle of stanza 24 is equally sudden. **9 part**: side.

Stanza 4
4–5 According to Plutarch, the priests of Isis wore linen robes and were shaven. In Ezek. 44.17–20, priests are enjoined to wear linen garments and 'not shaue their heades, nor suffre their lockes to growe long'. (The Geneva gloss adds 'as did the infideles and heathen', which would include the tonsured canonists of the Church of Rome, as Graziani 1964a:387 notes.) Although the chief priest is a man (20.4), the rest may be women as in the temple of Venus at IV x 38.9. If men, their **long locks** may indicate that they serve a goddess; and while a sign of lust at IV vii 7.3, **comely kemd** indicates control over desire. A sixteenth-century iconographical tradition identifies the Egyptian by his long hair, as Manning 1988:41 notes. **shaped like the Moone**: 'the horned moone' (IV vi 43.9) that marks the time of Artegall's departure on his quest. **7 portend**: signify. **9 like race in equall iustice**: as the moon and the sun are equally just (i.e. exact or regular) in their daily course from east to west, and as 'their annual course eventually accomplishes an *equal sharing* of the total hours of day and night' (A. Fowler 1964:81).

5

The Championesse them greeting, as she could,
    Was thence by them into the Temple led;
    Whose goodly building when she did behould,
    Borne vppon stately pillours, all dispred
    With shining gold, and arched ouer hed,
    She wondred at the workemans passing skill,
    Whose like before she neuer saw nor red;
    And thereuppon long while stood gazing still,
But thought, that she thereon could neuer gaze her fill.

6

Thence forth vnto the Idoll they her brought,
    The which was framed all of siluer fine,
    So well as could with cunning hand be wrought,
    And clothed all in garments made of line,
    Hemd all about with fringe of siluer twine.
    Vppon her head she wore a Crowne of gold,
    To shew that she had powre in things diuine;
    And at her feete a Crocodile was rold,
That with her wreathed taile her middle did enfold.

7

One foote was set vppon the Crocodile,
    And on the ground the other fast did stand,
    So meaning to suppresse both forged guile,
    And open force: and in her other hand
    She stretched forth a long white sclender wand.
    Such was the Goddesse; whom when *Britomart*
    Had long beheld, her selfe vppon the land
    She did prostrate, and with right humble hart,
Vnto her selfe her silent prayers did impart.

8

To which the Idoll as it were inclining,
    Her wand did moue with amiable looke,
    By outward shew her inward sence desining.
    Who well perceiuing, how her wand she shooke,
    It as a token of good fortune tooke.
    By this the day with dampe was ouercast,
    And ioyous light the house of *Ioue* forsooke:
    Which when she saw, her helmet she vnlaste,
And by the altars side her selfe to slumber plaste.

9

For other beds the Priests there vsed none,
    But on their mother Earths deare lap did lie,
    And bake their sides vppon the cold hard stone,
    T'enure them selues to sufferaunce thereby
    And proud rebellious flesh to mortify.
    For by the vow of their religion
    They tied were to stedfast chastity,
    And continence of life, that all forgon,
They mote the better tend to their deuotion.

10

Therefore they mote not taste of fleshly food,
    Ne feed on ought, the which doth bloud containe,
    Ne drinke of wine, for wine they say is blood,
    Euen the bloud of Gyants, which were slaine,
    By thundring Ioue in the Phlegrean plaine.
    For which the earth (as they the story tell)
    Wroth with the Gods, which to perpetuall paine
    Had damn'd her sonnes, which gainst them did rebell,
With inward griefe and malice did against them swell.

Stanza 5

1 as she could: i.e. as she knew how to do. **4 dispred**: overspread. **7 red**: also imagined. Cf. her wonder on seeing the statue of Cupid and the bas-reliefs in the house of Busirane at III xi 49.6–9, 53.1–4.

Stanza 6

1 Idoll: image; statue. **4 line**: linen. **8–9 a Crocodile**: its iconography is examined by Aptekar 1969:87–107. It is associated chiefly with 'forged guile' at 7.3, as suggested by the 'harmefull guile' of the 'craftie Crocodile' at I v 18. Particularly relevant here is the association of the virgin goddess Minerva with a dragon; see III xi 48.6–9*n*. **with her**: 'with his', conj. Church 1758, for the crocodile is identified with Osiris at 22.6, and in Britomart's dream at 15–16 with Artegall. S.'s point may be that the sexes are not distinguished in their union.

Stanza 7

1–4 forged guile, | And open force: the powers that besiege the castle of Alma at II xi 7.4, and through which Radigund subdues knights at iv 31.1. On this traditional pair, see II vii 25.3*n*. On their relation to the legend of justice, see Aptekar 1969:108–24. An iconographical tradition that shows Isis seated with her feet on a crocodile is noted by Hume 1984:131–32. **4–5 in her other hand**: i.e. in one of her hands, presumably the right hand, as Cambina holds the rod of peace at IV iii 42.1. Her **white . . . wand** is a symbol of royal power; cf. the 'white rod' held by the 'royall Virgin' (i.e.

Elizabeth) at III iii 49.6–9, and see *n*. **9 Vnto her selfe**: i.e. to Isis and therefore to herself. **impart**: communicate.

Stanza 8

2 amiable looke: cf. Venus's 'amiable grace' at IV x 56.3, which encourages Scudamour in his courtship of Amoret. **3 desining**: indicating by a sign. **6 dampe**: fog. At vi 21.8, fog and night lead to Dolon's treachery. **8–9** In contrast, Britomart refuses to doff her arms or even lie down in Dolon's castle (vi 23–26). Sleeping in a temple for oracular purposes – a practice called 'incubation' (*OED* 4) – is described by Diodorus 1.25 who records that Isis appears in sleep to those who seek her aid. In Geoffrey of Monmouth 1891:1.11, Brutus has a prophetic dream of his progeny when he sleeps before the altar in the temple of Diana.

Stanza 9

3 bake: harden. **4 sufferaunce**: patient endurance. **5** Cf. Col. 3.5: 'Mortifie therefore your members which are on the earth, fornication, vnclennes, the inordinate affection, euil concupiscence'. **mortify**: kill. **8 all forgon**: all things having been renounced.

Stanzas 10–11

A rare double-stanza linked by the 'b' and 'c' rhymes, marking an interruption of the narrative in which S. follows Plutarch 6 closely.

11

And of their vitall bloud, the which was shed
    Into her pregnant bosome, forth she brought
    The fruitfull vine, whose liquor bloudy red
    Hauing the mindes of men with fury fraught,
    Mote in them stirre vp old rebellious thought,
    To make new warre against the Gods againe:
    Such is the powre of that same fruit, that nought
    The fell contagion may thereof restraine,
Ne within reasons rule, her madding mood containe.

12

There did the warlike Maide her selfe repose,
    Vnder the wings of *Isis* all that night,
    And with sweete rest her heauy eyes did close,
    After that long daies toile and weary plight.
    Where whilest her earthly parts with soft delight
    Of sencelesse sleepe did deeply drowned lie,
    There did appeare vnto her heauenly spright
    A wondrous vision, which did close implie
The course of all her fortune and posteritie.

13

Her seem'd, as she was doing sacrifize
    To *Isis*, deckt with Mitre on her hed,
    And linnen stole after those Priestes guize,
    All sodainely she saw transfigured
    Her linnen stole to robe of scarlet red,
    And Moone-like Mitre to a Crowne of gold,
    That euen she her selfe much wondered
    At such a chaunge, and ioyed to behold
Her selfe, adorn'd with gems and iewels manifold.

14

And in the midst of her felicity,
    An hideous tempest seemed from below,
    To rise through all the Temple sodainely,
    That from the Altar all about did blow
    The holy fire, and all the embers strow
    Vppon the ground, which kindled priuily,
    Into outragious flames vnwares did grow,
    That all the Temple put in ieopardy
Of flaming, and her selfe in great perplexity.

15

With that the Crocodile, which sleeping lay
    Vnder the Idols feete in fearelesse bowre,
    Seem'd to awake in horrible dismay,
    As being troubled with that stormy stowre;
    And gaping greedy wide, did streight deuoure
    Both flames and tempest: with which growen great,
    And swolne with pride of his owne peerelesse powre,
    He gan to threaten her likewise to eat;
But that the Goddesse with her rod him backe did beat.

Stanza 10
1–2 Cf. Gen. 9.4: 'But flesh with the life thereof, I meane, with the bloud thereof, shal ye not eat'. Called 'natures first beheast' at VI iv 14.9. **4–5** See III vii 47.3–5*n*. **9 swell**: behave proudly. Also, swelling in pregnancy; cf. III vii 47.6–9.

Stanza 11
9 containe: keep under control.

Stanza 12
1–2 A biblical image; see, e.g. Ps. 36.7. **the warlike Maide**: this most common description of Britomart is poignantly used here; see 16.9*n*. **all that night**: because prophetic dreams come just before awakening. **7 heauenly spright**: as Genius 'Who wondrous things concerning our welfare, | And straunge phantomes doth lett vs ofte forsee' (II xii 47.5–6). **8–9 vision**: in the sense of the *visio* in Macrobius 1952:1.3.9, a dream that will come true, as is known from Merlin's prophecy at III iii 22.5–9. **close implie**: secretly express or contain.

Stanzas 13–16
On the relation of this dream to others in the poem, see 'dreams' in the *SEnc*. It may be interpreted psychologically to show Britomart's relationship with Artegall, assuming that 'The things that day most minds, at night doe most appeare' (IV v 43.9); see Woodhouse 1949:216*n*42. Or prophetically, as it is by the priest. As the celebration of a mystery, or 'the prophetic moment in its purest form', see Fletcher 1971:268– 73.

Stanza 13
4 All sodainely: as the masque in the house of Busirane began 'All suddeinly' (III xii 3.1). **transfigured**: significantly, its only other use in the poem refers to the moment when the disciples saw Christ 'in strange disguise | Transfigur'd' (VII vii 7.8–9). **5–6** She sees Isis changed, but also herself crowned like Isis wearing not priestly linen but the royal robe, such as Duessa wears at I ii 13.2.

Stanza 14
1 her: refers to Isis and to Britomart as they blend in the dream. **2–6 tempest**: the power assigned to the wind is called Osiris by Plutarch but here recalls the 'stormy whirlwind' in the house of Busirane which heralds the god of love's entrance and exit at III xii 2–3, 27. **from below** suggests that the force that secretly kindles the holy fire is demonic. In contrast, Una's father kindled the 'housling fire' at her betrothal to the Red Cross Knight at I xii 37.4. **7 outragious flames**: a common image to describe love's effects, e.g. III vii 16.1–2. Specifically, it describes Britomart's love for Artegall at III ii 37.3, 43.4, etc., and alludes to the flames at the entrance to Busirane's castle at III xi 21. **9 perplexity**: trouble.

Stanza 15
4 stowre: tumult. **5–8** The crocodile's mouth is described as the 'griesly gates of his devouring hell' in *Vanitie* 38. Traditionally, the dragon is the guardian of chastity – see 6.8–9*n* – but here **swolne with pride** (in the sexual sense) it has become its enemy. **9** The dream recalls the moment Britomart forced Artegall 'backward to retreat' at IV vi 15.3, preliminary to his wooing her. She is not said to hold a rod, as Walker 1998b:106 notes, but is saved by Isis's rod. On the relation of the rod to her magic spear, see Hieatt 1975a:141–42.

16

Tho turning all his pride to humblesse meeke,
   Him selfe before her feete he lowly threw,
   And gan for grace and loue of her to seeke:
   Which she accepting, he so neare her drew,
   That of his game she soone enwombed grew,
   And forth did bring a Lion of great might;
   That shortly did all other beasts subdew.
   With that she waked, full of fearefull fright,
And doubtfully dismayd through that so vncouth sight.

17

So thereuppon long while she musing lay,
   With thousand thoughts feeding her fantasie,
   Vntill she spide the lampe of lightsome day,
   Vp-lifted in the porch of heauen hie.
   Then vp she rose fraught with melancholy,
   And forth into the lower parts did pas;
   Whereas the Priestes she found full busily
   About their holy things for morrow Mas:
Whom she saluting faire, faire resaluted was.

18

But by the change of her vnchearefull looke,
   They might perceiue, she was not well in plight;
   Or that some pensiuenesse to heart she tooke.
   Therefore thus one of them, who seem'd in sight
   To be the greatest, and the grauest wight,
   To her bespake; Sir Knight it seemes to me,
   That thorough euill rest of this last night,
   Or ill apayd, or much dismayd ye be,
That by your change of cheare is easie for to see.

19

Certes (sayd she) sith ye so well haue spide
   The troublous passion of my pensiue mind,
   I will not seeke the same from you to hide,
   But will my cares vnfolde, in hope to find

Your aide, to guide me out of errour blind.
   Say on (quoth he) the secret of your hart:
   For by the holy vow, which me doth bind,
   I am adiur'd, best counsell to impart
To all, that shall require my comfort in their smart.

20

Then gan she to declare the whole discourse
   Of all that vision, which to her appeard,
   As well as to her minde it had recourse.
   All which when he vnto the end had heard,
   Like to a weake faint-hearted man he fared,
   Through great astonishment of that strange sight;
   And with long locks vp-standing, stifly stared
   Like one adawed with some dreadfull spright.
So fild with heauenly fury, thus he her behight.

21

Magnificke Virgin, that in queint disguise
   Of British armes doest maske thy royall blood,
   So to pursue a perillous emprize,
   How couldst thou weene, through that disguized hood,
   To hide thy state from being vnderstood?
   Can from th'immortall Gods ought hidden bee?
   They doe thy linage, and thy Lordly brood;
   They doe thy sire, lamenting sore for thee;
They doe thy loue, forlorne in womens thraldome see.

22

The end whereof, and all the long euent,
   They doe to thee in this same dreame discouer.
   For that same Crocodile doth represent
   The righteous Knight, that is thy faithfull louer,
   Like to *Osyris* in all iust endeuer.
   For that same Crocodile *Osyris* is,
   That vnder *Isis* feete doth sleepe for euer:
   To shew that clemence oft in things amis,
Restraines those sterne behests, and cruell doomes of his.

Stanza 16

The serpent lover is a traditional motif: Alexander the Great, Augustus Caesar, and Scipio were conceived by a dragon or serpent, as Upton 1758 notes. More familiar is Ovid's story of Cadmus transformed into a serpent embracing his wife, to the horror of all who watched (*Met.* 4.576–603). More pertinent is Apuleius's story of Psyche who feared that her lover, Cupid, was a serpent; see III vi 50*n*. The biblical analogue is the woman in Rev. 12.1–5 who, as she is giving birth, is confronted by the red dragon that threatens to devour her child, 'which shulde rule all nations with a rod of yron'. Beauty taming a beast is a common motif in the poem, e.g. Una and the lion at I iii 6, Venus and the boar at III vi 48, and Mercilla and the lion at V ix 33. **1–3** Refiguring Artegall's actions at IV vi 33. **humblesse**: humbleness. **5 game**: sexual play. **9 dismayd**: punning on the word, as Fletcher 1971:271 notes, for she has been seduced in her dream. Cf. 18.8.

Stanza 17

5 melancholy: her mood at vi 19.1. **8 morrow Mas**: the first mass of the day. On its place in the Protestant tradition, see Waters 1979. The priests' abstention from 'fleshly food' and 'bloud' (10.1–2) prevents any association with the Roman mass.

Stanza 18

8 ill apayd: ill-pleased.

Stanza 19

8 adiur'd: bound by oath.

Stanza 20

1 discourse: account. **3** . . . as she recalled it. **5 fared**: behaved. **8 adawed**: daunted. **9 heauenly fury**: prophetic frenzy inspired from above; cf. Merlin's 'halfe extatick stoure' at III iii 50.5 when he foresees Elizabeth's reign. **behight**: addressed.

Stanza 21

1 Magnificke: renowned. **queint**: strange, as Artegall appears 'In quyent disguise' at IV iv 39.3. **3 emprize**: enterprise. **4 hood**: the helmet that hides her identity as at IV i

23

That Knight shall all the troublous stormes asswage,
    And raging flames, that many foes shall reare,
    To hinder thee from the iust heritage
    Of thy sires Crowne, and from thy countrey deare.
    Then shalt thou take him to thy loued fere,
    And ioyne in equall portion of thy realme:
    And afterwards a sonne to him shalt beare,
    That Lion-like shall shew his powre extreame.
So blesse thee God, and giue thee ioyance of thy dreame.

24

All which when she vnto the end had heard,
    She much was eased in her troublous thought,
    And on those Priests bestowed rich reward:
    And royall gifts of gold and siluer wrought,
    She for a present to their Goddesse brought.
    Then taking leaue of them, she forward went,
    To seeke her loue, where he was to be sought;
    Ne rested till she came without relent
Vnto the land of Amazons, as she was bent.

25

Whereof when newes to *Radigund* was brought,
    Not with amaze, as women wonted bee,
    She was confused in her troublous thought,
    But fild with courage and with ioyous glee,
    As glad to heare of armes, the which now she
    Had long surceast, she bad to open bold,
    That she the face of her new foe might see.
    But when they of that yron man had told,
Which late her folke had slaine, she bad them forth to hold.

26

So there without the gate (as seemed best)
    She caused her Pauilion be pight;
    In which stout *Britomart* her selfe did rest,
    Whiles *Talus* watched at the dore all night.
    All night likewise, they of the towne in fright,
    Vppon their wall good watch and ward did keepe.
    The morrow next, so soone as dawning light
    Bad doe away the dampe of drouzie sleepe,
The warlike Amazon out of her bowre did peepe.

27

And caused streight a Trumpet loud to shrill,
    To warne her foe to battell soone be prest:
    Who long before awoke (for she ful ill
    Could sleepe all night, that in vnquiet brest
    Did closely harbour such a iealous guest)
    Was to the battell whilome ready dight.
    Eftsoones that warriouresse with haughty crest
    Did forth issue, all ready for the fight:
On th'other side her foe appeared soone in sight.

28

But ere they reared hand, the Amazone
    Began the streight conditions to propound,
    With which she vsed still to tye her fone;
    To serue her so, as she the rest had bound.
    Which when the other heard, she sternly frownd
    For high disdaine of such indignity,
    And would no lenger treat, but bad them sound.
    For her no other termes should euer tie
Then what prescribed were by lawes of cheualrie.

13.1; or, in a figurative sense, 'covering', 'mask' as at xi 56.7.
7 brood: offspring.

Stanza 22
1 euent: outcome, implying the course of events. **4 faithfull** dismisses her earlier fears about his 'breach of faith to her' (vi 12.9).

Stanza 23
1–4 The language suggests Artegall's aid to Britomart as prophesied by Merlin at III iii 27.6–28.4, and his quest to secure for Irena 'the heritage, which she did clame' (i 3.8). **5 fere**: husband. **8 Lion-like**: Merlin's simile at III iii 30.1.

Stanza 24
4 The gifts are **royall** as she gives them; as she gives them to the goddess whose colours are **gold** and **silver** (6.2–6); and as they are royal: see Hag. 2.9. **8 relent**: slackening of speed.

Stanza 25
2–3 I.e. she was not confused with amazement as women usually are. She shares Britomart's anti-womanly behaviour at vi 13.8–9. **6 surceast**: abandoned, after she became a lover. **to open**: referring to the city gates, as at iv 37.8. **9 forth to hold**: i.e. even though she knows Talus to be present, she

orders her forces to proceed; or she orders her forces to keep Britomart and Talus out of the city.

Stanza 26
2 She: apparently Radigund who sets up her pavilion for Britomart. Yet Artegall sets up his own tent at iv 46.4–5, and (by his own command) again at xii 10.1–4. **8 dampe**: the dew of sleep and its consequence, a dazed or stupefied condition (*OED* 4). **9 her bowre**: possibly her own pavilion, as at v 4.8–9.

Stanza 27
2 prest: ready. **3–5** A reversal of the first battle when Artegall 'did rest in safety' while Radigund 'Could take no rest' (iv 46.6, 47.3). Her jealousy prepares for 32.4–6: she knows that the disguised Britomart is a woman come to claim her lover. **6 whilome**: some time before. **7 haughty**: lofty, both literally and metaphorically.

Stanza 28
2–7 These terms are outlined to Artegall at iv 49.2–5, which he accepts affably at 51, in contrast to Britomart's indignant rejection. **streight**: strict. **8–9** The laws of chivalry do not impose preset conditions but leave the victor free to offer mercy, as Guyon does to the defeated Pyrochles at II v 12–13 and Arthur at viii 51–52.

29

The Trumpets sound, and they together run
  With greedy rage, and with their faulchins smot;
  Ne either sought the others strokes to shun,
  But through great fury both their skill forgot,
  And practicke vse in armes: ne spared not
  Their dainty parts, which nature had created
  So faire and tender, without staine or spot,
  For other vses, then they them translated;
Which they now hackt and hewd, as if such vse they hated,

30

As when a Tygre and a Lionesse
  Are met at spoyling of some hungry pray,
  Both challenge it with equall greedinesse:
  But first the Tygre clawes thereon did lay;
  And therefore loth to loose her right away,
  Doth in defence thereof full stoutly stond:
  To which the Lion strongly doth gainesay,
  That she to hunt the beast first tooke in hond;
And therefore ought it haue, where euer she it fond.

31

Full fiercely layde the Amazon about,
  And dealt her blowes vnmercifully sore:
  Which *Britomart* withstood with courage stout,
  And them repaide againe with double more.
  So long they fought, that all the grassie flore
  Was fild with bloud, which from their sides did flow,
  And gushed through their armes, that all in gore
  They trode, and on the ground their liues did strow,
Like fruitles seede, of which vntimely death should grow.

32

At last proud *Radigund* with fell despight,
  Hauing by chaunce espide aduantage neare,
  Let driue at her with all her dreadfull might,
  And thus vpbrayding said; This token beare
  Vnto the man, whom thou doest loue so deare;
  And tell him for his sake thy life thou gauest.
  Which spitefull words she sore engrieu'd to heare,
  Thus answer'd; Lewdly thou my loue deprauest,
Who shortly must repent that now so vainely brauest.

33

Nath'lesse that stroke so cruell passage found,
  That glauncing on her shoulder plate, it bit
  Vnto the bone, and made a griesly wound,
  That she her shield through raging smart of it
  Could scarse vphold; yet soone she it requit.
  For hauing force increast through furious paine,
  She her so rudely on the helmet smit,
  That it empierced to the very braine,
And her proud person low prostrated on the plaine.

34

Where being layd, the wrothfull Britonesse
  Stayd not, till she came to her selfe againe,
  But in reuenge both of her loues distresse,
  And her late vile reproch, though vaunted vaine,
  And also of her wound, which sore did paine,
  She with one stroke both head and helmet cleft.
  Which dreadfull sight, when all her warlike traine
  There present saw, each one of sence bereft,
Fled fast into the towne, and her sole victor left.

Stanza 29

2 faulchins: falchion, a curved sword like the 'Cemitare' (v 3.4). **5 practicke**: practised, cunning. **6–9 Their dainty parts**: modesty usually forbids naming them, as earlier when the dwarf revives Una by tossing and turning 'euerie tender part' (I vii 21.6), but here they refer primarily to the breasts: the 'dainty partes' that the two damzels expose to Guyon's gaze at II xii 63.9, suggested by an Amazon's mastectomy, according to the etymology: Gk ἀ + μαζός, without the breast.

Stanza 30

The **Tygre** is Radigund, a beast noted for its cruelty (e.g. viii 49.7–8), as she is; see iv 30.1–2*n*. The **Lionesse** is Britomart, the royal beast, which she carries on her shield; see III i 4.9*n*. (Since Radigund is the Queen of Amazons, she is properly compared to 'a fell Lionesse' at iv 39.6.) The extended simile is a brief allegory of Artegall's plight as they fight over the right of present possession (Radigund was **first** to claim him as her prey and holds him now) versus prior ownership (Britomart was the first to **hunt** him). On the relation between them, see Hamilton 1961a:183–85, and M. Suzuki 1989:177–90. Cf. the quarrel between Una and Duessa over the Red Cross Knight at I xii 27–34. **2 hungry pray**: also prey for which they hunger. **3 challenge**: claim. **7 gainesay**: oppose, claim in opposition.

Stanza 31

6 fild: also defiled.

Stanza 32

4–9 In seeking to give Britomart her death-blow as a message to take to Artegall, Radigund implies that she has slain him, a charge that Britomart calls a 'vile reproch' (34.4) because it implies that she has seduced him. Hence **Lewdly** means both 'wickedly' and 'lasciviously', **deprauest** both 'defame' and 'pervert', and **vainely** both 'in vain' and 'from vanity'. **brauest**: boasts.

Stanza 33

1 Nath'lesse: Radigund's slander of Artegall almost deprives Britomart of her faith in him.

Stanza 34

4 vaine: in vain; vainly; in vanity. **6** In having Britomart behead Radigund, S. deliberately departs from Ariosto, *Orl. Fur.* 36.47: in a similarly vicious fight, Bradamante is prevented from cutting off Marfisa's head; see vi 3–18*n*. For a comparison, see Bowman 1990:514–18. Decapitation is an appropriate death for one who, as an Amazon, denies that 'the man is the womans head' (1 Cor. 11.3), esp. for a usurping female head of state; see Quilligan 1987:169. On decapitation of the female head, see Eilberg-Schwartz and Doniger 1995:1–11. A literary analogy is the death of the Amazon Queen, Penthesilea, in Christine de Pisan, *La cité des dames*; see 'Christine de Pisan' in the *SEnc*. A possible political analogy is the execution of Mary, Queen of Scots; see 'Mary, Queen of Scots' in the *SEnc*, and Stump 1991.

35

But yet so fast they could not home retrate,
  But that swift *Talus* did the formost win;
  And pressing through the preace vnto the gate,
  Pelmell with them attonce did enter in.
  There then a piteous slaughter did begin:
  For all that euer came within his reach,
  He with his yron flale did thresh so thin,
  That he no worke at all left for the leach:
Like to an hideous storme, which nothing may empeach.

36

And now by this the noble Conqueresse
  Her selfe came in, her glory to partake;
  Where though reuengefull vow she did professe,
  Yet when she saw the heapes, which he did make,
  Of slaughtred carkasses, her heart did quake
  For very ruth, which did it almost riue,
  That she his fury willed him to slake:
  For else he sure had left not one aliue,
But all in his reuenge of spirite would depriue.

fury + justice?

37

Tho when she had his execution stayd,
  She for that yron prison did enquire,
  In which her wretched loue was captiue layd:
  Which breaking open with indignant ire,
  She entred into all the partes entire.
  Where when she saw that lothly vncouth sight,
  Of men disguiz'd in womanishe attire,
  Her heart gan grudge, for very deepe despight
Of so vnmanly maske, in misery misdight.

38

At last when as to her owne Loue she came,
  Whom like disguize no lesse deformed had,
  At sight thereof abasht with secrete shame,
  She turnd her head aside, as nothing glad,

To haue beheld a spectacle so bad:
  And then too well beleeu'd, that which tofore
  Iealous suspect as true vntruely drad,
  Which vaine conceipt now nourishing no more,
She sought with ruth to salue his sad misfortunes sore.

39

Not so great wonder and astonishment,
  Did the most chast *Penelope* possesse,
  To see her Lord, that was reported drent,
  And dead long since in dolorous distresse,
  Come home to her in piteous wretchednesse,
  After long trauell of full twenty yeares,
  That she knew not his fauours likelynesse,
  For many scarres and many hoary heares,
But stood long staring on him, mongst vncertaine feares.

40

Ah my deare Lord, what sight is this (quoth she)
  What May-game hath misfortune made of you?
  Where is that dreadfull manly looke? where be
  Those mighty palmes, the which ye wont t'embrew
  In bloud of Kings, and great hoastes to subdew?
  Could ought on earth so wondrous change haue wrought,
  As to haue robde you of that manly hew?
  Could so great courage stouped haue to ought?
Then farewell fleshly force; I see thy pride is nought.

41

Thenceforth she streight into a bowre him brought,
  And causd him those vncomely weedes vndight;
  And in their steede for other rayment sought,
  Whereof there was great store, and armors bright,
  Which had bene reft from many a noble Knight;
  Whom that proud Amazon subdewed had,
  Whilest Fortune fauourd her successe in fight,
  In which when as she him anew had clad,
She was reuiu'd, and ioyd much in his semblance glad.

Stanza 35
2 **win**: overtake. **4 Pelmell**: mingling. **9 empeach**: hinder, withstand.

Stanza 36
As Elizabeth complained about the actions of her Lord Deputy in Ireland; see xii 26–27*n*. **7 willed**: ordered.

Stanza 37
1–5 She imitates Arthur who rends the iron door of Orgoglio's dungeon with 'indignation fell' at I viii 39.6 to release the Red Cross Knight. **partes entire**: inner parts. 6–9 Cf. Deut. 22.5: 'nether shal a man put on womans raiment; for all that do so, are abominacion vnto the Lord thy God'. (S. must suppress the first part of the verse, which would condemn Britomart's cross-dressing.) **grudge**: complain. **in misery misdight**: i.e. ill-clad in women's clothes, which is their misery.

Stanza 38
6–8 Possibly, 'she sees now how untrue was her jealous suspicion (**suspect**)'; but more likely, 'the sight of him in drag leads her to believe what before she had only suspected, that he has

been unfaithful to her'. Either way, her fears are confirmed at the moment they are dismissed as **vaine conceipt**.

Stanza 39
Alluding to Homer, *Ody*. 23.93–95, 101–02. The comparison is supported only by inferring from 7–8 that Penelope would not have recognized Ulysses if he had been dressed as a woman, as was Hercules; see v 24. **3 drent**: drenched: drowned. **6 trauell**: also travail. 7 She did not know the likeness of his features.

Stanza 40
2 **May-game**: an object of ridicule, alluding to the popular custom of disguising a man as Maid Marian to take the place of the May Queen. 3–5 Britomart invokes her vision of him at III ii 24.4, and his prophetic role at III iii 28.1–2. **mighty palmes**: a variation of 'mightie hands' at iv 1.3 that are needed to administer justice. **embrew**: stain.

Stanza 41
8 **anew**: presumably his old armour, '*Achilles armes*' (III ii 25.6), which Radigund 'hang'd on high' (though breaking his sword) at v 21.7–8. Possibly new armour, for she fashions him anew.

42

So there a while they afterwards remained,
  Him to refresh, and her late wounds to heale:
  During which space she there as Princess rained,
  And changing all that forme of common weale,
  The liberty of women did repeale,
  Which they had long vsurpt; and them restoring
  To mens subiection, did true Iustice deale:
  That all they as a Goddesse her adoring,
Her wisedome did admire, and hearkned to her loring.

43

For all those Knights, which long in captiue shade
  Had shrowded bene, she did from thraldome free;
  And magistrates of all that city made,
  And gaue to them great liuing and large fee:
  And that they should for euer faithfull bee,
  Made them sweare fealty to *Artegall*.
  Who when him selfe now well recur'd did see,
  He purposd to proceed, what so be fall,
Vppon his first aduenture, which him forth did call.

44

Full sad and sorrowfull was *Britomart*
  For his departure, her new cause of griefe;
  Yet wisely moderated her owne smart,
  Seeing his honor, which she tendred chiefe,
  Consisted much in that aduentures priefe.
  The care whereof, and hope of his successe
  Gaue vnto her great comfort and reliefe,
  That womanish complaints she did represse,
And tempred for the time her present heauinesse.

45

There she continu'd for a certaine space,
  Till through his want her woe did more increase:
  Then hoping that the change of aire and place
  Would change her paine, and sorrow somewhat ease,
  She parted thence, her anguish to appease.
  Meane while her noble Lord sir *Artegall*
  Went on his way, ne euer howre did cease,
  Till he redeemed had that Lady thrall:
That for another Canto will more fitly fall.

Stanza 42
Britomart's role in Bk V (and in the poem) is concluded when she takes over Radigund's role as **Princess** (see iv 33.4) to rule her subjects, when she assumes Isis's role as a **Goddesse** (cf. 3.2) to be adored by them, when in Artegall's name she restores **true Iustice** (see i 3.2) to the commonwealth, and when she resumes Penelope's role of waiting for her lord to return. On the impact of her repeal of queenship on the later cantos, see Eggert 2000a:37–50. **5–7 The liberty of women**: called 'a licentious libertie' at v 25.6. Cf. 1 Tim. 2.12: 'I permit not a woman . . . to vsurpe autoritie ouer the man'; and God's curse upon woman: 'Thy desire shal be subiect to thine housband, and he shal rule ouer thee' (Gen. 3. 16). **9 loring**: instruction.

Stanza 43
4 liuing: estates. **fee**: possessions. **6** In doing so they swear fealty to her, for she joins Artegall 'in equall portion' (23.6); see Woods 1985:155. **7 recur'd**: recovered.

Stanza 44
4 tendred: cherished. **5 priefe**: proof.

Stanza 45
2 his want: want of him. **5 parted**: departed.

Cant. VIII.

Prince Arthure and Sir Artegall,
Free Samient from feare:
They slay the Soudan, driue his wife,
Adicia to despaire.

1

Nought vnder heauen so strongly doth allure
    The sence of man, and all his minde possesse,
  As beauties louely baite, that doth procure
  Great warriours oft their rigour to represse,
  And mighty hands forget their manlinesse;
  Drawne with the powre of an heart-robbing eye,
  And wrapt in fetters of a golden tresse,
  That can with melting pleasaunce mollifye
Their hardned hearts, enur'd to bloud and cruelty.

2

So whylome learnd that mighty Iewish swaine,
  Each of whose lockes did match a man in might,
  To lay his spoiles before his lemans traine:
  So also did that great Oetean Knight
  For his loues sake his Lions skin vndight:
  And so did warlike *Antony* neglect
  The worlds whole rule for *Cleopatras* sight.
  Such wondrous powre hath wemens faire aspect,
To captiue men, and make them all the world reiect.

3

Yet could it not sterne *Artegall* retaine,
  Nor hold from suite of his auowed quest,
  Which he had vndertane to *Gloriane*;
  But left his loue, albe her strong request,

Faire *Britomart* in languor and vnrest,
  And rode him selfe vppon his first intent:
  Ne day nor night did euer idly rest;
  Ne wight but onely *Talus* with him went,
The true guide of his way and vertuous gouernment.

4

So trauelling, he chaunst far off to heed
  A Damzell, flying on a palfrey fast
  Before two Knights, that after her did speed
  With all their powre, and her full fiercely chast
  In hope to haue her ouerhent at last:
  Yet fled she fast, and both them farre outwent,
  Carried with wings of feare, like fowle aghast,
  With locks all loose, and rayment all to rent;
And euer as she rode, her eye was backeward bent.

5

Soone after these he saw another Knight,
  That after those two former rode apace,
  With speare in rest, and prickt with all his might:
  So ran they all, as they had bene at bace,
  They being chased, that did others chase.
  At length he saw the hindmost ouertake
  One of those two, and force him turne his face;
  How euer loth he were his way to slake,
Yet mote he algates now abide, and answere make.

Book V Canto viii

Argument

Arthur intercedes as usual in the eighth canto to engage in a number of actions corresponding to the book's number; see I viii Arg.1–2*n*. He slays the Souldan (viii), captures Malengin (Guyle) with the aid of Artegall (ix), slays Geryoneo's Seneschall (x), Geryoneo, and his monster (xi). **3 Soudan:** Souldan or Sultan; see 24.7*n*.

Stanza 1

A seemingly retrospective moral comment on Artegall's first sight of Britomart's face framed by her yellow hair 'Like to a golden border', which causes him to drop his sword to worship 'so diuine a beauties excellence' (IV vi 20.3, 21.9). **2 possesse:** dominate, control absolutely. **3 procure:** induce, persuade. **7 wrapt:** also suggesting 'rapt'.

Stanza 2

To the biblical example of Samson yielding to Delilah in Judg. 16.17–19, S. adds the two classical examples of love's triumph over 'Great warriours' (1.4) portrayed on the gates of Armida's palace in Tasso, *Ger. Lib.* 16.3–7: the Greek Hercules – called **Oetean** because he died on Mount Oeta – spinning on a distaff for Iole who wore his lion's skin (see v 24*n*), and the Roman Antony who left the battle against Caesar and thereby gave up governing the world (*l'imperio del mondo*) to follow Cleopatra. **3 traine:** snare.

Stanza 3

2 suite: pursuit. **5 languor:** sorrow. **8–9** Repeating iv 3.6–9 and vii 43.7–9. As the Palmer is Guyon's guide and 'him gouerned' (II xii 38.5) in his final adventure, Talus is Artegall's **gouernment:** i.e. the instrument of his governing or his executive power, specifically the law; see i 12.1–6*n*.

Stanza 4

1 heed: see. **5 ouerhent:** overtaken. **8 all to rent:** entirely torn.

Stanza 5

4–5 bace: the children's game, prisoner's base, in which those who chase are chased; see III xi 5.5*n*. **8 slake:** slacken. **9 algates:** nevertheless.

6

But th'other still pursu'd the fearefull Mayd;
   Who still from him as fast away did flie,
   Ne once for ought her speedy passage stayd,
   Till that at length she did before her spie
   Sir *Artegall*, to whom she streight did hie
   With gladfull hast, in hope of him to get
   Succour against her greedy enimy:
   Who seeing her approch gan forward set,
To saue her from her feare, and him from force to let.

7

But he like hound full greedy of his pray,
   Being impatient of impediment,
   Continu'd still his course, and by the way
   Thought with his speare him quight haue ouerwent.
   So both together ylike felly bent,
   Like fiercely met. But *Artegall* was stronger,
   And better skild in Tilt and Turnament,
   And bore him quite out of his saddle, longer
Then two speares length; So mischiefe ouermatcht the
                   (wronger.

8

And in his fall misfortune him mistooke;
   For on his head vnhappily he pight,
   That his owne waight his necke asunder broke,
   And left there dead. Meane while the other Knight
   Defeated had the other faytour quight,
   And all his bowels in his body brast:
   Whom leauing there in that dispiteous plight,
   He ran still on, thinking to follow fast
His other fellow Pagan, which before him past.

9

In stead of whom finding there ready prest
   Sir *Artegall*, without discretion
   He at him ran, with ready speare in rest:
   Who seeing him come still so fiercely on,
   Against him made againe. So both anon
   Together met, and strongly either strooke
   And broke their speares; yet neither has forgon
   His horses backe, yet to and fro long shooke,
And tottred like two towres, which through a tempest quooke.

10

But when againe they had recouered sence,
   They drew their swords, in mind to make amends
   For what their speares had fayld of their pretence.
   Which when the Damzell, who those deadly ends
   Of both her foes had seene, and now her frends
   For her beginning a more fearefull fray,
   She to them runnes in hast, and her haire rends,
   Crying to them their cruell hands to stay,
Vntill they both doe heare, what she to them will say.

11

They stayd their hands, when she thus gan to speake;
   Ah gentle Knights, what meane ye thus vnwise
   Vpon your selues anothers wrong to wreake?
   I am the wrong'd, whom ye did enterprise
   Both to redresse, and both redrest likewise:
   Witnesse the Paynims both, whom ye may see
   There dead on ground. What doe ye then deuise
   Of more reuenge? if more, then I am shee,
Which was the roote of all, end your reuenge on mee.

12

Whom when they heard so say, they lookt about,
   To weete if it were true, as she had told;
   Where when they saw their foes dead out of doubt,
   Eftsoones they gan their wrothfull hands to hold,
   And Ventailes reare, each other to behold.
   Tho when as *Artegall* did *Arthure* vew,
   So faire a creature, and so wondrous bold,
   He much admired both his heart and hew,
And touched with intire affection, nigh him drew.

13

Saying, Sir Knight, of pardon I you pray,
   That all vnweeting haue you wrong'd thus sore,
   Suffring my hand against my heart to stray:
   Which if ye please forgiue, I will therefore
   Yeeld for amends my selfe yours euermore,
   Or what so penaunce shall by you be red.
   To whom the Prince; Certes me needeth more
   To craue the same, whom errour so misled,
As that I did mistake the liuing for the ded.

Stanza 6

9 . . . and prevent him (her pursuer) from using force (on her).

Stanza 7

4 ouerwent: overcome. **7** As said of him at III ii 9.8.
9 mischiefe: misfortune.

Stanza 8

1 mistooke: took wrongfully, i.e. seized disastrously. **5 faytour**: miscreant. **6 brast**: burst. **7 dispiteous**: cruel, deserving only contempt.

Stanza 9

1 prest: at hand. **2 discretion**: i.e. discerning who he was.
6–9 Their equal encounter demonstrates their equality; see
i 3*n*, and Dunseath 1968:184–88. **quooke**: quaked.

Stanza 10

3 pretence: intention.

Stanza 11

4 enterprise: undertake.

Stanza 12

3 out of doubt: without doubt. **5 Ventailes**: the movable
front of a helmet that may be lifted up to show the face.
8 hew: appearance. **9 intire**: sincere; complete; inner (as the
spelling indicates).

Stanza 13

6 red: decided, decreed. **8–9** Their **error** anticipates the plot
to destroy Adicia; cf. 25.4–5.

14

But sith ye please, that both our blames shall die,
  Amends may for the trespasse soone be made,
  Since neither is endamadg'd much thereby.
  So can they both them selues full eath perswade
  To faire accordaunce, and both faults to shade,
  Either embracing other louingly,
  And swearing faith to either on his blade,
  Neuer thenceforth to nourish enmity,
But either others cause to maintaine mutually.

15

Then *Artegall* gan of the Prince enquire,
  What were those knights, which there on ground were layd,
  And had receiu'd their follies worthy hire,
  And for what cause they chased so that Mayd.
  Certes I wote not well (the Prince then sayd)
  But by aduenture found them faring so,
  As by the way vnweetingly I strayd,
  And lo the Damzell selfe, whence all did grow,
Of whom we may at will the whole occasion know.

16

Then they that Damzell called to them nie,
  And asked her, what were those two her fone,
  From whom she earst so fast away did flie;
  And what was she her selfe so woe begone,
  And for what cause pursu'd of them attone.
  To whom she thus; Then wote ye well, that I
  Doe serue a Queene, that not far hence doth wone,
  A Princesse of great powre and maiestie,
Famous through all the world, and honor'd far and nie.

17

Her name *Mercilla* most men vse to call;
  That is a mayden Queene of high renowne,
  For her great bounty knowen ouer all,
  And soueraine grace, with which her royall crowne
  She doth support, and strongly beateth downe
  The malice of her foes, which her enuy,
  And at her happinesse do fret and frowne:
  Yet she her selfe the more doth magnify,
And euen to her foes her mercies multiply.

18

Mongst many which maligne her happy state,
  There is a mighty man, which wonnes here by
  That with most fell despight and deadly hate,
  Seekes to subuert her Crowne and dignity,
  And all his powre doth thereunto apply:
  And her good Knights, of which so braue a band
  Serues her, as any Princesse vnder sky,
  He either spoiles, if they against him stand,
Or to his part allures, and bribeth vnder hand.

19

Ne him sufficeth all the wrong and ill,
  Which he vnto her people does each day,
  But that he seekes by traytrous traines to spill
  Her person, and her sacred selfe to slay:
  That ô ye heauens defend, and turne away
  From her, vnto the miscreant him selfe,
  That neither hath religion nor fay,
  But makes his God of his vngodly pelfe,
And Idols serues; so let his Idols serue the Elfe.

20

To all which cruell tyranny they say,
  He is prouokt, and stird vp day and night
  By his bad wife, that hight *Adicia*,
  Who counsels him through confidence of might,
  To breake all bonds of law, and rules of right.
  For she her selfe professeth mortall foe
  To Iustice, and against her still doth fight,
  Working to all, that loue her, deadly woe,
And making all her Knights and people to doe so.

21

Which my liege Lady seeing, thought it best,
  With that his wife in friendly wise to deale,
  For stint of strife, and stablishment of rest
  Both to her selfe, and to her common weale,
  And all forepast displeasures to repeale.
  So me in message vnto her she sent,
  To treat with her by way of enterdeale,
  Of finall peace and faire attonement,
Which might concluded be by mutuall consent.

Stanza 14
3 endamadg'd: injured.   4 can: did. eath: easily.   5 shade: veil, conceal.

Stanza 15
6 aduenture: chance.

Stanza 16
4 what: why.

Stanza 17
1–2 As Elizabeth is about to enter the poem most transparently as Queen, she is explicitly named **a mayden Queene of high renowne**, one usually called **Mercilla** because of her **mercies**. See 'Mercilla' in the *SEnc*.   3 bounty: also goodness.   8–9 She makes herself greater by offering mercy even to her foes.

Stanza 18
1 maligne: regard with envy.   8 spoiles: destroys.

Stanza 19
3–4 traines: intrigues. spill: overthrow. The distinction between Mercilla's **person** and **her sacred selfe** relates to the claim in the *LR* 35 that the Queen 'beareth two persons'.   5 defend: avert, forbid.   7 fay: faith.   8 So Auarice 'of his wicked pelf his God he made' (I iv 27.6).   9 The Souldan sins as did the children of Israel when they 'serued idoles' (2 Kings 17.12).

Stanza 20
3 Adicia: Gk ἀδικία, Injustice. See 'Adicia, Souldan' in the *SEnc*, and cf. 49.8–9. She is identified as 'Popery' in a copy of the *1611* folio; see Manning 1984:226.

Stanza 21
5 repeale: give up.   6 in message: on the business of carrying a message (*OED* 2b).   7 enterdeale: mutual dealing.   8 attonement: concord.

22

All times haue wont safe passage to afford
    To messengers, that come for causes iust:
    But this proude Dame disdayning all accord,
    Not onely into bitter termes forth brust,
    Reuiling me, and rayling as she lust,
    But lastly to make proofe of vtmost shame,
    Me like a dog she out of dores did thrust,
    Miscalling me by many a bitter name,
That neuer did her ill, ne once deserued blame.

23

And lastly, that no shame might wanting be,
    When I was gone, soone after me she sent
    These two false Knights, whom there ye lying see,
    To be by them dishonoured and shent:
    But thankt be God, and your good hardiment,
    They haue the price of their owne folly payd.
    So said this Damzell, that hight *Samient*,
    And to those knights, for their so noble ayd,
Her selfe most gratefull shew'd, and heaped thanks repayd.

24

But they now hauing throughly heard, and seene
    Al those great wrongs, the which that mayd complained
    To haue bene done against her Lady Queene,
    By that proud dame, which her so much disdained,
    Were moued much thereat, and twixt them fained,
    With all their force to worke auengement strong
    Vppon the Souldan selfe, which it mayntained,
    And on his Lady, th'author of that wrong,
And vppon all those Knights, that did to her belong.

25

But thinking best by counterfet disguise
    To their deseigne to make the easier way,
    They did this complot twixt them selues deuise,
    First that sir *Artegall* should him array,

Like one of those two Knights, which dead there lay.
    And then that Damzell, the sad *Samient*,
    Should as his purchast prize with him conuay
    Vnto the Souldans court, her to present
Vnto his scornefull Lady, that for her had sent.

26

So as they had deuiz'd, sir *Artegall*
    Him clad in th'armour of a Pagan knight,
    And taking with him, as his vanquisht thrall,
    That Damzell, led her to the Souldans right.
    Where soone as his proud wife of her had sight,
    Forth of her window as she looking lay,
    She weened streight, it was her Paynim Knight,
    Which brought that Damzell, as his purchast pray;
And sent to him a Page, that mote direct his way.

27

Who bringing them to their appointed place,
    Offred his seruice to disarme the Knight;
    But he refusing him to let vnlace,
    For doubt to be discouered by his sight,
    Kept himselfe still in his straunge armour dight.
    Soone after whom the Prince arriued there,
    And sending to the Souldan in despight
    A bold defyance, did of him requere
That Damzell, whom he held as wrongfull prisonere.

28

Wherewith the Souldan all with furie fraught,
    Swearing, and banning most blasphemously,
    Commaunded straight his armour to be brought,
    And mounting straight vpon a charret hye,
    With yron wheeles and hookes arm'd dreadfully,
    And drawne of cruell steedes, which he had fed
    With flesh of men, whom through fell tyranny
    He slaughtred had, and ere they were halfe ded,
Their bodies to his beasts for prouender did spred.

Stanza 22
3 this proude Dame: pride characterizes her – cf. 24.4 and 26.5 – as it does all the enemies of justice; see iv 38.6*n*. **5 lust**: chose. **8 Miscalling**: reviling.

Stanza 23
1 And lastly: a variation of 22.6. Adicia exceeds her own utmost shame in seeking to shame others. **4 shent**: defiled. **7 Samient**: signifying 'bringing together', from 'sam' (I x 57.8), as she is an ambassador who seeks 'attonement (21.8) between Mercilla and Adicia; and as she unites Artegall and Arthur.

Stanza 24
5 fained: desired. **7 Souldan**: or Sultan, the title of a Mohammedan or Egyptian ruler; applied here to a pagan tyrant. The **great wrongs**, which he maintains, anticipate their final consolidation in Grantorto. Historically, England's chief enemy, Philip II of Spain, whose wife, Mary Tudor, may be merged with Mary Queen of Scots, the enemy with whom Elizabeth sought to be reconciled. Meyer 1991:104–05 notes that the sixteenth-century Süleyman the Magnificent, Sultan of the Ottoman Empire, had a wife noted for her ferocity.

Stanza 25
3 complot: plot; literally a plot between them; used only here, it marks their unified effort. **6 sad**: as their captive. **7 purchast**: got by conquest.

Stanza 26
4 right: domain, territory.

Stanza 27
4 doubt: fear. **5 straunge**: belonging to another.

Stanzas 28–45
Arthur's defeat of the Souldan, as Upton 1758 first noted, alludes to England's defeat of the Spanish Armada in 1588. For apocalyptic commentary on the event, see Mallette 1997:149–53.

Stanza 28
2 banning: anathematizing; cf. 39.4. Perhaps alluding specifically to the 1570 papal bull excommunicating Elizabeth but more generally to the apocalyptic Beast from the Sea that 'spake . . . blasphemies' (Rev. 13.5), as Mallette 1997:151

29

So forth he came all in a cote of plate,
    Burnisht with bloudie rust, whiles on the greene
    The Briton Prince him readie did awayte,
    In glistering armes right goodly well beseene,
    That shone as bright, as doth the heauen sheene;
    And by his stirrup *Talus* did attend,
    Playing his pages part, as he had beene
    Before directed by his Lord; to th'end
He should his flale to finall execution bend.

30

Thus goe they both together to their geare,
    With like fierce minds, but meanings different:
    For the proud Souldan with presumpteous cheare,
    And countenance sublime and insolent,
    Sought onely slaughter and auengement:
    But the braue Prince for honour and for right,
    Gainst tortious powre and lawlesse regiment,
    In the behalfe of wronged weake did fight:
More in his causes truth he trusted then in might.

31

Like to the *Thracian* Tyrant, who they say
    Vnto his horses gaue his guests for meat,
    Till he himselfe was made their greedie pray,
    And torne in peeces by *Alcides* great.
    So thought the Souldan in his follies threat,
    Either the Prince in peeces to haue torne
    With his sharpe wheeles, in his first rages heat,
    Or vnder his fierce horses feet haue borne
And trampled downe in dust his thoughts disdained scorne.

32

But the bold child that perill well espying,
    If he too rashly to his charet drew,
    Gaue way vnto his horses speedie flying,
    And their resistlesse rigour did eschew.

Yet as he passed by, the Pagan threw
    A shiuering dart with so impetuous force,
    That had he not it shun'd with heedfull vew,
    It had himselfe transfixed, or his horse,
Or made them both one masse withouten more remorse.

33

Oft drew the Prince vnto his charret nigh,
    In hope some stroke to fasten on him neare;
    But he was mounted in his seat so high,
    And his wingfooted coursers him did beare
    So fast away, that ere his readie speare
    He could aduance, he farre was gone and past.
    Yet still he him did follow euery where,
    And followed was of him likewise full fast;
So long as in his steedes the flaming breath did last.

34

Againe the Pagan threw another dart,
    Of which he had with him abundant store,
    On euery side of his embatteld cart,
    And of all other weapons lesse or more,
    Which warlike vses had deuiz'd of yore.
    The wicked shaft guyded through th'ayrie wyde,
    By some bad spirit, that it to mischiefe bore,
    Stayd not, till through his curat it did glyde,
And made a griesly wound in his enriuen side.

35

Much was he grieued with that haplesse throe,
    That opened had the welspring of his blood;
    But much the more that to his hatefull foe
    He mote not come, to wreake his wrathfull mood.
    That made him raue, like to a Lyon wood,
    Which being wounded of the huntsmans hand
    Can not come neare him in the couert wood,
    Where he with boughes hath built his shady stand,
And fenst himselfe about with many a flaming brand.

---

notes. **4–9** The chariot armed with hooks, called an 'embatteld cart' at 34.3, is classical in origin, as the scythed chariots in Quintus Curtius, *History* 4.9.5, but also biblical (2 Macc. 13.2), and contemporary. See representations of scythed battle-wagons in M. West 1988:674–75. **hye** alluding to the high-pooped Spanish galleons; cf. 33.3.

Stanza 29
2 greene: refers also to the sea; cf. 42.9. **6–9** Talus, seconded as Arthur's page, plays only a token role, for the Souldan is defeated by Arthur and the **finall execution** of his forces by Artegall acting alone.

Stanza 30
1 geare: business. **3 cheare**: mien. **4 sublime**: haughty, proud. **7 tortious**: illegal. **regiment**: rule.

Stanza 31
1–4 'The nynthe [of Hercules's labours] was the takyng of Diomedes kyng of Thracia, and castyng hym to his horses, who feeding them with mans fleshe, was himselfe of them deuoured' (T. Cooper 1565). In Boccaccio 1976:13.1, as Lotspeich 1932 notes, the victims were Diomedes's guests. Cf. Geryon's guest-eating cows at x 9.7–9, and the sacrifice-eating

monster at xi 20.1–4. The comparison indicates Arthur's role as Hercules, e.g. II xi 45–46*n*; for Bk V, see i 3.1*n*, ix 5.8*n*, x 9–11*n*. **9** . . . whom he disdained in thinking of him with scorn.

Stanza 32
1 child: on its application to Arthur, see IV viii 44.8*n*; cf. 'infant' (41.2). **4 rigour**: violence. **9** . . . without further delay or showing further pity.

Stanza 33
7–8 The game of prisoner's base, as at 5.4–5.

Stanza 34
4 lesse or more: smaller or greater. **6 wyde**: used as a substantive. **8 curat**: cuirass or breastplate.

Stanza 35
1 throe: the pain caused by the Souldan's throw. **5–9** Noting the lion's traditional fear of fire. This startling comparison of Arthur to a wounded lion, whose traditional fear of fire prevents it even from engaging its enemy, defines him here as one who trusts 'More in his causes truth . . . then in might' (30.9), and consequent reliance on grace alone. **wood**: mad.

36

Still when he sought t'approch vnto him ny,
    His charret wheeles about him whirled round,
    And made him backe againe as fast to fly;
    And eke his steedes like to an hungry hound,
    That hunting after game hath carrion found,
    So cruelly did him pursew and chace,
    That his good steed, all were he much renound
For noble courage, and for hardie race,
Durst not endure their sight, but fled from place to place.

37

Thus long they trast, and trauerst to and fro,
    Seeking by euery way to make some breach,
    Yet could the Prince not nigh vnto him goe,
    That one sure stroke he might vnto him reach,
    Whereby his strengthes assay he might him teach.
    At last from his victorious shield he drew
    The vaile, which did his powrefull light empeach,
And comming full before his horses vew,
As they vpon him prest, it plaine to them did shew.

38

Like lightening flash, that hath the gazer burned,
    So did the sight thereof their sense dismay,
    That backe againe vpon themselues they turned,
    And with their ryder ranne perforce away:
    Ne could the Souldan them from flying stay,
    With raynes, or wonted rule, as well he knew.
    Nought feared they, what he could do, or say,
But th'onely feare, that was before their vew;
From which like mazed deare, dismayfully they flew.

39

Fast did they fly, as them their feete could beare,
    High ouer hilles, and lowly ouer dales,
    As they were follow'd of their former feare.
    In vaine the Pagan bannes, and sweares, and rayles,
    And backe with both his hands vnto him hayles
    The resty raynes, regarded now no more:
    He to them calles and speakes, yet nought auayles;
They heare him not, they haue forgot his lore,
But go, which way they list, their guide they haue forlore.

40

As when the firie-mouthed steeds, which drew
    The Sunnes bright wayne to *Phaetons* decay,
    Soone as they did the monstrous Scorpion vew,
    With vgly craples crawling in their way,
    The dreadfull sight did them so sore affray,
    That their well knowne courses they forwent,
    And leading th'euer-burning lampe astray,
This lower world nigh all to ashes brent,
And left their scorched path yet in the firmament.

41

Such was the furie of these head-strong steeds,
    Soone as the infants sunlike shield they saw,
    That all obedience both to words and deeds
    They quite forgot, and scornd all former law;
    Through woods, and rocks, and mountaines they did draw
    The yron charet, and the wheeles did teare,
    And tost the Paynim, without feare or awe;
From side to side they tost him here and there,
Crying to them in vaine, that nould his crying heare.

Stanza 36
5 carrion: a beast inferior to **game** as flesh for hounds.

Stanza 37
1 trast, and trauerst: pursued, and turned aside when pursued. **5 assay**: proof. **6–9** At I viii 19.2, the veil is loosed 'by chaunce' when the covered shield is struck by Orgoglio. Against Pyrochles and Cymochles, the shield remains covered; see II viii 17.7. Now Arthur draws the veil back to indicate that the Armada was defeated 'by heauens high decree' (44.6). S.'s literary model is Ariosto, *Orl. Fur.* 10.109, where Ruggiero slays the Orc by raising the veil on his shield. Cf. the action at IV viii 42.6–9 and V xi 21.5. **empeach**: impede.

Stanza 38
1–2 S. continues the comparison – see I viii 21.8–9 – in terms appropriate to the Souldan as Phaethon. **8** They feared only what was before them. **9 mazed**: terrified. **dismayfully**: in dismay.

Stanza 39
6 resty: resisting control. **8 lore**: instruction. **9 forlore**: abandoned.

Stanza 40
Phaethon's story is told at I iv 9 and III xi 38 but here wittily varied, for the horses' terror, not his, is the subject. Details of their fiery mouths and their fear of the constellation Scorpio may be drawn directly from Ovid, *Met.* 2.85, 119, 195–97. Philip II's *impresa* depicted him as the sun-god driving his chariot over the world, with the motto *Iam illustrabit omnia* to indicate his claim to world empire and his divine mission to spread the light of the true faith everywhere. Now he is exposed as Phaethon, as Graziani 1964b notes. **2 wayne**: chariot, suggesting Lat. *plaustrum*, a threshing instrument with wheels (*OED* 3). **decay**: downfall. **3–4 Scorpion**: also a military engine for hurling stones, alluding to the English ships attacking the Spanish galleons. **craples**: conflating 'claws' and 'graples' (42.6). **6 forwent**: forsook. **9 their scorched path**: the Milky Way.

Stanza 41
The extended description alludes to the Spanish ships scattered and wrecked by storms, as shown in the Queen's Armada portrait. **2** By defeating Spanish power, Arthur assumes Philip II's title, *Infante* or Prince; see II viii 56.1–3*n*. **9 nould**: would not.

42

Yet still the Prince pursew'd him close behind,
  Oft making offer him to smite, but found
  No easie meanes according to his mind.
  At last they haue all ouerthrowne to ground
  Quite topside turuey, and the pagan hound
  Amongst the yron hookes and graples keene,
  Torne all to rags, and rent with many a wound,
  That no whole peece of him was to be seene,
But scattred all about, and strow'd vpon the greene.

43

Like as the cursed sonne of *Theseus*,
  That following his chace in dewy morne,
  To fly his stepdames loues outrageous,
  Of his owne steedes was all to peeces torne,
  And his faire limbs left in the woods forlorne;
  That for his sake *Diana* did lament,
  And all the wooddy Nymphes did wayle and mourne.
  So was this Souldan rapt and all to rent,
That of his shape appear'd no litle moniment.

44

Onely his shield and armour, which there lay,
  Though nothing whole, but all to brusd and broken,
  He vp did take, and with him brought away,
  That mote remaine for an eternall token
  To all, mongst whom this storie should be spoken,
  How worthily, by heauens high decree,
  Iustice that day of wrong her selfe had wroken,
  That all men which that spectacle did see,
By like ensample mote for euer warned bee.

45

So on a tree, before the Tyrants dore,
  He caused them be hung in all mens sight,
  To be a moniment for euermore.
  Which when his Ladie from the castles hight

Beheld, it much appald her troubled spright:
  Yet not, as women wont in dolefull fit,
  She was dismayd, or faynted through affright,
  But gathered vnto her her troubled wit,
And gan eftsoones deuize to be aueng'd for it.

46

Streight downe she ranne, like an enraged cow,
  That is berobbed of her youngling dere,
  With knife in hand, and fatally did vow,
  To wreake her on that mayden messengere,
  Whom she had causd be kept as prisonere,
  By *Artegall*, misween'd for her owne Knight,
  That brought her backe. And comming present there,
  She at her ran with all her force and might,
All flaming with reuenge and furious despight.

47

Like raging *Ino*, when with knife in hand
  She threw her husbands murdred infant out,
  Or fell *Medea*, when on *Colchicke* strand
  Her brothers bones she scattered all about;
  Or as that madding mother, mongst the rout
  Of *Bacchus* Priests her owne deare flesh did teare.
  Yet neither *Ino*, nor *Medea* stout,
  Nor all the *Mœnades* so furious were,
As this bold woman, when she saw that Damzell there.

48

But *Artegall* being thereof aware,
  Did stay her cruell hand, ere she her raught,
  And as she did her selfe to strike prepare,
  Out of her fist the wicked weapon caught:
  With that like one enfelon'd or distraught,
  She forth did rome, whether her rage her bore,
  With franticke passion, and with furie fraught;
  And breaking forth out at a posterne dore,
Vnto the wyld wood ranne, her dolours to deplore.

Stanza 42

5 topside turuey: topsyturvy. The Souldan may be called **the pagan hound** because summer's scorching heat (see 40.9), which is marked by Sirius, the Dog Star, has now ended; see I iii 31.6*n*. **6 graples**: grappling irons. **8–9** Recalls Ovid, *Met.* 15.528–29, to introduce the comparison to Hippolytus.

Stanza 43

For the story of Hippolytus, see I v 37–40. **7 wooddy**: woodland. **8 rapt**: carried off, pulled down. **all to rent**: entirely rent. **9** . . . no trace at all.

Stanza 44

2 . . . all entirely battered. **7 wroken**: wreaked, avenged.

Stanza 45

1–3 on a tree: as on a tree of chivalry; see I v 5.7*n*. W. Camden 1630:144 records that after the defeat of the Armada 'the banners taken from the Enemy were hung forth to bee seene'.

Stanza 46

1–3 The image of an angry cow running with knife in hand is not entirely obliterated by the comma. **6 misween'd**: mistaken.

Stanza 47

The three examples treat a woman's role as wife, sister, and mother. For the story of **Ino**, see IV xi 13.4–6. Conti 1616:8.4 may have suggested to S. that she threw not only herself and her child into the sea but also the child murdered by her husband, as Lotspeich 1932 notes. For **Medea**, see II xii 44.3–9*n*. As told by Ovid, *Met.* 3.701–33, the **madding** (frenzied) **mother** is Agave who, with the worshippers of Bacchus, tore her son, Pentheus, to pieces when he spied upon their sacred rites. **3 on Colchicke strand**: following Golding's tr. of *Iolciacos* (*Met.* 7.158), as Taylor 1986:344 notes.

Stanza 48

2 raught: reached; touched. **5 enfelon'd**: made furious; suggesting one caught in a felony. **6 whether**: whither.

49

As a mad bytch, when as the franticke fit
   Her burning tongue with rage inflamed hath,
   Doth runne at randon, and with furious bit
   Snatching at euery thing, doth wreake her wrath
   On man and beast, that commeth in her path.
   There they doe say, that she transformed was
   Into a Tygre, and that Tygres scath
   In crueltie and outrage she did pas,
To proue her surname true, that she imposed has.

50

Then *Artegall* himselfe discouering plaine,
   Did issue forth gainst all that warlike rout
   Of knights and armed men, which did maintaine
   That Ladies part, and to the Souldan lout:

[handwritten marginal note: Sultan – racial stereotyping]

All which he did assault with courage stout,
   All were they nigh an hundred knights of name,
   And like wyld Goates them chaced all about,
   Flying from place to place with cowheard shame,
So that with finall force them all he ouercame.

51

Then caused he the gates be opened wyde,
   And there the Prince, as victour of that day,
   With tryumph entertayn'd and glorifyde,
   Presenting him with all the rich array,
   And roiall pompe, which there long hidden lay,
   Purchast through lawlesse powre and tortious wrong
   Of that proud Souldan, whom he earst did slay.
   So both for rest there hauing stayd not long,
Marcht with that mayd, fit matter for another song.

Stanza 49
An accurate description of a rabid dog, as A.B. Gough 1921 notes. As told in *Met.* 13.567–69, Hecuba was so enraged by her son's murder that 'she finally waxed madde, and did byte and stryke all men that she mette, wherfore she was called dogge' (T. Cooper 1565). **7 scath**: harm; harmfulness. **9** Either the name Adicia was bestowed on her for her injustice, or she bestowed it on herself, 'For she her selfe professeth mortall foe | To Iustice' (20.6–7). Fittingly, she and her forces are expelled by the knight of justice rather than by Arthur.

Stanza 50
1 discouering: revealing. **4 lout**: make obeisance. **6 hundred**: at the marriage tournament at iii 11.5, he proved his worth by defeating this number of knights. **8 cowheard**: the etymological spelling suggests conduct befitting a cow-herder. **9 with finall force**: i.e. with force finally; but suggesting absolute force.

Stanza 51
3 tryumph: see iii 15.3*n*. **6 Purchast**: plundered.

Cant. IX.

Arthur and Artegall catch Guyle
whom Talus doth dismay,
They to Mercillaes pallace come,
and see her rich array.

1

WHat Tygre, or what other saluage wight
  Is so exceeding furious and fell,
As wrong, when it hath arm'd it selfe with might?
Not fit mongst men, that doe with reason mell,
But mongst wyld beasts and saluage woods to dwell;
Where still the stronger doth the weake deuoure,
And they that most in boldnesse doe excell,
  Are dreadded most, and feared for their powre:
Fit for *Adicia*, there to build her wicked bowre.

2

There let her wonne farre from resort of men,
  Where righteous *Artegall* her late exyled;
  There let her euer keepe her damned den,
  Where none may be with her lewd parts defyled,
  Nor none but beasts may be of her despoyled:
And turne we to the noble Prince, where late
We did him leaue, after that he had foyled
  The cruell Souldan, and with dreadfull fate
Had vtterly subuerted his vnrighteous state.

3

Where hauing with Sir *Artegall* a space
  Well solast in that Souldans late delight,
  They both resoluing now to leaue the place,
  Both it and all the wealth therein behight
Vnto that Damzell in her Ladies right,
And so would haue departed on their way.
But she them woo'd by all the meanes she might,
  And earnestly besought, to wend that day
With her, to see her Ladie thence not farre away.

4

By whose entreatie both they ouercommen,
  Agree to goe with her, and by the way,
  (As often falles) of sundry things did commen.
  Mongst which that Damzell did to them bewray
A straunge aduenture, which not farre thence lay;
To weet a wicked villaine, bold and stout,
Which wonned in a rocke not farre away,
  That robbed all the countrie there about,
And brought the pillage home, whence none could get it out.

5

Thereto both his owne wylie wit, (she sayd)
  And eke the fastnesse of his dwelling place,
  Both vnassaylable, gaue him great ayde:
  For he so crafty was to forge and face,
So light of hand, and nymble of his pace,
So smooth of tongue, and subtile in his tale,
That could deceiue one looking in his face;
  Therefore by name *Malengin* they him call,
Well knowen by his feates, and famous ouer all.

6

Through these his slights he many doth confound,
  And eke the rocke, in which he wonts to dwell,
  Is wondrous strong, and hewen farre vnder ground
  A dreadfull depth, how deepe no man can tell;
But some doe say, it goeth downe to hell.
And all within, it full of wyndings is,
And hidden wayes, that scarse an hound by smell
  Can follow out those false footsteps of his,
Ne none can backe returne, that once are gone amis.

Book V Canto ix

Argument
1 **Guyle**: i.e. Malengin.   2 **dismay**: defeat.

Stanza 1
4 **mell**: concern themselves.   5 **saluage**: wild, uncultivated; hence fierce, ungoverned.

Stanza 2
4 **lewd parts**: the sexual import of her conduct at viii 20.4–5.
8 **fate**: sentence, judgement.

Stanza 3
2 **solast**: comforted themselves.   4 **behight**: committed.   5 **in her Ladies right**: i.e. in Mercilla's name, being rightfully hers.

Stanza 4
3 **commen**: commune.   4 **bewray**: reveal.

Stanza 5
2 **fastnesse**: security from invasion.   4 **forge**: devise evil; deceive.   **face**: show a false face.   8 **Malengin**: personifying fraud or deceit (*OED*); from Lat. *mal* + *engin*, evil machinations; 'Guyle' (Arg.1). His labyrinthine bottomless den, described at 6.2–9, associates him with Cacus in Virgil, *Aen.* 8.193–95; and his defeat by Arthur with Hercules's defeat of Cacus, as Dunseath 1968:198–204 argues. In his cave which suggests the Irish *souterrain* (see Herron 2000), in his guerilla tactics, and esp. in his appearance (see 10.6–9*n*), he resembles the rebel Irish, as Upton 1758 first noted. In his guile at 12–14 and disguisings at 17–18, he resembles the Jesuit missionary priests who were much feared and vilified throughout the 1580s and 1590s for their guile, as Heale 1990:171–81 argues. See 'Malengin' in the *SEnc*, and Clegg 1998:251–55.

Stanza 6
1 **slights**: wiles.

7

Which when those knights had heard, their harts gan earne,
    To vnderstand that villeins dwelling place,
    And greatly it desir'd of her to learne,
    And by which way they towards it should trace.
    Were not (sayd she) that it should let your pace
    Towards my Ladies presence by you ment,
    I would you guyde directly to the place.
    Then let not that (said they) stay your intent;
For neither will one foot, till we that carle haue hent.

8

So forth they past, till they approched ny
    Vnto the rocke, where was the villains won,
    Which when the Damzell neare at hand did spy,
    She warn'd the knights thereof: who thereupon
    Gan to aduize, what best were to be done.
    So both agreed, to send that mayd afore,
    Where she might sit nigh to the den alone,
    Wayling, and raysing pittifull vprore,
As if she did some great calamitie deplore.

9

With noyse whereof when as the caytiue carle
    Should issue forth, in hope to find some spoyle,
    They in awayt would closely him ensnarle,
    Ere to his den he backward could recoyle,
    And so would hope him easily to foyle.
    The Damzell straight went, as she was directed,
    Vnto the rocke, and there vpon the soyle
    Hauing her selfe in wretched wize abiected,
Gan weepe and wayle, as if great griefe had her affected.

10

The cry whereof entring the hollow caue,
    Eftsoones brought forth the villaine, as they ment,
    With hope of her some wishfull boot to haue.
    Full dreadfull wight he was, as euer went

    Vpon the earth, with hollow eyes deepe pent,
    And long curld locks, that downe his shoulders shagged,
    And on his backe an vncouth vestiment
    Made of straunge stuffe, but all to worne and ragged,
And vnderneath his breech was all to torne and iagged.

11

And in his hand an huge long staffe he held,
    Whose top was arm'd with many an yron hooke,
    Fit to catch hold of all that he could weld,
    Or in the compasse of his clouches tooke;
    And euer round about he cast his looke.
    Als at his backe a great wyde net he bore,
    With which he seldome fished at the brooke,
    But vsd to fish for fooles on the dry shore,
Of which he in faire weather wont to take great store.

12

Him when the damzell saw fast by her side,
    So vgly creature, she was nigh dismayd,
    And now for helpe aloud in earnest cride.
    But when the villaine saw her so affrayd,
    He gan with guilefull words her to perswade,
    To banish feare, and with *Sardonian* smyle
    Laughing on her, his false intent to shade,
    Gan forth to lay his bayte her to beguyle,
That from her self vnwares he might her steale the whyle.

13

Like as the fouler on his guilefull pype
    Charmes to the birds full many a pleasant lay,
    That they the whiles may take lesse heedie keepe,
    How he his nets doth for their ruine lay:
    So did the villaine to her prate and play,
    And many pleasant trickes before her show,
    To turne her eyes from his intent away:
    For he in slights and iugling feates did flow,
And of legierdemayne the mysteries did know.

Stanza 7
1 earne: yearn. **4 trace**: travel. **5 let**: hinder. **6 ment**: intended. **9** For neither of us will go . . .

Stanza 8
2 won: accustomed dwelling-place. **5 aduize**: consider.

Stanza 9
3 in awayt: in ambush. **ensnarle**: entangle in a snarl or snare, a 'sting' operation that will trap him with the emblem of guile, which is a net, and thereby beguile the beguiler. **8 abiected**: cast down; hence literally downcast. **9** The alexandrine, repeated from 8.9 with its similar construction, emphasizes her guile.

Stanza 10
3 wishfull boot: wished-for booty. **6–9** As the rebel Irish wore 'mantles and longe glibs which is a thick curled bush of hair hanging down over their eyes, and monstrously disguising them' (*View* 50). **shagged**: hung in a shaggy manner. **all to**: entirely. **breech**: rump.

Stanza 11
Malengin is the false fisher of men described in Hab. 1.14: 'Thei take vp all with the angle [fish-hook]: thei catche it in their net', and in Jer. 16.16: 'thei shal hunt them . . . out of the caues of the rockes'. Accordingly, he displays the traditional emblem of guile: in Ripa, *Inganno* is shown as a man with long shaggy hair and strange jagged garments carrying a fishing net in one hand and three fish hooks in the other; rpt in the *SEnc*. See Aptekar 1969:129–31. **3 weld**: wield: prevail over. **4 compasse**: reach. **5 cast his looke** suggests that his glance nets his victims.

Stanza 12
6 Sardonian: sardonic. Forced laughter to hide bitterness is proverbial; see Smith 676. **7** As Dissemblance 'laught on' Suspect at III xii 15.3 to encourage him.

Stanza 13
2 Charmes: plays in order to fascinate, punning on 'charm', the bird-song which he imitates. **8 flow**: abound.

14

To which whilest she lent her intentiue mind,
　He suddenly his net vpon her threw,
　That ouersprad her like a puffe of wind;
　And snatching her soone vp, ere well she knew,
　Ran with her fast away vnto his mew,
　Crying for helpe aloud. But when as ny
　He came vnto his caue, and there did vew
　The armed knights stopping his passage by,
He threw his burden downe, and fast away did fly.

15

But *Artegall* him after did pursew,
　The whiles the Prince there kept the entrance still:
　Vp to the rocke he ran, and thereon flew
　Like a wyld Gote, leaping from hill to hill,
　And dauncing on the craggy cliffes at will;
　That deadly daunger seem'd in all mens sight,
　To tempt such steps, where footing was so ill:
　Ne ought auayled for the armed knight,
To thinke to follow him, that was so swift and light.

16

Which when he saw, his yron man he sent,
　To follow him; for he was swift in chace.
　He him pursewd, where euer that he went,
　Both ouer rockes, and hilles, and euery place,
　Where so he fled, he followd him apace:
　So that he shortly forst him to forsake
　The hight, and downe descend vnto the base.
　There he him courst a fresh, and soone did make
To leaue his proper forme, and other shape to take.

17

Into a Foxe himselfe he first did tourne;
　But he him hunted like a Foxe full fast:
　Then to a bush himselfe he did transforme,
　But he the bush did beat, till that at last

Into a bird it chaung'd, and from him past,
　Flying from tree to tree, from wand to wand:
　But he then stones at it so long did cast,
　That like a stone it fell vpon the land,
But he then tooke it vp, and held fast in his hand.

18

So he it brought with him vnto the knights,
　And to his Lord Sir *Artegall* it lent,
　Warning him hold it fast, for feare of slights.
　Who whilest in hand it gryping hard he hent,
　Into a Hedgehogge all vnwares it went,
　And prickt him so, that he away it threw.
　Then gan it runne away incontinent,
　Being returned to his former hew:
But *Talus* soone him ouertooke, and backward drew.

19

But when as he would to a snake againe
　Haue turn'd himselfe, he with his yron flayle
　Gan driue at him, with so huge might and maine,
　That all his bones, as small as sandy grayle
　He broke, and did his bowels disentrayle;
　Crying in vaine for helpe, when helpe was past.
　So did deceipt the selfe deceiuer fayle,
　There they him left a carrion outcast;
For beasts and foules to feede vpon for their repast.

20

Thence forth they passed with that gentle Mayd,
　To see her Ladie, as they did agree.
　To which when she approched, thus she sayd;
　Loe now, right noble knights, arriu'd ye bee
　Nigh to the place, which ye desir'd to see:
　There shall ye see my soucrayne Lady Queene
　Most sacred wight, most debonayre and free,
　That euer yet vpon this earth was seene,
Or that with Diademe hath euer crowned beene.

Stanza 14
1 intentiue: inwardly attentive.　**5 mew**: den, a place where a 'fouler' (13.1) keeps his prey.

Stanza 15
4 The epithet **wyld** is appropriate to goats, as at viii 50.7, but may allude to the 'wild Irish', i.e. those not subject to English rule (*OED* B1a); sugg. Maley 1996b:10.

Stanza 16
9 proper: own.

Stanzas 17–19
The first transformation marks his guile – 'the Foxe of al beasts is most wily and crafty' (E.K. on *SC May* 219) – while the others follow nursery-rhyme logic: the fox hiding in a bush becomes a bush; the bush being beaten becomes a bird (the logic of alliteration); the bird pelted with stones becomes a stone; and the tightly held stone becomes a rolled-up hedgehog, which is the prickly Devil in *Physiologus* 16, and associated with the fallen state in Isa. 24.11. With the sixth change into himself, he must be stopped, for the cycle would begin

again if he were allowed to transform himself into a snake, the archetype of guile.

Stanza 17
6 wand: shrub.

Stanza 18
2 lent: gave.　**7 incontinent**: immediately.　**8 hew**: shape.

Stanza 19
5 disentrayle: drag forth from their inner parts; in effect, unravel the 'wyndings' (6.6) of his labyrinthine cave.　**7 the selfe deceiuer**: i.e. the deceiver himself.　**fayle**: deceive, and cause to fail; with proverbial force, as at III xi 46.9.

Stanza 20
1–3 The transition from faery land to Mercilla's court is noted by Dunseath 1968:207. It opens the poem to the world of Elizabethan foreign affairs that involves Belgium, France, and Ireland.　**6–9** The most overt and hyperbolic praise in the poem (apart from the proems) of Elizabeth as the image of the Faerie Queene. Cf. Samient's praise of her at viii 16.8–9, and the poet's at x 3. **debonayre**: gracious. **free**: noble; gracious; magnanimous.

21

The gentle knights reioyced much to heare
  The prayses of that Prince so manifold,
  And passing litle further, commen were,
  Where they a stately pallace did behold,
  Of pompous show, much more then she had told;
  With many towres, and tarras mounted hye,
  And all their tops bright glistering with gold,
  That seemed to outshine the dimmed skye,
And with their brightnesse daz'd the straunge beholders eye.

22

There they alighting, by that Damzell were
  Directed in, and shewed all the sight:
  Whose porch, that most magnificke did appeare,
  Stood open wyde to all men day and night;
  Yet warded well by one of mickle might,
  That sate thereby, with gyantlike resemblance,
  To keepe out guyle, and malice, and despight,
  That vnder shew oftimes of fayned semblance,
Are wont in Princes courts to worke great scath and
                      (hindrance.

23

His name was *Awe*; by whom they passing in
  Went vp the hall, that was a large wyde roome,
  All full of people making troublous din,
  And wondrous noyse, as if that there were some,

Which vnto them was dealing righteous doome.
  By whom they passing, through the thickest preasse,
  The marshall of the hall to them did come;
  His name hight *Order*, who commaunding peace,
Them guyded through the throng, that did their clamors
                      (ceasse.

24

They ceast their clamors vpon them to gaze;
  Whom seeing all in armour bright as day,
  Straunge there to see, it did them much amaze,
  And with vnwonted terror halfe affray.
  For neuer saw they there the like array.
  Ne euer was the name of warre there spoken,
  But ioyous peace and quietnesse alway,
  Dealing iust iudgements, that mote not be broken
For any brybes, or threates of any to be wroken.

25

There as they entred at the Scriene, they saw
  Some one, whose tongue was for his trespasse vyle
  Nayld to a post, adiudged so by law:
  For that therewith he falsely did reuyle,
  And foule blaspheme that Queene for forged guyle,
  Both with bold speaches, which he blazed had,
  And with lewd poems, which he did compyle;
  For the bold title of a Poet bad
He on himselfe had ta'en, and rayling rymes had sprad.

cracking metaphor

Stanza 21

2 that Prince: used of Elizabeth only here and xii 3.3, except IV proem 4.9 where it is a biblical term, the usual address being 'Princesse', as viii 16.8, 18.7, etc. Perhaps deferring to her wishes, as Marcus 1988:56–57 suggests.   **4–9** Details of Mercilla's **stately pallace**, such as the gold, towers, and dazzling light, expose its parody in Lucifera's 'stately Pallace' at I iv 4. **pompous**: magnificent.   **tarras**: i.e. terraces or galleries.

Stanza 22

The entrance resembles that to Hampton Court; see *Var* 5.237–38. A.B. Gough 1921 notes that Elizabeth's porter was said to have been 8′6″.   **3–7** As the gates of Jerusalem 'shal be open continually: nether day nor night shal they be shut' (Isa. 60.11). Rev. 21.27 adds that no unclean thing may enter these open gates 'nether whatsoeuer worketh abomination or lies'.   **guyle** is associated with Malengin (Arg.1); **despight** with the Souldan and Adicia (viii 17.6, 18.3).   **9 scath**: harm. **hindrance**: injury.

Stanza 23

1 Awe: a complex personification representing the power to inspire dread mingled with veneration and a profound reverence in the presence of supreme authority (*OED* 2), such as royalty. See 'Awe' in the *SEnc*.   **4 some**: some one.   **8–9 Order** appears as Nature's 'Sergeant' at VII vii 4.6. His office is to summon persons to appear before the court (*OED* 4).

Stanza 24

3–7 Alluding to Elizabeth's highly praised peaceful reign; see 30.6–9*n*.   **amaze**: dazzle, bewilder.   **9 wroken**: i.e. wreaked: avenged.

Stanzas 25–26

The punishment of the poet, who is neither identified nor his **sin** revealed, is described in the two central stanzas of the canto, as Oram 1997:245 observes. While Elizabeth, like any ruler, was subject to slander – all the more being a woman: on dissing Elizabeth, see Walker 1998a *passim* – no contemporary poet is known who openly proclaimed himself a bad poet through his **forged guyle** in uttering presumptuous speeches and publishing licentious or seditious poems, or who wrote poems that accused her of **forged guyle** (a point noted by Farness 1996:182*n*8) which it would be her duty to suppress, as does Isis at vii 7.3. (Clegg 1998:256 argues that a case may be made for the recusant Stephen Vallenger, who was found guilty of publishing libels in verse.) If his tongue has been cut out, the punishment is biblical: 'The Lord cut of . . . the tongue that speaketh proude things' (Ps. 12.3); and also classical: Philomela whose tongue had been cut out was a common Renaissance emblem of a poet who feared being charged with slander, as in Gascoigne 1907–10:2.146–47. In naming the poet **BON FONT**, and renaming him **Malfont** either for the evil he did (Fr. *faire mal,* to do evil), or for being **a welhed | Of euill words**, S. may anticipate that James VI would regard him as one about to take on himself the title of a bad poet by treating the trial of his mother, Mary Queen of Scots; see 38–50*n*. So might Elizabeth, and Burghley; see IV proem 1.1–2*n*. See 'Bonfont, Malfont' in the *SEnc*. Flesh nailed to a cruciform post suggests a poet's martyrdom, as Bieman 1988:185 claims. On Elizabethan laws against slander, e.g. the 1581 statute against any 'defamation of the queenes majestie', see Kaplan 1997:12–19.

Stanza 25

1 Scriene: a room-divider fitted with a door; a place for the execution of justice at x 37.9.   **2–9** 'Thou shalt not raile vpon

26

Thus there he stood, whylest high ouer his head,
  There written was the purport of his sin,
  In cyphers strange, that few could rightly read,
  BON FONT: but *bon* that once had written bin,
  Was raced out, and *Mal* was now put in.
  So now *Malfont* was plainely to be red;
  Eyther for th'euill, which he did therein,
  Or that he likened was to a welhed
Of euill words, and wicked sclaunders by him shed.

27

They passing by, were guyded by degree
  Vnto the presence of that gratious Queene:
  Who sate on high, that she might all men see,
  And might of all men royally be seene,
  Vpon a throne of gold full bright and sheene,
  Adorned all with gemmes of endlesse price,
  As either might for wealth haue gotten bene,
  Or could be fram'd by workmans rare deuice;
And all embost with Lyons and with Flourdelice.

28

All ouer her a cloth of state was spred,
  Not of rich tissew, nor of cloth of gold,
  Nor of ought else, that may be richest red,
  But like a cloud, as likest may be told,

That her brode spreading wings did wyde vnfold;
  Whose skirts were bordred with bright sunny beams,
  Glistring like gold, amongst the plights enrold,
  And here and there shooting forth siluer streames,
Mongst which crept litle Angels through the glittering
                                              (gleames.

29

Seemed those litle Angels did vphold
  The cloth of state, and on their purpled wings
  Did beare the pendants, through their nimblesse bold:
  Besides a thousand more of such, as sings
  Hymnes to high God, and carols heauenly things,
  Encompassed the throne, on which she sate:
  She Angel-like, the heyre of ancient kings
  And mightie Conquerors, in royall state,
Whylest kings and kesars at her feet did them prostrate.

30

Thus she did sit in souerayne Maiestie,
  Holding a Scepter in her royall hand,
  The sacred pledge of peace and clemencie,
  With which high God had blest her happie land,
  Maugre so many foes, which did withstand.
  But at her feet her sword was likewise layde,
  Whose long rest rusted the bright steely brand;
  Yet when as foes enforst, or friends sought ayde,
She could it sternely draw, that all the world dismayde.

the Iudges, nether speake euil of the ruler of thy people' (Exod. 22.28; cited by Paul, Acts 23.5). **rayling rymes** suggests broadsides, which were strongly suppressed.

Stanza 26
4–9 few could rightly read: suggesting that **BON** was raced, i.e. erased, as in a palimpsest, but not entirely. **FONT**: FONS 1596, but the emendation sugg. by Upton 1758 is supported by 6: the poet had been named **BON FONT** in being a fount (Lat. *fons*), or maker (Fr. *font*), or publisher (Eng. font or type) of good words, as S. praises Chaucer as a 'well of English vndefyled' at IV ii 32.8 and the 'pure well head of Poesie' at VII vii 9.4, and in calling him 'that good Poet' at VI iii 1.1.

Stanza 27
2 They enter the presence chamber where a sovereign receives visitors (see I iv 7.2*n*) to come into her **presence**. **3 Who sate on high**: emblematic of her assumption of authority, as again at 30.1, 33.1, and 34.1, in contrast to Lucifera's display of herself for adoration at I iv 8. (It is noteworthy that Mercilla's person is not described.) Only in the canto's concluding phrase does she arise. **5 a throne of gold**: a replica of the mercy-seat of pure gold from which God speaks to the children of Israel (Exod. 25.17–18, 22). Its two cherubims, whose wings stretch across the seat, are linked with the angels who uphold the canopy of state in 29.1–2. **sheene**: shining. **6 price**: worth. **9** Mercilla displays the royal coat-of-arms of England and France because Elizabeth is Queen of both countries, as the poem's title-page declares. The setting may refer specifically to Parliament, the supreme court of justice, which was called on 29 Oct. 1586 to try Mary Queen of Scots; see Northrop 1968–69, Northrop 1973. Or to the court of com-

mon pleas at Westminster Hall, as suggested by 36.3–5; see Leslie 1983:65–68. On her court as a shrine of justice, in which she displays both classical equity and Christian mercy, see Stump 1982.

Stanza 28
1–3 As over Lucifera's throne 'a cloth of State was spred' (I iv 8.1). **tissew**: a rich cloth interwoven with gold. **red**: imagined. **4–9** The imagery is broadly scriptural, e.g. Ps. 97.2: 'Cloudes and darkenes are round about him: righteousnes and iudgement are the fundation of his throne'. The **cloud** suggests the cloud of glory in which God appeared to Moses (Exod. 24.18), and in which Christ will appear to judge the earth (Matt. 24.30). **plights**: pleats.

Stanza 29
3 pendants: ornamental fringe. **nimblesse**: nimbleness. **4–6** Cf. Rev. 7.11: 'And all the Angels stode rounde about the throne . . . and worshiped God'. Their singing here marks divine endorsement of Mercilla's government, as Wells 1994:29 notes. **9** Cf. Rev. 4.10: 'The foure and twentie elders fell downe before him that sate on the throne'.

Stanza 30
2 a Scepter: see III iii 49.6–9*n*. **5 Maugre**: despite. **6–9 her sword**: the emblem of royal power, with which Elizabeth was invested at her coronation; see the Portland portrait in Strong 1963: pl. 11. That it lies at her feet indicates that it is ready to be used, as it was against the nearly 700 rebels killed in the 1569 Rising of the North. (Elizabeth's poem, *ca.* 1570, warns the 'daughter of debate', evidently Mary Stuart, that her 'rusty sword' was ready to be used; see Nelson 1965:115.) Being **rusted** marks her peaceful reign.

31

And round about, before her feet there sate
  A beuie of faire Virgins clad in white,
  That goodly seem'd t'adorne her royall state,
  All louely daughters of high *Ioue*, that hight
  Litæ, by him begot in loues delight,
  Vpon the righteous *Themis*: those they say
  Vpon *Ioues* iudgement seat wayt day and night,
  And when in wrath he threats the worlds decay,
They doe his anger calme, and cruell vengeance stay.

32

They also doe by his diuine permission
  Vpon the thrones of mortall Princes tend,
  And often treat for pardon and remission
  To suppliants, through frayltie which offend.
  Those did vpon *Mercillaes* throne attend:
  Iust *Dice*, wise *Eunomie*, myld *Eirene*,
  And them amongst, her glorie to commend,
  Sate goodly *Temperance* in garments clene,
And sacred *Reuerence*, yborne of heauenly strene.

33

Thus did she sit in royall rich estate,
  Admyr'd of many, honoured of all,
  Whylest vnderneath her feete, there as she sate,
  An huge great Lyon lay, that mote appall
  An hardie courage, like captiued thrall,
  With a strong yron chaine and coller bound,
  That once he could not moue, nor quich at all;
  Yet did he murmure with rebellions sound,
And softly royne, when saluage choler gan redound.

34

So sitting high in dreaded souerayntie,
  Those two strange knights were to her presence brought;
  Who bowing low before her Maiestie,
  Did to her myld obeysance, as they ought,
  And meekest boone, that they imagine mought.
  To whom she eke inclyning her withall,
  As a faire stoupe of her high soaring thought,
  A chearefull countenance on them let fall,
Yet tempred with some maiestie imperiall.

35

As the bright sunne, what time his fierie teme
  Towards the westerne brim begins to draw,
  Gins to abate the brightnesse of his beme,
  And feruour of his flames somewhat adaw:
  So did this mightie Ladie, when she saw
  Those two strange knights such homage to her make,
  Bate somewhat of that Maiestie and awe,
  That whylome wont to doe so many quake,
And with more myld aspect those two to entertake.

36

Now at that instant, as occasion fell,
  When these two stranger knights arriu'd in place,
  She was about affaires of common wele,
  Dealing of Iustice with indifferent grace,
  And hearing pleas of people meane and base.
  Mongst which as then, there was for to be heard
  The tryall of a great and weightie case,
  Which on both sides was then debating hard:
But at the sight of these, those were a while debard.

Stanza 31

5 S. conflates the **Litæ** who personify prayer in Homer, *Iliad*
9.502–12, with the three *Horae* or Hours in Hesiod, *Theog.*
901–03, following Conti 1616: 2.1, as Lotspeich 1932 notes.
See VII vii **45***n*.

Stanza 32

6–9 Their order is climactic: just judgement upholds good law,
which brings peace, the true end of justice: 'And the worke of
iustice shalbe peace' (Isa. 32.17). They are described by Bodin
in *Six Bookes of a Commonweale* (1606) as three kinds of
justice: 'εὐνομία, ἐπιείκεια, εἰρήνη', that is to say Upright
Law, Equitie, and Peace'; cited Dunseath 1968:211. They may
be compared to three of the four daughters of God from Ps.
85:10: truth, righteousness (justice), and peace, the fourth
being mercy; see Aptekar 1969:18–19. On Elizabeth and the
imperial virtues, *justitia* and *clementia*, see Yates 1977:71–72;
cf. Gloriana's 'faire peace, and mercy' (II ii 40.9). On her
name signifying 'Peace of the Lord', see Hamilton 1973:110.
Iust Dice: epithet and name merge into 'justice' to suggest
'just saying' in contrast to Malfont.   **Temperance** ensures that
justice is tempered by mercy; see x 4.5. At I x 7, **Reuerence** (a
squire) leads Una and the Red Cross Knight to Dame Cælia.
strene: strain, lineage.

Stanza 33

3–9 One emblem of royal power, cited by Aptekar 1969:61–
69, shows a monarch attended by a lion. It is found in
Valeriano (1556); see Bath 1988:232–33. Cf. the dragon
beneath Lucifera's feet at I iv 10.   **quich**: stir, implying rebel-
lious stirring (*OED* 4c).   **rebellions**: indicating that rebellion
must be chained; see Fletcher 1971:238–42.   **royne**: growl,
specifically a lion's roar suggested by the sound of the Fr. *roi*,
king.   **gan redound**: overflowed.

Stanza 34

2 **two strange knights**: a designation used again at 35.6
and 36.2 – cf. 21.9, 24.3, and esp. 37.5 – for both are Britons.
5 **boone**: favour, as the Red Cross Knight 'falling before the
Queen of Faries desired a boone' (*LR* 53–54).   7 **stoupe**: the
swoop of a falcon; fig. condescension, in contrast to Lucifera's
conduct at I iv 14.1.

Stanza 35

2 **brim**: edge, horizon; sea.   4 **adaw**: subdue, as its flames are
extinguished in the sea.   8 **doe**: make.   9 **entertake**: receive.

Stanza 36

4 Using the language of the *BCP*: 'that they may truly and
indifferently [i.e. impartially] minister justice'.   9 **these**: i.e.
Arthur and Artegall.

37

But after all her princely entertayne,
  To th'hearing of that former cause in hand,
  Her selfe eftsoones she gan conuert againe;
  Which that those knights likewise mote vnderstand,
  And witnesse forth aright in forrain land,
  Taking them vp vnto her stately throne,
  Where they mote heare the matter throughly scand
  On either part, she placed th'one on th'one,
The other on the other side, and neare them none.

38

Then was there brought, as prisoner to the barre,
  A Ladie of great countenance and place,
  But that she it with foule abuse did marre;
  Yet did appeare rare beautie in her face,
  But blotted with condition vile and base,
  That all her other honour did obscure,
  And titles of nobilitie deface:
  Yet in that wretched semblant, she did sure
The peoples great compassion vnto her allure.

39

Then vp arose a person of deepe reach,
  And rare in-sight, hard matters to reuele;
  That well could charme his tongue, and time his speach
  To all assayes; his name was called *Zele*:

He gan that Ladie strongly to appele
  Of many haynous crymes, by her enured,
  And with sharpe reasons rang her such a pele,
  That those, whom she to pitie had allured,
He now t'abhorre and loath her person had procured.

40

First gan he tell, how this that seem'd so faire
  And royally arayd, *Duessa* hight
  That false *Duessa*, which had wrought great care,
  And mickle mischiefe vnto many a knight,
  By her beguyled, and confounded quight:
  But not for those she now in question came,
  Though also those mote question'd be aright,
  But for vyld treasons, and outrageous shame,
Which she against the dred *Mercilla* oft did frame.

41

For she whylome (as ye mote yet right well
  Remember) had her counsels false conspyred,
  With faithlesse *Blandamour* and *Paridell*,
  (Both two her paramours, both by her hyred,
  And both with hope of shadowes vaine inspyred)
  And with them practiz'd, how for to depryue
  Mercilla of her crowne, by her aspyred,
  That she might it vnto her selfe deryue,
And tryumph in their blood, whom she to death did dryue.

Stanza 37

1 entertayne: reception. **3 conuert**: turn; suggesting a change of role from queen to judge. **5** And bear witness abroad to the justice of her proceedings – as S. now undertakes to do. **7 scand**: examined. **8–9** With Artegall on one side and Arthur on the other, Mercilla appears as Astræa holding the scales of justice to balance their respective virtues, *justitia* and *clementia*; see A. Fowler 1964:197. Elizabeth is shown being crowned by justice and mercy in the woodcut border of the 1569 Bishops' Bible; see King 1990a:124.

Stanzas 38–50

In 1596, Robert Bowes in Edinburgh wrote to Lord Burghley that James VI complained that this canto contained 'some dishonorable effects (as the k. demeth thereof) against himself and his mother [Mary, Queen of Scots] deceassed . . . [and] desyreth that Edward Spenser for his faulte, may be dewly tryed and punished' (*Sp All* 45). See 'James I of England' and 'Mary, Queen of Scots' in the *SEnc*. For an account of the trial, see Goldberg 1989:1–17; and for a contemporary illustration, see Beckingsale 1967: facing 166. While certain details of her trial in 1586 are not reproduced – e.g. it was not presided over by Elizabeth, the jurors were not limited to two, and Mary defended herself vehemently – its broad outlines are retained with an emphasis on imperial law; see Parkin-Speer 1992:494–99. On S.'s difficulty in representing the trial, see McCabe 1987, and Gallagher 1991:233–61.

Stanza 38

2 countenance: position. **4 rare beautie**: an obvious historical allusion, for Mary's beauty was well known. **5 condition**:

behaviour. **7** Indicating that Mary had no claim to the English throne. **8 semblant**: outward appearance.

Stanza 39

3 charme his tongue: tune his tongue to fascinate those who hear him, using Malengin's ability (cf. 13.2) for just purposes. **4 assayes**: occasions. **Zele** initiates the Red Cross Knight's sojourn in the house of Holinesse at I x 6.4–9, and is manifest at V i 14.7 in Artegall's 'zeale of vengeance' and at 49.5 below in his 'zeale of Iustice'. **5 appele**: accuse. **6 enured**: committed. **9 procured**: caused.

Stanza 40

3 care: trouble, grief. **5 confounded**: destroyed. **6–9** The commission by which Mary was tried was not empowered to deal with anything that had occurred before 1585, for she was charged only with having 'conspired the destruction of the Queen of England and the subversion of religion'; noted A.B. Gough 1921.

Stanza 41

1–5 All that readers – as distinct from **ye**, who are the jury – may remember is their entrance at IV i 17 when Duessa was paired with Paridell, and Ate with Blandamour; their later exchanges as an exemplum of false friendship; and their last appearance at IV ix 20–31 when she and Ate provoked their lovers into a love-skirmish that only Arthur could end. **6 practiz'd**: schemed. **8 deryue**: transfer; in the legal sense, 'convey by right of descent', as the political allegory suggests.

42

But through high heauens grace, which fauour not
  The wicked driftes of trayterous desynes,
  Gainst loiall Princes, all this cursed plot,
  Ere proofe it tooke, discouered was betymes,
  And th'actours won the meede meet for their crymes.
  Such be the meede of all, that by such mene
  Vnto the type of kingdomes title clymes.
  But false *Duessa* now vntitled Queene,
Was brought to her sad doome, as here was to be seene.

43

Strongly did *Zele* her haynous fact enforce,
  And many other crimes of foule defame
  Against her brought, to banish all remorse,
  And aggrauate the horror of her blame.
  And with him to make part against her, came
  Many graue persons, that against her pled;
  First was a sage old Syre, that had to name
  The *Kingdomes care*, with a white siluer hed,
That many high regards and reasons gainst her red.

44

Then gan *Authority* her to appose
  With peremptorie powre, that made all mute;
  And then the law of *Nations* gainst her rose,
  And reasons brought, that no man could refute;
  Next gan *Religion* gainst her to impute
  High Gods beheast, and powre of holy lawes;
  Then gan the Peoples cry and Commons sute,
  Importune care of their owne publicke cause;
And lastly *Iustice* charged her with breach of lawes.

45   *Religion + Justice*

But then for her, on the contrarie part,
  Rose many aduocates for her to plead:
  First there came *Pittie*, with full tender hart,
  And with her ioyn'd *Regard* of womanhead;

And then came *Daunger* threatning hidden dread,
  And high alliance vnto forren powre;
  Then came *Nobilitie* of birth, that bread
  Great ruth through her misfortunes tragicke stowre;
And lastly *Griefe* did plead, and many teares forth powre.

46

With the neare touch whereof in tender hart
  The Briton Prince was sore empassionate,
  And woxe inclined much vnto her part,
  Through the sad terror of so dreadfull fate,
  That for great ruth his courage gan relent.
  Which when as *Zele* perceiued to abate,
  He gan his earnest feruour to augment,
And many fearefull obiects to them to present.

47

He gan t'efforce the euidence anew,
  And new accusements to produce in place:
  He brought forth that old hag of hellish hew,
  The cursed *Ate*, brought her face to face,
  Who priuie was, and partie in the case:
  She, glad of spoyle and ruinous decay,
  Did her appeach, and to her more disgrace,
  The plot of all her practise did display,
And all her traynes, and all her treasons forth did lay.

48

Then brought he forth, with griesly grim aspect,
  Abhorred *Murder*, who with bloudie knyfe
  Yet dropping fresh in hand did her detect,
  And there with guiltie bloudshed charged ryfe:
  Then brought he forth *Sedition*, breeding stryfe
  In troublous wits, and mutinous vprore:
  Then brought he forth *Incontinence* of lyfe,
  Euen foule *Adulterie* her face before,
And lewd *Impietie*, that her accused sore.

Stanza 42
2 driftes: aims. **4 proofe**: effect. **5 actours**: authors. **6 mene**: means. **7 type**: highest point. **8 vntitled Queene**: in answer to the claim that Mary was a queen and therefore above the law; noted Northrop 1968–69:281.

Stanza 43
1 fact: crime. **2 defame**: infamy. **7–9 Kingdomes care** may be identified as Burghley; see IV proem 1.1–2*n*. He is so identified in the marginalia of a copy of the *1611* folio; see Manning 1984:226. **high regards**: matters of great importance. **red**: declared.

Stanza 44
The historical matter relevant to four of the advocates is noted by A.B. Gough 1921: **Authority** refers to the Act of 1584, which set up penalties for any attempt upon the Queen's person and also authorized Mary's trial; **the law of Nations** was transgressed when Mary joined a conspiracy against Elizabeth, the head of a foreign state; **Religion** sought Mary's death to protect the Protestant faith; and the **Commons** twice petitioned the Queen to have Mary put to death. **1 appose**: examine; oppose. **5 impute**: adduce.

Stanza 45
Five reasons against Duessa in 43–44 are countered by five in her favour: '*Kingdomes care*': **Pittie**; '*Authority*': **Regard of womanhead**; 'the law of *Nations*': **Daunger** (of foreign power); the 'Commons': **Nobilitie**. The arguments against her by *Religion* cannot be countered. **8 stowre**: time of distress.

Stanza 46
Arthur is affected because 'pitee renneth soone in gentil herte' (Chaucer, *Knight's Tale* 1761), his **terror** and **ruth** being the specific tragic emotions aroused by Mary's fall. Artegall is not affected: though he rued Munera's plight, 'for no pitty would he change the course | Of Iustice' (ii 26.1–2). **1 neare touch**: deep impression, as Mercilla is 'touched nere' (50.1).

Stanza 47
1 efforce: urge more strongly. **2 accusements**: accusations. **3–9** Duessa is condemned through evidence brought by the spirit she herself had raised from hell at IV i 19.5–9. **hew**: form. **appeach**: accuse. **practise**: treachery. **traynes**: plots.

49

All which when as the Prince had heard and seene,
His former fancies ruth he gan repent,
And from her partie eftsoones was drawn cleene.
But *Artegall* with constant firme intent,
For zeale of Iustice was against her bent.
So was she guiltie deemed of them all.
Then *Zele* began to vrge her punishment,
And to their Queene for iudgement loudly call,
Vnto *Mercilla* myld for Iustice gainst the thrall.

50

But she, whose Princely breast was touched nere
With piteous ruth of her so wretched plight,
Though plaine she saw by all, that she did heare,
That she of death was guiltie found by right,
Yet would not let iust vengeance on her light;
But rather let in stead thereof to fall
Few perling drops from her faire lampes of light;
The which she couering with her purple pall
Would haue the passion hid, and vp arose withall.

Stanza 48

An additional five advocates testify against Mary/Duessa: **Murder**, with complicity in the murder of her husband, Henry Darnley; **Sedition**, her involvement in plots to overthrow the English government; **Adulterie**, her marriage to the Earl of Bothwell, the alleged assassin of Darnley; **Incontinence of lyfe** and **Impietie** in the charges against her by the House of Commons that she 'hath heaped up together all the Sins of the Licentious sons of David, Adulteries, Murders, Conspiracies, Treasons, and Blasphemies against God'. See Neill 1935:212. In the marginalia noted at 43.7–9*n*, Darnley and Bothwell are cited, and **Sedition** is glossed: 'Dk of Norfolk', whose proposed marriage to Mary was part of a conspiracy against the Queen; see Guy 1988:273–75. **3 detect**: expose.

Stanza 50

4 guiltie: deserving. **5 let**: prevent, obstruct (*OED* v.[2]) in contrast to its meaning 'allow' in 6; noted Roche 1978. **8 purple pall**: robe of state. While in her private person Mercilla shares Arthur's pity for Duessa at 46.1–2, as Queen she shares Artegall's 'zeale of Iustice' (49.5). On the need of justice to uphold her authority, in Ireland especially, see Lim 1995:46–47. On the distinction between mercy or clemency and *misericordia* or vain pity, see Phillips 1970:114–16. The usual interval between a verdict and the sentencing, which is carried out at x 4, is marked by a gap of three stanzas, corresponding to Elizabeth's delay of three months before consenting to Mary's execution.

Cant. X.

Prince Arthur takes the enterprize
for Belge for to fight:
Gerioneos Seneschall
he slayes in Belges right.

1

SOme Clarkes doe doubt in their deuicefull art,
   Whether this heauenly thing, whereof I treat,
   To weeten *Mercie*, be of Iustice part,
   Or drawne forth from her by diuine extreate.
   This well I wote, that sure she is as great,
   And meriteth to haue as high a place,
   Sith in th'Almighties euerlasting seat
   She first was bred, and borne of heauenly race;
From thence pour'd down on men, by influence of grace.

2

For if that Vertue be of so great might,
   Which from iust verdict will for nothing start,
   But to preserue inuiolated right,
   Oft spilles the principall, to saue the part;
   So much more then is that of powre and art,
   That seekes to saue the subiect of her skill,
   Yet neuer doth from doome of right depart:
   As it is greater prayse to saue, then spill,
And better to reforme, then to cut off the ill.

3

Who then can thee, *Mercilla*, throughly prayse,
   That herein doest all earthly Princes pas?
   What heauenly Muse shall thy great honour rayse
   Vp to the skies, whence first deriu'd it was,

And now on earth it selfe enlarged has,
   From th'vtmost brinke of the *Armericke* shore,
   Vnto the margent of the *Molucas*?
   Those Nations farre thy iustice doe adore:
But thine owne people do thy mercy prayse much more.

4

Much more it praysed was of those two knights;
   The noble Prince, and righteous *Artegall*,
   When they had seene and heard her doome a rights
   Against *Duessa*, damned by them all;
   But by her tempred without griefe or gall,
   Till strong constraint did her thereto enforce.
   And yet euen then ruing her wilfull fall,
   With more then needfull naturall remorse,
And yeelding the last honour to her wretched corse.

5

During all which, those knights continu'd there,
   Both doing and receiuing curtesies,
   Of that great Ladie, who with goodly chere
   Them entertayn'd, fit for their dignities,
   Approuing dayly to their noble eyes
   Royall examples of her mercies rare,
   And worthie paterns of her clemencies;
   Which till this day mongst many liuing are,
Who them to their posterities doe still declare.

Book V Canto x

Stanza 1

1–6 That '*Mercilla* myld' (ix 49.9) should be judge in a trial
that imposes capital punishment on one for whom even Arthur
felt 'great ruth' (ix 46.6) requires some statement about
the relation of mercy to justice. S. evades it by relying on what
he just knows to be true: that mercy has a place as high as
justice. **Clarkes**: scholars. **deuicefull**: cunning. **extreate**:
extraction. **7–8** God's throne is his mercy-seat: Exod. 25.22;
cf. Isa. 16.5: 'And in mercie shal the throne be prepared,
and he shal sit vpon it in stedfastnes'. **9** As love which the
heavens 'pourd into men' (III iii 1.4). **influence**: infusion,
literally inflowing.

Stanza 2

2 start: swerve. **4** Justice may need to sacrifice the human
principall in order to save the written **part**, i.e. the virtue itself
as codified by law, so Nelson 1963:268 suggests. O'Connell
1977:204n27 responds that if S. means 'principle', he has
reversed what he means to say. Gallagher 1991:252 cites the
proverb, *summa ius, summa iniuria*. Yet the gist of S.'s claim

is clear: mercy need not depart **from doome of right** in seek-
ing to save rather than spill, or to reform rather than **to cut off**
(though that phrase jars with Duessa's head cut off at 4.6).

Stanza 3

6 Armericke: i.e. 'America' (as spelled at II x 72.6) rather
than 'Armorick', i.e. Britanny (as II x 64.5 and III iii 41.4).
The earlier spelling, 'Armerica', is noted in *Var* 5.248.
7 Molucas: the Moluccas or Spice Islands.

Stanza 4

3 a rights: indicating that they endorsed Mercilla's judgement.
5 griefe: anger. **6 thereto**: i.e. to chop off her head, though
that is deliberately not said, nor need it be. **7 wilfull**: the
term is chosen to blame Duessa alone for her fall.

Stanza 5

5 Approuing: showing for their approval.

Stanzas 6–xi 35

Of the three episodes that allude to Elizabeth's foreign policy
in the three concluding cantos of Bk V – the other two involve

6

Amongst the rest, which in that space befell,
There came two Springals of full tender yeares,
Farre thence from forrein land, where they did dwell,
To seeke for succour of her and of her Peares,
With humble prayers and intreatfull teares;
Sent by their mother, who a widow was,
Wrapt in great dolours and in deadly feares,
By a strong Tyrant, who inuaded has
Her land, and slaine her children ruefully alas.

7

Her name was *Belgae*, who in former age
A Ladie of great worth and wealth had beene,
And mother of a frutefull heritage,
Euen seuenteene goodly sonnes; which who had seene
In their first flowre, before this fatall teene
Them ouertooke, and their faire blossomes blasted,
More happie mother would her surely weene,
Then famous *Niobe*, before she tasted
Latonaes childrens wrath, that all her issue wasted.

8

But this fell Tyrant, through his tortious powre,
Had left her now but fiue of all that brood:
For twelue of them he did by times deuoure,
And to his Idols sacrifice their blood,

Whylest he of none was stopped, nor withstood.
For soothly he was one of matchlesse might,
Of horrible aspect, and dreadfull mood,
And had three bodies in one wast empight,
And th'armes and legs of three, to succour him in fight.

9

And sooth they say, that he was borne and bred
Of Gyants race, the sonne of *Geryon*,
He that whylome in Spaine so sore was dred,
For his huge powre and great oppression,
Which brought that land to his subiection,
Through his three bodies powre, in one combynd;
And eke all strangers in that region
Arryuing, to his kyne for food assynd;
The fayrest kyne aliue, but of the fiercest kynd.

10

For they were all, they say, of purple hew,
Kept by a cowheard, hight *Eurytion*,
A cruell carle, the which all strangers slew,
Ne day nor night did sleepe, t'attend them on,
But walkt about them euer and anone,
With his two headed dogge, that *Orthrus* hight;
Orthrus begotten by great *Typhaon*,
And foule *Echidna*, in the house of night;
But *Hercules* them all did ouercome in fight.

France and Ireland – that involving the Netherlands is the most extended, perhaps because it was the most controversial. In all three, S. violates his rule to choose his matter 'furthest from . . . suspition of present time' (*LR* 12). Its 69 stanzas divide roughly into three parts showing how Arthur defeats first Geryoneo's Seneschall, then Geryoneo himself, and finally the monster under his idol. Kouwenhoven 1986:160 notes that cantos x and xi devote the same number of stanzas to the story. In the historical allegory, Belge (Lat. *Belgae*) refers to the Low Countries as a whole, and her seventeen sons to the seventeen provinces, twelve of which were ruled by Philip II of Spain who appears as Geryoneo. In 1585, the remaining five led by delegates from Holland and Zeeland – the 'two Springals' at 6.2 – signed the Treaty of Nonsuch with England. (A contemporary picture of this moment is reproduced in Morrill 1996:237.) England's intervention was justified because a foreign conqueror who ruled as a tyrant could be opposed by a foreign prince though not by his own subjects. In 1585, Elizabeth sent Leicester with an army to the Low Countries, thereby fulfilling Merlin's prophecy of the time when 'a royall Virgin . . . shall | Stretch her white rod ouer the *Belgicke* shore' (III iii 49.6–7). Early marginalia identified Arthur as both Leicester and Essex; see A. Fowler 1961c:417, and Kouwenhoven 152–55. The historical facts, which relate topically to the power of Spain and the Catholic Church in the Low Countries, are either misrepresented or exaggerated; see A.B. Gough 1921, Norbrook 1984:132–36, and 'Belge' in the *SEnc*. Their apocalyptic dimension is noted by Borris 1991:11–61 in arguing that the allegory is prophetic rather than simply topical. See also Mallette 1997:160–62. As an idealized account, see Gregory 2000:366–72.

Stanza 6

2 Springals: youths. 4 Peares: the nobility. 5 intreatfull: full of entreaty. 6 a widow: such naming of a desolate city – here a country – is biblical, e.g. Lam. 1.1. On aid owing a widow, see I x 43.2–3n. 8 Tyrant: a title that Geryoneo shares in Bk V with Grantorto. 9 ruefully: in a pitiable fashion.

Stanza 7

5 teene: harm, affliction. 7–9 For the story of Niobe, see IV vii 30.5–9. Belge is More happie because she has seventeen sons against Niobe's seven sons and seven daughters.

Stanza 8

1 tortious: wrongful. 3 by times: from time to time. 4 Idols: 'Idol', conj. Church 1758, to agree with 13.8, etc. 8–9 The Tyrant has the three bodies of his father Geryon, here representing (by one interpretation) Spain, Portugal, and the Low Countries, but chiefly Spain or the papacy. empight: implanted.

Stanzas 9–11

Most of the details are taken from Conti 1616:7.1, as Lotspeich 1932 notes. S. may have known that 'Geryon' is the guardian of the fraudulent in Dante, *Inf.* 17. His three bodies symbolize concord, which he parodies; see Aptekar 1969:146–49, and Hardin 1992:112–13. On 'Typhaon' and 'Echidna', see VI vi 10–12n.

Stanza 10

1 purple: crimson, the royal colour, as they belong to the King.

11

His sonne was this, *Geryoneo* hight,
　　Who after that his monstrous father fell
　　Vnder *Alcides* club, streight tooke his flight
　　From that sad land, where he his syre did quell,
　　And came to this, where *Belge* then did dwell,
　　And flourish in all wealth and happinesse,
　　Being then new made widow (as befell)
　　After her Noble husbands late decesse;
Which gaue beginning to her woe and wretchednesse.

12

Then this bold Tyrant, of her widowhed
　　Taking aduantage, and her yet fresh woes,
　　Himselfe and seruice to her offered,
　　Her to defend against all forrein foes,
　　That should their powre against her right oppose.
　　Whereof she glad, now needing strong defence,
　　Him entertayn'd, and did her champion chose:
　　Which long he vsd with carefull diligence,
The better to confirme her fearelesse confidence.

13

By meanes whereof, she did at last commit
　　All to his hands, and gaue him soueraine powre
　　To doe, what euer he thought good or fit.
　　Which hauing got, he gan forth from that howre
　　To stirre vp strife, and many a Tragicke stowre,
　　Giuing her dearest children one by one
　　Vnto a dreadfull Monster to deuoure,
　　And setting vp an Idole of his owne,
The image of his monstrous parent *Geryone*.

14

So tyrannizing, and oppressing all,
　　The woefull widow had no meanes now left,
　　But vnto gratious great *Mercilla* call
　　For ayde, against that cruell Tyrants theft,
　　Ere all her children he from her had reft.
　　Therefore these two, her eldest sonnes she sent,
　　To seeke for succour of this Ladies gieft:
　　To whom their sute they humbly did present,
In th'hearing of full many Knights and Ladies gent.

15

Amongst the which then fortuned to bee
　　The noble Briton Prince, with his braue Peare;
　　Who when he none of all those knights did see
　　Hastily bent, that enterprise to heare,
　　Nor vndertake the same, for cowheard feare,
　　He stepped forth with courage bold and great,
　　Admyr'd of all the rest in presence there,
　　And humbly gan that mightie Queene entreat,
To graunt him that aduenture for his former feat.

16

She gladly graunted it: then he straight way
　　Himselfe vnto his iourney gan prepare,
　　And all his armours readie dight that day,
　　That nought the morrow next mote stay his fare.
　　The morrow next appear'd, with purple hayre
　　Yet dropping fresh out of the *Indian* fount,
　　And bringing light into the heauens fayre,
　　When he was readie to his steede to mount,
Vnto his way, which now was all his care and count.

17

Then taking humble leaue of that great Queene,
　　Who gaue him roiall giftes and riches rare,
　　As tokens of her thankefull mind beseene,
　　And leauing *Artegall* to his owne care,
　　Vpon his voyage forth he gan to fare,
　　With those two gentle youthes, which him did guide,
　　And all his way before him still prepare.
　　Ne after him did *Artegall* abide,
But on his first aduenture forward forth did ride.

18

It was not long, till that the Prince arriued
　　Within the land, where dwelt that Ladie sad,
　　Whereof that Tyrant had her now depriued,
　　And into moores and marshes banisht had,
　　Out of the pleasant soyle, and citties glad,
　　In which she wont to harbour happily:
　　But now his cruelty so sore she drad,
　　That to those fennes for fastnesse she did fly,
And there her selfe did hyde from his hard tyranny.

Stanza 11
1 this: i.e. 'this fell Tyrant' (8.1). **Geryoneo** suggests 'Geryon-anew'. See 'Geryoneo' in the *SEnc*. **6 wealth**: well-being. **8 decesse**: decease. Perhaps alluding to the assassination of William the Silent, Prince of Orange, in 1584, which resulted in Spanish rule.

Stanza 13
5 stowre: time of distress.

Stanza 14
7 gieft: gift; giving. **9 gent**: high-born, gracious.

Stanza 15
2 Peare: companion; equal; see i 3*n*. **5 Their cowheard feare**, which contradicts Samient's praise of them at viii 18.6–7, may be intended to single out Leicester who died in

1588. **9** I.e. as a reward for defeating the Souldan (unless **former** means 'first').

Stanza 16
4 fare: going. **5–7** An elegant variation of Aurora spreading 'her purple robe' (I ii 7.3), or 'her purple pall' (iv 16.4), when rising out of the sea. It heralds the new morning at 20.8–9. **9 count**: consideration.

Stanza 17
3 beseene: provided; perhaps simply, 'to be seen'.

Stanza 18
8 fastnesse: security from invasion. **fly**: as the mother, in Rev. 12.14, persecuted by the serpent was given eagle's wings to fly into the wilderness; noted Borris 1991:13.

19

There he her found in sorrow and dismay,
   All solitarie without liuing wight;
   For all her other children, through affray,
   Had hid themselues, or taken further flight:
   And eke her selfe through sudden strange affright,
   When one in armes she saw, began to fly;
   But when her owne two sonnes she had in sight,
   She gan take hart, and looke vp ioyfully:
For well she wist this knight came, succour to supply.

20

And running vnto them with greedy ioyes,
   Fell straight about their neckes, as they did kneele,
   And bursting forth in teares; Ah my sweet boyes,
   (Sayd she) yet now I gin new life to feele,
   And feeble spirits, that gan faint and reele,
   Now rise againe, at this your ioyous sight.
   Alreadie seemes that fortunes headlong wheele
   Begins to turne, and sunne to shine more bright,
Then it was wont, through comfort of this noble knight.

21

Then turning vnto him; And you Sir knight
   (Said she) that taken haue this toylesome paine
   For wretched woman, miserable wight,
   May you in heauen immortall guerdon gaine
   For so great trauell, as you doe sustaine:
   For other meede may hope for none of mee,
   To whom nought else, but bare life doth remaine,
   And that so wretched one, as ye do see
Is liker lingring death, then loathed life to bee.

22

Much was he moued with her piteous plight,
   And low dismounting from his loftie steede,
   Gan to recomfort her all that he might,
   Seeking to driue away deepe rooted dreede,

With hope of helpe in that her greatest neede.
   So thence he wished her with him to wend,
   Vnto some place, where they mote rest and feede,
   And she take comfort, which God now did send:
Good hart in euils doth the euils much amend.

23

Ay me (sayd she) and whether shall I goe?
   Are not all places full of forraine powres?
   My pallaces possessed of my foe,
   My cities sackt, and their sky-threating towres
   Raced, and made smooth fields now full of flowres?
   Onely these marishes, and myrie bogs,
   In which the fearefull ewftes do build their bowres,
   Yeeld me an hostry mongst the croking frogs,
And harbour here in safety from those rauenous dogs.

24

Nathlesse (said he) deare Ladie with me goe,
   Some place shall vs receiue, and harbour yield;
   If not, we will it force, maugre your foe,
   And purchase it to vs with speare and shield:
   And if all fayle, yet farewell open field:
   The earth to all her creatures lodging lends.
   With such his chearefull speaches he doth wield
   Her mind so well, that to his will she bends
And bynding vp her locks and weeds, forth with him wends.

25

They came vnto a Citie farre vp land,
   The which whylome that Ladies owne had bene;
   But now by force extort out of her hand,
   By her strong foe, who had defaced cleene
   Her stately towres, and buildings sunny sheene;
   Shut vp her hauen, mard her marchants trade,
   Robbed her people, that full rich had beene,
   And in her necke a Castle huge had made,
The which did her commaund, without needing perswade.

Stanza 19
3 **affray**: terror.

Stanza 21
5 **trauell**: travail. 6 For other reward none may hope from me.

Stanza 22
3–5 Alluding to the Low Countries's deep suspicion of England's offered help. **recomfort**: console.

Stanza 23
5 **Raced**: razed. 6 **marishes**: marshes. 7 **ewftes**: efts or newts. 8 **hostry**: lodging.

Stanza 24
4 **purchase**: gain by conquest. 5–6 I.e. And if all military action fails, we may fare well in some unconquered place other

than the 'myrie bogs' (23.6), being assured that the earth gives lodging to everyone. (I owe this reading to Michael West.) Or **farewell** = 'welcome'; sugg. in Spenser 1912:652. A distinction is implied between **earth** and bogs, which provide no lodging, as S. knew well from living in Ireland. 7 **wield**: direct, sway.

Stanza 25
The **Citie** is Antwerp, which lies about 80 km from the mouth of the Scheldt. Before it was sacked by the Spanish in 1585, it was the wealthiest city in Europe and London's chief trading partner. Its prototype is the fallen Babylon in Rev. 18.10–19; see Borris 1991:15–18. The **Castle huge** refers to the citadel built on the river in 1567 by the Duke of Alva to keep the city in subjection. Merlin's prophecy, at III iii 49.8–9, that Elizabeth will cause its fall was not fulfilled: Leicester captured only the Veluwe fort near Zutphen. 3 **extort**: extorted, literally 'twisted out'. 8 **in her necke**: the traditional posture of conquest.

26

That Castle was the strength of all that state,
Vntill that state by strength was pulled downe,
And that same citie, so now ruinate,
Had bene the keye of all that kingdomes crowne;
Both goodly Castle, and both goodly Towne,
Till that th'offended heauens list to lowre
Vpon their blisse, and balefull fortune frowne.
When those gainst states and kingdomes do coniure,
Who then can thinke their hedlong ruine to recure.

27

But he had brought it now in seruile bond,
And made it beare the yoke of inquisition,
Stryuing long time in vaine it to withstond;
Yet glad at last to make most base submission,
And life enioy for any composition.
So now he hath new lawes and orders new
Imposd on it, with many a hard condition,
And forced it, the honour that is dew
To God, to doe vnto his Idole most vntrew.

28

To him he hath, before this Castle greene,
Built a faire Chappell, and an Altar framed
Of costly Iuory, full rich beseene,
On which that cursed Idole farre proclamed,
He hath set vp, and him his God hath named,
Offring to him in sinfull sacrifice
The flesh of men, to Gods owne likenesse framed,
And powring forth their bloud in brutishe wize,
That any yron eyes, to see it would agrize.

29

And for more horror and more crueltie,
Vnder that cursed Idols altar stone;
An hideous monster doth in darknesse lie,
Whose dreadfull shape was neuer seene of none
That liues on earth; but vnto those alone
The which vnto him sacrificed bee.
Those he deuoures, they say, both flesh and bone:
What else they haue, is all the Tyrants fee;
So that no whit of them remayning one may see.

30

There eke he placed a strong garrisone,
And set a Seneschall of dreaded might,
That by his powre oppressed euery one,
And vanquished all ventrous knights in fight;
To whom he wont shew all the shame he might,
After that them in battell he had wonne.
To which when now they gan approch in sight,
The Ladie counseld him the place to shonne,
Whereas so many knights had fouly bene fordonne.

31

Her fearefull speaches nought he did regard,
But ryding streight vnder the Castle wall,
Called aloud vnto the watchfull ward,
Which there did wayte, willing them forth to call
Into the field their Tyrants Seneschall.
To whom when tydings thereof came, he streight
Cals for his armes, and arming him withall,
Eftsoones forth pricked proudly in his might,
And gan with courage fierce addresse him to the fight.

32

They both encounter in the middle plaine,
And their sharpe speares doe both together smite
Amid their shields, with so huge might and maine,
That seem'd their soules they wold haue ryuen quight
Out of their breasts, with furious despight.
Yet could the Seneschals no entrance find
Into the Princes shield, where it empight;
So pure the mettall was, and well refynd,
But shiuered all about, and scattered in the wynd.

33

Not so the Princes, but with restlesse force,
Into his shield it readie passage found,
Both through his haberieon, and eke his corse:
Which tombling downe vpon the senselesse ground,
Gaue leaue vnto his ghost from thraldome bound,
To wander in the griesly shades of night.
There did the Prince him leaue in deadly swound,
And thence vnto the castle marched right,
To see if entrance there as yet obtaine he might.

Stanza 26
1 state: the three uses of the term in this stanza – the only use in the poem for a country – may reflect disapproval of its republicanism in its lack of a central monarchy; but see Hadfield 1998b. **3 ruinate**: reduced to ruins. **4 crowne**: dominion. **8 coniure**: conspire. **9 recure**: remedy; i.e. prevent.

Stanza 27
2 inquisition: specifically, the Papal Inquisition, which in 1568 condemned almost all the inhabitants to death. **5 composition**: agreement; specifically, terms of surrender, such as the Union of Brussels in 1577, which pledged support for the Church of Rome.

Stanza 28
2–5 The **Chappell** with its **Altar** and **Idole** refer to Roman Catholic worship imposed on the Low Countries; see xi

19–20*n*. **6–9** Alluding to the public burning of heretics. **agrize**: horrify.

Stanza 29
8 fee: property.

Stanza 30
2 Seneschall: a steward who administers justice; here the Spanish-appointed Regent of the Netherlands, either the Duke of Alva or the Prince of Parma. **6 wonne**: defeated. **9 fordonne**: ruined; killed.

Stanza 32
7–8 the Princes shield: called 'th'Adamantine shield' at xi 10.7 (see I vii 33.5–9), referring to the Protestant faith, as the Seneschall's shield refers to the Roman Catholic faith. The conflict of the two faiths results in thirteen uses of the word in canto xi. **where it empight**: where it might infix itself.

34

But as he nigher drew, three knights he spyde,
 All arm'd to point, issuing forth a pace,
 Which towards him with all their powre did ryde,
 And meeting him right in the middle race,
 Did all their speares attonce on him enchace.
 As three great Culuerings for battrie bent,
 And leueld all against one certaine place,
 Doe all attonce their thunders rage forth rent,
That makes the wals to stagger with astonishment.

35

So all attonce they on the Prince did thonder;
 Who from his saddle swarued nought asyde,
 Ne to their force gaue way, that was great wonder,
 But like a bulwarke, firmely did abyde,
 Rebutting him, which in the midst did ryde,
 With so huge rigour, that his mortall speare
 Past through his shield, and pierst through either syde,
 That downe he fell vppon his mother deare,
And powred forth his wretched life in deadly dreare.

36

Whom when his other fellowes saw, they fled
 As fast as feete could carry them away;
 And after them the Prince as swiftly sped,
 To be aueng'd of their vnknightly play.
 There whilest they entring, th'one did th'other stay,
 The hindmost in the gate he ouerhent,
 And as he pressed in, him there did slay:
 His carkasse tumbling on the threshold, sent
His groning soule vnto her place of punishment.

37

The other which was entred, laboured fast
 To sperre the gate; but that same lumpe of clay,
 Whose grudging ghost was thereout fled and past,
 Right in the middest of the threshold lay,
 That it the Posterne did from closing stay:
 The whiles the Prince hard preased in betweene,
 And entraunce wonne. Streight th'other fled away,
 And ran into the Hall, where he did weene
Him selfe to saue: but he there slew him at the skreene.

38

Then all the rest which in that Castle were,
 Seeing that sad ensample them before,
 Durst not abide, but fled away for feare,
 And them conuayd out at a Posterne dore.
 Long sought the Prince, but when he found no more
 T'oppose against his powre, he forth issued
 Vnto that Lady, where he her had lore,
 And her gan cheare, with what she there had vewed,
And what she had not seene, within vnto her shewed.

39

Who with right humble thankes him goodly greeting,
 For so great prowesse, as he there had proued,
 Much greater then was euer in her weeting,
 With great admiraunce inwardly was moued,
 And honourd him, with all that her behoued.
 Thenceforth into that Castle he her led,
 With her two sonnes, right deare of her beloued,
 Where all that night them selues they cherished,
And from her balefull minde all care he banished.

Stanza 33
1 restlesse: not resting, never ceasing; hence resistless. **4** . . . senseless upon the ground.

Stanza 34
1–5 If they, rather than the Seneschall, are Geryoneo's 'Champion' at xi 2.3, they unfold his 'three bodies in one' (8.8). They strike **attonce** (thrice repeated), i.e. as one. **to point**: completely. **a pace**: apace, quickly. **in the middle race**: at the midpoint of their chivalric course, as 32.1. **enchace**: enclose; or figuratively, 'set'. **6 Culuerings**: the culverin, a long cannon. **8 rent**: burst; describing also the effect of the shot.

Stanza 35
6 rigour: violence; referring also to his spear's stiffness. **7 either syde**: i.e. from one side of his body to the other. **9 deadly dreare**: the sorrow and horror of death.

Stanza 36
4 vnknightly: because all three attacked at once, and without the required challenge. **6 ouerhent**: overtook.

Stanza 37
2 sperre: bolt. **3 grudging**: complaining.

Stanza 38
7 lore: left.

Stanza 39
1 greeting: congratulating. **3 weeting**: knowledge. **4 admiraunce**: admiration. **8 cherished**: cheered. **9 balefull**: sorrowful.

Cant. XI.

Prince Arthure ouercomes the great
Gerioneo in fight:
Doth slay the Monster, and restore
Belge vnto her right.

1

I T often fals in course of common life,
   That right long time is ouerborne of wrong,
      Through auarice, or powre, or guile, or strife,
      That weakens her, and makes her party strong:
      But Iustice, though her dome she doe prolong,
      Yet at the last she will her owne cause right.
      As by sad *Belge* seemes, whose wrongs though long
      She suffred, yet at length she did requight,
And sent redresse thereof by this braue Briton Knight.

2

Whereof when newes was to that Tyrant brought,
   How that the Lady *Belge* now had found
      A Champion, that had with his Champion fought,
      And laid his Seneschall low on the ground,
      And eke him selfe did threaten to confound,
      He gan to burne in rage, and friese in feare,
      Doubting sad end of principle vnsound:
      Yet sith he heard but one, that did appeare,
He did him selfe encourage, and take better cheare.

3

Nathelesse him selfe he armed all in hast,
   And forth he far'd with all his many bad,
      Ne stayed step, till that he came at last
      Vnto the Castle, which they conquerd had.
      There with huge terrour, to be more ydrad,
      He sternely marcht before the Castle gate,
      And with bold vaunts, and ydle threatning bad
      Deliuer him his owne, ere yet too late,
To which they had no right, nor any wrongfull state.

4

The Prince staid not his aunswere to deuize,
   But opening streight the Sparre, forth to him came,
      Full nobly mounted in right warlike wize;
      And asked him, if that he were the same,
      Who all that wrong vnto that wofull Dame
      So long had done, and from her natiue land
      Exiled her, that all the world spake shame.
      He boldly aunswerd him, he there did stand
That would his doings iustifie with his owne hand.

5

With that so furiously at him he flew,
   As if he would haue ouerrun him streight,
      And with his huge great yron axe gan hew
      So hideously vppon his armour bright,
      As he to peeces would haue chopt it quight:
      That the bold Prince was forced foote to giue
      To his first rage, and yeeld to his despight;
      The whilest at him so dreadfully he driue,
That seem'd a marble rocke asunder could haue riue.

6

Thereto a great aduauntage eke he has
   Through his three double hands thrise multiplyde,
      Besides the double strength, which in them was:
      For stil when fit occasion did betyde,
      He could his weapon shift from side to syde,
      From hand to hand, and with such nimblesse sly
      Could wield about, that ere it were espide,
      The wicked stroke did wound his enemy,
Behinde, beside, before, as he it list apply.

Book V Canto xi

Argument

The Burbon episode, 43.6–65, is summarized in xii Arg.1–2. It may have been taken from there and inserted here after Bk V had been disposed into cantos. F.B. Evans 1965 cites bibliographical evidence which suggests that Artegall's meeting with Sergis (36–43.1–5) was inserted after some of the copy, originally intended at this point, had been set in type. For further speculation, see *Var* 5.372.

Stanza 1
4 her party: i.e. the party opposing her.   **5 prolong**: delay. **9 redresse**: aid.

Stanza 2
7 Doubting: fearing.   **principle vnsound**: evil beginning.

Stanza 3
2 many: company.   **9** . . . nor any title or claim except a wrong one.

Stanza 4
2 Sparre: bolt.

Stanza 5
2 ouerrun: trampled down.   **8–9 driue**: either 'drives' or the earlier form, 'drove'.   **riue**: riven.

Stanza 6
2 In having 'th'armes . . . of three' (x 8.9), he has **three double hands**; in having them **thrise multiplyde**, he has eighteen.   **6 nimblesse**: nimbleness.   **9** Geryoneo can literally surround his enemy.

7

Which vncouth vse when as the Prince perceiued,
  He gan to watch the wielding of his hand,
  Least by such slight he were vnwares deceiued;
  And euer ere he saw the stroke to land,
  He would it meete, and warily withstand.
  One time, when he his weapon faynd to shift,
  As he was wont, and chang'd from hand to hand,
  He met him with a counterstroke so swift,
That quite smit off his arme, as he it vp did lift.

8

Therewith, all fraught with fury and disdaine,
  He brayd aloud for very fell despight,
  And sodainely t'auenge him selfe againe,
  Gan into one assemble all the might
  Of all his hands, and heaued them on hight,
  Thinking to pay him with that one for all:
  But the sad steele seizd not, where it was hight,
  Vppon the childe, but somewhat short did fall,
And lighting on his horses head, him quite did mall.

9

Downe streight to ground fell his astonisht steed,
  And eke to th'earth his burden with him bare:
  But he him selfe full lightly from him freed,
  And gan him selfe to fight on foote prepare.
  Whereof when as the Gyant was aware,
  He wox right blyth, as he had got thereby,
  And laught so loud, that all his teeth wide bare
  One might haue seene enraung'd disorderly,
Like to a rancke of piles, that pitched are awry.

10

Eftsoones againe his axe he raught on hie,
  Ere he were throughly buckled to his geare,
  And can let driue at him so dreadfullie,
  That had he chaunced not his shield to reare,
  Ere that huge stroke arriued on him neare,
  He had him surely clouen quite in twaine.
  But th'Adamantine shield, which he did beare,
  So well was tempred, that for all his maine,
It would no passage yeeld vnto his purpose vaine.

11

Yet was the stroke so forcibly applide,
  That made him stagger with vncertaine sway,
  As if he would haue tottered to one side.
  Wherewith full wroth, he fiercely gan assay,
  That curt'sie with like kindnesse to repay;
  And smote at him with so importune might,
  That two more of his armes did fall away,
  Like fruitlesse braunches, which the hatchets slight
Hath pruned from the natiue tree, and cropped quight.

12

With that all mad and furious he grew,
  Like a fell mastiffe through enraging heat,
  And curst, and band, and blasphemies forth threw,
  Against his Gods, and fire to them did threat,
  And hell vnto him selfe with horrour great.
  Thenceforth he car'd no more, which way he strooke,
  Nor where it light, but gan to chaufe and sweat,
  And gnasht his teeth, and his head at him shooke,
And sternely him beheld with grim and ghastly looke.

13

Nought fear'd the childe his lookes, ne yet his threats,
  But onely wexed now the more aware,
  To saue him selfe from those his furious heats,
  And watch aduauntage, how to worke his care:
  The which good Fortune to him offred faire.
  For as he in his rage him ouerstrooke,
  He ere he could his weapon backe repaire,
  His side all bare and naked ouertooke,
And with his mortal steel quite throgh the body strooke.

14

Through all three bodies he him strooke attonce;
  That all the three attonce fell on the plaine:
  Else should he thrise haue needed, for the nonce
  Them to haue stricken, and thrise to haue slaine.
  So now all three one sencelesse lumpe remaine,
  Enwallow'd in his owne blacke bloudy gore,
  And byting th'earth for very deaths disdaine;
  Who with a cloud of night him couering, bore
Downe to the house of dole, his daies there to deplore.

Stanza 7

1 vncouth: strange. **6 faynd**: sought; desired.

Stanza 8

5 on hight: on high. **7 sad**: heavy. **hight**: directed. **8 childe**: as Arthur's title, see IV viii 44.8*n*. **9 mall**: knock down.

Stanza 9

1 astonisht: stunned. **6 got**: profited; gained the victory.

Stanza 10

2 Before he could properly prepare his armour 'to fight on foote' (9.4). **3 can**: began to. **7–9** As it resisted the Seneschall's spear at x 32.7–9. **maine**: strength.

Stanza 11

5 kindnesse: suggesting a stroke of like kind. **6 importune**: grievous; heavy. **8** . . . which a skilful stroke by a hatchet.

Stanza 12

1–2 He rages like a rabid dog, as did Adicia at viii 49.1–5. **3–4** He swears as did the Souldan at viii 28.2; and also curses his own gods as does Pollente at ii 18.7–9, and the monster at 20.6–9 and 28.1–5. Blasphemy is a dominant motif in this episode, which Borris 1991:12 links to the apocalyptic beast out of the sea upon whose seven heads (identified by the Geneva gloss as Rome) is written 'the name of blasphemie' (Rev.13.1). **7 it**: his blow.

Stanza 13

4 worke his care: cause him trouble. **6 ouerstrooke**: struck too far. **7 repaire**: draw. **8 ouertooke**: reached with a blow.

Stanza 14

3 for the nonce: for the purpose (of slaying him). **6 Enwallow'd**: lying prostrate. **7** See ii 18.6*n*. **9 dole**: pain, suffering.

15

Which when the Lady from the Castle saw,
    Where she with her two sonnes did looking stand,
    She towards him in hast her selfe did draw,
    To greet him the good fortune of his hand:
    And all the people both of towne and land,
    Which there stood gazing from the Cities wall
    Vppon these warriours, greedy t'vnderstand,
    To whether should the victory befall,
Now when they saw it falne, they eke him greeted all.

16

But *Belge* with her sonnes prostrated low
    Before his feete, in all that peoples sight,
    Mongst ioyes mixing some tears, mongst wele, some wo,
    Him thus bespake; O most redoubted Knight,
    The which hast me, of all most wretched wight,
    That earst was dead, restor'd to life againe,
    And these weake impes replanted by thy might;
    What guerdon can I giue thee for thy paine,
But euen that which thou sauedst, thine still to remaine?

17

He tooke her vp forby the lilly hand,
    And her recomforted the best he might,
    Saying; Deare Lady, deedes ought not be scand
    By th'authors manhood, nor the doers might,
    But by their trueth and by the causes right:
    That same is it, which fought for you this day.
    What other meed then need me to requight,
    But that which yeeldeth vertues meed alway?
That is the vertue selfe, which her reward doth pay.

18

She humbly thankt him for that wondrous grace,
    And further sayd; Ah Sir, but mote ye please,
    Sith ye thus farre haue tendred my poore case,
    As from my chiefest foe me to release,

That your victorious arme will not yet cease,
    Till ye haue rooted all the relickes out
    Of that vilde race, and stablished my peace.
    What is there else (sayd he) left of their rout?
Declare it boldly Dame, and doe not stand in dout.

19

Then wote you, Sir, that in this Church hereby,
    There stands an Idole of great note and name,
    The which this Gyant reared first on hie,
    And of his owne vaine fancies thought did frame:
    To whom for endlesse horrour of his shame,
    He offred vp for daily sacrifize
    My children and my people, burnt in flame;
    With all the tortures, that he could deuize,
The more t'aggrate his God with such his blouddy guize.

20

And vnderneath this Idoll there doth lie
    An hideous monster, that doth it defend,
    And feedes on all the carkasses, that die
    In sacrifize vnto that cursed feend:
    Whose vgly shape none euer saw, nor kend,
    That euer scap'd: for of a man they say
    It has the voice, that speaches forth doth send,
    Euen blasphemous words, which she doth bray
Out of her poysnous entrails, fraught with dire decay.

21

Which when the Prince heard tell, his heart gan earne
    For great desire, that Monster to assay,
    And prayd the place of her abode to learne.
    Which being shew'd, he gan him selfe streight way
    Thereto addresse, and his bright shield display.
    So to the Church he came, where it was told,
    The Monster vnderneath the Altar lay;
    There he that Idoll saw of massy gold
Most richly made, but there no Monster did behold.

Stanza 15

4 greet: offer congratulations on. **8 whether**: which.

Stanza 16

7 impes: offshoots; scions or descendants. **9** In the political allegory, she offers Leicester sovereignty of the Low Countries, which Elizabeth had refused in 1584, and was outraged when he accepted it in 1586.

Stanza 17

1 forby: by. **3–5** I.e. individuals should be judged (**scand**) by the truth of the causes they undertake, and their actions by their rightness. Cf. viii 30.9. **6 That same**: i.e. truth and right. **9** Proverbial: Smith 818.

Stanza 18

3 tendred: taken care of. **6 relickes**: alluding to objects of Roman Catholic worship. **9 dout**: fear.

Stanzas 19–20

Geryoneo's sacrificial idol on its altar is described at x 8.4 and 28–29 as a Saturn figure, but here under the altar there is a flesh-devouring and fire-consuming monster, such as the sacrificial fire before Molech at 2 Kings 23.10. The Geneva gloss to Lev. 18.21 explains that Molech is 'an idole of the Ammonites, vnto whome they burned and sacrificed their children'. Cf. the altar in Orgoglio's castle at I viii 36 under which slain Christian martyrs cry for justice. The image is biblical: 'all ye workers of iniquitie . . . eat vp my people' (Ps. 14.4). The topical reference is to the martyrs burned alive by the Duke of Alva's Council of Blood.

Stanza 19

4 At x 13.9, Geryoneo's **Idole** is called 'The image of his monstrous parent *Geryone*'; now it is called a god fashioned by his own fancy in his own image, in line with Edward VI's injunction against images 'devysed by mennes phantasies'. On the injunction, see King 1990a:78 and Kaske 1994:24. **9 aggrate**: gratify. **guize**: custom.

Stanza 20

9 decay: ruin, death.

22

Vpon the Image with his naked blade
　　Three times, as in defiance, there he strooke;
　　And the third time out of an hidden shade,
　　There forth issewd, from vnder th'Altars smooke,
　　A dreadfull feend, with fowle deformed looke,
　　That stretcht it selfe, as it had long lyen still;
　　And her long taile and fethers strongly shooke,
　　That all the Temple did with terrour fill;
Yet him nought terrifide, that feared nothing ill.

23

An huge great Beast it was, when it in length
　　Was stretched forth, that nigh fild all the place,
　　And seem'd to be of infinite great strength;
　　Horrible, hideous, and of hellish race,
　　Borne of the brooding of *Echidna* base,
　　Or other like infernall furies kinde:
　　For of a Mayd she had the outward face,
　　To hide the horrour, which did lurke behinde,
The better to beguile, whom she so fond did finde.

24

Thereto the body of a dog she had,
　　Full of fell rauin and fierce greedinesse;
　　A Lions clawes, with powre and rigour clad,
　　To rend and teare, what so she can oppresse;
　　A Dragons taile, whose sting without redresse
　　Full deadly wounds, where so it is empight;
　　And Eagles wings, for scope and speedinesse,
　　That nothing may escape her reaching might,
Whereto she euer list to make her hardy flight.

25

Much like in foulnesse and deformity
　　Vnto that Monster, whom the Theban Knight,
　　The father of that fatall progeny,
　　Made kill her selfe for very hearts despight,

That he had red her Riddle, which no wight
　　Could euer loose, but suffred deadly doole.
　　So also did this Monster vse like slight
　　To many a one, which came vnto her schoole,
Whom she did put to death, deceiued like a foole.

26

She comming forth, when as she first beheld
　　The armed Prince, with shield so blazing bright,
　　Her ready to assaile, was greatly queld,
　　And much dismayd with that dismayfull sight,
　　That backe she would haue turnd for great affright.
　　But he gan her with courage fierce assay,
　　That forst her turne againe in her despight,
　　To saue her selfe, least that he did her slay:
And sure he had her slaine, had she not turnd her way.

27

Tho when she saw, that she was forst to fight,
　　She flew at him, like to an hellish feend,
　　And on his shield tooke hold with all her might,
　　As if that it she would in peeces rend,
　　Or reaue out of the hand, that did it hend.
　　Strongly he stroue out of her greedy gripe
　　To loose his shield, and long while did contend:
　　But when he could not quite it, with one stripe
Her Lions clawes he from her feete away did wipe.

28

With that aloude she gan to bray and yell,
　　And fowle blasphemous speaches forth did cast,
　　And bitter curses, horrible to tell,
　　That euen the Temple, wherein she was plast,
　　Did quake to heare, and nigh asunder brast.
　　Tho with her huge long taile she at him strooke,
　　That made him stagger, and stand halfe agast
　　With trembling ioynts, as he for terrour shooke;
Who nought was terrifide, but greater courage tooke.

Stanza 21

1 earne: yearn.　**2 assay**: attack.　**5** For the first time Arthur's shield is unveiled from the beginning of a battle; see viii 37.6–9*n*. Cf. 26.2.

Stanza 22

7 As the dragon at I xi 9.5–7, his 'aery plumes doth rouze'.

Stanzas 23–25

Geryoneo's monster corresponds to Geryon's Orthrus at x 10.7–8 and resembles its mother, Echidna – see VI vi 10 – who was interpreted as learned error; see Steadman 1979:160–63. Lotspeich 1932 compares the Sphinx in Conti 1616:9.18, a beast described by T. Cooper 1565 as 'a monster which had the head and handes of a mayden, the bodie of a dogge, wynges lyke a byrde, nayles like a lyon, a tayle like a dragon, the voyce of a man'. S. also draws on his description of Errour at I i 14, error now being religious heresies investigated by the Spanish Inquisition.

Stanza 23

9 fond: foolish.

Stanza 24

4 oppresse: take by surprise; overwhelm.　**6 empight**: implanted.

Stanza 25

2–3 the Theban Knight is Oedipus; his **fatall progeny** inherited the curse against the house of Laius.　**6 loose**: undo. By solving the Sphinx's **Riddle**, Oedipus freed the Thebans from being strangled by her for not knowing the answer.　**deadly doole**: the pain (Lat. *dolor*) of death.　**8 her schoole**: referring to the Inquisitors to whom a false answer meant death.

Stanzas 26–35

S. recycles many details from his account of the Red Cross Knight's battle against Errour in I i, and against the dragon in xi followed by the victory celebration in xii.

Stanza 27

5 hend: hold.　**8 quite**: quit, free.　**stripe**: stroke.　**9 wipe**: cut off.

29

As when the Mast of some well timbred hulke
   Is with the blast of some outragious storme
   Blowne downe, it shakes the bottome of the bulke,
   And makes her ribs to cracke, as they were torne,
   Whilest still she stands as stonisht and forlorne:
   So was he stound with stroke of her huge taile.
   But ere that it she backe againe had borne,
   He with his sword it strooke, that without faile
He ioynted it, and mard the swinging of her flaile.

30

Then gan she cry much louder then afore,
   That all the people there without it heard,
   And *Belge* selfe was therewith stonied sore,
   As if the onely sound thereof she feard.
   But then the feend her selfe more fiercely reard
   Vppon her wide great wings, and strongly flew
   With all her body at his head and beard,
   That had he not foreseene with heedfull vew,
And thrown his shield atween, she had him done to rew.

31

But as she prest on him with heauy sway,
   Vnder her wombe his fatall sword he thrust,
   And for her entrailes made an open way,
   To issue forth; the which once being brust,
   Like to a great Mill damb forth fiercely gusht,
   And powred out of her infernall sinke
   Most vgly filth, and poyson therewith rusht,
   That him nigh choked with the deadly stinke:
Such loathly matter were small lust to speake, or thinke.

32

Then downe to ground fell that deformed Masse,
   Breathing out clouds of sulphure fowle and blacke,
   In which a puddle of contagion was,
   More loathd then *Lerna*, or then *Stygian* lake,

That any man would nigh awhaped make.
   Whom when he saw on ground, he was full glad,
   And streight went forth his gladnesse to partake
   With *Belge*, who watcht all this while full sad,
Wayting what end would be of that same daunger drad.

33

Whom when she saw so ioyously come forth,
   She gan reioyce, and shew triumphant chere,
   Lauding and praysing his renowmed worth,
   By all the names that honorable were.
   Then in he brought her, and her shewed there
   The present of his paines, that Monsters spoyle,
   And eke that Idoll deem'd so costly dere;
   Whom he did all to peeces breake and foyle
In filthy durt, and left so in the loathely soyle.

34

Then all the people, which beheld that day,
   Gan shout aloud, that vnto heauen it rong;
   And all the damzels of that towne in ray,
   Came dauncing forth, and ioyous carrols song:
   So him they led through all their streetes along,
   Crowned with girlonds of immortall baies,
   And all the vulgar did about them throng,
   To see the man, whose euerlasting praise
They all were bound to all posterities to raise.

35

There he with *Belgæ* did a while remaine,
   Making great feast and ioyous merriment,
   Vntill he had her settled in her raine,
   With safe assuraunce and establishment.
   Then to his first emprize his mind he lent,
   Full loath to *Belgæ*, and to all the rest:
   Of whom yet taking leaue, thenceforth he went
   And to his former iourney him addrest,
On which long way he rode, ne euer day did rest.

Stanza 29
1 hulke: a large, heavy ship. **3 bulke**: hull or hold. **6 stound**: stunned.

Stanza 30
4 the onely sound: the sound alone. **9 done to rew**: caused to regret not doing so.

Stanza 31
1 prest: alluding topically to the torture of heretics – cf. 19.8–9 – by pressing them to death. **sway**: force. **6 sinke**: womb or organs of excretion. **9 lust**: pleasure.

Stanza 32
1 that deformed Masse: an antipapist pun, noted by Borris 1991:53. **2 sulphure**: associated with hell, as at i v 31.5. **4 Lerna**: named here as the marsh inhabited by the Hydra slain by Hercules. **Stygian lake** is **loathd** because of its name and nature; see II v 22.5–9*n*. **5 awhaped**: terrified, utterly confounded.

Stanza 33
6 present: present occasion. **spoyle**: dead body. **8–9** Cf. Exod. 23.24: 'Thou shalt . . . vtterly ouerthrowe them [the idols], and breake in pieces their images'. He cleanses the altar by smashing the idol on it and killing the monster beneath it. Defiling an altar is the work of Antiochus at I v 47.8–9, Ate at IV i 21.5, and the Blatant Beast at VI xii 25.3. **foyle**: tread under foot; defile.

Stanza 34
Alluding to the two triumphal progresses to honour Leicester's arrival in the Low Countries; see Strong and van Dorsten 1964:37–49, 64–70. In the first, Leicester was heralded as a second Arthur. **3 ray**: array.

Stanza 35
3 raine: kingdom. **4 assuraunce**: suggests also securing her title to rule. **establishment**: settled constitution or government. **5 emprize**: enterprise or quest, his search for Gloriana, which he had renewed at IV ix 17.5 and renews again at VI vi 44.9. **7 thenceforth**: from that place.

36

But turne we now to noble *Artegall*;
　Who hauing left *Mercilla*, streight way went
　On his first quest, the which him forth did call,
　To weet to worke *Irenaes* franchisement,
　And eke *Grantortoes* worthy punishment.
　So forth he fared as his manner was,
　With onely *Talus* wayting diligent,
Through many perils and much way did pas,
Till nigh vnto the place at length approcht he has.

37

There as he traueld by the way, he met
　An aged wight, wayfaring all alone,
　Who through his yeares long since aside had set
　The vse of armes, and battell quite forgone:
　To whom as he approcht, he knew anone,
　That it was he which whilome did attend
　On faire *Irene* in her affliction,
When first to Faery court he saw her wend,
Vnto his soueraine Queene her suite for to commend.

38

Whom by his name saluting, thus he gan;
　Haile good Sir *Sergis*, truest Knight aliue,
　Well tride in all thy Ladies troubles than,
　When her that Tyrant did of Crowne depriue;
　What new ocasion doth thee hither driue,
　Whiles she alone is left, and thou here found?
　Or is she thrall, or doth she not suruiue?
To whom he thus; She liueth sure and sound;
But by that Tyrant is in wretched thraldome bound.

39

For she presuming on th'appointed tyde,
　In which ye promist, as ye were a Knight,
　To meete her at the saluage Ilands syde,
　And then and there for triall of her right
　With her vnrighteous enemy to fight,
　Did thither come, where she afrayd of nought,
　By guilefull treason and by subtill slight
Surprized was, and to *Grantorto* brought,
Who her imprisond hath, and her life often sought.

40

And now he hath to her prefixt a day,
　By which if that no champion doe appeare,
　Which will her cause in battailous array
　Against him iustifie, and proue her cleare
　Of all those crimes, that he gainst her doth reare,
　She death shall by. Those tidings sad
　Did much abash Sir *Artegall* to heare,
And grieued sore, that through his fault she had
Fallen into that Tyrants hand and vsage bad.

41

Then thus replide; Now sure and by my life,
　Too much am I to blame for that faire Maide,
　That haue her drawne to all this troublous strife,
　Through promise to afford her timely aide,
　Which by default I haue not yet defraide.
　But witnesse vnto me, ye heauens, that know
　How cleare I am from blame of this vpbraide:
For ye into like thraldome me did throw,
And kept from complishing the faith, which I did owe.

Stanzas 36–43.5
An interlude apparently designed to renew Artegall's quest, which is first mentioned at IV vi 42.3, formally given him at V i 3–4, undertaken at 13.1–5, renewed at ii 28.9, iv 3.6 and 20.9, vii 43.9, viii 3.6, and x 17.9, and repeated at xii 3.1–6. His delaying may relate to heaven's failure to keep its course, as noted in the proem. Yet he may proceed 'on his first aduenture' only 'as time . . . shall tend' (iii 40.8–9), i.e. in an apocalyptic fulfilling of time. Hence he arrives 'nigh vnto the place' (36.9) only to be deflected one final time, after which 'the terme [is] approching fast' to rescue Irena (65.9); cf. 'time drawing ny' (xii 3.6).

Stanza 36
4 **franchisement**: liberation.　7 **wayting**: attending as a servant.

Stanza 38
2 **Sergis**: from 'sergeant', one whose office is to summon persons to appear before the court (*OED* 4), as here he summons Artegall. A Nestor-figure – see II ix 48 – alluding most likely to some elderly civil servant, e.g. Sir Henry Sidney, thrice Lord Deputy Governor of Ireland who could advise his successor, Lord Grey, on his duties and also serve as aide-de-camp in battle, as he does at xii 10.7–9. Or Grey himself – Hardin 1992:230*n*45 reads the name as an anagram of *gris* – who could advise his successor, Sir John Perrot. Or some military figure who served the Lord Deputy and would attend the forces subduing Irish rebels, as at xii 6.1–3. A seventeenth-century reader suggested an aged soldier, Cosby, who advised Grey before his first defeat by the rebels; see *N&Q* (1957) 202:514. Maley 1994:101 suggests Sir William Pelham, Lord Justice of Ireland. That Sergis has 'close friends' (xii 10.8) in Ireland suggests that he may be one of the 'Old English' – on which see Hadfield 1997:21–25.　3 **than**: then.

Stanza 39
1 **presuming**: relying.　**tyde**: time.　3 **saluage**: wild, barbarous, full of savages. In *DS* 7.2, S. refers to Ireland's 'saluage soyl'; cf. *DS 10*.12. Probably **Ilands** echoes Ireland's.　7 **slight**: treachery.

Stanza 40
1 **prefixt**: appointed.　5 **crimes**: accusations.　6 **by**: suffer. The caesura of this rare tetrameter line heightens the effect of the tidings, as A.B. Gough 1921 notes.

Stanza 41
5 **default**: neglect of duty, implying the legal sense, 'failure to attend in a court on the day assigned'.　**defraide**: paid, discharged.　6–9 He excuses himself for a reason that he denied Terpine: 'faulty men . . . lay on heauen the guilt of their owne crimes' (iv 28.1–3).　**vpbraide**: reproach.　**complishing**: accomplishing; fulfilling.

42

But now aread, Sir *Sergis,* how long space,
   Hath he her lent, a Champion to prouide:
   Ten daies (quoth he) he graunted hath of grace,
   For that he weeneth well, before that tide
   None can haue tidings to assist her side.
   For all the shores, which to the sea accoste,
   He day and night doth ward both far and wide,
   That none can there arriue without an hoste:
So her he deemes already but a damned ghoste.

43

Now turne againe (Sir *Artegall* then sayd)
   For if I liue till those ten daies haue end,
   Assure your selfe, Sir Knight, she shall haue ayd,
   Though I this dearest life for her doe spend;
   So backeward he attone with him did wend.
   Tho as they rode together on their way,
   A rout of people they before them kend,
   Flocking together in confusde array,
As if that there were some tumultuous affray.

44

To which as they approcht, the cause to know,
   They saw a Knight in daungerous distresse
   Of a rude rout him chasing to and fro,
   That sought with lawlesse powre him to oppresse,
   And bring in bondage of their brutishnesse:
   And farre away, amid their rakehell bands,
   They spide a Lady left all succourlesse,
   Crying, and holding vp her wretched hands
To him for aide, who long in vaine their rage withstands.

45

Yet still he striues, ne any perill spares,
   To reskue her from their rude violence,
   And like a Lion wood amongst them fares,
   Dealing his dreadfull blowes with large dispence,

Gainst which the pallid death findes no defence.
   But all in vaine, their numbers are so great,
   That naught may boot to banishe them from thence:
   For soone as he their outrage backe doth beat,
They turne afresh, and oft renew their former threat.

46

And now they doe so sharpely him assay,
   That they his shield in peeces battred haue,
   And forced him to throw it quite away,
   Fro dangers dread his doubtfull life to saue;
   Albe that it most safety to him gaue,
   And much did magnifie his noble name.
   For from the day that he thus did it leaue,
   Amongst all Knights he blotted was with blame,
And counted but a recreant Knight, with endles shame.

47

Whom when they thus distressed did behold,
   They drew vnto his aide; but that rude rout
   Them also gan assaile with outrage bold,
   And forced them, how euer strong and stout
   They were, as well approu'd in many a doubt,
   Backe to recule; vntill that yron man
   With his huge flaile began to lay about,
   From whose sterne presence they diffused ran,
Like scattred chaffe, the which the wind away doth fan.

48

So when that Knight from perill cleare was freed,
   He drawing neare, began to greete them faire,
   And yeeld great thankes for their so goodly deed,
   In sauing him from daungerous despaire
   Of those, which sought his life for to empaire.
   Of whom Sir *Artegall* gan then enquire
   The whole occasion of his late misfare,
   And who he was, and what those villaines were,
The which with mortall malice him pursu'd so nere.

Stanza 42
1 aread: declare. **3 Ten daies**: the length of time may be suggested by 'the ten yeares siege of *Troy*' (III ix 36.2). **6 accoste**: provide the coast. **8 hoste**: the 'Great hostes of men' who oppose him at xii 4.8.

Stanzas 43.6–65
The matter of this episode is the English intervention in France in 1589 and 1591 to support Henri de Burbon, King of Navarre, who became Henri IV after the murder of Henri III. On Burbon as the Gallic Hercules, see Prescott 2000. As leader of the Huguenots, he opposed the Spanish-supported Catholic League. Its specific matter is his conversion to the Church of Rome in 1593 in order to gain Paris, seen here as his lady Flourdelis. At xii 1, S. condemns him for 'doing wrong' in his desire 'to raine'. His recantation is treated by Gallagher 1991:191–97 in terms of the casuistical principle of *dolus bonus,* the good deceit. On S.'s emphasis on religious compromise, see Gregory 2000:376–78. Artegall's historical counterpart would be Essex and/or Sir John Norris. See 'Burbon', with its illustration in the *SEnc.*

Stanza 43
5 attone: together. **7 kend**: caught sight of.

Stanza 44
6 rakehell: rascal.

Stanza 45
3 wood: raging. **4** . . . with lavish liberality.

Stanza 46
In lamenting Saul's overthrow, David says that 'the shield of the mightie is cast downe' (2 Sam. 1.21). Since one is enjoined to 'take the shield of faith' in Eph. 6.16, to throw it away means to renounce faith. Burbon is called **recreant** in the etymological sense: he has abandoned his faith.

Stanza 47
5 doubt: peril. **6 recule**: recoil. **8 sterne**: merciless. **diffused**: dispersed. **9** As Isa. 41.15–16: '[Thou] shalt make the hilles as chaffe. Thou shalt fanne them, and the winde shal carye them away'.

49

To whom he thus; My name is *Burbon* hight,
  Well knowne, and far renowmed heretofore,
  Vntill late mischiefe did vppon me light,
  That all my former praise hath blemisht sore;
  And that faire Lady, which in that vprore
  Ye with those caytiues saw, *Flourdelis* hight,
  Is mine owne loue, though me she haue forlore,
  Whether withheld from me by wrongfull might,
Or with her owne good will, I cannot read aright.

50

But sure to me her faith she first did plight,
  To be my loue, and take me for her Lord,
  Till that a Tyrant, which *Grandtorto* hight,
  With golden giftes and many a guilefull word
  Entyced her, to him for to accord.
  O who may not with gifts and words be tempted?
  Sith which she hath me euer since abhord,
  And to my foe hath guilefully consented:
Ay me, that euer guyle in wemen was inuented.

51

And now he hath this troupe of villains sent,
  By open force to fetch her quite away;
  Gainst whom my selfe I long in vaine haue bent,
  To rescue her, and daily meanes assay,
  Yet rescue her thence by no meanes I may:
  For they doe me with multitude oppresse,
  And with vnequall might doe ouerlay,
  That oft I driuen am to great distresse,
And forced to forgoe th'attempt remedilesse.

52

But why haue ye (said *Artegall*) forborne
  Your owne good shield in daungerous dismay?
  That is the greatest shame and foulest scorne,
  Which vnto any knight behappen may

don't lose your shield!

To loose the badge, that should his deedes display.
  To whom Sir *Burbon*, blushing halfe for shame,
  That shall I vnto you (quoth he) bewray;
  Least ye therefore mote happily me blame,
And deeme it doen of will, that through inforcement came.

53

True is, that I at first was dubbed knight
  By a good knight, the knight of the *Redcrosse*;
  Who when he gaue me armes, in field to fight,
  Gaue me a shield, in which he did endosse
  His deare Redeemers badge vpon the bosse:
  The same longwhile I bore, and therewithall
  Fought many battels without wound or losse;
  Therewith *Grandtorto* selfe I did appall,
And made him oftentimes in field before me fall.

54

But for that many did that shield enuie,
  And cruell enemies increased more;
  To stint all strife and troublous enmitie,
  That bloudie scutchin being battered sore,
  I layd aside, and haue of late forbore,
  Hoping thereby to haue my loue obtayned:
  Yet can I not my loue haue nathemore;
  For she by force is still fro me detayned,
And with corruptfull brybes is to vntruth mis-trayned.

55

To whom thus *Artegall*; Certes Sir knight,
  Hard is the case, the which ye doe complaine;
  Yet not so hard (for nought so hard may light,
  That it to such a streight mote you constraine)
  As to abandon, that which doth containe
  Your honours stile, that is your warlike shield.
  All perill ought be lesse, and lesse all paine
  Then losse of fame in disauentrous field;
Dye rather, then doe ought, that mote dishonour yield.

Stanza 48
4 . . . i.e. from danger which causes him to despair; cf.
'daungerous dismay' (52.2). **7 misfare**: misfortune. **8 vil-
laines**: see II ix 13.2*n*.

Stanza 49
6 Flourdelis: alluding to France (or Paris) by her royal arms.
7 forlore: forsaken. **9 read**: guess.

Stanza 50
8 consented: been in accord. **9 inuented**: found.

Stanza 51
3 bent: applied. **6 oppresse**: overwhelm. **7 ouerlay**: crush
by force. **9 remedilesse**: having no hope of succeeding.

Stanza 52
1–5 On the general response to Burbon's conversion, see
Prescott 2000:203–07. According to xii Arg., Artegall 'blames
[him] for changing shield' rather than having given it up (**for-
borne**) voluntarily, as he himself did at v 16.8. His charge

against Burbon turns against himself when he triumphs over
Grantorto only by 'loosing soone his shield, did it forgoe' (xii
22.7). Burbon's **inforcement** is seen at 46.1–4. **7 bewray**:
declare. **8 happily**: haply; perchance.

Stanza 53
1–5 Referring specifically to Henri IV being admitted to the
Order of the Garter in 1590, as Leslie 1983:195 notes, but
more generally to his education as a Protestant. **endosse**:
inscribe. **bosse**: the centre of the shield, here with 'The
sacred badge of my Redeemers death' (II i 27.6).

Stanza 54
1 **enuie**: dislike. **4 scutchin**: the shield with its 'bloodie
Crosse' (I i 2.1). **9 corruptfull**: corrupting; and suggesting
the effect of the bribes: making her corrupt. **mis-trayned**: led
astray; or simply, 'trained amiss'.

Stanza 55
3 **light**: happen. **6 honours stile**: title of honour; literally,
that upon which his honour is penned. **8 disauentrous field**:
unsuccessful conflict.

56

Not so; (quoth he) for yet when time doth serue,
   My former shield I may resume againe:
   To temporize is not from truth to swerue,
   Ne for aduantage terme to entertaine,
   When as necessitie doth it constraine.
   Fie on such forgerie (said *Artegall*)
   Vnder one hood to shadow faces twaine.
   Knights ought be true, and truth is one in all:
Of all things to dissemble fouly may befall.

57

Yet let me you of courtesie request,
   (Said *Burbon*) to assist me now at need
   Against these pesants, which haue me opprest,
   And forced me to so infamous deed,
   That yet my loue may from their hands be freed.
   Sir *Artegall*, albe he earst did wyte
   His wauering mind, yet to his aide agreed,
   And buckling him eftsoones vnto the fight,
Did set vpon those troupes with all his powre and might.

58

Who flocking round about them, as a swarme
   Of flyes vpon a birchen bough doth cluster,
   Did them assault with terrible allarme,
   And ouer all the fields themselues did muster,
   With bils and glayues making a dreadfull luster;
   That forst at first those knights backe to retyre:
   As when the wrathfull *Boreas* doth bluster,
   Nought may abide the tempest of his yre,
Both man and beast doe fly, and succour doe inquyre.

59

But when as ouerblowen was that brunt,
   Those knights began a fresh them to assayle,
   And all about the fields like Squirrels hunt;
   But chiefly *Talus* with his yron flayle,

Gainst which no flight nor rescue mote auayle,
   Made cruell hauocke of the baser crew,
   And chaced them both ouer hill and dale:
   The raskall manie soone they ouerthrew,
But the two knights themselues their captains did subdew.

60

At last they came whereas that Ladie bode,
   Whom now her keepers had forsaken quight,
   To saue themselues, and scattered were abrode:
   Her halfe dismayd they found in doubtfull plight,
   As neither glad nor sorie for their sight;
   Yet wondrous faire she was, and richly clad
   In roiall robes, and many Iewels dight,
   But that those villens through their vsage bad
Them fouly rent, and shamefully defaced had.

61

But *Burbon* streight dismounting from his steed,
   Vnto her ran with greedie great desyre,
   And catching her fast by her ragged weed,
   Would haue embraced her with hart entyre.
   But she backstarting with disdainefull yre,
   Bad him auaunt, ne would vnto his lore
   Allured be, for prayer nor for meed.
   Whom when those knights so forward and forlore
Beheld, they her rebuked and vpbrayded sore.

62

Sayd *Artegall*; What foule disgrace is this,
   To so faire Ladie, as ye seeme in sight,
   To blot your beautie, that vnblemisht is,
   With so foule blame, as breach of faith once plight,
   Or change of loue for any worlds delight?
   Is ought on earth so pretious or deare,
   As prayse and honour? Or is ought so bright
   And beautifull, as glories beames appeare,
Whose goodly light then *Phebus* lampe doth shine more cleare?

Stanza 56
1–5 To the implied charge that he is a time-server, Burbon claims first, that he is waiting until the fullness of time requires him to act, even as Artegall may proceed 'on his first aduenture' only 'as time . . . shall tend' (iii 40.8–9); and second, that he does not swerve from truth in accepting conditions forced on him by necessity. 6–8 Artegall answers Burbon's one proverb (Smith 891) with two: Smith 231, 791 (cf. ii 48.6). **forgerie**: deception. 9 May shame above all else befall those who dissemble.

Stanza 57
6 . . . although he lately blamed. His **yet** in response to Burbon's repeated use indicates his own **wauering mind**.

Stanza 58
2–3 Not a distinctively literary metaphor: flies are attracted to a birch's sugary sap. **allarme**: din. **5 bils and glayues**: Elizabethan infantry weapons with a blade fastened to a long handle. **7–9 Boreas**: the north wind. **yre**: with a pun on 'air'. **inquyre**: try to find.

Stanza 59
6 **baser**: most base. **8–9 raskall manie**: rabble mob, the 'pesants' (57.3); cf. iv 44.5. **they**: 'he', i.e. Talus, conj. Church 1758 rightly, because, as at ii 52.4–5, a knight does not fight with his social inferiors. **the two knights**: i.e. Artegall and Burbon, for Sergis is unarmed (cf. 2, 58.6, 61.8), though present at 43–44.

Stanza 61
4 **entyre**: sincere. 6 **lore**: speech or pleading (sugg. by the context); or 'religion' (*OED* 2c). 7 **meed**: 'hyre', conj. Church 1758, to fit the 'c' rhyme. Yet S.'s choice both fits the 'a' rhyme and hints at the bribery condemned at 54.9. 8 **forward**: the sense requires 'froward' (*1609*). J.C. Smith 1909 notes the distinction between the two words at II ii 38. 5, 7; see VI x 24.6–9*n*. **forlore**: led astray, morally lost.

Stanza 62
4–5 He echoes Britomart at III i 25.3–6.

63

Why then will ye, fond Dame, attempted bee
  Vnto a strangers loue, so lightly placed,
  For guiftes of gold, or any worldly glee,
  To leaue the loue, that ye before embraced,
  And let your fame with falshood be defaced?
  Fie on the pelfe, for which good name is sold,
  And honour with indignitie debased:
  Dearer is loue then life, and fame then gold;
But dearer then them both, your faith once plighted hold.

64

Much was the Ladie in her gentle mind
  Abasht at his rebuke, that bit her neare,
  Ne ought to answere thereunto did find;
  But hanging downe her head with heauie cheare,
  Stood long amaz'd, as she amated weare.
  Which *Burbon* seeing, her againe assayd,
  And clasping twixt his armes, her vp did reare
  Vpon his steede, whiles she no whit gainesayd,
So bore her quite away, nor well nor ill apayd.

65

Nathlesse the yron man did still pursew
  That raskall many with vnpittied spoyle,
  Ne ceassed not, till all their scattred crew
  Into the sea he droue quite from that soyle,
  The which they troubled had with great turmoyle.
  But *Artegall* seeing his cruell deed,
  Commaunded him from slaughter to recoyle,
  And to his voyage gan againe proceed:
For that the terme approching fast, required speed.

cruelty vs justice?

Stanza 63
1 **fond**: foolish. **attempted**: tempted, seduced. **3 glee**: glitter. **6–8** Cf. Prov. 22.1: 'A good name is to be chosen aboue great riches, and louing fauour is aboue siluer and aboue golde'. **indignitie**: disgraceful action.

Stanza 64
5 **amated**: confounded; perhaps also 'mated', for she recognizes her union with Burbon. **9 apayd**: pleased.

Stanza 65
2 **vnpittied spoyle**: merciless havoc. **7 recoyle**: draw back. **9 terme**: i.e. the tenth and final day by which a champion of Irena must appear; see 43.2.

Cant. XII.

Artegall doth Sir Burbon aide,
And blames for changing shield:
He with the great Grantorto fights,
And slaieth him in field.

1

O Sacred hunger of ambitious mindes,
And impotent desire of men to raine,
Whom neither dread of God, that deuils bindes,
Nor lawes of men, that common weales containe,
Nor bands of nature, that wilde beastes restraine,
Can keepe from outrage, and from doing wrong,
Where they may hope a kingdome to obtaine.
No faith so firme, no trust can be so strong,
No loue so lasting then, that may endure long.

2

Witnesse may *Burbon* be, whom all the bands,
Which may a Knight assure, had surely bound,
Vntill the loue of Lordship and of lands
Made him become most faithlesse and vnsound:
And witnesse be *Gerioneo* found,
Who for like cause faire *Belge* did oppresse,
And right and wrong most cruelly confound:
And so be now *Grantorto*, who no lesse
Then all the rest burst out to all outragiousnesse.

3

Gainst whom Sir *Artegall*, long hauing since
Taken in hand th'exploit, being theretoo
Appointed by that mightie Faerie Prince,
Great *Gloriane*, that Tyrant to fordoo,

Through other great aduentures hethertoo
Had it forslackt. But now time drawing ny,
To him assynd, her high beheast to doo,
To the sea shore he gan his way apply,
To weete if shipping readie he mote there descry.

4

Tho when they came to the sea coast, they found
A ship all readie (as good fortune fell)
To put to sea, with whom they did compound,
To passe them ouer, where them list to tell:
The winde and weather serued them so well,
That in one day they with the coast did fall;
Whereas they readie found them to repell,
Great hostes of men in order martiall,
Which them forbad to land, and footing did forstall.

5

But nathemore would they from land refraine,
But when as nigh vnto the shore they drew,
That foot of man might sound the bottome plaine,
Talus into the sea did forth issew,
Though darts from shore and stones they at him threw;
And wading through the waues with stedfast sway,
Maugre the might of all those troupes in vew,
Did win the shore, whence he them chast away,
And made to fly, like doues, whom the Eagle doth affray.

Book V Canto xii

Argument
1–2 See xi Arg.*n*. If originally placed here, the 22 stanzas plus 4 lines of the Burbon episode (xi 43.6–65) balanced the Irena episode of the same length (xii 3.6–25.9), with 26–27 serving as a transition to the concluding 16 stanzas on the slandering of Artegall, which introduces Bk VI.

Stanza 1
1–2 **Sacred hunger**: i.e. accursed, as Virgil's *sacra fames* (*Aen.* 3.57). Hadfield 1996a:32 adds the sense, 'proceeding from God', to note a taboo not to be violated, specifically Grantorto's aim to restore Catholicism in Ireland which, for Protestants, was an accursed threat. **impotent desire**: i.e. uncontrollable desire, as shown in Burbon's willingness to abandon his faith in order to rule, and as evident in his 'greedie great desyre' to embrace Flourdelis at xi 61.2; see II xi 23.8–9*n*. 3–9 Cf. Jas. 2.19: 'the deuils also beleue it [that there is one God] and tremble'. Ambition to rule is first related to the three forces of order – divine, civil, and natural – and then distributed: firm faith may bind, strong trust may con-taine (confine, keep under control), and lasting love may restrain. M.F.N. Dixon 1996:106 relates these forces to holiness, friendship, and chastity respectively.

Stanza 2
2 **assure**: make secure.

Stanza 3
1–4 As i 4. **Prince**: see ix 21.2*n*. **fordoo**: kill. 6 **forslackt**: neglected.

Stanza 4
3 **compound**: make terms. 6 I.e. they reached the (Irish) coast in one day, the usual crossing-time, as A.B. Gough 1921 notes. 9 **forstall**: prevent.

Stanza 5
6 **sway**: force. 9 Opposition between the eagle (or falcon) and dove is traditional, as III iv 49.4–9.

Stanza 6
1 **that old knight**: Sergis. See xi 38.2 and *n*. 7 **reare**: gather.

6

The whyles Sir *Artegall*, with that old knight
    Did forth descend, there being none them neare,
    And forward marched to a towne in sight.
    By this came tydings to the Tyrants eare,
    By those, which earst did fly away for feare
    Of their arriuall: wherewith troubled sore,
    He all his forces streight to him did reare,
    And forth issuing with his scouts afore,
Meant them to haue incountred, ere they left the shore.

7

But ere he marched farre, he with them met,
    And fiercely charged them with all his force;
    But *Talus* sternely did vpon them set,
    And brusht, and battred them without remorse,
    That on the ground he left full many a corse;
    Ne any able was him to withstand,
    But he them ouerthrew both man and horse,
    That they lay scattred ouer all the land,
As thicke as doth the seede after the sowers hand.

8

Till *Artegall* him seeing so to rage,
    Wild him to stay, and signe of truce did make:
    To which all harkning, did a while asswage
    Their forces furie, and their terror slake;
    Till he an Herauld cald, and to him spake,
    Willing him wend vnto the Tyrant streight,
    And tell him that not for such slaughters sake
    He thether came, but for to trie the right
Of fayre *Irenaes* cause with him in single fight.

9

And willed him for to reclayme with speed
    His scattred people, ere they all were slaine,
    And time and place conuenient to areed,
    In which they two the combat might darraine.
    Which message when *Grantorto* heard, full fayne
    And glad he was the slaughter so to stay,
    And pointed for the combat twixt them twayne
    The morrow next, ne gaue him longer day.
So sounded the retraite, and drew his folke away.

10

That night Sir *Artegall* did cause his tent
    There to be pitched on the open plaine;
    For he had giuen streight commaundement,
    That none should dare him once to entertaine:
    Which none durst breake, though many would right faine
    For fayre *Irena*, whom they loued deare.
    But yet old *Sergis* did so well him paine,
    That from close friends, that dar'd not to appeare,
He all things did puruay, which for them needfull weare.

11

The morrow next, that was the dismall day,
    Appointed for *Irenas* death before,
    So soone as it did to the world display
    His chearefull face, and light to men restore,
    The heauy Mayd, to whom none tydings bore
    Of *Artegalls* arryuall, her to free,
    Lookt vp with eyes full sad and hart full sore;
    Weening her lifes last howre then neare to bee,
Sith no redemption nigh she did nor heare nor see.

12

Then vp she rose, and on her selfe did dight
    Most squalid garments, fit for such a day,
    And with dull countenance, and with doleful spright,
    She forth was brought in sorrowfull dismay,
    For to receiue the doome of her decay.
    But comming to the place, and finding there
    Sir *Artegall*, in battailous array
    Wayting his foe, it did her dead hart cheare,
And new life to her lent, in midst of deadly feare.

13

Like as a tender Rose in open plaine,
    That with vntimely drought nigh withered was,
    And hung the head, soone as few drops of raine
    Thereon distill, and deaw her daintie face,
    Gins to looke vp, and with fresh wonted grace
    Dispreds the glorie of her leaues gay;
    Such was *Irenas* countenance, such her case,
    When *Artegall* she saw in that array,
There wayting for the Tyrant, till it was farre day.

Stanza 7
3 **sternely**: cruelly, as Grantorto at 19.6.   **4 brusht**: thrashed.
8–9 As a thresher at i 12.8–9 and xi 47.6–9, Talus separates seed from chaff. As a sower, he sows death.

Stanza 8
2 As he orders him at xi 65.7, and as Britomart does at vii 36.7–9.   **9** On trial by **single fight**, see i 25.1–4*n*.

Stanza 9
1 **reclayme**: recall (a hawking term).   **3 conuenient**: fitting.
areed: appoint.   **4 darraine**: engage.   **7 pointed**: appointed.

Stanza 10
3 **he**: i.e. Grantorto. **streight**: strict. **8 close**: secret.
9 puruay: provide.

Stanza 11
1 **dismall day**: unlucky or evil day, the day of death.
9 redemption: as his mission is to 'succour' (i 3.6), 'restore' (4.8), and redeem (cf. vii 45.8) her.

Stanza 12
2 **squalid**: see i 13.7*n*.   **5** To receive punishment or the judgement of death.

Stanza 13
A most obvious simile for a Tudor poet to use but it may be indebted to Ariosto, *Orl. Fur.* 32.108, as Upton 1758 notes. The rose has faded through drought rather than heat, in line with Ecclus. 35.19 where mercy is 'like a cloud of raine, that cometh in the time of a drought', as Hardin 1992:117 notes. Cf. Marinell's restoration at IV xii 34.6–9.   **9 farre day**: far on in the day.

14

Who came at length, with proud presumpteous gate,
   Into the field, as if he fearelesse were,
   All armed in a cote of yron plate,
   Of great defence to ward the deadly feare,
   And on his head a steele cap he did weare
   Of colour rustie browne, but sure and strong;
   And in his hand an huge Polaxe did beare,
   Whose steale was yron studded, but not long,
With which he wont to fight, to iustifie his wrong.

15

Of stature huge and hideous he was,
   Like to a Giant for his monstrous hight,
   And did in strength most sorts of men surpas,
   Ne euer any found his match in might;
   Thereto he had great skill in single fight:
   His face was vgly, and his countenance sterne,
   That could haue frayd one with the very sight,
   And gaped like a gulfe, when he did gerne,
That whether man or monster one could scarse discerne.

16

Soone as he did within the listes appeare,
   With dreadfull looke he *Artegall* beheld,
   As if he would haue daunted him with feare,
   And grinning griesly, did against him weld
   His deadly weapon, which in hand he held.
   But th'Elfin swayne, that oft had seene like sight,
   Was with his ghastly count'nance nothing queld,
   But gan him streight to buckle to the fight,
And cast his shield about, to be in readie plight.

17

The trompets sound, and they together goe,
   With dreadfull terror, and with fell intent;
   And their huge strokes full daungerously bestow,
   To doe most dammage, where as most they ment.
   But with such force and furie violent,
   The tyrant thundred his thicke blowes so fast,
   That through the yron walles their way they rent,
   And euen to the vitall parts they past,
Ne ought could them endure, but all they cleft or brast.

18

Which cruell outrage when as *Artegall*
   Did well auize, thenceforth with warie heed
   He shund his strokes, where euer they did fall,
   And way did giue vnto their gracelesse speed:
   As when a skilfull Marriner doth reed
   A storme approching, that doth perill threat,
   He will not bide the daunger of such dread,
   But strikes his sayles, and vereth his mainsheat,
And lends vnto it leaue the emptie ayre to beat.

19

So did the Faerie knight himselfe abeare,
   And stouped oft his head from shame to shield;
   No shame to stoupe, ones head more high to reare,
   And much to gaine, a litle for to yield;
   So stoutest knights doen oftentimes in field.
   But still the tyrant sternely at him layd,
   And did his yron axe so nimbly wield,
   That many wounds into his flesh it made,
And with his burdenous blowes him sore did ouerlade.

20

Yet when as fit aduantage he did spy,
   The whiles the cursed felon high did reare
   His cruell hand, to smite him mortally,
   Vnder his stroke he to him stepping neare,
   Right in the flanke him strooke with deadly dreare,
   That the gore bloud thence gushing grieuously,
   Did vnderneath him like a pond appeare,
   And all his armour did with purple dye;
Thereat he brayed loud, and yelled dreadfully.

21

Yet the huge stroke, which he before intended,
   Kept on his course, as he did it direct,
   And with such monstrous poise adowne descended,
   That seemed nought could him from death protect:
   But he it well did ward with wise respect,
   And twixt him and the blow his shield did cast,
   Which thereon seizing, tooke no great effect,
   But byting deepe therein did sticke so fast,
That by no meanes it backe againe he forth could wrast.

Stanza 14
3–9 As the Irish gallowglass or foot-soldier was armed 'in a long shirt of mail down to the calf of the leg with a long, broade axe in his hand' (*View* 71). **deadly feare**: i.e. fear of death. **steale**: handle.

Stanza 15
1 **hideous**: immense. 3 **sorts**: kinds; multitudes. 8 **gerne**: show the teeth (with open mouth); cf. 16.4.

Stanza 17
6 **thicke**: rapid.

Stanza 18
2 **auize**: perceive. 4 **gracelesse**: cruel. 5 **reed**: see. 8–9 I.e. he drops his smaller sails and loosens his mainsail to hold less wind.

Stanza 19
1 **abeare**: bear, conduct. 2 **from shame**: i.e. from shameful injury. 4 Proverbial: Smith 890. 9 **burdenous**: heavy. **ouerlade**: press hard.

Stanza 20
2 **felon**: villain; also one who has committed a felony. 5 **with deadly dreare**: i.e. with the pain and sorrow of death, as x 35.9.

Stanza 21
3 **poise**: weight, force. 5 **respect**: care.

Stanza 22
7 Artegall lets his shield go to prevent being defeated, unlike Burbon who threw his away to achieve peace. **forgoe** recalls 'forborne' (xi 52.1) and 'forbore' (54.5). Kaske 1999:75

22

Long while he tug'd and stroue, to get it out,
  And all his powre applyed thereunto,
  That he therewith the knight drew all about:
  Nathlesse, for all that euer he could doe,
  His axe he could not from his shield vndoe.
  Which *Artegall* perceiuing, strooke no more,
  But loosing soone his shield, did it forgoe,
  And whiles he combred was therewith so sore,
He gan at him let driue more fiercely then afore.

23

So well he him pursew'd, that at the last,
  He stroke him with *Chrysaor* on the hed,
  That with the souse thereof full sore aghast,
  He staggered to and fro in doubtfull sted.
  Againe whiles he him saw so ill bested,
  He did him smite with all his might and maine,
  That falling on his mother earth he fed:
  Whom when he saw prostrated on the plaine,
He lightly reft his head, to ease him of his paine.

24

Which when the people round about him saw,
  They shouted all for ioy of his successe,
  Glad to be quit from that proud Tyrants awe,
  Which with strong powre did them long time oppresse;
  And running all with greedie ioyfulnesse
  To faire *Irena*, at her feet did fall,
  And her adored with due humblenesse,
  As their true Liege and Princesse naturall;
And eke her champions glorie sounded ouer all.

25

Who streight her leading with meete maiestie
  Vnto the pallace, where their kings did rayne,
  Did her therein establish peaceablie,
  And to her kingdomes seat restore agayne;
  And all such persons, as did late maintayne
  That Tyrants part, with close or open ayde,
  He sorely punished with heauie payne;
  That in short space, whiles there with her he stayd,
Not one was left, that durst her once haue disobayd.

26

During which time, that he did there remaine,
  His studie was true Iustice how to deale,
  And day and night employ'd his busie paine
  How to reforme that ragged common-weale:
  And that same yron man which could reueale
  All hidden crimes, through all that realme he sent,
  To search out those, that vsd to rob and steale,
  Or did rebell gainst lawfull gouernment;
On whom he did inflict most grieuous punishment.

27

But ere he could reforme it thoroughly,
  He through occasion called was away,
  To Faerie Court, that of necessity
  His course of Iustice he was forst to stay,
  And *Talus* to reuoke from the right way,
  In which he was that Realme for to redresse.
  But enuies cloud still dimmeth vertues ray.
  So hauing freed *Irena* from distresse,
He tooke his leaue of her, there left in heauinesse.

---

argues that Artegall's shield, unlike Burbon's, has no religious meaning, thereby allowing him to temporize.

Stanza 23
1 pursew'd: harassed.   **2 Chrysaor**: see i 9.5–9*n*.   **3 souse**: heavy downward blow.   **4 sted**: state.   **7 he fed**: i.e. he bit the dust; see ii 18.6*n*.   **9 lightly**: easily; quickly; gently. The word marks a moment of high comedy, as the rest of the line indicates.

Stanza 24
8 I.e. she is the one to whom they owe allegiance as their legitimate ruler rather than Grantorto, and who may claim the 'heritage' (i 3.8) and 'franchisement' (xi 36.4) that he had denied her. Yet she is **Liege** in being the loyal subject of Gloriana.

Stanza 25
3 peaceablie: according to her name, Irena or Peace; see i 4.1*n*.   **7 heauie payne**: i.e. torturing to death.

Stanzas 26–27
The topical matter that informs these stanzas, the conduct of Lord Grey, the Lord Deputy Governor of Ireland, from 1580 until his recall in 1582, is given in *View* 106: 'I remember that in the late government of that good Lord Gray, when after long travail and many perilous assays, he had brought things almost to this pass that ye speak of [Irenius has been describing to Eudoxus the wasting of Ireland], that it was even made ready for reformation, and might have been brought to what Her Majesty would, like complaint was made against him, that he was a bloody man, and regarded not the life of her subjects, no more than dogs but had wasted and consumed all, so as now she had almost nothing left but to reign in their ashes'. He died in 1593. On S.'s career as one of his secretaries, see Chronology 1580, 1581, 1582, and *DS 10*. See also 'Grey, Arthur' in the *SEnc*.

Stanza 26
2 He imitates Britomart who, in restoring the women of Radegone to 'mens subiection, did true Iustice deale' (vii 42.6–7).

Stanza 27
2 through occasion: the deliberate evasiveness of the phrase is noted by Gallagher 1991:197–99. S. dare not blame the Queen; also, Grey pleaded many times to be recalled. Kaplan 1997:50 compares the role of slanderous Occasion in II iv 4–5.   **5 reuoke**: recall.   **7 still**: ever.

28

Tho as he backe returned from that land,
    And there arriu'd againe, whence forth he set,
    He had not passed farre vpon the strand,
    When as two old ill fauour'd Hags he met,
    By the way side being together set,
    Two griesly creatures; and, to that their faces
    Most foule and filthie were, their garments yet
    Being all rag'd and tatter'd, their disgraces
Did much the more augment, and made most vgly cases.

29

The one of them, that elder did appeare,
    With her dull eyes did seeme to looke askew,
    That her mis-shape much helpt; and her foule heare
    Hung loose and loathsomely: Thereto her hew
    Was wan and leane, that all her teeth arew,
    And all her bones might through her cheekes be red;
    Her lips were like raw lether, pale and blew,
    And as she spake, therewith she slauered;
Yet spake she seldom, but thought more, the lesse she sed.

30

Her hands were foule and durtie, neuer washt
    In all her life, with long nayles ouer raught,
    Like puttocks clawes: with th'one of which she scracht
    Her cursed head, although it itched naught;
    The other held a snake with venime fraught,
    On which she fed, and gnawed hungrily,
    As if that long she had not eaten ought;
    That round about her iawes one might descry
The bloudie gore and poyson dropping lothsomely.

31

Her name was *Enuie*, knowen well thereby,
    Whose nature is to grieue, and grudge at all,
    That euer she sees doen prays-worthily,
    Whose sight to her is greatest crosse, may fall,
    And vexeth so, that makes her eat her gall.
    For when she wanteth other thing to eat,
    She feedes on her owne maw vnnaturall,
    And of her owne foule entrayles makes her meat;
Meat fit for such a monsters monsterous dyeat.

32

And if she hapt of any good to heare,
    That had to any happily betid,
    Then would she inly fret, and grieue, and teare
    Her flesh for felnesse, which she inward hid:
    But if she heard of ill, that any did,
    Or harme, that any had, then would she make
    Great cheare, like one vnto a banquet bid;
    And in anothers losse great pleasure take,
As she had got thereby, and gayned a great stake.

33

The other nothing better was, then shee;
    Agreeing in bad will and cancred kynd,
    But in bad maner they did disagree:
    For what so *Enuie* good or bad did fynd,
    She did conceale, and murder her owne mynd;
    But this, what euer euill she conceiued,
    Did spred abroad, and throw in th'open wynd.
    Yet this in all her words might be perceiued,
That all she sought, was mens good name to haue bereaued.

34

For what soeuer good by any sayd,
    Or doen she heard, she would streightwayes inuent,
    How to depraue, or slaunderously vpbrayd,
    Or to misconstrue of a mans intent,
    And turne to ill the thing, that well was ment.
    Therefore she vsed often to resort,
    To common haunts, and companies frequent,
    To hearke what any one did good report,
To blot the same with blame, or wrest in wicked sort.

35

And if that any ill she heard of any,
    She would it eeke, and make much worse by telling,
    And take great ioy to publish it to many,
    That euery matter worse was for her melling.
    Her name was hight *Detraction*, and her dwelling
    Was neare to *Enuie*, euen her neighbour next;
    A wicked hag, and *Enuy* selfe excelling
    In mischiefe: for her selfe she onely vext;
But this same both her selfe, and others eke perplext.

Stanza 28
6–7 **to that**: i.e. to that end; besides that.   **yet**: in addition.
8 **disgraces**: ill-favouredness.

Stanza 29
2 Alluding to the etymology of Lat. *invidia*, to look maliciously upon. As Envie in the *Romaunt of the Rose* 291–92, 'ne lokide but awry | Or overthwart, all baggyngly [squintingly]'.
3 **mis-shape**: deformed shape.   5 **arew**: in a row.   6 **red**: seen.   9 Proverbial: Smith 471.

Stanza 31
1 For a description of **Enuie** here and in 32, see I iv 30–32 and *nn*.   2 **grudge**: grumble.

Stanza 32
2 **happily**: by good chance.   9 **got**: profited.

Stanza 33
2 **kynd**: nature.   5 **murder**: torment.

Stanza 34
2 **inuent**: plot.   3 **depraue**: defame; represent as bad; backbite (Ital. *depravare*), as seen at 39.9.

Stanza 35
2 **eeke**: extend; increase.   4 **melling**: meddling.   5 **Detraction**: see 'Sclaunder' in the *SEnc*.   9 **perplext**: tormented.

36

Her face was vgly, and her mouth distort,
   Foming with poyson round about her gils,
   In which her cursed tongue full sharpe and short
   Appear'd like Aspis sting, that closely kils,
   Or cruelly does wound, whom so she wils:
   A distaffe in her other hand she had,
   Vpon the which she litle spinnes, but spils,
   And faynes to weaue false tales and leasings bad,
To throw amongst the good, which others had disprad.

37

These two now had themselues combynd in one,
   And linckt together gainst Sir *Artegall*,
   For whom they wayted as his mortall fone,
   How they might make him into mischiefe fall,
   For freeing from their snares *Irena* thrall,
   Besides vnto themselues they gotten had
   A monster, which the *Blatant beast* men call,
   A dreadfull feend of gods and men ydrad,
Whom they by slights allur'd, and to their purpose lad.

38

Such were these Hags, and so vnhandsome drest:
   Who when they nigh approching, had espyde
   Sir *Artegall* return'd from his late quest,
   They both arose, and at him loudly cryde,
   As it had bene two shepheards curres, had scryde
   A rauenous Wolfe amongst the scattered flockes.
   And *Enuie* first, as she that first him eyde,
   Towardes him runs, and with rude flaring lockes
About her eares, does beat her brest, and forhead knockes.

39

Then from her mouth the gobbet she does take,
   The which whyleare she was so greedily
   Deuouring, euen that halfe-gnawen snake,
   And at him throwes it most despightfully.
   The cursed Serpent, though she hungrily
   Earst chawd thereon, yet was not all so dead,
   But that some life remayned secretly,
   And as he past afore withouten dread,
Bit him behind, that long the marke was to be read.

40

Then th'other comming neare, gan him reuile,
   And fouly rayle, with all she could inuent;
   Saying, that he had with vnmanly guile,
   And foule abusion both his honour blent,
   And that bright sword, the sword of Iustice lent,
   Had stayned with reprochfull crueltie,
   In guiltlesse blood of many an innocent:
   As for *Grandtorto*, him with treacherie
And traynes hauing surpriz'd, he fouly did to die.

41

Thereto the Blatant beast by them set on
   At him began aloud to barke and bay,
   With bitter rage and fell contention,
   That all the woods and rockes nigh to that way,
   Began to quake and tremble with dismay;
   And all the aire rebellowed againe.
   So dreadfully his hundred tongues did bray,
   And euermore those hags them selues did paine,
To sharpen him, and their owne cursed tongs did straine.

Stanza 36

3–4 As Sclaunder at IV viii 26.8–9. Cf. Ps. 140.3: 'Thei haue sharpened their tongues like a serpent: adders poyson is vnder their lippes'. **short**: i.e. easily prouoked; or speaking angrily. **closely**: secretly. 6 Detraction's **distaffe**, for which there is no iconographical analogue, according to Aptekar 1969:251*n*, may have been suggested by its use as the symbol of his subjection to Radigund at v 23.2, with which he is now mocked; or by the image of weaving, which associates Detraction with the spider, a symbol of envy; see *Muiopotmos* 337–52. **her other hand**: i.e. one of her hands; or her left hand. 7 What little she spins on her distaff, she destroys. 8 **faynes**: delights. **leasings**: lies.

Stanza 37

7 **the Blatant Beast**: from Lat. *blatero, blaterare*: 'to bable in vayne, to clatter out of measure' (T. Cooper 1565); or *blateratus*: barking; or Engl. 'blatter': 'to speak or prate volubly' (*OED* 1); or from the Gk: Wybarne 1609 writes that 'actions done by diuine instinct, haue euer found some . . . tongue of blattant beast, so called of βλάπτω, to hurt' (*Sp All* 120). In *View* 20, S. defends Grey 'however envy list to blatter against him'. The Beast may be compared to the 'glatysaunt [i.e. yelping] beest', in Malory 10.13: 'that is in Englysshe to saye the questynge beeste, for that beest, wheresomeuer he yede, he quested in the bely with suche a noyse as it hadde ben a thyrtty couple of houndes' (10.13). See 'Blatant Beast' in the *SEnc*. For its genealogy, see VI i 8. As the poem's most potent and elusive avatar of slander, see Gross 1999:102–04.

Stanza 38

5–6 The comparison of Artegall to a **rauenous Wolfe** reveals him to be 'a bloody man', as charged; see 26–27*n*. **scryde**: descried. 7 **first him eyde**: because of her nature; see 29.2*n*. 8 **flaring**: outspreading.

Stanza 39

1 **gobbet**: a piece of raw flesh. 9 **read**: seen.

Stanza 40

3–4 Detraction may allude to Artegall 'loosing soone his shield' at 22.7. **abusion**: outrage, corrupt practice. **blent**: corrupted. 5–7 Referring to Chrysaor given him by Astræa at i 9.1–2, and which he used, e.g. in his 'bloody slaughter' of the Amazons at iv 41.2–3. 9 May refer to the massacre of the Spanish invaders at Smerwick under Grey's command; see Chronology 1580, *9 Nov.* In *View* 107, Eudoxus reports the charge, 'some say that he promised them life', which Irenius denies. **traynes**: wiles.

Stanza 41

7 **hundred**: as VI xii 33.2. Reduced to one at 34.5, and multiplied to a thousand at VI i 9.3 and xii 27.1. 9 **sharpen**: goad. **straine**: use to the utmost.

Stanzas 42–43

As David was slandered by Shimei who cursed him, cast stones, and called him murderer and a wicked man for having brought upon himself all the blood of the house of Saul, and yet

42

And still among most bitter wordes they spake,
   Most shamefull, most vnrighteous, most vntrew,
   That they the mildest man aliue would make
   Forget his patience, and yeeld vengeaunce dew
   To her, that so false sclaunders at him threw.
   And more to make them pierce and wound more deepe,
   She with the sting, which in her vile tongue grew,
   Did sharpen them, and in fresh poyson steepe:
Yet he past on, and seem'd of them to take no keepe.

43

But *Talus* hearing her so lewdly raile,
   And speake so ill of him, that well deserued,
   Would her haue chastiz'd with his yron flaile,
   If her Sir *Artegall* had not preserued,
   And him forbidden, who his heast obserued.
   So much the more at him still did she scold,
   And stones did cast, yet he for nought would swerue
   From his right course, but still the way did hold
To Faery Court, where what him fell shall else be told.

restrained his servant from punishing him (2 Sam. 16.5–13); noted A.B. Gough 1921.

Stanza 42
1 among: all the while. **9** He illustrates Erasmus's adage, *frustra Herculi*: the great hero cannot be slandered.

Stanza 43
1 lewdly: wickedly. **6 So much the more**: as VI i 9.9. To ignore the Beast's attack only strengthens it. **8 right**: also direct. **9** A very open-ended ending, for what happened to him would be told only in the projected Bk XII or Bk XXIV. **else**: elsewhere; at another time.

THE SIXTE
BOOKE OF THE
FAERIE QVEENE.

Contayning
THE LEGEND OF S.CALIDORE
OR
OF COVRTESIE.

1

He waies, through which my weary steps I guyde,
In this delightfull land of Faery,
Are so exceeding spacious and wyde,
And sprinckled with such sweet variety,
Of all that pleasant is to eare or eye,
That I nigh rauisht with rare thoughts delight,
My tedious trauell doe forget thereby;
And when I gin to feele decay of might,
It strength to me supplies, and chears my dulled spright.

2

Such secret comfort, and such heauenly pleasures,
Ye sacred imps, that on *Parnasso* dwell,
And there the keeping haue of learnings threasures,
Which doe all worldly riches farre excell,
Into the mindes of mortall men doe well,
And goodly fury into them infuse;
Guyde ye my footing, and conduct me well
In these strange waies, where neuer foote did vse,
Ne none can find, but who was taught them by the Muse.

Book VI Title

S. is an accepted abbreviation of 'Sir'; used only in the title of this Bk, probably to make it fit the line.

Proem

Stanza 1
7 **trauell**: also travail. In *Am* 33.10, S. complains to Bryskett of the 'tædious toyle' of writing the first six books of his poem. At 80.5, he is ready to begin another six books 'as a steed refreshed after toyle'.

Stanza 2
1 **comfort**: also support, invigoration.   2 **imps**: the muses.
3 **learnings threasures**: its association with the muse's 'euerlasting scryne' (I proem 2.3) is noted by Anderson 1996:131–32.   4 Proverbial: Prov. 3.13–14, as at ix 30.7: 'wisedome is most riches'.   6 **fury**: poetic 'rage' (cf. I xi 6.2), or inspiration. **infuse**: pour; parallel to **well**, an image prompted by 'the sacred brooke | of *Helicon*' (*Am* 1.9–10) which flows from Parnassus.   8 On the topos, see I proem 1.6*n*.   **foote** implies the metrical sense, as at II proem 4.1–5, though now only the inspired poet, and the reader inspired by him, may find the way.

3

Reuele to me the sacred noursery
    Of vertue, which with you doth there remaine,
    Where it in siluer bowre does hidden ly
    From view of men, and wicked worlds disdaine.
    Since it at first was by the Gods with paine
    Planted in earth, being deriu'd at furst
    From heauenly seedes of bounty soueraine,
And by them long with carefull labour nurst,
Till it to ripenesse grew, and forth to honour burst.

4

Amongst them all growes not a fayrer flowre,
    Then is the bloosme of comely courtesie,
    Which though it on a lowly stalke doe bowre,
    Yet brancheth forth in braue nobilitie,
    And spreds it selfe through all ciuilitie:
    Of which though present age doe plenteous seeme,
    Yet being matcht with plaine Antiquitie,
Ye will them all but fayned showes esteeme,
Which carry colours faire, that feeble eies misdeeme.

5

But in the triall of true curtesie,
    Its now so farre from that, which then it was,
    That it indeed is nought but forgerie,
    Fashion'd to please the eies of them, that pas,

Which see not perfect things but in a glas:
    Yet is that glasse so gay, that it can blynd
    The wisest sight, to thinke gold that is bras.
    But vertues seat is deepe within the mynd,
And not in outward shows, but inward thoughts defynd.

6

But where shall I in all Antiquity
    So faire a patterne finde, where may be seene
    The goodly praise of Princely curtesie,
    As in your selfe, O soueraine Lady Queene,
    In whose pure minde, as in a mirrour sheene,
    It showes, and with her brightnesse doth inflame
    The eyes of all, which thereon fixed beene;
    But meriteth indeede an higher name:
Yet so from low to high vplifted is your name.

7

Then pardon me, most dreaded Soueraine,
    That from your selfe I doe this vertue bring,
    And to your selfe doe it returne againe:
    So from the Ocean all riuers spring,
    And tribute backe repay as to their King.
    Right so from you all goodly vertues well
    Into the rest, which round about you ring,
    Faire Lords and Ladies, which about you dwell,
And doe adorne your Court, where courtesies excell.

Stanza 3

1 noursery: nursery garden, as the nursery of virtue where Amoret 'to perfect ripenes grew' (III vi 52.1; cf. IV viii 33) before being brought into the world. It is parodied by the Stygian fen in which the Blatant Beast grew 'to perfect ripenesse' (i 8.5) before being sent into the world. On the poem as a garden of virtue planted in the mind, see Introduction. **3 siluer bowre**: the home of the angels at II viii 2.1, and of Cynthia at VII vi 18.7. **5 with paine**: with care, painstakingly, paralleling **with carefull labour**. The georgic emphasis on labour indicates the social nature of courtesy, as Low 1985:44 notes. **6–7** Cf. Jas. 1.17: 'Euerie good giuing, and euerie perfite gift is from aboue.'

Stanza 4

1–2 As courtesy is ranked highest in 1 Pet. 3.8: 'Finally, be ye all of one minde: one suffre with another: loue as brethren: be pitiful: be courteous'. **3 bowre**: lodge. **4 braue**: splendid. **5 ciuilitie**: civilized life, as Lat. *civilitas*, 'curteisie, ciuilitie, gentilnesse, humanitie' (T. Cooper 1565); cf. i 26.6, and see ii 1.6–7*n*. For Guazzo, 'to live civilly, is not sayde in respect of the citie, but of the quallities of the minde' (1925:1.56). **7 plaine Antiquitie**: see V proem 1*n*. **9 misdeeme**: form a wrong judgement of.

Stanza 5

1 triall suggests a formal examination, as does **defynd**, i.e. determined. **4–7 pas**: go by without really seeing, as those who 'se through a glasse darkely' (1 Cor. 13.12) and for whom the glass is only a self-reflecting mirror. **gay**: i.e. brilliant in its dazzling deception in showing 'a world of glas' (III ii 19.9).

Stanza 6

1 But: echoing the four uses of the word in stanza 5. Its openly adversative use is noted by Anderson 1982b:113. The implied contradiction – ideal courtesy is found only in antiquity: it is found now in the Queen – is noted by Shaver 1991:211. **5–7** Invoking 2 Cor. 3.18: '[we] beholde as in a mirrour the glorie of the Lord with open face', in contrast to the deceiving glass of the previous stanza. In I proem 4.2, the Queen is addressed as 'Mirrour of grace'. **sheene**: 'fayre and shining' (E.K. on *SC Nov.* 38). **8–9** The rule against duplicating a rhyme word with the same sense is followed if **name** means 'appellation' in 8 and 'character' in 9, as Church 1758 suggests; or if 'fame' is substituted in 9.

Stanza 7

The reciprocal movement of receiving and returning (1–5) and then of giving and receiving (6–9) is expressed in the traditional gloss on the dance of the Graces at x 24.8–9, as Snare 1974:3 observes. See also Bates 1992:157–59. Cf. Eccles. 1.7: 'All the riuers go into the sea, yet the sea is not ful: for the riuers go vnto the place, whence thei returne, and go'. The Geneva gloss adds: 'The sea which compasseth all the earth filleth the veines thereof, the which powre out springs and riuers into the sea againe'. Cf. the use at IV iii 27 and V x 3.3–7. On courtesy as freely giving and freely receiving, see D. Cheney 1966:203; and on gift-giving in the poem and in Elizabethan society, see Fumerton 1991:29–66, 214–26, and L.M. Klein 1997. D.L. Miller 1988:102 notes S.'s self-effacement. **6 well**: cf. 2.5.

Cant. I.

Calidore saues from Maleffort,
A Damzell vsed vylde:
Doth vanquish Crudor, and doth make
Briana wexe more mylde.

1

OF Court it seemes, men Courtesie doe call,
　For that it there most vseth to abound;
　And well beseemeth that in Princes hall
　That vertue should be plentifully found,
　Which of all goodly manners is the ground,
　And roote of ciuill conuersation.
　Right so in Faery court it did redound,
　Where curteous Knights and Ladies most did won
Of all on earth, and made a matchlesse paragon.

2

But mongst them all was none more courteous Knight,
　Then *Calidore*, beloued ouer all,
　In whom it seemes, that gentlenesse of spright
　And manners mylde were planted naturall;
　To which he adding comely guize withall,
　And gracious speach, did steale mens hearts away.
　Nathlesse thereto he was full stout and tall,
　And well approu'd in batteilous affray,
That him did much renowme, and far his fame display.

3

Ne was there Knight, ne was there Lady found
　In Faery court, but him did deare embrace,
　For his faire vsage and conditions sound,
　The which in all mens liking gayned place,
　And with the greatest purchast greatest grace:
　Which he could wisely vse, and well apply,
　To please the best, and th'euill to embase.
　For he loathd leasing, and base flattery,
And loued simple truth and stedfast honesty.

4

And now he was in trauell on his way,
　Vppon an hard aduenture sore bestad,
　Whenas by chaunce he met vppon a day
　With *Artegall*, returning yet halfe sad
　From his late conquest, which he gotten had.
　Who whenas each of other had a sight,
　They knew them selues, and both their persons rad:
　When *Calidore* thus first; Haile noblest Knight
Of all this day on ground, that breathen liuing spright.

Book VI Canto i

Argument
2 vylde: vilely.

Stanza 1
1 This commonly cited etymology, indicated by the spelling, is prompted by the closing line of the proem; cf. III vi 1.5–6. On the connection of the courtier, and therefore Calidore, with Puttenham's *Allegoria*, which he calls 'the Courtier or figure of faire semblant' (1936:299), see J. Miller 1991. **2 vseth**: implying '*was* accustomed'; hence the vb tenses: **should be** and **did redound**. See II iii 40.1–5. **6 ciuill conuersation**: 'an honest commendable and vertuous kinde of liuing in the world' (Guazzo 1925:1.56); civilized conduct or intercourse. **7 redound**: abound. **8** Where dwelt the most courteous knights, etc.

Stanza 2
2–5 Calidore: Gk καλός, beautiful + δῶρον, gift. 'Beauty' and 'gift' are key terms throughout Bk VI, culminating in a gift to Calidore: a vision of the Graces who 'to men all gifts of grace do graunt' (x 15.4). His virtue is **naturall** to him, as chastity is to Britomart, not one in which he is educated (as is the Red Cross Knight), or trained (as is Guyon), or its instrument (as is Artegall). Hence he is 'goodly gratious . . . by kind' (ii 2.2; cf. iii 15.5). Other suggested etymologies: Lat. *calidus*, living or spirited (Bennett 1942:215); *callidus*, skilful, experienced

(Tonkin 1972:95*n*13). See III viii 28.8–9*n*. **beloued ouer all**: as courtesy arouses love in others in contrast to prowess which arouses dread. **5–6** At ii 3.2–4, Calidore is said to steal hearts through the eyes and ears; cf. ix 18.3–4. In *As* 21–22, Sidney is praised because 'all mens hearts with secret ravishment | He stole away'. His model is Absalom whose physical beauty and eloquence 'stale the heartes of men of Israel' (2 Sam. 15.6). **comely guize**: pleasing appearance. **7–9 Nathlesse** indicates that courtesy and prowess may be at odds (cf. 41.2) though, at iii 40.8–9, Calepine maintains that it is seldom they ever disagree. The conjunction is found elsewhere only in Britomart (IV i 11.6) and in the three brothers (IV iii 2.6–9). **tall**: comely, handsome; brave, valiant. **approu'd**: tested. **batteilous affray**: warlike battle.

Stanza 3
3 For his pleasing behaviour and good qualities. **5 purchast**: gained. **7 embase**: put down. **8–9** As Chaucer's Knight 'loved chivalrie, | Trouthe and honour, fredom and curteisie'. **leasing**: lying.

Stanza 4
7 I.e. in knowing the other each knows himself, indicating the consonance of their virtues. For the first time eponymous heroes on their introduction need not be reconciled through conflict. **rad**: knew, recognized. **8 Haile noblest Knight**: an address used elsewhere only to Arthur: II xi 30.7; cf. II iii 18.3–4.

5
Now tell, if please you, of the good successe,
    Which ye haue had in your late enterprize.
    To whom Sir *Artegall* gan to expresse
    His whole exploite, and valorous emprize,
    In order as it did to him arize.
    Now happy man (sayd then Sir *Calidore*)
    Which haue so goodly, as ye can deuize,
    Atchieu'd so hard a quest, as few before;
That shall you most renowmed make for euermore.

6
But where ye ended haue, now I begin
    To tread an endlesse trace, withouten guyde,
    Or good direction, how to enter in,
    Or how to issue forth in waies vntryde,
    In perils strange, in labours long and wide,
    In which although good Fortune me befall,
    Yet shall it not by none be testifyde.
    What is that quest (quoth then Sir *Artegall*)
That you into such perils presently doth call?

7
The Blattant Beast (quoth he) I doe pursew,
    And through the world incessantly doe chase,
    Till I him ouertake, or else subdew:
    Yet know I not or how, or in what place
    To find him out, yet still I forward trace.
    What is that Blattant Beast? (then he replide.)
    It is a Monster bred of hellishe race,
    (Then answerd he) which often hath annoyd
Good Knights and Ladies true, and many else destroyd.

8
Of *Cerberus* whilome he was begot,
    And fell *Chimæra* in her darkesome den,
    Through fowle commixture of his filthy blot;
    Where he was fostred long in *Stygian* fen,
    Till he to perfect ripenesse grew, and then
    Into this wicked world he forth was sent,
    To be the plague and scourge of wretched men:
    Whom with vile tongue and venemous intent
He sore doth wound, and bite, and cruelly torment.

9
Then since the saluage Island I did leaue,
    Sayd *Artegall*, I such a Beast did see,
    The which did seeme a thousand tongues to haue,
    That all in spight and malice did agree,
    With which he bayd and loudly barkt at mee,
    As if that he attonce would me deuoure.
    But I that knew my selfe from perill free,
    Did nought regard his malice nor his powre,
But he the more his wicked poyson forth did poure.

10
That surely is that Beast (saide *Calidore*)
    Which I pursue, of whom I am right glad
    To heare these tidings, which of none afore
    Through all my weary trauell I haue had:
    Yet now some hope your words vnto me add.
    Now God you speed (quoth then Sir *Artegall*)
    And keepe your body from the daunger drad:
    For ye haue much adoe to deale withall.
So both tooke goodly leaue, and parted seuerall.

Stanza 5
4 emprize: adventure. **7** I.e. 'as you know well how to describe', praising Artegall's eloquence; or, 'as you could wish', praising his prowess.

Stanza 6
1–7 Recalling the Palmer's address to the Red Cross Knight on Guyon's quest: 'wretched we, where ye haue left your marke, | Must now anew begin' (II i 32.6–7). **an endlesse trace**, or way, marks the labyrinth in which Calidore wanders. Alone among S.'s knights, he goes on his quest unattended even by a groom, bound by his vow; see ii 37.5–8. For the custom, see IV vi 44.6–8. After his initial encounter with the discourteous knight at 33, he walks, rather than rides, as does Guyon after his encounter with Amavia. **Fortune**, good and bad, is another key term in the Bk VI: events seem governed by chance or accident, rather than by individual will or divine providence. It is used along with 'fate' and 'chance' eighty times, a ratio over the other books of 2:1. See M.F.N. Dixon 1996:165; cf. the compilation by Kinney 1992:92. **not by none**: i.e. by no one (the emphatic double negative), an important matter in a book that treats the evils of slander, and despairs of the rewards of virtuous action; cf. I ix 2.8–9, III xi 9.8–9. While the Red Cross Knight hopes 'To winne him worshippe, and her [Gloriana's] grace to haue' (I i 3.4), for Calidore good deeds are their own reward, as Arthur declares at II viii 56 and V xi 17.7–9. **9 presently**: immediately.

Stanza 7
1 Blattant Beast: see V xii 37.7*n*. **5 trace**: go.

Stanza 8
1–5 Cerberus: the triple-headed dog that guards the entrance to hell; see I v 34. **Chimæra**: a triple-formed monster that guards its outer gates (Virgil, *Aen.* 6.288). For a variant genealogy, see vi 10–12; and for a comparison, see Nohrnberg 1976:692–96. **commixture**: mingling of his stain with hers in copulation; cf. 'commixtion' (vi 12.1). **4 Stygian fen**: associated with discord at II v 22.6–8.

Stanza 9
1 saluage Island: see V xi 39.3*n*. **7–8** As he 'seem'd of them to take no keepe' at V xii 42.9.

Stanza 10
9 goodly: courteous. **seuerall**: separately, each going his separate way.

11

Sir *Calidore* thence trauelled not long,
  When as by chaunce a comely Squire he found,
  That thorough some more mighty enemies wrong,
  Both hand and foote vnto a tree was bound:
  Who seeing him from farre, with piteous sound
  Of his shrill cries him called to his aide.
  To whom approching, in that painefull stound
  When he him saw, for no demaunds he staide,
But first him losde, and afterwards thus to him saide.

12

Vnhappy Squire, what hard mishap thee brought
  Into this bay of perill and disgrace?
  What cruell hand thy wretched thraldome wrought,
  And thee captyued in this shamefull place?
  To whom he answerd thus; My haplesse case
  Is not occasiond through my misdesert,
  But through misfortune, which did me abase
  Vnto this shame, and my young hope subuert,
Ere that I in her guilefull traines was well expert.

13

Not farre from hence, vppon yond rocky hill,
  Hard by a streight there stands a castle strong,
  Which doth obserue a custome lewd and ill,
  And it hath long mayntaind with mighty wrong:
  For may no Knight nor Lady passe along
  That way, (and yet they needs must passe that way,)
  By reason of the streight, and rocks among,
  But they that Ladies lockes doe shaue away,
And that knights berd for toll, which they for passage pay.

14

A shamefull vse as euer I did heare,
  Sayd *Calidore*, and to be ouerthrowne.
  But by what meanes did they at first it reare,
  And for what cause, tell if thou haue it knowne.
  Sayd then that Squire: The Lady which doth owne
  This Castle, is by name *Briana* hight.
  Then which a prouder Lady liueth none:
  She long time hath deare lou'd a doughty Knight,
And sought to win his loue by all the meanes she might.

15

His name is *Crudor*, who through high disdaine
  And proud despight of his selfe pleasing mynd,
  Refused hath to yeeld her loue againe,
  Vntill a Mantle she for him doe fynd,
  With beards of Knights and locks of Ladies lynd.
  Which to prouide, she hath this Castle dight,
  And therein hath a Seneschall assynd,
  Cald *Maleffort*, a man of mickle might,
Who executes her wicked will, with worse despight.

16

He this same day, as I that way did come
  With a faire Damzell, my beloued deare,
  In execution of her lawlesse doome,
  Did set vppon vs flying both for feare:
  For little bootes against him hand to reare.
  Me first he tooke, vnhable to withstond;
  And whiles he her pursued euery where,
  Till his returne vnto this tree he bond:
Ne wote I surely, whether her he yet haue fond.

Stanza 11
7 stound: plight.   8 demaunds: questions.

Stanza 12
2 Into this bay: referring to the end of a chase when an exhausted quarry must turn to face its pursuers.   4 place: way or manner is suggested by the context; or the place may be shamefull because of the custom maintained there.   6 misdesert: ill-deserving, apparently coined by S.   9 traines: wiles.

Stanza 13
Cf. the description of this custome – it is lewd also in being wicked – at vi 34.4–9. One analogue is the toll levied at the Castle of Beards, which is also at a pass (streight), in *Perlesvaus* (see *Var* 6.365–66). In Malory 1.26, King Ryons, who trimmed a 'mantel with kynges berdes', came to Arthur for his beard; cf. Geoffrey of Monmouth 1891:10.3. S. adds the similarly degendering practice against the knight's lady who is shorn and half-stripped. On S.'s use of the custom of the castle topos to fashion courtesy, see Ross 1997:86–89. 6–7 Church 1758 includes line 7 in the parentheses.

Stanza 14
6 Briana: 'shrill voice', the meaning of 'Brian' noted by W. Camden 1984:61, befits her outcry against Calidore at 25. An obviously Irish name, as is Brianor; see IV iv 40.7–9n, and 'Briana' in the *SEnc*.

Stanza 15
1 Crudor: from Lat. *crudus*, raw, bloody, cruel; also 'undeveloped', giving hope of his reformation at 43. See 'Crudor' in the *SEnc*. 3 againe: in return. 6 dight: built. 7 Seneschall: steward. 8 Maleffort: evil endeavour' so called because he executes her wicked will.

Stanza 16
3 doome: decree.

17

Thus whiles they spake, they heard a ruefull shrieke
  Of one loud crying, which they streight way ghest,
  That it was she, the which for helpe did seeke.
  Tho looking vp vnto the cry to lest,
  They saw that Carle from farre, with hand vnblest
  Hayling that mayden by the yellow heare,
  That all her garments from her snowy brest,
  And from her head her lockes he nigh did teare,
Ne would he spare for pitty, nor refraine for feare.

18

Which haynous sight when *Calidore* beheld,
  Eftsoones he loosd that Squire, and so him left,
  With hearts dismay and inward dolour queld,
  For to pursue that villaine, which had reft
  That piteous spoile by so iniurious theft.
  Whom ouertaking, loude to him he cryde;
  Leaue faytor quickely that misgotten weft
  To him, that hath it better iustifyde,
And turne thee soone to him, of whom thou art defyde.

19

Who hearkning to that voice, him selfe vpreard,
  And seeing him so fiercely towardes make,
  Against him stoutly ran, as nought afeard,
  But rather more enrag'd for those words sake;
  And with sterne count'naunce thus vnto him spake.
  Art thou the caytiue, that defyest me,
  And for this Mayd, whose party thou doest take,
  Wilt giue thy beard, though it but little bee?
Yet shall it not her lockes for raunsome fro me free.

20

With that he fiercely at him flew, and layd
  On hideous strokes with most importune might,
  That oft he made him stagger as vnstayd,
  And oft recuile to shunne his sharpe despight.

But *Calidore*, that was well skild in fight,
  Him long forbore, and still his spirite spar'd,
  Lying in waite, how him he damadge might.
  But when he felt him shrinke, and come to ward,
He greater grew, and gan to driue at him more hard.

21

Like as a water streame, whose swelling sourse
  Shall driue a Mill, within strong bancks is pent,
  And long restrayned of his ready course;
  So soone as passage is vnto him lent,
  Breakes forth, and makes his way more violent.
  Such was the fury of Sir *Calidore*,
  When once he felt his foeman to relent;
  He fiercely him pursu'd, and pressed sore,
Who as he still decayd, so he encreased more.

22

The heauy burden of whose dreadfull might
  When as the Carle no longer could sustaine,
  His heart gan faint, and streight he tooke his flight
  Toward the Castle, where if need constraine,
  His hope of refuge vsed to remaine.
  Whom *Calidore* perceiuing fast to flie,
  He him pursu'd and chaced through the plaine,
  That he for dread of death gan loude to crie
Vnto the ward, to open to him hastilie.

23

They from the wall him seeing so aghast,
  The gate soone opened to receiue him in,
  But *Calidore* did follow him so fast,
  That euen in the Porch he him did win,
  And cleft his head asunder to his chin.
  The carkasse tumbling downe within the dore,
  Did choke the entraunce with a lumpe of sin,
  That it could not be shut, whilest *Calidore*
Did enter in, and slew the Porter on the flore.

Stanza 17
4 lest: list, listen.   **5 vnblest**: wicked.

Stanza 18
2 He had loosed him at 11.9 but then held him by his questions.   **5 spoile**: i.e. the maiden; or her locks taken from her as his booty, leaving her distressed.   **7 faytor**: miscreant, impostor.   **weft**: waif; stolen goods abandoned by a thief.   **8** 'To him who has a better legal claim to her'. Calidore addresses him on behalf of his client, the helpless youth.

Stanza 19
1 His posture suggests that of the reclining lover.   **7 party**: side.

Stanza 20
2 importune: grievous, heavy.   **3 vnstayd**: unstable.   **6 his spirite**: i.e. his own strength.   **8 to ward**: into a defensive posture.

Stanza 21
1–5 S. adapts Virgil's simile of a river that having broken its banks floods the land, *Aen.* 2.496–99, by adding the rural detail, **Shall driue a Mill**, and allegorical pointers, e.g. **ready** (i.e. direct, suggesting that Calidore has been restrained from rightful action), and **more violent** (suggesting that Maleffort's effort provokes his).   **7 relent**: slacken.

Stanza 22
7 Applying Virgil's image of the river rushing over all the plains (*camposque per omnis*).   **9 ward**: guards.

Stanza 23
Recalling Arthur's slaying of the knight at the gate of Geryoneo's castle, preventing it from being shut (V x 36–37), as even the language suggests: e.g. 'lumpe of clay' becomes **lumpe of sin**.   **4 win**: overtake.   **9 on the flore**: on the spot.

24

With that the rest, the which the Castle kept,
    About him flockt, and hard at him did lay;
    But he them all from him full lightly swept,
    As doth a Steare, in heat of sommers day,
    With his long taile the bryzes brush away.
    Thence passing forth, into the hall he came,
    Where of the Lady selfe in sad dismay
    He was ymett, who with vncomely shame
Gan him salute, and fowle vpbrayd with faulty blame.

25

False traytor Knight, (sayd she) no Knight at all,
    But scorne of armes that hast with guilty hand
    Murdred my men, and slaine my Seneschall;
    Now comest thou to rob my house vnmand,
    And spoile my selfe, that can not thee withstand?
    Yet doubt thou not, but that some better Knight
    Then thou, that shall thy treason vnderstand,
    Will it auenge, and pay thee with thy right:
And if none do, yet shame shal thee with shame requight.

26

Much was the Knight abashed at that word;
    Yet answerd thus; Not vnto me the shame,
    But to the shamefull doer it afford.
    Bloud is no blemish; for it is no blame
    To punish those, that doe deserue the same;
    But they that breake bands of ciuilitie,
    And wicked customes make, those doe defame
    Both noble armes and gentle curtesie.
No greater shame to man then inhumanitie.

27

Then doe your selfe, for dread of shame, forgoe
    This euill manner, which ye here maintaine,
    And doe in stead thereof mild curt'sie showe
    To all, that passe. That shall you glory gaine

More then his loue, which thus ye seeke t'obtaine.
    Wherewith all full of wrath, she thus replyde;
    Vile recreant, know that I doe much disdaine
    Thy courteous lore, that doest my loue deride,
Who scornes thy ydle scoffe, and bids thee be defyde.

28

To take defiaunce at a Ladies word
    (Quoth he) I hold it no indignity;
    But were he here, that would it with his sword
    Abett, perhaps he mote it deare aby.
    Cowherd (quoth she) were not, that thou wouldst fly,
    Ere he doe come, he should be soone in place.
    If I doe so, (sayd he) then liberty
    I leaue to you, for aye me to disgrace
With all those shames, that erst ye spake me to deface.

29

With that a Dwarfe she cald to her in hast,
    And taking from her hand a ring of gould,
    A priuy token, which betweene them past,
    Bad him to flie with all the speed he could,
    To *Crudor*, and desire him that he would
    Vouchsafe to reskue her against a Knight,
    Who through strong powre had now her self in hould,
    Hauing late slaine her Seneschall in fight,
And all her people murdred with outragious might.

30

The Dwarfe his way did hast, and went all night;
    But *Calidore* did with her there abyde
    The comming of that so much threatned Knight,
    Where that discourteous Dame with scornfull pryde,
    And fowle entreaty him indignifyde,
    That yron heart it hardly could sustaine;
    Yet he, that could his wrath full wisely guyde,
    Did well endure her womanish disdaine,
And did him selfe from fraile impatience refraine.

Stanza 24
5 **bryzes**: breezes, gadflies.   9 She greets him shamefully by foully reproaching him for wrong-doing.

Stanza 25
5 Her tone, implying 'surely you are going to ravish (**spoile**) me', and her claim that she cannot resist him, reveal her frustration in love.   7 **vnderstand**: come to know.

Stanza 26
1–3 Shamefastness, a state shared by Artegall at V xii 42.9, allows Calidore to ignore, and finally bind, the shame-producing Blatant Beast. In effect, he invokes the motto of the Order of the Garter, which Puttenham 1936:103 renders: 'Dishonored be he, who meanes vnhonorably'. **afford**: bestow, attach.   6–9 **ciuilitie**: see proem 4.5*n* and 1.6*n*. The **wicked customes** of the toll pass parallel the 'wicked customes' (V ii 28.8) of the toll bridge, which Artegall reforms by killing Pollente in contrast to Calidore who pardons Crudor.   **gentle** associates courtesy with the 'vertuous and gentle discipline' (*LR* 8) by which the poem fashions a gentle-

man or noble person.   **inhumanitie** signifies the want of courtesy proper to the civilized (*OED* 2). Cf. the praise of the Salvage Man's 'milde humanity, and perfect gentle mynd' at v 29.9.

Stanza 27
2 **manner**: custom.   8 **courteous lore**: doctrine of courtesy.

Stanza 28
2 **indignity**: disgraceful act.   4 **Abett**: uphold.   **it deare aby**: dearly suffer for it.   9 **deface**: defame.

Stanza 29
7 **hould**: custody.

Stanza 30
3 **threatned**: i.e. threatened against him, as 40.4.   4 The frequent association of discourtesy with pride in Bk VI is noted in *Var* 6.191, e.g. the unnamed 'proud discourteous knight' (ii Arg.).   5 **entreaty**: treatment.   **indignifyde**: treated with disdain, humiliated.

31

The morrow next, before the lampe of light,
    Aboue the earth vpreard his flaming head,
    The Dwarfe, which bore that message to her knight,
    Brought aunswere backe, that ere he tasted bread,
    He would her succour, and aliue or dead
    Her foe deliuer vp into her hand:
    Therefore he wild her doe away all dread;
    And that of him she mote assured stand,
He sent to her his basenet, as a faithfull band.

32

Thereof full blyth the Lady streight became,
    And gan t'augment her bitternesse much more:
    Yet no whit more appalled for the same,
    Ne ought dismayed was Sir *Calidore,*
    But rather did more chearefull seeme therefore.
    And hauing soone his armes about him dight,
    Did issue forth, to meete his foe afore;
    Where long he stayed not, when as a Knight
He spide come pricking on with al his powre and might.

33

Well weend he streight, that he should be the same,
    Which tooke in hand her quarrell to maintaine;
    Ne stayd to aske if it were he by name,
    But couch his speare, and ran at him amaine.
    They bene ymett in middest of the plaine,
    With so fell fury, and dispiteous forse,
    That neither could the others stroke sustaine,
    But rudely rowld to ground both man and horse,
Neither of other taking pitty nor remorse.

34

But *Calidore* vprose againe full light,
    Whiles yet his foe lay fast in sencelesse sound,
    Yet would he not him hurt, although he might:
    For shame he weend a sleeping wight to wound.
    But when *Briana* saw that drery stound,
    There where she stood vppon the Castle wall,
    She deem'd him sure to haue bene dead on ground,
    And made such piteous mourning therewithall,
That from the battlements she ready seem'd to fall.

35

Nathlesse at length him selfe he did vpreare
    In lustlesse wise, as if against his will,
    Ere he had slept his fill, he wakened were,
    And gan to stretch his limbs; which feeling ill
    Of his late fall, a while he rested still:
    But when he saw his foe before in vew,
    He shooke off luskishnesse, and courage chill
    Kindling a fresh, gan battell to renew,
To proue if better foote then horsebacke would ensew.

36

There then began a fearefull cruell fray
    Betwixt them two, for maystery of might.
    For both were wondrous practicke in that play,
    And passing well expert in single fight,
    And both inflam'd with furious despight:
    Which as it still encreast, so still increast
    Their cruell strokes and terrible affright;
    Ne once for ruth their rigour they release,
Ne once to breath a while their angers tempest ceast.

37

Thus long they trac'd and trauerst to and fro,
    And tryde all waies, how each mote entrance make
    Into the life of his malignant foe;
    They hew'd their helmes, and plates asunder brake,
    As they had potshares bene; for nought mote slake
    Their greedy vengeaunces, but goary blood,
    That at the last like to a purple lake
    Of bloudy gore congeal'd about them stood,
Which from their riuen sides forth gushed like a flood.

38

At length it chaunst, that both their hands on hie,
    At once did heaue, with all their powre and might,
    Thinking the vtmost of their force to trie,
    And proue the finall fortune of the fight:
    But *Calidore,* that was more quicke of sight,
    And nimbler handed, then his enemie,
    Preuented him before his stroke could light,
    And on the helmet smote him formerlie,
That made him stoupe to ground with meeke humilitie.

Stanza 31
9 In exchange for her ring at 29.2–3, which is her **faithfull band,** he sends her his helmet as a pledge to protect her. Accordingly, it figures in his defeat at 38.8–9.

Stanza 33
4 amaine: with full force; at once (stressing his failure to formally defy his opponent).

Stanza 34
2 sound: swoon. **5 drery stound:** grievous state of stupefaction.

Stanza 35
2 lustlesse: listless. **7 luskishnesse:** sluggishness. **9** To try if better fortune would follow being on foot.

Stanza 36
Their equal martial ability, which is registered in the grammatical parallelism in this stanza, comments on the need for courtesy to avoid violence; see Whigham 1984:79. **3 practicke:** experienced. **4 passing:** surpassing. **7 affright:** fearsomeness. **8 release:** moderated.

Stanza 37
1 trac'd and trauerst: pursued and then turned aside. **3 malignant:** evil; seeking to do evil to him. **5 potshares:** potsherds, fragments of a broken vessel. **7 lake:** pool (*OED* sb.[4] 2).

Stanza 38
7 Preuented: anticipated. **8 formerlie:** first.

39

And ere he could recouer foot againe,
 He following that faire aduantage fast,
 His stroke redoubled with such might and maine,
 That him vpon the ground he groueling cast;
 And leaping to him light, would haue vnlast
 His Helme, to make vnto his vengeance way.
 Who seeing, in what daunger he was plast,
 Cryde out, Ah mercie Sir, doe me not slay,
But saue my life, which lot before your foot doth lay.

40

With that his mortall hand a while he stayd,
 And hauing somewhat calm'd his wrathfull heat
 With goodly patience, thus he to him sayd;
 And is the boast of that proud Ladies threat,
 That menaced me from the field to beat,
 Now brought to this? By this now may ye learne,
 Strangers no more so rudely to intreat,
 But put away proud looke, and vsage sterne,
The which shal nought to you but foule dishonor yearne.

41

For nothing is more blamefull to a knight,
 That court'sie doth as well as armes professe,
 How euer strong and fortunate in fight,
 Then the reproch of pride and cruelnesse.
 In vaine he seeketh others to suppresse,
 Who hath not learnd him selfe first to subdew:
 All flesh is frayle, and full of ficklenesse,
 Subiect to fortunes chance, still chaunging new;
What haps to day to me, to morrow may to you.

42

Who will not mercie vnto others shew,
 How can he mercy euer hope to haue?
 To pay each with his owne is right and dew.
 Yet since ye mercie now doe need to craue,

I will it graunt, your hopelesse life to saue;
 With these conditions, which I will propound:
 First, that ye better shall your selfe behaue
 Vnto all errant knights, whereso on ground;
Next that ye Ladies ayde in euery stead and stound.

43

The wretched man, that all this while did dwell
 In dread of death, his heasts did gladly heare,
 And promist to performe his precept well,
 And whatsoeuer else he would requere.
 So suffring him to rise, he made him sweare
 By his owne sword, and by the crosse thereon,
 To take *Briana* for his louing fere,
 Withouten dowre or composition;
But to release his former foule condition.

44

All which accepting, and with faithfull oth
 Bynding himselfe most firmely to obay,
 He vp arose, how euer liefe or loth,
 And swore to him true fealtie for aye.
 Then forth he cald from sorrowfull dismay
 The sad *Briana*, which all this beheld:
 Who comming forth yet full of late affray,
 Sir *Calidore* vpcheard, and to her teld
All this accord, to which he *Crudor* had compeld.

45

Whereof she now more glad, then sory earst,
 All ouercome with infinite affect,
 For his exceeding courtesie, that pearst
 Her stubborne hart with inward deepe effect,
 Before his feet her selfe she did proiect,
 And him adoring as her liues deare Lord,
 With all due thankes, and dutifull respect,
 Her selfe acknowledg'd bound for that accord,
By which he had to her both life and loue restord.

Stanza 39
9 **lot**: fortune.

Stanza 40
4 **boast**: i.e. the one whom Briana boasted at 27.9 would defy him.   7 **intreat**: treat.   8 **sterne**: cruel.   9 **yearne**: earn.

Stanza 41
5 **suppresse**: subdue.   7 Proverbial: Smith 267.

Stanza 42
1–2 As Jas. 2.13: 'For there shalbe iudgement merciles to him that sheweth no mercie'.   3 Romans 13.7: 'Giue to all men therefore their duetie'.   7 **behaue**: conduct, bear.   9 . . . everywhere and at all times.

Stanza 43
2 **heasts**: 'conditions' (42.6).   3 **precept**: moral injunction. 6 Swearing by the sword is a common chivalric practice; see V viii 14.7. Swearing on the **crosse** formed by the hilt and blade of a sword in an act of mercy carries specifically Christian significance. That it leads Briana to be bound to Calidore at 45.8 and 46.8 emphasizes the central motif of binding in Bk VI; noted Bates 1992:158–59.   7 **fere**: wife.   8 **composition**: payment of money, in line with Calidore's rejection of 'hyre' at 47.2.   9 **release**: revoke.

Stanza 44
3 . . . however willing or unwilling.   7 **affray**: fright.   8 **teld**: told (an obs. form).

Stanza 45
2 **affect**: affection.   5 **proiect**: throw. *OED* credits S. with its first use in this sense.

46

So all returning to the Castle glad,
   Most ioyfully she them did entertaine,
   Where goodly glee and feast to them she made,
   To shew her thankefull mind and meaning faine,
   By all the meanes she mote it best explaine:
   And after all, vnto Sir *Calidore*
   She freely gaue that Castle for his paine,
   And her selfe bound to him for euermore;
So wondrously now chaung'd, from that she was afore.

47

But *Calidore* himselfe would not retaine
   Nor land nor fee, for hyre of his good deede,
   But gaue them streight vnto that Squire againe,
   Whom from her Seneschall he lately freed,
   And to his damzell as their rightfull meed,
   For recompence of all their former wrong:
   There he remaind with them right well agreed,
   Till of his wounds he wexed hole and strong,
And then to his first quest he passed forth along.

Stanza 46
4 meaning faine: well-disposed intentions, favourable disposition. **5 explaine**: display.

Stanza 47
2 Briana's gift to Calidore and his receiving it not for himself as **hyre** (i.e. reward) for what he has done but freely offering it to the squire and damsel express the mutual actions of offering, receiving, and giving in return, which is characteristic of courtesy; see proem 7*n*. **9 his first quest**: repeated at ii 1.6 to isolate the opening episode as an introductory exemplum of courtesy.

Cant. II.

*Calidore sees young Tristram slay
A proud discourteous knight,
He makes him Squire, and of him learnes
his state and present plight.*

1

WHat vertue is so fitting for a knight,
  Or for a Ladie, whom a knight should loue,
  As Curtesie, to beare themselues aright
  To all of each degree, as doth behoue?
  For whether they be placed high aboue,
  Or low beneath, yet ought they well to know
  Their good, that none them rightly may reproue
  Of rudenesse, for not yeelding what they owe:
Great skill it is such duties timely to bestow.

2

Thereto great helpe dame Nature selfe doth lend:
  For some so goodly gratious are by kind,
  That euery action doth them much commend,
  And in the eyes of men great liking find;
  Which others, that haue greater skill in mind,
  Though they enforce themselues, cannot attaine.
  For euerie thing, to which one is inclin'd,
  Doth best become, and greatest grace doth gaine:
Yet praise likewise deserue good thewes, enforst with paine.

3

That well in courteous *Calidore* appeares,
  Whose euery act and deed, that he did say,
  Was like enchantment, that through both the eyes,
  And both the eares did steale the hart away.

He now againe is on his former way,
  To follow his first quest, when as he spyde
  A tall young man from thence not farre away,
  Fighting on foot, as well he him descryde,
Against an armed knight, that did on horsebacke ryde.

4

And them beside a Ladie faire he saw,
  Standing alone on foot, in foule array:
  To whom himselfe he hastily did draw,
  To weet the cause of so vncomely fray,
  And to depart them, if so be he may.
  But ere he came in place, that youth had kild
  That armed knight, that low on ground he lay;
  Which when he saw, his hart was inly child
With great amazement, and his thought with wonder fild.

5

Him stedfastly he markt, and saw to bee
  A goodly youth of amiable grace,
  Yet but a slender slip, that scarse did see
  Yet seuenteene yeares, but tall and faire of face
  That sure he deem'd him borne of noble race.
  All in a woodmans iacket he was clad
  Of Lincolne greene, belayd with siluer lace;
  And on his head an hood with aglets sprad,
And by his side his hunters horne he hanging had.

Book VI Canto ii

Argument
2 discourteous knight: so named at 43.1 and iii 18.6, but otherwise, not named, nor his lady.

Stanza 1
6–7 know | Their good: know how to behave with the respect proper to each social class, a skill shown by the hermit at v 36.8, Reverence at I x 7.5, and Curtesie at IV x 51.4. Called 'civility' at x 23.7–9; see proem 4.5n.

Stanza 2
6 enforce: exert. **7–9** I.e. doing what comes naturally is done best, though good behaviour (**thewes**) practised with difficulty when against the grain, also deserves praise. On the distinction, see iii 1–2n.

Stanza 3
1 That: i.e. being 'so goodly gratious' (2.2). **2–4 act and deed**: 'act and word' conj. Church 1758. Calidore's eloquence is that of Hercules to whom he is compared at xii 32, 35.

Stanza 4
2 foule: soiled. **4 vncomely** because 'hit is not for one knyght to be on foote and the other on horsbak' (Malory 4.18–19). **5 depart**: separate.

Stanza 5
4 seuenteene yeares: the traditional age of attaining manhood or womanhood, e.g. of Pyrocles and Pamela in Sidney, *Old Arcadia* 10, 5. At 32.8, Tristram claims that he is 'yet past a boy'. **tall**: also handsome. **7 Lincolne greene**: a bright green material, reputed 'the best greene of *England*' (Drayton 1931–41:4.517) and worn by Robin Hood and his men (529). **belayd**: ornamented. **8 aglets**: tags or sequins.

6

Buskins he wore of costliest cordwayne,
    Pinckt vpon gold, and paled part per part,
    As then the guize was for each gentle swayne;
    In his right hand he held a trembling dart,
    Whose fellow he before had sent apart;
    And in his left he held a sharpe borespeare,
    With which he wont to launch the saluage hart
    Of many a Lyon, and of many a Beare
That first vnto his hand in chase did happen neare.

7

Whom *Calidore* a while well hauing vewed,
    At length bespake; What meanes this, gentle swaine?
    Why hath thy hand too bold it selfe embrewed
    In blood of knight, the which by thee is slaine,
    By thee no knight; which armes impugneth plaine?
    Certes (said he) loth were I to haue broken
    The law of armes; yet breake it should againe,
    Rather then let my selfe of wight be stroken,
So long as these two armes were able to be wroken.

8

For not I him, as this his Ladie here
    May witnesse well, did offer first to wrong,
    Ne surely thus vnarm'd I likely were;
    But he me first, through pride and puissance strong
    Assayld, not knowing what to armes doth long.
    Perdie great blame, (then said Sir *Calidore*)
    For armed knight a wight vnarm'd to wrong.
    But then aread, thou gentle chyld, wherefore
Betwixt you two began this strife and sterne vprore.

9

That shall I sooth (said he) to you declare.
    I whose vnryper yeares are yet vnfit
    For thing of weight, or worke of greater care,
    Doe spend my dayes, and bend my carelesse wit
    To saluage chace, where I thereon may hit
    In all this forrest, and wyld wooddie raine:
    Where, as this day I was enraunging it,
    I chaunst to meete this knight, who there lyes slaine,
Together with this Ladie, passing on the plaine.

10

The knight, as ye did see, on horsebacke was,
    And this his Ladie, (that him ill became,)
    On her faire feet by his horse side did pas
    Through thicke and thin, vnfit for any Dame.
    Yet not content, more to increase his shame,
    When so she lagged, as she needs mote so,
    He with his speare, that was to him great blame,
    Would thumpe her forward, and inforce to goe,
Weeping to him in vaine, and making piteous woe.

11

Which when I saw, as they me passed by,
    Much was I moued in indignant mind,
    And gan to blame him for such cruelty
    Towards a Ladie, whom with vsage kind
    He rather should haue taken vp behind.
    Wherewith he wroth, and full of proud disdaine,
    Tooke in foule scorne, that I such fault did find,
    And me in lieu thereof reuil'd againe,
Threatning to chastize me, as doth t'a chyld pertaine.

12

Which I no lesse disdayning, backe returned
    His scornefull taunts vnto his teeth againe,
    That he streight way with haughtie choler burned,
    And with his speare strooke me one stroke or twaine;
    Which I enforst to beare though to my paine,
    Cast to requite, and with a slender dart,
    Fellow of this I beare, throwne not in vaine,
    Strooke him, as seemeth, vnderneath the hart,
That through the wound his spirit shortly did depart.

13

Much did Sir *Calidore* admyre his speach
    Tempred so well, but more admyr'd the stroke
    That through the mayles had made so strong a breach
    Into his hart, and had so sternely wroke
    His wrath on him, that first occasion broke.
    Yet rested not, but further gan inquire
    Of that same Ladie, whether what he spoke,
    Were soothly so, and that th'vnrighteous ire
Of her owne knight, had giuen him his owne due hire.

Stanza 6
Tristram appears as a male Belphœbe wearing, e.g. the **cordwayne** that she wears at II iii 27.3. **2 Pinckt vpon gold**: ornamented by perforating with a design to reveal the gold backing. **paled part per part**: a heraldic term signifying marked with vertical bands of colour. **3 guize**: fashion. **4 trembling**: quivering with the tension of the intended thrust. **7 launch**: pierce.

Stanza 7
3 embrewed: stained. **5** I.e. which clearly violates the **law of armes** that only knights may fight each other. **armes** provokes Tristram's play on the word in 9. **9 wroken**: avenged.

Stanza 8
3 I.e. since I am unarmed, it is unlikely that I would first challenge him to fight. **5 long**: belong. **8 aread**: tell. **gentle chyld**: noble youth.

Stanza 9
4 carelesse: carefree. **6 wooddie raine**: woodland realm. **7 enraunging it**: roaming in it.

Stanza 11
8 And reviled me for reviling him.

Stanza 12
6 Cast: determined. **9 through**: to be taken literally, as at IV iii 12.7–9.

14

Of all which, when as she could nought deny,
  But cleard that stripling of th'imputed blame,
  Sayd then Sir *Calidore*; Neither will I
  Him charge with guilt, but rather doe quite clame:
  For what he spake, for you he spake it, Dame;
  And what he did, he did him selfe to saue:
  Against both which that knight wrought knightlesse
  For knights and all men this by nature haue,   (shame.
Towards all womenkind them kindly to behaue.

15

But sith that he is gone irreuocable,
  Please it you Ladie, to vs to aread,
  What cause could make him so dishonourable,
  To driue you so on foot vnfit to tread,
  And lackey by him, gainst all womanhead?
  Certes Sir knight (sayd she) full loth I were
  To rayse a lyuing blame against the dead:
  But since it me concernes, my selfe to clere,
I will the truth discouer, as it chaunst whylere.

16

This day, as he and I together roade
  Vpon our way, to which we weren bent,
  We chaunst to come foreby a couert glade
  Within a wood, whereas a Ladie gent
  Sate with a knight in ioyous iolliment,
  Of their franke loues, free from all gealous spyes:
  Faire was the Ladie sure, that mote content
  An hart, not carried with too curious eyes,
And vnto him did shew all louely courtesyes.

17

Whom when my knight did see so louely faire,
  He inly gan her louer to enuy,
  And wish, that he part of his spoyle might share.
  Whereto when as my presence he did spy
  To be a let, he bad me by and by

For to alight: but when as I was loth,
  My loues owne part to leaue so suddenly,
  He with strong hand down from his steed me throw'th,
And with presumpteous powre against that knight streight
                                          (go'th.

18

Vnarm'd all was the knight, as then more meete
  For Ladies seruice, and for loues delight,
  Then fearing any foeman there to meete:
  Whereof he taking oddes, streight bids him dight
  Himselfe to yeeld his loue, or else to fight.
  Whereat the other starting vp dismayd,
  Yet boldly answer'd, as he rightly might;
  To leaue his loue he should be ill apayd,
In which he had good right gaynst all, that it gainesayd.

19

Yet since he was not presently in plight
  Her to defend', or his to iustifie,
  He him requested, as he was a knight,
  To lend him day his better right to trie,
  Or stay till he his armes, which were thereby,
  Might lightly fetch. But he was fierce and whot,
  Ne time would giue, nor any termes aby,
  But at him flew, and with his speare him smot;
From which to thinke to saue himselfe, it booted not.

20

Meane while his Ladie, which this outrage saw,
  Whilest they together for the quarrey stroue,
  Into the couert did her selfe withdraw,
  And closely hid her selfe within the groue.
  My knight hers soone, as seemes, to daunger droue
  And left sore wounded: but when her he mist,
  He woxe halfe mad, and in that rage gan roue
  And range through all the wood, where so he wist
She hidden was, and sought her so long, as him list.

Stanza 13
5 . . . that had first caused the fight.

Stanza 14
4 **quite clame**: i.e. quitclaim, acquit. 7 **knightlesse**: unknightly. 8–9 He agrees with Tristram's claim at 11.4–5 but ignores S.'s claim at 2.2 that only 'some' are gracious 'by kind'; others, such as Crudor at i 42.9, must be compelled to treat women kindly.

Stanza 15
2 **aread**: declare. 5 **lackey**: run as a footman. 6–7 A proverbial sentiment: Smith 151.

Stanza 16
The motif in Bk VI of being surprised in a moment of diversion, e.g. iii 20–21, 23–24, iv 17, etc., is noted by Berger 1988:219. 4–6 Lovers 'Ioying together in vnblam'd delight' (43.3) are present in the garden of Adonis at III vi 41.5–9 and

in the garden surrounding the temple of Venus at IV x 26.1–2. Cf. Amoret in bed with Britomart at IV i 15.7–9. **gent**: gentle. 7–8 This remark suggests a jilted lady's own **too curious** (i.e. fastidious) or envious eyes. 9 **louely**: loving. **courtesyes**: courteous behaviour.

Stanza 17
5 **let**: hindrance. 7 **part**: side.

Stanza 18
4 **oddes**: advantage. **dight**: prepare. 8 **ill apayd**: ill-pleased.

Stanza 19
1 **plight**: physical condition. 2 **his**: i.e. his 'good right' (18.9). 6 **lightly**: quickly. 7–8 **with his speare** notes his double offence against courtesy: being mounted, he fights an unarmed man on foot. **aby**: abide.

21

But when as her he by no meanes could find,
  After long search and chauff, he turned backe
  Vnto the place, where me he left behind:
  There gan he me to curse and ban, for lacke
  Of that faire bootie, and with bitter wracke
  To wreake on me the guilt of his owne wrong.
  Of all which I yet glad to beare the packe,
  Stroue to appease him, and perswaded long:
But still his passion grew more violent and strong.

22

Then as it were t'auenge his wrath on mee,
  When forward we should fare, he flat refused
  To take me vp (as this young man did see)
  Vpon his steed, for no iust cause accused,
  But forst to trot on foot, and foule misused,
  Pounching me with the butt end of his speare,
  In vaine complayning, to be so abused.
  For he regarded neither playnt nor teare,
But more enforst my paine, the more my plaints to heare.

23

So passed we, till this young man vs met,
  And being moou'd with pittie of my plight,
  Spake, as was meet, for ease of my regret:
  Whereof befell, what now is in your sight.
  Now sure (then said Sir *Calidore*) and right
  Me seemes, that him befell by his owne fault:
  Who euer thinkes through confidence of might,
  Or through support of count'nance proud and hault
To wrong the weaker, oft falles in his owne assault.

24

Then turning backe vnto that gentle boy,
  Which had himselfe so stoutly well acquit;
  Seeing his face so louely sterne and coy,
  And hearing th'answeres of his pregnant wit,

He praysd it much, and much admyred it;
  That sure he weend him borne of noble blood,
  With whom those graces did so goodly fit:
  And when he long had him beholding stood,
He burst into these words, as to him seemed good.

25

Faire gentle swayne, and yet as stout as fayre,
  That in these woods amongst the Nymphs dost wonne,
  Which daily may to thy sweete lookes repayre,
  As they are wont vnto *Latonaes* sonne,
  After his chace on woodie *Cynthus* donne:
  Well may I certes such an one thee read,
  As by thy worth thou worthily hast wonne,
  Or surely borne of some Heroicke sead,
That in thy face appeares and gratious goodlyhead.

26

But should it not displease thee it to tell;
  (Vnlesse thou in these woods thy selfe conceale,
  For loue amongst the woodie Gods to dwell;)
  I would thy selfe require thee to reueale,
  For deare affection and vnfayned zeale,
  Which to thy noble personage I beare,
  And wish thee grow in worship and great weale.
  For since the day that armes I first did reare,
I neuer saw in any greater hope appeare.

27

To whom then thus the noble youth; May be
  Sir knight, that by discouering my estate,
  Harme may arise vnweeting vnto me;
  Nathelesse, sith ye so courteous seemed late,
  To you I will not feare it to relate.
  Then wote ye that I am a Briton borne,
  Sonne of a King, how euer thorough fate
  Or fortune I my countrie haue forlorne,
And lost the crowne, which should my head by right adorne.

Stanza 21
2 **chauff**: raging. 4 **ban**: revile. 5 **wracke**: vengeance; violence. 7 **packe**: the burden of his blows.

Stanza 23
3 **regret**: sorrow; or grief which she regrets to endure. 7 **confidence**: overboldness. 8 **hault**: haughty.

Stanza 24
3 **coy**: modest, reserved. 6 Repeating 5.5 to stress that noble blood is revealed in appearance and actions. 8–9 Calidore's admiring gaze on the 'sweete lookes' (25.3) of **that gentle boy**, which began at 3.6–9, and continued at 5.1 and 7.1, now proves overwhelming. It leads to his hope in Tristram's future expressed at 26.9 and repeated at 34.3 and 36.8.

Stanza 25
1 **stout**: brave. 4–5 **Latonaes sonne** is Apollo; **Cynthus** is the mountain in Delos where he and Diana were born. His counterpart, Belphœbe, is compared to Diana 'on *Cynthus*

greene' at II iii 31.1–5. 6 **read**: take to be. 9 **goodlyhead**: excellence; suggesting that noble birth is the source of his goodness.

Stanza 26
5 **zeale**: devotion. 7 **worship**: honour; good and honourable report. **weale**: well-being.

Stanzas 27–32
S. draws on Malory 8.1–3 chiefly for Tristram's name, place of birth, his education in hunting and hawking, his fear of his uncle, and the seven years spent in the woods. In Malory, Tristram's mother Elizabeth dies, not his father Melyodas; and his step-mother, not his uncle, threatens him. S. transfers the sadness of his birth, which gave him his name, to his father. See 'Tristram' in the *SEnc*.

Stanza 27
2 **estate**: state, rank. 7 **how euer**: although. 8 **forlorne**: left.

28

And *Tristram* is my name, the onely heire
    Of good king *Meliogras* which did rayne
    In Cornewale, till that he through liues despeire
    Vntimely dyde, before I did attaine
    Ripe yeares of reason, my right to maintaine.
    After whose death, his brother seeing mee
    An infant, weake a kingdome to sustaine,
    Vpon him tooke the roiall high degree,
And sent me, where him list, instructed for to bee.

29

The widow Queene my mother, which then hight
    Faire *Emiline*, conceiuing then great feare
    Of my fraile safetie, resting in the might
    Of him, that did the kingly Scepter beare,
    Whose gealous dread induring not a peare,
    Is wont to cut off all, that doubt may breed,
    Thought best away me to remoue somewhere
    Into some forrein land, where as no need
Of dreaded daunger might his doubtfull humor feed.

30

So taking counsell of a wise man red,
    She was by him aduiz'd, to send me quight
    Out of the countrie, wherein I was bred,
    The which the fertile *Lionesse* is hight,
    Into the land of *Faerie*, where no wight
    Should weet of me, nor worke me any wrong.
    To whose wise read she hearkning, sent me streight
    Into this land, where I haue wond thus long,
Since I was ten yeares old, now growen to stature strong.

31

All which my daies I haue not lewdly spent,
    Nor spilt the blossome of my tender yeares
    In ydlesse, but as was conuenient,
    Haue trayned bene with many noble feres
    In gentle thewes, and such like seemely leres.
    Mongst which my most delight hath alwaies been,
    To hunt the saluage chace amongst my peres,
    Of all that raungeth in the forrest greene;
Of which none is to me vnknowne, that eu'r was seene.

32

Ne is there hauke, which mantleth her on pearch,
    Whether high towring, or accoasting low,
    But I the measure of her flight doe search,
    And all her pray, and all her diet know.
    Such be our ioyes, which in these forrests grow:
    Onely the vse of armes, which most I ioy,
    And fitteth most for noble swayne to know,
    I haue not tasted yet, yet past a boy,
And being now high time these strong ioynts to imploy.

33

Therefore, good Sir, sith now occasion fit
    Doth fall, whose like hereafter seldome may,
    Let me this craue, vnworthy though of it,
    That ye will make me Squire without delay,
    That from henceforth in batteilous array
    I may beare armes, and learne to vse them right;
    The rather since that fortune hath this day
    Giuen to me the spoile of this dead knight,
These goodly gilden armes, which I haue won in fight.

34

All which when well Sir *Calidore* had heard,
    Him much more now, then earst he gan admire,
    For the rare hope which in his yeares appear'd,
    And thus replide; Faire chyld, the high desire
    To loue of armes, which in you doth aspire,
    I may not certes without blame denie;
    But rather wish, that some more noble hire,
    (Though none more noble then is cheualrie,)
I had, you to reward with greater dignitie.

35

There him he causd to kneele, and made to sweare
    Faith to his knight, and truth to Ladies all,
    And neuer to be recreant, for feare
    Of perill, or of ought that might befall:
    So he him dubbed, and his Squire did call.
    Full glad and ioyous then young *Tristram* grew,
    Like as a flowre, whose silken leaues small,
    Long shut vp in the bud from heauens vew,
At length breakes forth, and brode displayes his smyling hew.

Stanza 29

1 then: either 'then conceiving'; or implying that she is dead. **2 Emiline**: cf. Emmilen, one of the 'wemen valorous' cited by Glauce at III iii 54.9. **5 peare**: rival. **6 doubt**: danger. **9 doubtfull**: apprehensive, suspicious.

Stanza 30

1 . . . of a man esteemed wise. **4 Lionesse**: the fabled land west of Cornwall between Land's End and the Scillies. **7 read**: counsel.

Stanza 31

1 lewdly: foolishly. **2 spilt**: spoiled. **3 conuenient**: proper. **4 feres**: companions. **5 thewes**: manners. **leres**: lessons.

Stanza 32

1–4 Tristram began 'alle these termes we haue yet of haukyng and huntyng' (Malory), as he illustrates: **mantleth**: the

perched bird stretches one wing and then the other over the corresponding outstretched leg; **towring**: either mounting up in order to swoop down upon a quarry, or 'touring', i.e. turning, wheeling; **accoasting**: when a hawk skims the ground. **8 tasted**: experienced.

Stanza 33

9 gilden: gilded, as 44.7; or being of 'bright mettall' (39.4).

Stanza 34

4 Faire chyld marks Tristram's transition to manhood. At 11.9 he was treated as a child; at 36.3 he becomes 'Chyld *Tristram*'.

Stanza 35

7–9 The simile extends Tristram's reference at 31.2–3 to the unspoiled blossom of his youth, and refers back to the flower image in proem 3.

36

Thus when they long had treated to and fro,
    And *Calidore* betooke him to depart,
    Chyld *Tristram* prayd, that he with him might goe
On his aduenture, vowing not to start,
But wayt on him in euery place and part.
    Whereat Sir *Calidore* did much delight,
    And greatly ioy'd at his so noble hart,
    In hope he sure would proue a doughtie knight:
Yet for the time this answere he to him behight.

37

Glad would I surely be, thou courteous Squire,
    To haue thy presence in my present quest,
    That mote thy kindled courage set on fire,
And flame forth honour in thy noble brest:
But I am bound by vow, which I profest
    To my dread Soueraine, when I it assayd,
    That in atchieuement of her high behest,
    I should no creature ioyne vnto mine ayde,
For thy I may not graunt, that ye so greatly prayde.

38

But since this Ladie is all desolate,
    And needeth safegard now vpon her way,
    Ye may doe well in this her needfull state
To succour her, from daunger of dismay;
That thankfull guerdon may to you repay.
    The noble ympe of such new seruice fayne,
    It gladly did accept, as he did say.
    So taking courteous leaue, they parted twayne,
And *Calidore* forth passed to his former payne.

39

But *Tristram* then despoyling that dead knight
    Of all those goodly implements of prayse,
    Long fed his greedie eyes with the faire sight
Of the bright mettall, shyning like Sunne rayes;
Handling and turning them a thousand wayes.
    And after hauing them vpon him dight,
    He tooke that Ladie, and her vp did rayse
    Vpon the steed of her owne late dead knight,
So with her marched forth, as she did him behight.

40

There to their fortune leaue we them awhile,
    And turne we backe to good Sir *Calidore*;
    Who ere he thence had traueild many a mile,
Came to the place, whereas ye heard afore
This knight, whom *Tristram* slew, had wounded sore
    Another knight in his despiteous pryde;
    There he that knight found lying on the flore,
    With many wounds full perilous and wyde,
That all his garments, and the grasse in vermeill dyde.

41

And there beside him sate vpon the ground
    His wofull Ladie, piteously complayning
    With loud laments that most vnluckie stound,
And her sad selfe with carefull hand constrayning
To wype his wounds, and ease their bitter payning.
    Which sorie sight when *Calidore* did vew
    With heauie eyne, from teares vneath refrayning,
    His mightie hart their mournefull case can rew,
And for their better comfort to them nigher drew.

42

Then speaking to the Ladie, thus he sayd:
    Ye dolefull Dame, let not your griefe empeach
    To tell, what cruell hand hath thus arayd
This knight vnarm'd, with so vnknightly breach
Of armes, that if I yet him nigh may reach,
    I may auenge him of so foule despight.
    The Ladie hearing his so courteous speach,
    Gan reare her eyes as to the chearefull light,
And from her sory hart few heauie words forth sight.

43

In which she shew'd, how that discourteous knight
    (Whom *Tristram* slew) them in that shadow found,
    Ioying together in vnblam'd delight,
And him vnarm'd, as now he lay on ground,
Charg'd with his speare and mortally did wound,
    Withouten cause, but onely her to reaue
    From him, to whom she was for euer bound:
    Yet when she fled into that couert greaue,
He her not finding, both them thus nigh dead did leaue.

Stanza 36
1 treated: conversed. **3 Chyld**: applied to any youth of gentle birth but particularly to a squire awaiting knighthood. **4 start**: i.e. desert him. **9 behight**: addressed.

Stanza 37
5–9 As Artegall rejects the company of a squire at V i 30.6 in order to travel alone as he vowed at IV vi 44.6–9, according to 'custome ancient'. **assayd**: set out to do. **For thy**: therefore.

Stanza 38
6 fayne: glad.

Stanza 39
1–5 The discourteous knight had lusted after another's love; Tristram lusts after his arms, and gains both. Evidently 'loue of

armes' (34.5) by one worthy of them, and needing them, exempts him from the Palmer's injunction: 'To spoile the dead of weed | Is sacrilege, and doth all sinnes exceed' (II viii 16.4–5). **2** Arms are **implements of prayse** as they provide the means to get it; cf. II xii 80.1–2. **9 behight**: command.

Stanza 40
7 flore: ground.

Stanza 41
3 stound: troublous time. **4 constrayning**: forcing; exerting. **7 vneath**: with difficulty. **8 can rew**: did pity.

Stanza 42
2 empeach: hinder. **3 arayd**: afflicted; literally, 'dressed him in his wounds'. **9 heauie**: sad. **sight**: sighed.

44

When *Calidore* this ruefull storie had
 Well vnderstood, he gan of her demand,
 What manner wight he was, and how yclad,
 Which had this outrage wrought with wicked hand.
 She then, like as she best could vnderstand,
 Him thus describ'd, to be of stature large,
 Clad all in gilden armes, with azure band
 Quartred athwart, and bearing in his targe
A Ladie on rough waues, row'd in a sommer barge.

45

Then gan Sir *Calidore* to ghesse streight way
 By many signes, which she described had,
 That this was he, whom *Tristram* earst did slay,
 And to her said; Dame be no longer sad:
 For he, that hath your Knight so ill bestad,
 Is now him selfe in much more wretched plight;
 These eyes him saw vpon the cold earth sprad,
 The meede of his desert for that despight,
Which to your selfe he wrought, and to your loued knight.

46

Therefore faire Lady lay aside this griefe,
 Which ye haue gathered to your gentle hart,
 For that displeasure; and thinke what reliefe
 Were best deuise for this your louers smart,

And how ye may him hence, and to what part
 Conuay to be recur'd. She thankt him deare,
 Both for that newes he did to her impart,
 And for the courteous care, which he did beare
Both to her loue, and to her selfe in that sad dreare.

47

Yet could she not deuise by any wit,
 How thence she might conuay him to some place.
 For him to trouble she it thought vnfit,
 That was a straunger to her wretched case;
 And him to beare, she thought it thing too base.
 Which when as he perceiu'd, he thus bespake;
 Faire Lady let it not you seeme disgrace,
 To beare this burden on your dainty backe;
My selfe will beare a part, coportion of your packe.

48

So off he did his shield, and downeward layd
 Vpon the ground, like to an hollow beare;
 And powring balme, which he had long puruayd,
 Into his wounds, him vp thereon did reare,
 And twixt them both with parted paines did beare,
 Twixt life and death, not knowing what was donne.
 Thence they him carried to a Castle neare,
 In which a worthy auncient Knight did wonne:
Where what ensu'd, shall in next Canto be begonne.

Stanza 43
2 shadow: shady place. **3 vnblam'd**: blameless, unblameable; i.e. neither shameful in them nor deserving shameful attack. **6 reaue**: take by force. **8 greaue**: thicket. **9 She is nigh dead** through shame; see iii 11.6–8.

Stanza 44
7–9 The **azure band . . . athwart** suggests the blue diagonal St Andrew's Cross or saltire, though **Quartred** applies better to the Red Cross Knight's 'bloodie Crosse, that quartred all the field' (II i 18.9). The *impresa* on his shield alludes – mysteriously, as an *impresa* should – to the state of his lady, a Phædria in her **barge** (a small boat) come to grief, as happens to her at II xii 16.7–9.

Stanza 45
4–9 News of the death of the knight who had wounded her lover and harassed her seems to console her, for she thanks him for it at 46.6.

Stanza 46
3 displeasure: offence. **6 recur'd**: healed. **9 dreare**: dreary state.

Stanza 47
5 A bawdy sense may be implicit, as Cheney suggests in *SpN* 1978:24, but primarily her fear is social: in bearing him, and therefore being under him, she would be **base**, i.e. of low class. Cf. Turpine's response at iii 31.7–9 to the request that he bear the wounded Serena. While she may be too fastidious, not allowing that 'Entire affection hateth nicer hands' (I viii 40.3), she helps carry him on Calidore's shield. **9 coportion**: joint portion.

Stanza 48
3 long puruayd: provided long before. **5 parted paines**: shared labour.

Cant. III.

Calidore brings Priscilla home,
Pursues the Blatant Beast:
Saues Serena whilest Calepine
By Turpine is opprest.

nature or class?

1

True is, that whilome that good Poet sayd,
   The gentle minde by gentle deeds is knowne.
For a man by nothing is so well bewrayd,
As by his manners, in which plaine is showne
Of what degree and what race he is growne.
For seldome seene, a trotting Stalion get
An ambling Colt, that is his proper owne:
So seldome seene, that one in basenesse set
Doth noble courage shew, with curteous manners met.

2

But euermore contrary hath bene tryde,
   That gentle bloud will gentle manners breed;
   As well may be in *Calidore* descryde,
   By late ensample of that courteous deed,
   Done to that wounded Knight in his great need,
   Whom on his backe he bore, till he him brought
   Vnto the Castle where they had decreed,
   There of the Knight, the which that Castle ought,
To make abode that night he greatly was besought.

3

He was to weete a man of full ripe yeares,
   That in his youth had beene of mickle might,
   And borne great sway in armes amongst his peares:
   But now weake age had dimd his candle light.

Yet was he courteous still to euery wight,
   And loued all that did to armes incline,
   And was the father of that wounded Knight,
   Whom *Calidore* thus carried on his chine,
And *Aldus* was his name, and his sonnes *Aladine*.

4

Who when he saw his sonne so ill bedight,
   With bleeding wounds, brought home vpon a Beare,
   By a faire Lady, and a straunger Knight,
   Was inly touched with compassion deare,
   And deare affection of so dolefull dreare,
   That he these words burst forth; Ah sory boy,
   Is this the hope that to my hoary heare
   Thou brings? aie me, is this the timely ioy,
Which I expected long, now turnd to sad annoy?

5

Such is the weakenesse of all mortall hope;
   So tickle is the state of earthly things,
   That ere they come vnto their aymed scope,
   They fall too short of our fraile reckonings,
   And bring vs bale and bitter sorrowings,
   In stead of comfort, which we should embrace:
   This is the state of Keasars and of Kings.
   Let none therefore, that is in meaner place,
Too greatly grieue at any his vnlucky case.

Book VI Canto iii

Stanzas 1–2
The distinction between nature and nurture, i.e. between those gracious 'by kynd' (i.e. by nature) and those who have 'learn'd the art' (vi 43), is of central concern in a poem that seeks 'to fashion a gentleman or noble person in vertuous and gentle discipline' (*LR* 8). At II ii 6, the Palmer distinguishes between the virtues 'indewd | By great Dame Nature' and those added 'by guifte of later grace'. It is esp. important in the treatment of courtesy, being first mentioned at ii 7–9, and continued at v 1–2, vi 43.1–3, and vii 1. S. praises 'gentle bloud' again at v 1.2, and 'noble blood' at ii 24.6 and v 2.7, though he allows that God 'hathe made of one blood all mankinde' (Acts 17.26) by having Calepine say at iv 35–36 that those of unknown lineage may become worthy through proper nurture. See 'lineage', and 'nature and art' in the *SEnc*, and Schoenfeldt 1994:154–56.

Stanza 1
1–2 whilome: once upon a time.   **that good Poet** is Chaucer who writes in the *Wife of Bath's Tale* that 'he is gentil that dooth gentil dedis' (1170; cf. 1113–24), which is not quite

what S. says he says.   **3–4** Proverbial: Smith 516.   **5 degree**: rank.   **6–7** Proverbial: Smith 786.   **9 courage**: heart, nature. **met**: united.

Stanza 2
1 tryde: demonstrated.   **6 on his backe**, rather than hers, as he suggested at ii 47.8, or on his shield as at 48; cf. 4.2. **7 decreed**: decided.   **8 ought**: owned.

Stanza 3
8 chine: back.   **9 Aldus**: from 'ald' (a form of 'eld'), as he is of **weake age** and called 'old Knight' at 6.1 and 9.4. In Tasso, *Ger. Lib.* 1.83, Aladin is aged.   **Aladine**: 'like Aldus', i.e. as Aldus was in his youth, 'lusty' (7.6) and 'gentle' (8.4). See 'Aladine, Priscilla' in the *SEnc*.

Stanza 4
4 deare: heartfelt; for one dear to him.   **5 affection**: feeling. **dreare**: sorrow.   **6 sory**: wretched.   **8 timely**: i.e. brought in the fullness of time.

Stanza 5
2 tickle: uncertain.   **3 aymed scope**: mark aimed at.

6

So well and wisely did that good old Knight
    Temper his griefe, and turned it to cheare,
    To cheare his guests, whom he had stayd that night,
    And make their welcome to them well appeare:
    That to Sir *Calidore* was easie geare;
    But that faire Lady would be cheard for nought,
    But sigh'd and sorrow'd for her louer deare,
    And inly did afflict her pensiue thought,
With thinking to what case her name should now be brought.

7

For she was daughter to a noble Lord,
    Which dwelt thereby, who sought her to affy
    To a great pere; but she did disaccord,
    Ne could her liking to his loue apply,
    But lou'd this fresh young Knight, who dwelt her ny,
    The lusty *Aladine*, though meaner borne,
    And of lesse liuelood and hability,
    Yet full of valour, the which did adorne
His meanesse much, and make her th'others riches scorne.

8

So hauing both found fit occasion,
    They met together in that luckelesse glade;
    Where that proud Knight in his presumption
    The gentle *Aladine* did earst inuade,
    Being vnarm'd, and set in secret shade.
    Whereof she now bethinking, gan t'aduize,
    How great a hazard she at earst had made
    Of her good fame, and further gan deuize,
How she the blame might salue with coloured disguize.

9

But *Calidore* with all good courtesie
    Fain'd her to frolicke, and to put away
    The pensiue fit of her melancholie;
    And that old Knight by all meanes did assay,

To make them both as merry as he may.
    So they the euening past, till time of rest,
    When *Calidore* in seemly good array
    Vnto his bowre was brought, and there vndrest,
Did sleepe all night through weary trauell of his quest.

10

But faire *Priscilla* (so that Lady hight)
    Would to no bed, nor take no kindely sleepe,
    But by her wounded loue did watch all night,
    And all the night for bitter anguish weepe,
    And with her teares his wounds did wash and steepe.
    So well she washt them, and so well she wacht him,
    That of the deadly swound, in which full deepe
    He drenched was, she at the length dispacht him,
And droue away the stound, which mortally attacht him.

11

The morrow next, when day gan to vplooke,
    He also gan vplooke with drery eye,
    Like one that out of deadly dreame awooke:
    Where when he saw his faire *Priscilla* by,
    He deepely sigh'd, and groaned inwardly,
    To thinke of this ill state, in which she stood,
    To which she for his sake had weetingly
    Now brought her selfe, and blam'd her noble blood:
For first, next after life, he tendered her good.

12

Which she perceiuing, did with plenteous teares
    His care more then her owne compassionate,
    Forgetfull of her owne, to minde his feares:
    So both conspiring, gan to intimate
    Each others griefe with zeale affectionate,
    And twixt them twaine with equall care to cast,
    How to saue hole her hazarded estate;
    For which the onely helpe now left them last
Seem'd to be *Calidore*: all other helpes were past.

Stanza 6
3 stayd: caused to stay. **5 geare**: matter.

Stanza 7
3 disaccord: refuse assent. **6 lusty**: young; virile; handsome. **7 liuelood**: livelihood. **hability**: i.e. means. **9 meanesse**: humbler birth. Being only a knight, Aladine is **meaner borne** than the **great pere** who is a member of the aristocracy. Cf. Æmylia, daughter of 'a Lord of high degree' who falls in love with 'a Squire of low degree' (IV vii 15.2, 7).

Stanza 8
4 inuade: attack. **6 bethinking**: thinking over. **aduize**: reflect. **7 at earst**: lately. **9 salue**: smooth over, explain away. **coloured**: fair-seeming; feigned; cf. 16.9.

Stanza 9
2 Fain'd: desired. **7 array**: the preparations and ceremonies befitting his state. **9 trauell**: travail.

Stanza 10
1 Priscilla: dim. of Lat. *prisca*, 'antient' (W. Camden 1984:86), linking her to Aldus (see 3.9*n*), but for her loving care she may be named after one of Paul's 'fellow helpers in Christ Iesus' (Rom. 16.3). **2 kindely**: natural. **5–9 Tears**, being antiseptic, cleanse his wounds. **drenched**: overwhelmed. **dispacht**: relieved. **stound**: state of shock. **attacht**: seized.

Stanza 11
7 weetingly: i.e. wittingly, knowingly. **8 blam'd**: brought blame upon. **9 tendered**: cherished.

Stanza 12
1–3 I.e. she felt more compassion for him and his concern for her than for herself, forgetting her own fears to mind his. **4 conspiring**: agreeing in feeling. **intimate**: mutually share (sugg. by the context); or as each makes private grief known to the other. **7 estate**: state; specifically, her 'name' (6.9) or 'good fame' (8.8); or her status (*OED* 3) within her family, as Belt 1991:132*n*28 suggests.

13

Him they did deeme, as sure to them he seemed,
    A courteous Knight, and full of faithfull trust:
    Therefore to him their cause they best esteemed
    Whole to commit, and to his dealing iust.
    Earely, so soone as *Titans* beames forth brust
    Through the thicke clouds, in which they steeped lay
    All night in darkenesse, duld with yron rust,
    Calidore rising vp as fresh as day,
Gan freshly him addresse vnto his former way.

14

But first him seemed fit, that wounded Knight
    To visite, after this nights perillous passe,
    And to salute him, if he were in plight,
    And eke that Lady his faire louely lasse.
    There he him found much better then he was,
    And moued speach to him of things of course,
    The anguish of his paine to ouerpasse:
    Mongst which he namely did to him discourse,
Of former daies mishap, his sorrowes wicked sourse.

15

Of which occasion *Aldine* taking hold,
    Gan breake to him the fortunes of his loue,
    And all his disaduentures to vnfold;
    That *Calidore* it dearly deepe did moue.
    In th'end his kyndly courtesie to proue,
    He him by all the bands of loue besought,
    And as it mote a faithfull friend behoue,
    To safeconduct his loue, and not for ought
To leaue, till to her fathers house he had her brought.

16

Sir *Calidore* his faith thereto did plight,
    It to performe: so after little stay,
    That she her selfe had to the iourney dight,
    He passed forth with her in faire array,
    Fearelesse, who ought did thinke, or ought did say,
    Sith his own thought he knew most cleare from wite.
    So as they past together on their way,
    He can deuize this counter-cast of slight,
To giue faire colour to that Ladies cause in sight.

17

Streight to the carkasse of that Knight he went,
    The cause of all this euill, who was slaine
    The day before by iust auengement
    Of noble *Tristram*, where it did remaine:
    There he the necke thereof did cut in twaine,
    And tooke with him the head, the signe of shame.
    So forth he passed thorough that daies paine,
    Till to that Ladies fathers house he came,
Most pensiue man, through feare, what of his childe became.

18

There he arriuing boldly, did present
    The fearefull Lady to her father deare,
    Most perfect pure, and guiltlesse innocent
    Of blame, as he did on his Knighthood sweare,
    Since first he saw her, and did free from feare
    Of a discourteous Knight, who her had reft,
    And by outragious force away did beare:
    Witnesse thereof he shew'd his head there left,
And wretched life forlorne for vengement of his theft.

19

Most ioyfull man her sire was her to see,
    And heare th'aduenture of her late mischaunce;
    And thousand thankes to *Calidore* for fee
    Of his large paines in her deliueraunce
    Did yeeld; Ne lesse the Lady did aduaunce.
    Thus hauing her restored trustily,
    As he had vow'd, some small continuaunce
    He there did make, and then most carefully
Vnto his first exploite he did him selfe apply.

20

So as he was pursuing of his quest
    He chaunst to come whereas a iolly Knight,
    In couert shade him selfe did safely rest,
    To solace with his Lady in delight:
    His warlike armes he had from him vndight;
    For that him selfe he thought from daunger free,
    And far from enuious eyes that mote him spight.
    And eke the Lady was full faire to see,
And courteous withall, becomming her degree.

Stanza 13
5–7 This brief *chronographia*, which overlaps 11.1, is designed to herald Calidore's intervention to aid those in need.

Stanza 14
2 The passing of the night is linked to the passing of the crisis of his illness at 11.1–3.   **3 plight**: health.   **6 things of course**: everyday events.   7 **ouerpasse**: pass over by ignoring.   **8 namely**: particularly.

Stanza 15
1 Aldine: i.e. Aladine.   5 **kyndly**: natural, innate.

Stanza 16
5–6 I.e. he is shameproof, as is Artegall; see i 9.7–8 and cf. i 26. **wite**: blame.   **8–9 counter-cast of slight**: counterplot. Although Calidore 'loued simple truth' (i 3.9), he is econom-

ical with it to protect a lady from shame, for 'it is commendable to coyne a lye at some time, and in some place, so that it tend to some honest ende' (Guazzo 1925:1.97).   **in sight**: i.e. in sight of others.

Stanza 17
6 **signe of shame** because the knight's severed head shows that he suffered a shameful death.   **9 pensiue**: apprehensive.

Stanza 18
Calidore is careful not to swear to Priscilla's innocence *before* he saw her with Aladine 'in ioyous iolliment' (ii 16.5). Further, he swears to her innocence, not to the truth of what he says. The 'truth' of his story bears little reference to what he saw or what he was told had happened, but rather to the damsel 'reft' by Maleffort whom he did behead (i 18.4, 23.5).

21

To whom Sir *Calidore* approaching nye,
    Ere they were well aware of liuing wight,
    Them much abasht, but more him selfe thereby,
    That he so rudely did vppon them light,
    And troubled had their quiet loues delight.
    Yet since it was his fortune, not his fault,
    Him selfe thereof he labour'd to acquite,
    And pardon crau'd for his so rash default,
That he gainst courtesie so fowly did default.

22

With which his gentle words and goodly wit
    He soone allayd that Knights conceiu'd displeasure,
    That he besought him downe by him to sit,
    That they mote treat of things abrode at leasure;
    And of aduentures, which had in his measure
    Of so long waies to him befallen late.
    So downe he sate, and with delightfull pleasure
    His long aduentures gan to him relate,
Which he endured had through daungerous debate.

23

Of which whilest they discoursed both together,
    The faire *Serena* (so his Lady hight)
    Allur'd with myldnesse of the gentle wether,
    And pleasaunce of the place, the which was dight
    With diuers flowres distinct with rare delight,
    Wandred about the fields, as liking led
    Her wauering lust after her wandring sight,
    To make a garland to adorne her hed,
Without suspect of ill or daungers hidden dred.

24

All sodainely out of the forrest nere
    The *Blatant Beast* forth rushing vnaware,
    Caught her thus loosely wandring here and there,
    And in his wide great mouth away her bare,
    Crying aloud in vaine, to shew her sad misfare
    Vnto the Knights, and calling oft for ayde,
    Who with the horrour of her haplesse care
    Hastily starting vp, like men dismayde,
Ran after fast to reskue the distressed mayde.

25

The Beast with their pursuit incited more,
    Into the wood was bearing her apace
    For to haue spoyled her, when *Calidore*
    Who was more light of foote and swift in chace,
    Him ouertooke in middest of his race:
    And fiercely charging him with all his might,
    Forst to forgoe his pray there in the place,
    And to betake him selfe to fearefull flight;
For he durst not abide with *Calidore* to fight.

26

Who nathelesse, when he the Lady saw
    There left on ground, though in full euill plight,
    Yet knowing that her Knight now neare did draw,
    Staide not to succour her in that affright,
    But follow'd fast the Monster in his flight:
    Through woods and hils he follow'd him so fast,
    That he nould let him breath nor gather spright,
    But forst him gape and gaspe, with dread aghast,
As if his lungs and lites were nigh a sunder brast.

Stanza 20
The setting and situation parallel that of the discourteous knight who surprised Aladine and Priscilla in their love-making, e.g. **couert shade** and 'couert glade' (ii 16.3). **2 iolly**: gallant, handsome; 'lusty', as Aladine at 7.6.

Stanza 21
8–9 The repetition of **default**, the first meaning 'fault', 'error' and the second 'failure to fulfil an obligation', highlights the moment, for its consequence is that the Blatant Beast wounds Serena and Calidore first encounters it.

Stanza 22
5 measure suggests the tedium of travel. **7–9** The **delightfull pleasure** is either Calidore's in telling his story or the interrupted lover's in hearing it. Either way, Calidore has taken the place of Serena with whom her lover had taken 'delight' (20.4). Their pleasure leaves her to her pleasure and to her wounding. **debate**: conflict.

Stanza 23
2 Serena signifies tranquil (Lat. *serenus*, applied to the weather). The name is appropriate to one who responds to the **gentle wether** (see 24*n*); or whose usual epithet is **faire**, as at v 9.3, 27.1, etc. It is Raleigh's pet-name for Elizabeth Throckmorton in a ms. poem in which he urges her to enjoy 'sweete imbraces'; see IV vii 36.8–9*n*, and Morris 1997:45–49. See 'Serena' in the *SEnc*. In some *1596* copies, though only here, she is named '*Crispina*', i.e. smooth, shining, clear; and in all

copies, she is named '*Matilda*' at v Arg. Since all that happens to her only belies her name(s), S. may not have decided what to call her. **4 pleasaunce**: an ominous term; see I vii 4.2*n*. **dight**: adorned. **5 distinct**: distinguished each from the others. **7 lust**: desire, inclination; also sexual desire. **9** Her state corresponds to Amoret's at IV vii 4.1–2 just before she was seized by Lust. **suspect**: suspicion.

Stanza 24
The chief classical analogue to the plight of Serena is Proserpina who was seized by Pluto also while gathering flowers (Ovid, *Met.* 5.391–95). Her name may have been suggested, then, by Proserpina's association with temperate air, e.g. by Sandys 1970:254. **2 vnaware**: suddenly; as she was unaware. **3 loosely wandring** suggests moral erring. **5 in vaine**: omitted in *1612–13* to avoid the extra foot, but the phrase suggests the extent of her **haplesse care** (trouble). **misfare**: misfortune.

Stanza 25
3 spoyled: ravished; also make her his spoil, anticipating her encounter with the cannibals at viii 37–51.

Stanza 26
5 Calidore leaves in the middle line of the canto's middle stanza to continue his pursuit off-stage, remaining absent in the four middle cantos to return at ix 2. Cf. Britomart's absence from III iv 18 to ix 12. **7 nould**: would not. **spright**: breath. **9 lungs and lites**: a set term for the lungs.

27

And now by this Sir *Calepine* (so hight)
      Came to the place, where he his Lady found
      In dolorous dismay and deadly plight,
      All in gore bloud there tumbled on the ground,
      Hauing both sides through grypt with griesly wound.
      His weapons soone from him he threw away,
      And stouping downe to her in drery swound,
      Vprear'd her from the ground, whereon she lay,
And in his tender armes her forced vp to stay.

28

So well he did his busie paines apply,
      That the faint sprite he did reuoke againe,
      To her fraile mansion of mortality.
      Then vp he tooke her twixt his armes twaine,
      And setting on his steede, her did sustaine
      With carefull hands soft footing her beside,
      Till to some place of rest they mote attaine,
      Where she in safe assuraunce mote abide,
Till she recured were of those her woundes wide.

29

Now when as *Phœbus* with his fiery waine
      Vnto his Inne began to draw apace;
      Tho wexing weary of that toylesome paine,
      In trauelling on foote so long a space,
      Not wont on foote with heauy armes to trace,
      Downe in a dale forby a riuers syde,
      He chaunst to spie a faire and stately place,
      To which he meant his weary steps to guyde,
In hope there for his loue some succour to prouyde.

30

But comming to the riuers side, he found
      That hardly passable on foote it was:
      Therefore there still he stood as in a stound,
      Ne wist which way he through the foord mote pas.

Thus whilest he was in this distressed case,
      Deuising what to doe, he nigh espyde
      An armed Knight approaching to the place,
      With a faire Lady lincked by his syde,
The which themselues prepard through the foord to ride.

31

Whom *Calepine* saluting (as became)
      Besought of courtesie in that his neede,
      For safe conducting of his sickely Dame,
      Through that same perillous foord with better heede,
      To take him vp behinde vpon his steed,
      To whom that other did this taunt returne.
      Perdy thou peasant Knight, mightst rightly reed
      Me then to be full base and euill borne,
If I would beare behinde a burden of such scorne.

32

But as thou hast thy steed forlorne with shame,
      So fare on foote till thou another gayne,
      And let thy Lady likewise doe the same,
      Or beare her on thy backe with pleasing payne,
      And proue thy manhood on the billowes vayne.
      With which rude speach his Lady much displeased,
      Did him reproue, yet could him not restrayne,
      And would on her owne Palfrey him haue eased,
For pitty of his Dame, whom she saw so diseased.

33

Sir *Calepine* her thanckt, yet inly wroth
      Against her Knight, her gentlenesse refused,
      And carelesly into the riuer goth,
      As in despight to be so fowle abused
      Of a rude churle, whom often he accused
      Of fowle discourtesie, vnfit for Knight,
      And strongly wading through the waues vnused,
      With speare in th'one hand, stayd him selfe vpright,
With th'other staide his Lady vp with steddy might.

Stanza 27
1 Calepine: the first syllable links him to Calidore for whom
he functions as surrogate: he is 'this most courteous knight' (iv
1.6), which is Calidore's title at i 2.1. The final syllable links
him to his antagonist Turpine; see 40.1–4*n*. The name signifies
'sweetness of speech' (from Gk καλλι-επής, sugg. M. Parker
1960:233); or 'difficult' (from χαλεπός, sugg. Nohrnberg
1976:xiv). The first associates him with Calidore's 'gracious
speech', which is praised at i 2.6, the second distinguishes him
as one who must strive to acquire courtesy (see 1–2*n*); sugg.
Bernard 1989:225–26. He shares the name of Ambrogio
Calepino who edited the standard Latin dictionary; see
'Calepine' in the *SEnc*. **5 grypt**: seized, pierced; cf. 39.3 and
Claribell 'whose sides before with secret wound | Of loue to
Bellamoure empierced were' (xii 4.7–8). Her 'mortall wound'
of both body and mind (v 28.3–4) expresses her shame.
6 His natural gesture here – he must put his arms down to pick
her up **in his tender armes**, i.e. tenderly – relates to his earlier
unarming at 20.5 to make love to her. By 29.5, he has picked
them up again to his regret. Without his arms at iv 23.1, he
takes the bloody babe 'betwixt his armes'.

Stanza 28
2 reuoke: bring back.   **9 recured**: healed.

Stanza 29
2 As Calepine and Serena seek 'some place of rest' (28.7), so
does the sun.   **5 trace**: travel.

Stanza 30
3 stound: state of bewilderment.   **9 through**: emended in
later edns to 'thorough' to make the metre regular, though a
pause before 'through' gives fitting emphasis to the key word.

Stanza 31
7 peasant: base, a term of abuse.   **reed**: suppose.

Stanza 32
Turpine infers not only that Calepine has forfeited his horse in
losing a battle but also that Serena rides her own horse (though
that would be a lady's **Palfrey** rather than a knight's **steed**),
not recognizing Calepine's courtesy in setting her on his.
5 vayne: in vain.   **9 diseased**: afflicted.

34

And all the while, that same discourteous Knight,
    Stood on the further bancke beholding him,
    At whose calamity, for more despight
    He laught, and mockt to see him like to swim.
    But when as *Calepine* came to the brim,
    And saw his carriage past that perill well,
    Looking at that same Carle with count'nance grim,
    His heart with vengeaunce inwardly did swell,
And forth at last did breake in speaches sharpe and fell.

35

Vnknightly Knight, the blemish of that name,
    And blot of all that armes vppon them take,
    Which is the badge of honour and of fame,
    Loe I defie thee, and here challenge make,
    That thou for euer doe those armes forsake;
    And be for euer held a recreant Knight,
    Vnlesse thou dare for thy deare Ladies sake,
    And for thine owne defence on foote alight,
To iustifie thy fault gainst me in equall fight.

36

The dastard, that did heare him selfe defyde,
    Seem'd not to weigh his threatfull words at all,
    But laught them out, as if his greater pryde,
    Did scorne the challenge of so base a thrall:
    Or had no courage, or else had no gall.
    So much the more was *Calepine* offended,
    That him to no reuenge he forth could call,
    But both his challenge and him selfe contemned,
Ne cared as a coward so to be condemned.

37

But he nought weighing what he sayd or did,
    Turned his steede about another way,
    And with his Lady to the Castle rid,
    Where was his won; ne did the other stay,
    But after went directly as he may,
    For his sicke charge some harbour there to seeke;
    Where he arriuing with the fall of day,
    Drew to the gate, and there with prayers meeke,
And myld entreaty lodging did for her beseeke.

38

But the rude Porter that no manners had,
    Did shut the gate against him in his face,
    And entraunce boldly vnto him forbad.
    Nathelesse the Knight now in so needy case,
    Gan him entreat euen with submission base,
    And humbly praid to let them in that night:
    Who to him aunswer'd, that there was no place
    Of lodging fit for any errant Knight,
Vnlesse that with his Lord he formerly did fight.

39

Full loth am I (quoth he) as now at earst,
    When day is spent, and rest vs needeth most,
    And that this Lady, both whose sides are pearst
    With wounds, is ready to forgo the ghost:
    Ne would I gladly combate with mine host,
    That should to me such curtesie afford,
    Vnlesse that I were thereunto enforst.
    But yet aread to me, how hight thy Lord,
That doth thus strongly ward the Castle of the ford.

40

His name (quoth he) if that thou list to learne,
    Is hight Sir *Turpine*, one of mickle might,
    And manhood rare, but terrible and stearne
    In all assaies to euery errant Knight,
    Because of one, that wrought him fowle despight.
    Ill seemes (sayd he) if he so valiaunt be,
    That he should be so sterne to stranger wight:
    For seldome yet did liuing creature see,
That curtesie and manhood euer disagree.

41

But go thy waies to him, and fro me say,
    That here is at his gate an errant Knight,
    That house-rome craues, yet would be loth t'assay
    The proofe of battell, now in doubtfull night,
    Or curtesie with rudenesse to requite:
    Yet if he needes will fight, craue leaue till morne,
    And tell withall, the lamentable plight,
    In which this Lady languisheth forlorne,
That pitty craues, as he of woman was yborne.

Stanza 33
3 carelesly: without fear.   **7 vnused**: unfamiliar because he was unaccustomed to ford on foot.

Stanza 34
1–2 And all the while: i.e. while fording the stream, Calepine is mocked by Turpine who has already crossed. Turpine inherits the title **discourteous Knight** from the unnamed knight in canto ii; see Arg.2.   **6 carriage**: burden.

Stanza 36
3 greater: too great.   **5 gall**: the source of bitterness of spirit. **8 contemned**: treated with contempt.

Stanza 37
4 won: dwelling.   **9 beseeke**: beseech.

Stanza 38
9 formerly: beforehand. Since Turpine has already refused to fight him, Calepine is necessarily excluded.

Stanza 39
1 . . . just now.   **8 aread**: tell.

Stanza 40
1–4 Turpine: from Lat. *turpis*: 'fowle, filthie; dishonest, unhonorable; cruell' (T. Cooper 1565). His crime in refusing hospitality to those in need – cf. vi 21.3–5 – measures the turpitude of 'his base kind' (vii 1.9). Pitted against Calepine who is 'this most courteous knight' (iv 1.6), he is 'this most discourteous crauen' (2.6). See 'Blandina, Turpine' in the *SEnc*. His common title is 'recreant'; see iv 13.1*n*. **stearne**: cruel. **assaies**: combats.

42

The groome went streight way in, and to his Lord
　　Declar'd the message, which that Knight did moue;
　　Who sitting with his Lady then at bord,
　　Not onely did not his demaund approue,
　　But both himselfe reuil'd, and eke his loue;
　　Albe his Lady, that *Blandina* hight,
　　Him of vngentle vsage did reproue
And earnestly entreated that they might
Finde fauour to be lodged there for that same night.

43

Yet would he not perswaded be for ought,
　　Ne from his currish will awhit reclame.
　　Which answer when the groome returning, brought
　　To *Calepine*, his heart did inly flame
　　With wrathfull fury for so foule a shame,
　　That he could not thereof auenged bee:
　　But most for pitty of his dearest Dame,
　　Whom now in deadly daunger he did see;
Yet had no meanes to comfort, nor procure her glee.

44

But all in vaine; for why, no remedy
　　He saw, the present mischiefe to redresse,
　　But th'vthmost end perforce for to aby,
　　Which that nights fortune would for him addresse.
　　So downe he tooke his Lady in distresse,
　　And layd her vnderneath a bush to sleepe,
　　Couer'd with cold, and wrapt in wretchednesse,
　　Whiles he him selfe all night did nought but weepe,
And wary watch about her for her safegard keepe.

45

The morrow next, so soone as ioyous day
　　Did shew it selfe in sunny beames bedight,
　　Serena full of dolorous dismay,
　　Twixt darkenesse dread, and hope of liuing light,
　　Vprear'd her head to see that chearefull sight.
　　Then *Calepine*, how euer inly wroth,
　　And greedy to auenge that vile despight,
　　Yet for the feeble Ladies sake, full loth
To make there lenger stay, forth on his iourney goth.

46

He goth on foote all armed by her side,
　　Vpstaying still her selfe vppon her steede,
　　Being vnhable else alone to ride;
　　So sore her sides, so much her wounds did bleede:
　　Till that at length, in his extreamest neede,
　　He chaunst far off an armed Knight to spy,
　　Pursuing him apace with greedy speede,
　　Whom well he wist to be some enemy,
That meant to make aduantage of his misery.

47

Wherefore he stayd, till that he nearer drew,
　　To weet what issue would thereof betyde,
　　Tho whenas he approched nigh in vew,
　　By certaine signes he plainely him descryde,
　　To be the man, that with such scornefull pryde
　　Had him abusde, and shamed yesterday;
　　Therefore misdoubting, least he should misguyde
　　His former malice to some new assay,
He cast to keepe him selfe so safely as he may.

48

By this the other came in place likewise,
　　And couching close his speare and all his powre,
　　As bent to some malicious enterprise,
　　He bad him stand, t'abide the bitter stoure
　　Of his sore vengeaunce, or to make auoure
　　Of the lewd words and deedes, which he had done:
　　With that ran at him, as he would deuoure
　　His life attonce; who nought could do, but shun
The perill of his pride, or else be ouerrun.

49

Yet he him still pursew'd from place to place,
　　With full intent him cruelly to kill,
　　And like a wilde goate round about did chace,
　　Flying the fury of his bloudy will.
　　But his best succour and refuge was still
　　Behinde his Ladies backe, who to him cryde,
　　And called oft with prayers loud and shrill,
　　As euer he to Lady was affyde,
To spare her Knight, and rest with reason pacifyde.

Stanza 42

2 moue: make. **4, 7** The rhyme words are transposed in *1596*. **6 Blandina**: from Lat. *blandiri*, to flatter; or *blandus*, soothing. At vi 37.2, she is called 'that Ladie myld'. For further on her name and nature, see vi 41.3–9*n*.

Stanza 43

2 reclame: draw back.

Stanza 44

1 for why: because. **3 aby**: endure. **4 addresse**: prepare. **8–9** As Priscilla wept and watched over Aladine at 10.3–5.

Stanza 47

7 misdoubting: fearing.

Stanza 48

4 stoure: assault. **5–6 make auoure | Of**: confess; justify. **lewd words and deedes** may refer to Calepine's challenge at 35; or to his 'ioyous iolliment' at ii 16.5, which led to his and Serena's present plight. **7–8** The act of devouring is characteristic of the Blatant Beast, as at i 9.6 and 25.3 above. **nought could do**: because he is on foot.

Stanza 49

5 succour: shelter, protection. **8 affyde**: betrothed.

50

But he the more thereby enraged was,
   And with more eager felnesse him pursew'd,
   So that at length, after long weary chace,
   Hauing by chaunce a close aduantage vew'd,
   He ouer raught him, hauing long eschew'd
   His violence in vaine, and with his spere
   Strooke through his shoulder, that the blood ensew'd
   In great aboundance, as a well it were,
That forth out of an hill fresh gushing did appere.

51

Yet ceast he not for all that cruell wound,
   But chaste him still, for all his Ladies cry,
   Not satisfyde till on the fatall ground
   He saw his life powrd forth dispiteously:
   The which was certes in great ieopardy,
   Had not a wondrous chaunce his reskue wrought,
   And saued from his cruell villany.
   Such chaunces oft exceed all humaine thought:
That in another Canto shall to end be brought.

Stanza 50
5 ouer raught: overtook. **eschew'd**: avoided.

Stanza 51
8 Such chaunces are identified as 'The worke of heauens will'
at V iv 27.9 but as the work of fortune at VI iv 2.1.

Cant. IIII.

Calepine by a saluage man
from Turpine reskewed is,
And whylest an Infant from a Beare
he saues, his loue doth misse.

1
Like as a ship with dreadfull storme long tost,
  Hauing spent all her mastes and her ground-hold,
Now farre from harbour likely to be lost,
At last some fisher barke doth neare behold,
That giueth comfort to her courage cold.
Such was the state of this most courteous knight
Being oppressed by that faytour bold,
  That he remayned in most perilous plight,
And his sad Ladie left in pitifull affright.

2
Till that by fortune, passing all foresight,
  A saluage man, which in those woods did wonne,
Drawne with that Ladies loud and piteous shright,
Toward the same incessantly did ronne,
To vnderstand what there was to be donne.
There he this most discourteous crauen found,
As fiercely yet, as when he first begonne,
  Chasing the gentle *Calepine* around,
Ne sparing him the more for all his grieuous wound.

3
The saluage man, that neuer till this houre
  Did taste of pittie, neither gentlesse knew,
Seeing his sharpe assault and cruell stoure
Was much emmoued at his perils vew,
That euen his ruder hart began to rew,
And feele compassion of his euill plight,
Against his foe that did him so pursew:
  From whom he meant to free him, if he might,
And him auenge of that so villenous despight.

4
Yet armes or weapon had he none to fight,
  Ne knew the vse of warlike instruments,
Saue such as sudden rage him lent to smite,
But naked without needfull vestiments,
To clad his corpse with meete habiliments,
He cared not for dint of sword nor speere,
No more then for the stroke of strawes or bents:
  For from his mothers wombe, which him did beare,
He was invulnerable made by Magicke leare.

5
He stayed not t'aduize, which way were best
  His foe t'assayle, or how himselfe to gard,
But with fierce fury and with force infest
Vpon him ran; who being well prepard,
His first assault full warily did ward,
And with the push of his sharp-pointed speare
Full on the breast him strooke, so strong and hard,
  That forst him backe recoyle, and reele areare;
Yet in his bodie made no wound nor bloud appeare.

6
With that the wyld man more enraged grew,
  Like to a Tygre that hath mist his pray,
And with mad mood againe vpon him flew,
Regarding neither speare, that mote him slay,
Nor his fierce steed, that mote him much dismay.
The saluage nation doth all dread despize:
Tho on his shield he griple hold did lay,
  And held the same so hard, that by no wize
He could him force to loose, or leaue his enterprize.

Book VI Canto iv

Stanza 1
2 I.e. her masts are lost and her anchor is slipping.   7 **faytour**:
villain.

Stanza 2
2 **saluage man**: the traditional wild man or medieval wode-
wose or wild man of the woods, though his courteous
behaviour reveals that he is 'borne of noble blood' (v 2.7). The
obs. form of 'savage', f. *salvare*, to save, fits his role here.
See 'Salvage Man' in the *SEnc* and IV vii 5.1*n*. On his rela-
tion to the irascible faculty, see Hankins 1971:180–82, and
Borris 2000:156–60.   3 **shright**: shriek.   4 **incessantly**:
immediately.

Stanza 3
The Salvage Man belongs to the 'saluage nation' (6.6), and
responds as it does, moved with 'pitty and vnwonted ruth'
(I vi 12.7) on seeing Una in distress.   2 **gentlesse**: gentle-
ness; perhaps suggesting 'gentilesse': courtesy.   5 **ruder**: quite
rude.

Stanza 4
6 **dint**: blow.   7 **bents**: reeds or rushes.   9 **leare**: lore.

Stanza 5
1 **aduize**: consider.   3 **infest**: hostile.

Stanza 6
7 **griple**: gripping.

7

Long did he wrest and wring it to and fro,
    And euery way did try, but all in vaine:
    For he would not his greedie grype forgoe,
    But hayld and puld with all his might and maine,
    That from his steed him nigh he drew againe.
    Who hauing now no vse of his long speare,
    So nigh at hand, nor force his shield to straine,
    Both speare and shield, as things that needlesse were,
He quite forsooke, and fled himselfe away for feare.

8

But after him the wyld man ran apace,
    And him pursewed with importune speed,
    (For he was swift as any Bucke in chace)
    And had he not in his extreamest need,
    Bene helped through the swiftnesse of his steed,
    He had him ouertaken in his flight.
    Who euer, as he saw him nigh succeed,
    Gan cry aloud with horrible affright,
And shrieked out, a thing vncomely for a knight.

9

But when the Saluage saw his labour vaine,
    In following of him, that fled so fast,
    He wearie woxe, and backe return'd againe
    With speede vnto the place, whereas he last
    Had left that couple, nere their vtmost cast.
    There he that knight full sorely bleeding found,
    And eke the Ladie fearefully aghast,
    Both for the perill of the present stound,
And also for the sharpnesse of her rankling wound.

10

For though she were right glad, so rid to bee
    From that vile lozell, which her late offended,
    Yet now no lesse encombrance she did see,
    And perill by this saluage man pretended;

Gainst whom she saw no meanes to be defended,
    By reason that her knight was wounded sore.
    Therefore her selfe she wholy recommended
    To Gods sole grace, whom she did oft implore,
To send her succour, being of all hope forlore.

11

But the wyld man, contrarie to her feare,
    Came to her creeping like a fawning hound,
    And by rude tokens made to her appeare
    His deepe compassion of her dolefull stound,
    Kissing his hands, and crouching to the ground;
    For other language had he none nor speach,
    But a soft murmure, and confused sound
    Of senselesse words, which nature did him teach,
T'expresse his passions, which his reason did empeach.

12

And comming likewise to the wounded knight,
    When he beheld the streames of purple blood
    Yet flowing fresh, as moued with the sight,
    He made great mone after his saluage mood,
    And running streight into the thickest wood,
    A certaine herbe from thence vnto him brought,
    Whose vertue he by vse well vnderstood:
    The iuyce whereof into his wound he wrought,
And stopt the bleeding straight, ere he it staunched thought.

13

Then taking vp that Recreants shield and speare,
    Which earst he left, he signes vnto them made,
    With him to wend vnto his wonning neare:
    To which he easily did them perswade.
    Farre in the forrest by a hollow glade,
    Couered with mossie shrubs, which spredding brode
    Did vnderneath them make a gloomy shade;
    There foot of liuing creature neuer trode,
Ne scarse wyld beasts durst come, there was this wights abode.

Stanza 7
4 hayld: tugged.   **7 straine**: grip.   **8–9** The shame of his action is noted at V xi 55.3–9.

Stanza 8
2 importune: grievous, i.e. exceeding.   **7 succeed**: approach.

Stanza 9
5 . . . near death.   **8 stound**: moment of grief.   **9 rankling** defines the festering sore inflicted by the Blatant Beast whose bite is rabid, as at vi 2.9, 5.3, etc. The term defines the Red Cross Knight's 'infected sin'; see I x 25.1–5*n*.

Stanza 10
2 lozell: scoundrel.   **3 encombrance**: trouble.   **4 pretended**: held out, presented.   **7–9** When the Salvage Man offers her **succour**, she thanks God at 15.2.   **sole grace**: grace alone. In

the only other instance in the poem, 'Gods grace' preserves Britomart from Dolon's treachery at V vi 34.6.

Stanza 11
8–9 I.e. lack of language inhibited his reason, allowing him to express only his emotions.

Stanza 12
4 after: i.e. in accord with.   **6** As Belphœbe sought salvific herbs to cure Timias's wounds at III v 32.

Stanza 13
1 Recreant: Turpine first gained this title when he refused Calepine's challenge at iii 35.6, and confirmed it by violating the oath of chivalry, which is 'neuer to be recreant, for feare | Of perill' (ii 35.3–4), when he abandoned his shield at 7.8–9. Cf. vi 37.2, vii 26.8.

14

Thether he brought these vnacquainted guests;
   To whom faire semblance, as he could, he shewed
   By signes, by lookes, and all his other gests.
   But the bare ground, with hoarie mosse bestrowed,
   Must be their bed, their pillow was vnsowed,
   And the frutes of the forrest was their feast:
   For their bad Stuard neither plough'd nor sowed,
   Ne fed on flesh, ne euer of wyld beast
Did taste the bloud, obaying natures first beheast.

15

Yet howsoeuer base and meane it were,
   They tooke it well, and thanked God for all,
   Which had them freed from that deadly feare,
   And sau'd from being to that caytiue thrall.
   Here they of force (as fortune now did fall)
   Compelled were themselues a while to rest,
   Glad of that easement, though it were but small;
   That hauing there their wounds awhile redrest,
They mote the abler be to passe vnto the rest.

16

During which time, that wyld man did apply
   His best endeuour, and his daily paine,
   In seeking all the woods both farre and nye
   For herbes to dresse their wounds; still seeming faine,
   When ought he did, that did their lyking gaine.
   So as ere long he had that knightes wound
   Recured well, and made him whole againe:
   But that same Ladies hurts no herbe he found,
Which could redresse, for it was inwardly vnsound.

17

Now when as *Calepine* was woxen strong,
   Vpon a day he cast abrode to wend,
   To take the ayre, and heare the thrushes song,
   Vnarm'd, as fearing neither foe nor frend,

And without sword his person to defend.
   There him befell, vnlooked for before,
   An hard aduenture with vnhappie end,
   A cruell Beare, the which an infant bore
Betwixt his bloodie iawes, besprinckled all with gore.

18

The litle babe did loudly scrike and squall,
   And all the woods with piteous plaints did fill,
   As if his cry did meane for helpe to call
   To *Calepine*, whose eares those shrieches shrill
   Percing his hart with pities point did thrill;
   That after him, he ran with zealous haste,
   To rescue th'infant, ere he did him kill:
   Whom though he saw now somewhat ouerpast,
Yet by the cry he follow'd, and pursewed fast.

19

Well then him chaunst his heauy armes to want,
   Whose burden mote empeach his needfull speed,
   And hinder him from libertie to pant:
   For hauing long time, as his daily weed,
   Them wont to weare, and wend on foot for need,
   Now wanting them he felt himselfe so light,
   That like an Hauke, which feeling her selfe freed
   From bels and iesses, which did let her flight,
Him seem'd his feet did fly, and in their speed delight.

20

So well he sped him, that the wearie Beare
   Ere long he ouertooke, and forst to stay,
   And without weapon him assayling neare,
   Compeld him soone the spoyle adowne to lay.
   Wherewith the beast enrag'd to loose his pray,
   Vpon him turned, and with greedie force
   And furie, to be crossed in his way,
   Gaping full wyde, did thinke without remorse
To be aueng'd on him, and to deuoure his corse.

Stanza 14

1 **vnacquainted**: i.e. who did not know him or his dwelling.
2 **semblance**: demeanour. 3 **gests**: gestures. 5 **vnsowed**:
growing naturally because unsown. 6–9 He is a vegetarian, as
are Isis's priests (V vii 10.1–2), unlike his counterpart, the
flesh-eating 'saluage man' at IV vii 5. **bad**: improvident.

Stanza 15

7 **easement**: food and lodging.

Stanza 16

4 **faine**: glad. 8–9 Serena's wound in her mind and body is
'mortall' (v 28.4).

Stanza 17

1–5 As Serena enters the forest 'Allur'd with myldnesse of the
gentle wether' (iii 23.3), and Amoret walks through the wood
'for pleasure, or for need' (IV vii 4.2). Reference to the
thrushes song may have been suggested by **ayre** in the sense
of 'tune', a word-play found in *Proth* 1–2. The bird, which is
the mavis or song-thrush, is cited because, along with the
cuckoo, it is the 'messenger of Spring' (*Am* 19.1, and see

85.3), and therefore of birth. **cast**: determined. 9 **his
bloodie iawes**: since the baby is unwounded (see 23.9), the
blood may signal its recent birth, as do its swaddling-clothes at
23.7. Ross 1997:93 suggests that the baby is Serena's, which
was conceived at iii 20.

Stanza 18

1 **scrike**: shriek.

Stanza 19

1 'It was well for him that he lacked his heavy arms'. They had
wearied him at iii 29.5. 2 **empeach**: impede. 3 I.e. armour
would restrain him from – or cause – heavy breathing.
7–9 **bels and iesses**: the harness used to restrain a hawk's
flight. The simile **prepares** for an elaborate play: not encum-
bered with arms, Calepine may overtake the bear encumbered
with the child. When the bear is encumbered instead with the
stone (see 22.1), he is left 'Much . . . encombred' (25.1) with
the child.

Stanza 20

8 **without remorse**: also immediately.

21

But the bold knight no whit thereat dismayd,
    But catching vp in hand a ragged stone,
    Which lay thereby (so fortune him did ayde)
    Vpon him ran, and thrust it all attone
    Into his gaping throte, that made him grone
    And gaspe for breath, that he nigh choked was,
    Being vnable to digest that bone;
    Ne could it vpward come, nor downward passe,
Ne could he brooke the coldnesse of the stony masse.

22

Whom when as he thus combred did behold,
    Stryuing in vaine that nigh his bowels brast,
    He with him closd, and laying mightie hold
    Vpon his throte, did gripe his gorge so fast,
    That wanting breath, him downe to ground he cast;
    And then oppressing him with vrgent paine,
    Ere long enforst to breath his vtmost blast,
    Gnashing his cruell teeth at him in vaine,
And threatning his sharpe clawes, now wanting powre to
                        (straine.

23

Then tooke he vp betwixt his armes twaine
    The litle babe, sweet relickes of his pray;
    Whom pitying to heare so sore complaine,
    From his soft eyes the teares he wypt away,
    And from his face the filth that did it ray,
    And euery litle limbe he searcht around,
    And euery part, that vnder sweathbands lay,
    Least that the beasts sharpe teeth had any wound
Made in his tender flesh, but whole them all he found.

24

So hauing all his bands againe vptyde,
    He with him thought backe to returne againe:
    But when he lookt about on euery syde,
    To weet which way were best to entertaine,

To bring him to the place, where he would faine,
    He could no path nor tract of foot descry,
    Ne by inquirie learne, nor ghesse by ayme.
    For nought but woods and forrests farre and nye,
That all about did close the compasse of his eye.

25

Much was he then encombred, ne could tell
    Which way to take: now West he went a while,
    Then North; then neither, but as fortune fell.
    So vp and downe he wandred many a mile,
    With wearie trauell and vncertaine toile,
    Yet nought the nearer to his iourneys end;
    And euermore his louely litle spoile
    Crying for food, did greatly him offend.
So all that day in wandring vainely he did spend.

26

At last about the setting of the Sunne,
    Him selfe out of the forest he did wynd,
    And by good fortune the plaine champion wonne:
    Where looking all about, where he mote fynd
    Some place of succour to content his mynd,
    At length he heard vnder the forrests syde
    A voice, that seemed of some woman kynd,
    Which to her selfe lamenting loudly cryde,
And oft complayn'd of fate, and fortune oft defyde.

27

To whom approching, when as she perceiued
    A stranger wight in place, her plaint she stayd,
    As if she doubted to haue bene deceiued,
    Or loth to let her sorrowes be bewrayd,
    Whom when as *Calepine* saw so dismayd,
    He to her drew, and with faire blandishment
    Her chearing vp, thus gently to her sayd,
    What be you wofull Dame, which thus lament,
And for what cause declare, so mote ye not repent.

Stanza 21
4 it all atone: i.e. all of it.   **9 brooke**: endure; digest, continuing the joke in 7, possibly alluding to the story of Saturn who devoured all his sons at their birth, except Jove for whom a stone was substituted.

Stanza 22
6 oppressing: pressing down. **vrgent**: severe, heavy. **7 vtmost blast**: last breath. **9 straine**: seize.

Stanza 23
5 ray: soil. **6–9 sweathbands**: swaddling-clothes, associated with recent birth, as with Christ at Luke 2.7; cf. I x 65.7. The baby seems to be invulnerable, like the Salvage Man at his birth (4.8–9), as shown in its 'spotlesse spirit' (35.5).

Stanza 24
4 entertaine: take. **5 faine**: wish to be. **7 inquirie**: seeking. **ayme**: conjecture.

Stanza 25
2–3 His wandering first **West** and then **North** takes him in the direction of Sir Bruin's land; see 29.4*n*. In relation to Ireland, he is outside the English Pale and in the rebellious Tyrone county. **5 vncertaine**: futile.

Stanza 26
2 wynd: extricate. **3 champion**: open country, in contrast to being 'Farre in the forrest' at 13.5.

Stanza 27
3 doubted: feared. **4 bewrayd**: revealed. **7 gently**: courteously. **9 repent**: mourn.

miscegenation (handwritten, left margin)

28

To whom she thus, What need me Sir to tell,
  That which your selfe haue earst ared so right?
  A wofull dame ye haue me termed well;
  So much more wofull, as my wofull plight
  Cannot redressed be by liuing wight.
  Nathlesse (quoth he) if need doe not you bynd,
  Doe it disclose, to ease your grieued spright:
  Oftimes it haps, that sorrowes of the mynd
Find remedie vnsought, which seeking cannot fynd.

29

Then thus began the lamentable Dame;
  Sith then ye needs will know the griefe I hoord,
  I am th'vnfortunate *Matilde* by name,
  The wife of bold Sir *Bruin*, who is Lord
  Of all this land, late conquer'd by his sword
  From a great Gyant, called *Cormoraunt*;
  Whom he did ouerthrow by yonder foord,
  And in three battailes did so deadly daunt,
That he dare not returne for all his daily vaunt.

30

So is my Lord now seiz'd of all the land,
  As in his fee, with peaceable estate,
  And quietly doth hold it in his hand,
  Ne any dares with him for it debate.
  But to these happie fortunes, cruell fate
  Hath ioyn'd one euill, which doth ouerthrow
  All these our ioyes, and all our blisse abate;
  And like in time to further ill to grow,
And all this land with endlesse losse to ouerflow.

Succession (handwritten, right margin)

31

For th'heauens enuying our prosperitie,
  Haue not vouchsaft to graunt vnto vs twaine
  The gladfull blessing of posteritie,
  Which we might see after our selues remaine
  In th'heritage of our vnhappie paine:
  So that for want of heires it to defend,
  All is in time like to returne againe
  To that foule feend, who dayly doth attend
To leape into the same after our liues end.

32

But most my Lord is grieued herewithall,
  And makes exceeding mone, when he does thinke
  That all this land vnto his foe shall fall,
  For which he long in vaine did sweat and swinke,
  That now the same he greatly doth forthinke.
  Yet was it sayd, there should to him a sonne
  Be gotten, not begotten, which should drinke
  And dry vp all the water, which doth ronne
In the next brooke, by whom that feend shold be fordonne.

33

Well hop't he then, when this was propheside,
  That from his sides some noble chyld should rize,
  The which through fame should farre be magnifide,
  And this proud gyant should with braue emprize
  Quite ouerthrow, who now ginnes to despize
  The good Sir *Bruin*, growing farre in yeares;
  Who thinkes from me his sorrow all doth rize.
  Lo this my cause of griefe to you appeares;
For which I thus doe mourne, and poure forth ceaselesse teares.

Stanza 28

2 . . . have just now so rightly discerned.

Stanza 29

1 **lamentable**: lamenting.   3 **Matilde**: the name is suggested
by Matilda in Tasso, *Ger. Lib.* 1.59, to whom Rinaldo was
given by his mother to instruct him in the royal arts, as here the
baby is given to her to raise 'in goodly thewes' to become 'a
famous knight' (38.7–8). Or by Matilda who was 'wondrously
begotten' of Merlin by 'a guilefull Spright' (III iii 13.3–4). It
signifies 'Noble or honourable Ladie of Maides' (W. Camden
1984:85). See 'Bruin, Matilde' in the *SEnc*.   4 **Bruin**, or
brown bear, alluding to a family name. In *View* 64, Irenius
refers to the English living outside the Pale who had become
entirely Irish – see V i 4.1*n* – 'planted above towards the
west', and names the Macmahons 'in the north' who were
'descended from the Fitz-Ursulas', i.e. bear's sons. Implicit
word-play fulfils the prophecy at 32.7: Bruin will believe that
his wife begot his child which she got from a bear.   6 **Corm-
oraunt**: the voracious sea-raven; see II xii 8.5*n*.   7 **yonder
foord**: associated with Turpine's 'Castle of the ford' (iii 39.9),
and the river forded by Calepine at iii 30–34 to reach it.
8 **daunt**: subdue.

Stanza 30

1–4 I.e. my lord now possesses all the land legally, as
rightfully his, and rules it peaceably with no one contending

his rightful ownership.   7 **abate**: put an end to.   9 **losse**:
ruin.

Stanza 31

5 Inheriting the land we laboured to gain.   **vnhappie** because
lacking heirs.   7–9 **dayly** (cf. 29.9) and 'in time' (30.8) link
Cormoraunt with time through its variant, 'cornvorant', f. Lat.
vorant-em, devouring (*OED*), as in Shakespeare's reference
to 'cormorant devouring Time' (*Loves Labours Lost* 1.1.4).
Ovid's 'tempus edax rerum' (*Met.* 15.234) is rendered by S.
as 'devouring tyme' in *Am* 58.7. Implicit is Isaiah's vision of
ostriches inhabiting the fallen Babylon, and the pelican and
owl inhabiting the fallen Edom (Isa. 13.21, 34.11).   **attend**:
wait.

Stanza 32

5 **forthinke**: regret.   7–9 Referring to Matilde's 'ceaselesse
teares' (33.9), which dry up at 37.8–9 when she receives the
baby; or to a future battle when the giant who now threatens
to 'ouerflow' (30.9) the land will be **fordonne**, i.e. killed.
Implicit is John's vision of the time when 'there was no more
sea' (Rev. 21.1).

Stanza 33

2 **sides**: loins.   3 **magnifide**: extolled.   4 **emprize**: prowess.

34

Which when he heard, he inly touched was
    With tender ruth for her vnworthy griefe,
    And when he had deuized of her case,
    He gan in mind conceiue a fit reliefe
    For all her paine, if please her make the priefe.
    And hauing cheared her, thus said; Faire Dame,
    In euils counsell is the comfort chiefe,
    Which though I be not wise enough to frame,
Yet as I well it meane, vouchsafe it without blame.

35

If that the cause of this your languishment
    Be lacke of children, to supply your place,
    Lo how good fortune doth to you present
    This litle babe, of sweete and louely face,
    And spotlesse spirit, in which ye may enchace
    What euer formes ye list thereto apply,
    Being now soft and fit them to embrace;
    Whether ye list him traine in cheualry,
Or noursle vp in lore of learn'd Philosophy.

lack of lineage = good

36

And certes it hath oftentimes bene seene,
    That of the like, whose linage was vnknowne,
    More braue and noble knights haue raysed beene,
    As their victorious deedes haue often showen,
    Being with fame through many Nations blowen,
    Then those, which haue bene dandled in the lap.
    Therefore some thought, that those braue imps were
    Here by the Gods, and fed with heauenly sap, (sowen
That made them grow so high t'all honorable hap.

37

The Ladie hearkning to his sensefull speach,
    Found nothing that he said, vnmeet nor geason,
    Hauing oft seene it tryde, as he did teach.
    Therefore inclyning to his goodly reason,

Agreeing well both with the place and season,
    She gladly did of that same babe accept,
    As of her owne by liuerey and seisin,
    And hauing ouer it a litle wept,
She bore it thence, and euer as her owne it kept.

38

Right glad was *Calepine* to be so rid
    Of his young charge, whereof he skilled nought:
    Ne she lesse glad; for she so wisely did,
    And with her husband vnder hand so wrought,
    That when that infant vnto him she brought,
    She made him thinke it surely was his owne,
    And it in goodly thewes so well vpbrought,
    That it became a famous knight well knowne
And did right noble deedes, the which elswhere are showne.

39

But *Calepine*, now being left alone
    Vnder the greenewoods side in sorie plight,
    Withouten armes or steede to ride vpon,
    Or house to hide his head from heauens spight,
    Albe that Dame by all the meanes she might,
    Him oft desired home with her to wend,
    And offred him, his courtesie to requite,
    Both horse and armes, and what so else to lend,
Yet he them all refusd, though thankt her as a frend.

40

And for exceeding griefe which inly grew,
    That he his loue so lucklesse now had lost,
    On the cold ground, maugre himselfe he threw,
    For fell despight, to be so sorely crost;
    And there all night himselfe in anguish tost,
    Vowing, that neuer he in bed againe
    His limbes would rest, ne lig in ease embost,
    Till that his Ladies sight he mote attaine,
Or vnderstand, that she in safetie did remaine.

Stanza 34

2 **vnworthy**: undeserved. **3 deuized of**: considered.
5 priefe: proof; i.e. trial. **7** Proverbial: Smith 123.
9 vouchsafe: deign to accept.

Stanzas 35–36

Calepine's 'goodly reason' (37.4) concerning the role of art or nurture to supplement nature – see iii 1–2*n* – is supported by the popular belief that a bear licks its formless cubs into shape (from the assumed etymology, *orsus*, 'perfected after the littering'; see Topsell 1967:1.28). Of the three forces, 'nature, arte, | And heauen' (*Rome* 57–58), he stresses the third: there are those born and nurtured by the gods. Cf. Castiglione, *Courtier* 32: 'some there are borne indued with such graces, that they seeme not to have beene borne, but rather fashioned with the verie hand of some God, and abound in all goodnes both of bodie and minde'.

Stanza 35

1 **languishment**: suffering. **5 enchace**: engrave. **9 noursle vp**: educate. **learn'd Philosophy** recalls that the mother of Tasso's Rinaldo was Sophia; see 29.3*n*.

Stanza 37

2 **geason**: strange. **3 tryde**: proved. **5** The forest is a fitting **place** for fortune to produce a child, and the **season**, spring (see 17.1–5*n*), is a fitting time for its birth. **7 by liuerey and seisin**: a legal phrase ('livery of seisin') for the delivery of property into the corporal possession of a person; hence, by delivery and possession.

Stanza 38

2 **skilled**: understood; i.e. he did not know how to take care of the baby. **7 thewes**: manners.

Stanza 39

8 **lend**: give.

Stanza 40

3 **maugre himselfe**: in spite of himself, i.e. against his will; or 'to spite himself'. **7** . . . nor lie wrapped in ease. **8** He attains this sight when he sees Serena at viii 48, not **in safetie** but stripped and about to be eaten.

Cant. V.

*The saluage serues Matilda well
till she Prince Arthure fynd,
Who her together with his Squyre
with th'Hermit leaues behynd.*

1

OWhat an easie thing is to descry
  The gentle bloud, how euer it be wrapt
In sad misfortunes foule deformity,
And wretched sorrowes, which haue often hapt?
For howsoeuer it may grow mis-shapt,
Like this wyld man, being vndisciplynd,
That to all vertue it may seeme vnapt,
  Yet will it shew some sparkes of gentle mynd,
And at the last breake forth in his owne proper kynd.

2

That plainely may in this wyld man be red,
  Who though he were still in this desert wood,
Mongst saluage beasts, both rudely borne and bred,
Ne euer saw faire guize, ne learned good,
Yet shewd some token of his gentle blood,
By gentle vsage of that wretched Dame.
For certes he was borne of noble blood,
  How euer by hard hap he hether came;
As ye may know, when time shall be to tell the same.

3

Who when as now long time he lacked had
  The good Sir *Calepine*, that farre was strayd,
Did wexe exceeding sorrowfull and sad,
As he of some misfortune were afrayd:
And leauing there this Ladie all dismayd,
Went forth streightway into the forrest wyde,
To seeke, if he perchance a sleepe were layd,
  Or what so else were vnto him betyde:
He sought him farre and neare, yet him no where he spyde.

4

Tho backe returning to that sorie Dame,
  He shewed semblant of exceeding mone,
By speaking signes, as he them best could frame;
Now wringing both his wretched hands in one,
Now beating his hard head vpon a stone,
That ruth it was to see him so lament.
By which she well perceiuing, what was done,
  Gan teare her hayre, and all her garments rent,
And beat her breast, and piteously her selfe torment.

5

Vpon the ground her selfe she fiercely threw,
  Regardlesse of her wounds, yet bleeding rife,
That with their bloud did all the flore imbrew,
As if her breast new launcht with murdrous knife,
Would streight dislodge the wretched wearie life.
There she long groueling, and deepe groning lay,
As if her vitall powers were at strife
  With stronger death, and feared their decay,
Such were this Ladies pangs and dolorous assay.

6

Whom when the Saluage saw so sore distrest,
  He reared her vp from the bloudie ground,
And sought by all the meanes, that he could best
Her to recure out of that stony swound,
And staunch the bleeding of her dreary wound.
Yet nould she be recomforted for nought,
Ne cease her sorrow and impatient stound,
  But day and night did vexe her carefull thought,
And euer more and more her owne affliction wrought.

Book VI Canto v

Argument
1 Matilda: 'Serena' corr. Hughes 1715, an error occasioned
by its use at iv 29.3, as Upton 1758 notes.

Stanzas 1–2
Extending Calepine's argument at iv 35–36. **gentle bloud**,
i.e. noble lineage, will be manifest even when it lacks nurture.

Stanza 1
6 vndisciplynd: uneducated.

Stanza 2
1 red: seen. **4** I.e. he neither saw nor was taught how to

behave with the respect proper to each person; see ii 1.6–7n.
9 That time never comes, as with Tristram and his lady at ii
40.1.

Stanza 4
2 semblant: signs. **mone**: grief.

Stanza 5
3 flore: ground. **imbrew**: stain. **4 launcht**: pierced.
8 decay: destruction. **9 assay**: affliction.

Stanza 6
3 could: knew. **4 recure**: restore. **5 dreary**: bloody.
7 impatient: unendurable. Her 'dolefull stound' at iv 11.4 has
now worsened; cf. 28.5.

7

At length, when as no hope of his retourne
  She saw now left, she cast to leaue the place,
  And wend abrode, though feeble and forlorne,
  To seeke some comfort in that sorie case.
  His steede now strong through rest so long a space,
  Well as she could, she got, and did bedight,
  And being thereon mounted, forth did pace,
  Withouten guide, her to conduct aright,
Or gard her to defend from bold oppressors might.

8

Whom when her Host saw readie to depart,
  He would not suffer her alone to fare,
  But gan himselfe addresse to take her part.
  Those warlike armes, which *Calepine* whyleare
  Had left behind, he gan eftsoones prepare,
  And put them all about himselfe vnfit,
  His shield, his helmet, and his curats bare.
  But without sword vpon his thigh to sit:
Sir *Calepine* himselfe away had hidden it.

9

So forth they traueld an vneuen payre,
  That mote to all men seeme an vncouth sight;
  A saluage man matcht with a Ladie fayre,
  That rather seem'd the conquest of his might,
  Gotten by spoyle, then purchaced aright.
  But he did her attend most carefully,
  And faithfully did serue both day and night,
  Withouten thought of shame or villeny,
Ne euer shewed signe of foule disloyalty.

10

Vpon a day as on their way they went,
  It chaunst some furniture about her steed
  To be disordred by some accident:
  Which to redresse, she did th'assistance need

Of this her groome, which he by signes did reede,
  And streight his combrous armes aside did lay
  Vpon the ground, withouten doubt or dreed,
  And in his homely wize began to assay
T'amend what was amisse, and put in right aray.

11

Bout which whilest he was busied thus hard,
  Lo where a knight together with his squire,
  All arm'd to point came ryding thetherward,
  Which seemed by their portance and attire,
  To be two errant knights, that did inquire
  After aduentures, where they mote them get.
  Those were to weet (if that ye it require)
  Prince *Arthur* and young *Timias*, which met
By straunge occasion, that here needs forth be set.

12

After that *Timias* had againe recured
  The fauour of *Belphebe*, (as ye heard)
  And of her grace did stand againe assured,
  To happie blisse he was full high vprear'd,
  Nether of enuy, nor of chaunge afeard,
  Though many foes did him maligne therefore,
  And with vniust detraction him did beard;
  Yet he himselfe so well and wisely bore,
That in her soueraine lyking he dwelt euermore.

13

But of them all, which did his ruine seeke
  Three mightie enemies did him most despight,
  Three mightie ones, and cruell minded eeke,
  That him not onely sought by open might
  To ouerthrow, but to supplant by slight.
  The first of them by name was cald *Despetto*,
  Exceeding all the rest in powre and hight;
  The second not so strong but wise, *Decetto*;
The third nor strong nor wise, but spightfullest *Defetto*.

Stanza 7
2 cast: decided. **4 comfort**: aid, succour. **6 bedight**: harness.

Stanza 8
3 addresse: make ready. **7 curats**: cuirasses, body armour. **bare**: i.e. he put on.

Stanza 9
1 vneuen: unequal, ill-matched. **3–5** The folklore conjunction of Beauty and the Beast suggests that he conquered, i.e. raped, her rather than having won her by killing her knight.

Stanza 10
2 furniture: harness. **4 redresse**: put in order. **5 reede**: understand. **7 doubt**: fear.

Stanza 11
3 to point: completely. **4 portance**: bearing. **5 inquire**: seek. **7–9 require**: ask. They met last at IV vii 42 but Arthur left him after five stanzas unable to recognize him through his grief at having lost Belphœbe's favour. At 41, he leaves him again, now in the care of the Hermit.

Stanza 12
1–5 At IV viii 17–18, the reader learned that Belphœbe 'him receiu'd againe to former fauours state' causing him to become 'Fearlesse of fortunes chaunge or enuies dread'. **recured**: recovered. **6 maligne**: regard with hatred; slander.

Stanza 13
5 supplant: cause to fall. **slight**: wiles, deceit. **6–9 Despetto**: Ital. *despitto*, spite; **Decetto**: *decettione*, deception, deceit; **Defetto**: *difetto*, an offence, a blame (Florio 1598). See 'Despetto, Decetto, Defetto' in the *SEnc*. As a triad, they form a sequence: in their spite, Timias's enemies use deceit to expose him to blame. Their differences are acted out at 19.1–6 and 20.4–8. The first exceeds the other two in being personified eight times in the poem, as *Var* 6.207 notes: in the train of Wrath at I iv 35.4, the mother of Pyrochles and Cymochles at II iv 41.6, in the company sitting by Pluto's gate at II vii 22.2, in the company pursuing Malbecco at III x 55.5, one of the two villeins leading Amoret in the masque of Cupid at III xii 19.2, lying in ambush behind Daunger at IV x 20.6, and – together with 'foule *Infamie*' – testifying against Mirabella at the court of Cupid at VI vii 34.7. Cf. Enuie, Detraction, and

14

Oftimes their sundry powres they did employ,
  And seuerall deceipts, but all in vaine:
  For neither they by force could him destroy,
  Ne yet entrap in treasons subtill traine.
  Therefore conspiring all together plaine,
  They did their counsels now in one compound;
  Where singled forces faile, conioynd may gaine.
  The *Blatant Beast* the fittest meanes they found,
To worke his vtter shame, and throughly him confound.

15

Vpon a day as they the time did waite,
  When he did raunge the wood for saluage game,
  They sent that *Blatant Beast* to be a baite,
  To draw him from his deare beloued dame,
  Vnwares into the daunger of defame.
  For well they wist, that Squire to be so bold,
  That no one beast in forrest wylde or tame,
  Met him in chase, but he it challenge would,
And plucke the pray oftimes out of their greedy hould.

16

The hardy boy, as they deuised had,
  Seeing the vgly Monster passing by,
  Vpon him set, of perill nought adrad,
  Ne skilfull of the vncouth ieopardy;
  And charged him so fierce and furiously,
  That his great force vnable to endure,
  He forced was to turne from him and fly:
  Yet ere he fled, he with his tooth impure
Him heedlesse bit, the whiles he was thereof secure.

17

Securely he did after him pursew,
  Thinking by speed to ouertake his flight;
  Who through thicke woods and brakes and briers him drew,
  To weary him the more, and waste his spight,
  So that he now has almost spent his spright.
  Till that at length vnto a woody glade
  He came, whose couert stopt his further sight,
  There his three foes shrowded in guilefull shade,
Out of their ambush broke, and gan him to inuade.

18

Sharpely they all attonce did him assaile,
  Burning with inward rancour and despight,
  And heaped strokes did round about him haile
  With so huge force, that seemed nothing might
  Beare off their blowes, from percing thorough quite.
  Yet he them all so warily did ward,
  That none of them in his soft flesh did bite,
  And all the while his backe for best safegard,
He lent against a tree, that backeward onset bard.

19

Like a wylde Bull, that being at a bay,
  Is bayted of a mastiffe, and a hound,
  And a curre-dog; that doe him sharpe assay
  On euery side, and beat about him round;
  But most that curre barking with bitter sownd,
  And creeping still behinde, doth him incomber,
  That in his chauffe he digs the trampled ground,
  And threats his horns, and bellowes like the thonder,
So did that Squire his foes disperse, and driue asonder.

20

Him well behoued so; for his three foes
  Sought to encompasse him on euery side,
  And dangerously did round about enclose.
  But most of all *Defetto* him annoyde,
  Creeping behinde him still to haue destroyde:
  So did *Decetto* eke him circumuent,
  But stout *Despetto* in his greater pryde,
  Did front him face to face against him bent,
Yet he them all withstood, and often made relent.

21

Till that at length nigh tyrd with former chace,
  And weary now with carefull keeping ward,
  He gan to shrinke, and somewhat to giue place,
  Full like ere long to haue escaped hard;
  When as vnwares he in the forrest heard
  A trampling steede, that with his neighing fast
  Did warne his rider be vppon his gard;
  With noise whereof the Squire now nigh aghast,
Reuiued was, and sad dispaire away did cast.

---

the Blatant Beast who attack Artegall at V xii 28–43. On their relation to the three fosters who attack Timias at III v 18–25, see Bednarz 1984:66. As an anti-triad to the three Graces, see A. Fowler 1973:64–65.

Stanza 14
2 seuerall: different; separate.   **4 traine**: snare.   **5 plaine**: openly.   **9 confound**: destroy.

Stanza 15
5 defame: disgrace.

Stanza 16
4 Nor mindful of the unknown peril.   **9** On the possible topical reference to the scandal brought on Raleigh through his affair with Elizabeth Throckmorton, see IV vii 36.8–9*n*. **secure**: free from care; over-confident.

Stanza 17
1 Securely: over-confidently.   **5 spright**: breath.   **9 inuade**: attack.

Stanza 19
The simile refers to the popular Elizabethan sport of bull-baiting, as at II viii 42, and depends on the general contempt with which dogs were regarded. At IV viii 36.5–6, Sclaunder is compared to a cur. The simile is used again at vi 27.4–7 and vii 47.1–6.   **1 at a bay**: at bay, when it must turn to face its pursuers.   **3 assay**: assail.   **6 incomber**: harass.   **7 chauffe**: rage.   **8 threats**: threatens with.

Stanza 20
1 so: i.e. so to defend himself.   **9 relent**: slacken, yield.

Stanza 21
4 hard: with difficulty.

22

Eftsoones he spide a Knight approching nye,
  Who seeing one in so great daunger set
  Mongst many foes, him selfe did faster hye;
  To reskue him, and his weake part abet,
  For pitty so to see him ouerset.
  Whom soone as his three enemies did vew,
  They fled, and fast into the wood did get:
  Him booted not to thinke them to pursew,
The couert was so thicke, that did no passage shew.

23

Then turning to that swaine, him well he knew
  To be his *Timias*, his owne true Squire,
  Whereof exceeding glad, he to him drew,
  And him embracing twixt his armes entire,
  Him thus bespake; My liefe, my lifes desire,
  Why haue ye me alone thus long yleft?
  Tell me what worlds despight, or heauens yre
  Hath you thus long away from me bereft?
Where haue ye all this while bin wandring, where bene weft?

24

With that he sighed deepe for inward tyne:
  To whom the Squire nought aunswered againe,
  But shedding few soft teares from tender eyne,
  His deare affect with silence did restraine,
  And shut vp all his plaint in priuy paine.
  There they awhile some gracious speaches spent,
  As to them seemed fit time to entertaine.
  After all which vp to their steedes they went,
And forth together rode a comely couplement.

25

So now they be arriued both in sight
  Of this wyld man, whom they full busie found
  About the sad *Serena* things to dight,
  With those braue armours lying on the ground,
  That seem'd the spoile of some right well renownd.
  Which when that Squire beheld, he to them stept,
  Thinking to take them from that hylding hound:
  But he it seeing, lightly to him lept,
And sternely with strong hand it from his handling kept.

26

Gnashing his grinded teeth with griesly looke,
  And sparkling fire out of his furious eyne,
  Him with his fist vnwares on th'head he strooke,
  That made him downe vnto the earth encline;
  Whence soone vpstarting much he gan repine,
  And laying hand vpon his wrathfull blade,
  Thought therewithall forthwith him to haue slaine,
  Who it perceiuing, hand vpon him layd,
And greedily him griping, his auengement stayd.

27

With that aloude the faire *Serena* cryde
  Vnto the Knight, them to dispart in twaine:
  Who to them stepping did them soone diuide,
  And did from further violence restraine,
  Albe the wyld-man hardly would refraine.
  Then gan the Prince, of her for to demand,
  What and from whence she was, and by what traine
  She fell into that saluage villaines hand,
And whether free with him she now were, or in band.

28

To whom she thus; I am, as now ye see,
  The wretchedst Dame, that liue this day on ground,
  Who both in minde, the which most grieueth me,
  And body haue receiu'd a mortall wound,
  That hath me driuen to this drery stound.
  I was erewhile, the loue of *Calepine*,
  Who whether he aliue be to be found,
  Or by some deadly chaunce be done to pine,
Since I him lately lost, vneath is to define.

29

In saluage forrest I him lost of late,
  Where I had surely long ere this bene dead,
  Or else remained in most wretched state,
  Had not this wylde man in that wofull stead
  Kept, and deliuered me from deadly dread.
  In such a saluage wight, of brutish kynd,
  Amongst wilde beastes in desert forrests bred,
  It is most straunge and wonderfull to fynd
So milde humanity, and perfect gentle mynd.

Stanza 22
4 . . . and support the weaker side. **5 ouerset**: set upon by
superior numbers; oppressed.

Stanza 23
4 entire: heartily. **5 my lifes desire**: associating Timias,
whose name signifies 'honoured' (see III i 18.9*n*) with
'*Praysdesire*, | That by well doing sought to honour to aspyre',
with whom Arthur is identified at II ix 39.8–9. His homoerotic
desire is examined by Ellis 1994. **9 weft**: wafted, driven upon
water, as **wandring** refers to land.

Stanza 24
Timias is silent in his shame when Arthur discovers him at IV
vii 44.1–5, and again at VI viii 5.1–7, 27.3. **1 tyne**: sorrow.
4 affect: affection. **6 spent**: uttered. **9 couplement**: pair;

comely in contrast to the Salvage Man and Serena who make
'an vneuen payre' (9.1).

Stanza 25
3 dight: put in order. **5 some**: someone. **7 hylding
hound**: contemptible or worthless creature.

Stanza 27
7 traine: course of events, circumstances. **9 band**: bond,
bondage.

Stanza 28
8 . . . be put to death. 9 . . . it is difficult to decide.

Stanza 29
4 stead: place; situation. **5 deadly dread**: the dread of death,
or simply death. **9 humanity**: civility, good behaviour.

30
Let me therefore this fauour for him finde,
　That ye will not your wrath vpon him wreake,
　Sith he cannot expresse his simple minde,
　Ne yours conceiue, ne but by tokens speake:
　Small praise to proue your powre on wight so weake.
　With such faire words she did their heate asswage,
　And the strong course of their displeasure breake,
　That they to pitty turnd their former rage,
And each sought to supply the office of her page.

31
So hauing all things well about her dight,
　She on her way cast forward to proceede,
　And they her forth conducted, where they might
　Finde harbour fit to comfort her great neede.
　For now her wounds corruption gan to breed;
　And eke this Squire, who likewise wounded was
　Of that same Monster late, for lacke of heed,
　Now gan to faint, and further could not pas
Through feeblenesse, which all his limbes oppressed has.

32
So forth they rode together all in troupe,
　To seeke some place, the which mote yeeld some ease
　To these sicke twaine, that now began to droupe,
　And all the way the Prince sought to appease
　The bitter anguish of their sharpe disease,
　By all the courteous meanes he could inuent,
　Somewhile with merry purpose fit to please,
　And otherwhile with good encouragement,
To make them to endure the pains, did them torment.

33
Mongst which, *Serena* did to him relate
　The foule discourt'sies and vnknightly parts,
　Which *Turpine* had vnto her shewed late,
　Without compassion of her cruell smarts,
　Although *Blandina* did with all her arts
　Him otherwise perswade, all that she might;
　Yet he of malice, without her desarts,
　Not onely her excluded late at night,
But also trayterously did wound her weary Knight.

34
Wherewith the Prince sore moued, there auowd,
　That soone as he returned backe againe,
　He would auenge th'abuses of that proud
　And shamefull Knight, of whom she did complaine.
　This wize did they each other entertaine,
　To passe the tedious trauell of the way;
　Till towards night they came vnto a plaine,
　By which a little Hermitage there lay,
Far from all neighbourhood, the which annoy it may.

35
And nigh thereto a little Chappell stoode,
　Which being all with Yuy ouerspred,
　Deckt all the roofe, and shadowing the roode,
　Seem'd like a groue faire braunched ouer hed:
　Therein the Hermite, which his life here led
　In streight obseruaunce of religious vow,
　Was wont his howres and holy things to bed;
　And therein he likewise was praying now,
Whenas these Knights arriu'd, they wist not where nor how.

36
They stayd not there, but streight way in did pas.
　Whom when the Hermite present saw in place,
　From his deuotion streight he troubled was;
　Which breaking off he toward them did pace,
　With stayed steps, and graue beseeming grace:
　For well it seem'd, that whilome he had beene
　Some goodly person, and of gentle race,
　That could his good to all, and well did weene,
How each to entertaine with curt'sie well beseene.

37
And soothly it was sayd by common fame,
　So long as age enabled him thereto,
　That he had bene a man of mickle name,
　Renowmed much in armes and derring doe:
　But being aged now and weary to
　Of warres delight, and worlds contentious toyle,
　The name of knighthood he did disauow,
　And hanging vp his armes and warlike spoyle,
From all this worlds incombraunce did himselfe assoyle.

Stanza 30
4 tokens: signs, gestures.

Stanza 31
5 corruption: putrefaction.　**7 for lacke of heed**: as 16.9.

Stanza 32
7 purpose: conversation.　**9** . . . the pains that did torment them.

Stanza 33
2 parts: acts.　**7** . . . i.e. without her (Blandina's) good qualities.

Stanza 34
7–9 In contrast to Archimago's hermitage 'Downe in a dale, hard by a forests side' (I i 34.2), and Contemplation's her-
mitage on a hill with its chapel at the summit (I x 46.2–3).
neighbourhood: neighbours.

Stanza 35
3 roode: a crucifix. It is hidden in ivy to avoid being smashed by Reformation zealots.　**6 streight**: strict.　**7** Was accustomed to offer his canonical prayers and devotions.

Stanza 36
3 As Contemplation was distracted from heavenly thoughts at I x 49.2–3.　**5 stayed**: steady; or supported.　**8 could his good**: knew how to behave, which is the virtue of civility; see proem 4.5*n*.　**9** . . . with well-pleasing courtesy.

Stanza 37
A knight who has taken early retirement in order to start a second career as a hermit is a familiar figure in chivalric romance.

38

He thence them led into his Hermitage,
  Letting their steedes to graze vpon the greene:
  Small was his house, and like a little cage,
  For his owne turne, yet inly neate and clene,
  Deckt with greene boughes, and flowers gay beseene.
  Therein he them full faire did entertaine
  Not with such forged showes, as fitter beene
  For courting fooles, that curtesies would faine,
But with entire affection and appearaunce plaine.

39

Yet was their fare but homely, such as hee
  Did vse, his feeble body to sustaine;
  The which full gladly they did take in glee,
  Such as it was, ne did of want complaine,
  But being well suffiz'd, them rested faine.
  But faire *Serene* all night could take no rest,
  Ne yet that gentle Squire, for grieuous paine
  Of their late woundes, the which the *Blatant Beast*
Had giuen them, whose griefe through suffraunce sore
                          (increast.

40

So all that night they past in great disease,
  Till that the morning, bringing earely light
  To guide mens labours, brought them also ease,
  And some asswagement of their painefull plight.
  Then vp they rose, and gan them selues to dight
  Vnto their iourney; but that Squire and Dame
  So faint and feeble were, that they ne might
  Endure to trauell, nor one foote to frame:
Their hearts were sicke, their sides were sore, their feete
                          (were lame.

41

Therefore the Prince, whom great affaires in mynd
  Would not permit, to make there lenger stay,
  Was forced there to leaue them both behynd,
  In that good Hermits charge, whom he did pray
  To tend them well. So forth he went his way,
  And with him eke the saluage, that whyleare
  Seeing his royall vsage and array,
  Was greatly growne in loue of that braue pere,
Would needes depart, as shall declared be elsewhere.

See 'hermits' in the *SEnc.* **1 fame**: report. **4 derring doe**: daring deeds, 'manhoode and cheualrie' (E.K. on *SC Oct.* 65). **5 to**: the intensive, 'entirely,' as Todd 1805 suggests. **8 hanging vp his armes**: for the first time in the poem, this action is neither disgraceful as when Verdant's arms 'were hong vpon a tree' (II xii 80.2), nor dangerous as when Calepine doffed his arms at iii 20.5. **9 assoyle**: set free.

Stanza 38
3 The simile prepares for its use at vi 4.9. **4 turne**: needs. **5 gay beseene**: of gay appearance; or (paralleling **Deckt**) gaily furnished, adorned. **9 entire**: sincere.

Stanza 39
3 in glee: heartily. in gree *1609* (i.e. with good will) is supported by I v 16.4, etc. **5 faine**: gladly. **7 that gentle Squire**: Timias is so named from here on: e.g. vii 39.2, viii 3.1, etc. **9 griefe**: physical pain; or grief to them. **suffraunce**: delay in treating, neglect; see 31.7, vi 2.4.

Stanza 40
1 disease: discomfort. **8 frame**: support, direct.

Cant. VI.

The Hermite heales both Squire and dame
Of their sore maladies:
He Turpine doth defeate, and shame
For his late villanies.

1

NO wound, which warlike hand of enemy
    Inflicts with dint of sword, so sore doth light,
    As doth the poysnous sting, which infamy
    Infixeth in the name of noble wight:
    For by no art, nor any leaches might
    It euer can recured be againe;
    Ne all the skill, which that immortall spright
    Of *Podalyrius* did in it retaine,
Can remedy such hurts; such hurts are hellish paine.

2

Such were the wounds, the which that *Blatant Beast*
    Made in the bodies of that Squire and Dame;
    And being such, were now much more increast,
    For want of taking heede vnto the same,
    That now corrupt and curelesse they became.
    Howbe that carefull Hermite did his best,
    With many kindes of medicines meete, to tame
    The poysnous humour, which did most infest
Their ranckling wounds, and euery day them duely drest.

3

For he right well in Leaches craft was seene,
    And through the long experience of his dayes,
    Which had in many fortunes tossed beene,
    And past through many perillous assayes,

He knew the diuerse went of mortall wayes,
    And in the mindes of men had great insight;
    Which with sage counsell, when they went astray,
    He could enforme, and them reduce aright,
And al the passions heale, which wound the weaker spright.

4

For whylome he had bene a doughty Knight,
    As any one, that liued in his daies,
    And proued oft in many perillous fight,
    Of which he grace and glory wonne alwaies,
    And in all battels bore away the baies.
    But being now attacht with timely age,
    And weary of this worlds vnquiet waies,
    He tooke him selfe vnto this Hermitage,
In which he liu'd alone, like carelesse bird in cage.

5

One day, as he was searching of their wounds,
    He found that they had festred priuily,
    And ranckling inward with vnruly stounds,
    The inner parts now gan to putrify,
    That quite they seem'd past helpe of surgery,
    And rather needed to be disciplinde
    With holesome reede of sad sobriety,
    To rule the stubborne rage of passion blinde:
Giue salues to euery sore, but counsell to the minde.

Book VI Canto vi

Argument

3 He: i.e. Arthur.

Stanza 1

3–6 **infamy**: slander (Lat. *infamia*); personified at vii 34.7. It is the ultimate enemy of the heroic knight who seeks fame. **recured**: healed. 8 **Podalyrius**: 'one of the sonnes of Aesculapius, and a great surgeon' (T. Cooper 1565). 9 **hellish**: because the effects of slander are 'lasting' (II v 13.9) and 'endlesse' (IV i 53.6), slander being 'the wound that nothing healeth' (Shakespeare, *Lucrece* 731).

Stanza 2

5 **curelesse**: as indicated by 1.5–9, though at 15.6 she is said to be 'throughly heal'd'; cf. Arg.1. Possibly her body is cured but not her mind, a distinction made at v 28.3–4; or she may cured but not her reputation. 6 **Howbe**: howbeit, with the force of 'nevertheless'. 8 **infest**: infect. 9 **ranckling**: see iv 9.9*n*.

Stanza 3

The hermit exercises his twin traditional roles, healer of the body and counsellor of the mind. 1 **seene**: skilled. 4 **assayes**: trials. 5 **went**: courses. 8 **enforme**: instruct; guide. **reduce**: lead back. 9 **weaker**: too weak.

Stanza 4

Repeating the matter of v 37, perhaps to assure those readers suspicious of the contemplative life that this hermit should enjoy a life promised the Red Cross Knight only near the end of his life (I x 61); sugg. Bernard 1989:145. The stanza prepares for Calidore's retreat from the active life at ix 31. 5 **baies**: the garland of victory. 6 **attacht**: seized. 9 **carelesse**: carefree. A variant of this specious justification for caging birds is offered at *Am* 65.7–8.

Stanza 5

1 **searching**: probing. 3–4 In *SC March* 100–01, this accurate description of a gangrenous wound describes the effect of love. **vnruly**: violent; literally, not responding to discipline. **stounds**: paroxysms of pain. 7 **reede**: counsel. **sad**: serious.

6

So taking them apart into his cell,
    He to that point fit speaches gan to frame,
    As he the art of words knew wondrous well,
    And eke could doe, as well as say the same,
    And thus he to them sayd; Faire daughter Dame,
    And you faire sonne, which here thus long now lie
    In piteous languor, since ye hither came,
    In vaine of me ye hope for remedie,
And I likewise in vaine doe salues to you applie.

7

For in your selfe your onely helpe doth lie,
    To heale your selues, and must proceed alone
    From your owne will, to cure your maladie.
    Who can him cure, that will be cur'd of none?
    If therefore health ye seeke, obserue this one.
    First learne your outward sences to refraine
    From things, that stirre vp fraile affection;
    Your eies, your eares, your tongue, your talk restraine
From that they most affect, and in due termes containe.

8

For from those outward sences ill affected,
    The seede of all this euill first doth spring,
    Which at the first before it had infected,
    Mote easie be supprest with little thing:
    But being growen strong, it forth doth bring
    Sorrow, and anguish, and impatient paine
    In th'inner parts, and lastly scattering
    Contagious poyson close through euery vaine,
It neuer rests, till it haue wrought his finall bane.

9

For that beastes teeth, which wounded you tofore,
    Are so exceeding venemous and keene,
    Made all of rusty yron,ranckling sore,
    That where they bite, it booteth not to weene
    With salue, or antidote, or other mene
    It euer to amend: ne maruaile ought;
    For that same beast was bred of hellish strene,
    And long in darksome *Stygian* den vpbrought,
Begot of foule *Echidna*, as in bookes is taught.

10

Echidna is a Monster direfull dred,
    Whom Gods doe hate, and heauens abhor to see;
    So hideous is her shape, so huge her hed,
    That euen the hellish fiends affrighted bee
    At sight thereof, and from her presence flee:
    Yet did her face and former parts professe
    A faire young Mayden, full of comely glee;
    But all her hinder parts did plaine expresse
A monstrous Dragon, full of fearefull vglinesse.

11

To her the Gods, for her so dreadfull face,
    In fearefull darkenesse, furthest from the skie,
    And from the earth, appointed haue her place,
    Mongst rocks and caues, where she enrold doth lie
    In hideous horrour and obscurity,
    Wasting the strength of her immortall age.
    There did *Typhaon* with her company,
    Cruell *Typhaon*, whose tempestuous rage
Make th'heauens tremble oft, and him with vowes asswage.

---

9 Variations of two proverbs: 'There is a salve for every sore' (Smith 672) and 'Counsel is a sovereign remedy' (Smith 123). The first is invoked by Glauce at III ii 35.7; but since Serena's mind, like Britomart's, is wounded by love, **counsell** is needed.

Stanza 6
7 **languor**: illness.

Stanza 7
5 **one**: i.e. one rule.   7 **affection**: passion, called **fraile** because it makes us so.   9 From what they are most drawn to, and keep within proper limits.

Stanza 8
The hermit's moral lesson, 'nip evil in the bud', is also the Palmer's at II iv 35.   6 **impatient**: unendurable.   8 **close**: secretly.   9 **bane**: death.

Stanza 9
1–3 At xii 26.7, the Beast is said to have 'yron teeth in raunges twaine', similar to the dragon's 'Threeranckes of yron teeth' at I xi 13.2.   **tofore**: earlier.   5 **mene**: means.   7 **bred of hellish strene** (i.e. strain, race); cf. 'bred of hellishe race' (i 7.7).   8 As i 8.4.

Stanzas 10–12
One of the 'bookes' referred to at 9.9 is Hesiod, *Theogony*. **Echidna** appears as 'half a nymph with glancing eyes and fair cheeks, and half again a huge snake, great and awful' (295–332). Cf. Errour at I i 14.7–9, and see *n*. After her birth, the gods thrust her into a cave beneath the earth where, cohabiting with **Typhaon** – or Typhoeus, 'a great gyaunt, the sonne of Titan. . . . Also a great puissant wynde: a whirlwynde' (T. Cooper 1565) – she gave birth to Orthrus (see V x 10.7–9), Geryoneo's monster (see V xi 23.5–6), and the Hydra, to which the Blatant Beast is compared (see xii 32). At i 8.1–5, the beast is said to be the offspring of Cerberus and Chimæra. At Typhaon's rage, 'th'heauens tremble oft' because he waged war against the Olympians so successfully that he forced them to change their shapes and flee (see Ovid, *Met*. 5.325–31) until Jove imprisoned him under Mount Aetna. On his connection with Typhœus, the father of Argante (III vii 47.6), see Butler 1997:1–2.

Stanza 10
3 **hideous**: also immense.   6–9 **former**: front.   **professe**: have the appearance of.   **expresse**: reveal or display her to be.

Stanza 11
1 **face**: general appearance.   4 **enrold**: coiled.   7 **company**: copulate.

12

Of that commixtion they did then beget
  This hellish Dog, that hight the *Blatant Beast*;
  A wicked Monster, that his tongue doth whet
  Gainst all, both good and bad, both most and least,
  And poures his poysnous gall forth to infest
  The noblest wights with notable defame:
  Ne euer Knight, that bore so lofty creast,
  Ne euer Lady of so honest name,
But he them spotted with reproch, or secrete shame.

13

In vaine therefore it were, with medicine
  To goe about to salue such kynd of sore,
  That rather needes wise read and discipline,
  Then outward salues, that may augment it more.
  Aye me (sayd then *Serena* sighing sore)
  What hope of helpe doth then for vs remaine,
  If that no salues may vs to health restore?
  But sith we need good counsell (sayd the swaine)
Aread good sire, some counsell, that may vs sustaine.

14

The best (sayd he) that I can you aduize,
  Is to auoide the occasion of the ill:
  For when the cause, whence euill doth arize,
  Remoued is, th'effect surceaseth still.
  Abstaine from pleasure, and restraine your will,
  Subdue desire, and bridle loose delight,
  Vse scanted diet, and forbeare your fill,
  Shun secresie, and talke in open sight:
So shall you soone repaire your present euill plight.

15

Thus hauing sayd, his sickely patients
  Did gladly hearken to his graue beheast,
  And kept so well his wise commaundements,
  That in short space their malady was ceast,

And eke the biting of that harmefull Beast
  Was throughly heal'd. Tho when they did perceaue
  Their wounds recur'd, and forces reincreast,
  Of that good Hermite both they tooke their leaue,
And went both on their way, ne ech would other leaue.

16

But each th'other vow'd t'accompany,
  The Lady, for that she was much in dred,
  Now left alone in great extremity,
  The Squire, for that he courteous was indeed,
  Would not her leaue alone in her great need.
  So both together traueld, till they met
  With a faire Mayden clad in mourning weed,
  Vpon a mangy iade vnmeetely set,
And a lewd foole her leading thorough dry and wet.

17

But by what meanes that shame to her befell,
  And how thereof her selfe she did acquite,
  I must a while forbeare to you to tell;
  Till that, as comes by course, I doe recite,
  What fortune to the Briton Prince did lite,
  Pursuing that proud Knight, the which whileare
  Wrought to Sir *Calidore* so foule despight;
  And eke his Lady, though she sickely were,
So lewdly had abusde, as ye did lately heare.

18

The Prince according to the former token,
  Which faire *Serene* to him deliuered had,
  Pursu'd him streight, in mynd to bene ywroken
  Of all the vile demeane, and vsage bad,
  With which he had those two so ill bestad:
  Ne wight with him on that aduenture went,
  But that wylde man, whom though he oft forbad,
  Yet for no bidding, nor for being shent,
Would he restrayned be from his attendement.

Stanza 12
1 commixtion: copulation; literally, mixing of the two. Cf. i 8.3. **4 most and least**: the highest and lowest in rank. **5 infest**: infect, as 2.8. **6 notable defame**: notorious infamy.

Stanza 13
1–4 The hermit confirms his initial diagnosis at 5.5–9. Now Timias at least is ready of his 'owne will' (7.3) to follow his counsel.

Stanza 14
1–4 The hermit's counsel is proverbial: 'Avoid the occasion of evil' and 'The cause taken away, the effect vanishes' (Smith, 221, 89). In sum, take heed, which Timias and Serena had failed to do; see v 16.9, 31.7 and vi 2.4. **surceaseth**: comes to an end. **5 Abstaine from pleasure** is the lesson Medina learns from the story of Mordant at II ii 45.4. The complexities of the hermit's advice are noted by Gross 1999:106–08.

Stanza 15
7 forces: physical strength; moral strength, virtue.

Stanza 16
4 indeed: in deed. **6–9** A preview of the story of Mirabella told at vii 27.7–44, and again at viii 19–24. **iade**: as a term of abuse for a woman (*OED* 2; cf. II xi 31.2), it is a fitting mount for her. **lewd**: ill-mannered; wicked. **foole**: Scorn's common title.

Stanza 17
2 acquite: free. Since Mirabella gains her freedom by choosing not to free herself from her shame, the context suggests 'conduct' (cf. *OED* 13). Cf. viii Arg.2: Arthur 'Quites Mirabell from dreed'. **5 lite**: happen. **7 Calidore**: Calepine, corr. Hughes 1715. The error suggests their connection. **9 lewdly**: wickedly. **lately**: at iii 31–51.

Stanza 18
3 ywroken: avenged. **4 demeane**: behaviour. **8 shent**: reproved. **9 his attendement**: attendance on him.

19

Arriuing there, as did by chaunce befall,
    He found the gate wyde ope, and in he rode,
    Ne stayd, till that he came into the hall:
    Where soft dismounting like a weary lode,
    Vpon the ground with feeble feete he trode,
    As he vnable were for very neede
    To moue one foote, but there must make abode;
    The whiles the saluage man did take his steede,
And in some stable neare did set him vp to feede.

20

Ere long to him a homely groome there came,
    That in rude wise him asked, what he was,
    That durst so boldly, without let or shame,
    Into his Lords forbidden hall to passe.
    To whom the Prince, him fayning to embase,
    Mylde answer made; he was an errant Knight,
    The which was fall'n into this feeble case,
    Through many wounds, which lately he in fight,
Receiued had, and prayd to pitty his ill plight.

21

But he, the more outrageous and bold,
    Sternely did bid him quickely thence auaunt,
    Or deare aby, for why his Lord of old
    Did hate all errant Knights, which there did haunt,
    Ne lodging would to any of them graunt,
    And therefore lightly bad him packe away,
    Not sparing him with bitter words to taunt;
    And therewithall rude hand on him did lay,
To thrust him out of dore, doing his worst assay.

22

Which when the Saluage comming now in place,
    Beheld, eftsoones he all enraged grew,
    And running streight vpon that villaine base,
    Like a fell Lion at him fiercely flew,
    And with his teeth and nailes, in present vew,
    Him rudely rent, and all to peeces tore:
    So miserably him all helpelesse slew,
    That with the noise, whilest he did loudly rore,
The people of the house rose forth in great vprore.

23

Who when on ground they saw their fellow slaine,
    And that same Knight and Saluage standing by,
    Vpon them two they fell with might and maine,
    And on them layd so huge and horribly,
    As if they would haue slaine them presently.
    But the bold Prince defended him so well,
    And their assault withstood so mightily,
    That maugre all their might, he did repell,
And beat them back, whilest many vnderneath him fell.

24

Yet he them still so sharpely did pursew,
    That few of them he left aliue, which fled,
    Those euill tidings to their Lord to shew.
    Who hearing how his people badly sped,
    Came forth in hast: where when as with the dead
    He saw the ground all strow'd, and that same Knight
    And saluage with their bloud fresh steeming red,
    He woxe nigh mad with wrath and fell despight,
And with reprochfull words him thus bespake on hight.

25

Art thou he, traytor, that with treason vile,
    Hast slaine my men in this vnmanly maner,
    And now triumphest in the piteous spoile
    Of these poore folk, whose soules with black dishonor
    And foule defame doe decke thy bloudy baner?
    The meede whereof shall shortly be thy shame,
    And wretched end, which still attendeth on her.
    With that him selfe to battell he did frame;
So did his forty yeomen, which there with him came.

26

With dreadfull force they all did him assaile,
    And round about with boystrous strokes oppresse,
    That on his shield did rattle like to haile
    In a great tempest; that in such distresse,
    He wist not to which side him to addresse.
    And euermore that crauen cowherd Knight,
    Was at his backe with heartlesse heedinesse,
    Wayting if he vnwares him murther might:
For cowardize doth still in villany delight.

Stanza 19
1 there: i.e. at Turpine's 'Castle of the ford' (iii 39.9), so one infers.

Stanza 20
5 . . . pretending to humble himself. **6–9** The 'token' (18.1) which identifies the discourteous Knight is his refusal to offer hospitality to errant knights; see iii 38.7–9. On the law of hospitality, see III viii 52.4–6n. By feigning weakness, Arthur tempts his cowardice.

Stanza 21
3–4 'Because of one, that wrought him fowle despight' (iii 40.5). **aby**: suffer for it. **for why**: because. **6 lightly**: quickly.

Stanza 24
9 on hight: aloud; or as loudly as he could.

Stanza 25
1–2 At this same point in canto i, Briana makes the same charge against Calidore for slaying her servants. **7 her**: i.e. **treason**. **9 forty**: i.e. a large number.

Stanza 26
2 boystrous: violent. **oppresse**: harass. **6–7 cowherd**: the spelling marks a nature befitting a herder, as again at 33.4, 34.2, vii 25.7. **heedinesse**: heedfulness.

27

Whereof whenas the Prince was well aware,
  He to him turnd with furious intent,
  And him against his powre gan to prepare;
  Like a fierce Bull, that being busie bent
  To fight with many foes about him ment,
  Feeling some curre behinde his heeles to bite,
  Turnes him about with fell auengement;
  So likewise turnde the Prince vpon the Knight,
And layd at him amaine with all his will and might.

28

Who when he once his dreadfull strokes had tasted,
  Durst not the furie of his force abyde,
  But turn'd abacke, and to retyre him hasted
  Through the thick prease, there thinking him to hyde.
  But when the Prince had once him plainely eyde,
  He foot by foot him followed alway,
  Ne would him suffer once to shrinke asyde
  But ioyning close, huge lode at him did lay:
Who flying still did ward, and warding fly away.

29

But when his foe he still so eger saw,
  Vnto his heeles himselfe he did betake,
  Hoping vnto some refuge to withdraw:
  Ne would the Prince him euer foot forsake,
  Where so he went, but after him did make.
  He fled from roome to roome, from place to place,
  Whylest euery ioynt for dread of death did quake,
  Still looking after him, that did him chace;
That made him euermore increase his speedie pace.

30

At last he vp into the chamber came,
  Whereas his loue was sitting all alone,
  Wayting what tydings of her folke became.
  There did the Prince him ouertake anone,
  Crying in vaine to her, him to bemone;
  And with his sword him on the head did smyte,
  That to the ground he fell in senselesse swone:
  Yet whether thwart or flatly it did lyte,
The tempred steele did not into his braynepan byte.

31

Which when the Ladie saw, with great affright
  She starting vp, began to shrieke aloud,
  And with her garment couering him from sight,
  Seem'd vnder her protection him to shroud;
  And falling lowly at his feet, her bowd
  Vpon her knee, intreating him for grace,
  And often him besought, and prayd, and vowd;
  That with the ruth of her so wretched case,
He stayd his second strooke, and did his hand abase.

32

Her weed she then withdrawing, did him discouer,
  Who now come to himselfe, yet would not rize,
  But still did lie as dead, and quake, and quiuer,
  That euen the Prince his basenesse did despize,
  And eke his Dame him seeing in such guize,
  Gan him recomfort, and from ground to reare.
  Who rising vp at last in ghastly wize,
  Like troubled ghost did dreadfully appeare,
As one that had no life him left through former feare.

33

Whom when the Prince so deadly saw dismayd,
  He for such basenesse shamefully him shent,
  And with sharpe words did bitterly vpbrayd;
  Vile cowheard dogge, now doe I much repent,
  That euer I this life vnto thee lent,
  Whereof thou caytiue so vnworthie art;
  That both thy loue, for lacke of hardiment,
  And eke thy selfe, for want of manly hart,
And eke all knights hast shamed with this knightlesse part.

34

Yet further hast thou heaped shame to shame,
  And crime to crime, by this thy cowheard feare.
  For first it was to thee reprochfull blame,
  To erect this wicked custome, which I heare,
  Gainst errant Knights and Ladies thou dost reare;
  Whom when thou mayst, thou dost of arms despoile,
  Or of their vpper garment, which they weare:
  Yet doest thou not with manhood, but with guile
Maintaine this euill vse, thy foes thereby to foile.

Stanza 27
4–7 This simile is used at v 19 to describe Timias's turning
upon Defetto.   **ment**: joined in battle.

Stanza 28
1 tasted: felt.   **8** . . . dealt him heavy blows.

Stanza 29
1 eger: fierce.

Stanza 30
5 . . . i.e. to pity him, and therefore plead for him.   **8 thwart**:
crosswise.

Stanza 31
Fittingly, Turpine is shamed as he shamed Calepine by forcing
him to hide behind his lady at iii 49.5–6. He savagely wounded

him in contrast to Arthur who now lowers his sword. In accord
with the chivalric code upheld by the knights of the Round
Table, Arthur is willing 'to gyue mercy vnto hym that asketh
mercy' (Malory 3.15). Blandina's action carries biblical reson-
ance: 'I spred my skirtes ouer thee, and couered thy filthines'
(Ezek. 16.8).

Stanza 32
Lying on the ground totally shamed, Turpine is an emblem of
the **basenesse** of one 'basely borne' (36.5); cf. vii 1.9.

Stanza 33
8 manly: repaying Turpine's charge at 25.2.   **9 knightlesse**:
unknightly.   **part**: conduct; act.

Stanza 34
4–9 There is no earlier reference to Turpine's **wicked custome**
of despoiling a defeated knight and taking away his lady's outer

35

And lastly in approuance of thy wrong,
   To shew such faintnesse and foule cowardize,
   Is greatest shame: for oft it falles, that strong
   And valiant knights doe rashly enterprize,
   Either for fame, or else for exercize,
   A wrongfull quarrell to maintaine by fight;
   Yet haue, through prowesse and their braue emprize,
   Gotten great worship in this worldes sight.
For greater force there needs to maintaine wrong, then
                             (right.

36

Yet since thy life vnto this Ladie fayre
   I giuen haue, liue in reproch and scorne;
   Ne euer armes, ne euer knighthood dare
   Hence to professe: for shame is to adorne
   With so braue badges one so basely borne;
   But onely breath sith that I did forgiue.
   So hauing from his crauen bodie torne
   Those goodly armes, he them away did giue
And onely suffred him this wretched life to liue.

37

There whilest he thus was setling things aboue,
   Atwene that Ladie myld and recreant knight,
   To whom his life he graunted for her loue,
   He gan bethinke him, in what perilous plight
   He had behynd him left that saluage wight,
   Amongst so many foes, whom sure he thought
   By this quite slaine in so vnequall fight:
   Therefore descending backe in haste, he sought
If yet he were aliue, or to destruction brought.

38

There he him found enuironed about
   With slaughtred bodies, which his hand had slaine,
   And laying yet a fresh with courage stout
   Vpon the rest, that did aliue remaine;
   Whom he likewise right sorely did constraine,
   Like scattred sheepe, to seeke for safetie,
   After he gotten had with busie paine
   Some of their weapons, which thereby did lie,
With which he layd about, and made them fast to flie.

39

Whom when the Prince so felly saw to rage,
   Approching to him neare, his hand he stayd,
   And sought, by making signes, him to asswage:
   Who them perceiuing, streight to him obayd,
   As to his Lord, and downe his weapons layd,
   As if he long had to his heasts bene trayned.
   Thence he him brought away, and vp conuayd
   Into the chamber, where that Dame remayned
With her vnworthy knight, who ill him entertayned.

40

Whom when the Saluage saw from daunger free,
   Sitting beside his Ladie there at ease,
   He well remembred, that the same was hee,
   Which lately sought his Lord for to displease:
   Tho all in rage, he on him streight did seaze,
   As if he would in peeces him haue rent;
   And were not, that the Prince did him appeaze,
   He had not left one limbe of him vnrent:
But streight he held his hand at his commaundement.

41

Thus hauing all things well in peace ordayned,
   The Prince himselfe there all that night did rest,
   Where him *Blandina* fayrely entertayned,
   With all the courteous glee and goodly feast,
   The which for him she could imagine best.
   For well she knew the wayes to win good will
   Of euery wight, that were not too infest;
   And how to please the minds of good and ill,
Through tempering of her words and lookes by wondrous
                             (skill.

42

Yet were her words and lookes but false and fayned,
   To some hid end to make more easie way,
   Or to allure such fondlings, whom she trayned
   Into her trap vnto their owne decay:
   Thereto, when needed, she could weepe and pray,
   And when her listed, she could fawne and flatter;
   Now smyling smoothly, like to sommers day,
   Now glooming sadly, so to cloke her matter;
Yet were her words but wynd, and all her teares but water.

---

garments. It may be owing to Ariosto's cowardly Pinabello, in
Orl. Fur. 22.47–98, who forces four valiant knights to strip
errant knights of their arms and ladies of their clothing and
make them go on foot. See D. Cheney 1966:202–07. It recalls
Crudor's custom of shaving a lady's locks and a knight's beard
at i 13, and may inform Turpine's complaint against Arthur at
vii 4.3–5.

Stanza 35
1 approuance: proof. **3–9** This extraordinary claim applies
to the knights whom Pinabello forces to uphold his wicked
custom, and, in limited measure, to the two knights whom
Turpine hires at vii 3–5 to attack Arthur. **enterprize**: take in
hand. **emprize**: enterprise. **worship**: honour.

Stanza 36
4 Hence: henceforth. **6** I.e. I am allowing you only to live,
not to be a knight.

Stanza 38
6 As Talus is compared to a wolf slaughtering sheep at V iv
44.7–9 and vi 30.6.

Stanza 41
1 ordayned: set up. **3–9** Blandina displays one meaning of
her name, from Lat. *blandus*, merry. **fayrely**: courteously.
infest: hostile.

Stanza 42
Her flattering speech defines her nature; see iii 42.6*n*.
3 fondlings: foolish persons. **trayned**: beguiled.

43

Whether such grace were giuen her by kynd,
  As women wont their guilefull wits to guyde;
  Or learn'd the art to please, I doe not fynd.
  This well I wote, that she so well applyde
  Her pleasing tongue, that soone she pacifyde
  The wrathfull Prince, and wrought her husbands peace.
  Who nathelesse not therewith satisfyde,
  His rancorous despight did not releasse,
Ne secretly from thought of fell reuenge surceasse.

44

For all that night, the whyles the Prince did rest
  In carelesse couch, not weeting what was ment,
  He watcht in close awayt with weapons prest,
  Willing to worke his villenous intent
  On him, that had so shamefully him shent:
  Yet durst he not for very cowardize
  Effect the same, whylest all the night was spent.
  The morrow next the Prince did early rize,
And passed forth, to follow his first enterprize.

Stanza 43
1–3 On the distinction between nature (**kynd**) and nurture (**learn'd the art**), see iii 1–2*n*. The 'wyles of wemens wits' are mentioned at III viii 8.9. **8 releasse**: moderate. **9 surceasse**: leave off.

Stanza 44
2 carelesse: carefree. **3 close awayt**: secret ambush. **prest**: ready. **7 whylest**: until.

Cant. VII.

*Turpine is baffuld, his two knights
doe gaine their treasons meed,
Fayre Mirabellaes punishment
for loues disdaine decreed.*

1

Ike as the gentle hart it selfe bewrayes,
  In doing gentle deedes with franke delight,
  Euen so the baser mind it selfe displayes,
  In cancred malice and reuengefull spight.
  For to maligne, t'enuie, t'vse shifting slight,
  Be arguments of a vile donghill mind,
  Which what it dare not doe by open might,
  To worke by wicked treason wayes doth find,
By such discourteous deeds discouering his base kind.

2

That well appeares in this discourteous knight,
  The coward *Turpine*, whereof now I treat;
  Who notwithstanding that in former fight
  He of the Prince his life receiued late,
  Yet in his mind malitious and ingrate
  He gan deuize, to be aueng'd anew
  For all that shame, which kindled inward hate.
  Therefore so soone as he was out of vew,
Himselfe in hast he arm'd, and did him fast pursew.

3

Well did he tract his steps, as he did ryde,
  Yet would not neare approch in dauugers eye,
  But kept aloofe for dread to be descryde,
  Vntill fit time and place he mote espy,
  Where he mote worke him scath and villeny.
  At last he met two knights to him vnknowne,
  The which were arm'd both agreeably,
  And both combynd, what euer chaunce were blowne,
Betwixt them to diuide, and each to make his owne.

4

To whom false *Turpine* comming courteously,
  To cloke the mischiefe, which he inly ment,
  Gan to complaine of great discourtesie,
  Which a straunge knight, that neare afore him went,
  Had doen to him, and his deare Ladie shent:
  Which if they would afford him ayde at need
  For to auenge, in time conuenient,
  They should accomplish both a knightly deed,
And for their paines obtaine of him a goodly meed.

5

The knights beleeu'd, that all he sayd, was trew,
  And being fresh and full of youthly spright,
  Were glad to heare of that aduenture new,
  In which they mote make triall of their might,
  Which neuer yet they had approu'd in fight;
  And eke desirous of the offred meed,
  Said then the one of them; Where is that wight,
  The which hath doen to thee this wrongfull deed,
That we may it auenge, and punish him with speed?

6

He rides (said *Turpine*) there not farre afore,
  With a wyld man soft footing by his syde,
  That if ye list to haste a litle more,
  Ye may him ouertake in timely tyde.
  Eftsoones they pricked forth with forward pryde,
  And ere that litle while they ridden had,
  The gentle Prince not farre away they spyde,
  Ryding a softly pace with portance sad,
Deuizing of his loue more, then of daunger drad.

Book VI Canto vii

Stanza 1
See iii 1–2*n*. **1 bewrayes:** reveals. **5 maligne:** regard with hatred or envy. **slight:** wiles, deceit; cf. v 13.5. **6 arguments:** tokens, evidence.

Stanza 2
5 ingrate: ungrateful.

Stanza 3
1 tract: trace. **5 scath:** harm. **villeny:** shameful injury. **7 agreeably:** similarly; properly. **8–9** Each would take up the other's cause in fighting and share the spoils, for they are **combynd**, i.e. bound together, as 7.4–6 shows. Their sameness means that only one, Enias, need be named at viii 4.3.

Stanza 4
5 shent: disgraced. **7 conuenient:** due, proper. **9 meed:** a key term in the episode, as Arg.2 suggests. The chivalric model, 'doing gentle deedes with franke delight' (1.2), is violated by the two knights when they offer their services for hire at 5.6; cf. 12.7. One of them is almost killed for 'his former follies meed' (11.8; cf. 13.2), and confesses his fault at 15.1–4. The mercantile terminology is noted by Schoenfeldt 1994:162–63. The angels who act 'all for loue, and nothing for reward' at II viii 2.8 provide the pattern for Arthur, as he says at 56.1–6. That virtue is its own reward is esp. true of courtesy; see proem 7*n* and i 47.1–2. Borris 2000:146–55 finds a 'complex of christological motifs' in the story of Enias.

Stanza 5
5 approu'd: tested.

Stanza 6
4 timely tyde: fit time. **5 forward:** bold. Such pride leads them forward. **8 softly:** easy. **portance:** demeanour. **9 Deuizing:** meditating.

7

Then one of them aloud vnto him cryde,
　Bidding him turne againe, false traytour knight,
　Foule womanwronger, for he him defyde.
　With that they both at once with equall spight
　Did bend their speares, and both with equall might
　Against him ran; but th'one did misse his marke,
　And being carried with his force forthright,
　Glaunst swiftly by; like to that heauenly sparke,
Which glyding through the ayre lights all the heauens darke.

8

But th'other ayming better, did him smite
　Full in the shield, with so impetuous powre,
　That all his launce in peeces shiuered quite,
　And scattered all about, fell on the flowre.
　But the stout Prince, with much more steddy stowre
　Full on his beuer did him strike so sore,
　That the cold steele through piercing, did deuowre
　His vitall breath, and to the ground him bore,
Where still he bathed lay in his owne bloody gore.

9

As when a cast of Faulcons make their flight
　At an Herneshaw, that lyes aloft on wing,
　The whyles they strike at him with heedlesse might,
　The warie foule his bill doth backward wring;
　On which the first, whose force her first doth bring,
　Her selfe quite through the bodie doth engore,
　And falleth downe to ground like senselesse thing,
　But th'other not so swift, as she before,
Fayles of her souse, and passing by doth hurt no more.

10

By this the other, which was passed by,
　Himselfe recouering, was return'd to fight;
　Where when he saw his fellow lifelesse ly,
　He much was daunted with so dismall sight;
　Yet nought abating of his former spight,
　Let driue at him with so malitious mynd,
　As if he would haue passed through him quight:
　But the steele-head no stedfast hold could fynd,
But glauncing by, deceiu'd him of that he desynd.

11

Not so the Prince: for his well learned speare
　Tooke surer hould, and from his horses backe
　Aboue a launces length him forth did beare,
　And gainst the cold hard earth so sore him strake,
　That all his bones in peeces nigh he brake.
　Where seeing him so lie, he left his steed,
　And to him leaping, vengeance thought to take
　Of him, for all his former follies meed,
With flaming sword in hand his terror more to breed.

12

The fearefull swayne beholding death so nie,
　Cryde out aloud for mercie him to saue;
　In lieu whereof he would to him descrie,
　Great treason to him meant, his life to reaue.
　The Prince soone hearkned, and his life forgaue.
　Then thus said he, There is a straunger knight,
　The which for promise of great meed, vs draue
　To this attempt, to wreake his hid despight,
For that himselfe thereto did want sufficient might.

13

The Prince much mused at such villenie,
　And sayd; Now sure ye well haue earn'd your meed,
　For th'one is dead, and th'other soone shall die,
　Vnlesse to me thou hether bring with speed
　The wretch, that hyr'd you to this wicked deed.
　He glad of life, and willing eke to wreake
　The guilt on him, which did this mischiefe breed,
　Swore by his sword, that neither day nor weeke
He would surceasse, but him, where so he were, would seeke.

14

So vp he rose, and forth streight way he went
　Backe to the place, where *Turpine* late he lore;
　There he him found in great astonishment,
　To see him so bedight with bloodie gore,
　And griesly wounds that him appalled sore.
　Yet thus at length he said, How now Sir knight?
　What meaneth this, which here I see before?
　How fortuneth this foule vncomely plight,
So different from that, which earst ye seem'd in sight?

Stanza 7
3 **for**: i.e. for which.　5 **bend**: aim, level.

Stanza 8
5–9 Presumably Arthur kills the one who slanders him at
7.2–3, not the one called 'that courteous Knight' at viii 4.4.
stowre: blow, assault.

Stanza 9
1 **cast**: couple (a hawking term).　2 **Herneshaw**: a young
heron.　4–7 This defensive ploy appears in contemporary
emblem books; see Scoular 1965:pl. iv, and Harrison
1956:72–75.　**engore**: pierce.　9 **souse**: swoop.

Stanza 10
4 **dismall**: causing terror.

Stanza 11
1 **learned**: trained.

Stanza 12
3 **descrie**: reveal.　4 **reaue**: take away.

Stanza 13
1 **mused**: wondered.　8 **Swore by his sword**: a solemn oath,
as at i 43.6 and V viii 14.7.　9 **surceasse**: desist.

Stanza 14
2 **lore**: left.

Stanza 15
3 . . . i.e. to risk my life for money.　5 **lake**: pool, as i 37.7.
9 **yearned**: earned.

15

Perdie (said he) in euill houre it fell,
    That euer I for meed did vndertake
    So hard a taske, as life for hyre to sell;
    The which I earst aduentur'd for your sake.
    Witnesse the wounds, and this wyde bloudie lake,
    Which ye may see yet all about me steeme.
    Therefore now yeeld, as ye did promise make,
    My due reward, the which right well I deeme
I yearned haue, that life so dearely did redeeme.

16

But where then is (quoth he halfe wrothfully)
    Where is the bootie, which therefore I bought,
    That cursed caytiue, my strong enemy,
    That recreant knight, whose hated life I sought?
    And where is eke your friend, which halfe it ought?
    He lyes (said he) vpon the cold bare ground,
    Slayne of that errant knight, with whom he fought;
    Whom afterwards my selfe with many a wound
Did slay againe, as ye may see there in the stound.

17

Thereof false *Turpin* was full glad and faine,
    And needs with him streight to the place would ryde,
    Where he himselfe might see his foeman slaine;
    For else his feare could not be satisfyde.
    So as they rode, he saw the way all dyde
    With streames of bloud; which tracting by the traile,
    Ere long they came, whereas in euill tyde
    That other swayne, like ashes deadly pale,
Lay in the lap of death, rewing his wretched bale.

18

Much did the Crauen seeme to mone his case,
    That for his sake his deare life had forgone;
    And him bewayling with affection base,
    Did counterfeit kind pittie, where was none:
    For wheres no courage, theres no ruth nor mone.
    Thence passing forth, not farre away he found,
    Whereas the Prince himselfe lay all alone,
    Loosely displayd vpon the grassie ground,
Possessed of sweete sleepe, that luld him soft in swound.

19

Wearie of trauell in his former fight,
    He there in shade himselfe had layd to rest,
    Hauing his armes and warlike things vndight,
    Fearelesse of foes that mote his peace molest;
    The whyles his saluage page, that wont be prest,
    Was wandred in the wood another way,
    To doe some thing, that seemed to him best,
    The whyles his Lord in siluer slomber lay,
Like to the Euening starre adorn'd with deawy ray.

20

Whom when as *Turpin* saw so loosely layd,
    He weened well, that he in deed was dead,
    Like as that other knight to him had sayd:
    But when he nigh approcht, he mote aread
    Plaine signes in him of life and liuelihead.
    Whereat much grieu'd against that straunger knight,
    That him too light of credence did mislead,
    He would haue backe retyred from that sight,
That was to him on earth the deadliest despight.

21

But that same knight would not once let him start,
    But plainely gan to him declare the case
    Of all his mischiefe, and late lucklesse smart;
    How both he and his fellow there in place
    Were vanquished, and put to foule disgrace,
    And how that he in lieu of life him lent,
    Had vow'd vnto the victor, him to trace
    And follow through the world, where so he went,
Till that he him deliuered to his punishment.

22

He therewith much abashed and affrayd,
    Began to tremble euery limbe and vaine;
    And softly whispering him, entyrely prayd,
    T'aduize him better, then by such a traine
    Him to betray vnto a straunger swaine:
    Yet rather counseld him contrarywize,
    Sith he likewise did wrong by him sustaine,
    To ioyne with him and vengeance to deuize,
Whylest time did offer meanes him sleeping to surprize.

Stanza 16
5 ought: is owing; or ought to have. **9 againe**: in return. **stound**: 'place' (17.2); 'a state of stupefaction' (*OED* sb.2) describes Arthur's state at 19.8–9.

Stanza 17
1 faine: pleased. **6 tracting**: tracking; cf. 3.1. **7 tyde**: time. 9 Presumably his ghost laments his death at 8.7–9; cf. 13.3.

Stanza 18
1 Crauen: as the exemplar of discourtesy, the 'coward *Turpine*' (2.2) personifies cowardice; cf. iv 2.6, vi 36.7. **4 kind**: natural. **5 mone**: grief.

Stanza 19
1 trauell: travail. 5 . . . that usually was near at hand. **8–9 siluer slomber**: cf. 'siluer sleepe' (ix 22.8). **siluer**

because associated with the moon; **deawy ray** because the star rises out of the ocean (cf.II xii 65.2), and is therefore associated with the dew of sleep.

Stanza 20
4 aread: perceive. **5 liuelihead**: life.

Stanza 21
1 start: escape. **2 case**: what had happened to him; or in the legal sense.

Stanza 22
3 entyrely: earnestly. **4 traine**: trick. **8–9** Turpine's proposal to kill the sleeping Arthur is measured against Calidore's unwillingness even to wound the unconscious Crudor at i 34.4.

23

Nathelesse for all his speach, the gentle knight
  Would not be tempted to such villenie,
  Regarding more his faith, which he did plight,
  All were it to his mortall enemie,
  Then to entrap him by false treacherie:
  Great shame in lieges blood to be embrew'd.
  Thus whylest they were debating diuerslie,
  The Saluage forth out of the wood issew'd.
Backe to the place, whereas his Lord he sleeping vew'd.

24

There when he saw those two so neare him stand,
  He doubted much what mote their meaning bee,
  And throwing downe his load out of his hand,
  To weet great store of forrest frute, which hee
  Had for his food late gathered from the tree,
  Himselfe vnto his weapon he betooke,
  That was an oaken plant, which lately hee
  Rent by the root; which he so sternely shooke,
That like an hazell wand, it quiuered and quooke.

25

Whereat the Prince awaking, when he spyde
  The traytour *Turpin* with that other knight,
  He started vp, and snatching neare his syde
  His trustie sword, the seruant of his might,
  Like a fell Lyon leaped to him light,
  And his left hand vpon his collar layd.
  Therewith the cowheard deaded with affright,
  Fell flat to ground, ne word vnto him sayd,
But holding vp his hands, with silence mercie prayd.

26

But he so full of indignation was,
  That to his prayer nought he would incline,
  But as he lay vpon the humbled gras,
  His foot he set on his vile necke, in signe

Of seruile yoke, that nobler harts repine.
  Then letting him arise like abiect thrall,
  He gan to him obiect his haynous crime,
  And to reuile, and rate, and recreant call,
And lastly to despoyle of knightly bannerall.

27

And after all, for greater infamie,
  He by the heeles him hung vpon a tree,
  And baffuld so, that all which passed by,
  The picture of his punishment might see,
  And by the like ensample warned bee,
  How euer they through treason doe trespasse.
  But turne we now backe to that Ladie free,
  Whom late we left ryding vpon an Asse,
Led by a Carle and foole, which by her side did passe.

28 *not living up to expectations*

She was a Ladie of great dignitie,
  And lifted vp to honorable place,
  Famous through all the land of Faerie,
  Though of meane parentage and kindred base,
  Yet deckt with wondrous giftes of natures grace,
  That all men did her person much admire,
  And praise the feature of her goodly face,
  The beames whereof did kindle louely fire
In th'harts of many a knight, and many a gentle squire.

29

But she thereof grew proud and insolent,
  That none she worthie thought to be her fere,
  But scornd them all, that loue vnto her ment;
  Yet was she lou'd of many a worthy pere,
  Vnworthy she to be belou'd so dere,
  That could not weigh of worthinesse aright.
  For beautie is more glorious bright and clere,
  The more it is admir'd of many a wight,
And noblest she, that serued is of noblest knight.

Stanza 23
6 **lieges**: as one to whom he was bound by oath.   **embrew'd**: stained.

Stanza 24
2 **doubted**: feared.   **meaning**: intention.   7–9 An uprooted oak is the traditional weapon of the wild man, as IV vii 7.4. **plant**: young tree.

Stanza 26
3 . . . as he lay humbled on the grass.   4 Only Terpine at V iv 40.3 and Enias at VI viii 10.9 suffer such humiliation. 5 **repine**: disdain.   7 **obiect**: reproach.   9 **bannerall**: banderol, a pennant attached to the lance as an emblem of chivalry.

Stanza 27
1–6 On the ritual of baffling or degradation, inflicted also on Braggadocchio, see V iii 37.5–9*n*. The **tree** is the tree of chivalry; see I v 5.7*n*. Cf. Gal. 3.13: 'Cursed is euerie one that hangeth on tre'.   **How euer**: in any way whatever; to whatever extent. Turpine's **treason** is his plot to murder Prince Arthur.   7 **free**: a stock epithet for a lady of noble birth, as

Malecasta at III i 44.8; used here in the sense of being wilful, as 30.8, 31.5. Cf. the lady in *Am* 10.4 who scorns her lover and Cupid 'of her freewill'.   8 **late**: at vi 16.6–17.3.   **Asse**: a 'mangy iade' at vi 16.8 and 40.7 below.   9 The **Carle** who leads her is Disdaine; see 41–43*n*. The **foole** at her side, or following her (as at 39.7, viii 24.8, etc.), is Scorn.

Stanzas 28–31
At viii 20–22, Mirabella gives her own spin on how her beauty led knights to love her but led her in her disdain to scorn them. Disdain and scorn are her humours which now punish her, their counterparts being Modestie and Curtesie respectively in Amoret's womanhood; see IV x 50–51*n*. Cf. Beatrice in Shakespeare's *Much Ado* 3.1.51–52: 'Disdain and scorn ride sparkling in her eyes, | Misprising what they look on'; see Potts 1958:40–44. On her story, see 'Mirabella' in the *SEnc*.

Stanza 28
4 I.e. she is of low social rank.   8 **louely fire**: the fire of love.

Stanza 29
1 **insolent**: haughty.   2 **fere**: mate.   7–9 That a woman should display her beauty to the gaze of as many men as

30

But this coy Damzell thought contrariwize,
    That such proud looks would make her praysed more;
    And that the more she did all loue despize,
    The more would wretched louers her adore.
    What cared she, who sighed for her sore,
    Or who did wayle or watch the wearie night?
    Let them that list, their lucklesse lot deplore;
    She was borne free, not bound to any wight,
And so would euer liue, and loue her owne delight.

31

Through such her stubborne stifnesse, and hard hart,
    Many a wretch, for want of remedie,
    Did languish long in lifeconsuming smart,
    And at the last through dreary dolour die:
    Whylest she, the Ladie of her libertie,
    Did boast her beautie had such soueraine might,
    That with the onely twinckle of her eye,
    She could or saue, or spill, whom she would hight.
What could the Gods doe more, but doe it more aright?

32

But loe the Gods, that mortall follies vew,
    Did worthily reuenge this maydens pride;
    And nought regarding her so goodly hew,
    Did laugh at her, that many did deride,
    Whilest she did weepe, of no man mercifide.
    For on a day, when *Cupid* kept his court,
    As he is wont at each Saint Valentide,
    Vnto the which all louers doe resort,
That of their loues successe they there may make report.

33

It fortun'd then, that when the roules were red,
    In which the names of all loues folke were fyled,
    That many there were missing, which were ded,
    Or kept in bands, or from their loues exyled,

Or by some other violence despoyled.
    Which when as *Cupid* heard, he wexed wroth,
    And doubting to be wronged, or beguyled,
    He bad his eyes to be vnblindfold both,
That he might see his men, and muster them by oth.

34

Then found he many missing of his crew,
    Which wont doe suit and seruice to his might;
    Of whom what was becomen, no man knew.
    Therefore a Iurie was impaneld streight,
    T'enquire of them, whether by force, or sleight,
    Or their owne guilt, they were away conuayd.
    To whom foule *Infamie*, and fell *Despight*
    Gaue euidence, that they were all betrayd,
And murdred cruelly by a rebellious Mayd.

35

Fayre *Mirabella* was her name, whereby
    Of all those crymes she there indited was:
    All which when *Cupid* heard, he by and by
    In great displeasure, wild a *Capias*
    Should issue forth, t'attach that scornefull lasse.
    The warrant straight was made, and therewithall
    A Baylieffe errant forth in post did passe,
    Whom they by name there *Portamore* did call;
He which doth summon louers to loues iudgement hall.

36

The damzell was attacht, and shortly brought
    Vnto the barre, whereas she was arraynd:
    But she thereto nould plead, nor answere ought
    Euen for stubborne pride, which her restrayned.
    So iudgement past, as is by law ordayned
    In cases like, which when at last she saw,
    Her stubborne hart, which loue before disdayned,
    Gan stoupe, and falling downe with humble awe,
Cryde mercie, to abate the extremitie of law.

---

possible is a claim made in *HB* 183–89. Line 9 varies the usual formula (see IV iv 5.7–9*n*) that the strongest knight deserves the most beautiful lady. Mirabella's state is moralized at viii 1–2. **clere**: glorious.

Stanza 31
7 **the onely**: only the. **8 spill**: kill. **hight**: name.

Stanza 32
1–5 The gods scorn her as she scorns her lovers. They **Did laugh at her** as she 'Did laugh at those [her lovers]' (viii 21.8); and as she pitied none, none pities her. **hew**: appearance. 6–9 The literary tradition of the Court of Cupid held on Saint Valentine's Day, which S. would know best from Chaucer, *Parl. Fowls*, and which would seem to have been the subject of his *Court of Cupide* (see 'works, lost' in the *SEnc*), is described by E.B. Fowler 1921:103–06. A. Williams 1967:108 claims that the legal imagery belongs to an ecclesiastical court that judged sexual offences and assigned penances.

Stanza 33
1 **roules**: rolls, records. **7 doubting**: fearing.

Stanza 34
2 **suit and seruice**: a feudal term for attendance at court and the personal service owing to the lord. **5 sleight**: trickery. 7 **Despight**: cf. Despetto at v 13.6.

Stanza 35
1 **Mirabella**: Lat. *mira* + *bella*, wondrously beautiful, as she appears to others at 28.5–9 and to herself at viii 20.1–4. **3 by and by**: straightway. 4–9 He issued a warrant of arrest (**Capias** = 'thou mayest take') to require her appearance at court. **therewithall**: with that. **Baylieffe errant**: an officer of justice who executes writs. **in post**: in haste. **Portamore**: i.e. Messenger of Love.

Stanza 36
3–6 In English law at that time, not to answer charges was to acknowledge guilt, as Todd 1805 notes. **9 the extremitie of law** for her multiple murders would be death.

37

The sonne of *Venus* who is myld by kynd,
    But where he is prouokt with peeuishnesse,
    Vnto her prayers piteously enclynd,
    And did the rigour of his doome represse;
    Yet not so freely, but that nathelesse
    He vnto her a penance did impose,
    Which was, that through this worlds wyde wildernes
    She wander should in companie of those,
Till she had sau'd so many loues, as she did lose.

38

So now she had bene wandring two whole yeares
    Throughout the world, in this vncomely case,
    Wasting her goodly hew in heauie teares,
    And her good dayes in dolorous disgrace:
    Yet had she not in all these two yeares space,
    Saued but two, yet in two yeares before,
    Through her dispiteous pride, whilest loue lackt place,
    She had destroyed two and twenty more.
Aie me, how could her loue make half amends therefore?

39

And now she was vppon the weary way,
    When as the gentle Squire, with faire *Serene*,
    Met her in such misseeming foule array;
    The whiles that mighty man did her demeane
    With all the euill termes and cruell meane,
    That he could make; And eeke that angry foole
    Which follow'd her, with cursed hands vncleane
    Whipping her horse, did with his smarting toole
Oft whip her dainty selfe, and much augment her doole.

40

Ne ought it mote auaile her to entreat
    The one or th'other, better her to vse:
    For both so wilfull were and obstinate,
    That all her piteous plaint they did refuse,
    And rather did the more her beate and bruse.
    But most the former villaine, which did lead
    Her tyreling iade, was bent her to abuse;
    Who though she were with wearinesse nigh dead,
Yet would not let her lite, nor rest a little stead.

41

For he was sterne, and terrible by nature,
    And eeke of person huge and hideous,
    Exceeding much the measure of mans stature,
    And rather like a Gyant monstruous.
    For sooth he was descended of the hous
    Of those old Gyants, which did warres darraine
    Against the heauen in order battailous,
    And sib to great *Orgolio*, which was slaine
By *Arthure*, when as *Vnas* Knight he did maintaine.

42

His lookes were dreadfull, and his fiery eies
    Like two great Beacons, glared bright and wyde,
    Glauncing askew, as if his enemies
    He scorned in his ouerweening pryde;
    And stalking stately like a Crane, did stryde
    At euery step vppon the tiptoes hie,
    And all the way he went, on euery syde
    He gaz'd about, and stared horriblie,
As if he with his lookes would all men terrifie.

Stanza 37

1 kynd: nature. **2** Except when he is provoked by perverse behaviour. **8 those**: i.e. the Carl and Fool (27.9) who embody her disdain and scorn. **9** A similar penance is imposed on the Squire of Dames at III vii 56. **lose**: destroy.

Stanza 38

5–9 For two years she had destroyed one lover a month, but since she has saved only one lover a year over two years, she has 22 more years of penance. On the association of that number with the soul, see II ix 22*n*; and on her dilemma, see Shaver 1991:221. **place**: i.e. in her heart.

Stanza 39

2–3 As told at vi 16.6–9. **4–9 that mighty man**, who is said to ill-treat (**demeane**) her is Disdaine, and the **foole** following her – at vi 16.9 he leads her – is Scorn, whose **smarting toole** is not a fool's bauble, as one would expect, but a whip. **meane**: means. **doole**: grief.

Stanza 40

6 former: foremost, being in front. **9 stead**: while.

Stanzas 41–43

The description of Disdayne, the porter of Philotime's court at II vii 40.4–41.9, is varied to express Mirabella's state. He is called a 'Carle' (i.e. a churl) at 27.9 and 47.7, or 'villaine' at

46.1 and viii 8.1, both terms marking him as one of 'base kind' (1.9) and therefore the enemy of civility. In being descended from 'those old Gyants', which are 'of the *Titans* race' (II vii 41.6), he is 'sib' (akin) both to the giant Orgoglio (see I vii 9) and to Argante (see III vii 47.3–5). His 'fiery eies' are those of the dragon at I xi 14, and of Corflambo at IV viii 39, and are 'Glauncing askew' as Mammon's eyes (see II vii 7.5*n*). His dress links him to the Irish: in *View* 70, Irenius compares Irish apparel to Chaucer's description of Sir Thopas's apparel 'when he went to fight against the Geant in his robe of Checklatoun, which . . . is that kind of gilden leather, with which they use to embroider their Irish jacks [jackets]'. His headpiece is similar to the turbaned churl Dangier with his knotted club in a *Le Roman de la Rose* ms. noted by Tuve 1970:130 and shown in Fleming 1969:fig. 11. See 'Disdain' in the *SEnc*.

Stanza 41

1 sterne: cruel. **2 hideous**: immense. **6–9** On their wars, see III vii 47.3–5*n*. **darraine**: wage. **maintaine**: conduct himself, or maintain her cause.

Stanza 42

5–6 As the Ape, in *Mother Hubberd* 664–65, 'Upon his tiptoes, stalketh stately by, | As if he were some great *Magnifico*'.

Stanza 43

5 plight: folded. **8 voyded from before**: kept clear from his face.

43

He wore no armour, ne for none did care,
  As no whit dreading any liuing wight;
  But in a Iacket quilted richly rare,
  Vpon checklaton he was straungely dight,
  And on his head a roll of linnen plight,
  Like to the Mores of Malaber he wore;
  With which his locks, as blacke as pitchy night,
  Were bound about, and voyded from before,
And in his hand a mighty yron club he bore.

44

This was *Disdaine*, who led that Ladies horse
  Through thick and thin, through mountains and through
  Compelling her, wher she would not, by force (plains,
  Haling her palfrey by the hempen raines.
  But that same foole, which most increast her paines,
  Was *Scorne*, who hauing in his hand a whip,
  Her therewith yirks, and still when she complaines,
  The more he laughes, and does her closely quip,
To see her sore lament, and bite her tender lip.

45

Whose cruell handling when that Squire beheld,
  And saw those villaines her so vildely vse,
  His gentle heart with indignation sweld,
  And could no lenger beare so great abuse,
  As such a Lady so to beate and bruse;
  But to him stepping, such a stroke him lent,
  That forst him th'halter from his hand to loose,
  And maugre all his might, backe to relent:
Else had he surely there bene slaine, or fowly shent.

46

The villaine wroth for greeting him so sore,
  Gathered him selfe together soone againe,
  And with his yron batton, which he bore,
  Let driue at him so dreadfully amaine,
  That for his safety he did him constraine
  To giue him ground, and shift to euery side,
  Rather then once his burden to sustaine:
  For bootelesse thing him seemed, to abide,
So mighty blowes, or proue the puissaunce of his pride.

47

Like as a Mastiffe hauing at a bay
  A saluage Bull, whose cruell hornes doe threat
  Desperate daunger, if he them assay,
  Traceth his ground, and round about doth beat,
  To spy where he may some aduauntage get;
  The whiles the beast doth rage and loudly rore:
  So did the Squire, the whiles the Carle did fret,
  And fume in his disdainefull mynd the more,
And oftentimes by Turmagant and Mahound swore.

48

Nathelesse so sharpely still he him pursewd,
  That at aduantage him at last he tooke,
  When his foote slipt (that slip he dearely rewd,)
  And with his yron club to ground him strooke;
  Where still he lay, ne out of swoune awooke,
  Till heauy hand the Carle vpon him layd,
  And bound him fast: Tho when he vp did looke,
  And saw him selfe captiu'd, he was dismayd,
Ne powre had to withstand, ne hope of any ayd.

49

Then vp he made him rise, and forward fare,
  Led in a rope, which both his hands did bynd;
  Ne ought that foole for pitty did him spare,
  But with his whip him following behynd,
  Him often scourg'd, and forst his feete to fynd:
  And other whiles with bitter mockes and mowes
  He would him scorne, that to his gentle mynd
  Was much more grieuous, then the others blowes:
Words sharpely wound, but greatest griefe of scorning growes.

50

The faire *Serena*, when she saw him fall
  Vnder that villaines club, then surely thought
  That slaine he was, or made a wretched thrall,
  And fled away with all the speede she mought,
  To seeke for safety, which long time she sought:
  And past through many perils by the way,
  Ere she againe to *Calepine* was brought;
  The which discourse as now I must delay,
Till *Mirabellaes* fortunes I doe further say.

Stanza 44
7 yirks: lashes. **8 closely quip**: covertly taunt.

Stanza 45
8 maugre: in spite of. **relent**: give way. **9 fowly shent**: shamefully injured.

Stanza 46
3 batton: club. **7 burden**: bourdon or club; or its weight.

Stanza 47
1–6 When Timias fights Defetto at v 19, he is compared to a bull baited by a mastiff. **assay**: put to the proof.

9 Turmagant and Mahound: the Saracen god and Mohammed; see II viii 30.4n.

Stanza 48
3–4 As the context makes clear, when Timias's foot slips, Disdaine's club knocks him to the ground.

Stanza 49
5 . . . forced him to keep walking. **6 mowes**: derisive grimaces. **9 Words**: 'Swords', conj. Church 1758. For J.C. Smith 1909, alliteration favours the text; so does the proverb: 'Words cut deeper than swords' (Smith 879).

Cant. VIII.

Prince Arthure ouercomes Disdaine,
Quites Mirabell from dreed:
Serena found of Saluages,
By Calepine is freed.

1

YE gentle Ladies, in whose soueraine powre
  Loue hath the glory of his kingdome left,
  And th'hearts of men, as your eternall dowre,
  In yron chaines, of liberty bereft,
  Deliuered hath into your hands by gift;
  Be well aware, how ye the same doe vse,
  That pride doe not to tyranny you lift;
  Least if men you of cruelty accuse,
He from you take that chiefedome, which ye doe abuse.

2

And as ye soft and tender are by kynde,
  Adornd with goodly gifts of beauties grace,
  So be ye soft and tender eeke in mynde;
  But cruelty and hardnesse from you chace,
  That all your other praises will deface,
  And from you turne the loue of men to hate.
  Ensample take of *Mirabellaes* case,
  Who from the high degree of happy state,
Fell into wretched woes, which she repented late.

3

Who after thraldome of the gentle Squire,
  Which she beheld with lamentable eye,
  Was touched with compassion entire,
  And much lamented his calamity,

That for her sake fell into misery:
  Which booted nought for prayers, nor for threat
  To hope for to release or mollify;
  For aye the more, that she did them entreat,
The more they him misust, and cruelly did beat.

4

So as they forward on their way did pas,
  Him still reuiling and afflicting sore,
  They met Prince *Arthure* with Sir *Enias*,
  (That was that courteous Knight, whom he before
  Hauing subdew'd, yet did to life restore,)
  To whom as they approcht, they gan augment
  Their cruelty, and him to punish more,
  Scourging and haling him more vehement;
As if it them should grieue to see his punishment.

5

The Squire him selfe when as he saw his Lord,
  The witnesse of his wretchednesse, in place,
  Was much asham'd, that with an hempen cord
  He like a dog was led in captiue case,
  And did his head for bashfulnesse abase,
  As loth to see, or to be seene at all:
  Shame would be hid. But whenas *Enias*
  Beheld two such, of two such villaines thrall,
His manly mynde was much emmoued therewithall.

Book VI Canto viii

Argument
In this 'regeneration' canto, Arthur completes the six labours required by the book's number; see I viii Arg.1–2*n*. In v, he rescues Timias and succours Serena; in vi, he defeats Turpine; in vii, he defeats Turpine's knights and baffles him; and in viii, he overcomes Disdaine and offers Mirabella her freedom. **2 Quites**: frees; see 29.6–9*n*.

Stanza 1
3 The **eternall dowre** of Ladies is only conditional, as Shaver 1991:212 observes.

Stanza 2
1 kynde: nature.

Stanza 3
At vii 29.3, the disdainful Mirabella scorned all lovers; now she pities Timias. Yet because she pities him, she disdains and

scorns him all the more, particularly in the presence of others. **2 lamentable**: lamenting. **3 entire**: sincere.

Stanza 4
3 Enias: a variant of Aeneas, from Lydgate, *Troy Book*, where Eneas is a brave warrior but also a traitor who plots to give Troy to the Greeks if his life is saved (4.4539–61), and later plots to have his fellow-traitor, Antenor, murdered (5.450–510). The name echoes Timias, whose plight he shares at 11.9, because he has assumed the role of Arthur's squire.

Stanza 5
Ashamed to be seen by Arthur at IV vii 44 and VI v 24, Timias is now reduced to 'greatest shame' (6.2); cf. 27.3. **3 hempen cord**: as the hanging rope worn by Trevisan at I ix 22.7, and the cord by which Disdaine drags Mirabella's jade at vii 44.4. **5 bashfulnesse**: mortification through shame. **abase**: hang down. **7** The emblematic posture of Shame at II vii 22.9.

6

And to the Prince thus sayd; See you Sir Knight,
   The greatest shame that euer eye yet saw?
   Yond Lady and her Squire with foule despight
   Abusde, against all reason and all law,
   Without regard of pitty or of awe.
   See how they doe that Squire beat and reuile;
   See how they doe the Lady hale and draw.
   But if ye please to lend me leaue a while,
I will them soone acquite, and both of blame assoile.

7

The Prince assented, and then he streight way
   Dismounting light, his shield about him threw,
   With which approching, thus he gan to say;
   Abide ye caytiue treachetours vntrew,
   That haue with treason thralled vnto you
   These two, vnworthy of your wretched bands;
   And now your crime with cruelty pursew.
   Abide, and from them lay your loathly hands;
Or else abide the death, that hard before you stands.

8

The villaine stayd not aunswer to inuent,
   But with his yron club preparing way,
   His mindes sad message backe vnto him sent;
   The which descended with such dreadfull sway,
   That seemed nought the course thereof could stay:
   No more then lightening from the lofty sky.
   Ne list the Knight the powre thereof assay,
   Whose doome was death, but lightly slipping by,
Vnwares defrauded his intended destiny.

9

And to requite him with the like againe,
   With his sharpe sword he fiercely at him flew,
   And strooke so strongly, that the Carle with paine
   Saued him selfe, but that he there him slew:
   Yet sau'd not so, but that the bloud it drew,
   And gaue his foe good hope of victory.
   Who therewith flesht, vpon him set anew,
   And with the second stroke, thought certainely
To haue supplyde the first, and paide the vsury.

10

But Fortune aunswerd not vnto his call;
   For as his hand was heaued vp on hight,
   The villaine met him in the middle fall,
   And with his club bet backe his brondyron bright
   So forcibly, that with his owne hands might
   Rebeaten backe vpon him selfe againe,
   He driuen was to ground in selfe despight;
   From whence ere he recouery could gaine,
He in his necke had set his foote with fell disdaine.

11

With that the foole, which did that end awayte,
   Came running in, and whilest on ground he lay,
   Laide heauy hands on him, and held so strayte,
   That downe he kept him with his scornefull sway,
   So as he could not weld him any way.
   The whiles that other villaine went about
   Him to haue bound, and thrald without delay;
   The whiles the foole did him reuile and flout,
Threatning to yoke them two and tame their corage stout.

12

As when a sturdy ploughman with his hynde
   By strength haue ouerthrowne a stubborne steare,
   They downe him hold, and fast with cords do bynde,
   Till they him force the buxome yoke to beare:
   So did these two this Knight oft tug and teare.
   Which when the Prince beheld, there standing by,
   He left his lofty steede to aide him neare,
   And buckling soone him selfe, gan fiercely fly
Vppon that Carle, to saue his friend from ieopardy.

13

The villaine leauing him vnto his mate
   To be captiu'd, and handled as he list,
   Himselfe addrest vnto this new debate,
   And with his club him all about so blist,
   That he which way to turne him scarcely wist:
   Sometimes aloft he layd, sometimes alow;
   Now here, now there, and oft him neare he mist;
   So doubtfully, that hardly one could know
Whether more wary were to giue or ward the blow.

Stanza 6
9 I will soon set both free and release them from reproof.

Stanza 7
2 **light**: quickly. 4 **Abide**: stop, as in 8; but with its usual sense, 'endure', in 9. **treachetours**: traitors; see II x 51.3*n*. 6 **vnworthy**: not deserving.

Stanza 8
3 **sad**: heavy, as it refers to the club; but also the usual sense for the **message** is death. 4 **sway**: force.

Stanza 9
7 **flesht**: incited; also literally, having thrust his sword into his enemy's flesh. 9 **supplyde**: reinforced. **vsury**: interest.

Stanza 10
3 **in the middle fall**: i.e. in the middle of his downward stroke. 4 **brondyron**: sword. 5–7 The gesture indicates that Enias causes his own downfall, overcome by his own disdain at 6. Hence **in selfe despight**: in spite of himself, but also by his own despite.

Stanza 11
3 **strayte**: tightly. 4 **sway**: force. 5 **weld him**: move himself. 9 **them two**: i.e. Timias and Enias.

Stanza 12
1 **hynde**: servant. 4 . . . to bear the yoke obediently.

Stanza 13
3 **debate**: conflict. 4 **blist**: brandished.

14

But yet the Prince so well enured was
  With such huge strokes, approued oft in fight,
  That way to them he gaue forth right to pas.
  Ne would endure the daunger of their might,
  But wayt aduantage, when they downe did light.
  At last the caytiue after long discourse,
  When all his strokes he saw auoyded quite,
  Resolued in one t'assemble all his force,
And make one end of him without ruth or remorse.

15

His dreadfull hand he heaued vp aloft,
  And with his dreadfull instrument of yre,
  Thought sure haue pownded him to powder soft,
  Or deepe emboweld in the earth entyre:
  But Fortune did not with his will conspire.
  For ere his stroke attaynd his intent,
  The noble childe preuenting his desire,
  Vnder his club with wary boldnesse went,
And smote him on the knee, that neuer yet was bent.

16

It neuer yet was bent, ne bent it now,
  Albe the stroke so strong and puissant were,
  That seem'd a marble pillour it could bow,
  But all that leg, which did his body beare,
  It crackt throughout, yet did no bloud appeare;
  So as it was vnable to support
  So huge a burden on such broken geare,
  But fell to ground, like to a lumpe of durt,
Whence he assayd to rise, but could not for his hurt.

17

Eftsoones the Prince to him full nimbly stept,
  And least he should recouer foote againe,
  His head meant from his shoulders to haue swept.
  Which when the Lady saw, she cryde amaine;
  Stay stay, Sir Knight, for loue of God abstaine,
  From that vnwares ye weetlesse doe intend;
  Slay not that Carle, though worthy to be slaine:
  For more on him doth then him selfe depend;
My life will by his death haue lamentable end.

18

He staide his hand according her desire,
  Yet nathemore him suffred to arize;
  But still suppressing gan of her inquire,
  What meaning mote those vncouth words comprize,
  That in that villaines health her safety lies:
  That, were no might in man, nor heart in Knights,
  Which durst her dreaded reskue enterprize,
  Yet heauens them selues, that fauour feeble rights,
Would for it selfe redresse, and punish such despights.

19

Then bursting forth in teares, which gushed fast
  Like many water streames, a while she stayd;
  Till the sharpe passion being ouerpast,
  Her tongue to her restord, then thus she sayd;
  Nor heauens, nor men can me most wretched mayd
  Deliuer from the doome of my desart,
  The which the God of loue hath on me layd,
  And damned to endure this direfull smart,
For penaunce of my proud and hard rebellious hart.

20

In prime of youthly yeares, when first the flowre
  Of beauty gan to bud, and bloosme delight,
  And nature me endu'd with plenteous dowre,
  Of all her gifts, that pleasde each liuing sight,
  I was belou'd of many a gentle Knight,
  And sude and sought with all the seruice dew:
  Full many a one for me deepe groand and sight,
  And to the dore of death for sorrow drew,
Complayning out on me, that would not on them rew.

21

But let them loue that list, or liue or die;
  Me list not die for any louers doole:
  Ne list me leaue my loued libertie,
  To pitty him that list to play the foole:
  To loue my selfe I learned had in schoole.
  Thus I triumphed long in louers paine,
  And sitting carelesse on the scorners stoole,
  Did laugh at those that did lament and plaine:
But all is now repayd with interest againe.

Stanza 14
2 approued: tested. **4 daunger**: harm. **6 discourse**: running to and fro, as Ital. *discorso*.

Stanza 15
S. recycles details from Arthur's battle with Orgoglio, esp. I viii 22. **3** Such is the power of Orgoglio's blow at I vii 14.3. **4 entyre**: completely; or as adj., 'inner'. **7 childe**: applied only to Arthur; see IV viii 44.8n. **preuenting**: anticipating.

Stanza 17
1 nimbly: swiftly. **4–9** As Amoret appeals to Britomart not to slay Busirane at III xii 34 for their lives depend on their tormentors. **amaine**: with all her might. The **God** to whose love she appeals is 'the God of loue' (19.7).

Stanza 18
3 suppressing: pressing down. **4 comprize**: contain. **6–9** I.e. if knights were neither strong nor valorous enough to dare rescue me 'from dreed' (Arg.), the heavens, which support the rights of the weak, would do so.

Stanzas 20–22
To the story told of her at vii 28–31, Mirabella adds more on her natural gifts and the griefs of her lovers, and admits that she scorned them out of love of freedom and self-love.

Stanza 20
1–4 Mirabella's natural gifts contrast with Belphœbe's heavenly gifts at III vi 2, and Amoret's virtues at IV x 49–52. **6 sude**: wooed (*OED* I.15), as in the formulaic phrase, 'serue and sew' (II vii 9.1), i.e. give suit and service. **7 sight**: sighed. **9 out on me**: aloud against me; or an interjection of reproach.

22

For loe the winged God, that woundeth harts,
  Causde me be called to accompt therefore,
  And for reuengement of those wrongfull smarts,
  Which I to others did inflict afore,
  Addeem'd me to endure this penaunce sore;
  That in this wize, and this vnmeete array,
  With these two lewd companions, and no more,
  Disdaine and *Scorne*, I through the world should stray,
Till I haue sau'd so many, as I earst did slay.

23

Certes (sayd then the Prince) the God is iust,
  That taketh vengeaunce of his peoples spoile.
  For were no law in loue, but all that lust,
  Might them oppresse, and painefully turmoile,
  His kingdome would continue but a while.
  But tell me Lady, wherefore doe you beare
  This bottle thus before you with such toile,
  And eeke this wallet at your backe arreare,
That for these Carles to carry much more comely were?

24

Here in this bottle (sayd the sory Mayd)
  I put the teares of my contrition,
  Till to the brim I haue it full defrayd:
  And in this bag which I behinde me don,
  I put repentaunce for things past and gon.
  Yet is the bottle leake, and bag so torne,
  That all which I put in, fals out anon;
  And is behinde me trodden downe of *Scorne*,
Who mocketh all my paine, and laughs the more I mourn.

25

The Infant hearkned wisely to her tale,
  And wondred much at *Cupids* iudg'ment wise,
  That could so meekly make proud hearts auale,
  And wreake him selfe on them, that him despise.

Then suffred he *Disdaine* vp to arise,
  Who was not able vp him selfe to reare,
  By meanes his leg through his late luckelesse prise,
  Was crackt in twaine, but by his foolish feare
Was holpen vp, who him supported standing neare.

26

But being vp, he lookt againe aloft,
  As if he neuer had receiued fall;
  And with sterne eye-browes stared at him oft,
  As if he would haue daunted him withall:
  And standing on his tiptoes, to seeme tall,
  Downe on his golden feete he often gazed,
  As if such pride the other could apall;
  Who was so far from being ought amazed,
That he his lookes despised, and his boast dispraized.

27

Then turning backe vnto that captiue thrall,
  Who all this while stood there beside them bound,
  Vnwilling to be knowne, or seene at all,
  He from those bands weend him to haue vnwound.
  But when approching neare, he plainely found,
  It was his owne true groome, the gentle Squire,
  He threat wext exceedingly astound,
  And him did oft embrace, and oft admire,
Ne could with seeing satisfie his great desire.

28

Meane while the Saluage man, when he beheld
  That huge great foole oppressing th'other Knight,
  Whom with his weight vnweldy downe he held,
  He flew vpon him, like a greedy kight
  Vnto some carrion offered to his sight,
  And downe him plucking, with his nayles and teeth
  Gan him to hale, and teare, and scratch, and bite;
  And from him taking his owne whip, therewith
So sore him scourgeth, that the bloud downe followeth.

Stanza 21
1–4 **list**: the repetitions point to the contradiction between the claim that her lovers are free to love, even as she is free not to love, and their actual state: they are subject to love even as she is subject to disdain and scorn. **doole**: grief. 7 Cf. Ps. 1.1: 'The man is blest that hath not . . . sat in scorners chair' (Sternhold-Hopkins 1562).

Stanza 22
5 **Addeem'd**: adjudged. 7 **lewd**: evil.

Stanza 23
3 **lust**: chose; but not excluding the sexual sense. 4 **turmoile**: torment. 8 **arreare**: behind.

Stanza 24
1–2 **this bottle**: the tear-bottle of Ps. 56.8: 'Thou hast . . . put my teares into thy bottel', except that this bottle is leaky. 3 Until I have fully discharged my contrition by filling the bottle.

Stanza 25
1 **Infant**: Arthur's title; see II viii 56.1–3*n*. 3 **auale**: yield. 7 **By meanes**: because. **prise**: contest. 8 **foolish feare**: his companion, Scorn, who is the fool; see vii 39.4–9*n*.

Stanza 26
5 He resumes his posture at vii 42.5–6. 6 **his golden feete**: cf. the feet of Disdayne at II vii 40.7, and see *n*. 9 **boast**: ostentation; threatening.

Stanza 27
6–9 **gentle** is the first epithet to describe Timias when he first appears at I vii 37.1; the second is that he is Arthur's 'dearely loued Squire'. With this strongly erotic union, cf. v 23.5–9 where he is welcomed by Arthur as 'my lifes desire'. **admire**: gaze at with wonder.

Stanza 28
3 **vnweldy**: unwieldy, unless it applies to Enias who is unable to move at 11.5.

29

And sure I weene, had not the Ladies cry
  Procur'd the Prince his cruell hand to stay,
  He would with whipping, him haue done to dye:
  But being checkt, he did abstaine streight way,
  And let him rise. Then thus the Prince gan say;
  Now Lady sith your fortunes thus dispose,
  That if ye list haue liberty, ye may,
Vnto your selfe I freely leaue to chose,
Whether I shall you leaue, or from these villaines lose.

30

Ah nay Sir Knight (sayd she) it may not be,
  But that I needes must by all meanes fulfill
  This penaunce, which enioyned is to me,
  Least vnto me betide a greater ill;
  Yet no lesse thankes to you for your good will.
  So humbly taking leaue, she turnd aside,
  But *Arthure* with the rest, went onward still
On his first quest, in which did him betide
A great aduenture, which did him from them deuide.

31

But first it falleth me by course to tell
  Of faire *Serena*, who as earst you heard,
  When first the gentle Squire at variaunce fell
  With those two Carles, fled fast away, afeard
  Of villany to be to her inferd:
  So fresh the image of her former dread,
  Yet dwelling in her eye, to her appeard,
That euery foote did tremble, which did tread,
And euery body two, and two she foure did read.

32

Through hils and dales, through bushes and through breres
  Long thus she fled, till that at last she thought
  Her selfe now past the perill of her feares.
  Then looking round about, and seeing nought,

Which doubt of daunger to her offer mought,
  She from her palfrey lighted on the plaine,
  And sitting downe, her selfe a while bethought
  Of her long trauell and turmoyling paine;
And often did of loue, and oft of lucke complaine.

33

And euermore she blamed *Calepine*,
  The good Sir *Calepine*, her owne true Knight,
  As th'onely author of her wofull tine:
  For being of his loue to her so light,
  As her to leaue in such a piteous plight.
  Yet neuer Turtle truer to his make,
  Then he was tride vnto his Lady bright:
Who all this while endured for her sake,
Great perill of his life, and restlesse paines did take.

34

Tho when as all her plaints, she had displayd,
  And well disburdened her engrieued brest,
  Vpon the grasse her selfe adowne she layd;
  Where being tyrde with trauell, and opprest
  With sorrow, she betooke her selfe to rest.
  There whilest in *Morpheus* bosome safe she lay,
  Fearelesse of ought, that mote her peace molest,
False Fortune did her safety betray,
Vnto a straunge mischaunce, that menac'd her decay.

35

In these wylde deserts, where she now abode,
  There dwelt a saluage nation, which did liue
  Of stealth and spoile, and making nightly rode
  Into their neighbours borders; ne did giue
  Them selues to any trade, as for to driue
  The painefull plough, or cattell for to breed,
  Or by aduentrous marchandize to thriue;
  But on the labours of poore men to feed,
And serue their owne necessities with others need.

Stanza 29
2 **Procur'd**: prevailed upon. **6–9** While Arthur 'Quites Mirabell from dreed', according to the Arg., he does not kill Disdaine, for his death she fears would bring her own (17.9), and he saves Scorn from being killed. Since he claims, at IV ix 37.6–7, that ladies must be given freedom to choose their loves, he allows Mirabella freedom either to fulfil her penance or be freed from it. **lose**: loosen.

Stanza 30
Mirabella, who was 'the Ladie of her libertie' (vii 31.5), now chooses penance for fear of **a greater ill** (presumably death), 'as is by law ordayned' at vii 36.5. **9** This unidentified **great aduenture** divides him also from us until his great awakening.

Stanzas 31–51
The final episode of Serena's story parallels Amoret's story in Bk IV: as they wander fearlessly in the forest, Amoret is captured by a 'saluage man' (IV vii 5.1) and Serena by a 'saluage nation' (35.2 below), and both are threatened with being eaten. On the sources, see McNeir 1968; on the significance of the parallels, see D. Cheney 1966:108–16; on the possible theological satire on radical Reformers, see Borris 1990.

Stanza 31
1–6 Recalling vii 50, which promises the present 'discourse'. **to her inferd**: inflicted on her; also she fears that she will be accused of shameful conduct. She flees from **villany** only to be captured by 'villeins' (43.3). **her former dread** refers to the beginning of her story when the Blatant Beast intended 'to haue spoyled her' (iii 25.3). Her story comes full circle when she is 'spoyld of all attire' (48.5) by the Salvage Nation. **9 read**: take for.

Stanza 32
5 **doubt**: fear.

Stanza 33
3 **tine**: sorrow. **6 make**: mate. **7 tride**: proven faithful.

36

Thereto they vsde one most accursed order,
    To eate the flesh of men, whom they mote fynde,
    And straungers to deuoure, which on their border
    Were brought by errour, or by wreckfull wynde.
    A monstrous cruelty gainst course of kynde.
    They towards euening wandring euery way,
    To seeke for booty, came by fortune blynde,
    Whereas this Lady, like a sheepe astray,
Now drowned in the depth of sleepe all fearelesse lay.

37

Soone as they spide her, Lord what gladfull glee
    They made amongst them selues; but when her face
    Like the faire yuory shining they did see,
    Each gan his fellow solace and embrace,
    For ioy of such good hap by heauenly grace.
    Then gan they to deuize what course to take,
    Whether to slay her there vpon the place,
    Or suffer her out of her sleepe to wake,
And then her eate attonce; or many meales to make.

38

The best aduizement was of bad, to let her
    Sleepe out her fill, without encomberment:
    For sleepe they sayd would make her battill better.
    Then when she wakt, they all gaue one consent,
    That since by grace of God she there was sent,
    Vnto their God they would her sacrifize,
    Whose share, her guiltlesse bloud they would present,
    But of her dainty flesh they did deuize
To make a common feast, and feed with gurmandize.

39

So round about her they them selues did place
    Vpon the grasse, and diuersely dispose,
    As each thought best to spend the lingring space.
    Some with their eyes the daintest morsels chose;
    Some praise her paps, some praise her lips and nose;
    Some whet their kniues, and strip their elboes bare:
    The Priest him selfe a garland doth compose
    Of finest flowres, and with full busie care
His bloudy vessels wash, and holy fire prepare.

40

The Damzell wakes, then all attonce vpstart,
    And round about her flocke, like many flies,
    Whooping, and hallowing on euery part,
    As if they would haue rent the brasen skies.
    Which when she sees with ghastly grieffull eies,
    Her heart does quake, and deadly pallid hew
    Benumbes her cheekes: Then out aloud she cries,
    Where none is nigh to heare, that will her rew,
And rends her golden locks, and snowy brests embrew.

41

But all bootes not: they hands vpon her lay;
    And first they spoile her of her iewels deare,
    And afterwards of all her rich array;
    The which amongst them they in peeces teare,
    And of the pray each one a part doth beare.
    Now being naked, to their sordid eyes
    The goodly threasures of nature appeare:
    Which as they view with lustfull fantasyes,
Each wisheth to him selfe, and to the rest enuyes.

mirabella vs belphoebe = foils

Stanza 34
6 **safe**: either she is overconfident or she remains secure in the power of the god of sleep while suffering the ensuing nightmare; cf. 36.9.   9 . . . that threatened her death.

Stanza 35
2 **a saluage nation**: see 'Cannibals' in the *SEnc*. On their relation to the native peoples of the New World, see Hamlin 1995:85–87. On their relation to the Irish, see Cavanagh 1996:273–74. Their cannibalism is shared by the hyena 'That feeds on wemens flesh' (III vii 22.9) and by Lust that 'fed on fleshly gore' (IV vii 5.8), but more generally by male desire, e.g. Cymochles who 'with spoyle of beauty feedes' (II v 34.3) in the Bower of Bliss. As a critique of Petrarchism, see Rowe 1989:322–24, Krier 1990:114–18, Crewe 1992, and Dubrow 1995:259–60.   3 **stealth**: theft.   **rode**: raid.   5–6 A mark of their savage state: in *View* 157, Irenius urges that the Irish be driven 'unto the plough' to help civilize them; cf. x 39.4.   7 **marchandize**: trading.

Stanza 36
1 **order**: custom.   4 **errour**: wandering.   5 **kynde**: nature.

Stanza 37
5 **by heauenly grace**: as 38.5, though they found her 'by fortune blynde' (36.7).   7 **vpon the place**: on the spot, immediately.

Stanza 38
1 I.e. even their best plan was bad.   2 **encomberment**: disturbance.   3 **battill**: grow fat, as do cattle.   7–9 I.e. they would offer her blood to their god as his share, keeping the flesh for themselves to eat, as at Deut. 12.27.   **gurmandize**: gluttony.

Stanza 39
7–9 The **garland** is for Serena, as the sacrificial ox is garlanded at III iv 17. The priest's vessels are **bloudy** as they are prepared to hold her blood.

Stanza 40
2 **like many flies**: a common simile for a swarming attack, as xi 48; appropriate here for the fly is associated with lechery.   3 **part**: side.   9 **embrew**: moistens with tears, or stains with blood.

Stanza 41
9 **enuyes**: begrudges.

42
Her yuorie necke, her alablaster brest,
    Her paps, which like white silken pillowes were,
    For loue in soft delight thereon to rest;
    Her tender sides, her bellie white and clere,
    Which like an Altar did it selfe vprere,
    To offer sacrifice diuine thereon;
    Her goodly thighes, whose glorie did appeare
    Like a triumphall Arch, and thereupon
The spoiles of Princes hang'd, which were in battel won.

43
Those daintie parts, the dearlings of delight,
    Which mote not be prophan'd of common eyes,
    Those villeins vew'd with loose lasciuious sight,
    And closely tempted with their craftie spyes;
    And some of them gan mongst themselues deuize,
    Thereof by force to take their beastly pleasure.
    But them the Priest rebuking, did aduize
    To dare not to pollute so sacred threasure,
Vow'd to the gods: religion held euen theeues in measure.

44
So being stayd, they her from thence directed
    Vnto a litle groue not farre asyde,
    In which an altar shortly they erected,
    To slay her on. And now the Euentyde
    His brode black wings had through the heauens wyde
    By this dispred, that was the tyme ordayned
    For such a dismall deed, their guilt to hyde:
    Of few greene turfes an altar soone they fayned,
And deckt it all with flowres, which they nigh hand obtayned.

45
Tho when as all things readie were aright,
    The Damzell was before the altar set,
    Being alreadie dead with fearefull fright.
    To whom the Priest with naked armes full net
    Approching nigh, and murdrous knife well whet,
    Gan mutter close a certaine secret charme,
    With other diuelish ceremonies met:
    Which doen he gan aloft t'aduance his arme,
Whereat they shouted all, and made a loud alarme.

46
Then gan the bagpypes and the hornes to shrill,
    And shrieke aloud, that with the peoples voyce
    Confused, did the ayre with terror fill,
    And made the wood to tremble at the noyce:
    The whyles she wayld, the more they did reioyce.
    Now mote ye vnderstand that to this groue
    Sir *Calepine* by chaunce, more then by choyce,
    The selfe same euening fortune hether droue,
As he to seeke *Serena* through the woods did roue.

47
Long had he sought her, and through many a soyle
    Had traueld still on foot in heauie armes,
    Ne ought was tyred with his endlesse toyles,
    Ne ought was feared of his certaine harmes:
    And now all weetlesse of the wretched stormes,
    In which his loue was lost, he slept full fast,
    Till being waked with these loud alarmes,
    He lightly started vp like one aghast,
And catching vp his arms streight to the noise forth past.

Stanza 42
The blazon began with her face at 37.2–3 and now continues down her body in an erotic version of the blazon of Belphœbe at II iii 22–30 (e.g. referring to 'Those daintie parts' at 43.1). As a blazon, see Gregerson 1995:137–39. As preparation for the *sparagmos*, the tearing apart of her sacrificial body, see N. Frye 1957:148. Pitcher 1987:86–87 notes the contrast between the poetic conceits and how the savages see her. **4 clere**: bright, shining. **5** In a context that involves the fantasies of a woman in love, the **Altar** suggests the nuptial bed on which the bride awaits the groom 'Like an appointed lambe, when tenderly | The priest comes on his knees t'embowell her' (Donne, 'Epithalamion made at Lincolnes Inne' 89–90) before becoming the physical altar on which she is to be sacrificed. **7–9** In Song Sol. 4.4, the beloved's neck is compared to a tower upon which 'a thousand shields hang . . . and all the targates of the strong men'.

Stanza 43
4 closely: secretly. **tempted**: made trial of. **spyes**: eyes or glances. **9 measure**: moderation.

Stanza 44
7 dismall: terrible, dreadful. **8** Repeating line 3 to stress that the altar is **fayned**, i.e. fashioned and false, in being used for an obscene religious ritual.

Stanza 45
4 net: clean or bare, for the purpose of sacrifice. **6 close**: covertly. **7 met**: meet, fitting; or (if a vb), united.

Stanza 46
1–4 bagpypes: a traditional emblem of lust from their shape, as at III x 43.2, sounding here as part of epithalamic ritual to drown out the bride's cry on being penetrated, as Puttenham 1936:51 records. **Confused**: mingled together. **4–6** His state corresponds to Serena's at 34.4–5, sleeping soundly at 47.6 as she slept at 34.6–7, thus sharing her nightmare. On his role as voyeur, see Linton 1998:110–17.

Stanza 47
2 still: because he began doing so at iii 29.5. **4 feared of**: alarmed by.

48

There by th'vncertaine glims of starry night,
    And by the twinkling of their sacred fire,
    He mote perceiue a litle dawning sight
    Of all, which there was doing in that quire:
    Mongst whom a woman spoyld of all attire
    He spyde, lamenting her vnluckie strife,
    And groning sore from grieued hart entire;
    Eftsoones he saw one with a naked knife
Readie to launch her brest, and let out loued life.

49

With that he thrusts into the thickest throng,
    And euen as his right hand adowne descends,
    He him preuenting, layes on earth along,
    And sacrifizeth to th'infernall feends.
    Then to the rest his wrathfull hand he bends,
    Of whom he makes such hauocke and such hew,
    That swarmes of damned soules to hell he sends:
    The rest that scape his sword and death eschew,
Fly like a flocke of doues before a Faulcons vew.

50

From them returning to that Ladie backe,
    Whom by the Altar he doth sitting find,
    Yet fearing death, and next to death the lacke
    Of clothes to couer, what they ought by kind,
    He first her hands beginneth to vnbind;
    And then to question of her present woe;
    And afterwards to cheare with speaches kind.
    But she for nought that he could say or doe,
One word durst speake, or answere him a whit thereto.

51

So inward shame of her vncomely case
    She did conceiue, through care of womanhood,
    That though the night did couer her disgrace,
    Yet she in so vnwomanly a mood,
    Would not bewray the state in which she stood.
    So all that night to him vnknowen she past.
    But day, that doth discouer bad and good,
    Ensewing, made her knowen to him at last:
The end whereof Ile keepe vntill another cast.

Stanza 48

1 glims: glimpse, glimmering.   **2 twinkling** refers either to the light of the stars or the 'holy fire' (39.9), which is **sacred** in being consecrated.   **4 quire**: chorus, either as a band or as singers, referring to their yelling.   **6 strife**: distress.   **7 entire**: 'wholly', if an adv.; describing her unpierced heart if an adj.   **9 launch**: pierce.

Stanza 49

2 On this dramatic intervention, stressed by **adowne** ('down' would better serve the metre), see I ix 51.9*n*.   **3–4 preuenting**: also 'anticipating'. The irony of the sacrificer being sacrificed is noted in *Var* 6.235.   **6 hew**: hewing, slaughter.   **8 eschew**: evade.

Stanza 50

4 . . . what they are naturally intended to cover.

Stanza 51

The end of Serena's story contrasts with its beginning at iii 20–21 when Calepine was seen 'To solace with [her] in delight'. That first moment when they were 'much abasht' by Calidore's sight of them is now renewed in her. The sight of her sitting in shamed silence unknown to her lover is the opposite pole to the vision of the hundred naked and dancing maidens who surround the three Graces who both dance and sing at x 11–12.   **1 her vncomely case**: her evil plight; or her 'daintie parts' which are compared to 'a triumphall Arch' at 42.8–9.   **4–5** In a state so contrary to the modesty of womanhood, she would not **bewray** (i.e. identify) herself; or **vnwomanly** because she remains silent, as Nelson 1973:91 suggests. See Stephens 1998:132–34.   **8 knowen**: the sexual meaning is suggested.   **9 cast**: throw; or in the fig. sense, 'time'.

Cant. IX.

Calidore hostes with Melibæ
and loues fayre Pastorell;
Coridon enuies him, yet he
for ill rewards him well.

1

Now turne againe my teme thou iolly swayne,
  Backe to the furrow which I lately left;
I lately left a furrow, one or twayne
Vnplough'd, the which my coulter hath not cleft:
Yet seem'd the soyle both fayre and frutefull eft,
  As I it past, that were too great a shame,
  That so rich frute should be from vs bereft;
Besides the great dishonour and defame,
Which should befall to *Calidores* immortall name.

2

Great trauell hath the gentle *Calidore*
  And toyle endured, sith I left him last
Sewing the *Blatant beast*, which I forbore
To finish then, for other present hast.
Full many pathes and perils he hath past,
  Through hils, through dales, throgh forests, and throgh plaines
  In that same quest which fortune on him cast,
Which he atchieued to his owne great gaines,
Reaping eternall glorie of his restlesse paines.

3

So sharply he the Monster did pursew,
  That day nor night he suffred him to rest,
Ne rested he himselfe but natures dew,
  For dread of daunger, not to be redrest,

If he for slouth forslackt so famous quest.
  Him first from court he to the citties coursed,
  And from the citties to the townes him prest,
And from the townes into the countrie forsed,
And from the country back to priuate farmes he scorsed.

4

From thence into the open fields he fled,
  Whereas the Heardes were keeping of their neat,
And shepheards singing to their flockes, that fed,
Layes of sweete loue and youthes delightfull heat:
  Him thether eke for all his fearefull threat
  He followed fast, and chaced him so nie,
That to the folds, where sheepe at night doe seat,
And to the litle cots, where shepherds lie
In winters wrathfull time, he forced him to flie.

5

There on a day as he pursew'd the chace,
  He chaunst to spy a sort of shepheard groomes,
Playing on pypes, and caroling apace,
The whyles their beasts there in the budded broomes
Beside them fed, and nipt the tender bloomes:
  For other worldly wealth they cared nought.
  To whom Sir *Calidore* yet sweating comes,
And them to tell him courteously besought,
If such a beast they saw, which he had thether brought.

Book VI Canto ix

Argument
1 **hostes**: lodges.

Stanza 1
The georgic topos of conclusion used at III xii 47.3–6, IV v 46.8–9, and V iii 40.6–9 to express the poet's tiredness is adapted to announce his fresh beginning. It is wittily varied: a ploughboy guides the **teme** (the muses) while the poet guides the plough. Its use here may have been prompted by the Salvage Nation that did not drive 'The painefull plough' (viii 35.6). **5 eft**: also. **8–9 dishonour and defame** are brought upon Calidore when he now abandons his quest, and last until he resumes it at xii 12, thereby 'Reaping eternall glorie' (2.9).

Stanza 2
2 **left him last**: at iii 26.5. **3 Sewing**: pursuing.

Stanza 3
3 **but natures dew**: i.e. only the sleep required by nature, the 'kindely sleepe' at iii 10.2, in contrast to his willing rest in the pastoral retreat. **4 redrest**: remedied, atoned for. **5 forslackt**: neglected, as xii 12.3–9 where the **daunger** is named 'reprochfull blame' and 'foule dishonour'. **6–9** In her search for Cupid at III vi 13–16, Venus follows a similar sequence: from court to cities to country and finally to the woods where she finds Amoret instead, much as Calidore finds love in Pastorella. **scorsed**: caused to exchange; chased.

Stanza 4
2 **Heardes**: herdsmen. **neat**: cattle. **7 seat**: lie down. **8 cots**: cotes or shelters. **9 time**: 'tine', conj. Upton 1758, which IV iii 23.7 and xii 34.6 support.

Stanza 5
2 **sort**: company. **9** I.e. his quest for the Beast brought him to the shepherds. The suggestion that he brought it to them is denied by 6.1–3.

6

They answer'd him, that no such beast they saw,
  Nor any wicked feend, that mote offend
  Their happie flockes, nor daunger to them draw:
  But if that such there were (as none they kend)
  They prayd high God them farre from them to send.
  Then one of them him seeing so to sweat,
  After his rusticke wise, that well he weend,
  Offred him drinke, to quench his thirstie heat,
And if he hungry were, him offred eke to eat.

7

The knight was nothing nice, where was no need,
  And tooke their gentle offer: so adowne
  They prayd him sit, and gaue him for to feed
  Such homely what, as serues the simple clowne,
  That doth despise the dainties of the towne.
  Tho hauing fed his fill, he there besyde
  Saw a faire damzell, which did weare a crowne
  Of sundry flowres, with silken ribbands tyde,
Yclad in home-made greene that her owne hands had dyde.

8

Vpon a litle hillocke she was placed
  Higher then all the rest, and round about
  Enuiron'd with a girland, goodly graced,
  Of louely lasses, and them all without
  The lustie shepheard swaynes sate in a rout,
  The which did pype and sing her prayses dew,
  And oft reioyce, and oft for wonder shout,
  As if some miracle of heauenly hew
Were downe to them descended in that earthly vew.

9

And soothly sure she was full fayre of face,
  And perfectly well shapt in euery lim,
  Which she did more augment with modest grace,
  And comely carriage of her count'nance trim,

That all the rest like lesser lamps did dim:
  Who her admiring as some heauenly wight,
  Did for their soueraine goddesse her esteeme,
  And caroling her name both day and night,
The fayrest *Pastorella* her by name did hight.

10

Ne was there heard, ne was there shepheards swayne
  But her did honour, and eke many a one
  Burnt in her loue, and with sweet pleasing payne
  Full many a night for her did sigh and grone:
  But most of all the shepheard *Coridon*
  For her did languish, and his deare life spend;
  Yet neither she for him, nor other none
  Did care a whit, ne any liking lend:
Though meane her lot, yet higher did her mind ascend.

11

Her whyles Sir *Calidore* there vewed well,
  And markt her rare demeanure, which him seemed
  So farre the meane of shepheards to excell,
  As that he in his mind her worthy deemed,
  To be a Princes Paragone esteemed,
  He was vnwares surprisd in subtile bands
  Of the blynd boy, ne thence could be redeemed
  By any skill out of his cruell hands,
Caught like the bird, which gazing still on others stands.

12

So stood he still long gazing thereupon,
  Ne any will had thence to moue away,
  Although his quest were farre afore him gon;
  But after he had fed, yet did he stay,
  And sate there still, vntill the flying day
  Was farre forth spent, discoursing diuersly
  Of sundry things, as fell, to worke delay;
  And euermore his speach he did apply
To th'heards, but meant them to the damzels fantazy.

Stanza 6
2 **offend**: attack.   7 . . . as he thought best.

Stanza 7
1 . . . was not at all fastidious.   4 **what**: thing.   **clowne**:
rustic.

Stanza 8
1–5 This grouping anticipates x 12 where a hundred maidens
encircle the three Graces with the garlanded damsel at the
centre. The shepherds (and Calidore) remain **all without** as
does Colin Clout (though see x 10.7–9*n*). **lustie**: joyful,
vigorous; the masculine equivalent of **louely**. **rout**: company.
8 **hew**: form.

Stanza 9
4 **count'nance trim**: pleasing appearance or 'demeanure'
(11.2). 9 **Pastorella**: Ital. *pastorella*, 'a shepheardesse'
(Florio 1598), a name linked to the medieval genre, *pastourelle*
(see H. Cooper 1977:164), which treats a knight's seduction
of a beautiful but lowly born shepherdess. See 'Pastorella' in
the *SEnc*. **fayrest**: 'fair' is her stock epithet.

Stanza 10
Pastorella is like Mirabella at viii 20–21 in being (apparently)
lowly born, in her beauty, and in her rejection of lovers, but
lacks her ruling passions of disdain and scorn (though see
35.9). 5 **Coridon**: a traditional pastoral name, perhaps derived
from Theocritus, *Idyll* 4, where his namesake is a cowherd; or
Virgil, *Ecl.* 2, where he is the rejected lover. See 'Coridon' in
the *SEnc*.

Stanza 11
3 **meane**: or mien; playing on her 'meane' lot (10.9) and on
her **demeanure**, and suggesting the mean or norm, as x 27.3.
5 **Paragone**: consort in marriage; companion. 6–9 **subtile**:
thin, fine; crafty. **the blynd boy**: Cupid. **the bird** may be
the 'darred Larke' (VII vi 47.5 and see *n*), or a parrot, which
becomes paralysed at the sight of a hawk.

Stanza 12
To emphasize this moment of ecstatic admiration, **still** turns back
(**stood he still**) and then forward (**still long gazing**), its effect
being further emphasized by the internal rhymes, as Borris
1985:225 notes. Cf. his rapt gazing on Tristram at ii 24.8, and
on the Graces at x 17.1–4. 8 **apply**: address. 9 **fantazy**: fancy.

13

By this the moystie night approching fast,
  Her deawy humour gan on th'earth to shed,
  That warn'd the shepheards to their homes to hast
  Their tender flocks, now being fully fed,
  For feare of wetting them before their bed;
  Then came to them a good old aged syre,
  Whose siluer lockes bedeckt his beard and hed,
  With shepheards hooke in hand, and fit attyre,
That wild the damzell rise; the day did now expyre.

14

He was to weet by common voice esteemed
  The father of the fayrest *Pastorell*,
  And of her selfe in very deede so deemed;
  Yet was not so, but as old stories tell
  Found her by fortune, which to him befell,
  In th'open fields an Infant left alone,
  And taking vp brought home, and noursed well
  As his owne chyld; for other he had none,
That she in tract of time accompted was his owne.

15

She at his bidding meekely did arise,
  And streight vnto her litle flocke did fare:
  Then all the rest about her rose likewise,
  And each his sundrie sheepe with seuerall care
  Gathered together, and them homeward bare:
  Whylest euerie one with helping hands did striue
  Amongst themselues, and did their labours share,
  To helpe faire *Pastorella*, home to driue
Her fleecie flocke; but *Coridon* most helpe did giue.

16

But *Melibœ* (so hight that good old man)
  Now seeing *Calidore* left all alone,
  And night arriued hard at hand, began
  Him to inuite vnto his simple home;
  Which though it were a cottage clad with lome,
  And all things therein meane, yet better so
  To lodge, then in the saluage fields to rome.
  The knight full gladly soone agreed thereto,
Being his harts owne wish, and home with him did go.

17

There he was welcom'd of that honest syre,
  And of his aged Beldame homely well;
  Who him besought himselfe to disattyre,
  And rest himselfe, till supper time befell.
  By which home came the fayrest *Pastorell*,
  After her flocke she in their fold had tyde,
  And supper readie dight, they to it fell
  With small adoe, and nature satisfyde,
The which doth litle craue contented to abyde.

18

Tho when they had their hunger slaked well,
  And the fayre mayd the table ta'ne away,
  The gentle knight, as he that did excell
  In courtesie, and well could doe and say,
  For so great kindnesse as he found that day,
  Gan greatly thanke his host and his good wife;
  And drawing thence his speach another way,
  Gan highly to commend the happie life,
Which Shepheards lead, without debate or bitter strife.

Stanza 13
2 deawy humour: dew.

Stanza 14
4 as old stories tell: a set phrase – see III vi 6.3*n* – used here to give impersonal authority to the romance motif of the foundling, as in the story of the Red Cross Knight at I x 65–66. On S.'s use of that motif in the poem, see Estrin 1985:70–106. **9 tract of time**: the passage or course of time (*tractus temporum*).

Stanza 15
4 seuerall: individual.

Stanza 16
1 Melibœ: a traditional pastoral name, as 'Good *Melibœ*' in *Time* 436, used here for its etymological meanings: 'one who has the care of cattle' (Gk μέλω + βοῦς; so Servius; cited Belson 1964:252), noting his pastoral care; and 'honey-toned' (μέλι+βοή), from Chaucer's *Tale of Melibee* VII 1410: 'Thy name is Melibee, this is to seyn, "a man that drynketh hony"'. See 'Melibœ' in the *SEnc*; and for S.'s use of Chaucer's tale, see Anderson 1995. **5 lome**: clay.

Stanza 17
2 homely: kindly. **3 disattyre**: unarm.

Stanza 18
2 table: food.

Stanzas 19–25
S. draws on the conversation between Erminia and the aged shepherd in Tasso, *Ger. Lib.* 7.7–13, at times very closely. (About 1610, William Drummond of Hawthornden wrote in the margin of this passage: 'all . . . Tasso's'; noted Fowler and Leslie 1981.) Like Melibœ, Tasso's shepherd once scorned the simple life and chose to live at the court where he wasted his youth until he decided to return. Persuaded by his praise of the pastoral life, Erminia is prepared to offer him jewels or gold (as does Calidore at 32.5–9), goes to his cottage where he lives with his aged wife, and assumes pastoral disguise. See 'Tasso' in the *SEnc*. For S.'s use of pastoral to formulate a rhetoric of colonial power, see Fogarty 1989:92–104.

Stanza 19
4–5 Cf. Isa. 54:11: 'O thou afflicted and tossed with tempest, that hast no comfort'; noted Shaheen 1976:165. **rest**: in a double sense. **disease**: distress.

Stanza 20
1 againe: in return. **2 intent**: sense. **5–7** Confirming 17.8–9. This argument is used by Guyon to reject Mammon's offer of abundant wealth at II vii 15.3–6.

19

How much (sayd he) more happie is the state,
   In which ye father here doe dwell at ease,
   Leading a life so free and fortunate,
   From all the tempests of these worldly seas,
   Which tosse the rest in daungerous disease?
   Where warres, and wreckes, and wicked enmitie
   Doe them afflict, which no man can appease,
   That certes I your happinesse enuie,
And wish my lot were plast in such felicitie.

20

Surely my sonne (then answer'd he againe)
   If happie, then it is in this intent,
   That hauing small, yet doe I not complaine
   Of want, ne wish for more it to augment,
   But doe my selfe, with that I haue, content;
   So taught of nature, which doth litle need
   Of forreine helpes to lifes due nourishment:
   The fields my food, my flocke my rayment breed;
No better doe I weare, no better doe I feed.

21

Therefore I doe not any one enuy,
   Nor am enuyde of any one therefore;
   They that haue much, feare much to loose thereby,
   And store of cares doth follow riches store.
   The litle that I haue, growes dayly more
   Without my care, but onely to attend it;
   My lambes doe euery yeare increase their score,
   And my flockes father daily doth amend it.
What haue I, but to praise th'Almighty, that doth send it?

22

To them, that list, the worlds gay showes I leaue,
   And to great ones such follies doe forgiue,
   Which oft through pride do their owne perill weaue,
   And through ambition downe themselues doe driue
   To sad decay, that might contented liue.
   Me no such cares nor combrous thoughts offend,
   Ne once my minds vnmoued quiet grieue,
   But all the night in siluer sleepe I spend,
And all the day, to what I list, I doe attend.

23

Sometimes I hunt the Fox, the vowed foe
   Vnto my Lambes, and him dislodge away;
   Sometime the fawne I practise from the Doe,
   Or from the Goat her kidde how to conuay;
   Another while I baytes and nets display,
   The birds to catch, or fishes to beguyle:
   And when I wearie am, I downe doe lay
   My limbes in euery shade, to rest from toyle,
And drinke of euery brooke, when thirst my throte doth boyle.

24

The time was once, in my first prime of yeares,
   When pride of youth forth pricked my desire,
   That I disdain'd amongst mine equall peares
   To follow sheepe, and shepheards base attire:
   For further fortune then I would inquire.
   And leauing home, to roiall court I sought;
   Where I did sell my selfe for yearely hire,
   And in the Princes gardin daily wrought:
There I beheld such vainenesse, as I neuer thought.

25

With sight whereof soone cloyd, and long deluded
   With idle hopes, which them doe entertaine,
   After I had ten yeares my selfe excluded
   From natiue home, and spent my youth in vaine,
   I gan my follies to my selfe to plaine,
   And this sweet peace, whose lacke did then appeare.
   Tho backe returning to my sheepe againe,
   I from thenceforth haue learn'd to loue more deare
This lowly quiet life, which I inherite here.

26

Whylest thus he talkt, the knight with greedy eare
   Hong still vpon his melting mouth attent;
   Whose sensefull words empierst his hart so neare,
   That he was rapt with double rauishment,
   Both of his speach that wrought him great content,
   And also of the obiect of his vew,
   On which his hungry eye was alwayes bent;
   That twixt his pleasing tongue, and her faire hew,
He lost himselfe, and like one halfe entraunced grew.

Stanza 21
2 of any one: i.e. of anyone in his pastoral world, answering Calidore's envy at 19.8. **6 attend**: tend. His carefree state is stressed by **onely**. **7 score**: number.

Stanza 22
2 forgiue: give over; grant. **5 decay**: ruin. **6 combrous**: troublesome. **7 grieue**: trouble; vex. **8 siluer sleepe**: see vii 19.8–9n.

Stanza 23
2 dislodge: drive out of its lair. **3–4** At times I scheme how to steal, etc. **8, 9 euery**: any; to indicate that none is dangerous or polluted.

Stanza 24
3 peares: companions. **5 inquire**: seek. **6 sought**: went.

Stanza 25
2 them: i.e. the courtiers. **entertaine**: engage. **5 plaine**: lament; deplore. **9 inherite**: possess. The term suggests his proper lot in contrast to Calidore's chivalric life.

Stanza 26
2 melting mouth: alluding to one etymology of his name; see 16.1n. **attent**: attentive. **3 sensefull**: full of sense or meaning (*OED* 1), as iv 37.1; but also appealing to his senses rather than his reason. His two nobler senses, sight and hearing, are overcome. **4** Since he gazes upon Pastorella's 'heauenly hew' (8.8), **rapt** may suggest the religious sense, 'carried up to heaven', for he is taken out of himself and prepared for his vision at x 11–17. **rauishment** and **hungry eye** invoke the cannibals when they anticipate eating Serena at viii 37. Unlike Meliboe, Calidore is not content with what he has.

27

Yet to occasion meanes, to worke his mind,
  And to insinuate his harts desire,
He thus replyde; Now surely syre, I find,
  That all this worlds gay showes, which we admire,
  Be but vaine shadowes to this safe retyre
Of life, which here in lowlinesse ye lead,
  Fearelesse of foes, or fortunes wrackfull yre,
  Which tosseth states, and vnder foot doth tread
The mightie ones, affrayd of euery chaunges dread.

28

That euen I which daily doe behold
  The glorie of the great, mongst whom I won,
And now haue prou'd, what happinesse ye hold
  In this small plot of your dominion,
  Now loath great Lordship and ambition;
And wish th'heauens so much had graced mee,
  As graunt me liue in like condition;
  Or that my fortunes might transposed bee
From pitch of higher place, vnto this low degree.

29

In vaine (said then old *Meliboe*) doe men
  The heauens of their fortunes fault accuse,
Sith they know best, what is the best for them:
  For they to each such fortune doe diffuse,
  As they doe know each can most aptly vse.
For not that, which men couet most, is best,
  Nor that thing worst, which men do most refuse;
  But fittest is, that all contented rest
With that they hold: each hath his fortune in his brest.

30

It is the mynd, that maketh good or ill,
  That maketh wretch or happie, rich or poore:
For some, that hath abundance at his will,
  Hath not enough, but wants in greatest store;

And other, that hath litle, askes no more,
  But in that litle is both rich and wise.
For wisedome is most riches; fooles therefore
  They are, which fortunes doe by vowes deuize,
Sith each vnto himselfe his life may fortunize.

31

Since then in each mans self (said *Calidore*)
  It is, to fashion his owne lyfes estate,
Giue leaue awhyle, good father, in this shore
  To rest my barcke, which hath bene beaten late
  With stormes of fortune and tempestuous fate,
In seas of troubles and of toylesome paine,
  That whether quite from them for to retrate
  I shall resolue, or backe to turne againe,
I may here with your selfe some small repose obtaine.

32

Not that the burden of so bold a guest
  Shall chargefull be, or chaunge to you at all;
For your meane food shall be my daily feast,
  And this your cabin both my bowre and hall.
  Besides for recompence hereof, I shall
You well reward, and golden guerdon giue,
  That may perhaps you better much withall,
  And in this quiet make you safer liue.
So forth he drew much gold, and toward him it driue.

33

But the good man, nought tempted with the offer
  Of his rich mould, did thrust it farre away,
And thus bespake; Sir knight, your bounteous proffer
  Be farre fro me, to whom ye ill display
  That mucky masse, the cause of mens decay,
That mote empaire my peace with daungers dread.
  But if ye algates couet to assay
  This simple sort of life, that shepheards lead,
Be it your owne: our rudenesse to your selfe aread.

Stanza 27

1–2 Yet to gain what he wants (i.e. contentment), and what his heart desires (i.e. Pastorella) . . . **5 to:** compared to. **7 wrackfull:** destructive. **8 states:** those of high rank or office.

Stanza 28

3 prou'd: experienced. **8 transposed:** removed; transferred.

Stanzas 29–30

Befitting a stock pastoral figure, Meliboe's speech is a tissue of familiar proverbs – Anderson 1995:38 lists at least nine – and stock sayings that may be found almost anywhere. E.g. 29.1–2: see V iv 28.1–3. 29.3–6: Juvenal, *Satire* 10.347–49: 'Leave it to the gods themselves to provide what is good for us, and what will be serviceable for our state; for, in place of what is pleasing, they will give us what is best'. 30.1: Shakespeare, *Hamlet* 2.2.249–50: 'there is nothing either good or bad, but thinking makes it so'. 30.7: Prov. 3.13–14. 30.9: Boethius, *De Cons. Phil.* 4 Prosa 7: 'For it is set in your hand . . . what fortune yow is levest' (noted Lewis 1964:87).

Stanza 29

4 diffuse: send forth.

Stanza 30

2 wretch: wretched. The noun is uniquely used as an adj. to echo **rich**. **8** . . . which scheme to make their fortune by their own will. **9 fortunize:** control the fortunes of. Cf. the hermit's advice at vi 7.1–3.

Stanza 31

1–2 In choosing to fashion himself, Calidore comments on the poet's intention in the poem 'to fashion a gentleman or noble person in vertuous and gentle discipline' (*LR* 8). He interprets **estate** in physical, rather than ethical, terms, as Mikics 1994:236 notes. **3–6** The metaphor of a ship in a storm extends 19.4–5. **7–9** As the hermit gives up the active life at v 37.5–9, and the Red Cross Knight wishes to do at I x 63.1–4. By x 2.1–2, Calidore has decided never to turn back.

34

So there that night Sir *Calidore* did dwell,
  And long while after, whilest him list remaine,
  Dayly beholding the faire *Pastorell*,
  And feeding on the bayt of his owne bane.
  During which time he did her entertaine
  With all kind courtesies, he could inuent;
  And euery day, her companie to gaine,
  When to the field she went, he with her went:
So for to quench his fire, he did it more augment.

35

But she that neuer had acquainted beene
  With such queint vsage, fit for Queenes and Kings,
  Ne euer had such knightly seruice seene,
  But being bred vnder base shepheards wings,
  Had euer learn'd to loue the lowly things,
  Did litle whit regard his courteous guize,
  But cared more for *Colins* carolings
  Then all that he could doe, or euer deuize:
His layes, his loues, his lookes she did them all despize.

36

Which *Calidore* perceiuing, thought it best
  To chaunge the manner of his loftie looke;
  And doffing his bright armes, himselfe addrest
  In shepheards weed, and in his hand he tooke,
  In stead of steelehead speare, a shepheards hooke,
  That who had seene him then, would haue bethought
  On *Phrygian Paris* by *Plexippus* brooke,
  When he the loue of fayre *Oenone* sought,
What time the golden apple was vnto him brought.

37

So being clad, vnto the fields he went
  With the faire *Pastorella* euery day,
  And kept her sheepe with diligent attent,
  Watching to driue the rauenous Wolfe away,
  The whylest at pleasure she mote sport and play;
  And euery euening helping them to fold:
  And otherwhiles for need, he did assay
  In his strong hand their rugged teats to hold,
And out of them to presse the milke: loue so much could.

38

Which seeing *Coridon*, who her likewise
  Long time had lou'd, and hop'd her loue to gaine,
  He much was troubled at that straungers guize,
  And many gealous thoughts conceiu'd in vaine,
  That this of all his labour and long paine
  Should reap the haruest, ere it ripened were,
  That made him scoule, and pout, and oft complaine
  Of *Pastorell* to all the shepheards there,
That she did loue a stranger swayne then him more dere.

39

And euer when he came in companie,
  Where *Calidore* was present, he would loure,
  And byte his lip, and euen for gealousie
  Was readie oft his owne hart to deuoure,
  Impatient of any paramoure:
  Who on the other side did seeme so farre
  From malicing, or grudging his good houre,
  That all he could, he graced him with her,
Ne euer shewed signe of rancour or of iarre.

Stanza 32
As the Red Cross Knight offers 'goodly meed' to Contempla-tion at I x 68.4–5. **2 chargefull**: burdensome. **9 driue**: drove, i.e. pushed.

Stanza 33
1 good man: a moral description; or his title either as a man of substance or head of the household. **2–5 mould**: dirt, a fittingly pejorative term for **mucky masse**, i.e. 'filthy lucre' (cf. 'worldly mucke' at II vii 10.5). **proffer**: offer. **7 algates**: nevertheless. **9** . . . i.e. commit yourself to our simple life.

Stanza 34
4 bayt: also food.

Stanza 35
2 queint vsage: elegant or refined behaviour. **6 guize**: man-ner. **9 loues**: loving deeds.

Stanza 36
3 addrest: clothed. **6–9** Two episodes in Paris's pastoral sojourn are conflated: his love for **Oenone** (see III ix 36.3–4), and his judgement on Mount Ida: of the three goddesses, he presented Venus with the **golden apple** (see II vii 55.4–8 and *n*). Together they explain why he chose Venus over Minerva

and Juno. The comparison is suggested because Calidore steals Coridon's love as his prize, even as Paris abducted Menelaus's Helen as his prize. **Phrygian**: Trojan, a term chosen either because Phrygia is west of Troy, as is Mount Ida; or because it is associated with Oenone. **Plexippus**: its etymology, 'horse-taming' or 'horse-striking', may be S.'s coinage for the clas-sical Hippocrene, the fountain of the horse on Mount Helicon which first flowed when struck by Pegasus's hooves; cf. *Teares* 271. D. Cheney 1966:223n8 suggests that S. conflates Mount Ida with Helicon as a haunt of the muses. P. Cheney 1993:207 sees a reference to S.'s shift from epic to pastoral. On S.'s return to pastoral, see Shore 1985:132–46.

Stanza 37
3 attent: attention. **7 otherwhiles**: at other times. **9** . . . love could do so much.

Stanza 38
5 this: i.e. Calidore.

Stanza 39
3–4 On jealousy expressed as eating one's heart, see I ii 6.3; on biting the lip, repeated at 41.9, see II vii 22.4–5. **5 paramoure**: rival lover. **7 malicing**: regarding with malice. **good houre**: good luck or fortune.

40

And oft, when *Coridon* vnto her brought
  Or litle sparrowes, stolen from their nest,
  Or wanton squirrels, in the woods farre sought,
  Or other daintie thing for her addrest,
  He would commend his guift, and make the best.
  Yet she no whit his presents did regard,
  Ne him could find to fancie in her brest:
This newcome shepheard had his market mard.
Old loue is litle worth when new is more prefard.

41

One day when as the shepheard swaynes together
  Were met, to make their sports and merrie glee,
  As they are wont in faire sunshynie weather,
  The whiles their flockes in shadowes shrouded bee,
  They fell to daunce: then did they all agree,
  That *Colin Clout* should pipe as one most fit;
  And *Calidore* should lead the ring, as hee
That most in *Pastorellaes* grace did sit.
Thereat frown'd *Coridon*, and his lip closely bit.

42

But *Calidore* of courteous inclination
  Tooke *Coridon*, and set him in his place,
  That he should lead the daunce, as was his fashion;
  For *Coridon* could daunce, and trimly trace.
  And when as *Pastorella*, him to grace,
  Her flowry garlond tooke from her owne head,
  And plast on his, he did it soone displace,
  And did it put on *Coridons* in stead:
Then *Coridon* woxe frollicke, that earst seemed dead.

43

Another time, when as they did dispose
  To practise games, and maisteries to try,
  They for their Iudge did *Pastorella* chose;
  A garland was the meed of victory.
  There *Coridon* forth stepping openly,

Did chalenge *Calidore* to wrestling game:
  For he through long and perfect industry,
  Therein well practisd was, and in the same
Thought sure t'auenge his grudge, and worke his foe
                (great shame.

44

But *Calidore* he greatly did mistake;
  For he was strong and mightily stiffe pight,
  That with one fall his necke he almost brake,
  And had he not vpon him fallen light,
  His dearest ioynt he sure had broken quight.
  Then was the oaken crowne by *Pastorell*
  Giuen to *Calidore*, as his due right;
  But he, that did in courtesie excell,
Gaue it to *Coridon*, and said he wonne it well.

45

Thus did the gentle knight himselfe abeare
  Amongst that rusticke rout in all his deeds,
  That euen they, the which his riuals were,
  Could not maligne him, but commend him needs:
  For courtesie amongst the rudest breeds
  Good will and fauour. So it surely wrought
  With this faire Mayd, and in her mynde the seeds
  Of perfect loue did sow, that last forth brought
The fruite of ioy and blisse, though long time dearely
                (bought.

46

Thus *Calidore* continu'd there long time,
  To winne the loue of the faire *Pastorell*;
  Which hauing got, he vsed without crime
  Or blamefull blot, but menaged so well,
  That he of all the rest, which there did dwell,
  Was fauoured, and to her grace commended.
  But what straunge fortunes vnto him befell,
  Ere he attain'd the point by him intended,
Shall more conueniently in other place be ended.

Stanza 40
2–3 At III vii 17, the witch's son woos Florimell with birds and a squirrel. The sparrow is notorious for its lechery. **wanton:** frisky; also the erotic sense. **4 addrest:** prepared. 9 Proverbial: Smith 497.

Stanza 41
6 **Colin Clout:** 'Under which name this Poete secretly shadoweth himself' (E.K. on *SC Jan.* 1). On the formation of the name, see 'Colin Clout' in the *SEnc*.

Stanza 42
4 **trimly trace:** neatly step.

Stanza 43
1 **dispose:** prepare. **2 maisteries:** competitions of strength.

Stanza 44
2 . . . and was very firmly fixed on his legs. **6 oaken crowne:** seen by Borris 1985:251 as the classical *corona civica* given to

one who saved another's life, as Calidore does here in the sense that he does not kill Coridon. It is an appropriate token of victory in the pastoral world, as at VII vii 11.5, for the oak is associated with strength.

Stanza 45
1 **abeare:** bear. **4 needs:** i.e. must needs, of necessity. 7–9 Referring to the harvest that Coridon hoped to enjoy (38.6) but is enjoyed instead by Calidore at x 38.5. **last:** at last.

Stanza 46
3–4 In contrast to Scudamour who got the shield of love but failed to 've his blis' (IV x 8.8). **without crime:** without giving occasion for reproach. **menaged:** in the technical sense, putting a horse through its paces (cf. II iv 2.2), here referring to the handling of his emotions. **5 of all:** above all.

Cant. X.

Calidore sees the Graces daunce,
To Colins melody:
The whiles his Pastorell is led,
Into captiuity.

1

Who now does follow the foule *Blatant Beast*,
  Whilest *Calidore* does follow that faire Mayd,
  Vnmyndfull of his vow and high beheast,
  Which by the Faery Queene was on him layd,
  That he should neuer leaue, nor be delayd
  From chacing him, till he had it attchieued?
  But now entrapt of loue, which him betrayd,
  He mindeth more, how he may be relieued
With grace from her, whose loue his heart hath sore engrieued.

2

That from henceforth he meanes no more to sew
  His former quest, so full of toile and paine;
  Another quest, another game in yew
  He hath, the guerdon of his loue to gaine:
  With whom he myndes for euer to remaine,
  And set his rest amongst the rusticke sort,
  Rather then hunt still after shadowes vaine
  Of courtly fauour, fed with light report,
Of euery blaste, and sayling alwaies on the port.

3

Ne certes mote he greatly blamed be,
  From so high step to stoupe vnto so low.
  For who had tasted once (as oft did he)
  The happy peace, which there doth ouerflow,
  And prou'd the perfect pleasures, which doe grow
  Amongst poore hyndes, in hils, in woods, in dales,
  Would neuer more delight in painted show
  Of such false blisse, as there is set for stales,
T'entrap vnwary fooles in their eternall bales.

4

For what hath all that goodly glorious gaze
  Like to one sight, which *Calidore* did vew?
  The glaunce whereof their dimmed eies would daze,
  That neuer more they should endure the shew
  Of that sunne-shine, that makes them looke askew,
  Ne ought in all that world of beauties rare,
  (Saue onely *Glorianaes* heauenly hew
  To which what can compare?) can it compare;
The which as commeth now, by course I will declare.

Book VI Canto x

Argument
3 The whiles: since the two events are not concurrent in the narrative, the phrase suggests that Calidore's vision which immediately vanishes replicates Pastorella's sudden seizure by the Brigants.

Stanza 1
That Calidore's quest was assigned to him by the Faerie Queene is first noted here, and repeated at xii 12.4–5. Precedents for his abandoning his quest through love of Pastorella are noted by Upton 1758: e.g. Ulysses for Calypso (Homer, *Ody*. 5; Circe in *Ody*. 10 is a better example), Aeneas for Dido (Virgil, *Aen*. 4), Ruggiero for Alcina (Ariosto, *Orl. Fur*. 7), and Rinaldo for Armida (Tasso, *Ger. Lib*. 16). In all other ways, they differ: e.g. Calidore woos Pastorella, and she is not an enchantress. On the implications of Calidore abandoning his quest, see D.L. Miller 1979.

Stanza 2
1 sew: pursue. **3 game**: the hunted animal, applied to the Beast; sport, amusement, applied to Pastorella. Yet he is the prey at ix 11.9 and 31.9 below. **5 myndes**: intends. **6 set his rest**: take up permanent abode (*OED* sb[2] 7f), in contrast to his earlier pursuit in which he never 'suffred him [the Beast] to rest' (ix 3.2); and implying that no longer will he set his spear in its rest in a chivalric charge (for that sense, see, e.g. II i

26.3). The reference to **game** adds the sense, 'hazard all' (*OED* 7a); as a gaming phrase, see Dodge 1908. On the dualism of the chivalric code, with its split between public service and private impulse, see McCoy 1989:146–47. **sort**: company.
7–9 The reference to Calidore's earlier hunt for **courtly fauour** relates to his hunt for the Blatant Beast which began at the court (ix 3.6). **on the port**: i.e. towards the port without ever gaining safety there; cf. 'gladsome port' at 9.4, and the theme of seeking the shore at ix 31.3–9 and xi 44.6–9. **in the port** 1609, i.e. port-bound. J.C. Smith 1909 cites the proverb *in portu nauigare*, 'to be out of daunger' (T. Cooper 1565); hence being so concerned with the direction of the wind that one never leaves port.

Stanza 3
5 prou'd: experienced; cf. ix 28.3. **6 hyndes**: rustics. **8 there**: in the court, in opposition to its use in 4 to refer to the pastoral world. The courtly life is rejected in the terms given by Calidore at ix 27. **stales**: decoys; snares. **9 . . .** to their eternal suffering. As those who 'Fell from high Princes courtes' (I v 51.6) into the dungeon beneath the house of Pride.

Stanza 4
1 gaze: that which is looked at, referring to the 'painted show' (3.7) and obliquely to **that world of beauties rare** in Elizabeth's court. Also the act of looking, or the visual milieu itself, as D.L. Miller 1993:756–57 notes. **5 askew**: to the side. **8 . . .** can be compared to it. **9 declare**: describe.

5

One day as he did raunge the fields abroad,
  Whilest his faire *Pastorella* was elsewhere,
  He chaunst to come, far from all peoples troad,
  Vnto a place, whose pleasaunce did appere
  To passe all others, on the earth which were:
  For all that euer was by natures skill
  Deuized to worke delight, was gathered there,
  And there by her were poured forth at fill,
As if this to adorne, she all the rest did pill.

6

It was an hill plaste in an open plaine,
  That round about was bordered with a wood
  Of matchlesse hight, that seem'd th'earth to disdaine,
  In which all trees of honour stately stood,
  And did all winter as in sommer bud,
  Spredding pauilions for the birds to bowre,
  Which in their lower braunches sung aloud;
  And in their tops the soring hauke did towre,
Sitting like King of fowles in maiesty and powre.

7

And at the foote thereof, a gentle flud
  His siluer waues did softly tumble downe,
  Vnmard with ragged mosse or filthy mud,
  Ne mote wylde beastes, ne mote the ruder clowne

Thereto approch, ne filth mote therein drowne:
  But Nymphes and Faeries by the bancks did sit,
  In the woods shade, which did the waters crowne,
  Keeping all noysome things away from it,
And to the waters fall tuning their accents fit.

8

And on the top thereof a spacious plaine
  Did spred it selfe, to serue to all delight,
  Either to daunce, when they to daunce would faine,
  Or else to course about their bases light;
  Ne ought there wanted, which for pleasure might
  Desired be, or thence to banish bale:
  So pleasauntly the hill with equall hight,
  Did seeme to ouerlooke the lowly vale;
Therefore it rightly cleeped was mount *Acidale.*

9

They say that *Venus,* when she did dispose
  Her selfe to pleasaunce, vsed to resort
  Vnto this place, and therein to repose
  And rest her selfe, as in a gladsome port,
  Or with the Graces there to play and sport;
  That euen her owne Cytheron, though in it
  She vsed most to keepe her royall court,
  And in her soueraine Maiesty to sit,
She in regard hereof refusde and thought vnfit.

Stanza 5

3 . . . i.e. far from the trodden way. **4 pleasaunce**: usually an ominous setting because it suggests that **natures skill** is abused by art – see I vii 4.2*n* and VI iii 23.4 – but no longer; cf. its use at 9.2 and 17.4. Cf. the garden of Adonis, which is 'So faire a place, as Nature can deuize' (III vi 29.3) without art (44.2) except S's. **8 at fill**: at full, fully. **9 pill**: pillage, plunder.

Stanzas 6–9

Mount Acidale is described at IV v 5.4–6 as the place where Venus plays with the Graces. It recalls the traditional features of the earthly paradise, esp. Eden, which is often placed on a mountain top walled by trees, and the hill with its wide plain to which Orpheus brings all the trees with their shade (Ovid, *Met.* 10.86–142). Its connection with the description in Boccaccio 1976:14.11, of the lonely haunts sought by poets as favourable to contemplation, is noted by Hardin 1979:14–15. Within the poem it relates to Venus's 'stately Mount' at III vi 43–46, the 'second paradise' which surrounds the temple of Venus at IV x 21–25, Belphœbe's forest home at III v 39–40, and esp. 'that pleasant Mount' at I x 54.6–9 where the muses play and sing. See 'Acidale' in the *SEnc.* It is read neoplatonically by Bellamy 1990. Colin's reference to it as 'this pleasant groue' (22.3; cf. 4, 6) indicates that it is a local habitation.

Stanza 6

4 all trees of honour: as the garden of Eden has 'euerie tre pleasant to the sight, and good for meat' (Gen. 2.9). **5** A variation of a traditional feature of the *locus amoenus*, on which see III vi 42.1–6*n*. **6 bowre**: lodge. **8 towre**: perch high; but also 'mount up', as at ii 32.2.

Stanza 7

In *Epith* 310, S. refers to 'the Acidalian brooke', which is described by T. Cooper 1565 as 'a wel in Orchomenum, dedicated unto Venus, and the Graces'. Cf. Narcissus's pool with its silver water to which neither shepherds nor beasts dare approach and whose clear surface is never ruffled (Ovid, *Met.* 3.407–10). **1 flud**: stream. **4 the ruder clowne**: the rude rustic; rude in being a rustic. **5 drowne**: sink. **6 Nymphes** appear because they are 'Daughters of the Flood' (*Proth* 21). **Faeries**: at last the aboriginals of the heavily colonized faery land make their debut. **9** S.'s signature announces his presence in his poem as Colin Clout. It first appeared – prominently as an alexandrine in otherwise pentameter verse – in *Theatre, epigram* 4.6–7, and then in *SC Apr.* 36 and *June* 8. See Hollander 1988:174–77 who also notes that **fall** has the musical sense of cadence, and **tuning** means both singing and sounding. **accents**: sounds; words. On S.'s use of the hexameter line, see Gross 1983: 23–27.

Stanza 8

3 faine: desire. **4** On the game of prisoner's base, see III xi 5.5*n*. **light**: quickly. **7 equall**: level. **9 Acidale**: 'the surname of Venus' (T. Cooper 1565). Its etymology, Gk ἀκίς, a pointed, rising object + δῆλος, conspicuous, indicates a hill rising from a valley; or, as **Therefore** suggests, Lat. *acies*, look + dale, i.e. valley-view; or ἀκηδής, free from care (from Hesiod, *Theog.*; sugg. Renwick 1923); or med. Lat. *accidia*, the sin of sloth, of which Calidore is guilty (sugg. Nelson 1963:293).

Stanza 9

1 dispose: prepare. **6–8 Cytheron**: see III vi 29.4–5*n*. **9 in regard hereof**: compared to this place.

10

Vnto this place when as the Elfin Knight
　　Approcht, him seemed that the merry sound
　　Of a shrill pipe he playing heard on hight,
　　And many feete fast thumping th'hollow ground,
　　That through the woods their Eccho did rebound.
　　He nigher drew, to weete what mote it be;
　　There he a troupe of Ladies dauncing found
　　Full merrily, and making gladfull glee,
And in the midst a Shepheard piping he did see.

11

He durst not enter into th'open greene,
　　For dread of them vnwares to be descryde,
　　For breaking of their daunce, if he were seene;
　　But in the couert of the wood did byde,
　　Beholding all, yet of them vnespyde.
　　There he did see, that pleased much his sight,
　　That euen he him selfe his eyes enuyde,
　　An hundred naked maidens lilly white,
All raunged in a ring, and dauncing in delight.

12

All they without were raunged in a ring,
　　And daunced round; but in the midst of them
　　Three other Ladies did both daunce and sing,
　　The whilest the rest them round about did hemme,
　　And like a girlond did in compasse stemme:
　　And in the middest of those same three, was placed
　　Another Damzell, as a precious gemme,
　　Amidst a ring most richly well enchaced,
That with her goodly presence all the rest much graced.

13

Looke how the Crowne, which *Ariadne* wore
　　Vpon her yuory forehead that same day,
　　That *Theseus* her vnto his bridale bore,
　　When the bold *Centaures* made that bloudy fray
　　With the fierce *Lapithes*, which did them dismay;
　　Being now placed in the firmament,
　　Through the bright heauen doth her beams display,
　　And is vnto the starres an ornament,
Which round about her moue in order excellent.

Stanza 10
1 the Elfin Knight: on the epithet, see I i 17.1*n*.　**3 pipe**: the 'bag-pipe' (18.5). To S.'s musical ear, the bagpipe is usually **shrill**, as at viii 46.1.　**on hight**: loudly; the context suggests 'on the height'.　**4** In Horace, *Odes* 1.4.5–7, the Cytherean Venus leads the dance with the nymphs and Graces whose feet shake the ground.　**6 to weete**: to know. Calidore is not content simply to see and hear; cf. 17.8, 18.9.　**7–9** On folktales involving fairy dances, see Tonkin 1972:131–36.　**in the midst**: the repetition of the phrase – see 12.2*n* – suggests a shifting of focus. The shepherd is seen with the damsel encircled by the Graces and the nymphs; or he may be encircled only by the nymphs who 'him daunst about' (16.5); or he may be outside the two circles.

Stanza 11
3 For breaking: i.e. for dread of breaking.　**7 eyes enuyde**: playing on the etymology of envy; see I iv 31.2*n*.　**8 hundred**: the number of Graces sitting on each eyelid of the lady in *Am* 40.4; also the number of maidens in the temple of Venus at IV x 38. As a Pythagorean commonplace, see S. Weiner 1985:99–100. This fittingly round number may be borrowed from Tasso, *Ger. Lib.* 18.22–38: 100 dancing wood-nymphs surround Rinaldo in an enchanted forest but disappear when he strikes a myrtle tree; sugg. P. Cheney 1984.

Stanza 12
The **Damzell**, apparently still and silent (though see 25.2*n*), occupies Venus's traditional place at the centre of the dancing and singing Graces. Encompassed by the naked, dancing ladies, she invokes images of Diana enclosed 'like a girlond' by her nymphs at III vi 19.9, of Amoret in the ring of feminine virtues at IV x 52, of the Queen surrounded by her court at VI proem 7.7, and of Pastorella with her garland of shepherdesses at ix 8. As in *SC Apr.* 109–17, the three Graces dance and sing, and to their number the poet adds his lady as a fourth Grace.

See 27*n*.　**2 in the midst**: repeated at 6, 14.3, 15.7, and 25.2.　**4 did hemme**: enclosed, in the sense of being decorated with a border.　**5 in compasse**: in a circular movement.　**stemme**: encircle, coined by S. from Lat. *stemma*, 'a garlande of flowers' (T. Cooper 1565); or they form the stem of the flower, which is composed of the Graces and the damsel. Nature becomes art, for she is **enchaced**, i.e. set as a jewel in a ring, adorned by the Graces.

Stanza 13
After Ariadne was abandoned by Theseus, Bacchus placed her bridal crown among the stars as the constellation Corona Borealis (see Ovid, *Met.* 8.169–82). Since that constellation was 'culminant in her [Elizabeth's] nativitie', as W. Camden 1984:190 records, it was associated with her (see Yates 1977:73–74), and appropriate for S. to cite. He may be indebted to Thomas Watson, *Hekatompathia* 1582, sonnet 33: if his mistress had lived in earlier times she would have been preferred before the three Graces and been placed in the heavens 'where nowe the Crowne of *Ariadne* called *Corona Gnosia* doth shine continuallie'. As a hieroglyph of the stars and planets in their circular course, see A. Fowler 1964:226; as a schematic model of the Ptolemaic universe, see P. Cheney and Klemp 1984. By associating the battle between the **Centaures** and **Lapithes** (see IV i 23.1–5) with the wedding of **Ariadne** and **Theseus**, rather than that of Pirithous and Hippodamia at which Theseus fought the Centaurs (see *Met.* 12.210–535), S. conflates the two.　**1 Looke how**, rather than the formulaic 'Like as', shows the poet caught up in his vision. As a vision of 'the sacred noursery | Of vertue' (proem 3.1–2), which inspires S. to fashion his virtues, see Hamilton 1961a:201. As a visionary experience, not imagining but pure seeing, see Guillory 1983:43.　**3 bridale**: wedding-feast.　**5 dismay**: defeat by sudden onslaught.　**9** The Corona Borealis takes the place of the North Star around which the other stars revolve; or they may be grouped, as they are by Dante in *Paradiso* 13.4–15.

14

Such was the beauty of this goodly band,
   Whose sundry parts were here too long to tell:
   But she that in the midst of them did stand,
   Seem'd all the rest in beauty to excell,
   Crownd with a rosie girlond, that right well
   Did her beseeme. And euer, as the crew
   About her daunst, sweet flowres, that far did smell,
   And fragrant odours they vppon her threw;
But most of all, those three did her with gifts endew.

15

Those were the Graces, daughters of delight,
   Handmaides of *Venus*, which are wont to haunt
   Vppon this hill, and daunce there day and night:
   Those three to men all gifts of grace do graunt,
   And all, that *Venus* in her selfe doth vaunt,
   Is borrowed of them. But that faire one,
   That in the midst was placed parauaunt,
   Was she to whom that shepheard pypt alone,
That made him pipe so merrily, as neuer none.

16

She was to weete that iolly Shepheards lasse,
   Which piped there vnto that merry rout,
   That iolly shepheard, which there piped, was
   Poore *Colin Clout* (who knowes not *Colin Clout?*)
   He pypt apace, whilest they him daunst about.
   Pype iolly shepheard, pype thou now apace
   Vnto thy loue, that made thee low to lout;
   Thy loue is present there with thee in place,
Thy loue is there aduaunst to be another Grace.

17

Much wondred *Calidore* at this straunge sight,
   Whose like before his eye had neuer seene,
   And standing long astonished in spright,
   And rapt with pleasaunce, wist not what to weene;

Whether it were the traine of beauties Queene,
   Or Nymphes, or Faeries, or enchaunted show,
   With which his eyes mote haue deluded beene.
   Therefore resoluing, what it was, to know,
Out of the wood he rose, and toward them did go.

18

But soone as he appeared to their vew,
   They vanisht all away out of his sight,
   And cleane were gone, which way he neuer knew;
   All saue the shepheard, who for fell despight
   Of that displeasure, broke his bag-pipe quight,
   And made great mone for that vnhappy turne.
   But *Calidore*, though no lesse sory wight,
   For that mishap, yet seeing him to mourne,
Drew neare, that he the truth of all by him mote learne.

19

And first him greeting, thus vnto him spake,
   Haile iolly shepheard, which thy ioyous dayes
   Here leadest in this goodly merry make,
   Frequented of these gentle Nymphes alwayes,
   Which to thee flocke, to heare thy louely layes;
   Tell me, what mote these dainty Damzels be,
   Which here with thee doe make their pleasant playes?
   Right happy thou, that mayst them freely see:
But why when I them saw, fled they away from me?

20

Not I so happy, answerd then that swaine,
   As thou vnhappy, which them thence didst chace,
   Whom by no meanes thou canst recall againe,
   For being gone, none can them bring in place,
   But whom they of them selues list so to grace.
   Right sory I, (saide then Sir *Calidore*,)
   That my ill fortune did them hence displace.
   But since things passed none may now restore,
Tell me, what were they all, whose lacke thee grieues so sore.

Stanza 15

1–2 Traditionally, the Graces are handmaids of Venus; in calling them **daughters of delight**, S. follows Conti 1616:4.15 for whom they signify *hilaritas et laetitia*, as Lotspeich 1932 notes. See 'Graces' in the *SEnc*. **7 parauaunt**: pre-eminently. **9** . . . as none had ever piped before.

Stanza 16

4 As this address and the exhortation at 6 indicate, S. distances himself from his persona. His question would seem to imply that Colin Clout is a household name, as he asks of Rosalind in *SC Aug.* 141, but it may be taken as self-promotional (as by Alwes 1990), or as ironical (as by Hadfield 1994:171–72). On the variety of responses to it, see Farness 1996:18–21. **7 lout**: stoop in submission. **9** This compliment is paid to 'fayre *Elisa*, Queene of shepheardes all' in *SC Apr.* 113–17. On the fourth Grace, see *27 n*.

Stanza 17

8 Stress and punctuation emphasize the final phrase: not content with enjoying the vision, Calidore is determined **to know**

– its carnal sense is present – much as did Arthur at I ix 15 and Britomart at III i 8.6–9.

Stanza 18

1–4 S. draws on Chaucer, *Wife of Bath's Tale*: when the knight sees a dance 'under a forest syde . . . | Of ladyes foure and twenty, and yet mo', he draws near 'In hope that som wysdom sholde he lerne. | But certeinly, er he cam fully there, | Vanysshed was this daunce, he nyste where. | No creature saugh he that bar lyf, | Save on the grene he saugh sittynge a wyf' who is the transformed 'elf-queene, [who] with hir ioly compaignye, | Daunced ful ofte in many a grene mede' (990–98, 860–61). Like him, Calidore comes forward in order to understand. **5–6** As Colin Clout breaks his pipe in *SC Jan.* 72, and hangs it upon a tree in *Dec.* 141. **6 vnhappy turne**: unlucky event; also alluding to the breaking of the dance.

Stanza 19

2 Haile: a respectful form of address used when he met Artegall. **3 merry make**: merry-making. **5 louely layes**: lays of love. **9** Calidore is more affable than honest: at 11.3,

21

Tho gan that shepheard thus for to dilate;
    Then wote thou shepheard, whatsoeuer thou bee,
    That all those Ladies, which thou sawest late,
    Are *Venus* Damzels, all within her fee,
    But differing in honour and degree:
    They all are Graces, which on her depend,
    Besides a thousand more, which ready bee
    Her to adorne, when so she forth doth wend:
But those three in the midst, doe chiefe on her attend.

22

They are the daughters of sky-ruling Ioue,
    By him begot of faire *Eurynome*,
    The Oceans daughter, in this pleasant groue,
    As he this way comming from feastfull glee,

Of *Thetis* wedding with *Æacidee*,
    In sommers shade him selfe here rested weary.
    The first of them hight mylde *Euphrosyne*,
    Next faire *Aglaia*, last *Thalia* merry:
Sweete Goddesses all three which me in mirth do cherry.

23

These three on men all gracious gifts bestow,
    Which decke the body or adorne the mynde,
    To make them louely or well fauoured show,
    As comely carriage, entertainement kynde,
    Sweete semblaunt, friendly offices that bynde,
    And all the complements of curtesie:
    They teach vs, how to each degree and kynde
    We should our selues demeane, to low, to hie;
To friends, to foes, which skill men call Ciuility.

---

he knows that the dance would end if he were seen, and later acknowledges that he 'rashly sought that, which I mote not see' (29.7). Accordingly, Colin Clout retorts that he 'them thence didst chace' (20.2). On Calidore's affability, see Krier 1990:236. On the significance of their encounter in the poem, see Shore 1985:148–59.

Stanza 20
A rare instance of a poet under his well-known *persona* entering into his fiction to reprimand one of his own characters, so ticked off that he tells Calidore to expect considerable unhappiness when the story continues. In the next stanza, he denies even knowing him. **4 in place**: back again; cf. 16.8. **5 grace**: be gracious to. **8–9** As iii 21–22 where Calidore consoles another victim of his inadvertent intrusion.

Stanza 21
1 dilate: relate at length, as the eight stanzas indicate. **4 within her fee**: in her service, being her followers. **6 on her depend**: belong to her, literally surround her as her train.

Stanza 22
The major classical source of S.'s genealogy of the Graces is Hesiod, *Theog*, 907–11, as mediated by T. Cooper 1565 (see Starnes and Talbert 1955:53–54), to which he adds that they were begotten by Jove on his return from the marriage of Peleus and Thetis. At II viii 6.6, they are said to be sisters of Cupid. See 'Peleus, Thetis' in the *SEnc*. Jove's epithet **sky-ruling** suggests the etymology of **Eurynome** (Gk 'wide rule'), and since she ruled with Ophion before both were deposed by Saturn and Ops, her union with Jove signifies a healing of division and a restoration of original rule. At VII vii 12, S. links the assembly of the gods on Hæmus hill to their previous assembly at the marriage of Peleus and Thetis. He need not mention that at this marriage Ate produced the golden apple which led to the fall of Troy – see II vii 55.4–9*n* – for she is 'present' even in the initials of the Graces in their traditional order in Cooper: Aglaia, Thalia, and Euphrosyne. **4 feastfull**: festive. **5 Æacidee**: Peleus, son of Aeacus; so named to link him to his father who was a son of Jove and so famed for his justice that Pluto made him judge over the dead. **7–9 Euphrosyne**: Gk εὐφροσύνη, 'Cheerfulness'. **Aglaia** is **faire** because her

name, ἀγλαΐα, 'is interpreted brightnesse, cleerenesse, beautie, pleasure, or maiestie' (Cooper). **Thalia**, θαλία, is **merry** because she is the muse of comedy; cf. 'Ioyous *Thalia*' (IV xi 49.2). **cherry**: a nonce-word that signifies 'cheer' (*OED*).

Stanzas 23–24
As does E.K. in his gloss to *SC Apr.* 109, S. follows T. Cooper's (1565) account of the Graces: 'Some men suppose that there were three Graces deuised to signifie that men ought to be both bountifull and gracious to other, and secondly to take benefites at other mens handes, and thirdly thankefully to requite benefites receiued: whiche are three sundrie actes in the vse of liberalitie. Other say they imagined three graces to signifie liberall thankefulnesse, and that we shoulde plentifully requite benefite with vantage more then we receiued. Wherfore they painte the Graces in this maner, that the ones backe should be towarde vs, and hir face fromward, as proceding from vs, the other twoo towarde vs: noting double thanke to bee due for the benefite we haue done. They weare also painted naked, to dooe men to witte, that pleasures should be done vnfeinedly without cloke or dissimulation: they weare made yonge, to note that the memory of a benefite should in no tyme weare awaye and decaye: they weare descriued laughing, because pleasures ought to be donne with a chereful and glad minde: finally their armes weare painted as it weare linked one within an other, to teach that kyndnesse should be vndissoluble, and one benefite so to prouoke an other, as it may make the league of loue and frendship sure and perpetuall.'

Stanza 23
1 all gracious gifts: literally 'all gifts of grace' (15.4). **4–5 carriage**: demeanour; behaviour. **entertainement kynde**: courteous manners in treating others. **semblaunt**: demeanour shown to others. **friendly offices that bynde**: acts of kindness that establish bonds of friendship. **6 complements**: ceremonies; accomplishments; also that which perfects courtesy, as chastity and courtesy in Belphœbe 'did make in her a perfect complement' (III v 55.9). **7–9 Ciuility**: as courtesy is praised as the virtue by which knights and ladies 'beare themselues aright | To all of each degree, as doth behoue' (ii. 1.3–4). See proem 4.5*n*.

24

Therefore they alwaies smoothly seeme to smile,
  That we likewise should mylde and gentle be,
  And also naked are, that without guile
  Or false dissemblaunce all them plaine may see,
  Simple and true from couert malice free:
  And eeke them selues so in their daunce they bore,
  That two of them still forward seem'd to bee,
  But one still towards shew'd her selfe afore;
That good should from vs goe, then come in greater store.

25

Such were those Goddesses, which ye did see;
  But that fourth Mayd, which there amidst them traced,
  Who can aread, what creature mote she bee,
  Whether a creature, or a goddesse graced
  With heauenly gifts from heuen first enraced?
  But what so sure she was, she worthy was,
  To be the fourth with those three other placed:
  Yet was she certes but a countrey lasse,
Yet she all other countrey lasses farre did passe.

26

So farre as doth the daughter of the day,
  All other lesser lights in light excell,
  So farre doth she in beautyfull array,
  Aboue all other lasses beare the bell,

Ne lesse in vertue that beseemes her well,
  Doth she exceede the rest of all her race,
  For which the Graces that here wont to dwell,
  Haue for more honor brought her to this place,
And graced her so much to be another Grace.

27

Another Grace she well deserues to be,
  In whom so many Graces gathered are,
  Excelling much the meane of her degree;
  Diuine resemblaunce, beauty soueraine rare,
  Firme Chastity, that spight ne blemish dare;
  All which she with such courtesie doth grace,
  That all her peres cannot with her compare,
  But quite are dimmed, when she is in place.
She made me often pipe and now to pipe apace.

28

Sunne of the world, great glory of the sky,
  That all the earth doest lighten with thy rayes,
  Great *Gloriana*, greatest Maiesty,
  Pardon thy shepheard, mongst so many layes,
  As he hath sung of thee in all his dayes,
  To make one minime of thy poore handmayd,
  And vnderneath thy feete to place her prayse,
  That when thy glory shall be farre displayd
To future age of her this mention may be made.

Stanza 24

2, 9 **That**: teaching us that.   **6–9** In their traditional order, as in Botticelli's *Primavera* and E.K.'s gloss noted above, one Grace has her back to us, facing the other two who come towards us, as **forward** suggests. Or they may be seen dancing in a ring, as Spens 1958:68 suggests: one gives the **good** to the Grace on her left; in turn, she gives it and her own contribution to the third; the third adds her contribution and returns the threefold gift to the first, thus returning it **in greater store**. Cf. IV iii 27.8–9. Some editors emend **forward** to 'froward' *1611*, an elision of 'fromward' (i.e. away from us), claiming that S. reverses the traditional order. (Cf. the play on 'froward' and 'forward' at II ii 38.5–8 and III v 7.4.) One Grace would then face us and the other two would have their backs to us, which is the order in Pico della Mirandola, as Geller 1972:273 notes. For a summary account supporting the *1611* reading, see Tung 1972. Bates 1992:154–55 suggests that the Graces face outward with their backs to one another, indicating a threefold reward as each, dancing in a circle, faces the viewer. For the *1596* text, **then** in 9 is an adv.; for *1611*, it is the conjunction 'than' (i.e. rather than). It may be best to allow, with Roche 1978, that the description is genuinely ambiguous. Line 9 provides an excellent moral comment on the traditional order of the Graces: if good goes out from us, it will return **in greater store**, agreeing with the parable of the talents and with Christ's words, as reported by Paul in Acts 20.35: 'It is a blessed thing to giue, rather then to receiue'. Cf. Matt. 10.8: 'Frely ye haue receiued, frely giue'.

Stanza 25

The past tense is stressed throughout the stanza.   **2 traced**: danced. At 12.6, she is seen 'placed' in the midst of the three Graces, and at 14.3 she 'in the midst of them did stand', i.e.

'remain', as though she were the still centre about which the others revolve.   **3 aread**: declare; conjecture.   **5 enraced**: implanted; cf. III v 52.1–5.

Stanza 26

1–4 As Pastorella outshines the other shepherdesses at ix 9.5. **the daughter of the day**: a periphrastic expression for Venus as either the evening or morning star, and naming her as one of 'The children of day' (III iv 59.5). Cf. the praise of Elizabeth at 28.1.   **9 another Grace**: as 16.9, 25.7. The same claim is made in the next line and at 25.6–7.

Stanza 27

In his gloss to *SC Apr.* 109, E.K. notes that Homer adds a fourth, 'Pasithea', which suggests that she contains them all. On the tradition of the fourth Grace, see Snare 1971. **3 meane**: average; also playing on 'mien', demeanour, as ix 11.2–3.   **4–6** These three features are one: her **beauty** is shown in her **Diuine resemblaunce**, for 'beautie . . . was made to represent | The great Creatours owne resemblance bright' (IV viii 32.1–2); and it also manifests her virtues expressed in her **Firme Chastity**. Either spite does not dare blemish her, or neither spite nor blemish dares confront her. On the relation of chastity to courtesy in Belphœbe, see III v 55.1–5. **7 peres**: companions.

Stanza 28

6–7 This praise and apology are offered in *Am* 80.13–14; cf. 4.7–8. They underline Elizabeth's displacement in Bk VI (apart from proem 6–7).   **minime**: a half note (half the time value of a semibreve), which in a song of 4,000+ stanzas to Elizabeth, the two given Colin's country lass amount to just one note. The term also acknowledges that the lass, who may

29

When thus that shepherd ended had his speach,
　Sayd *Calidore*; Now sure it yrketh mee,
　That to thy blisse I made this luckelesse breach,
　As now the author of thy bale to be,
　Thus to bereaue thy loues deare sight from thee:
　But gentle Shepheard pardon thou my shame,
　Who rashly sought that, which I mote not see.
Thus did the courteous Knight excuse his blame,
And to recomfort him, all comely meanes did frame.

30

In such discourses they together spent
　Long time, as fit occasion forth them led;
　With which the Knight him selfe did much content,
　And with delight his greedy fancy fed,
　Both of his words, which he with reason red;
　And also of the place, whose pleasures rare
　With such regard his sences rauished,
That thence, he had no will away to fare,
But wisht, that with that shepheard he mote dwelling share.

31

But that enuenimd sting, the which of yore,
　His poysnous point deepe fixed in his hart
　Had left, now gan afresh to rancle sore,
　And to renue the rigour of his smart:
　Which to recure, no skill of Leaches art
　Mote him auaile, but to returne againe
　To his wounds worker, that with louely dart
Dinting his brest, had bred his restlesse paine,
Like as the wounded Whale to shore flies from the maine.

32

So taking leaue of that same gentle swaine,
　He backe returned to his rusticke wonne,
　Where his faire *Pastorella* did remaine:
　To whome in sort, as he at first begonne,

He daily did apply him selfe to donne,
　All dewfull seruice voide of thoughts impure:
　Ne any paines ne perill did he shonne,
　By which he might her to his loue allure,
And liking in her yet vntamed heart procure.

33

And euermore the shepheard *Coridon*,
　What euer thing he did her to aggrate,
　Did striue to match with strong contention,
　And all his paines did closely emulate;
　Whether it were to caroll, as they sate
　Keeping their sheepe, or games to exercize,
　Or to present her with their labours late;
　Through which if any grace chaunst to arize
To him, the Shepheard streight with iealousie did frize.

34

One day as they all three together went
　To the greene wood, to gather strawberies,
　There chaunst to them a dangerous accident;
　A Tigre forth out of the wood did rise,
　That with fell clawes full of fierce gourmandize,
　And greedy mouth, wide gaping like hell gate,
　Did runne at *Pastorell* her to surprize:
　Whom she beholding, now all desolate
Gan cry to them aloud, to helpe her all too late.

35

Which *Coridon* first hearing, ran in hast
　To reskue her, but when he saw the feend,
　Through cowherd feare he fled away as fast,
　Ne durst abide the daunger of the end;
　His life he steemed dearer then his frend.
　But *Calidore* soone comming to her ayde,
　When he the beast saw ready now to rend
　His loues deare spoile, in which his heart was prayde,
He ran at him enraged in stead of being frayde.

---

be identified as S.'s wife, Elizabeth Boyle (see Chronology 1594 *11 June*), is a creature of least importance (*OED* 4) compared to Elizabeth. For a detailed gloss on the word's musical sense in the sixteenth century – it was the note on which the musical beat was based – see S. Weiner 1985:91–97.

Stanza 29
2 **yrketh**: troubles, grieves.

Stanza 30
5 **red**: spoke. 7 **regard**: sight. 8–9 As at ix 26, the 'double rauishment' of sight and hearing persuades Calidore to retreat within his present retreat.

Stanza 31
4 **rigour**: violence. 5 **recure**: an intensive form used by S. for mortal wounds, as I xi 30.4, II xi 21.9, etc. 7 **louely dart**: the dart of love. 8 **Dinting**: striking. 9 Like the whale, then, he seeks his own death.

Stanza 32
4 **sort**: manner. 6 **dewfull**: due.

Stanza 33
2 **aggrate**: please. 6 **exercize**: practise.

Stanza 34
2 **strawberies**: traditionally, the fruit of the golden age, as in Ovid, *Met.* 1.104, and therefore associated with the serpent. 4–7 The **Tigre** is always associated with savage cruelty and fierce greediness. **gourmandize**: voraciousness, as the cannibals threaten Serena at viii 38.9. Its mouth is like the dragon's mouth which 'Wyde gaped, like the griesly mouth of hell' (I xi 12.8). **surprize**: seize. 9 **all too late**: i.e. before it was too late.

Stanza 35
2 **feend**: so called because its mouth gapes 'like hell gate' (34.6). 5 As **frend** suggests, Coridon is being judged by Christ's injunction to love one another, for 'greater loue then this hathe no man, when any man bestoweth his life for his friends' (John 15.13). **steemed**: esteemed. 8 **His loues deare spoile**: i.e. Pastorella's body, which is the reward (or plunder) that his love seeks to possess. Clearly two beasts seek her as their spoil. Yet Calidore himself becomes the spoil: through his love for her, his own heart is preyed upon; and the tiger, in seeking to spoil her body, is about to spoil his heart.

36

He had no weapon, but his shepheards hooke,
  To serue the vengeaunce of his wrathfull will,
  With which so sternely he the monster strooke,
  That to the ground astonished he fell;
  Whence ere he could recou'r, he did him quell,
  And hewing off his head, it presented
  Before the feete of the faire *Pastorell*;
Who scarcely yet from former feare exempted,
A thousand times him thankt, that had her death preuented.

37

From that day forth she gan him to affect,
  And daily more her fauour to augment;
  But *Coridon* for cowherdize reiect,
  Fit to keepe sheepe, vnfit for loues content:
  The gentle heart scornes base disparagement.
  Yet *Calidore* did not despise him quight,
  But vsde him friendly for further intent,
  That by his fellowship, he colour might
Both his estate, and loue from skill of any wight.

38

So well he woo'd her, and so well he wrought her,
  With humble seruice, and with daily sute,
  That at the last vnto his will he brought her;
  Which he so wisely well did prosecute,
  That of his loue he reapt the timely frute,
  And ioyed long in close felicity:
  Till fortune fraught with malice, blinde, and brute,
  That enuies louers long prosperity,
Blew vp a bitter storme of foule aduersity.

39

It fortuned one day, when *Calidore*
  Was hunting in the woods (as was his trade)
  A lawlesse people, *Brigants* hight of yore,
  That neuer vsde to liue by plough nor spade,

unskilled, can't take care of sheep
VI, 11

But fed on spoile and booty, which they made
  Vpon their neighbours, which did nigh them border,
  The dwelling of these shepheards did inuade,
  And spoyld their houses, and them selues did murder;
And droue away their flocks, with other much disorder.

40

Amongst the rest, the which they then did pray,
  They spoyld old *Melibee* of all he had,
  And all his people captiue led away,
  Mongst which this lucklesse mayd away was lad,
  Faire *Pastorella*, sorrowfull and sad,
  Most sorrowfull, most sad, that euer sight,
  Now made the spoile of theeues and *Brigants* bad,
  Which was the conquest of the gentlest Knight,
That euer liu'd, and th'onely glory of his might.

41

With them also was taken *Coridon*,
  And carried captiue by those theeues away;
  Who in the couert of the night, that none
  Mote them descry, nor reskue from their pray,
  Vnto their dwelling them close conuay.
  Their dwelling in a little Island was,
  Couered with shrubby woods, in which no way
  Appeard for people in nor out to pas,
Nor any footing fynde for ouergrowen gras.

42

For vnderneath the ground their way was made,
  Through hollow caues, that no man mote discouer
  For the thicke shrubs, which did them alwaies shade
  From view of liuing wight, and couered ouer:
  But darkenesse dred and daily night did houer
  Through all the inner parts, wherein they dwelt,
  Ne lightned was with window, nor with louer,
  But with continuall candlelight, which delt
A doubtfull sense of things, not so well seene, as felt.

Stanza 36
4 astonished: stunned. **5 quell**: kill. **6** A rare metrically faulty line which requires **head** to be disyllabic, or three stresses on **presented**, which only intensifies the ugly internal echo. S. may have been distracted by wondering how Calidore could decapitate a tiger with a shepherd's crook.

Stanza 37
1 affect: love. **3 cowherdize**: the spelling suggests base conduct befitting a herder; cf. 35.3. **5 disparagement**: the disgrace of a relationship with one of inferior rank. **6–9** His subterfuge is needed to defend himself from the Blatant Beast. By claiming Coridon as a friend, he may disguise (**colour**) his higher rank (**estate**), and the consummation of his love from the knowledge (**skill**) of everyone.

Stanza 38
4 prosecute: take advantage of. **5** Coridon had feared that Calidore 'Should reap the haruest, ere it ripened were' (ix 38.6), as now has happened. Calidore sowed the seeds of love at ix 45.7–8 and 'got' her love at 46.3. Her heart was

'vntamed' at x 32.9; but now she is his 'conquest' (40.8). The repeated **long** separates their love's fulfilment from her seizure by the Brigants. **7 brute**: dumb, insensible.

Stanza 39
2 trade: custom. Not now a shepherd, then, but a hunter. **3–4 Brigants**: corresponding to the 'saluage nation' that seizes Serena as its spoil at viii 35, which also does not 'driue | The painefull plough'. S. may allude to the 'auncient people in the North part of Englande' (T. Cooper 1565), or to the 'spoyle-full Picts', or 'neighbour Scots' (II x 63.2, 5); or, more likely, to the Irish (see Hadfield 1997:184). See 'Brigands' in the *SEnc*. Dubrow 2000 relates their spoiling to thievery in S.'s England. **8 spoyld**: plundered.

Stanza 40
6 sight: sighed. **9 th'onely**: the chief or greatest.

Stanza 41
4 pray: preying. **5 close**: secretly.

43

Hither those *Brigants* brought their present pray,
  And kept them with continuall watch and ward,
  Meaning so soone, as they conuenient may,
  For slaues to sell them, for no small reward,
  To merchants, which them kept in bondage hard,
  Or sold againe. Now when faire *Pastorell*
  Into this place was brought, and kept with gard
  Of griesly theeues, she thought her self in hell,
Where with such damned fiends she should in darknesse
                               (dwell.

44

But for to tell the dolefull dreriment,
  And pittifull complaints, which there she made,
  Where day and night she nought did but lament
  Her wretched life, shut vp in deadly shade,
  And waste her goodly beauty, which did fade
  Like to a flowre, that feeles no heate of sunne,
  Which may her feeble leaues with comfort glade.
  But what befell her in that theeuish wonne,
Will in an other Canto better be begonne.

Stanza 42

1–2 For: 'Far', conj. Upton 1758, is supported by II i 22.3, IV i 20.4, etc. **5 daily night**: night even during the day, as endured by Florimell at IV xi 4.2. In *Teares* 256, '*Cymerians* dailie night' is cited as extreme darkness; used here it associates the Brigants with the Cimmerians who lived in caves where 'was supposed to be a descente into hell' (T. Cooper 1565). See Starnes and Talbert 1955:76–77, and Borris 1985:406–07. On the cave as an Irish *souterrain*, see Herron 2000:306–08.

It is identified by Hadfield 1997:184 as an Irish crannog. **7 louer**: louver or lantern to admit light. **9** As the darkness of God's curse upon Egypt, 'euen darcknes that may be felt' (Exod. 10.21).

Stanza 44

1609 attempted to improve the syntax by bracketing 3–7, removing the period after **glade**, and beginning 8 with And. **7 glade**: gladden.

Cant. XI.

The theeues fall out for Pastorell,
Whilest Melibee is slaine:
Her Calidore from them redeemes,
And bringeth backe againe.

1

THe ioyes of loue, if they should euer last,
   Without affliction or disquietnesse,
   That worldly chaunces doe amongst them cast,
   Would be on earth too great a blessednesse,
   Liker to heauen, then mortall wretchednesse.
   Therefore the winged God, to let men weet,
   That here on earth is no sure happinesse,
   A thousand sowres hath tempred with one sweet,
To make it seeme more deare and dainty, as is meet.

2

Like as is now befalne to this faire Mayd,
   Faire *Pastorell*, of whom is now my song,
   Who being now in dreadfull darknesse layd,
   Amongst those theeues, which her in bondage strong
   Detaynd, yet Fortune not with all this wrong
   Contented, greater mischiefe on her threw,
   And sorrowes heapt on her in greater throng;
   That who so heares her heauinesse, would rew
And pitty her sad plight, so chang'd from pleasaunt hew.

3

Whylest thus she in these hellish dens remayned,
   Wrapped in wretched cares and hearts vnrest,
   It so befell (as Fortune had ordayned)
   That he, which was their Capitaine profest,
   And had the chiefe commaund of all the rest,
   One day as he did all his prisoners vew,
   With lustfull eyes, beheld that louely guest,
   Faire *Pastorella*, whose sad mournefull hew
Like the faire Morning clad in misty fog did shew.

4

At sight whereof his barbarous heart was fired,
   And inly burnt with flames most raging whot,
   That her alone he for his part desired
   Of all the other pray, which they had got,
   And her in mynde did to him selfe allot,
   From that day forth he kyndnesse to her showed,
   And sought her loue, by all the meanes he mote;
   With looks, with words, with gifts he oft her wowed:
And mixed threats among, and much vnto her vowed.

5

But all that euer he could doe or say,
   Her constant mynd could not a whit remoue,
   Nor draw vnto the lure of his lewd lay,
   To graunt him fauour, or afford him loue.
   Yet ceast he not to sew and all waies proue,
   By which he mote accomplish his request,
   Saying and doing all that mote behoue;
   Ne day nor night he suffred her to rest,
But her all night did watch, and all the day molest.

6

At last when him she so importune saw,
   Fearing least he at length the raines would lend
   Vnto his lust, and make his will his law,
   Sith in his powre she was to foe or frend,
   She thought it best, for shadow to pretend
   Some shew of fauour, by him gracing small,
   That she thereby mote either freely wend,
   Or at more ease continue there his thrall:
A little well is lent, that gaineth more withall.

Book VI Canto xi

Argument

The romance motif of a beautiful maiden captured and then sold as a slave by pirates who quarrel when their lustful captain claims her for himself is found, e.g. in Heliodorus, *An Æthiopian History* and Achilles Tatius, *Clitophon and Leucippe*. **3 redeemes**: as the word signifies the rescue of someone from the threat of death, as the Red Cross Knight at I ix 1.9, Amoret at III xi 16.4, and Irena at V vii 45.8, almost inevitably in a romance it shadows (Christian) redemption.

Stanza 1

3 worldly chaunces: mishaps; mischances of life, as in the *BCP*: 'All the changes and chances of this mortal life'. **6–9** Cupid is given fortune's usual role, as 2.5. 'That blisse may not abide in state of mortall men' (I viii 44.9) is a common motif in the poem but never illustrated more poignantly than here. While the odds against happiness in love have been subject to a tenfold inflation since IV x 1, **tempred** implies 'controlled' (*OED* II 7) rather than 'mixed' (*OED* 3), as Borris 1985:294 suggests. **dainty**: precious.

Stanza 2

8 heauinesse: grief.

Stanza 3

1 these hellish dens: a key detail that extends x 43.8–9 and is repeated at 41.2, in part to gain the chiaroscuro effect at 13.1–5 and 21.6–9.

Stanza 4

3 part: share.

Stanza 5

2 remoue: move; persuade. **5 proue**: try.

7

So from thenceforth, when loue he to her made,
    With better tearmes she did him entertaine,
    Which gaue him hope, and did him halfe perswade,
    That he in time her ioyaunce should obtaine.
    But when she saw, through that small fauours gaine,
    That further, then she willing was, he prest,
    She found no meanes to barre him, but to faine
    A sodaine sickenesse, which her sore opprest,
And made vnfit to serue his lawlesse mindes behest.

8

By meanes whereof she would not him permit
    Once to approch to her in priuity,
    But onely mongst the rest by her to sit,
    Mourning the rigour of her malady,
    And seeking all things meete for remedy.
    But she resolu'd no remedy to fynde,
    Nor better cheare to shew in misery,
    Till Fortune would her captiue bonds vnbynde,
Her sickenesse was not of the body but the mynde.

9

During which space that she thus sicke did lie,
    It chaunst a sort of merchants, which were wount
    To skim those coastes, for bondmen there to buy,
    And by such trafficke after gaines to hunt,
    Arriued in this Isle though bare and blunt,
    T'inquire for slaues; where being readie met
    By some of these same theeues at the instant brunt,
    Were brought vnto their Captaine, who was set
By his faire patients side with sorrowfull regret.

10

To whom they shewed, how those marchants were
    Arriu'd in place, their bondslaues for to buy,
    And therefore prayd, that those same captiues there
    Mote to them for their most commodity
    Be sold, and mongst them shared equally.
    This their request the Captaine much appalled;
    Yet could he not their iust demaund deny,
    And willed streight the slaues should forth be called,
And sold for most aduantage not to be forstalled.

11

Then forth the good old *Melibœ* was brought,
    And *Coridon*, with many other moe,
    Whom they before in diuerse spoyles had caught:
    All which he to the marchants sale did showe.
    Till some, which did the sundry prisoners knowe,
    Gan to inquire for that faire shepherdesse,
    Which with the rest they tooke not long agoe,
    And gan her forme and feature to expresse,
The more t'augment her price, through praise of comlinesse.

12

To whom the Captaine in full angry wize
    Made answere, that the Mayd of whom they spake,
    Was his owne purchase and his onely prize,
    With which none had to doe, ne ought partake,
    But he himselfe, which did that conquest make;
    Litle for him to haue one silly lasse:
    Besides through sicknesse now so wan and weake,
    That nothing meet in marchandise to passe.
So shew'd them her, to proue how pale and weake she was.

13

The sight of whom, though now decayd and mard,
    And eke but hardly seene by candle-light,
    Yet like a Diamond of rich regard,
    In doubtfull shadow of the darkesome night,
    With starrie beames about her shining bright,
    These marchants fixed eyes did so amaze,
    That what through wonder, and what through delight,
    A while on her they greedily did gaze,
And did her greatly like, and did her greatly praize.

14

At last when all the rest them offred were,
    And prises to them placed at their pleasure,
    They all refused in regard of her,
    Ne ought would buy, how euer prisd with measure,
    Withouten her, whose worth aboue all threasure
    They did esteeme, and offred store of gold.
    But then the Captaine fraught with more displeasure,
    Bad them be still, his loue should not be sold:
The rest take if they would, he her to him would hold.

Stanza 6
4 . . . to treat as a foe or as a friend.   **5 for shadow**: for
protection from danger, i.e. by dissimulating.   6–7 I.e. by
showing him slight favour, she might either go free, etc.
9 Proverbial: Smith 890.

Stanza 7
4 **her ioyaunce**: his sexual enjoyment of her.

Stanza 8
2 **in priuity**: privately.   9 I.e. the **sickenesse** she feigns is her
'constant mynd' (5.2), referring to her love for Calidore.

Stanza 9
2 **sort**: company.   **3 skim**: scour.   5 . . . though desolate and
barren.   7 . . . at the very outset.

Stanza 10
4 . . . for their greatest profit.   9 I.e. all the slaves were to be
sold, none to be reserved.

Stanza 11
3 **spoyles**: raids.   **8 expresse**: describe.

Stanza 12
3 **purchase**: booty, spoil.   **his onely**: only his.   6 **silly**: sim-
ple.   8 That she was not fit for sale.

Stanza 13
3 **regard**: value.   6 **amaze**: dazzle, bewilder.

Stanza 14
2 **prises**: prices.   **3 in regard of her**: on account of her, as she
is 'like a Diamond of rich regard' (13.3).   4 . . . i.e. however
moderately priced the others were.

15

Therewith some other of the chiefest theeues
   Boldly him bad such iniurie forbeare;
   For that same mayd, how euer it him greeues,
   Should with the rest be sold before him theare,
   To make the prises of the rest more deare.
   That with great rage he stoutly doth denay;
   And fiercely drawing forth his blade, doth sweare,
   That who so hardie hand on her doth lay,
It dearely shall aby, and death for handsell pay.

16

Thus as they words amongst them multiply,
   They fall to strokes, the frute of too much talke,
   And the mad steele about doth fiercely fly,
   Not sparing wight, ne leauing any balke,
   But making way for death at large to walke:
   Who in the horror of the griesly night,
   In thousand dreadful shapes doth mongst them stalke,
   And makes huge hauocke, whiles the candlelight
Out quenched, leaues no skill nor difference of wight.

17

Like as a sort of hungry dogs ymet
   About some carcase by the common way,
   Doe fall together, stryuing each to get
   The greatest portion of the greedie pray;
   All on confused heapes themselues assay,
   And snatch, and byte, and rend, and tug, and teare;
   That who them sees, would wonder at their fray,
   And who sees not, would be affrayd to heare.
Such was the conflict of those cruell *Brigants* there.

18

But first of all, their captiues they doe kill,
   Least they should ioyne against the weaker side,
   Or rise against the remnant at their will;
   Old *Melibœ* is slaine, and him beside
   His aged wife, with many others wide,
   But *Coridon* escaping craftily,
   Creepes forth of dores, whilst darknes him doth hide,
   And flyes away as fast as he can hye,
Ne stayeth leaue to take, before his friends doe dye.

19

But *Pastorella*, wofull wretched Elfe,
   Was by the Captaine all this while defended,
   Who minding more her safety then himselfe,
   His target alwayes ouer her pretended;
   By meanes whereof, that mote not be amended,
   He at the length was slaine, and layd on ground,
   Yet holding fast twixt both his armes extended
   Fayre *Pastorell*, who with the selfe same wound
Launcht through the arme, fell down with him in drerie
                               (swound.

20

There lay she couered with confused preasse
   Of carcases, which dying on her fell.
   Tho when as he was dead, the fray gan ceasse,
   And each to other calling, did compell
   To stay their cruell hands from slaughter fell,
   Sith they that were the cause of all, were gone.
   Thereto they all attonce agreed well,
   And lighting candles new, gan search anone,
How many of their friends were slaine, how many fone.

21

Their Captaine there they cruelly found kild,
   And in his armes the dreary dying mayd,
   Like a sweet Angell twixt two clouds vphild:
   Her louely light was dimmed and decayd,
   With cloud of death vpon her eyes displayd;
   Yet did the cloud make euen that dimmed light
   Seeme much more louely in that darknesse layd,
   And twixt the twinckling of her eye-lids bright,
To sparke out litle beames, like starres in foggie night.

22

But when they mou'd the carcases aside,
   They found that life did yet in her remaine:
   Then all their helpes they busily applyde,
   To call the soule backe to her home againe;
   And wrought so well with labour and long paine,
   That they to life recouered her at last.
   Who sighing sore, as if her hart in twaine
   Had riuen bene, and all her hart strings brast,
With dreary drouping eyne lookt vp like one aghast.

Stanza 15
9 **aby**: suffer for.   **handsell**: reward, with a play on **hand**: lay a hand on her and you will be handed death as your reward.

Stanza 16
4 **balke**: exception; a figurative sense from the literal, a piece missed in ploughing.   9 **skill**: distinction.

Stanza 17
1 **sort**: pack.   4 **greedie pray**: prey for which they are greedy.
5 **assay**: assail.

Stanza 18
5 **wide**: round about.   9 Said in scorn of his cowardice, though at 32.6–9 he is said to regret his flight.

Stanza 19
1 **Elfe**: poor creature.   4 **target**: shield.   **pretended**: held, stretched.   9 **Launcht**: pierced.   **drerie**: also 'bloody'. The captain is permitted 'to approch to her in priuity' (8.2) only when dying.

Stanza 20
1–2 This startling image of Pastorella buried under the dead is highlighted by the metre: **couered** or **confused** may be trisyllabic.

Stanza 21
2 **dreary**: sad; yet cf. 'drerie' (19.9).

23

There she beheld, that sore her grieu'd to see,
   Her father and her friends about her lying,
   Her selfe sole left, a second spoyle to bee
   Of those, that hauing saued her from dying,
   Renew'd her death by timely death denying:
   What now is left her, but to wayle and weepe,
   Wringing her hands, and ruefully loud crying?
   Ne cared she her wound in teares to steepe,
Albe with all their might those *Brigants* her did keepe.

24

But when they saw her now reliu'd againe,
   They left her so, in charge of one the best
   Of many worst, who with vnkind disdaine
   And cruell rigour her did much molest;
   Scarse yeelding her due food, or timely rest,
   And scarsely suffring her infestred wound,
   That sore her payn'd, by any to be drest.
So leaue we her in wretched thraldome bound,
And turne we backe to *Calidore*, where we him found.

25

Who when he backe returned from the wood,
   And saw his shepheards cottage spoyled quight,
   And his loue reft away, he wexed wood,
   And halfe enraged at that ruefull sight,
   That euen his hart for very fell despight,
   And his owne flesh he readie was to teare,
   He chauft, he grieu'd, he fretted, and he sight,
   And fared like a furious wyld Beare,
Whose whelpes are stolne away, she being otherwhere.

26

Ne wight he found, to whom he might complaine,
   Ne wight he found, of whom he might inquire;
   That more increast the anguish of his paine.
   He sought the woods; but no man could see there:
   He sought the plaines; but could no tydings heare.
   The woods did nought but ecchoes vaine rebound;
   The playnes all waste and emptie did appeare:
   Where wont the shepheards oft their pypes resound,
And feed an hundred flocks, there now not one he found.

27

At last as there he romed vp and downe,
   He chaunst one comming towards him to spy,
   That seem'd to be some sorie simple clowne,
   With ragged weedes, and lockes vpstaring hye,
   As if he did from some late daunger fly,
   And yet his feare did follow him behynd:
   Who as he vnto him approched nye,
   He mote perceiue by signes, which he did fynd,
That *Coridon* it was, the silly shepherds hynd.

28

Tho to him running fast, he did not stay
   To greet him first, but askt where were the rest;
   Where *Pastorell*? who full of fresh dismay,
   And gushing forth in teares, was so opprest,
   That he no word could speake, but smit his brest,
   And vp to heauen his eyes fast streming threw.
   Whereat the knight amaz'd, yet did not rest,
   But askt againe, what ment that rufull hew:
Where was his *Pastorell*? where all the other crew?

29

Ah well away (sayd he then sighing sore)
   That euer I did liue, this day to see,
   This dismall day, and was not dead before,
   Before I saw faire *Pastorella* dye.
   Die? out alas, then *Calidore* did cry:
   How could the death dare euer her to quell?
   But read thou shepheard, read what destiny,
   Or other dyrefull hap from heauen or hell
Hath wrought this wicked deed, doe feare away, and tell.

30

Tho when the shepheard breathed had a whyle,
   He thus began: Where shall I then commence
   This wofull tale? or how those *Brigants* vyle,
   With cruell rage and dreadfull violence
   Spoyld all our cots, and caried vs from hence?
   Or how faire *Pastorell* should haue bene sold
   To marchants, but was sau'd with strong defence?
   Or how those theeues, whilest one sought her to hold,
Fell all at ods, and fought through fury fierce and bold.

Stanza 23
8 I.e. since she did not want to live, she did not care to heal her wound by steeping it in tears, as at iii 10.5–9.

Stanza 24
1 **reliu'd**: restored again to life. 6 **infestred**: festered inwardly.

Stanza 25
4 **halfe enraged**: almost maddened. 5–6 The language but not the meaning of Joel 2.13: 'rent your heart'. 7–9 Cf. 2 Sam. 17.8: 'they be strong men, and are chafed in minde as a beare robbed of her whelpes'. **sight**: sighed. **fared**: acted.

Stanza 26
On the witty use of echo in this stanza to mark the breaking of communion with the pastoral world, see 'echo, resonance' in the *SEnc*.

Stanza 27
4 **vpstaring**: standing on end. 9 **hynd**: servant.

Stanza 29
3 **dismall day**: unlucky or evil day. 6 **quell**: kill. 7 **read**: tell. 9 **doe**: put.

31

In that same conflict (woe is me) befell
   This fatall chaunce, this dolefull accident,
   Whose heauy tydings now I haue to tell.
   First all the captiues, which they here had hent,
   Were by them slaine by generall consent;
   Old *Meliboe* and his good wife withall
   These eyes saw die, and dearely did lament:
   But when the lot to *Pastorell* did fall,
Their Captaine long withstood, and did her death forstall.

32

But what could he gainst all them doe alone?
   It could not boot; needs mote she die at last:
   I onely scapt through great confusione
   Of cryes and clamors, which amongst them past,
   In dreadfull darknesse dreadfully aghast;
   That better were with them to haue bene dead,
   Then here to see all desolate and wast,
   Despoyled of those ioyes and iollyhead,
Which with those gentle shepherds here I wont to lead.

33

When *Calidore* these ruefull newes had raught,
   His hart quite deaded was with anguish great,
   And all his wits with doole were nigh distraught,
   That he his face, his head, his brest did beat,
   And death it selfe vnto himselfe did threat;
   Oft cursing th'heauens, that so cruell were
   To her, whose name he often did repeat;
   And wishing oft, that he were present there,
When she was slaine, or had bene to her succour nere.

34

But after griefe awhile had had his course,
   And spent it selfe in mourning, he at last
   Began to mitigate his swelling sourse,
   And in his mind with better reason cast,
   How he might saue her life, if life did last;
   Or if that dead, how he her death might wreake,
  · Sith otherwise he could not mend thing past;
   Or if it to reuenge he were too weake,
Then for to die with her, and his liues threed to breake.

35

Tho *Coridon* he prayd, sith he well knew
   The readie way vnto that theeuish wonne,
   To wend with him, and be his conduct trew
   Vnto the place, to see what should be donne.
   But he, whose hart through feare was late fordonne,
   Would not for ought be drawne to former drede,
   But by all meanes the daunger knowne did shonne:
   Yet *Calidore* so well him wrought with meed,
And faire bespoke with words, that he at last agreed.

36

So forth they goe together (God before)
   Both clad in shepheards weeds agreeably,
   And both with shepheards hookes: But *Calidore*
   Had vnderneath, him armed priuily.
   Tho to the place when they approched nye,
   They chaunst, vpon an hill not farre away,
   Some flockes of sheepe and shepheards to espy;
   To whom they both agreed to take their way,
In hope there newes to learne, how they mote best assay.

37

There did they find, that which they did not feare,
   The selfe same flocks, the which those theeues had reft
   From *Meliboe* and from themselues whyleare,
   And certaine of the theeues there by them left,
   The which for want of heards themselues then kept.
   Right well knew *Coridon* his owne late sheepe,
   And seeing them, for tender pittie wept:
   But when he saw the theeues, which did them keepe,
His hart gan fayle, albe he saw them all asleepe.

38

But *Calidore* recomforting his griefe,
   Though not his feare: for nought may feare disswade;
   Him hardly forward drew, whereas the thiefe
   Lay sleeping soundly in the bushes shade,
   Whom *Coridon* him counseld to inuade
   Now all vnwares, and take the spoyle away;
   But he, that in his mind had closely made
   A further purpose, would not so them slay,
But gently waking them, gaue them the time of day.

Stanza 31
4 **hent**: seized.   9 **forstall**: prevent; here, postpone.

Stanza 32
8 **iollyhead**: merriment.

Stanza 33
1 **raught**: received.

Stanza 34
3 **his swelling sourse**: alluding to the well of tears, as II ii 8.7. 6 **wreake**: avenge.   9 Alluding to the role of Atropos, as at IV ii 48.7–9.

Stanza 35
3 **conduct**: guide.   5 **fordonne**: overcome.   8 **meed**: bribes.

Stanza 36
1 **God before**: as the Red Cross Knight proceeds on his quest 'with God to frend' at I i 28.7, and Artegall seeks Pollente with 'God to guide' at V ii 10.5, and used here to support the claim that Pastorella is one 'whom high God did saue' (xii 17.9). 2 **agreeably**: similarly.   9 **assay**: act.

Stanza 37
1 **feare**: expect, anticipate; cf. 41.5.   5 **heards**: herdsmen. 7 He pities the sheep because not being in their fold they would get wet with the dew; see ix 13.5.

Stanza 38
1 **recomforting**: consoling.   2 **disswade**: advise against, and so remove.   3 **hardly**: forcibly; with difficulty.   5 **inuade**: attack.   7 **closely**: secretly.   9 I.e. he woke them up to tell

39
Tho sitting downe by them vpon the greene,
   Of sundrie things he purpose gan to faine;
   That he by them might certaine tydings weene
   Of *Pastorell*, were she aliue or slaine.
   Mongst which the theeues them questioned againe,
   What mister men, and eke from whence they were.
   To whom they answer'd, as did appertaine,
That they were poore heardgroomes, the which whylere
Had from their maisters fled, and now sought hyre elswhere.

40
Whereof right glad they seem'd, and offer made
   To hyre them well, if they their flockes would keepe:
   For they themselues were euill groomes, they sayd,
   Vnwont with heards to watch, or pasture sheepe,
   But to forray the land, or scoure the deepe.
   Thereto they soone agreed, and earnest tooke,
   To keepe their flockes for litle hyre and chepe:
For they for better hyre did shortly looke,
So there all day they bode, till light the sky forsooke.

41
Tho when as towards darksome night it drew,
   Vnto their hellish dens those theeues them brought,
   Where shortly they in great acquaintance grew,
   And all the secrets of their entrayles sought.
   There did they find, contrarie to their thought,
   That *Pastorell* yet liu'd, but all the rest
   Were dead, right so as *Coridon* had taught:
Whereof they both full glad and blyth did rest,
But chiefly *Calidore*, whom griefe had most possest.

42
At length when they occasion fittest found,
   In dead of night, when all the theeues did rest
   After a late forray, and slept full sound,
   Sir *Calidore* him arm'd, as he thought best,
   Hauing of late by diligent inquest,
   Prouided him a sword of meanest sort:
   With which he streight went to the Captaines nest.
But *Coridon* durst not with him consort,
Ne durst abide behind, for dread of worse effort.

43
When to the Caue they came, they found it fast:
   But *Calidore* with huge resistlesse might,
   The dores assayled, and the locks vpbrast.
   With noyse whereof the theefe awaking light,
   Vnto the entrance ran: where the bold knight
   Encountring him with small resistance slew;
   The whiles faire *Pastorell* through great affright
Was almost dead, misdoubting least of new
Some vprore were like that, which lately she did vew.

44
But when as *Calidore* was comen in,
   And gan aloud for *Pastorell* to call,
   Knowing his voice although not heard long sin,
   She sudden was reuiued therewithall,
   And wondrous ioy felt in her spirits thrall:
   Like him that being long in tempest tost,
   Looking each houre into deathes mouth to fall,
At length espyes at hand the happie cost,
On which he safety hopes, that earst feard to be lost.

45
Her gentle hart, that now long season past
   Had neuer ioyance felt, nor chearefull thought,
   Began some smacke of comfort new to tast,
   Like lyfull heat to nummed senses brought,
   And life to feele, that long for death had sought;
   Ne lesse in hart reioyced *Calidore*,
   When he her found, but like to one distraught
And robd of reason, towards her him bore,
A thousand times embrast, and kist a thousand more.

46
But now by this, with noyse of late vprore,
   The hue and cry was raysed all about;
   And all the *Brigants* flocking in great store,
   Vnto the caue gan preasse, nought hauing dout
   Of that was doen, and entred in a rout.
   But *Calidore* in th'entry close did stand,
   And entertayning them with courage stout,
Still slew the formost, that came first to hand,
So long till all the entry was with bodies mand.

---

them what time it was, as a way of courteous greeting
(see 'time' *OED* 28b). Calidore has a special gift of surprising
others in the privacy of love, inspiration, or sleep, and then
striking up a conversation. On the role of privacy in relation to
courtesy, see Rowe 1989.

Stanza 39
2 purpose: conversation. **5 againe**: in return. **6 mister**:
sort of. **7** . . . i.e. as was suitable to their disguises as herdsmen.

Stanza 40
3 euill: unskilled. **6 soone**: straightway. **earnest**: pledge.
7 . . . for low wages and upkeep.

Stanza 41
2 hellish dens: as 3.1. **4 entrayles**: 'the inner parts' (x 42.6)
of the cave.

Stanza 42
5 inquest: search.

Stanza 43
4 light: quickly. **8 misdoubting**: fearing. **of new**: anew.

Stanza 44
3 long sin: i.e. for a long time. **5 thrall**: thrilled, pierced; or
enthralled.

Stanza 45
4 lyfull: life-giving, vital.

Stanza 46
7 entertayning: encountering. **9 mand**: piled with men.

47

Tho when no more could nigh to him approch,
    He breath'd his sword, and rested him till day:
    Which when he spyde vpon the earth t'encroch,
    Through the dead carcases he made his way,
    Mongst which he found a sword of better say,
    With which he forth went into th'open light:
    Where all the rest for him did readie stay,
    And fierce assayling him, with all their might
Gan all vpon him lay: there gan a dreadfull fight.

48

How many flyes in whottest sommers day
    Do seize vpon some beast, whose flesh is bare,
    That all the place with swarmes do ouerlay,
    And with their litle stings right felly fare;
    So many theeues about him swarming are,
    All which do him assayle on euery side,
    And sore oppresse, ne any him doth spare:
    But he doth with his raging brond diuide
Their thickest troups, and round about him scattreth wide.

49

Like as a Lion mongst an heard of dere,
    Disperseth them to catch his choysest pray;
    So did he fly amongst them here and there,
    And all that nere him came, did hew and slay,

Till he had strowd with bodies all the way;
    That none his daunger daring to abide,
    Fled from his wrath, and did themselues conuay
    Into their caues, their heads from death to hide,
Ne any left, that victorie to him enuide.

50

Then backe returning to his dearest deare,
    He her gan to recomfort, all he might,
    With gladfull speaches, and with louely cheare,
    And forth her bringing to the ioyous light,
    Whereof she long had lackt the wishfull sight,
    Deuiz'd all goodly meanes, from her to driue
    The sad remembrance of her wretched plight.
    So her vneath at last he did reuiue,
That long had lyen dead, and made againe aliue.

51

This doen, into those theeuish dens he went,
    And thence did all the spoyles and threasures take,
    Which they from many long had robd and rent,
    But fortune now the victors meed did make;
    Of which the best he did his loue betake;
    And also all those flockes, which they before
    Had reft from *Meliboe* and from his make,
    He did them all to *Coridon* restore.
So droue them all away, and his loue with him bore.

Stanza 47
5 of better say: of better temper, to replace the one 'of meanest sort' obtained at 42.6.

Stanza 48
The simile expands i 24.4–5 and adapts its use at I i 23.

Stanza 49
3 fly: the term links the two similes.   **6 daunger**: power to inflict injury.   **9 enuide**: refused.

Stanza 50
3 louely: loving.   **8–9 vneath**: with difficulty. Pastorella's resurrection is rendered as though entirely natural, marking the transition from pastoral innocence to worldly experience. See Snyder 1998:6–7.

Stanza 51
5 betake: give to.   **7 make**: mate.   **8 restore**: because the sheep are Coridon's 'owne' (37.6).

Cant. XII.

Fayre Pastorella by great hap
her parents vnderstands,
Calidore doth the Blatant beast
subdew, and bynd in bands.

1

Ike as a ship, that through the Ocean wyde
        Directs her course vnto one certaine cost,
    Is met of many a counter winde and tyde,
    With which her winged speed is let and crost,
    And she her selfe in stormie surges tost;
    Yet making many a borde, and many a bay,
    Still winneth way, ne hath her compasse lost:
    Right so it fares with me in this long way,
Whose course is often stayd, yet neuer is astray.

2

For all that hetherto hath long delayd
    This gentle knight, from sewing his first quest,
    Though out of course, yet hath not bene mis-sayd,
    To shew the courtesie by him profest,
    Euen vnto the lowest and the least.
    But now I come into my course againe,
    To his atchieuement of the *Blatant beast*;
    Who all this while at will did range and raine,
Whilst none was him to stop, nor none him to restraine.

3

Sir *Calidore* when thus he now had raught
    Faire *Pastorella* from those *Brigants* powre,
    Vnto the Castle of *Belgard* her brought,
    Whereof was Lord the good Sir *Bellamoure*;
    Who whylome was in his youthes freshest flowre
    A lustie knight, as euer wielded speare,
    And had endured many a dreadfull stoure
    In bloudy battell for a Ladie deare,
The fayrest Ladie then of all that liuing were.

4

Her name was *Claribell*, whose father hight
    The Lord of *Many Ilands*, farre renound
    For his great riches and his greater might.
    He through the wealth, wherein he did abound,
    This daughter thought in wedlocke to haue bound
    Vnto the Prince of *Picteland* bordering nere,
    But she whose sides before with secret wound
    Of loue to *Bellamoure* empierced were,
By all meanes shund to match with any forrein fere.

Book VI Canto xii

Argument
The two episodes are equally matched at 19 stanzas each.
1 hap: good fortune.

Stanza 1
On S.'s comparison of writing his poem to a ship making a perilous voyage, see I xii 1*n*. **2 cost**: coast (apparently suggested by xi 44.8); direction. **4 let**: hindered. **6–9** I.e. by tacking and turning often before the wind. A ship at **bay** needs to turn into the wind, as a hunted animal at bay is forced to confront its pursuers. When it is **stayd**, it must turn windward to tack (*OED* v.³ 3). **compasse**: implying 'correct way' or **course**.

Stanza 2
The poet's course and his knight's are parallel, 'often stayd, yet neuer . . . astray' (1.9). S. has not **mis-sayd** because Calidore's conduct continues to reveal the nature of courtesy. **2 sewing**: pursuing.

Stanza 3
1 raught: seized. **3 Belgard**: Ital. *bel + guard*, goodly or loving view, as Belphœbe's 'belgardes' at II iii 25.3, i.e. loving glances; or goodly guard for Pastorella's beauty, as earlier it was a prison for Claribell. The **Castle** may allude to Morgan le Fay's castle, La Beale Regard, in Malory 10.37; or the Earl of Rutland's Belvoir Castle, as Upton 1758 suggests; or Winchester Castle, as Clifford-Amos 1999:314–23 argues. **4 Bellamoure**: as II vi 16.7, 'fair lover', for he is his lady's 'loued Lord' (22.1), as their joint name, Clari-Bellamoure, indicates; see Nohrnberg 1976:607. The rhyme with **flowre** suggests a flower of that name at *Am* 64.7, and hence Pastorella's birthmark at 7.7–9. Or Lat. *bellum* + Fr. *amour*, lover of war; or a knight who is also a lover. See 'Bellamour' in the *SEnc*. **6 lustie**: vigorous. **7 stoure**: encounter.

Stanza 4
1 Claribell: famous or shining in beauty, from Lat. *clara* + *bella*, being the 'fayrest Ladie' (3.9). **2–6 Many Islands** may refer to Britain, which was among the Fortunate Isles: see Bennett 1956; or to the Hebrides, as Wayne Erickson and Willy Maley have suggested to me; or to the Gaelic borderlands north of England, in Ireland and Scotland, ruled by the MacDonald Lord of the Isles. **Picteland** refers to Scotland, or more generally to the border lands, which would include Ireland. **9 fere**: husband.

5

And *Bellamour* againe so well her pleased,
    With dayly seruice and attendance dew,
    That of her loue he was entyrely seized,
    And closely did her wed, but knowne to few.
    Which when her father vnderstood, he grew
    In so great rage, that them in dongeon deepe
    Without compassion cruelly he threw;
    Yet did so streightly them a sunder keepe,
That neither could to company of th'other creepe.

6

Nathlesse Sir *Bellamour*, whether through grace
    Or secret guifts so with his keepers wrought,
    That to his loue sometimes he came in place,
    Whereof her wombe vnwist to wight was fraught,
    And in dew time a mayden child forth brought.
    Which she streight way for dread least, if her syre
    Should know thereof, to slay he would haue sought,
    Deliuered to her handmayd, that for hyre
She should it cause be fostred vnder straunge attyre.

7

The trustie damzell bearing it abrode
    Into the emptie fields, where liuing wight
    Mote not bewray the secret of her lode,
    She forth gan lay vnto the open light
    The litle babe, to take thereof a sight.
    Whom whylest she did with watrie eyne behold,
    Vpon the litle brest like christall bright,
    She mote perceiue a litle purple mold,
That like a rose her silken leaues did faire vnfold.

8

Well she it markt, and pittied the more,
    Yet could not remedie her wretched case,
    But closing it againe like as before,
    Bedeaw'd with teares there left it in the place:
    Yet left not quite, but drew a litle space
    Behind the bushes, where she her did hyde,
    To weet what mortall hand, or heauens grace
    Would for the wretched infants helpe prouyde,
For which it loudly cald, and pittifully cryde.

9

At length a Shepheard, which there by did keepe
    His fleecie flocke vpon the playnes around,
    Led with the infants cry, that loud did weepe,
    Came to the place, where when he wrapped found
    Th'abandond spoyle, he softly it vnbound;
    And seeing there, that did him pittie sore,
    He tooke it vp, and in his mantle wound;
    So home vnto his honest wife it bore,
Who as her owne it nurst, and named euermore.

10

Thus long continu'd *Claribell* a thrall,
    And *Bellamour* in bands, till that her syre
    Departed life, and left vnto them all.
    Then all the stormes of fortunes former yre
    Were turnd, and they to freedome did retyre.
    Thenceforth they ioy'd in happinesse together,
    And liued long in peace and loue entyre,
    Without disquiet or dislike of ether,
Till time that *Calidore* brought *Pastorella* thether.

11

Both whom they goodly well did entertaine;
    For *Bellamour* knew *Calidore* right well,
    And loued for his prowesse, sith they twaine
    Long since had fought in field. Als *Claribell*
    No lesse did tender the faire *Pastorell*,
    Seeing her weake and wan, through durance long.
    There they a while together thus did dwell
    In much delight, and many ioyes among,
Vntill the damzell gan to wex more sound and strong.

12

Tho gan Sir *Calidore* him to aduize
    Of his first quest, which he had long forlore,
    Asham'd to thinke, how he that enterprize,
    The which the Faery Queene had long afore
    Bequeath'd to him, forslacked had so sore;
    That much he feared, least reprochfull blame
    With foule dishonour him mote blot therefore;
    Besides the losse of so much loos and fame,
As through the world thereby should glorifie his name.

Stanza 5
1 againe: in return. **3 seized**: possessed. **4 closely**: secretly.
8 streightly: strictly.

Stanza 6
1 grace: favour. **4 fraught**: burdened.

Stanza 7
3 bewray: reveal. **8 mold**: mole; pattern.

Stanza 8
1 the more: greatly. **3 it**: referring metaphorically to the rose
whose leaves unfold again when Pastorella is restored to her
mother at 19.5. **5 drew**: withdrew.

Stanza 9
6 pittie: move to pity. **9 named**: i.e. called her own.

Stanza 10
5 retyre: return.

Stanza 11
5 tender: cherish. **6 durance**: imprisonment.

Stanza 12
1 aduize: consider. **2 forlore**: abandoned. **5 Bequeath'd**:
entrusted. **forslacked**: neglected. **8 loos**: renown.

13

Therefore resoluing to returne in hast
  Vnto so great atchieuement, he bethought
  To leaue his loue, now perill being past,
  With *Claribell*, whylest he that monster sought
  Throughout the world, and to destruction brought.
  So taking leaue of his faire *Pastorell*,
  Whom to recomfort, all the meanes he wrought,
  With thanks to *Bellamour* and *Claribell*,
He went forth on his quest, and did, that him befell.

14

But first, ere I doe his aduentures tell,
  In this exploite, me needeth to declare,
  What did betide to the faire *Pastorell*,
  During his absence left in heauy care,
  Through daily mourning, and nightly misfare:
  Yet did that auncient matrone all she might,
  To cherish her with all things choice and rare;
  And her owne handmayd, that *Melissa* hight,
Appointed to attend her dewly day and night.

15

Who in a morning, when this Mayden faire
  Was dighting her, hauing her snowy brest
  As yet not laced, nor her golden haire
  Into their comely tresses dewly drest,
  Chaunst to espy vpon her yuory chest
  The rosie marke, which she remembred well
  That litle Infant had, which forth she kest,
  The daughter of her Lady *Claribell*,
The which she bore, the whiles in prison she did dwell.

16

Which well auizing, streight she gan to cast
  In her conceiptfull mynd, that this faire Mayd
  Was that same infant, which so long sith past
  She in the open fields had loosely layd

To fortunes spoile, vnable it to ayd.
  So full of ioy, streight forth she ran in hast
  Vnto her mistresse, being halfe dismayd,
  To tell her, how the heauens had her graste,
To saue her chylde, which in misfortunes mouth was plaste.

17

The sober mother seeing such her mood,
  Yet knowing not, what meant that sodaine thro,
  Askt her, how mote her words be vnderstood,
  And what the matter was, that mou'd her so.
  My liefe (sayd she) ye know, that long ygo,
  Whilest ye in durance dwelt, ye to me gaue
  A little mayde, the which ye chylded tho;
  The same againe if now ye list to haue,
The same is yonder Lady, whom high God did saue.

18

Much was the Lady troubled at that speach,
  And gan to question streight how she it knew.
  Most certaine markes, (sayd she) do me it teach,
  For on her brest I with these eyes did vew
  The litle purple rose, which thereon grew,
  Whereof her name ye then to her did giue.
  Besides her countenaunce, and her likely hew,
  Matched with equall yeares, do surely prieue
That yond same is your daughter sure, which yet doth liue.

19

The matrone stayd no lenger to enquire,
  But forth in hast ran to the straunger Mayd;
  Whom catching greedily for great desire,
  Rent vp her brest, and bosome open layd,
  In which that rose she plainely saw displayd.
  Then her embracing twixt her armes twaine,
  She long so held, and softly weeping sayd;
  And liuest thou my daughter now againe?
And art thou yet aliue, whom dead I long did faine?

Stanza 13
4 whylest: indicates that he intends to return for her.

Stanza 14
4 care: grief. **5 misfare**: misfortune (in having gone astray).
8 Melissa: Gk 'honey-bee'. The name associates her with
Meliboe to whom she delivered Pastorella; see ix 16.1*n*. Also,
it suggests her attraction to the 'purple rose' (18.5), which is
Pastorella's birthmark. It is the name of the nurse and goddess
of childbirth: 'a woman, who with hir sister *Amalthea*
nouryshed Jupiter' (T. Cooper 1565). Appropriately, then, she
assists in Pastorella's rebirth.

Stanza 15
2 dighting: dressing.

Stanza 16
1 auizing: observing. **2 conceiptfull**: perceptive. **9 in misfortunes mouth**: an unusual personification of fortune but
consonant with the Blatant Beast's devouring mouth.

Stanza 17
2 thro: throe, anguish or agony of emotion. The sense, 'pain
of childbirth', is relevant since Pastorella is 'born' again.
7 chylded: gave birth to. **tho**: then.

Stanza 18
6 The **name** is a variant of 'Rose', as 15.5–6 indicates. It may
well be Rosalind, as Cheney 1997/98:157 claims; see x 16.4*n*.
It is withheld in accord with pastoral convention, as Rosalinde
in *SC* is 'a feigned name' (E.K. on *Jan.* 60), though 'who
knowes not Rosalend?' (*SC Aug.* 141). The identifying birthmark on the breast of an abandoned royal infant is a romance
motif. **7 likely hew**: similar appearance. **8** I.e. their ages
correspond.

Stanza 19
8–9 Invoking Luke 15.24: 'For this my sonne was dead, and is
aliue againe'; noted Shaheen 1976:168. **faine**: imagine.

20

Tho further asking her of sundry things,
    And times comparing with their accidents,
    She found at last by very certaine signes,
    And speaking markes of passed monuments,
    That this young Mayd, whom chance to her presents
Is her owne daughter, her owne infant deare.
    Tho wondring long at those so straunge euents,
A thousand times she her embraced nere,
With many a ioyfull kisse, and many a melting teare.

21

Who euer is the mother of one chylde,
    Which hauing thought long dead, she fyndes aliue,
    Let her by proofe of that, which she hath fylde
    In her owne breast, this mothers ioy descriue:
    For other none such passion can contriue
In perfect forme, as this good Lady felt,
    When she so faire a daughter saw suruiue,
As *Pastorella* was, that nigh she swelt
For passing ioy, which did all into pitty melt.

22

Thence running forth vnto her loued Lord,
    She vnto him recounted, all that fell:
    Who ioyning ioy with her in one accord,
    Acknowledg'd for his owne faire *Pastorell*.
    There leaue we them in ioy, and let vs tell
Of *Calidore*, who seeking all this while
    That monstrous Beast by finall force to quell,
Through euery place, with restlesse paine and toile
Him follow'd, by the tract of his outragious spoile.

23

Through all estates he found that he had past,
    In which he many massacres had left,
    And to the Clergy now was come at last;
    In which such spoile, such hauocke, and such theft
He wrought, that thence all goodnesse he bereft,
    That endlesse were to tell. The Elfin Knight,
    Who now no place besides vnsought had left,
At length into a Monastere did light,
Where he him found despoyling all with maine and might.

24

Into their cloysters now he broken had,
    Through which the Monckes he chaced here and there,
    And them pursu'd into their dortours sad,
    And searched all their cels and secrets neare;
    In which what filth and ordure did appeare,
Were yrkesome to report; yet that foule Beast
    Nought sparing them, the more did tosse and teare,
And ransacke all their dennes from most to least,
Regarding nought religion, nor their holy heast.

25

From thence into the sacred Church he broke,
    And robd the Chancell, and the deskes downe threw,
    And Altars fouled, and blasphemy spoke,
    And th'Images for all their goodly hew,
    Did cast to ground, whilest none was them to rew;
So all confounded and disordered there.
    But seeing *Calidore*, away he flew,
Knowing his fatall hand by former feare;
But he him fast pursuing, soone approched neare.

Stanza 20

2 accidents: occurrences. **4 passed monuments**: commemorative records.

Stanza 21

3 fylde: felt; or the past tense of 'file': recorded. **4 descriue**: describe. **5 contriue**: come to understand; imagine. **6 perfect forme**: the perfect pattern or idea. **8 swelt**: swooned. **9 passing**: surpassing.

Stanza 22

7 quell: kill. **8 Through euery place**: as it is 'the questynge beeste' (see V xii 37.7*n*), i.e. the 'searching' beast pursued by Calidore 'through the world' (i 7.2), as described at ix 3.6–9. **9 tract**: track. **spoile**: plundering.

Stanzas 23–25

The defence by Irenius, in *View* 163, of 'the seemly form and comely order of the church' in answer to 'whatever some of our late too nice fools say' suggests a general reference here to the continuing desecration of the church by iconoclasts. Reformation iconoclasm in relation to S. is examined by Gilman 1986:61–83; King 1990:56–58, 108–09; and Kaske 1994:22–27. See also Moroney 1998:124–27. A particular reference here to the Puritans is indicated by Jonson's remark, recorded by Drummond: 'by ye Blating beast the Puritans were vnderstood' (1925–52:1.137). For Kirkrapine's compar-

able sacrilegious acts, see I iii 22.3*n*; and of Ate, see IV i 21.5. In so concluding the *1596* poem, S. would seem to have been influenced by the conclusion of Langland, *Piers Plowman*: Holichurch is besieged from without by Antichrist and betrayed from within by false prelates.

Stanza 23

1 Through all estates: through all sorts of people, specifically the three estates: knights, commons, and clergy. **8 Monastere**: the OF spelling of monastery associates the hideout with the monster. On the significance of the association, see Moroney 1998:125–26.

Stanza 24

3 dortours: dormitories. **sad**: referring to their orderly life (*OED* A 4). **4 secrets neare**: adjoining secret places. Or **neare**: closely (*OED* adv.² I 7). **6 yrkesome**: loathsome. 7 I.e. far from sparing them (because they were religious figures), he tossed and tore them all the more. Kaske 1994: 23 reads **yet . . . the more** to mean 'more than this sin would deserve'. **9 heast**: vow.

Stanza 25

2–3 Chancell: where the communion table is placed. **deskes**: stalls or choir-seats. **blasphemy**: as the many-headed dragon in Rev. 13.5 'spake . . . blasphemies'.

26

Him in a narrow place he ouertooke,
  And fierce assailing forst him turne againe:
  Sternely he turnd againe, when he him strooke
  With his sharpe steele, and ran at him amaine
  With open mouth, that seemed to containe
  A full good pecke within the vtmost brim,
  All set with yron teeth in raunges twaine,
  That terrifide his foes, and armed him,
Appearing like the mouth of *Orcus* griesly grim.

27

And therein were a thousand tongs empight,
  Of sundry kindes, and sundry quality,
  Some were of dogs, that barked day and night,
  And some of cats, that wrawling still did cry;
  And some of Beares, that groynd continually,
  And some of Tygres, that did seeme to gren,
  And snar at all, that euer passed by:
  But most of them were tongues of mortall men,
Which spake reprochfully, not caring where nor when.

28

And them amongst were mingled here and there,
  The tongues of Serpents with three forked stings,
  That spat out poyson and gore bloudy gere
  At all, that came within his rauenings,
  And spake licentious words, and hatefull things
  Of good and bad alike, of low and hie;
  Ne Kesars spared he a whit, nor Kings,
  But either blotted them with infamie,
Or bit them with his banefull teeth of iniury.

29

But *Calidore* thereof no whit afrayd,
  Rencountred him with so impetuous might,
  That th'outrage of his violence he stayd,
  And bet abacke, threatning in vaine to bite,

And spitting forth the poyson of his spight,
  That fomed all about his bloody iawes.
  Tho rearing vp his former feete on hight,
  He rampt vpon him with his rauenous pawes,
As if he would haue rent him with his cruell clawes.

30

But he right well aware, his rage to ward,
  Did cast his shield atweene, and therewithall
  Putting his puissaunce forth, pursu'd so hard,
  That backeward he enforced him to fall,
  And being downe, ere he new helpe could call,
  His shield he on him threw, and fast downe held,
  Like as a bullocke, that in bloudy stall
  Of butchers balefull hand to ground is feld,
Is forcibly kept downe, till he be throughly queld.

31

Full cruelly the Beast did rage and rore,
  To be downe held, and maystred so with might,
  That he gan fret and fome out bloudy gore,
  Striuing in vaine to rere him selfe vpright.
  For still the more he stroue, the more the Knight
  Did him suppresse, and forcibly subdew;
  That made him almost mad for fell despight.
  He grind, hee bit, he scratcht, he venim threw,
And fared like a feend, right horrible in hew.

32

Or like the hell-borne *Hydra*, which they faine
  That great *Alcides* whilome ouerthrew,
  After that he had labourd long in vaine,
  To crop his thousand heads, the which still new
  Forth budded, and in greater number grew.
  Such was the fury of this hellish Beast,
  Whilest *Calidore* him vnder him downe threw;
  Who nathemore his heauy load releast,
But aye the more he rag'd, the more his powre increast.

Stanza 26
3 **Sternely**: fiercely. **5** In the dedication to *Colin Clout*, S. seeks Raleigh's protection 'against the malice of evill mouthes, which are alwaies wide open to carpe at and misconstrue my simple meaning'. **7 raunges**: rows. **9 Orcus**: Pluto, god of hell: 'sometyme taken for hell' (T. Cooper 1565), as here. Earlier Calidore saved Pastorella from the Tiger with its mouth 'wide gaping like hell gate' (x 34.6), and from the brigand's 'hellish dens' (xi 3.1). The present battle marks his third and final victory over hell.

Stanza 27
1 **empight**: placed. **4 wrawling**: caterwauling. **still**: ceaselessly. **5 groynd**: growled. **6 gren**: show their teeth in anger. **7 snar**: snarl. **9 reprochfully**: abusively.

Stanza 28
3 **gere**: foul matter. **9 iniury**: offensive speech; insult; calumny.

Stanza 29
1 Calidore displays his invulnerability at iii 16.5–6. **2 Rencountred**: charged in return. **3 outrage**: fury. **7–9** The Beast assumes a heraldic posture, as suggested by **rampt**: reared up on his hind legs with his fore (**former**) feet on high (**on hight**).

Stanza 30
1 **aware**: wary.

Stanza 31
8 **grind**: either baring teeth in anger, as 27.6, or gnashing them as does Furor when he is bound at II iv 15.3. **9 fared**: acted.

Stanza 32
The **Hydra** that Hercules fought was also an offspring of Typhaon and Echidna (see vi 10–12), and was identified as Invidia or evil speaking which only death may slay; see Aptekar 1969:208–10. **1 hell-borne**: because she dwells in hell; see Virgil, *Aen.* 6.576–77. **8 nathemore**: nevermore. **release**: removed.

33

Tho when the Beast saw, he mote nought auaile,
   By force, he gan his hundred tongues apply,
   And sharpely at him to reuile and raile,
   With bitter termes of shamefull infamy;
   Oft interlacing many a forged lie,
   Whose like he neuer once did speake, nor heare,
   Nor euer thought thing so vnworthily:
Yet did he nought for all that him forbeare,
But strained him so streightly, that he chokt him neare.

34

At last when as he found his force to shrincke,
   And rage to quaile, he tooke a muzzell strong
   Of surest yron, made with many a lincke;
   Therewith he mured vp his mouth along,
   And therein shut vp his blasphemous tong,
   For neuer more defaming gentle Knight,
   Or vnto louely Lady doing wrong:
   And thereunto a great long chaine he tight,
With which he drew him forth, euen in his own despight.

35

Like as whylome that strong *Tirynthian* swaine,
   Brought forth with him the dreadfull dog of hell,
   Against his will fast bound in yron chaine,
   And roring horribly, did him compell
   To see the hatefull sunne, that he might tell
   To griesly *Pluto*, what on earth was donne,
   And to the other damned ghosts, which dwell
   For aye in darkenesse, which day light doth shonne.
So led this Knight his captyue with like conquest wonne.

36

Yet greatly did the Beast repine at those
   Straunge bands, whose like till then he neuer bore,
   Ne euer any durst till then impose,
   And chauffed inly, seeing now no more

Him liberty was left aloud to rore:
   Yet durst he not draw backe; nor once withstand
   The proued powre of noble *Calidore*,
   But trembled vnderneath his mighty hand,
And like a fearefull dog him followed through the land.

37

Him through all Faery land he follow'd so,
   As if he learned had obedience long,
   That all the people where so he did go,
   Out of their townes did round about him throng,
   To see him leade that Beast in bondage strong,
   And seeing it, much wondred at the sight;
   And all such persons, as he earst did wrong,
   Reioyced much to see his captiue plight,
And much admyr'd the Beast, but more admyr'd the Knight.

38

Thus was this Monster by the maystring might
   Of doughty *Calidore*, supprest and tamed,
   That neuer more he mote endammadge wight
   With his vile tongue, which many had defamed,
   And many causelesse caused to be blamed:
   So did he eeke long after this remaine,
   Vntill that, whether wicked fate so framed,
   Or fault of men, he broke his yron chaine,
And got into the world at liberty againe.

39

Thenceforth more mischiefe and more scath he wrought
   To mortall men, then he had done before;
   Ne euer could by any more be brought
   Into like bands, ne maystred any more:
   Albe that long time after *Calidore*,
   The good Sir *Pelleas* him tooke in hand,
   And after him Sir *Lamoracke* of yore,
   And all his brethren borne in Britaine land;
Yet none of them could euer bring him into band.

Stanza 33
1 **auaile**: prevail. 8 **forbeare**: spare. 9 **strained**: pressed down. **streightly**: tightly.

Stanza 34
1 **shrincke**: collapse, fail. 2 **quaile**: lessen, fail. 4 **mured**: walled up. **along**: i.e. along its whole length. 6 I.e. to prevent him from evermore . . . 8 **tight**: tied. 9 . . . in spite of his defiance; or, even though he was outraged.

Stanza 35
The **dog of hell** is Cerberus that sired the Blatant Beast (i 8.1–3) and was chained and dragged from hell by Hercules, who is called the **Tirynthian swaine** because he performed his twelve labours while living in Tiryns. See Ovid, *Met.* 7.408–15. As the most difficult of his labours, which was interpreted as a victory over death, it is fittingly compared to the last labour of S.'s knight. 4–8 In *Vita Herculis*, Giraldi compares the conquest to the purification of infection by the sun, and hidden truth brought to light, as Nohrnberg 1976:696 notes. S. adds details drawn from Plato's myth of the cave, *Republic* 514–18, as Borris 1985:364 notes. 9 **like conquest**: because Hercules

chained Cerberus without using arms even as Calidore subdues the Blatant Beast using only his shield and an iron muzzle. *Invidia* was Hercules's last opponent, and the only one he did not destroy; see Dunseath 1968:232. That labour is left to Calidore.

Stanza 37
9 **admyr'd**: wondered at. A fitting response to Calidore's royal progress.

Stanza 38
3 **endammadge**: injure. 7–9 As Archimago escapes at the end of Bk I; see I xii 36.1–5n.

Stanza 39
1–2 The Geneva gloss to Rev. 20.3 notes that 'Satan had greater power then he had before'; noted Borris 1987:135. **scath**: harm. 3 **by any more**: i.e. again. 6–9 In Malory 9.12, **Lamoracke** meets Palomydes alone pursuing 'the questynge beest'. **Pelleas**, another knight of Arthur's Round Table, lacks even this connection.

40

So now he raungeth through the world againe,
    And rageth sore in each degree and state;
    Ne any is, that may him now restraine,
    He growen is so great and strong of late,
    Barking and biting all that him doe bate,
    Albe they worthy blame, or cleare of crime:
    Ne spareth he most learned wits to rate,
    Ne spareth he the gentle Poets rime,
But rends without regard of person or of time.

41

Ne may this homely verse, of many meanest,
    Hope to escape his venemous despite,
    More then my former writs, all were they clearest
    From blamefull blot, and free from all that wite,
    With which some wicked tongues did it backebite,
    And bring into a mighty Peres displeasure,
    That neuer so deserued to endite.
    Therfore do you my rimes keep better measure,
And seeke to please, that now is counted wisemens threasure.

FINIS.

Stanza 40
2 in each degree: against every social class. **state**: i.e. the 'estates' (23.1). **5 bate**: attack; beat back. **6 Albe**: whether. 7–9 The action of Enuie at I iv 32.6–8. **most**: modifies **learned**, but may suggest 'almost all', and also imply that the **wits** are least spared, as Kaplan 1997:59 suggests.

Stanza 41
The three added books of the *1596* edition end as they began, with S. lamenting the blame his writings have incurred. He always feared that envy would destroy his verse, right from the opening of the *SC* in which he appeals to Sidney to protect him from the barking of envy. See D. Cheney 1986:271. The **mighty Pere** is generally taken to be Lord Burghley; see IV proem i.1–2*n*. **3 clearest**: 'cleanest', sugg. Hughes 1715, for the rhyme and the meaning. **7** I.e. my former writings never deserved so to be charged. S. may refer to *Mother Hubberd*: in March 1591, it was 'by Superior awthoritie called in'; see Peterson 1998:7. **9** In the *LR* 24–25, S. anticipated that his 'darke conceit' would not satisfy 'the vse of these dayes, seeing all things accounted by their showes, and nothing esteemed of, that is not delightfull and pleasing to commune sence'. Hence **seeke to please**: i.e. seek only to please his readers rather than educate them, and to please them only superficially rather than having them share – as they have been invited to do throughout the poem – his state of being 'nigh rauisht with rare thoughts delight' (VI proem 1.6). Or, seek only to please myself, reverting to his role in *SC June* 72: in not daring to aspire to the heroic, he is resigned, Narcissus-like, to 'play to please my selfe'. As this ending to Bk VI challenges Sidney's literary theory, see Philmus 1995. The final line seems to be S.'s resigned acceptance of what even the wise must value in a world infected by the Blatant Beast, leading him to abandon his task as a poet. Or he may be planning to renew it more aggressively. On conflicting readings of the line, see, e.g. Neuse 1968:368 and Belt 1991:128; and on the implications of **threasure**, see D.L. Miller 1996:170–71.

TWO CANTOS
OF
MVTABILITIE:

VVhich, both for Forme and Matter, appeare
to be parcell of some following Booke of the
FAERIE QVEENE,
(·.·)

VNDER THE LEGEND
OF
Constancie.

Neuer before imprinted.

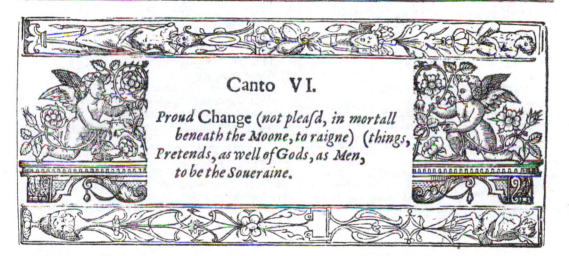

Canto VI.

Proud Change *(not pleas'd, in mortall*
beneath the Moone, to raigne) (things,
Pretends, as well of Gods, as Men,
to be the Soueraine.

1

VVHat man that sees the euer-whirling wheele
Of *Change*, the which all mortall things doth sway,
But that therby doth find, and plainly feele,
How *MVTABILITY* in them doth play

Her cruell sports, to many mens decay?
Which that to all may better yet appeare,
I will rehearse that whylome I heard say,
How she at first her selfe began to reare,
Gainst all the Gods, and th'empire sought from them to beare.

Book VII Canto vi

Argument
1 Change: i.e. Mutabilitie. **2 beneath the Moone**: the
appearance of a new star in Nov. 1572 – see I iii 16.1–3*n* –
challenged the traditional Renaissance cosmology that only the

sublunary realm was subject to change. See Meyer
1984:118–19. **3 Pretends**: claims.

Stanza 1
1–2 Mutabilitie's **wheele** is usually fortune's, as at V x 20.7–8.
See 'Fortune' and 'mutability' in the *SEnc*. **sway**: rule. **5**
decay: downfall. **7 rehearse**: relate.

2

But first, here falleth fittest to vnfold
   Her antique race and linage ancient,
   As I haue found it registred of old,
   In *Faery* Land mongst records permanent:
   She was, to weet, a daughter by descent
   Of those old *Titans*, that did whylome striue
   With *Saturnes* sonne for heauens regiment.
   Whom, though high *Ioue* of kingdome did depriue,
Yet many of their stemme long after did surviue.

3

And many of them, afterwards obtain'd
   Great power of *Ioue*, and high authority;
   As *Hecaté*, in whose almighty hand,
   He plac't all rule and principality,
   To be by her disposed diuersly,
   To Gods, and men, as she them list diuide:
   And drad *Bellona*, that doth sound on hie
   Warres and allarums vnto Nations wide,
That makes both heauen and earth to tremble at her pride.

4

So likewise did this *Titanesse* aspire,
   Rule and dominion to her selfe to gaine;
   That as a Goddesse, men might her admire,
   And heauenly honours yield, as to them twaine.
   And first, on earth she sought it to obtaine;
   Where she such proofe and sad examples shewed
   Of her great power, to many ones great paine,
   That not men onely (whom she soone subdewed)
But eke all other creatures, her bad dooings rewed.

5

For, she the face of earthly things so changed,
   That all which Nature had establisht first
   In good estate, and in meet order ranged,
   She did pervert, and all their statutes burst:

And all the worlds faire frame (which none yet durst
   Of Gods or men to alter or misguide)
   She alter'd quite, and made them all accurst
   That God had blest; and did at first prouide
In that still happy state for euer to abide.

6

Ne shee the lawes of Nature onely brake,
   But eke of Iustice, and of Policie;
   And wrong of right, and bad of good did make,
   And death for life exchanged foolishlie:
   Since which, all liuing wights haue learn'd to die,
   And all this world is woxen daily worse.
   O pittious worke of *MVTABILITIE!*
   By which, we all are subiect to that curse,
And death in stead of life haue sucked from our Nurse.

7

And now, when all the earth she thus had brought
   To her behest, and thralled to her might,
   She gan to cast in her ambitious thought,
   T'attempt th'empire of the heauens hight,
   And *Ioue* himselfe to shoulder from his right.
   And first, she past the region of the ayre,
   And of the fire, whose substance thin and slight,
   Made no resistance, ne could her contraire,
But ready passage to her pleasure did prepaire.

8

Thence, to the Circle of the Moone she clambe,
   Where *Cynthia* raignes in euerlasting glory,
   To whose bright shining palace straight she came,
   All fairely deckt with heauens goodly story;
   Whose siluer gates (by which there sate an hory
   Old aged Sire, with hower-glasse in hand,
   Hight *Tyme*) she entred, were he liefe or sory:
   Ne staide till she the highest stage had scand,
Where *Cynthia* did sit, that neuer still did stand.

Stanza 2
4 records permanent: i.e. the 'antique rolles' (I proem 2.4) which are not subject to mutability. **5–9** On the war between the **Titans** and **Ioue**, who is **Saturnes sonne**, see III vii 47.3–5*n*. **regiment**: rule; kingdom. **stemme**: stock.

Stanza 3
3 Hecaté: an infernal deity; see I i 43.3*n*. **7–9 Bellona**: the Roman goddess of war; see III ix 22.1*n*. For her powers, see 32.4–8 below. S. calls her one of the Titans because he assumes, in *Bellay* 200, that she was du Bellay's 'la sœur du grand Typhée'; noted Lotspeich 1932.

Stanza 4
1 Titanesse: coined by S. from the Gk Τιτανίς. **3 admire**: wonder at. **4 twaine**: i.e. Hecaté and Bellona.

Stanza 5
3 estate: state. **4 pervert**: overturn. **statutes**: decrees. **5 frame**: applied to the heavens, earth, and universe regarded as structures fashioned by God (*OED* 7). **9 still**: ever, continually.

Stanza 6
2 Policie: government; the art of prudent statecraft. **5** Change is usually seen to be a consequence of the 'fall' (11.5) of Adam and Eve but here becomes its cause; see Weatherby 1994:155–56. **6** As V proem 1.7–9. **9 our Nurse**: i.e. Nature (5.2), 'nurse of every living thing' (*Daph* 337).

Stanza 7
3 cast: resolve. **4–5** She imitates the Titans who sought 'To scale the skyes, and put *Ioue* from his right' (III vii 47.5). **attempt**: attack, assault. **6–7** In the hierarchical order of the four elements above the earth (omitting water), **ayre** is the middle region; the region of **fire** is next under the moon; and beyond is 'the purest sky' (23.7) of the empyrean which mortals may not enter. See *HL* 78–91. **8 contraire**: oppose.

Stanzas 8–10
Details of the 'bright shining palace' with its 'siluer gates' and of the enthroned deity surrounded by attendants are taken from Ovid's story, in *Met.* 2.1–328, of Phaethon's similarly proud ascent into the heavens; noted Cumming 1931:243–45. **glory** at 8.2 and 10.6 is a code word, like the name Gloriana, to refer to Elizabeth, as Christian 1993:210 notes.

9

Her sitting on an Iuory throne shee found,
    Drawne of two steeds, th'one black, the other white,
    Environd with tenne thousand starres around,
    That duly her attended day and night;
    And by her side, there ran her Page, that hight
    Vesper, whom we the Euening-starre intend:
    That with his Torche, still twinkling like twylight,
    Her lightened all the way where she should wend,
And ioy to weary wandring trauailers did lend:

10

That when the hardy *Titanesse* beheld
    The goodly building of her Palace bright,
    Made of the heauens substance, and vp-held
    With thousand Crystall pillors of huge hight,
    Shee gan to burne in her ambitious spright,
    And t'envie her that in such glorie raigned.
    Eftsoones she cast by force and tortious might,
    Her to displace, and to her selfe to haue gained
The kingdome of the Night, and waters by her wained.

11

Boldly she bid the Goddesse downe descend,
    And let her selfe into that Ivory throne;
    For, shee her selfe more worthy thereof wend,
    And better able it to guide alone:

Whether to men, whose fall she did bemone,
    Or vnto Gods, whose state she did maligne,
    Or to th'infernall Powers, her need giue lone
    Of her faire light, and bounty most benigne,
Her selfe of all that rule shee deemed most condigne.

12

But shee that had to her that soueraigne seat
    By highest *Ioue* assign'd, therein to beare
    Nights burning lamp, regarded not her threat,
    Ne yielded ought for fauour or for feare;
    But with sterne countenaunce and disdainfull cheare,
    Bending her horned browes, did put her back:
    And boldly blaming her for comming there,
    Bade her attonce from heauens coast to pack,
Or at her perill bide the wrathfull Thunders wrack.

13

Yet nathemore the *Giantesse* forbare:
    But boldly preacing-on, raught forth her hand
    To pluck her downe perforce from off her chaire;
    And there-with lifting vp her golden wand,
    Threatned to strike her if she did with-stand.
    Where-at the starres, which round about her blazed,
    And eke the Moones bright wagon, still did stand,
    All beeing with so bold attempt amazed,
And on her vncouth habit and sterne looke still gazed.

Stanza 8
1 Circle: sphere. **4 story**: 'any work of pictorial or sculptural art containing figures' (*OED* sb.[1] 8); referring here to the constellations. **5–7 Tyme** belongs here because the moon marks the boundary between the temporal and eternal worlds. **liefe or sory**: willing or unwilling. **8 stage**: celestial station or 'seat' (12.1). **scand**: climbed. **9** Referring to the moon's continual waxing and waning: **sit** as she is always enthroned in authority, and yet she **neuer still did stand** or remain; i.e. she is ever-moving.

Stanza 9
2 The black and white steeds refer to the two phases of the moon, as in Boccaccio 1976:4.16; and to an emblem of the moon itself, as in Conti 1616:3.17. Since Elizabeth was commonly praised as Diana or Cynthia, **black** and **white** allude to her personal colours; see I i 4*n*. **6 Vesper**: or Hesperus, the evening star, as at III iv 51.6–9. **intend**: call.

Stanza 10
7–9 tortious: wrongful, illegal. The phrase is linked to the common legal formula, *vi et armis*, for trespass to a person and territory; noted Parkin-Speer 1992:500. **to her selfe**: in contrast to sharing her power at 4.4. Her ambition extends to all kingdoms by 18.9. **kingdome of the Night**: 'The moone and the starres . . . gouerne the night' (Ps. 136.9). **wained**:

drawn (sugg. Zitner 1968), possibly alluding to the moon's wain or chariot and referring to the moon's control over the tides; or 'diminished', alluding to the moon's waning.

Stanza 11
3 wend: weened, i.e. thought. **5–8** Referring to the three aspects of the moon: Diana on earth, Luna in heaven, and Hecate in hell. **maligne**: envy; regard with malice. **lone | Of her faire light**: when not visible in the sky, the moon was thought to shine in hell. **9 condigne**: worthy.

Stanza 12
5 cheare: aspect. **6 horned browes**: interpreting the horned moon as bending her brows in anger. As an iconographical detail of Isis as the moon, see V vii 4.5–7. **8 heauens coast**: as the moon marks heaven's boundary. **9 Thunders wrack**: the destruction or vengeance of Jupiter Tonans.

Stanza 13
2 raught: reached. **3 perforce**: forcibly. **chaire**: the symbol of power. **4** At V vii 7.5, the white wand is a symbol of royal power. It may be **golden** here to indicate that Mutabilitie's power derives from Mammon; cf. Philotime's golden chain of ambition at II vii 46.2. **7 still did stand**: cf. 8.9, and Josh. 10.13: 'and the moone stode stil'.

14

Meane-while, the lower World, which nothing knew
  Of all that chaunced here, was darkned quite;
  And eke the heauens, and all the heauenly crew
  Of happy wights, now vnpurvaide of light,
  Were much afraid, and wondred at that sight;
  Fearing least *Chaos* broken had his chaine,
  And brought againe on them eternall night:
  But chiefely *Mercury*, that next doth raigne,
Ran forth in haste, vnto the king of Gods to plaine.

15

All ran together with a great out-cry,
  To *Ioues* faire Palace, fixt in heauens hight;
  And beating at his gates full earnestly,
  Gan call to him aloud with all their might,
  To know what meant that suddaine lack of light.
  The father of the Gods when this he heard,
  Was troubled much at their so strange affright,
  Doubting least *Typhon* were againe vprear'd,
Or other his old foes, that once him sorely fear'd.

16

Eftsoones the sonne of *Maia* forth he sent
  Downe to the Circle of the Moone, to knowe
  The cause of this so strange astonishment,
  And why shee did her wonted course forslowe;
  And if that any were on earth belowe
  That did with charmes or Magick her molest,
  Him to attache, and downe to hell to throwe:
  But, if from heauen it were, then to arrest
The Author, and him bring before his presence prest.

17

The wingd-foot God, so fast his plumes did beat,
  That soone he came where-as the *Titanesse*
  Was striuing with faire *Cynthia* for her seat:
  At whose strange sight, and haughty hardinesse,
  He wondred much, and feared her no lesse.

Yet laying feare aside to doe his charge,
  At last, he bade her (with bold stedfastnesse)
  Ceasse to molest the Moone to walke at large,
Or come before high *Ioue*, her dooings to discharge.

18

And there-with-all, he on her shoulder laid
  His snaky-wreathed Mace, whose awfull power
  Doth make both Gods and hellish fiends affraid:
  Where-at the *Titanesse* did sternely lower,
  And stoutly answer'd, that in euill hower
  He from his *Ioue* such message to her brought,
  To bid her leaue faire *Cynthias* siluer bower;
  Sith shee his *Ioue* and him esteemed nought,
No more then *Cynthia's* selfe; but all their kingdoms
                      (sought.

19

The Heauens Herald staid not to reply,
  But past away, his doings to relate
  Vnto his Lord; who now in th'highest sky,
  Was placed in his principall Estate,
  With all the Gods about him congregate:
  To whom when *Hermes* had his message told,
  It did them all exceedingly amate,
  Saue *Ioue*; who, changing nought his count'nance bold,
Did vnto them at length these speeches wise vnfold;

20

Harken to mee awhile yee heauenly Powers;
  Ye may remember since th'Earths cursed seed
  Sought to assaile the heauens eternall towers,
  And to vs all exceeding feare did breed:
  But how we then defeated all their deed,
  Yee all doe knowe, and them destroied quite;
  Yet not so quite, but that there did succeed
  An off-spring of their bloud, which did alite
Vpon the fruitfull earth, which doth vs yet despite.

Stanza 14
1–5 Alluding to the lunar eclipse of 14 April 1595, according to Meyer 1984:125, who suggests that the 100 minutes of the total eclipse corresponds to the 100 lines from 12.6 to 23.6. **vnpurvaide**: unprovided.   6–7 As Mutabilitie is 'great *Chaos* child' (26.6), and Chaos is associated with 'hatefull darknes' (III vi 36.7). **chaine**: the 'inuiolable bands' by which the 'Almightie maker' binds the elements (IV x 35.3–4). 8–9 **Mercury** or '*Hermes*' (19.6), the messenger of the gods, is identified with the planet of that name, which is **next** because its sphere is next beyond the moon's in the Ptolemaic system. On S.'s use of the classical motif of the celestial messenger's descent from heaven, see Greene 1963:314–27. **plaine**: complain.

Stanza 15
1–2 **All ran together**: referring to the near conjunction of Mars and Venus with Jove in his **faire Palace** (the zodiacal sign of Pisces) during the 1594 eclipse, as Meyer 1984:124 notes. 8–9 **Doubting**: fearing. **Typhon**, or Typhœus; see VI vi 10–12*n*. **fear'd**: frightened, made afraid; or feared him, as 20.4.

Stanza 16
1 **the sonne of Maia**: Mercury.   4 **forslowe**: delay.   6 Cf. I vii 34.8–9.   7 **attache**: seize.   9 **prest**: promptly.

Stanza 17
4 **hardinesse**: boldness; effrontery.   8 . . . from moving abroad.   9 **discharge**: clear from the charge; justify.

Stanza 18
2–3 **snaky-wreathed Mace**: on Mercury's caduceus and its powers, see II xii 41.1–3*n* and IV iii 42.1–7*n*.

Stanza 19
4 **Estate**: his position of state in the assembly or senate of the gods, cf. 'his soueraine throne' (24.7).   7 **amate**: confound.

Stanza 20
The story is told in Ovid, *Met.* 1.151–62.   2 **since**: the time when. **th'Earths cursed seed**: the giants, whose assault on the Olympians is linked with that of the Titans; see 2.5–9. 9 **which** may refer to the earth, though Ovid refers to the new race of giants as *contemptrix superum*.

21

Of that bad seed is this bold woman bred,
  That now with bold presumption doth aspire
  To thrust faire *Phœbe* from her siluer bed,
  And eke our selues from heauens high Empire,
  If that her might were match to her desire:
  Wherefore, it now behoues vs to advise
  What way is best to driue her to retire;
  Whether by open force, or counsell wise,
Areed ye sonnes of God, as best ye can deuise.

22

So hauing said, he ceast; and with his brow
  (His black eye-brow, whose doomefull dreaded beck
  Is wont to wield the world vnto his vow,
  And euen the highest Powers of heauen to check)
  Made signe to them in their degrees to speake:
  Who straight gan cast their counsell graue and wise.
  Meane-while, th'Earths daughter, thogh she nought
  Of *Hermes* message; yet gan now advise,   (did reck
What course were best to take in this hot bold emprize.

23

Eftsoones she thus resolv'd; that whil'st the Gods
  (After returne of *Hermes* Embassie)
  Were troubled, and amongst themselues at ods,
  Before they could new counsels re-allie,
  To set vpon them in that extasie;
  And take what fortune time and place would lend:
  So, forth she rose, and through the purest sky
  To *Ioues* high Palace straight cast to ascend,
To prosecute her plot: Good on-set boads good end.

24

Shee there arriuing, boldly in did pass;
  Where all the Gods she found in counsell close,
  All quite vnarm'd, as then their manner was.
  At sight of her they suddaine all arose,

In great amaze, ne wist what way to chose.
  But *Ioue*, all fearelesse, forc't them to aby;
  And in his soueraine throne, gan straight dispose
  Himselfe more full of grace and Maiestie,
That mote encheare his friends, and foes mote terrifie.

25

That, when the haughty *Titanesse* beheld,
  All were she fraught with pride and impudence,
  Yet with the sight thereof was almost queld;
  And inly quaking, seem'd as reft of sense,
  And voyd of speech in that drad audience;
  Vntill that *Ioue* himselfe, her selfe bespake:
  Speake thou fraile woman, speake with confidence,
  Whence art thou, and what doost thou here now make?
What idle errand hast thou, earths mansion to forsake?

26

Shee, halfe confused with his great commaund,
  Yet gathering spirit of her natures pride,
  Him boldly answer'd thus to his demaund:
  I am a daughter, by the mothers side,
  Of her that is Grand-mother magnifide
  Of all the Gods, great *Earth*, great *Chaos* child:
  But by the fathers (be it not envide)
  I greater am in bloud (whereon I build)
Then all the Gods, though wrongfully from heauen exil'd.

27

For, *Titan* (as ye all acknowledge must)
  Was *Saturnes* elder brother by birth-right;
  Both, sonnes of *Vranus:* but by vniust
  And guilefull meanes, through *Corybantes* slight,
  The younger thrust the elder from his right:
  Since which, thou *Ioue*, iniuriously hast held
  The Heauens rule from *Titans* sonnes by might;
  And them to hellish dungeons downe hast feld:
Witnesse ye Heauens the truth of all that I haue teld.

Stanza 21
3 **Phœbe**: the moon as the sister of Phœbus Apollo.
6 **advise**: consider. 9 **Areed**: declare.

Stanza 22
2–4 A traditional description of Jove; e.g. his 'blacklidded eye' in *Mother Hubberd* 1228, derives from Homer, *Iliad* 1.528. **beck**: nod of command. **wield**: direct, sway. **vow**: desire. 6 **cast**: deliver. 9 **emprize**: enterprise.

Stanza 23
4 **re-allie**: rally, form again. 5 **extasie**: confused state of astonishment. Mutabilitie's ambition to replace them adds its etymological sense, 'withdrawn from their proper place'. 7–8 **purest sky**: the empyrean, beyond the *primum mobile*. She takes the path of Juno at I iv 17.7, and of Cybele at IV xi 28.3. 9 Proverbial: Smith 51.

Stanza 24
5 **amaze**: bewilderment; panic. 6 **aby**: remain.

Stanza 25
5 **audience**: with the legal sense, judicial hearing to consider her claims. 7 **fraile**: a frequent epithet throughout the poem for

the mortal state, but only here addressed specifically to a female character. It may extend to all women, as in Hamlet's complaint, 'Frailty, thy name is woman'. As an expression of Elizabethan misogyny, see Berleth 1995:37–38. 8 **make**: intend; want.

Stanza 26
5–6 **Earth** is called the mother of the gods by Boccaccio 1976:1.8, as Lotspeich 1932 notes. As the offspring of **Chaos**, see III vi 36.3–9*n*. **magnifide**: extolled. 7 **envide**: begrudged.

Stanza 27
This less familiar account of how Saturn gained Titan's throne is found in Conti 1616:6.20, as Lotspeich 1932 notes. **Titan** was persuaded to abdicate his throne by his younger brother, **Saturn**, who promised to devour his own male children so that, lacking any descendants, Titan and his issue would succeed him. The infant **Ioue** escaped by the **slight** or cunning device of the **Corybantes** who beat their shields to drown his birth-cries, tricking Saturn into devouring instead a stone wrapped in swaddling-clothes. In the more familiar account, Saturn devoured his children because of the prophecy that one of them would displace him. See 'Jove' in the *SEnc*. 6 **iniuriously**: wrongfully.

28

Whil'st she thus spake, the Gods that gaue good eare
 To her bold words, and marked well her grace,
 Beeing of stature tall as any there
 Of all the Gods, and beautifull of face,
 As any of the Goddesses in place,
 Stood all astonied, like a sort of Steeres;
 Mongst whom, some beast of strange and forraine race,
 Vnwares is chaunc't, far straying from his peeres:
So did their ghastly gaze bewray their hidden feares.

29

Till hauing pauz'd awhile, *Ioue* thus bespake;
 Will neuer mortall thoughts ceasse to aspire,
 In this bold sort, to Heauen claime to make,
 And touch celestiall seates with earthly mire?
 I would haue thought, that bold *Procrustes* hire,
 Or *Typhons* fall, or proud *Ixions* paine,
 Or great *Prometheus*, tasting of our ire,
 Would haue suffiz'd, the rest for to restraine;
And warn'd all men by their example to refraine:

30

But now, this off-scum of that cursed fry,
 Dare to renew the like bold enterprize,
 And chalenge th'heritage of this our skie;
 Whom what should hinder, but that we likewise
 Should handle as the rest of her allies,
 And thunder-driue to hell? With that, he shooke
 His Nectar-deawed locks, with which the skyes
 And all the world beneath for terror quooke,
And eft his burning levin-brond in hand he tooke.

31

But, when he looked on her louely face,
 In which, faire beames of beauty did appeare,
 That could the greatest wrath soone turne to grace
 (Such sway doth beauty euen in Heauen beare)
 He staide his hand: and hauing chang'd his cheare,
 He thus againe in milder wise began;
 But ah! if Gods should striue with flesh yfere,
 Then shortly should the progeny of Man
Be rooted out, if *Ioue* should doe still what he can:

32

But thee faire *Titans* child, I rather weene,
 Through some vaine errour or inducement light,
 To see that mortall eyes haue neuer seene;
 Or through ensample of thy sisters might,
 Bellona; whose great glory thou doost spight,
 Since thou hast seene her dreadfull power belowe,
 Mongst wretched men (dismaide with her affright)
 To bandie Crownes, and Kingdomes to bestowe:
And sure thy worth, no lesse then hers doth seem to showe.

33

But wote thou this, thou hardy *Titanesse*,
 That not the worth of any liuing wight
 May challenge ought in Heauens interesse;
 Much lesse the Title of old *Titans* Right:
 For, we by Conquest of our soueraine might,
 And by eternall doome of Fates decree,
 Haue wonne the Empire of the Heauens bright;
 Which to our selues we hold, and to whom wee
Shall worthy deeme partakers of our blisse to bee.

Stanza 28
5 in place: present.   **6–9** An astonishing simile even though applied to pagan gods.   **Steeres** implies their impotence, as at IV vi 37.4–5.   **sort**: herd.

Stanza 29
5–9 Jove names those whom he punished for rebellion against his rule: for **Typhon**, see 15.8–9; for **Ixion**, see I v 35.1–2; for **Prometheus**, see II x 70.5–9. He adds **Procrustes** whom Theseus punished by treating him as he treated his victims, which was to fit them to a bed by stretching or lopping off their limbs. This action and the epithet, **bold**, are provoked by Mutabilitie's boldness in seeking 'To thrust faire *Phœbe* from her siluer bed' (21.3).   **mortall** and **earthly** remind Mutabilitie of her maternal ancestry.   **hire**: reward, i.e. punishment.

Stanza 30
1 Mutabilitie is the **off-scum** or dross; **fry**, the brood of Titans.   **3 challenge**: lay claim to.   **6–9** S. invokes the opening episode of the major classical poem on mutability, Ovid's *Metamorphoses* 151–81: angered by the attempt of the giants to invade heaven, Jove consults with the other gods. His angry shaking of his locks moves the land, sea, and sky, and he threatens to destroy the human race with a bolt of lightning (**levin-brond**).   **eft**: afterwards.

Stanza 31
7–9 Cf. Gen. 6.3: 'The Lord said, My Spirit shal not alway striue with man, because he is but flesh'.   **with flesh yfere**: i.e. against flesh.

Stanza 32
5 Bellona: see 3.7–9n.   **spight**: feel annoyed at; envy.
7 with her affright: through fear of her.

Stanza 33
3 May claim any legal right or title to heaven.   **5–9** The doctrine that 'all is the conqueror's' is invoked by Irenius in *View* 9 to justify England's right to rule Ireland, and here by Jove to answer Mutabilitie's charge at 27.6–7 that he inherited his kingdom wrongfully. Jove adds that he inherited it also by **Fates decree**, referring to the prophecy – see 27*n* – that Saturn would be deposed by one of his sons, namely, himself.

34

Then ceasse thy idle claime thou foolish gerle,
    And seeke by grace and goodnesse to obtaine
    That place from which by folly *Titan* fell;
    There-to thou maist perhaps, if so thou faine
    Haue *Ioue* thy gratious Lord and Soueraigne.
    So, hauing said, she thus to him replide;
    Ceasse *Saturnes* sonne, to seeke by proffers vaine
    Of idle hopes t'allure mee to thy side,
For to betray my Right, before I haue it tride.

35

But thee, ô *Ioue*, no equall Iudge I deeme
    Of my desert, or of my dewfull Right;
    That in thine owne behalfe maist partiall seeme:
    But to the highest him, that is behight
    Father of Gods and men by equall might;
    To weet, the God of Nature, I appeale.
    There-at *Ioue* wexed wroth, and in his spright
    Did inly grudge, yet did it well conceale;
And bade *Dan Phœbus* Scribe her Appellation seale.

36

Eftsoones the time and place appointed were,
    Where all, both heauenly Powers, and earthly wights,
    Before great Natures presence should appeare,
    For triall of their Titles and best Rights:

That was, to weet, vpon the highest hights
    Of *Arlo-hill* (Who knowes not *Arlo-hill*?)
    That is the highest head (in all mens sights)
    Of my old father *Mole*, whom Shepheards quill
Renowmed hath with hymnes fit for a rurall skill.

37

And, were it not ill fitting for this file,
    To sing of hilles and woods, mongst warres and Knights,
    I would abate the sternenesse of my stile,
    Mongst these sterne stounds to mingle soft delights;
    And tell how *Arlo* through *Dianaes* spights
    (Beeing of old the best and fairest Hill
    That was in all this holy-Islands hights)
    Was made the most vnpleasant, and most ill.
Meane while, ô *Clio*, lend *Calliope* thy quill.

38

Whylome, when *IRELAND* florished in fame
    Of wealths and goodnesse, far aboue the rest
    Of all that beare the *British* Islands name,
    The Gods then vs'd (for pleasure and for rest)
    Oft to resort there-to, when seem'd them best:
    But none of all there-in more pleasure found,
    Then *Cynthia*; that is soueraine Queene profest
    Of woods and forrests, which therein abound,
Sprinkled with wholsom waters, more then most on ground.

Stanza 34

1 gerle: to remind her of her inferior sex and age. On the sexual politics implicit in their conflict, see Laws 1992:25–29. **foolish**: links her with Titan's folly. **7 Saturnes sonne**: to remind him of her superior right by the laws of primogeniture, though the many OT examples of a younger son triumphing over the elder undercuts her claim. **9 tride**: i.e. by legal trial.

Stanza 35

1–3 equall: impartial. She appeals to the common law maxim that one may not be a judge in one's own case, as Parkin-Speer 1992:501 notes. **4–6** Being androgynous, Nature may appear later as feminine. **by equall might**: i.e. ruling equally over gods and men. **9 Dan Phœbus Scribe**: i.e. Apollo. Apparently his role as secretary of the gods was invented by S., and since he soon appears in his traditional role as the 'god of Poets' (vii 12.6), S. may be patterning Apollo's career on his own. **Appellation**: appeal to a higher court.

Stanza 36

6–9 The question may be rhetorical, like the parallel question, 'who knowes not *Colin Clout*?' at VI x 16.4 (and see *n*); or perhaps witty in prompting a rhetorical question in response: 'Apart from a small circle of friends, who could possibly know that Arlo Hill is S.'s name for Galtymore, the highest peak of the Galtee mountains, about 30 km north-east of his residence at Kilcolman Castle, esp. since he transfers to the mountain the name of the glen of Aherlow, a notorious haunt of rebels, beneath?' Or it may be defiant: readers ought to know that S.

is the shepherd who praises the Mole in *Colin Clout* 104–05 as 'that mountain gray | That walls the Northside of *Armulla* dale', aka the Awbeg valley. See 'Arlo Hill' in the *SEnc*. As the setting marks S.'s double stance as an exile from England and home-maker in Ireland, see Lupton 1990 and 1993:10. Joyce 1911:96 suggests that the **Mole** refers here to the entire range, including the Galtys and the Ballyhoura Mountains.

Stanza 37

1 file: thread (Lat. *filum*) or course of the story, referring to the 'records' of 2.4. The poet imitates Calidore who left wars and knights to live 'in hils, in woods, in dales' (VI x 3.6). **4 stounds**: conflicts. **7 this holy-Island**: in *View* 92, Irenius notes that Ireland has been called '*Banno* or *Sacra Insula*, taking *sacra* for *accursed*'. Diana's curse is pronounced at 55.3. **8 the most vnpleasant**: cf. 'fowle *Arlo*' (*As* 96). See Coughlan 1996:326–28. **9** Deliberately ambiguous: either Calliope (the muse of epic) takes the place held until now by Clio (the muse of history) to tell the story, or she lends her powers to Clio to tell the story herself. See Roche 1989:185. Cf. the reference at vii 1.1 to 'thou greater Muse'. Such ambiguity prepares for the poet's witty reversal of intent.

Stanza 38

1–3 '[I]t is certain that Ireland hath had the use of letters very anciently, and long before England' (*View* 40). **7 Cynthia**: the preferred name for the moon, as at 8.2, etc., but referring here to the moon's role on earth as Diana, the virgin goddess of the forest.

39

But mongst them all, as fittest for her game,
   Either for chace of beasts with hound or boawe,
   Or for to shroude in shade from *Phœbus* flame,
   Or bathe in fountaines that doe freshly flowe,
   Or from high hilles, or from the dales belowe,
   She chose this *Arlo*; where shee did resort
   With all her Nymphes enranged on a rowe,
   With whom the woody Gods did oft consort:
For, with the Nymphes, the Satyres loue to play and sport.

40

Amongst the which, there was a Nymph that hight
   Molanna; daughter of old father *Mole*,
   And sister vnto *Mulla*, faire and bright:
   Vnto whose bed false *Bregog* whylome stole,
   That Shepheard *Colin* dearely did condole,
   And made her lucklesse loues well knowne to be.
   But this *Molanna*, were she not so shole,
   Were no lesse faire and beautifull then shee:
Yet as she is, a fairer flood may no man see.

41

For, first, she springs out of two marble Rocks,
   On which, a groue of Oakes high mounted growes,
   That as a girlond seemes to deck the locks
   Of som faire Bride, brought forth with pompous showes

Out of her bowre, that many flowers strowes:
   So, through the flowry Dales she tumbling downe,
   Through many woods, and shady coverts flowes
   (That on each side her siluer channell crowne)
Till to the Plaine she come, whose Valleyes shee doth drowne.

42

In her sweet streames, *Diana* vsed oft
   (After her sweatie chace and toilesome play)
   To bathe her selfe; and after, on the soft
   And downy grasse, her dainty limbes to lay
   In couert shade, where none behold her may:
   For, much she hated sight of liuing eye.
   Foolish God *Faunus*, though full many a day
   He saw her clad, yet longed foolishly
To see her naked mongst her Nymphes in priuity.

43

No way he found to compasse his desire,
   But to corrupt *Molanna*, this her maid,
   Her to discouer for some secret hire:
   So, her with flattering words he first assaid;
   And after, pleasing gifts for her puruaid,
   Queene-apples, and red Cherries from the tree,
   With which he her allured and betraid,
   To tell what time he might her Lady see
When she her selfe did bathe, that he might secret bee.

Stanza 39
1–6 The syntax is clarified if lines 2–5 are read as a parenthetical catalogue, as Zitner 1968 proposes. More simply, Diana chose **Arlo** over all other **hilles** and **dales** as a place to hunt, rest, and bathe.   7 As Diana's nymphs are seen sitting 'in a rew' at III vi 17.4.

Stanzas 40–41
Joyce 1911:101 concludes that S. describes the rivers with such exactness and detail that he must have written from personal knowledge.

Stanza 40
2 **Molanna**: S.'s name for the Behanna by combining it with Mole. See 'Fanchin, Molanna' in the *SEnc*.   3–6 S. tells the story of the union of these rivers in *Colin Clout* 104–55. On **Mulla**, see IV xi 41.9, and 'Bregog, Mulla' in the *SEnc*. **bed**: the pun is repeated at 53.6.   **false Bregog**: 'So hight because of this deceitfull traine, | Which he with *Mulla* wrought to win delight' (*Colin Clout* 118–19). The Irish name signifies 'deceitful' (Joyce 1911:111).   **dearely did condole**: keenly or lovingly bewailed.   7 **shole**: shallow.

Stanza 41
2 **a groue of Oakes** may have crowned the rocks out of which the Behanna rises, as Joyce 1911:103 conjectures, but it is cited because the oak being 'sole king of forrests all' (I i 8.8) was associated with Cynthia as 'soueraine Queene profest | Of woods and forrests' (38.7–8 above). Its bridal garland heralds

Molanna's marriage when she reaches the plain at 53.7–9.
4 pompous: magnificent, ceremonious.

Stanzas 42–53
S. conflates three Ovidian stories of metamorphosis – Actaeon's accidental sight of the naked Diana (*Met.* 3.155–252); Diana's banishment of the pregnant Callisto (*Met.* 2.463–65), though only punishment for betrayal is common; and the union of the brook Alpheus with the nymph Arethusa (*Met.* 5.572–641) – into an etiological story of how Ireland was reduced to a waste land. Also he uses Ovid, *Fasti* 2.267–538, which tells how Faunus was ridiculed when he attempted to rape Omphale (see Ringler 1965–66), and may have used Irish folktale (see R. Smith 1935). The questions arising from this amalgam as they involve the *topos* of the sight of a numinous woman are examined by Krier 1990:241–50. On S.'s use of Ovid in this episode, see Holahan 1976:246–62. On his use of the myth of Actaeon, see 'Actaeon' in the *SEnc*; on its allegorical interpretation in relation to Faunus, see Hall 1995.

Stanza 42
1–6 For the grotto where Diana was surprised by Venus, see III vi 17–18.   7–9 On Faunus, see II ii 7.5*n*. He is **Foolish** by nature: in his note to Virgil, *Aen.* 7.47, Servius relates the name to Fatuus, 'the foolish one'; noted Nelson 1963:300.

Stanza 43
3 **discouer**: reveal.   5 **puruaid**: provided.   6 Apples are traditionally associated with temptation (see 'apples' in the *SEnc*), as are cherries.   **Queene-apples**: a variety noted for its size and redness.

44

There-to hee promist, if shee would him pleasure
 With this small boone, to quit her with a better;
 To weet, that where-as shee had out of measure
 Long lov'd the *Fanchin*, who by nought did set her,
 That he would vndertake, for this to get her
 To be his Loue, and of him liked well:
 Besides all which, he vow'd to be her debter
 For many moe good turnes then he would tell;
The least of which, this little pleasure should excell.

45

The simple maid did yield to him anone;
 And eft him placed where he close might view
 That neuer any saw, saue onely one;
 Who, for his hire to so foole-hardy dew,
 Was of his hounds devour'd in Hunters hew.
 Tho, as her manner was on sunny day,
 Diana, with her Nymphes about her, drew
 To this sweet spring; where, doffing her array,
She bath'd her louely limbes, for *Ioue* a likely pray.

46

There *Faunus* saw that pleased much his eye,
 And made his hart to tickle in his brest,
 That for great ioy of some-what he did spy,
 He could him not containe in silent rest;
 But breaking forth in laughter, loud profest
 His foolish thought. A foolish *Faune* indeed,
 That couldst not hold thy selfe so hidden blest,
 But wouldest needs thine owne conceit areed.
Babblers vnworthy been of so diuine a meed.

47

The Goddesse, all abashed with that noise,
 In haste forth started from the guilty brooke;
 And running straight where-as she heard his voice,
 Enclos'd the bush about, and there him tooke,
 Like darred Larke; not daring vp to looke
 On her whose sight before so much he sought.
 Thence, forth they drew him by the hornes, and shooke
 Nigh all to peeces, that they left him nought;
And then into the open light they forth him brought.

48

Like as an huswife, that with busie care
 Thinks of her Dairie to make wondrous gaine,
 Finding where-as some wicked beast vnware
 That breakes into her Dayr'house, there doth draine
 Her creaming pannes, and frustrate all her paine;
 Hath in some snare or gin set close behind,
 Entrapped him, and caught into her traine,
 Then thinkes what punishment were best assign'd,
And thousand deathes deuiseth in her vengefull mind:

49

So did *Diana* and her maydens all
 Vse silly *Faunus*, now within their baile:
 They mocke and scorne him, and him foule miscall;
 Some by the nose him pluckt, some by the taile,
 And by his goatish beard some did him haile:
 Yet he (poore soule) with patience all did beare;
 For, nought against their wils might countervaile:
 Ne ought he said what euer he did heare;
But hanging downe his head, did like a Mome appeare.

Stanza 44
1–5 Faunus's desire to see Diana naked prompts an unprecedented sequence of 'a' and 'b' feminine rhymes, as C. Burrow 1993:143 notes. **quit**: requite. **Fanchin**: the Funsheon which joins the Molanna; called the 'Funchin' in *Colin Clout* 301 but the spelling here links him etymologically with Faunus; sugg. J.C. Smith, Spenser 1912:653. **set**: esteem. **8 good turnes**: fancifully referring to delightful bends into which he would lead the river.

Stanza 45
1 anone: instantly; soon. **2 close**: secretly; close-up. **3** The **one** is Actaeon. Faunus is also like Mutabilitie, the 'foolish gerle' (34.1) who sought 'To see that mortall eyes haue neuer seene' (32.3). **4** Who as a reward due to one so fool-hardy. **5** . . . in the shape of a deer to be hunted. **9 likely**: likable, proper.

Stanza 46
2 tickle: be thrilled. **3 some-what**: some thing, in the bawdy sense. **5** Cf. Lust's loud 'grenning laughter' at IV vii 24.9 as he carries off Amoret as his spoil. **6–9** The poet's surprising intrusion into his narrative shows that he still fumes over

Calidore's similar failure to contain himself. **conceit**: thought; also personal vanity or pride, since only one before him had seen Diana naked. **areed**: make known.

Stanza 47
2 guilty brooke: Molanna, the 'sweet spring' (45.8) in which Diana was bathing, is now guilty of betraying her. **5 Like darred Larke**: referring to the practice of capturing larks by paralysing them by the sight of some glittering object. The simile sets up a verbal echo – one who dared to look now does not dare to look – that extends into 'Dairie' and 'Dayr'house' in the next stanza, as Harrison 1956:71 notes. **8 nought**: good for nothing.

Stanza 48
7 traine: snare.

Stanza 49
2 baile: power, custody. **3 miscall**: revile. **9 Mome**: dolt; specifically, Momus 'whose propertie it is . . . with curious eyes to beholde the doynges of other' (T. Cooper 1565).

50

At length, when they had flouted him their fill,
    They gan to cast what penaunce him to giue.
    Some would haue gelt him, but that same would spill
    The Wood-gods breed, which must for euer liue:
    Others would through the riuer him haue driue,
    And ducked deepe: but that seem'd penaunce light;
    But most agreed and did this sentence giue,
    Him in Deares skin to clad; and in that plight,
To hunt him with their hounds, him selfe saue how hee might.

51

But *Cynthia's* selfe, more angry then the rest,
    Thought not enough, to punish him in sport,
    And of her shame to make a gamesome iest;
    But gan examine him in straighter sort,
    Which of her Nymphes, or other close consort,
    Him thither brought, and her to him betraid?
    He, much affeard, to her confessed short,
    That 'twas *Molanna* which her so bewraid.
Then all attonce their hands vpon *Molanna* laid.

52

But him (according as they had decreed)
    With a Deeres-skin they couered, and then chast
    With all their hounds that after him did speed;
    But he more speedy, from them fled more fast
    Then any Deere: so sore him dread aghast.
    They after follow'd all with shrill out-cry,
    Shouting as they the heauens would haue brast:
    That all the woods and dales where he did flie,
Did ring againe, and loud reeccho to the skie.

53

So they him follow'd till they weary were;
    When, back returning to *Molann'* againe,
    They, by commaund'ment of *Diana*, there
    Her whelm'd with stones. Yet *Faunus* (for her paine)
    Of her beloued *Fanchin* did obtaine,
    That her he would receiue vnto his bed.
    So now her waues passe through a pleasant Plaine,
    Till with the *Fanchin* she her selfe doe wed,
And (both combin'd) themselues in one faire riuer spred.

54

Nath'lesse, *Diana*, full of indignation,
    Thence-forth abandond her delicious brooke;
    In whose sweet streame, before that bad occasion,
    So much delight to bathe her limbes she tooke:
    Ne onely her, but also quite forsooke
    All those faire forrests about *Arlo* hid,
    And all that Mountaine, which doth over-looke
    The richest champian that may else be rid,
And the faire *Shure*, in which are thousand Salmons bred.

55

Them all, and all that she so deare did way,
    Thence-forth she left; and parting from the place,
    There-on an heauy haplesse curse did lay,
    To weet, that Wolues, where she was wont to space,
    Should harbour'd be, and all those Woods deface,
    And Thieues should rob and spoile that Coast around.
    Since which, those Woods, and all that goodly Chase,
    Doth to this day with Wolues and Thieues abound:
Which too-too true that lands in-dwellers since haue found.

Stanza 50
2 cast: consider. **3–4** To punish Faunus by having him **gelt**, i.e. gelded by losing his own 'some-what' (46.3), would be appropriate but would **spill**, i.e. destroy, the species. **8 plight**: attire; condition, state. **9 their hounds**: in contrast to the hunter Actaeon who, transformed into a stag, became the hunted, and was torn apart by his own hounds. S. follows Conti 1616:6.24 in having the voyeur only clad in a deer skin, but while Actaeon in Conti's version is mauled by his dogs, Faunus is only chased. Guilt for his act is transferred to Molanna and through her to Arlo Hill and Ireland.

Stanza 51
4 in straighter sort: more strictly. **5 close consort**: secret confederate. **7 short**: soon. **8 bewraid**: betrayed.

Stanza 52
5 I.e. he is terrified of what he sorely dreaded, namely, being devoured.

Stanza 53
4 whelm'd: overwhelmed. The story explains why the river is 'so shole' (40.7). As Joyce 1911:104 notes, during winter floods the river brings down large quantities of stones and gravel from its mountain source. In *Colin Clout* 149–55, Bregog is similarly punished.

Stanza 54
8–9 champian: champaign, open country, referring to the vale of Aherlow in County Tipperary. **else be rid**: anywhere else be seen.

Stanza 55
1 way: value. **4 space**: walk. **7 Chase**: hunting-ground. **8** In *Colin Clout* 318–19, S. laments that wolves and outlaws infect Ireland. He is himself one of **that lands in-dwellers** in being 'an inhabitant' or 'a sojourner' (*OED* b) in Ireland. There may be a topical reference: Elizabeth withdrew the English forces in 1598 after they were routed in Tyrone's rebellion; or more generally to the desolation in Ireland brought by her policies, as Norbrook 1984:152 suggests.

Canto VII.

Pealing, from Ioue, *to* Natur's *Bar,*
bold Alteration *pleades*
Large Euidence: but Nature *soone*
her righteous Doome areads.

1

AH! whither doost thou now thou greater Muse
  Me from these woods and pleasing forrests bring?
  And my fraile spirit (that dooth oft refuse
  This too high flight, vnfit for her weake wing)
  Lift vp aloft, to tell of heauens King
  (Thy soueraine Sire) his fortunate successe,
  And victory, in bigger noates to sing,
  Which he obtain'd against that *Titanesse,*
That him of heauens Empire sought to dispossesse.

2

Yet sith I needs must follow thy behest,
  Doe thou my weaker wit with skill inspire,
  Fit for this turne; and in my feeble brest
  Kindle fresh sparks of that immortall fire,
  Which learned minds inflameth with desire
  Of heauenly things: for, who but thou alone,
  That art yborne of heauen and heauenly Sire,
  Can tell things doen in heauen so long ygone;
So farre past memory of man that may be knowne.

3

Now, at the time that was before agreed,
  The Gods assembled all on *Arlo* hill;
  As well those that are sprung of heauenly seed,
  As those that all the other world doe fill,
  And rule both sea and land vnto their will:
  Onely th'infernall Powers might not appeare;
  Aswell for horror of their count'naunce ill,
  As for th'vnruly fiends which they did feare;
Yet *Pluto* and *Proserpina* were present there.

4

And thither also came all other creatures,
  What-euer life or motion doe retaine,
  According to their sundry kinds of features;
  That *Arlo* scarsly could them all containe;
  So full they filled euery hill and Plaine:
  And had not *Natures* Sergeant (that is *Order*)
  Them well disposed by his busie paine,
  And raunged farre abroad in euery border,
They would haue caused much confusion and disorder.

Book VII Canto vii

Argument
1 Pealing: appealing. **2 bold Alteration**: Mutabilitie is named 'Proud *Change*' at vi Arg. **3 Large**: extensive, copious. **soone**: to note her deliberation at 57.1–3, 8. **4 areads**: declares.

Stanza 1
1 thou greater Muse: Calliope, possibly Clio (see vi 37.9*n*). She is not named because she assumes the role of Urania in revealing 'heauenly things' (2.6); see Roche 1989:186. **greater**: very great. **5–9** Nature's verdict, but not her judgement, is revealed before the trial begins. **Lift** has imperative force rather than simply acknowledging the muse's power. **Thy soueraine Sire**: Jove; see I xi 5.6–9*n*. **bigger**: louder. In *SC Oct.* 46, 'bigger notes' refers to the poet's heroic song.

Stanza 2
2 weaker: too weak, as he allows at I proem 2.2. **3 turne**: task. **4** Referring to remnants of God's image in the fallen state; cf. *HL* 107. **8–9** As the muse invoked at IV xi 10.1–2 is the offspring of Jove and Memory.

Stanza 3
The Gods are invoked in their order: first the heavenly gods; then those of **the other world**, i.e. the earth, such as the nymphs, dryads, and nereids who 'haue the sea in charge to them assinde' (IV xi 52.2); and finally **th'infernall Powers** represented by Pluto, who was once a heavenly god, and by his consort Proserpina who is connected with the earth through her mother Ceres, the last two being the only named gods, as Thomsen 1994:456 notes in arguing the influence on the Mutabilitie Cantos of Claudian, *De Raptu Proserpinae.* **8** Referring either to the fiends held in fear by the infernal powers or to the heavenly and earthly powers that fear them. Cf. vi 15.9.

Stanza 4
As in Chaucer, *Parl. Fowls*, birds of every kind assemble to fill all the space, and Nature herself, sitting on a hill of flowers, orders her creatures. S. calls it an 'assembly' at 59.8, after its title, *Assemble of Fowles*, in Thynne's 1561 edition; noted Hieatt 1975a:19–24. **6–9** As Nature first established earthly things 'in meet order ranged' (vi 5.3).

Stanzas 5–6
For the extended tradition that informs S.'s vision of Nature, appearing here as 'the God of Nature' (vi 35.6), see 'Nature' in the *SEnc*, and Weatherby 1996a:245–53. Her veiled androgyny relates her to Venus at IV x 41.6–9.

5

Then forth issewed (great goddesse) great dame *Nature*,
  With goodly port and gracious Maiesty;
  Being far greater and more tall of stature
  Then any of the gods or Powers on hie:
  Yet certes by her face and physnomy,
  Whether she man or woman inly were,
  That could not any creature well descry:
For, with a veile that wimpled euery where,
Her head and face was hid, that mote to none appeare.

6

That some doe say was so by skill deuized,
  To hide the terror of her vncouth hew,
  From mortall eyes that should be sore agrized;
  For that her face did like a Lion shew,
  That eye of wight could not indure to view:
  But others tell that it so beautious was,
  And round about such beames of splendor threw,
  That it the Sunne a thousand times did pass,
Ne could be seene, but like an image in a glass.

7

That well may seemen true: for, well I weene
  That this same day, when she on *Arlo* sat,
  Her garment was so bright and wondrous sheene,
  That my fraile wit cannot deuize to what
  It to compare, nor finde like stuffe to that,
  As those three sacred *Saints*, though else most wise,
  Yet on mount *Thabor* quite their wits forgat,
  When they their glorious Lord in strange disguise
Transfigur'd sawe; his garments so did daze their eyes.

8

In a fayre Plaine vpon an equall Hill,
  She placed was in a pauilion;
  Not such as Craftes-men by their idle skill
  Are wont for Princes states to fashion:
  But th'earth her self of her owne motion,
  Out of her fruitfull bosome made to growe
  Most dainty trees; that, shooting vp anon,
  Did seeme to bow their bloosming heads full lowe,
For homage vnto her, and like a throne did shew.

9

So hard it is for any liuing wight,
  All her array and vestiments to tell,
  That old *Dan Geffrey* (in whose gentle spright
  The pure well head of Poesie did dwell)
  In his *Foules parley* durst not with it mel,
  But it transferd to *Alane*, who he thought
  Had in his *Plaint of kindes* describ'd it well:
  Which who will read set forth so as it ought,
Go seek he out that *Alane* where he may be sought.

10

And all the earth far vnderneath her feete
  Was dight with flowres, that voluntary grew
  Out of the ground, and sent forth odours sweet,
  Tenne thousand mores of sundry sent and hew,
  That might delight the smell, or please the view:
  The which, the Nymphes, from all the brooks thereby
  Had gathered, which they at her foot-stoole threw;
  That richer seem'd then any tapestry,
That Princes bowres adorne with painted imagery.

Stanza 5
5 physnomy: countenance.   **8 wimpled**: covered.

Stanza 6
2 vncouth hew: strange form.   **3 agrized**: terrified.   **4** As Una whose face 'As the great eye of heauen shyned bright', and who is attended by a lion whose look 'her [Abessa] cast in deadly hew' (I iii 4.7, 11.9).   **6** These **others** include, notably, Jean de Meun, *Roman de la Rose* 16230–48.   **7–9** As Wisdom is 'the brightnes of the euerlasting light, the vndefiled mirroure of the maiestie of God' (Wisdom 7.26); cf. 2 Cor. 3.18.

Stanza 7
1 That: i.e. what 'others tell' (6.6).   **2 sat**: i.e. in judgement.   **3 sheene**: shining.   **4–9 those three sacred Saints** are Peter, James, and John who on **mount Thabor** first saw Jesus in his divinity so transfigured that 'his face did shine as the sunne, and his clothes were as white as the light' (Matt. 17.2). On the significance of the simile in the seventh stanza of the seventh canto of the seventh book, see Weatherby 1994:90.   **quite their wits forgat**: as Peter 'knewe not what he said' (Mark 9.6). What N. Frye 1990a:183 cites as the one biblical image in the Mutabilitie Cantos – there is another: the balancing reference to Christ's birth at 41.4 – is chosen because **Transfigur'd** renders μετεμορφώθη in the Gk text; because the transfiguration, unlike the resurrection, is a mountain-top epiphany, which suggests the highest order of nature; and because it represents the identity of the Word as the person of Christ with the Word as the Bible. For the claim that Nature is an image of God, Lewis 1967:15 cites Nicholas of Cusa;

Weatherby 76–94 cites the Greek Church Fathers; and Harvey in a letter to S. cites 'the olde Philosophers' who refer to God as 'very Nature selfe . . . *Natura Naturans*' (Spenser 1912:617).

Stanza 8
1 equall: level-topped.   **4 states**: the throne of state with its canopy; cf. Jove 'in his principall Estate' at vi 19.4.   **5 of her owne motion**: i.e. spontaneously, 'voluntary' (10.2).   **7 anon**: straightway.

Stanza 9
Since the stanza interrupts the narrative, Padelford, *Var* 6.478, suggests that it belongs after 7.   **3–6** At IV ii 32.8, Chaucer is described as the 'well of English vndefyled'.   **Poesie**: the poet's 'skill, or Crafte of making' (Jonson 1925–52:8.636) rather than poetry itself.   **old** is Chaucer's epithet in *SC*, Epistle. S.'s point is that even Chaucer in *Parl. Fowls* 316–18 chooses not to **mel**, i.e. meddle, with the matter but defers to **Alane**. See 'Alanus de Insulis' in the *SEnc*.   **7 Plaint of kindes**: properly, *Plaint of kinde*, as in Chaucer. Since the work remained in manuscript, it is unlikely that S. would have read it (though see Quilligan 1983:162); hence the tone of exasperation in 9.

Stanza 10
1–3 Spontaneous flowering in honour of the gods is a common classical motif.   **4 mores**: roots. Perhaps used poetically for 'plant', as *OED* suggests; but in this fertile earth, root and flower are one.

11

And *Mole* himselfe, to honour her the more,
    Did deck himself in freshest faire attire,
    And his high head, that seemeth alwaies hore
    With hardned frosts of former winters ire,
    He with an Oaken girlond now did tire,
    As if the loue of some new Nymph late seene,
    Had in him kindled youthfull fresh desire,
    And made him change his gray attire to greene;
Ah gentle *Mole*! such ioyance hath thee well beseene.

12

Was neuer so great ioyance since the day,
    That all the gods whylome assembled were,
    On *Hæmus* hill in their diuine array,
    To celebrate the solemne bridall cheare,
    Twixt *Peleus*, and dame *Thetis* pointed there;
    Where *Phœbus* self, that god of Poets hight,
    They say did sing the spousall hymne full cleere,
    That all the gods were rauisht with delight
Of his celestiall song, and Musicks wondrous might.

13

This great Grandmother of all creatures bred
    Great *Nature*, euer young yet full of eld,
    Still moouing, yet vnmoued from her sted;
    Vnseene of any, yet of all beheld;

Thus sitting in her throne as I haue teld,
    Before her came dame *Mutabilitie*;
    And being lowe before her presence feld,
    With meek obaysance and humilitie,
Thus gan her plaintif Plea, with words to amplifie;

14

To thee ô greatest goddesse, onely great,
    An humble suppliant loe, I lowely fly
    Seeking for Right, which I of thee entreat;
    Who Right to all dost deale indifferently,
    Damning all Wrong and tortious Iniurie,
    Which any of thy creatures doe to other
    (Oppressing them with power, vnequally)
    Sith of them all thou art the equall mother,
And knittest each to'each, as brother vnto brother.

15

To thee therefore of this same *Ioue* I plaine,
    And of his fellow gods that faine to be,
    That challenge to themselues the whole worlds raign;
    Of which, the greatest part is due to me,
    And heauen it selfe by heritage in Fee:
    For, heauen and earth I both alike do deeme,
    Sith heauen and earth are both alike to thee;
    And, gods no more then men thou doest esteeme:
For, euen the gods to thee, as men to gods do seeme.

Stanza 11
5 From the 'groue of Oakes' at vi 41.2. **tire**: adorn his head. 8 **gray**: as in *Colin Clout* 104. 9 . . . well becomes you.

Stanza 12
At the marriage of **Peleus** and **Thetis**, Ate incited the quarrel that led to the fall of Troy; see II vii 55.4–9. The marriage was the occasion of the birth of the Graces (see VI x 22); but chiefly, as N. Frye 1963:85–86 notes, Jove was 'confirm'd in his imperiall see' (59.7) by removing the threat to his power from a son of Thetis, and it led to his reconciliation with Prometheus, the originator of the elves and fays (II x 70–71). 3 **Hæmus hill**: 'a great mountain in Thrace, in height vi miles' (T. Cooper 1565), which S. associates with Jove's battle against the giants at III ix 22. Traditionally, it took place on Mount Pelion. If the change is not intentional, S. may have been misled by Ovid's account of Peleus's seduction of Thetis which opens: *Est sinus Haemoniae* (*Met.* 11.229), as Upton 1758 conjectures. 4 **solemne**: sacred, holy. 5 **pointed**: appointed.

Stanza 13
2–4 Three notable paradoxes: 1. 'old yet young' or the 'Old Woman and Girl' topos, which is traced by Curtius 1953:101–05, is particularly appropriate to Nature; 2. 'moving yet unmoved' is associated with the god of nature by Boethius, *De Consol. Phil.* 3 Met. 9.3: 'thow that duellest thiselve ay stedefast and stable, and yevest alle othere thynges to ben meved' (tr. Chaucer); 3. 'unseen yet seen' relates God whom 'no man [shall] se . . . and liue' (Exod. 33.20) to nature, for 'the inuisible things of him . . . are seene by the creation of the worlde' (Rom. 1.20). **Still**: a term used almost obsessively in the canto to indicate that Mutabilitie understands movement but not its relation to stillness, as Kermode 1965:226 notes. See also Anderson 1996:133–34. 7 **feld**: having fallen. 9 **to**

amplifie: 'to make more impressive' through rhetorical figures, as Tuve 1947:90 suggests.

Stanzas 14–26
In her formal 'plaintif Plea' (13.9), Mutabilitie shows how the four elements in their traditional order – earth (17–19), water (20–21), air (22–23), and fire (24) – are subject to change both in themselves and, through transmutation, into each other (25). On their stable yet constantly changing system of contrarieties and agreements, see 'cosmogony' in the *SEnc*. She concludes her case by claiming that her rule extends to their heavenly counterparts (26). Their revised order in this stanza allows a final stress on water, the traditional emblem of change. See 26.4–7n, and 'elements' in the *SEnc*. While her arguments are too common to attribute to any specific source, they are esp. close to Ovid, *Met.* 15 in Golding's tr., as Taylor 1985:18–20 demonstrates.

Stanza 14
1 Mutabilitie concludes her defence with a similar address to 'thou greatest goddesse trew' (56.6) in order to set Nature above Jove, and also herself as one 'greater . . . | Then all the Gods' (vi 26.8–9). 4 **indifferently**: impartially. 7–9 Despite her obeisance to Nature as **onely great**, Mutabilitie, like the Giant with the Scales, 'all things would reduce vnto equality' (V ii 32.9). Hence **vnequally**: unfairly, implying that all should be treated as equal. **equall mother**: unlike Jove whom she rejects as 'no equall Iudge' at vi 35.1.

Stanza 15
1 **plaine**: complain. 2–3 Cf. her claim at 26.2. **faine**: pretend. **challenge**: claim. 4 By claiming only **the greatest part** rather than **the whole worlds raign**, she excludes the lower world ruled by Pluto and Proserpina to which she properly belongs. 5 **Fee**: absolute possession.

16

Then weigh, ô soueraigne goddesse, by what right
  These gods do claime the worlds whole soueranty;
  And that is onely dew vnto thy might
  Arrogate to themselues ambitiously:
  As for the gods owne principality,
  Which *Ioue* vsurpes vniustly; that to be
  My heritage, *Ioue's* self cannot deny,
  From my great Grandsire *Titan*, vnto mee,
Deriv'd by dew descent; as is well knowen to thee.

17

Yet mauger *Ioue*, and all his gods beside,
  I doe possesse the worlds most regiment;
  As, if ye please it into parts diuide,
  And euery parts inholders to conuent,
  Shall to your eyes appeare incontinent.
  And first, the Earth (great mother of vs all)
  That only seems vnmov'd and permanent,
  And vnto *Mutability* not thrall;
Yet is she chang'd in part, and eeke in generall.

18

For, all that from her springs, and is ybredde,
  How-euer fayre it flourish for a time,
  Yet see we soone decay; and, being dead,
  To turne again vnto their earthly slime:
  Yet, out of their decay and mortall crime,
  We daily see new creatures to arize;
  And of their Winter spring another Prime,
  Vnlike in forme, and chang'd by strange disguise:
So turne they still about, and change in restlesse wise.

19

As for her tenants; that is, man and beasts,
  The beasts we daily see massacred dy,
  As thralls and vassalls vnto mens beheasts:
  And men themselues doe change continually,

From youth to eld, from wealth to pouerty,
From good to bad, from bad to worst of all.
Ne doe their bodies only flit and fly:
But eeke their minds (which they immortall call)
Still change and vary thoughts, as new occasions fall.

20

Ne is the water in more constant case;
  Whether those same on high, or these belowe.
  For, th'Ocean moueth stil, from place to place;
  And euery Riuer still doth ebbe and flowe:
  Ne any Lake, that seems most still and slowe,
  Ne Poole so small, that can his smoothnesse holde,
  When any winde doth vnder heauen blowe;
  With which, the clouds are also tost and roll'd;
Now like great Hills; and, streight, like sluces, them vnfold.

21

So likewise are all watry liuing wights
  Still tost, and turned, with continuall change,
  Neuer abyding in their stedfast plights.
  The fish, still floting, doe at randon range,
  And neuer rest; but euermore exchange
  Their dwelling places, as the streames them carrie:
  Ne haue the watry foules a certaine grange,
  Wherein to rest, ne in one stead do tarry;
But flitting still doe flie, and still their places vary.

22

Next is the Ayre: which who feeles not by sense
  (For, of all sense it is the middle meane)
  To flit still? and, with subtill influence
  Of his thin spirit, all creatures to maintaine,
  In state of life? O weake life! that does leane
  On thing so tickle as th'vnsteady ayre;
  Which euery howre is chang'd, and altred cleane
  With euery blast that bloweth fowle or faire:
The faire doth it prolong; the fowle doth it impaire.

Stanza 16

3 And what is due only . . .   **5 principality**: sovereignty.
8–9 As she claims at vi 27.1–5.

Stanza 17

2 **most regiment**: chief rule.   **4 inholders**: inhabitants, with
the implication that they 'doe the world in being hold' (27.3).
conuent: assemble.   **5 incontinent**: immediately.   **6–9 great
mother** is earth's traditional epithet as *omniparens*, see I vii
9.1*n*.   **only**: alone. It also modifies **seems**.

Stanza 18

1–4 The giant uses this argument at V ii 37.6–7, and is
answered by Artegall at 40.1–5.   **5 mortall crime**: sin of
mortality, i.e. death and corruption; or, from Lat. *crimen*,
judgement and sentence (of death).   **6** On abiogenesis, see I i
21.6–9*n*.   **7 Prime**: spring.

Stanza 19

1 tenants: as her address is directed to mortals – shown by the

use of 'we' in 18.3, 6, 24.3, 25.3 – the term reminds us that
life is only loaned, not held in freehold.   **8** As *HL* 103: 'man,
that breathes . . . [an] immortall mynd'.

Stanza 20

2 Following Gen. 1.7 on the waters under and above the
firmament.

Stanza 21

4 still floting: continually swimming.   **7 certaine grange**:
fixed dwelling-place.

Stanza 22

2 middle meane: as the intermediary between the senses
and what is perceived. Not **all** because air was not considered
the means of touch or taste, as A. Fowler 1970:59*n*1 observes.
3 influence: in the etymological sense, literally 'flowing'.
5–9 On the need of air to 'feed' the vital spirits, see 'psycho-
logy' in the *SEnc*.   **tickle**: changeable.

23
Therein the changes infinite beholde,
    Which to her creatures euery minute chaunce;
    Now, boyling hot: streight, friezing deadly cold:
    Now, faire sun-shine, that makes all skip and daunce:
    Streight, bitter storms and balefull countenance,
    That makes them all to shiuer and to shake:
    Rayne, hayle, and snowe do pay them sad penance,
    And dreadfull thunder-claps (that make them quake)
With flames and flashing lights that thousand changes make.

24
Last is the fire: which, though it liue for euer,
    Ne can be quenched quite; yet, euery day,
    Wee see his parts, so soone as they do seuer,
    To lose their heat, and shortly to decay;
    So, makes himself his owne consuming pray.
    Ne any liuing creatures doth he breed:
    But all, that are of others bredd, doth slay;
    And, with their death, his cruell life dooth feed;
Nought leauing, but their barren ashes, without seede.

25
Thus, all these fower (the which the ground-work bee
    Of all the world, and of all liuing wights)
    To thousand sorts of *Change* we subiect see:
    Yet are they chang'd (by other wondrous slights)
    Into themselues, and lose their natiue mights;
    The Fire to Aire, and th'Ayre to Water sheere,
    And Water into Earth: yet Water fights
    With Fire, and Aire with Earth approaching neere:
Yet all are in one body, and as one appeare.

26
So, in them all raignes *Mutabilitie*;
    How-euer these, that Gods themselues do call,
    Of them doe claime the rule and souerainty:
    As, *Vesta*, of the fire æthereall;
    Vulcan, of this, with vs so vsuall;
    Ops, of the earth; and *Iuno* of the Ayre;
    Neptune, of Seas; and Nymphes, of Riuers all.
    For, all those Riuers to me subiect are:
And all the rest, which they vsurp, be all my share.

27
Which to approuen true, as I haue told,
    Vouchsafe, ô goddesse, to thy presence call
    The rest which doe the world in being hold:
    As, times and seasons of the yeare that fall:
    Of all the which, demand in generall,
    Or iudge thy selfe, by verdit of thine eye,
    Whether to me they are not subiect all.
    Nature did yeeld thereto; and by-and-by,
Bade *Order* call them all, before her Maiesty.

28
So, forth issew'd the Seasons of the yeare;
    First, lusty *Spring*, all dight in leaues of flowres
    That freshly budded and new bloosmes did beare
    (In which a thousand birds had built their bowres
    That sweetly sung, to call forth Paramours):
    And in his hand a iauelin he did beare,
    And on his head (as fit for warlike stoures)
    A guilt engrauen morion he did weare;
That as some did him loue, so others did him feare.

Stanza 23
The three regions of air are listed in ascending order: the lowest (3–4) produces heat and cold alternately; the middle (5–8) produces storms; the highest (9), which is next to the region of fire, produces comets or blazing stars. These regions with their effect on mortal creatures are treated by du Bartas 1979:1.2.411–64. **2 minute**: the smallest unit of time in the sixteenth century. **7 penance**: because the seasons punish mortals for Adam and Eve's sin.

Stanza 24
According to traditional Elizabethan cosmology, the 'natiue seat' (II xi 32.6) of the sublunary region of fire was situated above the region of air and therefore apart from 'vsuall' fire (26.5), i.e. fire as we know it. See 'fire' in the *SEnc*. By the late sixteenth century it was known that contrary to Mutabilitie's claim in 1–2, 'The Element of fire is quite put out' (Donne, 'The First Anniversary' 206).

Stanza 25
4–6 slights: devices. **Into themselues**, i.e. one into another, with only fire not replenished. On such transmutation, see Heninger 1974:160–66; on the resultant discord, see *HL* 78–84. **sheere**: bright, clear.

Stanza 26
4–7 Vesta, the Roman goddess of the hearth and hence of fire,

is linked with the sphere of sublunary fire; **Vulcan** is the god of fire as we know it on earth; **Ops**, or Rhea, is the goddess of the earth; and **Iuno** is the goddess of the air, the element in which we live.

Stanza 27
1 approuen: prove; suggesting 'sanction'. **6 verdit**: the spelling suggests the etymology, 'to speak true'. **8 by-and-by**: immediately; one by one in order (*OED* 1): cf. 'in order went' (32.1).

Stanzas 28–31
Mutabilitie's pageant begins with the seasons as the largest measurement of the year but also because Jove's defeat of Saturn, who had usurped the rule of her ancestor Titan, ended the timeless golden age. Now time governs the seasons in their change, as described by Ovid, *Met.* 1.113–18. See 'time' in the *SEnc*.

Stanza 28
This experiment in employing only two rhymes serves to introduce the notion of a cycle. See 44.2*n*. **2 lusty**: vigorous. **7–9 stoures**: encounters. **guilt**: gilded. **morion**: a helmet worn by the warlike Minerva in *Muiopotmos* 322. Since it lacks a beaver or visor, it leaves the face open to glances of love or hate.

29

Then came the iolly *Sommer*, being dight
   In a thin silken cassock coloured greene,
   That was vnlyned all, to be more light:
   And on his head a girlond well beseene
   He wore, from which as he had chauffed been
   The sweat did drop; and in his hand he bore
   A boawe and shaftes, as he in forrest greene
   Had hunted late the Libbard or the Bore,
And now would bathe his limbes, with labor heated sore.

30

Then came the *Autumne* all in yellow clad,
   As though he ioyed in his plentious store,
   Laden with fruits that made him laugh, full glad
   That he had banisht hunger, which to-fore
   Had by the belly oft him pinched sore.
   Vpon his head a wreath that was enrold
   With eares of corne, of euery sort he bore:
   And in his hand a sickle he did holde,
To reape the ripened fruits the which the earth had yold.

31

Lastly, came *Winter* cloathed all in frize,
   Chattering his teeth for cold that did him chill,
   Whil'st on his hoary beard his breath did freese;
   And the dull drops that from his purpled bill

As from a limbeck did adown distill.
   In his right hand a tipped staffe he held,
   With which his feeble steps he stayed still:
   For, he was faint with cold, and weak with eld;
That scarse his loosed limbes he hable was to weld.

32

These, marching softly, thus in order went,
   And after them, the Monthes all riding came;
   First, sturdy *March* with brows full sternly bent,
   And armed strongly, rode vpon a Ram,
   The same which ouer *Hellespontus* swam:
   Yet in his hand a spade he also hent,
   And in a bag all sorts of seeds ysame,
   Which on the earth he strowed as he went,
And fild her womb with fruitfull hope of nourishment.

33

Next came fresh *Aprill* full of lustyhed,
   And wanton as a Kid whose horne new buds:
   Vpon a Bull he rode, the same which led
   Europa floting through th'*Argolick* fluds:
   His hornes were gilden all with golden studs
   And garnished with garlonds goodly dight
   Of all the fairest flowres and freshest buds
   Which th'earth brings forth, and wet he seem'd in sight
With waues, through which he waded for his loues delight.

Stanza 29
5 chauffed: heated.   **8** The **Bore** is cited as the traditional object of the hunt but the **Libbard** (leopard) is sometimes, as here, just a leopard.

Stanza 30
7 corne: grain.   **9 yold**: yielded.

Stanza 31
1 frize: coarse woollen cloth. The pun is reinforced by the rhyme.   **4–5 bill**: nose.   **limbeck**: alembic, the 'beak' of an alchemist's still. Linden 1996:93 notes that this description of alchemists was a current joke.   **7 stayed still**: always supported.   **9 loosed**: weakened.   **weld**: i.e. wield, move.

Stanzas 32–43
Each month represents the age of human life appropriate to its time of year and in a role appropriate to its agricultural labour. Most carry a tool associated with sowing or harvesting. Since they pass more quickly than the seasons, they ride rather than walk, except for August, September, and January. (February does not ride but is driven.) Each is associated with the zodiacal sign or 'house' occupied by the sun during its month. (On the signs, see V proem 5–6.) Except for June, September, and February, each is associated with a classical myth. Each is allotted a whole stanza, except March, which begins at line 3, possibly because it is the third month in the popular Julian calendar used in the *SC*; see Cooke 1995. February loses the final line because it is the shortest month. On the iconographical tradition that informs this pageant, see Ruskin, *Stones of Venice*

2.7.52, the illustrations to the *SC* in the *SEnc* (esp. fig. 1), and Heninger 1977:110–15; and on S.'s adaptation of it, see S. Hawkins 1961:88–98. On their processional form, see 'pageants' in the *SEnc*. Instead of showing only random change, being summoned by Order, they demonstrate repeated cyclical order, an irony noted by Hawkins 90.

Stanza 32
1–2 softly: slowly, as do the seasons. Appropriately, March's stanza opens with **marching**.   **3 First**: because 'the yeare beginneth in March', as E.K. explains in the 'General Argument' to the *SC*.   **sturdy**: stern, surly.   **4–5 armed strongly**: befitting the month of Mars, and the season spring at 28.7–9.   **rode vpon a Ram**: Jove disguised as a ram bore Helle in flight from her stepmother until she fell into the water that now bears her name (see V proem 5.6–7); here the zodiacal sign Aries which is associated with the fruitfulness of spring.   **7 ysame**: together.

Stanza 33
3–4 Jove, disguised as a bull, carried Europa on his back over the sea; cf. III xi 30.6–9. Here the zodiacal sign Taurus, an identification made by Ovid, *Fasti* 5.617.   **Argolick**: the gulf of Argolis.   **5–8** In Ovid, *Met.* 2.856, 867–68, the bull's horns, which are 'More cleare . . . than is the Christall stone', are offered 'with flowers to be drest' (tr. Golding).   **golden studs** suggest stars.   **freshest buds** allude to the traditional etymology of April, from Lat. *aperire*, to open, referring to the time when buds open, as shown in the woodcut to *SC* Apr.   **wet**: referring to April showers, as Ruskin observes.

34

Then came faire *May*, the fayrest mayd on ground,
  Deckt all with dainties of her seasons pryde,
  And throwing flowres out of her lap around:
  Vpon two brethrens shoulders she did ride,
  The twinnes of *Leda*; which on eyther side
  Supported her like to their soueraine Queene.
  Lord! how all creatures laught, when her they spide,
  And leapt and daunc't as they had rauisht beene!
And *Cupid* selfe about her fluttred all in greene.

35

And after her, came iolly *Iune*, arrayd
  All in greene leaues, as he a Player were;
  Yet in his time, he wrought as well as playd,
  That by his plough-yrons mote right well appeare:
  Vpon a Crab he rode, that him did beare
  With crooked crawling steps an vncouth pase,
  And backward yode, as Bargemen wont to fare
  Bending their force contrary to their face,
Like that vngracious crew which faines demurest grace.

36

Then came hot *Iuly* boyling like to fire,
  That all his garments he had cast away:
  Vpon a Lyon raging yet with ire
  He boldly rode and made him to obay:
  It was the beast that whylome did forray
  The Nemæan forrest, till th'*Amphytrionide*
  Him slew, and with his hide did him array;
  Behinde his back a sithe, and by his side
Vnder his belt he bore a sickle circling wide.

37

The sixt was *August*, being rich arrayd
  In garment all of gold downe to the ground:
  Yet rode he not, but led a louely Mayd
  Forth by the lilly hand, the which was cround
  With eares of corne, and full her hand was found;
  That was the righteous Virgin, which of old
  Liv'd here on earth, and plenty made abound;
  But, after Wrong was lov'd and Iustice solde,
She left th'vnrighteous world and was to heauen extold.

38

Next him, *September* marched eeke on foote;
  Yet was he heauy laden with the spoyle
  Of haruests riches, which he made his boot,
  And him enricht with bounty of the soyle:
  In his one hand, as fit for haruests toyle,
  He held a knife-hook; and in th'other hand
  A paire of waights, with which he did assoyle
  Both more and lesse, where it in doubt did stand,
And equall gaue to each as Iustice duly scann'd.

39

Then came *October* full of merry glee:
  For, yet his noule was totty of the must,
  Which he was treading in the wine-fats see,
  And of the ioyous oyle, whose gentle gust
  Made him so frollick and so full of lust:
  Vpon a dreadfull Scorpion he did ride,
  The same which by *Dianaes* doom vniust
  Slew great *Orion*: and eeke by his side
He had his ploughing share, and coulter ready tyde.

Stanza 34
1 faire May: the epithet and name prepare for her personification and the play upon her name. **2 pryde**: most flourishing state. **4–6 twinnes of Leda**: Castor and Pollux; here the zodiacal sign Gemini. They are so named in order to stress Jove's amorous exploits: he seduced Leda in the disguise of a swan; see III xi 32. May rides on their shoulders because Gemini 'hath mastry in mans body, of the shoulders, armes, and handes' (Bartholomaeus 1582:8.12). **7–8** Suggesting the festivities of May-day about the may-pole.

Stanza 35
2 greene leaues: the attire of an actor appearing as the wild or savage man. **5–7 Crab**: the zodiacal sign Cancer in which the sun begins to move backwards. **7–9** Those who out of excessive politeness walk backwards as they leave a room are like rowers who face opposite to the direction they are moving. They feign grace but are **vngracious**, i.e. devoid of grace.

Stanza 36
2 As Summer appears naked in Ovid, *Met.* 2.28. **3–4** As Wrath rides upon a lion at I iv 33.2. **5–7** The Nemean lion was slain by Hercules as the first of his labours (see II v 31.1–5); here the zodiacal sign Leo. **th'Amphytrionide**: an epithet of Hercules because he was the reputed son of Amphitryon, so called here because his real father was Jove (see III xi 33.6–9). The associative links are noteworthy: July, who

has taken off his garments because he is hot and appears on a raging lion, suggests Hercules raging in death when he sought to take off his burning garment. **8–9** He both reaps and mows, as Ruskin notices.

Stanza 37
1–2 August is appropriately august in the sense of Lat. *augustus*, consecrated, venerable. **4–9 the righteous Virgin**: Astræa, the goddess of Justice, here seen as Virgo, August's zodiacal sign; see V i 5.4n. In *Mother Hubberd* 1–8, she leaves the earth to return to heaven in this month. She was associated with Ceres and therefore with corn; on her flight and stellification, see V i 11. **extold**: raised.

Stanza 38
1 September walks because he bears the scales of the Virgin who also walks, and marks their measured pace. **3 boot**: booty. **7 waights**: scales; the zodiacal sign Libra. See V i 11.8–9. **assoyle**: solve or determine. **9 equall**: what was equitable. **scann'd**: judged.

Stanza 39
2 For his head was always tipsy with new wine. **3 wine-fats see**: the sea of liquor in the wine vats. **4 gust**: taste. **6–8** By one account, Diana sent a scorpion to kill Orion because he had boasted that he could kill any earthly creature; here the zodiacal sign **Scorpio**. See II ii 46.1–3.

40

Next was *Nouember*, he full grosse and fat,
  As fed with lard, and that right well might seeme;
  For, he had been a fatting hogs of late,
  That yet his browes with sweat, did reek and steem,
  And yet the season was full sharp and breem;
  In planting eeke he took no small delight:
  Whereon he rode, not easie was to deeme;
  For it a dreadfull *Centaure* was in sight,
The seed of *Saturne*, and faire *Nais*, *Chiron* hight.

41

And after him, came next the chill *December*:
  Yet he through merry feasting which he made,
  And great bonfires, did not the cold remember;
  His Sauiours birth his mind so much did glad:
  Vpon a shaggy-bearded Goat he rode,
  The same wherewith *Dan Ioue* in tender yeares,
  They say, was nourisht by th'*Idæan* mayd;
  And in his hand a broad deepe boawle he beares;
Of which, he freely drinks an health to all his peeres.

42

Then came old *Ianuary*, wrapped well
  In many weeds to keep the cold away;
  Yet did he quake and quiuer like to quell,
  And blowe his nayles to warme them if he may:
  For, they were numbd with holding all the day
  An hatchet keene, with which he felled wood,
  And from the trees did lop the needlesse spray:
  Vpon an huge great Earth-pot steane he stood;
From whose wide mouth, there flowed forth the Romane
                             (floud.

43

And lastly, came cold *February*, sitting
  In an old wagon, for he could not ride;
  Drawne of two fishes for the season fitting,
  Which through the flood before did softly slyde
  And swim away: yet had he by his side
  His plough and harnesse fit to till the ground,
  And tooles to prune the trees, before the pride
  Of hasting Prime did make them burgein round:
So past the twelue Months forth, and their dew places found.

44

And after these, there came the *Day*, and *Night*,
  Riding together both with equall pase,
  Th'one on a Palfrey blacke, the other white;
  But *Night* had couered her vncomely face
  With a blacke veile, and held in hand a mace,
  On top whereof the moon and stars were pight,
  And sleep and darknesse round about did trace:
  But *Day* did beare, vpon his scepters hight,
The goodly Sun, encompast all with beames bright.

45

Then came the *Howres*, faire daughters of high *Ioue*,
  And timely *Night*, the which were all endewed
  With wondrous beauty fit to kindle loue;
  But they were Virgins all, and loue eschewed,
  That might forslack the charge to them fore-shewed
  By mighty *Ioue*; who did them Porters make
  Of heauens gate (whence all the gods issued)
  Which they did dayly watch, and nightly wake
By euen turnes, ne euer did their charge forsake.

Stanza 40

5 breem: rough, stormy; 'chill, bitter' (E.K. on *SC Feb*. 43).
7–9 November's zodiacal sign is Sagittarius, the Archer who
on earth was a centaur; here named **Chiron**, as in Conti
1616:4.12. **Nais**: 'a nymphe of the water' (T. Cooper 1565);
at III xi 43.7, she is named '*Philliras*' (Philyra). Since Chiron
was reputed to be either the son of Saturn and Philyra or the
son of Magnes and Nais, who he is **not easie was to deeme**.

Stanza 41

4 His Sauiours birth: cf II x 50.2–7. This second reference
to Christ in the Mutabilitie Cantos – see 7.4–9*n* – links the
nativity to the transfiguration as epiphanies that comprehend
his double nature, and comes, appropriately, in a stanza that
begins in the 365th line of the canto (including the Arg.),
as Walls notes in an unpublished paper. **5–7** December's
zodiacal sign is Capricorn, identified with the goat whose milk
fed the infant Jove when he was tended by **th'Idæan mayd**,
Amalthea, a nymph on Mount Ida. The connection is made by
Conti 1616:7.7. Jove's birth implies the renewal of the months
which celebrate his later deeds.

Stanza 42

3 like to quell: as if he were perishing. **8 steane**: jar, urn;
here the zodiacal sign Aquarius, the water-bearer. **9 the
Romane floud** should be the Tiber, which, in *Bellay* 114–20,

appears 'full of Saturnlike awe' leaning on a pot from which
pours a flood associated with Rome's corruption. Zitner 1968
suggests that S. recalls *Rome* 178–80: the overflowing Tiber
washes away Rome's pride. Of the months, only January is said
to stand, possibly referring to his role of ushering in the year.

Stanza 43

3 The **two fishes** represent the zodiacal sign Pisces, a suitable
symol for Lent, as Renwick 1923 notes. **4–5** This **flood** is
the water flowing from Aquarius's urn.

Stanza 44

1–2 Day, and Night ride as a pair to illustrate the seasonal
balancing of diurnal and nocturnal hours about the equinoxes,
as A. Fowler 1964:232 notes. Their balance is demonstrated
by the single pair of rhymes in the stanza. **3–5** Cf. Night at
I v 20. The **mace** brings sleep, as at I iv 44.6. **7 trace**: go.

Stanza 45

On the **Howres**, or Horae, who mark the rising and setting
of the planets, see Hieatt 1960:33–38, 111–13. In *Epith* 99,
as here, they are daughters of 'Day [i.e. Jove] and Night'
who allot the seasons, and 'by the Poets are fained to be the
Guardians of Heaven's gates' (*Entertainment at Elvetham*,
1591, in Nichols 1823:3.108). Traditionally, like the Litæ at
V ix 31, they are daughters of Jove and Themis. **1–2 high**:

46

And after all came *Life*, and lastly *Death*;
   Death with most grim and griesly visage seene,
   Yet is he nought but parting of the breath;
   Ne ought to see, but like a shade to weene,
   Vnbodied, vnsoul'd, vnheard, vnseene.
   But *Life* was like a faire young lusty boy,
   Such as they faine *Dan Cupid* to haue beene,
   Full of delightfull health and liuely ioy,
Deckt all with flowres, and wings of gold fit to employ.

47

When these were past, thus gan the *Titanesse*;
   Lo, mighty mother, now be iudge and say,
   Whether in all thy creatures more or lesse
   CHANGE doth not raign and beare the greatest sway:
   For, who sees not, that *Time* on all doth pray?
   But *Times* do change and moue continually.
   So nothing here long standeth in one stay:
   Wherefore, this lower world who can deny
But to be subiect still to *Mutabilitie*?

48

Then thus gan *Ioue*; Right true it is, that these
   And all things else that vnder heauen dwell
   Are chaung'd of *Time*, who doth them all disseise
   Of being: But, who is it (to me tell)
   That *Time* himselfe doth moue and still compell
   To keepe his course? Is not that namely wee
   Which poure that vertue from our heauenly cell,
   That moues them all, and makes them changed be?
So them we gods doe rule, and in them also thee.

49

To whom, thus *Mutability*: The things
   Which we see not how they are mov'd and swayd,
   Ye may attribute to your selues as Kings,
   And say they by your secret powre are made:
   But what we see not, who shall vs perswade?
   But were they so, as ye them faine to be,
   Mov'd by your might, and ordred by your ayde;
   Yet what if I can proue, that euen yee
Your selues are likewise chang'd, and subiect vnto mee?

50

And first, concerning her that is the first,
   Euen you faire *Cynthia*, whom so much ye make
   Ioues dearest darling, she was bred and nurst
   On *Cynthus* hill, whence she her name did take:
   Then is she mortall borne, how-so ye crake;
   Besides, her face and countenance euery day
   We changed see, and sundry forms partake,
   Now hornd, now round, now bright, now brown and gray:
So that *as changefull as the Moone* men vse to say.

51

Next, *Mercury*, who though he lesse appeare
   To change his hew, and alwayes seeme as one;
   Yet, he his course doth altar euery yeare,
   And is of late far out of order gone:
   So *Venus* eeke, that goodly Paragone,
   Though faire all night, yet is she darke all day;
   And *Phœbus* self, who lightsome is alone,
   Yet is he oft eclipsed by the way,
And fills the darkned world with terror and dismay.

---

empyrean, eternal, in contrast to **timely**: temporal, belonging to time. **5 forslack**: cause the neglect of. **fore-shewed**: showed beforehand, ordained. **8–9 wake**: guard. **euen turnes** suggests regular movement in a circle.

Stanza 46

1 lastly Death: significantly, however, Time's pageant concludes with the celebration of Life even as Day follows Night in 44. See 'Life and Death' in the *SEnc*. Heberle 1987 notes that the ambiguity of the line – either death follows life or life follows death – indicates that both are integral to a larger natural process. **5** This brilliant example of asyndeton, i.e. the omission of grammatical connections between words, which here share the same prefix, is made memorable by the two introductory iambs of **Vnbodied** and by being placed as the stanza's central line.

Stanza 47

5 As does 'wicked *Tyme*' in the garden of Adonis at III vi 39–41. S.'s phrase stands as a succinct final statement of a theme that haunts the poem: *tempus edax rerum*. See V iv 8.1 and VI iv 31.7–9*n*.

Stanza 48

1–4 Cf. *View* 45: 'time working alteration of all things'; for the proverb, see Smith 770. Bulger 1994:128 interprets **Ioue** as the World Soul confronted by disorder and change. **disseise**: deprive wrongfully. **5 still**: always; referring to Mutabilitie's

use of the term at 47.9. **6 namely**: above all, alone. **7 vertue**: power, influence.

Stanza 49

1–5 Mutabilitie is answered by her allusion to 2 Cor. 4.18: 'the things which are not sene, are eternal'.

Stanzas 50–53

Mutabilitie's review of the seven planets in the order of their distance from the earth follows the Ptolemaic system except that Jove usurps Saturn's role as the last. The planetary week recalls the week of creation, which proves her undoing for it invokes God's control over time, as A. Fowler 1964:233 notes. See also Grimm 1986:30–31.

Stanza 50

1 the first in being closest to the earth. **2 you**: 'yon', sugg. Birch 1751, for Cynthia is not addressed, as Jove is at 53.1. **3–4 Ioues dearest darling**: this slander of the virgin Diana – Jove is her father – is without classical warrant. She is seen 'on *Cynthus* greene' at II iii 31.2; her birth is described at II xii 13. **5 crake**: boast. **8 brown**: dark.

Stanza 51

4 of late: apparently referring to some recent confirmation of Mercury's notorious eccentricity, e.g. in du Bartas 1979:2.4.2.966–68. See V proem 8.8–9*n*. **8 by the way**: in his course.

52

Now *Mars* that valiant man is changed most:
    For, he some times so far runs out of square,
    That he his way doth seem quite to haue lost,
    And cleane without his vsuall sphere to fare;
    That euen these Star-gazers stonisht are
    At sight thereof, and damne their lying bookes:
    So likewise, grim Sir *Saturne* oft doth spare
    His sterne aspect, and calme his crabbed lookes:
So many turning cranks these haue, so many crookes.

53

But you *Dan Ioue*, that only constant are,
    And King of all the rest, as ye do clame,
    Are you not subiect eeke to this misfare?
    Then let me aske you this withouten blame,
    Where were ye borne? some say in *Crete* by name,
    Others in *Thebes*, and others other-where;
    But wheresoeuer they comment the same,
    They all consent that ye begotten were,
And borne here in this world, ne other can appeare.

54

Then are ye mortall borne, and thrall to me,
    Vnlesse the kingdome of the sky yee make
    Immortall, and vnchangeable to be;
    Besides, that power and vertue which ye spake,
    That ye here worke, doth many changes take,
    And your owne natures change: for, each of you
    That vertue haue, or this, or that to make,
    Is checkt and changed from his nature trew,
By others opposition or obliquid view.

55

Besides, the sundry motions of your Spheares,
    So sundry waies and fashions as clerkes faine,
    Some in short space, and some in longer yeares;
    What is the same but alteration plaine?
    Onely the starrie skie doth still remaine:
    Yet do the Starres and Signes therein still moue,
    And euen it self is mov'd, as wizards saine.
    But all that moueth, doth mutation loue:
Therefore both you and them to me I subiect proue.

56

Then since within this wide great *Vniuerse*
    Nothing doth firme and permanent appeare,
    But all things tost and turned by transuerse:
    What then should let, but I aloft should reare
    My Trophee, and from all, the triumph beare?
    Now iudge then (ô thou greatest goddesse trew!)
    According as thy selfe doest see and heare,
    And vnto me addoom that is my dew;
That is the rule of all, all being rul'd by you.

57

So hauing ended, silence long ensewed,
    Ne *Nature* to or fro spake for a space,
    But with firme eyes affixt, the ground still viewed.
    Meane while, all creatures, looking in her face,
    Expecting th'end of this so doubtfull case,
    Did hang in long suspence what would ensew,
    To whether side should fall the soueraigne place:
    At length, she looking vp with chearefull view,
The silence brake, and gaue her doome in speeches few.

Stanza 52
1 As V proem 8.8: 'most is *Mars* amisse of all the rest'. **4 without**: outside. The planets were assumed to be embedded in a sphere whose rolling caused their motion. 7–8 Saturn's baleful influence is modified by its conjunction with other planets. **aspect**: punning on the astrological sense. **9 cranks**: winding paths, apparently referring to Saturn's irregularities in the Ptolemaic system; or to the imagined turnings of his aspect compared to the faster-moving planets (the moon's 28 days and Saturn's 30 years), as Mutabilitie's **oft** suggests; see Eade 1984b:3–5. **turning**: alluding to his name.

Stanza 53
3 misfare: going astray. **5–9** The conflicting traditions of Jove's birthplace are noted by Conti 1616:2.1, who concludes that there can be no certainty. **comment**: devise.

Stanza 54
1–6 Mutabilitie's **Vnlesse** undoes her case by invoking a higher kingdom which is **vnchangeable**. Her claim that a god's nature changes applies to her, for the time will come when 'none no more change shall see' (59.5). **which ye spake**: at 48.6–8. 6–9 The power and influence (**vertue**) of a planet is affected by its position relative to the other planets, being either opposite (and then **checkt**) or oblique (and then **changed**). **obliquid** is a S. coinage used only here.

Stanza 55
2 clerkes: scholars. 4 alteration: which she personifies in the Arg. 5 the starrie skie: the crystalline sphere of fixed stars which encloses the seven concentric spheres of the planets. doth still remaine: remains constant. Mutabilitie's repeated use of **still** now reaches a climax: the stars, the zodiacal signs, and the sphere move **still**, i.e. continually. She refers to the precession of the equinoxes; see V proem 4.6–9*n*.

Stanza 56
2 That nothing is **permanent** caps her opening claim that the earth 'only seems vnmov'd and permanent' (17.7). 3 Her claim that all things are **turned by transuerse**, i.e. 'turned awry', points to the etymology of **Vniuerse**: 'one turning' (Lat. *unus* + *versus*), allowing Nature to invoke the notion of things 'all turning', i.e. 'turning to themselues at length againe' (58.6), i.e. turning-to-one. Cf. II xii 34.8–9. In Petrarch, *Trionfi*, accordingly, the **triumph** of time leads to the triumph of eternity. **4–5** Mutabilitie fulfils her ambition to rival her sister Bellona in power (vi 32.4–5). **let**: prevent. 8 Ironically, she invokes judgement against herself: she receives her due but not in the way she expects. **addoom**: judge.

Stanza 57
2 to or fro: for or against the question. 4 In effect, Nature's veil is removed by the clarity of her final judgement. 5 Expecting: awaiting. 7 whether: which.

58

I well consider all that ye haue sayd,
　　And find that all things stedfastnes doe hate
　　And changed be: yet being rightly wayd
　　They are not changed from their first estate;
　　But by their change their being doe dilate:
　　And turning to themselues at length againe,
　　Doe worke their owne perfection so by fate:
　　Then ouer them Change doth not rule and raigne;
But they raigne ouer change, and doe their states maintaine.

59

Cease therefore daughter further to aspire,
　　And thee content thus to be rul'd by me:
　　For thy decay thou seekst by thy desire;
　　But time shall come that all shall changed bee,
　　And from thenceforth, none no more change shall see.
　　So was the *Titaness* put downe and whist,
　　And *Ioue* confirm'd in his imperiall see.
　　Then was that whole assembly quite dismist,
And *Natur's* selfe did vanish, whither no man wist.

Stanza 58

2 find: also in the legal sense (*OED* 17), 'deliver a verdict'. **3–7 first estate** refers to the original (unfallen) state, so that change either leads to **perfection** (as III vi 3.9) or returns to it. In changing, things **dilate**, i.e. expand as they fulfil their natures, showing that change is not random but purposeful (see N. Frye 1990b:160–61), acting in accord with the Pauline concept of sowing a natural body to raise a spiritual body (1 Cor. 15.36–44). It is not circular, then, but spiral in returning creation to its beginning but at a higher level. The complexity of the term **dilate** and its importance in the poem are explored by P.A. Parker 1979:54–64. Nature's verdict finally answers Despaire's claim that 'strong necessitie, | . . . holds the world in his still chaunging state' (I ix 42.6–7).

Stanza 59

1 daughter: Nature claims as her own one who claimed at vi 26.4–6 to be the daughter of Chaos. **further**: further than the earth; or, 'any longer'. **2 me**: placed emphatically here, though Mutabilitie has allowed that Nature 'is the rule of all' (56.9). **3 decay**: downfall. **4–5** 'Beholde, I shewe you a secret thing . . . we shal all be changed . . . when this corruptible hathe put on incorruption, and this mortal hathe put on immortalitie, then shal be broght to passe the saying that is written, Death is swallowed vp into victorie' (1 Cor. 15.51, 54). **6 put downe**: also literally, below the moon. **whist**: silenced. **7** While Jove's sovereign power in his **see** (throne) is confirmed, it remains subordinate to Nature's authority.

The VIII.
Canto, *vnperfite.*

1

WHen I bethinke me on that speech whyleare,
    Of *Mutability*, and well it way:
  Me seemes, that though she all vnworthy were
  Of the Heav'ns Rule; yet very sooth to say,
  In all things else she beares the greatest sway.
  Which makes me loath this state of life so tickle,
  And loue of things so vaine to cast away;
  Whose flowring pride, so fading and so fickle,
Short *Time* shall soon cut down with his consuming sickle.

2

Then gin I thinke on that which Nature sayd,
    Of that same time when no more *Change* shall be,
  But stedfast rest of all things firmely stayd
  Vpon the pillours of Eternity,
  That is contrayr to *Mutabilitie*:
  For, all that moueth, doth in *Change* delight:
  But thence-forth all shall rest eternally
  With Him that is the God of Sabbaoth hight:
O that great Sabbaoth God, graunt me that Sabaoths sight.

FINIS.

Book VII Canto viii

Traditional number symbolism would seem to determine the numbering of the Mutabilitie Cantos: 6 on Mutabilitie's reign in the world; 7 on Nature's control over it; and 8 on redemption from it. See A. Fowler 1964:58 and Weatherby 1994:88–89.

Title

vnperfite: imperfect.

Stanza 1

6–7 loath: implying also 'reluctant', as Berger 1988:269 suggests. **9 Short Time**: brief, referring primarily to cyclical or planetary time in contrast to eternity, as Hieatt 1960:56–59 argues.

Stanza 2

3–4 The apt echo of the concluding lines of *Theatre, sonn* 1 – 'So I knowing the worldes unstedfastnesse, | Sith only God surmountes the force of tyme, | In God alone do stay my confidence' – is noted by Prescott 1996:144–45. **5 contrayr**: the opposite of. **6** Even in this stanza, which is meant to complement Mutabilitie's 'speech' with what **Nature sayd**, S. recalls Mutabilitie's claim at vii 55.8, which Nature endorsed at 58.2. **7–9** Alluding to the announcement of the Seventh Angel: 'that time shulde be no more' (Rev. 10.6). S. is responding to the voice heard by John that told him to 'seale vp those things which the seuen thondres haue spoken, and write them not', which the Geneva Bible glosses: 'there is no nede to write more for the vnderstanding of Gods children'. Nor is there for him. The distinction between 'Sabaoth' as 'hostes' (in Rom. 9.29) and 'Sabbath' as 'rest' was first noticed by Upton 1758. The second is esp. appropriate because 'Elizabeth' signifies 'Peace of the Lord, or Quiet Rest of the Lord' (W. Camden 1984:83); see Hamilton 1973:110. S. prays for the sight of the Lord on the last day: both for the sight of the host, the body of the redeemed, and for his place of rest after the six days of creating the six books of the *FQ.*

LETTER TO RALEIGH

The placing of the *LR* at the end of *1590* Bk III is moot. In giving 'better light in reading' the poem, it would best be prefatory. Yet the signatures allow no place before the 'A' gathering, which begins with the title and dedication to Elizabeth, and its signatures, Pp1^r-Pp3^r, suggest that it was intended to be where it is. In revealing S.'s 'general intention and meaning', which allows the reader to stand back from the poem and 'in a handfull gripe al the discourse', it is best 'hereunto annexed'. If we assume that S. originally planned to fashion the private virtues in the first six books, the *Letter* would appear 'in middest of the race' (I vii 5.4; see 12–13*n*) to afford a perspective on the whole. In the *1596* edition, however, it has no place at all, nor in the *1609* folio, and one may only speculate why. (It first appeared again in the 1611 folio.) Possibly, and most likely, the cancellation of the five concluding stanzas of Bk III led to its accidental deletion along with all but three of the *CV* and all the *DS*; or because its original position was effaced when Bks IV–VI were added, as Teskey 1990:39 argues; or because with six books now published it was no longer needed. For an analysis of the *Letter*, see Kouwenhoven 1983:1–71, 'Raleigh, Letter to' in the *SEnc*, and Erickson 1992.

S.'s principal model is Tasso's *Allegoria del poema*, which was placed at the beginning of the two 1581 editions of the *Gerusaleme Liberata* and the 1584 edition. Like the *Letter*, it shows how the poem may be read as an allegory; see 'Tasso' in the *SEnc*. A second model is the introductory essay to Renaissance editions of Virgil's *Aeneid*, as Nelson 1963:118–19 argues. A third is Crowley's introduction to his 1550 editions of *Piers Plowman* in which he urges that the book be read 'to amende thyne owne wille'. Since 'the sence [is] somewhat darcke', he adds notes 'geuynge light to the Reader' and 'a brief summe of all the principall matters spoken of in the boke'.

A
Letter of the Authors expounding his
whole intention in the course of this worke: which
for that it giueth great light to the Reader,
for the better vnderstanding is hereunto
annexed.

1   *To the Right noble, and Valorous, Sir Walter* Raleigh knight, Lo. Wardein of the Stanneryes, and her
Maiesties liefetenaunt of the County of Cornewayll.

*SIR knowing how doubtfully all Allegories may be construed, and this booke of mine, which I haue entituled
the Faery Queene, being a continued Allegory, or darke conceit, I haue thought good aswell for auoyding of*
5   *gealous opinions and misconstructions, as also for your better light in reading therof, (being so by you com-
manded,) to discouer vnto you the general intention and meaning, which in the whole course thereof I haue
fashioned, without expressing of any particular purposes or by-accidents therein occasioned. The generall end
therefore of all the booke is to fashion a gentleman or noble person in vertuous and gentle discipline: Which*

Title: on the Elizabethan conventions of letter-writing, see 'letter as genre' in the *SEnc*, and Rambuss 1993:30–41. For Raleigh's titles, see *DS 14* and *n*. The introductory statement of the letter's subject may be by the printer who has taken the phrase 'whole intention in the course of this worke' from S.'s account in the *Letter* of his 'general intention' in the poem and 'the whole course thereof'; and the phrase 'great light to the Reader' from its 'better light in reading'.

3 doubtfully: ambiguously; dangerously.

4 a continued Allegory, or darke conceit: on the genre in which one thing is said but another is meant, see 'allegory' and 'allegory, historical' in the *SEnc*. Except for Dante, S. is the only major poet who deliberately wrote his major poem as an allegory. Its place in the biblical culture of the sixteenth century was especially controversial. Although in the Bible, 'darke things were writt, hard to be vnderstood . . . | That none could read, except she [Fidelia] did them teach' (I x 13.9, 19.2), for Protestants its literal truth was primary and allegorical readings were eschewed. In contrast, poets wrote fiction that conceals truth, as Richard Mulcaster taught S.: 'when the *poetes* write sadly and soberly, without counterfeiting though they write in verse, yet they be no *poetes* in that kinde of their writing: but where they cover a truth with a fabulous veele, and resemble with alteration' (1994:266). S. refers to his poem's veil as 'dim' (*DS* 2.10), and 'shady' (*DS* 3.7), and in II proem declares it to be 'couert' in order to reveal, rather than conceal, the Queen's glory; see II proem 5.1–2*n*. The allegory is said to be **continued** because its presence is neither restricted to an episode nor intermittent but continuous, as Chapman found 'the Allegorie driven through the whole *Odysses*' (*Chapman's Homer* 2.14). On the rhetorical definition of allegory as a continued metaphor, which leads S. to use metaphor to reveal divine truth, see Wood 1997; and on the poem as 'a material manifestation of divine knowledge', see Pendergast 1996:268. On the traditional fourfold exegesis applied to Bk I, see W.R. Davis 1977.

As the poem is an allegory, not an allegory *of* any one thing, its literal level must be read in its depth, and not translated into separate horizontal layers of something else; see Hamilton 1961a:7–14. For a countering argument that it is to be read 'as an intervention into Elizabethan political thought', see Hadfield 1997:125.

4 or: S.'s prose, like his poetry, is characterized by a deeply obsessive doubling of terms.

4 darke conceit: a variation of what Sidney calls a poem's '*idea* or fore-conceit' (*Defence* 79) by which the poet's skill is to be judged rather than by the poem itself. For an extended account of the works of Spenser and Sidney in terms of Aristotelian *mimesis*, see Heninger 1988.

7 by-accidents: incidental matter.

7 generall end: i.e. to fashion readers in the virtues fashioned by the poem, as Caxton printed Malory in 1485 'to the entente that noble men may see and lerne the noble actes of chyualrye . . . used in tho dayes' (2); as Elyot recommended the books of Homer 'where with the reders shall be so all inflamed, that they most feruently shall desire and coueite, by the imitation of their vertues, to acquire semblable glorie' (1907:36–37); and as Harington translated Ariosto to make readers 'capable of vertue and good discipline' (1972:2). See 'reader in *The Faerie Queene*' and 'poetics, Elizabethan' in the *SEnc*, Meyer 1991, and the argument by Teskey 1996:99: 'By drawing the reader into its system, the poem "fashions" an intellectual habit'.

8 fashion: represent; train; mould, create, as *Am* 8.9: 'You . . . fashion me within'. The poem's sub-title, '*Fashioning* XII. Morall vertues', indicates that the poem fashions a virtue by showing a hero fashioning or fashioned by it, as Castiglione in the *Courtier* 16 intends to 'fashion such a Courtier, as the Prince that shall be worthie to have him in his service, although his state be but small, may notwithstanding be called a mighty Lord'.

8 a gentleman or noble person: the two social orders may be distinguished, as they are in the order of the *DS*; or they

for that I conceiued shoulde be most plausible and pleasing, being coloured with an historicall fiction, the
10 *which the most part of men delight to read, rather for variety of matter, then for profite of the ensample:*
  I chose the historye of king Arthure, as most fitte for the excellency of his person, being made famous by
  many mens former workes, and also furthest from the daunger of enuy, and suspition of present time. In which
  I haue followed all the antique Poets historicall, first Homere, who in the Persons of Agamemnon and Vlysses
  hath ensampled a good gouernour and a vertuous man, the one in his Ilias, the other in his Odysseis: then
15 *Virgil, whose like intention was to doe in the person of Aeneas: after him Ariosto comprised them both in his*
  Orlando: and lately Tasso disseuered them againe, and formed both parts in two persons, namely that part
  which they in Philosophy call Ethice, or vertues of a priuate man, coloured in his Rinaldo: The other named
  Politice in his Godfredo. By ensample of which excellente Poets, I labour to pourtraict in Arthure, before he was
  king, the image of a braue knight, perfected in the twelue priuate morall vertues, as Aristotle hath deuised,
20 *the which is the purpose of these first twelue bookes: which if I finde to be well accepted, I may be perhaps encor-*
  aged, to frame the other part of pollitike vertues in his person, after that hee came to be king. To some I know

may overlap as they do in Mulcaster 1994:197–99, though, for him, 'to become a *gentleman* is to beare the cognisance of vertue' (195). The phrase may include women: in the *Courtier* 188–89, Lord Julian resolves 'to fashion . . . a perfect gentle-woman of the Court', and Mulcaster urged that women be educated. See Quilligan 1983:38–40. Most likely, though, **noble person** refers to the nobly born.

9 plausible: 'acceptable, pleasaunte' (T. Cooper 1565 on Lat. *plausibilis*), and hence 'deserving of applause' (*OED*); also 'credible', as suggested by S.'s praise of Xenophon for offering what 'might best be'. In offering **discipline** that is **pleasing**, S. follows the Horatian commonplace that the poet seeks to profit (*prodesse*) and to delight (*delectare*), mingling the useful (*utile*) with the sweet (*dulce*).

9 coloured with an historicall fiction: referring primarily to the colours of rhetoric by which the history is feigned, in general accord with Boccaccio's claim that poetry veils truth 'in a fair and fitting garment of fiction' (1930:14.7), but more with Sidney's claim that readers, turning to poetry 'looking but for fiction . . . shall use the narration but as an imaginative ground-plot of a profitable invention' (*Defence* 103). On S.'s fiction as history, see Steadman 1995:101–22 and Galbraith 2000:31–74.

11 the historye of king Arthure: see 'Arthur, legend of', in the *SEnc*. Of the three Christian worthies of the traditional nine, Charlemagne had been chosen by Ariosto in *Orl. Fur.*, and Godfrey of Boulogne by Tasso in *Ger. Lib.*, leaving Arthur for S., an appropriate but also fitting choice since his history as the last Emperor of the West helped legitimize Tudor rule. See III iii 26–50*n*, and Millican 1932:37–105; and as S. renovates a British Arthurian tradition, see Summers 1997. In claiming that Arthur was **most fitte for the excellency of his person**, S. agrees with Caxton that he is 'the moost renomed Crysten kyng, fyrst and chyef of the thre best Crysten and worthy' (1). See 'Arthur in *The Faerie Queene*' in the *SEnc*, and McCabe 1993b. Since the poem's fiction treats Arthur before he was king, for which there was little historical evidence, S. is free from **enuy, and suspition of present time** as shown, e.g. by E.K. in condemning 'certain fine fablers and lowd lyers, such as were the Authors of King Arthure' (gloss to *SC Apr.* 120).

12 many mens former workes: chiefly Geoffrey of Monmouth, *Historia regum Britanniae*, and Malory, *Le Morte Darthur*.

13–18 the antique Poets historicall: on the four who are named, and on the traditional interpretation of their works, see the appropriate entries in the *SEnc*. They are invoked because 'Poesie historicall is of all other next the diuine most honorable and worthy' (Puttenham 1936:39). **Orlando** is the hero of

Ariosto's *Orlando Furioso* (1532); and **Rinaldo** and **Godfredo** refer either to the characters or to the works in which they appear: Tasso, *Rinaldo* (1562) and *Gerusalemme Liberata* (1581, first published in 1580 as *Il Goffredo* in which Rinaldo also appears); see IV iii 45.2–6. Harvey remarked in 1580 that Spenser 'flatly professed' to him that he intended 'to emulate, and hope to ouergo' *Orlando Furioso* (Spenser 1912:628), possibly prompted by the canonization of his poem in the sixteenth century; see Javitch 1991. For his imitation of Ariosto and Tasso, see Fichter 1982:70–155, Kirkpatrick 1995:182–92, and Alistair Fox 1997:136–80. On Ariosto, see also Alpers 1967:160–99; on Tasso, see also Helgerson 1992:44–50, Rhu 1993a:57–76, and Treip 1994:270–74. For imitation as emulation that seeks to surpass its model, see Pigman III 1980:22–26.

19 twelue priuate morall vertues: when asked by Lodowick Bryskett if he would 'vouchsafe to open unto us the goodly cabinet, in which this excellent treasure of vertues lieth locked up from the vulgar sort', S. declined, saying 'I have already undertaken a work tending to the same effect, which is in *heroical verse*, under the title of a *Faerie Queene*, to represent all the moral vertues, assigning to every vertue, a Knight to be the patron and defender of the same; in whose actions and feates of armes and chivalry, the operations of that vertue, whereof he is the protector, are to be expressed, and the vices & unruly appetites that oppose themselves against the same, to be beaten downe and overcome' (Bryskett 1970:22). Arthur is **perfected** in the twelve virtues because he contains each in its perfected state integrated with the rest to constitute his 'magnificence' (38), much as in *Ger. Lib.*, as Tasso explains in 'The Allegorie of the Poem', 'the *Army* compounded of diuers Princes, and of other Christian souldiers, signified *Man*'.

19 as Aristotle hath deuised: in the *Nicomachean Ethics*, Aristotle distinguishes the **priuate morall vertues** from the **polliticke** (public) virtues, which he treats in the *Politics*. On the distinction, see Nohrnberg 1976:60–65, Horton 1978:124–37, and 'virtues' in the *SEnc*. Or if the phrase modifies **pourtraict**, as J.L. Mills 1977:247 suggests, S. refers to his *Poetics*, specifically to his claim that poetry deals with the universal rather than the particular, as Kouwenhoven 1983:14 claims. S. may refer to **twelue** virtues because that number is the traditional number of books in an epic; or is associated with the cosmic pattern, as Demaray 1991:100 suggests. (That his model was not Aristotle but the *Corpus Hermeticum*, see Cummings 1990.)

21 after that hee came to be king: possibly later books would treat the public virtues shown perfected in Arthur in his conquest of Rome; see I xi 7.2–6*n*.

this Methode will seeme displeasaunt, which had rather haue good discipline deliuered plainly in way of pre-
cepts, or sermoned at large, as they vse, then thus clowdily enwrapped in Allegoricall deuises. But such, me
seeme, should be satisfide with the vse of these dayes, seeing all things accounted by their showes, and nothing
25 *esteemed of, that is not delightfull and pleasing to commune sence. For this cause is Xenophon preferred before*
Plato, for that the one in the exquisite depth of his iudgement, formed a Commune welth such as it should be,
but the other in the person of Cyrus and the Persians fashioned a gouernement such as might best be: So much
more profitable and gratious is doctrine by ensample, then by rule. So haue I laboured to doe in the person of
Arthure: whome I conceiue after his long education by Timon, to whom he was by Merlin deliuered to be
30 *brought vp, so soone as he was borne of the Lady Igrayne, to haue seene in a dream or vision the Faery Queen,*
with whose excellent beauty rauished, he awaking resolued to seeke her out, and so being by Merlin armed, and
by Timon throughly instructed, he went to seeke her forth in Faerye land. In that Faery Queene I meane glory
in my generall intention, but in my particular I conceiue the most excellent and glorious person of our
soueraine the Queene, and her kingdome in Faery land. And yet in some places els, I doe otherwise shadow
35 *her. For considering she beareth two persons, the one of a most royall Queene or Empresse, the other of a most*
vertuous and beautifull Lady, this latter part in some places I doe express in Belphœbe, fashioning her name
according to your owne excellent conceipt of Cynthia, (Phœbe and Cynthia being both names of Diana.) So
in the person of Prince Arthure I sette forth magnificence in particular, which vertue for that (according to
Aristotle and the rest) it is the perfection of all the rest, and conteineth in it them all, therefore in the whole
40 *course I mention the deedes of Arthure applyable to that vertue, which I write of in that booke. But of the xii.*
other vertues, I make xii. other knights the patrones, for the more variety of the history: Of which these three
bookes contayn three. The first of the knight of the Redcrosse, in whome I express Holynes: The seconde of Sir
Guyon, in whome I sette forth Temperaunce: The third of Britomartis a Lady knight, in whome I picture
Chastity. But because the beginning of the whole worke seemeth abrupte and as depending vpon other
45 *antecedents, it needs that ye know the occasion of these three knights seuerall aduentures. For the Methode of*
a Poet historical is not such, as of an Historiographer. For an Historiographer discourseth of affayres orderly
as they were donne, accounting as well the times as the actions, but a Poet thrusteth into the middest, euen
where it most concerneth him, and there recoursing to the thinges forepaste, and diuining of things to come,

---

22 this Methode, which is to offer **good discipline** not **in way of precepts, or sermoned at large** (see 'homiletics' in the *SEnc*) but **clowdily enwrapped in Allegoricall deuises**, is consonant with Sidney's claim, in *Defence* 93, that the poet teaches readers not by instructing them by moral precepts but by delighting them with images of the virtues in order to move them to 'see the form of goodness (which seen they cannot but love)'.

25–28 Xenophon preferred before Plato: while S. may be expected to prefer Plato to Xenophon because the *Republic* presents what **should be** while the *Cyropaedia* presents what **might best be**, he praises Plato only for his judgement in forming a commonwealth by **rule** while Xenophon is praised for having **fashioned** his commonwealth by **ensample**, i.e. by images of virtues and vices. Sidney makes much the same distinction: the *Cyropaedia* is not 'wholly imaginative' (as is the *Republic*) but works substantially 'to bestow a Cyrus upon the world to make many Cyruses' (79). On the distinction, see Nohrnberg 1976:26–28; on S.'s severely qualified praise of Xenophon, see Erickson 1992:148–51.

29–30 after his long education: on Arthur's birth and education, see I ix 3–5; on his **dream or vision**, see I ix 13–15.

32–35 glory: on **that Faery Queene**, or Gloriana, as **glory**, see I i 3.2–3n. On her **Faery land**, see 'fairyland' in the *SEnc*, and Erickson 1996:3–8. Her **two persons** correspond to the distinction between 'a good gouernour and a vertuous man' (14), referring here to the concept of the Queen's two bodies,

as Elizabeth acknowledged that she was 'but one bodye naturallye considered though by his [God's] permission a bodye politique to governe' (cited M. Axton 1977:38), and as the poem shows in Belphœbe and Gloriana (see III proem 5.7–9). On the concept, see Kantorowicz 1957:7, Hardin 1992:22–28, and Marcus 1988:53–66; and on the extension of the concept to the poem's two bodies, see D.L. Miller 1988:68–119.

37 Cynthia: see III proem 4.3–9.

38 magnificence: see 'magnanimity, magnificence' in the *SEnc*; also Armbrust 1990. The etymological sense of the first term, *magnus* + *animus*, 'great-souled', is expressed in etymological sense of the second, *magnus* + *facere*, 'greatly doing': Arthur's virtue is shown in his virtuous actions. Cf. the dedication of the poem to the Queen as 'magnificent empresse'.

39 Aristotle and the rest: on the medieval exegesis of Aristotle's *Ethics*, see 'Aristotle and his Commentators' in the *SEnc*.

39 perfection of all the rest refers to the description of Arthur 'perfected in the twelue priuate morall vertues' (19).

45 Methode: see 'logic' in the *SEnc*.

47 thrusteth into the middest: a commonplace that derives from Horace, *Ars Poetica* 146–52.

48 diuining of things to come: on S.'s prophetic role, see 'prophecies' in the *SEnc*. The cyclical structure given the narrative by relating its beginning at the end is discussed by Steadman 1995:80–85.

maketh a pleasing Analysis of all. The beginning therefore of my history, if it were to be told by an
50 *Historiographer should be the twelfth booke which is the last, where I deuise that the Faery Queene kept her Annuall feaste xii. dayes, vppon which xii. seuerall dayes, the occasions of the xii. seuerall aduentures hapned, which being vndertaken by xii. seuerall knights, are in these xii books seuerally handled and discoursed. The first was this. In the beginning of the feast, there presented him selfe a tall clownishe younge man, who falling before the Queen of Faries desired a boone (as the manner then was) which during that feast she might not*
55 *refuse: which was that hee might haue the atchieuement of any aduenture, which during that feaste should happen, that being graunted, he rested him on the floore, vnfitte through his rusticity for a better place. Soone after entred a faire Ladye in mourning weedes, riding on a white Asse, with a dwarfe behind her leading a warlike steed, that bore the Armes of a knight, and his speare in the dwarfes hand. Shee falling before the Queene of Faeries, complayned that her father and mother an ancient King and Queene, had bene by an huge*
60 *dragon many years shut vp in a brasen Castle, who thence suffred them not to yssew: and therefore besought the Faery Queene to assygne her some one of her knights to take on him that exployt. Presently that clownish person vpstarting, desired that aduenture: whereat the Queene much wondering, and the Lady much gaine-saying, yet he earnestly importuned his desire. In the end the Lady told him that vnlesse that armour which she brought, would serue him (that is the armour of a Christian man specified by Saint Paul v. Ephes.) that*
65 *he could not succeed in that enterprise, which being forthwith put vpon him with dewe furnitures thereunto, he seemed the goodliest man in al that company, and was well liked of the Lady. And eftsoones taking on him knighthood, and mounting on that straunge Courser, he went forth with her on that aduenture: where begin-neth the first booke, vz.*

A gentle knight was pricking on the playne. &c.

70 *The second day ther came in a Palmer bearing an Infant with bloody hands, whose Parents he complained to haue bene slayn by an Enchaunteresse called Acrasia: and therfore craued of the Faery Queene, to appoint him some knight, to performe that aduenture, which being assigned to Sir Guyon, he presently went forth with that same Palmer: which is the beginning of the second booke and the whole subiect thereof. The third day there*

50–51 her Annuall feaste: described by Guyon as 'An yearely solemne feast she [the Faerie Queene] wontes to make | The day that first doth lead the yeare around' (II ii 42.6–7). Most likely, **xii. dayes** refers to twelve days of the Christmas season from 25 Dec. to 6 Jan., the only twelve-day festivity in the calendar, as Wall 1987 notes. At this time Christ's birth returns 'the compasse of expired yeres to theyr former date and first commencement' (E.K., *Arg.* to *SC*). Possibly the feast coincides with the Queen's Accession Day tilts on 17 Nov. (see A. Fowler 1964:170n1, and Eade 1984a:178–79); or 25 March, the beginning of the calendar year, 'for it is wel known . . . that the yeare beginneth in March' (E.K., *Arg.* to *SC*); or 25 April, St George's Day, celebrated by the Order of the Garter of which the Queen was the head. The choice of date may be determined by the *chronographia* in Bk II; see II ii 44.1–4n and 46.1–3n. According to S.'s entirely schematic statement, a knight leaves on each day of the annual feast: 'In the beginning of the feast . . . The second day ther came in . . . The third day there came in'; or on successive feasts over twelve years, each knight taking a year to accomplish a quest. The latter suggests a relay race: Guyon begins his quest just when the Red Cross Knight has ended his (II i 32.6–7) and intends to return to the court (I xii 18, 41); and Calidore meets Artegall at a similar moment (VI i 4). On the narrative chronology, see McCabe 1989a:84–91.

52 seuerally handled and discoursed: differently, as the four uses of the word in this sentence suggests, in order to note each book's distinctive structure. In devoting a book to the exploits of one knight, S. imitates Malory; see Rovang 1996:40–49.

54 desired a boone: on the folklore motif of 'the rash promise', which is linked here to the licensed misrule of May Day or the Whitsunday festival when access to the Queen by commoners was allowed, see Laroque 1991:148–54. Yates 1977:99 notes that in an idealized picture of the Accession Day tournaments shown in the Ditchley Ms., the Queen is introduced to a company of homely people led by a 'clownishly clad' knight. S.'s model seems to be Malory's tale of Gareth or the Fair Unknown, as Rovang 1996:23–32 argues. The details presented here are consonant with Bk I, the dwarf serving as a squire (as at I vii 19), and the steed called **straunge** (67) because it comes from another country (*OED* 1).

61 Presently: immediately. **clownish**: rustic.

64 v. Ephes: i.e. see (*vide*) Eph. 6.11–17.

65 dewe furnitures: proper weapons.

70 The second day: the inconsistency in the narrative about the occasion of Guyon's quest described here, and at II i 61 where he vows to avenge the deaths of the parents of the bloody-handed babe only after he and the Palmer find him with his dying mother and dead father, has been variously explained: e.g. that S. had forgotten what he had recently written; that the occasion is here described schematically (Hamilton 1961a:53–54); or that he invites the reader to reread in order to understand his allegory (Herman 1998:207–11).

73 The third day: the occasion is described at III xi 7–19. The differences are noted by Roche in the *SEnc* 270.

75   *came in, a Groome who complained before the Faery Queene, that a vile Enchaunter called Busirane had in*
hand a most faire Lady called Amoretta, whom he kept in most grieuous torment, because she would not yield
him the pleasure of her body. Whereupon Sir Scudamour the louer of that Lady presently tooke on him that
aduenture. But being vnable to performe it by reason of the hard Enchauntments, after long sorrow, in the
end met with Britomartis, who succoured him, and reskewed his loue.

But by occasion hereof, many other aduentures are intermedled, but rather as Accidents, then intendments.
80   *As the loue of Britomart, the ouerthrow of Marinell, the misery of Florimell, the vertuousnes of Belphœbe, the*
lasciuiousnes of Hellenora, and many the like.

Thus much Sir, I haue briefly ouerronne to direct your vnderstanding to the wel-head of the History, that
from thence gathering the whole intention of the conceit, ye may as in a handfull gripe al the discourse, which
otherwise may happily seeme tedious and confused. So humbly crauing the continuaunce of your honorable
85   *fauour towards me, and th'eternall establishment of your happines, I humbly take leaue.*

23. Ianuary. 1589.

Yours most humbly affectionate.
Ed. Spenser.

---

79 intermedled: referring to the interlacing of stories in a romance. Those listed include the chief matter of the first ten cantos of Bk III in their narrative order as **Accidents** – called 'particular purposes or by-accidents' at 7 – as distinct from its **intendments**, namely, the fashioning of the virtue of chastity seen in Britomart's freeing of Amoret from Busirane after Scudamour had failed. See Roche 1964:196–98. On the conflict in the poem between epic and chivalric romance, see Helgerson 1992:48–59 and C. Burrow 1993.

84 happily: haply.

86 23. Ianuary. 1589: i.e. OS = 1590 NS. In the sixteenth century the new year did not officially begin until 25 March. Brink 1994b argues for 1589. Books I–III were entered in the Stationers' Register on 1 Dec. 1589.

COMMENDATORY VERSES AND DEDICATORY SONNETS

For a general account, see 'The Faerie Queene, commendatory verses and dedicatory sonnets' in the *SEnc*. It is not known why these poems do not precede the *FQ* where they could more directly lure prospective buyers. Perhaps because the present prefatory matter – the title page backed by the dedication to the Queen signed '*Ed. Spenser*' who on the second leaf of signature A introduces himself as 'Lo I the man . . .' – could not be more startlingly effective. Perhaps the printer, who usually set up prefatory matter last, lacked copy of the *CV* and *DS* and proceeded with the title page and dedication. What might have served the reader as a threshold, a liminal space to introduce the reader to the poem, becomes instead an epilogue, remaining apart from it as a commentary on its publication as a literary and social event; see Erickson 1997. F.R. Johnson 1933:17 suggests that possibly four presses and probably two were used, and 'that it seems highly probable that in 1590 the second largest printing-house in London was devoting at least half its resources [two presses] to the rapid printing of Spenser's *Faerie Queene*'. As a consequence, matter usually printed first, if it were not available, was tacked on at the end. Nor is it known why the *DS* exist in several states in the copies examined by Johnson 15–16: some have ten sonnets ending with 'Finis'; some add seven new sonnets to eight of these and in a new order; and some include all ten of the first state, making a total of seventeen. The simplest but most unlikely explanation is that Spenser forgot to include Burghley, and in adding a sonnet to him decided to add six more. Nor is it known why all were omitted – together with the *LR* and all but three of the *CV* – in the *1596* edition. The simplest and most likely explanation is that six years after the appearance of the first three books, the poem no longer needed an appendix: 'Who knows not the *FQ*?' Or that the *DS* were omitted because the dedication to the Queen had proven sufficient; and that *CV* 1–3 were included only to fill in the otherwise blank eighth leaf of the signature Oo, as Johnson 19 suggests. (For a thorough investigation of the different states of the DS, see Brink's article forthcoming in *RES*.) Finally, it is not known when they were written except for *DS 12*: since Walsingham died on 2 Apr. 1590, presumably the sonnet to him was written before that date.

COMMENDATORY VERSES

The signature **W.R.** at the end of *CV 2* applies also to *CV 1*, and identifies its author as Walter Raleigh, as his wife acknowledged in her folio copy of S.'s works for their son, 'both thes of your fathar's making' (Oakeshott 1971:4); see IV vii 36.8–9*n*. The author of *CV 3*, **Hobynoll**, is Gabriel Harvey, who is named as S.'s 'especiall good freend Hobbinoll' by E.K. in his gloss to *SC Sept*. 176. The other four remain unidentified. John Worthington complained in 1660 that those 'whose initial letters of their names only are set down . . . [would] need some Oedipus to discover them' (*Sp All* 252). Possibly **R.S.** is the compiler of *The Phoenix Nest* (1593); or the one who commends Wilfrid Holme's *The Fall . . . of Rebellion* (1572), and Gascoigne's *Hundreth Sundrie Flowres* (1575); or (though unlikely, for he was a Catholic exile on the continent) the Irish translator and historian Richard Stanyhurst. An **H.B.** commends Speght's *Works of Chaucer* (1598). (I owe this information to Steven May.) **W.L.** may be William Lisle, who comments on S.'s stanzas in his *c.* 1596 tr. of du Bartas, and praises the *Gnat* in his tr. of Virgil's *Eclogues* in 1628 (*Sp All* 44, 178). **Ignoto** is unusual – F.B. Williams 1962 lists only three dedicatory or commendatory verses so signed in English books before 1641, this being the first – but appropriate to conclude the praise of a poet whose first poem appeared anonymously as the work of one 'unknown to most men' (*Epistle* to *SC*). On the uses of anonymity in early modern England, see North 1994.

The variety and grouping of stanza forms in the seven poems may be deliberate. The first two are carefully balanced quatorzaines: *CV 1* is modishly Italianate with its pentameter lines in three alternately rhymed quatrains rounded out with a couplet; *CV 2* is native and old-fashioned in using the poulter's measure (twelve syllables followed by fourteen), while preserving the sonnet's division into eight and six lines.

CV 3 stands alone with its six six-line stanzas rhyming *ababcc*. As 'Hobynoll' is Colin Clout's special friend in the *SC*, his verse uses the stanza form of that poem's opening and closing eclogues. In contrast, the grouped *CV 4* and *CV 5* use a single ten-line stanza, the first rhyming *abab abab cc*, the second *abab cdcd ee*. Both *CV 6* and *CV 7* use four six-line stanzas rhyming *ababcc* (except the latter's third stanza which rhymes *ababaa*).

For ease of reference, the verses are numbered: *CV 1* and *CV 2* by Raleigh; *CV 3* by Hobynoll; *CV 4* by R.S.; *CV 5* by H.B.; *CV 6* by W.L.; *CV 7* by Ignoto.

CV1

¶A Vision vpon this conceipt of the
Faery Queene.

ME thought I saw the graue, where *Laura* lay,
Within that Temple, where the vestall flame
Was wont to burne, and passing by that way,
To see that buried dust of liuing fame,
Whose tumbe faire loue, and fairer vertue kept,
All suddeinly I saw the Faery Queene:
At whose approch the soule of *Petrarke* wept,
And from thenceforth those graces were not seene.
For they this Queene attended, in whose steed
Obliuion laid him downe on *Lauras* herse:
Hereat the hardest stones were seene to bleed,
And grones of buried ghostes the heuens did perse.
    Where *Homers* spright did tremble all for griefe,
    And curst th'accesse of that celestiall theife.

CV2

Another of the same.

THe prayse of meaner wits this worke like profit brings,
As doth the Cuckoes song delight when Philumena *sings.*
If thou hast formed right true vertues face herein:
Vertue her selfe can best discerne, to whome they writen bin.
If thou hast beauty praysd, let her sole lookes diuine
Iudge if ought therein be amis, and mend it by her eine.
If Chastitie want ought, or Temperaunce her dew,
Behold her Princely mind aright, and write thy Queene *anew.*
Meane while she shall perceiue, how far her vertues sore
Aboue the reach of all that liue, or such as wrote of yore:
And thereby will excuse and fauour thy good will:
Whose vertue can not be exprest, but by an Angels quill.
    Of me no lines are lou'd, nor letters are of price,
    Of all which speak our English tongue, but those of thy deuice.
                            W.R.

CV 1 and CV 2

Companion poems, as their shared title indicates. The first offers Raleigh's vision of the Faerie Queene as she approaches; in the second, she has arrived to receive his compliments, the vision of her now replaced by praise of 'her Princely mind'. Both are self-serving: in the first, Raleigh's vision of the Faerie Queene displaces Arthur's vision of her, which is the originary vision of the *FQ*. S. himself creeps in only in the concluding phrase as 'that celestiall theife'. In the second, the repeated 'If thou hast' implies that S. has not, leading to the advice that if (or since) his treatment of the virtues in Bks II and III is lacking, he should write his poem **anew**, i.e. either write those books over again, or (more likely) continue writing. *CV 2* is sufficiently reminiscent of *FQ* III proem to suggest that in 1589 S. read it to the Queen in Raleigh's presence.

CV 1

Title: since **Faery Queene** is in italics, the title may refer to S.'s poem, or to Elizabeth as that poem's 'darke conceit', though for Raleigh there may be no difference because he has his 'owne excellent concept of Cynthia' (i.e. Elizabeth), as S. acknowledges in the *LR* 37. See May 1989:35. His reference to Petrarch's love and virtue may have been designed to place himself as a major subject of Spenser's poem, specifically III v 41–50 where the love-stricken Timias is overcome by his vision of Belphœbe whose beauty is guarded by her virtue; see III v 32*n*, IV vii 36.8–9*n*. On this poem, see Cousins 1983 and Bednarz 1996. **2 that Temple**: the temple of Vesta at Rome with its virgins serving the Roman goddess of the earth. As she is 'of the fire

æthereall' (VII vii 26.4), she is the keeper of poetic fame, alluding to Elizabeth who is seen as the Vestal Virgin, e.g. in the Sieve portrait. **5 faire loue, and fairer vertue**: their conjunction is evident in Sidney's phrase: 'who could see virtue would be wonderfully ravished with the love of her beauty' (*Defence* 98), and in III iii 1 where love is defined as the emotion that responds to true beauty and chooses virtue as his dearest dame. Raleigh's 1588 portrait, which is designed to compliment the Queen, bears the motto *Amor et Virtute*; noted Strong 1977:74. **13–14** S. was praised as 'the only Homer living'; see *Sp All* 37. **that celestiall theife**: Hermes or Mercury, the 'God of . . . thefte' (T. Cooper 1565); hence associated with 'cunning theeveries' in *Mother Hubberd* 1287.

CV 2

1–2 Philumena: i.e. Philomela, the traditional figure for the pastoral poet, as in *SC Aug.* 183–86. In *Nov.* 25, S. is praised as 'the nightingale . . . sovereigne of song'; as it is Colin's bird, see P. Cheney 1993:80. There may be a topical allusion: in a lyric written in 1590 or 1591 in praise of the Queen as virtue and beauty personified, Essex attacked Raleigh as 'that cursed cuckowe's throate, | That so hath crost sweete Philomela's note'; noted May 1989:36. **4–5** The conjunction of **Vertue** and **beauty** in the Queen is consonant with Sidney's praise of her as one 'in whom the whole storie of vertue is written with the language of Beautie' (*The Four Foster Children of Desire*, in J. Wilson 1980:70–71). **14 of thy deuice**: i.e. lines devised by you, alluding to his lines 'clowdily enwrapped in Allegoricall deuises', as S. explains to Raleigh in the *LR* 23.

CV3

To the learned Shepeheard.

COllyn I see by thy new taken taske,
    some sacred fury hath enricht thy braynes,
That leades thy muse in haughty verse to maske,
    and loath the layes that longs to lowly swaynes.
That lifts thy notes from Shepheardes vnto kinges,
So like the liuely Larke that mounting singes.

Thy louely Rosolinde seemes now forlorne,
    and all thy gentle flockes forgotten quight,
Thy chaunged hart now holdes thy pypes in scorne,
    those prety pypes that did thy mates delight.
Those trusty mates, that loued thee so well,
Whom thou gau'st mirth: as they gaue thee the bell.

Yet as thou earst with thy sweete roundelayes,
    didst stirre to glee our laddes in homely bowers:
So moughtst thou now in these refyned layes,
    delight the daintie eares of higher powers.
And so mought they in their deepe skanning skill
Alow and grace our Collyns flowing quyll.

And fare befall that Faery Queene *of thine,*
    in whose faire eyes loue linckt with vertue sittes:
Enfusing by those bewties fyers deuyne,
    such high conceites into thy humble wittes,
As raised hath poore pastors oaten reede,
From rustick tunes, to chaunt heroique deedes.

So mought thy Redcrosse knight *with happy hand*
    victorious be in that faire Ilands right:
Which thou dost vayle in Type of Faery land
    Elyzas blessed field, that Albion *hight.*
That shieldes her friendes, and warres her mightie foes,
Yet still with people, peace, and plentie flowes.

But (iolly shepheard) though with pleasing style,
    thou feast the humour of the Courtly trayne:
Let not conceipt thy setled sence beguile,
    ne daunted be through enuy or disdaine.
Subiect thy dome to her Empyring spright,
From whence thy Muse, and all the world takes light.

                                             Hobynoll.

CV 3
Harvey's poem answers Raleigh's by recalling S.'s role as the pastoral poet when 'our pypes . . . shrild as lowde as Larke' (*SC Nov.* 71). **3–7** The alliterative play on 'l' imitates S.'s pastoral style, perhaps mockingly – esp. in the fourth line – because Harvey disliked the excessive use of the figure. **15–18** On S.'s appeal for patronage by writing the *FQ*, see 'patronage' in the *SEnc*. **20** Appropriating Raleigh's praise of 'faire loue, and fairer vertue' in Laura (*CV* 1.5). **25 thy Redcrosse knight**: here seen as '*Saint George* of mery England' (I x 61.9) in the service of the Queen. **35 her Emypring spright**: i.e. the Queen's absolute and empowering rule.

CV4

FAyre *Thamis* streame, that from *Ludds* stately towne,
Runst paying tribute to the Ocean seas,
Let all thy Nymphes and Syrens of renowne
Be silent, whyle this Bryttane *Orpheus* playes:
Nere thy sweet bankes, there liues that sacred crowne,
Whose hand strowes Palme and neuer-dying bayes,
Let all at once, with thy soft murmuring sowne
Present her with this worthy Poets prayes.
For he hath taught hye drifts in shepeherdes weedes,
And deepe conceites now singes in *Faeries* deedes.

R.S.

CV5

GRaue Muses march in triumph and with prayses,
Our Goddesse here hath giuen you leaue to Land:
And biddes this rare dispenser of your graces
Bow downe his brow vnto her sacred hand.
Desertes findes dew in that most princely doome,
In whose sweete brest are all the Muses bredde:
So did that great Augustus erst in Roome
With leaues of fame adorne his Poets hedde.
Faire be the guerdon of your Faery Queene,
Euen of the fairest that world hath seene.

H.B.

CV 4

1 Ludds   stately towne: i.e. London; see II x 46.   **4 this Bryttane Orpheus**: as Orpheus's song gathered trees around him (Ovid, *Met.* 10.86–105), S. has such power over the nymphs of the Thames, apparently referring to his lost *Epithalamium Thamesis*. See the account in his letter to Harvey (Spenser 1912:612). On S. as an Orphic poet, see P. Cheney 1993:7, 117, and esp. 294*n*22.   **10 deepe conceites**: cf. S.'s reference to the *FQ* as a 'darke conceit' (*LR* 4).

CV 5

3 this rare dispenser: for the play on S.'s name, see II ix 27.5–9*n*.   **7–10** Praise of S. as the English Virgil is designed to supplement (and correct) praise of him as the English Petrarch, Homer, and Orpheus.

CV6

WHen stout *Achilles* heard of *Helens* rape
And what reuenge the States of Greece deuisd:
Thinking by sleight the fatall warres to scape,
In womans weedes him selfe he then disguisde:
But this deuise *Vlysses* soone did spy,
And brought him forth, the chaunce of warre to try.

When *Spencer* saw the same was spredd so large,
Through Faery land of their renowned Queene:
Loth that his Muse should take so great a charge,
As in such haughty matter to be seene,
To seeme a shepeheard then he made his choice,
But *Sydney* heard him sing, and knew his voice.

And as *Vlysses* brought faire *Thetis* sonne
From his retyred life to menage armes:
So *Spencer* was by *Sidneys* speaches wonne,
To blaze her fame not fearing future harmes:
For well he knew, his Muse would soone be tyred
In her high praise, that all the world admired.

Yet as *Achilles* in those warlike frayes,
Did win the palme from all the *Grecian* Peeres:
So *Spencer* now to his immortall prayse,
Hath wonne the Laurell quite from all his feres.
What though his taske exceed a humaine witt,
He is excus'd, sith *Sidney* thought it fitt.

W.L.

CV 6
Ovid's story, *Met.* 13.162–64, of how Achilles's mother fore-seeing his death in battle had him disguised as a woman only to be discovered by Ulysses, provides the comparison to Spenser who disguised himself as a shepherd to write the *SC* believing he was not ready to write of 'Fierce warres' (I proem 1.9) in the *FQ* only to be discovered by Sidney when the *SC* was dedicated to him. In *DS* 15.6, S. acknowledges Sidney as the one 'Who first my Muse did lift out of the flore'. As S.'s choice of epic genre constitutes a renunciation of feminine disguise, see W. Wall 1993:227–33. **17–18** These lines seem to belong after 11: S. decided to be a pastoral poet because he knew that his muse could not **take so great a charge** of praising the Queen as she deserved. Or, if they belong here: Sidney knew that S.'s muse would soon be attired in heroic garb to praise her.

CV7

TO looke vpon a worke of rare deuise
The which a workman setteth out to view,
And not to yield it the deserued prise,
That vnto such a workmanship is dew,
　　Doth either proue the iudgement to be naught
　　Or els doth shew a mind with enuy fraught.

To labour to commend a peece of worke,
Which no man goes about to discommend,
Would raise a iealous doubt that there did lurke,
Some secret doubt, whereto the prayse did tend.
　　For when men know the goodnes of the wyne,
　　T'is needlesse for the hoast to haue a sygne.

Thus then to shew my iudgement to be such
As can discerne of colours blacke, and white,
As alls to free my minde from enuies tuch,
That neuer giues to any man his right,
　　I here pronounce this workmanship is such,
　　As that no pen can set it forth too much.

And thus I hang a garland at the dore,
Not for to shew the goodnes of the ware:
But such hath beene the custome heretofore,
And customes very hardly broken are.
　　And when your tast shall tell you this is trew,
　　Then looke you giue your hoast his vtmost dew.

　　　　　　　　　　　　　　　　Ignoto.

CV 7

The poem fittingly concludes the *CV*, and remains fittingly anonymous, by dismissing any commendation of S.'s poem in four carefully argued stanzas: not to praise the *FQ* suggests either lack of judgement or envy; to praise it suggests that it needs to be praised; to show his judgement and lack of envy, Ignoto declares that the poem is beyond praise; and since it does not need the 'prayse of meaner wits' (*CV* 2.1), even as 'Good wine needs no bush' (Tilley W462), he offers his verse as a vintner displays only a bush for his wines.

DEDICATORY SONNETS

Addressing 'heauenlie *Spencer*', Nashe refers to the *DS* as 'that honourable catalogue of our English *Heroes*, which insueth the conclusion of thy famous Fairie Queene', but since it failed to include an unnamed (feigned?) 'piller of Nobilitie' (adapting the term from *DS 1*.2), he adds a sonnet in his praise in which he relates how he found at the end of the poem lines penned 'to sundry Nobles . . . | Whom he as speciall Mirrours singled fourth, | To be the Patrons of his Poetry' (1904–10:1.243–44). As F.R. Johnson 1933:15 notes, one issue of the poem has ten sonnets distributed by page as follows: to Hatton, Essex, / Oxford, Northumberland, / Ormond, Howard, / Grey, Raleigh, / Lady Carew, and 'All the Ladies'. Another issue adds seven new sonnets mingled among the first eight of the first issue: to Burghley, Cumberland, Hunsdon, Buckhurst, Walsingham, Norris, and the Countess of Pembroke. Since there would be no reason to exclude Lady Carew and 'All the Ladies', the full second series would have seventeen sonnets in the order given here. Of those who receive dedicatory sonnets, as Adams in *SEnc* 194 notes, eight belong to the Queen's inner circle either as major officeholders or privy councillors (Burghley, Hatton, Howard, Buckhurst, Essex, Walsingham, Hunsdon, and Raleigh); of the six other males, three were prominent in Irish affairs (Ormond, Grey, and Norris) and three were heirs of older noble families (in their order of ancestry: Oxford, Northumberland, and Cumberland). Stillman 1985 has demonstrated that their order follows heraldic rules for preference according to the rank and dignity of families, offices, and titles, with chief officials of the crown preceding others of their rank. Accordingly, the Lord High Chancellor (Hatton) comes first and before the Lord High Treasurer (Burghley); Oxford comes before Howard and Hunsdon because he is an earl and they are only barons, and they are first among the barons because of their offices (Lord High Admiral and Lord Chamberlain of the Household, respectively); Grey precedes Buckhurst because his title is older; Walsingham is first among the knights because of his office; and Norris comes before Raleigh because of his nobler ancestry and office. By even more rigid gender rules, ladies make up the rear and appear in

their order: Pembroke as a countess precedes Carew who is only a baronet's wife. Røstvig 1994:362–65 argues that the first sixteen sonnets are ordered symmetrically; McNamara 2000 argues that all seventeen sonnets form a symmetrical pageant to the Queen.

To each of his dedicatees, S. offers his poem as a 'present' (*DS 4*.14, *16*.12) or 'guift' (*DS 10*.8) with the expectation that he will receive something in return, as *DS 4* and *DS 13* spell out, and as Raleigh suggests in telling S. that the Queen may 'fauour thy good will' (*CV 2*.11). More broadly, the sonnets constitute a 'Pageaunt' (*DS 8*.6), which D.L. Miller 1988:50 terms 'a pageant of the body politic' because of their ordered hierarchy. As the Queen sustains the nobility who sustain her, so Spenser supports them as they should support him. On the network of patronage in the series, see Finke 1994:215–19.

Except for *DS 10* and *DS 15*, most sonnets are impersonal and interchangeable. Their form, which became known as Spenserian, was invented by S. in his sonnet to Harvey in 1586: fourteen iambic pentameter lines of three interlinked rhyming quatrains and a couplet, rhymed *abab bcbc cdcd ee*. Five – *DS 7*, *9*, *14*, *15*, *17* – conclude with the six-stressed alexandrine, the trademark of the Spenserian stanza. (See 'alexandrine' in the *SEnc* and VI x 7.9*n*.) Loewenstein 1996:107 argues that all seventeen form a sequence organized in part by their succession as groups of two on a page (*DS 1* and *DS 2*, *DS 3* and *DS 4*, etc.) except *DS 15* on one page, as indicated below.

For ease of reference, the sonnets are numbered:

DS 1	Hatton	*DS 10*	Grey
DS 2	Burghley	*DS 11*	Buckhurst
DS 3	Oxford	*DS 12*	Walsingham
DS 4	Northumberland	*DS 13*	Norris
DS 5	Cumberland	*DS 14*	Raleigh
DS 6	Essex	*DS 15*	Pembroke
DS 7	Ormond		————————
DS 8	Howard	*DS 16*	Carey
DS 9	Hunsdon	*DS 17*	Ladies

For the poetry of Hatton, Oxford, Clifford, Essex, Sackville, Raleigh, and Pembroke, see May 1991.

DS1

To the right honourable Sir Christopher Hatton,
Lord high Chauncelor of England. &c.

THose prudent heads, that with theire counsels wise
   Whylom the Pillours of th'earth did sustaine,
   And taught ambitious *Rome* to tyrannise,
   And in the neck of all the world to rayne,
Oft from those graue affaires were wont abstaine,
   With the sweet Lady Muses for to play:
   So *Ennius* the elder Africane,
   So *Maro* oft did *Cæsars* cares allay.
So you great Lord, that with your counsell sway
   The burdeine of this kingdom mightily,
   With like delightes sometimes may eke delay,
   The rugged brow of carefull Policy:
And to these ydle rymes lend litle space,
   Which for their titles sake may find more grace.

DS2

*To the right honourable the Lo. Burleigh Lo. high
Threasurer of England.*

TO you right noble Lord, whose carefull brest
   To menage of most graue affaires is bent,
   And on whose mightie shoulders most doth rest
   The burdein of this kingdomes gouernement,
As the wide compasse of the firmament,
   On *Atlas* mighty shoulders is vpstayd;
   Vnfitly I these ydle rimes present,
   The labor of lost time, and wit vnstayd:
Yet if their deeper sence be inly wayd,
   And the dim vele, with which from comune vew
   Their fairer parts are hid, aside be layd,
   Perhaps not vaine they may appeare to you.
Such as they be, vouchsafe them to receaue,
   And wipe their faults out of your censure graue.

                           E.S.

DS 1

Hatton (1540–91) was the Queen's highest ranking minister. Being so favoured, he was a chief means of S.'s access to her. 7 The first Latin epic poet **Ennius**, 'for his learning and most honest conditions . . . was entierly beloved of Scipio Affrican' (T. Cooper 1565). **8 Maro**: Virgil, *Vergilius Maro*, who wrote his *Aeneid* at the request of Augustus, Caesar Octavianus. **12 rugged brow**: cf. the 'rugged forhead' (IV proem 1.1), apparently Burghley's. **Policy**: the art of statecraft. **13 these ydle rymes**: S.'s disparagement of his own verse, repeated at *DS* 2.7, anticipates the hostility to poetry shared by most political and religious figures in the 1580s; see Belt 1991.

DS 2

See 'Burghley, William Cecil, Lord' (1520–98) in the *SEnc*. Closely paired with *DS 1* for both Hatton and Burghley uphold the burden of the kingdom, one being compared to a pillar of the Roman empire and the other to Atlas; see D.L. Miller 1988:53, and Finke 1994:216. Burghley's apparent hostility to S.'s poetry, which is dismissed in IV proem, is now answered by the traditional defence of poetry: its surface is a **dim vele** that conceals a **deeper sence** hidden from the common reader. Cf. II proem 5.1–5. The appeal is appropriately directed to Burghley who, as the Queen's secretary, was privy to her secrets. On S.'s obsessive fear of idleness, which was a national fear, see S. Miller 1998:26–49.

DS3

To the right Honourable the Earle of Oxenford,
Lord high Chamberlayne of England. &c.

REceiue most Noble Lord in gentle gree,
  The vnripe fruit of an vnready wit:
  Which by thy countenaunce doth craue to bee
  Defended from foule Enuies poisnous bit.
Which so to doe may thee right well besit,
  Sith th'antique glory of thine auncestry
  Vnder a shady vele is therein writ,
  And eke thine owne long liuing memory,
Succeeding them in true nobility:
  And also for the loue, which thou doest beare
  To th'*Heliconian* ymps, and they to thee,
  They vnto thee, and thou to them most deare:
Deare as thou art vnto thy selfe, so loue
  That loues and honours thee, as doth behoue.

DS4

To the right honourable the Earle of
Northumberland.

THe sacred Muses haue made alwaies clame
  To be the Nourses of nobility,
  And Registres of euerlasting fame,
  To all that armes professe and cheualry.
Then by like right the noble Progeny,
  Which them succeed in fame and worth, are tyde
  T'embrace the seruice of sweete Poetry,
  By whose endeuours they are glorifide,
And eke from all, of whom it is enuide,
  To patronize the authour of their praise,
  Which giues them life, that els would soone haue dide,
  And crownes their ashes with immortall baies.
To thee therefore right noble Lord I send
  This present of my paines, it to defend.

DS 3
See 'Oxford, Edward deVere, seventeenth Earl of' (1550–
1604) in the rev. *SEnc.* As his was the most ancient earldom in
England, he most deserves to be addressed **most Noble Lord.**
Since his ancestry began early in the first millennium, it may
well be hidden under the **shady vele** of Merlin's chronicle at
III iii 27–50.   **1 gree:** goodwill, as I v 16.4.   **2 vnripe fruit:**
cf. 'wilde fruit' (*DS* 7.2).   **3–4** Being a poet himself, Oxford
may be called upon by his **countenaunce,** i.e. his patronage or
appearance of favour (*OED* 8), to defend poets against the
poisnous bit of envy (cf. *DS* 4.9 and *DS* 11.13–14). See D.L.
Miller 1988:61. On S.'s fear of envy throughout his career, see
I iv 32.6–8. Cf. *DS* 6.13, and his appeal to Raleigh in the ded-
ication to *Colin Clout* for his 'good countenance' to protect his

poem 'against the malice of evill mouthes'.   **11 th'Heliconian**
ymps: the muses of poetry – cf. 'th'*Heliconian* maides' at II xii
31.2 – who dwell either on Mount Helicon, or by its fountain
as *SC June* 60.

DS 4
Henry Percy, ninth Earl of Northumberland (1564–1632).
He is addressed, though not directly, only in the concluding
couplet, perhaps because there is little to be said about him
except that he was known as the Wizard Earl for his interest in
alchemy – he seems to have been an outsider at court – but
chiefly because S. wants to spell out the mutual obligation of
poet and patron.   **1 The sacred Muses** are 'th'*Heliconian*
ymps' of the previous sonnet.

DS5
To the right honourable the Earle of Cumberland.

REdoubted Lord, in whose corageous mind
   The flowre of cheualry now bloosming faire,
   Doth promise fruite worthy the noble kind,
   Which of their praises haue left you the haire;
To you this humble present I prepare,
   For loue of vertue and of Martiall praise,
   To which though nobly ye inclined are,
   As goodlie well ye shew'd in late assaies,
Yet braue ensample of long passed daies,
   In which trew honor yee may fashiond see,
   To like desire of honor may ye raise,
   And fill your mind with magnanimitee.
Receiue it Lord therefore as it was ment,
   For honor of your name and high descent.
                            E.S.

DS6
To the most honourable and excellent Lo. the Earle of Essex. Great Maister of the Horse to her Highnesse, and knight of thr Noble order of the Garter. &c.

MAgnificke Lord, whose vertues excellent
   Doe merit a most famous Poets witt,
   To be thy liuing praises instrument,
   Yet doe not sdeigne, to let thy name be writt
In this base Poeme, for thee far vnfitt.
   Nought is thy worth disparaged thereby,
   But when my Muse, whose fethers nothing flitt
   Doe yet but flagg, and lowly learne to fly
With bolder wing shall dare alofte to sty
   To the last praises of this Faery Queene,
   Then shall it make more famous memory
   Of thine Heroicke parts, such as they beene:
Till then vouchsafe thy noble countenaunce,
   To these first labours needed furtheraunce.

DS 5
George Clifford (1558–1605). As the third Earl of Cumberland, he may be praised for **the noble kind** of which he is the heir but chiefly because of his **late assaies**, referring to his military exploits in the Azores in 1589; or for his role in the Accession Day tournament in 1587. **9–12** S. assumes, with Calidore, that 'in each mans self . . . | It is, to fashion his owne lyfes estate' (VI ix 31.1–2). In effect, he urges the still youthful earl to imitate the **brave ensample**[s] in his poem in order to achieve its end, which is is 'to fashion a gentleman or noble person in vertuous and gentle discipline' (*LR* 8), and thereby share Arthur's **magnanimitee**.

DS 6
See 'Essex, Robert Devereux, second Earl of' (1565–1601) in the *SEnc*. Since he was taking Leicester's place as the Queen's favourite and was only 25 in 1590, S. may be proposing to celebrate him as a future embodiment of Arthur when he continues his **last praises** of the Queen in future books. **Magnificke Lord** associates him with Arthur's 'magnificence' as described in the *LR* 38. See Hieatt 1988:187. In *Proth* 146, S. praises him as 'Great *Englands* glory and the Worlds wide wonder', and in *View* 168 singles him out, though not by name, as the one who may subdue the Irish. On his career, see McCoy 1989:79–102. **9 sty**: mount.

DS7
To the right Honourable the Earle of
Ormond and Ossory.

REceiue most noble Lord a simple taste
    Of the wilde fruit, which saluage soyl hath bred,
    Which being through long wars left almost waste,
    With brutish barbarisme is ouerspredd:
And in so faire a land, as may be redd,
    Not one *Parnassus,* nor one *Helicone*
    Left for sweete Muses to be harboured,
    But where thy selfe hast thy braue mansione;
There in deede dwel faire Graces many one.
    And gentle Nymphes, delights of learned wits,
    And in thy person without Paragone
    All goodly bountie and true honour sits,
Such therefore, as that wasted soyl doth yield,
    Receiue dear Lord in worth, the fruit of barren field.

DS8
To the right honourable the Lo. Ch. Howard, Lo. high
Admiral of England, knight of the noble order of the
Garter, and one of her Maiesties priuie Counsel. &c.

ANd ye, braue Lord, whose goodly personage,
    And noble deeds each other garnishing,
    Make you ensample to the present age,
    Of th'old Heroes, whose famous offspring
The antique Poets wont so much to sing,
    In this same Pageaunt haue a worthy place,
    Sith those huge castles of Castilian king,
    That vainly threatned kingdomes to displace,
Like flying doues ye did before you chace;
    And that proud people woxen insolent
    Through many victories, didst first deface:
    Thy praises euerlasting monument
Is in this verse engrauen semblably,
    That it may liue to all posterity.

DS 7
Thomas Butler, tenth Earl of Ormond and Ossory (1531–1614), appointed Governor of Munster in 1583. He deserves a place as a cousin of the Queen though, as one of the Old English in Ireland, he was antagonistic towards the New English, such as Lord Grey (see *Var* 10.384) and S. himself (see *SEnc* 406). On the clash between the two factions, see Canny 1983:7–13, and 'Ireland, the historical context' in the *SEnc*. On his political power in Ireland in the 1580s, see Brady 1989b. He may appear in the guise of Sir Orimont at V iii 5.1–2. In *View* 30, he may be the one called 'that right noble man . . . [doing] all that he may to yield equal justice unto all', or the 'noble personage' (106). **1–7** Ireland is seen to suffer under Diana's 'heauy haplesse curse' uttered at VII vi 55.3, reducing it to 'sauadge soyle, far from Parnasso mount' (*DS* 10.12). **redd**: seen. **Parnassus** is the mountain from which the **Helicone** flows, both being haunts of the muses. **8–12** If S. was with Grey in 1580, he may have stayed in his **braue mansione** in Kilkenny, as Judson 1945:89 speculates.

DS 8
Charles, Lord Howard of Effingham (1536–1624). **1 And ye**: an abrupt beginning, for the sonnet shares the page with Ormond. He is called a **braue Lord** because he was known as conqueror of the Spanish Armada. The **Castilian king** refers to Philip II, **those huge castles** to his ships. The battle is **in this verse engrauen semblably** in Arthur's defeat of the Souldan at V viii 28–45.

DS9

To the right honourable the Lord of Hunsdon, high Chamberlaine to her Maiesty.

REnowmed Lord, that for your worthinesse
   And noble deeds haue your deserued place,
   High in the fauour of that Emperesse,
   The worlds sole glory and her sexes grace,
Here eke of right haue you a worthie place,
   Both for your nearnes to that Faerie Queene,
   And for your owne high merit in like cace,
   Of which, apparaunt proofe was to be seene,
When that tumultuous rage and fearfull deene
   Of Northerne rebels ye did pacify,
   And their disloiall powre defaced clene,
   The record of enduring memory.
Liue Lord for euer in this lasting verse,
   That all posteritie thy honor may reherse.

                        E.S.

DS10

To the most renowmed and valiant Lord, the Lord Grey of Wilton, knight of the Noble order of the Garter, &c.

MOst Noble Lord the pillor of my life,
   And Patrone of my Muses pupillage,
   Through whose large bountie poured on me rife,
   In the first season of my feeble age,
I now doe liue, bound yours by vassalage:
   Sith nothing euer may redeeme, nor reaue
   Out of your endlesse debt so sure a gage,
   Vouchsafe in worth this small guift to receaue,
Which in your noble hands for pledge I leaue,
   Of all the rest; that I am tyde t'account:
   Rude rymes, the which a rustick Muse did weaue
   In sauadge soyle, far from Parnasso mount,
And roughly wrought in an vnlearned Loome:
   The which vouchsafe dear Lord your fauorable doome.

DS 9

Henry Carey, first Lord Hunsdon (1526–96). As **high Chamberlaine**, he became patron of Lord Chamberlain's Men in 1594.   **2 noble deeds**: a phrase used of Howard at *DS 8.2* and repeated to praise Hunsdon for his role in defeating the **Northerne rebels** in 1569–70. **Emperesse**: as Elizabeth is called in the Dedication of the *FQ* and *LR* 35.   **5 a worthie place**: repeating *DS 8.6*, being modelled on that sonnet, as Loewenstein 1996:114 notes.   **6 nearnes** in being a first cousin to the Queen.   **7 in like cace**: also; equally; or 'in any case'.   **9 deene**: din.

DS 10

See 'Grey, Arthur, fourteenth Baron of Wilton' (1536–93) in the *SEnc*. Since S. served as one of his secretaries, he addresses him as a friend to whom he was deeply loyal. Hence his praise of him as **the pillor of my life** rather than as one of 'the Pillours of th' earth' (*DS 1.2*).   **8–10 this small guift**, i.e. this sonnet (or the *1590 FQ*), which is a token **Of all the rest** of his poetry which he owes to Grey, possibly alluding to his plan to defend Grey's actions as Lord Deputy of Ireland; see V xii 26–27n, 37n.   **11 a rustick Muse**: as S. names himself at III proem 5.2, though only here does he use the apt metaphor of weaving the stanzas of the *FQ*.

DS11

*To the right honourable the Lord of Buckhurst, one
of her Maiesties priuie Counsell.*

IN vain I thinke right honourable Lord,
    By this rude rime to memorize thy name;
    Whose learned Muse hath writ her owne record,
    In golden verse, worthy immortal fame:
Thou much more fit (were leasure to the same)
    Thy gracious Souerains praises to compile.
    And her imperiall Maiestie to frame,
    In loftie numbers and heroicke stile.
But sith thou maist not so, giue leaue a while
    To baser wit his power therein to spend,
    Whose grosse defaults thy daintie pen may file,
    And vnaduised ouersights amend.
But euermore vouchsafe it to maintaine
    Against vile Zoilus backbitings vaine.

DS12

*To the right honouorable Sir Fr. Walsingham knight,
principall Secretary to her Maiesty, and of her
honourable priuy Counsell.*

THat Mantuane Poetes incompared spirit,
    Whose girland now is set in highest place,
    Had not *Mecænas* for his worthy merit,
    It first aduaunst to great *Augustus* grace,
Might long perhaps haue lien in silence bace,
    Ne bene so much admir'd of later age.
    This lowly Muse, that learns like steps to trace,
    Flies for like aide vnto your Patronage;
That are the great *Mecenas* of this age,
    As wel to al that ciuil artes professe
    As those that are inspird with Martial rage,
    And craues protection of her feeblenesse:
Which if ye yield, perhaps ye may her rayse
    In bigger tunes to sound your liuing prayse.

                                                    E.S.

DS 11

In contrast to the political dedicatees, S. addresses Thomas
Sackville, Lord Buckhurst (1536–1608), as a revered fellow-
poet.   **golden verse** may refer to his 'Induction' to 'The com-
playnt of Henrye duke of Buckingham' in the 1563 edition of
A Mirror for Magistrates. He did not have **leasure** to praise the
Queen in his poetry because he was appointed to her Privy
Council in 1585 and served on many diplomatic missions.
2 memorize: make memorable.   **14 Zoilus**: 'a malicious
poete, that wrate a booke of railing verses against the noble
wourkes of Homer. . . . Of him, all malicious carpers of other
mens wourkes be called Zoili' (T. Cooper 1565).

DS 12

Sir Francis Walsingham (1530?–90) served as Secretary of State
from 1573. S.'s muse fled too late to him for his patronage for
he died in Apr. 1590. The only sonnet of the first fourteen that
does not address the recipient directly. In keeping with his rank
as a gentleman (as with Raleigh), he is not addressed as 'Lord'.
1 The Mantuane Poet is Virgil (of Mantua) whose patron
Mecœnas was vice-regent of Octavian, surnamed **Augustus** on
becoming the first emperor of Rome. Cf. *DS 1.8*, and see *SC
Oct.* 55–60. 'All favourers and succourers of learned men be so
called' (T. Cooper 1565). **incompared**: incomparable (evid-
ently coined by S).   **7 like steps to trace**: in *SC Oct.* 55–60,
Cuddie laments the lack of a Mecœnas whose patronage would
allow him to follow Virgil's career in moving from eclogues
to georgics to epic; see E.K.'s gloss to 55, 57.   **10–11** The
'*Antiquitee* of *Faery* lond' (II ix 60.2) records the deeds of
princes remembered as examples 'both of martiall, | And ciuil
rule to kinges and states imperiall' (II x 74.8–9).   **14 bigger**:
louder; see VII vii 1.5–9*n*.

DS13

To the right noble Lord and most valiaunt Captaine,
Sir Iohn Norris knight, Lord president of Mounster.

WHo euer gaue more honourable prize
   To the sweet Muse, then did the Martiall crew;
   That their braue deeds she might immortalize
   In her shril tromp, and sound their praises dew?
Who then ought more to fauour her, then you
   Moste noble Lord, the honor of this age,
   And Precedent of all that armes ensue?
   Whose warlike prowesse and manly courage,
Tempred with reason and aduizement sage
   Hath fild sad Belgicke with victorious spoile,
   In *Fraunce* and *Ireland* left a famous gage,
   And lately shakt the Lusitanian soile,
Sith then each where thou hast dispredd thy fame,
   Loue him, that hath eternized your name.

                  E.S.

DS14

To the right noble and valorous knight, Sir Walter
Raleigh, Lo. Wardein of the Stanneryes, and
lieftenaunt of Cornewaile.

TO thee that art the sommers Nightingale,
   Thy soueraine Goddesses most deare delight,
   Why doe I send this rusticke Madrigale,
   That may thy tunefull eare vnseason quite?
Thou onely fit this Argument to write,
   In whose high thoughts Pleasure hath built her bowre,
   And dainty loue learned sweetly to endite.
   My rimes I know vnsauory and sowre,
To tast the streames, that like a golden showre
   Flow from thy fruitfull head, of thy loues praise,
   Fitter perhaps to thonder Martiall stowre,
   When so thee list thy lofty Muse to raise:
Yet till that thou thy Poeme wilt make knowne,
   Let thy faire Cinthias praises bee thus rudely showne.

                  E.S.

DS 13
The argument of *DS 4* is now well applied to the military profession, for Sir John Norris (1547?–97) fought in France (see V xi 43.6–65*n*), in the Netherlands to aid **sad Belgicke** in 1585–87 (see V x 6–xi 35*n*), and sailed with Drake in his expedition against Portugal (**Lusitanian soile**) in 1589. He served as Lord President of Munster from 1584. **7 Precedent**: pattern; guardian.

DS 14
See 'Raleigh, Walter' (1554–1618) in the *SEnc*. He was appointed warden of the Stanneries (an area of tin mines and smelting works in Cornwall and Devon) and steward of the Duchy of Cornwall in 1587. See his titles in the dedication to *Colin Clout*. While his rank places him last of the male recipients, praise of him as a courtier and poet of love balances praise of Norris as a soldier on the same page and appropriately introduces the sonnets to the courtly ladies. He deserves his place as one who befriended S., was his neighbour in Ireland, and presented him to the Queen, as S. records in *Colin Clout*. **1** S. is returning Raleigh's compliment in *CV 2*, but more pointedly since the nightingale was the type of the unhappy lover. **3–5 this rusticke Madrigale**: referring to the *FQ* written by 'a rustick Muse' (*DS 10*.11); **this Argument** refers to its subject, specifically the Queen, as at I proem 4.8. **9–10 like a golden showre**: referring to Raleigh's 'Would I wer chaungde, into that goulden Showre' (*Poems* 81), as Oakeshott 1960:95 suggests. **13 thy Poeme**: cf. the title of *CV 1* where 'this' suggests that Raleigh's subject is his own conceit of the Queen in *The Ocean to Scinthia*. On S.'s praise of this poem, see III proem 4–5.

DS15

To the right honourable and most vertuous Lady,
the Countesse of Penbroke.

REmembraunce of that most Heroicke spirit,
   The heuens pride, the glory of our daies,
   Which now triumpheth through immortall merit
   Of his braue vertues, crownd with lasting baies,
Of heuenlie blis and euerlasting praies;
   Who first my Muse did lift out of the flore,
   To sing his sweet delights in lowlie laies;
   Bids me most noble Lady to adore

His goodly image liuing euermore,
   In the diuine resemblaunce of your face;
   Which with your vertues ye embellish more,
   And natiue beauty deck with heuenlie grace:
For his, and for your owne especial sake,
   Vouchsafe from him this token in good worth to take.
                       E.S.

DS 15

See 'Pembroke, Mary Sidney, Countess of' (1561–1621) in the *SEnc*. She is praised here and in the Envoy to *Time* as she wished to be remembered, as Philip Sidney's sister. On her patronage for which S. appeals, see Hannay 1990:78–83. **6** The gesture reproduces the beginning of the *FQ* as described in the *LR*, the occasion when 'a tall clownishe younge man . . . rested him on the floore' (53, 56) until he was chosen Una's knight. In the dedication of her and Sidney's tr. of the Psalms,

she speaks of herself being 'First rais'de by thy blest hand, and what is mine | inspird by thee, thy secrett power imprest'. In dedicating *Time* to her, S. refers to Sidney as 'the Patron of my young *Muses*'. **9–10** In the dedication to *The Third Part of the Countess of Pembrokes Yuychurch*, Fraunce refers to her similarly as '*morientis imago Philippi*' though **diuine** suggests God's image in her face as Sidney's **goodly image** is embellished with the heavenly grace of her virtues and beauty.

DS16

**To the most vertuous, and beautifull Lady,
the Lady Carew.**

NE may I, without blot of endlesse blame,
   You fairest Lady leaue out of this place,
   But with remembraunce of your gracious name,
   Wherewith that courtly garlond most ye grace,
And deck the world, adorne these verses base:
   Not that these few lines can in them comprise
   Those glorious ornaments of heuenly grace,
   Wherewith ye triumph ouer feeble eyes,
And in subdued harts do tyranyse:
   For thereunto doth need a golden quill,
   And siluer leaues, them rightly to deuise,
   But to make humble present of good will:
Which whenas timely meanes it purchase may,
   In ampler wise it selfe will forth display.

                      E.S.

                  FINIS.

DS17

To all the gratious and beautifull Ladies in the Court.

THe Chian Peincter, when he was requirde
   To pourtraict Venus *in her perfect hew,*
   To make his worke more absolute, desird
   Of all the fairest Maides to haue the vew.
Much more me needs to draw the semblant trew,
   Of beauties Queene, the worlds sole wonderment,
   To sharpe my sence with sundry beauties vew,
   And steale from each some part of ornament.
If all the world to seeke I ouerwent,
   A fairer crew yet no where could I see,
   Then that braue court doth to mine eie present,
   That the worlds pride seemes gathered there to bee.
Of each a part I stole by cunning thefte:
   Forgiue it me faire Dames, sith lesse ye haue not lefte.

                      E.S.

DS 16

Elizabeth Carew or Carey (1552–1618), daughter of Sir John Spencer of Althorp, the family of the Despencers with which S. claimed kinship in *Colin Clout* 537–38. He fulfils his promise to celebrate her **In ampler wise** in dedicating *Muiopotmos* to her in 1590, and in praising her as Phyllis in *Colin Clout* 544–47. **10 golden quill**: the instrument of pastoral poetry, or love poetry, as at *Am* 85.10, in contrast to the epic trumpet used 'to thonder Martiall stowre' (*DS14.*11).

DS 17

The *DS* may conclude here, and be assigned to the court ladies, because seventeen signified the age of innocence poised at the moment of maturity; see VI ii 5.4*n*. **1–8 Chian Peincter**: see IV v 12.6–8*n*. **absolute**: paradigmatic in approaching the conceit or idea of Venus. Fittingly, these last words of the *1590* poem explain and justify S.'s attempt to make his poem 'absolute' by presenting his vision of the Faerie Queene as the idea of Elizabeth. The concluding reference to his **cunning thefte** is designed to confirm Raleigh's reference to him as 'that celestiall theife' (*CV 1.*14).

TEXTUAL NOTES

by Hiroshi Yamashita and Toshiyuki Suzuki

Abbreviations and Symbols:

F.E. 'Faults escaped in the Print' in 1590
P.V. press variant
~   the same word/words that appears/appear before the bracket
∧   the absence of a punctuation mark

Copies Collated:

1590 Quarto (Bks I–III): Bodleian Lib. (Malone 615); British Lib. 1 (C12h17); British Lib. 2 (G11536); Folger Sh. Lib. 1 (*STC* 23080); Folger Sh. Lib. 2 (*STC* 23081); Harvard Univ. (H.E.W. 6.9.32); Huntington Lib. (RB 56742); Meisei Univ. Tokyo; National Lib. of Wales; Seitoku Univ. Tokyo; Yale Univ. (Beinecke 1976 1671); Yamashita

1596 Quarto (Bks IV–VI): Bodleian Lib. (4o S.22.ART SELD); British Lib. 1 (C12h18); British Lib. 2 (G11536–2); British Lib. 3 (G11537); Cambridge Univ. (Trinity IV.2.63); Edinburgh Univ. (De7 108); Folger Sh. Lib.; Huntington Lib.; Newberry Lib. (Case 4A 923); Scolar Press (T. Hofmann); Seitoku Univ. Tokyo; Univ. of Texas; Univ. of Washington (821 SP3fl 1596); Yale Univ. 1 (Vanderbilt 150 2); Yale Univ. 2 (Beinecke Ig SP35 590b 2); Yamashita

1609 Folio (Book VII): British Lib. (G57f6); Bodleian Lib. (Douce S.817); Harvard Univ. (Harper 14446.7.2); Newberry Lib. (Case fy 185 S776); National Lib. of Scotland (Hall 169.d); Scolar Press (T. Hofmann); Yamashita

Code *a* 1590 *b* 1596 *c* 1609 *d* 1611

Book I

Proem
4.5 my] *b, c;* mine *a.*

Canto i
2.1 And] *a;* But *b, c.*
3.3 Glorious] *a, b;* glorious *c. F.E.:* glorious *for* Glorius. Glorious *in copies of a.*

5.1 and] *a;* an *b, c.*
8.4 sky.] ~∧ *P.V. in a.*
10.4 They] *a, c;* The *b.*
12.5 stroke] *F.E.;* hardy stroke *a, b, c.*
17.9 glaunst.] *b, c;* ~∧ *a.*
19.2 bee,] *b, c;* ~∧ *a.*
20.5 from] *b, c;* ftom *a.*
21.5 spring gins to auale] *F.E.;* ebbe gins t'auale *a, b* (to auale), *c* (to avale).
24.9 corse.] *b, c;* ~∧ *a.*
28.8 passed] *a, c;* passeth *b.*
31.2 euil] *a, c;* euill euill *b.*
31.6 thee] *a;* you *b, c.*
41.3 euer drizling] *F.E.;* euery drizling *a;* euer-drizling *b, c.*
42.8 sights] *F.E., b, c;* sighes *a.*
46.7 vsage] *a, b;* visage *c.*
48.9 her with Yuie] *a;* her Yuie *b, c.*
49.3 starteth] *a;* started *b, c.*
49.9 took.] *b, c;* ~∧ *a.*

Canto ii
Arg.1 *parts*∧] *b, c;* ~. *a.*
Arg.3 *stead*] *F.E., b, c;* *steps a.*
1.4 But] *b, c;* Bur *a.*
5.5 embracement] *b, c;* enbracement *a.*
7.5 off] *b, c;* of *a.*
8.9 loued] *a, c;* louest *b.*
12.8 limbe] *b, c;* lim be *a.*
14.4 off] *b, c;* of *a.*
14.7 day,] *b, c;* ~. *a.*
15.6 Their] *b, c;* Theit *a.*
16.4 shocke∧] *b, c;* ~. *a.*
16.5 stand sencelesse] *F.E., b, c;* stands fencelesse *a.*
     blocke,] *b, c;* ~. *a.*
17.5 cruell spies] *F.E.;* cruelties *a, b, c.*
18.1 quoth] *b, c;* qd. *a passim.*
21.2 show] showe *P.V. in a.*
22.5 thy] *a;* your *b, c.*
22.6 was?] *a;* ~! *b, c.*
24.5 soule assaid] *b, c;* soulea ssaid *a.*
26.8 Faire] *c;* faire *a, b.*
29.2 shade him] *a;* shade *b;* shadow *c.*
29.3 ymounted] *F.E.;* that mounted *a, b, c.*

29.9   tide.] *b, c*;   ~, *a*.

32.9   ruefull] *F.E., b, c*;   tuefull *a*.
plaints] *b, c*;   plants *a*.

39.1   Fye] *Smith*;   fye *a, b*; Phy *c*.

40.1   Thens forth] *F.E., c* (Thenceforth);   Then
forth *a, b*.

40.2   vnweeting] *a*;   vnweening *b, c*.

41.5   Thens forth] *F.E., c* (Thenceforth);   Then
forth *a, b*.

Canto iii

1.5   brightnes] *F.E., b, c*;   brightne *a*.

2.4   thinke,] ~∧ *P.V. in a*.
guyleful] *guylefull P.V. in a*.
handeling,] ~∧ *P.V. in a*.

3.6   wrought,] *b, c*;   ~∧ *a*.

3.9   vnto] vn1o *P.V. in a*.

7.1   field,] *c*;   ~∧ *a, b*.

7.5   pittie] *b, c*;   pit tie *a*.

7.6   Lord,] *b, c*;   ~∧ *a*.

9.9   her intent] *b, c*;   heri ntent *a*.

13.5   darkesome] *b, c*;   darkfome *a*.

16.9   criminall.] *b, c*;   ~, *a*.

18.3   daughter] *b, c*;   daghter *a*.

29.5   deface:] *b, c*;   ~, *a*.

34.5   feare] *a, c*;   fea *b*.

34.9   spurd] *a*;   spurnd *b, c*.

36.7   mourning] *a, c*;   morning *b*.

37.9   not depriue] notd epriue *P.V. in a*.

38.7   that] *F.E., Smith*;   the *a, b, c*.

41.6   sharp rending clawes] sharprending claw es
P.V. in a.

44.7   off] *b, c*;   of *a*.

Canto iv

1.9   proue.] *b, c*;   ~∧ *a*.

2.3   false] fale *P.V. in a*.

3.5   case] *F.E., b, c*;   care *a*.

12.2   a Queene] *a, c*;   Queene *b*.

12.7   Realme] *a*;   Realmes *b, c*.

13.1   Elfin] *a, c*;   Elfing *b*.

15.7   knightly] knighly *P.V. in a*.

16.9   glitterand] *a*;   glitter and *b, c*.

18.2   Counsellours] Cosunellours *P.V. in a*.

20.3   From] *a*;   For *b, c*.

22.8   corse] *F.E., b, c*;   course *a*.

23.1   wordly] *a*;   worldly *b, c*.

27.3   coffers] *b, c*;   coffets *a*.

27.6   pelf] *F.E., b, c*;   pelpe *a*.

29.9   fourth] *b, c*;   forth *a*.

31.8   great] *b, c*;   gteat *a*.

32.9   fifte] *F.E.*;   first *a, b, c*.

37.6   *Lucifer'*] *a*;   *Lucifera b, c*.

45.5   of my new ioy] *F.E., c*;   of new ioy *a, b*.

46.6   *Sansfoy*] *b, c*;   *Sanfoy a*.

49.1   Faire] *Smith*;   faire *a, b, c*.

49.7   grone:] *b, c*;   ~∧ *a*.

Canto v

1.9   did he wake] *a, c*;   did wake *b*.
light.] *b, c*;   ~, *a*.

2.4   hayre:] *b, c*;   ~:, *a*.

2.5   hurld] *F.E.*;   hurls *a, b, c*.

7.9   helmets hewen] *b, c*;   hewen helmets *a*.

9.5   show,] *Smith*;   ~∧ *a, b, c*.

13.9   shrowd.] *b, c*;   ~∧ *a*.

15.2   thristy] *a*;   thirstie *b, c*.

17.5   gan] *a*;   can *b, c*.

18.9   anothers] *b, c*;   an others *a*.

21.8   Yet] *Smith*;   yet *a, b, c*.

23.9   forlone?] *b, c*;   ~. *a*.

24.9   for] *a*;   and *b, c*.

27.7   falshood] *b, c*;   fashood *a*.

30.1   ground] *b, c*;   grouud *a*.

35.7   *Typhoeus*] *Typhæus P.V. in a*.

35.9   leke] *F.E., b, c*;   lete *a*.

38.6   cliffs] *a, F.E.*;   clifts *b, c. P.V. in a*.

40.2   reuiue] reviue *P.V. in a*.

40.9   fire] *a, b, c. F.E.:* fire *for* sire. *P.V. in a*.

41.2   nigh] *a*;   high *b, c*.

43.6   renowmed] *F.E., b, c*;   renouned *a*.

50.9   fill.] *b, c*;   ~∧ *a*.

51.5   that] *F.E., Smith*;   the *a, b, c*.

Canto vi

1.5   in] *F.E.*;   it *a, b, c*.

5.5   win] *a*;   with *b, c*.

7.9   sownd.] *b*;   ~, *a*; sound: *c*.

8.7   mishapen] *b*;   mishappen *a*; misshapen *c*.

12.4   ensu'th:] *This edn*;   ~, *a, b, c*.

15.2   Or] *a*;   Of *b, c*.

18.9   find.] *b, c*;   ~∧ *a*.

23.8   noursled] *b, c*;   nousled *a*.

25.8   Libbard] *b, c*;   Libbatd *a*.

26.5   fierce and fell] *a, b, c. F.E.:* fiers and fell *for*
swift and cruell. *P.V. in a*.

26.9   a tyrans] *a*;   tyrans *b*; proud tyrants *c*.

29.9   blown.] *b, c*;   ~∧ *a*.

30.7   Straunge] *b, c*;   Sraunge *a*.

33.9   woods] *b, c*;   wods *a*.

39.3   might] *b, c*;   migh *a*.

39.7   quoth he] *b, c*;   qd. she *a*.

44.1 fell] *b, c;*   full *a.*
45.2 retourne,] *b, c;*   ~. *a.*
45.8 thrown,] *c;*   ~: *a, b.*
47.2 fate] *a, c;*   fete *b.*
47.8 to] *a;*   two *b, c.*
47.9 afrayd.] *b, c;*   ~∧ *a.*
48.5 Damsell] Damfell *P.V. in a.*

Canto vii
1.6 frame,] *c;*   ~; *a, b.*
3.5 mynd:] *b, c;*   ~, *a.*
4.7 fade:] *b, c;*   ~∧ *a.*
5.5 her] *a, c;*   he *b.*
5.9 drinke] *a;*   drunke *b, c.*
      do] *a;*   did *b, c.*
10.3 presumption] presu mption *P.V. in a.*
11.4 hopelesse,] *c;*   ~; *a, b.*
11.6 inwardly] inwarldly *P.V. in a.*
12.6 blow:] *b, c;*   ~∧ *a.*
13.2 Hell,] *b, c;*   ~,, *a.*
16.6 dreaded] *b, c;*   dteaded *a.*
20.3 that] *a;*   the *b, c.*
22.9 sad sight fro] *b, c;*   sad fro *a.*
25.4 feele] seele *P.V. in a.*
32.8 Whose] *b, c;*   Her *a.*
33.3 steele] *F.E., b, c;*   steeld *a.*
36.1 seeme] *F.E., b, c;*   seene *a.*
37.7 amble] *a;*   trample *b, c.*
37.8 chauft] *F.E., b, c;*   chanst *a.*
41.7 staid] ıJaid *P.V. in a.*
42.5 said;] *b, c;*   ~∧ *a.*
      Faire] *c;*   faire *a, b.*
43.4 whiles] *a;*   whilest *b;* whil'st *c.*
43.5 ronne] *F.E., b, c;*   come *a.*
43.9 *Gehons*] *a;*   *Gebons b, c.*
47.3 hands] *F.E., b, c;*   hand *a.*
47.5 ground] *b, c;*   gtound *a.*
48.9 yee] *a;*   you *b, c.*
50.1 forsooke] *b, c;*   forfooke *a.*

Canto viii
Arg.3 the *Gyaunt*] *F.E.;*   that *Gyaunt a, b, c.*
3.1 his Squire] *a;*   the Squire *b, c.*
5.5 fownd,] *b;*   ~. *a;* found) *c.*
7.6 wise] *F.E., b, c;*   wist *a.*
8.1 might:] *b, c;*   ~, *a.*
10.6 off] *b, c;*   of *a.*
11.9 murmur ring] *F.E.;*   murmuring *a, b, c.*
14.9 dismayd.] *b;*   ~∧ *a, c.*
15.3 nigh] *a, c;*   night *b.*
17.1 exceeding] *b, c;*   excecding *a.*

18.8 low:] *Smith;*   ~∧ *a, b;* lowe, *c.*
24.6 his] *b, c;*   her *a.*
27.7 eye] *a;*   eyes *b, c.*
30.2 An] *a;*   And *b, c.*
33.5 sits] *a;*   fits *b, c.*
38.8 vew:] *c;*   ~, *a, b.*
41.7 and helmets] *a, c;*   helmets *b*
43.3 fie] *a, b, c. F.E.:* fye *for* sie. fie *in copies of a.*
46.9 told.] *b, c;*   ~, *a.*

Canto ix
Arg.1 *tells:*] *Smith;*   ~∧ *a, b;* ~, *c.*
Arg.2 *bands*] *F.E., b, c;*   *hands a.*
4.8 billowes] dillowes *P.V. in a.*
5.2 mee:] *b, c;*   ~∧ *a.*
8.9 the] *F.E., b, c;*   that *a.*
      respyre.] *b, c;*   ~∧ *a.*
9.3 that] *a;*   the *b, c.*
9.5 *Timons*] *F.E., b, c;*   *Cleons a.*
12.9 on] *F.E., c;*   at *a, b.*
15.8 vowd] *a;*   vow *b, c.*
16.9 grownd.] *b, c;*   ~∧ *a.*
18.9 as] *a;*   the *b, c.*
19.7 his] *F.E., b, c;*   this *a.*
26.5 nye.] *Smith;*   ~? *a, b, c.*
31.5 mealt'th] *Smith;*   mealt'h *a, b, c.*
33.3 ypight] *b, c;*   yplight *a.*
34.6 cliffs] *F.E.;*   clifts *a, b, c.*
35.9 Were] *a, c;*   Where *b.*
41.2 life is limited] *F.E., b, c;*   life limited *a.*
43.8 way,] *b, c;*   ~. *a.*
46.7 falsed] *b, c;*   falsest *a.*
52.1 saw] *b, c;*   heard *a.*
53.1 feeble] *a;*   seely *b;* silly *c.*

Canto x
2.7 daint,] *b, c;*   ~. *a.*
15.4 for] *a;*   well *b, c.*
16.8 her] *F.E.;*   be *a, b, c.*
17.4 whyle∧] *b, c;*   ~. *a.*
20.5 Dry-shod . . . tway;] *c;*   *not in a, b. This line appears for the first time in c.*
21.9 dismayes.] *b, c;*   ~ , *a.*
22.9 perplexity.] *b, c;*   ~∧ *a.*
24.4 relief∧] *c;*   ~. *a, b.*
25.6 extirpe] *b, c;*   extirp e *a.*
27.6 His blamefull body . . . sore] *a;*   His bodie in salt water smarting sore *b, c.*
36.6 Their] *c;*   There *a, b.*
36.9 in commers-by] *c;*   in-commers by *a, b.*
50.1 she] *a, c;*   he *b.*

52.6 Brings] *c*; Bring *a*, *b*.
56.2 descendʌ] *b*, *c*; ~. *a*.
57.5 pretious] *F.E.*; piteous *a*, *b*, *c*. *F.E.* '150' *refers to the wrong page.*
58.3 dwell,] *Smith*; ~ʌ *a*, *b*, *c*.
59.2 frame] *F.E.*; fame *a*, *b*, *c*.
61.3 thy] *a*, *c*; to thy *b*.
62.4 As wretched men, and liued] *a*; (Quoth he) as wretched, and liu'd *b*, *c*.
62.8 bitter battailes all are] *This edn*; bitter battailes all ate *a*; battailes none are to be *b*, *c*.
62.9 they'are] *a*; are *b*, *c*.
64.7 doen nominate] *a*, *c*; doen then nominate *b*.
65.3 place] *b*, *c*; face *a*.
65.4 Britans] *a*; *Britane b*, *c*.
66.5 brought] *b*, *c*; btought *a*.

Canto xi

1.1 fayre] *c*; *fayre a*, *b*.
2.4 at] *F.E.*, *b*, *c*; it *a*.
3.1–9 And . . . misery.] *b*, *c*; *not in a. This stanza appears for the first time in b.*
4.5 stretcht] *a*, *c*; stretch *b*.
5.1 his] *F.E.*; this *a*, *b*, *c*.
5.5 wyde.] *b*, *c*; ~, *a*.
6.9 scared] *F.E.*; feared *a*, *b*, *c*.
8.7 vaste] *a*, *c*; wast *b*.
10.5 lynd] *b*, *c*; kynd *a*.
11.5 as] *F.E.*; all *a*, *b*, *c*.
12.9 fell.] *b*, *c*; ~, *a*.
14.4 off] *b*, *c*; of *a*.
22.7 augmented] *b*, *c*; angmented *a*.
23.8 off] *b*, *c*; of *a*.
25.5 pight.] *b*, *c*; ~, *a*.
27.2 vaunt] *a*; daunt *b*, *c*.
30.5 one] *F.E.*; it *a*, *b*, *c*.
39.4 sting] *a*; string *b*, *c*.
39.7 string] *a*; sting *b*, *c*.
41.4 Nor] *c*; For *a*, *b*.
42.9 thereby] *b*, *c*; threby *a*.
43.1 shield,] *c*; ~ʌ *a*, *b*.
47.5 ouerthrow] *b*, *c*; ouerthow *a*.
50.5 (might] ~ *placed after line 2. P.V. in a.*
51.2 the] *a*; her *b*, *c*.
51.7 spred,] *Smith*; ~; *a*, *b*, *c*.
51.8 darke;] *Smith*; ~, *a*, *b*, *c*.
55.6 off-shaking] *b*, *c*; of-shaking *a*.

Canto xii

2.9 fall.] *c*; ~, *a*, *b*.
8.1 merimentʌ] *b*, *c*; ~. *a*.
9.5 wonderment.] *b*, *c*; ~, *a*.

11.2 too] *b*, *c*; to *a*.
11.4 gossibs] *a*; gossips *b*, *c*.
11.5 talants] *F.E.*; talents *a*, *b*, *c*. *F.E.* '170' *refers to the wrong page.*
13.4 street:] *b*, *c*; ~ʌ *a*.
13.8 Bespredd] *b*, *c*; Be spredd *a*.
14.5 contayne] *F.E.*, *b*, *c*; vntayne *a*.
16.1 pleasure] *a*; pleasures *b*, *c*.
17.1 that] *a*; the *b*, *c*.
21.7 that] *a*; the *b*, *c*.
drawing] *a*; dawning *b*, *c*.
25.9 read] *a*, *c*; red *b*.
27.7 of] *a*; and *b*, *c*.
28.7 her] *a*; his *b*, *c*.
31.7 strayd] *F.E.*, *b*, *c*; stayd *a*.
32.5 t'inueigle] *F.E.*; to inueigle *a*, *b*, *c*.
34.2 vaine] *F.E.*, *b*, *c*; faine *a*.
34.9 who] *F.E.*, *c*; wo *a*, *b*.
38.4 odours] *b*, *c*; odo urs *a*.
40.4 Suffice] *b*, *c*; Snffice *a*.
40.9 His] *a*; Her *b*, *c*.
41.5 sea] fea *P.V. in a.*
41.7 In case] *b*, *c*; Incase *a*.

Book II

Proem

2.5 mentioned.] *b*, *c*; ~, *a*.
2.6 *Peru?*] *b*, *c*; ~ʌ *a*.
2.8 *Amazons*] *b*, *c*; Amazon *F.E.*; *Amarons a*.
trew?] *b*, *c*; ~ʌ *a*.
2.9 vew?] *b*, *c*; ~. *a*.
3.1 know,] *This edn*; ~‹ *a*; ~; *b*, *c*.
3.3 show.] *b*, *c*; ~ʌ *a*.
3.6 spheare,] *This edn*, ~ *a*; ~? *b*, *c*.
3.8 heare?] *b*, *c*; ~ʌ *a*.
3.9 appeare.] *b*, *c*; ~ʌ *a*.
4.5 no'te] n'ote *P.V. in a.*
trace.] *b*, *c*; ~ʌ *a*.
4.6 thou] *b*, *c*; then *a*.
sky,] *b*, *c*; ~ʌ *a*.
4.8 Faery,] *b*, *c*; ~ʌ *a*.
5.2 light,] *b*, *c*; ~ʌ *a*.
5.5 light.] *b*, *c*; ~ʌ *a*.

Canto i

Arg.2 *knight*] *kniggt P.V. in a.*
2.7 natiue] *a*; natiues *b*, *c*.
4.1 lay,] *c*; ~. *a*, *b*.
4.6–7 But . . . knight | By . . . cares,] *a*; *Lines 6 and 7 transposed in b*, *c*.
6.6 land;] *b*, *c*; ~, *a*.

8.5 with faire] *a, c;* with a faire *b.*
8.7 spoyle,] *c;* ~. *a, b.*
11.1 sayd] sdyd *P.V. in a.*
11.7 he] *a, c;* be *b.*
11.9 Tounge] Tongue *P.V. in a.*
16.1 liefe] *b, c;* life *a.*
18.2 plight;] *c;* ~. *a, b.*
18.6 he did] *a;* did he *b, c.*
20.7 blotted] *b, c;* blotting *a.*
26.9 betide] *a;* betidde *b, c.*
27.9 breath.] *b, c;* ~∧ *a.*
29.1 at one] *a;* attone *b, c.*
31.2 handling] *a, c;* handing *b.*
31.4 on] *b, c;* one *a.*
31.7 Fayre] *c;* fayre *a, b.*
32.7 Must] *b, c;* Most *a.*
33.8 thrise] *F.E.;* these *a, b, c.*
39.4 dolour] *a;* labour *b, c.*
40.4 gore] *a;* gold *b, c.*
42.1 *Guyon*] *b, c; Guyou a.*
44.6 auenging] *a;* reuenging *b, c.*
47.6 off] *b, c;* of *a.*
48.9 griefe.] *b, c;* ~, *a.*
49.9 *Mortdant*] *This edn;* Mortdant *a, b; Mordant c.*
51.6 is;] *c;* ~, *a, b.*
52.5 liefest] *a;* lifest *b, c.*
52.9 dreed.] *b, c;* ~∧ *a.*
53.9 too] *b, c;* to *a.*
     sought.] *b, c;* ~∧ *a.*
55.6 *lincke*:] *c;* ~, *a, b.*
56.2 off] *b, c;* of *a.*
56.6 abstayne,] *b;* ~. *a;* abstaine; *c.*
57.6 part:] ~, *P.V. in a.*
57.7 infirmitie,] ~: *P.V. in a.*
59.1 equall] *a;* euill *b, c.*

Canto ii

Arg.3 *Extremities*∧] *Smith;* ~: *a, b, c.*
4.5 hat'th] hat'h *P.V. in a.*
5.3 hard] *b, c;* hart *a.*
6.9 place to place] *F.E., b, c;* place place *a.*
9.1 whose] *a;* those *b, c.*
9.8 be] *a, c;* he *b.*
12.7 seas;] *c;* ~, *a, b.*
12.8 fame] *b, c;* frame *a.*
21.1 cald] *a;* calth *b, c.*
23.2 boldly] *a;* bloudy *b;* boldy *c.*
28.2 their] *b, c;* her *a.*
     champions] *a;* champion *b, c.*
29.2 *Erinnys,*] *c;* ~∧ *a, b.*
     harts∧] *c;* harts, *a, b.*

30.1 there] *c;* their *a, b.*
31.3 makes] *F.E., b, c;* make *a.*
34.9 thought her] *This edn;* though ther *a;*
     thought their *b, c.*
37.1 Fast] *F.E.;* First *a, b, c.*
40.5 peaceably] *a;* peaceable *b, c.*
41.4 eye,] *c;* ~. *a, b.*
42.5 found:] *c;* ~, *a, b.*
42.6 An yearely] *b, c;* An y earely *a.*
43.9 employes.] *b, c;* ~, *a.*
44.7 told,] *c;* ~∧ *a, b.*
44.9 fordonne.] *b, c;* ~, *a.*
46.9 hyes.] *b, c;* ~∧ *a.*

Canto iii

2.6 raught] *F.E., b, c;* rought *a.*
3.7 heard] *b, c;* hard *a.*
4.5 he] *a;* vaine *b, c.*
5.9 t'aduaunce] *a;* t'auaunce *b, c.*
9.8 flattery] *b, c;* slattery *a.*
11.4 courser] *b, c;* course *a.*
18.6 deuice] *a;* aduise *b, c.*
19.5 off] *b, c;* of *a.*
20.5 does greatly them affeare] *F.E.;* does vnto
     them affeare *a;* their haire on end does reare *b, c.*
27.8 the] *a;* their *b, c.*
28.1 were] *F.E., b, c;* did *a.*
33.7 But] *b, c;* Bur *a.*
38.4 I haue] *a;* haue I *b, c.*
42.1 court.] *a;* ~, *b, c.*
45.4 on] *a, b;* one *c.*

Canto iv

Arg.2 *Occasion*] *c; occasion a, b.*
Arg.3 *Phaon*] *a; Phedon b, c.*
Arg.4 *Strife*] *c; strife a, b.*
1.2 (what)] *a;* what *b, c.*
1.4 valorous pretence] *b, c;* valorours preten ce *a.*
4.3 walke,] *c;* ~. *a, b.*
9.3 threat,] *b, c;* ~. *a.*
9.5 menace] menaee *P.V. in a.*
10.4 not,] *F.E.;* no, *a, b, c.*
10.9 despight.] *b, c;* ~∧ *a.*
12.8 tonge] *F.E.;* tongue *a, c;* tong *b.*
17.3 surpryse?] *c;* ~∧ *a, b.*
17.6 weakest wretch] *a;* weakest one *b, c.*
17.8 her guilful trech] *a;* occasion *b, c.*
17.9 wandring ketch] *a;* light vpon *b, c.*
22.1 ere] *b, c;* ear *a.*
22.3 disposd,] *c;* ~∧ *a, b.*
28.7 assayd?] *b;* ~: *a;* ~! *c.*

34.1 Most] *c*;   most *a, b.*
35.7 outweed,] *c*;   ~∧ *a, b.*
36.2 into] *a, c*;   vnto *b.*
36.7 *Phaon*] *a*;   *Phedon b, c.*
41.2 *Pyrochles*] *F.E.*;   *Pyrrhochles a, b, c.*
42.4 and] *b, c*;   aud *a.*
43.1 concerne,] *b*;   ~. *a*; ~∧ *c.*
45.5 that did] *a*;   thus to *b, c.*

Canto v

Arg.2 *vntyes,*] *a*;   *vnbinds b, c.*
Arg.3 *Who . . . , whiles Atin to*] *a*;   *Of whom sore hurt, for his reuenge b, c.*
Arg.4 *Cymochles for ayd flyes.*] *a*;   *Attin Gymochles finds. b, c.*
4.4   glauncing fell] *b, c*;   glaun cingfell *a.*
5.4   innocent] *b, c*;   innnocent *a.*
5.9   me not much fayl] *a*;   not much me faile *b, c.*
8.7   hurtle] *a*;   hurle *b*; hurlen *c.*
10.7 enimyes] *b, c*;   enimye *a.*
11.5 great] *b, c*;   grear *a.*
13.4 know;] *b, c*;   ~. *a.*
17.8 *Occasion*] *Smith*;   occasion *a*; Occasion *b, c.*
18.5 emboyling] *F.E., b, c*;   embayling *a.*
19.4 shee] *c*;   hee *a, b.*
19.7 garre] *a*;   do *b, c.*
22.9 withstond.] *b, c*;   ~∧ *a.*
27.3 her] *a, c*;   his *b.*
27.6 transforme] *b, c*;   trasforme *a.*
29.5 prickling] *a*;   pricking *b, c.*
29.9 shew.] *b, c*;   ~∧ *a.*
30.8 slomber] *b, c*;   sl omber *a.*
31.5 In *Nemus* gayned] *F.E.*;   In *Netmus* gayned *a*; Gaynd in *Nemea b, c.*
33.3 lights,] *Smith*;   ~∧ *a, b*; ~; *c.*
36.2 Vp, vp,] *c*;   vp, vp, *a, b.*

Canto vi

1.7   abstaine] *a*;   restraine *b, c.*
1.8   her] *a*;   their *b, c.*
3.4   as merry as Pope Ione] *a*;   that nigh her breth was gone *b, c.*
3.6   to her might] *a*;   might to her *b, c.*
4.1   off] *b, c*;   of *a.*
7.7   of] *b, c*;   off *a.*
12.9 throwe her sweete smels] *a*;   her sweet smels throw *b, c.*
14.8 slumbred,] *b, c*;   ~∧ *a.*
14.9 loue] *a*;   loud *b, c.*
15.5 no man] *b, c*;   noman *a.*
18.2 wordly] *a*;   worldly *b, c.*

18.7 griesy] *a*;   griesly *b, c.*
22.2 that] *b, c*;   thar *a.*
24.3 fruitfulnesse] *b, c*;   fuitfulnesse *a.*
27.9 there] *c*;   their *a, b.*
29.2 importune] *a*;   importance *b*; important *c.*
29.9 falles.] *b, c*;   ~∧ *a.*
35.2 shend] *a, c*;   shent *b.*
38.8 There by] *c*;   Thereby *a, b.*
39.4 Shepheards] Shepheardes *P.V. in a.*
      eueninges] eueniges *P.V. in a.*
40.9 delayd.] *b, c*;   ~∧ *a*
43.7 but this his] *a*;   this *b, c.*
43.8 damnifyde?] *c*;   ~∧ *a, b.*
44.8 marre:] *b, c*;   ~∧ *a.*
45.3 Burning] *a, c*;   But *b.*
47.7 came] *b, c*;   ca me *a.*
48.6 man∧ saw,] *F.E., b, c*;   man, saw∧ *a*
51.5 fier inly] *a*;   fire too inly *b, c.*

Canto vii

2.6   So long] *a, b, c*;   Long so *Var. Var. reports P.V. in a.*
3.6   bleard,] *b, c*;   ~∧ *a.*
4.4   yet] *a*;   it *b, c.*
4.9   And] *a, c*;   A *b.*
5.1   him lay] him lay lay *P.V. in a.*
5.4   *Mulcibers*] *b, c*;   *Malcibers a.*
7.3   hils] *a*;   heapes *b, c.*
11.5 kingdomes] kingdowes *P.V. in a.*
11.6 and throw] *a, c*;   throw *b.*
12.9 as] *b, c*;   in *a.*
18.2 of that antique] *a, c*;   of antique *b.*
20.5 and by∧] *b, c*;   ~. *a.*
21.5 internall] *a*;   infernall *b, c.*
24.7 nought] *a*;   ought *b, c.*
24.8 Betwixt] Betwtxt *P.V. in a.*
32.6 *Mammon*] *F.E., b, c*;   *Hammon a.*
36.4 yron] dying *P.V. in a.*
37.1 an] *a*;   as *b, c.*
39.8 mesprise] *a*;   mespise *b, c.*
40.5 As if] *a, c*;   As *b.*
      that] *F.E., Smith*;   the *a, b, c.*
40.7 And] *a*;   But *b, c.*
      yron] *a*;   golden *b, c.*
41.3 his] *a*;   to *b, c.*
45.8 fall;] *b, c*;   ~, *a.*
45.9 Thenceforth] Thencforth *P.V. in a.*
48.3 aspyre.] ~, *P.V. in a.*
48.6 is;] *b, c*;   ~, *a.*
50.1 *Mammon*] *b, c*;   *Mammom a.*
50.4 mate∧] ~, *P.V. in a.*

50.9 knight.] *b*, *c*;   ~∧ *a*.
52.6 With which] *Smith*;   Which with *a*, *b*; Which-
      with *c*.
53.7 great,] ~. *P.V. in a*.
54.8 th'*Eubœan*] *F.E.*, *b*, *c*;   the *Eubœan a*.
56.7 round;] *b*, *c*;   ~, *a*.
60.4 more temperate] *a*;   intemperate *b*, *c*.
64.9 his] *a*;   the *b*, *c*.

Canto viii

1.1   there loue] *b*, *c*;   their loue *a*.
2.5   militant?] *b*, *c*;   ~: *a*.
2.9   regard?] *b*, *c*;   ~. *a*.
5.2   wondrous] *b*, *c*;   wondtous *a*.
12.5 ere while] *b*, *c*;   ere whfle *a*.
18.5 distresse,] *b*, *c*;   ~. *a*.
21.9 might.] *b*, *c*;   ~∧ *a*.
25.1 his cruell] *F.E.*;   same *a*, *b*, *c*.
31.9 defast.] *b*, *c*;   ~∧ *a*.
32.2 Pagans] *F.E.*, *b*, *c*;   Pagons *a*.
32.6 to ward] *b*, *c*;   toward *a*.
33.9 dispossest.] *b*, *c*;   ~∧ *a*.
35.8 double] *F.E.*, *b*, *c*;   doubly *a*.
39.4 and] *b*, *c*;   aud *a*.
40.3 Fayre] *c*;   fayre *a*, *b*.
40.4 well, as he] *a*;   wisely as *b*, *c*.
43.2 before,] *b*, *c*;   ~. *a*.
44.8 not thore] *a*;   no more *b*, *c*.
45.3 empierst] *F.E.*, *b*, *c*;   empiest *a*.
46.8 Harrow] *F.E.*, *c*;   Horrow *a*, *b*.
48.8 Sir *Guyon*] *a*, *b*;   Prince *Arthur c*.
49.9 cast.] *b*, *c*;   ~∧ *a*.
50.4 aw;] *b*, *c*;   ~, *a*.
53.6 Had] *a*, *c*;   Hast *b*.
54.4 Fayre] *c*;   fayre *a*, *b*.
54.7 had,] ~. *P.V. in a*.
55.3 bowing] *F.E.*;   with bowing *a*, *b*, *c*.

Canto ix

Arg.4 *flight*] *a*;   *fight b*, *c*.
1.5   indecent] *F.E.*, *b*, *c*;   incedent *a*.
3.9   poure] *b*, *c*;   ponre *a*.
4.3   chastity] *b*, *c*;   ehastity *a*.
6.3   and] *b*, *c*;   add *a*.
6.9   *Arthogall*] *a*;   *Arthegall b*, *c*.
7.5   Seuen times] *a*;   Now hath *b*, *c*.
7.6   Hath walkte] *a*;   Walkt round *b*, *c*.
13.5 threatning] *b*, *c*;   threaning *a*.
15.2 fownd;] ~, *P.V. in a*.
15.3 Captaine] *a*, *b*;   Capitaine *c*.
16.8 wind with blustring] *a*, *c*;   wind blustring *b*.

18.3 of many] *b*, *c*;   ofmany *a*.
18.7 of her] *b*, *c*;   ofher *a*.
19.9 crowned] *F.E.*, *b*, *c*;   crownd *a*.
20.6 Then] *a*;   There *b*, *c*.
21.1 them] *b*, *c*;   him *a*.
21.3 fensible] *a*;   sensible, *b*, *c*.
21.7 lenger time] *F.E.*, *b*, *c*;   lenger a time *a*.
22.9 diapase] *F.E.*;   *Dyapase a*, *b*, *c*.
26.1 syde∧] *b*, *c*;   ~. *a*.
36.9 spright.] *b*, *c*;   ~∧ *a*.
37.8 you loue] *c*;   your loue *a*, *b*.
38.3 aduise?] *b*, *c*;   ~. *a*.
38.9 three years] *a*;   twelue moneths *b*, *c*.
41.7 Castory.] *F.E.*;   lastery∧ *a*; lastery. *b*, *c*.
42.1 cheare] *b*, *c*;   cleare *a*.
43.6 Why] *c*;   why *a*, *b*.
48.3 this] *a*;   these *b*, *c*.
49.9 would] *a*;   could *b*, *c*.
55.9 well is] *F.E.*, *b*, *c*;   welis *a*.
57.1 to] *b*, *c*;   so *a*.
58.8 Therefore] *b*, *c*;   Theresore *a*.
60.2 *Antiquitee*] *Antiquitiee P.V. in a*.

Canto x

4.3   Who] *F.E.*, *c*;   Whom *a*, *b*.
4.6   and great] *F.E.*, *b*, *c*;   and thy great *a*.
      old] *F.E.*, *b*, *c*;   gold *a*.
5.9   from] *b*, *c*;   ftom *a*.
6.6   safety] *a*;   safeties sake *b*, *c*.
7.7   liueden] *a*;   liued then *b*, *c*.
10.7 besprincled] beprincled *P.V. in a*.
11.5 monstrous] *b*, *c*;   monstrons *a*.
12.6 *Deuonshyre*] *Deuon shyre P.V. in a*.
13.8 surrender] surtender *P.V. in a*.
16.7 Chiefetain] Cheifetain *P.V. in a*.
17.2 wox] wax *P.V. in a*.
18.7 remaind;] *b*, *c*;   ~∧ *a*.
19.5 vpon the present floure] *a*;   in that impatient
      stoure *b*, *c*.
22.9 retyre.] *b*, *c*;   ~, *a*.
24.8 *Scuith guiridh*] *blank space. P.V. in a. F.E.*:
      Scuith *for* Seuith.
      it] *b*, *c*;   he *a*.
      bee,] *c*;   ~. *a*, *b*.
24.9 rather *y Scuith gogh*, signe of sad crueltee.]
      blank space. P.V. in a.
26.6 their] *F.E.*;   her *a*, *b*, *c*.
28.7 forth,] *b*, *c*;   ~,, *a*.
29.5 *Celtica.*] *b*, *c*;   ~∧ *a*.
31.8 an] *b*, *c*;   au *a*.
31.9 bereau'd.] *b*, *c*;   ~∧ *a*.

34.1 *Riuall'*] *a*, *c*; *Riuallo b*.
34.7 Then] *a*; Till *b*; When *c*.
  ambitious] *b*, *c*; Ambitious *a*.
37.3 with] *a*, *c*; vp *b*.
38.2 of] *a*; or *b*, *c*.
41.1 *Gurgunt*] *b*, *c*; *Gurgiunt a*.
43.1 sonne] *a*; sonnes *b*, *c*.
  Sisillus] *Smith*; *Sifillus a*, *b*, *c*.
44.1 sonnes] *a*, *c*; sonne *b*.
46.4 reædifye] reædisye *P.V. in a*.
48.9 foyle.] *b*, *c*; ~∧ *a*.
49.8 defrayd] *a*; did defray *b*, *c*.
51.7 in his armes] *a*; in armes *b*, *c*.
57.3 fled:] ~∧ *P.V. in a*.
59.4 bright,] *b*, *c*; ~. *a*.
61.8 withstand,] *b*, *c*; ~. *a*.
63.4 bordragings∧] *b*, *c*; ~. *a*.
65.9 haue forst] *a*; enforst *b*, *c*.
67.9 entombed] *b*, *c*; ento mbed *a*.
68.7 seemed] *a*; seemeth *b*, *c*.

Canto xi
2.9 and for delight] *a*, *c*; and delight *b*.
4.4 And he] *a*, *c*; And *b*.
6.1 dispart,] ~∧ *P.V. in a*.
7.1 fiue,] *b*, *c*; fine, *a*.
9.9 against that Bulwarke lent] *a*; that Bulwarke
  sorely rent *b*, *c*.
10.2 assignment] *a*; dessignment *b*, *c*.
13.2 is] *a*; was *b*, *c*.
13.5 assayed] *a*; assayled *b*, *c*.
17.7 rablement] rablcment *P.V. in a*.
17.9 outrageous] outragous *P.V. in a*.
19.4 withered leaues] witheredleaues *P.V. in a*.
19.9 breed.] *c*; ~∧ *a*, *b*.
23.8 support] *a*; disport *b*, *c*.
27.5 But] *a*; Who *b*, *c*.
30.7 *Britayne*] *F.E.*; *Britom a*; *Briton b*, *c*.
30.9 suruiue] *F.E.*; reuiue *a*, *b*, *c*.
32.5 infest] *a*; vnrest *b*, *c*.
37.8 his] hi *P.V. in a*.
44.3 this] *F.E.*, *b*, *c*; his *a*.
49.8 sumptuous] *b*, *c*; sumptuons *a*.
49.9 dressing] *b*, *c*; dressiing *a*.
  stayd.] *b*, *c*; ~∧ *a*.

Canto xii
Arg.1 *through*] *a*; *by b*, *c*.
Arg.2 *through passing*] *a*; *passing through b*, *c*.
1.6 that vertue] *F.E.*; this vertue *a*, *b*, *c*.
3.9 doe] *F.E.*, *b*, *c*; did *a*.
5.5 dryue∧] ~, *P.V. in a*.

8.6 wayting] *F.E.*; weiting *a*; waiting *b*, *c*.
8.9 drift.] *b*, *c*; ~, *a*.
9.2 Behold] *c*; behold *a*, *b*.
13.9 temple] *a*; honor *b*, *c*.
  herried] *b*, *c*; her ried *a*.
15.5 afore:] ~∧ *P.V. in a*.
15.7 withouten] *b*, *c*; wihtouten *a*; wirhouten *a*.
  P.V. in a.
17.1 *Phædria*] *This edn*; *Phœdria a*, *b*, *c*.
20.8 their] *a*; the *b*, *c*.
21.1 th'earnest] *a*; th'heedfull *b*, *c*.
27.3 pittifully] *a*, *c*; pittifull *b*.
32.4 That] *a*, *c*; Thou *b*.
37.3 but] hut *P.V. in a*.
37.7 Palmer,] *b*, *c*; ~∧ *a*
38.4 *Guyon*] *Guyou P.V. in a*.
39.8 vpstaring] *a*; vpstarting *b*, *c*.
42.7 dayntest] *a*; dayntiest *b*, *c*.
43.2 their] iheir *P.V. in a*.
43.7 mightiest] *b*, *c*; migtest *a*.
44.6 conquest] couquest *P.V. in a*.
46.3 there] *b*, *c*; their *a*.
48.7 of this] *b*, *c*; oft his *a*.
48.9 formalitee.] *b*, *c*; ~∧ *a*.
51.1 Therewith] *a*; Thereto *b*, *c*.
  the] rhe *P.V. in a*.
52.9 Or *Eden* selfe] *a*; Of *Eden b*, *c*.
54.7 *Hyacint*] *Hyacine P.V. in a*.
57.9 nought] *a*; not *b*, *c*.
58.2 sober] sobcr *P.V. in a*.
60.9 ioyes,] *a*; ~. *b*, *c*.
61.4 vew,] *b*, *c*; ~. *a*.
61.8 fearefully] *a*; tenderly *b*, *c*.
62.4 to] into *P.V. in a*.
65.9 secret] *b*, *c*; sccret *a*.
66.4 avise] *a*, *c*; a vise *b*.
76.8 That] *b*, *c*; Thot *a*.
77.4 uele] *a*; vele *b*; veile *c*.
81.4 that] *a*; the *b*, *c*.
82.9 applyde.] *b*, *c*; ~, *a*.
83.7 spoyle] *a*; spoyld *b*, *c*.
85.1 These] *c*; these *a*, *b*.
87.4 chooseth] chooseh *P.V. in a*.

Book III

Proem
1.2 The] *a*; That *b*, *c*.
2.3 *Praxiteles*] *b*, *c*; *Praxitcles a*.
4.2 Thy selfe thou] *a*; Your selfe you *b*, *c*.

Canto i

Arg.3 *Malecastaes*] F.E.;   *Materastaes a, b, c.*
4.2   towards] *b, c;*   towatds *a.*
6.5   But] *b, c;*   Rut *a.*
7.6   thee] *b, c;*   the *a.*
8.7   aduenture] *b, c;*   aduentnre *a.*
12.9   ryde.] *b, c;*   ~, *a.*
14.8   creature] *a;*   creatures *b, c.*
17.2   rush,] ~' *P.V. in a.*
24.5   vnto] unro *P.V. in a.*
29.8   truth] *b, c;*   trurh *a.*
29.9   fight.] *b, c;*   ~, *a.*
30.6   mard] F.E.;   shard *a, b, c.*
31.6   and of many] *a;*   and many *b, c.*
44.5   brethren] brethen *P.V. in a.*
47.1   wight,] *c;*   ~. *a, b.*
47.7   that] *a;*   which *b, c.*
53.2   griefe,] *b, c;*   ~. *a.*
53.3   inburning] *a, c* (in-burning);   in burning *b.*
54.1   for] fot *P.V. in a.*
54.7   annexe] aunexe *P.V. in a.*
55.4   request] reqnest *P.V. in a.*
56.8   *Bascimano*] *a;*   *Basciomani b, c.*
60.8   wary] *c;*   weary *a, b.*
61.6   spake,] *b, c;*   ~. *a.*
67.6   knights] *b, c;*   knighcs *a.*
67.9   went.] *b, c;*   ~∧ *a.*

Canto ii

1.9   all,] *a, b;*   ~: *c.*
3.6   too] *b, c;*   to *a.*
4.1   *Guyon*] *a, b, c;*   *Redcrosse MS corr. in the Bodleian copy* (Malone 615).
6.8   thread;] *b, c;*   ~, *a.*
8.5   to proue, I] *a;*   I to proue, *b, c.*
25.6   *Arthogall*] *a;*   *Arthegall b, c.*
30.5   her in her warme bed] *a;*   in her warme bed her *b, c.*
       dight;] *b, c;*   ~, *a.*
32.9   confused] *b, c;*   confufed *a.*
33.9   debarre,] *b;*   ~. *a;* ~; *c.*
36.1   other] *a;*   others *b, c.*
41.2   Nor] F.E.;   Not *a, b, c.*
42.7   alablaster] *a, c;*   alablasted *b.*
47.8   oyl] oyi *P.V. in a.*
50.1   off] *b, c;*   of *a.*
50.2   Them] F.E., *b, c;*   Then *a.*

Canto iii

1.8   Dame,] *b, c;*   ~. *a.*
2.9   moniments.] *b, c;*   ~∧ *a.*

4.8   protense] *a;*   pretence *b, c.*
15.6   Let] *c;*   let *a, b.*
22.9   *Greeke*] *a;*   *Greece b, c.*
29.1   With] *a;*   Where *b, c.*
33.6   subdewd] subdeʌd *P.V. in a.*
35.1   thy] *a;*   the *b, c.*
36.4   false] *b, c;*   falfe *a.*
37.7   their] *a;*   the *b, c.*
39.9   guifts] *b, c;*   guists *a.*
43.9   from off the earth] F.E.;   from th'earth *a, b, c.*
44.5   hundreth yeares shalbe] *a;*   hundreth shalbe *b, c.*
44.6   vnto their former] *a;*   to former *b, c.*
       shalbee,] *c;*   ~. *a, b.*
46.4   outronne] *a, c;*   ouerronne *b.*
49.1   Thenceforth] Thənce forth *P.V. in a.*
50.9   Hee] F.E., *c;*   Shee *a, b.*
       looks did shew] *a, b;*   looks as earst shew *c.*
51.9   disguise] *a;*   deuise *b, c.*
53.3   (need . . . schollers)] *a;*   (whom need new strength shall teach∧] *b, c;*   ~. *a.*
55.1   sway,] *b, c;*   ~∧ *a.*
57.5   vnweeting] *a, c;*   vnmeeting *b.*
60.9   fit.] *c;*   ~∧ *a, b.*

Canto iv

4.9   meed.] *b, c;*   ~∧ *a.*
5.8   she] *b, c;*   he *a.*
6.9   to the] *b, c;*   tot he *a.*
8.4   Why] *a;*   Who *b, c.*
8.9   thy] *a;*   these *b, c.*
13.9   did into] *a;*   into *b, c.*
14.3   prepayre] pɹepayre *P.V. in a.*
15.6   speares] *a, b;*   speare *c.*
18.9   all; for all∧] all, for all;   *P.V. in a.*
20.9   sonne.] *b, c;*   ~∧ *a.*
27.6   fleshly] *b, c;*   fleshy *a.*
28.1   this that] *b, c;*   this thar *a.*
28.3   which] wich *P.V. in a.*
29.9   shade,] *a;*   ~; *b, c.*
30.4   gamesome] *c;*   gameson *a, b.*
30.6   swowne] *b, c;*   swownd *a.*
30.9   girlond] gitlond *P.V. in a.*
33.9   their] rheir *P.V. in a.*
39.9   till we againe may] *a;*   sith we no more shall *b, c.*
41.3   craft] crafe *P.V. in a.*
41.7   there] *c;*   their *a, b.*
48.1   off] *b;*   of *a, c.*
48.2   steed] steəd *P.V. in a.*
49.7   nimble] nimblle *P.V. in a.*

53.4 dismayd;] *b, c;* ~, *a.*
56.9 handmaide,] ~∧ *P.V. in a.*
59.5 The children of day] *a;* Dayes dearest children *b, c.*
60.4 bright,] *c;* ~? *a, b.*
60.9 rowme] *b, c;* ro wme *a.*

Canto v
5.1 wight∧] ~, *P.V. in a.*
5.5 A] *a;* And *b, c.*
6.9 where?] *c;* ~. *a, b.*
8.2 debonaire] dkbonaire *P.V. in a.*
8.8 of many a] *a, c;* of a many, *b.*
11.1 ye] *a;* you *b, c.*
14.2 beast,] *c;* ~; *a, b.*
16.9 despight.] *b, c;* ~∧ *a.*
17.3 wade] *F.E., b, c;* made *a.*
19.3 habericon] haberieon *P.V. in a.*
19.5 no] *b, c;* now *a.*
20.2 will;] *b, c;* ~, *a.*
21.9 bloud] *b, c;* flood *a.*
28.7 the] rhe *P.V. in a.*
28.9 her] het *P.V. in a.*
29.2 deformed] deforwed *P.V. in a.*
30.7 better] *b, c;* bitter *a.*
30.8 soft] sofe *P.V. in a.*
31.8 habericon] haberieon *P.V. in a.*
33.2 peeces] *b, c;* peeces *a.*
37.6 followd] *a;* follow *b, c.*
38.1 with] *b, c;* wlth *a.*
39.9 murmure] mnrmure *P.V. in a.*
       his] *b, c;* their *a.*
40.4 sweet loues] *a;* loues sweet *b, c.*
40.9 liuing] *b, c;* liking *a.*
41.2 rest;] *This edn;* ~, *a, b;* ~. *c.*
41.4 drest;] *b, c;* ~, *a.*
46.5 restore?] *Smith;* ~: *a, b, c.*
50.2 him remedy] hitu remedy *P.V. in a.*
52.6 admyre:] *c;* ~∧ *a, b.*
53.3 Reames] *a;* Realmes *b, c.*
53.9 weare] *b, c;* were *a.*
55.9 complement.] *b, c;* ~; *a.*

Canto vi
3.9 was] *b, c;* were *a.*
4.4 *Belphœbe*] *c; Belphœbe a, b.*
5.3 bore] *a;* bare *b, c.*
8.7 invndation] *a, b;* inundation *c.*
8.8 creatures] *a, c;* creature *b.*
12.4 beautie] *a;* beauties *b, c.*
17.6 off] *b, c;* of *a.*

21.5 apayd.] *b, c;* ~, *a.*
25.5 From which] *a, b;* Which as *c.*
25.8 Through] *b, c;* Thtough *a.*
       place,] *b, c;* ~. *a.*
26.4 fugitiue,] *b, c;* ~. *a.*
       both farre and nere.] *b, c;* *not in a.*
28.3 *Phœbe*] *c; Phœbe a, b.*
28.6 thence] *a;* hence *b, c.*
29.5 *Gnidus*] *b, c; Gnidas a.*
34.2 or] *a, c;* of *b.*
42.5 heauenly] *a;* heauy *b, c.*
44.2 Arber] Arbcr *P.V. in a.*
45.4 And dearest loue,] *c;* *not in a, b. This line appears for the first time in c.*
45.5 *Narcisse*] *b, c; Marcisse a.*
52.9 launched] *b;* launch *a;* launced *c.*

Canto vii
Arg.1 *witches*] *b, c;* witehes *a.*
Arg.3 *Squyre*] *b, c;* *Sqnyre a.*
Arg.4 *Gyaunts*] *b, c;* *Gynunt a.*
1.8 she did] *b, c;* he did *a.*
1.9 escapt] *b, c;* eseapt *a.*
13.6 hath] *a;* had *b, c.*
15.8 mind;] *b, c;* ~, *a.*
17.7 conquered] *b, c;* conpuered *a.*
18.5 by the witch or by] *a;* be the witch or that *b, c.*
23.4 he] *b, c;* she *a.*
27.8 the shallop] rhe ~ *P.V. in a.*
29.2 hellish] *a, c;* bellish *b.*
36.3 beast,] *b;* ~. *a;* Beast∧ *c.*
37.2 off] *b, c;* of *a.*
38.6 But] Bnt *P.V. in a.*
39.9 tare.] *b, c;* ~∧ *a.*
42.6 hee] *F.E., b, c;* she *a. F.E. '500' refers to the wrong page.*
       stund] *F.E., b, c;* stuned *a. F.E. '500' refers to the wrong page.*
43.8 nere] *F.E., b, c;* were *a. F.E. 'ibid.' refers to the wrong page.*
45.1 the good] *a;* good *b, c.*
46.8 the] *a;* that *b, c.*
48.4 Till him Chylde *Thopas* to confusion] *a;* And many hath to foule confusion *b, c.*
49.4 deuoure∧] *b, c;* ~: *a.*
49.5 staine] *a;* straine *b, c.*
50.2 thrust] *a;* thurst *b, c.*
52.4 is] *b, c;* it *a.*
53.3 ta'ne.] *This edn;* ~, *a;* ~? *b, c.*
53.5 amis.] *b, c;* ~, *a.*
55.4 Three] *b, c;* Thre *a.*

58.3 a doe] *b* (a do); adoe *a*; a-do *c*.
60.3 sound] souud *P.V. in a.*
61.5 backe] *b, c*; bace *a*.

Canto viii

2.7 golden] *a*; broken *b, c*.
5.1 deuice] *a*; aduise *b, c*.
7.4 to womens] *a*; a womans *b, c*.
8.3 somewhyle] *c*; lomewhyle *a, b*.
9.9 who] *a, b*; whom *c*.
11.6 knight he was] *a, c*; knight was *b*.
13.2 trembling] tremblring *P.V. in a.*
18.5 said,] *b, c*; ~∧ *a*.
23.1 perceiu'd] *b, c*; peceiu'd *a*.
23.8 this] *a*; the *b, c*.
24.5 befell.] *b, c*; ~, *a*.
25.9 reprou'd] *a*; reproued *b, c*.
        rudenes] *b, c*; ru denes *a*.
28.4 that] thae *P.V. in a.*
30.3 frory] *c*; frowy *a, b*.
31.9 so] *b, c*; fo *a*.
33.9 her by] *a*; thereby *b, c*.
37.9 *Nymph*] *Nymph P.V. in a.*
        hight] *b, c*; high *a*.
42.1 thraldome] thaldome *P.V. in a.*
42.9 that] rhat *P.V. in a.*
44.1 *Squyre*] *Squyre P.V. in a.*
46.9 (vnworthy')] *a*; (vnworthy) *b, c*.
49.2 To haue] *a*; T'haue *b, c*.
        quoth] Quoth *P.V. in a.*
50.1 *Paridell*] *b, c*; *Pauidell a*.
50.6 succeed] *b, c*; succed *a*.

Canto ix

2.4 attone] *b, c*; attonce *a*.
5.2 supply;] *b, c*; ~, *a*.
6.4 Is] *a*; It *b, c*.
7.3 misdonne] *b, c*; disdonne *a*.
9.7 haynous] *b, c*; hayno us *a*.
13.9 And so defyde them] *a*; And defide them *b*;
        And them defied *c*.
14.7 in] *a*; to *b, c*.
16.9 throw.] *b, c*; ~∧ *a*.
18.7 call.] *b, c*; ~, *a*.
20.1 rest,] *c*; ~; *a, b*.
22.1 *Bellona*] *a*; *Minerua b, c*.
22.5 her] *a*; the *b, c*.
24.5 But most they] *a, c*; But they *b*.
27.5 that] *b, c*; with *a*.
32.8 yglad] *a*; glad *b, c*.
40.8 cities] cites *P.V. in a.*

45.3 neck] *b, c*; necks *a*.
46.2 Hygate] *a, c*; Hygate gate *b*.
47.3 heard] *b, c*; hard *a*.
48.6 to sea] *a, c*; to the sea *b*.
48.9 sayne.] *b, c*; ~∧ *a*.
53.8 measured] measurd *P.V. in a.*

Canto x

Arg.2 *Malbecco*] *b, c*; *Malbceco a*; *Malbeeco a. P.V.
        in a.*
1.3 *Aurora*] *Anrora P.V. in a.*
2.2 grieuously] *b, c*; griuously *a*.
8.9 with] *a*; to *b, c*.
10.4 driue;] *b, c*; ~, *a*.
11.7 told.] *b, c*; ~, *a*.
13.1 *Hellenore*] *b, c*; *Hcllenore a*.
13.3 before,] *b, c*; ~. *a*.
13.8 did] *a*; would *b, c*.
14.8 place;] *b, c*; ~. *a*.
16.7 safe conduct] *b, c*; safeconduct *a*.
17.6 despight;] *b, c*; ~, *a*.
18.4 So] *a*; Then *b, c*.
24.6 Thou] *Smith*; thou *a, b, c*.
29.2 treasure] *b, c*; treasute *a*.
29.6 Thy] *c*; thy *a, b*.
30.4 rownded] *a, c*; grounded *b*.
31.3 that with] *a*; with thy *b, c*.
31.7 vertuous pray] *a*; vertues pray *b*; vertues pay *c*.
32.1 more] *b, c*; mote *a*.
40.1 They] *a, c*; The *b*.
40.3 wastefull] *b, c*; faithfull *a*.
41.4 You] *c*; you *a, b*.
45.8 fedd,] *c*; ~. *a, b*.
46.4 abound.] *b, c*; ~, *a*.
46.5 grownd∧] *b, c*; ~. *a*.
47.2 hands] *a, c*; hand *b*.
50.6 her] *b, c*; he r *a*.
51.9 wonne.] *b, c*; ~∧ *a*.
52.1 spring] *a, c*; springs *b*.
54.1 he,] *b, c*; h e, *a*.

Canto xi

Arg.4 *exprest.*] *b, c*; ~, *a*.
2.3 golden] *c*; golding *a, b*.
4.4 vse all, that I euer] *a*; vse that I did euer *b, c*.
4.9 did him] *a*; him did *b, c*.
7.6 off] *b, c*; of *a*.
9.6 hast∧ thou,] *c*; hast, thou∧ *a, b*.
12.1 singulfes] *a, b*; singultes *c*.
14.3 grace some] *b, c*; gracesome *a*.
15.6 At] *a, c*; And *b*.

19.7 dy.] *b, c*; ~, *a*.
20.3 enterprise;] *b*; ~: *a*; ~. *c*.
22.8 the Earthes] *a*; th'Earthes *b, c*.
   which] *a*; the which *b, c*.
23.3 dempt,] *b, c*; ~. *a*.
23.5 This is] *a, c*; This *b*.
26.7 and with] *a*; and *b*; and his *c*.
27.7 decked] *a*; entred *b, c*.
28.8 Like to] *a*; Like *b, c*.
31.3 And] *b, c*; Ant *a*.
33.7 entire;] *b, c*; ~, *a*.
36.7 thee] *b, c*; the *a*.
37.4 beare] breare *P.V. in a*.
37.5 breare] beare *P.V. in a*.
39.6 his] *a*; each *b, c*.
39.8 Stag] *Smith conj. Jortin*; Hag *a, b, c*.
43.4 proue.)] *b, c*; ~.^ *a*.
48.1 cruell] craell *P.V. in a*.
50.2 sted,] *c*; ~^ *a, b*.
50.4 ouer-red,] *b, c*; ~^ *a*.

Canto xii
1.9 some] fome *P.V. in a*.
7.3 ether] *a*; either *b, c*.
7.8 wood] *b, c*; word *a*.
8.1 nether] *a*; neither *b, c*.
9.3 other] *c*; others *a, b*.
11.4 shade;] *b, c*; ~, *a*.
12.2 not] nnt *P.V. in a*.
12.3 to] *b, c*; too *a*.
   or] *a*; and *b, c*.
12.6 winged heeld] *a*; wingyheeld *b, c*.
15.3 *Dissemblaunce*] *Dissemblaunee P.V. in a*.
17.8 embost] *b, c*; emhost *a*.
18.5 dread] *a*; drad *b, c*.
18.7 had,] *This edn*; ~^ *a, b*; ~: *c*.
18.8 Bee;] *b, c*; ~, *a*.
18.9 degree.] *b, c*; ~^ *a*.
20.9 sanguine] sangine *P.V. in a*.
21.8 still] *b, c*; skill *a*.
23.5 right hand] *F.E., c*; right *a, b. F.E. '502'*
   refers to the wrong page.
25.4 *Vnthriftyhead*] *Vnthriftybead P.V. in a*.
26.6 All] *a*; And *b, c*.
26.7 chamber] camber *P.V. in a*.
   by the] *a*; with that *b, c*.
27.3 nothing did remayne] *a*; and bore all away *b, c*.
27.8 rigorous] rigorons *P.V. in a*.
28.1 there] *c*; their *a, b*.
28.7 exercize] *b, c*; ezercize *a*.
33.3 the next] *a*; her selfe *b, c*.

34.4 her] *c*; him *a, b*.
38.5 sor'd] *a*; bor'd *b, c*.
38.9 grownd.] *b*; ~, *a*; ground: *c*.
39.4 deed?] *b, c*; ~; *a*.
40.6 Lady] *b, c*; Lad *a*.
42.2 She] *F.E., b, c*; He *a*.
42.4 She] *F.E., b, c*; He *a*.
42.5 her] *F.E., b, c*; him *a*.
43*.4 succour] *F.E.*; fuccour *a*.
44*.5 loathed] *This edn*; loath ed *a*.

Book IV

Proem
5.5   thereof] *b*; whereof *c*.

Canto i
7.9   excesse.] *c*; ~^ *b*.
11.5 since] *b*; sith *c*.
11.6 then] *b*; and *c*.
16.7 none] *b*; one *c*.
20.3 amisse:] *c*; ~, *b*.
38.5 ply^] *c*; ~. *b*.
46.1 knight,] *c*; ~^ *b*.
51.5 rotten.] *c*; ~, *b*.

Canto ii
3.5   As] *b*; And *c*.
6.8   torne;] *c*; ~^ *b*.
13.2 by day;] *c*; ~, *b*.
22.2 *Florimell.*] *c*; ~, *b*.
22.4 tell.] *c*; ~, *b*.
23.6 late^] ~, *P.V. in b*.
23.8 state.] *c*; ~, *b*.
27.5 Since] *b*; Sith *c*.
44.4 creature,] *c*; ~: *b*.
46.9 stout.] *c*; ~^ *b*.
50.9 came.] *c*; ~^ *b*.
51.5 Fond dame] *Smith*; fond dame *b*; Fond
   Dame *c*.
52.1 since] *b*; sith *c*.
53.5 assynd,] *c*; ~,, *b*.

Canto iii
Arg.2 *Canacee:*] *Smith*; ~^ *b*; ~. *c*.
4.7   fortune] *c*; fortnne *b*.
6.3   *Priamond*] *c*; *Priumond b*.
   worth,] *c*; ~: *b*.
7.4   skill] *c*; sill *b*.
8.4   disaduaunce:] *c*; ~, *b*.
9.6   not] *b*; n'ote *c*.
9.9   of] *b*; at *c*.

18.2 deadly it was] *b*;   deadly was it *c*.
20.2 ere] *c*;   erc *b*.
26.1 blowes:] *c*;   ~, *b*.
32.2 in] *c*;   ın *b*.
48.7 mighty] mighly *P.V. in b*.
50.3 To] *c*;   Too *b*.
51.7 *Canacee*] *Canace P.V. in b*.
52.1 feast] *b*;   feasts *c*.
      theire] there *P.V. in b*.
52.9 elswere] *b*;   elswhere *c*.

Canto iv

1.4   depends,] *Smith*;   ~. *b*; ~; *c*.
2.3   els] *b*;   als *c*.
2.4   *Scudamour*] *b*, *c*;   *Blandamour Var. corr.* 1679.
7.1   seeing] seeming *P.V. in b*.
7.9   somwhere] some wher *P.V. in b*.
8.2   *Ferrau*] *Ferrat P.V. in b*.
9.5   sight∧] *c*;   ~. *b*.
10.5 worse] *c*;   worst *b*.
11.4 refus'd] refuse *P.V. in b*.
11.6 *Ate*] *Atc P.V. in b*.
11.9 nor friendship] no friendship *P.V. in b*.
19.7 an] *b*;   a *c*.
21.5 *Palimord*] *Paliumord*;   *Dabumord P.V. in b*.
21.6 them] you *P.V. in b*.
21.7 increst] in crest *P.V. in b*.
22.4 When as] Whereas *P.V. in b*.
      affray,] *c*;   ~. *b*.
22.6 Maidenhead,] ~. *P.V. in b*.
23.5 glode,] *c*;   ~. *b*.
23.7 lode,] ~. *P.V. in b*.
24.1 beamlike] brauelike *P.V. in b*.
24.4 guide,] *c*;   ~. *b*.
24.5 side,] *c*;   ~. *b*.
27.3 behalue,] *c*;   ~. *b*.
27.8 misdid,] *Smith*;   ~: *b*; ~; *c*.
27.9 fight.] *c*;   ~∧ *b*.
34.6 makes;] *c*;   ~. *b*.
35.5 wexed] *b*;   waxed *c*.
45.2 t'auenge] *c*;   t'euenge *b*.

Canto v

5.5   *Acidalian*] *b*;   *Aridalian c. P.V. in b*.
6.1   *Cestus*] *b*;   *Cestas c. P.V. in b*.
8.1   that] *b*;   the *c*.
9.8   Then] *b*;   The *c*.
14.3 Phebes] *b*;   *Phœbés c*.
16.1 that] *b*;   the *c*.
23.7 sens] *b*;   since *c*.
24.5 strifull] *b*;   strifefull *c*.

25.1 auiz'd,] *c*;   ~: *b*.
25.5 one] *c*;   once *b*.
27.9 bore] *c*;   borc *b*.
30.8 stryfull] *b*;   stryfefull *c*.
31.3 his] *c*;   her *b*.
37.2 *Pyracmon*] *c*;   *Pynacmon b*.
37.7 hammer] *c*;   ham mer *b*.
38.8 heare:] *c*;   ~, *b*.
44.3 therewith∧] ~, *P.V. in b*.

Canto vi

23.5 vnlesse] *c*;   vnlessc *b*.
24.8 turning his feare] *b*;   turning feare *c*.
28.6 He] *c*;   Her *b*.
      Certes] *c*;   certes *b*.
31.5 withstand.] *c*;   ~∧ *b*.
35.1 Certes] *c*;   certes *b*.
40.5 launcht] *b*;   launc't *c*.
44.4 in] *b*;   on *c*.
46.4 mind,] *c*;   ~. *b*.

Canto vii

1.1   dart] *b*;   darts *c*.
1.8   lanchedst] *b*;   launcedst *c*.
4.6   snatched] *b*;   snatcht *c*.
      ground] *b*;   the ground *c*.
10.9 ouersight] *b*;   ore-sight *c*.
21.2 the vtmost] *b*;   th'vtmost *c*.
25.1 Which] *c*;   With *b*.
33.1 Thenceforth] *b*;   Thence, forth *c*.
34.1 sad] *c*;   said *b*.
36.8 faith,] *c*;   ~∧ *b*.
41.6 euer] *b*;   neuer *c*.

Canto viii

2.9   decay;] *c*;   ~∧ *b*.
10.4 ribbands] *b*;   ribband *c*.
30.4 then] *c*;   them *b*.
38.2 flie,] *This edn*;   ~∧ *b*; ~; *c*.
62.9 hapned] *c*;   hapncd *b*.
63.5 And] *c*;   and *b*.

Canto ix

Arg.2 *Pœana*] *b*, *c*;   *Æmylia conj. Church*.
Arg.3 *Knights*,] *c*;   ~∧ *b*.
1.8   vertuous] *c*;   vertues *b*.
3.3   these] *b*;   this *c*.
3.7   trustie Squire] *c*;   Trustie squire *b*.
17.1 perfectly] pefectly *P.V. in b*.
17.5 quest] *Smith*;   guest *b*, *c*.
18.8 represse,] *c*;   ~. *b*.

24.4 straid,] *Smith*; ~∧ *b*, *c*.
26.1 There] *c*; Their *b*.
30.7 the other] *b*; th'other *c*.
30.8 repayed] *c*; repayred *b*.
35.9 repeat,] *This edn*; ~. *b*; ~; *c*.
39.8 a wretch I and] *b*; a wretch, and *c*.

Canto x
Arg.1 *conquest*] *c*; *conqust b*.
1.8 launcht] *b*; launc't *c*.
2.8 Since] *b*; Sith *c*.
7.8 manner] *c*; nanner *b*.
7.9 ancient] *c*; ancients *b*.
8.8 *his*] *this P.V. in b*.
8.9 *be his*] *ée his P.V. in b*.
19.1 meanest] *c*; nearest *b*.
23.2 ghesse] *b*; bee *c*. *P.V. in b*.
23.8 bee] *b*; ghesse *c*. *P.V. in b*.
25.1 alleyes] *c*; all eyes *b*.
27.1 *Hylas*] *Smith*; *Hyllus b*; *Hylus c*.
36.3 *Loue*] *c*; loue *b*.
37.9 May] *c*; may *b*.
42.6 eldest] *b*; elder *c*.
56.4 at] *b*; on *c*.

Canto xi
Arg.3 *Medway*] *c*; *Medw ay b*.
4.5 Grandame] *c*; Gramdame *b*.
4.6 seuen] *b*; three *c*. *P.V. in b*.
21.5 Ooraxes] *b*; Oraxes *c*. *P.V. in b*.
23.7 *Ægæan*] *Smith*; *Agæan b*, *c*.
24.4 became,] *c*; ~; *b*.
27.9 That] *c*; Thaɪ *b*.
30.5 none] *b*; one *c*.
34.5 Grant] *Smith*; Guant *b*, *c*.
35.7 Nene] *Smith*; *Nene b*, *c*.
40.5 see?] *c*; ~. *b*.
41.8 Allo] *Smith*; *Allo b*, *c*.
41.9 Mulla] *Smith*; *Mulla b*, *c*.
45.1 louely] *b*; louing *c*.
48.8 *Eudore*] *Smith*; *Endore b*, *c*.
52.4 vpbinde,] *c*; ~. *b*.

Canto xii
1.9 numbers,] ~,, *P.V. in b*.
5.4 none,] *c*; ~. *b*.
5.5 bemone.] *c*; ~, *b*.
10.4 shall] *b*; should *c*.
13.1 Thus . . . ruth∧] *b*; Thus whilst his stony heart was touched with tender ruth, *c*. *P.V. in b*.

13.2 Was . . . mollifide] *b*; And mighty courage something mollifide *c*. *P.V. in b*.
18.3 seeing, *Marinell*∧] *c*; seeing∧ *Marinell*, *b*.
26.9 seene] *c*; seenc *b*.
28.4 sayd] *c*; fayd *b*.

Book V

Proem
1.3 prime,] *c*; ~. *b*.
11.2 place] *b*; stead *c*.

Canto i
4.1 *Eirena*] *b*; *Irena c*.
16.2 why?] *c*; ~, *b*.
19.7 it's] *b*; its *c*.
24.9 the] *c*; thc *b*.
25.1 Now] *c*; now *b*.
26.9 is] *b*; his *c*.
30.5 aduenture] *c*; adueuturc *b*.

Canto ii
Arg.3 *Munera*] *Smith*; *Momera b*, *c*.
2.7 As] *c*; And *b*.
4.1 hee] *c*; she *b*.
6.2 way,] *c*; ~; *b*.
7.9 ouersight.] *c*; ~∧ *b*.
11.8 Loe] *Smith*; loe *b*; lo *c*.
17.5 *Artegall*] *Artoe gall P.V. in b*.
18.9 dight.] *c*; ~∧ *b*.
26.2 lye;] ~, *P.V. in b*.
28.8 refourmed.] *c*; ~∧ *b*.
32.4 earth] *c*; eare *b*.
35.4 right.] *c*; ~, *b*.
37.7 be?] *c*; ~. *b*.
38.1 these] *b*; those *c*.
41.5 sit] fit *P.V. in b*.
46.9 way] *b*; lay *c*.
47.4 Be] *c*; bc *b*.
50.5 make] *c*; makes *b*.
51.6 good,] *c*; ~; *b*.

Canto iii
19.1 the azure] *b*; th'azure *c*.
24.2 image] *c*; imagc *b*.
36.8 hee:] *c*; ~∧ *b*.
40.6 we] *c*; were *b*.

Canto iv
2.6 president] *b*; precedent *c*.
6.5 readinesse∧] *c*; ~: *b*.

7.7 degree;] ~, *P.V. in b.*
26.1 *Turpine*] *b*; *Terpine c.*
33.1 *Artegall*)?] *c*; ~?) *b.*
35.1 repryu'd *c*; repry'ud *b.*
36.1 watchmen] *b*; watchman *c.*
36.8 her selfe, halfe] *Smith*; her selfe∧ halfe, *b*; her self, arm'd *c.*
39.3 diuide] *c*; dauide *b.*
48.3 *Clarin*] *b*; *Clarind' c passim.*

Canto v
Arg.3 *her*] *c*; hcr *b.*
Arg.4 *Clarins*] *b*; *Clarind's c.*
18.4 to'a] *b*; to a *c.*
20.8 a napron] *b*; an apron *c.*
38.8 vnlike,] *b*; (~) *c.*
41.2 he] *b*; she *c.*
55.7 maladie,] *c*; ~; *b.*

Canto vi
4.7 from] *b*; for *c.*
13.9 singulfs] *b*; singults *c.*
17.5 Heard] Here *P.V. in b.*
19.3 th'euen-tide] *b*; the euen-tide *c.*
20.1 salute∧] *c*; ~. *b.*
21.9 empeach.] *c*; ~∧ *b.*
24.1 their] *b*; her *c.*
24.4 of her] *c*; ofher *b.*
27.2 of his] *c*; ofhis *b.*
29.2 arm'd] *b*; armed *c.*
30.5 euer] *c*; eucr *b.*
31.3 to abide] *b*; t'abide *c.*
34.7 their] *b*; that *c.*
35.5 family.] *c*; ~∧ *b.*

Canto vii
Arg.1 *comes*] *b*; come *c.*
13.1 seem'd, as] *c*; seem', das *b.*
13.5 red,] *c*; ~. *b.*
21.4 couldst] *c* (could'st); coulst *b.*
25.9 hold.] *c*; ~∧ *b.*
28.8 tie∧] *c*; ~. *b.*
38.5 bad] *b*; sad *c.*
42.3 Princess] *c*; Princes *b.*

Canto viii
8.1 him] *c*; hm *b.*
13.1 Sir] *Smith*; sir *b, c.*
14.3 Since] *b*; Sith *c.*
16.1 them] *c*; then *b.*

24.2 complained∧] *c*; ~. *b.*
40.6 knowne] *b*; knowen *c.*
43.3 loues] *b*; loue *c.*
45.2 caused] *c*; causcd *b.*
48.6 whether] *b*; whither *c.*
49.1 mad] *b*; bad *c.*

Canto ix
18.4 hard] *c*; hart *b.*
26.4 FONT] *Smith*; FONS *b, c.*
31.4 hight∧] *c*; ~, *b.*
31.5 *Litæ,*] *c*; ~∧ *b.*
33.8 rebellions] *b*; rebellious *c.*
41.5 inspyred∧] *c*; ~. *b.*
44.1 appose] *b*; oppose *c.*
45.7 *Nobilitie*] *c*; Nobilitie *b.*
45.9 *Griefe*] *c*; Griefe *b.*
48.4 there with] with there *P.V. in b.*

Canto x
Arg.2 *fight:*] *c*; ~, *b.*
1.3 *Mercie,*] *c*; ~∧ *b.*
6.4 and of her] *b*; and her *c.*
16.8 mount,] *c*; ~; *b.*
17.4 care,] *c*; ~; *b.*
17.8 *Artegall*] *c*; *Artigall b.*
22.7 where] *c*; wherc *b.*
37.3 past,] *c*; ~; *b.*
37.6 hard] *b*; had *c.*

Canto xi
16.2 sight,] *c*; ~; *b.*
24.7 And] *b*; An *c.*
30.3 stonied] stonished *P.V. in b.*
39.5 vnrighteous] *c*; vnrigteous *b.*
40.5 reare,] *c*; ~∧ *b.*
41.2 to] *Smith*; too *b, c.*
41.6 know] *Smith*; knew *b, c.*
51.1 this] *b*; his *c.*
56.9 dissemble] *c*; disscmble *b.*
57.9 with all] *c*; withall *b.*
60.2 had] *b*; haue *c.*
61.8 forward] *b*; froward *c.*
62.1 What] *c*; what *b.*
63.5 defaced?] *c*; ~. *b.*
63.9 hold.] *c*; ~; *b.*

Canto xii
1.9 endure] *b*; enduren *c.*
3.5 hethertoo] hether too *P.V. in b.*

5.9 the Eagle] *b*; th'Eagle *c*.
14.4 to ward] *b*; toward *c*.
16.6 sight] *c*; fight *b*.
17.5 such] *b*; sure *c*.
30.6 hungrily] *b*; hungerly *c*.
40.5 sword, the sword∧] *c*; sword∧ the sword, *b*.
   lent,] *c*; ~∧ *b*.

Book VI

Proem
1.9 It] tI *P.V. in b*.
3.5 Since] *b*; Sith *c*.

Canto i
7.6 replide.)] *Smith*; ~∧) *b*; ~? *c*.
9.1 leaue,] *c*; ~∧ *b*.
10.8 withall.] *Smith*; ~, *b*; ~; *c*.
13.9 pay.] *c*; ~∧ *b*.
23.6 carkasse] *c* (carcasse); carkarsse *b*.
24.4 day,] *c*; ~. *b*.
25.9 requight.] *c*; ~∧ *b*.
28.6 Ere he] *c*; Ere thou *b*.
42.4 since] *b*; sith *c*.

Canto ii
3.2 act and deed] *b*; deed, and word *c*.
5.7 Lincolne] *c*; lincolne *b*.
6.7 launch] *b*; launce *c*.
7.2 What] *c*; what *b*.
8.1 him,] *c*; ~∧ *b*.
14.3 Sayd] *b*; Staid *c*.
   Neither] *Smith*; neither *b*, *c*.
15.8 since] *b*; sith *c*.
19.1 since] *b*; sith *c*.
27.1 May] *c*; may *b*.
30.6 wrong.] *c*; ~∧ *b*.
33.7 since] *b*; sith *c*.
34.4 Faire] *c*; faire *b*.
39.2 implements] *b*; ornaments *c*.
44.4 this] his *P.V. in b*.
46.9 loue,] *c*; ~; *b*.

Canto iii
3.6 incline,] *c*; ~. *b*.
10.2 to no] *b*; not to *c*.
13.7 rust,] *c*; ~. *b*.
23.2 *Serena*] Crispina *P.V. in b*.
23.5 delight,] *Smith*; ~; *b*, *c*.
24.4 bare,] *Smith*; ~. *b*; *c*.

24.8 starting∧ vp,] starting, vp∧ *P.V. in b*.
28.6 soft footing] *Smith*; softing foot *b*, *c*.
30.9 ride.] *c*; ~∧ *b*.
32.6 displeased,] *c*; ~. *b*.
33.6 Knight,] *Smith*; ~∧ *b*; ~; *c*.
35.3 Which] That *P.V. in b*.
35.5 forsake;] ~, *P.V. in b*.
37.9 did for her] for her did *P.V. in b*.
39.3 whose] *b*; wose *c*.
41.7 withall] *c*; with all *b*.
42.4 approue] *c*; reproue *b*.
42.7 reproue] *c*; approue *b*.

Canto iv
4.7 stroke] *b*; strokes *c*.
4.8 beare,] *c*; ~∧ *b*.
5.1 t'aduize] *b*; to aduize *c*.
13.4 perswade.] *c*; ~∧ *b*.
13.8 There] *b*; Where *c*.
28.1 What] *c*; what *b*.
30.5 these] *b*; those *c*.
30.6 ouerthrow] ouerthow *P.V. in b*.
33.2 sides] *b*; side *c*.
34.6 Faire] *c*; faire *b*.
35.3 Lo] *c*; Low *b*.
40.9 vnderstand,] ~; *P.V. in b*.

Canto v
Arg.1 *Matilda*] *a*, *c*; *Serena Var. corr. Hughes*
1.2 be wrapt] *c*; bewrapt *b*.
5.4 launcht] *b*; launc't *c*.
5.6 and] *c*; aud *b*.
11.7 require] *c*; requre *b*.
13.2 enemies] *b*; en'mies *c*.
28.2 liue] *b*; liues *c*.
28.9 Since] *b*; Sith *c*.
34.9 neighbourhood] *c*; neighbourhoood *b*.
36.4 off] *c*; of *b*.
36.7 Some] *c*; Soome *b*.
39.3 glee] *b*; gree *c*.
39.7 Squire,] *c*; ~∧ *b*.
41.2 there] *c*; their *b*.

Canto vi
6.5 Faire] *c*; faire *b*.
7.8 talk restraine] talke restaine *P.V. in b*.
16.1 th'other] *b*; the other *c*.
17.7 *Calidore*] *b*, *c*; *Calepine Var. corr. Hughes*.
30.7 ground] *c*; gound *b*.

35.6 fight] *c*;   right *b*.
36.1 since] *b*;   sith *c*.
   · thy] *b*;   this *c*.
41.9 Through] *b*;   Trough *c*.

Canto vii
1.1   the] *b*;   a *c*.
3.7   arm'd] *b*;   armed *c*.
5.7   Where] *c*;   where *b*.
6.4   tyde.] *Smith*;   ~: *b, c*.
13.5 deed.] *c*;   ~, *b*.
14.6 How] *c*;   how *b*.
17.6 tracting] *b*;   tracking *c*.
33.2 which] *b*;   wich *c*.
35.8 there] *b*;   their *c*.
38.7 Through] Throgh *P.V. in b*.
38.9 therefore?] *Smith*;   ~. *b, c*.
44.3 not,] *Smith*;   ~∧ *b, c*.
47.6 rore:] *c*; ~, *b*.

Canto viii
3.8   entreat,] *c*;   ~∧ *b*.
11.9 two] *c*;   tow *b*.
15.3 pownded] *b*;   powned *c*.
17.6 From] *c*;   For *b*.
26.4 withall] *Smith*;   with all *b*; with-all *c*.
32.4 nought,] *c*;   ~. *b*.
38.5 since] *b*;   sith *c*.
39.4 daintest] *b*;   daintiest *c*.
41.2 iewels] *c*;   iewls *b*.
42.4 sides,] *Smith*;   ~∧ *b, c*.
45.9 a loud] *b*;   aloud *c*.
47.3 toyles] *b*;   toyle *c*.
50.4 they] *b*;   shee *c*.
50.9 a whit] *Smith*;   awhit *b, c*.

Canto ix
6.5   God them] *b*;   God him *c*.
7.8   tyde,] *c*;   ~. *b*.
12.7 fell,] *c*;   ~∧ *b*.
26.1 eare] *b*;   care *c*.
36.8 *Oenone*] *Smith*;   *Benone b, c*.
39.2 present] *b*;   pesent *c*.
41.6 *Clout*] *c*;   clout *b*.
45.5 breeds∧] *c*;   ~: *b*.
46.5 dwell] *d*;   well *b, c*.

Canto x
2.9   on] *b*;   in *c*.
13.4 fray∧] ~. *P.V. in b*.

18.7 wight,] *c*;   ~,, *b*.
20.1 happy,] *c*;   ~∧ *b*.
21.4 within] *c*;   with in *b*.
22.5 *Æacidee*,] *c*;   AEcidee. *b*.
22.6 selfe] *c*;   felfe *b*.
25.8 countrey] counrtey *P.V. in b*.
31.5 Which] *c*;   Whch *b*.
32.6 impure:] *c*;   impare∧ *b*.
38.1 woo'd] wood *P.V. in b*.
39.9 flocks] *b*;   flocke *c*.
44.8 But] *b*;   And *c*.

Canto xi
9.7   the instant] *b*;   th'instant *c*.
10.8 be] *b*;   he *c*.
11.6 that] *b*;   the *c*.
24.1 reliu'd] *b*;   reuiv'd *c*.
26.4 there:] *c*;   ~, *b*.
29.5 alas,] *This edn*;   ~∧ *b, c*.
30.2 Where] *c*;   where *b*.
32.1 alone?] *c*;   ~: *b*.
32.8 iollyhead] *Smith*;   iolly head *b, c*.
36.5 they] *b*;   him *c*.
37.3 themselues] *c*;   themseles *b*.
37.8 keepe,] *c*;   ~∧ *b*.
45.4 lyfull] *b*;   lifefull *c*.

Canto xii
12.8 loos] *b*;   praise *c*.
13.5 Throughout] *c*;   Troughout *b*.
16.3 sith] *b*;   since *c*.
18.9 liue.] *c*;   ~∧ *b*.
19.9 faine?] *c*;   ~. *b*.
22.9 tract] *b*;   track *c*.
25.4 th'Images] *b*;   the Images *c*.
27.4 cry;] *This edn*;   ~. *b*; ~: *c*.
36.5 rore:] ~˙ *P.V. in b*.
40.7 learned] *b*;   gentle *c*.
41.2 Hope] *c*;   H'ope *b*.
41.5 tongues] *c*;   tongnes *b*.

Book VII

Canto vi
7.4   th'empire] *c*;   the empire *d*.
29.5 *Procrustes*] *Smith*;   *Procustes c, d*.

Canto vii
2.3   feeble] *Smith*;   sable *c, d*.
4.5   euery] *d*;   cuery *c*.

7.8   they] *d*; thcy *c*.

8.3   as] *d*; ar *c*.

9.1   hard] *d*; heard *c*.

12.1 neuer] *d*; neucr *c*.

12.5 *Peleus*] *d*; *Pelene c*.

14.9 to'each] *c*; to each *d*.

15.6 I] *c*; are *d*.

      do] *c*; to *d*.

15.8 esteeme] *d*; esteeeme *c*.

16.3 thy] *c*; my *d*.

17.2 worlds] *c*; world *d*.

28.3 bloosmes did beare] *c*; bloosomes beare *d*.

36.7 array;] *d*; ~: *c*.

40.1 full] *d*; full full *c*.

41.7 th'*Idæan*] *Smith*; th'*Iæan c, d*.

48.3 disseise] *d*; disseife *c*.

49.8 if] *d*; If *c*.

55.7 saine] *c*; faine *d*.

Canto viii

1.7   to] *c*; and *d*.

2.9   O∧] ~! *P.V. in c*.

      graunt] grant *P.V. in c*.

LR

7   *by-accidents*] *d*; *by accidents a*.

36   *expresse*] *d*; *ezpresse a*.

56   *through*] *d*; *throngh a*.

CV

7.4   *dew*,] *Smith*; ~. *a, d*.

DS

1.10   The] *a* (*1st issues*); he *a* (*2nd issue*).

2.11   layd,] *d* (laid,); ~. *a*.

3.Head.2 Chamberlayne] *a* (*2nd issue*); Chamber-layne *a* (*1st issue*).

5.7   are,] *d*; ~; *a*.

6.1   *excellent*] *d*; *exellent a*.

6.14   *furtheraunce.*] *d* (*furtherance.*); ~, *a*.

9.3   Emperesse,] *d*; ~. *a*.

10.14 doome.] *a* (*1st issue*); ~∧ *a* (*2nd issue*).

11.6   Souerains] *d* (Soueraignes); Souerain *a*.

13.   Mounster.] *d*; ~, *a*.

14.Head.3 leiftenaunt] *a* (*2nd issue*); liefenaunt *a* (*1st issue*).

BIBLIOGRAPHY

Unless otherwise indicated, texts and translations of classical writers are cited from the Loeb Classical Library, and biblical references from *The Geneva Bible* 1560 facs by Lloyd E. Berry, Madison, WI, 1969.

Abbreviations of Periodicals

AHR	American Historical Review
AN&Q	American Notes and Queries
BJJ	Ben Jonson Journal
BuR	Bucknell Review
CahiersE	Cahiers Elizabéthains
CL	Comparative Literature
C&L	Christianity and Literature
CLS	Comparative Literature Studies
CML	Classical and Modern Literature
ContempR	Contemporary Review
EETS	Early English Text Society
EIC	Essays in Criticism
EIRC	Explorations in Renaissance Culture
Éire	Éire-Ireland: A Journal of Irish Studies
ELH	Journal of English Literary History
ELN	English Language Notes
ELR	English Literary Renaissance
EM	English Miscellany
ES	English Studies
ESC	English Studies in Canada
Expl	Explicator
GHJ	George Herbert Journal
HLQ	Huntington Library Quarterly
HTR	Harvard Theological Review
IHR	Irish Historical Review
IUR	Irish University Review
JDJ	John Donne Journal
JEGP	Journal of English and Germanic Philology
JELL	Journal of English Language and Literature
JMEMS	Journal of Medieval and Early Modern Studies
JMRS	Journal of Medieval and Renaissance Studies
JRMMRA	Journal of the Rocky Mountain Medieval and Renaissance Association
JWCI	Journal of the Warburg & Courtauld Institutes
L&H	Literature and History
LJHum	Lamar Journal of the Humanities
MiltonS	Milton Studies
MLN	Modern Language Notes
MLQ	Modern Language Quarterly
MLR	Modern Language Review
MLS	Modern Language Studies
MP	Modern Philology
N&Q	Notes and Queries
NLH	New Literary History
NS	Die Neueren Sprachen
PBA	Proceedings of the British Academy
PLL	Papers on Language and Literature
PMLA	Publications of the Modern Language Association of America
PQ	Philological Quarterly
Ren&R	Renaissance and Reformation
RenD	Renaissance Drama
RenN	Renaissance News
RenP	Renaissance Papers
RenSt	Renaissance Studies
RES	Review of English Studies
RP	Romance Philology
RQ	Renaissance Quarterly
SAQ	South Atlantic Quarterly
SB	Studies in Bibliography
SCJ	Sixteenth Century Journal
SCN	Seventeenth Century News
SEL	Studies in English Literature, 1500–1900
SN	Studia Neophilologica
SNew	Sidney Newsletter & Journal
SP	Studies in Philology
SpN	Spenser Newsletter
SSt	Spenser Studies
TCAAS	Transactions of the Connecticut Academy of the Arts and Sciences
TLS	Times Literary Supplement
TSE	Tulane Studies in English
TSLL	Texas Studies in Literature and Language
UTQ	University of Toronto Quarterly
WS	Women's Studies
YES	Yearbook of English Studies

ADLER, DORIS 1981 'Imaginary Toads in Real Gardens' *ELR* 11:235–60

ALCIATI, ANDREAS ALCIATUS 1985 *The Latin Emblems*, vol. 1 of *Index Emblematicus* (1531), ed. Peter M. Daly with Virginia W. Callahan, 2 vols, Toronto

ALLEN, DON CAMERON 1960 *Image and Meaning: Metaphoric Traditions in Renaissance Poetry*, Baltimore

ALPERS, PAUL J. 1967 *The Poetry of 'The Faerie Queene'*, Princeton

ALWES, DEREK B. 1990 ' "Who knowes not Colin Clout?": Spenser's Self-Advertisement in *The Faerie Queene*, Book VI' *MP* 88:26–42

ANDERSON, JUDITH H. 1971 'Whatever Happened to Amoret? The Poet's Role in Book IV of *The Faerie Queene*' *Criticism* 13:180–200

ANDERSON, JUDITH H. 1976 *The Growth of a Personal Voice: 'Piers Plowman' and 'The Faerie Queene'*, New Haven

ANDERSON, JUDITH H. 1982a ' "In liuing colours and right hew": The Queen of Spenser's Central Books', in *Poetic Traditions of the English Renaissance*, ed. Maynard Mack and George deForest Lord, New Haven, 47–66; rpt M. Suzuki 1996:168–82

ANDERSON, JUDITH H. 1982b 'What Comes After Chaucer's *But*: Adversative Constructions in Spenser', in *Acts of Interpretation: The Text in its Contexts, 700–1600*, ed. Mary J. Carruthers and Elizabeth D. Kirk, Norman, OK, 105–18

ANDERSON, JUDITH H. 1985 ' "A Gentle Knight was pricking on the plaine": The Chaucerian Connection' *ELR* 15:166–74

ANDERSON, JUDITH H. 1987 'The Antiquities of Fairyland and Ireland' *JEGP* 86:199–214

ANDERSON, JUDITH H. 1988 'Arthur, Argante, and the Ideal Vision: An Exercise in Speculation and Parody', in *The Passing of Arthur: New Essays in Arthurian Tradition*, ed. Christopher Baswell and William Sharpe, New York, 193–206

ANDERSON, JUDITH H. 1989 ' "Myn auctour": Spenser's Enabling Fiction and Eumnestes' "immortall scrine" ', in Logan and Teskey, 16–31

ANDERSON, JUDITH H. 1994 'The "couert vele": Chaucer, Spenser, and Venus' *ELR* 24:638–59

ANDERSON, JUDITH H. 1995 'Prudence and her Silence: Spenser's use of Chaucer's *Melibee*' *ELH* 62:29–46

ANDERSON, JUDITH H. 1996 *Words That Matter: Linguistic Perception in Renaissance English*, Stanford

ANDERSON, JUDITH H. 1998 'Narrative Reflections: Re-envisaging the Poet in *The Canterbury Tales* and *The Faerie Queene*', in Krier, 87–105

ANDERSON, JUDITH H., DONALD CHENEY, and DAVID A. RICHARDSON eds 1996 *Spenser's Life and the Subject of Biography*, Amherst

ANGLO, SYDNEY 1969 *Spectacle, Pageantry, and Early Tudor Policy*, Oxford; rpt 1997

APTEKAR, JANE 1969 *Icons of Justice: Iconography and Thematic Imagery in Book V of 'The Faerie Queene'*, New York

APULEIUS, LUCIUS tr. 1566 *The Golden Asse (Metamorphoses)* by William Adlington; facs of 1639 edn, Watergate Library, London, n.d.

ARCHER, MARK 1987 'The Meaning of "Grace" and "Courtesy": Book VI of *The Faerie Queene*' *SEL* 27:17–34

ARIOSTO, LUDOVICO 1619 *Orlando Furioso*, Venice

ARIOSTO, LUDOVICO 1972 '*Orlando Furioso': Translated into English Heroical Verse* by Sir John Harington (1591), ed. Robert McNulty, Oxford

ARISTOTLE 1941 *Basic Works*, ed. Richard McKeon, New York

ARMBRUST, CRYS 1990 'Humanist Re-Presentations of "Glory" and "Magnificence" in Spenser's *Faerie Queene*' *RenP*, 27–40

ASHELFORD, JANE 1988 *Dress in the Age of Elizabeth I*, London

ATKINSON, DOROTHY F. 1937 *Edmund Spenser: A Bibliographical Supplement*, Baltimore

AXTON, MARIE 1977 *The Queen's Two Bodies: Drama and the Elizabethan Succession*, London

AXTON, RICHARD 1990 'Spenser's "faire hermaphrodite": Rewriting *The Faerie Queene*', in *A Day Estivall: Essays on the Music, Poetry, and History of Scotland and England*, ed. Alisoun Gardner-Medwin and Janet Hadley Williams, Aberdeen, 35–47

BAILEY, HAROLD 1912 *The Lost Language of Symbolism*, London

BAKER, DAVID J. 1997 *Between Nations: Shakespeare, Spenser, Marvell, and the Question of Britain*, Stanford

BARCLAY, ALEXANDER 1955 *The Life of St. George* (*c.* 1515), ed. William Nelson, EETS os 230, London

BARKAN, LEONARD 1975 *Nature's Work of Art: The Human Body as Image of the World*, New Haven

BARKAN, LEONARD 1986 *The Gods Made Flesh: Metamorphosis and the Pursuit of Paganism*, New Haven

BARTHOLOMAEUS ANGLICUS 1582 *Batman vppon Bartholome His Booke 'De Proprietatibus Rerum'*, tr. Stephen Bateman, London; facs Hildesheim 1976

BATES, CATHERINE 1989 'Images of Government in *The Faerie Queene*, Book II' *N&Q* 234:314–15

BATES, CATHERINE 1992 *The Rhetoric of Courtship in Elizabethan Language and Literature*, Cambridge

BATH, MICHAEL 1988 'Collared Stags and Bridled Lions: Queen Elizabeth's Household Accounts', in *The English Emblem and the Continental Tradition*, ed. Peter M. Daly, New York, 225–57

BAYBAK, MICHAEL, PAUL DELANY, and A. KENT HIEATT 1969 'Placement "In the Middest" in *The Faerie Queene*' *PLL* 5:227–34; rpt *EA*, 389–94

BAYLEY, P.C. ed. *The Faerie Queene, Book I*, 1966

BAYLEY, P.C. ed. *The Faerie Queene, Book II*, 1965

BEAL, PETER 1980 *Index of English Literary Manuscripts*, vol. 1:1450–1625, London

BECKINGSALE, B.W. 1967 *Burghley: Tudor Statesman 1520–1598*, London

BEDNARZ, JAMES P. 1984 'Ralegh in Spenser's Historical Allegory' *SSt* 4 (for 1983):49–70

BEDNARZ JAMES P. 1996 'The Collaborator as Thief: Ralegh's (Re)Vision of *The Faerie Queene*' *ELH* 63:279–307

BELLAMY, ELIZABETH JANE 1985 'The Broken Branch and the "Liuing Well": Spenser's Fradubio and Romance Error in *The Faerie Queene*' *RenP*, 1–12

BELLAMY, ELIZABETH JANE 1987 'The Vocative and the Vocational: The Unreadability of Elizabeth in *The Faerie Queene*' *ELH* 54:1–30

BELLAMY, ELIZABETH JANE 1989 'Reading Desire Backwards: Belatedness and Spenser's Arthur' *SAQ* 88:789–809

BELLAMY, ELIZABETH JANE 1990 'Colin and Orphic Interpretation: Reading Neoplatonically on Spenser's Acidale' *CLS* 27:172–92

BELLAMY, ELIZABETH JANE 1992 *Translations of Power: Narcissism and the Unconscious in Epic History*, Ithaca

BELLAMY, ELIZABETH JANE 1997 'Waiting for Hymen: Literary History as "Symptom" in Spenser and Milton' *ELH* 64:391–414

BELLAMY, ELIZABETH JANE 2000 'Spenser's Faeryland and "The Curious Genealogy of India" ', in P. Cheney and Silberman, 177–92

BELSEY, CATHERINE 1994 *Desire: Love Stories in Western Culture*, Oxford

BELSON, JOEL JAY 1964 'The Names in *The Faerie Queene*', Columbia University diss.

BELT, DEBRA 1991 'Hostile Audiences and the Courteous Reader in *The Faerie Queene*, Book VI' *SSt* 9 (for 1988):107–35

BENDER, JOHN B. 1972 *Spenser and Literary Pictorialism*, Princeton

BENGSTON, JONATHAN 1997 'Saint George and the Formation of English Nationalism' *JMEMS* 27:317–40

BENNETT, JOSEPHINE WATERS 1942 *The Evolution of 'The Faerie Queene'*, Chicago; rpt New York 1960

BENNETT, JOSEPHINE WATERS 1956 'Britain among the Fortunate Isles' *SP* 53:114–40

BENSON, PAMELA J. 1986 'Florimell at Sea: The Action of Grace in *Faerie Queene*, Book III' *SSt* 6 (for 1985):83–94

BENSON, PAMELA J. 1992 *The Invention of the Renaissance Woman: The Challenge of Female Independence in the Literature and Thought of Italy and England*, University Park, PA

BERETTA, ILVA 1993 *'The World's a Garden': Garden Poetry of the English Renaissance*, Uppsala

BERGER, HARRY, JR 1957 *The Allegorical Temper: Vision and Reality in Book II of Spenser's 'Faerie Queene'*, New Haven

BERGER, HARRY, JR ed. 1968 *Spenser: A Collection of Critical Essays*, Englewood Cliffs, NJ

BERGER, HARRY, JR 1988 *Revisionary Play: Studies in the Spenserian Dynamics*, Berkeley

BERGER, HARRY, JR 1989 ' "Kidnapped Romance": Discourse in *The Faerie Queene*', in Logan and Teskey, 208–56

BERGER, HARRY, JR 1991 'Narrative as Rhetoric in *The Faerie Queene*' *ELR* 21:3–48

BERGER, HARRY, JR 1994 'Actaeon at the Hinder Gate: The Stag Party in Spenser's Gardens of Adonis', in *Desire in the Renaissance: Psychoanalysis and Literature*, ed. Valeria Finucci and Regina Schwartz, Princeton, 91–119

BERGER, HARRY, JR 1998 'Displacing Autophobia in *Faerie Queene* I: Ethics, Gender, and Oppositional Reading in the Spenserian Text' *ELR* 28:163–82

BERGVALL, ÅKE 1993 'The Theology of the Sign: St. Augustine and Spenser's Legend of Holiness' *SEL* 33:21–42

BERGVALL, ÅKE 1997 'Between Eusebius and Augustine: Una and the Cult of Elizabeth' *ELR* 27:3–30

BERLETH, RICHARD J. 1973 'Heavens Favorable and Free: Belphoebe's Nativity in *The Faerie Queene*' *ELH* 40:479–500

BERLETH, RICHARD J. 1995 'Fraile Woman, Foolish Gerle: Misogyny in Spenser's *Mutabilitie Cantos*' *MP* 93:37–53

BERMAN, RUTH 1983 'Blazonings in *The Faerie Queene*' *CahiersE* 23:1–14

BERNARD, JOHN D. 1989 *Ceremonies of Innocence: Pastoralism in the Poetry of Edmund Spenser*, Cambridge

BERRY, CRAIG A. 1994 'Borrowed Armor / Free Grace: The Quest for Authority in *The Faerie Queene* 1 and Chaucer's *Tale of Sir Thopas*' *SP* 91:136–66

BERRY, CRAIG A. 1998 ' "Sundrie Doubts": Vulnerable Understanding and Dubious Origins in Spenser's Continuation of the Squire's Tale', in Krier, 106–27

BERRY, PHILIPPA 1989 *Of Chastity and Power: Elizabethan Literature and the Unmarried Queen*, London

BETTS, HANNAH 1998 ' "The Image of this Queene so quaynt": The Pornographic Blazon 1588–1603', in Walker, 153–84

BIEMAN, ELIZABETH 1988 *Plato Baptized: Towards the Interpretation of Spenser's Mimetic Fictions*, Toronto

BIOW, DOUGLAS 1996 *'Mirabile Dictu': Representations of the Marvelous in Medieval and Renaissance Epic*, Ann Arbor

BLACK, LYNETTE C. 1999 'Prudence in Book II of *The Faerie Queene*' *SSt* 13:65–88

BLISSETT, WILLIAM 1964 'Spenser's Mutabilitie', in *Essays in English Literature from the Renaissance to the Victorian Age*, ed. Millar MacLure and F.W. Watt, Toronto, 26–42; rpt *EA*, 253–66; rpt EA, 253–66

BLISSETT, WILLIAM 1989 'Caves, Labyrinths, and *The Faerie Queene*', in Logan and Teskey, 281–311

BLOOM, HAROLD 1986 'Introduction', in *Modern Critical Views: Edmund Spenser*, New York, 1–21

BLOOMFIELD, MORTON W. 1952 *The Seven Deadly Sins*, East Lansing; rpt 1967

BOCCACCIO, GIOVANNI 1930 *Boccaccio on Poetry: Being the Preface and the Fourteenth and Fifteenth Books of Boccaccio's 'Genealogia Deorum Gentilium' in an English Version* by Charles G. Osgood, Princeton; rpt New York 1956

BOCCACCIO, GIOVANNI 1976 *Genealogiae*; facs of 4th edn, Venice 1494

BOEHRER, BRUCE THOMAS 1992 *Monarchy and Incest in Renaissance England: Literature, Culture, Kinship, and Kingship*, Philadelphia

BOIARDO, MATTEO MARIA (1989) *Orlando Innamorato* (1495), tr. Charles Stanley Ross, Berkeley

BOLTON, W.F. 1967 *A Short History of Literary English*, London

BONO, BARBARA J. 1984 *Literary Transvaluation: From Vergilian Epic to Shakespearean Tragicomedy*, Berkeley

BORRIS, KENNETH 1985 'A Commentary on Book Six of *The Faerie Queene*', Edinburgh University diss.

BORRIS, KENNETH 1987 'Fortune, Occasion, and the Allegory of the Quest in Book Six of *The Faerie Queene*' *SSt* 7 (for 1986):123–45

BORRIS, KENNETH 1990 ' "Diuelish Ceremonies": Allegorical Satire of Protestant Extremism in *The Faerie Queene* VI. viii. 31–51' *SSt* 8 (for 1987):175–209

BORRIS, KENNETH 1991 *Spenser's Poetics of Prophecy in 'The Faerie Queene' V*, Victoria, BC

BORRIS, KENNETH 2000 *Allegory and Epic in English Renaissance Literature: Heroic form in Sidney, Spenser, and Milton*, Cambridge

BOWMAN, MARY R. 1990 ' "She there as Princess rained": Spenser's Figure of Elizabeth' *RQ* 43:509–28

BRADBROOK, M.C. 1936 *The School of Night: A Study in the Literary Relationships of Sir Walter Ralegh*, Cambridge

BRADEN, GORDON 1975 'riverrun: An Epic Catalogue in *The Faerie Queene*' *ELR* 5:25–48

BRADSHAW, BRENDAN, ANDREW HADFIELD, and WILLY MALEY eds 1993 *Representing Ireland: Literature and the Origins of Conflict, 1534–1660*, Cambridge

BRADY, CIARÁN 1989a 'The Road to the *View*: On the Decline of Reform Thought in Tudor Ireland', in Coughlan, 25–45

BRADY, CIARÁN 1989b 'Thomas Butler, Earl of Ormond (1531–1614) and Reform in Tudor Ireland', in *Worsted in the Game: Losers in Irish History*, ed. C. Brady, Dublin, 49–59

BREEN, JOHN 1996 '*The Faerie Queene*, Book I and the Theme of Protestant Exile' *IUR* 26:226–36

BRIGGS, K.M. 1962 *Pale Hecate's Team: An Examination of the Beliefs on Witchcraft and Magic among Shakespeare's Contemporaries and his Immediate Successors*, London

BRILL, LESLEY 1994 'Other Places, Other Times: The Sites of the Proems to *The Faerie Queene*' *SEL* 34:1–17

BRINK, JEAN R. 1972 'The Masque of the Nine Muses: Sir John Davies's Unpublished "Epithalamion" and the "Belphoebe-Ruby" Episode in *The Faerie Queene*' *RES* 23:445–47

BRINK, JEAN R. 1991 'Who Fashioned Edmund Spenser?: The Textual History of *Complaints*' *SP* 88:153–68

BRINK, JEAN R. 1994a 'Constructing the *View of the Present State of Ireland*' *SSt* 11 (for 1990):203–28

BRINK, JEAN R. 1994b 'Dating Spenser's "Letter to Ralegh"' *Library* Sixth Series 16:219–24

BRINK, JEAN R. 1996 '"All his minde on honour fixed": The Preferment of Edmund Spenser', in Anderson, 45–64

BRINK, JEAN R. 1997a 'Edmund Spenser's Family: Two Notes and a Query' *N&Q* 242:49–51

BRINK, JEAN R. 1997b 'Appropriating the Author of *The Faerie Queene*: The Attribution of the *View of the Present State of Ireland* and *A Brief Note of Ireland* to Edmund Spenser', in *Soundings of Things Done: Essays in Early Modern Literature in Honor of S.K. Heninger, Jr*, ed. Peter E. Medine and Joseph Wittreich, Newark, 93–136

BROADDUS, JAMES W. 1995 *Spenser's Allegory of Love: Social Vision in Books III, IV, and V of The Faerie Queene*, Madison

BROOKS-DAVIES, DOUGLAS 1983 *The Mercurian Monarch: Magical Politics from Spenser to Pope*, Manchester

BROWN, JAMES NEIL 1973 '"Lyke Phoebe": Lunar Numerical and Calendrical Patterns in Spenser's *Amoretti*' *Gypsy Scholar* 1:5–15

BROWN, RICHARD DANSON 1999 *'The New Poet': Novelty and Tradition in Spenser's 'Complaints'*, Liverpool

BROWNE, SIR THOMAS 1981 (1646) *Pseudodoxia Epidemica*, ed. Robin Robbins, 2 vols, Oxford

BRUCE, DONALD 1985 'Spenser's Welsh' *N&Q* 230:465–67

BRUCE, DONALD 1994 'Edmund Spenser: The Boyhood of a Poet' *ContempR* 264:70–79

BRUCE, DONALD 1995a 'Spenser's Birth and Birthplace' *N&Q* 240:283–85

BRUCE, DONALD 1995b 'Edmund Spenser and the Irish Wars' *ContempR* 266:129–38

BRUCE, DONALD 1997 'Spenser in Westminster: His Marriage and his Death' *N&Q* 241:51–53

BRUHN, MARK J. 1995 'Approaching Busyrane: Episodic Patterning in *The Faerie Queene*' *SP* 92:275–90

BRYSKETT, LODOWICK 1970 *A Discourse of Civill Life* (1606), ed. Thomas E. Wright, Northridge, CA

BUHLER, STEPHEN M. 1999 'Pre-Christian Apologetics in Spenser and Sidney: Pagan Philosophy and the Process of *Metanoia*' *SSt* 13:223–43

BULGER, THOMAS 1987 'Britomart and Galahad' *ELN* 25:10–17

BULGER, THOMAS 1994 'Platonism in Spenser's *Mutabilitie Cantos*', in *Platonism and the English Imagination*, ed. Anna Baldwin and Sarah Hutton, Cambridge, 126–38

BULL, MALCOLM 1997a 'Pagan Names in *The Faerie Queene*, I' *N&Q* 242:471–72

BULL, MALCOLM 1997b 'Calumny in *The Faerie Queene*, II. iv' *N&Q* 242:473–77

BULL, MALCOLM 1998 'Spenser, Seneca, and the Sibyl: Book V of *The Faerie Queene*' *RES* 49:416–23

BULLOUGH, GEOFFREY ed. 1957–75 *Narrative and Dramatic Sources of Shakespeare*, 8 vols, London

BURCHMORE, DAVID W. 1981 'The Medieval Sources of Spenser's Occasion Episode' *SSt* 2:93–120

BURCHMORE, DAVID W. 1985 'Triamond, Agape, and the Fates: Neoplatonic Cosmology in Spenser's Legend of Friendship' *SSt* 5 (for 1984):45–64

BURROW, COLIN 1988 'Original Fictions: Metamorphoses in *The Faerie Queene*', in *Ovid Renewed: Ovidian Influences on Literature and Art from the Middle Ages to the Twentieth Century*, ed. Charles Martindale, Cambridge, 99–119

BURROW, COLIN 1993 *Epic Romance: Homer to Milton*, Oxford

BURROW, COLIN 1996 *Edmund Spenser*, Plymouth

BURROW, J.A. 1986 *The Ages of Man: A Study in Medieval Writing and Thought*, Oxford

BURTON, ROBERT 1896 (1621) *The Anatomy of Melancholy*, ed. A.R. Shilleto, 3 vols, London

BUTLER, GEORGE F. 1997 'Milton's Typhon: Typhaon and Typhoeus in the 'Nativity Ode' and *Paradise Lost*' *SCN* 55 (1–2):1–5

CAIN, THOMAS H. 1978 *Praise in 'The Faerie Queene'*, Lincoln, NE

CAMDEN, CARROLL 1943 'The Architecture of Spenser's "House of Alma"' *MLN* 58:262–65

CAMDEN, WILLIAM 1630 *Annales. The history of the princesse Elizabeth* (1615), tr. R. Norton, London

CAMDEN, WILLIAM 1637 *Britain, or a chorographicall description of England, Scotland, and Ireland*, tr. of *Britannia* (1586) by Philemon Holland, London

CAMDEN, WILLIAM 1984 *Remains Concerning Britain* (1605), ed. R.D. Dunn, Toronto

CANDIDO, JOSEPH 1977 'The Compositional History of Cantos ii and iii in Book III of *The Faerie Queene*' *AN&Q* 16:50–52

CANNY, NICHOLAS 1983 'Edmund Spenser and the Development of an Anglo-Irish Identity' *YES* 13:1–19

CAREW, RICHARD 1602 *Survay of Cornwall*, London

CAREY, VINCENT P. and CLARE L. CARROLL 1996 'Factions and Fictions: Spenser's Reflections of and on Elizabethan Politics', in Anderson, 31–44

CARPENTER, FREDERIC IVES 1923 *A Reference Guide to Edmund Spenser*, Chicago

CARROLL, CLARE 1990 'The Construction of Gender and the Cultural and Political Other in *The Faerie Queene* 5 and *A View of the Present State of Ireland*: the Critics, the Context, and the Case of Radigund' *Criticism* 32:163–92

CARROLL, CLARE 1996 'Spenser and the Irish Language: The Sons of Milesio in *A View of the Present State of Ireland, The Faerie Queene*, Book V, and the *Leabhar Gabhála*' *IUR* 26:281–90

CARROLL, WILLIAM MEREDTTH 1954 *Animal Conventions in English Renaissance Non-religious Prose (1550–1600)*, New York

CARTIGNY, JEAN 1951 *The Wandering Knight* (1581), tr. William Goodyear, ed. Dorothy Atkinson Evans, Seattle

CASTIGLIONE, BALDASSARE 1928 *The Book of the Courtier* (1561) tr. Sir Thomas Hoby, London

CAVANAGH, SHEILA T. 1994a *Wanton Eyes and Chaste Desires: Female Sexuality in 'The Faerie Queene'*, Bloomington, IN

CAVANAGH, SHEILA T. 1994b '"That Savage Land": Ireland in Spenser's Legend of Justice', in Miller and Dunlop, 143–52

CAVANAGH, SHEILA T. 1996 '"Licentious Barbarism": Spenser's View of the Irish and *The Faerie Queene*' *IUR* 26:268–280

CELOVSKY, LISA 1994–95 'Vanquished by Marriage: Tournaments in *The Faerie Queene* (1596) and the *New Arcadia* (1590)' *SNew* 13:20–34

CHAMBERS, A.B. 1966 'The Fly in Donne's "Canonization"' *JEGP* 65:252–59

CHANG, H.C. 1955 *Allegory and Courtesy in Spenser: A Chinese View*, Edinburgh

CHAPMAN, GEORGE 1941 *Poems*, ed. Phyllis Brooks Bartlett, New York; rpt New York 1962

CHAPMAN, GEORGE 1888 tr. Hesiod's *Works and Days*, ed. Richard Hooper, London

CHAPMAN, GEORGE 1956 *Chapman's Homer*, ed. Allardyce Nicoll, 2 vols, Princeton

CHAUCER, GEOFFREY 1933 *Works*, ed. F.N. Robinson, Boston; rev edn 1957

CHENEY, DONALD 1966 *Spenser's Image of Nature: Wild Man and Shepherd in 'The Faerie Queene'*, New Haven

CHENEY, DONALD 1972 'Spenser's Hermaphrodite and the 1590 *Faerie Queene*' *PMLA* 87:192–200

CHENEY, DONALD 1984 'Spenser's Fortieth Birthday and Related Fictions' *SSt* 4 (for 1983):3–31

CHENEY, DONALD 1986 'Envy in the Middest of the 1596 *Faerie Queene*', in Bloom, 267–83

CHENEY, DONALD 1996 'Afterword', in Anderson, 172–77

CHENEY, DONALD 1997/98 'Colin Clout's Homecoming: The Imaginative Travels of Edmund Spenser' *Connotations* 7:146–58

CHENEY, PATRICK 1984 'Spenser's Dance of the Graces and Tasso's Dance of the Sylvan Nymphs' *ELN* 22:5–9

CHENEY, PATRICK 1985 'Spenser's Completion of *The Squire's Tale*: Love, Magic, and Heroic Action in the Legend of Cambell and Triamond' *JMRS* 15:135–55

CHENEY, PATRICK 1988 '"Secret Powre Unseene": Good Magic in Spenser's Legend of Britomart' *SP* 85:1–28

CHENEY, PATRICK 1989 '"And Doubted Her to Deeme an Earthly Wight": Male Neoplatonic "Magic" and the Problem of Female Identity in Spenser's Allegory of the Two Florimells' *SP* 86:310–40

CHENEY, PATRICK 1993 *Spenser's Famous Flight: A Renaissance Idea of a Literary Career*, Toronto

CHENEY, PATRICK 1997 *Marlowe's Counterfeit Profession: Ovid, Spenser, Counter-Nationhood*, Toronto

CHENEY, PATRICK and P.J. KLEMP 1984 'Spenser's Dance of the Graces and the Ptolemaic Universe' *SN* 56:27–33

CHENEY, PATRICK and LAUREN SILBERMAN eds 2000 *Worldmaking Spenser: Explorations in the Early Modern Age*, Lexington

CHEW, SAMUEL C. 1937 *The Crescent and the Rose: Islam and England during the Renaissance*, London; rpt New York 1965

CHEW, SAMUEL C. 1947 *The Virtues Reconciled: An Iconographic Study*, Toronto

CHEW, SAMUEL C. 1962 *The Pilgrimage of Life*, New Haven

CHRISTIAN, MARGARET 1991 '"The ground of Storie": Genealogy in *The Faerie Queene*' *SSt* 9 (for 1988):61–79

CHRISTIAN, MARGARET 1993 '"Now lettest thou thy servant depart": Scriptural Tradition and the Close of *The Faerie Queene*' *C&L* 42:205–220

CHRISTIAN, MARGARET 2000 '"Waves of weary wretchednesse": Florimell and the Sea' *SSt* 14:133–61

CINCOTTA, MARY ANN 1983 'Reinventing Authority in *The Faerie Queene*' *SP* 80:25–52

CLEGG, CYNDIA SUSAN 1998 'Justice and Press Censorship in Book V of Spenser's *Faerie Queene*' *SP* 95:237–62

CLIFFORD-AMOS, TERENCE 1999 'The Geography of *The Faerie Queene*', doct. diss., University of Glasgow

COHEE, GAIL E. 2000 '"To Fashion a Noble Person": Spenser's Readers and the Politics of Gender' *SSt* 14:83–105

CONTI, NATALE [Natalis Comes] 1616 *Mythologiae sive explicationum fabularum libri decem* (1567), Padua

COOK, PATRICK J. 1996 *Milton, Spenser and the Epic Tradition*, Aldershot

COOKE, JESSICA 1995 'The Beginning of the Year in Spenser's *Mutabilitie Cantos*' *N&Q* 240:285–86

COONEY, HELEN 2000 'Guyon and his Palmer: Spenser's Emblem of Temperance' *RES* 51:169–92

COOPER, HELEN 1977 *Pastoral: Mediaeval into Renaissance*, Ipswich

COOPER, THOMAS 1565 'Dictionarium Historicum Poeticum', in *Thesaurus linguae Romanae et Britannicae*, London

COTGRAVE, RANDLE 1611 *A Dictionarie of the French and English Tongues*; facs Columbia, NC 1950

COUGHLAN, PATRICIA ed. 1989a *Spenser and Ireland: An Interdisciplinary Perspective*, Cork

COUGHLAN, PATRICIA 1989b '"Some secret scourge which shall by her come unto England": Ireland and Incivility in Spenser', in Coughlan, 46–74

COUGHLAN, PATRICIA 1996 'The Local Context of Mutabilitie's Plea' *IUR* 26:320–41

COUSINS, A.D. 1983 'Ralegh's "A Vision vpon this conceipt of the Faery Qveene"' *Expl* 41:14–16

CRAIG, JOANNE 1988 '"As if but one soule in them all did dwell": Busyrane, Scudamour, and Radigund' *ESC* 14:15–25

CRAIG, JOANNE 2000 '"All Flesh Doth Frailtie Breed": Mothers and Children in *The Faerie Queene*' *TSLL* 42:16–32

CRAIG, MARTHA 1967 'The Secret Wit of Spenser's Language', in *Elizabethan Poetry: Modern Essays in Criticism*, ed. Paul J. Alpers, New York, 447–72; rpt *EA*, 313–33

CRAIG, MARTHA J. 1996 'The Protocol of Submission: Ralegh as Timias' *Genre* 29:325–39

CRAMPTON, GEORGIA RONAN 1974 *The Condition of Creatures: Suffering and Action in Chaucer and Spenser*, New Haven

CRAUN, EDWIN D. 1994 '"Most Sacred Vertue She": Reading Book 5 alongside Aristotle and Thomas Aquinas on Justice', in Miller and Dunlop, 153–61

CREWE, JONATHAN 1992 'Spenser's Saluage Petrarchanism: *Pensées Sauvages* in *The Faerie Queene*' *BuR* 35:89–103

CROSSETT, JOHN M. and DONALD V. STUMP 1984 'Spenser's Inferno: The Order of the Seven Deadly Sins at the Palace of Pride' *JMRS* 14:203–18

CROSSLEY, BRIAN and PAUL EDWARDS 1973 'Spenser's Bawdy: A Note on *The Faerie Queene* II vi' *PLL* 9:314–19

CROWLEY, LESLIE-ANNE 1992 *The Quest for Holiness: Spenser's Debt to Langland*, Milan

CULLEN, PATRICK 1974 *Infernal Triad: The Flesh, the World, and the Devil in Spenser and Milton*, Princeton

CUMMING, WILLIAM P. 1931 'The Influence of Ovid's *Metamorphoses* on Spenser's "Mutabilitie" Cantos' *SP* 28:241–56

CUMMINGS, ROBERT M. 1971 *Spenser: The Critical Heritage*, London

CUMMINGS, ROBERT M. 1990 'Spenser's "Twelve Private Morall Virtues"' *SSt* 8 (for 1987):35–59

CURRAN, JOHN E., JR 1996 'Spenser and the Historical Revolution: Briton Moniments and the Problem of Roman Britain' *Clio* 25:273–92

CURRAN, JOHN E., JR 1998 'Florimell's "Vaine Feare": Horace's Ode 1.23 in *The Faerie Queene* 3.7.1' *SSt* 12 (for 1991): 215–18

CURTIUS, ERNST ROBERT 1953 *European Literature and the Latin Middle Ages*, tr. Willard R. Trask, New York

DALY, JOHN P. S.J. 1960 '"Talus" in Spenser's *Faerie Queene*' *N&Q* 205:49

DANIELS, EDGAR F. 1990 'Spenser's *The Faerie Queene* 2.12.65' *Expl* 48:173–75

DANNER, BRUCE 1998 'Courteous *Virtù* in Spenser's Book 6 of *The Faerie Queene*' *SEL* 38:1–18

DASENBROCK, REED WAY 1991 *Imitating the Italians: Wyatt, Spenser, Synge, Pound, Joyce*, Baltimore

DAUBER, ANTOINETTE B. 1980 'The Art of Veiling in the Bower of Bliss' *SSt* 1:163–75

DAVIES, STEVIE 1986 *The Feminine Reclaimed: The Idea of Woman in Spenser, Shakespeare and Milton*, Lexington, KY

DAVIS, NICK 1999 *Stories of Chaos: Reason and its Displacement in Early Modern English Narrative*, Aldershot

DAVIS, WALTER R. 1977 'Arthur, Partial Exegesis, and the Reader' *TSLL* 18:553–76

DAVIS, WALTER R. 1981 'The Houses of Mortality in Book II of *The Faerie Queene*' *SSt* 2:121–40

DEACON, RICHARD 1968 *John Dee: Scientist, Geographer, Astrologer and Secret Agent to Elizabeth I*, London

DE GROOT, H.B. and ALEXANDER LEGGATT eds 1990 *Craft and Tradition: Essays in Honour of William Blissett*, Calgary

DE LACY, HUGH 1934 'Astrology in the Poetry of Edmund Spenser' *JEGP* 33:520–43

DE LORRIS, GUILLAUME and JEAN de MEUN 1965–70 *Le Roman de la Rose*, ed. Félix Lecoy, 3 vols, Paris

DE MARLY, DIANA 1985 'A Note on *FQ* III.xii.10: ". . . sleeves dependant Albanese-wyse . . ."' *SpN* 16:15–16

DEMARAY, JOHN G. 1991 *Cosmos and Epic Representation: Dante, Spenser, Milton and the Transformation of Renaissance Heroic Poetry*, Pittsburgh

DENEEF, A. LEIGH 1982a *Spenser and the Motives of Metaphor*, Durham, NC

DENEEF, A. LEIGH 1982b 'Ploughing Virgilian Furrows: The Genres of *Faerie Queene* VI' *JDJ* 1:151–66

DENEEF, A. LEIGH 1994 'Rethinking the Spenserian Gaze', in Miller and Dunlop, 162–71

DESENS, MARLISS C. 1994 *The Bed-Trick in English Renaissance Drama: Explorations in Gender, Sexuality, and Power*, Newark, DE

DE TERVARENT, GUY 1958 *Attributs et symboles dans l'art profane, 1450–1600: Dictionnaire d'un langage perdu*, Geneva; *Supplément et Index* 1964

D'EWES, SIMONDS 1682 *The Journals of all the Parliaments during the Reign of Queen Elizabeth*, London

DIEHL, HUSTON 1986 'Into the Maze of Self: The Protestant Transformation of the Image of the Labyrinth' *JMRS* 16:281–99

DILLON, GRACE L. 1998 'Mocking Imperialism: A Lively Hyperbolical Amplification in Spenser's *Faerie Queene*' *RenP*, 19–28

DIMATTEO, ANTHONY 1992 'Spenser's Venus-Virgo: The Poetics and Interpretive History of a Dissembling Figure' *SSt* 10 (for 1989):37–70

DIXON, JOHN 1964 *The First Commentary on 'The Faerie Queene'*, ed. Graham Hough, London

DIXON, MICHAEL F.N. 1996 *The Polliticke Courtier: Spenser's 'The Faerie Queene' as a Rhetoric of Justice*, Montreal

DOBIN, HOWARD 1990 *Merlin's Disciples: Prophecy, Poetry, and Power in Renaissance England*, Stanford

DOLLERUP, CAY 1985 'Spenser's Concord and the Danish Princess Anna' *N&Q* 230:23–25

DOLVEN, JEFF 1999 'Spenser and the Troubled Theaters' *ELR* 29:179–200

DONNE, JOHN 1912 *Poems*, ed. Herbert J.C. Grierson, 2 vols, London

DOWNING, CRYSTAL NELSON 1982 'The "charmes backe to reverse": Deconstructing Architectures in Books II and III of *The Faerie Queene*' *Comitatus* 13:64–83

DRAPER, JOHN W. 1932 'Classical Coinage in the *Faerie Queene*' *PMLA* 47:97–108

DRAYTON, MICHAEL 1931–41 *Works*, ed. J. William Hebel, Kathleen Tillotson, and Bernard H. Newdigate, 5 vols, Oxford; corr edn 1961

DU BARTAS, GUILLAUME DE SALUSTE 1979 *The Divine Weeks and Works*, tr. Joshua Sylvester, ed. Susan Snyder, 2 vols, Oxford

DUBOIS, PAGE ANN 1980 '"The devil's gateway": Women's Bodies and the Earthly Paradise' *WS* 7 (3):43–58

DUBOIS, PAGE ANN 1982 *History, Rhetorical Description and the Epic: From Homer to Spenser*, Woodbridge

DUBROW, HEATHER 1990 'The Arraignment of Paridell: Tudor Historiography in *The Faerie Queene*, III.ix' *SP* 87:312–28

DUBROW, HEATHER 1995 *Echoes of Desire: English Petrarchism and its Counterdiscourses*, Ithaca

DUBROW, HEATHER 2000 ' "A doubtfull sense of things": Thievery in *The Faerie Queene* 6.10 and 6.11', in P. Cheney and Silberman, 204–16

DUGHI, THOMAS A. 1997 'Redcrosse's "Springing Well" of Scriptural Faith' *SEL* 37:21–38

DUNDAS, JUDITH 1993 *Pencils Rhetorique: Renaissance Poets and the Art of Painting*, Newark, DE

DUNSEATH, T.K. 1968 *Spenser's Allegory of Justice in Book Five of 'The Faerie Queene'*, Princeton

DURLING, ROBERT M. 1954 'The Bower of Bliss and Armida's Palace' *CL* 6:335–47; rpt *EA*, 113–24

DUROCHER, RICHARD J. 1984 'Arthur's Gift, Aristotle's Magnificence, and Spenser's Allegory: A Study of *Faerie Queene* 1.9.19' *MP* 82:185–90

DUROCHER, RICHARD J. 1993 'Guiding the Glance: Spenser, Milton, and "Venus looking glas" ' *JEGP* 92:325–41

EADE, J.C. 1984a *The Forgotten Sky: A Guide to Astrology in English Literature*, Oxford

EADE, J.C. 1984b 'Spenser's *Faerie Queene*, VII.vii.52' *Expl* 42 (2):3–5

EDWARDS, PHILIP 1997 *Sea-Mark: The Metaphorical Voyage, Spenser to Milton*, Liverpool

EGGERT, KATHERINE 2000a *Showing Like a Queen: Female Authority and Literary Experiment in Spenser, Shakespeare, and Milton*, Philadelphia

EGGERT, KATHERINE 2000b 'Spenser's Ravishment: Rape and Rapture in *The Faerie Queene*' *Representations* 70:1–26

EILBERG-SCHWARTZ, HOWARD and WENDY DONIGER eds 1995 *Off with Her Head!: The Denial of Women's Identity in Myth, Religion, and Culture*, Berkeley

ELDEVIK, RANDI 1998 '*The Faerie Queene* II.x.18–19' *SSt* 12 (for 1991):207–14

ELIOT, T.S. 1932 *Selected Essays 1917–1932*, London

ELLIS, JIM 1994 'Desire in Translation: Friendship in the Life and Work of Spenser' *ESC* 20:171–85

ELLRODT, ROBERT 1960 *Neoplatonism in the Poetry of Spenser*, Geneva; rpt Folcraft, PA 1969

ELYOT, THOMAS 1907 *The Boke Named The Governour* (1531), ed. Foster Watson, London

ELYOT, THOMAS 1946 *Of the Knowledge Which Maketh a Wise Man* (1533), ed. Edwin Johnston Howard, Oxford, OH

ERICKSON, WAYNE 1992 'Spenser's Letter to Ralegh and the Literary Politics of *The Faerie Queene*'s 1590 Publication' *SSt* 10 (for 1989):139–74

ERICKSON, WAYNE 1996 *Mapping 'The Faerie Queene': Quest Structures and the World of the Poem*, New York

ERICKSON, WAYNE 1997 'Spenser and His Friends Stage a Publishing Event: Praise, Play, and Warning in the Commendatory Verses to the 1590 *Faerie Queene*' *RenP*, 13–22

ERSKINE, JOHN 1915 'The Virtue of Friendship in the *Faerie Queene*' *PMLA* 30:831–50

ESOLEN, ANTHONY M. 1990 'The Disingenuous Poet Laureate: Spenser's Adoption of Chaucer' *SP* 87:285–311

ESOLEN, ANTHONY M. 1993 'Spenser's "Alma Venus": Energy and Economics in the Bower of Bliss' *ELR* 23:267–86

ESOLEN, ANTHONY M. 1994 'Spenserian Chaos: Lucretius in *The Faerie Queene*' *SSt* 11 (for 1990):31–51

ESTRIN, BARBARA L. 1985 *The Raven and the Lark: Lost Children in Literature of the English Renaissance*, Lewisburg

ETTIN, ANDREW V. 1982 'The Georgics in *The Faerie Queene*' *SSt* 3:57–71

EVANS, FRANK B. 1965 'The Printing of Spenser's *Faerie Queene* in 1596' *SB* 18:49–67

EVANS, MAURICE 1967 *English Poetry in the Sixteenth Century*, London

EVANS, MAURICE 1970 *Spenser's Anatomy of Heroism: A Commentary on 'The Faerie Queene'*, Cambridge

EVETT, DAVID 1982 'Mammon's Grotto: Sixteenth-Century Visual Grotesquerie and Some Features of Spenser's *Faerie Queene*' *ELR* 12:180–209

EVETT, DAVID 1990 *Literature and the Visual Arts in Tudor England*, Athens, GA

FALCONER, ALEXANDER FREDERICK 1964 *Shakespeare and the Sea*, London

FARMER, NORMAN K., JR 1993 'The World's New Body: Spenser's *Faerie Queene* Book II, St Paul's Epistles and Reformation England', in *Renaissance Culture in Context: Theory and Practice*, ed. Jean R. Brink and William F. Gentrup, Brookfield, VT, 75–85

FARNESS, JAY 1996 'Disenchanted Elves: Biography in the Text of *Faerie Queene* V', in Anderson, 18–30

FERRY, ANNE 1988 *The Art of Naming*, Chicago

FICHTER, ANDREW 1982 *Poets Historical: Dynastic Epic in the Renaissance*, New Haven

FIKE, MATTHEW A. 1997 ' "Not without Theseus": The Mythic Weave of *The Faerie Queene*, Book I' *CML* 17:231–49

FIKE, MATTHEW A. 1999 'Spenser's Merlin Reconsidered' *SSt* 13:89–99.

FINCH, MARY E. 1956 *The Wealth of Five Northamptonshire Families 1540–1640*, Oxford

FINKE, LAURIE A. 1994 'Spenser for Hire: Arthurian History as Cultural Capital in *The Faerie Queene*', in *Culture and the King: The Social Implications of the Arthurian Legend*, ed. Martin B. Shichtman and James P. Carley, Albany, 211–33

'*Firumbras*' and '*Otuel and Roland*' 1935 ed. Mary Isabelle O'Sullivan, EETS os 198, London

FISHER, JAMES R. 1993a 'The Seven Deadly Passions: Edmund Spenser, Architectonike and Genre Critic' *EIRC* 19:135–46

FISHER, JAMES R. 1993b 'Certaine Signes of the Zodiac: The Shape of Spenser's Allegory in Book II of *The Faerie Queene*' *Constructions* 8:9–35

FISHER, JAMES R. 1993c 'Signs and Seasons in Edmund Spenser's *Faerie Queene*' *J Interdisciplinary St* 5:57–76

FLEMING, JOHN V. 1969 '*The Roman de la Rose*': A Study in Allegory and Iconography', Princeton

FLETCHER, ANGUS 1964 *Allegory: The Theory of a Symbolic Mode*, Ithaca

FLETCHER, ANGUS 1971 *The Prophetic Moment: An Essay on Spenser*, Chicago

FLORIO, JOHN 1598 *A Worlde of Wordes*, London; facs New York 1972

FOGARTY, ANNE 1989 'The Colonization of Language: Narrative Strategy in *A View of the Present State of*

Ireland and *The Faerie Queene*, Book VI', in Coughlan, 75–108

FORSTE-GRUPP, SHERYL L. 1999 'A Possible Irish Source for the Giant Coulin of Spenser's *Faerie Queene*' *SP* 96:42–50

FOWLER, ALASTAIR 1959 'Six Knights at Castle Joyous' *SP* 56:583–99

FOWLER, ALASTAIR 1960a 'The river Guyon' *MLN* 75:289–92

FOWLER, ALASTAIR 1960b 'Emblems of Temperance in *The Faerie Queene*, Book II' *RES* 11:143–49

FOWLER, ALASTAIR 1961a 'The Image of Mortality: *The Faerie Queene*, II.i–ii' *HLQ* 24:91–110; rpt *EA*, 139–52

FOWLER, ALASTAIR 1961b 'Spenser and Renaissance Iconography' *EIC* 11:235–38

FOWLER, ALASTAIR 1961c 'Oxford and London Marginalia to *The Faerie Queene*' *N&Q* 206:416–19

FOWLER, ALASTAIR 1964 *Spenser and the Numbers of Time*, London

FOWLER, ALASTAIR 1970 *Triumphal Forms: Structural Patterns in Elizabethan Poetry*, Cambridge

FOWLER, ALASTAIR 1973 'Emanations of Glory: Neoplatonic Order in Spenser's *Faerie Queen*', in Kennedy and Reither, 53–82

FOWLER, ALASTAIR 1989a 'Spenser's Names', in Logan and Teskey, 32–48

FOWLER, ALASTAIR 1989b 'Spenser and War', in *War, Literature and the Arts in Sixteenth-Century Europe* ed. J.R. Mulryne and Margaret Shewring, London, 147–64

FOWLER, ALASTAIR 1996 *Time's Purpled Masquers: Stars and the Afterlife in Renaissance English Literature*, Oxford

FOWLER, ALASTAIR 1999 'The Emblem as a Literary Genre', in *Deviceful Settings: The English Renaissance Emblem and its Contexts*, ed. Michael Bath and Daniel Russell, New York, pp. 1–31

FOWLER, ALASTAIR and MICHAEL LESLIE 1981 'Drummond's Copy of *The Faerie Queene*' *TLS* July 17:821–22

FOWLER, EARLE BROADUS 1921 *Spenser and the Courts of Love*, Menasha

FOWLER, ELIZABETH 1995 'The Failure of Moral Philosophy in the Work of Edmund Spenser' *Representations* 51:47–76

FOX, ALICE 1975 'More on Terwin and Trevisan' *SpN* 6:39–40

FOX, ALISTAIR 1997 *The English Renaissance: Identity and Representation in Elizabethan England*, Oxford

FRACASTORO, GIROLAMO 1984 *Syphilis* (1555), ed. Geoffrey Eatough, Liverpool

FRANKE, PAUL C. 1980–81 'The Heraldry of *The Faerie Queene*' Coat of Arms 4:317–23

FRANTZ, DAVID O. 1986 'The Union of Florimell and Marinell: The Triumph of Hearing' *SSt* 6 (for 1985): 115–27

FRANTZ, DAVID O. 1989 '*Festum Voluptatis*': A Study of Renaissance Erotica, Columbus, OH

FRASER, ANTONIA 1984 *The Weaker Vessel: Woman's Lot in Seventeenth-Century England*, London

FRAUNCE, ABRAHAM 1950 *The Arcadian Rhetorike* (1588), ed. Ethel Seaton, Oxford

FRAUNCE, ABRAHAM 1967 *The Lamentations of Amyntas* (1587), ed. Franklin M. Dickey, Chicago

FRAUNCE, ABRAHAM 1975 *The Third Part of the Countesse of Pembrokes Yuychurch. Entitled 'Amintas Dale'* (1592), ed. Gerald Snare, Northridge

FREEMAN, LOUIS GILBERT 2000 'The Metamorphosis of Malbecco: Allegorical Violence and Ovidian Change' *SP* 97:308–30

FREEMAN, ROSEMARY 1970 '*The Faerie Queene*': A Companion for Readers, London

FRIED, DEBRA 1981 'Spenser's Caesura' *ELR* 11:261–80

FRIEDMAN, LIONEL J. 1965–66 'Gradus amoris' *RP* 19:167–77

FRUEN, JEFFREY P. 1987 ' "True Glorious Type": The Place of Gloriana in *The Faerie Queene*' *SSt* 7 (for 1986):147–73

FRUEN, JEFFREY P. 1994 'The Faery Queen Unveiled? Five Glimpses of Gloriana' *SSt* 11 (for 1990):53–88

FRUSHELL, RICHARD C. 1999 *Edmund Spenser in the Early Eighteenth Century: Education, Imitation, and the Making of a Literary Model*, Pittsburgh

FRUSHELL, RICHARD C. and BERNARD J. VONDERSMITH eds 1975 *Contemporary Thought on Edmund Spenser*, Carbondale

FRYE, NORTHROP 1957 *Anatomy of Criticism: Four Essays*, Princeton

FRYE, NORTHROP 1963 'The Structure of Imagery in *The Faerie Queene*', in *Fables of Identity: Studies in Poetic Mythology*, New York, 69–87; rpt *EA*, 153–70

FRYE, NORTHROP 1976a *The Secular Scripture: A Study of the Structure of Romance*, Cambridge, MA

FRYE, NORTHROP 1976b *Spiritus Mundi: Essays on Literature, Myth, and Society*, Bloomington, IN

FRYE, NORTHROP 1990a *Words With Power: Being a Second Study of 'The Bible and Literature'*, New York

FRYE, NORTHROP 1990b *Myth and Metaphor: Selected Essays, 1974–1988*, Charlottesville

FRYE, SUSAN 1993 *Elizabeth I: The Competition for Representation*, New York

FRYE, SUSAN 1994 'Of Chastity and Violence: Elizabeth I and Edmund Spenser in the House of Busirane' *Signs* 20:49–78

FUJII, HARUHIKO 1974 *Time, Landscape and the Ideal Life: Studies in the Pastoral Poetry of Spenser and Milton*, Kyoto

FUKUDA, SHOHACHI 1997 'A List of Pronunciations and Etymologies of Spenser's Names in *The Faerie Queene*' *Memoirs of the Faculty of Education, Kumamoto University* 46:225–29.

FULGENTIUS 1971 *Fulgentius the Mythographer*, tr. Leslie George Whitbread, Columbus, OH

FUMERTON, PATRICIA 1991 *Cultural Aesthetics: Renaissance Literature and the Practice of Social Ornament*, Chicago

GALBRAITH, DAVID 2000 *Architectonics of Imitation in Spenser, Daniel, and Drayton*, Toronto

GALLAGHER, LOWELL 1991 *Medusa's Gaze: Casuistry and Conscience in the Renaissance*, Stanford

GARRETT, MARTIN ed. 1996 *Sidney: The Critical Heritage*, London

GASCOIGNE, GEORGE 1907–10 *Complete Works*, ed. John W. Cunliffe, 2 vols, Cambridge

GELLER, LILA 1972 'The Acidalian Vision: Spenser's Graces in Book VI of *The Faerie Queene*' *RES* 23:267–77

GEOFFREY OF MONMOUTH 1891 (*c.* 1135) *British History*, in *Six Old English Chronicles*, ed. J.A. Giles, London, 89–292

GIAMATTI, A. BARTLETT 1966 *The Earthly Paradise and the Renaissance Epic*, Princeton

GIAMATTI, A. BARTLETT 1984 *Exile and Change in Renaissance Literature*, New Haven

GIL, ALEXANDER 1621 *Logonomia Anglica* (1619), London; rpt Menston 1969

GILBERT, BISHOP OF SARUM 1850 *An Exposition of the Thirty-Nine Articles of the Church of England* (1699), London

GILBERT, ALLAN H. 1933 'Spenser's Cymocles' *MLN* 48:230

GILBERT, ALLAN H. 1955 ' "Those two brethren giants": the *Faerie Queene* II xi 15' *MLN* 70:93–94

GILMAN, ERNEST B. 1986 *Iconoclasm and Poetry in the English Reformation: Down Went Dagon*, Chicago

GIROUARD, MARK 1983 *Robert Smythson & The Elizabethan Country House*, New Haven

GLESS, DARRYL J. 1994 *Interpretation and Theology in Spenser*, Cambridge

GOEGLEIN, TAMARA A. 1994 'Utterances of the Protestant Soul in *The Faerie Queene*: The Allegory of Holiness and the Humanist Discourse of Reason' *Criticism* 36:1–19

GOHLKE, MADELON S. 1978 'Embattled Allegory: Book II of *The Faerie Queene*' *ELR* 8:123–40

GOLDBERG, JONATHAN 1975 'The Mothers in Book III of *The Faerie Queene*' *TSLL* 17:5–26

GOLDBERG, JONATHAN 1981 *Endlesse Worke: Spenser and the Structures of Discourse*, Baltimore

GOLDBERG, JONATHAN 1989 *James I and the Politics of Literature: Jonson, Shakespeare, Donne, and Their Contemporaries*, Stanford

Golden Legend c. 1483. See ARTHUR

GOLDING, ARTHUR. See OVID

GOUGH, MELINDA J. 1999 ' "Her filthy feature open showne" in Ariosto, Spenser, and *Much Ado about Nothing*' *SEL* 39:41–67

GOWER, JOHN 1980 *Confessio Amantis*, ed. Russell A. Peck, Toronto (edited by Caxton 1483)

GRAY, M.M. 1930 'The Influence of Spenser's Irish Experiences on *The Faerie Queene*' *RES* 6:413–28

GRAZIANI, RENÉ 1964a 'Elizabeth at Isis Church' *PMLA* 79:376–89

GRAZIANI, RENÉ 1964b 'Philip II's *impresa* and Spenser's Souldan' *JWCI* 27:322–24

GREENBLATT, STEPHEN 1980 *Renaissance Self-Fashioning: From More to Shakespeare*, Chicago

GREENBLATT, STEPHEN 1990a *Learning to Curse: Essays in Early Modern Culture*, New York

GREENBLATT, STEPHEN 1990b 'Culture', in *Critical Terms for Literary Study*, ed. Frank Lentricchia and Thomas McLaughlin, Chicago, 225–32

GREENE, ROLAND 2000 'A Primer of Spenser's Worldmaking: Alterity in the Bower of Bliss', in P. Cheney and Silberman, 9–31

GREENE, THOMAS 1963 *The Descent from Heaven: A Study in Epic Continuity*, New Haven

GREENFIELD, SAYRE N. 1989 'Reading Love in the Geography of *The Faerie Queene*, Book Three' *PQ* 68:425–42

GREENFIELD, SAYRE N. 1998 *The Ends of Allegory*, Newark, NJ

GREGERSON, LINDA 1993 'Narcissus Interrupted: Specularity and the Subject of the Tudor State' *Criticism* 35:1–40

GREGERSON, LINDA 1995 *The Reformation of the Subject: Spenser, Milton, and the English Protestant Epic*, Cambridge

GREGORY, TOBIAS 2000 'Shadowing Intervention: On the Politics of *The Faerie Queene* Book 5 Cantos 10–12' *ELH* 67:365–97

GRIERSON, H.J.C. 1929 *Cross Currents in English Literature of the XVIIth Century*, London

GRIMM, NADINE G. 1986 'Mutabilitie's Plea before Dame Nature's Bar' *Comitatus* 17:22–34

GROSS, KENNETH 1983 ' "Each Heav'nly Close": Mythologies and Metrics in Spenser and the Early Poetry of Milton' *PMLA* 98:21–36

GROSS, KENNETH 1985 *Spenserian Poetics: Idolatry, Iconoclasm, and Magic*, Ithaca

GROSS, KENNETH 1999 'Reflections on the Blatant Beast' *SSt* 13:101–23

GUAZZO, STEFANO 1925 *The Civile Conversation*, tr. George Pettie 1581 and Bartholomew Young 1586, ed. Edward Sullivan, 2 vols, London

GUILLORY, JOHN 1983 *Poetic Authority: Spenser, Milton, and Literary History*, New York

GUILPIN, EVERARD 1974 *Skialetheia* (1598), ed. D. Allen Carroll, Chapel Hill, NC

GURR, ANDREW 1987 *Playgoing in Shakespeare's London*, Cambridge

GUY, JOHN 1988 *Tudor England*, Oxford

HACKETT, HELEN 1995 *Virgin Mother, Maiden Queen: Elizabeth I and the Cult of the Virgin Mary*, London

HADFIELD, ANDREW 1994 *Literature, Politics and National Identity: Reformation to Renaissance*, Cambridge

HADFIELD, ANDREW 1996a 'The "sacred hunger of ambitious minds": Spenser's savage religion', in *Religion, Literature, and Politics in Post-Reformation England, 1540–1688*, ed. Donna B. Hamilton and Richard Strier, Cambridge, 27–45

HADFIELD, ANDREW 1996b 'Introduction', to *Edmund Spenser, Longman Critical Readers*, London

HADFIELD, ANDREW 1997 *Edmund Spenser's Irish Experience: 'Wilde Fruit and Salvage Soyl'*, Oxford

HADFIELD, ANDREW 1998a 'Certainties and Uncertainties: By Way of Response to Jean Brink' *SSt* 12 (for 1991):197–202

HADFIELD, ANDREW 1998b 'Was Spenser a Republican?' *English* 47:169–82

HADFIELD, ANDREW 1999 'Spenser's Description of the Execution of Murrogh O'Brien: An Anti-Catholic Polemic?', *N&Q* 244:195–97

HADFIELD, ANDREW and WILLY MALEY eds 1997 *A View of the State of Ireland*, by Edmund Spenser, Oxford

HAGEMAN, ELIZABETH H. 1971 'Alma, Belphoebe, Maleger, and the Number 22: Another Note on Symbolic Stanza Placement' *N&Q* 216:225–26

HAKLUYT, RICHARD 1903–05 *The Principal Navigations*, 12 vols, Glasgow (3 vols, 1598–1600)

HALE, JOHN K. 1977 *Milton's Languages: The Impact of Multilingualism on Style*, Cambridge

HALL, ANNE D. 1995 'The Actaeon Myth and Allegorical Reading in Spenser's "Two Cantos of Mutabilitie"' *SCJ* 26:561–75

HAMILTON, A.C. 1959 'Spenser's Treatment of Myth' *ELH* 26:335–54

HAMILTON, A.C. 1961a *The Structure of Allegory in 'The Faerie Queene'*, Oxford

HAMILTON, A.C. 1961b 'The Visions of *Piers Plowman* and *The Faerie Queene*', in Nelson, 1–34

HAMILTON, A.C. ed. 1966 *Edmund Spenser: Selected Poetry*, New York

HAMILTON, A.C. 1967 *The Early Shakespeare*, San Marino, CA

HAMILTON, A.C. 1968 '*The Faerie Queene*', in *Critical Approaches to Six Major English Works: 'Beowulf' through 'Paradise Lost'*, ed. R.M. Lumiansky and Herschel Baker, Philadelphia, 132–66

HAMILTON, A.C. 1973 'Our New Poet: Spenser, "well of English undefyld"', in Kennedy and Reither, 101–23; rpt *EA*, 488–506

HAMILTON, A.C. 1975 'On Annotating Spenser's *Faerie Queene* : A New Approach to the Poem', in Frushell and Vondersmith, 41–60

HAMILTON, A.C. 1981 'The Philosophy of the Footnote', in *Editing Poetry from Spenser to Dryden*, ed. A.H. deQuehen, New York, 127–63

HAMILTON, A.C. 1990 'Closure in Spenser's *The Faerie Queene*', in de Groot and Leggatt, 23–34

HAMILTON, A.C. 1992 'The Bible and Spenser's *Faerie Queene*: Sacred and Secular Scripture' *JELL* 38:667–81

HAMILTON, A.C. 1995 'The Renaissance of the Study of the English Literary Renaissance' *ELR* 25:372–87

HAMILTON, A.C. 1996 'Problems in Reconstructing an Elizabethan Text: The Example of Sir Philip Sidney's "Triumph"' *ELR* 26:451–81

HAMILTON, A.C. 1999 'Northrop Frye as a Cultural Theorist', in *Rereading Frye: The Published and Unpublished Works*, ed. David Boyd and Imre Salusinszky, Toronto, 103–21

HAMLIN, WILLIAM M. 1994 'Attributions of Divinity in Renaissance Ethnography and Romance; or, Making Religion of Wonder' *JMRS* 24:415–47

HAMLIN, WILLIAM M. 1995 *The Image of America in Montaigne, Spenser, and Shakespeare: Renaissance Ethnography and Literary Reflection*, New York

HANKINS, JOHN ERSKINE 1971 *Source and Meaning in Spenser's Allegory: A Study of 'The Faerie Queene'*, Oxford

HANNA III, RALPH 1991 'Annotation as Social Practice', in *Annotation and Its Texts*, ed. Stephen A. Barney, New York, 178–84

HANNAY, MARGARET P. 1990 *Philip's Phoenix: Mary Sidney, Countess of Pembroke*, New York

HARDIN, RICHARD F. 1979 'The Pastoral Moment', in *Survivals of Pastoral*, ed. R.F. Hardin, Lawrence, KS, 1–17

HARDIN, RICHARD F. 1992 *Civil Idolatry: Desacralizing and Monarchy in Spenser, Shakespeare, and Milton*, Newark

HARDYNG, JOHN 1812 *The Chronicle* (1543), ed. Henry Ellis, London; facs New York 1974

HARINGTON 1591 See ARIOSTO

HARPER, CARRIE ANNA 1910 *The Sources of the British Chronicle History in Spenser's 'Faerie Queene'*, Philadelphia; rpt New York 1964

HARRIS, JONATHAN GIL 1998 *Foreign Bodies and the Body Politic: Discourses of Social Pathology in Early Modern England*, Cambridge

HARRISON, THOMAS P. 1956 *They Tell of Birds: Chaucer, Spenser, Milton, Drayton*, Austin

HARVEY, ELIZABETH D. 1992 *Ventriloquized Voices: Feminist Theory and English Renaissance Texts*, London

HARVEY, GABRIEL 1884 *Letter-Book A.D. 1573–1580*, ed. Edward John Long Scott, Camden Society, London

HARVEY, GABRIEL 1884–85 *Works*, ed. Alexander B. Grosart, London

HARVEY, GABRIEL 1913 *Marginalia*, ed. G.C. Moore Smith, Stratford-upon-Avon

HASKER, RICHARD 1947 'Spenser's "vaine delight"' *MLN* 62:334–35

HAWKINS, PETER S. 1981 'From Mythography to Mythmaking: Spenser and The *Magna Mater* Cybele', *SCJ* 12:51–64

HAWKINS, SHERMAN 1961 'Mutabilitie and the Cycle of the Months', in Nelson, 76–102

HAZARD, MARK 2000 'The Other Apocalypse: Spenser's Use of 2 Esdras in the Book of Justice' *SSt* 14:163–87

HAZLITT, WILLAM 1910 *Lectures on the English Poets* (1818), London

HEAL, FELICITY 1990 *Hospitality in Early Modern England*, Oxford

HEALE, ELIZABETH 1987 *'The Faerie Queene': A Reader's Guide*, Cambridge

HEALE, ELIZABETH 1990 'Spenser's Malengine, Missionary Priests, and the Means of Justice' *RES* 41:171–84

HEALY, THOMAS 1992 *New Latitudes: Theory and English Renaisance Literature*, London

HEBERLE, MARK A. 1987 'Spenser's *The Faerie Queene*, VII.7.46' *Expl* 45 (3):4–6

HEBERLE, MARK A. 1989 'Pagans and Saracens in Spenser's *The Faerie Queene*', in *Comparative Literature East and West: Traditions and Trends*, ed. Cornelia N. Moore and Raymond A. Moody, Honolulu, 81–87

HEBERLE, MARK A. 1990 'The Limitations of Friendship' *SSt* 8 (for 1987): 101–18

HEBERT, C.A. 1974 'In Despair over Trevisan and Terwin: A Query' *SpN* 5 (3):18

HEDLEY, JANE 1988 *Power in Verse: Metaphor and Metonymy in the Renaissance Lyric*, University Park, PA

HEFFERNAN, JAMES A.W. 1993 *Museum of Words: The Poetics of Ekphrasis from Homer to Ashbery*, Chicago

HEFFNER, RAY 1933 'Did Spenser Die in Poverty?' *MLN* 48:221–26

HELGERSON, RICHARD 1983 *Self-Crowned Laureates: Spenser, Jonson, Milton, and the Literary System*, Berkeley

HELGERSON, RICHARD 1992 *Forms of Nationhood: The Elizabethan Writing of England*, Chicago

HENDRIX, HOWARD V. 1990 *The Ecstasy of Catastrophe*, New York

HENDRIX, HOWARD V. 1992 ' "Those Wandring Eyes of His": Watching Guyon Watch The Naked Damsels Wrestling' *Assays* 7:71–85

HENDRIX, LAUREL L. 1993 '"Mother of laughter, and welspring of blisse": Spenser's Venus and the Poetics of Mirth' *ELR* 23:113–33

HENINGER, S.K., JR 1959 'The Orgoglio Episode in *The Faerie Queene*' *ELH* 26:171–87; rpt *EA*, 125–38

HENINGER, S.K., JR 1960 *A Handbook of Renaissance Meteorology*, Durham, NC

HENINGER, S.K., JR 1974 *Touches of Sweet Harmony: Pythagorean Cosmology and Renaissance Poetics*, San Marino

HENINGER, S.K., JR 1977 *The Cosmographical Glass: Renaissance Diagrams of the Universe*, San Marino

HENINGER, S.K., JR 1987 'Words and Meter in Spenser and Scaliger' *HLQ* 50:309–22

HENINGER, S.K., JR 1988 *Sidney and Spenser: The Poet as Maker*, University Park, PA

HENINGER, S.K., JR 1991 'Spenser, Sidney, and Poetic Form' *SP* 88:140–52

HENLEY, PAULINE 1928 *Spenser in Ireland*, Cork

HERENDEEN, WYMAN H. 1986 *From Landscape to Literature: The River and the Myth of Geography*, Pittsburgh

HERMAN, PETER C. 1998 '"With-hold till further triall": Spenser's Letter to Ralegh and Modes of Rereading in the 1590 *Faerie Queene*', in *Second Thoughts: A Focus on Rereading*, ed. David Galef, Detroit, 196–227

HERRON, THOMAS 2000 'Irish Den of Thieves: Souterrains (and a Crannog?) in Books V and VI of Spenser's *Faerie Queene*' *SSt* 14:303–17

HIEATT, A. KENT 1960 *Short Time's Endless Monument: The Symbolism of the Numbers in Edmund Spenser's 'Epithalamion'*, New York

HIEATT, A. KENT 1962 'Scudamour's Practice of *Maistrye* upon Amoret' *PMLA* 77:509–10; rpt *EA* 199–201

HIEATT, A. KENT 1973 'Three Fearful Symmetries and the Meaning of *Faerie Queene* II', in Kennedy and Reither, 19–52

HIEATT, A. KENT 1975a *Chaucer, Spenser, Milton: Mythopoeic Continuities and Transformations*, Montreal

HIEATT, A. KENT 1975b 'A Spenser to Structure Our Myths (Medina, Phaedria, Proserpina, Acrasia, Venus, Isis)', in Frushell and Vondersmith, 99–120

HIEATT, A. KENT 1988 'The Passing of Arthur in Malory, Spenser, and Shakespeare: The Avoidance of Closure', in *The Passing of Arthur: New Essays in Arthurian Tradition*, ed. Christopher Baswell and William Sharpe, New York, 173–92

HIEATT, A. KENT 1990 'The Projected Continuation of *The Faerie Queene*: Rome Delivered?' *SSt* 8 (for 1987):335–42

HIEATT, A. KENT 1991 'Arthur's Deliverance of Rome? (Yet Again)' [Rejoinder to Roche 1990a] *SSt* 9 (for 1988):243–48

HIEATT, A. KENT 1992 'The Alleged Early Modern Origin of the Self and History:Terminate or Regroup?' *SSt* 10 (for 1989):1–35

HIEATT, A. KENT 1998 'Room of One's Own for Decisions: Chaucer and *The Faerie Queene*', in Krier, 147–64

HIEATT, A. KENT 1999 'Male Boldness and Female Rights: What the Isle of Venus Proposes' *SSt* 13:269–72

HIGGINS, ANNE 1990 'Spenser Reading Chaucer: Another Look at the *Faerie Queene* Allusions' *JEGP* 89:17–36

HIGHLEY, CHRISTOPHER 1997 *Shakespeare, Spenser, and the Crisis in Ireland*, Cambridge

HOENIGER, F. DAVID 1992 *Medicine and Shakespeare in the English Renaissance*, Newark

HOLAHAN, MICHAEL 1976 '*Iamque opus exegi*: Ovid's Changes and Spenser's Brief Epic of Mutability' *ELR* 6:244–70

HOLINSHED, RAPHAEL 1807–08 *Chronicles* (1577, rev. 1587), ed. Henry Ellis *et al.*, 6 vols, London; facs New York 1965

HOLLANDER, JOHN 1970 *The Untuning of the Sky: Ideas of Music in English Poetry, 1500–1700*, New York

HOLLANDER, JOHN 1971 'Spenser and the Mingled Measure' *ELR* 1:226–38

HOLLANDER, JOHN 1981 *The Figure of Echo: A Mode of Allusion in Milton and After*, Berkeley

HOLLANDER, JOHN 1988 *Melodious Guile: Fictive Patterns in Poetic Language*, New Haven

HOLLANDER, JOHN 1995 *The Gazer's Spirit: Poems Speaking to Silent Works of Art*, Chicago

HOOKER, RICHARD 1888 *Works*, ed. John Keble, rev. R.W. Church and F. Paget, 3 vols, Oxford

HOOPES, ROBERT 1962 *Right Reason in the English Renaissance*, Cambridge, MA

HORTON, RONALD ARTHUR 1978 *The Unity of 'The Faerie Queene'*, Athens, GA

HORTON, RICHARD ARTHUR 1991 'The Argument of Spenser's Garden of Adonis', in *Love and Death in the Renaissance*, ed. Kenneth R. Bartlett, Konrad Eisenbichler, and Janice Liedl, Ottawa, 61–72

HUFFMAN, CLIFFORD CHALMERS 1988 *Elizabethan Impressions: John Wolfe and His Press*, New York

HULSE, CLARK 1990 *The Rule of Art: Literature and Painting in the Renaissance*, Chicago

HULSE, CLARK 1994 '"Painted Forgery": Visual Approaches to *The Faerie Queene*', in Miller and Dunlop, 93–105

HUME, ANTHEA 1984 *Edmund Spenser: Protestant Poet*, Cambridge

HUTSON, LORNA 1996 'Chivalry for Merchants; or, Knights of Temperance in the Realms of Gold' *JMEMS* 26:29–59

HYDE, THOMAS 1986 *The Poetic Theology of Love: Cupid in Renaissance Literature*, Newark

IMBRIE, ANN E. 1987 '"Playing Legerdemaine with the Scripture": Parodic Sermons in *The Faerie Queene*' *ELR* 17:142–55

IVIC, CHRISTOPHER 1999 'Spenser and the Bounds of Race' *Genre* 32:141–73

JARDINE, LISA 1993 'Encountering Ireland: Gabriel Harvey, Edmund Spenser, and English Colonial Ventures', in Bradshaw *et al.*, 60–75

JARDINE, LISA 1996 *Worldly Goods*, London

JAVITCH, DANIEL 1991 *Proclaiming a Classic: The Canonization of 'Orlando Furioso'*, Princeton

JOHNSON, FRANCIS R. 1933 *A Critical Bibliography of the Works of Edmund Spenser Printed Before 1700*, Baltimore; rpt London 1966

JOHNSON, FRANCIS R. 1937 *Astronomical Thought in Renaissance England: A Study of the English Scientific Writings from 1500 to 1645*, Baltimore; rpt New York 1968

JOHNSON, WILLIAM C. 1992 'Spenser in the House of Busyrane: Transformations of Reality in *The Faerie Queene* III and *Amoretti*' *ES* 73:104–20

JONES, H.S.V. 1930 *A Spenser Handbook*, New York

JONSON, BEN 1925–52 *Ben Jonson [Works]* ed. C.H. Herford, Percy Simpson, and Evelyn Simpson, 11 vols, Oxford

JONSON, BEN 1995. For his annotations on the *FQ*, see Riddell and Stewart, 164–87

JORDAN, RICHARD DOUGLAS 1977 'Una among the Satyrs: *The Faerie Queene*, 1.6' *MLQ* 38:123–31

JORDAN, RICHARD DOUGLAS 1989 *The Quiet Hero: Figures of Temperance in Spenser, Donne, Milton, and Joyce*, Washington

JORTIN, JOHN 1734 *Remarks on Spenser's Poems*, London; facs New York 1970

JOYCE, P.W. 1911 *The Wonders of Ireland and Other Papers on Irish Subjects*, London

JUDSON, ALEXANDER CORBIN 1933 *Spenser in Southern Ireland*, Bloomington

JUDSON, ALEXANDER CORBIN 1945 *The Life of Edmund Spenser*, Baltimore

KANE, SEAN 1989 *Spenser's Moral Allegory*, Toronto

KANE, SEAN 1990 'Spenser's Broken Symmetries', in de Groot and Leggatt, 13–22

KANTOROWICZ, ERNST H. 1957 *The King's Two Bodies: A Study in Mediaeval Political Theology*, Princeton

KAPLAN, M. LINDSAY 1997 *The Culture of Slander in Early Modern England*, Cambridge

KASKE, CAROL V. 1969 'The Dragon's Spark and Sting and the Structure of Red Cross's Dragon-fight: *The Faerie Queene*, I.xi–xii' *SP* 66:609–38; rpt *EA*, 425–46

KASKE, CAROL V. 1975 'Spenser's Pluralistic Universe: The View from the Mount of Contemplation (*F.Q.* I.x)', in Frushell and Vondersmith, 121–49

KASKE, CAROL V. 1976 'The Bacchus Who Wouldn't Wash: *Faerie Queene* II.i–ii' *RQ* 29:195–209

KASKE, CAROL V. 1979 '"Religious reuerance doth buriall teene": Christian and Pagan in *The Faerie Queene*, II. i–ii' *RES* 30:129–43

KASKE, CAROL V. 1989 'How Spenser Really Used Stephen Hawes in the Legend of Holiness', in Logan and Teskey, 119–36

KASKE, CAROL V. 1994 'The Audiences of *The Faerie Queene*: Iconoclasm and Related Issues in Books I, V, and VI' *L&H* 3:15–35

KASKE, CAROL V. 1999 *Spenser and Biblical Poetics*, Ithaca

KEATS, JOHN 1978 *Complete Poems*, ed. Jack Stillinger, Cambridge, MA; rev edn 1982

KENDRICK, T.D. 1950 *British Antiquity*, London

KENNEDY, JUDITH M. and JAMES A. REITHER eds 1973 *A Theatre for Spenserians*, Toronto

KENNEDY, WILLIAM J. 1973 'Rhetoric, Allegory, and Dramatic Modality in Spenser's Fradubio Episode' *ELR* 3:351–68

KENNEDY, WILLIAM J. 2000 'Spenser's Squire's Literary History', in P. Cheney and Silberman, 45–62

KERMODE, FRANK 1971 *Shakespeare, Spenser, Donne: Renaissance Essays*, London

KERMODE, FRANK 1975 *The Classic*, London

KIEFER, FREDERICK 1979 'The Conflation of Fortuna and Occasio in Renaissance Thought and Iconography' *JMRS* 9:1–27

KING, JOHN N. 1982 *English Reformation Literature: The Tudor Origins of the Protestant Tradition*, Princeton

KING, JOHN N. 1985 '*The Faerie Leveller*: A 1648 Royalist Reading of *The Faerie Queene*, V.ii.29–54' *HLQ* 48:297–308

KING, JOHN N. 1989 *Tudor Royal Iconography: Literature and Art in an Age of Religious Crisis*, Princeton

KING, JOHN N. 1990a *Spenser's Poetry and the Reformation Tradition*, Princeton

KING, JOHN N. 1990b 'Queen Elizabeth I: Representations of the Virgin Queen' *RQ* 43:30–74

KINNEY, CLARE REGAN 1992 *Strategies of Poetic Narrative: Chaucer, Spenser, Milton, Eliot*, Cambridge

KIRKPATRICK, ROBIN 1995 *English and Italian Literature from Dante to Shakespeare: A Study of Source, Analogue and Divergence*, London

KLEIN, JOAN LARSEN 1985 'The Demonic Bacchus in Spenser and Milton' *MiltonS* 21:93–118

KLEIN, LISA M. 1997 'Your Humble Handmaid: Elizabethan Gifts of Needlework' *RQ* 50:459–93

KLIBANSKY, RAYMOND, ERWIN PANOFSKY and FRITZ SAXL 1964 *Saturn and Melancholy: Studies in the History of Natural Philosophy, Religion and Art*, London

KNAPP, JEFFREY 1992 *An Empire Nowhere: England, America, and Literature from 'Utopia' to 'The Tempest'*, Berkeley

KNIGHT, W. NICHOLAS 1970 'The Narrative Unity of Book V of *The Faerie Queene*: "That Part of Justice which is Equity"' *RES* 21:267–94

KOCHER, PAUL H. 1953 *Science and Religion in Elizabethan England*, San Marino

KOSAKO, MASARU 1993 'Double Syntax in *The Faerie Queene* as a Bearer of Allegory', in *Essays on English Language and Literature in Honour of Michio Kawai*, Tokyo, 129–36

KOSAKO, MASARU 1995 'Some Historical Observations on Collocation of Noun plus Adjective in Rhyme Position of *The Faerie Queene*' *Bul Fac of Education, Okayama Univ.* 100:197–221

KOSAKO, MASARU 1998 'Parts of Speech in Rhyme Words of *The Faerie Queene* (from Book I to Book III): Verbal Icons in the Prominent Distributions', in *A Love of Words: English Philological Studies in Honour of Akira Wada*, ed. Masahiko Kanno *et al.*, Tokyo, 145–60

KOUWENHOVEN, JAN KAREL 1983 *Apparent Narrative as Thematic Metaphor: The Organization of 'The Faerie Queene'*, Oxford

KOUWENHOVEN, JAN KAREL 1986 'Sidney, Leicester, and *The Faerie Queene*', in *Sir Philip Sidney: 1586 and the Creation of a Legend*, ed. Jan van Dorsten, Dominic Baker-Smith, and Arthur F. Kinney, Leiden, 149–69

KRAMNICK, JONATHAN BRODY 1998 *Making the English Canon: Print-Capitalism and the Cultural Past, 1700–1770*, Cambridge

KRIER, THERESA M. 1990 *Gazing on Secret Sights: Spenser, Classical Imitation, and the Decorums of Vision*, Ithaca

KRIER, THERESA M. 1994 ' "The Form and Gait of the Body": Physical Carriage, Genre, and Spenserian Allegory', in Miller and Dunlop, 72–81

KRIER, THERESA M. ed. 1998 *Refiguring Chaucer in the Renaissance*, Gainesville

LAMB, MARY ELLEN 1990 *Gender and Authorship in the Sidney Circle*, Madison

LAMB, MARY ELLEN 2000 'Gloriana, Acrasia, and the House of Busirane: Gendered Fictions in *The Faerie Queene* as Fairy Tale', in P. Cheney and Silberman, 81–100

LANGLAND, WILLIAM 1869 *The Vision of William Concerning 'Piers the Plowman'* (the Crowley text; or Text B, first pub. 1550), ed. Walter W. Skeat, London

LA PRIMAUDAYE, PETER DE 1586 *The French Academie*, facs New York 1972

LAROQUE, FRANÇOIS 1991 *Shakespeare's Festive World: Elizabethan Seasonal Entertainment and the Professional Stage*, tr. Janet Lloyd, Cambridge

LAWS, JENNIFER 1992 'Sexual Politics and the Interpretation of Nature in Spenser's *Two Cantos of Mutabilitie*' *Ren&R* 28:21–35

LEE, SIR SIDNEY 1916 'Bearbaiting, Bullbaiting, and Cockfighting', in *Shakespeare's England: An Account of the Life & Manners of his Age*, Oxford, 2:428–36

LEMMI, C.W. 1929 'The Symbolism of the Classical Episodes in *The Faerie Queene*' *PQ* 8:270–87

LESLIE, MICHAEL 1983 *Spenser's 'Fierce Warres and Faithfull Loves': Martial and Chivalric Symbolism in 'The Faerie Queene'*, Cambridge

LESLIE, MICHAEL 1985 'The Dialogue Between Bodies and Souls: Pictures and Poesy in the English Renaissance' *Word & Image* 1:16–30

LESLIE, MICHAEL 1991 'Edmund Spenser: Art and *The Faerie Queene*' *PBA* 76:73–107

LESLIE, MICHAEL 1992 'Spenser, Sidney, and the Renaissance Garden' *ELR* 22:3–36

LETHBRIDGE, J.B. 1992 'Raleigh in Books III and IV of *The Faerie Queene*: The Primacy of Moral Allegory' *SN* 64:55–66

LEVIN, RICHARD A. 1991 'The Legende of the Redcrosse Knight and Una, or Of the Love of a Good Woman' *SEL* 31:1–24

LEVY, F.J. 1967 *Tudor Historical Thought*, San Marino

LEVY, F.J. 1996 'Spenser and Court Humanism', in Anderson, 65–80

LEWIS, C.S. 1936 *The Allegory of Love: A Study in Medieval Tradition*, London

LEWIS, C.S. 1954 *English Literature in the Sixteenth Century Excluding Drama*, Oxford

LEWIS, C.S. 1964 *The Discarded Image: An Introduction to Medieval and Renaissance Literature*, Cambridge

LEWIS, C.S. 1966 *Studies in Medieval and Renaissance Literature*, Cambridge

LEWIS, C.S. 1967 *Spenser's Images of Life*, Cambridge

LIM, WALTER S.H. 1995 'Figuring Justice: Imperial Ideology and the Discourse of Colonialism in Book V of *The Faerie Queene* and *A View of the Present State of Ireland*' *Ren&R* 19:45–70

LINDEN, STANTON J. 1996 *Darke Hierogliphicks: Alchemy in English Literature from Chaucer to the Restoration*, Lexington

LINTON, JOAN PONG 1998 *The Romance of the New World: Gender and the Literary Formations of English Colonialism*, Cambridge

LOCKERD, BENJAMIN G., JR 1987 *The Sacred Marriage: Psychic Integration in 'The Faerie Queene'*, Lewisburg

LOEWENSTEIN, JOSEPH 1988 'For a History of Literary Property: John Wolfe's Reformation' *ELR* 18:389–412

LOEWENSTEIN, JOSEPH 1996 'Spenser's Retrography: Two Episodes in Post-Petrarchan Bibliography', in Anderson, 99–130

LOGAN, GEORGE M. and GORDON TESKEY eds 1989 *Unfolded Tales: Essays on Renaissance Romance*, Ithaca

LOTSPEICH, HENRY GIBBONS 1932 *Classical Mythology in the Poetry of Edmund Spenser*, Princeton

LOW, ANTHONY 1985 *The Georgic Revolution*, Princeton

LOW, ANTHONY 1998 'Sin, Penance, and Privatization in the Renaissance: Redcrosse and the True Church' *BJJ* 5:1–35

LUBORSKY, RUTH SAMSON and ELIZABETH MORLEY INGRAM 1998 *A Guide to English Illustrated Books 1536–1603*, 2 vols, Tempe, AZ

LUPTON, JULIA REINHARD 1990 'Home-Making in Ireland: Virgil's Eclogue I and Book VI of *The Faerie Queene*' *SSt* 8 (for 1987):119–45

LUPTON, JULIA REINHARD 1993 'Mapping Mutability: or, Spenser's Irish Plot', in Bradshaw *et al.*, 93–115

LYDGATE, JOHN 1906–35 *Troy Book*, ed. Henry Bergen, EETS es 97, 103, 106, 126, London

LYDGATE, JOHN 1911 *The Minor Poems*, ed. Henry Noble MacCracken, EETS es 107, London

LYLY, JOHN 1902 *Complete Works*, ed. R. Warwick Bond, 3 vols, Oxford; rpt 1967

MacCAFFREY, ISABEL G. 1976 *Spenser's Allegory: The Anatomy of Imagination*, Princeton

MacCOLL, ALAN 1989 'The Temple of Venus, the Wedding of the Thames and the Medway, and the end of *The Faerie Queene*, Book IV' *RES* 40:26–47

MACFIE, PAMELA POYSTON 1990 'Text and *Textura*: Spenser's Arachnean Art', in *Traditions and Innovations: Essays on British Literature of the Middle Ages and the Renaissance*, ed. David G. Allen and Robert A. White, Newark, 88–96

MACEY, J. DAVID, JR 1999 ' "Fowle Idolatree" and Fair: Apuleius and the Idol of Isis Church' *CLS* 36:279–93

MacGILLIVRAY, S.R. 1992 'Spenser's *Faerie Queene* [I xi 28.1–2]' *Expl* 50:131–32

MacLACHLAN, HUGH 1980 'The "carelesse heauens": A Study of Revenge and Atonement in *The Faerie Queene*' *SSt* 1:135–61

MacLACHLAN, HUGH 1984 'The Death of Guyon and the Elizabethan Book of Homilies' *SSt* 4 (for 1983):93–114

MACROBIUS 1952 *Commentary on the Dream of Scipio*, tr. William Harris Stahl, New York

MAGILL, A.J. 1970 'Spenser's Guyon and the Mediocrity of the Elizabethan Settlement' *SP* 67:167–77

MALEY, WILLY 1991 'Spenser and Ireland: A Select Bibliography' *SSt* 9 (for 1988):227–42

MALEY, WILLY 1994 *A Spenser Chronology*, London

MALEY, WILLY 1996a 'Spenser and Ireland: An Annotated Bibliography, 1986–96' *IUR* 26:342–53

MALEY, WILLY 1996b 'Spenser and Scotland: The *View* and the Limits of Anglo-Irish Identity' *Prose Studies* 19:1–18

MALEY, WILLY 1997 *Salvaging Spenser: Colonialism, Culture and Identity*, London

MALLETTE, RICHARD 1997 *Spenser and the Discourses of Reformation England*, Lincoln, NE

MALORY 1983 *Caxton's Malory*, ed. James W. Spisak and William Matthews, 2 vols, Berkeley

MANLEY, LAWRENCE 1995 *Literature and Culture in Early Modern London*, Cambridge

MANN, JILL 1991 *Geoffrey Chaucer*, Hempstead

MANNING, JOHN 1984 'Notes and Marginalia in Bishop Percy's Copy of Spenser's *Works* (1611)' *N&Q* 229:225–27

MANNING, JOHN 1985 ' "Deuicefull Sights": Spenser's Emblematic Practice in *The Faerie Queene*, V. 1–3' *SSt* 5 (for 1984):65–89

MANNING, JOHN 1988 'Spenser and the Long-Haired Egyptians' *N&Q* 233:40–41

MANNING, JOHN and ALASTAIR FOWLER 1976 'The Iconography of Spenser's Occasion' *JWCI* 39:263–66

MAPLET, JOHN 1930 *A Greene Forest, or A Naturall Historie* (1567), London

MARCUS, LEAH S. 1988 *Puzzling Shakespeare: Local Reading and its Discontents*, Berkeley

MARCUS, LEAH S. 1996 *Unediting the Renaissance: Shakespeare, Marlowe, Milton*, London

MARESCA, THOMAS E. 1979 *Three English Epics: Studies of 'Troilus and Criseyde', 'The Faerie Queene', and 'Paradise Lost'*, Lincoln, NE

MARPRELATE, MARTIN (pseud.) 1588–89 'Hay any Worke for Cooper', in *The Marprelate Tracts* (1588–1589), London; facs Leeds 1967

MARTIN, ELLEN E. 1987 'Spenser, Chaucer, and the Rhetoric of Elegy' *JMRS* 17:83–109

MAY, STEVEN W. 1989 *Sir Walter Ralegh*, Boston

MAY, STEVEN W. 1991 *The Elizabethan Courtier Poets: The Poems and Their Contexts*, Columbia, MO; rpt Asheville, NC 1999

MAZZOLA, ELIZABETH 1994 ' "Most Strong in Most Infirmitee": Ritual Sequences and Consequences in *The Faerie Queene* Book II' *LJHum* 20:5–25

MAZZOLA, ELIZABETH 1995 'Apocryphal Texts and Epic Amnesia: The Ends of History in *The Faerie Queene*' *Soundings* 78:131–42

MAZZOLA, ELIZABETH 1996 'The Implied Arthur: Mass Publics and Splintered Subjects in Spenser's *Faerie Queene*, Book II', in *Word and Image in Arthurian Literature*, ed. Keith Busby, New York, 132–50

MAZZOLA, ELIZABETH 1998 *The Pathology of the English Renaissance: Sacred Remains and Holy Ghosts*, Leiden

MCAULEY, JAMES 1974 'The Form of Una's Marriage Ceremony in "The Faerie Queene" ' *N&Q* 219:410–11

MCCABE, RICHARD A. 1987 'The Masks of Duessa: Spenser, Mary Queen of Scots, and James VI' *ELR* 17:224–42

MCCABE, RICHARD A. 1989a *The Pillars of Eternity: Time and Providence in 'The Faerie Queene'*, Dublin

MCCABE, RICHARD A. 1989b 'The Fate of Irena: Spenser and Political Violence', in Coughlan, 109–25

MCCABE, RICHARD A. 1993a 'Edmund Spenser, Poet of Exile' *PBA* 80:73–103

MCCABE, RICHARD A. 1993b 'Prince Arthur's "Vertuous and Gentle Discipline" ', in Ní Cuilleanáin and Pheifer, 221–43

MCCABE, RICHARD A. 1999 ed. *Edmund Spenser: The Shorter Poems*, London

MCCARTHY, PENNY 2000 'E.K. was only the Postman' *N&Q* 245:28–31

MCCLURE, PETER AND ROBIN HEADLAM WELLS 1990 'Elizabeth I as a Second Virgin Mary' *RenSt* 4:38–70

MCCOY, RICHARD C. 1989 *The Rites of Knighthood: The Literature and Politics of Elizabethan Chivalry*, Berkeley

MCDERMOTT, JOHN V. 1996 'Spenser's *Faerie Queene*, 1.11.52 and 53' *Expl* 54:198–99

MCEACHERN, CLAIRE 1996 *The Poetics of English Nationhood, 1590–1612*, Cambridge

MCKERROW, RONALD B. 1913 *Printers' and Publishers' Devices in England and Scotland, 1485–1640*, London

MCLEOD, BRUCE 1999 *The Geography of Empire in English Literature, 1580–1745*, Cambridge

MCMANUS, CAROLINE 1997 'The "carefull Nourse": Female Piety in Spenser's Legend of Holiness' *HLQ* 60:381–406

MCNAMARA, RICHARD 2000 'The Numerological Patterning of Spenser's Dedicatory Sonnets to *The Faerie Queene*' *Journal of Sapporo International University* 31:19–23

MCNEIR, WALDO F. 1966 'Trial by Combat in Elizabethan Literature' *NS* 15:101–12

MCNEIR, WALDO F. 1968 'The Sacrifice of Serena: *The Faerie Queene*, VI.viii.31–51', in *Festschrift für Edgar Mertner*, ed. Bernhard Fabian and Ulrich Suerbaum, Munich, 117–56

MEYER, RUSSELL J. 1975 'From Thérouanne to Terwin?' *SpN* 6:18–19

MEYER, RUSSELL J. 1984 ' "Fixt in heauens hight": Spenser, Astronomy, and the Date of the *Cantos of Mutabilitie*' *SSt* 4 (for 1983):115–29

MEYER, RUSSELL J. 1991 *'The Faerie Queene': Educating the Reader*, Boston

MIKALACHKI, JODI 1998 *The Legacy of Boadicea: Gender and Nation in Early Modern England*, London

MIKICS, DAVID 1994 *The Limits of Moralizing: Pathos and Subjectivity in Spenser and Milton*, Lewisburg

MILLER, DAVID LEE 1979 'Abandoning the Quest' *ELH* 46:173–92

MILLER, DAVID LEE 1988 *The Poem's Two Bodies: The Poetics of the 1590 'Faerie Queene'*, Princeton

MILLER, DAVID LEE 1993 'Spenser and the Gaze of Glory', in Maclean and Prescott, 756–64

MILLER, DAVID LEE 1996 'The Earl of Cork's Lute', in Anderson, 146–71

MILLER, DAVID LEE and ALEXANDER DUNLOP eds 1994 *Approaches to Teaching Spenser's 'Faerie Queene'*, New York

MILLER, JACQUELINE T. 1986a *Poetic License: Authority and Authorship in Medieval and Renaissance Contexts*, New York

MILLER, JACQUELINE T. 1986b 'The Omission in Red Cross Knight's Story: Narrative Inconsistencies in *The Faerie Queene*' *ELH* 53:279–88

MILLER, JACQUELINE T. 1991 'The Courtly Figure: Spenser's Anatomy of Allegory' *SEL* 31:51–68

MILLER, JACQUELINE T. 1997 'Mother Tongues: Language and Lactation in Early Modern Literature', *ELR* 27:177–96

MILLER, SHANNON 1998 *Invested with Meaning: The Raleigh Circle in the New World*, Philadelphia

MILLER, W. IAN 1997 'Gluttony' *Representations* 60:92–112

MILLICAN, CHARLES BOWIE 1932 *Spenser and the Table Round: A Study in the Contemporaneous Background for Spenser's Use of the Arthurian Legend*, Cambridge, MA; rpt New York 1967

MILLS, JERRY LEATH 1967 'Spenser's Castle of Alma and the Number 22: A Note on Symbolic Stanza Placement' *N&Q* 212:456–57

MILLS, JERRY LEATH 1973 'Spenser, Lodowick Bryskett, and the Mortalist Controversy: The Faerie Queene, II.ix.22' *PQ* 52:173–86

MILLS, JERRY LEATH 1976 'Spenser and the Numbers of History: A Note on the British and Elfin Chronicles in *The Faerie Queene*' *PQ* 55:281–87

MILLS, JERRY LEATH 1977 'Spenser's Letter to Raleigh and the Averroistic *Poetics*', *ELN* 14:246–49.

MILLS, JERRY LEATH 1978 'Prudence, History, and the Prince in *The Faerie Queene*, Book II' *HLQ* 41:83–101

MILLS, LAURENS J. 1937 *One Soul in Bodies Twain: Friendship in Tudor Literature and Stuart Drama*, Bloomington

MILTON, JOHN 1953–82 *Complete Prose Works*, ed. Don M. Wolfe *et al.*, 8 vols, New Haven

MILTON, JOHN 1968 *Poems*, ed. John Carey and Alastair Fowler, London

MONTROSE, LOUIS ADRIAN 1986 'The Elizabethan Subject and the Spenserian Text', in *Literary Theory / Renaissance Texts*, ed. Patricia Parker and David Quint, Baltimore, 303–40

MONTROSE, LOUIS ADRIAN 1993 'The Work of Gender in the Discourse of Discovery', in *New World Encounters*, ed. Stephen Greenblatt, Berkeley, 177–217

MONTROSE, LOUIS ADRIAN 1996 'Spenser's Domestic Domain: Poetry, Property, and the Early Modern Subject', in *Subject and Object in Renaissance Culture*, ed. Margreta de Grazia, Maureen Quilligan, and Peter Stallybrass, Cambridge, 83–130

MORGAN, GERALD 1981 'Spenser's Conception of Courtesy and the Design of the *Faerie Queene*' *RES* 32:17–36

MORGAN, GERALD 1986a 'Holiness as the First of Spenser's Aristotelian Moral Virtues' *MLR* 81:817–37

MORGAN, GERALD 1986b 'The Idea of Temperance in the Second Book of *The Faerie Queene*' *RES* 37:11–39

MORGAN, GERALD 1993 'The Meaning of Spenser's Chastity as the Fairest of Virtues', in Ní Cuilleanáin and Pheifer, 245–63

MORLEY, LORD 1971 *Lord Morley's 'Tryumphes of Fraunces Petrarcke': The First English Translation of the 'Trionfi'*, ed. D.H. Carnicelli, Cambridge, MA

MORONEY, MARYCLAIRE 1998 'Spenser's Dissolution: Monasticism and Ruins in *The Faerie Queene* and *The View of the Present State of Ireland*' *SSt* 12 (for 1991):105–32

MORRILL, JOHN ed. 1996 *The Oxford Illustrated History of Tudor and Stuart Britain*, Oxford

MORRIS, JEFFREY B. 1997 'To (Re)fashion a Gentleman: Ralegh's Disgrace in Spenser's Legend of Courtesy' *SP* 94:38–58

MOSELEY, CHARLES ed. 1989 *A Century of Emblems: An Introductory Anthology*, Aldershot

MUELLER, ROBERT J. 1991 '"Infinite Desire": Spenser's Arthur and the Representation of Courtly Ambition' *ELH* 58:747–71

MULCASTER, RICHARD 1994 *Positions Concerning the Training Up of Children* (1581), ed. William Barker, Toronto

MURRIN, MICHAEL 1969 *The Veil of Allegory: Some Notes toward a Theory of Allegorical Rhetoric in the English Renaissance*, Chicago

MURRIN, MICHAEL 1980 *The Allegorical Epic: Essays in its Rise and Decline*, Chicago

MURRIN, MICHAEL 1997 'The Audience of *The Faerie Queene*' *EIRC* 23:1–21

NASHE, THOMAS 1904–10 *Works*, ed. Ronald B. McKerrow, 5 vols, London; rev edn F.P. Wilson, Oxford 1958

NEILL, KERBY 1935 'The *Faerie Queene* and the Mary Stuart Controversy' *ELH* 2:192–214

NELSON, WILLIAM ed. 1961 *Form and Convention in the Poetry of Edmund Spenser*, New York

NELSON, WILLIAM 1963 *The Poetry of Edmund Spenser: A Study*, New York

NELSON, WILLIAM 1965 'Queen Elizabeth, Spenser's Mercilla, and a Rusty Sword' *RenN* 18:113–17

NELSON, WILLIAM 1973 'Spenser *ludens*', in Kennedy and Reither, 83–100

NEUSE, RICHARD 1968 'Book VI as Conclusion to *The Faerie Queene*' *ELH* 35:329–53; rpt *EA*, 366–88

NEUSE, RICHARD 1990 'Planting Words in the Soul: Spenser's Socratic Garden of Adonis' *SSt* 8 (for 1987):79–100

NICHOLS, JOHN 1823 *The Progresses and Public Processions of Queen Elizabeth*, 3 vols, London; rpt New York 1965

NICOLSON, MARJORIE 1936 *A World in the Moon: A Study of the Changing Attitude toward the Moon in the Seventeenth and Eighteenth Centuries*, Northampton, MA

NÍ CUILLEANÁIN, EILÉAN and J.D. PHEIFER eds 1993 *Noble and Joyous Histories: English Romances, 1375–1650*, Dublin

NOHRNBERG, JAMES 1976 *The Analogy of 'The Faerie Queene'*, Princeton

NOHRNBERG, JAMES 1998 'Orlando's Opportunity: Chance, Luck, Fortune, Occasion, Boats, and Blows in Boiardo's *Orlando Innamorato*', in *Fortune and Romance: Boiardo in America*, ed. Jo Ann Cavallo and Charles Ross, Tempe, AZ, 31–75

NORBROOK, DAVID 1984 *Poetry and Politics in the English Renaissance*, London

NORTH, MARCY 1994 'Ignoto in the Age of Print: The Manipulation of Anonymity in Early Modern England' *SP* 91:390–416

NORTHROP, DOUGLAS A. 1968–69 'Spenser's Defence of Elizabeth' *UTQ* 38:277–94

NORTHROP, DOUGLAS A. 1973 'Mercilla's Court as Parliament' *HLQ* 36:153–58

NORTHROP, DOUGLAS A. 2000 'The Uncertainty of Courtesy in Book VI of *The Faerie Queene*' *SSt* 14:215–32

OAKESHOTT, WALTER 1960 *The Queen and the Poet*, London; New York 1961

OAKESHOTT, WALTER 1971 'Carew Ralegh's Copy of Spenser' *Library* 5th ser 26:1–21

OATES, MARY I. 1984 '*Fowre Hymnes*: Spenser's Retractations of Paradise' *SSt* 4 (for 1983):143–69

O'BRIEN, ROBERT VIKING 1999 'Astarte in the Temple of Venus: An Allegory of Idolatry' *SP* 93:144–58

O'CONNELL, MICHAEL 1977 *Mirror and Veil: The Historical Dimension of Spenser's 'Faerie Queene'*, Chapel Hill

O'CONNOR, JOHN J. 1970 '*Amadis de Gaule' and its Influence on Elizabethan Literature*, New Brunswick, NJ

O'CONNOR, JOHN J. 1990 'Terwin, Trevisan, and Spenser's Historical Allegory' *SP* 87:328–40

O'DAY, ROSEMARY 1995 *The Longman Companion to The Tudor Age*, London

OLMSTED, WENDY RAUDENBUSH 1994 'Deconstruction and Spenser's Allegory' *SSt* 11 (for 1990):111–27

ORAM, WILLIAM A. 1984 'Elizabethan Fact and Spenserian Fiction' *SSt* 4 (for 1983):33–47

ORAM, WILLIAM A. 1990 'Spenser's Raleghs' *SP* 87:341–62

ORAM, WILLIAM A. 1997 *Edmund Spenser*, New York

ORANGE, LINWOOD E. 1958 'Spenser's *Faerie Queene* IV ix 30.5–9' *Expl* 17: item 22

OSGOOD, CHARLES GROSVENOR 1920 'Spenser's English Rivers' *TCAAS* 23:65–108

OVID 1904 *Shakespeare's Ovid, Being Arthur Golding's Translation of the 'Metamorphoses'* (1567), ed. W.H.D. Rouse, London; rpt New York 1966

PADELFORD, FREDERICK MORGAN 1938 'The Punctuation of *The Faerie Queene*', in *The Works of Edmund Spenser, a Variorum Edition* 6:480–503

PAGLIA, CAMILLE A. 1979 'The Apollonian Androgyne and the *Faerie Queene*' *ELR* 9:42–63

PAGLIA, CAMILLE A. 1990 *Sexual Personae: Art and Decadence from Nefertiti to Emily Dickinson*, New Haven; cited from Vintage Books Edition, New York 1991

PAINTER, WILLIAM 1813 *The Palace of Pleasure* (1566–75), ed. Joseph Haslewood, 3 vols, London; facs New York 1966

PANOFSKY, ERWIN 1955 *Meaning in the Visual Arts: Papers in and on Art History*, New York

PANOFSKY, ERWIN 1962 *Studies in Iconology: Humanistic Themes in the Art of the Renaissance*, New York

PARKER, M. PAULINE 1960 *The Allegory of the 'Faerie Queene'*, Oxford

PARKER, PATRICIA A. 1979 *Inescapable Romance: Studies in the Poetics of a Mode*, Princeton

PARKER, PATRICIA A. 1987 *Literary Fat Ladies: Rhetoric, Gender, Property*, London

PARKIN-SPEER, DIANE 1992 'Allegorical Legal Trials in Spenser's *The Faerie Queene*' *SCJ* 23:494–505

PASK, KEVIN 1996 *The Emergence of the English Author: Scripting the Life of the Poet in Early Modern England*, Cambridge

PASTER, GAIL KERN 1993 *The Body Embarrassed: Drama and the Disciplines of Shame in Early Modern England*, Ithaca

PATRIDES, C.A. 1982 *Premises and Motifs in Renaissance Thought and Literature*, Princeton

PATTERSON, ANNABEL 1993 *Reading between the Lines*, Madison

PAXSON, JAMES J. 1994 *The Poetics of Personification*, Cambridge

PENDERGAST, JOHN S. 1996 'Christian Allegory and Spenser's "General Intention"' *SP* 93:267–87

PERRY, NANDRA 1997 'Elizabeth I as Holy Church in Spenser's *Faerie Queene*' *RenP*, 33–48

PETERSON, RICHARD S. 1998 'Laurel Crown and Ape's Tail: New Light on Spenser's Career from Sir Thomas Tresham' *SSt* 12 (for 1991):1–35

PHEIFER, J.D. 1984 'Errour and Echidna in *The Faerie Queene*: A Study in Literary Tradition', in *Literature and Learning in Medieval and Renaissance England*, ed. John Scattergood, Dublin, 127–74

PHILLIPS, JAMES E., JR 1941–42 'The Background of Spenser's Attitude Toward Women Rulers' *HLQ* 5:5–32

PHILLIPS, JAMES E., JR 1970 'Renaissance Concepts of Justice and the Structure of *The Faerie Queene*, Book V' *HLQ* 33:103–20; rpt *EA*, 471–87

PHILMUS, MARIA R. ROHR 1995 '*The Faerie Queene* and Renaissance Poetics: Another Look at Book VI as "Conclusion" to the Poem' *ES* 6:497–519

Physiologus 1979, tr. Michael J. Curley, Austin

PIGMAN III, G.W. 1980 'Versions of Imitation in the Renaissance' *RQ* 33:1–32

PITCHER, JOHN 1987 'Tudor Literature, 1485–1603', in *An Outline of English Literature*, ed. Pat Rogers, Oxford, 58–91

PLATO 1961 *Collected Dialogues*, ed. Edith Hamilton and Huntington Cairns, New York

POTTS, ABBIE FINDLAY 1958 *Shakespeare and 'The Faerie Queene'*, Ithaca

PRESCOTT, ANNE LAKE 1986 'The Thirsty Deer and the Lord of Life: Some Contexts for *Amoretti* 67–70' *SSt* 6 (for 1985):33–76

PRESCOTT, ANNE LAKE 1989 'Spenser's Chivalric Restoration: From Bateman's *Travayled Pylgrime* to the Redcrosse Knight' *SP* 86:166–97; extract in Suzuki 1996:77–94

PRESCOTT, ANNE LAKE 1994 'Triumphing over Death and Sin' *SSt* 11 (for 1990):231–32

PRESCOTT, ANNE LAKE 1996 'Spenser (Re)Reading du Bellay: Chronology and Literary Response', in Anderson, 131–45

PRESCOTT, ANNE LAKE 2000 'Foreign Policy in Fairyland: Henri IV and Spenser's Burbon' *SSt* 14:189–214

PURDON, LIAM O. 1988 'A Reconsideration of the Ass Image in Book I of *The Faerie Queen*' *ELN* 26:18–21

PUTTENHAM, GEORGE 1936 *The Arte of English Poesie* (1589), ed. Gladys Doidge Willcock and Alice Walker, Cambridge

QUILLIGAN, MAUREEN 1979 *The Language of Allegory: Defining the Genre*, Ithaca

QUILLIGAN, MAUREEN 1983 *Milton's Spenser: The Politics of Reading*, Ithaca

QUILLIGAN, MAUREEN 1987 'The Comedy of Female Authority in *The Faerie Queene*' *ELR* 17:156–71

QUILLIGAN, MAUREEN 1990 'Feminine Endings: The Sexual Politics of Sidney's and Spenser's Rhyming', in *The Renaissance Englishwoman in Print: Counterbalancing the Canon*, ed. Anne M. Haselkorn and Betty S. Travitsky, Amherst, 311–26

QUINT, DAVID 1983 *Origin and Originality in Renaissance Literature: Versions of the Source*, New Haven

QUINT, DAVID 1992 'Bragging Rights: Honor and Courtesy in Shakespeare and Spenser', in *Creative Imitation: New Essays on Renaissance Literature in Honor of Thomas M. Greene*, ed. David Quint, Margaret W. Ferguson, G.W. Pigman III, and Wayne A. Rebhorn, Binghamton, 391–430

QUINT, DAVID 2000 'Archimago and Amoret: The Poem and its Doubles', in P. Cheney and Silberman, 32–42

QUITSLUND, JON A. 1996 'Questionable Evidence in the *Letters* of 1580 between Gabriel Harvey and Edmund Spenser', in Anderson, 81–98

QUITSLUND, JON A. 1997 'The Work of Mourning in Spenser's Garden of Adonis' *RenP*, 23–31

RADCLIFFE, DAVID HILL 1996 *Edmund Spenser: A Reception History*, Columbia, SC

RAJAN, BALACHANDRA 1985 *The Form of the Unfinished: English Poetics from Spenser to Pound*, Princeton

RALEGH, SIR WALTER 1999 *Poems: A Historical Edition*, ed. Michael Rudick, Tempe, AZ

RALEIGH, SIR WALTER 1965 *The Discovery of Guiana* (1596), in *Selected Prose and Poetry*, ed. Agnes M.C. Latham, London, pp. 102–68

RAMBUSS, RICHARD 1993 *Spenser's Secret Career*, Cambridge

RAMBUSS, RICHARD 1996 'Spenser's Lives, Spenser's Careers', in Anderson, 1–17

RAPAPORT, HERMAN 1986 'The Phenomenology of Spenserian Ekphrasis', in *Murray Krieger and Contemporary Critical Theory*, ed. Bruce Henricksen, New York, 157–75

RATHBORNE, ISABEL E. 1937 *The Meaning of Spenser's Fairyland*, New York; rpt New York 1965

READ, DAVID T. 2000 *Temperate Conquests: Spenser and the Spanish New World*, Detroit·

REID, ROBERT L. 1981 'Alma's Castle and the Symbolization of Reason in *The Faerie Queene* *JEGP* 80:512–27

RHU, LAWRENCE F. 1993a *The Genesis of Tasso's Narrative Theory: English Translations of the Early Poetics and a Comparative Study of Their Significance*, Detroit

RHU, LAWRENCE F. 1993b 'Agons of Interpretation: Ariostan Source and Elizabethan Meaning in Spenser, Harington, and Shakespeare' *RenD* 24:171–88

RHU, LAWRENCE F. 1993c 'Romancing Eliza: The Political Decorum of Ariostan Imitation in *The Faerie Queene*' *RenP*, 31–39

RHU, LAWRENCE F. 1994 'Romancing the Word: Pre-Texts and Contexts for the Errour Episode' *SSt* 11 (for 1990):101–109

RICHARDSON, J. MICHAEL 1989 *Astrological Symbolism in Spenser's 'The Shepheardes Calender': The Cultural Background of a Literary Text*, Lewiston, NY

RICHEY, ESTHER GILMAN 1998 *The Politics of Revelation in the English Renaissance*, Columbia, MO

RIDDELL, JAMES A. and STANLEY STEWART 1995 *Jonson's Spenser: Evidence and Historical Criticism*, Pittsburgh

RINGLER, RICHARD N. 1965–66 'The Faunus Episode' *MP* 63:12–19; rpt *EA*, 289–98

RIPA, CESARE 1603 *Iconologia* Rome; facs New York 1970

ROBBINS, ROSSELL HOPE ed. 1952 *Secular Lyrics of the XIVth and XVth Centuries*, Oxford

ROBERTS, GARETH 1978 'Three Notes on Uses of Circe by Spenser, Marlowe and Milton' *N&Q* 223:433–35

ROBERTS, GARETH 1992 *The Faerie Queene*, 'Open Guides to Literature Series', Buckingham

ROBERTS, GARETH 1997 'Women and Magic in English Renaissance Love Poetry', in *Representing Women in Renaissance England*, ed. Claude J. Summers and Ted-Larry Pebworth, Columbia, MO, 59–75

ROBIN, P. ANSELL 1911 *The Old Physiology in English Literature*, London

ROBIN, P. ANSELL 1932 *Animal Lore in English Literature*, London

ROBINSON, LILLIAN S. 1985 *Monstrous Regiment: The Lady Knight in Sixteenth-Century Epic*, New York

ROCHE, THOMAS P., JR 1964 *'The Kindly Flame': A Study of the Third and Fourth Books of Spenser's 'Faerie Queene'*, Princeton

ROCHE, THOMAS P., JR 1984 'The Menace of Despair and Arthur's Vision, *Faerie Queene* I.9' *SSt* 4 (for 1983):71–92

ROCHE, THOMAS P., JR 1989 'Spenser's Muse', in Logan and Teskey, 162–88

ROCHE, THOMAS P., JR 1990a 'A Response to A. Kent Hieatt' [Hieatt 1990] *SSt* 8 (for 1987):343–47

ROCHE, THOMAS P., JR 1990b 'Typology, Allegory, and Protestant Poetics' *GHJ* 13 (1):1–17

ROCHE, THOMAS P., JR 1995 'Spenser, Milton, and the Representation of Evil', in *Heirs of Fame: Milton and Writers of the English Renaissance*, ed. Margo Swiss and David A. Kent, Lewisburg, 14–33

ROCHE, THOMAS P., JR with C. PATRICK O'DONNELL, JR eds 1978 *Edmund Spenser: 'The Faerie Queene'*, Harmondsworth

ROLLINSON, PHILIP 1987 'Arthur, Maleger, and the Interpretation of *The Faerie Queene*' *SSt* 7 (for 1986):103–21

Romance of the Rose, see de Lorris and de Meun 1965–70

Romaunt of the Rose, in Chaucer 1933, 565–637

ROOKS, JOHN 1988 'Art, Audience and Performance in the Bowre of Bliss' *MLS* 18:23–36

ROSE, MARK 1968 *Heroic Love: Studies in Sidney and Spenser*, Cambridge, MA

ROSE, MARK 1975 *Spenser's Art: A Companion to Book I of 'The Faerie Queene'*, Cambridge, MA

ROSS, CHARLES 1997 *The Custom of the Castle: From Malory to 'Macbeth'*, Berkeley

ROSSI, JOAN WARCHOL 1985 '*Britons moniments*: Spenser's Definition of Temperance in History' *ELR* 15:42–58

ROSTON, MURRAY 1987 *Renaissance Perspectives in Literature and the Visual Arts*, Princeton

RØSTVIG, MAREN-SOFIE 1994 *Configurations: A Topomorphical Approach to Renaissance Poetry*, Oslo

ROVANG, PAUL R. 1996 *Refashioning 'Knights and Ladies Gentle Deeds': The Intertextuality of Spenser's 'Faerie Queene' and Malory's 'Morte Darthur'*, Madison

ROWE, GEORGE E. 1989 'Privacy, Vision, and Gender in Spenser's Legend of Courtesy' *MLQ* 50:309–36

ROWLAND, BERYL 1973 *Animals with Human Faces: A Guide to Animal Symbolism*, Knoxville

ROWLAND, BERYL 1978 *Birds with Human Souls: A Guide to Bird Symbolism*, Knoxville

RUDAT, WOLFGANG E.H. 1983 'Spenser's "Angry Ioue": Vergilian Allusion in the First Canto of *The Faerie Queene*' *JRMMRA* 3:89–98

RYDÉN, MATS 1978 *Shakespearean Plant Names: Identifications and Interpretations*, Stockholm

RYDÉN, MATS 1984 'The Contextual Significance of Shakespeare's Plant Names' *SN* 56:155–62

SADOWSKI, PIOTR 2000 'Spenser's "golden squire" and "golden Meane": Numbers and Proportions in Book II of *The Faerie Queene*' *SSt* 14:107–31

SANDERS, ARNOLD A. 1992 'Ruddymane and Canace, Lost and Found: Spenser's Reception of Gower's *Confessio Amantis* 3 and Chaucer's *Squire's Tale*', in *Work of Dissimilitude*, ed. David G. Allen and Robert A. White, Newark, 196–215

SANDYS, GEORGE 1615 *A Relation of a Journey begun anno Dom, 1610*, London

SANDYS, GEORGE 1970 *Ovid's 'Metamorphosis' Englished, Mythologized, and Represented in Figures* (1632), ed. Karl K. Hulley and Stanley T. Vandersall, Lincoln, NE

SAWDAY, JONATHAN 1995 *The Body Emblazoned: Dissection and the Human Body in Renaissance Culture*, London

SCHIAVONI, JAMES 1992 'Predestination and Free Will: The Crux of [Book I] Canto Ten' *SSt* 10 (for 1989):175–95

SCHLEINER, WINFRIED 1978 '*Divina virago*: Queen Elizabeth as an Amazon' *SP* 75:163–80

SCHOENFELDT, MICHAEL C. 1994 'The Poetry of Conduct: Accommodation and Transgression in *The Faerie Queene*, Book 6', in *Enclosure Acts: Sexuality, Property, and Culture in Early Modern England*, ed. Richard Burt and John Michael Archer, Ithaca, 151–69

SCHOENFELDT, MICHAEL C. 1999 *Bodies and Selves in Early Modern England: Physiology and Inwardness in Spenser, Shakespeare, Herbert, and Milton*, Cambridge

SCHOENFELDT, MICHAEL C. 2000 'The Construction of Inwardness in *The Faerie Queene*, Book 2', in P. Cheney and Silberman, 234–43

SCOTT, SHIRLEY CLAY 1987 'From Polydorus to Fradubio: The History of a *Topos*' *SSt* 7 (for 1986):27–57

SCOULAR, KITTY W. 1965 *Natural Magic: Studies in the Presentation of Nature in English Poetry from Spenser to Marvell*, Oxford

SEDINGER, TRACEY 2000 'Women's Friendship and the Refusal of Lesbian Desire in *The Faerie Queene*' *Criticism* 42:91–113

SESSIONS, WILLIAM A. 1980 'Spenser's Georgics' *ELR* 10:202–38

SEZNEC, JEAN 1953 *The Survival of the Pagan Gods: The Mythological Tradition and Its Place in Renaissance Humanism and Art*, tr. Barbara F. Sessions, New York

SHAHEEN, NASEEB 1976 *Biblical References in 'The Faerie Queene'*, Memphis

SHAKESPEARE, WILLIAM 1974 *The Riverside Shakespeare*, ed. G. Blakemore Evans *et al.*, Boston

SHAVER, ANNE 1991 'Rereading Mirabella' *SSt* 9 (for 1988):211–26

SHEPHERD, SIMON 1989 *Spenser*, New York

SHIRE, HELENA 1978 *A Preface to Spenser*, London

SHORE, DAVID R. 1985 *Spenser and the Poetics of Pastoral: A Study of the World of Colin Clout*, Montreal

SHORE, DAVID R. 1987 'Spenser, Gabriel Harvey, and "*Hobgoblin* runne away with the garland from *Apollo*"' *CahiersE* 31:59–61

SHROEDER, JOHN W. 1962 'Spenser's Erotic Drama: The Orgoglio Episode' *ELH* 29:140–59

SHUGER, DEBORA 1997 'Irishmen, Aristocrats, and Other White Barbarians' *RQ* 50:494–525

SIDNEY, PHILIP 1962 *Poems*, ed. William A. Ringler, JR, Oxford

SIDNEY, PHILIP 1973a *The Countess of Pembroke's Arcadia (The Old Arcadia)* [*c.* 1580], ed. Jean Robertson, Oxford

SIDNEY, PHILIP 1973b *A Defence of Poetry* [1595], in *Miscellaneous Prose of Sir Philip Sidney*, ed. Katherine Duncan-Jones and Jan van Dorsten, Oxford

SIDNEY, PHILIP 1987 *The Countess of Pembroke's Arcadia (The New Arcadia)* [*c.* 1590], ed. Victor Skretkowicz, Oxford

SIDNEY, PHILIP and THE COUNTESS OF PEMBROKE 1963 *The Psalms*, ed. J.C.A. Rathmell, New York

SILBERMAN, LAUREN 1988a '*The Faerie Queene*, Book II and the Limitations of Temperance' *MLS* 25:9–22

SILBERMAN, LAUREN 1988b 'Spenser and Ariosto: Funny Peril and Comic Chaos' *CLS* 25:23–34

SILBERMAN, LAUREN 1995 *Transforming Desire: Erotic Knowledge in Books III and IV of 'The Faerie Queene*, Berkeley

SINFIELD, ALAN 1983 *Literature in Protestant England, 1560–1660*, London

SINGLETON, CHARLES S. ed. 1968 *A Dictionary of Proper Names and Notable Matters in the Works of Dante* by Paget Toynbee, Oxford

SIRLUCK, ERNEST 1949–50 'A Note on the Rhetoric of Spenser's "Despair"' *MP* 47:8–11

SKELTON, JOHN 1980 (*c.* 1516) *Magnificence*, ed. Paula Neuss, Baltimore

SKRETKOWICZ, VICTOR 1980 'Hercules in Sidney and Spenser' *N&Q* 225:306–10

SKULSKY, HAROLD 1981 *Metamorphosis: The Mind in Exile*, Cambridge, MA

SMITH, CHARLES G. 1935 *Spenser's Theory of Friendship*, Baltimore; rpt New York 1969

SMITH, G. GREGORY 1904 *Elizabethan Critical Essays*, 2 vols, London

SMITH, JOHN 1970 *A Sea Grammar* (1627), ed. Kermit Goell, London

SMITH, ROLAND M. 1935 'Spenser's Irish river stories' *PMLA* 50:1047–56

SMITH, ROLAND M. 1942 'Spenser's Tale of the Two Sons of Milesio' *MLQ* 3:547–57

SMITH, ROLAND M. 1944 'Spenser's "stony Aubrian"' *MLN* 59:1–5

SMITH, ROLAND M. 1955 'Origines Arthurianae: The Two Crosses of Spenser's Red Cross Knight' *JEGP* 54:670–83

SMITH, ROLAND M. 1958 'Spenser's Scholarly Script and "Right Writing"' in D.C. Allen, ed. *Studies in Honor of T.W. Baldwin*, Urbana, 66–111.

SNARE, GERALD 1970 'Satire, Logic, and Rhetoric in Harvey's Earthquake Letter to Spenser' *TSE* 18:17–33

SNARE, GERALD 1971 'Spenser's Fourth Grace' *JWCI* 34:350–55

SNARE, GERALD 1974 'The Poetics of Vision: Patterns of Grace and Courtesy in *The Faerie Queene*, VI' *RenP*, 1–8

SNARE, GERALD 1995 'The Practice of Glossing in Late Antiquity and the Renaissance' *SP* 92:439–59

SNYDER, SUSAN 1998 *Pastoral Process: Spenser, Marvell, Milton*, Stanford

SPENS, JANET 1934 *Spenser's 'Faerie Queene': An Interpretation*, London; rpt New York 1967

SPENS, JANET 1958 Review of *Allegory and Courtesy in Spenser* by H.C. Chang, *RES* 9:66–69

STAMBLER, PETER D. 1977 'The Development of Guyon's Christian Temperance' *ELR* 7:51–89

STAPLETON, M.L. 1998 '"Loue my lewd Pilot": The *Ars Amatoria* in *The Faerie Queene*' *TSLL* 40:328–46

STARNES, DEWITT T. and ERNEST WILLIAM TALBERT 1955 *Classical Myth and Legend in Renaissance Dictionaries*, Chapel Hill

STATON, SHIRLEY F. 1987 'Reading Spenser's *Faerie Queene* – In a Different Voice', in *Ambiguous Realities: Women in the Middle Ages and Renaissance*, ed. Carole Levin and Jeanie Watson, Detroit, 145–62

STEADMAN, JOHN M. 1979 *Nature into Myth: Medieval and Renaissance Moral Symbols*, Pittsburgh

STEADMAN, JOHN M. 1995 *Moral Fiction in Milton and Spenser*, Columbia, MO

STEADMAN, JOHN M. 1996 '"Respects of Fortune": Dowries and Inheritances in Shakespeare, Spenser and Marvell – an Overview', in *Shakespeare's Universe: Renaissance Ideas and Conventions*, ed. John M. Mucciolo, Aldershot, 71–94

STEGGLE, MATTHEW 2000 'Spenser's Ludgate: A Topical Reference in *The Faerie Queene* II.x' *N&Q* 245:34–37

STEPHENS, DOROTHY 1998 *The Limits of Eroticism in Post-Petrarchan Narrative: Conditional Pleasure from Spenser to Marvell*, Cambridge

STEPPAT, MICHAEL 1990 *Chances of Mischief: Variations of Fortune in Spenser*, Köln

STERN, VIRGINIA F. 1979 *Gabriel Harvey: His Life, Marginalia, and Library*, Oxford

STERNHOLD, THOMAS, JOHN HOPKINS et al., 1562 *The Whole Booke of Psalmes*, London

STEVENS, PAUL 1995 'Spenser and Milton on Ireland: Civility, Exclusion, and the Politics of Wisdom' *Ariel* 26:151–67

STEVENS, WALLACE 1951 *The Necessary Angel: Essays on Reality and the Imagination*, New York

STEWART, STANLEY 1966 *The Enclosed Garden: The Tradition and the Image in Seventeenth-Century Poetry*, Madison

STEWART, STANLEY 1991 'Spenser and the Judgment of Paris' *SSt* 9 (for 1988):161–209

STEWART, STANLEY 1997 *'Renaissance' Talk: Ordinary Language and the Mystique of Critical Problems*, Pittsburgh

STILLMAN, CAROL 1981 'Nobility and Justice in Book Five of *The Faerie Queene*' *TSLL* 23:535–54

STILLMAN, CAROL 1985 'Politics, Precedence, and the Order of the Dedicatory Sonnets in *The Faerie Queene*' *SSt* 5 (for 1984):143–48

STOW, JOHN 1956 *A Suruay of London* (1598), London

STRAUSS, PAUL 1995 'Allegory and the Bower of Bliss' *BJJ* 2:59–71

STRONG, ROY C. 1963 *Portraits of Queen Elizabeth I*, Oxford

STRONG, ROY C. 1977 *The Cult of Elizabeth: Elizabethan Portraiture and Pageantry*, London

STRONG, ROY C. and J.A. VAN DORSTEN 1964 *Leicester's Triumph*, London

STUBBLEFIELD, JAY 1998 'A Note on Spenser's *Faerie Queene IV* and Chaucer's *Squire's Tale*' *ELN* 36:9–10

STUMP, DONALD V. 1982 'Isis Versus Mercilla: The Allegorical Shrines in Spenser's Legend of Justice' *SSt* 3:87–98

STUMP, DONALD V. 1991 'The Two Deaths of Mary Stuart: Historical Allegory in Spenser's Book of Justice' *SSt* 9 (for 1988):81–105

STUMP, DONALD V. 1999 'A Slow Return to Eden: Spenser on Women's Rule' *ELR* 29:401–21

SUMMERS, DAVID A. 1997 *Spenser's Arthur: The British Arthurian Tradition and 'The Faerie Queene'*, Lanham

SUMMERSON, JOHN 1963 *Architecture in Britain 1530–1830*, Harmondsworth

SUTTIE, PAUL 1998 'Edmund Spenser's Political Pragmatism' *SP* 95:56–76

SUZUKI, MIHOKO 1989 *Metamorphoses of Helen: Authority, Difference, and the Epic*, Ithaca

SUZUKI, MIHOKO ed. 1996 *Critical Essays on Edmund Spenser*, New York

SUZUKI, TOSHIYUKI 1983 'The Spelling of the Rhymes in 1590 Quarto of *The Faerie Queene*', *Treatises and Studies by the Faculty of Kinjo Gakuin University* 100, 24: 83–101

SUZUKI, TOSHIYUKI 1993 'Irregular Visual Rhymes in *The Faerie Queene*, Part I (Books I–III)', *Treatises and Studies by the Faculty of Kinjo Gakuin University* 149, 34: 61–80

SUZUKI, TOSHIYUKI 1997 'A Note on the Errata to the 1590 quarto of *The Faerie Queene*', *Treatises and Studies by the Faculty of Kinjo Gakuin University* 169:38, 105–29

SUZUKI, TOSHIYUKI 1999 'The Punctuation of *The Faerie Queene* Reconsidered' *Treatises and Studies by the Faculty of Kinjo Gakuin University* 179, 40: 151–71

SZÖNYI, GY.E. 1984 '"O Worke Diuine": The Iconography and Intellectual Background of Alma's House in *The Faerie Queene*', in *Shakespeare and the Emblem: Studies in Renaissance Iconography and Iconology*, Szeged, 353–94

TASSO, TORQUATO 1963 *Gerusalemme Liberata* (1581), in *Opere*, ed. Bruno Maier, 5 vols, Milan

TASSO, TORQUATO 1981 *Jerusalem Delivered*, tr. Edward Fairfax as *Godfrey of Bulloigne* (1600), ed. Kathleen M. Lea and T.M. Gang, Oxford, includes 'The Allegorie of the Poem', 87–93

TAYLOR, ANTHONY BRIAN 1985 'Spenser and Arthur Golding' *N&Q* 230:18–21

TAYLOR, ANTHONY BRIAN 1986 'Spenser and Golding: Further Debts in *The Faerie Queene*' *N&Q* 231:342–45

TAYLOR, ANTHONY BRIAN 1987a 'The Elizabethan Seneca and Two Notes on Shakespeare and Spenser' *N&Q* 232:193–95

TAYLOR, ANTHONY BRIAN 1987b 'The Faerie Queene Book I and Golding's Translation of *Metamorphoses*' *N&Q* 232:197–99

TESKEY, GORDON 1990 'Positioning Spenser's "Letter to Raleigh"', in de Groot and Leggatt, 35–46

TESKEY, GORDON 1996 *Allegory and Violence*, Ithaca

THAON, BRENDA 1985 'Spenser's Neptune, Nereus and Proteus: Renaissance Mythography Made Verse', in *Acta Conventus Neo-Latini Bononiensis*, ed. R.J. Schoeck, Binghamton, 630–37

Thirty-Nine Articles, see Gilbert, Bishop of Sarum

THOMPSON, ROGER 1979 *Unfit for Modest Ears: A Study of Pornographic, Obscene and Bawdy Works Written or Published in England in the Second Half of the Seventeenth Century*, Totowa, NJ

THOMSEN, KERRI LYNNE 1994 'Spenser's Use of Claudian's *De Raptu Proserpinae*' *N&Q* 239:456–59

TILNEY, EDMUND 1992 *The Flower of Friendship* [1568]: *A Renaissance Dialogue Contesting Marriage*, ed. Valerie Wayne, Ithaca

TONKIN, HUMPHREY 1972 *Spenser's Courteous Pastoral: Book VI of the 'Faerie Queene'*, Oxford

TONKIN, HUMPHREY 1989 *The Faerie Queene*, London

TOPSELL, EDWARD 1967 *The History of Four-Footed Beasts and Serpents and Insects* (1607–08), 3 vols, New York

TRAPP, J.B. 1968 'The Iconography of the Fall of Man', in *Approaches to 'Paradise Lost'*, ed. C.A. Patrides, Toronto, 223–65

TRATNER, MICHAEL 1990 '"The thing S. Paule ment by . . . the courteousness that he spake of": Religious Sources for Book VI of *The Faerie Queene*' *SSt* 8 (for 1987):147–74

TREIP, MINDELE ANNE 1994 *Allegorical Poetics and the Epic: The Renaissance Tradition to 'Paradise Lost'*, Lexington

TRIBBLE, EVELYN B. 1993 *Margins and Marginality: The Printed Page in Early Modern England*, Charlottesville

TRIBBLE, EVELYN B. 1996 'The Partial Sign: Spenser and the Sixteenth-Century Crisis of Semiotics', in *Ceremony and Text in the Renaissance*, ed. Douglas F. Rutledge, Newark, 23–34

TUNG, MASON 1972 'Spenser's Graces and Costalius' "Pegma"' *EM* 23:9–14

TUNG, MASON 1985 'Spenser's "Emblematic" Imagery: A Study in Emblematics' *SSt* 5 (for 1984):185–207

TUVE, ROSEMOND 1947 *Elizabethan and Metaphysical Imagery: Renaissance Poetic and Twentieth-Century Critics*, Chicago

TUVE, ROSEMOND 1966 *Allegorical Imagery: Some Mediaeval Books and their Posterity*, Princeton

TUVE, ROSEMOND 1970 *Essays by Rosemond Tuve: Spenser, Herbert, Milton*, ed. Thomas P. Roche, JR, Princeton

UNDERWOOD, VERNE 1996 'Who Paid for Spenser's Funeral?' *SpN* 27 (2):22–24

VANCE, EUGENE 1986 *Mervelous Signals: Poetics and Sign Theory in the Middle Ages*, Lincoln, NE

VAN DER NOOT, JAN 1569 *A Theatre [for] Voluptuous Worldlings*, London; facs New York 1939, Delmar, NY 1977

VAN DYKE, CAROLYNN 1985 *The Fiction of Truth: Structures of Meaning in Narrative and Dramatic Allegory*, Ithaca

VAN ES, BART 2000 '"Priuie to his Counsell and Secret Meaning": Spenser and Political Prophecy' *ELR* 30:3–31

VICKERS, BRIAN 1970 *Classical Rhetoric in English Poetry*, London

VILLEPONTEAUX, MARY 1993 '*Semper Eadem*: Belphoebe's Denial of Desire', in *Renaissance Discourses of Desire*, ed. Claude J. Summers and Ted-Larry Pebworth, Columbia, MO, 29–45

VILLEPONTEAUX, MARY 1995 'Displacing Feminine Authority in *The Faerie Queene*' *SEL* 35:53–67

VILLEPONTEAUX, MARY 1998 '"*Not as women wonted be*": Spenser's Amazon Queen', in Walker 1998a:209–25

VINK, JAMES 1990 'Spenser's "Easterland" as the Columban Church of Ancient Ireland' *Éire* 25:96–106

VIVES, JUAN LUIS 1912 *Instruction of a Christian Woman* (1533), in *Vives and the Renascence Education of Women*, ed. Foster Watson, London

VORAGINE, JACOBUS DE 1900 *The Golden Legend, or Lives of the Saints*, tr. William Caxton, ed. F.S. Ellis, 7 vols, London

VOSS, PAUL J. 1996 '*The Faerie Queene* 1590–1596: The Case of Saint George' *BJJ* 3:59–73

WALKER, JULIA M. ed. 1998a *Dissing Elizabeth: Negative Representations of Gloriana*, Durham, NC

WALKER, JULIA M. 1998b *Medusa's Mirrors: Spenser, Shakespeare, Milton, and the Metamorphosis of the Female Self*, Newark, NJ

WALL, JOHN N. 1984 '"Fruitfullest Virginia": Edmund Spenser, Roanoke Island, and the Bower of Bliss' *RenP*, 1–17

WALL, JOHN N. 1987 'Orion's Flaming Head: Spenser's *Faerie Queene*, II.ii.46 and the Feast of the Twelve Days of Christmas' *SSt* 7 (for 1986):93–101

WALL, JOHN N. 1988 *Transformations of the Word: Spenser, Herbert, Vaughan*, Athens, GA

WALL, JOHN N. 1990 'Orion Once More: Revisiting the Sky over Faerieland' *SSt* 8 (for 1987):331–34

WALL, WENDY 1993 *The Imprint of Gender: Authorship and Publication in the English Renaissance*, Ithaca

WALLER, GARY 1994 *Edmund Spenser: A Literary Life*, New York

WALLS, KATHRYN 1984 'Spenser's Kirkrapine and John Foxe's Attack on Rome' *N&Q* 229:173–75

WALLS, KATHRYN 1985 'Abessa and the Lion: *The Faerie Queene*, I.3.1–12' *SSt* 5 (for 1984):3–30

WARNER, MARINA 1976 *Alone of All Her Sex: The Myth and Cult of the Virgin Mary*, London

WARTON, THOMAS 1762 *Observations on the Fairy Queen of Spenser* (1754), 2 vols, London; rpt Westmead, Hants 1969

WASWO, RICHARD 1987–88 'The History that Literature Makes' *NLH* 19:541–64

WATERS, D. DOUGLAS 1970 *Duessa as Theological Satire*, Columbia, MO

WATERS, D. DOUGLAS 1979 'Spenser and the "Mas" at the Temple of Isis' *SEL* 19:43–53

WATKINS, JOHN 1995 *The Specter of Dido: Spenser and Virgilian Epic*, New Haven

WATKINS, JOHN 2000 '"And yet the end was not": Apocalyptic Deferral and Spenser's Literary Afterlife', in P. Cheney and Silberman, 156–73

WATKINS, W.B.C. 1961 *Shakespeare and Spenser*, Cambridge, MA First pub. 1950

WATSON, ELIZABETH PORGES 1999 'Mr. Fox's Mottoes in the House of Busirane' *SSt* 13:285–90

WATSON, ELIZABETH SEE 2000 'Spenser's Flying Dragon and Pope Gregory XIII' *SSt* 14:293–301

WEATHERBY, HAROLD L. 1986 '*Axiochus* and the Bower of Bliss: Some Fresh Light on Sources and Authorship' *SSt* 6 (for 1985):95–113

WEATHERBY, HAROLD L. 1994 *Mirrors of Celestial Grace: Patristic Theology in Spenser's Allegory*, Toronto

WEATHERBY, HAROLD L. 1996a 'Dame Nature and the Nymph' *ELR* 26:243–58

WEATHERBY, HAROLD L. 1996b 'Spenser's Legend of Ἐγκράτεια' *SP* 93:207–17

WEATHERBY, HAROLD L. 1999 'Holy Things' *ELR* 29:422–42

WEBER, BURTON J. 1993 'The Interlocking Triads of the First Book of *The Faerie Queene*' *SP* 90:176–212

WEBSTER, JOHN 1976 'Oral Form and Written Craft in Spenser's *Faerie Queene*' *SEL* 16:75–93

WEBSTER, JOHN 1994 'Challenging the Commonplace: Teaching as Conversation in Spenser's Legend of Temperance', in Miller and Dunlop, 82–92

WEINER, ANDREW D. 1991 'Sidney / Spenser / Shakespeare: Influence / Intertextuality / Intention', in *Influence and Intertextuality in Literary History*, ed. Jay Clayton and Eric Rothstein, Madison, 245–70

WEINER, SETH 1985 'Minims and Grace Notes: Spenser's Acidalian Vision and Sixteenth-Century Music' *SSt* 5 (for 1984):91–112

WELD, J.S. 1951 'The Complaint of Britomart: Word-play and Symbolism' *PMLA* 66:548–51

WELLS, ROBIN HEADLAM 1983 *Spenser's 'Faerie Queene' and the Cult of Elizabeth*, London

WELLS, ROBIN HEADLAM 1994 *Elizabethan Mythologies: Studies in Poetry, Drama and Music*, Cambridge

WEST, MICHAEL 1973 'Spenser, Everard Digby, and the Renaissance Art of Swimming' *RQ* 26:11–22

WEST, MICHAEL 1988 'Spenser's Art of War: Chivalric Allegory, Military Technology, and the Elizabethan Mock-Heroic Sensibility' *RQ* 41:654–704

WEST, ROBERT H. 1955 *Milton and the Angels*, Athens, GA

WHIGHAM, FRANK 1984 *Ambition and Privilege: The Social Tropes of Elizabethan Courtesy Theory*, Berkeley

WHITE, R.S. 1996 *Natural Law in English Renaissance Literature*, Cambridge

WHITE, T.H. 1954 *The Book of Beasts* [tr. from a medieval bestiary], London

WHITNEY, GEFFREY 1586 *A Choice of Emblemes*, facs with an Introduction by John Manning, Aldershot 1989

WHITNEY, LOIS 1921–22 'Spenser's Use of the Literature of Travel in the *Faerie Queene*' *MP* 19:143–62

WIGGINS, PETER DESA 1988 'Spenser's Anxiety' *MLN* 103:75–86

WIGGINS, PETER DESA 1991 'Spenser's Use of Ariosto: Imitation and Allusion in Book I of the *Faerie Queene*' *RQ* 44:257–79

WILKIN, GREGORY 1994 'Spenser's Rehabilitation of the Templars' *SSt* 11 (for 1990):89–100

WILLIAMS, ARNOLD 1967 *Flower on a Lowly Stalk: The Sixth Book of the 'Faerie Queene'*, East Lansing, MI

WILLIAMS, FRANKLIN B., JR 1962 *Index of Dedications and Commendatory Verses in English Books before 1641*, London

WILLIAMS, KATHLEEN 1966 *Spenser's 'Faerie Queene': The World of Glass*, London

WILLIAMS, KATHLEEN 1969 'Vision and Rhetoric: The Poet's Voice in *The Faerie Queene*' *ELH* 36:131–44

WILSON, ELKIN CALHOUN 1939 *England's Eliza*, Cambridge, MA; rpt London 1966

WILSON, JEAN 1980 *Entertainments for Elizabeth I*, Woodbridge

WILSON, SCOTT 1995 *Cultural Materialism: Theory and Practice*, Oxford

WIMSATT, W.K., JR and MONROE C. BEARDSLEY 1954 *The Verbal Icon: Studies in the Meaning of Poetry*, London

WIND, EDGAR 1967 *Pagan Mysteries in the Renaissance*, Harmondsworth

WINSTANLEY, LILIAN ed. 1915 *Edmund Spenser: The Faerie Queene, Book I*, Cambridge

WOFFORD, SUSANNE LINDGREN 1987 'Britomart's Petrarchan Lament: Allegory and Narrative in *The Faerie Queene* III, iv' *CL* 39:28–57

WOFFORD, SUSANNE LINDGREN 1988 'Gendering Allegory: Spenser's Bold Reader and the Emergence of Character in *The Faerie Queene* III' *Criticism* 30:1–21

WOFFORD, SUSANNE LINDGREN 1992 *The Choice of Achilles: The Ideology of Figure in the Epic*, Stanford

WOOD, RUFUS 1997 *Metaphor and Belief in 'The Faerie Queene'*, London

WOODHOUSE, A.S.P. 1949 'Nature and Grace in *The Faerie Queene*' *ELH* 16:194–228; rpt *EA*, 58–83

WOODS, SUSANNE 1985 'Spenser and the Problem of Women's Rule' *HLQ* 48:141–58

WOODS, SUSANNE 1991 'Amazonian Tyranny: Spenser's Radigund and Diachronic Mimesis', in *Playing with Gender: A Renaissance Pursuit*, ed. Jean R. Brink *et al.*, Urbana, 52–61

WRIGHT, CELESTE TURNER 1940 'The Amazons in Elizabethan Literature' *SP* 37:433–56

WURTSBAUGH, JEWEL 1936 *Two Centuries of Spenserian Scholarship (1609–1805)*, Baltimore

WYNNE-DAVIES, MARION 1996 *Women and Arthurian Literature: Seizing the Sword*, New York

YAMASHITA, HIROSHI 1981 'The Printing of The First Part (Books I–III) of *The Faerie Queene* in 1590 (I)', *Studies in Languages and Cultures* (University of Tsukuba) 11:143–178

YAMASHITA, HIROSHI 1982 'The Printing of The First Part (Books I–III) of *The Faerie Queene* in 1590 (II)', *Studies in Languages and Cultures* (University of Tsukuba) 13:231–284

YAMASHITA, HIROSHI *et al.* 1990 *A Comprehensive Concordance to 'The Faerie Queene' 1590*, Tokyo

YAMASHITA, HIROSHI *et al.* 1993 *A Textual Companion to 'The Faerie Queene' 1590*, Tokyo

YATES, FRANCES A. 1977 *Astraea: The Imperial Theme in the Sixteenth Century*, London

YIAVIS, KOSTAS P. 1998 'Life-Giving Waters and the Waters of the Cephise: *Fairie Queene* 1.11.29–30' *CML* 19:77–82

YOUNG, ALAN 1987 *Tudor and Jacobean Tournaments*, London

THE CHARACTERS OF
THE FAERIE QUEENE

by Shohachi Fukuda

How they are placed in the poem. The bracketed number at the end of an entry refers to the meaning of the name as it may be reconstructed from its implied etymology. The list is indebted to Charles Huntington Whitman, *A Subject-Index to the Poems of Edmund Spenser*, 1919, reissued 1966 New York. For the pronunciations of the names, see Fukuda 1997.

Abessa see **Una**   (I iii 18)

Acrasia the false enchantress who enthrals Mordant, and poisons him with her magic cup after he is freed by Amavia, II i 50–55; enthrals Cymochles who is seen by Atin with her damsels in the Bower of Bliss, but provoked by him to leave to aid Pyrochles, v 26–38; seen in her Bower by Guyon and the Palmer with her lover, Verdant, xii 72–80; bound by Guyon who destroys the Bower and restores her lovers who have been transformed into beasts, 81–86; sent to the Faerie Queene, III i 2.   (II xii 69)

Adicia incites her husband, Souldan, against Mercilla, and mistreats Samient, Mercilla's messenger, V viii 20–24; mistakes Artegall for one of her knights, 25–26; transformed into a tiger, 45–49, ix 1–2.   (V viii 20)

Adonis enjoys/enjoyed by Venus in the Garden of Adonis where he sports with Cupid, III vi 46–49.

Æmylia confined in Lust's cave when she seeks to join her lover, Amyas, as she tells Amoret, IV vii 10–19; freed by Britomart, 33–34; befriended by Arthur and, with Amoret, taken to Sclaunder's house, viii 19–36; the story of her love for Amyas is told by his friend, Placidas, to Arthur, 50–51; greets Placidas, 63–64; reunited with Amyas, ix 9.   (IV vii 18)

Aesculapius son of Apollo who restores Hippolytus to life, I v 36–40; heals Sansjoy, 41–44.

Agape the fay mother of Priamond, Diamond, and Triamond, whose lives she prolongs by interceding with the Fates (Clotho, Lachesis, and Atropos), IV ii 41–54; instructs her daughter, Cambina, in magic, iii 40.   (IV ii 41)

Agdistes see **Genius** (2)   (II xii 46–48)

Aladine (Aldine) son of Aldus, surprised by the discourteous knight while making love to Priscilla and wounded by him, VI ii 16–21; carried by Calidore and Priscilla to Aldus's castle, 46–48, iii 2–9; the story of his love for Priscilla, 7–8; persuades Calidore to save Priscilla's reputation, 10–19.   (VI iii 3)

Aldus see **Aladine**   (VI iii 3)

Alma welcomes Arthur and Guyon into her besieged castle and entertains them in the castle hall, II ix 17–20; guides them on a tour through the castle, 21–60; feasts them, x 77; attends the wounded Arthur, xi 49.   (II ix 18)

Amavia mother of the bloody-handed babe, Ruddymane, who stabs herself through grief after telling Guyon how Acrasia poisoned her husband, Mordant, whom she had rescued from her, II i 35–55; dies, 56; buried with Mordant, 60–61; her story told by Guyon to Medina, ii 44–45, and to Artegall, V iii 31.   (II i 55)

Amidas see **Bracidas**   (V iv 9)

Amoret her birth as daughter of Chrysogone and the later-born twin of Belphœbe, III vi 4–10, 26–27; adopted by Venus in place of Cupid to be nurtured in the Garden of Adonis 28–29; raised by Psyche together with her daughter, Pleasure, 51–52; taken to the court of the Faerie Queene where she is loved by many but loves only Scudamour, 52–53; imprisoned and tortured for seven months by Busirane to make her yield to him, as Scudamour complains to Britomart, xi 9–17; appears in Cupid's masque, 19–21; seen bound and tortured by Busirane, xii 30–31; about to be stabbed by him, rescued by Britomart, 32–38; in *1590*, reunited with Scudamour, 43–47, but in *1596*, remains in Britomart's company, 43–45; how she was seized by Busirane at her marriage festivities, IV i 2–4; fears Britomart until she learns her sex, 5–16; puts on Florimell's girdle at Satyrane's tournament, v 19–20; wanders away at night, as Britomart tells Scudamour, and both seek her, vi 34–38, 46–47; seized by Lust and imprisoned in his cave along with Æmylia, vii 4–20; escapes from the cave but, seized by Lust, is wounded by Timias, 21–35; befriended by Arthur who heals her wounds, viii 19–21; slandered when they stay in Sclaunder's cottage, 23–28, 35–36; accompanies Arthur, ix 17–20, but apparently not present after he reconciles the quarrelling lovers (see 39*n*, x 3*n*); in Scudamour's story of his conquest of her in the Temple of Venus, seen in the lap of Womanhood in the circle of the virtues, x 52–58.   (III vi 28)

Amphisa see **Belphœbe**   (III vi 4)

Amyas the Squire of low degree loved by Æmylia, IV vii 15–18; imprisoned by Corflambo when he seeks a tryst with her, viii 50–51; loved by Pœana, 52–54; mistaken by her for his look-alike friend, Placidas, 55–61; rescued by Arthur, ix 4–8; united to Æmylia and Placidas, 9.   (IV viii 59)

Anamnestes see **Eumnestes**   (II ix 58)

Angel see **Guyon**   (II viii 5, 6)

Apollo see **Marinell**   (I v 43)

Archimago called 'Hypocrisie', I i Arg.; disguised as a hermit, hosts the Red Cross Knight and Una, 29–35;

provokes him to leave her with a dream of her lust for him, 45–55, and a vision of her copulating with a squire, ii 3–6; disguises himself as the Red Cross Knight, 11; directed by Corceca, finds Una who accepts him as her knight, iii 24–32; as her champion, defeated by Sansloy, 33–39; disguised as a pilgrim, leads Una to believe that her knight was killed by Sansloy, vi 34–39, provoking Satyrane to attack him, 40–47; while they fight, pursues Una, 48; as Duessa's messenger, delivers her letter to Una's father claiming that the Red Cross Knight is betrothed to her, xii 24–28; exposed by Una and imprisoned, 33–36; escapes, II i 1; as Duessa's squire, deceives Guyon into believing that the Red Cross Knight has violated her, 5–23; guides him to the knight, 24–25; tells Braggadocchio that the two killed Mordant and Amavia, iii 13, and promises to get him Arthur's sword to fight them, 14–19; with Arthur's sword in hand, comes upon the drowning Pyrochles and heals his wounds, vi 47–51; incites Pyrochles and Cymochles to attack the unconscious Guyon, viii 11; yields the former Arthur's sword, 22; flees with Atin after Arthur kills Pyrochles and Cymochles, 56; pursues Britomart, III iv 45. (I i 43)

Argante the giant nymphomaniac and twin of Ollyphant, III vii 48 (cf. xi 3–4) who, having seized the Squire of Dames and fleeing from the virgin, Palladine, seizes Satyrane but forced to abandon him, 37–52. (III vii 47)

Armeddan see **Marinell** (V iii 5)

Artegall aka the Salvage Knight, with Sophy, honoured by the Faerie Queene, II ix 6; praised by the Red Cross Knight, III ii 10, 13–14; first seen in Achilles' arms by Britomart in Merlin's magic mirror, 17–25; birth, upbringing, marriage, and death revealed to her by Merlin, iii 26–28; triumphs in Satyrane's tournament by defeating Sangliere, Brianor and seven other knights until overthrown by Britomart, IV iv 39–44; meets Scudamour and with him, seeks revenge, vi 2–8, but in fighting her, yields to her beauty, 11–23; learns who she is, 25–33; woos and wins her troth before leaving on his quest, 40–46; chosen by the Faerie Queene to aid Irena, V i 3–4; as a boy, trained in justice by Astraea, who arms him with the sword, Chrysaor, and Talus as groom, 5–12; punishes Sangliere, 13–29; from Dony, learns of the impending marriage of Florimell and Marinell, ii 2–4, and of Pollente's toll bridge and his daughter, Munera, whom he supports by his tolls, 4–10; kills Pollente's groom, Guizor and then Pollente, 11–19; bids Talus to attack Munera, dismember her, and raze her castle, 20–28; debates with the Giant with the Scales, 29–48, until Talus shoulders him from his rock, 49–50; fights with Braggadocchio's shield to rescue Marinell at the tournament to celebrate his marriage to Florimell, iii 10–12; exposes Braggadocchio's villainy, 15–22; exposes the False Florimell, restores Florimell's girdle to her, returns Guyon's horse to him, and baffles Braggadocchio, 22–39; pacifies the quarrelling Bracidas and Amidas, iv 4–20; saves Terpine from being hanged by Amazons, 21–25; hears his story, 26–34; with him, seeks to enter Radegone, 35–38; prevents Radigund from killing Terpine, 39–43; accepts her conditions for battle proposed by her maid, Clarinda, 47–51; in fighting Radigund, yields to her beauty, v 6–18; submits to her degradation of him, 20–25; resists her wooing through

Clarinda, 26–57; rescued by Britomart after she defeats Radigund, vii 29–41; with Arthur, saves Samient from two of Adicia's knights, viii 3–8; through her, recognizes Arthur and learns of the plots against Mercilla by Adicia and the Souldan, 9–23; with Samient appearing as a captive, enters the Souldan's castle disguised as a pagan knight, 25–27; prevents Adicia from slaying Samient, and kills her followers, 46–50; praises Arthur, 51; with Arthur and Talus, kills Malengin, ix 3–19; visits Mercilla's court and witnesses Duessa's trial, 22–48; judges against her, 49; meets Sergis and learns of Irena's plight, xi 36–42; aids Burbon and restores Flourdelis to him, 43–65; frees Irena by slaying Grantorto, xii 3–23; on being recalled to the court of the Faerie Queene, attacked by Envie and Detraction aided by the Blatant Beast, 28–43; learns more about the Blatant Beast from Calidore, VI i 4–10. (V i 3)

Arthur befriends Una, I vii 29–52; wounds Orgoglio's dragon, and slays him, viii 2–24; enters his castle to confront Ignaro, 29–36; frees the Red Cross Knight from its dungeon and restores him to Una, 37–44; helps despoil Duessa, 46–50; at Una's request, relates his birth, and nurture by Timon through Merlin, ix 2–5; relates his dream of the Faerie Queene's love for him, 13–14, which occasions his quest to seek her, 15–17, 20 (cf. II ix 7, IV ix 17); exchanges gifts with the Red Cross Knight, 18–20; intercedes on behalf of Guyon to save him from Pyrochles and Cymochles, II viii 17–29; wounds Pyrochles who wields his (Arthur's) sword and defends himself with Guyon's shield, 30–32; unseated by Cymochles, wounds him but is wounded himself, 33–39; kills Cymochles with Guyon's sword given him by the Palmer, 40–45; slays Pyrochles, 46–52; pledges friendship with Guyon, 53–56; converses with him about the Faerie Queene, ix 2–9; disperses Maleger's villeins who attack them when they seek to enter Alma's castle, 10–16; with him, enters and tours the castle, 17–35; converses with Praysdesire who embodies his desire for praise, 36–39; in Eumnestes's chamber, reads British history up to the rule of his father, Uther Pendragon, and learns the prophecy that he will even the account with Rome, x 5–68.2; fights Maleger who is aided by two hags, Impotence and Impatience, and whose twelve troops besiege Alma's castle, xi 5–28; saved by Timias, 29–31; slays Maleger by drowning him, 34–46; succoured by Timias and nursed by Alma, 48–49; with Guyon, leaves his castle to undertake many adventures until Guyon asks to fight Britomart, III i 1–5; helps reconcile them, 11–12; pursues Florimell, 18, iv 45–54; complains against night, 55–61; learns about Florimell from her dwarf and continues to seek her, v 3–12; fails to recognize the love-lorn Timias, IV vii 42–47; succours the abandoned Amoret (and Æmylia), curing her wounds, and with them, enters Sclaunder's cottage where they endure her slanders, viii 19–37; kills Corflambo who is pursuing Placidas, 38–45; learns about Amyas's imprisonment in Corflambo's dungeon, 46–64; forces Pœana's dwarf to guide him to Corflambo's castle, tricks the watch to let him enter, releases Amyas, restores him to Æmylia and arranges the marriage of Placidas to Pœana, ix 4–16 (but see Arg.1–2*n*); accompanies Amoret, 17–19; restores peace among six knights including

Britomart and Scudamour, 20–37; with Artegall, saves
Samient from pagan knights, V viii 4–23; slays the
Souldan, 27–45; with Artegall and Talus, helps kill
Malengin, ix 3–19; visits Mercilla's court and witnesses
Duessa's trial, 22–50; pities her, 46, then repents, 49;
aids Belge by killing Geryoneo's Seneschall and his three
knights, x 15–39, Geryoneo, xi 1–14, and his monster,
21–35; reunited with Timias after rescuing him from his
enemies, VI v 11–24; meets Serena with the Salvage
Man, 25–33; leaves Timias and Serena to be counselled
by the Hermit, 34–41; in the company of the Salvage
Man, slays Turpine's forces and shames him before his
lady, Blandina, vi 17–39; entertained by her, 41–43; foils
Turpine who has hired two hit men to kill him in
revenge but he kills one and baffles Turpine, vii 2–27; in
the company of the other, Enias, sees Timias abused by
Disdain and Scorn, viii 4–5; after Enias intervenes but is
defeated, defeats Disdain but spares him at Mirabella's
request, 6–25; restored to Timias, 27; leaves on his quest
for the Faerie Queene, 30. (I vii 29–36, *LR*)

Astræa see **Artegall** (V i 5)

Ate goddess of discord who provoked the war against
Troy, II vii 52; raised from her house in hell by Duessa
to be mated with Blandamour and accompany her and
Paridell, IV i 17–32; provokes jealousy in Scudamour,
47–54 (cf. v 30–31); provokes discord between
Blandamour and Paridell, ii 3, 11–19; provokes
Blandamour to fight Cambell, iv 3–4; attempts to pro-
voke Braggadocchio to fight, 11; provokes discord at
Satyrane's tournament, v 22–23 (cf. ix 24); serves as
a witness against Duessa at the trial at Mercilla's court,
V ix 47. (IV i 19–30)

Atin Pyrochles's squire who warns Guyon of his approach,
II iv 39–46; rescues Cymochles from Acrasia's Bower of
Bliss to avenge Pyrochles's apparent death, v 25–38;
prevented by Phædria from entering her boat with
Cymochles, vi 4; rails at Guyon, 38–40; saves Pyrochles
from drowning, 41–47; appeals to Archimago to help
him, 48; stirs up strife against Guyon, viii 11; flees with
Archimago, 56. (II iv 42)

Bacchante see **Malecasta** (III i 45)

Basciante see **Malecasta** (III i 45)

Bead-men, The seven see **Cælia** (I x 36)

Belge two of her sons ask Mercilla to aid her against
Geryoneo, V x 6–14; comforted by Arthur, 18–24; thanks
him for killing Geryoneo's Seneschall, 39, Geryoneo, xi
15–18, and his monster, 33–35 (cf. 19–20). (V x 6-xi 35)

Bellamoure Lord of the Castle of Belgard, imprisoned
earlier because he married Claribell against the wishes
of her father, Lord of Many Ilands, VI xii 3–5; their
child, Pastorella, abandoned, 6–9; after the Lord's death,
inherits his castle, 10. (VI xii 3)

Bellisont see **Marinell** (V iii 5)

Bellodant see **Radigund** (V iv 30)

Belphœbe seen by Trompart, II iii 21–33, and then by
Braggadocchio who attempts to embrace her, 34–42;
heals Timias's wounds but wounds his heart by love of
her, III v 27–50; her virginity, 51–55; her birth, with
that of her later-born twin, Amoret, to Chrysogone,
daughter of Amphisa, vi 2–4, 10, 26–27; nurtured by
Diana's/Phœbe's nymph, 28; after hunting with Timias,
kills Lust who had seized Amoret, IV vii 23, 29–32; frees

Æmylia and Lust's hag, 33–34; offended by Timias's
handling of Amoret, 35–36; reconciled to him, viii 2–18.
(II iii Arg.)

Blandamour mated with Ate, IV i 32; unhorsed by
Britomart, 35–36; provokes Paridell to fight Scudamour,
38–40; defeats Ferraugh to win the False Florimell, ii
4–11; his quarrel with Paridell ended by the Squire of
Dames, 12–29; quarrels with Braggadocchio over the
False Florimell until reconciled by Cambell, iv 6–12;
with his false friends, takes one side of Satyrane's tourna-
ment, 14; defeated by Ferramont, 19, and by Britomart,
45; quarrels, esp. with Erivan, over the False Florimell, v
22–27; fights Druon, Paridell, and Claribell over the
False Florimell, ix 20–37; with Claribell, fights Britomart
until pacified by Arthur, 30–37; with Duessa and Paridell,
conspires against Mercilla, V ix 41. (IV i 32)

Blandina see **Turpine** (VI iii 42)

Blatant Beast incited by Envie and Detraction, attacks
Artegall, V xii 37–41; pursued by Calidore who tells
Artegall about her, VI i 7–10; seizes and wounds Serena
but abandons her when pursued by Calidore, iii 24–26;
wounds Timias and exposes him to be ambushed by
Defetto, Decetto, and Despetto, v 14–21; descended
from Echidna and Typhaon, vi 9–12 (cf. i 8); still pur-
sued by Calidore, ix 2–6; after rampaging through
society, caught, muzzled and chained by him, xii 22–37;
escapes to be pursued by Pelleas, Lamoracke, and others,
38–40. (V xii 37)

Bloody-handed Babe see **Guyon** (II ii 3–4)

Bracidas elder son of Milesio who quarrels with his
brother, Amidas, over ownership of alluvion and flotsam,
V iv 4–8; abandoned by his lady, Philtera, for Amidas
after most of his island is washed by the sea onto his
brother's island, 9; joined by Amidas's lady, Lucy, who
sought to drown herself but is saved by Philtera's lost
floating dowry, 10–14; his quarrel is resolved by
Artegall, 16–20. (V iv 18)

Braggadoc[c]hio steals Guyon's horse and his spear, II iii
4–5; dubs Trompart his liegeman, 6–10; meets
Archimago who promises to bring him Arthur's sword to
defeat the Red Cross Knight and Guyon, 11–19; hides
from the approach of Belphœbe, 20–21, but forced to
appear, 34–36; rebuffed when he seeks to embrace her
and she flees, 42; leaves with Trompart, 43–46 (cf. III
v 27); seizes the False Florimell from the witch's son but
loses her to Ferraugh when he flees from him, III viii
11–18; promises to help Malbecco gain Hellenore from
Paridell, x 20–33; covets his wealth, 34; refuses to fight
Paridell, 38; flees from the satyrs, 43; has stolen Malbecco's
wealth, 54; refuses to fight Blandamour over the False
Florimell, IV iv 8–11; refuses to fight in Satyrane's tourna-
ment but his spear, wielded by Triamond, defeats four
knights, 20–21; claims the False Florimell, is chosen by
her, and leaves with her, v 23–27; arrives at the marriage
tournament with Artegall who, fighting with his shield,
allows him to claim the prize for chivalry for himself and
the prize of beauty for his lady, V iii 10–19, but then
exposes his false claims to chivalry, his lady's false claims
to beauty, and his theft of Guyon's horse, 20–36; baffled
by Talus, 37–39. (II iii 10)

Briana see **Crudor** (VI i 14)

Brianor see **Artegall** (IV iv 40)

Brigants capture Pastorella along with others and imprison her in their cave, VI x 39–44; claiming her as his own, their captain dies in defending her, xi 3–21; slay Melibœ and others, 18; many slain by Calidore, 43–49. (VI x 39)

Britomart unhorses Guyon but reconciled to him by the Palmer and Arthur, III i 4–12; saves the Red Cross Knight from Malecasta's six knights, 20–29; entertained in Castle Joyeous, 31–46; rejects Malecasta from her bed, 47–62; wounded by Gardante, 65; aided by the Red Cross Knight, forces Malecasta's knights to flee, 66–67; asks him about Artegall, whom she accuses of violating her, ii 4–16; earlier, saw Artegall in Merlin's mirror, 17–26; overcome by unconsolable love for him, 27–52; with Glauce also in disguise, seeks Merlin to help find Artegall, iii 5–7, 14–20; learns from him about their descendants, 21–50; disguises herself as a Saxon knight, 51–62; leaves the Red Cross Knight and arrives at the rich strond where she laments her love, iv 4–11; wounds Marinell, 12–17; outside Malbecco's castle, fights Paridell, ix 12–16; doffs her disguise on entering the castle, 20–24; discusses with Paridell the Trojan ancestry of Britons, 38–51; in pursuing Ollyphant, finds Scudamour, hears him complain that Amoret is imprisoned by Busirane, and promises to free her, xi 3–20; passes through the flames at the porch to Busirane's castle, 21–25; in the first room, views the tapestries of the loves of the gods, the statue of Cupid, and the motto over the door, '*Be bold*', 28–50; in the second room, wonders at the bas-relief, the spoils of war, and the same motto on the other side of the door, and on the far door, '*Be not too bold*', 51–54, and sees Amoret in Cupid's masque, xii 1–27; in the third room, sees Busirane torturing Amoret, wounded by him, overturns his power and releases her, 29–40; binds him with Amoret's chain, 41; restores her to Scudamour, 43–47 (*1590*), but (in *1596*) with Scudamour gone, keeps Amoret who is fearful of her until she reveals her sex, IV i 5–15; meets Duessa and Paridell, Ate and Blandamour, 17; unhorses Blandamour, 35–36; defends the Knights of Maidenhead at the marriage tournament, unhorses Artegall, Cambell, Triamond, Blandamour and many others, iv 44–48; reveals Amoret and refuses the False Florimell as her prize, v 13–20; leaves with Amoret, 29; unhorses Scudamour, vi 9–10; battles Artegall until he yields at the sight of her beauty and she yields on learning who he is, 11–33; tells Scudamour how Amoret wandered away from her, and vows to help him find her, 34–38; wooed and won by Artegall, 40–41; with Scudamour seeks Amoret, 46–47; battles four knights until their conflict is resolved by Arthur, ix 20–37; learns from Talus of Artegall's subjection to Radigund, V vi 3–17; in journeying to free him, avoids Dolon's trap and kills his two sons on Pollente's bridge, 19–40; enters the Temple of Isis and prostrates herself before the crowned idol of Isis with a crocodile (Osiris) at her feet, vii 3–8; sleeping under its aegis has a vision of herself royally transfigured, threatened by the crocodile until Isis beats it back, but wooed and impregnated by it, gives birth to a lion, 12–16; leaves after the vision is interpreted by Isis's Priest, 17–24; defeats Radigund and decapitates her, 29–34, releases Artegall and her other prisoners, and

restores him, 37–41; restores Radegone to male rule while he leaves on his quest, 42–45. (III i 8)

Bruin see **Matilde** (VI iv 29)

Bruncheval see **Satyrane** (IV iv 17)

Brunell see **Marinell** (V iii 5)

Burbon rescued by Artegall and Talus from Grantorto's villeins, admonished for abandoning his battered shield, and has the wavering Flourdelis restored to him, V xi 44–65. (V xi 43.6–65)

Busirane holds Amoret captive, III xi 10–11; seen torturing her, xii 30–31; his magic undone by Britomart who binds him with Amoret's chain and leads him captive, 32–41. (III xi 10)

Cælia (**Cœlia**) receives the Red Cross Knight and Una in her house of Holinesse to which they are admitted by Humiltá and Reverence, I x 3–11, and where he is instructed by her daughters, Fidelia and Speranza, 18–22, by Patience and others in the house of Penance, 24–29, and by Charissa, 30–31, and calls on Mercie who guides him first to the holy Hospital with its seven Beadmen, 34–44, where she instructs him in the charitable life, 45, and then to the hill of Contemplation, 46. (I x 4)

Calepine interrupted by Calidore while making love to Serena, VI iii 20–21; cares for her after she was carried off and wounded by the Blatant Beast, 27–28; refused help by Turpine to cross a river, and at nightfall refused entry into his Castle of the Ford, 29–44; wounded by him, 46–51, and rescued by the Salvage Man who dresses their wounds, iv 2–16; rescues an infant from a bear and leaves him with Matilde, 17–38; loses Serena, 39–40; finds her about to be killed and eaten by the Salvage Nation, viii 46–51. (VI iii 27)

Calidore in his quest for the Blatant Beast (assigned to him by the Faerie Queene, x 1; cf. xii 12), meets Artegall who says he has been attacked by it, VI i 4–10; saves a squire and his lady by killing Maleffort, who, at Briana's bidding, seeks his beard and her locks, 11–23; invades Briana's castle, 23–24, and endures her shaming him while waiting for her knight, Crudor, 25–31; defeats him and requires him to marry Briana, 32–47; sees Tristram slay a discourteous knight and dubs him his squire, ii 3–35; hears Priscilla tell how this discourteous knight wounded Aladine, 40–45; with her, bears Aladine to Aldus's castle, 46–48, iii 2; conducts her to her home and upholds her honour, 15–19; interrupts Calepine making love to Serena, 20–21; rescues Serena from the Blatant Beast, which he then pursues, 22–26; abandons the pursuit to stay with Melibœ and woo Pastorella, ix 2–46; on Mount Acidale, sees the Graces dance and converses with Colin, x 5–30; returns to woo and win Pastorella after killing a tiger that has attacked her, 31–38; rescues her from the Brigants, xi 25–51; takes her to her parents at Belgard Castle, xii 3–11; renews his quest of the Blatant Beast, 12–13; captures it, 22–38. (VI i 2)

Cambell (**Cambello**) agrees to fight the three brothers, Priamond, Diamond, and Triamond, the suitors of his sister, Canacee, IV ii 30–41; kills the first two, and his battle with the third is ended by their sister, Cambina, iii 3–48; becomes his friend and marries her, 49–52; the four travel to Satyrane's tournament, iv 2–13; fights Satyrane in Triamond's armour, aided by Triamond in his armour, 27–36; unhorsed by Britomart, 44; displays Cambina in the ensuing beauty contest, v 10. (IV ii 31)

Cambina see **Triamond**   (IV ii 31)

Canacee see **Cambell**   (IV ii 31)

Care the giant blacksmith who with his six servants prevents Scudamour from sleeping, IV v 32–45.

Charissa see **Red Cross Knight**   (I x 29)

Chrysogone see **Belphœbe**   (III vi 4)

Claribell (1) see **Phaon**   (II iv 26)

Claribell (2) see **Blandamour**   (IV ix 20)

Claribell (3) see **Bellamoure**   (VI xii 4)

Clarinda (**Clarin**) see **Radigund**   (V iv 48)

Cœlia see **Cælia**

Colin Clout his songs enjoyed by Pastorella, VI ix 35; pipes for the shepherds, 41; pipes for the Graces, x 15–16; converses with Calidore, 18–32; laments the loss of Bregog and Mulla, VII vi 40.   (VI x 16)

Columbell see **Squire of Dames**   (III vii 51)

Concord see **Scudamour**   (IV x 34)

Contemplation receives the Red Cross Knight at his hermitage, I x 46–52; leads him to the highest mount to see the New Jerusalem, 53–59; reveals his future role as St George of England, 60–61; counsels him to serve the Faerie Queene, and only after that may he seek the path to the New Jerusalem, 63; reveals his Saxon ancestry, 65–66.   (I x 46)

Coradin see **Phaon**   (II iv 36)

Corceca see **Una**   (I iii 18)

Corflambo pursues Placidas fleeing with the dwarf of his daughter, Pœana, strikes them down but is decapitated by Arthur, IV viii 38–45; had imprisoned Amyas, 50–51; his body with its head restored and bound to his dromedary, tricks Pœana into admitting Arthur into her castle where he releases Amyas, ix 4–8.   (IV viii 49)

Coridon the shepherd who is Calidore's rival for Pastorella's love, VI ix 10, 38–44, x 33–37; captured by the Brigants, 41; escapes, xi 18; helps Calidore rescue Pastorella, 27–42; rewarded with Melibœ's sheep, 51. (VI ix 10)

Cormoraunt see **Matilde**   (VI iv 29)

Crudor refuses to love Briana until her seneschal, Maleffort, gathers enough beards of knights and locks of ladies to line a mantle for him, VI i 14–15; after being summoned by her dwarf, defeated by Calidore, 29–39; instructed by him, agrees to love her, causing her to become courteous, 40–46.   (VI i 15)

Cupid son of Venus, god of love who plays unarmed in Alma's castle, II ix 34; kindles lust in Castle Joyeous, III i 39; sought by Venus, vi 11–23, also by Diana, 25–26; sports with Adonis in the Garden of Adonis, and with Psyche and their daughter, Pleasure, 49–50; his altar and image, xi 47–49; rejoices in Amoret's suffering in his masque, xii 22–23; with his elder brother, Hatred, accompanies Concord in the Temple of Venus, IV x 32; punishes Mirabella at his court, VI vii 32–37.   (I proem 3)

Cymochles leaves Acrasia's Bower of Bliss when Atin reports the death of his brother, Pyrochles, his lust changing to wrath, II v 25–38; ferried to Phædria's island, lapses into lust, vi 2–18; becomes wrathful when Guyon arrives and fights him until pacified by Phædria, 27–36; with Pyrochles, seeks to disarm the unconscious

Guyon, viii 10–17; opposes Arthur who defends Guyon, 28; wounds him but is killed by him, 33–45.   (II iv 41)

Cymodoce (aka **Cymoent** in Bk III) advised by Proteus's prophecy, warns her son, Marinell, to avoid woman's love, III iv 25–28; on learning that he has been wounded, bears him to her underwater bower to be healed, 29–43; attends the marriage of the Thames and the Medway, IV xi 53; when Marinell languishes, appeals first to Tryphon who diagnoses a new wound, xii 20–24, and then to Apollo who reveals that her son is wounded by love, 25; on learning from him that he loves Florimell, appeals to Neptune to force Proteus to release her and then takes her to him, 26–33.   (III iv 19)

Cynthia see **Mutabilitie**

Daunger see **Scudamour**   (IV x 17)

Decetto see **Timias**   (VI v 13)

Defetto see **Timias**   (VI v 13)

Despaire persuades Terwin to take his own life and causes Trevisan to flee, I ix 21–32; almost persuades the Red Cross Knight to take his own life but saved by Una, 37–53; tries to take his own life but forever fails, 54.

Despetto see **Timias**   (VI v 13)

Detraction see **Artegall**   (V xii 35, 36)

Devon see **Triamond**   (IV iv 21)

Diamond see **Triamond**   (IV ii 41)

Diana (aka **Phœbe**) curses the nymph of the fountain from which the Red Cross Knight drinks, I vii 4–5; while bathing, seen by Venus searching for Cupid, III vi 17–19, in helping her to find him, finds Belphœbe, whom she has her nymph nurture, 26–28; was seen naked by Faunus who bribed her maid, Molanna, with a promise to gain Fanchin as her love, VII vi 38–46; punishes him, 47–53; deserts Arlo hill, 54–55.

Disdain (1) see **Guyon**   (II vii 41)

Disdain (2) see **Mirabella**   (VI vii 41–43)

Dolon mistakes Britomart for Artegall who had killed his son, Guizor, and in his castle tries to trap her in bed, V vi 19–34, but she escapes and kills his two other sons, 36–40.   (V vi 32)

Dony Florimell's dwarf who accompanies Arthur in his search for her, III v 3–12; tells Artegall that she has been found, V ii 2–3, and directs him to Pollente who prevents him from attending her impending marriage to Marinell, 4–10.   (V ii 3)

Douglas see **Triamond**   (IV iv 21)

Dragon see **Red Cross Knight**   (I xi Arg.)

Druon see **Blandamour**   (IV ix 20)

Duessa as Fidessa, accompanies Sansfoy, I ii 13–14, and after he is killed, accompanies the Red Cross Knight, 20–27; having encountered Fradubio and Fralissa whom she had transformed into trees, 28–45, leads him to the house of Pride, iv 2–3; accompanies Lucifera in the procession of the sins, 37; counsels Sansjoy in his forthcoming battle with the Red Cross Knight, 44–51, but her intervention leads to his defeat, v 11–12, though she saves his life through her magic, 13; descends into hell in Night's chariot to have him restored by Æsculapius, 20–44; joins the Red Cross Knight, vii 2–4; becomes Orgoglio's mistress after he imprisons him, 14–18; flees after Orgoglio is killed by Arthur but captured by Timias, viii 25, and stripped to expose her ugliness, 46–49; through Archimago, delivers a letter to Una's father to forbid Una's betrothal to the Red Cross Knight, xii 24–28; their duplicity is exposed by Una, 33–36; shown to Guyon by Archimago as a virgin violated by the Red Cross Knight but their duplicity is exposed, II i 8–30; paired with Paridell, and Blandamour with Ate, as an exemplum of false friendship, IV i 17–18, 32; shown by Paridell at the beauty contest, v 11; tried in Mercilla's court and condemned to death, V ix 36–50; executed, x 4. (I ii 34)

Dumarin see **Marinell**   (III iv 19)

Dwarf, Briana's see **Crudor**

Dwarf, Florimell's see **Dony**

Dwarf, Pœana's see **Placidas**

Dwarf, Una's accompanies her, bearing her needments, I i 6; urges the Red Cross Knight to flee Errour, 13; accompanies him when he flees Una, ii 6; reveals to him those imprisoned in the dungeon of the house of Pride, v 45, 52; takes his armour to Una, vii 19–27; leads her to find him, and, on meeting Arthur, leads both to Orgoglio's castle, 28, 52.

Ecastor see **Marinell**   (V iii 5)

Eden, King of see **Una**   (I xii 3)

Elissa see **Medina**   (II ii 35)

Emiline see **Tristram**   (VI ii 29)

Enias with another (unnamed) knight, hired by Turpine to kill Arthur but, defeated by him, reveals Turpine's treachery, VI vii 3–23; accompanies Arthur, viii 4; overcome by Disdain and bound by Scorn, 5–11, provoking Arthur to attack Disdain, 12–18, and the Salvage Man to attack Scorn, 28–29; leaves with Arthur, 30.   (VI viii 4)

Envie see **Artegall**

Erivan see **Blandamour**   (IV v 24)

Errour killed by the Red Cross Knight, I i 14–24; her brood die by drinking her blood, 25–26.   (I i 14)

Eumenias see **Radigund**   (V v 34)

Eumnestes the third of Alma's three counsellors, II ix 47–49; associated with memory, 55–58; aided by Anamnestes, 58.   (II ix 58)

Excesse see **Guyon**

Faerie Queene (aka Gloriana and Tanaquill) assigns the Red Cross Knight to aid Una by killing the dragon who imprisons her parents, I i 3 (cf. vii 46–47, *LR* 52–63); brings Arthur's arms to faery land, vii 36; appears to Arthur in a dream promising him her love, leading him to search for her, ix 13–15; praise of her city, Cleopolis, x 58–59 (cf. III ix 51); her future war against a pagan king, xi 7 (cf. xii 18); the Red Cross Knight journeys to her court, xii 41 (cf. II i 1); her image on Guyon's shield, II i 28 (cf. v 11, viii 43, ix 2, 4); praised by Guyon to Medina, ii 40–41; at her annual feast, had assigned Guyon to capture Acrasia, 42–43 (cf. *LR* 70–73); praised by Guyon to Arthur, ix 3–6; her lineage in the rolls of Elfin emperors, x 70–76; to be presented with the bound Acrasia, III i 2; praise of her wisdom, ii 3; her lineage from Britomart, iv 3; her image on Satyrane's shield, IV iv 17; assigns Artegall to restore Irena's rights usurped by Grantorto, V i 3–4 (cf. viii 3, xi 37, xii 3); assigns Calidore to capture the Blatant Beast, VI x 1 (cf. xii 12); praise of her beauty, 4, and her glory, 28. (I i 3)

Fanchin see **Diana**   (VII vi 44)

Fates see **Agape**   (IV ii 48)

Faunus see **Diana**   (VII vi 42)

Ferramont see **Triamond**   (IV iv 19)

Ferraugh (**Ferrau**) seizes the False Florimell from Braggadocchio, III viii 15–19 (cf. IV ii 8); seized from him by Blandamour, IV ii 4–7.   (IV ii 4)

Ferryman see **Guyon**   (II xii 10)

Fidelia see **Red Cross Knight**   (I x 12)

Fidessa see **Duessa**   (I ii 26)

Fisher see **Florimell**   (III viii 23–33)

Florimell flees from the Foster from whom Arthur and Guyon seek to rescue her, III i 15–18, iv 45–46; flees from Arthur, 47–53; as told by her dwarf to Arthur, the story of her love of Marinell and search for him on hearing at the court of the Faerie Queene that he has been slain, v 4–10; sought by Arthur, 11–12; finds refuge in a witch's cottage until she must flee her son, vii 1–19, and then her hyena, 22–26; escapes in a fisher's boat, 27; feared dead by Satyrane on seeing her palfrey being devoured by the hyena and finding her girdle, 29–32 (cf. IV ii 25); harassed by the Fisher, viii 20–27; saved by Proteus, 29–36; harassed by him and cast into his dungeon, 37–43; sought by all the knights at the court, notably Satyrane who tells Paridell how he found her girdle and the hyena devouring her palfrey, 44–50; how she brought her girdle (named 'Cestus') from Mount Acidale where she was nurtured by the Graces, IV v 2–6; complains that Marinell does not love her, xii 6–11; through Cymodoce's intercession, freed from Proteus's dungeon by Neptune's command and restored to Marinell, 28–35; her impending marriage is told to Artegall, V ii 2–4; praises Braggadocchio's victory at the marriage tournament, but is shamed by him and the False Florimell until they are exposed by Artegall, iii 14–26, and her girdle restored by him to her, 27. (III v 8)

Florimell, False (or **Snowy**) created by the witch for her son to replace Florimell, III viii 5–10; taken from him by Braggadocchio, 11–13; taken from him by Ferraugh, 15–19; taken from him by Blandamour, IV ii 3–10, and fought over with Paridell, 11–19; claimed by Braggadocchio in rejecting Blandamour's proposal that he win her, iv 7–11; wins the beauty contest at Satyrane's tournament and awarded Florimell's girdle but cannot wear it, v 13–20; awarded in succession to Britomart, Artegall, Triamond, and Satyrane, 21–22; claimed by Braggadocchio whom she chooses and leaves secretly with him, 23–27; presented by Braggadocchio at the marriage tournament and judged to win the prize for beauty until placed beside Florimell and dissolves, V iii 17–26.   (III viii 6)

Flourdelis see **Burbon**   (V xi 49)

Foster pursues Florimell, III i 17–18; pursued by Timias, 18, iv 47; with his two brothers, killed by Timias, v 15–25.   (III i 17)

Fradubio with his lady, Fralissa, transformed by Duessa into trees after he leaves Fralissa for her and sees her in her naked ugliness, I ii 28–44.   (I ii 33)

Fralissa see **Fradubio**   (I ii 37)

Furor seen with his mother, Occasion, attacking Phaon, II iv 3–5; bound by Guyon after he locks her tongue and binds her hands, 12–15; overcomes Pyrochles after he frees them, v 18–23 (cf. vi 50). (II iv 10)

Gardante see **Malecasta** (III i 45)

Genius (1) porter of the Bower of Bliss, II xii 46–49. (II xii 46–48)

Genius (2) porter of the Garden of Adonis, III vi 31–33. (III vi 31)

Georgos see **Red Cross Knight** (I x 66)

Geryoneo oppresses Belge and devours most of her children, V x 6–13; defeated when Arthur kills his Seneschall and three knights, 30–37, him, xi 1–14, and his monster, 21–32. (V x 6-xi 35)

Giant with the Scales attempts to reduce all things to equality as measured by his scales, provoking Artegall to engage him in a debate that ends when Talus shoulders him into the sea and disperses his followers, V ii 29–54. (V ii 30)

Glauce the aged nurse who counsels Britomart in her love-sickness, III ii 30–47; fails to cure her by charms and herbal medicines, 48–52; advises her to visit Merlin, iii 6; intercedes on her behalf, 15–21, 25; proposes that they disguise themselves in armour to seek Artegall in faery land, 52–62; comforts Britomart, iv 11; in *1596*, leaves with Scudamour fearing that Britomart has failed to free Amoret from Busirane, xii 44–45; threatened with death by the jealous Scudamour for reports of Britomart's intimacy with Amoret, IV i 50–54; tries to calm him, ii 3, v 31; visits the house of Care with him, 32–33; reconciles Britomart, Artegall, and Scudamour, vi 25–32. (III ii 30)

Gloriana see **Faerie Queene** (I i 3)

Graces sisters of Cupid, II viii 6; rock Belphœbe's cradle, III vi 2; foster Florimell on Mount Acidale, IV v 5, where they sport with Venus, VI x 9; surrounded by 100 naked, dancing maidens, dance and sing around Colin Clout's damsel, 12; as handmaids of Venus, their gifts of grace, 15, 23–24; daughters of Jove and Eurynome, named Euphrosyne, Aglaia, Thalia, 22. (VI x 15)

Grantorto oppresses Irena, V i 3 (cf. xi 36–43); seduces Burbon's Flourdelis and plans to take her away from him, xi 50–51; defeated often by Burbon, 53; killed by Artegall, xii 14–23. (V i 3)

Grille regrets that the Palmer restored him from being a hog to being human, II xii 86–87. (II xii 86)

Guizor son of Dolon who as Pollente's groom, plunders and pillages the poor, V ii 6; slain by Artegall when he demands toll for crossing Pollente's bridge, 11 (cf. vi 33, 37). (V vi 33)

Guyle see **Malengin**

Guyon dubbed knight by Sir Huon, II i 6; guided by the Palmer, 7; confronted by Archimago who complains that the Red Cross Knight sexually abused his lady, Duessa, 8–11; shows her to him, 12–23, and then guides him to the knight, 24–25; recognizing him, they are reconciled, 26–34; succours the dying Amavia, vows revenge on Acrasia who killed Mordant, and buries her and Mordant, 35–61; fails to cleanse the bloody-handed babe, Ruddymane, ii 1–10; bears Mordant's arms, 11; journeys on foot to Medina's castle, 12; fights Huddibras and Sansloy until they are reconciled by Medina, 21–33; tells her that the Faerie Queene has appointed him to capture

Acrasia, 40–44; tells the story of Amavia and Mordant, 45–46, and on leaving Ruddymane to be nurtured by her, discovers that his horse, Brigadore, and spear have been stolen, iii 2–4 (cf. ii 11); rescues Phaon from Occasion and Furor by binding them, iv 3–15; advises him to be temperate, 33, 36; confronted by Atin who rails at him, 37–46; overcomes Pyrochles, v 2–12, and advises him to be temperate, 13–16; allows him to unbind Occasion and Furor who attack him but, advised by the Palmer, refuses to intercede, 17–25; taken by Phædria to her island in the Idle Lake where he fights Cymochles until they are pacified by her, vi 19–36; on leaving, confronted by Atin but now ignores his railing, 38–40; debates with Mammon over the need of wealth, vii 7–18; descends into his cave to be tempted by wealth, 19–34, and by the source of all wealth, 35–39; confronted by Disdain, 40–42; refuses worldly advancement through marriage to Mammon's daughter, Philotime, 43–50, enters the Garden of Proserpina where he meets Tantalus and Pilate, 51–62; refuses to eat its fruit and sit on its stool, 63–64; requests Mammon to return him to the world where he faints, 65–66; saved by the angel sent by God who summons the Palmer, viii 1–8; about to be disarmed by Pyrochles and Cymochles, 10–16, Arthur arrives and kills them both, 17–52; awakes to thank him, 53–56; talks with him, about the Faerie Queene, ix 2–7, and, after dispersing the villeins who assault Alma's castle, 13–17, with him, enters the castle to be welcomed by her and taken on a guided tour, 17–35; meets Shamefastnes, 40–44; in Eumnestes's chamber, reads 'Antiquitie of *Faerie* lond', 60, x 70–76; leaves for Acrasia's island, rowed by the Ferryman, xi 3–4, and on the third day, passes its dangers, xii 2–41; nearing her bower, rejects the wine offered by Genius, 46–49, and by Excesse, 56–57; falters briefly on seeing the antics of two naked maidens wrestling in a fountain, 60–69; sees Acrasia with Verdant, binds and releases him, 72–82; destroys her Bower, 83, moralizes on her transformed lovers, 84–87; with Arthur, leaves Alma's castle, sends Acrasia to the Faerie Queene, and undertakes many adventures with him, III i 1–3; asks leave of Arthur to fight Britomart and is unhorsed by her, 4–8; reconciled to her, 9–12; pursues Florimell, 18, iv 45–46; claims his horse from Braggadocchio, V iii 29–35, and pacifies Artegall, 36–37. (II proem 5)

Hellenore young wife of the aged and impotent Malbecco, seduced by Paridell, III ix 25–31, 52, x 5–11; elopes with him taking much of her husband's wealth, sets fire to his castle, but because he prefers to save it with the rest of his wealth, escapes with Paridell, 12–17; abandoned by him, 35, becomes the May-lady of satyrs, 43–49; free at last, chooses them over Malbecco, 50–52. (III ix 6)

Hermit at Arthur's request, tends Timias and Serena wounded by the Blatant Beast, VI v 34–41; heals them through his advice, and they leave, vi 1–15. (VI v 37)

Huddibras see **Medina** (II ii 17)

Humiltá see **Cælia** (I x 5)

Ignaro foster-father of Orgoglio and porter of his castle but lacks the key to unlock the door that imprisons the Red Cross Knight, I viii 30–34, 37. (I viii 31)

Impatience see **Maleger** (II xi 23)

Impotence see **Maleger** (II xi 23)

Irena petitions the Faerie Queene to free her from Grantorto's tyranny, V i 3–4 (cf. 13, xii 3); imprisoned by Grantorto and threatened with death, as her servant, Sergis, tells Artegall, unless saved by a champion within ten days, xi 36–42; freed by Artegall, xii 3–27. (V i 4)

Isis see **Britomart** (V vii 2–4)

Jocante see **Malecasta** (III i 45)

Jove his rule challenged by Mutabilitie, VII vi 7–27; makes his case to rule, 33; accedes to her demand that her right to rule be judged by Nature, 35; makes his case in answer to hers, vii 48; his rule confirmed by Nature, 58–59.

Kirkrapine robs churches to support Abessa, I iii 16–19; killed by Una's lion, 20. (I iii 22)

Labryde see **Satyrane** (I iii 21)

Lamoracke see **Blatant Beast** (VI xii 39)

Lansack see **Marinell** (V iii 5)

Liagore see **Marinell** (III iv 41)

Lion befriends Una, I iii 5–9; kills Kirkrapine, 20; killed by Sansloy, 41–42. (I iii 9)

Lord of Many Ilands see **Bellamoure** (VI xii 4)

Lucida her beauty displayed by Ferramont at Satyrane's tournament, IV v 11.

Lucifera receives the Red Cross Knight and Duessa into her house of Pride, I iv 13–14; with Duessa, heads the procession of the seven deadly sins driven by Sathan (Satan), 16–37; arranges the joust between the Knight and Sansjoy, 38–43; conducts the joust and accepts the Knight's obeisance to her, v 5–16; the sight of those imprisoned in her dungeon causes him and the dwarf to flee, 45–53. (I iv 12)

Lucy see **Bracidas** (V iv 9)

Lust the savage man named 'greedie lust', IV vii Arg.; takes Amoret to his cave where he rapes, kills, and eats women, 4–8, 12–13; chases her when she flees, 21–24; uses her as a shield against Timias's attack, 26–28; flees from Belphœbe but is killed by her, 29–32. (IV vii 5)

Malbecco aged and jealous miser, III ix 3–6, forced to admit Paridell and others into his castle, 18–19; forced to show them his wife, Hellenore, 25–26; chooses his money over her, allowing her to flee with Paridell, x 12–15; engages Braggadocchio and Trompart to find her, 17–33; learns from Paridell that he has abandoned her, 35–38; finds her among the satyrs, but fails to persuade her to leave with him, 43–52; discovers that Braggadocchio and Trompart have stolen his hidden wealth, 54; transformed into Jealousy, 55–60. (III ix 6)

Malecasta Lady of Delight, the Lady of Castle Joyeous whose law imposing infidelity is enforced by her knights born of one parent (Gardante, Parlante, Jocante, Basciante, Bacchante, Noctante), III i 20–45; lusts after Britomart believing her to be a man, 47–56; rebuffed when she steals into her bed, 57–62; defended by her knights until Britomart and the Red Cross Knight force them to flee, 63–67. (III i 57)

Maleffort see **Crudor** (VI i 15)

Maleger with his villeins in twelve troops, besieges Alma's castle, II ix 12, xi 5–15; attacks Arthur and Guyon when they seek to enter, ix 13–17; aided by Impotence and Impatience, fights Arthur but is killed by him when

crushed and drowned in a standing lake, xi 20–46. (II xi 23)

Malengin called 'Guyle', Vix Arg.; the wily pillager, 4–6; lured from his den by Samient, 8–11; captures her, 14; pursued by Artegall, barred from his den by Arthur, and, despite his transformations, killed by Talus, 15–19. (V ix 5)

Malfont see **Mercilla** (V ix 25–26)

Mammon see **Guyon** (II vii 8)

Marinell wounded by Britomart on his rich strond, III iv 12–18; was conceived when his mother, Cymoent, was raped by Dumarin, 19–20, given wealth by his grandfather, Nereus, 21–23; warned by his mother to avoid woman's love because of Proteus's prophecy that he would be overthrown or killed by a virgin, 25–28; carried to her underwater bower to be attended by Liagore, 29–43; loved by Florimell and sought by her, v 8–10, vi 54, viii 46; cured of his wounds by Tryphon, IV xi 6–7; attends the marriage of the Thames and the Medway, xii 3; overhears Florimell's complaint that he does not return her love, 6–11; falls ill through love of her and grief that he cannot free her, 12–19; attended again by Tryphon, 23–24; diagnosed by Apollo, god of medicine, as suffering from love-sickness, 25; cured when his mother gains Florimell's release and presents her to him, 33–35; marries her, V iii 2–3 (cf. iv 3); defends her at their marriage tournament aided by six knights (Orimont, Bellisont, Brunell, Ecastor, Armeddan, and Lansack), 4–5; triumphs on the first two days, 6–7; captured on the third but rescued by Artegall, 8–12; takes the False Florimell for the true until she is exposed by Artegall, 17–26. (III iv 20)

Matilda see **Merlin** (III iii 13)

Matilde wife of Sir Bruin who laments their lack of offspring to inherit the land won from the giant, Cormoraunt, VI iv 28–33; accepts as her own the new-born child taken by Calepine from the bear, 34–38. (VI iv 29)

Medina welcomes Guyon (and the Palmer) to her castle, II ii 14–15; resolves his battle with Huddibras who courts her elder sister (Elissa), and Sansloy who courts her younger sister (Perissa), 27–33; persuades them all to feast together, 34–38; asks Guyon to tell the story of his quest, 39; agrees to nurture Ruddymane, iii 2. (II ii 14)

Medway see **Thames**

Meliboe had found Pastorella abandoned as a baby and nurtured her, VI ix 14 (cf. xii 9); invites Calidore to lodge with him, 16; discusses the pastoral life, 19–33; imprisoned by the Brigants, x 40–43; killed by them, xi 18 (cf. 31). (VI ix 16)

Meliogras see **Tristram** (VI ii 27–32)

Melissa see **Pastorella** (VI xii 14)

Mercie see **Cælia**

Mercilla praised by her messenger, Samient, V viii 16–17; seeks through her to be reconciled to Adicia who provokes her husband, Souldan, against her, 18–21; her porter, Awe, receives Arthur and Artegall into her court, ix 22–23; her marshall, Order, brings them into the hall where by the screen is displayed the tongue of Malfont nailed to a post, 25–26; seen enthroned with the royal sceptre in her hand and a rusty sword and a lion at her feet, attended by the Litae (Dice, Eunomie, and Eirene),

Temperance, and Reverence, 28–33; receives Arthur and Artegall graciously, 34–35; conducts the trial of Duessa, 38–49; grieves for the judgment against her, 50; grieves when she has been executed, x 4; on hearing Belge's petition, sends Arthur to defend her, 6–16. (V viii 17)

Mercury sent by Jove to learn why Cynthia has been eclipsed, either to throw her molester into hell or bring him to heaven, VII vi 14–16; reports that Mutabilitie threatens to unseat Cynthia, 19. (VII vi 14)

Merlin fashions Arthur's sword, Morddure (cf. II viii 20), shield, and armour, I vii 36; in charge of his nurturing and tutoring, ix 5; fashions a magic crystal ball in which Britomart's father, King Ryence, may see anything that pertains to him, III ii 18–21, and in which she sees Artegall, 22–26; betrayed by the Lady of the Lake, iii 10–11; his magical powers and birth to Matilda, 12–13; hears Glauce's complaint, 15–21, and tells Britomart of Artegall's birth, upbringing, his marriage to her, and death, 26–28, and their descendants, 29–50 (cf. iv 11); directs them to faery land, 62. (I vii 36)

Milesio see **Bracidas** (V iv 7–8)

Mirabella seen by Timias and Serena, riding a jade and led by a fool (Scorn), VI vi 16–17; has scorned her many lovers in her desire to be free, vii 28–31; summoned to Cupid's court and required to save as many lovers as she has destroyed, 32–37; saves only two in two years while two years earlier had destroyed twenty-four, 38; punished in being led by Disdain and whipped from behind by Scorn, 39–44; defended by Timias, but he is defeated by Disdain, 45–49; defended by Enias but he is defeated by Disdain and Scorn, viii 6–12; defended by Arthur who defeats Disdain, 13–16; asks Arthur not to kill him, 17; tells him her story, and how she must fill the leaky bottle of contrition with her tears, 18–24; offered her freedom but chooses to be punished, 29–30. (VI vii 35)

Mnemon see **Paridell** (III ix 47)

Molanna see **Diana** (VII vi 40)

Monster, Geryoneo's see **Geryoneo** (V xi 23–25)

Mordant see **Amavia** (II i 55)

Munera see **Pollente** (V ii 9)

Mutabilitie the Titaness who aspires to usurp Jove's rule, VII vi 2–4; assaults Cynthia, goddess of the moon, to usurp her rule, 7–13; summoned by Mercury to appear before Jove, refuses, then appears of her own will, 16–24; defies Jove and demands that her right to rule heaven be judged by Nature, 26–35; argues her case to Nature, vii 14–47, 49–56; loses, and is put down, 58–59.

Nature holds court on Arlo hill attended by all the gods, VII vii 3–13; hears Mutabilitie's case and Jove's, 14–56; judges against her, confirms him in his imperial see, and vanishes, 57–59. (VII vii 5–6)

Neptune god of the sea who leads the procession at the marriage of the Thames and the Medway, IV xi 11; at Cymodoce's petition, orders Proteus to release Florimell, xii 32.

Nereides fifty sea nymphs, daughters of Nereus and Doris, who attend the marriage of the Thames and the Medway, IV xi 48–52. (IV xi 48–52)

Night at Duessa's request, conveys Sansjoy to Æsculapius in hell to be cured, I v 20–44.

Noctante see **Malecasta** (III i 45)

Occasion see **Furor** (II iv 4–5)

Ollyphant offspring of Typhœus and his mother, Earth, twin of Argante, III vii 48, xi 3–4; seen by Britomart and Satyrane pursuing a young man, and escapes, 3–6; their pursuit leads her to Scudamour, 7. (III vii 48)

Orgoglio offspring of Earth and Æolus, I vii 9; defeats the Red Cross Knight and imprisons him in his dungeon, 10–15; takes Duessa as his mistress and places her on his dragon, 16–18; killed by Arthur, viii 3–24. (I vii 14)

Orimont see **Marinell** (V iii 5)

Osiris see **Britomart** (V vii 2–4)

Palimord see **Triamond** (IV iv 21)

Palladine see **Argante** (III vii 52)

Palmer Guyon's guide, II i 7, 34 (cf. iv 2); praises the Red Cross Knight, 31–32; advocates temperance, 58; helps bury Amavia and Mordant, 60; tells Guyon why the well cannot cleanse Ruddymane's bloody hands, ii 5–10; carries the babe to Medina's castle, 11, where Guyon tells her how the Palmer's complaint against Acrasia led the Faerie Queene to assign him his quest, 43 (cf. ix 9, *LR* 70–73); informs Guyon of the nature of Furor and Occasion, iv 10–11; admonishes Phaon for his intemperance, 34–35; advises Guyon not to help Pyrochles, v 24; refused entry into Phædria's boat, vi 19–20; summoned by the angel, finds Guyon in a swoon, viii 3–9; defends him against Pyrochles and Cymochles, 12–16; asks Arthur to succour Guyon, 25; gives him Guyon's sword, 40; tells the awakened Guyon what happened, 53–54; steers the boat that takes Guyon to Acrasia's Bower of Bliss, xii 3; moralizes on their dangers, 9; rebukes Phædria, 16; disperses the sea monsters with his staff, 26; warns Guyon not to pity a wailing maiden, 28–29; subdues the land monsters with his staff, 40; warns Guyon not to dally with the two naked damsels wrestling in the fountain, 69; with Guyon, captures Acrasia and Verdant with a net he has made, 81; pacifies Acrasia's beasts and changes them back into men, 84–87; persuades Guyon not to seek revenge against Britomart, III i 9–11. (II i 7)

Panope see **Proteus** (III viii 37)

Paridell in seeking Florimell, meets Satyrane and the Squire of Dames, III viii 44–51; jousts with Britomart, ix 14–16; courts Hellenore in Malbecco's castle, 27–31, 52; recounts his Trojan lineage from Paris, 33–37, 41–43, and the Trojan settlement of England as told to him by Mnemon, 47–51; persuades Hellenore to elope with him, x 1–16; tells Malbecco that he has abandoned her, 35–38; seen as a companion of Duessa, Blandamour, and Ate, IV i 17, 32; gains Ate as his companion, 37; defeated by Scudamour, 40–43; quarrels with Blandamour over the False Florimell until pacified by the Squire of Dames, ii 7–29; defeated by Ferramont at Satyrane's tournament, iv 19; exhibits Duessa at the beauty contest, v 11; quarrels with Blandamour and Erivan over the False Florimell, 24; fights Druon, Claribell, and Blandamour over the False Florimell, ix 20–27; with Druon, fights Scudamour, 29–30, until pacified by Arthur, fights Scudamour, 33–37. (III viii 45)

Parlante see **Malecasta** (III i 45)

Pastorella a shepherdess adored by the shepherds and by Calidore, VI ix 7–12; had been found by Melibœ as a baby, 14; prefers Colin for his songs until Calidore assumes pastoral attire, 35–37; wooed by the jealous Coridon, 38–44, x 33; loves Calidore after he saves her from a tiger, 34–37, and yields to him, 38; taken captive by the Brigants and imprisoned in their underground den, 39–44; loved by their captain who is killed defending her, xi 3–21; mistreated by her guard, 24; rescued by Calidore, 25–51; taken by him to Belgard Castle where Bellamoure and Claribell, through their maid, Melissa, are revealed to be her parents, xii 3–22.   (VI ix 9)

Patience see **Red Cross Knight** (I x 23)
Pelleas see **Blatant Beast** (VI xii 39)
Perissa see **Medina** (II ii 36)
Phædria ferries Cymochles to her island in the Idle Lake where he yields to her, II vi 2–18; brings Guyon there but he resists her, 19–26; pacifies them when they fight, 27–36; ferries Guyon to the farther shore, 37–38; tries to allure him to her floating island, xii 14–17.   (II vi 9)
Phantastes the first of Alma's three counsellors, II ix 47–49; associated with what is known through foresight, and therefore with fancy or imagination, 49–52.   (II ix 52)
Phaon or **Phedon** (*1596*) descendant of Coradin, rescued by Guyon from Occasion and Furor, II iv 3–15; tells him how his friend, Philemon, tricked him into believing that he saw his lady, Claribell, having an affair with him (what he saw was her maid, Pryene, in her clothes), 18–28; kills her, and on learning the truth from Pryene, poisons his friend, and seeks to kill her, 29–32; counselled by Guyon and the Palmer not to be intemperate, 34–36.   (II iv 36)
Philemon see **Phaon** (II iv 20)
Philotime see **Guyon** (II vii 49)
Philtera see **Bracidas** (V iv 8)
Phœbe see **Diana**
Pilate with Tantalus, seen by Guyon in the Cocytus trying vainly to wash their hands, II vii 61–62.
Placidas rescued by Arthur from Corflambo, IV viii 38–46; tells him how his look-alike friend, Amyas, imprisoned by Corflambo, was wooed by his daughter, Pœana, but resisted her, 47–54; loved by her after he exchanged places with Amyas, 55–60; escapes by carrying off her dwarf, 61–62; marries her (but see Arg.*n*) after Arthur captures and reforms her, ix 4–15.   (IV viii 59)
Pleasure see **Amoret**
Pœana see **Placidas** (IV viii 49)
Pollente aided by Guizor, exacts toll from those who cross his bridge in order to support his daughter, Munera, and then causes them to fall through a trap to be drowned or killed by him, V ii 4–10; killed by Artegall, 11–19; his daughter dismembered by Talus, drowned, and her castle razed, 20–28.   (V ii 7)
Praysdesire see **Arthur** (II ix 39)
Priamond see **Triamond** (IV ii 41)
Priest, Isis's see **Britomart** (V vii 4)
Priscilla see **Aladine** (VI iii 10)
Proteus warns Cymoent that her son, Marinell, will be overthrown or killed by a virgin, III iv 25; rescues Florimell from the Fisher, punishes him, and takes her to his bower to be kept by Panope, viii 30–37; woos her unsuccessfully, 38–42, IV xi 2–4; commanded by Neptune to release her, xii 32.   (III viii 30)

Pryene see **Phaon** (II iv 25)
Psyche see **Amoret** (III vi 50)
Pyrochles his ancestry, II iv 41; attacks Guyon but is subdued by him and counselled in temperance, v 2–16; persuades Guyon to release Occasion only to be abused by her and Furor, 17–24; saved by Atin from drowning after he seeks to quench his inner flames in the Idle Lake, vi 41–47; healed by Archimago, 48–51; with his brother, Cymochles, seeks to disarm the unconscious Guyon, viii 10–17; wielding Arthur's sword, attacks Arthur, 30, but is wounded by him even though he bears Guyon's shield, 31–32; killed by Arthur after Cymochles is killed, 46–52.   (II iv 41)
Radigund Queen of the Amazons whose maids are about to hang Terpine when he is rescued by Artegall and Talus, V iv 21–24; seeks revenge against the Knights of Maidenhead because she had been rebuffed by Bellodant, despoiling them of their arms and dressing them as women to do women's work, 29–32; almost slays Terpine after he guides Artegall to her city, Radegone, 39–42; sends her maid, Clarinda, to propose a single combat with Artegall on the condition that the vanquished submit to the conqueror, which he accepts, 46–51; defeats him, v 1–17; having hanged Terpine, makes Artegall her thrall, 18–25; falling in love with him, 26–28, arranges to have her jailer, Eumenias, allow Clarinda access to him to intercede on her behalf, but is deceived by her because she loves him herself, 29–57; defeated by Britomart and decapitated, vii 25–34.   (V iv 33)
Red Cross Knight assigned by the Faerie Queene to slay the dragon that besieges Una's parents, I i 3 (cf. *LR* 52–63); travels with Una and her dwarf, 4–6; encounters and kills Errour in the Wandering Wood, 7–27; deceived by Archimago, 29–35, who betrays him first by a dream of a lustful Una, 45–55, and then by the false sight of her in bed with a squire, ii 3–6; fleeing from her, meets and kills Sansfoy, 12–19, but thereby gains his companion, Duessa, 20–27; fails to be warned by Fradubio who tells how he and Fralissa were transformed into trees after choosing Duessa as his companion, 28–45; led by her to the house of Pride, iv 2–3; makes obeisance to Lucifera, 13; accompanies her on her progress but estranges himself, 37; challenged by Sansjoy for Sansfoy's shield, 38–43; defeats him, v 6–13; fêted as Lucifera's knight, 16; flees on being told by the dwarf about the victims in her dungeon, 52–53; after yielding to Duessa, defeated by Orgoglio and imprisoned in his dungeon, vii 2–15; freed by Arthur and restored to Una, viii 37–43; vows his love for the Faerie Queene, ix 17; exchanges gifts with Arthur, 18–19; meets Trevisan fleeing from Despaire, 21–32; meets Despaire, 33–36; overcome by his arguments to despair, is about to stab himself, 37–51; until rescued by Una, 52–53; guided by her to the house of Holinesse, x 2–3; meets Cælia, 8–11; taught doctrine by Fidelia in her schoolhouse, and hope for salvation by Speranza, 18–22; instructed by Patience who takes him to the house of Penance to be purged of sin, 23–28; meets Charissa who teaches him to live righteously, 30–33; led by Mercie at Una's request first to the Holy Hospital to be perfected, 34–45, and then to Contemplation, who leads him to the top of the mountain, 53–54, shows him the way to the New Jerusalem, 55–58, tells him his

duty to the Faerie Queene by aiding Una, 58–59, fore-tells his future role among the saints as 'Saint *George* of mery England' (61), and reveals his Saxon ancestry, which was unknown to him because he was a changeling, and his name, *Georgos*, 65–66; fights the dragon for two days, xi 8–50, slays it on the third, 52–55; welcomed by Una's parents, xii 5–6, 12–14; relates his adventures, 15–16; betrothed to Una despite Duessa's forbidding the banns, 17–41; reconciled to Guyon who had been deceived by Archimago into believing that he had violated Duessa, II i 26–31; aided by Britomart, fights Malecasta's six knights, III i 20–29, and aids her against them, 66–67; praises Artegall to her, ii 9–15; pledges affectionate friendship with her, iii 62, and perpetual love, iv 4; had dubbed Burbon a knight, V xi 53. (I i 1–6)

Ruddymane see **Guyon**   (II iii 2)

St George see **Red Cross Knight**   (I x 61)

Salvage Knight see **Artegall**   (IV iv 39)

Salvage Man rescues Calepine from Turpine, VI iv 2–8; serves him and Serena, 9–16, v 1–9; meets Arthur and Timias, 10–11; saved by Serena from an attack by Timias, 25–30; as Arthur's groom, kills Turpine's groom, vi 22; slaughters his forces, 38–39; defends Arthur against Turpine and Enias, vii 24; attacks Scorn, viii 28–29. (VI iv 2)

Salvage Nation captures Serena whom they intend to sacrifice and eat, VI viii 35–46; slaughtered by Calepine, 49.   (VI viii 35)

Samient Mercilla's messenger, saved by Arthur and Artegall from Adicia's knights, V viii 4–12; tells them of Mercilla and the Souldan's wrongs against her, 16–23; to trick Adicia, led by the disguised Artegall into the Souldan's castle as though his prisoner, 25–26; saved by him from being stabbed by her, 46–48; guides Arthur and Artegall to Malengin's cave, ix 7–8, where she acts as bait to lure him out, 9–14; guides them to Mercilla's palace, 20–22.   (V viii 23)

Sangliere unhorsed by Artegall in Satyrane's tournament, IV iv 40; seizes a squire's lady, and cuts off his own lady's head when she asks to die rather than be abandoned, V i 14–18; captured by Talus, 20–22; forced by Artegall to carry her head for twelve months, 29.   (V i 20)

Sansfoy eldest of the three Sans brothers, killed by the Red Cross Knight, who thereby gains his shield and his lady, Duessa, I ii 12–19.   (I ii 25)

Sansjoy youngest of the three who challenges the Red Cross Knight for Sansfoy's shield, I iv 38–41; befriended by Duessa, 44–51; wounded by the Red Cross Knight, v 5–13; through Duessa's intercession, conveyed by Night to Æsculapius to be cured, 20–44.   (I ii 25)

Sansloy the middle son who wounds Archimago disguised as the Red Cross Knight, I iii 33–39; seizes Una and kills her lion, 41–42; attempts to rape her but flees when the fawns and satyrs appear, vi 4–8; fights Satyrane, 40–47; in Medina's castle, courts Perissa, II ii 18; fights Hud-dibras, and then both attack Guyon, 20–26.   (I ii 25)

Sathan see **Lucifera**   (I iv 36)

Satyrane son of Thyamis (daughter of Labryde and wife of Therion who was raped by a satyr), I vi 20–22; nurtured by satyrs and visited by his mother, 23–29; befriends Una and helps her escape the satyrs, 30–33; seeks

Sansloy, believing that he has killed the Red Cross Knight, 36–40; fights him while Una flees, 41–47; binds the witch's monster with Florimell's girdle, III vii 29–36 (cf. viii 49); allows it to escape in order to rescue the Squire of Dames from Argante but is seized by her, 37–43; freed when she flees Palladine, 44–45; aids the Squire who tells him about Argante, 46–52; amused by his story of how he tried to find chaste women, 53–61; joins Paridell in seeking Florimell, viii 44–50; reconciles Britomart and Paridell, ix 17; dines in Malbecco's castle, 27; leaves with Britomart, x 1; pursues Ollyphant with her, xi 3–6; finds Florimell's girdle, wears it for her sake, and plans a feast and tournament at which it will be awarded to the fairest lady who, in turn, will be awarded to the best knight, IV ii 25–27; at his tournament, dis-plays the girdle in an ark of gold as the prize of beauty and of might, iv 15–16; fights Bruncheval to a draw, 17–18, but revives to lead the Knights of Maidenhead to victory on the first day, 22–25; defeated by Cambell on the second day but rescued by his forces, 26–31; triumphs on the third day until his forces are defeated by Artegall, 37–44; awarded the False Florimell but Braggadocchio claims her, v 22; seeks to resolve quarrels over her by allowing her to choose, 25–26.   (I vi 28)

Satyrs save Una from Sansloy, I vi 7–8, and worship her, 9–19; adopt Hellenore as their May-lady, III x 43–46. (I vi 7)

Sclaunder see **Arthur**   (IV viii 24)

Scorn see **Mirabella**   (VI vii 28–31)

Scudamour loved by Amoret, III vi 53; while grieving, because he cannot rescue her from being imprisoned and tortured by Busirane, found by Britomart while pursuing Ollyphant, xi 7–17; promised by her to free Amoret, 18–19; unlike her, forced to retreat by the flames at the gate of Busirane's castle, 26; restored to Amoret (*1590*), xii 43–47; leaves with Glauce (*1596*) despairing of Britomart's success, 43–45; had lost Amoret to Busirane during their wedding celebrations, IV i 3–4; defeats Paridell, 40–43; made jealous by Duessa and Ate who report that Amoret is intimate with Britomart, 46–49; vents his jealous rage on Glauce, 52–54; spends a sleep-less night in the house of Care, v 30–46; joins Artegall to plot revenge against Britomart, vi 2–8; unhorsed by her, 9–10; learns from her that Amoret has wandered away, 34–37; promised her help to find her, 38, 46–47; with Britomart, sees four knights skirmishing, two of whom, Paridell and Druon, attack him until Arthur intervenes, ix 22, 28–35; complains of his loss of Amoret, 38–39; persuaded chiefly by Britomart, 41, tells how he won the shield of love, x 5–10; overcame Doubt, Delay, and Daunger who guard the bridge's gates to Venus's island, 11–20, and passed by its bands of lovers, 21–27; confronted by Love and Hatred, and aided by Concord at the porch of Venus's temple, 31–36, enters it to see her veiled idol, 37–42, hears lovers praise her, 43–47; seeing Amoret in the lap of Womanhood with her attendant virtues, and encouraged by Venus, seizes her against her will, 48–58.   (III xi 7)

Seneschall, Geryoneo's see **Geryoneo**   (V x 30)

Serena seen by Calidore while making love to Calepine, VI iii 20–21; seized and wounded by the Blatant Beast as she wanders but is saved by Calidore, 23–25; tended by

Calepine in spite of Turpine who refuses to help them cross the river, forces them to spend the night outdoors, and wounds him, 27–51; saved by the Salvage Man who cures his wounds but not hers, iv 2–16; accompanied by the Salvage Man in Calepine's absence, meets Arthur and Timias, v 2–11, and tells them her story, 25–34; left with Timias to be tended by the Hermit, 35–41; their wounds cured by his advice, vi 2–15, travelling with Timias, meets Mirabella led by Scorn, 16 (cf. vii 39); flees when he is overcome by Disdain, vii 50; seized by a Salvage nation, stripped, and, about to be sacrificed and eaten, saved by Calepine, viii 31–51.   (VI iii 23)

Sergis servant of Irena who tells Artegall that her life is threatened unless a champion defends her within ten days, V xi 37–42; accompanies him when he rescues Burbon, 43–59; accompanies him to Irena's land, xii 4–6; arranges for his provisions, 10.   (V xi 38)

Shamefastnes see **Guyon**   (II ix 43)

Sophy see **Artegall**   (II ix 6)

Souldan opposes Mercilla, being provoked by his wife, Adicia, V viii 18–20; defeated by Arthur whose uncovered shield causes his horses to flee, tearing him to pieces, 28–43.   (V viii 24)

Speranza see **Red Cross Knight**   (I x 14)

Squire of Dames bound on Argante's horse to be taken to serve her lust but discarded when she is attacked by Satyrane, III vii 37–38; required by his mistress, Columbell, to prove his faithful love to her by seducing as many women as possible within a year, 54; having serviced 300 with a possible 900 more, ordered to find as many chaste women, 55–56, but in three years, has found only three, 57–60; with Satyrane, meets Paridell, viii 45–46; suggests that they spend the night in Malbecco's castle, 51; explains why they may not be admitted, ix 3–6; pacifies Blandamour and Paridell by persuading them to attend Satyrane's tournament with Florimell's girdle as its prize, IV ii 20–28; serves as their squire to introduce Cambell and Triamond, Canacee and Cambina, 31; mocks the shamed ladies at Satyrane's tournament, v 18.   (III vii 51)

Sylvanus see **Una**   (I vi 7)

Talus the iron man appointed Artegall's groom by Astræa, V i 12; captures Sangliere and binds him, 20–22; finds, dismembers, and drowns Munera, and razes her castle, ii 20–28; shoulders the Giant with the Scales into the sea and disperses his followers, 49–54; baffles Braggadocchio and scourges Trompart, iii 37–38; disperses the Amazons about to hang Terpine, iv 24; disperses those who protect Radigund, 44; conducts Clarinda to Artegall, 51; disperses the Amazons after they hang Terpine, v 19; reports Artegall's imprisonment to Britomart and guides her to Radegone, vi 9–18; guards her against Dolon's treachery, 26, and routs his men, 29–30; refused entry into Isis Church, vii 3; after Radigund's death, slaughters her Amazons until ordered to stop by Britomart, 35–36; serves as Arthur's page ready to exterminate the Souldan's forces, viii 29; captures and kills Malengin, ix 16–19; disperses the mob that attacks Burbon, xi 47, 59, 65; establishes a beach-head for Artegall to land on Irena's savage island, and slaughters the defenders until he orders him to stop, xii 5–8; searches the country to flush out robbers and rebels, 26–27; prevented by Artegall from attacking Detraction, 43.   (V i 12)

Tanaquill see **Faerie Queene**   (I proem 2)

Tantalus see **Pilate**   (II vii 61)

Terpine see **Radigund**   (V iv 26)

Terwin see **Despaire**   (I ix 27)

Thames his marriage to the Medway becomes the occasion for the procession of waters, IV xi 8–53.

Therion see **Satyrane**   (I vi 21)

Thyamis see **Satyrane**   (I vi 21)

Timias Arthur's beloved squire who carries his spear, I vii 37; blows his horn that opens the doors of Orgoglio's castle, viii 3–5; defends him against Duessa's dragon but, weakened by her magic potion, is almost overcome until rescued by him, 12–16; catches the fleeing Duessa and guards her, 25, 29; accompanies him, bearing his spear and shield, when they meet Pyrochles and Cymochles, II viii 17; blows his horn that shakes Alma's castle, ix 11; saves him when overcome by Impotence and Impatience, xi 29–31; helps him on his horse and leads him back to Alma's castle, 48; pursues the Foster who pursues Florimell, III i 18 (cf. iv 47, v 13); kills him and his two brothers, v 13–25; tended by Belphœbe who binds his wounds, 26–36; taken to her bower where she heals his wounds only to wound his heart by loving her, leaving him in despair, 37–50; while hunting with her, they are separated, and he saves Amoret from being carried off by Lust, IV vii 23–25; wounds her when fighting Lust who uses her as a shield, 25–28; abandoned by Belphœbe when she sees him fondling Amoret, 35–37, retires into the forest, so pined away and struck dumb that he is not recognized by Arthur, 38–47; regains Belphœbe's favour through the intercession of a turtle dove, viii 2–18; lured to chase the Blatant Beast, is bitten and ambushed by Despetto, Decetto, and Defetto, who flee when Arthur arrives, VI v 12–24; meets Serena with the Salvage Man, 25–26; left with her to be tended by the Hermit, 35–41; cured by his advice, vi 2–15, travelling with her, meets Mirabella led by Scorn, 16, vii 39; bound by Disdain, 45–49; in his shameful state, meets Arthur, viii 5, and freed by him, 27.   (III i 18)

Trevisan see **Despaire**   (I ix 32)

Triamond one of Agape's triplets, whose brothers are Priamond and Diamond, IV ii 41–43, born to her after being raped by a knight, 44–46; his life is prolonged when she persuades the Fates to add his brothers' lives to his, 47–53; their love of Canacee leads them to challenge her brother, Cambell, for her, 54; sustained by his brothers' lives, fights Cambell until they are reconciled by his own sister, Cambina, iii 5–49; marries Canacee, 52; wielding the spear that Braggadocchio stole from Guyon, defeats Ferramont, Deuon, Douglas, and Palimord, iv 20–21; being wounded by Satyrane, 24, his shield and arms are used by Cambell to defeat Satyrane, 26–32; wearing Cambell's arms, they triumph on the second day of the tournament, 33–36; defeated by Britomart, 45; displays Canacee at the contest, v 10; refuses the False Florimell, 21.   (IV ii 41)

Tristram seen by Calidore killing the discourteous knight, VI ii 3–6; justifies having done so, 7–12, as does the knight's lady, 14–23; at Calidore's request, reveals that he is the son of the dead Meliogras, King of Cornwall, 26–28; sent as a youth by his mother, Emiline, to be raised in faery land, 29–32; dubbed by Calidore as his squire but not allowed to accompany him, 33–38; despoils the discourteous knight of his armour and rides off with his lady, 39.   (VI ii 27–32)

Trompart made Braggadocchio's liege-man, II iii 6–10; frightened by Archimago's flight to get Arthur's sword, 18–19; dismayed at the sight of Belphœbe but addresses her as a goddess, 32–33; advises Braggadocchio not to pursue her, 44; advises Malbecco to appeal to Braggadocchio to help him recover Hellenore, III x 23–32; advises him to hide his wealth for security, 40–42; steals it after they flee the satyrs' bagpipes, 54; keeps the False Florimell from open sight, V iii 17; scourged by Talus, 38.   (II iii 10)

Tryphon see **Marinell**   (III iv 43)

Turpine refuses to help Calepine by taking the wounded Serena on his horse to cross the river though reproved by his lady, Blandina (cf. v 33), VI iii 31–33; taunts him while he struggles across, 34–36; refuses to let them enter his Castle of the Ford at nightfall, 37–44; on his horse, chases Calepine on foot, and wounds him, 46–51, but forced to flee without his spear and shield by the Salvage Man, iv 1–8; his discourtesy revealed by Serena to Arthur who vows to punish him, v 33–34; his servants killed by Arthur when he enters his castle, vi 17–24; with forty yeomen, confronts Arthur but forced to flee to Blandina for protection, 25–32; for her sake, allowed to live in disgrace, 33–36; his servants slaughtered by the Salvage Man, 38–40; hires two knights to kill Arthur, but one is killed by him and the other, Enias, tricks him into coming to Arthur who baffles him, 44, vii 3–27.   (VI iii 40)

Una accompanies the Red Cross Knight, I i 4–5; advises caution when he approaches Errour's cave, 12–13; supports him in his fight against Errour, 19, and congratulates him on his victory, 27; searches for him after he flees from her, ii 6–8; befriended by a lion, iii 5–8; sees Abessa, the deaf mute daughter of Corceca, who flees from her, 10–12; spends the night in their cottage, and on leaving is pursued by them, 13–23; deluded by Archimago who disguises himself as her knight, 24–32; seized by Sansloy after he wounds Archimago and kills her lion, 33–44; rescued by satyrs who worship her, vi 7–13; her beauty astonishes their god, Sylvanus, 14–17; teaches them truth, 19; escapes from them aided by Satyrane, 33; deceived by Archimago's claim that Sansloy killed her knight, 34–40, and flees when Satyrane fights him, 47; told by her dwarf of her knight's capture by Orgoglio, vii 20–27; meets Arthur, 29, at whose request, 38–41, tells her story, 43–51; congratulates him and Timias after Orgoglio has been slain, viii 26–28; welcomes the Red Cross Knight on his release, 42–43; asks that Duessa be stripped of her robe and let go, 45–46; saves her knight from Despaire, ix 52–53; takes him to the house of Holinesse, x 2–4, where she is greeted by Cælia, 8–9, and then by Fidelia and Speranza, 15; asks Fidelia to teach her knight, 18; asks Cælia to comfort him, 23; shares his anguish and welcomes him on his recovery, 28–29; asks Charissa to instruct him in the virtuous life, 32; awaits his return from Contemplation, 68; guides him to her native land, and watches as he fights the dragon, xi 1–5; prays for him when he falls at the end of the first day, 32, and again at the end of the second day, 50; congratulates him on his victory, 55; crowned by virgins as a maiden Queen, xii 8; greeted by her father, the King of Eden, 12; appears unveiled to become the Red Cross Knight's bride, 20–23; discloses Duessa's and Archimago's deception, 33–34; betrothed by her father, 37–41.   (I i 4–5)

Venus 'Queene of beautie and of grace' (IV x 44), invoked by Spenser to inspire him, I proem 3; searches for Cupid, III vi 11–16; meets Diana and both search for him, 17–27; adopts Amoret in his place, 28; enjoys Adonis, 46–49; her temple, IV x 29–38, with her veiled idol on its altar, 39–42, with lovers praising her, 43–47, and with Amoret and the virtues at her feet, 48–52.

Verdant see **Acrasia**   (II xii 82)

Villeins see **Maleger**   (II ix 13)

Witch accepts Florimell into her hovel, III vii 7–11; sends a hyena to devour her when she leaves, 22–23; fashions the False Florimell to console her son, viii 1–10.   (III vii 6)

Womanhood see **Amoret**   (IV x 50–51)

CPSIA information can be obtained
at www.ICGtesting.com
Printed in the USA
LVHW101700070321
680816LV00006B/188

9 781405 832816